YEARBOOK OF THE
UNITED NATIONS
2001

Volume 55

Yearbook of the United Nations, 2001

Volume 55   Sales No. E.03.I.1

Prepared by the Yearbook Section of the Department of Public Information, United Nations, New York. Although the *Yearbook* is based on official sources, it is not an official record.

Chief Editor: Kathryn Gordon

Senior Editors: Elizabeth Baldwin-Penn, Melody C. Pfeiffer

Editors/Writers: Barbara Christiani, Peter Jackson, Federigo Magherini, John R. Sebesta, Jullyette Ukabiala

Contributing Editors/Writers: Luisa Balacco, Eugene Forson, Itai Madamombe, Juanita B. Phelan, Nancy Seufert-Barr

Senior Copy Editor: Alison M. Koppelman

Copy Editor: Peter Homans

Production Coordinators: Rodney Pascual, Leonard M. Simon

Editorial Assistants: Jingbo Huang, Lawri Moore, Margaret O'Donnell

Senior Typesetter: Sunita Chabra

Indexer: David Golante

Jacket design by James Eschinger

YEARBOOK
OF THE
UNITED
NATIONS
2001

Volume 55

Department of Public Information
United Nations, New York

Yearbook of the United Nations, 2001
Vol. 55
ISBN: 92-1-100897-2
ISSN: 0082-8521

UNITED NATIONS PUBLICATIONS
SALES NO. E.03.I.1

Printed in the United States of America

Foreword

On 11 September 2001, devastating terrorist attacks in the United States of America, including on the host city of the United Nations, dramatized the global threat of international terrorism and highlighted the need for a common, and multifaceted, strategy to combat it. While the most direct result of 11 September was the conflict in Afghanistan and the beginnings of United Nations efforts to assist in the transformation of that country, the international community also focused on strengthening international law and cooperation to prevent and suppress terrorism.

Yet the other social, economic and political problems that blighted so much of our planet and so many of its peoples were rendered no less important by 11 September, and they also demanded the attention of the international community throughout the year. During a special session on HIV/AIDS, the General Assembly adopted the Declaration of Commitment—the first global battle plan against the epidemic. The Assembly also held a special session on human settlements, while major conferences discussed racism, the illicit trade in small arms and the problems of the least developed countries. Conflict continued to plague Africa, though in some countries—most notably in Sierra Leone—there were signs of improvement. Steady progress was made in the transition to independence in East Timor and towards local control in Kosovo. Yet the Georgian-Abkhaz conflict escalated, and a terrible cycle of violence and reprisals plagued the lives of Israelis and Palestinians.

In this year of trial and toil, the Norwegian Nobel Committee, in awarding the United Nations the centennial Nobel Peace Prize, recognized the work of the Organization for "a better-organized and more peaceful world".

I trust that this *Yearbook of the United Nations* for 2001 bears out this theme by showing the crucial role of the United Nations in addressing pressing global problems and strengthening international cooperation, as well as the magnitude of the challenges that lie before us as we continue our common efforts to achieve the goals of the Charter. As the year showed, so many of our problems are common problems, and international cooperation is more necessary than ever if we are to address the dangers, spread the burdens and share the opportunities of our age.

KOFI A. ANNAN

Secretary-General of the United Nations
New York, June 2003

Contents

Part One: *Political and security questions*

Part Two: *Human Rights*

Part Three: *Economic and social questions*

Part Four: *Legal questions*

Part Six: *Intergovernmental organizations related to the United Nations*

Appendices

Indexes

About the 2001 edition of the *Yearbook*

This volume of the *YEARBOOK OF THE UNITED NATIONS* continues the tradition of providing the most comprehensive coverage of the activities of the United Nations. It is an indispensable reference tool for the research community, diplomats, government officials and the general public seeking readily available information on the UN system and its related organizations.

Efforts by the Department of Public Information to achieve a more timely publication have resulted in having to rely on provisional documentation and other materials to prepare the relevant articles. Largely, Security Council resolutions and presidential statements, Economic and Social Council resolutions and some other texts in the present volume are provisional.

Structure and scope of articles

The *Yearbook* is subject-oriented and divided into six parts covering political and security questions; human rights issues; economic and social questions; legal questions; institutional, administrative and budgetary questions; and intergovernmental organizations related to the United Nations. Chapters and topical headings present summaries of pertinent UN activities, including those of intergovernmental and expert bodies, major reports, Secretariat activities and, in selected cases, the views of States in written communications.

Activities of United Nations bodies. All resolutions, decisions and other major activities of the principal organs and, on a selective basis, those of subsidiary bodies are either reproduced or summarized in the appropriate chapter. The texts of all resolutions and decisions of substantive nature adopted in 2001 by the General Assembly, the Security Council and the Economic and Social Council are reproduced or summarized under the relevant topic. These texts are preceded by procedural details giving date of adoption, meeting number and vote totals (in favour–against–abstaining) if any; and an indication of their approval by a sessional or subsidiary body prior to final adoption. The texts are followed by details of any recorded or roll-call vote on the resolution/decision as a whole.

Major reports. Most reports of the Secretary-General, in 2001, along with selected reports from other UN sources, such as seminars and working groups, are summarized briefly.

Secretariat activities. The operational activities of the United Nations for development and humanitarian assistance are described under the relevant topics. For major activities financed outside the UN regular budget, selected information is given on contributions and expenditures.

Views of States. Written communications sent to the United Nations by Member States and circulated as documents of the principal organs have been summarized in selected cases, under the relevant topics. Substantive actions by the Security Council have been analysed and brief reviews of the Council's deliberations given, particularly in cases where an issue was taken up but no resolution was adopted.

Related organizations. The *Yearbook* also briefly describes the 2001 activities of the specialized agencies and other related organizations of the UN system.

Multilateral treaties. Information on signatories and parties to multilateral treaties and conventions is taken from *Multilateral Treaties Deposited with the Secretary-General: Status as at 31 December 2001* (ST/LEG/SER.E/20 (vols. I & II)), Sales No. E.02.V.4.

Terminology

Formal titles of bodies, organizational units, conventions, declarations and officials are given in full on first mention in an article or sequence of articles. They are also used in resolution/decision texts, and in the SUBJECT INDEX under the key word of the title. Short titles may be used in subsequent references.

How to find information in the *Yearbook*

The user may locate information on the United Nations activities contained in this volume by the use of the Table of Contents, the Subject Index, the Index of Resolutions and Decisions and the Index of Security Council Presidential Statements. The volume also has five appendices: Appendix I comprises a roster of Member States; Appendix II reproduces the Charter of the United Nations, including the Statute of the International Court of Justice; Appendix III gives the structure of the principal organs of the United Nations; Appendix IV provides the agenda for each session of the principal organs in 2001; and Appendix V gives the addresses of the United Nations information centres and services worldwide.

For more information on the United Nations and its activities, visit our Internet site at:

http://www.un.org

ABBREVIATIONS COMMONLY USED IN THE *YEARBOOK*

ACABQ	Advisory Committee on Administrative and Budgetary Questions
ACC	Administrative Committee on Coordination
CEB	United Nations System Chief Executives Board for Coordination
CIS	Commonwealth of Independent States
DPKO	Department of Peacekeeping Operations
DPRK	Democratic People's Republic of Korea
DRC	Democratic Republic of the Congo
ECA	Economic Commission for Africa
ECE	Economic Commission for Europe
ECLAC	Economic Commission for Latin America and the Caribbean
ECOWAS	Economic Community of West African States
ESC	Economic and Social Council
ESCAP	Economic and Social Commission for Asia and the Pacific
ESCWA	Economic and Social Commission for Western Asia
EU	European Union
FAO	Food and Agriculture Organization of the United Nations
FRY	Federal Republic of Yugoslavia
FYROM	The former Yugoslav Republic of Macedonia
GA	General Assembly
GDP	gross domestic product
GNP	gross national product
HIPC	heavily indebted poor countries
IAEA	International Atomic Energy Agency
ICAO	International Civil Aviation Organization
ICJ	International Court of Justice
ICRC	International Committee of the Red Cross
ICTR	International Criminal Tribunal for Rwanda
ICTY	International Tribunal for the Former Yugoslavia
IDA	International Development Association
IFAD	International Fund for Agricultural Development
IFC	International Finance Corporation
ILO	International Labour Organization
IMF	International Monetary Fund
IMO	International Maritime Organization
INCB	International Narcotics Control Board
ITC	International Trade Centre (UNCTAD/WTO)
ITU	International Telecommunication Union
JIU	Joint Inspection Unit
LDC	least developed country
MINUGUA	United Nations Verification Mission in Guatemala
MINURSO	United Nations Mission for the Referendum in Western Sahara
MONUC	United Nations Mission in the Democratic Republic of the Congo
NATO	North Atlantic Treaty Organization
NGO	non-governmental organization
NSGT	Non-Self-Governing Territory
OAS	Organization of American States
OAU	Organization of African Unity
OCHA	Office for the Coordination of Humanitarian Affairs
ODA	official development assistance
OECD	Organisation for Economic Cooperation and Development
OHCHR	Office of the United Nations High Commissioner for Human Rights
OIOS	Office of Internal Oversight Services
OSCE	Organization for Security and Cooperation in Europe
PA	Palestinian Authority
PLO	Palestine Liberation Organization
SC	Security Council
UN	United Nations
UNAIDS	Joint United Nations Programme on HIV/AIDS
UNAMSIL	United Nations Mission in Sierra Leone
UNCTAD	United Nations Conference on Trade and Development
UNDCP	United Nations International Drug Control Programme
UNDOF	United Nations Disengagement Observer Force (Golan Heights)
UNDP	United Nations Development Programme
UNEP	United Nations Environment Programme
UNESCO	United Nations Educational, Scientific and Cultural Organization
UNFICYP	United Nations Peacekeeping Force in Cyprus
UNFPA	United Nations Population Fund
UNHCR	Office of the United Nations High Commissioner for Refugees
UNIC	United Nations Information Centre
UNICEF	United Nations Children's Fund
UNIDO	United Nations Industrial Development Organization
UNIFIL	United Nations Interim Force in Lebanon
UNIKOM	United Nations Iraq-Kuwait Observation Mission
UNMEE	United Nations Mission in Ethiopia and Eritrea
UNMIBH	United Nations Mission in Bosnia and Herzegovina
UNMIK	United Nations Interim Administration Mission in Kosovo
UNMOGIP	United Nations Military Observer Group in India and Pakistan
UNMOVIC	United Nations Monitoring, Verification and Inspection Commission
UNOMIG	United Nations Observer Mission in Georgia
UNOPS	United Nations Office for Project Services
UNRWA	United Nations Relief and Works Agency for Palestine Refugees in the Near East
UNTAET	United Nations Transitional Administration in East Timor
UNTSO	United Nations Truce Supervision Organization
UPU	Universal Postal Union
WFP	World Food Programme
WHO	World Health Organization
WIPO	World Intellectual Property Organization
WMO	World Meteorological Organization
WTO	World Trade Organization
YUN	*Yearbook of the United Nations*

EXPLANATORY NOTE ON DOCUMENTS

References in square brackets in each chapter of Parts One to Five of this volume give the symbols of the main documents issued in 2001 on the topic. The following is a guide to the principal document symbols:

A/- refers to documents of the General Assembly, numbered in separate series by session. Thus, A/56/- refers to documents issued for consideration at the fifty-sixth session, beginning with A/56/1. Documents of special and emergency special sessions are identified as A/S- and A/ES-, followed by the session number.

A/C.- refers to documents of the Assembly's Main Committees, e.g. A/C.1/- is a document of the First Committee, A/C.6/-, a document of the Sixth Committee. A/BUR/- refers to documents of the General Committee. A/AC.- documents are those of the Assembly's ad hoc bodies and A/CN.-, of its commissions; e.g. A/AC.105/- identifies documents of the Assembly's Committee on the Peaceful Uses of Outer Space, A/CN.4/-, of its International Law Commission. Assembly resolutions and decisions since the thirty-first (1976) session have been identified by two arabic numerals: the first indicates the session of adoption; the second, the sequential number in the series. Resolutions are numbered consecutively from 1 at each session. Decisions of regular sessions are numbered consecutively, from 301 for those concerned with elections and appointments, and from 401 for all other decisions. Decisions of special and emergency special sessions are numbered consecutively, from 11 for those concerned with elections and appointments, and from 21 for all other decisions.

E/- refers to documents of the Economic and Social Council, numbered in separate series by year. Thus, E/2001/- refers to documents issued for consideration by the Council at its 2001 sessions, beginning with E/2001/1. E/AC.-, E/C.- and E/CN.-, followed by identifying numbers, refer to documents of the Council's subsidiary ad hoc bodies, committees and commissions. For example, E/CN.5/- refers to documents of the Council's Commission for Social Development, E/C.2/-, to documents of its Committee on Non-Governmental Organizations. E/ICEF/- documents are those of the United Nations Children's Fund (UNICEF). Symbols for the Council's resolutions and decisions, since 1978, consist of two arabic numerals: the first indicates the year of adoption and the second, the sequential number in the series. There are two series: one for resolutions, beginning with 1 (resolution 2001/1); and one for decisions, beginning with 201 (decision 2001/201).

S/- refers to documents of the Security Council. Its resolutions are identified by consecutive numbers followed by the year of adoption in parentheses, beginning with resolution 1(1946).

ST/-, followed by symbols representing the issuing department or office, refers to documents of the United Nations Secretariat.

Documents of certain bodies bear special symbols, including the following:

ACC/-	Administrative Committee on Coordination
CD/-	Conference on Disarmament
CERD/-	Committee on the Elimination of Racial Discrimination
DC/-	Disarmament Commission
DP/-	United Nations Development Programme
HS/-	Commission on Human Settlements
ITC/-	International Trade Centre
TD/-	United Nations Conference on Trade and Development
UNEP/-	United Nations Environment Programme

Many documents of the regional commissions bear special symbols. These are sometimes preceded by the following:

E/ECA/-	Economic Commission for Africa
E/ECE/-	Economic Commission for Europe
E/ECLAC/-	Economic Commission for Latin America and the Caribbean
E/ESCAP/-	Economic and Social Commission for Asia and the Pacific
E/ESCWA/-	Economic and Social Commission for Western Asia

"L" in a symbol refers to documents of limited distribution, such as draft resolutions; "CONF." to documents of a conference; "INF." to those of general information. Summary records are designated by "SR.", verbatim records by "PV.", each followed by the meeting number.

United Nations sales publications each carry a sales number with the following components separated by periods: a capital letter indicating the language(s) of the publication; two arabic numerals indicating the year; a Roman numeral indicating the subject category; a capital letter indicating a subdivision of the category, if any; and an arabic numeral indicating the number of the publication within the category. Examples: E.01.II.A.2; E/F/R.01.II.E.7; E.01.X.1.

Report of the Secretary-General

Report of the Secretary-General on the work of the Organization

*Following is the Secretary-General's report on the work of the Organization, submitted to the fifty-sixth session of the General Assembly. The Assembly took note of it on 26 September (**decision 56/404**). On 24 December, the Assembly decided that the agenda item would remain for consideration during the resumed fifty-sixth (2002) session (**decision 56/464**).*

Introduction

1. My annual report on the work of the Organization reviews the efforts of the United Nations to find constructive solutions to the fundamental problems of our age. It is a sober recognition of the complexities of the tasks facing the Organization. At the same time, it underlines the enduring significance of the United Nations as an instrument of global cooperation for the common good.

2. The dawn of the new millennium brought an historic reaffirmation by Member States of the purposes and principles of their Organization. At the Millennium Summit, held from 6 to 8 September 2000 in New York, 147 heads of State and Government, and 189 Member States in total, adopted the Millennium Declaration, pledging their collective responsibility to uphold the principles of human dignity, equality and equity at the global level. In my report to the General Assembly entitled "Road map towards the implementation of the Millennium Declaration", I offer a programme for meeting those ambitious objectives.

3. One of the United Nations strengths is its capacity to adjust to changing international conditions. We must preserve this tradition of innovation while maintaining the principles of the Charter, which have guided the Organization for 56 years. We must prepare for the possibilities of the future and meet the new demands made on the United Nations.

4. During the past year, we have witnessed striking contrasts on the international scene, both encouraging developments and dangerous threats. These mixed global trends are a reminder that the pursuit of international peace and progress requires the sustained commitment and engagement of the community of nations.

5. Today, universal ideas—the sovereignty of the people, accountability of leaders, individual rights and the rule of law—are spreading around the world. Yet there is no guarantee that these values will not be reversed, and that some nations will not once again succumb to tyranny and oppression.

6. The chapters of this report present a comprehensive review of the various activities of the United Nations system in pursuit of common objectives. The United Nations role in peace and security remains an essential part of its global responsibilities. Conflict prevention is of critical importance and requires a comprehensive understanding of the underlying causes and dynamics of violent conflict. The Organization's authority as a credible instrument to prevent conflict depends on its capacity to address the root causes of deadly conflict.

7. The United Nations is about much more than peace and security. The value of the Organization in providing humanitarian assistance to the vulnerable in natural disasters and complex emergencies has frequently been affirmed.

8. As I have stressed often, development co-operation is a solid foundation on which to build stability, economic justice and social development. The nature and scope of the development challenge will require an unprecedented level of financial commitment and international co-operation. The United Nations has assisted in developing policies and tools to tackle the problems involved and to construct the building blocks of sustainable peace.

9. The quest of the United Nations to build a world of order and justice can be achieved only through respect for the rule of law in international affairs. The growth of international law, the ratification of international treaties and the

prosecution of war criminals by international tribunals will help to ensure that ruthless force does not prevail.

10. Management reform within the United Nations should always be viewed as a work in progress in which constant efforts are made to enhance the Organization's effectiveness, efficiency and relevance.

11. In an increasingly globalized world, none of the critical issues we are dealing with can be resolved within a solely national framework. All of them require cooperation, partnership and burden-sharing among Governments, the United Nations, regional organizations, nongovernmental organizations, the private sector and civil society. The United Nations has made important efforts to forge global partnerships to promote the international interest, but we need to reach out still further.

12. On 29 June 2001, Member States did me great honour in appointing me to a second term as Secretary-General. We have achieved a great deal over the past five years. I firmly believe, however, that we can and must do better.

13. The United Nations is an embodiment of the will of humankind to defeat violence with the power of reason and to achieve some betterment of the human condition. Its Member States work together to make principle and justice prevail in world affairs. I am confident that, with the active support of Member States and the peoples of the world, the United Nations will fulfil its promise as an indispensable institution for international cooperation.

10 September 2001

On 11 September, less than 24 hours after my annual report was issued, our host city was subjected to a cold-blooded and vicious terrorist attack. I wish to express my profound sympathy to the victims, to their loved ones and to the people and Government of the United States. Terrorist acts are never justified. I condemn these deliberate acts of terrorism and those who planned and carried them out in the strongest possible terms.

14 September 2001

Chapter I

Achieving peace and security

14. The United Nations activities in peace and security have been conducted against a background of suffering caused by virulent conflicts across the world. These conflicts involve a preponderance of civilian rather than combatant victims, many of them women and children; massive movements of refugees and internally displaced persons; increasingly complex (though widely varying) conflict-sustaining economies; and a ready access to weapons of all kinds, particularly small arms, which have a devastating impact on people and societies throughout the world. Such conflicts threaten stability, undermine human security, inflict suffering on many millions of people and damage local and regional economies, infrastructures and the environment, in ways that will have consequences for decades to come.

15. The United Nations has an obligation to prevent the outbreak of armed conflict wherever and whenever possible. To this end, I have reinforced my efforts to move the United Nations from a culture of reaction to one of prevention. In June 2001, I submitted a major report on the prevention of armed conflict to the General Assembly and the Security Council (A/55/985-S/2001/574 and Corr.1), in which I reviewed the progress that has been achieved in developing the capacity of the United Nations to prevent conflict and presented specific recommendations to enhance the efforts of the United Nations system in this field.

16. Where the United Nations is involved in peacekeeping or peace-building, preventing the recurrence of conflict is a central priority. In most cases today, our mandates for peacekeeping extend beyond the classic missions of the past, where lightly armed forces were interposed between armies, and involve providing assistance to local authorities in a wide range of areas. They may include humanitarian relief and mine action; disarmament, demobilization and reintegration of combatants; training of the police and judiciary; monitoring human rights; providing electoral assistance; and strengthening national institutions to ensure that future problems can be resolved by democratic means without recourse to violence. In East Timor and the Federal Republic of Yugoslavia, where the United Nations heads transitional administrations, our responsibilities are still greater.

17. The field operations that conduct this broad array of tasks rely upon the support structures of the United Nations Secretariat to achieve their goals. As was ably documented by the report of the Panel on United Nations Peace Operations (A/55/305-S/2000/809), the current structures came into being through improvisation. In many respects they are insufficient, or poorly adapted to real needs. While many peacekeeping successes have been achieved, those involved have often had to make enormous efforts to overcome the deficiencies of existing structures.

18. As a result of the findings of the Panel on Peace Operations, the international community has begun to work towards the creation of secure and adequate foundations for an effective structure to support United Nations peace operations. Part of my own contribution has been to submit to the General Assembly a comprehensive review of all the elements within the Secretariat that play a role in peacekeeping operations (A/55/977). I have also charged my staff with the preparation of a draft plan of action on peace-building. The plan, now being finalized, is a practical guide for the United Nations system on how Headquarters can best support colleagues in the field in the formulation and implementation of coherent peace-building strategies.

19. In this respect, I warmly endorse the observation made by the President of the Security Council in his statement of 20 February 2001 that "a well-planned and coordinated peace-building strategy can play a significant role in conflict prevention" (S/PRST/2001/5). I welcome the Security Council's growing interest in the protection of civilians, in particular of women and children, and its focused attention on issues such as HIV/AIDS. We have learned that, within the United Nations system, efforts to prevent conflict and to keep and build peace must be driven by realities in the field, underpinned by rigorous situation analysis, and sustained by timely and targeted support from Headquarters as well as adequate resources from Member States. I am optimistic that the efforts made in the last year to lay out our requirements for achieving peace and security will contribute substantially to achieving the pledges made in the Millennium Declaration, provided the necessary resources are made available by Member States.

Conflict prevention and peacemaking

20. While comprehensive and coherent conflict prevention strategies offer the greatest potential for promoting lasting peace, they have never been easy to formulate or to implement. I have been gratified to note that in recent years Member States are turning increasing attention and providing more assistance to conflict prevention. For the United Nations, the concept of conflict prevention must be put into practice, and the rhetoric matched by action.

21. My report on the prevention of armed conflict contains concrete recommendations to enhance the effectiveness of various United Nations organs, bodies, agencies and Secretariat departments and to strengthen cooperation between the United Nations, regional organizations, non-governmental organizations and civil society in conflict prevention. It underlines that

the development and humanitarian agencies of the United Nations system, together with the Bretton Woods institutions, have a vital role to play in creating a peaceful environment, as well as in addressing the root causes of conflicts at the early stages of prevention. I intend to continue dispatching United Nations interdisciplinary fact-finding and confidence-building missions to volatile regions; to start submitting periodic regional or subregional reports to the Security Council on disputes that may potentially threaten international peace and security; to develop regional prevention strategies with regional partners, and organs and agencies of the United Nations, as appropriate; to establish an informal network of eminent persons for conflict prevention; and to improve the capacity and resource base for preventive action in the Secretariat. I look forward to constructive dialogue with Member States on the contributions that we may make together in the effort to ensure that a culture of prevention takes root in the international community.

22. In West Africa, the United Nations has intensified its partnership with the countries of the region. Collectively, we have concentrated on identifying potential threats to peace and are cooperating to prevent such challenges from deteriorating into violent conflict. This was the goal of the multidisciplinary missions I sent to the Gambia in November 2000 and to West Africa in March 2001. The Gambia's international partners have since undertaken to work closely with the country, within the framework of an integrated preventive strategy, to help strengthen the Gambia's capacity to avert a worsening of conditions. As a result of the second mission, a United Nations Office in West Africa will be established, headed by a Special Representative. The office will aim to enhance the United Nations capacity for monitoring, early warning and conflict prevention in the subregion and work closely with the Economic Community of West African States (ECOWAS) and other partners.

23. In an effort to expand the benefits of an integrated regional approach, I dispatched senior envoys to the Central African Republic and Côte d'Ivoire at moments when the two countries faced acute tension and friction late in 2000. Their respective efforts gave us a more detailed understanding of the situation. The International Commission of Inquiry for Côte d'Ivoire, which I set up at the request of the Government to look into the violence that followed the presidential elections held on 22 October 2000, has completed its work. Its mission was to facilitate justice and prevent impunity, and also to promote healing and reconciliation within Ivorian

society. In December 2000, I sent my Special Envoy to assess the impact of the conflict in the Democratic Republic of the Congo on two of its immediate neighbours, the Central African Republic and the Republic of the Congo. The mission was also designed as a confidence-building measure to promote cooperation among the countries concerned in addressing common challenges along their shared borders.

24. The Millennium Declaration called for enhanced institutional cooperation between the United Nations and regional and subregional organizations. The utility of such an approach has been demonstrated in West Africa. Nowhere was this more evident than in the Mano River basin, where the United Nations, in collaboration with the three Mano River Union countries and ECOWAS, actively participated in addressing complex humanitarian, political and security situations affecting Guinea, Liberia and Sierra Leone. I have particularly supported ECOWAS initiatives to promote dialogue among the three countries, in the belief that, without such dialogue, efforts to address the root causes of the subregion's problems will remain insufficient and ineffective. Since the imposition of sanctions in May 2001, I have also stressed the importance of remaining engaged with Liberia in the pursuit of durable peace in the subregion.

25. Elsewhere in Africa, impetus was given to efforts to resolve two long-standing conflicts. In Burundi, the signing of the Arusha Agreement on Peace and Reconciliation on 28 August 2000 brought new momentum to the peace process. As stipulated in the Agreement, an Implementation Monitoring Committee was established under United Nations chairmanship to follow up, monitor, supervise, coordinate and ensure the effective implementation of all provisions of the Agreement. I appointed my Special Representative for the Great Lakes region as its chairman. The issue of the transitional leadership has since been resolved and a transitional government is expected to be established on 1 November 2001. However, the absence of a ceasefire remains an impediment to the implementation of the Arusha Agreement. I remain hopeful that the negotiations between the armed rebel groups and the Government of Burundi, facilitated by the Deputy President of South Africa, Jacob Zuma, on behalf of former President Nelson Mandela, will soon prove successful.

26. The establishment of the Transitional National Government of Somalia, as a result of the Djibouti initiative, and its move to Mogadishu in October 2000, marked an important step in the effort to end the conflict in Somalia. Unfortunately, the lack of progress in completing the peace process and the precarious security situation in much of Somalia have so far prevented me from recommending to the Security Council the establishment of a United Nations peace-building mission in the country. We remain ready to assist whenever conditions permit and I urge the international community to remain engaged in the search for an end to Somalia's long nightmare.

27. I cannot report significant changes in Angola, where the war continues to cause intense suffering. The Government has indicated a willingness to resume dialogue with UNITA with a view to completing the remaining tasks under the Lusaka Protocol. Both sides have reiterated their commitment to the Lusaka Protocol, although they continue to disagree on how to complete its implementation. My Adviser for Special Assignments in Africa continues to pay special attention to Angola. The United Nations remains ready to assist the Government and others concerned to end the war, and to provide technical assistance for the elections to be held in 2002 and maintain its programmes of humanitarian relief and capacity-building in the field of human rights.

28. In the Middle East, the deteriorating situation in the region, resulting in the worst crisis since the signing of the Oslo Agreement in 1993, remains a source of great concern for the international community. The outbreak of violence in the occupied Palestinian territory and in Israel late in September 2000 has brought extensive loss of life and serious decline in the economic conditions on both sides, as well as a devastating deterioration in the humanitarian situation of the Palestinians. In view of the gravity of the situation and its negative implications for international peace and security, I have devoted much of my personal attention to this issue. I have maintained close and regular contacts with the parties and other leaders in the region and the international community to find a way forward. I visited the region in October 2000 to explore avenues to end the violence and to revive the peace process. I worked with the parties and the leaders of the United States of America, the European Union, Egypt and Jordan to reach an understanding at the Sharm el-Sheikh Summit on the steps required to end the confrontation. The report of the Sharm el-Sheikh Fact-finding Committee, known as the Mitchell report, which was released in April, provided a viable basis for a return to the negotiating table, and I fully endorsed its recommendations. In June 2001, I went again to the Middle East to encourage the parties to consolidate the ceasefire agreement and move towards full implementation of the Mitchell report.

29. The conflict between Israelis and Palestinians can be resolved only through a political settlement. To this end, I once again urge both sides to end violence, adhere to the security agreements already agreed upon and restart a viable political process leading to peace and reconciliation.

30. The dramatic developments during the year under review and the tragic loss of life have underlined the urgency of reaching a comprehensive, just and lasting solution to the Middle East conflict on the basis of Security Council resolutions 242(1967) and 338(1973).

31. In view of Iraq's continuing non-compliance with Security Council resolutions, in particular resolution 1284(1999), the United Nations Monitoring, Verification and Inspection Commission has not been deployed. It remains a great concern that, since December 1998, the United Nations has not been able to verify Iraq's adherence to Security Council resolutions regarding weapons of mass destruction. Moreover, Iraq continues its non-cooperation with the High-level Coordinator, who is seeking to repatriate all Kuwaiti and third-country nationals and secure the return of Kuwaiti property. I deeply regret the continuing suffering of the Iraqi people and share their hopes that sanctions can be lifted sooner rather than later. While I am prepared to resume my dialogue with the Government of Iraq, a first round of which was held in February 2001, Iraq must reconsider its non-cooperation with the Security Council if it wishes to make progress towards an eventual lifting of the sanctions.

32. Little or no progress has been made towards ending the conflict in Afghanistan, despite the tireless efforts of my Personal Representative to bring the warring parties to the negotiating table. In the year under review, a severe drought has added to the woes of the Afghan people and the humanitarian crisis now afflicting the country has contributed to a sense of hopelessness, further aggravating the plight of Afghan civilians, particularly women and girls, under the harsh policies of the Taliban regime. This conflict, like so many others we face around the world, cannot be considered in isolation from its regional context. A solution can be advanced only with the active and coordinated support of neighbouring States, especially the Islamic Republic of Iran and Pakistan, and other members of the "six plus two" group of countries. A more coordinated approach by the international community will be required if significant progress in addressing the problems of Afghanistan is to be achieved.

33. Over the past two years, sporadic fighting, including hostage-taking, initiated by extremist and terrorist forces, has affected some countries in Central Asia. These isolated but worrisome developments are related in part to the situation in Afghanistan and in part to other factors such as deteriorating economic conditions and the resulting social tensions. In cooperation with Member States in the region and other interested parties, the United Nations is prepared to offer assistance in the political, developmental and humanitarian fields in order to address the root causes of instability.

34. In March 2001, I visited several countries in South Asia. In my meetings with the leaders of India and Pakistan, I urged them to resume their bilateral dialogue with a view to reducing tensions in the region, including Kashmir. I was greatly encouraged that the leaders of India and Pakistan held a summit meeting at Agra in July. I hope that the useful discussions held there will continue and develop into a sustained dialogue. While I remain concerned at the unresolved civil war in Sri Lanka, I hope that the good offices of Norway will soon result in the initiation of peace talks.

35. In East Asia, I am pleased to report that a peaceful settlement of the conflict in Bougainville has been reached. Following talks between the Government of Papua New Guinea and the Bougainville parties, facilitated by the United Nations Political Office in Bougainville, a comprehensive agreement covering the issues of autonomy, referendum and weapons disposal was reached on 22 June 2001. The involvement of regional countries and the consistent support of the Security Council were crucial to the achievement of this agreement.

36. In the implementation of the mandate entrusted to me by the General Assembly, my Special Envoy and I have continued to encourage the Government of Myanmar to engage in a substantive dialogue with Daw Aung San Suu Kyi in order to achieve national reconciliation and to return the country to democratic rule. During the year under review, a number of steps have been taken to build confidence between the two sides. The United Nations is committed to continuing to facilitate the dialogue and looks forward to further progress.

37. Together with relevant agencies and programmes of the United Nations system, I intend to enhance our efforts to assist Indonesia as it seeks to establish a democratic society and to address the wide range of complex issues facing the country. It is my firm belief that Indonesia's territorial integrity can best be assured by adherence to democratic norms and the promotion of

human rights. To this end, efforts should be made to support the reform process that the Government is implementing, as well as to help find peaceful resolutions to the problems in regions such as Aceh, Maluku and West Papua.

38.   I shall also continue to search for ways and means to contribute to inter-Korean rapprochement and other positive developments in the region. I believe that the international community should take active measures to foster peace and stability in this region and urge Member States to consider further support for promoting dialogue, trust and reconciliation on the peninsula.

39.   In Europe, proximity talks on Cyprus with the parties, led by Glafcos Clerides and Rauf Denktash, proceeded under my auspices until November 2000. However, Mr. Denktash asked that no date be set for talks early in 2001. Although it was not possible to resume talks immediately, my Special Adviser continued to hold consultations with a number of Governments and organizations, making preparations to be of further assistance to the parties at the appropriate time. Late in August, I met Mr. Denktash at Salzburg with a view to moving towards an early resumption of the process.

40.   My Special Representative for Georgia, in cooperation with the Russian Federation as facilitator, the members of the group of Friends of the Secretary-General for Georgia, and the Organization for Security and Cooperation in Europe, has continued his efforts to pursue a comprehensive settlement of the Georgian/Abkhaz conflict. The two sides were able to agree on a series of concrete confidence-building steps at the Third High-level Meeting on Confidence-building Measures, which was held at Yalta in March 2001 at the invitation of the Government of Ukraine.

41.   In Latin America, my Special Adviser on International Assistance to Colombia maintained regular contacts in Colombia and abroad. Peace talks between the Government and the two largest guerrilla groups proceeded intermittently throughout the year. Nevertheless, the violence intensified, resulting in frequent violations of human rights and in growing numbers of internally displaced persons. Analysts have warned that fighting, displacement and drug cultivation are likely to increase and spread further beyond the borders of Colombia. The United Nations stands ready, at the request of the parties to the conflict, to assist further in promoting a peaceful resolution. It is my hope that the parties will take urgent measures to cease violence against the unarmed civilian population and to ensure full respect for human rights and international humanitarian law. I also remain concerned at the adverse environmental effects that the cultivation of drug crops, the processing of narcotics and forced eradication efforts have had. The combination of counter-narcotics and counter-insurgency efforts poses the risk of a regional arms race and could lead to a spread of fighting, displacement and drug cultivation beyond the borders of Colombia.

Peacekeeping and peace-building

42.   While the conflicts that United Nations peacekeeping operations seek to address are complex and daunting, I am gratified to report that the international community has shown a renewed appreciation for the value of United Nations peacekeeping, a determination to acknowledge openly and learn from peacekeeping failures and successes, and an increased commitment to give peacekeepers the tools and resources they need to accomplish their missions.

43.   The key factors for successful peacekeeping remain the will of parties on the ground; realistic mandates based on a well-understood and common overall strategy; and readiness to support those mandates politically and through the provision of appropriate human and material resources. To have a lasting impact, peacekeeping must be supported and accompanied by a process of peace-building, to prevent the recurrence of armed conflict and permit recovery and development.

44.   Over the past year, the Secretariat has sought to lay secure and adequate foundations for an effective peacekeeping structure while providing daily direction and support to the operations in the field. The report of the Panel on Peace Operations and its subsequent endorsement by the Millennium Summit gave this reform process, rooted in an ongoing dialogue with Member States, renewed focus and momentum. My initial report on the implementation of the Panel's recommendations, presented in October 2000, offered a number of practical measures to support the broad objectives identified by the Panel. Member States responded positively to many of my suggestions and provided significant additional resources to the Secretariat for peacekeeping. They also requested more detail in a number of areas, however, and underlined their interest in a further, comprehensive review of the Secretariat's peacekeeping capacity. In response, on 1 June 2001, I issued a second report (A/55/977).

45.   My second report adopted the comprehensive approach requested by Member States, and proposed further steps for improving peacekeeping capacity. These included proposals for enhancing the Secretariat's planning capacity at

three levels—strategic, policy and operational—in order to move from a reactive mode towards advanced planning. In addition, I outlined measures to develop a more effective relationship between Headquarters and the field; to ensure a closer collaboration between the Department of Peacekeeping Operations and other departments in the Secretariat engaged in supporting peacekeeping; to enhance logistical support for operations in order to achieve the 30-day to 90-day time frames for deployment recommended by the Panel on Peace Operations; to develop within the Secretariat a more effective capacity for analysis that can draw upon the wealth of information available from open sources and from within the Organization; and to improve the safety and security of peacekeepers in the field.

46. Implementation of these reforms will make demands upon the Secretariat and on Member States. Some of the measures proposed will require immediate investment for future benefits, while others will require political compromise. Nonetheless, I am convinced that their adoption will improve our capacity to respond to the demands that will be made of us.

47. In addition to underlining the need to enhance United Nations peacekeeping capacity, the Member States resolved, in the section of the Millennium Declaration on meeting the special needs of Africa, "to encourage and sustain regional and subregional mechanisms for preventing conflict and promoting political stability, and to ensure a reliable flow of resources for peacekeeping operations on the continent".

48. While African States and regional and subregional organizations have shown a growing interest in playing a role in peacekeeping operations in Africa, the limited resources available to them continue to be a major impediment. Support for building African peacekeeping capacity can take the form of assistance to specific operations or of incremental steps to enhance capability—for example, provision by the international community of information, expertise and logistical and financial resources. The Secretariat's efforts in this regard have included cooperation with the Organization of African Unity, the Economic Community of West African States, the Southern African Development Community and, more recently, the Economic Community of Central African States in areas such as training, information-sharing, staff exchanges and participation in regional peacekeeping exercises, as well as the strengthening of the United Nations standby arrangements system and mine action programmes. The Secretariat has also continued to facilitate contacts between African troop contributors to United Nations operations and do-

nor States, and to promote agreement between African and non-African States regarding assistance.

49. The international community should be conscious, however, that efforts to enhance African peacekeeping capacity cannot become a justification for reduced engagement in the continent. Support by non-African States for peacemaking and peacekeeping efforts in Africa, including deployment of peacekeeping troops, will remain essential in the foreseeable future. The experience of United Nations peacekeeping operations in Africa during the year under review demonstrates this most vividly.

50. In the Democratic Republic of the Congo, President Laurent-Désiré Kabila was succeeded in January 2001 by his son, General Joseph Kabila. Since then, the situation has undergone a marked change. The ceasefire under the Lusaka Agreement was re-established and has remained in force without major violations. Deployment of the United Nations Organization Mission in the Democratic Republic of the Congo (MONUC) has continued without incident. Prospects also improved on the political front after President Joseph Kabila invited Sir Ketumile Masire to resume his work as facilitator of the inter-Congolese dialogue, upon which peace and stability in the country depend.

51. MONUC is now entering the phase of the implementation of the Lusaka Ceasefire Agreement during which all foreign forces should be withdrawn from the Democratic Republic of the Congo and the armed groups disarmed, demobilized and reintegrated or repatriated. The Security Council has authorized the expansion of the civilian components of MONUC to enable it to play a larger role, particularly in the political, humanitarian, human rights and child-protection areas. This is an important development as the humanitarian problems faced by the country, all of them exacerbated by the conflict, are very serious. Some 16 million people are affected by severe shortages of food; millions of children suffer from malnutrition; more than a third of the population lacks access to even basic medical care, and half has no access to clean water; and serious violations of human rights continue to be reported throughout the country.

52. In implementing its peacekeeping mandate in Sierra Leone and in cooperation with regional leaders, the United Nations has continued to pursue a dual-track approach, combining credible military pressure with constructive political dialogue. With the recent arrival of additional troops, the United Nations Mission in Sierra Leone (UNAMSIL) has consolidated its presence in nearly all parts of the country. Con-

siderable progress has been made in the implementation of the Agreement on the Ceasefire and Cessation of Hostilities between the Government and the Revolutionary United Front (RUF), signed at Abuja in November 2000, as a result of a number of follow-up meetings between the parties, UNAMSIL and ECOWAS. The ceasefire has held, and over 13,000 combatants from both pro-Government forces and RUF were disarmed from May to August 2001 under a disarmament, demobilization and reintegration programme. Peace consolidation and confidence-building measures taken by the Government have included the release of some RUF detainees and other steps to help facilitate the transformation of RUF into a political party. In July 2001, the Government indicated its intention to seek Parliamentary approval for a second six-month extension of its current term of office, which will expire at the end of September 2001. The Government has just announced an indefinite postponement of elections. In the area of addressing impunity and promoting reconciliation, planning for the establishment of the Special Court and a Truth and Reconciliation Commission is under way. As the deployment of UNAMSIL nears completion and the disarmament, demobilization and reintegration programme makes further progress, the Government will be expected to step up its efforts to extend its authority across the country, particularly in the diamond-producing areas. Sustained international support remains vital to the success of the disarmament, demobilization and reintegration process. Moreover, the underlying political problems of the country, which the civil war has exacerbated, will need to be addressed by the Government and people of Sierra Leone.

53. The United Nations Mission in Ethiopia and Eritrea (UNMEE) was launched in September 2000, and has played a key role in helping the two countries emerge from their tragic and destructive war. The tasks of the peacekeepers include the monitoring of the ceasefire, verification of the redeployment of Ethiopian and Eritrean troops, establishment of mine and unexploded ordnance clearance operations, and monitoring of a Temporary Security Zone between the two countries in accordance with the Agreement on Cessation of Hostilities signed at Algiers on 18 June 2000. A second Agreement, reached on 12 December 2000, provided for the establishment of a Boundary Commission to delimit and demarcate the common border and so resolve the border dispute which was the immediate cause of the war. The conclusion of the delimitation and demarcation of the border will lead to termination of the peacekeeping mission. The Boundary Commission has now been formally constituted, and it has agreed to a tentative timeline for the first phase of its work, namely, the delimitation of the border.

54. The search for a mutually acceptable solution between the parties in Western Sahara remained the focus of the United Nations efforts to overcome the multiple problems impeding implementation of the settlement plan. After meeting with officials of the Government of Morocco to determine if Morocco, as the administrative Power in Western Sahara, was prepared to offer or support some devolution of authority to the Territory that would be substantial and in keeping with international norms, my Personal Envoy presented a draft framework agreement on the status of Western Sahara to the Frente POLISARIO and to the Government of Algeria. In view of the adoption of resolution 1359(2001) by the Security Council, the parties are expected to meet directly or through proximity talks under the auspices of my Personal Envoy to discuss the draft framework agreement and negotiate specific changes to the document, and to discuss any other proposal for a political solution, that may be put forward by the parties, in order to arrive at a mutually acceptable agreement. The official proposals submitted by the Frente POLISARIO to overcome the obstacles to the implementation of the settlement plan will also be considered.

55. The situation along the border between Israel and Lebanon is volatile. While the situation over the past year along the withdrawal line, or "Blue Line", was generally calm, there were tensions and serious breaches of the line connected to the dispute over the Shab'a farms area. The Government of Lebanon has yet to take all the necessary steps to ensure the return of its effective authority throughout the south down to the Blue Line, where the activities of armed elements keep the situation unstable. Persistent Israeli violations of Lebanese airspace have created additional tension. The Security Council has repeatedly called for all parties concerned to respect fully the Blue Line, most recently in resolution 1365(2001).

56. The functions of the United Nations Interim Force in Lebanon are now largely those of an observer mission. Accordingly, the Force has commenced a reconfiguration exercise and is reducing its numbers.

57. The United Nations Mission in Bosnia and Herzegovina (UNMIBH) has made important strides in ensuring that its core police reforms will be completed by the end of the Mission's mandate. Registration of the country's 24,007 police personnel was completed in May 2001, while final certification with appropriate background checks continues. The Mission's police

training programmes are nearing conclusion. The Mission also issued a new policy for monitoring police performance. In response to incidents of mob violence, UNMIBH has taken the lead in establishing training support units, and is seeking to obtain anti-riot equipment. However, the percentage of minority representation in the local police force remains very low. The Mission is in need of donor assistance to meet minority police representation targets in both entities.

58. In the second year of its mandate, the United Nations Interim Administration Mission in Kosovo (UNMIK) has focused on the progressive transfer of public administration responsibilities to local control. Steps to ensure this were the holding of municipal elections in October 2000 and my Special Representative's promulgation, early in 2001, of a Constitutional Framework for Provisional Self-Government. This has paved the way for the Kosovo-wide elections that will be held on 17 November 2001. UNMIK continues to encourage all communities, particularly the Kosovo Serb community, to participate in the existing UNMIK-led structures and is urging them to register for elections. With a view to strengthening law and order, one of the major challenges in Kosovo, UNMIK established a new pillar,[1] which combines UNMIK police and the Department of Judicial Affairs into a single structure.

59. UNMIK continues to face critical challenges, such as the protection of the rights of all communities, the return of refugees and internally displaced persons, the issue of the missing and detainees, the adoption of confidence-building measures vis-à-vis the Kosovo Serb community, the development of constructive dialogue with the authorities of the Federal Republic of Yugoslavia, the fight against terrorism and organized crime, and the impact of the deteriorating security situation in the former Yugoslav Republic of Macedonia.

60. The serious threat posed by mines and unexploded ordnance in Kosovo is being successfully addressed and mitigated; mine action operations are moving towards implementation of an exit strategy in the coming year.

61. The situation in the former Yugoslav Republic of Macedonia is a source of grave concern. The country is riven by an ethnic conflict that threatens to spiral into civil war. The recent crisis, which began last February with a military campaign by ethnic Albanian armed groups, is a result of festering inter-ethnic demographic

---

[1] The pillars of UNMIK are police and justice (United Nations); civil adminstration (United Nations); institution-building (Organization for Security and Cooperation in Europe); and reconstruction (European Union), each pillar relying on the capabilities and expertise of the lead organization.

pressures, internal political dynamics and the links between the former Yugoslav Republic of Macedonia and its neighbours, including Kosovo. The crisis is continuing, despite several cessation of hostilities agreements and mediation efforts by the European Union and the North Atlantic Treaty Organization, which remains in the lead. These efforts have my personal support. The Security Council remains seized of the situation in the former Yugoslav Republic of Macedonia. I have continued to exchange views on the situation while exploring areas where the United Nations may be of assistance.

62. I reported last year that positive developments on the ground had allowed for two peacekeeping operations, in Tajikistan and the Central African Republic, to be closed down and replaced with smaller peace-building support offices. These offices, like others in Africa and in Guatemala, have continued to lead United Nations efforts to consolidate peace and promote democratization and the rule of law.

63. The United Nations Tajikistan Office of Peace-building (UNTOP) provides a political framework and leadership for a variety of peace-building activities in Tajikistan. Together with the country team, in particular the United Nations Development Programme (UNDP), the Office has made a significant contribution to mobilizing international support for programmes that create employment and train former irregular fighters as part of their reintegration into civilian life. In May 2001, UNTOP, UNDP and the World Bank convened a successful donor conference in Tokyo, where pledges exceeded $400 million.

64. Working in close cooperation with Governments and civil society, the three United Nations post-conflict peace-building support offices currently operating in Africa, in the Central African Republic, Guinea-Bissau and Liberia, are trying to create an enabling political environment for addressing the post-conflict priorities facing the three countries and their fragile democratic institutions. This includes providing the political framework and leadership for integrating the peace-building activities of the United Nations country team, mobilizing international assistance to address pressing economic and social problems, and promoting national reconciliation and dialogue and strengthening local capacities for managing crises. Efforts continue to assist the rebuilding of the judiciary and the legislature, in promoting the rule of law and respect for human rights, and enhancing relations between each country and its neighbours.

65. The United Nations Verification Mission in Guatemala (MINUGUA) has continued to verify compliance with the peace agreements reached

in 1996. The President of Guatemala has frequently reiterated his Government's commitment to the peace process. Yet implementation of the agreements continues to face numerous obstacles and pending commitments have been rescheduled until the end of 2004. In a context of increasing polarization, MINUGUA has encouraged political alliances around the peace agenda in order to foster cooperation between the Government and civil society. At my request, my Chief of Staff travelled to Guatemala recently to underline my concern about the faltering peace process. He expressed my hope that the Government and influential sectors of civil society, specifically the private sector, would enter into a constructive dialogue to overcome the growing polarization in the country. I am convinced that at this political juncture it is necessary to mobilize all efforts to ensure the irreversibility of the peace process. However, unless the Government assumes ownership of and leads that process, democracy in Guatemala will remain fragile and social discontent may increase. While the United Nations will continue to support the implementation of the peace agreements, it cannot and should not become a substitute for the social and political commitments required of Guatemalans to build their future.

66. The International Civilian Support Mission in Haiti (MICAH) has faced serious obstacles during this year. In my final report on the Mission (A/55/905), the mandate of which ended on 6 February 2001, I provided a sobering assessment of the situation in the country and expressed my hope that the Government and the opposition would enter into a political dialogue aimed at reconciliation. For the post-MICAH period, the United Nations has put in place a comprehensive transition programme coordinated by UNDP. The programme emphasizes human rights, favours consensus-building and conflict reduction, and seeks strong civil society participation. Since the closure of MICAH, the Organization of American States (OAS) and the Caribbean Community (CARICOM) have taken the lead in international efforts to improve the prospects for negotiations between the Government and the opposition. I welcome the efforts of OAS at mediation and negotiation, and look forward to the outcome of its joint initiative with CARICOM.

67. The engagement of OAS in Haiti exemplifies the close cooperation and coordination of efforts between the United Nations and regional organizations that are required for peace-building. In order to further such cooperation, in February 2001, I convened the fourth high-level meeting between the United Nations and regional organizations on cooperation for peace-building. The meeting adopted a Framework for Cooperation in Peace-building, in which we agreed on guiding principles for cooperation in this field, as well as on possible joint activities.

68. In less than two years since its inception, the United Nations Transitional Administration in East Timor (UNTAET), in partnership with the East Timorese people and in close coordination with United Nations agencies, funds and programmes, has made considerable progress towards fulfilling the broad mandate entrusted to it by the Security Council to assist the country in its transition to self-government and to establish conditions for sustainable development, while ensuring security, law and order throughout the territory and providing humanitarian assistance. The 12 months under review have seen intensive activity. Through power-sharing arrangements with UNTAET, the East Timorese have gradually taken charge of government responsibilities. They have also been vested with executive power in a mixed international/Timorese Cabinet, and have exercised legislative responsibilities in an all-Timorese National Council.

69. On 15 September 2001, following the election on 30 August of a Constituent Assembly to prepare a Constitution for an independent and democratic East Timor, the country will enter the final transition phase, with the formation of a new and expanded all-Timorese Cabinet and the convening of the Constituent Assembly. If so decided by its members, the Constituent Assembly may in due course become the first legislature of an independent East Timor. Once the Constitution is approved and the necessary elections are held, perhaps early in 2002, East Timor will be ready to declare independence, with the Security Council's endorsement. Independence will not, however, precipitate East Timor's abandonment by the international community. Plans are under way for a possible United Nations mission to succeed UNTAET. This new mission would continue to provide a military and police presence and to assist the new Government in those areas that could not be consolidated during UNTAET.

70. I am aware of concern among Member States regarding the level of resources committed to this operation. I am also aware of the comprehensive responsibility the United Nations has assumed in East Timor. I therefore favour a prudent approach that seeks to safeguard the international community's considerable investment in East Timor's future. In the interest of effectiveness, and to ensure that the population of East Timor can build upon the investment made, I believe that once UNTAET is closed down, and after the independence of East Timor is declared, substantial international support should

continue to be provided, through an integrated and well-coordinated mission led by a Special Representative, mandated by the Security Council and funded from assessed contributions.

71. United Nations peace-building activities continue to be strengthened by increasingly dynamic cooperation and coordination across the system. This cooperation is perhaps best exemplified at the field level, where peace operations interact regularly with the different entities of the United Nations system engaged in peace-building and preventive work, including emergency operations led by the Office of the United Nations High Commissioner for Refugees and other relief agencies, and the long-term work of entities like UNDP. Work in the field of human rights is of particular importance for both early warning and peace-building. In this regard, cooperation with the Office of the United Nations High Commissioner for Human Rights by the human rights component of a peacekeeping operation or with the High Commissioner's own field presence is of paramount importance to the Organization's work.

Electoral assistance

72. Requests for United Nations electoral assistance have increased during the year under review. Major electoral missions were conducted in the Democratic Republic of the Congo, East Timor and Sierra Leone. In November 2000, local elections were successfully held in Kosovo, where area-wide elections are currently being prepared. Assistance to the Peruvian electoral process culminated in the completion of the second round of presidential voting early in June 2001.

73. Several elections that have been held during the past year suggest important progress towards democratization. In Côte d'Ivoire, the Federal Republic of Yugoslavia and Peru, incumbent regimes organized elections in the expectation that voters would simply renew their mandates as they had done in the past. In each case, the electorate voted out the regime or protested so strongly against attempts by the incumbents to remain in office that they eventually submitted their resignations. In the Philippines, popular protests spurred by allegations of corruption toppled the President. These examples suggest that public awareness of democratic rights—such as freedom of the press, the rule of law, and free and fair elections—is rising, and that citizens are beginning to act upon this awareness. They are holding their leaders accountable. Moreover in the era of globalization, when information moves instantaneously around the world, each instance of successful popular action reinforces and invigorates others.

74. This change has had important repercussions for United Nations electoral assistance. The emphasis on capacity-building will continue, but assistance will also be more specifically targeted to supporting particular institutions and stimulating greater local participation. In Nigeria, for example, an innovative project is providing encouragement and support to Nigerian civil society in designing and implementing civic education programmes.

Disarmament

75. In the Millennium Declaration, world leaders resolved to strive to eliminate weapons of mass destruction, particularly nuclear weapons, and to reduce the global risks posed by small arms and landmines. Uncertainties about the status of the strategic relationship between the leading nuclear-weapon Powers and continuing divergence of views among States on priorities and perspectives, however, continue to inform the debate and block further movement on global security and disarmament.

76. Global military expenditures have continued to rise, the increase occurring in some industrialized countries and in a number of developing countries. Although official development assistance levels have continued to fall during the year, military budgets have risen persistently. Conservative estimates suggest that annual military expenditures exceed $800 billion, or 80 per cent of average cold war global military expenditures.

77. The level of international cooperation in disarmament remains disappointingly low. This is especially evident in the Conference on Disarmament—a crucial part of the multilateral disarmament machinery—where in 2001 no consensus on a programme of work could be reached. I hope that the appointment by the Conference of three special coordinators will help to bring about some forward movement next year. Several multilateral agreements still await either entry into force or effective implementation. The historic agreements reached at the 2000 Review Conference of the Parties to the Treaty on the Non-Proliferation of Nuclear Weapons have yet to be fully realized.

78. Although 161 States have signed and 79 States have ratified the Comprehensive Nuclear-Test-Ban Treaty, the challenges that confront its entry into force still persist. At the request of the majority of the States parties, I have decided to convene the second Conference on Facilitating the Entry into Force of the Treaty, which will be held in New York from 25 to 27 September 2001. It is my hope that the prevailing global morato-

rium on nuclear testing will be strictly observed pending the Treaty's entry into force.

79. I am concerned that plans to deploy national missile defences threaten not only current bilateral and multilateral arms control agreements but also ongoing and future disarmament and non-proliferation efforts. In order to avert a new arms race, I encourage continuing consultation on these issues. Multilateral negotiations towards legally binding, irreversible and verifiable disarmament agreements are essential.

80. Multilaterally negotiated norms against missile proliferation would considerably reduce the threat posed by ballistic missiles armed with conventional weapons or weapons of mass destruction. At the General Assembly's request, I have convened a panel of governmental experts to review and report in 2002 on the issue of missiles in all its aspects.

81. Negotiations on a verification protocol to strengthen the Biological Weapons Convention, enhance its effectiveness and promote a higher degree of transparency have not led to agreement. It is expected that the work to strengthen the Convention will be addressed at the Fifth Review Conference of the Parties, scheduled to begin on 19 November 2001. The Chemical Weapons Convention has played a vital role in international efforts to eliminate the dangers posed by weapons of mass destruction, to curb their proliferation and to achieve their elimination. Increased effort is required to ensure the Convention's universality, and continued political and financial support for the Organization for the Prohibition of Chemical Weapons is vital to ensuring that its mandated tasks are effectively and efficiently carried out.

82. The dangerous global prevalence of small arms and light weapons has attracted increasing attention in recent years. The United Nations Conference on the Illicit Trade in Small Arms and Light Weapons in All Its Aspects, held from 9 to 20 July 2001, mobilized Governments, regional organizations, United Nations agencies, non-governmental organizations and civil society, and provided an historic opportunity for international debate on the illicit small arms trade. The Programme of Action, which was adopted by consensus, is a significant first step towards the goal of preventing, combating and eradicating the illicit trade in small arms and light weapons. It included guidelines for practical action at the national, regional and international levels. The Conference did not achieve consensus on all issues, however. I encourage Governments to continue work on those issues and urge Member States to act upon the key recommendations of the Conference.

83. Member States are increasingly requesting the Secretariat to implement practical disarmament measures in the context of peace-building efforts. Weapons collection projects and disarmament, demobilization and reintegration programmes have been developed in Africa, Asia, Europe and Latin America. Although a lack of adequate resources continues to hamper their work, regional centres for peace and disarmament have expanded their activities and initiated the provision of advisory and training services. Efforts are under way to seek more contributions from interested Member States in order to cope with growing requests for assistance.

84. Adherence to the amended Protocol II to the Convention on Certain Conventional Weapons has grown, the total number of States which have adhered to the amended Protocol II now being 58. An additional 12 countries acceded to or ratified the Convention on the Prohibition of Anti-personnel Mines, while States parties continued to work towards its implementation. It is estimated that production of landmines has all but ceased, transfer of anti-personnel landmines has sharply dropped, and existing stockpiles in many countries are steadily being destroyed. By the Second Meeting of States Parties to the Convention, in September 2000, 25 States parties had completed the destruction of their mines, and elimination was ongoing in 24 others.

Sanctions

85. The risk of adverse effects of sanctions on innocent populations or third parties highlights the tension inherent in the Organization's dual mandate to preserve international peace and to protect human needs. Sanctions should be forceful enough to persuade targeted leaders to move towards political compliance, but not so severe as to precipitate humanitarian distress that undermines the viability of the policy and of the instrument itself.

86. I welcome the continued development of the concept of targeted sanctions, evident in the sanctions measures that the Security Council has imposed during the year under review. In December 2000, by resolution 1333(2000), the Council extended the flight ban and added an arms embargo to the targeted financial sanctions previously imposed against the Taliban regime in Afghanistan. In March 2001, by resolution 1343 (2001), the Council imposed a travel ban and an embargo on diamonds from Liberia. In both cases, the Security Council sought to focus pressure on those responsible for behaviour that contravened international norms of peace and security, while minimizing the impact of its action on civilian populations and affected third States.

87. The recommendations of the Security Council informal Working Group on General Issues on Sanctions should prove a valuable contribution to the sanctions debate. In the meantime, I warmly welcome the continued use of investigative panels to document sanctions violations, including illicit arms trafficking and illegal sales of diamonds.

Chapter II

Meeting humanitarian commitments

88. Sadly, the turn of the millennium has not been accompanied by a reduction in the suffering caused by natural disasters and complex emergencies throughout the world. Protracted conflicts continue in Afghanistan, Angola, the Democratic Republic of the Congo, Somalia and the Sudan, while crises escalated or erupted in Burundi, Indonesia, Liberia and the former Yugoslav Republic of Macedonia, to mention several prominent examples. Vulnerable civilian populations continue to be deliberate targets of violence and to bear the brunt of the suffering caused by conflict. The deplorable attacks on humanitarian workers have also persisted. Heads and representatives of all 189 Member States paid tribute to those victims of violence at the Millennium Summit in New York in September 2000.

89. The scale and number of natural disasters continue to grow, escalating the demand for humanitarian assistance. During the past year, continuing drought in the Horn of Africa, Central America and Central and South Asia left a trail of devastation. Severe floods wrought destruction and large-scale displacement in Southern Africa and Asia. North-East Asia experienced devastating cold. Massive earthquakes struck in El Salvador and India, causing enormous loss of life and damage to infrastructure. This growing need for humanitarian assistance requires greater efficiency in relief efforts carried out by the aid community, civil society and national Governments.

Coordinating humanitarian action and the protection of civilians

90. Coordination, both within the humanitarian community and between humanitarian initiatives and peace and security efforts, has continued to improve during the year. Special attention has been paid to improving coordination between humanitarian action and peace operations, in accordance with my note guiding the relationship between Representatives of the Secretary-General, resident coordinators and humanitarian coordinators.

91. In my second report to the Security Council on the protection of civilians in armed conflict (S/2001/331), I stated that the realities of distressed populations had not changed. Little progress had been made in implementing the 40 recommendations in my first report (S/1999/957) or in the two subsequent Security Council resolutions on the subject (resolutions 1265(1999) and 1296(2000)). I therefore urged the Security Council to shift the focus from reporting on this issue to implementing agreed recommendations.

92. Progress in protecting civilians threatened by armed conflict is measured in lives and livelihoods, and freedom from fear. Success depends on the willingness of Member States and international actors, including the Security Council and the General Assembly, to take appropriate and necessary action to protect civilians in armed conflict, particularly women, children and the elderly. The efforts to build the "culture of protection" that I called for in my second report should extend beyond the United Nations, and will require continued action and cooperation on the part of Governments, regional organizations, international and domestic nongovernmental organizations, the media, the private sector and academia and civil society as a whole.

93. In the report and its recommendations it is argued that international action must complement, rather than serve as a substitute for, the responsibilities of States. The primary responsibility for protecting civilians in armed conflict rests with States, as recognized by the Member States when they pledged in the Millennium Declaration "to expand and strengthen the protection of civilians in complex emergencies, in conformity with international humanitarian law". Given the predominantly internal nature of today's armed conflicts, my report also highlighted the need to engage armed groups in protecting distressed populations.

94. Of the tens of millions of persons displaced worldwide, roughly half have been displaced by armed conflict. During the past year, the United Nations continued to strengthen humanitarian responses to crises of internal displacement. In July 2000, the Inter-Agency Standing Committee mandated a Senior Inter-Agency Network on Internal Displacement to carry out reviews of particular countries with internally displaced populations, in order to make recommendations to improve the situation in those countries and offer proposals for enhancing the international response to their basic needs. The Network complements the continuing advocacy efforts of my Representative on Internally Displaced Persons, and uses the Guiding Principles

on Internal Displacement, formulated under his direction, as its overarching framework. Indeed, the mandate of my Representative is also represented on Network review missions.

95. Representatives of the Network visited Afghanistan, Angola, Burundi, Colombia, Eritrea, Ethiopia and Indonesia from October 2000 to August 2001. The review missions undertaken confirmed that there are serious gaps in the United Nations humanitarian response to the needs of internally displaced persons that have to be addressed, particularly with regard to protection. These gaps arise from the absence of clear agency responsibility in some sectors, and from what would appear to be insufficient efforts by some agencies in their designated areas. In many cases, the major constraint to an improved inter-agency response remains a lack of sustained funding. Work is under way to bridge the gaps that were identified. Over the long term, the Office for the Coordination of Humanitarian Affairs will be strengthened to support the responses of operational agencies to the needs of the internally displaced. This will be done through the establishment of a small, inter-agency, non-operational Internally Displaced Persons Unit that will advise the Emergency Relief Coordinator.

Delivering humanitarian services and dealing with underfunded emergencies

96. During the year under review, humanitarian assistance from the United Nations has reached a number of vulnerable populations, in Afghanistan, Angola, Burundi, Colombia, the Democratic Republic of the Congo, Eritrea, Ethiopia, Guinea, Indonesia, Liberia, Mongolia, Mozambique, the occupied Palestinian territory, the Russian Federation, Sierra Leone, Somalia, the Sudan, Tajikistan, the former Yugoslav Republic of Macedonia and the Great Lakes region in Africa, among others.

97. The United Nations Children's Fund (UNICEF) is playing an increasingly important emergency role in over 35 countries. Its humanitarian action this past year included the immunization of more than 47 million children against polio on National Immunization Days, for which special ceasefires were negotiated in Afghanistan, Angola, the Democratic Republic of the Congo, the Sudan and Sri Lanka. More than 7 million children have benefited from UNICEF education support, and its response in East Timor, Kosovo and the United Republic of Tanzania highlighted the importance of emergency education as important means of bringing normalcy to a traumatized population.

98. Of the 17 countries most affected by HIV/AIDS, 13 are experiencing conflict. UNICEF has numerous programmes in these countries, including peer education and awareness-raising activities targeting young people through mass media and non-formal education. UNICEF programmes and partnerships for the protection of children and women in emergencies have expanded during the year. In the Democratic Republic of the Congo and the Sudan, progress was made towards demobilizing child soldiers while, in Sierra Leone, 1,000 of a total 1,700 demobilized children were reunited with their families. United Nations peacekeeping missions have also been used as both channels and targets for education and awareness-raising on HIV/AIDS.

99. The World Health Organization (WHO) contributes to overall humanitarian coordination by informing all partners on the determinants of survival and health in emergencies, and works to put coordinated public health actions in place for all affected populations, including the forcibly displaced. The priorities remain needs assessment, immunization, improved nutrition, providing pharmaceuticals, controlling communicable as well as non-communicable diseases, reproductive health and mental health. WHO also supports inter-agency action for HIV/AIDS control in emergencies, for the elderly in humanitarian emergencies and for the health of humanitarian workers.

100. The presence and field operational ability of WHO can ensure optimal impact in coordinated public health management, collective learning and health sector accountability. To this end, WHO provides country-specific technical guidance, situation reports and epidemiological surveillance data to all those partners that by their action in health or related sectors can contribute to the common goal of reducing avoidable mortality and suffering. In October 2000, WHO organized an International Consultation on the Mental Health of Refugees and Displaced Populations in Conflict and Post-Conflict Situations that endorsed a declaration of cooperation between operational agencies, Member States and academic and research institutions. WHO validated technical instruments for assessment and evaluation, and is organizing an international conference to examine how the response of local health-care systems to the needs of internally displaced persons can be improved.

101. As the food aid arm of the United Nations, the World Food Programme (WFP) continued to use food aid to save lives, alleviate hunger and enable poor people whose food supply is insecure to make investments to help themselves in the longer term. In response to emergencies in

2000, WFP delivered over 3.5 million tons of food, assisting 83 million people, including over 60 million people affected by natural disasters and complex emergencies. WFP continued to work with other United Nations entities to secure safe and unimpeded access to vulnerable populations and areas for the assessment, delivery, distribution and monitoring of food aid. WFP uses food aid to support livelihoods, reduce vulnerability to future food scarcities and support durable solutions, and strives to channel food through women in order to ensure that food aid meets the needs of families, particularly children. It seeks to provide 80 per cent of relief food directly to women, ensure full participation of women in decision-making groups, and facilitate equal access of women to resources, employment, markets and trade. WFP also works to understand the particular needs of food-insecure internally displaced people and help to ensure for them the same rights and freedoms as other people in their country, as well as addressing the food needs of refugees in a manner that builds self-reliance.

102. About 50 per cent of WFP food assistance in 2000 was targeted to vulnerable populations and groups affected by civil strife or conflicts in one of the many protracted emergencies plaguing Africa, Central Asia, the Balkans and Latin America. While in global terms WFP increased its food assistance to affected civilians by 3 per cent in 2000, it has experienced problems in some underfunded, "forgotten" emergencies, such as Angola, Somalia or the Great Lakes region. Timely contributions allowed the provision of humanitarian aid efficiently in a number of extremely complex and volatile situations. In some cases, however, resources were made available too late to avert or mitigate unfolding crises, or to avoid breaks in the food distribution chain, with the result that WFP had to resort to reducing the rations of affected populations.

103. The Global Information and Early Warning System of the Food and Agriculture Organization of the United Nations (FAO), a comprehensive international warning system for threats to crop and food supply conditions, continued, in the wake of dramatic increases in food emergencies, to alert the international community to imminent crop failures and food crises. During the period 1998-2000, virtually all regions were seriously affected by natural or man-made disasters. Using field and satellite data, the system monitors crop and food supply and demand conditions in all countries, identifies those where food shortages may be imminent and maintains continuous assessments of possible emergency food needs.

104. In 2000, FAO provided emergency agriculture and livelihood recovery assistance to people affected by natural disasters and complex emergencies in 41 countries. FAO distributed seeds and tools to vulnerable groups, including internally displaced persons, ex-combatants and women. In the Horn of Africa and in Mongolia, FAO supplied animal feed and veterinary drugs to safeguard the health of livestock, upon which the local rural populations rely heavily. In countries, such as Afghanistan and Tajikistan, that have undergone protracted periods of conflict, FAO implemented longer-term rehabilitation projects, including the development of private veterinary services, the establishment of seed multiplication schemes and the restoration of farming machinery. To enhance the sustainability of these efforts, FAO placed special emphasis on the technical training and capacity-building elements of these projects.

105. FAO plays a central coordination role in the agricultural sector. A comprehensive relief and rehabilitation agricultural programme was implemented in Kosovo where, owing primarily to the presence of the FAO Emergency Coordination Unit, rehabilitation activities were able to expand in scope as immediate food relief was scaled down, successfully linking the relief and recovery stages of humanitarian assistance.

106. The United Nations Development Programme has continued to provide technical assistance through country offices, both to facilitate the reintegration of displaced populations and to rehabilitate crisis-affected communities through socio-economic initiatives. UNDP is introducing transitional recovery teams to strengthen the capacity of its country offices and resident coordinator system to support early recovery efforts and to advance effective transitions from situations of conflict and disaster.

107. UNDP also seeks to reduce demand for illicit arms by confronting the root causes of violence. It has collected and destroyed tens of thousands of weapons and encouraged authorities in countries emerging from crisis to destroy tons of ammunition and explosives used in conflict. In the past year, it achieved some success in Albania, the Republic of the Congo and El Salvador. In Albania, some 14,000 weapons were collected and destroyed, and 10,000 weapons were collected and destroyed in the Republic of the Congo.

108. The United Nations Relief and Works Agency for Palestine Refugees in the Near East provides education, health, relief and social services, and implements income-generation programmes aimed at over 4 million refugees. Funding has not kept pace with the rapidly growing demand for services in this area, however. On the

basis of donor pledges so far, the Agency faces an estimated deficit of $67 million against a budget of $311 million approved by the General Assembly. The deficit seriously jeopardizes the quality and extent of the Agency's services.

109. During the past year the "oil-for-food" programme, established by the Security Council in 1996, and administered by the Office of the Iraq Programme, has continued to assist the Iraqi people in meeting their basic needs in the areas of food and nutrition, health, water and sanitation, agriculture and shelter. Since the adoption of Security Council resolution 1330(2000) on 5 December 2000, 72 per cent of Iraqi oil revenue is now available for the humanitarian programme, instead of the 66 per cent available during earlier phases. The additional funds will address the needs of the most vulnerable groups of the population. The Government of Iraq's delays in contracting humanitarian supplies and equipment are of great concern, as are the delays in submitting applications by contractors, and the decision to place a large number of contracts on hold by the Security Council sanctions committee.

110. The United Nations system, under the co-ordination of the United Nations Mine Action Service, has continued to address the threat of landmines in over 20 countries. Affected land is surveyed, marked, mapped and cleared, while awareness of the risks is raised within the communities concerned. Assistance to victims has focused on rehabilitation and reintegration. The United Nations has continued to mobilize resources to support these activities, and more than 30 countries now seek funding assistance through various United Nations mechanisms. It is estimated that, in 2000, international donors provided over $200 million for mine action in addition to the resources committed by mine-affected States themselves. At the international level, considerable advancements have been made, including the development and dissemination of the International Mine Action Standards, the further deployment of the Information Management System for Mine Action, and work on the socio-economic impact of landmine contamination. While significant progress has been achieved in reducing the threat posed by landmines in several countries, the most severely affected States will require consistent levels of international support for a number of years to come.

111. Underfunding, access restrictions and staff security issues have seriously constrained the emergency response capacity of agencies during the year. Underfunding is an ongoing and critical limitation for humanitarian action in a number of countries. In the absence of immediate and realistic funding, emergency planning, preparedness and stockpiling can do little to accelerate the humanitarian response to a crisis.

112. The consolidated appeals process brings the United Nations humanitarian community together to develop common strategies for complex emergencies in the most acute crises, often characterized by political or economic failure in the State concerned. For 2001, consolidated appeals were issued for humanitarian crises in Afghanistan, Angola, Burundi, the Democratic People's Republic of Korea, the Democratic Republic of the Congo, the Republic of the Congo, Eritrea, Ethiopia, Maluku in Indonesia, the northern Caucasus in the Russian Federation, Sierra Leone, Somalia, South-Eastern Europe, the Sudan, Tajikistan, the United Republic of Tanzania, Uganda and West Africa.

113. The 2001 consolidated appeals sought $2.8 billion to reach an estimated 44 million people in need of humanitarian assistance in countries affected by conflict. As at June 2001, less than a third of the requirements listed in the consolidated appeals had been met, even lower in percentage terms than pledges made to the 2000 consolidated appeals at the same time last year.

The challenge of protecting and assisting refugees

114. The year 2000 marked the fiftieth anniversary of the Office of the United Nations High Commissioner for Refugees (UNHCR). At this important milestone, UNHCR faces serious challenges. They include ensuring the availability and quality of asylum; revitalizing the refugee protection system; providing effective assistance to refugees; promoting durable solutions for refugees; and fostering partnerships in support of the international protection system and in pursuit of durable solutions.

115. The global population of concern to UNHCR decreased from 22.3 million at the start of 2000 to 21.1 million at the start of 2001. This population includes refugees, asylum seekers, returning refugees in the early stages of their reintegration, and internally displaced persons. Ongoing or renewed conflicts, coupled with stagnating peace processes, generated continuing outflows of refugees. Repeated violations in the Democratic Republic of the Congo of the Lusaka Ceasefire Agreement displaced an estimated 1.8 million people internally, and led over 100,000 people to flee, mostly to the Republic of the Congo, the United Republic of Tanzania and Zambia. Despite the signing in August 2000 of the Arusha Agreement on Peace and Reconciliation, continued violence prompted 80,000 people to leave Burundi for the United Republic of Tanzania. In the first seven months of 2001, the arrival of some 880,000 Afghans in Pakistan

made Pakistan host to the largest refugee population in the world, estimated at some 2 million people.

116. In September 2000, we witnessed the brutal killings of three UNHCR staff members in West Timor and one staff member in Guinea. To address the inextricably linked issues of refugee and staff security, UNHCR undertook a comprehensive review of its emergency preparedness and response structures, as well as the management of its security services, increasing its coordination with the office of the United Nations Security Coordinator and other United Nations agencies, funds and programmes.

117. Access to safety and continued protection in host countries remain vital for the world's refugees. The quality of asylum has, however, deteriorated in a number of countries, including in several regions with traditionally generous asylum policies. This is a result of the economic and social difficulties in hosting large refugee populations, national security considerations and concerns about the use of asylum procedures by illegal immigrants and the trafficking and smuggling of persons.

118. In December 2000, after consultations with key partners, in particular the International Committee of the Red Cross, UNHCR produced policy guidelines on the question of combatants and former combatants with particular reference to the situations in the Democratic Republic of the Congo, Namibia and Zambia.

119. UNHCR has continued to monitor implementation of the 1951 Convention relating to the Status of Refugees and its 1967 Protocol, notably through involvement in national procedures for the determination of refugee status. When a State is not a party to international law regarding refugees, or has not established the relevant procedures, UNHCR carries out refugee status determinations under its mandate. Fifty years after the establishment of UNHCR, a major challenge still lies in persuading more States to accede to and comply with the Convention and Protocol. At the end of 2000, 140 States, including most recently Mexico and Trinidad and Tobago, had acceded to the instruments.

120. UNHCR has played a leading role in facilitating and coordinating voluntary repatriation, which includes providing assistance to returnees during reintegration and rehabilitation. In total, over 790,000 persons returned to their countries during 2000, including 290,000 returning to Afghanistan mostly from the Islamic Republic of Iran and Pakistan, and 125,000 to Kosovo, from other parts of the Federal Republic of Yugoslavia.

121. Apart from being an important protection tool, resettlement has increasingly become a mechanism for sharing responsibility and seeking durable solutions. The traditional resettlement countries continue each year to provide resettlement opportunities to some 30,000 refugees referred by UNHCR, usually from the Middle East and increasingly from Africa. In a welcome development over recent years, Argentina, Benin, Brazil, Burkina Faso, Chile, Iceland, Ireland and Spain have joined the list of countries willing to provide resettlement opportunities.

122. Underfunding has also seriously affected UNHCR operations and, in some cases, led to a scaling-down of assistance. In Angola, for example, lack of funding curtailed the procurement of building materials for the completion of houses in camps ahead of the rainy season. In Afghanistan, unpredictable and insufficient funding undermined the ability of UNHCR to cope with repatriation rates that more than doubled in the past year, and to alleviate the suffering of some 500,000 internally displaced persons.

Natural disaster response: engaging developing countries and building capacities

123. Although natural disasters can occur anywhere, a number of factors such as poverty, food insecurity, wars, social strife, lack of community planning and environmental degradation make developing countries more vulnerable to their devastating impact. The United Nations has been working closely with Governments, at national and regional levels, to strengthen their preventive and response capacities in order to minimize the risks and impact of disasters.

124. In cooperation with the Governments of affected countries, the United Nations intensified its efforts to draw lessons from previous relief operations and to strengthen preventive strategies, including early warning mechanisms, at national and regional levels. In the Americas and the Caribbean regions, thanks to 25 years of efforts spearheaded by the Pan American Health Organization/WHO, most countries have made significant progress in the disaster field. They have developed country hazard maps, and have improved and expanded seismic monitoring networks and early warning systems. World Food Programme assistance to victims of natural disasters has increased steadily in recent years. Globally, one third of WFP food aid in 2000 was targeted to these vulnerable populations, marking a 20 per cent increase over the preceding year. UNDP cooperated with developing countries to mainstream disaster management within broader development strategies, and integrate

disaster response preparedness initiatives into a framework of support for disaster reduction.

125. The Disaster Management Training Programme, managed by UNDP in collaboration with 26 partner United Nations agencies, programmes and funds, and international organizations, aims to provide training to capacity-building programmes. Country-level training activities under the Programme have been integrated into the Comprehensive Disaster Management Strategy in the Southern Africa region. Other training activities have focused on countries of the Mekong River Commission, and have provided capacity-building support for individual countries at vital stages of long-term disaster management strategy in Central America.

126. The United Nations disaster assessment and coordination system, managed by the Office for the Coordination of Humanitarian Affairs, has been building expertise in disaster-prone regions to coordinate international assistance in major disasters. The Military and Civil Defence Unit of the Office is conducting training to improve relationships and coordination between humanitarian actors and the military and civil defence resources that are employed in emergency response. It also coordinates international exercises when military and civil defence assets are used.

127. In partnership with the United Nations Environment Programme, the Office for the Coordination of Humanitarian Affairs is focusing on upgrading the humanitarian community's capacity to respond rapidly to the environmental consequences of natural disasters. Specifically, it has developed a global network of officially designated national focal points to serve as the conduit for accessing information and assistance. This continuously expanding global network currently includes representatives of more than 100 countries in all major regions.

128. Events in 2001 once again confirmed the need to plan effective disaster reduction measures in order to strike a better balance between, on the one hand, funds spent on intervention and relief and, on the other, resources which could be devoted to enhance prevention capacities. The first year of operation of the International Strategy for Disaster Reduction has demonstrated that many countries and a large number of United Nations agencies and organizations, non-governmental organizations, regional entities and representatives of civil society are willing to engage in broad efforts to promote a global culture of prevention. Building and strengthening effective early warning systems, and providing adequate education and training, as well as appropriate technology, are a few major areas where decisive action is required.

Chapter III

Cooperating for development

Overview: extreme poverty

129. At the Millennium Summit, the international community resolved to wage war on poverty by launching a sustained campaign to make the right to development a reality for everyone. The effort to render globalization inclusive and equitable will pose a daunting challenge in the years ahead. If the international community is to meet its goals of development and poverty eradication, economic growth in developing economies must accelerate. At the same time, disparities in prevailing poverty rates both within and between countries will require targeted attention. We will need to work together, with adequate financial resources, to advance appropriate economic, social and financial policies and to bolster supporting institutions at the national and international levels.

Cooperating effectively to eradicate poverty

130. Through its development cooperation efforts, the United Nations continues to dedicate substantial resources to supporting Governments in the implementation of their development objectives and priorities, including those articulated in the Millennium Declaration. The United Nations Strategy for Halving Extreme Poverty, endorsed by the Administrative Committee on Coordination in October 2000, recognizes the multidimensional nature of poverty. It incorporates a rights-based approach embodying principles of equity, non-discrimination (among ethnic, gender and geographical groups), accountability and participation into development and poverty reduction efforts. United Nations entities have cooperated in the formulation of national poverty reduction strategies in 60 countries and the writing of comprehensive poverty reduction strategy papers in others. The United Nations has carried out assessments of the social and economic effects of liberalization and globalization in 17 countries of Latin America and the Caribbean. Common country assessments and the United Nations Development Assistance Frameworks, drafted in 81 countries and completed in 34, are the principal vehicles by means of which the United Nations is contributing to achieving the millennium development goals. To date, 71 countries have aligned their activities to those goals.

131. The United Nations Development Group, under the chairmanship of UNDP, continues to manage development activities. Since my last report, I am pleased to announce that the Food

and Agriculture Organization of the United Nations, the United Nations Educational, Scientific and Cultural Organization (UNESCO) and the World Health Organization have joined the United Nations Development Group.

132. Early in 2001, the International Fund for Agricultural Development (IFAD) released its *Rural Poverty Report 2001: The Challenges of Ending Rural Poverty*, a comprehensive review of the causes and dynamics of rural poverty and effective approaches to poverty reduction. The report concludes that the poor themselves are the most potent agents of change. Evidence shows that poverty decreases faster when the poor participate actively in poverty reduction. Access to assets such as land, water, markets, information and technology enables the poor to take charge of their lives and allows them to escape poverty permanently. In 2000, IFAD approved 27 new rural development projects expected to benefit an estimated 13.6 million people. Those projects are implemented in collaboration with United Nations entities, bilateral and multilateral donors, non-governmental organizations and partners in the private sector. Joint operations based on complementary expertise and shared objectives have proved invaluable in achieving project goals and thus contributing to poverty eradication.

133. The United Nations has also reached out in other areas to help people lift themselves out of poverty. Through the use of vulnerability assessment and mapping tools, the World Food Programme has identified the food-insecure and marginalized, targeted its food aid and sought to ensure that each of its interventions involves investment in physical or human assets of lasting value. Meanwhile, UNDP has increased the availability of sustainable microfinance services. Together with the United Nations Capital Development Fund, it operates the MicroStart programme. As at 31 March 2001, MicroStart had begun operations in 20 countries and 62 projects in 14 countries had received grants. Collectively, the 62 projects have increased the number of active clients served from a baseline of 67,026 to 192,881. The percentage of women clients served by the projects has increased from 57 per cent to 84 per cent.

134. No effort to reduce poverty can succeed without first ensuring the well-being of children and the enjoyment of their rights. Education, and especially education of girls, will contribute significantly to poverty reduction and achievement of the millennium development goals. At my request, UNICEF is leading an inter-agency task force to develop and implement the United Nations Girls' Education Initiative and United Nations staff in 50 countries are involved in collaborative activities related to girls' education. In 2000, WFP fed more than 12 million schoolchildren in 54 countries. This year, it will aim to increase funding for food aid, while also creating alliances to combine food with sanitation, health and education assistance.

135. Ensuring gender equality and women's empowerment are equally critical to the reduction of poverty. The United Nations Population Fund (UNFPA) has worked closely with partner agencies, the World Bank, civil society and private sector partners to reduce maternal mortality by three quarters between 1990 and 2015 through the Safe Motherhood Initiative. In 2000, the United Nations Development Fund for Women (UNIFEM) focused on strengthening women's economic capacity, rights and bargaining power; promoting legal and regulatory changes that safeguard women's equal ownership and access to economic assets; enhancing Governments' capacities to manage economic transitions without marginalizing poor women; and supporting gender-responsive government budgets and macroeconomic policy frameworks.

136. At the intergovernmental level, the twenty-fourth special session of the General Assembly, held at Geneva from 26 June to 1 July 2000, provided a broad mandate for a global campaign to eradicate poverty, with emphasis on the need for consolidation of the many ongoing initiatives. The Administrative Committee on Coordination has proposed that the Assembly discuss a framework for a global campaign to eradicate poverty. The campaign, a common advocacy effort, would underline the United Nations system-wide commitment to reducing poverty through concerted action in social, educational, nutritional, health and cultural dimensions, as well as in the promotion of gender equality and empowerment.

137. The twenty-fifth special session of the General Assembly for an overall review and appraisal of the implementation of the outcome of the United Nations Conference on Human Settlements (Habitat II), held in New York from 6 to 8 June 2001, provided a further vehicle for poverty reduction. The concluding Declaration on Cities and Other Human Settlements in the New Millennium emphasizes that improvements in shelter and related urban infrastructure and services, as well as the sustainable development of human settlements, will contribute to eliminating poverty. The implementation of the Habitat Agenda and the pursuit of sustainable development are an integral part of the overall fight for the eradication of poverty. As poverty is a main obstacle in implementing the Habitat Agenda, the Declaration stresses the need to ad-

dress, in an integrated manner, poverty, homelessness, unemployment, lack of basic services, exclusion of women and of children and marginalized groups. This will help achieve better, more liveable and inclusive human settlements. The Declaration also highlights the need to empower the poor and vulnerable by promoting greater security of tenure, including awareness of legal rights, and by promoting the upgrading of slums and regularization of squatter settlements, within the legal framework of each country. In particular, it re-emphasizes the aim of the Cities without Slums initiative to make a significant improvement in the lives of at least 100 million slum-dwellers by 2020.

Mobilizing resources for development and poverty eradication

138. World leaders at the Millennium Summit resolved to make every effort to ensure the success of a unique intergovernmental process called financing for development. All the major international actors that deal with the interrelated issues of finance, trade and development have decided to search collectively for solutions to common problems. The preparatory meetings for the International Conference on Financing for Development, which is to be held at Monterrey, Mexico, from 18 to 22 March 2002, include regional meetings organized by the five regional commissions in collaboration with the United Nations Conference on Trade and Development (UNCTAD) and regional development banks. The Coordinating Secretariat for Financing for Development, established in 2000, is located in the Department of Economic and Social Affairs of the Secretariat, and includes staff seconded from the World Bank, UNCTAD and UNDP. Staff from the International Monetary Fund and the World Trade Organization have also worked actively with the Coordinating Secretariat. Last January I issued a report that offered a comprehensive set of 87 recommendations on all key aspects of financing for development. To further assist the preparatory process, I requested a High-level Panel on Financing for Development, chaired by the former President of Mexico, Ernesto Zedillo, to produce a report that will help Governments refine their proposals for the Monterrey Conference.

139. The aim of the special high-level meeting of the Economic and Social Council with the Bretton Woods institutions, held on 1 May 2001, was to promote coherence and cooperation in international development and, in particular, in poverty reduction. The meeting stressed the crucial need to ensure sustained economic growth, but noted that economic growth would not advance sustainable development in the absence of social justice. The meeting recognized that halving the number of people living in poverty by 2015 would require lasting debt relief to the poorest countries and stressed that a stable and well-managed international financial system was vital in the context of increasing globalization. Of equal importance was the recognition that protectionism in trade measures, in particular for the agricultural sector of developed countries, had prevented developing countries from benefiting fully from trade. Increased market access for developing countries was fundamental to ensuring poverty reduction. Participants welcomed efforts to open the new round of trade talks in 2001. These issues will also be discussed at the International Conference on Financing for Development.

Least developed countries: giving the poorest nations a chance

140. Of the 49 countries classified as least developed, 34 are in Africa, 13 are located in the region of Asia and the Pacific, one is in Western Asia and one is in the region of Latin America and the Caribbean. Those countries face formidable obstacles to their development, which include external debt problems, declining external resource flows, declining terms of trade, barriers to market access for their products, high population growth, inadequate social development, lack of infrastructure and environmental constraints, including water shortages.

141. The progress of the least developed countries towards international targets for human and social development has been disappointingly slow. Special measures are therefore needed to lend momentum to their development efforts. The *World Economic and Social Survey 2000*, prepared by the Department of Economic and Social Affairs, reviewed a number of issues that least developed countries will need to address in order to achieve rapid and sustained growth that improves living standards. Focusing on domestic conditions, the *Survey* stressed the pivotal role of agriculture, the importance of human capital development, the need to improve technological capabilities and the prime role of institutions and institutional change in the development process.

142. Against this backdrop, I conducted the preparatory process for, and convened, the Third United Nations Conference on the Least Developed Countries at Brussels from 14 to 20 May 2001. Preparing African countries for the Conference was of particular importance. The Economic Commission for Africa (ECA) organized a high-level consultative meeting in Novem-

ber 2000. The meeting reviewed progress in the implementation of the Programme of Action for the Least Developed Countries for the 1990s and considered policies to ensure the progressive, sustainable integration of least developed countries into the global economy. The Conference of African Ministers of Finance considered the expert recommendations and adopted a common declaration calling for an increase in external resource flows, including official development assistance and foreign direct investment; expansion of current debt relief initiatives; wider preferential market access for products originating in least developed countries; and technical assistance to strengthen capacity to address supply-side constraints, including those relating to infrastructure and institutions.

143. The Third United Nations Conference on the Least Developed Countries adopted a political declaration, the Brussels Declaration, and the Programme of Action for the Least Developed Countries for the Decade 2001-2010. The Brussels Declaration reaffirms the collective responsibility of the international community to uphold the principles of human dignity, equality and equity and to ensure that globalization becomes a positive force for all the world's people, as set out in the Millennium Declaration.

144. The Programme of Action provides specific goals and targets along with action-oriented commitments in seven critically important areas: fostering a people-centred policy framework; good governance at the national and international levels; building human and institutional capacities; building productive capacities to make globalization work for least developed countries; enhancing the role of trade in development; reducing vulnerability and protecting the environment; and mobilizing financial resources.

145. In both the Political Declaration and the Programme of Action, development partners agreed to increase market access for least developed countries; to provide adequate financial resources for the full implementation of the enhanced Heavily Indebted Poor Countries Initiative; and to contribute to the integrated framework for trade-related technical assistance. UNCTAD, the Multilateral Investment Guarantee Agency, the World Bank Group's Foreign Investment Advisory Service and the United Nations Industrial Development Organization also launched a technical assistance programme on foreign direct investment in a pilot group of countries. Drawing on the experience of United Nations field teams, UNCTAD will lead the implementation of the Programme of Action.

Battling HIV/AIDS

146. The HIV/AIDS pandemic is a catastrophe of global proportions. It is destroying the social fabric in the most affected countries, reversing years of declining death rates and causing dramatic rises in mortality among young adults. By late 2000, over 36 million adults and children were living with HIV/AIDS, while nearly 22 million had died of the virus. According to the Joint United Nations Programme on HIV/AIDS (UN-AIDS) *Epidemic Update* of December 2000, 5.3 million new infections occurred last year and the number of children orphaned by AIDS had reached nearly 15 million.

147. Africa is the continent most profoundly affected by the spread of AIDS. In sub-Saharan Africa, where 25.3 million people are living with HIV/AIDS, the epidemic is now the leading cause of death. HIV prevalence rates among people aged 15 to 49 have reached or exceeded 10 per cent in 16 sub-Saharan countries. The virus is also spreading with alarming speed in other parts of the world. A rapid increase in the number of HIV infections in Eastern Europe and South and East Asia is also cause for serious concern.

148. Participants in the Millennium Summit resolved to halt and begin to reverse the spread of HIV/AIDS by 2015; to provide special assistance to children orphaned by HIV/AIDS; and to help Africa build its capacity to tackle the spread of the HIV/AIDS pandemic and other infectious diseases. The United Nations has pursued numerous initiatives to assist Governments in defeating the epidemic. The depth of the health crisis in sub-Saharan Africa, in particular, has generated concerted action in numerous forums. African Governments, partners of the Organisation for Economic Cooperation and Development, United Nations entities, non-governmental organizations and private sector partners intensified efforts to mobilize additional resources under the auspices of the Framework for Action of the International Partnership against AIDS in Africa.

149. The Economic Commission for Africa organized the African Development Forum in December 2000 around the theme "AIDS: the greatest leadership challenge". The Forum called for leadership and action by all stakeholders to fight HIV/AIDS in Africa in the African Consensus and Plan of Action: Leadership to Overcome HIV/AIDS. The Plan of Action served as an important input for the Special Summit on HIV/AIDS, Tuberculosis and Other Related Infectious Diseases of the Organization of African Unity (OAU) held at Abuja in April 2001, where African leaders committed themselves to devot-

ing at least 15 per cent of their annual budgets to improving health-care systems.

150. In June 2001, the General Assembly held its twenty-sixth special session, on HIV/AIDS, to review and address the problem of HIV/AIDS in all its aspects and to secure a global commitment to enhancing coordination and intensification of national, regional and international efforts to combat it in a comprehensive manner. The special session constituted a culminating point in the efforts of the United Nations to combat HIV/AIDS. In that framework and with the assistance of UNAIDS and its co-sponsors, I called for a major new global campaign in the fight against HIV/AIDS at the OAU Special Summit on HIV/AIDS, Tuberculosis and Other Related Infectious Diseases. The Plan of Action adopted at the Summit is intended to translate into concrete initiatives the commitments made by African leaders to intensify efforts to mobilize resources for prevention, care and treatment of the diseases and to develop strategies to mitigate the impact of the epidemic on Africa's socio-economic development. I also proposed the establishment of a Global AIDS and Health Fund in order to mobilize the $7 billion to $10 billion necessary to appropriately address the AIDS epidemic.

151. In order to strengthen coordination within the United Nations system, I also established a High-level Inter-Agency Task Force on HIV/AIDS, chaired by the Deputy Secretary-General and composed of all relevant funds, programmes and agencies. System-wide efforts to address the various aspects of the HIV/AIDS crisis continue.

Social development

152. Social objectives are integral to the struggle against poverty. The United Nations is continuing, through its own operational activities and through partnerships and networks, to promote improved access to basic social services and health care, to advance gender equality, to safeguard respect for human rights, to facilitate good governance, to expand access to information and communication technologies, to combat the scourge of illegal drugs and to support data collection and analyses on a wide range of policy issues.

Basic social services

153. The Task Force on Basic Social Services for All of the Administrative Committee on Coordination, chaired by UNFPA, has strengthened the United Nations system's capacity to deliver coordinated assistance, including policies, plans and programmes at the national and regional levels. In October 2000, the Task Force completed new or revised Guidelines for the United Nations

Resident Coordinator System on basic education, maternal mortality, primary health care and HIV/AIDS.

Health

154. Global immunization coverage (the major childhood diseases covered are measles, poliomyelitis, pertussis, diphtheria, tetanus and tuberculosis) stands at 74 per cent, although many countries in sub-Saharan Africa, as well as those in conflict, report coverage rates far below 50 per cent. The Global Alliance for Vaccines and Immunization is playing a critical role in improving coverage. In 2000, only 2,800 cases of polio were confirmed, as compared with 7,100 cases in 1999. National immunization days, typically organized in partnership with UNICEF, WHO, Rotary International and the United States Centers for Disease Control and Prevention, remain vital to improved coverage. In 2000, a record 550 million children under five years of age were immunized during intensified national immunization days in 82 countries. For example, in India, 152 million children were vaccinated in three days, and across West and Central Africa 76 million children were immunized in 17 countries. Within Africa, the Roll Back Malaria initiative, led by WHO, UNDP, the World Bank and UNICEF, emphasizes partnerships with all stakeholders, including Governments of countries where the disease is endemic, donor Governments, the private sector and civil society, in malaria prevention and control.

Gender and population

155. The new biennial report of UNIFEM, *Progress of the World's Women 2000*, offers revealing insights into advances and challenges in women's economic, social and political status and rights. *Progress 2000* documents the advances many countries have made on behalf of women and also examines remaining social, economic and political gaps. The report found that, during the last decade, only eight countries had successfully met global agreements to achieve both gender equality in secondary education enrolment and at least a 30 per cent share for women of seats in parliament. It strongly recommends the adoption of a globally agreed goal specific to women's paid employment, such as raising women's share of administrative and managerial positions.

156. Gender inequality has direct consequences for women's health, education and social and economic participation. At its twenty-first special session, in 1999, at which it reviewed the implementation of the Programme of Action of

the International Conference on Population and Development, the General Assembly reconfirmed gender equality and women's empowerment as central goals of the Programme of Action and recommended a number of key initiatives such as zero tolerance for all forms of violence, including rape, incest, sexual violence and sex trafficking, against women and children. This entails developing an integrated approach that addresses the need for widespread social, cultural and economic change, in addition to legal reforms, and the close monitoring of the gender-differentiated impact of the globalization of the economy and the privatization of basic social services, in particular reproductive health.

157. In 2000, the UNIFEM Trust Fund in Support of Actions to Eliminate Violence against Women continued to serve as the basis for learning about gender-based violence and support for initiatives aimed at ending such violence. UNIFEM funded 17 new Trust Fund projects addressing a variety of issues, including addressing "honour killings" in Jordan, building local capacity to protect women from trafficking and domestic violence in the Republic of Moldova, training human rights lawyers on domestic violence issues in Peru and educating the public and sensitizing law enforcement agents about domestic violence laws in the United Republic of Tanzania.

158. In March 2000, the Commission on Human Rights adopted a resolution on women's equal ownership of, access to and control over land and the equal rights to own property and to adequate housing. Introduced by the Committee on Housing Rights and Evictions, a recipient of UNIFEM funding, the resolution constitutes a milestone in recognizing the gender dimensions of economic, social and cultural rights, drawing connections between women's property ownership, housing and inheritance rights.

159. The United Nations Development Programme worked in more than 100 countries to address issues of gender equality and empowerment. It facilitated dialogue between Governments and civil society stakeholders on gender issues, drew up action plans addressing gender equality, and established networks of gender focal points in Government and within the wider community of national stakeholders. It also helped to augment national capacities for data collection and analysis, mainly to facilitate national reporting on the implementation of the Beijing Platform for Action and the Convention on the Elimination of All Forms of Discrimination against Women.

Youth employment

160. Social integration is a fundamental dynamic of social development. It continues to evolve under the influence of demographic change, most noticeably in changing family structures and the ageing of populations. In my report to the Millennium Assembly, I highlighted the urgency of finding decent work for the more than 70 million young women and men actively but unsuccessfully seeking employment, as well as for the many others underemployed in the informal economy. The Member States, in the Millennium Declaration, accepted the challenge of youth employment when they resolved to "develop and implement strategies that give young people everywhere a real chance to find decent and productive work".

161. As a first step in meeting that challenge, I have, together with the heads of the World Bank and the International Labour Organization, convened a high-level network—drawing on the experience and creativity of private industry and civil society—on youth unemployment and economic policy. The network will formulate a set of recommendations on youth employment directed at world leaders, disseminate information on good practices and identify a series of collaborative youth employment initiatives for implementation with partners.

162. "Empowering Youth for Action" was the theme of the fourth session of the World Youth Forum of the United Nations, held at Dakar in August 2001. Pursuant to the General Assembly's decision to proclaim 12 August International Youth Day, Member States and youth organizations worldwide recognized the day as an opportunity to strengthen youth involvement in development activities.

Ageing

163. Ageing remains one of the most complex social development issues confronting countries today. The *World Ageing Situation 2001* questions conventional wisdom that ageing is a problem and offers fresh approaches to the issue. The Second World Assembly on Ageing, to be held at Madrid in April 2002, will offer an opportunity to adopt a revised version of the International Plan of Action on Ageing, originally adopted in 1982, focusing on humanitarian and developmental aspects of ageing, aligned with modern, sociocultural, economic and demographic realities.

People with disabilities

164. Promoting equal opportunities for persons with disabilities and ensuring respect for

their rights and full participation in all spheres of social life also remains a priority. In 2001, the Secretariat supported an initiative to develop an effective policy framework and programme interventions for children and young adults with disabilities in Latin America in preparation for the special session of the General Assembly on children, to be held from 19 to 21 September 2001. Through the United Nations Voluntary Fund on Disability, it has also sponsored activities of the African Decade of Disabled People (2000-2009), an innovative partnership between Governments and the non-governmental community to bring disability to the forefront of Africa's development agenda.

The promotion of human rights and good governance

165. Rights-based programming underpins much of the operational activity undertaken by the United Nations. Last year, UNDP supported the development of national human rights action plans, invested in civic education and awareness-raising campaigns, and established and strengthened ombudsman offices and national human rights institutions. In several countries, UNDP also carried out a range of activities to bolster democratic governance. For example, support was made available to 38 parliaments, 34 justice systems and 21 electoral systems in 2000. A $6 million global initiative funded by the Government of Belgium was launched to strengthen parliaments, while a global network of 350 civil society organizations was established to promote judicial reform. Public sector management programmes in 78 countries resulted in civil service reform, national action to tackle corruption and promote transparency, and the adoption by some Governments of results-based management to advance public sector efficiency and accountability. Decentralization programmes involving capacity-building, resource mobilization, service delivery and community empowerment were ongoing in 37 countries.

Reduction of the demand for drugs

166. The United Nations International Drug Control Programme (UNDCP) continues to lead the United Nations system in supporting government efforts to combat the scourge of illegal drug abuse. To that end, the Programme has organized the Global Youth Network against Drug Abuse and assisted Governments and non-governmental organizations in involving young people in policy-making and programme activities. The UNDCP Global Assessment Programme on Drug Abuse has assisted countries in Africa

and Asia to collect and analyse data, while the joint UNDCP/WHO Global Initiative on Primary Prevention of Substance Abuse has supported community-level prevention in Belarus, the Philippines, the Russian Federation, South Africa, Thailand, the United Republic of Tanzania, Viet Nam and Zambia.

Access to information and communication technologies

167. Information and communication technology is an important instrument for reaping the potential benefits of globalization. In the past year, the United Nations forged important partnerships to bridge the "digital divide" and harness the power of technology to promote development. I will launch, on 14 September 2001, the United Nations Information and Communication Technologies Task Force, which resulted from the high-level segment of the Economic and Social Council in July 2000 (resolution 2000/29). The Task Force, created for an initial period of three years, consists of representatives of 18 countries, 8 private corporations, 6 multilateral organizations (International Telecommunication Union, United Nations, UNDP, UNESCO, World Intellectual Property Organization and the World Bank) and 4 non-governmental organizations. The principal mission of the Task Force is to harness the power of information and communication technologies for advancing the millennium development goals, in particular the eradication of poverty. It should achieve this by acting as an effective and useful facilitator, catalyst and accelerator, a global forum and a means to raise awareness and mobilize resources.

168. UNDP has been actively involved in a number of public and private multisectoral initiatives to focus attention on the issues, undertake advocacy and provide mechanisms for follow-up at the country level. It has also, with the World Bank, provided for the secretariat of the Digital Opportunity Task Force, or DOT Force, which was set up in the wake of the meeting of the Group of Eight summit, held at Okinawa in July 2000. The final report of the DOT Force, *Digital Opportunities for All: Meeting the Challenge*, with a nine-point action plan, was fully endorsed by the G-8 leaders in their final communiqué at Genoa in July 2001. UNDP has also endeavoured to strengthen the voice of developing countries by means of a multisectoral task force which is a partnership between G-8 countries, developing countries, the private sector and non-governmental organizations. To support the work of the DOT Force, UNDP, in collaboration with the Markle Foundation and Accenture, also completed the first phase of the Digital Opportu-

nity Initiative in July 2001, which makes the case for information and communication technology for development and will continue to assist developing countries in preparing national e-strategies. As also announced at Okinawa, and completed in July 2001, the United Nations Volunteers, UNDP, the United States Peace Corps and Cisco Systems deployed a programme to provide Internet training in 24 least developed countries worldwide. UNDP will work with other United Nations entities, Governments, non-governmental organizations and the private sector in implementing the DOT Force Plan of Action.

Data collection and analysis for advocacy and policy

169. The United Nations produces a wealth of reports and analyses that enable Governments to track the progress made in different aspects of social development. That data collection provides an excellent basis for advocacy and policy development. In the area of population, for example, UNFPA and the Statistics Division of the Department of Economic and Social Affairs have collaborated to enhance national capacities for statistical collection and analysis, especially in relation to conducting population censuses and surveys. This is fundamental to the construction of population-based indicators with a view to monitoring progress towards the goals set by global conferences.

170. With support from UNDP, more than 56 national human development reports are in various stages of preparation. Long-term studies were completed in Cameroon, Namibia and Sierra Leone, and another 30 such exercises are under way elsewhere. Courses on human development were introduced in 11 universities across Europe and the Commonwealth of Independent States. Advocacy has begun to produce new policies and programmes across all regions. Examples of recent progress include the participation of members of the think tank on human development in the formulation of the new National Charter in Bahrain; the Government of Brazil's adoption of the Human Development Index as a prerequisite to all federal resource allocation for social development; the use of the municipal Human Development Index in Bulgaria to focus public assistance; and the amendment of the rules and regulations of the Social Fund for Development in Egypt to incorporate best practices on poverty reduction.

Sustainable development

171. Nearly a decade has passed since the United Nations Conference on Environment and Development was convened in 1992. Since then, Governments and civil society groups have brought tremendous energy to the implementation of Agenda 21 and other outcomes of the Conference. Governments in both developed and developing countries have taken legislative and regulatory action to strengthen national policy frameworks for sustainable development. Around the world, numerous communities have implemented local versions of Agenda 21 and a growing number of companies have adopted sustainable development as an essential element of corporate stewardship.

172. Within the United Nations system, diverse initiatives in support of Member States' efforts to pursue country-specific sustainable development plans have been launched through project financing, policy advice and technical assistance aimed at strengthening human, institutional, technical and productive capacities of developing countries.

173. Notwithstanding those efforts, the challenge of achieving sustainability remains. The *World Resources Report 2000-01: People and Ecosystems, the Fraying Web of Life*, produced in September 2000 by the World Resources Institute, UNDP, the United Nations Environment Programme (UNEP) and the World Bank, concluded that increased resource demands continued to cause global ecosystems to deteriorate, with potentially devastating results for human development and the welfare of all species. The report was based largely on information collected in the preparatory phase of the Millennium Ecosystem Assessment from 1998-2000, a major international collaborative effort to map the health of our planet, generate new information, develop methodological tools, inform public policies and increase public awareness. It led to the launching of a Poverty-Environment Initiative designed to identify practical policy measures that advance the twin goals of poverty reduction and environmental regeneration. The World Energy Assessment, co-sponsored by UNDP, the Department of Economic and Social Affairs and the World Energy Council, was also launched in the period under review.

174. An important landmark will be the convening, at the instigation of the General Assembly, of the World Summit on Sustainable Development at Johannesburg, South Africa, in 2002. The Summit is intended to reinvigorate global commitment to sustainable development by identifying accomplishments and constraints as well as new challenges and opportunities in the

implementation of Agenda 21 and other out-comes of the United Nations Conference on Environment and Development. The regional commissions and UNEP have been organizing regional meetings with this in mind.

175. In order to successfully address new and emerging challenges in promoting sustainable development, the international community needs strong, focused and effective institutional arrangements that ensure coherent and integrated international environmental policy. To that end, and in line with the Malmö Ministerial Declaration, adopted by the First Global Ministerial Environment Forum, held at Malmö, Sweden, in May 2000, and the decisions of the Governing Council of UNEP, a review of international environmental governance, involving Governments, financial institutions, civil society and experts, is under way. It will take full account of the environmental components of the Millennium Declaration and provide substantive inputs to the preparatory process for the World Summit on Sustainable Development.

176. International cooperation for sustainable development at the intergovernmental level continues under the auspices of the Commission on Sustainable Development, which held its ninth session in April 2001. The Commission placed its policy review in a broad development context and highlighted the linkages between atmospheric issues and other problems, including unsustainable consumption and production patterns, rapid urbanization and the interdependence of energy, transport and the atmosphere. In its deliberations on energy, the Commission emphasized that meeting the energy challenge would require financial resources, technology transfer and commitment to innovative ways of applying energy-efficient, environmentally sound and cost-effective technologies to all sectors of the economy.

177. The first Meeting of the Parties to the Convention on the Transboundary Effects of Industrial Accidents was held in November 2000. Negotiations were initiated for a new legally binding instrument on pollutant release and transfer registers under the Convention on Access to Information, Public Participation in Decision-making and Access to Justice in Environmental Matters (the "Aarhus Convention") for possible adoption at the Fifth Ministerial Conference on Environment for Europe, to be held at Kiev in 2003. The Aarhus Convention, negotiated under the auspices of the Economic Commission for Europe, was adopted in June 1998 and enters into force in October 2001.

178. During the year under review, the Commission on Sustainable Development success-fully concluded the work of the Intergovernmental Forum on Forests. By its resolution 2000/35, the Economic and Social Council decided to establish the United Nations Forum on Forests to promote the implementation of internationally agreed actions on forests at the national, regional and global levels. In June 2001, the Forum held its first substantive session to develop a plan of action and to initiate the Forum's work by means of a collaborative partnership on forests.

179. Implementation of multilateral environmental agreements is essential in the protection of our common environment. The adoption and signing at Stockholm in May 2001 of the Convention for Implementing International Action on Certain Persistent Organic Pollutants, with a view to minimizing and eliminating some of the most toxic chemicals, was an important milestone. Environmental experts have hailed the Convention, which sets out control measures covering the production, trade, disposal and use of such pollutants, as an historic step towards making the planet safer.

180. In the field of climate change, summaries of the third assessment report of the Intergovernmental Panel on Climate Change were released early in 2001. The Panel concluded that there was strong evidence that most of the warming over the past 50 years was attributable to human activities and projected a global average temperature rise of 1.4° to 5.8° C over the next 100 years. To alleviate the problem, efforts by the United Nations system to promote renewable energy technologies and facilitate the required reductions in emissions of greenhouse gases continue, as do attempts to ensure the entry into force of the Kyoto Protocol by 2002.

181. Efforts towards sustainable development also continue at the regional level. The Economic and Social Commission for Asia and the Pacific organized a Ministerial Conference on Environment and Development at Kitakyushu, Japan, in September 2000. The Conference adopted a Ministerial Declaration and a Regional Action Programme 2001-2005, which commit regional Governments to pursuing common priorities to promote sustainable development. The Conference also launched the Kitakyushu Initiative for a Clean Environment, the first attempt at twinning cities of developing countries with the City of Kitakyushu to improve urban environmental management.

182. The Economic Commission for Latin America and the Caribbean is working with the Department of Economic and Social Affairs and UNEP in assisting countries in the region to prepare for the World Summit on Sustainable Development. Participants in the preparatory meet-

ings reported a high level of adherence to international environmental agreements, both those approved at the United Nations Conference on Environment and Development in 1992 and those negotiated subsequently.

183. Most countries of the region of the Economic and Social Commission for Western Asia (ESCWA) have formulated national environmental strategies and action plans aimed at integrating environmental concerns into economic development plans and setting priorities to achieve sustainable development. ESCWA is also emphasizing assessment and identification of options to facilitate sustainable approaches to energy resource management and the development of mechanisms to support regional and subregional cooperation. By October 2000, 11 ESCWA member States had agreed to join the mechanism and had nominated concerned national authorities to represent them as national focal points. The region is facing a critical situation with respect to water resources. It must work to increase the efficiency of water use and water management, including water recycling and desalination; to induce more regional cooperation, especially in the management of shared water resources; and to utilize its abundant energy resources in increasing the availability of water resources and protecting our common environment.

Africa

184. In the Millennium Declaration, Member States devoted special attention to Africa and called on the United Nations system to play a catalytic role in mobilizing resources in the cause of African development.

185. The recommendations contained in my report on the causes of conflict and the promotion of durable peace and sustainable development in Africa (A/52/871-S/1998/318) remain an important point of departure. The implementation of those recommendations has been entrusted to the General Assembly Ad Hoc Working Group, whose progress report of November 2000 contained a concise overview of the progress in and constraints to their implementation. The Working Group met again in May and June 2001 to focus on conflict prevention, post-conflict peace-building and education.

186. At the high-level segment of the Economic and Social Council, in July 2001, the New African Initiative adopted by the Organization of African Unity at Lusaka, also in July, was the principal focus of attention. The ministerial declaration adopted by the Council at the conclusion of the session gives clear direction to the United Nations system to rally behind the unified framework that African leaders have launched. Through the declaration, the Council established itself as the main global forum for mobilizing the support of the United Nations system and the international community at large for the Initiative and the newly created African Union. I am pleased at the high-level participation of Africa and the clear demonstration of its intention to take control of its own destiny.

187. The Economic and Social Council placed particular emphasis on the link between peace and development and the need to ensure that the momentum towards democracy and economic reform was sustained. It called for effective international support for Africa, including in addressing the HIV/AIDS crisis, improving market access and providing deeper and broader debt relief and increased official development assistance. The United Nations system will have to play a central role in mobilizing international support in order to achieve those objectives.

188. In its ministerial declaration, the Council noted in particular the call made by African heads of State for a special session of the General Assembly to consider how best to support the New African Initiative and requested me to explore the feasibility of creating a subregional coordinating capacity for peace-building and an ad hoc advisory group of the Economic and Social Council on countries emerging from conflict.

189. While international support remains essential, ultimately African countries themselves are best placed to overcome the pressing challenges that confront the continent, and it is encouraging to see the renewed determination of Africans to do so. The full engagement of the Economic Commission for Africa is especially important. The Compact for African Recovery, presented to ECA at its thirty-fourth session, held at Algiers in May 2001, represents an important component of the ECA response to the implementation of the Millennium Declaration.

190. The priority areas of the Compact include promoting good governance, peace and security; tackling diseases that accentuate poverty; developing human resources; promoting infrastructure expansion; advancing regional integration; enhancing Africa's competitiveness through the utilization of information and communication technologies and economic diversification; sustaining high economic growth rates; expanding market access and trade; and ensuring external resource flows, including debt relief.

191. United Nations entities remain deeply involved in a wide range of African development issues. In 2000, WFP assisted almost 35 million people with food deliveries, 51 per cent of them women, in sub-Saharan Africa. Its operations in

that area now include 76 development projects, 20 long-term relief and recovery operations and 47 emergency operations.

192. UNDP continues to promote participatory approaches to poverty reduction through partnership arrangements with civil society organizations. Moreover, in countries in special development situations, such as Angola and Burundi, UNDP has played an important role in ensuring that humanitarian concerns do not eclipse broader dialogue on poverty eradication or environmental protection. Together with other partners, UNDP has also invested in democratic governance in Africa by supporting electoral processes and parliaments.

193. UNIFEM has implemented a series of strategies to address the multidimensional nature of poverty in Africa. It has emphasized the importance of building the capacity of small-scale businesses owned by women. Linking women producers and entrepreneurs with external markets, the initiative also supports women's participation in non-traditional fields and assists with microfinance projects. The UNIFEM project Promoting Women's Rights to Economic Security in countries of the Southern African Development Community safeguards women's economic security by strengthening their capacity and skills at the local, national and regional levels.

194. A number of United Nations entities, including UNFPA, UNICEF, WHO and UNESCO, have worked to provide sexual and reproductive health information, counselling and services to youth and adolescents in Africa. With funding from the Bill and Melinda Gates Foundation, and in cooperation with Pathfinder International, UNFPA has created the African Youth Alliance to reduce the rate of HIV/AIDS infection among adolescents. Support from the United Nations Foundation has permitted UNFPA to support similar programmes in Benin, Burkina Faso, Mali, Sao Tome and Principe, and Senegal. UNDP, UNICEF, UNFPA, UNESCO, WHO and UNIFEM are working together to build on the success of UNIFEM in promoting alternative rites of passage to combat female genital mutilation. To date, 16 countries have outlawed the practice.

195. Child survival and improvements in child and maternal health remain a priority in Africa. Sub-Saharan Africa continued to receive the greatest share of UNICEF programme expenditure, which in 2000 amounted to $391 million, or 38 per cent of total spending. This represents an increase of 15 per cent over 1999 expenditure. Under its Bamako Initiative, UNICEF is contributing to the revitalization of health systems and community participation. The Initiative has improved the quality of services and access to basic health care in 7,000 health centres in 13 countries. The UNICEF African Girls' Education Initiative, implemented in partnership with the Government of Norway, has afforded an increasing number of African girls in, for example, Cameroon, Chad, Eritrea, Senegal and Uganda the opportunity to attend school and receive an improved basic education. The Initiative will expand its support to 31 African countries, including some torn by civil strife.

Chapter IV

The international legal order and human rights

Human rights development

196. Bridging the gap between human rights norms and their implementation continues to pose a substantial challenge for the United Nations. The Commission on Human Rights plays a crucial role in meeting this challenge by providing a forum for discussion, in which more than 60 heads of State or Government, Ministers for Foreign Affairs or other Ministers participated in the past year. In addition to the 53 States members of the Commission, almost all the remaining Members of the United Nations now attend meetings of the Commission as observers. Nearly all the United Nations agencies, 10 intergovernmental organizations and about 250 non-governmental organizations participated in the Commission's fifty-seventh session. Forty-two special rapporteurs, independent experts, and chairpersons of bodies and groups submitted country and thematic reports. Those reports painted a bleak picture of the status of human rights in the world today.

197. Some progress was made during the Commission's fifty-seventh session, but the task of achieving universal respect for human rights remains daunting. Eighty-two resolutions, 19 decisions, and three statements by the Chairperson were adopted, addressing the human rights situation in more than 20 countries and territories; they focused on numerous themes such as summary executions, torture, religious intolerance, violence against women, the right to development, and human rights and extreme poverty. This year, the Commission addressed new topics and made particular advances in the protection of the human rights of indigenous peoples by appointing a special rapporteur on the situation of human rights and fundamental freedoms of indigenous people. The Special Rapporteur will gather, request, receive and exchange informa-

tion and communications from all relevant sources, including Governments, indigenous people themselves, and their communities and organizations, on violations of their human rights and fundamental freedoms. This is a particularly appropriate step in view of the General Assembly's emphasis on enhancing the rights of vulnerable groups, as expressed in the Millennium Declaration, and the designation of the period 1995-2004 as the International Decade of the World's Indigenous People. To stress the specific human rights dimension of indigenous matters, I designated the Office of the United Nations High Commissioner for Human Rights as the lead agency for the Permanent Forum on Indigenous Issues, established by the Economic and Social Council in July 2000. In addition to its work on indigenous issues, the Commission adopted a timely resolution concerning access to medication in the context of pandemics such as HIV/AIDS. It also requested the appointment of an independent expert to examine the question of a draft optional protocol, under which individual communications could be considered, to the International Covenant on Economic, Social and Cultural Rights, and established a working group to draft a legally binding instrument for the protection of all persons from enforced disappearance.

198. In addressing the Commission on 30 March 2001, I gave my full support to the High Commissioner for Human Rights in her efforts to ensure the success of the World Conference against Racism, Racial Discrimination, Xenophobia and Related Intolerance, held at Durban, South Africa, from 31 August to 7 September 2001. Racial discrimination, xenophobia and intolerance are scourges that must be fought and defeated. The High Commissioner, acting in her capacity as the Secretary-General of the Conference, and her Office have organized five regional seminars of experts, at Geneva, Warsaw, Bangkok, Addis Ababa and Santiago. Four regional intergovernmental conferences have already been held at Strasbourg, Santiago, Dakar and Tehran. The Durban Conference has great potential to give people around the world both help and hope in the fight against discrimination.

199. During the Millennium Summit, I renewed my call upon States to ratify the six core United Nations human rights treaties, and many have done so. Protecting the vulnerable is a crucial task. One significant development is the entry into force, on 22 December 2000, of the Optional Protocol to the Convention on the Elimination of All Forms of Discrimination against Women. The Protocol contains a communications procedure that allows submission of claims of violations of rights protected under the Convention, and an inquiry procedure enabling the Committee to initiate inquiries into situations of grave or systematic violations of women's rights. Progress has also been made with regard to the two Optional Protocols to the Convention on the Rights of the Child. Both protocols were adopted by the General Assembly on 25 May 2000. The Protocol on the involvement of children in armed conflict has already been signed by 80 States, with four States parties. The Protocol on the sale of children, child prostitution and child pornography has been signed by 73 States, three of which have already become parties. Each Protocol requires ratification or accession by 10 States parties to become enforceable.

200. The six United Nations treaty bodies continue to provide a framework for national action to enhance the protection of human rights. New general recommendations have been adopted by various committees addressing issues such as the right to education, HIV/AIDS, equality and the gender-related dimension of racial discrimination.

201. The Office of the United Nations High Commissioner for Human Rights continued its technical cooperation efforts to assist States in the protection and promotion of human rights. At present, the Office is responding directly to requests from some 60 Member States to create or strengthen national human rights capacities and infrastructures. As the system-wide focal point for human rights, democracy and the rule of law, and in an effort to continue mainstreaming human rights, the Office has strengthened its partnerships with other parts of the system. Creating new linkages between human rights policy expertise and field-level development, peacekeeping and humanitarian capacities has proved useful in these endeavours. In response, 2001 has seen more rights-based development programmes, more rights-sensitive humanitarian operations and more rights-attentive peacekeeping operations.

202. The dissemination of information on human rights issues has improved in 2000-2001. The Office's strategy for securing, processing and sharing human rights information has involved human rights research activities, reference and documentation services, publications and web-publishing efforts. The web site of the Office offers comprehensive information on the United Nations human rights programme and activities and gives access to essential human rights documents. In June 2001, the web site received a record high of 5 million hits.

The International Criminal Court

203.   The Preparatory Commission for the International Criminal Court held its sixth session in November/December 2000, and its seventh session in February/March 2001. The eighth session will be held from 24 September to 5 October 2001. At its sixth session, the Preparatory Commission considered issues relating to the financing, privileges and immunities, and relationship agreements of the Court, as well as the crime of aggression. At its seventh session, it considered the rules of procedure of the Assembly of States Parties. Substantial progress was made on all five of these items. At its eighth session, the Preparatory Commission will consider the budget of the Court for its first financial year and the basic principles of a headquarters agreement between the Court and the host country.

204.   A total of 139 States had signed the Rome Statute of the International Criminal Court by 31 December 2000, the last day on which it was open for signature. To date, 37 States have ratified the statute. These figures are encouraging and there is no doubt that the statute will enter into force soon. The adoption of the Rome Statute has opened a new chapter in international law. A comprehensive legal and institutional regime now exists in the field of international criminal justice, something that will certainly affect the conduct of States but, more importantly, will guide and shape the behaviour of individuals. Much remains to be done to operationalize that regime and make it effective. I appeal to States not only to establish their consent to be bound by the Rome Statute as soon as possible but also to support, by every means, the important cause of the Court.

205.   Some Governments and their peoples remain wary of this enterprise. I find it hard to believe, though, that their scepticism flows from any disagreement with the importance of compliance with international humanitarian law, much less from any principled opposition to the notion that those who are guilty of the most atrocious crimes known to humanity should be tried and punished. I would encourage those who remain unconvinced by the project of a permanent International Criminal Court to reflect on the central principle of Nürnberg and Tokyo, namely, that those who commit or authorize war crimes and other serious violations of international humanitarian law are individually accountable for their crimes, and the community of States can and should bring them to justice.

The International Tribunals

International Tribunal for the Former Yugoslavia

206.   During the past year, there were several major developments in the work of the International Tribunal for the Former Yugoslavia. These developments should significantly enhance the Tribunal's ability to discharge its mandate to prosecute those responsible for serious violations of international humanitarian law in the former Yugoslavia, and to contribute to the maintenance of peace and security in the region, while enabling the Tribunal to complete its work by 2008.

207.   Major reforms enhancing the efficiency of the Tribunal's operations and expediting the commencement and completion of trials have been made. In November 2000, the Security Council amended the statute of the International Tribunal to provide for a pool of 27 judges to help its 16 permanent judges to conduct and complete trials as the need arises. In a major demonstration of support for the Tribunal, 34 States in all regions of the world responded to my invitation for nominations and, among them, proposed no fewer than 64 candidates for election. In June 2001, the General Assembly elected 27 of those candidates to the Tribunal. Other significant reforms have included an increase in the capacity of the Tribunal's Appeals Chamber, and a series of amendments to the Tribunal's Rules of Procedure and Evidence, the most noteworthy of which is that barring "interlocutory" or provisional appeals.

208.   As regards States' cooperation with the Tribunal, the most notable event over the past year was the apprehension and subsequent transfer to the Tribunal of the former President of the Federal Republic of Yugoslavia, Slobodan Milosevic, on 28 June 2001. This marked the beginning of a new era in the development of international criminal justice. The surrender, arraignment and forthcoming trial of an accused person who was, until very recently, a head of State, represent a major victory in the international community's fight against impunity and a decisive step towards a world governed in accordance with the rule of law. The voluntary surrender of Biljana Plavsic and the transfer of Momcilo Krajišnik, two former high-ranking political figures, also represented major developments in the Tribunal's relations with the authorities of the Federal Republic of Yugoslavia.

209.   There are currently 39 accused persons held in the United Nations Detention Unit. Four trials, involving a total of 10 accused, are under way before the Tribunal's three Trial Chambers, and 10 other cases, involving a total of 16 accused,

are in the pre-trial phase. Over the past year, the Tribunal has tried and sentenced five individuals. Each of the five has appealed against the sentence. One other accused has pleaded guilty and is awaiting sentencing. The Tribunal transferred three convicted persons to Member States to serve their sentences: two to Finland and one to Germany.

210. Following the electoral defeat of Mr. Milosevic, the Prosecutor reopened the Tribunal's field office in Belgrade in order to help investigators to resume their work in the Federal Republic of Yugoslavia. Meanwhile, investigators completed work on exhumations in Kosovo that resulted in the discovery of the remains of some 4,000 individuals. The Prosecutor also commenced investigations into allegations against ethnic Albanian rebels in southern Serbia, the Kosovo Liberation Army, and groups involved in hostilities in the former Yugoslav Republic of Macedonia. Over the past year, the Prosecutor has personally dedicated a considerable amount of time and effort to encouraging Governments to arrest persons indicted by the Tribunal and to transfer them to The Hague to stand trial. It is gratifying that those efforts are now beginning to bear fruit.

International Tribunal for Rwanda

211. The Tribunal made significant advances during the past year. Amendments to the Rules of Procedure and Evidence, which lay down a framework for the admission of statements from other trials and impose stricter judicial controls on motions, will all help to speed up court proceedings. A generally more vigorous approach to the Tribunal's caseload has begun to yield positive results. The Appeals Chamber handed down final judgements in three cases, bringing the total number of cases disposed of on appeal to five. Meanwhile, Trial Chamber I completed the trial of one accused, who received the Tribunal's first acquittal.

212. Following the implementation of a "twin-track" approach, whereby each of the three Trial Chambers simultaneously conducts two trials, a total of 15 accused persons are now on trial before the Tribunal in five cases. One of these cases, known as the Butare case, is the largest to date at the Tribunal, involving no less than six accused. Another trial, involving two accused, is scheduled to commence in September 2001, at which time the number of persons on trial will total 17. As these figures show, the Tribunal is discharging its mandate as effectively as possible given current resources.

213. At the same time, four accused were arrested and transferred to the Tribunal's detention facility in Arusha. They were Samuel Musabyimana, a former Bishop of the Anglican Church in Rwanda; Simeon Nshamihigo, a defence investigator; and two former mayors, Sylvestre Gabumbitsi and Jean Mpambara.

214. In November 2000, the Security Council decided to increase the number of judges in the Appeals Chambers of the two International Tribunals. Following the amendment of the Tribunal's statute, the General Assembly elected two new judges to the Tribunal on 24 April 2001, and the President of the Tribunal transferred two existing judges to the Appeals Chambers on 1 June 2001. It is hoped that this increase in the judicial capacity of both International Tribunals will expedite the disposition of the increasing numbers of appeals.

215. Regrettably, the first President of the Tribunal and the Presiding Judge of Trial Chamber II, Judge Laïty Kama of Senegal, passed away in Nairobi on 6 May 2001. Judge Kama was a man of the highest professional competence who was devoted to the cause of justice and the promotion and protection of human rights, and who fulfilled his duties with dignity and integrity. On 31 May 2001, I appointed Judge Andrésia Vaz, President of the Court of Cassation of Senegal, to fill the position.

Enhancing the rule of law

216. Over the past year, the Organization has taken further decisive steps towards strengthening respect for the rule of law in international affairs. In August 2000, the Security Council charged me with negotiating and concluding an agreement with the Government of Sierra Leone for the establishment of an independent special court. It will try persons bearing the greatest responsibility for serious violations of international humanitarian law, as well as crimes under relevant Sierra Leonean law. At my request, the Office of Legal Affairs prepared a draft Agreement between the United Nations and the Government of Sierra Leone on the Establishment of the Special Court, and a draft statute for the Court, and negotiated both of these instruments with the Government of Sierra Leone. The members of the Security Council have given their agreement, in principle, to their contents.

217. At my request, the Office of Legal Affairs has also initiated a process of informal consultations with a group of interested States on practical arrangements for the implementation of the Agreement, including establishing a management committee, budget estimates and Court premises. In view of the response to my appeal for voluntary contributions in funds, personnel and equipment, initial arrangements for the operation of the Court have been modified, to align

them with the level of available funding. Once the resources are sufficient to fund the establishment and operation of the Court, the Agreement will be concluded with the Government of Sierra Leone, and the legal framework needed for the Court to begin to function will be established.

218. At the Millennium Summit, I encouraged States to sign, ratify and accede to treaties of which I am the depositary. Specific attention was paid to a core group of 25 multilateral treaties that represent the objectives of the Charter and reflect the Organization's values. I was deeply gratified by the success of this initiative. During the Summit, no less than 84 States performed a total of 274 treaty actions—187 signatures and 87 ratifications and accessions—in respect of 40 of the more than 500 treaties for which I act as the depositary. Particularly satisfying were the 12 signatures and four ratifications of the Rome Statute of the International Criminal Court, and the seven ratifications of, or accessions to, the Convention on the Safety of United Nations and Associated Personnel. In view of this positive response, I have decided to organize a similar event, albeit on a somewhat smaller scale, during the special session of the General Assembly on children and the general debate at the fifty-sixth session of the General Assembly. This event will focus on 23 multilateral treaties relating to the advancement of the rights of women.

219. Many States fail to sign or ratify treaties, not because of any lack of political will, but because of a simple shortage of technical expertise when it comes to the implementation of treaty provisions. Consequently, the Office of Legal Affairs is preparing a handbook that will provide guidance to Governments on the execution of treaty formalities. This practical guide will be issued in the six official languages of the Organization and will be supplemented by training sessions for government lawyers, organized with the United Nations Institute for Training and Research. It is not enough simply for States to establish their consent to be bound by treaties, however; States must also implement and respect the obligations which those treaties impose.

220. One of the central objectives of the United Nations is to assist Governments in establishing the necessary conditions for compliance with treaty commitments. The Organization already undertakes a broad range of actions to this end, helping Governments to draft national implementing legislation and supporting training programmes for those involved in its application. Over the past year, the Office of Legal Affairs has worked to increase awareness of the various forms of technical assistance that the Organization can provide to Governments in this respect.

221. That the law should be accessible to those whom it is meant to guide is a central precept of the rule of law. Mindful of this, the Office of Legal Affairs is working to make the entire corpus of modern international treaty law directly available to legal practitioners, diplomats, nongovernmental organizations and ordinary citizens by publishing on the Internet the complete texts of more than 50,000 treaties that were registered with the Secretariat prior to May 1998. Ordinary citizens, civil society and corporations should thus be in a better position to ensure that they are accorded their rights and benefits and that they, in turn, respect their duties, under international law.

Legal affairs

222. The past year was particularly productive for the International Law Commission. The Commission adopted a set of draft articles on responsibility of States for internationally wrongful acts, thus concluding work that had been on its agenda for almost 50 years. The Commission also adopted a set of draft articles on the prevention of transboundary harm from hazardous activities and advanced work on a number of other topics, notably, reservations to treaties, unilateral acts of States and diplomatic protection.

223. At its session in 2001, the United Nations Commission on International Trade Law adopted two major texts, the draft Convention on Assignment of Receivables in International Trade and the Model Law on Electronic Signatures. The draft Convention, which was referred to the General Assembly for conclusion, will enhance the availability of credit at more affordable rates, thus facilitating international trade and a more equitable distribution of the benefits of international trade among all peoples. The Model Law on Electronic Signatures is aimed at facilitating electronic commerce by promoting a safe environment for all participants to share in the benefits of modern technology. The Commission also took note of ongoing work on arbitration and insolvency and decided to begin work in the fields of electronic contracting, transport law, privately financed infrastructure projects and secured transactions.

224. The past year has seen no less than 83 ratifications of, and accessions to, the 12 existing global conventions for the prevention and suppression of international terrorism. Particularly gratifying is the fact that 16 States ratified or acceded to the International Convention for the Suppression of Terrorist Bombings, which, as a result, entered into force on 23 May 2001. The Ad Hoc Committee and the Sixth Committee of the General Assembly commenced work on a compre-

hensive convention on international terrorism. Efforts to resolve outstanding issues regarding plans for an international convention for the suppression of acts of nuclear terrorism continue.

225. In 1999, the General Assembly launched consultations to facilitate its annual review of developments in the field of ocean affairs and the law of the sea. The second series was held in May 2001 and addressed illegal, unreported and unregulated fishing, marine science, piracy and the economic and social impacts of marine degradation, particularly in coastal areas.

226. The Office of Legal Affairs advised UNMIK and UNTAET on the exercise of their legislative and executive authority. In particular, it assisted the two Administrations in establishing legal frameworks for transitional, democratic and autonomous self-governing institutions. The Office continued to provide legal advice to the Organization's other peacekeeping missions. In particular, it participated in the negotiation of several status-of-forces and status-of-mission agreements, the finalization of the Agreement between the United Nations and Ethiopia concerning the United Nations Mission in Ethiopia and Eritrea and the Agreement between the United Nations and the former Yugoslav Republic of Macedonia concerning the United Nations Interim Administration Mission in Kosovo. Further, the Office provided legal advice to participants in the Burundi peace process under former President Nelson Mandela's facilitation, and contributed to implementing recommendations made by the Panel on United Nations Peace Operations.

227. The Office of Legal Affairs successfully defended the Organization in complex arbitration proceedings involving a $20 million claim; assisted in the resolution of claims against the Organization arising out of its peacekeeping operations; cooperated with host State authorities in recovering nearly $750,000 worth of Member States' contributions to the United Nations Environment Programme that had erroneously been credited to a private individual's bank account; assisted in negotiating a number of agreements with the private sector; and provided advice on implementation of the "oil-for-food" programme, including negotiation of agreements to facilitate the diversification and better protection of its assets.

Chapter V

Enhancing management

Administration and management

228. Member States have continued to support management reform within the United Na-

tions and have endorsed detailed proposals in three priority areas: human resources reform, information technology policy, and the capital master plan. The Organization is now equipped to operate more efficiently and effectively and to make the best use of its financial and human resources.

Human resources reform

229. Comprehensive human resources reform, unanimously agreed to by Member States, will change the Organization's management culture. It will enable the Secretariat to be more flexible and responsive in its use of human resources, a necessity given the evolution of the United Nations from a headquarters-based organization into one with a strong field presence. The reforms will modernize the Organization's human resources management standards and strengthen its capacity to recruit, develop and manage its staff.

Capitalizing on technology

230. The United Nations information technology strategy, designed to promote access to and sharing of information, support field operations, strengthen technical infrastructure, build human resources capacity and launch an e-administration, will ensure a coordinated approach to technical challenges. An example of work already under way is the Integrated Management Information System (IMIS). This electronic administration system for human resources, finance, accounts and procurement is being installed throughout the Secretariat, and will serve to anchor future technological improvements in this rapidly changing field. We are poised to establish field connectivity so that we can use IMIS for the Organization's operations around the globe. Ongoing efforts to render the system more user-friendly will encourage its use and therefore increase productivity.

Capital master plan

231. The capital master plan, including its financing components, was submitted to the General Assembly at its fifty-fifth session. Member States supported its plans for the proactive refurbishing of the Headquarters complex, and a comprehensive design plan and detailed cost analysis are in preparation.

Future challenges

232. Numerous other reform initiatives, at various stages of implementation, are under way. Procurement reform has been successfully completed, and the simplification and streamlining

of the Organization's rules and procedures is progressing smoothly. The electronic personnel manual is now available through the Intranet, and has proved to be an invaluable tool for responsible, consistent and uniform managerial action. We are continually shifting to a more results-based mode of operation. Performance indicators are being introduced at all levels; for example, in the financial area, through the introduction of results-based budgeting, and in the personnel area, through refinements in the performance evaluation system.

233. The Secretariat will continue to implement comprehensive management reform, introducing best management practices and technologies, so that limited resources are made available for priorities. It will complete and implement a Key Item Management Reporting System, make productivity a managerial responsibility, and extend IMIS, with its far-reaching management control functions, to all major duty stations and peacekeeping missions. Innovations will continue to be introduced in the context of the overall information technology strategy. Human resources management reform will also continue. The introduction and refinement of performance measurements, through the performance appraisal system, and through the introduction of results-based budgeting, are geared towards ensuring the delivery of high-priority services identified by Member States.

234. The introduction of sunset provisions in all of the Organization's legislative directives, another important step towards revitalizing the Organization, still awaits acceptance by Member States. Once adopted, sunset provisions will orient the Organization's work programme to high-priority tasks as they evolve.

Financial situation

235. In the area of fiscal responsibility, the United Nations has demonstrated consistent budgetary discipline. There has been no budgetary growth over the last four bienniums and there has even been a reduction in the Organization's budget. The Organization has absorbed the effects of inflation and a large number of unfunded mandates. At the same time, it has succeeded in reallocating resources from low-priority areas and administrative services to higher-priority programmes identified by Member States. While many Member States have responded to Secretariat efforts to improve the collection of current and outstanding assessments, a number of major contributors have paid none or only part of their dues. This has forced the United Nations to borrow from peacekeeping accounts to offset the earlier and larger-than-usual deficit currently being experienced. It is clear that the United Nations cannot function effectively unless all Member States pay their dues, in full, on time and without conditions.

Accountability and oversight

236. Since its creation in 1994, the Office of Internal Oversight Services has evolved from a collection of small autonomous units reporting to the Administration into an independent, integrated Office providing a comprehensive range of internal oversight services. It is now recognized—both within and outside the Organization—as an objective source of reliable information and an agent of change in the United Nations.

237. The work of the Office of Internal Oversight Services extends from audits to consulting, evaluations, monitoring, inspections and investigations. It produces semi-annual overall performance assessments of the departments and offices under my charge. During the past year, oversight activities resulted in over 2,000 recommendations related to strengthening internal controls and improving management performance, and identified some $58 million in potential cost savings and recoveries. The number of recommendations is significantly higher than that reported in previous years. In order to reflect its widening global coverage, the Office is for the first time also making recommendations issued through observations made at the operating level in the field. The emphasis of the Office on full implementation of its recommendations results in ongoing dialogue between it and the rest of the Organization. To focus on areas that warrant special monitoring, the Office has recently developed criteria to identify those of its recommendations that have a critical and far-reaching impact on the Organization's operations.

238. The Office of Internal Oversight Services has convened several senior staff workshops to address strategic oversight planning issues such as maximizing the value added to the Organization, making greater use of information technology, and improving staff competencies. Achievement of the Office's oversight goals ultimately depends on the quality of the work it produces and the significance and impact of its recommendations. It is therefore critical for the Office to use the most up-to-date oversight techniques and procedures, such as those used by advanced private and public sector oversight entities.

239. As a result of a strategic planning exercise, which began last year, the Office of Internal Oversight Services proposes to merge its moni-

toring, evaluation, inspection and consulting functions. This will allow for a more synthesized gathering of qualitative data, facilitating the preparation of programme performance reports, as requested by the intergovernmental bodies. The Office also proposes to strengthen the investigations subprogramme to cope with the increasing number of cases received, and to establish an office at Geneva to deliver more responsive and coordinated oversight services there.

240. As the United Nations has become more field-based, it has delegated increased levels of authority in areas such as procurement and human resources management. This obliges us to ensure that proper controls are in place in the field, and that adequate checks and balances exist. It is encouraging to note that the Office of Internal Oversight Services has increased its oversight of field activities, including the operations of the Office of the United Nations High Commissioner for Human Rights, the Office of the United Nations High Commissioner for Refugees and the Office of the Iraq Programme.

Audit and management consulting

241. The Audit and Management Consulting Division placed special emphasis on audits of peacekeeping operations, humanitarian and related activities, human resources management and procurement of goods and services. The Division also conducted management audits addressing some of the major reform issues facing the Organization, such as recruitment.

242. The Division has expanded audit coverage of the Department of Peacekeeping Operations. Audits were conducted at Headquarters and numerous field missions during the past year. Resident auditors assigned to major peacekeeping missions provided continuous audit coverage and assisted management in establishing appropriate internal controls. Resident auditors have been posted to Abidjan and Nairobi to cover the decentralized operations of UNHCR in Africa, and to provide audit and management advice to the regional directors. As a temporary measure, resident auditors have also been assigned to UNHCR emergency operations in East Timor and Kosovo.

Investigations

243. The Investigations Section carries out internal oversight responsibilities by examining reports of violations of United Nations regulations, rules and pertinent administrative issuances to ensure greater staff member accountability and to protect the Organization's resources. During the reporting period, the Section received over 400 new cases and produced 36 reports containing its recommendations to the relevant programme. Recommendations were also made in several cases where staff members were cleared of allegations of wrongdoing, as the evidence gathered during the investigations did not substantiate the report received.

244. At the invitation of my Special Representatives in Kosovo and in East Timor, the Section opened Resident Investigator offices in UNMIK and UNTAET to provide a range of investigative services to the missions, and help to train staff to build the investigation capacity of the civilian administration.

245. Major investigations conducted during the reporting period included the misdirection of funds at UNEP and an investigation into allegations of fee-splitting between defence counsel and indigent detainees at the International Tribunals for Rwanda and the former Yugoslavia. The Office of Internal Oversight Services also led an international task force investigating bribery and extortion of refugees in Kenya seeking resettlement, which resulted in the arrest of nine people.

Central monitoring and inspection

246. The Central Monitoring and Inspection Unit conducted inspections of the Department of Economic and Social Affairs, the Department of General Assembly Affairs and Conference Services, and the United Nations Office for Drug Control and Crime Prevention. From the inspection of the Department of Economic and Social Affairs it was concluded that the Department had promoted greater policy and programme coherence and provided more effective substantive support to the intergovernmental and interagency machineries. Improvements need to be made in evaluating development cooperation activities and implementing organization-wide executive decisions.

247. The inspection of Conference Services showed that streamlining technical support services had allowed for improved planning and more rational resource allocation, and enhanced the efficiency of services provided to intergovernmental and expert bodies. Further feedback mechanisms, such as surveys, would improve the quality of its services. In its inspection of the Office for Drug Control and Crime Prevention, the Office of Internal Oversight Services observed that that Office was being run in a highly centralized and arbitrary manner. No consistent system for programme oversight was in place, and the absence of clearly defined delegation of authority clouded accountability. Member States, in-

cluding donors and recipients of services, indicated that this had adversely affected fulfilment of its mandates and implementation of some projects. The Office for Drug Control and Crime Prevention accepted all of the recommendations of the Office of Internal Oversight Services and initiated a series of measures to improve the situation.

Central evaluation

248. The Central Evaluation Unit examined the population and sustainable development programmes of the Department of Economic and Social Affairs in the past year. The examination found that the value of the Population Division's reports and publications as reference work, and their comprehensiveness and technical quality, is well recognized, and that the Division has made a significant contribution to the understanding of international migration. The evaluation of the sustainable development programme focused on current programme implementation issues. The Office of Internal Oversight Services recommended actions to improve support for intergovernmental processes, streamline reporting and enhance the quality of information presented. All the evaluation recommendations were endorsed by the Committee for Programme and Coordination at its forty-first session, in June 2001.

249. The Unit also completed triennial reviews of the implementation of the recommendations resulting from in-depth evaluations of the United Nations Crime Prevention and Criminal Justice Programme and the United Nations International Drug Control Programme. The Office of Internal Oversight Services found that, although some of the recommendations were implemented satisfactorily, the overall level of implementation was somewhat disappointing, as the Drug Control Programme had not addressed the underlying problems identified in the evaluation. The Office of Internal Oversight Services is monitoring implementation of those recommendations that have not yet been implemented.

Chapter VI

Partnerships

Communications

250. As I noted in my previous annual report, the United Nations has succeeded in forging global partnerships that would hardly have been conceivable even a decade ago. These partnerships continue to be strengthened by the Organization's communications and information strategy, which rests on a clear understanding that the goals of the United Nations can be met only if an informed public understands its mission.

251. The world is assailed by an information overload, and yet we are charged with the responsibility of giving a public face and discernible meaning to the activities and programmes of the Organization. For the Department of Public Information, this has meant integrating otherwise diverse operations into strategic global advocacy campaigns. The Department has highlighted tangible results of the major international conferences convened by the United Nations over the past year. Several initiatives, including the "UN works" campaign, capturing the direct impact of the Organization on the lives of people; a documentary film on light weapons, *Armed to the Teeth*; and a United Nations in Action report on human rights and special features on health issues in Africa in the *United Nations Chronicle* have contributed to articulating the importance of achieving the goals of the Millennium Declaration.

252. As the Millennium Declaration affirms, the benefits of new information and communication technologies must be available to all. This mandate drives our efforts to provide developing countries with immediate access to news developments at the United Nations. The global growth in Internet and e-mail access, including in the least developed countries, has allowed us to communicate rapidly and in real time with the media of developing countries. Most of those media entities have no representation at the United Nations, and e-mail and web-based news services are of enormous service and interest to them.

253. A daily news service has been established on the United Nations web site, reporting on and providing links to United Nations activities, operations, documents and other sources of information available electronically, including direct links from the field, complete with digital images. The news service is part of the United Nations News Centre, specifically designed to be an electronic gateway to news throughout the United Nations system, helping to ensure timely and global access to information on the Organization. In addition, an e-mail news alert system is being put in place as a more direct and proactive means of electronic communication to target audiences. A similar system is already regularly used to alert media in all parts of the world to important developments.

254. The launch of daily news bulletins by United Nations Radio in the six official languages of the Organization is a further dramatic example of the Department reaching out to cross

the "digital divide" between developed and developing countries. Transmitted to hundreds of radio stations in all regions of the world, these live radio broadcasts have a daily audience of tens of millions. More than 100 radio and television networks have received public service announcements relating to the commemoration of this Year of Dialogue among Civilizations. The United Nations web site, also in all official languages, has averaged 4 million hits a day this year, twice the number in 2000. The multilingualism essential to this success is being fostered creatively: an agreement is being finalized, for instance, with a number of universities in Spain to provide translations of material on the web site into Spanish. United Nations information centres expand the site's outreach further, with creatively tailored messages in the languages of their areas of operation.

255. Technology facilitates the channelling of traditional forms of information outreach, notably print, in a manner that is attractive, accessible and yet economical. Articles by outside contributors have highlighted the successes and the limitations of United Nations activities. Republishing individual articles in other media has also promoted a multiplier effect of the content.

256. Media outreach programmes continue to expand awareness of United Nations activities. United Nations information centres nurture relationships with local media, non-governmental organizations and the broader public to ensure that the Organization's concerns are widely understood. With generous support from the Government of Japan, 15 journalists from Asia attended high-level briefings at United Nations Headquarters, and 19 participants joined the Department's annual training programme for broadcasters and journalists from developing countries.

257. In the Dag Hammarskjöld Library, digitalization of documents and creation of resource databases have rendered this world-class repository of information more accessible. In the past year, the Library responded to 60,000 individual reference queries and delivered electronic journals via e-mail to readers.

258. The Department of Public Information continues to work actively to implement the Millennium Declaration's goal of giving "greater opportunities to the private sector, non-governmental organizations and civil society, in general, to contribute to the realization of the Organization's goals and programmes". Those partners include 1,600 non-governmental organizations formally associated with the Department; participants in guided tours for whom a new, comprehensive "visitors' experience" is be-

ing planned; school students who have enthusiastically joined programmes devised on the electronic *CyberSchoolBus*; and the business community, which accesses procurement opportunities in developing countries through the print and online editions of *Development Business*. Further, the Department supports the political, economic and humanitarian actors within the United Nations through the Cartographic Section, which remains a vital resource to the Organization as a whole.

259. The communication revolution has thrown open new, and increasingly accessible, technologies, even as it offers fresh possibilities to enhance and energize existing means of dissemination. Today's resources are essential to redeem tomorrow's promise, however. As the Department of Public Information moves beyond reorientation to modernization, it is essential that it should not be compelled, by a multiplicity of mandates and a lack of realistic resources, to spread itself too thin.

United Nations Fund for International Partnerships

260. The United Nations continues to benefit from an ever-expanding range of partnerships with the business community, philanthropic foundations and civil society organizations. Private sector interest in cooperating with the United Nations is intensifying and my office is increasingly called upon to develop innovative partnerships with a wide range of civil society actors. The United Nations Fund for International Partnerships (UNFIP) plays a vital role in developing networks to benefit the United Nations system. The Fund identifies new avenues for partnership with a wide range of external partners; provides advice on programme design; offers guidance on United Nations rules of procedure and funding modalities; and supports the creation of an enabling environment for corporate and individual philanthropy.

261. The Fund entered its fourth year in March 2001. As the counterpart of the United Nations Foundation, it has programmed nearly $385 million in support of more than 170 projects, involving 32 United Nations organizations in more than 100 countries. In 2001, the Fund added a peace, security and human rights portfolio to its ongoing programmes in children's health, environment, and women and population. In the past year, an additional $63 million in programme funds was mobilized from a wide range of partners. Together with the United Nations Foundation, UNFIP also encourages complementarity and coordination by bringing to-

gether United Nations organizations in joint programming.

262. The Fund has developed and continues to develop collaborative arrangements with the private sector and foundations, including the Bill and Melinda Gates Foundation, the Rockefeller Foundation, the Coca-Cola Company, Cisco Systems, Ericsson, the Canadian Imperial Bank of Commerce World Markets, United Way International and others. In collaboration with UNAIDS and the Global Business Council on HIV/AIDS, for example, UNFIP served as a private sector interlocutor to support fund-raising efforts for HIV/AIDS. It also helped in the creation of a facility for the receipt of private sector funds by the United Nations Foundation, pending the establishment of the Global AIDS and Health Fund. UNFIP continues to provide coordination for the Health InterNetwork, administered by WHO, and the United Nations Information Technology Service, administered by the United Nations Volunteers. It will continue to focus on promoting partnerships to advance the goals of the Millennium Declaration.

Project services

263. The only completely self-financing entity in the United Nations system, the United Nations Office for Project Services (UNOPS), finances itself on a fee-for-service basis. In 2000, UNOPS acquired new business valued at $948 million and delivered more than $471 million in services in over 2,600 projects worldwide. It also approved disbursement of $193 million in loans for projects it is supervising on behalf of the International Fund for Agricultural Development.

264. During the year, UNOPS worked predominantly to diversify its client base, building on its core relationship with UNDP. In 2000, acquisition of projects from new United Nations partners totalled an unprecedented $132 million, exceeding project acquisition from the regular resources of UNDP. In the first six months of 2001, demand for project services from clients other than UNDP approached a record $200 million.

265. New clients requesting UNOPS services included UNEP, the Economic and Social Commission for Asia and the Pacific (ESCAP), the International Atomic Energy Agency (IAEA), UNMIK and UNTAET. In both East Timor and Kosovo, major procurement operations were carried out to support the United Nations efforts to establish interim governing structures. Its operations yielded a substantial cost savings to clients and contributed to building local capacity for reconstruction.

266. As project work on behalf of non-traditional clients grows, so do new partnerships characterized by a clear division of labour. While project funders retain responsibility for the expertise provided in the area of their mandate, UNOPS acts as a project manager, assuming responsibility for operational and commercial activity and managing the financial risks and liabilities inherent in the contracting process. The Office's comparative advantage in results-based management, and the potential to transfer this knowledge to the United Nations system at large, is increasingly recognized. In 2000, UNOPS provided management consultancy services to ESCAP to support its revitalization programme and to the Department of Technical Cooperation of IAEA to analyse workload pressures. Consulting services were also provided in Guatemala, where WFP asked the Office for assistance in formulating its country programme; at the request of the United Nations Verification Mission in Guatemala, UNOPS provided consulting services to the Soros Foundation, the Centre for Legal Action and Human Rights and the Government of Norway on issues relating to the implementation of peace agreements and the follow-up of the Commission for Historical Clarification.

267. UNOPS efforts are expected to yield great results in 2001. Under its dedicated partnership regime, a new services offering, United Nations organizations may hire UNOPS to broker partnerships or to implement projects under existing partnership agreements. To date, 11 agreements have been signed with non-governmental organizations and private sector firms. One such partnership, funded by UNFIP, is bringing HIV/AIDS education to remote communities in Nepal. Another is transferring trade and business skills to local artisans in Mozambique. Such partnerships strengthen project delivery and attract new stakeholders whose support is critical to the global mandates of the United Nations.

Partnerships with civil society

268. Over the past year, cooperation with civil society, including a wide range of non-governmental organizations and the private sector, has continued to develop. Existing initiatives in the areas of policy dialogue and advocacy for United Nations values and activities are being consolidated. At the same time we are building new partnerships with the business community, non-governmental organizations and other civil society actors in order to promote information-sharing and learning, to support operational delivery and to mobilize private funds.

269. At the policy level, two notable developments have been the launch of the Information

and Communication Technologies Task Force and the establishment of the high-level Policy Network on Youth Employment. Both of these cooperative efforts are drawing on the expertise and resources of non-governmental organizations, the private sector and academia, to help us increase our effectiveness in addressing critical development issues. Non-governmental organizations, the private sector and other civil society actors, including parliamentarians, are also providing valuable input to the preparations for the International Conference on Financing for Development and the World Summit on Sustainable Development to be held in 2002, working closely with the relevant United Nations bodies to share expertise, learn from existing experience and propose future joint action.

270. My Global Compact initiative continues to evolve as a multi-stakeholder network focused on three core areas of activity, namely, learning, dialogue and action. The network now consists of several hundred companies, business associations, academic institutions and non-governmental organizations active in the areas of environment, labour, human rights and development. A key focus during the past 12 months has been to involve more companies and business associations from developing countries, and almost two thirds of our private sector participants are now from those countries. The International Labour Organization, UNEP, the Office of the United Nations High Commissioner for Human Rights and UNDP continue to play a central role, and other United Nations bodies are involved in specific areas of the initiative. UNCTAD, for example, is working with the International Chamber of Commerce and individual companies on a programme of investment deliverables for the least developed countries, including investment guides, linkages and advisory councils. The International Organization of Employers is working with the International Labour Organization to develop training materials on the Compact's nine principles for its national organizations in over 100 countries, and is cooperating with UN-AIDS to strengthen the capacity of employers organizations to tackle HIV/AIDS, especially in Africa. Several regional commissions are using the Global Compact as a framework for dialogue and partnerships with the private sector in their regions. A learning forum has been established, managed by a consortium of academic institutions, and a policy dialogue has been initiated on the role of the private sector in zones of conflict. Individual companies are supporting development projects in partnership with the United Nations in areas such as HIV/AIDS, microcredit, digital divide, diversity, and humanitarian and refugee support.

271. We continue to mobilize funds, product donations and volunteer support through the work of UNFIP, as well as advocacy and fund-raising programmes initiated by individual United Nations bodies, including UNICEF, UNDP, UNAIDS, the Office for the Coordination of Humanitarian Affairs, the United Nations International Drug Control Programme and UNHCR. These range from long-standing initiatives, such as the UNICEF Change for Good programme, to more recent cooperative efforts, such as NetAid and corporate support for our *UN works* cyber-magazine.

PART ONE

Political and security questions

Chapter I

International peace and security

The year 2001 witnessed new and extraordinary challenges to international peace and security, dramatized by the 11 September terrorist attacks in the United States. Both the General Assembly and the Security Council immediately condemned the attacks, expressed condolences and solidarity with the people and Government of the United States and called for urgent international action to eradicate terrorism and to hold the organizers, perpetrators and sponsors accountable. Towards that end, the Council, in September, adopted a number of measures designed to stifle international terrorist activities and established a committee to monitor implementation of those measures by Member States. In November, the Council adopted a declaration on the global effort to combat terrorism, in which it proposed further measures, including the provision of assistance to Member States.

Although the 11 September attacks dominated international attention, the United Nations was no less preoccupied with other threats to international peace and security and with its own efforts to consolidate its peacekeeping, peacemaking and peace-building efforts. In recognition of those efforts, the Norwegian Nobel Committee, on 12 October, announced the joint award of the Nobel Peace Prize to the United Nations and its Secretary-General, Kofi A. Annan, for their work for a better organized and more peaceful world. On the same day, the Security Council congratulated the recipients and paid tribute to the men and women who worked for the United Nations in the service of peace.

In the context of the need to enhance the Organization's conflict prevention efforts, the Council, in February, held a debate on a comprehensive approach to peace-building, during which it supported the formulation of an integrated strategy in that regard. In June, the Secretary-General submitted to the Council and the General Assembly a number of recommendations on how to further develop the UN system's conflict prevention capacity, with the cooperation and involvement of Member States.

The United Nations political and peace-building missions continued to lead UN efforts to consolidate peace and promote democratization and the rule of law. In 2001, the number of such missions in operation rose to 12. At the same time, efforts continued to strengthen and streamline the management and operation of UN peacekeeping missions through the implementation of the recommendations made in 2000 by the Panel on United Nations Peace Operations in the Brahimi report. As part of those efforts, the Secretariat conducted the first in-depth managerial examination of UN peacekeeping operations and identified core capacities that required further strengthening. During the year, the United Nations deployed no new peacekeeping missions, with the total number of missions remaining at 15 (4 in Africa, 3 in Asia, 5 in Europe and 3 in the Middle East). However, the number of military personnel and civilian police serving under UN command increased to some 47,000 compared to 37,719 the year before; they were supported by some 12,800 international and local civilian staff.

The Council, in January, established a working group on peacekeeping operations to address generic peacekeeping issues and technical aspects of individual peacekeeping operations. It also adopted measures to improve consultations among the Council, troop-contributing countries and the Secretariat.

The Special Committee on Peacekeeping Operations, the body responsible for reviewing UN peacekeeping operations in all their aspects, met in June and recommended action to enhance UN peacekeeping capacity and to fulfil peacekeeping responsibilities in the field. It approved most of the recommendations of the in-depth management review of peacekeeping operations.

The cost of UN peacekeeping operations increased to $2,378.7 million for the period 1 July 2000 to 30 June 2001, compared with $1,756.8 million during the previous 12-month period. Unpaid assessed contributions for peacekeeping operations also increased to $2,352.3 million, compared with $2,128.9 million during the previous period. The Assembly considered various aspects of peacekeeping financing, financial performance reports and proposed budgets, including the peacekeeping support account and the United Nations Logistics Base in Brindisi, Italy. It considered the Secretary-General's report on the use of resident auditors at peacekeeping missions and endorsed further recommendations on reform procedures for determining reimbursement of contingent-owned equipment and troop costs. The Secretariat clarified for Member States the procedures adopted in 2000 for apportioning the expenses of peacekeeping operations.

Promotion of international peace and security

Nobel Peace Prize

On 12 October, the Norwegian Nobel Committee announced that it would award the 2001 Nobel Peace Prize, in two equal portions, to the United Nations and its Secretary-General, Kofi A. Annan, for their work for a better organized and more peaceful world.

The Committee stated that the United Nations was at the forefront of efforts to achieve peace and security in the world, and of the international mobilization aimed at meeting the world's economic, social and environmental challenges. As Secretary-General, the Committee said, Mr. Annan had been pre-eminent in bringing new life to the United Nations. While clearly underlining the Organization's traditional responsibility for peace and security, he had also emphasized its obligations with regard to human rights, risen to new challenges such as HIV/AIDS and international terrorism, and brought about more efficient utilization of the Organization's modest resources.

At a 12 October meeting of the General Assembly [A/56/PV.24], several Member States congratulated the Organization and the Secretary-General on the award of the Peace Prize. Addressing the Assembly, the Secretary-General quoted the Nobel Committee's statement that it had used the prize "to proclaim that the only negotiable route to global peace and cooperation goes by way of the United Nations". He observed that, in a world that was growing ever closer and more interconnected, yet still torn by brutal conflicts and cruel injustice, it was more important than ever that humanity travelled that route and that everyone should work hard to pave the road ahead of it.

Also on 12 October, the Security Council held a special meeting on the award of the Nobel Peace Prize.

SECURITY COUNCIL ACTION

On 12 October [meeting 4390], following consultations among Security Council members, the President made statement **S/PRST/2001/28** on behalf of the Council:

> The Security Council today celebrates, together with the rest of the United Nations family, the award

of the 2001 Nobel Peace Prize to the United Nations and to its Secretary-General, Kofi Annan.

> The United Nations is the embodiment of co-operation among States in safeguarding peace, advancing international development, and in combating common threats to the dignity and well-being of peoples everywhere.

> The United Nations remains today, in its activities around the world and in the ideals it sets, the best hope for a future in which peoples everywhere can work together to meet common challenges and to advance common goals.

> The Security Council today pays special tribute to all the men and women who work for the United Nations, whatever their tasks of duty, wherever they may be in the service of peace.

> The decision of the Nobel Committee to award the 2001 Nobel Peace Prize to the United Nations and to the Secretary-General reflects the high esteem shared by people throughout the world for Secretary-General Kofi Annan. It rightly honours his exceptional achievements in the service of the United Nations and of the entire international community as well as honouring the achievements of the United Nations itself.

> In warmly congratulating the Secretary-General, Kofi Annan, the Council reiterates its own strong support for his efforts in upholding the purposes and principles of the United Nations Charter and for his role in assuring to the Organization its full and rightful place in the world and in leading its search for new ways forward for all men and women in all countries to live their lives with dignity and peace.

Following delivery of the statement, the Secretary-General congratulated Council members past and present, stating that the Nobel Committee, in awarding the Peace Prize to the United Nations, had honoured the Council and, indeed, all parts of the Organization, above all the men and women who worked in the service of peace. All who worked at the United Nations should feel proud, but also humble, because even more would be expected of them in the future, perhaps in the near future.

On 10 December, the Secretary-General received the Nobel Peace Prize for 2001 in Oslo. He was accompanied by the General Assembly President, who accepted the Prize on behalf of the United Nations. Delivering the Nobel Lecture, the Secretary-General said that in the twenty-first century the mission of the United Nations would be defined by a new, more profound awareness of the sanctity of every human being, regardless of race or religion. Peace had to be sought because it was the condition for every member of the human family to live a life of dignity and security. He added that from the vision of the UN role in the next century flowed three key priorities—eradicting poverty, preventing conflict and promoting democracy.

Follow-up to Millennium Summit (2000)

In his September report "Road map towards the implementation of the United Nations Millennium Declaration" [A/56/326], submitted in response to General Assembly resolution 55/162 [YUN 2000, p. 62], the Secretary-General outlined action taken to implement the millennium development goals contained in the Declaration [ibid., p. 49] adopted at the Assembly's Millennium Summit, including those related to peace and security. In a section of the report on strengthening United Nations capacities for resolving armed conflict, the Secretary-General described progress in implementing the goal of making the United Nations more effective in maintaining peace and security by giving it the resources and tools for conflict prevention, the peaceful resolution of disputes, peacekeeping, and post-conflict peace-building and reconstruction. Those challenges, he said, required action to replace the culture of reaction by one of prevention, as reflected in the measures designed to limit armed conflict, including preventive arms control and marking and tracking "blood diamonds" (see p. 52); completing the ongoing management reforms in UN peacekeeping; and supporting peace-building efforts on the ground with regard to disarmament, demobilization and reintegration, while providing electoral assistance and promoting reconciliation.

He proposed, as strategies for moving forward, earlier and more sustained action to address the underlying causes of conflict, development of improved integrated prevention strategies with a regional focus, and enhancing the capacity of Member States, regional organizations and the UN system for effective prevention; encouraging States to ensure equitable distribution of assets and access to resources; urging States to act on the Secretary-General's recommendations on the prevention of armed conflict (see p. 48); strengthening national capacities for addressing structural risk factors by providing advisory services and technical assistance; and utilizing multidisciplinary fact-finding missions, encouraging the use of preventive deployments and establishing an informal network of eminent persons for conflict prevention.

In peacekeeping, the Secretary-General recommended ensuring the expeditious completion of peacekeeping reform, particularly by reaching, in 2001, an agreement on the decisions required for further progress, including on financial resources (see p. 74); increasing collaboration between the United Nations and regional organizations; and paying greater attention to gender, humanitarian and disarmament issues in peacekeeping operations.

As to peace-building, the Secretary-General recommended securing adequate international resources to permit recovery and development for post-conflict societies; strengthening the capacity of UN resident coordinators and country teams to undertake effective peace-building; preventing the recurrence of conflict through disarmament, demobilization and reintegration measures; and improving the functioning of UN peace-building support offices.

In the area of international terrorism, he proposed encouraging States to sign, ratify and implement the conventions and protocols relating to terrorism (see p. 69); supporting international efforts to finalize the draft convention for the suppression of nuclear terrorism and to draw up a comprehensive convention on international terrorism (see p. 1224); and continuing efforts to develop and adopt corresponding laws and administrative procedures at the national level.

The Assembly, on 14 December, adopted **resolution 56/95** on the follow-up to the outcome of the Millennium Summit (see p. 1279).

Follow-up to Security Council Summit (2000)

On 7 March [meeting 4288], the Security Council held an open debate on the agenda item "Ensuring an effective role of the Security Council in the maintenance of international peace and security, particularly in Africa". In a 28 February letter [S/2001/185], Ukraine, as Council President, informed the Secretary-General of its intention to convene the meeting, stating that the objective was to evaluate progress achieved in implementing the Council's declaration contained in resolution 1318(2000) [YUN 2000, p. 64], adopted at its high-level meeting in 2000, and to explore further ways to enhance the Council's role in that regard.

In an explanatory memorandum, Ukraine recalled the commitments set out in resolution 1318(2000) to enhance the effectiveness of the United Nations in addressing the challenges to peace and security and posed a number of questions regarding the Council's practical implementation of those commitments. Specifically, it asked how effectively was the promotion of peace and sustainable development being translated into practical action; whether there were "forgotten" conflicts or situations that needed greater attention; whether there were any specific tasks related to the strengthening of peacekeeping that required more energetic efforts by the Council; what specific areas had been overlooked in enhancing UN effectiveness in addressing conflict; how effectively was the Council contributing to the development of comprehensive strategies to address the root causes of conflicts; and what progress had been achieved in strengthening cooperation and communication between the United Nations and regional and subregional organizations and was there any need for institutional reinforcement. Appended to the note was a summary of the major ideas, initiatives and messages presented during the Summit.

On 22 March [meeting 4302], following consultations among Security Council members, the President made statement **S/PRST/2001/10** on behalf of the Council:

The Security Council recalls the decisions and recommendations contained in the declaration on ensuring an effective role for the Security Council in the maintenance of international peace and security, particularly in Africa, adopted at its meeting at the level of heads of State and Government in the course of the Millennium Summit (resolution 1318(2000) of 7 September 2000, annex), and the open debate held on 7 March 2001 to review its implementation. The Council takes note with interest of the important views expressed by non-members at this debate.

The Council notes the progress achieved in translating the commitments made at its Summit meeting into practical results and expresses its determination to intensify efforts to this end. The Council underlines the importance of the declaration as a contribution towards the development of a well-targeted strategy and shared vision in the maintenance of international peace and security and of the deeper and broader involvement of Member States and the wider international community in that regard.

The Council will consider and take appropriate action on the Secretary-General's forthcoming report on conflict prevention, his recommendations on the strengthening of the United Nations capacity to develop peace-building strategies, the report prepared by its Working Group on General Issues of Sanctions, and the recommendations on improving the three-way relationship between the Council, the troop-contributing countries and the Secretariat to be prepared by its Working Group on Peacekeeping Operations, and reiterates its intention to review periodically the implementation of its resolution 1327(2000) of 13 November 2000 on strengthening peacekeeping operations.

The Council underlines the need for closer cooperation and interaction within the United Nations system in addressing the challenges to peace and security, including the root causes of conflicts, and intends to continue taking concrete steps in advancing this goal. The Council also expresses its willingness to continue to develop productive working relationships with regional and subregional organizations in addressing conflict.

The Council decides to conduct a further review, with the active participation of non-members, of the implementation of the commitments made at its meeting at the level of heads of State and Government.

Implementation of 1970 Declaration

The General Assembly, by **decision 56/417** of 29 November, decided to include in the provisional agenda of its fifty-eighth (2003) session the item entitled "Review of the implementation of the Declaration on the Strengthening of International Security" [YUN 1970, p. 105].

Conflict prevention

Prevention of armed conflict

Report of Secretary-General. In response to Security Council presidential statement S/PRST/2000/25 [YUN 2000, p. 73], the Secretary-General submitted to the Council and the General Assembly a June report on the prevention of armed conflict [A/55/985-S/2001/574 & Corr.1], in which he reviewed progress in developing a conflict prevention capacity in the United Nations and made recommendations on how UN system efforts could be further enhanced, with the cooperation and involvement of Member States.

The Secretary-General stated that the primary responsibility for conflict prevention rested with national Governments and other local actors; without a sense of national ownership, prevention was unlikely to succeed. It required early action by national actors and, where appropriate, by the international community. However, for early prevention to be effective, the multidimensional causes of conflict needed to be identified and addressed. Of great importance were a deep understanding of the importance of local circumstances and traditions and the identification of fundamental socio-economic inequities.

Prevention fell into two categories: operational prevention, or measures applicable in the face of immediate crisis; and structural prevention, which consisted of measures to ensure that crises did not arise in the first place or, if they did, that they did not recur. An investment in long-term structural prevention was ultimately an investment in sustainable development, which, when it addressed the root causes of conflict, played an important role in preventing conflict and in promoting peace.

In the current era of diminishing international development assistance, the donor community was increasingly reluctant to provide development support to States that were on the brink of or in the midst of conflict. However, investing in conflict prevention offered the potential for multiple returns for national development over the long term and would save hundreds of thousands of lives and billions of dollars. Funds currently spent on military action could instead be available for poverty reduction and equitable sustainable development, which would further reduce the risks of war and disaster.

The Secretary-General noted that many of the UN system's development and other programmes and projects already had preventive effects or preventive potential, though they were often disparate and inchoate. The challenge therefore was how to mobilize that collective potential with greater coherence and focus, without major new resources.

The Secretary-General recommended that the General Assembly consider both more active use of its powers, in accordance with Articles 10, 11 and 14 of the Charter, in the prevention of armed conflicts, and ways to enhance its interaction with the Security Council, particularly in developing long-term conflict prevention and peace-building strategies. He encouraged the Council to consider establishing a mechanism for discussing prevention cases on a continuing basis, in addition to early warning or prevention cases brought to its attention by Member States. He further suggested that the Economic and Social Council, at a future high-level segment of its annual substantive session, address the root causes of conflict and the role of development in promoting long-term conflict prevention.

The Secretary-General urged Member States to resort to the International Court of Justice (ICJ) earlier and more often to settle their disputes; accept the Court's jurisdiction or, where necessary, agree on matters to present to the Court; and when adopting multilateral treaties under UN auspices, include clauses providing for disputes to be referred to ICJ. He recommended that the Assembly authorize the Secretary-General and other UN organs to take advantage of the Court's advisory competence and that those organs that already enjoyed such authorization resort to the Court more frequently.

As to the role of his own office, the Secretary-General indicated his intention to increase the use of interdisciplinary fact-finding and confidence-building missions to volatile regions; develop regional prevention strategies with regional partners and appropriate UN organs and agencies; establish an informal network of eminent persons for conflict prevention; and improve the capacity and resource base for preventive action in the Secretariat.

With regard to the UN system, funds and programmes and specialized agencies should consider how best to integrate a conflict prevention perspective into their mandated activities, the Assembly should provide the Department of Political Affairs with adequate resources to carry out its conflict prevention and peace-building responsibilities, and Member States and the Security Council should make more use of preventive deployments before the onset of conflict. The Secretary-General urged the Council to support peace-building components within peacekeeping operations and strengthen the Secretariat's capacity in that regard through, among other actions, the measures outlined in the Secretary-General's report on the implementation of the recommendations of the Special Committee on Peacekeeping Operations and of the Panel on United Nations Peace Operations [A/55/977] (see p. 71).

The Secretary-General also recommended greater transparency by Member States on military matters and called on the Assembly and other UN disarmament bodies to strengthen disarmament-related early warning and transparency mechanisms, particularly with regard to small arms and light weapons. He encouraged the Council to include a disarmament, demobilization and reintegration component in the mandates of UN peacekeeping and peace-building operations.

The Secretary-General also made recommendations regarding human rights, development assistance, humanitarian action, media and public information, gender equality, drug control and crime prevention and interaction between the United Nations and other international actors in the prevention of armed conflict.

In his conclusions, the Secretary-General addressed measures for overcoming the obstacles to conflict prevention, including the refusal by some Governments to admit that they had a problem that could lead to violent conflict and their rejection of offers of assistance, ways in which Member States defined their national interests in any given crisis, the intractability of conflicts and the obduracy of warring parties, and the many instances of local warlords and other non-State actors who did not consider themselves constrained by Security Council decisions and the wishes of the international community. The time had come, he said, to intensify efforts to move from a culture of reaction to a culture of prevention, and he proposed 10 principles to guide the future approach of the United Nations to conflict prevention.

Related issues. Sweden, on 29 June [A/55/1013-S/2001/683], transmitted to the Secretary-General a 15 June statement on the European Union Programme for the Prevention of Violent Conflicts.

The United Nations Conference on the Illicit Trade in Small Arms and Light Weapons in All Its Aspects (New York, 9-20 July) [A/CONF.192/15 & Corr.1] adopted the Programme of Action to Prevent, Combat and Eradicate the Illicit Trade in Small Arms and Light Weapons in All Its Aspects (see p. 499).

The United Nations Standing Advisory Committee on Security Questions in Central Africa organized a Subregional Conference on the Protection of Women and Children in Armed Conflict in Central Africa (Kinshasa, Democratic Republic of the Congo, 14-16 November) [A/56/680-S/2001/1155].

GENERAL ASSEMBLY ACTION

On 1 August [meeting 110], the General Assembly adopted **resolution 55/281** [draft: A/55/L.91] without vote [agenda item 10].

Prevention of armed conflict

The General Assembly,

Having received the report of the Secretary-General on prevention of armed conflict and the recommendations contained therein,

Recalling its debate on the report on 12 and 13 July 2001,

1. *Calls upon* Governments to consider the report of the Secretary-General and the recommendations contained therein;

2. *Calls upon* regional and subregional organizations to consider the report and the recommendations therein addressed to them;

3. *Calls upon* all relevant organs, organizations and bodies of the United Nations system to consider, in accordance with their mandates, the recommendations addressed to them and to inform the General Assembly, preferably during its fifty-sixth session, of their views in this regard;

4. *Invites* relevant civil society actors to consider the report and the recommendations therein addressed to them;

5. *Decides* to continue to consider the report and the recommendations contained therein at its fifty-sixth session, taking into account, as appropriate, any views and comments received pursuant to paragraphs 1 to 4 above.

SECURITY COUNCIL ACTION

On 30 August [meeting 4360], the Security Council unanimously adopted **resolution 1366(2001)**. The draft [S/2001/828] was prepared in consultations among Council members.

The Security Council,

Recalling its resolutions 1196(1998) of 16 September 1998, 1197(1998) of 18 September 1998, 1208(1998) of 19 November 1998, 1209(1998) of 19 November 1998, 1265(1999) of 17 September 1999, 1296(2000) of 19 April 2000, 1318(2000) of 7 September 2000, 1325 (2000) of 31 October 2000 and 1327(2000) of 13 November 2000,

Recalling also the statements of its President of 16 September 1998 (S/PRST/1998/28), 24 September 1998 (S/PRST/1998/29), 30 November 1998 (S/PRST/1998/35), 24 September 1999 (S/PRST/1999/28), 30 November 1999 (S/PRST/1999/34), 23 March 2000 (S/PRST/2000/10), 20 July 2000 (S/PRST/2000/25), 20 February 2001 (S/PRST/2001/5) and 22 March 2001 (S/PRST/2001/10),

Having considered the report of the Secretary-General on the prevention of armed conflict and in particular the recommendations contained therein relating to the role of the Security Council,

Reiterating the purposes and principles enshrined in the Charter of the United Nations and reaffirming its commitment to the principles of the political independence, sovereign equality and territorial integrity of all States,

Mindful of the consequences of armed conflict on relations between and among States, the economic burden on the nations involved as well as on the international community, and, above all, the humanitarian consequences of conflicts,

Bearing in mind its primary responsibility under the Charter of the United Nations for the maintenance of international peace and security and reaffirming its role in the prevention of armed conflicts,

Stressing the need for the maintenance of regional and international peace and stability and friendly relations among all States, and underlining the overriding political, humanitarian and moral imperatives as well as the economic advantages of preventing the outbreak and escalation of conflicts,

Emphasizing the importance of a comprehensive strategy comprising operational and structural measures for prevention of armed conflict, and recognizing the ten principles outlined by the Secretary-General in his report on prevention of armed conflicts,

Noting with satisfaction the increased recourse, with consent of receiving Member States, to Security Council missions to areas of conflict or potential conflict, which among others, can play an important role in the prevention of armed conflicts,

Reiterating that conflict prevention is one of the primary responsibilities of Member States,

Recognizing the essential role of the Secretary-General in the prevention of armed conflict and the importance of efforts to enhance his role in accordance with Article 99 of the Charter of the United Nations,

Recognizing the role of other relevant organs, offices, funds and programmes and the specialized agencies of the United Nations, and other international organizations including the World Trade Organization and the Bretton Woods institutions, as well as the role of non-governmental organizations, civil society actors and the private sector in the prevention of armed conflict,

Stressing the necessity of addressing the root causes and regional dimensions of conflicts, recalling the recommendations contained in the report of the Secretary-General on causes of conflicts and the promotion of durable peace and sustainable development in Africa of 13 April 1998 and underlining the mutually supportive relationship between conflict prevention and sustainable development,

Expressing serious concern over the threat to peace and security caused by the illicit trade in and the excessive and destabilizing accumulation of small arms and light weapons in areas of conflict and their potential to exacerbate and prolong armed conflicts,

Emphasizing the importance of adequate, predictable and properly targeted resources for conflict prevention and of consistent funding for long-term preventive activities,

Reiterating that early warning, preventive diplomacy, preventive deployment, practical disarmament measures and post-conflict peace-building are interdependent and complementary components of a comprehensive conflict prevention strategy,

Underlining the importance of raising awareness of and ensuring respect for international humanitarian law, stressing the fundamental responsibility of Member States to prevent and end impunity for genocide, crimes against humanity and war crimes, recognizing the role of the ad hoc tribunals for the former Yugoslavia and Rwanda in deterring the future occurrence of such crimes thereby helping to prevent armed conflict, and stressing the importance of international efforts in accordance with the Charter of the United Nations in this regard,

Reiterating the shared commitment to save people from the ravages of armed conflicts, acknowledging the lessons to be learned for all concerned from the failure of preventive efforts that preceded such tragedies as the genocide in Rwanda and the massacre in Srebrenica, and resolving to take appropriate action within its competence, combined with the efforts of Member States, to prevent the recurrence of such tragedies,

1. *Expresses its determination* to pursue the objective of prevention of armed conflict as an integral part of its primary responsibility for the maintenance of international peace and security;

2. *Stresses* that the essential responsibility for conflict prevention rests with national Governments, and that the United Nations and the international community can play an important role in support of national efforts for conflict prevention and can assist in building national capacity in this field and recognizes the important supporting role of civil society;

3. *Calls upon* Member States as well as regional and subregional organizations and arrangements to support the development of a comprehensive conflict prevention strategy as proposed by the Secretary-General;

4. *Emphasizes* that for the success of a preventive strategy, the United Nations needs the consent and support of the Government concerned and, if possible, the cooperation of other key national actors and underlines in this regard that the sustained political will of neighbouring States, regional allies or other Member States who would be well placed to support United Nations efforts, is necessary;

5. *Expresses its willingness* to give prompt consideration to early warning or prevention cases brought to its attention by the Secretary-General and in this regard, encourages the Secretary-General to convey to the Security Council his assessment of potential threats to international peace and security with due regard to relevant regional and subregional dimensions, as appropriate, in accordance with Article 99 of the Charter of the United Nations;

6. *Undertakes* to keep situations of potential conflict under close review as part of a conflict prevention strategy and expresses its intention to consider cases of potential conflict brought to its attention by any Member State, or by a State not a Member of the United Nations or by the General Assembly or on the basis of information furnished by the Economic and Social Council;

7. *Expresses its commitment* to take early and effective action to prevent armed conflict and to that end to employ all appropriate means at its disposal including, with the consent of the receiving States, its missions to areas of potential conflict;

8. *Reiterates* its call to Member States to strengthen the capacity of the United Nations in the maintenance of international peace and security and in this regard urges them to provide the necessary human, material and financial resources for timely and preventive measures including early warning, preventive diplomacy, preventive deployment, practical disarmament measures and peace-building as appropriate in each case;

9. *Reaffirms* its role in the peaceful settlement of disputes and reiterates its call upon the Member States to settle their disputes by peaceful means as set forth in Chapter VI of the Charter of the United Nations including by use of regional preventive mechanisms and more frequent resort to the International Court of Justice;

10. *Invites* the Secretary-General to refer to the Council information and analyses from within the United Nations system on cases of serious violations of international law, including international humanitarian law and human rights law, and on potential conflict situations arising, inter alia, from ethnic, religious and territorial disputes, poverty and lack of development and expresses its determination to give serious consideration to such information and analyses regarding situations which it deems to represent a threat to international peace and security;

11. *Expresses its intention* to continue to invite the Office of the United Nations Emergency Relief Coordinator and other relevant United Nations agencies to brief its members on emergency situations which it deems to represent a threat to international peace and security and supports the implementation of protection and assistance activities by relevant United Nations agencies in accordance with their respective mandates;

12. *Expresses its willingness* to consider preventive deployment upon the recommendation of the Secretary-General and with the consent of the Member States concerned;

13. *Calls upon* all Member States to ensure timely and faithful implementation of the United Nations Programme of Action to Prevent, Combat and Eradicate the Illicit Trade in Small Arms and Light Weapons in All Its Aspects adopted on 20 July 2001 and to take all necessary measures at national, regional and global levels to prevent and combat the illicit flow of small arms and light weapons in areas of conflict;

14. *Expresses its willingness* to make full use of information from the Secretary-General provided to him, inter alia, under paragraph 33 section II of the Programme of Action in its efforts to prevent armed conflict;

15. *Stresses* the importance of the inclusion, as part of a conflict prevention strategy, of peace-building components including civilian police within peace-keeping operations on a case-by-case basis to facilitate a smooth transition to the post-conflict peace-building phase and the ultimate conclusion of the mission;

16. *Decides* to consider inclusion, as appropriate, of a disarmament, demobilization and reintegration component in the mandates of United Nations peace-keeping and peace-building operations with particular attention to the rehabilitation of child soldiers;

17. *Reiterates* its recognition of the role of women in conflict prevention and requests the Secretary-General to give greater attention to gender perspectives in the implementation of peacekeeping and peace-building mandates as well as in conflict prevention efforts;

18. *Supports* the enhancement of the role of the Secretary-General in conflict prevention including by increased use of United Nations interdisciplinary fact-finding and confidence-building missions to regions of tension, developing regional prevention strategies with regional partners and appropriate United Nations organs and agencies, and improving the capacity and resource base for preventive action in the Secretariat;

19. *Endorses* the call of the Secretary-General for support to the follow-up processes launched by the Third and Fourth High-level United Nations–Regional Organizations Meetings in the field of conflict prevention and peace-building, and to provide increased resources for the development of regional capacities in these fields;

20. *Calls* for the enhancement of the capacity for conflict prevention of regional organizations, in particular in Africa, by extending international assistance to, inter alia, the Organization of African Unity and its successor organization, through its Mechanism of Conflict Prevention, Management and Resolution, as well as to the Economic Community of West African States and its Mechanism for Prevention, Management and Resolution of Conflicts, Peacekeeping and Security;

21. *Stresses* the need to create conditions for durable peace and sustainable development by addressing the root causes of armed conflict and, to this end, calls upon Member States and relevant bodies of the United Nations system to contribute to the effective implementation of the United Nations Declaration and Programme of Action for a Culture of Peace ;

22. *Looks forward to* further consideration of the report of the Secretary-General on prevention of armed conflict by the General Assembly and the Economic and Social Council, as well as other actors including the Bretton Woods institutions, and supports the development of a system-wide coordinated and mutually supportive approach to prevention of armed conflict;

23. *Decides* to remain actively seized of the matter.

In related action, the Council, in presidential statement **S/PRST/2001/21** of 31 August, noted with concern, among other things, that the destabilizing accumulation and uncontrolled spread of small arms and light weapons in many regions of the world increased the intensity and duration of armed conflicts, impeded success at peace-building, frustrated efforts to prevent armed conflict and compromised the effectiveness of the Council in discharging its responsibility for the maintenance of international peace and security (see p. 500).

Conflict diamonds

Kimberly Process. The Kimberly Process on conflict diamonds, established in 2000 [YUN 2000, p. 76] to stem the flow of rough diamonds used by rebels to finance armed conflict, protect the legitimate diamond industry and create and implement an international certification scheme for rough diamonds based on national certification schemes and internationally agreed minimum standards, held six meetings in 2001 under the chairmanship of South Africa (Windhoek, Namibia, 13-16 February; Brussels, Belgium, 25-27 April; Moscow, 3-5 July; Twickenham, United Kingdom, 11-13 September; Luanda, Angola, 30 October–1 November; and Gaborone, Botswana, 26-29 November).

In an October provisional report [A/56/502], submitted in response to General Assembly resolution 55/56 [YUN 2000, p. 77], it was stated that the Windhoek meeting, which also included a technical workshop, had adopted a road map to guide future meetings in devising an implementable, simple and workable international certification scheme for rough diamonds. The Brussels meeting produced a consolidated paper outlining elements of a model certificate of origin and considered the need for non-producing countries to certify their rough diamond exports. It requested that a non-paper be drafted containing all the elements of the envisaged certification scheme. The Moscow meeting [A/56/186] agreed in principle on the basic elements of an international system for certification of rough diamonds, which was to be elaborated further to include the format and content of certificates accompanying rough diamonds, plus the minimum standards to support those certificates and underpin the whole system.

At the Twickenham meeting, it was agreed to assess the relationship between proposed elements and the envisaged certification scheme and international trade obligations, plus elements relating to its implementation in the European Community (EC). It also examined the type of instrument necessary to establish the certification scheme, its implementation and maintenance.

The meeting in Luanda [A/56/675] agreed on internal controls, provisions for cooperation and transparency and the content of the certificate to accompany shipments of rough diamonds. Agreement was also reached on the preamble of the working document on the certification scheme, which set out the scheme in context. The meeting considered proposals from the World Diamond Council for a comprehensive system of warranties and industry self-regulation, the essential elements of which were incorporated into the draft certification scheme.

The Gaborone meeting, held at the ministerial level [A/56/675] and attended also by representatives of the world's leading rough diamond-producing, -exporting and -importing States, the EC, the Southern African Development Community and other concerned States, issued a statement in which it declared that the 28 November working document entitled "Essential elements of an international scheme of certification for rough diamonds, with a view to breaking the link between armed conflict and the trade in rough diamonds" provided a good basis for the envisaged certification scheme. The scheme should be established through an international understanding as soon as possible. Those in a position to issue the Kimberly Process Certificate should do so immediately. All others were encouraged to do so by 1 June 2002 and full and simultaneous implementation was scheduled for the end of 2002. The mandate of the Kimberly Process should be extended until that time in order to finalize the international understanding. The widest possible participation in the certification scheme should be encouraged and facilitated. The ministers also recognized the need to ensure that the measures taken to implement the scheme were consistent with international law governing international trade, and agreed that a progress report should be submitted to the General Assembly.

The ministers recommended that the United Nations support the implementation of the certification scheme for rough diamonds as an instrument to help promote legitimate trade and ensure the effective implementation of the relevant Security Council resolutions relating to sanctions on the trade in conflict diamonds that were contributing to the promotion of international peace and security and relevant Assembly resolutions.

The Security Council, in **resolution 1385 (2001)** of 19 December (see p. 178), welcomed the efforts by interested States, the diamond industry, in particular the World Diamond Council, and non-governmental organizations (NGOs) to break the link between illicit trade in rough diamonds and armed conflict, particularly through the Kimberly Process, and encouraged further progress in that regard. It also welcomed the establishment of a certification regime in relation to the export of rough diamonds from Guinea and Sierra Leone and the efforts of the Economic Community of West African States to develop a region-wide certification regime.

The General Assembly, by **decision 56/464** of 24 December, decided that the item on the role of diamonds in fuelling conflict would remain for consideration during its resumed fifty-sixth (2002) session.

Preventive diplomacy and peacemaking

While comprehensive and coherent conflict prevention strategies offered the greatest poten-tial for promoting lasting peace, they had never been easy to formulate or to implement, the Secretary-General said in his annual report on the work of the Organization [A/56/1 & Add.1]. Member States were turning increasing attention and providing more assistance to conflict prevention; for the United Nations, the concept had to be put into practice, and the rhetoric matched by action. The Secretary-General recalled his 1998 recommendations [YUN 1998, p. 66] on enhancing the effectiveness of and strengthening cooperation in conflict prevention and emphasized that UN development and humanitarian agencies, together with the Bretton Woods institutions (the World Bank Group and the International Monetary Fund), had a vital role to play in creating a peaceful environment and addressing the root causes of conflicts at the early stages of prevention. The Secretary-General said that he would continue to dispatch UN interdisciplinary fact-finding and confidence-building missions to volatile regions; start submitting periodic regional or subregional reports to the Security Council on disputes that might potentially threaten international peace and security; develop regional prevention strategies with regional partners and UN organs and agencies to establish an informal network of eminent persons for conflict prevention; and improve the capacity and resource base for preventive action in the Secretariat.

The Secretary-General noted that the Millennium Declaration [YUN 2000, p. 49] called for enhanced institutional cooperation between the United Nations and regional and subregional organizations. The utility of such an approach had been demonstrated in West Africa, where the Organization had intensified its partnership with the countries of that region to identify potential threats to peace and was cooperating to prevent such challenges from deteriorating into violent conflict.

International symposium on conflict prevention

The International Symposium on Conflict Prevention, entitled "Culture of Prevention: Multi-Actor Coordination from UN to Civil Society", organized by Japan (Tokyo, 13-14 March), was held as a follow-up to the G-8 (Group of eight major industrialized States) Miyazaki Initiatives for Conflict Prevention [YUN 2000, p. 75]. The Symposium considered how to achieve successful coordination among various actors engaged in conflict prevention activities and specifically addressed the themes of small arms and light weapons in the case of Cambodia and conflict and development in the case of East Timor.

In his summary of the Symposium's deliberations [A/55/875-S/2001/322], submitted to the

Secretary-General by Japan on 2 April, the Chairman said that there was inadequate coordination and insufficient communication among the multiple actors working on conflict prevention, resulting in ineffectiveness and failure, with the actions of some actors cancelling out those of others. To eliminate those difficulties and achieve solid coordination, the Symposium recommended a number of measures for action by the United Nations, other international organizations and Governments.

Women's role in conflict prevention and resolution

On 8 March—the United Nations Day for Women's Rights and International Peace—the Security Council held informal consultations on women and peace and security [A/56/2]. In a press statement, the Council President reiterated the call to Member States to ensure increased representation of women in decision-making for the prevention, management and resolution of conflicts and to all parties to armed conflicts to take specific measures to protect women and girls from gender-based violence in situations of armed conflict. The need for early and full implementation of resolution 1325(2000) [YUN 2000, p. 1113] on women in armed conflict was stressed and UN agencies and bodies were urged to take it into account in their work. The President noted the launch of the first Millennium Peace Prize for Women, which recognized and highlighted women's leadership in ending war and building sustainable peace.

SECURITY COUNCIL ACTION

On 31 October [meeting 4402], following consultations among Security Council members, the President made statement **S/PRST/2001/31** on behalf of the Council:

The Security Council reaffirms its commitment to the implementation of its resolution 1325(2000) of 31 October 2000 and welcomes the efforts by the United Nations system, Member States, civil society organizations and other relevant actors in promoting the equal participation and full involvement of women in the maintenance and promotion of peace and security and in implementing the provisions of resolution 1325(2000).

The Council further reaffirms its strong support for increasing the role of women in decision-making with regard to conflict prevention and resolution and renews its call on States to include women in the negotiation and implementation of peace accords, constitutions and strategies for resettlement and re-building and to take measures to support local women's groups and indigenous processes for conflict resolution. In this regard it recognizes the efforts of the Mano River Women's Peace Network in facilitating peace and dialogue in the Mano River

Union region. It is also encouraged by the inclusion of women in the political decision-making bodies in Burundi, Somalia and East Timor.

The Council underscores the importance of promoting an active and visible policy of mainstreaming a gender perspective in all policies and programmes while addressing armed conflicts, in particular peacekeeping operations in keeping with the statement of the President of the Security Council on 8 March 2000.

The Council therefore reiterates its request to the Secretary-General to include, where appropriate, in his reporting to the Security Council, progress in gender mainstreaming throughout United Nations peacekeeping missions and on other aspects relating to women and girls. It expresses its intention to give full consideration to these reports and to take appropriate action. The Council also reaffirms its call for the inclusion of gender components, as appropriate, in peacekeeping operations.

The Council renews its support for gender-sensitive training guidelines and material on the protection, rights and the particular needs of women, as well as on the importance of involving women in all peacekeeping and peace-building measures. The Council calls upon all troop-contributing countries to include these elements in their national training programmes for peacekeepers.

The Council welcomes the specific proposals made by the Secretary-General aimed at strengthening the Best Practices Unit of the Department of Peacekeeping Operations with the appointment of gender advisers at sufficiently senior levels.

It also welcomes the practical efforts, including the preparation of complementary reports, already made by the United Nations and its agencies, funds, programmes and regional bodies, in particular those participating in the Administrative Committee on Coordination Inter-agency Task Force on Women, Peace and Security to implement all aspects of resolution 1325(2000), as well as the timely issuance of the publication *Gender Perspective in Disarmament*, which gives a clear indication of ways in which women can be fully involved and the benefits to the parties concerned.

The Council notes with satisfaction that the Secretary-General's study requested under paragraph 16 of its resolution 1325(2000) on the impact of armed conflict on women and girls, the role of women in peace-building and the gender dimensions of peace processes and conflict resolution is under way and welcomes the coordinated comprehensive input of the United Nations and all the relevant agencies, funds and programmes of the United Nations system and looks forward to its review.

The Council is concerned that there are still no women appointed as Special Representatives or Special Envoys of the Secretary-General to peace missions, and urges Member States to redouble their efforts to nominate women candidates to the Secretary-General. The Council also urges the Secretary-General to appoint women as Special Representatives and Envoys to pursue good offices on his behalf in accordance with his strategic plan of action.

The Council recognizes the need to implement fully international humanitarian and human rights law that protects the rights of civilians, including women and girls, during and after conflicts and calls on all parties to armed conflicts to take special measures to protect women and girls from gender-based violence and all other forms of violence.

The Council remains actively seized of the matter and expresses its willingness to consider, as appropriate, the gender dimensions of armed conflict in carrying out its responsibility of maintaining international peace and security under the Charter of the United Nations.

Peace-building

In his report on the work of the Organization [A/56/1 & Add.1], the Secretary-General said that UN peace-building activities continued to be strengthened by increasingly dynamic co-operation and coordination across the system, especially at the field level, where peace operations interacted regularly with the different UN system entities engaged in peace-building and preventive work, including emergency operations led by the Office of the United Nations High Commissioner for Refugees and other relief agencies, and the long-term work of entities like the United Nations Development Programme (UNDP). Work in human rights was of particular importance for both early warning and peace-building. In that regard, cooperation with the Office of the United Nations High Commissioner for Human Rights (OHCHR) by the human rights component of a peacekeeping operation or with the High Commissioner's own field presence was of paramount importance to the Organization's work.

Comprehensive approach to peace-building

On 5 February [meeting 4272], the Security Council held an open debate on the topic "Peace-building: towards a comprehensive approach". In a 25 January letter [S/2001/82], Tunisia, in its capacity as Council President, informed the Secretary-General of its intention to organize such a debate, noting that it would give the international community an opportunity to reaffirm its political will and commitment to define a common approach to peace-building, to focus on various aspects of peace-building and the problems involved and to work towards a comprehensive strategy for peace-building and conflict prevention. In an attached working paper, it examined the concept of peace-building and proposed points for discussion during the Council's debate, including the disarmament, demobilization and reintegration of former combatants; refugees and displaced persons; poverty eradication and the promotion of sustainable development; and strengthening the rule of law and dem-

ocratic institutions. Tunisia also made proposals for a comprehensive peace-building strategy.

Addressing the Council on 5 February, the Secretary-General said that peace-building in the broadest sense was about helping a country to put back in place the rudiments of normal life after a period of conflict, the resumption of economic activity, the rejuvenation of institutions, the restoration of basic services, the reconstruction of clinics and schools, the revamping of public administration and the resolution of differences through dialogue, not violence. The overarching challenge was to move societies towards sustainable peace.

Peace-building done well was a powerful deterrent to violent conflict. It was not the dramatic imposition of a grand plan, but rather the process of building the pillars of peace from the ground up, bit by bit. Virtually every part of the UN system, including the Bretton Woods institutions, was currently engaged in one form of peace-building or another through the disarmament, demobilization and reintegration of former combatants; human rights education; the repatriation of refugees; the promotion of conflict resolution and reconciliation techniques, as well as cultural exchanges. To ensure the coherence of those efforts, the United Nations was trying to improve its internal arrangements, so that peace-building was comprehensive and integrated and duplication of effort and confusion were avoided.

Although peace-building was thought of primarily in post-conflict settings, it was also a preventive instrument, which could address the underlying root causes of conflict, and which could be used before the actual outbreak of war. While peace-building should be seen as a long-term exercise, there was also an element of urgency to achieve tangible progress on a number of fronts in a short period of time. It was an extremely difficult undertaking, often starting almost from ground zero, under clouds of bitterness and loss. It required persistence and vision, as well as the courage to pursue reconciliation in societies still fractured by suspicion and mistrust.

The Secretary-General undertook to do his utmost operationally to improve peace-building projects and to exploit to the best possible effect the expertise within the UN system and among many partners. He would also ask Council members to do more politically to give peace-building a higher priority and a higher profile by bringing it closer to the forefront of their awareness. Peace-building should not be seen as an add-on or an afterthought, something to save for later when conditions or resources or politics permitted. It was a central tool of proven worth and

Council members should pledge to develop and improve it, and to use it in good time.

UN–regional organizations meeting on peace-building

The Fourth High-level United Nations–Regional Organizations Meeting (New York, 6-7 February) discussed UN peace-building efforts. The Secretary-General, as Chairman of the meeting, transmitted to the Council President on 12 February [S/2001/138] his summary of the meeting's deliberations entitled "Framework for cooperation in peace-building", which included the "Guiding principles for cooperation in peace-building" agreed on at the meeting.

The Secretary-General said that participants emphasized that peace-building should be a home-grown process, in which the role of the United Nations and regional organizations was to support national endeavours and its fundamental goal was to promote self-reliance. The meeting recognized that there were a number of constraints to effective peace-building activities, in particular a lack of political support by the international community for long-term peace-building; mandates given to the United Nations and regional organizations that frequently exceeded their capacities; and the limited availability of resources, which were often drawn from funds provided for other activities.

The guiding principles for cooperation in peace-building advocated the promotion of self-reliance as a fundamental goal of all cooperative peace-building activities, which should be a home-grown process supported by the United Nations and regional organizations. The aim was to ensure speedy operational response and optimum mobilization of resources geared to the priority needs of the affected countries. In addition, joint peace-building activities should be directed at preventing the outbreak or recurrence of conflict, with the cooperation of the parties concerned; cooperation should be based on the comparative advantages of the United Nations and regional organizations leading to complementarity of efforts; and multidisciplinary actions could encompass five key areas of peace-building: negotiation and implementation of peace agreements; security stabilization; good governance, democratization and human rights; justice and reconciliation; and humanitarian relief and sustainable development. Also needed were the coordinated mobilization of international assistance, peace-building assistance guided by needs rather than by geographic preferences and efforts to ensure that peace-building was undertaken on the basis of international legitimacy.

Possible cooperative activities could be undertaken in the areas of capacity-building, strategic development, operational interaction, monitoring, mobilization of political will and financial resources, and follow-up activities.

Annexed to the report was the Secretary-General's statement at the concluding session of the meeting, in which he highlighted some of the main points of discussion that commanded broad agreement.

SECURITY COUNCIL ACTION

On 20 February [meeting 4278], following consultations among Security Council members, the President made statement **S/PRST/2001/5** on behalf of the Council:

The Security Council recalls the open debate held at its 4274th meeting on 5 February 2001 on "Peace-building: towards a comprehensive approach". The Council recalls also the statements of its President in relation to activities of the United Nations in preventive diplomacy, peacemaking, peacekeeping and post-conflict peace-building. The Security Council welcomes the convening by the Secretary-General of the Fourth High-level United Nations–Regional Organizations Meeting and notes with interest its results, in particular the "Framework for cooperation in peace-building" as conveyed by the Secretary-General to the President of the Security Council in his letter of 12 February 2001.

The Council reaffirms its primary responsibility under the Charter of the United Nations for the maintenance of international peace and security. The Council emphasizes the need for full respect for the purposes and principles of the Charter of the United Nations and the relevant provisions of international law, in particular those related to prevention of armed conflicts and settlement of disputes by peaceful means.

The Council reaffirms that the quest for peace requires a comprehensive, concerted and determined approach that addresses the root causes of conflicts, including their economic and social dimensions.

The Council recognizes that peacemaking, peace-keeping and peace-building are often closely interrelated. The Council stresses that this interrelationship requires a comprehensive approach in order to preserve the results achieved and prevent the recurrence of conflicts. To this effect, the Council reiterates the value of including, as appropriate, peace-building elements in the mandates of peacekeeping operations.

The Council recognizes that peace-building is aimed at preventing the outbreak, the recurrence or continuation of armed conflict and therefore encompasses a wide range of political, developmental, humanitarian and human rights programmes and mechanisms. This requires short- and long-term actions tailored to address the particular needs of societies sliding into conflict or emerging from it. These actions should focus on fostering sustainable institutions and processes in areas such as sustainable development, the eradication of poverty and inequalities, transparent and accountable governance, the promotion of democracy, respect for human rights and the rule of law and the promotion of a culture of peace and non-violence.

The Council further reaffirms that a comprehensive and integrated strategy in peace-building must involve all the relevant actors in this field, taking into account the unique circumstances of each conflict situation. The Council emphasizes that a well-planned and coordinated peace-building strategy can play a significant role in conflict prevention. In this connection, the Council underlines that international efforts in peace-building must complement and not supplant the essential role of the country concerned.

The Council notes that the experiences of the United Nations and regional organizations and other actors in peace-building point to the need for enhancing peace-building activities by formulating a strategy based on the interdependence between sustainable peace, security and development in all its dimensions.

The Council stresses that, to be successful, such a peace-building strategy should meet, inter alia, the following basic criteria: relevance, coherence and consistency of programmes and actions; the consent and cooperation of the authorities of the State concerned where they exist; continuity in and conclusion of the process; cooperation and coordination among organizations and other actors involved; and cost-effectiveness of the overall peace-building operation.

The Council strongly encourages the United Nations system and regional and subregional organizations, donor countries and the international financial institutions to consider undertaking initiatives such as: utilization of the mechanism of consolidated appeals, the joint holding of pledging conferences to mobilize expeditiously international political support and the essential resource requirements; ensuring prompt financing of quick start-up peace-building projects; and strengthening mechanisms that promote development and self-reliance by improving capacity-building activities.

The Council also underlines that successful peace-building is predicated on an effective and an unambiguous division of labour, based on the comparative advantage of different implementing bodies, between all the international partners, including the United Nations system, the international financial institutions, regional and subregional organizations, non-governmental organizations and the wider international community. In this regard, the Council strongly encourages all those actors to enhance their cooperation in areas such as the early identification of situations where peace-building is required; the definition of objectives and priority areas of peace-building; the development of an integrated operational response through mutual consultation; joint monitoring of peace-building activities; and establishing repertories of best practices and lessons learned in the area of peace-building.

The Council stresses the importance of mainstreaming a gender perspective into peace agreements and peace-building strategies and of involving women in all peace-building measures.

The Council further encourages the United Nations and regional and subregional organizations to establish consultative processes to ensure that peace settlements and agreements mediated by these organizations include commitments by the parties to the conflict to concerted action in different areas of peace-building, and stresses the need to identify such areas at early stages of the negotiation of peace agreements.

The Council recognizes that the repatriation and resettlement of refugees and internally displaced persons as well as the disarmament, demobilization and reintegration of ex-combatants should not be seen in isolation but must be carried out in the context of a broader search for peace, stability and development, with special emphasis on the revival of economic activities and reparation of the social fabric.

The Council considers it essential to provide speedy operational solutions to the exceptional and urgent needs of countries emerging from or on the verge of conflict, through innovative and flexible means, including quick impact programmes which translate into concrete and visible improvements in the daily lives of their local populations.

To enhance further the effectiveness of the United Nations in addressing conflicts at all stages, from prevention to settlement to post-conflict peace-building, the Security Council reiterates its willingness to consider ways to improve its cooperation with other United Nations bodies and organs directly concerned by peace-building, in particular the General Assembly and the Economic and Social Council which have a primary role in this field.

The Security Council recalls the essential role of the Secretary-General in peace-building, in particular in the establishment of strategies in this field and their implementation and recognizes the need to strengthen the coordination and analysis capacity of the Secretariat in order to allow the Secretary-General to fulfil his responsibilities in this area.

The Council recognizes the need for the early involvement on the ground of peace-building actors and an orderly assumption of their responsibilities. To this effect and in order to avoid any gap between peacekeeping and peace-building, the Council expresses its determination, where appropriate, to consult at various stages of any peacekeeping operation that includes peace-building elements and in particular when the operation is being established, with the State concerned and with relevant actors who are primarily responsible for coordinating and implementing aspects of peace-building activities, such as the General Assembly, the Economic and Social Council, the United Nations funds and programmes, the international financial institutions, regional organizations and major donor countries.

The Security Council recognizes that troop-contributing countries may be involved in peace-building activities and that, within the existing system of consultations with these countries, relevant peace-building activities should be discussed.

The Council encourages close cooperation between the authorities of the State concerned and the international community in elaborating programmes of peace-building activities where the commitment by the parties could be formalized in written communications.

The Council underlines the importance of the presence of special representatives of the Secretary-General or other suitable United Nations coordination arrangements, such as the resident coordinator system, in coordinating the elaboration and implementation of peace-building programmes by international organizations and donor countries in close cooperation with local authorities, taking into account ongoing activities. The Council stresses that any United Nations peace-building presence should have the necessary personnel and financial resources to discharge its mandate.

The Council stresses the importance of its being kept regularly informed of the progress achieved as well as of difficulties encountered in peace-building in countries where a peacekeeping operation had been mandated by the Security Council.

The Council reiterates that efforts to ensure lasting solutions to conflicts and to maintain the momentum for peace in any given country or region require an increased solidarity, sustained political will and timely and adequate resources on the part of the international community.

The Council recalls the decision by the Secretary-General to instruct the Executive Committee on Peace and Security to formulate a plan on the strengthening of the United Nations capacity to develop peace-building strategies and to implement programmes in support of them, and looks forward to the submission by him of recommendations to the Security Council and the General Assembly on the basis of this plan.

The Council will remain seized of the matter.

In November [S/2001/1054], the Netherlands transmitted to the Council President the report of a seminar "The United Nations system in the new millennium: fostering substantive and operational linkages in the implementation of Peace" (Tarrytown, United States, 19-20 October). Hosted by the International Peace Academy and funded by the Netherlands, the seminar brought together 30 Permanent and Deputy Permanent Representatives of Security Council and Economic and Social Council member States to discuss the respective roles of the primary UN intergovernmental bodies and how they could be better coordinated to increase UN effectiveness in peace-building.

Political and peace-building missions in 2001

During 2001, 12 political and peace-building missions were in operation: 8 in Africa, 2 in the Americas and 2 in Asia and the Pacific.

In Africa, the United Nations Office in Angola continued to explore measures for restoring peace and assisted in capacity-building, humanitarian assistance and the promotion of human rights. The Security Council extended its mandate until 15 October 2001 and again until 15 April 2002. The United Nations Office in Burundi continued to assist the parties to the peace process with regard to the building of an internal political partnership within the context of the Arusha peace process (see p. 145). In 2001, the Secretary-General proposed that the Office undertake additional responsibilities in the post-conflict peace-building phase to help in the consolidation of peace and security and that the staff and resources of the Office be restructured and strengthened. The Security Council extended the mandate of the United Nations Peace-building Support Office in the Central African Republic until 31 December 2002 and agreed with the Secretary-General's proposals for strengthening its mandate to support national reconciliation and create a political environment conducive to peace and development. The mandate of the United Nations Peace-building Support Office in Guinea-Bissau was extended until 31 December 2002. On 21 November, the Council noted the Secretary-General's intention to extend the United Nations Political Office for Somalia for a further two years (2002-2003) to continue to assist him to advance the cause of peace and reconciliation, to monitor the situation and support the formation of the Transitional National Government. The mandate of the Office of the Special Representative of the Secretary-General for the Great Lakes Region and that of the United Nations Peace-building Support Office in Liberia were extended until 31 December 2002. In November, the Council noted the Secretary-General's intention to establish the Office of the Special Representative of the Secretary-General for West Africa for three years from January 2002.

In the Americas, the Organization continued to support the United Nations Verification Mission in Guatemala, whose mandate was extended until 24 December 2002 by the General Assembly. The International Civilian Support Mission in Haiti, which assisted in that country's economic rehabilitation and reconstruction, ended on 6 February.

In Asia and the Pacific, the United Nations Tajikistan Office of Peace-building (UNTOP) was extended until 1 June 2002 and the United Nations Political Office in Bougainville (UNPOB) (Papua New Guinea) was extended until 31 December 2002, with an expanded mandate to assist with weapons collection and disposal. The United Nations Special Mission in Afghanistan (UNSMA) continued to facilitate a political process aimed at achieving a lasting political settlement of the internal conflict there. The General Assembly, in **resolution 56/220 A** of 21 December, supported the Mission's enhanced role in helping the Afghan Interim Authority to implement the Bonn agreement (see p. 263) until UNSMA could be integrated in a new UN mission in Afghanistan. In the Democratic People's Republic of Korea, the United Nations Command continued to implement the maintenance of the 1953 Armistice Agreement [YUN 1953, p. 136].

Other related missions authorized by the Assembly and the Council during 2001 included the United Nations Electoral Observer Mission to monitor the general elections in Fiji and the post-election environment (see p. 314); and an International Security Assistance Force to assist the Afghan Interim Authority in the maintenance of security in Kabul and its surrounding areas so as to allow it to operate in a secure environment **(resolution 1386(2001))** (see p. 267).

(For the financing of UN peace-building missions, see PART FIVE, Chapter II.)

Roster of peace-building offices

UNOB

United Nations Office in Burundi
Established: 25 October 1993.
Mandate: To assist the parties to the peace process with regard to the building of an internal political partnership within the context of the Arusha peace process; extended in 2001 to help in the consolidation of peace and security.
Head of Mission: Jean Arnault (France) (until August).
Officer-in-Charge: Amadou Keita (Guinea) (from 1 September).
Strength: 10 international civilian staff, 17 local civilian staff.

MINUGUA

United Nations Verification Mission in Guatemala
Established: 19 September 1994.
Mandate: To verify implementation of the Comprehensive Agreement on Human Rights.
Chief of Mission: Gerd D. Merrem (Germany).
Strength: 64 international civilian staff, 11 civilian police observers, 4 military liaison officers, 117 local civilian staff.

UNPOS

United Nations Political Office for Somalia
Established: 15 April 1995.
Mandate: To monitor the situation in Somalia and keep the Security Council informed, particularly about developments affecting the humanitarian and security situation, repatriation of refugees and impacts on neighbouring countries.
Representative of the Secretary-General and Head of Office: David Stephen (United Kingdom).
Strength: 5 international civilian staff.

UNOL

United Nations Peace-building Support Office in Liberia
Established: 1 November 1997.
Mandate: To act as focal point for peace-building, support reconciliation efforts and the establishment of democratic institutions.
Representative of the Secretary-General and Head of Office: Felix C. Downes-Thomas (Gambia).
Strength: 7 international civilian staff, 15 local civilian staff.

Great Lakes Region

Office of the Special Representative of the Secretary-General for the Great Lakes Region
Established: 19 December 1997.
Mandate: To monitor developments in the region and their implications for peace and security and contribute to regional efforts in the prevention or peaceful settlement of conflicts.
Special Representative of the Secretary-General: Berhanu Dinka (Ethiopia).
Strength: 6 international civilian staff, 3 local civilian staff.

UNPOB

United Nations Political Office in Bougainville (Papua New Guinea)
Established: 15 June 1998.
Mandate: To assist in the promotion of the political process under the Lincoln Agreement.
Head of Office: Noel Sinclair (Guyana).
Strength: 5 international civilian staff, 1 military adviser, 3 local civilian staff.

UNOGBIS

United Nations Peace-building Support Office in Guinea-Bissau
Established: 3 March 1999.
Mandate: To assist in the transition from conflict management to post-conflict peace-building and reconstruction.
Head of Office: Samuel C. Nana-Sinkam (Cameroon).
Strength: 15 international civilian staff, 2 military advisers, 1 civilian police adviser, 13 local civilian staff.

UNSCO

Office of the United Nations Special Coordinator for the Middle East
Established: 1 October 1999.
Mandate: To act as the focal point for the United Nations contribution to the implementation of the peace agreements and to enhance UN assistance.

Special Coordinator and Special Representative:
Terje Roed-Larsen (Norway).
Strength: 25 international civilian staff, 18 local
civilian staff.

UNOA

United Nations Office in Angola
Established: 15 October 1999.
Mandate: To explore effective measures for restoring peace and assisting in capacity-building
and the promotion of human rights.
Head of Office: Mussagy Jeichande (Mozambique).
Strength: 41 international civilian staff, 1 civilian police, 72 local civilian staff.

BONUCA

United Nations Peace-building Office in the
Central African Republic
Established: 15 February 2000.
Mandate: To support efforts to consolidate
peace and national reconstruction and economic
recovery.
Head of Office: Cheik Tidiane Sy (Senegal) (until May), General Lamine Cissé (Senegal) (from
16 July).
Strength: 20 international civilian staff, 3 military advisers, 5 civilian police, 2 UN Volunteers,
24 local civilian staff.

UNTOP

United Nations Tajikistan Office of Peace-
building
Established: 1 June 2000.
Mandate: To provide a political framework and
leadership for post-conflict peace-building.
Special Representative of the Secretary-General: Ivo
Petrov (Bulgaria).
Strength: 7 international civilian staff, 19 local
civilian staff.

Threats to
international peace and security

International terrorism

Terrorist attacks in the United States

On 11 September, four civilian aeroplanes
were hijacked by terrorists in the United States of
America and deliberately crashed in New York,
Washington, D.C., and Pennsylvania, resulting
in the loss of thousands of innocent lives.

The Secretary-General, in a statement to the
press on the same day [SG/SM/7948], expressed his
profound condolences to the victims and their
families, and to the people and Government of
the United States. The attacks, he said, were un-
doubtedly deliberate acts of terrorism, carefully
planned and coordinated, and he condemned
them utterly. Terrorism had to be fought resolutely wherever it appeared; no just cause could
be advanced by terror.

In a statement on behalf of the Security Council [SC/7141], the President said that Council members condemned in the strongest terms the horrifying attacks and expressed their deepest
sympathy and condolences to the victims and
their families and to the people and Government
of the United States. They called on all States to
work together urgently to bring to justice the perpetrators, organizers and sponsors, and on the international community to redouble its efforts to
prevent and suppress terrorist acts by increased
cooperation and full implementation of relevant
international anti-terrorist conventions and
Council resolutions. Council members expressed
their readiness to take urgent further steps in
accordance with their responsibilities under the
Charter.

On 12 September [A/56/350], Mongolia resolutely condemned the terrorist attacks against the
United States and stated that the tragic events
demonstrated that international terrorism posed
a real threat and a serious challenge to all humanity. Mongolia asked the Secretary-General to
convene immediately an emergency session of
the General Assembly to deliberate the issue of
international terrorism.

Also on 12 September, the fifty-sixth session of
the Assembly, at its first plenary meeting, heard
statements on the terrorist attacks from the Presidents of the fifty-fifth and fifty-sixth sessions,
the Secretary-General and representatives of the
Asian Group, the Group of Eastern European
States, the Group of Latin American and Caribbean States, the Group of Western European and
Other States and the United States [A/56/PV.1].

GENERAL ASSEMBLY ACTION

On 12 September [meeting 1], the General Assembly adopted **resolution 56/1** [draft: A/56/L.1]
without vote [agenda item 8].

**Condemnation of terrorist attacks in the
United States of America**

The General Assembly,

Guided by the purposes and principles of the Charter
of the United Nations,

1. *Strongly condemns* the heinous acts of terrorism,
which have caused enormous loss of human life, destruction and damage in the cities of New York, host
city of the United Nations, and Washington, D.C., and
in Pennsylvania;

2. *Expresses its condolences and solidarity* with the people and Government of the United States of America in these sad and tragic circumstances;

3. *Urgently calls* for international cooperation to bring to justice the perpetrators, organizers and sponsors of the outrages of 11 September 2001;

4. *Also urgently calls* for international cooperation to prevent and eradicate acts of terrorism, and stresses that those responsible for aiding, supporting or harbouring the perpetrators, organizers and sponsors of such acts will be held accountable.

SECURITY COUNCIL ACTION

On 12 September [meeting 4370], the Security Council, in accordance with the understanding reached in prior consultations, met to consider the agenda item "Threats to international peace and security caused by terrorist acts". Before hearing statements by the Council members and the Secretary-General, the Council observed a minute of silence in memory of the victims of the 11 September terrorists acts. The Council President, because of the Council's decision to limit the list of speakers to the 15 members of the Council, invited those delegations wishing to have their planned statements included in the official records to submit them to the Secretariat. Statements from Australia, Belgium (on behalf of the European Union (EU)), Brazil, Cuba, Israel, Japan, New Zealand, Romania, Slovenia and Yugoslavia were annexed to a 13 September note of the Council President [S/2001/864].

The Council unanimously adopted **resolution 1368(2001)**. The draft [S/2001/861] was prepared in consultations among Council members.

The Security Council,

Reaffirming the principles and purposes of the Charter of the United Nations,

Determined to combat by all means threats to international peace and security caused by terrorist acts,

Recognizing the inherent right of individual or collective self-defence in accordance with the Charter,

1. *Unequivocally condemns* in the strongest terms the horrifying terrorist attacks which took place on 11 September 2001 in New York, Washington, D.C., and Pennsylvania and regards such acts, like any act of international terrorism, as a threat to international peace and security;

2. *Expresses its deepest sympathy and condolences* to the victims and their families and to the people and Government of the United States of America;

3. *Calls* on all States to work together urgently to bring to justice the perpetrators, organizers and sponsors of these terrorist attacks and stresses that those responsible for aiding, supporting or harbouring the perpetrators, organizers and sponsors of these acts will be held accountable;

4. *Calls also* on the international community to redouble their efforts to prevent and suppress terrorist acts including by increased cooperation and full implementation of the relevant international anti-terrorist conventions and Security Council resolutions, in particular resolution 1269(1999) of 19 October 1999;

5. *Expresses its readiness* to take all necessary steps to respond to the terrorist attacks of 11 September 2001, and to combat all forms of terrorism, in accordance with its responsibilities under the Charter of the United Nations;

6. *Decides* to remain seized of the matter.

On 17 September [A/56/377-S/2001/885], the United States, in identical letters to the Presidents of the Assembly and the Council, conveyed its appreciation for the expressions of sympathy and support contained in the resolutions passed by the Assembly and the Council in connection with the 11 September terrorist attacks.

Measures to eliminate international terrorism

On 28 September [meeting 4385], the Security Council continued consideration of the item on threats to international peace and security caused by terrorists acts, during which it adopted a series of measures aimed at countering international terrorism. The Council had before it communications from Afghanistan [A/56/365-S/2001/870], China [A/56/410-S/2001/914], Georgia [A/56/387-S/2001/893], Iraq [S/2001/888], Mali [S/2001/895], Pakistan [A/56/368-S/2001/877], Qatar [A/56/363-S/2001/869] and the United Arab Emirates [A/56/401-S/2001/903] (see p. 65), and statements issued by the GUUAM States (Azerbaijan, Georgia, Republic of Moldova, Ukraine, Uzbekistan) [A/56/405-S/2001/906] and the EU [S/2001/894].

Also before the Council was the text of a plan of action to combat terrorism, adopted at an extraordinary session of the European Council on 21 September [A/56/407-S/2001/909]. The plan provided for the introduction of a European arrest warrant and the adoption of a common definition of terrorism, the identification of presumed terrorists in Europe and of their support organizations, the sharing by States with Europol (the European Police Organization) of all useful data regarding terrorism and the establishment of a specialist anti-terrorism team within Europol to cooperate closely with the United States. The European Council also supported the development of a general UN convention against international terrorism and measures to combat the financing of terrorist activities.

The Council unanimously adopted **resolution 1373(2001)**. The draft [S/2001/921] was prepared in consultations among Council members.

The Security Council,

Reaffirming its resolutions 1269(1999) of 19 October 1999 and 1368(2001) of 12 September 2001,

Reaffirming also its unequivocal condemnation of the terrorist attacks which took place in New York, Washington, D.C., and Pennsylvania on 11 September 2001, and expressing its determination to prevent all such acts,

Reaffirming further that such acts, like any act of international terrorism, constitute a threat to international peace and security,

Reaffirming the inherent right of individual or collective self-defence as recognized by the Charter of the United Nations as reiterated in resolution 1368(2001),

Reaffirming the need to combat by all means, in accordance with the Charter of the United Nations, threats to international peace and security caused by terrorist acts,

Deeply concerned by the increase, in various regions of the world, of acts of terrorism motivated by intolerance or extremism,

Calling on States to work together urgently to prevent and suppress terrorist acts, including through increased cooperation and full implementation of the relevant international conventions relating to terrorism,

Recognizing the need for States to complement international cooperation by taking additional measures to prevent and suppress, in their territories through all lawful means, the financing and preparation of any acts of terrorism,

Reaffirming the principle established by the General Assembly in its declaration of October 1970 (resolution 2625(XXV)) and reiterated by the Security Council in its resolution 1189(1998) of 13 August 1998, namely that every State has the duty to refrain from organizing, instigating, assisting or participating in terrorist acts in another State or acquiescing in organized activities within its territory directed towards the commission of such acts,

Acting under Chapter VII of the Charter of the United Nations,

1. *Decides* that all States shall:

(a) Prevent and suppress the financing of terrorist acts;

(b) Criminalize the wilful provision or collection, by any means, directly or indirectly, of funds by their nationals or in their territories with the intention that the funds should be used, or in the knowledge that they are to be used, in order to carry out terrorist acts;

(c) Freeze without delay funds and other financial assets or economic resources of persons who commit, or attempt to commit, terrorist acts or participate in or facilitate the commission of terrorist acts; of entities owned or controlled directly or indirectly by such persons; and of persons and entities acting on behalf of, or at the direction of such persons and entities, including funds derived or generated from property owned or controlled directly or indirectly by such persons and associated persons and entities;

(d) Prohibit their nationals or any persons and entities within their territories from making any funds, financial assets or economic resources or financial or other related services available, directly or indirectly, for the benefit of persons who commit or attempt to commit or facilitate or participate in the commission of terrorist acts, of entities owned or controlled, directly or indirectly, by such persons and of persons and entities acting on behalf of or at the direction of such persons;

2. *Decides also* that all States shall:

(a) Refrain from providing any form of support, active or passive, to entities or persons involved in terror-

ist acts, including by suppressing recruitment of members of terrorist groups and eliminating the supply of weapons to terrorists;

(b) Take the necessary steps to prevent the commission of terrorist acts, including by provision of early warning to other States by exchange of information;

(c) Deny safe haven to those who finance, plan, support, or commit terrorist acts, or provide safe havens;

(d) Prevent those who finance, plan, facilitate or commit terrorist acts from using their respective territories for those purposes against other States or their citizens;

(e) Ensure that any person who participates in the financing, planning, preparation or perpetration of terrorist acts or in supporting terrorist acts is brought to justice and ensure that, in addition to any other measures against them, such terrorist acts are established as serious criminal offences in domestic laws and regulations and that the punishment duly reflects the seriousness of such terrorist acts;

(f) Afford one another the greatest measure of assistance in connection with criminal investigations or criminal proceedings relating to the financing or support of terrorist acts, including assistance in obtaining evidence in their possession necessary for the proceedings;

(g) Prevent the movement of terrorists or terrorist groups by effective border controls and controls on issuance of identity papers and travel documents, and through measures for preventing counterfeiting, forgery or fraudulent use of identity papers and travel documents;

3. *Calls upon* all States to:

(a) Find ways of intensifying and accelerating the exchange of operational information, especially regarding actions or movements of terrorist persons or networks; forged or falsified travel documents; traffic in arms, explosives or sensitive materials; use of communications technologies by terrorist groups; and the threat posed by the possession of weapons of mass destruction by terrorist groups;

(b) Exchange information in accordance with international and domestic law and cooperate on administrative and judicial matters to prevent the commission of terrorist acts;

(c) Cooperate, particularly through bilateral and multilateral arrangements and agreements, to prevent and suppress terrorist attacks and take action against perpetrators of such acts;

(d) Become parties as soon as possible to the relevant international conventions and protocols relating to terrorism, including the International Convention for the Suppression of the Financing of Terrorism of 9 December 1999;

(e) Increase cooperation and fully implement the relevant international conventions and protocols relating to terrorism and Security Council resolutions 1269(1999) and 1368(2001);

(f) Take appropriate measures in conformity with the relevant provisions of national and international law, including international standards of human rights, before granting refugee status, for the purpose of ensuring that the asylum-seeker has not planned, facilitated or participated in the commission of terrorist acts;

(g) Ensure, in conformity with international law, that refugee status is not abused by the perpetrators, organizers or facilitators of terrorist acts, and that claims of political motivation are not recognized as grounds for refusing requests for the extradition of alleged terrorists;

4. *Notes with concern* the close connection between international terrorism and transnational organized crime, illicit drugs, money-laundering, illegal arms-trafficking, and illegal movement of nuclear, chemical, biological and other potentially deadly materials, and in this regard emphasizes the need to enhance coordination of efforts on national, subregional, regional and international levels in order to strengthen a global response to this serious challenge and threat to international security;

5. *Declares* that acts, methods and practices of terrorism are contrary to the purposes and principles of the United Nations and that knowingly financing, planning and inciting terrorist acts are also contrary to the purposes and principles of the United Nations;

6. *Decides* to establish, in accordance with rule 28 of its provisional rules of procedure, a Committee of the Security Council, consisting of all the members of the Council, to monitor implementation of this resolution, with the assistance of appropriate expertise, and calls upon all States to report to the Committee, no later than 90 days from the date of adoption of this resolution and thereafter according to a timetable to be proposed by the Committee, on the steps they have taken to implement this resolution;

7. *Directs* the Committee to delineate its tasks, to submit a work programme within 30 days of the adoption of this resolution, and to consider the support it requires, in consultation with the Secretary-General;

8. *Expresses* its determination to take all necessary steps in order to ensure the full implementation of this resolution, in accordance with its responsibilities under the Charter;

9. *Decides* to remain seized of this matter.

Several communications were addressed to the Secretary-General on other measures taken by countries and international and regional organizations to combat terrorism. Those included communications from Uzbekistan [A/56/354-S/2001/866]; Argentina [A/56/414-S/2001/917]; Belarus [A/56/496-S/2001/996]; Qatar [A/56/519-S/2001/1033]; the five permanent Security Council members, transmitting the 12 November statement of their Ministers for Foreign Affairs [A/56/613-S/2001/1066]; Chile, transmitting statements of the Ministers for Foreign Affairs of the Rio Group (Latin American and Caribbean States) [A/56/637-S/2001/1091, A/56/636-S/2001/1090]; Senegal, transmitting the Dakar Declaration against Terrorism adopted at the African conference on terrorism (Dakar, 17 October) [A/56/513-S/2001/1021]; Chile, transmitting the press communiqué of the meeting of the "troika" of Ministers for Foreign Affairs of the Rio Group (Chile, Colombia, Costa Rica) with the Minister for Foreign Affairs of Ukraine (New York, 13 November) [A/56/635- S/2001/1088];

Poland, transmitting the Declaration and Action Plan adopted by the Warsaw Conference on Combating Terrorism (Warsaw, 6 November) (see p. 66) [A/56/671-S/2001/1142]; the United Arab Emirates [A/56/463-S/2001/964]; and Cuba [A/56/520-S/2001/1037].

GENERAL ASSEMBLY ACTION

From 1 to 5 October [meetings 12-22], the General Assembly considered in plenary the agenda item "Measures to eliminate international terrorism" in the context of the importance and urgency of the issue in the aftermath of the 11 September terrorist attacks in the United States. The Assembly had before it the Secretary-General's report on measures to eliminate international terrorism [A/56/160 & Corr.1 & Add.1] (see p. 1225).

Addressing the Assembly on 1 October [A/56/PV.12], the Secretary-General recalled that Security Council resolution 1373(2001) (see p. 61) required States to cooperate in a wide range of areas, from suppressing the financing of terrorism to providing early warning, cooperating in criminal investigations and exchanging information on possible terrorist acts. Implementation of that resolution required technical expertise at the national level and the Secretary-General encouraged States that could offer such assistance to do so urgently.

In meeting to deliberate on its own response to the events of 11 September, the Assembly's task was to build on the wave of human solidarity to ensure that the momentum was not lost and to develop a broad, comprehensive and sustained strategy to combat and eradicate terrorism. Member States had a clear agenda before them, beginning with ensuring that the 12 conventions and protocols on international terrorism, drafted and adopted under UN auspices, were signed, ratified and implemented without delay by all States (see p. 69). It would also be important to obtain agreement on a comprehensive convention on international terrorism.

While the world was unable to prevent the 11 September attacks, there was much it could do to prevent future terrorist acts carried out with weapons of mass destruction. The global norm against the use or proliferation of weapons of mass destruction should be strengthened, by redoubling efforts to ensure the universality, verification and full implementation of key related treaties; promoting cooperation among international organizations dealing with such weapons; tightening national legislation over exports of goods and technologies needed to manufacture weapons of mass destruction and their means of delivery; and developing new efforts to criminalize their acquisition and use by non-State groups.

Controls over other types of weapons that posed grave dangers through terrorist use should also be strengthened, including a ban on the sale of small arms to non-State groups; making progress in eliminating landmines; improving the physical protection of sensitive industrial facilities, including nuclear and chemical plants; and increased vigilance against cyber-terrorist threats.

The Assembly President, summarizing the debate on 5 October [A/56/PV.22], said that it was unprecedented in the history of the United Nations for 167 Member States and 4 observers to participate in a debate on a single agenda item. That fact alone demonstrated how seriously all Member States and the international community regarded the acts of terrorism that took place on 11 September.

During the deliberations, Member States condemned international terrorism as a threat to international peace and security and a crime against humanity. It was one of the formidable challenges to the world community in the twenty-first century, and the United Nations should play the key role in intensifying international efforts to eliminate it. Member States also recognized the urgency of dealing with all forms and manifestations of international terrorism and those who harboured and supported the perpetrators, organizers and sponsors. They stressed the need to enhance international cooperation and to promptly take all necessary measures to prevent and suppress terrorist activities.

Member States concurred that a primary task facing the international community was to ensure that an effective legal framework for the prevention and elimination of international terrorism was in place. To that end, the President called on Member States that had not done so to become, as a matter of priority, parties to existing international conventions relating to terrorism. Many Member States also expressed their intention to take measures to implement international conventions within their domestic jurisdiction.

The President urged Member States to accelerate the Assembly's work, with a view to the early conclusion of the pending conventions on international terrorism, in order to enhance the capacity of the international community to combat terrorism. He requested the Assembly's Sixth (Legal) Committee to expedite its work and report to the Assembly by 15 November (see p. 1225).

Member States also shared the view that the international community should resolve to fight terrorism as a phenomenon separate from any religion or ethnic group. In that regard, the necessity for dialogue among civilizations was stressed. Also, some representatives had suggested a high-level conference on international terrorism, while others called on the international community to address the root causes of terrorism. At the same time, the need for a clearer definition of terrorism was raised as an issue for further consideration.

On 12 December, the Assembly adopted **resolution 56/88** on measures to eliminate international terrorism (see p. 1226).

Responsibility for 11 September attacks

Communications. In a 7 October letter to the Security Council President [S/2001/946], the United States said that it had clear and compelling information that the Al-Qa'idah organization, which was supported by the Taliban regime in Afghanistan, had a central role in the 11 September attacks. Although there was much the United States did not know as its inquiry was in its early stages, it was clear that the attacks and the ongoing threat posed by the Al-Qa'idah organization had been made possible by the Taliban regime's decision to allow parts of Afghanistan under its control to be used by that organization as a base of operation to train and support agents of terror.

That position was supported by the United Kingdom, which, on 8 October [S/2001/949], submitted to the Council President a document setting out the case against Osama bin Laden for the 11 September terrorist attacks against the United States based on intelligence information. The United Kingdom stressed that the document did not purport to provide a prosecutable case against Osama bin Laden in a court of law, but on the basis of all information available it was confident of the conclusions reached: that Osama bin Laden and Al-Qa'idah, the terrorist network which he headed, planned and carried out the atrocities on 11 September; they retained the will and resources to carry out further atrocities; the United Kingdom and its nationals were potential targets; and Osama bin Laden and Al-Qa'idah were able to commit those atrocities because of their close alliance with the Taliban regime, which allowed them to operate with impunity in pursuing terrorist activities. The United Kingdom stated that the document did not contain the totality of the material known to it, given the continuing and absolute need to protect intelligence sources.

In earlier communications, Côte d'Ivoire, on 2 October [A/56/429], drew attention to an article in *The Times* of the United Kingdom that alleged the existence of a cell of the bin Laden network in Côte d'Ivoire and accused the country of harbouring a terrorist training camp. Côte d'Ivoire formally advised the Secretary-General that it harboured no terrorist training camps, much less terrorists from the bin Laden network, and unequivocally denied any close or remote involvement in the tragedy that struck the United States.

Afghanistan's President, B. Rabbani, on 13 September [A/56/365-S/2001/870], said that the 11 September acts of terrorism in the United States, which followed the suicide bombing aimed at Ahmad Shah Massoud, Vice-President and Defence Minister of the Islamic State of Afghanistan, on 9 September, well established how terrorism constituted a threat to international peace and security, freedom and liberty. Afghanistan recalled its earlier warnings of the threats of terrorist activities by the Pakistan-Taliban–bin Laden axis in the Taliban-occupied parts of Afghanistan. The time had come, it said, for the international community to put pressure on Pakistan, the Taliban's main backer, to cease immediately its aggression in Afghanistan, withdraw its armed personnel, put an end to the use of Afghan soil for perpetrating subversive acts against other States and close down all terrorist training camps and centres of indoctrination within Pakistan.

The Secretary-General, in a 17 September press statement [SG/SM/7959], said that he was saddened at the assassination of Commander Massoud. That act of terrorism had eliminated a key Afghan leader, and both the method and apparent involvement of non-Afghan elements in the crime further complicated the efforts of the international community to end the conflict.

The United Arab Emirates, on 24 September [A/56/401-S/2001/903], informed the Secretary-General of its decision to break off diplomatic relations with the Taliban Government of Afghanistan following its failure to respond to the Security Council's request to hand over Osama bin Laden to face a fair international trial on the accusations made against him in connection with the terrorist attacks of 11 September in the United States.

Action against the Taliban and Al-Qa'idah

Action under Article 51 of the Charter

On 7 October [S/2001/946], the United States reported to the Security Council President that, in accordance with Article 51 of the Charter of the United Nations, it had, together with other States, initiated action in the exercise of its inherent right of individual and collective self-defence following the armed attacks against it on 11 September, resulting in the death of more than 5,000 persons, including nationals of 81 countries, and the destruction of four civilian aircraft, the World Trade Center towers and a section of the Pentagon (United States military headquarters). The actions of the United States military were

designed to prevent or deter further attacks on the United States and included measures against Al-Qa'idah terrorist training camps and Taliban military installations in Afghanistan. In carrying out those actions, the United States was committed to minimizing civilian casualties and damage to civilian property and would continue its humanitarian efforts to alleviate the suffering of the people of Afghanistan. (For information on the resulting military, political and humanitarian developments in Afghanistan, see PART ONE, Chapter IV, and PART THREE, Chapter III.)

On 8 October [S/2001/967], the EU declared its full solidarity with the United States and wholehearted support for the action it was taking in Afghanistan. It stressed that the targeted action launched on 7 October was an attack neither against Islam nor against the people of Afghanistan. The military action was part of a wider multilateral strategy in which the EU was committed to playing its part, including a comprehensive assault on the organizations and financing structures that underpinned terrorism.

Invoking Article 51 of the Charter, several other countries informed the Council President of action they had taken following the 11 September attacks, clarifying that such action was not in any way directed against the people of Afghanistan or Islam. Canada, on 24 October [S/2001/1005], reported that it was deploying naval ships, surveillance and transport aircraft, military personnel and other assets. On 23 November [S/2001/1103], France announced that it was undertaking action involving the participation of military air, land and naval forces. On the same date [S/2001/1104], Australia said that it was invoking the 1951 Security Treaty between Australia, New Zealand and the United States (ANZUS Treaty), under which it would contribute elements of the Australian Defence Force, including land, air and naval units, to assist the United States–led military operations. As approved by its Federal Parliament, Germany announced on 29 November [S/2001/1127] that it was providing nuclear, biological and chemical defence units, medical and specialized units, air-transport capacities and naval forces. The Netherlands, on 6 December [S/2001/1171], stated that it was providing air-transport capacity, naval forces, navy aviation and support. Some of its units would be deployed as backfill for American military forces in the Caribbean. On 17 December [S/2001/1193], New Zealand indicated its willingness to make a military contribution.

United States policy on terrorism

On 6 November [S/2001/1052], United States President George W. Bush, in a telecast statement to the Warsaw Conference on Combating Terrorism [A/56/671-S/2001/1142], said that Al-Qa'idah was operating in more than 60 nations, including some in Central and Eastern Europe. Those terrorist groups were seeking chemical, biological and nuclear weapons and, given the means, they would be a threat to every nation and eventually to civilization itself. Therefore, the United States was determined to fight that evil until it was rid of it and would not wait for the authors of mass murder to gain weapons of mass destruction. The United States military was systematically pursuing its mission, destroying many terrorist training camps, severing communication links and taking out air defences, and was currently attacking the Taliban front lines.

It was a difficult struggle of uncertain duration and Afghanistan was only the beginning of United States efforts in the world. The United States would not rest until terrorist groups of global reach had been found, stopped and defeated. That goal would not be achieved until all nations stopped harbouring and supporting such terrorists within their borders.

The defeat of terror required an international coalition of unprecedented scope and co-operation, and no nation could be neutral in that conflict, because no civilized nation could be secure in a world threatened by terror.

Implementation of resolution 1373(2001)

Counter-Terrorism Committee

In a 4 October note [S/2001/935], the Security Council President announced that, after consultations among Council members, it was agreed to elect the chairperson (Sir Jeremy Greenstock (United Kingdom)) and vice-chairpersons (Colombia, Mauritius, Russian Federation) of the Security Council Committee established pursuant to resolution 1373(2001) (known as the Counter-Terrorism Committee). The Committee would submit a work programme by 28 October. The Council would review the Committee's structure and activities not later than 4 April 2002.

On 19 October [S/2001/986], the Chairman of the Counter-Terrorism Committee submitted the Committee's work programme to the Council. Recognizing that many areas of counter-terrorism were inherently sensitive, the Committee undertook to ensure the highest level of confidentiality and would develop rules to that effect.

On 23 October [S/2001/999], the Council President informed the Chairman that the Council agreed to the work programme.

On 30 November [S/2001/1134], the Committee submitted to the Council a directory of contact points in each State and in a number of international/regional organizations and agencies and the Secretariat. The directory was updated in December [S/2001/1134/Add.1]. A revised consolidated version would be submitted in January 2002 and every two months subsequently.

Reports of Member States. The Chairman of the Counter-Terrorism Committee submitted to the Council President reports received from Member States containing information on action they had taken or intended to take to implement Council resolution 1373(2001). On 30 November, the Committee submitted reports from Honduras [S/2001/1136], Mongolia [S/2001/1135], Norway [S/2001/1138] and Venezuela [S/2001/1137]; on 10 December, from Myanmar [S/2001/1144]; on 13 December, from the Dominican Republic [S/2001/1200] and Lebanon [S/2001/1201]; on 14 December, from Bahrain [S/2001/1210], Canada [S/2001/1209] and the Syrian Arab Republic [S/2001/1204]; on 19 December, from Slovakia [S/2001/1225] and the United States [S/2001/1220]; on 20 December, from the Bahamas [S/2001/1236], Egypt [S/2001/1237], Singapore [S/2001/1234], Sweden [S/2001/1233] and Uruguay [S/2001/1235]; on 21 December, from Andorra [S/2001/1244], Australia [S/2001/1247], Austria [S/2001/1242], Cyprus [S/2001/1243], the Democratic People's Republic of Korea [S/2001/1248], El Salvador [S/2001/1249], Finland [S/2001/1251], Indonesia [S/2001/1245], Ireland [S/2001/1252], Liechtenstein [S/2001/1253], Malta [S/2001/1250], Mexico [S/2001/1254] and Spain [S/2001/1246]; on 27 December, from Albania [S/2001/1309], Algeria [S/2001/1280], Barbados [S/2001/1276], Belgium [S/2001/1266], Belize [S/2001/1265], Bosnia and Herzegovina [S/2001/1313], Botswana [S/2001/1267], Brazil [S/2001/1285], Bulgaria [S/2001/1273], China [S/2001/1270], Colombia [S/2001/1318], Costa Rica [S/2001/1279], Croatia [S/2001/1271], the Czech Republic [S/2001/1302], Denmark [S/2001/1303], Djibouti [S/2001/1311], Estonia [S/2001/1315], France [S/2001/1274], Guatemala [S/2001/1272], Iceland [S/2001/1308], India [S/2001/1278], Iraq [S/2001/1291], Israel [S/2001/1312], Jamaica [S/2001/1314], Japan [S/2001/1306], Kazakhstan [S/2001/1307], Mauritius [S/2001/1286], Morocco [S/2001/1288], Mozambique [S/2001/1319], Namibia [S/2001/1305], Pakistan [S/2001/1310], Paraguay [S/2001/1293], Poland [S/2001/1275], Romania [S/2001/1339], the Russian Federation [S/2001/1284], San Marino [S/2001/1292], Slovenia [S/2001/1277], Somalia [S/2001/1287], South Africa [S/2001/1281], the Sudan [S/2001/1317], Tunisia [S/2001/1316], Turkey [S/2001/1304], Venezuela [S/2001/1289] and the EU [S/2001/1297]; and on 28 December, from Argentina [S/2001/1340], Azerbaijan [S/2001/1325], Burundi [S/2001/1322], Cape Verde [S/2001/1329], the Cook Islands [S/2001/1324], the Democratic Republic of the Congo [S/2001/1331], Ecuador [S/2001/1327], Iran [S/2001/1332], the Libyan Arab Jamahiriya [S/2001/1323], Nepal [S/2001/1326], the former Yugoslav Republic of Macedonia [S/2001/1333], Ukraine [S/2001/1330] and the Federal Republic of Yugoslavia [S/2001/1328].

Terrorism and human rights

The Director of the New York Office of OHCHR, on behalf of the High Commissioner, in a statement to the Counter-Terrorism Committee [S/2001/1227] transmitted to the Security Council President on 14 December by the Committee Chairman, said that, while pursuing the objective of eradicating terrorism under resolution 1373(2001), efforts should be made to avoid innocent people becoming the victims of counter-terrorism measures. States should strictly adhere to their international obligations to uphold human rights and fundamental freedoms.

The Director hoped that the Counter-Terrorism Committee would assist States in ensuring the compatibility of measures taken under resolution 1373(2001) with States' obligations under human rights law. OHCHR was committed to advising Governments on the content of human rights standards in the light of international norms and jurisprudence that might be relevant in the context of anti-terrorism measures.

OHCHR was aware of the Committee's guidance for States in the reporting requirements under resolution 1373(2001). To avoid the misapplication of the resolution, the High Commissioner was recommending that further complementary guidance be issued to assist States to comply with their international human rights obligations. The suggested "further guidance", based on States' obligations under international human rights law, was available to the Committee members. The misapplication of resolution 1373(2001) could lead to unwarranted infringement on civil liberties, and there was evidence that some Governments were introducing measures that might erode core human rights safeguards. In some countries, non-violent activities had been considered as terrorism and excessive measures had been taken to suppress or restrict individual rights, including the presumption of innocence, the right to a fair trial, freedom from torture, privacy rights, freedom of expression and assembly, and the right to seek asylum. That was clearly not the aim of resolution 1373(2001) and it was important to ensure that such unintended and undesirable consequences of the global effort against terrorism were avoided. The High Commissioner was urging the Committee therefore to ensure that those assisting it in its crucial monitoring task had strong human rights expertise; she stood ready to assist the Committee in identifying such experts.

(For further information on human rights and terrorism, see p. 648.)

IAEA action

In a 7 December letter to the Security Council President [S/2001/1164], the Director General of the International Atomic Energy Agency (IAEA) stated that, pursuant to resolution 1373(2001), the IAEA General Conference, in a resolution adopted at its forty-fifth regular session (Vienna, 17-21 September) (see p. 1401), requested him to strengthen the Agency's work relevant to preventing acts of terrorism involving nuclear material and other radioactive materials.

In response to that request, he reported to the IAEA Board of Governors on protection against nuclear terrorism, summarizing the Agency's work in areas relevant to the prevention and mitigation of the consequences of terrorist acts and outlining proposals for enhanced and additional activities, excerpts of which were contained in an attachment to the Director General's letter. The Board had directed him to proceed urgently with approved activities, to review the Agency's proposed response to the threat of nuclear terrorism and to submit the outcome for consideration in 2002.

Security Council declaration on the global effort to combat terrorism

On 12 November [meeting 4413], the Security Council met at the ministerial level to continue consideration of threats to international peace and security caused by terrorist acts. It had before it a statement by Japan outlining its positions on counter-terrorism [S/2001/1062].

A number of other communications on the question of terrorism were addressed to the Secretary-General or the Council President by Member States and intergovernmental organizations: Belgium transmitted the conclusions of the General Affairs Council of the EU of 8 October [S/2001/968] and of 17 October [S/2001/980]; Slovenia, also on 17 October [S/2001/987], transmitted a declaration of its National Assembly; Armenia transmitted the statement of the participants in the extraordinary meeting of the Committee of Secretaries of the Security Councils of the States parties to the Treaty on Collective Security (Dushanbe, 9 October) [S/2001/1020]; Iraq transmitted a letter from its President of 29 October [S/2001/1034]; and Zambia forwarded a communiqué issued by the fifth extraordinary session of the Central Organ of the Organization of African Unity Mechanism for Conflict Prevention, Management and Resolution (New York, 11 November) [S/2001/1061].

Addressing the Council [S/PV.4413], the Secretary-General noted that the reports submitted by Member States to the Counter-Terrorism Committee (see p. 66) would play an indispensable role in identifying and cataloguing existing policies and instruments, and provide the benchmark for the international community as it assessed its ability to combat international terrorism. He encouraged all States to ensure the full implementation of resolution 1373(2001) (see p. 61) and to submit their reports by December.

The Secretary-General announced that he had established a working group, comprising senior officials from the UN system, as well as outside experts, to identify the longer-term implications and broad policy dimensions of terrorism for the United Nations and to formulate recommendations on steps the UN system might take.

The United Nations was uniquely placed to facilitate cooperation between Governments in the fight against terrorism and to ensure that the greatest number of States were able and willing to take the necessary and difficult steps—diplomatic, legal and political—that were needed to defeat terrorism.

France drew attention to the plan of action adopted on 21 September by the EU (see p. 61), which included a European arrest warrant and other legal, police and aviation-security measures, and to the "special recommendations" adopted on 30 October in Washington, D.C., by the intergovernmental Financial Action Task Force on Money Laundering (FATF), established in 1989 by the G-7 countries, to apply to the sources of financing of terrorism methods that had been successfully used to combat money-laundering. France proposed the establishment of a forum on the financing of terrorism, with a broader membership than that of FATF.

United States Secretary of State Colin Powell stated that his country had declared war on all terrorist organizations with a global reach, and, as a result, it needed the support of all of its partners in the international community, and specifically the help of police forces, intelligence services and banking systems around the world to isolate and eradicate the common enemies.

Council resolution 1373(2001) was a mandate to change fundamentally how the international community responded to terrorism. States were starting to work together to cut off the financial resources that were the oxygen of terrorist groups, and Council members had supported the immediate freezing of the assets of over 120 persons and entities that the United States had identified to the UN Committee established pursuant

to resolution 1267(1999) [YUN 1999, p. 265] (Afghan sanctions committee) (see p. 270). The Council was well situated to coordinate specialized training and assistance to help countries deal with rapid financial flows and regulatory loopholes.

The war on terrorism would be fought also with increased support for democracy programmes, judicial reform, conflict resolution, poverty alleviation, economic reform and health and education programmes. The United States stood ready to provide technical assistance, ranging from aviation security to financial tracking measures and law enforcement. It welcomed initiatives by others in those field, and was ready to exchange information about terrorism and to cooperate in other ways. The integrity of international transmission systems, such as the mail system, should also be taken into account, as should the Internet. In each of those areas, there were important roles for the United Nations and for each country to play.

SECURITY COUNCIL ACTION

On 12 November [meeting 4413], the Security Council unanimously adopted **resolution 1377 (2001)**. The draft [S/2001/1060] was prepared in consultations among Council members.

The Security Council
Decides to adopt the attached declaration on the global effort to combat terrorism.

ANNEX

The Security Council,
Meeting at the ministerial level,
Recalling its resolutions 1269(1999) of 19 October 1999, 1368(2001) of 12 September 2001 and 1373(2001) of 28 September 2001,
Declares that acts of international terrorism constitute one of the most serious threats to international peace and security in the twenty-first century;
Further declares that acts of international terrorism constitute a challenge to all States and to all of humanity;
Reaffirms its unequivocal condemnation of all acts, methods and practices of terrorism as criminal and unjustifiable, regardless of their motivation, in all their forms and manifestations, wherever and by whomever committed;
Stresses that acts of international terrorism are contrary to the purposes and principles of the Charter of the United Nations, and that the financing, planning and preparation of as well as any other form of support for acts of international terrorism are similarly contrary to the purposes and principles of the Charter of the United Nations;
Underlines that acts of terrorism endanger innocent lives and the dignity and security of human beings everywhere, threaten the social and economic development of all States and undermine global stability and prosperity;
Affirms that a sustained, comprehensive approach involving the active participation and collaboration of all

Member States of the United Nations, and in accordance with the Charter of the United Nations and international law, is essential to combat the scourge of international terrorism;

Stresses that continuing international efforts to broaden the understanding among civilizations and to address regional conflicts and the full range of global issues, including development issues, will contribute to international cooperation and collaboration, which themselves are necessary to sustain the broadest possible fight against international terrorism;

Welcomes the commitment expressed by States to fight the scourge of international terrorism, including during the General Assembly plenary debate from 1 to 5 October 2001, calls on all States to become parties as soon as possible to the relevant international conventions and protocols relating to terrorism, and encourages Member States to take forward work in this area;

Calls on all States to take urgent steps to implement fully resolution 1373(2001), and to assist each other in doing so, and underlines the obligation on States to deny financial and all other forms of support and safe haven to terrorists and those supporting terrorism;

Expresses its determination to proceed with the implementation of that resolution in full cooperation with the whole membership of the United Nations, and welcomes the progress made so far by the Counter-Terrorism Committee established by paragraph 6 of resolution 1373(2001) to monitor implementation of that resolution;

Recognizes that many States will require assistance in implementing all the requirements of resolution 1373(2001), and invites States to inform the Counter-Terrorism Committee of areas in which they require such support;

In that context, invites the Counter-Terrorism Committee to explore ways in which States can be assisted, and in particular to explore with international, regional and subregional organizations:

—The promotion of best-practice in the areas covered by resolution 1373(2001), including the preparation of model laws as appropriate;

—The availability of existing technical, financial, regulatory, legislative or other assistance programmes which might facilitate the implementation of resolution 1373(2001);

—The promotion of possible synergies between these assistance programmes;

Calls on all States to intensify their efforts to eliminate the scourge of international terrorism.

Treaty Event

The Treaty Event: Multilateral Treaties on Terrorism was held at United Nations Headquarters from 10 to 16 November, with the participation of 66 heads of State and Government and Ministers for Foreign Affairs. The Secretary-General, in his 4 October letter of invitation to Member States, said that, having witnessed the horror and devastation caused by the recent terrorist attacks in the host State of the United Nations and consistent with the calls made by the General Assembly and the Security Council, he was urging States to reaffirm their

abhorrence of terrorism by becoming party, if they had not done so, to the 12 global conventions that addressed various aspects of terrorism, four of which were deposited with him. Those four conventions deposited with the Secretary-General were the Convention on the Prevention and Punishment of Crimes against Internationally Protected Persons, including Diplomatic Agents, adopted by General Assembly resolution 3166(XXVIII) [YUN 1973, p. 775]; the International Convention against the Taking of Hostages, adopted by Assembly resolution 34/146 [YUN 1979, p. 1144]; the International Convention for the Suppression of Terrorist Bombings, adopted by Assembly resolution 52/164 [YUN 1997, p. 1348]; and the International Convention for the Suppression of the Financing of Terrorism, adopted by Assembly resolution 54/109 [YUN 1999, p. 1233]. The other conventions adopted under UN auspices were the Convention on Offences and Certain Other Acts Committed on Board Aircraft (Tokyo, 1963); the Convention for the Suppression of Unlawful Seizure of Aircraft (The Hague, 1970); the Convention for the Suppression of Unlawful Acts against the Safety of Civil Aviation (Montreal, 1971); the Convention on the Physical Protection of Nuclear Material (Vienna, 1980); the Protocol on the Suppression of Unlawful Acts of Violence at Airports Serving International Civil Aviation, supplementary to the Convention for the Suppression of Unlawful Acts against the Safety of Civil Aviation (Montreal, 1988); the Convention for the Suppression of Unlawful Acts against the Safety of Maritime Navigation (Rome, 1988); the Protocol for the Suppression of Unlawful Acts against the Safety of Fixed Platforms Located on the Continental Shelf (Rome, 1988); and the Convention on the Marking of Plastic Explosives for the Purpose of Detection (Montreal, 1991).

The Secretary-General said that States also needed to take measures to implement the obligations under those treaties within their domestic jurisdictions. In reaffirming their commitment to the treaty framework dealing with terrorism, by signing and ratifying or acceding to those treaties to which they were not already party, Member States would also contribute to strengthening the international legal framework.

In a 16 November report on the Event, the Office of Legal Affairs indicated that 79 States participated and undertook 180 treaty actions relating to 41 treaties (110 signatures and 70 ratifications/accessions and other actions). The highest number of treaty actions related to the International Convention for the Suppression of the Financing of Terrorism (48 signatures and 8 ratifications/accessions), followed by the International Convention for the Suppression of Terrorist Bombings (15 ratifications/accessions) and the Convention on the Prevention and Punishment of Crimes against Internationally Protected Persons, including Diplomatic Agents (4 ratifications/accessions).

(For further information on treaties and conventions relating to terrorism, see PART FOUR, Chapter III.)

Other terrorist incidents

On 15 August [S/2001/793], Angola reported that, on 10 August, a train carrying some 500 civilian passengers was attacked by rebel forces near the town of Zenza do Itombe in Kwanza Norte province, resulting in the deaths of 252 people, with more than 165 injured. Some 90 days earlier, after having killed and brutally mistreated civilians in the city of Caxito, the rebels kidnapped 61 children. Angola called on the international community and the United Nations to take action to isolate those who waged war and refused to respect Security Council decisions.

In a 14 August press release [SG/SM/7916], the Secretary-General condemned the 10 August attack and noted that the National Union for the Total Independence of Angola (UNITA) had claimed, and therefore bore responsibility for, that indefensible loss of life.

The Security Council, in presidential statement **S/PRST/2001/24** of 20 September (see p. 226), condemned the terrorist attacks by UNITA forces on the civilian population of Angola and stressed that such attacks were unacceptable and could not be justified by any political goals.

In a series of communications submitted to the Secretary-General throughout 2001, Israel reported on violent incidents committed against Israeli civilians, including suicide bombings, and armed attacks allegedly committed by Palestinian gunmen, resulting in the deaths of hundreds of Israeli civilians and damage to property. Israel called on the Palestinian leadership to bring an end to the violence.

In a 4 December letter [A/56/678-S/2001/1150], Israel, in reporting new atrocities, listed those communications. It reported that, on the evening of 1 December, two Palestinian suicide bombers detonated their charges in a crowded pedestrian mall in Jerusalem, killing 10 Israelis and wounding 180, several of them seriously. In a similar act committed 12 hours later in Haifa, 15 civilians were killed and 38 others wounded. Israel recalled its previous letters to the Secretary-General detailing Palestinian terrorist atrocities of the past 14 months and said that it held Chairman Yasser Arafat and the Palestinian Authority

(PA) fully responsible for those attacks. Israel maintained that there could be no return to normalcy in the region until the PA fulfilled its signed commitments to renounce the use of terror and violence. The international community should therefore make it clear to the Palestinian leadership that its inaction would not be tolerated and that any regime that lent support to terrorism or allowed its territory to serve as a haven for terrorist murderers was unwelcome in the family of civilized nations.

The Secretary-General, in a 2 December press statement [SG/SM/8056], expressed shock and horror at the bombings in Jerusalem and Haifa. No cause and no motive could ever justify the deliberate murder of innocent civilians, he said. The Secretary-General unequivocally condemned those acts of terrorism and called on the PA to take immediate and decisive action to arrest and bring to justice those responsible for those and earlier acts of terrorism.

The Permanent Observer of Palestine to the United Nations, in a January letter [A/ES-10/54-S/2001/7], referring to previous Israeli accusations of terrorism, reiterated that the Palestinian side remained opposed to terrorist actions by any side and definitely did not condone the actions referred to. (For further information on the Israel/Palestine situation, see PART ONE, Chapter VI.)

Qatar, on 29 October [A/56/519-S/2001/1033], condemned attacks on several churches in Pakistan, which had resulted in a number of civilian fatalities. Qatar reaffirmed its condemnation of terrorism in all its forms and manifestations.

Peacekeeping operations

In 2001, the United Nations, in the context of its continuing review of peacekeeping operations and follow-up to the recommendations of the 2000 report of the Panel on United Nations Peace Operations (the Brahimi report), conducted the first in-depth managerial examination of those operations, which resulted in proposals for further steps for improving UN peacekeeping capacity, including the provision of additional financial and human resources.

The Special Committee on Peacekeeping Operations, whose mandate was to review the whole question of peacekeeping operations in all their aspects, held a general debate on 18 and 19 June, during which it approved a number of recommendations for submission to the General Assembly. The Special Committee also considered other general issues related to peacekeeping operations and made recommendations for improving their effectiveness.

On 7 September, by **decision 55/492**, the Assembly included in the draft agenda of its fifty-sixth session the item "Comprehensive review of the whole question of peacekeeping operations in all their aspects". On 10 December, by **decision 56/418**, the Assembly took note of the report of the Fourth (Special Political and Decolonization) Committee [A/56/551].

In-depth examination of UN peacekeeping operations

Report of Secretary-General. In response to General Assembly resolutions 54/81 B [YUN 2000, p. 96], 55/2 [ibid., p. 49] and 55/135 [ibid., p. 90], the Secretary-General submitted a June report on implementation of the recommendations of the Special Committee on Peacekeeping Operations and the Panel on United Nations Peace Operations [A/55/977]. The 2000 resolutions contained the Assembly's response to four interlinked reports produced over the preceding 12 months on strengthening the capacity of the United Nations for peacekeeping: the report of the Special Committee [YUN 2000, p. 95]; the Brahimi report [ibid., p. 83]; the Secretary-General's report on the implementation of the Brahimi report [ibid., p. 85]; and the Special Committee response to the Brahimi report and the implementation plan contained in that report [ibid., p. 89].

The Secretary-General's June 2001 report contained the findings of the first in-depth and comprehensive managerial examination of UN peacekeeping operations. The review, which was conducted in-house, benefited from the input of external management consultants and former senior UN and Member States' officials with extensive exposure to UN peacekeeping, and from the External Review Board and the Office of Internal Oversight Services (OIOS). It examined the Department of Peacekeeping Operations (DPKO), the need for enhanced interrelationships with other parts of the Secretariat, the security management system (DPKO and the Office of the United Nations Security Coordinator), and system-wide information, analysis and decision-making capacities.

The report contended that DPKO's core capacities required considerable strengthening, including its management practices and culture; its ability to translate legislative guidance into strategic plans for future peacekeeping operations, bearing in mind lessons learned and best practices from previous operations; the priority and effort it dedicated to developing the requisite policies and capacities to enable peacekeeping

operations to function efficiently and effectively; and internal coordination for the planning, conduct and support of specific operations.

In assessing the implications of the Brahimi report's recommendation [YUN 2000, p. 84] that the United Nations set as an objective the ability to fully and effectively deploy peacekeeping missions within 30 to 90 days of the adoption of a Security Council resolution establishing them, the Secretary-General outlined three options for achieving that objective: a "heavy strategic reserve" of equipment and materiel at the United Nations Logistics Base (UNLB) in Brindisi, Italy (which could entail an initial investment of some $350 million); a "light strategic reserve" option, with substantially lower up-front investments (some $30 million), which would rely on extensive "retainer" contracts for the "just-in-time" delivery of goods and services, but with very large annual recurring costs (over $100 million per annum); and a "medium strategic reserve" option, with approximately $170 million up-front investment and some $40 million annual recurring costs. The Secretary-General recommended the "medium strategic reserve" option as the most economical and practical. Any of the options to meet the 30-to-90-day deployment time frames would require a one-time expenditure budget to enhance the strategic deployment stocks at UNLB and to cater for annual recurring costs; entry into pre-arranged contracts and letters of assist for key services; increased reliability of standby arrangements with Member States, especially for support units; and improved personnel surge capacity, particularly for administrative support staff. Pre-commitment authority to initiate spending to procure essential goods and services prior to the adoption of a resolution establishing an operation could greatly enhance the Organization's ability to meet the stated deployment objectives.

However, although those proposals could go a long way to ensure a military and civilian police capacity in parallel with a rapid military deployment, none of the options would guarantee 30-to-90-day deployment time frames, unless fully self-sustaining and completely self-sufficient troops were provided by Member States with the means to do so.

The report also outlined progress with regard to proposals for enhancing the standby arrangements system for military and civilian police personnel, including for the creation of a revolving list of "on call" officers to be deployed at short notice. In that regard, it referred to the 19 March letter to Member States from the Under-Secretary-General for Peacekeeping Operations (annex G to the report), containing the profiles of required expertise and the proposed mechanism for enhancing the standby arrangements system. The report also presented the outlines of a global strategy for civilian staffing of peace-keeping operations (see p. 106) to address critical shortcomings in the current system.

The Secretary-General argued that to strengthen DPKO's core capacities and meet the challenges of rapid and effective deployment, adjustments would be required to DPKO's organizational structure and staffing levels. He therefore proposed creating a new position of Director for Strategic Planning and Management in the Office of the Under-Secretary-General for Peace-keeping Operations, with responsibilities for overseeing improvements to the management infrastructure, including information management, as well as an enhanced lessons learned and strategic planning capacity; increasing the number of Assistant Secretaries-General in DPKO from two to three, with the addition of an Assistant Secretary-General for Military/Civilian Police Affairs and Mine Action; and upgrading the rank of the Civilian Police Adviser. He also proposed restructuring the Office of Logistics, Management and Mine Action, by dividing the Field Administration and Logistics Division into two separate divisions (one for administrative support and the other for logistics support), reporting directly to the Assistant Secretary-General, whose title would be changed to the Assistant Secretary-General for Mission Support. The Office of Mission Support would have enhanced capacities for administrative planning and civilian training, plus contracts management (annexes E and H).

The Secretary-General stated that DPKO needed to be strengthened to bring to completion the myriad of policies, standard operating procedures, systems and training programmes that were critical for efficient and effective performance in the field. Additional resources were also necessary to give DPKO the time and flexibility to interact with Member States more frequently, particularly Security Council members and troop, police and financial contributors. Strengthening DPKO could entail some 150 new posts, the additional resources for which would be justified in a subsequent report, on a post-by-post basis.

The Secretary-General further proposed measures to strengthen DPKO's collaboration with other departments, agencies, funds and programmes that played a role in peacekeeping, but recommended against delegating procurement and budgeting authority from the Department of Management to DPKO, proposing instead that the two Departments should interact with one another with much greater frequency and depth.

The roles and responsibilities of DPKO and the Department of Political Affairs were clarified (annex L), with the suggestion that the physical co-location of the political affairs officers in both Departments was desirable to promote cohesion and cultural change. The need to strengthen the capacities of the Department of Management, OIOS, OHCHR and the Office of Legal Affairs to more effectively support UN peacekeeping operations was underlined, as was the need for increased collaboration between DPKO and the Department of Public Information. Greater attention needed to be paid to gender issues in peacekeeping operations and there should be more involvement of the Office for the Coordination of Humanitarian Affairs, operational funds and programmes and the Department for Disarmament Affairs in all aspects of peacekeeping, from planning to liquidation.

The report recommended that, to optimize the Organization's resources in conflict zones, enhanced analytical capacities, better executive-level decision-making systems and the ability to devise coherent and comprehensive mid-to-long-term strategies were required. It proposed strengthening the Executive Committee on Peace and Security by creating a small new multi-disciplinary policy and analysis unit to support the Committee's work (see p. 76).

In his concluding remarks, the Secretary-General observed that most of the findings confirmed that the overall peacekeeping capacities of the Secretariat had not developed at the pace they should have because sufficient time, energy and resources had not been dedicated to planning for the future. Furthermore, if the United Nations continued to define its capacities strictly based on current minimum needs, it would be no better off two to three years later. It should not lose the opportunity to invest in the future. Performance could significantly improve if changes were brought to structures, systems and procedures, and if additional resources were provided, but the United Nations could no longer afford to continue with the "gifted amateurism" that had characterized its approach to peacekeeping. Higher professional standards were required, as were enhanced mechanisms to monitor performance and progress more effectively.

However, strengthening DPKO and other parts of the Secretariat was not the only answer to the challenge. The decisions of the Council and its willingness to ensure that operations did not fail were determining factors, as was the political will of Member States to match mandates with the required human, material, financial and political support.

Special Committee on Peacekeeping Operations. The Special Committee on Peacekeeping Operations, at its 2001 session (18-19 June) [A/55/1024 & Corr.1], considered the Secretary-General's report (see p. 71) and encouraged the Secretariat to conduct regular and systematic reviews. It recognized the need to further strengthen DPKO's capacity to undertake its core functions and, especially, to reinforce management, planning and mission support.

In the area of management, the Special Committee recommended the creation of the position of Director for Management in the Office of the Under-Secretary-General for Peacekeeping Operations. The Director would also supervise the work of the restructured Peacekeeping Best Practices Unit. The Committee recognized the need to strengthen the front offices of the respective assistant secretaries-general, and requested the Secretary-General to report in his budget proposals on specific measures taken to address the problems related to DPKO's management or organizational culture. The Special Committee recommended that the capacity of the Best Practices Unit be strengthened and its mandate broadened, and that the Unit be renamed to reflect better its responsibilities.

As to policy and capacity development, the Special Committee concurred that additional resources should be allocated to the Department. It welcomed the proposal to create a small new unit in the Office of Mission Support and stressed that the training of civilian personnel in DPKO should be done in coordination with the Office of Human Resources Management.

With regard to operational planning, the Special Committee welcomed the improvement in coordination and cooperation through the establishment of Integrated Mission Task Forces (IMTFs) and called on the Secretariat to fully embrace the IMTF concept. It recommended increasing the capacity of the Office of Operations to fulfil its mission planning and support responsibilities to better enable the Secretariat to consult with Member States and troop-contributing countries. Stressing the importance of having the entire leadership of a mission participate in key aspects of the mission-planning process at Headquarters and in the field, the Special Committee expressed concern over the practicality of having potential mission leaders as heads of future IMTFs. It recognized the Secretariat's efforts to develop a "mission headquarters orientation programme".

The Special Committee supported the "task team" approach to mission support and encouraged the Secretary-General to ensure greater communication and coordination between the Office of Operations, the Office of Mission Support, and the Military and Civilian Police Divisions. The Situation Centre should be responsible for producing comprehensive fact sheets and status reports in support of DPKO's reporting requirements, supplemented during crises by timely military and political assessments. The Special Committee agreed that additional resources and staff training were required to enhance the capacity of the Situation Centre in the overall strengthening of the Office of Operations.

With regard to rapid deployment, the Special Committee urged the Secretariat to continue working towards the 30-to-90-day goal for deploying peacekeeping operations and endorsed the concept of a medium strategic reserve at UNLB as the most appropriate and practical option. The Secretariat, in preparing mission budget proposals, should develop a common understanding with Member States of the financial, equipment and personnel requirements needed to meet set deployment objectives. The Special Committee concurred with the Secretary-General's assessment that the rapid deployment time frame could be achieved only if Member States provided fully self-sustaining and completely self-sufficient troops within current contingent-owned equipment procedures. The Secretariat should make recommendations on how the strategic air and sea lift for rapid deployment of peacekeeping missions could be better pre-arranged. It supported efforts to enhance and strengthen the United Nations standby arrangements system (see p. 77) and looked forward to consultations between the Secretariat and Member States on its improvement, including the creation of "on call" lists of military and civilian police personnel. The Special Committee also supported the further development of pre-mandate commitment authority given to the Secretary-General prior to a mission's full authorization by the Security Council.

The Special Committee endorsed the separation of the Civilian Police Division from the Military Division and supported the upgrading of the post of Civilian Police Adviser, the further strengthening of the Civilian Police Division and the creation of a limited capability in the Division to assist in criminal law and judicial issues, the upgrading of the Mine Action Service to a Division, the reorganization of the Field Administration and Logistics Division, the creation of two separate divisions within the new Office of Mission Support, and the establishment of a Contracts Management Section within the Logistics Support Division to strengthen procurement planning (see p. 103). It recommended that active service military officers be included in the re-organized Office of Mission Support.

However, the Special Committee remained unconvinced about the exact role of a third assistant secretary-general as proposed by the Secretary-General and requested him to elaborate on the matter in his next report.

Resource requirements

Report of Secretary-General. On 2 August [A/C.4/55/L.24], the Secretary-General stated that implementation of the Special Committee's recommendations on strengthening UN peacekeeping operations would require additional resources of not more than $30 million under the support account for peacekeeping operations budget for the period 1 July 2001 to 30 June 2002, approved in General Assembly **resolution 55/271** (see p. 95) and in the 2002-2003 programme budget. Detailed resource requirements would be provided to the Fifth (Administrative and Budgetary) Committee.

On 9 August [A/C.5/55/46 & Corr.1 & Add.1], the Secretary-General informed the Fifth Committee that the consequential changes in the 2002-2003 programme budget would amount to $2,696,200 gross, inclusive of an increase of nine posts. The change in the support account would amount to $23,129,600, inclusive of an increase of 207 posts, of which 129 posts were requested for DPKO. The increase represented 0.9 per cent of the level of peacekeeping costs for the 2000-2001 biennium, which were projected at slightly in excess of $3 billion.

Report of ACABQ. In October [A/56/478], the Advisory Committee on Administrative and Budgetary Questions (ACABQ) noted that, should the Assembly adopt the draft resolution on the comprehensive review of the whole question of peacekeeping operations in all their aspects (see resolution 56/241 below), additional requirements of $1,575,700 would arise under the 2002-2003 programme budget (section 3: $376,400; section 22: $888,800; section 27D: $127,900; section 32: $182,600). Additional requirements of $16,215,450 would also arise under the support account for 1 July 2001 to 30 June 2002. ACABQ recommended approval of seven additional posts under the regular budget (three under section 3, Political affairs, and four under section 22, Human rights) and 122 additional posts under the support account (92 under section 5, Peacekeeping operations; 26 under section 27, Management and central support services; and 4 under section 28, Internal oversight).

On 4 December [A/C.4/56/5], in response to queries from Nigeria and other interested Mem-ber States, the Under-Secretary-General for Peacekeeping Operations transmitted to the Chairman of the Fourth Committee a list containing the number and nationalities of candidates selected in the first round of the recruitment process following the issuance of the Brahimi report [YUN 2000, p. 83] and subsequent documents [ibid., p. 91]. The list showed that 88 of the 93 posts approved by the Assembly in resolution 55/238 had been filled [ibid., p. 1300].

GENERAL ASSEMBLY ACTION

On 24 December [meeting 92], the General Assembly, on the recommendation of the Fifth Committee [A/56/738], adopted **resolution 56/241** without vote [agenda items 122 & 133].

Comprehensive review of the whole question of peacekeeping operations in all their aspects

The General Assembly,

Having considered the statement submitted by the Secretary-General on the comprehensive review of the whole question of peacekeeping operations and the related report of the Advisory Committee on Administrative and Budgetary Questions,

Taking account of the report of the Special Committee on Peacekeeping Operations on the comprehensive review of the whole question of peacekeeping operations in all their aspects,

Recalling its resolutions 45/258 of 3 May 1991, 47/218 A of 23 December 1992, 48/226 A of 23 December 1993, 48/226 B of 5 April 1994, 48/226 C of 29 July 1994, 49/250 of 20 July 1995, 50/11 of 2 November 1995, 50/221 A of 11 April 1996, 50/221 B of 7 June 1996, 51/226 of 3 April 1997, 51/239 A of 17 June 1997, 51/239 B and 51/243 of 15 September 1997, 52/220 of 22 December 1997, 52/234 and 52/248 of 26 June 1998, 53/12 A of 26 October 1998, 53/208 B of 18 December 1998, 53/12 B of 8 June 1999, 54/243 A of 23 December 1999, 54/243 B of 15 June 2000, 55/238 of 23 December 2000 and 55/271 of 14 June 2001 and its decisions 48/489 of 8 July 1994, 49/469 of 23 December 1994 and 50/473 of 23 December 1995,

Noting with appreciation the comments and observations contained in paragraph 6 of the report of the Advisory Committee, concerning the Panel on United Nations Peace Operations and the determination of resources, and in paragraph 26, concerning the role and responsibilities of the head of the Department of Peacekeeping Operations of the Secretariat and his senior staff in the area of management,

1. *Attaches* great importance to the provision of adequate resources for peacekeeping operations and their backstopping as well as for all priority activities of the Organization, in particular activities in the area of development, and underlines the need for genuine and meaningful partnership between the Security Council, the troop-contributing Governments and other Member States and the Secretariat;

2. *Reaffirms* that the expenses of the Organization, including the backstopping of peacekeeping operations, shall be borne by Member States;

3. *Requests* the Secretary-General, when making first-time use of the results-based budgeting technique

in the presentation of the support account budget estimates for peacekeeping operations for the period from 1 July 2002 to 30 June 2003, to undertake a complete rethinking of how post and non-post resources for the support account are justified and presented and, in this regard, to take full account of paragraphs 9 and 10 of the report of the Advisory Committee on Administrative and Budgetary Questions;

4. *Reaffirms* the decision in paragraph 2 of its resolution 49/250 that the support account funds shall be used for the sole purpose of financing human and non-human resource requirements for backstopping and supporting peacekeeping operations at Headquarters, and that any changes to this limitation will require the prior approval of the General Assembly;

5. *Requests* the Secretary-General to review the issue of capacity in the Peacekeeping Best Practices Unit for policy support in peacekeeping operations in the area of demobilization, disarmament and reintegration, taking into account the views of the Advisory Committee;

6. *Stresses* that the creation of small units in the Department of Peacekeeping Operations to fulfil various functions which duplicate the responsibilities of other departments must be avoided, and shares the caution expressed by the Advisory Committee on Administrative and Budgetary Questions that an increase in the number of organizational units in the Department does not necessarily facilitate coordination or enhance administrative and management capacity;

7. *Requests* the Secretary-General to prevent duplication of work between the Department of Peacekeeping Operations and the Department of Political Affairs of the Secretariat and to further clarify the relationships and interactions between the Department of Peacekeeping Operations and other offices in the Department of Management of the Secretariat, especially those dealing with personnel, financial administration and control, management of procurement activities and monitoring of delegated authority;

8. *Also requests* the Secretary-General to report, in the context of the annual support account budget estimates, on action taken by the Department of Peacekeeping Operations to develop and implement a comprehensive information technology systems strategy that integrates field missions with the Secretariat's overall information and communication technology strategy;

9. *Expresses concern* about the effect of scattering the units of the Department of Peacekeeping Operations in a number of different physical locations on its operational effectiveness, and requests the Secretary-General to investigate and report on ways and means of achieving co-location of such units;

10. *Also expresses concern* over the delay in the recruitment and staffing of the 93 support account posts approved in December 2000 on an urgent basis;

11. *Reaffirms* section I, paragraph 6, of its resolution 55/238, in which it agreed with paragraph 36 of the report of the Special Committee on Peacekeeping Operations relating to proper representation of troop-contributing countries in the Department of Peacekeeping Operations;

12. *Expresses concern* over the imbalance in the geographical representation of Member States in the Department of Peacekeeping Operations, and urges the

Secretary-General to take immediate measures to improve the representation of underrepresented and unrepresented Member States in future recruitment;

13. *Also expresses concern* over the lack of compliance by the Department of Peacekeeping Operations with the rules, regulations and procedures pertaining to human resources management, and in this regard reaffirms the role of the Office of Human Resources Management of the Secretariat as set out in General Assembly resolutions 53/221 of 7 April 1999 and 55/258 of 14 June 2001, in particular the General Assembly decision that the Office of Human Resources Management should remain the central authority for the monitoring and approval of the recruitment and placement of staff and for the interpretation of the regulations and rules of the Organization and their enforcement;

14. *Welcomes* the emphasis on training, planning and establishment of rosters, which would provide the capacity to manage and monitor personnel actions in the Department of Peacekeeping Operations and the Office of Human Resources Management, and encourages the utilization of information technology in reducing the current recruitment period below 180 days;

15. *Regrets* the inordinate delay in the certification of write-off claims from some liquidated peacekeeping operations, and requests the Secretary-General to finalize the certification of those claims by 30 June 2002 and to submit a progress report on this issue to the General Assembly at its resumed fifty-sixth session;

16. *Urges* the Secretary-General to give priority to the reimbursement of claims from liquidated missions, including maintaining adequate reserves to settle claims once certified;

17. *Endorses* the conclusions and recommendations contained in the report of the Advisory Committee, subject to the provisions of the present resolution, and decides not to establish at this time the D-2 post of Director of Change Management mentioned in paragraph 28 of the report of the Advisory Committee and to keep the matter under review for consideration at the second part of its resumed fifty-sixth session, and, in the light of the development of a coherent policy, to review the P-5 post for gender issues at the second part of its resumed fifty-sixth session;

18. *Requests* the Secretary-General to entrust the Office of Internal Oversight Services of the Secretariat with the task of conducting an evaluation of the impact of the recent restructuring of the Department of Peacekeeping Operations on its backstopping of peacekeeping operations performance, and the impact on efficient and effective use of the resources of the Department, and to report to the General Assembly at its resumed fifty-eighth session;

19. *Decides* to appropriate an additional amount of 1,575,700 United States dollars under the following sections of the proposed programme budget for the biennium 2002-2003: 376,400 dollars under section 3, Political affairs; 888,800 dollars under section 22, Human rights; 127,900 dollars under section 27, Management and central support services; and 182,600 dollars under section 32, Staff assessment, to be offset by a corresponding amount (182,600 dollars) under income section 1, Income from staff assessment, of the proposed programme budget for the biennium 2002-2003;

20. *Approves* an additional 121 support account–funded posts and their related post and non-post requirements in the amount of 16,103,750 dollars gross (14,889,500 dollars net) for the period from 1 July 2001 to 30 June 2002;

21. *Requests* the Secretary-General to conduct, through the Office of Internal Oversight Services, an audit of the policies and procedures of the Organization for recruiting staff for the Department of Peacekeeping Operations and to report thereon to the General Assembly for its consideration at its resumed fifty-sixth session.

General aspects of UN peacekeeping

Establishment of Security Council Working Group on Peacekeeping Operations

On 31 January, the Security Council, by presidential statement **S/PRST/2001/3** (see p. 79), established a Working Group of the whole on UN peacekeeping operations to address generic peacekeeping issues relevant to the Council's responsibilities and technical aspects of individual peacekeeping operations, without prejudice to the competence of the Special Committee on Peacekeeping Operations.

The Council President, in a 14 February note [S/2001/135], indicated that, after consultations, it had been agreed that Curtis A. Ward (Jamaica) would serve as the Working Group's Chairman until 31 December.

The Working Group held three sessions in 2001. In May [S/2001/546], it examined the relationship between the Council, troop-contributing countries and the Secretariat (see p. 80); in September [S/2001/900], it examined the Secretary-General's report "No exit without strategy: Security Council decision-making and the closure or transition of United Nations peacekeeping operations" [S/2001/394] (see p. 89); and in December [S/2001/1335], it assessed the efficiency and effectiveness of the measures set out in resolution 1353(2001) for meetings with troop-contributing countries with a view to improving the system (see p. 84).

Information, analysis and decision-making

In his June report on the implementation of the recommendations of the Special Committee on Peacekeeping Operations and the Panel on United Nations Peace Operations [A/55/977] (see p. 71), the Secretary-General stated that he had directed the Secretariat, working closely with the relevant agencies, funds and programmes, to reassess the formation of the Information and Strategic Analysis Secretariat (EISAS), as proposed in the Brahimi report [YUN 2000, p. 84]. The findings of that review, together with observations by the management consultants and the External Review Board, reaffirmed several weaknesses: that during the planning and operation of peacekeeping operations, mission planners and senior mission leadership did not always operate with the benefit of a comprehensive assessment of the political, socio-economic, development, human rights and humanitarian factors that contributed to the conflict concerned, which affected their credibility with the parties to the conflict and also affected the Organization's ability to carry out its mandate effectively; where the information did exist, there was no organizational unit within the system to pull that information together into a coherent whole, to identify gaps in knowledge and synthesize it into a digestible format for those concerned; contrary to perceptions, the desk officers in the Department of Political Affairs were not performing that knowledge management function from a multidisciplinary perspective because their numbers were few, their time limited and their expertise mainly restricted to political analysis; and greater use needed to be made of modern information systems.

Convinced that the original idea behind the creation of EISAS would substantially address those shortcomings, the Secretary-General proposed creating a more modest unit for system-wide policy and analysis, which would maintain some of the objectives previously articulated for EISAS, but would be half the proposed size and would not absorb the information technology, cartographic and media monitoring capabilities from the Department of Public Information. The Peace-building Unit would be de-linked from it. The new unit would serve as the secretariat for the Executive Committee on Peace and Security (ECPS); undertake medium and long-term analyses of cross-cutting issues that were fundamental to the successful planning and support of peacekeeping operations, peace-building offices, special political missions and peacemaking/diplomatic activities; and prepare proposals for mid-to-long-term strategies. The new unit would be autonomous and headed by a Director, with a small support staff.

Special Committee action. The Special Committee on Peacekeeping Operations, in June [A/55/1024 & Corr.1], recommended that a capability to analyse information relevant to each peacekeeping operation, and to disseminate its analysis to senior mission leadership, troop-contributing countries and other countries involved should not be established in support of ECPS. Instead, it requested the Secretary-General to consider placing it within DPKO or in his Executive Office. The

Secretariat should revisit the concept of establishing information technology systems in support of the proposed analytical capability. The Special Committee requested that the Secretary-General address those issues.

Standby arrangements and rapid deployment

The Secretary-General, in a December report [A/56/732] on the implementation of the recommendations of the Special Committee on Peacekeeping Operations [YUN 2000, p. 95] and the Panel on United Nations Peace Operations [ibid., p. 83], said that he had appealed to Member States to consider committing specialized enabling resources, together with strategic lift capabilities, to the UN standby arrangements system (UNSAS). In that regard, DPKO had initiated specific requests to certain Member States. In response to his further request that UNSAS participants indicate the availability or not of their currently listed assets, only nine replies had so far been received. In addition, since very few participants had been reporting monthly on the status of their commitments and many States had indicated a preference for reporting quarterly, the initiative was being re-examined.

The Secretariat welcomed the creation and identification of peacekeeping forces through regional partnerships, and had sought the views of Member States on the deployment of coherent brigade-sized units to UN peacekeeping operations. Following the creation of a generic mission headquarters of some 100 military officers, deployable on seven days' notice as a means of enhancing planning capability, Member States were requested in March to provide staffing nominations. As at December, 22 States had responded positively. Individuals serving under the system would be rotated every two years. A model civilian police headquarters had also been designed and would be reviewed by Member States in 2002. The Secretary-General encouraged Member States to participate in the on-call lists and to submit their staffing nominations. The Mine Action Service was developing an emergency response plan, which would be supported by standing arrangements currently being developed with mine action organizations. Stocks of mine action–related equipment would be established within the United Nations Humanitarian Response Depot in Brindisi, while a database of experts for deployment on short notice was also being developed. Those arrangements were expected to be completed by the end of 2002.

Consultations held with Member States in October on the enhancement of rapid deployment capabilities and the development of a common understanding of the requirements to meet the 30- to 90-day deployment time lines had advanced the planning assumptions and rationale supporting the proposed strategic deployment stock (SDS) equipment lists and the attendant financial requirements and methodologies. The aim was to make SDS fully deployable by the end of 2002 or early 2003. DPKO was also reviewing ways to enhance the timely availability of strategic air- and sea-lift capabilities, including options for establishing a long-term standing Letter of Assist arrangement for large cargo aircraft (AN-124) with two Member States. The Procurement Division was reviewing whether standby commercial contracts could be established with commercial AN-124 operators. The Secretariat had established a surge roster of key administrative staff for the rapid and effective start-up of new missions.

HIV/AIDS and peacekeeping operations

On 19 January [meeting 4259], the Security Council considered the agenda item "The responsibility of the Security Council in the maintenance of international peace and security: HIV/AIDS and international peacekeeping operations". Briefing the Council, the Under-Secretary-General for Peacekeeping Operations acknowledged that UN peacekeepers ran the risk of transmitting or contracting HIV, but observed that it was difficult to quantify the extent of the risk. He reported on measures taken by DPKO to implement resolution 1308(2000) [YUN 2000, p. 82] and to mitigate the risks that peacekeepers presented or were exposed to. They included heightened awareness of the problem among peacekeepers and training in preventive measures, such as the development of a training module on medical issues for senior-level trainers, including AIDS prevention and awareness, the production and distribution of a number of publications to peacekeeping missions and to Member States, and the production of a "pocket card" with basic facts on codes of conduct and HIV/AIDS awareness and prevention in various languages. In addition, DPKO had proposed to Member States, within the context of the post–Phase V Working Group on Peacekeeping Operations (see p. 99), that the United Nations reimburse contributor States for the cost of conducting HIV testing of their personnel. On 19 January, DPKO and the Joint United Nations Programme on HIV/AIDS (UNAIDS) signed a memorandum of understanding that further developed and institutionalized the relationship between the organizations.

The UNAIDS Executive Director updated the Council on action taken to fulfil his commitment to address HIV/AIDS in emergencies and the uniformed services, including assessment missions by the UNAIDS Humanitarian Coordination Unit to Burundi, East Timor, Eritrea and Ethiopia to assess locally specific risk factors, prepare HIV prevention strategies and train trainers in prevention and behaviour change so that peacekeepers could become agents of change and HIV prevention. With the UNDP Administrator, he had written to UN resident coordinators in countries affected by conflict to ensure that AIDS, as a humanitarian and security issue, was at the top of the UN system's agenda in those countries. UNAIDS was also working with its co-sponsors and DPKO to focus on the elevated risk of HIV in conflict and humanitarian situations and was establishing with DPKO an expert panel to analyse and formulate a comprehensive position on HIV testing for peacekeepers and humanitarian personnel.

General Assembly special session on HIV/AIDS

The General Assembly, at its twenty-sixth special session (25-27 June) on the problem of HIV/AIDS in all its aspects, adopted the Declaration of Commitment on HIV/AIDS (**resolution S-26/2**) (see p. 1126), which, among other things, addressed the issue of HIV/AIDS in conflict and disaster-affected regions.

SECURITY COUNCIL ACTION

On 28 June [meeting 4339], following consultations among Security Council members, the President made statement **S/PRST/2001/16** on behalf of the Council:

The Security Council welcomes the successful holding of the twenty-sixth special session of the General Assembly on HIV/AIDS and encourages further action to address the problem of HIV/AIDS.

The Council recalls its resolution 1308(2000) of 17 July 2000, in which the Council, bearing in mind its primary responsibility for the maintenance of international peace and security, and emphasizing the important roles of the General Assembly and the Economic and Social Council in addressing the social and economic factors that lead to the spread of HIV/AIDS, inter alia, recognized that the HIV/AIDS pandemic is also exacerbated by conditions of violence and instability, and stressed that the HIV/AIDS pandemic, if unchecked, may pose a risk to stability and security.

The Security Council therefore welcomes the fact that the declaration adopted at the twenty-sixth special session of the General Assembly addresses HIV/AIDS in conflict and disaster-affected regions, and contains a number of practical measures at the national and international levels, to be met within given time frames, to reduce the impact of conflict and disasters on the spread of HIV/AIDS, including the provision of awareness and training for personnel employed by United Nations agencies and other relevant organizations, the development of national strategies to address the spread of HIV amongst national uniformed services, as required, and the inclusion of HIV/AIDS awareness and training into guidelines designed for personnel involved in international peacekeeping operations.

The Council also recalls its open debate on 19 January 2001, taking stock of progress made since the adoption of resolution 1308(2000). The Council notes the progress made in the implementation of the resolution, and commends the increased cooperation in this regard between the Department of Peacekeeping Operations (DPKO) and the Joint United Nations Programme on HIV/AIDS (UNAIDS) through the Memorandum of Understanding between them signed in January 2001. Further, the Council welcomes the efforts to develop practical measures, such as the planned joint United Nations field assessment missions to major peacekeeping operations, and the development of the HIV/AIDS Awareness Card for Peacekeeping Operations to be distributed to all peacekeeping operations after testing in the United Nations Mission in Sierra Leone. The Council also welcomes the fact that the cooperation framework signed in May this year between UNAIDS and the United Nations Development Fund for Women (UNIFEM) expresses their intention to cooperate in the follow-up to resolution 1308 (2000), as well as resolution 1325(2000) of 31 October 2000 on women, peace and security.

The Council recognizes that further efforts are necessary to reduce the negative impact of conflict and disasters on the spread of HIV/AIDS, and to develop the capacity of peacekeepers to become advocates and actors for awareness and prevention of HIV transmission. The Council encourages continued efforts with regard to relevant training for peacekeeping, pre-deployment orientation, and increased international cooperation by interested Member States in areas such as prevention, voluntary and confidential testing and counselling, treatment for personnel, and the exchange of best practices and countries' policies in this regard. The Council encourages UNAIDS and DPKO to further pursue the implementation of resolution 1308(2000), including through the consideration of further efforts to enhance cooperation, such as the inclusion of HIV/AIDS advisers in peacekeeping operations, and revision, as required, of relevant codes of conduct.

The Council expresses its intention to contribute within its competence to the attainment of the relevant objectives in the declaration adopted at the twenty-sixth special session of the General Assembly in carrying out the Council's work, in particular in its follow-up to resolution 1308(2000).

Consultations with troop contributors

Singapore, in an 8 January letter [S/2001/21], informed the Secretary-General that, during its Presidency of the Security Council, it would organize an open debate on strengthening cooperation with troop-contributing countries (TCCs). In background papers attached to its letter, Singapore stated that the guidelines for meetings of TCCs established by the Council in S/PRST/1994/62 [YUN 1994, p. 120] and

S/PRST/1996/13 [YUN 1996, p. 18] continued to be valid if they were fully implemented. Unfortunately, the meetings between the Council, the Secretariat and troop-contributing countries had become pro forma and ritualistic and had fallen short of expectations. Singapore also referred to resolution 1327(2000) [YUN 2000, p. 87], in which the Council had stated its commitment to hold private meetings with TCCs at various stages of the establishment and implementation of peacekeeping operations, which was a significant improvement over the earlier arrangement.

In introducing the item on 16 January [meeting 4257], the Council President said that the success of peacekeeping operations depended on a healthy relationship between the Council, the Secretariat and TCCs. The Council and the Secretariat had already initiated action to strengthen consultations with TCCs in follow-up to the Brahimi report [YUN 2000, p. 83], but more needed to be done to strengthen cooperation among all three partners. Several questions regarding the relations between TCCs, the Council and the Secretariat should be addressed, including the usefulness of meeting with TCCs prior to the adoption of Council resolutions; other mechanisms and channels that could be used to strengthen the link between the Council and TCCs; and better cooperation among the three partners to address peacekeeping problems, including commitment gaps in the contribution of troops to all peacekeeping operations and the safety and security of UN peacekeepers.

On 23 January [S/2001/73], Canada proposed that for each mission the Council should establish an operation-specific cooperative committee with TCCs, including those countries contributing formed military units and/or senior command personnel, when they were not the same. The proposed operation-specific committee would be a decision-making body, but the Council would retain its ultimate decision-making authority. The committee would be presided over by a Council member with a natural lead interest in the situation. All other Council members and those TCCs meeting participation criteria would be full members. Participation by the relevant UN agencies would be essential. The parties to the conflict would be excluded, but modalities for consultations with them would be developed on a case-by-case basis.

SECURITY COUNCIL ACTION

On 31 January [meeting 4270], following consultations among Security Council members, the President made statement **S/PRST/2001/3** on behalf of the Council:

The Security Council has given further consideration to the question of strengthening cooperation between the Council, the troop-contributing countries and the Secretariat. In this connection, the Council stresses the importance of full implementation of provisions of resolution 1327(2000) of 13 November 2000 and in the statements of its President of 28 March 1996 (S/PRST/1996/13) and 3 May 1994 (S/PRST/1994/22). The Council takes note of the views expressed at its debate on the subject "Strengthening cooperation with troop-contributing countries" at its 4257th meeting on 16 January 2001. The Council recognizes the scope for further improvement in its relations with troop-contributing countries and the need to work together with a common purpose towards shared goals.

The Council recognizes that in view of the increasing complexity of peacekeeping operations, there is a need for a transparent three-way relationship between the Security Council, the Secretariat and the troop-contributing countries that will foster a new spirit of partnership, cooperation and confidence.

Recognizing that the experience and expertise of troop-contributing countries in theatres of operation can greatly assist the planning process, the Council reiterates its agreement to hold consultations with troop-contributing countries in a timely manner at different stages of a United Nations peacekeeping operation, in particular when the Secretary-General has identified potential troop-contributing countries for a new or ongoing peacekeeping operation, during the implementation phase of an operation, when considering a change to, or renewal of, or completion of a peacekeeping mandate, or when a rapid deterioration in the situation on the ground threatens the safety and security of United Nations peacekeepers.

The Council will seek to ensure that all private meetings as provided for in resolution 1327(2000) between members of the Council, the troop-contributing countries and the Secretariat are substantive, representative, meaningful and provide for a full exchange of views. The Council stresses the importance of full participation by all those involved and encourages troop-contributing countries to take the initiative to call for meaningful exchanges of information. The President of the Council will provide, where appropriate, a detailed report of consultations with the troop-contributing countries to the Council.

The Council stresses the usefulness of full and comprehensive briefings by the Secretariat at private meetings with the troop-contributing countries, including, where appropriate, military factors.

The Council encourages the Secretary-General to continue his efforts to improve coordination and cooperation on peacekeeping issues within the United Nations system and the Secretariat.

The Council encourages the Secretary-General to raise public awareness globally of the positive contribution of peacekeeping operations and the role played by peacekeepers from various troop-contributing countries.

The Council acknowledges that the Secretariat must be able to rely on sufficient human and financial resources to respond to the demands placed on it. It underlines the importance of follow-up to the report of the Panel on Peace Operations with a view to strengthening the Department of Peacekeeping Operations and other relevant departments of the Secretariat involved in peacekeeping.

The Council reiterates that the problem of the commitment gap with regard to personnel and equipment for peacekeeping operations requires the assumption by all Member States of the shared responsibility to support United Nations peace-keeping.

The Council acknowledges that the delay in reim-bursement causes severe budgetary constraints to troop-contributing countries. It urges all Member States to pay their assessed contributions in full and on time, so that peacekeeping operations can stand on a solid financial basis.

The Council decides to establish a Working Group of the whole on United Nations peace-keeping operations. The Working Group will not replace the private meetings with the troop-contributing countries. The Working Group will ad-dress both generic peacekeeping issues relevant to the responsibilities of the Council, and technical as-pects of individual peacekeeping operations, with-out prejudice to the competence of the Special Committee on Peacekeeping Operations. Where appropriate, the Working Group will seek the views of the troop-contributing countries, including through meetings between the Working Group and the troop-contributing countries, with a view to their views being taken into account by the Council.

As a first step, the Working Group is tasked to un-dertake an in-depth consideration of, inter alia, all the proposals made in the course of the Council's public meeting on 16 January 2001, including ways to improve the three-way relationship between the Council, the troop-contributing countries and the Secretariat and to report to the Council by 30 April 2001. An indicative list of all the ideas and proposals arising from the meeting on 16 January 2001 will be forwarded to the Working Group for its considera-tion.

Meeting of Working Group on Peacekeeping Operations. The Working Group established pursuant to presidential statement S/PRST/ 2001/3 submitted its first report to the Security Council in May [S/2001/546]. The Group's first task was to examine the relationship between the Council, TCCs and the Secretariat. An indicative list of the proposals made by Member States dur-ing the Council's 16 January meeting, prepared by Singapore [S/2001/130], formed the basis of the Group's working document. The Group also had before it a paper submitted on 30 May [S/2001/535] by Argentina, Canada, Ghana, India, Jordan, the Netherlands and New Zealand elaborating fur-ther Canada's proposals on cooperation with TCCs, on participation in the mission planning process, the establishment of a mission-specific cooperative management committee and on

managing the mission, including during its ter-mination phase.

The Group was briefed by the Under-Secretary-General for Peacekeeping Operations on the Secretariat's perspectives on measures that could enhance the quality of consultations be-tween the Council, TCCs and the Secretariat. He also apprised the Group of the Secretariat's limi-tations in carrying out those measures, and the importance of support for the resources to do so effectively.

The Working Group's recommendations were contained in a draft resolution, which it recom-mended to the Council for adoption.

On 13 June [meeting 4326], the Security Council unanimously adopted **resolution 1353(2001)**. The draft [S/2001/573] was prepared in consulta-tions among Council members, on the basis of the Working Group's draft.

The Security Council,

Reaffirming its resolutions 1318(2000) of 7 September 2000 and 1327(2000) of 13 November 2000 and the statements by its President of 3 May 1994 (S/PRST/1994/22) and 28 March 1996 (S/PRST/ 1996/13), and all other relevant statements by its Presi-dent,

Recalling also the statement by its President of 31 January 2001 (S/PRST/2001/3),

Taking into consideration the views expressed at its de-bate on the subject "Strengthening cooperation with troop-contributing countries" at its 4257th meeting on 16 January 2001,

Reaffirming its commitment to the Purposes of the Charter of the United Nations as set out in Article 1, paragraphs 1 to 4, of the Charter, and to the Principles of the Charter as set out in Article 2, paragraphs 1 to 7, of the Charter, including its commitment to the princi-ples of the political independence, sovereign equality and territorial integrity of all States, and to respect for the sovereignty of all States,

Reaffirming its primary responsibility under the Charter of the United Nations for the maintenance of international peace and security, reiterating its com-mitment to enhance the capacity of the United Nations in this area, and emphasizing its willingness to take all necessary steps within its competence to that end,

Recalling the relevant recommendations in the re-port of the Panel on United Nations Peace Operations, and reaffirming its support for all efforts to strengthen the efficiency and effectiveness of United Nations peacekeeping operations,

Stressing the need to ensure the safety and security of peacekeepers and other United Nations and associated personnel, including humanitarian personnel,

Stressing the need to improve the relationship be-tween the Security Council, the troop-contributing countries and the Secretariat to foster a spirit of part-nership, cooperation, confidence and mutual trust,

Recognizing the need to strengthen cooperation with troop-contributing countries, as part of a series of measures to ensure more coherent and integrated concepts of operations and to enhance managerial efficiency and operational effectiveness of United Nations peacekeeping operations,

Noting that relevant provisions contained in the annexes to the present resolution pertain also to strengthening cooperation with countries contributing civilian police and other personnel,

1. *Agrees* to adopt the decisions and recommendations contained in the annexes to the present resolution;

2. *Requests* its Working Group on Peacekeeping Operations to continue its work on strengthening the capacity of the United Nations to establish and support efficient and effective peacekeeping operations;

3. *Undertakes* to follow closely the implementation of the agreed measures for cooperation with troop-contributing countries, and requests its Working Group on Peacekeeping Operations to assess within six months of the adoption of this resolution the efficiency and effectiveness of the agreed measures, consider their further improvement taking into account the proposals of the troop-contributing countries and to report to the Council on these matters;

4. *Decides* to remain actively seized of the matter.

ANNEX I

A

Statement of principles on cooperation with troop-contributing countries

The Security Council

1. *Recognizes* that its partnership with troop-contributing countries can be strengthened by the assumption by Member States, in particular those with the greatest capacity and means to do so, of their shared responsibility to provide personnel, assistance and facilities to the United Nations for the maintenance of international peace and security;

2. *Encourages* Member States to take steps to bridge the commitment gap with regard to personnel and equipment for specific United Nations peacekeeping operations;

3. *Emphasizes* the importance of troop-contributing countries taking the necessary and appropriate steps to ensure the capability of their peacekeepers to fulfil the missions' mandate, and underlines the importance of bilateral and international cooperation in this regard, including in the area of training, logistics and equipment;

4. *Underlines* the importance of ensuring that national contingents participating in United Nations peacekeeping operations receive effective and appropriate support from the Secretariat, including in the area of training, logistics and equipment;

5. *Stresses* the need to ensure that the Secretariat is given sufficient human and financial resources to fulfil these tasks, and that these resources be used efficiently and effectively;

6. *Underlines* that consultations between the Security Council, the Secretariat and troop-contributing countries should enhance the ability of the Security Council to make appropriate, effective and timely decisions in fulfilling its responsibilities;

7. *Underlines also* the need to maintain a comprehensive approach to improving the effectiveness of peacekeeping operations from their conception, including in preparing contingency plans for volatile situations, and promoting cohesive exit strategies;

B

Operational issues

1. *Encourages* international cooperation and support for peacekeeping training, including the establishment of regional peacekeeping training centres, and stresses the need for technical support from the Secretary-General to such centres;

2. *Requests* the Secretary-General to include information on his consultations with troop-contributing countries in his regular reports to the Security Council on individual peacekeeping operations, and undertakes to take account of the views expressed in these consultations and in its meetings with troop-contributing countries when taking decisions on such operations;

3. *Also requests* the Secretary-General to convene assessments meetings with interested delegations, in particular troop-contributing countries, at appropriate stages of each peacekeeping operation as a part of his efforts to draw the lessons that can be learned, which should be taken into account in the conduct and planning of current and future operations;

4. *Further requests* the Secretary-General to take into account in the conduct of peacekeeping operations and in the regular lessons-learned process, the operational experiences of national contingents while in the field or following departure;

5. *Undertakes* to inform troop-contributing countries fully of the terms of reference of missions of the Security Council involving peacekeeping operations and subsequently of the conclusions of the missions;

6. *Expresses its view* that the conduct of reconnaissance visits to the mission area by countries committing troops can be highly valuable in preparing for effective participation in peacekeeping operations, and encourages support for such visits;

7. *Urges* the Secretary-General to take further steps to implement the proposal of the Panel on United Nations Peace Operations to create integrated mission task forces, and to pursue other related capabilities to improve United Nations planning and support capacities;

8. *Stresses* the need to improve the information and the analysis capacity of the United Nations Secretariat, with a view to improving the quality of advice to the Secretary-General, the Security Council and the troop-contributing countries;

9. *Stresses also* that the Secretariat's advice to the Security Council and the troop-contributing countries should include a range of recommendations for action on the basis of an objective assessment of the situation on the ground, rather than what Member States are presumed to be willing to support;

10. *Underlines* the importance of an effective mission-specific public information and communications capacity within peacekeeping operations, in particular through campaigns to improve awareness of the objectives and scope of the mission within the local population in the mission area;

11. *Stresses* the need for an effective public information programme to generate international public support for United Nations peacekeeping operations, and stresses also in this regard the need for special pro-

grammes, in particular in troop-contributing countries, to project the contribution of peacekeepers;

12. *Underlines* in this regard the need for an effective public information capacity within the United Nations, and takes note in this regard of the proposals made by the Secretary-General to strengthen Secretariat planning and support for public information in peacekeeping operations;

C
Other mechanisms

1. *Undertakes* to continue to consider the possibility of using the Military Staff Committee as one of the means of enhancing United Nations peacekeeping operations;

2. *Expresses its belief* that Groups of Friends of the Secretary-General, as well as other informal mechanisms which might include troop-contributing countries, Security Council members, donors and the countries in the region, can play a useful role in increasing the coherence and effectiveness of United Nations action, and stresses that they should conduct their work in close cooperation with the Security Council;

D
Follow-up

1. *Expresses its intention* to assess within six months the efficiency and effectiveness of its meetings with troop-contributing countries, with a view to the possibility of further improvement to the current system, including through the consideration of specific proposals of troop-contributing countries for new mechanisms;

2. *Decides* to strengthen cooperation with the troop-contributing countries in addition to and on the basis of the principles and provisions contained in the resolution and the present annex by improving and expanding existing consultation mechanisms as elaborated in annex II, with a view to ensuring proper reflection of the views and concerns of troop-contributing countries.

ANNEX II
Format, procedures and documentation of meetings with the troop-contributing countries

The consultations with troop-contributing countries will take place in the following formats:

A. Public or private meetings of the Security Council with the participation of troop-contributing countries;

B. Consultation meetings with the troop-contributing countries;

C. Meetings between the Secretariat and troop-contributing countries.

A
Public or private meetings of the Security Council

1. The Security Council will hold public or private meetings with the participation of troop-contributing countries, including at their request, and without prejudice to the provisional rules of procedure of the Security Council, in order to ensure a full and high-level consideration of issues of critical importance to a specific peacekeeping operation.

2. Such meetings may be held, in particular, when the Secretary-General has identified potential troop-contributing countries for a new or ongoing peacekeeping operation, when considering a change in, or

renewal or completion of a peacekeeping mandate, or when there is a rapid deterioration in the situation on the ground, including when it threatens the safety and security of United Nations peacekeepers.

B
Consultation meetings with the troop-contributing countries

1. Consultation meetings with troop-contributing countries will continue as the principal means of consultation, and will continue to be convened and chaired by the President of the Security Council.

2. Such consultation meetings may be convened, including at the request of troop-contributing countries, as appropriate at different stages of peacekeeping operations, including:

(*a*) Mission planning, including the development of the concept of operations and the elaboration of the mandate of a new operation;

(*b*) Any change in the mandate, in particular the broadening or narrowing of the scope of the mission, the introduction of new or additional functions or components, or a change in the authorization to use force;

(*c*) The renewal of a mandate;

(*d*) Significant or serious political, military or humanitarian developments;

(*e*) A rapid deterioration of the security situation on the ground;

(*f*) The termination, withdrawal or scaling down in size of the operation, including the transition from peacekeeping to post-conflict peace-building;

(*g*) Before and after Council missions to a specific peacekeeping operation.

3. The following parties will be invited to these meetings:

(*a*) Countries contributing troops, military observers or civilian police to the peacekeeping operation;

(*b*) Prospective troop-contributing countries as identified by the Secretary-General;

(*c*) Relevant United Nations bodies and agencies, when they have specific contributions to make to the issue under discussion;

(*d*) Other bodies and agencies, as observers, as appropriate;

(*e*) Countries that make special contributions, such as other civilian personnel, contributions to trust funds, logistics, equipment and facilities and other contributions, as appropriate;

(*f*) The host country/countries, as observers, as appropriate;

(*g*) The representative of a regional or subregional organization or arrangement, contributing troops as appropriate;

(*h*) Regional organizations, as observers when not contributing troops, as appropriate.

4. Such consultation meetings will, as appropriate, include consideration of:

(*a*) Preparations for the establishment of a peacekeeping mandate by the Security Council;

(*b*) Operational issues, including the concept of operations, mission planning, authorization to use force, the chain of command, force structure, the unity and cohesion of the force, training and equipment, risk assessment and deployment;

(c) Significant concerns of or recommendations by the Secretary-General, as set out in his report, a briefing note from the Secretariat or the Secretariat's oral briefing;

(d) The specific concerns of troop-contributing countries, including those communicated to the President of the Security Council;

(e) Progress in the accomplishment of the mission's tasks in different areas or mission components.

5. The following measures will be ensured to improve the quality and effectiveness of such consultations:

(a) An informal paper setting out the agenda, including issues to be covered and drawing attention to relevant background documentation, will be circulated by the President of the Security Council to the participants when inviting them to attend these meetings;

(b) The Secretary-General should ensure, within the constraints of the Security Council's programme of work, that reports requested by the Security Council on specific peacekeeping operations are issued in good time to allow the timely holding of meetings with troop-contributing countries before discussion among Security Council members;

(c) The Secretariat should also make fact sheets available to all participants at the beginning of these meetings;

(d) The Secretary-General should ensure, where possible, that briefings are given by senior personnel working with the mission in the field;

(e) The Secretary-General should ensure that briefings consist of an objective assessment and analysis of the political, military, humanitarian and human rights situations, where appropriate;

(f) The Secretary-General should add value to the briefings by making them more user-friendly, including through the exploitation of information technology.

6. The following arrangements will be made to ensure timely and appropriate communication of the concerns and views of troop-contributing countries, as expressed at the consultation meetings, to the members of the Security Council so that these concerns and views can receive due consideration:

The President of the Security Council will prepare, with the assistance of the Secretariat, and make available a summary of the content of such meetings;

The summary of discussion will be distributed to Council members in advance of informal consultations or of the next meeting on the relevant peacekeeping operation, where appropriate.

C
Meetings between the Secretariat and troop-contributing countries

The Security Council supports the existing practice of meetings between the Secretariat and troop-contributing countries to discuss matters concerning specific peacekeeping operations, and also the participation at such meetings, where appropriate, of Special Representatives of the Secretary-General, Force Commanders and Civilian Police Commissioners.

Other forms of consultations

The Security Council notes that the forms of consultations mentioned herein are not exhaustive and that consultations may take a variety of other forms, including formal or informal communication between the President of the Council or its members, the Secretary-General and the troop-contributing countries and, as appropriate, with other countries especially affected, including countries from the region concerned.

Special Committee consideration. The Special Committee on Peacekeeping Operations, at its 2001 session (18-19 June) [A/55/1024 & Corr.1], requested the Council to consider implementing the recommendations contained in the Brahimi report [YUN 2000, p. 83] that pertained to the strengthening of cooperation between TCCs, the Council and the Secretariat and to consider seriously the proposals for a new mechanism of consultations between the Council and TCCs.

It asked DPKO to provide Member States, semi-annually, with updated lists of the names of key personnel and officers and their responsibilities in the relevant offices, divisions, units and sections within the Department who maintained regular contacts with the permanent missions of Member States on all issues related to the participation, deployment and reimbursement of their personnel in peacekeeping operations.

Follow-up to Council resolution 1353(2001)

Communications. On 22 June [S/2001/626], Pakistan submitted to the Security Council further proposals on strengthening cooperation with TCCs, which, it said, were intended to improve on those already put forward by other Member States. On 6 July [S/2001/671], the Russian Federation put forward suggestions for enhancing the activities of the Military Staff Committee.

Bangladesh made proposals on 18 August [S/2001/811] concerning the holding of meetings by the Council with TCCs prior to review or renewal of a peacekeeping mandate, with Secretariat participation, and other periodic meetings as required to review a situation, assess progress, address difficulties faced by the mission and consider concerns of TCCs.

Report of Secretary-General. The Secretary-General, in his December report on the implementation of the Special Committee's 2000 recommendations [A/56/732], said that assessment meetings were being held between the Secretariat and TCCs to draw out lessons learned and benefit from the operational experiences of national contingents. The Secretariat planned to engage TCCs in further discussions on how their national systems recorded those experiences and was seeking to improve its support to the Council's meetings with TCCs within the new format outlined in resolution 1353(2001) (see p. 80).

Working Group on Peacekeeping Operations.
In December, the Working Group on Peacekeeping Operations submitted its third report to the Security Council [S/2001/1335]. The Group had assessed the efficiency and effectiveness of the measures for meetings with TCCs with a view to further improving the system. It reviewed the consultation process during the past six months, including the conduct of Council meetings with those countries, and considered specific proposals by TCCs for new mechanisms [S/2001/535, S/2001/626].

The Working Group concluded that six months was not sufficient time to evaluate fully the effectiveness of resolution 1353(2001) and that a further in-depth review should take place. However, the format of meetings conducted under that resolution did provide a better process for information exchange than previous arrangements. Consultation meetings chaired by the Council President should be the principal means of consultations with TCCs. A position paper submitted by the Russian Federation on the use of the Military Staff Committee (see p. 83) and a United Kingdom proposal to enhance military advice to the Council would require further consideration.

The Working Group proposed for the Council's consideration a draft note by the Council President on setting up a new mechanism. The draft text stated that the new mechanism would provide for, among other things, joint meetings of the Working Group, TCCs and the Secretariat for a closer and more interactive dialogue over issues pertaining to peacekeeping operations as set out in paragraphs 2 and 4 of section B of annex II of resolution 1353(2001) (see p. 82) so as to complement the ongoing process of consultation meetings pursuant to that resolution.

The Working Group would continue to assess the implementation of resolution 1353(2001) and any other new mechanism, and agreed that meetings held under any new mechanism should complement and not supplant those held pursuant to resolution 1353(2001).

Civilian police

In March [A/55/812], the Secretary-General transmitted to the General Assembly the OIOS report on the management audit of UN civilian police operations. The audit, which reviewed civilian police operations with a view to enhancing their effectiveness and efficiency, was conducted at Headquarters and at the three missions with the largest civilian police components—the United Nations Mission in Bosnia and Herzegovina, the United Nations Transitional Administration in East Timor and the United Nations Interim Administration Mission in Kosovo.

OIOS observed that the civilian police component of UN peacekeeping operations had increased in both size and scope of operations, from some 2,200 less than two years previously to more than 8,600. Although there had been several positive accomplishments, many of the previous recommendations concerning civilian police had not been implemented. DPKO continued to "reinvent" civilian police management and administrative systems with each new mission, and had not developed a comprehensive civilian police strategy. Selection criteria remained unchanged throughout the life of a mission, regardless of its stage and skills needed; frequent rotations, particularly at senior management levels, were detrimental to operations; and the DPKO Civilian Police Unit had not been proactive in recruiting from Member States with language and culture similar to those of the mission area. The qualifying grade for the English proficiency test had been standardized, although it was clear that, in certain missions, a higher level of proficiency would be more appropriate. Further, no programme was in place to train and develop civilian police for rapid deployment. In addition, civilian police were deployed in several non-policing roles, such as guarding prisons, protecting dignitaries, providing security, and performing customs duties and other administrative functions. The audit also revealed inefficiencies in transporting large civilian police contingents to and from missions.

OIOS recommended that DPKO reclassify the post of Civilian Police Adviser to the same level as the military counterpart; strengthen staff capabilities within the Civilian Police Unit to develop strategic plans and policies and to manage information systems and technology; develop civilian police mission start-up kits (including standard operating procedures, organizational structures, job descriptions, management information systems and equipment specifications) to facilitate rapid and effective deployment to new missions; and standardize civilian police designations, uniforms, equipment and patrol vehicle markings.

DPKO should train and develop a cadre of "UN-certified" civilian police ready for rapid deployment; improve the effectiveness of the selection assistance teams by expanding their use to additional contributing countries and incorporating induction training into team visits; identify essential civilian police positions and offer regular UN appointments to attract higher-calibre candidates and to help retain institutional memory; and target the recruitment of civilian police from countries with languages, cultures or legal systems similar to those of the mission area.

OIOS further recommended that DPKO: ask Member States to contribute skilled civilian or non-commissioned civilian police officers to perform administrative functions, as well as specialists in the other non-policing activities currently being performed by civilian police; appoint a central coordinator within the Civilian Police Unit to manage rotations and repatriations; and establish an information technology focal point within that Unit to manage central integrated databases and to develop and support standard civilian police applications in areas such as logistics, crime and incident reporting.

The Department's management should, in addition, reassess current civilian police responsibilities and determine which of those functions were critical to mission success.

The Secretary-General, in his letter of transmittal, said that DPKO had already taken measures to address many of the issues identified in the review.

Special Committee consideration. The Special Committee on Peacekeeping Operations, in June [A/55/1024 & Corr.1], said that it appreciated the efforts to promote standardization and professionalism in the civilian police operations and welcomed the issuance of the "Principles and guidelines for United Nations police operations" to support Member States in training police for participation in UN operations.

The Special Committee noted the Secretariat's intention to draft other rules and procedures, including disciplinary measures, and recommended that the Secretariat finalize that exercise in consultation with Member States.

Safety and security

In his June report on the implementation of the recommendations of the Special Committee on Peacekeeping Operations and the Panel on United Nations Peace Operations [A/55/977], the Secretary-General said that DPKO had completed in May a comprehensive review of security requirements in peacekeeping missions, as requested by the Special Committee [YUN 2000, p. 93]. The purpose of the review was to assess security management in peacekeeping and identify weaknesses and ways to rectify such deficiencies. The review benefited from the deliberations of the Seminar on the Safety of United Nations Peacekeepers and Associated Personnel Working in Conflict Zones (Tokyo, Japan, 15-16 March) [A/55/950-S/2001/512].

The review found that, unlike the personnel of UN agencies, funds and programmes, the security of peacekeeping personnel was the responsibility of the head of mission, and not the United Nations Security Coordinator (UNSECOORD).

DPKO did draw on UNSECOORD technical expertise, but the Coordinator lacked the staff to participate fully in the entire planning process for each mission or address the full range of security implications and requirements. As a result, the initial threat/risk assessments tended to focus on political and military considerations and paid less attention to security management issues.

The review noted that there were no templates or guidelines for minimum equipment required for security purposes, and mission personnel were often deployed before such items as communications equipment, vehicles, protective gear and medical evacuation aircraft were available in sufficient quantities. The review urged that the responsibilities of managers for the safety of staff should be clearly recorded in their terms of reference; all staff should receive security awareness training; and negligent performance or non-compliance with security management should be identified and those involved held accountable. More attention should be paid to the outlying team sites and regional headquarters where the majority of security incidents occurred. To better protect staff in the most vulnerable areas, missions should allocate equipment according to security needs, ensure the full integration of regional sites into security planning and improve information exchange among all locations and components. Personnel should not be deployed to areas where speedy evacuation could not be guaranteed in an emergency.

The review emphasized the importance of better information collection and analysis, and the development of integrated strategies to guide the implementation of mandates, based on continuous threat/risk assessments. It recommended strengthening the Situation Centre at Headquarters as part of the DPKO management reforms. The review also made recommendations for improving the security oversight processes at Headquarters, particularly the further clarification of the relationship between DPKO and the UNSECOORD, and for increasing staffing at Headquarters to support peacekeeping security management.

Special Committee consideration. The Special Committee on Peacekeeping Operations, in June [A/55/1024 & Corr.1], stressed the need for host countries and others concerned to ensure the safety and security of UN and associated personnel, and urged those States that had not done so to consider becoming party as soon as possible to the 1994 Convention on the Safety of United Nations and Associated Personnel, adopted by General Assembly resolution 49/59 [YUN 1994, p. 1289], which had entered into force on 15 January 1999 [YUN 1999, p. 1336]. It noted the Secretary-General's report on the scope of legal protection under the Convention [YUN 2000, p. 1347]. The Special Committee emphasized that status-of-forces agreements should include specific measures to enhance personnel safety and security, based on the Convention.

The Special Committee welcomed the comprehensive review of security requirements in peacekeeping missions (see above), but remained concerned about their deficiencies. It urged DPKO and UNSECOORD to pursue as a matter of urgency better information collection, analysis and dissemination at Headquarters and in the field, and stressed the importance of Member States and the Secretariat sharing safety and security "best practices". The Special Committee asked the Secretary-General to include in his next report steps taken to address those concerns. It invited the Security Council to pay special attention to personnel safety and security when establishing a new operation or changing peacekeeping mandates. The Special Committee also recommended that the Secretariat and Member States accept responsibility for improved preparation of personnel, including better training. All peacekeeping personnel should receive security briefings upon arrival in the mission area, particularly regarding potential threats, and given specific guidelines for avoiding hazardous situations.

The Special Committee stressed the critical role played by the DPKO Air Safety/Transport Unit regarding safety awareness and accident prevention within UN peacekeeping operations. It welcomed the review by the International Civil Aviation Organization of UN peacekeeping air operations and supported its recommendations concerning safety and security. It was concerned about the standards of UN-chartered aircraft contracted for the transportation of UN peacekeepers and called on the Secretariat to take remedial measures.

Report of Secretary-General. In his December report on the implementation of the recommendations of the Special Committee on Peacekeeping Operations and the Panel on United Nations Peace Operations [A/56/732], the Secretary-General said that, as follow-up to the comprehensive review of security requirements in peacekeeping operations (see p. 85), DPKO, in collaboration with the UNSECOORD Office, had developed a proposal for implementing the review's recommendations, and the minimum resources required had been identified in the peacekeeping support account budget submission (see p. 94). Pending the approval of those resources, DPKO was assisting field missions in improving their ability to respond to the specific threats associated with the upsurge in global terrorism. Missions had been reminded to raise awareness among staff of basic precautions and to ensure that updated security plans were in place and complied with. Exceptional measures, including the relocation of dependants and restrictions on operational activities, were implemented in a number of missions, and particular attention was being paid to protection from nuclear, biological and chemical threats. DPKO was working to formalize a policy on such threats in the field, including the integration of related measures into mission security plans. During the year, pre-mission security and safety training was supported through the distribution of publications to Member States, peacekeeping training centres and field missions. Security Awareness Aides-Memoires and Hostage Incident Cards were also circulated, as were health and safety publications. DPKO also reviewed its short-term aircraft specifications, and made a number of amended proposals on various aircraft-related issues, to be implemented in 2002.

The General Assembly, in **resolution 56/255, section VIII** (see p. 1320), requested the Secretary-General to submit in 2002 a report on the establishment of a clear mechanism of accountability and responsibility. He was also asked to evaluate the UN security system, including the new security arrangements and the relationship and interaction between DPKO and the UNSECOORD Office, and to report in 2003.

(For more information on the safety and security of UN and associated personnel, see p. 1347.)

Comprehensive review of peacekeeping

Special Committee on Peacekeeping Operations

As requested by the General Assembly in resolution 54/81 B [YUN 2000, p. 96], the Special Committee on Peacekeeping Operations continued its comprehensive review of peacekeeping operations in all their aspects [A/55/1024 & Corr.1]. In response to the Committee's request, the Secretary-General submitted two reports on the implementation of the Special Committee's recommendations: one in June [A/55/977] and the other in December [A/56/732].

The Special Committee held an organizational meeting on 18 June and a general debate on 18 and 19 June.

The Special Committee noted that, since the end of the cold war, the number of complex peacekeeping operations had increased, and that the Security Council had recently mandated peacekeeping operations which, in addition to the traditional tasks of monitoring and reporting, included other activities. In that regard, it stressed the importance of an effective, efficiently structured and adequately staffed DPKO. The Special Committee stressed the importance of applying the principles and standards of establishing and conducting peacekeeping operations and emphasized the need to continue considering those principles, together with peacekeeping definitions, systematically. New proposals or conditions concerning peacekeeping operations should be discussed in the Special Committee.

The Special Committee noted the statements of the Security Council President in 1998 [YUN 1998, p. 37] and S/PRST/2001/5 (see p. 56) with regard to the inclusion of peace-building elements in peacekeeping mandates to ensure a smooth transition to a successful post-conflict phase, and emphasized that, before doing so, those elements should be explicitly defined and clearly identified. Peacekeeping operations should be provided with clearly defined mandates, objectives and command structures and secure financing, and congruity should be ensured between mandates, resources and objectives. Changes in mandates should be accompanied by commensurate resource changes and should be based on a thorough and timely reassessment by the Council, including military advice, of the implications on the ground.

The Special Committee recognized the importance of coordinating measures in the field with regard to conflict prevention, peacekeeping and peace-building, and reiterated the importance of early planning and regular coordination for peacekeeping operations and other mandated activities designed to reduce the risk of resumption of conflicts and to contribute to reconciliation, reconstruction and recovery. The Special Committee also stressed the importance of formulating appropriate exit strategies in future peacekeeping operations (see p. 89).

The Special Committee recommended that Member States concerned be fully consulted and provided on a timely basis with a copy of all UN internal investigations or inquiries into incidents, including the final outcome, that involved the death of or injury to personnel from Member States or loss/theft of property of Member States. In cases of alleged gross misconduct, Member States concerned should be invited to take part in the investigation, bearing in mind the need to maintain discipline in the mission area and the desirability of justice being done in all such cases. The Special Committee welcomed the circulation of sample rules of engagement and looked forward to further consultation on their finaliza-tion. It also underlined the importance of further consultation with Member States regarding the Secretary-General's bulletin [ST/SGB/1999/13] on observance by UN forces of international humanitarian law.

The Special Committee reiterated the importance of issuing training materials in all UN official languages and urged that funding be made available for that purpose. It encouraged the Secretariat to provide increased assistance for regional training programmes. Disarmament, demobilization and reintegration programmes should be provided with adequate and timely resources, which should be included in the assessed budgets of relevant peacekeeping operations during its start-up phase. Funding for such programmes would be reviewed during examination of the mission's budget.

With regard to DPKO participation in the Executive Committee on Peace and Security, the Special Committee acknowledged the need for greater coordination among UN departments and agencies to avoid duplication and improve effectiveness in the conduct of peacekeeping operations; it recommended that the Secretary-General establish a small support secretariat to service the Executive Committee (see p. 76).

The Special Committee supported a review of the personal baggage allowance for a peace-keeper and stated that consideration should be given to providing senior staff, officers, military observers and civilian police with the same travel arrangements as UN personnel at Headquarters.

GENERAL ASSEMBLY ACTION

On 24 December [meeting 92], the General Assembly, on the recommendation of the Fourth Committee [A/55/572/Add.1], adopted **resolution 56/225** without vote [agenda item 89].

Comprehensive review of the whole question of peacekeeping operations in all their aspects

The General Assembly,

Recalling its resolution 2006(XIX) of 18 February 1965 and all other relevant resolutions,

Recalling in particular its resolutions 54/81 B of 25 May 2000 and 55/135 of 8 December 2000,

Affirming that the efforts of the United Nations in the peaceful settlement of disputes, inter alia, through its peacekeeping operations, are indispensable,

Convinced of the need for the United Nations to continue to improve its capabilities in the field of peacekeeping and to enhance the effective and efficient deployment of its peacekeeping operations,

Considering the contribution that all States Members of the Organization make to peacekeeping,

Noting the widespread interest in contributing to the work of the Special Committee on Peacekeeping Operations expressed by many Member States, in particular troop-contributing countries,

Bearing in mind the continuous necessity of preserving the efficiency and strengthening the effectiveness of the work of the Special Committee,

1. *Welcomes* the report of the Special Committee on Peacekeeping Operations;

2. *Endorses* the proposals, recommendations and conclusions of the Special Committee, contained in paragraphs 33 to 136 of its report;

3. *Urges* Member States, the Secretariat and relevant organs of the United Nations to take all necessary steps to implement the proposals, recommendations and conclusions of the Special Committee;

4. *Reiterates* that those Member States that become personnel contributors to United Nations peacekeeping operations in years to come or that participate in the future in the Special Committee for three consecutive years as observers shall, upon request in writing to the Chairman of the Special Committee, become members at the following session of the Special Committee;

5. *Decides* that the Special Committee, in accordance with its mandate, shall continue its efforts for a comprehensive review of the whole question of peacekeeping operations in all their aspects and shall review the implementation of its previous proposals and consider any new proposals so as to enhance the capacity of the United Nations to fulfil its responsibilities in this field;

6. *Requests* the Special Committee to submit a report on its work to the General Assembly at its fifty-sixth session;

7. *Decides* to include in the provisional agenda of its fifty-seventh session the item entitled "Comprehensive review of the whole question of peacekeeping operations in all their aspects"

Also on 24 December, the Assembly decided that the agenda item "Comprehensive review of peacekeeping operations in all their aspects" would remain for consideration during its resumed fifty-sixth (2002) session (**decision 56/464**).

Peacekeeping exit strategies

In response to a Security Council request [YUN 2000, p. 97], the Secretary-General submitted an April report entitled "No exit without strategy: Security Council decision-making and the closure or transition of United Nations peacekeeping operations" [S/2001/394]. The report examined guidelines for an exit strategy and the role of the Council and other principal organs in that regard.

The Secretary-General said that, more than once during the preceding 10 years, the United Nations had withdrawn a peacekeeping operation, or dramatically altered its mandate, only to see the situation remain unstable or sink into renewed violence. The central issue was what factors the Council should assess in deciding to launch, close or significantly alter a UN peacekeeping operation. Discussions on whether to "exit" or significantly alter an operation might be prompted by three circumstances: the successful completion of the mandate, failure or partial success.

In terms of the completion of a mandate, the Secretary-General stated that the ultimate purpose of a peacekeeping operation was the achievement of a sustainable peace, both internationally, through a mutually agreed settlement, and domestically, when the natural conflicts of society could be resolved peacefully through the exercise of State sovereignty, and warring parties helped to move their political and economic struggles from the battlefield into an institutional framework where a settlement process could be engaged. To facilitate such a transition, a mission's mandate should include peace-building, incorporating such elements as institution-building and the promotion of good governance and the rule of law. Related to the success of the transition was the availability of resources to implement the mandate and address critical elements of the programme, such as re-establishing civil administration and basic civil infrastructure, and effective disarmament, demobilization and reintegration.

The UN system had recently identified three key objectives whose fulfilment had often brought about successful, comprehensive peace-building: consolidating internal and external security; strengthening political institutions and good governance; and promoting economic and social rehabilitation and transformation. A successful exit depended on a collaborative and inclusive UN system and the effectiveness of other international actors, including the international financial institutions and NGOs. A carefully planned exit was also essential so that the gains made during a peacekeeping deployment could be sustained. Withdrawal of a large operation could have a highly visible, negative effect on mission support businesses and local mission staff. However, such a comprehensive exit strategy was not always possible in the short run, since there were occasions when the most that could be hoped for was to establish a stabilizing presence based on a limited agreement. Even when a mandate had been successfully completed, the Council might still wish to review the situation to ascertain whether current achievements were sustainable in the wake of a withdrawal, if they could be consolidated in a follow-on mission and if the requisite capacity and resources were assured.

In other cases, the Council might decide on withdrawal in recognition of the fact that failure sometimes occurred because conditions for an orderly transition to post-conflict peace-building did not materialize. However, mission closure as a result of the failure of the parties to abide by their agreements did not represent an end to UN and Council responsibility or involvement. When a mission could not be seen through to a successful completion, the focus should be on the alternatives to a UN peace operation. In the past decade, the experiences of the United Nations Preventive Deployment Force in the former Yugoslav Republic of Macedonia and the United Nations Assistance Mission for Rwanda, one inter-State and the other intra-State but both exiting without a follow-on strategy, had shown that closure could be costly in both financial and human terms.

Between clear-cut success and failure was the ambiguous situation where the Council might consider withdrawing an operation that was making a positive contribution in some respects but was stymied in others. The decision-making process was further complicated where the mission had a less encouraging record and an uncertain outlook, and/or casualties and other costs had exceeded expectations. In such cases, the Council should critically re-evaluate the mission's mandate to determine if a lower profile but open-ended mission was the best alternative. If the decision was to stay the course, was it possible to deter emerging war entrepreneurs or spoilers and what redesigns in the exit strategy might assist a transition to a more stable situation or sustainable peace?

The Secretary-General highlighted the weak link of voluntary funding to support programmes that were not part of a peacekeeping operation per se, but on which its ultimate success depended, as the critical hindrance to the United Nations ability to implement successfully the type of long-term, multiphase mandate that he was suggesting. The Council would have to address that funding gap if it was to enjoy a record of achievement in helping to foster successful peacekeeping exits as well as self-sustaining peace in their aftermath. He also identified the cases of the Kosovo province of the Federal Republic of Yugoslavia (see PART ONE, Chapter V) and East Timor (see PART ONE, Chapter IV), which reflected important differences in circumstances and illustrated the challenges of a successful exit strategy. In Kosovo, no agreement commanding the support of the parties and the international community appeared in sight. In East Timor, the situation was much clearer—the mandate was to prepare East Timor for independence, after which the mission would be closed.

The Secretary-General outlined the roles of the Council and other principal organs and agencies in formulating and implementing those vital decisions, the requirements for designing a strategically informed mandate, including efficient information gathering and analysis, and the conditions necessary for its implementation.

Working Group on Peacekeeping Operations. The Security Council Working Group on Peacekeeping Operations transmitted in September its second report [S/2001/900], which dealt with its consideration of the issues raised and recommendations made in the Secretary-General's report on exit strategies (see p. 88). The Working Group recommended to the Council a draft statement setting out the agreement and commitment of Council members in decision-making in creating a peacekeeping mandate, changing the mandate of a current mission and closing a mission, and recognizing the importance of achieving a sustainable peace through a UN peace mission.

SECURITY COUNCIL ACTION

The Security Council President, in a 25 September note [S/2001/905], indicated that Council members, having discussed the Secretary-General's report, recognized the importance of achieving a sustainable peace through a UN peace mission and had indicated their agreement and commitment as follows:

1. The Security Council recalls its resolutions 1327(2000) and 1353(2001), all relevant Council resolutions and all relevant statements of its President, and takes note of the respective roles of the Council, the Secretariat and the General Assembly, including the Council's relationship with troop-contributing countries and the use of Council missions in conflict areas, in formulating and implementing decisions with respect to a United Nations mission.

2. The Council acknowledges that a good exit strategy is facilitated by a good entrance strategy.

3. The Council agrees that it is essential that all relevant parts of the United Nations system, as well as the Government of the host country, be fully engaged during the life of a mission, that clear direction is given and milestones are established that support a comprehensive and integrated approach to peace-building, where peace-building is appropriate, as well as the operation's exit strategy, and to that end encourages the Secretary-General to make recommendations to the Council as appropriate.

4. The Council undertakes to include, as appropriate, peace-building elements in a mission's mandate to support the transition from peacekeeping to post-conflict peace-building, and underlines the importance of necessary coordination with the General Assembly and the Economic and Social Council and the relevant funds, programmes and specialized agencies of the United Nations system, as well as the Bretton Woods institutions, particularly in respect of transition from peacekeeping to post-conflict peace-building.

5. The Council recognizes that a more systematic assessment of certain basic factors, including political objectives, strategic analysis, the commitment of

parties, the role of regional actors and the availability of resources, in particular troops and equipment, will be important in deciding on the authorization of, making significant changes to, the withdrawal of and the closure and transition of United Nations peacekeeping operations.

6. The Council agrees that a major criterion for the Council's decision on the scaling down or withdrawal of a peacekeeping operation is the successful completion of its mandate, resulting in the establishment of a requisite political and security environment conducive to durable peace and/or a follow-on post-conflict peace-building process.

7. The Council welcomes the expressed commitment of the Secretary-General to providing the best, most pertinent information available to the Secretariat, including that obtained through the early dispatch of fact-finding and technical surveys to potential mission areas.

8. The Council reiterates that the Secretary-General should possess the capacity for efficient information-gathering and analysis to provide credible, objective analyses and sound advice to support the Council's deliberations during mandate formation, periodic or episodic review of a mandate and consideration of withdrawal of a mission.

9. The Council supports the expressed intention of the Secretary-General to include comprehensive disarmament, demobilization and reintegration programmes in his plans for future peacekeeping operations, as appropriate, so that the Council can consider, on a case-by-case basis, the inclusion of aspects of disarmament, demobilization and reintegration in the operations' mandates, and encourages the Secretary-General to do so.

10. The Council reiterates its commitment contained in its resolution 1353(2001) to strengthen its partnership with troop-contributing countries, in particular the role of troop-contributing countries in the process of mandate formation, review and termination, taking into account the views of troop-contributing countries for the extension of co-operation between them and the Council.

11. The Council undertakes to give consideration in its deliberations on the launch, review, closure or significant alteration of the mandate of a peacekeeping operation to the questions presented by the Secretary-General in his report, and also to the observations made by Member States during the debate of the Council on 15 November 2000.

12. The Council, pursuant to Chapter VIII of the Charter, and without compromising the Security Council's prerogative to act, undertakes to encourage cooperation with regional organizations, where appropriate, and stresses, in particular, that the views of those who will be responsible for the implementation of a peace agreement should be considered during the negotiation phase, that the main actors in negotiations should assess realistically the capacity and comparative advantage of different implementing bodies and that the lines of reporting and the division of labour must be unambiguous, and recognizes the importance of regional organizations that contribute to peacekeeping operations, seeking to develop their capacity to provide peace-keeping operations not only with military peace-keepers, but also with other relevant personnel, such as police and judicial or penal experts, and calls upon the international community to extend support in that regard.

13. The Council recognizes that the timely contribution and deployment of personnel, material and funds is vital to the successful implementation of a mission and to the withdrawal of a mission on the basis of an accomplished mandate, agrees to undertake a major role in accordance with its Charter responsibilities in consolidating support for the mission among the parties, regional actors, troop-contributing countries and Member States, and reiterates that the support and political will of each can be crucial to a mission's ultimate success.

Operations in 2001

On 1 January, 15 UN peacekeeping operations were in place—4 in Africa, 3 in Asia, 5 in Europe and 3 in the Middle East. That number remained unchanged as no missions were launched or terminated during the year.

Africa

In Africa, the mandate of the United Nations Mission in Sierra Leone (UNAMSIL) was twice extended by the Security Council for six months, the second time to 31 March 2002. In November, the Security Council supported the launching of phase III of the deployment of the United Nations Organization Mission in the Democratic Republic of the Congo (MONUC), especially in the east of the country, in conformity with its new concept of operation. The United Nations Mission for the Referendum in Western Sahara (MINURSO) continued to monitor the ceasefire and otherwise conduct peacekeeping tasks. In November, the Council extended its mandate until 28 February 2002. It also extended the mandate of the United Nations Mission in Ethiopia and Eritrea (UNMEE) until 15 March 2002.

Asia

In Asia, the United Nations Iraq-Kuwait Observation Mission (UNIKOM) continued to monitor the demilitarized zone along the border between the two countries. In October, the Security Council concurred with the Secretary-General's recommendation to maintain the mission and to review the question of its continuation or termination by April 2002. The United Nations Military Observer Group in India and Pakistan (UNMOGIP) remained in place to monitor the ceasefire in Jammu and Kashmir. In January, the Council extended the mandate of the United Nations Transitional Administration in East Timor (UNTAET) until 31 January 2002. In October, it noted that UNTAET's mandate was being extended until independence and endorsed a plan for adjusting its size and configuration in the months prior to independence and for a reduced UN integrated mission in the post-independence period.

Europe

In Europe, the Security Council extended the mandates of the United Nations Observer Mission in Georgia (UNOMIG) until 31 January 2002; the United Nations Mission of Observers in Prevlaka (UNMOP) until 15 January 2002; the United Nations Peacekeeping Force in Cyprus (UNFICYP) until 15 June 2002; and the United Nations Mission in Bosnia and Herzegovina (UNMIBH), including the International Police Task Force (IPTF), until 21 June 2002.

The United Nations Interim Administration Mission in Kosovo (UNMIK), Federal Republic of Yugoslavia, remained in place.

Middle East

Three long-standing operations continued in the Middle East: the United Nations Truce Supervision Organization (UNTSO) continued to observe the truce in Palestine; the United Nations Interim Force in Lebanon (UNIFIL), whose mandate was extended until 31 January 2002 under new reconfiguration and deployment arrangements; and the United Nations Disengagement Observer Force (UNDOF), whose mandate was renewed until 31 May 2002.

Roster of 2001 operations

UNTSO

United Nations Truce Supervision Organization
Established: June 1948.
Mandate: To assist in supervising the observance of the truce in Palestine.
Strength as at December 2001: 152 military observers.

UNMOGIP

United Nations Military Observer Group in India and Pakistan
Established: January 1949.
Mandate: To supervise the ceasefire between India and Pakistan in Jammu and Kashmir.
Strength as at December 2001: 45 military observers.

UNFICYP

United Nations Peacekeeping Force in Cyprus
Established: March 1964.

Mandate: To prevent the recurrence of fighting between the two Cypriot communities.
Strength as at December 2001: 1,196 troops, 35 civilian police.

UNDOF

United Nations Disengagement Observer Force
Established: June 1974.
Mandate: To supervise the ceasefire between Israel and the Syrian Arab Republic and the disengagement of Israeli and Syrian forces in the Golan Heights.
Strength as at December 2001: 1,036 troops.

UNIFIL

United Nations Interim Force in Lebanon
Established: March 1978.
Mandate: To restore peace and security and assist the Lebanese Government in ensuring the return of its effective authority in the area.
Strength as at December 2001: 3,639 troops.

UNIKOM

United Nations Iraq-Kuwait Observation Mission
Established: April 1991.
Mandate: To monitor the demilitarized zone along the border between Iraq and Kuwait.
Strength as at December 2001: 906 troops, 193 military observers.

MINURSO

United Nations Mission for the Referendum in Western Sahara
Established: April 1991.
Mandate: To monitor and verify the implementation of a settlement plan for Western Sahara and assist in the holding of a referendum in the Territory.
Strength as at December 2001: 27 troops, 204 military observers, 22 civilian police.

UNOMIG

United Nations Observer Mission in Georgia
Established: August 1993.
Mandate: To verify compliance with a ceasefire agreement between the parties to the conflict in Georgia and investigate ceasefire violations; expanded in 1994 to include monitoring the implementation of an agreement on a ceasefire and separation of forces and observing the operation of a multinational peacekeeping force.
Strength as at December 2001: 106 military observers.

UNMIBH

United Nations Mission in Bosnia and Herzegovina (including the International Police Task Force (IPTF))

Established: December 1995.

Mandate: To monitor and facilitate law enforcement activities in Bosnia and Herzegovina, train and assist law enforcement personnel in carrying out their responsibilities, advise government authorities on the organization of civilian law enforcement agencies and assess threats to public order and the agencies' capability to deal with such threats.

Strength as at December 2001: 1,674 civilian police, 4 military observers.

UNMOP

United Nations Mission of Observers in Prevlaka

Established: January 1996.

Mandate: To monitor the demilitarization of the Prevlaka peninsula.

Strength as at December 2001: 27 military observers.

UNMIK

United Nations Interim Administration Mission in Kosovo

Established: June 1999.

Mandate: To promote, among other things, the establishment of substantial autonomy and self-government in Kosovo, perform basic civilian administrative functions, organize and oversee the development of provisional institutions, facilitate a political process to determine Kosovo's future status, support reconstruction of key infrastructure, maintain civil law and order, protect human rights and assure the return of refugees and displaced persons.

Strength as at December 2001: 4,519 civilian police, 37 military observers.

UNTAET

United Nations Transitional Administration in East Timor

Established: October 1999.

Mandate: To provide security and maintain law and order, establish an effective administration, assist in the development of civil and social services, ensure the coordination and delivery of humanitarian, rehabilitation and development assistance, support capacity-building for self-government and assist in the establishment of conditions for sustainable development.

Strength as at December 2001: 7,110 troops, 1,316 civilian police, 102 military observers.

UNAMSIL

United Nations Mission in Sierra Leone

Established: October 1999.

Mandate: To cooperate with the Government of Sierra Leone and other parties in the implementation of the Peace Agreement signed in Lomé, Togo, on 7 July 1999, including, among other things, to assist in the implementation of the disarmament, demobilization and reintegration plan, monitor adherence to the ceasefire agreement of 18 May 1999 and facilitate the delivery of humanitarian assistance.

Strength as at December 2001: 17,105 troops, 261 military observers, 54 civilian police.

MONUC

United Nations Organization Mission in the Democratic Republic of the Congo

Established: November 1999.

Mandate: To establish contacts with the signatories to the Ceasefire Agreement, provide technical assistance in implementation of the Agreement, provide information on security conditions, plan for the observation of the ceasefire, facilitate the delivery of humanitarian assistance and assist in the protection of human rights.

Strength as at December 2001: 2,924 troops, 449 military observers, 13 civilian police.

UNMEE

United Nations Mission in Ethiopia and Eritrea

Established: July 2000.

Mandate: To establish and put into operation the mechanism for verifying the cessation of hostilities and prepare for the establishment of the Military Coordination Commission.

Strength as at December 2001: 3,722 troops, 217 military observers.

Financial and administrative aspects of peacekeeping operations

Financing

Expenditures for peacekeeping activities amounted to $2,378.7 million for the period 1 July 2000 to 30 June 2001, compared to $1,756.8 million during the previous 12-month period. The increase of $621.9 million, or 35.4 per cent, was mainly the result of the start-up mission in Ethiopia and Eritrea, expanded operations in Sierra Leone and the Democratic Republic of the Congo and a full year of operations in East Timor.

The financial situation of UN peacekeeping operations continued to be affected by serious cash shortages, necessitating borrowing from and among peacekeeping funds, while substantial amounts of obligations for reimbursement to Member States for troop costs and contingent-owned equipment remained unpaid.

As at 30 June 2001, total unpaid assessed contributions for peacekeeping operations were $2,352.3 million, up from $2,128.9 million in the previous period. Available cash for all operations totalled $979.8 million, while total liabilities were twice as much at $2,247.1 million.

Notes of Secretary-General. In accordance with General Assembly resolution 49/233 A [YUN 1994, p. 1338], the Secretary-General submitted to the Assembly's Fifth Committee a February note [A/C.5/55/37] updating the budgetary information on requirements for all peacekeeping operations from 1 July 2000 to 30 June 2001 and reflecting the appropriations provided to date by the Assembly for those operations for that period, inclusive of requirements for the peacekeeping support account and the United Nations Logistics Base in Brindisi (UNLB). The updated level of requirements totalled $2.4 billion gross, compared to the initial estimate of $2,072,562,000 [YUN 2000, p. 101].

In April [A/55/874], the Secretary-General submitted estimated gross budgetary requirements for seven missions (MINURSO, UNDOF, UNFICYP, UNIKOM, UNMIBH, UNMIK and UNOMIG) whose budgets had been submitted for the period 1 July 2001 to 30 June 2002 in the amount of $799,398,000, and gross estimates for five missions (UNIFIL, UNAMSIL, UNMEE, UNTAET and MONUC) whose budgets for the same period would be submitted to the Assembly's fifty-sixth session amounting to $1,633,416,900, excluding support account requirements (see p. 94) and requirements for UNLB (see p. 104). The Secretariat estimated that the total overall requirements would probably be around $2.6 billion, but could be significantly higher should the Security Council approve large-scale deployment contingents for MONUC.

Financial performance and proposed budgets

In April [A/55/874], ACABQ considered the financial performance reports for the period 1 July 1999 to 20 June 2000 and the proposed budgets for the period 1 July 2001 to 30 June 2002 of UNDOF, UNIKOM, UNFICYP, UNOMIG, UNMIBH (which included UNMOP and liaison offices in Belgrade and Zagreb), UNMIK, MINURSO and UNLB. It also considered the financial performance reports for the period 1 July 1999 to 30 June 2000 of the United Nations Civilian Police Mission in Haiti (MIPONUH) and the reports on the final disposition of the assets of the United Nations Support Mission in Haiti, the United Nations Transition Mission in Haiti and MIPONUH; and of the United Nations Preventive Deployment Force (UNPREDEP).

ACABQ further considered the financial performance reports for the period 1 July 1999 to 30 June 2000 of the United Nations Mission of Observers in Tajikistan, the United Nations Observer Mission in Angola and MINURCA; the financial performance reports for the period 1 July 1999 to 30 June 2000 and the revised budgets for the period 1 July 2000 to 30 June 2001 of UNIFIL and UNAMSIL; the financial performance reports for the period 1 January to 31 December 2000 of the United Nations Protection Force, the United Nations Confidence Restoration Operation in Croatia, UNPREDEP and the United Nations Peace Forces headquarters; the proposed budget for the establishment of UNMEE for the period 31 July 2000 to 30 June 2001; and the report of the Board of Auditors to the General Assembly on the accounts of UN peacekeeping operations for the period ended 30 June 2000 [A/55/878].

ACABQ was informed by the United Nations Controller that the initial maintenance budgets for UNIFIL, UNMEE, UNAMSIL, UNTAET and MONUC for the period 1 July 2001 to 30 June 2002, to be submitted to the Assembly's resumed fifty-fifth (2001) session, would probably have to be recosted and resubmitted. The financial performance report for UNTAET for 1 July 1999 to 30 June 2000 and the budgets for UNIFIL, UNMEE, UNAMSIL and UNTAET for 1 July 2001 to 30 June 2002 would be submitted to the Assembly's fifty-sixth (2001) session. ACABQ recommended that, pending submission of the budgets for those missions to its fifty-sixth session, the Assembly's resumed fifty-fifth session should approve, as a bridging action, commitment authority with assessment for the period 1 July to 31 December 2001 as follows: UNIFIL, $99,548,960 gross ($97,558,500 net) based on a revised budget of $199,097,919 gross ($195,117,090 net) for 1 July 2000 to 30 June 2001; UNMEE, $90 million gross ($88,933,450 net) based on an authorized budget of $180 million gross ($177,866,900 net); UNAMSIL, $275 million gross ($273,375,000 net) based on a revised budget of $550 million gross ($546,750,000 net), as approved by General Assembly resolution 55/251 B (see p. 173); and UNTAET, $282 million gross ($273,025,800 net) based on a budget of $563 million gross ($546,051,600 net), as approved by Assembly resolution 55/228 A [YUN 2000, p. 291].

ACABQ, while acknowledging that the exigencies that led to the Secretary-General's proposals for bridging action were unavoidable, observed that their simultaneous application during the same budgetary period placed a considerable strain on the system for considering and approving performance reports and budgets for peacekeeping operations, including the Assembly's programme of work. It stressed the importance of not letting those exceptions affect the discipline required to maintain the system.

ACABQ recommended that a summary of actions taken to implement the relevant recommendations of the internal and external oversight bodies be annexed to the performance reports of peacekeeping operations and that the Secretariat study the process with respect to memorandums of understanding on arrangements for contingent-owned equipment and identify the reasons for delays.

ACABQ, having reviewed UNAMSIL's estimates, concluded that an effective procedure should be put in place for ascertaining the capacity of TCCs to meet the requirements for wet-lease and self-sustainment provisions of contingent-owned equipment arrangements and for ensuring consistent implementation of the standards set out in the contingent-owned equipment manual. It was concerned that some TCCs might be experiencing difficulties in meeting the required level of equipment and self-sustainment, and encouraged the Secretary-General to review the wet-lease arrangements and the anticipated efficiency gains.

With regard to civilian personnel, ACABQ asked that expenditures on staff security should be clearly identified in performance reports and budgets of all peacekeeping operations. It reiterated its request that the Secretary-General analyse the problems of staff recruitment and retention, and recommended that personnel contracts be issued to staff for periods longer than a mission's mandate, with proper safeguards should the mandate not be renewed. Staff travel expenditures should be justified and explained in performance reports and proposed budget estimates.

ACABQ believed that there was a need for close cooperation with United Nations Volunteers at early mission stages, especially in planning. Volunteers should not, however, be a cheap labour source for peacekeeping operations. Their contribution in any mission operation should be recognized and they should be given the same functional access to services in the mission area as UN international staff.

As to procurement and inventory management, ACABQ expressed concern about weaknesses in inventory management and asset control and stressed that steps should be taken to ensure that adequate qualified staff were assigned, trained and retained to perform procurement and inventory management functions in field missions. The restructuring of logistics units to report directly to the mission civilian component should be addressed as a matter of urgency in all peacekeeping operations, with a view to introducing appropriate changes. Future peacekeeping budget submissions should justify significant investments ($1 million and above) in non-UN-owned premises.

With regard to the short- and long-term solutions to problems relating to the Secretariat's capacity to handle mission liquidation and to eliminate the backlog in areas such as claims and information and personnel management support services, ACABQ recommended that they should be addressed and that future requests for resources for mission liquidation be accompanied by a detailed plan, including a timetable for completion. Future transfers of assets to a host Government under "temporary possession" arrangements should be submitted to ACABQ for review prior to finalization. The Assembly should approve any disposition of mission assets free of charge to Governments, and the sale of equipment on credit to a Member State should be discouraged.

ACABQ recommended that experience gained in some missions regarding public information programmes should be examined to determine its applicability to other missions. An examination should be conducted as to whether maximum use was being made of existing UN facilities and resources and the possibility of using local public information facilities and reported on in the next budget submission.

ACABQ believed that there should be better planning for training personnel in mission areas and the subjects covered in training programmes and their costs should be clearly stated in programme budgets.

Peacekeeping support account

The Secretary-General, in March [A/55/861], submitted the financial performance report of the support account for peacekeeping operations for the period 1 July 1999 to 30 June 2000. Of the revised total resources of $38,388,700 for post and non-post requirements authorized by General Assembly resolutions 53/12 B [YUN 1999, p. 64] and 54/243 B [YUN 2000, p. 106], expenditures amounted to $38,360,800, resulting in an unutilized balance of $27,900.

Also in March [A/55/862], in response to Assembly resolution 54/243 B, the Secretary-General submitted support account resource requirements for the period 1 July 2001 to 30 June 2002, estimated at $73,645,500 gross ($64,361,800 net), which provided for a staffing establishment of

562 posts and related non-post costs. The Secretary-General recommended that the Assembly approve that amount, as well as the $3,501,600 originally authorized by resolution 54/243 B, and that the amount of $1,300,900, comprising the unencumbered balance from the 1 July 1999 to 30 June 2000 period, plus interest and miscellaneous income be applied to the 1 July 2001 to 30 June 2002 period. The total amount of $75,846,200 gross ($66,562,500 net) would be prorated among the individual peacekeeping operation budgets.

In April [A/55/882], ACABQ recommended that the Assembly approve the Secretary-General's recommendations.

GENERAL ASSEMBLY ACTION

On 14 June [meeting 103], the General Assembly, on the recommendation of the Fifth Committee [A/55/534/Add.2], adopted **resolution 55/271** without vote [agenda item 153 (a)].

Support account for peacekeeping operations
The General Assembly,

Recalling its resolutions 45/258 of 3 May 1991, 47/218 A of 23 December 1992, 48/226 A of 23 December 1993, 48/226 B of 5 April 1994, 48/226 C of 29 July 1994, 49/250 of 20 July 1995, 50/11 of 2 November 1995, 50/221 A of 11 April 1996, 50/221 B of 7 June 1996, 51/226 of 3 April 1997, 51/239 A of 17 June 1997, 51/239 B and 51/243 of 15 September 1997, 52/220 of 22 December 1997, 52/234 and 52/248 of 26 June 1998, 53/12 A of 26 October 1998, 53/208 B of 18 December 1998, 53/12 B of 8 June 1999, 54/243 A of 23 December 1999, 54/243 B of 15 June 2000 and 55/238 of 23 December 2000 and its decisions 48/489 of 8 July 1994, 49/469 of 23 December 1994 and 50/473 of 23 December 1995,

Having considered the report of the Secretary-General on the financial performance of the support account for peacekeeping operations for the period from 1 July 1999 to 30 June 2000, his report on the budget for the support account for the period from 1 July 2001 to 30 June 2002 and the related report of the Advisory Committee on Administrative and Budgetary Questions,

Reaffirming the need to continue to improve the administrative and financial management of peacekeeping operations,

Recognizing the need for adequate support during all phases of peacekeeping operations, including the liquidation and termination phases,

1. *Takes note* of the report of the Secretary-General on the financial performance of the support account for peacekeeping operations for the period from 1 July 1999 to 30 June 2000 and of his report on the budget for the support account for the period from 1 July 2001 to 30 June 2002;

2. *Recognizes* the importance of the United Nations being able to respond and deploy rapidly a peacekeeping operation upon the adoption of a Security Council mandate;

3. *Endorses* the conclusions and recommendations contained in the report of the Advisory Committee on Administrative and Budgetary Questions, and requests the Secretary-General to ensure their full implementation;

4. *Affirms* the need for adequate funding for the backstopping of peacekeeping operations;

5. *Reaffirms* that the expenses of the Organization, including the backstopping of peacekeeping operations, shall be borne by Member States and, to that effect, that the Secretary-General should request adequate funding to maintain the capacity of the Department of Peacekeeping Operations of the Secretariat;

6. *Decides* to maintain for the period from 1 July 2001 to 30 June 2002 the funding mechanism for the support account used in the current period, from 1 July 2000 to 30 June 2001, as approved in paragraph 3 of its resolution 50/221 B;

7. *Also decides* to continue the five hundred and sixty-two support account–funded temporary posts;

8. *Reaffirms* the need for the Secretary-General to ensure that delegation of authority to the Department of Peacekeeping Operations and field missions is in strict compliance with relevant resolutions and decisions, as well as relevant rules and procedures of the General Assembly on this matter;

9. *Notes* the intention of the Secretary-General to submit revised resource requirements for the support account prior to the opening of the fifty-sixth session of the General Assembly;

10. *Notes with appreciation* the intention of the Secretary-General, as reflected in paragraph 12 of the report of the Advisory Committee, to introduce changes in the presentation of the support account budget document in conformity with General Assembly resolution 55/231 of 23 December 2000 on results-based budgeting;

11. *Requests* the Secretary-General to ensure a more consistent and balanced presentation of proposals for all the departments;

12. *Also requests* the Secretary-General, as a matter of urgency, to address the need for streamlining the contingent-owned equipment procedures, including processing claims and memoranda of understanding, and to strengthen the Finance Management and Support Service in the area of claims processing, and to submit to the General Assembly, at its fifty-sixth session, concrete remedial proposals to address adequately the concerns raised in paragraph 15 of the report of the Advisory Committee;

13. *Decides* to appropriate the commitment authority of 3,501,600 United States dollars approved by the General Assembly in its resolution 54/243 A;

14. *Approves* the support account post and non-post requirements in the amount of 73,645,500 dollars gross (64,361,800 dollars net) for the period from 1 July 2001 to 30 June 2002;

15. *Decides* to apply the unencumbered balance of 1,300,900 dollars in respect of the period from 1 July 1999 to 30 June 2000, inclusive of 1,273,000 dollars in miscellaneous and interest income, and to prorate the balance of 75,846,200 dollars gross (66,562,500 dollars net) among the individual active peacekeeping operation budgets, to meet the resources required for the support account for the period from 1 July 2001 to 30 June 2002.

In December [A/C.5/56/34], the Secretary-General submitted additional support account requirements totalling $16,103,750 gross ($14,889,500 net) in respect of the budgets of UNIFIL, UNAMSIL, UNMEE, UNTAET and MONUC for the 12-month period 1 July 2001 to 30 June 2002, which were discussed by the Assembly during its consideration of the implementation of the recommendations of the Panel on United Nations Peace Operations (see p. 74).

Appropriations

In May [A/C.5/55/43], the Secretary-General submitted to the General Assembly initial 2001/02 appropriations and commitment authorities with assessment, including the support account for peacekeeping operations and UNLB, totalling $1,772,825,760 gross ($1,699,425,550 net).

In August [A/C.5/55/48], the Secretary-General submitted updated information on the total budgetary requirements for peacekeeping operations for the period 1 July 2000 to 30 June 2001 amounting to $2.63 billion; and for the period 1 July 2001 to June 2002 totalling $1.77 billion. However, in the light of the revised budgets under preparation for UNIFIL, UNAMSIL, UNMEE, UNTAET, MONUC and UNMIK and for the support account and UNLB, the overall level of budgetary requirements for active peacekeeping missions was likely to be in excess of $3 billion. Also included in the Secretary-General's note were indicative consolidated summary information on amounts to be apportioned among Member States for the period 1 July 2001 to 30 June 2002 amounting to $1,275,143,380 gross ($1,223,471,543 net) and unencumbered balances to be credited to Member States for closed peacekeeping operations amounting to $4,826,222 gross ($4,760,450 net).

Apportionment of costs

In March [A/C.5/55/38], the Secretary-General, following numerous queries from Member States regarding changes in the system for the apportionment of peacekeeping expenses among Member States set out in resolutions 55/235 [YUN 2000 p. 102] and 55/236 [ibid., p. 104], provided information to Member States on the implementation of those resolutions based on the Secretariat's understanding of their provisions. Annexed to the report (annex II) was a tabulated assignment of contribution levels, voluntary movements and transitional phasing for the period 1 July 2001 to 31 December 2003. Another annex (annex III) provided the effective rates of assessment for peacekeeping operations for the same period, based on the information contained in annex II

and the regular budget scale of assessments for 2001-2003 set out in resolution 55/5 B [ibid., p. 1311].

It was the Secretariat's understanding that the new structure of 10 levels (A to J) for determining rates of assessment from July 2001 would be reviewed by the Assembly in 2009. Regarding the triennial updating of the composition of those levels, in conjunction with the reviews of the regular budget scale of assessments, the Secretary-General would inform the Assembly in 2003 and 2006 of the composition of the 10 levels during the periods 2004-2006 and 2007-2009, respectively. After 2009, it would presumably be considered in the context of the Assembly's review of the structure of the levels. Movement between categories would be based on Member States' per capita gross national product (GNP) based on the same statistical data used in preparing the regular budget scale of assessments. Subject to the provisions of resolutions 55/5 B and 55/5 C [YUN 2000, p. 1314], the scale of assessments for the 2004-2006 regular budget period would be based on the average of the results of machine scales using base periods of six (1996-2001) and three (1999-2001) years.

For 2001-2003, the Assembly had decided that the average used for determining the composition of the 10 levels should be that for the six-year (1993-1998) base period. In updating the composition of those levels, average per capita GNP figures for the six-year (1996-2001) base period for the regular budget scale of assessments for the period 2004-2006 should also be used.

After 2001-2003, the Assembly had stated that two-year transition periods would apply to countries moving up by two levels and three-year transition periods would apply to countries moving up by three levels or more, while transitions specified for 2001-2003 would occur in equal increments over the transition period. It was the Secretariat's understanding that any transitional measures applied for 2004-2006 would also occur in equal annual increments, and changes involving a two-year transition would involve an increase of 50 per cent of the change in the percentage of the respective regular budget rates payable by each of the Member States concerned from 1 January to 31 December 2004, and a second 50 per cent from 1 January 2005 onwards. For those moving up by three levels or more, the transitional three-year phasing would involve equal instalments of one third of the respective regular budget rates payable from 1 January to 31 December 2004, an additional one third from 1 January to 31 December 2005 and a final one third from 1 January 2006 onwards.

The Assembly had listed the Member States assigned to level C for 2001-2003 in resolution 55/235 [YUN 2000, p. 102] but did not specify parameters for their inclusion in that level. Therefore, it was the Secretariat's understanding that, in updating the composition of the 10 levels used in 2001-2003 for 2004-2006 and for 2007-2009, the countries listed under level C would remain at that level until the 2009 review of the structure of levels, subject to any subsequent decisions by the Assembly or voluntary movements to level B by any of the countries concerned.

The Secretariat also understood that, notwithstanding the average per capita GNP of Hungary and the Republic of Korea for the six-year (1996-2001) base period used for the regular budget scale of assessments for 2004-2006, the transitional periods would continue to 1 January 2005 in the case of the Republic of Korea, and to 1 July 2005 in the case of Hungary.

With regard to the voluntary upward movements, the Assembly had welcomed Turkey's commitment to move to level H (paying 30 per cent of its regular budget rate of assessment) from 1 July 2001 until 2002, and to level F for the remainder of the scale period. It was therefore the Secretariat's understanding that, when the Secretary-General updated the composition of levels and informed the Assembly thereon at its fifty-eighth (2003) session, Turkey would revert to the level corresponding to its average per capita GNP for the six-year (1996-2001) base period used for the regular budget scale of assessments for the period 2004-2006. That would be subject to any further voluntary decision by its Government to be assessed at a higher level. The position with regard to the assessment rates for 2007-2009 would depend on decisions made with respect to the period 2004-2006.

The upward movement of the Republic of Korea and the voluntary upward movement of other Member States were not similarly time-limited. The Secretariat understood that, in updating the composition of the 10 levels in 2003 and 2006, the Secretary-General should include those countries at their voluntarily established levels for 2001-2003 unless their revised levels would otherwise be higher, or unless they wished to revert to a lower level for which they were eligible in the new scale period (2004-2006 or 2005-2007). As regards the current scale period (2001-2003), it was the Secretariat's understanding that resolution 55/235 did not provide for reversal of a voluntary upward movement during a scale period, except by specific decision of the Assembly.

Regarding the Assembly's decision that a Member State might voluntarily contribute at a rate higher at any time during the scale period, it was the Secretariat's understanding that, unless any such new commitments were time-limited, they would be considered open-ended, that the provisions of paragraph 6 of resolution 55/236 [YUN 2000, p. 104] related specifically to the current scale period (2001-2003), and that voluntary movements might still be considered by the Assembly in the context of the triennial updating of the composition of the levels. The Assembly might also make additional decisions on changes in the level of specific Member States at any time.

In a May addendum [A/C.5/55/38/Add.1], the Secretary-General recalled that the Assembly, in **resolution 55/253** (see p. 773), had endorsed the Economic and Social Council recommendations that Senegal be added to the list of least developed countries (LDCs) and that consideration of the graduation of Maldives from that list be deferred. In accordance with the provisions of resolution 55/235, when the composition of the levels was updated in 2003 for the 2004-2006 triennium, Senegal would move to level J (LDCs), together with any other Member State that might be added to the list of LDCs by 2003. Similarly, any Member State graduating from the list during that same period would move up from level J.

The Secretary-General observed that, had Senegal been on the list of LDCs prior to the adoption of resolution 55/235, its effective rate of assessment for peacekeeping during the period 1 July 2001 to 31 December 2003 would have been 0.0005 per cent, rather than 0.0010 per cent, and the share of Member States in level A would have been higher as a result by 0.0005 per cent.

The Fifth Committee considered the Secretary-General's reports in May and agreed that no action should be taken on them [A/55/712/Add.1]. By **decision 55/487** of 14 June, the Assembly took note of the Fifth Committee's report.

On 24 December, the Assembly decided that the item on the administrative and budgetary aspects of the financing of the UN peacekeeping operations would remain for consideration during its resumed fifty-sixth (2002) session (**decision 56/464**) and that the Fifth Committee would continue consideration of the item at that session (**decision 56/458**).

Accounts and auditing

At its resumed fifty-fifth session, the General Assembly considered the financial report and audited financial statements for UN peacekeeping operations for the 12-month period 1 July 1999 to 30 June 2000 [A/55/5, vol. II], the Secretary-General's March report on the implementation of the recommendations of the Board of Auditors [A/55/380/Add.2] and the related report of ACABQ [A/55/878].

On 14 June [meeting 103], the General Assembly, on the recommendation of the Fifth Committee [A/55/689/Add.2], adopted **resolution 55/220 C** without vote [agenda item 115].

Financial reports and audited financial statements, and reports of the Board of Auditors

The General Assembly,

Having considered the financial report and audited financial statements for the twelve-month period from 1 July 1999 to 30 June 2000 and the report of the Board of Auditors on United Nations peacekeeping operations, the related report of the Advisory Committee on Administrative and Budgetary Questions and the first report of the Secretary-General on the implementation of the recommendations of the Board of Auditors concerning United Nations peacekeeping operations for that period,

1. *Accepts* the audited financial statements on the United Nations peacekeeping operations for the period from 1 July 1999 to 30 June 2000;

2. *Endorses* the recommendations of the Board of Auditors contained in its report;

3. *Takes note* of the observations, and endorses the recommendations contained in the report of the Advisory Committee on Administrative and Budgetary Questions;

4. *Also takes note* of the first report of the Secretary-General on the implementation of the recommendations of the Board of Auditors concerning United Nations peacekeeping operations for the financial period ending 30 June 2000;

5. *Requests* the Secretary-General to ensure the use of objective-setting by the administrations of peacekeeping missions and also to ensure that the development and attainment of such objectives are reported on to the General Assembly through the financial performance reports of the missions;

6. *Requests* the Board of Auditors to monitor the process of objective-setting by missions and the measurement of their use, whether effective or otherwise, and to report thereon to the General Assembly in its annual audit report on the financial statements of peacekeeping missions;

7. *Notes with concern* the late issuance of the financial report and audited financial statements for the twelve-month period from 1 July 1999 to 30 June 2000 and the report of the Board of Auditors on United Nations peacekeeping operations, and requests the Board of Auditors and the Secretary-General to work together to implement ways to ensure its timely and simultaneous issuance in all six official languages of the United Nations, including streamlining the format and content of the report as well as the related financial information contained in the performance reports.

Resident auditors at peacekeeping missions

As requested by the General Assembly in resolution 54/241 A [YUN 1999, p. 168], the Secretary-General submitted a January report on experiences learned from the use of resident auditors at peacekeeping missions [A/55/735]. He stated that the main concept behind resident auditors—OIOS staff members deployed to missions but reporting to the OIOS Director, Audit and Management Consulting Division—was that their continuous physical presence in peacekeeping missions would provide reasonable assurance to management that established internal controls were functioning effectively. They would also be an additional deterrent against mismanagement, waste, abuse or fraud in high-risk missions; enable OIOS to gain more in-depth knowledge of mission operations and be better able to react promptly to "audit-worthy" events; and facilitate the OIOS process for providing management advice.

OIOS and DPKO agreed that the practice had been useful and should be continued. During 1994 to 1999, 15 resident auditors were deployed in 10 missions, serving a total of 209 staff-months and issuing more than 1,500 recommendations, 80 per cent of which were implemented. Other corrective actions included the recovery of $9.5 million in fraud-related and other overpayments and the adoption of cost-saving or income-enhancement measures amounting to $9.3 million, the installation of stronger internal controls and other improvements to ensure the quality of administrative and logistical support operations and the efficient and effective use of mission resources.

However, the use of resident auditors presented a number of challenges, including recruiting qualified candidates; ensuring adequate training and exposure to best auditing practices; maintaining an effective working relationship with mission management without compromising their independence; and assisting and motivating the resident auditors to perform effectively.

To ensure adequate internal audit coverage, ACABQ had endorsed the OIOS recommendation that a resident auditor at the P-4 or P-3 level be assigned for each $100 million of annual budgeted expenditure and, for those missions with annual budgets exceeding $200 million, that an auditing assistant at the G-6 or G-7 level be assigned also. OIOS was also proposing that the resident audit teams in large missions, namely, UNMIK and UNAMSIL, be headed by resident auditors at the P-5 level.

As at 31 December 2000, 13 resident auditor posts and three auditing assistant posts had been authorized in six peacekeeping missions (UNMIK, UNAMSIL, MONUC, UNMIBH, UNTAET and UNMEE). If the OIOS formula were fully implemented, it would result in: the inclusion of one additional mission (UNIFIL) under the resident auditor arrangement; and the establishment of up to five additional resident auditor posts at the P-5, P-4 or P-3 level and one auditing assistant post at the G-7 or G-6 level. The recruitment and deployment of additional resident auditors would be made only after OIOS had made a detailed assessment of the risks and corresponding audit requirements pertaining to each affected mission.

The work of the resident auditors had become even more important in the light of the implementation of the recommendations of the Panel on United Nations Peace Operations (see p. 71), which provided for greater delegation of administrative authority to peacekeeping missions.

The Secretary-General said that the use of OIOS resident auditors in peacekeeping missions should be strengthened, and endorsed the formula for determining their number and salary levels.

ACABQ report. In March [A/55/828], ACABQ said that, in its report on the report of the Board of Auditors on the financial statements for UN peacekeeping operations for the period ended 30 June 2000 [A/55/878], it had requested the Board, in its next submission, to include information on the adequacy of the resident audit function in the missions to be audited. ACABQ was of the opinion that a proper selection process for all eligible candidates and a strict definition of functions were essential. It also advised that other challenges could be surmounted by rotating resident auditors among different missions and at Headquarters at regular intervals and by strengthening the synergy of communication and coordination between the field and Headquarters.

GENERAL ASSEMBLY ACTION

On 14 June [meeting 103], the General Assembly, on the recommendation of the Fifth Committee [A/55/534/Add.2], adopted **resolution 55/273** without vote [agenda item 153 (a)].

Experiences learned from the use of resident auditors at peacekeeping missions

The General Assembly,

Recalling paragraph 9 of its resolution 54/241 A of 23 December 1999,

Having considered the report of the Secretary-General on experiences learned from the use of resident auditors at peacekeeping missions and the related report of the Advisory Committee on Administrative and Budgetary Questions,

1. *Takes note* of the report of the Secretary-General;

2. *Endorses* the observations contained in the report of the Advisory Committee on Administrative and Budgetary Questions.

Reimbursement issues

Equipment

Report of post–Phase V Working Group. The post–Phase V Working Group on reformed procedures for determining reimbursement of contingent-owned equipment (15-26 January) [A/C.5/55/39 & Corr.1] reviewed the reimbursement rates for contingent-owned equipment and the methodology for review of the troop cost rates (see p. 100). Convened in response to General Assembly resolutions 54/19 B [YUN 2000, p. 109] and 55/229 [ibid., p. 108], the Working Group examined issues related to major equipment, self-sustainment, medical support services, troop costs and other issues, including inland transport costs and updating the model memorandum of understanding.

The Working Group validated the methodology and agreed on revised reimbursement rates for major equipment and self-sustainment; rates for some special cases and new categories of major equipment; generic reimbursement for painting and repainting of major equipment; and a new rate for level II services provided by level III medical facilities. It also adopted principles regarding liability for damage to major equipment used by one country and owned by another; a policy for reimbursing inland transportation claims; and a modular approach to reimbursement of medical facilities. In addition, it reviewed self-sustainment categories and standards; and the provision of level I medical support, medical aspects contained in the contingent-owned equipment manual and the provision of blood and blood products. The Working Group proposed options on troop costs reimbursement for the consideration of the Assembly (see p. 100).

Report of Secretary-General. In a March report [A/55/815], the Secretary-General said that, while recognizing that the post–Phase V Working Group could not arrive at a consensus on some issues, such as the review of the policy on vaccination costs and pre- and post-deployment examinations, he welcomed its achievements. The enhanced procedures and policies developed for major equipment, self-sustainment and medical support services would greatly facilitate the reimbursement of troop contributors for their contingent-owned equipment.

The Secretary-General agreed with the Working Group's recommendations and recommended that the Assembly: adopt a revised methodology of applying the statistical tool of standard deviation to the indices for generic categories to all major equipment and self-sustainment categories listed in the reports of the Phase II and Phase III Working Groups [YUN 1995, p. 311]; increase reimbursement rates using a maximum standard deviation of 25 per cent for major equipment and self-sustainment, as set out in annexes I.A and II.C of the Working Group's report; adopt the reimbursement rates for new categories of major equipment contained in annex I.B; request the United Nations to conduct training to ensure users were qualified to operate unique major equipment belonging to other countries; hold the user country responsible for reimbursing the providing country through the United Nations for major equipment damage; and adopt generic rates of reimbursement for painting and repainting of major equipment, as set out in annex I.C.

The Secretary-General also recommended that the Assembly adopt the new procedures on reimbursement of inland transportation costs for major equipment; adopt the amendment of the performance standards for catering, office, electrical, laundry and cleaning, tentage, observation and field defence stores; adopt the definitions for high- and normal-risk missions in the context of medical support; apply the term "force asset" in the context of medical support; adopt the modular approach to reimbursement for medical facilities; approve the occasional provision of level I medical support in an emergency to all members of a UN mission; include suggested changes, as set out in the contingent-owned equipment manual; confirm the rate for the provision of blood and blood products; adopt the new rate for the provision of level II services by level III medical facilities; replace the terms "major medical equipment" and "minor medical equipment" by the term "medical equipment"; adopt a maintenance cost of 0.5 per cent of the generic fair-market value per month for the medical modules in all levels of medical support; endorse the existing medical self-sustainment rates; accept the new methodology for collecting and interpreting medical data; and decide on the modalities for the conduct of a triennial review of rates and standards of related policy issues.

Report of ACABQ. ACABQ, in April [A/55/887], recommended that the Assembly approve the Working Group's recommendations as outlined in the Secretary-General's report.

Troops

The post–Phase V Working Group [A/C.5/55/39 & Corr.1] considered the methodology for calculating standard rates of reimbursement to troop-contributing States, including ways to produce timely and more representative data, as requested by the General Assembly in resolution 55/229 [YUN 2000, p. 108]. The Working Group considered two proposals: that troop contributors be reimbursed on an equal basis for identical services, on the basis of a standard cost reimbursement formula, and for additional costs incurred for the participation of their troops in UN peacekeeping operations, with some Governments not being fully reimbursed on any standard cost-reimbursement formula; or, as an alternative to the creation of a standard rate, an arbitrary definition of the "cost of a soldier" could serve as a new starting point.

The Working Group recommended that the Assembly consider all aspects of the methodologies proposed. A number of delegations did not believe that establishing a rate was within the Working Group's mandate; the majority of troop-contributing countries supported the adoption of the second option as an interim measure.

In April [A/55/887], ACABQ, pending a comprehensive review of the methodology of reimbursement of troop costs, recommended that the Assembly consider, as an ad hoc arrangement, increasing the standard monthly rates of reimbursement by 4 to 6 per cent, and that a group of qualified individuals study and make proposals on the methodology and the elements on which it was based.

Annexed to ACABQ's report was a table showing the impact of the increase on the reimbursement rates for UN peacekeeping operations. ACABQ recommended that, should the Assembly approve the increases, they should be reflected either in the proposed 2001-2002 budgets for those operations that were yet to be considered by the Assembly or in the performance reports for those peacekeeping budgets already approved.

GENERAL ASSEMBLY ACTION

On 14 June [meeting 103], the General Assembly, on the recommendation of the Fifth Committee [A/55/534/Add.2], adopted **resolution 55/274** without vote [agenda item 153 (a)].

Reformed procedures for determining reimbursement to Member States for contingent-owned equipment and troop costs

The General Assembly,

Recalling its resolutions 49/233 A of 23 December 1994, 50/222 of 11 April 1996, 51/218 E of 17 June 1997, 54/19 A of 29 October 1999 and 54/19 B of 15 June 2000,

Recalling also its decision 55/452 of 23 December 2000, by which the Secretary-General was requested to convene the post–Phase V Working Group,

Having considered the report of the post–Phase V Working Group on reformed procedures for determining reimbursement of contingent-owned equipment, as transmitted by the Chairman of the Working Group to the Chairman of the Fifth Committee, the report of the Secretary-General, and the related report of the Advisory Committee on Administrative and Budgetary Questions, on the reform of the procedures for determining reimbursement to Member States for contingent-owned equipment and troop costs,

1. *Endorses* the recommendations of the post–Phase V Working Group on reform procedures for determining reimbursement of contingent-owned equipment and troop costs, as outlined in paragraph 17 of the report of the Secretary-General, subject to the provisions of the present resolution;

2. *Takes note* of the recommendations contained in the report of the Advisory Committee on Administrative and Budgetary Questions;

3. *Affirms* the importance of conducting peacekeeping operations with the maximum of efficiency and effectiveness and the need to minimize delays in processing reimbursements to troop- and equipment-contributing countries;

4. *Recognizes* the fact that delay and uncertainty in reimbursements to troop-contributing countries of troop and contingent-owned equipment costs adversely impact on the ability of current and potential troop-contributing countries to participate effectively in United Nations peacekeeping operations, and in this context emphasizes the need for all Member States to pay their assessed contributions to all peacekeeping operations in full, on time and without preconditions;

5. *Stresses* that necessary resources should be provided to the Secretariat to allow verifications to be conducted to confirm, before deployment, the preparedness of each potential troop contributor and to ensure that standards continue to be met in accordance with the provisions of the relevant memoranda of understanding;

6. *Notes* that the evaluation and standardization of United Nations peacekeeping training are currently being developed by the Secretariat in consultation with troop-contributing countries, and requests the Secretary-General to submit a report on this important issue to the General Assembly at its fifty-sixth session, through the Special Committee on Peacekeeping Operations, for approval of these standards;

7. *Recognizes* the need for providing specific guidance on the methodology of reimbursement for troop costs;

8. *Requests* the Secretary-General to submit to the General Assembly for its approval at its resumed fifty-sixth session, taking into account the views expressed by Member States, a methodology for reimbursement for troop costs, covering troops and formed police units, and a questionnaire to be submitted to troop-contributing countries, on the basis of the following elements and guidelines:

(a) Troops, formed civilian police units and staff officers serving in United Nations peacekeeping operations shall be reimbursed on an equal basis for identical services;

(b) Reimbursement for troop costs shall take into consideration, inter alia, general principles such as simplicity, equity, transparency, comprehensiveness, portability, financial control and audit and confirmed delivery of specified services, all of which shall be built into the agreements entered into by the United Nations with the participating States;

(c) The data for this survey shall identify the common and essential additional costs from existing troop levels related to personnel that are incurred by troop-contributing countries due to their participation in United Nations peacekeeping operations, including the establishment of a standard vaccination package and identification of mission-specific vaccines and mission-specific medical and biochemical examinations, using the data available from the World Health Organization and the United Nations Children's Fund, that could be liable for reimbursement;

(d) The methodology shall ensure that no double payment is made with respect to reimbursement between the various levels of self-sustainment, components of troop costs and any other allowances;

9. *Decides* that a future standard rate of reimbursement for troop costs should be based on new survey data that is representative of the costs incurred by around 60 per cent of countries that have contributed troops to peacekeeping operations;

10. *Decides also*, on an interim and ad hoc basis, to increase the standard rate of reimbursement for troop costs to troop-contributing countries by 2 per cent, effective 1 July 2001;

11. *Decides further* that an additional 2 per cent increase, on an interim and ad hoc basis, will be effective as of 1 January 2002, bringing the total increase of the current rate of reimbursement for troop costs to 4 per cent;

12. *Requests* the Secretary-General to review the practical aspects of the wet-lease, dry-lease and self-sustainment arrangements, including the effectiveness of the contingent-owned equipment procedures to ascertain the capacity of troop-contributing countries to meet the requirements for wet-lease and self-sustainment provisions of the contingent-owned equipment arrangements and the need to ensure the effectiveness of peacekeeping operations, including through a consistent implementation of the standards set out in the contingent-owned equipment manual, and to report thereon to the General Assembly at its fifty-sixth session;

13. *Stresses* the need for the Secretariat to meet its obligations, in full, as agreed upon in the memoranda of understanding, in a timely manner, so as to ensure operational effectiveness of the troops in United Nations peacekeeping operations;

14. *Takes note* of the views of the Secretariat regarding the possibility of reviewing, subject to future experience, the procedures for settlement of liability for damages for major equipment used by one country and owned by another country, and decides that the liability for damage to major equipment used by one country and owned by another country should be based on the relevant provisions of their memoranda of understanding in accordance with the applicable rules and regulations of the United Nations;

15. *Requests* the Secretary-General to convene in 2004 an open-ended working group of experts, for a period of no less than ten working days, to hold a triennial review of reimbursement rates for contingent-owned equipment and self-sustainment, including medical services;

16. *Decides* to keep this matter under review at its fifty-sixth session.

In an August note [A/C.5/55/47], the Secretary-General, in the light of the adoption by the Assembly in resolution 55/274 of interim and ad hoc measures for the reimbursement of troop costs, including increasing the standard rate of reimbursement for troop costs to troop-contributing countries by 2 per cent effective 1 July 2001 and an additional 2 per cent increase effective 1 January 2002, submitted a table setting out the applicable revised reimbursement rates effective 1 July 2001 and 1 January 2002.

Special Committee consideration. In its July report [A/55/1024 & Corr.1], the Special Committee on Peacekeeping Operations expressed concern at the delay in reimbursement of troop contributors and the hardships caused for all troop- and equipment-contributing countries, especially developing countries. It encouraged the Secretariat to continue to expedite the processing of all claims and reiterated its request that the Secretary-General present a progress report to the Committee in 2002.

Management of peacekeeping assets

Liquidation

By **decision 55/485** of 14 June, the General Assembly noted the OIOS report on the audit of the liquidation of peacekeeping operations [YUN 1999, p. 69].

The Assembly, in **resolution 56/246** (see p. 1284) of 24 December, requested the Secretary-General to present an update on the implementation of OIOS recommendations on UN mission liquidation activities, in particular with regard to write-offs, at its resumed fifty-sixth (2002) session.

Field assets control system

In March [A/55/845], the Secretary-General reported on progress in the implementation of the field assets control system (FACS), which was developed in 1997 [YUN 1997, p. 56] to help manage non-expendable UN-owned equipment in the field. He stated that the Secretariat had successfully prototyped and developed the mission-critical online inventory tracking and management system using Lotus Notes. FACS was successfully implemented in 28 field missions, and over 800 staff members had been trained in its use. There were currently over 500 daily users of the system, which helped to improve the efficiency of peacekeeping inventory management through standardized work flow and inventory management procedures, the explicit definition of roles and responsibilities of organizational units, data issues and the accommodation of areas requiring extra security, such as financial data and purchase value. It also provided each mission with full visibility of its inventory and

enabled an informed procurement planning process. FACS provided a detailed transaction history of transferred inventory from a liquidated mission to a current one, thereby enabling online monitoring and follow-up of asset shipments.

In 2000, FACS was used for the first time as the mission-wide, sole repository for the non-expendable inventory data of all field missions. The information available from it had already assisted contingents serving specific missions to identify, analyse and make adjustments to essential financial parameters such as costs of maintenance. A variety of operational support information could be obtained on numerous parameters used to identify bottlenecks and problem areas and to provide feedback for mission preparedness and procurement planning.

In terms of its future development, FACS would be closely integrated with the field expendable and supplies system, which was being designed to control UN-owned expendable property. It would continue to be deployed in all new peacekeeping missions and implemented in missions operated by the Department of Political Affairs. As new systems were developed and deployed, the number of databases requiring management and control was expected to grow significantly, increasing the complexity of managing the entire operation and the load on the data and communications infrastructure. The introduction of knowledge management tools and techniques within the system would be necessary to enable its proper management and control. Consideration was also being given to interfacing FACS with other major systems in the field.

As to resources, the requirement for a long-term decentralized maintenance strategy with centralized planning, coordination and control needed to be taken into account. It was planned to outsource specific maintenance and support activities of the field mission logistics system, while retaining specialist activities, with overall planning and coordination of the whole project. There was also an increasing need to provide for enhanced security measures at operational and database levels and during transmission, and to maintain well-developed contingency plans in the event of failure or disaster.

By **decision 55/480** of 14 June, the General Assembly deferred consideration of the Secretary-General's report on progress in the implementation of FACS.

ACABQ, in August [A/56/7], in its first report on the proposed 2002-2003 programme budget, welcomed the progress achieved in the implementation of FACS and requested that steps be taken to ensure that qualified personnel were available in all missions to use and maintain the system so as to avoid disruptions resulting from frequent staff rotation. It requested that FACS be reviewed to determine its applicability to the inventory management of the rest of the Organization's assets. Priority should be given to developing a capacity to archive electronically records of mission inventory that had been liquidated. In that regard, closer cooperation should exist between DPKO's Field Administration and Logistics Division and the Archives and Records Management Section in the Office of Central Support Services.

ACABQ reiterated that adequate maintenance should be provided for and that further development should be envisaged to ensure the effectiveness of the system. It trusted that proper use of FACS would result in better control of UN property in peacekeeping missions and minimize the loss of UN inventory assets.

Procurement

The Secretary-General, in his June report [A/55/977] on the implementation of the recommendations of the Special Committee on Peacekeeping Operations and the Panel on United Nations Peace Operations, outlined the current division of labour between DPKO and the Department of Management in procurement (annex J) and presented a flow chart of the entire acquisition and deployment process within which procurement fell (annex K).

The Secretary-General said he had deferred action on the recommendation of the Panel that the Department of Management delegate authority and responsibility for peacekeeping procurement to DPKO on a two-year trial basis, bearing in mind the substantial changes that might be required to the entire logistics support system to meet 30- to 90-day rapid deployment timelines and the impact they would have on existing procurement arrangements and procedures. A number of procedural reviews had already been conducted and others were still in process, and the two Departments had jointly identified areas that could be streamlined and/or improved through the increased delegation of procurement authority to the field, fast-track procurement and other mechanisms to speed response, while ensuring independent monitoring of adherence to financial regulations and rules, through the missions' resident auditors (see p. 98).

With or without increased delegated authority to the field, additional training for procurement officers in the field was required and pilot courses were to begin in September. In order to meet the 30- to 90-day deployment timelines, a major undertaking was required to create a strategic reserve of equipment and materiel and to expand the breadth, scope and numbers of systems contracts. In that connection, the Secretary-General agreed with the consultants' recommendation not to delegate procurement authority from the Department of Management to DPKO. However, since the planning of procurement activities needed to be strengthened, the Secretary-General proposed establishing a Contracts Management Section within the proposed Logistics Support Division to strengthen those capacities. The section would liaise with the Procurement Division and the Office of Mission Support to facilitate smooth procurement-related activities through advance planning and requisition, bidding and selection, including technical evaluation and contract management, and contractors' performance evaluation.

The two Departments needed to work more closely to ensure that the stringent deployment timelines were met, including the out-posting of procurement officers from the Procurement Division to the Office of Mission Support and their participation in coordination meetings within DPKO and visits to the field missions. The Procurement Division should consult more frequently with DPKO when designing system-wide policies and procedures to ensure their flexibility to cater for the unique aspects of peacekeeping procurement. The two Departments should treat as a shared responsibility and priority the building of capacity in the field to assume greater levels of authority for local procurement.

The General Assembly, in **resolution 55/247** of 12 April on procurement reform (see p. 1280), requested the Secretary-General to ensure that there was capacity in field missions to perform the procurement functions properly, as well as effective mechanisms at Headquarters for monitoring procurement in the field, including remedial measures to address the problems identified with regard to peacekeeping operations and their standardization.

By **decision 55/485** of 14 June, the Assembly noted the OIOS reports on the investigation into the award of a fresh rations contract in a UN peacekeeping mission [YUN 1999, p. 70] and on the audit of the management of service and rations contracts in peacekeeping missions [ibid.].

Special Committee consideration. The Special Committee on Peacekeeping Operations, in June [A/55/1024 & Corr.1], welcomed the review of procurement procedures with regard to peacekeeping operations and stressed the need for efficiency, propriety, accountability and transparency in the procurement process. In that regard, it took note of General Assembly resolution 55/247 and other relevant Assembly resolutions.

UN Logistics Base

The resumed fifty-fifth session of the General Assembly had before it the financial performance report of the United Nations Logistics Base (UNLB) in Brindisi, Italy, for the period 1 July 1999 to 30 June 2000 [YUN 2000, p. 112].

In March 2001 [A/55/830], the Secretary-General submitted the proposed budget for UNLB for the period 1 July 2001 to 30 June 2002 in the amount of $8,982,600 gross ($8,174,400 net), representing a 3.6 per cent decrease in resources from the 2000/01 budget period. The decrease reflected a 4.2 per cent drop in civilian personnel costs, a 3.2 per cent drop in operational costs and a 0.5 per cent drop in staff assessment. There was an 18.6 per cent increase under other programmes. The budget provided for 23 international and 83 local staff.

The Secretary-General indicated that he proposed submitting a revised budget after the submission of the review of UNLB's concept of operation and related requirements and the Headquarters capacity study and comprehensive review to the General Assembly's fifty-sixth session.

In relation to the financial performance report, ACABQ, in April [A/55/874/Add.8], recommended acceptance of the Secretary-General's proposal regarding the unencumbered balance and interest and miscellaneous income.

Regarding the 2001/02 cost estimates, ACABQ recommended approval of the proposed budget. It was of the opinion that, unless the proposed budget revisions entailed significant changes in financial requirements, the results of the reviews should be reported in the next performance report and budget for UNLB.

In February [A/C.5/55/37] and May [A/C.5/55/43], the Secretary-General submitted to the Fifth Committee notes on the amounts to be apportioned in respect of each peacekeeping mission, including the prorated share of UNLB for the periods 1 July 2000 to 30 June 2001 and for the period 1 July 2001 to 30 June 2002, respectively.

GENERAL ASSEMBLY ACTION

On 14 June [meeting 103], the General Assembly, on the recommendation of the Fifth Committee [A/55/534/Add.2], adopted **resolution 55/272** without vote [agenda item 153 (a)].

Financing of the United Nations Logistics Base at Brindisi, Italy

The General Assembly,

Recalling section XIV of its resolution 49/233 A of 23 December 1994,

Recalling also its decision 50/500 of 17 September 1996 on the financing of the United Nations Logistics

Base at Brindisi, Italy, and its subsequent resolutions thereon, the latest of which was resolution 54/278 of 15 June 2000,

Having considered the reports of the Secretary-General on the financing of the United Nations Logistics Base and the related reports of the Advisory Committee on Administrative and Budgetary Questions,

Reiterating the importance of establishing an accurate inventory of assets,

1. *Takes note* of the reports of the Secretary-General on the financing of the United Nations Logistics Base at Brindisi, Italy;

2. *Endorses* the observations and recommendations contained in the report of the Advisory Committee on Administrative and Budgetary Questions;

3. *Reiterates* the need to implement, as a matter of priority, an effective inventory management standard, especially in respect of peacekeeping operations involving high inventory value;

4. *Approves* the cost estimates for the United Nations Logistics Base amounting to 8,982,600 United States dollars gross (8,174,400 dollars net) for the period from 1 July 2001 to 30 June 2002;

5. *Decides* to apply the unencumbered balance of 430,500 dollars in respect of the period from 1 July 1999 to 30 June 2000, the interest income of 289,000 dollars and miscellaneous income of 340,000 dollars, that is, a total of 1,059,500 dollars, to the resources required for the period from 1 July 2001 to 30 June 2002;

6. *Also decides* to prorate the balance of 7,923,100 dollars gross (7,114,900 dollars net) among the individual active peacekeeping operation budgets to meet the financing requirements of the United Nations Logistics Base for the period from 1 July 2001 to 30 June 2002;

7. *Authorizes* the Secretary-General to provide for a civilian establishment consisting of ten Professional, thirteen Field Service and eighty-three locally recruited staff;

8. *Decides* to consider during its fifty-sixth session the question of the financing of the United Nations Logistics Base.

Personnel matters

Mission subsistence allowance

In November [A/56/648], the Secretary-General transmitted an OIOS report on the audit of the establishment and management by the Department of Management and DPKO of mission subsistence allowance (MSA) rates—a daily allowance paid to UN international civilian staff, military observers and civilian police in special peacekeeping missions to cover subsistence costs. MSA constituted a significant portion of overall peacekeeping costs. In general, the MSA rate reflected subsistence costs (including food, lodging and incidental items) based on the conditions that peacekeeping staff were exposed to in each mission area. It was generally lower than, or at least did not exceed, the daily subsistence allowance (DSA) rates established by the International Civil Service Commission for short-term travel to the same locations. The audit reviewed MSA rates in effect as at September 2000 in 10 peacekeeping missions (MINURSO, MONUC, UNAMSIL, UNIKOM, UNMEE, UNMIBH, UNMOP, UNMIK, UNOMIG and UNTAET) to determine whether they were reasonable and justified. For the 2000/01 financial period, those costs made up 17 per cent ($350 million) of the total expenditures of the 10 missions reviewed.

The audit revealed that the MSA rates in seven of the missions (MINURSO, UNAMSIL, UNOMIG, MONUC, UNMEE, UNMIK and UNIKOM) were found to be excessive and should be reduced. The UNMIBH rate appeared to be unduly low. The reviews by the Office of Human Resources Management (OHRM) of the MSA rates at UNMEE, UNOMIG, MINURSO, MONUC, UNAMSIL and UNIKOM, made in conjunction with the audit, had reduced the MSA rates payable in those missions, resulting in projected savings of approximately $33.7 million per year. The audit also found that there was a need for a regular OHRM review of MSA rates to ensure their continued reasonableness in comparison with actual subsistence costs in the various mission areas. That would also mitigate the inherent conflict of interest in the collection of relevant data on those costs, which was mainly based on questionnaires filled out by mission personnel. In order to introduce a stable and reliable means of setting MSA rates, consideration should be given to using DSA rates as a standard or benchmark for establishing and adjusting MSA rates in the same geographical locations.

The Secretary-General, in his letter of transmittal, concurred with the audit recommendations and noted that the Department of Management and DPKO were undertaking a more proactive approach in establishing and managing MSA.

The General Assembly, in **resolution 56/246** (see p. 1284) of 24 December, requested the Secretary-General to ensure that the OIOS recommendations on MSA were fully and expeditiously implemented and to report on the matter in the context of the performance reports of the relevant peacekeeping operations.

Death and disability benefits

In a March note [A/C.5/55/40 & Corr.1], the Secretary-General, pursuant to General Assembly decision 54/459 B [YUN 2000, p. 113] and ACABQ recommendations [ibid.], submitted the first annual report on death and disability claims, indicating that, in 2000, 145 claims were received and 318 processed, including 19 claims from the backlog of claims received before 1997, with 90 claims pending at the end of the year. Annexed to the note were tables showing claims received by country and by mission as at 31 December 2000 and the total number of casualties reported and claims submitted for incidents occurring between 1 January 1995 and 31 December 2000.

The information by country and mission did not contain the dollar amounts as requested by ACABQ, since claims were submitted in different currencies, were subject to exchange rate fluctuations, and the original claimed amount might be adjusted, creating a difference between the amount claimed and that paid. Inclusion of dollar amounts would therefore give a misleading description of the value of pending claims.

ACABQ, in April [A/55/883], while noting the Secretariat's position on the matter of dollar amounts, requested that a column be added to the tables showing claims by country and mission, indicating the dollar amount of claims settled and paid during the specific reporting year, and that information be included in the next report on the complete process for the settlement of death and disability claims. It believed that permanent missions accredited to the United Nations should be involved from the outset of the exercise to facilitate and accelerate the process.

By **decision 55/486** of 14 June, the General Assembly noted the Secretary-General's note on death and disability benefits and the related ACABQ report.

Recruitment policies and procedures

Report of Secretary-General (June). In his June report on the implementation of the recommendations of the Special Committee on Peacekeeping Operations and the Panel on United Nations Peace Operations [A/55/977], the Secretary-General stated that consultants had observed that mission staff members had expressed concern about staff shortages and the quality of staff assigned to missions. In addition, the roster for civilian peacekeepers was ineffective and inadequately supported, advertising of vacancies was limited, the grading system for newly recruited staff was inflexible, the interview process was inadequate and missions seldom participated in the selection process for international staff.

Other observations were: that there was lack of career development and no real succession planning; insufficient attention to the gender issue; and no priority accorded to ensuring proper care of civilian, military and civilian police personnel, particularly those serving in unsafe environments. The staffing constraints within DPKO's Personnel Management and Support Service had contributed to those problems, as had the structure of the Service.

Concerning the proposed global strategy for civilian staffing that would correct current weaknesses and prepare for the future, senior UN system managers had outlined the main elements of that strategy, the resources required and potential implementation timelines. Some of those weaknesses were also addressed in the Organization's human resources management reforms (see p. 1336). Considerable progress had been made in the design of a new recruitment roster system, and DPKO and OHRM had collaborated in the establishment of the Galaxy Project for automating UN staff recruitment and selection procedures. A key facet of the staffing strategy would be to delegate additional recruitment authority to field missions. OHRM and DPKO concluded that written procedures, policy guidelines and monitoring mechanisms needed to be developed and the further delegation of recruitment authority to field missions required established recruitment standards, qualified recruitment specialists at the missions and appropriate Headquarters oversight. DPKO would set up a monitoring function with OHRM based on agreed parameters. To develop further and implement the global strategy for civilian staffing, the Secretary-General proposed creating a new section in the restructured Personnel Management and Support Service, which would include gender expertise to ensure equitable gender distribution in recruitment strategies for peacekeeping operations.

Special Committee consideration. In June [A/55/1024 & Corr.1], the Special Committee on Peacekeeping Operations supported the creation of a new section in the restructured Personnel Management and Support Service to undertake civilian workforce planning and analysis, expand recruitment sources, expedite recruitment, manage the rapid civilian deployment capability and manage the careers of civilian staff in peacekeeping operations. It looked forward to the further development and wider use of the Galaxy Project to standardize civilian personnel recruitment and provide for greater transparency. The Special Committee recognized the benefits of further delegation of recruitment authority to the field, but stressed the necessity of proper policy guidelines, monitoring mechanisms and adequately trained and experienced human resources staff. It believed that greater mobility of personnel, especially between Headquarters and the field, was required for improving DPKO's management and planning capacities.

Report of Secretary-General (December). In December [A/56/732], the Secretary-General reported that the Secretariat had undertaken a number of strategies to implement the global staffing strategy. The Galaxy Project was being modified to meet the full range of recruitment needs and the prototype of the "Galaxy 1 a" roster component had been released. Mission templates would further assist in refining a surge roster of middle/senior administrative staff for mission start-up phases and the succession planning phase, and generic profiles were being formulated for 30 key professional-level job profiles in peacekeeping operations. In August, DPKO reviewed the applicant databases of the United Nations Volunteers, the World Food Programme and the Office of the United Nations High Commissioner for Refugees in an ongoing effort to develop a compendium of existing and potential recruitment sources and to create tools to enhance standby capacities. New procedures were concluded with OHCHR to streamline and shorten the selection process of human rights officers in field missions. DPKO had approached OHRM with regard to developing a mechanism for identifying and securing the release of suitable and sufficient numbers of staff to field operations, who would be entered in a sub-roster of pre-selected personnel ready to deploy on short notice. Work was under way to codify the policy and procedure of granting special post allowances for field staff and to simplify administrative entitlements, and consideration was being given to reducing differences in emoluments and benefits of mission appointees and staff seconded from a parent UN department, programme or agency. DPKO, in consultation with the Field Staff Union, continued work on the concept and structure of a Field Service category. To provide career prospects for qualified field personnel, DPKO, in its support account budget, had requested the establishment of a civilian training section and human resources management and development section in the Personnel Management and Support Service of the Field Administration and Logistics Division.

OIOS report

In July, the Secretary-General transmitted to the General Assembly the OIOS report on the audit of the policies and procedures of DPKO for the recruitment of international civilian staff for field missions [A/56/202]. The audit reviewed selected mission appointments processed by DPKO's Personnel Management and Support Service between January 1999 and October 2000.

Among the shortcomings identified by OIOS were: the absence of benchmarks and proper analysis of workload; the limited functionality of the candidate roster and the yet to be fully developed standard job descriptions for mission posts; a selection process that did not ensure the competitive selection of candidates; and inconsistencies in determining the salary levels and lack of reference checks of their qualifications and experience in most cases. The audit also found that DPKO's recruitment practices and procedures needed to be substantially improved to enhance transparency and to meet the staffing needs of field missions more effectively. OIOS supported the proposal of the Panel on United Nations Peace Operations [YUN 2000, p. 83] for the delegation of recruitment authority to field missions, but advised that it should be preceded by the establishment of recruitment standards, the deployment of qualified recruitment specialists in the affected missions and the implementation of appropriate monitoring mechanisms at Headquarters.

OIOS recommended that: OHRM should implement an effective monitoring mechanism to ensure that the recruitment authority delegated to DPKO was exercised with transparency and in accordance with the Organization's human resources policies; the Personnel Management and Support Service should establish a functional roster of qualified, pre-screened candidates and selection decisions should be delegated to field missions; the Service should develop standard job descriptions for all posts; to promote transparency and fairness in determining salary levels, the Service should apply grading criteria consistently and record reasons for deviations from those criteria; the Service should ensure that checks of candidates' educational qualifications and work experience were completed before appointment or before extending initial appointments; to improve the management of recruitment functions, the Service should strengthen its case for additional resources by fully justifying its posts based on reliable workload indicators and benchmarks, presenting a risk analysis highlighting the potential impact of lower resource levels; the Service should prepare written procedures for recruiting international civilian staff for field missions; and DPKO should deploy qualified human resources specialists and train existing field mission staff before recruitment authority was fully delegated.

DPKO and OHRM agreed with the report's recommendations and were working together to strengthen the policies and procedures for recruiting international civilian staff for field missions.

Behavioural issues

In his December report on implementation of the recommendations of the Special Committee on Peacekeeping Operations and the Panel on United Nations Peace Operations [A/56/732], the Secretary-General stated that DPKO had recognized that problems sometimes occurred with the behaviour of military, civilian and civilian police peacekeeping personnel. A working group had been constituted to review all guidelines, including those on disciplinary issues, the investigation of alleged gross misconduct and investigations or inquiries into incidents involving the death of or injury to personnel from Member States or loss of property, and to identify areas for improvement. Another working group was constituted to review, among other things, the administrative procedures on discipline for UN police personnel in peacekeeping missions and to submit recommendations for their incorporation into a revised version of the guidelines. The Civilian Police Division was drafting guidelines for the development of rules of engagement and guidelines for generic standard operating procedures for civilian police and was introducing a standard disciplinary process in all field missions with a UN civilian police component. It intended to make current codes of conduct, policies and guidelines electronically available and part of the Division's start-up kit for newly established peacekeeping missions.

The sample Rules of Engagement for military personnel were revised by DPKO and the Department of Legal Affairs based on comments and observations received from Member States. The revised document was being used by military planning staff to guide them in preparing mission-specific Rules of Engagement.

Other peacekeeping matters

Cooperation with regional organizations

The Special Committee on Peacekeeping Operations [A/55/1024 & Corr.1] recognized the need to strengthen cooperation between the United Nations and regional organizations. As those arrangements posed considerable challenges, it reiterated its recommendation that the Secretary-General elaborate in his next progress report on how they could best be confronted. The Special Committee stressed that efforts to enhance the collective capacity of African countries to participate in peacekeeping operations should focus on increasing the institutional capacity of the Organization of African Unity (OAU), particularly its Mechanism for Conflict Prevention, Management and Resolution. Member States were urged to contribute to the OAU Peace Fund and to the trust fund established by the Secretary-General for enhancing the participation of African countries in peacekeeping operations. They were also urged to provide financial and other support to the study of peacekeeping operations conducted by African subregional organizations.

The Special Committee looked forward to the establishment of a group on the enhancement of African peacekeeping capacity and urged the Secretariat to continue its consultations on the group's terms of reference with a view to its timely establishment. It urged that discussion on the exchange of staff between the secretariats of the United Nations and OAU be concluded at the earliest opportunity, and encouraged the Secretariat to extend its efforts in subregional peacekeeping training and seminars to all African subregional organizations.

The Secretary-General, in his December report on the implementation of the recommendations of the Special Committee and the Panel on United Nations Peace Operations [A/56/732], said that, pursuant to the calls of the General Assembly and the Security Council for strengthening the UN partnership in peacekeeping activities with regional and subregional organizations, he had convened four high-level meetings of the United Nations and regional organizations aimed at establishing a clearer framework for cooperation in peace and security areas, including conflict prevention and peace-building. DPKO had prepared draft terms of reference for the proposed working group on the enhancement of African peacekeeping capacity and would resume consultations in order to fine-tune its provisions and seek agreement on the remaining elements for the establishment of the working group.

Over the preceding 14 months, DPKO had expended 30 per cent of its training efforts on enhancing peacekeeping capacity in Africa, including courses in Ghana, Kenya and Zimbabwe, UN military observer training in South Africa, leadership seminars/strategic studies in Botswana, a senior mission management seminar in Zimbabwe, gender and peacekeeping training courses for UNMEE, UNAMSIL and MONUC, assistance to a Southern African Development Community (SADC) planning seminar and the coordination of a disarmament, demobilization and reintegration seminar in Canada to enhance the African capacity. Support was also given to the French Reinforcement of African Peacekeeping Capacities project "Exercise Tanzanite", involving a military exercise for forces from all SADC countries, planned for 2002.

DPKO continued to facilitate contacts with African troop contributors to UN operations and donor States that could provide support in making up for the shortfalls in contingent-owned equipment and self-sustainment. Cooperation between DPKO and OAU in various aspects of peacekeeping activities had been growing steadily and comprised information exchange, peacekeeping training and the promotion of greater African participation in the UN standby arrangement system (see p. 77).

Within its staff exchange programme with OAU, DPKO arranged orientation/training in New York for the head of the OAU Early Warning Unit in the Conflict Management Centre (31 January–9 February) and was preparing to send an officer to OAU headquarters in Addis Ababa, Ethiopia, in early 2002, to train staff and assist in strengthening the OAU Situation Room. The United Nations maintained a liaison office at OAU headquarters.

The United Nations also maintained close working relations with SADC and the Economic Community of West African States (ECOWAS) with regard to peace efforts in the Democratic Republic of the Congo and Sierra Leone and cooperated with them in carrying out various joint activities aimed at enhancing African peacekeeping capacity. A coordination mechanism between the United Nations, ECOWAS and the Government of Sierra Leone was set up in 2000 at the initiative of the Secretary-General.

Over the preceding five years, the Balkans had been the stage for growing cooperation between DPKO and regional organizations, such as the European Union, the Organization for Security and Cooperation in Europe (OSCE) and the North Atlantic Treaty Organization (NATO). Both in Bosnia and Herzegovina and Yugoslavia's Kosovo province, NATO troops provided overall security and cooperated with UN civilian police, while OSCE had electoral and institution-building tasks. UNMIK's four-pillar structure (see PART ONE, Chapter V) offered a unique coordination model, which had prompted intensification of contacts between the Secretariat and the headquarters of European organizations in Brussels and Vienna. A NATO Liaison Officer had been assigned to DPKO, and the establishment of a United Nations Liaison Office in Brussels was under discussion.

Chapter II

Africa

Although Africa continued to be plagued by numerous conflicts in 2001, several of them showed signs of amelioration as political situations evolved and diplomatic efforts, including those by the United Nations, began to take effect and show positive results. The situation in war-affected countries was further complicated by problems of economic stagnation, flows of refugees and internally displaced persons, and the spread of HIV/AIDS. In some cases, for example Angola, the Democratic Republic of the Congo (DRC) and Sierra Leone, warfare was fuelled by the illegal trade in raw diamonds, known as "conflict" or "blood" diamonds, and the exploitation of other natural resources. Various UN bodies investigated that issue.

The General Assembly's working group on ways to implement the 1998 recommendations of the Secretary-General on the causes of conflict and the promotion of durable peace and sustainable development in Africa focused in 2001 on two themes—education, and conflict prevention and post-conflict peace-building—and made suggestions for further action in both areas. The Secretary-General issued his own report on follow-up action in the area of peace and security and reviewed UN action with regard to governance and sustainable development. The Assembly endorsed the working group's proposals for further action.

The area of major conflict continued to be the Great Lakes region, which was again dominated by events in the DRC, where war involved several opposition forces and troops from six neighbouring countries. Burundi, Rwanda and Uganda supported opposition groups in the DRC, and the Government was supported by Angola, Namibia and Zimbabwe. The Security Council dispatched a mission to eight countries of the region in May to assess the situation and make recommendations for resuming the road to peace. In January, President Laurent-Désiré Kabila was assassinated, and his son, Joseph Kabila, replaced him. Those events and statements by the new President were followed by a reduction in fighting; the opposing sides began disengaging from the confrontation line and Namibia and Uganda had withdrawn many of their troops from DRC territory by the end of the year. The United Nations Organization Mission in the Democratic Republic of the Congo (MONUC) was thus able to take up the next phase of its mandate—the observation and monitoring of the disarmament, demobilization and resettlement of combatants—which required the expansion of its peacekeeping force, and the Council extended the Mission's mandate until 15 June 2002. The ceasefire held in most of the country, with the exception of eastern DRC, where violations increased in late 2001. The factions and other interested parties met in an inter-Congolese dialogue on 15 October, but did not consider substantive issues.

In Burundi, the conflict between government forces and armed opposition groups continued, despite their agreement in 2000 to cease hostilities. The Facilitator of the peace process in that country, Nelson Mandela, intensified efforts to resolve the conflict and was able to bring the parties together to agree on a transitional government, which was installed on 1 November under a power-sharing formula.

The conflict in the DRC also continued to affect Rwanda, which maintained that its troops in the DRC were necessary to preserve its own security. The situation inside Rwanda remained calm and the Government focused on a transition to democracy and overhauling the justice system.

The internal situation of the Central African Republic deteriorated in 2001 as a result of an attempted coup d'état in May and other manifestations of political opposition. The lack of dialogue between the country's political stakeholders was a serious obstacle to the sustainability of the democratic institutions established a year before, and the country's economic situation was dire. The United Nations Peace-building Support Office in the Central African Republic, established in 2000, continued to support the Government's efforts to consolidate peace and national reconciliation.

Tensions also rose in West Africa in early 2001, especially in Guinea-Bissau, Liberia and Sierra Leone. However, there was encouraging progress towards peace and stability later in the year, especially in Sierra Leone. The Secretary-General dispatched an inter-agency mission to the region in March, which visited 11 countries and remarked on the stability of the political and security situation in the Mano River Union countries (Guinea, Liberia and Sierra Leone), Côte d'Ivoire, Guinea-Bissau and the Casamance region of Senegal. The mission urged the international community to adopt an integrated regional approach to prevent, manage and contribute to resolving the many conflicts in the region. Acting on its recommendations, the Secretary-General decided to establish the Office of the Special Representative for West Africa, as from January 2002.

The United Nations Mission in Sierra Leone (UNAMSIL), the size and scope of which was expanded by the Council during 2001, maintained contacts with the Government and the main rebel group to follow up on the implementation of the 2000 Abuja Ceasefire Agreement. Progress was reported, and the withdrawal of forces and disarmament were nearly completed by the end of the year. In September, the Council extended UNAMSIL's mandate until March 2002. Cross-border fighting along Sierra Leone's boundaries with Guinea and Liberia flared up in early 2001 but abated following a dialogue among the three countries. Acting on the Government's suggestion, the Secretary-General pursued efforts to establish a Special Court for Sierra Leone and decided to send a planning mission to that country in January 2002. In addition, the United Nations provided support for the establishment of a Truth and Reconciliation Commission in Sierra Leone, also expected to begin work in 2002.

Fighting in northern Liberia in early 2001 threatened the border regions in Guinea and Sierra Leone, as did Liberia's assistance to rebels in Sierra Leone. Liberia's support included exporting rough diamonds obtained in Sierra Leone, which reportedly financed the rebels' military efforts. The Council, in March, demanded that Liberia cease its support of the rebels and imposed an arms embargo against Liberia and sanctions against importing diamonds from Liberia. The tension between the Mano River Union countries decreased following ministerial meetings that began in August.

The Government of Guinea-Bissau, which had been formed in 2000 in accordance with the 1998 Abuja Peace Accord, remained precarious in 2001. The United Nations Peace-building Support Office in Guinea-Bissau continued to report on developments within the country and along its border with Senegal.

The Horn of Africa remained calm but tense in 2001. The subregion was beset by problems and struggled to overcome disputes, both bilateral, as in the case of the border dispute between Eritrea and Ethiopia, and internal, as in Somalia. Eritrea and Ethiopia generally continued to abide by the Peace Agreement they had signed in December 2000, but progress in its implementation was slow, particularly with regard to the demarcation of the boundary. The United Nations Mission in Ethiopia and Eritrea (UNMEE) monitored the ceasefire and the Temporary Security Zone between the two countries. In late 2001, Eritrea restricted movement of UNMEE in certain areas.

The humanitarian situation in Angola deteriorated significantly in 2001 as the conflict between the Government and the National Union for the Total Independence of Angola (UNITA) intensified and UNITA guerrilla attacks, particularly against civilians, increased in frequency. The number of people displaced as a result of the civil strife rose to 4.1 million by the end of the year. Matters changed towards the latter part of the year when the Government gained the upper hand in the fighting and reportedly moved into much of the area previously under UNITA control. The United Nations hoped that the new situation would provide a window of opportunity to advance the peace process and set the stage for elections. The Security Council, through its Sanctions Committee and the Monitoring Mechanism, continued to investigate violations of the sanctions against UNITA.

The United Nations pursued efforts to hold a referendum in Western Sahara for the self-determination of its people, as agreed in 1990 by Morocco and the Frente Popular para la Liberación de Saguia el-Hamra y de Río de Oro (POLISARIO), but progress was negligible. The Secretary-General's Personal Envoy proposed a different approach—for Morocco to retain responsibility for foreign relations, national security and defence, while executive, legislative and judicial bodies in the Territory would have competence over local issues. Morocco indicated its support for the plan, while POLISARIO and Algeria objected to it on the grounds that it provided for the integration of Western Sahara into Morocco. Meanwhile, the United Nations continued its work on identifying eligible voters for holding a referendum.

In January, the Scottish Court sitting in the Netherlands concluded its trial of two nationals of the Libyan Arab Jamahiriya accused of plotting the 1988 bombing of Pan Am flight 103 over Lockerbie, Scotland. One of the accused was found guilty and the other not guilty.

The Council, in September, having taken into account the Sudan's efforts to cooperate with the international community by acceding to anti-terrorism conventions, to improve relations with neighbouring countries and to discharge its obligations under various Council resolutions, terminated the sanctions it had imposed against that country in 1996.

Promotion of peace in Africa

During 2001, the General Assembly considered ways to implement the recommendations made by the Secretary-General in his 1998 report on the causes of conflict and the promotion of durable peace and sustainable development in Africa [YUN 1998, p. 66]. The Assembly's open-ended working group to follow up the recommendations, the mandate of which had been extended in late 2000 [YUN 2000, p. 116], focused on two themes—education, and conflict prevention and post-conflict peace-building—and made suggestions for further action in those areas. The Secretary-General also issued a progress report on the recommendations, describing specific action by UN organizations in the promotion of peace and security and developments in governance and sustainable development.

The Assembly endorsed the recommendations of the working group and requested the Secretary-General to designate the already established interdepartmental/inter-agency task force as the permanent focal point within the Secretariat to monitor their implementation.

In March, the Security Council held an open debate on ensuring its effective role in the maintenance of peace and security, particularly in Africa (see p. 47).

Working Group report. The Open-ended Ad Hoc Working Group on the Causes of Conflict and the Promotion of Durable Peace and Sustainable Development in Africa, established by General Assembly resolution 53/92 [YUN 1998, p. 77] to monitor implementation of the Secretary-General's 1998 recommendations on the topic, submitted a report on its 2001 activities to the Assembly [A/56/45], as requested by the Assembly in resolution 55/217 [YUN 2000, p. 117]. The Working Group held one organizational session (20 March) and two substantive sessions (29 May–1 June, 30 July–3 August) during the year. It adopted two themes as the focus of its discussions—education, and conflict prevention and post-conflict peace-building—and made suggestions for further action in those areas.

With regard to education for durable peace and sustainable development, the Working Group focused on the role of education in addressing the challenges of globalization and poverty eradication; development of technical, vocational and professional skills to respond to the knowledge-based economy and society; employability in a globalized world economy; contribution to science and technology; preventing the spread of HIV/AIDS; preventing and managing

conflicts; and promoting sustainable development in Africa. UN system programmes for education, including a number aimed at expanding access to education, especially at the primary level, and improving the quality of education, were considered. While such efforts were commendable, the Working Group observed, the human resources capacity in many African countries remained inadequate to respond to challenges; the low enrolment rates in primary education (77 per cent) and the low school enrolment rates of girls (under 75 per cent) in many African countries would undermine economic growth and sustainable development.

As to conflict prevention and post-conflict peace-building, the Working Group noted the large number of ongoing conflicts in Africa, estimated at 17. To address those conflicts, the Secretary-General had used a variety of mechanisms, including the appointment of special envoys and representatives who worked closely with regional and subregional organizations and others to address the conflicts, as was the case with the Ethiopia-Eritrea conflict and conflicts in the Democratic Republic of the Congo (DRC) and Burundi. The Secretary-General's establishment in March of the Inter-Agency Mission to West Africa was an important initiative to develop a coordinated and global approach to conflict prevention. It aimed to mobilize UN bodies to address the multifaceted problems confronting the Mano River Union countries and to integrate UN efforts with those of the Economic Community of West African States (ECOWAS). It would focus on issues that might threaten peace and security in the region, such as arms flows, the illegal exploitation of strategic natural resources, mass refugee movements, mercenaries and terrorist activities. A number of UN offices had been established in Africa, including in Burundi, the Central African Republic, Guinea-Bissau and Liberia, to promote peace and national reconciliation, the strengthening of democratic institutions and governance structures, the harmonization of UN peace-building activities, international support for post-conflict peace-building activities, the facilitation of communications between the Governments of neighbouring countries, the coordination of activities of regional organizations and bilateral donors, and assistance in disarmament and the demobilization and reintegration of ex-combatants into civilian life. The United Nations also cooperated with the Organization of African Unity (OAU) in developing specific capacities in OAU for conflict prevention, management and resolution. The United Nations Development Fund for Women provided support to strengthen women's leadership role in the peace process at the regional and interregional levels; for example, it supported women's participation in the peace processes in Burundi and Somalia.

The Working Group made suggestions for further action in the two thematic areas. It encouraged the Assembly to call on the international community to provide assistance to African countries to achieve universal primary education, eliminate gender disparities in primary and secondary education by 2005 and achieve gender equality in education by 2015. The Group welcomed innovative programmes that increased access to education and retention of children in schools by providing incentives and called on countries to share successful experiences. It recognized the need to increase the use of information and communications technology in training, institutional capacity-building and education, and to develop the skills required by the new knowledge-based world economy. The role of education was also emphasized in preventing the spread of HIV/AIDS, malaria, tuberculosis and other diseases. As Africa's external debt continued to divert its resources from development activities, including education, the Working Group called for the implementation of the enhanced Heavily Indebted Poor Countries Initiative for eligible African countries through new resources. Developed countries were urged to grant more development assistance. The Working Group proposed that UN system organizations assist interested African countries in developing curricula that provided access to information and communications technology.

With respect to conflict prevention and post-conflict peace-building, the Working Group called for international support for African countries that were promoting regional peace and resolution of conflicts and proposed the collaboration of civil society with organizations making such efforts. The Group believed that economic growth supportive of poverty eradication and development should be at the core of conflict-prevention strategies. All partners should support economic growth, reconstruction and recovery, national peace-building efforts in promoting good governance and strengthening the rule of law. The root causes of conflict were numerous, but poverty was nearly always a related issue and it needed to be addressed in the peace process. The international community should increase support for African efforts in that regard by addressing poverty eradication through debt cancellation, improved market access, enhanced official development assistance, increased flows of foreign direct investment and transfer of technology; making linkages between

the economic and social dimensions of poverty reduction strategies, and assisting in monitoring and analysis; promoting policies that were pro-poor and gender-sensitive; and supporting African policies towards job creation. Demobilization, disarmament and reintegration programmes should also be supported, in particular through the regular budget of peacekeeping operations. The Group further recommended that post-conflict peace-building be supported by international assistance to UN offices in Africa; assistance to African countries for including peace-building activities in their planning and budgetary processes; support for the efforts of civil society to work for peace; mechanisms to address illicit trade in natural resources and arms; support for rehabilitation; and promotion of good governance and transparency in financial and trading systems.

Having considered the multiplicity of initiatives in the UN system to address the recommendations in the Secretary-General's report, the Working Group recommended that the Assembly suspend the Group's activities during the Assembly's fifty-sixth (2001) session to allow Member States to appraise the outcome of other UN initiatives on Africa. It proposed that a permanent focal point be established within the Secretariat to monitor progress by the UN system in implementing the Secretary-General's recommendations.

Report of Secretary-General. In response to General Assembly resolution 55/217 [YUN 2000, p. 117], the Secretary-General, in a September report [A/56/371], updated the 1999 progress report [YUN 1999, p. 78] on the implementation of his 1998 recommendations on the causes of conflict and promotion of durable peace and sustainable development in Africa. Affirming that the recommendations remained valid, he described specific follow-up action, mainly by UN organizations, in the matters of peace and security and gave an overview of developments in governance and sustainable development.

Concerning peacemaking, the Secretary-General continued to appoint special mediators and representatives. Commissions of inquiry had also been established to investigate allegations of massacres in Togo and killings in Côte d'Ivoire after the 2000 presidential elections [YUN 2000, p. 230]. The key objective of such commissions was to discourage a sense of impunity and to deter similar action. The UN system was mobilizing the international community to support post-conflict countries by convening donor conferences, including those held for Burundi, the Central African Republic and the DRC in 2000. The Secretariat was continuing efforts to improve the effectiveness of sanctions, and consultations had been held with a number of African States with a view to encouraging them to pass legislation making the violation of a Security Council arms embargo a criminal offence. Efforts were also made to stop the proliferation of arms and reduce the purchase of arms and munitions to below 1.5 per cent of gross domestic product while maintaining a zero-growth budget for military expenditure, through, for example, support for various disarmament registers, declarations and activities. The United Nations remained committed to supporting disarmament initiatives, such as the Declaration concerning Firearms, Ammunition and Other Related Materials in the Southern African Development Community (SADC), adopted in March [A/CONF.192/PC/35].

UN peacekeeping efforts included support for African peacekeeping capacity, in consultation with OAU, ECOWAS, SADC and others. The United Nations provided specific services to support Africa's own initiatives to resolve disputes and the Secretary-General continued to urge Member States to contribute bilaterally and multilaterally to UN and OAU trust funds for peacekeeping. Protecting civilians in situations of conflict had become an important aspect of UN peacekeeping operations, and the mandates of the UN missions in the DRC and Sierra Leone included the responsibility for providing protection to civilians under imminent threat of physical violence. To address refugee security, which was also a concern in conflict situations, the Office of the United Nations High Commissioner for Refugees (UNHCR) had decided to establish arrangements with some Governments to provide law and order and public security experts to be deployed at the beginning of a refugee crisis and to work with local public security institutions. Programmes were already in place in Kenya and the United Republic of Tanzania, where UNHCR provided material support for the deployment of police forces to ensure law and order in and around refugee camps.

Post-conflict peace-building included UN provision of emergency assistance to create the preconditions necessary for reconstruction and development. Such assistance was being provided by the peace-building support offices in the Central African Republic, Guinea-Bissau and Liberia. Their activities included encouraging reconciliation and respect for human rights; fostering political inclusiveness; promoting national unity; ensuring repatriation and resettlement of refugees and displaced persons; reintegrating ex-combatants; and curtailing the availability of arms.

With regard to good governance, the Secretary-General, in his 1998 report [YUN 1998, p. 66], had urged African countries to enact legislation to combat bribery and set out a uniform African convention on the conduct of public officials and the transparency of public administration. While very little progress had been made in that regard, the United Nations continued to encourage African countries to implement the Secretary-General's recommendations and to advocate the repatriation of the illegally acquired wealth that was transferred to Western banks by some corrupt African leaders and officials, and the adequate remuneration of African civil servants for their work. The United Nations was also promoting good governance by strengthening the administrative capacity of African countries.

UN efforts to promote sustainable development in Africa included projects that created a positive environment for investment and economic growth; investing in human resources; pursuing public health priorities, such as reduction of HIV/AIDS and malaria; eliminating all forms of discrimination against women; restructuring international aid and reducing the debt burden; opening international markets to African products; providing support for regional cooperation and integration; and harmonizing current international and bilateral initiatives.

The Secretary-General observed that the fact that a significant number of the least developed countries in Africa were also conflict-prone countries underlined the interrelationship between peace and development. In proposing a new global partnership with their development partners (see p. 899), African leaders had committed themselves to strengthening mechanisms for conflict prevention, management and resolution, and to promoting and protecting democracy and human rights by developing standards of accountability, transparency and participative governance. Such goals could be achieved more quickly with support from the international community. The Group of Eight industrialized countries, at their summit meeting (Genoa, Italy, July) [A/56/222-S/2001/736], adopted a Plan for Africa, which the United Nations hoped would complement its efforts. The obstacles remained immense—the reversals in human development over the previous 15 years, increased poverty levels, the devastation caused by HIV/AIDS and the destruction of infrastructure caused by conflict. Since his previous report [YUN 1999, p. 78], the Secretary-General noted, the war in Ethiopia and Eritrea had ended and a UN peacekeeping operation was patrolling the ceasefire line and helping to solidify peaceful relations, and there were signs of better prospects in Burundi, the DRC and Sierra Leone, although the crisis in Liberia and Sierra Leone was spreading to Guinea. Progress had been made in implementing many of the earlier recommendations, but much more needed to be done to improve political and economic governance and to stop the proliferation of small arms in Africa. Reducing poverty continued to be the biggest challenge for the region, and mobilization of domestic and external resources was urgent. The region would continue to rely on a strong and committed international partnership.

Communications. On 29 October [S/2001/1031], the Secretary-General informed the Security Council President of his decision to extend the appointment of his Special Adviser on Africa, Mohamed Sahnoun (Algeria), until 31 December 2002. He stated that Mr. Sahnoun had been following developments in the Horn of Africa subregion (see p. 191), especially Somalia and the Sudan, and had provided assessment and advice on a possible UN role in those countries. He had also represented the Secretary-General in meetings of the Intergovernmental Authority on Development (IGAD) and the IGAD Partners Forum devoted to the two countries. On 31 October [S/2001/1032], the Council President replied that the Council had taken note of his decision.

GENERAL ASSEMBLY ACTION

On 4 December [meeting 74], the General Assembly adopted **resolution 56/37** [draft: A/56/L.28 & Add.1, orally revised] without vote [agenda item 48].

Causes of conflict and the promotion of durable peace and sustainable development in Africa

The General Assembly,

Having considered the report of the Open-ended Ad Hoc Working Group on the Causes of Conflict and the Promotion of Durable Peace and Sustainable Development in Africa and the progress report of the Secretary-General,

Recalling its resolutions 53/92 of 7 December 1998, 54/234 of 22 December 1999 and 55/217 of 21 December 2000 on the causes of conflict and the promotion of durable peace and sustainable development in Africa,

Recalling also its resolution 46/151 of 18 December 1991, the annex to which contains the United Nations New Agenda for the Development of Africa in the 1990s, its resolutions 48/214 of 23 December 1993, 49/142 of 23 December 1994 and 51/32 of 6 December 1996, on the midterm review of the New Agenda, and its resolution 53/90 of 7 December 1998 on the implementation of the New Agenda, as well as chapter VII of the United Nations Millennium Declaration,

Reaffirming that the implementation of the recommendations contained in the report of the Secretary-General constitutes a priority that must remain high on the agenda of the United Nations system and Member States,

Reaffirming also that the General Assembly, as the chief policy-making and representative organ of the United Nations, must continue to play the primary role in monitoring the implementation of the recommendations contained in the report of the Secretary-General and assessing the progress made,

Emphasizing the need to strengthen further the political will to ensure the political, financial, technical and other support critical for the effective implementation of the recommendations contained in the report of the Secretary-General not only in the two thematic areas—education and conflict prevention and post-conflict peace-building—of the deliberations of the Working Group in 2001, but also in all the areas mentioned in the report,

Welcoming the adoption by the Assembly of Heads of State and Government of the Organization of African Unity at its thirty-seventh ordinary session, held at Lusaka from 9 to 11 July 2001, of the New African Initiative (now called New Partnership for Africa's Development),

Mindful of the ministerial declaration of the high-level segment of the substantive session of 2001 of the Economic and Social Council, on the role of the United Nations system in supporting the efforts of African countries to achieve sustainable development,

1. *Takes note with appreciation* of the report of the Open-ended Ad Hoc Working Group on the Causes of Conflict and the Promotion of Durable Peace and Sustainable Development in Africa and the progress report of the Secretary-General;

2. *Notes with deep concern* that access to education at all levels in Africa remains low, despite the recognition that education plays a central role in conflict prevention and the promotion of durable peace and sustainable development;

3. *Also notes with deep concern* that, while some efforts have been made in the prevention and settlement of conflicts, such efforts have not often brought positive results;

4. *Endorses* the recommendations entitled "Suggestions for further action and measures", contained in paragraphs 35 to 56 of the report of the Working Group;

5. *Decides* to suspend the activities of the Working Group during the fifty-sixth session of the General Assembly in order to consider further measures for the implementation and monitoring of initiatives on Africa, including the ministerial declaration of the high-level segment of the substantive session of 2001 of the Economic and Social Council, in the light of the forthcoming review of the United Nations New Agenda for the Development of Africa in the 1990s and related initiatives, all of which should be guided by the New Partnership for Africa's Development;

6. *Invites* the Working Group to re-examine its mandate during the fifty-seventh session of the General Assembly, including the most appropriate way to proceed with the deliberations of the Working Group as well as the scope and nature of its work;

7. *Decides* to continue to monitor the implementation of the recommendations contained in the report of the Secretary-General on causes of conflict and the promotion of durable peace and sustainable development in Africa;

8. *Requests* the Secretary-General to submit to the General Assembly at its fifty-seventh session a comprehensive report on the implementation of the recommendations contained in his report, including concrete measures needed to ensure a coordinated and

integrated approach to the full and early implementation of the recommendations;

9. *Requests* that the Secretary-General designate the already established interdepartmental/inter-agency task force as the permanent focal point within the Secretariat mandated to monitor the implementation of the recommendations contained in his report, and also requests that the task force be strengthened with the necessary human, managerial and administrative resources effectively to carry out this task;

10. *Also requests* that the task force provide Member States, on an annual basis, with updated matrices indicating the current status of implementation of the various recommendations contained in the report of the Secretary-General.

Central Africa and Great Lakes region

The situation in the Great Lakes region of Africa in 2001 continued to be shaped by events in the Democratic Republic of the Congo (DRC), where the conflict involved a number of opposition forces, most of them based on ethnic groups, and troops from six neighbouring States. There was a significant improvement in security as the result of the partial withdrawal of foreign troops from the DRC and the change in leadership of that country following the assassination of President Laurent-Désiré Kabila in January. His son, Joseph Kabila, assumed his father's position. Those changes gave grounds for cautious hope for positive change and resumption of the peace process under the 1999 Lusaka Ceasefire Agreement [YUN 1999, p. 87]. Under the improved circumstances, the opposing sides began disengaging from the confrontation line and redeploying to new defensive positions, as verified by the United Nations Organization Mission in the Democratic Republic of the Congo (MONUC). That move allowed the Mission to begin the next phase of its mandate—to observe and monitor the disarmament, demobilization and resettlement of the combatants—with an expanded peacekeeping force of nearly 3,000 troops by the end of the year. Efforts were made to bring the opposing political factions together at an inter-Congolese dialogue to discuss re-establishment of the State administration in all areas of the DRC; however, that goal remained elusive at the end of the year. Throughout 2001, the ceasefire was observed by the opposing forces in most of the country with the exception of eastern DRC, where fighting intensified in the later months. Much of the conflict focused on control of natural resources in that area, and it benefited many of the opposing

parties to prolong rather than end the fighting. The plundering of the DRC's natural resources was the subject of a report by an expert panel set up by the Security Council to investigate the phenomenon.

Progress in peacemaking efforts was also achieved in Burundi, where armed factions, generally divided into two ethnic groups, and government forces continued the conflict despite most of them having signed the Arusha Agreement on Peace and Reconciliation in 2000 [YUN 2000, p. 146]. That Agreement, a framework for political reform, served as the basis for negotiations in 2001 under the UN-appointed Facilitator, Nelson Mandela. Although no ceasefire was in place, the parties were able to reach agreement on establishing a transitional government, which was installed on 1 November under a power-sharing formula.

In Rwanda, the situation remained generally calm as the country made efforts to overcome the ill-effects of the 1994 genocide through changes in government and the justice system and promoting human rights. The Government, which maintained troops in the DRC, expressed concern about the security of its borders with that country.

In May, the Security Council dispatched a mission to the Great Lakes region to assess the situation and make recommendations for resuming the peace process. At that time, the ceasefire in the DRC was holding and the mission stressed the urgency of taking advantage of the window of opportunity to move the peace process forward. At the same time, the Council was struck by the intractability of the situation in Burundi.

The Central African Republic was affected by events in the DRC, but its problems stemmed mainly from civil unrest and lack of dialogue between the Government and opposition parties that had contributed to internal tension since a 1996 army rebellion. Efforts to achieve national reconciliation were set back in May following an attempted coup d'état and the Government's questions about the loyalty of certain members of the armed forces.

Security Council consideration. At a 7 February meeting [meeting 4273], during which it considered the situation in the Great Lakes region, the Security Council was addressed by the Secretary-General and President Paul Kagame of Rwanda. The Secretary-General pointed out that President Kagame had met the previous week in Washington, D.C., with DRC President Joseph Kabila to discuss the challenges facing both countries and the entire region. The issues of governance, national dialogue, democracy, accountability and reconciliation needed to be addressed in the DRC and in the region as a whole if there was to be a lasting solution in the Great Lakes. There was also the issue of the continued existence of predatory armed groups. All countries of the region, in particular Rwanda, had legitimate security concerns. Council members had expressed the need to seize the current opportunity in the DRC to implement the Lusaka Ceasefire Agreement. The withdrawal of Rwandan forces and their allies from the town of Pweto, currently under discussion between the MONUC Force Commander and the authorities in Kigali and the DRC, would serve as a confidence-building measure and as an important step towards compliance with Council resolution 1304(2000) [YUN 2000, p. 131]. The Secretary-General expressed the hope that the resolution of the conflict in the DRC would bring peace to the entire Great Lakes region and in particular to Rwanda.

Confirming his country's willingness to fulfil its obligations under the Lusaka peace process, President Kagame pointed to three core issues that needed to be addressed to have that process succeed: the inter-Congolese dialogue, called for in the Lusaka Agreement, to find a stable internal situation so that DRC problems would not affect the neighbouring countries; the problem of former Rwandan Armed Forces (ex-FAR) and Interahamwe forces, which threatened security in the region; and the withdrawal of foreign forces from the DRC [S/PV.4273].

Security Council mission. Following consultations, Security Council members agreed to dispatch a mission to the Great Lakes region in late May. The Council President, in a letter of 25 April [S/2001/408], requested the Secretary-General to ensure that the Secretariat made all the necessary arrangements. The President also forwarded the mission's terms of reference, which pertained specifically to the situations in the DRC (see below) and Burundi (see p. 145). The mission's report [S/2001/521 & Add.1] contained recommendations on ways to pursue the peace process in the two countries (see p. 124).

Addressing the Council on 30 May [meeting 4323], the head of the mission (French Ambassador Jean-David Levitte) explained that 12 Council members had visited eight countries and in 10 days met with 10 heads of State and two Facilitators—former Presidents Ketumile Masire of Botswana, for the inter-Congolese dialogue, and Nelson Mandela of South Africa, for Burundi—and with representatives of political parties, civil society and armed groups. There was a feeling that a real window of opportunity existed for the DRC to move towards peace, particularly in view of the leadership of President Joseph Kabila and

the fact that the ceasefire had been holding for four months. The Secretary-General commented on the change in the political climate within the DRC and progress in the inter-Congolese dialogue, the linkage between the conflicts in the DRC and Burundi, the disengagement of troops and the liberalization of political life [S/PV.4323].

Communications. The DRC, in a 26 June letter to the Security Council President [S/2001/634], expressed the readiness of President Joseph Kabila to meet his Burundian, Rwandan and Ugandan counterparts to discuss the withdrawal of foreign troops from Congolese territory and the pacification of the region. The Presidency of the European Union (EU), in a 9 October statement on the Great Lakes region transmitted to the Secretary-General on 15 October [S/2001/979], welcomed the August meeting led by the Facilitator for the DRC, Sir Ketumile Masire, that had opened up the way for the inter-Congolese dialogue on 15 October. The EU underlined the need for the signatory States and other parties to the Lusaka Agreement to demonstrate the political will required to end support for the negative forces. With regard to Burundi, the agreement reached in late July on guiding the transition in Burundi, led by the Facilitator, Mr. Mandela, also opened up new prospects, although those were still fragile in the absence of a ceasefire.

On 16 November [S/2001/1095], the Secretary-General informed the Council President of his intention to extend the mandate of his Special Representative for the Great Lakes Region, Berhanu Dinka, for another year, until 31 December 2002. Mr. Dinka had been soliciting the views of countries in the region regarding the proposed organization of an International Conference on the Great Lakes; representing the Secretary-General at meetings under the Arusha peace process on Burundi; and addressing the regional dimensions of the conflict in the DRC through interaction with the Special Representative in that country. The Council, on 21 November [S/2001/1096], took note of the Secretary-General's intention.

Democratic Republic of the Congo

The DRC remained at the centre of regional strife in 2001, albeit at reduced levels of fighting, as it had since the beginning of the conflict in 1998, which eventually involved seven neighbouring countries and numerous rebel groups. Burundi, Rwanda and Uganda, at times allied with various rebel factions, supported opposition to the DRC Government, which in turn was supported, at its request, by Angola, Namibia and Zimbabwe.

On 16 January, President Laurent-Désiré Kabila was assassinated. His son, Major General Joseph Kabila, was nominated as President. The change in leadership provided a window of opportunity for renewed efforts to pursue the implementation of the 1999 Lusaka Ceasefire Agreement [YUN 1999, p. 87] signed by the Government of the DRC, one of the two main rebel movements and five regional States. The Agreement provided for a ceasefire to be monitored by MONUC, OAU and Zambia; withdrawal of foreign forces from the country; and re-establishment of State administration throughout the country. MONUC, with a mandate to facilitate the implementation of the Agreement, began expanding its force from 200 troops at the beginning of the year. With a mandated force of 5,500, MONUC reached a total of approximately 3,000 troops by the end of 2001, and the Security Council extended its mandate until 15 June 2002. The rapid expansion of MONUC was made possible by the disengagement of forces from the confrontation line and their redeployment to new defensive positions, as verified by the Mission. MONUC began establishing four coordination centres to provide command for the military observers in areas distant from its headquarters in Kinshasa. At the same time, some foreign forces were withdrawn from Congolese territory and the Government began to demobilize some of its troops. By the end of the year, Namibia and Uganda had greatly reduced their forces in the DRC, and Angola had announced its intention to withdraw some troops. Rwandan troops remained in the country. Having verified the disengagement and redeployment of opposing forces, MONUC was able to commence the third phase of its operations and began to plan disarmament, demobilization, repatriation, resettlement and reintegration of the combatants.

In general, the ceasefire held throughout the year in much of the country, with the exception of eastern DRC, where violations were on the rise by late 2001. The Secretary-General, who visited the region in September, and the neutral Facilitator, Sir Ketumile Masire, urged the Governments of both the DRC and Rwanda to use all their influence to end the fighting in the east and to open a dialogue.

Efforts were made to bring the warring factions and other interested parties together at an inter-Congolese dialogue, which took place on 15 October in Addis Ababa, Ethiopia. The meeting did not address any substantive issues, which led the Facilitator to adjourn the dialogue until 2002. An informal meeting in preparation for the dialogue was held in Abuja, Nigeria, from 6 to 8 December.

An expert panel established by the Security Council to investigate the illegal exploitation of natural resources of the DRC reported in 2001 that the plundering of those resources continued unabated. Over the years of conflict, the exploitation had become systematic and systemic, with networks having been developed for channelling extracted resources, first by Rwanda and Uganda and later by individual actors, including army commanders, businessmen and government structures. The panel made a number of recommendations for halting the illegal exploitation, including sanctions against countries and individuals involved in those activities.

On 7 September, the General Assembly decided to include in the draft agenda of its fifty-sixth (2001) session the item on armed aggression against the DRC (**decision 55/502**). On 24 December, it decided that the item would remain for consideration at its resumed fifty-sixth (2002) session (**decision 56/464**).

Political and military developments

Change in leadership

At the beginning of 2001, the political and military situation in the DRC was at a standstill despite intense diplomatic activity and personal initiatives of heads of State in the region during 2000. Broad agreement on the key questions to put the peace process back on track had not been achieved, and military activity, although relatively quiet, was observed in several areas throughout the country. The situation changed on 16 January with the assassination of President Laurent-Désiré Kabila in Kinshasa by a member of the presidential bodyguard.

Report of Secretary-General (February). The Secretary-General reported that event and consequent political and military developments in his sixth report on MONUC [S/2001/128], issued in February, as requested by the Security Council in resolution 1332(2000) [YUN 2000, p. 139]. On 17 January, Major General Joseph Kabila, the son of the former President, was entrusted with the powers of head of State and Commander-in-Chief of the Congolese Armed Forces (FAC) by ministers and senior military officers, a decision approved by the Congolese transitional parliament but rejected by both rebel groups and some elements of the Congolese political class.

On 21 January, the heads of State of Angola, Namibia and Zimbabwe issued a communiqué in which they undertook to maintain their respective military forces in the DRC and reinforce the security of the population. They encouraged all parties to search for a political solution to the conflict and called on the United Nations to deploy additional military observers. The new President, in meetings with the Secretary-General's Special Representative, Kamel Morjane (Tunisia), affirmed his desire to implement Council resolutions, particularly those relating to the process of disengagement of forces, the withdrawal of foreign forces and the inter-Congolese dialogue. Addressing the Congolese people on 26 January, Mr. Kabila called for the immediate withdrawal of Burundian, Rwandan and Ugandan forces from Congolese territory, and advocated a policy of dialogue and reconciliation with neighbouring States. He committed himself to working to relaunch the Lusaka Agreement and indicated that he would seek national reconciliation through political dialogue. He called for further engagement of OAU in a process of co-facilitation of the inter-Congolese dialogue. Once peace was established, he envisaged that elections would be held.

Addressing the Security Council on 2 February [meeting 4271], Mr. Kabila said that, despite many efforts over the previous two years, forces from Burundi, Rwanda and Uganda remained on DRC soil. Expressing hope for relaunching the Lusaka Agreement, he added that, to be effective, the Agreement needed to be reinforced by a mechanism that could punish the parties that violated the ceasefire and did not respect the deployment and disengagement measures. He sought the Council's agreement in four areas: the disengagement of opposing troops; the deployment of UN troops; the unconditional withdrawal of uninvited forces; and the withdrawal of troops from countries that were invited.

Following the assassination, the rebel movements denied any involvement and reaffirmed their commitment to the Lusaka Agreement. All rebel leaders called for progress in convening the inter-Congolese dialogue stipulated in the Agreement and denounced the installation of Joseph Kabila as President. Rebel leaders were unanimous in demanding the establishment of a transitional government. On 17 January, three rebel movements merged to form the Front de libération du Congo (FLC), comprising the Mouvement pour la libération du Congo (MLC), the Rassemblement congolais pour la démocratie-Mouvement de libération (RCD-ML) and RCD-National (RCD-N). The new group envisaged a single military force opposing the government side.

Continuing in his role as neutral Facilitator of the inter-Congolese dialogue, Sir Ketumile Masire enjoyed the support of the rebel movements and main political parties. Although the new President did not withdraw the Government's rejection of Sir Ketumile, he called for a francophone co-facilitator.

The Secretary-General described military developments in the DRC during the reporting period (December 2000–February 2001). Though much of the country remained quiet, military action was observed in border areas. As called for in Security Council resolution 1304(2000) [YUN 2000, p. 131], Rwanda and Uganda kept their forces at a distance of some 100 kilometres from Kisangani. However, RCD military elements remained in the city, with their leaders maintaining that security concerns did not allow them to withdraw their forces before the arrival of UN troops. The area around the city had been de facto divided into quadrants, each occupied by rebel factions. The areas were generally respected, except for isolated skirmishes between RCD and MLC/RCD-N in the diamond mining area north of the city. The opposition parties, with the exception of MLC, ratified the detailed sub-plans for disengagement and redeployment in Harare, Zimbabwe, on 6 December. However, there had been no movement in that regard. Nor had there been any indication of withdrawal of Rwandan and Ugandan forces from the DRC, estimated to number 20,000 and 10,000, respectively, as the Council had called for in resolution 1304(2000). On the government side, it was estimated that there were approximately 12,000 Zimbabwean, 7,000 Angolan and 2,000 Namibian troops deployed in the DRC.

As at 8 February, MONUC had a total of 200 military personnel deployed to the headquarters of the rebel movements (Bunia, Gbadolite, Goma), the four regional joint military commissions (Boende, Kabalo, Kabinda, Lisala) and six other locations (Gemena, Isiro, Kananga, Kindu, Kisangani, Mbandaka). A team was also deployed in Nchelenge, northern Zambia. Twenty-three liaison officers were stationed in the capitals of surrounding countries and one was with OAU in Addis Ababa. In South Kivu, attacks by armed groups had forced international agencies to suspend many of their operations; that threat precluded MONUC deployment in the eastern provinces.

The number of internally displaced persons in the DRC was 2 million and was expected to rise further; when added to the refugee population, the total was estimated to be over 2,335,000. Fewer than half received humanitarian assistance (see also pp. 833 and 1117). Numerous human rights violations had continued with impunity (see p. 697), compounded by renewed outbreaks of political and ethnic tensions, which took the form of clashes between various armed groups and ethnic groups.

On the basis of experience gained since MO-NUC's first deployment in the DRC in 1999 [YUN 1999, p. 94], the UN Secretariat developed a revised draft concept of operations for the monitoring of actions taken by the parties in compliance with the disengagement and redeployment plan signed in Harare on 6 December 2000. The deployment of up to 550 military observers was envisaged, together with 1,900 armed personnel. Two riverine units were also planned with the necessary rotary and fixed-wing air assets. The military personnel required would total 3,000 officers and other ranks. The Harare disengagement plan allowed two weeks for the verification phase, which would begin once the parties had disengaged and moved to designated areas; thereafter MONUC would verify and monitor the plan across the four areas. The Secretary-General also intended to deploy civilian staff, including political, human rights, humanitarian, public information and child protection officers, to the Mission area as the operation proceeded.

In general, the Secretary-General found that the change in President had marked a new stage in the UN consideration of the DRC conflict and gave grounds for cautious optimism regarding the peace process. One hopeful sign was that the DRC Government might be willing to accept Sir Ketumile Masire, the neutral Facilitator.

Communications. The DRC, on 10 January [S/2001/29], informed the Security Council President that Rwanda was still waging an offensive in the DRC province of Katanga and had tried to involve Zambia in the war of aggression against the DRC. The DRC welcomed the neutrality displayed by Zambia. On 12 January [S/2001/41], Rwanda asserted that the DRC Government and its allies continued to violate the Lusaka Agreement and were poised to attack the Rwandan forces in Katanga province. Referring to a charge made by the DRC in 2000 [YUN 2000, p. 141] that Zambian territory was being used by Rwandan and other forces to launch attacks into the DRC, Zambia, on 12 January [S/2001/77], asserted that it had been and would remain neutral with regard to the conflict in the DRC.

Following the assassination of President Laurent-Désiré Kabila, Uganda, on 18 January [S/2001/60], refuted charges by the DRC Defence Minister that Uganda was involved, and appealed to the new leadership to follow the Lusaka peace process. On 19 January [S/2001/65], Rwanda also denied charges about its involvement in the assassination and expressed support for the peace process. The EU, in a 22 January statement [S/2001/97], expressed support for the Lusaka Agreement as the consensual basis for peace and called on all parties to show restraint.

Lusaka summit

The heads of State of the signatory countries to the Lusaka Peace Agreement met in Lusaka, Zambia, on 15 February, reviving hopes for progress in the peace process. At the meeting, the new DRC President gave assurances of his acceptance of Sir Ketumile Masire as the neutral Facilitator of the inter-Congolese dialogue. The parties also committed themselves to the Kampala plan [YUN 2000, p. 126] and the Harare sub-plans for disengagement and redeployment of forces, signed in April and December 2000, respectively.

Rwanda, on 18 February [S/2001/147], taking note of the statement issued at the conclusion of the Lusaka summit, welcomed the declaration of the DRC President that the neutral Facilitator would be invited to begin consultations with the interested parties with a view to beginning the dialogue as soon as possible, and the announced deployment of the second phase of MONUC by 26 February. Rwanda also reaffirmed its earlier offer to pull back the Rwanda Patriotic Army (RPA) to new positions, not less than 200 kilometres from all forward positions, beginning on 28 February in Pweto. It hoped that other parties would remain committed to the disarmament of the ex-FAR and Interahamwe, as stipulated in the Agreement.

On 20 February [S/2001/150], Uganda issued a statement on the Lusaka summit in which it expressed support for the Kampala disengagement plan and subsequent sub-plans. It welcomed the improved rapport of the DRC Government with MONUC; the DRC commitment to dialogue facilitated by Sir Ketumile; the planned deployment of MONUC observers; and the consensus reached at the summit to implement area-to-area disengagement and redeployment plans. As a demonstration of its commitment to the peace process, Uganda would withdraw two battalions from the DRC in addition to the five already withdrawn in August 2000, and it hoped the other parties would follow so as to make possible a total withdrawal of all foreign forces.

Implementation of Lusaka Agreement

The Security Council considered the Secretary-General's February report on MONUC at meetings on 21 and 22 February, which were attended by members of the Political Committee for the Implementation of the Lusaka Ceasefire Agreement (the parties to the Agreement, OAU and the United Nations), and discussed further deployment of MONUC.

Addressing the Council on 21 February [meeting 4279], the Secretary-General noted the recent positive changes in the DRC: the parties had been talking to each other at the highest levels; the

Congolese people were able to take part in the governance of their country; and a cessation of hostilities prevailed throughout much of the country. Although the country remained divided by a line of confrontation between the forces of five foreign armies, agreement had been reached for them to pull back as a first step towards a withdrawal of all foreign forces from the DRC. Under his concept of operations, MONUC would monitor and verify the disengagement. The dire humanitarian crisis also needed to be addressed.

In official communiqués on private meetings of the Council with the Political Committee on 21 [S/PV.4280] and 22 [S/PV.4281] February, it was stated that a constructive dialogue had taken place and that Sir Ketumile Masire had responded to questions posed by Council members.

SECURITY COUNCIL ACTION

On 22 February [meeting 4282], the Security Council unanimously adopted **resolution 1341 (2001)**. The draft [S/2001/157] was prepared in consultations among Council members.

The Security Council,

Recalling its resolutions 1234(1999) of 9 April 1999, 1258(1999) of 6 August 1999, 1265(1999) of 17 September 1999, 1273(1999) of 5 November 1999, 1279(1999) of 30 November 1999, 1291(2000) of 24 February 2000, 1296(2000) of 19 April 2000, 1304(2000) of 15 June 2000, 1323(2000) of 13 October 2000 and 1332(2000) of 14 December 2000 and the statements by its President of 13 July 1998 (S/PRST/1998/20), 31 August 1998 (S/PRST/1998/26), 11 December 1998 (S/PRST/1998/36), 24 June 1999 (S/PRST/1999/17), 26 January 2000 (S/PRST/2000/2), 5 May 2000 (S/PRST/2000/15), 2 June 2000 (S/PRST/2000/20) and 7 September 2000 (S/PRST/2000/28),

Reaffirming the sovereignty, territorial integrity and political independence of the Democratic Republic of the Congo and of all States in the region,

Reaffirming also the obligation of all States to refrain from the use of force against the territorial integrity and political independence of any State, or in any other manner inconsistent with the purposes of the United Nations,

Reaffirming further the sovereignty of the Democratic Republic of the Congo over its natural resources, and noting with concern reports of the illegal exploitation of the country's assets and the potential consequences of these actions for security conditions and the continuation of hostilities,

Expressing its alarm at the dire consequences of the prolonged conflict for the civilian population throughout the territory of the Democratic Republic of the Congo, in particular the increase in the number of refugees and displaced persons and stressing the urgent need for substantial humanitarian assistance to the Congolese population,

Expressing its deep concern at all violations of human rights and international humanitarian law, including

atrocities against civilian populations, especially in the eastern provinces,

Deeply concerned at the increased rate of HIV/AIDS infection, in particular amongst women and girls as a result of the conflict,

Gravely concerned by the continued recruitment and use of child soldiers by armed forces and groups, including cross-border recruitment and abduction of children,

Reaffirming its primary responsibility under the Charter of the United Nations for the maintenance of international peace and security,

Reaffirming its support for the Lusaka Ceasefire Agreement, as well as the Kampala plan and the Harare sub-plans for disengagement and redeployment,

Stressing the importance of giving new impetus to the peace process in order to secure the full and definitive withdrawal of all foreign troops from the Democratic Republic of the Congo,

Also stressing the importance of advancing the political process called for under the Lusaka Ceasefire Agreement and facilitating national reconciliation,

Recalling the responsibilities of all parties to cooperate in the full deployment of the United Nations Organization Mission in the Democratic Republic of the Congo, and noting with satisfaction the recent statements by the President of the Democratic Republic of the Congo and his assurances of support for the deployment of the Mission,

Welcoming the participation of the members of the Political Committee of the Lusaka Ceasefire Agreement in its meetings of 21 and 22 February 2001, and stressing the need for the parties to honour the commitments they made to take concrete steps to advance the peace process,

Commending the outstanding work of Mission personnel in challenging conditions, and noting the strong leadership of the Special Representative of the Secretary-General,

Taking note of the report of the Secretary-General of 12 February 2001 and his conclusion that the necessary conditions of respect for the ceasefire, a valid plan for disengagement and cooperation with the Mission are being met,

Determining that the situation in the Democratic Republic of the Congo continues to pose a threat to international peace and security in the region,

Acting under Chapter VII of the Charter of the United Nations,

1. *Notes* the recent progress made in achieving respect for the ceasefire, and urgently calls on all parties to the Lusaka Ceasefire Agreement not to resume hostilities and to implement this agreement, as well as the agreements reached in Kampala and Harare and the relevant Security Council resolutions;

2. *Demands once again* that Ugandan and Rwandan forces and all other foreign forces withdraw from the territory of the Democratic Republic of the Congo in compliance with paragraph 4 of its resolution 1304 (2000) and the Lusaka Ceasefire Agreement, and urges these forces to take urgent steps to accelerate this withdrawal;

3. *Demands* that the parties implement fully the Kampala plan and the Harare sub-plans for disengagement and redeployment of forces without reservations

within the 14-day period stipulated in the Harare Agreement, starting from 15 March 2001;

4. *Welcomes* the commitment by the Rwandan authorities in their letter of 18 February 2001 to withdraw their forces from Pweto in accordance with the Harare Agreement, calls on them to implement this commitment, and calls on other parties to respect this withdrawal;

5. *Welcomes also* the commitment of the Ugandan authorities to reduce immediately by two battalions the strength of their forces in the territory of the Democratic Republic of the Congo, calls on the Ugandan authorities to implement this commitment, and calls on the United Nations Organization Mission in the Democratic Republic of the Congo to verify it;

6. *Urges* the parties to the Lusaka Ceasefire Agreement to prepare and adopt not later than 15 May 2001, in close liaison with the Mission, a precise plan and schedule which, in accordance with the Lusaka Ceasefire Agreement, would lead to the completion of the orderly withdrawal of all foreign troops from the territory of the Democratic Republic of the Congo, and requests the Secretary-General to report to it by 15 April 2001 on the progress of these efforts;

7. *Demands* that all the parties refrain from any offensive military action during the process of disengagement and withdrawal of foreign forces;

8. *Urges* all the parties to the conflict, in close liaison with the Mission, to prepare by 15 May 2001 for immediate implementation prioritized plans for the disarmament, demobilization, reintegration, repatriation or resettlement of all armed groups referred to in annex A, chapter 9.1, of the Lusaka Ceasefire Agreement, and demands that all parties cease all forms of assistance and cooperation with these groups and use their influence to urge such groups to cease their activities;

9. *Condemns* the massacres and atrocities committed in the territory of the Democratic Republic of the Congo, and demands once again that all the parties concerned put an immediate end to violations of human rights and international humanitarian law;

10. *Demands* that all armed forces and groups concerned bring an effective end to the recruitment, training and use of children in their armed forces, calls upon them to extend full cooperation to the Mission, the United Nations Children's Fund and humanitarian organizations for speedy demobilization, return and rehabilitation of such children, and requests the Secretary-General to entrust the Special Representative of the Secretary-General for Children and Armed Conflict with pursuing these objectives on a priority basis;

11. *Calls upon* all parties to ensure the safe and unhindered access of relief personnel to all those in need, and recalls that the parties must also provide guarantees for the safety, security and freedom of movement of United Nations and associated humanitarian relief personnel;

12. *Calls also upon* all the parties to respect the principles of neutrality and impartiality in the delivery of humanitarian assistance;

13. *Calls upon* the international community to increase its support to humanitarian relief activities within the Democratic Republic of the Congo and in neighbouring countries affected by the crisis in the Democratic Republic of the Congo;

14. *Reminds* all parties of their obligations with respect to the security of civilian populations under the Fourth Geneva Convention relative to the Protection of Civilian Persons in Time of War of 12 August 1949 and stresses that occupying forces should be held responsible for human rights violations in the territory under their control;

15. *Welcomes* the expressed willingness of the authorities of the Democratic Republic of the Congo to proceed with the inter-Congolese dialogue under the aegis of the neutral Facilitator, Sir Ketumile Masire, and in this regard welcomes the announcement by the President of the Democratic Republic of the Congo at the Summit in Lusaka on 15 February 2001 that the Facilitator has been invited to Kinshasa, and calls upon all Congolese parties to take immediate concrete steps to take forward the inter-Congolese dialogue;

16. *Reiterates* that the Mission shall cooperate closely with the Facilitator of the inter-Congolese dialogue, provide support and technical assistance to him, and coordinate the activities of other United Nations agencies to this effect;

17. *Calls upon* all the parties to the conflict to cooperate fully in the deployment and operations of the Mission including through full implementation of the provisions and the principles of the Status-of-Forces Agreement throughout the territory of the Democratic Republic of the Congo, and reaffirms that it is the responsibility of all the parties to ensure the security of United Nations personnel, together with associated personnel;

18. *Requests* the parties, as a follow-up to the discussions on this matter at the Lusaka Summit on 15 February 2001, to relocate the Joint Military Commission to Kinshasa, co-locating it at all levels with the Mission, and calls upon the authorities of the Democratic Republic of the Congo to ensure the security of all the Commission members;

19. *Reaffirms* the authorization contained in resolution 1291(2000) and the mandate set out in its resolution for the expansion and deployment of the Mission, and endorses the updated concept of operations put forward by the Secretary-General in his report of 12 February 2001, with a view to the deployment of all the civilian and military personnel required to monitor and verify the implementation by the parties of the ceasefire and disengagement plans, stressing that this disengagement is a first step towards the full and definitive withdrawal of all foreign troops from the territory of the Democratic Republic of the Congo;

20. *Emphasizes* that it will be prepared to consider a further review of the concept of operations for the Mission, when appropriate and in the light of developments, in order to monitor and verify the withdrawal of foreign troops and the implementation of the plan mentioned in paragraph 8 above and, in coordination with existing mechanisms, to enhance security on the border of the Democratic Republic of the Congo with Rwanda, Uganda and Burundi, and requests the Secretary-General to make proposals when appropriate;

21. *Reaffirms* that it is ready to support the Secretary-General if and when he deems that it is necessary and it determines that conditions allow it to deploy troops in the border areas in the east of the Demo-

cratic Republic of the Congo, including possibly in Goma or Bukavu;

22. *Welcomes* the dialogue initiated between the authorities of the Democratic Republic of the Congo and Burundi, urges them to continue their efforts, and emphasizes in this respect that the settlement of the crisis in Burundi would contribute positively to the settlement of the conflict in the Democratic Republic of the Congo;

23. *Welcomes also* the recent meetings of the parties, including the meeting of the Presidents of the Democratic Republic of the Congo and Rwanda, encourages them to intensify their dialogue with the goal of achieving regional security structures based on common interest and mutual respect for the territorial integrity, national sovereignty and security of both States, and emphasizes in this respect that the disarmament and demobilization of and cessation of any support to the ex-Rwandese Armed Forces and Interahamwe forces will facilitate the settlement of the conflict in the Democratic Republic of the Congo;

24. *Expresses its full support* for the work of the expert panel on the illegal exploitation of natural resources and other forms of wealth in the Democratic Republic of the Congo, and once again urges the parties to the conflict in the Democratic Republic of the Congo and the other parties concerned to cooperate fully with it;

25. *Reaffirms* that it attaches the highest importance to the cessation of the illegal exploitation of the natural resources of the Democratic Republic of the Congo, affirms that it is ready to consider the necessary actions to put an end to this exploitation, and awaits with interest in this respect the final conclusions of the expert panel, including the conclusions relating to the level of cooperation of States with the expert panel;

26. *Reaffirms also* that an international conference on peace, security, democracy and development in the Great Lakes region, with participation by all the Governments of the region and all the other parties concerned, should be organized at the appropriate time under the aegis of the United Nations and the Organization of African Unity with a view to strengthening stability in the region and working out conditions that will enable everyone to enjoy the right to live peacefully within national borders;

27. *Expresses its intention* to monitor closely progress by the parties in implementing the requirements of the present resolution and to undertake a mission to the region, possibly in May 2001, to monitor progress and discuss the way forward;

28. *Expresses its readiness* to consider possible measures which could be imposed, in accordance with its responsibilities and obligations under the Charter of the United Nations, in case of failure by parties to comply fully with this resolution;

29. *Decides* to remain actively seized of the matter.

Referring to resolution 1341(2001), the Secretary-General proposed to the Council on 18 April [S/2001/405] the names of 40 States to be included in the list of countries contributing military personnel to MONUC. The Council took note of the proposal on 24 April [S/2001/406].

Communications (February-April). On 26 February [S/2001/174], the DRC welcomed Security Council resolution 1341(2001) and reaffirmed its position on the inter-Congolese dialogue, disengagement, cooperation with MONUC, the co-location of MONUC and the Joint Military Commission (JMC) of the Political Committee, respect for human rights, provision of humanitarian aid and further deployment of MONUC along the borders with Rwanda. Referring to that letter, Uganda, on 14 March [S/2001/224], said that the reason for insecurity along the borders of the DRC was the presence of armed groups who were using the DRC as a base against neighbouring countries. Uganda refuted the charge that it was directly involved in the inter-ethnic fighting between the Hema and the Lendu and expressed support for the DRC peace process.

The EU, in a 27 February statement [S/2001/200], welcomed the Council's action, noted the commitment of the parties to implement the Lusaka Ceasefire Agreement and called on them to take immediate measures to permit the disengagement and withdrawal of their troops. It would consider appropriate measures if parties failed to honour their commitments.

On 19 March [S/2001/246], Namibia claimed that MLC rebels in the DRC had attacked an allied forces' ferry on a supply mission, in violation of the Lusaka Ceasefire Agreement.

The DRC stated on 3 April [S/2001/320] that it had received information concerning Burundi's announcement that it was withdrawing three of its battalions from the towns of Pweto and Kalemie, in the province of Katanga, which demonstrated the extent to which Burundi was involved in destabilizing the DRC. The DRC called on the Council to demand that Burundi, which was not a party to the Lusaka Agreement, withdraw immediately its remaining troops from the DRC. On 4 May [S/2001/441], Burundi denied that it had announced the withdrawal of any troops as the DRC claimed. It intended to pursue the dialogue with the DRC on security along the common border and on implementing the Lusaka Agreement.

On 16 April [S/2001/361], the DRC requested the Council to hold an emergency meeting to discuss recent developments concerning the deployment of MONUC, including the blocking by Rwanda and RCD-Goma of the landing of a UN aircraft carrying peacekeepers. In addition, RCD-Goma had not withdrawn from the front line as agreed in the disengagement plan and had hindered the movement of MONUC forces. The DRC urged the Council to apply sanctions against Rwanda and RCD-Goma.

Report of Secretary-General (April). In response to resolution 1341(2001), the Secretary-General issued his seventh report on MONUC on 17 April [S/2001/373]. He noted that President

Kabila had reaffirmed his acceptance of Sir Ketumile Masire as Facilitator of the inter-Congolese dialogue and President Kagame had confirmed Rwanda's intention to disengage its forces 200 kilometres from forward positions.

In an effort to pursue the inter-Congolese dialogue, President Kabila had met with Sir Ketumile in March and they agreed that the process for national dialogue would be as inclusive as possible. On 12 March, President Kabila met with Congolese political and civil society representatives to review the regulation of political activity. However, some main opposition groups did not attend. Subsequently, the Government recommended amendments to laws, which, if adopted, would allow all political parties to operate.

The military situation remained generally calm with significant ceasefire violations reported only around Bolomba in Equateur province. Government and allied forces alleged repeated attacks by FLC against their postions and against resupply ferries in that area. Meanwhile, RPA troops began withdrawing from positions around Pweto in Katanga province on 28 February. The withdrawal was monitored by MONUC military observers. At the same time, three battalions of the Burundian army were reportedly repatriated, leaving two battalions in the DRC. The repatriation of one Ugandan battalion was completed on 11 April. Beginning on 15 March, the date set for the start of disengagement in Security Council resolution 1341(2001), RCD forces withdrew from Pweto to 15 kilometres to the east, as observed by MONUC. On 23 March, the JMC adopted a supplementary protocol to the Harare disengagement sub-plans to take into account RCD's decision to withdraw its forces to a distance of 15 rather than 200 kilometres. The protocol included arrangements for new RCD defensive positions, including at Pweto and Ikela airport. Withdrawals by FAC were observed, despite delays, but there was no indication of disengagement by FLC. Rwanda and Uganda maintained their forces some 100 kilometres from Kisangani. However, RCD elements, citing security concerns, remained in the city, blocking the deployment of MONUC.

The Political Committee, on 6 April, endorsed the concept of operations and timetable for the first phase of the draft plan prepared by JMC for the disarmament, demobilization, reintegration, repatriation and/or resettlement of armed groups (DDRRR), and approved the concept of the orderly withdrawal of all foreign forces from the country, including a calendar. JMC and MONUC would monitor the withdrawal.

As at 11 April, MONUC had a total of 288 liaison officers and military observers. The most serious threat to the security of UN personnel stemmed from lawlessness and the actions of armed groups. While freedom of movement had improved for MONUC, it continued to experience difficulties in negotiations with RCD over deployment locations of sector headquarters and guard units in Goma, Kalemie and Kisangani, and with FLC over deployment to Basankusu. In accordance with the Harare disengagement sub-plan, a 56-day period of verification began on 29 March, during which MONUC military observers would verify the disengagements and redeployments across four areas, a task that was complicated by the danger of mines and the increase in defensive positions in the revised Harare sub-plans, possibly requiring additional MONUC military observers.

The humanitarian situation in the DRC continued to be a cause for grave concern despite some marginal improvements, including a slight reduction in the total number of displaced persons (1.89 million). The number of persons in critical need of food remained at an estimated 16 million. There had been discernible improvements in the Government's attitude regarding respect for human rights as well as some reduction in violence and ethnic tension in the eastern provinces.

The Secretary-General reported that considerable additional work would need to be done in order to produce plans for a MONUC mandate in an eventual third phase of deployment. The second phase, essentially a technical military operation of limited scope, had been launched, whereas the third could require a significant expansion in mandate and size for DDRRR functions, ensuring the withdrawal of all foreign forces and securing the borders. The Secretary-General mentioned some of the anticipated difficulties, including the need for an interim civilian administration, the provision of humanitarian assistance and basic services, security of local populations following the withdrawal of forces, repair of infrastructure and averting human rights violations.

In general, the Secretary-General found that much had changed since the beginning of the year. It was time for all parties to pull back to their new defensive positions, as some had done, so that MONUC could continue its verification operations under phase II and begin the more difficult phase III, currently being planned. He welcomed the bilateral contacts that had taken place between the DRC and Uganda, as well as between the other parties.

Communications (April/May). On 27 April [S/2001/420], the DRC informed the Security Council of the murder of six staff of the International Committee of the Red Cross near the town of

Bunia, close to the Ugandan border; it alleged that Ugandan troops were most likely responsible. Uganda denied those charges on 8 May [S/2001/452]. On 7 May [S/2001/461], Uganda announced it would completely withdraw its forces from 10 positions in the DRC, examine whether to maintain a presence in two other locations, and maintain deployment in the Rwenzori mountains until security concerns had been addressed. Rwanda, on 7 May [S/2001/469], also objected to claims made by the DRC in the 27 April letter, in particular claims linking Rwandan authorities to criminal and mafia elements.

On 10 May [S/2001/466], Zambia issued the text of the Declaration of Fundamental Principles of the Inter-Congolese Political Negotiations, signed in Lusaka on 4 May by the Congolese signatories to the Lusaka Agreement (the DRC Government, MLC, RCD and RCD-ML). Among the principles were national reconciliation and a new political order as a basis for rebuilding the DRC; inclusion of the political opposition and representatives of the *Forces Vives* to designate their representatives to the inter-Congolese dialogue; the organization of free and transparent elections; and the formation of a restructured, integrated army.

Security Council mission to Great Lakes

The Security Council, following consultations and in response to its resolution 1341(2001) (see p. 120), sent a 12-member mission to the Great Lakes region (15-26 May) to monitor progress by the parties to the Lusaka Ceasefire Agreement in implementing the resolution [S/2001/521]. It held extensive talks with leaders of several States, as well as opposition forces and others involved in the peace process. The mission noted that, for the first time since the outbreak of the DRC conflict, the outlines of a solution appeared to be taking shape; it stressed the urgency of taking advantage of that window of opportunity. Among the positive signs was the attitude displayed by President Kabila towards the peace process and MONUC. The mission observed that the ceasefire had held for four months and that the belligerents' forces had disengaged from the confrontation line, enabling MONUC to deploy its guard units and military observers to their designated locations. President Kabila's repeal of a law banning political parties was a significant step toward ameliorating the political environment. Nonetheless, obstacles remained. The mission expressed concern about the reluctance of Jean-Pierre Bemba, the leader of FLC, to disengage his forces, which were some 100 kilometres beyond the positions agreed to under the Harare disengagement plan. The DDRRR plans for armed groups needed to be finalized, operational sub-plans needed to be drawn up and signed by the military commanders of all parties, and the withdrawal of foreign forces needed to be conducted in a phased and orderly manner.

The mission recommended that the Council approve a transition to phase III of MONUC operations on the basis of forthcoming recommendations by the Secretary-General. During that phase, MONUC would assist the parties in carrying out phased withdrawal of all foreign forces and for DDRRR of armed groups. The co-location of JMC with MONUC would help them to coordinate military planning for operations. The mission impressed upon RCD and the Political Committee the need to demilitarize Kisangani, the presence of RCD forces there being a violation of resolution 1304(2000) [YUN 2000, p. 131].

Aware of the security concerns of the civilian population in the areas to be evacuated by foreign forces, the mission said that some form of civil administration, including police, would be essential. Such concerns needed to be addressed by the Congolese parties in the context of the inter-Congolese dialogue. In the mission's view, DDRRR of armed groups was the key to ending the conflict in the DRC. The Political Committee members had assured the mission that they would provide the necessary information on the armed groups to JMC in order to facilitate planning for that goal. The mission affirmed that peace could not be restored until all foreign forces had departed and welcomed indications that some foreign contingents had already withdrawn. The mission considered it indispensable for the return to peace to be accompanied by increased economic activity, which the international community should mobilize to assist. MONUC could play an important role in reopening the riverine network to stimulate trade and facilitate the movement of persons and goods, including MONUC supplies. The Security Council looked forward to receiving further details concerning the proposed Congo River Basin Commission comprising the Congolese parties, UN agencies and the Governments of the Republic of the Congo and the Central African Republic, under the chairmanship of MONUC. The mission also called for a halt to the illegitimate exploitation of the natural resources of the DRC (see p. 140), respect for human rights by all the parties and cessation of the use of child soldiers. In that regard, it recommended the deployment of additional human rights observers in the DRC. The mission proposed that, at the appropriate time, an international conference on the Great Lakes region be held to promote peace, security and development.

Annexed to the mission's report [S/2001/521/Add.1] were a statement issued in Kinshasa on 21 May by the mission at the close of its visit to that city; a communiqué issued after a joint meeting of the Political Committee and the mission in Lusaka on 22 May [S/2001/525]; a draft plan issued by JMC on DDRRR of all armed groups in the DRC, the handing over of mass killers, perpetrators of crimes against humanity and other war criminals, and disarmament of all Congolese civilians who were illegally armed; and a plan issued by JMC for the orderly withdrawal of all foreign forces from the DRC.

During the Security Council consideration of the mission's report on 30 May [meeting 4323], the head of the mission, Mr. Levitte, said that the mission had obtained assurances from Mr. Bemba, on the one hand, and the Political Committee, on the other, that on 1 June FLC forces would withdraw from the zones they were occupying to the agreed positions set out in the communiqué adopted by the Political Committee and the mission. There was a parallel decision to send humanitarian observers to Equateur province, as elsewhere throughout the DRC, in order to improve the human rights and humanitarian situations. In the economic field, the mission had announced some 40 small quick-impact projects, to be carried out in areas where MONUC troops were deployed, and the reopening on 7 June of the Congo River to commercial navigation as a result of the presence of a MONUC riverine unit. Urgent matters that needed to be dealt with included the withdrawal of foreign troops from and demilitarization of Kisangani, the co-location of JMC and MONUC and a transition to the third phase of MONUC deployment. In that regard, Mr. Levitte observed that the ceiling of 5,537 forces, as decided by the Council in resolution 1291(2000) [YUN 2000, p. 123], remained adequate but further planning was required.

Extension of MONUC mandate

Report of Secretary-General (June). The Secretary-General, in his eighth report on MONUC, dated 8 June [S/2001/572], described developments since his previous report and made recommendations for future activities of the Mission, whose mandate was due to expire the following week. He reported that Under-Secretary-General for Peacekeeping Operations Jean-Marie Guéhenno visited the area in mid-April and urged all parties to cooperate with MONUC. In the region, there had been signs of rapprochement, including a number of visits by heads of State for talks on implementation of the Lusaka Agreement and security concerns. A meeting of the Central Organ of the OAU Mechanism for Conflict Prevention, Management and Resolution (Lomé, Togo, 19 May) expressed satisfaction at the new disposition of the DRC Government and other parties to the Lusaka Agreement. President Museveni of Uganda, in a note verbale dated 3 May [S/2001/357], said that Ugandan forces would soon be withdrawn from the DRC and advised that his Government was considering withdrawing from the Lusaka peace process. The Secretary-General appealed to President Museveni not to abandon the process. Uganda later affirmed that it would remain party to the Lusaka Agreement but reserved the right to withdraw if it remained dissatisfied with the Agreement's implementation [S/2001/461].

Following intensive consultations by Sir Ketumile Masire, the neutral Facilitator, representatives of the DRC Government and the rebel movements agreed on 4 May on a set of principles to serve as the framework for the inter-Congolese dialogue. A preparatory meeting to the dialogue was scheduled for 16 July. As a result of the new political climate, some exiled political opponents returned to the DRC.

The military situation remained generally calm, with significant ceasefire violations reported only around Bolomba in Equateur province in early May, allegedly between FLC and FAC. As at 8 June, MONUC had a total of 2,366 military personnel, including 497 liaison officers and military observers, stationed throughout the country and in capitals of surrounding countries. Although MONUC enjoyed good cooperation with the Government and its allies, it experienced difficulties and delays from RCD on many issues, specifically the procurement of goods and services due to RCD's insistence on local suppliers. FLC had also caused unreasonable delays for MONUC deployment.

MONUC's verification process expanded to include all four sectors in its supervision of the movements of the forces; cooperation from the parties varied but was generally satisfactory. Logistics presented problems, in some cases requiring the establishment of forward refuelling bases because of the remote location of some of the new defensive positions. Disengagement and verification were almost complete in three of the four sectors. As at 4 June, 69 of the designated 96 redeployment positions had been visited and the disengagement of forces in those areas had been verified. The one area where disengagement had been unsatisfactory was Equateur province, where the rebel forces were controlled by FLC leader Mr. Bemba, who cited fears for the safety of the civilian populations in the areas to be evacuated by his troops. MONUC worked with the parties to secure the withdrawal of Ugandan and

Zimbabwean troops and equipment from certain areas.

The security situation in the eastern provinces remained highly volatile. RCD announced on 29 May that its forces had captured the airfield of Kilembwe in South Kivu, which, it alleged, had been used by FAC to resupply ex-FAR and Interahamwe militias. RCD accused the Government of seeking to transfer the war to the eastern regions, alleging a sharp increase in the number of attacks by armed groups since the President had assumed office. An envoy from Burundi, at a meeting of the Political Committee on 21 May, reported that a large-scale eastward movement of rebels of the Front pour la défense de la démocratie (FDD) had taken place over the preceding few months, with a third of the FDD rebels having returned to Burundi, where they were responsible for the upsurge in violence in and around Bujumbura. Rwanda and Uganda continued to maintain their forces some 100 kilometres from Kisangani, but RCD military elements remained in the city.

JMC, in collaboration with MONUC, was developing plans for the withdrawal of foreign forces and for DDRRR of the armed groups identified in the Lusaka Agreement. In that regard, the Security Council mission had insisted that the parties should provide information concerning numbers, locations, assembly areas, withdrawal routes and timetables in order to allow the United Nations to make its own plans to assist the parties and to monitor the withdrawal. On the basis of that information, MONUC would draw up plans and modalities for UN assistance. As at 8 June, only Angola and Uganda had provided information on their forces in the DRC. Further progress in developing a detailed plan for approval by the parties could not be made until Namibia, Rwanda and Zimbabwe provided information on their forces. During the reporting period, the four regional Joint Military Commissions had co-located with the MONUC sector headquarters, enabling members to be involved in the verification of the disengagement and redeployment of forces.

The Secretary-General cautioned that it would be precipitous to enter a third phase of MONUC deployment before the completion of the disengagement and verification phase and without the benefit of realistic and approved plans; nevertheless, the momentum generated by the disengagement of forces and the withdrawal of foreign forces must not be lost. The Secretariat had therefore updated MONUC's concept of operations to ensure that the Mission had the necessary resources to complete the current phase and to prepare for the next one, which would involve continuing to monitor the presence of forces in the new defensive positions, as well as any further withdrawals of foreign contingents, and would require additional military personnel and equipment. An expansion of MONUC's presence in the sector headquarters in Kisangani, Kalemie, Kananga and Mbandaka was also necessary in the form of civilian (political, humanitarian, human rights, child protection and public information staff) and military personnel. A mine action centre should be established in MONUC headquarters, with subsidiary cells in each sector headquarters. Due to a lack of trained police and a vacuum in the security situation that would follow the withdrawal of foreign forces, the deployment of a small civilian police component with MONUC was envisaged, to prepare recommendations for an expanded civilian police component wherever MONUC military personnel were deployed and to advise local authorities. MONUC would also support the opening of the internal waterway system, including through the deployment of two riverine units. Since MONUC would be called upon to assist with DDRRR functions, military and civilian support staff would need to be deployed as part of the transition to phase III. As part of its public information capability, it was envisaged that a radio studio would be set up in Kinshasa with transmitters in five locations. Programming would cover MONUC activities, the peace process, the DDRRR programme and the inter-Congolese dialogue. To strengthen the civilian component, the Secretary-General intended to appoint a Deputy Special Representative with responsibility for coordination within the Mission, as well as between MONUC and other UN agencies and donors operating in the DRC.

Given the scale of the country and the degraded infrastructure, the revised concept of operations provided for a progressive build-up of capabilities in personnel, logistics and equipment in order to position MONUC to respond in an effective manner once the parties began withdrawal of foreign troops and DDRRR. The revised concept envisaged an increase of up to 2,500 military personnel over the 3,000 authorized under the current MONUC mandate, thus remaining within the force level of 5,537 approved by the Security Council in resolution 1291(2000).

The Secretary-General was gratified to note that the parties continued to adhere to the ceasefire; however, reports of the eastward movement of armed groups and their recent incursions into Burundi, Rwanda and the United Republic of Tanzania were disturbing. There was speculation that the armed groups were moving out of the DRC to evade participation in the DDRRR programme. The Secretary-General said that there could be no lasting peace in the DRC without a comprehensive settlement in Burundi and he was gratified by the recent meetings of regional heads of State. He welcomed the DRC Government's cooperation with MONUC and called on the rebel movements to extend the same level of cooperation. The substantial compliance of the parties with the Harare disengagement plan, as monitored and verified by MONUC, was also a matter for encouragement. However, the reluctance of FLC to disengage its forces in Equateur province remained a concern. The plans drawn up by JMC and the Political Committee, in consultation with MONUC, on troop withdrawal and DDRRR did not constitute a sufficient basis for further action by the United Nations at that point, the Secretary-General said. He called on the parties to provide, as soon as possible, the information requested. Though incomplete, the progress made in the disengagement of forces (phase II of MONUC) demanded a follow-up; therefore, the Secretary-General recommended that the Council authorize a transition to the third phase of MONUC deployment that would not require an increase in the authorized military strength. A transition with an enlarged civilian component and a new civilian police unit would eventually lead to the third phase, DDRRR. The Secretary-General, emphasizing that MONUC would be engaged in the DRC for a considerable time to come, recommended that the Council extend its mandate for a year, until 15 June 2002.

SECURITY COUNCIL ACTION (June)

On 15 June [meeting 4329], the Security Council unanimously adopted **resolution 1355(2001)**. The draft [S/2001/587] was prepared in consultations among Council members.

The Security Council,

Recalling its resolutions 1234(1999) of 9 April 1999, 1258(1999) of 6 August 1999, 1265(1999) of 17 September 1999, 1273(1999) of 5 November 1999, 1279(1999) of 30 November 1999, 1291(2000) of 24 February 2000, 1296(2000) of 19 April 2000, 1304(2000) of 15 June 2000, 1323(2000) of 13 October 2000, 1332(2000) of 14 December 2000 and 1341(2001) of 22 February 2001 and the statements by its President of 13 July 1998 (S/PRST/1998/20), 31 August 1998 (S/PRST/1998/26), 11 December 1998 (S/PRST/1998/36), 24 June 1999 (S/PRST/1999/17), 26 January 2000 (S/PRST/2000/2), 5 May 2000 (S/PRST/2000/15), 2 June 2000 (S/PRST/2000/20), 7 September 2000 (S/PRST/2000/28) and 3 May 2001 (S/PRST/2001/13),

Reaffirming the sovereignty, territorial integrity and political independence of the Democratic Republic of the Congo and of all States in the region,

Reaffirming also the obligation of all States to refrain from the use of force against the territorial integrity and political independence of any State, or in any other manner inconsistent with the purposes of the United Nations,

Reaffirming further the sovereignty of the Democratic Republic of the Congo over its natural resources,

Expressing its alarm at the dire consequences of the prolonged conflict for the civilian population throughout the territory of the Democratic Republic of the Congo, in particular the increase in the number of refugees and displaced persons, and stressing the urgent need for substantial humanitarian assistance to the Congolese population,

Expressing its deep concern at all violations of human rights and international humanitarian law, including atrocities against civilian populations, especially in the eastern provinces,

Deeply concerned at the increased rate of HIV/AIDS infection, in particular amongst women and girls in the Democratic Republic of the Congo,

Gravely concerned by the continued recruitment and use of child soldiers by armed forces and groups, including cross-border recruitment and abduction of children,

Reaffirming its primary responsibility under the Charter of the United Nations for the maintenance of international peace and security,

Reaffirming its support for the Lusaka Ceasefire Agreement, as well as the Kampala plan and the Harare sub-plans for disengagement and redeployment,

Reaffirming that the primary responsibility for implementing the Lusaka Ceasefire Agreement lies with the parties,

Reiterating its support for the inter-Congolese dialogue and the Facilitator, and stressing the need for the parties to resolve outstanding substantive and procedural issues,

Recalling the responsibilities of all parties to cooperate in the full deployment of the United Nations Organization Mission in the Democratic Republic of the Congo,

Endorsing the report of the Security Council mission to the Great Lakes region, and recalling the communiqué of the joint meeting of the Political Committee for the Implementation of the Lusaka Ceasefire Agreement in the Democratic Republic of the Congo and the United Nations Security Council mission to the Great Lakes region,

Taking note of the report of the Secretary-General of 8 June 2001 and its recommendations,

Determining that the situation in the Democratic Republic of the Congo continues to pose a threat to international peace and security in the region,

A

Acting under Chapter VII of the Charter of the United Nations,

1. *Notes with satisfaction* that the ceasefire among the parties to the Lusaka Ceasefire Agreement has been respected, welcomes the progress on disengagement and redeployment noted in the Secretary-General's report of 8 June 2001, and reiterates its urgent call on all parties to the Lusaka Ceasefire Agreement to implement this agreement, as well as the agreements reached in Kampala and Harare and all relevant Security Council resolutions;

2. *Demands* that the Front de Libération du Congo disengage and redeploy its forces in accordance with

the Harare sub-plans and the commitment it made to the Security Council mission to the Great Lakes region, in their meeting of 25 May 2001, and expresses its intention to monitor this process;

3. *Demands once again* that Ugandan and Rwandan forces and all other foreign forces withdraw from the territory of the Democratic Republic of the Congo in compliance with paragraph 4 of its resolution 1304 (2000) and the Lusaka Ceasefire Agreement, urges those forces to take the necessary steps to accelerate this withdrawal, and welcomes in this regard the decision by Ugandan authorities to start withdrawing their troops from the territory of the Democratic Republic of the Congo;

4. *Calls upon* all the parties to refrain from any offensive action during the process of disengagement and withdrawal of foreign forces, and expresses concern at recent reports of military operations in the Kivus;

5. *Demands* that the Rassemblement Congolais pour la Démocratie demilitarize Kisangani in accordance with resolution 1304(2000), and that all parties respect the demilitarization of the city and its environs;

6. *Demands* that all parties, including the Government of the Democratic Republic of the Congo, cease immediately all forms of assistance and cooperation with all armed groups referred to in annex A, chapter 9.1, of the Lusaka Ceasefire Agreement;

7. *Takes note* of the plans drafted by the Political Committee for the orderly withdrawal of all foreign forces from the territory of the Democratic Republic of the Congo and for the disarmament, demobilization, repatriation and reintegration of all armed groups in the Democratic Republic of the Congo, and calls upon the parties to finalize these plans and to implement them as a matter of urgency;

8. *With a view to ensuring the finalization of these plans, requests* all parties that have not already done so to provide the Joint Military Commission, as soon as possible, with all necessary operational information on the withdrawal, including, inter alia, the numbers and locations of the foreign forces, their assembly areas and withdrawal routes and the timetable, and on disarmament, demobilization, repatriation and reintegration, including, inter alia, the numbers, location and armaments of the armed groups, and the proposed sites of their demobilization areas, in order to facilitate United Nations planning to assist the parties in the implementation of these plans;

9. *Encourages* the Presidents and Governments of the Democratic Republic of the Congo and Rwanda to intensify their dialogue with the goal of achieving regional security structures based on common interest and mutual respect for the territorial integrity, national sovereignty and security of both States, and emphasizes in this respect that the disarmament and demobilization of, and cessation of any support to, the ex-Forces Armées Rwandaises and Interahamwe forces are essential to the settlement of the conflict in the Democratic Republic of the Congo;

10. *Condemns* the recent incursions by armed groups into Rwanda and Burundi;

11. *Welcomes* the dialogue initiated between the authorities of the Democratic Republic of the Congo and Burundi, strongly urges them to continue their efforts, calls on all States in the region to bring to bear their influence on Burundian armed groups to encourage them to refrain from violence, to enter negotiations for a political settlement and to join the Arusha peace process, and demands that all States in the region cease any military support to such groups;

12. *Stresses* that a durable peace in the Democratic Republic of the Congo should not be achieved at the expense of peace in Burundi, and requests the Secretary-General as well as interested Member States to make proposals, on an urgent basis, on how best to address these interrelated crises;

13. *Welcomes* the announcement by the facilitator of the inter-Congolese dialogue of the organization of the preparatory meeting of the inter-Congolese dialogue on 16 July 2001, calls on all Congolese parties to commence that dialogue as soon as possible, preferably on Congolese soil, and to ensure a successful outcome, and welcomes in this regard the initial measures taken by the authorities of the Democratic Republic of the Congo towards the liberalization of political activities;

14. *Calls upon* all relevant parties to ensure that urgent child protection concerns, including disarmament, demobilization, repatriation and reintegration of child soldiers, the plight of girls affected by the conflict, the protection and safe return of refugee and internally displaced children, and the registration and reunification of unaccompanied or orphaned children, are addressed in all national, bilateral and regional dialogues, and that solutions are designed in accordance with international best practice;

15. *Condemns* the massacres and atrocities committed in the territory of the Democratic Republic of the Congo, demands once again that all the parties to the conflict put an immediate end to violations of human rights and international humanitarian law, and stresses that those responsible will be held accountable;

16. *Reminds* all parties of their obligations with respect to the security of civilian populations under the Fourth Geneva Convention relative to the Protection of Civilian Persons in Time of War of 12 August 1949, and stresses that all forces present on the territory of the Democratic Republic of the Congo are responsible for preventing violations of international humanitarian law in the territory under their control;

17. *Condemns strongly* the attacks against the personnel of humanitarian organizations, and demands that the perpetrators be brought to justice;

18. *Condemns* the use of child soldiers, demands that all armed forces and groups concerned bring an end to all forms of recruitment, training and use of children in their armed forces, calls upon all parties to collaborate with the United Nations, humanitarian organizations and other competent bodies to ensure the expeditious demobilization, rehabilitation and reintegration of children abducted or enrolled in armed forces or groups and to allow their reunification with their families, and urges Member States to ensure adequate and sustained resources for long-term reintegration;

19. *Calls upon* all parties to ensure, in accordance with relevant international law, the full, safe and unhindered access of relief personnel to all those in need and the delivery of humanitarian assistance, in particular to all children affected by the conflict, and recalls that the parties must also provide guarantees for the safety, security and freedom of movement of

United Nations and associated humanitarian personnel;

20. *Calls upon* the international community to increase its support for humanitarian relief activities within the Democratic Republic of the Congo and in neighbouring countries affected by the conflict in the Democratic Republic of the Congo;

21. *Expresses its full support* for the work of the Expert Panel on the illegal exploitation of natural resources and other forms of wealth in the Democratic Republic of the Congo, and notes that the report of the Expert Panel of 12 April 2001 contains disturbing information about the illegal exploitation of Congolese resources by individuals, Governments and armed groups involved in the conflict and the link between the exploitation of the natural resources and other forms of wealth in the Democratic Republic of the Congo and the continuation of the conflict;

22. *Reaffirms* that it attaches the highest importance to the cessation of the illegal exploitation of the natural resources of the Democratic Republic of the Congo, and reaffirms that it is ready to consider the necessary actions to put an end to this exploitation;

23. *Awaits* in this respect the publication of the addendum to the report of the Expert Panel which should contain an updated evaluation of the situation, again urges all the parties to the conflict in the Democratic Republic of the Congo and the other parties concerned to cooperate fully with the Expert Panel while ensuring necessary security for the experts, and welcomes the action taken by Ugandan authorities in setting up a commission of inquiry in this regard;

24. *Stresses* the link between the progress in the peace process and economic recovery of the Democratic Republic of the Congo, welcomes initial economic reforms undertaken by the Government of the Democratic Republic of the Congo, and underlines the urgent need for international economic assistance;

25. *Stresses* the importance of the restoration of river traffic, welcomes the reopening of the Congo and the Oubangui Rivers, calls urgently on all parties, and in particular the Rassemblement Congolais pour la Démocratie in the light of its recent public comments, to cooperate further in order to permit the re-establishment of economic links between, inter alia, Kinshasa, Mbandaka and Kisangani, and expresses its support for the proposed establishment of a Congo River Basin Commission comprising the Congolese parties, United Nations agencies and some neighbouring countries under the chairmanship of the United Nations Organization Mission in the Democratic Republic of the Congo;

26. *Stresses* that durable peace can only be achieved if all the countries of the region are successful in defining amongst themselves the rules by which to promote security and development, and reaffirms in this regard that an international conference on peace, security, democracy and development in the region, with participation by all the Governments of the region and all the other parties concerned, should be organized at the appropriate time under the aegis of the United Nations and the Organization of African Unity;

27. *Expresses its intention* to monitor closely progress by the parties in implementing the requirements and demands of the present resolution;

28. *Expresses again its readiness* to consider possible measures which could be imposed, in accordance with its responsibilities and obligations under the Charter of the United Nations, in case of failure by parties to comply fully with the present resolution and other relevant resolutions;

B

29. *Decides* to extend the mandate of the United Nations Organization Mission in the Democratic Republic of the Congo until 15 June 2002, and also decides to review progress at least every four months based on reporting by the Secretary-General;

30. *Requests* the Secretary-General to submit to the Council, once all necessary information has been provided by the parties to the Lusaka Ceasefire Agreement, and subject to the continuing cooperation of the parties, proposals concerning the way the Mission could assist in, monitor and verify the implementation by the parties of the plans referred to in paragraphs 7 and 8 above;

31. *Approves* the updated concept of operations put forward by the Secretary-General in paragraphs 84 to 104 of his report of 8 June 2001, including, for further planning purposes, the creation of a civilian police component and of an integrated civilian/military section to coordinate disarmament, demobilization, repatriation and reintegration operations, the strengthening of the Mission presence in Kisangani, and the strengthening of the Mission logistic support capability to support current and foreseen future deployment, with a view to preparing the transition towards the third phase of the deployment of the Mission after the necessary information has been provided by the parties;

32. *Authorizes* in this regard the Mission, consistent with the Secretary-General's report, to assist, upon request, and within its capabilities, in the early implementation, on a voluntary basis, of the disarmament, demobilization, repatriation and reintegration of armed groups, and requests the Secretary-General to deploy military observers in locations where early withdrawal is implemented, with a view to monitoring the process;

33. *Reiterates* the authorization contained in resolution 1291(2000) for up to 5,537 Mission military personnel, including observers as deemed necessary by the Secretary-General;

34. *Requests* the Secretary-General to expand the civilian component of the Mission, in accordance with the recommendations in his report, in order to assign to areas in which the Mission is deployed human rights personnel, so as to establish a human rights monitoring capacity, as well as civilian political affairs and humanitarian affairs personnel;

35. *Calls upon* the Secretary-General to ensure sufficient deployment of child protection advisers to ensure consistent and systematic monitoring and reporting on the conduct of the parties to the conflict as concerns their child protection obligations under humanitarian and human rights law and the commitments they have made to the Special Representative of the Secretary-General for Children and Armed Conflict;

36. *Stresses* the need for an increased public information capacity, including the establishment of United Nations radio stations to promote understand-

ing of the peace process and of the role of the Mission among local communities and the parties;

37. *Calls upon* all the parties to the conflict to cooperate fully in the deployment and operations of the Mission, including through full implementation of the provisions of the Status-of-Forces Agreement throughout the territory of the Democratic Republic of the Congo, and reaffirms that it is the responsibility of all the parties to ensure the security of United Nations personnel, together with associated personnel;

38. *Stresses* the need for the co-location of the Joint Military Commission with the Mission in Kinshasa;

39. *Reaffirms* that it is ready to support the Secretary-General if and when he deems it necessary and when conditions allow it, in the context of viable security frameworks, to further deploy military personnel in the border areas in the east of the Democratic Republic of the Congo;

40. *Expresses* its appreciation for the partnership established with the parties to the Lusaka Ceasefire Agreement, which was strengthened during the last Security Council mission to the Great Lakes region, and reiterates that it is firmly determined to continue to provide assistance to the parties in their efforts to achieve peace;

41. *Commends* the outstanding work of Mission personnel who operate in challenging conditions, and expresses its strong support for the Special Representative of the Secretary-General;

42. *Decides* to remain actively seized of the matter.

Communications (June/July). In mid-2001, the DRC drew the Security Council's attention to increased violence and tension in the country and the region. On 25 June [S/2001/634], it issued a statement on reports of a resurgence of violence in Burundi and Rwanda due to infiltrations from Congolese territory of Interahamwe and ex-FAR and Burundian rebels; it denied allegations that it was facilitating those infiltrations. Uganda, in a 3 July response [S/2001/665], denied allegations that it was harbouring those opposed to the Rwandan Government. On 27 June [S/2001/646], the DRC transmitted a press release issued after a meeting between President Kabila and President Denis Sassou-Nguesso of the Republic of the Congo, during which they discussed prospects for peace and the inter-Congolese dialogue, among other things.

On 5, 11, 13 and 18 July [S/2001/666, S/2001/685, S/2001/694, S/2001/709], the DRC alerted the Council to the lack of compliance by opposition groups to its resolutions calling for the disengagement and redeployment of forces; in particular the DRC mentioned FLC, the Uganda People's Defence Force and RCD-Goma, assisted by Rwanda. It charged Rwanda and RCD-Goma with trying to create a secessionist State in eastern DRC and said that Rwanda and its allies refused to demilitarize Kisangani. Responding on 19 July [S/2001/716],

Rwanda stated that the DRC was using delaying tactics, including provocation, to sabotage the implementation of the Lusaka Agreement.

The EU General Affairs Council, in a 16 July statement [S/2001/729], said it considered the window of opportunity that had opened up earlier in regard to peacemaking efforts in the DRC to be still available in spite of risks of a deterioration in the situation. The EU intended to encourage a gradual and balanced resumption of aid and cooperation in the DRC; such engagement would depend on progress in implementing the Lusaka Agreement.

SECURITY COUNCIL ACTION (July)

On 24 July [meeting 4349], following consultations among Security Council members, the President made statement **S/PRST/2001/19** on behalf of the Council:

The Security Council takes note with satisfaction of the progress made so far in the peace process in the Democratic Republic of the Congo.

The Council calls on all the parties to the conflict to fulfil all their commitments, implement fully the Lusaka Ceasefire Agreement and complete the disengagement and redeployment of their forces in accordance with the Kampala plan and the Harare sub-plans, which the United Nations Organization Mission in the Democratic Republic of the Congo will verify.

The Council finds it unacceptable that more than one year after the adoption of its resolution 1304 (2000) of 15 June 2000 containing the demand to completely demilitarize Kisangani, reiterated in resolution 1355(2001) of 15 June 2001, the Rassemblement Congolais pour la Démocratie has thus far failed to comply with it. The Council calls on the Rassemblement Congolais pour la Démocratie to implement fully and immediately its obligation under resolution 1304(2000), and notes that continued failure to do so may have future implications.

The Council reminds all the parties of their obligation to cooperate fully with the Organization Mission and of their obligations with respect to the security of civilian populations under the fourth Geneva Convention relative to the Protection of Civilian Persons in Time of War of 12 August 1949. The Council urges the relevant parties to expedite the conclusion of their investigation into the killing of six International Committee of the Red Cross staff in eastern Democratic Republic of the Congo, to report their findings to the Committee and to bring the perpetrators to justice.

The Council calls on all parties to facilitate and support humanitarian efforts of the United Nations and non-governmental organizations. It stresses the importance of the work of the United Nations Humanitarian Coordinator.

The Council reiterates its call for the cessation of the illegal exploitation of the natural resources of the Democratic Republic of the Congo. In this regard, it calls on all parties to cooperate fully with the Expert Panel and, looking forward to the addendum to the report of the Panel, reiterates its readiness to consider the necessary actions to put an end to this exploitation.

The Council reiterates its demand on all parties to accelerate the finalization and the implementation of comprehensive plans for the orderly withdrawal of all foreign troops from the territory of the Democratic Republic of the Congo, and the disarmament, demobilization, reintegration, repatriation and resettlement of all armed groups referred to in annex A, chapter 9.1, of the Lusaka Ceasefire Agreement.

The Council expresses serious concern over the activities of the armed groups in the east of the country. It takes note with interest of the invitation by the President of the Democratic Republic of the Congo to the Mission to visit the camps where some members of the armed groups have reportedly been quartered by the Forces Armées Congolaises, and stresses the importance of the Mission assisting, within its capabilities, in the early implementation, on a voluntary basis, of the disarmament, demobilization, reintegration, repatriation and resettlement of these armed groups, in accordance with the authorization given in its resolution 1355(2001). The Council requests in this regard the donor community, in particular the World Bank and the European Union, to provide financial and in-kind contributions as soon as possible to the Mission in the implementation of this mission.

The Council reiterates its firm support for the inter-Congolese dialogue and the efforts of the Facilitator and his team in the field. It emphasizes the importance of an open, representative and inclusive dialogue, free from outside interference and involving civil society, leading to a consensus settlement. It calls on the Congolese parties to the Lusaka Ceasefire Agreement to cooperate fully with the Facilitator to enable him to conduct the process in a swift and constructive manner. It expresses the hope that the dialogue can be held on Congolese soil, respecting the choice that the Congolese actors themselves will make. It encourages donors to continue to provide support to the Facilitator's mission.

The Council welcomes the recent high-level meetings between the Presidents of the Democratic Republic of the Congo, Rwanda and Uganda and encourages them further to pursue the dialogue to find solutions to their common security concerns in accordance with the Lusaka Ceasefire Agreement.

The Council reiterates its commitment to support full implementation of the Lusaka Ceasefire Agreement. It reaffirms that the primary responsibility for implementing the Agreement lies with the parties. The Council urges them to demonstrate the necessary political will by cooperating with each other and with the Mission in achieving this goal. It expresses its readiness to consider, subject to necessary progress made by the parties and to recommendations of the Secretary-General the possible expansion of the Mission if and when the mission enters its third phase.

The Council commends the Special Representative of the Secretary-General, Ambassador Kamel Morjane, for his outstanding work and invaluable contribution to the peace process in the Democratic Republic of the Congo.

Appointment. The Secretary-General, on 31 July [S/2001/760], informed the Security Council of his intention to appoint Amos Namanga Ngongi (Cameroon) as his Special Representative for the DRC, replacing Kamel Morjane (Tunisia). The Council took note of the decision on 2 August [S/2001/761].

Communications (August). The DRC, on 1 August [S/2001/759], condemned an alleged attempt by RCD-Goma to establish "federalism" in Congolese territories under Rwandan and Ugandan occupation, which, it said, was aimed at ending the peace process and undermining the chances for an inter-Congolese dialogue; it called on the Security Council to take enforcement action. Responding on 8 August [S/2001/774], Rwanda said that the DRC, frustrated because three quarters of the country was under the control of various Congolese rebels, was trying to convince international public opinion that its claims of secessionism and expansionism were true.

The sixteenth ministerial meeting of the United Nations Standing Advisory Committee on Security Questions in Central Africa (Kinshasa, 13-17 August) [A/56/378-S/2001/890] welcomed the forthcoming preparatory meeting of the inter-Congolese dialogue and appealed to the Council to move ahead as soon as possible with the implementation of phase III of MONUC deployment.

Inter-Congolese dialogue

The preparatory meeting for the inter-Congolese dialogue was held in Gabarone, Botswana, from 20 to 24 August. Approximately 70 delegates from the Congolese signatory parties to the Lusaka Ceasefire Agreement, as well as from civil society and every DRC province, took part. The Assistant Secretary-General for Peacekeeping Operations, Hédi Annabi, addressing the Security Council on 30 August [meeting 4361], described the meeting as remarkably successful. The parties agreed to conduct the dialogue itself in Addis Ababa, starting on 15 October, for an estimated period of 45 days. In a Declaration of Commitment, the participants agreed on key issues such as liberalization of political life in the DRC, respect for human rights, release of political prisoners and prisoners of war, freedom of movement of people and goods throughout the country, re-establishment of communication links and the rehabilitation of infrastructure, restitution of seized property, protection from arbitrary arrests, protection of natural resources from illegal exploitation, and the withdrawal of foreign troops in accordance with the Lusaka Agreement. Another key development that emerged in the margins of the preparatory talks was a meeting between President Kabila and rebel leaders, Mr. Bemba of FLC and Adolphe Onusumba of RCD. The Secretary-General, in his October report on MONUC (see below), described the outcome as an important exercise in confidence-building during which the parties were able to develop unofficial channels of communication. As requested by the Facilitator, the United Nations would help organize the dialogue [S/PV.4361].

The EU issued two statements on the inter-Congolese dialogue, on 17 and 30 August [S/2001/815, S/2001/836], welcoming the meeting and encouraging the parties to continue to work in the same spirit of compromise and conciliation as that which prevailed in Gaborone.

SECURITY COUNCIL ACTION (September)

Following a private meeting on 5 September [meeting 4364], the Security Council issued a communiqué [S/PV.4364] stating that it had heard a briefing by Sir Ketumile Masire, Facilitator of the inter-Congolese dialogue, who had responded to questions posed by Council members.

Also on 5 September [meeting 4365], following consultations among Council members, the President made statement **S/PRST/2001/22** on behalf of the Council.

> The Security Council welcomes the success of the preparatory meeting of the inter-Congolese dialogue, held in Gaborone on 20-24 August 2001.
> The Council reiterates its strong support for the inter-Congolese dialogue and for the efforts of the Facilitator and his team in the field. It calls on all the Congolese parties to further cooperate with each other and the Facilitator in the constructive spirit of Gaborone to ensure the successful outcome of the inter-Congolese dialogue starting on 15 October 2001, in Addis Ababa.
> The Council stresses the importance for the dialogue to be free from outside interference, open, representative and inclusive, and emphasizes the need to ensure adequate representation of Congolese women in the process.
> The Council encourages donors to provide further support to the Facilitator for the inter-Congolese dialogue and, in due course, the process of implementing a new political dispensation in the Democratic Republic of the Congo.
> The Council urges all the parties to the Lusaka Ceasefire Agreement to press forward with the full and early implementation of that Agreement, including disarmament, demobilization, reintegration, repatriation and resettlement of the armed groups, and the withdrawal of foreign forces.

The inter-Congolese dialogue began in Addis Ababa on 15 October. However, because of insufficient resources, 80 participants attended instead of the more than 300 expected. The Secretary-General's Special Representative explained the circumstances to the Security Council on 24 October [meeting 4395]. The DRC raised objections about the reduced number of participants and refused to allow substantive issues to be addressed. On 21 October, the neutral Facilitator announced that the dialogue would be postponed until a later date. In a letter of 23 October [S/2001/998], the DRC gave its position on the Addis Ababa talks, emphasizing the need for them to be inclusive. South Africa offered to host the dialogue within one month and to assume most of the cost, a proposal to which the DRC and all the other component groups responded positively.

Communication. On 18 September [S/2001/884], the DRC alleged that RCD-Goma had appointed what they called "provincial assemblies" aimed at establishing federalism or a secessionist State in the Congolese territories occupied by Rwanda.

MONUC phase III

Report of Secretary-General (October). The Secretary-General, in his ninth report on MONUC, issued on 16 October [S/2001/970], stated that the overall situation in the DRC continued to develop in a largely positive direction. The ceasefire had held and the disengagement of forces and their redeployment to new defensive positions was effectively complete. Some foreign forces had been withdrawn from the territory. The preparatory meeting of the inter-Congolese dialogue was held successfully. At the same time, outbreaks of fighting had continued in the east of the country, where the ceasefire violations were mainly attributed to armed groups.

During a visit to the region from 1 to 5 September, the Secretary-General urged the DRC to bring an end to the fighting in the east, open a dialogue with Rwanda and cooperate with MONUC in preparing for the demobilization of the soldiers of Rwandan origin located at Kamina. In that regard, President Kabila announced that some 3,000 soldiers at that location would be demobilized shortly. The Secretary-General also met with representatives of civil society and with the RCD leadership in Kisangani, where he insisted on the earliest possible demilitarization of the town. In Kigali, he met with President Paul Kagame and urged him to use his influence to halt the fighting in eastern DRC. The President expressed his Government's willingness to take back the Rwandan former combatants currently in the DRC.

At a meeting of the Political Committee (Kigali, 14-15 September), the JMC decision to co-locate to Kinshasa with MONUC was endorsed. The Political Committee criticized the United Nations for its "hesitancy" in deploying forces to the DRC.

On 29 September, armed elements, believed to be Mayi-Mayi militia (a term applied to local armed Congolese groups in opposition to Rwandan forces), attacked Kindu, apparently aiming for the RPA command headquarters and the airport. The attacks were repulsed by RCD troops occupying the town. On 16 August, a MONUC helicopter was hit by 14 bullets, fired by unidentified armed men, but the occupants were unhurt.

As at 15 October, MONUC's strength stood at 2,408 military personnel. A total of 77 military observer teams were inside the DRC, of which 46 were static and 31 were mobile. MONUC completed the verification of disengagement and redeployment of the parties. All but one of the 96 new defensive positions were verified, thereby effectively ending that element of the Lusaka process. While much progress had been made in the south-eastern areas, there were some violations of the disengagement plan at Moliro, Pweto and Mani. Uganda had largely withdrawn its troops from Equateur province but had declared its intention to maintain three battalions in the country until a peace agreement was reached. The Namibian authorities indicated that they had withdrawn their troops except for two small elements. Zimbabwe declared the withdrawal of three battalions from Equateur province and the eastern part of the country. There had been no withdrawals by RPA.

In general, the parties provided satisfactory security for MONUC military and civilian personnel. However, RCD, which filed most of the allegations of ceasefire violations, did not in many cases provide timely security guarantees for investigation by MONUC. RCD continued to reject the demilitarization of Kisangani and maintained forces there, allegedly to counter the threat by the Mayi-Mayi and FAC.

The humanitarian situation in the DRC remained grave, with humanitarian agencies having access to fewer than half of the estimated 2,041,000 displaced people due to security constraints. The human rights situation, on the other hand, had improved as a result of the Government's efforts to establish human rights laws and standards.

At the time of the report, MONUC had nearly completed the second phase of its deployment and was faced with the tasks of the next phase—the total withdrawal of foreign forces and the disarmament and demobilization of armed groups. It would also be necessary to find durable solutions to the problem of armed groups, including the repatriation, resettlement and reintegration of ex-combatants into society. With regard to Rwandan former combatants, the objective would be to repatriate them to Rwanda as soon as possible after they were disarmed, rather than accommodating them for long periods in camps on Congolese territory. Screening of ex-combatants would largely be organized by the host country with the support of the United Nations. In that regard, the Secretary-General warned, it should be borne in mind that some members of ex-FAR and Interahamwe had taken part in the Rwandan genocide of 1994. He also cautioned that the armed groups operating in eastern DRC had not signed the Lusaka Agreement and continued to take part in armed hostilities.

The main role of MONUC in phase III would be to establish temporary reception centres where combatants could surrender their weapons to MONUC. They would then be demobilized, perhaps accompanied by their dependants, and transported back to Rwanda for reintegration. MONUC would assume a coordinating role in organizing the DDRRR effort but would rely on UN programmes and agencies for such practical tasks as camp management, medical support and provision of food, water and sanitation. MONUC would adopt a step-by-step approach in the eastern part of the DRC. It needed to assess the security situation in the area before deploying troops. Its initial objective would be to establish a mixed civilian and military presence, as well as a forward support base, probably at Kindu, and strengthen its presence in Kisangani once it was demilitarized. An initial group of 400 would have responsibility for establishing the necessary infrastructure for subsequent deployments, as well as investigating ceasefire violations, gathering information on the size and movement of armed groups, and facilitating disarmament and demobilization. The base would be gradually expanded to some 2,000 troops, including an aviation regiment with armed helicopters, an engineering unit, and riverine and ferry services. UN civilian personnel would work to increase humanitarian access, draw attention to human rights problems, gather information about armed groups, keep the local population informed through radio broadcasts about MONUC, and plan for disarmament and demobilization of armed groups, including child soldiers. A public information component would prepare for a UN radio network capable of broadcasting to the entire country.

To sustain the momentum in the peace process, the Secretary-General recommended that the Security Council authorize MONUC to enter phase III of its deployment in accordance with the concept of operations he outlined. The initial deployment of troops in Kindu would remain within the limit of 5,537 troops already authorized. Significant assistance and funding would be required for peace-related operations.

SECURITY COUNCIL ACTION (October/November

Following a closed meeting on 18 and 22 October [meeting 4391], the Security Council issued a communiqué [S/PV.4391] stating that it had heard briefings from the Special Representative of the Secretary-General for the DRC and Major General Mountaga Diallo, MONUC Force Commander. The Special Representative had responded to questions by Council members and representatives of troop-contributing countries.

On 24 October [meeting 4396], following consultations among Council members, the President made statement **S/PRST/2001/29** on behalf of the Council:

> The Security Council welcomes the recommendations of the Secretary-General on the next phase in the deployment of the United Nations Organization Mission in the Democratic Republic of the Congo, as contained in his report of 16 October 2001.
>
> The Council supports the initiation of phase III of the deployment of the Mission within the currently mandated ceiling and, in particular, its deployment towards the east of the Democratic Republic of the Congo.
>
> The Council reminds the parties to the conflict that they are responsible for the continuation of the peace process. It is up to them to create and to maintain conditions conducive to the start of phase III of the Mission by fully implementing the commitments they have undertaken. The Council will take its decisions on the future of phase III of the Mission after ascertaining that the parties to the Lusaka Ceasefire Agreement are committed to continuing, in a spirit of partnership, to make the efforts necessary to advance the peace process. The next meeting between the Security Council and members of the Political Committee established by the Lusaka Ceasefire Agreement will provide an opportunity to discuss these issues.
>
> The Council recalls the importance it places on the implementation of the Lusaka Ceasefire Agreement and the relevant resolutions of the Council. In particular the Council:
>
> —Calls on those States which have not yet done so to withdraw from the territory of the Democratic Republic of the Congo in accordance with the Lusaka Ceasefire Agreement and the relevant Security Council resolutions;
>
> —Calls on all parties to cease any support for armed groups and to implement the process of disarmament, demobilization, repatriation, resettlement and reintegration of the groups referred to in annex A, chapter 9.1; of the Lusaka Ceasefire Agreement;
>
> —Emphasizes the importance of the inter-Congolese dialogue and calls on the Congolese parties to work together for the success of this process; and

> —Demands the demilitarization of Kisangani, in conformity with its resolution 1304(2000).
>
> The Council expresses serious concern at the worsening humanitarian and human rights situation, particularly in the eastern part of the Democratic Republic of the Congo, and reiterates its call for all the parties to urgently address the human rights abuses, including those raised in the ninth report of the Secretary-General, in the Government-controlled territory, the territory controlled by the Front de Libération du Congo and the territory controlled by the Rassemblement Congolais pour la Démocratie.

Following a closed meeting on 9 November [meeting 4411], the Security Council issued a communiqué [S/PV.4411] stating that it had held a frank and constructive discussion with members of the Political Committee of the Lusaka Agreement. Also on 9 November [meeting 4412], the Council unanimously adopted **resolution 1376 (2001)**. The draft [S/2001/1058] was prepared in consultations among Council members.

> *The Security Council,*
>
> *Recalling* its previous resolutions and statements by its President,
>
> *Reaffirming* the obligation of all States to refrain from the use of force against the territorial integrity and political independence of any State, or in any other manner inconsistent with the purposes of the United Nations, and reaffirming also the political independence, the territorial integrity and the sovereignty of the Democratic Republic of the Congo, including over its natural resources,
>
> *Taking note* of the report of the Secretary-General of 16 October 2001 and its recommendations,
>
> *Welcoming* the participation of the Political Committee for the implementation of the Lusaka Ceasefire Agreement in joint meetings held on 9 November 2001,
>
> *Determining* that the situation in the Democratic Republic of the Congo continues to pose a threat to international peace and security in the region,
>
> 1. *Welcomes* the general respect for the ceasefire among the parties to the Lusaka Ceasefire Agreement, expresses nonetheless its concern at the hostilities in areas of the eastern Democratic Republic of the Congo and calls on the parties to cease any form of support to the armed groups, particularly in the east of the country;
>
> 2. *Welcomes* the withdrawal of some foreign forces from the Democratic Republic of the Congo, including the full Namibian contingent, as a positive step towards the full withdrawal of all foreign forces, and requests all States that have not yet done so to begin to implement, without delay, their full withdrawal in accordance with resolution 1304(2000) of 16 June 2000;
>
> 3. *Demands once again* that Kisangani be demilitarized rapidly and unconditionally in accordance with Security Council resolution 1304(2000), takes note of the pledge by the RCD-Goma during the 4411th meeting of 9 November 2001 fully to demilitarize the city, welcomes the decision of the Secretary-General to further deploy Mission personnel in this city, notably to contribute to the training of police, stresses that, once

demilitarized, no party will be permitted to reoccupy the city militarily and welcomes in this regard the pledge by the Government of the Democratic Republic of the Congo, during the same meeting, to respect this provision;

4. *Expresses its support* for the inter-Congolese dialogue, one of the key elements of the peace process, and for all efforts to promote this process, calls on the Congolese parties to work together for the success of the dialogue, and expresses its support for the facilitator and his call on the parties to make the dialogue fully inclusive;

5. *Expresses its grave concern* at the repeated human rights violations throughout the Democratic Republic of the Congo in particular in the territories under the control of the rebel groups party to the Lusaka Ceasefire Agreement, and calls on all parties to put an end to such violations;

6. *Expresses its serious concern* with regard to the humanitarian situation in the Democratic Republic of the Congo and calls on the international community to increase, without delay, its support for humanitarian activities;

7. *Expresses its serious concern* with regard to the economic difficulties facing the Democratic Republic of the Congo, stresses that progress in the peace process and the economic recovery and development of the country are interdependent, and in this regard underlines the urgent need for increased international economic assistance in support of the peace process;

8. *Reiterates* its condemnation of all illegal exploitation of the natural resources of the Democratic Republic of the Congo, demands that such exploitation cease and stresses that the natural resources of the Democratic Republic of the Congo should not be exploited to finance the conflict in that country;

9. *Emphasizes* that there are links between the peace processes in Burundi and in the Democratic Republic of the Congo and, welcoming the recent progress in the Burundi process, invites the parties to the Lusaka Ceasefire Agreement to work with the Burundian authorities to advance these two processes;

10. *Supports* the launching of phase III of the deployment of the United Nations Organization Mission in the Democratic Republic of the Congo on the basis of the concept of operations detailed in paragraphs 59 to 87 of the Secretary-General's report and stresses, in this regard, the importance it attaches to the deployment of the Mission in the east of the Democratic Republic of the Congo, in conformity with the new concept of operation and within the overall ceiling, including in the cities of Kindu and Kisangani;

11. *Notes with concern* the joint communiqué issued on 4 November 2001 by the Secretaries-General of the Mouvement de Libération du Congo and of the Rassemblement Congolais pour la Démocratie concerning the deployment of a joint special force in Kindu, and stresses that appropriate conditions will be necessary to allow the Mission to fulfil its role in Kindu and to ensure that discussions on the voluntary disarmament and demobilization of concerned armed groups take place in a neutral environment;

12. *Affirms* that the implementation of phase III of the deployment of the Mission requires the following steps from the parties and requests the Secretary-General to report on progress thereon:

(i) The transmission to the Mission, as soon as possible and in accordance with its resolution 1355(2001) of 15 June 2001, of the necessary operational information for the planning of Mission support for the process of total withdrawal of foreign troops present in the territory of the Democratic Republic of the Congo, including the number of foreign military personnel in the territory of the Democratic Republic of the Congo, their equipment and armament, their exit routes, and a precise timetable for implementation;

(ii) The transmission to the Mission, as soon as possible and in accordance with its resolution 1355(2001), of the necessary operational information for the planning of the Mission's mandated role in the process of disarmament, demobilization, repatriation, resettlement and reintegration programme for the armed groups referred to in annex A, chapter 9.1, of the Lusaka Ceasefire Agreement, including the number of persons concerned, their equipment and armament, their location, their intentions, as well as a precise timetable for implementation;

(iii) The establishment of a direct dialogue between the Governments of the Democratic Republic of the Congo and Rwanda leading to confidence-building and a joint mechanism for coordination, and exchanges of information regarding the disarmament, demobilization, repatriation, resettlement and reintegration process;

(iv) The establishment by the Governments of the countries concerned, in particular Rwanda, and noting steps taken so far, of conditions conducive to voluntary disarmament, demobilization, repatriation, resettlement and reintegration of the members of the armed groups concerned, in particular, by assuring the protection of the personal safety of the members of these armed groups, their civil rights and their economic reintegration including with the assistance of the donor community;

(v) The demilitarization of Kisangani;

(vi) The full restoration of freedom of movement for persons and goods between Kinshasa and Kisangani and throughout the country;

(vii) The full cooperation by the parties with Mission military and logistical operations, as well as its humanitarian, human rights and child protection activities, including by permitting unrestricted access to ports and airports, and by refraining from introducing administrative and other impediments;

13. *Expresses its satisfaction* at the partnership established with the parties to the Lusaka Ceasefire Agreement, strengthened by regular contacts between the Political Committee for the implementation of that Agreement and the Council, and reiterates its firm determination to continue to provide assistance to the parties in their efforts to achieve peace;

14. *Commends* the outstanding work of Mission personnel in challenging conditions, and pays tribute in particular to the efforts of the Special Representative of the Secretary-General;

15. *Decides* to remain actively seized of the matter.

Communications (November/December). The Sudan, in a 20 November letter to the Security Council President [S/2001/1113], referred to an allegation by Uganda in a statement to the Council that the objective of Ugandan forces in the DRC was to ensure that the Democratic Alliance, a Ugandan opposition group supported by the Sudan and trained by Al-Qa'idah, did not obtain assistance for the purpose of launching terrorist operations in Uganda across the Ruwenzori mountains. The Sudan said Uganda was trying to divert attention from its invasion of DRC territory and its plundering of resources.

On 3 December [S/2001/1143], the DRC informed the Council of recent developments that might jeopardize the peace process, including the refusal of RCD-Goma to demilitarize Kisangani, the deployment of RPA in eastern DRC, the resumption of fighting in areas under Ugandan control, and repression of workers in the occupied provinces. The DRC called on the Council to take action. In another letter of the same date [S/2001/1146], the DRC stated that Rwanda was substantially increasing its military presence in eastern DRC at a time when the Congolese people were focusing on the inter-Congolese negotiations and when the allied forces of Namibia had completed their withdrawal and Angola and Zimbabwe had begun a significant withdrawal of their forces. In its view, Rwanda was seeking to restart the war. Rwanda, on 10 December [S/2001/1168], denied that it had made any changes to its troops' deployment in the DRC, adding that they were in the new defensive positions, as agreed, and in other places in Katanga. It claimed that the DRC was supporting Rwandan opposition forces. The DRC, on 27 December [S/2001/1299], refuting a claim by President Kagame of Rwanda that he had already withdrawn half of his troops from the DRC, noted that the Secretary-General's Special Representative had recently reported a build-up of Rwandan forces in eastern DRC.

Situation at year's end. On 4 November, RCD and MLC leaders announced their intention to create a joint military force to forcibly disarm rebel groups in eastern DRC; a force of 4,102 soldiers, based in Kindu, would track, disarm and neutralize "negative forces". Addressing the Security Council on 9 November [meeting 4410], the Secretary-General expressed concern about that decision and warned that Kindu must not be used as a base for launching military operations.

Late 2001 was marked by a realignment of political and military alliances of armed rebel groups, resulting in intensified fighting in the north-eastern part of the country [S/2002/169]. Following the dissolution of the former FLC

(merger of MLC and RCD-K/ML), a shift of alliances on the ground involving MLC and factions of RCD-K/ML was reflected in military confrontations between the forces of the two movements. On 16 November, RCD-K/ML took over administrative control of Bunia, forcing MLC to retreat to Equateur province. Other clashes between the two factions also occurred. On 29 December, MONUC reported firing for much of that day in Kindu. RCD/RPA claimed that Mayi-Mayi fighters had attacked the town with the aim of gaining control of the airfield, allegedly killing 21 civilians.

At the invitation of President Kabila, MONUC observed the demobilization at Kamina of nearly 2,000 combatants, said to be Rwandans, who were interviewed by MONUC. MONUC was working with the Governments of the DRC and Rwanda to facilitate repatriation and resettlement of those men. Meanwhile, Uganda claimed that it had reduced its troops in the DRC by 6,655 since 29 July 2000. However, it insisted that three battalions would remain in eastern DRC.

In an effort to pave the way for substantive discussions at the next inter-Congolese dialogue (planned for 2002), the Assistant Secretary-General for Political Affairs, Ibrahima Fall, in consultation with the neutral Facilitator, held talks with the Government, MLC and RCD on 9 and 12 November in New York and from 6 to 8 December in Abuja. It was agreed to reduce the number of participants in the 2002 round of talks to 300 and participation was extended to representatives of the Mayi-Mayi, religious groups, traditional chiefs, internal and external opposition not present at the preparatory talks in Gaborone, and the Congolese diaspora.

The overall humanitarian situation continued to be characterized by grievous human rights violations, chronic food insecurity, population displacement and serious health problems, aggravated by restrictions on humanitarian agencies due to the prevailing insecurity.

MONUC financing

In a 10 May report [A/55/935], the Secretary-General submitted the financial performance of MONUC from 6 August 1999 to 30 June 2000, the proposed budget for its operation from 1 July 2000 to 30 June 2001 and its estimated initial requirements for 1 July to 31 December 2001. He recommended that the General Assembly: appropriate $58,681,000 gross ($58,441,000 net) as authorized in resolution 54/260 B [YUN 2000, p. 142] for the operation of the Mission from 6 August 1999 to 30 June 2000; decide on the treatment of the unencumbered balance of $3,409,600 gross ($3,605,300 net) for the period ending 30 June 2000; appropriate $273,119,600 gross ($270,085,600 net) for operations from 1 July 2000 to 30 June 2001; assess $131,800,600 gross ($129,258,500 net) for 1 July 2000 to 30 June 2001; and approve a commitment authority, with assessment, of $209,965,600 gross ($204,788,900 net) for the maintenance of MONUC from 1 July to 31 December 2001.

The Advisory Committee on Administrative and Budgetary Questions (ACABQ) commented on that report on 15 May [A/55/941] and made general comments on the financing of UN peacekeeping operations in a 6 April report [A/55/874].

GENERAL ASSEMBLY ACTION (June)

On 14 June [meeting 103], the General Assembly, on the recommendation of the Fifth (Administrative and Budgetary) Committee [A/55/962], adopted **resolution 55/275** without vote [agenda item 167].

Financing of the United Nations Organization Mission in the Democratic Republic of the Congo

The General Assembly,

Having considered the report of the Secretary-General on the financing of the United Nations Organization Mission in the Democratic Republic of the Congo and the related reports of the Advisory Committee on Administrative and Budgetary Questions,

Bearing in mind Security Council resolutions 1258 (1999) of 6 August 1999 and 1279(1999) of 30 November 1999 regarding, respectively, the deployment to the Congo region of military liaison personnel and the establishment of the United Nations Organization Mission in the Democratic Republic of the Congo, and the subsequent resolutions by which the Council extended the mandate of the Mission, the latest of which was resolution 1332(2000) of 14 December 2000,

Recalling its resolutions 54/260 A of 7 April 2000 and 54/260 B of 15 June 2000 on the financing of the Mission,

Reaffirming the general principles underlying the financing of United Nations peacekeeping operations, as stated in General Assembly resolutions 1874(S-IV) of 27 June 1963, 3101(XXVIII) of 11 December 1973 and 55/235 of 23 December 2000,

Mindful of the fact that it is essential to provide the Mission with the necessary financial resources to enable it to fulfil its responsibilities under the relevant resolutions of the Security Council,

1. *Reaffirms* its resolution 49/233 A of 23 December 1994, in particular those paragraphs regarding the peacekeeping budgetary cycles, which should be adhered to in the future budgeting process, where possible;

2. *Takes note* of the status of contributions to the United Nations Organization Mission in the Democratic Republic of the Congo as at 30 April 2001, including the contributions outstanding in the amount of 32.7 million United States dollars, representing some 16 per cent of the total assessed contributions, notes that some 64 per cent of the Member States have paid their assessed contributions in full, and urges all other Member States concerned, in particular those in ar-

rears, to ensure the payment of their outstanding assessed contributions;

3. *Expresses its appreciation* to those Member States which have paid their assessed contributions in full;

4. *Expresses concern* about the financial situation with regard to peacekeeping activities, in particular as regards the reimbursements to troop contributors that bear additional burdens owing to overdue payments by Member States of their assessments;

5. *Urges* all other Member States to make every possible effort to ensure the payment of their assessed contributions to the Mission in full and on time;

6. *Expresses concern* at the delay experienced by the Secretary-General in deploying and providing adequate resources to some recent peacekeeping missions, in particular those in Africa;

7. *Emphasizes* that all future and existing peacekeeping missions shall be given equal and non-discriminatory treatment in respect of financial and administrative arrangements;

8. *Also emphasizes* that all peacekeeping missions shall be provided with adequate resources for the effective and efficient discharge of their respective mandates;

9. *Reiterates its request* to the Secretary-General to make the fullest possible use of facilities and equipment at the United Nations Logistics Base at Brindisi, Italy, in order to minimize the costs of procurement for the Mission;

10. *Endorses* the conclusions and recommendations contained in the report of the Advisory Committee on Administrative and Budgetary Questions, and requests the Secretary-General to ensure their full implementation;

11. *Expresses concern* about the high level of unliquidated obligations in the Mission as at 30 June 2000;

12. *Requests* the Secretary-General to take all necessary action to ensure that the Mission is administered with a maximum of efficiency and economy;

13. *Also requests* the Secretary-General, in order to reduce the cost of employing General Service staff, to continue efforts to recruit local staff for the Mission against General Service posts, commensurate with the requirements of the Mission;

14. *Decides* to appropriate to the Special Account for the United Nations Organization Mission in the Democratic Republic of the Congo the amount of 58,681,000 dollars gross (58,441,000 dollars net), as previously authorized and apportioned under the terms of General Assembly resolutions 54/260 A and B for the establishment and operation of the Mission for the period from 6 August 1999 to 30 June 2000;

15. *Decides also* to appropriate the amount of 232,119,600 dollars gross (229,085,600 dollars net) for the maintenance of the Mission for the period from 1 July 2000 to 30 June 2001, inclusive of the amount of 141,319,000 dollars gross (140,827,100 dollars net) previously authorized under the terms of General Assembly resolution 54/260 B and of 49,865,400 dollars gross (49,530,700 dollars net) authorized by the Advisory Committee under the terms of section IV of General Assembly resolution 49/233 A, and authorizes the Secretary-General to enter into additional commitments for the Mission for the same period in the amount not exceeding 41 million dollars gross and net;

16. *Decides further,* taking into account the amount of 141,319,000 dollars gross (140,827,100 dollars net) already apportioned under the terms of its resolution 54/260 A, to apportion among Member States the additional amount of 83,233,883 dollars gross (80,903,625 dollars net) for the Mission for the period from 1 July 2000 to 15 June 2001 in accordance with the levels set out in General Assembly resolution 55/235, as adjusted by the Assembly in its resolution 55/236 of 23 December 2000, and taking into account the scale of assessments for the year 2001, as set out in its resolution 55/5 B of 23 December 2000;

17. *Decides* that, in accordance with the provisions of its resolution 973(X) of 15 December 1955, there shall be set off against the apportionment among Member States, as provided for in paragraph 16 above, their respective share in the Tax Equalization Fund of the estimated additional staff assessment income of 2,330,258 dollars approved for the Mission for the period from 1 July 2000 to 15 June 2001;

18. *Decides also* to apportion among Member States the amount of 7,566,717 dollars gross (7,354,875 dollars net) for the period from 15 to 30 June 2001, in accordance with paragraph 16 above, subject to the decision of the Security Council to extend the mandate of the Mission beyond 15 June 2001;

19. *Decides further* that, in accordance with the provisions of its resolution 973(X), there shall be set off against the apportionment among Member States, as provided for in paragraph 18 above, their respective share in the Tax Equalization Fund of the estimated additional staff assessment income of 211,842 dollars approved for the Mission for the period from 15 to 30 June 2001;

20. *Decides* that, for Member States that have fulfilled their financial obligations to the Mission, there shall be set off against the apportionment, as provided for in paragraph 16 above, their respective share of the unencumbered balance of 3,409,600 dollars gross (3,605,300 dollars net) in respect of the period ending 30 June 2000, in accordance with the composition of groups set out in paragraphs 3 and 4 of General Assembly resolution 43/232 of 1 March 1989 and as adjusted by the Assembly in subsequent relevant resolutions and decisions for the ad hoc apportionment of peacekeeping appropriations, the latest of which were resolution 52/230 of 31 March 1998 and decisions 54/456 to 54/458 of 23 December 1999 for the period 1998-2000, and taking into account the scale of assessments for the year 2000, as set out in its resolutions 52/215 A of 22 December 1997 and 54/237 A of 23 December 1999;

21. *Decides also* that, for Member States that have not fulfilled their financial obligations to the Mission, their share of the unencumbered balance of 3,409,600 dollars gross (3,605,300 dollars net) in respect of the period ending 30 June 2000 shall be set off against their outstanding obligations, in accordance with paragraph 20 above;

22. *Decides further* to appropriate for the maintenance of the Mission for the period from 1 July to 31 December 2001 the amount of 200 million dollars gross (194,823,300 dollars net) to be apportioned among Member States in accordance with paragraph 16 above, at the monthly rate of 33,333,333 dollars gross (32,470,550 dollars net), subject to the decision of the Security Council to extend the mandate of the Mission beyond 30 June 2001;

23. *Decides* that, in accordance with the provisions of its resolution 973(X), there shall be set off against the apportionment among Member States, as provided for in paragraph 22 above, their respective share in the Tax Equalization Fund of the estimated staff assessment income of 5,176,700 dollars approved for the Mission for the period from 1 July to 31 December 2001;

24. *Decides also* to appropriate to the Special Account for the Mission the amount of 8,260,509 dollars gross (7,249,409 dollars net) for the support account for peacekeeping operations and the amount of 862,915 dollars gross (774,893 dollars net) for the United Nations Logistics Base for the period from 1 July 2001 to 30 June 2002, to be apportioned among Member States in accordance with paragraph 16 above, and taking into account the scale of assessments for the years 2001 and 2002, as set out in General Assembly resolution 55/5 B, the scale of assessments for the year 2001 to be applied against a portion thereof, that is, 4,130,254 dollars gross (3,624,704 dollars net) for the support account and 431,457 dollars gross (387,446 dollars net) for the Logistics Base for the period from 1 July to 31 December 2001, and the scale of assessments for the year 2002 to be applied against the balance, that is, 4,130,255 dollars gross (3,624,705 dollars net) for the support account and 431,458 dollars gross (387,447 dollars net) for the Logistics Base for the period from 1 January to 30 June 2002;

25. *Decides further* that, in accordance with the provisions of its resolution 973(X), there shall be set off against the apportionment among Member States, as provided for in paragraph 24 above, their respective share in the Tax Equalization Fund of the estimated staff assessment income of 1,011,100 dollars for the support account and 88,022 dollars for the United Nations Logistics Base approved for the period from 1 July 2001 to 30 June 2002, 505,550 dollars for the support account and 44,011 dollars for the Logistics Base being amounts pertaining to the period from 1 July to 31 December 2001, and the balance, that is, 505,550 dollars for the support account and 44,011 dollars for the Logistics Base pertaining to the period from 1 January to 30 June 2002;

26. *Emphasizes* that no peacekeeping mission shall be financed by borrowing funds from other active peacekeeping missions;

27. *Encourages* the Secretary-General to continue to take additional measures to ensure the safety and security of all personnel under the auspices of the United Nations participating in the Mission;

28. *Invites* voluntary contributions to the Mission in cash and in the form of services and supplies acceptable to the Secretary-General, to be administered, as appropriate, in accordance with the procedure and practices established by the General Assembly;

29. *Decides* to include in the provisional agenda of its fifty-sixth session the item entitled "Financing of the United Nations Organization Mission in the Democratic Republic of the Congo".

On 27 November, the Secretary-General reported on the budget for MONUC for 1 July 2001 to 30 June 2002 [A/56/660], which amounted to

$537,051,200 gross ($528,531,800 net). It was based on an authorized strength of up to 5,537 military personnel, as authorized in part B of Security Council resolution 1355(2001) (see p. 129). Of the total budget, some 13 per cent of resources related to civilian personnel costs. Operational costs accounted for 59 per cent of the budget, military personnel costs reflected 25 per cent, while staff assessment comprised 2 per cent. The Secretary-General recommended that the General Assembly: appropriate $337,051,200 gross ($333,708,500 net) for the maintenance of the Mission from 1 July 2001 to 30 June 2002, in addition to the amount of $200 million gross ($194,823,300 net) appropriated under Assembly resolution 55/275 (see p. 137) for 1 July to 31 December 2001; assess the additional amount of $68,526,600 gross ($69,422,600 net) for the maintenance of MONUC for 1 July to 31 December 2001; assess $246,148,500 gross ($242,243,700 net) for 1 January to 15 June 2002; and assess $22,377,100 gross ($22,022,200 net) for 16 to 30 June 2002 should the Council decide to continue the Mission's mandate beyond 15 June 2002.

ACABQ reviewed MONUC financing in a report of 7 December [A/56/688]. It noted that a report of the size and complexity of the MONUC budget required more time than was available to the Committee to properly fulfil its function. It would revert to the issue in 2002.

GENERAL ASSEMBLY ACTION (December)

On 24 December [meeting 92], the General Assembly, on the recommendation of the Fifth Committee [A/56/713], adopted **resolution 56/252** without vote [agenda item 158].

Financing of the United Nations Organization Mission in the Democratic Republic of the Congo

The General Assembly,

Having considered the report of the Secretary-General on the financing of the United Nations Organization Mission in the Democratic Republic of the Congo and the related report of the Advisory Committee on Administrative and Budgetary Questions,

Bearing in mind Security Council resolution 1258 (1999) of 6 August 1999, by which the Council established the United Nations Organization Mission in the Democratic Republic of the Congo, and the subsequent resolutions by which the Council revised and extended the mandate of the Mission, the latest of which was resolution 1376(2001) of 9 November 2001,

Recalling its resolution 54/260 A of 7 April 2000 as well as subsequent resolutions on the financing of the Mission, the latest of which was resolution 55/275 of 14 June 2001,

Reaffirming the general principles underlying the financing of United Nations peacekeeping operations, as stated in General Assembly resolutions 1874(S-IV) of 27 June 1963, 3101(XXVIII) of 11 December 1973 and 55/235 of 23 December 2000,

Noting with appreciation that voluntary contributions have been made to the Mission,

Mindful of the fact that it is essential to provide the Mission with the necessary financial resources to enable it to fulfil its responsibilities under the relevant resolutions of the Security Council,

1. *Reiterates* paragraph 1 of its resolution 55/275;

2. *Takes note* of the status of contributions to the United Nations Organization Mission in the Democratic Republic of the Congo as at 15 November 2001, including the contributions outstanding in the amount of 152.6 million United States dollars, representing, regrettably, some 40 per cent of the total assessed contributions, notes that some 22 per cent of Member States have paid their assessed contributions in full, and urges all other Member States concerned, in particular those in arrears, to ensure payment of their outstanding assessed contributions;

3. *Expresses its appreciation* to those Member States that have paid their assessed contributions in full and on time, and urges all other Member States to make every possible effort to ensure payment of their assessed contributions to the Mission in full;

4. *Expresses concern* about the financial situation with regard to peacekeeping activities, in particular as regards the reimbursements to troop contributors that bear additional burdens owing to overdue payments by Member States of their assessments;

5. *Also expresses concern* at the delay experienced by the Secretary-General in deploying and providing adequate resources to some recent peacekeeping missions, in particular those in Africa;

6. *Emphasizes* that all future and existing peacekeeping missions shall be given equal and non-discriminatory treatment in respect of financial and administrative arrangements;

7. *Also emphasizes* that all peacekeeping missions shall be provided with adequate resources for the effective and efficient discharge of their respective mandates;

8. *Reiterates its request* to the Secretary-General to make the fullest possible use of facilities and equipment at the United Nations Logistics Base at Brindisi, Italy, in order to minimize the costs of procurement for the Mission;

9. *Endorses* the conclusions and recommendations contained in the report of the Advisory Committee on Administrative and Budgetary Questions, and requests the Secretary-General to ensure their full implementation;

10. *Requests* the Secretary-General to take all necessary action to ensure that the Mission is administered with a maximum of efficiency and economy;

11. *Also requests* the Secretary-General, in order to reduce the cost of employing General Service staff, to continue efforts to recruit local staff for the Mission against General Service posts, commensurate with the requirements of the Mission;

12. *Decides* to appropriate the additional amount of 196,593,590 dollars gross (193,819,705 dollars net) for the maintenance of the Mission for the nine-month period from 1 July 2001 to 31 March 2002, inclusive of the amount of 3,351,190 dollars gross (3,098,505 dollars net) for the support account for peacekeeping operations, in addition to the amount of 8,260,509 dollars gross (7,249,409 dollars net) already appropriated for the support account, the amount of 862,915 dollars

gross (774,893 dollars net) already appropriated for the United Nations Logistics Base and the amount of 200 million dollars gross (194,823,300 dollars net) for the maintenance of the Mission for the period from 1 July to 31 December 2001 appropriated and assessed by the General Assembly in its resolution 55/275;

13. *Decides also*, taking into account the amount of 200 million dollars gross (194,823,300 dollars net) already apportioned for the period from 1 July to 31 December 2001 in accordance with the provisions of its resolution 55/275, to apportion among Member States the additional amount of 196,593,590 dollars gross (193,819,705 dollars net) for the period from 1 January to 31 March 2002 in accordance with the levels set out in General Assembly resolution 55/235 as adjusted by the Assembly in its resolution 55/236 of 23 December 2000, and taking into account the scale of assessments for the years 2001 and 2002 as set out in its resolution 55/5 B of 23 December 2000;

14. *Decides further* that, in accordance with the provisions of its resolution 973(X) of 15 December 1955, there shall be set off against the apportionment among Member States, as provided for in paragraph 13 above, their respective share in the Tax Equalization Fund of the estimated staff assessment income of 2,773,885 dollars approved for the Mission for the period from 1 January to 31 March 2002;

15. *Emphasizes* that no peacekeeping mission shall be financed by borrowing funds from other active peacekeeping missions;

16. *Encourages* the Secretary-General to continue to take additional measures to ensure the safety and security of all personnel under the auspices of the United Nations participating in the Mission;

17. *Invites* voluntary contributions to the Mission in cash and in the form of services and supplies acceptable to the Secretary-General, to be administered, as appropriate, in accordance with the procedure and practices established by the General Assembly;

18. *Decides* to keep under review during its fifty-sixth session the item entitled "Financing of the United Nations Organization Mission in the Democratic Republic of the Congo".

The Assembly, on 24 December, decided that the agenda item on MONUC financing would remain for consideration during its resumed fifty-sixth (2002) session (**decision 56/464**), and that the Fifth Committee would continue to consider the item at that session (**decision 56/458**).

Exploitation of natural resources

Reports of Expert Panel. The Secretary-General submitted to the Security Council, on 16 January [S/2001/49], the interim report of the Panel of Experts on the Illegal Exploitation of Natural Resources and Other Forms of Wealth of the Democratic Republic of the Congo. The Expert Panel, established by the Secretary-General in response to a Council request contained in presidential statement S/PRST/2000/20 [YUN 2000, p. 128], had the mandate to collect information on illegal exploitation and to analyse the

links between such exploitation and the continuation of the conflict in the DRC. It described its activities, including difficulties encountered, and its meetings with government leaders in Burundi, the DRC, Kenya, Rwanda, Uganda and Zimbabwe. It also sent members to meet with officials in Cameroon, South Africa and the United Republic of Tanzania and conducted meetings with government officials, the diplomatic community, non-governmental organizations (NGOs), members of civil society and private individuals in Brussels, London and Paris. One of the most serious problems facing the Panel was the paucity of detailed and reliable information, including statistics, as to the nature, extent, location, yield and value of the DRC's natural resources. Decades of government neglect, mismanagement and corruption, including widespread evasion of taxes and customs duties, as well as the effects of conflict since 1996, made it almost impossible to establish a precise and impartial factual picture of the country's natural resource base and exploitation patterns. Mines and other sources were remote and heavily guarded, roads were few and ill-maintained and communications poor.

The Panel intended to follow up information it had received, in particular to examine the links between the exploitation of the natural resources and other forms of wealth in the DRC and the continuation of the conflict. However, the Panel concluded that it could not assemble a coherent picture of the situation in the three months remaining due to the complexity of the situation, the vast territories, the multiplicity of the actors involved, the difficulties of travel and communications, the lack of cooperation on the part of some Governments and other sources of information, and the security risks arising from the conflict. It therefore proposed that its mandate be extended for three months, until mid-June.

On 25 January [S/2001/84], Uganda protested some aspects of the interim report, including the Panel's interpretation of its mandate, its description of meetings with Ugandan officials and allegations by the DRC that Uganda had been involved in exploitation of minerals, agricultural products and protected species.

In a 23 March letter [S/2001/288], the Secretary-General recommended, in view of the need for extra time, that the Panel submit its final report by 3 April; he later requested a deadline of 16 April [S/2001/338]. The Council, on 28 March [S/2001/289] and 6 April [S/2001/339], took note of those recommendations.

On 12 April [S/2001/357], the Secretary-General submitted to the Security Council the final report of the Panel of Experts. The report stated that illegal exploitation of the mineral and forest resources of the DRC was taking place at an alarming rate. Two phases could be distinguished: mass-scale looting and the systematic exploitation of natural resources. During the first phase, stockpiles of minerals, coffee, wood, livestock and money that were available in territories conquered by the armies of Burundi, Rwanda and Uganda were taken and either transferred to those countries or exported to international markets by their forces or nationals. In the second phase, exploitation became systematic and systemic, requiring planning and organization. Systematic exploitation flourished because of the pre-existing structures developed during the 1996 conquest of power by the Alliance of Democratic Forces for the Liberation of Congo-Zaire, led by the late Laurent-Désiré Kabila. Those structures were improved and new networks for channelling extracted resources were put in place. However, the systemic exploitation used the existing systems of control established by Rwanda and Uganda. In both cases, exploitation was often carried out in violation of the DRC's sovereignty, the national legislation and sometimes international law. Key individual actors, including army commanders, businessmen and government structures, had been the engines of the systematic and systemic exploitation.

The illegal exploitation had resulted in massive availability of financial resources for RPA and the individual enrichment of top Ugandan military commanders and civilians, as well as the emergence of illegal networks headed by military commanders or businessmen. Other contributing factors included the roles played by some entities, private companies and individuals, including some decision makers in the DRC and Zimbabwe and some leaders in the region.

The conflict in the DRC had become mainly about access to and control and trade of five key mineral resources—coltan (columbo-tantalite, used in communications equipment), diamonds, copper, cobalt and gold. Plundering, looting and racketeering and the constitution of criminal cartels were becoming commonplace in occupied territories. Those cartels had ramifications worldwide, and they represented the next serious security problem in the region. The private sector had also contributed in the exploitation, whether directly or indirectly. The conflict in the DRC, because of its lucrative nature, had created a "win-win" situation for all belligerents. Adversaries and enemies were at times partners in business.

The Panel concluded that tough measures needed to be taken to end the cycle of exploitation of the natural resources and the continuation of the conflict in the DRC. It made a number of recommendations regarding: sanctions against countries and individuals involved in the illegal activities; preventive measures to avoid a recurrence of the current situation; reparations to the victims of the illegal exploitation of natural resources; design of a framework for reconstruction; improvement of international mechanisms and regulations governing some natural resources; and security issues. Proposed measures included: that a Security Council embargo be imposed on the import or export of coltan, niobium, pyrochlore, cassiterite, timber, gold and diamonds from or to Burundi, Rwanda and Uganda until those countries' involvement in the exploitation of DRC natural resources was made clear; that all countries should abstain from facilitating the import or export of those resources or face sanctions; that Member States should freeze the financial assets of the rebel movements and their leaders; that an embargo on weapons supply to rebel groups should be established; that Member States should suspend balance-of-payments support to those countries involved in illegal exploitation; that to curb the flow of illicit diamonds, the DRC should liberalize the diamond trade; and that all diamond dealers operating in the territories occupied by foreign forces should immediately stop doing business with rebels and with Burundi, Rwanda and Uganda; failure to do so should lead to action through the World Diamond Council. The Panel endorsed all the relevant recommendations on diamonds made in 2000 by the expert panel investigating the diamond trade in relation to Sierra Leone [YUN 2000, p. 204]. The Panel proposed that countries with seaports and transit facilities report to the United Nations Forum on Forests on the transit of timber through their territory and called for an improved certification system. It recommended that individuals, groups and companies whose properties were damaged or expropriated by the Burundian, Rwandan or Ugandan armed forces and their allies be compensated by the States concerned. The Panel further recommended that the Council establish an international mechanism to investigate and prosecute individuals involved in economic criminal activities and companies and government officials whose activities harmed powerless people and weak economies, and a permanent mechanism to investigate the illicit trafficking of natural resources in armed conflicts so as to monitor cases already subject to the investigation of other panels, such as those of Angola, the DRC and Sierra Leone.

The Security Council considered the Panel's report on 3 May [meetings 4317, 4318].

Communications (April/May). In letters of 16 and 24 April and 1 May [S/2001/378, S/2001/402,

S/2001/433], Uganda, Rwanda and Burundi, respectively, raised objections to the Expert Panel's report. Uganda expanded on its objections in letters of 4 and 25 May [S/2001/458, S/2001/522], stating that the report suffered from a number of fundamental flaws and that Uganda had appointed a commission to investigate the allegations.

Action plan. As requested by the Security Council at informal consultations on 18 April, the Chairperson of the Panel of Experts presented, on 24 April [S/2001/416], an action plan for the extension of its mandate by three months, until the end of July 2001. In transmitting its final report, the Panel indicated that approximately 70 per cent of the information and work had been covered. On that basis, the Panel wished to work on the remaining 30 per cent, mainly on two themes: the activities of criminal cartels and the mining of and deals on copper and cobalt. In addition, the Panel would compile comments and reactions from various stakeholders and actors cited in the report and prepare answers to those parties. The first theme, on criminal cartels, covered a wide range of issues related to continuation of the conflict, including money-laundering, counterfeit currency and its use for purchasing natural resources, financial networks, and arms transactions to support the continuation of the conflict. With regard to the second theme, the Panel would work primarily on investigating the stocks of copper and cobalt that existed in some regions of the DRC before the beginning of the war.

SECURITY COUNCIL ACTION (May)

On 3 May [meeting 4318], following consultations among Security Council members, the President made statement **S/PRST/2001/13** on behalf of the Council:

The Security Council recalls the statement of its President of 2 June 2000 (S/PRST/2000/20). It expresses its intention to give full consideration to the report of the Panel of Experts on the Illegal Exploitation of Natural Resources and Other Forms of Wealth of the Democratic Republic of the Congo. It takes note of the action plan of the Expert Panel for the extension of its mandate.

The Council notes that the report contains disturbing information about the illegal exploitation of Congolese resources by individuals, Governments and armed groups involved in the conflict, and the link between the exploitation of the natural resources and other forms of wealth in the Democratic Republic of the Congo and the continuation of the conflict.

The Council condemns the illegal exploitation of the natural resources of the Democratic Republic of the Congo and expresses its serious concern at those economic activities that fuel the conflict. It urges the Governments named in the report in this regard to conduct their own inquiries into this information, cooperate fully with the Expert Panel while ensuring necessary security for the experts, and take immediate steps to end illegal exploitation of the natural resources by their nationals or others under their control.

The Council notes with concern the terrible toll the conflict is taking on the people, economy and environment of the Democratic Republic of the Congo.

The Council believes that the only viable solution to the crisis in the Democratic Republic of the Congo remains the full implementation of the Lusaka Ceasefire Agreement and the relevant Security Council resolutions.

The Council emphasizes the importance of a comprehensive approach addressing all the root causes of the conflict to achieve a lasting peace settlement in the Democratic Republic of the Congo.

The Council requests the Secretary-General to extend the mandate of the Expert Panel for a final period of three months, and requests also that the Expert Panel submit to the Council, through the Secretary-General, an addendum to its final report which shall include the following:

(a) An update of relevant data and an analysis of further information, including as pointed out in the action plan submitted by the Panel to the Security Council;

(b) Relevant information on the activities of countries and other actors for which the necessary quantity and quality of data were not made available earlier;

(c) A response, based as far as possible on corroborated evidence, to the comments and reactions of the States and actors cited in the final report of the Expert Panel;

(d) An evaluation of the situation at the end of the extension of the mandate of the Panel, and of its conclusions, assessing whether progress has been made on the issues which come under the responsibility of the Panel.

The Council expresses its intention to examine and respond to the recommendations of the report in the light of the addendum submitted by the Panel, so as to advance the peace process in the Democratic Republic of the Congo.

The Secretary-General, on 25 June [S/2001/632], informed the Council of his intention to appoint Mahmoud Kassem (Egypt) as Chairperson of the Expert Panel.

On 3 October [S/2001/950], the Secretary-General said that the Panel would need extra time to complete its work; he therefore recommended that the Panel's mandate be extended until 30 November 2001. The Council, on 8 October [S/2001/951], took note of the recommendation.

Addendum to Panel report. On 10 November, the Expert Panel issued the addendum [S/2001/1072] to its April report. It remarked that the history of the DRC, regardless of the political authority, had been marked by systematic abuse of its natural and human resources, almost always backed by brutal use of force and directed to the benefit of a few. The mismanagement and plunder of the country's natural resources led to an informal economy based on barter, smuggling and fraudulent trade that reinforced preexisting ties based on ethnicity, kinship and colonial structures between DRC regions and neighbouring States such as Burundi and Rwanda, as well as Angola, Kenya, Uganda, the United Republic of Tanzania and Zambia. The result was that a country with vast natural wealth was reduced to one of the poorest States by the early 1990s. That was the situation when the war began in August 1998.

The Panel described a pattern of continued exploitation since the 12 April ceasefire by both State and non-State actors, including the rebel forces and armed groups. Some exploitation activities were conducted as joint ventures and others were carried out by the de facto authority in the area. The Panel limited its latest investigations to specific resources—coltan, gold, copper, cobalt, diamonds and timber. Human resources were also exploited by all parties to the conflict, resulting in systematic violations of human rights.

The Panel found indications that clashes during the previous seven months in the eastern areas between the Mayi-Mayi, who were better equipped and coordinated than before, and the Ugandan troops and the MLC rebel group were directly related to the control of coltan and gold. Similar battles were fought by the Mayi-Mayi with RPA over access to coltan. The Panel concluded that Zimbabwe's arming of Burundian rebel groups was contributing to sustaining the war by proxy, allowing the ceasefire to remain intact while creating a "controllable" conflict in the occupied zone in the east that satisfied the interests of many parties. With the low-intensity conflict dragging on, a certain status quo was maintained whereby many resources could continue to be extracted, traded and routed for export. Rwanda and Zimbabwe had the most important commercial presence in the DRC as a result of their involvement in the war. It was thought that Zimbabwe's role in continuing the conflict might be shared with the DRC Government, or some elements in it, as well as others. The profiteering of private businesses of all kinds in illicit and criminal activities gave them vested interests in seeing the continuation of the conflict, in particular businesses in Kenya, South Africa and the United Republic of Tanzania.

The report described the military involvement and economic interests in the DRC of the allied countries—Angola, the DRC, Namibia and Zimbabwe—and the uninvited forces of Burundi, Rwanda and Uganda. It explored the role in exploitation of some of the neighbouring countries in the region, which it called the transit countries—the Central African Republic, the Republic of the Congo, Kenya, South Africa, the United Republic of Tanzania and Zambia—and provided background information on the national armed groups (RCD-Goma, RCD-ML, MLC/FLC and the Mayi-Mayi) and the foreign armed groups or negative forces (FDD, the Interahamwe and ex-FAR, currently known as ALIR I and II).

The Panel concluded that the systematic exploitation of the DRC's natural resources continued unabated, resulting in the further enrichment of individuals and institutions. A primary reason for the continuing exploitation was the collapse of State institutions and structures. Initially, foreign countries and rebel movements were motivated to intervene for political and security concerns, but the primary motivation had become financial benefits. The military operations and presence of all sides had been transformed into self-financing activities, whereby no real budgetary burden was borne by the parties concerned. Contrary to its protestations, the DRC Government had been involved in allowing some foreign companies to continue the exploitation of resources in rebel-occupied areas without cancelling any concessions.

The Panel stated that the international community should assist in formulating a plan of action for rebuilding the DRC State institutions as a means of enabling it to control its territory and to protect its natural resources. Such assistance should be linked to the convening of an international conference on peace and development in the Great Lakes region. The Panel recommended that: all concessions, commercial agreements and contracts signed during the 1997-2001 era of Laurent-Désiré Kabila and subsequently in the rebel-held areas should be reviewed and revised to correct all irregularities, under the auspices of a Security Council body; MONUC should accelerate the disarmament, demobilization and reintegration process in order to reduce the security concerns of regional States, including the DRC; a temporary moratorium should ban the purchase of products such as coltan, diamonds, gold, copper, cobalt, timber and coffee originating in areas in the DRC under the control of foreign troops or rebel groups; and countries involved in the conflict should investigate and prosecute illicit traffickers of high-value products from the DRC, and technical measures to control trade should be finalized, such as the standardization of certificates of production, harmonization of tax regimes and verification regulations, and analysis of diamond production and trade statistics. The Panel further recommended that the Council consider sanctions, depending on future trends in exploitation of DRC natural resources and developments in the Great Lakes region, and, in the meantime, establish a monitoring mechanism to report on progress in reducing exploitation.

Communications (November/December). During November and December, a number of countries transmitted comments on and/or reservations with regard to the Expert Panel's April report and November addendum. On 5 and 6 December [S/2001/1156, S/2001/1175], the DRC commented on the report and expressed support for the Panel's recommendations. Having conducted an inquiry on the reports, Uganda, on 14 and 21 November and 10 December [S/2001/1080, S/2001/1107, S/2001/1163], commented on the findings and recommendations, covering what it considered to be both positive conclusions and areas of concern, including what it called false allegations against Uganda. On 23 November and 7 December [S/2001/1102, S/2001/1161], Rwanda welcomed many key elements of the report but denied any involvement by its armed forces in commercial activities in the DRC. Burundi, on 13 December [S/2001/1197], welcomed the Panel's finding that Burundi was cleared of all suspicion of illegally exploiting the wealth of the DRC and requested the international community to focus efforts on obtaining a ceasefire. Namibia, on 14 December [S/2001/1212], listed its objections to specific claims about its involvement in exploitation. On the same date [S/2001/1214], Zimbabwe forwarded the communiqué of the Southern African Development Community Ministerial Task Force on Developments in Zimbabwe (Harare, 10-11 December) to counter misleading observations concerning Zimbabwe raised in the November addendum.

SECURITY COUNCIL ACTION (December)

The Security Council considered the Panel's addendum on 14 [meeting 4437] and 19 [meeting 4441] December. Following consultations among Council members on 19 December, the President made statement **S/PRST/2001/39** on behalf of the Council:

The Security Council notes with concern that the plundering of the natural resources and other forms of wealth of the Democratic Republic of the Congo continues unabated. The Council strongly condemns these activities, which are perpetuating the conflict in the country, impeding the economic development of the Democratic Republic of the Congo and exacerbating the suffering of its people, and reaffirms the territorial integrity, political independence and sovereignty of the Democratic Republic of the Congo, including over its natural resources.

The Council stresses that:

—No external parties, or groups or individuals under their control, should benefit from the exploitation of the natural resources of the Democratic Republic of the Congo at the Democratic Republic of the Congo's expense;

—The Democratic Republic of the Congo's natural resources should not serve as an incentive for any State, group or individual to prolong the conflict;

—External parties, and groups or individuals under their control, must not use the natural resources of the Democratic Republic of the Congo to finance the conflict in the country;

—The resources should be exploited legally and on a fair commercial basis to benefit the country and people of the Democratic Republic of the Congo.

The Council thanks the Expert Panel for its recommendations on the institutional, financial and technical aspects of the issue, and for its advice on possible measures to be imposed by the Security Council. It reaffirms its support to the Lusaka Ceasefire Agreement, and reiterates its commitment to take any appropriate action to help put an end to the plundering of the resources of the Democratic Republic of the Congo, in support of the peace process, once it has been established that such actions will have no serious and unmanageable negative impact on the disastrous humanitarian and economic situation of the country.

The Council stresses the importance of continuing the monitoring of the situation regarding the illegal exploitation of the natural resources of the Democratic Republic of the Congo and the link between the exploitation of these natural resources in the Democratic Republic of the Congo and the continuation of the conflict, in order to keep the necessary pressure to put an end to the illegal exploitation of the resources of the Democratic Republic of the Congo, including the exploitation of human resources, at the expense of the Congolese people and of the peace process.

Therefore, the Council, having heard the views expressed at its open debate on 14 December 2001, requests the Secretary-General to renew the mandate of the Expert Panel for a period of six months at the end of which the Expert Panel should report to the Council. The panel should submit an interim report after three months.

The next reports of the panel should include the following elements:

—An update of relevant data and an analysis of further information from all relevant countries, including in particular from those which thus far have not provided the panel with the requested information;

—An evaluation of the possible actions that could be taken by the Council, including those recommended by the panel in its report and in its addendum, in order to help bring to an end the plundering of natural resources of the Democratic Republic of the Congo, taking into account the impact of such actions on the financing of the conflict and their potential impact on the humanitarian and economic situation of the Democratic Republic of the Congo;

—Recommendations on specific actions that the international community, in support of the Government of the Democratic Republic of the Congo, might take, working through existing international organizations, mechanisms and United Nations bodies, to address the issues in the report and its addendum;

—Recommendations on possible steps that may be taken by transit countries as well as end-users to contribute to ending illegal exploitation of the natural resources and other forms of wealth of the Democratic Republic of the Congo.

The Council stresses the importance of the panel maintaining a high level of collaboration with all the Congolese players, governmental as well as nongovernmental, throughout the national territory.

The Council once again urges the Governments named in the previous reports to conduct their own inquiries, cooperate fully with the Expert Panel and take, on an urgent basis, the necessary steps to end all illegal exploitation of the natural resources of the Democratic Republic of the Congo, by their nationals or others under their control, and inform the Council accordingly. The Council also calls on those countries that have not yet provided the Panel with the requested information to do so as a matter of urgency.

Burundi

Throughout the year, efforts to revive the Burundi peace process based on the 2000 Arusha Agreement on Peace and Reconciliation [YUN 2000, p. 146], a framework for political reform, were led by former President Nelson Mandela of South Africa, whom the Secretary-General appointed in 1999 as Facilitator of the peace process. The main obstacles to implementation of the Agreement were the continued hostilities and the lack of agreement on leadership of a transitional government. The conflict between armed groups and government forces intensified at several points in 2001, despite the fact that most political parties had signed the Agreement in August 2000. Some of the main combatant rebel forces, however, were not parties to the Agreement although they had joined the negotiations.

The Implementation Monitoring Committee, set up by the Arusha Agreement under the chairmanship of the Facilitator, met five times in 2001 to follow up on implementation, arbitrate on disputes among signatories and consider draft legislation on political activity, among other things. Although his efforts were complicated by ongoing civil conflict and lack of a formal ceasefire, Mr. Mandela was successful in bringing the parties together to agree on and install a broad-based transitional government on 1 November under a power-sharing formula, thus ushering in a new and promising chapter in the search for lasting peace and stability in the country. Peacemaking efforts were also carried out by regional leaders who met four times in 2001 as the Regional Peace

Initiative and agreed to provide forces to assist Burundi in protecting exiled political leaders once they returned to the country.

Political and military developments

The intensification of fighting following the August 2000 signing of the Arusha Agreement severely hampered efforts to carry out tasks of the transitional phase as stipulated in the Agreement, including the return and resettlement of refugees and displaced people, and the reform of military and security institutions. It also exacerbated the humanitarian situation in a country already afflicted with a malaria epidemic and widespread malnutrition and hunger. Efforts to reach a ceasefire were stymied by the fact that two main armed groups, the National Council for the Defence of Democracy–Front for the Defence of Democracy (CNDD-FDD) and the Party for the Liberation of the Hutu People–National Liberation Forces (PALIPEHUTU-FNL), were not part of the Arusha peace process.

Communications (January). Burundi, on 16 January [S/2001/51], called on the Security Council to condemn the rebel groups in Burundi for the violence committed against the civilian population, urge them to join the peace process, and urge all countries bordering Burundi to ensure that their territories were not used by the Burundian rebels against their country of origin. The Council was also requested to welcome the 9 January meeting in Libreville, Gabon, between Burundi President Pierre Buyoya and Jean Bosco Ndayikengurukiye, head of CNDD-FDD, to discuss the peace process. Annexed to the letter were a communiqué issued after that meeting and a list of armed attacks against civilians that occurred in December 2000 and January 2001.

The DRC drew the Council's attention to the wider implications of the Burundi conflict in a 10 January letter [S/2001/30]. Welcoming the Libreville meeting, the DRC stated that President Laurent-Désiré Kabila had offered his good offices in the resolution of the Burundian crisis, in the light of the consequences of Burundi's ethnic conflicts on DRC territory. The DRC also welcomed President Buyoya's commitment to withdraw his troops from Congolese territory.

Regional peace initiative. The fourteenth Summit Meeting of the Regional Peace Initiative on Burundi (Arusha, United Republic of Tanzania, 26 February) [A/55/850-S/2001/265] was attended by the Presidents of Burundi, the DRC, Kenya, Rwanda and the United Republic of Tanzania, and the Vice-Presidents of Gabon, South Africa and Uganda. The meeting considered the Facilitator's progress report on the Burundi negotiations and his recommendations on the outstanding issues, namely, cessation of hostilities and leadership of the transition. It took note of the establishment of the Arusha Agreement's Implementation Monitoring Committee and its Executive Council and expressed support for the work of the Committee and its UN-appointed Chairman, Berhanu Dinka.

In view of the absence of agreement on leadership of the transition, the Summit recommended a scheme by which the three-year period of transition would be divided into two phases of 18 months. In the first phase, the parties would agree on a Transitional President from the G-10 group of parties (Tutsi) and the Vice-President from the G-7 group (Hutu); in the second phase, the positions would be reversed. The signatory parties would agree on the 26 ministerial posts in the proportions already agreed and the Security Council would provide assistance to the Regional Initiative and the Facilitator, in particular by dispatching peacekeepers and protection aides to Burundi as soon as hostilities were suspended or by financing any countries willing to contribute peacekeepers. The Summit held three more meetings in 2001 in efforts to arrange negotiations leading to a ceasefire.

SECURITY COUNCIL ACTION (March)

On 2 March [meeting 4285], following consultations among Security Council members, the President made statement **S/PRST/2001/6** on behalf of the Council:

> The Security Council strongly condemns the recent attacks by armed groups in Burundi, particularly those launched on Bujumbura by the Forces for National Liberation. The timing of these actions is of particular concern since they were launched during the meeting of the parties to the Arusha Peace and Reconciliation Agreement (the Arusha Agreement) on Burundi convened by the Facilitator, Nelson Mandela, on 25 February 2001 in Arusha, United Republic of Tanzania. The Council calls for the immediate cessation of these attacks.
>
> The Council expresses its strong disapproval of all acts aimed at undermining the peace process in Burundi. The Council urges all sides to exercise restraint and to refrain from any action that may exacerbate the situation.
>
> The Council condemns the deliberate targeting of the civilian population by the armed groups and calls upon all parties to abide by international humanitarian law and in particular to refrain from any further attacks or any military action that endangers the civilian population.
>
> The Council reiterates its call on the Forces for National Liberation and the Forces for the Defence of Democracy to cease hostilities immediately and to join the peace process. The Council recalls the meeting in Libreville on 9 January 2001 between the President of the Republic of Burundi and the leader of the Forces for the Defence of Democracy and

urges the continuation of this process. The Council calls on all the parties, including the armed groups, to engage in dialogue immediately so as to allow an early cessation of hostilities and to reach agreement on a permanent ceasefire.

> The Council stresses the importance of providing urgent humanitarian assistance to civilians displaced by the hostilities, and calls upon all parties to guarantee safe and unhindered access by humanitarian personnel to those in need. The Council reiterates its request to the donor community to help the Government of Burundi, United Nations agencies and the humanitarian community to respond effectively to the needs of the population of Burundi. The Council also urges donors to deliver on the commitments made at the Paris Donors Conference on 11 and 12 December 2000.
>
> The Council takes note of the scheme for power-sharing arrangements among parties to the Arusha Agreement worked out by the fourteenth Summit Meeting of the Regional Peace Initiative on Burundi, held in Arusha on 26 February 2001, and calls on all the parties to reach early agreement on the outstanding issues related to the transitional power-sharing arrangements and to give their full cooperation to the Facilitator.
>
> The Council stresses that the key to achieving lasting peace in Burundi lies with the Burundian parties. It is convinced that compromise is the only means to resolve the conflict, and to this end urges all parties to work towards settling outstanding differences over the peace accord, and to proceed to its implementation.
>
> The Council reaffirms its full support for the continuing efforts of the Facilitator, the Regional Peace Initiative and the Implementation Monitoring Committee to bring peace to Burundi. The Council also emphasizes the role of the Implementation Monitoring Committee in advancing the peace process. It takes note of the communiqué of the 14th Summit Meeting of the Regional Peace Initiative on Burundi held in Arusha on 26 February 2001. It also reiterates its readiness to consider practical ways in which it can best support the peace process, and the implementation of the Arusha Agreement.
>
> The Council will remain seized of the matter.

Communications (March-May). On 14 March [S/2001/221], Burundi requested the Security Council to meet in order to condemn once again the recent attacks by PALIPEHUTU-FNL and CNDD-FDD, supported by the other "negative forces" fighting in the DRC, and call on the signatories to the Arusha Agreement to give priority to a ceasefire instead of establishing the transitional institutions. Reviewing the evolution of the peace process, Burundi said that progress was currently hindered because of the ongoing offensive by FDD in the south-east of the country on the Tanzanian border and a two-week urban guerrilla warfare campaign in Bujumbura. The situation in the DRC had brought about a realignment of armed factions, Burundi said, which could cause grave danger not just for Burundi but also for neighbouring countries, which would be drawn into the conflict because of the Hutu-Tutsi sensitivities that existed throughout the region and in some Southern African countries. In Burundi's view, priority should be given to ensuring security and combating the rebellion. Pending the ceasefire, activities could proceed on drafting laws on provisional immunity, the transitional legislature and political parties. The Government supported the Facilitator's request for international observation and protection forces.

At a private meeting on 16 March, the Security Council considered Burundi's 14 March letter. In an official communiqué [S/PV.4297], the Council stated that its members and the representative of Burundi had had a constructive discussion.

On the eve of the Security Council's mission to the region (see below), Burundi, on 11 May [S/2001/472], transmitted to the Council President the "Memorandum on the peace process in Burundi: the security challenge", which stated that the situation urgently required action by the international community because the regional efforts of Mr. Mandela were not enough. Burundi saw a correlation between developments in the DRC conflict and those in the Burundi conflict: the further the former moved towards peace, the more adversely the Burundi conflict was affected. The Burundi conflict was the work of armed rebel groups (FDD and FNL) who trained in and operated from the DRC. Some rebel groups were also operating from the United Republic of Tanzania, but that Government had remained passive to the problem. Burundi believed the Arusha Agreement to be in jeopardy and made a number of suggestions for the Council mission, including calling for short-term sanctions against the rebel groups, urging Tanzania to look into Burundi's security concerns, and urging the DRC to hold a bilateral dialogue with Burundi in a more positive spirit.

Security Council mission

The Security Council, having agreed to dispatch a mission to the Great Lakes region in May (see p. 116), informed the Secretary-General on 25 April of its terms of reference [S/2001/408].

Reporting to the Council on 29 May [S/2001/521], the mission stated that it was struck by the complexity and intractability of the situation in Burundi and its potential for large-scale violence. It delivered a strong message to all its Burundian interlocutors that peace could be achieved only through negotiations within the framework of the Arusha Agreement. The mission suggested that the regional heads of State should remain involved and that the Government and FNL should hold a dialogue; urgent attention should be paid to the situation along the border between Burundi and the United Republic of Tanzania, which could ignite a serious deterioration in the crisis, and a joint commission should be established to deal with refugee issues. It also proposed the establishment of a permanent negotiating mechanism involving the Secretary-General's Representative in Bujumbura to deal with such issues as the reform of the armed forces and the judiciary, human rights and refugees and displaced persons. The mission observed that the movements of rebel fighters from the DRC eastwards in order to evade being disarmed and demobilized might aggravate the Burundi crisis. The Council supported a global solution to restore peace to both countries and to the region.

The Security Council discussed the report on 30 May [meeting 4323].

Communications (June/July). In a joint communiqué [S/2001/633] issued following consultations in Dar es Salaam (23-24 June), the Defence Ministers of Burundi and the United Republic of Tanzania expressed concern about the illegal movements and criminal activities along the common border between the two countries and directed local authorities to meet to solve the problem of cross-border crimes. Concerning the repatriation of refugees, they commended the signing of a tripartite agreement between Burundi, Tanzania and UNHCR in May and directed that the meeting of the Technical Working Group be held in early July in Kigoma, Tanzania, as scheduled, so as to put in place the operational plan for repatriating refugees and to propose further measures facilitating repatriation, including the creation of safe zones in Burundi.

On 26 June [S/2001/634], the DRC stated that the preceding few weeks had seen a resurgence of violence in Burundi and Rwanda, where governmental sources were reportedly attributing the upsurge to infiltrations from Congolese territory of Interahamwe and ex-FAR, with the support of the DRC authorities. The DRC asserted that such claims were baseless. Burundi responded on 6 July [S/2001/672], alleging Congolese support to factions opposing the Burundi authorities.

The EU, in statements of 6 and 24 July [S/2001/684, S/2001/739], noted the worsening of the political and security situation in Burundi, expressed support for Mr. Mandela's efforts and condemned the coup attempt by a group of mutineers from the Burundian armed forces on 22-23 July.

SECURITY COUNCIL ACTION (July)

On 29 June [meeting 4341], following consultations among Security Council members, the

President made statement **S/PRST/2001/17** on behalf of the Council:

The Security Council calls for an immediate suspension of hostilities in Burundi.

The Council calls on the armed groups to enter into negotiations.

The Council reiterates its profound concern at the continuation of the conflict in Burundi and its toll on the civilian population. In that context, the Council stresses once again its support for the Arusha process and the efforts of the Facilitator, Nelson Mandela.

The Council strongly emphasizes to the parties to the Arusha Peace and Reconciliation Agreement of August 2000 (Arusha Agreement) the need to implement all the immediately applicable provisions of the Agreement, including the provisions for the establishment of new institutions.

The Council calls upon the parties to the Arusha Agreement to continue searching, together with all parties concerned, for solutions to outstanding issues in the Agreement.

The Council expresses grave concern at continuing human rights abuses and violations of humanitarian law, and stresses the need for all parties to ensure respect for human rights and humanitarian law. In particular, it urges the belligerents to commit themselves immediately to the protection of civilians, in particular their life, physical integrity and the means necessary for their survival. It also reiterate its call for safe and unhindered access for the delivery of humanitarian aid to all people in need.

The Council encourages the Secretary-General through his Representatives to continue to engage the armed groups and contribute to coordinated efforts to bring about a political settlement of the conflict.

The Council reiterates its call to the donor community to increase its humanitarian and development assistance to the people of Burundi, in keeping with their pledges given at the Paris Donor Conference on 11-12 December 2000.

The Council remains actively seized of the situation in Burundi and, in this context, will continue to receive regular reporting from the Secretariat on developments in and around the country. The Council stands ready to consider, in the light of progress in the above areas, further contributions to the peace process, and the implementation of the Arusha Agreement.

Installation of Transitional Government

The Facilitator convened two meetings in July in an effort to break the impasse in the transitional arrangements: the first with leaders of the Regional Peace Initiative in Lusaka on 8 July and the second with the signatories of the Arusha Agreement in Johannesburg two days later [S/2001/1076]. At the first meeting, the Facilitator proposed, due to the lack of consensus within the G-10 (Tutsi) group of parties and the position taken by the army, that Mr. Buyoya would be the transitional leader for the first phase. The lead-

ers agreed, but insisted on certain conditions that were also agreed to by Mr. Buyoya: inclusion of representatives of the signatory parties in the transitional government; full implementation of the Agreement; reforming the army and integrating the armed groups into it; collaborating with UNHCR on repatriation of refugees and resettlement of internally displaced persons; protection of all political leaders; refraining from reprisals against political opponents; release of political prisoners; appealing for regional and international troops for maintaining peace and security; establishing a special protection unit for political leaders consisting of an equal number of soldiers/policemen and people appointed by the G-7 (Hutu) and G-10 groups; working towards an equitable representation of Burundian communities in all public offices; collaborating with the Implementation Monitoring Committee; and ceasing the functions of President after the 18-month period.

The fifteenth Summit Meeting of the Regional Peace Initiative on Burundi (Arusha, 23 July) took note of Mr. Mandela's proposal on the transitional leadership and Mr. Buyoya signed a document agreeing to fulfil all the conditions. The Summit agreed that a special protection unit should be deployed in Burundi as soon as possible to protect returning exiled leaders. Half of the unit would be contributed by the G-7 group. It would be assisted by Ghana, Nigeria, Senegal and South Africa. Reform of the army would begin immediately after installation of the transitional government. It was also decided that cabinet members would be nominated in accordance with the agreed quota of posts (60 per cent for G-7, 40 per cent for G-10) and the allocation of those posts would be determined through negotiations among the participating signatories.

Burundi, in a statement [S/2001/752] issued after the fifteenth Summit Meeting, described recent developments and the next stages of the peace process. It announced that the Facilitator and the Summit, following a process of consultation with the people, had designated the current President and Domitien Ndayizeye to serve as President and Vice-President, respectively, for the first 18 months of the transitional government. On the issue of a ceasefire, contacts were made in South Africa between the Government and CNDD-FDD to launch negotiations. However, Burundi acknowledged that difficulties stemmed not only from the persistence of the war in a number of localities but also from the issue of the transitional leadership. The search for a ceasefire remained the top priority. The draft laws necessary for the formation of a new Government and Parliament would soon be adopted, which would allow those institutions to be operational by 1 November.

SECURITY COUNCIL ACTION (September)

On 26 September [meeting 4383], following consultations among Security Council members, the President made statement **S/PRST/2001/26** on behalf of the Council:

The Security Council reaffirms its strong support for the Facilitation of Former President Nelson Mandela, and urges all Burundians of goodwill to join in the cause of peace, democracy and national reconciliation in their country. It also calls upon all parties to cooperate fully with the Implementation Monitoring Committee.

The Council looks forward to and strongly supports the 1 November 2001 installation of the transitional government in Burundi. The Council believes that this event, the creation of a broad-based and inclusive government, will mark a critical turning point in the Burundi peace process. It will also encourage the donors to provide additional assistance, including by honouring fully the pledges they made during the Paris Donors' Conference in December 2000.

The Council calls on the Burundian parties to reach agreement swiftly on the establishment of a special protection unit entrusted solely with the police function of providing personal security for politicians returning from exile. It welcomes the convening by the Facilitation of a pre-implementation stakeholders meeting in Arusha and urges the international community to provide, on an urgent basis, support for the training and deployment of this special protection unit.

Deeply concerned by the increase of violence recently, the Council recalls the urgent need to bring about a negotiated settlement of the conflict and calls upon the Facilitation, the Regional Peace Initiative for Burundi, the Government of Burundi, the signatory parties and the armed groups to devote their full attention to the achievement of a definitive ceasefire. The Council once again calls on the Forces pour la Défense de la Démocratie (FDD) and Forces Nationales de Libération (FNL) to suspend hostilities, to continue negotiations and to join the peace process. The Council believes that the installation of a broad-based government on the basis of an internationally sanctioned peace process makes armed rebellion an unacceptable means of political expression. It calls on the FNL and FDD, together with the Burundi Government, to observe strictly the rights of the civilian population and other provisions of international humanitarian law.

The Council calls on all States, in particular those in the region, to cease all forms of support to the FNL and FDD, and urges all Member States to encourage the armed groups to join the peace process.

The Council calls on the States of the Regional Initiative to mark the installation of the transitional government by further enhancing their bilateral and regional cooperation with the new government. The Council believes that this cooperation is particularly important in the area of regional security and calls on the Governments of Burundi and its neighbouring States to increase their cooperation in this regard.

The Council expresses its concern at the deteriorating humanitarian situation and calls on all parties to create the conditions for the voluntary return of refugees, and for the safe and unhindered activities of the humanitarian relief community. It also calls upon the donor community to increase their humanitarian assistance to Burundi and to accelerate its delivery.

The sixteenth Summit of the Initiative was held on 1 October. In view of the disagreement between the Burundian Government and the G-7 group on a number of issues, including the composition of the transitional government and the transitional constitution, as well as the composition and size of the special protection unit, the Summit urged both parties to solve their differences and to report to the next Summit 10 days later. In a 10 October press statement [AFR/342-SC/7170], the Security Council condemned the continuing violence in Burundi and expressed concern at the appalling humanitarian situation there. The Council reiterated its strong support for the installation of the transitional government on 1 November and called on the signatories to the Arusha Agreement to cooperate fully with the Facilitator and the Implementation Monitoring Committee. At the seventeenth Summit (Pretoria, South Africa, 11 October), Mr. Mandela reported that Mr. Buyoya and the G-7 group had agreed on the legal framework of the transitional government, the composition of the cabinet, the structure of government and the composition of the Senate and the transitional National Assembly. With regard to the special protection unit, Ghana, Nigeria, Senegal and South Africa offered to provide protection for the returning exiled political leaders until an all-Burundi unit was trained and deployed. South Africa confirmed its offer on 25 October [S/2001/1013]. The first contingent of South African troops arrived in Bujumbura on 27 October.

In a 9 October statement transmitted to the Council on 15 October [S/2001/979], the EU commented that the agreement reached in July on guiding the transition in Burundi led by the Facilitator, Mr. Mandela, also opened up new prospects although they were still fragile in the absence of a ceasefire.

In a 16 October press statement [SC/7176], the Council welcomed the progress made at the seventeenth Summit and called on the Burundian parties to resolve outstanding issues so that the installation of the transitional government could proceed on 1 November.

On 29 October [meeting 4399], the Security Council unanimously adopted **resolution 1375 (2001)**. The draft [S/2001/1016] was prepared in consultations among Council members.

The Security Council,

Recalling all its previous resolutions and statements by its President on the situation in Burundi, in particular the statement by its President of 26 September 2001 (S/PRST/2001/26),

Reaffirming that the Arusha Peace and Reconciliation Agreement of August 2000 (Arusha Agreement) remains the most viable basis for a resolution of the conflict together with the continued efforts to build an internal political partnership in Burundi,

Expressing deep concern at the ongoing violence and insecurity in Burundi,

Noting with concern the implications of the situation in Burundi for the region as well as the consequences for Burundi of continued regional instability,

Reiterating its strong support for the facilitation of former President Nelson Mandela in his efforts to achieve a peaceful solution to the conflict in Burundi,

Supporting the efforts of the Secretary-General to enhance the role of the United Nations in Burundi, and in particular the continued work of his Special Representative for the Great Lakes region, as well as in his capacity as Chairman of the Implementation Monitoring Committee,

Commending the continued efforts of and support from the Organization of African Unity/African Union for a peaceful resolution of the conflict,

Welcoming the agreement reached at the Summit of the Regional Initiative on 11 October 2001 in Pretoria, South Africa, on the legal framework and the structure of the transitional government, and the composition of the cabinet, the senate and the transitional national assembly,

Also welcoming the letter from the Foreign Minister of South Africa to the President of the Security Council of 23 October 2001 and the letter from the President of Burundi to the President of South Africa annexed thereto,

1. *Reaffirms* its strong support for the 1 November 2001 installation of the transitional government in Burundi;

2. *Calls upon* the parties to the Arusha Agreement and the armed groups, namely the Forces pour la Défense de la Démocratie (FDD) and Forces Nationales de Libération (FNL), to put an end immediately to all acts of violence against civilians;

3. *Calls upon* the FDD and FNL to cease immediately all hostilities, enter into negotiations and join the peace process, and calls upon all the States of the region to support fully the process;

4. *Endorses* the efforts of the Government of South Africa and other member States to support the implementation of the Arusha Agreement, and strongly supports in this regard the establishment of an interim multinational security presence in Burundi, at the request of its Government, to protect returning political leaders and train an all-Burundian protection force;

5. *Requests* the Government of Burundi to keep the Council informed of progress to establish an all-Burundian protection force;

6. *Reiterates* its willingness to consider, in the light of progress in the peace process, further contributions to the peace process and the implementation of the Arusha Agreement;

7. *Urges* the international community, with the installation of the transitional government, to provide additional assistance, including by honouring fully the pledges made by donors during the Paris Conference of December 2000;

8. *Decides* to remain actively seized of the matter.

On 1 November, the Transitional Government of national unity was installed in Burundi. The occasion was witnessed by the Presidents of Malawi, Nigeria, Rwanda, the United Republic of Tanzania and Zambia, the Deputy Presidents of South Africa and Uganda, the OAU Secretary-General and representatives of the United Nations and the EU.

On 8 November [meeting 4408], following consultations among Security Council members, the President made statement **S/PRST/2001/33** on behalf of the Council:

The Security Council welcomes the 1 November 2001 inauguration of Burundi's Transitional Government, and calls on all Burundians to support it and work together to ensure the success of this broad-based and inclusive government's fulfilling its functions in accordance with the agreements that led to its establishment.

The Council welcomes the continued engagement of the Regional Initiative and, in this regard, also welcomes the deployment of the first elements of the multinational security presence tasked with the protection of returning political leaders. The Council calls on all the Burundian parties to support this undertaking, and expresses its gratitude to the Government of South Africa for its contribution to the cause of peace in Burundi.

The Council expresses its deep appreciation to former President Nelson Mandela for his dedicated service as Facilitator of the Arusha Peace Process, and reiterates its hope that the region and the international community may continue to rely on his moral leadership. The Council welcomes the efforts of the Secretary-General and his Special Representative for the Great Lakes, through the Implementation Monitoring Committee.

The Council condemns the recent attacks by the FDD and FNL on civilians, and is gravely concerned that the frequency of such attacks has increased. The Council once again states that the installation of a broad-based government in accordance with an internationally supported peace process makes armed rebellion an unacceptable means of political expression.

The Council reiterates its call for an immediate suspension of hostilities in Burundi and for the armed groups to enter into negotiations to reach a definitive ceasefire, which is the priority issue. In this regard, the Council welcomes the involvement of President Bongo of Gabon and Deputy President

Zuma of South Africa and expresses its full support for their efforts.

The Council expresses its concern at the human rights and humanitarian situation in Burundi and once again calls on the responsible parties to ensure full compliance with the relevant international conventions.

The Council calls on the international community to increase its humanitarian assistance, as well as to assist in Burundi's economic recovery and development through, inter alia, honouring the pledges made at the Paris donors' conference.

Report of Secretary-General. The Secretary-General, in his November interim report on the situation in Burundi [S/2001/1076], said that the indefatigable efforts of the Facilitator and leaders of the region had finally succeeded in bringing about the installation of a broad-based Transitional Government of national unity, on 1 November. Mr. Mandela announced that although his role as Facilitator had come to an end, and responsibility for ensuring the implementation of the Arusha Agreement rested with the Implementation Monitoring Committee, under the chairmanship of the United Nations, he would continue to act as moral guarantor to the Agreement and would be represented on the Committee.

The establishment of the Transitional Government made it possible for the peace process to be repatriated from Arusha to Bujumbura where Implementation Committee meetings would be held once adequate security measures were in place for the protection of Committee members and other returning exiled leaders. The primary role of the United Nations Office in Burundi (UNOB), the mandate of which had been extended until December 2001 [YUN 2000, p. 147], would need to be adjusted and refocused. The Office's staffing and resources would have to be increased to provide it with the expertise and the capability needed to support the work of the Implementation Committee and related activities. The net additional staff requirements would amount to 16 international posts, including the Committee Chairman, and a small number of military advisers and civilian police to plan for possible deployment of a peacekeeping mission.

The Secretary-General reported that the progress made on the Transitional Government highlighted the need to cease hostilities to allow the full implementation of the Arusha Agreement, and he called for the international community to increase its contribution in support of that goal by providing assistance for humanitarian, development and reconstruction efforts.

As the Transitional Government was being established, negotiations on a cessation of hostili-

ties/ceasefire continued. Deputy President Jacob Zuma of South Africa, who assisted the Facilitator in the negotiations, addressed the fifteenth and sixteenth Summit Meetings of the Regional Peace Initiative and asked the leaders to call on the armed groups to negotiate seriously. They called on CNDD-FDD and PALIPEHUTU-FNL to cease hostilities and to enter into negotiations on a ceasefire. Despite some positive indications that they would cooperate with the Transitional Government, both groups increased their attacks on civilians, killing more than 30 and forcing scores to flee.

The prolonged conflict continued to disrupt social and economic development. The gross domestic product (GDP) per capita, which averaged $240 from 1980 to 1985, was estimated at $120 in 2001. The external debt exceeded $1 billion (175 per cent of GDP), while the debt service amounted to 124 per cent of the total value of exports of goods and services. Those conditions had had a devastating impact on social services, national health, access to clean water and agricultural production. Life expectancy had declined from 53.8 years in 1993 to 42.8 years, and 58 per cent of the population lived below the poverty line, compared with 39 per cent in 1993. The humanitarian situation suffered due to the increased hostilities.

SECURITY COUNCIL ACTION (15 November)

Following a closed meeting on 15 November, the Security Council issued a communiqué [S/PV.4416], in which it stated that it had had a useful exchange of views with Mr. Mandela, Facilitator of the Arusha Peace Process. The Council thanked Mr. Mandela and commended his efforts on behalf of Burundi. Also on 15 November [meeting 4417], following consultations among Council members, the President made statement **S/PRST/2001/35** on behalf of the Council:

The Security Council expresses its deep gratitude to Madiba Nelson Mandela of South Africa for his dedicated service to the people of Burundi and the cause of peace in Central Africa. Building on the work of his predecessor, the late Mwalimu Julius Nyerere of the United Republic of Tanzania, Madiba has helped to give Burundi a chance for lasting peace, democracy, economic development and national reconciliation.

The Council had, in the statement of its President on 8 November 2001 (S/PRST/2001/33), welcomed the 1 November 2001 inauguration of Burundi's Transitional Government and expressed its appreciation for the instrumental role played by Madiba towards the creation of the Transitional Government. The Council had also expressed the hope that the region and the international community could continue to rely on his moral leadership and ingenious spirit that are essential for progress towards peace in Burundi.

The Council acknowledges the sterling contribution of Madiba as Facilitator of the Arusha Peace Process in bringing together all the parties, including the armed groups, to engage in dialogue in order to facilitate an early cessation of hostilities in accordance with the Arusha Agreement. The Council commends Madiba for his tenacity and unwavering commitment towards political reconciliation in Burundi.

The Council expresses its appreciation to Madiba and the South African Government for initiating the deployment of the first elements of the multinational security presence tasked with the protection of returning political leaders, without which the conditions would not have been conducive for the inauguration of the Burundi Transitional Government. These key successes have confirmed the trust and confidence which the Council and the international community have always had in Madiba.

The Council expresses its concern about the recent increase in violence and reiterates its call for an immediate cessation of hostilities in Burundi. The Council calls on all Burundians to reject violence and to pursue their objectives through the institutions and mechanisms of the transition process. The Council appeals to all Burundians and United Nations Member States to build on the momentum created through the efforts of Madiba and to support the Regional Peace Initiative and the Transitional Government and the Implementation Monitoring Committee.

Communications (December). On 7 December [S/2001/1207], the Security Council informed the Secretary-General that it had taken note of his November report [S/2001/1076] and, in particular, the information on UNOB. The members supported his proposal to strengthen the Office to help implement the Arusha Peace Agreement.

The Netherlands, on 6 December [S/2001/1158], said that in view of the importance of supporting the peace process, in particular the deployment of a multinational security force as recommended by the Secretary-General, it would contribute 1.8 million euros to the Burundi protection force and would consider an additional contribution in 2002.

Rwanda

Rwanda continued to undergo significant changes in 2001 in the areas of decentralization of government and transition to democracy, the drawing up of a new constitution, overhauling of the justice system, and the promotion of a culture of human rights, unity and reconciliation. Such strides were possible as Rwanda moved beyond the aftermath of the 1994 genocide [YUN 1994, p. 2991].

Those efforts were clouded by the insecurity in the region largely due to the ongoing conflict in

the DRC. During the Security Council's mission to the Great Lakes region in May [S/2001/521 & Add.1] (see p. 124), President Paul Kagame stated that Rwandan troops were in the DRC because of his Government's concern about the security of its borders. He mentioned recent cross-border incursions and said that some actors were taking advantage of the peace process to push fighters eastwards from the DRC towards Burundi and Rwanda.

Arms embargo

The Chairman of the Security Council Committee established pursuant to resolution 918 (1994) concerning the arms embargo against Rwanda [YUN 1994, p. 285] submitted to the Council a report on its 2001 activities [S/2002/49]. In the absence of a specific monitoring mechanism to ensure the implementation of the arms embargo, the Committee repeated its observation that it relied solely on the cooperation of States and organizations to provide it with information on violations of the arms embargo. No violations were brought to the Committee's attention during the reporting period.

Financing of UNAMIR

The General Assembly, by **decision 55/500** of 7 September, included in the draft agenda of its fifty-sixth (2001) session the item on financing of the United Nations Assistance Mission for Rwanda (UNAMIR). The Mission had been withdrawn from Rwanda in 1996 [YUN 1996, p. 62] and the liquidation process was begun at that time. On 24 December, the Assembly decided that the agenda item would remain for consideration at its resumed fifty-sixth (2002) session (**decision 56/464**) and that the Fifth Committee should continue to consider the item at that session (**decision 56/458**).

Central African Republic

The United Nations Peace-building Support Office in the Central African Republic (BONUCA), established by Security Council presidential statement S/PRST/2000/5 [YUN 2000, p. 162] to take over from the United Nations Mission in the Central African Republic, the peacekeeping mission that had been in place since 1998 [YUN 1998, p. 134], continued to support the Government's efforts to consolidate peace and national reconciliation in the wake of a 1996 army rebellion [YUN 1996, p. 808]. Despite efforts to implement the 1997 Bangui Agreements [YUN 1997, p. 91] and the 1998 National Reconciliation Pact [YUN 1998, p. 133], the Government, under President

Ange-Félix Patassé, and the numerous opposition parties found little ground for cooperation or dialogue, and the political situation was dominated by considerable tension in their relationship. The situation was further clouded by social tension and a precarious economic and security situation.

In May, the political situation was exacerbated by an attempted coup d'état led by General André Kolingba, a former President. The Government quickly regained control and worked to restore security in the capital; many of the main instigators fled to the DRC. Most of the army remained loyal and it therefore appeared unlikely that the attempt would jeopardize the restructuring of the defence and security forces upon which the Government had embarked. The security situation contributed to the refugee problem and it was estimated that 20,000 people had fled the Central African Republic for the DRC. The presence of putschists among the refugees was a matter of concern for the Central African Republic, which closed the border between the two States on 17 July.

In the light of the heightened tension in the country, the Secretary-General, in September, recommended strengthening the mandate of BO-NUCA to focus on activities to bring about political dialogue and national reconciliation, to monitor the security situation, to ensure respect for human rights, and to provide political support for the mobilization of resources for economic reconstruction. The Security Council considered those recommendations and noted the Secretary-General's intention to extend BONUCA's mandate for another year, until 31 December 2002.

The political situation, which had been precarious since the attempted coup, suffered another blow on 26 October when President Patassé dismissed General François Bozizé, the Chief of Staff of the Central African Republic armed forces, following the discovery of a cache of weapons at his residence. As a result of the affair, the situation in the Central African Republic, which was gradually returning to normal, encountered setbacks at the end of the year, further weakening the State's economic recovery efforts.

Political situation and BONUCA activities

Report of Secretary-General (January). The Secretary-General, in response to a request contained in the Security Council's presidential statement S/PRST/2000/5 [YUN 2000, p. 162], reported on 11 January on the situation in the Central African Republic and on BONUCA activities for the previous six months [S/2001/35]. He stated that late 2000 had been dominated by considerable tension in the relationship between the rul-ing party and the 15 opposition parties [YUN 2000, p. 164]. The lack of dialogue between the country's political stakeholders was a serious obstacle to the sustainability of the democratic institutions established barely a year before. Prolonged civil service strikes, brought about by the accumulation of unpaid salary arrears and current salaries, increased the risk of social upheaval, and the negative economic and social impact of the conflict in the DRC was compromising the progress made towards the consolidation of the fragile peace and stability in the country. The economy as a whole had never recovered from the destruction of the socio-economic infrastructure that took place during the mutinies of 1996 and 1997 and, even more damaging, the continuing fuel crisis that began in June 2000.

SECURITY COUNCIL ACTION (January)

The Security Council met twice on 23 January [meetings 4261, 4262] to consider the situation in the Central African Republic. At the second meeting, following consultations among Council members, the President made statement **S/PRST/2001/2** on behalf of the Council:

The Security Council has considered the report of the Secretary-General dated 11 January 2001, submitted in accordance with the statement by the President of the Council of 10 February 2000 (S/PRST/2000/5).

The Council commends the United Nations Peace-building Support Office in the Central African Republic and the Representative of the Secretary-General for the efforts they have constantly made to contribute to peace and stability in the Central African Republic. In this connection, the Council welcomes the additional progress made in certain areas since the previous report of the Secretary-General of 29 June 2000, particularly in the area of disarmament and the restructuring of the security and defence forces, and as regards respect for human rights by the police.

The Council welcomes the mission to the region of the Special Envoy of the Secretary-General, to assess the impact of the conflict in the Democratic Republic of the Congo on the Central African Republic and the Republic of the Congo, in particular its humanitarian, economic, social and security implications. The Council is looking forward to discussing the findings of that mission in the very near future.

The Council expresses its concern at the political and social tensions which have recently resurfaced in the Central African Republic, which threaten the national reconciliation process undertaken four years ago with the active support of the international community. The Council notes with concern the absence of dialogue between the Government and the opposition. The Council is also disturbed by the deterioration of the economic situation, partly because of the repercussions of the conflict in the Democratic Republic of the Congo and the resulting fuel crisis.

The Council welcomes the contributions already received and calls upon bilateral and multilateral donors to provide full support to the efforts of the Government of the Central African Republic. The Council appreciates the release by the World Bank of the second tranche of credit for the consolidation of public finances and welcomes the recent decision by the International Monetary Fund to release additional funds. The Council calls upon Member States which made pledges at the special meeting in New York co-chaired by the Secretariat, Germany and the United Nations Development Programme in May 2000 to fulfil their commitments. The Council also stresses the importance of international assistance to refugees and displaced persons in the Central African Republic and in the other countries of the region in order to contribute to regional stability.

The Council reaffirms that it is first up to the Central Africans to summon the necessary political will for national reconciliation. The Council strongly encourages the Government of the Central African Republic to do everything in its power to strengthen democratic institutions and broaden the scope of national reconciliation. The Council urges all political actors in the Central African Republic to contribute each in their own way to the reduction of the existing tension between the Government and the opposition. In this respect, while it welcomes the release, on 8 January 2001, of 62 persons who had been arrested during the prohibited demonstration of 19 December 2000, the Council nevertheless notes with concern certain constraints on the peaceful public assembly of opposition and labour groups.

The Council calls upon the Government of the Central African Republic to take concrete measures to implement economic reforms and to ease social tensions. The Council stresses the priority need for the payment of salary arrears in the civil service and welcomes the recent announcement by the Government of the Central African Republic that it will take steps in this direction. The Council also encourages the Government of the Central African Republic to take all the financial measures that are necessary to relaunch the demobilization and reintegration programme.

The Council requests the Secretary-General to continue to keep it regularly informed about the activities of the United Nations Peace-building Support Office, the situation in the Central African Republic, and in particular the progress made in the political, economic and social reforms, and to submit a report by 30 June 2001, in accordance with the statement of the President of the Council dated 10 February 2000.

Report of Secretary-General (July). In his 2 July report to the Council on the situation in the Central African Republic and on BONUCA [S/2001/660], the Secretary-General stated that the political situation was exacerbated by the completely unexpected attempted coup d'état on the night of 27-28 May when a group of soldiers attempted to overthrow the regime of President Ange-Félix Patassé and to seize power. The putschists simultaneously attacked the residence of the head of State, the national radio and the headquarters of the Presidential Guard. They were repulsed by loyalist forces and the coup attempt failed, thanks to the support of Libyan troops sent to Bangui and to the support of elements of the Congolese rebel movement of Jean-Pierre Bemba. The Secretary-General and the President of the Council issued statements condemning the coup attempt.

On 30 May, General André Kolingba, a former President of the Republic, claimed responsibility for the attempted coup. The next day, President Patassé instituted charges against all those involved. On 1 June, General Kolingba called on his supporters to cease fighting, but clashes continued until 6 June. According to authorities, 59 persons were killed (25 military and 34 civilians) and 88,765 displaced. The President announced that the trial of the putschists would be held under transparent conditions and international observers would be allowed to monitor it.

The situation in Bangui was gradually returning to normal, and international organizations were mobilizing to provide appropriate humanitarian assistance, which was estimated to cost $3.6 million. In view of the new crisis, the Secretary-General dispatched General Amadou Toumani Touré, former President of Mali, as his Special Envoy to the Central African Republic from 12 June to 1 July to hold talks on the political situation, assess the humanitarian consequences of the fighting, consider how best the needs of those affected could be met and encourage a resumption of the political dialogue in the country.

Despite the gradual return to normalcy in the capital, a civil service strike had not ended as an announced salary payment was interrupted by the attempted coup. The human rights situation was markedly affected by the events following the attempted coup in that thousands of persons were displaced from one district to another in Bangui. Cases of exactions and of the summary executions of civilian and military personnel were reported; the Government pledged to put an end to those acts.

Since the attempted coup was supported by only a small number of participants, roughly 100, it was unlikely that it had jeopardized the restructuring of the defence and security forces upon which the Government had embarked. The reporting period was marked by heightened insecurity in certain provinces where there were attacks on travellers, military convoys and cattle farmers, and pillaging of refugee camps and villages. In Bangui itself, a number of acts of armed banditry were reported, thus highlighting the situation in respect of the proliferation of illegally owned weapons. BONUCA undertook a fact-finding mission on the border between the Central African Republic and Cameroon in March, following the tensions that had arisen between the two countries in February. That initiative resulted in an easing of tensions that led to the discussion of the demarcation of the common border within the framework of their mixed commission on cooperation. BONUCA's civilian police organized a number of training programmes for the police and gendarmerie of the Central African Republic. The economic situation suffered further as a result of the attempted coup d'état, and the Government's reform efforts were set back. The consequences for the Central African Republic of the crisis in the DRC were also felt in the economic (interruption of traffic on the Ubangui River, supply difficulties), humanitarian (refugee flows) and security (risk of illegal circulation of weapons) areas.

The Secretary-General concluded that the Central African Republic was in a crisis situation which was not fundamentally different from the situation caused by the 1996-1997 mutinies. The attempted coup d'état had jeopardized the efforts the international community had been making for five years to restore and consolidate peace, and had endangered the democratic process and economic recovery. The Secretary-General called on the international community to provide support for the restructuring of the defence and security forces, the collection of weapons and the redeployment plan drawn up by the Government. The continuation and completion of the restructuring of the armed forces was a priority task. The efforts already made in that sphere and the training provided by BONUCA had enabled the army to demonstrate its loyalty during the attempt. The people of the Central African Republic were urged to re-establish political dialogue, restore confidence, foster consultations and promote tolerance.

Appointment. On 9 July [S/2001/690], the Secretary-General informed the Security Council of his intention to appoint General Lamine Cissé (Senegal) as his Representative in the Central African Republic and Head of BONUCA. He would succeed Cheikh Tidiane Sy (Senegal), who resigned in May. The Council, on 12 July [S/2001/691], took note of the Secretary-General's intention.

SECURITY COUNCIL ACTION (July)

On 17 July [meeting 4347], following consultations among Security Council members, the President made statement **S/PRST/2001/18** on behalf of the Council:

The Security Council has examined the report of the Secretary-General of 2 July 2001 on the activities of the United Nations Peace-building Support Office in the Central African Republic and the situation in the Central African Republic.

The Council expresses its appreciation to the Special Envoy of the Secretary-General, General Amadou Toumani Touré, for the mission he conducted in Bangui from 9 June to 1 July 2001. It notes with satisfaction that the mission has contributed to easing tensions in the Central African Republic.

The Council welcomes the appointment of the new Representative of the Secretary-General in the Central African Republic. It looks forward to his assuming the active leadership of the Peace-building Support Office at an early date.

The Council reiterates its condemnation of the recent attempted coup in the Central African Republic. It recognizes the importance of the Central African Republic to subregional stability. It expresses its deep concern at the precarious situation in the country and the persisting acts of violence, in particular against certain ethnic groups. The Council notes that such a climate is not conducive to encouraging the continuation of the return home of the thousands of Central Africans that were displaced or took refuge in neighbouring countries as a result of the events at the end of May. It calls upon the Government of the Central African Republic to take urgent steps to bring an end to all acts of violence.

The Council strongly condemns the killing of the security coordinator for the United Nations system in the Central African Republic. It takes note of the condemnation of this act by the Central African authorities and of their intention to carry out an investigation and urges them to bring those responsible to justice.

The Council calls for respect for human rights, national reconciliation and political dialogue in the spirit of the 1998 National Reconciliation Pact.

The Council requests the Secretary-General to submit to it by 30 September 2001 recommendations on how the United Nations might further contribute to the recovery of the Central African Republic, paying particular attention to the following questions:

(a) Strengthening the Peace-building Support Office, in particular in areas such as human rights monitoring, assistance to the judicial system and capacity-building, and enhancing the effectiveness of its early warning capacity;

(b) Exploring with the Government of the Central African Republic, in cooperation with the relevant institutions, the provision of expertise in the area of public administration and finances, in particular by making available experts in such matters;

(c) The continued and improved restructuring of the Central African armed forces and the implementation of an effective arms-collection programme.

The Council expresses its willingness to study, in cooperation with the relevant institutions, particularly the International Monetary Fund and World Bank, the recommendations of the Secretary-General.

The Council stresses that an enhanced international effort will be necessary to help in the recovery of the Central African Republic. It urges all States that made pledges at the special donor meeting in

New York in May 2000 to fulfil them. It calls on the Bretton Woods institutions to take into account the specific nature of the situation in order to conclude programmes with the Central African authorities at an early date. The Council stresses the crucial importance of poverty eradication, debt payment and payment of arrears of salary for civil servants which requires in the long term heightened efforts on the part of the Government of the Central African Republic in the management of public finances and administration.

The Council again recalls that responsibility for national reconciliation, stability and the reconstruction of the country lies primarily with the political leaders and the people of the Central African Republic. It emphasizes in this regard that the full effectiveness of the assistance of the international community depends on the implementation in parallel of appropriate structural reforms.

Report of Secretary-General (September). On 18 September [S/2001/886], the Secretary-General, in response to the Council's request (above), submitted a report on the situation in the Central African Republic, which, he said, was in a situation of crisis since the attempted coup d'état in May and required immediate and increased levels of external assistance. The repercussions of the fighting in the capital had been disastrous for the economy, and the World Bank had suspended disbursements for non-payment of amounts due. The State was unable to pay the salaries of its public servants on a regular basis. In addition, political dialogue no longer seemed to be on the agenda. In the area of security, the chief instigators of the attempted coup and a large number of soldiers had fled to the DRC and posed a threat to stability in the country. For that reason, any solution to the DRC crisis should take into account the situation in the Central African Republic. The Central African Republic's stability was threatened by the proliferation of weapons in the subregion and in areas adjacent to the DRC's Equateur region under the control of the Front de libération du Congo of Jean-Pierre Bemba. The refugee problem was a further illustration of the connection between the situations in the DRC and the Central African Republic. At the time of the report, approximately 20,000 refugees from the Central African Republic were residing in the DRC, and the putschists were reportedly among them. The Central African authorities closed the common border on 17 July.

At the domestic level, the situation was gradually returning to normal. The investigation by the Government into the killing of the security coordinator for the UN system was under way. The human rights situation was gradually improving, with a reduction in the number of exactions.

In order to ensure that security and peace were restored in the Central African Republic, the Secretary-General called on States and other partners to provide assistance in disarmament and redeployment, and in the restructuring of the defence and security forces.

Due to the situation since the attempted coup d'état, the Secretary-General, as the Council had requested, proposed that BONUCA's mandate, originally set out in 1999 [YUN 1999, p. 128], should be expanded in the areas of political support, security, civilian police, human rights and economic recovery. Its tasks would include monitoring the political situation; supporting initiatives to strengthen national unity and reconciliation; strengthening democratic institutions; monitoring the military and security situation; promoting the restructuring of the defence and security forces and the redeployment plan; promoting arms collection; promoting, within the armed forces, a culture of peace and respect for national institutions; helping to mobilize external resources for restructuring of the defence and security forces; monitoring the public security situation; supporting the Government's training of police and gendarmerie; providing technical assistance to police and gendarmerie in public order and crime control; monitoring the human rights situation; contributing to national capacity-building in respect for human rights; supporting activities in strengthening the judicial system and the rule of law; providing political support for UN efforts to promote national reconstruction, combat poverty and promote good governance; and contributing to mobilizing political support and resources to implement social and economic programmes agreed upon with the Bretton Woods institutions (the World Bank Group and the International Monetary Fund (IMF)). Should the Council approve those new tasks, the Secretary-General suggested that BONUCA's mandate be extended for an additional year, until 31 December 2002.

SECURITY COUNCIL ACTION (September)

The Security Council considered the Secretary-General's report at two meetings, on 21 and 26 September [meetings 4380, 4382]. At the second meeting, following consultations among Security Council members, the President made statement **S/PRST/2001/25** on behalf of the Council:

The Security Council has considered the report of the Secretary-General of 19 September 2001 submitted in accordance with the statement of its President on 17 July 2001 (S/PRST/2001/18), particularly his recommendations on how the United

Nations might further contribute to the recovery of the Central African Republic.

The Council expresses its appreciation of the continuing work of the Secretary-General's Representative, General Lamine Cissé, and of the United Nations Peace-building Support Office in the Central African Republic.

The Council expresses its continued deep concern at the precarious situation in the Central African Republic. It reiterates its call on all parties for political dialogue, national reconciliation and respect for human rights in the spirit of the 1998 National Reconciliation Pact. In this respect it has taken note of the appeals for national unity made by the Central African authorities.

The Council calls on the Central African authorities to follow the internationally accepted standards for due process in the course of investigations and court trials of individuals involved in the coup attempt in May 2001. These procedures should be transparent and should not be allowed to aggravate the inter-ethnic relations in the Central African Republic. The refugees who left the country after the failed coup should be able to return in safety without fear of persecution on ethnic basis.

The Council encourages the international community to make a substantial and urgent contribution to the recovery of the Central African Republic and emphasizes that the efficiency of such a contribution will greatly depend on the efforts the Government of the Central African Republic itself makes to this end. The Council emphasizes that the crucial issues of external debt and payment of arrears of salary for civil servants need to be urgently addressed.

The Council encourages the United Nations Development Programme and the international financial institutions, particularly the World Bank, the International Monetary Fund and the African Development Bank, to consider, in consultation with the Government of the Central African Republic and the Secretary-General's Representative, ways of strengthening the capacities of the Government of the Central African Republic in the management of its economic and financial affairs, including through secondment of high-level experts. The Council invites the Secretary-General to keep it informed of actions taken in this regard when he presents his next report on the Central African Republic. In addition, the Council urges the Bretton Woods institutions to show exceptional solicitude towards the Central African Republic.

The Council takes note with interest of the intention of the Secretary-General, in coordination with the Government of the Central African Republic, to extend the mandate of the Peace-building Support Office and to strengthen it in accordance with paragraph 29 of his report of 19 September 2001.

The Council underlines the need to continue the restructuring of the Central African armed forces to enable them to fulfil their role effectively, loyally and impartially, in the service of the Central African people. It also recalls the importance of implementing an effective arms-collection programme. In this regard, it supports the recommendations in paragraphs 17 and 18 of the report of the Secretary-General.

The Council requests the Secretary-General to continue to keep it regularly informed of the activities of the Support Office and the situation in the Central African Republic, particularly in the areas of political dialogue, national reconciliation and respect for human rights.

At that meeting, the President informed the Council that the Secretariat's assessment of the cost of strengthening BONUCA would be $1.4 million; extending its mandate for the year 2002 would cost approximately $4.9 million.

Communications. On 19 November [S/2001/1117], the Sudan forwarded to the Secretary-General a Declaration issued by the meeting of the Community of Sahelo-Saharan States on Central Africa (New York, 15 November). Expressing concern about the deteriorating security conditions in the Central African Republic, the Community emphasized solidarity with the legitimate elected Government and commended efforts by Colonel Muammar Qaddafi, the Libyan Arab Jamahirya leader, to promote stability in Central Africa within the framework of the mandate assigned to him by the Community as its coordinator for peace and security.

The Sudan, on 4 December [S/2001/1148], transmitted the final communiqué issued by the African mini-summit on peace and stability in the Central African Republic (Khartoum, 3 December). Attended by the heads of State of Chad, the Central African Republic, the Sudan and Zambia, and the Libyan Secretary of Defence, together with representatives of OAU and the United Nations, the meeting decided to establish, for an interim period, a peacekeeping force to ensure security in the country and appealed to OAU, the United Nations, and friendly countries to support it. The mini-summit also decided to form a political committee of foreign ministers of Burkina Faso, Chad, Gabon, Libya and the Sudan, the OAU Secretary-General, the Representative of the UN Secretary-General and the Secretary-General of the Community of Sahelo-Saharan States to maintain contacts with a view to achieving national conciliation in Central Africa.

Further developments. In a report covering the situation in the Central African Republic in the last three months of 2001 [S/2002/12], the Secretary-General said that the situation there continued to be marked by the repercussions of the attempted coup d'état in May. On 9 October, the Joint Commission of Judicial Inquiry submitted its partial conclusions to President Patassé and to the competent judicial authorities. It was expected that the trial of the putschists would commence in December and would involve about 700 individuals, of whom 70 were in custody and

628 were fugitives. The political situation deteriorated further on 26 October when the President relieved General François Bozizé of his duties as Chief of Staff of the Central African Republic's armed forces after a cache of weapons was discovered in his residence. When the General resisted arrest, the Secretary-General's Representative undertook a good offices mission. The President promised to appoint General Bozizé to another position and to consider granting a pardon once the judicial procedure was completed, while the General stated that he would remove barricades that had a stranglehold on Bangui. Despite the verbal agreement, government troops attacked the General's positions, and the General and some of his supporters fled to Chad. The President of Chad refused to consider extraditing General Bozizé and proposed negotiations, with OAU and UN involvement. The General claimed to be willing to negotiate with his country's authorities, a claim supported by Chad, which granted him political asylum.

Efforts were made at the regional level, through the Community of Sahelo-Saharan States and OAU, to reach a negotiated solution to the new crisis. Libya proposed sending international observers and an African peacekeeping force to the Central African Republic.

Internally, the Bozizé affair contributed to the persistent tension between the majority and the opposition, who sought an amnesty for General Bozizé and his men. A peaceful end to the affair was desired, and the Secretary-General supported all subregional initiatives that sought to restore stability to the Central African Republic.

Responding to calls for calm, the Central African Republic authorities put an end, on 24 December, to all judicial proceedings against former General Bozizé and his men. The former General set a number of conditions for his return to Bangui, including the proclamation of a general amnesty, the departure of foreign troops, cancellation of the sending of a peacekeeping force to the Central African Republic and the holding of a national dialogue. A meeting between President Patassé and the opposition leaders was planned. With the assistance of UN agencies, a committee was set up on 29 November to consider the modalities for receiving refugees returning from the DRC. Only a few returned officially, but many returned to Bangui quietly.

During the reporting period, instances of extrajudicial execution and arbitrary detention were reported to BONUCA, and the situation in the prisons remained troubling. The failed coup and the Bozizé affair had a serious impact on the country's armed forces, with the army losing 1,300 soldiers. Most of the deserters fled to the DRC and the remainder to Chad, leaving the army in a state of disarray. The Bozizé affair led to a worsening in the security situation and also had adverse consequences for the economy, as the blocking of the main supply route for nearly a week and the closure of offices, banks and businesses led to a major loss of income for the State.

The Secretary-General observed that the process of returning to normal in the Central African Republic had been slowed down by the Bozizé affair. The national reconciliation that was expected after the failed coup in May had still not taken place by the end of the year, partly because of the continuing judicial investigations. It was hoped that President Patassé's call for the return of refugees would contribute to an easing of tension.

MINURCA financing

In March [A/55/849], the Secretary-General submitted the financial performance report of the United Nations Mission in the Central African Republic (MINURCA) for the period 1 July 1999 to 30 June 2000. The Mission, which at the end of its mandate in 2000 [YUN 2000, p. 161], was replaced with BONUCA, remained in the process of liquidation. The General Assembly, by resolutions 53/238 [YUN 1999, p. 129] and 54/277 [YUN 2000, p. 166], had appropriated a total amount of $41,098,075 gross ($40,069,275 net) for the maintenance and liquidation of the Mission for that period, inclusive of $1,659,640 for the support account for peacekeeping operations and $325,435 for the United Nations Logistics Base in Brindisi, Italy. Expenditures for the period totalled $39,900,975 gross ($38,916,875 net), resulting in an unencumbered balance of $1,197,100 gross ($1,152,400 net). The unencumbered balance resulted mainly from lower actual costs for military contingents and civilian personnel, as well as reduced operational requirements under premises/accommodation, air operations and other programmes.

ACABQ considered the financial performance report and made comments in two of its own reports, both issued in April: one on financing of UN peacekeeping operations in general [A/55/874] and the other on the financial report of MINURCA [A/55/884].

GENERAL ASSEMBLY ACTION

On 14 June [meeting 103], the General Assembly, on the recommendation of the Fifth Committee [A/55/960], adopted **resolution 55/270** without vote [agenda item 152].

Financing of the United Nations Mission in the Central African Republic

The General Assembly,

Having considered the report of the Secretary-General on the financing of the United Nations Mission in the Central African Republic and the related reports of the

Advisory Committee on Administrative and Budgetary Questions,

Bearing in mind Security Council resolution 1159 (1998) of 27 March 1998, by which the Council established the United Nations Mission in the Central African Republic, and the subsequent resolutions by which the Council extended the mandate of the Mission, the last of which was resolution 1271(1999) of 22 October 1999,

Recalling its resolution 52/249 of 26 June 1998 on the financing of the Mission and its subsequent resolutions thereon, the latest of which was resolution 54/277 of 15 June 2000,

Reaffirming that the costs of the Mission are expenses of the Organization to be borne by Member States in accordance with Article 17, paragraph 2, of the Charter of the United Nations,

Recalling its previous decisions regarding the fact that, in order to meet the expenditures caused by the Mission, a different procedure is required from that applied to meet expenditures of the regular budget of the United Nations,

Taking into account the fact that the economically more developed countries are in a position to make relatively larger contributions and that the economically less developed countries have a relatively limited capacity to contribute towards such an operation,

Bearing in mind the special responsibilities of the States permanent members of the Security Council, as indicated in General Assembly resolution 1874(S-IV) of 27 June 1963, in the financing of such operations,

Noting with appreciation that voluntary contributions have been made to the Mission,

Mindful of the fact that it is essential to provide the Mission with the necessary financial resources to enable it to meet its outstanding liabilities,

1. *Takes note* of the status of contributions to the United Nations Mission in the Central African Republic as at 30 April 2001, including the contributions outstanding in the amount of 36.7 million United States dollars, representing 32 per cent of the total assessed contributions, notes that some 44 per cent of the Member States have paid their assessed contributions in full, and urges all other Member States concerned, in particular those in arrears, to ensure payment of their outstanding assessed contributions in full;

2. *Expresses its appreciation* to those Member States which have paid their assessed contributions in full;

3. *Expresses concern* about the financial situation with regard to peacekeeping activities, in particular as regards the reimbursements to troop contributors that bear additional burdens owing to overdue payments by Member States of their assessments;

4. *Also expresses concern* at the delay experienced by the Secretary-General in deploying and providing adequate resources to some recent peacekeeping missions, in particular those in Africa;

5. *Emphasizes* that all future and existing peacekeeping missions shall be given equal and non-discriminatory treatment in respect of financial and administrative arrangements;

6. *Also emphasizes* that all peacekeeping missions shall be provided with adequate resources for the effective and efficient discharge of their respective mandates;

7. *Endorses* the conclusions and recommendations contained in the report of the Advisory Committee on Administrative and Budgetary Questions, and requests the Secretary-General to ensure their full implementation;

8. *Requests* the Secretary-General to take all necessary action to ensure that the liquidation of the Mission is administered with a maximum of efficiency and economy;

9. *Decides* that Member States that have fulfilled their financial obligations to the Mission shall be credited their respective share of the unencumbered balance of 1,197,100 dollars gross (1,152,400 dollars net) in respect of the period ending 30 June 2000, in accordance with the composition of groups set out in paragraphs 3 and 4 of General Assembly resolution 43/232 of 1 March 1989, as adjusted by the Assembly in subsequent relevant resolutions and decisions for the ad hoc apportionment of peacekeeping appropriations, the latest of which were resolution 52/230 of 31 March 1998 and decisions 54/456 to 54/458 of 23 December 1999 for the period 1998-2000, and taking into account the scale of assessments for the year 2000, as set out in its resolutions 52/215 A of 22 December 1997 and 54/237 A of 23 December 1999;

10. *Also decides* that, for Member States that have not fulfilled their financial obligations to the Mission, their share of the unencumbered balance of 1,197,100 dollars gross (1,152,400 dollars net) in respect of the period ending 30 June 2000 shall be set off against their outstanding obligations in accordance with the scheme set out in paragraph 9 above;

11. *Emphasizes* that no peacekeeping mission shall be financed by borrowing funds from other active peacekeeping missions;

12. *Decides* to include in the provisional agenda of its fifty-sixth session the item entitled "Financing of the United Nations Mission in the Central African Republic".

On 24 December, the Assembly decided that the item on MINURCA financing would remain for consideration during its resumed fifth-sixth (2002) session (**decision 56/464**) and that the Fifth Committee would continue to consider the item at that session (**decision 56/458**).

West Africa

In response to rising tensions in West Africa, particularly in the Mano River Union countries (Guinea, Liberia and Sierra Leone), the Secretary-General, in March, sent an inter-agency mission to the subregion, led by Ibrahima Fall, Assistant Secretary-General for Political Affairs. The mission underscored the fragility of the political, security, social and humanitarian situation, as well as the precarious governance and economic development conditions in West Africa, particularly in the Mano River Union countries and Côte d'Ivoire, Guinea-Bissau and the Casamance region of Senegal. It recommended that the United Nations and the international community adopt an integrated and comprehensive regional approach to prevent, manage and contribute to resolving the many conflicts in the region, and made recommendations in political, security, economic and humanitarian areas to that end. As proposed by the mission, the Secretary-General established the Office of the Special Representative for West Africa, as of January 2002.

Following the mission, some tangible improvement in parts of West Africa was noted: the peace process in Sierra Leone saw significant progress followed by an improvement in the humanitarian situation; in Côte d'Ivoire, the Government organized a dialogue for national reconciliation, which was attended by all the major political leaders; Guinea decided not to force through legislative elections that could have escalated the internal political crisis following a controversial referendum in November on the extension of the President's term of office; a UN mission was dispatched to Guinea-Bissau to develop an overall peace-building and development plan; and elections were held in the Gambia. There was also a reduction in tension among the Mano River Union countries following progress in the ministerial dialogue among ministers for foreign affairs, defence and the interior, which began in August. The ministers discussed restoring confidence at the highest political level, security problems along the common borders and preparations for a summit of heads of State, planned for early 2002. Despite those improvements, the overall political situation remained volatile, and the threat of insecurity and instability remained real in the Mano River Union and other countries.

Inter-Agency Mission to West Africa

The Inter-Agency Mission to West Africa, led by Assistant Secretary-General for Political Affairs, Ibrahima Fall, visited 11 West African countries (Côte d'Ivoire, Gambia, Ghana, Guinea, Guinea-Bissau, Liberia, Mali, Nigeria, Senegal, Sierra Leone, Togo) from 6 to 27 March [S/2001/434]. The Secretary-General's decision to dispatch the mission in response to security problems in the subregion, particularly along the borders between Guinea, Liberia and Sierra Leone, had been welcomed by the Security Council in presidential statement S/PRST/2000/41 [YUN 2000, p. 182]. During the Mission's meetings with high-level government officials, UN country teams, members of the diplomatic corps, parliamentarians, political party representatives, religious leaders, representatives of civil society groups, NGOs, and staff of the Economic Community of West African States (ECOWAS), the Mano River Union secretariat, the Commission of the West African Economic and Monetary Union, the African Development Bank and the Central Bank of West African States, the idea of a comprehensive and integrated approach to the priority needs and challenges of the subregion was extensively discussed. Within that context, views were exchanged on a range of issues, including peace and security, governance, national reconciliation, promoting political dialogue, human rights, humanitarian issues, subregional integration, enhancing cooperation with ECOWAS and other organizations, the HIV/AIDS epidemic, alleviating poverty and external debt, illegal arms trafficking and its connection to the sale of "conflict diamonds", landmines, the proliferation of arms and militias, and issues affecting children, including the problem of child soldiers.

Throughout the Mission's visit, the gravity of the political and security situation in West Africa and the potential for the rapid spread of insecurity and instability were repeatedly underscored. Most interlocutors foresaw deterioration in the Mano River Union countries, Côte d'Ivoire, Guinea-Bissau and the Casamance region of Senegal, and the possibility of a "domino effect", with instability spreading from one country to another, which was a source of deep and widespread concern. The importance of approaching conflict resolution from a regional perspective was stressed. Likewise, humanitarian problems within single countries could not be viewed as specific and internal. It was repeatedly noted that problems had been compounded by a lack of political dialogue among leaders and a lack of national reconciliation, persistent economic decline and high levels of poverty, the trade in arms and proliferation of militias, narcotics trafficking, disease, resource scarcity and the often violent and aggressive attempts at transnational control of natural resources by State and non-State actors. In some countries, the Mission noted wide disparities in perception of the situation between the Government and other interlocutors. Ethnic affinities, which transcended national boundaries in countries such as the Gambia, Guinea, Guinea-Bissau, Liberia, Senegal and Sierra Leone, had contributed to the spread of conflicts in border areas, especially where militia groups and others had carved out territories for control. Of particular concern were tensions between the Mano River Union countries and the alleged involvement of State and non-State actors in supporting the Revolutionary United Front in Sierra Leone, among them dealers in conflict diamonds, mercenaries and international arms dealers. Interlocutors stressed the importance of efforts by ECOWAS leaders and the United Nations to promote reconciliation between the leaders of the three Mano River Union countries.

ECOWAS had played a significant role in conflict prevention and resolution and had sent peacekeeping forces to several of its member States where conflict had broken out. The possible deployment of an interposition force along the borders between Guinea, Liberia and Sierra Leone to prevent further armed incursions remained under consideration. While ECOWAS countries were generally willing to contribute peacekeeping forces to either an ECOWAS or UN force, they lacked equipment, training, logistical and technical capacities.

The Mission found that reports of violations of human rights, ranging from the broader rights of people to peace, security and development to abuses against the rights of individuals, were widespread within the subregion. In addition, the economies of West African countries were generally fragile, despite abundant natural resources, and the issue of the external debt burden was raised as a major concern by both government and non-governmental interlocutors. As a result of the many conflicts, the subregion was confronted with a serious refugee problem, with well over half a million refugees and over 670,000 internally displaced persons. Insecurity had, in a number of areas, severely constrained humanitarian operations and the prevalence of HIV/AIDS was increasing.

The Mission recommended enhancement of institutional arrangements and mechanisms within the UN system, including the establishment of a UN office for West Africa to develop policies for activities and monitor political, security, human rights, humanitarian and development issues in the subregion; closer consultations between the United Nations, Governments and ECOWAS; and a subregional UN development assistance framework to target issues of a cross-border nature. In the area of peace and security, the Mission proposed that the mandate of the United Nations Mission in Sierra Leone be expanded to cover Guinea and Liberia to take into account the interrelations between the implementation of the Lomé Peace Agreement [YUN 1999, p. 159] and implementation of UN sanctions on Liberia and the monitoring of borders between the three countries. As to conflict prevention and resolution, it was recommended that the UN system and the international community strengthen the ECOWAS Mechanism for Conflict Prevention, Management, Resolution, Peacekeeping and Security. Cooperation with the UN

system should be enhanced to develop the ECOWAS early warning system, including a central observer office and zonal bureaux, and the ECOWAS secretariat should be supported to enable it to provide electoral assistance to member States. The United Nations needed to be more involved in national reconciliation activities as soon as signs of a potential crisis in the subregion were evident and should follow up on the efforts of national leaders, in particular those of Côte d'Ivoire, Guinea, Guinea-Bissau, Liberia and Sierra Leone, to honour their commitments to reconciliation with opposition groups. Preventive and post-conflict peace-building measures should be among primary activities in national and subregional programmes, with particular emphasis on the political dimensions of peace-building. Disarmament, demobilization and reintegration programmes should be implemented simultaneously in post-conflict situations, in particular in the Mano River Union countries, Côte d'Ivoire Guinea-Bissau and the Casamance area of Senegal. The United Nations should assist ECOWAS in implementing its peacekeeping programmes, including through strengthening ECOWAS headquarters arrangements and training centres, and providing logistical and technical support. Other recommendations concerned stopping the proliferation of arms in the subregion; ending the use of child soldiers, child trafficking and child labour; women and armed conflict; peacekeeping arrangements; implementing targeted sanctions; governance; human rights; refugees; ensuring safe access and safe passage for humanitarian assistance; internally displaced persons and host communities; funding; and economic integration.

Security Council consideration. On 10 April, the Security Council received a briefing from Assistant Secretary-General Fall on the findings of the Mission. The Council considered the Mission's report on 14 May [meeting 4319], when it was again briefed by Mr. Fall and other Mission members. The report was again considered by the Council on 18 and 19 December [meetings 4439, 4440] when the President made a statement on the situation in West Africa (see p. 162).

Communications. The ECOWAS heads of State and Government, at an extraordinary summit on the security situation in West Africa (Abuja, Nigeria, 11 April) [S/2001/353], expressed concern at the continuing tension along the common boundaries of Guinea, Liberia and Sierra Leone, and the presence of several irregular armed groups in the region. They appealed to the Mano River Union States to take individual and collective measures to curb the activities of armed rebel groups operating on their territories. They reaffirmed their wish to deploy troops along the borders.

In a 24 September statement [S/2001/922], the EU expressed satisfaction about progress made in the dialogue among the Mano River Union countries, particularly recent meetings of their Foreign Ministers held in the three capitals. The EU welcomed commitments concerning joint action against the groups involved in events destabilizing the region, the establishment of a joint patrol along the borders of the three countries and combating the proliferation of small arms. It welcomed the prospect of a meeting between the heads of State of those countries in January 2002.

Establishment of UN office for West Africa

The Secretary-General informed the Security Council President on 26 November [S/2001/1128] that he intended to establish the Office of the Special Representative of the Secretary-General for West Africa. It would be entrusted with the functions of: promoting an integrated subregional approach in the work of the United Nations and other partners; liaising with and assisting ECOWAS and the Mano River Union; carrying out good offices roles and special assignments, including in conflict prevention and peace-building; and reporting to Headquarters on key developments. The Office, which would have seven international staff headed by an Under-Secretary-General, would be established in Dakar, Senegal, for three years from January 2002, subject to a review after its first year. On 29 November [S/2001/1129], the Council welcomed the Secretary-General's intention.

SECURITY COUNCIL ACTION

On 19 December [meeting 4440], following consultations among Security Council members, the President made statement **S/PRST/2001/38** on behalf on the Council:

The Security Council has considered, during its public meetings of 14 May and 18 December 2001, the report of the Inter-Agency Mission to West Africa.

The Council welcomes with satisfaction the above report and fully supports initiatives taken with a view to implementing its recommendations. It welcomes, in particular, the establishment of the Office of the Special Representative of the Secretary-General for West Africa to ensure, inter alia, the strengthening of harmonization and coordination of the activities of the United Nations system in an integrated regional perspective and to the development of a fruitful partnership with the Economic Community of West African States, other subregional organizations and international and national actors, including civil society.

The Council emphasizes that greater subregional integration must remain a key goal for the United Nations system in the search for lasting solutions to the conflicts in West Africa and to the human suffering to which these give rise. It stresses the need to further strengthen the capacities of the Economic Community of West African States in the areas which should enable it to act as the engine of subregional integration and increased cooperation with the United Nations system.

The Council underlines the importance of taking steps to develop cooperation and coordination among the intergovernmental bodies and entities of the United Nations system which can influence the situation in West Africa, and expresses its intention to consider measures to coordinate its action with these bodies and entities.

The Council emphasizes the need to maintain regional peace and stability and, in that connection, welcomes the progress made in the Mano River Union area. It also emphasizes the need to see to the effective implementation of the confidence-building and cooperation measures agreed on by Guinea, Liberia and Sierra Leone and strongly encourages these three countries to do their utmost to hold a summit meeting of their heads of State and to ensure its success. It commends the role of the civil society particularly the Mano River Union Women's Peace Network for their instrumental role in facilitating dialogue among the leaders of the region.

The Council also emphasizes the need to strengthen the capacity of the Economic Community of West African States to monitor and to stem the illicit flows of small arms and the establishment of militia. In this connection it welcomes the extension for a period of three years, starting on 5 July 2001, of the Moratorium on the Importation, Exportation and Manufacture of Small Arms and Light Weapons in West Africa. It appeals to the international community to provide appropriate financial assistance to the Programme for Coordination and Assistance for Security and Development and to the national mechanisms involved in the fight against the proliferation of small arms in West Africa.

The Council also emphasizes the urgent need to solve the problem of refugees and displaced persons in the subregion by permitting voluntary returns as soon as possible, under acceptable security conditions.

The Council reiterates its condemnation of the use, by State and non-State actors, of children as combatants in violation of the relevant international instruments on the rights of the child and the Accra Declaration on War-Affected Children in West Africa and the related Plan of Action. It calls for the immediate demobilization of all child soldiers.

The Council welcomes the holding in New York, on 16 November 2001, of the fifth meeting of the United Nations–Economic Community of West African States–Sierra Leone coordination mechanism and the progress made in the peace process in Sierra Leone. It appeals to the international community for substantial financial assistance for the programme for the disarmament, demobilization and reintegration of former combatants and other peace-consolidating activities in Sierra Leone.

The Council welcomes the holding of the twenty-fifth conference of heads of State and of Government of the Economic Community of West African States. It pays tribute to that organization for its major contribution to the restoration of peace, stability, democracy and development in West Africa.

The Council will remain actively seized of this matter.

Communication. The twenty-fifth session of the Authority of Heads of State and Government of ECOWAS (Dakar, 20-21 December) [A/56/849-S/2002/219] reviewed the political and security situation in West Africa and commended Sierra Leone for its progress in restoring peace and security. It also took note of the evolution of the situation in the Mano River Union region and appealed to member States of the Union to intensify the dialogue they had initiated.

Sierra Leone

The United Nations Mission in Sierra Leone (UNAMSIL) continued throughout 2001 to maintain its contacts with the Government of Sierra Leone and the main rebel group, the Revolutionary United Front (RUF), to follow up on the implementation of the Agreement on the Ceasefire and Cessation of Hostilities (Abuja Agreement), signed in November 2000 [YUN 2000, p. 210]. Although the situation in Sierra Leone had remained relatively stable since the signing of the Agreement, concerns remained about continuing incursions and violence along the borders of Guinea, Liberia and Sierra Leone (see above). Progress towards implementing the terms of the Abuja Agreement was slow but discernible in the early months of the year, beginning with the disarmament and demobilization of ex-combatants. UNAMSIL began patrols into RUF-held territory to carry out its aim of assisting the Government to extend its authority and restore law and order throughout the country, to promote a political process, and to renew the disarmament, demobilization and reintegration programme.

In March, the Security Council increased UNAMSIL's military component to 17,500 and welcomed the Mission's revised concept of operations that foresaw a progressive expansion of its area of operations leading to eventual government control of the entire country and political inclusion of opposing groups.

By midyear, the pace of implementation of the Abuja Agreement picked up and progress continued to be made throughout the rest of 2001. The Secretary-General reported in September that there were grounds for cautious optimism on the peace process. The ceasefire, although fragile, was generally observed, and by December withdrawal of forces and disarmament had been accomplished in 10 of the 12 districts. As disarm-

ament progressed, the Government began preparations for elections in December, later postponed to May 2002. RUF was permitted to register as a political party and was invited to participate in electoral discussions. Security in the country remained a serious concern, and the Secretary-General noted that the establishment of adequate disarmament, demobilization and reintegration facilities remained an urgent task.

In January, the Security Council considered the 2000 report of the Panel of Experts established to investigate possible violations of the sanctions against Sierra Leone—the arms embargo and the ban on rough diamond exports. According to the Panel, the trade in rough diamonds was a major source of income for RUF and had enabled it to sustain its military activities. Sierra Leone informed the Council of steps it had taken to end transactions of such "conflict" or "blood" diamonds by, among other measures, establishing a certificate-of-origin regime to halt illicit mining and smuggling of diamonds, action that was welcomed by the Council.

The Secretary-General pursued efforts to establish a Special Court for Sierra Leone to try crimes against humanity, war crimes and other violations of international humanitarian law. He raised questions concerning some aspects of the draft agreement between the United Nations and Sierra Leone and the proposed statute, particularly on the personal jurisdiction of the Special Court and funding. Having received indications of sufficient, if not total, funding for the first three years, the Secretary-General authorized the commencement of the operation of the Court, beginning with a planning mission to Freetown in January 2002.

Initiatives were under way to establish a Truth and Reconciliation Commission in Sierra Leone, which was expected to begin work in 2002.

UNAMSIL

Report of Secretary-General (March). In a 14 March report [S/2001/228], his ninth on UNAMSIL, the Secretary-General described developments in Sierra Leone since his December 2000 report [YUN 2000, p. 211]. The Secretary-General's Special Representative, Oluyemi Adeniji, and UNAMSIL representatives held several meetings and maintained contacts with the Government and RUF to follow up on the implementation of the 2000 Abuja Agreement. UNAMSIL discussed military issues with the rebel group, in particular the return of weapons seized from UNAMSIL contingents in May 2000 [ibid., p. 195] and the reopening of roads to facilitate the free movement of people and goods in RUF-held areas. RUF was also urged to disengage from the conflict at Sierra Leone's border with Guinea, to begin disarming and demobilizing its fighters and to accept the deployment of government officials. Those contacts yielded some results—RUF reopened several roads, UNAMSIL was able to expand its patrol areas and RUF returned some of the UNAMSIL weapons and equipment it had seized.

The Government established its own indirect contacts with RUF, but the slow pace at which RUF was implementing aspects of the Abuja Agreement did not help to remove apprehension about the rebels' intentions. The RUF leadership indicated that it would not disarm unless the Government was replaced by an inclusive interim government when its term of office expired on 28 March. On 13 February, the Parliament agreed to extend the Government's term so that it could work towards accelerating the disarmament, demobilization and reintegration programme for all combatants, with the exception of the Sierra Leone Army, repatriating and resettling refugees and internally displaced persons, extending government authority to all RUF-held areas and preparing for elections. The Electoral Commission completed its plan for holding parliamentary and presidential elections by 31 December; however, there appeared to be consensus both among Sierra Leoneans and in the international community that free and fair elections would not be possible until security conditions were in place and the Government's authority was extended throughout the country. Other issues needed to be addressed, such as the choice of an electoral system, a review of the electoral law, restructuring of constituency boundaries, registration of voters and printing of the electoral roll.

During the reporting period, the ceasefire between the Government and the rebels continued to hold and the military situation remained relatively calm. However, there was increased fighting at the border areas with Guinea, and the Sierra Leone Army attempted to move towards RUF positions in some areas, which caused local tensions. In the meantime, the Army continued its training and restructuring programme with the assistance of the United Kingdom. UNAMSIL maintained liaison with the Army and the United Kingdom Task Force.

As to the situation with neighbouring countries (see also above), fighting escalated in the areas along Sierra Leone's border with Guinea. In response to cross-border attacks, Guinean forces intensified shelling and launched helicopter gunship attacks on RUF positions deep inside Sierra Leone, causing civilian casualties and flows of internally displaced persons. There were also reports of incursions by armed elements into Liberia, with Liberia accusing Guinea of providing support to those armed elements. A joint Guinea–Sierra Leone military body was set up to ensure that Guinean forces avoided causing civilian casualties during military operations against RUF positions. In an effort to arrest further escalation, the Special Representative met with the Presidents of Guinea and Liberia and the Chairman of ECOWAS to convey the Security Council's concern at the widening crisis. Liberia, under increasing international pressure, on 12 January publicly renounced its support for RUF and expelled RUF elements. The Security Council, by **resolution 1343(2001)** of 7 March (see p. 181), outlined the steps that Liberia had to take with a view to ending its support for RUF and other armed rebel groups in the region.

As at 14 March, the military strength of UNAMSIL was 10,356 personnel and was expected to reach 12,700 by the end of March. UNAMSIL had consolidated its presence in the south and west of the country and had begun patrolling into RUF-controlled areas. The Mission revised its concept of operations to take into account the Abuja Agreement, the changes in its military structure and circumstances on the ground. UNAMSIL's main objectives remained to assist the Government to extend its authority and restore law and order throughout the country, and to promote a political process that would lead to a renewed disarmament, demobilization and reintegration programme and the holding of free and fair elections. The updated concept of operations integrated military and civilian aspects and envisaged the deployment, in successive phases, into RUF-controlled areas of UNAMSIL troops, UN civil affairs, civilian police and human rights personnel, representatives of humanitarian agencies and government personnel. The Mission's rules of engagement allowed it to respond robustly to any attack or threat of attack, including in a pre-emptive manner. In the first stage of forward deployment, which was under way, UNAMSIL was expanding its area of operations by conducting long-range patrols into RUF-controlled areas; it was continuing to maintain liaison with RUF. On the arrival of significant reinforcements, UNAMSIL would enter its second phase of forward deployment by expanding into new areas to ensure freedom of movement along the east-west supply routes and to create the conditions for the resumption of organized disarmament and demobilization by ex-combatants. In the third stage, subject to the availability of troops, UNAMSIL would deploy further forward to the diamond-producing regions and to some border areas, and ensure the orderly conduct of the disarmament, demobilization and reintegration programme and the extension of government authority and basic services. At the next stage, UNAMSIL might need to establish a presence at all key towns and areas to create the necessary conditions for holding elections. The Secretary-General continued to seek contributions to UNAMSIL of additional well-trained and well-equipped troops. When new contingents were deployed, UNAMSIL's total military strength would reach 17,500. Once State authority was extended, the international community could shift its focus to development and humanitarian assistance, and the establishment of security would facilitate the return of Sierra Leonean refugees and internally displaced persons.

The disarmament programme continued, and at the time of the report some 20,000 ex-combatants had been disarmed and demobilized, with some 28,000 ex-combatants, mainly RUF and Civil Defence Forces (CDF)—a militia group allied to the Government—remaining to be disarmed. Reintegration projects existed for some ex-combatants, but thousands had not reported to regional reintegration offices. UNAMSIL was expected to assume a broader responsibility in those efforts.

While the situation in Sierra Leone had remained relatively stable since the signing of the Abuja Agreement, there were continuing incursions and violence at the borders of Guinea, Liberia and Sierra Leone. The Secretary-General called on those Governments to work with ECOWAS and the United Nations to end the crisis and stated that it was imperative that RUF leaders and their backers stop further incursions across the borders. RUF, which continued to delay its disarmament, was apparently ready to implement only those aspects of the Abuja Agreement that posed no threat to its military strength and to its exploitation of the country's natural resources. In the Secretary-General's view, the two-track approach continued to offer the best chances of achieving a durable peace through a combination of a strong military deterrent and a political dialogue between the parties. The forward deployment of UNAMSIL in sufficient strength was an important element in that approach; the Secretary-General recommended that the authorized strength of the Mission be increased and that the mandate be extended for another six months, until 30 September 2001. It was also important for the Government and all other parties involved to formulate more clearly their approaches to the peace process, including a clearer picture of the future status of members of armed groups, as well as the impact of the Truth and Reconciliation Commission and of the planned Special Court (see p. 179). The current

cessation of hostilities provided an opportunity for the parties to restore dialogue and build confidence. The decision by RUF to establish a political body in Freetown was a step in the right direction, and the Secretary-General commended the Government for consenting to the RUF presence in the capital, which should facilitate the opening of a meaningful political dialogue.

(see p. 179)

SECURITY COUNCIL ACTION (March)

On 30 March [meeting 4306], the Security Council unanimously adopted **resolution 1346(2001)**. The draft [S/2001/293] was prepared in consultations among Council members.

The Security Council,

Recalling its previous resolutions and the statements of its President concerning the situation in Sierra Leone,

Affirming the commitment of all States to respect the sovereignty, political independence and territorial integrity of Sierra Leone,

Expressing its continued concern at the fragile security situation in Sierra Leone and neighbouring countries, and in particular at the continued fighting on the border regions of Sierra Leone, Guinea and Liberia and at the grave humanitarian consequences for the civilian, refugee and internally displaced populations in those areas,

Recognizing the importance of the progressive extension of State authority throughout the entire country, political dialogue and national reconciliation, the full implementation of a disarmament, demobilization and reintegration programme, the legitimate exploitation of the natural resources of Sierra Leone for the benefit of its people, full respect for the human rights of all and the rule of law, effective action on the issues of impunity and accountability, the voluntary and unhindered return of refugees and internally displaced persons, the holding by the Government of Sierra Leone of free, fair and transparent elections, and the formulation of a long-term plan for the peace process in order to achieve sustainable peace and security in Sierra Leone, and stressing that the United Nations should continue to support the fulfilment of these objectives,

Having considered the report of the Secretary-General of 14 March 2001,

1. *Decides* that the mandate of the United Nations Mission in Sierra Leone, established in its resolutions 1270(1999) of 22 October 1999 and 1289(2000) of 7 February 2000, shall be extended for a period of six months from the date of the adoption of the present resolution;

2. *Further decides* to increase the military component of the Mission to a strength of 17,500, including the 260 military observers already deployed, as recommended by the Secretary-General in paragraphs 99 and 100 of his report;

3. *Welcomes* the revised concept of operations for the Mission as set out in paragraphs 57 to 67 of the report of the Secretary-General and the progress already made towards its implementation, and encourages the Secretary-General to proceed to its completion;

4. *Expresses its appreciation* to those Member States providing additional troops and support elements to the Mission and those who have made commitments to do so, encourages the Secretary-General to continue his efforts to seek, if necessary, further properly trained and equipped forces to strengthen the military components of the Mission in order to enable the Mission to implement fully its revised concept of operations, and requests the Secretary-General to inform the Council upon receipt of firm commitments to that end;

5. *Requests* the Secretary-General to inform the Council at regular intervals on progress made by the Mission in the implementation of key aspects of its concept of operations, and further requests him to provide an assessment in his next report on steps taken to improve the effectiveness of the Mission;

6. *Expresses its deep concern* at the reports of human rights abuses committed by the Revolutionary United Front and others, including other military groups, against the civilian population, in particular the harassment and forced recruitment of adults and children for fighting and forced labour, demands that these acts cease immediately, and requests the Secretary-General to ensure all human rights monitoring positions within the Mission are filled in order to address the concerns raised in paragraphs 44 to 51 of the report of the Secretary-General;

7. *Expresses also its deep concern* that the Ceasefire Agreement signed in Abuja on 10 November 2000 between the Government of Sierra Leone and the Revolutionary United Front has not been fully implemented, and demands that the Front take immediate steps to fulfil its commitments under that Agreement to ensure full liberty for the United Nations to deploy its troops throughout the country, the free movement of persons and goods, unimpeded movement of humanitarian agencies, refugees and displaced persons and the immediate return of all seized weapons, ammunition and other equipment, and to recommence active participation in the disarmament, demobilization and reintegration programme;

8. *Requests*, in this respect, the Mission to maintain its support, within its capabilities and areas of deployment, for returning refugees and displaced persons and to encourage the Revolutionary United Front to cooperate to this end in fulfilment of its commitments under the Abuja Ceasefire Agreement;

9. *Requests* the Secretary-General to submit to the Council his views on how to take forward the issue of refugees and internally displaced persons, including their return;

10. *Calls upon* all the parties to the Sierra Leone conflict to intensify their efforts towards the full and peaceful implementation of the Abuja Ceasefire Agreement and the resumption of the peace process, taking into account the basis of the Abuja Ceasefire Agreement and relevant Security Council resolutions, and urges Governments and regional leaders concerned to continue their full cooperation with the Economic Community of West African States and the United Nations to promote these efforts, and, in particular, to use their influence with the leaders of the Revolutionary United Front to obtain their cooperation towards achievement of the above-mentioned goals;

11. *Encourages* the efforts of the Economic Community towards a lasting and final settlement of the crisis in the Mano River Union region caused by the continued fighting in the border areas of Sierra Leone, Guinea and Liberia, and underlines the importance of the political support that the United Nations can provide to these efforts in order to stabilize the region;

12. *Takes note* of the responsibilities to be undertaken by the Mission in support of the Government of Sierra Leone's disarmament, demobilization and reintegration programme, notably the decision to provide an enhanced management role as referred to in paragraphs 76 to 79 of the report of the Secretary-General, commends the Government of Sierra Leone for the improvements it has already brought about in the programme, encourages it to take the necessary urgent decisions to allow finalization of the programme and dissemination of information on its benefits and conditions to proceed expeditiously, and also encourages international organizations and donor countries to support generously the efforts of the Government of Sierra Leone in this regard;

13. *Emphasizes* that the development and extension of the administrative capacities of Sierra Leone are also essential to sustainable peace and development in the country, and therefore urges the Government of Sierra Leone to take the necessary practical steps to prepare for and bring about the restoration of civil authority and basic public services throughout its territory, including in the locations where the Mission is expected to deploy in accordance with its concept of operations, and encourages States, other international organizations and non-governmental organizations to provide appropriate assistance in this regard;

14. *Encourages* the Government of Sierra Leone, together with the Secretary-General, the United Nations High Commissioner for Human Rights and other relevant international actors, to expedite the establishment of the Truth and Reconciliation Commission and the Special Court envisaged by resolution 1315(2000) of 14 August 2000, bearing in mind in particular the need to ensure the appropriate protection of children;

15. *Welcomes* the intention of the Secretary-General to keep the security, political, humanitarian and human rights situation in Sierra Leone under close review and to report to the Council, after due consultations with troop-contributing countries, with any additional recommendations, including, if necessary, for a further strengthening of the military component of the Mission for the completion of the planned concept of operations to fulfil the overall objective of assisting the Government of Sierra Leone to re-establish its authority throughout the country, including the diamond-producing areas, and to create the necessary conditions for the conduct of free, fair and transparent elections in due course under the authority of the Government of Sierra Leone;

16. *Decides* to remain actively seized of the matter.

Communications (March). In a 30 March letter [S/2001/301], Guinea referred to the Secretary-General's 14 March report on UNAMSIL, in particular his statement on ensuring the conditions for repatriating Sierra Leonean refugees. Such an operation would require the cooperation of

UNAMSIL, Guinea said, and therefore the Mission should consider deploying its forces in the security zones that would receive the refugees. For a decade Guinea had accepted refugees in its territory and was determined to cooperate in order to ensure the success of a repatriation operation.

Sierra Leone, on 21 March [S/2001/253], expressed its dismay at Liberia's decision to expel Sierra Leone's Ambassador to that country and indicated that it had responded in kind. Sierra Leone further noted Liberia's closure of the border between the two countries.

Refugee situation. In response to resolution 1346(2001) (see p. 165), the Secretary-General reported, on 23 May, on refugees and internally displaced persons in and around Sierra Leone [S/2001/513 & Corr.1]. In total, there were over 1 million refugees, internally displaced persons and other war-affected victims in Guinea, Liberia and Sierra Leone. The crisis had its roots in the civil wars in Liberia and Sierra Leone, continuing RUF control over large areas of Sierra Leone, and the ongoing instability and violence on the borders between the Mano River Union countries. The movements and presence of large numbers of refugees and internally displaced persons in the subregion had serious humanitarian, political and security implications and had become a contentious issue, especially in Guinea. The heavy burden on Guinea as host State, the worsening security situation on the border, and the suspicion that refugee communities might be harbouring rebels had led to calls for their early repatriation. Consequently, UNHCR had encountered problems in providing protection to many refugees in Guinea. Also, a large number of Liberians had recently crossed into Sierra Leone to flee fighting in northern Liberia.

With regard to the refugee situation in Guinea, the Secretary-General stated that the High Commissioner for Refugees had visited the region in February. Since then, the security situation had improved, and UNHCR and other agencies had accessed camps in the Parrot's Beak area of Guinea to provide emergency relief and to commence the relocation of refugees to sites further inland. Since that relocation exercise began, UNHCR had relocated some 43,600 Sierra Leonean refugees from Parrot's Beak to safer areas further north. UNHCR had also assisted voluntary repatriation to Sierra Leone. With the deterioration of the situation in Guinea and Liberia and the gradual improvement of the security situation in Sierra Leone, Sierra Leonean refugees had begun to make their way back to Sierra Leone. Since September 2000, more than 55,000 Sierra Leoneans had returned from Guinea.

The Secretary-General stated his opinion that the conditions for the immediate return of all refugees to Sierra Leone did not exist at the current time. A large part of Sierra Leone remained under RUF control and largely beyond the reach of humanitarian assistance. He called on the international community to support UN and others' efforts to assist in the protection, relocation and return of refugees and internally displaced persons.

The Presidents of Guinea and Sierra Leone, having met at Pamelap, Guinea, on 3 June, issued a communiqué [S/2001/579] stating they had reviewed the security situation along the border. They expressed satisfaction with the imposition of sanctions on Liberia and appealed for international assistance in the repatriation and resettlement of refugees and displaced people from both countries.

Report of Secretary-General (June). In his tenth report on UNAMSIL, dated 25 June [S/2001/627], the Secretary-General said that significant progress had been achieved in the Sierra Leone peace process. On 10 April, the joint committee comprising ECOWAS, the Government and the United Nations met in Abuja, and decided to meet with RUF to review implementation of the Abuja Agreement. That review meeting (Abuja, 2 May) concluded that the ceasefire had been largely observed, with the exception of some attacks by CDF on RUF in eastern Sierra Leone. The Government and RUF agreed to remove all roadblocks in areas under their control. RUF pledged to return, by 30 May, all weapons and equipment it had seized from UNAMSIL and the ECOWAS Monitoring Group (ECOMOG). The meeting, which led to an affirmation that CDF and RUF should disarm simultaneously, called on the fighting groups to release all abductees, in particular child combatants, and urged the parties to create an atmosphere conducive to the return of refugees and internally displaced persons. The Government declared its readiness to address some of RUF's political concerns, including releasing some detained RUF leaders and transforming RUF into a political party. Nearly all the meeting's decisions were implemented, including withdrawal and disarmament plans in certain districts. However, RUF handed over only a negligible amount of UNAMSIL weapons.

ECOWAS leaders continued efforts to advance the peace process in Sierra Leone and to address the conflicts affecting the Mano River Union. At a summit meeting on 11 April (see p. 161), a mediation committee was established to encourage dialogue between the heads of State of Guinea, Liberia and Sierra Leone.

The overall military and security situation in Sierra Leone during March and April remained volatile, with reports of ceasefire violations by CDF, but the situation improved after the 2 May Abuja meeting. UNAMSIL's troop strength increased to 12,718 as at 21 June, enabling the Mission to implement the second phase of its concept of operations and to prepare for the third by maintaining a patrol presence in Koidu, a diamond-producing centre. The disarmament, demobilization and reintegration programme, to be monitored by a mechanism with the participation of CDF and RUF, was resumed on 18 May. UNAMSIL worked with the Government to extend civil authority to all areas of the country. With the progress in disarmament, it appeared likely that the Government would be able to organize elections during the next dry season (October 2001 to May 2002), and it began preparations for elections in December. To plan for its involvement in elections, the Secretariat sent an assessment mission to Sierra Leone in May to discuss its participation.

The Secretary-General, while remarking on positive developments in the previous two months, cautioned that challenges remained, in particular the need to establish security throughout the country. The security situation in the subregion remained difficult, and he urged the Mano River Union countries to start a political dialogue. He also called on the international community to contribute to the disarmament, demobilization and reintegration programme, which was crucial to all aspects of the peace process, including the creation of conditions conducive to holding free and fair elections. The most urgent tasks that needed to be addressed in the short term were the establishment of adequate disarmament, demobilization and reintegration facilities and the development of a realistic timetable for implementing the programme in the remaining districts and for the timely creation of reintegration opportunities. UNAMSIL could play an enhanced role in providing training and advice to Sierra Leonean law enforcement officials, in cooperation with the team of Commonwealth police advisers in the country. To that end, the Secretary-General intended to bring the civilian police component of UNAMSIL to its authorized strength of 60 and to assess further needs.

The Security Council considered the Secretary-General's report on UNAMSIL on 28 June [meeting 4340].

Report of Secretary-General (September). On 7 September, the Secretary-General, in his eleventh report on UNAMSIL [S/2001/857 & Add.1], said that the Sierra Leone peace process had continued to make encouraging progress during the period since his last report. The disarmament of RUF and CDF combatants had so far been completed in four districts, including the diamond-producing Kono district. With the exception of skirmishes between those two groups, which marred the initial stages of disarmament in Kono district, the ceasefire had continued to hold. The cross-border fighting between RUF and Guinean forces in the northern and eastern border areas had also ceased. The deployment of UNAMSIL covered much of the country, including Kabala in the north and Koidu in the east. Consequently, more areas had become accessible to humanitarian workers and the civilian population. The Government had begun to restore civil authority in some areas formerly controlled by RUF. The joint committee on disarmament, demobilization and reintegration had met twice and agreed on a schedule for the programme. The Government and RUF took additional confidence-building measures, including RUF's release of more abductees and child combatants, participation by both sides in sensitization and reconciliation campaigns, enrolment of some RUF ex-combatants in the military reintegration programme, the provisional registration of the RUF party by the National Electoral Commission and an invitation to the party to participate in discussions on the electoral process. The Government announced its intention to seek six-month extensions of its term of office and that of Parliament, which were due to expire on 30 September and 1 October, respectively.

The peace process in Sierra Leone had a positive impact on the situation in the Mano River Union region. Since the relaunching of the disarmament process in May, no further cross-border fighting between RUF and Guinean armed forces had been reported. The Special Representative, on 7 August, took part in a meeting of the Presidents of Mali, Nigeria and Sierra Leone and the Executive Secretary of ECOWAS. The three Presidents met in Koidu on 3 September [S/2001/838] with Issa Sesay, the RUF leader, the first direct meeting between President Ahmad Tejan Kabbah and Mr. Sesay. At the meeting, the RUF leadership reiterated its commitment to the peace process but expressed concern for the personal security of the movement's members after disarmament. The Foreign Ministers of the Mano River Union countries met in Monrovia, Liberia, from 13 to 15 August. On 22 and 23 August, the Ministers, together with the Defence and Security Ministers, met in Freetown to review the security situation in the subregion. Preparations were begun for a summit meeting.

The overall military and security situation remained calm and stable, despite some clashes.

UNAMSIL visited trouble spots in Kono district where RUF and CDF combatants were disarmed. The Mission's troop strength stood at 16,664 as at 5 September. UNAMSIL patrols reached most areas of the country and military observers played a role in the disarmament process by receiving and processing combatants. Since the disarmament, demobilization and reintegration process resumed on 18 May, a total of 16,097 combatants had been disarmed, out of an estimated 25,000. A total of 6,502 weapons had been collected. The reintegration programme, operating from four regional offices, had provided assistance to over 10,600 ex-combatants. UNAMSIL personnel were also involved in community reconciliation, rehabilitation of health, education and local administration structures, human rights–related activities, HIV/AIDS sensitization and public information activities.

On 5 September, the Government announced that the parliamentary and presidential elections would be held on 14 May 2002. In response to a request from the Government, the Secretary-General dispatched an electoral needs assessment mission to Sierra Leone from 18 to 28 August. The pre- and post-electoral period would require security arrangements and coordination among all entities involved in the electoral process, including UNAMSIL, which would provide security and logistical assistance.

In general, the Secretary-General found that the continued progress achieved during the period under review, in particular in the disarmament, demobilization and reintegration programme and the eastward deployment of UNAMSIL, including into the diamond-producing areas, gave grounds for cautious optimism concerning the peace process. The potentially destabilizing clashes between RUF and CDF elements had been addressed by UNAMSIL and the parties. The shortfalls in the budget for disarmament, demobilization and reintegration under the multidonor trust fund, some $5 million for 2001, remained a source of concern, and long-term needs remained crucial to the entire process. The Secretary-General urged the Government to restore civil authority throughout the country, extend services to long-neglected communities, deploy the police and the army, and increase its capacity to regulate better the diamond mining industry. He welcomed the preparatory work for holding elections, but stressed that certain benchmarks should be achieved before then—the completion of the disarmament, demobilization and reintegration programme; the restoration of civil authority throughout the country; the transformation of RUF into a political party; the deployment of UNAMSIL; and the guarantee of freedom of movement throughout the country. In that context, the Secretary-General recommended that the Mission's mandate be extended for six months. UNAMSIL would seek to complete the disarmament, demobilization and reintegration programme, continue to assist in implementing the Abuja Agreement and support preparations for elections.

SECURITY COUNCIL ACTION (September)

On 18 September [meeting 4374], the Security Council unanimously adopted **resolution 1370 (2001)**. The draft [S/2001/874] was prepared in consultations among Council members.

The Security Council,

Recalling its resolutions 1270(1999) of 22 October 1999, 1289(2000) of 7 February 2000, 1313(2000) of 4 August 2000, 1317(2000) of 5 September 2000, 1321(2000) of 20 September 2000 and 1346(2001) of 30 March 2001, and the statement of its President of 3 November 2000 (S/PRST/2000/31), and all other relevant resolutions and statements of its President concerning the situation in Sierra Leone,

Affirming the commitment of all States to respect the sovereignty, political independence and territorial integrity of Sierra Leone,

Expressing its concern at the fragile security situation in the Mano River countries, in particular the continued fighting in Liberia, and at the humanitarian consequences for the civilian, refugee and internally displaced populations in those areas,

Welcoming the progress made in the peace process aimed at achieving sustainable peace and security in Sierra Leone and commending the positive role of the United Nations Mission in Sierra Leone in advancing the peace process,

Recognizing the importance of the progressive extension of State authority throughout the entire country, political dialogue and national reconciliation, the holding by the Government of Sierra Leone of free, fair and transparent elections, the transformation of the Revolutionary United Front into a political party, full respect for the human rights of all and the rule of law, effective action on the issues of impunity and accountability, the voluntary and unhindered return of refugees and internally displaced persons, the full implementation of a disarmament, demobilization and reintegration programme, the legitimate exploitation of the natural resources of Sierra Leone for the benefit of its people, and stressing that the United Nations should continue to support the fulfilment of these objectives,

Having considered the report of the Secretary-General of 7 September 2001,

1. *Decides* that the mandate of the United Nations Mission in Sierra Leone shall be extended for a period of six months from 30 September 2001;

2. *Expresses its appreciation* to those Member States providing troops and support elements to the Mission and those who have made commitments to do so;

3. *Requests* the Secretary-General to inform the Council at regular intervals on progress made by the

Mission in the implementation of key aspects of its concept of operations, and further requests him to provide an assessment in his next report on steps taken to improve the effectiveness of the Mission;

4. *Expresses its continued deep concern* at the reports of human rights abuses and attacks committed by the Revolutionary United Front, the Civil Defence Forces and other armed groups and individuals against the civilian population, in particular the widespread violation of the human rights of women and children, including sexual violence, demands that these acts cease immediately, and requests the Secretary-General to ensure that all human rights monitoring positions within the Mission are filled in order to address the concerns raised in paragraphs 40 to 43 of the report of the Secretary-General;

5. *Welcomes* the efforts made by the Government of Sierra Leone and the Revolutionary United Front towards full implementation of the Ceasefire Agreement signed in Abuja on 10 November 2000 between the Government of Sierra Leone and the Revolutionary United Front and reaffirmed at the meeting of the Economic Community of West African States, the United Nations, the Government of Sierra Leone and the Revolutionary United Front at Abuja on 2 May 2001, and encourages them to continue those efforts;

6. *Urges*, in particular, the Revolutionary United Front to step up its efforts to fulfil its commitment under the Abuja Ceasefire Agreement to ensure full liberty for the United Nations to deploy its troops throughout the country and also, with a view to restoring the authority of the Government of Sierra Leone throughout the country, to ensure the free movement of persons, goods and humanitarian assistance, unimpeded and safe movement of humanitarian agencies, refugees and displaced persons and the immediate return of all seized weapons, ammunition and other equipment;

7. *Encourages* the Government of Sierra Leone and the Revolutionary United Front to continue to take steps towards furthering of dialogue and national reconciliation, and, in this regard, stresses the importance of the reintegration of the Revolutionary United Front into Sierra Leone society and the transformation of the Front into a political party, and demands that the Front cease any effort at maintaining options for military action;

8. *Requests* the Mission to continue to support, within its capabilities and areas of deployment, returning refugees and displaced persons and urges the Revolutionary United Front to cooperate to this end in fulfilment of its commitments under the Abuja Ceasefire Agreement;

9. *Requests* the Secretary-General to provide the Council, further to his report of 23 May 2001, an update of his views on how to take forward the issue of refugees and internally displaced persons, including their return;

10. *Urges* Governments and regional leaders concerned to continue their full cooperation with the Economic Community of West African States and the United Nations to promote the efforts of all parties to the Sierra Leone conflict towards the full and peaceful implementation of the Abuja Ceasefire Agreement, and to provide assistance to that end;

11. *Encourages* the ongoing efforts of the Economic Community of West African States towards a lasting and final settlement of the crisis in the Mano River Union region, and underlines the importance of the continuing political and other support that the United Nations provides to these efforts in order to stabilize the region;

12. *Welcomes* the positive impact of progress made in the Sierra Leone peace process on the situation in the Mano River basin, including the recent ministerial meetings of the Mano River Union and the prospects for a summit meeting of Mano River Union Presidents, and in this regard, encourages the efforts of the Mano River Union Women's Peace Network towards regional peace;

13. *Emphasizes* the importance of a successful disarmament, demobilization and reintegration programme to long-term stability in Sierra Leone, welcomes the progress made in that process and urges the Revolutionary United Front, the Civil Defence Forces and other groups to continue their commitment to, and active participation in, the programme;

14. *Expresses concern* at the serious financial shortfall in the multi-donor trust fund for the disarmament, demobilization and reintegration programme, and urges international organizations and donor countries to support generously and urgently the efforts of the Government of Sierra Leone in this regard, as well as provide additional funds for the wide range of urgently needed post-conflict activities, including humanitarian and rehabilitation requirements;

15. *Emphasizes* the importance of free, fair, transparent and inclusive elections for the long-term stability of Sierra Leone and takes note of the Mission's readiness to provide support, within its capabilities, to facilitate the smooth holding of the elections;

16. *Emphasizes* that the development and extension of the administrative capacities of Sierra Leone are essential to sustainable peace and development in the country, and to the holding of free, fair and transparent elections, and therefore urges the Government of Sierra Leone, with the assistance of the Mission, in accordance with its mandate, to accelerate and coordinate efforts to restore civil authority and basic public services throughout the country (including in the diamond mining areas), including by the deployment of key administrative officials and the Sierra Leone police and the progressive involvement of the Sierra Leone Army in providing border security against external forces, and encourages States, other international organizations and non-governmental organizations to provide appropriate assistance in this regard;

17. *Encourages* the Government of Sierra Leone, together with the Secretary-General, the United Nations High Commissioner for Human Rights and other relevant international actors, to expedite the establishment of the Truth and Reconciliation Commission and the Special Court envisaged by resolution 1315(2000) of 14 August 2000, bearing in mind in particular the need to ensure the appropriate protection of children, and urges donors urgently to commit funds for the Truth and Reconciliation Commission and to disburse their financial pledges to the Trust Fund for the Special Court;

18. *Welcomes* the Secretary-General's intention to keep the security, political, humanitarian and human

rights situation in Sierra Leone under close review and to report to the Council, after due consultations with troop-contributing countries, with any additional recommendations, including on how the Mission will provide support to the Government of Sierra Leone in holding elections;

19. *Decides* to remain actively seized of the matter.

Report of Secretary-General (December). In his twelfth report on UNAMSIL, issued on 13 December [S/2001/1195 & Add.1], the Secretary-General stated that there had been further progress in the Sierra Leone peace process. The ceasefire continued to hold and the disarmament of RUF and CDF combatants was completed in 10 of the 12 districts. UNAMSIL's troop strength reached the authorized ceiling of 17,500, and the Mission was deployed in all districts. The Government continued to take steps to extend its authority to areas formerly controlled by RUF. The joint committee on disarmament, demobilization and reintegration, comprising UNAMSIL, the Government and RUF, held three meetings to review the disarmament process. It declared the disarmament exercise completed in the main diamond-producing district of Kono and in Bonthe and agreed to a programme for collecting shotguns, which had been excluded from the original disarmament plan. Meanwhile, the political parties were preparing for elections. Eight opposition parties held meetings and discussed the possibility of uniting. With the assistance of the Government, RUF acquired offices for its party in Freetown, Bo and Makeni. Although the overall security situation remained generally stable, there were clashes between disarmed CDF and RUF cadres over mining claims in Kono district in September. In coordination with UNAMSIL, the Sierra Leone Army deployed in key areas on the borders with Guinea and Liberia.

As at 9 December, a total of 36,741 combatants had disarmed, a number that far exceeded the initial estimate; the final figure was expected to reach 40,000. Some 13,500 weapons were collected during the reporting period. Payment of reinsertion benefits, which were intended to enable disarmed combatants to resettle in their communities while awaiting long-term reintegration, started on 15 October, with over 17,000 former combatants receiving payments. Following the deployment of UNAMSIL and the completion of disarmament, district and ministry officials returned to three districts, and a number of displaced chiefs returned to their districts.

Preparations were under way for national elections on 14 May 2002. The National Electoral Commission drew up an electoral plan and a National Consultative Conference (13-15 November) addressed core electoral issues. The identification of voter registration centres was expected to be completed by the end of the year, to be followed by voter registration, including the registration of refugees and internally displaced persons. It was proposed that 5,400 polling stations be established at about 3,000 locations. UNAMSIL would provide technical and logistical assistance and general security support for the electoral process, and its public information section would assist the National Electoral Commission in carrying out civic education on elections.

The Mission's human rights officers investigated allegations of abuses, confirming the existence of mass graves and attacks by RUF on a village in Koinadugu district. They facilitated the release of persons detained by RUF. At the beginning of December, an estimated 510,000 Sierra Leonean refugees were living in countries of the subregion, with some 200,000 in Guinea and Liberia. Within Sierra Leone, some 247,590 people were displaced. UNHCR registered 60,000 returnees in Sierra Leone and thousands of others had spontaneously returned.

The Secretary-General reported that the peace process in Sierra Leone had reached an important juncture. A secure environment with increased freedom of movement, a gradual return of refugees and a resurgence of economic activity in the provinces were emerging as a result of UNAMSIL's full deployment and progress in disarmament. At the same time, problems remained concerning the extension of the Government's authority throughout the country, the reintegration of disarmed combatants and the return and resettlement of refugees and internally displaced persons. Regrettably, RUF had slowed down the disarmament of its combatants in the two remaining districts. The international community needed to assist Sierra Leone in rehabilitating its infrastructure, establishing national reconciliation and addressing impunity and accountability, as well as in resettling returnees and internally displaced persons. The situation in the subregion, in particular within the Mano River Union, also deserved attention, and it was important to support the dialogue among Guinea, Liberia and Sierra Leone.

UNAMSIL financing

The Secretary-General, in February [A/55/805 & Corr.1], presented to the General Assembly the budget for UNAMSIL for 1 July 2000 to 30 June 2001, which had been revised following the Security Council's expansion, by resolution 1299 (2000) [YUN 2000, p. 196], of the military component of the Mission to 13,000 military personnel from the previously authorized strength of 11,100. The revised budget amounted to $561,996,400 gross ($558,128,000 net), exclusive of a budgeted voluntary contribution in kind of $2,025,200, and represented an increase of $85,270,000 or 17.9 per cent in gross terms over the budget already appropriated for UNAMSIL.

In a March report [A/55/839], ACABQ reviewed the Secretary-General's report on the revised budget and made recommendations for reducing costs. It recommended that the Assembly approve an appropriation of $550,000,000 gross for the maintenance of UNAMSIL for the same period, inclusive of the appropriation of $476,726,400 gross already made by the Assembly in resolution 54/241 B [YUN 2000, p. 213].

GENERAL ASSEMBLY ACTION (April)

On 12 April [meeting 98], the General Assembly, on the recommendation of the Fifth Committee [A/55/891], adopted **resolution 55/251 A** without vote [agenda item 132].

Financing of the United Nations Mission in Sierra Leone

The General Assembly,

Having considered the report of the Secretary-General on the financing of the United Nations Mission in Sierra Leone and the related report of the Advisory Committee on Administrative and Budgetary Questions,

Bearing in mind Security Council resolution 1270 (1999) of 22 October 1999, by which the Council established the United Nations Mission in Sierra Leone, and the subsequent resolutions by which the Council revised and extended the mandate of the Mission, the latest of which was resolution 1346(2001) of 30 March 2001,

Recalling its resolution 53/29 of 20 November 1998 on the financing of the United Nations Observer Mission in Sierra Leone and its resolutions 54/241 A and B of 23 December 1999 and 15 June 2000, respectively, on the financing of the Observer Mission and the United Nations Mission in Sierra Leone,

Reaffirming that the costs of the Mission are expenses of the Organization to be borne by Member States in accordance with Article 17, paragraph 2, of the Charter of the United Nations,

Recalling its previous decisions regarding the fact that, in order to meet the expenditures caused by the Mission, a different procedure is required from that applied to meet expenditures of the regular budget of the United Nations,

Taking into account the fact that the economically more developed countries are in a position to make relatively larger contributions and that the economically less developed countries have a relatively limited capacity to contribute towards such an operation,

Bearing in mind the special responsibilities of the States permanent members of the Security Council, as indicated in General Assembly resolution 1874(S-IV) of 27 June 1963, in the financing of such operations,

Noting with appreciation that voluntary contributions have been made to the Mission,

Mindful of the fact that it is essential to provide the Mission with the necessary financial resources to enable it to fulfil its responsibilities under the relevant resolutions of the Security Council,

1. *Takes note* of the status of contributions to the United Nations Observer Mission in Sierra Leone and the United Nations Mission in Sierra Leone as at 28 February 2001, including the contributions outstanding in the amount of 242.1 million United States dollars, representing some 41 per cent of the total assessed contributions, notes that some 11 per cent of the Member States have paid their assessed contributions in full, and urges all other Member States concerned, in particular those in arrears, to ensure the payment of their outstanding assessed contributions;

2. *Expresses its appreciation* to those Member States which have paid their assessed contributions in full;

3. *Expresses concern* about the financial situation with regard to peacekeeping activities, in particular as regards the reimbursements to troop contributors that bear additional burdens owing to overdue payments by Member States of their assessments;

4. *Urges* all other Member States to make every possible effort to ensure payment of their assessed contributions to the Mission in full and on time;

5. *Expresses concern* at the delay experienced by the Secretary-General in deploying and providing adequate resources to some recent peacekeeping missions, in particular those in Africa;

6. *Emphasizes* that all future and existing peacekeeping missions shall be given equal and non-discriminatory treatment in respect of financial and administrative arrangements;

7. *Also emphasizes* that all peacekeeping missions shall be provided with adequate resources for the effective and efficient discharge of their respective mandates;

8. *Reiterates its request* to the Secretary-General to make the fullest possible use of facilities and equipment at the United Nations Logistics Base at Brindisi, Italy, in order to minimize the costs of procurement for the Mission, and for this purpose requests the Secretary-General to speed up the implementation of the asset management system at all peacekeeping missions in accordance with General Assembly resolution 52/1 A of 15 October 1997;

9. *Endorses* the conclusions and recommendations contained in the report of the Advisory Committee on Administrative and Budgetary Questions, and requests the Secretary-General to ensure their full implementation;

10. *Requests* the Secretary-General to take all necessary action to ensure that the Mission is administered with a maximum of efficiency and economy;

11. *Also requests* the Secretary-General, in order to reduce the cost of employing General Service staff, to continue efforts to recruit local staff for the Mission against General Service posts, commensurate with the requirements of the Mission;

12. *Decides* to appropriate to the Special Account for the United Nations Mission in Sierra Leone the amount of 73,273,600 dollars gross (73,784,400 dollars net) for the maintenance of the Mission for the period from 1 July 2000 to 30 June 2001, in addition to the amount of 504,399,051 dollars gross (496,545,461 dollars net) already appropriated under the terms of General Assembly resolution 54/241 B, inclusive of the amount of 23,931,281 dollars gross (20,250,873 dollars

net) for the support account for peacekeeping operations and the amount of 3,741,370 dollars gross (3,328,988 dollars net) for the United Nations Logistics Base;

13. *Decides also,* as an ad hoc arrangement, taking into account the amount of 504,399,051 dollars gross (496,545,461 dollars net) already apportioned under the terms of its resolution 54/241 B, to apportion among Member States an additional amount of 36,636,800 dollars gross (36,892,200 dollars net) for the period from 1 July 2000 to 30 June 2001, in accordance with the composition of groups set out in paragraphs 3 and 4 of General Assembly resolution 43/232 of 1 March 1989, as adjusted by its subsequent relevant resolutions and decisions, for the apportionment of peacekeeping appropriations, the latest of which were its resolution 52/230 of 31 March 1998 and its decisions 54/456 to 54/458 of 23 December 1999 for the period 1998-2000, and its resolutions 55/235 and 55/236 of 23 December 2000 for the period 2001-2003, the scale of assessments for 2000 to be applied against a portion thereof, that is, 18,318,400 dollars gross (18,446,100 dollars net), which is the amount pertaining to the period ending 31 December 2000, and the scale of assessments for 2001 to be applied against the balance, that is, 18,318,400 dollars gross (18,446,100 dollars net) for the period from 1 January to 30 June 2001;

14. *Decides further* that, in accordance with the provisions of its resolution 973 A (X) of 15 December 1955, the apportionment among Member States, as provided for in paragraph 13 above, shall take into consideration the decrease in their respective share in the Tax Equalization Fund of the estimated staff assessment income of 255,400 dollars approved for the Mission for the period from 1 July 2000 to 30 June 2001, 127,700 dollars being the amount pertaining to the period ending 31 December 2000 and the balance, that is, 127,700 dollars, pertaining to the period from 1 January to 30 June 2001;

15. *Emphasizes* that no peacekeeping mission shall be financed by borrowing funds from other active peacekeeping missions;

16. *Encourages* the Secretary-General to continue to take additional measures to ensure the safety and security of all personnel under the auspices of the United Nations participating in the Mission;

17. *Invites* voluntary contributions to the Mission in cash and in the form of services and supplies acceptable to the Secretary-General, to be administered, as appropriate, in accordance with the procedure and practices established by the General Assembly;

18. *Decides* to keep under review during its fifty-fifth session the item entitled "Financing of the United Nations Mission in Sierra Leone".

In March, the Secretary-General reported on the financial performance of UNAMSIL from 1 July 1999 to 30 June 2000 [A/55/853]. UNAMSIL had taken over the civilian and military components and functions of the United Nations Observer Mission in Sierra Leone (UNOMSIL) in October 1999 [YUN 1999, p. 164]; accordingly, the report incorporated expenditures related to the operation of UNOMSIL. For the period covered by the report, the General Assembly had appropri-

ated for the missions in Sierra Leone a total of $265,789,000 gross ($264,371,600 net), exclusive of voluntary contributions in kind of $1,550,020. Expenditures for the period totalled $263,338,200 gross ($262,035,200 net), resulting in an unencumbered balance of $2,450,800 gross ($2,336,400 net).

ACABQ reviewed the report and issued its comments in April [A/55/869]. It recommended that the unencumbered balance be credited to Member States in a manner to be decided by the Assembly. Also in April [A/55/874], ACABQ reported on general aspects of financing of UN peacekeeping operations.

GENERAL ASSEMBLY ACTION (June)

On 14 June [meeting 103], the General Assembly, on the recommendation of the Fifth Committee [A/55/891/Add.1], adopted **resolution 55/251 B** without vote [agenda item 132].

Financing of the United Nations Mission in Sierra Leone

The General Assembly,

Having considered the report of the Secretary-General on the financing of the United Nations Mission in Sierra Leone and the related reports of the Advisory Committee on Administrative and Budgetary Questions,

Bearing in mind Security Council resolution 1270 (1999) of 22 October 1999, by which the Council established the United Nations Mission in Sierra Leone, and the subsequent resolutions by which the Council revised and extended the mandate of the Mission, the latest of which was resolution 1346(2001) of 30 March 2001,

Recalling its resolution 53/29 of 20 November 1998 on the financing of the United Nations Observer Mission in Sierra Leone and subsequent resolutions on the financing of the United Nations Mission in Sierra Leone, the latest of which was resolution 55/251 A of 12 April 2001,

Reaffirming the general principles underlying the financing of United Nations peacekeeping operations as stated in General Assembly resolutions 1874(S-IV) of 27 June 1963, 3101(XXVIII) of 11 December 1973 and 55/235 of 23 December 2000,

Noting with appreciation that voluntary contributions have been made to the Mission,

Mindful of the fact that it is essential to provide the Mission with the necessary financial resources to enable it to fulfil its responsibilities under the relevant resolutions of the Security Council,

1. *Reaffirms* its resolution 49/233 A of 23 December 1994, in particular those paragraphs regarding the peacekeeping budgetary cycles, which should be adhered to in the future budgeting process, where possible;

2. *Takes note* of the status of contributions to the United Nations Observer Mission in Sierra Leone and the United Nations Mission in Sierra Leone as at 30 April 2001, including the contributions outstanding in the amount of 165.8 million United States dollars, representing some 28 per cent of the total assessed contri-

butions, notes that some 19 per cent of the Member States have paid their assessed contributions in full, and urges all other Member States concerned, in particular those in arrears, to ensure payment of their outstanding assessed contributions;

3. *Expresses its appreciation* to those Member States which have paid their assessed contributions in full;

4. *Expresses concern* about the financial situation with regard to peacekeeping activities, in particular as regards the reimbursements to troop contributors that bear additional burdens owing to overdue payments by Member States of their assessments;

5. *Urges* all other Member States to make every possible effort to ensure payment of their assessed contributions to the United Nations Mission in Sierra Leone in full and on time;

6. *Expresses concern* at the delay experienced by the Secretary-General in deploying and providing adequate resources to some recent peacekeeping missions, in particular those in Africa;

7. *Emphasizes* that all future and existing peacekeeping missions shall be given equal and non-discriminatory treatment in respect of financial and administrative arrangements;

8. *Also emphasizes* that all peacekeeping missions shall be provided with adequate resources for the effective and efficient discharge of their respective mandates;

9. *Reiterates its request* to the Secretary-General to make the fullest possible use of facilities and equipment at the United Nations Logistics Base at Brindisi, Italy, in order to minimize the costs of procurement for the Mission;

10. *Endorses* the conclusions and recommendations contained in the reports of the Advisory Committee on Administrative and Budgetary Questions, and requests the Secretary-General to ensure their full implementation;

11. *Requests* the Secretary-General to take all necessary action to ensure that the Mission is administered with a maximum of efficiency and economy;

12. *Also requests* the Secretary-General, in order to reduce the cost of employing General Service staff, to continue efforts to recruit local staff for the Mission against General Service posts, commensurate with the requirements of the Mission;

13. *Approves*, on an exceptional basis, the special arrangements for the Mission with regard to the application of article IV of the financial regulations of the United Nations, whereby appropriations required in respect of obligations owed to Governments providing contingents and/or logistic support to the Mission shall be retained beyond the period stipulated under financial regulations 4.3 and 4.4, as set out in the annex to the present resolution;

14. *Authorizes* the Secretary-General to enter into commitments in the amount of 275 million dollars gross (273,375,000 dollars net) for the maintenance of the Mission for the period from 1 July to 31 December 2001, and decides to appropriate the amount of 16,634,763 dollars gross (14,598,640 dollars net) for the support account for peacekeeping operations and the amount of 1,737,712 dollars gross (1,560,456 dollars net) for the United Nations Logistics Base representing the prorated share of the Mission in the support

account and Logistics Base requirements for the period from 1 July 2001 to 30 June 2002;

15. *Decides* to apportion among Member States the amount of 137.5 million dollars gross (136,687,500 dollars net) for the Mission for the period from 1 July to 30 September 2001, in accordance with the levels set out in General Assembly resolution 55/235, as adjusted by the Assembly in its resolution 55/236 of 23 December 2000, and taking into account the scale of assessments for the year 2001, as set out in its resolution 55/5 B of 23 December 2000;

16. *Decides also* that, in accordance with the provisions of its resolution 973(X) of 15 December 1955, there shall be set off against the apportionment among Member States, as provided for in paragraph 15 above, their respective share in the Tax Equalization Fund of the estimated staff assessment income of 812,500 dollars approved for the Mission for the period from 1 July to 30 September 2001;

17. *Decides further* to apportion among Member States the amount of 137.5 million dollars gross (136,687,500 dollars net) for the period from 1 October to 31 December 2001, at a monthly rate of 45,833,333 dollars gross (45,562,500 dollars net) in accordance with paragraph 15 above, and taking into account the scale of assessments for the year 2001 as set out in General Assembly resolution 55/5 B, subject to the decision of the Security Council to extend the mandate of the Mission beyond 30 September 2001;

18. *Decides* that, in accordance with the provisions of its resolution 973(X), there shall be set off against the apportionment among Member States, as provided for in paragraph 17 above, their respective share in the Tax Equalization Fund of the estimated staff assessment income of 812,500 dollars approved for the Mission for the period from 1 October to 31 December 2001;

19. *Decides also* to apportion among Member States the amount of 16,634,763 dollars gross (14,598,640 dollars net) for the support account and the amount of 1,737,712 dollars gross (1,560,456 dollars net) for the United Nations Logistics Base for the period from 1 July 2001 to 30 June 2002 in accordance with paragraph 15 above, and taking into account the scale of assessments for the years 2001 and 2002, as set out in General Assembly resolution 55/5 B, the scale of assessments for the year 2001 to be applied against a portion thereof, that is, 8,317,382 dollars gross (7,299,320 dollars net) for the support account and 868,856 dollars gross (780,228 dollars net) for the Logistics Base for the period from 1 July to 31 December 2001, and the scale of assessments for the year 2002 to be applied against the balance, that is, 8,317,381 dollars gross (7,299,320 dollars net) for the support account and 868,856 dollars gross (780,228 dollars net) for the Logistics Base for the period from 1 January to 30 June 2002;

20. *Decides further* that, in accordance with the provisions of its resolution 973(X), there shall be set off against the apportionment among Member States, as provided for in paragraph 19 above, their respective share in the Tax Equalization Fund of the estimated staff assessment income of 2,036,123 dollars for the support account and 177,256 dollars for the United Nations Logistics Base approved for the period from 1 July 2001 to 30 June 2002, 1,018,062 dollars for the

support account and 88,628 dollars for the Logistics Base, being amounts pertaining to the period from 1 July to 31 December 2001, and the balance, that is, 1,018,061 dollars for the support account and 88,628 dollars for the Logistics Base pertaining to the period from 1 January to 30 June 2002;

21. *Decides* that, for Member States that have fulfilled their financial obligations to the Mission, there shall be set off against the apportionment, as provided for in paragraph 15 above, their respective share of the unencumbered balance of 2,450,800 dollars gross (2,336,400 dollars net) in respect of the period ending 30 June 2000, in accordance with the composition of groups set out in paragraphs 3 and 4 of General Assembly resolution 43/232 of 1 March 1989, as adjusted by the Assembly in subsequent relevant resolutions and decisions, for the ad hoc apportionment of peacekeeping appropriations, the latest of which were resolution 52/230 of 31 March 1998 and decisions 54/456 to 54/458 of 23 December 1999 for the period 1998-2000, and taking into account the scale of assessments for the year 2000, as set out in its resolutions 52/215 A of 22 December 1997 and 54/237 A of 23 December 1999;

22. *Decides also* that, for Member States that have not fulfilled their financial obligations to the Mission, their share of the unencumbered balance of 2,450,800 dollars gross (2,336,400 dollars net) in respect of the period ending 30 June 2000, shall be set off against their outstanding obligations in accordance with the scheme set out in paragraph 21 above;

23. *Emphasizes* that no peacekeeping mission shall be financed by borrowing funds from other active peacekeeping missions;

24. *Encourages* the Secretary-General to continue to take additional measures to ensure the safety and security of all personnel under the auspices of the United Nations participating in the Mission;

25. *Invites* voluntary contributions to the Mission in cash and in the form of services and supplies acceptable to the Secretary-General, to be administered, as appropriate, in accordance with the procedure and practices established by the General Assembly;

26. *Decides* to include in the provisional agenda of its fifty-sixth session the item entitled "Financing of the United Nations Mission in Sierra Leone".

ANNEX

Special arrangements with regard to the application of article IV of the financial regulations of the United Nations

1. At the end of the twelve-month period provided for in financial regulation 4.3, any unliquidated obligations of the financial period in question relating to goods supplied and services rendered by Governments for which claims have been received or which are covered by established reimbursement rates shall be transferred to accounts payable; such accounts shall remain recorded in the Special Account for the United Nations Mission in Sierra Leone until payment is effected.

2. In addition:

(a) Any other unliquidated obligations of the financial period in question owed to Governments for provision of goods and services rendered but not yet verified, as well as other obligations owed to Governments, for which claims have not yet been received shall remain valid for an additional period of four years following the end of the twelve-month period provided for in financial regulation 4.3;

(b) Claims received during this four-year period as well as approved verification reports shall be treated as provided for under paragraph 1 of the present annex, if appropriate;

(c) At the end of the additional four-year period, any unliquidated obligations shall be cancelled and the then remaining balance of any appropriations retained therefor shall be surrendered.

The Secretary-General, in October [A/56/487], proposed a budget for UNAMSIL for 1 July 2001 to 30 June 2002 of $722,134,800 gross ($716,498,400 net), exclusive of budgeted voluntary contributions in kind amounting to $1,350,133. His proposal was based on an authorized force strength of 17,500 military personnel, including 260 military observers, as authorized by the Security Council in resolution 1346(2001) (see p. 165). The Secretary-General recommended that the Assembly appropriate the total amount for the maintenance of UNAMSIL for that period, inclusive of $275 million gross ($273,375,000 net) already assessed under resolution 55/251 B (see p. 173) for 1 July to 31 December 2001.

In November [A/56/621], ACABQ recommended that the Assembly approve an appropriation of $692 million gross for UNAMSIL for 1 July 2001 to 30 June 2002, inclusive of the amount already appropriated.

GENERAL ASSEMBLY ACTION (December)

On 24 December [meeting 92], the General Assembly, on the recommendation of the Fifth Committee [A/56/712], adopted **resolution 56/251** without vote [agenda item 141].

Financing of the United Nations Mission in Sierra Leone

The General Assembly,

Having considered the report of the Secretary-General on the financing of the United Nations Mission in Sierra Leone and the related report of the Advisory Committee on Administrative and Budgetary Questions,

Bearing in mind Security Council resolution 1270 (1999) of 22 October 1999, by which the Council established the United Nations Mission in Sierra Leone, and the subsequent resolutions by which the Council revised and extended the mandate of the Mission, the latest of which was resolution 1370(2001) of 18 September 2001,

Recalling its resolution 53/29 of 20 November 1998 on the financing of the United Nations Observer Mission in Sierra Leone and subsequent resolutions on the financing of the United Nations Mission in Sierra Leone, the latest of which was resolution 55/251 B of 14 June 2001,

Reaffirming the general principles underlying the financing of United Nations peacekeeping operations, as stated in General Assembly resolutions 1874(S-IV) of

27 June 1963, 3101(XXVIII) of 11 December 1973 and 55/235 of 23 December 2000,

Noting with appreciation that voluntary contributions have been made to the Mission,

Mindful of the fact that it is essential to provide the Mission with the necessary financial resources to enable it to fulfil its responsibilities under the relevant resolutions of the Security Council,

1. *Takes note* of the status of contributions to the United Nations Observer Mission in Sierra Leone and the United Nations Mission in Sierra Leone as at 15 November 2001, including the contributions outstanding in the amount of 317.1 million United States dollars, representing, regrettably, some 30 per cent of the total assessed contributions, notes that some 11 per cent of Member States have paid their assessed contributions in full, and urges all other Member States concerned, in particular those in arrears, to ensure payment of their outstanding assessed contributions;

2. *Expresses its appreciation* to those Member States which have paid their assessed contributions in full and on time, and urges all other Member States to make every possible effort to ensure the payment of their assessed contributions to the United Nations Mission in Sierra Leone in full and on time;

3. *Expresses concern* about the financial situation with regard to peacekeeping activities, in particular as regards the reimbursements to troop contributors that bear additional burdens owing to overdue payments by Member States of their assessments;

4. *Also expresses concern* at the delay experienced by the Secretary-General in deploying and providing adequate resources to some recent peacekeeping missions, in particular those in Africa;

5. *Emphasizes* that all future and existing peacekeeping missions shall be given equal and non-discriminatory treatment in respect of financial and administrative arrangements;

6. *Also emphasizes* that all peacekeeping missions shall be provided with adequate resources for the effective and efficient discharge of their respective mandates;

7. *Reiterates its request* to the Secretary-General to make the fullest possible use of facilities and equipment at the United Nations Logistics Base at Brindisi, Italy, in order to minimize the costs of procurement for the Mission;

8. *Endorses* the conclusions and recommendations contained in the report of the Advisory Committee on Administrative and Budgetary Questions, and requests the Secretary-General to ensure their full implementation;

9. *Requests* the Secretary-General to take all necessary action to ensure that the Mission is administered with a maximum of efficiency and economy;

10. *Also requests* the Secretary-General, in order to reduce the cost of employing General Service staff, to continue efforts to recruit local staff for the Mission against General Service posts, commensurate with the requirements of the Mission;

11. *Decides* to appropriate the amount of 699,230,584 dollars gross (693,126,185 dollars net) for the maintenance of the Mission for the twelve-month period from 1 July 2001 to 30 June 2002, inclusive of the amount of 7,230,584 dollars gross (6,685,385 dollars net) for the support account for peacekeeping operations, in addi-

tion to the amount of 16,634,763 dollars gross (14,598,640 dollars net) already appropriated for the support account, and the amount of 1,737,712 dollars gross (1,560,456 dollars net) already appropriated for the United Nations Logistics Base by the General Assembly in its resolution 55/251 B, inclusive also of the amount of 275 million dollars gross (273,375,000 dollars net) authorized by the Assembly in resolution 55/251 B;

12. *Decides also*, taking into account the amount of 275 million dollars gross (273,375,000 dollars net) already apportioned for the period from 1 July to 31 December 2001 and the amount of 18,372,475 dollars gross (16,159,096 dollars net) already apportioned for the period from 1 July 2001 to 30 June 2002, in accordance with the provisions of its resolution 55/251 B, to apportion among Member States the amount of 251,230,584 dollars gross (248,140,985 dollars net) for the period from 1 July 2001 to 31 March 2002, in accordance with the levels set out in General Assembly resolution 55/235, as adjusted by the Assembly in its resolution 55/236 of 23 December 2000, and taking into account the scale of assessments for the years 2001 and 2002 as set out in its resolution 55/5 B of 23 December 2000, the scale of assessments for the year 2001 to be applied against a portion thereof, that is, 71 million dollars gross (69,845,400 dollars net) for the period from 1 July to 31 December 2001, and the scale of assessments for the year 2002 to be applied against the balance, that is, 180,230,584 dollars gross (178,295,585 dollars net) for the period from 1 January to 31 March 2002;

13. *Decides further* that, in accordance with the provisions of its resolution 973(X) of 15 December 1955, there shall be set off against the apportionment among Member States, as provided for in paragraph 12 above, their respective share in the Tax Equalization Fund of the estimated staff assessment income of 3,089,599 dollars approved for the Mission for the period from 1 July 2001 to 31 March 2002, 1,154,600 dollars being the amount pertaining to the period from 1 July to 31 December 2001, and the balance, that is, 1,934,999 dollars pertaining to the period from 1 January to 31 March 2002;

14. *Decides* to apportion among Member States the amount of 132 million dollars gross (130,938,600 dollars net) for the period from 1 April to 30 June 2002, at a monthly rate of 44 million dollars gross (43,646,200 dollars net) in accordance with the scheme set out in the present resolution and taking into account the scale of assessments for the year 2002 as set out in General Assembly resolution 55/5 B, subject to the decision of the Security Council to extend the mandate of the Mission beyond 31 March 2002;

15. *Decides also* that, in accordance with the provisions of its resolution 973(X), there shall be set off against the apportionment among Member States, as provided for in paragraph 14 above, their respective share in the Tax Equalization Fund of the estimated staff assessment income of 1,061,400 dollars approved for the Mission for the period from 1 April to 30 June 2002;

16. *Emphasizes* that no peacekeeping mission shall be financed by borrowing funds from other active peacekeeping missions;

17. *Encourages* the Secretary-General to continue to take additional measures to ensure the safety and security of all personnel under the auspices of the United Nations participating in the Mission;

18. *Invites* voluntary contributions to the Mission in cash and in the form of services and supplies acceptable to the Secretary-General, to be administered, as appropriate, in accordance with the procedure and practices established by the General Assembly;

19. *Decides* to keep under review during its fifty-sixth session the item entitled "Financing of the United Nations Mission in Sierra Leone".

On 24 December, the Assembly decided that the agenda item on UNAMSIL financing would remain for consideration during its resumed fifty-sixth (2002) session (**decision 56/464**) and that the Fifth Committee should continue to consider the item at that session (**decision 56/458**).

Sanctions and justice system

Efforts by the United Nations to find a peaceful solution to the Sierra Leone conflict included Security Council action to control the illicit trade in diamonds from that country, which it found was linked to the trade in arms and related materiel. The Council considered the report of the Panel of Experts to investigate possible violations of the arms embargo and the ban on rough diamond exports and welcomed the establishment of the certificate-of-origin regime for trade in rough diamonds in and their export from Sierra Leone.

The Council's arms sanctions against non-governmental forces in Sierra Leone, imposed by resolution 1132(1997) [YUN 1997, p. 135] and revised by resolution 1171(1998) [YUN 1998, p. 169], remained in force and were monitored by the Council Committee established for that purpose.

The Secretary-General continued his efforts to establish a Special Court to bring to justice those responsible for committing serious crimes against the people of Sierra Leone and to establish a Truth and Reconciliation Commission.

Role of diamonds in conflict

On 25 January [meeting 4264], the Security Council considered the 2000 report of the Panel of Experts on Sierra Leone Diamonds and Arms [YUN 2000, p. 204]. The Panel, established by the Secretary-General in accordance with resolution 1306(2000) [ibid., p. 201], examined how and why Sierra Leone's conflict diamonds were able to find their way into the legitimate diamond trade with relative ease and how weapons reached RUF in Sierra Leone, in spite of UN arms embargoes being in place. The Panel made recommendations on control of the illegal diamond trade and a ban on weapons trade and transport.

In letters to the Council, the Gambia [S/2001/74], Liberia [S/2001/78] and the Libyan Arab Jamahiriya [S/2001/421] rejected some findings or methods of work of the Panel. Guinea, in letters of 26 February [S/2001/173, S/2001/279], said that the report rightly implicated the Liberian authorities in arms trafficking in Sierra Leone and in the subregion and that the imposition of sanctions against Liberia was justified (see p. 181); Guinea also announced its decision to establish a certificate-of-origin regime for the diamonds it exported. On 29 March [S/2001/303], Saudi Arabia said that it had taken measures to prohibit the direct or indirect import of all rough diamonds from Sierra Leone except those controlled through the certificate-of-origin regime.

Sierra Leone informed the Security Council Sanctions Committee on Sierra Leone (see p. 178) that it had made efforts to comply with the terms of resolution 1306(2000). On 7 February [S/2001/127], Sierra Leone submitted a 90-day review of its new certificate-of-origin regime for trade in Sierra Leone diamonds, the main objective of which was to end transactions in what were described as "conflict" or "blood" diamonds by halting illicit mining and smuggling. The Government outlined steps it had taken to strengthen regulations in the mining and marketing sectors, as well as revision of related banking guidelines for diamond exports. As at 31 January, the Government's buying office had issued 34 certificates of origin under the new regulations. Control mechanisms included an electronic database on exports and digital photographs of rough diamonds. The Government believed the regime, though still in its infancy, was a modest success and that it had demonstrated the potential of serving as a model for other national certification systems, particularly in other areas of conflict in Africa. The real success of the certification regime would depend on implementation of resolution 1306(2000) by all States, in particular the diamond-importing States. On 28 March [S/2001/300], the Security Council Sanctions Committee stated that Sierra Leone's new certificate-of-origin regime for trade in diamonds was effectively in operation. The Committee would pursue several issues relating to the operation of the certification regime directly with the Government of Sierra Leone.

Sierra Leone conducted a second 90-day review of the certificate-of-origin regime, which was forwarded to the Council on 13 August [S/2001/794]. The review stated that a total of 113 certificates had been issued and further measures had strengthened controls. After nine months in operation, $19.1 million in diamonds had been exported and the certification system was considered a major success; by the end of the year, the export total had reached $24 million [S/2002/38]. The Government shared the Council's view that the peace process in Sierra Leone was entering a crucial phase as UNAMSIL and the Government moved into the main diamond-producing areas. It believed that the positive trends in the peace process augured well for further success for the certification system. Sierra Leone welcomed the establishment of a similar certification system in Guinea (see p. 177), and it supported efforts to establish standards for an international certification system to break the link between the illicit transaction of rough and uncut diamonds and armed conflict. On 27 August [S/2001/827], the Council received a statement from Sierra Leone on a police investigation of suspected transactions in illicit diamonds in the Freetown area. The action, Sierra Leone said, demonstrated the Government's commitment to ensuring implementation of resolution 1306 (2000).

SECURITY COUNCIL ACTION (December)

On 19 December [meeting 4442], the Security Council unanimously adopted **resolution 1385 (2001)**. The draft [S/2001/1216] was prepared in consultations among Council members.

The Security Council,

Recalling its previous resolutions and the statements of its President concerning the situation in Sierra Leone, and in particular its resolutions 1132(1997) of 8 October 1997, 1171(1998) of 5 June 1998, 1299(2000) of 19 May 2000 and 1306(2000) of 5 July 2000,

Affirming the commitment of all States to respect the sovereignty, political independence and territorial integrity of Sierra Leone,

Welcoming the significant progress made in the peace process in Sierra Leone, including in the disarmament, demobilization and reintegration programme, and the efforts of the Government to extend its authority over the diamond-producing areas, with the assistance of the United Nations Mission in Sierra Leone, but noting that it has not yet established effective authority over those areas,

Expressing its continued concern at the role played by the illicit trade in diamonds in the conflict in Sierra Leone,

Welcoming General Assembly resolution 55/56 of 1 December 2000, as well as ongoing efforts by interested States, the diamond industry, in particular the World Diamond Council, and non-governmental organizations to break the link between illicit trade in rough diamonds and armed conflict, particularly through the significant progress made by the Kimberley Process, and encouraging further progress in this regard,

Welcoming the establishment of a certification regime in relation to Guinea's exports of rough diamonds and the continued efforts of the Economic Community of West African States as well as West African countries towards developing a region-wide certification regime,

Emphasizing the responsibility of all member States, including diamond importing countries, for fully implementing the measures in resolution 1306(2000),

Taking note of the views of the Government of Sierra Leone on the extension of the measures imposed by paragraph 1 of resolution 1306(2000),

Determining that the situation in Sierra Leone continues to constitute a threat to international peace and security in the region,

Acting under Chapter VII of the Charter of the United Nations,

1. *Welcomes* the establishment and implementation of the Certificate of Origin regime for trade in diamonds in Sierra Leone, and the export of rough diamonds from Sierra Leone certified under that regime;

2. *Welcomes* reports that the Certificate of Origin regime is helping to curb the flow of conflict diamonds out of Sierra Leone;

3. *Decides* that the measures imposed by paragraph 1 of resolution 1306(2000) shall remain in force for a new period of 11 months from 5 January 2002, except that, pursuant to paragraph 5 of resolution 1306(2000), rough diamonds controlled by the Government of Sierra Leone under the Certificate of Origin regime shall continue to be exempt from these measures, and affirms that, in addition to its six-monthly review in accordance with paragraph 15 of resolution 1306(2000), at the end of this period it will review the situation in Sierra Leone, including the extent of the Government's authority over the diamond-producing areas, in order to decide whether to extend these measures for a further period and, if necessary, to modify them or adopt further measures;

4. *Decides also* that the measures imposed by paragraph 1 of resolution 1306(2000), as extended by paragraph 3 above, shall be terminated immediately if the Council determines that it would be appropriate to do so;

5. *Requests* the Secretary-General to publicize the provisions of the present resolution and the obligations imposed by it;

6. *Decides* to remain actively seized of the matter.

Sanctions Committee

The Chairman of the Security Council Committee established pursuant to resolution 1132 (1997) [YUN 1997, p. 135] concerning Sierra Leone reported to the Council several times in 2001 on the arms embargo and the question of the export of rough diamonds (see p. 177). By four letters [S/2001/105, S/2001/261, S/2001/493, S/2001/718], the Chairman forwarded information he had received from the United Kingdom on arms and related materiel sent to Sierra Leone for use by the Sierra Leone Army or by UNAMSIL. Three other letters [S/2001/126, S/2001/492, S/2001/664] conveyed reports from Sierra Leone on weapons it had imported for use by its Army and police. On 7 August [S/2001/771, S/2001/772], the Chairman forwarded lists of countries that had responded since December 2000 to the Security Council's request for information on implementation of certain aspects of resolution 1306(2000).

On 29 November [S/2001/1130], the President of the Council affirmed that the members had elected the Chairman and Vice-Chairmen of the Committee for a term ending on 31 December 2001. The Chairman was Iftekhar Ahmed Chowdhury (Bangladesh), who succeeded Anwarul Karim Chowdhury (Bangladesh), and the Vice-Chairmen were from Mali and Singapore.

In a summary of the Committee's activities for the year [S/2002/50], the Chairman said that five meetings were held in 2001, at which the Committee reviewed trade and transfer of both arms and diamonds with Sierra Leone and considered travel requests for leaders of rebel groups. The Committee received a total of 23 replies from States on implementation of paragraph 17 (on the arms embargo) and 43 replies on implementation of paragraph 8 (on restrictions on diamond trade) of resolution 1306(2000). The report noted that the President of the Council, in a statement to the press on 13 December, welcomed the efforts of the West African countries to develop a region-wide certification regime for diamonds, and the establishment of the certificate-of-origin regime by Sierra Leone, and the effect of those actions on curbing the flow of illicit diamonds out of Sierra Leone. The President had added, however, that RUF and CDF continued to mine diamonds illegally, giving them access to funds that might be used to buy weapons. He indicated the readiness of the Council to extend the ban on the export of Sierra Leone diamonds. In the absence of a specific monitoring mechanism to ensure the implementation of the sanctions regime, the Committee urged States and organizations in a position to provide it with pertinent information to do so.

Proposal for Special Court

The Secretary-General in 2001 pursued efforts to establish a Special Court for Sierra Leone to try crimes against humanity, war crimes and other serious violations of international humanitarian law, as well as crimes under relevant Sierra Leonean law. The Court was first proposed by Sierra Leone and recommended by the Security Council in resolution 1315(2000) [YUN 2000, p. 205]. In a January letter [S/2001/40], the Secretary-General commented on the Council's proposed amendments [YUN 2000, p. 206] to the draft Agreement between the United Nations and the Government of Sierra Leone and the proposed Statute. He also presented his understanding of the meaning, scope and legal effect of some proposals pertaining to the personal jurisdiction of the Special Court, its funding and the reduced size

of the Court. On 31 January [S/2001/95], the Council said it agreed in general with the Secretary-General's views on personal jurisdiction and his analysis of the importance and role of the phrase "persons who bear the greatest responsibility". However, Council members did not agree that the President of the Court should be empowered to seek the Council's intervention with regard to intervening with third States on surrendering accused individuals. The Council agreed with the Secretary-General's proposal to seek information from States on their preparedness to contribute resources before the entry into force of the Agreement with the Government of Sierra Leone.

The Secretary-General informed the Council on 12 July [S/2001/693] that he consulted with Sierra Leone on the changes to the proposed Agreement and draft Statute of the Court. He provided details of financing for the Court, noting that the requirements for the first three years of operation amounted to $114.6 million. Having appealed to States for possible contributions, he stated that, as at 6 July, $15 million would likely be available for the first year—a shortfall of approximately $1.8 million—and pledges for the following two years of $20.4 million—a shortfall of $19.6 million. Considering that the amount pledged was sufficient to commence the establishment and operation of the Special Court, he would seek payment of those pledges; when funds were deposited, he would ask the Legal Counsel to conclude on behalf of the United Nations the Agreement on the Establishment of the Special Court with the Government of Sierra Leone. On 23 July [S/2001/722], the President of the Council said that the members welcomed the developments as described by the Secretary-General as a step towards bringing justice to the people of Sierra Leone and supported informal consultations between the Secretariat and interested States to plan for the Court.

On 26 December [S/2001/1320], the Secretary-General recalled that the Council and the Secretariat had an understanding that the implementation of the Agreement would commence only after sufficient contributions were in hand to finance the Court's establishment and 12 months of operation and pledges had been received to cover expenses for the following 24 months. He stated that, while the first year of the Court's operation was virtually funded, the shortfall in the pledges for the second and third years of operation remained high. He was persuaded, however, of the political will of States to the success of the Court, and therefore had decided to authorize the commencement of its operation, beginning with the dispatch of a planning mission to Freetown from 7 to 18 January 2002 to discuss practical arrangements, including premises, the provision of local personnel and services, and the launching of the investigative and prosecutorial process. The Secretary-General remarked that the last pending issue between the Secretariat and the Government—the question of the temporal jurisdiction of the Court—had been resolved, with the two parties agreeing to the temporal jurisdiction set as of 30 November 1996. It was expected that the Agreement would be signed at the conclusion of the mission, thus establishing the legal framework for the establishment and operation of the Court. The Secretary-General expressed concern about the difficulties inherent in securing funds on the basis of voluntary contributions. Once the Court was established, he noted, the United Nations would assume certain obligations, including vis-à-vis persons detained under the Court's authority or in regard to contractual relationship.

Truth and Reconciliation Commission

Preparations for the establishment of the Truth and Reconciliation Commission in Sierra Leone continued throughout 2001.

By December [S/2001/1195], the United Nations High Commissioner for Human Rights and the Special Representative had selected the four national and three international members of the Commission; their names were being forwarded to President Kabbah for approval. UNAMSIL engaged the RUF leadership on the issue of the Commission and began a sensitization campaign in the Northern Province in August. Although RUF appeared receptive to the Commission, leaders expressed concern over its independence and the relationship between it and the Special Court.

The budget for the planned 15 months of operation of the Commission was estimated at $8.5 million. The Commission was expected to commence operations in the first half of 2002.

Liberia

In early 2001, fighting in the north-east and north-west of Liberia intensified, threatening peace not only internally but also in the border regions with Guinea and Sierra Leone. The situation was complicated by Liberian support to the RUF rebels in Sierra Leone, as reported in 2000 by the Panel of Experts established to investigate violations of the arms embargo and the ban on rough diamond exports in relation to Sierra Leone [YUN 2000, p. 204]. According to the Panel, the bulk of RUF diamonds left Sierra Leone through Liberia, which would not be possible without the involvement of Liberian government officials at the highest levels. The illicit trade in

diamonds represented a major source of income for RUF.

In March, the Security Council demanded that Liberia take certain specific measures to cease its support of RUF in its opposition struggle with the Government of Sierra Leone (see p. 181). The Council also imposed an arms embargo against Liberia, sanctions against importing diamonds from Liberia and a travel ban on senior members of the Government and armed forces.

By December, the tension among Guinea, Liberia and Sierra Leone had decreased following ministerial meetings beginning in August to consider security problems along the common borders (see p. 168). The United Nations Peacebuilding Support Office in Liberia (UNOL) continued to work towards peace in the country and to monitor the situation.

Border situation

In early 2001, the Security Council received letters alerting it to the deteriorating security situation along the borders of the Mano River Union countries (Guinea, Liberia and Sierra Leone) (see also p. 161) and particularly between Guinea and Liberia. On 5 February [S/2001/106], Germany noted that the border situation between the two countries was characterized by armed cross-border incursions and a deteriorating humanitarian situation. It expressed its readiness to contribute to the efforts of the Council, ECOWAS and other States to maintain international peace and security in the region.

President Charles Taylor of Liberia, in a 23 February letter to the Secretary-General [S/2001/167], complained of remarks attributed to Guinea's Army Chief of Staff about intended aggressive action against Liberia. Liberia had been the victim of five armed incursions by Guinean-based Liberian dissidents supported by the Government of President Lansana Conteh, according to President Taylor. Liberia called on the United Nations to urge Guinea to exercise restraint and to support the deployment of ECOWAS monitoring forces along the Liberian-Guinean border.

On 26 February [S/2001/173], Guinea said that it agreed with the Expert Panel report [YUN 2000, p. 204] that implicated the Liberian authorities in arms trafficking in Sierra Leone and in the subregion, which was fuelled by diamonds being exploited by RUF. Guinea added that the recent rebel attacks on Guinea's borders by rebel groups from Liberia and Sierra Leone were part of the destabilization of the countries of the subregion, which had been organized by the Government of Liberia and the RUF rebels. In Guinea's view, the imposition of sanctions against Liberia would be justified. Guinea, on 20 March [S/2001/283], said that its Ambassador in Monrovia had been declared persona non grata by Liberia and that the movement of its diplomatic personnel had been restricted. Liberia had already withdrawn its Ambassador in Guinea. Nevertheless, Guinea remained committed to improving relations with Liberia.

Sierra Leone informed the Council President on 27 February [S/2001/176] that Liberia had unilaterally taken control of operations over the airspace of the Roberts Flight Information Region, of which Guinea, Liberia and Sierra Leone were the members, by expelling the Guinean and Sierra Leonean telecommunications operators from Liberia.

Imposition of sanctions

Sierra Leone, on 23 February [S/2001/166], noting that the Security Council had discussed the 2000 report of the Panel of Experts on Sierra Leone Diamonds and Arms [YUN 2000, p. 204] almost a month earlier (see p. 177), listed the reasons why it believed that sanctions should be imposed against Liberia without further delay. For instance, Liberia had failed to show that it had taken steps to disengage itself from RUF, it continued to harbour senior RUF members and their families and it also continued to violate the arms embargo imposed by Council resolution 788 (1992) [YUN 1992, p. 192].

SECURITY COUNCIL ACTION

On 7 March [meeting 4287], the Security Council unanimously adopted **resolution 1343(2001)**. The draft [S/2001/188] was prepared in consultations among Council members.

The Security Council,

Recalling its resolutions 1132(1997) of 8 October 1997, 1171(1998) of 5 June 1998, 1306(2000) of 5 July 2000 and its other resolutions and statements of its President on the situation in Sierra Leone and the region,

Welcoming General Assembly resolution 55/56 of 1 December 2000, in particular its call for measures engaging all concerned parties including diamond producing, processing, exporting and importing countries as well as the diamond industry to break the link between diamonds and armed conflict, and its call upon all States to implement fully Security Council measures targeting the link between the trade in conflict diamonds and the supply to rebel movements of weapons, fuel or other prohibited materiel,

Taking note of the report of the United Nations Panel of Experts established pursuant to paragraph 19 of resolution 1306(2000) in relation to Sierra Leone,

Taking note of the findings of the Panel of Experts that diamonds represent a major and primary source of income for the Revolutionary United Front, that the bulk of Revolutionary United Front diamonds leave Sierra Leone through Liberia, and that such illicit trade cannot be conducted without the permission and involvement of Liberian government officials at the highest levels, and expressing its deep concern at the unequivocal and overwhelming evidence presented by the report of the Panel of Experts that the Government of Liberia is actively supporting the Revolutionary United Front at all levels,

Recalling the Economic Community of West African States Moratorium on the Importation, Exportation and Manufacture of Small Arms and Light Weapons in West Africa adopted in Abuja on 31 October 1998,

Taking note of the measures announced by the Government of Liberia since the publication of the report of the Panel of Experts established pursuant to resolution 1306(2000), and welcoming the intention of the Economic Community of West African States to monitor their implementation in close cooperation with the United Nations and to report thereon after a period of two months,

Recalling its concern already expressed in resolution 1306(2000) at the role played by the illicit diamond trade in fuelling the conflict in Sierra Leone and at reports that such diamonds transit neighbouring countries, including Liberia,

Reiterating its call made in the statement of its President of 21 December 2000 (S/PRST/2000/41) on all States in West Africa, particularly Liberia, immediately to cease military support for armed groups in neighbouring countries and prevent armed individuals from using their national territory to prepare and commit attacks in neighbouring countries,

Determining that the active support provided by the Government of Liberia for armed rebel groups in neighbouring countries, and in particular its support for the Revolutionary United Front in Sierra Leone, constitutes a threat to international peace and security in the region,

Acting under Chapter VII of the Charter of the United Nations,

A

Recalling its resolutions 788(1992) of 19 November 1992 and 985(1995) of 13 April 1995,

Noting that the conflict in Liberia has been resolved, that national elections have taken place within the framework of the Yamoussoukro IV Agreement of 30 October 1991 and that the final communiqué of the informal consultative group meeting of the Economic Community of West African States Committee of Five on Liberia issued in Geneva on 7 April 1992 has been implemented, and determining therefore that the embargo imposed by paragraph 8 of resolution 788(1992) should be terminated,

1. *Decides* to terminate the prohibitions imposed by paragraph 8 of resolution 788(1992) and to dissolve the Committee established under resolution 985(1995);

B

2. *Demands* that the Government of Liberia immediately cease its support for the Revolutionary United Front in Sierra Leone and for other armed rebel groups in the region, and in particular take the following concrete steps:

(a) Expel all Revolutionary United Front members from Liberia, including such individuals as are listed by the Committee established by paragraph 14 below, and prohibit all Revolutionary United Front activities on its territory, provided that nothing in this paragraph

shall oblige Liberia to expel its own nationals from its territory;

(b) Cease all financial and, in accordance with resolution 1171(1998), military support to the Revolutionary United Front, including all transfers of arms and ammunition, all military training and the provision of logistical and communications support, and take steps to ensure that no such support is provided from the territory of Liberia or by its nationals;

(c) Cease all direct or indirect import of Sierra Leone rough diamonds which are not controlled through the Certificate of Origin regime of the Government of Sierra Leone, in accordance with resolution 1306 (2000);

(d) Freeze funds or financial resources or assets that are made available by its nationals or within its territory directly or indirectly for the benefit of the Revolutionary United Front or entities owned or controlled directly or indirectly by the Revolutionary United Front;

(e) Ground all Liberia-registered aircraft operating within its jurisdiction until it updates its register of aircraft pursuant to Annex VII to the Chicago Convention on International Civil Aviation of 1944 and provides to the Council the updated information concerning the registration and ownership of each aircraft registered in Liberia;

3. *Stresses* that the demands in paragraph 2 above are intended to lead to further progress in the peace process in Sierra Leone, and, in that regard, calls upon the President of Liberia to help ensure that the Revolutionary United Front meet the following objectives:

(a) Allow the United Nations Mission in Sierra Leone free access throughout Sierra Leone;

(b) Release all abductees;

(c) Enter their fighters in the disarmament, demobilization and reintegration process;

(d) Return all weapons and other equipment seized from the Mission;

4. *Demands* that all States in the region take action to prevent armed individuals and groups from using their territory to prepare and commit attacks on neighbouring countries and refrain from any action that might contribute to further destabilization of the situation on the borders between Guinea, Liberia and Sierra Leone;

5. (a) *Decides* that all States shall take the necessary measures to prevent the sale or supply to Liberia, by their nationals or from their territories or using their flag vessels or aircraft, of arms and related materiel of all types, including weapons and ammunition, military vehicles and equipment, paramilitary equipment and spare parts for the aforementioned, whether or not originating in their territories;

(b) *Decides* that all States shall take the necessary measures to prevent any provision to Liberia by their nationals or from their territories of technical training or assistance related to the provision, manufacture, maintenance or use of the items in subparagraph (a) above;

(c) *Decides* that the measures imposed by subparagraphs (a) and (b) above shall not apply to supplies of non-lethal military equipment intended solely for humanitarian or protective use, and related technical assistance or training, as approved in advance by the Committee established by paragraph 14 below;

(d) *Affirms* that the measures imposed by subparagraph (a) above do not apply to protective clothing, including flak jackets and military helmets, temporarily exported to Liberia by United Nations personnel, representatives of the media and humanitarian and development workers and associated personnel, for their personal use only;

6. *Decides further* that all States shall take the necessary measures to prevent the direct or indirect import of all rough diamonds from Liberia, whether or not such diamonds originated in Liberia;

7. (a) *Decides also* that all States shall take the necessary measures to prevent the entry into or transit through their territories of senior members of the Government of Liberia and its armed forces and their spouses and any other individuals providing financial and military support to armed rebel groups in countries neighbouring Liberia, in particular the Revolutionary United Front in Sierra Leone, as designated by the Committee established by paragraph 14 below, provided that nothing in this paragraph shall oblige a State to refuse entry into its territory to its own nationals, and provided that nothing in this paragraph shall impede the transit of representatives of the Government of Liberia to United Nations Headquarters to conduct United Nations business or the participation of the Government of Liberia in the official meetings of the Mano River Union, the Economic Community of West African States and the Organization of African Unity;

(b) *Decides* that the measures imposed by subparagraph (a) above shall not apply where the Committee established by paragraph 14 below determines that such travel is justified on the grounds of humanitarian need, including religious obligation, or where the Committee concludes that exemption would otherwise promote Liberian compliance with the demands of the Council, or assist in the peaceful resolution of the conflict in the subregion;

8. *Further decides* that the measures imposed by paragraphs 6 and 7 above shall come into force at 0001 eastern daylight time two months after the date of adoption of this resolution, unless the Security Council determines before that date that Liberia has complied with the demands in paragraph 2 above, taking into account the report of the Secretary-General referred to in paragraph 12 below, inputs from the Economic Community of West African States, relevant information provided by the Committee established by paragraph 14 below and the Committee established pursuant to resolution 1132(1997) and any other relevant information;

9. *Decides* that the measures imposed by paragraph 5 are established for 14 months and that, at the end of the period, the Council will decide whether the Government of Liberia has complied with the demands in paragraph 2 above, and, accordingly, whether to extend these measures for a further period with the same conditions;

10. *Decides further* that the measures imposed by paragraphs 6 and 7 above are established for a period of 12 months, and that at the end of this period the Council will decide whether the Government of Liberia has complied with the demands in paragraph 2 above, and, accordingly, whether to extend these measures for a further period with the same conditions;

11. *Decides also* that the measures imposed by paragraphs 5 to 7 above shall be terminated immediately if the Council, taking into account, inter alia, the reports of the Panel of Experts referred to in paragraph 19 below and of the Secretary-General referred to in paragraph 12 below, inputs from the Economic Community of West African States, any relevant information provided by the Committee established by paragraph 14 below and the Committee established pursuant to resolution 1132(1997) and any other relevant information, determines that the Government of Liberia has complied with the demands in paragraph 2 above;

12. *Requests* the Secretary-General to submit a first report to the Council by 30 April 2001 and thereafter at six-month intervals from that date, drawing on information from all relevant sources, including the United Nations Office in Liberia, the United Nations Mission in Sierra Leone and the Economic Community of West African States, on whether Liberia has complied with the demands in paragraph 2 above and on any progress made towards the objectives set out in paragraph 3 above, and calls on the Government of Liberia to support United Nations efforts to verify all information on compliance which is brought to the United Nations notice;

13. *Requests* the Secretary-General to provide to the Council six months from the date of the adoption of this resolution:

(*a*) A preliminary assessment of the potential economic, humanitarian and social impact on the Liberian population of possible follow-up action by the Council in the areas of investigation indicated in paragraph 19 (*c*) below;

(*b*) A report on the steps taken by the Government of Liberia to improve its capacity in air traffic control and surveillance in accordance with the recommendations of the Panel of Experts established pursuant to resolution 1306(2000) and any advice which may be provided by the International Civil Aviation Organization;

14. *Decides* to establish, in accordance with rule 28 of its provisional rules of procedure, a Committee of the Security Council, consisting of all the members of the Council, to undertake the following tasks and to report on its work to the Council with its observations and recommendations:

(*a*) To seek from all States information regarding the actions taken by them to implement effectively the measures imposed by paragraphs 5 to 7 above, and thereafter to request from them whatever further information it may consider necessary;

(*b*) To consider, and to take appropriate action on, information brought to its attention by States concerning alleged violations of the measures imposed by paragraphs 5 to 7 above, identifying where possible persons or entities, including vessels or aircraft, reported to be engaged in such violations, and to make periodic reports to the Council;

(*c*) To promulgate expeditiously such guidelines as may be necessary to facilitate the implementation of the measures imposed by paragraphs 5 to 7 above;

(*d*) To give consideration to and decide upon requests for the exemptions set out in paragraphs 5 (*c*) and 7 (*b*) above;

(*e*) To designate the individuals subject to the measures imposed by paragraph 7 above, and to update this list regularly;

(*f*) To make information it considers relevant, including the list referred to in subparagraph (*e*) above, publicly available through appropriate media, including through the improved use of information technology;

(*g*) To make recommendations to the Council on ways of increasing the effectiveness of the measures imposed by paragraphs 5 to 7 above and on ways to limit unintended effects, if any, of these measures on the Liberian population;

(*h*) To cooperate with other relevant Security Council Sanctions Committees, in particular that established pursuant to resolution 1132(1997) and that established pursuant to resolution 864(1993);

(*i*) To establish a list of Revolutionary United Front members present in Liberia as referred to in paragraph 2 (*a*) above;

15. *Calls upon* the Government of Liberia to establish an effective Certificate of Origin regime for trade in rough diamonds that is transparent and internationally verifiable and has been approved by the Committee established by paragraph 14 above, to come into operation after the measures imposed by paragraphs 5 to 7 above have been terminated in accordance with this resolution;

16. *Urges* all diamond-exporting countries in West Africa to establish Certificate of Origin regimes for the trade in rough diamonds similar to that adopted by the Government of Sierra Leone, as recommended by the Panel of Experts established pursuant to resolution 1306(2000), and calls upon States, relevant international organizations and other bodies in a position to do so to offer assistance to those Governments to that end;

17. *Calls upon* the international community to provide the necessary assistance to reinforce the fight against the proliferation and illicit trafficking of light weapons in West Africa, in particular the implementation of the Economic Community of West African States Moratorium on the Importation, Exportation and Manufacture of Small Arms and Light Weapons in West Africa, and to improve air traffic control in the West African subregion;

18. *Requests* all States to report to the Committee established by paragraph 14 above, within 30 days of the promulgation of the list referred to in paragraph 14 (*e*) above, on the actions they have taken to implement the measures imposed by paragraphs 5 to 7 above;

19. *Requests* the Secretary-General to establish, within one month from the date of adoption of the present resolution, in consultation with the Committee established by paragraph 14 above, a Panel of Experts for a period of six months consisting of no more than five members, drawing, as much as possible and as appropriate, on the expertise of the members of the Panel of Experts established pursuant to resolution 1306(2000), with the following mandate:

(*a*) To investigate any violations of the measures imposed by paragraphs 5 to 7 above;

(*b*) To collect any information on the compliance by the Government of Liberia with the demands in paragraph 2 above, including any violations by the Government of Liberia of the measures imposed by paragraph

2 of resolution 1171(1998) and paragraph 1 of resolution 1306(2000);

(c) To further investigate possible links between the exploitation of natural resources and other forms of economic activity in Liberia, and the fuelling of conflict in Sierra Leone and neighbouring countries, in particular those areas highlighted by the report of the Panel of Experts established pursuant to resolution 1306(2000);

(d) To collect any information linked to the illegal activities of the individuals referred to in paragraph 21 below and to any other alleged violations of this resolution;

(e) To report to the Council through the Committee established by paragraph 14 above no later than six months from the date of adoption of this resolution with observations and recommendations in the areas set out in subparagraphs (a) to (d) above;

(f) To keep the Committee established by paragraph 14 above updated on their activities as appropriate;

and further requests the Secretary-General to provide the necessary resources;

20. *Requests* the Panel of Experts referred to in paragraph 19 above, as far as possible, to bring any relevant information collected in the course of its investigations conducted in accordance with its mandate to the attention of the States concerned for prompt and thorough investigation and, where appropriate, corrective action, and to allow them the right of reply;

21. *Calls upon* all States to take appropriate measures to ensure that individuals and companies in their jurisdiction, in particular those referred to in the report of the Panel of Experts established pursuant to resolution 1306(2000), act in conformity with United Nations embargoes, in particular those established by resolutions 1171(1998), 1306(2000) and the present resolution, and, as appropriate, take the necessary judicial and administrative action to end any illegal activities by those individuals and companies;

22. *Calls upon* all States and all relevant international and regional organizations to act strictly in accordance with the provisions of the present resolution notwithstanding the existence of any rights or obligations entered into or any licence or permit granted prior to the date of adoption of this resolution;

23. *Decides* to conduct reviews of the measures imposed by paragraphs 5 to 7 above not more than sixty days after the adoption of this resolution, and every six months thereafter;

24. *Urges* all States, relevant United Nations bodies and, as appropriate, other organizations and interested parties to cooperate fully with the Committee established by paragraph 14 above and the Panel of Experts referred to in paragraph 19 above, including by supplying information on possible violations of the measures imposed by paragraphs 5 to 7 above;

25. *Decides* to remain actively seized of the matter.

The Council, on 12 March [S/2001/215], elected Kishore Mahbubani (Singapore) as Chairman and Ireland and Mauritius as Vice-Chairmen of the Council Committee established pursuant to resolution 1343(2001) (Sanctions Committee for Liberia). On 23 March [S/2001/268], the Secretary-General informed the Council that, in accordance with resolution 1343(2001), he had established a five-member Panel of Experts to investigate violations of measures imposed by paragraphs 5 to 7 of that resolution, among other things. The Panel would be chaired by Martin Chungong Ayafor (Cameroon).

Liberia, on 22 March [S/2001/264], called on the United Nations to put in place a credible mechanism to verify Liberia's compliance with resolution 1343(2001), including establishing a UNAMSIL presence in Liberia. It also requested the United Nations to provide technical assistance to set up a diamond certification regime and to engage ECOWAS in a partnership in conflict management in West Africa, and in particular Sierra Leone. Consistent with the Council's demands in resolution 1343(2001), Liberia had taken the following measures: all RUF fighters had been expelled from Liberian territory; the border with Sierra Leone had been closed; the entry of uncertified rough diamonds from countries with certification regimes had been banned; systems were being put in place to freeze RUF financial assets; and Liberian-registered aircraft had been ordered grounded.

Liberia expressed concern about the threat to its security being posed by former combatants of the United Liberation Movement for Democracy in Liberia (ULIMO), dissidents who were waging war against Liberia from Guinea and whose presence in Guinea was a destabilizing force in the Mano River Union countries. Liberia claimed that its territorial integrity was again under attack from Guinea.

Report of Secretary-General (April). On 30 April, the Secretary-General issued his first report pursuant to Security Council resolution 1343(2001) regarding Liberia [S/2001/424], in which he listed steps taken by Liberia to comply with that text, as reported by UNOL, UNAMSIL, ECOWAS and other sources. Among measures reported by UNAMSIL were that Liberia issued a statement renouncing all support for RUF and calling on RUF to lay down its arms and announced the expulsion of the former RUF field commander, Sam Bockarie, and all persons associated with RUF from Liberia and the closure of the RUF office in Monrovia. However, the whereabouts of Mr. Bockarie was not known and there were reports he was in RUF-held territory in Sierra Leone. UNAMSIL was informed that the Government of Liberia continued to maintain relations with RUF. UNAMSIL reported that it had been able to deploy to some RUF-held areas as called for in resolution 1343(2001).

ECOWAS reported that it had sent a mission of its Mediation and Security Council (19-24 April) to verify Liberia's compliance with resolution 1343(2001). The mission expressed doubts about the departure of all RUF members. It considered that the United Nations should accept Liberia's request to deploy UNAMSIL monitors and observers on Liberia's side of the border with Sierra Leone and at all points of entry into Liberia. As to the banning of rough uncertified diamonds into Liberia and the 120-day ban on the export of Liberian diamonds, the mission stated that Liberia's efforts to institute its own certification-of-origin regime were commendable and warranted UN assistance. The Secretary-General said that the Secretariat had received information indicating that Mr. Bockarie was still living in Liberia and that the Liberian Government had not severed relations with RUF in Sierra Leone. He noted the ECOWAS mission's comment that the United Nations could not demand that Liberia expel RUF and at the same time request it to influence RUF to cooperate with UNAMSIL. In conclusion, the Secretary-General urged the international community to remain engaged with Liberia and the Security Council to continue to work with ECOWAS.

Communications. Between April and November, Liberia raised with the Secretary-General and the Security Council President a number of concerns or objections about the terms of resolution 1343(2001) [S/2001/429, S/2001/474, S/2001/516, S/2001/519, S/2001/562, S/2001/593, S/2001/595, S/2001/675, S/2001/727, S/2001/851, S/2001/924, S/2001/1035]. It protested that the arms embargo was unfair at a time when Liberia was coming under attack and needed to defend itself; that Guinea was aiding ULIMO rebels in their war against Liberia; that the attackers had occupied portions of Liberia's northern territory; that certain RUF members named by the Sanctions Committee for Liberia were not in Liberia despite claims to the contrary; that Guinea, Sierra Leone and the United Kingdom were supplying arms to the ULIMO rebels; that there was no justification for the Sanctions Committee to have banned many persons from international travel; and that Liberia's humanitarian situation was suffering as a result of the sanctions.

On 9 May [S/2001/467], Sierra Leone said that it was taking measures to comply with resolution 1343(2001), by preventing the import through Sierra Leone of all rough diamonds from Liberia, and banning the travel into or transit through Sierra Leone of Liberian individuals and their spouses who supported armed rebel groups. The United Kingdom, on 18 June [S/2001/625], stated that it had not supplied any arms to dissident movements in the Mano River Union region. The British Government was supplying equipment and training to the Sierra Leone Army.

The Sanctions Committee established pursuant to resolution 1343(2001), by a 13 September letter to the Council President [S/2001/867], rejected Liberia's request [S/2001/593] that the travel ban list be suspended. It affirmed its willingness to continue its policy of constructive engagement with Liberia. On 9 July [S/2001/704], the Gambia protested the inclusion of a Gambian national on the travel ban list. Bulgaria notified the Council President on 14 August [S/2001/795] that it had tightened the arms embargo against Liberia.

Reports of Secretary-General (October). In October, the Secretary-General issued three reports in response to resolution 1343(2001).

On 5 October [S/2001/939], he provided a preliminary assessment of the potential economic, humanitarian and social impact on the Liberian population of possible covert action with regard to the timber extraction industry, rubber production and the Liberian ship register. The report described the current economic and social conditions in the country, which was classified as a least developed country due to its low average per capita GDP ($177 in 2000, less than half the value in the 1980s), lack of economic diversification and poor prospects for sustained economic development. Since sanctions were imposed by resolution 1343(2001), the Liberian dollar had weakened markedly and public confidence in the Liberian economy had declined. The timber industry generated about 9 per cent of the total national budget. If that revenue was lost, all sectors of the budget would come under further pressure, income taxes might be increased, salary payment arrears would grow, the prices of imported goods would rise and new taxes on petty traders and foreigners would probably be introduced. International sanctions on Liberian rubber would directly affect more Liberians than sanctions on timber, and the effects of reduced revenues to the Government would be similar to those of the timber industry. Although the Liberian ship register generated 20 per cent of the national budget, its staff numbered only 100 people and little direct impact on the Liberian population was anticipated from possible restrictions on the register. In general, any restrictions would probably have negative effects on the financial environment, with worsening exchange rates, increasing prices for essential commodities, decreased savings and more capital flight.

In an 11 October report [S/2001/965], the Secretary-General described steps taken by Liberia to improve its capacity in air traffic control and surveillance and to obtain assistance in that regard from the International Civil Aviation Organization (ICAO). Liberia, as a member of the Roberts Flight Information Region, adhered to the African–Indian Ocean air navigation plan and other navigational and air traffic operation requirements and protocols. The Government had decided, however, as a result of cross-border incursions by dissident forces and increased national security concerns, to assume temporarily independent management of Liberian airspace, pending an improvement in relations among the Mano River Union countries. That plan required the installation of equipment at the Roberts International Airport Air Traffic Control Centre in Monrovia, reactivation of telecommunication equipment and a team of exclusively Liberian air control technicians under the supervision of the Liberian Civil Aviation Authority. The Authority remained in contact with ICAO to seek assistance in reforming its air traffic management within the Roberts Flight Information Region and held informal talks with ICAO in Dakar on 26 and 27 March to discuss the implications of Liberia's decision.

On 31 October [S/2001/1025], the Secretary-General issued his second report on steps Liberia had taken to cease support for RUF and other rebel groups, based on information from UNOL, UNAMSIL, ECOWAS and other sources. According to Liberia, it remained disengaged from RUF, its border with Sierra Leone remained closed, the ban on import of Sierra Leone rough diamonds remained in force and RUF funds remained frozen. UNAMSIL reported that it had free access throughout the country and that RUF continued to release abducted persons, including child combatants. RUF cooperation with the disarmament programme since 18 May had been encouraging and was expected to be completed on 31 October. However, RUF had returned only 87 weapons, 10 vandalized vehicles and 20 stripped armoured personnel carriers of the equipment taken from UNAMSIL. The Secretary-General noted the remark by ECOWAS that even though some of the socio-economic problems being experienced by the Liberian people predated the sanctions, they had been aggravated by their imposition. He reported that Liberia had actively participated in recent ministerial meetings of the Mano River Union, and he reiterated his appeal to the Council to remain engaged with Liberia whatever decision it might take with regard to sanctions.

Panel of Experts

On 26 October [S/2001/1015], the Chairman of the Sanctions Committee for Liberia submitted to the Council the report of the Panel of Experts appointed by the Secretary-General, in response to resolution 1343(2001), to investigate violations of the measures imposed by paragraphs 5 to 7 of that resolution. In the six months since its formation, the Panel noted significant signs of improvement in the Mano River Union region. Regional diplomatic efforts were currently under way to further improve bilateral relations among the three members of the Union. Conflict still existed, however, in Lofa County in Liberia, and there remained a possibility of Sierra Leone gravitating back into conflict if RUF did not release its hold on some of the best diamond areas.

There had been a proliferation of the use of non-State actors in the conflicts in the Mano River Union area, and their actions could destabilize the region again. Those groups obtained weapons from State supporters, from their trade in diamonds, gold, cocoa and coffee or from their military action. The junction of the borders of Guinea, Liberia and Sierra Leone had been the fault zone where those groups had thrived. RUF's relationship with Liberia, as described in the 2000 Panel of Experts report on Sierra Leone [YUN 2000, p. 204], continued, although a split was reported among RUF units that were willing to disarm in Sierra Leone and others that continued to fight in the war that had shifted to the Guinean and Liberian borders. Throughout 2001, RUF units were fighting with Liberian units in Lofa County.

The Panel proposed, among other things, that the Security Council: lift the grounding order against all Liberian-registered aircraft; extend the arms embargo on Liberia; impose an arms embargo on the armed non-State actors in the three Mano River Union countries; and impose a ban on all round log exports from Liberia from July 2002. The Liberian Government was urged to: consolidate revenues in a central account before allocating money to authorized agencies for approved expenditures; with IMF agreement, commission an independent report on revenue from timber concessions from January 2001 to July 2002; put in place a credible and transparent certification scheme for rough diamonds, which would be independently audited; and agree with IMF on auditing revenues generated from the shipping and corporate registry, and on using those funds for development purposes. The Panel further suggested that information about the travel ban on certain individuals should be made available on the Internet; the UN Secretariat should monitor compliance with resolution 1343(2001) and develop databases on violations; and the Panel should conduct assessment missions to Liberia and neighbouring States in April and September 2002.

With regard to other countries of the region, the Panel, noting that there were fraudulent aircraft registrations in the Central African Republic and Equatorial Guinea, as well as in Liberia, recommended that those countries and ICAO take action to cancel or ground such aircraft.

In the context of the travel ban, the Panel noted that most violations were through Abidjan; it urged the Council to encourage the Côte d'Ivoire authorities to adopt a less passive attitude to implementing the ban.

Singapore, in a 2 November letter [S/2001/1043], requested additional information about a Singapore-registered company mentioned in the Panel's report in connection with alleged weapons deliveries.

Sanctions Committee

The Security Council Committee established pursuant to resolution 1343(2001) concerning Liberia, reporting on its activities from 7 March to 31 December [S/2002/83], stated that it had received 13 notifications of travel and considered 35 requests for travel ban waivers, of which 28 were granted. It also received 13 requests for deletion from the list of persons banned; it retained 7 names, deleted 5 and deferred 1 to its next quarterly review. The Committee received information from 42 countries on action taken to implement the ban.

The Committee received information from only one State regarding a possible violation of the sanctions regime. However, its Chairman would seek information from States cited in the Panel of Experts report as having committed alleged violations.

Prior to the imposition of the sanctions regime on 7 May, the Committee Chairman conducted a fact-finding mission to the region (13-20 April) to ascertain its possible impact.

Extension of UNOL

The Secretary-General informed the Security Council on 12 October [S/2001/981] that the mandate of the United Nations Peace-building Support Office in Liberia would end on 31 December. Despite the difficult political and security circumstances prevailing in the country and the subregion and the limited resources available to it, the Office continued to make worthwhile contributions in the areas of national reconciliation, respect for human rights and the rule of law through good offices and training programmes. It provided a useful political link between Liberia and the international community, particularly since the imposition of sanctions, and gave support to the Sierra Leone peace process. In that

light and following consultations with the Government of Liberia, the Secretary-General recommended that UNOL's mandate be extended for another year, to 31 December 2002. He intended to conduct a review of the Office during 2002 and make proposals to the Council.

On 18 October [S/2001/982], the Council took note of his recommendation.

UNOMIL financing

By **decision 55/499** of 7 September, the General Assembly included in the draft agenda of its fifty-sixth (2001) session the item on financing of the United Nations Observer Mission in Liberia (UNOMIL), whose mandate ended in 1997 [YUN 1997, p. 123]. On 24 December, the Assembly decided that the item would remain for consideration during its resumed fifty-sixth (2002) session (**decision 56/464**) and that the Fifth Committee should continue to consider the item at that session (**decision 56/458**).

Guinea-Bissau

The political situation in Guinea-Bissau remained volatile throughout 2001. Early in the year, the authorities foiled an assassination plot against President Kumba Yala, elected in January 2000 [YUN 2000, p. 183], to topple his Government, which was formed in accordance with the 1998 Abuja Peace Accord [YUN 1998, p. 153], ending the internal conflict in the country. In addition, armed confrontations took place between government forces and rival factions of the separatist Movement of Democratic Forces of Casamance (MFDC) in the north-west of the country.

The United Nations Peace-building Support Office in Guinea-Bissau (UNOGBIS) continued to report on developments in the country as well as the situation along the border with Senegal. The Secretary-General described its activities and developments in the country in four reports issued during the year.

Developments and UNOGBIS activities

The democratic transition in Guinea-Bissau failed to yield tangible results in early 2001, according to the inter-agency mission sent to West Africa in March by the Secretary-General [S/2001/434] (see p. 160). With little technical expertise within government institutions, deep levels of poverty, an undeveloped private sector with few prospects for investment, few avenues for employment and an oversized army dependent on the State for resources, the situation remained fragile. The mission said that collapse of the State was possible, with security and humanitarian implications for neighbouring countries, specifically Guinea, the Gambia and the Casamance area of Senegal.

Report of Secretary-General (March). In response to resolution 1233(1999) [YUN 1999, p. 140], the Secretary-General, in a 16 March report [S/2001/237], provided to the Security Council an update of developments in Guinea-Bissau and UNOGBIS activities since his previous report in September 2000 [YUN 2000, p. 186].

Following the attempted coup d'état in November 2000 [ibid.], which ended in the death of the head of the former military junta, General Ansoumane Mane, the direct challenge to the constitutional order by the military appeared to decrease in early 2001. However, the overall situation in the country grew more unstable. Frictions within the coalition Government intensified, resulting in a mass resignation from the Government, on 23 January, of all members of the Guinea-Bissau Resistance, the coalition partner of the Party of Social Renewal (PRS) of President Yala. The President's subsequent appointment of a minority PRS Cabinet created further political uncertainty, since that party lacked the parliamentary majority to rule alone.

Against a background of ethnic and religious discontent, the President attempted to form a new coalition Government following demands to replace Prime Minister N'Chama. On 18 February, the authorities said they had foiled another plot to assassinate President Yala. Despite the climate of tension, Guinea-Bissau continued efforts to consolidate its fragile democratization process. The National Assembly, which resumed its annual session on 28 February, focused on the revision of the Constitution. To facilitate that debate, UNOGBIS organized a seminar that included discussion of such issues as norms and principles of constitutions in multiparty systems. The National Assembly was preparing the necessary legislation for holding municipal elections in June. The United Nations provided the services of an electoral expert.

The situation along Guinea-Bissau's border with Senegal became more tense as fighting between rival factions of the separatist MFDC increased in the north-west of Guinea-Bissau, and those fighters pursued their rebellion in Casamance province, Senegal. MFDC's cross-border infiltration into Guinea-Bissau led to armed clashes with that country's forces, and there were charges that MFDC was involved in a failed plot to assassinate Mr. Yala. The situation was further complicated by the presence in the border area of some 3,460 registered Casamance refugees. With much international assistance, the Government continued its mine-clearing pro-

gramme and commenced its demobilization, reinsertion and reintegration programme by completing a census of ex-combatants and paramilitary forces and demobilizing 948 of them.

The economy of Guinea-Bissau was in dire straits, and the Government was unable to meet the most basic social needs of the population. A World Bank mission visited the country from 26 January to 9 February to assess the implementation of the economic rehabilitation and recovery credit.

The Security Council considered the report during informal consultations on 29 March and received a briefing by the Secretariat on economic, social and security matters and the consolidation of democratic institutions and processes in Guinea-Bissau. In a statement to the press that day, the President, on behalf of the members, welcomed the authorities' efforts to form a broad-based Government and called on all parties to cooperate to that end. While noting the tense situation along Guinea-Bissau's border with Senegal, the President welcomed the signing of the peace agreement between the Government of Senegal and MFDC and expressed the hope that the situation would be addressed through peaceful means within Senegal, and would no longer be a destabilizing factor in Guinea-Bissau.

Report of Secretary-General (June). On 22 June, the Secretary-General submitted another report on developments in Guinea-Bissau and on UNOGBIS activities [S/2001/622 & Corr.1]. The political situation was dominated in the period since his March report by strong and prolonged friction between the executive and legislative branches of government over the choice of Prime Minister. Faustino Imbali, whom President Yala appointed on 20 March, was opposed by parliamentarians, mainly from opposition parties but also including members of the President's party, PRS. The National Assembly repeatedly refused to confirm Mr. Imbali and his Government, and the country practically operated without a government throughout April and May. Another foiled coup attempt took place in mid-April. During that unstable period, civil society, led by the Bishop of Bissau, called on political actors to engage in dialogue in order to stabilize the country. The Secretary-General's Representative, Samuel C. Nana-Sinkam (Cameroon), continued to provide his good offices to facilitate compromise. On 17 May, the National Assembly approved the work programme of Mr. Imbali's Government. UNOGBIS, in a follow-up to a previous meeting, organized a seminar on the consolidation of multiparty democracy in collaboration with the country's 17 political parties and the parliament (Bissau, 28 May–1 June).

The activities of the MFDC rebels remained the most serious security challenge to Guinea-Bissau. Since Guinea-Bissau forces launched a military offensive against the separatist rebels in March to force them from the north-west region, the border situation remained tense and skirmishes between rival MFDC factions continued, sometimes within Guinea-Bissau territory. The presence of an estimated 3,000 refugees from Casamance, some alleged to have links with the rebels, complicated the situation further. UNHCR sent a mission to Guinea-Bissau in April to assess the refugee situation. Tensions within the armed forces contributed to delays in implementing the demobilization, reinsertion and reintegration programme. However, with World Bank assistance, 571 former combatants were demobilized in May.

The volatility of the political and military situation was both a cause and a consequence of the country's economic deterioration; foreign assistance accounted for some 80 per cent of the national budget. The United Nations Development Programme (UNDP), on 17 April, signed a three-year financial assistance agreement in the amount of $3.7 million to support the Government's governance programme, and other UN agencies provided aid. UNOGBIS continued to promote respect for human rights and the rule of law. During the period under review, it focused on supporting the Government's efforts to ensure due process for persons detained on suspicion of complicity in the failed 2000 coup attempt. By 13 June, only 11 of the original 169 persons detained remained in detention, the rest having been released pending trial.

The Secretary-General expressed relief that the governmental impasse had been overcome, and he called for continued financial support for the country's newly restored democratic institutions in order to enable them to function effectively.

The Security Council considered the report on 10 July, following which the President, in a statement to the press, reaffirmed the Council's support for efforts to promote national reconciliation and strengthen democratic institutions and the rule of law. The Council also expressed concern about the unstable situation in the country and called for assistance to Guinea-Bissau in its economic rehabilitation and reconstruction efforts.

Report of Secretary-General (September). In a 27 September report on developments in Guinea-Bissau and on UNOGBIS [S/2001/915], the Secretary-General stated that the overall situation in the country remained volatile. The Government faced an institutional crisis resulting from differences among various institutions, representing different branches of power, over their constitutional responsibilities. The opposition continued to demand the resignation of both the Government and Prime Minister Imbali. By mid-September, a rift had formed between President Yala and his own party, due to a number of his controversial decisions, which also provoked strong resistance from major political actors, especially the judiciary. Despite the difficult political climate, the National Assembly continued efforts to assert its role as a check on the executive, including its oversight responsibilities in the management of the national treasury. The report of its commission to investigate the alleged embezzlement of $17 million and to recommend procedures on fiscal control of the national treasury was completed, but not made public. The National Assembly approved draft revisions to the Constitution and the revised Constitution was awaiting the President's approval. All political parties agreed that municipal elections should be held in early 2002. Electoral preparations continued, although planning was hampered by financial constraints. The Secretary-General's Representative continued to promote dialogue and to mobilize civil society groups and individuals, especially the Bishop of Bissau, to lessen tensions and stabilize the situation.

Along the border with Senegal, the situation remained precarious, as the withdrawal of regular Guinea-Bissau troops from the border region, with only border guards left in place to provide security, left the situation there tense and delicate. The volatility of the border regions continued to hamper progress in the reorganization of the army and caused delays in the demobilization, reinsertion and reintegration programme. The census for that programme was completed, with 23,803 candidates counted. The next stage would be demobilization of 5,000 persons. The mine-clearing process continued; 1,600 mines were removed, with an estimated 5,000 remaining.

The country's widespread economic and social problems prevented the few democratic advances achieved over the previous months from taking root. The Secretary-General explored with ECOWAS and others ways to assist the Government to stabilize the political situation, and he appealed to the international community for urgent technical and financial assistance to the weak judiciary.

The Security Council members, having considered the report on 22 October, issued a statement to the press in which they called on all government institutions to engage in dialogue, to respect the Constitution and to promote national reconciliation. They also called for an integrated and coordinated approach by the UN system, including the Bretton Woods institutions, and called on bilateral donors to help Guinea-Bissau create income-generating capacity.

Report of Secretary-General (December). On 14 December [S/2001/1211], the Secretary-General submitted his fourth and last report of the year on developments in Guinea-Bissau and UNOGBIS. The political situation continued to be difficult and volatile. The Government reported that it had foiled a coup attempt on 3 December, and the opposition called repeatedly for the President's resignation and for the dismissal of Prime Minister Imbali. The Foreign Minister was removed from office on 21 November, and the Prime Minister was dismissed on 7 December. The new 24-member Cabinet of Prime Minister Alhamara N'Tchia Nhasse took office on 11 December. The political process continued to be marked by multiple crises among various institutions. According to the opposition, the arrest and detention of the President of the Supreme Court on allegations of misappropriation of funds were politically motivated and should be rescinded. The executive insisted that National Assembly rules and procedures did not allow parliament to declare executive acts as unconstitutional. The different perceptions of the constitutionality or otherwise of executive decisions had engendered harsh rhetoric in parliament, including initiatives from the opposition for the removal of the President from office. The executive sought to strip some opposition legislators of their parliamentary immunity in order to bring them to trial on charges of corruption and misappropriation of funds, which opposition parties said were false. Meanwhile, UNOGBIS continued to promote dialogue and national reconciliation, including through a television forum and seminars to enhance the capacity of civil society to play a more active role in building a stable political environment. The Secretary-General discussed the situation in Guinea-Bissau with heads of State in the region and with ECOWAS. The Community of Portuguese-speaking Countries and ECOWAS explored the possibility of embarking on a joint initiative to contribute to the quest for peace in Guinea-Bissau.

Although security along the border with Senegal improved during the reporting period, occasional forays into Guinea-Bissau's territory by MFDC continued. Although no major factional fighting by rival MFDC groups was reported in Guinea-Bissau territory, armed attacks against civilian vehicles continued, resulting in theft and

civilian casualties. Internally, the military authorities continued to pledge loyalty to the constitutional order, although there were growing indications of concern about the apparent inability of the Government to move the democratic process forward. Military personnel to be demobilized in early 2002 were identified, following the completion of the census of the armed forces. Demining activities continued, and the Government established a Centre for Anti-Mine Action, which estimated that 2,500 mines had been removed and about 20,000 remained in the country.

The political instability continued to affect economic performance, including the flow of aid. Widespread poverty added to social instability and generated scepticism about the dividends of democracy. As the principal employer in the country, the Government's inability to pay civil service salaries on time, including months of accumulated arrears, generated enormous social and economic hardship and tensions. The drop in price of the principal cash crop, cashew nuts, and reported corruption at different levels of State administration were also factors. Against that backdrop, President Yala threatened to dismiss 60 per cent of civil servants for corruption and fraud, and the Government decided to set up an anti-corruption unit in the Ministry of Justice. UNOGBIS organized a seminar on ways to improve the functioning of anti-corruption mechanisms. The Bretton Woods institutions remained engaged with Guinea-Bissau in such areas as demobilization, reintegration, education, health and public finances. The human rights area showed signs of improvement. By late November, all detainees linked to the attempted military uprising in 2000 had reportedly been released. However, following a coup attempt on 3 December, a number of people, including military officers, were said to have been detained. Relations between the Government and the media, which had been strained, improved as discussions on a draft press code began. UNOGBIS prepared a reference document on principles and practices of journalism in a democratic society, and, with assistance from Germany, made available modern broadcasting equipment to State television and to government and private radio services. UNOGBIS also continued to organize training programmes for military and police staff, with a view to sensitizing them with regard to respect for human rights; it also organized courses for magistrates and Ministry of Justice staff members. In an effort to enhance coordination among UN bodies, UNOGBIS and the UN country team developed a "strategic vision" to assist Guinea-Bissau's peace-building process in the short to medium term. The immediate goal was to help prevent the country from relapsing into armed conflict by addressing the root causes of its crises.

By the end of the year, the situation in Guinea-Bissau remained a source of deep concern due to lack of stability and little progress in democratization. Appealing to political actors to resolve their differences through dialogue and within the framework of the Constitution, the Secretary-General said that consolidation of peace would help to create conditions in which economic growth and better living conditions could take place. He urged the international community to remain engaged with and supportive of Guinea-Bissau, and specifically to contribute to the round-table conference of donors, scheduled for early 2002.

Extension of UNOGBIS mandate

The Secretary-General, on 5 October [S/2001/960], proposed that the UNOGBIS mandate, which was due to expire on 31 December 2001, be extended until 31 December 2002. The Security Council, on 10 October [S/2001/961], took note of the proposal.

On 5 December [S/2001/1180], the Secretary-General informed the Council of his intention to appoint David Stephen (United Kingdom) as his Special Representative for Guinea-Bissau and Chief of UNOGBIS as from 1 February 2002. Mr. Stephen would succeed Samuel C. Nana-Sinkam (Cameroon). The Council, on 12 December [S/2001/1181], took note of that intention.

Horn of Africa

Eritrea-Ethiopia

During the year, Eritrea and Ethiopia generally continued to abide by the terms of the Algiers Peace Agreement that they had signed in December 2000 [YUN 2000, p. 180] and made efforts to implement it, even though progress in the peace process was slow and marked by disagreement, in particular on demarcation of the boundary between the two countries. The border dispute was the original cause of the conflict, which had first erupted in 1998 [YUN 1998, p. 144].

The United Nations Mission in Ethiopia and Eritrea (UNMEE), which was established in July 2000, continued to monitor the ceasefire throughout 2001. The formal declaration of the Temporary Security Zone in April, as called for in the 2000 Agreement on Cessation of Hostilities [YUN 2000, p. 173], gave momentum to the peace

process and made possible the return of civilians to their places of origin in that area. While the parties had reservations regarding the Zone's boundaries, they respected it on the ground. UNMEE continued to patrol and observe throughout the Zone, contributing to stability there. However, in the last few months of the year, tension rose considerably in the Mission area, with each party accusing the other of building up militarily. In addition, Eritrea failed to provide the Mission with information on its militia and police or to allow UNMEE complete freedom of movement in areas adjacent to the Zone. Other outstanding issues included the release of prisoners of war, establishment of a direct air corridor between Addis Ababa and Asmara, and the conclusion of a status-of-forces agreement between Eritrea and the United Nations. UNMEE's mandate was extended twice by the Security Council in 2001, the second time until March 2002.

The Boundary Commission began its work on delimitation and demarcation of the border, a complex and costly enterprise that required extensive demining.

Implementation of Algiers agreement

The Secretary-General, in response to Security Council resolution 1320(2000) [YUN 2000, p. 176], submitted five reports on Ethiopia and Eritrea in 2001. He provided updated information on political and humanitarian developments and on the status of UNMEE.

Report of Secretary-General (January). In his report of 12 January [S/2001/45], the Secretary-General welcomed the Peace Agreement between Eritrea and Ethiopia, which was signed in Algiers on 12 December 2000 [YUN 2000, p. 180], and described it as a major achievement for Africa. He stated that the strength of UNMEE's military component stood at 3,432 personnel as at 11 January, including 153 observers. UNMEE expected to be fully deployed and operational by the end of February, with a total strength of 4,200 troops. Civilian staff members totalled 194.

The presence of landmines and unexploded ordnance in the future Temporary Security Zone and adjacent areas was a threat not only to UNMEE personnel but also to the populations concerned. UNMEE was establishing a mine-action priority-setting coordination group at its Asmara office.

The Secretary-General said that the Algiers Peace Agreement underlined the commitment of both countries to the consolidation of the peace process. He was encouraged by the fact that the parties had already taken steps towards implementation. Noting that the Algiers Agreement required the parties to respect and implement fully the Agreement on Cessation of Hostilities of 18 June 2000 [YUN 2000, p. 173], the Secretary-General, while acknowledging UNMEE's rapid deployment, expressed concern about the delay in establishing the Temporary Security Zone. He recalled that disagreements between the parties in that regard had arisen during the second meeting of the Military Coordination Commission (MCC) in December 2000 [ibid., p. 181]. A few matters pertaining to UNMEE's deployment also remained to be resolved, including the status-of-forces agreements between the United Nations and Ethiopia and Eritrea. The Secretary-General hoped that the parties would work towards establishing the Boundary Commission, which, under the Algiers Agreement, had been entrusted with the delimitation and demarcation of the border, and would provide the required financing as soon as possible. He also called for contributions to the trust fund established under Security Council resolution 1177 (1998) [YUN 1998, p. 147] for establishing the border. Subject to the availability of the resources, the United Nations was prepared to assist the Boundary Commission.

SECURITY COUNCIL ACTION (February)

On 9 February [meeting 4275], following consultations among Security Council members, the President made statement **S/PRST/2001/4** on behalf of the Council:

The Security Council, recalling all previous resolutions and statements of its President regarding the situation in Eritrea and Ethiopia, notes with appreciation the Secretary-General's progress report of 12 January 2001 and subsequent update pertaining to the matter.

The Council reaffirms the commitment of all Member States to the sovereignty, independence and territorial integrity of Eritrea and Ethiopia, and further reaffirms its continued commitment to a peaceful definitive settlement of the conflict.

The Council, reiterating its strong support for the Agreement of Cessation of Hostilities signed by the parties in Algiers on 18 June 2000, strongly welcomes and supports the subsequent Peace Agreement between the Government of the State of Eritrea and the Government of the Federal Democratic Republic of Ethiopia signed in Algiers on 12 December 2000 ("Algiers Agreement"). It commends the efforts of the Organization of African Unity, the President of Algeria and his Special Envoy, as well as the United States of America and the European Union for their role in achieving the Algiers Agreement.

The Council encourages both parties to continue working towards the full and prompt implementation of the Algiers Agreement. In this connection, it further welcomes the agreement reached by the parties on 6 February 2001 to move forward with the es-

tablishment of the Temporary Security Zone on 12 February 2001.

The Council expresses its strong support for the Secretary-General's role in continuing to help implement the Algiers Agreement, including through his own good offices, for the efforts of his Special Representative and for the contributions of relevant United Nations entities.

The Council notes with satisfaction that the Algiers Agreement includes mechanisms for the delimitation and demarcation of the common border and for addressing claims and compensation, and that the parties are cooperating with the Secretary-General in these matters in accordance with agreed schedules. It draws the urgent attention of Member States to the fact that funds provided to date for border delimitation and demarcation, through the United Nations Trust Fund established under resolution 1177(1998) of 26 June 1998, remain clearly inadequate to meet the expenses of the Boundary Commission for the work entrusted to it under the Algiers Agreement. While expressing appreciation to those Member States that have already contributed financially, the Council calls upon Member States to consider providing further support to the peace process, including through contributions to the voluntary Trust Fund in order to assist the parties in rapid delimitation and demarcation of the common border in accordance with resolution 1312(2000) of 31 July 2000 and in accordance with the Algiers Agreement.

The Council notes with appreciation the expeditious deployment of the United Nations Mission in Ethiopia and Eritrea allowing the parties to redeploy and rearrange their forces as scheduled. It expresses appreciation to the troop-contributing countries and to those Member States that have provided the Mission with additional assets.

The Council urges the parties to cooperate fully and expeditiously with the Mission in the implementation of its mandate, including through the complete redeployment of troops consistent with the Algiers Agreement, the establishment of a direct air corridor between Addis Ababa and Asmara to ensure freedom of movement for Mission flights, and the conclusion of the necessary status-of-forces agreements, including identifying suitable accommodation sites for the Mission.

The Council further urges the parties to facilitate mine action in coordination with the United Nations Mine Action Service, including through exchanging and providing existing maps and any other relevant information to the United Nations. It notes with concern that mines and unexploded ordnance remain the pre-eminent threat to the safety and security of Mission troops and the population in and around the future Temporary Security Zone. It calls upon the international community to support generously non-governmental organizations with resources, skills and expertise in demining so that, in coordination with the Mission and the United Nations country teams, they can assist both Governments in this undertaking.

The Council encourages both parties to continue to exercise restraint and to implement confidence-building measures, to continue the release and voluntary and orderly return under the auspices of the International Committee of the Red Cross of civilians that remain interned, to release remaining prisoners of war and facilitate their return under the auspices of the International Committee of the Red Cross, and to fulfil their commitments under the Algiers Agreement to afford humane treatment to each other's nationals and persons of each other's national origin.

The Council calls on the parties to ensure the continued safe and unhindered access of humanitarian assistance to those in need, to guarantee the safety and security of all Mission, International Committee of the Red Cross and other humanitarian personnel and to respect strictly the relevant provisions of international humanitarian law.

The Council recognizes that the effects of the war have exacted a heavy toll on the civilian populations of Eritrea and Ethiopia, including through the internal displacement and outflow of refugees. It urges the respective Governments to continue to redirect their efforts towards the reconstruction and development of both economies, to work towards reconciliation with a view to normalizing their relations, and to engage in constructive cooperation with the other neighbouring States in the Horn of Africa, with a view to achieving stability in the subregion. It further urges contributions from the international community, including the United Nations agencies and the international financial institutions, in support of the reconstruction efforts of both countries.

The Council remains seized of the matter.

Report of Secretary-General (March). In a 7 March report [S/2001/202], the Secretary-General updated the Council on political and humanitarian developments in Eritrea and Ethiopia and recommended an extension of UNMEE's mandate. He stated that major strides towards establishing the Temporary Security Zone envisaged in the Agreement on Cessation of Hostilities were made by the parties at the third MCC meeting (Nairobi, Kenya, 6 February). The Zone, which was temporary and in no way prejudged the final status of any contested areas, was a first step to instil confidence, disengage troops and allow both Governments to arrange for the return of refugees and internally displaced persons. It would also enable humanitarian organizations to begin their activities in the area. The parties accepted in general terms UNMEE's proposal for the southern boundary of the Zone, although both expressed reservations about its location. The Force Commander translated the agreed map into a larger-scale operational map for use by the United Nations and the parties on the ground. Ethiopia began redeploying its forces on 12 February and Eritrea began to rearrange its forces northward on 17 February, while registering strong objections to the operational map. UNMEE established control of all sensitive locations inside the Zone and monitored the redeployment

and repositioning of the armed forces of both parties. At the fourth MCC meeting on 28 February, held for the first time inside the Zone, the parties agreed to cooperate with the UNMEE verification process and to allow UNMEE complete freedom of movement for that purpose.

Despite Eritrea's stated intention to abide by earlier understandings, on 1 March it announced a halt in the repositioning of its forces, due to objections to adjustments to the original map. It still maintained a substantial military presence in all three sectors of the Zone. Consequently, as at 6 March, UNMEE was not in a position to declare the formal establishment of the Zone, thus creating a potentially dangerous vacuum of authority in the Zone areas. UNMEE was also concerned about restrictions on its freedom of movement by the two parties; several requests for low flights over the Zone were denied, and some patrols in the Zone and adjacent areas were restricted. During the reporting period, the military situation between the two armed forces generally remained calm, despite some small-arms firings and destruction of property by one or the other party.

Some progress was made on the boundary demarcation issue, with both countries submitting to the Boundary Commission's Secretary, who was the Chief of the Cartographic Section of the UN Secretariat, their claims and supporting evidence. However, Ethiopia challenged one of the Eritrea-appointed Commissioners. In addition to the arbitral proceedings to be held by the Commission, the delimitation and demarcation of the border would require on-site technical work for which UNMEE would provide support. With regard to detained persons, Ethiopia had released a total of 614 prisoners of war and 989 civilian internees, and Eritrea had released 628 of the former and 4,357 of the latter since December 2000.

As at 1 March, the strength of UNMEE stood at 4,143 military personnel and 273 civilian staff. Negotiations between Ethiopia and the Secretariat over a few outstanding issues, particularly exemption from taxation and freedom of movement to and from the Temporary Security Zone, were still ongoing. The Mission's public information programme initiated radio broadcasts on recent developments and the peace process. UNMEE continued to receive frequent reports of landmine explosions on both sides of the border. However, neither side had provided complete information on minefields. The Mine Action Coordination Centre began training 150 local personnel. The difficult humanitarian situation caused by the impact of three years of drought was compounded by the effects of the war. Eritrea and the UN country team launched a humanitarian appeal for $217 million to stabilize the situation of the most vulnerable, in particular internally displaced persons and recently returned refugees (see p. 831). It was estimated that 6,240,000 people were affected by the drought and needed assistance and 400,000 had been displaced as a consequence of the war.

The Secretary-General proposed that the costs related to the work of the Secretary of the Boundary Commission, who was a UN staff member, as well as any support required from UNMEE, be included in the Mission's budget. To reduce the risks associated with mines for displaced persons returning to their homes, adequate mine-clearance and mine-awareness programmes would be required. The Secretary-General appealed to donors to contribute to the Mine Action Coordination Centre established by UNMEE. Noting that UNMEE had achieved significant progress since its establishment, the Secretary-General recommended that its mandate be extended for six months, until 15 September 2001.

Communications. On 8 March [S/2001/204], Eritrea transmitted to the Security Council a press release in which it called on the United Nations to rectify the alleged mistakes made in the location of the southern boundary of the Temporary Security Zone. Japan announced on 15 March [S/2001/240] a pledge of $1,083,000 for the Trust Fund in Support of the Delimitation and Demarcation of the Ethiopia/Eritrea Border. Eritrea, on 15 March [S/2001/229], said that although it broadly concurred with the Secretary-General's report, in particular the recommendation for the extension of UNMEE's mandate, it felt that a number of points had not been addressed adequately and took exception to the implication that a consensus was reached at MCC for an adjustment of the Zone to take account of reservations expressed by both parties. Also, Eritrea did not receive a larger-scale operational map as stated, but received a second map that put additional areas of sovereign Eritrean territory outside the Zone and under the military occupation of Ethiopia without consulting Eritrea; therefore, Eritrea had stopped its rearrangement of troops after having informed UNMEE. Ethiopia, on 20 March [S/2001/250], also commended the report and stated its willingness to resolve the issues of freedom of movement for the United Nations and sign a status-of-forces agreement; it called on Eritrea to do likewise. Ethiopia also rebutted some claims made by Eritrea.

SECURITY COUNCIL ACTION (March)

On 15 March [meeting 4294], the Security Council unanimously adopted **resolution 1344(2001)**. The draft [S/2001/233] was prepared in consultations among Council members.

The Security Council,

Recalling resolutions 1298(2000) of 17 May 2000, 1308(2000) of 17 July 2000, 1312(2000) of 31 July 2000, and 1320(2000) of 15 September 2000, the statement of its President of 9 February 2001 (S/PRST/2001/4), and all relevant previous resolutions and statements of its President pertaining to the Ethiopia-Eritrea conflict,

Reaffirming the commitment of all Member States to the sovereignty, independence and territorial integrity of Ethiopia and Eritrea,

Further reaffirming the need for both parties to fulfil all of their obligations under international humanitarian, human rights and refugee law,

Recalling the relevant principles contained in the Convention on the Safety of United Nations and Associated Personnel adopted by the General Assembly in its resolution 49/59 of 9 December 1994,

Reaffirming its strong support for the Agreement of Cessation of Hostilities signed between the Government of the State of Eritrea and the Government of the Federal Democratic Republic of Ethiopia in Algiers on 18 June 2000 and the subsequent Comprehensive Peace Agreement signed by the parties in Algiers on 12 December 2000,

Welcoming the progress made thus far in the implementation of these agreements,

Reaffirming its strong support for the Secretary-General's role in continuing to help implement the Agreements, including through his good offices, for the continuing efforts of his Special Representative and for the contributions of relevant United Nations entities,

Expressing its strong support for the role played by the United Nations Mission in Ethiopia and Eritrea in the implementation of its mandate,

Having considered the report of the Secretary-General of 7 March 2001,

1. *Decides* to extend the mandate of the United Nations Mission in Ethiopia and Eritrea at the troop and military observer levels authorized by its resolution 1320(2000) until 15 September 2001;

2. *Calls upon* the parties to continue working towards the full and prompt implementation of their Agreements, including an expeditious completion of the remaining steps, in particular the rearrangement of forces necessary for the establishment of the Temporary Security Zone, and to fulfil the following obligations:

(*a*) To ensure freedom of movement and access for the Mission;

(*b*) To establish a direct air corridor between Addis Ababa and Asmara in the interests of the safety of United Nations personnel;

(*c*) To conclude status-of-forces agreements with the Secretary-General;

(*d*) To facilitate mine action in coordination with the United Nations Mine Action Service, in particular through exchanging and providing existing maps and any other relevant information to the United Nations;

3. *Stresses* that the Agreements link the termination of the United Nations peacekeeping mission with the completion of the process of delimitation and demarcation of the Ethiopia-Eritrea border, which is a key element of the peace process;

4. *Notes* the primary responsibility of the parties under the Comprehensive Peace Agreement to fund the Boundary Commission and urges them to fulfil their financial obligations in this regard;

5. *Stresses* the importance of the close relationship between the Mission and the Boundary Commission and, noting the recommendations contained in paragraphs 50 and 53 of the Secretary-General's report, encourages the Mission to provide appropriate support to the Boundary Commission;

6. *Decides* to consider the recommendations in paragraphs 50 and 53 of the Secretary-General's report upon receipt of more detailed information;

7. *Calls upon* all States and international organizations to consider providing further support to the peace process, including through contributions to the voluntary Trust Fund to facilitate the rapid delimitation and demarcation of the common border, as well as to assist and participate in the longer-term tasks of reconstruction and development, and the economic and social recovery of Ethiopia and Eritrea;

8. *Decides* to remain seized of the matter.

The Security Council, on 16 March [S/2001/233], informed the Secretary-General that it shared his views on the importance of the Boundary Commission to the successful implementation of the UNMEE mandate. In order to make decisions on that matter, the Council requested quantified and detailed proposals on the recommendations contained in his March report (see p. 194).

Communications. Ethiopia and Eritrea, in letters to the Council, accused each other of impeding progress towards a peaceful settlement. On 29 March [S/2001/312], Eritrea transmitted a press release, which stated that the mines that had exploded around Tserona that resulted in an injury to an UNMEE peacekeeper had been laid by Ethiopia, which continued to reject appeals to provide minefield information to UNMEE. On 4 April [S/2001/327], Ethiopia countered that it had submitted information on minefields to UNMEE. Eritrea's claims were an effort to divert attention from its not having signed the status-of-forces agreement and its refusal to allow UNMEE to fly directly between Asmara and Addis Ababa.

Ethiopia, on 7 May [S/2001/448], said that Eritrea was violating the Algiers Agreement by reintroducing its troops into the Temporary Security Zone under the guise of militia. Eritrea, on 14 May [S/2001/477], denied that claim and said that Ethiopia's objective was to destabilize Eritrea; it had done so by using terrorist armed groups to harass the population in the occupied areas and to loot property. Meanwhile, Ethiopia refused to redeploy its troops from certain areas in the Temporary Security Zone, refused to provide UNMEE with information on landmines and impeded agreement on high-altitude flights. Also on 14 May [S/2001/480], Eritrea reported the results of

an inquiry into an incident in which its forces had turned back an UNMEE vehicle travelling on a road in Eritrea. It maintained that movement outside the Temporary Security Zone and within restricted military zones required observance of notification procedures. On 18 June [S/2001/609], Eritrea protested what it described as an attack by the Ethiopian Army on an Eritrean police station inside the Temporary Security Zone. Another protest was made by Eritrea on 28 June [S/2001/648], when it accused Ethiopia of having deported 722 Eritreans and one Ethiopian on 25 June. It added that over the past years, Ethiopia had deported over 76,000 Eritreans and Ethiopians of Eritrean origin.

Establishment of Temporary Security Zone

The Temporary Security Zone was established on 18 April, marking the formal separation of the Ethiopian and Eritrean forces, as the UN Under-Secretary-General for Peacekeeping Operations, Jean-Marie Guéhenno, announced to the Security Council the following day [S/PV.4310 & Corr.1]. Mr. Guéhenno stated that that step, as called for in the Algiers Agreement, was an important stage that would allow for the restoration of the Eritrean civil administration, including police and local militia, and the return of displaced persons to the Zone. In his announcement of the event, the Secretary-General's Special Representative, Legwaila Joseph Legwaila, had said that UNMEE continued to work with both countries to resolve a number of problems concerning the southern boundary of the Zone. The Special Representative reminded the parties that it was their obligation to ensure that all returnees were able to go back to their villages of origin. In addition, UNMEE reported that some Ethiopian military forces had moved forward slightly in the Zone from the confirmed redeployment position and discussions on the subject with the Ethiopian authorities were ongoing.

On 17 April, Mr. Guéhenno informed the Council, UNMEE and Eritrea had signed a protocol that would govern relations between the Mission and the police and militia units that would return to the Zone. That protocol established that police and militia should be clearly identifiable and allowed to carry only personal weapons. The most immediate challenge, he said, was the return of displaced persons to the Zone, and Eritrea was anxious that the move should be completed prior to the rainy season. Accordingly, Eritrea was planning for the return of 300,000 displaced persons within the next six to eight weeks. UNMEE made clear that a precipitous return could put returnees in a dire humanitarian situation. Linked to those returns was the threat posed by landmines and unexploded ordnance in the areas of return, where only limited mine-clearance activities were being carried out. The issue of direct flights between Addis Ababa and Asmara was still unresolved, and UNMEE faced repeated restrictions of movement.

Mr. Guéhenno noted that the Boundary Commission held its first informal meeting (The Hague, Netherlands, 25-26 March), with the participation of agents for both Ethiopia and Eritrea, at which a tentative time line of activities was presented. The Commission was drawing up a plan of action for the on-site activities required for delimitation and demarcation of the border. However, the formal orders to commence the work of the Commission could be issued only after Ethiopia's objection to one of the Commissioners was resolved. The President of the Commission had asked the Secretary-General to resolve Ethiopia's challenge, and he had a similar responsibility with regard to objections posed by both parties to three out of five members of the Claims Commission. The Presidents of both Commissions had requested the parties to make deposits to cover the initial costs of those two bodies, pursuant to commitments made in the Algiers Agreement. Some contributions were made to the Claims Commission, but the parties had not made any to the Boundary Commission.

SECURITY COUNCIL ACTION (May)

On 15 May [meeting 4320], following consultations among Security Council members, the President made statement **S/PRST/2001/14** on behalf of the Council:

Recalling all previous resolutions and statements of its President regarding the situation between Ethiopia and Eritrea, the Security Council emphasizes the importance of the commitments undertaken by the Government of the State of Eritrea and the Government of the Federal Democratic Republic of Ethiopia to the Agreement of Cessation of Hostilities signed in Algiers on 18 June 2000 and the subsequent Peace Agreement between the parties signed in Algiers on 12 December 2000 ("Algiers Agreements").

The Council reiterates its strong support for the Secretary-General's role in helping to implement the Agreements, including through his own good offices, and for the efforts of his Special Representative. It further expresses its appreciation for the continued role of the Organization of African Unity in helping to implement the Algiers Agreements.

The Council also reiterates its appreciation for the continued deployment of the United Nations Mission in Ethiopia and Eritrea both to the troop-contributing countries and to those Member States that have provided the Mission with additional assets.

The Council encourages both parties to continue working towards the full and prompt implementa-

tion of the Agreements and, in this context, to take concrete confidence-building measures. The Council further reaffirms its continued commitment to a peaceful definitive settlement of the conflict. In this connection, the Council notes with satisfaction that the parties have agreed to the Secretary-General's proposal of 1 May 2001, on the composition of the Boundary and Claims Commissions, critical components to the peaceful definitive settlement of the conflict. It now calls on the parties to fully cooperate with the Boundary Commission and to fulfil their financial responsibilities regarding the Boundary Commission's work.

The Council stresses that the parties must provide free movement and access for the Mission and its supplies as required throughout the territories of the parties, without any restrictions, including within the Temporary Security Zone and the 15-kilometre-wide adjacent area. Free and unhindered access for the Mission is a fundamental condition for the success of the peacekeeping operation. The Council emphasizes further that the purpose of the Temporary Security Zone is to separate the parties' armed forces. The Temporary Security Zone must be completely demilitarized. The civilian populations inside the Temporary Security Zone should be supported by an appropriate but limited number of Eritrean civilian militia and police.

The Council calls on the parties to cooperate fully and expeditiously with the Mission in the implementation of its mandate and to abide scrupulously by the letter and spirit of their agreements, particularly regarding the inviolability of the Temporary Security Zone. It also calls on both parties to exercise restraint in their public statements.

The Council further calls on the parties to continue to facilitate mine action in coordination with the United Nations Mine Action Service. It encourages the parties to exercise caution in returning civilians to the Temporary Security Zone before it has been adequately demined. The Council further calls for the immediate establishment of a secure air corridor between Addis Ababa and Asmara that does not require a detour through other countries. It also calls on Eritrea to conclude the necessary status-of-forces agreement for the Mission.

The Council notes that, in accordance with paragraph 16 of resolution 1298(2000) of 17 May 2000, the arms embargo on the parties expires on 16 May 2001. The Council recognizes that the Algiers Agreements are consistent with paragraphs 2 through 4 of resolution 1298(2000). Under the current circumstances, the measures imposed by paragraph 6 of the same resolution have not been extended by the Council beyond 16 May 2001.

The Council urges the parties to ensure that efforts are redirected from weapons procurement and other military activities towards the reconstruction and development of both economies, and regional reconciliation, with a view to achieving stability in the Horn of Africa. The Council reiterates its encouragement of Member States to exercise the highest degree of responsibility in discouraging arms flows to countries and regions emerging from armed conflicts.

The Council remains vigilant and expresses its intention to take appropriate measures if the situation between Eritrea and Ethiopia again threatens regional peace and security.

The Council will remain seized of the matter.

Report of Secretary-General (June). In his 19 June progress report on Ethiopia and Eritrea [S/2001/608], the Secretary-General welcomed the establishment of the Temporary Security Zone as a milestone in the peace process, making possible the return of civilians seeking to resume their lives in their places of origin. Despite differing views concerning the exact boundaries and its regime, in particular as it referred to the restoration of Eritrean militia and police, the situation on the ground remained generally calm. Nonetheless, there was a growing concern at the possibility of incidents resulting from the proximity between the Eritrean militia and police and the Ethiopian forces in the area of the southern boundary of the Zone.

UNMEE had attempted to define a precise southern boundary of the Zone that took into account the concerns of the parties of an administrative, military or humanitarian nature. It investigated the situation along several segments of that boundary, including clarification of the location and status of over a hundred villages in the area, resulting in a number of mutually acceptable adjustments of the boundary. Given the need for operational clarity, UNMEE had completed a finalized map showing the southern and northern boundaries of the Zone. UNMEE was concerned at the continued presence of Ethiopian troops inside the Zone in one location, despite Ethiopian assurances that those troops would be withdrawn. UNMEE had received recent indications that Ethiopia considered that the redeployment position corresponded to the 6 May 1998 line. That was not acceptable to the Mission, long after an understanding had been reached on the Ethiopian troops' redeployment positions in that area. Eritrea had not informed UNMEE of past or planned redeployment numbers, despite repeated requests and the fact that it was required to do so under the 2000 ceasefire Agreement. As at 13 June, UNMEE estimated that over 5,500 Eritrean militia and 3,100 police had already deployed inside the Zone. Both militia and police were apparently being organized along the lines of a military structure.

On 16 April, the Special Representative and the Eritrean Commissioner signed a Protocol Agreement on the functioning of local militia and police inside the Zone. The Protocol outlined the terms under which Eritrean militia and police were expected to operate and limited the types of weapons that they could carry. It also provided for the storage of certain types of weapons in predetermined locations. As at 13 June, UNMEE had lodged 31 protests with the Eritrean authorities concerning violations of the Protocol. Notwithstanding those problems, UNMEE had received good cooperation from both police and militia.

Ethiopia, on 21 April, issued a statement in which it rejected key elements of the Protocol Agreement on police and militia. It objected to the number of Eritrean militia to be deployed in the Zone, the type of weapons they would be allowed to carry and the fact that militia members would wear distinctive uniforms; Ethiopia said that was evidence that the Zone had not been demilitarized. It expressed similar concerns on 7 May [S/2001/448]. Eritrea said that its deployment of police and militias, dispersed over such a vast area, could not pose a cause of concern to Ethiopia [S/2001/477]. In the absence of any information on the pre-conflict strength and configuration of Eritrean local militia and police, UNMEE was attempting to determine what would constitute an appropriate but limited number of Eritrean civilian police and militia.

Freedom of movement for UNMEE, as required in the ceasefire Agreement, remained a problem; as at 13 June, the Mission had recorded and protested 113 restrictions on its movement by Eritrea and 30 by Ethiopia. Eritrea argued that UNMEE's freedom of movement should be limited to the Zone and to the main supply/access routes, and that it should not extend to the 15-kilometre-wide area adjacent to the Zone. Those restrictions impeded the Mission's monitoring mandate, which required the United Nations to monitor both the Zone and the forces of the two parties after redeployment and repositioning in the vicinity of the Zone. There had been no progress regarding the establishment of a direct high-altitude flight route between Asmara and Addis Ababa for UNMEE aircraft.

The United Nations continued to build confidence between the parties through MCC, which remained the only channel for direct contacts between them. Meetings were held on 6 April and 21 May in Djibouti and Nairobi, respectively. The meetings discussed the restoration of Eritrean militia and police in the Zone, freedom of movement, mine information, and the need for customs and immigration control along the southern boundary of the Zone. The parties agreed in principle to establish a joint mechanism, with the participation of OAU and UNMEE, to repatriate remains of soldiers from the Zone. They also agreed to establish three sector-level MCCs.

On 22 March, Ethiopia signed the status-of-forces agreement (SOFA) for UNMEE; however, the SOFA with Eritrea remained under negotiation.

The landmine and unexploded ordnance situation in the Zone was slowly but steadily becoming clearer since more information was provided by the parties and on-site surveying progressed. In March, Eritrea handed over to UNMEE 313 mine records covering 175,000 anti-personnel mines and 45,000 anti-tank mines. Ethiopia provided 17 reports to the Mine Action Coordination Centre and maintained that it had no central records of mines laid in the Zone. The Centre entered the relevant information on its database. The threat to both Mission personnel and the civilian population was great. Mine-awareness leaflets were distributed throughout the Zone and adjacent areas.

The Boundary Commission and the Claims Commission had begun their work, the initial difficulties regarding the nomination of some of the Commissioners having been resolved. Information on the main activities of the two Commissions was annexed to the Secretary-General's report.

In the humanitarian area, significant numbers of internally displaced persons had moved back to their home areas, either spontaneously or through returns organized by the Government with UNHCR assistance. Approximately 160,000 such persons were in camps and another 100,000 to 150,000 were living in host communities. Eritrea drew up plans for the second phase of government-organized returns, and UNMEE participated in village assessments of infrastructure in preparation for their arrival. Following a March agreement among Eritrea, the Sudan and UNHCR on the voluntary repatriation of Eritrean refugees from the Sudan, the first group of 900 Eritrean refugees returned to their home villages in May. The Sudan estimated that 174,000 Eritrean refugees remained there. During the period under review, Ethiopia released 242 Eritrean prisoners of war, and Eritrea released one Ethiopian prisoner of war, on health grounds. According to the International Committee of the Red Cross (ICRC), some 400 prisoners of war remained in Eritrea and some 1,300 in Ethiopia. The human rights component of UNMEE became operational with the arrival of five of the expected seven human rights officers. They began investigating allegations of violations in the Zone area and monitoring the return of displaced persons.

The Secretary-General commended the two Governments for their commitment to the peace process and their overall compliance with their obligations under the Algiers Agreement, in spite of the fact that serious difficulties remained. It was imperative, he said, for the parties to resolve the outstanding issues, in particular those pertaining to the Temporary Security Zone, so as to ensure that it was clearly defined and effectively demilitarized. In letters to the leaders of the two countries, the Secretary-General appealed to Eritrea to pay attention to the deployment of an excessive number of militia and police in the Zone and to the fact that a SOFA had not been signed, and expressed concern to Ethiopia over the continued presence of its troops in parts of the eastern sector of the Zone. The continuing restrictions on UNMEE's freedom of movement and the establishment of a direct high-altitude route between Asmara and Addis Ababa were mentioned in both letters. The Secretary-General regretted that neither Government had displayed publicly much openness to a normalization of relations between them.

Report of Secretary-General (September). On 5 September [S/2001/843], the Secretary-General issued an update of his previous report on Ethiopia and Eritrea; he recommended that the Council extend UNMEE's mandate for six months.

On 21 and 22 June, UNMEE presented its final map of the Temporary Security Zone to the Eritrean and Ethiopian authorities. The Special Representative urged the parties to accept the map despite their objections to some parts of the boundary. Ethiopia stated that the map was unacceptable because of two "errors". It asserted that an 8-kilometre-wide pocket at the eastern end of Sector East should be returned to Ethiopia, and that the Zone should be uniformly 25 kilometres wide, which was not the case in Sector Centre. For its part, Eritrea indicated that it could not accept the map as it was a departure from the proposals originally presented to the parties on 30 January; in particular, the Zone could not be considered as "fully established" until Eritrea's concerns regarding the southern boundary had been addressed. The Secretary-General noted that, while neither party had formally accepted the map, they had in fact based their operations on it and cooperated with UNMEE in the management of the Zone, in accordance with the parameters established in the map. However, on several occasions, Eritrea invoked its disagreement with the southern boundary by refusing to cooperate on other issues, thus delaying resolution of matters such as restrictions on UNMEE's freedom of movement, signing a SOFA, convening sector-level meetings of MCC and providing information on the number of militia and police inside the Zone. With regard to the last, UNMEE had not been able to determine whether the number of Eritrean police and militia deployed in the Zone was commensurate with the size of the population. Nevertheless, UNMEE estimated that 6,800 Eritrean militia and 3,000 police were deployed inside the Zone, a significant rise in militia since June (5,500), but the police number was unchanged. Despite appeals from UNMEE not to deploy police and militia close to the southern boundary of the Zone, on at least one occasion their deployment in that area led to increased tensions between the parties in some sections of the boundary. In addition, UNMEE protested several violations by the police and militia of the Protocol Agreement on the Presence of Police and Militia in the Temporary Security Zone, signed between UNMEE and Eritrea on 16 April. In particular, the Eritrean militia and police contravened the provisions of the Protocol relating to the type of weapons they could carry and to stockpiling of weapons in the Zone. Despite those concerns, cooperation and communication between UNMEE and the police at the field level were relatively good.

Eritrea continued to hamper UNMEE's freedom of movement, thereby reducing its ability to monitor the area north of the Zone where Eritrean Defence Forces were positioned. On a few occasions, movement was restricted by the Ethiopian Armed Forces owing to insufficient coordination among some of their elements.

The seventh meeting of MCC (Nairobi, 27 June) discussed plans for opening the Mereb River Bridge, the challenges faced by civilians returning to their homes and UNMEE's freedom of movement. Eritrea continued to maintain that it was premature to hold sector MCC meetings until the Zone was "fully established", and its representative questioned the holding of future MCC meetings in either Addis Ababa or Asmara. The parties continued discussions on a draft procedure for collecting and exchanging the remains of soldiers killed during the conflict. The eighth MCC meeting (Nairobi, 8 August) focused on border security and the return of internally displaced persons. As at 31 August, the strength of UNMEE's military component stood at 3,870 military personnel.

Landmines remained a major threat in the Zone and adjacent areas, with eight civilians killed and 24 injured from 1 June to 31 August. On 18 August, eight Jordanian peacekeepers were injured when their truck hit a mine. A positive step in mine action was Eritrea's 27 August signature of the 1997 Convention on the Prohibition of the Use, Stockpiling, Production and Transfer of Anti-personnel Mines and on Their Destruction [YUN 1997, p. 503]. Ethiopia, which said it did not possess centralized mine records, agreed to facilitate an UNMEE-organized infor-

mation collection project in three sectors. However, the project was tested in Sector East and found to be unsatisfactory. Mine-clearance teams continued their work, and training of humanitarian demining teams progressed.

The composition of the Boundary Commission and of the Claims Commission was completed, and a report on the Boundary Commission's activities was annexed to the Secretary-General's report. The parties had made initial contributions towards the expenses of the Boundary Commission, and voluntary contributions from various Member States to the Trust Fund for the Delimitation and Demarcation of the Border totalled $5.4 million.

As a result of UNMEE's patrolling, the return of civilian administration, police and militia to the Zone, and the efforts of the humanitarian community, security conditions in the Zone improved. A total of 170,000 internally displaced persons had returned to their villages from camps by the time of the report. A total of 70,000 persons still lived in camps, as their home areas remained inaccessible because of mines and unexploded ordnance, insecurity caused by the proximity of villages to the southern boundary of the Zone, or the fact that some villages were in areas under Ethiopian administration. UN agencies, NGOs and the Eritrean Relief and Refugee Committee began programmes to provide housing materials to villages. The release and repatriation of prisoners of war came to a halt, despite the commitment made by both parties under the Algiers Agreement. According to ICRC, some 1,800 prisoners of war remained in Ethiopia and 400 in Eritrea. During the reporting period, ICRC assisted the repatriation of 3,522 persons of Ethiopian descent from Eritrea. Since December 2000, a total of 19,853 persons had been repatriated to Ethiopia. On 25 June, 704 persons of Eritrean descent, mostly long-term residents of the Tigray region in Ethiopia, were sent to Eritrea in a manner, which ICRC determined was not in accordance with international humanitarian law and which UNMEE protested. The Secretary-General expressed his concern over those circumstances in a letter of 2 August to the Prime Minister. In a reply of 8 August, the Government of Ethiopia maintained that the persons were repatriated to Eritrea of their own free will. UNMEE interviewed individuals repatriated by both countries and found serious human rights concerns, including the issue of long-term detention without due process, allegations of ill-treatment, discrimination in access to social services and employment, and harassment. UNMEE carried out human rights monitoring activities within the Zone and adjacent areas. The Secretary-General appealed to both countries to reconsider their positions on the eviction of each other's nationals.

The three-month period under review, which completed the first year of the Mission's operations, had seen the gradual consolidation of progress achieved earlier. For the first time in three years, the armies of Eritrea and Ethiopia had been fully separated and some of their soldiers were beginning to return home. The outstanding issues remained freedom of movement for UNMEE, high-altitude flights between Asmara and Addis Ababa, the unconditional release of prisoners of war, Eritrea's non-acceptance of a SOFA, the presence of landmines and the human rights and humanitarian situations.

SECURITY COUNCIL ACTION (September)

On 14 September [meeting 4372], the Security Council unanimously adopted **resolution 1369 (2001)**. The draft [S/2001/862] was prepared in consultations among Council members.

The Security Council,

Recalling resolutions 1298(2000) of 17 May 2000, 1308(2000) of 17 July 2000, 1312(2000) of 31 July 2000, 1320(2000) of 15 September 2000 and 1344(2001) of 15 March 2001, the statements of its President of 9 February 2001 (S/PRST/2001/4) and of 15 May 2001 (S/PRST/2001/14) and all relevant previous resolutions and statements pertaining to the situation between Ethiopia and Eritrea,

Reaffirming the commitment of all Member States to the sovereignty, independence and territorial integrity of Ethiopia and Eritrea,

Further reaffirming the need for both parties to fulfil their obligations under international law, international humanitarian law, human rights law and refugee law, and to ensure the safety of all personnel of the United Nations, the International Committee of the Red Cross and other humanitarian organizations,

Reaffirming its strong support for the Comprehensive Peace Agreement between the Government of the State of Eritrea and the Government of the Federal Democratic Republic of Ethiopia, signed in Algiers on 12 December 2000, and the preceding Agreement of Cessation of Hostilities, signed in Algiers on 18 June 2000 (hereafter referred to collectively as the Algiers Agreements),

Further reaffirming its strong support for the help in implementing the Algiers Agreements continuously provided by the Secretary-General and his Special Representative, including through their good offices, and by the Organization of African Unity,

Reaffirming its strong support for the role played by the United Nations Mission in Ethiopia and Eritrea in the implementation of its mandate, as well as by the Organization of African Unity Liaison Mission in Ethiopia-Eritrea,

Welcoming the progress made thus far in implementing the Algiers Agreements, including in the establishment and functioning of the Temporary Security Zone and the constitution of the Boundary and Claims Commissions, respectively,

Having considered the report of the Secretary-General of 5 September 2001,

1. *Decides* to extend the mandate of the United Nations Mission in Ethiopia and Eritrea at the troop and military observer levels authorized by its resolution 1320(2000) until 15 March 2002;

2. *Calls upon* the parties to cooperate fully and expeditiously with the Mission in the implementation of its mandate and to abide scrupulously by the letter and spirit of their agreements, including regarding cooperation with the Boundary Commission and facilitation of its work;

3. *Emphasizes* that the Algiers Agreements link the termination of the Mission with the completion of the work of the Boundary Commission related to delimitation and demarcation of the Ethiopia-Eritrea border;

4. *Further emphasizes* that the Temporary Security Zone must be completely demilitarized;

5. *Calls upon* the parties to urgently resolve the outstanding issues in accordance with the Algiers Agreements and fulfil the following obligations:

(a) The parties must provide freedom of movement and access for Mission personnel and its supplies as required for the performance of the Mission's duties; Eritrea must without restrictions allow the Mission to monitor the 15-kilometre area north of the Temporary Security Zone, and Ethiopia must avoid creating restrictions on the freedom of movement of the Mission in the 15-kilometre area south of the Temporary Security Zone;

(b) The parties must facilitate the establishment of a secure and practicable air corridor between Addis Ababa and Asmara, which does not require a detour through other countries, by accepting the proposal made in this regard by the Special Representative of the Secretary General;

(c) Eritrea must provide the Mission with information on the local militia and police inside the Temporary Security Zone, including their weapons, necessary for the mission to verify that the functions and configuration of the militia and police do not exceed that which prevailed before the outbreak of the conflict;

(d) Ethiopia must provide the Mission with full information and maps concerning all minefields so as to facilitate the work of the Mine Action Coordination Centre with a view, inter alia, to allow internally displaced persons to return safely to homes within the Temporary Security Zone;

(e) Eritrea must, without further delay, conclude the status-of-forces agreement with the Secretary-General;

(f) The parties must, unconditionally and without further delay, and in accordance with the 1949 Geneva Conventions, release and return the remaining prisoners of war and detainees under the auspices of the International Committee of the Red Cross;

(g) The parties must fulfil their financial responsibilities regarding the Boundary Commission;

6. *Further calls upon* the parties, where relevant in cooperation with the Mission, to explore and pursue a range of confidence-building measures, including the following:

(a) Affording humane treatment to each other's nationals and persons of each other's national origin and allowing each other's nationals to remain, without discrimination, in locations where they have decided to settle;

(b) Assisting relevant initiatives and contacts between organizations and groups, including those of the civil society, in the two countries;

(c) Exercising restraint in public statements;

7. *Encourages* all States and international organizations to support the peace process, including through:

(a) Contributions to the voluntary Trust Fund to Support the Peace Process in Ethiopia and Eritrea to facilitate quick-impact projects for emergency reconstruction and confidence-building measures;

(b) Contributions to the voluntary Trust Fund for the Delimitation and Demarcation of the Border between Ethiopia and Eritrea;

(c) Contributions to the United Nations country teams' consolidated appeals for humanitarian assistance to Eritrea and Ethiopia;

(d) Assistance to facilitate sustainable reintegration of demobilized soldiers, internally displaced persons and refugees;

(e) Assistance in the longer-term tasks of reconstruction and development, and the economic and social recovery of Ethiopia and Eritrea;

(f) Exercising the highest degree of responsibility in discouraging arms flows to the region;

8. *Urges* the parties to ensure that efforts are redirected from weapons procurement and other military activities towards the reconstruction and development of their economies and encourages both countries to continue and enhance the efforts to improve their relations in order to promote regional peace and security;

9. *Expresses its intention* to continue to monitor closely progress by the parties in implementing the provisions of the Algiers Agreements and the requirements of the present resolution, and to consider a mission to the two countries before agreeing to a further mandate renewal in order to monitor progress and discuss possible further steps towards reconciliation;

10. *Decides* to remain actively seized of the matter.

The Security Council held private meetings separately with the Foreign Ministers of Eritrea and Ethiopia on 16 November [meetings 4420 & 4421].

Report of Secretary-General (December). On 13 December [S/2001/1194], the Secretary-General submitted his last progress report of the year on Ethiopia and Eritrea. He described the situation as having remained calm and said that both parties had generally respected the Zone, even though Eritrea disputed the southern boundary and therefore considered that the Zone was "not fully established". There were isolated instances of small units or patrols of both parties crossing into the Zone, but they did not have a negative impact on its overall integrity. UNMEE, which had reached a military strength of 4,117, patrolled and observed effectively throughout the Zone, contributing an important element of stability to the situation. However, during the period under review, UNMEE experienced increased restrictions on its freedom of movement in the area

north of the Zone, hindering its ability to monitor the Eritrean Defence Forces in their redeployment positions. The Mission refined its monitoring activities to overcome those restrictions. Compounding those problems, a series of allegations in late November contributed to an escalation in tensions. On 14 November, Ethiopian Prime Minister Meles Zenawi, in letters to the Secretary-General and the Security Council, alleged that Eritrea was accelerating the "further militarization" of the Zone and was building up its troops along the border, and claimed that UNMEE might have adopted a "policy of appeasement to secure Eritrea's compliance". Ethiopia, he said, reserved the right of self-defence in the face of what it perceived as a growing threat. President Isaias Afwerki of Eritrea reacted in a letter of 20 November to the Secretary-General, asserting that Ethiopia's allegations were groundless and that its motive was to influence the delimitation process. The Special Representative ordered an investigation of the entire northern boundary and determined that the allegations were unfounded. On 30 November, Prime Minister Zenawi expressed concern to the Secretary-General over Eritrea's non-compliance with the ceasefire, stating that Eritrea continued to violate the Zone and that its troops were present under the guise of police and militia.

Despite repeated requests, Eritrea had not provided UNMEE with the necessary information (strength, disposition and structure before the outbreak of the conflict and currently) on its militia and police deployed inside the Zone, but had offered to provide overall numbers of militia and police against a guarantee of confidentiality, which UNMEE was unable to do given its policy of transparency. UNMEE estimated that there were 6,400 Eritrean militia and 3,000 police currently inside the Zone, and those numbers had remained roughly constant since the Secretary-General's September report. In certain areas, militia and police checkpoints, observation posts and other installations were located close to the southern boundary of the Zone. UNMEE increased the number of its observation posts on the southern boundary.

UNMEE continued to enjoy good access to the positions of the redeployed Ethiopian forces in the area south of the Zone. At the same time, there had been an increase in restrictions on freedom of movement by the Eritrean authorities north of the Zone where Eritrean forces were positioned, in violation of the ceasefire Agreement. After long discussions between UNMEE and the Eritrean authorities, Eritrea began to allow UNMEE to visit locations in the area north of the Zone upon 24 hours' prior notification. No progress was made on establishing a direct high-altitude flight between Asmara and Addis Ababa. Eritrea continued to maintain that UNMEE should fly the most direct route, while Ethiopia insisted that UNMEE should make a brief deviation to steer clear of anti-aircraft installations. At MCC meetings on 29 October (Djibouti) and 28 November (Mereb River Bridge), outstanding issues were discussed but little progress was made.

Minefields continued to be a problem in the Zone and caused the death of six people, mostly civilians, and injured many more. Ethiopia, in October, handed over to the United Nations maps of minefields inside the Zone and in adjacent areas. UNMEE was seeking further details on the types of mines used and more specific information on minefields already cleared by the Ethiopian Armed Forces. Demining operations continued to expand during the reporting period, by UNMEE and a number of other organizations. UNMEE also continued its mine-risk education programmes.

Since the last report, the Boundary Commission's work had proceeded in accordance with the programme adopted soon after its establishment. Information on its activities was contained in an annex to the Secretary-General's report. The demarcation process was expected to be complex, large and costly and required extensive mine clearance, and the Secretary-General appealed for contributions to the UN Trust Fund established for that purpose.

The humanitarian situation throughout the Zone and adjacent areas in Eritrea and Ethiopia remained stable, and many of the internally displaced persons and refugees who had returned were rebuilding their lives. At the time of the report, an estimated 55,000 internally displaced persons remained in nine camps; that figure included 9,300 persons living outside camps. The voluntary repatriation of Eritrean refugees from the Sudan, which was suspended owing to heavy rains, resumed on 20 October. As at the end of November, over 26,700 refugees had returned with UNHCR and Eritrean assistance. UN agencies assisted with the reintegration of returning refugees by providing aid for agricultural, water and sanitation, health, education and community services projects.

Eritrea and Ethiopia both released a number of prisoners of war on health grounds. Since December 2000, a total of 879 Eritrean and 653 Ethiopian prisoners of war had been repatriated under ICRC auspices. ICRC continued to assist the repatriation of persons of Ethiopian descent from Eritrea; since December 2000, 21,255 such persons had been repatriated to Ethiopia. Following the forced repatriation of persons of Eritrean descent by Ethiopia in June, no further such repatriations were reported. UNMEE continued to carry out human rights monitoring activities within the Zone and adjacent areas and investigated some allegations of abductions by militia, police or military personnel. UNMEE's public information component conducted regular press briefings in the capitals of both countries and facilitated access to the Zone for media members. It had not yet gained access to Ethiopian radio for its own broadcasts, and its weekly transmissions on Radio Eritrea were suspended by the Eritrean authorities in October. Radio UNMEE posted its programmes on UN web sites in English and six local languages. The UNMEE HIV/AIDS Task Force continued to pursue its programme, and training of the Mission's military contingents was ongoing.

The Secretary-General observed that the absence of mutual confidence left the relationship between the two countries in a potentially volatile situation. He appealed to Eritrea to cooperate with UNMEE by giving it freedom of movement in the areas north of the Zone and urged both parties to exercise restraint, as recent public allegations of major military preparations and further rhetoric did not help the cause of peace. He called on them to facilitate the establishment of a direct air corridor between the capitals and release all prisoners of war. The Secretary-General again urged Eritrea to conclude a SOFA.

Arms embargo

On 9 January [S/2001/23], Ethiopia protested to the Security Council that the arms embargo the Council had imposed against Ethiopia and Eritrea under resolution 1298(2000) [YUN 2000, p. 170] was unfair because it denied Ethiopia the means to defend itself and hindered the demining effort. On 26 January [S/2001/100], Malta informed the Secretary-General of measures it had taken to implement the arms embargo.

The Chairman of the Security Council Committee established pursuant to resolution 1298 (2000) concerning the situation between Eritrea and Ethiopia, on 16 May [S/2001/503], transmitted the Committee's report describing its activities from 1 January to 16 May, during which time it had held one informal meeting and one formal meeting. On 7 March, the Committee adopted guidelines for conducting its work. In accordance with provisions of resolution 1298(2000), the Committee expected to receive further replies from States concerning measures they had instituted to meet their obligations set out in that resolution. Two replies were received, from France and New Zealand. During the reporting period, the Committee received no reports from international/regional organizations on violations of the established prohibitions. It did, however, receive press reports that a Ukrainian aircraft carrying eight people and 30 tons of rifles and ammunition, originating from the Czech Republic and officially destined for Georgia, had been seized by the Bulgarian authorities at Bourgas Airport after the pilot requested permission to take off for Eritrea. The Committee requested Bulgaria, the Czech Republic, Eritrea, Georgia, Israel and Ukraine to undertake investigations. On 10 May, the Committee received letters from Bulgaria and Ukraine informing it of the current stage of their investigations.

The Committee observed that it did not have any specific monitoring mechanism to ensure the implementation of the arms embargo and relied solely on the cooperation of States and organizations to provide pertinent information.

UNMEE financing

2000-2001 budget

ACABQ report (March). In a March report [A/55/688/Add.1], ACABQ reviewed the report of the Secretary-General on the financing of UNMEE for the period from 31 July 2000 to 30 June 2001 [A/55/666 & Corr.1]. ACABQ had first reviewed the Secretary-General's report in 2000 [YUN 2000, p. 179] and had decided to resume consideration in 2001. Having received further information from the Secretariat on the structure of UNMEE and on financial requirements based on revised staffing estimates, ACABQ recommended that the General Assembly approve an appropriation and assessment of $180 million gross for 31 July 2000 to 30 June 2001, inclusive of the commitment authority of $150 million gross approved by the Assembly in resolution 55/237 [YUN 2000, p. 179]. The Committee expected to examine resources for the period 1 July 2001 to 30 June 2002 during the autumn of 2001, based on actual experience during the period ending 30 June 2001.

GENERAL ASSEMBLY ACTION (April)

On 12 April [meeting 98], the General Assembly, on the recommendation of the Fifth Committee [A/55/711/Add.1], adopted **resolution 55/252 A** without vote [agenda item 176].

Financing of the United Nations Mission in Ethiopia and Eritrea

The General Assembly,

Having considered the report of the Secretary-General on the financing of the United Nations Mission in Ethiopia and Eritrea and the related reports of the Advisory Committee on Administrative and Budgetary Questions,

Bearing in mind Security Council resolution 1312 (2000) of 31 July 2000, regarding the establishment of the United Nations Mission in Ethiopia and Eritrea, and the subsequent resolutions by which the Council extended the mandate of the Mission, the latest of which was its resolution 1344(2001) of 15 March 2001,

Recalling its resolution 55/237 of 23 December 2000 on the financing of the Mission,

Reaffirming that the costs of the Mission are expenses of the Organization to be borne by Member States in accordance with Article 17, paragraph 2, of the Charter of the United Nations,

Recalling its previous decisions regarding the fact that, in order to meet the expenditures caused by the Mission, a different procedure is required from that applied to meet expenditures of the regular budget of the United Nations,

Taking into account the fact that the economically more developed countries are in a position to make relatively larger contributions and that the economically less developed countries have a relatively limited capacity to contribute towards such an operation,

Bearing in mind the special responsibilities of the States permanent members of the Security Council, as indicated in General Assembly resolution 1874(S-IV) of 27 June 1963, in the financing of such an operation,

Mindful of the fact that it is essential to provide the Mission with the necessary financial resources to enable it to fulfil its responsibilities under the relevant resolutions of the Security Council,

1. *Takes note* of the status of contributions to the United Nations Mission in Ethiopia and Eritrea as at 28 February 2001, including the contributions outstanding in the amount of 101.9 million United States dollars, representing 92 per cent of the total assessed contributions, notes that some 13 per cent of the Member States have paid their assessed contributions in full, and urges all other Member States concerned to ensure the payment of their outstanding assessed contributions;

2. *Expresses its appreciation* to those Member States which have paid their assessed contributions in full;

3. *Expresses concern* about the financial situation with regard to peacekeeping activities, in particular as regards the reimbursements to troop contributors that bear additional burdens owing to overdue payments by Member States of their assessments;

4. *Urges* all other Member States to make every possible effort to ensure the payment of their assessed contributions to the Mission in full and on time;

5. *Expresses concern* at the delay experienced by the Secretary-General in deploying and providing adequate resources to some recent peacekeeping missions, in particular those in Africa;

6. *Emphasizes* that all future and existing peacekeeping missions shall be given equal and non-discriminatory treatment in respect of financial and administrative arrangements;

7. *Also emphasizes* that all peacekeeping missions shall be provided with adequate resources for the effective and efficient discharge of their respective mandates;

8. *Reiterates its request* to the Secretary-General to make the fullest possible use of facilities and equipment at the United Nations Logistics Base at Brindisi, Italy, in order to minimize the costs of procurement

for the Mission, and for this purpose requests the Secretary-General to speed up the implementation of the asset management system at all peacekeeping missions in accordance with its resolution 52/1 A of 15 October 1997;

9. *Endorses* the conclusions and recommendations contained in the report of the Advisory Committee on Administrative and Budgetary Questions, and requests the Secretary-General to ensure their full implementation;

10. *Requests* the Secretary-General to take all necessary action to ensure that the Mission is administered with a maximum of efficiency and economy;

11. *Also requests* the Secretary-General to report to the General Assembly at the earliest possible time on how the concept of operations affects and can justify the proposed structure of the Mission, including its senior staff component;

12. *Further requests* the Secretary-General, in order to reduce the cost of employing General Service staff, to continue efforts to recruit local staff for the Mission against General Service posts, commensurate with the requirements of the Mission;

13. *Decides* to appropriate the amount of 180 million dollars gross (177,866,900 dollars net) for the operation of the Mission for the period from 31 July 2000 to 30 June 2001, inclusive of the amount of 150 million dollars gross (148,220,200 dollars net) authorized by the General Assembly in its resolution 55/237;

14. *Decides also*, as an ad hoc arrangement, taking into account the amount of 150 million dollars gross (148,220,200 dollars net) already apportioned under the terms of its resolution 55/237, to apportion the additional amount of 30 million dollars gross (29,646,700 dollars net) for the period from 31 July 2000 to 30 June 2001 among Member States in accordance with the composition of groups set out in paragraphs 3 and 4 of its resolution 43/232 of 1 March 1989, as adjusted by subsequent relevant resolutions and decisions, for the apportionment of peacekeeping appropriations, the latest of which were its resolution 52/230 of 31 March 1998 and its decisions 54/456 to 54/458 of 23 December 1999 for the period 1998-2000, and its resolutions 55/235 and 55/236 of 23 December 2000 for the period 2001-2003, the scale of assessments for 2000 to be applied against a portion thereof, that is, 13,791,045 dollars gross (13,628,632 dollars net), which is the amount pertaining to the period ending 31 December 2000, and the scale of assessments for 2001 to be applied against the balance, that is, 16,208,955 dollars gross (16,018,068 dollars net) for the period from 1 January to 30 June 2001;

15. *Decides further* that, in accordance with the provisions of its resolution 973 A (X) of 15 December 1955, there shall be set off against the apportionment among Member States, as provided for in paragraph 14 above, their respective share in the Tax Equalization Fund of the estimated additional staff assessment income of 353,300 dollars approved for the Mission for the period from 31 July 2000 to 30 June 2001, 162,413 dollars being the amount pertaining to the period ending 31 December 2000 and the balance, that is, 190,887 dollars, pertaining to the period from 1 January to 30 June 2001;

16. *Emphasizes* that no peacekeeping mission shall be financed by borrowing funds from other active peacekeeping missions;

17. *Encourages* the Secretary-General to continue to take additional measures to ensure the safety and security of all personnel under the auspices of the United Nations participating in the Mission;

18. *Invites* voluntary contributions to the Mission in cash and in the form of services and supplies acceptable to the Secretary-General, to be administered, as appropriate, in accordance with the procedure and practices established by the General Assembly;

19. *Decides* to keep under review during its fifty-fifth session the item entitled "Financing of the United Nations Mission in Ethiopia and Eritrea".

ACABQ report (April). ACABQ reported in April on financing of the UN peacekeeping operations [A/55/874] (see p. 93). With regard to UN-MEE and four other missions, the Secretariat had informed the Committee that, although it was possible to prepare initial maintenance level budgets for the period from 1 July 2001 to 30 June 2002 for submission to the Assembly during the resumed fifty-fifth (2001) session, the initial budgets would be overtaken by events and would have to be prepared anew, recosted and resubmitted at a later date. The UNMEE budget would be submitted to the Assembly during its fifty-sixth session, later in the year. ACABQ therefore recommended that the Assembly approve bridging action for UNMEE for 1 July to 31 December 2001, based on the authorized budget of $180 million gross ($177,866,900 net) for 1 July 2000 to 30 June 2001, in the amount of $90 million gross ($88,933,450 net).

GENERAL ASSEMBLY ACTION (June)

On 14 June [meeting 103], the General Assembly, on the recommendation of the Fifth Committee [A/55/711/Add.2], adopted **resolution 55/252 B** without vote [agenda item 176].

Financing of the United Nations Mission in Ethiopia and Eritrea

The General Assembly,

Having considered the report of the Advisory Committee on Administrative and Budgetary Questions,

Bearing in mind Security Council resolution 1312 (2000) of 31 July 2000, regarding the establishment of the United Nations Mission in Ethiopia and Eritrea, and the subsequent resolutions by which the Council extended the mandate of the Mission, the latest of which was resolution 1344(2001) of 15 March 2001,

Recalling its resolutions 55/237 of 23 December 2000 and 55/252 A of 12 April 2001 on the financing of the Mission,

Reaffirming the general principles underlying the financing of United Nations peacekeeping operations, as stated in General Assembly resolutions 1874(S-IV) of 27 June 1963, 3101(XXVIII) of 11 December 1973 and 55/235 of 23 December 2000,

Mindful of the fact that it is essential to provide the Mission with the necessary financial resources to enable it to fulfil its responsibilities under the relevant resolutions of the Security Council,

1. *Reaffirms* its resolution 49/233 A of 23 December 1994, in particular those paragraphs regarding the peacekeeping budgetary cycles, which should be adhered to in the future budgeting process, where possible;

2. *Takes note* of the status of contributions to the United Nations Mission in Ethiopia and Eritrea as at 30 April 2001, including the contributions outstanding in the amount of 127.8 million United States dollars, representing some 81 per cent of the total assessed contributions, notes that some 10 per cent of the Member States have paid their assessed contributions in full, and urges all other Member States concerned to ensure payment of their outstanding assessed contributions;

3. *Expresses its appreciation* to those Member States which have paid their assessed contributions in full;

4. *Expresses concern* about the financial situation with regard to peacekeeping activities, in particular as regards the reimbursements to troop contributors that bear additional burdens owing to overdue payments by Member States of their assessments;

5. *Urges* all other Member States to make every possible effort to ensure payment of their assessed contributions to the Mission in full and on time;

6. *Expresses concern* at the delay, in general, experienced by the Secretary-General in deploying and providing adequate resources to some recent peacekeeping missions, in particular those in Africa, and notes with satisfaction the comments of the Advisory Committee on Administrative and Budgetary Questions in paragraph 24 of its report, regarding the quick and efficient deployment of the military contingents of the Mission;

7. *Emphasizes* that all future and existing peacekeeping missions shall be given equal and non-discriminatory treatment in respect of financial and administrative arrangements;

8. *Also emphasizes* that all peacekeeping missions shall be provided with adequate resources for the effective and efficient discharge of their respective mandates;

9. *Reiterates its request* to the Secretary-General to make the fullest possible use of facilities and equipment at the United Nations Logistics Base at Brindisi, Italy, in order to minimize the costs of procurement for the Mission;

10. *Endorses* the recommendation contained in paragraph 10 *(b)* of the report of the Advisory Committee;

11. *Requests* the Secretary-General to report to the General Assembly at the earliest possible time on how the concept of operations affects and can justify the proposed structure of the Mission, including its senior staff component;

12. *Also requests* the Secretary-General to take all necessary action to ensure that the Mission is administered with a maximum of efficiency and economy;

13. *Further requests* the Secretary-General, in order to reduce the cost of employing General Service staff, to continue efforts to recruit local staff for the Mission against General Service posts, commensurate with the requirements of the Mission;

14. *Authorizes* the Secretary-General to enter into commitments in the amount of 90 million dollars gross (88,933,450 dollars net) for the maintenance of the Mission for the period from 1 July to 31 December 2001, and decides to appropriate the amount of 5,444,104 dollars gross (4,777,737 dollars net) for the support account for peacekeeping operations and the amount of 568,706 dollars gross (510,695 dollars net) for the United Nations Logistics Base, representing the prorated share of the Mission in the support account and Logistics Base requirements for the period from 1 July 2001 to 30 June 2002;

15. *Decides* to apportion among Member States the amount of 37.5 million dollars gross (37,055,604 dollars net) for the period from 1 July to 15 September 2001, in accordance with the levels set out in General Assembly resolution 55/235 and adjusted by the Assembly in its resolution 55/236 of 23 December 2000, and taking into account the scale of assessments for the year 2001, as set out in its resolution 55/5 B of 23 December 2000;

16. *Decides also* that, in accordance with the provisions of its resolution 973(X) of 15 December 1955, there shall be set off against the apportionment among Member States, as provided for in paragraph 15 above, their respective share in the Tax Equalization Fund of the estimated staff assessment income of 444,396 dollars approved for the Mission for the period from 1 July to 15 September 2001;

17. *Decides further* to apportion among Member States the amount of 52.5 million dollars gross (51,877,846 dollars net) for the period from 16 September to 31 December 2001, at a monthly rate of 15 million dollars gross (14,822,242 dollars net), in accordance with paragraph 15 above, subject to the decision of the Security Council to extend the mandate of the Mission beyond 15 September 2001;

18. *Decides* that, in accordance with the provisions of its resolution 973(X), there shall be set off against the apportionment among Member States, as provided for in paragraph 17 above, their respective share in the Tax Equalization Fund of the estimated staff assessment income of 622,154 dollars approved for the Mission for the period from 16 September to 31 December 2001;

19. *Decides also* to apportion among Member States the amount of 5,444,104 dollars gross (4,777,737 dollars net) for the support account and the amount of 568,706 dollars gross (510,695 dollars net) for the United Nations Logistics Base for the period from 1 July 2001 to 30 June 2002, in accordance with paragraph 15 above, and taking into account the scale of assessments for the years 2001 and 2002, as set out in General Assembly resolution 55/5 B, the scale of assessments for the year 2001 to be applied against a portion thereof, that is, 2,722,052 dollars gross (2,388,869 dollars net) for the support account and 284,353 dollars gross (255,348 dollars net) for the Logistics Base for the period from 1 July to 31 December 2001, and the scale of assessments for the year 2002 to be applied against the balance, that is, 2,722,052 dollars gross (2,388,868 dollars net) for the support account and 284,353 dollars gross (255,347 dollars net) for the Logistics Base for the period from 1 January to 30 June 2002;

20. *Decides further* that, in accordance with the provisions of its resolution 973(X), there shall be set off against the apportionment among Member States, as provided for in paragraph 19 above, their respective share in the Tax Equalization Fund of the estimated staff assessment income of 666,367 dollars for the sup-

port account and 58,011 dollars for the United Nations Logistics Base approved for the period from 1 July 2001 to 30 June 2002, 333,183 dollars for the support account and 29,005 dollars for the Logistics Base being amounts pertaining to the period from 1 July to 31 December 2001 and the balance, that is, 333,184 dollars for the support account and 29,006 dollars for the Logistics Base, pertaining to the period from 1 January to 30 June 2002;

21. *Emphasizes* that no peacekeeping mission shall be financed by borrowing funds from other active peacekeeping missions;

22. *Encourages* the Secretary-General to continue to take additional measures to ensure the safety and security of all personnel under the auspices of the United Nations participating in the Mission;

23. *Invites* voluntary contributions to the Mission in cash and in the form of services and supplies acceptable to the Secretary-General, to be administered, as appropriate, in accordance with the procedure and practices established by the General Assembly;

24. *Decides* to include in the provisional agenda of its fifty-sixth session the item entitled "Financing of the United Nations Mission in Ethiopia and Eritrea".

2001-2002 budget

On 8 November, the Secretary-General submitted to the General Assembly the proposed UNMEE budget for the period from 1 July 2001 to 30 June 2002 [A/56/610], which amounted to $208,879,800 gross ($204,969,700 net). Additionally, non-budgeted voluntary contributions in kind amounted to $200,000. The Secretary-General recommended that the Assembly approve an appropriation for the proposed budget, assess the additional amount of $14,439,900 gross ($13,551,400 net) for 1 July to 31 December 2001, assess $43,516,625 gross ($42,702,021 net) for 1 January to 15 March 2002, and assess $60,923,275 gross ($59,782,829 net) for 16 March to 30 June 2002, should the Security Council decide to continue the Mission's mandate.

Having reviewed the Secretary-General's proposed budget, ACABQ, on 28 November [A/56/661], taking into consideration the pattern of expenditure for 1 July to 31 December 2001, which showed an unspent balance of $38.6 million, compared with the apportionment of $90 million, recommended that the Assembly approve an appropriation and assessment of $198.4 million gross for 1 July 2001 to 30 June 2002, inclusive of $90 million gross appropriated and assessed by the Assembly in resolution 55/252 B (above) for 1 July to 31 December 2001.

GENERAL ASSEMBLY ACTION

On 24 December [meeting 92], the General Assembly, on the recommendation of the Fifth Committee [A/56/714 & Corr.1], adopted **resolution 56/250** without vote [agenda item 137].

Financing of the United Nations Mission in Ethiopia and Eritrea

The General Assembly,

Having considered the report of the Secretary-General on the financing of the United Nations Mission in Ethiopia and Eritrea and the related report of the Advisory Committee on Administrative and Budgetary Questions,

Bearing in mind Security Council resolution 1312 (2000) of 31 July 2000, by which the Council established the United Nations Mission in Ethiopia and Eritrea, and the subsequent resolutions by which the Council extended the mandate of the Mission, the latest of which was resolution 1369(2001) of 14 September 2001,

Recalling its resolution 55/237 of 23 December 2000 on the financing of the Mission and its subsequent resolutions thereon, the latest of which was resolution 55/252 B of 14 June 2001,

Reaffirming the general principles underlying the financing of United Nations peacekeeping operations, as stated in General Assembly resolutions 1874(S-IV) of 27 June 1963, 3101(XXVIII) of 11 December 1973 and 55/235 of 23 December 2000,

Noting with appreciation that voluntary contributions have been made to the Mission,

Mindful of the fact that it is essential to provide the Mission with the necessary financial resources to enable it to fulfil its responsibilities under the relevant resolutions of the Security Council,

1. *Takes note* of the status of contributions to the United Nations Mission in Ethiopia and Eritrea as at 15 November 2001, including the contributions outstanding in the amount of 100.3 million United States dollars, representing, regrettably, 36 per cent of the total assessed contributions, notes that some 12 per cent of the Member States have paid their assessed contributions in full, and urges all other Member States concerned, in particular those in arrears, to ensure payment of their outstanding assessed contributions;

2. *Expresses its appreciation* to those Member States that have paid their assessed contributions in full and on time and urges all other Member States to make every possible effort to ensure payment of their assessed contributions to the Mission in full and on time;

3. *Expresses concern* about the financial situation with regard to peacekeeping activities, in particular as regards the reimbursements to troop contributors, that bear additional burdens owing to overdue payments by Member States of their assessments;

4. *Also expresses concern* at the delay experienced by the Secretary-General in deploying and providing adequate resources to some recent peacekeeping missions, in particular those in Africa;

5. *Emphasizes* that all future and existing peacekeeping missions shall be given equal and non-discriminatory treatment in respect of financial and administrative arrangements;

6. *Also emphasizes* that all peacekeeping missions shall be provided with adequate resources for the effective and efficient discharge of their respective mandates;

7. *Reiterates its request* to the Secretary-General to make the fullest possible use of facilities and equipment at the United Nations Logistics Base at Brindisi,

Italy, in order to minimize the costs of procurement for the Mission;

8. *Endorses* the conclusions and recommendations contained in the report of the Advisory Committee on Administrative and Budgetary Questions, and requests the Secretary-General to ensure their full implementation;

9. *Requests* the Secretary-General to take all necessary action to ensure that the Mission is administered with a maximum of efficiency and economy;

10. *Also requests* the Secretary-General, in order to reduce the cost of employing General Service staff, to continue efforts to recruit local staff for the Mission against General Service posts, commensurate with the requirements of the Mission;

11. *Decides* to appropriate the amount of 200,279,308 dollars gross (196,227,505 dollars net) for the maintenance of the Mission for the twelve-month period from 1 July 2001 to 30 June 2002, inclusive of the amount of 1,879,308 dollars gross (1,737,605 dollars net) for the support account for peacekeeping operations, in addition to the amount of 5,444,104 dollars gross (4,777,737 dollars net) already appropriated for the support account, and the amount of 568,706 dollars gross (510,695 dollars net) already appropriated for the United Nations Logistics Base by the General Assembly in its resolution 55/252 B, and inclusive of the amount of 90 million dollars gross (88,933,450 dollars net) authorized by the Assembly in resolution 55/252 B;

12. *Decides also*, taking into account the amount of 90 million dollars gross (88,933,450 dollars net) already apportioned for the period from 1 July to 31 December 2001 and the amount of 6,012,810 dollars gross (5,288,432 dollars net) already apportioned for the period from 1 July 2001 to 30 June 2002 in accordance with the provisions of its resolution 55/252 B, to apportion among Member States the amount of 52,412,641 dollars gross (50,567,834 dollars net) for the period from 1 July 2001 to 15 March 2002 in accordance with the levels set out in General Assembly resolution 55/235, as adjusted by its resolution 55/236 of 23 December 2000, and taking into account the scale of assessments for the years 2001 and 2002 as set out in its resolution 55/5 B of 23 December 2000, the scale of assessments for the year 2001 to be applied against a portion thereof, that is, 9.2 million dollars gross (8,311,500 dollars net) for the period from 1 July to 31 December 2001, and the scale of assessment for the year 2002 to be applied against the balance, that is, 43,212,641 dollars gross (42,256,334 dollars net) for the period from 1 January to 15 March 2002;

13. *Decides further* that, in accordance with the provisions of its resolution 973(X) of 15 December 1955, there shall be set off against the apportionment among Member States, as provided for in paragraph 12 above, their respective share in the Tax Equalization Fund of the estimated staff assessment income of 1,844,807 dollars approved for the Mission for the period from 1 July 2001 to 15 March 2002, 888,500 dollars being the amount pertaining to the period from 1 July to 31 December 2001, and the balance, that is, 956,307 dollars, pertaining to the period from 1 January to 15 March 2002;

14. *Decides* to apportion among Member States the amount of 57,866,667 dollars gross (56,726,221 dollars net) for the period from 16 March to 30 June 2002, at a monthly rate of 16,533,333 dollars gross (16,207,492 dollars net) in accordance with the scheme set out in the present resolution and taking into account the scale of assessments for the year 2002 as set out in General Assembly resolution 55/5 B, subject to any decision by the Security Council to extend the mandate of the Mission beyond 15 March 2002;

15. *Decides also* that, in accordance with the provisions of its resolution 973(X), there shall be set off against the apportionment among Member States, as provided for in paragraph 14 above, their respective share in the Tax Equalization Fund of the estimated staff assessment income of 1,140,446 dollars approved for the Mission for the period from 16 March to 30 June 2002;

16. *Emphasizes* that no peacekeeping mission shall be financed by borrowing funds from other active peacekeeping missions;

17. *Encourages* the Secretary-General to continue to take additional measures to ensure the safety and security of all personnel under the auspices of the United Nations participating in the Mission;

18. *Invites* voluntary contributions to the Mission in cash and in the form of services and supplies acceptable to the Secretary-General, to be administered, as appropriate, in accordance with the procedure and practices established by the General Assembly;

19. *Decides* to keep under review during its fifty-sixth session the item entitled "Financing of the United Nations Mission in Ethiopia and Eritrea".

Also on 24 December, the Assembly decided that the agenda item on UNMEE financing would remain for consideration during its resumed fifty-sixth (2002) session (**decision 56/464**) and that the Fifth Committee should continue its consideration of the item at that session (**decision 56/458**).

Somalia

In 2001, Somalia continued to struggle for national reconciliation and restoration in the wake of the Arta (Djibouti) Peace Conference, which took place in 2000 [YUN 2000, p. 215]. The Conference, an initiative of the Government of Djibouti, brought together the Somali factions, with the exception of Puntland and Somaliland, and resulted in the formation of a Transitional National Assembly and the election of President Abdikassim Salad Hassan to head Somalia's Transitional National Government (TNG). President Hassan continued his efforts to bring on board the factions that had remained outside the Arta process, including those that formed the Somali Reconciliation and Restoration Council in March. He was also instrumental in initiating conferences with faction leaders in Kenya, under the auspices of President Daniel arap Moi. In October, the Security Council reiterated its support for the Arta peace process, which, it believed, was the most viable basis for peace and national reconciliation in Somalia.

Having completed a security assessment of Mogadishu, as requested by the Council in January, the Secretary-General was unable to recommend the deployment of a post-conflict peace-building mission in Somalia. However, he did propose that the mandate of the United Nations Political Office for Somalia (UNPOS), with its headquarters in Nairobi, be renewed for the biennium 2002-2003.

The humanitarian situation in Somalia continued to be of concern, due to poor harvests and internal conflict. Despite efforts by the United Nations and other humanitarian and development agencies, the unfavourable security conditions prevented assistance from reaching the needy on a continuous and unimpeded basis. In December, the General Assembly, in **resolution 56/106**, called on the Secretary-General to continue to mobilize international humanitarian, rehabilitation and reconstruction assistance for Somalia (see p. 834).

SECURITY COUNCIL ACTION (January)

On 11 January [meeting 4254], the Security Council held a private meeting to consider the Secretary-General's 19 December 2000 report on the situation in Somalia [YUN 2000, p. 217]. It also heard a briefing by the Prime Minister of the Transitional Government of Somalia, Ali Khalif Galaydh. The Prime Minister responded to questions posed by Council members.

On the same day [meeting 4255], following consultations among Council members, the President made statement **S/PRST/2001/1** on behalf of the Council:

The Security Council notes with appreciation the Secretary-General's report of 19 December 2000 on the situation in Somalia and reaffirms its commitment to a comprehensive and lasting settlement of the situation in Somalia, consistent with the principles of the Charter of the United Nations, bearing in mind respect for the sovereignty, territorial integrity, political independence and unity of Somalia.

The Council welcomes and supports the outcome of the Arta peace conference, the establishment of the Transitional National Assembly and the Transitional National Government. It expresses gratitude for the efforts undertaken by the Government and people of Djibouti in convening the peace conference. Furthermore, it recognizes with appreciation the impetus provided to the process by the Intergovernmental Authority on Development, including the mandate extended by the ministerial meeting in Djibouti in March 2000.

The Council further welcomes the efforts of the Transitional National Government to promote reconciliation within Somalia. It strongly urges all political groups in the country, in particular those which have remained outside the Arta peace process, to engage in peaceful and constructive dialogue with the Transitional National Government in order to promote national reconciliation and facilitate the democratic elections scheduled for 2003 as called for in the Transitional National Charter. It further calls upon all groups, in particular armed movements, to support and participate in the demobilization efforts undertaken by the Transitional National Government. It encourages the Transitional National Government to continue, in a spirit of constructive dialogue, the process of engaging all groups in the country, including in the north-eastern and north-western areas, with the view to preparing for the installation of permanent governance arrangements through the democratic process.

The Council underlines the massive challenges facing Somalia with respect to reconstruction and development, and the immediate need for urgent assistance, particularly in the areas of demobilization (with special attention to measures to combat HIV/AIDS and other communicable diseases), disarmament and rehabilitation of basic infrastructure. It calls upon the United Nations, its Member States and specialized agencies, non-governmental organizations as well as the Bretton Woods institutions to assist in addressing these challenges.

The Council, emphasizing the importance of respect for human rights and international humanitarian law, notes with concern that the humanitarian and security situation remains fragile in several parts of Somalia, including Mogadishu. It strongly condemns attacks by armed groups on civilians and humanitarian personnel and calls upon all Somalis to respect fully the security and safety of personnel of the United Nations and its specialized agencies, the International Committee of the Red Cross and of non-governmental organizations, and to guarantee their complete freedom of movement and safe access throughout Somalia.

The Council reiterates to all States their obligation to comply with the measures imposed by resolution 733(1992) of 23 January 1992 and urges each State to take the necessary steps to ensure full implementation and enforcement of the arms embargo. It strongly condemns the illegal supply of weapons to recipients in Somalia. It reiterates its call upon all States, the United Nations and other international organizations and entities to report to the Committee established by resolution 751(1992) of 24 April 1992 information on possible violations of the arms embargo.

The Council insists that all States should refrain from any military intervention in the internal situation in Somalia and that the territory of Somalia should not be used to undermine the stability in the subregion.

The Council welcomes the Secretary-General's intention to put in place a trust fund for peace-building in Somalia. It notes that despite the recent positive developments in Somalia, the security situation in the country is still a cause for serious concern. The Council therefore invites the Secretary-General to prepare a proposal for a peace-building mission for Somalia. Such a proposal should, with specific attention to the security situation in the country, outline possible ways to advance the peace process further.

The Council remains seized of the matter.

Communications. On 8 January [S/2001/19], Ethiopia informed the Security Council of its concern regarding the situation in Somalia. As a country sharing a 2,000-kilometre border with Somalia and a haven for tens of thousands of Somalian refugees, Ethiopia would be the second greatest beneficiary from a stable and peaceful Somalia. It would be a tragedy if an effort was not made to build on the momentum for peace and national reconciliation created at the Arta Peace Conference. On 10 January [S/2001/27], Ethiopia referred to an 8 January British Broadcasting Corporation report that Somalia's Prime Minister had criticized Ethiopia for interfering in the affairs of Somalia. It observed that there was real hope for peace in Somalia but only if TNG ceased trying to create artificial enemies.

In a 21 March letter to the Security Council President [S/2001/263], Somalia's Prime Minister described some actions taken to engage the factions that were not part of the Arta Conference. He also listed activities by Ethiopia that he viewed as interferences in Somalia's internal affairs and as posing a threat to Somalia's unity, territorial integrity and political independence.

In a 4 April response [S/2001/325], Ethiopia rejected Somalia's portrayal of it as a State bent on "destabilizing" Somalia and stated that its spirit of goodwill towards Somalia would continue.

On 10 August [S/2001/792], the EU Presidency expressed concern about the recent outbreak of conflict in Mogadishu and other parts of Somalia. It welcomed the creation of the National Commission for Reconciliation and Property Settlement (NCRPS) and drew the attention of all parties involved to the need for guaranteed safety of all humanitarian agencies and their personnel operating in Somalia.

Report of Secretary-General (October). In an 11 October report [S/2001/963], submitted in response to a request contained in Security Council presidential statement S/PRST/1999/16 [YUN 1999, p. 171], the Secretary-General described events in Somalia since his December 2000 report [YUN 2000, p. 217].

TNG, led by President Hassan, appointed a 25-member NCRPS, and the Transitional National Assembly approved a Chief Justice of the Supreme Court. It also succeeded in bringing on board two of the five faction leaders in Mogadishu who had originally opposed the Arta peace process. Although TNG negotiated with the militias holding the Mogadishu seaport in early 2001, it remained closed because some faction leaders

would not agree to its reopening. TNG also sent delegations to various parts of Somalia for talks with clan leaders; while they met with some success in the Hiran region, they were ambushed by opposition militia in Gedo and Bakool. TNG claimed that the attacks were carried out with Ethiopia's backing, allegations that Ethiopia denied. On 18 June, the Chairman of the Lower Juba Alliance announced the formation of an 11-member inter-clan council which allied itself with TNG. However, several faction leaders who attended the Arta Conference subsequently joined those opposed to TNG. The Mogadishu faction leaders and the others hostile to the Arta peace process announced on 23 March the formation of the Somali Reconciliation and Restoration Council, which aimed to hold an all-inclusive national reconciliation conference, within six months, to form a representative Transitional Government of National Unity. That conference was postponed until 2002.

On 17 April, the Djibouti Government closed its border with "Somaliland", which claimed to have separated from the rest of Somalia, following its administration's destruction of a consignment of cigarettes allegedly belonging to a Djibouti businessman. Since then there had been no air, land or sea communications between Djibouti and Somaliland, despite an attempt by Mohamed Ibrahim Egal, Somaliland's leader, to improve relations. On 31 May, the Somaliland administration carried out a referendum on a new constitution, the first article of which asserted the region's independence. Officials claimed that 97 per cent of 1.3 million voters endorsed the new constitution. Mr. Egal then called on the international community to recognize Somaliland. The "Puntland" administration and TNG opposed the referendum, citing the 1960 Act of Union. In July, Mr. Egal announced the formation of a new political party, the Allied People's Democratic Party (UDUB), in preparation for parliamentary and presidential elections in 2002. Elders remained divided on UDUB's constitutionality.

The "Puntland" administration's mandate expired on 30 June. The administration, headed by Colonel Abdullahi Yusuf, rather than undertake presidential and parliamentary elections as stipulated in the 1998 Transitional Charter of Puntland, requested and received a three-year extension from the House of Representatives. The Chairman of the Supreme Court declared the extension unconstitutional and, as provided for in the Charter, assumed office as the legal interim President of Puntland. That decision was upheld by a meeting of elders despite Colonel Yusuf's attempt to unseat the Chairman by suspending him from the Supreme Court. The interim President organized a conference (Garowe, 26 August) to set the future course of Puntland. Meanwhile, Colonel Yusuf announced on 12 August that he was still President of Puntland and declared the Garowe conference to be illegal.

Regional and other peace initiatives on Somalia included a call by the summit meeting of the League of Arab States (Amman, Jordan, 26-27 March) for funding of $54 million for the absorption and resettlement of militias and the restoration of State institutions. In early April, President Omar Hassan al-Bashir of the Sudan, as Chairman of the Intergovernmental Authority on Development (IGAD), appointed a Special Envoy for Somalia, renewing expectations that the IGAD mechanism for the peace process in Somalia would be put in place. The OAU Secretary-General, following OAU's thirty-seventh summit (Lusaka, Zambia, 2-7 July), announced his intention to field a mission to consult with all parties to the conflict. While attending that summit, the UN Secretary-General took the opportunity to meet President Hassan and encouraged him to make further efforts towards the completion of the Arta process. The Secretary-General's Representative continued to meet with all parties in Somalia and with regional actors.

Economic and social systems sustaining lives and livelihoods in Somalia continued to be disrupted by more than a decade of conflict, exacerbated by recurrent drought and flooding. UN agencies adopted a four-part humanitarian and development strategy, the accomplishment of which, the Secretary-General stated, was possible only if adequate financial and material resources were available. To support the humanitarian, recovery and development activities, the consolidated inter-agency appeal for 2001, requesting $129.6 million, was launched (see p. 834).

The security situation in Somalia remained tenuous and included a militia attack on the Spanish Médecins sans frontières (MSF-Spain) compound that resulted in the abduction of six UN staff and the MSF-Spain workers, who were later released. Numerous clashes took place between militias, and fighting in Puntland and Somaliland resulted in the temporary suspension of UN activities in those regions. The United Nations conducted two more security assessments in Mogadishu in August and September, which showed that the situation had improved somewhat and that there were fewer weapons in the streets. However, the Secretary-General concluded that the security situation did not make it possible to deploy a post-conflict peace-building mission in Somalia at that time. He recommended that the mandate of UNPOS be extended for a further two years (2002-2003) (see p. 212). The Secretary-General stated his intention to consult all concerned on the feasibility and usefulness of setting up a Committee of Friends of Somalia to focus on ways and means of drawing attention to Somalia's needs and to help mobilize funds.

SECURITY COUNCIL ACTION (October)

On 31 October [meeting 4401], following consultations among Security Council members, the President made statement **S/PRST/2001/30** on behalf of the Council:

The Security Council, having considered the report of the Secretary-General of 11 October 2001 and having held a public meeting on 19 October 2001 (S/PV.4392 and S/PV.4392 resumption 1), reaffirms its commitment to a comprehensive and lasting settlement of the situation in Somalia, consistent with the principles of the Charter of the United Nations, and bearing in mind its respect for the sovereignty, territorial integrity, political independence and unity of Somalia.

The Council reiterates its support for the outcome of the Arta peace conference, the establishment of the Transitional National Assembly and the Transitional National Government. It encourages the Transitional National Government to continue, in the spirit of constructive dialogue, the process of engaging all groups in the country, including in the north-eastern and north-western areas, with the view to preparing for the installation of permanent governance arrangements through the democratic process.

The Council believes that the Arta peace process continues to be the most viable basis for peace and national reconciliation in Somalia. It urges the Transitional National Government, political and traditional leaders and factions in Somalia to make every effort to complete, without preconditions, the peace and reconciliation process through dialogue and involvement of all parties in a spirit of mutual accommodation and tolerance. It calls on all parties to refrain from actions that undermine the Arta peace process. The Council emphasizes that while the search for a national solution continues, unwavering attention must be paid to achieving local political settlements as well.

The Council expresses its support for the Transitional National Government's ongoing efforts to enhance security in the Mogadishu area and to make operational the National Commission for Reconciliation and Property Settlement, which should be independent, as foreseen in the Transitional National Charter. The Council emphasizes the necessity for efforts against international terrorism in accordance with resolution 1373(2001) of 28 September 2001 and welcomes the stated intention of the Transitional National Government to take steps in this regard. The Council urges the international community, including through the Counterterrorism Committee established pursuant to resolution 1373(2001), to provide assistance to Somalia for the implementation of the aforementioned resolution.

The Council calls on the concerned States in the Horn of Africa to contribute constructively to the peace efforts in Somalia. It emphasizes that the situation in Somalia and the objective of long-term regional stability can most effectively be addressed if neighbouring States play a positive role, including in the process of rebuilding national institutions in Somalia.

The Council acknowledges Djibouti's major contribution to the Arta peace process and welcomes its continued role in this regard. It encourages the Intergovernmental Authority on Development, the Organization of African Unity/African Union and the League of Arab States to enhance their efforts to promote peace in Somalia.

The Council calls on all States and other actors to comply scrupulously with the arms embargo established by resolution 733(1992) of 23 January 1992. The Council insists that all States, in particular those of the region, should not interfere in the internal affairs of Somalia. Such interference could jeopardize the sovereignty, territorial integrity, political independence and unity of Somalia.

The Council insists that the territory of Somalia should not be used to undermine stability in the subregion.

The Council strongly condemns the attack on 13 October 2001 on a police station in Mogadishu, in which a number of officers and civilians were killed. It reiterates its condemnation of the attack on 27 March 2001 on the compound of Médecins sans Frontières in Mogadishu and the subsequent abduction of international personnel, and demands that those responsible must be brought to justice. The Council notes that these attacks were launched at the same time as the consideration of a possible United Nations peace-building mission for Somalia.

The Council emphasizes that no measure of violence can alleviate the plight of the Somali people nor bring stability, peace or security to their country. It calls for an immediate end to all acts of violence in Somalia. Deliberate acts of violence should not be allowed to prevent the rehabilitation of Somalia's governing structures and the restoration of the rule of law throughout the country. In this context, the Council condemns the leaders of those armed factions who remain outside the peace process and continue to be obstacles to peace and stability in Somalia.

The Council expresses concern about the humanitarian situation in Somalia, in particular in southern areas, and in the Bay, Bakool, Gedo and Hiran regions due to the expected food insecurity and lack of rainfall in the October-December period. It draws attention to the urgent need for international assistance, inter alia, in covering food and water shortfalls, thereby also combating potentially further destabilizing stress migration and prevalence of disease. Noting that problems in livestock exports have also been a major influence in worsening the economic and humanitarian situation, the Council calls on all States and on all authorities within Somalia to cooperate in efforts to allow the resumption of such exports.

The Council notes with satisfaction that the United Nations, the Red Cross movement and non-governmental organizations continue to provide humanitarian and development assistance to all areas of Somalia. The Council calls upon all parties in Somalia to respect fully the security and safety of personnel of the United Nations, the International Committee of the Red Cross and non-governmental organizations, and to guarantee their complete freedom of movement and access throughout Somalia. The Council calls on Member States to respond urgently and generously to the United Nations consolidated inter-agency appeal for 2001, for which only 16 per cent of the identified needs have been financially provided thus far.

The Council requests the Secretary-General to take the following steps in support of the peace process in Somalia:

(i) Dispatch a headquarters-led inter-agency mission to carry out a comprehensive assessment, based on the existing general United Nations standards, of the security situation in Somalia, including in Mogadishu;

(ii) Prepare proposals for how the United Nations may further assist in the demobilization of militia members, and the training of police personnel from the Transitional National Government;

(iii) Invite donors to make contributions to the trust fund for peace-building in Somalia, to be put in place as proposed in the 19 December 2000 report of the Secretary-General, with a view to facilitate targeted activities in line with proposals developed pursuant to paragraph (ii) above;

(iv) Consider the scope for adjustments, as appropriate, to the mandate for the United Nations Political Office for Somalia;

(v) Consult all concerned on finding practical and constructive ways of achieving the following objectives:

(a) Promoting coherency of policy approaches towards Somalia and consolidating support for peace and reconciliation in the country;

(b) Facilitating exchange of information; and

(c) Finding ways and means of drawing attention to Somalia's needs related to national reconciliation and development.

The effort to achieve the objectives stated in subparagraphs (a), (b) and (c) above should have a focus in the region and include close interaction with the Intergovernmental Authority on Development and its Partners Forum, the Organization of African Unity/African Union, the League of Arab States and the Security Council;

(vi) Intensify, through urgent contacts with donor countries and relevant non-governmental organizations, the efforts for humanitarian and development assistance in Somalia; and

(vii) Submit reports, at least every four months, on the situation in Somalia and the efforts to promote the peace process, including updates on the scope and contingency planning for launching a peace-building mission for Somalia. The next report, due on 31 January 2002, should provide an update on the activities undertaken pursuant to paragraphs (i) to (vi) above.

The Council remains seized of the matter.

Communication. On 6 November [S/2001/1063], Somalia transmitted to the Security Council President the communiqué that was issued following the Somalia Reconciliation Meeting (Nairobi, 1-4 November), which was attended by TNG and the Somali Reconciliation and Restoration Council. The two parties adopted an agenda as the basis for future deliberations.

Later developments. In a later report that covered developments in Somalia towards the end of 2001 [S/2002/189], the Secretary-General stated that, on 12 October, the Transitional National Assembly put forward a motion of no-confidence in TNG, accusing it of failing to move the national reconciliation process forward. The motion passed on 28 October and, on 12 November, Hassan Abshir Farah was named the new Prime Minister. With regard to the political crisis in "Puntland", the protracted Garowe conference of elders finally elected Jama Ali Jama as the new President of the "Puntland State of Somalia" on 14 November. Colonel Yusuf rejected the outcome and returned with his forces to Garowe. Mr. Jama retreated to Bosasso claiming that Ethiopian troops had crossed into Somalia in support of Colonel Yusuf, an allegation that Ethiopia dismissed as baseless.

As to the situation in "Somaliland", Mr. Egal continued to state that he was not interested in participating in any reconciliation talks on Somalia. His administration had attempted to institute a multiparty system, as opposed to governance under the guidance of the traditional council of elders, an effort that was being resisted. Seven registered political organizations were expected to compete in municipal elections, which were to have been held on 20 December following the passing of an electoral law on 17 November. However, the elections were postponed, and Mr. Egal was given a one-year extension by the upper house of the "Somaliland Parliament".

President Moi of Kenya convened two rounds of meetings (Nairobi, 1-4 November and 13-24 December) between TNG and some factions outside the Arta process. Agreements signed in December called for an all-inclusive government to be formed. As a result, TNG proposed to the Transitional National Assembly that the number of cabinet members and parliamentarians be increased to facilitate a broader-based government, and the Kenyan authorities announced their intention to establish an international secretariat on Somalia.

Following the Joint IGAD Partners Forum (Addis Ababa, 20 November), the Special Envoy of the President of the Sudan on Somalia led a joint IGAD mission to Somalia and Addis Ababa (20-31 December). Its recommendations included a call for a national reconciliation conference.

In the wake of the 11 September terrorist attacks in the United States, the United States President signed an executive order on 23 September blocking the assets of organizations and individuals linked to terrorism, including Al-Itihaad al-Islamiya, a Somali organization. The list was further expanded to include a number of Somali individuals and Al-Barakaat Group of Companies Somalia, Ltd. On 31 October, President Hassan met with the Secretary-General's Representative for Somalia and denied any linkage between his administration and Al-Itihaad al-Islamiya. When the United States Treasury shut down the Al-Barakaat Group offices in the United States, on 7 November, claiming the Group to be a principal source of funding for Osama bin Laden, President Hassan set up a commission to look into the Group's records.

UNPOS

On 16 November [S/2001/1097], the Secretary-General proposed to the Security Council that the mandate for UNPOS, established in 1995 [YUN 1995, p. 400], be renewed for the biennium 2002-2003, pending an improvement in the security situation that would allow him to submit a proposal for a peace-building office in Somalia.

On 21 November [S/2001/1098], the Council President informed the Secretary-General that his decision concerning UNPOS had been noted by the Council.

Arms embargo

The Security Council Committee established pursuant to resolution 751(1992) [YUN 1992, p. 202] concerning Somalia continued throughout 2001 to monitor the arms embargo against Somalia imposed by resolution 733(1992) [ibid., p. 199]. In June, the Council decided that the embargo would not apply to non-lethal military equipment intended solely for humanitarian or protective use.

In a 6 June note [S/2001/564], the Council President announced the election of Noureddine Mejdoub (Tunisia) as Chairman of the Committee, with Jamaica and Norway as Vice-Chairmen. Their terms were to end on 31 December 2001.

SECURITY COUNCIL ACTION

On 19 June [meeting 4332], the Security Council unanimously adopted **resolution 1356(2001)**. The draft [S/2001/589] was prepared in consultations among Council members.

The Security Council,

Reaffirming its resolutions 733(1992) of 23 January 1992 and 751(1992) of 24 April 1992,

Expressing its desire to see peace and security return to Somalia,

Recognizing the ongoing efforts of the United Nations, its specialized agencies and humanitarian organizations to deliver humanitarian assistance to Somalia,

Acting under Chapter VII of the Charter of the United Nations,

1. *Reiterates* to all States their obligation to comply with the measures imposed by resolution 733(1992), and urges each State to take the necessary steps to ensure full implementation and enforcement of the arms embargo;

2. *Decides* that the measures imposed by paragraph 5 of resolution 733(1992) shall not apply to protective clothing, including flak jackets and military helmets, temporarily exported to Somalia by United Nations personnel, representatives of the media and humanitarian and development workers and associated personnel for their personal use only;

3. *Decides also* that the measures imposed by paragraph 5 of resolution 733(1992) shall not apply to supplies of non-lethal military equipment intended solely for humanitarian or protective use, as approved in advance by the Committee established pursuant to resolution 751(1992) (the Committee);

4. *Requests* the Committee to give consideration to and decide upon requests for the exemptions set out in paragraph 3 above;

5. *Decides* to remain seized of the matter.

Security Council Committee. On 21 December, the Chairman of the Security Council Committee concerning Somalia submitted to the Council a report covering its activities in 2001 [S/2001/1259]. Following the adoption of Council resolution 1356(2001), the Committee approved draft new consolidated guidelines for the conduct of its work. On 20 July, the Committee approved a United Kingdom request to export specialized demining equipment to Somalia. The Committee reiterated that, in the absence of a specific monitoring mechanism to ensure the effective implementation of the arms embargo, it relied solely on the cooperation of States and organizations in a position to provide information on violations of the embargo.

UNOSOM II financing

The United Nations Operation in Somalia (UNOSOM), established by Security Council resolution 751(1992) [YUN 1992, p. 202], was withdrawn from Somalia in March 1995 [YUN 1995, p. 400].

On 7 September, the General Assembly decided to include in the draft agenda of its fifty-sixth session the item entitled "Financing of the United Nations Operation in Somalia II" (**decision 55/496**).

On 24 December, the Assembly decided that the item would remain for consideration at its resumed (2002) fifty-sixth session (**decision 56/464**) and that the Fifth Committee should continue its consideration of the item at that session (**decision 56/458**).

North Africa

Western Sahara

In 2001, the United Nations considered new alternatives to holding a referendum for the people of Western Sahara, a Non-Self-Governing Territory, to choose between independence or integration with Morocco, as outlined in the 1990 settlement plan. That plan, approved by Security Council resolution 658(1990) [YUN 1990, p. 920], outlined terms for a referendum and was agreed to by Morocco and the Frente Popular para la Liberación de Saguia el-Hamra y de Río de Oro (POLISARIO). Progress on its implementation over the following decade had been slow, despite the continuous efforts of the United Nations. The United Nations Mission for the Referendum in Western Sahara (MINURSO), established by Council resolution 690(1991) [YUN 1991, p. 794] to implement the plan, continued to monitor the 1991 ceasefire between Morocco and POLISARIO [ibid., p. 796] and to report on developments.

Tension in Western Sahara mounted in the early months of the year when POLISARIO restricted the movement of MINURSO patrols in western areas of the Territory.

In May, the Secretary-General's Personal Envoy, James A. Baker III (United States), proposed a draft framework agreement on the status of Western Sahara, by which the population of Western Sahara, through their executive, legislative and judicial bodies, would have competence over local issues while Morocco would be responsible for foreign relations, national security and defence. The executive powers would be held by an Executive, elected by a vote of those identified by the MINURSO Identification Commission, and an Assembly. Morocco indicated its support for the plan, while POLISARIO objected to it on the grounds that it provided for the integration of Western Sahara into Morocco. Algeria also protested that it would confirm the illegal occupation of the Territory by Morocco and would violate the right of the Saharan people to self-determination.

The Identification Commission continued its work on establishing a list of voters by considering appeals following the issuance in 1999 and 2000 of provisional parts of the list.

On 29 June, the Council extended MINURSO's mandate until 30 November in order to allow the Secretary-General's Personal Envoy to meet with Morocco, POLISARIO, Algeria and Mauritania to discuss the proposed draft framework agreement. On 27 November, MINURSO's mandate was extended until 28 February 2002 to allow the Personal Envoy more time for those consultations.

Report of Secretary-General (February). The Secretary-General, in response to Security Council resolution 1324(2000) [YUN 2000, p. 227], on 20 February submitted a report on the situation concerning Western Sahara [S/2001/148], which covered developments since his previous report of 25 October 2000 [YUN 2000, p. 225]. He observed that the reporting period was marked by a deterioration in relations between the two parties and there was no progress in implementing the settlement plan.

The crossing, in early January, of the Paris-Dakar car rally into Western Sahara contributed to an increase in tensions. On previous occasions, the rally had crossed Western Sahara with prior consultations by the organizers with the two parties. For the 2001 crossing, however, only Morocco was contacted for permission. In a communiqué of 22 December 2000, POLISARIO indicated that the passage of the rally would constitute a violation of the ceasefire and that it would resume military activities. Morocco responded with an equally strong statement. As the rally date neared, MINURSO reported a partial mobilization and military movements by POLISARIO. In a 5 January statement, the Secretary-General's Special Representative, William Eagleton (United States), emphasized that any military action by either party would constitute a violation of the ceasefire. On 7 January, the rally crossed into the Territory and POLISARIO stated that the event was a breach of the ceasefire, for which it held Morocco responsible, but it would suspend its decision regarding the resumption of military activities. While no action was taken, the event increased animosity between the parties and raised tensions in the area.

The Identification Commission continued its work on establishing a list of voters, specifically on consolidation of files and data quality control, with particular attention to preparations for the technical review of the appeals admissibility and for appeal hearings on substance. The Commission had received a total of 131,038 appeals, following the issuance of the first part of the provisional voter list in July 1999 (containing the names of 84,251 applicants identified as eligible to vote, out of 144,369 interviewed by the Com-

mission) and of the second part of the list in January 2000 (containing the names of 2,161 eligible applicants, out of 51,220 interviewed). The overwhelming majority of the appeals filed (115,645) was against exclusion from the provisional voter list, with most of the appeals (108,708) falling under the article of the Appeals Procedures dealing with applicants rejected by the Identification Commission who were bringing new evidence. Most of those appellants had listed one or two witnesses to support their claims, with only limited documentary evidence, especially regarding appellants from tribal groupings H41, H61 and J51/52. The remaining appeals were based on claims that the Commission failed to convoke or to identify them (1,260), that they were blocked by force majeure (5,079), or that they were not identified although they were on the 1991 revised census list (643). Another category of appellants included those who were contesting the inclusion of other persons on the provisional voter list (15,393). Regarding potential additional appellants, Morocco estimated that those who reached 18 years of age after 31 December 1993 might number about 30,000, while POLISARIO estimated that number at 11,000, including 5,000 in Tindouf, Algeria.

As at 16 February, the strength of MINURSO's military component stood at 230 military personnel. It continued to monitor the 1991 ceasefire between the Royal Moroccan Army and POLISARIO military units and to implement the military agreements between MINURSO and the two parties on the marking and disposal of mines and unexploded ordnance, and the exchange of related information, until December 2000. On 31 December, POLISARIO liaison officers advised MINURSO that it would not be allowed within 800 metres of POLISARIO unit locations. On 17 January, POLISARIO announced restrictions on the movement of MINURSO air and ground reconnaissance patrols and, since 3 January, all POLISARIO units had deployed outside their confinement locations without prior notification to MINURSO. Both decisions were in violation of the military agreements between MINURSO and the two parties. On 6 January, POLISARIO protested to MINURSO that a Royal Moroccan Army unit had entered the buffer zone (a 5-kilometre strip from the berm), thus violating the military agreements pertaining to the ceasefire. Morocco rejected the allegation. The MINURSO civilian police component, at a strength of 47 officers, protected files and other materials at the Identification Commission centres at Laayoune and Tindouf.

The Secretary-General regretted that he could not report any progress in implementing the settlement plan or towards determining whether Morocco, as administering Power, was prepared to support some devolution of authority for all inhabitants and former inhabitants of Western Sahara. On the advice of his Personal Envoy, the Secretary-General recommended that the MINURSO mandate be extended for two months, until 30 April 2001, to see whether Morocco was prepared to support some devolution of authority. Failing such support, MINURSO would be directed to begin hearing the pending appeals from the identification process on an expedited basis. The Personal Envoy also advised the Secretary-General that that was the last request he would support for a mandate extension to provide extra time for Morocco to decide on devolution of authority.

Communications (February/March). In a 21 February letter to the Security Council President [S/2001/155], Algeria said that since there had not been any progress in the quest for a mutually acceptable political solution, MINURSO should begin hearing the pending appeals from the identification process, thereby resuming the implementation of the settlement plan. Algeria believed that the question of the appeals should and could be settled if the United Nations decided to mobilize the necessary resources, thereby enabling the holding of a referendum.

Morocco, on 27 February [S/2001/178], said that since the beginning of the referendum process, the adversaries of Morocco's territorial integrity had waged a campaign against the identification of Saharans who were not in the Territory at the time of the 1974 Spanish census, though they were aware that many were in northern Morocco, Mauritania and other places. However, it was unrealistic to attempt to reduce to the appeals process alone the many problems that had hampered the implementation of the settlement plan.

Cuba, in its capacity as Chairman of the Group of Latin American and Caribbean States, on 30 March [A/55/867-S/2001/308], commenting on Western Sahara, reaffirmed that the settlement plan, including the holding of a referendum, was the only choice accepted by both parties to ensure the right to self-determination and achieve a just and lasting peace.

SECURITY COUNCIL ACTION (February)

On 27 February [meeting 4284], the Security Council unanimously adopted **resolution 1342 (2001)**. The draft [S/2001/165] was prepared in consultations among Council members.

The Security Council,

Reaffirming all its previous resolutions on Western Sahara, in particular resolutions 1108(1997) of 22 May

1997, 1292(2000) of 29 February 2000, 1301(2000) of 31 May 2000, 1309(2000) of 25 July 2000 and 1324(2000) of 30 October 2000, and also its resolution 1308(2000) of 17 July 2000,

Recalling the relevant principles contained in the Convention on the Safety of United Nations and Associated Personnel of 9 December 1994,

Welcoming the report of the Secretary-General of 20 February 2001 and the observations and recommendations contained therein, and expressing full support for the role and work of the Personal Envoy,

Reiterating full support for the continued efforts exerted by the United Nations Mission for the Referendum in Western Sahara to implement the settlement plan and agreements adopted by the parties to hold a free, fair and impartial referendum for the self-determination of the people of Western Sahara,

Noting that fundamental differences between the parties over the interpretation of the main provisions of the settlement plan remain to be resolved,

1. *Decides* to extend the mandate of the United Nations Mission for the Referendum in Western Sahara until 30 April 2001, with the expectation that the parties, under the auspices of the Personal Envoy of the Secretary-General, will continue to try to resolve the multiple problems relating to the implementation of the settlement plan and try to agree upon a mutually acceptable political solution to their dispute over Western Sahara;

2. *Requests* the Secretary-General to provide an assessment of the situation before the end of the present mandate;

3. *Decides* to remain seized of the matter.

Report of Secretary-General (April). In response to Council resolution 1342(2001), the Secretary-General submitted a 24 April report on the situation concerning Western Sahara [S/2001/398]. During the period since his February report, the Secretary-General's Personal Envoy consulted with the two parties and other interested parties and his Special Representative also pursued consultations.

Following the passage of the Paris-Dakar car rally, tensions remained high and the integrity of the ceasefire was called into question by unmonitored deployment of POLISARIO forces and their restrictions on the movement of MINURSO military observers. MINURSO ground patrols continued to be restricted to areas not closer than 800 metres to POLISARIO combat units and observation posts, and its air reconnaissance was limited to the 30-kilometre area immediately east of the berm. On 15 March, Moroccan military authorities informed MINURSO of plans to begin construction of an asphalt road in the south-west corner of the Territory, across the 5-kilometre buffer strip and into Mauritania near Nouadhibou. On the same day, the Royal Moroccan Army deployed troops in the Guerguerat area, allegedly to provide security for contractors working on the road. The Special Representative and the Force Commander warned Morocco that the proposed road building could be in violation of the ceasefire agreement. At the time of the report, there was no evidence of road construction.

The Identification Commission completed the consolidation and quality control of the files received during the second round of appeals and corrected some minor errors on the provisional voter list. The first draft of a manual on hearings on the substance was produced, and its usefulness and practicability tested in simulation sessions with actual appeal files.

UNHCR continued to carry out its responsibilities for the Saharan refugees in the four Tindouf camps in Algeria, monitoring their welfare and coordinating activities with the host Government and implementing partners. It held a meeting on 22 February with the World Food Programme and the European Community Humanitarian Office in Geneva on redressing the basic food situation in the camps. UNHCR held a workshop in Algiers from 1 to 4 April to discuss its 2001 and 2002 implementation and operations plan with the host Government, NGO partners, donor countries, UN agencies and refugees.

The Secretary-General saw no progress towards overcoming the obstacles to implementation of the settlement plan during the reporting period. However, he believed that substantial progress had been made towards determining whether Morocco, as the administering Power in Western Sahara, was prepared to offer or support some devolution of authority for all the inhabitants and former inhabitants of the Territory. Because of that progress, his Personal Envoy recommended that MINURSO's mandate be extended for two months, until 30 June, to provide time to consult further with the parties concerning both a possible devolution of authority and a possible solution to implementation of the settlement plan. The Secretary-General shared those views.

SECURITY COUNCIL ACTION (April)

On 27 April [meeting 4315], the Security Council unanimously adopted **resolution 1349(2001)**. The draft [S/2001/413] was prepared in consultations among Council members.

The Security Council,

Reaffirming all its previous resolutions on Western Sahara, in particular resolutions 1108(1997) of 22 May 1997, 1292(2000) of 29 February 2000, 1301(2000) of 31 May 2000, 1309(2000) of 25 July 2000, 1324(2000) of 30 October 2000 and 1342(2001) of 27 February 2001, and also its resolution 1308(2000) of 17 July 2000,

Recalling the relevant principles contained in the Convention on the Safety of United Nations and Associated Personnel of 9 December 1994,

Welcoming the report of the Secretary-General of 24 April 2001 and the observations and recommendations contained therein, and expressing full support for the role and work of the Personal Envoy,

Reiterating full support for the continued efforts exerted by the United Nations Mission for the Referendum in Western Sahara to implement the settlement plan and agreements adopted by the parties to hold a free, fair and impartial referendum for the self-determination of the people of Western Sahara,

Noting that fundamental differences between the parties over the interpretation of the main provisions of the settlement plan remain to be resolved,

1. *Decides* to extend the mandate of the United Nations Mission for the Referendum in Western Sahara until 30 June 2001, with the expectation that the parties, under the auspices of the Personal Envoy of the Secretary-General, will continue to try to resolve the multiple problems relating to the implementation of the settlement plan and try to agree upon a mutually acceptable political solution to their dispute over Western Sahara;

2. *Requests* the Secretary-General to provide an assessment of the situation before the end of the present mandate;

3. *Decides* to remain seized of the matter.

Report of Secretary-General (June). On 20 June [S/2001/613], the Secretary-General described developments in Western Sahara since his April report. During that period, his Personal Envoy met with officials of Morocco to determine if it was prepared to offer or support some devolution of authority for all inhabitants and former inhabitants. He also met with President Abdelaziz Bouteflika and other Algerian officials to present a draft "Framework agreement on the status of Western Sahara", which was annexed to the Secretary-General's report. The draft stated that the population of Western Sahara, through their executive, legislative and judicial bodies, would have exclusive competence over internal issues, while Morocco would have exclusive competence over external matters, such as foreign relations, national security, defence, weapons and the preservation of territorial integrity. The flag, currency, customs, postal and telecommunication systems of Morocco would be the same for Western Sahara. The executive authority would be vested in an Executive, who would be elected by individuals identified by the Identification Commission as qualified, for a term of four years, and thereafter by majority vote of the Assembly. Assembly members would be directly elected for terms of four years. Judges would be from Western Sahara. All laws and court decisions would comply with the Moroccan constitution. Within five years, a referendum on the final status of the Territory would be held.

On 22 May, President Bouteflika transmitted Algeria's comments on the proposed agreement, which were also annexed to the Secretary-General's report. In Algeria's view, the proposal presented certain weaknesses and imbalances. The UN Secretariat, in a statement annexed to the report, analysed Algeria's remarks. The Algerian memorandum made three points: that the proposed agreement favoured and prepared the ground for eventual integration of Western Sahara with Morocco; that the framework went against the principle of self-determination; and that the Personal Envoy was not following his mandate but was focusing instead solely on a political solution.

The Personal Envoy met with the POLISARIO Secretary-General, Mohamed Abdelaziz, and other members of his party in Tindouf to review the proposed agreement. Mr. Abdelaziz stated that anything other than independence meant integration with Morocco and that he would not discuss the proposal. In a letter of 28 May to the Personal Envoy, also annexed to the Secretary-General's report, he offered some proposals to overcome obstacles preventing the implementation of the settlement plan, dealing with the appeals issue, the repatriation of refugees, respect for the outcome of the referendum, humanitarian issues and confidence-building measures, and post-referendum guarantees. The UN Secretariat analysed the proposals in comments annexed to the Secretary-General's report, stating that they raised three kinds of difficulties: some proposals, while offering concessions, attached conditions; other proposals would require action by the Security Council; and others would require clarification. Overall, some of them sought to provide technical solutions, but they did not address the main problem with the implementation of the settlement plan as a whole, namely the inability of the United Nations to implement any measures unless both parties agreed to cooperate.

The Secretary-General reported that Morocco had resumed construction of an asphalt road in the south-western corner of the Territory. In mid-May, MINURSO and several Member States contacted the Moroccan authorities and requested them to suspend the road construction. Subsequent MINURSO patrols confirmed that no roadwork was under way.

The Identification Commission continued with simulation workshops, and feedback from those sessions was used in preparing a manual on the hearings on the substance. A meeting in Agadir (26-27 May) evaluated the Commission's activities and adopted the Manual on Hearings on the Substance.

Discussions continued between MINURSO and POLISARIO on easing or lifting the restrictions on the Mission's freedom of movement east of the berm, but no progress was reported. On the western side of the berm, MINURSO patrols continued to visit Royal Moroccan Army ground units greater than company size. From 7 to 22 May, MINURSO confirmed the destruction, by the Royal Moroccan Army, of about 3,000 anti-tank mines, 37,000 anti-personnel mines and 27,000 detonators and munitions in the Ankesh area, near Smara. In total, 7.5 tons of mines and explosives were destroyed.

UNHCR continued its activities in the Tindouf camps for Western Saharan refugees. It undertook an assessment of their humanitarian welfare and concluded that their overall situation was precarious, particularly for the weak, the elderly, women and children.

The Secretary-General reviewed the implementation process since the 1991 adoption of the settlement plan. With the exception of the monitoring of the ceasefire, none of the main provisions of the plan had been fully implemented because of fundamental differences between the parties over its interpretation. The establishment of the electorate body for the referendum in Western Sahara had been, and remained, the most contentious issue. The difficulties in determining who was eligible to take part in the referendum were due in large part to the nomadic tradition of the Saharan people and the tribal structure of the society.

The Secretary-General observed that the United Nations had gone through an arduous process over 10 years to implement the settlement plan, involving his efforts and those of two previous Secretaries-General, five Special Representatives and his Personal Envoy. Because of the parties' unwillingness to work together to resolve problems, the United Nations had submitted proposals to bridge their differences, which the parties revised or diluted through long negotiations. The process had become a zero-sum game, which each side felt it had to win since the referendum would produce only one winner. That resulted in successive deadlocks in the identification process, which was the only substantial element of the settlement plan after the establishment of the ceasefire in 1991 that the United Nations began to try to implement. All other key issues remained unresolved, namely: the release of prisoners of war and Saharan political detainees; the repatriation of refugees, including security concerns; the code of conduct for the referendum campaign; and the lack of an enforcement mechanism for the results of the referendum. More significantly, implementation of the settlement plan required the cooperation of the two parties and the two neighbouring countries, Algeria and Mauritania. After four years of attempting to find ways to implement the settlement plan, and confronted with the failure of the parties to come up with any concrete proposals during the three rounds of consultations held from June to September 2000 [YUN 2000, p. 223], the Personal Envoy concluded that there were serious doubts as to whether the settlement plan could be implemented in its current form, and the Secretary-General concurred with that view. Adjustments to the plan proved just as contentious as other provisions and did not resolve the long-term problems.

The Secretary-General and his Personal Envoy hoped that Morocco, POLISARIO, Algeria and Mauritania would agree to meet, either directly or through proximity talks under the auspices of the Personal Envoy, to discuss with specificity the elements of the proposed framework agreement, which aimed at reaching a resolution of the Western Sahara conflict in a way that did not foreclose self-determination, but provided for it. The Secretary-General especially invited Algeria, which had indicated its willingness to offer clarifications on the imbalances it found in the proposed framework agreement, to engage in those discussions and to negotiate changes. As the Personal Envoy had informed the parties, should they agree to discuss a political solution other than the settlement plan, they would not prejudice their final positions since nothing would be agreed until everything had been agreed. While the discussions on the proposed framework went on, the settlement plan would not be abandoned, but put on hold. The Identification Commission would suspend its activities, after safely storing all records.

Over the next five months, the Personal Envoy would invite the two parties, Algeria and Mauritania, to discuss the proposed framework agreement. Should he decide to continue those discussions after that period, the Secretary-General would recommend to the Security Council that MINURSO's mandate be extended. If the Personal Envoy concluded otherwise, the Council could review the Mission's mandate and consider its future role under the circumstances. The Secretary-General therefore recommended that the Council extend MINURSO's mandate for five months, until 30 November.

Communication (June). Algeria, on 21 June [S/2001/623], forwarded comments to the Security Council on the Secretary-General's report, claiming that the Secretariat had deliberately set out to prove that the settlement plan, which had been accepted by the parties and was supported by the international community, was not workable. The Secretariat had taken it upon itself to champion an autonomy plan and had decided to reject Algeria's objections. By those actions, the Secretariat was taking sides and intruding in an area that was strictly within the competence of Member States and the Council. On the substance of the recommendations in the report, Algeria, while it had indicated its willingness to support the Personal Envoy's efforts, could not accept that the settlement plan should be dismissed in such a cavalier manner and that the POLISARIO proposals for relaunching its implementation should be set aside without serious consideration by Morocco and the Council. Algeria called on the Council to reaffirm its commitment to the settlement plan and reiterate MINURSO's mandate in the same terms it had used for a year.

SECURITY COUNCIL ACTION (June)

On 29 June [meeting 4342], the Security Council unanimously adopted **resolution 1359(2001)**. The draft [S/2001/641] was prepared in consultations among Council members.

The Security Council,

Recalling all its previous resolutions on Western Sahara, in particular resolution 1108(1997) of 22 May 1997, and the statement by its President of 19 March 1997 (S/PRST/1997/16),

Recalling also its resolution 1308(2000) of 17 July 2000, and the relevant principles contained in the Convention on the Safety of United Nations and Associated Personnel of 9 December 1994,

Reaffirming the provisions contained in paragraph 2 of Article 1 of the Charter of the United Nations,

Having considered the report of the Secretary-General of 20 June 2001,

Expressing full support for the role and work of the Personal Envoy,

Reiterating full support for the ongoing efforts of the United Nations Mission for the Referendum in Western Sahara to implement the settlement plan and agreements adopted by the parties to hold a free, fair and impartial referendum for the self-determination of the people of the Western Sahara,

Taking into consideration the official proposals submitted by the Polisario Front in order to overcome the obstacles preventing the implementation of the settlement plan contained in annex IV to the report of the Secretary-General,

Taking into consideration also the draft Framework Agreement on the Status of Western Sahara contained in annex I to the report of the Secretary-General, which would provide for a substantial devolution of authority, which does not foreclose self-determination, and which indeed provides for it,

Taking into consideration further the memorandum of the Government of Algeria on the draft status for Western Sahara contained in annex II to the report of the Secretary-General,

Reaffirming its commitment to assist the parties to achieve a just and lasting solution to the question of Western Sahara,

1. *Decides*, as recommended by the Secretary-General in his report of 20 June 2001, to extend the mandate of the United Nations Mission for the Referendum in Western Sahara until 30 November 2001;

2. *Supports fully* the efforts of the Secretary-General to invite all the parties to meet directly or through proximity talks, under the auspices of his Personal Envoy, and encourages the parties to discuss the draft Framework Agreement and to negotiate any specific changes they would like to see in this proposal, as well as to discuss any other proposal for a political solution, which may be put forward by the parties, to arrive at a mutually acceptable agreement;

3. *Affirms* that while discussions referred to above go on, the official proposals submitted by the Polisario Front to overcome the obstacles preventing implementation of the Settlement Plan will be considered;

4. *Recalls* that according to the rules of the consultations established by the Personal Envoy nothing would be agreed until everything had been agreed, and therefore emphasizes that by engaging in these negotiations the parties will not prejudice their final positions;

5. *Urges* the parties to solve the problem of the fate of people unaccounted for, and calls on the parties to abide by their obligations under international humanitarian law to release without further delay all those held since the start of the conflict;

6. *Requests* the Secretary-General to provide an assessment of the situation before the end of the present mandate, and, as appropriate, recommendations on the future mandate and composition of the Mission;

7. *Decides* to remain seized of the matter.

Communications (October/November). The Secretary-General, on 30 October [S/2001/1041], informed the Security Council of his intention to appoint William Lacy Swing (United States) as his Special Representative for Western Sahara, with effect from 1 December. Mr. Swing would succeed William Eagleton (United States). On 2 November [S/2001/1042], the Council took note of his intention.

In a 12 November letter [S/2001/1067], the Secretary-General briefly described the activities of his Personal Envoy pursuant to Council resolution 1359(2001) (above). Mr. Baker informed the Secretary-General that he would need additional time for his consultations with the parties; accordingly, the Secretary-General proposed that the Council authorize a technical extension of MINURSO's mandate for two months, to 31 January 2002. The Secretary-General would report to the Council before that date.

SECURITY COUNCIL ACTION (November)

On 27 November [meeting 4427], the Security Council unanimously adopted **resolution 1380 (2001)**. The draft [S/2001/1109] was prepared in consultations among Council members.

The Security Council,
Reaffirming its resolution 1359(2001) of 29 June 2001 and its previous resolutions on the question of Western Sahara,
Taking note of the letter of the Secretary-General of 12 November 2001,
1. *Decides* to extend the mandate of the United Nations Mission for the Referendum in Western Sahara until 28 February 2002;
2. *Requests* the Secretary-General to keep the Council informed of all significant developments in an interim report by 15 January 2002 and to provide an assessment of the situation by 18 February 2002;
3. *Decides* to remain seized of the matter.

Further developments. The Personal Envoy held talks on the draft framework agreement with delegations of Algeria, Mauritania and POLISARIO in Pinedale, Wyoming, United States, from 27 to 29 August [S/2002/41]. Morocco was not invited to the meeting, since it had indicated its support of the document. The Personal Envoy had sought clarification from POLISARIO on its proposals of 28 May (see p. 217) and pointed out that Morocco's concurrence would be required for some proposals to be implemented and Council action would be required for others.

On 4 October, POLISARIO submitted a memorandum containing its position on the draft framework agreement, objecting to it on the grounds that it set the stage for integrating Western Sahara into Morocco. It urged the United Nations to continue trying to implement the settlement plan at all costs. Three days later, President Bouteflika forwarded Algeria's comments on the draft, stating its view that the draft framework would confirm the illegal occupation of the Territory by providing for its integration into Morocco and would thereby constitute a violation of the right of the Saharan people to self-determination. In order to overcome the disagreements between the two parties, and rather than resort to a period of so-called autonomy, Algeria said it would be better for the United Nations to take sovereign responsibility for the implementation of its own settlement plan for Western Sahara. It could do that by initiating a short transition period leading up to a referendum, during which the Territory would be placed under its exclusive authority and administration. Before such a transition period, certain conditions would have to be met, including the withdrawal of Moroccan troops from the Territory and the cantonment of the personnel authorized to remain there under the supervision of MINURSO, along with the cantonment of POLISARIO military forces. Morocco, in comments submitted on 10 November, stated that the legality of its presence and the legal grounds for its sovereignty had been well established for over

25 years. Algeria, it said, was attempting to escalate the situation by, among other things, entrusting the administration and security of the Territory to the United Nations instead of actively pursuing a peaceful settlement.

The situation of prisoners of war, persons unaccounted for and detainees remained a serious concern towards the end of 2001. In November, an ICRC representative interviewed 23 former POLISARIO combatants in Laayoune who had been unaccounted for, and the spouse of another. On 6 November, Morocco released 25 Saharan detainees, including 24 civilians arrested since 1999 and one military person arrested in 1979 and serving a life sentence. From 20 November to 3 December, an ICRC team visited the remaining 1,477 prisoners of war held by POLISARIO, providing them with medical and mail services. POLISARIO informed the team that one prisoner had recently died and another had escaped.

GENERAL ASSEMBLY ACTION

On 10 December [meeting 82], the General Assembly, having considered the Secretary-General's report summarizing developments in Western Sahara from 31 August 2000 to 30 June 2001 [A/56/159], on the recommendation of the Fourth (Special Political and Decolonization) Committee [A/56/557], adopted **resolution 56/69** without vote [agenda item 18].

Question of Western Sahara

The General Assembly,

Having considered in depth the question of Western Sahara,

Reaffirming the inalienable right of all peoples to self-determination and independence, in accordance with the principles set forth in the Charter of the United Nations and in General Assembly resolution 1514(XV) of 14 December 1960, containing the Declaration on the Granting of Independence to Colonial Countries and Peoples,

Recalling its resolution 55/141 of 8 December 2000,

Recalling also the agreement in principle given on 30 August 1988 by the Kingdom of Morocco and the Frente Popular para la Liberación de Saguia el-Hamra y de Río de Oro to the proposals of the Secretary-General of the United Nations and the Chairman of the Assembly of Heads of State and Government of the Organization of African Unity in the context of their joint mission of good offices,

Recalling further Security Council resolutions 658(1990) of 27 June 1990 and 690(1991) of 29 April 1991, by which the Council approved the settlement plan for Western Sahara,

Reaffirming the responsibility of the United Nations towards the people of Western Sahara, as provided for in the settlement plan,

Recalling all Security Council and General Assembly resolutions relating to the question of Western Sahara,

Noting with satisfaction the entry into force of the ceasefire in accordance with the proposal of the Secretary-General, and stressing the importance it attaches to the maintenance of the ceasefire as an integral part of the settlement plan,

Noting also with satisfaction the agreements reached by the two parties during their private direct talks aimed at the implementation of the settlement plan, and stressing the importance it attaches to a full, fair and faithful implementation of the settlement plan and the agreements aimed at its implementation,

Noting that, despite the progress achieved, difficulties remain in the implementation of the settlement plan which must be overcome,

Taking note of the resolutions of the Security Council relating to the question, including resolution 1359 (2001) of 29 June 2001,

Taking note also of the efforts of the Secretary-General and his Personal Envoy in search of a mutually acceptable political solution on the question of Western Sahara,

Welcoming the acceptance by the two parties of the detailed modalities for the implementation of the Secretary-General's package of measures relating to the identification of voters and the appeals process,

Having examined the relevant chapter of the report of the Special Committee on the Situation with regard to the Implementation of the Declaration on the Granting of Independence to Colonial Countries and Peoples,

Having also examined the report of the Secretary-General,

1. *Takes note* of the report of the Secretary-General;

2. *Commends* the Secretary-General and his Personal Envoy for their outstanding efforts and the two parties for the spirit of cooperation they have shown in the support they provide for those efforts;

3. *Takes note* of the agreements reached between the Kingdom of Morocco and the Frente Popular para la Liberación de Saguia el-Hamra y de Río de Oro for the implementation of the settlement plan during their private direct talks under the auspices of James Baker III, the Personal Envoy of the Secretary-General, and urges the parties to implement those agreements fully and in good faith;

4. *Urges* the two parties to continue their cooperation with the Secretary-General and his Personal Envoy, as well as with his Special Representative, and to refrain from undertaking anything that would undermine the implementation of the settlement plan and the agreements reached for its implementation and the continued efforts of the Secretary-General and his Personal Envoy;

5. *Calls upon* the two parties to cooperate fully with the Secretary-General, his Personal Envoy and his Special Representative in implementing the various phases of the settlement plan and in overcoming the difficulties that remain despite the progress so far achieved;

6. *Encourages* the parties to continue their discussions under the auspices of the Personal Envoy of the Secretary-General with a view to reaching a mutually acceptable agreement on the question of Western Sahara;

7. *Urges* the two parties to implement faithfully and loyally the Secretary-General's package of measures re-

lating to the identification of voters and the appeals process;

8. *Reaffirms* the responsibility of the United Nations towards the people of Western Sahara, as provided for in the settlement plan;

9. *Reiterates its support* for further efforts of the Secretary-General for the organization and supervision by the United Nations, in cooperation with the Organization of African Unity, of a referendum for self-determination of the people of Western Sahara that is impartial and free of all constraints, in conformity with Security Council resolutions 658(1990) and 690(1991), by which the Council approved the settlement plan for Western Sahara;

10. *Takes note* of the relevant resolutions of the Security Council, including resolutions 1349(2001) of 27 April 2001 and 1359(2001) of 29 June 2001;

11. *Urges* the parties to solve the problem of the fate of people unaccounted for, and calls on the parties to abide by their obligations under international humanitarian law to release without further delay all those held since the start of the conflict;

12. *Requests* the Special Committee on the Situation with regard to the Implementation of the Declaration on the Granting of Independence to Colonial Countries and Peoples to continue to consider the situation in Western Sahara, bearing in mind the positive ongoing implementation of the settlement plan, and to report thereon to the General Assembly at its fifty-seventh session;

13. *Invites* the Secretary-General to submit to the General Assembly at its fifty-seventh session a report on the implementation of the present resolution.

MINURSO

The military component of the United Nations Mission for the Referendum in Western Sahara (MINURSO), under the command of General Claude Buze (Belgium), continued to monitor the ceasefire between the Royal Moroccan Army and the POLISARIO military forces that came into effect in 1991 [YUN 1991, p. 796]. The Mission's military strength remained at the authorized figure of 230 throughout the year. The civilian police, under the command of Inspector General Om Prakash Rathor (India), fell from 47 officers to 26 at the end of the year. MINURSO civilian police officers continued to protect files and materials at the Identification Commission centres in Laayoune and Tindouf and to undertake training and planning activities.

MINURSO financing

In February [A/55/764], the Secretary-General reported to the General Assembly on MINURSO's financial performance for the period 1 July 1999 to 30 June 2000. Expenditures totalled $49,211,511 gross ($45,860,511 net), resulting in an unutilized balance of $2,913,400 gross ($2,312,800 net).

In another February report [A/55/794], the Secretary-General presented the proposed budget to maintain MINURSO from 1 July 2001 to 30 June 2002, which amounted to $48,849,600 gross ($45,280,800 net). In April [A/55/874/Add.7], ACABQ reviewed the proposed budget and recommended that the Assembly assess the requested amount at a monthly rate of $4,070,800 gross ($3,773,400 net), should the Security Council decide to extend MINURSO's mandate beyond 30 April 2001.

GENERAL ASSEMBLY ACTION

On 14 June [meeting 103], the General Assembly, on the recommendation of the Fifth Committee [A/55/966], adopted **resolution 55/262** without vote [agenda item 135].

Financing of the United Nations Mission for the Referendum in Western Sahara

The General Assembly,

Having considered the reports of the Secretary-General on the financing of the United Nations Mission for the Referendum in Western Sahara and the related reports of the Advisory Committee on Administrative and Budgetary Questions,

Bearing in mind Security Council resolution 690 (1991) of 29 April 1991, by which the Council established the United Nations Mission for the Referendum in Western Sahara, and the subsequent resolutions by which the Council extended the mandate of the Mission, the latest of which was resolution 1349(2001) of 27 April 2001,

Recalling its resolution 45/266 of 17 May 1991 on the financing of the Mission and its subsequent resolutions and decisions thereon, the latest of which was resolution 54/268 of 15 June 2000,

Reaffirming the general principles underlying the financing of United Nations peacekeeping operations, as stated in General Assembly resolutions 1874(S-IV) of 27 June 1963, 3101(XXVIII) of 11 December 1973 and 55/235 of 23 December 2000,

Noting with appreciation that voluntary contributions have been made to the Mission,

Mindful of the fact that it is essential to provide the Mission with the necessary financial resources to enable it to fulfil its responsibilities under the relevant resolutions of the Security Council,

1. *Takes note* of the status of contributions to the United Nations Mission for the Referendum in Western Sahara as at 30 April 2001, including the contributions outstanding in the amount of 89 million United States dollars, representing some 20 per cent of the total assessed contributions, notes that some 10 per cent of the Member States have paid their assessed contributions in full, and urges all other Member States concerned, in particular those in arrears, to ensure payment of their outstanding assessed contributions;

2. *Expresses its appreciation* to those Member States which have paid their assessed contributions in full;

3. *Expresses concern* about the financial situation with regard to peacekeeping activities, in particular as regards the reimbursements to troop contributors that

bear additional burdens owing to overdue payments by Member States of their assessments;

4. *Urges* all other Member States to make every possible effort to ensure payment of their assessed contributions to the Mission in full and on time;

5. *Expresses concern* at the delay experienced by the Secretary-General in deploying and providing adequate resources to some recent peacekeeping missions, in particular those in Africa;

6. *Emphasizes* that all future and existing peacekeeping missions shall be given equal and non-discriminatory treatment in respect of financial and administrative arrangements;

7. *Also emphasizes* that all peacekeeping missions shall be provided with adequate resources for the effective and efficient discharge of their respective mandates;

8. *Reiterates its request* to the Secretary-General to make the fullest possible use of facilities and equipment at the United Nations Logistics Base at Brindisi, Italy, in order to minimize the costs of procurement for the Mission;

9. *Endorses* the conclusions and recommendations contained in the report of the Advisory Committee on Administrative and Budgetary Questions, and requests the Secretary-General to ensure their full implementation;

10. *Requests* the Secretary-General to take all necessary action to ensure that the Mission is administered with a maximum of efficiency and economy;

11. *Also requests* the Secretary-General, in order to reduce the cost of employing General Service staff, to continue efforts to recruit local staff for the Mission against General Service posts, commensurate with the requirements of the Mission;

12. *Decides* to appropriate the amount of 50,481,396 dollars gross (46,716,010 dollars net) for the maintenance of the Mission for the period from 1 July 2001 to 30 June 2002, inclusive of the amount of 1,477,457 dollars gross (1,296,614 dollars net) for the support account for peacekeeping operations and the amount of 154,339 dollars gross (138,596 dollars net) for the United Nations Logistics Base, to be apportioned among Member States at a monthly rate of 4,206,783 dollars gross (3,893,001 dollars net) in accordance with the levels set out in General Assembly resolution 55/235, as adjusted by resolution 55/236 of 23 December 2000, and taking into account the scale of assessments for the years 2001 and 2002, as set out in its resolution 55/5 B of 23 December 2000, subject to the decision of the Security Council to extend the mandate of the Mission beyond 30 June 2001;

13. *Decides also* that, in accordance with the provisions of its resolution 973(X) of 15 December 1955, there shall be set off against the apportionment among Member States, as provided for in paragraph 12 above, their respective share in the Tax Equalization Fund of the estimated staff assessment income of 3,765,386 dollars approved for the Mission for the period from 1 July 2001 to 30 June 2002;

14. *Decides further* that, for Member States that have fulfilled their financial obligations to the Mission, there shall be set off against the apportionment, as provided for in paragraph 12 above, their respective share of the unencumbered balance of 2,913,400 dollars gross (2,312,800 dollars net) in respect of the period ending 30 June 2000, in accordance with the composition of groups set out in paragraphs 3 and 4 of General Assembly resolution 43/232 of 1 March 1989, as adjusted by subsequent relevant resolutions and decisions, for the ad hoc apportionment of peacekeeping appropriations, the latest of which were resolution 52/230 of 31 March 1998 and decisions 54/456 to 54/458 of 23 December 1999 for the period 1998-2000, and taking into account the scale of assessments for the year 2000, as set out in its resolutions 52/215 A of 22 December 1997 and 54/237 A of 23 December 1999;

15. *Decides* that, for Member States that have not fulfilled their financial obligations to the Mission, their share of the unencumbered balance of 2,913,400 dollars gross (2,312,800 dollars net) in respect of the period ending 30 June 2000 shall be set off against their outstanding obligations in accordance with the scheme set out in paragraph 14 above;

16. *Emphasizes* that no peacekeeping mission shall be financed by borrowing funds from other active peacekeeping missions;

17. *Encourages* the Secretary-General to continue to take additional measures to ensure the safety and security of all personnel under the auspices of the United Nations participating in the Mission;

18. *Invites* voluntary contributions to the Mission in cash and in the form of services and supplies acceptable to the Secretary-General, to be administered, as appropriate, in accordance with the procedure and practices established by the General Assembly;

19. *Decides* to include in the provisional agenda of its fifty-sixth session the item entitled "Financing of the United Nations Mission for the Referendum in Western Sahara".

On 24 December, the Assembly decided that the item on MINURSO financing would remain for consideration at its resumed fifty-sixth (2002) session (**decision 56/464**) and that the Fifth Committee should continue its consideration of the item at that session (**decision 56/458**).

Libyan Arab Jamahiriya

In January, the Scottish Court sitting in the Netherlands concluded the trial of two Libyan Arab Jamahiriya nationals accused of plotting the 1988 bombing of Pan Am flight 103 over Lockerbie, Scotland, which caused the deaths of 259 passengers and crew and 11 Lockerbie residents. The verdict was that one of the accused was guilty and the other was not. A number of regional organizations made comments on the case in letters to the Security Council and called on the Council to lift entirely the sanctions against Libya imposed by resolution 748(1992) [YUN 1992, p. 55] and suspended in 1999 [YUN 1999, p. 149].

Trial of Pan Am 103 bombing suspects

The Scottish Court sitting in the Netherlands gave its verdict on 31 January in the case against

Abdelbaset Ali Mohmed Al Megrahi and Al Amin Khalifa Fhimah, both nationals of the Libyan Arab Jamahiriya, accused of the Lockerbie crime. The three judges of the Court, by a unanimous decision, found the former guilty and the latter not guilty. On the same date, the United Kingdom forwarded to the Security Council President a copy of the Opinion of the Court on the case [S/2001/94].

On 7 February [S/2001/118], the Movement of Non-Aligned Countries expressed its satisfaction that Libya had fulfilled its commitments in accordance with the relevant Council resolutions and requested the Council to lift the sanctions against Libya. On 13 November [S/2001/1108], the Movement's six-member committee established to follow up the Lockerbie question reiterated that request. The African Group, on 14 February [S/2001/140], also called on the Council to lift the sanctions, as did the Community of Sahel Saharan States in a 13 February resolution [S/2001/182]. The Community also requested the immediate release of Abdelbaset Ali Mohmed Al Megrahi, who, it said, had been sentenced on political grounds unrelated to law or justice. In letters of 21 March and 9 April [S/2001/257, S/2001/349], the League of Arab States transmitted resolutions by its Foreign Ministers and its Council, respectively, demanding the release of the Libyan citizen convicted for political reasons unrelated to the law, demanding that the Security Council lift the sanctions, urging the Arab States to declare the sanctions null and void, and expressing support for Libya's right to obtain compensation for damage and suffering caused by the sanctions. In November [S/2001/1074], the League's Committee of Seven entrusted with monitoring the Lockerbie issue reaffirmed those resolutions. In similar action, the heads of State of OAU adopted an 11 July resolution [S/2001/769] calling on the Council to lift sanctions against Libya, demanding the release of the unjustly convicted Libyan citizen and reaffirming Libya's right to compensation. The OAU committee established to follow up the Lockerbie issue reiterated that position on 4 December [S/2001/1152].

1986 attack against Libya

The Libyan Arab Jamahiriya, on 21 June [S/2001/624], protested to the Security Council that it had failed to take action against the United States when it attacked Libya on 15 April 1986 [YUN 1986, p. 252]. In contrast, the Council had acted speedily when the United States made demands regarding the Lockerbie affair, despite a lack of any legal basis or any evidence. Libya stated that the case of the United States attack would remain open before the Council until it adopted a resolution calling for those responsible to be brought to trial and the victims' families compensated.

The General Assembly, by **decision 56/449** of 21 December, deferred consideration of the item "Declaration of the Assembly of Heads of State and Government of the Organization of African Unity on the aerial and naval military attack against the Socialist People's Libyan Arab Jamahiriya by the present United States Administration in April 1986" and included it in the provisional agenda of its fifty-seventh (2002) session.

Sudan

During 2001, the Sudan continued the efforts it began in 2000 [YUN 2000, p. 218] to cooperate with the international community, among other things, acceding to anti-terrorism conventions, improving relations with neighbouring countries and discharging its obligations under various Security Council resolutions. As a result, the Council, in September, terminated the sanctions it had imposed against the Sudan in 1996.

Sanctions

On 9 April [S/2001/341], the League of Arab States transmitted to the Security Council President a resolution, adopted by the thirteenth Arab Summit Conference (Amman, Jordan, 28-29 March), which endorsed the call made by the Sudan in 2000 [YUN 2000, p. 218] for the sanctions against it to be lifted. That call had also been endorsed by several other groups in 2000 [ibid., p. 219]. Those sanctions, imposed under Council resolutions 1044(1996) [YUN 1996, p. 129], 1054 (1996) [ibid., p. 130] and 1070(1996) [ibid., p. 131], called for States to reduce the level of diplomatic staff in the Sudan and restrict travel of Sudanese government officials and armed forces into or through their territories, and to deny Sudanese aircraft the right to use other countries' airspace.

SECURITY COUNCIL ACTION

On 28 September [meeting 4384], the Security Council adopted **resolution 1372(2001)** by vote (14-0-1). The draft [S/2001/916] was submitted by Bangladesh, Colombia, Jamaica, Mali, Mauritius, Singapore, Tunisia and Ukraine.

The Security Council,

Recalling its resolutions 1044(1996) of 31 January 1996, 1054(1996) of 26 April 1996 and 1070(1996) of 16 August 1996,

Noting the steps taken by the Government of the Sudan to comply with the provisions of resolutions 1044 (1996) and 1070(1996),

Noting in that respect the communications from the Permanent Representative of South Africa on behalf of the Non-Aligned Movement, and the Permanent Representative of Algeria on behalf of the League of Arab States and the Permanent Representative of Gabon on behalf of the African Group, and from the Secretary-General of the Organization of African Unity dated 20 June 2000,

Noting further the letter of the Acting Minister for Foreign Affairs of the Federal Democratic Republic of Ethiopia, dated 5 June 2000, and the letter of the Minister for Foreign Affairs of the Arab Republic of Egypt, dated 9 June 2000 supporting the lifting of sanctions imposed on the Republic of the Sudan,

Noting also the contents of the letter dated 1 June 2000 from the Minister of External Relations of the Republic of the Sudan addressed to the Secretary-General of the United Nations,

Welcoming the accession of the Republic of the Sudan to the relevant international conventions for the elimination of terrorism, its ratification of the 1997 International Convention for the Suppression of Terrorist Bombing and its signing of the 1999 International Convention for the Suppression of Financing of Terrorism,

Acting under Chapter VII of the Charter of the United Nations,

Decides to terminate, with immediate effect, the measures referred to in paragraphs 3 and 4 of resolution 1054(1996) and paragraph 3 of resolution 1070 (1996).

VOTE ON RESOLUTION 1372(2001):

In favour: Bangladesh, China, Colombia, France, Ireland, Jamaica, Mali, Mauritius, Norway, Russian Federation, Singapore, Tunisia, Ukraine, United Kingdom.
Against: None.
Abstaining: United States.

Speaking after the vote, the United States said that, although the Sudan had taken substantial steps to meet the specific demands of Security Council resolution 1054(1996) [YUN 1996, p. 130], it was concerned that the suspects wanted in connection with the 1995 assassination attempt on Egyptian President Hosni Mubarak in Addis Ababa [YUN 1995, p. 412] had not been turned over to the appropriate authorities; however, the United States believed, as did Egypt and Ethiopia, that the suspects were no longer in the Sudan. The United States welcomed the Sudan's recent efforts to apprehend extremists within the country who might have contributed to international terrorism and welcomed the fact that the Sudan was engaged in discussions with the United States Government on ways to combat terrorism. However, the United States had continuing concerns about the civil war in the Sudan, which had lasted some 18 years, and the abuse of human rights. For those reasons, the United States had abstained in the vote.

The Sudan said that resolution 1372(2001) provided an impetus for it to cooperate further in efforts to eliminate terrorism and to engage in the work of the international community.

Sudan-Uganda

On 25 January [S/2001/84], Uganda, in comments on the interim report of the United Nations Expert Panel on the Illegal Exploitation of Natural Resources and Other Forms of Wealth of the DRC (see p. 140), stated it had become involved in the DRC in order to protect its legitimate national security interests against Sudanese-backed rebels in the DRC. Responding to those comments on 4 February [S/2001/113], the Sudan stated that the excuses advanced by Uganda for its invasion of the DRC represented an attempt to distract attention from the plunder of the DRC's wealth—gold, diamonds and hardwoods—by members of the corrupt clique in Uganda.

Southern Africa

Angola

The armed conflict in Angola between the Government and the National Union for the Total Independence of Angola (UNITA) continued unabated in 2001, causing further population displacement. The estimated number of displaced persons rose to 4.1 million by the end of the year as guerrilla attacks forced people from their homes and into neighbouring countries, creating serious humanitarian situations. In late 2001, the Government was apparently gaining the upper hand in the struggle; it reported that UNITA's strength was weakened and the area under its control greatly reduced. UN officials expressed the view that there was a window of opportunity for the United Nations to advance the peace process. In talks with the United Nations, the Government said it would seek UN assistance in the electoral process for elections in 2002 and humanitarian aid.

There was no progress in implementing the 1994 Lusaka Protocol [YUN 1994, p. 348], by which the Government and UNITA had agreed that the State administration would be extended. However, by the end of the year both sides indicated a willingness to reopen discussions on achieving its terms. The Security Council held UNITA and its leader primarily responsible for the failure to implement the Protocol, which it regarded as the only viable basis for a political settlement of the conflict.

Sanctions against UNITA remained in force in 2001 and violations were investigated by the

Monitoring Mechanism established by resolution 1295(2000) [YUN 2000, p. 155]. That body issued two reports in 2001 on sanctions-busting in such areas as arms brokering and transport, petroleum sales, diamond trading and travel and residence of senior UNITA officials and their families. On three occasions during the year, the Security Council extended the mandate of the Mechanism. Angola affirmed that the sanctions had been effective in reducing UNITA's capacity to wage war.

The United Nations Office in Angola (UNOA) continued to monitor the situation in the country and to urge the parties to carry out their obligations under the Lusaka Protocol.

Political and military developments

Report of Secretary-General (April). The Secretary-General, in response to Security Council resolution 1294(2000) [YUN 2000, p. 152], submitted an April report on developments in Angola [S/2001/351]. The security situation remained tense in the early part of the year as government troops pursued residual UNITA forces and took control of municipalities previously under UNITA control. Reports indicated that UNITA soldiers were deserting in large numbers, taking advantage of the amnesty law announced in November 2000 [YUN 2000, p. 154] and transmitted to the Security Council President on 11 January 2001 [S/2001/36]. Nevertheless, UNITA retained the capacity to attack government positions, was still the dominant power in some localities in the north and north-east of the country and had safe havens in the Malange and Cuango basins.

On 15 March, the Government announced a four-point plan for the completion of the peace process. It called for an unconditional cessation of hostilities by UNITA, the handover of its weapons to the United Nations, the conclusion of tasks pending under the Lusaka Protocol and UNITA participation in the general elections to be held in 2002.

Another opposition group, the Front for the Liberation of the Enclave of Cabinda, reiterated its call for negotiations with the Governments of Angola and Portugal, both for the right of the people of the Cabinda enclave to self-determination and for the release of seven Portuguese nationals taken hostage in May 2000 and March 2001. Angolan authorities were reported to be making contacts with the various separatist movements of Cabinda province, aimed at initiating discussions on how to resolve the concerns of the population.

Relations between Angola and Zambia, which had deteriorated due to the military offensive of the Angolan Armed Forces in the eastern region

and the resulting influx of refugees into Zambia, improved in early 2001. On 10 February, Presidents Frederick Chiluba of Zambia and Sam Nujoma of Namibia attended a mini-summit with President José Eduardo dos Santos in Luanda and discussed border security issues. They agreed to set up a tripartite security mechanism to prevent the illegal circulation of people and goods and the unlawful trade in diamonds and ivory, as well as illicit arms trafficking.

Breaking a long period of silence, UNITA leader Jonas Savimbi, in an interview on 22 March, said that his movement was ready for dialogue, reiterated the validity of the Lusaka Protocol and noted that both parties still had to conclude the implementation of some of its key provisions. He expressed doubts about the sincerity of the Government in granting him amnesty. He indicated that UNITA had no objections to the disarmament plan under the Protocol but would like to discuss its modalities beforehand.

The Secretary-General's representative in Angola and head of UNOA, Mussagy Jeichande, met with President dos Santos and other officials, who reaffirmed the continuing validity of the Lusaka Protocol and called on UNOA to seek the completion of its implementation. The representative also maintained contacts with opposition parties and other civil society groups.

The human rights situation continued to be undermined by the direct consequences of the ongoing conflict and structural weaknesses in government institutions. Civilians, in particular villagers and farmers, were often victims of serious and recurring human rights abuses, and abuses and attacks were perpetrated by both UNITA members and soldiers and policemen acting outside the parameters of the official code of conduct.

The humanitarian situation in Angola remained precarious due to the large number of internally displaced persons. By the end of February, the number of those displaced since the resumption of hostilities in January 1998 reached 2.9 million, of whom 2.2 million lived in areas accessible to humanitarian agencies. Efforts were made to increase the registration of the internally displaced persons for humanitarian assistance. Increases in cases of malaria, respiratory infections and diarrhoea were reported. Significant efforts were made to resettle displaced populations in safe areas in order to protect them from guerrilla and counter-insurgency activity.

The Secretary-General welcomed the positive measures taken by the Government of Angola. He said that it was imperative that UNITA abandon its military option and seek a resolution of the conflict in the context of the Lusaka Protocol. He appealed to all concerned to facilitate the delivery of emergency relief assistance and urged the donor community to respond as generously as possible to the 2001 UN consolidated inter-agency appeal for Angola (see p. 831). He noted encouraging signs of a nascent democratic process involving broad segments of Angolans, including civil society, and the need for drafting a new constitution and holding free and fair elections. UNOA would continue to report on developments in the country and to provide assistance to Angola in human rights and capacity-building. The Secretary-General therefore recommended that the Security Council extend UNOA's mandate for a further six months, until 15 October. The Council, on 19 April [S/2001/387], informed the Secretary-General that it concurred with his recommendation.

Communications (June-August). Côte d'Ivoire, in an 18 June letter to the Secretary-General [S/2001/607], said that, although in the past it had maintained contacts with UNITA leaders, it had frozen its relations with that organization; that message had been conveyed by President Laurent Gbagbo during an official visit to Angola in late May.

On 15 August [S/2001/793], Angola reported that on 10 August UNITA forces had attacked a train, killing 252 people and injuring more than 165. UNITA had begun to pursue a policy of avoiding confrontations with government military forces and had resorted to violence against defenceless communities. Angola called on the United Nations to take action.

Security Council consideration. On 20 September, the Security Council met in private and was briefed by Angola's Minister of the Interior. The Council issued a communiqué [S/PV.4376] stating that it had had a constructive interactive discussion with the Minister. The United States transmitted to the Council President a statement it had made on behalf of the Troika of Observer States to the Lusaka Protocol (Portugal, Russian Federation, United States) to the Council meeting [S/2001/908]. The Troika condemned the 10 August attack on the passenger train, called on UNITA to re-enter the dialogue on implementing the Lusaka Protocol, and expressed support for further work on a judicial framework in advance of Angola's next election.

SECURITY COUNCIL ACTION (September)

On 20 September [meeting 4377], following consultations among Security Council members, the President issued statement **S/PRST/2001/24** on behalf of the Council:

The Security Council remains concerned at the continuing conflict in Angola. It reiterates its position that the primary responsibility for the continued fighting lies with the leadership of the armed faction of the União Nacional para a Independência Total de Angola (UNITA) headed by Mr. J. Savimbi which is refusing to fulfil its obligations under the "Accordos de Paz", the Lusaka Protocol and relevant resolutions of the Security Council, which remain the only viable basis for political settlement of the conflict in Angola.

The Council considers the four-point agenda for peace proposed by the Government of Angola a useful indication of areas where an agreement or progress should be reached. It calls on the UNITA armed faction headed by Mr. J. Savimbi to cease all military action and to enter into a dialogue with the Government of Angola on how to conclude the implementation of the Lusaka Protocol on this basis.

The Council condemns in the strongest terms the terrorist attacks by UNITA forces on the civilian population of Angola. It stresses that such attacks are unacceptable and cannot be justified by any political goals. The Council reminds their perpetrators that such acts are in violation of international law and may have further implications.

The Council reaffirms that the failure by the armed faction of UNITA to implement its obligations under the "Accordos de Paz", the Lusaka Protocol, and its relevant resolutions remains the reason for the Security Council sanctions against UNITA. The Council is determined to keep sanctions in place until it is convinced that the conditions in its relevant resolutions are met. It reiterates its call on all States to implement strictly the sanctions regime against UNITA and urges them to strengthen, where appropriate, their internal legislation related to application of sanction measures imposed by the Council. The Council reaffirms its intention to keep sanctions under close monitoring and periodic review in order to raise their effectiveness, including as they relate to UNITA activity abroad.

The Council notes with satisfaction that, at their recent summit, the heads of State and Government of the Southern African Development Community countries undertook to prepare a report on how the Community countries implement Security Council resolution 1295(2000). The Council encourages the Community countries to cooperate fully in their efforts to implement the Security Council's measures against UNITA.

The Council encourages the Government of Angola to promote the peace process and in this regard welcomes the initiatives by the Government of Angola, as well as by the Angolan people, including the civil society and the churches. It calls on the Angolan authorities to continue efforts aimed at national reconciliation and stabilization of the situation in the country in consultation with all segments of the Angolan society, including the civil society and the churches. These should focus on re-establishment of the State administration, improvement of the social and economic situation of the population, promotion of the rule of law, protection of human rights, and the activity of the Inter-Agency Committee and of the Peace and Reconciliation Fund.

The Council supports the intention of the Government of Angola to hold elections as a part of the ongoing democratization process in Angola in conformity with the universally accepted democratic principles and standards. It stresses the need to create the necessary conditions for elections to be free and fair. The Council requests the Secretary-General to provide appropriate support, in coordination with the Government of Angola, in preparation of elections, including through the work of the ongoing United Nations technical assistance mission.

The Council notes the positive contribution that the United Nations Office in Angola is making towards finding the solution to the Angolan conflict. It reiterates its full support for the work of the Office and the Representative of the Secretary-General.

The Council is seriously concerned with the plight of the Angolan population particularly the internally displaced persons and, in order to alleviate its suffering, calls again on all parties concerned to facilitate the delivery of emergency relief assistance. The work of the United Nations agencies and other international organizations delivering assistance to those in the affected areas is of the utmost importance and must continue unobstructed with the financial support of the international community.

Communication (September). On 24 September [S/2001/904], Burkina Faso categorically denied an assertion by the Angolan Minister of Defence that Mr. Savimbi was in Burkina Faso.

Report of Secretary-General (October). The Secretary-General, in an October report on Angola [S/2001/956], provided an update on the situation there since his previous (April) report. During that six-month period, deep animosity and distrust had persisted between the Government and UNITA. Despite increasing pressure from the civil society for a political settlement of the conflict, fighting continued unabated with dire humanitarian consequences. UNITA guerrilla activities included the killing of 150 persons and the kidnapping of 60 children in Bengo province (north-east of Luanda), shooting at a World Food Programme (WFP) plane near Kuito in June, and the attack on a passenger train in Kwanza Norte province in August. In both the train and plane attacks, UNITA alleged that government forces and war materiel were being transported, charges denied by the Government.

In a speech in Luanda during the opening of a peace conference on 2 May [S/2001/470], President dos Santos explained that his Government had opted for a military solution to the conflict as a matter of legitimate self-defence. He affirmed that the Government's four-point peace plan (see p. 225) reinforced the Lusaka Protocol and its determination to hold general elections. He added that Mr. Savimbi, having declared that he accepted the Lusaka Protocol, needed to announce how he intended to implement its terms.

In a June interview with the British Broadcasting Corporation, Mr. Savimbi said UNITA could neither declare a unilateral ceasefire nor disarm because there were no verification mechanisms in place. UNITA proposed the establishment of a transitional government and the creation of a High Council of Peace to include many political and civil society leaders. Meanwhile, the Government maintained its intention to hold general elections in the second half of 2002, and the President said he would be a candidate again.

Replying on 15 May to a message from the Secretary-General, Mr. dos Santos acknowledged the positive impact of sanctions against UNITA and sought the assistance of the United Nations for the forthcoming electoral process, a pilot project for the resettlement of former combatants, and the Fund for Peace and National Reconciliation.

Relations between the Angolan Government and neighbouring countries improved, with the Côte d'Ivoire President proposing to respect the sanctions against UNITA (see p. 226). There were a number of exchange visits by the Foreign Affairs and Defence Ministers of Angola and Zambia and, at a tripartite summit meeting of Angola, Namibia and Zambia on 26 June, President dos Santos expressed satisfaction with the situation along the Angolan-Zambian border and acknowledged the contributions of Namibia and Zambia towards peace in Angola.

The human rights situation continued to be undermined by the ongoing conflict. Humanitarian principles were largely ignored, with civilians subjected to a wide range of human rights abuses. Ambushes on roads and landmines endangered the lives of civilians and limited freedom of movement. UNITA had begun to target civilians with greater intensity. Through partnerships with government authorities and civil society, the UNOA human rights programme helped establish a mechanism to enable Angolans to exercise their rights while supporting the government institutions that were responsible for their protection.

The humanitarian situation remained serious, particularly in inaccessible regions. At the end of August, the number of persons reportedly displaced since the resumption of hostilities in December 1998 reached over 3 million, of whom 1.3 million had been confirmed by humanitarian organizations. More than 165,000 persons had been displaced since March by war-related activity and food insecurity. April floods in southern Angola and attacks during May led to the temporary displacement of about 100,000 people during a three-month period. In addition, growing insecurity in Uíge province in July and August forced at least 10,000 Angolan refugees to flee to the DRC. Malnutrition was a serious problem in several provinces and was compounded by lack of health facilities and water and sanitation. Despite intermittent insecurity, a new corridor was opened into Camacupa and a major humanitarian operation was launched. Although plans were made to relocate 500,000 internally displaced persons during the year, only 67,000 people were resettled between March and September because of deteriorating security conditions.

Despite the intensification of guerrilla attacks, the Secretary-General noted encouraging signs towards the resolution of the conflict led by civil society's call for a political settlement. Both the Government and UNITA had reaffirmed the validity of the Lusaka Protocol as a basis for peace, although they differed with respect to the ways its provisions should be implemented. The Secretary-General's Special Adviser on Africa, Ibrahim Gambari, having visited Angola in early May, led UN efforts to search for a solution and ways in which the United Nations could assist the Government. UNOA, in addition to promoting a peaceful resolution of the conflict, provided assistance in humanitarian aid, human rights and capacity-building, and also monitored the situation. For those reasons, the Secretary-General recommended that the Security Council extend the UNOA mandate for another six months, until 15 April 2002. The Council, on 16 October [S/2001/973], informed the Secretary-General that it concurred with that recommendation.

Security Council consideration. The Secretary-General's Special Adviser on Africa, Mr. Gambari, addressed the Security Council on 15 November [meeting 4418] as it considered the situation in Angola. He stated that the Angolan Government had recently launched a number of military offensives, especially in the eastern province of Moxico, where it reportedly destroyed UNITA's operational command centres and took hundreds of prisoners. A total of 4.1 million people were estimated to be displaced and a tenth of all Angolans depended on food assistance to survive.

Concerning the peace process, the Government had reaffirmed its commitment to peace within the framework of the Lusaka Protocol. The UNITA leadership, while appearing to accept the validity of the Protocol, had made a number of specific proposals to solve the conflict that appeared to lie outside the Protocol's framework. Both the Church and the National Assembly were

actively involved in the search for a settlement. In a speech on 23 August, President dos Santos announced his intention not to stand as a candidate in the next general elections; however, he also indicated that there were several preconditions before elections could take place, including revision of the electoral law, a new constitution, a census, resettlement of displaced populations and security guarantees.

Addressing the Council, Angola affirmed that it was working towards peace and national reconciliation, a process that included meetings with political parties and civil society, including churches, NGOs and civic associations, as well as with representatives of the international community. In the military arena, the Government had taken forceful measures to complete the terms of the Lusaka Protocol, particularly the disarmament of UNITA forces and the extension of State authority throughout the national territory. The sanctions imposed by the international community had been effective in reducing the capacity of UNITA's military wing to wage war and, consequently, a number of UNITA members had been persuaded to lay down their weapons. Angola called on the international community to tighten the sanctions, particularly in the area of telecommunications.

SECURITY COUNCIL ACTION (November)

On 15 November [meeting 4419], following consultations among Security Council members, the President made statement **S/PRST/2001/36** on behalf of the Council:

> The Security Council remains deeply concerned about the ongoing conflict in Angola. It holds Mr. Jonas Savimbi and the armed faction of the União Nacional para a Independência Total de Angola (UNITA) primarily responsible for the failure to implement the Lusaka Protocol. It expresses its deep concern at the resulting human rights and international humanitarian law violations, and the humanitarian crisis.
>
> The Council reaffirms that the Lusaka Protocol remains the only viable basis for a political settlement of the conflict in Angola. The failure by UNITA to implement the Lusaka Protocol, the "Accordos de Paz" and the relevant resolutions of the Security Council are the basis for the continuation of the Security Council sanctions against UNITA.
>
> The Council once again reaffirms its intention to keep sanctions under close and ongoing monitoring with a view to improving their effectiveness until it is convinced that the conditions in the relevant resolutions are met. It welcomes, in this regard, the ongoing review by the Sanctions Committee of the recommendations of the Monitoring Mechanism on sanctions against UNITA.
>
> The Council reiterates its call on Member States to comply fully with the implementation of the sanctions regime against UNITA. The Council notes the

positive contribution of the Security Council Sanctions Committee established pursuant to resolution 864(1993) and, in this regard, calls upon the Member States to cooperate fully with the Security Council Committee and the Monitoring Mechanism on sanctions against UNITA.

The Council supports the Government of Angola in its efforts to implement the Lusaka Protocol including through the Fund for Peace and National Reconciliation. The Security Council supports the Government's intention to hold free and fair elections when appropriate conditions are in place. It encourages the Angolan authorities to continue, in consultation with all the political parties and the full participation of the civil society, their efforts for peace, stability and national reconciliation. The Council further encourages the Government of Angola to work for economic reform and to ensure transparent and accountable governance to provide a positive climate for peace.

The Council expresses its concern that the continuing conflict in Angola is leading to a large number of internally displaced persons and a dire humanitarian situation. It welcomes the efforts of the Government of Angola to improve the humanitarian situation and the resettlement of the displaced population and calls upon it to increase its efforts to this end. It also calls upon the international community to continue to provide necessary humanitarian assistance. It stresses that humanitarian assistance should be provided to the population in need, throughout Angola.

The Council supports the efforts of the civil society and the churches to alleviate the humanitarian situation and to facilitate national reconciliation.

The Council welcomes the upcoming visit of the Secretary-General's Special Adviser on Africa to Angola for consultations with the Government, political parties and civil society representatives on how the United Nations could help in the advancement of the peace process. It also reiterates its support for the work of the United Nations Office in Angola in finding the solution to the Angolan conflict.

The Russian Federation requested that the statement it had made to the Council on 15 November on behalf of the Troika of Observer States to the Lusaka Protocol be circulated [S/2001/1116]. The Troika pointed out that one of the new voices in Angola calling for dialogue in pursuit of peace was that of the growing civil society movement within government-controlled areas of the country, which should be encouraged. The Troika believed that the principles of the Lusaka Protocol should remain intact: the State administration should be extended to all areas of the country; UNITA should disarm and be demobilized; and UNITA should be able to enter politics as a political party.

Later developments. Following a mission to Angola from 8 to 14 December, Mr. Gambari reported to the Security Council on 21 December [meeting 4444] that progress was being made on all fronts. With regard to the peace process, he reported that, for the first time, there was a convergence of opinion among those consulted that the United Nations should play a more proactive role. The Government had no objection to the role of the churches in facilitating contacts with UNITA, but said that should be done through the United Nations as mediator. According to the Government, UNITA's military capacity had been nearly destroyed, it controlled no territory and was facing numerous defections. However, the Government recognized that UNITA was still capable of conducting terror attacks. UNITA parliamentarians reiterated the organization's commitment to peace through a dialogue within the framework of the Lusaka Protocol, but cautioned that it should not be used as a platform to obtain UNITA's surrender and that a final decision still lay in the hands of Mr. Savimbi.

The Government had indicated that the United Nations should assume responsibility for the collection and destruction of weapons; that would involve an adjustment to UNOA's mandate, which was to promote humanitarian assistance and capacity-building in human rights. Mr. Gambari said there was a window of opportunity to advance the peace process in Angola, which the United Nations should explore; under the guidance of the Secretary-General, he would seek to accelerate the peace process in the context of the Lusaka Protocol.

With regard to the proposed national elections, the Government continued to express its commitment to hold them soon. In Mr. Gambari's view, however, that was not realistic, as the discussions of the fundamental principles for a new constitution appeared deadlocked. The humanitarian situation had worsened in a number of areas, and the number of internally displaced persons and refugees was estimated to have reached 4.1 million out of a total population of about 12 million. The rapid increase was due to the "mop-up" operation by the Angolan Armed Forces, a strategy of moving people from their areas of origin into camps for internally displaced persons with the aim of depriving UNITA of its support base. Nevertheless, the Government had made enormous efforts to improve the humanitarian situation by, among other things, increasing funds to provide for the humanitarian needs of displaced persons who had moved into urban areas.

Sanctions

In 2001, the Security Council continued to monitor sanctions against UNITA through the Committee established pursuant to resolution 864(1993) [YUN 1993, p. 256] and the Monitoring

Mechanism on Sanctions against UNITA, which was established by resolution 1295(2000) [YUN 2000, p. 155] to investigate violations of the sanctions. The first set of sanctions under resolution 864(1993)—arms and petroleum embargoes—was expanded several times in the following years to include bans on diamond trading and travel by high UNITA officials and their families.

In January and February, the Council considered the December 2000 report of the Monitoring Mechanism [YUN 2000, p. 158], which presented findings on countries involved in arms and military equipment shipments, travel by UNITA representatives and trade in illegal diamonds and financial assets. In January, the Council extended the Mechanism's mandate for three months and, in April, extended it for a further six months, until 19 October. On that date, the Council again extended the Mechanism's mandate for six months, until 19 April 2002.

Monitoring Mechanism

SECURITY COUNCIL ACTION (January)

On 23 January [meeting 4263], the Security Council unanimously adopted **resolution 1336 (2001)**. The draft [S/2001/69] was prepared in consultations among Council members.

The Security Council,

Reaffirming its resolution 864(1993) of 15 September 1993 and all subsequent relevant resolutions, in particular resolutions 1127(1997) of 28 August 1997, 1173 (1998) of 12 June 1998, 1237(1999) of 7 May 1999 and 1295(2000) of 18 April 2000,

Reaffirming also its commitment to preserve the sovereignty and territorial integrity of Angola,

Expressing its continued concern regarding the humanitarian effects of the present situation on the civilian population of Angola,

Determining that the situation in Angola constitutes a threat to international peace and security in the region,

Acting under Chapter VII of the Charter of the United Nations,

1. *Takes note* of the final report of the Monitoring Mechanism established pursuant to resolution 1295 (2000);

2. *Expresses its intention* to give full consideration to the final report pursuant to paragraph 5 of resolution 1295(2000);

3. *Decides* to extend the mandate of the Monitoring Mechanism as set out in resolution 1295(2000) for a period of three months;

4. *Requests* the Monitoring Mechanism to report periodically to the Committee established pursuant to resolution 864(1993), and to provide a written addendum to the final report, by 19 April 2001;

5. *Requests* the Secretary-General, upon adoption of this resolution and acting in consultation with the Committee, to reappoint up to five of the experts appointed by him pursuant to resolution 1295(2000) to serve on the Monitoring Mechanism, and further requests the Secretary-General to make the necessary financial arrangements to support the work of the Monitoring Mechanism;

6. *Requests* the Chairman of the Committee established pursuant to resolution 864(1993) to submit the written addendum to the final report to the Council by 19 April 2001;

7. *Calls upon* all States to cooperate fully with the Monitoring Mechanism in the discharge of its mandate;

8. *Decides* to remain actively seized of the matter.

The Secretary-General, on 29 January [S/2001/91], informed the Council that he had reappointed the five experts to the Monitoring Mechanism in accordance with resolution 1336(2001).

Angola, in an 8 February letter [S/2001/123], urged the Security Council to uphold the sanctions against UNITA, which, in Angola's view, constituted the most effective means to maintain pressure on UNITA's armed wing. Angola remained concerned over the systematic violations of sanctions, noting in particular the diamond traffic that sustained rebel groups in Africa, especially in Angola. Angola stressed the need to strengthen the sanctions against UNITA, enlarge the Monitoring Mechanism's mandate to bring about judicial prosecution of companies and individuals violating the sanctions, adopt measures to combat the support of diamond and arms traffickers, and adopt measures against countries involved in violating sanctions.

Security Council consideration (February). On 22 February [meeting 4283], the Council again considered the Monitoring Mechanism's report and heard a statement by the Chairman of the Committee established pursuant to resolution 864(1993) [YUN 1993, p. 256] to monitor sanctions against UNITA. He noted that the recommendations of the Monitoring Mechanism required action by and financial support from the United Nations, individual States and the international community. The findings of the Monitoring Mechanism and of the Panel of Experts [YUN 2000, p. 154] had demonstrated the involvement of the same people, organizations and corporations in two and probably more of the major conflicts in Africa. The United Nations lacked the necessary permanent capacity for following up on those findings. The UN sanctions regime against UNITA was working; it was currently more expensive and difficult for UNITA to conduct business with the suppliers of essential materials, and it was riskier for State and commercial suppliers to engage in business with UNITA. With the Council's support, the Committee would work with others to erode UNITA's remaining military capacity.

Expressing support for the Committee's report, Angola said that the primary impact of the sanctions was reflected in the significant reduction of the military capacity of the rebels. Former rebels had accepted the Government's amnesty offer and joined national reconciliation efforts. Angola called on the Council to reinforce the Monitoring Mechanism and to adopt concrete measures to combat transnational organized crime networks in Africa.

April report. In an April addendum [S/2001/363] to its December 2000 report, submitted in response to resolution 1336(2001), the Monitoring Mechanism provided information obtained during its visit to a number of countries, from printouts from captured UNITA computers and from responses to questionnaires sent to Member States.

The Mechanism identified a number of companies that had played a key role in brokering arms transactions between Bulgaria and Romania and UNITA and observed that there was an urgent need to tighten the regulations governing the activities and operations of such companies. It recommended that the establishment of an international register of dubious companies involved in sanctions-busting should be considered. As to the travel of senior UNITA officials, the Mechanism stated that, in addition to carrying out public relations activities and political lobbying, UNITA representatives were also essential to UNITA supply lines, diamond sales and logistics. The Mechanism had been informed about UNITA links/branches in Latin America and Scandinavia. With regard to diamond trading, the Mechanism observed that many countries had not passed national laws enacting the implementation of Security Council resolution 1173(1998) [YUN 1998, p. 108] as it related to diamonds from Angola. Even in countries that had enacted laws and strengthened diamond-trading controls, illicit diamonds were still reaching the market. However, the sanctions had brought about reform of official Angola diamond-trading structures and produced a novel approach to resolving problems on the ground, which should be considered for application in other African diamond-mining countries. In the area of petroleum and petroleum products, the Mechanism was informed by Namibia that 32 full 5,000-litre petroleum containers had been unearthed in southern Angola. However, their source was unknown. The Mechanism also learned that small UNITA guerrilla groups still used trucks for rapid deployment, which highlighted the need for continued vigilance by the Government of Angola and countries in the subregion to ensure that fuel was not smuggled to UNITA.

As a result of the vigilance and systematic investigations undertaken by the Mechanism, Governments that had violated the sanctions in the past were distancing themselves from UNITA and taking measures to implement the sanctions. Companies and individuals were under pressure and constant scrutiny. The Mechanism believed that it would not be prudent to abandon its work when indications showed that UNITA was finally being hurt by the sanctions even if it had not given up.

SECURITY COUNCIL ACTION (April)

On 19 April [meeting 4311], the Security Council unanimously adopted **resolution 1348(2001)**. The draft [S/2001/379] was prepared in consultations among Council members.

The Security Council,

Reaffirming its resolution 864(1993) of 15 September 1993 and all subsequent relevant resolutions, in particular resolutions 1127(1997) of 28 August 1997, 1173 (1998) of 12 June 1998, 1237(1999) of 7 May 1999, 1295(2000) of 18 April 2000 and 1336(2001) of 23 January 2001,

Reaffirming also its commitment to preserve the sovereignty and territorial integrity of Angola,

Expressing once again its concern regarding the humanitarian effects of the present situation on the civilian population of Angola,

Recognizing the importance attached, inter alia, to the monitoring, for as long as it is necessary, of the implementation of the provisions contained in resolutions 864(1993), 1127(1997) and 1173(1998),

Determining that the situation in Angola continues to constitute a threat to international peace and security in the region,

Acting under Chapter VII of the Charter of the United Nations,

1. *Takes note* of the written addendum provided pursuant to paragraph 4 of resolution 1336(2001) to the final report of the Monitoring Mechanism established pursuant to resolution 1295(2000);

2. *Expresses its intention* to give full consideration to the written addendum and to the final report, pursuant to paragraph 5 of resolution 1295(2000);

3. *Decides* to extend the mandate of the Monitoring Mechanism for a further period of six months, ending on 19 October 2001;

4. *Requests* the Monitoring Mechanism to report periodically to the Committee established pursuant to resolution 864(1993), and to provide a supplementary report by 19 October 2001;

5. *Requests* the Secretary-General, upon adoption of the present resolution and acting in consultation with the Committee, to appoint up to five experts to serve on the monitoring mechanism, and further requests the Secretary-General to make the necessary financial arrangements to support the work of the monitoring mechanism;

6. *Requests* the Chairman of the Committee established pursuant to resolution 864(1993) to submit the supplementary report to the Council by 19 October 2001;

7. *Calls upon* all States to cooperate fully with the Monitoring Mechanism in the discharge of its mandate;

8. *Decides* to remain actively seized of the matter.

The Secretary-General, on 30 May [S/2001/537], informed the Council President of his decision to reappoint four experts to serve on the Monitoring Mechanism. On 9 July [S/2001/676], he announced the appointment of the fifth member.

Angola, on 3 October [S/2001/933], requested the Council to extend the mandate of the Monitoring Mechanism, as that body had played a crucial role in reducing the violations of sanctions against UNITA. Angola reiterated that request on 10 October [S/2001/958] and called on the Council to impose new restrictive measures against UNITA's military wing, namely in the area of telecommunications.

October report. On 12 October, in accordance with resolution 1348(2001), the Monitoring Mechanism transmitted to the Security Council a supplementary report on sanctions against UNITA [S/2001/966]. During the reporting period, it had pursued allegations of sanctions violations and continued to examine the role of criminal elements instrumental to UNITA's capacity to sustain its guerrilla war. In addition, the Mechanism expanded its base of inquiry by drawing on the expertise of professional asset tracers to identify UNITA's financial resources.

The Mechanism believed that deliveries of arms and ammunition had been drastically reduced due to the sanctions. Although UNITA had lost control over airstrips, cross-border supplies still reached it from the DRC. The Mechanism received repeated allegations that the DRC remained a major transit country for UNITA diamonds.

The Monitoring Mechanism described its further investigations concerning violations of arms sanctions, which centred on collecting additional information regarding the arms brokering companies, particularly the financial trail related to arms purchases; the determination of the origin of UNITA equipment seized in Togo; and the assessment of other possible sources of arms supply.

As to the diamond sanctions, the Mechanism stated that the Chief Executive Officer of the Angola Selling Corporation had informed it that between $1 million and $1.2 million of embargoed diamonds were leaving Angola each day. The Government had stated that the major problem was no longer diamonds produced by UNITA but illicit diamonds being smuggled by other players, as mining areas previously held by UNITA were recaptured. In investigating the rough diamond trading companies said to be involved in violating

the sanctions, the Mechanism noted the almost total lack of transparency, the relative absence of traceable paper trails and the protection of what data were available by commercial confidentiality or law, which created difficulties in finding hard evidence of dealers' activities. However, it had been possible to construct a chain of evidence in some cases. The Mechanism had identified one dealer in Antwerp that appeared to be implicated in illicit diamond trading with UNITA. It would provide the Government of Belgium with its findings and documentation, and request a thorough investigation, the outcome of which would be given to the Security Council Committee.

During the review period, the Mechanism had conducted investigations aimed at establishing the financial resources and network at the disposal of UNITA. Certain assets held in the names of senior UNITA officials had been located in six countries. The three main categories of assets identified were bank accounts, real estate properties and business entities. Offshore financial centres continued to play a major role as havens for UNITA funds and in facilitating financial transactions. The Mechanism had established that, since the announcement of sanctions, the UNITA network had experienced a decrease in liquidity; travel restrictions had proved particularly important in that regard.

With respect to improving the effectiveness of the sanctions, the Mechanism observed that, with few exceptions, measures aimed at enacting legislation to make the violation of Security Council sanctions a criminal offence were very limited. On the other hand, the Southern African Development Community and OAU, among other African subregional and regional organizations, had taken significant measures.

SECURITY COUNCIL ACTION (October)

On 19 October [meeting 4393], the Security Council unanimously adopted **resolution 1374(2001)**. The draft [S/2001/985] was prepared in consultations among Council members.

The Security Council,

Reaffirming its resolution 864(1993) of 15 September 1993 and all subsequent relevant resolutions, in particular resolutions 1127(1997) of 28 August 1997, 1173 (1998) of 12 June 1998, 1237(1999) of 7 May 1999, 1295 (2000) of 18 April 2000, 1336(2001) of 23 January 2001 and 1348(2001) of 19 April 2001,

Reaffirming also its commitment to preserve the sovereignty and territorial integrity of Angola,

Expressing once again its concern regarding the humanitarian effects of the present situation on the civilian population of Angola,

Recognizing the importance attached, inter alia, to the monitoring, for as long as it is necessary, of the implementation of the provisions contained in resolutions 864(1993), 1127(1997) and 1173(1998),

Determining that the situation in Angola continues to constitute a threat to international peace and security in the region,

Acting under Chapter VII of the Charter of the United Nations,

1. *Takes note* of the supplementary report of 12 October 2001 provided pursuant to paragraph 4 of resolution 1348(2001);

2. *Expresses its intention* to give full consideration to this supplementary report;

3. *Decides* to extend the mandate of the Monitoring Mechanism for a further period of six months, ending on 19 April 2002;

4. *Calls upon* the Committee established pursuant to resolution 864(1993) to undertake a review to be completed by 31 December 2001 of the final report of the Monitoring Mechanism, the addendum to the final report and the supplementary report with a view to examining the recommendations contained in these reports and to offer guidance to the Monitoring Mechanism on its future work;

5. *Requests* the Monitoring Mechanism to provide the Committee within 60 days of the adoption of this resolution with a detailed action plan for its future work, in particular, but not exclusively, on sanctions on UNITA diamonds, violations of arms sanctions, and on UNITA finances;

6. *Requests further* the Monitoring Mechanism to report periodically to the Committee and to provide an additional report by 19 April 2002;

7. *Requests* the Secretary-General, upon adoption of this resolution and acting in consultation with the Committee, to appoint four experts to serve on the Monitoring Mechanism and further requests the Secretary-General to make the necessary financial arrangements to support the work of the Monitoring Mechanism;

8. *Requests* the Chairman of the Committee established pursuant to resolution 864(1993) to submit the additional report to the Council by 19 April 2002;

9. *Calls upon* all States to cooperate fully with the Monitoring Mechanism in the discharge of its mandate;

10. *Decides* to remain actively seized of the matter.

In response to resolution 1374(2001), the Secretary-General, on 24 October [S/2001/1009], informed the Security Council that he had appointed four experts to the Monitoring Mechanism.

Sanctions Committee

The Security Council Committee established pursuant to resolution 864(1993) [YUN 1993, p. 256] concerning the situation in Angola, in a report on its 2001 activities [S/2002/243], stated that it had held 11 formal and 6 informal meetings during the year.

At those meetings, the Committee considered the reports of the Monitoring Mechanism (see pp. 231 and 232), and the Mechanism's activities

were summarized in the Committee's report. The Committee Chairman visited a number of countries in Africa and Europe and reported to the Committee on his discussions. Early in the year, the Chairman requested Member States to provide details of action taken to follow up on the conclusions and recommendations contained in the December 2000 report of the Monitoring Mechanism [YUN 2000, p. 158]; as at 31 December 2001, a limited number of responses had been received. On 20 February, the Committee Chairman wrote to the EU and ECOWAS, drawing their attention to concerns expressed by the Monitoring Mechanism regarding possible abuse by UNITA officials of the Schengen Agreement (on lifting of passport controls among EU members) and ECOWAS travel documents. A further request for information was sent to the two organizations on 4 December. On 28 September, the Committee approved an updated list of senior UNITA officials and family members, which was forwarded to all 189 Member States and relevant international organizations, requesting them to inform the Committee of action taken in the light of resolutions 1127(1997) [YUN 1997, p. 106] and 1173(1998) [YUN 1998, p. 108], which imposed representation, travel and financial sanctions. A further request was made in that regard on 4 December. At an 11 December meeting, the Committee stressed the importance of efforts made outside the UN framework for implementing the sanctions against UNITA. In that regard, it expressed its interest in progress being made at the Kimberley Process with regard to conflict diamonds (see p. 52).

The members of the Committee found a broad consensus that, in 2001, the sanctions against UNITA continued to be effective in helping to reach their main objective—preventing UNITA from pursuing its objectives through military means. The Committee reaffirmed the importance of closely monitoring the sanctions with a view to sustaining and improving their effectiveness until conditions in the relevant Council resolutions were met.

Financing of UN missions

In March [A/55/844 & Corr.1], the Secretary-General reported on the financial performance of the United Nations Observer Mission in Angola (MONUA), whose mandate expired in February 1999 [YUN 1999, p. 106], for the period 1 July 1999 to 30 June 2000. Expenditures totalled $14,231,340 gross ($13,402,740 net), resulting in an unutilized balance of $818,100 gross ($903,800 net) of the amount the General Assembly had appropriated for the liquidation of the Mission. Action by the Assembly was required to decide on the treatment of the unencumbered balance for both the reported period and the period 1 July 1998 to 30 June 1999, which totalled $967,600 gross ($116,200 net).

Having considered the Secretary-General's report on MONUA's financial performance, ACABQ, in an April report [A/55/879], recommended that the Assembly accept the Secretary-General's proposals.

GENERAL ASSEMBLY ACTION

On 14 June [meeting 103], the General Assembly, on the recommendation of the Fifth Committee [A/55/964], adopted **resolution 55/260** without vote [agenda item 129].

Financing of the United Nations Angola Verification Mission and the United Nations Observer Mission in Angola

The General Assembly,

Having considered the report of the Secretary-General on the financing of the United Nations Observer Mission in Angola and the related reports of the Advisory Committee on Administrative and Budgetary Questions,

Bearing in mind Security Council resolutions 626 (1988) of 20 December 1988, by which the Council established the United Nations Angola Verification Mission, 696(1991) of 30 May 1991, by which the Council decided to entrust a new mandate to the United Nations Angola Verification Mission (thenceforth called the United Nations Angola Verification Mission II), 976(1995) of 8 February 1995, by which the Council authorized the establishment of a peacekeeping operation (thenceforth called the United Nations Angola Verification Mission III), 1118(1997) of 30 June 1997, by which the Council decided to establish, as from 1 July 1997, the United Nations Observer Mission in Angola, and its subsequent resolutions, the latest of which was resolution 1229(1999) of 26 February 1999,

Recalling its resolution 43/231 of 16 February 1989 on the financing of the Verification Mission and its subsequent resolutions and decisions thereon, and its resolution 54/17 B of 15 June 2000 on the financing of the Observer Mission,

Reaffirming that the costs of the Observer Mission are expenses of the Organization to be borne by Member States in accordance with Article 17, paragraph 2, of the Charter of the United Nations,

Recalling its previous decisions regarding the fact that, in order to meet the expenditures caused by the Observer Mission, a different procedure is required from that applied to meet expenditures of the regular budget of the United Nations,

Taking into account the fact that the economically more developed countries are in a position to make relatively larger contributions and that the economically less developed countries have a relatively limited capacity to contribute towards such an operation,

Bearing in mind the special responsibilities of the States permanent members of the Security Council, as indicated in General Assembly resolution 1874(S-IV) of 27 June 1963, in the financing of such operations,

Noting with appreciation that voluntary contributions have been made to the Observer Mission,

Mindful of the fact that it is essential to provide the Observer Mission with the necessary financial resources to enable it to meet its outstanding liabilities,

1. *Takes note* of the status of contributions to the United Nations Angola Verification Mission and the United Nations Observer Mission in Angola as at 30 April 2001, including the contributions outstanding in the amount of 75.8 million United States dollars, representing 5 per cent of the total assessed contributions, notes that some 45 per cent of the Member States have paid their assessed contributions in full, and urges all other Member States concerned, in particular those in arrears, to ensure payment of their outstanding assessed contributions in full;

2. *Expresses its appreciation* to those Member States which have paid their assessed contributions in full;

3. *Expresses concern* about the financial situation with regard to peacekeeping activities, in particular as regards the reimbursements to troop contributors that bear additional burdens owing to overdue payments by Member States of their assessments;

4. *Also expresses concern* at the delay experienced by the Secretary-General in deploying and providing adequate resources to some recent peacekeeping missions, in particular those in Africa;

5. *Emphasizes* that all future and existing peacekeeping missions shall be given equal and non-discriminatory treatment in respect of financial and administrative arrangements;

6. *Also emphasizes* that all peacekeeping missions shall be provided with adequate resources for the effective and efficient discharge of their respective mandates;

7. *Endorses* the conclusions and recommendations contained in the report of the Advisory Committee on Administrative and Budgetary Questions, and requests the Secretary-General to ensure their full implementation;

8. *Requests* the Secretary-General to take all necessary action to ensure that the liquidation of the Observer Mission is administered with a maximum of efficiency and economy;

9. *Decides* that, for Member States that have fulfilled their financial obligations to the Observer Mission, there shall be credited their respective share of the unencumbered balance of 967,600 dollars gross (116,200 dollars net) in respect of the period from 1 July 1998 to 30 June 2000, comprising an unencumbered balance of 149,500 dollars gross and additional requirements of 787,600 dollars net in respect of the period from 1 July 1998 to 30 June 1999, and an unencumbered balance of 818,100 dollars gross (903,800 dollars net) in respect of the period from 1 July 1999 to 30 June 2000, in accordance with the composition of groups set out in paragraphs 3 and 4 of General Assembly resolution 43/232 of 1 March 1989, as adjusted by subsequent relevant resolutions and decisions, for the ad hoc apportionment of peacekeeping appropriations, the latest of which were resolution 52/230 of 31 March 1998 and decisions 54/456 to 54/458 of 23 December 1999 for the period 1998-2000, and taking into account the scale of assessments for the years 1998, 1999 and 2000, as set out in its resolutions 52/215 A of 22 December 1997 and 54/237 A of 23 December 1999;

10. *Decides also* that, for Member States that have not fulfilled their obligations to the Observer Mission,

their share of the unencumbered balance of 967,600 dollars gross (116,200 dollars net) in respect of the period from 1 July 1998 to 30 June 2000 shall be set off against their outstanding obligations in accordance with the scheme set out in paragraph 9 above;

11. *Emphasizes* that no peacekeeping mission shall be financed by borrowing funds from other active peacekeeping missions;

12. *Decides* to include in the provisional agenda of its fifty-sixth session the item entitled "Financing of the United Nations Angola Verification Mission and the United Nations Observer Mission in Angola".

On 24 December, the Assembly decided that the agenda item on the financing of MONUA would remain for consideration at its resumed fifty-sixth (2002) session (**decision 56/464**) and that the Fifth Committee should continue to consider the item at that session (**decision 56/458**).

Other questions

Comoros

On 21 December, the General Assembly deferred consideration of the item "Question of the Comorian island of Mayotte" and included it in the provisional agenda of its fifty-seventh (2002) session (**decision 56/454**).

Côte d'Ivoire

In connection with the violence that erupted in Côte d'Ivoire in late 2000 following the presidential elections [YUN 2000, p. 230], Mali, on 9 January [S/2001/25], transmitted to the Security Council President a communiqué from its President, Alpha Oumar Konaré, who currently held the Presidency of ECOWAS. President Konaré, concerned by recent violence, reaffirmed his faith in the political settlement of all disputes and strongly condemned any form of the assumption of power by force.

In February, the Secretary-General established an International Commission of Inquiry on Côte d'Ivoire. The Commission, which stayed in Côte d'Ivoire for two months, found, among other things, that members of the gendarmerie and military had been involved in the deaths of civilians.

Mozambique

In accordance with decision 55/458 [YUN 2000, p. 230], the General Assembly retained for consideration at its resumed fifty-fifth (2001) session the item "Financing of the United Nations Operation in Mozambique" (ONUMOZ). ONUMOZ began operations in 1992 [YUN 1992, p. 196] and was liquidated in 1995 [YUN 1995, p. 368].

On 7 September 2001, the Assembly included the item in the draft agenda of its fifty-sixth session (**decision 55/497**).

On 24 December, the Assembly decided that the item would remain for consideration at its resumed fifty-sixth (2002) session (**decision 56/464**) and that the Fifth Committee should continue to consider the item at that session (**decision 56/458**).

Cooperation between OAU and the UN system

In response to General Assembly resolution 55/218 [YUN 2000, p. 231], the Secretary-General submitted an October report [A/56/489] on cooperation between the United Nations and the Organization of African Unity (OAU).

A major development that could affect the structure and content of the programme of cooperation between the United Nations and OAU was the coming into force of the Constitutive Act of the African Union on 26 May. OAU would thus be phased out within a year, with the possibility of an extension of the period of transition. Proposals would be evolved on the orientation and structure of the new African Union for the consideration of the member States. That situation posed a number of questions for the programme of action that was agreed upon by the United Nations and OAU in April 2000 [YUN 2000, p. 230], especially those aspects that called for the international community's support for developing OAU institutional capacity in various areas, particularly in conflict prevention, management and resolution. The dismantling of OAU and the establishment of the African Union would require the re-evaluation and possible reformulation of many of the existing cooperation arrangements between the two organizations.

A leadership change also took place in 2001, with Amara Essy replacing Salim Ahmed Salim as Secretary-General on 20 September. The United Nations intended to undertake with the new OAU Secretary-General a review of the UN/OAU programme of cooperation to determine how it could be adapted to support OAU as it developed the structural concept of the African Union.

The Secretary-General noted that the United Nations and OAU continued to expand collaboration in peace and security, an area in which the UN Liaison Office with OAU remained a useful instrument in facilitating communication and consultation. He described cooperation between

OAU and the UN Departments of Political Affairs and of Peacekeeping Operations in maintaining peace and security, including providing electoral assistance, in a number of African countries. In the humanitarian area, both the Office for the Coordination of Humanitarian Affairs and the Office of the United Nations High Commissioner for Refugees (UNHCR) maintained regular contact with OAU.

The OAU Secretary-General and the High Commissioner for Refugees signed a revised OAU/UNHCR cooperation agreement on 9 April, which emphasized the need to address the underlying causes of refugee problems by the competent political organs within OAU. The report described collaborative work in economic and social development involving the Economic Commission for Africa (ECA) in the areas of environment, population, gender issues and regional cooperation and integration, and the United Nations Development Programme in promoting Africa's economic cooperation and integration and capacity-building for the OAU Mechanism for Conflict Prevention, Management and Resolution. Other cooperative activities included public information on HIV/AIDS, especially with the UN Department of Public Information and the United Nations Educational, Scientific and Cultural Organization (UNESCO). UNESCO also cooperated with OAU in the areas of education and culture.

Other UN bodies involved in the programme of cooperation with OAU included the United Nations Conference on Trade and Development, the Food and Agriculture Organization of the United Nations and the World Health Organization. The Secretary-General also provided information on collaboration by the International Organization for Migration with OAU.

The programme of cooperation between the United Nations and OAU was one of the most extensive formal arrangements concluded between the United Nations and regional organizations in the world, the Secretary-General observed. Not only had a tradition of regular consultation with OAU on issues of peace and security affecting the African continent evolved, but many of the UN agencies and programmes had developed extensive bilateral programmes with OAU in their various areas of work. The programme of action agreed upon at the April 2000 meeting between the two organizations had provided a valuable framework for the two organizations to work together to address a wide range of issues and problems.

On 9 October [A/56/457], the Sudan transmitted to the Secretary-General the decisions and declarations adopted by the OAU Assembly of Heads of State and Government at its thirty-seventh ordinary session (Lusaka, 9-11 July) and the decisions of the Council of Ministers at its seventy-fourth ordinary session (Lusaka, 5-8 July).

On 12 November [S/2001/1061], Zambia forwarded to the Security Council President a communiqué issued by the Central Organ of the OAU Mechanism for Conflict Prevention, Management and Resolution at its fifth extraordinary session, at the ministerial level (New York, 11 November).

GENERAL ASSEMBLY ACTION

On 7 December [meeting 80], the General Assembly adopted **resolution 56/48** [draft: A/56/L.37 & Add.1] without vote [agenda item 21 (j)].

Cooperation between the United Nations and the Organization of African Unity

The General Assembly,

Having considered the report of the Secretary-General,

Bearing in mind the decisions and declarations adopted by the Assembly of Heads of State and Government of the Organization of African Unity at its thirty-seventh ordinary session, held in Lusaka from 9 to 11 July 2001, in particular decision AHG/Dec.160 (XXXVII) on the establishment of the African Union on the basis of the Constitutive Act and a period of transition from Organization of African Unity and African Economic Community to African Union, to allow for the creation of the organs of the African Union,

Taking note of declaration AHG/Decl.1(XXXVII), adopted by the Assembly of Heads of State and Government of the Organization of African Unity at its thirty-seventh ordinary session, concerning the adoption of the New African Initiative, now called New Partnership for Africa's Development, following the review by the Implementation Committee of Heads of State and Government in Abuja on 23 October 2001 on sustainable development in Africa,

Recalling the provisions of Chapter VIII of the Charter of the United Nations and the agreement on cooperation between the United Nations and the Organization of African Unity, as well as all its resolutions on cooperation between the United Nations and the Organization of African Unity, including resolutions 54/94 of 8 December 1999 and 55/218 of 21 December 2000,

Taking note of the declarations and decisions adopted by the Assembly of Heads of State and Government of the Organization of African Unity at its thirty-sixth ordinary session, held in Lomé from 10 to 12 July 2000, in particular declaration AHG/Decl.4(XXXVI), the Solemn Declaration on the Conference on Security, Stability, Development and Cooperation in Africa,

Emphasizing the importance of the effective, coordinated and integrated implementation of the United Nations Millennium Declaration, and welcoming in this regard the commitments of Member States to respond to the special needs of Africa,

Taking note of the Organization of African Unity Convention on the Prevention and Combating of Terrorism, adopted by the Assembly of Heads of State and Government of the Organization of African Unity at its thirty-fifth ordinary session, held in Algiers from 12 to 14 July 1999, and the communiqué issued by the Central Organ of the Mechanism for Conflict Prevention, Management and Resolution of the Organization of African Unity, at its fifth extraordinary session, at the ministerial level, held in New York on 11 November 2001,

Taking note also of the declaration of the extraordinary summit meeting of the Assembly of Heads of State and Government of the Organization of African Unity on HIV/AIDS, tuberculosis and other related infectious diseases, held in Abuja from 24 to 27 April 2001,

Acknowledging the need for continued and closer cooperation between the United Nations and its specialized agencies and the Organization of African Unity and its specialized agencies in the peace and security, political, economic, social, technical, cultural and administrative fields,

Acknowledging also the contribution of the United Nations Liaison Office in strengthening coordination and cooperation between the Organization of African Unity and the United Nations since its establishment in Addis Ababa in April 1998 and the need for its consolidation in order to enhance its performance,

Emphasizing the need to implement the ministerial declaration of the high-level segment of the substantive session of the Economic and Social Council of 18 July 2001 on the role of the United Nations in support of the efforts of African countries to achieve sustainable development,

Emphasizing also the need to implement urgently its resolution S-26/2 of 27 June 2001 containing the Declaration of Commitment on HIV/AIDS, adopted at its special session on HIV/AIDS, and acknowledging in this respect the commitments of Member States to address the special needs of Africa,

Noting the efforts being made by the Organization of African Unity and its specialized agencies and member States in the area of economic integration, and the need to accelerate the process of implementation of the Treaty establishing the African Economic Community,

Noting also the progress made by the Organization of African Unity in developing the capacity of its Mechanism for Conflict Prevention, Management and Resolution, and acknowledging in this regard the assistance of the United Nations and the international community,

Stressing the urgent need to address the plight of refugees and internally displaced persons in Africa, and noting in this context the efforts made to implement the recommendations of the Organization of African Unity Ministerial Meeting on Refugees, Returnees and Displaced Persons in Africa, held in Khartoum on 13 and 14 December 1998, as well as the endorsement by the Council of Ministers of the Organization of African Unity at its seventy-second session of the Comprehensive Implementation Plan, adopted at the Special Meeting of Governmental and Non-Governmental Technical Experts organized by the Organization of African Unity and the Office of the United Nations High Commissioner for Refugees in Conakry from 27 to 29 March 2000,

Recognizing the importance of developing and maintaining a culture of peace, tolerance and harmonious relationships based on the promotion of economic development, democratic principles, good governance, the rule of law, human rights, social justice and international cooperation,

Recognizing also the need to improve coordination and harmonization among the various United Nations initiatives established to assist the development of Africa,

1. *Takes note with satisfaction* of the report of the Secretary-General;

2. *Welcomes* the cooperation existing between the Organization of African Unity and the United Nations and, in this respect, the continuing participation in and constructive contribution of the Organization of African Unity and its specialized agencies to the work of the United Nations, its organs and specialized agencies, and calls upon the two organizations to enhance the involvement of the Organization of African Unity in all United Nations activities concerning Africa;

3. *Calls upon* the Secretary-General closely to involve the Organization of African Unity and its specialized agencies in the implementation of the commitments contained in the United Nations Millennium Declaration, especially those that relate to meeting the special needs of Africa;

4. *Requests* the Secretary-General, together with the Organization of African Unity, to take the necessary measures for the speedy and effective implementation of the recommendations of the biennial meeting of the Organization of African Unity and the United Nations, held in Addis Ababa on 10 and 11 April 2000, in particular those priority areas specified in section III of the report of the Secretary-General submitted to the General Assembly at its fifty-fifth session;

5. *Stresses* the need for closer cooperation and coordination between the Organization of African Unity and the United Nations in the area of peace and security, particularly with regard to conflict prevention, peacekeeping, peace-making, post-conflict reconstruction and peace-building and support for the democratization processes and good governance;

6. *Requests* the United Nations to extend full cooperation and support to the Organization of African Unity in the implementation of the Solemn Declaration on the Conference on Security, Stability, Development and Cooperation in Africa, an initiative which creates a synergy between the various activities currently undertaken by the Organization of African Unity and provides a policy development forum for the elaboration and advancement of common values within the policy organs of the Organization of African Unity;

7. *Encourages* the Secretary-General to strengthen the capacity of the United Nations Liaison Office with the Organization of African Unity;

8. *Requests* the United Nations, while acknowledging its primary role in the promotion of international peace and security, to intensify its assistance to the Organization of African Unity in strengthening the institutional and operational capacity of its Mechanism for Conflict Prevention, Management and Resolution, in particular in the following areas:

(a) Development of its early warning system, including the Situation Room of the Conflict Management Centre;

(b) Technical assistance and training of civilian and military personnel, including a staff exchange programme;

(c) Regular and continued exchange and coordination of information, including between the early warning systems of the two organizations;

(d) Provision of assistance to field missions of the Organization of African Unity in its various member States, in particular, in the area of communication and other related logistical support;

(e) Mobilization of financial support, including through the trust funds of the United Nations and the Organization of African Unity;

9. *Urges* the United Nations to encourage donor countries, in consultation with the Organization of African Unity, to contribute to adequate funding, training and logistical support for African countries in their efforts to enhance their peacekeeping capabilities, with a view to enabling those countries to participate actively in peacekeeping operations within the framework of the United Nations;

10. *Also urges* the United Nations to contribute, where appropriate, to the enhancement of the capacity of the Organization of African Unity to deploy peace support missions;

11. *Requests* the agencies of the United Nations system working in Africa to include in their programmes at the national, subregional and regional levels activities to support African countries in their efforts to enhance regional economic cooperation and integration;

12. *Stresses* the urgent need for the United Nations and the Organization of African Unity to develop close cooperation and concrete programmes, aimed at addressing the problems posed by the proliferation of small arms and light weapons and anti-personnel mines, within the framework of the relevant declarations and resolutions adopted by the two organizations, including the Plan of Action on Landmines, adopted at the First Continental Conference of African Experts on Landmines, held at Kempton Park, South Africa, from 19 to 21 May 1997, the Bamako Declaration of 1 December 2000 on an African Common Position on the Illicit Proliferation, Circulation and Trafficking of Small Arms and Light Weapons and the Programme of Action to Prevent, Combat and Eradicate the Illicit Trade in Small Arms and Light Weapons in All Its Aspects, adopted by the United Nations Conference on the Illicit Trade in Small Arms and Light Weapons in All Its Aspects, held in New York from 9 to 20 July 2001;

13. *Welcomes* the intention of the United Nations, set out in section I of the report of the Secretary-General, to review the programme of cooperation between the United Nations and the Organization of African Unity in order to address the needs of the African Union during the transitional period;

14. *Calls upon* United Nations agencies to continue to cooperate with the Organization of African Unity in order to facilitate the transition from the Organization of African Unity to the African Union, to intensify the coordination of their regional programmes in Africa

to ensure the effective harmonization of their programmes with those of the African regional and subregional economic organizations and to contribute to creating a positive environment for economic development and investment;

15. *Welcomes* the leadership efforts of African leaders to develop an African-owned and African-led framework for action towards the sustainable development of the African continent, and calls upon the United Nations system and the international community to support the New Partnership for Africa's Development and the ministerial declaration of the high-level segment of the substantive session of the Economic and Social Council, and the enhancement of the capacity of African countries to take advantage of the opportunities offered by globalization and overcome the challenges it poses, as a means of ensuring sustained economic growth and sustainable development;

16. *Encourages* the United Nations and the Organization of African Unity to collaborate closely in the global fight against terrorism and the implementation of the Organization of African Unity Convention on the Prevention and Combating of Terrorism and the communiqué issued by the Central Organ of the Mechanism for Conflict Prevention, Management and Resolution;

17. *Calls upon* the United Nations to support actively the efforts of the Organization of African Unity in urging the donor community and, where appropriate, multilateral institutions to strive to meet the agreed target of 0.7 per cent of gross national product for official development assistance, to implement fully, speedily and effectively the enhanced programme of debt relief for the heavily indebted poor countries, and to achieve the goal of securing debt relief in a comprehensive and effective manner in favour of African countries through various national and international measures designed to make their debt sustainable in the long term;

18. *Calls upon* all Member States and regional and international organizations, in particular those of the United Nations system, as well as non-governmental organizations, to provide additional assistance to the Organization of African Unity and those Governments in Africa concerned with the problems of refugees, returnees and displaced persons;

19. *Calls upon* the relevant organizations of the United Nations system to ensure the effective and equitable representation of African men and women at senior and policy levels at their respective headquarters and in their regional fields of operation;

20. *Requests* the Secretary-General to report to the General Assembly at its fifty-seventh session on the implementation of the present resolution.

Portuguese-speaking countries

By a 16 April note verbale [S/2001/366], Angola transmitted to the Security Council President the final communiqué of the summit meeting of the African Countries Using Portuguese as an Official Language (PALOP) (Luanda, 10 April).

Chapter III

Americas

During 2001, the United Nations continued to advance the cause of lasting peace, human rights, sustainable development and the rule of law in the Americas. The Organization monitored the political and security situation in Central America, where, despite delays in the implementation of the peace agreements in Guatemala, progress was made in the consolidation of greater democratization throughout the subregion. Peaceful general elections were held in November in both Honduras and Nicaragua.

The United Nations Verification Mission in Guatemala (MINUGUA) continued to fulfil its mandate of verifying compliance with the 1996 peace accords between the Government of Guatemala and the Unidad Revolucionaria Nacional Guatemalteca. In December, the General Assembly extended MINUGUA's mandate until 31 December 2002. In order to reactivate and speed up the implementation of pending commitments on the peace agenda, the Commission to Follow Up the Implementation of the Peace Agreements defined priority agendas for the State's executive, legislative and judiciary branches.

In Haiti, a political and security crisis continued to stall the implementation of essential structural reforms, which undermined social and economic development. The inauguration of Jean-Bertrand Aristide on 7 February as Haiti's President further polarized political and civil society, leading to major outbreaks of violence throughout the year. The mandate of the International Civilian Support Mission in Haiti (MICAH) ended on 6 February. The United Nations Development Programme assumed responsibility for formulating a post-MICAH transition programme and other UN agencies continued to provide assistance to Haiti throughout 2001.

In November, the Assembly again called on States to refrain from promulgating laws and measures such as the ongoing United States economic embargo against Cuba.

Central America

In response to General Assembly resolution 55/178 [YUN 2000, p. 237], the Secretary-General submitted a September report on the situation in Central America [A/56/416], describing progress achieved by Central American countries in the areas of peace, freedom, democracy and development since October 2000.

The Secretary-General said that the consolidation of democratic systems in Central America continued as elections unfolded peacefully throughout the region. General elections were held in Nicaragua on 4 November; Enrique Bolaños was elected President. A United Nations technical monitoring team provided advice and assistance in the pre- and post-electoral periods. General elections were held in Honduras on 25 November, resulting in the election of Ricardo Maduro Joest to the presidency. For the first time, Hondurans living abroad were entitled to vote following modifications in the Electoral Law.

With the end of armed conflict throughout the region, human rights violations were no longer systematic nor the norm, yet violations did occur and the institutions designed to protect human rights were still weak and required strengthening. In July, a new ombudsman was elected in El Salvador. With a solid mandate from the Legislative Assembly, the new ombudsman should be in a position to extend protection throughout the country and to shape the office and its agenda to play its envisioned role. The growth of the ombudsman's office in Nicaragua was also a source of optimism, as three special ombudsmen had been appointed for women, indigenous peoples and youth, respectively. The United Nations Development Programme (UNDP) and the Office of the United Nations High Commissioner for Human Rights were working with the police on developing a strategic human rights plan for the force.

Human rights compliance and public security deteriorated in Guatemala with an increase in crime, including armed assault and lynchings. There was also a growing incidence of attacks and intimidation against judicial officials, human rights activists and journalists. UNDP promoted the involvement of civil society organizations in fulfilling the 1999 Commission for Historical Clarification's recommendations [YUN 1999, p. 199].

According to the Economic Commission for Latin America and the Caribbean, the per capita gross domestic product (GDP) for the Central American region, excluding Belize and Panama, grew by only 0.7 per cent in 2000. That trend was strongly influenced by the downturn in the Costa Rican economy. The GDP of El Salvador, Guatemala, Honduras and Nicaragua in fact increased 3.6 per cent in 2000, having grown by 3.2 per cent in 1999. Although the region's financial situation continued to stabilize and structural reforms were implemented, Central America was still burdened by heavy external debt. Strengthening regional economic cooperation among the countries continued to be a challenge for development in the region. In March, Mexico launched the Puebla-Panama Plan, a comprehensive initiative involving nine states in southern Mexico and all the Central American countries. The Plan envisioned, among other things, new investment in infrastructure, human development, disaster prevention and environmental protection. Heads of State from all the countries involved met in San Salvador in June and decided to implement the Plan.

In March, the Regional Consultative Group of Central America met in Spain to follow up on a similar meeting held in Sweden in 1999 [YUN 1999, p. 195]. After extensive consultations, Central American Governments submitted the "Madrid proposal", a strategic framework for the transformation and modernization of Central America in the twenty-first century. In particular, the proposal aimed to enhance development and improve living conditions through sustained economic growth. The areas of focus included the reduction of social, economic and environmental vulnerabilities; transformation of the productive sector; sustainable management of natural resources; and increased civil society participation in development.

Heads of State from every country in the western hemisphere, with the exception of Cuba, met at the Third Summit of the Americas (Quebec City, Canada, 20-22 April) to consider an extensive agenda that included political, human rights and economic issues. Among other things, participants agreed that negotiations on a Free Trade Agreement of the Americas should be concluded no later than January 2005, and adopted a number of resolutions that should provide a firm foundation for the consolidation of institutional human rights guarantees.

The General Assembly of the Organization of American States (OAS) (San José, Costa Rica, 3-5 June) debated and considered a series of proposed reforms to the inter-American human rights system. Central American heads of State attended the Rio Group Summit (Santiago, Chile, 17-18 August) and discussed the economic crisis in Argentina and the widening technology gap between the developed and the developing world.

In early 2001, a series of earthquakes ravaged El Salvador. A severe drought that began in June affected the whole region as large parts of the harvest were damaged or destroyed, causing hunger and disastrous conditions, especially in Honduras and Nicaragua. Throughout the year, several regional initiatives were undertaken to reduce the region's social and ecological vulnerability.

The United Nations continued to support the process of peace-building and development in Central America. In El Salvador, UNDP monitored pending aspects of the 1992 Peace Agreement [YUN 1992, p. 222]. The major outstanding area of the accords remained the Fund for the Protection of the War Wounded and War Disabled, particularly the difficulty in establishing the total number of potential beneficiaries.

In Guatemala, the United Nations continued to verify compliance with the 1996 Agreement on a Firm and Lasting Peace [YUN 1996, p. 168]. General dissatisfaction with the peace process, increasing public insecurity and an economic crisis provoked escalating social and political tension.

The Secretary-General observed that as important as ensuring the foundations for good governance was the need to improve other human development indicators and combat poverty. Such a national strategy was best situated within a framework of consensus-building, effective participation and political pluralism. It was from the constant interaction of those factors that democratic political culture was built. He added that Central America had been transformed by the strides taken in the last decade. While armed conflict and the consistent violation of human rights had ended, the region had a long way to go before the poverty and structural inequalities that gave rise to conflict were overcome.

Communication. El Salvador transmitted to the Secretary-General the text of the Political Agreement between the Government and the associations representing the war wounded and disabled, adopted on 18 December [A/56/804]. The Agreement rectified the shortcomings of the Fund for the Protection of the War Wounded and War Disabled and satisfied the last outstanding commitment for the full implementation of the 1992 Peace Agreement.

GENERAL ASSEMBLY ACTION

On 24 December [meeting 92], the General Assembly adopted **resolution 56/224** [draft: A/56/L.45/Rev.1 & Add.1] without vote [agenda item 44].

The situation in Central America: procedures for the establishment of a firm and lasting peace and progress in fashioning a region of peace, freedom, democracy and development

The General Assembly,

Considering the relevant resolutions of the Security Council, particularly resolution 637(1989) of 27 July 1989, and its own resolutions, particularly resolution 43/24 of 15 November 1988, in which it requests the Secretary-General to continue his good offices and to afford the fullest possible support to the Central American Governments in their efforts to achieve the objectives of peace, reconciliation, democracy, development and justice established in the agreement on "Procedures for the establishment of a firm and lasting peace in Central America" of 7 August 1987,

Reaffirming its resolutions in which it recognizes and stresses the importance of international economic, financial and technical cooperation and assistance, both bilateral and multilateral, aimed at promoting economic and social development in the region with a view to furthering and supplementing the efforts of the Central American peoples and Governments to achieve peace and democratization, particularly resolution 52/169 G of 16 December 1997, concerning international assistance to and cooperation with the Alliance for the Sustainable Development of Central America, and the relevant resolutions concerning emergency assistance to the Central American countries, as a consequence of the destruction caused by natural disasters,

Emphasizing the importance of the development of the Central American Integration System, which has as its main objective the promotion of the integration process, the Alliance for the Sustainable Development of Central America as the integrated programme for national and regional development, which contains the commitments and priorities of the countries of the area for the promotion of sustainable development, the establishment of the subsystem and of the regional social policy, the model of democratic Central American security, and the implementation of other agreements adopted at the presidential summit meetings, which taken together constitute the global frame of reference for consolidating peace, freedom, democracy and development and the basis for the promotion of mutually advantageous relations between Central America and the international community,

Recognizing the considerable success achieved in the fulfilment of the commitments contained in the Guatemala peace agreements, implementation of which is being verified by the United Nations Verification Mission in Guatemala,

Noting with concern the deterioration in the Central American economies, mainly due to an unfavourable international economic climate and its negative effects on the efforts of the peoples and Governments of the region to achieve sustainable economic development,

Noting at the same time the delays in the fulfilment of some of the commitments contained in the Guatemala peace agreements, which have led the Commission to Follow Up the Implementation of the Peace Agreements to reschedule its fulfilment for the period 2001-2004, and having considered the report of the Secretary-General on the work of the United Nations Verification Mission in Guatemala and the recommendations contained therein aimed at ensuring that the Mission is able to respond adequately to the demands of the peace process until December 2002,

Taking note with satisfaction of the successful implementation of the peace agreements and the continuous consolidation of the process of democratization in El Salvador, as a result of the efforts of its people and Government,

Recognizing with satisfaction the role played by the peacekeeping operations and observer and monitoring missions of the United Nations, which carried out successfully their mandate in Central America pursuant to the relevant resolutions of the Security Council and the General Assembly, respectively,

Recognizing with satisfaction also the organization and holding of general elections in 2001, in Nicaragua on 4 November and in Honduras on 25 November,

Emphasizing the importance of the end of a critical period in Central American history and the start of a new phase free from armed conflict, with freely elected Governments in each country and with political, economic, social and other changes which are creating a climate conducive to the promotion of economic growth and further progress towards the consolidation and further development of democratic, just and equitable societies,

Noting that the Third Meeting of the States Parties to the Convention on the Prohibition of the Use, Stockpiling, Production and Transfer of Anti-personnel Mines and on Their Destruction was held in Nicaragua in September 2001,

Reaffirming that the consolidation and establishment of firm and lasting peace and democracy in Central America is a dynamic and ongoing process that faces serious structural challenges,

Stressing the importance of progress in human development, especially the alleviation of extreme poverty, the promotion of economic and social justice, judicial reform, the promotion and safeguarding of human rights and fundamental freedoms, respect for minorities and the satisfaction of the basic needs of the most vulnerable groups among the peoples in the region, issues which have been a primary source of tension and conflict and which deserve to be discussed with the same urgency and dedication as was the case in the settlement of armed conflicts,

Considering with concern that it has not yet been possible to overcome the devastating effects of hurricanes Mitch and Keith on certain countries of the region, which are causing setbacks in the progress made by the peoples and Governments of Central America, a situation which is aggravated by the earthquakes in El Salvador and the drought afflicting the entire region in 2001, especially Honduras and Nicaragua,

Emphasizing the solidarity of the international community with the victims of hurricane Mitch, as demonstrated by the Stockholm Declaration, the subsequent meetings of the Regional Consultative Group for the transformation and modernization of Central America and, in particular, by the meeting of the Group, held in Madrid on 8 and 9 March 2001, at which the requirements of the Central American countries affected by natural disasters, including the earthquakes in El Salvador early in 2001, were considered,

Bearing in mind the efforts made by the Central American Governments to reduce the risks and mitigate the consequences of natural disasters in the region, as demonstrated by the adoption, by the Presidents of the Isthmus, of the Declaration of Guatemala II of 19 October 1999, the subsequent adoption of the Strategic Framework for the Reduction of Vulnerability and Disasters in Central America, as well as the adoption of the Central American Five-Year Plan for the Reduction of Vulnerability to and the Impact of Disasters, 2000 to 2004,

1. *Takes note with appreciation* of the report of the Secretary-General on the situation in Central America;

2. *Commends* the efforts of the peoples and the Governments of the Central American countries to re-establish peace and democracy throughout the region and promote sustainable development by implementing the commitments adopted at the summit meetings in the region, and supports the decision of the Presidents that Central America should become a region of peace, freedom, democracy and development;

3. *Reaffirms* the need to continue to improve the electoral processes that have been taking place in Central America, which are conducive to the consolidation of democracy in the region;

4. *Recognizes* the need to continue to follow closely the situation in Central America according to the objectives and principles established in the Stockholm Declaration in order to support national and regional efforts to overcome the underlying causes that have led to armed conflicts, avoid setbacks and consolidate peace and democratization in the area and promote the objectives of the Alliance for the Sustainable Development of Central America;

5. *Takes note with satisfaction* of the results of the meeting of the Regional Consultative Group for the transformation and modernization of Central America which will continue to help to consolidate the transformation and modernization of Central America through the implementation of measures to reform and harmonize the legislation and institutions of the region, and through specific development projects;

6. *Reaffirms* the importance of the Puebla-Panama Plan as a means of promoting the economic and social development of the Mesoamerican region, and in that connection recognizes the progress made in implementing the Plan and invites the friendly countries of the Mesoamerican region, international agencies and international businessmen and investors to support the Mesoamerican countries in the implementation of the projects prioritized in the Plan;

7. *Recognizes* the efforts made by the Government of El Salvador to deal effectively with the requirements deriving from the earthquakes in that country early in 2001;

8. *Welcomes* the valuable and speedy response of the international community to the serious natural disasters which have affected the region, in particular the earthquakes in El Salvador early in 2001, which demonstrates the permanent solidarity that unites the peoples of the world, and also urges the cooperating international community to continue to make the necessary contributions to supplement national efforts to reconstruct the country;

9. *Also welcomes* the Declaration of Guatemala II which provides for the necessary measures to prevent vulnerability to and mitigate the effects of natural disasters;

10. *Further welcomes* the progress achieved in implementing the Guatemala peace agreements, calls upon all parties to take further measures to implement the commitments in the peace agreements, in particular with regard to the Fiscal Pact for a Future with Peace and Development, the Agreement on Identity and Rights of Indigenous Peoples, and the recommendations of the Commission for Historical Clarification, and urges all sectors of society to combine efforts and work with courage and determination to consolidate peace;

11. *Requests* the Secretary-General, the bodies and programmes of the United Nations system and the international community to continue to support and verify in Guatemala the implementation of all the peace agreements signed under United Nations auspices, compliance with which is an essential condition for a firm and lasting peace in that country, and to consider the implementation of the peace agreements as the framework for their technical and financial assistance programmes and projects, stressing the importance of constant and close cooperation among them in the context of the United Nations Development Assistance Framework for Guatemala;

12. *Expresses its appreciation and satisfaction* to the people and the Government of El Salvador for their successful efforts to fulfil the commitments set forth in the peace agreements, which have made a substantial contribution to the strengthening of the process of democratization in that country;

13. *Recognizes* the importance of the Central American Integration System as the body set up to coordinate and harmonize efforts to achieve integration, and calls upon the international community, the United Nations system and other international organizations, both governmental and non-governmental, to extend effective cooperation with a view to improving the competence and efficiency of the Integration System in the fulfilment of its mandate;

14. *Underlines* the efforts carried out in the Central American region towards integration, such as the Trinational Declaration between Guatemala, El Salvador and Nicaragua, as well as the Customs Union between those countries, as means for promoting integration while respecting different stages of development, through a pragmatic mechanism open to the participation of the other countries of the region; underlines also the most recent progress in the form of the frontier post in Peñas Blancas, Nicaragua, common to four countries (El Salvador, Guatemala, Honduras and Nicaragua), which became operational in October 2001; this customs unification, involving twelve frontier posts, entailed bilateral, trinational and quadrinational unifications;

15. *Encourages* the Central American Governments to continue to carry out their historic responsibilities by implementing fully the commitments they have assumed under national, regional or international agreements, especially the agreements for the promotion and safeguarding of human rights, and the commitments to implement the social programme to overcome poverty and unemployment, establish a more just and equitable society, improve public safety, strengthen the judiciary, consolidate a modern and transparent public

administration and eliminate corruption, impunity, acts of terrorism and drug and arms trafficking, all of which are necessary and urgent measures for consolidating a firm and lasting peace in the region;

16. *Reiterates its deep appreciation* to the Secretary-General, his special representatives, the groups of countries for the peace processes in El Salvador (Colombia, Mexico, Spain, United States of America and Venezuela), and Guatemala (Colombia, Mexico, Norway, Spain, United States of America and Venezuela), to the Support Group for Nicaragua (Canada, Mexico, Netherlands, Spain and Sweden), to the European Union and to other countries that have contributed significantly and to the international community in general for its support and solidarity in the building of peace, democracy and development in Central America;

17. *Reaffirms* the importance of international cooperation, in particular cooperation with the bodies, funds and programmes of the United Nations system and the donor community in the new stage of consolidating firm and lasting peace and democracy in Central America, and urges them to continue to support Central American efforts to achieve those goals;

18. *Notes with satisfaction* the firm determination of the Central American Governments to settle their disputes through peaceful means, thereby avoiding any setback in the efforts to consolidate firm and lasting peace in the region;

19. *Requests* the Secretary-General to continue to lend his full support to the initiatives and activities of the Central American Governments, particularly their efforts to consolidate peace and democracy through the promotion of integration and the implementation of the comprehensive sustainable development programme, emphasizing, inter alia, the potential repercussions of natural disasters, in particular the persisting effects of hurricane Mitch, for the peace processes and the vulnerable economies of the region, and to report to the General Assembly at its fifty-seventh session on the implementation of the present resolution;

20. *Decides* to include in the provisional agenda of its fifty-seventh session the item entitled "The situation in Central America: procedures for the establishment of a firm and lasting peace and progress in fashioning a region of peace, freedom, democracy and development".

On 24 December, the Assembly decided that the agenda item on the situation in Central America would remain for consideration during its resumed fifty-sixth (2002) session (**decision 56/464**).

Guatemala

The peace process in Guatemala made little progress in 2001. However, with the aim of establishing targeted sectoral partnerships on urgent topics, the Commission to Follow Up the Implementation of the Peace Agreements submitted priority agendas for the three branches of government. The Congress of the Republic approved some measures provided for in the 1999

Fiscal Pact [YUN 1999, p. 202], such as an increase in some taxes and the strengthening of the State's sanctioning capacity. The approval of those measures polarized the political debate, leading to anti-Government demonstrations. In August, the private sector staged protest strikes, which turned violent in some provinces. The Government, in turn, declared a state of siege in the department of Totonicapán. The Secretary-General's Chef de Cabinet, Iqbal Riza, in a visit to Guatemala in June, tried to reactivate a dialogue among all social and political parties, but to no avail.

The United Nations Verification Mission in Guatemala (MINUGUA) continued to verify the implementation of the 1996 Agreement on a Firm and Lasting Peace [YUN 1996, p. 168], signed by the Government of Guatemala and the Unidad Revolucionaria Nacional Guatemalteca (URNG), and monitored compliance with the 2000-2004 verification timetable [YUN 2000, p. 239]. The calendar established in the 1997 Agreement on the Implementation, Compliance and Verification Timetable for the Peace Agreements [YUN 1997, p. 176] for the period 1997-2000, also signed by the Government and URNG, expired in December 2000. Since much of the peace agenda remained outstanding, the Commission to Follow Up the Implementation of the Peace Agreements rescheduled pending commitments in an implementation timetable for 2000-2004, which recognized that the basis of the Timetable Agreement and the peace agreements as a whole remained valid.

MINUGUA

The mandate of MINUGUA, which was extended to 31 December 2001 by General Assembly resolution 55/177 [YUN 2000, p. 247], included verification of all agreements signed by the Government of Guatemala and URNG, covering human rights, the parties' compliance with the ceasefire, separation and concentration of the respective forces, and disarmament and demobilization of former URNG combatants. The Mission's functions also comprised verifying compliance with the 2000-2004 timetable for the implementation of pending commitments under the Peace Agreements, in addition to good offices, advisory and support services and public information.

Report of Secretary-General. In response to Assembly resolution 55/177, the Secretary-General submitted a September report [A/56/391] covering the state of implementation of the peace agreements (see below) and the structure and staffing of MINUGUA. It also contained recommendations for assisting the peace-building process and continuing the gradual scaling-down of MINUGUA's operations, especially in 2002.

Since the rescheduling of the pending commitments in December 2000, the peace process made little progress, heightening social polarization and political conflict. In view of the standstill in the implementation process, the Commission to Follow Up the Implementation of the Peace Agreements defined a reactivation strategy that involved preparing and presenting priority agendas for the main sectors of State activity. The agenda for the executive branch included commitments relating to national reconciliation, socio-economic aspects, public security and the armed forces, and human rights and justice. The agenda for the legislative branch called on Congress to consider laws on participation, modernization, the electoral system, human rights, indigenous peoples' rights, social development and other fiscal initiatives. The agenda for the judicial system suggested giving priority to the drafting of a State policy against crime and to expanding access to justice for the entire population. The Secretary-General said that, in 2002, compliance with the rescheduled timetable would have to speed up and important reforms would have to go into effect, such as the amendments to the Elections and Political Parties Act, which would govern the general elections to be held in 2003.

During 2001, MINUGUA had to provide increased support, facilitation and good offices at the request of the parties, in order to exert a positive influence on the prevention and resolution of many local and national conflicts. Among other things, the Mission provided technical assistance to the Presidential Office for Conflict Resolution, the function of which was to coordinate a comprehensive approach to multiple sources of tension. Systematic, across-the-board impunity for crimes and human rights violations remained the principal obstacle to the enjoyment of those rights. At the same time, there was a need to expand access to the media, especially for indigenous people, avoid media concentration and safeguard the public's right to receive objective, unbiased information.

The scaling back of MINUGUA [YUN 2000, p. 240] had an impact on the Mission's territorial deployment, bringing the number of its regional offices down from eight to six and its regional sub-offices down from five to four, and forced it to prioritize its activities, especially verification and institution-building. During the period 2002-2003, MINUGUA would have to meet new challenges, such as the deteriorating human rights situation; the growing climate of conflict in the country's interior; the need to give priority to promoting compliance with the Agreement on

Identity and Rights of Indigenous Peoples; and the tasks of verifying the exercise of political rights and providing technical assistance for the new electoral legislation that would govern the holding of the 2003 general elections. The Secretary-General proposed that the reduction envisaged for 2002 should not affect or alter the territorial deployment planned for 2001 and that all the mobile teams envisaged should be put into operation. Concomitantly, the regional offices would be reinforced by redeploying posts from MINUGUA headquarters. In 2001, MINUGUA headquarters was structured around four substantive areas: human rights; juridical affairs; socio-economic affairs, resettlement and integration; and public security and the armed forces. In 2002, the substantive areas would not include juridical affairs, as the human rights section would take over the verification of the justice system and the juridical affairs section would cease to function. The new human rights and justice section would be responsible for verifying compliance with all the commitments made under the 1994 Comprehensive Agreement on Human Rights [YUN 1994, p. 407] with regard to the administration of justice and the right to justice. It would also coordinate with the UN system the monitoring of the overall process of reform and modernization of the administration of justice.

In 2001, the offices of the police and military advisers were merged with the public security and armed forces section and the number of police and military personnel was reduced from 51 to 10 police observers and from 20 to 4 military liaison officers. Of the two special units established on cross-cutting themes, the women's unit would cease to function and its monitoring and institution-building tasks would be transferred to the UN system, while the socio-economic affairs section would maintain a focal point on the agrarian situation and coordinate with MINUGUA. The indigenous affairs unit would become an Indigenous Affairs Advisory Service and a new conflict-resolution and State reform unit would be set up to meet the new challenges posed by electoral reform.

In anticipation of the Mission's withdrawal, a Transition Group, composed of officials appointed by the Secretary-General's Special Representative and by the resident coordinator of the UN system for operational activities for development, would be set up to establish policy guidelines for projects being transferred to UN agencies and provide legal advice.

The Secretary-General observed that 2002 would be decisive for progress in complying with the Guatemalan peace agreements and reiterated the commitment of the United Nations to the peace process. Accordingly, he recommended that the Assembly authorize the renewal of MINU-GUA's mandate for a further period of one year, until 31 December 2002.

Verification of compliance

In response to General Assembly resolution 55/177 [YUN 2000, p. 247], the Secretary-General in June submitted his sixth report [A/55/973] on the verification of compliance with the agreements signed by the Government of Guatemala and URNG [YUN 1996, p. 168].

The implementation of the commitments entered into by the two parties was governed by the Timetable Agreement [YUN 1997, p. 176], which expired in December 2000. The Commission to Follow Up the Implementation of the Peace Agreements rescheduled pending commitments in an implementation timetable for 2000-2004 [YUN 2000, p. 239], which recognized the validity of the Timetable Agreement.

The Secretary-General expressed concern about the scant progress made in the implementation of the agreements, citing the lengthy time it took the Government to effect the transition, replace officials in charge of institutions central to the peace process and formulate public policies. An overall assessment of the peace agreements showed that the process of sustainable resettlement and definitive integration of demobilized combatants had not gone far enough and there was still no comprehensive development strategy that would ensure the sustainability of the overall integration of those population groups. In the social development area, huge gaps remained between the indigenous and non-indigenous population, between rural and urban areas and between men and women. The formulation of public policies on such issues as education, housing and health, which in some cases involved consultations with civil society, represented significant progress. On the other hand, the formulation of a policy for sustainable development of production and the creation of institutions capable of promoting it were still in the early stages and progress had been made on only a few specific issues.

The work done by the National Commission for Monitoring and Supporting the Strengthening of the Justice System [YUN 2000, p. 244] had fostered dialogue between civil society and State institutions. However, the justice system's performance showed no signs of significant improvements, especially regarding the investigations of human rights violations. Commitments in the areas of public security, police reform and transformation of the armed forces' role faced the challenges of a society in transition from war

to peace. The situation of insecurity and the limitations of the National Civil Police (PNC) continued to be invoked to justify maintaining an active role for the armed forces in public security tasks. That represented a setback in the demilitarization of public security and was not conducive to the strengthening of either civilian power or the police. Fulfilment of the commitments on the armed forces had been uneven, since, although progress had been made in their restructuring and deployment, the commitments on military intelligence and the formulation of a new military doctrine had not moved forward.

The sustainable, equitable development of resettlement areas and the integration of uprooted and demobilized population groups continued to face major constraints. The integration phase for demobilized combatants was still moving very slowly, due, in part, to the lack of progress in complying with other agreements, especially the 1996 Agreement on Social and Economic Aspects and Agrarian Situation [YUN 1996, p. 165]. Some progress had been made in land and housing projects, but projects related to integration in production, health care for the disabled and exhumation of URNG's combatants started very late. The Peace Secretariat continued to implement pilot compensation projects in some departments of the country, but, overall, little progress had been made in compensating victims of human rights violations.

The execution of public spending was slow; it accelerated in the closing months of the reporting period, but only in the education and health sectors. In housing, the effective spending rate was inadequate, owing to lack of access to funds budgeted and appropriated. In 2001, social funds managed approximately 25 per cent of the State's social investment, which underscored the need to completely overhaul them in order to improve investment efficiency and returns.

The concentration of land ownership, low wages and the adverse conditions resulting from the decline in the international price for some of the country's main exports, mainly coffee, continued to challenge the sustainability of the peace-building process. A promising development was the adoption by the Congress of 36 amendments to the Labour Code, which represented major progress in complying with the peace agreements and bringing domestic legislation into line with the recommendations of the International Labour Organization. In addition, the Ministry of Agriculture created a Gender, Women and Rural Youth Unit to add a gender perspective to its work and to promote women's equal access to land ownership.

The modernization of the State, which focused on strengthening social participation and consensus-building, remained a key element in the implementation and consolidation of the peace agreements. The decentralization process, however, experienced uncertainty and considerable delays. In early 2001, the Presidential Commissioner for the Modernization and Decentralization of the State assumed overall responsibility for the decentralization process, in order to better coordinate and accelerate its implementation. The National Women's Forum made great progress in promoting participation by indigenous and non-indigenous women, though it still faced constraints on their participation in development planning forums. Although some progress had been made on taxation and other aspects which improved tax collection by curbing tax evasion, not enough had been done to implement the commitments made in the 1999 Fiscal Pact [YUN 1999, p. 202]. In particular, the Government failed to make progress on issues such as assessment and oversight of public spending and fiscal decentralization.

Public spending in the justice sector increased and considerable efforts were made to give indigenous people access to justice and to recognize their customary law. Public security remained an issue of concern, even though the spending target for it been exceeded. PNC made progress by creating and setting up specialized units and by increasing its efforts to prevent lynchings. However, the units' incomplete territorial deployment and lack of human and material resources undermined their effectiveness. In the reporting period, proposals were made for promoting the formulation of rules and structures for the intelligence services, as well as for their oversight and functioning. The process of formulating a new doctrine for the armed forces was ongoing. The television frequency allocated to the armed forces was reassigned to the Office of the President of the Republic, thereby complying with the corresponding agreement. The redeployment of military units continued and the reassignment of troops would enable available resources to be used more appropriately. The commitment to replace the Presidential General Staff was rescheduled to the first half of 2003.

The Secretary-General observed that substantial, sustained progress on the pending agenda was essential for overcoming the profound social inequalities that existed in Guatemala. Lack of equity in employment, ethnic discrimination, lack of access to basic services and the fact that large sectors of the population continued to live in extreme poverty threatened the gains and sustainability of the peace process. Resolving that situation was the basic prerequisite for guaranteeing peace and eliminating the considerable potential for conflict that still characterized Guatemalan society.

In a later report [A/56/1003], the Secretary-General said that, as of the end of 2001, many of the commitments that had been rescheduled for that year had not been fulfilled. In October, the Productive Projects Trust was set up to deal with the sustainable resettlement of the uprooted population and the integration of URNG's former combatants, but the Government had yet to allocate the necessary financial resources to the Trust. The end of 2001 was set as the deadline for fulfilment of the rescheduled commitments concerning information and intelligence. However, no bills had been drafted for the creation of a civil intelligence department in the Ministry of the Interior, nor had any progress been made on the law that was supposed to establish procedures for the legislative oversight of State intelligence agencies. The Secretary-General noted that PNC, as at December, had met the target of 200,000 members, 12 per cent of whom were indigenous and 10 per cent women.

Human rights

In August [A/56/273], the Secretary-General transmitted to the General Assembly MINUGUA's twelfth report on human rights, which described the Mission's activities between 1 July 2000 and 30 June 2001.

During the period under review, the Mission received 352 complaints, compared with 285 during the previous reporting period [YUN 2000, p. 245]. There was a decrease in the number of alleged violations of the rights accorded priority under the 1994 Comprehensive Agreement on Human Rights [YUN 1994, p. 407]. Despite the Government's repeated assertions that it was willing to promote a human rights agenda, institutional shortcomings and insufficient action caused delays and impunity. There was an increase in the involvement of municipal authorities in right-to-life violations, especially auxiliary mayors, who were responsible for the bulk of violations, and of former members of the Voluntary Civil Defence Committees, who were mainly responsible for lynchings. There were also further cases of executions by PNC members. On 8 June, the Third Trial Court convicted State agents of Monsignor Juan José Gerardi Conedera's murder [YUN 1998, p. 219] and determined that it had been a political crime. The sentence contained a direct reference to the existence of a modus operandi, tolerated and abetted by State structures, in the planning, execution and subsequent cover-up of Monsignor Gerardi's assassination.

The practice of torture, cruel, inhuman and degrading treatment and ill-treatment persisted. The main characteristic of the period under review was the large number of complaints of threats, harassment and intimidation against persons and institutions working for the protection of human rights, civil servants and persons involved in judicial proceedings, which had been neither investigated nor punished. In some cases of intimidation, political motives could not be ruled out. In other cases, pressure was used to prevent the clarification and judicial punishment of serious violations and offences, especially when they were attributed to State agents. On his visit to the country in May, the Special Rapporteur of the United Nations Commission on Human Rights on the independence of judges and lawyers expressed concern for the security and independence of persons involved in judicial proceedings and expressed regret at the failure to implement most of the recommendations made following his August 1999 visit [YUN 1999, p. 627]. Violations of the right to freedom of association and assembly continued, and the right to freedom of expression was affected by alleged threats against communications media and journalists.

In June, inmates of the Escuintla maximum security prison, including those indicted and convicted in cases that had had a major impact on society, escaped with the cooperation and complicity of most of the prison staff. The escape, a serious setback for efforts to combat impunity, further exacerbated the public's feeling that it was defenceless against crime and discouraged those witnesses, judges and prosecutors who had played an effective role in the punishment of dangerous criminals. At the same time, attacks on police stations, acts of mob violence and lynchings, the release of alleged criminals and serious clashes between communities occurred with alarming frequency, seriously undermining governance in various municipalities.

The influence and involvement of illegal security forces and clandestine structures in criminal activities increased, though the complicity that they enjoyed made them difficult to verify. Clandestine groups also operated within prisons and conducted illegal parallel investigations without proper authorization. The existence of criminal groups within private security companies was also reported. The problem was complicated by the fact that such companies employed over 25,000 people, many of whom were alleged to have committed serious human rights violations. Little progress was made in providing compensation for victims of human rights violations, even

though a Commission for Peace and Harmony was set up in June.

In a later report [A/57/336], MINUGUA stated that the armed forces continued to expand their role in public security and other spheres of government action. In November, the Defence Minister, then a general on active duty, was nominated by the President of Guatemala to head the Ministry of the Interior, in charge of PNC. Military and former military officers were later appointed to key positions in the Ministry, the National Security Commission, the prison system, the civil aviation authority and the tourism institute. Also in November, Congress approved the Law on Mandatory Professional Membership, prompting some concerns that it was an attempt to restrict journalists' freedom of expression. However, the Constitutional Court ruled provisionally that there was no requirement of professional membership in order to exercise freedom of expression.

GENERAL ASSEMBLY ACTION

On 24 December [meeting 92], the General Assembly adopted **resolution 56/223** [draft: A/56/L.42/Rev.1] without vote [agenda item 44].

United Nations Verification Mission in Guatemala

The General Assembly,

Recalling its resolution 55/177 of 19 December 2000, in which it decided to authorize the renewal of the mandate of the United Nations Verification Mission in Guatemala from 1 January to 31 December 2001,

Taking into account the fact that the Government of Guatemala has expressed its commitment to the full implementation of the peace agreements,

Underlining the fact that substantive aspects of the peace agreements have yet to be implemented and that the Commission to Follow Up the Implementation of the Peace Agreements has approved a new schedule for their implementation from 2000 until the end of 2004,

Taking into account that the parties have requested the United Nations to support the consolidation of the peace-building process until 2003,

Taking into account also the twelfth report of the Mission on human rights,

Taking into account further the sixth report of the Secretary-General on the verification of compliance with the peace agreements,

Taking into account the report of the Commission for Historical Clarification,

Stressing the positive role played by the Mission in support of the Guatemala peace process, and emphasizing the need for the Mission to continue to enjoy the full support of all parties concerned,

Having considered the report of the Secretary-General on the work of the Mission,

1. *Welcomes* the twelfth report of the United Nations Verification Mission in Guatemala on human rights;

2. *Also welcomes* the sixth report of the Secretary-General on the verification of compliance with the peace agreements;

3. *Recalls* the report of the Commission for Historical Clarification and the recommendations contained therein;

4. *Welcomes* the commitment made by the Government of Guatemala to the full implementation of the peace agreements through the adoption of social policies anchored to the agreements;

5. *Recalls* that the Commission to Follow Up the Implementation of the Peace Agreements has rescheduled the pending commitments and included others not initially scheduled;

6. *Takes note* of the recommendations contained in the report of the Secretary-General aimed at ensuring that the Mission can respond adequately to the demands of the peace process until 31 December 2002, as well as of his proposals relating to the changes in the structure and staffing of the Mission for the period 2001-2003;

7. *Also takes note* of the agreement reached by the parties regarding the importance of the continuing presence of the Mission in Guatemala until 2003;

8. *Notes with satisfaction* the progress made in the implementation of the peace agreements, in particular the partial fulfilment of the Fiscal Pact for a Future with Peace and Development which establishes the basis for increased public spending on the peace agenda and paves the way for the modernization of the economic system, and stresses the need to complete its implementation, in particular as regards measures to enhance public confidence in Government spending;

9. *Also notes with satisfaction* the significant reforms introduced in labour laws and the reinforcement of the operational capacities, training and full deployment of the National Civil Police;

10. *Underlines with concern* the fact that key commitments remain outstanding in the areas of fiscal, judicial, military, electoral and land reform, as well as decentralization and rural development, and therefore urges that those commitments be implemented without further delay;

11. *Notes* that the consolidation of the peace-building process remains a significant challenge that requires a concerted national effort to guarantee the irreversibility of the peace process;

12. *Also notes* that the present Government has taken a significant step forward by signing and ratifying various important international human rights instruments;

13. *Encourages* the Government to implement the recommendations contained in the reports of the Mission on human rights, in particular those related to the systematic impunity for crimes and human rights violations and the alarming increase in incidents directed at individuals working on human rights and judicial issues;

14. *Underlines* the importance of implementing fully the Agreement on Identity and Rights of Indigenous Peoples as a key to fighting discrimination and consolidating peace and equality in Guatemala, and highlights the need to implement fully the Agreement on Social and Economic Aspects and Agrarian Situation as a means of addressing the root causes of the armed conflict;

15. *Calls upon* the Government to implement the recommendations of the Commission for Historical Clarification with a view to promoting national reconciliation, upholding the right to truth and providing redress for the victims of human rights abuses and violence committed during the thirty-six-year conflict, and calls upon Congress to establish, as recommended, the Commission for Peace and Harmony;

16. *Invites* the international community and, in particular, the agencies, programmes and funds of the United Nations to continue to support the consolidation of the peace-building process, with the peace agreements as the framework for their technical and financial assistance programmes and projects, and stresses the continued importance of close cooperation among them in the context of the United Nations Development Assistance Framework for Guatemala;

17. *Urges* the international community to support financially, through existing mechanisms of international cooperation, the strengthening of national capacities to ensure the consolidation of the peace process in Guatemala;

18. *Also urges* the international community to support financially the strengthening of the capacities of the United Nations agencies and programmes as the Mission will transfer some of its activities and projects to these agencies to support the national efforts to comply with the commitments of the peace agreements;

19. *Stresses* that the Mission has a key role to play in promoting the consolidation of peace and the observance of human rights and in verifying compliance with the revised timetable for the implementation of pending commitments under the peace agreements;

20. *Decides* to authorize the renewal of the mandate of the Mission from 1 January to 31 December 2002;

21. *Requests* the Secretary-General to submit, as early as possible, an updated report to the General Assembly at its fifty-seventh session, together with his recommendations regarding the continuation of the peace-building phase after 31 December 2002;

22. *Also requests* the Secretary-General to keep the General Assembly fully informed of the implementation of the present resolution.

Haiti

During 2001, Haiti continued to experience a political and security crisis, which stalled the implementation of essential structural reforms and undermined social and economic development. The general human rights situation again deteriorated, with growing intimidation and attacks on journalists and human rights activists. The year was marked by several major security incidents, including assaults against the Police Academy in July and against the Presidential Palace in December, followed, in both cases, by violence against opposition members and the media.

The International Civilian Support Mission in Haiti (MICAH) was closed at the end of its mandate on 6 February. UNDP assumed responsibility for the implementation of a post-MICAH transition programme and other UN agencies continued to provide assistance to Haiti throughout the year. OAS took the lead in trying to mediate a solution to the political crisis, though little progress was made.

International Civilian Support Mission

In April [A/55/905], the Secretary-General submitted the last report on the activities of MICAH, covering developments in the Mission's area from 10 November 2000 to 6 February 2001. MICAH had been established by General Assembly resolution 54/193 [YUN 1999, p. 218] to consolidate the results achieved by the OAS/UN International Civilian Mission in Haiti (MICIVIH), the United Nations Civilian Police Mission in Haiti (MIPONUH) and previous UN missions.

The period under review was marked by the holding of the November 2000 elections for President and a third of the Senate [YUN 2000, p. 255] and its aftermath, which saw a concerted civil society effort to promote political dialogue, questionable opposition moves to form an alternative government, and a climate of tension and threats accompanied by intermittent bombings. The elections resulted in a landslide victory for the ruling party Fanmi Lavalas and the election of its leader and former President, Jean-Bertrand Aristide, to the presidency. The opposition parties boycotted the elections over a dispute with Fanmi Lavalas pertaining to irregularities committed during the parliamentary and municipal elections of May 2000 [ibid., p. 253]. After Fanmi Lavalas proposed the eight-point accord with the United States on 27 December 2000 [ibid., p. 255] as the starting point for any dialogue, talks between Fanmi Lavalas and the Democratic Convergence (a 15-member opposition party coalition) started on 3 February, but discussions broke down three days later due to lack of significant concessions by either side. Mr. Aristide was installed as President on 7 February.

MICAH was closed at the end of its mandate on 6 February and the first group of advisers began leaving on 19 January. The Mission was created with a mandate of 11 months, three of which were lost because of delays in obtaining the necessary voluntary contributions. The brevity of the working period limited MICAH's overall effectiveness, especially as it was mandated to work in areas where multi-year programmes were called for, such as judicial reform and strengthening of police command. The Mission's ability to be effective was also limited by a difficult and tense political context following the May and November 2000 elections. MICAH's capacity to contribute to the institutional reinforcement of the justice and human rights sectors, and especially public secu-

rity, was also hampered by an insufficient determination within the country to strengthen those institutions. Nonetheless, MICAH contributed to some advances in all of the mandated areas.

MICAH's programme for the Haitian National Police focused on central command, administrative and control structures, including the Inspectorate General, and the departmental command centres. Activities included developing and putting into place key management and administrative tools and procedures, strengthening decentralized command and management capacities, helping to launch a permanent recruitment programme and drafting a career incentive and development plan for police officers. However, those developments were undercut by, among other things, highly centralized command structures; politicization, demoralization and a wait-and-see attitude; and corruption and involvement of police officers in criminal activity. The Mission also contributed towards the improvement of human rights training at the Police Academy, the Prison Authority's training centre and the Judges School, and supported the drafting of a law defining the Ombudsman's Office mandate and structure.

As work continued on the formulation of a United Nations Development Assistance Framework (UNDAF) [YUN 2000, p. 254], three working groups were established in the areas of education for all, human resources and access to social services; governance and rule of law; and food security and sustainable rural development. UNDP, in close coordination with the Friends of the Secretary-General for Haiti, MICAH and the UN Department of Political Affairs, developed a post-MICAH transition programme, for which funding was being sought. The programme would build on UNDP's ongoing activities related to the rule of law, while consolidating activities initiated by MICAH. Its five main objectives were: strengthening national capacities in the justice sector; facilitating a participatory judicial reform process; improving access to justice; consolidating the institutional development of the police and prison systems; and strengthening national capacities in human rights monitoring and promotion. Unfortunately, sufficient funding was not found to allow for an immediate handover of MICAH's tasks.

In a statement to the press on 13 February, the Security Council called on the Haitian authorities and politicians actively to continue their efforts at reconciliation and resolve their differences through dialogue. The Council also encouraged OAS to continue to identify options and recommendations aimed at resolving the political situation and requested UN agencies, especially UNDP, to work with Haitian authorities on the restructuring of the security forces and the judicial system and on strengthening human rights.

The Secretary-General observed that all the UN missions had contributed effectively to the reinforcement of Haiti's democratic institutions and to the respect for human rights, although strong countervailing forces often reduced those gains. He noted that President Aristide had expressed interest in a continuation of UN assistance in projects related to the rule of law. In order to respond to that request, it would be necessary to devise new forms of technical assistance that might better allow the UN system to support the Haitian people. President Aristide had also expressed interest in maintaining the position of the Representative of the Secretary-General with the mandate of facilitating dialogue between the various political actors and promoting peace. The Secretary-General would consult with relevant parties to assess how to respond to that request. Though the democratic process in Haiti had been undermined, the United Nations would continue to support the Haitian people in their difficult transition towards democracy.

On 7 September, the General Assembly decided to include in the draft agenda of its fifty-sixth (2001) session the item on the situation of democracy and human rights in Haiti (**decision 55/489**). On 24 December, the Assembly decided that the item would remain for consideration at its resumed fifty-sixth (2002) session (**decision 56/464**).

Post-MICAH activities

In a report to the Economic and Social Council [E/2002/56], the Secretary-General said that on 1 March the Haitian Parliament approved the appointment of Jean-Marie Chérestal as Prime Minister. Following MICAH's closure in February and the departure of the Special Representative of the Secretary-General for Haiti, OAS took the lead responsibility for providing international support for the negotiation process between Fanmi Lavalas and the Democratic Convergence on reaching an agreement to end the political crisis. Despite the fact that numerous OAS mediation missions took place throughout 2001, little progress was made.

The UN resident coordinator withdrew from his functions in Haiti in July. In August, the candidacy of a new resident coordinator was presented to the Haitian Government, which gave its approval in December. Prior to his departure, the outgoing resident coordinator had placed significant emphasis on the completion of the UN-DAF document and focused on the implementa-

tion of mechanisms for ensuring an efficient post-MICAH transition.

Owing to its special role in the transition phase and its responsibility for providing a degree of institutional memory to the UN system in Haiti, UNDP had continued to follow the development of the political situation through regular contact with OAS. UNDP's transition programme took place under difficult circumstances, marked by, among other things, increased political polarization and the near-complete withdrawal of bilateral donors' support to the rule of law. The post-MICAH transition programme was launched without the allocation of any additional resources and, therefore, it had been impossible to implement the full range of activities originally foreseen. Despite those difficulties, UNDP and other UN agencies continued to provide assistance to Haiti throughout 2001 (see p. 856).

Financing of missions

In January [A/55/753], the Secretary-General submitted to the General Assembly MIPONUH's financial performance report for the period from 1 July 1999 to 30 June 2000. Expenditures for the period totalled $18,082,500 gross ($16,952,200 net), resulting in an unencumbered balance of $559,116 gross ($666,216 net).

In April [A/55/881], the Advisory Committee on Administrative and Budgetary Questions (ACABQ) reviewed the Secretary-General's reports on MIPONUH's financial performance (see above) and on the final disposition of the assets of the United Nations Support Mission in Haiti (UNSMIH), which ended in July 1997, the United Nations Transition Mission in Haiti (UNTMIH), which terminated in November 1997, and MIPONUH, which terminated in March 2000 (liquidation phase was completed in September 2000) [YUN 2000, p. 257]. ACABQ suggested that the Assembly should authorize the Secretary-General to utilize an amount of $164,200 gross ($142,900 net) in order to meet the cost of completing the liquidation tasks at UN Headquarters.

GENERAL ASSEMBLY ACTION

On 14 June [meeting 103], the General Assembly, on the recommendation of the Fifth (Administrative and Budgetary) Committee [A/55/963], adopted **resolution 55/269** without vote [agenda item 150].

Financing of the United Nations Civilian Police Mission in Haiti

The General Assembly,

Having considered the reports of the Secretary-General on the financing of the United Nations Support Mission in Haiti, the United Nations Transition Mission in Haiti and the United Nations Civilian Police Mission in Haiti and the related report of the Advisory Committee on Administrative and Budgetary Questions,

Bearing in mind Security Council resolution 1063 (1996) of 28 June 1996, by which the Council established the United Nations Support Mission in Haiti, and resolution 1086(1996) of 5 December 1996, by which the Council extended the mandate of the Mission until 31 July 1997,

Bearing in mind also Security Council resolution 1123(1997) of 30 July 1997, by which the Council established the United Nations Transition Mission in Haiti for a single four-month period,

Bearing in mind further Security Council resolution 1141(1997) of 28 November 1997, by which the Council established the United Nations Civilian Police Mission in Haiti, and resolution 1277(1999) of 30 November 1999, by which the Council continued the Mission until 15 March 2000,

Recalling its resolution 51/15 A of 4 November 1996 on the financing of the Support Mission and its subsequent resolutions and decisions thereon, the latest of which was resolution 54/276 of 15 June 2000,

Reaffirming that the costs of the Missions are expenses of the Organization to be borne by Member States in accordance with Article 17, paragraph 2, of the Charter of the United Nations,

Recalling its previous decisions regarding the fact that, in order to meet the expenditures caused by the Missions, a different procedure is required from that applied to meet expenditures of the regular budget of the United Nations,

Taking into account the fact that the economically more developed countries are in a position to make relatively larger contributions and that the economically less developed countries have a relatively limited capacity to contribute towards such an operation,

Bearing in mind the special responsibilities of the States permanent members of the Security Council, as indicated in General Assembly resolution 1874(S-IV) of 27 June 1963, in the financing of such operations,

Noting with appreciation that voluntary contributions have been made to the United Nations Civilian Police Mission in Haiti by certain Governments,

Mindful of the fact that it is essential to continue to provide the account of the Missions with the necessary financial resources to enable them to meet their outstanding liabilities,

1. *Takes note* of the status of contributions to the United Nations Support Mission in Haiti, the United Nations Transition Mission in Haiti and the United Nations Civilian Police Mission in Haiti as at 30 April 2001, including the contributions outstanding in the amount of 19.9 million United States dollars, representing 22 per cent of the total assessed contributions from the inception of the Support Mission to the period ending 30 June 2000, notes that some 65 per cent of the Member States have paid their assessed contributions in full, and urges all other Member States concerned, in particular those in arrears, to ensure payment of their outstanding contributions in full;

2. *Expresses its appreciation* to those Member States which have paid their assessed contributions in full;

3. *Expresses concern* about the financial situation with regard to peacekeeping activities, in particular as regards the reimbursements to troop contributors that bear additional burdens owing to overdue payments by Member States of their assessments;

4. *Also expresses concern* at the delay experienced by the Secretary-General in deploying and providing adequate resources to some recent peacekeeping missions, in particular those in Africa;

5. *Emphasizes* that all future and existing peacekeeping missions shall be given equal and non-discriminatory treatment in respect of financial and administrative arrangements;

6. *Also emphasizes* that all peacekeeping missions shall be provided with adequate resources for the effective and efficient discharge of their respective mandates;

7. *Endorses* the conclusions and observations contained in the report of the Advisory Committee on Administrative and Budgetary Questions, and requests the Secretary-General to ensure their full implementation;

8. *Notes* that the commitment authority of 2,201,284 dollars gross (1,987,784 dollars net) authorized by the Advisory Committee under the terms of section IV of General Assembly resolution 49/233 A of 23 December 1994 was not utilized;

9. *Authorizes* the Secretary-General to utilize an amount of 164,200 dollars gross (142,900 dollars net) from the resources provided for the period ending 30 June 2000 in order to meet the cost of completing the liquidation tasks at Headquarters;

10. *Decides* that Member States that have fulfilled their financial obligations to the Civilian Police Mission shall be credited their respective share of the remaining unencumbered balance of 394,916 dollars gross (523,316 dollars net) in respect of the period ending 30 June 2000, in accordance with the composition of groups as set out in paragraphs 3 and 4 of General Assembly resolution 43/232 of 1 March 1989 and adjusted by subsequent relevant General Assembly resolutions and decisions for the ad hoc apportionment of peacekeeping appropriations, the latest of which were resolution 52/230 of 31 March 1998 and decisions 54/456 to 54/458 of 23 December 1999 for the period 1998-2000, and taking into account the scale of assessments for the year 2000, as set out in its resolutions 52/215 A of 22 December 1997 and 54/237 A of 23 December 1999;

11. *Also decides* that, for Member States that have not fulfilled their obligations to the Civilian Police Mission, their share of the remaining unencumbered balance of 394,916 dollars gross (523,316 dollars net) in respect of the period ending 30 June 2000 shall be set off against their outstanding obligations in accordance with the scheme set out in paragraph 10 above;

12. *Takes note* of the report of the Secretary-General on the final disposition of the assets of the Missions;

13. *Emphasizes* that no peacekeeping mission shall be financed by borrowing funds from other active peacekeeping missions;

14. *Decides* to include in the provisional agenda of its fifty-sixth session the item entitled "Financing of the United Nations Support Mission in Haiti, the United Nations Transition Mission in Haiti and the United Nations Civilian Police Mission in Haiti".

On 7 September, the Assembly decided to include in the draft agenda of its fifty-sixth (2001) session the item on the financing of the United Nations Mission in Haiti (UNMIH) (**decision 55/498**).

On 24 December, the Assembly decided that the items on the financing of UNMIH and of UNSMIH, UNTMIH and MIPONUH would remain for consideration at its resumed fifty-sixth (2002) session (**decision 56/464**), and that the Fifth Committee should continue its consideration of those items at that session (**decision 56/458**).

Other questions

Costa Rica–Panama

Costa Rica and Panama transmitted to the Secretary-General the text of a document entitled "Proclamation for peace, human security and demilitarization", which was signed in Panama by the Presidents of the two countries on 29 November [A/56/917]. The proclamation, among other things, called on Latin America's heads of State to work towards the progressive elimination of military forces through their gradual conversion into civilian police institutions.

Cuba-Panama

On 26 October [S/2001/1039], Cuba transmitted to the Secretary-General a background paper on the alleged terrorist activities of Luis Posada Carriles and three other Cuban-Americans. Mr. Carriles and his associates were arrested in Panama in November 2000 as they were allegedly planning to assassinate President Fidel Castro during the Ibero-American Summit. On 14 May 2001, Panama denied Cuba's extradition request.

By a 12 November letter to the Secretary-General [S/2001/1073], Panama replied that Cuba's request for the extradition of Mr. Carriles and his alleged accomplices was denied as inadmissible, since the accused were the subject of judicial proceedings in the territory of Panama and because there was no reciprocity by Cuba vis-à-vis Panama in that regard.

Cuba– United States

In August [A/56/276 & Add.1], the Secretary-General, in response to General Assembly resolution 55/20 [YUN 2000, p. 257], submitted information received from 74 States, the European Union and 12 UN bodies and agencies on the imple-mentation of the resolution, by which the Assembly had called on States to refrain from unilateral application of economic and trade measures against States, and urged them to repeal or invalidate such measures. The preamble to resolution 55/20 had made particular reference to the Helms-Burton Act, promulgated by the United States in 1996, which had strengthened sanctions against Cuba.

GENERAL ASSEMBLY ACTION

On 27 November [meeting 64], the General Assembly adopted **resolution 56/9** [draft: A/56/L.9] by recorded vote (167-3-3) [agenda item 34].

Necessity of ending the economic, commercial and financial embargo imposed by the United States of America against Cuba

The General Assembly,

Determined to encourage strict compliance with the purposes and principles enshrined in the Charter of the United Nations,

Reaffirming, among other principles, the sovereign equality of States, non-intervention and non-interference in their internal affairs and freedom of international trade and navigation, which are also enshrined in many international legal instruments,

Recalling the statements of the heads of State or Government at the Ibero-American Summits concerning the need to eliminate the unilateral application of economic and trade measures by one State against another that affect the free flow of international trade,

Concerned at the continued promulgation and application by Member States of laws and regulations, such as that promulgated on 12 March 1996 known as the "Helms-Burton Act", the extraterritorial effects of which affect the sovereignty of other States, the legitimate interests of entities or persons under their jurisdiction and the freedom of trade and navigation,

Taking note of declarations and resolutions of different intergovernmental forums, bodies and Governments that express the rejection by the international community and public opinion of the promulgation and application of regulations of the kind referred to above,

Recalling its resolutions 47/19 of 24 November 1992, 48/16 of 3 November 1993, 49/9 of 26 October 1994, 50/10 of 2 November 1995, 51/17 of 12 November 1996, 52/10 of 5 November 1997, 53/4 of 14 October 1998, 54/21 of 9 November 1999 and 55/20 of 9 November 2000,

Concerned that, since the adoption of its resolutions 47/19, 48/16, 49/9, 50/10, 51/17, 52/10, 53/4, 54/21 and 55/20, further measures of that nature aimed at strengthening and extending the economic, commercial and financial embargo against Cuba continue to be promulgated and applied, and concerned also at the adverse effects of such measures on the Cuban people and on Cuban nationals living in other countries,

   1. *Takes note* of the report of the Secretary-General on the implementation of resolution 55/20;

   2. *Reiterates its call upon* all States to refrain from promulgating and applying laws and measures of the kind referred to in the preamble to the present resolu-

tion in conformity with their obligations under the Charter of the United Nations and international law, which, inter alia, reaffirm the freedom of trade and navigation;

3. *Once again urges* States that have and continue to apply such laws and measures to take the necessary steps to repeal or invalidate them as soon as possible in accordance with their legal regime;

4. *Requests* the Secretary-General, in consultation with the appropriate organs and agencies of the United Nations system, to prepare a report on the implementation of the present resolution in the light of the purposes and principles of the Charter and international law and to submit it to the General Assembly at its fifty-seventh session;

5. *Decides* to include in the provisional agenda of its fifty-seventh session the item entitled "Necessity of ending the economic, commercial and financial embargo imposed by the United States of America against Cuba".

RECORDED VOTE ON RESOLUTION 56/9:

In favour: Afghanistan, Albania, Algeria, Andorra, Angola, Antigua and Barbuda, Argentina, Armenia, Australia, Austria, Azerbaijan, Bahamas, Bahrain, Bangladesh, Barbados, Belarus, Belgium, Belize, Benin, Bhutan, Bolivia, Botswana, Brazil, Brunei Darussalam, Bulgaria, Burkina Faso, Burundi, Cambodia, Cameroon, Canada, Cape Verde, Chad, Chile, China, Colombia, Comoros, Congo, Costa Rica, Côte d'Ivoire, Croatia, Cuba, Cyprus, Czech Republic, Democratic People's Republic of Korea, Democratic Republic of the Congo, Denmark, Djibouti, Dominica, Dominican Republic, Ecuador, Egypt, Equatorial Guinea, Eritrea, Estonia, Ethiopia, Fiji, Finland, France, Gabon, Gambia, Georgia, Germany, Ghana, Greece, Grenada, Guatemala, Guinea, Guyana, Haiti, Honduras, Hungary, Iceland, India, Indonesia, Iran, Ireland, Italy, Jamaica, Japan, Jordan, Kazakhstan, Kenya, Kuwait, Lao People's Democratic Republic, Lebanon, Lesotho, Libyan Arab Jamahiriya, Liechtenstein, Lithuania, Luxembourg, Madagascar, Malawi, Malaysia, Maldives, Mali, Malta, Mauritania, Mauritius, Mexico, Monaco, Mongolia, Mozambique, Myanmar, Namibia, Nauru, Nepal, Netherlands, New Zealand, Nigeria, Norway, Oman, Pakistan, Panama, Papua New Guinea, Paraguay, Peru, Philippines, Poland, Portugal, Qatar, Republic of Korea, Republic of Moldova, Romania, Russian Federation, Rwanda, Saint Kitts and Nevis, Saint Lucia, Saint Vincent and the Grenadines, Samoa, San Marino, Saudi Arabia, Senegal, Seychelles, Sierra Leone, Singapore, Slovakia, Slovenia, South Africa, Spain, Sri Lanka, Sudan, Suriname, Swaziland, Sweden, Syrian Arab Republic, Thailand, The former Yugoslav Republic of Macedonia, Togo, Tonga, Trinidad and Tobago, Tunisia, Turkey, Turkmenistan, Tuvalu, Uganda, Ukraine, United Arab Emirates, United Kingdom, United Republic of Tanzania, Uruguay, Vanuatu, Venezuela, Viet Nam, Yemen, Yugoslavia, Zambia, Zimbabwe.

Against: Israel, Marshall Islands, United States.

Abstaining: Latvia, Micronesia, Nicaragua.

Communications. By letters of 26 October [A/56/522-S/2001/1040] and 29 October [A/56/521-S/2001/1038] to the Secretary-General, Cuba transmitted documentation pertaining to alleged terrorist acts committed by the United States Central Intelligence Agency against Cuba.

Chapter IV

Asia and the Pacific

The United Nations addressed major political and security challenges in the Asia and the Pacific region in 2001, especially in Afghanistan, East Timor and Iraq.

In Afghanistan, the military conflict between the Taliban and the United Front continued for most of the year. The restrictions imposed on the delivery of humanitarian assistance and other acts committed by the Taliban, such as the destruction of non-Islamic statues and shrines, further deteriorated an already tenuous relationship between the authorities in Kabul and the international community. The Secretary-General, during a visit to the region in March, called attention to the plight of Afghan refugees and strongly exhorted the Taliban to refrain from destroying non-Islamic statues, but to no avail. However, the 11 September attacks in the United States, carried out by Afghanistan-based Osama bin Laden and his terrorist network Al-Qa'idah, changed the Afghan political landscape. The Taliban's refusal to abide by Security Council resolutions and to hand over bin Laden to the proper authorities brought about a United States–led military intervention (Operation Enduring Freedom), which resulted in the overthrow of that regime. A UN-sponsored conference in Bonn, Germany, attended by various Afghan ethnic groups, laid the foundations for the beginning of a process of transition towards a freely elected and constitutional government. An Afghan Interim Administration, headed by Hamid Karzai, was established in December and the Security Council authorized the establishment of the International Security Assistance Force to help maintain security in Kabul and its surrounding areas. Lakhdar Brahimi was appointed as the Secretary-General's Special Representative for Afghanistan, supported by an Integrated Management Task Force. The United Nations Special Mission to Afghanistan continued to promote political dialogue throughout the year, despite the restrictions imposed by the Taliban.

In East Timor, substantial progress was made in the transition towards independence and self-government. The first Constituent Assembly, which was elected in August, recommended 20 May 2002 as the date for independence and started the Constitution-drafting process. The United Nations Transitional Administration in East Timor, which had been entrusted with full governing and military power over the territory, guided the transition process by devolving power to East Timorese institutions. The Security Council endorsed the Secretary-General's recommendations for a reduced UN integrated mission in the post-independence period and expressed concern at the continued presence of large numbers of East Timorese refugees in West Timor.

UN activities to verify Iraq's compliance with its weapons-related obligations under Council resolution 687(1991), which brought a formal ceasefire to the 1991 Gulf war, continued to be stalled following the withdrawal in December 1998 of the United Nations Special Commission (UNSCOM) and the International Atomic Energy Agency. The United Nations Monitoring, Verification and Inspection Commission, which assumed UNSCOM's monitoring and verification activities in 2000, was not able to carry out its activities inside Iraqi territory. The United Nations Iraq-Kuwait Observation Mission continued to monitor the demilitarized zone between the two countries. The Council extended the humanitarian programme in Iraq, based on the oil-for-food formula, and worked on securing improvements to the sanctions regime and on modifications to the oil-for-food programme based on a goods review list. In November, it pledged to adopt such a list for implementation starting in May 2002.

In Fiji, a United Nations Electoral Observer Mission monitored the general elections in August, which represented a major step towards a return to full constitutional democracy following the May 2000 coup d'état. The activities of the United Nations Tajikistan Office of Peacebuilding were extended for another year, until June 2002, in order to continue to support Tajikistan in its post-conflict peace-building efforts.

Among other concerns brought to the attention of the United Nations were the longstanding dispute between India and Pakistan over Jammu and Kashmir; violations reported by Iran and Iraq of their 1988 ceasefire agreement and the 1991 agreement on the area of separation between them; and reciprocal accusations of border violations reported by Saudi Arabia and Iraq.

Afghanistan

Unending war and drought in Afghanistan made 2001 a long and difficult year both for the Afghans and for the United Nations, which had to confront numerous obstacles put in place by the Taliban regime concerning a variety of political and humanitarian issues. However, the 11 September attacks in the United States by Osama bin Laden's Al-Qa'idah terrorist network and the Taliban's refusal to abide by Security Council demands to hand over bin Laden to the proper authorities in order to bring him to justice led to an October military intervention in Afghanistan by a United States–led international force (Operation Enduring Freedom) together with the United Front (UF). The UF, a coalition of Afghan groups opposing the Taliban, represented the Government driven from power by the Taliban in 1996 and was still recognized by the United Nations as representing the State of Afghanistan. On 13 November, UF troops entered the capital, Kabul, and officially brought to an end the Taliban regime, though pockets of resistance continued in other parts of the country.

In October, the Secretary-General reappointed Lakhdar Brahimi (Algeria) as his Special Representative for Afghanistan. Francesc Vendrell (Spain), the Secretary-General's Personal Representative, was also nominated Deputy Special Representative and continued his political functions as Head of the United Nations Special Mission to Afghanistan (UNSMA). Mr. Brahimi assumed a leading role in coordinating international efforts to establish a stable post-conflict governing administration and peaceful society. A UN-sponsored conference, convened in Bonn, Germany, at the end of November, culminated in the Bonn Agreement of 5 December, in which Afghan parties pledged to engage in a process of transition to a freely elected constitutional and democratic government. On 22 December, an Interim Administration was established in Afghanistan under the chairmanship of Hamid Karzai.

Following the 11 September attacks, much of the Security Council's attention, and that of the UN system at large, focused on Afghanistan. The Council expressed its support for a transitional administration in Afghanistan, endorsed the Bonn Agreement and authorized the establishment of an International Security Assistance Force to assist the Afghan Interim Administration in the maintenance of security in Kabul and its surrounding areas. The United Kingdom agreed to lead that force for the first three months.

During a visit to South Asia in March, the Secretary-General met with heads of State and senior officials, including Taliban leaders. He focused his discussions on the plight of the Afghan refugees in the countries bordering Afghanistan and on the continued presence of bin Laden in Taliban-held territory. Together with the international community at large, he tried to dissuade the Taliban from carrying out an edict issued by the Taliban leader, Mullah Mohammad Omar, calling for the destruction of all non-Islamic statues and shrines in Afghanistan. Despite that appeal, the order was carried out and two statues of Buddha in Bamian province were destroyed.

During the year, the humanitarian situation of the population of Afghanistan worsened drastically due to the combined effects of chronic poverty, hunger, war, drought, displacement and abuse of civilians. In the months before its overthrow, the Taliban regime hampered the implementation of assistance programmes by restricting access to people in need, especially women.

The Afghanistan Sanctions Committee continued to monitor the implementation of sanctions against the Taliban regime and the Secretary-General submitted four progress reports on the humanitarian implications of those measures. In July, the Security Council introduced a mechanism to monitor the implementation of sanctions against the Taliban, as recommended by a committee of experts established to study how the arms embargo could be monitored and terrorist training camps closed. With the Taliban's collapse, the sanctions framework no longer applied.

Situation in Afghanistan

The situation in Afghanistan during 2001 was described by the Secretary-General in three progress reports, submitted in response to General Assembly resolution 55/174 A [YUN 2000, p. 266]. The first two were issued on 19 April [A/55/907-S/2001/384] and 17 August [A/55/1028-S/2001/789]; the third was an annual report issued in the last quarter of the year (see p. 264). The reports described the political and military developments in the country; the peacemaking activities of the Secretary-General's Personal Representative, of UNSMA and at UN Headquarters in New York; UN assistance and programmes to alleviate the progressively deteriorating humanitarian and human rights situations of the war victims; and UN efforts to curb terrorism within and from Afghanistan, and to reduce the illicit cultivation, production and trafficking of drugs. The annual report also detailed the situation in Afghanistan following the 11 September terrorist attacks in the United States and the military action launched on 7 October.

Communications (23 January–6 April). In identical letters of 23 January [A/55/740-S/2001/70] to the Secretary-General and the Security Council President, the Acting Minister for Foreign Affairs of the Islamic State of Afghanistan reported that a number of new commando and artillery units of the Pakistan Army had been deployed in northern Afghanistan in support of the Taliban–Osama bin Laden coalition and in preparation for attacks on UF forces. The Acting Minister stated that Pakistan's military involvement in Afghanistan manifested its belligerence towards Council resolutions that placed an embargo on military aid to the Taliban and called for the immediate withdrawal of foreign military personnel from Afghanistan.

In a 7 February letter to the Secretary-General [A/55/775-S/2001/121], the President of the Islamic State of Afghanistan, Burhanuddin Rabbani, said that Pakistan had forcibly expelled thousands of Afghan refugee families. Instead of deporting oppressed refugees, he said, Pakistan should prevent the crossing of armed contingents, which continued to enter Afghanistan from Pakistan on a regular basis with the aim of carrying out mass executions. The Islamic State of Afghanistan was ready to put an end to the conflict and to start negotiations with the Taliban under the supervision of the United Nations.

In March, a number of States transmitted communications in which they urged the Taliban not to destroy the statues of Buddha in Bamian (see below and p. 1019).

In a 4 April letter to the Secretary-General [A/55/896-S/2001/346], Pakistan expressed its disappointment that UN agencies had yet to take steps to establish camps and mobilize relief efforts inside Afghanistan to stop the further influx of Afghan refugees into Pakistan. Consequently, it could not accept the intention of the Office of the United Nations High Commissioner for Refugees (UNHCR) to allow the registration of refugees at the Jalozai camp without the provision of relief inside Afghanistan, as such registration would only induce Afghans to move in greater numbers to Pakistan.

On 6 April [A/55/897-S/2001/347], Pakistan forwarded to the Secretary-General additional comments on the Afghan refugee issue.

Report of Secretary-General (April). In his 19 April report [A/55/907-S/2001/384], submitted in response to General Assembly resolution 55/174 A [YUN 2000, p. 266], the Secretary-General said that from 10 to 12 March he visited Pakistan as part of a tour in the South Asian region. His stay in Pakistan included a meeting with Afghan refugees in

the Shamshattoo refugee camp in the north-western part of the country. During discussions with Pakistan's Chief Executive, General Pervez Musharraf, it was agreed that Afghans who had recently entered Pakistan would be allowed to remain and that, while Pakistan would facilitate the provision of immediate relief assistance to the nearly 80,000 refugees at the Jalozai camp, the UN system would redouble its efforts to provide assistance to Afghans inside Afghanistan in order to discourage further outflows.

In discussions with the Taliban Foreign Minister, Wakil Ahmad Mutawakkil, in Islamabad, Pakistan, the Secretary-General urged the Taliban to reconsider its rejection, following the imposition of further sanctions under Security Council resolution 1333(2000) [YUN 2000, p. 273], of the 2 November 2000 written agreement [ibid., p. 270], whereby the two parties to the conflict agreed to pursue a process of dialogue under his auspices. Other topics covered included the humanitarian situation, the Taliban's progress towards eradicating poppy cultivation and the continued presence of Osama bin Laden in Afghanistan. A considerable portion of the discussion dealt with the order to destroy all statues and other objects of "un-Islamic worship". The Secretary-General asked that implementation of the order be halted and offered alternative solutions to the problem, including the possible removal of the statues for safekeeping outside Afghanistan. Despite that appeal, and many others made by Governments, Islamic ulemas (scholars), the United Nations Educational, Scientific and Cultural Organization (UNESCO) and the General Assembly in resolution 55/243 (see p. 1019), Taliban authorities carried out the order and destroyed two statues of Buddha in Bamian province. The Secretary-General said that those artefacts were part of the common heritage of mankind. Moreover, they not only symbolized the multifaceted history of the Afghan nation, but also embodied the values of religious, political and ethnic tolerance—the strongest foundation for a better, more peaceful and tolerant future for all Afghans.

The Secretary-General's Personal Representative for Afghanistan and Head of UNSMA, Francesc Vendrell, continued to pursue his contacts with the two Afghan warring sides and other Afghans, as well as with the Governments of the region, including some members of the "six plus two" group—the countries bordering Afghanistan (China, Iran, Pakistan, Tajikistan, Turkmenistan and Uzbekistan) plus the Russian Federation and the United States.

UNSMA's Civil Affairs Unit continued its efforts to promote peace and human rights awareness in Afghanistan by conducting a regular dialogue with political authorities, engaging various sectors of civil society and observing political, human rights, social and economic trends in the country. The process of consolidating an UNSMA presence in the field had faced renewed difficulties following the closure of the Taliban office in New York in February and what the Taliban perceived as the uncertainty of its liaison presence at the United Nations.

Following the imposition of further sanctions by the Security Council in resolution 1333(2000) and as requested in that resolution, the Secretary-General appointed a committee of five experts to make recommendations on how the arms embargo and closure of terrorist camps could be monitored. On 31 March, the committee began a four-week visit to countries in the region to consult with government officials (see p. 269).

From late December 2000, fighting had been continuous throughout Afghanistan. That indicated that fighting in the country was no longer seasonal, the two sides being better equipped and prepared for winter warfare. Troop movements on both sides and the concentration of units along the main confrontation line and in the central part of Afghanistan suggested that large-scale fighting could be expected to resume in the spring and summer.

During the reporting period, there was further dramatic deterioration in the humanitarian situation. The combination of ongoing war and drought on an already impoverished population was pushing hundreds of thousands of people into destitution. The number of people displaced from rural areas to cities had grown to 500,000, as they searched for food, shelter, security and assistance. A further estimated 200,000 people had sought refuge and protection in neighbouring countries. Of that number, 170,000 had crossed into Pakistan, an unknown number had entered Iran and 10,000 remained on the border with Tajikistan. The strategy of the United Nations and its partners had been to assist families in their areas of origin to help prevent involuntary displacement. Although that strategy had worked well where it could be implemented, the widespread impact of both the drought and the conflict, together with insufficient financial resources, a limited humanitarian presence and the unwillingness of the authorities to provide assistance, had contributed to dismal conditions for the majority of the displaced. In February, the Secretary-General requested his Emergency Relief Coordinator, Kenzo Oshima, to visit Afghanistan to review the humanitarian situation and to highlight critical funding short-

falls. Over $250 million was required to address the tide of involuntary displacement, but only $85 million had been made available as at April 2001 (see also p. 838).

A preliminary assessment of the implementation of the decree banning all opium poppy cultivation in Afghanistan indicated that it was being implemented. However, the ban had brought serious economic and social consequences to the former growing areas, with farmers and their communities bearing the economic burden of the conversion to other types of cultivation. It had also contributed to displacement of people inside Afghanistan and to the influx of new refugees to Pakistan and Iran. The Secretary-General said that, for whatever motive, the Taliban regime had done what the international community had asked: it had drastically curtailed poppy cultivation. It was therefore incumbent on the international community to respond positively to that progress, or face an equally rapid increase in production at the end of the year if farmers were to return to poppy cultivation.

In the first quarter of 2001, the United Nations had been attempting to improve access to protection and assistance for the large numbers of Afghan refugees in Iran and Pakistan and along the border with Tajikistan. In the biggest influx since the early 1990s, more than 170,000 Afghans had sought assistance in Pakistan, the majority arriving during the first months of 2001. An estimated 80,000 were camped out in the open in the squalid Jalozai camp. In November 2000, Pakistan, which hosted 1.2 million Afghan refugees, had closed its borders and imposed a ban on new arrivals, citing social, economic and security reasons. Permission to carry out any verification exercises had been withheld and the authorities maintained that no additional land could be made available to relieve the intense overcrowding that already existed in the camps. Thus, it was extremely difficult to provide protection assistance to those of most concern to UNHCR. The Secretary-General and General Musharraf, in their discussions in March, agreed on a two-pronged approach to address the refugee problem. The United Nations would continue to expand its assistance activities inside Afghanistan in order to avoid any further involuntary displacement and would remain committed to providing assistance within Pakistan to ensure the protection of genuine refugees. In return, Pakistan would support and facilitate assistance and protection support for refugees. In Iran, negotiations between UNHCR and the Government on a mechanism to identify Afghans in need of protection continued. With regard to the 10,000 Afghans on the border with Tajikistan, UNHCR was negotiating with local authorities to ensure un-hindered access, protection at a safe location and the separation of civilians from combatants to allow for assistance to the civilians to continue.

The human rights problems faced by the Afghan people continued to be compounded by the war, by deep-rooted and widespread poverty and by the policies and practices of the authorities. In particular, the situation of women and girls remained unacceptable. The law that banned Afghan women from working in aid agencies, except in the health sector, which was issued by the Taliban in July 2000 [YUN 2000, p. 272], continued to be a major obstacle. It narrowed considerably the ability of the assistance community to reach Afghan women, since only women aid workers could directly reach female beneficiaries. In January 2001, Mullah Omar declared conversion or propagation of conversion of Muslims to Christianity or Judaism punishable by death, an edict that led to restrictions on the activities of non-governmental organizations (NGOs) for fear that their association with the Afghan people might be misinterpreted.

The Secretary-General observed that the situation in Afghanistan had continued to deteriorate and that the humanitarian crisis had reached alarming proportions. Conditions were liable to deteriorate further soon due to the likely increase in the fighting and the continuing effects of the drought. He therefore urged Member States to respond generously to the consolidated appeal for Afghanistan (see p. 838). If humanitarian assistance was not to continue indefinitely in Afghanistan, a new commitment was needed from Member States to find a comprehensive political solution. In the absence of a settlement, no significant voluntary return of refugees and internally displaced persons would occur. While the sanctions were not responsible for the humanitarian situation, the Taliban had sought to blame them, with mixed success among the local population, for the deteriorating internal situation, and had used them as an argument to suspend participation in the UN-sponsored dialogue process agreed to in 2000 [YUN 2000, p. 270]. One unintentional fallout from the sanctions was the precarious position of UNSMA's offices and staff working inside Afghanistan, especially since the Taliban had threatened to close the UNSMA office in Kabul.

Communications (26 April–31 July). By a 26 April letter to the Secretary-General [A/55/916-S/2001/419], Kazakhstan proposed, in a document entitled "The conceptual approaches of Kazakhstan to resolving the situation in Afghanistan", that it should assist as a mediator in reactivating the negotiation process by organizing a round of peace talks between the warring Afghan groups in the city of Almaty.

On 14 May [A/55/939-S/2001/481], in identical letters to the Secretary-General and the Security Council President, the Ministry of Foreign Affairs of the Islamic State of Afghanistan declared, in principle, its readiness to attend, under the aegis of the United Nations, the proposed peace negotiations with the Taliban in Almaty.

In a 31 May letter [A/55/980-S/2001/553], Sweden, on behalf of the European Union (EU), informed the Secretary-General that Mullah Omar had ordered all Hindus in Afghanistan to wear identity marks. The EU stressed that forcing persons belonging to ethnic and religious minorities to wear distinctive clothing or identity marks was a form of discrimination prohibited by international human rights law.

By identical letters of 1 June to the Secretary-General and the Council President [A/55/978-S/2001/549], Afghanistan's representative to the United Nations transmitted a letter from the Acting Minister for Foreign Affairs, stating that Pakistan continued to supply arms to the Taliban and to provide them with planning, logistical and recruitment support. In addition, Pakistan maintained in Afghanistan thousands of military personnel, armed nationals belonging to numerous Pakistan-based extremist organizations and volunteers from religious schools called the Madrassa, who were fighting alongside the Taliban mercenaries.

On 25 July [A/55/1021-S/2001/735], Mali transmitted to the Secretary-General the texts of the final communiqué and resolutions adopted at the twenty-eighth session of the Islamic Conference of Foreign Ministers (Bamako, Mali, 25-27 June). The Conference, among other things, emphasized the impossibility of resolving the Afghan problem by military means and called on the Afghan parties to the conflict to put an end to hostilities. It also called on all States to refrain from providing weapons and ammunition to all Afghan parties. Member States and Islamic institutions were urged to extend assistance to the Afghan refugees in Pakistan and Iran.

Report of Secretary-General (August). In his 17 August report [A/55/1028-S/2001/789], the Secretary-General stated that his Personal Representative had been in frequent contact with the two warring sides, but there had been no talks, direct or indirect, between them. He also described contacts with non-belligerent Afghans and concerned Governments and noted that there had been a plethora of diplomatic activities related to Afghanistan since April. However, fighting had intensified since the beginning of May and the humanitarian situation had reached alarming proportions owing to the combined effects of 22 years of conflict and the worst drought in living memory. He observed that, after so many years of fruitless endeavours, the Security Council might wish to consider adopting a comprehensive approach to the settlement of the situation in Afghanistan, in its political, military, humanitarian and human rights dimensions, setting forth the basic requirements for a settlement of the conflict and the principles on which it should be based, together with a coherent strategy to achieve those objectives, including incentives and disincentives.

Communications (August). On 28 August [S/2001/829], Iran informed the Secretary-General that the Taliban, using armed forces and military equipment, had violated the Iranian border on 27 August and taken an Iranian border kiosk onto Afghan territory.

By a 31 August letter to the Secretary-General [A/56/332-S/2001/841], Pakistan denied that it was ejecting Afghan refugees from the Jalozai or Shamshattoo camps, where a joint screening by Pakistani officials and UNHCR was taking place. However, Pakistan was not in a position to absorb any further flows of Afghan refugees and it called on the international community to provide relief to displaced Afghans inside Afghanistan.

Post–11 September developments

Following the 11 September terrorist attacks in the United States (see p. 60), the United Kingdom and the United States informed the Security Council President that they had compelling information that Osama bin Laden and the Al-Qa'idah terrorist network, supported by the Taliban regime in Afghanistan, bore responsibility for the attacks and posed an ongoing threat (see p. 64). On 7 October [S/2001/946], the United States reported to the Council President that, in accordance with Article 51 of the Charter of the United Nations, it had, together with other States, initiated action to prevent or deter further attacks on the United States, including measures against Al-Qa'idah terrorist training camps and Taliban military installations in Afghanistan (see p. 65).

Special Representative. In identical letters of 3 October to the Presidents of the General Assembly and the Security Council [A/56/432-S/2001/934], the Secretary-General said that, in view of the grave humanitarian and political situation affecting Afghanistan and the surrounding region, it was his intention to reappoint Lakhdar Brahimi (Algeria) as his Special Representative for Afghanistan, with overall authority for the humanitarian, political and rehabilitation endeavours of the United Nations in that country. The Special Representative would be supported by the two existing pillars of the UN system responsible for activities in Afghanistan: UNSMA and the Office for the Coordination of Humanitarian Affairs. Mr. Brahimi's terms of reference were annexed to the letter. In 1999, the Secretary-General had decided to freeze Mr. Brahimi's activities as Special Envoy until conditions warranted his renewed intervention [YUN 1999, p. 262].

On 4 October [S/2001/937], the Council took note of the Secretary-General's intention.

Communications (13 September–26 October). In identical letters of 13 September to the Secretary-General and the Council President [A/56/365-S/2001/870], the President of the Islamic State of Afghanistan, Mr. Rabbani, said that, after the terrorist attacks of 11 September and the 9 September assassination of Vice-President and Minister of Defence Ahmad Shah Massoud, the time had come for the international community to consider all aspects of terrorism in the Taliban-occupied territories and to put effective pressure on Pakistan, the Taliban's main backer, to cease immediately its aggression in Afghanistan. There was also a need to close down all terrorist training camps and centres of indoctrination within Pakistan, especially religious schools, so as to end the teaching of bigotry and hatred against humanity, which ran counter to Islam's genuine message. President Rabbani proposed the convening of a special meeting of the Security Council to address the presence of foreign military and armed personnel in Afghanistan.

On 8 October [S/2001/967], Belgium, on behalf of the EU, drew the Secretary-General's attention to the statement of the EU General Affairs Council, which said that all the information pointed clearly and convincingly to the responsibility of Osama bin Laden and the Al-Qa'idah network for the 11 September terrorist attacks in the United States. The Taliban regime had refused to take responsibility for handing over those suspected so that they could be brought to justice. The Taliban and Al-Qa'idah were now facing the consequences of their action. The EU stressed that the carefully targeted action launched on 7 October was an attack neither against Islam nor against the people of Afghanistan. The military action was one part of a wider multilateral strategy that involved a comprehensive assault on the organizations and financing structures that underpinned terrorism.

On 26 October [S/2001/1018], the text of the statement adopted at the meeting of heads of State of the Russian Federation, Tajikistan and the Islamic State of Afghanistan (Dushanbe, Tajikistan, 22 October) was transmitted to the Secretary-General. The participants stated that an essential precondition for the transfer of the resolution of the situation in Afghanistan to the political channel was the unconditional fulfilment of the demands set forth by the antiterrorist coalition, including the handover of those responsible for the 11 September terrorist attacks in the United States, the removal of the Taliban regime, and the disbandment and complete disarmament of its armed units. Tajikistan and Russia confirmed their readiness to support Afghanistan in its struggle against the Taliban regime.

Establishment of transitional administration

Six plus two group. On 12 November, Foreign Ministers and senior representatives of the "six plus two" group—the countries bordering Afghanistan (China, Iran, Pakistan, Tajikistan, Turkmenistan and Uzbekistan) plus the Russian Federation and the United States—held a meeting in New York under the chairmanship of the Secretary-General. The meeting concluded with the adoption of a joint statement [A/56/681-S/2001/1157, annex], in which the members pledged their support to efforts of the Afghan people to find a political solution to the crisis and agreed that a broad-based, multi-ethnic, politically balanced, freely chosen administration should be established in Afghanistan. They welcomed the central role of the United Nations in assisting the Afghan people and pledged continued support for the Organization's humanitarian efforts to alleviate their suffering, both inside the country and in refugee camps in neighbouring countries.

Security Council consideration. On 13 November [meeting 4414], the Security Council discussed the situation in Afghanistan. With the Council's consent, the President invited, at their request, representatives of Afghanistan, Argentina, Australia, Belgium, Canada, Egypt, Germany, India, Indonesia, Iran, Italy, Japan, Kazakhstan, Malaysia, Mexico, the Netherlands, New Zealand, Pakistan, the Republic of Korea, Tajikistan, Turkey and Uzbekistan to participate in the discussion without the right to vote. He also invited the Special Representative of the Secretary-General for Afghanistan, Mr. Brahimi, to brief the Council on latest developments.

In his opening statement, the Secretary-General said that the 11 September terrorist attacks in the United States and the consequent military action in Afghanistan had created a new environment that presented daunting challenges to the international community, but also new opportunities. First and foremost, the humanitarian needs of the Afghan people had to be met, especially since winter was closing in, and thus there was a need to feed and shelter as many people as possible. Next, urgent action had to be taken to avoid a political and security vacuum in the post-Taliban period. A stable Afghanistan, living in peace, carrying out its international obligations and posing no threat to its neighbours, had to be the international community's common objective. To achieve it, any arrangement arrived at had to reflect the will, needs and interests of the Afghan people. That required the end of interference in Afghanistan's affairs by neighbouring countries, without which there could be little hope of lasting stability in Afghanistan. The Secretary-General added that UN agencies and NGOs had stepped up cross-border delivery and distribution of food and non-food assistance, though many areas, particularly in the north, remained inaccessible.

Mr. Brahimi said that the united international reaction to the 11 September terrorist attacks had transformed the conditions for international action in Afghanistan. During his visit to Pakistan, Iran and Saudi Arabia in late October, he held talks with heads of State, senior officials and Afghan groups and individuals, including women and students. Presidents Pervez Musharraf of Pakistan and Mohammad Khatami of Iran had stated that they would like the United Nations to play a pivotal role in the process of finding a political solution, one that would prevent Afghanistan from being used again as a breeding and staging ground for acts of terror. The six plus two group, at a 12 November meeting (see above), had also confirmed that a broad-based, multi-ethnic, politically balanced and freely chosen Afghan administration should be established.

Mr. Brahimi said that consensus among Afghanistan's neighbours was essential; without it, Afghans themselves would find it extremely difficult to achieve a durable solution. The international community also would need to make a massive political and financial commitment to the long-term stability of Afghanistan. It was therefore necessary to strengthen other mechanisms for multilateral cooperation and coordination in Afghanistan. The United Nations had, over the years, convened several groups of interested countries in addition to the six plus two group, such as the Group of 21, which comprised a broader range of countries that had been directly or indirectly affected by the Afghan crisis and could help contribute to its resolution. Mr. Brahimi was of the view that the Group of 21 should be reactivated and reinvigorated. The United Nations also participated in the Afghanistan Support Group convened by donor countries, the Geneva Initiative in support of peace efforts seeking to legitimize a transition through a loya jirga (the Afghan council of elders) and other initiatives.

Mr. Brahimi stressed that the strategic objective of the international community's efforts was to help the people of Afghanistan to establish a responsible, representative, accountable Government; to promote respect for human rights; to foster good relations between Afghanistan and its neighbours; and to ensure that Afghanistan would never be used again as a breeding and staging ground for terrorists or drug traffickers. There was agreement among Afghan parties, and in the international community, on the goal of creating a broad-based Government that would be representative of all groups in the country, accountable to its citizens and friendly to its neighbours. The difficulty was in securing agreement among interested parties to design a series of concrete steps to reach that goal. The bitter experience of the previous 10 years had shown that the solution had to be carefully put together and home-grown so that it enjoyed the support of all internal and external players.

Discussions among Afghans themselves on how to achieve those objectives were taking place in many forums both inside and outside Afghanistan, including between former Afghan King Mohammad Zahir Shah and representatives of the United Islamic and National Front for the Salvation of Afghanistan (the Northern Alliance) and within the Cyprus process and at the Peshawar Conference (see p. 265). In those forums, Afghans had proposed a series of steps and mechanisms to establish a transitional administration that would pave the way for a stable Government, a common theme of which had been the emphasis on the convening role of the United Nations in order to bring the parties together. Mr. Brahimi said the Secretary-General was of the view that, instead of continuing with shuttle diplomacy, the Northern Alliance and the representatives of the existing initiatives should meet with the United Nations as early as possible so that a common framework could be created and enlarged to allow for fair representation for all Afghan communities.

Mr. Brahimi suggested, therefore, that the approach to solve the Afghan crisis could follow a sequence of events: the United Nations would convene a meeting of the Northern Alliance's representatives and existing processes to agree on a framework for the process of political transition; the meeting would suggest concrete steps for the convening of a provisional council—to be composed of a fairly large and representative group of Afghans drawn from all ethnic and regional communities, and chaired by an individual recognized as a symbol of national unity—the

credibility and legitimacy of which would be enhanced by the participation of those individuals and groups, including women, who had not been engaged in armed conflict; the provisional council would propose the composition of a transitional administration and a programme of action for the period of political transition, to last no more than two years, and arrangements for security; an emergency loya jirga would then be convened to approve the transitional administration, its programme of action and proposals for security, and to authorize the transitional administration to prepare a constitution; and the transitional phase would result in the convening of a second loya jirga, which would approve the constitution and create the Government of Afghanistan.

For the Government to be sustainable, Afghans themselves had to be engaged in creating institutions and good governance. Working with UN agencies and international and local NGOs had given many Afghans wide experience in managing accountable organizations. There was also significant capacity among a new generation of Afghans in the diaspora, particularly in Iran and Pakistan. It was those Afghans who could help constitute a transitional administration that would be far more credible, acceptable and legitimate in the eyes of the country's population than a transitional administration run by the United Nations or another constellation of foreigners. Parachuting a large number of international experts into Afghanistan could overwhelm the nascent transitional administration and interfere with the building of local capacity.

However, without genuine and lasting security nothing would be possible. Even in a political settlement among Afghans, the parties could not ensure security on their own. The pervasive presence of non-Afghan armed and terrorist groups with no interest in a lasting peace would necessitate the introduction of a robust security force, able to deter and, if possible, defeat challenges to its authority. Three options were available for such a force, presented in order of desirability: an all-Afghan security force; a multinational force; or a UN peacekeeping force. Although work to establish an all-Afghan force should start as early as possible, it was unlikely that it could be constituted in the near term, which suggested that consideration would need to be given to the deployment of a national security presence that, if adequately trained and armed, could ensure security in the major city and preserve the political space in which negotiations towards the resolution of many problems could proceed.

An armed UN peacekeeping force was not recommended. The Secretary-General would require several months to obtain from Member States sufficient numbers of troops to pose a credible military deterrent and, subsequently, to deploy them. Furthermore, UN peacekeepers had proved most successful when deployed to implement an existing political settlement among willing parties, not to serve as a substitute for one.

As far as the humanitarian situation was concerned (see also p. 838), the challenge was clear: it was necessary to ship to the country, and distribute, at least 52,000 tonnes of food per month over the forthcoming months. The international community had to provide health care for 7.5 million people and shelter for over 1 million internally displaced persons, and to provide protection for those at risk from persecution. During the first week of November, the United Nations and its partners had improved the delivery of humanitarian aid to Afghanistan, though the challenges remained immense. Of special concern was the almost complete lack of information on new internal displacement.

Mr. Brahimi observed that the reconstruction of Afghanistan was going to be key in bringing peace and stability and was at the heart of the political transition. It would also provide opportunities for the absorption of large numbers of men engaged in war and opportunities for Afghan women. However, reconstruction would require a clear strategy and the subordination of the interests of individual agencies or donors to the overall agenda of peace and stability.

Addressing the Council, the United States said that all Member States had to support the United Nations in its efforts to bring Afghans together to form an interim authority in the liberated areas. That authority had to be representative of and acceptable to Afghans and had to be supported by all Member States, especially the countries of the region. An international presence had to be re-established as soon as possible. The United States called for restraint on the part of the Afghan liberation forces as they took up their new positions and continued their offensive.

The Russian Federation said that the United Nations should play the central role in facilitating the transformation of Afghanistan into a stable and prosperous State—not only because averting the threat to regional and international security emanating from the Taliban-controlled territory fell within the purview of the Security Council and the General Assembly, but also because only within the context of the United Nations could practical solutions, acceptable to all parties, be found, thereby ensuring the parties' cooperation in the peace process.

Pakistan endorsed the four-step approach proposed by Mr. Brahimi. However, it stressed that speed was of the essence. Withdrawal of the Taliban from Kabul had created a dangerous political vacuum. Unless the United Nations was able to put together a political dispensation that was representative of all segments of the Afghan population, conflict and turmoil would continue to afflict Afghanistan.

SECURITY COUNCIL ACTION

On 14 November [meeting 4415], the Security Council unanimously adopted **resolution 1378 (2001)**. The draft [S/2001/1075] was prepared in consultations among Council members.

The Security Council,

Reaffirming its previous resolutions on Afghanistan, in particular resolutions 1267(1999) of 15 October 1999, 1333(2000) of 19 December 2000 and 1363(2001) of 30 July 2001,

Supporting international efforts to root out terrorism, in keeping with the Charter of the United Nations, and reaffirming also its resolutions 1368(2001) of 12 September 2001 and 1373(2001) of 28 September 2001,

Recognizing the urgency of the security and political situation in Afghanistan in the light of the most recent developments, particularly in Kabul,

Condemning the Taliban for allowing Afghanistan to be used as a base for the export of terrorism by the Al-Qa'idah network and other terrorist groups and for providing safe haven to Osama bin Laden, Al-Qa'idah and others associated with them, and in this context supporting the efforts of the Afghan people to replace the Taliban regime,

Welcoming the intention of the Special Representative to convene an urgent meeting of the various Afghan processes at an appropriate venue and calling on the United Front and all Afghans represented in those processes to accept his invitation to that meeting without delay, in good faith and without preconditions,

Welcoming the Declaration on the Situation in Afghanistan by the Foreign Ministers and other Senior Representatives of the Six plus Two of 12 November 2001, as well as the support being offered by other international groups,

Taking note of the views expressed at the meeting of the Security Council on the situation in Afghanistan on 13 November 2001,

Endorsing the approach outlined by the Special Representative of the Secretary-General at the meeting of the Security Council on 13 November 2001,

Reaffirming its strong commitment to the sovereignty, independence, territorial integrity and national unity of Afghanistan,

Deeply concerned by the grave humanitarian situation and the continuing serious violations by the Taliban of human rights and international humanitarian law,

1. *Expresses* its strong support for the efforts of the Afghan people to establish a new and transitional administration leading to the formation of a government, both of which:

—Should be broad-based, multi-ethnic and fully representative of all the Afghan people and committed to peace with Afghanistan's neighbours,

—Should respect the human rights of all Afghan people, regardless of gender, ethnicity or religion,

—Should respect Afghanistan's international obligations, including by cooperating fully in international efforts to combat terrorism and illicit drug trafficking within and from Afghanistan, and

—Should facilitate the urgent delivery of humanitarian assistance and the orderly return of refugees and internally displaced persons, when the situation permits;

2. *Calls upon* all Afghan forces to refrain from acts of reprisal, to adhere strictly to their obligations under human rights and international humanitarian law, and to ensure the safety and security and freedom of movement of United Nations and associated personnel, as well as personnel of humanitarian organizations;

3. *Affirms* that the United Nations should play a central role in supporting the efforts of the Afghan people to establish urgently such a new and transitional administration leading to the formation of a new government and expresses its full support for the Special Representative of the Secretary-General in the accomplishment of his mandate, and calls on Afghans, both within Afghanistan and among the Afghan diaspora, and Member States to cooperate with him;

4. *Calls upon* Member States to provide:

—Support for such an administration and government, including through the implementation of quick-impact projects,

—Urgent humanitarian assistance to alleviate the suffering of Afghan people both inside Afghanistan and Afghan refugees, including in demining, and

—Long-term assistance for the social and economic reconstruction and rehabilitation of Afghanistan and welcomes initiatives towards this end;

5. *Encourages* Member States to support efforts to ensure the safety and security of areas of Afghanistan no longer under Taliban control, and in particular to ensure respect for Kabul as the capital for all the Afghan people, and especially to protect civilians, transitional authorities, United Nations and associated personnel, as well as personnel of humanitarian organizations;

6. *Decides* to remain actively seized of the matter.

Bonn Agreement

A UN-sponsored conference on Afghanistan (the Bonn Conference) took place in Bonn from 27 November to 5 December. Attended by delegations representing different Afghan groups, the Conference culminated in the signing of the Agreement on provisional arrangements in Afghanistan pending the re-establishment of permanent government institutions, which the Secretary-General transmitted to the Security Council on 5 December [S/2001/1154].

The implementation period of the Agreement was envisaged to last for two to three years and was intended to lead to a full-fledged government, chosen freely by the entire Afghan elector-

ate. The Interim Authority would be succeeded by a Transitional Authority, selected through an emergency loya jirga that would convene within six months of the establishment of the Interim Authority. The participants in the loya jirga would be drawn from all segments of society, and the representation of women and all ethnic and religious communities would be ensured. The Transitional Authority would lead Afghanistan until a fully representative government could be elected through free and fair elections, which were to be held no later than two years after the date of the convening of the emergency loya jirga. A constitutional loya jirga to ratify a new constitution would convene within 18 months of the establishment of the Transitional Authority. The parties to the Agreement also called for the deployment of an international security force to assist in the maintenance of security for Kabul and its surrounding areas. Such a force could be progressively expanded to other urban centres and areas. Among other things, the Agreement provided for the establishment of a number of commissions, namely, a special independent commission for the convening of the emergency loya jirga, a human rights commission, a civil service commission and a judicial commission.

SECURITY COUNCIL ACTION

On 6 December [meeting 4434], the Security Council unanimously adopted **resolution 1383 (2001)**. The draft [S/2001/1153] was prepared in consultations among Council members.

The Security Council,

Reaffirming its previous resolutions on Afghanistan, in particular its resolution 1378(2001) of 14 November 2001,

Reaffirming its strong commitment to the sovereignty, independence, territorial integrity and national unity of Afghanistan,

Stressing the inalienable right of the Afghan people themselves freely to determine their own political future,

Determined to help the people of Afghanistan to bring to an end the tragic conflicts in Afghanistan and promote national reconciliation, lasting peace, stability and respect for human rights, as well as to cooperate with the international community to put an end to the use of Afghanistan as a base for terrorism,

Welcoming the letter of 5 December 2001 from the Secretary-General informing the Council of the signature in Bonn on 5 December 2001 of the Agreement on provisional arrangements in Afghanistan pending the re-establishment of permanent government institutions,

Noting that the provisional arrangements are intended as a first step towards the establishment of a broad-based, gender sensitive, multi-ethnic and fully representative government,

1. *Endorses* the Agreement on provisional arrangements in Afghanistan pending the re-establishment of

permanent government institutions as reported in the Secretary-General's letter of 5 December 2001;

2. *Calls upon* all Afghan groups to implement this Agreement in full, in particular through full co-operation with the Interim Authority which is due to take office on 22 December 2001;

3. *Reaffirms* its full support to the Special Representative of the Secretary-General and endorses the missions entrusted to him in annex 2 of the abovementioned Agreement;

4. *Declares* its willingness to take further action, on the basis of a report by the Secretary-General, to support the interim institutions established by the abovementioned Agreement and, in due course, to support the implementation of the Agreement and its annexes;

5. *Calls upon* all Afghan groups to support full and unimpeded access by humanitarian organizations to people in need and to ensure the safety and security of humanitarian workers;

6. *Calls upon* all bilateral and multilateral donors, in coordination with the Special Representative of the Secretary-General, United Nations agencies and all Afghan groups, to reaffirm, strengthen and implement their commitment to assist with the rehabilitation, recovery and reconstruction of Afghanistan, in coordination with the Interim Authority and as long as the Afghan groups fulfil their commitments;

7. *Decides* to remain actively seized of the matter.

Communications (27 November–18 December). In letters of 27 November to the Secretary-General [A/56/657-S/2001/1114, A/56/658-S/2001/1115], Qatar expressed concern about the fate of Arabs and others in Afghanistan. It called on the Northern Alliance to treat captured Taliban fighters and other groups as prisoners of war.

On 7 December [A/56/693-S/2001/1169], the Russian Federation transmitted to the Secretary-General the text of the statement by the heads of State of the Commonwealth of Independent States (CIS) on the situation in Afghanistan, adopted on 30 November in Moscow. CIS assessed positively the conduct of the anti-terrorist operation by the international coalition in Afghanistan and noted that its coordination with UF forces had made it possible to strike a serious blow at the infrastructure of terrorism and extremism inside Afghanistan. CIS advocated that the struggle against global terrorism should be conducted on a comprehensive and long-term basis in accordance, first and foremost, with the Charter of the United Nations. In order to eradicate the hotbeds of instability in Afghanistan, it was necessary to combine, in a flexible manner, measures based on force and political, legal and economic measures in order to bring pressure to bear on the sources of the terrorist, extremist and drug threats. CIS declared its support for the process of a political settlement in Afghanistan, under the auspices of the United Nations, leading to the replacement of the Taliban regime and

to the formation in the country of a multi-ethnic and broadly representative government.

On 10 December [A/56/691], the Islamic State of Afghanistan transmitted to the Secretary-General a newspaper article published in the United States entitled "Pakistan ended aid to Taliban only hesitantly".

On 18 December [A/56/719-S/2001/1213], Uzbekistan expressed its support for UN efforts to bring about peace and a stable situation in Afghanistan and for the Bonn Agreement and the establishment of a provisional administration. As part of Uzbekistan's efforts to facilitate the provision of humanitarian assistance to the Afghan people, approximately 6,000 tons of various humanitarian supplies had been transported into Afghanistan from its territory. Uzbekistan expressed concern that large arsenals of military equipment remained at the disposal of various uncontrollable groups and armed units within Afghanistan.

Report of Secretary-General (December). In his 6 December annual report on the situation in Afghanistan [A/56/681-S/2001/1157], which covered developments since the issuance of his 20 November 2000 annual report [YUN 2000, p. 269] until 15 November 2001, the Secretary-General stated that, since the terrorist attacks of 11 September, much of his attention, and that of the UN system at large, had been focused on Afghanistan. An Integrated Management Task Force had been established to support Mr. Brahimi in his efforts as Special Representative. The Secretary-General's Personal Representative, Mr. Vendrell, would continue his political functions as Deputy Special Representative and Head of UNSMA.

The Secretary-General again described the situation in Afghanistan during the first half of 2001, as outlined in his earlier reports (see pp. 256 and 258). With regard to the United States–led coalition air strikes that began on 7 October, the Secretary-General reported that the first week of precision engagement was conducted by night, targeting mainly air defence and command centres. That was followed by daytime flights, after which strikes were conducted against concentrations of Taliban troops along the main confrontation line. On 9 November, UF troops captured the city of Mazar-e-Sharif and started a southern drive towards the capital, Kabul, which they occupied without a battle on 13 November, since the Taliban had already abandoned the city.

Since his reappointment on 3 October 2001, the Special Representative for Afghanistan, Mr. Brahimi, had undertaken numerous contacts with a wide range of Afghans and concerned Governments in order to accelerate the political process in the light of the rapidly changing circumstances. In addition to meeting with heads of

State, Foreign Ministers and other senior officials in Saudi Arabia, Pakistan and Iran during a visit to the region from 27 October to 7 November, he also went to Rome, where he met with former King Mohammad Zahir Shah, who informed him that he was willing to help in a manner that was useful and acceptable to everyone.

The offices of UNSMA's Civil Affairs Unit, established by Council resolution 1214(1998) [YUN 1998, p. 297] to monitor the situation in Afghanistan, promote and support respect for minimum humanitarian standards, and deter massive and systematic violations of human rights, were closed in May when the Taliban implemented their earlier threat of closure as a reaction to the imposition of sanctions under Council resolution 1333(2000) [YUN 2000, p. 273]. The Unit's presence was then restricted to Kabul and Faizabad, until September, when all international UN staff left the country. In early November, UNSMA resumed its presence in Kabul and would return to other major cities as soon as the security situation permitted. In view of the challenges ahead for the United Nations in Afghanistan, the Secretary-General said that it was his intention to recommend in due time that the Mission be strengthened and its role enlarged, in particular its presence on the ground. As an immediate step, the Mission's administrative and logistical capacity needed to be enhanced.

By the second half of September, the Council for Peace and National Unity of Afghanistan (the "Bonn process") was fully merged with the Rome process, led by former King Zahir Shah, who initiated a large number of contacts with Afghan and foreign delegations. An agreement in principle was reached between Zahir Shah and the UF to form a 120-member Supreme Council for National Unity. The Cyprus Meeting for Implementation of Peace in Afghanistan (the "Cyprus process") decided, at a meeting of its executive committee on 20 and 21 October, to send a delegation to Rome to explore closer cooperation with the former King's loya jirga initiative. In Peshawar, Pakistan, on 24 and 25 October, a Conference for Peace and National Unity was attended by almost 1,000 representatives, the largest gathering to date of Pashtun tribal elders supporting a political solution to the conflict. Both events were attended by UNSMA representatives.

A central theme that the Secretary-General pursued during the course of the year was the need for the Security Council to adopt a comprehensive approach to Afghanistan, as the only way of ending the conflict, while at the same time addressing the specific concerns of the international community, such as terrorism, narcotics, human rights and the refugee crisis. Such an approach had two objectives: enabling the Afghans to exercise their right freely to determine their form of government through an internationally acceptable mechanism, such as elections or a fully representative loya jirga; and ensuring a stable and unified Afghanistan at peace with its neighbours. That approach, complemented by the creation of a rehabilitation and reconstruction plan for Afghanistan as an incentive to achieve and cement a political settlement, would address two major root causes of the Afghan conflict, namely, the lack of legitimacy of successive regimes since the 1970s and the continued degradation of Afghan institutions and infrastructure. The Secretary-General designated the Administrator of the United Nations Development Programme (UNDP), Mark Malloch Brown, to take on the responsibility of leading the early recovery effort in Afghanistan in his capacity as Chairman of the United Nations Development Group.

The dramatic changes brought about by the terrorist attacks of 11 September had made the objectives of the comprehensive approach easier to achieve. The international community's renewed focus on Afghanistan after years of neglect, and the realization that a military campaign to root out terrorism from Afghanistan required a simultaneous political process leading to the formation of a legitimate Afghan government, offered renewed hope that the Afghan people might at last get the kind of government to which they had long aspired. The challenge that faced the international community was to speed up the delivery of humanitarian assistance, to help chart a path that would lead to a stable and unified Afghanistan and to rebuild a country shattered by over two decades of war.

Later developments. In a later report on the situation in Afghanistan [A/56/875-S/2002/278], the Secretary-General said that the Interim Authority was established on 22 December, with Hamid Karzai as its Chairman. The following day, Mr. Karzai held the first cabinet meeting. He also met with the Secretary-General's Special Representative for Afghanistan and sought UN assistance in a broad range of areas in order to facilitate the work of the Interim Administration.

GENERAL ASSEMBLY ACTION

On 21 December [meeting 91], the General Assembly adopted **resolution 56/220 A** [draft: A/56/L.62 & Add.1] without vote [agenda items 20 (f) & 43].

The situation in Afghanistan and its implications for international peace and security

The General Assembly,

Recalling its resolution 55/174 A of 19 December 2000 and all its previous relevant resolutions,

Recalling also all relevant Security Council resolutions and statements by the President of the Council on the situation in Afghanistan, in particular resolutions 1267(1999) of 15 October 1999, 1333(2000) of 19 December 2000, 1378(2001) of 14 November 2001 and 1383(2001) of 6 December 2001,

Reaffirming its continued strong commitment to the sovereignty, independence, territorial integrity and national unity of Afghanistan, and respecting its multicultural, multi-ethnic and historical heritage,

Reaffirming its condemnation of the use of Afghan territory for terrorist activities and the exporting of international terrorism from Afghanistan, and welcoming the successful efforts of the Afghan people to remove the Taliban regime, as well as the terrorist organizations it hosted, and to decide their own future,

Expressing its appreciation and strong support for the ongoing efforts of the Secretary-General, his Special Representative and the head of the United Nations Special Mission to Afghanistan to promote peace and a lasting political settlement in Afghanistan,

Convinced that the main responsibility for finding a political solution lies ultimately with the Afghan people themselves, and strongly welcoming and endorsing therefore the agreement reached among various Afghan groups in Bonn, Germany, on 5 December 2001,

Convinced also that only a political settlement aimed at the establishment of a broad-based, gender-sensitive, multi-ethnic and fully representative government, which respects the human rights of all Afghans and the international obligations of Afghanistan and is committed to peace with its neighbours, can lead to durable peace and reconciliation,

Reiterating that the United Nations must continue to play its central and impartial role in the international efforts towards a peaceful resolution of the Afghan conflict as well as in efforts to provide humanitarian assistance, to provide for rehabilitation and reconstruction and to facilitate the orderly return of refugees, and therefore endorsing the request to the United Nations by the participants at the United Nations–sponsored talks on Afghanistan contained in annex III to the Bonn agreement,

Recognizing that the collapse of the Afghan economy requires, in addition to emergency assistance, integrated and multisectoral programmes of rehabilitation and reconstruction with a view to ensuring economic and social recovery and the sustainable development of the country, and that a strong international commitment to this end can serve as an incentive for the Afghan groups to implement the Bonn agreement,

Deeply concerned by the grave humanitarian situation and the serious violations of human rights and international humanitarian law in Afghanistan, especially against women and children, committed, in particular, by the Taliban, and recognizing that the accountability of perpetrators of grave human rights violations is a key factor in ensuring reconciliation and stability,

Deeply disturbed by the use of Afghan territory for the cultivation, production and trafficking of narcotic drugs, which has dangerous repercussions in the region and far beyond,

1. *Takes note* of the report of the Secretary-General;

2. *Expresses its concern* that the unstable situation in Afghanistan poses a continuing risk to peace and stability in the region, and expresses its determination to assist the efforts of the interim authority to prevent the use of Afghan territory for international terrorism;

3. *Calls upon* all Afghan groups to cooperate fully with the United Nations and the Special Representative of the Secretary-General to promote peace and a lasting political settlement in Afghanistan;

4. *Strongly supports* the efforts of the Afghan people, consistent with the agreement reached in Bonn, Germany, to establish an interim authority, leading, through the convening of loya jirgas and free and fair elections, to the formation of a new government, which should all be broad-based, multi-ethnic, fully representative and committed to peace with Afghanistan's neighbours;

5. *Calls upon* all Afghan groups, in particular the interim authority, to implement the Bonn agreement fully;

6. *Strongly supports* the enhanced role of the United Nations Special Mission to Afghanistan in helping the interim authority to implement the Bonn agreement until it is integrated in a new United Nations mission in Afghanistan;

7. *Supports* the efforts of groups of interested States and international organizations, underlines the importance of ensuring complementarity among these efforts, and towards this end calls upon all parties to coordinate closely with the Special Representative of the Secretary-General;

8. *Strongly urges* all Afghan groups to refrain from acts of reprisal, to respect human rights and to adhere to their obligations under international humanitarian law;

9. *Stresses* the importance of the full, equal and effective participation of women in civil, cultural, economic, political and social life and decision-making processes throughout the country at all levels, and calls upon all Afghan groups to protect and promote the equal rights of men and women, especially in the fields of education, work and health care;

10. *Calls upon* the international community to reinforce assistance to alleviate the urgent humanitarian needs of Afghanistan and, as long as the interim authority fulfils its commitments, to support generously post-conflict rehabilitation and reconstruction;

11. *Calls upon* all concerned countries to continue to provide assistance and protection to Afghan refugees and internally displaced persons in need of it and to work with the United Nations to facilitate their orderly return and effective reintegration, in safety and dignity, as soon as conditions permit;

12. *Calls upon* the interim authority to respect fully the international obligations of Afghanistan with regard to narcotic drugs, and calls upon the international community to increase its assistance for programmes aimed at reducing poppy cultivation in Afghanistan, including capacity-building for drug control, drug control monitoring systems and crop substitution programmes, as part of a comprehensive food security strategy and drug demand reduction support;

13. *Requests* the Secretary-General to report to the General Assembly every three months during its fifty-sixth session on the progress of the United Nations and the efforts of his Special Representative to promote peace in Afghanistan, and to report to the Assembly at its fifty-seventh session on the progress made in the implementation of the present resolution;

14. *Decides* to include in the provisional agenda of its fifty-seventh session the item entitled "The situation in Afghanistan and its implications for international peace and security".

Also on 21 December, the Assembly adopted **resolution 56/220 B** on emergency international assistance for peace, normalcy and reconstruction of war-stricken Afghanistan (see p. 839).

On 24 December, the Assembly decided that the agenda item on the situation in Afghanistan and its implications for international peace and security would remain for consideration at its resumed fifty-sixth (2002) session (**decision 56/464**).

International Security Assistance Force

By a 19 December letter to the Council President [S/2001/1223], the Islamic State of Afghanistan confirmed that it had agreed to the deployment of multinational security forces inside its territory. It reiterated that, in each case of deployment of forces, previously recommended coordination terms were to be agreed upon with Afghan authorities in Kabul regarding the nationality and the size of the military units, their intended location on Afghan territory, the duration and the timetable of their assignment and the modalities of the role on the ground.

On the same day [S/2001/1217], the United Kingdom informed the Council President that it was willing to become the initial lead nation for the International Security Assistance Force (ISAF) for Kabul and its surrounding area for a period of approximately three months under the terms of the Bonn Agreement (see p. 263) and upon receiving Council authorization. ISAF would assist the interim Afghan administration in the maintenance of security. The United Kingdom would transfer responsibility as the lead nation three months from the declaration of initial operational capability and no later than 30 April 2002. The United Kingdom requested the Council President to support efforts to identify a successor lead nation by asking Member States to consider urgently the possibility of taking over as the next lead nation.

The United Kingdom envisaged that the force's tasks could include: liaison with the new interim administration in Afghanistan to help in its establishment and with the Secretary-General's Special Representative; providing advice and support to the interim administration and to the United Nations on security issues; and assessing future requirements for helping the Afghan authorities in the establishment and training of new Afghan security and armed forces, key infrastructure development tasks and

possible future expanded security assistance in other areas of Afghanistan. ISAF would have a particular mission authorized by a Council resolution that was distinct from Operation Enduring Freedom. The United Kingdom, as the lead nation, would exercise command of ISAF, which would include troops and equipment contributed by other nations and would have the support of the United States. For reasons of effectiveness, the United States Central Command would have authority over ISAF to avoid conflict between ISAF operations and those of Operation Enduring Freedom. A joint coordinating body would be developed with representatives from the United States Central Command, the Afghan interim administration and ISAF to deal with operational issues. To ensure political-military coordination, ISAF would establish a committee of contributors with the lead nation as the chair.

SECURITY COUNCIL ACTION

On 20 December [meeting 4443], the Security Council unanimously adopted **resolution 1386 (2001)**. The draft [S/2001/1228] was prepared in consultations among Council members.

The Security Council,

Reaffirming its previous resolutions on Afghanistan, in particular its resolutions 1378(2001) of 14 November 2001 and 1383(2001) of 6 December 2001,

Supporting international efforts to root out terrorism, in keeping with the Charter of the United Nations, and reaffirming also its resolutions 1368(2001) of 12 September 2001 and 1373(2001) of 28 September 2001,

Welcoming developments in Afghanistan that will allow for all Afghans to enjoy inalienable rights and freedom unfettered by oppression and terror,

Recognizing that the responsibility for providing security and law and order throughout the country resides with the Afghan people themselves,

Reiterating its endorsement of the Agreement on provisional arrangements in Afghanistan pending the re-establishment of permanent government institutions, signed in Bonn on 5 December 2001 (the Bonn Agreement),

Taking note of the request to the Security Council in annex 1, paragraph 3, to the Bonn Agreement to consider authorizing the early deployment to Afghanistan of an international security force, as well as the briefing on 14 December 2001 by the Special Representative of the Secretary-General on his contacts with the Afghan authorities in which they welcome the deployment to Afghanistan of a United Nations–authorized international security force,

Taking note of the letter dated 19 December 2001 from Dr. Abdullah Abdullah to the President of the Security Council,

Welcoming the letter from the Secretary of State for Foreign and Commonwealth Affairs of the United Kingdom of Great Britain and Northern Ireland to the Secretary-General of 19 December 2001, and taking note of the United Kingdom offer contained therein to take the lead in organizing and commanding an International Security Assistance Force,

Stressing that all Afghan forces must adhere strictly to their obligations under human rights law, including respect for the rights of women, and under international humanitarian law,

Reaffirming its strong commitment to the sovereignty, independence, territorial integrity and national unity of Afghanistan,

Determining that the situation in Afghanistan still constitutes a threat to international peace and security,

Determined to ensure the full implementation of the mandate of the International Security Assistance Force, in consultation with the Afghan Interim Authority established by the Bonn Agreement,

Acting for these reasons under Chapter VII of the Charter of the United Nations,

1. *Authorizes,* as envisaged in annex 1 to the Bonn Agreement, the establishment for six months of an International Security Assistance Force to assist the Afghan Interim Authority in the maintenance of security in Kabul and its surrounding areas, so that the Afghan Interim Authority as well as the personnel of the United Nations can operate in a secure environment;

2. *Calls upon* Member States to contribute personnel, equipment and other resources to the International Security Assistance Force, and invites those Member States to inform the leadership of the Force and the Secretary-General;

3. *Authorizes* the Member States participating in the International Security Assistance Force to take all necessary measures to fulfil its mandate;

4. *Calls upon* the International Security Assistance Force to work in close consultation with the Afghan Interim Authority in the implementation of the force mandate, as well as with the Special Representative of the Secretary-General;

5. *Calls upon* all Afghans to cooperate with the International Security Assistance Force and relevant international governmental and non-governmental organizations, and welcomes the commitment of the parties to the Bonn Agreement to do all within their means and influence to ensure security, including to ensure the safety, security and freedom of movement of all United Nations personnel and all other personnel of international governmental and non-governmental organizations deployed in Afghanistan;

6. *Takes note* of the pledge made by the Afghan parties to the Bonn Agreement in annex 1 to that Agreement to withdraw all military units from Kabul, and calls upon them to implement this pledge in cooperation with the International Security Assistance Force;

7. *Encourages* neighbouring States and other Member States to provide to the International Security Assistance Force such necessary assistance as may be requested, including the provision of overflight clearances and transit;

8. *Stresses* that the expenses of the International Security Assistance Force will be borne by the participating Member States concerned, requests the Secretary-General to establish a trust fund through which contributions could be channelled to the Member States or operations concerned, and encourages Member States to contribute to such a fund;

9. *Requests* the leadership of the International Security Assistance Force to provide periodic reports on progress towards the implementation of its mandate through the Secretary-General;

10. *Calls upon* Member States participating in the International Security Assistance Force to provide assistance to help the Afghan Interim Authority in the establishment and training of new Afghan security and armed forces;

11. *Decides* to remain actively seized of the matter.

Communications (December). By a 21 December letter to the Secretary-General [S/2001/1238], Germany said that, together with Denmark and the Netherlands, it was willing to contribute to ISAF for a period of up to six months with a combined contingent of some 1,450 troops, subject to the completion of constitutional requirements in all three countries. An advance party of some 200 troops would be on 48-hour notice to move immediately after the Bundestag (Parliament) had authorized German participation.

On the same day [A/56/754-S/2001/1255], Kazakhstan transmitted to the Secretary-General a document entitled "Position of Kazakhstan with regard to resolving the situation in Afghanistan", in which it reaffirmed, among other things, that all peacekeeping efforts in Afghanistan should be carried out under UN auspices in order to avert the renewed outbreak of civil war and ensure the delivery of humanitarian aid. It offered to supply food, fuel and construction materials as part of the humanitarian aid mobilized by the donor community; to set up in its territory, under the auspices of the United Nations and the international coalition, forward-based humanitarian warehouses; and to send its civilian specialists—doctors, teachers, builders and engineers—to Afghanistan. Kazakhstan would also consider participation by its peacekeeping battalion in ISAF in the post-conflict period.

Also on 21 December [S/2001/1257], France informed the Secretary-General that it was willing to participate in ISAF, for the same period of time as envisaged and expressed by the United Kingdom in its 19 December letter (see p. 267). For that purpose, France intended to deploy special units immediately available to help provide security for individuals and protection for the premises of the interim Afghan administration in Kabul. In addition, France was willing to help train Afghan demining teams and could participate in training Afghan security and armed forces in the future.

By a 27 December note verbale to the Secretary-General [S/2001/1296], Spain said that its Council of Ministers had authorized the participation of a maximum of 485 army and air force personnel in ISAF to be deployed in Afghanistan under UN auspices. The duration of that authorization would be three months from when the Force was ready to operate in the zone. The Spanish contingent would comprise a national liaison component and signals, helicopter, bomb disposal and aviation deployment support units, supported by a Logistics Support Unit.

On 28 December [S/2001/1321], Italy informed the Secretary-General that it had decided to contribute approximately 600 military personnel to ISAF.

Oman transmitted to the Secretary-General the text of the final communiqué adopted at the Twenty-second Summit of the Supreme Council of the Gulf Cooperation Council (Muscat, Oman, 30-31 December) [A/56/797-S/2001/125]. The Supreme Council welcomed the formation of the Afghan interim administration under the chairmanship of Mr. Karzai and affirmed its readiness to cooperate with the new authorities.

Sanctions

Committee of Experts

Pursuant to Security Council resolution 1333 (2000) [YUN 2000, p. 273], the Secretary-General, on 8 March [S/2001/206], informed the Council President that he had established a committee of five experts to study for a 60-day period how to monitor the arms embargo against the Taliban and the closure of terrorist training camps in the Taliban-held areas of Afghanistan, as called for in Council resolutions 1267(1999) [YUN 1999, p. 265] and 1333(2000), and to make recommendations.

On 21 May [S/2001/511], the Secretary-General transmitted to the Council President the report of the Committee of Experts. The Committee, which commenced work on 19 March, undertook a programme of visits to the region, holding fact-finding and information-gathering meetings with those States bordering Afghanistan (China, Iran, Pakistan, Tajikistan, Turkmenistan and Uzbekistan) and with the other members of the six plus two group (Russian Federation and United States).

The Committee observed that the sanctions against the Taliban had to be seen and implemented as part of an overall package pursued by the United Nations to ensure peace and stability in Afghanistan. The enforcement of the sanctions had to rely on the will and initiative, primarily, of the six countries bordering Afghanistan. However, the capacities of most of those countries were inadequate and a hands-on engagement with them was absolutely essential to strengthen and develop their monitoring mechanisms, at the same time permitting continuous as-

sessment of capacity and follow-up of sanctions enforcement. The six countries had stated to the Committee that they would abide by the relevant Council resolutions and that they were implementing the resolutions' requirements with their border-control services, which, for the most part, were made up of customs, border guards or police and security service personnel. The effectiveness of the border services varied, depending on their training, the equipment they possessed and other local parameters, for example, supporting legislation. All six countries stated that they would welcome the international community's assistance in improving their monitoring capabilities.

The Committee concluded that the arms embargo and the closure of the terrorist training camps could be monitored by making use of mechanisms already in place in each of Afghanistan's neighbours, enhancing those mechanisms with a sanctions enforcement support team in each country. Those teams, made up of customs, border-security and counter-terrorism experts, should form the basis of a United Nations Office for Sanctions Monitoring and Coordination—Afghanistan. The Office, to be headed by a Director and staffed with specialist officers, would support the work of the teams in the field, as well as task the teams to verify and report to the Security Council Committee established pursuant to resolution 1267(1999) (the Afghanistan Sanctions Committee) (see p. 270) on allegations of sanctions-busting and progress being made in each of the countries to improve the effectiveness of their border-control and counter-terrorism services. In the interest of safety and security and speed of implementation, the Committee recommended that the proposed sanctions enforcement support teams be based within the existing UN offices in the countries neighbouring Afghanistan.

Security Council consideration. On 5 June [meeting 4325], the Security Council considered the Committee of Experts' report. With the Council's consent, the President invited the representatives of Afghanistan, Iran, Pakistan and Uzbekistan, at their request, to participate in the discussion without the right to vote. He also invited the Chairman of the Afghanistan Sanctions Committee and the Chairman of the Committee of Experts to brief the Council on the report's contents. Members of the Council expressed support for the proposal to establish a monitoring mechanism to oversee the sanctions regime and indicated their readiness to work on a draft resolution to realize that objective. They were also in agreement as to the importance of the commitment of the neighbouring countries if the sanctions were to succeed.

SECURITY COUNCIL ACTION

On 30 July [meeting 4352], the Security Council unanimously adopted **resolution 1363(2001)**. The draft [S/2001/741] was submitted by Colombia.

The Security Council,

Reaffirming its previous resolutions, in particular resolution 1267(1999) of 15 October 1999 and resolution 1333(2000) of 19 December 2000, as well as the statements by its President on the situation in Afghanistan,

Determining that the situation in Afghanistan constitutes a threat to international peace and security in the region,

Acting under Chapter VII of the Charter of the United Nations,

1. *Stresses* the obligation under the Charter of the United Nations of all Member States to comply fully with the measures imposed by resolutions 1267(1999) and 1333(2000);

2. *Welcomes* the report of the Committee of Experts established pursuant to resolution 1333(2000), and notes the conclusions and recommendations contained therein, following consultations with the States bordering the territory of Afghanistan under Taliban control which it had visited;

3. *Requests* the Secretary-General to establish, in consultation with the Committee established pursuant to resolution 1267(1999), within thirty days of the date of adoption of this resolution and for a period running concurrently with the application of the measures imposed by resolution 1333(2000), a mechanism:

(a) To monitor the implementation of the measures imposed by resolutions 1267(1999) and 1333(2000);

(b) To offer assistance to States bordering the territory of Afghanistan under Taliban control and other States, as appropriate, to increase their capacity regarding the implementation of the measures imposed by resolutions 1267(1999) and 1333(2000);

(c) To collate, assess, verify wherever possible, report and make recommendations on information regarding violations of the measures imposed by resolutions 1267(1999) and 1333(2000);

4. *Decides* that the composition of the monitoring mechanism, bearing in mind inter alia equitable geographical distribution, should comprise:

(a) A Monitoring Group in New York of up to five experts, including a Chairman, to monitor the implementation of all the measures imposed by resolutions 1267(1999) and 1333(2000), including in the fields of arms embargoes, counter-terrorism and related legislation and, in view of the link to the purchase of arms and financing of terrorism, money-laundering, financial transactions and drug trafficking;

(b) A Sanctions Enforcement Support Team, under the coordination of the Monitoring Group, of up to fifteen members with expertise in areas such as: customs, border security and counter-terrorism, to be located in those States referred to in paragraph 2 above, in full consultation and in close cooperation with those States;

5. *Requests* the Monitoring Group to report to the Committee established pursuant to resolution 1267 (1999) including through briefings of experts of the monitoring mechanism regarding the work of the monitoring mechanism as established in paragraph 3

above, and requests also the Sanctions Enforcement Support Team to report at least once a month to the Monitoring Group;

6. *Requests also* the Committee established pursuant to resolution 1267(1999) to report to the Security Council on the implementation of the present resolution at regular intervals;

7. *Calls upon* all States, the United Nations and concerned parties to cooperate in a full and timely manner with the monitoring mechanism;

8. *Urges* all States to take immediate steps to enforce and strengthen through legislative enactments or administrative measures, where appropriate, the measures imposed under their domestic laws or regulations against their nationals and other individuals or entities operating on their territory, to prevent and punish violations of the measures imposed by resolutions 1267 (1999) and 1333(2000), and to inform the Committee established pursuant to resolution 1267(1999) of the adoption of such measures, and invites States to report the results of all related investigations or enforcement actions to the Committee unless to do so would compromise the investigation or enforcement action;

9. *Requests* the Secretary-General to make the necessary arrangements to support the work of the monitoring mechanism, as an expense of the Organization and through a United Nations Trust Fund established for this purpose, affirms that this Trust Fund will be established by the Secretary-General, encourages States to contribute to the Fund and to contribute, through the Secretary-General, personnel, equipment and services to the monitoring mechanism and further requests the Secretary-General to keep the Committee established pursuant to resolution 1267(1999) informed on a regular basis of the financial arrangements supporting the mechanism;

10. *Expresses its intention* to review the implementation of the measures imposed by resolutions 1267(1999) and 1333(2000) on the basis of the information provided by the monitoring mechanism through the Committee established pursuant to resolution 1267(1999);

11. *Decides* to remain seized of the matter.

Pursuant to resolution 1363(2001) and in consultation with the Sanctions Committee, the Secretary-General, on 18 September, appointed five experts to serve on the Monitoring Group in New York [S/2001/887].

On 5 October [S/2001/952], the Secretary-General informed the Council President that, due to the fact that two experts were unable to assume their functions, he had appointed two new experts to replace them. On 7 November [S/2001/1056], the Secretary-General replaced one more expert.

Sanctions Committee activities

The Security Council Committee established pursuant to resolution 1267(1999) [YUN 1999, p. 265] (the Afghanistan Sanctions Committee) submitted a report [S/2002/101] covering its activities from 29 December 2000 to 31 December 2001. During that period, the Committee held five meetings and numerous informal consultations at the expert level. After the terrorist attacks of 11 September in the United States, the Committee's activities concentrated on the lists of individuals and entities associated with Al-Qa'idah.

The Committee established lists of entry and landing areas for aircraft within Taliban-held territory and of organizations and governmental relief agencies providing humanitarian assistance that were exempted from the flight ban. It also approved several humanitarian flights and shipment of demining equipment, solely for use in the Humanitarian Demining Programme. Among other activities, it published lists of individuals and entities whose assets should be frozen and authorized requests made by the Taliban for the transport of Afghan pilgrims to Saudi Arabia for the purpose of performing the hajj.

On 4 April [S/2001/326], the Chairman transmitted to the Council a list of 46 Member States that had responded to his request for information regarding the measures imposed against the Taliban. On 21 November [S/2001/326/Add.1], the Chairman transmitted 20 additional replies. Three more replies were received from Burkina Faso [S/2001/462], Saudi Arabia [S/2001/302] and the United Arab Emirates [S/2001/455].

By a 14 December letter to the Council President [S/2001/1226], the Sanctions Committee Chairman said that, in the light of the rapidly changing situation in Afghanistan, maps of Afghan territory under Taliban control were either obsolete or rapidly becoming obsolete. The Committee reminded Member States of their continuing obligations under Council resolutions not to provide assistance to the Taliban, Al-Qa'idah or Osama bin Laden or to individuals and entities associated with them.

Humanitarian implications

In accordance with Security Council resolution 1333(2000) [YUN 2000, p. 273], the Secretary-General submitted four progress reports on the humanitarian implications of the sanctions regime against Afghanistan during 2001.

In his 20 March report [S/2001/241], the Secretary-General focused primarily on the reporting methodology and examined the implications for the humanitarian situation in the first 60 days of the sanctions regime. He observed that the vulnerability of the Afghan population was compounded by the continuing effects of the drought, the escalating conflict, massive internal displacement, the disruption of the livelihood of farmers and labourers normally engaged in poppy cultivation, the absence of significant economic recovery and the lack of a single effective national authority. That acute vulnerability provided the context within which sanctions were being monitored. There was widespread recognition of the importance of protecting the international humanitarian assistance programme from any possible adverse effects of the sanctions. Exemption mechanisms to achieve that appeared to have functioned smoothly, and humanitarian assistance operations had been able to continue largely unhindered by the sanctions. Urgent steps had to be taken to facilitate procurement of aircraft spare parts, and maintenance flights, for the Ariana Afghan Airlines fleet in order to meet internationally recognized safety standards. Other restrictions on the Taliban, including diplomatic restrictions, financial measures aimed at Osama bin Laden and the ban on acetic anhydride (the indispensable chemical precursor in refining heroin), did not have any noticeable humanitarian implications.

In his 13 July report [S/2001/695], the Secretary-General said that although the monitoring process had identified adverse humanitarian effects from the sanctions regime, those effects were limited and their scope and magnitude were greatly exceeded by other factors causing humanitarian suffering, most notably the unprecedented drought, the continuation of the conflict and the widespread deprivation of human rights. The clearest direct effects of the UN sanctions were still on civil aviation, through the reduced ability of the national airline to operate its planes, maintain safety, generate employment and income, and render services. A simple technical solution was developed for certification of requests by Ariana for exemptions from the aviation sanctions. Humanitarian exemption mechanisms had worked relatively well and agencies had faced no delays or obstacles arising directly from the sanctions. With regard to exemptions of humanitarian agencies from the aviation restrictions, the Secretary-General suggested that the Sanctions Committee should intervene with the Pakistani authorities to explain the limitations of the air ban and agency exemption procedures. With regard to Ariana's frozen overseas accounts, the Sanctions Committee should consider granting supervised access to those assets for approved maintenance work and crew training. Taliban sources were promoting the idea that the sanctions were causing widespread humanitarian effects, something which was believed by most Afghans. Thus, there was a clear need for the United Nations to be more proactive in providing public information regarding sanctions.

In his 19 November report [S/2001/1086], the Secretary-General said that, owing to the precarious security situation in Afghanistan, the United

Nations had to relocate its international staff on 12 September. Consequently, the personnel and researchers assigned to monitor and assess the humanitarian implications of the sanctions regime had not been able to discharge their functions within Afghanistan. As a result, the Secretary-General was not in a position to submit the report envisaged for the third quarter of 2001.

In his 18 December report [S/2001/1215], the Secretary-General said that the latest political developments and the formation of an interim government for Afghanistan had fundamentally affected the framework under which sanctions were adopted. With the collapse of the Taliban, most sanctions measures appeared to have no focus. Therefore, he was not in a position to submit any further assessment of the humanitarian implications of the sanctions regime. He remarked that the frequent and efficient communication and interaction between the Sanctions Committee, the Office for the Coordination of Humanitarian Affairs and the humanitarian programmes in the field had facilitated the effective handling of the humanitarian exemption procedure and functioned as a troubleshooting mechanism for humanitarian problems linked to the sanctions. Throughout the monitoring process, the exemption procedures worked well and in a timely and efficient manner. The established monitoring and assessment mechanism and the regular reviews of the sanctions' impact, as well as the subsequent briefings and consultations with the Security Council and its Sanctions Committee, had resulted in useful reflections and discussions on sanctions and their implications. The Secretary-General noted that the Council might wish to consider establishing such a procedure for future sanctions regimes to monitor and assess possible unintended negative effects on the civilian population of targeted countries.

East Timor

During 2001, the people of East Timor, in partnership with the United Nations, made great advances on the path to independence and self-government. The first elections for a Constituent Assembly were held peacefully in August. Soon afterwards, the Assembly recommended a date for independence—20 May 2002—and started the constitution-drafting process.

The United Nations Transitional Administration in East Timor (UNTAET), which had been entrusted with a governance operation with full administrative and military power over the territory, had evolved, by the end of 2001, into a support structure for the embryonic government of East Timor and other institutions of State. At the heart of that process was UNTAET's devolution of power to East Timorese institutions. Full transfer of executive, legislative and judicial authority would occur on independence day. The Secretary-General proposed a plan for a continued and appropriately reduced UN integrated mission in the post-independence period.

The Security Council held nine open meetings during the year to discuss the situation in East Timor [meetings 4265, 4268, 4308, 4321, 4351, 4367, 4368, 4403, 4404], plus two closed ones [meetings 4358, 4397], at which it was briefed on the developments in the territory by the Special Representative of the Secretary-General and Transitional Administrator of East Timor, Sergio Vieira de Mello, the Under-Secretary-General for Peacekeeping Operations, Jean-Marie Guéhenno, and the Assistant Secretary-General for Peacekeeping Operations, Hédi Annabi. The General Assembly President, Harri Holkeri, also briefed the Council on his visit to East Timor, Indonesia and Singapore from 10 to 17 January. The Council extended UNTAET's mandate until 31 January 2002, and issued two presidential statements welcoming the successful staging of the national elections and endorsing 20 May 2002 as independence day. It also endorsed the Secretary-General's recommendations for a post-UNTAET presence in East Timor. However, the Council expressed concern at the continued presence of large numbers of East Timorese refugees in the province of East Nusa Tenggara (West Timor).

In December, the General Assembly, by **resolution 56/104** (see p. 841), called on the international community to continue to address the remaining humanitarian relief needs of East Timor and to support the transition from relief and rehabilitation to development in preparation for independence.

UN Transitional Administration in East Timor

UNTAET, established under Security Council resolution 1272(1999) [YUN 1999, p. 293], continued to carry out its mandate in East Timor, which included the maintenance of law and order, assistance in the development of civil and social services, coordination and delivery of humanitarian assistance and capacity-building support for self-government. At the same time, as part of the transitional process towards independence, it gradually devolved governing authority to East Timorese institutions by strengthening local participation in the administration of the territory.

On 18 May [S/2001/509], the Secretary-General proposed that Slovakia be added to the list of Member States contributing military personnel to UNTAET. On 22 May [S/2001/510], the Council took note of the Secretary-General's proposal.

On 7 August [S/2001/781], the Secretary-General informed the Council of his intention to appoint Lieutenant General Winai Phattiyakul (Thailand) as the Force Commander of UNTAET with effect from 1 September. Lieutenant General Boonsrang Niumpradit (Thailand), who had served as Force Commander since July 2000, would relinquish his post on 31 August. On 13 August [S/2001/782], the Council took note of the Secretary-General's intention.

Report of Secretary-General (January). In a January report [S/2001/42], the Secretary-General described developments in East Timor and UNTAET's activities during the latter part of 2000 [YUN 2000, p. 286], and recommended that UNTAET's mandate be extended until 31 December 2001.

Communications (January). On 25 January [S/2001/83], Portugal provided the Security Council President with an overview of the support it had extended to UNTAET and to the transition of East Timor to independence. Portugal's contributions included substantial donations to the consolidated humanitarian appeal for East Timor (see p. 826); some 800 men in the military component of UNTAET with plans to raise the national contingent to about 1,000; and participation in UNTAET's plans to establish an East Timorese Defence Force (ETDF).

By a 29 January letter [S/2001/90] to the Council President, Indonesia said that it was committed to building a mutually beneficial and harmonious relationship with an independent, democratic and stable East Timor, and to resolving all outstanding issues, including the question of East Timorese refugees in the province of East Nusa Tenggara (West Timor). In that regard, Indonesia had provided food, medicine and shelter and had confiscated weapons from the camps. The steady rate of spontaneous return of refugees during recent months attested to the fact that they were able to decide their future freely. In addition, Indonesia was collaborating with UN agencies in preparation for the formal registration of refugees through which they would be able to decide whether to repatriate to East Timor or resettle in Indonesia. However, the situation in East Timor itself was a matter of relevance to the return of refugees as the issues of safety and security, and uncertainty surrounding the matter of property, were a commonly expressed concern among them. Indonesia reiterated its commitment to bring to justice those suspected of involvement in human rights violations in East Timor. The trial of six suspects involved in the killings of three UNHCR workers [YUN 2000, p. 282] was under way at the South Jakarta District Court. In addition, effective channels of communication had been established between Indonesia and UNTAET at all levels of governance. Links had also been promoted between East Timorese and Indonesian officials.

SECURITY COUNCIL ACTION (January)

On 31 January [meeting 4268], the Security Council unanimously adopted **resolution 1338 (2001)**. The draft [S/2001/92] was prepared in consultations among Council members.

The Security Council,

Reaffirming its previous resolutions on the situation in East Timor, in particular resolutions 1272(1999) of 25 October 1999 and 1319(2000) of 8 September 2000, and the relevant statements of its President, in particular those of 3 August 2000 (S/PRST/2000/26) and of 6 December 2000 (S/PRST/2000/39),

Having considered the report of the Secretary-General of 16 January 2001,

Commending the work of the United Nations Transitional Administration in East Timor and the leadership of the Special Representative of the Secretary-General,

Expressing support for the steps taken by the Transitional Administration to strengthen the involvement and direct participation of the East Timorese people in the administration of their territory, and urging further measures to delegate authority to the East Timorese people as an essential part of the transition to independence,

Encouraging efforts to achieve the goal of independence for East Timor by the end of 2001, as set out in paragraphs 4 and 50 of the report of the Secretary-General, and acknowledging that it is the responsibility of the Transitional Administration to ensure free and fair elections in collaboration with the East Timorese people,

Reiterating its endorsement of the recommendations contained in the report of the Security Council Mission to East Timor and Indonesia of 21 November 2000, in particular the view of the Mission that a strong international commitment will be required in East Timor after independence,

Underlining its concern at the continued presence of large numbers of refugees from East Timor in the camps in the province of East Nusa Tenggara (West Timor), and at the security situation there, particularly as it relates to militia activity and the effect on refugees, and stressing the need to find a comprehensive solution to the problem,

Recalling the relevant principles contained in the Convention on the Safety of United Nations and Associated Personnel adopted on 9 December 1994, and emphasizing the need to take further steps to ensure the safety and security of international personnel in East Timor and Indonesia, in view of the dangers faced,

Welcoming and encouraging efforts by the United Nations to sensitize international personnel in the prevention and control of HIV/AIDS and other communicable diseases in all its peacekeeping operations,

Emphasizing the need for continued international financial support to East Timor, and urging all those who have made pledges to the Trust Fund for East Timor to make their contributions expeditiously,

1. *Welcomes* the report of the Secretary-General of 16 January 2001;

2. *Decides* to extend the current mandate of the United Nations Transitional Administration in East Timor until 31 January 2002, bearing in mind the possible need for adjustments related to the independence timetable;

3. *Requests* the Special Representative of the Secretary-General to continue to take steps to delegate progressively further authority within the East Timor Transitional Administration to the East Timorese people until authority is fully transferred to the government of an independent State of East Timor, as set out in the report of the Secretary-General;

4. *Encourages* the United Nations Transitional Administration in East Timor, bearing in mind the need to support capacity-building for self-government, to continue to support fully the transition to independence, including through development and training for the East Timorese people;

5. *Calls upon* the international financial institutions, the United Nations funds and programmes and bilateral donors who have committed resources to East Timor to fulfil their commitments and to accelerate disbursements, in particular in areas relevant to peace-building and development assistance, and reaffirms in this regard the continued need for effective coordination of development assistance to East Timor;

6. *Urges* the international community to provide financial and technical assistance to the creation of an East Timor Defence Force, and encourages and welcomes the coordinating role of the Transitional Administration in this endeavour;

7. *Underlines* that the Transitional Administration should respond robustly to the militia threat in East Timor, consistent with its resolution 1272(1999);

8. *Emphasizes* the need, in the light of the recommendations in the report of the Security Council Mission, for measures to address shortcomings in the administration of justice in East Timor, particularly with a view to bringing to justice those responsible for serious crimes in 1999, and for urgent action to expedite the training of the Timor Lorasa'e Police Service and to attract sufficient resources to develop this police service and the judicial system;

9. *Encourages* the Government of Indonesia, while acknowledging their efforts so far, to continue to take steps, in cooperation with the Transitional Administration and relevant international agencies, in accordance with its resolution 1319(2000) and the relevant recommendations in the statement by its President of 6 December 2000;

10. *Requests* the Secretary-General to submit to the Security Council by 30 April 2001 a report on the implementation of the mandate of the Transitional Administration, which should include in particular military and political assessments of the situation on the ground and their implications for the size, struc-

ture and deployment of the Administration, and expresses its intention to take appropriate steps on the basis of this report expeditiously, taking into account the views of troop-contributing countries;

11. *Stresses* the need for a substantial international presence in East Timor after independence, and requests the Secretary-General to make detailed recommendations in this regard to the Council within six months of the adoption of the present resolution, which should be developed in close consultation with the East Timorese people and in coordination with other relevant international and bilateral actors, in particular the international financial institutions and the United Nations funds and programmes;

12. *Decides* to remain actively seized of the matter.

Communication (March). By a 7 March letter [S/2001/198] to the Security Council President, Indonesia said that any effort to depict the East Timorese refugees as continuing to languish in the camps in West Timor because they were being held against their will was without foundation. It had never been the policy of the Indonesian Government to condone the illegal actions taken by the militia to intimidate the refugees and/or to undermine security on the ground. Indonesia added that reconciliation among the East Timorese was vital, as it was the key to removing any actual or perceived hindrance for the refugees' return. Equally important was the issue of international humanitarian assistance. The security designation of West Timor as "Phase V" (evacuation) by the United Nations (see p. 275) had virtually prevented international agencies from providing assistance to the refugees there. Indonesia therefore called on the United Nations to dispatch its security experts from the Office of the United Nations Security Coordinator (UNSECOORD) to West Timor in order to re-rate the "Phase V" security designation of the West Timorese refugee camps.

Report of Secretary-General (May). In response to resolution 1338(2001), the Secretary-General submitted to the Security Council, on 2 May, an interim report [S/2001/436] on the implementation of UNTAET's mandate, including military and political assessments of the situation on the ground and their implications for the size, structure and deployment of UNTAET.

The main development in East Timor's political transition to independence since January was the promulgation, on 16 March, of the regulation on the election of the Constituent Assembly, which would form the basis for the preparation of the electoral roll. While the Assembly had been given a target of 90 days to complete the constitution, the date of independence would become clearer only when the Assembly had made some headway in its deliberations. In order to encourage public participation in the constitutional development process and to facilitate a broad public consultation, a national civic education framework was developed in close consultation with major civil society groups, which provided for widespread civic education through mass information and multiple civil society initiatives. UNTAET also supported initiatives by NGOs to facilitate public participation in the development of the constitution. In preparation for the election, to be held in August, UNTAET had launched a comprehensive voter education programme, utilizing printed media, radio and television. The political parties were beginning to establish district and subdistrict offices, build their membership and prepare for national congresses at which manifestos would be adopted and candidates selected. However, only the East Timor National Liberation Front (FRETILIN) was well advanced in that process.

During the preceding year, gross domestic product (GDP) grew by an estimated 15 per cent and crop production reached over 70 per cent of the pre-September 1999 level. However, much of the economic growth occurred in the capital, Dili, in service-sector enterprises and in trade and construction related to donor-funded reconstruction programmes. Unemployment remained substantial, especially in urban areas where the ranks of the unemployed had been swelled by migrants from the rural districts. In order to slow that migration, World Bank programmes were seeking to channel investments to rural areas.

The issue of refugees in West Timor remained unresolved. After a brief upsurge in March, when 2,735 refugees returned, less than 400 returned in April, despite increased information efforts by UNTAET, culminating in a tour of four camps by its Chief of Staff from 9 to 11 April. The United Nations was working with Indonesian authorities on an appeal for donations to meet the costs of disseminating information in the camps, registering the refugees, repatriation and resettlement. Security "Phase V" (evacuation), which was put into effect in West Timor after the murder of three UNHCR workers in 2000 [YUN 2000, p. 282], remained in place. Thus, there was no permanent presence of internationally recruited UN staff in West Timor. Although Indonesia had not implemented all the measures called for by the Security Council in resolution 1319(2000) [ibid., p. 283], including the disarmament and disbandment of the militias, UNSECOORD had decided to organize and lead an inter-agency security assessment mission to West Timor as soon as possible.

The East Timorese had readily accepted back into local communities returning refugees who had supported integration with Indonesia. At the same time, they agreed that those who had committed major crimes had to be prosecuted. In that connection, the Indonesian Parliament's decision to establish an ad hoc tribunal to deal with gross violations of human rights in East Timor was seen as a positive step. However, the relevant decree, signed by President Abdurrahman Wahid on 24 April, limited the jurisdiction of the tribunal to acts committed after the ballot on 30 August 1999 [YUN 1999, p. 280]. Therefore, a number of massacres and serious crimes, on which the Indonesian Attorney-General had been conducting investigations, would not be prosecuted.

Although the security situation had been generally good, both on the border and inside the territory, it remained unpredictable. In March, there had been violence in Baucau and Viqueque, including attacks on a Timorese District Administrator and other UN staff. The pro-Indonesian militias based in West Timor continued to advocate armed struggle to bring East Timor into Indonesia and had not laid down their arms. The involvement of the militias in illegal cross-border trade had increased, providing them with contacts and intelligence. The Secretary-General recommended maintaining UNTAET's military component until the East Timorese Government had established itself. The force stood at 8,162 all ranks as at 1 May, compared to its authorized strength of 8,950.

The Secretary-General stressed that East Timor would continue to need significant assistance after attaining independence, in order to ensure the country's stability. Towards that end, the Special Representative, in March, established a working group on post-UNTAET planning. The group initiated a complete review of the estimated level and skills of international staffing required to support the future Government and began consultations with Timorese authorities to ensure that any recommendations would be acceptable to the future Government. The working group noted that, although there was scope for reductions in the number of international civilian personnel, there remained a need for a significant international presence in the post-independence period. That presence should comprise international experts who would act as advisers to East Timorese civil servants and who had demonstrated skills in training and mentoring. In some cases, international staff would be needed to perform line functions that had a high technical content for which expertise was not available locally. Those needs were being assessed and evaluated within the framework of the overall allocation of resources. At UN Headquarters, an integrated mission task force had been established to support and complement the working group and to carry out coordination among the organizations concerned.

The development and training of the Timor Lorasa'e Police Service was proceeding in accordance with a plan that provided for the achievement of its full strength of 3,000 by the end of April 2003. Until that time, an international civilian police presence would be needed, at a level that would be gradually reduced, to provide assistance for the maintenance of law and order.

Once the new Government had established itself, and subject to the conditions prevailing at that time, it was envisaged that the troops deployed in the east could be gradually withdrawn, while those in the western sector and the Oecussi enclave would be maintained. In the meantime, the first ETDF battalion was undergoing introductory training by Portuguese personnel, using equipment provided by Australia.

Communication (June). On 20 June [S/2001/621], Indonesia transmitted to the Security Council President a document containing the findings of 12 international observers on the registration of East Timorese in Nusa Tenggara Timur, which was conducted on 6 June. The objective of the registration was to ascertain the precise number of East Timorese refugees there and to determine how many wished to remain in Indonesia and how many wished to return to East Timor. The international observers, including one from UNTAET, were present in five districts on the day of registration. The results of the registration process reflected that, from a total of 113,791 participants, 1,250 (1.1 per cent) East Timorese refugees elected to return to East Timor, while 111,540 (98.02 per cent) opted to remain in Indonesia and 1,010 (0.88 per cent) abstained.

Report of Secretary-General (July). In accordance with resolution 1338(2001), the Secretary-General submitted a 24 July report [S/2001/719] on the activities of UNTAET, developments in East Timor and progress made in planning for an international presence in East Timor after independence, covering the period since his May report.

With the dissolution of the National Council and the start of a six-week election campaign on 15 July, a new phase of organized political activity had begun. Sixteen parties registered with the Independent Electoral Commission to field candidates in the election for the 88-member Constituent Assembly, scheduled for 30 August. In early July, 14 of the 16 parties contesting in the election signed a pact of national unity by which they committed themselves to respect the outcome of the election, to conduct themselves in a peaceful and mutually respectful fashion and to

defend multiparty democracy. The refusal by two minor parties to sign was not seen as detrimental to the positive stance that was being adopted overall in the campaign period. In June and July, nearly 10 per cent of the electorate took part in hearings, convened by the 13 district constitutional commissions, on systems of government, basic rights and other issues to be included in the constitution. The views, along with those of political parties, would be conveyed to the Constituent Assembly. The Assembly would meet from 15 September, with a target of 90 days in which to draft a constitution. It would also perform essential legislative functions under the authority of the Transitional Administrator, who would continue to exercise ultimate executive and legislative authority until independence. During the preceding six months, the nine-member Cabinet composed of East Timorese and UN staff members, and presided over by the Special Representative, continued to direct the work of the East Timor Transitional Administration (ETTA) and determine policy. The Special Representative intended to appoint, on 15 September, a new and enlarged transitional Cabinet composed entirely of East Timorese. The composition of the Cabinet of National Unity, expected to see East Timor through to independence, would broadly reflect the outcome of the election.

As the political process moved towards independence, ETTA's work was focused on the achievement of a series of key benchmarks that set out the steps in the transition of the Administration to independence. The benchmarks, contained in an annex to the report, covered the period from December 2000 to December 2001 and included the following areas: political affairs; administrative handover; defence force; foreign affairs; law and order; public finances; agriculture/economy; health; education; and infrastructure. East Timorese had been integrated into all major decision-making areas within ETTA, with 9,266 of the 10,554 civil service positions having been filled and 20 East Timorese having taken on senior management responsibilities. During the first half of 2001, steady progress had been made in achieving targets in civil service recruitment and training, and, among other things, adopting legislation on employment and labour administration. Although economic growth remained strong, sustained private sector growth continued to be limited. In July, Australian and East Timorese Cabinet ministers initialled the Timor Sea Arrangement, which provided East Timor with 90 per cent of the oil and gas production in the area covered under the 1989 Australia-Indonesia Timor Gap Treaty. The Arrangement also gave East Timor control over the development of its own fiscal scheme for future developments and taxation in the area.

The fourth donors' meeting on East Timor (Canberra, Australia, 14-15 June) endorsed a combined-sources budget of $65 million for East Timor for the fiscal year 2001-2002 (see also p. 841). While the meeting was not a pledging session, some donors indicated that they would provide additional contributions to the budget. Donors accepted their responsibility to take recurrent expenditures and future budgetary implications into account when designing their assistance programmes, but emphasized the need for fiscal sustainability and to strengthen revenues. Expenditure under the UNTAET Consolidated Trust Fund and the World Bank-administered Trust Fund for East Timor for 2000-2001 reached about $110 million. With regard to the consolidated budget, roughly 60 per cent was financed by donor contributions and 40 per cent from tax revenues or other income.

Agriculture remained the single largest contributor to the East Timorese gross national product. Efforts to increase crop production with the aim of ensuring food self-sufficiency and food security, together with a relatively favourable climate in early 2001, caused the volume of agriculture production to continue to recover, approaching the levels before the outbreak of the 1999 post-ballot violence [YUN 1999, p. 288]. Although the education sector received a significant portion of the budget allocations and bilateral assistance, considerable obstacles remained, including a need for teacher training and equipping of schools. In the health sector, the first half of 2001 saw an increase in reproductive health services, and a national polio immunization programme had achieved 80 per cent coverage. However, overall national immunization rates, at 15 per cent, were still low.

The East Timorese leadership and UNTAET stepped up their reconciliation efforts with militia leaders in West Timor and, in June, the National Council endorsed the establishment of the Commission for Reception, Truth and Reconciliation in East Timor, which would enable the East Timorese to create a public record of human rights abuses since 1975, to facilitate the reintegration of returning refugees and to promote community reconciliation by dealing with low-level offences committed in 1999. Despite persistent efforts by UNTAET, the memorandum of understanding on cooperation in legal, judicial and human rights matters, concluded with Indonesia in 2000 [YUN 2000, p. 280], had failed to yield results. In fact, Indonesian authorities had yet to transfer persons for purposes of prosecution, as

called for in the memorandum, and the establishment of a special human rights tribunal in Indonesia for the prosecution of serious crimes against the East Timorese people remained outstanding. In addition, the Indonesian Attorney-General had not appealed the light sentences handed down by a Jakarta court to six men in connection with the murder of three UNHCR workers in 2000 [ibid., p. 282]. The Serious Crimes Investigation Unit of the Office of the East Timor General Prosecutor continued to focus on the investigation of priority cases. The first trial on charges of crimes against humanity began in July with 11 persons accused of war crimes in the killings of clergy and other persons and the deportation of the civilian population in the Lautem district from April to September 1999. The UN civilian police, with a presence of 1,419 officers, continued its dual role of maintaining law and order and building the East Timor Police Service.

The UNTAET Human Rights Unit continued to assist in the development of East Timor's national institutions, such as the police and the courts, and to protect and promote human rights, in addition to facilitating and monitoring the safe reintegration of refugees returning from West Timor. It also worked in cooperation with other UNTAET units to support the constitutional consultative process.

A five-year plan for the future development of ETDF was presented at the second international conference of interested parties on the establishment of ETDF, held in June. The first battalion of 408 soldiers was scheduled for operational deployment in mid-2002. While training, infrastructure and equipment for ETDF depended on voluntary contributions, personnel, operating and maintenance costs would be borne by East Timor's Government.

The Secretary-General noted that Indonesia's registration of the refugees in Nusa Tenggara Timur (see p. 276) indicated that the overwhelming majority of them opted to remain in Indonesia. He said that continued disinformation and intimidation in the camps prior to the registration process, feelings of uncertainty on the part of the refugees about the political process in East Timor, and a lack of clarity as to whether the benefits to which they were entitled in Indonesia would continue in East Timor might have contributed to their reluctance to return. A UN interagency security assessment mission visited West Timor from 6 to 14 July and would soon report to the Secretary-General on its findings.

With regard to the security situation, there had been an overall decrease in the level of direct contact between militia forces and the UNTAET military component since December 2000. However, there was an aggressive attack against UNTAET troops in April 2001, which was followed by a number of other incidents. Illegal cross-border trade and movement had been associated with serious security incidents and remained of considerable concern. Also of concern was the ability of militias to operate and train unhindered in some areas. Within East Timor, there remained the potential for communal or inter-party violence over the transition period. Sporadic incidents in East Timor had developed rapidly into larger clashes and house burnings. Many East Timorese remained afraid of multiparty politics, associating them with the confrontation and violence of the past. In response, UNTAET and ETTA continued to upgrade the security measures entailing a coordinated approach between the civilian, military and police components.

With regard to a successor mission to UNTAET, the working group on post-UNTAET planning in East Timor (see p. 275), together with an integrated mission task force in New York, continued to plan for an international presence after independence. The civilian component of the mission would include the essential elements of a sizeable operation headed by a Special Representative of the Secretary-General. It was envisaged that the UNDP resident representative/UN resident coordinator would be appointed as the Deputy Special Representative and be supported by a small political office. A legal adviser's office, a gender focal point, an office of public affairs and an office of administration were also foreseen, as was the retention of a liaison office in Jakarta. The Secretary-General was of the view that an effective human rights component should be an essential part of the mission and that an electoral assistance component would be required. It would also be necessary to maintain within the mission a small team of professionals in various fields, to continue the work of Timorization and skills transfer. UNTAET was completing an assessment of the total skills package that would be available from all donor sources, to keep to an absolute minimum the number of staff needed within the new mission. By the end of UNTAET's current mandate (January 2002), it was expected that about 75 per cent of ETTA's international staff and up to 20 per cent of UNTAET's administrative staff could be eliminated. The development and training of the East Timor Police Service were proceeding according to schedule, the Secretary-General stated. The UN civilian police's role would continue to be one of executive policing, gradually shifting to one of mentoring and monitoring as the East Timorese police assumed increased responsibility for public security functions. A UN force would need to continue, in close cooperation with the Government of East Timor, to maintain a secure environment, with a particular emphasis on a strong presence in the border areas with West Timor. In the eastern sector, the number of infantry battalions could be reduced from three to one, provided the security situation remained stable. Subsequently, a similar reduction could take place in the central sector.

The Secretary-General observed that during the first half of 2001 the East Timorese people, in partnership with the United Nations, but increasingly on their own, had made broad advances towards independence and self-government. While a number of serious incidents had occurred, the overall security situation in the country had been stable. It was clear that the debate on the future constitution was drawing intense interest from broad segments of the population. The East Timorese leaders had acted with great responsibility to promote peace, tolerance and mutual respect. Many difficulties and challenges, however, remained. A key task was the establishment of effective administrative institutions that were fiscally sustainable. It was essential to ensure the smooth formation of the Constituent Assembly and the new Cabinet and to maintain a peaceful environment for the debate over the first constitution and the transition to independence.

Communications (August). By a 9 August letter [S/2001/779], Indonesia informed the Security Council President that its President, Megawati Soekarnoputri, had issued a presidential decree, which amended a previous decree (see p. 275) on the establishment of the ad hoc human rights courts. The new decree authorized the ad hoc human rights courts to investigate and render judicial decisions on cases of gross human rights violations that took place in the districts of Liquica, Dili and Suai, in East Timor, during the months of April and September 1999. Indonesia was in the process of appointing ad hoc judges to preside over those cases.

On 22 August [S/2001/817], Indonesia informed the Council President that, as part of the ongoing disarmament process, the police authorities in East Nusa Tenggara had confiscated large numbers of weapons and explosives.

Elections for Constituent Assembly

The Security Council held a closed meeting on 23 August to discuss the situation in East Timor, at which it heard a briefing by the Assistant Secretary-General for Peacekeeping Operations, Hédi Annabi. Mr. Annabi gave details of the arrangements for the elections for East Timor's first Constituent Assembly, to be held on 30 August. He informed the Council that the electoral campaign had been conducted in a peaceful manner, with political parties and the population at large showing strong support for the pact of national unity.

In an official communiqué [S/PV.4358], the members of the Council emphasized the importance of the peaceful conduct of the elections. They believed that a peaceful, democratic process would be a major first step towards East Timor's independence in a complex process of stabilization. Speakers encouraged a spirit of peace, democracy and tolerance throughout the electoral process and beyond, and joined the Secretary-General in supporting the heroic efforts of the East Timorese people and in urging a large voter turnout.

SECURITY COUNCIL ACTION

On 10 September [meeting 4368], following consultations among Security Council members, the President made statement **S/PRST/2001/23** on behalf of the Council:

> The Security Council recalls its previous resolutions and the statements of its President on the situation in East Timor.
>
> The Council warmly welcomes the successful staging on 30 August 2001 of the elections for East Timor's first Constituent Assembly, in particular the orderly and peaceful conduct of the elections and the very high voter turnout, which demonstrated the wish of the East Timorese people to establish a full participatory democracy. In that regard, the Council recognizes with appreciation the important role of the East Timorese leadership and welcomes the cooperation extended by the Government of Indonesia during the election period.
>
> The Council expresses its appreciation to the United Nations Transitional Administration in East Timor for facilitating a smooth and representative election process. The Council calls on all parties to fully respect and implement the election results which provide the basis for a broad-based Constituent Assembly. The Council looks forward to the establishment on 15 September of the Constituent Assembly and the new Cabinet within the framework of resolution 1272(1999). The Council calls upon all parties to work together to draft a constitution which reflects the will of the East Timorese people and to cooperate for the successful completion of the final steps towards independence, in a complex process of stabilization in East Timor which will take some time and will involve many actors.
>
> The Council reiterates the importance of a substantial international presence in East Timor post-independence.
>
> The Council looks forward to receiving the Secretary-General's October report focusing on the transition and post-independence periods.

Post-election developments

Report of Secretary-General (October). In accordance with resolution 1388(2001), the Secretary-General submitted a report [S/2001/983 & Corr.1] on the activities of UNTAET and developments in East Timor from 25 July to 15 October. The report also gave an update on efforts to support economic and social developments in East Timor and outlined the proposed structure for the successor mission to UNTAET.

The Secretary-General said that three crucial steps had been taken since his last report: the election of a Constituent Assembly; the start of the 90-day constitution-drafting process; and the formation of an all-Timorese Council of Ministers. After the peaceful elections for the Constituent Assembly on 30 August, in which 91.3 per cent of eligible voters participated, the Independent Electoral Commission announced the final certified results on 10 September, and assessed that the criteria for a free and fair election had been met. On 15 September, the Special Representative swore in the 88 members of the Assembly. A committee was established by the Assembly to make recommendations on the constitution and to oversee its drafting. The 13 Constitutional Commissions had prepared reports that summarized the views expressed by over 36,000 Timorese on such topics as national and territorial sovereignty; the country's name and flag; systems of government; the economy and taxation; and language and citizenship. On 20 September, the Special Representative appointed an all-Timorese "Second Transitional Government", which reflected the outcome of the elections of 30 August. A Council of Ministers, led by a Chief Minister, presided over the Transitional Government and supervised the East Timor Public Administration. For the first time, the executive branch of government in East Timor was controlled by East Timorese, albeit under the overall authority of the Special Representative.

The building of an all-Timorese civil service and its institutions from the ground up continued. By mid-September, UNTAET had recruited some 9,500 East Timorese civil servants, about 90 per cent of the revised target of 10,500. However, since the professional bureaucratic skills and capacity of many civil servants remained limited, the civil administration of East Timor was still highly reliant on international staff. Of particular concern were the areas of public finances, the judiciary, senior management and the development and maintenance of the central administrative systems of government. Maintaining the delivery of government services while diminishing dependence on UNTAET support would require realistic and sustainable standards of service to be set prior to independence. Following independence, the management of public finances would require a minimum level of international technical support, as mismanagement could threaten the overall functioning of the administration and undermine donor confidence in East Timor.

The Office of the Deputy Prosecutor for Ordinary Crimes continued to direct investigations into more than 400 criminal cases for offences committed since November 1999. The justice system, which was still in a nascent state, would continue to require significant international support, particularly judicial expertise, beyond independence.

The UN civilian police (1,485 officers) continued its dual role of maintaining law and order and training the East Timor Police Service. The reported crime rate remained low. A medium-term plan for the development of the Service was being finalized. The headquarters of ETDF had been established in Dili and a new training centre was fully functional. A code of military discipline had been developed, as well as other administrative procedures.

The amount of militia activity on the East Timor side of the Tactical Coordination Line (the informal boundary agreed to by UNTAET and the Indonesian armed forces (TNI), pending formal demarcation of the border) continued to decline. However, the frequency and size of illegal markets in the vicinity of that Line had grown, creating substantial security concerns, as various armed groups attempted to control and regulate those markets for their own ends. UNTAET and the Indonesian authorities had commenced discussion on a comprehensive border regime between East Timor and Indonesia. Reports of misinformation and intimidation in the refugee camps continued to be received and a core of hard-line militia in West Timor would continue to pose a potential threat to East Timor after independence, the Secretary-General stated. TNI and the Indonesian police had carried out operations to restrict the militia's movement, and had conducted sweeps for weapons in the refugee camps in West Timor. On 28 August, UNTAET and TNI signed the Military Technical Arrangement, a security agreement that would improve information-sharing and the coordination of military activity in the vicinity of the border.

A lack of experienced East Timorese investigators, prosecutors and a sufficient number of experienced judges had inhibited the issuance of indictments and prosecutions for serious crimes. The Office of the Deputy Special Representative had taken a direct role in addressing the problems of the Serious Crimes Unit. If fully provided with resources, the Unit should be able to complete the investigations and indictments for 10 priority cases of crimes against humanity by mid-2002.

Since July, more than 2,600 refugees had returned to East Timor. As anticipated, after the elections of 30 August both organized and spontaneous refugee returns began to increase. Since October 1999, 185,519 refugees had returned to East Timor and an estimated 60,000 to 80,000 remained in Indonesia. Indonesia had announced that after December 2001 it would no longer provide humanitarian assistance for the refugees. The priority was to ensure that the refugees were free to return voluntarily to East Timor, voluntary local resettlement in Indonesia being a secondary option. Negotiations between the United Nations and Indonesia regarding a memorandum of understanding delineating security responsibilities and requirements were ongoing.

UNTAET continued to prepare the populations in the districts for returnees, to facilitate their peaceful reintegration and longer-term reconciliation. Although there remained some concern over reprisals against some returnees, incidents of violence had been minimal. While perpetrators of serious crimes had to be dealt with by the courts, those implicated in lesser crimes would be dealt with by the Commission for Reception, Truth and Reconciliation. The Commission was also empowered to hold hearings and seek evidence in order to establish the truth about all relevant events that occurred in East Timor from 25 April 1974 to 25 October 1999. It would have a mandate of two years and would report, and make recommendations based on its findings, to the Government. The Commission would be predominantly staffed by East Timorese, assisted by an international technical assistance unit, and would be funded from voluntary contributions, which had yet to reach the target amount.

Significant progress in the fields of economic and social development in East Timor had been made during the transitional period. The administrative structures provided by UNTAET had assisted a range of humanitarian and development partners to implement wide-ranging recovery and development cooperation activities throughout the territory. The decrease of UN personnel and expenditure would inevitably have an adverse impact on growth, and special efforts, including poverty reduction initiatives and structural reforms, might be required to counteract a sudden reduction in the demand for labour and consumption expenditure linked to UNTAET's presence. Other structural constraints likely to inhibit sustained future growth, such as legislation on property rights and on land claims, would also have to be addressed. The newly established Commission on Planning within the East Timor

Public Administration continued to work on the development of a plan for medium-term expenditures to help ensure fiscal sustainability, with an emphasis on reducing poverty.

Much progress had been achieved in the education sector. The severity of the damage to educational facilities, however, meant that the support of international development programmes would need to continue well past independence to restore infrastructure and accommodate a fast-growing population and expanding enrolment rates. In the health sector, progress continued to be seen under the sector-wide approach to restoring access to basic services and establishing the policies, systems and human resources needed for a sustainable health system.

With regard to the transition to the successor mission, the reduction of UNTAET's military component was to commence in November. The plan was to reduce the authorized strength from 8,950 troops (actual deployment, 7,947) to some 5,000 military personnel, including 120 military observers, by independence. Commensurate reductions would be made in the military engineering, medical, aviation and support units, to be achieved through scheduled troop rotations. Likewise, it was envisaged that the civilian police component would be reduced to 1,250 from 1,640 by independence. By late September, UNTAET had already achieved the October target of reducing the staff of the East Timor Public Administration by 35 per cent; plans for a total reduction of 75 per cent were expected to be achieved by the end of the transition period. That reduction would be implemented in a phased manner to minimize the negative effect on the delivery of basic government services and on the local economy.

The primary focus of the successor mission would be to ensure the security of East Timor and the viability and stability of its government structures, allowing for the completion of UNTAET's mandate. The mission would be based on the premise that operational responsibilities had to be fully devolved to the East Timorese authorities as soon as it was feasible. A continuing process of assessment and downsizing was therefore envisaged over a period of two years, starting from independence.

The military component of the western sector would continue to have a two-battalion group with a sector headquarters, while the Oecussi enclave would retain a battalion group, and the central and eastern sectors would be reduced to only one mobile battalion. Further staged reductions would take place during the life of the successor mission, subject to ongoing security assessments and progress achieved in the development of

ETDF. In the border area, the force would continue to take measures to deter unlawful armed groups and ensure security, pending the full deployment of ETDF. The mission's military observers would play a role in maintaining liaison with both the Indonesian and East Timor defence forces. As to the development of ETDF, it was envisaged that a battalion would be ready for operational tasks in the eastern sector in June 2002; a second battalion would be ready by late 2003. However, the schedule for the development of ETDF could be shortened, subject to the provision of donor funds for the necessary capital investments. It was foreseen that East Timor would take over full responsibility for its own defence arrangements by mid-2004 at the latest.

The United Nations would continue its police work to ensure that the East Timor Police Service was developed as a service and an institution that was credible, accountable and professional. Drawing on the lessons learned from other operations, the main objective of the successor mission's police component would be to promote the capacity and integrity of the Service and its personnel. The civilian police component would be led by an international police commissioner, and would continue to perform a dual role of executive policing, while supporting the development of the East Timor Police Service. UNTAET expected that 1,500 East Timorese police officers would be operationally deployed by 31 January 2002. If the projected East Timorese police force of 3,000 was reduced, depending on consultations with and decisions taken by the new East Timorese Government, there would be corresponding reductions within the UN civilian police component. It was also expected that reductions in the civilian police component would occur throughout the life of the successor mission as the East Timorese police force acquired the capacity to assume full executive responsibilities. In order to ensure the viability of the East Timor Police Service—which had only a rudimentary infrastructure and no logistical or administrative framework, and continued to be almost completely reliant on UNTAET resources for transport, communication and administration—it would be essential for additional resources that could not be transferred from UNTAET to be secured through bilateral and multilateral donors. The Secretary-General said that since the strategy and implementation plan of the new mission would depend largely on the successful preparation of ETDF and the Police Service to take over the responsibility for East Timor's external and internal security, it was essential that those two organizations be properly funded and that their operations be sustainable under the budget of the new administration. He therefore appealed to Member States to support an adequate and sustainable capital programme to equip both organizations.

As to the civilian component, the United Nations had identified approximately 100 core functions for which local expertise did not exist, but which were essential to the stability and functioning of government; those core functions therefore required assured funding for a short period after independence to permit the completion of the Security Council mandate and to ensure that the investments made to date were not jeopardized. Two thirds of those positions were intended as mentoring functions (advisory and training), and one third would primarily cover public finance and banking, justice, and central and common services necessary to maintaining government functioning. In the justice sector, the successor mission would include court of appeal judges, special panel judges, court administrators and public defenders, as well as prison staff advisers and trainers. Other core civilian functions within the new mission would focus on strengthening internal administration and the infrastructure sector. Experts would also provide capacity-building in management, procurement, supplies and inventory in the area of central administrative services and assist in the drafting of legislative documents and in ensuring compliance with international human rights instruments. Expert advisers would be required to assist the new State in establishing demographic information, conducting foreign affairs, formulating economic policy, undertaking donor coordination and supporting decision-making by constitutional organs. With the support of UNDP, the Transitional Administration had prepared an overall framework for governance and public sector management, identifying priority areas in the short, medium and long term which would require funding from voluntary contributions.

The Secretary-General observed that the essential requirement in the case of East Timor was to ensure that the enormous sacrifices of the East Timorese, the substantial investments of the international community, and the cooperation of the parties required to bring about a successful transition to independence were not squandered for lack of international attention and support for the new State. At the same time, it was important to move towards a normal development assistance framework as quickly as was responsibly possible. The Secretary-General would recommend to the Security Council a date for East Timor's independence, following consultations with his Special Representative and the Constitu-

ent Assembly. The successor mission would be established on that date. The responsibility for establishing a viable State in East Timor belonged to its people, who had amply demonstrated the depth of their commitment to that task through sacrifice, imagination and determination.

SECURITY COUNCIL ACTION

On 31 October [meeting 4404], following consultations among Security Council members, the President made statement **S/PRST/2001/32** on behalf of the Council:

> The Security Council welcomes the Secretary-General's report of 18 October 2001.
>
> The Council expresses its appreciation to the Secretary-General's Special Representative in East Timor and to the United Nations Transitional Administration in East Timor for their efforts in developing detailed plans for the future United Nations presence in East Timor.
>
> The Council welcomes the political progress achieved to date towards establishing an independent East Timorese State and endorses the recommendation by the Constituent Assembly that independence be declared on 20 May 2002.
>
> The Council recalls resolutions 1272(1999) of 25 October 1999 and 1338(2001) of 31 January 2001 and other relevant resolutions. It agrees with the Secretary-General's assessment that premature withdrawal of the international presence could have a destabilizing effect in a number of crucial areas. It further agrees with the Secretary-General's assessment that the United Nations should remain engaged in East Timor to protect the major achievements so far realized by the Transitional Administration, to build upon those achievements in cooperation with other actors, and to assist the East Timorese Government in ensuring security and stability.
>
> The Council takes note of the Secretary-General's observation that the mandate of the Transitional Administration should be extended until independence and endorses his plans for adjusting the size and configuration of the Transitional Administration in the months prior to independence.
>
> The Council endorses the Secretary-General's recommendations for a continued and appropriately reduced United Nations integrated mission in the post-independence period, and requests the Secretary-General to continue planning and preparation for this mission, in consultation with the East Timorese people, and to submit further and more detailed recommendations to the Council. The Council agrees that the successor mission would be headed by a Special Representative of the Secretary-General and comprise a military component, a civilian police component and a civilian component, including experts who would provide crucial assistance to the emergent East Timorese administration. The Council notes that a core number of civilian positions will be critical to the stability of the independent East Timorese Government and agrees that these limited positions will require assessed funding for a period of between six months and two years after independence. The Coun-

cil agrees that the new mission should be based on the premise that operational responsibilities should be devolved to the East Timorese authorities as soon as this is feasible, and it supports a continuing process of assessment and downsizing over a period of two years, starting from independence. In this regard, the Council recognizes the essential role of the General Assembly in peace-building and expresses its intention to continue planning for peace-building in close cooperation with the General Assembly. The Council acknowledges the importance of a strong focus on justice and human rights in the successor mission and, where appropriate, in other assistance provided to East Timor.

The Council agrees with the Secretary-General's assessment that it will be vital that the United Nations contribution is supplemented by multilateral and bilateral arrangements. The Council looks forward to receiving information on the financial implications of the follow-on mission and a detailed assessment of shared responsibilities among the principal interacting players, i.e. the United Nations system, international financial institutions, regional mechanisms and national donors, in their efforts to assist East Timor in its unprecedented transition to self-government.

Further report of Secretary-General. In a later report [S/2002/80 & Corr.1], the Secretary-General described UNTAET's activities and developments in East Timor during the latter part of 2001. He assessed progress made in the implementation of UNTAET's mandate and proposed measures to consolidate that progress, including detailed planning for an integrated UN mission that would be deployed in East Timor after independence. Annexed to the report was the proposed framework for the successor mission to UNTAET.

A milestone on the road towards East Timor's independence was the Security Council's endorsement, in its presidential statement of 31 October (see p. 282), of the Constituent Assembly's proposal that independence be declared on 20 May 2002. Other important political advances were made and steady gains achieved in the establishment of a public administration for East Timor. The security environment had continued to improve, and policies were being implemented that favoured economic and social development. At the same time, the comparative fragility of the political foundations of the new country, its very limited pool of professional and administrative expertise, the lack of strong independent security mechanisms and a nascent state of economic development meant that East Timor would continue to require significant assistance from the international community well after independence.

The Constituent Assembly had started in December to consider the new draft constitution; the review process was expected to be completed in late January 2002. The draft constitution would establish a unitary democratic State, based on the rule of law and the principle of separation of powers. Representative organs would be elected through direct and universal suffrage. It proposed a President, who would also be commander-in-chief of the armed forces, a Prime Minister, who would head a Council of Ministers, and a Parliament. The President's powers would be limited by Parliament, and the President would be required to consult the latter, as well as the Council of State and a Supreme Council on Defence and Security, before declaring a state of emergency or siege. Pursuant to the Constituent Assembly's resolution in support of direct presidential elections, adopted on 28 November, the Transitional Administrator announced that the election for East Timor's first President would take place on 14 April 2002. The Assembly was also considering transforming itself into a legislative body in an arrangement whereby its 88 seats would be maintained for a first term, and later reduced to between 52 and 65. However, opposition parties and some civil society organizations had called for new legislative elections, to be held either concurrently with the presidential elections or soon after independence.

The third meeting of the East Timor–Indonesia Joint Border Committee took place in Dili from 19 to 21 November 2001. As the first visit by an Indonesian delegation since the visit of former President Wahid in February 2000 [YUN 2000, p. 280], the meeting represented a significant step in building relations between the two neighbours.

During the reporting period, the East Timorese Public Administration continued to play an increasing role in running the daily affairs of the country. By the end of 2001, it had recruited 9,633 East Timorese civil servants, representing 91.2 per cent of the total budgeted positions. The education and health sectors remained the largest public service employers. The East Timorese were working to strengthen their administrative structures through, among other things, the activities of an Inspector General's Office. An East Timorese Adviser on Equality assumed her functions on 1 November. Over 180 customs officers were present in Dili, in Oecussi and on the border with West Timor, providing customs, immigration and quarantine services.

The East Timorese justice system still lacked experienced and trained judges, public defenders and prosecutors, while support services for the courts remained limited. The prison population increased by nearly one third during the last six months of 2001, reflecting a rise in criminal activity, particularly violence by delinquent groups.

The first ETDF infantry battalion was provisionally organized in October and would begin operations in 2002. The progress achieved in training was the result of effective and coordinated bilateral assistance. The Secretary-General said that such a level of support would need to be maintained up to and beyond independence, in order to permit the gradual downsizing and ultimate withdrawal of UN peacekeepers.

The United Nations civilian police (CIVPOL) continued to maintain law and order while training the East Timor Police Service. Peter Miller (Canada) assumed the functions of CIVPOL Commissioner in November. The East Timor police force had reached a level of 1,453 officers. Donor countries had organized overseas and in-country training programmes in areas ranging from criminal investigation and maritime policing to police management and crowd control. However, the development of the East Timor Police Service continued to be constrained by the lack of resources.

Although there had been few sightings of militia along the Tactical Coordination Line, hard-line militia could still pose a long-term threat. Stability along the border would require substantial progress in East Timor's discussions with Indonesia regarding a comprehensive border regime.

Security in East Timor also meant addressing the legacy of violence that was committed in 1999, including the return of refugees, support for reconciliation and effective prosecution of serious crimes. The rate of refugee returns accelerated in spite of misinformation and continuing intimidation in the camps. In 2001, 17,900 refugees returned to East Timor, for a total of 192,000 returns. An estimated 60,000 to 75,000 refugees remained in camps in West Timor. Continued monitoring and protection of returnees were needed to ensure a high rate of returns. It appeared that the most significant deterrents to further returns were economic concerns, rather than security issues and militia intimidation. In November, the Indonesian Government started paying a repatriation incentive, and the World Food Programme doubled the rice component of the reintegration package. Additionally, the question of pension payments for East Timorese formerly employed by Indonesia in its civil, military and police service appeared to be a factor in delaying the return of some 8,500 families. The United Nations was working towards the establishment of a special fund to compensate for loss of employment and/or pension benefits. Local settlement activities in West Timor began in late November, with the building of housing units for some 6,500 East Timorese refugees wishing to remain in the area. Also in November, the United Nations and the Indonesian Government launched a joint appeal, which included UNHCR/UNDP plans to support Indonesia in the local settlement of 3,010 refugee families in East Nusa Tenggara, outside West Timor, through contributions towards housing and economic livelihood packages for refugees and support to host communities.

Work continued towards the establishment of the Commission for Reception, Truth and Reconciliation. National Commissioners were nominated by an independent panel in December. Some progress had been made with the prosecution of serious crimes. The Office of the General Prosecutor had filed 33 indictments charging 83 individuals with crimes committed between 1 January and 25 October 1999. However, progress in the courts was slow due to limited human and financial resources. Judgement was passed in December 2001 on a case concerning the operations of the Tim Alfa militia in 1999; that was the first trial for crimes against humanity to take place in East Timor, and the first example worldwide of the application of laws originally formulated for the International Criminal Court. Ten men received sentences ranging from 4 to 33 years for crimes of torture, murder, forced deportation and persecution. Indonesia announced that 30 judges for the Ad Hoc Human Rights Court had been selected in October/November.

The reported crime rate in East Timor remained low. However, there was a drastic increase in reports of violence against women and children, which led to the launching of a series of workshops on domestic violence.

The growth of East Timor's GDP was estimated at 18 per cent in 2001, with annual inflation estimated to be less than 3 per cent. Some uncertainty in the economy prior to the August election had been resolved and economic activity continued to expand. Forward projections for external financing requirements in the three years after independence were presented to the Oslo donors' conference (Oslo, Norway, 11-12 December). Rehabilitation of the educational system was advancing rapidly and, with the gradual departure of international professionals, East Timorese workers were taking on increased responsibilities in the health sector, at both the national and district levels. Progress also continued in the restoration of public buildings and road and port repairs, drawing on support from the Trust Fund for East Timor and the Consolidated Fund for East Timor. East Timorese officials had reached an understanding with the petroleum companies operating in the Joint Petroleum Development Area of the Timor Sea on a gas and fiscal package that would allow gas development to proceed.

In preparation for the downsizing of UNTAET, the Planning Commission completed its assessment of the scale, timing and economic effect of the international drawdown, and recommended a series of measures to limit the impact, including an information strategy directed towards local UN employees, the establishment of a legal framework to support the private sector, improved access to information about skilled vacancies and a short-term job creation programme.

The Secretary-General said that several elements were key to a smooth transition to an independent government: the phased reduction of international staff; the incorporation within the government of essential common services and the transfer of UN assets supporting those services; the transfer of some residual functions of government from UNTAET; the development of the essential legislative and procedural machinery for the operation of government at independence; and the timely recruitment of civilian advisers for the post-independence government. In November, the stable security environment enabled UNTAET to begin reducing its military component from the current 7,212 troops to some 5,000 soldiers at the time of independence. As downsizing progressed, the peacekeeping force was being reconfigured to enable it to continue to promote stability both along the border and internally throughout East Timor. UNTAET was working with the East Timorese Public Administration to ensure that immediately upon independence the Government would conclude with the United Nations a status-of-forces agreement that would address the role of the military component and its relationship with ETDF. Similar legal arrangements would also need to be agreed and implemented with regard to the performance of police functions by CIVPOL and the East Timor Police Service.

Reduction of civilian staffing assisting the East Timorese Public Administration was under way. Approximately 200 international staff and 60 UN Volunteers would remain in place until independence, representing a 75 per cent reduction from the original authorized strength of that component. The East Timorese Public Administration was gradually developing and taking on the responsibility for essential common services that underpinned the operations of government.

Planning for the successor mission continued both at UN Headquarters and in the field. The need for assured funding for some 100 key functions within the administration, for periods ranging from 12 to 24 months after independence, was confirmed by a skills audit undertaken by UNDP, which was completed in late October. Based on extensive consultations with donors and with other relevant actors, it had been determined that the only way those needs could be met on an assured basis was through their inclusion in the assessed funding of the successor mission.

Further reductions of the military component were envisaged over two broad stages. The first would begin once normalization of border activity was achieved. That would require that two conditions be met: agreement between the Governments of Indonesia and East Timor on the location of the border and its subsequent demarcation; and the establishment of an adequate national border security and control system. Those conditions would permit withdrawal of the military component from the immediate vicinity of the border, constituting a reduction to a two-battalion force of 2,500-3,000 troops. Complete withdrawal of the military component would take place when ETDF became fully capable of responding to external threats.

Planning for the development of the East Timor Police Service envisioned a force of 2,600 officers. Should the Service be given the responsibility for border security, an additional border service component of 200 officers would be created. It was projected that the international civilian police strength would be reduced by an average of 5 per cent every month, leaving by January 2004 about 100 officers, who would have purely advisory functions.

The Secretary-General stated that the people of East Timor and the international community had much to be proud of in all that had been accomplished in laying the political foundations for a new State, in providing the elements of the practical machinery that it required, in successfully addressing challenges to security and in setting out the basis for economic development. Close partnership between East Timor and the international community would remain essential for the continued stability and development of the country. Throughout the UN engagement in East Timor, the international community's efforts to promote political reconciliation and address security risks were complemented by wide-ranging support for new administrative structures and assistance with development for appropriate economic and social policies. The Secretary-General said that it was important that international assistance to East Timor reverted to a normal development model as soon as feasible. In that context, it would be essential for all elements of the UN system to work in a coordinated manner, together with bilateral assistance.

On 24 December, the General Assembly decided that the agenda item on the situation in East Timor during its transition to independence would remain for consideration during its resumed fifty-sixth (2002) session (**decision 56/464**).

Financing of UN operations

During 2001, the General Assembly considered the financing of two UN missions in East Timor—UNTAET and the United Nations Mission in East Timor (UNAMET). UNTAET was established by Security Council resolution 1272(1999) [YUN 1999, p. 293] to administer East Timor during its transition to independence. UNAMET was established by Council resolution 1246(1999) [ibid., p. 283] to conduct the 1999 popular consultation on East Timor's autonomy [ibid., p. 288]; its mandate ended on 30 November 1999, in accordance with resolution 1262(1999) [ibid., p. 287].

UNTAET

In April [A/55/874], the Advisory Committee on Administrative and Budgetary Questions (ACABQ) recommended, pending the submission of UNTAET's budget, that the General Assembly approve and assess $282 million gross ($273,025,800 net) for UNTAET for the period from 1 July to 31 December 2001. That amount was based on the budget of $563 million gross ($546,051,600 net) approved by the Assembly in resolution 55/228 A [YUN 2000, p. 291].

In May [A/55/925], the Secretary-General submitted to the Assembly UNTAET's financial performance report for the period from 1 December 1999 to 30 June 2000. Expenditures for the period totalled $292,010,000 gross ($287,968,200 net), resulting in an unencumbered balance of $57,990,000 gross ($53,116,100 net) that was attributable to the delayed deployment of international staff, which, in turn, resulted in a higher vacancy rate, reduced requirements under air operations and lower requirements for utilities, construction/prefabricated buildings, communications equipment and transport of contingent-owned equipment.

GENERAL ASSEMBLY ACTION (June)

On 14 June [meeting 103], on the recommendation of the Fifth (Administrative and Budgetary) Committee [A/55/664/Add.1], the General Assembly adopted **resolution 55/228 B** without vote [agenda item 134].

Financing of the United Nations Transitional Administration in East Timor

The General Assembly,

Having considered the report of the Secretary-General on the financing of the United Nations Transitional Administration in East Timor and the related reports of the Advisory Committee on Administrative and Budgetary Questions,

Bearing in mind Security Council resolution 1272 (1999) of 25 October 1999 regarding the establishment of the United Nations Transitional Administration in East Timor and resolution 1338(2001) of 31 January 2001, by which the Council extended the mandate of the Transitional Administration,

Recalling its resolution 54/246 A of 23 December 1999 on the financing of the Transitional Administration and its subsequent resolutions thereon, the latest of which was resolution 55/228 A of 23 December 2000,

Reaffirming the general principles underlying the financing of United Nations peacekeeping operations, as stated in General Assembly resolutions 1874(S-IV) of 27 June 1963, 3101(XXVIII) of 11 December 1973 and 55/235 of 23 December 2000,

Noting with appreciation that voluntary contributions have been made to the trust fund for the multinational force,

Also noting with appreciation that voluntary contributions have been made to the Trust Fund for the United Nations Transitional Administration in East Timor, and inviting further such contributions to the Trust Fund,

Mindful of the fact that it is essential to provide the Transitional Administration with the necessary financial resources to enable it to fulfil its responsibilities under the relevant resolutions of the Security Council,

1. *Reaffirms* its resolution 49/233 A of 23 December 1994, in particular those paragraphs regarding the peacekeeping budgetary cycles, which should be adhered to in the future budgetary process, where possible;

2. *Takes note* of the status of contributions to the United Nations Transitional Administration in East Timor as at 30 April 2001, including the contributions outstanding in the amount of 315.9 million United States dollars, representing some 35 per cent of the total assessed contributions from the inception of the Transitional Administration to the period ending 30 June 2001, notes that some 12 per cent of the Member States have paid their assessed contributions in full, and urges all other Member States concerned, in particular those in arrears, to ensure the payment of their outstanding assessed contributions;

3. *Expresses its appreciation* to those Member States which have paid their assessed contributions in full;

4. *Expresses concern* about the financial situation with regard to peacekeeping activities, in particular as regards the reimbursements to troop contributors that bear additional burdens owing to overdue payments by Member States of their assessments;

5. *Urges* all other Member States to make every possible effort to ensure payment of their assessed contributions to the Transitional Administration in full and on time;

6. *Expresses concern* at the delay experienced by the Secretary-General in deploying and providing adequate resources to some recent peacekeeping missions, in particular those in Africa;

7. *Emphasizes* that all future and existing peacekeeping missions shall be given equal and non-discriminatory treatment in respect of financial and administrative arrangements;

8. *Also emphasizes* that all peacekeeping missions shall be provided with adequate resources for the effec-

tive and efficient discharge of their respective mandates;

9. *Reiterates its request* to the Secretary-General to make the fullest possible use of facilities and equipment at the United Nations Logistics Base at Brindisi, Italy, in order to minimize the costs of procurement for the Transitional Administration;

10. *Endorses* the conclusions and recommendations contained in the reports of the Advisory Committee on Administrative and Budgetary Questions, and requests the Secretary-General to ensure their full implementation;

11. *Requests* the Secretary-General to take all necessary action to ensure that the Transitional Administration is administered with a maximum of efficiency and economy;

12. *Also requests* the Secretary-General, in order to reduce the cost of employing General Service staff, to continue efforts to recruit local staff for the Transitional Administration against General Service posts, commensurate with the requirements of the Transitional Administration;

13. *Approves*, on an exceptional basis, the special arrangements for the Transitional Administration with regard to the application of article IV of the financial regulations of the United Nations, whereby appropriations required in respect of obligations owed to Governments providing contingents and/or logistic support for the Transitional Administration shall be retained beyond the period stipulated under financial regulations 4.3 and 4.4, as set out in the annex to the present resolution;

14. *Authorizes* the Secretary-General to enter into commitments in the amount of 282 million dollars gross (273,025,800 dollars net) for the maintenance of the Transitional Administration for the period from 1 July to 31 December 2001, and decides to appropriate the amount of 17,027,947 dollars gross (14,943,699 dollars net) for the support account for peacekeeping operations and the amount of 1,778,786 dollars gross (1,597,340 dollars net) for the United Nations Logistics Base, representing the prorated share of the Transitional Administration in the support account and Logistics Base requirements for the period from 1 July 2001 to 30 June 2002;

15. *Decides* to apportion among Member States the amount of 282 million dollars gross (273,025,800 dollars net) for the period from 1 July to 31 December 2001 in accordance with the levels set out in General Assembly resolution 55/235, as adjusted by the Assembly in its resolution 55/236 of 23 December 2000, and taking into account the scale of assessments for the year 2001, as set out in its resolution 55/5 B of 23 December 2000;

16. *Decides also* that, in accordance with the provisions of its resolution 973(X) of 15 December 1955, there shall be set off against the apportionment among Member States, as provided for in paragraph 15 above, their respective share in the Tax Equalization Fund of the estimated staff assessment income of 8,974,200 dollars approved for the Transitional Administration for the period from 1 July to 31 December 2001;

17. *Decides further* to apportion among Member States the amount of 17,027,947 dollars gross (14,943,699 dollars net) for the support account and the amount of 1,778,786 dollars gross (1,597,340 dollars net) for the United Nations Logistics Base for the pe-

riod from 1 July 2001 to 30 June 2002 in accordance with paragraph 15 above, and taking into account the scale of assessments for the years 2001 and 2002, as set out in General Assembly resolution 55/5 B, the scale of assessments for the year 2001 to be applied against a portion thereof, that is, 8,513,974 dollars gross (7,471,850 dollars net) for the support account and 889,393 dollars gross (798,670 dollars net) for the Logistics Base for the period from 1 July to 31 December 2001, and the scale of assessments for the year 2002 to be applied against the balance, that is, 8,513,973 dollars gross (7,471,849 dollars net) for the support account and 889,393 dollars gross (798,670 dollars net) for the Logistics Base for the period from 1 January to 30 June 2002;

18. *Decides* that, in accordance with the provisions of its resolution 973(X), there shall be set off against the apportionment among Member States, as provided for in paragraph 17 above, their respective share in the Tax Equalization Fund of the estimated staff assessment income of 2,084,248 dollars for the support account and 181,446 dollars for the United Nations Logistics Base approved for the period from 1 July 2001 to 30 June 2002, 1,042,124 dollars for the support account and 90,723 dollars for the Logistics Base being amounts pertaining to the period from 1 July to 31 December 2001 and the balance, that is, 1,042,124 dollars for the support account and 90,723 dollars for the Logistics Base, pertaining to the period from 1 January to 30 June 2002;

19. *Decides also* that, for Member States that have fulfilled their financial obligations to the Transitional Administration, there shall be set off against the apportionment, as provided for in paragraph 15 above, their respective share of the unencumbered balance of 57,990,000 dollars gross (53,116,100 dollars net) in respect of the period ending 30 June 2000, in accordance with the composition of groups set out in paragraphs 3 and 4 of General Assembly resolution 43/232 of 1 March 1989, as adjusted by the Assembly in subsequent relevant resolutions and decisions for the ad hoc apportionment of peacekeeping appropriations, the latest of which were resolution 52/230 of 31 March 1998 and decisions 54/456 to 54/458 of 23 December 1999 for the period 1998-2000, and taking into account the scale of assessments for the year 2000, as set out in its resolutions 52/215 A of 22 December 1997 and 54/237 A of 23 December 1999;

20. *Decides further* that, for Member States that have not fulfilled their financial obligations to the Transitional Administration, their respective share in the unencumbered balance of 57,990,000 dollars gross (53,116,100 dollars net) in respect of the period ending 30 June 2000 shall be set off against their outstanding obligations in accordance with the scheme set out in paragraph 19 above;

21. *Emphasizes* that no peacekeeping mission shall be financed by borrowing funds from other active peacekeeping missions;

22. *Encourages* the Secretary-General to continue to take additional measures to ensure the safety and security of all personnel under the auspices of the United Nations participating in the Transitional Administration;

23. *Invites* voluntary contributions to the Transitional Administration in cash and in the form of serv-

ices and supplies acceptable to the Secretary-General, to be administered, as appropriate, in accordance with the procedure and practices established by the General Assembly;

24. *Decides* to include in the provisional agenda of its fifty-sixth session the item entitled "Financing of the United Nations Transitional Administration in East Timor".

ANNEX
Special arrangements with regard to the application of article IV of the financial regulations of the United Nations

1. At the end of the twelve-month period provided for in financial regulation 4.3, any unliquidated obligations of the financial period in question relating to goods supplied and services rendered by Governments for which claims have been received or which are covered by established reimbursement rates shall be transferred to accounts payable; such accounts shall remain recorded in the Special Account for the United Nations Transitional Administration in East Timor until payment is effected.

2. In addition:

(*a*) Any other unliquidated obligations of the financial period in question owed to Governments for provision of goods and services rendered but not yet verified, as well as other obligations owed to Governments, for which claims have not yet been received shall remain valid for an additional period of four years following the end of the twelve-month period provided for in financial regulation 4.3;

(*b*) Claims received during this four-year period as well as approved verification reports shall be treated as provided for under paragraph 1 of the present annex, if appropriate;

(*c*) At the end of the additional four-year period, any unliquidated obligations shall be cancelled and the then remaining balance of any appropriations retained therefor shall be surrendered.

In November [A/56/624], the Secretary-General submitted a report containing UNTAET's proposed budget for the period from 1 July 2001 to 30 June 2002, which amounted to $490,060,000 gross ($475,780,000 net), inclusive of budgeted voluntary contributions in kind amounting to $60,000.

In December [A/56/685], ACABQ, taking into account the fact that the Secretary-General's next report on UNTAET's budget would contain the requirements of the successor mission and the assistance needed for the new Government after independence, recommended that the Assembly approve an appropriation of $455 million gross for UNTAET's operations for the period from 1 July 2001 to 30 June 2002, inclusive of the amount of $282 million gross ($273,025,800 net) already authorized and assessed by the Assembly in its resolution 55/228 B for the period 1 July 2001 to 31 December 2001. The recommended amount reflected a reduction of 7 per cent from the amount proposed by the Secretary-General. The Committee also recommended that the Assembly approve an additional assessment of $120 million gross for the period 1 January to 30 June 2002, at a monthly rate of $20 million gross, for a total assessment of $402 million gross for the period 1 July 2001 to 30 June 2002, and authorize the Secretary-General to enter into commitments (without assessment) in the amount of $53 million should the Security Council decide to extend UNTAET's mandate beyond 31 January 2002.

GENERAL ASSEMBLY ACTION (December)

On 24 December [meeting 92], the General Assembly, on the recommendation of the Fifth Committee [A/56/715], adopted **resolution 56/249** without vote [agenda item 136].

Financing of the United Nations Transitional Administration in East Timor

The General Assembly,

Having considered the report of the Secretary-General on the financing of the United Nations Transitional Administration in East Timor and the related report of the Advisory Committee on Administrative and Budgetary Questions,

Bearing in mind Security Council resolution 1272(1999) of 25 October 1999 regarding the establishment of the United Nations Transitional Administration in East Timor and Council resolution 1338 (2001) of 31 January 2001, by which the Council extended the mandate of the Transitional Administration,

Recalling its resolution 54/246 A of 23 December 1999 on the financing of the Transitional Administration and its subsequent resolutions thereon, the latest of which was resolution 55/228 B of 14 June 2001,

Reaffirming the general principles underlying the financing of United Nations peacekeeping operations, as stated in General Assembly resolutions 1874(S-IV) of 27 June 1963, 3101(XXVIII) of 11 December 1973 and 55/235 of 23 December 2000,

Noting with appreciation that voluntary contributions have been made to the trust fund for the multinational force,

Also noting with appreciation that voluntary contributions have been made to the Trust Fund for the United Nations Transitional Administration in East Timor, and inviting further such contributions to the Trust Fund,

Mindful of the fact that it is essential to provide the Transitional Administration with the necessary financial resources to enable it to fulfil its responsibilities under the relevant resolutions of the Security Council,

1. *Takes note* of the status of contributions to the United Nations Transitional Administration in East Timor as at 15 November 2001, including the contributions outstanding in the amount of 239.9 million United States dollars, representing some 20 per cent of the total assessed contributions from the inception of the Transitional Administration to the period ending 31 December 2001, notes that some 19 per cent of the Member States have paid their assessed contributions in full, and urges all other Member States concerned, in particular those in arrears, to ensure the payment of their outstanding assessed contributions;

2. *Expresses its appreciation* to those Member States which have paid their assessed contributions in full and on time, and urges all other Member States to make every possible effort to ensure payment of their assessed contributions to the Transitional Administration in full and on time;

3. *Expresses concern* about the financial situation with regard to peacekeeping activities, in particular as regards the reimbursements to troop contributors that bear additional burdens owing to overdue payments by Member States of their assessments;

4. *Expresses concern* at the delay experienced by the Secretary-General in deploying and providing adequate resources to some recent peacekeeping missions, in particular those in Africa;

5. *Emphasizes* that all future and existing peacekeeping missions shall be given equal and non-discriminatory treatment in respect of financial and administrative arrangements;

6. *Also emphasizes* that all peacekeeping missions shall be provided with adequate resources for the effective and efficient discharge of their respective mandates;

7. *Reiterates its request* to the Secretary-General to make the fullest possible use of facilities and equipment at the United Nations Logistics Base at Brindisi, Italy, in order to minimize the costs of procurement for the Transitional Administration;

8. *Endorses* the conclusions and recommendations contained in the report of the Advisory Committee on Administrative and Budgetary Questions, and requests the Secretary-General to ensure their full implementation;

9. *Requests* the Secretary-General to take all necessary action to ensure that the Transitional Administration is administered with a maximum of efficiency and economy;

10. *Also requests* the Secretary-General, in order to reduce the cost of employing General Service staff, to continue efforts to recruit local staff for the Transitional Administration against General Service posts, commensurate with the requirements of the Transitional Administration;

11. *Decides* to appropriate the amount of 458,000,128 dollars gross (445,193,514 dollars net) for the operation of the Transitional Administration for the period from 1 July 2001 to 30 June 2002, inclusive of the amount of 3,000,128 dollars gross (2,773,914 dollars net) for the support account for peacekeeping operations, in addition to the amount of 17,027,947 dollars gross (14,943,699 dollars net) already appropriated for the support account and the amount of 1,778,786 dollars gross (1,597,340 dollars net) already appropriated for the United Nations Logistics Base by the General Assembly in its resolution 55/228 B, and inclusive of the amount of 282 million dollars gross (273,025,800 dollars net) authorized by the Assembly in resolution 55/228 B;

12. *Decides also*, taking into account the amount of 282 million dollars gross (273,025,800 dollars net) already apportioned for the period from 1 July to 31 December 2001 and the amount of 18,806,733 dollars gross (16,541,039 dollars net) already apportioned for the period from 1 July 2001 to 30 June 2002, in accordance with the provisions of its resolution 55/228 B, to apportion among Member States the amount of 23,000,128 dollars gross (22,220,931 dollars net) for the period from 1 to 31 January 2002, in accordance with the levels set out in General Assembly resolution 55/235, as adjusted by the Assembly in its resolution 55/236 of 23 December 2000, and taking into account the scale of assessments for the year 2002, as set out in its resolution 55/5 B of 23 December 2000;

13. *Decides further* that, in accordance with the provisions of its resolution 973(X) of 15 December 1955, there shall be set off against the apportionment among Member States, as provided for in paragraph 12 above, their respective share in the Tax Equalization Fund of the estimated staff assessment income of 779,197 dollars approved for the Transitional Administration for the period from 1 to 31 January 2002;

14. *Decides* to apportion among Member States the amount of 100 million dollars gross (97,235,083 dollars net) for the period from 1 February to 30 June 2002, at a monthly rate of 20 million dollars gross (19,447,016 dollars net), in accordance with the scheme set out in the present resolution and taking into account the scale of assessments for the year 2002, as set out in General Assembly resolution 55/5 B, subject to the decision of the Security Council to extend the mandate of the Transitional Administration beyond 31 January 2002;

15. *Decides also* that, in accordance with the provisions of its resolution 973(X), there shall be set off against the apportionment among Member States, as provided for in paragraph 14 above, their respective share in the Tax Equalization Fund of the estimated staff assessment income of 2,764,917 dollars approved for the Transitional Administration for the period from 1 February to 30 June 2002;

16. *Emphasizes* that no peacekeeping mission shall be financed by borrowing funds from other active peacekeeping missions;

17. *Encourages* the Secretary-General to continue to take additional measures to ensure the safety and security of all personnel under the auspices of the United Nations participating in the Transitional Administration;

18. *Invites* voluntary contributions to the Transitional Administration in cash and in the form of services and supplies acceptable to the Secretary-General, to be administered, as appropriate, in accordance with the procedure and practices established by the General Assembly;

19. *Decides* to keep under review during its fifty-sixth session the item entitled "Financing of the United Nations Transitional Administration in East Timor".

On 24 December, the Assembly decided that the agenda item on the financing of UNTAET would remain for consideration during its resumed fifty-sixth (2002) session (**decision 56/464**) and that the Fifth Committee should continue consideration of the item at that session (**decision 56/458**).

UNAMET

On 7 September, the General Assembly decided to include in the draft agenda of its fifty-sixth (2001) session the item on UNAMET's financing (**decision 55/494**). On 24 December, the Assembly decided that the item would remain for consideration at its resumed fifty-sixth (2002) session (**decision 56/464**) and that the Fifth Committee should continue consideration of the item at that session (**decision 56/458**).

Iraq

The stalemate between the United Nations and Iraq concerning Iraq's refusal to allow the Organization to verify compliance with Iraq's weapons-related obligations continued throughout 2001. The stalemate was precipitated by the withdrawal in December 1998 [YUN 1998, p. 262] of the United Nations Special Commission (UNSCOM) and the International Atomic Energy Agency (IAEA)—both mandated by the Security Council's ceasefire resolution 687(1991) [YUN 1991, p. 172] to disarm Iraq of its weapons of mass destruction and to ensure that it did not reconstitute or reacquire them. UNSCOM's monitoring and verification responsibilities had been assumed in 2000 by the United Nations Monitoring, Verification and Inspection Commission (UNMOVIC), which was established by resolution 1284(1999) [YUN 1999, p. 230]. However, since Iraq refused to accept that resolution, UNMOVIC had not been able to carry out its work inside Iraqi territory. The Council received four quarterly reports on UNMOVIC activities and two biannual reports from IAEA. In January, IAEA inspectors were able to verify the presence of known material under safeguards during an inspection carried out in Iraq.

The Secretary-General transmitted three reports on the repatriation or return of all Kuwaiti and third-country nationals from Iraq, and on the return of all Kuwaiti property seized by Iraq during its 1990 invasion and occupation of Kuwait [YUN 1990, p. 189]. The Secretary-General's high-level Coordinator for missing Kuwaiti and third-country nationals, Yuli M. Vorontsov, briefed the Security Council regularly on his work.

The United Nations Iraq-Kuwait Observation Mission (UNIKOM) continued to carry out its functions of surveillance, control and investigation in the demilitarized zone between Iraq and Kuwait, and maintained liaison with authorities from both countries. The Council, on the Secretary-General's recommendation, decided to maintain UNIKOM and to review its functions in 2002.

In the context of the continuing sanctions against Iraq, the temporary arrangements for the humanitarian programme for the Iraqi people, based on an oil-for-food formula, was extended three times during the year—the first time for a month in order to consider new arrangements for the sale or supply of commodities and products to Iraq, the second time for 150 days and the last time for 180 days. Throughout the year, the Council focused on securing improvements to the sanctions regime and on modifications to the oil-for-food programme based on a goods review list. In November, the Council pledged to adopt the proposed goods review list and procedures for its application for implementation beginning in May 2002.

By **decisions 56/450** and **56/451** of 21 December, the General Assembly deferred consideration of, respectively, armed Israeli aggression against Iraqi nuclear installations and its grave consequences for the established international system on the peaceful uses of nuclear energy, the non-proliferation of nuclear weapons and international peace and security; and the consequences of Iraq's occupation of and aggression against Kuwait. It included both items in the provisional agenda of its fifty-seventh (2002) session.

UN Monitoring, Verification and Inspection Commission and IAEA activities

UNMOVIC

In 2001, UNMOVIC continued its attempts, in the absence of Iraqi cooperation and refusal to allow field operations, to monitor Iraq's compliance with its weapons-related obligations under resolution 687(1991) [YUN 1991, p. 172] and other relevant resolutions. UNMOVIC, which was a successor body to UNSCOM, prepared itself for full monitoring and verification operations in the field by recruiting and training new staff and examining information received from sources other than Iraq.

By letters dated 26 October [S/2001/1029] and 2 November [S/2001/1064], the Secretary-General proposed to the Security Council President that John S. Wolf (United States) and Li Junhua (China) be appointed to the UNMOVIC College of Commissioners as replacements for Robert Einhorn (United States) and Cong Guang (China), respectively. By letters dated 31 October [S/2001/1030] and 12 November [S/2001/1065], the Council President replied that the Council had taken note of the Secretary-General's proposals.

Reports of UNMOVIC (February, May, August, November). As called for by Security Council resolution 1284(1999) [YUN 1999, p. 230],

UNMOVIC submitted to the Council, through the Secretary-General, four quarterly reports on its activities. Throughout the year, the Executive Chairman continued his practice of providing monthly briefings to the Council President and kept the Secretary-General informed about UNMOVIC's preparatory activities. UNMOVIC staff training courses were held throughout the year.

The February report [S/2001/177], covering the period from 1 December 2000 to 28 February 2001, noted that Iraq's failure to accept resolution 1284(1999) meant that the Commission had been unable to commence inspections on the ground. The fourth meeting of UNMOVIC's College of Commissioners (Vienna, 21-22 February) discussed, among other things, unresolved disarmament issues in each of the three disciplines for which UNMOVIC was responsible (chemical weapons, biological weapons and proscribed missiles). As on previous occasions, observers from IAEA and the Organization for the Prohibition of Chemical Weapons also attended. The College received a briefing on progress made on revising and updating the lists of dual-use items and material to which the export/import monitoring mechanism, approved in Council resolution 1051 (1996) [YUN 1996, p. 218], applied. The College also had before it a draft of the UNMOVIC handbook, which provided guidance for the conduct of inspections in Iraq, and heard a briefing on the planned use of overhead imagery as a complement to on-site inspections.

The May report [S/2001/515], which covered the period from 1 March to 31 May, stated that UNMOVIC was continuing to prepare for work in Iraq, particularly by training staff, seeking to identify issues that would need special attention through monitoring and inspection, and consolidating the archives inherited from UNSCOM. The Commission's core staff had, by and large, been recruited. The completion of both the inventory of unresolved disarmament issues and the identification of the key remaining disarmament tasks would be possible only after the Commission's experts had commenced work in Iraq and had been able to assess what changes might have occurred during almost two and a half years of no on-site inspections or monitoring within the country. Nevertheless, the experts were able to make considerable progress through analysing and assessing the large volume of material taken over from UNSCOM. UNMOVIC experts had completed their review of the criteria for the classification of inspection facilities and sites throughout Iraq. They also continued to link IAEA and UNMOVIC databases, in particular with respect to information relevant to the operation of the joint unit established to implement the export/import

monitoring mechanism. The new system would also integrate information held by IAEA and UNMOVIC on sites and facilities subject to inspection in Iraq. UNMOVIC held two meetings with representatives of interested Member States on suggested revisions to the missile, chemical and biological lists of dual-use items and materials to which the export/import monitoring mechanism applied. The fifth meeting of the College of Commissioners (New York, 21-22 May) focused on the identification of unresolved disarmament issues. Although UNMOVIC had not been able to conduct work in Iraq, it had undertaken as much preparatory work as was possible without incurring major financial commitments and without employing a large number of staff; it was ready to take up the full tasks mandated to it by the Council.

The August report [S/2001/833], which covered the period from 1 June to 31 August, noted that UNMOVIC had completed the review and updating of the lists of dual-use items to which the export/import monitoring mechanism applied. The Executive Chairman had forwarded to the Security Council on 1 June [S/2001/560] the revised lists of chemical, biological and missile-related items subject to notification under resolution 1051(1996); the new lists entered into force on 13 July. In the absence of on-site inspection and monitoring, UNMOVIC was seeking other sources of information based on overhead imagery and had diversified its sources by obtaining imagery from a commercial provider. The College of Commissioners, at its sixth meeting (New York, 28-29 August), continued to discuss key remaining disarmament tasks and unresolved disarmament issues, and received a briefing on UNMOVIC's plans for the implementation of a reinforced system of ongoing monitoring and verification (OMV) in Iraq.

The November report [S/2001/1126], covering the period 1 September to 30 November, stated that the first phase of analytical work on a draft inventory of unresolved disarmament issues had been completed. The second phase, which would try to obtain a better overall picture of Iraq's weapons of mass destruction, the gaps in knowledge and what remained to be verified, had begun. UNMOVIC continued to analyse the imagery that it was receiving through a commercial satellite, principally for infrastructure changes at sites in Iraq previously subject to monitoring. The new images were compared with those already in the Commission's database. The data were also being used to create line diagrams of sites for inspection purposes. UNMOVIC also continued to carry out analysis of open-source information, such as newspapers, academic journals and other published material, as well as television and radio broadcasts. The UNMOVIC/IAEA joint unit continued to receive notifications from Member States of supplies to Iraq of dual-use items. Technologies that might be relevant to future inspection and monitoring work were being explored by UNMOVIC staff. A draft handbook, describing systematically the policies and technical procedures for inspectors, was largely complete. The seventh meeting of UNMOVIC's College of Commissioners (New York, 26-27 November) discussed, among other things, international efforts to prevent the proliferation of weapons of mass destruction by all States and non-State actors. Views were expressed that the terrorist attacks of 11 September in the United States had brought a new urgency to those efforts.

IAEA

Safeguards inspection

On 12 February [S/2001/129], the Secretary-General transmitted to the Council President a letter from the IAEA Director General concerning a safeguards inspection carried out by the Agency in Iraq in accordance with the safeguards agreement concluded between Iraq and IAEA, pursuant to the 1968 Treaty on the Non-Proliferation of Nuclear Weapons, adopted by the General Assembly in resolution 2373(XXII) [YUN 1968, p. 17]. Between 20 and 23 January, a four-person IAEA team carried out a physical inventory verification of the declared nuclear material remaining in Iraq under IAEA seal. The inspectors were able to verify the presence of the nuclear material subject to safeguards, which consisted of low enriched, natural and depleted uranium. Iraq provided the necessary co-operation for the inspection team to perform its activities effectively and efficiently. As was the case with the 2000 inventory verification [YUN 2000, p. 295], the inspection had the limited objective of verifying the presence of the nuclear material in question. It was not intended nor could it serve as a substitute for IAEA's activities under the relevant Council resolutions.

IAEA reports (April and October). In accordance with Security Council resolution 1051(1996) [YUN 1996, p. 218], IAEA submitted to the Council, through the Secretary-General, two consolidated six-monthly reports, on 6 April [S/2001/337] and on 5 October [S/2001/945], on the Agency's verification activities in Iraq. The Agency had not been in a position, since its withdrawal from Iraq on 16 December 1998 [YUN 1998, p. 267], to implement its mandate in Iraq. It was thus unable to provide any measure of assurance with regard to

Iraq's compliance with its obligations under relevant Council resolutions. In that context, IAEA had not received from Iraq the semi-annual declarations required by the Agency's OMV plan. Those declarations were the principal means for Iraq to provide information regarding the use and any changes in the use of certain facilities, installations and sites and regarding the inventory and location of certain materials, equipment and isotopes.

In the April report, IAEA noted that, pursuant to Council resolution 1284(1999) [YUN 1999, p. 230] and in consultation with UNMOVIC and Member States, the Agency had revised and updated the nuclear-related list of items and technology to which the export/import mechanism, approved by resolution 1051(1996), applied. That document also constituted annex 3 to the Agency's OMV plan approved by resolution 715(1991) [YUN 1991, p. 194], and listed those nuclear and nuclear-related items that were prohibited to Iraq or were subject to certain controls, including reporting by Iraq of their location and use. IAEA would forward the revision to the Council prior to 5 June, as requested by resolution 1330(2000) [YUN 2000, p. 310]. The Agency had continued to expand and refine the structure and content of its information system in the areas of computer support to inspections and analytical tools. Advances in commercially available satellite imagery had led to its integration in the Agency's Iraq-related information system. An enhanced analysis of the available original Iraqi documentation and results accumulated through the past inspection process had also continued. IAEA remained prepared to resume its verification activities in Iraq at short notice, with UNMOVIC's assistance and cooperation.

In October, IAEA noted that the revised and updated list of items and technology to which the export/import mechanism applied was submitted to the Council, through the Secretary-General, on 4 June [S/2001/561], and that the new list had been operative since 1 September [S/2001/818].

Iraq-Kuwait

POWs, Kuwaiti property and missing persons

Reports of Secretary-General (June, August, December). Pursuant to Council resolution 1284 (1999) [YUN 1999, p. 230], the Secretary-General submitted reports in June [S/2001/582], August [S/2001/796] and December [S/2001/1196] on compliance by Iraq with its obligations regarding the repatriation or return of all Kuwaiti and third-country nationals or their remains, and on the return of all Kuwaiti property, including archives, seized by Iraq.

In June, the Secretary-General said that Iraq continued to maintain that it had returned a large part of the Kuwaiti property found in Iraq and had expressed its readiness to return what it might find in the future. Kuwait maintained that the return of the national archives, military equipment and museum items remained the highest priority and that there had been no progress on those issues. The Secretary-General had discussed the issue of Kuwaiti property during a meeting in February with an Iraqi delegation [S/2001/715] and subsequently briefed the Security Council, as well as Kuwaiti high officials, on those discussions. The Iraqi delegation had promised to continue the search for Kuwaiti property.

The high-level Coordinator for compliance by Iraq with its obligations regarding the return of Kuwaiti nationals and property, Yuli M. Vorontsov (Russian Federation), continued to visit countries and international organizations to further intensify efforts aimed at the resolution of humanitarian and property issues. The Coordinator reported that no substantive progress had been made in the implementation of his mandate, owing to Iraq's unwillingness to cooperate with him. The Secretary-General observed that groundless Iraqi claims that the Coordinator was, among other things, not playing an impartial role and making statements that were hostile to Iraq (see p. 294) had to be rejected in the strongest possible terms. He added that the Coordinator's activities would not yield positive results until and unless a substantial change of attitude on the part of the Iraqi leadership occurred, and that the continuing absence of a credible explanation by Iraq with regard to the Kuwaiti archives, military material and museum items delayed the closure of that file.

In August, the Secretary-General described developments related to the repatriation of all Kuwaiti and third-country nationals or their remains in the period since December 2000. While briefing the Security Council on 20 April, the Coordinator stated that one year after his appointment to the post, he had been unable to report a breakthrough on the issue of the repatriation of all Kuwaiti and third-country nationals. The Council President, addressing the press, had said that the Council unanimously supported the Coordinator's work and hoped that there would be some progress on that strictly humanitarian issue.

During the reporting period, the Coordinator continued to visit countries and international organizations to further intensify efforts to resolve the issue of the repatriation of all Kuwaiti and third-country nationals or their remains. The outcome of the Tripartite Commission's meeting (Geneva, 19 July) again demonstrated that the International Committee of the Red Cross (ICRC) remained committed to resolving the issue of repatriation. The meeting also addressed the issue of the missing pilots Muhammad Salih Nazirah (Saudi Arabia) and Michael Speicher (United States) (see p. 294). The Tripartite Commission, established in 1991 under ICRC auspices, dealt with the question of persons still unaccounted for, and was made up of representatives of France, Iraq, Kuwait, Saudi Arabia, the United Kingdom and the United States. A Technical Subcommittee was established in 1994 to expedite the search for all persons for whom inquiry files had been opened. However, at the end of 1998, Iraq decided not to participate in the Commission's work, arguing that it no longer held captive Kuwaiti prisoners in its territory and, thus, the issue had become one of missing persons, not prisoners of war (POWs).

The Secretary-General observed that it was regrettable that Iraq was still unwilling to cooperate with the high-level Coordinator on the grounds that it rejected resolution 1284(1999). He added that Iraq should appreciate the fact that the international community was not selective and that all cases of missing persons, whether Kuwaiti, Saudi, Iraqi or others, would be addressed. (The nationals to be repatriated or returned included 570 Kuwaitis, 3 Lebanese, 1 Indian, 4 Iranians, 5 Egyptians, 4 Syrians, 1 Bahraini, 1 Omani and 14 Saudi Arabians. Iraq claimed 1,142 missing nationals.) As Iraq said it wished to seek a resolution to the issue of its own nationals, it was essential that it exercised an appropriate understanding of the position held by Kuwait and other countries concerned. Initiatives taken by the League of Arab States (LAS) and the Organization of the Islamic Conference (OIC) in support of the Coordinator's efforts were welcomed and highly appreciated.

In December, the Secretary-General reported on activities related to repatriation of all Kuwaiti and third-country nationals or their remains, and the return of Kuwaiti property. He had continued to raise the issue of repatriation or return of all Kuwaiti and third-country nationals with representatives of Member States and heads of international organizations, among others. In pursuance of his mandate, the high-level Coordinator maintained close contacts with LAS and OIC. On 15 August, the Coordinator addressed letters to Bahrain, Egypt, India, Iran, Lebanon, Oman, Saudi Arabia and the Syrian Arab Republic, in which he provided information on their nationals who were yet to be repatriated, or their remains returned.

Regarding the return of Kuwaiti property, the Coordinator, in June, had reaffirmed to the Security Council his readiness to travel to Baghdad in order to facilitate the return of archives and military equipment, as well as other items belonging to Kuwait. Members of the Council, in their interventions, had pointed out, among other things, that it was legitimate for Kuwait to demand the return of the national archives and called on Iraq to cooperate fully with the Coordinator. The Coordinator met with the Executive Secretary of the Compensation Commission, Rolf G. Knutsson, in October and discussed the problem of the return of Kuwaiti property, including its financial aspects.

In his observations, the Secretary-General said that it was most regrettable that during the past two years not a single item had been returned to Kuwait from Iraq, and that the most disturbing aspect in that regard remained Iraq's refusal to address the issue of Kuwait's national archives.

Communications. In identical letters of 5 February to the Secretary-General and the Council President [S/2001/117], Iraq said that it had cooperated with ICRC and Saudi authorities in finding the remains of Saudi pilot Muhammad Salih Nazirah, whose aircraft was shot down by Iraq in 1991. Iraq affirmed its readiness to continue to investigate the fate of missing persons with the Tripartite Commission and its Technical Subcommittee. It also called attention to the issue of the 1,142 missing Iraqis and to the fact that Kuwaiti and Saudi authorities had provided no information in that regard.

Responding in identical letters of 26 March [S/2001/274], Saudi Arabia said, among other things, that Iraq had not cooperated in the finding of the Saudi pilot and had not provided the positive information required to demonstrate its seriousness in devising solutions to the humanitarian predicament of missing persons. Referring to that letter on 7 April [S/2001/340], Iraq objected to the use of the term "prisoners" in referring to the issue of missing Kuwaitis and Saudis. Iraq reiterated that it had cooperated with ICRC and the Tripartite Commission on the humanitarian issue of missing persons, but questioned Mr. Vorontsov's role, which, it said, could only be political. Responding to that letter on 21 May [S/2001/517], Saudi Arabia questioned the compliance by Iraqi authorities with their obligation to hand over all of the remains of the Saudi pilot to ICRC and reaffirmed that, on humanitarian grounds, it backed, endorsed, supported and welcomed any stance, role or effort that was conducive to addressing the issue of the Saudi,

Kuwaiti and other prisoners, detainees and missing persons in Iraq.

On 1 May [S/2001/439], in identical letters to the Secretary-General and the Council President, Iraq said, among other things, that from the outset it had worked with ICRC, through the Tripartite Commission, in the search for missing Kuwaitis, but had stopped attending the Commission's meetings because of the military aggression committed by the United Kingdom and the United States against it in December 1998 [YUN 1998, p. 262]. Iraq added that the appointment of Mr. Vorontsov had been contrived by the United Kingdom and the United States in deference to Kuwait's desire to obstruct the work on the humanitarian issue of missing persons.

By a 23 May letter [S/2001/528], Iraq informed the Secretary-General that the Secretariat had never responded to its requests that a specific time should be designated for the return of itemized Kuwaiti property that had been found on the local Iraqi market. It called on the Secretary-General to designate a time and place for the handover of the property without reference to the mechanisms established by resolution 1284(1999), whose true objective was to impose a long series of conditions on the lifting of the embargo maintained against Iraq.

On 24 May [A/55/956-S/2001/526], Bahrain submitted to the Secretary-General the joint communiqué of the eleventh session of the Ministerial Council of the Gulf Cooperation Council (GCC) and the EU (Manama, Bahrain, 23 April). Both sides underlined their concern at the continuing uncertainty over the Kuwaiti and other POWs and persons unaccounted for and held by Iraq after the Gulf war.

In letters to the Secretary-General of 17 [S/2001/804] and 20 August [S/2001/809], Iraq confirmed its desire to cooperate with ICRC and with those States that held files of missing persons. It also called on the Secretary-General to intervene with the United Kingdom and the United States regarding their insistence on participating in the Tripartite Commission's work.

On 12 December [S/2001/1188], Kuwait informed the Secretary-General that Iraq had yet to respond to his appeals concerning Kuwaitis and third-country nationals being held in Iraq. Kuwait also stated that Iraq did not need any new mechanism to solve the issue of missing persons, as the appropriate mechanisms (the Tripartite Commission and its Technical Subcommittee, ICRC, the Secretary-General and the high-level Coordinator) already existed. Kuwait affirmed its willingness to permit ICRC to conduct a free and thorough search in its territory for the missing Iraqis whose presence was alleged by Baghdad, on the understanding that Kuwait would obtain in return full and precise information from Iraq on the fate of the Kuwaitis and third-country nationals detained in Iraqi territory.

In a later document [A/56/797-S/2002/125], Oman transmitted to the Secretary-General the final communiqué adopted by the GCC Supreme Council at its twenty-second session (Muscat, Oman, 30-31 December). The Council, among other things, urged Iraq to discharge all of its obligations under relevant resolutions, with a view to devising a definitive solution to the problem of Kuwaiti and third-country prisoners.

UN Iraq-Kuwait Observation Mission

The United Nations Iraq-Kuwait Observation Mission (UNIKOM), established by Security Council resolution 687(1991) [YUN 1991, p. 172], continued in 2001 to discharge its functions in accordance with its terms of reference, as expanded by resolution 806(1993) [YUN 1993, p. 406].

UNIKOM operations involved surveillance, control, investigation and liaison. Surveillance of the demilitarized zone (DMZ), an area about 200 to 240 kilometres long and extending 10 kilometres into Iraq and 5 kilometres into Kuwait, was based on ground and air patrols and observation points. Control operations included static checkpoints, random checks and maintenance of a mobile reserve force. For operational purposes, the DMZ was divided into the northern and southern sectors, with 10 and 7 patrol/observation bases, respectively. Investigation teams were stationed in those sectors and at UNIKOM headquarters. Continuous liaison was maintained with Iraqi and Kuwaiti authorities at all levels.

The military observers were responsible for patrol, observation, investigation and liaison activities. The infantry battalion, deployed at Camp Khor, Kuwait, at a company camp in Al-Abdali, at platoon camps in two DMZ sectors, and in the easternmost patrol/observation base on the DMZ's Iraqi side, conducted armed patrols within those areas and manned checkpoints at border-crossing sites, making random checks in cooperation with Iraqi and Kuwaiti liaison officers. It also provided security for UNIKOM personnel and installations.

UNIKOM maintained headquarters at Umm Qasr in Iraq, liaison offices in Baghdad and Kuwait City and a support centre at Camp Khor.

Communications. On 17 January [S/2001/53], 25 April [S/2001/412] and 21 August [S/2001/813], Kuwait said that senior Iraqi officials, including President Saddam Hussein, and the Iraqi satellite television channel had made threatening statements against Kuwait. By a 26 May letter to the Secretary-General [S/2001/533], Iraq re-

sponded to Kuwait's allegations. On 17 February [S/2001/146], Iraq informed the Secretary-General that British and United States aircraft had carried out attacks in the vicinity of Baghdad and its suburbs on 16 February, causing the death and injury of Iraqi civilians as well as the destruction of civilian property. Iraq said that UNIKOM had failed to fulfil its responsibilities, since one of the Mission's main functions was to monitor acts of military aggression carried out inside the DMZ and immediately to inform the Secretary-General thereof, taking action to prevent their recurrence.

By a 17 February statement [S/2001/149], Belarus expressed concern at the air strikes carried out by the United Kingdom and the United States against targets to the south-west of Baghdad. Such actions represented violations of international law, undermined the UN Charter and exacerbated the situation, both in the region and at the global level.

On 20 February [S/2001/152], Iraq informed the Secretary-General that the air strikes against its territory by American and British aircraft had been launched from Saudi and Kuwaiti territory, thus making Saudi Arabia and Kuwait partners in the aggression.

By a 21 February letter to the Iraqi Foreign Minister [S/2001/160], the Secretary-General said that since 1999 UNIKOM had recorded over 200 aerial violations. In the majority of cases, it had not been possible for the Mission to identify the aircraft involved or to determine their nationality. UNIKOM's inability to identify the States responsible for conducting such flights was in no way to be understood to constitute condonation of them. The Secretary-General noted that, in view of the fact that the United Kingdom and the United States had been conducting military air operations in the region, the United Nations had intervened with representatives of those States, urging them to respect the DMZ. He added that only the Security Council was competent to determine whether or not its resolutions were of such a nature and effect as to provide a lawful basis for the no-fly zones and for the actions that had been taken for their enforcement.

On 25 February [S/2001/169], Iraq transmitted a letter to the Secretary-General concerning the position that had to be taken under the UN Charter with regard to the British and United States aggression against Iraq on 16 February and with regard to the no-fly zones.

On 21 September [S/2001/899], Iraq drew the Secretary-General's attention to Kuwait's excessive exploitation of the Iraqi Rumailah oilfield, which was situated on the border and was an extension of a shared oilfield, in violation of international agreements and practice relating to the exploitation of frontier oilfields. Replying on 1 October [S/2001/925], Kuwait noted, among other things, that it alone retained the absolute sovereignty to exploit and develop its natural resources at any location in its territory and within its internationally recognized boundaries. On 10 December [S/2001/1208], Iraq said that any unilateral action by Kuwait to exploit and develop transboundary oilfields in a manner that damaged the corresponding fields in Iraqi territory was in violation of international conventions and customs.

On 21 October [S/2001/994], Iraq informed the Secretary-General of the increasing number of armed assaults carried out by Kuwaiti naval units on Iraqi fishing boats in Iraq's territorial waters.

By a 12 November letter to the Council President [S/2001/1070], Kuwait said that, on 11 November, Iraqi border forces had fired a number of projectiles in the direction of Kuwaiti territory. Replying on 10 December [S/2001/1176], Iraq refuted Kuwait's allegations.

Reports of Secretary-General (March and September). UNIKOM's activities were described in two reports of the Secretary-General, covering the periods 22 September 2000 to 27 March 2001 [S/2001/287] and 28 March to 24 September 2001 [S/2001/913].

The reports noted that the situation in the DMZ remained generally calm. However, there had been no UNIKOM helicopter flights over the Iraqi side of the DMZ since they were suspended in December 1998 [YUN 1998, p. 262], when Iraqi authorities informed UNIKOM that they could not guarantee the safety of such flights due to Iraq's conflict with the United Kingdom and the United States regarding the no-fly zone.

DMZ violations increased to 267 during the first period and decreased slightly to 255 during the second period. Most of the ground violations along the border involved Iraqi vehicles using the gravel road, which crossed in and out of Kuwaiti territory. During the reporting periods, UNIKOM received 43 official complaints, 5 from Kuwait and 38 from Iraq. Of the incidents reported by UNIKOM, several involved unexploded mines and other ordnance, which still posed a danger in the DMZ and injured a number of Iraqi civilians. A high level of activity was observed at the oil installations on the Kuwaiti side of the DMZ. Iraqi oil production in the same vicinity also expanded considerably during the first reporting period. UNIKOM continued to provide security and logistical support for ICRC's humanitarian activities.

The Secretary-General observed that UNIKOM received the cooperation of the Iraqi and Kuwaiti authorities in the performance of its tasks and recommended that it be maintained in view of its continued contribution to the maintenance of calm and stability in the DMZ.

SECURITY COUNCIL ACTION

The Security Council informed the Secretary-General on 5 April [S/2001/328] and on 4 October [S/2001/936] that, in the light of his reports, it concurred with his recommendation that UNIKOM be maintained. The Council would review the question again by 6 April 2002.

Composition

As at 20 September, UNIKOM had an overall strength of 1,319, comprising 192 military observers from 31 Member States; an infantry battalion of 775 from Bangladesh; 129 support personnel, including a 50-member engineering unit and a 30-member logistics unit from Argentina, a helicopter unit of 35 from Bangladesh and a medical unit of 14 from Germany; plus a civilian staff of 223, of whom 56 were recruited internationally.

On 13 November [S/2001/1082], the Secretary-General informed the Council of his intention to appoint General Miguel Angel Moreno (Argentina) as the new Force Commander of UNIKOM. Major General John Augustine Vize (Ireland), who had served as Force Commander since 1 December 1999, would relinquish his post on 30 November. On 16 November [S/2001/1083], the Council took note of the Secretary-General's intention.

Financing

On 14 June [meeting 103], the General Assembly considered the Secretary-General's reports on the financial performance of UNIKOM for the period 1 July 1999 to 30 June 2000 [A/55/810] and its proposed budget for 1 July 2001 to 30 June 2002 [A/55/811], together with the related report of ACABQ [A/55/874/Add.2]. On the recommendation of the Fifth Committee [A/55/971], the Assembly adopted **resolution 55/261** without vote [agenda item 130 (a)].

Financing of the United Nations Iraq-Kuwait Observation Mission

The General Assembly,

Having considered the reports of the Secretary-General on the financing of the United Nations Iraq-Kuwait Observation Mission and the related reports of the Advisory Committee on Administrative and Budgetary Questions,

Recalling Security Council resolutions 687(1991) of 3 April 1991 and 689(1991) of 9 April 1991, by which the Council decided to establish the United Nations Iraq-Kuwait Observation Mission and to review the question of its termination or continuation every six months,

Recalling also its resolution 45/260 of 3 May 1991 on the financing of the Observation Mission and its subsequent resolutions and decisions thereon, the latest of which was resolution 54/18 B of 15 June 2000,

Reaffirming the general principles underlying the financing of United Nations peacekeeping operations, as stated in General Assembly resolutions 1874(S-IV) of 27 June 1963, 3101(XXVIII) of 11 December 1973 and 55/235 of 23 December 2000,

Expressing its appreciation for the substantial voluntary contributions made to the Observation Mission by the Government of Kuwait and the contributions of other Governments,

Mindful of the fact that it is essential to provide the Observation Mission with the necessary financial resources to enable it to fulfil its responsibilities under the relevant resolutions of the Security Council,

1. *Takes note* of the status of contributions to the United Nations Iraq-Kuwait Observation Mission as at 30 April 2001, including the contributions outstanding in the amount of 13.3 million United States dollars, representing some 5 per cent of the total assessed contributions from the inception of the Mission to the period ending 30 April 2001, notes that some 22 per cent of the Member States have paid their assessed contributions in full, and urges all other Member States concerned, in particular those in arrears, to ensure the payment of their outstanding assessed contributions;

2. *Expresses its continued appreciation* of the decision of the Government of Kuwait to defray two thirds of the cost of the Observation Mission, effective 1 November 1993;

3. *Expresses its appreciation* to those Member States which have paid their assessed contributions in full;

4. *Expresses concern* about the financial situation with regard to peacekeeping activities, in particular as regards the reimbursements to troop contributors that bear additional burdens owing to overdue payments by Member States of their assessments;

5. *Urges* all other Member States to make every possible effort to ensure payment of their assessed contributions to the Observation Mission in full and on time;

6. *Expresses concern* at the delay experienced by the Secretary-General in deploying and providing adequate resources to some recent peacekeeping missions, in particular those in Africa;

7. *Emphasizes* that all future and existing peacekeeping missions shall be given equal and non-discriminatory treatment in respect of financial and administrative arrangements;

8. *Also emphasizes* that all peacekeeping missions shall be provided with adequate resources for the effective and efficient discharge of their respective mandates;

9. *Reiterates its request* to the Secretary-General to make the fullest possible use of facilities and equipment at the United Nations Logistics Base at Brindisi, Italy, in order to minimize the costs of procurement for the Observation Mission;

10. *Endorses* the conclusions and recommendations contained in the report of the Advisory Committee on Administrative and Budgetary Questions, and requests the Secretary-General to ensure their full implementation;

11. *Requests* the Secretary-General to take all necessary action to ensure that the Observation Mission is administered with a maximum of efficiency and economy;

12. *Also requests* the Secretary-General, in order to reduce the cost of employing General Service staff, to continue efforts to recruit local staff for the Observation Mission against General Service posts, commensurate with the requirements of the Mission;

13. *Decides* to appropriate to the Special Account for the United Nations Iraq-Kuwait Observation Mission the amount of 52,815,237 dollars gross (50,478,961 dollars net) for the maintenance of the Observation Mission for the period from 1 July 2001 to 30 June 2002, inclusive of the amount of 1,545,763 dollars gross (1,356,558 dollars net) for the support account for peacekeeping operations and the amount of 161,474 dollars gross (145,003 dollars net) for the United Nations Logistics Base, a two-thirds share of this amount, equivalent to 33,652,640 dollars, to be funded through voluntary contributions from the Government of Kuwait, subject to the review by the Security Council with regard to the question of termination or continuation of the Mission;

14. *Decides also*, taking into consideration the funding through voluntary contributions from the Government of Kuwait of the two-thirds share of the cost of the Observation Mission, equivalent to 33,652,640 dollars, to apportion among Member States the amount of 19,162,597 dollars gross (16,826,321 dollars net), representing one third of the cost of the maintenance of the Mission for the period from 1 July 2001 to 30 June 2002, the said amount to be apportioned at a monthly rate of 1,596,883 dollars gross (1,402,193 dollars net) in accordance with the levels set out in General Assembly resolution 55/235, as adjusted by the Assembly in its resolution 55/236 of 23 December 2000, and taking into account the scale of assessments for the years 2001 and 2002, as set out in its resolution 55/5 B of 23 December 2000, subject to the review by the Security Council with regard to the question of termination or continuation of the Mission;

15. *Decides further* that, in accordance with the provisions of its resolution 973(X) of 15 December 1955, there shall be set off against the apportionment among Member States, as provided for in paragraph 14 above, their respective share in the Tax Equalization Fund of the estimated staff assessment income of 2,336,276 dollars approved for the Observation Mission for the period from 1 July 2001 to 30 June 2002;

16. *Decides* that, taking into consideration the funding through voluntary contributions from the Government of Kuwait of the two-thirds share of the cost of the Observation Mission, for Member States that have fulfilled their financial obligations to the Mission, there shall be set off against the apportionment, as provided for in paragraph 14 above, their respective share of the unencumbered balance of 1,216,833 dollars gross (884,833 dollars net), representing one third of the unencumbered balance of 2,986,500 dollars gross (2,654,500 dollars net) in respect of the period ending 30 June 2000, in accordance with the composition of groups as set out in paragraphs 3 and 4 of General Assembly resolution 43/232 of 1 March 1989 and adjusted by the Assembly in subsequent relevant resolutions and decisions for the ad hoc apportionment of peacekeeping appropriations, the latest of which were its resolution 52/230 of 31 March 1998 and its decisions 54/456 to 54/458 of 23 December 1999 for the period 1998–2000, and taking into account the scale of assess-

ments for the year 2000, as set out in its resolutions 52/215 A of 22 December 1997 and 54/237 A of 23 December 1999;

17. *Decides also* that, for Member States that have not fulfilled their financial obligations to the Observation Mission, their share of the unencumbered balance of 1,216,833 dollars gross (884,833 dollars net) in respect of the period ending 30 June 2000 shall be set off against their outstanding obligations in accordance with the scheme set out in paragraph 16 above;

18. *Decides further* that two thirds of the net unencumbered balance of 2,654,500 dollars, equivalent to 1,769,667 dollars, shall be returned to the Government of Kuwait;

19. *Emphasizes* that no peacekeeping mission shall be financed by borrowing funds from other active peacekeeping missions;

20. *Encourages* the Secretary-General to continue to take additional measures to ensure the safety and security of all personnel under the auspices of the United Nations participating in the Observation Mission;

21. *Invites* voluntary contributions to the Observation Mission in cash and in the form of services and supplies acceptable to the Secretary-General, to be administered, as appropriate, in accordance with the procedure and practices established by the General Assembly;

22. *Decides* to include in the provisional agenda of its fifty-sixth session, under the item entitled "Financing of the activities arising from Security Council resolution 687(1991)", the sub-item entitled "United Nations Iraq-Kuwait Observation Mission".

On 24 December, the Assembly decided that the agenda item on the financing of the activities arising from Security Council resolution 687 (1991) would remain for consideration during its resumed fifty-sixth (2002) session (**decision 56/464**) and that the Fifth Committee should continue consideration of the item at that session (**decision 56/458**).

Arms and related sanctions

The Security Council's reviews of the sanctions provisions against Iraq for the purpose of determining whether to reduce or lift the prohibitions against it imposed under resolution 687 (1991) [YUN 1991, p. 172] remained suspended in 2001, in accordance with resolution 1194(1998) [YUN 1998, p. 257]. As it later reaffirmed in resolution 1205(1998) [ibid., p. 258], the Council would act in accordance with the relevant provisions of resolution 687(1991) on the duration of the prohibitions referred to in that resolution.

Communications. By a 3 April statement [S/2001/323] transmitted to the Secretary-General, the Russian Federation proposed that all States interested in a comprehensive settlement of the Iraqi issue should unite their efforts on the basis of a "package" approach entailing the suspension and then the lifting of economic sanctions in ex-

change for the re-establishment in Iraqi territory of an international disarmament monitoring system. Within a short period of time, Iraq and the Secretary-General could draw up a concrete formula for giving effect to that idea, which would include, among other things, the objectives and modalities of inspection activity. If within a clearly defined reasonable period the monitoring organ found no activity by Iraq associated with prohibited military programmes, the Council would take a decision on the lifting of sanctions against Iraq. On 5 November [S/2001/1047], Kuwait alerted the Council President to the fact that Iraq had for some years engaged in the large-scale smuggling of petroleum and petroleum products through the waterways and seaports of the Arabian Gulf.

Sanctions Committee activities

The Security Council Committee established by resolution 661(1990) [YUN 1990, p. 192] (Sanctions Committee for Iraq), in its annual report [S/2002/647], described its activities from 1 December 2000 to 31 December 2001. In addition to its implementation activities under Council resolutions 986(1995) [YUN 1995, p. 475] and 1175(1998) [YUN 1998, p. 274] relating to the humanitarian programme for the Iraqi people (see p. 300), the Committee processed 6,352 notifications and applications from States and international organizations to send humanitarian goods to Iraq under resolutions 661(1990) and 687(1991). Some 2,168 of those requests, with an estimated value of $8,041,384,653, were approved; 682, valued at $2,009,426,507, were placed on hold for further information or clarification; 3,313, valued at $27,550,806,741, were blocked; and 8, valued at $2,574,551, were withdrawn or annulled.

The Committee processed and responded to 447 communications concerning flights to Iraq. In September, it discussed the plan by Syrian Arab Airlines to start operating charter flights twice a week between Damascus and Baghdad. In the absence of consensus, the Committee continued to follow its practice of considering flight communications on a case-by-case basis, pending a solution with regard to the procedures for flights to Iraq.

As to financial matters, no agreement was reached by the Committee on the proposal by Iraq to donate 1 billion euros of oil revenue to the Palestinian people. The Committee decided to request further clarification on a proposal by UNESCO to open a bank account in Iraqi dinars to finance activities in Iraq. Concerning a request by Jordan that its share in a private joint venture held in Baghdad be released, the Committee decided that it needed further information on the matter. It also expressed the view that resolution 661(1990) prohibited a Jordanian company from providing insurance to a company in Baghdad. The UN Treasurer, in a briefing to the Committee, confirmed that an account in euros had been opened with the BNP-Paribas bank and cited administrative costs of $2.6 million for the change-over from dollars to euros in pricing Iraq's oil exports. The Treasurer also briefed the Committee on the diversification of banking services for the UN Iraq account and appealed to it to encourage States to transfer proceeds from the sale of illegal Iraqi oil cargoes into the escrow account established by resolution 778(1992) [YUN 1992, p. 320]. The Committee decided to request the Multinational Interception Force (MIF) to provide information regarding ships seized and diverted in the Gulf.

Concerning reported violations, the Committee sent letters to the United Arab Emirates and Qatar to ascertain whether a United Arab Emirates subsidiary of a Qatari company had donated an aeroplane to Iraq. Likewise, it had sent letters to the Libyan Arab Jamahiriya, the Syrian Arab Republic and the United Arab Emirates regarding flights to Iraq that had taken place without notification to the Committee. Two flights to Iraq, from Bulgaria and Syria, had allegedly taken place without being brought to the Committee's attention. There had also been reports of Iraqi aircraft landing in other countries; the Committee did not reach a consensus on how to proceed with the matter. During a November briefing to the Committee, the MIF Coordinator noted that oil smuggling in the Persian Gulf continued, as did the unauthorized use of passenger ferries by certain States to carry cargo to and from Iraq. The Committee considered a letter from the captain of the turbine tanker *Essex*, forwarded by the Executive Director of the Office of the Iraq Programme (OIP), which stated that a large quantity of Iraqi crude oil had been exported outside the framework of the UN humanitarian programme. The Committee agreed: that OIP should make recommendations on improving the monitoring of oil loading at the oil pumping stations, and address letters to all States whose companies had been involved in the incident (Bahamas, France, Netherlands, United Kingdom, United States, Venezuela); and that the oil overseers, who advised the Committee on oil-related matters, should forward to the Committee for review contracts of the oil companies implicated in the incident. France notified the Committee that it planned to withdraw Ibex Energy from the list of companies that could make approved national oil purchases until French authorities completed investigations of its activi-

ties, particularly its alleged involvement in the *Essex* case. In December, the Committee considered and approved an OIP proposal for additional operating procedures for crude oil monitoring at the Mina al-Bakr facility in Iraq.

The Committee considered a number of requests from Gulf States to open marine service lines to Iraq. Although most Committee members indicated that they would be positively inclined to approve ferry services, provided that effective controls to prevent the transport of prohibited commodities could be developed, no consensus was reached. While the Committee had agreed in principle to the 2001 aerial pesticide campaign of the Food and Agriculture Organization of the United Nations (FAO), Iraq refused to accept the Committee's condition that FAO observers be allowed aboard the flights. The Committee decided that it would continue to discuss the application of Article 50 of the UN Charter in relation to India's claim that it had lost $25 billion to $30 billion as a result of UN sanctions against Iraq.

With regard to new projects, the Committee approved an IAEA request for seven technical co-operation projects in Iraq; endorsed the International Civil Aviation Organization's intention to initiate contacts with Iraq as part of the Universal Safety Oversight Audit Programme; agreed to a UN Secretariat request concerning the transfer to Iraq of equipment and spare parts used for the implementation of projects by UNDP; and approved a request from the Organization for the Protection of the Marine Environment to clean up the polluted waters of the Arabian Gulf and to prevent oil leakage from sunken Iraqi ships.

Concerning a request for the opening of a border crossing to allow humanitarian goods to pass from Saudi Arabia to Iraq, the Committee decided to seek further clarification from Saudi authorities. The request was also forwarded to the Secretary-General for his consideration. No agreement was reached by the Committee on requests from Jordan and Tunisia to transfer Iraqi civilian aircraft held in their territories since the Gulf war.

During the year, the Committee issued four reports on the implementation of the arms and related sanctions against Iraq, in accordance with the guidelines approved by Council resolution 700(1991) [YUN 1991, p. 198] for facilitating full international implementation of resolution 687 (1991). The reports were transmitted to the Council on 23 January [S/2001/72], 23 April [S/2001/400], 20 July [S/2001/721] and 23 October [S/2001/1003]. The October report indicated that the United Kingdom, on 7 September, had brought to the Committee's attention some German press articles reporting the alleged Iraqi attempt to develop its weapons of mass destruction programmes. The other three reports indicated that no other State had brought to the Committee's attention any information relating to possible violations of the arms and related sanctions against Iraq committed by other States or foreign nationals. All of the reports noted that no State or international organization had consulted the Committee on whether certain items fell within the provisions of paragraph 24 of resolution 687 (1991), or on cases relating to dual-use or multiple-use items; and no international organization had reported any relevant information requested under the guidelines.

Oil-for-food programme

In accordance with Security Council resolutions 1330(2000) [YUN 2000, p. 310] and 1360(2001) (see p. 305), extending for a 180-day period and a 150-day period, respectively, the provisions of resolution 986(1995) [YUN 1995, p. 475], which authorized States to import Iraqi petroleum and petroleum products as a temporary measure to finance a humanitarian programme to alleviate the adverse consequences of the sanctions regime on the Iraqi people (also known as the oil-for-food programme) [YUN 1996, p. 225], the Secretary-General and the Sanctions Committee for Iraq separately submitted a report 90 days after entry into force of each resolution and again before the end of the respective periods. The 180-day period under the first resolution was extended from 6 December 2000 to 31 May 2001, and again by resolution 1352(2001) (see p. 303) from 1 June to 3 July (phase IX) in order to complete a review of the programme, more specifically to consider new arrangements for the sale or supply of commodities and products to Iraq and for the facilitation of civilian trade and economic cooperation with Iraq in civilian sectors. The 150-day period under resolution 1360(2001) was extended from 4 July to 30 November (phase X).

The reports described progress in implementing the arrangements specified by the resolutions, taking account of the provisions of the 1996 Memorandum of Understanding between the UN Secretariat and the Government of Iraq [YUN 1996, p. 226] and the procedures established by the Sanctions Committee [ibid., p. 228] for the implementation of resolution 986(1995). They also described the distribution of humanitarian relief, on behalf of Iraq, in the three northern governorates of Erbil, Dahuk and Sulaymaniyah under the United Nations Inter-Agency Humanitarian Programme, to complement government distribution in central and southern Iraq, thereby en-suring equitable distribution to all segments of the Iraqi population. However, throughout 2001, the effective implementation of the programme continued to face a number of difficulties and obstacles, partly due to the fact that Iraqi oil exports under the oil-for-food programme had suffered significant financial losses.

The provisions of resolution 986(1995) were extended for a further 180-day period beginning on 1 December by resolution 1382(2001) (see p. 308), inaugurating phase XI of the programme.

Pursuant to resolution 1352(2001), the Council met in June to consider new arrangements for the sale or supply of commodities and products to Iraq and for the facilitation of civilian trade and economic cooperation with Iraq in civilian sectors on the basis of a goods review list. No agreement was reached on a proposal submitted by the United Kingdom on a new set of arrangements. In November, by resolution 1382(2001), the Council pledged to adopt the proposed goods review list and procedures for its application, subject to any refinements to them agreed by the Council, for implementation beginning on 30 May 2002.

A team of experts visited Iraq in March to assist the Secretary-General in formulating modalities for the use of cash in meeting programme requirements.

Allocation for oil-production equipment

Team of experts report. In response to resolution 1330(2000) [YUN 2000, p. 310], the Secretary-General submitted to the Council on 6 June [S/2001/566] the report of the team of experts established to assist him in developing the necessary arrangements to allow funds up to 600 million euros deposited in the escrow account created by resolution 986(1995) [YUN 1995, p. 475] to be used for the cost of installation and maintenance, including training services, of equipment and spare parts for the Iraqi oil industry. The team visited Iraq from 18 March to 1 April 2001 and received full cooperation from Iraqi authorities.

As at 1 June 2001, the total value of oil spare parts and equipment delivered to Iraq was over $716 million. Additional supplies, valued at over $800 million under already approved applications, were in the production and delivery pipeline. The team of experts reiterated the views expressed in previous reports by expert missions that the oil industry in Iraq continued to face significant technical and infrastructural problems, which, unless addressed, would inevitably result in the reduction of crude oil production. The peak levels of production recorded in phases VI (1999) and VIII (2000) of the programme were only achieved at the expense of long-term damage to the oil-bearing structures utilized, and with increasing collateral damage to surface facilities operating beyond recommended and safe maintenance periods. It was therefore essential to take all necessary measures to address the rapid decline of oil-production capabilities of existing fields, as well as to ensure additional production capabilities in order to sustain production and export levels.

The team of experts formulated a set of arrangements and a budget for the utilization of the funds from the escrow account, which followed normal oil company methodology and addressed the cash component requirements of the Iraq oil industry over a period of 12 months. It also correlated the proposed projects with the oil spare parts and equipment already delivered. In a number of cases, however, proposed projects were based on the expectation of the Iraqi Ministry of Oil of the early delivery of spare parts and equipment not yet approved. According to the team of experts, the expectation of the Ministry of Oil for the renewal of the allocation of 600 million euros with each extension of the programme's mandate by the Council was commensurate with the size and complexity of the projects that were required to be installed, commissioned and maintained. It was proposed that the funds be initially transferred from the UN escrow account to the Rafidain Bank in Amman, Jordan. Subsequently, the funds would be transferred in euros, in monthly instalments, to the Ministry of Oil, for transfer to the operating companies in Iraqi dinars against the agreed cash flow requirements.

The Secretary-General welcomed the team's main conclusions and recommended that the Council approve the proposed arrangements for the utilization of the 600 million euros.

Phase IX

On 13 February [S/2001/134], the Secretary-General informed the Security Council that he had approved the distribution plan for the purchase of humanitarian supplies during phase IX. The plan, submitted by Iraq, proposed spending $5.556 billion on food, medicines, education, infrastructure and spare parts and equipment for the Iraqi oil industry. Approval was given on the understanding that the implementation would be governed by Council resolutions 986(1995) [YUN 1995, p. 475], 1281(1999) [YUN 1999, p. 250], 1284(1999) [ibid., p. 230], 1302(2000) [YUN 2000, p. 307] and 1330(2000) [ibid., p. 310] and the 1996 Memorandum of Understanding between the UN Secretariat and Iraq [YUN 1996, p. 226] and would be without prejudice to the Sanctions Committee procedures.

Reports of Secretary-General (March and May). Pursuant to resolution 1330(2000), the Secretary-General issued two progress reports, each covering a 90-day period under phase IX, which began on 6 December 2000. The reports, issued on 2 March [S/2001/186 & Corr.1] and 18 May [S/2001/505], provided information on all implementation aspects, including progress made in meeting the humanitarian needs of the Iraqi people, up to 31 January and 30 April, respectively.

The reports reviewed revenue generation, including the status of the oil industry, UN accounts pertaining to the Iraq programme, and processing and approval of applications for contracts; observation and monitoring activities; and the effectiveness, equitability and adequacy of programme implementation in central and southern Iraq and in the three northern governorates of Dahuk, Erbil and Sulaymaniyah, by focusing on food, health, agriculture, water and sanitation, education, electricity, telecommunications, housing and mine action.

In his March report, the Secretary-General said that he was concerned that the funds required for the implementation of the distribution plan for phase IX (see above) might not be available, due to the substantial drop in oil exports from Iraq under the programme since December 2000. Although the programme was never meant to meet all the needs of the Iraqi people, it had contributed to arresting the decline of, and in some parts improving, living conditions in Iraq. However, its impact had not been uniform, as the existing disparities between Baghdad and the rest of the country, as well as between rural and urban areas, persisted. The nutritional situation of the Iraqi population had improved since the start of the programme's implementation in December 1996 and the average caloric value of the food ration provided had risen. Nevertheless, purchasing power had steadily declined and, while food items were readily available in markets, they were unaffordable to the average Iraqi citizen. In the three northern governorates, there had been considerable improvement in the nutritional status of children under five years of age. In the central and southern governorates, however, chronic malnutrition rates remained higher overall.

The Secretary-General observed that the programme could not be a substitute for normal economic activity in Iraq. However, as long as sanctions were in place, there was no alternative to the programme in providing for the humanitarian needs of the Iraqi people. He recommended that Iraq clarify how the limited resources allocated in the distribution plan for phase IX would satisfy its own objectives to improve the nutritional status of children. He also urged Iraq to increase its daily average rate of oil exports to at least the levels in the previous phase, as it had lost about 2 billion euros in revenue due to the substantial drop in exports since December 2000. He regretted that the Sanctions Committee had not heeded the Council's urging, in resolution 1330(2000), to review applications in an expeditious manner and to decrease the level of applications on hold. The Secretary-General welcomed Iraq's confirmation of its willingness to cooperate with the programme and to allow UN personnel to observe throughout the country the equitable distribution of humanitarian supplies imported under the distribution plan, but expressed concern over the delays in the issuance of visas by Iraq to UN personnel. In connection with the killing of two FAO staff members and the injuring of eight others in June 2000 [YUN 2000, p. 309], the Secretary-General said that a criminal court in Baghdad was considering the case, though Iraq had yet to submit a report to him on its investigation into the deaths.

The Secretary-General said that, with the increased funding for the humanitarian component of the programme, the time had come to review the validity of applying procedures and practices, originally designed to cover food and medicine, to a vastly more expanded and more complex array of activities and equipment. It was essential not only to improve the process of the preparation and timely submission of the plan, but also to prepare a more targeted and result-oriented plan, with a clear statement of objectives to be achieved during a given phase, including benchmarks, which would improve the evaluation of the performance, achievements and effectiveness of the programme. In that context, a project approach, with a clear indication of targets and performance indicators, had been adopted for the implementation of the programme by UN agencies and programmes in the three northern governorates.

In his May report, the Secretary-General confirmed that, despite the increase in the daily average rate of oil exports under the programme to at least the levels of the previous phase, it was estimated that the total revenue of oil exports under the programme during phase IX would reach only 6.5 billion euros, or about $5.7 billion, which would provide only about $3.5 billion for the programme's implementation, after the deductions pursuant to relevant Council resolutions. An annex to the report gave the status of the UN Iraq Account established under resolution 986(1995), indicating that, by 30 April 2001, 3,253.8 million euros had been deposited into the account for phase IX, bringing total oil sales since the inception of the programme to $37,333.9 million and 4,833.4 million euros. The authorization for Iraq to export unlimited amounts of oil and to import a wider range of goods had transformed the programme's nature and range of activities from providing emergency humanitarian relief to encompassing many aspects of rehabilitation of essential civilian infrastructure. The Secretary-General recommended that the list of items already approved, relating to different sectors, be expanded to include all items, with the exception of those covered under resolution 1051(1996) [YUN 1996, p. 218]. Notwithstanding the range of opinions and discussions on a broader framework for the programme, the Secretary-General appealed to all parties concerned to preserve the distinct humanitarian identity of the programme.

A number of major difficulties continued to be encountered in the effective implementation of the programme, due to the absence of a viable arrangement for local procurement of goods and services and the provision of a cash component. An increasing range of equipment was being imported, with insufficient local resources available to undertake installation, training and maintenance. The Secretary-General appealed to Iraq to work with the United Nations in developing necessary and viable working arrangements for local procurement and a cash component, which would ultimately serve to stimulate local production. He informed the Council that he had instructed the Executive Director of the Iraq Programme, in consultation with the UN Humanitarian Coordinator for Iraq and the UN agencies and programmes concerned, to provide him with a list of essential medicines in short supply and measures required to resolve that problem. The total value of applications received during phase IX, as at 14 May, was $1.8 billion, including $1.2 billion for items for the food basket. Not a single application under the health, water and sanitation, education and oil sectors had been received. The Secretary-General appealed to Iraq to provide information to OIP and the UN Office of the Humanitarian Coordinator for Iraq on contracts signed, as such information would expedite the processing of the applications received. He also expressed concern over the visa situation and the negative impact that the interruption in essential activities was having on the humanitarian situation in the three northern governorates, and called on Iraq to issue the required visas to UN officials, experts and other personnel. He informed the Council that the criminal trial proceedings concerning the death of two FAO staff members in June 2000 was postponed, for the seventh time, to 28 May.

SECURITY COUNCIL ACTION

On 1 June [meeting 4324], the Security Council unanimously adopted **resolution 1352(2001)**. The draft [S/2001/545] was prepared in consultations among Council members.

The Security Council,

Recalling its previous relevant resolutions, including its resolutions 986(1995) of 14 April 1995, 1284(1999) of 17 December 1999 and 1330(2000) of 5 December 2000,

Convinced of the need, as a temporary measure, to provide for the civilian needs of the Iraqi people until the fulfilment by the Government of Iraq of the relevant resolutions, including notably resolutions 687(1991) of 3 April 1991 and 1284(1999), allows the Council to take further action with regard to the prohibitions referred to in resolution 661(1990) of 6 August 1990, in accordance with the provisions of those resolutions,

Recalling the Memorandum of Understanding between the United Nations and the Government of Iraq of 20 May 1996,

Determined to improve the humanitarian situation in Iraq,

Reaffirming the commitment of all Member States to the sovereignty and territorial integrity of Iraq,

Acting under Chapter VII of the Charter of the United Nations,

1. *Decides* to extend the provisions of resolution 1330(2000) until 3 July 2001;

2. *Expresses its intention* to consider new arrangements for the sale or supply of commodities and products to Iraq and for the facilitation of civilian trade and economic cooperation with Iraq in civilian sectors, based on the following principles:

(a) That such new arrangements will improve significantly the flow of commodities and products to Iraq, other than commodities and products referred to in paragraph 24 of resolution 687(1991), and subject to review by the Committee established by resolution 661(1990) of the proposed sale or supply to Iraq of commodities and products on a Goods Review List to be elaborated by the Council;

(b) That such new arrangements will improve the controls to prevent the sale or supply of items prohibited or unauthorized by the Council, in the categories referred to in paragraph 2 *(a)* above, and to prevent the flow of revenues to Iraq outside the escrow account established pursuant to paragraph 7 of resolution 986(1995) from the export of petroleum and petroleum products from Iraq, and also expresses its intention to adopt and implement such new arrangements, and provisions on various related issues under discussion in the Council, for a period of 190 days beginning at 0001 hours on 4 July 2001;

3. *Decides* to remain seized of the matter.

Communication. On 18 June [S/2001/603], Iraq transmitted to the Secretary-General a letter concerning the Security Council's consultations on the extension of the Memorandum of Understanding and review of the oil-for-food programme. According to Iraq, the Secretary-General had stated to the press on 4 June that the Council had not completed the review in the time required and that an automatic extension of the programme for one month had therefore been decided. Iraq said that the United Kingdom and the United States were endeavouring to terminate the Memorandum of Understanding and the humanitarian programme and to replace them with a so-called regime of smart sanctions that would impose international tutelage on Iraq for decades to come, would prevent it from using its resources and would ultimately lead to a further deterioration in the humanitarian situation in Iraq.

Security Council consideration. At the request of the Russian Federation [S/2001/597], the Security Council, on 26 and 28 June, discussed the situation between Iraq and Kuwait [meeting 4336]. With the Council's consent, the President invited the representative of LAS, at the request of Tunisia [S/2001/631], to participate in the discussion without the right to vote. The President also drew attention to Iraq's 18 June letter (see above).

Addressing the Council, the Russian Federation said that a draft resolution prepared by the United Kingdom, which proposed a goods review list for deliveries to Iraq, would preserve the sanctions regime with unacceptable consequences for the people and economy of Iraq. According to Russia, the United Kingdom proposal included goods from the so-called Wassenaar Arrangements, which brought together a limited group of countries on a voluntary basis and which were already being applied in practice in respect of Iraq. Giving those Arrangements a sanctions status under Chapter VII of the UN Charter would have serious legal and political consequences. The proposal also included a list of goods defined in such a way that it would be possible, through vague procedures for considering contracts, to block essential projects for the recovery of the energy, oil, industrial and other areas of Iraq's economy. In addition, the introduction of new sanctions, as proposed by the United Kingdom, could seriously damage the trade and economic interests of many countries. Consequently, Russia had introduced a specific proposal for suspending and then lifting sanctions (see p. 298) that was tied to the deployment in Iraq of the OMV system on the basis of implementation of existing Council resolutions.

The United Kingdom said its draft resolution contained a series of proposals to allow Iraq to import the full range of civilian goods without restriction. The Council, in resolution 1352 (2001) (see above), had agreed to spend a month examining and refining those proposals and, at the end of that month, to agree to a new set of arrangements. The aim was not to replace resolution 1284(1999) [YUN 1999, p. 230], but to set in place measures to liberalize the flow of goods to Iraq and, at the same time, to examine ways to make sure that military-related items were not exported to Iraq. The new proposals contained in the draft text would make a significant difference to the flow of goods to Iraq, as all types of exports would be allowed, except for a very limited range of items that had to be reviewed by the Sanctions Committee on the basis of criteria related to their potential military use. Even for those items, there would be no presumption of denial. There was no intention in the draft resolution to harm the economic interests of neighbouring States or others doing legitimate business with Iraq. On the contrary, the United Kingdom expected to see an expansion of civilian trade, which would benefit all. However, Iraq continued to export oil outside the UN system to build up illegal revenue with which it could purchase weapons and other proscribed items. The traffic of such items to Iraq had to be controlled if the Council resolutions were to have their intended effect. The draft resolution would ask the Secretary-General to consult and cooperate with the neighbouring States to address those problems and there would also be obligations on supplier countries. Other elements in the draft would move the situation forward: Iraq would be allowed to pay its UN dues from the escrow account, aircraft frozen and held in other States would be allowed to return to Iraq, and steps would be taken to address the problem of the illegal oil surcharge levied by Iraq on purchasers of Iraqi oil.

Kuwait said that, despite the strict humanitarian nature of the oil-for-food programme, Iraq had not worked to ensure the success of the programme or to ensure benefits from its modalities. Iraq's implementation of all relevant Council resolutions was the primary guarantee of the security and stability of the region. If Iraq had implemented its commitments under resolution 1284(1999), in all probability the sanctions would have been suspended, if not lifted, as had happened to other States subjected to a sanctions regime.

At the resumed meeting, on 28 June, Iraq said it had implemented all the obligations enshrined in the relevant Council resolutions. It had also recognized Kuwait's sovereignty and territorial integrity, its independence and its borders as delineated by the United Nations. While the Council continued to call on Iraq to comply with its resolutions, it had shown no reaction to the no-fly zones imposed on Iraq by the United Kingdom and the United States without any Council resolution authorizing those operations. In addi-

tion, the humanitarian objectives of the oil-for-food programme had not been achieved because of the complexity of the measures adopted by the Council for the implementation of the Memorandum of Understanding and interference by the United Kingdom and the United States in its implementation; unfairness in the distribution of revenues from the sale of Iraqi oil; and the persistence of the United Kingdom and the United States in putting contracts on hold on imaginary pretexts. With regard to the draft resolution proposed by the United Kingdom, Iraq said, among other things, that it would lead to an intervention in the pricing of Iraqi crude oil, which would entail the destruction of the relationship between supplier and buyer. The end result would be to use Iraqi oil as leverage, because it would be under tight control, and to transform the oil market and maintain it at all times as a buyer's market.

Sanctions Committee report (September). The Sanctions Committee report for phase IX, which was extended by one month to 3 July by resolution 1352(2001), was transmitted to the Security Council on 4 September [S/2001/842]. Issues considered by the Committee included the sale of petroleum and petroleum products; humanitarian supplies to Iraq; and matters relating to oil spare parts and equipment for Iraq. The Committee also held informal meetings on sectoral activities on a monthly basis, with presentations by UN agencies and programmes concerned, as well as discussions on holds in each sector. The oil overseers continued to advise the Committee on oil pricing mechanisms, oil contract approval and amendments, management of revenue objectives and other pertinent questions related to export and monitoring.

During the initial period of phase IX, some 100 million barrels of crude oil export from Iraq, valued at some $2.5 billion, were lost as a result of erratic exports and a decline in market prices. A further $1.3 billion was lost during the latter part of phase IX due to Iraq's decision to suspend oil exports for about a month after the adoption of resolution 1352(2001). Applications received as at 30 June for the export of humanitarian supplies to Iraq (under phase VIII) totalled 2,650. Of the 1,565 circulated to the Committee, 1,257 were approved for payment from the UN Iraq Account, totalling some $3.2 billion. Pursuant to resolution 1330(2000), the Committee also approved a number of expanded lists of humanitarian items. The work of goods-arrival confirmation by the UN independent inspection agents continued according to the established procedures at four entry points to Iraq. As in previous phases, the Iraqi authorities had accorded the agents full co-operation in their work.

Communications. A number of communications on various subjects were received from Iraq during phase IX. In identical letters of 22 January to the Secretary-General and the Security Council President [S/2001/68], Iraq, in the light of Council resolution 1314(2000) on children and armed conflict [YUN 2000, p. 723], transmitted a study on the impact of the embargo on Iraqi children.

In a 25 February statement [S/2001/170], Iraq said that the United Kingdom and the United States were attempting to rewrite resolution 687(1991) in order to erase paragraph 14, which referred to the goal of establishing in the Middle East a zone free from weapons of mass destruction, and paragraph 22, which provided for the lifting of the economic sanctions imposed on Iraq.

On 3 April [S/2001/324], Iraq informed the Secretary-General that OIP had abused its power to request entry visas, had caused a great waste of Iraqi funds and had ignored the provisions of the Memorandum of Understanding requiring consultation with the Iraqi side with respect to the Programme's operations. Iraq had cooperated with the UN Office of the Humanitarian Coordinator in granting 991 entry visas in the year 2000 to UN personnel, despite a sense that the visa requests were excessive.

In a 6 May letter to the Secretary-General [S/2001/451], Iraq said that the Council, in resolution 1330(2000), allowed the sum of $15 million drawn from the sub-account of the Iraq Account designated for operational and administrative expenses to be used for the payment of the arrears in Iraq's contributions to the UN budget. That provision had not been applied, despite the fact that there was a sum of some half billion dollars lying dormant in the account.

On 2 July [S/2001/659], Iraq transmitted to the Secretary-General a number of tables containing statistical data for the health sector.

SECURITY COUNCIL ACTION

On 3 July [meeting 4344], the Security Council unanimously adopted **resolution 1360(2001)**. The draft [S/2001/652] was prepared in consultations among Council members.

The Security Council,

Recalling its previous relevant resolutions, including its resolution 986(1995) of 14 April 1995, 1284(1999) of 17 December 1999, 1330(2000) of 5 December 2000 and 1352(2001) of 1 June 2001, as they relate to the improvement of the humanitarian programme for Iraq,

Convinced of the need as a temporary measure to continue to provide for the humanitarian needs of the Iraqi people until the fulfilment by the Government of Iraq of the relevant resolutions, including notably resolution 687(1991) of 3 April 1991, allows the Council to take further action with regard to the prohibitions referred to in resolution 661(1990) of 6 August 1990, in accordance with the provisions of those resolutions,

Convinced also of the need for equitable distribution of humanitarian supplies to all segments of the Iraqi population throughout the country,

Determined to improve the humanitarian situation in Iraq,

Reaffirming the commitment of all Member States to the sovereignty and territorial integrity of Iraq,

Acting under Chapter VII of the Charter of the United Nations,

1. *Decides* that the provisions of resolution 986(1995), except those contained in paragraphs 4, 11 and 12 and subject to paragraph 15 of resolution 1284 (1999), shall remain in force for a new period of 150 days beginning at 0001 hours eastern daylight time on 4 July 2001;

2. *Also decides* that from the sum produced from the import by States of petroleum and petroleum products originating in Iraq, including financial and other essential transactions related thereto, in the 150-day period referred to in paragraph 1 above, the amounts recommended by the Secretary-General in his report of 1 February 1998 for the food/nutrition and health sectors should continue to be allocated on a priority basis in the context of the activities of the Secretariat, of which 13 per cent of the sum produced in the period referred to above shall be used for the purposes referred to in paragraph 8 *(b)* of resolution 986(1995);

3. *Requests* the Secretary-General to continue to take the actions necessary to ensure the effective and efficient implementation of the present resolution, and to continue to enhance as necessary the United Nations observation process in Iraq in such a way as to provide the required assurance to the Council that the goods produced in accordance with the present resolution are distributed equitably and that all supplies authorized for procurement, including dual-usage items and spare parts, are utilized for the purpose for which they have been authorized, including in the housing sector and related infrastructure development;

4. *Decides* to conduct a thorough review of all aspects of the implementation of the present resolution 90 days after the entry into force of paragraph 1 above and again prior to the end of the 150-day period, and expresses its intention, prior to the end of the 150-day period, to consider favourably renewal of the provisions of this resolution as appropriate, provided that the reports referred to in paragraphs 5 and 6 below indicate that those provisions are being satisfactorily implemented;

5. *Requests* the Secretary-General to provide a comprehensive report to the Council 90 days after the date of entry into force of this resolution on its implementation and again at least one week prior to the end of the 150-day period, on the basis of observations of United Nations personnel in Iraq, and of consultations with the Government of Iraq, on whether Iraq has ensured the equitable distribution of medicine, health supplies, foodstuffs, and materials and supplies for essential civilian needs, financed in accordance with paragraph 8 *(a)* of resolution 986(1995), including in his

reports any observations which he may have on the adequacy of the revenues to meet Iraq's humanitarian needs;

6. *Requests* the Committee established by resolution 661(1990), in close consultation with the Secretary-General, to report to the Council 90 days after the entry into force of paragraph 1 above and prior to the end of the 150-day period on the implementation of the arrangements in paragraphs 1, 2, 6, 8, 9 and 10 of resolution 986(1995);

7. *Decides* that from the funds produced pursuant to this resolution in the escrow account established by paragraph 7 of resolution 986(1995), up to a total of 600 million United States dollars may be used to meet any reasonable expenses, other than expenses payable in Iraq, which follow directly from the contracts approved in accordance with paragraph 2 of resolution 1175(1998) of 19 June 1998 and paragraph 18 of resolution 1284(1999), and expresses its intention to consider favourably the renewal of this measure;

8. *Requests* the Secretary-General to take the necessary steps to transfer the excess funds drawn from the account created pursuant to paragraph 8 *(d)* of resolution 986(1995) for the purposes set out in paragraph 8 *(a)* of resolution 986(1995) in order to increase the funds available for humanitarian purchases, including as appropriate the purposes referred to in paragraph 24 of resolution 1284(1999);

9. *Decides* that the effective deduction rate of the funds deposited in the escrow account established by resolution 986(1995) to be transferred to the Compensation Fund in the 150-day period shall be 25 per cent, further decides that the additional funds resulting from this decision will be deposited into the account established under paragraph 8 *(a)* of resolution 986 (1995) to be used for strictly humanitarian projects to address the needs of the most vulnerable groups in Iraq as referred to in paragraph 126 of the report of the Secretary-General of 29 November 2000, requests the Secretary-General to report on the use of these funds in his reports referred to in paragraph 5 above, and expresses its intention to establish a mechanism to review, before the end of the 150-day period, the effective deduction rate of the funds deposited in the escrow account to be transferred to the Compensation Fund in future phases, taking into account the key elements of the humanitarian needs of the Iraqi people;

10. *Urges* all States, and in particular the Government of Iraq, to provide their full cooperation in the effective implementation of the present resolution;

11. *Calls upon* the Government of Iraq to take the remaining steps necessary to implement paragraph 27 of resolution 1284(1999), and further requests the Secretary-General to include in his reports under paragraph 5 above a review of the progress made by the Government of Iraq in the implementation of these measures;

12. *Stresses* the need to continue to ensure respect for the security and safety of all persons directly involved in the implementation of the present resolution in Iraq;

13. *Appeals* to all States to continue to cooperate in the timely submission of applications and expeditious issue of export licences, facilitating the transit of humanitarian supplies authorized by the Committee established by resolution 661(1990), and to take all other appropriate measures within their competence in order to ensure that urgently needed humanitarian supplies reach the Iraqi people as rapidly as possible;

14. *Decides* to remain seized of the matter.

Speaking after the vote, the United States said that it had worked hard to adopt a different sort of draft resolution from the one that the Council finally adopted. The goods review list, which was central to a new approach in the humanitarian programme, was supported by four of the five permanent members, and it merited the support of all Council members, including Russia. Although the Council had not reached agreement on the new set of arrangements proposed by the United Kingdom, that draft remained under active consideration. The United States agreed to the rollover of the oil-for-food programme for a further 150 days while continuing to work towards the adoption of the new list as soon as possible.

Tunisia said that, in supporting the adopted resolution, it stressed the importance of using the new rollover period in the humanitarian programme to intensify recent discussions within the Council, with a view to finding a comprehensive solution to the Iraqi problem in all its aspects and dimensions.

Communication from Secretary-General. The Secretary-General transmitted to the Council a 5 July exchange of letters [S/2001/682] between the UN Secretariat and Iraq extending, in the light of resolution 1360(2001), the provisions of the 1996 Memorandum of Understanding between them on the implementation of resolution 986(1995) for a new 150-day period, effective 4 July.

Phase X

Pursuant to paragraph 1 of Council resolution 1360(2001), the new 150-day extension (phase X) of the humanitarian programme established by resolution 986(1995) began on 4 July. The corresponding distribution plan was approved by the Secretary-General on 1 August [S/2001/758], on the understanding that its implementation would be governed by resolutions 986(1995), 1281(1999), 1284(1999), 1302(2000), 1330(2000) and 1360(2001) and the 1996 Memorandum of Understanding between the UN Secretariat and Iraq, and without prejudice to Sanctions Committee procedures. The accompanying list of supplies and goods was made available to that Committee, which concluded that, based on the information provided in the annexes, no prohibited items could be identified.

Communication. By a 17 July letter to the Council President [S/2001/703], Malaysia said that, like other countries, it had suffered enormous economic losses as a result of the implementation of the Council's sanctions against Iraq and that it was seeking to address those problems in accordance with the provisions of Article 50 of the UN Charter.

Reports of Secretary-General (September and November). Pursuant to resolution 1360(2001), the Secretary-General submitted two progress reports on phase X. The reports, issued on 28 September [S/2001/919] and 19 November [S/2001/1089], provided information on all implementation aspects up to 31 August and 31 October, respectively.

In his September report, the Secretary-General observed that, with the increased funding level and the growing magnitude and scope of the programme, which involved not only, as initially intended, the provision of food, health and medical supplies, but also the rehabilitation of infrastructure, including the oil sector, considerable difficulties were being faced in its effective implementation, especially in the three northern governorates. The difficulties had been compounded by the continuing impasse within the Sanctions Committee on a number of crucial matters, as well as the excessive number of holds placed on applications, the total value of which was $4.05 billion as at 15 September. Programme implementation had also suffered considerably because of the substantial reduction in revenues received from oil exports when the volume of oil exports under the programme had been reduced or totally suspended by Iraq, despite the lifting of the ceiling on oil revenues by the Council. The Secretary-General reiterated that the responsibility for the sectoral allocations in the distribution plans remained with the Iraqi Government, which was also responsible for the selection of its suppliers and contracting. The UN Secretariat was involved only after applications were submitted to OIP by the suppliers through their respective permanent and/or observer missions to the United Nations. The Secretary-General said that despite all the difficulties encountered and the criticisms levelled by various quarters against the programme, it had made a considerable difference to the average Iraqi citizen.

In his November report, the Secretary-General noted that the substantial shortfall in the funds available for programme implementation, particularly during phase X, continued to be a major concern. Although the distribution plan for that phase was budgeted at $5.5 billion, only about $2.2 billion was available for funding supplies and equipment, due mainly to the sharp decline in oil market prices during the preceding two months and the lower rate of export of Iraqi oil under the programme. Furthermore, because of the substantial drop in revenues received during the previous phase, over $1.6 billion worth of approved applications had been transferred to phase X for funding purposes. Accordingly, it was recommended that Iraq further review the relative sectoral allocations in the distribution plan for phase X and submit revised sectoral allocations in order to ensure the funding of priority sectors. The programme's implementation continued to experience difficulties, particularly in the electricity and demining sectors in the three northern governorates. The Secretary-General appealed to all parties to refrain from politicizing the implementation of the programme and instead to concentrate their efforts on maximizing the full benefits of the programme to the Iraqi people. An annex to the report noted that, as at 31 October, 3.78 billion euros had been deposited in the account for phase X, bringing total oil sale revenues since the inception of the programme to $37.33 billion and 12.03 billion euros.

Sanctions Committee report. The Sanctions Committee report on its activities during phase X, from 4 July to 30 November, was transmitted to the Council on 31 December [S/2001/1341]. The Committee reviewed the sale of petroleum and petroleum products; humanitarian supplies to Iraq; and matters relating to oil spare parts and equipment for Iraq. The oil overseers continued to advise the Committee on oil pricing mechanisms, oil contract approval and amendments, management of revenue objectives and other pertinent questions related to export and monitoring. The overseers had worked with the independent inspection agents (Saybolt Nederland BV) to ensure the effective monitoring of the relevant oil installations and the liftings. In that regard, they continued to receive the full cooperation of the Iraqi authorities.

Applications received under phase IX as at 30 November for the export of humanitarian supplies to Iraq totalled 1,967. Of the 855 circulated to the Committee for action, 601 were found eligible for payment from the UN Iraq Account, in the amount of approximately $1.64 billion. From the beginning of phase X until 30 November, the Committee approved 305 applications for the export of humanitarian supplies to Iraq, totalling approximately $1.28 billion. During the reporting period, 379 applications were released from hold with a total value of $1.28 billion. As at 30 November, a total of 1,113 applications were still on hold with a total value of $3.79 billion. The Committee approved, on 15 November, a list of oil spare parts and equipment submitted by OIP pursuant to resolution 1284(1999). From the beginning of the process, the total allocation for oil spare parts and equipment amounted to $3.6 billion.

Among other activities, the Committee, on 17 October, sent a letter to OIP's Executive Director conveying the Committee's agreement, in principle, with the approach and direction taken by the Secretary-General in his report to the Council on the issue of the cash component for the oil sector (see p. 300). OIP provided the Committee with a brief update on the situation of holds on contracts. On 6 November, the Committee considered a letter from the captain of the turbine tanker *Essex*, which stated that a large quantity of crude oil had been exported outside the United Nations humanitarian programme (see p. 299). The Multinational Interception Force (MIF) Coordinator updated the Committee on MIF activities in the Persian Gulf. While noting a substantial decrease in Iraqi oil smuggling through Iranian territorial waters, he said oil smuggling activities continued to destinations in India, the United Arab Emirates, Yemen and the Horn of Africa, as well as the unauthorized use of passenger ferries by certain States to carry cargo to and from Iraq.

Communication. On 27 November [S/2001/1120], the United States submitted to the Council President the dual-use goods and technologies list.

Phase XI

On 29 November [meeting 4431], the Security Council unanimously adopted **resolution 1382 (2001)**. The draft [S/2001/1123] was prepared in consultations among Council members.

The Security Council,

Recalling its relevant resolutions, including resolutions 986(1995) of 14 April 1995, 1284(1999) of 17 December 1999, 1352(2001) of 1 June 2001 and 1360(2001) of 3 July 2001, as they relate to the improvement of the humanitarian programme for Iraq,

Convinced of the need as a temporary measure to continue to provide for the civilian needs of the Iraqi people until the fulfilment by the Government of Iraq of the relevant resolutions, including notably resolutions 687(1991) of 3 April 1991 and 1284(1999), allows the Council to take further action with regard to the prohibitions referred to in resolution 661(1990) of 6 August 1990 in accordance with the provisions of those resolutions,

Determined to improve the humanitarian situation in Iraq,

Reaffirming the commitment of all Member States to the sovereignty and territorial integrity of Iraq,

Acting under Chapter VII of the Charter of the United Nations,

1. *Decides* that the provisions of Security Council resolution 986(1995), except those contained in paragraphs 4, 11 and 12 and subject to paragraph 15 of resolution 1284(1999), and the provisions of paragraphs 2, 3 and 5 to 13 of resolution 1360(2001) shall remain in force for a new period of 180 days beginning at 0001 hours eastern standard time on 1 December 2001;

2. *Notes* the proposed Goods Review List as contained in annex 1 to the present resolution, and the procedures for its application, as contained in annex 2 to the present resolution, and decides that it will adopt the List and the procedures, subject to any refinements to them agreed by the Council in the light of further consultations, for implementation beginning on 30 May 2002;

3. *Reaffirms* the obligation of all States, pursuant to resolution 661(1990) and subsequent relevant resolutions, to prevent the sale or supply to Iraq of any commodities or products, including weapons or any other military equipment, and to prevent the making available to Iraq of any funds or any other financial or economic resources, except as authorized by existing resolutions;

4. *Stresses* the obligation of Iraq to cooperate with the implementation of the present resolution and other applicable resolutions, including by respecting the security and safety of all persons directly involved in their implementation;

5. *Appeals* to all States to continue to cooperate in the timely submission of technically complete applications and the expeditious issuing of export licences, and to take all other appropriate measures within their competence in order to ensure that urgently needed humanitarian supplies reach the Iraqi population as rapidly as possible;

6. *Reaffirms* its commitment to a comprehensive settlement on the basis of the relevant resolutions of the Council, including any clarification necessary for the implementation of resolution 1284(1999);

7. *Decides* that, for the purposes of the present resolution, references in resolution 1360(2001) to the 150-day period established by that resolution shall be interpreted to refer to the 180-day period established pursuant to paragraph 1 above;

8. *Decides* to remain seized of the matter.

ANNEX 1
Proposed Goods Review List

(Note: Arms and munitions are prohibited under Security Council resolution 687(1991), paragraph 24, and thus are not included on the review list.)

A. Items subject to the provisions of Security Council resolution 1051(1996).

B. The List contained in the annex to document S/2001/1120, (to the extent, if any, that the items on these lists are not covered by Council resolution 687(1991), paragraph 24). The List includes the following general categories and includes clarifying notes and statements of understanding: (1) advanced materials; (2) materials processing; (3) electronics; (4) computers; (5) telecommunications and information security; (6) sensors and lasers; (7) navigation and avionics; (8) marine; and (9) propulsion.

C. The following individual items, as further described in the annex:

Command, Control, Communication and Simulation

1. Specific advanced telecommunications equipment.

2. Information security equipment.

Sensors, Electronic Warfare, and Night Vision

3. Specialized electronic instrumentation and test equipment.

4. Image intensifier night vision systems, tubes, and components.

Aircraft and Related Items

5. Specialized radar equipment.

6. Non-civil-certified aircraft; all aero gas turbine engines; unmanned aerial vehicles; and parts and components.

7. Non-x-ray explosive detection equipment.

Naval-related Items

8. Air independent propulsion engines and fuel cells specially designed for underwater vehicles, and specially designed components therefor.

9. Marine acoustic equipment.

Explosives

10. Charges and devices specially designed for civil projects, and containing small quantities of energetic materials.

Missile-related Items

11. Specialized vibration test equipment.

Conventional Weapons Manufacturing

12. Specialized semiconductor manufacturing equipment.

Heavy Military Transport

13. Low-bed trailers/loaders with a carrying capacity greater than 30 metric tonnes and width equal to or greater than 3 metres.

Biological Weapons Equipment

14. Certain Biological Equipment.

**Annex to Proposed Goods Review List
Technical Parameters for Individual Items**

1. Specific advanced telecommunication equipment

a. Any type of telecommunications equipment, specially designed to operate outside the temperature range from 218 K (-55° C) to 397 K (124° C);

b. Phased array antennas, containing active elements and distributed components, and designed to permit electronic control of beam shaping and pointing, except for landing systems with instruments meeting International Civil Aviation Organization standards (microwave landing systems);

c. Radio relay communications equipment designed for use at frequencies of 7.9 through 10.55 GHz or exceeding 40 GHz and assemblies and components therefor;

d. Optical fiber cables of more than 5 metres in length, and preforms or drawn fibers of glass or other materials optimized for manufacture and use as optical telecommunications transmission medium. Optical terminals and optical amplifiers;

e. Software specially designed for the development or production of the components or equipment in a to d above;

f. Technology for the design, development or production of the components, software, or equipment in a to d above.

2. Information security equipment

Information security equipment having any of the following characteristics:

a. A symmetric encryption algorithm;

b. An asymmetric encryption algorithm;

c. A discrete-log encryption algorithm;

d. Analog encryption or scrambling;

e. TCSEC B1, B2, B3, or A1 or equivalent Multilevel Secure computer systems;

f. Software specially designed for the development or production of a to d above;

g. Technology for the development design, or production of a to d above.

Note 1: This entry does not require review of items that meet all the following conditions:

a. Items are generally available to the public, by being sold, without restriction, from stock at retail selling points by means of any of the following:

a.1. Over the counter transactions;

a.2. Mail order transactions;

a.3. Electronic transactions;

a.4. Telephone call transactions;

b. The cryptographic functionality cannot easily be changed by the user;

c. Items are designed for installation by the user without further substantial support by the supplier; and

d. When necessary, details of the items are accessible and will be provided, upon request, to the appropriate authority in the exporter's country in order to ascertain compliance with conditions described in paragraphs a to c above.

Note 2: This entry does not require review of:

a. "Personalized smart cards" where the cryptographic capability is restricted for use in equipment or systems excluded from control under paragraphs b to f of this note. If a "personalized smart card" has multiple functions, the control status of each function is addressed individually;

b. Receiving equipment for radio broadcast, pay television, or similar restricted audience broadcast of the consumer type, without digital encryption except that exclusively used for sending the billing or programme-related information back to the broadcast providers;

c. Equipment where the cryptographic capability is not user-accessible and which is specially designed and limited to allow any of the following:

c.1. Execution of copy-protected software;

c.2. Access to any of the following:

c.2.a. Copy-protected contents stored on read-only media; or

c.2.b. Information stored in encrypted form on media (e.g. in connection with intellectual property rights) where the media is offered for sale in identical sets to the public;

c.2.c. One-time copying of copyright protected audio or video data;

d. Cryptographic equipment specially designed and limited for banking use or money transactions;

Technical Note: "Money transactions" includes the collection and settlement of fares or credit functions.

e. Portable or mobile radio-telephones for civil use (e.g. for commercial civil cellular radio-communications systems) that are not capable of end-to-end encryption;

f. Cordless telephone equipment not capable of end-to-end encryption where the maximum effective range of unboosted cordless operation (i.e., a single, unrelayed hop between terminal and home base-station) is less than 400 metres according to the manufacturer's specifications.

3. Specialized electronic instrumentation and test equipment

a. Signal analysers from 4 through 31 GHz;

b. Microwave test receivers from 4 through 40 GHz;

c. Network analysers from 4 through 40 GHz;

d. Signal generators from 4 through 31 GHz;

e. Travelling wave tubes, pulsed or continuous wave, as follows:

e.1. Coupled cavity tubes, or derivatives thereof;

e.2. Helix tubes, or derivatives thereof, having any of the following characteristics:

e.2.a.1. An "instantaneous bandwidth" of half an octave or more; and

e.2.a.2. The product of the rated average output power (expressed in kW) and the maximum operating frequency (expressed in GHz) of more than 0.2;

e.2.b.1. An "instantaneous bandwidth" of less than half an octave; and

e.2.b.2. The product of the rated average output power (expressed in kW) and the maximum operating frequency (expressed in GHz) of more than 0.4;

f. Equipment specially designed for the manufacture of electron tubes, optical elements and specially designed components therefor;

g. Hydrogen/hydrogen-isotope thyratrons of ceramic-metal construction and rate for a peak current of 500 A or more;

h. Digital instrumentation data recorders having any of the following characteristics:

h.1. A maximum digital interface transfer rate exceeding 175 Mbit/s; or

h.2. Space qualified;

i. Radiation and radioisotope detection and simulation equipment, analysers, software, and Nuclear Instrumentation Module (NIM) componentry and mainframes;

j. Software specially designed for the development or production of the components or equipment in a to i above;

k. Technology for the design, development or production of the components or equipment in a to i above.

Note: Items a to e above do not require review when contained in contracts for civil telecommunications projects, including ongoing maintenance, operation, and repair of the system, certified for civil use by the supplier government.

4. Image intensifier night vision systems, tubes, and components

a. Night vision systems (i.e., cameras or direct view imaging equipment) using an image intensifier tube that utilizes a microchannel plate and an S-20, S-25, GaAs, or GaInAs photocathode;

b. Image intensifier tubes that utilize a microchannel plate and an S-20, S-25, GaAs, or GaInAs photocathode with a sensitivity of 240 μA/lm and below;

c. Microchannel plates of 15 μm and above;

d. Software specially designed for the development or production of the components or equipment in a to c above;

e. Technology for the design, development or production of the components or equipment in a to c above.

5. Specialized radar equipment

a. All airborne radar equipment and specially designed components therefor, not including radars specially designed for meteorological use or Mode 3, Mode C, and Mode S civilian air traffic control equipment specially designed to operate only in the 960 to 1215 MHz band;

Note: This entry does not require initial review of airborne radar equipment installed as original equipment in civil-certified aircraft operating in Iraq.

b. All ground-based primary radar systems that are capable of aircraft detection and tracking;

c. Software specially designed for the development or production of the components or equipment in a and b above;

d. Technology for the design, development or production of the components or equipment in a and b above.

6. Non-civil-certified aircraft; all aero gas turbine engines; unmanned aerial vehicles; and parts and components

a. Non-civil-certified aircraft and specially designed parts and components therefor. This does not include parts and components solely designed to accommodate a carrying of passengers including seats, food services, environmental conditioning, lighting systems, and passenger safety devices;

Note: Civil-certified aircraft consist of aircraft that have been certified for general civil use by the civil aviation authorities of the original equipment manufacturer's government.

b. All gas turbine engines except those designed for stationary power generation applications, and specially designed parts and components therefor;

c. Unmanned aerial vehicles and parts and components therefor having any of the following characteristics:

c.1. Capable of autonomous operation;

c.2. Capable of operating beyond line of sight;

c.3. Incorporating a satellite navigation receiver (i.e. Global Positioning System);

c.4. A gross take-off weight greater than 25 kg (55 lbs);

d. Parts and components for civil-certified aircraft (not including engines);

Note 1: This does not include parts and components for normal maintenance of non-Iraqi owned or leased civil-certified aircraft that were originally qualified or certified by the original equipment manufacturer for that aircraft.

Note 2: For Iraqi-owned or leased civil aircraft, review of parts and components for normal maintenance is not required if the maintenance is performed in a country other than Iraq.

Note 3: For Iraqi-owned or leased aircraft, parts and components are subject to review except for equivalent one-for-one replacement of parts and components that have been certified or qualified by the original equipment manufacturer for use on that aircraft.

Note 4: Any specially designed parts or components that improve the performance of the aircraft remain subject to review.

e. Technology, including software, for the design, development and production of equipment and parts/components for the items in sub-items a to d above.

9. Marine acoustic equipment

a. Marine acoustic systems, equipment and specially designed components therefor, as follows:

a.1. Active (transmitting or transmitting-and-receiving) systems, equipment and specially designed components therefor, as follows:

a.1.a. Wide-swath bathymetric survey systems designed for seabed topographic mapping designed to measure depths less than 600 m below the water surface;

a.2. Passive (receiving, whether or not related in normal application to separate active equipment) systems, equipment and specially designed components thereof as follows:

a.2.a. Hydrophones with sensitivity better than minus 220 dB at any depth with no acceleration compensation;

a.2.b. Towed acoustic hydrophone arrays designed or able to be modified to operate at depths exceeding 15 metres but not exceeding 35 metres;

a.2.b.1. Heading sensors with an accuracy better than +/- 0.5°;

a.2.c. Processing equipment specially designed for towed acoustic hydrophone arrays;

a.2.d. Processing equipment, specially designed for bottom or bay cable systems;

b. Correlation-velocity sonar log equipment designed to measure the horizontal speed of the equipment carrier relative to the seabed.

Technical Note: Hydrophone sensitivity is defined as twenty times the logarithm to the base 10 of the ratio of rms output voltage to a 1 V rms reference, when the hydrophone sensor, without a pre-amplifier, is placed in a plane wave acoustic field with an rms pressure of 1μPa. For example, a hydrophone of -160 dB(reference 1 V per μPa) would yield an output voltage of 10^{-8} V in such a field, while one of -180 dB sensitivity would yield only 10^{-9} V output. Thus -169 dB is better than -180 dB.

10. Charges and devices specially designed for civil projects, and containing small quantities of the following energetic materials:

1. Cyclotetramethylenetetranitramine (HMX) (CAS 2691–41-0) octahydro-1,3,5,7-tetra-nitro-1,3,5,7-tetrazine; 1,3,5,7-tetranitro-1,3,5,7-tetraza-cyclooctane; (octogen, octogene);

2. Hexanitrostilbene (HNS) (CAS 20062—22-0);

3. Triaminotrinitrobenzene (TATB) (CAS 3058—38-6);

4. Triaminoguanidinenitrate (TAGN) (CAS 4000—16-2);

5. Dinitroglycoluril (DNGU, DINGU) (CAS 55510—04-8): tetranitroglycoluril (TNGU, SORGUYL) (CAS 55510—03-7);

6. Tetranitrobenzotriazolobenzotriazole (TACOT) (CAS 25243—36-1);

7. Diaminohexanitrobiphenyl (DIPAM) (CAS 17215—44-0);

8. Picrylaminodinitropyridine (PYX) (CAS 38082—89-2);

9. 3-nitro-1,2,4-triazol-5-one (NTO or ONTA) (CAS 932—64-9);

10. Cyclotrimethylenetrinitramine (RDX) (CAS 121—82-4); cyclonite; T4; hexahydro-1,3,5-trinitro-1, 3, 5-triazine; 1, 3, 5-trinitro-1, 3, 5-triaza-cyclohexane (hexogen, hexogene);

11. 2-(5-cyanotetrazolato) penta amine-cobalt (III) -perchlorate (or CP) (CAS 70247—32-4);

12. cis-bis (5-nitrotetrazolato) tetra amine-cobalt (III)-perchlorate (or BNCP);

13. 7-Amino-4,6-dinitrobenzofurazane-1-oxide (ADNBF) (CAS 97096—78-1); amino dinitrobenzofuroxan;

14. 5,7-diamino-4,6-dinitrobenzofurazane-1-oxide (CAS 117907—74-1), (CL-14 or diamino dinitrobenzofuroxan);

15. 2,4,6-trinitro-2,4,6-triazacyclohexanone (K-6 or Keto-RDX) (CAS 115029—35-1);

16. 2,4,6,8-tetranitro-2,4,6,8-tetraazabicyclo [3,3,0]-octanone-3 (CAS 130256—72-3) (tetranitrosemiglycouril, K-55 or keto-bicyclic HMX);

17. 1,1,3-trinitroazetidine (TNAZ) (CAS 97645—24-4);

18. 1,4,5,8-tetranitro-1,4,5,8-tetraazadecalin (TNAD) (CAS 135877—16-6);

19. Hexanitrohexaazaisowurtzitane (CAS 135285—90-4) (CL-20 or HNIW); and chlathrates of CL-20;

20. Trinitrophenylmethylnitramine (tetryl) (CAS 479—45-8);

21. Any explosive with a detonation velocity exceeding 8,700 m/s or a detonation pressure exceeding 34 GPa (340 kbar);

22. Other organic explosives yielding detonation pressures of 25 GPa(250 kbar) or more that will remain stable at temperatures of 523 K (250°C) or higher for periods of 5 minutes or longer;

23. Any other United Nations-Class 1.1 solid propellant with a theoretical specific impulse (under standard conditions) of more than 250 seconds for non-metallized, or more than 270 seconds for aluminized compositions; and

24. Any United Nations-Class 1.3 solid propellant with a theoretical specific impulse of more than 230 seconds for non-halogenized, 250 seconds for non-metallized and 266 seconds for metallized compositions.

Note: When not part of a charge or device specifically designed for civil projects in small quantities, the energetic materials above are considered military items and are subject to Security Council resolution 687(1991), paragraph 24.

11. Specialized vibration test equipment

Vibration test equipment and specially designed parts and components capable of simulating flight conditions of less than 15,000 metres:

a. Software specially designed for the development or production of the components or equipment above;

b. Technology for the design, development or production of the components or equipment above.

12. Specialized semiconductor manufacturing equipment

a. Items specially designed for the manufacture, assembly, packaging, test, and design of semiconductor devices, integrated circuits and assemblies with a minimum feature size of 1.0 μm, including:

a.1. Equipment and materials for plasma etching, chemical vapor deposition, lithography, mask lithography, masks, and photoresists;

a.2. Equipment specially designed for ion implantation, ion-enhanced or photo-enhanced diffusion, having any of the following characteristics:

a.2.a. Beam energy (accelerating voltage) exceeding 200 keV; or

a.2.b. Optimized to operate at a beam energy (accelerating voltage) of less than 10 keV;

a.3. Surface finishing equipment for the processing of semiconductor wafers as follows:

a.3.a. Specially designed equipment for backside processing of wafers thinner than 100 µm and the subsequent separation thereof; or

a.3.b. Specially designed equipment for achieving a surface roughness of the active surface of a processed wafer with a two-sigma value of 2 µm or less, total indicator reading;

a.4. Equipment, other than general-purpose computers, specially designed for computer-aided design of semiconductor devices or integrated circuits;

a.5. Equipment for the assembly of integrated circuits, as follows:

a.5.a. "Stored program controlled" die bonders having all of the following characteristics:

a.5.a.1. Specially designed for "hybrid integrated circuits";

a.5.a.2. X-Y stage positioning travel exceeding 37.5 x 37.5 mm; and

a.5.a.3. Placement accuracy in the X-Y plane of finer than +10 µm;

a.5.b. Stored program controlled equipment for producing multiple bonds in a single operation (e.g., beam lead bonders, chip carrier bonders, tape bonders);

a.5.c. Semi-automatic or automatic hot cap sealers, in which the cap is heated locally to a higher temperature than the body of the package, specially designed for ceramic microcircuit packages and that have a throughput equal to or more than one package per minute;

b. Software specially designed for the development or production of the components or equipment in a above;

c. Technology for the development, design or production of the components or equipment in a above.

14. Certain Biological Equipment

a. Equipment for the microencapsulation of live micro-organisms and toxins in the range of 1 to 15 µm particle size, to include interfacial polycondensors and phase separators.

ANNEX 2
Procedures

1. Applications for each export of commodities and products should be forwarded to the Office of the Iraq Programme by the exporting States through permanent or observer missions, or by United Nations agencies and programmes. Each application should include technical specifications and end-user information in order for a determination to be made on whether the contract contains any item referred to in paragraph 24 of Security Council resolution 687(1991) of 3 April 1991 or any item on the Goods Review List. A copy of the concluded contractual arrangements should be attached to the application.

2. Each application and the concluded contractual arrangements will be reviewed by customs experts in the Office of the Iraq Programme and experts from the United Nations Monitoring, Verification and Inspection Commission, consulting the International Atomic Energy Agency as necessary, in order to determine whether the contract contains any item referred to in paragraph 24 of resolution 687(1991) or included on the Goods Review List. The Office will identify an official to act as a contact point on each contract.

3. In order to verify that the conditions set out in paragraph 2 above are met, the experts may request additional information from the exporting States or Iraq. The exporting States or Iraq should provide the additional information requested within a period of sixty days. If the experts do not require any additional information within four working days, the procedure under paragraphs 5, 6 and 7 below applies.

4. If the experts determine that the exporting State or Iraq has not provided the additional information within the period set out in paragraph 3 above, the application will not proceed further until the necessary information has been provided.

5. If the experts of the Commission, consulting the Agency as necessary, determine that the contract contains any item referred to in paragraph 24 of resolution 687(1991), the application shall be considered lapsed and be returned to the mission or agency which submitted it.

6. If the experts of the Commission, consulting the Agency as necessary, determine that the contract contains any item referred to on the Goods Review List, they will forward to the Security Council Committee established by resolution 661(1990) full details of such items, including the technical specifications of the items and the associated contract. In addition, the Office of the Iraq Programme and the Commission, consulting the Agency as necessary, shall provide to the Committee an assessment of the humanitarian, economic and security implications, of the approval or denial of the items referred to on the List, including the viability of the whole contract in which the listed item appears and the risk of diversion of the item for military purposes. The Office shall also provide information on the possible end-use monitoring of such items. The Office will immediately inform the missions or agencies concerned. The remaining items in the contract, which are determined as not included in the List, will be processed according to the procedure in paragraph 7 below.

7. If the experts of the Commission, consulting the Agency as necessary, determine that the contract does not contain any item referred to in paragraph 2 above, the Office of the Iraq Programme will immediately inform the Government of Iraq and the exporting State in written form. The exporter will be eligible for payment upon verification by Cotecna that the goods have arrived as contracted in Iraq.

8. If the mission or agency submitting a contract disagrees with the decision to refer the contract to the Committee, it may appeal against that decision within two business days to the Executive Director of the Office of the Iraq Programme. In that event, the Executive Director of the Office, in consultation with the Executive Chairman of the United Nations Monitoring; Verification and Inspection Commission, will appoint experts to reconsider the contract in accordance with the procedures set out above. Their decision, endorsed by the Executive Director and Executive Chairman,

will be final and no further appeals will be permitted. The application shall not be forwarded to the Committee until the appeal period has expired without an appeal being filed.

9. Experts from the Office of the Iraq Programme and the Commission who review contracts should be drawn from the broadest possible geographical base.

10. The Secretariat will report to the Committee at the end of each 180-day phase on the contracts submitted and approved for export to Iraq during this period and provide to any member of the Committee at the member's request copies of applications for information purposes only.

11. Any Committee member may call for an urgent meeting of the Committee to consider revising or revoking these procedures. The Committee will keep these procedures under review and, in the light of experience, will amend them as appropriate.

In the light of the new 180-day extension of the humanitarian programme (phase XI) from 1 December, the UN Secretariat and Iraq, by a 1 December exchange of letters [S/2001/1172], agreed to extend for the same period the provisions of the 1996 Memorandum of Understanding between them on the implementation of Council resolution 986(1995).

UN Compensation Commission and Fund

The United Nations Compensation Commission, established in 1991 [YUN 1991, p. 195] for the resolution and payment of claims against Iraq for losses and damage resulting from its 1990 invasion and occupation of Kuwait [YUN 1990, p. 189], continued in 2001 to expedite the prompt settlement of claims through the United Nations Compensation Fund, which was established at the same time as the Commission.

Governing Council. The Governing Council held four sessions during the year—the thirty-ninth (13-15 March) [S/2001/403], which was adjourned until 2 April [S/2001/404]; the fortieth (19-21 June) [S/2001/763]; the forty-first (25-27 September) [S/2001/1069]; and the forty-second (11-13 December) [S/2002/152]—at which it considered the reports and recommendations of the Panels of Commissioners appointed to review specific instalments of various categories of claims. The Governing Council also acted on the Executive Secretary's report submitted at each session, which, in addition to providing a summary of the previous period's activities, covered corrections to approved claim awards, claim withdrawals, the processing and payment of approved claims, and the 2001 progress report on the Commission's 1997-2003 work programme.

Other matters considered by the Council throughout the year included the distribution of payments and transparency, and the return of undistributed funds; the late filing of Palestinian claims; and the procedure for commencing the determination of interest rates on awards of compensation. At its resumed thirty-ninth session, on 2 April, which was convened to consider the provision of technical assistance to Iraq with respect to claims for environmental damage filed with the Commission, the Council agreed, in principle, that funds be made available for the purpose of hiring experts, through the Commission's budget, whose work would be of assistance to Iraq in responding to environmental claims.

Other issues

Iraqi complaints

Reaffirming its absolute rejection of the northern and southern air exclusion (no-fly) zones imposed by the United States, Iraq reported regularly on the issue to the Secretary-General and the Security Council throughout 2001. Iraq also alleged wanton military attacks by British and United States aircraft against Iraqi civilians and property, and condemned those countries that provided the logistic support for those attacks, namely Kuwait, Saudi Arabia and Turkey [S/2001/18, S/2001/37, S/2001/79, S/2001/116, S/2001/122, S/2001/141, S/2001/161, S/2001/168, S/2001/227, S/2001/248, S/2001/297, S/2001/316, S/2001/369, S/2001/484, S/2001/536, S/2001/559, S/2001/620, S/2001/638, S/2001/650, S/2001/692, S/2001/726, S/2001/756, S/2001/773, S/2001/805, S/2001/807, S/2001/816, S/2001/846, S/2001/850, S/2001/927, S/2001/954, S/2001/995, S/2001/1014, S/2001/1027, S/2001/1068, S/2001/1106, S/2001/1229, S/2001/1263].

In a further series of communications to the Secretary-General, Iraq detailed violations of its international boundaries committed by British and United States warplanes flying across the DMZ monitored by UNIKOM [S/2001/85, S/2001/115, S/2001/151, S/2001/230, S/2001/285, S/2001/329, S/2001/370, S/2001/475, S/2001/583, S/2001/602, S/2001/649, S/2001/702, S/2001/755, S/2001/786, S/2001/847, S/2001/879, S/2001/898, S/2001/955, S/2001/1026, S/2001/1057, S/2001/1105, S/2001/1145, S/2001/1230]. On 3 June [S/2001/554], Iraq claimed that United States aircraft had intercepted and trailed an Iraqi civilian plane, jeopardizing the safety of civilian passengers. On 7 September [S/2001/859], and again on 17 September [S/2001/878], Iraq said that British and United States aircraft engaged on 29 and 30 August in concentrated bombardment of civilian and military locations in Iraq, including the radar system of Basrah International Airport.

During the year, Iraq also alleged violations of its territorial waters and interceptions of Iraqi vessels by the United States [S/2001/32, S/2001/57, S/2001/647, S/2001/929].

In other letters to the Secretary-General [S/2001/109, S/2001/179, S/2001/259, S/2001/637, S/2001/724], Iraq alleged that humanitarian contracts had been placed on hold by the United Kingdom and the United States and requested the lifting of such holds.

Iraq submitted several reports [S/2001/163, S/2001/410, S/2001/658, S/2001/845, S/2001/974, S/2001/1260] concerning the finding and disposal of unexploded ordnance—left behind by what it called the 1991 30-Power aggression against it—which continued to be found in large quantities in the country.

By a 14 January letter to the Secretary-General [S/2001/44], Iraq requested an inquiry into the use of depleted-uranium munitions by the United Kingdom and the United States in their 1991 military campaign against Iraq. On 10 July [S/2001/687], Iraq informed the Secretary-General that, due to the lack of the necessary UN security clearances, the visit by a team of specialists from the World Health Organization (WHO) to Iraq had been postponed. WHO had agreed to dispatch experts to Iraq in order to finalize with Iraqi authorities project proposals for studies on the impact of depleted-uranium munitions. In addition, on 28 March [S/2001/298], Iraq drew the Secretary-General's attention to the outbreak of foot-and-mouth disease in neighbouring countries and to the great efforts that had been made to guard against the spread of the disease to Iraq; those efforts were being thwarted by UNSCOM's destruction in 1996 of laboratories that produced the vaccine and the inhuman position of the United Kingdom and United States in placing holds on contracts for the importation of serums and vaccines.

Iraq also protested, throughout 2001, continuing air incursions and armed aggression in its northern territory by Turkey [S/2001/31, S/2001/61, S/2001/1010].

On 9 August [S/2001/776], Iraq claimed that the United States naval forces stationed in the Arabian Gulf had searched vessels carrying goods of a humanitarian nature to Iraq, including goods being imported under the Memorandum of Understanding and the oil-for-food programme.

In other communications, Iraq alleged that the United Kingdom and the United States were funding and training terrorist groups for the purpose of undermining Iraq's security and territorial integrity [S/2001/532]; refuted allegations made by an American newspaper that it had tested a radiological bomb [S/2001/450]; and transmitted to the Secretary-General a 1 November letter on the question of disarmament from President Hussein to the peoples and Governments of the West, including the United States [A/C.1/56/6].

Other matters

Cambodia

Throughout 2001, the United Nations continued to negotiate with the Government of Cambodia with regard to establishing a tribunal to try top Khmer Rouge leaders for crimes against humanity committed during the period of Democratic Kampuchea (1975-1979). The Law on the Establishment of Extraordinary Chambers in the Courts of Cambodia for the Prosecution of Crimes Committed during the Period of Democratic Kampuchea was promulgated on 10 August and the official translations from Khmer into English and French were submitted to the UN Secretariat on 30 August. During the remainder of the year, the Secretariat communicated to the Cambodian Government a number of issues of concern regarding the conduct of the Extraordinary Chambers.

In **resolution 56/169** of 19 December (see p. 600), the General Assembly welcomed the promulgation of the Law and urged the Government and the United Nations to conclude an agreement without delay so that the Extraordinary Chambers could start to function promptly.

(For the situation of human rights in Cambodia, see p. 598.)

UNTAC financing and liquidation

On 7 September, the General Assembly decided to include the item on the financing and liquidation of the United Nations Transitional Authority in Cambodia (UNTAC), which terminated in 1993 [YUN 1993, p. 371], in the draft agenda of its fifty-sixth (2001) session (**decision 55/495**). On 24 December, it decided that the item would remain for consideration at the resumed fifty-sixth (2002) session (**decision 56/464**) and that the Fifth Committee would continue its consideration of the item at that session (**decision 56/458**).

Fiji

In 2001, the caretaker Government of Fiji organized general elections from 25 August to 1 September, in an effort to restore a system of constitutional democracy that was derailed by a coup d'état on 19 May 2000, one year after Fiji's Labour Party and its coalition partners had won the elections. As a result of the coup, the President had declared a state of emergency and Parliament was suspended. The Commander of the Fiji Military Forces subsequently took over executive authority and Laisenia Qarase was appointed Prime Minister of an interim caretaker Government. The caretaker Government requested the United Nations to attend and observe the general elections. The Organization dispatched an assessment mission to Fiji from 11 to 15 June. With the authorization of the General Assembly, the United Nations Electoral Observer Mission, together with observers from the EU and the Commonwealth, monitored the elections and the immediate post-election environment. The Secretary-General subsequently reported to the Assembly that the elections were credible and reflected the will of the people of Fiji.

Communication. On 13 July [A/55/1016], Fiji requested the Secretary-General to provide assistance and help to ensure that its general elections were conducted in a just and orderly manner and invited the United Nations to attend and observe those elections.

GENERAL ASSEMBLY ACTION

On 25 July [meeting 109], the General Assembly adopted **resolution 55/280** [draft: A/55/L.90 & Add.1] without vote [agenda item 39].

United Nations Electoral Observer Mission for the general elections in Fiji in August 2001

The General Assembly,

Noting the request of the caretaker Government of the Republic of the Fiji Islands to the Secretary-General for the participation of the United Nations in the observation of the general elections in Fiji,

Recalling its resolution 54/173 of 17 December 1999 on strengthening the role of the United Nations in enhancing the effectiveness of the principle of periodic and genuine elections and the promotion of democratization,

Noting with satisfaction that increasing numbers of Member States are using elections as a peaceful means of national decision-making and confidence-building, thereby contributing to greater national peace and stability,

Taking note of the letter dated 31 October 2000 from the Permanent Representative of New Zealand to the United Nations, on behalf of the Pacific Islands Forum, addressed to the Secretary-General, which transmitted the communiqué of the thirty-first meeting of the Forum, held at Tarawa from 27 to 30 October 2000, and recognizing and endorsing the need to address the fundamental causes of political instability in the region,

Taking into account the positive impact on the regional promotion of democracy, peace and well-being that a stable democracy in Fiji will provide,

Taking note of the letter from the Minister for Foreign Affairs, External Trade and Sugar of the caretaker Government addressed to the President of the General Assembly, which registers the commitment of the caretaker Government to return Fiji to a full constitutional democracy through free and fair elections and invites the United Nations to observe the elections,

Reaffirming the Universal Declaration of Human Rights, which provides that everyone has the right to take part in the government of his or her country, directly or through freely chosen representatives, that everyone has the right of equal access to public service in his or her country, that the will of the people shall be the basis of the authority of the government and that this will shall be expressed in periodic and genuine elections which shall be by universal and equal suffrage and shall be held by secret vote or by equivalent free voting procedures,

Taking into account the requested assistance provided by the United Nations in 1995, supporting the revision of the 1990 Constitution of Fiji leading to the promulgation of the Constitution Amendment Act 1997 of the Republic of the Fiji Islands,

Recalling that the verification of free and fair elections should cover the entire time span of the electoral process, and noting that assistance by the United Nations to Member States should continue on a case-by-case basis in accordance with the evolving needs of requesting countries,

Recognizing existing time constraints, which allow the Organization to observe only the election environment, polling, counting, computation of results, complaints and resolution mechanisms, the announcement of results and the post-election acceptance of results,

Welcoming the early exercise of free and fair elections by the caretaker Government seeking to reinstate constitutional democracy,

1. *Decides* to authorize the Secretary-General to establish the United Nations Electoral Observer Mission to monitor the general elections in Fiji and the immediate post-election environment;

2. *Requests* the Secretary-General to arrange, as soon as possible, for the deployment of the Electoral Observer Mission so that it may commence its monitoring functions;

3. *Calls upon* the authorities directly concerned to extend their fullest cooperation to the Electoral Observer Mission in order to facilitate the accomplishment of its task, as requested by the United Nations;

4. *Requests* the Secretary-General to report to the General Assembly at its fifty-sixth session on the implementation of the present resolution under the agenda item entitled "Support by the United Nations system of the efforts of Governments to promote and consolidate new or restored democracies".

Report of Secretary-General. Pursuant to resolution 55/280, the Secretary-General reported on 10 November on the United Nations Electoral Observer Mission for the general elections in Fiji [A/56/611], stating that the core team had arrived in Suva by mid-August and 38 international observers had been deployed across the Fiji Islands by 23 August. The observers visited 96 per cent of the 818 polling stations during the week of voting and monitored the entire counting process, the announcement of the results on 7 September and the post-election period.

The Secretary-General stated that the elections were conducted in a credible manner and that the results reflected the will of the people. However, during the post-election observation, a number of concerns were registered regarding the formation of the Government. In contravention of Fiji's Constitution, a multiparty Cabinet was not formed, resulting in a legal challenge. Given those circumstances, the Secretary-General stated that there was still an opportunity to assist and support Fiji in its expressed determination to return to full constitutional democracy. Continued participation by the United Nations was made viable, and its potential to contribute well served, by the credibility established by the Observer Mission.

With regard to complaints and a number of technical problems, including serious issues related to the electoral rolls, the Mission made recommendations to the Fijian authorities, which it hoped would prove useful for the future.

India-Pakistan

The United Nations Military Observer Group in India and Pakistan (UNMOGIP) continued in 2001 to monitor the situation in Jammu and Kashmir. As at 31 December, UNMOGIP had a strength of 45 military observers. On 13 July [S/2001/710], the Secretary-General informed the Security Council of his intention to appoint Major General Hermann K. Loidolt (Austria) as Chief Military Observer of UNMOGIP, replacing Major General Manuel L. Saavedra (Uruguay), who served in that position until 10 July. The Council took note of the Secretary-General's intention on 18 July [S/2001/711].

Communications. On 30 May [S/2001/594], Sweden drew the Secretary-General's attention to a 29 May statement by the Presidency of the EU welcoming the invitation by India's Prime Minister, Atal Behari Vajpayee, to Pakistan's Chief Executive, General Pervez Musharraf, to visit India. By a 12 June letter to the Security Council President [S/2001/584], the Libyan Arab Jamahiriya also expressed its satisfaction with the initiative taken by India's Prime Minister and the acceptance of the invitation by Pakistan's Chief Executive. Annexed to the letter were the texts of the letters sent by Colonel Muammar Qaddafi to both parties.

In the final communiqué of the annual coordination meeting of the Ministers for Foreign Affairs of the States members of the Organization of the Islamic Conference (New York, 15 November) [A/56/779-S/2002/82], appreciation was expressed for Pakistan's initiative in participating in a results-oriented dialogue with India with a view to resolving all outstanding disputes, and the summit-level talks between the two parties (Agra, India, July) were welcomed.

Oman transmitted to the Secretary-General the text of the final communiqué adopted at the twenty-second Summit of the Gulf Cooperation Council (Muscat, 30-31 December) [A/56/797-S/2002/125], in which it condemned the 13 December terrorist attack on India's Parliament House. The Council expressed concern about the tension between India and Pakistan and hoped that the two parties would exercise self-restraint and return to the positive atmosphere that had accompanied the contacts between the two leaders.

Iran-Iraq

Throughout 2001, Iran and Iraq continued to inform the Secretary-General of alleged repeated violations of their 1988 ceasefire agreement [YUN 1988, p. 193] and 1991 Tehran agreements [YUN 1991, p. 163] concerning the area of separation between them. They also alleged cross-border attacks and terrorist activities in each other's territory.

Iran alleged ceasefire violations by Iraq in an 8 January letter [S/2001/28]; Iraq made counter-allegations on 15 February [S/2001/144], 12 April [S/2001/368] and 23 May [S/2001/529]. Iran alleged violation of internal waters by Iraq on 17 January [S/2001/57] and Iraqi aggression at sea on 20 February [S/2001/159]. Iran further alleged terrorist attacks on its territory by an Iraqi-based organization on 22 March [S/2001/271] and 18 April [S/2001/381].

On 6 February [S/2001/124], Iraq stated that a book by a former UN employee disclosed that Iraq had been assigned responsibility for initiating the Iraq-Iran war in a deal to release Western hostages in Lebanon.

Korea question

By a 17 May letter to the Security Council President [S/2001/495], the Democratic People's Republic of Korea (DPRK) transmitted a report on the delay in the construction of the light-water reactor (LWR) project under the 1994 DPRK–United States Agreed Framework [YUN 1994, p. 442]. Under the Framework, which was a step towards denuclearizing the Korean peninsula and maintaining peace and security in the region, the parties had agreed to cooperate in replacing the DPRK's graphite-moderated reactors and related facilities with LWR power plants; move towards full normalization of political and economic relations; and work together to strengthen the international nuclear non-proliferation regime. The DPRK indicated that it had complied with the Framework and entered into a complete freeze on the graphite-moderated reactors. It had also fully cooperated with IAEA and allowed it to monitor the freeze, and had completed the safe storage of spent-fuel rods out of an experimental atomic reactor. The DPRK expressed concern that LWR power plants the United States had pledged to complete by 2003 had witnessed too much delay and stated that, in the light of the DPRK–United States relations, the delay in the LWR project might lead to the scrapping of the Agreed Framework.

On 10 August [A/56/194], the Republic of Korea requested that an item on peace, security and reunification on the Korean peninsula be included in the agenda of the fifty-sixth (2001) session of the General Assembly. It explained that, following the inter-Korean summit in 2000 [YUN 2000, p. 321], the DPRK and itself had been committed to the implementation of the inter-Korean agreements towards peace and stability in the Korean peninsula.

On 24 December, the Assembly decided that the item requested would remain for consideration at its resumed fifty-sixth (2002) session (**decision 56/464**).

IAEA safeguards inspections

Pursuant to the agreement between IAEA and the DPRK for the application of safeguards in connection with the 1968 Treaty on the Non-Proliferation of Nuclear Weapons, adopted by the General Assembly in resolution 2373(XXII) [YUN 1968, p. 17], IAEA continued to maintain an inspector presence in Nyongbyon to monitor the freeze of the DPRK's graphite-moderated reactors instituted in 1994 [YUN 1994, p. 442]. The DPRK continued to accept IAEA's activities in that regard solely within the context of the 1994 Agreed Framework between it and the United States [ibid.] and not under its safeguards agreement with the Agency [S/2002/211].

IAEA, in May, proposed concrete steps to be taken towards verifying the DPRK's initial declaration of nuclear material, which it had thus far been unable to do. At a technical meeting in November, the DPRK did not agree to begin implementing those proposals, citing the delay in implementing the Agreed Framework (see p. 316).

In a 21 September resolution, the IAEA General Conference again urged the DPRK to comply fully with its safeguards agreement and strongly encouraged it to respond positively and at an early date to the Agency's detailed proposals for the first concrete steps needed to implement the generic requirements for the verification of the correctness and completeness of the DPRK's initial declaration.

Saudi Arabia–Iraq

Saudi Arabia informed the Secretary-General and the Security Council on 29 May [S/2001/547] that, on 23 May, an Iraqi patrol crossed the Saudi border and opened fire on Saudi border personnel, wounding a number of them. An Iraqi soldier was killed during the exchange of fire. Saudi Arabia also listed a number of other alleged Iraqi violations and infringements of Saudi territory. In a 6 June reply [S/2001/568], Iraq said that Saudi soldiers had ambushed and opened fire first on the Iraqi soldiers in the 23 May incident. It also refuted Saudi Arabia's other claims of violations.

By a 4 June letter to the Secretary-General [S/2001/567], Saudi Arabia said that, in view of the fact that Iraq had not maintained neighbourly relations or respected fraternal ties, it had decided to seize full control of the Iraqi pipeline built to carry Iraqi crude oil across Saudi territory. Responding on 13 June [S/2001/588], Iraq said that Saudi Arabia's confiscation of the Iraqi pipeline constituted an illegal seizure of the assets of another State in breach of a bilateral agreement and the norms of international law.

On 10 July, in identical letters to the Secretary-General and the Council President [S/2001/689], Saudi Arabia protested the entry into its territory of Iraqi citizens in possession of hashish on 11 June. In a 23 July reply [S/2001/725], Iraq refuted Saudi Arabia's allegations.

On 27 August [S/2001/823], Iraq informed the Secretary-General and the Council President that Saudi patrol personnel had violated Iraq's territorial integrity and had attacked units of the Iraqi Border Guard Force. Replying on 26 September [S/2001/923], Saudi Arabia said that Iraqi authorities were continuing their practice of violating Saudi territory.

Solomon Islands

On 25 October [A/56/508], Solomon Islands submitted a note verbale to the Secretary-General requesting a UN observer mission to monitor its general elections to be held on 5 December and to provide assistance to help ensure that its elections were conducted in a fair and orderly manner. The Expert Election Monitoring Team was deployed to carry out that task, interacting with international observers, including those from the Pacific Islands Forum.

Tajikistan

On 2 May [S/2001/445], the Secretary-General informed the Security Council of his intention to continue the activities of the United Nations Tajikistan Office of Peace-building (UNTOP) for another year, until 1 June 2002, in view of its role over the preceding year and Tajikistan's need for continuing support in its post-conflict peace-building efforts. The Council took note of the Secretary-General's intention on 7 May [S/2001/446].

UNTOP, which was established in 2000 [YUN 2000, p. 315], focused on facilitating the process of reconciliation and broadening national consensus in the political environment after a prolonged civil war conflict. Together with the UN country team, it contributed to the mobilization of international support for targeted programmes aimed at the creation of employment and the retraining of former irregular fighters and their integration into civilian life.

UNMOT financing

On 14 June [meeting 103], the General Assembly, having considered the Secretary-General's report on the financial performance of the United Nations Mission of Observers in Tajikistan (UN-MOT) from 1 July 1999 to 30 June 2000 [A/55/816 & Corr.1], together with ACABQ's related reports [A/55/874 & A/55/880], and on the recommendation of the Fifth Committee [A/55/972], adopted **resolution 55/263** without vote [agenda item 136].

Financing of the United Nations Mission of Observers in Tajikistan

The General Assembly,

Having considered the report of the Secretary-General on the financing of the United Nations Mission of Observers in Tajikistan and the related reports of the Advisory Committee on Administrative and Budgetary Questions,

Recalling Security Council resolution 968(1994) of 16 December 1994, by which the Council established the United Nations Mission of Observers in Tajikistan, and the subsequent resolutions by which the Council extended the mandate of the Mission of Observers, the latest of which was resolution 1274(1999) of 12 November 1999,

Recalling also Security Council resolution 1138(1997) of 14 November 1997, by which the Council authorized the Secretary-General to expand the size of the Mission of Observers,

Recalling further its resolution 49/240 of 31 March 1995 on the financing of the Mission of Observers and its subsequent resolutions and decisions thereon, the latest of which was resolution 54/272 of 15 June 2000,

Reaffirming that the costs of the Mission of Observers are expenses of the Organization to be borne by Member States in accordance with Article 17, paragraph 2, of the Charter of the United Nations,

Recalling its previous decisions regarding the fact that, in order to meet the expenditures caused by the Mission of Observers, a different procedure is required from that applied to meet expenditures of the regular budget of the United Nations,

Taking into account the fact that the economically more developed countries are in a position to make relatively larger contributions and that the economically less developed countries have a relatively limited capacity to contribute towards such an operation,

Bearing in mind the special responsibilities of the States permanent members of the Security Council, as indicated in General Assembly resolution 1874(S-IV) of 27 June 1963, in the financing of such operations,

Noting with appreciation that voluntary contributions have been made to the Mission of Observers,

Mindful of the fact that it is essential to provide the Mission of Observers with the necessary financial resources to enable it to fulfil its responsibilities under the relevant resolutions of the Security Council,

1. *Takes note* of the status of contributions to the United Nations Mission of Observers in Tajikistan as at 30 April 2001, including the contributions outstanding in the amount of 2.1 million United States dollars, representing some 3 per cent of the total assessed contributions from the inception of the Mission of Observers to the period ending 15 May 2000, notes that some 32.8 per cent of the Member States have paid their assessed contributions in full, and urges all other Member States concerned, in particular those in arrears, to ensure payment of their outstanding assessed contributions in full;

2. *Expresses concern* about the financial situation with regard to peacekeeping activities, in particular as regards the reimbursements to troop contributors that bear additional burdens owing to overdue payments by Member States of their assessments;

3. *Expresses its appreciation* to those Member States which have paid their assessed contributions in full;

4. *Urges* all other Member States to make every possible effort to ensure payment of their assessed contributions to the Mission of Observers in full;

5. *Expresses concern* at the delay experienced by the Secretary-General in deploying and providing adequate resources to some recent peacekeeping missions, in particular those in Africa;

6. *Emphasizes* that all future and existing peacekeeping missions shall be given equal and non-discriminatory treatment in respect of financial and administrative arrangements;

7. *Also emphasizes* that all peacekeeping missions shall be provided with adequate resources for the effective and efficient discharge of their respective mandates;

8. *Endorses* the conclusions and recommendations contained in the report of the Advisory Committee on Administrative and Budgetary Questions, and requests the Secretary-General to ensure their full implementation;

9. *Decides* to reduce the appropriation approved by the General Assembly in its resolution 53/19 B of 8 June 1999 to 16,370,309 dollars gross (15,291,434 dollars net);

10. *Decides also* that, for Member States that have fulfilled their financial obligations to the Mission of Observers, there shall be set off against the apportion-

ment, their respective share of the consequential un-encumbered balance of 2,416,109 dollars gross (2,180,934 dollars net), in respect of the period ending 30 June 2000, in accordance with the composition of groups set out in paragraphs 3 and 4 of General Assembly resolution 43/232 of 1 March 1989, as adjusted by the Assembly in subsequent relevant resolutions and decisions for the ad hoc apportionment of peace-keeping appropriations, the latest of which were resolution 52/230 of 31 March 1998 and decisions 54/456 to 54/458 of 23 December 1999 for the period 1998-2000, and taking into account the scale of assessments for the year 2000, as set out in its resolutions 52/215 A of 22 December 1997 and 54/237 A of 23 December 1999;

11. *Decides further* that, for Member States that have not fulfilled their financial obligations to the Mission of Observers, their share of the unencumbered balance of 2,416,109 dollars gross (2,180,934 dollars net)

in respect of the period ending 30 June 2000 shall be set off against their outstanding obligations;

12. *Emphasizes* that no peacekeeping mission shall be financed by borrowing funds from other active peacekeeping missions;

13. *Encourages* the Secretary-General to continue to take additional measures to ensure the safety and security of all personnel under the auspices of the United Nations participating in the Mission of Observers;

14. *Decides* to include in the provisional agenda of its fifty-sixth session the item entitled "Financing of the United Nations Mission of Observers in Tajikistan".

On 24 December, the Assembly decided that the item on the financing of UNMOT would remain for consideration at the resumed fifty-sixth (2002) session (**decision 56/464**) and that the Fifth Committee would continue its consideration of the item at that session (**decision 56/458**).

Chapter V

Europe and the Mediterranean

In 2001, there were encouraging signs that a number of countries in Europe and the Mediterranean were moving closer towards achieving their goal of peace and security. In the Balkans, the contentious issue of State succession was finally settled on 29 June, when the States successors to the former Socialist Federal Republic of Yugoslavia (SFRY) signed the Agreement on Succession Issues, providing for the distribution of SFRY's rights, obligations, assets and liabilities. Following the change of Government in the Federal Republic of Yugoslavia (FRY) in 2000, relations with Croatia improved, leading to their joint statement of intent to further normalize bilateral relations and to elaborate a protocol on the identification of borders and the delimitation on land and sea, for which they established an inter-State border commission on 10 December.

The United Nations Mission in Bosnia and Herzegovina continued to pursue its Mandate Implementation Plan, which was due to be completed by the end of 2002. In anticipation of the Plan's completion, the Security Council began to consider proposals as to what form continued UN and international civilian presences in Bosnia and Herzegovina would take thereafter.

Between March and May, the United Nations Interim Administration Mission in Kosovo, headed by the Special Representative of the Secretary-General, began laying the foundations for the interim period of self-government in the FRY province of Kosovo. That culminated in the Special Representative's promulgation on 16 May of a Constitutional Framework for Provisional Self-Government, which paved the way for Kosovo-wide elections on 17 November. Formation of a coalition Government and establishment of the provisional self-government institutions followed.

On the Secretary-General's recommendation, the Security Council, on 10 September, terminated the sanctions imposed on FRY and dissolved the committee that had been monitoring them. With the improved situation in the ground safety zone—the buffer zone between Kosovo and Serbia proper—the North Atlantic Treaty Organization allowed the phased return of Yugoslav forces to the area.

In the former Yugoslav Republic of Macedonia, the President and the leaders of the four main political parties signed a Framework Agreement on 13 August. Among its main provisions were the cessation of hostilities, the voluntary disarmament and disbandment of the ethnic Albanian armed groups, an unconditional ceasefire and the development of a decentralized Government.

In Cyprus, the leaders of the Greek and Turkish Cypriot communities, in a 4 December face-to-face meeting in the presence of the Secretary-General's Personal Adviser for Cyprus, agreed to hold direct talks under the auspices of the Secretary-General's mission of good offices. They further agreed on the conditions for such talks, which would begin on 16 January 2002.

In Georgia, however, the peace process aimed at resolving the Georgian/Abkhaz armed conflict remained stalled. The long-awaited paper on the basic principles for the distribution of competencies between Tbilisi and Sukhumi was finalized in mid-December. The paper, which the Special Representative of the Secretary-General transmitted to the parties, was to serve as the basis for substantial negotiations towards a comprehensive settlement, including a definition of the political status of Abkhazia within the State of Georgia. Adamant in its rejection of any suggestion that Abkhazia was within the State of Georgia, the Abkhaz party was not prepared to receive the paper.

Attempts to bring about a settlement in the Nagorny-Karabakh region of Azerbaijan also proved unsuccessful. Both sides of the conflict remained entrenched in their positions: Azerbaijan maintained that Nagorny Karabakh was an integral part of the State of Azerbaijan, while Nagorny Karabakh's leadership considered the region a separate, independent entity, referring to it as the "Nagorno-Karabakh Republic".

The former Yugoslavia

UN operations

The United Nations continued efforts to restore peace and stability in the territories of the former Yugoslavia through its peacekeeping missions: the United Nations Mission in Bosnia and Herzegovina (UNMIBH), the United Nations Mission of Observers in Prevlaka (UNMOP) and the

United Nations Interim Administration Mission in the FRY province of Kosovo (UNMIK). The Secretary-General's Special Envoys for the Balkans, Carl Bildt (Sweden) and Eduard Kukan (Slovakia), also continued in their functions.

The Security Council extended the mandates of UNMIBH, which included the International Police Task Force, until 21 June 2002 and of UNMOP until 15 January 2002.

The Secretary-General, on 1 March [S/2001/194], informed the Security Council President that he had asked his Special Envoys to continue their efforts until midyear, and beyond if required, to promote peace and stability in the Balkans. The Council noted that request on 6 March [S/2001/195].

Financing of previous peacekeeping operations

UNPF and UNPF-HQ

In March [A/55/840], the Secretary-General, in response to General Assembly resolution 54/269 [YUN 2000, p. 325], submitted the financial performance report of the United Nations Protection Force (UNPROFOR), which ended in 1999, the United Nations Confidence Restoration Operation in Croatia (UNCRO), which ended in 1996, the United Nations Preventive Deployment Force (UNPREDEP), which ended in 1999—known collectively as the United Nations Peace Forces (UNPF)—and UNPF headquarters (UNPF-HQ).

Reimbursements to troop-contributing Governments for troop costs had been made in full, apart from $1,358,146 being held in accounts payable awaiting payment instructions from one Government. Also being held in accounts payable were certified claims totalling $219,991,166 for amounts owed for contingent-owned equipment and $15,022,361 for related losses. An estimated $29 million in additional claims for equipment losses was awaiting approval. Claims for goods and services amounting to $12.8 million were recorded in accounts payable as at 31 December 2000.

The unencumbered balance of appropriations stood at $174,743,027 gross ($175,519,370 net); however, there was no corresponding cash balance. In addition, although the operating deficit decreased from $353,288,018 in 1999 to $305,889,451 in 2000, the shortage of cash in the UNPF special account remained a critical problem, owing to the high level of unpaid assessed contributions to UNPF, which, at 31 December 2000, totalled $616,724,373. Consequently, certified government claims had had to be placed in accounts payable.

In the light of the chronic cash shortage of the combined forces, the Secretary-General sought the Assembly's agreement to the continued temporary suspension of financial regulations 4.3, 4.4 and 5.2 (d) in respect of the remaining surplus of $174,743,027 gross ($175,519,370 net). The Advisory Committee on Administrative and Budgetary Questions (ACABQ), in its April report [A/55/886], concurred with the Secretary-General's recommendation.

GENERAL ASSEMBLY ACTION

On 14 June [meeting 103], the General Assembly, on the recommendation of the Fifth (Administrative and Budgetary) Committee [A/55/961], adopted **resolution 55/265** without vote [agenda item 140].

Financing of the United Nations Protection Force, the United Nations Confidence Restoration Operation in Croatia, the United Nations Preventive Deployment Force and the United Nations Peace Forces headquarters

The General Assembly,

Having considered the report of the Secretary-General on the financing of the United Nations Protection Force, the United Nations Confidence Restoration Operation in Croatia, the United Nations Preventive Deployment Force and the United Nations Peace Forces headquarters and the related report of the Advisory Committee on Administrative and Budgetary Questions,

Recalling Security Council resolutions 727(1992) of 8 January 1992 and 740(1992) of 7 February 1992, in which the Council endorsed the sending of a group of military liaison officers to Yugoslavia to promote maintenance of the ceasefire,

Recalling also Security Council resolution 743(1992) of 21 February 1992, by which the Council established the United Nations Protection Force, and the subsequent resolutions by which the Council extended and expanded its mandate,

Recalling further Security Council resolution 981 (1995) of 31 March 1995, by which the Council established the United Nations Confidence Restoration Operation in Croatia, to be known as UNCRO,

Recalling Security Council resolution 983(1995) of 31 March 1995, by which the Council decided that the United Nations Protection Force within the former Yugoslav Republic of Macedonia should be known as the United Nations Preventive Deployment Force,

Recalling also Security Council resolution 1025(1995) of 30 November 1995, in which the Council decided to terminate the mandate of the United Nations Confidence Restoration Operation in Croatia on 15 January 1996,

Recalling further Security Council resolution 1031 (1995) of 15 December 1995, in which the Council decided to terminate the mandate of the United Nations Protection Force on the date on which the Secretary-General reported that the transfer of authority from the United Nations Protection Force to the Implementation Force had taken place,

Recalling the letter dated 1 February 1996 from the President of the Security Council to the Secretary-General, informing him of the Council's concurrence in principle that the United Nations Preventive Deployment Force should become an independent mission,

Recalling also its resolution 46/233 of 19 March 1992 on the financing of the United Nations Protection Force and its subsequent resolutions and decisions thereon, the latest of which was resolution 54/269 of 15 June 2000,

Reaffirming that the costs of the combined Forces are expenses of the Organization to be borne by Member States in accordance with Article 17, paragraph 2, of the Charter of the United Nations,

Recalling its previous decisions regarding the fact that, in order to meet the expenditures caused by the combined Forces, a different procedure is required from that applied to meet expenditures of the regular budget of the United Nations,

Taking into account the fact that the economically more developed countries are in a position to make relatively larger contributions and that the economically less developed countries have a relatively limited capacity to contribute towards such operations,

Bearing in mind the special responsibilities of the States permanent members of the Security Council, as indicated in General Assembly resolution 1874(S-IV) of 27 June 1963, in the financing of such operations,

Noting with appreciation that voluntary contributions have been made to the combined Forces by certain Governments,

Mindful of the fact that it is essential to provide the combined Forces with the necessary financial resources to enable them to meet their outstanding liabilities,

1. *Takes note* of the status of contributions to the combined Forces as at 30 April 2001, including the contributions outstanding in the amount of 615.8 million United States dollars, representing 13 per cent of the total assessed contributions from the inception of the United Nations Protection Force to the period ending 30 June 1997, notes that some 63 per cent of the Member States have paid their assessed contributions in full, and urges all other Member States concerned, in particular those in arrears, to ensure payment of their outstanding assessed contributions in full;

2. *Expresses its appreciation* to those Member States which have paid their assessed contributions in full;

3. *Expresses concern* about the financial situation with regard to peacekeeping activities, in particular as regards the reimbursements to troop contributors that bear additional burdens owing to overdue payments by Member States of their assessments;

4. *Also expresses concern* at the delay experienced by the Secretary-General in deploying and providing adequate resources to some recent peacekeeping missions, in particular those in Africa;

5. *Emphasizes* that all future and existing peacekeeping missions shall be given equal and non-discriminatory treatment in respect of financial and administrative arrangements;

6. *Also emphasizes* that all peacekeeping missions shall be provided with adequate resources for the effective and efficient discharge of their respective mandates;

7. *Endorses* the conclusions and recommendations contained in the report of the Advisory Committee on Administrative and Budgetary Questions, and requests the Secretary-General to ensure their full implementation;

8. *Decides* to suspend for the immediate future the provisions of regulations 4.3, 4.4 and 5.2 *(d)* of the financial regulations of the United Nations in respect of the remaining surplus of 174,743,027 dollars gross (175,519,370 dollars net) in order to allow for reimbursements to troop contributors and in the light of the cash shortage of the combined Forces, and requests the Secretary-General to provide an updated report in one year;

9. *Emphasizes* that no peacekeeping mission shall be financed by borrowing funds from other active peacekeeping missions;

10. *Decides* to include in the provisional agenda of its fifty-sixth session the item entitled "Financing of the United Nations Protection Force, the United Nations Confidence Restoration Operation in Croatia, the United Nations Preventive Deployment Force and the United Nations Peace Forces headquarters".

On 24 December, the Assembly decided that the item on the financing of UNPROFOR, UNCRO, UNPREDEP and UNPF-HQ would remain for consideration during its resumed fifty-sixth (2002) session (**decision 56/464**) and that the Fifth Committee should continue to consider the item at that session (**decision 56/458**).

UNTAES and UN Civilian Police Support Group

By **decision 55/501** of 7 September, the General Assembly included in the draft agenda of its fifty-sixth session the item on financing of the United Nations Transitional Administration for Eastern Slavonia, Baranja and Western Sirmium (UNTAES) and the Civilian Police Support Group.

On 24 December, the Assembly decided that the item on the financing of UNTAES and the Civilian Police Support Group would remain for consideration during its resumed fifty-sixth (2002) session (**decision 56/464**) and that the Fifth Committee should continue to consider the item at that session (**decision 56/458**).

UNPREDEP

The General Assembly, at its resumed fifty-fifth (2001) session, considered the Secretary-General's September 2000 report [A/55/390] on the final disposition of UNPREDEP's assets [YUN 2000, p. 328], seeking authority from the Assembly for the transfer to the Government of the former Yugoslav Republic of Macedonia (FYROM) of assets consisting of observation towers and non-expendable equipment within the observation posts with an inventory value of $1,705,200.

ACABQ, in its related report [A/55/870], recommended approval of the transfer. Noting, however, that the transfer had already been made under "temporary possession" arrangements pending the Assembly's approval, ACABQ observed that such proposals should be submitted to it before the actual transfer, whether under "temporary possession" or otherwise. Noting also that assets of $79,600 had been written off as unaccounted for due to the liquidation team's inability to identify the names of military officials who received some of the equipment provided to the battalions, ACABQ trusted that, since the field assets control system (see p. 102) was fully operational, such instances would be reduced, pointing out that, as a general rule, UN officials should be designated to receive, inspect and report on equipment provided to missions.

By **decision 55/484** of 14 June, the Assembly took note of the Secretary-General's report and the related ACABQ report, and approved the donation of observation towers and non-expendable equipment within the observation posts to FYROM.

On 24 December, the Assembly decided that the item on UNPREDEP's financing would remain for consideration at its resumed fifty-sixth (2002) session (**decision 56/464**) and that the Fifth Committee should continue to consider the item at that session (**decision 56/458**).

State succession issues

The High Representative for the Implementation of the Peace Agreement on Bosnia and Herzegovina [YUN 1995, p. 544] reported in July [S/2001/723] that, in accordance with his mandate, he, together with the Special Negotiator, Sir Arthur Watts (United Kingdom), mediated the final round of negotiations for the succession of the Socialist Federal Republic of Yugoslavia (SFRY) in Vienna. That resulted in the Agreement on Succession Issues, providing for the distribution of the rights, obligations, assets and liabilities of SFRY, which its five successor States—Bosnia and Herzegovina, Croatia, Slovenia, FYROM and the Federal Republic of Yugoslavia (FRY)—initialled on 25 May. The High Representative reported in September [S/2001/868] that the five States had formally signed the Agreement on 29 June in Vienna.

The General Assembly, in **resolution 56/215** (see p. 327), welcomed the Agreement and its implementation.

Prevlaka peninsula

In 2001, the United Nations continued to explore ways to advance the political process relating to the dispute over the Prevlaka peninsula, particularly through the United Nations Mission of Observers in Prevlaka (UNMOP), which monitored the demilitarization of the peninsula and neighbouring territories in Croatia and FRY. The Security Council renewed UNMOP's mandate until 15 January 2002.

As relations between the two countries improved and with their declarations of intent to work towards a negotiated settlement, bilateral negotiations on Prevlaka, which had been stalled for two years, resumed in June 2001. The leaders of the two countries also issued a joint statement on the further normalization of bilateral relations, in accordance with the 1996 Agreement on Normalization of Relations between them [YUN 1996, p. 340]. In November, their Foreign Ministers agreed to elaborate a protocol on the identification of borders and the delimitation on land and sea. As a follow-up, the first meeting was held on 10 December, at which an inter-State border commission was established.

Despite the long-standing violations of the agreed security regime in the UN-controlled zones, including limitations on the free movement of UN military observers, the situation there remained stable and calm. In June, Croatia disbanded its Special Police stationed on its side of the demilitarized zone (DMZ), replacing it with a Police Intervention Unit, and also significantly reduced the number of its regular police there.

Bilateral negotiations

On 5 January [S/2001/13], Croatia said that the emergence of the new Government in FRY [YUN 2000, p. 384] raised hopes that an overall lasting solution could be reached on the question of Prevlaka through bilateral contacts between Croatia and FRY and its Republic of Montenegro. Croatia expected bilateral talks to commence as soon as possible and declared its intention to take account of FRY's security concerns and to endeavour to resolve the issue in the spirit of good-neighbourliness. The Secretary-General's April report on UNMOP [S/2001/350] indicated, however, that no further meetings of the negotiating teams had taken place and the parties continued to hold divergent views on resolving the dispute.

FRY stated its belief on 3 July [S/2001/668] that conditions existed for the two countries to arrive at a satisfactory solution through negotiations, with full respect for the interests of both sides. Regardless of their differing views, FRY continued to believe that gradualism, the strengthening of confidence and the taking of specific steps aimed at creating conditions conducive to reaching a final agreement on the determination of land, water and sea borders between FRY and Croatia were the best way to proceed.

In his July report on UNMOP [S/2001/661], the Secretary-General said that the two countries had held meetings on bilateral issues, including Prevlaka. In addition to working-level discussions, Croatian and Yugoslav officials had met in the Yugoslav capital of Belgrade on 11 June and in Vienna on 28 June. The United Nations did not participate in those meetings, during which the Prevlaka issue was broached.

On 9 July [S/2001/680], Croatia welcomed the resumption of bilateral contacts. It said that it was encouraged by FRY's political will to engage actively in the quest for a solution to the Prevlaka issue and was ready to start negotiations on the delimitation of the maritime border based on international law as soon as possible.

In a later report on UNMOP [S/2002/1], the Secretary-General said that Croatia and FRY continued to maintain contacts. Their Foreign Ministers met on 11 November in New York and issued a joint statement declaring their intention to set up an inter-State commission to address outstanding issues concerning their common land and sea borders and to examine further the issue of demilitarization. In separate meetings with the Secretary-General on 14 November, they expressed their Governments' commitment to continue working bilaterally towards a peaceful, negotiated solution to the Prevlaka dispute. The Secretary-General assured them of UN assistance, should it be required.

On 28 December [S/2001/1301], FRY informed the Security Council President that, as a follow-up to the Foreign Ministers' November decision to elaborate a protocol on the principle of the identification of borders and the delimitation on land and sea, a meeting was held on 10 December, at which an inter-State border commission was established.

Normalization of relations

The Presidents of Croatia, Stjepan Mesic, and of FRY, Vojislav Kostunica, issued a joint statement on their talks on 8 June in Verbania, Italy [A/56/116-S/2001/617], on the state of relations between their countries and on the situation in the broader region. They announced their readiness to continue to maintain periodic contacts in order to give a fresh impetus to the region's stabilization and reaffirmed their commitment in principle to a policy of peace and resolution of all outstanding questions through negotiations.

The Presidents acknowledged that Croatia-FRY relations should be built with a view to achieving full normalization and be expanded in all areas of mutual interest. To that end, special emphasis should be placed on facilitating the free movement of persons, commodities and ideas. Implementation of existing bilateral agreements should continue and measures undertaken to ensure the equal protection of minorities in both countries. All obstacles to the return of refugees and expelled persons should be removed, and maximum efforts exerted to ensure that persons missing in action were accounted for.

They acknowledged that a stable and democratic Bosnia and Herzegovina based on the General Framework Agreement for Peace in Bosnia and Herzegovina [YUN 1995, p. 544] was in the lasting interest, not only of their two countries, but also of the region as a whole, and reaffirmed that Croatia and FRY had no claims to any part of the territory of Bosnia and Herzegovina.

UN Mission of Observers in Prevlaka (UNMOP)

The United Nations Mission of Observers in Prevlaka continued in 2001 to monitor the demilitarization of the disputed Prevlaka peninsula and the neighbouring areas in Croatia and FRY, to hold periodic meetings with local authorities and to maintain contact with the Belgrade and Zagreb authorities. It further maintained cooperation with the multinational Stabilization Force (SFOR) in Bosnia and Herzegovina (see p. 344). UNMOP's areas of responsibility were in two UN-designated zones: the DMZ (Yellow Zone) and the UN-controlled zone (Blue Zone). Until 15 September, UNMOP, which comprised 27 military observers, had been under the command of Chief Military Observer Colonel Graeme Roger Williams (New Zealand). He was replaced by Colonel Rodolfo Sergio Mujica (Argentina), who was appointed through an exchange of letters between the Secretary-General [S/2001/872] and the Security Council [S/2001/873].

The Council extended UNMOP's mandate twice during the year, to 15 July 2001 and to 15 January 2002.

Although an independent mission, UNMOP was, for administrative and budgetary purposes, treated as part of UNMIBH. (For the financing of UNMOP, see p. 337.)

SECURITY COUNCIL ACTION

On 12 January [meeting 4256], the Security Council, having considered the Secretary-General's December 2000 report on UNMOP [YUN 2000, p. 335], unanimously adopted **resolution 1335 (2001)**. The draft [S/2001/34] was prepared in prior consultations.

The Security Council,
Recalling all its earlier relevant resolutions, including resolutions 779(1992) of 6 October 1992, 981(1995) of 31 March 1995, 1088(1996) of 12 December 1996, 1147(1998) of 13 January 1998, 1183(1998) of 15 July 1998, 1222(1999) of 15 January 1999, 1252(1999) of 15

July 1999, 1285(2000) of 13 January 2000, 1305(2000) of 21 June 2000 and 1307(2000) of 13 July 2000,

Having considered the report of the Secretary-General of 29 December 2000 on the United Nations Mission of Observers in Prevlaka,

Recalling the letters addressed to its President from the Chargé d'affaires a.i. of the Permanent Mission of the Federal Republic of Yugoslavia of 22 December 2000 and from the Permanent Representative of Croatia of 5 January 2001, concerning the disputed issue of Prevlaka,

Reaffirming once again its commitment to the independence, sovereignty and territorial integrity of the Republic of Croatia within its internationally recognized borders,

Noting once again that the Joint Declaration signed at Geneva on 30 September 1992 by the Presidents of the Republic of Croatia and the Federal Republic of Yugoslavia, in particular articles 1 and 3 thereof, the latter reaffirming their agreement concerning the demilitarization of the Prevlaka peninsula,

Noting with satisfaction that the overall situation in the area of responsibility of the Mission has remained stable and calm,

Reiterating its concern about continuing violations of the demilitarization regime, including limitations placed on the free movement of United Nations military observers,

Noting with satisfaction that the opening of crossing points between Croatia and the Federal Republic of Yugoslavia in the demilitarized zone continues to facilitate civilian and commercial traffic in both directions without security incidents and continues to represent a significant confidence-building measure in the normalization of relations between the two parties, and urging the parties to utilize these openings as a basis for further confidence-building measures to achieve the normalization of relations between them,

Welcoming the commitment of the democratic governments of Croatia and the Federal Republic of Yugoslavia, as expressed by the Prime Minister of the Federal Government of the Federal Republic of Yugoslavia and the Foreign Minister of Croatia, to resume as soon as possible bilateral talks on the disputed issue of Prevlaka pursuant to the Agreement on Normalization of Relations between the Republic of Croatia and the Federal Republic of Yugoslavia of 23 August 1996, which would end a long period during which no substantive progress was made on the issue,

Expressing its concern over the delay in putting in place a comprehensive demining programme by the parties,

Commending the role played by the Mission, and noting that the presence of the United Nations military observers continues to be essential to maintaining conditions that are conducive to a negotiated settlement of the disputed issue of Prevlaka,

Recalling the relevant principles contained in the Convention on the Safety of the United Nations and Associated Personnel of 9 December 1994 and the statement of its President of 10 February 2000,

Welcoming and encouraging efforts by the United Nations to sensitize peacekeeping personnel in the prevention and control of HIV/AIDS and other communicable diseases in all its peacekeeping operations,

1. *Authorizes* the United Nations military observers to continue monitoring the demilitarization of the Prevlaka peninsula, in accordance with resolutions 779(1992) and 981(1995) and paragraphs 19 and 20 of the report of the Secretary-General of 13 December 1995, until 15 July 2001;

2. *Reiterates its call* upon the parties to cease all violations of the demilitarized regime in the United Nations designated zones, to take steps further to reduce tension and to improve safety and security in the area, to cooperate fully with the United Nations military observers and to ensure their safety and full and unrestricted freedom of movement;

3. *Calls upon* the parties to resume talks on the disputed issue of Prevlaka as soon as possible and encourages them to make use of the recommendations and options to develop confidence-building measures with which they were provided pursuant to its request in resolution 1252(1999) with a view to, inter alia, further facilitating the freedom of movement of the civilian population, and requests the Secretary-General to report by 15 April 2001;

4. *Urges once again* that the parties abide by their mutual commitments and implement fully the Agreement on Normalization of Relations between the Republic of Croatia and the Federal Republic of Yugoslavia, and stresses in particular the urgent need for them to fulfil rapidly and in good faith their commitment to reach a negotiated resolution of the disputed issue of Prevlaka in accordance with article 4 of the Agreement;

5. *Requests* the parties to continue to report at least bimonthly to the Secretary-General on the status of their bilateral negotiations;

6. *Reiterates its call* upon the parties to put a comprehensive demining programme in place in the identified minefields in the area of responsibility of the United Nations Mission of Observers in Prevlaka;

7. *Requests* the United Nations military observers and the multinational Stabilization Force authorized by the Council in resolution 1088(1996) of 12 December 1996 and extended by resolution 1305(2000) of 21 June 2000 to cooperate fully with each other;

8. *Decides* to remain seized of the matter.

Reports of Secretary-General (April and July). The Secretary-General, in his April report on UNMOP [S/2001/350], said that the situation in the DMZ and the UN-controlled zone remained stable and calm. In the latter zone, the long-standing violations of the security regime remained unchanged, with both parties continuing to maintain police positions on their respective sides of the zone and manned Croatian and Montenegrin checkpoints at Cape Kobila. On 21 March, the Chief Military Observer, escorting a visiting representative of a Security Council member, was denied permission to proceed through the Croatian-erected checkpoint. In violation of the regime forbidding entry of civilians into the zone, a civilian van was observed within it on 17 March, reportedly conducting a survey on behalf of the Croatian telecommunications authorities.

No new developments were reported concerning the 1999 package of recommendations and options for confidence-building [YUN 1999, p. 312] conveyed to the parties by the Secretariat. During recent consultations with UNMOP, neither party expressed an interest in pursuing the options that formed part of the package.

The Secretary-General said it was incumbent on the parties to resume discussions aimed at reaching a negotiated solution. In that regard, the package for confidence-building mentioned above remained available as a way of achieving progress, and UNMOP stood ready to assist in the development of practical arrangements to give effect to any agreement that the parties might reach. He intended to explore with them ways to move the political process forward.

In his July report [S/2001/661], the Secretary-General advised the Council that UNMOP had been informed by Croatia that it was disbanding the Special Police that helped to maintain control of the DMZ and replacing it with a newly formed Police Intervention Unit and regular uniformed police. The number of Croatian police stationed in the DMZ had since been significantly reduced. However, there was no change in the disposition of the Montenegrin Border Police and Special Police personnel stationed on the Yugoslav side. On 19 and 22 June, Croatian officials at the Brgat/Ivancia crossing point between Bosnia and Herzegovina and Croatia prevented UN vehicles carrying administrative supplies from UNMIBH to UNMOP from transiting through Croatia.

In the UN-controlled zone, where the number of Croatian police stationed had also been reduced, each side currently maintained a strength of 10 police. The agreed security regime in the zone continued to be violated by both sides permitting the unauthorized entry of civilians, including: police-escorted busloads of some 100 sightseers from Croatia on 16 April; a vehicle bearing Croatian military licence plates on 25 April; and, on 29 April, some 60 vehicles from Croatia carrying about 120 persons protesting a government decision on land ownership.

The Secretary-General concluded that, while the parties remained committed to reaching a negotiated solution on Prevlaka, he was of the view that more time was required for progress to be made. Croatia's reduction of the number of its police in the DMZ reflected its confidence that the area was likely to remain calm and stable—an assessment that accorded with UNMOP's. To ensure that calm and to maintain the stability essential for meaningful progress towards a political settlement, the Secretary-General recommended that UNMOP's mandate be extended for a further six months, to 15 January 2002.

That recommendation was supported by Croatia and FRY in letters of 9 [S/2001/680] and 3 [S/2001/668] July, respectively, to the Council President.

SECURITY COUNCIL ACTION

On 11 July [meeting 4346], the Security Council unanimously adopted **resolution 1362(2001)**. The draft [S/2001/681] was prepared in consultations among Council members.

The Security Council,

Recalling all its earlier relevant resolutions, including resolutions 779(1992) of 6 October 1992, 981(1995) of 31 March 1995, 1088(1996) of 12 December 1996, 1147(1998) of 13 January 1998, 1183(1998) of 15 July 1998, 1222(1999) of 15 January 1999, 1252(1999) of 15 July 1999, 1285(2000) of 13 January 2000, 1307(2000) of 13 July 2000, 1335(2001) of 12 January 2001 and 1357(2001) of 21 June 2001,

Having considered the report of the Secretary-General of 3 July 2001 on the United Nations Mission of Observers in Prevlaka,

Recalling the letters to its President from the Chargé d'affaires a.i. of the Federal Republic of Yugoslavia of 5 July 2001 and from the Chargé d'affaires a.i. of the Republic of Croatia of 9 July 2001 addressed to the President of the Security Council concerning the disputed issue of Prevlaka,

Reaffirming once again its commitment to the independence, sovereignty and territorial integrity of the Republic of Croatia within its internationally recognized borders,

Noting once again the Joint Declaration signed at Geneva on 30 September 1992 by the Presidents of the Republic of Croatia and the Federal Republic of Yugoslavia, in particular articles 1 and 3, the latter reaffirming their agreement concerning the demilitarization of the Prevlaka peninsula, and the Agreement on Normalization of Relations between the Republic of Croatia and the Federal Republic of Yugoslavia of 23 August 1996,

Noting with satisfaction that the overall situation in the area of responsibility of the Mission has remained stable and calm despite continuing violations of the demilitarization regime, including limitations placed on the free movement of United Nations military observers,

Noting with satisfaction that the opening of crossing points between Croatia and the Federal Republic of Yugoslavia in the demilitarized zone continues to facilitate civilian and commercial traffic in both directions without security incidents and continues to represent a significant confidence-building measure in the normalization of relations between the two parties, and urging the parties to utilize these openings as a basis for further confidence-building measures to achieve the normalization of relations between them,

Welcoming the joint statement by the Presidents of the Republic of Croatia and the Federal Republic of Yugoslavia issued in Verbania, Italy, on 8 June 2001 in which they expressed their commitment to normalize the bilateral relations between their countries, with a special emphasis on facilitating the free movement of persons, commodities and ideas, and to implement bilateral agreements already signed,

Commending the role played by the Mission, and noting that the presence of the United Nations military observers continues to be essential to maintaining conditions that are conducive to a negotiated settlement of the disputed issue of Prevlaka,

Recalling the relevant principles contained in the Convention on the Safety of the United Nations and Associated Personnel of 9 December 1994 and the statement by its President of 9 February 2000,

Welcoming and encouraging efforts by the United Nations to sensitize peacekeeping personnel in the prevention and control of HIV/AIDS and other communicable diseases in all its peacekeeping operations,

1. *Authorizes* the United Nations military observers to continue monitoring the demilitarization of the Prevlaka Peninsula, in accordance with resolutions 779(1992) and 981(1995) and paragraphs 19 and 20 of the report of the Secretary-General of 13 December 1995, until 15 January 2002, and requests the Secretary-General to continue to report to the Council where appropriate;

2. *Reiterates its call* upon the parties to cease all violations of the demilitarized regime in the United Nations designated zones, to cooperate fully with the United Nations military observers and to ensure their safety and full and unrestricted freedom of movement;

3. *Welcomes* the resumption of talks between the Governments of the Republic of Croatia and the Federal Republic of Yugoslavia, and urges the parties to continue their talks with the aim of fulfilling rapidly and in good faith their commitment to a negotiated resolution on the disputed issue of Prevlaka in accordance with article 4 of the Agreement on Normalization of Relations;

4. *Encourages* the parties to consider all confidence-building measures, including the options provided to them pursuant to resolution 1252(1999), that could help facilitate a solution to the disputed issue of Prevlaka;

5. *Requests* the parties to continue to report at least bimonthly to the Secretary-General on the status of their bilateral negotiations;

6. *Requests* the United Nations military observers and the multinational Stabilization Force authorized by the Council in resolution 1088(1996) of 12 December 1996 and extended by resolution 1357(2001) of 21 June 2001 to cooperate fully with each other;

7. *Decides* to remain seized of the matter.

Further developments. In a later report on UNMOP [S/2002/1], the Secretary-General said that more than 85 per cent of the recorded unauthorized entries in the UN-controlled zone in 2001 had occurred from the Croatian side. On 21 September, a twin-engine jet originating from Montenegro overflew the zone, and, on 8 November, Croatian workmen employed a trench-digger to lay a communications cable in the zone.

In November, Croatia began a demining programme in a section of the northern DMZ, which was to continue until May 2002. There was no systematic demining on the Yugoslav side.

Bosnia and Herzegovina

In 2001, the United Nations Mission in Bosnia and Herzegovina (UNMIBH) continued its efforts to bring about as complete a fulfilment as possible of the provisions set forth in the 1995 General Framework Agreement for Peace in Bosnia and Herzegovina and the annexes thereto (collectively the Peace Agreement) [YUN 1995, p. 544] by the two multi-ethnic entities of the Republic of Bosnia and Herzegovina: the Federation of Bosnia and Herzegovina (where mainly Bosnian Muslims (Bosniacs) and Bosnian Croats resided); and Republika Srpska (where mostly Bosnian Serbs resided).

As designated by the 1995 Peace Implementation Conference [ibid., p. 547] and with the Security Council's agreement in resolution 1031(1995) [YUN 1995, p. 548], the High Representative for the Implementation of the Peace Agreement on Bosnia and Herzegovina, under the overall management of the Peace Implementation Council and its Steering Board and in cooperation with UNMIBH, continued to monitor, mobilize and coordinate the implementation activities by the parties of the Peace Agreement's civilian aspects [ibid., p. 547]. The multinational Stabilization Force (SFOR), under the command of the North Atlantic Treaty Organization (NATO), likewise continued to oversee their compliance with the Agreement's military aspects, in addition to lending support to UNMIBH.

Progress in the peace implementation process and related political developments in the country during the year (detailed in the following sections) was reported at regular intervals to the Council by the Secretary-General and by the High Representative and SFOR through the Secretary-General.

In anticipation of the completion of UNMIBH's core mandate by the end of 2002 as scheduled, the Council, in addition to extending UNMIBH until July of that year, began to consider what form a continued UN and international civilian presence in the country would take beyond 2002.

GENERAL ASSEMBLY ACTION

On 21 December [meeting 91], the General Assembly adopted **resolution 56/215** [draft: A/56/L.65 & Add.1] without vote [agenda item 40].

The situation in Bosnia and Herzegovina

The General Assembly,

Recalling its resolution 55/24 of 14 November 2000 and all previously adopted resolutions, as well as all relevant resolutions of the Security Council, regarding the situation in Bosnia and Herzegovina,

Reaffirming its support for the independence, sovereignty, legal continuity and territorial integrity of Bosnia and Herzegovina, within its internationally recognized borders, and also reaffirming its support for the equality of the three constituent peoples and others in Bosnia and Herzegovina as a united country, with two multi-ethnic entities, according to the General Framework Agreement for Peace in Bosnia and Herzegovina and the annexes thereto (collectively the "Peace Agreement"), signed in Paris on 14 December 1995, which constitute the key mechanism for the achievement of a durable and just peace in Bosnia and Herzegovina,

Noting the significant progress that has been made since 1995 in implementing the provisions of the Peace Agreement, strengthening the rule of law in all of Bosnia and Herzegovina, and consolidating Bosnia and Herzegovina as a modern democratic State and civic society, fully respectful of the rule of law and committed to encouraging economic growth and promoting well-being for all its citizens,

Welcoming the commitment of the Government to speeding up the overall process of the reconstruction and democratization of Bosnia and Herzegovina, and noting the gradual progress that has been made in the development of efficient common institutions of Bosnia and Herzegovina,

Noting that corruption and the lack of transparency seriously hamper the economic development of Bosnia and Herzegovina, reiterating the need to combat all corruption, welcoming the important contribution made in that regard by the Customs and Fiscal Assistance Office, and expressing its full support for the efforts of the Council of Ministers of Bosnia and Herzegovina and local bodies and of others that are supportive in that regard,

Welcoming the overall progress that has been made in supporting the return of refugees to all parts of the country, and reaffirming the most important principle that all who were forced to leave should feel free and secure to return to their homes,

Noting the importance for the future of Bosnia and Herzegovina for prosecutors to conclude successfully their investigation of war crimes and the whereabouts of those still missing after the war in Bosnia and Herzegovina, as well as the importance of full cooperation with the International Tribunal for the Prosecution of Persons Responsible for Serious Violations of International Humanitarian Law Committed in the Territory of the Former Yugoslavia since 1991, especially with regard to surrendering all already indicted war criminals to the Tribunal,

Welcoming the efforts of the High Representative for the Implementation of the Peace Agreement on Bosnia and Herzegovina, reaffirming the fundamental importance of strengthening all aspects of the rule of law, and noting in that regard the ruling of the Constitutional Court of Bosnia and Herzegovina on the equality of the three constituent peoples throughout the territory of Bosnia and Herzegovina and progress made by the United Nations Mission in Bosnia and Herzegovina in ensuring a fully representative police force, free of corruption and dedicated to enforcing the laws of the country in an impartial way,

Reaffirming the importance for the future of Bosnia and Herzegovina of its successful integration into Europe, noting in that regard the progress made in ful-filling the conditions for entry into the Council of Europe, especially the adoption of the electoral law, welcoming the progress made in fulfilling conditions towards participation in the European Union Stabilization and Association Agreement, and stressing that the Stability Pact for South-Eastern Europe provides an additional contribution to the improvement of regional cooperation,

Welcoming the significant improvement of the overall mutual cooperation among the successor States of former Yugoslavia and the region as a whole, also welcoming the Memorandum of Understanding on intra-regional trade liberalization signed on 27 June 2001 in Brussels, the agreement reached in Vienna regarding the succession of former Yugoslavia and its implementation, and underlining the importance of the establishment of diplomatic relations between the Federal Republic of Yugoslavia and Bosnia and Herzegovina,

Reaffirming the need to combat corruption, smuggling, human trafficking, organized crime, and extremism and other illegal activities, and noting in that regard the establishment of the State Border Service, which is expected to be completed in 2002,

Recognizing the importance of demining and assistance to mine victims for the safety of citizens of Bosnia and Herzegovina, and for the return of refugees and internally displaced persons,

Welcoming the achievements, and encouraging further efforts, in reducing military assets in line with the Agreement on Subregional Arms Control, welcoming the finalizing of the negotiations led by the Organization for Security and Cooperation in Europe within the framework of article V of annex 1-B of the Peace Agreement, and emphasizing the importance of the declaration issued by the Joint Presidency of Bosnia and Herzegovina to commence the process of the formal admission of Bosnia and Herzegovina to the Partnership for Peace,

1. *Notes* that it is the people and the Council of Ministers of Bosnia and Herzegovina who are ultimately responsible for the future of the country, and urges them to work rapidly and intently on economic reform, refugee returns, joint State institution-building and full respect for the rule of law;

2. *Calls* for the full and early implementation of the General Framework Agreement for Peace in Bosnia and Herzegovina and the annexes thereto (collectively the "Peace Agreement") which is essential for stability and cooperation in the region and the reintegration of Bosnia and Herzegovina at all levels;

3. *Welcomes* the progress that has been made towards the implementation of the Peace Agreement by the Government and its commitment to the full, comprehensive and consistent implementation thereof;

4. *Also welcomes* the prompt action of the State and entity institutions in adopting the comprehensive plan of action to prevent terrorist activities, increase security and protect people and property in Bosnia and Herzegovina, further welcomes the active role of Bosnia and Herzegovina in global efforts against terrorism, and in that regard calls upon Bosnia and Herzegovina to work with the international community to establish the State Border Service and have it fully deployed by the end of 2002, in accordance with the

time frame of the United Nations Mission in Bosnia and Herzegovina;

5. *Supports fully* the efforts of the High Representative for the Implementation of the Peace Agreement on Bosnia and Herzegovina, in accordance with the Peace Agreement and subsequent declarations of the Peace Implementation Council, and notes the continuing need for the High Representative to use fully the authority of his office to deal with obstructionists, reaffirming the concept of "partnership" between the newly elected authorities of Bosnia and Herzegovina and the international community;

6. *Encourages* the political leadership of Bosnia and Herzegovina to extend cooperation with the States of South-Eastern Europe so as to promote and strengthen stability and confidence in the region;

7. *Urges* the entity parliaments and cantonal assemblies to implement promptly and fully the provisions of the ruling of the Constitutional Court of Bosnia and Herzegovina on the equality of all three constituent peoples throughout the territory of Bosnia and Herzegovina, and also urges the Constitutional Court to rule further on the status of those other than the three constituent peoples;

8. *Demands* that all the parties to the Peace Agreement fulfil their obligations towards the International Tribunal for the Prosecution of Persons Responsible for Serious Violations of International Humanitarian Law Committed in the Territory of the Former Yugoslavia since 1991, and encourages the authorities of Bosnia and Herzegovina to develop, in close cooperation with the international community, national court capacities to investigate and prosecute cases of war crimes;

9. *Urges* Member States, taking into account the orders and requests of the International Tribunal, to cooperate fully with it, in particular with regard to surrendering indictees, and to provide adequate financial support to the Tribunal;

10. *Reaffirms* the right of refugees and displaced persons to return voluntarily to their homes of origin in accordance with annex 7 of the Peace Agreement, encourages the acceleration of the peaceful, orderly and phased return of refugees and displaced persons, including in areas where they would be the ethnic minority, strongly condemns all acts of intimidation, violence and killings, including those acts designed to discourage the voluntary return of refugees and displaced persons, demands that such acts be investigated and prosecuted, supporting the effective engagement of the Commission for Real Property Claims of Displaced Persons and Refugees, and calls upon all sides to implement the property laws imposed on 27 October 1999, in particular by evicting illegal occupants from the homes of returning refugees, and to ensure respect for individual rights to return and the establishment of the rule of law;

11. *Encourages* all concerned parties to provide information on all persons unaccounted for through the tracing mechanisms of the International Committee of the Red Cross and to cooperate fully with the Committee in its efforts to determine the identities, whereabouts and fate of those persons;

12. *Welcomes* the efforts of international and regional organizations, Member States and non-governmental organizations in Bosnia and Herzegovina, including through the Board of Donors and the Slovenian International Trust Fund for Demining and Mine Victims Assistance, and calls upon Member States to continue to support mine-action activities in Bosnia and Herzegovina;

13. *Stresses* the importance of establishing, strengthening and expanding throughout Bosnia and Herzegovina a free and pluralistic media, and deplores any actions that seek to intimidate or restrict the freedom of the media;

14. *Also stresses* the importance of the restoration and rebuilding of the historical and cultural heritage of Bosnia and Herzegovina in its original form;

15. *Further stresses* the need for a more comprehensive approach to implementing economic reforms, and underlines the fact that a self-sustainable, market-oriented economy operating in a single economic space, expeditious and transparent privatization, improved banking and capital markets, reformed financial systems, the provision of adequate social protection and the adoption by both entities of a law on pension reforms that meet economic standards are crucial for achieving lasting peace and stability in Bosnia and Herzegovina;

16. *Supports* the efforts by the High Representative and the Commander of the multinational Stabilization Force to weaken the continued political and economic influence of remaining parallel structures obstructing peace implementation;

17. *Notes* that the authorities of Bosnia and Herzegovina have defined the common defence policy of Bosnia and Herzegovina, affirming the importance for the national development of Bosnia and Herzegovina of creating, on the basis of agreed principles, a joint military command and seeking to establish a military structure of the appropriate size based on future projections and the legitimate security needs of Bosnia and Herzegovina which will contribute to regional security, and encourages them to carry out its conclusions promptly, fully and in full accordance with the Peace Agreement;

18. *Commends* the efforts of the international community, recognizes the continued importance of its role, welcomes its readiness to continue and streamline its efforts towards a self-sustainable peace, and recalls that the responsibility for consolidating peace and security lies with the authorities of Bosnia and Herzegovina;

19. *Decides* to include in the provisional agenda of its fifty-seventh session the item entitled "The situation in Bosnia and Herzegovina".

On 24 December, the Assembly decided that the item on the situation in Bosnia and Herzegovina would remain for consideration during its resumed fifty-sixth (2002) session (**decision 56/464**).

Implementation of Peace Agreement

Communications. The Croat member of the Bosnia and Herzegovina Joint Presidency, Ante Jelavic, by a 6 February letter [S/2001/114] to the Secretary-General and the Security Council

President, protested the recent decision by the Mission of the Organization for Security and Cooperation in Europe (OSCE) in Bosnia and Herzegovina that revised election rules and procedures in respect of the 11 November 2000 national elections [YUN 2000, p. 349], specifically the mode of electing Croat representatives to the House of Peoples of the Federation of Bosnia and Herzegovina. He claimed the decision deprived the Federation's Croat constituency of the right to elect its own representatives to that legislative body, in clear violation of the concept of equal power-sharing established by the 1995 Peace Agreement.

That the OSCE Mission's representative had characterized the decision as "unconstitutional but democratic" and that the country's Constitutional Court had expressed itself as not competent to assess the decision's constitutional status pointed to the inconsistency in the interpretation of the Peace Agreement and thus to the need for its reformulation. In the circumstances, Mr. Jelavic called on the Council to mandate a conference to review the Agreement's implementation and necessary revision.

The European Union (EU), in a 22 February statement [S/2001/181], welcomed the formation on that date of the new Council of Ministers in Bosnia and Herzegovina and called on it to undertake serious reforms to improve the country's social and economic situation and work for the benefit of all its peoples. The EU also called on all political parties to respect the results of the November 2000 elections [YUN 2000, p. 349], adding that it expected no further delay either in the formation of governments at all other levels or in the election of delegates to the House of Peoples at the State and Federation levels.

In an 8 March declaration [S/2001/212], the EU condemned recent unilateral moves by the so-called Croat National Congress of Bosnia and Herzegovina led by the Croat Democratic Union (HDZ) to place itself outside the provisions of the Peace Agreement (see p. 339). It said such efforts were in vain and detrimental to the interests of the Bosnian Croats and all other peoples in Bosnia and Herzegovina. It called, in particular, on the Bosnian Croats to work within that country's legal institutions to defend their legitimate interests.

Security Council consideration. The Security Council, on 22 March [meeting 4303], was briefed by Wolfgang Petritsch (Austria), High Representative for the Implementation of the Peace Agreement on Bosnia and Herzegovina. He said that, while the results of the November 2000 general elections in Bosnia and Herzegovina were seen as a disappointment, the shift to more moderate

parties was both real and encouraging. That change had led to the formation of the country's first non-nationalist Government at the State level, as well as in the mainly Bosniac-Croat Federation. In the predominantly Serb entity of Republika Srpska, a moderate technocrat headed the Government. The country's new State-level Prime Minister, Bozidar Matic, had announced plans to implement market reforms, create jobs and get the hundreds of thousands of citizens who remained Bosnian refugees or displaced persons to return to their homes.

However, the High Representative was forced to remove Ante Jelavic, in March, as a member of the Joint Presidency and had banned his involvement with any political party, including HDZ, which he had led until recently. Three of his hard-line deputies were under the same ban. Mr. Jelavic had threatened the country's constitutional order and peace. In particular, his HDZ party, claiming to speak for the Bosnian Croats, had announced a plan for self-rule. HDZ was subsequently banned by OSCE for breaching election rules.

A record number of refugees (more than 67,000) returned home in 2000, despite criminal incidents aimed at scaring them away. In January 2001, the payments bureaux, the old communist monopoly on financial transactions, were finally closed down and replaced by commercial banks. The controversial law to end the cycle of pension payment arrears was working and the angry protests had stopped. The High Representative said that, unfortunately, he had had to impose too many of the positive advances in Bosnia and Herzegovina, but he believed that, with new administrations in place, the country for the first time had leaders who wanted to get on with the process of governing themselves. Both the new State and entity governments had ambitious plans to further the reforms to attract domestic and foreign investors and to balance official budgets.

Unfortunately, the High Representative also had to remove Edhem Bicakcic in February, until recently the Federation's Prime Minister and a senior member of the Bosniac Party of Democratic Action (SDA), from his post as director of the power utility, Elektroprivreda. Mr. Bicakcic was under four separate criminal investigations for fraud and abuse of public office. His removal sent a clear signal to officials to clean up their acts and, along with the State-level court created to arbitrate international trade disputes, had done much to bolster investor confidence.

The High Representative further reported that he had decided to set up constitutional commissions in both entities to ensure that the 2000 Constitutional Court decision on the so-called constituent peoples' case [YUN 2000, p. 349] was put in place on an interim basis until full implementation later in the year. Additionally, he had established the Independent Judicial Commission [ibid., p. 351] to effect reforms in the courts and prosecutors' offices across the country.

SECURITY COUNCIL ACTION

On 22 March [meeting 4304], following consultations among Security Council members, the President made statement **S/PRST/2001/11** on behalf of the Council:

The Security Council welcomes the briefing by the High Representative for the implementation of the General Framework Agreement on Peace in Bosnia and Herzegovina and the annexes thereto (collectively the Peace Agreement) on the situation in Bosnia and Herzegovina and commends his efforts in implementing this agreement.

The Council encourages further regional political and economic cooperation, in compliance with the principles of the sovereignty and territorial integrity and the inviolability of the borders of Bosnia and Herzegovina and the other States of the region.

The Council welcomes the new State-level and entity-level Governments formed after the general elections of 11 November 2000 and calls on them to take active measures to make further progress on the return of refugees, consolidation of the State institutions, and economic reform. It welcomes the progress on creating a State Level Defence Identity in full compliance with the relevant provisions of the Peace Agreement and encourages the Presidency of Bosnia and Herzegovina to finalize the unresolved details without delay.

The Council welcomes the establishment of Constitutional Commissions to protect the vital interest of the constituent peoples to facilitate the implementation of the "Constituent Peoples decision" of the Constitutional Court of Bosnia and Herzegovina of 1 July 2000 and calls upon the entity parliaments to engage in the debate about the necessary amendments to their respective constitutions in the light of proposals examined by the Constitutional Commissions.

The Council notes the recent conclusion of the Agreement on a Special Relationship between the Federal Republic of Yugoslavia and the Republika Srpska and urges the High Representative to monitor its implementation and any amendments to it, in order to ensure that it remains consistent with the territorial integrity and sovereignty of Bosnia and Herzegovina as a whole and with the Peace Agreement.

The Council condemns recent unilateral moves by the so-called Croat National Congress to establish Croat self-rule in open contradiction of the provisions of the Peace Agreement, and calls on all parties to work within the legal institutions and constitutional framework of Bosnia and Herzegovina and the entities. It expresses its support for the High Representative in taking actions against persons holding public office who are found to be in viola-

tion of legal commitments made under the Peace Agreement or the terms for its implementation.

The Council welcomes the progress made on the return of refugees and property law implementation in the year 2000, but remains concerned at the slow pace of refugee return, particularly in urban areas. The Council insists on the responsibility of the local authorities to accelerate the rate of return and property law implementation.

The Council urges all political parties in Bosnia and Herzegovina and their respective leaders to engage constructively within the legal institutions of that country in order to implement fully the Peace Agreement.

Civilian aspects

The civilian aspects of the 1995 Peace Agreement [YUN 1995, p. 544] entailed a wide range of activities, including humanitarian aid, infrastructure rehabilitation, establishment of political and constitutional institutions, the promotion of respect for human rights and the holding of free and fair elections. The High Representative, who chaired the Steering Board of the Peace Implementation Council (PIC) and other key implementation bodies, was the final authority with regard to implementing the civilian aspects of the Peace Agreement. UNMIBH, which comprised a UN civilian office, the International Police Task Force (IPTF) and the Mine Action Centre (MAC), reported to the Secretary-General through the Special Representative and Coordinator of United Nations Operations in Bosnia and Herzegovina, Jacques Paul Klein (United States).

The PIC Steering Board, which met regularly at the political-director level, held meetings on 21 June, 12 September, 30 October and 6 December, during which it discussed streamlining the international civilian implementation of the Peace Agreement (see p. 337).

Reports of High Representative. During the year, the High Representative issued progress reports covering the periods from 1 October 2000 to 23 February 2001 [S/2001/219], 24 February to 11 June [S/2001/723] and 12 June to 25 August [S/2001/868]. A later report covered activities from 26 August to the end of the year [S/2002/209]. All described activities in the civilian implementation of the Peace Agreement, which he had been mandated to monitor, mobilize and coordinate. (For details, see below under specific subjects.)

UN Mission in Bosnia and Herzegovina (UNMIBH)

Report of Secretary-General (June). On 7 June [S/2001/571 & Corr.1], the Secretary-General, reporting on UNMIBH activities, said that, in the area of police reform, registration of all police personnel, including prison staff, court police, the State Border Service and local Interpol, had been completed by May. Of the 24,007 law enforcement personnel registered, over 9,300 had been granted provisional authorization to exercise police powers. The core reform programme would be completed by late 2002, with every law enforcement officer appropriately vetted before receiving final certification. A criterion for certification was the regularization of the housing status of police personnel, which continued, with 1,129 of them having done so in the preceding year. UNMIBH had repeatedly requested the High Representative to raise the salaries of police to enable them to rent private housing and to give them priority allocation of alternative municipal accommodation. Meanwhile, UNMIBH had been helping them, on a case-by-case basis, to repossess their own property, qualify for reconstruction assistance or find other legal accommodation.

UNMIBH's police training programme was nearing conclusion, with compulsory courses expected to be completed by June/July. Specialized training had been concluded, while training in handling hazardous materials and exercises in inter-entity police cooperation were ongoing. In February, UNMIBH issued a new policy for monitoring and sanctioning local police performance, comprising "performance reports", which recorded minor acts of inadequate performance, and "non-compliance reports", which recorded serious lapses of duty or violations of law requiring disciplinary measures and placement under intensive IPTF scrutiny. Officers issued with more than one non-compliance report were automatically considered for de-authorization. In February, the Bratunac Police Chief and the Chief Criminal Investigator were de-authorized and several police received non-compliance reports after repeated failures to respond adequately to serious crimes against returning Bosniac refugees and displaced persons. Six police chiefs were also de-authorized for signing a statement renouncing the Federation's authority following the 6 April mob violence in Mostar and Grude over the change of administration at the Herzegovacka Bank, funded and controlled by Croat separatist elements (see p. 344). Police failure to maintain public order during the stone-laying ceremonies for new mosques in Trebinje and Banja Luka in early May resulted in the removal of Trebinje's Public Security Centre Chief and the issuance of a non-compliance report to the town's Chief of Crime Investigation; five Banja Luka police officers were suspended. UNMIBH took the lead in establishing and training police support units for dealing with mob violence, which, to be effective, required vehicles and other equipment.

Police performance had improved, but investigation of incidents of return-related violence remained lethargic and inadequate, particularly in eastern Republika Srpska. Operational capacity and political will were too deficient to deal with violent demonstrations, as in Mostar, Banja Luka and Trebinje. Seriously impairing police performance were three endemic problems: irregular payment of already inadequate wages; the consequent inability of officers to resolve their housing status and unwillingness of minority officers to redeploy across entity lines; and lack of efficient and impartial judicial follow-up to police work, creating a disincentive to professionalism and allowing ethnic extremists and criminals to remain at large. Continuing political interference aggravated those problems.

As for police restructuring, a comprehensive IPTF co-location project called "Manage the Managers", launched in February to address the institutional capacity of law enforcement institutions, was under way in eight Federation cantons and was being extended to public security centres in Republika Srpska. Under the project, IPTF monitors were also being co-located with crime, legal, personnel, finance and budget departments. In February, the pilot project launched in Canton 9 (Sarajevo) under the UNMIBH police commissioner project, aimed at creating an apolitical police service, had to be suspended pending revisions to the Law on Internal Affairs to depoliticize selection procedures. Legislative amendments were also being prepared in three other cantons.

On 20 March, a Bosnian Croat was designated interim Director of the Federation's Ministry of the Interior, whom certain Bosniac political leaders sought to undermine and remove, along with his deputy. No progress was made in establishing a Director of Police for Republika Srpska.

The proportion of minorities in local police forces remained low: 5.7 per cent of a targeted 28 per cent in the Federation and 2.2 per cent of a targeted 20 per cent in Republika Srpska. Representation of females of all ethnicities was also low, averaging 3 per cent in both entities. Since the initiation of minority police officers projects in 1999, the police academies had enrolled or graduated over 830 minority cadets. The first four rounds of UNMIBH's voluntary redeployment programme had resulted in the transfer of 54 minority officers. Thirty-four minority members had completed refresher courses for former police officers; another such course was currently in progress.

UNMIBH's Criminal Justice Advisory Unit, besides continuing its primary task of advising IPTF on criminal procedure and the criminal justice process, instituted a major project whose goal was to improve the quality of police crime reports by using selected prosecutors to train key local police officers. Progress was slowly being made in the establishment of a court police service as a multi-ethnic Federation police force.

The State Border Service had made appreciable progress towards becoming a viable multi-ethnic State-level law enforcement institution, expanding from 376 personnel deployed at four border crossings in 2000 to over 1,180 deployed across 62 per cent of the 1,666-kilometre border. Wide deployment and full effectiveness of the service continued to be hampered, however, by a lack of financial and material resources.

Major strides were also made in fostering cooperation among police forces in Bosnia and Herzegovina and at the regional level. In March, under the auspices of the UNMIBH-chaired Ministerial Consultative Meeting on Police Matters (MCMPM), all domestic police organizations signed a Cooperative Law Enforcement Arrangement for a Border Police Academy in Suhodol, outside Sarajevo. Through MCMPM, UNMIBH concluded the regional Cooperative Law Enforcement Arrangement Combating Illegal Migration and Organized Crime. A document formalizing that Arrangement was signed on 14 May by the Bosnia and Herzegovina entities, Croatia, FRY and the State Border Service.

A campaign called "Your Police Serving You" was launched nationwide on 26 March to increase public awareness of the principles of democratic policing. Each police organization was encouraged to develop its own public relations programme. In June, another multi-ethnic police recruitment campaign was launched, aimed at increasing the percentage of female applicants to police academies.

The Secretary-General observed that, despite the difficult political environment, UNMIBH continued to make measurable progress in implementing its mission. In view of the progress it had achieved so far and of the planned completion of its core tasks by December 2002, he recommended that its mandate be extended for a further 12-month period, to June 2002.

SECURITY COUNCIL ACTION

On 15 [meeting 4330] and 21 [meeting 4333] June, the Security Council met to consider the Secretary-General's report on UNMIBH. On 21 June, the Council unanimously adopted **resolution 1357(2001)**. The draft [S/2001/610] was prepared in consultations among Council members.

The Security Council,

Recalling all its previous relevant resolutions concerning the conflicts in the former Yugoslavia, including resolutions 1031(1995) of 15 December 1995, 1035(1995) of 21 December 1995, 1088(1996) of 12 December 1996, 1144(1997) of 19 December 1997, 1168 (1998) of 21 May 1998, 1174(1998) of 15 June 1998, 1184(1998) of 16 July 1998, 1247(1999) of 18 June 1999 and 1305(2000) of 21 June 2000,

Reaffirming its commitment to the political settlement of the conflicts in the former Yugoslavia, preserving the sovereignty and territorial integrity of all States there within their internationally recognized borders,

Underlining its commitment to supporting implementation of the General Framework Agreement for Peace in Bosnia and Herzegovina and the annexes thereto (collectively the "Peace Agreement"),

Emphasizing its appreciation to the High Representative for the Implementation of the Peace Agreement on Bosnia and Herzegovina, the Commander and personnel of the multinational Stabilization Force, the Special Representative of the Secretary-General and the personnel of the United Nations Mission in Bosnia and Herzegovina, including the Commissioner and personnel of the International Police Task Force, the Organization for Security and Cooperation in Europe, and the personnel of other international organizations and agencies in Bosnia and Herzegovina for their contributions to the implementation of the Peace Agreement,

Noting that the States in the region must play a constructive role in the successful development of the peace process in Bosnia and Herzegovina, and noting especially the obligations of the Republic of Croatia and the Federal Republic of Yugoslavia in this regard as signatories to the Peace Agreement,

Welcoming, in this regard, the positive steps taken by the Governments of the Republic of Croatia and the Federal Republic of Yugoslavia to strengthen their bilateral relations with Bosnia and Herzegovina, as well as their increasing cooperation with all relevant international organizations in implementing the Peace Agreement,

Emphasizing that a comprehensive and coordinated return of refugees and displaced persons throughout the region continues to be crucial to lasting peace,

Recalling the declarations of the Ministerial meetings of the Peace Implementation Conference,

Noting the reports of the High Representative, including his latest report of 13 March 2001,

Having considered the report of the Secretary-General of 7 June 2001, and welcoming the Mandate Implementation Plan of the Mission,

Determining that the situation in the region continues to constitute a threat to international peace and security,

Determined to promote the peaceful resolution of the conflicts in accordance with the purposes and principles of the Charter of the United Nations,

Recalling the relevant principles contained in the Convention on the Safety of United Nations and Associated Personnel of 9 December 1994 and the statement by its President of 9 February 2000,

Welcoming and encouraging efforts by the United Nations to sensitize peacekeeping personnel in the pre-

vention and control of HIV/AIDS and other communicable diseases in all its peacekeeping operations,
Acting under Chapter VII of the Charter,

I

1. *Reaffirms once again its support* for the General Framework Agreement for Peace in Bosnia and Herzegovina and the annexes thereto (collectively the "Peace Agreement"), as well as for the Dayton Agreement on Implementing the Federation of Bosnia and Herzegovina of 10 November 1995, calls upon the parties to comply strictly with their obligations under those Agreements, and expresses its intention to keep the implementation of the Peace Agreement and the situation in Bosnia and Herzegovina under review;

2. *Reiterates* that the primary responsibility for the further successful implementation of the Peace Agreement lies with the authorities in Bosnia and Herzegovina themselves and that the continued willingness of the international community and major donors to assume the political, military and economic burden of implementation and reconstruction efforts will be determined by the compliance and active participation by all the authorities in Bosnia and Herzegovina in implementing the Peace Agreement and rebuilding a civil society, in particular in full cooperation with the International Tribunal for the Prosecution of Persons Responsible for Serious Violations of International Humanitarian Law Committed in the Territory of the Former Yugoslavia since 1991, in strengthening joint institutions and in facilitating returns of refugees and displaced persons;

3. *Reminds* the parties once again that, in accordance with the Peace Agreement, they have committed themselves to cooperate fully with all entities involved in the implementation of this peace settlement, as described in the Peace Agreement, or which are otherwise authorized by the Security Council, including the International Tribunal for the Former Yugoslavia, as it carries out its responsibilities for dispensing justice impartially, and underlines that full cooperation by States and entities with the International Tribunal includes, inter alia, the surrender for trial of all persons indicted by the Tribunal and provision of information to assist in Tribunal investigations;

4. *Emphasizes its full support* for the continued role of the High Representative for the Implementation of the Peace Agreement on Bosnia and Herzegovina in monitoring the implementation of the Peace Agreement and giving guidance to and coordinating the activities of the civilian organizations and agencies involved in assisting the parties to implement the Peace Agreement, and reaffirms that the High Representative is the final authority in theatre regarding the interpretation of annex 10 on civilian implementation of the Peace Agreement and that in case of dispute he may give his interpretation and make recommendations, and make binding decisions as he judges necessary on issues as elaborated by the Peace Implementation Council in Bonn on 9 and 10 December 1997;

5. *Expresses its support* for the declarations of the ministerial meetings of the Peace Implementation Council;

6. *Recognizes* that the parties have authorized the multinational force referred to in paragraph 10 below to take such actions as required, including the use of necessary force, to ensure compliance with annex 1-A of the Peace Agreement;

7. *Reaffirms its intention* to keep the situation in Bosnia and Herzegovina under close review, taking into account the reports submitted pursuant to paragraphs 18 and 25 below, and any recommendations those reports might include, and its readiness to consider the imposition of measures if any party fails significantly to meet its obligations under the Peace Agreement;

II

8. *Pays tribute* to those Member States which participated in the multinational Stabilization Force established in accordance with its resolution 1088(1996), and welcomes their willingness to assist the parties to the Peace Agreement by continuing to deploy a multinational Stabilization Force;

9. *Notes* the support of the parties to the Peace Agreement for the continuation of the Stabilization Force, set out in the declaration of the ministerial meeting of the Peace Implementation Council in Madrid on 16 December 1998;

10. *Authorizes* the Member States acting through or in cooperation with the organization referred to in annex 1-A of the Peace Agreement to continue for a further planned period of 12 months the Stabilization Force as established in accordance with resolution 1088(1996) under unified command and control in order to fulfil the role specified in annexes 1-A and 2 of the Peace Agreement, and expresses its intention to review the situation with a view to extending this authorization further as necessary in the light of developments in the implementation of the Peace Agreement and the situation in Bosnia and Herzegovina;

11. *Also authorizes* the Member States acting under paragraph 10 above to take all necessary measures to effect the implementation of and to ensure compliance with annex 1-A of the Peace Agreement, stresses that the parties shall continue to be held equally responsible for compliance with that annex and shall be equally subject to such enforcement action by the Stabilization Force as may be necessary to ensure implementation of that annex and the protection of the Force, and notes that the parties have consented to the Force taking such measures;

12. *Authorizes* Member States to take all necessary measures, at the request of the Stabilization Force, either in defence of the Force or to assist the Force in carrying out its mission, and recognizes the right of the Force to take all necessary measures to defend itself from attack or threat of attack;

13. *Authorizes* the Member States acting under paragraph 10 above, in accordance with annex 1-A of the Peace Agreement, to take all necessary measures to ensure compliance with the rules and procedures established by the Commander of the Stabilization Force, governing command and control of airspace over Bosnia and Herzegovina with respect to all civilian and military air traffic;

14. *Requests* the authorities in Bosnia and Herzegovina to cooperate with the Commander of the Stabilization Force to ensure the effective management of the airports of Bosnia and Herzegovina, in the light of the responsibilities conferred on the Force by annex 1-A of the Peace Agreement with regard to the airspace of Bosnia and Herzegovina;

15. *Demands* that the parties respect the security and freedom of movement of the Stabilization Force and of other international personnel;

16. *Invites* all States, in particular those in the region, to continue to provide appropriate support and facilities, including transit facilities, for the Member States acting under paragraph 10 above;

17. *Recalls* all the agreements concerning the status of forces as referred to in appendix B to annex 1-A of the Peace Agreement, and reminds the parties of their obligation to continue to comply therewith;

18. *Requests* the Member States acting through or in cooperation with the organization referred to in annex 1-A of the Peace Agreement to continue to report to the Council, through the appropriate channels and at least at monthly intervals;

* *

Reaffirming the legal basis in the Charter of the United Nations on which the International Police Task Force was given its mandate in resolution 1035(1995),

III

19. *Decides* to extend the mandate of the United Nations Mission in Bosnia and Herzegovina, which includes the International Police Task Force, for an additional period terminating on 21 June 2002, and also decides that the Task Force shall continue to be entrusted with the tasks set out in annex 11 of the Peace Agreement, including the tasks referred to in the conclusions of the London, Bonn, Luxembourg, Madrid and Brussels Peace Implementation Conferences and agreed by the authorities in Bosnia and Herzegovina;

20. *Requests* the Secretary-General to keep the Council regularly informed and to report at least every six months on the implementation of the mandate of the Mission as a whole;

21. *Reiterates* that the successful implementation of the tasks of the International Police Task Force rests on the quality, experience and professional skills of its personnel, and once again urges Member States, with the support of the Secretary-General, to ensure the provision of such qualified personnel;

22. *Reaffirms* the responsibility of the parties to cooperate fully with, and to instruct their respective responsible officials and authorities to provide their full support to, the International Police Task Force on all relevant matters;

23. *Reiterates its call* upon all concerned to ensure the closest possible coordination between the High Representative, the Stabilization Force, the Mission and the relevant civilian organizations and agencies so as to ensure the successful implementation of the Peace Agreement and of the priority objectives of the civilian consolidation plan, as well as the security of International Police Task Force personnel;

24. *Urges* Member States, in response to demonstrable progress by the parties in restructuring their law enforcement institutions, to intensify their efforts to provide, on a voluntary-funded basis and in coordination with the International Police Task Force, training, equipment and related assistance for local police forces in Bosnia and Herzegovina;

25. *Requests* the Secretary-General to continue to submit to the Council reports from the High Representative, in accordance with annex 10 of the Peace Agreement and the conclusions of the Peace Implementation Conference held in London on 4 and 5 December 1996, and later Peace Implementation Conferences, on the implementation of the Peace Agreement and in particular on compliance by the parties with their commitments under that Agreement;

26. *Decides* to remain seized of the matter.

Report of Secretary-General (November). In his November report on UNMIBH [S/2001/1132 & Corr.1], the Secretary-General said that the number of police officers granted provisional authorization to exercise police powers had risen to 15,491 (6,625 in Republika Srpska, 8,229 in the Federation, 312 in Brcko District and the remainder in State institutions). Full certification would begin in early 2002 and be completed late that year. However, UNMIBH had identified a significant number of personnel serving in law enforcement positions without proper authorization. Moreover, de-authorized officers were often retained on the payroll or moved to administrative positions outside UNMIBH's authority or to public companies. Only rarely had local officials initiated disciplinary or criminal proceedings.

Under UNMIBH monitoring, local police conducted the majority of basic training courses, while UNMIBH conducted the first management training course for mid-level and senior-level police personnel and completed training programmes in a number of specialized areas. Training in hazardous materials and in anti-terrorism measures continued. With SFOR, UNMIBH developed a practical curriculum for joint training in riot control. In July, it established the Special Trafficking Operations Programme to address human trafficking, under which 90 victims had so far been assisted and seven individuals convicted. However, overall progress in combating that illegal trade was being hampered by weaknesses in the legal system.

Under the police commissioner project, ad interim commissioners had been appointed in the Federation's Ministry of the Interior and six of its cantons, and in Republika Srpska's Ministry of the Interior. However, the related ongoing project introducing necessary amendments to the Laws on Internal Affairs at the cantonal level and in Republika Srpska, in order to create a non-political police service, faced obstruction in the mixed Croat-Bosniac Canton 6 and in three Croat-majority cantons.

To improve internal management and accountability, UNMIBH introduced a disciplinary code that the State Border Police had already adopted and that would serve as a model for Republika Srpska. It also carried out a pilot audit of one canton, to be followed by comprehensive audits of all law enforcement institutions in 2002, with a view to developing modalities for police force restructuring.

Under UNMIBH's minority recruitment programmes, 934 provisionally authorized minority police (11.3 per cent of a total 8,229) were working in the Federation and 211 (3.2 per cent of a total 6,625) in Republika Srpska by November. The State Border Service and the Brcko District police services were totally multi-ethnic. A positive step towards further minority police deployment to Srebrenica was the appointment of a Bosniac as Deputy Station Commander at the newly opened Srebrenica police station.

The slow provision of donated vehicles and the lack of adequate funding had delayed deployment of the State Border Service field offices and mobile support units. At UNMIBH's request, the International Monetary Fund (IMF) had agreed to give priority to funding the Service in 2002 donor appeals. A joint Entity Task Force, created under MCMPM auspices, had developed a national anti-terrorist plan, following the 11 September 2001 terrorist attacks in the United States (see p. 60). The Service had put into effect tighter border controls and had drafted amendments to the Law on Immigration and Asylum to further assist in counter-terrorism activities. In the international fight against crime, UNMIBH facilitated the preparation of a draft law, currently before the Bosnia and Herzegovina Presidency, to create a State Information Protection Agency.

The Secretary-General observed that UNMIBH continued to make progress towards completing its core mandate by December 2002, as envisaged in its Mandate Implementation Plan [YUN 2000, p. 345]; thereafter, continued monitoring and assistance necessary to preserve what had been achieved could be undertaken by a police mission one fourth the size of UNMIBH's current strength, with regional actors assuming responsibility for it. Accordingly, he had instructed his Special Representative to cooperate fully with the organizations assessing requirements for a follow-on police mission. An early decision on the matter was important to ensure timely planning and a smooth transition. UNMIBH was also participating in discussions on streamlining the international presence in Bosnia and Herzegovina (see below).

Later developments. In a later report [S/2001/618], the Secretary-General stated that, in December, UNMIBH launched a nationwide systems analysis to complete the restructuring of key areas of internal police administration, involving the development of a manual of law enforcement standards and procedures and local self-assessment of compliance with them; on-site assessment by IPTF; the establishment of local police Change Management Teams within each law enforcement agency to consult with UNMIBH on the formulation of recommendations; and the implementation of the Teams' short- and long-term recommendations.

Future UNMIBH and international civilian presence

Security Council consideration (September). The Secretary-General's Special Representative and UNMIBH Coordinator told the Security Council on 21 September [meeting 4379] that UNMIBH was making good headway on its core mandate, notwithstanding the difficulties it faced. It had completed 30 out of 64 projects under the Mandate Implementation Plan [YUN 2000, p. 345], 28 were ongoing and eight were in the planning stage. However, as long as the international community continued its piecemeal approach to the Balkans, opportunities to close a tragic decade of war and instability would be missed. He advocated streamlining the structure and activities of the current international presence in Bosnia and Herzegovina, based on an agreed international strategic plan authorized and supported by the Council. Streamlining should therefore be based on certain elements, among them a comprehensive 2002-2005 Dayton Implementation Plan, with benchmarks and time lines endorsed by key international bodies—the United Nations, the Peace Implementation Council (PIC), the EU, OSCE and NATO—and guaranteed multi-year funding of the agreed programmes. In the medium term, activities for the core programmes—rule of law, refugee return, institution-building and economic development—should be functionally consolidated so that one organization would have primary responsibility for each programme and be held accountable for its execution. SFOR should be included in the process.

In view of the scheduled completion of UNMIBH's core mandate in December 2002, urgent decisions were required for its downsizing and liquidation and to enable the successor organizations to plan the future mission.

In that regard, a post-2002 intrusive police-monitoring mission would be needed to ensure that UNMIBH's achievements were not lost and that the international community's ongoing work was not compromised. The Special Representative proposed two options: a stand-alone police-monitoring mission or a comprehensive rule-of-law mission. The first would ensure the intensive monitoring of local police planning and performance in respect of returnee security, public order and human rights, the maintenance of internal and regional coordination and cooperation, continued minority recruitment, and that police structures were not compromised.

That suggested a mission of between 450 and 500 international police personnel. The second option would bring together under one roof the police, the judiciary and the penal system, consistent with the principle of one organization and one responsibility, which would facilitate the introduction of a more efficient "pillar" structure for the organization of the international effort in Bosnia and Herzegovina. Peace implementation by the international community would continue to be a collective endeavour among the five key organizations, but with clearer mandates and responsibilities.

Security Council consideration (December). At the Security Council's 5 December meeting [meeting 4433], the Assistant Secretary-General for Peacekeeping Operations, Hedi Annabi, updated information on UNMIBH operations and plans for a post-UNMIBH mission. He said that, of the Mandate Implementation Plan's 66 specific projects, 43 had been completed and 23 were ongoing, indicating that UNMIBH was on track to complete its mandate in December 2002. At the same time, important political and operational challenges still lay ahead. Some projects, including those for the removal of police officers based on their wartime record, faced political opposition; legislation for the police commissioner project was still opposed by nationalist parties, mainly in Croat-dominated cantons; and voluntary redeployment of minority police officers remained slow and difficult. Other projects, such as the State Border Service, or the training of riot-control units, depended on securing additional financial assistance. In addition, projects that were designed to establish ongoing mechanisms and structures, such as those for minority recruitment or for inter-entity and regional police cooperation, would require nurturing in a post-UNMIBH setting and continued monitoring and assistance.

Mr. Annabi noted the Secretary-General's belief that regional actors should assume responsibility for a follow-up mission with the capacity to preserve UNMIBH's accomplishments, bring to fruition those ongoing projects that would be left by UNMIBH and combine under one roof responsibilities for the police, the judiciary and the penal system. He assessed that that task could be carried out by a mission one fourth the strength of UNMIBH, to include some 450 police officers.

He said the United Nations welcomed the initial steps taken by the High Representative, the EU and OSCE in planning a post-UNMIBH international police-monitoring presence. The Special Representative was cooperating fully with those organizations. The issue was also being discussed at the PIC Steering Board meeting currently in progress in Brussels, Belgium. The Council would be kept informed of developments (see below).

Consideration by PIC Steering Board. At its meeting in Stockholm, Sweden, on 21 June, the PIC Steering Board reviewed progress in the implementation of the 1995 Peace Agreement [YUN 1995, p. 544], discussing, among other issues, the streamlining of current international civilian implementation structures in Bosnia and Herzegovina. To facilitate the process, it agreed on a strictly functional and phased approach that should be fully transparent.

Accordingly, at its 6 December meeting in Brussels, the Board endorsed the High Representative's draft action plan for such streamlining, which called for policy coordination task forces on the rule of law, institution-building, economic policy, and return and reconstruction, as well as for a situation group. At the top of the coordinating structure was a cabinet of lead agencies chaired by the High Representative. The plan also integrated mechanisms to implement the concept of partnership between the international community and the newly elected Bosnia and Herzegovina authorities at various levels, the main one being a consultative partnership forum. The Office of the High Representative subsequently refined the plan to include an assessment of matching multi-year funding requirements and options for the follow-on police mission, for presentation to the Board's next meeting, scheduled for 28 February 2002.

UNMIBH financing

In June, the General Assembly considered the Secretary-General's reports on the financial performance of UNMIBH for the period 1 July 1999 to 30 June 2000 [A/55/683] and the proposed budget for its maintenance and that of UNMOP (see p. 324) and the UN liaison offices in Belgrade and Zagreb for the period 1 July 2001 to 30 June 2002 [A/55/752], together with ACABQ's related comments and recommendations [A/55/874/Add.5].

GENERAL ASSEMBLY ACTION

On 14 June [meeting 103], the General Assembly, on the recommendation of the Fifth Committee [A/55/965], adopted **resolution 55/268** without vote [agenda item 148].

Financing of the United Nations Mission in Bosnia and Herzegovina

The General Assembly,

Having considered the reports of the Secretary-General on the financing of the United Nations Mission in Bosnia and Herzegovina and the related reports of the Advisory Committee on Administrative and Budgetary Questions,

Recalling Security Council resolution 1035(1995) of 21 December 1995, by which the Council established the United Nations Mission in Bosnia and Herzegovina for an initial period of one year, and Council resolution 1305(2000) of 21 June 2000, by which the Council extended the mandate of the Mission until 21 June 2001,

Recalling also Security Council resolution 1335(2001) of 12 January 2001, in which the Council authorized the United Nations military observers to continue to monitor the demilitarization of the Prevlaka peninsula until 15 July 2001,

Recalling further its decision 50/481 of 11 April 1996 on the financing of the Mission and its subsequent resolutions and decisions thereon, the latest of which was resolution 54/273 of 15 June 2000,

Reaffirming the general principles underlying the financing of United Nations peacekeeping operations, as stated in General Assembly resolutions 1874(S-IV) of 27 June 1963, 3101(XXVIII) of 11 December 1973 and 55/235 of 23 December 2000,

Noting with appreciation that voluntary contributions have been made to the Mission,

Mindful of the fact that it is essential to provide the Mission with the necessary financial resources to enable it to fulfil its responsibilities under the relevant resolutions of the Security Council,

1. _Takes note_ of the status of contributions to the United Nations Mission in Bosnia and Herzegovina as at 30 April 2001, including the contributions outstanding in the amount of 78.1 million United States dollars, representing 9 per cent of the total assessed contributions from the inception of the Mission to the period ending 21 June 2001, notes that some 17 per cent of the Member States have paid their assessed contributions in full, and urges all other Member States concerned, in particular those in arrears, to ensure payment of their outstanding assessed contributions;

2. _Expresses its appreciation_ to those Member States which have paid their assessed contributions in full;

3. _Urges_ all other Member States to make every possible effort to ensure payment of their assessed contributions to the Mission in full and on time;

4. _Expresses concern_ at the delay experienced by the Secretary-General in deploying and providing adequate resources to some recent peacekeeping missions, in particular those in Africa;

5. _Emphasizes_ that all future and existing peacekeeping missions shall be given equal and non-discriminatory treatment in respect of financial and administrative arrangements;

6. _Also emphasizes_ that all peacekeeping missions shall be provided with adequate resources for the effective and efficient discharge of their respective mandates;

7. _Reiterates its request_ to the Secretary-General to make the fullest possible use of facilities and equipment at the United Nations Logistics Base at Brindisi, Italy, in order to minimize the costs of procurement for the Mission;

8. _Endorses_ the conclusions and recommendations contained in the report of the Advisory Committee on Administrative and Budgetary Questions, and requests the Secretary-General to ensure their full implementation;

9. _Requests_ the Secretary-General to take all necessary action to ensure that the Mission is administered with a maximum of efficiency and economy;

10. _Also requests_ the Secretary-General, in order to reduce the cost of employing General Service staff, to continue efforts to recruit local staff for the Mission against General Service posts, commensurate with the requirements of the Mission;

11. _Decides_ to appropriate the amount of 144,676,630 dollars gross (135,728,725 dollars net) for the maintenance of the Mission for the period from 1 July 2001 to 30 June 2002, inclusive of the amount of 4,234,303 dollars gross (3,716,018 dollars net) for the support account for peacekeeping operations and the amount of 442,327 dollars gross (397,207 dollars net) for the United Nations Logistics Base, to be apportioned among Member States at a monthly rate of 12,056,385 dollars gross (11,310,727 dollars net) in accordance with the levels set out in General Assembly resolution 55/235, as adjusted by the Assembly in its resolution 55/236 of 23 December 2000, and taking into account the scale of assessments for the years 2001 and 2002, as set out in its resolution 55/5 B of 23 December 2000, subject to the decision of the Security Council to extend the mandate of the Mission beyond 30 June 2001;

12. _Decides also_ that, in accordance with the provisions of its resolution 973(X) of 15 December 1955, there shall be set off against the apportionment among Member States, as provided for in paragraph 11 above, their respective share in the Tax Equalization Fund of the estimated staff assessment income of 8,947,905 dollars approved for the Mission for the period from 1 July 2001 to 30 June 2002;

13. _Decides further_ that, for Member States that have fulfilled their financial obligations to the Mission, there shall be set off against the apportionment, as provided for in paragraph 11 above, their respective share in the unencumbered balance of 25,990,381 dollars gross (24,826,081 dollars net) in respect of the period ending 30 June 2000, in accordance with the composition of groups set out in paragraphs 3 and 4 of General Assembly resolution 43/232 of 1 March 1989 and adjusted by the Assembly in subsequent relevant resolutions and decisions for the ad hoc apportionment of peacekeeping appropriations, the latest of which were resolution 52/230 of 31 March 1998 and decisions 54/456 to 54/458 of 23 December 1999 for the period 1998-2000, and taking into account the scale of assessments for the year 2000, as set out in its resolutions 52/215 A of 22 December 1997 and 54/237 A of 23 December 1999;

14. _Decides_ that, for Member States that have not fulfilled their financial obligations to the Mission, their share of the unencumbered balance of 25,990,381 dollars gross (24,826,081 dollars net) in respect of the period ending 30 June 2000 shall be set off against their outstanding obligations in accordance with the scheme set out in paragraph 13 above;

15. _Emphasizes_ that no peacekeeping mission shall be financed by borrowing funds from other active peacekeeping missions;

16. _Encourages_ the Secretary-General to continue to take additional measures to ensure the safety and security of all personnel under the auspices of the United Nations participating in the Mission;

17. *Invites* voluntary contributions to the Mission in cash and in the form of services and supplies acceptable to the Secretary-General, to be administered, as appropriate, in accordance with the procedure and practices established by the General Assembly;

18. *Decides* to include in the provisional agenda of its fifty-sixth session the item entitled "Financing of the United Nations Mission in Bosnia and Herzegovina".

On 12 December [A/56/698], the Secretary-General submitted the UNMIBH financial performance report for the period from 1 July 2000 to 30 June 2001.

The General Assembly decided, on 24 December, that the item on the financing of UNMIBH would remain for consideration during its resumed fifty-sixth (2002) session (**decision 56/464**) and that the Fifth Committee should continue to consider the item at that session (**decision 56/458**).

International Police Task Force

During 2001, the IPTF component of UNMIBH remained below its authorized strength of 2,057 due to difficulties faced by police-contributing countries in meeting the requirements of all peacekeeping missions. As at 31 December, its actual strength stood at 1,674. The overall mandate completion target was predicated on maintaining IPTF strength at 1,850 until July 2002.

Led by Commissioner Vincent Coeurderoy (France), IPTF continued to assist in the restructuring and reform of the police services in the Federation and to monitor local police. To that end, it launched in February a comprehensive co-location project that extended to legal, personnel, finance and budget departments.

Civil affairs

The High Representative reported in March [S/2001/219] that, following the November 2000 elections in Bosnia and Herzegovina [YUN 2000, p. 349], lengthy delays in establishing the Parliamentary Assembly and the Council of Ministers hampered the functioning of State institutions. Forming a State Government also proved difficult. The House of Representatives rejected the nomination of a Croat, Bozidir Matic, as Chairman of the new Council of Ministers. Nonetheless, the Alliance for Change, a post-election coalition of moderate non-nationalist parties, made important gains that eventually led to the formation, on 22 February, of the new Council, chaired by Mr. Matic. HDZ, which had chosen to boycott the election implementation process and prevented the selection of cantonal delegates to the House of Peoples of the Federation and of Bosnia and Herzegovina, agreed, following the High

Representative's intervention, to implement the election results in the cantonal assemblies it controlled. However, unhappy with the Constitutional Court's decision that it had no jurisdiction over the Provisional Election Commission and its decision-making body, the Election Appeals Sub-commission, HDZ vowed to continue its boycott of the Federation House of Peoples. On 9 February, the High Representative issued a legal opinion, stating that both the House of Peoples and the cantonal assemblies could be constituted by those delegates who had taken their seats, and that boycotting parties and individuals had no right to block the functioning of those bodies.

On 11 January, the High Representative issued a decision restructuring the constitutional commissions in the Federation and the Republika Srpska Parliaments. The commissions would propose amendments to the constitutions of both entities and provisionally protect the constituent peoples and others against discrimination.

In July [S/2001/723], the High Representative further reported that, on 27 March, the Bosnia and Herzegovina House of Representatives elected Beriz Belkic and Jozo Krizanovic as the Bosniac and Croat members, respectively, of the Bosnia and Herzegovina Presidency; the House of Peoples confirmed the election on 30 March. The new Council of Ministers had begun functioning, making progress in implementing its work programme. However, legislative activities and the implementation process were regularly challenged and obstructed by Republika Srpska authorities on the grounds that the Council's legislative agenda invaded Republika Srpska competencies. Progress in the Bosnia and Herzegovina Parliamentary Assembly was less satisfactory, as it had passed no new legislation of major importance. In the House of Representatives, holding together the Alliance for Change coalition was proving difficult; the HDZ delegates, on the other hand, had ended their several months' boycott.

On 12 March, the Alliance for Change coalition formed the Federation's first non-nationalist Government. However, the new Government was challenged by the HDZ leadership and the "Croat National Assembly", which, on 3 March, voted to establish the unconstitutional "Croat Self-Rule in Bosnia and Herzegovina". In late March, HDZ radicals in Mostar tried but failed to oust that city's Mayor, considered an obstacle to the establishment of a separate Croat entity. The "Croat National Assembly" also rejected the Federation Government. On 13 March, HDZ officials ordered the Croat components of the Federation Army to disband; on 28 March, Croat officers and soldiers walked out of their barracks.

On 16 May, the Federation Defence Minister and some Bosnia and Herzegovina Croat Generals brokered a tentative agreement giving Croat soldiers one month to return to their barracks.

In February, the High Representative imposed binding arbitration on Republika Srpska and the Federation to resolve their dispute over the delineation of the inter-entity boundary line in the Bobrinja suburb of Sarajevo. The Arbitrator issued the award on 24 April.

As reported by the High Representative in September [S/2001/868], the Chairman of the Council of Ministers resigned on 22 June, due to the failure of the House of Representatives to adopt the Election Law. He was replaced on 18 July by Foreign Minister Zlatko Lagumdzija of the Social Democratic Party. The High Representative continued to deal with the issue of the so-called Croat Self-Rule, by chipping away at HDZ's financial resources, while assuring the Bosnia and Herzegovina Croats that the international community was aware of and responsive to their legitimate concerns. One result was that a significant but indeterminate number of Bosnian Croat officers and soldiers had renewed their contracts with the Federation Army by the 15 June deadline.

On 23 August, the Bosnia and Herzegovina Parliamentary Assembly finally passed the Election Law, paving the way for the formation of an Election Commission.

To develop a relationship on shared responsibility between the Office of the High Representative and the Council of Ministers, a Consultative Partnership Forum was established for the discussion and resolution of urgent issues, mainly related to the 2000 PIC agenda for accelerating the Peace Agreement's implementation [YUN 2000, p. 338]. The Forum held its first meeting on 2 August. The High Representative also undertook to consult with civil society representatives through a separate consultative structure called the Civic Forum. On 17 July, he imposed harmonizing amendments to both entities' laws on privatization and socially-owned apartments, to eliminate provisions in the Republika Srpska law that disadvantaged returnees in the privatization process and to remove the Federation's rule requiring two years' occupancy following repossession prior to purchasing a pre-war apartment. On 13 July, the Presidency officially transmitted to NATO Bosnia and Herzegovina's wish to join the Partnership for Peace Programme. Under the auspices of the High Representative, Bosniac and Croat representatives signed an agreement on 2 August reuniting the municipalities of Gornji Vakuf and Uskoplje.

In a later report [S/2002/209], the High Representative stated that, at the HDZ Party Congress in Mostar on 6 October, Ante Jelavic, whom he had removed as party president (see p. 330), ran unopposed and was re-elected president, as were most of the vice-presidents who were removed at the same time. Nevertheless, significant changes had occurred to make the so-called Croat/HDZ issue less dangerous for peace implementation: the imposition of a Provisional Administrator in Hercegovacka Banka (the financial backbone of the illegal Bosnia and Herzegovina Croat structures) (see p. 344); the loss of financial and political support from Croatia; and the policy of the Alliance Government of dismantling parallel institutions. By returning to the Federation House of Representatives on 28 November, HDZ had implicitly acknowledged that the self-rule project was untenable. Moreover, the successful implementation of the agreements on the unification of Gornji Vakuf (Bosniac) and Uskoplje (Croat) and on the integration of the Croat-majority municipality of Zepce into the Bosniac-majority canton of Zenica-Doboj, the unification of the Pension Fund in the Federation, progress in the divided city of Mostar and the Alliance Government's outreach to the Croat stronghold of Herzegovina, all indicated that the old bipolar world of ethnic politics was slowly moving to a more functional approach. At the third Congress of the main nationalist Bosniac party, the Party of Democratic Action (Sarajevo, 13 October), Alija Izetbegovic stepped down as a party president; he was succeeded by Sulejman Tihic, Deputy Speaker of the Republika Srpska National Assembly.

The Federation Law on Citizenship was finally adopted in September, thereby enabling citizens of the former Yugoslavia who had taken up permanent residence in Bosnia and Herzegovina before 1998 and were eligible for Bosnia and Herzegovina citizenship to exercise that right.

Responding to the PIC Steering Board's call in October for the Bosnia and Herzegovina authorities to accelerate the pace of preparation for the general elections scheduled for 5 October 2002, the High Representative, on 16 November, appointed the four national members of the Bosnia and Herzegovina Election Commission to work with its three international members, whom he had appointed on 27 September.

Republika Srpska issues

The High Representative, reporting in March [S/2001/219] on issues related specifically to Republika Srpska, the Serb-majority entity of the Republic of Bosnia and Herzegovina, stated that implementation of the election results in that entity had advanced relatively quickly. Mladen Ivanic of the moderate Party of Democratic Progress was appointed Prime Minister on 12 January and formed a "Government of experts" free of senior Serb Democratic Party (SDS) figures, which, with the support of several other parties, had a comfortable majority in the entity's parliament. In his June report [S/2001/723], the High Representative stated that the Prime Minister had managed to stabilize the socio-economic situation by improving tax collection and fiscal discipline. Important constitutional progress was made in April as the reshaped Constitutional Commission agreed on draft amendments to the Republika Srpska Constitution. Unfortunately, the reconstruction of mosques demolished during the war was set back when cornerstone-laying ceremonies for new mosques in Trebinje and Banja Luka were disrupted by violent protests and had to be postponed. Subsequently, the High Representative made several demands of Republika Srpska: an investigation into the violence; immediate changes of leadership in the Ministry of Interior; public condemnation and an apology by top officials; the reconvening of the ceremonies; and the establishment of a multi-ethnic Reform and Reconciliation Committee under the President's auspices. Most of those demands had been complied with.

On 5 March, Republika Srpska and FRY signed an agreement on special parallel relations, as provided for in the Peace Agreement, the implementation of which was to be supervised by the Office of the High Representative. The agreement was ratified on 7 June by the Republika Srpska National Assembly, despite the opposition of some Bosniac and Croat members of the Constitutional Commission who claimed that the agreement should be between Bosnia and Herzegovina and FRY. The High Representative's September report [S/2001/868] noted that the agreement had given rise to two annexes, one on defence issues and the other on sports. However, since the procedures specified in article 9 of the agreement were not complied with, the annex on defence issues had no legal effect. Acknowledging the suspension of the annex, both parties agreed on a way ahead on the issue. The Office of the High Representative had also reviewed the annex on sports and proposed holding a meeting to discuss amendments to it.

In September, the Republika Srpska National Assembly passed the draft Law on Cooperation with the International Tribunal for the Former Yugoslavia (ICTY). However, the entity's cooperation with ICTY had yet to yield any specific results, the High Representative later reported

[S/2002/209]. Not a single indicted war criminal had been apprehended, and Republika Srpska officials had let it be known that the most-wanted Bosnian Serb indictees, Radovan Karadzic and Ratko Mladic, would have to be arrested by the international community alone.

The socio-economic situation in Republika Srpska remained gloomy, as the many strikes by teachers and medical workers and protests by pensioners illustrated. Little had been done to advance the reconciliation process among the three constituent peoples. The Reconciliation and Reform Committee, set up after the May outbreak of violence in Banja Luka and Trebinje (see above), had met only once. Although SDS took tentative steps towards reform during its Congress on 24 December, its new platform remained devoid of a clear commitment to the State of Bosnia and Herzegovina.

Brcko District

In July [S/2001/723], the High Representative reported his continued satisfaction with developments in the Brcko District since its establishment in 2000 [YUN 2000, p. 350]. The entities comprising Bosnia and Herzegovina (the Bosniac-Croat Federation and Republika Srpska) and the District government were enacting a joint housing reconstruction programme for returning displaced persons, with an anticipated 500 housing units reconstructed during 2001. Under the Property Law Implementation Programme, the District was reinstating 100 properties a month on average. A modern judicial system, established on 1 April and consisting of a basic court, an appellate court, a legal aid centre and a judicial commission, was in place and functioning well. A transparent budget was adopted in April and, with improved revenue collection, the District was financially self-sustainable. In general, the entity governments had been supportive of the District and had appointed liaison officers to facilitate dialogue and communication among them. In September [S/2001/868], the High Representative observed that the commencement of reconstruction of the destroyed White Mosque in the Brcko town centre was an encouraging sign of increasing inter-ethnic tolerance.

In a later report [S/2002/209], he stated that reorganization of the District government was completed by the end of 2001, together with the hiring and rehiring of public employees in an open, competitive process.

Refugee/displaced person returns

In 2001, the Office of the United Nations High Commissioner for Refugees (UNHCR) registered the return of 92,061 persons to their pre-war home areas where they were in the ethnic minority—a 36.5 per cent rise from the final minority return figure of 67,445 in 2000. A promising increase in cooperation had emerged between the Bosnia and Herzegovina entities, particularly in information exchange on returnees and property repossession, and in the initiation of entity-funded reconstruction projects [S/2002/209].

The High Representative reported that, in June [S/2001/868], Croatia and international representatives in that country established a legal working group aimed at removing impediments to cross-border returns. He was encouraged by the adoption, under the Regional Return Initiative of the Stability Pact for South-Eastern Europe [YUN 1999, p. 398], of an Agenda for Regional Action providing for a framework to facilitate cross-border returns and the identification of lasting solutions for refugees yet to return to their pre-war homes.

Human rights

The High Representative reported in July [S/2001/723] that the 1997 Mostar "Liska Street" incident [YUN 1997, p. 307] was under criminal investigation by Mostar judicial authorities, as recommended by the Bosnia and Herzegovina Ombudsman. The Office of the High Representative was developing policies and strategies to remedy discriminatory practices in health care and access to utilities and employment. It continued to monitor implementation of the Bosniac-Croat Federation labour laws relating to re-employment or compensation for those dismissed during the war and to work towards establishing an equitable employment market. The Office also helped to facilitate a system allowing returnee pensioners to receive their pensions in their place of return, drafted the Bosnia and Herzegovina Plan of Action to Combat Trafficking in Human Beings, which was pending before Parliament, and assisted in reviewing draft legislation on minority rights and gender equality. In March, the boundaries of the Potocari site, designated by the High Representative in 2000 [YUN 2000, p. 353] for the burial and commemoration of the victims of the 1995 Srebrenica massacre [YUN 1995, p. 529], were identified and marked. The Foundation for the Srebrenica/Potocari Memorial and Cemetery was created and registered and had agreed on the design and location for a stone to mark the site.

Implementation of the Human Rights Chamber's decisions had increased from 33 per cent in late 1999 to 73 per cent by the end of 2001, noted the High Representative in a later report [S/2002/209]. The Federation registered significant progress in implementing occupancy rights and compensation awards. While Republika Srpska showed progress by paying monetary compensation in some 10 cases, its overall implementation rate was far from satisfactory.

As to social, economic and gender rights, the Office of the High Representative assisted in preparing Fair and Equal Employment Principles and in revising the Fair Employment Practices Strategy Policy Paper, both of which articulated standards for employment practices and outlined mechanisms to ensure compliance with inclusive, non-discriminatory hiring practices. It also contributed to finalizing the Inter-Entity Agreement on Health Care for insured persons in Bosnia and Herzegovina, which was signed on 3 December.

In collaboration with ICTY, the Office continued to pressure the Bosnia and Herzegovina authorities, especially those of Republika Srpska, into full cooperation with ICTY. The High Representative said he was considering having a team of experts address what needed to be done if future domestic war crimes were to be tried in the soon-to-be-established Bosnia and Herzegovina Court. An appropriate strategy was under formulation in response to the ICTY Prosecutor's proposal to the Security Council on 27 November [meeting 4429] to remit ICTY cases to a special court in Bosnia and Herzegovina during or following completion of ICTY's mandate. That would ensure that ICTY concerns with the Bosnia and Herzegovina judicial system relating to war crimes prosecutions were addressed and that domestic war crimes prosecutions met the highest professional standards and were expedited.

Judicial reform

The High Representative issued a decision on 14 March [S/2001/723] providing the Independent Judicial Commission (IJC), established in 2000 [YUN 2000, p. 351], with a comprehensive mandate regarding the promotion of the rule of law and judicial reform. An internal directive clarified the scope of administrative competencies and powers between his Office and IJC. Headquartered in Sarajevo, with field offices in Banja Luka, Mostar, Sarajevo and Tuzla, and a fifth to be opened in Bihac, IJC had started implementing its strategic plan and identified areas of particular importance to the strengthening of the rule of law: the review of laws on the appointment of judges and prosecutors; criminal and civil procedure reform; the review of legislation on the enforcement of civil judgements; and court administration and management. It had also begun to monitor and guide the work of the national commissions and councils established to improve the recruitment of judges and prosecutors and to conduct a comprehensive review of all those currently serving.

In July [S/2001/868], the High Representative approved IJC's Strategy Paper for 2001-2002. Its major priorities were: completion of the review of judges and prosecutors; reform of the judiciary appointment process; reform of court administration and management; and revision of legislation in civil procedure and enforcement of judgements. Also in July, the two entities of Bosnia and Herzegovina signed a memorandum of understanding regulating the appointment process for judges and prosecutors throughout the country. On 3 August, the High Representative imposed amendments to the Federation Law on Judicial and Prosecutorial Service to eliminate political obstruction, streamline the appointment and dismissal processes and strengthen the role of the Federation commissions dealing with the nomination of candidates for judicial and prosecutorial service.

Economic reform and reconstruction

The High Representative stated, in July [S/2001/723], that his Office was devoting a great deal of attention and resources to the major priorities of the privatization and restructuring of public utilities and the creation of a favourable investment climate. In Republika Srpska, through a voucher offer that ran from November 2000 to 15 March 2001, citizens and 13 privatization investment funds were offered 55 per cent of State equity in 830 enterprises. Of the 49 million vouchers issued, over 84 per cent were utilized. In a later report [S/2002/209], the High Representative said that, for the first time, three of the 50 largest enterprises in Republika Srpska were sold successfully to international investors. The sale of the remaining State-owned capital in every company was ongoing. In the Federation, the first public offering of shares was completed on 28 March; 542 enterprises were offered to certificate holders, with a subscription of 4.25 billion konvertible marka (KM). The second round was completed by the end of the year, with one or two more rounds to follow. A new Directorate of Privatization was established.

The Office of the High Representative, through the International Advisory Group on Taxation, accelerated the process of tax reform. An agreement on the harmonization of sales taxes was concluded between the two entity governments under the IMF project on the subject, which ended in April. Agreement was also reached for the Brcko District to harmonize its sales tax law with those of the entities by August. A harmonized income tax law was expected to be in place throughout Bosnia and Herzegovina by January 2002.

The report of the Foreign Investment Advisory Service on Bosnia and Herzegovina outlining investment impediments and recommendations for improving the situation was officially presented in Sarajevo and Banja Luka on 29 and 30 June, respectively.

In the transport sector, the Railway Public Corporation was legally registered in both entities. A 61 million euro railway recovery loan was signed on 11 June for the reconstruction of 750 kilometres of main track in Bosnia and Herzegovina. The High Representative's Office organized on 4 May an international conference on the Bosnia and Herzegovina rail transport situation, which recommended drastic reorganization. As a tangible sign of recovery, international passenger service on the Sarajevo–Banja Luka–Zagreb and Doboj–Banja Luka–Zagreb–Ljubljana railway lines reopened on 10 June, after a nine-year hiatus. The Federation and Republika Srpska were in negotiation with the European Investment Bank for a 60 million euro road improvement loan, while the World Bank was preparing a new road management and safety project worth $30 million. Bosnia and Herzegovina signed an agreement with Central European Air Traffic Services on 14 September and a contract with Croatia Control Limited to provide air traffic control services to the country effective 27 December. Deployment of the State Border Service was completed at the Banja Luka and Mostar airports. Recently passed transport legislation included a Federation law creating (from two old companies) the new Railways of the Bosnia and Herzegovina Federation and a State law providing for State-level licensing and regulation of international and inter-entity truck and bus transport.

In the telecommunications sector, the High Representative issued a 2 March decision establishing the Communications Regulatory Agency. The World Bank offered technical assistance for the sector's restructuring, privatization and other transition measures relating to postal services, radio transmission infrastructure and e-commerce.

In the energy sector, the State's Commission on Public Corporations agreed on 17 April to move forward with the analysis and design of new public corporations for gas transportation, power transmission, radio transmission infrastructure and posts. The World Bank and the European Bank for Reconstruction and Development approved a $230 million loan for a power generation and distribution project, conditional on the adoption by the Council of Ministers of a State electricity law providing for a regulatory commission for electricity transmission, an independent service operator and a single transmission company. That condition was fulfilled and the project was under way.

Anti-corruption and transparency issues

The High Representative reported in July [S/2001/723] that the emergence of so-called "Croat Self-Rule" (see p. 339) and its proclamation that it would take over Federation revenues forced him to take action against the financial centre of that illegal parallel structure by placing the Croat-controlled Hercegovacka Banka under his provisional administration. The takeover of the bank on 6 April was resisted by HDZ-organized riots, during which staff of the High Representative's Office and other international and local staff were injured, threatened and taken hostage. The bank was eventually taken over on 18 April with SFOR backing. Although an investigation was initiated by the Federation, the High Representative transferred jurisdiction for the investigation and prosecution to the Cantonal Court of Sarajevo because of well-grounded suspicion of local police involvement and doubts about the impartiality of the local prosecutors and judges. The bank's provisional administrator was faced with lack of management and shareholder cooperation, thus slowing down the consolidation of accounts and the investigative process.

Due to the lack of transparency and continuing suspicion of corruption in the public finance system, the High Representative appointed a Special Auditor to audit and report on the condition of government finances. As a result of the report's confirmation that the system was susceptible to fraud and corruption and lacked appropriate control mechanisms, the High Representative's Office was developing a strategy to reform administrative accounting procedures and to strengthen the Supreme Audit Institution (SAI), and treasury and parliamentary control mechanisms.

In September [S/2001/868], the High Representative stated that, with the assistance of the United States Treasury, his Office had presented to both entity governments a strategy for restructuring the Financial Police Agency, a critical pillar of an independent and effective investigative mechanism against high-level corruption, fraud and money-laundering.

The High Representative subsequently indicated that, following the SAI comprehensive audit early in the year, charges were filed against former and serving officials of Republika Srpska in five cases involving the misappropriation of some KM 300,000 (150,000 euros) in government funds [S/2002/209]. He also reported that, on 6 November, he issued a decision amending the Federation Law on Banks to allow provisional bank administrators to make payouts of up to KM 5,000 before completing their financial reports. That would enable the provisional administrator of Hercegovacka Banka to start paying in December those small depositors whose savings had been frozen since April.

Media issues

The continuing restructuring of the public broadcasting system (PBS) of Bosnia and Herzegovina saw the simultaneous launch on 7 May of PBS radio (broadcasting over the whole territory) and Federation radio, giving the country, for the first time since the disintegration of the former Yugoslavia, a Statewide broadcasting capability. Subject to funding, work would continue to extend the radio signal's reach to 85 per cent of the population, from its current coverage of 72 per cent. The Communications Regulatory Agency continued to evaluate broadcasters. By September, 126 had qualified for full licences. The evaluation was expected to be concluded by year's end, and consultations had begun to ensure that opportunities for new licences met citizens' needs. A working group had drafted a law for Republika Srpska Radio-Television. The Law on Federation Radio-Television was being amended and a PBS State law was in the drafting stage. On 27 October, the new Federation TV was launched and significant measures were taken to enfranchise Croats by improving signal coverage and developing a Croat component. The top managers for the State-level PBS had been appointed and the High Representative's Broadcasting Agent was working closely with them to create a PBS for the entire country that was financially viable and journalistically professional.

The draft Law on Freedom of Access to Information, prepared by an expert group in 2000 [YUN 2000, p. 352], was adopted by the State and entity governments. In June, the Federation Parliament adopted the draft Defamation Act.

Military aspects

Stabilization Force

Under the command of NATO, the multinational Stabilization Force (SFOR), also known as Operation Joint Guard, continued in 2001 to oversee the implementation of the military aspects of the 1995 Peace Agreement. Its activities from 13 November 2000 to 31 October 2001 were recorded in nine reports [S/2001/16, S/2001/290, S/2001/437, S/2001/542, S/2001/688, S/2001/820, S/2001/911, S/2001/1001, S/2001/1167], submitted by the NATO Secretary-General through the UN Secretary-

General to the Security Council, in accordance with Council resolution 1088(1996) [YUN 1996, p. 310]. Activities during the remainder of 2001 were covered in later reports [S/2002/17, S/2002/154].

The strength of SFOR fell from 22,000 in December 2000 to some 18,000 in December 2001. The troops, deployed in Bosnia and Herzegovina and Croatia, were contributed by all NATO members and 15 non-NATO countries. The Council, by **resolution 1357(2001)** of 21 June (see p. 333), authorized the continuation of SFOR for a further period of 12 months.

During the year, SFOR continued to conduct reconnaissance and surveillance, by means of ground and air patrols, to: monitor the border with FRY and the entity armed forces (EAF); conduct weapons storage site inspections; provide support to the international organizations operating in Bosnia and Herzegovina, including the Office of the High Representative; and collect weapons and ammunition. In addition, it assisted the local police and IPTF in providing a safe and secure environment in the Sarajevo suburb of Dobrinja before and after the international arbitrator's final ruling on the disposition of the inter-entity boundary line; conducted operations to ensure a safe and secure environment throughout Bosnia and Herzegovina to counter the destabilizing effects of Croat action to create a third entity (see p. 339); and supported IPTF and local police in their efforts to quell mob violence and maintain police order. Other major activities included an information campaign to reassure the population and deter support for terrorist acts. It discovered two underground bunkers containing military equipment and ammunition near Han Pijesak, north-east of Sarajevo.

The SFOR/OSCE Joint Restructuring Steering Board, on 13 March in Sarajevo, presented to the entities the master plan for restructuring EAF. The Federation and the Joint Presidency endorsed the Common Defence Policy Paper, a key element in that restructuring, and established several working groups. In the meantime, SFOR was verifying the reported 15 per cent troop reduction of EAF in 2000. It continued to support UNHCR efforts to encourage the return of Bosnian Serbs living in Republika Srpska to their home areas.

Federal Republic of Yugoslavia

The year 2001 saw a number of positive developments in the Federal Republic of Yugoslavia (FRY) and in its province of Kosovo. In early March, NATO informed the Secretary-General of its decision, in anticipation of the ultimate abolition of the ground safety zone—the buffer zone between Kosovo and Serbia proper—to allow the controlled return of FRY forces into the zone, which took place between March and May.

Also during that period, the United Nations Interim Administration in Kosovo (UNMIK) began to lay the foundations for Kosovo's interim period of self-government, as envisaged in Security Council resolution 1244(1999) [YUN 1999, p. 353]. The main achievement in that effort was the promulgation on 16 May by the Special Representative of the Secretary-General and Head of UNMIK of the Constitutional Framework for Provisional Self-Government, which determined the new provisional government institutions and their powers and responsibilities. That paved the way for the Kosovo-wide elections on 17 November, in which all communities participated. Since none of the contending parties gained enough Assembly seats to govern alone, negotiations began for the formation of a coalition Government. Accordingly, UNMIK assisted in the establishment of the necessary provisional institutions in accordance with the Constitutional Framework and engaged all communities in the transitional process, aimed at the progressive transfer of public administration to local control. UNMIK also, in cooperation with the EU, OSCE and UNHCR, stepped up measures relating to the reform of Kosovo's police and justice system, economic reform and reconstruction, the return of refugees and displaced persons and the improvement of security, in particular along the border with the the former Yugoslav Republic of Macedonia. In support of UNMIK's efforts, the Council had sent a mission to Kosovo in June to convey a strong message to its local leaders and all concerned to reject violence and promote inter-ethnic reconciliation.

In September, the Secretary-General informed the Council of the constructive cooperation of the new FRY authorities with the international community to bring peace and stability to the Balkan region and expressed his belief that FRY had complied with Council resolution 1160(1998) [YUN 1998, p. 369]. Accordingly, on 10 September, the Council lifted all sanctions imposed against FRY and dissolved the committee it had established to monitor them.

Situation in Kosovo

The United Nations continued to work towards the full implementation of Security Council resolution 1244(1999) [YUN 1999, p. 353], which set out the modalities for a political solution to the crisis in the FRY province of Kosovo, as well as resolutions 1160(1998) [YUN 1998, p. 369], 1199 (1998) [ibid., p. 377], 1203(1998) [ibid., p. 382] and 1239(1999) [YUN 1999, p. 349]. The civilian aspects of resolution 1244(1999) were being implemented by UNMIK and the military aspects by the international security presence (KFOR).

Ground safety zone and southern Serbia

In 2001, the security situation in the ground safety zone (GSZ) (the buffer zone between Kosovo and the rest of Serbia) and in southern Serbia, first brought to the Security Council's attention in December 2000 [YUN 2000, p. 378], continued to deteriorate. On 27 January [S/2001/86], FRY reported to the Council that, on the previous day, Albanian terrorists attacked an army unit on the Bujanovac-Presevo road in the vicinity of Gomja Susaja village, near Bujanovac, outside the GSZ. A soldier was seriously wounded and later died. FRY said those activities were aimed at endangering security, sowing terror among the civilians in the Bujanovac, Presevo and Medvedja municipalities in southern Serbia and provoking the Yugoslav police and army. It called for an urgent Council meeting so that measures could be taken to find the perpetrators and bring them to justice.

FRY also requested the Council to ensure that the provisions of its statement S/PRST/2000/40 [YUN 2000, p. 380] were fully implemented and that the GSZ regime was fully respected.

Security Council consideration (January). The Council, during informal consultations of the whole on 30 January, was briefed by the Assistant Secretary-General for Peacekeeping Operations on the situation in the Presevo Valley, including the foregoing incident [A/56/2]. He stated that, between 18 and 28 January, there was a notable increase in small-scale attacks on FRY forces by elements of the Liberation Army of Presevo, Medvedja and Bujanovac (UCPMB) and a splinter group (the ethnic Albanian armed groups). Eighteen attacks on FRY forces were reported in the central and northern parts of the GSZ. The fighting created a flow of internally displaced persons into Kosovo. Although KFOR continued to conduct proactive operations to interdict and prevent armed groups from crossing into the GSZ, tension in the area was rising.

In a statement to the press on behalf of the Council, the President said that the Council condemned the attacks and stressed the need to bring the perpetrators to justice. The Council recalled the call made in its December 2000 statement [YUN 2000, p. 380] for the immediate and complete cessation of violence, the dissolution of ethnic Albanian extremist groups and the immediate withdrawal from the GSZ of all non-

residents engaged in extremist activities. Welcoming FRY's commitment to work towards a peaceful settlement, the Council also called on ethnic Albanian leaders in southern Serbia to work with the FRY Government to achieve a peaceful settlement. It welcomed the measures taken by KFOR and called on it to continue to address the problem.

Security Council consideration (February). On 13 February [meeting 4277], the Under-Secretary-General for Peacekeeping Operations reported to the Council that there had been increased clashes, illegal checkpoints and training activities in the GSZ. UNMIK and KFOR continued to take action against persons and activities inside Kosovo known to support the ethnic Albanian fighters using the GSZ as a staging area. They were also working in selected areas along the Kosovo side of the administrative boundary to control more effectively the movements of individuals attempting to support ethnic Albanian fighters. KFOR had over 100 suspected ethnic Albanian fighters in detention.

Discussions were continuing with FRY and Serbia and with ethnic Albanian leaders on halting the displacement of persons and on encouraging returns to the Presevo area. An inter-agency team of representatives from the United Nations Development Programme, UNHCR, the Office for the Coordination of Humanitarian Affairs, the United Nations Children's Fund and the Office of the United Nations High Commissioner for Human Rights had been sent to the region to assess basic humanitarian needs in the Presevo Valley area.

Addressing the Council, the FRY representative said his Government had recently adopted a three-phase plan for resolving the crisis in the Bujanovac, Presevo and Medvedja municipalities. Also known as the Covic Plan, it included the establishment of the State sovereignty and territorial integrity of Serbia and FRY in that part of their territory, the preservation and development of the region's multi-ethnic character, respect for all civil and human rights of the ethnic Albanian community, protection of the basic interests of Serbs and of their personal property and security, and the building of a multi-ethnic democratic society, with the viable economic development of the three municipalities. In the first phase, already under way, an appeal had been sent to the ethnic Albanian community to refrain from any terrorist acts during negotiations, with FRY's army and police undertaking only defensive activity. The second phase, to be preceded by the reduction or total elimination of the GSZ, would include the permanent cessation of all terrorist acts, the disarmament of terrorists and dismantling of fortifications, followed by the withdrawal of military and police forces; regular mixed local police and military units would remain. Those who had not taken part in violent action up to the end of the second phase would not be prosecuted.

In the third phase, full security and peace in the region would be established, enabling the ethnic Albanian community to be integrated into the political, State and social systems and to have their human rights respected. That integration would reflect the local ethnic composition in the State institutions, economy and social activity, entailing appropriate representation on the executive boards of municipalities and in the Government of Serbia, the elimination of all forms of human rights violations through more effective control of police and other government bodies and free access for accredited human rights organizations.

Communication. The EU, on 15 February [S/2001/153], welcomed the plan adopted by FRY and Serbia on 8 February, which had been presented to it by Serbia's Deputy Prime Minister Nebojsa Covic on 15 February as a comprehensive response to the crisis. The EU looked forward to the implementation by Serbia and FRY of measures to fully integrate the ethnic Albanian community as soon as possible, and expected the ethnic Albanian community in southern Serbia to designate representatives to engage in constructive dialogue with Serbia and FRY. That implied an immediate cessation of violence by armed extremist Albanian groups in the GSZ.

NATO decision

On 8 March [S/2001/214], the NATO Secretary-General informed the UN Secretary-General that, following the previous week's fact-finding mission to southern Serbia and visits of a NATO political-military team to Skopje, FYROM, the North Atlantic Council (NAC) had decided on a number of steps regarding the GSZ to be implemented in the near future, together with confidence-building measures, including a ceasefire to be agreed between FRY and Serbian and ethnic Albanian representatives, and the initiation of direct negotiations between the parties. NAC confirmed NATO's intention ultimately to abolish the GSZ, but reaffirmed that the KFOR Commander should retain authority over it and the air safety zone under the terms of the 1999 military-technical agreement [YUN 1999, p. 356]. As a first step in a phased and conditioned reduction of the GSZ, NAC authorized the Commander to allow the controlled return of FRY forces into the GSZ sector along Serbia's border with FYROM

(Sector C (East)). Further controlled return should continue rapidly thereafter along the northern boundary of Kosovo with Serbia proper (Sector A), including the strip of the FRY border with Albania (Sector C (West)). That part of the GSZ in the municipality of Medvedja (Sector D) could be released at the same time as Sector A or later.

Further returns of FRY/Serbian forces were authorized on 22 March [S/2001/267] to Sectors A and C (West) of the GSZ, subject to FRY's agreement to the specific conditions set by the KFOR Commander on 24 March; on 11 April [S/2001/360] to Sector D with effect from 12 April; and on 14 May [S/2001/497] to Sector B with effect from 24 May. The return to Sector B completed the phased and conditioned reduction of the GSZ. NAC also noted the FRY/Serbia proposals on key capacity-building measures contained in the "Outline of the Plan for the Joint Security Forces Entry into the GSZ Sector Bravo" and further assurances made by Serbia's Deputy Prime Minister in his letters of 4 and 13 May.

Ceasefire agreement

During the Security Council's meeting on 16 March [meeting 4296], the FRY representative informed the Council of the agreement on a ceasefire in the GSZ in southern Serbia and the agreement between FRY and KFOR on the entry of Yugoslav forces into that part of the GSZ bordering FYROM. FRY considered that conditions had been created for the full implementation of the Council's repeated requests to end the violence and to have armed Albanian groups disarmed, disbanded and withdrawn from the GSZ. Steps towards a gradual and complete elimination of the GSZ would contribute to a comprehensive implementation of the FRY/Serbia plan for a resolution of the crisis (see p. 346).

The Council, in statement **S/PRST/2001/8** (see p. 350) of the same date, welcomed the ceasefire agreement and called for strict compliance with its provisions. It also welcomed FRY's plan for southern Serbia and NATO's decision to authorize the controlled return of FRY forces to the GSZ.

Other developments

Communication. The EU, in a 22 May statement on the demobilization of ethnic Albanian armed groups in the Presevo Valley [S/2001/539], welcomed the commitment by representatives of ethnic Albanian armed groups to full demobilization in southern Serbia, signed on 21 May by UCPMB Commander Shefket Musliu. The EU urged all concerned to fully respect that commitment and to hand over their weapons to KFOR and return to civilian life. It encouraged FRY/Serbian authorities and ethnic Albanian representatives to continue talks to consolidate implementation of confidence-building measures, including the early establishment of a multi-ethnic police force.

UN Interim Administration Mission in Kosovo

The United Nations Interim Administration Mission in Kosovo, established in June 1999 [YUN 1999, p. 357], set up, for the purpose of executing its tasks, what were referred to as pillars, concerned with interim administration (led by the United Nations), institution-building (led by OSCE), economic reconstruction (led by the EU), humanitarian affairs (led by UNHCR), and police and justice (formally launched by the United Nations on 21 May). UNMIK was headed by the Special Representative of the Secretary-General, Hans Haekkerup (Denmark), who replaced Bernard Kouchner (France) on 13 January.

Upon assuming office, the new Special Representative laid out the following priorities for UNMIK: to establish a legal framework for provisional self-government in Kosovo as a precondition for the holding of Kosovo-wide elections; to develop further an effective law enforcement and judicial system; and to advance economic reconstruction. The Special Representative would foster regular dialogue with FRY and Serbia and open an UNMIK office in Belgrade to contribute to the implementation of those priorities. In addition, UNMIK continued to address a number of serious challenges related to the security of all Kosovo communities, to the ongoing struggle to establish durable and universal law and order, and to the preparation of joint administrative structures.

UNMIK's efforts were facilitated and advanced by the series of regulations that the Special Representative issued during the year. In that connection, the Secretary-General submitted to the Security Council in March [S/2001/218/Add.1] the texts of regulations 2000/62-69 and 2001/1-4 and, in October [S/2001/926/Add.1], those of regulations 2001/23 and 2001/24.

Security Council consideration (January, February, March). The Council met on 18 January and 13 February to consider the implementation of its resolutions relating to the situation in Kosovo. On 18 January [meeting 4258], the Under-Secretary-General for Peacekeeping Operations updated the Council on UNMIK's progress in discharging its priority tasks, as identified by the new Special Representative. He also briefed the Council on the return of Albanian Kosovars detained in FRY, the situation in the Presevo Valley and the problem of depleted uranium.

In a further briefing to the Council on 13 February [meeting 4277], the Under-Secretary-General reported that the elaboration of the key principles for discussions on the legal framework for a provisional self-government was in progress. When completed, UNMIK would begin consultations with local interlocutors and the international community on mechanisms for the transfer of governmental powers. OSCE estimated that preparations for province-wide elections would take eight months. Therefore, decisions on key elements of the legal framework had to be completed by April for elections to take place in 2001. Progress had already been made in updating voter lists. Meanwhile, UNMIK had begun to restructure the Joint Interim Administrative Structure (JIAS) to take account of the 2000 municipal election results [YUN 2000, p. 367] and to prepare for a smooth transition to a locally managed structure. In the continued implementation of those results, 18 of Kosovo's 30 municipalities had appointed their chief executive officers and seven had set up their boards of directors.

To enhance the rule of law, UNMIK had under consideration a more unified judicial, police and civil administration coordination structure. To improve the quality of the judiciary, it had begun assessing the performance of 400 local judges and prosecutors who had been urgently appointed when UNMIK started. On the police side, UNMIK established the Police Organized Crime Intelligence Unit and 3,138 cadets had graduated from the Kosovo Police Service School.

The democratic changes in FRY and Serbia proper [YUN 2000, p. 384] provided an opportunity for a more constructive relationship with Belgrade. In that regard, the establishment of an UNMIK office there to facilitate dialogue had been agreed in principle. Negotiations were continuing with FRY on detainees and missing persons from Kosovo, as well as on a prepared amnesty bill, which UNMIK said should be extended to all Kosovo Albanian detainees.

UNMIK was working to improve economic regulation and decrease Kosovo's economic isolation by encouraging direct foreign investment. Plans were being made to restore the viability of the Trepca industrial complex [YUN 2000, p. 377]. A number of policy issues were being considered, as well as issues of interim management, ownership and debt claims, environmental damage reconciliation, restructuring and worker retraining, and the establishment of appropriate mining laws.

As to security issues, recent demonstrations in south Mitrovica, sparked by the death of a Kosovo Albanian youth in a 29 January grenade attack, became the focus for protests by Kosovo Albanians wanting to show that they did not trust KFOR to provide them with the necessary security. While the protests drew little reaction from the Kosovo Serbs, threats against the Kosovo Albanian minority in north Mitrovica were reported. To defuse tensions, the Special Representative and the KFOR Commander visited Mitrovica to hold discussions with the local Albanian and Serb leaders. A joint declaration was signed by the Special Representative, the KFOR Commander, the Mitrovica Municipal Assembly and local political representatives, calling for enhanced security and expansion of the zone of confidence to ensure freedom of movement for residents, the return of displaced persons and the establishment of functioning political structures. However, representatives of all local Serb factions signed a statement of non-concurrence, arguing that the plan excluded Kosovo Serbs and that expansion of the zone of confidence was only for north Mitrovica.

Another security concern related to tension in the Presevo Valley and in southern Serbia (see p. 346). Besides an increase in attacks on Kosovo Serbs and their property in Prizren, Mitrovica, Gnjilane and Pristina, pressure on Kosovo Serbs to sell their property remained high, particularly in mixed municipalities. Dialogue had begun with FRY, Serbian and Kosovo Serb and Kosovo Albanian political and community leaders on the envisioned framework for Serb returns to Kosovo.

On the question of depleted uranium, a draft report on its effects, prepared by a World Health Organization assessment team, concluded that its threat to public health and the environment was minimal. It recommended an information campaign to encourage public reporting of discoveries of depleted-uranium rounds, improved medical health data and an effective information system on the health situation in Kosovo to help monitor all of its aspects, including with respect to depleted uranium.

On 6 March [meeting 4286], the Security Council held a private meeting with the participation of FRY's Prime Minister, Zoran Zizic, to exchange views on the Kosovo situation and on the implementation of resolution 1244(1999). In a statement to the press [A/56/2], the President said that Council members welcomed the Special Representative's ongoing efforts to implement fully resolution 1244(1999), including the development of an institutional framework for the provisional self-governing institutions of Kosovo. They called on all parties to support UNMIK in building a stable and multi-ethnic democracy in Kosovo and to ensure suitable conditions for Kosovo-wide elections for those institutions as soon as feasible, including through the registration of all habitual residents of Kosovo, the return of refugees and adequate security for all.

Council members also welcomed the continued improvement of relations between the FRY Government and UNMIK and KFOR, and supported the early opening of an UNMIK office in Belgrade. They stressed the importance of substantial dialogue between Kosovo political leaders and the FRY Government.

Council members called for an end to all acts of violence in Kosovo, in particular those ethnically motivated, and urged all Kosovo political leaders to condemn those acts and to increase efforts to create inter-ethnic tolerance. They welcomed the adoption of an amnesty law in FRY, and stressed the importance of the immediate release of all Kosovo Albanian prisoners held without charge or on political grounds as a confidence-building measure.

They further welcomed the efforts undertaken, in particular by the EU and NATO, to support FRY in solving the problems in southern Serbia (see p. 347).

Report of Secretary-General (March). The Secretary-General, reporting in March on UNMIK [S/2001/218], stated that the current political situation among Kosovo Albanians was characterized by tensions between the two major parties, the Democratic League of Kosovo (LDK), which had a majority in 24 municipalities, and the Democratic Party of Kosovo (PDK), which had a majority in three. Tensions arose from the two parties' inability to reach agreement on co-governance, highlighting the continuing mistrust between them. Nevertheless, they were united in their desire for Kosovo-wide elections in 2001 and in their condemnation of the most recent violence against Kosovo Serbs.

The Kosovo Serb community was likewise divided. The recent change of government in Belgrade [YUN 2000, p. 384] contributed to a further decrease in the influence of the Serb National Council–Gracanica in central Kosovo and of the Serb National Council in north Mitrovica. Although the former continued to participate in UNMIK's Kosovo-wide institutions, its standing among the Kosovo Serb community had diminished. On the other hand, particularly in the Mitrovica region, those forces associated with the Democratic Opposition of Serbia (DOS) had consolidated. Triggered by the violent events in Mitrovica in January and February (see p. 350), the positions of some Kosovo Serb leaders had hardened, with the creation of a self-styled "Committee for the Defence of Mitrovica". UNMIK had made an intense effort to re-engage Kosovo Serb leaders in the Mitrovica region on key issues affecting their communities.

To ensure the representative nature of the provincial institutions, UNMIK had been examining ways to reform JIAS.

Persistent instances of ethnically and politically motivated violence continued to pose a threat to the fulfilment of UNMIK's mandate. In late January and early February, violent protests by the Kosovo Albanian population in south Mitrovica resulted in the burning of KFOR and UNMIK police vehicles. To put an end to the demonstrations, UNMIK and KFOR persuaded Kosovo Albanian leaders to sign a joint declaration and plan of action. In Prizren and Pristina, violence between Kosovo Serbs and Kosovo Albanians was on the rise. On 24 January, in Velika Hoca, near Orahovac municipality (Prizren region), six Kosovo Serb–owned houses were damaged by mortar fire. In early February, several attacks on Kosovo Serb homes and churches occurred, including an explosion that destroyed an Orthodox church west of Gnjilane on 7 February, as well as a number of attacks against Kosovo Serb houses, many of them potential dwellings for Kosovo Serb returnees, and cultural sites in the Gnjilane, Prizren and Pristina regions. A spate of more serious attacks targeting Kosovo Serbs occurred in mid-February, the worst being the 16 February attack near Podujevo on a KFOR-escorted convoy of civilian buses en route from Nis in Serbia proper to Gracanica near Pristina [S/2001/145].

Further Security Council consideration. At a 16 March Security Council meeting [meeting 4296], which had before it the Secretary-General's March report, the Special Representative stated that, in order to accelerate the process of defining a legal framework, he had established on 6 March a working group of international and Kosovar legal experts, including representatives of the major ethnic groups, to elaborate the structure of the future institutions of provisional self-government in Kosovo. The group would indicate clearly those powers and competencies to be transferred and those to remain under his control, but would not address the question of sovereignty. Nor would the legal framework address or in any way prejudge the final political settlement on Kosovo's status. The Special Representative regretted the withdrawal of the group's Kosovo Serb member.

The Special Representative further reported that FRY's Parliament had passed an amnesty law, covering, however, only a small number of the Kosovo Albanian detainees, of whom close to 500 remained imprisoned in Serbia. He called on Belgrade to transfer all detainees to UNMIK for a review of their cases according to international standards. To further the normalization process, the Special Representative said two clear messages from Belgrade were needed: one to the Kosovo Albanians, that Belgrade's new democratic Government was prepared to take the steps necessary to normalize relations between it and Pristina; and another to the Kosovo Serbs, that their future lay in Kosovo and that they should therefore participate in the structures established to govern the area.

According to the Special Representative, extremist actions in FYROM (see p. 368) were destabilizing the situation in the region. Although the problem was an internal one, it was important for KFOR and UNMIK to support FYROM in its efforts to solve it, including sealing off the border.

The Special Representative stated later in the meeting that he would welcome a visit by the Security Council to Kosovo, which should help in addressing the implementation of resolution 1244(1999).

SECURITY COUNCIL ACTION

On 16 March [meeting 4298], following consultations among Security Council members, the President made statement **S/PRST/2001/8** on behalf of the Council:

> The Security Council welcomes the briefing by the Special Representative of the Secretary-General on progress in the implementation of its resolution 1244(1999) of 10 June 1999.
>
> The Council commends the Special Representative of the Secretary-General and the commander of the Kosovo Force for their ongoing efforts to implement fully resolution 1244(1999), undertaken under difficult circumstances, and welcomes the priority areas of work identified by the Special Representative of the Secretary-General.
>
> The Council welcomes the establishment of a working group under the authority of the Special Representative of the Secretary-General aimed at developing a legal framework for provisional institutions for democratic and autonomous self-government in Kosovo and stresses the need for all ethnic groups to be represented in the work of this group. It underlines the need to keep the Government of the Federal Republic of Yugoslavia informed on the process. It calls on all parties to support the efforts of the United Nations Mission in Kosovo to build a stable multi-ethnic democratic society in Kosovo and to ensure suitable conditions for Kosovo-wide elections. It stresses the importance of a number of steps being taken for the holding of these elections: the establishment of the legal framework, in particular the definition of the functions and powers of the elected bodies; the development of an integrated voter registry which should include the refugees and internally displaced persons; full involvement of all the communities in the ballot; and a high security environment for the voting.
>
> The Council welcomes close contact between the Government of the Federal Republic of Yugoslavia

and the Mission and the international security presence, in particular the steps taken towards the opening of a Mission office in Belgrade, which will facilitate these consultations. It stresses the importance of substantial dialogue between Kosovo political leaders and the Government of the Federal Republic of Yugoslavia.

The Council calls for an end to all acts of violence in Kosovo, in particular those which are ethnically motivated and urges all political leaders in Kosovo to condemn these acts and to increase their efforts to create inter-ethnic tolerance. It reiterates the importance of resolving the problem of the missing and detainees and notes that this would be a major confidence-building measure. It welcomes the initial steps taken by the Government of the Federal Republic of Yugoslavia in this regard.

The Council remains concerned about the security situation in certain municipalities in southern Serbia as a result of the violent actions of ethnic Albanian armed groups. It welcomes the ceasefire agreements signed on 12 March 2001 and calls for strict compliance with their provisions. It stresses that a peaceful settlement of this crisis can only be achieved through substantial dialogue. It commends the continued restraint of the authorities of the Federal Republic of Yugoslavia and Serbia. The Security Council welcomes the plan of the Government of the Federal Republic of Yugoslavia for southern Serbia and supports its initiative to find a peaceful and durable solution through a process of dialogue and confidence-building measures. It expresses the opinion that the swift implementation of confidence-building measures would be an important element in a peaceful settlement, and underlines the importance of continued political and financial support for this process by the international community.

The Council welcomes the decision taken by the North Atlantic Treaty Organization to authorize the commander of the international security presence to allow the controlled return of forces of the Federal Republic of Yugoslavia to the Ground Safety Zone as defined in the military-technical agreement signed in Kumanovo on 9 June 1999, referred to in annex II of resolution 1244(1999), as a first step in a phased and conditioned reduction of the Ground Safety Zone.

The Council reiterates its strong support for the former Yugoslav Republic of Macedonia as set out in the statement of its President of 7 March 2001. It strongly condemns the continuing extremist violence in parts of the former Yugoslav Republic of Macedonia, supported from outside the country, which constitutes a threat to the stability and security of the entire region, and underlines the importance of maintaining the territorial integrity of the former Yugoslav Republic of Macedonia and all other States in the region. It supports efforts by the Government of the former Yugoslav Republic of Macedonia to cooperate with the North Atlantic Treaty Organization and other international organizations to end this violence in a manner consistent with the rule of law.

The Security Council will remain actively seized of the matter.

Communications. On 19 April [S/2001/382], FRY reported that, the previous day, a bomb activated by remote control went off in front of the offices of the Committee of the Yugoslav Government for Cooperation with UNMIK in Pristina, killing one person and wounding three others. On the same date [S/2001/386], the FRY President, Vojislav Kostunica, expressed his exasperation over the incident, which, he said, was further evidence of the extremely poor security situation in Kosovo, particularly affecting the few remaining non-Albanians, and of the failure of UNMIK and KFOR to fulfil their tasks in accordance with Security Council resolution 1244(1999). He recalled that at his 30 March meeting with the Secretary-General, he had pointed out the escalation of terrorism among Albanian extremists, who had been reinforced and, to all appearances, encouraged or at least incited by insufficient UNMIK and KFOR measures.

Serbia's National Assembly, by a 4 May resolution [S/2001/443], stated that, two years after the establishment of civil and security presences, the security situation in Kosovo and Metohija was becoming increasingly serious. The return of expelled persons was more uncertain than ever, and the daily life of the remaining Serbs and other non-Albanians was uncertain and risky. International representatives were working more for the adoption of regulations on interim self-governance than on ensuring the population's safety and security. The National Assembly demanded that UNMIK conduct an investigation within a month into the fate of all abducted and missing persons and inform their families as well as the public about the results. It appealed to all international human rights institutions to intensify their efforts to ascertain the fate of 1,300 abducted and missing Serbs and other non-Albanians.

The establishment of customs points at the administrative boundary of Kosovo and Metohija with central Serbia caused added concern and violated resolution 1244(1999) (see p. 363). The Assembly fully supported the population's resistance to that gross breach of Yugoslav customs laws and Serbia's tax legislation.

Moreover, the basic text of the draft legal framework for provisional self-government for Kosovo, as prepared by UNMIK, did not provide even minimum guarantees for protecting the rights of Serbs and other non-Albanian communities. It was unacceptable to adopt any "legal framework for provisional self-government for Kosovo", or to contemplate the holding of elections, without the prior fulfilment of all obligations stemming from paragraph 9 of resolution 1244(1999), particularly those relating to the full demilitarization of the so-called Kosovo Liberation Army and other armed groups, as well as to the establishment of a safe environment in which displaced persons could return to their homes in conditions of full public safety and order.

The National Assembly demanded that the working group on the elaboration of the legal framework adopt Serbia's amendments ensuring the maintenance of a multi-ethnic Kosovo and Metohija within Serbia and FRY and guaranteeing the rights of ethnic communities, and the establishment of an interim system of consensual democracy in which national and ethnic differences were institutionally safeguarded.

Constitutional Framework for Provisional Self-Government

The Secretary-General, in his June report on UNMIK activities [S/2001/565], informed the Security Council that the joint working group constituted on 6 March had, over a nine-week period, elaborated a constitutional framework for Kosovo's provisional self-government. Represented in the group were the three ethnic Albanian political parties, a Kosovo Serb member and a Bosniac representing other minorities, in addition to a civil society representative, an independent expert and seven international members, including the chairman. The final document reflected the large measure of agreement reached in the group, including comprehensive provisions on the structure and powers of the legislature, the judiciary and the executive branch. Five issues on which there had been no agreement (the title of the document, the request for a directly elected President, a Constitutional Court, a referendum and a sunset clause spelling out the time period of provisional self-government) were resolved by the Special Representative, in consultation with the Secretary-General. On 16 May, the Special Representative signed into law Regulation 2001/9 on the Constitutional Framework for Provisional Self-Government and established, on 18 May, the Steering Group on Issues of Implementation of the Constitutional Framework to coordinate the efforts of five working groups dealing with implementation.

The Constitutional Framework provided for a 120-seat Assembly based on proportional representation, with the first 100 seats reserved for all registered parties and 10 seats each for Kosovo Serbs and other communities. A seven-member presidency of the Assembly would guide its work. The Assembly would elect a President, who in turn would nominate a Prime Minister. The Framework contained extensive safeguards for the protection of communities and human rights, including: an extensive list of guaranteed rights of communities and their members in such areas as language, education, employment, media and public services, with a reservation giving the Special Representative the power to intervene to protect those rights; strong human rights provisions, including one on the right of all refugees and displaced persons to return to their homes and to recover their property, and another requiring that competent institutions had to facilitate returns; the creation of a Committee on the Rights and Interests of Communities in the Assembly with guaranteed and equal representation of communities and special rights to review proposed legislation to ensure that the communities' rights and interests were adequately addressed and to enable the Special Representative strictly to monitor the legislative process; guaranteed set-aside seats for Kosovo Serbs and other communities in the Assembly to ensure adequate representation, as well as guaranteed representation of all communities in the Assembly presidency and other bodies, including main and functional committees; full control and authority by the Special Representative over the judiciary, including the power to determine the assignment of international judges and prosecutors to cases so as to ensure the fair administration of justice, particularly in sensitive cases involving communities; and broad authority for the Special Representative to intervene and correct any actions of the provisional institutions of self-government that were inconsistent with resolution 1244(1999), including the power to veto Assembly legislation where necessary.

The Framework also provided for the following mechanisms to address Kosovo Serb concerns: a procedure enabling the Assembly's community members to object to legislation they felt violated their "vital interests" and to initiate a special process to avoid adoption of legislation without prior scrutiny by a panel in which a representative of the Special Representative and a community representative would have a majority; a requirement that the Ombudsperson give priority to allegations of discrimination against communities and their members and allegations of violations of community rights; preambular language reaffirming the commitment to the safe return of refugees and displaced persons and to freedom of movement; and preambular language stressing the importance of a free, safe and open political environment for members of the communities.

The Secretary-General said that key to the success of the Constitutional Framework was local acceptance of the document. In the main, reactions to its signing among Kosovo Albanian members of the Interim Administrative Council were encouraging. Ibrahim Rugova and Ramush Haradinaj, leaders of LDK and the Alliance for the Future of Kosovo, respectively, expressed their support for the document, despite the exclusion of certain key requests that they intended to pursue. However, the PDK president, Hashim Thaci, said the document would hold hostage the aim of Kosovo's people, which was political independence. According to local media reports, the FRY authorities and the Kosovo Serbs considered the Framework "unacceptable". On 14 May, the Special Representative appeared on local television to announce the promulgation of the Constitutional Framework and 17 November as the date for Kosovo-wide elections.

Communications. The EU, on 16 May [S/2001/538], welcomed the promulgation of the Constitutional Framework and the announcement of a date for elections. The EU urged all individuals and communities to participate in the elections and to refrain from violence in the process leading to them.

FRY, on 5 June [S/2001/563], informed the Security Council that, while it supported the establishment of provisional institutions of self-government and was ready to cooperate fully with the United Nations, UNMIK and the Special Representative, it had serious concerns and reservations regarding the Constitutional Framework and the holding of general elections, stressing that certain of the Framework's elements disregarded the principle of respect for FRY's territorial integrity and sovereignty. In particular, it omitted any express reference to Kosovo and Metohija as being part of FRY and Serbia—an unacceptable omission; the term "constitutional" in the title implied that the document was a constitution of a State, which it was not nor could it be; references to "the people of Kosovo" could neither bear nor imply any connection with the notion of "peoples" or the principle of "equal rights and self-determination of peoples" as contained in the UN Charter or in the Declaration on Principles of International Law concerning Friendly Relations and Cooperation among States in accordance with the Charter of the UN, adopted by General Assembly resolution 2625(XXV) [YUN 1970, p. 789]; and the provisions on the President of Kosovo and Metohija and his/her responsibilities "in the field of external relations", as well as the related provisions concerning certain responsibilities of provisional institutions, were contrary to the letter and the spirit of resolution 1244(1999). As a part of FRY and Serbia, Kosovo and Metohija was represented in international relations by the FRY Government, or by the Special Representative to the extent allowed under

that resolution. The reference to "the will of the people" in the Framework's preamble had to be interpreted without prejudice to the respect for the principle of sovereignty and territorial integrity and should be understood as including the will of all citizens of Serbia and FRY, expressed directly or through their elected representatives.

In addition, the Framework did not contain sufficient institutional guarantees for the protection of rights and interests of national communities. It was premature to transfer judicial responsibilities to provisional institutions of self-government, since conditions for a truly independent and impartial judiciary did not exist; therefore, judicial affairs should have remained within the reserved powers of the Special Representative. Also, any reference to the Kosovo Protection Corps [YUN 2000, p. 364] was unacceptable.

FRY emphasized its support in principle for the elections, provided the conditions necessary for the holding of truly all-inclusive, free and fair elections existed well before the election date.

Report of Secretary-General (June). Reporting on the political situation in his June report on UNMIK [S/2001/565], the Secretary-General said that the political engagement of the Kosovo Serb community remained a major challenge for UNMIK, rendered more difficult by the branding of the Constitutional Framework as "unacceptable" by FRY authorities and by the continuing divisions within the community itself. In the Mitrovica region, the self-styled Political Committee for the Defence of Kosovska Mitrovica, formed in February, had gained influence, with radical Kosovo Serb leaders seizing on the issue of UNMIK tax collection points along the northern administrative boundary line (see p. 363) to further harden the stance of the Kosovo Serb community in the region. The ensuing roadblocks and the linkage made between the tax collection points and the Constitutional Framework made progress on the issues in the divided city of Mitrovica and on Kosovo Serb cooperation with UNMIK very difficult. Faced with those difficulties, UNMIK made efforts to re-engage Kosovo Serb leaders in the Mitrovica region and to encourage FRY to use its influence in that regard. To that end, the Secretary-General met with FRY President Kostunica in New York on 8 May, resulting in some recent positive indications, including encouragement by FRY authorities of Kosovo Serb participation in civil registration and an agreement on tax collection points.

Continuing instances of ethnically and politically motivated violence, as well as organized crime, remained of great concern. Tensions in the Mitrovica, Gnjilane and Pristina regions had increased, as had targeted attacks on specific individuals, particularly of the Kosovo Serb community. There was a severe limitation on freedom of movement as a result of the temporary suspension of UNHCR-operated bus lines and the interruption of train services. The single most disturbing and extreme act of violence was the 18 April bomb attack in the centre of Pristina (see p. 351). Kosovo Albanian leaders were swift to condemn that attack, reflecting their relatively recent readiness to condemn such terrorist acts. Violence against the international community was on the rise. Openly aggressive behaviour towards law enforcement and security personnel had become commonplace, taking the form of threats and assaults against members of the Kosovo Police Service, UNMIK police and KFOR. On 11 April, a Russian KFOR soldier was fatally shot in the Kamenica area.

The Mitrovica region continued to be a focal point for violence and civil disobedience within the Kosovo Serb community. Following the arrest by UNMIK police of three Kosovo Serbs on 14 March, the level of violence escalated, resulting in the injury of 21 UNMIK police officers and damage to seven police vehicles and several houses. UNMIK police temporarily suspended patrols in northern Mitrovica, resuming them in early May with KFOR assistance. The blockades of critical road junctions in the largely Kosovo Serb–controlled northern municipalities of Leposavic, Zubin Potok, Zvecan and north Mitrovica from mid-April to early May further exacerbated the situation in the region. On 24 May, the Special Representative promulgated regulation 2001/10 on the prohibition of unauthorized border/boundary crossings, making crossing at locations other than at authorized border or boundary crossings a criminal offence.

In an effort to minimize the effect on Kosovo of the instability in the region, UNMIK fostered close cooperation with neighbouring States. In that context, the Special Representative met with Albanian representatives on 15 and 16 April and again on 16 May, as well as with FYROM authorities on 7 May.

An outbreak of inter-ethnic violence in FYROM and the resulting month-long closure of its border with Kosovo until 3 April adversely affected the political and security situation in Kosovo and severely limited UNMIK's freedom of movement and the delivery of essential supplies.

Although UNMIK was concerned over the phased re-entry into the GSZ of the joint Yugoslav forces, particularly the last phased re-entry into sector B effective 24 May (see p. 347), all phased redeployments went smoothly. Under consideration were programmes for the social rehabilitation of former UCPMB fighters to avoid further

activity should they remain unemployed. To reduce the possibility of their becoming engaged in the ongoing conflict in FYROM, KFOR was also increasing its efforts at the border with that country.

Communication. In an 8 June press release [S/2001/601], the Russian Federation stated that, since the adoption of resolution 1244(1999), the overall situation in Kosovo had remained tense. Despite the massive international presence there, an unacceptably high level of violence persisted, and ethnic Albanian extremists and separatists continued to intimidate and force out Serbs and other non-Albanians, and persisted in aggravating the situation in southern Serbia and FYROM.

UNMIK and KFOR efforts to ensure safe living conditions for all communities and to achieve stability had so far failed to bring about the expected results. The UNMIK leadership had taken decisions and actions without properly clearing them with the Yugoslav leadership; it neither took full account of the lawful interests of the Serb and other Kosovo communities, nor respected FRY's sovereignty and territorial integrity, in particular the promulgation by UNMIK's head of the Constitutional Framework for Provisional Self-Government in Kosovo and his announcement of the holding of province-wide elections in November.

The Russian Federation was convinced that the Kosovo problem could be settled only on the basis of the strict and full implementation of resolution 1244(1999); it intended to do everything possible to contribute to that goal.

Security Council mission

A Security Council mission on the implementation of resolution 1244(1999) visited Kosovo, FRY, from 16 to 18 June [S/2001/600]. Organized pursuant to the Council's 15 May decision [S/2001/482], the mission was to: find ways to enhance support for the implementation of the resolution; observe the situation on the ground and UNMIK's operations, including the difficult challenges facing it; look at the impact of the regional situation on UNMIK's work; convey a strong message to local leaders and all others concerned about the need to reject all violence, ensure public safety and order, promote stability, safety and security, inter-ethnic reconciliation and inclusion, support the full and effective implementation of resolution 1244(1999) and fully cooperate with UNMIK to those ends; and review ongoing implementation of the prohibitions imposed by the Council in resolution 1160(1998) [YUN 1998, p. 369].

The mission comprised the Permanent Representatives to the United Nations of Bangladesh (head of mission), China, Colombia, France, Ireland, Jamaica, Mauritius, Norway, the Russian Federation, Tunisia, the United Kingdom and the United States, a Counsellor of Mali and Minister-Counsellors of Singapore and Ukraine.

The mission held discussions with: the Special Representative and other related UN, OSCE and EU officials; a representative group of Kosovo women; members of the Yugoslav Committee on Kosovo and the Kosovo Serb representative in the joint working group on the drafting of the Constitutional Framework; the UN regional administration in Mitrovica and, separately, Kosovo Albanian and Kosovo Serb representatives; the Russian Federation President, who was visiting the region; the KFOR Commander; and the FRY President, Foreign Minister and Interior Minister.

The mission found that, in the two years since its inception, UNMIK had made considerable progress in implementing resolution 1244(1999), although much remained to be done. At the current critical stage of its mandate, the continued effectiveness of UNMIK required a major effort on its part and by KFOR and UNMIK police, backed up by the Council and by a sustained input of resources from the international community.

While the mission was left in no doubt that strong reservations existed about the difficulties involved in advancing preparations for the Kosovo elections on the basis of the Constitutional Framework, it recognized that the status quo was unacceptable and that a political process had to be taken forward in accordance with resolution 1244(1999). In underscoring that elections would enhance the democratic process in Kosovo and the region's stability, the mission stressed that secure conditions for holding them should be ensured. The participation of all communities in the elections, as well as the return of refugees and displaced persons so that they might also participate, should be encouraged.

The mission supported UNMIK's efforts to create a multi-ethnic Kosovo and emphasized the need to remove current obstacles to it, such as inadequate physical, social and economic security, and lack of freedom of movement and equal access to public services. It welcomed the Special Representative's establishment of the new UNMIK police and justice pillar (see p. 348) and legislation to combat organized crime, illegal weapons possession and terrorism. It noted the consequent additional resources required for justice and policing, an Assistant Secretary-General position to head the new pillar, increasing the number of international judges and prosecutors and additional detention facilities. It

recommended that KFOR regularly provide detailed information on weapons seized so as to enable the Security Council Committee established pursuant to resolution 1160(1998) to pursue possible violations.

The mission also recommended that intensified efforts be exerted towards resolving the issue of missing and detained persons (see p. 351). It supported the development of a comprehensive strategy to resolve the complex situation in Mitrovica, and emphasized the need for multi-ethnic initiatives in the social, economic and religious areas to start rebuilding confidence between the communities.

The mission underlined the responsibility of the Kosovo leadership for creating conditions conducive to improving inter-communal relations and promoting reconciliation. It conveyed to all community leaders that the responsibility lay with them clearly and openly to reject violence, extremism and terrorism, and that the majority should ensure respect for the rights of the minority communities. It advised the Kosovo Albanian leadership to be more forthcoming with regard to improving the treatment of the minority communities. In turn, minority communities should realize that there was no alternative to establishing a multi-ethnic society. The mission acknowledged that those communities had legitimate grievances, which it urged UNMIK and KFOR to address, but believed that participation was the only viable future for all communities. The Kosovo Serb community, in particular, should integrate into the structures being set up by UNMIK, rather than attempt to set up parallel ones. UNMIK should enhance its dialogue with the FRY authorities, whose influence in Kosovo was key in the implementation of resolution 1244(1999). Further efforts to ensure full implementation of that resolution remained a high priority of the Council.

The mission's report was presented to the Council on 19 June [meeting 4331] and debated on 22 June [meeting 4335], during the Council's consideration of the Secretary-General's June report on UNMIK (see p. 353).

Further developments

Security Council consideration (July, August, September). The Security Council, at its meetings on 26 July [meeting 4350] and 28 August [meeting 4359] and a private meeting on 17 September [meeting 4373], continued to review the political and security developments in Kosovo and the effects on it of the security situation in FYROM.

At the July meeting, the Under-Secretary-General for Peacekeeping Operations informed the Council that, in terms of implementing the

Constitutional Framework, UNMIK was continuing to determine its provisions and to prepare for the transfer of authority after the elections. Specifically, UNMIK's focus was on the development of the institutions of the executive branch, as they were not spelled out in the Constitutional Framework, and on the support and oversight UNMIK was to provide to those institutions. Preparations for the transition had stressed the "Kosovarization" of senior management and the capacity-building of local staff in administration, procurement, market management policy, budget and finance.

The Under-Secretary-General also touched on relations with Belgrade, which, he said, continued to intensify. The appointment of Serbia's Deputy Prime Minister as the Coordinator for Kosovo added a new dimension to that relationship. Those relations were being complicated, however, by the increasingly direct activity of the authorities of FRY and Serbia in Kosovo, including attempts by the Federal Committee for Kosovo to establish its own executive functions and business registration activities in Kosovo, as well as the opening of regional offices without UNMIK consent. An additional complicating factor was the humanitarian convoy organized on 14 July by the Kosovo Albanian party, PDK.

In his briefing of the Council at the August meeting, the Under-Secretary-General said that UNMIK was finalizing the structure of the institutions of provisional self-government, in which the JIAS departments would be streamlined into a more manageable number of government ministries. To build political consensus on the future structures, the Special Representative consulted the local leadership, who had expressed support for the streamlining. Along with preparations at the central level, the consolidation of municipal structures continued, with further efforts to devolve authority to municipalities. He informed the Council that relations with Belgrade had improved. A step forward was the 15 August meeting between the Special Representative, the KFOR Commander and Serbia's Deputy Prime Minister, at which the Special Representative reiterated the need to implement resolution 1244(1999) in all of Kosovo and to ensure that no parallel security and administrative structures were in place, especially in Mitrovica and northern Kosovo. UNMIK was currently exploring administrative ways to improve working relations with FRY's Joint Coordination Centre for Kosovo. In keeping with the parties' agreement to meet regularly, they held another meeting near Pristina on 21 August.

At the private meeting on 17 September, the Council was briefed by Serbia's Deputy Prime Minister, who was also head of FRY's Coordination Centre for Kosovo. He expressed concern about the continuing violence in Kosovo, the very small number of displaced persons returning to the province and the certification of extremist parties. He appealed for cooperation between UNMIK and FRY authorities along the lines of the cooperation developed between KFOR and Yugoslav authorities in the GSZ (see p. 347).

Communication. On 25 July [S/2001/740], the FRY Foreign Minister, in a letter addressed to the Special Representative, complained that the "Guidelines for visits of government officials and political entity representatives from the Federal Republic of Yugoslavia" to Kosovo, adopted by UNMIK and conveyed to him on 17 July, were likely to impede rather than facilitate visits of government officials and political party representatives. The formalities required, including conditions for approval and periods for the submission of requests for visits, contained serious restrictions that implied relations between sovereign States, which were clearly inappropriate for visits by individuals from the rest of FRY to Kosovo and Metohija, an integral part of FRY and its constituent Republic of Serbia. Those measures were not conducive to fruitful cooperation with the international community. The Foreign Minister asked the Special Representative to reconsider the Guidelines, and expressed FRY's readiness to settle that and other matters by an agreement on cooperation with, and on the status of, UNMIK.

Report of Secretary-General (October). In his October report on UNMIK [S/2001/926], the Secretary-General noted that, despite PDK's initial reticence in respect of the Constitutional Framework, all major Kosovo Albanian political forces appeared to have lent their support to important political and security initiatives and crucial legislation to combat terrorism and organized crime.

On the sensitive issue of the Framework for Return of Kosovo Serbs, the stated preference of the Kosovo Albanian members of the Interim Administrative Council was for that return process to start after the November elections. In public statements, however, they acknowledged the role of the Kosovo Serb community in Kosovo's future, marking a significant departure from the previously held position of the main political parties. They moreover joined UNMIK in calling on the Kosovo Serb community to register and participate in the November elections and agreed that special measures had to be taken to protect the Kosovo Serb community and guarantee its presence in Kosovo.

The political engagement of the Kosovo Serb communities was an ongoing challenge, as their political entities continued to look to Belgrade for sponsorship and direction. The communities remained divided and reluctant to participate in the administrative structures. Progress in incorporating minority communities in the municipal assemblies and related structures was mixed, although recent advances were noted, particularly the assumption of seats in the Pristina Municipal Assembly by three Kosovo Serb appointees.

Ethnically motivated violence against Kosovo minority communities continued, including an increase in the number of attacks at the beginning of August and of September. Nevertheless, freedom of movement of minority communities incrementally improved, following UNMIK's full assumption of operational responsibility for the bus lines, hitherto sponsored by UNHCR, and for the "freedom of movement" trains between key Kosovo communities. The number of incidents involving the use of weapons remained alarming. UNMIK and KFOR continued to eliminate unauthorized weapons in Kosovo and, in a Kosovo-wide operation, KFOR continued to confiscate weapons and seek out suspected members of armed groups. Following a number of apparently politically motivated criminal incidents, including the attempted assassination of an LDK politician in Srbica (Mitrovica region), UNMIK reestablished the Political Violence Task Force to coordinate response to any such future attempts.

UNMIK worked with KFOR to reduce the impact on FYROM of ethnic Albanian armed groups operating from Kosovo and to sever possible ties between radical elements in Kosovo and the so-called National Liberation Army operating in FYROM (see p. 372). More than 1,200 people had been detained and processed under regulation 2001/10 on the prohibition of unauthorized border/boundary crossings. KFOR reported no evidence of any involvement of the Kosovo Protection Corps in FYROM. UNHCR estimated that 26,000 refugees from FYROM remained in Kosovo as at 30 September, mainly in the Gnjilane region. UNMIK was increasingly concerned about the potential impact on inter-ethnic relations of ethnic Albanian refugees from FYROM taking up residence in Kosovo. It feared that the presence of those refugees in the Gnjilane and Prizren regions, where the majority were interspersed among mixed and minority communities, could affect areas being considered for minority returns.

Substantial progress had been made in the preparations for the transfer of authority to the institutions of provisional self-government. On 13 September, the Special Representative promulgated regulation 2001/19 on the Executive Branch, setting out the functions and competencies of the ministries of the provisional self-government. Work was under way to streamline the 20 JIAS departments into 10 ministries, covering the executive functions listed in chapter 5 of the Constitutional Framework. The regulation also defined the functions and responsibilities of the senior civil service of the provisional institutions of self-government and laid out general principles for its establishment, including a requirement that its composition should generally reflect the participation of Kosovo's various communities in the Assembly.

UNMIK continued preparations for the elections to the Kosovo Assembly. Voter and civil registrations were conducted from 30 July to 22 September. New Kosovo Albanian registrants totalled 23,940, while new minority community registrants (mainly Kosovo Serbs) totalled 69,349. In Serbia proper, 98,380 people registered, and 5,873 in Montenegro. Mail-in registration applications numbered 58,456. The institution-building pillar estimated that over 170,000 new registrants from non-Albanian Kosovo communities had registered, some 150,000 of whom were Kosovo Serbs.

To encourage participation of all communities in the electoral process and in the ensuing institutions of provisional self-government, the institution-building pillar established a special task group with five mobile teams to reach out to Kosovo Serbs and communities of internally displaced persons currently living in and outside Kosovo. A call on Kosovo Serbs to register by FRY's President and by Serbia's Prime Minister at the end of August gave momentum to the process, triggering an average daily registration of 3,000 to 4,000 Kosovo Serbs.

Between 22 June and 20 July, 33 political entities applied for certification, of which 25 had so far been certified by the Central Election Commission. An estimated 12,000 to 14,000 candidates were expected to run for office. The Commission had adopted electoral rules covering the role of municipal election commissions, the status of observers during the electoral process, the issue of candidate registration and equitable media access for political entities. The Commission had also determined that one third of the candidates in the first two thirds of the registration list should be women. The institution-building pillar re-established the Political Party Consultative Forum, which had proved effective in disseminating election information for the 2000 municipal elections [YUN 2000, p. 367]. OSCE continued its educational project, "Voters' voices", to hear voters' concerns about Kosovo-wide issues.

SECURITY COUNCIL ACTION (October)

On 5 October [meeting 4388], following consultations among Security Council members, the President made statement **S/PRST/2001/27** on behalf of the Council:

The Security Council welcomes the report of the Secretary-General and commends the Special Representative of the Secretary-General and the commander of the international security presence (KFOR) for their ongoing efforts to implement fully resolution 1244(1999).

The Council welcomes the elections to be held on 17 November as a basis for the establishment of democratic self-governing institutions as specified in the Constitutional Framework for Provisional Self-Government, under which the people of Kosovo, Federal Republic of Yugoslavia, will enjoy substantial autonomy in accordance with resolution 1244 (1999). It emphasizes the responsibility of Kosovo's elected leaders to respect fully the final status provisions of resolution 1244(1999). It reaffirms its commitment to the full implementation of resolution 1244(1999), which remains the basis for building Kosovo's future.

The Council supports the continuing efforts by the United Nations Mission in Kosovo and KFOR to improve public security, including through the confiscation of weapons and the package of legislation to combat violence, and to facilitate the return of displaced Serbs and members of other communities. It calls on Kosovo Albanian leaders to actively support these efforts to promote security and return, and to combat extremism, including terrorist activities. It further calls on all Kosovo leaders to publicly condemn violence and ethnic intolerance. It calls on them to exert all their influence and assume their responsibility for actively ensuring that the campaign and the elections are peaceful, democratic and inclusive. It stresses the need for proper organization and adequate security for the elections on 17 November, and welcomes continuing steps taken in that regard.

The Council calls on all women and men of Kosovo to vote in the elections of 17 November. This will provide for the broadest possible representation of views in the institutions of the provisional self-government. The Council commends the authorities of the Federal Republic of Yugoslavia, particularly President Kostunica, for their encouragement to the Kosovo Serb community to register, which confirms the multi-ethnic character of Kosovo, and calls on them to also actively encourage the fullest possible participation in the vote. It underlines the importance, for the Kosovo Serb community, to integrate in the structures set up by the Mission. It encourages the further development of a constructive dialogue between UNMIK and the authorities of the Federal Republic of Yugoslavia.

The Security Council will remain actively seized of the matter.

Communications. FRY's President, in a 6 November letter [S/2001/1051], drew the Secretary-General's attention to the FRY-UNMIK joint document known as the Common Document, signed the previous day, defining issues and cooperation between FRY and UNMIK for the consistent and comprehensive implementation of resolution 1244(1999). The President noted that the Document included agreement on provisions related to the judiciary and to the police in the Serb-majority areas, without which the Document would not have been complete. The President said he was convinced that implementation of the Document, together with the establishment of the related high-ranking working group, would ensure better communication and open institutional cooperation between UNMIK, FRY and Serbia to resolve accumulated problems in Kosovo and Metohija, in compliance with resolution 1244(1999) and FRY's territorial integrity and sovereignty. He also referred to his and Serbia's call on Kosovo Serbs to take part in the 17 November elections, which he believed was in their best interest.

In a 6 November statement [S/2001/1081], the EU welcomed the 3 November call on Kosovo Serbs to participate in the 17 November elections and the signing on 5 November of the UNMIK-FRY joint document.

SECURITY COUNCIL ACTION (November)

On 9 November [meeting 4409], following consultations among Security Council members, the President made statement **S/PRST/2001/34** on behalf of the Council:

The Security Council welcomes the progress made in preparing the Kosovo-wide elections on 17 November 2001 and calls on the Special Representative of the Secretary-General and all parties concerned to continue to strive for full implementation of resolution 1244(1999) of 10 June 1999. It further calls upon all women and men of Kosovo, Federal Republic of Yugoslavia, to vote.

The Council welcomes the helpful role played by the President of the Federal Republic of Yugoslavia and the Governments of the Federal Republic of Yugoslavia and the Republic of Serbia in recommending Kosovo Serb participation in the elections. Participation will allow them to take part in shaping Kosovo's multi-ethnic future.

The Council welcomes the signing on 5 November 2001 of the UNMIK-FRY Common Document by the Special Representative of the Secretary-General and the Special Representative of the President of the Federal Republic of Yugoslavia and the Government of the Federal Republic of Yugoslavia and the Government of the Republic of Serbia. This document is consistent with resolution 1244(1999) and the Constitutional Framework for Provisional Self-Government in Kosovo.

The Council reaffirms the statement of its President of 5 October 2001. It encourages the further development of a constructive dialogue between the United Nations Interim Administration Mission in Kosovo and the authorities of the Federal Republic of Yugoslavia. It emphasizes the responsibility of the provisional institutions of self-government and all concerned to respect fully the final status provisions of resolution 1244(1999). It underlines its continued commitment to the full implementation of resolution 1244(1999), which remains the basis for building Kosovo's future.

Transitional arrangements

The Special Representative, reporting to the Security Council on 5 October [meeting 4387], said that UNMIK was moving into a determining phase of interim administration in Kosovo. After the November elections, its role of direct administrative responsibility would evolve into one of oversight. UNMIK would transfer many of its interim administrative responsibilities to the provisional institutions of self-government, but would continue closely to monitor and support those institutions to ensure compliance with resolution 1244(1999), the Constitutional Framework and other relevant UNMIK regulations. During that period, its overarching mandate would remain the same, as would the Special Representative's ultimate authority.

In accordance with UNMIK regulation 2001/19, ten ministries would compose the Executive Branch of the provisional self-government (see p. 357). One of the ministers would come from the Kosovo Serb community and one from the non-Albanian community. To lay the groundwork for the transfer of responsibility to the ministries, the JIAS departments were merged into transitional administrative departments, whose composition reflected the distribution of responsibilities set out in regulation 2001/19. From 3 October until the certification of the general elections, UNMIK would continue to consolidate the transitional administrative departments, while preparing for their separation into provisional self-government ministries and reserved UNMIK structures. Also on 3 October, the function of "Co-heads" ceased and all Co-heads were given leave with pay until 17 November.

As part of the transition, the Kosovo Transitional Council concluded its activities on 2 October, but the Interim Administrative Council would continue to operate until the date of the transfer of powers to the provisional institutions. Functional responsibility for the administration of Kosovo would be divided between UNMIK and the provisional institutions of self-government. The transfer once made, the UNMIK structures and the provisional institutions of self-government would become separate and distinct entities. The future Assembly, however, would be able to pass legislation only within the transferred areas of responsibility.

The Executive Branch would consist of the Office of the Prime Minister and the Ministries of Finance and Economy; Trade and Industry; Education, Science and Technology; Culture, Youth and Sports; Health, Environment and Spatial Planning; Labour and Social Welfare; Transport and Communications; Public Services; and Agriculture, Forestry and Rural Development. The Ministers would be political appointees selected by the Prime Minister and confirmed by the Assembly. They would be responsible for setting policy and political direction for the Ministries but would not exercise direct administrative control over them. The Ministers would be assisted by up to five political appointees, one or more of whom would serve as a Vice-Minister, to whom the Minister could delegate authority in the latter's absence. Although most structures associated with JIAS would be absorbed into the Ministries, some, such as law enforcement, the judiciary and emergency preparedness, would remain under UNMIK's immediate control.

International staff members would be placed in the reserved and transferred structures. In the former, they would implement reserved functions, in line with resolution 1244(1999) and chapter 8 of the Constitutional Framework. In addition, a number of international staff members would be seconded to the provisional institutions of self-government, mostly to the Ministries, to oversee and monitor compliance with resolution 1244(1999), the Constitutional Framework and key UNMIK regulations. To that end, a senior international officer would sit next to each Minister to oversee, monitor and advise the Minister.

Other international staff members would sit in actual line management positions within the Ministry, where they would implement certain transferred functions for a limited time under the authority of the local Minister. They would gradually exchange their functional responsibilities for a purely advisory and oversight role as additional qualified Kosovo civil servants were identified and recruited.

Although there would be a clear functional and organizational separation between UNMIK and the provisional institutions of self-government, procedures would be in place to ensure that the Assembly and the Government fully respected resolution 1244(1999) and the Constitutional Framework for Provisional Self-Government.

Kosovo-wide elections

The Assistant Secretary-General for Peacekeeping Operations, in his briefing of the Security Council on 27 November [meeting 4430], said that the period leading up to the elections was relatively calm and free of violence. All parties carried out rallies throughout Kosovo that were peaceful and that largely adhered to the electoral rules.

Eligible voters totalled 1,250,318 (1,108,787 in Kosovo, 105,159 in Serbia and Montenegro and 36,372 by mail), of whom an estimated 150,000 were Kosovo Serbs. More than 1,300 candidates from 26 political parties contested the elections, including 60 from the Kosovo Serb Return Coalition. The signing of the UNMIK-FRY Common Document (see p. 358) largely made it possible for that Coalition to decide to participate in the elections and to provide its list of candidates. FRY's and Serbia's 3 November endorsement of Kosovo Serb participation in the elections also helped. At the same time, it was agreed that a memorandum of understanding would be signed with the respective commissariats for refugees, enabling UNMIK's OSCE-led institution-building pillar to carry out technical preparations for the elections in Serbia and Montenegro in conjunction with the International Organization for Migration (IOM).

The election for the Assembly went smoothly. There were 13,286 local observers from all communities, as well as several hundred others from the Belgrade-based Centre for Free Elections and Democracy. The overall turnout was 64.3 per cent of Kosovo's 1.25 million registered voters, with an estimated 65 per cent in primarily Kosovo Albanian areas and about 46 per cent in non-Albanian areas. Kosovo Serb participation was patchy, with a higher turnout in the enclaves than in northern Mitrovica.

On 24 November, the Special Representative certified the final results of the vote as follows: the Democratic League of Kosovo (LDK) received 45.65 per cent (359,851 votes); the Democratic Party of Kosovo (PDK), 25.7 per cent (202,622 votes); the Return Coalition, 11.34 per cent (89,388 votes); and the Alliance for the Future of Kosovo (AAK), 7.83 per cent (61,688 votes).

Seven smaller political parties, including three from the minority communities, received enough votes to obtain one seat each in the Assembly: the VATAN Coalition, a coalition of Bosniacs and Gorani; the National Movement for the Liberation of Kosovo (LKCK); the Turkish People's Party of Kosovo (KDTP); the Christian Democratic Party of Kosovo (PSHDK); the Justice Party (PD); the People's Movement of Kosovo (LPK); and the New Democratic Initiative of Kosovo (IRDK), a new Egyptian political party.

On the basis of those results, 14 parties would be represented in the Assembly, 11 through direct elections and 3 with set-aside seats. LDK would be allocated 47 seats; PDK 26; the Return Coalition 22, which included the 10 seats set aside for the Kosovo Serb community in the Constitutional Framework; AAK 8; VATAN 4, including 3 set-aside seats; KDTP 3, including 2 set-aside seats; the Ashkali Albanian Democratic Party 2 set-aside seats; IRDK 2, including 1 set-aside seat; LKCK 1; LPK and PD 1; PSHDK 1; and 1 set-aside each for the United Roma Party of Kosovo and the Bosniac Party of Democratic Action of Kosovo.

The Assistant Secretary-General said it was clear from the results that no party would be able to govern alone, since 61 seats in the Assembly were required for a majority. Negotiations had therefore begun on coalition-building.

The Council, in a 19 November press statement by its President [S/2002/160], welcomed the 17 November elections, which were held in peaceful and orderly conditions and with a good turnout of all communities. It was an important step in the implementation of resolution 1244(1999) and would make possible the establishment of democratic institutions of self-government. The Council recalled the responsibility of Kosovo's elected leaders to respect that resolution fully, in particular its final status provisions, and to comply with the Constitutional Framework, which would contribute to building a democratic, pluralist and prosperous future for all of Kosovo's communities.

Establishment of provisional institutions of self-government

In a later report on UNMIK [S/2002/62], the Secretary-General stated that, since no party gained enough seats in the Assembly to govern alone, attention was focused on forming a coalition. The main efforts concentrated on a power-sharing arrangement between the three main Kosovo Albanian parties. On 7 December, UNMIK arranged a meeting between Mr. Rugova, leader of LDK, and Mr. Thaci, leader of PDK. Representatives of foreign Governments also hosted meetings with the main party representatives in the Assembly.

On 10 December, the Assembly held its inaugural session, at which both the seven-member presidency of the Assembly and the President of Kosovo were to be elected; the latter would then nominate a Prime Minister for endorsement by the Assembly. However, PDK did not submit candidates for the two presidency seats reserved for it, and the Assembly elected only its President, Nexhet Daci of LDK, and four other members (one from LDK, two from the Kosovo Serb Return Coalition and one from the United Roma Party). On 13 December, the Assembly met again to elect the President of Kosovo. The only candidate was

Mr. Rugova, who received 49 votes—well short of the 80 votes required.

The Secretary-General also reported that security and freedom of movement for Kosovo minority communities remained a serious concern. On 1 December, KFOR and UNMIK police launched the largest simultaneous weapons search operation, involving 3,000 soldiers from all five multinational brigades, which resulted in the arrest of 12 people and the seizure of an assorted range of weaponry.

Sectoral developments

Kosovo minority communities

The number of persons returning to Kosovo continued to decline. In January, IOM assisted some 430 persons to return voluntarily, while the UNMIK border police reported that some 530 persons had been forcibly returned. The Framework on Return of Kosovo Serbs, adopted in January by the Joint Committee on Returns of Kosovo Serbs in Gracanica, outlined measures for establishing conditions conducive to safe and sustainable return, such as the provision of basic services and effective policing. Consultations on the Framework had begun with Kosovo Albanian political and community leaders, as well as with human rights activists, religious leaders and journalists. To further create conditions conducive to returns, the Joint Committee adopted an action plan for the 10 most advanced potential return locations in Kosovo, which was set in motion by local working groups. The first organized returns began on a small scale, with the voluntary return on 13 August of 53 Kosovo Serbs to the Osojane Valley (Pec region), one of the 10 sites identified in the action plan, followed by the return of 30 more internally displaced persons on 22 August. More returns to Osojane followed and more were expected. Mixed returns began at the end of August in the Leshtar area near Kamenica (Gnjilane region). UNHCR, with funding from the European Agency for Reconstruction and bilateral donors, was providing temporary shelter and basic needs while the returnees reconstructed their houses. Work also continued to facilitate the potential return of members of the Kosovo Roma, Ashkali and Egyptian communities.

However, the non-Albanian communities, particularly the Kosovo Serbs, continued to suffer disproportionately from major crimes and ethnically motivated acts of intimidation, eroding the confidence of minority communities and undermining the Special Representative's efforts to include all of Kosovo's inhabitants in the current administrative structures and in the future self-government. Some progress was made in incorporating Kosovo minority communities at the municipal level. Most Kosovo Turks, Roma, Ashkali, Egyptians and Bosniacs had taken up their reserved seats in the municipal assemblies and had been generally accepted by their Kosovo Albanian colleagues. The participation of Kosovo Serbs, however, had been uneven at best.

To coordinate UNMIK's approach towards engaging the Kosovo Serb community, several priority initiatives were being pursued to address that community's day-to-day concerns, including the allocation of revenues from taxes collected in Kosovo to minority communities; the implementation of employment-generating projects; improved public services and utilities; integration of the 24 local community offices as part of the local administration structure to ensure equal access to public services; and the provision of more educational and health facilities, as well as social welfare benefits. In addition, the OSCE-led institution-building pillar had established the Small Investment Minorities Fund for particularly vulnerable minority groups, which focused on income-generating projects or projects related to health, education and culture.

Multi-ethnic capacity-building was also promoted through the Kosovo Police Service, where 15 per cent of the cadets were from minority communities. In addition, Kosovo Albanians and Kosovo Serbs were cooperating in fire and rescue services and in demining activities. At the end of April, the first two Kosovo Serbs, alongside two Kosovo Turks, were inducted into the Kosovo Protection Corps.

A major advance on the issue of missing persons was the establishment on 19 June of the UNMIK/FRY contact groups on missing persons and detainees, which had since met twice monthly in Pristina and Belgrade. Their work resulted in increased Kosovo Serb participation in the judicial system and support for the UNMIK recruitment campaign in Serbia proper for judges and prosecutors; the development of mechanisms to coordinate administrative and operational support for defence counsels, witnesses and family members; the assistance of Serbian forensic pathologists in the confirmation of post-mortem results; the production of a consolidated list of missing Kosovo Serbs and other minorities; and the development of protocols for joint verification and forensic teams and for the cross-boundary repatriation of identified remains. Another key development was the signing of a memorandum of understanding between UNMIK and the International Commission for Missing Persons on 24 July to begin the process of DNA testing to facilitate the identification of missing persons.

Investigations continued on a number of mass graves in Serbia proper, believed to contain the remains of Kosovo Albanians. UNMIK had been provided with some details on the graves' contents and on recent post-mortem findings.

Regarding the problem of Kosovo Albanian detainees in Serbia proper, discussions were in progress on the possible handing over of their cases to UNMIK for judicial review. Talks were also in progress with the Belgrade authorities about Kosovo Serb detainees in Kosovo, addressing concerns of bias, miscarriage of justice and security.

The main strategy to deal with education issues focused on building a sustainable Kosovo Serb education system, with full recognition of the structures under the Constitutional Framework and maintaining strong ties with educational reforms in Serbia. A delegation headed by the international joint head of the Department of Education visited Belgrade to discuss issues relating to Kosovo Serb schools, teachers' contracts and curricula. The core curriculum would allow the Kosovo Serb community to retain its special syllabus for general and vocational education. The language issue had also come close to a practicable solution: Albanian would be offered as an option in Kosovo Serb schools, but would not be compulsory.

Judicial system and rule of law

A major focus of UNMIK efforts was on improving the quality and functioning of the judiciary in Kosovo. The credentials and performance of current judges and prosecutors were undergoing rigorous assessment, while screening of prospective candidates continued. The institution-building pillar had begun taking steps towards the provision of advocacy and legal aid. A working group was set up to coordinate plans to systematize and expand legal aid and guarantee minority access to it. The problem of access to the judiciary was compounded by difficulties in recruiting non-Albanian Kosovo judges and prosecutors, especially in the light of security threats against those groups. The ombudsperson institution was fully operational and currently investigating cases pertaining to employment disputes, to violations of property rights, social rights and equal access to public services, and to discriminatory practices.

The institution-building pillar, UNMIK police and the Department of Justice were jointly endeavouring to bring the practices and procedures of the Kosovo law enforcement and judicial authorities in line with international human rights standards. It established a working group with the Department of Justice to implement the recommendations set out in its Six-month Review of the Criminal Justice System. A review of the criminal code, juvenile law and commercial legislation in Kosovo was under way. The Kosovo Law Centre was cooperating with the University of Pristina Law Faculty in the implementation of academic reform and development of the law curriculum.

The creation of the new police and justice pillar (see p. 348) coincided with robust measures by UNMIK to bolster the legislative basis for prosecuting serious crime, including terrorism and organized crime. On 24 May, the Special Representative signed regulation 2001/10 on the prohibition of unauthorized border/boundary crossings, which came into effect on 4 June, together with regulation 2001/7 on the authorization of possession of weapons in Kosovo, following a month-long amnesty. Other initiatives included the elaboration of legislation to combat terrorism, the creation of more robust mechanisms for detaining alleged criminals, and implementation of systems to make the criminal prosecution institutions more just.

Key to UNMIK efforts to improve the justice system were its activities, through the Prosecution Services and Court Administration (PSCA), to coordinate and implement local judiciary reform. Currently employed in local courts and other non-correctional judicial institutions were 325 local judges, with 51 prosecutors plus a further 617 lay judges and about 1,000 operational support staff. PSCA developed a comprehensive inspection system to ensure the judiciary's independence and impartiality. Administrative direction 2001/4, issued on 11 May, established the Judicial Inspection Unit to conduct inspections, audits and investigations within the judicial system.

On the legislative front, three key regulations were signed on measures against organized crime, on cooperative witnesses and on the protection of injured parties and witnesses in criminal proceedings. Work started on refurbishing a witness protection office; a witness protection director was appointed, who had begun developing a witness protection programme. Progress was also made in forming the Kosovo Organized Crime Bureau. On 25 August, regulation 2001/18 on the establishment of a detention review commission for extrajudicial detention based on executive orders was promulgated, providing a mechanism for the review of extrajudicial detentions based on such orders, additional procedural protection and enhanced transparency.

The Department of Justice continued its recruitment efforts to increase the number of international judicial personnel, currently comprising eight international judges and six international prosecutors. An additional four judges and four prosecutors were under recruitment and, in August, an international prosecutor was appointed to the Office of the Public Prosecutor.

To raise the quality of the domestic judicial system, the Kosovo Judicial and Prosecutorial Council began the first disciplinary hearings in mid-September against local judges and prosecutors, stemming from investigations by the Judicial Inspection Unit. Progress was also made in the selection of judges and prosecutors, establishment of codes of conduct, judicial evaluations and the bar examination.

A more complex prison infrastructure was developing: five detention centres and two prisons were in operation and housed 664 inmates. The quick-build detention facility project to provide an additional 200 beds was proceeding, together with the refurbishment of Dubrava prison, providing another 300 beds. The construction of a special secure unit at Dubrava prison for high-risk prisoners was nearing completion. The Department of Justice had also begun implementing basic programmes in education and vocational training in the Lipljan and Dubrava prisons. Two urgent priorities were the development of a parole and probation service and addressing the needs of mentally ill inmates.

Communication. On 26 April [S/2001/428], the EU issued a statement welcoming the decision by Serbia's Supreme Court to release 145 Kosovo Albanians of the so-called Djakova/Djakovica group, sentenced in May 2000 to prison terms of between seven and 13 years for acts of terrorism allegedly carried out during the NATO campaign in 1999. The EU expected Serbia to complete the review of the remaining cases as rapidly as possible in order to correct the injustices of the Milosevic era.

Economic reconstruction and development

Through the UNMIK economic reconstruction pillar, Kosovo's emergency reconstruction needs had been largely met, so that emphasis began shifting towards developing economic sustainability. International donors, led by the EU and its member States, the United States and Japan, continued to support Kosovo's development drive. The 2001 Kosovo consolidated budget sought 700 million deutsche mark (DM) in new commitments to fund public reconstruction and investment programme activity, of which some DM 381 million had been committed by the end of March.

Meanwhile, domestically generated revenue increased as tax collection improved. That was achieved through UNMIK's tax policy, notified to FRY in February, under which tax collection points were set up on 15 April along Kosovo's borders and boundary lines, where a 15 per cent sales tax was levied on all saleable goods (except wheat, flour, fruit and vegetables) and an excise tax on alcohol, cigarettes and fuel. A 10 per cent customs duty was also levied, except for goods originating in FYROM and the rest of FRY. Despite efforts to explain the legality and necessity of the tax collection points to the public, the Kosovo Serb population interpreted their emplacement as compromising FRY's sovereignty and Security Council resolution 1244(1999). At the end of May, FRY authorities, in a joint statement signed with UNMIK's economic reconstruction pillar, agreed to the tax collection points along the administrative boundary line in northern Kosovo. By October, 90 per cent of the official commercial traders were reporting to tax collection offices in Mitrovica, approaching the level of compliance in the rest of Kosovo. Businesses in northern Kosovo were also registering with UNMIK to pay tax. As part of the strategy for creating a sustainable tax system for Kosovo, a 15 per cent value added tax (VAT) on most goods and services to replace the previous sales tax of the same rate came into effect in July. As donor funding tapered off, VAT would become the main tax in Kosovo and was expected to support growth in the export sector.

In the private sector, efforts were made to attract investment and foster industry through commercialization projects. Some 58 commercialization tenders had been issued, for about half of which bids had been received. Extra investment had come into Kosovo as a result of the commercialization process. The economic reconstruction pillar made progress in creating a banking sector. The Banking and Payments Authority of Kosovo approved two new branches for the New Bank of Kosovo in Orahovac (Prizren region) and Djakovica (Pec region). On 1 September, the Micro Enterprise Bank opened a branch in the "Confidence Zone" in Mitrovica.

Progress was also made in the communications and transportation sectors. Under a project to upgrade the communications network, transmission links were restored in many municipalities. A new digital telephone exchange, with a capacity of 23,000 lines, was installed in Pristina and the extension of the mobile network was continuing. Improvements in the transportation and communications infrastructure had also facilitated economic development and interaction between the different areas. Pristina airport was undergoing expansion and improvement of services. The experimental Pristina-Pec passenger train service had become permanent and freight rail traffic between FYROM and Kosovo had been running with increased frequency and payload. Work was also ongoing to improve Kosovo's power supply.

UNMIK police

At the end of 2001, UNMIK's police strength stood at 4,465 from 24 countries, out of the 1999 authorized strength of 4,718 [YUN 1999, p. 360]. Its priorities remained to increase success in solving serious crimes, in particular ethnically and politically motivated crimes. Work continued to reduce non-critical policing functions to allow an increased concentration of resources on core police priorities. Greatly helping that effort was the entry into force on 25 April of legislation on the operation of security service providers, which would free up UNMIK police resources.

With the launching in May of the police and justice pillar, the UNMIK police and the Department of Judicial Affairs were realigned into a single structure. That structure, headed by a Deputy Special Representative, who assumed duty on 16 August, had as its objectives to: consolidate a law and order structure that was responsive to peacekeeping and peace-building objectives and contributed to the promotion of the rule of law institutions in Kosovo; maintain effective international control and oversight over police and justice activities during the transition period; increase the short-term impact of law and order efforts through enhanced coordination of information and work; enable effective police and judicial response against destabilizing serious criminal activity in Kosovo; and establish an unbiased judicial process through initial international participation and reform of the judicial system.

The police and justice pillar would oversee the planned expansion of the Kosovo Police Service (KPS) from the current target of 4,000 police officers to a total of 6,000 by the end of 2002. The focus of training activities would shift from basic training to more supervisory and special training, anticipating the handover strategy of supervisory responsibility by UNMIK police to the KPS officers.

Communications. On 16 March [S/2001/238], Zimbabwe, a police-contributing country to UN-MIK, informed the Security Council President that the United Kingdom had constrained Zimbabwe's efforts to deliver arms and ammunition to its civilian police in Kosovo, because British Airways, the only airline flying to Kosovo, refused to transport them. The reason given for the airline's refusal was that it was consistent with the British Government's current policies on the Government of Zimbabwe. Zimbabwe felt that UN peacekeeping operations should not be held

hostage to bilateral relations between Member States. It asked that the Secretary-General bring the matter to the attention of relevant UN authorities with a view to its speedy resolution.

The United Kingdom replied on 20 March [S/2001/260] that that was the first time it had heard of the matter. Its investigation revealed that British Airways, a private company totally independent of the British Government, had informed Zimbabwe of its inability to carry the equipment in question because of the United Kingdom embargo on arms exports to Zimbabwe and concerns over their transport across London, but had suggested alternative carriers. The United Kingdom said it was unlikely that its arms embargo would have applied in that case, and its Acting High Commissioner, when informed of the matter, had advised that it appeared to be a minor, practical problem and he was ready to find a solution if contacted. No subsequent contact was made by Zimbabwe's Foreign Ministry or police. The United Kingdom remained open to discussing the matter directly with the Zimbabwe authorities and in no way wished to obstruct Zimbabwe's participation in UNMIK.

UNMIK financing

In June, the General Assembly considered the Secretary-General's report on UNMIK financial performance for the period 10 June 1999 to 30 June 2000 [A/55/724], the proposed budget for UNMIK's maintenance for the period 1 July 2001 to 30 June 2002 and ACABQ's related observations and recommendations [A/55/874/Add.6]. On 14 June [meeting 103], the Assembly, on the recommendation of the Fifth Committee [A/55/663/Add.1], adopted **resolution 55/227 B** without vote [agenda item 133].

Financing of the United Nations Interim Administration Mission in Kosovo

The General Assembly,

Having considered the reports of the Secretary-General on the financing of the United Nations Interim Administration Mission in Kosovo and the related reports of the Advisory Committee on Administrative and Budgetary Questions,

Bearing in mind Security Council resolution 1244 (1999) of 10 June 1999 regarding the establishment of the United Nations Interim Administration Mission in Kosovo,

Recalling its resolution 53/241 of 28 July 1999 on the financing of the Mission and its subsequent resolutions thereon, the latest of which was resolution 55/227 A of 23 December 2000,

Acknowledging the complexity of the Mission,

Reaffirming the general principles underlying the financing of United Nations peacekeeping operations as stated in General Assembly resolutions 1874(S-IV) of 27 June 1963, 3101(XXVIII) of 11 December 1973 and 55/235 of 23 December 2000,

Noting with appreciation that voluntary contributions have been made to the Mission by certain Governments,

Mindful of the fact that it is essential to provide the Mission with the necessary financial resources to enable it to fulfil its responsibilities under the relevant resolution of the Security Council,

1. *Takes note* of the status of contributions to the United Nations Interim Administration Mission in Kosovo as at 30 April 2001, including the contributions outstanding in the amount of 202.4 million United States dollars, representing 24 per cent of the total assessed contributions from the inception of the Mission to the period ending 30 June 2001, notes that some 20 per cent of the Member States have paid their assessed contributions in full, and urges all other Member States concerned, in particular those in arrears, to ensure payment of their outstanding assessed contributions;

2. *Expresses its appreciation* to those Member States which have paid their assessed contributions in full;

3. *Expresses concern* about the financial situation with regard to peacekeeping activities, in particular as regards the reimbursements to troop contributors that bear additional burdens owing to overdue payments by Member States of their assessments;

4. *Urges* all other Member States to make every possible effort to ensure payment of their assessed contributions to the Mission in full and on time;

5. *Expresses concern* at the delay experienced by the Secretary-General in deploying and providing adequate resources to some recent peacekeeping missions, in particular those in Africa;

6. *Emphasizes* that all future and existing peacekeeping missions shall be given equal and non-discriminatory treatment in respect of financial and administrative arrangements;

7. *Also emphasizes* that all peacekeeping missions shall be provided with adequate resources for the effective and efficient discharge of their respective mandates;

8. *Reiterates its request* to the Secretary-General to make the fullest possible use of facilities and equipment at the United Nations Logistics Base at Brindisi, Italy, in order to minimize the costs of procurement for the Mission;

9. *Endorses* the conclusions and recommendations contained in the report of the Advisory Committee on Administrative and Budgetary Questions, in particular paragraph 9, and requests the Secretary-General to ensure their full implementation;

10. *Expresses concern* about the high level of unliquidated obligations in the Mission as at 30 June 2000;

11. *Requests* the Secretary-General to improve the timeliness and accuracy of the expenditure data for the Mission;

12. *Approves*, on an exceptional basis, the special arrangements for the Mission with regard to the application of article IV of the financial regulations of the United Nations, whereby appropriations required in respect of obligations owed to Governments providing formed units and/or logistic support to the Mission shall be retained beyond the period stipulated under financial regulations 4.3 and 4.4, as set out in the annex to the present resolution;

13. *Requests* the Secretary-General to take all necessary action to ensure that the Mission is administered with a maximum of efficiency and economy;

14. *Also requests* the Secretary-General, in order to reduce the cost of employing General Service staff, to continue efforts to recruit local staff for the Mission against General Service posts, commensurate with the requirements of the Mission;

15. *Decides* to appropriate the amount of 413,361,800 dollars gross (385,256,870 dollars net) for the maintenance of the Mission for the period from 1 July 2001 to 30 June 2002, inclusive of the amount of 12,098,009 dollars gross (10,617,193 dollars net) for the support account for peacekeeping operations and the amount of 1,263,791 dollars gross (1,134,877 dollars net) for the United Nations Logistics Base, to be apportioned among Member States in accordance with the levels set out in General Assembly resolution 55/235, as adjusted by the Assembly in its resolution 55/236 of 23 December 2000, the scale of assessments for the year 2001 to be applied against a portion thereof, that is, 206,680,900 dollars gross (192,628,435 dollars net), which is the amount pertaining to the period ending 31 December 2001, and the scale of assessments for the year 2002 to be applied against the balance, that is, 206,680,900 dollars gross (192,628,435 dollars net) for the period from 1 January to 30 June 2002;

16. *Decides also* that, in accordance with the provisions of its resolution 973(X) of 15 December 1955, there shall be set off against the apportionment among Member States, as provided for in paragraph 15 above, their respective share in the Tax Equalization Fund of the estimated staff assessment income of 28,104,930 dollars approved for the Mission for the period from 1 July 2001 to 30 June 2002;

17. *Decides further* that, for Member States that have fulfilled their financial obligations to the Mission, there shall be set off against the apportionment, as provided for in paragraph 15 above, their respective share of the unencumbered balance of 65,272,000 dollars gross (57,860,300 dollars net) in respect of the period ending 30 June 2000, in accordance with the composition of groups as set out in paragraphs 3 and 4 of General Assembly resolution 43/232 of 1 March 1989 and as adjusted by the Assembly in subsequent relevant resolutions and decisions for the ad hoc apportionment of peacekeeping appropriations, the latest of which were resolution 52/230 of 31 March 1998 and decisions 54/456 to 54/458 of 23 December 1999 for the period 1998-2000, and taking into account the scale of assessments for the year 2000, as set out in its resolutions 52/215 A of 22 December 1997 and 54/237 A of 23 December 1999;

18. *Decides* that, for Member States that have not fulfilled their financial obligations to the Mission, their share of the unencumbered balance of 65,272,000 dollars gross (57,860,300 dollars net) in respect of the period ending 30 June 2000 shall be set off against their outstanding obligations in accordance with the scheme set out in paragraph 17 above;

19. *Emphasizes* that no peacekeeping mission shall be financed by borrowing funds from other active peacekeeping missions;

20. *Encourages* the Secretary-General to continue to take additional measures to ensure the safety and secu-

rity of all personnel under the auspices of the United Nations participating in the Mission;

21. *Invites* voluntary contributions to the Mission in cash and in the form of services and supplies acceptable to the Secretary-General, to be administered, as appropriate, in accordance with the procedure and practices established by the General Assembly;

22. *Decides* to include in the provisional agenda of its fifty-sixth session the item entitled "Financing of the United Nations Interim Administration Mission in Kosovo".

ANNEX
Special arrangements with regard to the application of article IV of the financial regulations of the United Nations

1. At the end of the twelve-month period provided for in financial regulation 4.3, any unliquidated obligations of the financial period in question relating to goods supplied and services rendered by Governments for which claims have been received or which are covered by established reimbursement rates shall be transferred to accounts payable; such accounts shall remain recorded in the Special Account for the United Nations Interim Administration Mission in Kosovo until payment is effected.

2. In addition:

(a) Any other unliquidated obligations of the financial period in question owed to Governments for provision of goods and services rendered but not yet verified, as well as other obligations owed to Governments, for which claims have not yet been received shall remain valid for an additional period of four years following the end of the twelve-month period provided for in financial regulation 4.3;

(b) Claims received during this four-year period as well as approved verification reports shall be treated as provided for under paragraph 1 of the present annex, if appropriate;

(c) At the end of the additional four-year period, any unliquidated obligations shall be cancelled and the then remaining balance of any appropriations retained therefor shall be surrendered.

The Assembly further decided on 24 December that the item on UNMIK financing would remain for consideration during its resumed fifty-sixth (2002) session (**decision 56/464**) and that the Fifth Committee should consider the item at that session (**decision 56/458**).

International security presence (KFOR)

During the year, the Secretary-General submitted to the Security Council, in accordance with resolution 1244(1999) [YUN 1999, p. 353], reports on the activities of KFOR, also known as Operation Joint Guardian, covering the period 23 November 2000 to 31 October 2001 [S/2001/52, S/2001/205, S/2001/333, S/2001/465, S/2001/578, S/2001/707, S/2001/832, S/2001/910, S/2001/1002, S/2001/1131]. Two later reports covered activities during the remainder of the year [S/2002/122, S/2002/183]. As at 31 December, the force, which operated under NATO leadership, comprised 38,500 troops from all NATO countries, as well as from non-NATO countries.

KFOR continued to uncover and confiscate significant amounts of weapons, ammunition and explosives, ranging from rifles to rockets and mines, during search operations. As at December, the total number of weapons destroyed under the weapons destruction programme stood at 10,132. The programme, temporarily suspended to allow repairs to be made to the destruction facility, was scheduled to resume in January 2002. KFOR continued to support UNMIK in the restoration of law and order. From mid-April, KFOR had to deal with public disorder in Mitrovica and northern Kosovo, in reaction to the implementation of the UNMIK excise and sales tax collection policy (see p. 363). On 18 May, it carried out jointly with UNMIK a search operation in Pec that resulted in the arrest of 26 persons and the confiscation of large amounts of weapons, documents and computer hardware and software. KFOR forces continued to provide appropriate control of Kosovo's internal boundaries, external borders and recognized crossing points. In reinforcing its presence along the border with FYROM, KFOR interdicted the movement of personnel and weapons into and out of the northern part of FYROM and between Albania and Kosovo. At the end of August, KFOR established mobile weapons collection teams close to the border with FYROM to collect weapons and screen suspected members of the National Liberation Army.

On 17 August, the KFOR Commander signed temporary operating procedures with FRY setting conditions for future cooperation and coordination on ending the conflict in the GSZ, following the North Atlantic Council's decision on the relaxation of the Zone (see p. 347). KFOR also supported UNMIK and OSCE during the Kosovo-wide elections on 17 November.

KFOR continued to provide regular assistance on request to international organizations and non-governmental organizations (NGOs) throughout Kosovo and to provide framework security in support of UNMIK police operations targeting organized crime, prostitution and smuggling. In addition, it continued to support safe conditions for minority returns. On 9 May, the KFOR Commander promulgated a directive, "KFOR and KPC (Kosovo Protection Corps)—Partners for the Future", setting out guidelines for the future relationship between them.

Sanctions against FRY

On 14 June [S/2001/592], FRY requested the Security Council to terminate the prohibitions relating to the shipment of arms imposed against it by resolution 1160(1998) [YUN 1998, p. 369]. It said that, since all the reasons that had led to the imposition of the prohibitions specified in paragraph 8 of that resolution no longer existed, FRY expected a favourable review of its request.

On 6 September [S/2001/849], the Secretary-General informed the Council that, since the adoption of resolution 1160(1998), the political and security situation in the region had changed considerably. The new FRY authorities were cooperating constructively with the international community in efforts to bring peace and stability to the Balkan region. The Council, in statement S/PRST/2001/8 (see p. 350), had welcomed the close contact between FRY and UNMIK and KFOR and stressed the importance of dialogue between Kosovo political leaders and FRY. Accordingly, he believed that FRY had complied with the provisions of resolution 1160(1998); the Council might therefore wish to reconsider the prohibitions in paragraph 8 of that resolution.

SECURITY COUNCIL ACTION

On 10 September [meeting 4366], the Security Council unanimously adopted **resolution 1367 (2001)**, based on a draft [S/2001/854] prepared in consultations among Council members.

The Security Council,

Recalling its resolutions 1160(1998) of 31 March 1998, 1199(1998) of 23 September 1998 and 1203(1998) of 24 October 1998, and reaffirming, in particular, its resolutions 1244(1999) of 10 June 1999 and 1345(2001) of 21 March 2001,

Noting with satisfaction that the conditions listed in paragraph 16 *(a)* to *(e)* of its resolution 1160(1998) have been satisfied,

Noting, in that respect, the letter of the Secretary-General dated 6 September 2001,

Noting further the difficult security situation along Kosovo's administrative boundary and parts of the border of the Federal Republic of Yugoslavia and emphasizing the continuing authority of the Secretary-General's Special Representative as head of the international civil presence and of the Commander of the international security presence (KFOR) to restrict and strictly control the flow of arms into, within and out of Kosovo, pursuant to resolution 1244(1999),

Acting under Chapter VII of the Charter of the United Nations,

1. *Decides* to terminate the prohibitions established by paragraph 8 of resolution 1160(1998);

2. *Decides further* to dissolve the Committee established by paragraph 9 of resolution 1160(1998).

Sanctions Committee final report. In October, the Chairman of the Security Council Committee established pursuant to resolution 1160(1998) (Sanctions Committee) submitted a final report covering the Committee's activities from 1 January to 10 September 2001 [S/2001/931].

According to the report, the Committee had approved Bulgaria's request to export 2,000 tons per month of industrial explosives to several mining companies in FRY. Switzerland brought to the Committee's attention the case of an arms shipment to FRY reported in the Chinese press, stating that criminal proceedings had been conducted by the Geneva authorities and two persons were arrested on 13 July 2000 and charged. The Committee approved under the no-objection procedure a request by the United Kingdom to transfer demining equipment to humanitarian demining organizations working for UNMIK.

The Committee drew attention to the Council's mission to Kosovo in June (see p. 354) and its request that KFOR provide detailed information on weapons seized to enable the Committee to pursue any possible violations. The Secretary-General informed NATO's Secretary-General of that request but no such information had been provided to the Committee by 10 September.

The Committee received no reports on actual violations or alleged violations of sanctions measures from States and relevant regional and international organizations. It sought and received additional information on the case of violations under investigation by the Geneva authorities. Reports on the activities of KFOR and the Stabilization Force in Bosnia and Herzegovina contained no information on violations.

Other issues

Arrest of Slobodan Milosevic

The Secretary-General, in a press statement on 2 April [SG/SM/7761], said that the arrest of Slobodan Milosevic, former FRY President, was an important step in the healing process in the Balkans and commended the FRY authorities for that decisive action. The Secretary-General noted that the FRY authorities had an obligation to cooperate with the International Tribunal for the Former Yugoslavia (ICTY) and urged them immediately to discuss with the Tribunal how that cooperation could be extended.

In a press release issued on 28 June [SG/SM/7870], the Secretary-General welcomed the decision of the FRY authorities to transfer Mr. Milosevic to ICTY in The Hague, saying it was a victory for accountability over impunity. He hoped that that day would mark a true break with the past and the beginning of a new spirit of coexistence throughout the former Yugoslavia. (For further details, see PART FOUR, Chapter II.)

Relations with Montenegro

The European Council, at its meeting in Stockholm, Sweden (23-24 March) [S/2001/305], among its concluding statements, called on Montenegro and FRY/Serbian authorities to agree on new constitutional arrangements within the federal framework through an open and democratic process in order to contribute to stability in the region.

The EU, in a 23 April statement [S/2001/415], welcomed the orderly conduct of the 22 April parliamentary elections in Montenegro, FRY, and looked forward to the formation of a Government that would continue the path of democratic reform. The EU urged the new Montenegrin Government to resume dialogue with Belgrade without delay towards an agreed definition of federal relations. The successful outcome of that dialogue, which should exclude any unilateral action, would enable the EU to continue its political, economic and financial support to Montenegro.

Former Yugoslav Republic of Macedonia

The situation along the border of the FRY province of Kosovo with the former Yugoslav Republic of Macedonia (FYROM), which had been brought to the Security Council's attention in 2000 [YUN 2000, p. 384], escalated in 2001 as armed ethnic Albanian insurgent groups launched attacks on FYROM forces across the border. In the FYROM capital of Skopje, on 23 February [A/56/60- S/2001/234], FRY President Vojislav Kostunica and FYROM President Boris Trajkovski signed the "Agreement for the delineation of the borderline between the Republic of Macedonia and the Federal Republic of Yugoslavia" demarcating the border between their two countries.

The EU, in a 28 February statement of its Presidency [S/2001/203], urged all parties to respect the border demarcation agreement and reiterated its strong attachment to the principle of inviolability of borders, including FYROM's territorial integrity. It also expressed concern about the recent escalation of violence in the border region between FRY/Kosovo and FYROM, particularly in the village of Tanusevci.

The Tanusevci incident, involving the landmine and sniper killing of three FYROM soldiers, was reported to the Council by FYROM in a 4 March letter [S/2001/191], calling for an urgent Council meeting and KFOR action to clear the Kosovo border area near Tanusevci. FYROM's President, at a meeting that included the Prime Minister, the Speaker of the Parliament, the ambassadors of EU and NATO countries and OSCE representatives, also proposed that NATO and the EU support his request for immediate KFOR action, as well as public support for FYROM's self-defence and preservation of its territorial integrity and sovereignty. It was the intention of FYROM's Foreign Minister to present to the Council meeting an action plan for the cessation of violence and lasting stabilization on the Kosovo section of the border with FRY and to prevent a spillover of violence into FYROM.

Action plan

FYROM's Minister for Foreign Affairs, in briefing the Security Council on 7 March [meeting 4289], said that in the past few weeks, his country had been confronted with a serious problem caused by unidentified extremist militant groups stationed on its northern border, which had occupied the village of Tanusevci from where they had been continuously provoking armed incidents; on 4 March, three FYROM soldiers were killed.

The extremists had not put forth their demands or requests, and were holding the local Albanian population hostage, and, as the border belt with Kosovo was inhabited mostly by ethnic Albanians, they were also affecting the interethnic relations in FYROM. Tanusevci was a serious warning that the FYROM border area with Kosovo could be used constantly for provoking those kinds of incidents, thus threatening the peace, security and stability of FYROM and the entire region.

FYROM was undertaking numerous activities to find a peaceful solution in close cooperation with the international community, and had undertaken a measured security response to the provocations. KFOR activities in the initial stage were not as effective as necessary, thus causing additional problems for the operations of FYROM's security forces. However, those cooperation difficulties had been overcome.

To resolve the situation, the Government adopted an action plan to prevent a spillover of the conflict from both sides of the border. Specifically, the plan proposed full observance of Council resolution 1244(1999) [YUN 1999, p. 353]; the immediate establishment of a ground safety area along the entire Kosovo side of the FYROM-Yugoslav border by KFOR and willing countries; the undertaking of urgent actions by KFOR for strict compliance of the provisions related to the movement of military and paramilitary formations, arms shipments and a ban on the movement and gathering of larger groups in the ground safety zone; strengthening the coordination of activities between FYROM's armed forces and KFOR, disarming paramilitary extremist groups and bringing them to justice; and creating conditions for the return of the inhabitants of Tanusevci to their homes. The action plan also proposed that the FYROM Government strengthen the existing measures along the border and undertake additional ones to prevent a spillover of the conflict, especially by reinforcing police control with new border police units.

The seriousness of the problem and the timing of its occurrence demanded prompt preventive action, the Foreign Minister said. The Council should be aware that the incident in Tanusevci should be seen in the broader context of the Balkan region and its transformation into a peaceful, stable, democratic and prosperous European region. He called on the Council to support the measures proposed so as to reaffirm the preconditions for a peaceful and democratic development of the Balkans, with inviolable, stable and transparent borders.

SECURITY COUNCIL ACTION

On 7 March [meeting 4290], following consultations among Security Council members, the President made statement **S/PRST/2001/7** on behalf of the Council:

The Security Council welcomes the participation of the Foreign Minister of the former Yugoslav Republic of Macedonia in its meeting on 7 March 2001 and carefully listened to him.

The Council strongly condemns recent violence by ethnic Albanian armed extremists in the north of the former Yugoslav Republic of Macedonia, in particular the killing of three soldiers of the armed forces of the former Yugoslav Republic of Macedonia in the area of Tanusevci. The Council regrets that the violence continues and calls for an immediate end to it.

The Council expresses its deep concern at those events, which constitute a threat to the stability and security not only of the former Yugoslav Republic of Macedonia but also of the entire region. It calls on all political leaders in the former Yugoslav Republic of Macedonia and Kosovo, Federal Republic of Yugoslavia, who are in a position to do so to isolate the forces behind the violent incidents and to shoulder their responsibility for peace and stability in the region.

The Council underlines the responsibility of the Government of the former Yugoslav Republic of Macedonia for the rule of law in its territory. It supports actions by the Government of the former Yugoslav Republic of Macedonia to address the violence with an appropriate level of restraint and to preserve the political stability of the country and foster harmony between all ethnic components of the population.

The Council recalls the need to respect the sovereignty and territorial integrity of the former Yugoslav Republic of Macedonia. In this context it emphasizes that the border demarcation agreement, signed in Skopje on 23 February 2001, and ratified by the Parliament of the former Yugoslav Republic of Macedonia on 1 March 2001, must be respected by all.

The Council welcomes the steps taken by the international security presence (KFOR) to control the border between Kosovo, Federal Republic of Yugoslavia, and the former Yugoslav Republic of Macedonia in accordance with the military-technical agreement signed in Kumanovo on 9 June 1999. It welcomes the ongoing dialogue between the Government of the former Yugoslav Republic of Macedonia and KFOR on practical steps to address the immediate security situation and to prevent crossing of the border by extremists as well as possible violations of resolution 1160(1998) of 31 March 1998. It welcomes the efforts of all relevant international organizations in cooperation with the Government of the former Yugoslav Republic of Macedonia to promote stability and to create conditions for a return of the inhabitants to their homes.

The Council will continue to follow the developments on the ground closely, and requests to be briefed regularly on the outcome of the efforts referred to above.

EU communications. On 8 March [S/2001/211], Sweden transmitted to the Secretary-General a declaration by the EU Presidency condemning the ethnic Albanian extremist attacks on 4 March near Tanusevci and calling for such acts to stop immediately. It also called on all FYROM political leaders to isolate the forces behind such attacks and shoulder their responsibility for peace and stability in the region. The EU reiterated its strong attachment to the principle of the inviolability of borders, including FYROM's territorial integrity and sovereignty.

In a further statement issued on 9 March [S/2001/217], the EU said that its Political and Security Committee had discussed FYROM's action plan for ending the violence and ensuring lasting stability on its border with FRY, and supported its policy of restraint, while preserving the country's political stability and fostering harmony and cooperation among all ethnic groups. It called on all neighbouring countries and international organizations active in the area to examine what support they could provide. The EU underlined the role played by KFOR, the EU and its monitoring mission, as well as the OSCE Spillover Monitor Mission to Skopje, especially in monitoring along FYROM's border.

NATO action. On 8 March [S/2001/214], the NATO Secretary-General informed the UN Secretary-General that, following a fact-finding mission by his Personal Representative, as well as visits of a NATO political-military team to Skopje, the North Atlantic Council (NAC) had, on the same day, taken a number of decisions concerning the ground safety zone in southern Serbia (see p. 347) and FYROM. Concerning FYROM, NAC welcomed the recent measures taken by the KFOR Commander, but charged its military authorities with identifying additional measures to enhance security along the FYROM border with Kosovo, FRY. NAC was also considering the findings of the Advisory Mission on Border Security, which recently returned from Skopje, as well as further bilateral and multilateral assistance to the Government. It promised to further study ways of showing political support to the FYROM Government, in the light of the recommendations by NATO's Deputy Assistant Secretary-General for Political Affairs, who recently visited Skopje. NAC would also meet with FYROM's Foreign Minister on 9 March, at his request, during which it hoped to address FYROM's concerns and to encourage continuation of its measured response to the situation at its northern border.

Security Council consideration. The Security Council, in statement **S/PRST/2001/8** of 16 March on Kosovo (see p. 350), reiterated its strong support for FYROM, as expressed by the Council President in his statement on 7 March (see p. 369). It condemned the continuing extremist violence and supported FYROM's efforts to cooperate with NATO and other international organizations to end that violence.

Communications. On 20 March [S/2001/251], FYROM transmitted to the Secretary-General the conclusions of its Assembly following discussion of the current security situation from 16 to 18 March. The Assembly, noting the deteriorating security situation, said that FYROM's authorities, its Assembly, Government and defence-security structures would undertake adequate measures to secure peace and stability in the country and the security of all its citizens, as well as urgent measures to impede further escalation of the situation. It appealed to international organizations to continue their unconditional support for FYROM in preserving its stability, territorial integrity and sovereignty, and to provide that assistance without the presence of military forces from neighbouring countries on its territory. It called on all political parties to refrain from any destructive scenarios and to direct their activities to the service of the State and to peace, stability and democracy. It condemned the statements made in support of violence. The Assembly also asked for KFOR's greater presence and strong engagement along the whole stretch of the northern border and indicated its intention immediately to intensify the broad political dialogue through its institutions with all relevant political bodies in the country to facilitate the settlement of all problems.

Albania's Foreign Minister, in a 20 March statement [S/2001/249] issued in his capacity as Chairman-in-Office of the South-East European Cooperation Process, expressed concern about developments in FYROM and reaffirmed his full support for the safeguard of that country's sovereignty and territorial integrity. He appreciated the self-restraint of the FYROM Government and the constructive attitude of all Albanian political parties in dealing with the crisis, and encouraged them to advance ethnic coexistence through institutional solution of the existing problems. The Chairman-in-Office demanded the immediate cessation of the armed actions, stating that any legitimate demand of the Albanian community should be resolved peacefully and democratically.

SECURITY COUNCIL ACTION

On 21 March [meeting 4301], the Security Council unanimously adopted **resolution 1345(2001)**, based on a draft [S/2001/256] prepared in consultations among Council members.

The Security Council,

Recalling its resolutions 1160(1998) of 31 March 1998, 1199(1998) of 23 September 1998, 1203(1998) of 24 October 1998, 1239(1999) of 14 May 1999 and 1244 (1999) of 10 June 1999 and the statements by its President of 19 December 2000 (S/PRST/2000/40), 7 March 2001 (S/PRST/2001/7) and 16 March 2001 (S/PRST/2001/8),

Welcoming the steps taken by the Government of the former Yugoslav Republic of Macedonia to consolidate a multi-ethnic society within its borders, and expressing its full support for the further development of this process,

Also welcoming the plan put forward by the Government of the Federal Republic of Yugoslavia to resolve peacefully the crisis in certain municipalities in southern Serbia, and expressing encouragement for the implementation of political and economic reforms designed to reintegrate the ethnic Albanian population as full members of civil society,

Welcoming international efforts, including those of the United Nations Interim Administration Mission in Kosovo, the international security presence in Kosovo (KFOR), the European Union, the North Atlantic Treaty Organization, and the Organization for Security and Cooperation in Europe in cooperation with the Governments of the former Yugoslav Republic of Macedonia, the Federal Republic of Yugoslavia and other States, to prevent the escalation of ethnic tensions in the area,

Further welcoming the contribution of the European Union to a peaceful solution to the problems in certain municipalities in southern Serbia, its decision substantially to increase the presence of the European Union Monitoring Mission there on the basis of its existing mandate, and its wider contribution to the region,

W*elcoming* the cooperation between the North Atlantic Treaty Organization and the authorities of the former Yugoslav Republic of Macedonia and the Federal Republic of Yugoslavia in addressing the security problems in parts of the former Yugoslav Republic of Macedonia and certain municipalities in southern Serbia,

1. *Strongly condemns* extremist violence, including terrorist activities, in certain parts of the former Yugoslav Republic of Macedonia and certain municipalities in southern Serbia, Federal Republic of Yugoslavia, and notes that such violence has support from ethnic Albanian extremists outside these areas and constitutes a threat to the security and stability of the wider region;

2. *Reaffirms* its commitment to the sovereignty and territorial integrity of the Federal Republic of Yugoslavia, the former Yugoslav Republic of Macedonia and the other States of the region, as set out in the Helsinki Final Act;

3. *Reiterates* its strong support for the full implementation of resolution 1244(1999);

4. *Demands* that all those who are currently engaged in armed action against the authorities of those States immediately cease all such actions, lay down their weapons and return to their homes;

5. *Supports* the Government of the former Yugoslav Republic of Macedonia and the Federal Republic of Yugoslavia in their efforts to end the violence in a manner consistent with the rule of law;

6. *Underlines* the need for all differences to be resolved by dialogue among all legitimate parties;

7 *Further underlines* the requirement for all parties to act with restraint and full respect for international humanitarian law and human rights;

8. *Welcomes* the efforts of the Government of Albania to promote peace in the region and isolate extremists working against peace, and encourages it and all States to take all possible concrete steps to prevent support for extremists, taking also into account resolution 1160(1998);

9. *Calls upon* Kosovo Albanian political leaders, and leaders of the ethnic Albanian communities in the former Yugoslav Republic of Macedonia, southern Serbia and elsewhere, publicly to condemn violence and ethnic intolerance and to use their influence to secure peace, and calls upon all those who have contact with the extremist armed groups to make clear that they have no support from any quarter in the international community;

10. *Welcomes* the efforts of KFOR to implement resolution 1244(1999) in cooperation with the authorities of the former Yugoslav Republic of Macedonia and the Federal Republic of Yugoslavia, and calls upon KFOR to continue further to strengthen its efforts to prevent unauthorized movement and illegal arms shipments across borders and boundaries in the region, to confiscate weapons within Kosovo, Federal Republic of Yugoslavia, and to continue to keep the Council informed in accordance with resolution 1160(1998);

11. *Calls upon* States and appropriate international organizations to consider how they can best give practical help to efforts in the region further to strengthen democratic, multi-ethnic societies in the interests of all and to assist the return of displaced persons in the areas in question;

12. *Calls upon* all States in the region to respect each other's territorial integrity and to cooperate on measures that foster stability and promote regional political and economic cooperation in accordance with the Charter of the United Nations, the basic principles of the Organization for Security and Cooperation in Europe and the Stability Pact for South-East Europe;

13. *Decides* to monitor developments on the ground carefully and remain actively seized of the matter.

EU communications. The EU, in a 3 May statement [S/2001/442], condemned the renewed acts of violence by ethnic Albanian extremists in FYROM's northern region, including the killing of two soldiers, the occupation of several villages and the taking of hostages. It called on the extremists to stop the violence, release the hostages and withdraw immediately. The EU supported the inter-ethnic dialogue recently launched by FYROM authorities and urged ethnic Albanian leaders in Kosovo, FRY, and Albania's political leaders to condemn unambiguously those acts of terrorism and to use their influence to prevent violence.

On 11 May [S/2001/498], the EU welcomed the agreement on a broad coalition Government in FYROM, expressed hope that the new Government would serve as a solid platform for handling the hard political decisions that lay ahead and assured it of EU support in that difficult task.

In a further statement issued on 26 July [S/2001/751], the EU condemned the violation of the ceasefire in FYROM and appealed for its restoration. It enjoined the parties to relaunch negotiations and to show a spirit of compromise. It reiterated its support for a new mission to Skopje by the EU High Representative (the EU President), who would be accompanied by the NATO Secretary-General and the OSCE Chairman-in-Office.

Framework Agreement

On 13 August, President Boris Trajkovski of FYROM and the leaders of the country's four main political parties signed the "Framework Agreement in the former Yugoslav Republic of Macedonia".

The Agreement laid out the principles basic to a modern democratic FYROM: the rejection of the use of violence to pursue political aims; the preservation of the State's sovereignty and territorial integrity and the multi-ethnic character of its society; the evolution of its Constitution so as to meet citizens' needs and conform with international standards; and the development of local self-government.

The Agreement provided for: the cessation of hostilities, an unconditional ceasefire, the voluntary disarmament and disbandment of ethnic Albanian armed groups, and the parties' acceptance of those conditions under which NATO would operate in the country; the development of a decentralized Government; non-discrimination and equal treatment for all, to be embodied in laws, particularly those regulating employment in public administration; special parliamentary procedures for the adoption of legislation; the Macedonian language as the country's official language and in international relations, with specific rules on the use of other native languages, in addition to Macedonian, in education and in units of local self-government; rules regarding the expression of identity in terms of State and local emblems; and timetables for the implementation of the constitutional amendments (within 45 days of the Agreement's signature), the legislative modifications and confidence-building measures, contained in annexes A, B and C, respectively, to the Agreement.

On the date of the Agreement's signature, the EU issued a statement [S/2001/802] welcoming the event as representing a crucial stage in FYROM's ongoing political process. It urged all parties to abide by the Agreement and to take all the measures for its speedy implementation. It reiterated its call for the scrupulous observance of the ceasefire and expressed readiness to convene a donors' conference soon after the Agreement's constitutional and legislative provisions had been adopted by the Parliament. It indicated that a reconstruction and rehabilitation programme to help in implementing the reforms was in preparation.

SECURITY COUNCIL ACTION

On 13 August [meeting 4356], following consultations among Security Council members, the President made statement **S/PRST/2001/20** on behalf of the Council:

> The Security Council welcomes the signing of the Framework Agreement in the former Yugoslav Republic of Macedonia by President Trajkovski and the leaders of four political parties on 13 August 2001. The Council calls for the full and immediate implementation of the Agreement, which promotes the peaceful and harmonious development of civil society while respecting the ethnic identity and the interests of all Macedonian citizens.
>
> The Council calls for the full implementation of its resolution 1345(2001) and reaffirms the sovereignty and territorial integrity of the former Yugoslav Republic of Macedonia.
>
> The Council calls again on all those concerned, including on leaders of ethnic Albanian communities in the region, publicly to condemn violence and ethnic intolerance and to use their influence to secure peace. It reiterates its call to all who have contact with extremist groups to make clear to them that they have no support from any quarter in the international community. The Council condemns the ongoing violence by extremists and calls on all parties

to respect the ceasefire. The Council rejects any attempt to use violence including the use of landmines to undermine the Framework Agreement, which has been negotiated by the democratically elected political leadership of the former Yugoslav Republic of Macedonia.

> The Council supports the actions of the President and Government of the former Yugoslav Republic of Macedonia aimed at resolving the crisis, and assuring a stable and democratic future for all of the citizens of the former Yugoslav Republic of Macedonia, including through continued dialogue with the full representation of all legitimate political parties to strengthen democracy and preserve the multi-ethnic character of Macedonian society and the stability of the country.
>
> The Council welcomes the efforts of the European Union, the Organization for Security and Co-operation in Europe and the North Atlantic Treaty Organization in support of the Framework Agreement. It also calls on the international community to consider how best to assist the Government of the former Yugoslav Republic of Macedonia in facilitating its full implementation.
>
> The Council will continue to follow closely developments on the ground.

During the Council's consideration on 28 August [meeting 4359] of the situation in the FRY province of Kosovo, the FYROM representative said that the signing of the Framework Agreement was a significant step towards a peaceful outcome of the political and security crisis in his country and noted that the Secretary-General had underlined UN readiness to assist in implementing it.

Drawing the Council's attention to the security dimension of the Agreement related to developments in Kosovo, he referred to recent UNMIK and KFOR activities along the border with Kosovo as contributing to a more efficient control of illegal border traffic and infiltration into FYROM. He stressed that, for the Agreement's security component to be effective, a complete cessation of the activities of ethnic Albanian insurgency instigators and supporters from Kosovo, including members of the Kosovo Protection Corps (KPC), had to be ensured. He reiterated his country's expectation that UNMIK and KFOR would put a stop to the infiltration and to all mobilization activities of former KPC fighters, including their joining the so-called National Liberation Army operating in FYROM. That was of particular importance for the success of the ongoing NATO operation in FYROM to disarm ethnic Albanian groups and to ensure their complete, voluntary disbandment.

Further developments

On 21 September [S/2001/897], FYROM transmitted to the Security Council the separate letters it had addressed to NATO and OSCE. By the former, FYROM thanked NATO for its response to FYROM's efforts to find a way out of its current crisis provoked by Albanian terrorists and illegal armed groups. Their disarmament and elimination were the foremost steps in the normalization of the country. FYROM would host an OSCE and EU monitoring mission and would support a light presence of NATO in the country upon the conclusion of its Operation Essential Harvest, to provide additional security for the mission. The modalities for such a security presence could be specified in a memorandum of understanding.

In its letter to OSCE, FYROM indicated its decision of 11 September to enhance the OSCE Spillover Monitor Mission to Skopje by increasing the number of monitors so as to assist the Government with the Framework Agreement's implementation, in particular with its confidence-building measures. As a priority, FYROM requested a rapid deployment of OSCE monitors and police advisers in sufficient numbers to provide a visible presence throughout the sensitive areas. It invited OSCE also to assist in other areas, especially the programmes of police training, media and inter-ethnic relations, as set out in the Agreement. It would further welcome OSCE involvement, through its Office for Democratic Institutions and Human Rights, in the conduct of the forthcoming censuses and elections in FYROM.

SECURITY COUNCIL ACTION

On 26 September [meeting 4381], the Security Council unanimously adopted **resolution 1371 (2001)**, based on a draft [S/2001/902] prepared in consultations among Council members.

The Security Council,

Recalling its resolutions 1244(1999) of 10 June 1999 and 1345(2001) of 21 March 2001 and the statements by its President of 7 March 2001 (S/PRST/2001/7), 16 March 2001 (S/PRST/2001/8) and 13 August 2001 (S/PRST/2001/20),

Welcoming the steps taken by the Government of the former Yugoslav Republic of Macedonia to consolidate a multi-ethnic society within its borders, and expressing its full support for the further development of this process,

Welcoming in this regard the signing of the Framework Agreement at Skopje on 13 August 2001 by the President of the former Yugoslav Republic of Macedonia and the leaders of four political parties,

Welcoming international efforts, including those of the Organization for Security and Cooperation in Europe, the European Union and the North Atlantic Treaty Organization, in cooperation with the Government of the former Yugoslav Republic of Macedonia and other States, to prevent the escalation of ethnic tensions in the area and to facilitate the full implementation of the Framework Agreement, thus contributing to peace and stability in the region,

Welcoming the letter from the Permanent Representative of the former Yugoslav Republic of Macedonia to the President of the Security Council of 21 September 2001,

1. *Reaffirms* its commitment to the sovereignty and territorial integrity of the former Yugoslav Republic of Macedonia and other States of the region;

2. *Calls* for the full implementation of resolution 1345(2001);

3. *Supports* the full and timely implementation of the Framework Agreement, rejects the use of violence in pursuit of political aims and stresses that only peaceful political solutions can assure a stable and democratic future for the former Yugoslav Republic of Macedonia;

4. *Welcomes* the efforts of the European Union and the Organization for Security and Cooperation in Europe to contribute to the implementation of the Framework Agreement, in particular through the presence of international observers;

5. *Endorses* the efforts of Member States and relevant international organizations to support the implementation of the Framework Agreement and strongly supports in that regard the establishment of a multinational security presence in the former Yugoslav Republic of Macedonia at the request of its Government to contribute towards the security of the observers, and invites the Government of the former Yugoslav Republic of Macedonia to keep the Council informed;

6. *Demands* that all concerned ensure the safety of international personnel in the former Yugoslav Republic of Macedonia;

7. *Welcomes* the efforts of the United Nations Interim Administration Mission in Kosovo and the international security presence to implement fully resolution 1244(1999), in particular by further strengthening its efforts to prevent unauthorized movement and illegal arms shipments across borders and boundaries, to confiscate illegal weapons within Kosovo, Federal Republic of Yugoslavia, and to keep the Council informed;

8. *Decides* to remain seized of the matter.

Communications. In a 9 October statement [S/2001/978], the EU expressed concern about the insufficient progress made by FYROM in implementing the Framework Agreement. The EU expected all democratic forces in the country to continue to engage fully and constructively in the parliamentary process and appealed to the Parliament to approve all of the Agreement's constitutional and legislative provisions. It was waiting for the Government to find an effective solution to the problem of amnesty for the rebels and for the return of the security forces to be coordinated with the international community's representatives. The EU stressed that its assistance in the reforms being carried out by the FYROM authorities was conditional upon the satisfactory conclusion of the parliamentary process of constitutional revision. In that regard, it noted that the conditions for the convening of a donors' conference had not yet been fulfilled.

The EU appreciated UN support for a multinational security presence in FYROM and welcomed NATO's decision to authorize the deployment of the Operation Amber Fox force to provide that presence and contribute to the security of the international monitors deployed by OSCE and the EU, whose number would be increased.

On 16 November [A/56/640-S/2001/1094], following adoption of the amendments to the FYROM Constitution, FYROM's President issued a statement welcoming those changes, saying the country had a great deal of work before it: immediate re-establishment of the State's sovereignty and rule of law throughout the country; the return of displaced persons to their homes before the winter; the reconstruction of their homes and repair of the infrastructure; the return of children to school; and initiating the process of healing and of overcoming differences. The President called on the international community to fulfil its commitments, including support for and involvement in the return of the security forces to the crisis regions. He also called for the early organization of the donors' conference. He welcomed the United States characterization of acts of armed provocation by Albanian groups in FYROM as acts of terrorism and called on all who considered violence as a solution to the problems to lay down their arms and to reintegrate into the community.

Georgia

During 2001, the Special Representative of the Secretary-General and Head of the United Nations Observer Mission in Georgia (UNOMIG), with the assistance of the Russian Federation in its capacity as facilitator, the Group of Friends of the Secretary-General (France, Germany, Russian Federation, United Kingdom, United States) and OSCE, continued efforts to engage the Georgian and Abkhaz parties in negotiations towards a comprehensive settlement of their conflict, including a definition of the political status of Abkhazia as a sovereign entity within the State of Georgia. The long-awaited paper on the Basic Principles for the Distribution of Competences between Tbilisi (Georgia's Government) and Sukhumi (the Abkhaz leadership), intended to serve as the basis for substantial negotiations, was finalized in mid-December and transmitted to the parties. Adamant in its rejection of any suggestion that Abkhazia was within the State of Georgia, the Abkhaz party was not prepared to

receive the paper. Consequently, the peace process remained stalled.

The successful holding of the third meeting on confidence-building measures between Georgia and Abkhazia in Yalta, Ukraine, in March yielded the Yalta Declaration and a Programme of Action on Confidence-building Measures. While those documents held promise of helping to narrow down the parties' divergent positions, by year's end, no significant implementation of the commitments and proposals they contained had been made. Furthermore, neither the parties' commitments on the voluntary return of refugees and displaced persons nor the recommendations of the 2000 joint assessment mission to the Gali district had been fulfilled. As noted by the Secretary-General, the parties neglected active work within the mechanisms of the UN-led Geneva peace process [YUN 1997, p. 365], in particular the Coordinating Council, thus threatening to defeat the purpose of that negotiating forum.

The month of October was marked by the shooting down of a UN helicopter on its way to resume patrolling in the upper Kodori Valley, as well as by large-scale hostilities in the conflict zone. Nonetheless, the Special Representative and UNOMIG, with the support of the Collective Peacekeeping Force of the Commonwealth of Independent States (CIS peacekeeping force), remained steadfast in the discharge of their mandates and in their determination to de-escalate hostilities and stabilize the situation in that zone. The Security Council strongly supported those efforts and, recognizing the contributions of UNOMIG to the peace process in Georgia, extended its mandate twice during the year, the second time until 31 January 2002.

UN Observer Mission in Georgia

The United Nations Observer Mission in Georgia (UNOMIG), established by Security Council resolution 858(1993) [YUN 1993, p. 509], continued to monitor and verify compliance with the 1994 Agreement on a Ceasefire and Separation of Forces (Moscow Agreement) [YUN 1994, p. 583] and to fulfil other tasks as mandated by resolution 937(1994) [ibid., p. 584]. Monitoring involved daily ground and regular helicopter patrols. UNOMIG operated in close collaboration with the CIS peacekeeping force that had been in the zone of conflict, at the request of the parties, since 1994 [ibid., p. 583]. The Council extended UNOMIG's mandate twice during the year, the first time until 31 July 2001 and the second until 31 January 2002.

UNOMIG's main headquarters was located in Sukhumi (Abkhazia, Georgia), with some admin-

istrative headquarters in Pitsunda, a liaison office in the Georgian capital of Tbilisi and team
bases and a sector headquarters in both the Gali
and Zugdidi sectors. A team base in the Kodori
Valley was manned by observers operating from
Sukhumi.

UNOMIG was headed by the Secretary-
General's Special Representative for Georgia,
Dieter Boden (Germany), who was assisted by the
Chief Military Observer, Major General Anis
Ahmed Bajwa (Pakistan). As at 31 December
2001, it had a strength of 106 military observers.

Activities

Report of Secretary-General (January). In his
January 2001 report [S/2001/59] describing the
situation in Abkhazia, Georgia, and UNOMIG
operations there from October to the end of
2000, summarized in 2000 [YUN 2000, p. 397], the
Secretary-General, observing that the continued
lack of progress on the fundamental issue of the
future political status of Abkhazia within the
State of Georgia could jeopardize the whole
peace process, called on both sides to muster
enough political will to overcome the impasse.
He appealed in particular to the Abkhaz side to
demonstrate more flexibility and willingness to
address the core political questions of the conflict and called for the early finalization of the
draft document on basic principles for the distribution of competences between Tbilisi and
Sukhumi [ibid., p. 391] and for its presentation to
the parties by the Special Representative and the
Group of Friends of the Secretary-General,
whose consensus position was deemed essential.
The Secretary-General called on the two sides to
enable the dignified, safe and secure return of
people to the Gali district, and urged them to implement the recommendations of the 2000 joint
assessment mission to that district [ibid., p. 397].
Together with the Resident Coordinator and
Humanitarian Coordinator, UNOMIG would explore possibilities for increasing humanitarian
aid to the population, including the allocation of
a sum in the UNOMIG budget for limited ad hoc
assistance.

Stressing that both sides bore primary responsibility for the security of UNOMIG's military and
civilian personnel, the Secretary-General appealed to the Government of Georgia to bring to
justice the perpetrators of the hostage-taking incidents of October 1999 [YUN 1999, p. 382] and of
June [YUN 2000, p. 392] and December 2000 [ibid.,
p. 397]. He said the Government also needed to
create the necessary security conditions in the
upper Kodori Valley to allow UNOMIG to carry
out its mandate fully in that area. Convinced of

UNOMIG's crucial role in stabilizing the zone of
conflict and in furthering the negotiation process, he recommended that the UNOMIG mandate
be extended for a further six-month period, until
31 July.

Communication. On 29 January [S/2001/89],
Georgia informed the Security Council about recent violations by the Abkhaz separatists of the
1994 Agreement on a Ceasefire and Separation
of Forces [YUN 1994, p. 583]. The first violation took
place on 25 January, when unidentified gunmen
opened fire on a civilian gasoline transportation
truck in the village of Chuburkhindgi, killing
one civilian and seriously injuring two others,
one of whom was kidnapped by the gunmen, who
retreated with the truck to Abkhaz-controlled
territory. The second violation took place on 26
January, when an anti-tank rocket was launched
from Abkhaz-controlled territory on the left
bank of the Inguri River towards Georgian-
controlled territory, hitting a moving car near the
CIS peacekeepers' checkpoint No. 301; the car exploded, seriously injuring four civilians.

SECURITY COUNCIL ACTION (January)

On 31 January [meeting 4269], the Security Council unanimously adopted **resolution 1339(2001)**,
based on a draft [S/2001/93] prepared in consultations among Council members.

The Security Council,

Recalling all its relevant resolutions, in particular
resolution 1311(2000) of 28 July 2000, and the statement of its President of 14 November 2000 (S/PRST/
2000/32),

Having considered the report of the Secretary-General
of 18 January 2001,

Recalling the conclusions of the Lisbon and Istanbul
summits of the Organization for Security and
Cooperation in Europe regarding the situation in
Abkhazia, Georgia,

Stressing that the continued lack of progress on key
issues of a comprehensive settlement of the conflict in
Abkhazia, Georgia, is unacceptable,

Deeply concerned that, although currently mostly
calm, the general situation in the conflict zone remains
very volatile,

Noting the holding of the twelfth session of the Coordinating Council of the Georgian and Abkhaz sides
on 23 January 2001,

Recalling the relevant principles contained in the
Convention on the Safety of United Nations and Associated Personnel adopted on 9 December 1994,

Welcoming the important contributions that the
United Nations Observer Mission in Georgia and the
collective peacekeeping force of the Commonwealth of
Independent States continue to make in stabilizing the
situation in the conflict zone, noting that the working
relationship between the Mission and the collective
peacekeeping force has remained very close, and
stressing the importance of close cooperation between
them in the performance of their respective mandates,

1. *Welcomes* the report of the Secretary-General of 18 January 2001;

2. *Strongly supports* the sustained efforts of the Secretary-General and his Special Representative, with the assistance of the Russian Federation, in its capacity as facilitator, as well as of the Group of Friends of the Secretary-General and of the Organization for Security and Cooperation in Europe, to promote the stabilization of the situation and the achievement of a comprehensive political settlement, which must include a settlement of the political status of Abkhazia within the State of Georgia;

3. *Strongly supports*, in particular, the intention of the Special Representative to submit, in the near future, the draft paper containing specific proposals to the parties on the question of the distribution of constitutional competences between Tbilisi and Sukhumi as a basis for meaningful negotiations;

4. *Stresses* the need to accelerate work on the draft protocol on the return of the refugees to the Gali region and measures for economic rehabilitation, as well as on the draft agreement on peace and guarantees for the prevention and for the non-resumption of hostilities;

5. *Calls upon* the parties, in particular the Abkhaz side, to undertake immediate efforts to move beyond the impasse and to engage in negotiations on the core political questions of the conflict and all other outstanding issues in the United Nations–led peace process;

6. *Welcomes* the readiness of the Government of Ukraine to host the third meeting on confidence-building measures, welcomes also the commitment of both sides to the conflict to meet in Yalta in March 2001, and notes the important contribution a successful conference would make to the peace process;

7. *Reaffirms* the unacceptability of the demographic changes resulting from the conflict, and reaffirms also the inalienable right of all refugees and displaced persons affected by the conflict to return to their homes in secure and dignified conditions, in accordance with international law and as set out in the Quadripartite Agreement on the Voluntary Return of Refugees and Displaced Persons of 4 April 1994;

8. *Urges* the parties, in this context, to address urgently and in a concerted manner, as a first step, the undefined and insecure status of spontaneous returnees to the Gali district, which remains an issue of serious concern;

9. *Expresses its satisfaction* with the joint assessment mission to the Gali district, carried out under the aegis of the United Nations, and looks forward to the careful consideration of the mission's recommendations regarding human rights, law enforcement and education;

10. *Condemns* all violations of the Moscow Agreement of 14 May 1994 on a Ceasefire and Separation of Forces, and notes with particular concern the Abkhaz military exercise conducted in November 2000;

11. *Deplores* the rise in criminality and activities of armed groups in the conflict zone, which constitutes a major destabilizing factor affecting the overall situation, calls upon the parties to increase their efforts at curbing them and to cooperate in good faith using the means provided by the Coordinating Council mechanism, condemns the recent killings of civilians and Abkhaz militiamen, and calls upon both sides, in particular the Georgian side, to investigate these incidents and bring to justice those responsible;

12. *Condemns* the abduction of two military observers of the United Nations Observer Mission in Georgia on 10 December 2000, recalls that the Georgian and the Abkhaz sides bear the primary responsibility for the security of the Mission, the collective peacekeeping force of the Commonwealth of Independent States and other international personnel, and appeals to them to bring to justice the perpetrators of the hostage-taking incidents of October 1999, June 2000 and December 2000;

13. *Calls upon* the parties to ensure security and freedom of movement of the United Nations and other international personnel;

14. *Welcomes* the fact that the Mission is keeping its security arrangements under constant review in order to ensure the highest possible level of security for its staff;

15. *Decides* to extend the mandate of the Mission for a new period terminating on 31 July 2001, subject to a review by the Council of the mandate of the Mission in the event of any changes that may be made in the mandate or in the presence of the collective peacekeeping force, and expresses its intention to conduct a thorough review of the operation at the end of its current mandate, in the light of steps taken by the parties to achieve a comprehensive settlement;

16. *Requests* the Secretary-General to continue to keep the Council regularly informed and to report three months from the date of the adoption of the present resolution on the situation in Abkhazia, Georgia, and requests also the Secretary-General to provide for a briefing within three months on the progress of the political settlement, including on the status of the draft paper his Special Representative intends to submit to the parties as referred to in paragraph 3 above;

17. *Decides* to remain actively seized of the matter.

Prior to the vote on the resolution, Georgia made a statement to the effect that the introduction of a new operative paragraph—paragraph 4—might jeopardize the upcoming third meeting on confidence-building measures and put the entire peace process on hold. The draft protocol and the draft agreement on peace guarantees referred to in that paragraph were unacceptable. The draft agreement, which it labelled dubious in many respects, was neither referred to in the Secretary-General's report nor discussed by the Council. Furthermore, it was not convinced that paragraph 4 as proposed would not be interpreted as exerting Council pressure on a Member State to enter into a peace agreement with a separate region, thus setting a dangerous precedent from the standpoint of international law. Stress should be placed, rather, on the need to accelerate work on the return of refugees and internally displaced persons to the Gali district, on the region's economic rehabilitation and on guarantees for the non-resumption of hostilities.

Communications. By a 27 February statement [S/2001/196], Georgia's Foreign Ministry stated that the Abkhaz regime's decision to hold self-styled local elections on 10 March was illegal and their results should be declared void. More than half the region's population had been expelled; the security and safety of the remaining Georgians were under constant threat, their basic human rights were regularly violated and free expression of the people's will was non-existent. It recalled the Security Council's reiteration in resolution 1287(2000) [YUN 2000, p. 387] that it considered unacceptable and illegitimate the holding of the self-styled referendum and elections in Abkhazia, Georgia. It further stated its belief that those unlawful elections created additional obstacles to the peace process, counteracted the good will of the Georgian Government and people, and undermined the international community's efforts to find a peaceful resolution, with full respect for the sovereignty and territorial integrity of Georgia.

In a 19 March letter to the Council [S/2001/245], Georgia's President, Eduard Shevardnadze, noted that the deadlocked peace process in Abkhazia had led to the eviction of tens of thousands of people from their homes. He stated that further efforts should be directed towards reaching an agreement on the political status of Abkhazia, with full respect for Georgia's sovereignty and territorial integrity, and towards the unconditional and dignified return of all refugees and internally displaced persons to their homes. To those ends, Georgia proposed that the United Nations draft a document setting forth the basic principles on the distribution of constitutional competences between Tbilisi and Sukhumi, to be debated and approved by the Security Council prior to its presentation to the two sides as a basis for further negotiations; and that decisive action be taken to ensure fulfilment of the Abkhaz regime's primary responsibility to secure the unconditional return of displaced persons, while asserting that there could be no linkage between the issue of Abkhazia's political status and the inalienable right of refugees and displaced persons to return home.

Ukraine, on 17 March [S/2001/242], transmitted to the Secretary-General the final documents of the third meeting on confidence-building measures between Georgia and Abkhazia (Yalta, 15-16 March), held under UN auspices within the framework of the Geneva peace process [YUN 1997, p. 365]. One was the Yalta Declaration, by which the two sides reaffirmed their commitments to the non-use of force in resolving their disputes and to create the conditions necessary for the safe return of refugees and internally displaced persons to their homes, the first phase being to the Gali district within the old borders. They asked the Special Representative to appeal to the United Nations, the Group of Friends of the Secretary-General, OSCE and CIS to guarantee the implementation of those commitments. The two sides further reaffirmed their commitment to observe their ceasefire accords and to prevent threats to the life and security of UNOMIG and CIS peacekeeping personnel.

The second document was a Programme of Action on confidence-building measures, to which was annexed a list of 15 specific measures in various fields, for the implementation of which they would provide organizational and technical support and create reporting channels and a database to record progress.

Ukraine, on 19 March [S/2001/247], referred to the foregoing meeting as having created a good platform for the conflicting sides to reach accord.

SECURITY COUNCIL ACTION (March)

The Security Council met twice on 21 March regarding the outcome of the third Georgia-Abkhaz meeting on confidence-building measures. The first Council meeting was held in private [meeting 4299], at which Ukraine briefed the Council on the subject.

At the second meeting [meeting 4300], following consultations among Council members, the President made statement **S/PRST/2001/9** on behalf of the Council:

The Security Council welcomes the successful holding of the third meeting on confidence-building measures between the Georgian and Abkhaz sides in Yalta on 15 and 16 March 2001 and the resumption of dialogue between them, and notes the documents signed there. It hopes that action flowing from the Yalta meeting will lead to a narrowing of the positions of the two sides and stimulate further constructive dialogue aimed at achieving a comprehensive political settlement of the conflict, including a settlement of the political status of Abkhazia within the State of Georgia and other key issues. The Council underlines the contribution that confidence-building measures can bring to the peace process and commends the efforts by the Government of Ukraine in ensuring the success of the Yalta meeting.

The Council reaffirms its support for the efforts by the Special Representative of the Secretary-General to enhance contacts at all levels between the Georgian and Abkhaz sides, in close cooperation with the Russian Federation, in its capacity as facilitator, the Group of Friends of the Secretary-General and the Organization for Security and Cooperation in Europe.

The Council encourages the two sides to engage with renewed commitment in the peace process. The Council notes the stated willingness of the two sides to ensure favourable conditions for the continuation of the peace process, their stated commitment to the non-use of force and their stated determination to intensify efforts in order to create the necessary climate for the voluntary return of internally displaced persons and refugees in secure and dignified conditions. The Council also notes the important contribution that the United Nations Observer Mission in Georgia and the collective peacekeeping force of the Commonwealth of Independent States continue to make in stabilizing the situation in the zone of conflict.

The Council underlines the unacceptability of the holding of self-styled local elections in Abkhazia, Georgia, on 10 March 2001, which it deems illegitimate and unhelpful. The organization of these elections represents an additional obstacle to the attempts to reach a comprehensive settlement of the conflict based on international law.

The Council stresses the importance of negotiations on the core political questions of the conflict. In this regard, it looks forward to the briefing to be provided by the Secretary-General on the progress of the political settlement, including on the status of the draft paper his Special Representative intends to submit to the two sides, as referred to in paragraph 16 of its resolution 1339(2001) of 31 January 2001.

The Council will remain actively seized of the matter and reaffirms its commitment to advancing the peace process.

Report of Secretary-General (April). In April [S/2001/401], the Secretary-General reported that no progress was achieved either on the fundamental issue of Abkhazia's future political status within the State of Georgia or on reaching agreement among the Group of Friends on the draft paper concerning the distribution of competences between Tbilisi and Sukhumi, considered a prerequisite for presenting the text as a basis for negotiations. Moreover, in a 12 March letter, the Abkhaz leader, Vladislav Ardzinba, repeated his rejection of any discussion on the status question on the basis of an eventual draft paper. Nevertheless, key aspects of the question were addressed at a seminar (Pitsunda, Georgia, 12-13 February), which gave the Abkhaz and Georgian sides an opportunity to argue their positions on statehood and self-determination.

Referring to the third meeting on confidence-building measures, the Secretary-General observed that good-faith implementation by the two sides of their commitments would mark a qualitatively new stage in the confidence-building component of the peace process and would give a strong impetus to the settlement effort.

The Coordinating Council, chaired by the Special Representative, held its twelfth session (Sukhumi, 12 January). The two sides continued to use that Council's Working Groups I and III to expand direct bilateral contacts on security and economic issues. With UNHCR support, efforts were under way to revive Working Group II on refugees and internally displaced persons, but the Abkhaz side withdrew its agreement to participate in the scheduled April session of the Coordinating Council due to a serious deterioration in relations brought about by that month's violent events (see below).

The Abkhaz de facto authorities held "local elections" on 10 March, which the Special Representative, in a public statement, characterized as unacceptable and illegitimate. Similar statements were issued by the Council of Europe, OSCE and the Russian Federation's Ministry of Foreign Affairs. An exchange of letters took place between UNOMIG and the Abkhaz side concerning the violation of UNOMIG's freedom of movement in November 2000, when the Abkhaz side prohibited the overflight of territory under its control [YUN 2000, p. 397].

As to UNOMIG operations, the Secretary-General reported that the Special Representative obtained adequate security assurances from the Georgian authorities for patrolling in the upper Kodori Valley, which had been suspended following the December 2000 abduction of UNOMIG military observers [ibid.]. Based on those assurances and under revised UNOMIG security regulations, the Chief Military Observer decided to resume helicopter patrols over the Kodori Valley on 13 April. UNOMIG was also ready to resume ground patrols in the lower Valley in cooperation with the CIS peacekeeping force.

The overall situation in the conflict zone, particularly in the Gali region, remained volatile: 45 shooting incidents, 12 killings, 9 abductions, 8 mine blasts and 40 robberies were recorded. None directly targeted UNOMIG personnel. In response to a number of January clashes between Abkhaz and Georgian armed groups and attacks targeting the CIS peacekeeping force, UNOMIG increased patrols and defused tensions through its Joint Fact-finding Group and regular weekly quadripartite meetings with the two sides, UNOMIG and the CIS peacekeeping force. March saw incidents of recently laid landmines, as well as two bomb attacks on "election" day in the Gali district.

During April, a CIS vehicle was ambushed. An anti-tank mine was discovered on the beach some 400 metres from UNOMIG headquarters in Sukhumi, which a United Kingdom–based demining NGO dismantled. To stop an escalating cycle of violence between armed groups from the two sides that had been triggered by an ambush from the Georgian side on the main road north of Gali, the Special Representative, on 16 April, convened a meeting of the two sides at the main bridge over the Inguri River. In a signed Protocol, they agreed to verify the physical condition of all persons held, to transfer them to the custody of official structures and to hand over the bodies of those killed. In subsequent consultations with the two sides and separate meetings with Georgia's President and the Abkhaz de facto "Prime Minister", Anri Jergenia, the Special Representative urged them to implement the Protocol. The Abkhaz side had since reported to UNOMIG sightings of several armed groups crossing the ceasefire line into Abkhaz-controlled territory.

Faced with an increasing threat from landmines, UNOMIG enhanced its security measures to include the use of heavier mine- and ballistic-protected vehicles. In that regard, the Chief Military Observer took up with both sides the discovery of armour-piercing small arms ammunition at the site of the April firefights. UNOMIG introduced new security regulations for its staff in the Zugdidi sector in response to warnings from the Security Services there of possible abductions or hostage-taking by anti-Government groups.

Despite the continuing grave humanitarian situation in Abkhazia, humanitarian agencies continued to provide for much of the population's acute food and medical needs and to conduct mine clearance and small-scale rehabilitation programmes. UNHCR resumed limited operations in the Gali district, distributing building materials, school kits and hygiene parcels to schools serving returnee children. The work of NGOs continued to be hampered by border-crossing restrictions in the region.

The human rights situation in Abkhazia continued to be precarious. The killing in August 2000 of a legal assistant to the United Nations Human Rights Office in Sukhumi [YUN 2000, p. 395] remained unsolved. Nevertheless, that Office continued to monitor the practices of law enforcement agencies during pre-trial detention and criminal trials; to provide advisory services to the local population, mostly in cases involving the violation of ownership and property rights; and to conduct human rights education and training programmes. Particular attention was paid to the situation in the Gali district.

The Secretary-General observed that the attitude of blanket rejection adopted by the Abkhaz side was short-sighted and counterproductive. He appealed to all concerned to clear the way for the start of meaningful talks aimed at defining the status of Abkhazia within the State of Georgia. He called on the two sides to implement without delay the recommendations of the 2000 joint assessment mission to the Gali district [ibid., p. 397], which were being finalized in consultation with

the participating organizations, as well as their obligations under the 16 April 2001 Protocol, in particular the Georgian side's commitment to take effective measures to stop the activities of illegal armed groups crossing into the Gali district from the Georgian-controlled side of the ceasefire line. The Secretary-General stated that violations of UNOMIG's freedom of movement and the failure to bring to justice the perpetrators of the hostage-taking incidents that had targeted UNOMIG were not acceptable.

Communication. Georgia, in a 16 April statement [S/2001/377], while noting the positive developments aimed at reaching a settlement to the conflict in Abkhazia, Georgia, expressed concern over the recent violent events in the Gali district: the renewed activity of Abkhaz armed groups; a bus explosion that killed one civilian; a mine explosion that severely injured five children; the detainment of five civilians, two of whom were murdered; and the capture of a fishing boat with its five fishermen on the grounds that the boat was "in violation of Abkhaz territorial waters". Georgia thus called on the United Nations, the Group of Friends of the Secretary-General, OSCE, the Council of Europe, CIS and other international organizations to take immediate steps to improve the situation and not allow the escalating hostilities to jeopardize the peace process.

SECURITY COUNCIL ACTION (April)

The Security Council met twice on 24 April to consider the agenda item on the situation in Georgia. At the first meeting [meeting 4313], held in private, the Council heard a briefing by the Special Representative of the Secretary-General and Head of UNOMIG; at the second [meeting 4314], the President, following consultations among Council members, made statement **S/PRST/2001/12** on behalf of the Council:

> The Security Council welcomes the briefing provided by the Special Representative of the Secretary-General, on 24 April 2001, in accordance with paragraph 16 of its resolution 1339(2001) of 31 January 2001. It welcomes also the presence of the Minister for Special Affairs of Georgia at its meeting.
>
> The Council stresses that the continued lack of progress on key issues of a comprehensive settlement of the conflict in Abkhazia, Georgia, is unacceptable. It underlines the decisive importance of early negotiations on the core political questions of the conflict. It strongly supports, in this context, the efforts of the Special Representative of the Secretary-General to promote the achievement of a comprehensive political settlement based on the resolutions of the Security Council, which must include a settlement of the political status of Abkhazia within the State of Georgia.

The Council strongly supports, in particular, the intention of the Special Representative to submit, in the near future, his draft paper containing specific proposals to the parties on the question of the distribution of constitutional competences between Tbilisi and Sukhumi. It calls on all those concerned to use their influence with a view to facilitating this process.

The Council welcomes the intention of the Special Representative to submit the draft paper to the parties soon, as a starting point for negotiation, and not as an attempt to impose or dictate any possible solution. It calls upon the parties constructively to accept the paper in this light and work towards a mutually acceptable settlement.

The Council will remain actively seized of the matter and reaffirms its commitment to advancing the peace process.

Communication. Belarus, on 20 June [S/2001/618], informed the Security Council of the 1 June decision of the Council of Heads of State of the Commonwealth of Independent States to extend the mandate of the CIS peacekeeping force in the conflict zone in Abkhazia, Georgia, until 31 December 2001.

Report of Secretary-General (July). The Secretary-General reported in July [S/2001/713] that, through the efforts of the Special Representative and the UNOMIG Chief Military Observer, the Georgian and Abkhaz sides, on 11 May, handed over the remains of those killed in the April firefights and exchanged all detainees. The lessening of tensions that followed allowed the seventh session of the Coordinating Council's Working Group I on security matters to be held (Sukhumi, 10 July) under the chairmanship of the Chief Military Observer. In a joint statement, the sides resolved to work together in a spirit of mutual trust in order to avoid further breaches of the 1994 Moscow Agreement [YUN 1994, p. 583], to reduce criminal activity and to bring criminals to justice.

On 8 and 9 July, two serious incidents in the Gulripshi area resulted in six people dead and two taken hostage outside UNOMIG's area of responsibility. In a 12 July statement, the Abkhaz side accused the Georgian side of involvement in those incidents. It cancelled its participation in the upcoming Coordinating Council session and refused to take part in a planned 16 July seminar on "State-legal aspects" of the settlement of the conflict—a follow-up to the February Pitsunda seminar (see p. 378)—to be held under the auspices of the Council of Europe.

Work on the issue of the future status of Abkhazia within the State of Georgia intensified following Security Council statement S/PRST/2001/12 (see p. 379). The Group of Friends, in close consultation with the Special Representa-tive, had accelerated the finalization of the draft paper on the distribution of competences between Tbilisi and Sukhumi. The Special Representative visited Moscow in mid-July, where he met with high-ranking representatives of the Russian Federation, in its capacity as facilitator. The Abkhaz authorities reiterated their well-known position that any discussion of Abkhazia's political status was obsolete given its 1999 "Act on State Independence of the Republic of Abkhazia" [YUN 1999, p. 373].

Despite the unstable security situation in the zone of conflict, a steady return of internally displaced persons to the Gali region continued. In early May, the Special Representative submitted to the two sides the report of the 2000 joint assessment mission to the Gali district [YUN 2000, p. 397]; both sides informally indicated that the report was an objective representation of the situation and expressed willingness to discuss the implementation of its recommendations. On 15 June, in a major step towards confidence-building, the Abkhaz side handed over to the Georgian side the remains of the 15 Georgian soldiers killed in combat near Sukhumi in 1993.

UNOMIG continued its ground patrols from Sukhumi and the two sector headquarters in Gali and Zugdidi, along with its helicopter patrols. For security reasons, patrolling remained suspended in the upper Kodori Valley. A detailed regime for patrolling that region had been agreed upon between the Chief Military Observer and Georgia's Minister of Defence and was to be implemented as soon as the security situation allowed.

A series of hostage-taking incidents started in early April, and extensive UNOMIG efforts were required to bring the two sides together at the highest political level to prevent further escalation of the situation. Two Abkhaz delegates refused to attend the meetings of the Joint Fact-finding Group due to the failure of the Georgian authorities to take adequate measures to prevent the activities of illegal armed groups in the Gali region and to provide essential evidence in some investigation cases, which constituted a breach of the 2000 protocol for the joint investigation of violations of the Moscow Agreement [YUN 2000, p. 387]. Following the joint statement signed during the seventh session of Working Group I, however, both sides expressed readiness to strengthen their cooperation with the Joint Fact-finding Group, which had concluded its investigations in three cases: the 25 January fuel truck ambush; the 26 January anti-tank missile attack (see p. 375); and the April mine explosion in which five children were injured (see p. 379).

On 6 May, an Abkhaz customs officer driving a vehicle was stopped and taken by a group of armed men to the Georgian side of the ceasefire line. A meeting of the two sides, facilitated by UNOMIG and chaired by its Chief Military Observer, was held on 11 May at the main bridge over the Inguri River. That meeting led to the signing of a protocol in which the Georgian side agreed to consider evidence gathered by the Abkhaz side against three Georgians suspected of murder. It was also agreed that UNOMIG would verify the protocol's implementation. Immediately following the meeting, an exchange of hostages took place.

The reporting period saw the repeated violation of the Moscow Agreement. During a June NATO/Partnership for Peace military exercise, hosted by Georgia's armed forces and conducted in the Kulevi military manoeuvre area, UNOMIG's freedom of movement in that site was restricted. Georgian armoured personnel carriers and helicopters were observed operating in the restricted weapons zone. On 23 June, two Abkhaz armoured vehicles entered the restricted weapons zone during a military exercise and, on 7 July, a Georgian armoured personnel carrier was seen in the security zone. UNOMIG lodged protests with both sides for all those violations. The Georgian law enforcement agencies had begun a criminal case against two individuals suspected of involvement in the hostage-taking of UN observers, and measures were under way to arrest others involved.

A disturbing tendency by the two sides to restrict the movement of UNOMIG personnel had developed, thereby hindering UNOMIG's ability to fulfil its mandate. A serious instance of obstruction occurred on 30 April, when Abkhaz military personnel aimed a grenade launcher at a UNOMIG helicopter circling an Abkhaz observation post. On 14 June, the Georgian side prevented UNOMIG military observers from entering part of the restricted weapons zone. The next day, the same side advised UNOMIG against conducting helicopter flights over parts of its area of responsibility due to the ongoing military exercises; the situation was rectified following UNOMIG's protest.

On 30 April, the UNOMIG Zugdidi liaison team was detained for about four hours by a demonstration of some 100 internally displaced persons waiting to receive allowances from the Zugdidi Post Bank. The demonstrators demanded that the team contact the Minister for Distribution of Allowances to request that he negotiate with them. The team was released upon the arrival of the police and local authorities, but the demonstrators threatened to destroy UNOMIG's Zugdidi

sector headquarters on 11 May if they had not received their allowances by 10 May. Despite UNOMIG's repeated requests, Georgian authorities failed to take measures to safeguard against that threat. On 11 May, quick police response to a demonstration outside the sector headquarters forestalled any damage.

With respect to the continued serious humanitarian situation in Abkhazia, Georgia, UNHCR initiated community-based rehabilitation of 14 schools requiring urgent attention in the upper and lower Gali regions and planned to expand its assistance to others. Despite the deplorable conditions found at many schools, they were attended by nearly 4,000 pupils in the 2000/01 school year. The rehabilitation of selected dispensaries and water purification systems would also be considered in 2001.

Violations of the right to life, the right to physical integrity and the right to liberty and security of person remained major issues of concern to the United Nations Human Rights Office in Abkhazia. The Office reported new cases of evictions and violations of the right to property, along with complaints about religious persecution. The number of abductions had markedly increased. The human rights situation remained particularly precarious in the Gali region, where the joint assessment mission had recommended the opening of a human rights branch office [YUN 2000, p. 397].

Encouraged by progress achieved within the Group of Friends on streamlining its position with regard to the draft paper on the distribution of competences, the Secretary-General appealed to the Group to complete that process with the cooperation of the Special Representative and said that the Abkhaz side should reconsider its position not to address the status question. He said both sides should work together to clarify the 8 and 9 July incidents (see p. 380), release the hostages and bring the perpetrators to justice. He further urged them to resume their work in the Coordinating Council as soon as possible.

The Secretary-General called on both sides to fulfil their commitments under the 1994 Quadripartite Agreement on the voluntary return of refugees and displaced persons [YUN 1994, p. 581] with renewed determination; invited them to implement the Yalta Programme of Action (see p. 377); and appealed for their full compliance with the Moscow Agreement. The Secretary-General concluded his report by recommending that UNOMIG's mandate be extended until 31 January 2002.

Communication. On 24 July [S/2001/733], Georgia expressed serious concern regarding the disruption by the Abkhaz side of the thirteenth

Georgian-Abkhaz Coordinating Council session scheduled for 17 July in Tbilisi. It said that such actions, designed to halt the peace process, were becoming routine. At the seventh session of Working Group I, the Georgian side had again underscored the need to create a joint action mechanism for the improvement of security conditions in the region. However, the Abkhaz side rejected all previous agreements and Georgian initiatives. Georgia claimed that returnees were being subjected to continuous violations of their fundamental rights by criminal elements and by the so-called law enforcement agencies of the illegitimate regime. Georgia also appealed for the resumption of dialogue between the sides.

SECURITY COUNCIL ACTION (July)

On 31 July [meeting 4353], the Security Council unanimously adopted **resolution 1364(2001)**, based on a draft [S/2001/747] prepared in consultations among Council members.

The Security Council,

Recalling all its relevant resolutions, in particular resolution 1339(2001) of 31 January 2001, and the statements by its President of 21 March 2001 (S/PRST/2001/9) and 24 April 2001 (S/PRST/2001/12),

Having considered the report of the Secretary-General of 19 July 2001,

Recalling the conclusions of the Lisbon and Istanbul summits of the Organization for Security and Cooperation in Europe regarding the situation in Abkhazia, Georgia,

Stressing that the continued lack of progress on key issues of a comprehensive settlement of the conflict in Abkhazia, Georgia, is unacceptable,

Deeply concerned by the interruption of negotiating activities following the killings and hostage-taking incidents in April and May 2001 in the district of Gali, on 8 and 9 July 2001 in the Gulripshi area and again on 22 July 2001 in Primorsk,

Expressing its regrets at the cancellation of the thirteenth session of the Coordinating Council of the Georgian and Abkhaz sides, initially scheduled for 17 July 2001, due to the withdrawal of the Abkhaz side following those incidents,

Recalling the relevant principles contained in the Convention on the Safety of United Nations and Associated Personnel adopted on 9 December 1994,

Welcoming the important contributions that the United Nations Observer Mission in Georgia and the collective peacekeeping force of the Commonwealth of Independent States continue to make in stabilizing the situation in the zone of conflict, noting that the working relationship between the Mission and the collective peacekeeping force has remained very close, and stressing the importance of close cooperation between them in the performance of their respective mandates,

Noting the invitation of the Georgian Government for the Security Council to dispatch a mission to the region,

1. *Welcomes* the report of the Secretary-General of 19 July 2001;

2. *Regrets* the deterioration of the situation in the zone of conflict due to the ongoing violence, hostage-taking incidents, the rise in criminality and the activities of illegal armed groups in the conflict zone, which constitutes a constant threat to the peace process;

3. *Strongly supports* the sustained efforts of the Secretary-General and his Special Representative, with the assistance of the Russian Federation, in its capacity as facilitator, as well as of the Group of Friends of the Secretary-General and of the Organization for Security and Cooperation in Europe, to promote the stabilization of the situation and the achievement of a comprehensive political settlement, which must include a settlement of the political status of Abkhazia within the State of Georgia;

4. *Recalls* the intention of the Special Representative to submit the draft paper on the question of the distribution of constitutional competences between Tbilisi and Sukhumi as a basis for meaningful negotiations, and not as an attempt to impose or dictate any specific solution to the parties;

5. *Stresses* the importance of early submission to the parties of the paper as a starting point and significant catalyst for negotiations on a comprehensive political settlement, and deeply regrets that the Special Representative of the Secretary-General has not been in a position to do so;

6. *Stresses also* the need to accelerate work on the draft protocol on the return of the refugees to the Gali region and measures for economic rehabilitation, as well as on the draft agreement on peace and guarantees for the prevention and for the non-resumption of hostilities;

7. *Calls upon* the parties, in particular the Abkhaz side, to undertake immediate efforts to move beyond the impasse and to engage into negotiations on the core political questions of the conflict and all other outstanding issues in the United Nations–led peace process;

8. *Welcomes* the documents signed at the Yalta meeting on confidence-building measures in March 2001, and urges the Georgian and Abkhaz sides to implement the proposals agreed in those documents in a purposeful and cooperative manner;

9. *Calls upon* the parties to resume their work in the Coordinating Council and its relevant mechanisms as soon as possible;

10. *Urges* the parties to work together, through more effective use of existing arrangements within the Coordinating Council mechanisms, in order to clarify the incidents of 8, 9 and 22 July 2001, bring about the release of the hostages still being held and bring the perpetrators to justice;

11. *Reaffirms* the unacceptability of the demographic changes resulting from the conflict, and reaffirms also the inalienable right of all refugees and internally displaced persons affected by the conflict to return to their homes in secure and dignified conditions, in accordance with international law and as set out in the Quadripartite Agreement of 4 April 1994;

12. *Further urges* the parties, in this context, to address urgently and in a concerted manner, as a first step, the undefined and insecure status of spontaneous returnees to the Gali district, which remains an issue of serious concern;

13. *Welcomes* measures undertaken by the Government of Georgia, the United Nations Development Programme, the Office of the United Nations High Commissioner for Refugees, the Office for the Coordination of Humanitarian Affairs and the World Bank to improve the situation of refugees and internally displaced persons to develop their skills and to increase their self-reliance with full respect for their inalienable right to return to their homes in secure and dignified conditions;

14. *Recalls with satisfaction* the joint assessment mission to the Gali district, carried out under the aegis of the United Nations, and looks forward to a discussion by the parties of practical steps to implement the mission's recommendations;

15. *Deplores* all violations of the Moscow Agreement of 14 May 1994 on a Ceasefire and Separation of Forces, and notes with particular concern the military exercises conducted by both parties in June and July 2001 in violation of the Moscow Agreement;

16. *Expresses its concern* at the disturbing tendency by the parties to restrict the freedom of movement of the United Nations Observer Mission in Georgia, thereby hindering the ability of the Mission to fulfil its mandate, urges both sides to return immediately to full compliance with the Moscow Agreement, which remains a cornerstone of the United Nations peace effort, and calls upon the parties to ensure the security and freedom of movement of United Nations and other international personnel;

17. *Recalls* that the Georgian and the Abkhaz sides bear the primary responsibility for the security of the Mission, the collective peacekeeping force of the Commonwealth of Independent States and other international personnel and for full compliance with all security arrangements agreed between them to preclude any further aggravation of the situation, and urges both parties to bring to justice the perpetrators of all hostage-taking incidents, particularly the abduction of two military observers of the Mission in the Kodori Valley on 10 December 2000;

18. *Reminds* the Georgian side in particular to uphold its commitment to put a stop to the activities of illegal armed groups crossing into Abkhazia, Georgia, from the Georgian-controlled side of the ceasefire line;

19. *Welcomes* the fact that the Mission is keeping its security arrangements under constant review in order to ensure the highest possible level of security for its staff;

20. *Decides* to extend the mandate of the Mission for a new period terminating on 31 January 2002, subject to a review by the Council of the mandate of the Mission in the event of any changes that may be made in the mandate or in the presence of the collective peacekeeping force of the Commonwealth of Independent States, and expresses its intention to conduct a thorough review of the operation at the end of its current mandate, in the light of steps taken by the parties to achieve a comprehensive settlement;

21. *Requests* the Secretary-General to continue to keep the Council regularly informed and to report three months from the date of the adoption of the present resolution on the situation in Abkhazia, Georgia, and requests also the Secretary-General to provide for a briefing within three months on the progress of the political settlement, including on the status of the draft paper his Special Representative intends to submit to the parties as referred to in paragraph 4 above;

22. *Decides* to remain actively seized of the matter.

Communication. In a 16 July statement [S/2001/762], transmitted on 1 August, Georgia drew the international community's attention to the increasingly dangerous scale of the illegal exploitation of natural resources and other properties in the territory controlled by the separatist regime in Abkhazia, Georgia. It claimed that the Abkhaz separatist leadership continued, for the purpose of personal enrichment, to break up and plunder industrial and agricultural complexes and sell them to foreign entities, and that it misappropriated medical/resort facilities and adjacent territories. The international community and the Government of Georgia had unequivocally asserted on numerous occasions that the separatist regime's decisions regarding the utilization of real estate or any other property in the territory of Abkhazia were illegal and void. The scale of natural resources exploitation in Abkhazia violated Georgia's sovereign rights and caused serious damage to the environment. The felling of certain varieties of trees and forests protected under Georgia's endangered species list caused irreversible damage to the entire region's unique ecosystems. Georgia appealed to the international community and the global environment society to take steps to halt the irresponsible exploitation of the natural resources in Abkhazia, Georgia.

Security Council consultations. Following informal consultations on 8 October, the Security Council issued a press statement [S/2001/1298] strongly condemning the shooting down on that date of a UNOMIG helicopter near the Kodori Valley in Abkhazia, killing four UN observers, two local staff and three crew members. The Council offered its condolences to the bereaved families, and called for a speedy investigation into the incident and for bringing the perpetrators to justice. It underlined the importance of keeping security arrangements under constant review to ensure the highest possible level of security for UNOMIG personnel. It recalled that providing appropriate security conditions for UNOMIG's functioning at all times was the primary responsibility of both sides, pursuant to relevant Council resolutions and to their mutual obligations, including under the Yalta Declaration.

In further informal Council consultations on 12 and 29 October, the Secretariat gave a briefing on developments surrounding the incident. The remains of all nine victims had been recovered; UNOMIG had restricted movement in the region and drawn up preliminary staff relocation plans should they be needed. The investigation team, constituted on 14 October, was headed by Ukraine, the helicopter's country of registration. Its preliminary findings suggested that the crash had been caused by the impact of a surface-to-air missile fired from a portable launcher, probably by an armed infiltrator.

Report of Secretary-General (October). In an October report [S/2001/1008], the Secretary-General said the UNOMIG helicopter shot down on 8 October (see above) in the Gulripshi district of Abkhazia, Georgia, was on its way to resume patrolling in the upper Kodori Valley. The incident, he noted, marked a new low point in the situation in Georgia, which had been deteriorating in the past six months, adding that both sides had contributed to the current deplorable state of affairs. They had neglected essential political work within the mechanisms of the Geneva peace process, particularly the Coordinating Council; disregarded the implementation of agreed protocols; and failed to contain a situation with a clear potential for armed clashes. Since direct political contacts between the two sides had been reduced to a minimum, the efforts of the Special Representative and the Chief Military Observer since mid-August had focused on crisis management rather than on the promotion of a political settlement. The Special Representative was attempting through high-level political contacts with the two sides to re-establish dialogue between them and to revitalize existing negotiating mechanisms.

In August, the Russian Federation presented new proposals for the draft paper on distribution of competences between Tbilisi and Sukhumi that suggested the inclusion of security guarantees. Following a series of meetings between the Special Representative and the Group of Friends in New York, Moscow and Tbilisi, it was further suggested that security guarantees be dealt with on a parallel track, based on the Yalta Declaration (see p. 377). The Group of Friends had yet to reach agreement on the basic paper for negotiations on the future political status of Abkhazia within the State of Georgia. A 1 August letter from the Abkhaz de facto "Prime Minister" repeated the Abkhaz leadership's refusal to participate in any negotiations based on such a paper, claiming "State-legal relations" between Abkhazia and Georgia had broken off when the Union of Soviet Socialist Republics was still in existence.

The thirteenth session of the Coordinating Council, rescheduled for 9 October in Tbilisi, was postponed for the third time by the Special Representative due to insufficient political will

on either side to engage in serious dialogue and to an increasing tendency to hold the peace process hostage to political demands. The implementation of agreed projects had almost come to a standstill, although some preparatory work within the framework of the Coordinating Council continued (see below).

On 18 October, the Abkhaz de facto "Prime Minister" publicly suggested a closer association between Abkhazia and the Russian Federation. Russian officials at the highest levels, however, reaffirmed their commitment to Georgia's territorial integrity. Earlier, on 11 October, Georgia's Parliament adopted a resolution to replace the CIS peacekeeping force with an international peacekeeping mission without specifying its modalities.

Turning to UNOMIG's operations, the Secretary-General reported that, following abductions and counter-abductions in July and August, the Special Representative chaired an extraordinary ministerial meeting of both sides on 14 August, during which the parties agreed to locate, take into protective custody and return all abducted persons, and to combat illegal activities in the security zone. The first hostages were released two days later. The two sides increased their cooperation in the Joint Fact-finding Group, and participation by all parties in the Group's investigations markedly improved.

On 18 and 19 August, clashes between armed irregulars and Abkhaz security forces near the upper Kodori Valley, outside UNOMIG's area of responsibility, resulted in the death of four irregulars. According to local authorities in Tbilisi, the Abkhaz forces used two helicopters and a jet aircraft in the fighting, leading to Georgian accusations of Russian involvement. On 22 August, the Abkhaz de facto "Prime Minister" claimed that 700 armed irregulars were massed on the Georgian side of the ceasefire line, in the northern part of UNOMIG's area of responsibility, poised to invade. The Abkhaz authorities responded with a partial military mobilization. To defuse tensions, UNOMIG's Chief Military Observer held meetings with top-level officials in Tbilisi and Sukhumi and received assurances that Georgia would prevent armed groups from crossing the ceasefire line. He further facilitated a meeting between the Abkhaz de facto "Prime Minister" and the Georgian Minister of Special Affairs on 24 August in Sukhumi, followed by direct telephone contact between the former and Georgia's President. The armed irregulars appeared to withdraw from their positions and the Abkhaz authorities called off their partial mobilization. They also expressed readiness to return to the Coordinating Council.

Working Group I on security matters convened on 11 September in Tbilisi, during which the parties reaffirmed their commitment to the 1994 Moscow Agreement and recommended that: UNOMIG and the CIS peacekeeping force should resume regular patrols in the Kodori Valley; in the case of suspected summary execution during detention, UNOMIG medical personnel should be granted immediate access to conduct independent examination of the bodies; the Georgian side should report on criminal proceedings against the persons handed over to them on 11 May (see p. 381); both sides should locate persons still missing according to the 14 August protocol; and both sides should exchange written information about cases for investigation by the Joint Fact-finding Group during the weekly quadripartite meetings.

The situation worsened anew in the second week of September, when Georgian armed irregulars, together with fighters from the North Caucasus of predominantly Chechen origin, were in or near the Georgian-controlled upper Kodori Valley, as reported to UNOMIG by the Abkhaz side, at the same time that the Georgian authorities informed of the movement of three Abkhaz armoured vehicles to the Abkhaz-controlled lower Kodori Valley. A special UNOMIG helicopter patrol confirmed the presence of a field howitzer and two armoured personnel carriers at the Abkhaz checkpoint. At a UNOMIG-facilitated meeting on 28 September in Tbilisi, Georgia's President and the Abkhaz de facto "Prime Minister" agreed to take steps to avert new fighting in and around the Kodori Valley. The Georgian side reportedly pledged to disperse the armed irregulars; the Abkhaz side pledged restraint in dealing with those irregulars, except in cases of criminal or unlawful activities, and appealed to the Group of Friends to help prevent new hostilities and provide security guarantees as requested in the Yalta Declaration. The Special Representative repeatedly urged Georgian officials to provide the necessary security guarantees for the resumption of UNOMIG patrols in the upper Kodori Valley.

Despite those undertakings, armed irregulars attacked an Abkhaz checkpoint in the village of Georgievskoe in the Abkhaz-controlled lower Kodori Valley on 3 and 4 October. One Abkhaz soldier and four civilians were killed, with five others reported missing. The Special Representative and the Chief Military Observer immediately held a series of meetings with senior government officials in Tbilisi to halt the escalation of violence. On 6 October, unknown irregulars attacked the Abkhaz security post in Tagiloni, near the ceasefire line; no casualties resulted. The as-sailants fled to the Georgian side of the ceasefire line.

Following the 8 October shooting down of the UNOMIG helicopter, the Special Representative travelled to Sukhumi to oversee rescue efforts and to meet with the Abkhaz leadership. On 9 October, he urged the Abkhaz de facto "Prime Minister" to exercise restraint and not allow the fighting to spread to the upper Kodori Valley. The Abkhaz leadership and Georgia's President agreed to meet on the condition that the only issue to be addressed would be the de-escalation and the end of the ongoing fighting. Meanwhile, 12 local residents were killed in the village of Naa in continued fighting. On 9 October, two unidentified fighter aircraft attacked the villages of Georgievskoe and Chiena in the Abkhaz-controlled lower Kodori Valley and, later, two other aircraft bombed the village of Omarishara in the Georgian-controlled upper Kodori Valley. On 11 October, the Abkhaz side used artillery and airpower to drive the irregulars out of the lower valley, and, on 17 October, the Abkhaz side was again reported to have used helicopters and planes extensively against retreating irregulars about 10 kilometres from the border with the Russian Federation. The Georgian side again voiced suspicion of Russian involvement.

The Special Representative met with Georgia's President on 11 October to urge him to meet with the Abkhaz de facto "Prime Minister" to avoid larger-scale hostilities, but no response had been received. The Georgian side was also urged not to send reinforcements or supplies into the area of fighting. Since 9 October, UNOMIG's Sukhumi headquarters and the Gali sector had been placed on high alert; operational patrolling from those sectors was suspended, but resumed on 18 October after the fighting had largely ended. Casualty estimates, in addition to civilians and UN staff, put those killed at 60 armed elements and about 16 Abkhaz troops; taken prisoner by Abkhaz forces were 10 irregulars.

Levels of crime remained high in the zone of conflict, especially in lower Gali. In some areas on the Abkhaz-controlled side of the ceasefire line, joint patrolling by Abkhaz militia, local residents and the CIS peacekeeping force helped reduce the level of lawlessness, and joint patrolling by Georgian police, local residents and the CIS peacekeeping force led to similar reductions on the Georgian side.

Due to the fighting in the Kodori Valley area and the volatile situation in Gali, many NGOs suspended their activities after 8 October. UNHCR expanded its school rehabilitation programme to 22 schools in the Gali district, as well as three schools in the Ochamchira district on a self-help basis; however, it still could not operate in the more remote and dangerous areas, such as Primorsk, where humanitarian needs were particularly urgent and only UNOMIG patrols had access. Restrictions on border crossings continued to hamper international NGOs, thus complicating the delivery of assistance and emergency evacuation planning.

Widespread organized crime, lack of effective law enforcement and the continuing stalemate regarding language policy in schools in the predominantly Georgian-speaking Gali district had adversely affected the return of displaced persons to their homes. Reports of human rights violations included harassment on ethnic and religious grounds, violations of fair trial standards and arbitrary and illegal detentions. The United Nations Human Rights Office handled individual complaints and monitored court sessions and detention facilities.

As a follow-up to the November 2000 joint assessment mission to the Gali district [YUN 2000, p. 397], Georgian and Abkhaz representatives and participants of the mission, on 24 September, explored ways to implement the mission's recommendations (see p. 380). Specific attention was given to progress in the return of displaced persons to the Gali district, human rights, public security and language of instruction. The issue of language was also taken up during a 20 September joint visit to the Gali district by the Georgian and Abkhaz Ministers of Education.

In his observations, the Secretary-General reminded both sides of their obligation to provide for the safety and security of UN personnel and to make it their top priority, emphasizing that perpetrators of criminal acts targeted against UNOMIG had to be brought to justice. He noted that the parties had neglected active work within the Geneva peace process mechanisms [YUN 1997, p. 365] and warned that the cancellation on three occasions of the Coordinating Council's thirteenth session over the past six months, twice at the Abkhaz side's request, threatened to defeat the purpose of that negotiating forum. Since the mechanisms had been set up to serve the parties' own security, especially in times of crises, he urged their immediate return to full participation in the Coordinating Council and in all its working groups.

The Secretary-General regretted the absence of meaningful negotiations on the future political status of Abkhazia within the State of Georgia, as well as on the issue of facilitating the safe, secure and dignified return of the refugees and internally displaced persons to their homes. He noted that the promising Programme of Action on confidence-building measures had come to a

standstill. In addition, he reminded the parties of their obligation to comply with the Moscow Agreement, the protocols agreed within the Coordinating Council framework and the commitments made during the weekly quadripartite meetings.

Security Council consideration. On 30 October, the Council held a private meeting [meeting 4400], during which the Special Representative, the Minister of Special Affairs of Georgia and the representative of Belgium held a constructive discussion on the situation in Georgia.

Further report of Secretary-General. In a later report [S/2002/88], the Secretary-General stated that the Special Representative, in consultation with the Group of Friends, was able to finalize in mid-December the paper on the "Basic Principles for the Distribution of Competences between Tbilisi and Sukhumi", which was to be presented to the Georgian and Abkhaz parties as a basis for substantive negotiations on the future status of Abkhazia within the State of Georgia. In preparation for those negotiations, the Special Representative held consultations in Sukhumi and Tbilisi; the Special Envoy of the Russian Federation also visited Sukhumi. At those consultations, the Abkhaz de facto "Prime Minister" rejected any suggestion that Abkhazia was "within the State of Georgia" and was not prepared to receive the letter transmitting the paper.

A major stumbling block had been the deployment since October of Georgian troops in the Kodori Valley because of the fighting and bombardments in the area. The Abkhaz side affirmed its unwillingness to discuss any subject with the Georgian side as long as those forces remained. The Special Representative repeatedly urged the Georgian side to withdraw its troops in compliance with the 1994 Moscow Agreement; the Group of Friends undertook a similar démarche on 14 December.

In the wake of the October hostilities in the Kodori Valley (see p. 385), contacts between the sides came practically to a standstill. No meetings within the Coordinating Council framework were held and no progress could be made on the implementation of the recommendations of the 2000 joint assessment mission to the Gali district. The lack of movement was partly attributable to internal developments on both sides. The dismissal of the Georgian Government on 1 November effectively immobilized the executive until mid-December. In Sukhumi, the Abkhaz leader was incapacitated by illness and the de facto "Prime Minister" faced a no-confidence vote in the Parliament on 31 October, which he overcame by 28 votes to 7.

UNOMIG continued regular patrolling in its area of responsibility, except in the Georgian-controlled upper Kodori Valley, and, on 20 December, with the CIS peacekeeping force, resumed joint ground patrols in the Abkhaz-controlled lower Kodori Valley, which had been suspended owing to the October hostilities.

The Abkhaz side took responsibility for the 27 to 31 October air raids on the Marukh pass, near the Russian border, which had rendered the area relatively calm although unstable. On 10 November, an Abkhaz official was killed and another seriously wounded in an attack on the Tagiloni customs post on the Abkhaz side of the ceasefire line. On 17 November, an armed group ambushed a CIS peacekeeping force patrol northeast of Zugdidi, injuring one soldier. On 29 December, an armed group attacked the head of Pirveli Gali administration, who returned fire, killing one of the assailants. On three occasions in the second half of December, CIS peacekeeping force checkpoints came under small arms fire, injuring two soldiers.

As in the past, crime escalated in the Gali area with the beginning of the mandarin harvest, highlighting the weakness of law enforcement there. Abductions continued on both sides of the ceasefire line. Direct negotiations between Georgian and Abkhaz local authorities resulted in an exchange, on 15 and 31 December, of four Abkhaz and the remains of two for the remains of five Georgians. The Abkhaz side still held at least four civilians and five fighters taken prisoner in October.

Two mine incidents in the Gali region involving local civilians, and two in the Kodori Valley involving CIS patrols, led UNOMIG to suspend its patrolling in those sites until mine searches were undertaken by the CIS patrols. Restrictions were also imposed in the Zugdidi sector following the discovery of two containers with radioactive materials near Potskhoztseri at the end of December.

UNHCR had almost completed the rehabilitation of 24 schools in the Gali district and provided assistance to elderly displaced persons in Sukhumi. In November, the United Nations Development Programme (UNDP) and the German Government signed an agreement whereby UNDP would implement a telecommunications rehabilitation programme, which would serve displaced persons and returnees on both sides of the ceasefire line, extend links to Sukhumi and connect Tbilisi and the upper Kodori Valley. The Georgian and Abkhaz sides jointly identified the programme needs under the auspices of Working Group III of the Coordinating Council on socio-economic issues, for which the German Government granted an initial contribution of $150,000.

From 12 to 16 December, the United Nations Human Rights Office in Abkhazia conducted a human rights training seminar for de facto Abkhaz law enforcement agencies. Violation of the right to freedom of speech had been of serious concern, in particular a harassment campaign against the editor of a weekly publication and members of her family.

Financing

On 14 June [meeting 103], the General Assembly, having considered the Secretary-General's reports on UNOMIG's financial performance for the period 1 July 1999 to 30 June 2000 [A/55/682], the proposed budget for the Mission's maintenance from 1 July 2001 to 30 June 2002 [A/55/768] and ACABQ's comments and recommendations thereon [A/55/874/Add.4], adopted without vote, on the recommendation of the Fifth Committee [A/55/968], **resolution 55/267** [agenda item 144].

Financing of the United Nations Observer Mission in Georgia

The General Assembly,

Having considered the reports of the Secretary-General on the financing of the United Nations Observer Mission in Georgia and the related reports of the Advisory Committee on Administrative and Budgetary Questions,

Recalling Security Council resolution 854(1993) of 6 August 1993, by which the Council approved the deployment of an advance team of up to ten United Nations military observers for a period of three months and the incorporation of the advance team into a United Nations observer mission if such a mission was formally established by the Council,

Recalling also Security Council resolution 858(1993) of 24 August 1993, by which the Council decided to establish the United Nations Observer Mission in Georgia, and the subsequent resolutions by which the Council extended the mandate of the Observer Mission, the latest of which was resolution 1339(2001) of 31 January 2001,

Recalling further its decision 48/475 A of 23 December 1993 on the financing of the Observer Mission and subsequent resolutions and decisions thereon, the latest of which was resolution 54/271 of 15 June 2000,

Reaffirming the general principles underlying the financing of United Nations peacekeeping operations, as stated by the General Assembly in its resolutions 1874(S-IV) of 27 June 1963, 3101(XXVIII) of 11 December 1973 and 55/235 of 23 December 2000,

Noting with appreciation that voluntary contributions have been made to the Observer Mission,

Mindful of the fact that it is essential to provide the Observer Mission with the necessary financial resources to enable it to fulfil its responsibilities under the relevant resolutions of the Security Council,

1. *Takes note* of the status of contributions to the United Nations Observer Mission in Georgia as at 30 April 2001, including the contributions outstanding in the amount of 19.8 million United States dollars, representing 14 per cent of the total assessed contributions

from the inception of the Observer Mission to the period ending 30 June 2001, notes that some 16 per cent of the Member States have paid their assessed contributions in full, and urges all other Member States concerned, in particular those in arrears, to ensure payment of their outstanding assessed contributions;

2. *Expresses its appreciation* to those Member States which have paid their assessed contributions in full;

3. *Urges* all other Member States to make every possible effort to ensure payment of their assessed contributions to the Observer Mission in full and on time;

4. *Expresses concern* at the delay experienced by the Secretary-General in deploying and providing adequate resources to some recent peacekeeping missions, in particular those in Africa;

5. *Emphasizes* that all future and existing peacekeeping missions shall be given equal and non-discriminatory treatment in respect of financial and administrative arrangements;

6. *Also emphasizes* that all peacekeeping missions shall be provided with adequate resources for the effective and efficient discharge of their respective mandates;

7. *Reiterates its request* to the Secretary-General to make the fullest possible use of facilities and equipment at the United Nations Logistics Base at Brindisi, Italy, in order to minimize the costs of procurement for the Observer Mission;

8. *Endorses* the conclusions and recommendations contained in the report of the Advisory Committee on Administrative and Budgetary Questions, and requests the Secretary-General to ensure their full implementation;

9. *Requests* the Secretary-General to take all necessary action to ensure that the Observer Mission is administered with a maximum of efficiency and economy;

10. *Also requests* the Secretary-General, in order to reduce the cost of employing General Service staff, to continue efforts to recruit local staff for the Observer Mission against General Service posts, commensurate with the requirements of the Mission;

11. *Decides* to appropriate to the Special Account for the United Nations Observer Mission in Georgia the amount of 27,896,341 dollars gross (26,175,806 dollars net) for the maintenance of the Observer Mission for the period from 1 July 2001 to 30 June 2002, inclusive of the amount of 816,452 dollars gross (716,517 dollars net) for the support account for peacekeeping operations and the amount of 85,289 dollars gross (76,589 dollars net) for the United Nations Logistics Base;

12. *Decides also* to apportion among Member States the amount of 2,324,695 dollars gross (2,181,317 dollars net) for the period from 1 to 31 July 2001 in accordance with the levels set out in General Assembly resolution 55/235, as adjusted by the Assembly in its resolution 55/236 of 23 December 2000, and taking into account the scale of assessments for the year 2001, as set out in its resolution 55/5 B of 23 December 2000;

13. *Decides further* that, in accordance with the provisions of its resolution 973(X) of 15 December 1955, there shall be set off against the apportionment among Member States, as provided for in paragraph 12 above, their respective share in the Tax Equalization Fund of the estimated staff assessment income of 143,378 dollars approved for the Observer Mission for the period from 1 to 31 July 2001;

14. *Decides* to apportion among Member States the amount of 25,571,646 dollars gross (23,994,489 dollars net) for the period from 1 August 2001 to 30 June 2002, at a monthly rate of 2,324,695 dollars gross (2,181,317 dollars net), in accordance with paragraph 12 above, and taking into account the scale of assessments for the years 2001 and 2002, as set out in General Assembly resolution 55/5 B, subject to the decision of the Security Council to extend the mandate of the Observer Mission beyond 31 July 2001;

15. *Decides also* that, in accordance with the provisions of its resolution 973(X), there shall be set off against the apportionment among Member States, as provided for in paragraph 14 above, their respective share in the Tax Equalization Fund of the estimated staff assessment income of 1,577,157 dollars approved for the period from 1 August 2001 to 30 June 2002;

16. *Decides further* that, for Member States that have fulfilled their financial obligations to the Observer Mission, there shall be set off against the apportionment, as provided for in paragraphs 12 and 14 above, their respective share of the unencumbered balance of 5,996,479 dollars gross (5,775,479 dollars net) in respect of the period ending 30 June 2000, of which 2,324,695 dollars gross (2,181,317 dollars net) pertains to the period from 1 to 31 July 2001 and 3,671,784 dollars gross (3,594,162 dollars net) pertains to the period from 1 August 2001 to 30 June 2002, in accordance with the composition of groups as set out in paragraphs 3 and 4 of General Assembly resolution 43/232 of 1 March 1989 and adjusted by the Assembly in subsequent relevant resolutions and decisions for the ad hoc apportionment of peacekeeping appropriations, the latest of which were resolution 52/230 of 31 March 1998 and decisions 54/456 to 54/458 of 23 December 1999 for the period 1998-2000, and taking into account the scale of assessments for the year 2000, as set out in its resolutions 52/215 A of 22 December 1997 and 54/237 A of 23 December 1999;

17. *Decides* that, for Member States that have not fulfilled their financial obligations to the Observer Mission, their share of the unencumbered balance of 5,996,479 dollars gross (5,775,479 dollars net) for the period ending 30 June 2000, of which 2,324,695 dollars gross (2,181,317 dollars net) pertains to the period from 1 to 31 July 2001 and 3,671,784 dollars gross (3,594,162 dollars net) pertains to the period from 1 August 2001 to 30 June 2002, shall be set off against their outstanding obligations in accordance with the scheme set out in paragraph 16 above;

18. *Emphasizes* that no peacekeeping mission shall be financed by borrowing funds from other active peacekeeping missions;

19. *Encourages* the Secretary-General to continue to take additional measures to ensure the safety and security of all personnel under the auspices of the United Nations participating in the Observer Mission;

20. *Invites* voluntary contributions to the Observer Mission in cash and in the form of services and supplies acceptable to the Secretary-General, to be administered, as appropriate, in accordance with the procedure and practices established by the General Assembly;

21. *Decides* to include in the provisional agenda of its fifty-sixth session the item entitled "Financing of the United Nations Observer Mission in Georgia".

The Assembly decided, on 24 December, that the item on UNOMIG financing would remain for consideration at its resumed fifty-sixth (2002) session (**decision 56/464**) and that the item would be considered by the Fifth Committee at that session (**decision 56/458**).

Also in December [A/56/721 & Corr.1], the Secretary-General submitted the UNOMIG financial performance report for the period 1 July 2000 to 30 June 2001.

Georgia–Russian Federation

On 29 October [S/2001/1022], Georgia claimed violation of its airspace and bombing of its territory on 28 and 29 October by warplanes from the Russian Federation. Georgia's repeated demands for an explanation and joint investigation into previous such violations had had no response. It therefore appealed to the Security Council and the world community to assess the situation and take steps to prevent aggression against Georgia.

On 15 November [A/56/633-S/2001/1085], the Russian Federation noted that it had fulfilled the key obligations specified in its 17 November 1999 joint statement with Georgia concerning the modalities for fulfilling the conditions laid down in the adapted Treaty on Conventional Armed Forces in Europe (CFE) and for regulating military bilateral ties. The remaining Russian weapons and equipment in Georgia subject to the CFE Treaty were withdrawn before 31 December 2000 or partially disposed of on the spot in conditions of transparency and under international monitoring. The disbandment and withdrawal of Russian military bases at Vaziani and Gudauta were completed in November in accordance with bilateral Georgia–Russian Federation agreements. The departure of Russian military personnel from the Gudauta base, located within the Georgian-Abkhaz conflict area, was protested by Abkhazia's population, who considered their presence a security guarantee in times of armed conflict. The facilities left behind were currently in use by the CIS peacekeeping force for its operations, which were under UNOMIG monitoring. Moscow and Tbilisi had yet to reach an agreement regarding the Russian military bases at Batumi and Akhalkalaki and other military facilities within Georgia; meanwhile, account should be taken of the considerable preparatory arrangements to be made for the return of the servicemen at those bases to the Russian Federation.

Georgia reported further violations of its airspace on 28 November [A/56/664-S/2001/1124] by two Russian military jets that overflew the Kodori gorge, and, on the previous night, by six jets that penetrated 50 kilometres into Georgia's airspace, bombing the territory adjacent to Birkani village, in the Akmeta district, as well as by military helicopters that carried out several air strikes on Georgian territory near the Chechnya and Ingushetia sections of the Georgia–Russian Federation border, including the outskirts of six villages in the area. Calling those violations undisguised aggression, Georgia warned that, if not suppressed, they could exacerbate the instability in the Caucasus. It was imperative for the international community to raise its voice against the violation of internationally accepted principles of peaceful coexistence. It demanded that the Russian Federation cease its repeated acts of aggression against Georgia, which reserved its right to take adequate steps as provided by international law.

Armenia-Azerbaijan

In 2001, Armenia and Azerbaijan were no closer to reaching a settlement of the armed conflict between them, which had erupted in 1992 [YUN 1992, p. 388] over the Nagorny-Karabakh region in Azerbaijan. The Minsk Group of OSCE (France, the Russian Federation and the United States) continued efforts to advance the peace process. In that context, the United States, one of the co-chairs of the Minsk Group, convened a meeting of the parties in Florida. Both sides addressed communications to the Secretary-General during the year regarding developments in the conflict. Nagorny Karabakh's communications were transmitted by Armenia.

Communications. On 4 April [A/56/62-S/2001/334], Azerbaijan transmitted to the Secretary-General a statement by its President, Heydar Aliyev, made at a meeting (Key West, Florida, 3 April) with the United States Secretary of State, Colin Powell, the Presidents of Armenia and Azerbaijan and co-chairs of the Minsk Group. President Aliyev said it was the first time the OSCE Minsk Group had convened with the Presidents of Armenia and Azerbaijan and other participants to discuss the question of the peaceful settlement of the Armenian-Azerbaijani Nagorny-Karabakh conflict. He hoped the meeting would play a positive role in resolving the 12-year conflict.

The President outlined the reasons preventing a settlement of the conflict, tracing its history from 1921. He recalled the direct meetings between the Presidents of Armenia and Azerbaijan that began in April 1999 on the initiative of the United States in a search for mutually acceptable compromises, pointing out that, at the end of that year, they were close to doing so. Armenia, however, reneged on the agreement reached. Unfortunately, as a result of those meetings, the co-chairs of the Minsk Group had adopted a wait-and-see position and had based their activities on the principle "What the Presidents agree upon will be acceptable to OSCE".

Azerbaijan did not consider the Presidents' meetings as replacing the activities of the co-chairs of the Minsk Group, but as mutually complementary to ensure progress in the negotiations towards a final settlement of the conflict. Azerbaijan remained committed to peace and the observance of the 1994 ceasefire regime [YUN 1994, p. 577], and would continue to strive for a complete and peaceful settlement of the conflict. The President called on the co-chairs of the Minsk Group to step up efforts to halt the armed conflict and establish stable peace.

Azerbaijan also requested that the item "The situation relating to Nagorny Karabakh" be retained on the list of matters of which the Security Council was seized [S/2001/422].

In response, the "Minister for Foreign Affairs of Nagorny Karabakh", in a 30 April letter transmitted by Armenia [A/56/64-S/2001/431], submitted a memorandum outlining Nagorny Karabakh's version of the region's history in order to prevent a one-sided interpretation of past events and to establish an objective historical basis in the search for a settlement to the conflict. The "Republic of Nagorny Karabakh" had refrained from discussing the problems of the past in the belief that it was unproductive and that both sides should concentrate on building a peaceful and stable future for the region.

On 16 May [A/56/75-S/2001/489], Azerbaijan rejected references to "Nagorny Karabakh" as a country and any attempt to disseminate within the United Nations the notion of Nagorny Karabakh as an independent entity. Armenia's circulation of the memorandum above was testimony to its direct participation in the conflict and to its aggressive and annexationist plans towards Azerbaijan.

By a 31 August statement [S/2001/844], the Chairman of the Milli Mejlis (Parliament) of Azerbaijan reported that "elections" were to be held on 5 September for local self-government bodies in the so-called "Nagorno-Karabakh Republic". The "elections", aimed at "legitimizing" the so-called "Nagorno-Karabakh Republic", contradicted the principles and norms of international law, the Constitution and laws of Azerbaijan and commonly accepted moral norms and values; they were null and void and had no legal consequences. It was another act of political provocation that would negatively affect the ongoing negotiations on the peaceful settlement of the Nagorny-Karabakh problem, in particular the mediation efforts of the Minsk Group.

The Chairman urged the international community not to remain indifferent to the fact that the occupation forces in Nagorny Karabakh were flagrantly defying the sovereignty and territorial integrity of the Republic of Azerbaijan. He called on the Parliamentary Assembly of the Council of Europe, the Inter-Parliamentary Union, the OSCE Parliamentary Assembly, the Parliamentary Assembly of the Black Sea Economic Cooperation, the CIS Inter-Parliamentary Assembly and the Parliamentary Union of the Member States of the Organization of the Islamic Conference, as well as the European Parliament and the North Atlantic Assembly, to condemn the act of political provocation and to support the just cause of Azerbaijan.

Cyprus

The year 2001 saw a significant breakthrough in UN efforts, through the Secretary-General's mission of good offices, in preparing the groundwork for meaningful negotiations towards a comprehensive settlement of the Cyprus question. For the first time, the President of Cyprus, Glafcos Clerides, and the Turkish Cypriot leader, Rauf R. Denktas, agreed to begin direct talks without preconditions until a comprehensive settlement was achieved. Those talks were scheduled to begin in January 2002 in Cyprus.

The United Nations Peacekeeping Force in Cyprus (UNFICYP) continued to assist in the restoration of normal conditions and in humanitarian functions. No progress was made during the year in removing the restrictions imposed in 2000 on UNFICYP by the Turkish Cypriot authorities and Turkish forces. The Security Council twice extended the UNFICYP mandate, the second time until 15 June 2002.

By **decision 55/491** of 7 September, the General Assembly included in the draft agenda of its fifty-sixth (2001) session the item entitled "Question of Cyprus". On 24 December, by **decision 56/464**, it decided that the item would remain for consideration during its resumed fifty-sixth (2002) session.

Incidents

Communications. Throughout 2001, the Secretary-General received numerous letters from the Government of Cyprus and from the Turkish Cypriot authorities containing charges and countercharges, protests and accusations, and explanations of position regarding the question of Cyprus. The letters from the "Turkish Republic of Northern Cyprus" were transmitted by Turkey.

In communications dated between 30 January and 2 November, Cyprus alleged massive violations of its national airspace and unauthorized intrusions into Nicosia's flight information region by Turkish military aircraft, while those from the "Representative of the Turkish Republic of Northern Cyprus" claimed, in refutation, the existence of two independent States in Cyprus and that the flights took place within the sovereign airspace of the "Turkish Republic of Northern Cyprus" [A/55/755-S/2001/96, A/55/776-S/2001/119, A/55/854-S/2001/272, A/55/893-S/2001/343, A/55/990-S/2001/599, A/55/1025-S/2001/765, A/55/476-S/2001/972, A/55/525-S/2001/1044].

In other communications, Cyprus, on 13 February [A/55/782-S/2001/133], responding to a December 2000 letter from Turkey [A/55/715-S/2000/1231], described events that had led to Security Council resolution 186(1964) [YUN 1964, p. 165] and affirmed the continued operation of the 1960 Constitution of Cyprus, subject to necessary temporary modifications. Cyprus also protested what it called the illegal visit of Turkey's Minister for Foreign Affairs to the Turkish occupied areas of Cyprus between 16 and 18 April [A/55/909-S/2001/395].

The "Turkish Republic of Northern Cyprus" gave its own position on various aspects of the Cyprus situation and drew attention to statements made by the representatives of what it called the Greek Cypriot administration in several UN bodies, which it described as containing misrepresentations [A/55/1004-S/2001/645, A/56/504-S/2001/1006, A/55/790-E/2001/6, A/55/865-S/2001/229, A/55/976-S/2001/548, A/55/987-S/2001/576, A/56/669-S/2001/1139, A/56/690-S/2001/1165, A/56/700-S/2001/1187, A/56/755-S/2001/1256]. Both sides also made claims and counterclaims regarding: the arrest and sentencing of a Greek Cypriot, Panicos Tsiakourmas, and the arrest of a Turkish Cypriot, Omer Gazi Tekogul [A/55/737-S/2001/58, A/55/895-S/2001/345, A/55/922-S/2001/427, A/55/932-S/2001/457, A/55/993-S/2001/628]; the issue of the excavations at the archaeological site of Salamis [A/55/1026-S/2001/778, A/55/1032-S/2001/853]; the 10

October judgement in the case of *Cyprus v. Turkey* by the European Court of Human Rights [A/55/986-S/2001/575, A/55/1012-S/2001/678 & Corr.1, A/55/1030-S/2001/824]; and the application of Cyprus for membership in the EU [A/55/899-S/2001/356, A/56/451-S/2001/953, A/56/669-S/2001/1186, A/56/723-S/2001/1222]. On the last issue, the United Kingdom, on 5 November [A/56/612-S/2001/1059], disagreed with Turkey's assertions that Cyprus's application for EU membership was illegal and that the United Kingdom was obliged by the terms of the 1960 Treaty of Guarantee to veto that application.

Good offices mission

Proximity talks

The Secretary-General's Special Adviser on Cyprus, Alvaro de Soto, continued efforts during 2001 to convene the sixth round of proximity talks, scheduled for January, in Geneva, between the two Cyprus parties, led by Cyprus President Glafcos Clerides and Turkish Cypriot leader Rauf R. Denktas, to prepare for meaningful negotiations towards a comprehensive settlement. In his May report on UNFICYP [S/2001/534], the Secretary-General reported that Mr. de Soto travelled to the island in January for meetings with the two leaders, as well as to Greece and Turkey. Mr. Denktas had asked that no date be set for proximity talks. However, the Special Adviser continued to consult with a number of Governments and organizations and was proceeding with preparations so as to be of assistance to the parties when appropriate.

The Secretary-General later reported that he had met with Mr. Denktas in Salzburg, Austria, on 28 August [S/2001/1122], while his Special Adviser returned to Cyprus, remaining there from 29 August to 5 September. On 4 September, the Special Adviser conveyed to Mr. Clerides and Mr. Denktas the Secretary-General's invitation to resume the search for a comprehensive settlement in a new and reinvigorated phase of his good offices, beginning with separate meetings with the two leaders in New York on 12 September. That invitation was accepted by Mr. Clerides, but declined by Mr. Denktas.

Security Council consideration. On 26 September [S/2001/976], the Security Council President issued a press statement in which the Council expressed disappointment at the unjustified decision by the Turkish side to decline the Secretary-General's invitation and reaffirmed that progress could be made only at the negotiating table. The Council encouraged the Secretary-General and his Special Adviser to continue their efforts in accordance with resolution 1250(1999) [YUN 1999, p. 388] and gave full support to those efforts. It urged all concerned to cooperate with the Secretary-General and his Special Adviser and to show confidence in their judgement.

Communications. Mr. Denktas, "President of the Turkish Republic of Northern Cyprus", in a 10 September letter transmitted by Turkey on 9 October [A/56/461-S/2001/959], informed the Secretary-General that he had declined to attend the proposed New York talks because he considered them premature. He reiterated that the Greek Cypriot's rejection of the Secretary-General's 12 September 2000 statement [SG/SM/7546], setting out his understanding of the status of the parties to the negotiations, had left no common ground for engaging in meaningful talks. The treatment of the Greek Cypriot side by all concerned as the legitimate Government of Cyprus and frequent statements to the effect that, "agreement or not", Cyprus would be accepted as an EU member, left no will or wish on the part of the Greek Cypriot leadership to share anything with the Turkish Cypriot side. Those developments had undermined the chances of success of the Secretary-General's mission of good offices. While convinced of the imperative to prepare the ground for meaningful negotiations, Mr. Denktas needed proof that the ground was really prepared so that the parties would not engage in yet another futile exercise. For those reasons, he was insisting on "common ground" with respect to the objective (the establishment of a new partnership) and guiding principles (the equal status of the parties and that neither could represent the other or the whole of Cyprus) before starting a new phase of reinvigorated and meaningful negotiations. Thus, securing a commitment from the two parties that the purpose of the UN-facilitated talks was the establishment of a new partnership based on the equal status of both would prepare the ground for the proposed reinvigorated phase of the talks.

The EU, in a 23 October statement on Cyprus [S/2001/1017], supported the Council President's 26 September statement (see p. 391), in particular the disappointment expressed at the Turkish side's refusal to take part in the 12 September meeting. It backed the Secretary-General's efforts to resume, without preconditions, the search for a comprehensive and lasting settlement and called on all parties involved to cooperate in the process for achieving a political settlement before the end of negotiations for the accession of Cyprus to the EU.

Agreement on direct talks

Turkey, on 14 November [A/56/622-S/2001/1077], transmitted a 12 November letter from Mr. Denktas, enclosing a paper entitled "Objectives and basic parameters of a Cyprus settlement", which formed the basis of his position during the 28 August meeting with the Secretary-General (see p. 391). According to Mr. Denktas, those parameters were in line with the ideas and principles that had emerged from the Secretary-General's good offices mission and reflected the realities of the island, as well as the objective of establishing a new partnership between the two parties.

The Secretary-General reported in November [S/2001/1122] that, following a proposal made directly to Mr. Clerides by Mr. Denktas for a face-to-face meeting without preconditions on the island, the two agreed through an exchange of letters to meet on 4 December in the United Nations Protected Area, in the presence of the Special Adviser.

On 10 December [S/2001/1162], the Secretary-General informed the Security Council that, at the 4 December meeting, the two leaders agreed that: the Secretary-General, in the exercise of his good offices mission, would invite them to direct talks to be held in Cyprus in mid-January 2002 on UN premises, with no preconditions; all issues would be on the table; negotiations would continue in good faith until a comprehensive settlement was achieved; and nothing would be agreed until everything was agreed. In transmitting the agreement to the Council, the Secretary-General indicated that the talks would begin on 16 January 2002.

The Council, in a 12 December press statement by its President [SC/7237], welcomed the agreement reached by the two leaders to begin direct talks and other positive developments and hoped that progress would be achieved resulting in a comprehensive settlement. The Council gave its full support to the Secretary-General's mission of good offices and encouraged him and his Special Adviser to continue to be of assistance to the parties.

Continuation of good offices mission

The Secretary-General, on 31 May [S/2001/556], drew the Security Council's attention to the fact that efforts related to his mission of good offices in Cyprus would continue at least throughout 2001. In furtherance of that mission, his Special Adviser would continue to be assisted by a small team. He asked the Council President to alert Council members to the importance of continuing support for his efforts in discharging his mission. The Council took note of the Secretary-General's letter on 5 June [S/2001/557].

The Secretary-General, on 5 December [S/2001/1182], informed the Council that the efforts relating to his mission would continue at least throughout 2002, which the Council took note of on 12 December [S/2001/1183].

UNFICYP

The United Nations Peacekeeping Force in Cyprus, established by Security Council resolution 186(1964) [YUN 1964, p. 165], continued in 2001 to monitor the ceasefire lines between the Turkish and Turkish Cypriot forces on the northern side and the Cypriot National Guard on the southern side of the island; to maintain the military status quo and prevent a recurrence of fighting; and to undertake humanitarian and economic activities. In the absence of a formal ceasefire agreement, the military status quo, as recorded by UNFICYP in 1974, remained the standard by which the Force judged whether changes constituted violations of the status quo.

UNFICYP, under the overall authority of the Acting Special Representative and Chief of Mission, Zbigniew Wlosowicz, continued to keep the area between the ceasefire lines, known as the buffer zone, under constant surveillance through a system of observation posts, and through air, vehicle and foot patrols.

During 2001, Alvaro de Soto continued as the Secretary-General's Special Adviser on Cyprus. On 6 December [S/2001/1184], the Secretary-General informed the Council of his intention to appoint Major General Jin Ha Hwang (Republic of Korea) as Force Commander, to succeed Major General Victory Rana (Nepal), whose tour of duty would end on 15 December. The Council noted that intended appointment on 12 December [S/2001/1185].

As at 31 December, UNFICYP, under the command of Major General Jin Ha Hwang, comprised 1,196 troops and 35 civilian police.

Activities

Report of Secretary-General (May). The Secretary-General, in his report covering developments and UNFICYP activities from 28 November 2000 to 29 May 2001 [S/2001/534], said that, except for a few minor incidents, the situation along the ceasefire line remained calm. Air violations in the UN buffer zone had decreased from 47 during the last reporting period [YUN 2000, p. 404] to 33. Since December 2000, the National Guard had developed two major defensive works on its ceasefire line just outside the UN buffer zone near Pyla. In response, the Turkish forces constructed two berms and dug 120 metres of a new trench between existing positions at a Turkish forces post. Despite repeated UNFICYP demands, the Turkish forces had refused to return that post to the status quo ante and had recently added a barbed wire fence to the north of that position. Reinforced concrete firing positions were also being installed along much of the National Guard ceasefire line.

Crossings of the maritime security lines (the seaward extensions of the median line of the buffer zone) continued as well. Restrictions imposed on UNFICYP by Turkish Cypriot authorities and Turkish forces in 2000 [ibid.] remained in force, including violation of the military status quo by the Turkish forces/Turkish Cypriot security forces in the village of Strovilia. Restrictions imposed along the Famagusta-Dherinia road continued to prevent UNFICYP from monitoring the whole of the fenced area of Varosha, limiting UNFICYP's observation to areas visible from static observation posts and from a short patrol route well away from the fence. Within Varosha, Turkish forces continued renovations of some buildings and flew flags on one of them in violation of the military status quo. Some tension developed in April in the mixed village of Pyla in the buffer zone as a result of the raising of Turkish and Turkish Cypriot flags in several locations, in violation of the agreement reached among the two communities in the village and UNFICYP.

UNFICYP assisted civilian activities in the buffer zone, by, for example, facilitating work to improve the water supply to the north and escorting farmers working on their land. In April, it also facilitated a visit by some 250 Greek Cypriots to a church in the buffer zone near Varisha, north-west of Lefka, to mark Saint George's Day. UNDP, through the United Nations Office for Project Services (UNOPS), continued to implement its programme to promote good will by encouraging Greek and Turkish Cypriots to work together in preparing and implementing projects of mutual concern, notably in public health, environment, sanitation, water, urban renovation, preservation of cultural heritage, natural resources and education.

The Secretary-General remarked that the conditions under which UNFICYP operated remained difficult owing to the restrictions imposed on it by the Turkish Cypriot authorities and Turkish forces. He considered the presence of UNFICYP essential for the maintenance of the ceasefire on the island and recommended that the Council extend its mandate for a further six months, until 15 December 2001.

Communications. In letters to the Secretary-General between February and June, the Government of Cyprus, representatives of the "Turkish Republic of Northern Cyprus" and Turkey continued to debate the legal necessity for approval by both sides of the extension of UNFICYP's mandate [A/55/784-S/2001/136, A/55/866-S/2001/307, A/55/949-S/2001/507, A/55/970-S/2001/541, A/55/1003-S/2001/644].

SECURITY COUNCIL ACTION

On 15 June [meeting 4328], the Security Council unanimously adopted **resolution 1354(2001)**. The draft [S/2001/581] was prepared in consultations among Council members.

The Security Council,

Welcoming the report of the Secretary-General of 30 May 2001 on the United Nations operation in Cyprus, in particular the call to the parties to assess and address the humanitarian issue of missing persons with due urgency and seriousness,

Noting that the Government of Cyprus has agreed that in view of the prevailing conditions in the island it is necessary to keep the United Nations Peacekeeping Force in Cyprus beyond 15 June 2001,

Welcoming and encouraging efforts by the United Nations to sensitize peacekeeping personnel in the prevention and control of HIV/AIDS and other communicable diseases in all its peacekeeping operations,

1. *Reaffirms* all its relevant resolutions on Cyprus, in particular resolutions 1251(1999) of 29 June 1999 and subsequent resolutions;

2. *Decides* to extend the mandate of the United Nations Peacekeeping Force in Cyprus for a further period ending 15 December 2001;

3. *Requests* the Secretary-General to submit a report, by 1 December 2001, on the implementation of the present resolution;

4. *Urges* the Turkish Cypriot side and Turkish forces to rescind the restrictions imposed on 30 June 2000 on the operations of the United Nations Peacekeeping Force in Cyprus, and to restore the military status quo ante at Strovilia;

5. *Decides* to remain actively seized of the matter.

Report of Secretary-General (November). In November [S/2001/1122], the Secretary-General reported fewer incidents along the ceasefire lines. However, the restrictions imposed on UNFICYP operations continued, including the violation of the military status quo in Strovilia. Patrols to Varosha, which were prevented under those restrictions, resumed in September but under escort by Turkish Cypriot security forces. The number of air violations remained about the same, and crossings of the maritime security lines totalled about 250 crossings by Turkish forces of the western line and some 3,000 in the east near Famagusta from the south. Incursions in the buffer zone by Greek Cypriot hunters increased significantly in November with the beginning of the winter hunting season.

The National Guard continued to develop and strengthen the two defensive positions (see p. 393) just outside the buffer zone south of Pyla,

reportedly to compensate for the minefield linking the two positions, which was being demined. The Turkish forces, for their part, reinforced their observation post adjacent to Pyla.

UNFICYP helped to facilitate monthly meetings of political party representatives from both sides, media gatherings, music rehearsals and a business forum at Ledra Palace. It continued its humanitarian support to 427 Greek Cypriots and 165 Maronites in the northern part of the island and those Turkish Cypriots in the southern part who had made themselves known to UNFICYP. It also facilitated the rotation of teachers at the Greek elementary school in Rizokarpaso in the Karpas peninsula. UNFICYP support of civilian activities in the buffer zone continued, including farming, liaison with local representatives to solve water problems, coordinating maintenance work on utilities, extending the Klimos river wall in Sector 2 to prevent flooding and reconstruction of a 73-bed hospital in Paralimni in Sector 4. UNFICYP also designated land in the buffer zone west of Nicosia for civilian use, mainly for housing. In Pyla, it brokered an agreement between Greek and Turkish Cypriot village leaders on road safety measures.

Efforts continued in overcoming obstacles to enable the Committee on Missing Persons to resume its activities, including specific proposals by the leaders of both sides concerning the Committee's work. Meanwhile, the Government of Cyprus continued to implement its unilateral programme of exhumation and identification of human remains.

The Secretary-General recommended that the Council extend the UNFICYP mandate for a further six months, until 15 June 2002.

SECURITY COUNCIL ACTION

On 14 December [meeting 4436], the Security Council unanimously adopted **resolution 1384 (2001)**. The draft [S/2001/1190] was prepared in consultations among Council members.

The Security Council,

Welcoming the report of the Secretary-General of 30 November 2001 on the United Nations operation in Cyprus, in particular the call to the parties to assess and address the humanitarian issue of missing persons with due urgency and seriousness,

Noting that the Government of Cyprus has agreed that in view of the prevailing conditions in the island it is necessary to keep the United Nations Peacekeeping Force in Cyprus beyond 15 December 2001,

Welcoming and encouraging efforts by the United Nations to sensitize peacekeeping personnel in the prevention and control of HIV/AIDS and other communicable diseases in all its peacekeeping operations,

1. *Reaffirms* all its relevant resolutions on Cyprus, in particular resolution 1251(1999) of 29 June 1999 and subsequent resolutions;

2. *Decides* to extend the mandate of the United Nations Peacekeeping Force in Cyprus for a further period ending on 15 June 2002;

3. *Requests* the Secretary-General to submit a report, by 1 June 2002, on the implementation of the present resolution;

4. *Urges* the Turkish Cypriot side and Turkish forces to rescind the restrictions imposed on 30 June 2000 on the operations of the United Nations Peacekeeping Force in Cyprus, and to restore the military status quo ante at Strovilia;

5. *Decides* to remain actively seized of the matter.

Financing

On 14 June [meeting 103], the General Assembly, having considered the Secretary-General's report on UNFICYP's financial performance for the period 1 July 1999 to 30 June 2000 [A/55/739], the proposed budget for UNFICYP's maintenance for the period 1 July 2001 to 30 June 2002 [A/55/788] and ACABQ's comments and recommendations thereon [A/55/874/Add.3], adopted, on the recommendation of the Fifth Committee [A/55/969], **resolution 55/266** without vote [agenda item 143].

Financing of the United Nations Peacekeeping Force in Cyprus

The General Assembly,

Having considered the reports of the Secretary-General on the financing of the United Nations Peacekeeping Force in Cyprus and the related reports of the Advisory Committee on Administrative and Budgetary Questions,

Recalling Security Council resolution 186(1964) of 4 March 1964, by which the Council established the United Nations Peacekeeping Force in Cyprus, and the subsequent resolutions by which the Council extended the mandate of the Force, the latest of which was resolution 1331(2000) of 13 December 2000,

Recalling also its resolution 54/270 of 15 June 2000 on the financing of the Force,

Reaffirming the general principles underlying the financing of United Nations peacekeeping operations as stated in General Assembly resolutions 1874(S-IV) of 27 June 1963, 3101(XXVIII) of 11 December 1973 and 55/235 of 23 December 2000,

Noting with appreciation that voluntary contributions have been made to the Force by certain Governments,

Noting that voluntary contributions were insufficient to cover all the costs of the Force, including those incurred by troop-contributing Governments prior to 16 June 1993, and regretting the absence of an adequate response to appeals for voluntary contributions, including that contained in the letter dated 17 May 1994 from the Secretary-General to all Member States,

Mindful of the fact that it is essential to provide the Force with the necessary financial resources to enable it to fulfil its responsibilities under the relevant resolutions of the Security Council,

1. *Takes note* of the status of contributions to the United Nations Peacekeeping Force in Cyprus as of 30 April 2001, including the contributions outstanding in the amount of 20.3 million United States dollars, representing some 10.7 per cent of the total assessed contributions from 16 June 1993 to the period ending 15 June 2001, notes that some 15.3 per cent of the Member States have paid their assessed contributions in full, and urges all other Member States concerned, in particular those in arrears, to ensure payment of their outstanding assessed contributions;

2. *Expresses concern* about the financial situation with regard to peacekeeping activities, in particular as regards the reimbursements to troop contributors that bear additional burdens owing to overdue payments by Member States of their assessments;

3. *Expresses its appreciation* to those Member States which have paid their assessed contributions in full;

4. *Urges* all other Member States to make every possible effort to ensure payment of their assessed contributions to the Force in full and on time;

5. *Expresses concern* at the delay experienced by the Secretary-General in deploying and providing adequate resources to some recent peacekeeping missions, in particular those in Africa;

6. *Emphasizes* that all future and existing peacekeeping missions shall be given equal and non-discriminatory treatment in respect of financial and administrative arrangements;

7. *Also emphasizes* that all peacekeeping missions shall be provided with adequate resources for the effective and efficient discharge of their respective mandates;

8. *Reiterates its request* to the Secretary-General to make the fullest possible use of facilities and equipment at the United Nations Logistics Base at Brindisi, Italy, in order to minimize the costs of procurement for the Force;

9. *Endorses* the conclusions and recommendations contained in the report of the Advisory Committee on Administrative and Budgetary Questions, and requests the Secretary-General to ensure their full implementation;

10. *Requests* the Secretary-General to take all necessary action to ensure that the Force is administered with a maximum of efficiency and economy;

11. *Also requests* the Secretary-General, in order to reduce the cost of employing General Service staff, to continue efforts to recruit local staff for the Force against General Service posts, commensurate with the requirements of the Force;

12. *Decides* to appropriate to the Special Account for the United Nations Peacekeeping Force in Cyprus the amount of 42,389,220 dollars gross (40,697,146 dollars net) for the maintenance of the Force for the period from 1 July 2001 to 30 June 2002, inclusive of the amount of 1,240,621 dollars gross (1,088,767 dollars net) for the support account for peacekeeping operations and the amount of 129,599 dollars gross (116,379 dollars net) for the United Nations Logistics Base, a one-third share of this amount, equivalent to 13,565,715 dollars, to be funded through voluntary contributions from the Government of Cyprus, and an amount of 6.5 million dollars from the Government of Greece, subject to the review by the Security Council with regard to the question of termination or continuation of the Force;

13. *Decides also,* taking into consideration the funding through voluntary contributions from the Government of Cyprus of a one-third share of the cost of the Force, equivalent to 13,565,715 dollars, and of 6.5 million dollars from the Government of Greece, to apportion among Member States the amount of 22,323,505 dollars gross (20,631,431 dollars net), the said amount to be apportioned at a monthly rate of 1,860,292 dollars gross (1,719,286 dollars net) in accordance with the levels set out in General Assembly resolution 55/235, as adjusted by the Assembly in its resolution 55/236 of 23 December 2000, and taking into account the scale of assessments for the years 2001 and 2002, as set out in its resolution 55/5 B of 23 December 2000, subject to the review by the Security Council with regard to the question of termination or continuation of the Force;

14. *Decides further* that, in accordance with the provisions of its resolution 973(X) of 15 December 1955, there shall be set off against the apportionment among Member States, as provided for in paragraph 13 above, their respective share in the Tax Equalization Fund of the estimated staff assessment income of 1,692,074 dollars approved for the Force for the period from 1 July 2001 to 30 June 2002;

15. *Decides* that, taking into consideration the funding through voluntary contributions from the Government of Cyprus of a one-third share of the cost of the Force, equivalent to 14,630,809 dollars, and of 6.5 million dollars from the Government of Greece, for Member States that have fulfilled their financial obligations to the Force, there shall be set off against the apportionment, as provided for in paragraph 13 above, their respective share of the amount of 280,800 dollars gross (261,400 dollars net) of the unencumbered balance of 523,400 dollars gross (504,000 dollars net) in respect of the period ending 30 June 2000, in accordance with the compositions of groups set out in paragraphs 3 and 4 of General Assembly resolution 43/232 of 1 March 1989, as adjusted by the Assembly in its subsequent relevant resolutions and decisions for the ad hoc apportionment of peacekeeping appropriations, the latest of which were resolution 52/230 of 31 March 1998 and decisions 54/456 to 54/458 of 23 December 1999 for the period 1998-2000, and taking into account the scale of assessments for the year 2000, as set out in its resolutions 52/215 A of 22 December 1997 and 54/237 A of 23 December 1999;

16. *Decides also* that, for Member States that have not fulfilled their financial obligations to the Force, their share of the unencumbered balance of 280,800 dollars gross (261,400 dollars net) in respect of the period ending 30 June 2000 shall be set off against their outstanding obligations in accordance with the scheme set out in paragraph 15 above;

17. *Decides further* that 168,000 dollars shall be returned to the Government of Cyprus and 74,600 dollars shall be returned to the Government of Greece;

18. *Decides* to continue to maintain as separate the account established for the Force for the period prior to 16 June 1993, invites Member States to make voluntary contributions to that account, and requests the Secretary-General to continue his efforts in appealing for voluntary contributions to the account;

19. *Emphasizes* that no peacekeeping mission shall be financed by borrowing funds from other active peacekeeping missions;

20. *Encourages* the Secretary-General to continue to take additional measures to ensure the safety and security of all personnel under the auspices of the United Nations participating in the Force;

21. *Invites* voluntary contributions to the Force in cash and in the form of services and supplies acceptable to the Secretary-General, to be administered, as appropriate, in accordance with the procedures and practices established by the General Assembly;

22. *Decides* to include in the provisional agenda of its fifty-sixth session the item entitled "Financing of the United Nations Peacekeeping Force in Cyprus".

On 24 December, the Assembly decided that the item on UNFICYP's financing would remain for consideration at its resumed fifty-sixth (2002) session (**decision 56/464**) and that the Fifth Committee would continue consideration of the item at that session (**decision 56/458**).

Other issues

Cooperation with OSCE

In response to General Assembly resolution 55/179 [YUN 2000, p. 408], the Secretary-General submitted a June report [A/56/125] describing cooperation between the United Nations and the Organization for Security and Cooperation in Europe (OSCE).

During the year, a number of meetings took place between the United Nations and OSCE, including attendance by the OSCE Secretary-General at the fourth high-level meeting with heads of regional organizations in February on "Cooperation for peace-building" (see p. 56) and participation in the annual high-level tripartite meeting of the United Nations, OSCE and the Council of Europe (Vienna, February) on the subject of good governance.

The United Nations and OSCE continued to practise a division of labour based on their comparative advantages: the United Nations retained the lead in Abkhazia, Georgia, and in Tajikistan; OSCE had the lead in the Republic of Moldova, South Ossetia, Georgia, and in the resolution of the conflict in and around the Nagorny-Karabakh region of Azerbaijan. Specific efforts were also made to improve consultation and cooperation in the field and between the respective headquarters, resulting in enhanced coordination aimed at making better use of international resources in the interests of the countries being assisted. The report listed specific cooperation activities by UN departments and programmes.

On 21 December [meeting 91], the General Assembly adopted **resolution 56/216** [draft: A/56/L.66 & Add.1] by recorded vote (123-0-4) [agenda item 21 (*i*)].

Cooperation between the United Nations and the Organization for Security and Cooperation in Europe

The General Assembly,

Recalling the framework for cooperation and coordination between the United Nations and the Conference on Security and Cooperation in Europe, which was signed on 26 May 1993, as well as its resolutions on cooperation between the two organizations,

Recalling also the principles embodied in the Helsinki Final Act and in the declaration at the 1992 Helsinki Summit by the heads of State or Government of the participating States of the Conference on Security and Cooperation in Europe of their understanding that the Conference is a regional arrangement in the sense of Chapter VIII of the Charter of the United Nations and as such provides an important link between European and global security,

Acknowledging the increasing contribution of the Organization for Security and Cooperation in Europe to the establishment and maintenance of international peace and security in its region through activities in early warning and preventive diplomacy, including through the activities of the High Commissioner on National Minorities, crisis management and post-conflict rehabilitation, as well as arms control and disarmament,

Recalling the Charter for European Security adopted at the Summit in Istanbul, Turkey, in November 1999, which reaffirms the Organization for Security and Cooperation in Europe as a primary organization for the peaceful settlement of disputes within its region and as a key instrument for early warning, conflict prevention, crisis management and post-conflict rehabilitation,

Recalling also the special ties between the Organization for Security and Cooperation in Europe and the Mediterranean Partners for Cooperation, as well as between that organization and the Asian Partners for Cooperation, Japan, the Republic of Korea and Thailand, which have been enhanced further in 2001,

Underlining the continued importance of enhanced cooperation and coordination between the United Nations and the Organization for Security and Cooperation in Europe,

1. *Welcomes* the report of the Secretary-General;

2. *Notes with appreciation* the further improvement of cooperation and coordination between the United Nations and its agencies and the Organization for Security and Cooperation in Europe, including at the level of activities in the field;

3. *Welcomes*, in this context, the meetings of the Secretary-General of the United Nations with the Chairman-in-Office and the Secretary-General of the Organization for Security and Cooperation in Europe, the participation of the Chairman-in-Office at a meeting of the Security Council in January 2001, the participation of the Director-General of the United Nations Office at Geneva in a meeting of the Ministerial Council of the Organization for Security and Cooperation in

Europe, which was held in Bucharest on 3 and 4 December 2001, and the participation of high-level United Nations representatives in meetings of the Organization for Security and Cooperation in Europe;

4. *Encourages* further efforts of the Organization for Security and Cooperation in Europe to foster security and stability in its region through early warning, conflict prevention, crisis management and post-conflict rehabilitation, as well as through continued promotion of democracy, the rule of law, human rights and fundamental freedoms;

5. *Welcomes* the documents of the meeting of the Ministerial Council in Bucharest confirming the determination of the participating States of the Organization for Security and Cooperation in Europe to strengthen and deepen their cooperation with a view to protecting their citizens from new challenges to their security while safeguarding the rule of law, individual liberties and the right to equal justice under the law;

6. *Commends* the adoption of the decision and Action Plan on Terrorism, whereby participating States pledged to reinforce and develop bilateral and multilateral cooperation among themselves, with the United Nations and with other international and regional organizations in order to combat terrorism in all its forms and manifestations, wherever and by whomever committed, to contribute to the fulfilment of international obligations as enshrined, inter alia, in Security Council resolution 1373(2001) of 28 September 2001, to act in conformity with the purposes and principles of the Charter of the United Nations, and to become parties to all twelve United Nations conventions and protocols related to terrorism as soon as possible;

7. *Notes* the review of the structures of the Organization for Security and Cooperation in Europe, undertaken at the initiative of the Romanian Chairmanship, with the goal of strengthening its efficiency, and the adoption of decisions to foster its role as a forum for political dialogue on issues of security and cooperation in Europe which promotes a more effective use of the means and mechanisms of the Organization for Security and Cooperation in Europe to counter threats and challenges to security and stability in its region;

8. *Welcomes* the decisions to strengthen cooperation in the economic and environmental sphere and to enhance the role of the Organization for Security and Cooperation in Europe in police-related activities;

9. *Also welcomes* the documents of the Ministerial Council meeting in Bucharest on enhancing the effectiveness of the human dimension meetings of the Organization for Security and Cooperation in Europe, promoting tolerance and non-discrimination, combating trafficking in human beings, improving the situation of Roma and Sinti, and on promoting equal opportunities for women and men and the continued close cooperation between the Organization for Security and Cooperation in Europe, the Office of the United Nations High Commissioner for Refugees and the Office of the United Nations High Commissioner for Human Rights;

10. *Notes with appreciation* the active involvement of the Organization for Security and Cooperation in Europe in Albania, Bosnia and Herzegovina, Croatia, the Federal Republic of Yugoslavia and the former Yugoslav Republic of Macedonia and its commitment to continue to contribute substantially to conflict pre-

vention, crisis management, and post-conflict stabilization in the region, thereby fostering peace and stability in the area;

11. *Welcomes* the establishment and the work of the Mission of the Organization for Security and Cooperation in Europe to the Federal Republic of Yugoslavia to assist further progress in the consolidation of democracy, the strengthening of the rule of law and respect for human rights and fundamental freedoms, including the rights of persons belonging to national minorities;

12. *Expresses its appreciation* for the contribution by the Organization for Security and Cooperation in Europe to implementing Security Council resolution 1244(1999) of 10 June 1999, in particular for its substantial role in the preparation and organization of the Kosovo-wide election on 17 November 2001, in view of the consolidation of stability and prosperity in Kosovo, Federal Republic of Yugoslavia, on the basis of substantial autonomy, respecting the sovereignty and territorial integrity of the Federal Republic of Yugoslavia, pending a final settlement, in accordance with resolution 1244(1999);

13. *Salutes* the commitment of participating States of the Organization for Security and Cooperation in Europe to the sovereignty, territorial integrity and unitary character of the former Yugoslav Republic of Macedonia and their offer to assist and support strongly the full and timely implementation of the Framework Agreement concluded on 13 August 2001, including the programmes on police training and reform, media and inter-ethnic relations;

14. *Supports* the priorities of the work of the Organization for Security and Cooperation in Europe for the continuous development of civil society and for increasing local ownership of the reform process in Bosnia and Herzegovina;

15. *Commends* the efforts to improve the coordination and efficiency of international engagement in the field of civilian implementation of the Dayton/Paris peace accords, as well as a timely decision on the best options for the succession of the United Nations International Police Task Force to allow for a smooth and comprehensive transition;

16. *Underlines* the importance of regional cooperation as a means of fostering good-neighbourly relations, stability and economic development, welcomes the implementation of the Stability Pact for South-Eastern Europe under the auspices of the Organization for Security and Cooperation in Europe as an important long-term and comprehensive initiative to promote good-neighbourly relations, stability and economic development, and also welcomes the commitment of participating States of the Organization for Security and Cooperation in Europe to contribute further to the goals of the Stability Pact;

17. *Notes* the efforts undertaken in 2001 by the Republic of Moldova and the mediators of the Organization for Security and Cooperation in Europe, the Russian Federation and Ukraine towards negotiation for a comprehensive political settlement of the Transdniestrian issue, based on full respect of the sovereignty and territorial integrity of the Republic of Moldova, welcomes the fulfilment by the Russian Federation, ahead of the agreed time, of the commitments undertaken at the summit of the Organization for Security and Cooperation in Europe held in Istanbul, Turkey, in 1999 on the withdrawal and disposal of the equipment limited by the Treaty on Conventional Armed Forces in Europe located in the Transdniestrian region of the Republic of Moldova by the end of 2001, and encourages the timely fulfilment of other commitments concerning the Republic of Moldova undertaken by the participating States of the Organization for Security and Cooperation in Europe in Istanbul in 1999;

18. *Welcomes* the developments in the peace process in the Tshkhinvali region/South Ossetia, Georgia, and the steps to reduce the quantities of small arms and light weapons in that region, as well as the progress made in 2001 towards meeting the commitments made in Istanbul on the future of Russian forces in Georgia, including the closure of the Russian base at Vaziani and the withdrawal of the equipment from the Russian base at Gudauta, encourages the implementation of the other Istanbul commitments, and with regard to Abkhazia, Georgia, calls for the resumption of a constructive dialogue aimed at achieving a comprehensive settlement, including a definition of the political status of Abkhazia as a sovereign entity within the State of Georgia;

19. *Acknowledges* the significant contribution to stability and confidence in the region made by the border monitoring operation of the Organization for Security and Cooperation in Europe along the border between Georgia and the Chechen Republic of the Russian Federation;

20. *Notes with satisfaction* the engagement of the Organization for Security and Cooperation in Europe towards cooperation with the five participating States of Central Asia, which has continued to grow in all dimensions, thus contributing to stability and prosperity in the region, as well as the commitment of the Organization for Security and Cooperation in Europe to assist in addressing specific threats to stability and security for the Central Asian participating States, and appreciates the valuable contribution of the Bishkek International Conference on enhancing security and stability in Central Asia, held on 13 and 14 December 2001, to addressing those problems, which are shared concerns among the participating States of the Organization for Security and Cooperation in Europe;

21. *Fully supports* the activities of the Organization for Security and Cooperation in Europe to achieve a peaceful solution to the conflict in and around the Nagorny-Karabakh region of the Republic of Azerbaijan, and welcomes cooperation between the United Nations and the Organization for Security and Cooperation in Europe in this regard;

22. *Expresses deep concern* at the failure to achieve a settlement of the Nagorny-Karabakh conflict despite the intensified dialogue between the parties and the active support of the Co-Chairmen of the Minsk Group of the Organization for Security and Cooperation in Europe, reaffirms that the prompt resolution of that protracted conflict will contribute to lasting peace, security, stability and cooperation in the South Caucasus region, reiterates the importance of continuing the peace dialogue, calls upon the sides to continue their efforts to achieve an early resolution of the conflict based on the norms and principles of international law, encourages the parties to explore further measures that would enhance mutual confidence and trust, in-

cluding the release of prisoners of war, welcomes the commitment of the parties to the ceasefire and to achieving a peaceful and comprehensive settlement, and encourages the parties to continue their efforts, with the active support of the Co-Chairmen, to reach a just and enduring settlement;

23. *Decides* to include in the provisional agenda of its fifty-seventh session the item entitled "Cooperation between the United Nations and the Organization for Security and Cooperation in Europe", and requests the Secretary-General to submit to the General Assembly at its fifty-seventh session a report on cooperation between the United Nations and the Organization for Security and Cooperation in Europe in implementation of the present resolution.

RECORDED VOTE ON RESOLUTION 56/216:

In favour: Albania, Algeria, Andorra, Argentina, Austria, Azerbaijan, Bahamas, Bahrain, Bangladesh, Belgium, Benin, Bhutan, Bolivia, Bosnia and Herzegovina, Brazil, Brunei Darussalam, Bulgaria, Burkina Faso, Cambodia, Canada, Chile, China, Colombia, Costa Rica, Côte d'Ivoire, Croatia, Cyprus, Czech Republic, Denmark, Djibouti, Dominica, Ecuador, Egypt, El Salvador, Equatorial Guinea, Eritrea, Estonia, Ethiopia, Finland, France, Gabon, Georgia, Germany, Ghana, Greece, Grenada, Guatemala, Hungary, Iceland, India, Indonesia, Iran, Ireland, Israel, Italy, Jamaica, Japan, Jordan, Kazakhstan, Kenya, Kuwait, Latvia, Lebanon, Libyan Arab Jamahiriya, Liechtenstein, Lithuania, Luxembourg, Malaysia, Maldives, Malta, Mauritius, Mexico, Monaco, Mongolia, Morocco, Mozambique, Myanmar, Namibia, Nepal, Netherlands, New Zealand, Nicaragua, Norway, Oman, Pakistan, Panama, Papua New Guinea, Paraguay, Peru, Philippines, Poland, Portugal, Qatar, Republic of Korea, Republic of Moldova, Romania, Russian Federation, San Marino, Saudi Arabia, Senegal, Singapore, Slovakia, Slovenia, Spain, Sri Lanka, Sudan, Suriname, Sweden, Syrian Arab Republic, Thailand, The former Yugoslav Republic of Macedonia, Togo, Tunisia, Turkey, Uganda, Ukraine, United Kingdom, United States, Uruguay, Venezuela, Yemen, Yugoslavia, Zambia.

Against: None.

Abstaining: Armenia, Belarus, South Africa, United Republic of Tanzania.

Before the adoption of the resolution, a recorded vote (34-1-85) was taken on an amendment adding paragraph 21, introduced by Azerbaijan [A/56/L.67], stating specifically that Nagorny Karabakh was a region of Azerbaijan.

Cooperation with the Council of Europe

In response to resolution 55/3 [YUN 2000, p. 410], the Secretary-General submitted an August report on cooperation between the United Nations and the Council of Europe [A/56/302].

The Secretary-General reported that cooperation continued through direct contact between the secretariats of the two organizations, the Council's observer status in the General Assembly and the cooperation agreements between the Council and various UN specialized agencies and bodies, and meetings of the Secretaries-General of the two organizations. He highlighted specific cooperation activities between the Council and UN programmes and the Secretariat.

The Secretary-General observed that both organizations continued to have shared interests that lent themselves to cooperation in such areas as conflict prevention, post-conflict peace-building and confidence-building measures for increasing tolerance and understanding between people belonging to different ethnic groups, es-

pecially those within countries in crisis. He recommended that such cooperation be reported to the Assembly every other year, the next report to be submitted to its fifty-eighth (2003) session, and that the item be included in that session's provisional agenda.

GENERAL ASSEMBLY ACTION

On 7 December [meeting 80], the General Assembly adopted **resolution 56/43** [draft: A/56/L.31 & Add.1] without vote [agenda item 21 *(c)*].

Cooperation between the United Nations and the Council of Europe

The General Assembly,

Recalling the Agreement between the Council of Europe and the Secretariat of the United Nations signed on 15 December 1951 and the Arrangement on Cooperation and Liaison between the secretariats of the United Nations and the Council of Europe of 19 November 1971,

Acknowledging the contribution of the Council of Europe to the protection and strengthening of democracy, human rights and fundamental freedoms and the rule of law on the European continent, including its activities against racism and intolerance, the promotion of gender equality, social development and a common cultural heritage,

Acknowledging also that, with its significant expertise in the field of human rights, democratic institutions and the rule of law, the Council of Europe is contributing to conflict prevention, confidence-building and long-term post-conflict peace-building through political, legal and institutional reform,

Stressing the importance of adherence to the standards and principles of the Council of Europe and its contribution to the solution of conflicts throughout the whole of Europe,

Acknowledging the contribution of the Council of Europe to the development of international law, inter alia, international criminal law,

Noting the increasing openness of the Council of Europe, through its legal instruments, to the participation of States of other regions,

1. *Welcomes* the report of the Secretary-General;

2. *Notes with appreciation* the further improvement of cooperation and coordination between the United Nations and its agencies and the Council of Europe, both at the level of headquarters and in the field;

3. *Welcomes* the increasingly close cooperation between the Council of Europe, the Office of the United Nations High Commissioner for Human Rights and the Office of the United Nations High Commissioner for Refugees;

4. *Welcomes also* the efforts of the Council of Europe to assist States in the ratification and implementation of the Rome Statute of the International Criminal Court, in particular the most recent meeting, held in Strasbourg, France, on 13 and 14 September 2001;

5. *Expresses its appreciation* to the Council of Europe for its contribution to the World Conference against Racism, Racial Discrimination, Xenophobia and Related Intolerance, held in Durban, South Africa, from 31 August to 8 September 2001;

6. *Welcomes* the contribution of the Council of Europe to the preparations for the special session of the General Assembly on children, to be held in 2002;

7. *Commends strongly* the contribution of the Council of Europe to international action against terrorism, as defined by the Committee of Ministers of the Council in the conclusions of its session of 7 and 8 November 2001 in Strasbourg, taking into account Security Council resolutions 1368(2001) of 12 September 2001 and 1373(2001) of 28 September 2001, including the intensification of legal cooperation to combat terrorism;

8. *Welcomes* the participation of the Council of Europe in the implementation of Security Council resolution 1244(1999) of 10 June 1999, in its cooperation with the United Nations Interim Administration Mission in Kosovo, notably with regard to the reform of the judiciary, the promotion and protection of human rights, including the rights of minorities, property rights, population registration, childhood and youth programmes, education policies and the protection and restoration of cultural heritage;

9. *Commends* the role of the Council of Europe in the capacity-building programme of the United Nations Interim Administration Mission in Kosovo, especially with regard to the electoral process in preparation for the Kosovo Assembly elections on 17 November 2001;

10. *Welcomes* the activities of the Council of Europe aimed at fulfilling the role assigned to it, under the General Framework Agreement for Peace in Bosnia and Herzegovina, with regard to the protection and promotion of human rights, and judicial and prison reform;

11. *Welcomes also* the major contribution of the Council of Europe to the Stability Pact for South-Eastern Europe, launched at the initiative of the European Union, and to the development of regional projects to support its aims;

12. *Welcomes further* the active role of the Council of Europe in the tripartite meetings between the United Nations, the Organization for Security and Cooperation in Europe and the Council of Europe;

13. *Requests* the Secretary-General to continue exploring, with the Chairman of the Committee of Ministers and the Secretary-General of the Council of Europe, possibilities for further enhancement of cooperation, information exchange and coordination between the United Nations and the Council of Europe;

14. *Decides* to include in the provisional agenda of its fifty-seventh session the sub-item entitled "Cooperation between the United Nations and the Council of Europe", and requests the Secretary-General to submit to the General Assembly at its fifty-seventh session a report on cooperation between the United Nations and the Council of Europe in implementation of the present resolution.

Strengthening of security and cooperation in the Mediterranean

In response to General Assembly resolution 55/38 [YUN 2000, p. 411], the Secretary-General submitted in July [A/56/153] replies received from Algeria, Mexico and Sweden, on behalf of the EU,

to his note verbale requesting their views on ways to strengthen security and cooperation in the Mediterranean region.

GENERAL ASSEMBLY ACTION

On 29 November [meeting 68], the General Assembly, on the recommendation of the First (Disarmament and International Security) Committee [A/56/541], adopted **resolution 56/29** without vote [agenda item 79].

Strengthening of security and cooperation in the Mediterranean region

The General Assembly,

Recalling its previous resolutions on the subject, including resolution 55/38 of 20 November 2000,

Reaffirming the primary role of the Mediterranean countries in strengthening and promoting peace, security and cooperation in the Mediterranean region,

Bearing in mind all the previous declarations and commitments, as well as all the initiatives taken by the riparian countries at the recent summits, ministerial meetings and various forums concerning the question of the Mediterranean region,

Recognizing the indivisible character of security in the Mediterranean and that the enhancement of cooperation among Mediterranean countries with a view to promoting the economic and social development of all peoples of the region will contribute significantly to stability, peace and security in the region,

Recognizing also the efforts made so far and the determination of the Mediterranean countries to intensify the process of dialogue and consultations with a view to resolving the problems existing in the Mediterranean region and to eliminating the causes of tension and the consequent threat to peace and security, and their growing awareness of the need for further joint efforts to strengthen economic, social, cultural and environmental cooperation in the region,

Recognizing further that prospects for closer Euro-Mediterranean cooperation in all spheres can be enhanced by positive developments worldwide, in particular in Europe, in the Maghreb and in the Middle East,

Reaffirming the responsibility of all States to contribute to the stability and prosperity of the Mediterranean region and their commitment to respecting the purposes and principles of the Charter of the United Nations, as well as the provisions of the Declaration on Principles of International Law concerning Friendly Relations and Cooperation among States in accordance with the Charter of the United Nations,

Noting the peace negotiations in the Middle East, which should be of a comprehensive nature and represent an appropriate framework for the peaceful settlement of contentious issues in the region,

Expressing its concern at the persistent tension and continuing military activities in parts of the Mediterranean that hinder efforts to strengthen security and cooperation in the region,

Taking note of the report of the Secretary-General,

1. *Reaffirms* that security in the Mediterranean is closely linked to European security as well as to international peace and security;

2. *Expresses its satisfaction* at the continuing efforts by Mediterranean countries to contribute actively to the elimination of all causes of tension in the region and to the promotion of just and lasting solutions to the persistent problems of the region through peaceful means, thus ensuring the withdrawal of foreign forces of occupation and respecting the sovereignty, independence and territorial integrity of all countries of the Mediterranean and the right of peoples to self-determination, and therefore calls for full adherence to the principles of non-interference, non-intervention, non-use of force or threat of use of force and the inadmissibility of the acquisition of territory by force, in accordance with the Charter and the relevant resolutions of the United Nations;

3. *Commends* the Mediterranean countries for their efforts in meeting common challenges through coordinated overall responses, based on a spirit of multilateral partnership, towards the general objective of turning the Mediterranean basin into an area of dialogue, exchanges and cooperation, guaranteeing peace, stability and prosperity, and encourages them to strengthen such efforts through, inter alia, a lasting multilateral and action-oriented cooperative dialogue among States of the region;

4. *Recognizes* that the elimination of the economic and social disparities in levels of development and other obstacles, as well as respect and greater understanding among cultures in the Mediterranean area will contribute to enhancing peace, security and cooperation among Mediterranean countries through the existing forums;

5. *Calls upon* all States of the Mediterranean region that have not yet done so to adhere to all the multilaterally negotiated legal instruments related to the field of disarmament and non-proliferation, thus creating the necessary conditions for strengthening peace and cooperation in the region;

6. *Encourages* all States of the region to favour the necessary conditions for strengthening the confidence-building measures among them by promoting genuine openness and transparency on all military matters, by participating, inter alia, in the United Nations system for the standardized reporting of military expenditures and by providing accurate data and information to the United Nations Register of Conventional Arms;

7. *Encourages* the Mediterranean countries to strengthen further their cooperation in combating terrorism in all its forms and manifestations, taking into account the relevant resolutions of the United Nations, and in combating international crime and illicit arms transfers and illicit drug production, consumption and trafficking, which pose a serious threat to peace, security and stability in the region and therefore to the improvement of the current political, economic and social situation and which jeopardize friendly relations among States, hinder the development of international cooperation and result in the destruction of human rights, fundamental freedoms and the democratic basis of pluralistic society;

8. *Requests* the Secretary-General to submit a report on means to strengthen security and cooperation in the Mediterranean region;

9. *Decides* to include in the provisional agenda of its fifty-seventh session the item entitled "Strengthening of security and cooperation in the Mediterranean region".

Stability and development in South-Eastern Europe

On 23 February [A/55/809-S/2001/172], the former Yugoslav Republic of Macedonia (FYROM) submitted to the Secretary-General the text of the Summit Declaration of the Heads of State and Government of South-East European Countries at their fourth meeting (Skopje, 23 February) and the Action Plan for Regional Economic Cooperation.

On 10 October [A/56/466], Bulgaria transmitted the Declaration of Solidarity adopted by the heads of State of Albania, Bulgaria, Croatia, Estonia, Latvia, Lithuania, Romania, Slovakia, Slovenia and FYROM during the Summit meeting of NATO candidate countries (Sofia, 5 October).

GENERAL ASSEMBLY ACTION

On 29 November [meeting 68], the General Assembly, on the recommendation of the First Committee [A/56/530], adopted **resolution 56/18** without vote [agenda item 68].

Maintenance of international security— good-neighbourliness, stability and development in South-Eastern Europe

The General Assembly,

Recalling the purposes and principles of the Charter of the United Nations and the Final Act of the Conference on Security and Cooperation in Europe, signed at Helsinki on 1 August 1975,

Recalling also the United Nations Millennium Declaration,

Recalling further its resolutions 48/84 B of 16 December 1993, 50/80 B of 12 December 1995, 51/55 of 10 December 1996, 52/48 of 9 December 1997, 53/71 of 4 December 1998, 54/62 of 1 December 1999 and 55/27 of 20 November 2000,

Convinced of the necessity of enhancing the overall conflict prevention and resolution capability of the United Nations system and other relevant regional organizations to prevent the outbreak of conflicts,

Emphasizing the crucial importance of the full implementation of Security Council resolution 1244(1999) of 10 June 1999 on Kosovo, Federal Republic of Yugoslavia, and stressing, inter alia, the role and responsibility of the United Nations Interim Administration Mission in Kosovo, supported by the Organization for Security and Cooperation in Europe and the European Union, and of the Kosovo Force in that regard, as well as the importance of the implementation of Security Council resolutions 1345(2001) of 21 March 2001 and 1371(2001) of 26 September 2001,

Commending the significant progress made by the people and the authorities of the Federal Republic of Yugoslavia towards establishing democracy and the important steps taken to cooperate with the International Tribunal for the Prosecution of Persons Responsible for Serious Violations of International Humanitarian

Law Committed in the Territory of the Former Yugoslavia since 1991,

Recalling the Stability Pact for South-Eastern Europe, and stressing the importance of the implementation of its objectives, with emphasis on regional cooperation,

Noting the importance of the activities of international organizations, such as the European Union, the Organization for Security and Cooperation in Europe and the Council of Europe, as well as the contribution of the Central European Initiative and the Black Sea Economic Cooperation, for the implementation of the Stability Pact,

Welcoming the normalization of relations among all States of the Balkan region, and noting, in this respect, the Agreement for the delineation of the borderline between the former Yugoslav Republic of Macedonia and the Federal Republic of Yugoslavia, signed at Skopje on 23 February 2001, as well as the re-establishment of diplomatic relations between Albania and the Federal Republic of Yugoslavia,

Welcoming also the agreement of 29 June 2001 on succession issues among the States successors to the former Socialist Federal Republic of Yugoslavia,

Welcoming further the signing of stabilization and association agreements and/or European agreements between the countries of the region and the European Union and its member States,

Reiterating the importance of the South-East European Cooperation Process and its contribution to security, stability and good-neighbourly relations in South-Eastern Europe, and recalling in particular the Summit Declaration and the Action Plan for Regional Economic Cooperation, adopted by the heads of State and Government of the participating and observer countries of the South-East European Cooperation Process at Skopje on 23 February 2001,

Emphasizing the crucial importance of strengthening regional efforts in South-Eastern Europe on arms control, demining, disarmament and confidence-building measures, and concerned that, in spite of the ongoing efforts, the illicit trade in small arms and light weapons in all its aspects persists,

Mindful of the importance of national and international activities of all relevant organizations aimed at the creation of peace, security, stability, democracy, cooperation and economic development and the observance of human rights and good-neighbourliness in South-Eastern Europe,

Taking note of the Declaration of Solidarity adopted by the heads of State participating in the Summit Meeting of the North Atlantic Treaty Organization candidate countries held at Sofia on 5 October 2001,

Reaffirming its determination that all nations should live together in peace with one another as good neighbours,

1. *Reaffirms* the need for full observance of the Charter of the United Nations;

2. *Calls upon* all States, the relevant international organizations and the competent organs of the United Nations to respect the principles of territorial integrity and sovereignty of all States and the inviolability of international borders, to continue to take measures in accordance with the Charter and the commitments of the Organization for Security and Cooperation in Europe and through further development of regional arrangements, as appropriate, to eliminate threats to international peace and security and to help to prevent conflicts in South-Eastern Europe, which can lead to the violent disintegration of States;

3. *Reaffirms* the urgency of consolidating South-Eastern Europe as a region of peace, security, stability, democracy, cooperation and economic development and for the promotion of good-neighbourliness and the observance of human rights, thus contributing to the maintenance of international peace and security and enhancing the prospects for sustained development and prosperity for all peoples in the region as an integral part of Europe, and recognizes the role of the United Nations, the Organization for Security and Cooperation in Europe and the European Union in promoting regional disarmament;

4. *Calls upon* all participants in the Stability Pact for South-Eastern Europe, as well as all concerned international organizations, to continue to support the efforts of the States of South-Eastern Europe towards regional stability and cooperation so as to enable them to pursue sustainable development and integration into European structures;

5. *Calls upon* all States and relevant international organizations to contribute to the full implementation of Security Council resolution 1244(1999) on Kosovo, Federal Republic of Yugoslavia, as well as Council resolutions 1345(2001) and 1371(2001);

6. *Rejects* the use of violence in pursuit of political aims, and stresses that only peaceful political solutions can assure a stable and democratic future for South-Eastern Europe;

7. *Welcomes* the signing of the Framework Agreement at Ohrid, the former Yugoslav Republic of Macedonia, on 13 August 2001, and supports its full and timely implementation by the parties to the Agreement;

8. *Stresses* the importance of good-neighbourliness and the development of friendly relations among States, and calls upon all States to resolve their disputes with other States by peaceful means, in accordance with the Charter;

9. *Urges* the strengthening of relations among the States of South-Eastern Europe on the basis of respect for international law and agreements, in accordance with the principles of good-neighbourliness and mutual respect;

10. *Recognizes* the efforts of the international community, and welcomes in particular the assistance already provided by the European Union, other contributors and the Stability Pact for South-Eastern Europe in promoting the long-term process of democratic and economic development of the region;

11. *Stresses* that the rapprochement of the South-Eastern European States with the European Union will favourably influence the security, political and economic situation in the region, as well as good-neighbourly relations among the States;

12. *Stresses also* the importance of regional efforts aimed at preventing conflicts that endanger the maintenance of international peace and security and, in this regard, notes with satisfaction the role of the Multinational Peace Force for South-Eastern Europe;

13. *Emphasizes* the importance of continuous regional efforts and intensified dialogue in South-Eastern Europe aimed at arms control, disarmament and confidence-building measures as well as strength-

ening cooperation and undertaking appropriate measures at the national, subregional and regional levels to prevent and suppress acts of terrorism;

14. *Welcomes* the adoption, on 18 July 2001, of the Concluding Document of the negotiations under article V of annex 1.B to the General Framework Agreement for Peace in Bosnia and Herzegovina;

15. *Recognizes* the seriousness of the problem of anti-personnel mines in some parts of South-Eastern Europe, welcomes, in this context, the efforts of the international community in support of mine action, and encourages States to join and support these efforts;

16. *Urges* all States to take effective measures against the illicit trade in small arms and light weapons in all its aspects and to help programmes and projects aimed at the collection and safe destruction of surplus stocks of small arms and light weapons, and stresses the importance of closer cooperation among States, inter alia, in crime prevention, combating terrorism, illicit trade in people, organized crime, drug trafficking and money-laundering;

17. *Calls upon* all States and the relevant international organizations to communicate to the Secretary-General their views on the subject of the present resolution;

18. *Decides* to include in the provisional agenda of its fifty-seventh session the item entitled "Maintenance of international security—good-neighbourliness, stability and development in South-Eastern Europe".

Chapter VI

Middle East

The work of the United Nations in the Middle East in 2001 was affected by an ever-growing cycle of violence and retaliation in the Occupied Palestinian Territory and by the standstill in the peace negotiations between Israel and the Palestine Liberation Organization (PLO), despite many international efforts to revive the process. The Palestinian intifada (uprising), which erupted in September 2000 following the visit of the then Israeli opposition leader, Ariel Sharon, to a holy Islamic site in the Old City of Jerusalem, continued in waves throughout the year.

Israeli and Palestinian negotiators met in late January in Taba, Egypt, and agreed on a number of issues with respect to the situation on the ground, but failed to achieve a comprehensive agreement. The deteriorating situation in the occupied territories and the election on 6 February of a new Israeli Government, headed by Mr. Sharon, led to a breakdown of bilateral negotiations between the two parties.

On 30 April, the Sharm el-Sheikh Fact-Finding Committee, established following the 2000 summit in Sharm el-Sheikh (Egypt) and chaired by former United States Senator George Mitchell, reported to the President of the United States and the Secretary-General on the nature and causes of the ongoing violence. The Committee recommended a number of steps to end the violence, starting with the implementation of an unconditional ceasefire and the resumption of security cooperation. The report was accepted by both parties and a ceasefire was brokered in June by the Director of the Central Intelligence Agency of the United States, George Tenet. In June, the Secretary-General visited the region and encouraged the parties to consolidate the ceasefire and implement the Mitchell Committee's recommendations.

In late September, a meeting took place between Israeli Foreign Minister Shimon Peres and President of the Palestinian Authority (PA) and PLO Chairman Yasser Arafat. Although the meeting achieved some progress, the assassination of an Israeli cabinet minister in October brought about a new wave of violence and reprisals. The Israeli Government refused to pursue further talks with Chairman Arafat and occupied and shelled PA buildings; at the same time, a number of Palestinian suicide bombers killed and injured Israeli civilians.

Concerned about the deteriorating situation in the region, the Security Council convened four times, twice in March, once in August and once in December, to discuss the situation in the Middle East, including the Palestinian question. On 27 March, a draft resolution, by which the Council would have expressed its determination to establish a UN observer force in the territories occupied by Israel, was not adopted due to the negative vote of the United States, a permanent Council member. On 15 December, a draft resolution, by which the Council would have encouraged the establishment of a monitoring mechanism to help the parties implement the Mitchell recommendations, was also not adopted due to the negative vote of the United States.

In December, the General Assembly resumed its tenth emergency special session, which first convened in 1997, to discuss the item "Illegal Israeli actions in Occupied East Jerusalem and the rest of the Occupied Palestinian Territory". The Assembly adopted the text that had not been adopted by the Council on 15 December. The resolution called for, among other things, the establishment of a monitoring mechanism. Another resolution, adopted on the same day, reiterated the applicability of the 1949 Geneva Convention relative to the Protection of Civilian Persons in Time of War (Fourth Geneva Convention) in the Occupied Palestinian Territory.

The Conference of High Contracting Parties to the Fourth Geneva Convention on Measures to Enforce the Convention in the Occupied Palestinian Territory, including Jerusalem, convened in December in Geneva, under the chairmanship of Switzerland as the depositary of the Geneva Conventions. The Conference adopted a declaration which, among other things, called on Israel to respect the Convention's provisions.

In southern Lebanon, Israeli troops and their main Lebanese opponents, the paramilitary group Hizbullah, faced each other along the so-called Blue Line, the provisional border drawn by the United Nations following the withdrawal of Israeli troops from south Lebanon in June 2000. The dispute, which centred on control of the Shab'a farmland, also brought about increased tensions between Israel and the Syrian Arab Republic.

The mandates of the United Nations Interim Force in Lebanon (UNIFIL) and of the United Nations Disengagement Observer Force (UN-DOF) in the Golan Heights were extended twice during the year, and the United Nations Truce Supervision Organization (UNTSO) continued to assist both peacekeeping operations in their tasks. In 2001, having fulfilled most of its mandate with regard to observing the Israeli withdrawal from southern Lebanon, UNIFIL started a gradual reconfiguration and redeployment phase.

The United Nations Relief and Works Agency for Palestine Refugees in the Near East, despite severe financial difficulties, continued to provide a wide-ranging programme of education, health relief and social services to over 3.8 million Palestinian refugees living both in and outside camps in the West Bank and the Gaza Strip, as well as in Jordan, Lebanon and the Syrian Arab Republic. In 2001, the Agency was forced to shift its focus from development to humanitarian emergency assistance due to the increased violence and deteriorating socio-economic situation in the occupied territories. Two emergency appeals were launched to provide short-term emergency employment opportunities for refugees, in addition to food, shelter and health services.

During the year, the Special Committee to Investigate Israeli Practices Affecting the Human Rights of the Palestinian People and Other Arabs of the Occupied Territories reported to the Assembly on the situation in the West Bank, including East Jerusalem, the Gaza Strip and the Golan Heights. The Committee on the Exercise of the Inalienable Rights of the Palestinian People continued to mobilize international support for the Palestinians. In July, together with the UN Division for Palestinian Rights, it organized an international meeting on the question of Palestine in Madrid, Spain, at which participants called for, among other things, the implementation of the Mitchell Committee's recommendations and for the establishment of an international presence to protect civilians and to monitor the implementation of agreements reached between the two parties.

By **decision 56/450** of 21 December, the General Assembly deferred consideration of the agenda item "Armed Israeli aggression against the Iraqi nuclear installations and its grave consequences for the established international system concerning the peaceful use of nuclear energy, the non-proliferation of nuclear weapons and international peace and security" and included it in the provisional agenda of its fifty-seventh (2002) session. The item had been inscribed yearly on the Assembly's agenda since 1981, following the bombing by Israel of a nuclear research centre near Baghdad [YUN 1981, p. 275].

Peace process

Overall situation

Report of Secretary-General. In a November report [A/56/642-S/2001/1100], the Secretary-General said that the Israeli-Palestinian crisis had entered its second year with an escalation of violence that continued throughout 2001.

Following the Sharm el-Sheikh Middle East Peace Summit of October 2000 [YUN 2000, p. 415] and in a further effort to reach agreement before the prime ministerial elections in Israel (6 February), senior Israeli and Palestinian negotiators held talks in Taba, Egypt, from 21 to 27 January 2001. In a joint statement, the two sides declared that they had never been closer to reaching an agreement. Substantial progress was achieved in each of the issues discussed: refugees, security, borders and Jerusalem. However, given the circumstances and time constraints, it proved impossible to reach a final understanding on all issues. As the parties remained deadlocked, further international efforts were made to revive the political process. In March, a discussion was generated by a joint Egyptian-Jordanian non-paper proposing steps to end the crisis and to restart negotiations. However, prior to the submission of the paper, new circumstances had evolved, including the establishment of a national unity Government in Israel, headed by Prime Minister Ariel Sharon. The new Government declared that it would honour previous diplomatic agreements approved by the Knesset (Parliament), but it would not conduct negotiations while the violence continued.

On 27 and 28 March, the Secretary-General took part in the Summit of the League of Arab States (LAS) in Amman, Jordan, where he discussed the crisis in the Middle East with heads of State and foreign ministers. In his statement to the Summit, he stressed that the international community and the Arab world had the right to criticize Israel for its continued occupation of Palestinian and Syrian territory, and for its excessively harsh response to the intifada. However, those points could be made more effectively if many Israelis did not believe that their existence was under threat: Israel had a right, enshrined in numerous UN resolutions, to exist in safety within internationally recognized borders. The

Secretary-General emphasized that what was needed was movement towards an agreement that responded both to the legitimate desire of the Palestinians for national independence and to the legitimate claims of the Israelis to recognition and security.

The 30 April report of the Sharm el-Sheikh Fact-Finding Committee, known as the Mitchell report, provided a viable basis for a return to the negotiating table; the Secretary-General fully endorsed its recommendations (see p. 409). Both parties accepted and reached agreement on a 13 June ceasefire, which was brokered by the Director of the Central Intelligence Agency of the United States, George Tenet. The Secretary-General visited the region from 12 to 18 June to encourage the parties to consolidate the ceasefire and move towards full implementation of the Mitchell report.

Israeli Foreign Minister Shimon Peres and PA President Yasser Arafat met on 26 September 2001 and agreed to resume full security cooperation and to exert maximum efforts to sustain the ceasefire. The meeting was made possible by international efforts, in particular those of the Russian Federation, the United States, the European Union (EU) and the United Nations, with the full support of Egypt and Jordan. The level of violent incidents declined and Israel took several positive steps, including the lifting of some internal closures. Significant statements were also made by a number of Member States, including the United States, envisioning the creation of a Palestinian State provided that Israel's right to exist was respected. However, that progress was sharply disrupted when Israeli cabinet minister Rehavam Zeevi was assassinated on 17 October by gunmen belonging to the Popular Front for the Liberation of Palestine. Following the assassination, Israeli forces launched a major incursion into Palestinian-controlled areas. In order to defuse the situation, a "Quartet", composed of the United Nations (represented by the Special Coordinator for the Middle East Peace Process and Personal Representative of the Secretary-General to the PLO and the PA), the United States, the Russian Federation and the EU, issued a joint statement on 25 October, which was supported in a statement to the press on the same day by the Security Council President [SC/7188]. On 11 November, the Secretary-General met in New York with the United States Secretary of State, the Foreign Minister of the Russian Federation and the High Representative for Common Foreign and Security Policy of the EU. The Quartet welcomed United States President George W. Bush's statement to the General Assembly on 10 November, in which he pledged to work towards the day when two States, Israel and Palestine, would live peacefully together within secure and recognized borders.

The Ministers for Foreign Affairs of the five permanent members of the Security Council met with the Secretary-General on 12 November and issued a statement strongly encouraging Israelis and Palestinians to take the necessary security, economic and political steps to move from confrontation to the resumption of the political process. The Ministers, among other things, called on Israel to withdraw from all areas into which it had made incursions and to ensure greater restraint by the Israel Defence Forces (IDF). They also called on the PA to take all possible steps to put an end to violence and called on both parties to implement the Tenet plan and the recommendations of the Mitchell report.

In **resolution 56/36** of 3 December (see p. 429), the General Assembly expressed its full support for the peace process, which began in Madrid in 1991 [YUN 1991, p. 221], the 1993 Declaration of Principles on Interim Self-Government Arrangements [YUN 1993, p. 521] and the 1995 Israeli-Palestinian Interim Agreement on the West Bank and the Gaza Strip [YUN 1995, p. 626]. It also called on the concerned parties to take the necessary steps to reverse all measures taken since 28 September 2000 and to implement the Fact-Finding Committee's recommendations.

Committee on Palestinian Rights. In its annual report [A/56/35 & Corr.1], the Committee on the Exercise of the Inalienable Rights of the Palestinian People (Committee on Palestinian Rights) expressed concern over Israel's policies and actions in the Occupied Palestinian Territory, including the illegal settlement policy; military incursions unprecedented in scope into various parts of the Territory, including areas under full Palestinian control; harsh and disproportionate attacks by IDF against Palestinians protesting the occupation; the widespread policy of targeted extrajudicial assassinations of Palestinian activists; and the overall harmful effect of the occupation on the Palestinians' living conditions. At the core of the conflict was the continuing Israeli occupation of the Palestinian Territory. The Committee called for the comprehensive implementation of the Mitchell Committee's recommendations, which afforded the most practicable route back to the peace process.

Occupied Palestinian Territory

Communications (3 January–12 March). In a series of letters dated between 3 January and 12 March [A/ES-10/54-S/2001/7, A/ES-10/55-S/2001/33,

A/ES-10/56-S/2001/50, A/ES-10/57-S/2001/101, A/ES-10/58-S/2001/131, A/ES-10/59-S/2001/156, A/ES-10/60-S/2001/175, A/ES-10/61-S/2001/189, A/ES-10/64-S/2001/209, A/ES-10/65-S/2001/226], the Permanent Observer of Palestine informed the Secretary-General and the Security Council President of the killing and injuring of Palestinians by Israeli forces and submitted lists of the names of those killed. He also referred to acts of violence and destruction by armed settlers, the bombardment of refugee camps, and the imposition of severe restrictions on the movement of persons and goods throughout the Occupied Palestinian Territory.

In a series of communications dated between 8 January and 6 March [A/55/730-S/2001/24, A/55/742-S/2001/71, A/55/748-S/2001/81, A/55/762-S/2001/103, A/55/777-S/2001/125, A/55/781-S/2001/132, A/55/787-S/2001/137, A/55/819-S/2001/187, A/55/821-S/2001/193, A/55/823-S/2001/197], Israel responded to the Palestinian allegations and detailed Palestinian attacks against Israeli civilians. Israel called on the Palestinian leadership to abide by its commitments to control terrorist elements in the territory under its control.

In identical letters of 1 February [A/55/760-S/2001/98] to the Secretary-General and the Security Council President, the Permanent Observer of Palestine expressed concern regarding the possible use by Israeli forces of depleted uranium shells against Palestinian targets. Responding on 21 February [A/55/799-S/2001/158], Israel denied the Palestinian allegations regarding the use of depleted uranium. In a 16 February follow-up [A/55/793-S/2001/139], the Permanent Observer said that Israeli forces had used, on 12 February, an unknown type of gas against Palestinian civilians, which resulted in the admission of 40 Palestinians to local hospitals.

On 13 February [A/55/795], the Presidency of the EU deplored the practice of extrajudicial killings of Palestinians carried out by Israeli security forces. According to the EU, the existence of such a policy had been confirmed by Israel.

Security Council consideration (14-19 March). At the request of the United Arab Emirates, on behalf of the Arab Group and LAS [S/2001/216], and Malaysia, on behalf of the Islamic Group at the United Nations [S/2001/231], the Security Council, on 15 and 19 March [meeting 4295], discussed the situation in the Middle East, including the Palestinian question. With the Council's consent, the President invited, among others, Egypt and Israel, at their request, to participate in the discussion without the right to vote. The President also invited the Permanent Observer of Palestine, at his own request [S/2001/225]. The Chairman of the Committee on Palestinian Rights was also invited to attend, at his own re-

quest. On 19 March, the Permanent Observer of the Organization of the Islamic Conference (OIC), at the request of Malaysia [S/2001/235], and the Deputy Permanent Observer of LAS, at the request of the United Arab Emirates [S/2001/236], were invited to participate in the discussion without the right to vote.

On 14 March, the Council had held private meetings on the subject with the Deputy Prime Minister and Minister for Foreign Affairs of Israel [meeting 4292] and with the Permanent Observer of Palestine [meeting 4293], who had requested to participate in the discussion [S/2001/222].

Addressing the Council on 15 March [S/PV.4295], the Permanent Observer of Palestine said that since 18 December 2000, when the Council failed to adopt a draft resolution that would have expressed its determination to establish a UN observer force in the territories occupied by Israel [YUN 2000, p. 426], Israeli forces had killed more than 80 Palestinians and had wounded several thousand. He stressed that the underlying cause of the violence in the region was the Israeli occupation of Palestinian territory and the measures taken by Israeli forces, such as the confiscation of territory and the building of settlements. Since the beginning of the crisis on 28 September 2000 [ibid., p. 416], other measures had included the presence of the Israeli army and the use of its huge military machinery; the presence of the settlers and their use of weapons against Palestinians; the destruction of the Palestinian economy; and the transforming of the lives of the Palestinians into a veritable hell. With regard to the peace process, reasonable progress was achieved by the two parties in the Taba talks (see p. 405). However, the policies of the new Israeli Government, elected on 6 February, contradicted the bases of the peace process and the agreements concluded between the two parties. The Israeli Government in fact claimed that it could not negotiate while the violence persisted, though it continued to occupy Palestinian territory. At the same time, it also refused to negotiate from the point that was reached by the two sides in Taba and was reluctant to negotiate a final settlement in favour of new interim arrangements and solutions. The Permanent Observer called on the Council to restore control as a prelude to the resuscitation of the peace process through practical measures, including the establishment of an observer force.

Israel stated that the Palestinian intifada, as it had existed for nearly six months, was incompatible with international protection. The situation in the Palestinian territories was not one of a threatened people in dire need of protection. In fact, the only thing that Palestinians needed protection from was the consequences of their own actions, since the responsibility for the violence lay with the Palestinian authorities. The new Israeli Government had frozen settlement construction and had decided against any acts of collective punishment, out of a real desire for peace, which was its chief objective. The Palestinian request for an international observer mission was unnecessary, as Chairman Arafat had the ability to protect Palestinian lives by publicly calling on his people to stop the confrontation. Though he had promised Israeli officials repeatedly that he would take such a step, he had ignored his many opportunities to do so. The United Nations could not be called upon to put out fires on behalf of the same party that had kindled the flames. Such a precedent would send a message to the Palestinians—and every other aggrieved people of the world—that violence and aggression would lead to international protection. The Council had to recognize that sending UN personnel to the territories while the intifada continued had the potential to actually escalate the violence and further destabilize the region. In addition, the Mitchell Committee, with which Israel had expressed its willingness to cooperate fully, was expected to arrive in the region the following week and to report to the President of the United States and the Secretary-General on the nature and causes of the ongoing violence. As to the security situation, citizens had experienced abductions and murders on a daily basis both in the territories and inside Israel. It was irresponsible to portray Israel's response to that constantly looming threat as punitive action taken against the Palestinian people.

The United Arab Emirates, on behalf of the Arab Group, said that since December 2000 Israeli military forces had implemented a design of deliberate killing, siege and closure of Palestinian villages and cities. They were also implementing policies aimed at destroying the human, social and economic infrastructure of the Palestinian people. The intifada was a reflection of Palestinian desperation and frustration and one of the simplest means of self-defence against the Israeli war machine and the heavily armed settlers. The Council, among other things, should adopt the draft resolution that was submitted in December 2000 for the formation of an international observer force to provide protection to the Palestinian people.

The United States stated that it was firmly committed to ensuring that the Council did not adopt any resolution that was not supported by both the Israelis and the Palestinians. The Council, in December 2000, had acted wisely by not adopting a resolution calling for the premature establishment of an international presence in the region. The United States looked forward to a time when the parties would reach an agreement and turn to the Council for support and assistance in implementing it. It was entirely possible that an international presence that had an achievable mandate would be a part of that implementation effort. At that time of prospective peace, the United States would join with the rest of the Council in giving full support to the parties' own efforts to secure peace. Suggesting that the Council could somehow impose itself between the parties and play a constructive role by observing violence only served to divert the parties from the absolute necessity to meet and shape their shared destiny, which was a just and lasting peace.

Addressing the Council on 19 March, the Chairman of the Committee on Palestinian Rights said that more than 360 Palestinian civilians had been killed and some 15,000 wounded since the beginning of the crisis in September 2000. Israel was systematically responding with disproportionate force to every outbreak of protest throughout the Palestinian territory. Furthermore, groups of armed settlers regularly harassed and physically assaulted Palestinian civilians, destroying their property. Paradoxically, on the one hand, a state of affairs had been created that was fuelled by confrontation and a cycle of violence; on the other hand, unarmed populations were being asked to end the violence that was triggered by provocation and punitive expeditions on the part of the occupier.

Communications (16-27 March). In letters of 16 [A/ES-10/66-S/2001/239] and 21 [A/ES-10/67-S/2001/255] March, the Permanent Observer of Palestine informed the Secretary-General and the Council President that the killing and injuring of Palestinians continued; he submitted lists of the names of those killed.

In letters to the Secretary-General of 19 [A/55/842-S/2001/244], 26 [A/55/858-S/2001/278] and 27 [A/55/860-S/2001/280] March, Israel detailed Palestinian terrorist acts against Israeli civilians, including a mortar attack near a kibbutz, a shooting at a playground, a car bomb and a suicide bomb.

Security Council consideration (27 March). On 27 March [meeting 4305], the Security Council discussed the situation in the Middle East, including the Palestinian question, and considered the text of a draft resolution [S/2001/270] submitted by Bangladesh, Colombia, Jamaica, Mali, Mauritius, Singapore and Tunisia. By that draft, the Council would have expressed its determination to establish an appropriate mechanism to protect Palestinian civilians, including through the establishment of a UN observer force.

With the Council's consent, the President invited the Israeli representative to participate in the meeting. He also invited the Permanent Observer of Palestine to participate, at his own request [S/2001/282].

Speaking before the vote, in his capacity as the representative of Ukraine, the Council President said that, despite efforts made by all Council members, there was no common ground on the draft resolution. Without the necessary unanimity, he did not believe that the vote on the draft resolution would either achieve its original goal as regards the protection of Palestinian civilians or send any positive signal to the people in the region. Therefore, while supporting the contents of the draft text and being well aware of the outcome of the voting exercise that the Council was about to take, Ukraine would not take part in the vote.

Speaking after the Council's vote (9-1-4) on the draft resolution, which was not adopted owing to the negative vote of a permanent Council member, the United States said that it had opposed the draft text because it was unbalanced and unworkable and hence unwise. By the text, some States would call on the Council to impose a solution in the absence of an agreement between the parties. Instead, the Council should have called on the parties to end all violence and resume negotiations. The United States supported much of the substance that the Council had been discussing in the preceding week, but it could not allow the Council to adopt a draft resolution that risked damaging simultaneously the prospects for peace and the Council's own credibility.

The Permanent Observer of Palestine said that the failure to adopt the draft resolution meant that the Council was prevented by one of its permanent members from carrying out its duties to preserve international peace and security in accordance with the Charter. It also meant that the Council had failed to provide the support necessary to revive what was left of the Middle East peace process. The Permanent Observer supported the convening of the Arab summit in Amman and the participation of the Secretary-General in that meeting (see p. 405), but said that the Council's action had failed to send the right message to the summit, one that would promote interdependence and harmony between Arab action and international legitimacy in addressing the deteriorating situation in the region.

Communications (28 March–26 April). In a series of letters to the Secretary-General and the Security Council President [A/ES-10/68-S/2001/284, A/ES-10/69-S/2001/295, A/ES-10/70-S/2001/304, A/ES-10/71-S/2001/314, A/ES-10/72-S/2001/332, A/ES-10/75-S/2001/352, A/ES-10/76-S/2001/372, A/ES-10/79-S/2001/418], the Permanent Observer of Palestine said that the killing and injuring of Palestinians continued and that Israel was employing excessive use of force; he submitted lists of the names of those killed.

In letters of 28 March [A/55/863-S/2001/291] and 23 April [A/55/910-S/2001/396], Israel said that Palestinian suicide bombers had killed and injured Israeli civilians.

On 18 April [S/2001/393], Morocco, as Chairman of the Al-Quds Committee, condemned Israel's use of force against unarmed Palestinians. The United Nations was called on to assume its responsibilities for implementing UN resolutions on the protection of civilians and of the Holy Places of Al-Quds al-Sharif, which had been threatened by the head of the Israeli Government.

Mitchell Committee report. On 30 April, the report of the Sharm el-Sheikh Fact-Finding Committee, chaired by former United States Senator George Mitchell, was released under the auspices of the President of the United States. The Committee was established in November 2000 by the United States, in consultation with Israel and the PA, as agreed upon at the October 2000 Sharm el-Sheikh Summit [YUN 2000, p. 420], to look into the nature and causes of the ongoing violence in the Middle East since September 2000.

The Committee recommended a number of steps to end the violence by implementing an unconditional ceasefire and resuming security cooperation, rebuilding confidence by establishing a meaningful "cooling-off period" and implementing additional confidence-building measures, including a freeze by Israel of all settlement activity, to be followed by the resumption of negotiations.

The report was accepted by both parties, which, on 13 June, agreed to a ceasefire, brokered by the Director of the United States Central Intelligence Agency.

Communications (1 May–16 August). In letters dated between 1 May and 16 August [A/ES-10/80-S/2001/432, A/ES-10/81-S/2001/447, A/ES-10/83-S/2001/471, A/ES-10/84-S/2001/479, A/ES-10/85-S/2001/486, A/ES-10/86-S/2001/496, A/ES-10/87-S/2001/504, A/ES-10/88-S/2001/508, A/ES-10/89-S/2001/544, A/ES-10/90-S/2001/586, A/ES-10/91-S/2001/605, A/ES-10/92-S/2001/629, A/ES-10/93-S/2001/657, A/ES-10/94-S/2001/669, A/ES-10/95-S/2001/686, A/ES-10/96-S/2001/697, A/ES-10/97-S/2001/708, A/ES-10/98-S/2001/717, A/ES-10/99-S/2001/742, A/ES-10/100-S/2001/754, A/ES-10/102-S/2001/785, A/ES-10/103-S/2001/798], the Permanent Observer of Palestine detailed attacks on

Palestinians by Israeli forces, including extrajudicial killings and the use of F-16 warplanes to fire missiles and rockets against Palestinian targets; he submitted lists of the names of those killed.

In letters dated between 1 May and 13 August [A/55/924-S/2001/435, A/56/69-S/2001/459, A/56/72-S/2001/473, A/56/78-S/2001/506, A/56/80-S/2001/524, A/56/81-S/2001/540, A/56/85-S/2001/555, A/56/91-S/2001/580, A/56/92-S/2001/585, A/56/97-S/2001/604, A/56/98-S/2001/611, A/56/119-S/2001/619, A/56/131-S/2001/656, A/56/138-S/2001/662, A/56/184-S/2001/696, A/56/201-S/2001/706, A/56/223-S/2001/737, A/56/225-S/2001/743, A/56/272-S/2001/768, A/56/280-S/2001/775, A/56/294-S/2001/787], Israel stated that the killing and injuring of Israeli civilians by Palestinian terrorists, including suicide bombers, continued. On 1 June, a Palestinian suicide bomber blew himself up near a Tel Aviv nightclub, killing 20 people and wounding 90 more.

In identical letters of 9 May [A/ES-10/82-S/2001/463] to the Secretary-General and the Council President, the Permanent Observer of Palestine said that the Israeli Prime Minister, Mr. Sharon, in a statement to the press on 8 May, claimed that the Palestinian territory occupied by Israel since 1967 was disputed and not occupied. He further rejected the cessation of settlement activities and made the resumption of negotiations conditional upon the total cessation of violence.

On 15 May [A/55/944-S/2001/491], the Permanent Observer transmitted to the Secretary-General the text of a resolution entitled "Dubious attempts by Israel to have a number of archaeological sites in East Jerusalem inscribed on the World Heritage List", adopted by the Council of LAS at its one hundred and fifteenth session at the level of ministers for foreign affairs (Cairo, Egypt, 12 March).

By a 24 May letter [A/55/956-S/2001/526], Bahrain transmitted to the Secretary-General the joint communiqué of the eleventh session of the Ministerial Council of the Cooperation Council of the Gulf Arab States and the EU (Manama, Bahrain, 23 April). Both organizations noted with deep concern the escalation of violence in the Middle East and, in particular, the use of excessive force against civilians.

On 29 May [A/55/974-S/2001/543], Qatar transmitted the final communiqué adopted by the extraordinary meeting of the Foreign Ministers of OIC on the grave situation in the Occupied Palestinian Territories (Doha, Qatar, 26 May). The meeting, among other things, called on the Security Council to secure the necessary international protection for the Palestinian people and to establish an international criminal tribunal to try those responsible for war crimes committed against the Palestinians. It also decided to stop all political contacts with the Israeli Government as long as the aggression and blockade against the Palestinian people and its National Authority continued. Qatar also transmitted to the Secretary-General the statement made by the Emir of Qatar at the extraordinary meeting [A/55/974/Add.1-S/2001/543/Add.1]. A summary of the outcome of the meeting was forwarded to the General Assembly President by Qatar [A/55/1022].

On 12 July [A/55/1017-S/2001/698], Bahrain transmitted to the Secretary-General the press communiqué of the Ministerial Council of the Cooperation Council of the Gulf Arab States (Jeddah, Saudi Arabia, 11 July). The Council said, among other things, that the settlements constituted the major danger to security and were preventing the achievement and advancement of the peace process.

On 30 July [A/55/1023-S/2001/750], Qatar condemned as a provocation against religious sentiments the decision by an Israeli religious group to lay a cornerstone for a temple at the Haram al-Sharif in Jerusalem, an act that was to be regarded as an affront to the sanctity of the Islamic Holy Places.

By a 7 August letter [A/56/275-S/2001/770] to the Secretary-General, Israel said that the Temple Mount Faithful, a small Israeli fringe group, had annually attempted to place a cornerstone on the Temple Mount. The Israeli high court had barred the group from entering the Mount and the Israeli police had actively enforced the decision. At no time did the group attempt to enter the Temple Mount compound and the cornerstone itself never entered the city. The Palestinian leadership, on the other hand, decided to capitalize on the event, declaring in advance a "day of rage" and calling on its people to defend the Mount. Consequently, crowds of Palestinians showered Jewish worshippers gathered below at the Western Wall with rocks and stones, forcing the evacuation of the site on the day when the Jewish people observed the holy day of Tish'a b'Av. With no efforts exerted by the Palestinian leadership to restore calm, Israeli soldiers were forced to enter the Mount to quell the disturbances; they did not enter the Al-Aqsa mosque.

On 1 August [S/2001/790], Belgium, on behalf of the EU, expressed concern with regard to the deteriorating situation in the region and the renewed escalation of violence. It called once again for the implementation of the Mitchell Committee's recommendations and for the rapid establishment of a third-party monitoring mechanism.

On 9 August [A/56/286-S/2001/780], Israel said that a Palestinian suicide bomber had that day detonated powerful explosives inside a restaurant in the centre of Jerusalem, killing 15 people and injuring 130 more. Two other Israelis had been shot and killed by Palestinians on the same day.

On the same day [S/2001/791], Belgium, on behalf of the EU, condemned the bombing in Jerusalem on 9 August and called on both sides to the conflict to regain their self-control and adopt a resolutely forward-looking approach.

In identical letters of 13 August to the Secretary-General and the Council President [A/ES-10/101-S/2001/783], the Permanent Observer of Palestine said that, on 10 August, Israeli security forces raided and closed down Orient House (PA offices in East Jerusalem) along with nine other buildings belonging to Palestinian institutions in and around Occupied East Jerusalem. The Israeli action represented an assault on Palestinian national dignity and Palestinian rights in Jerusalem.

On 13 August [A/55/1027-S/2001/784], Qatar, in its capacity as Chairman of OIC, condemned Israel's occupation of Orient House.

By letters of 15 [S/2001/797] and 16 [A/55/1029] August, Mali and Qatar informed the Security Council President and the Secretary-General that, at two urgent and successive meetings, the first of the Follow-up Committee of the Ninth Islamic Summit Conference and the second of the Islamic Group, both held on 15 August at the ambassadorial level, grave concern was expressed over the deteriorating situation that had developed in the Occupied Palestinian Territory as a result of Israel's seizure of Orient House and the closure of the PA's political and security offices.

Security Council consideration (20-21 August). At the request of Mali and Qatar on behalf of the Islamic Group [S/2001/797], the Security Council, on 20 and 21 August, discussed the situation in the Middle East, including the Palestinian question [meeting 4357]. With the Council's consent, the Council President invited, among others, Egypt and Israel, at their request, to participate in the discussion without the right to vote. The President also invited the Permanent Observer of Palestine to participate, at his request [S/2001/799]. The Chairman of the Committee on Palestinian Rights was also invited at his own request. In addition, invitations were extended to the Acting Permanent Observer of OIC to the United Nations, at the request of Mali [S/2001/800], and to the Deputy Permanent Observer of LAS, at the request of Tunisia [S/2001/801].

The Permanent Observer of Palestine said that Israel's military campaign and other measures,

such as the withholding of Palestinian funds, had placed the Palestinian people, in essence, in a collective prison. The PA condemned the bombings that had taken place in Israel, but observed that the wave of explosions started long after the beginning of the Israeli military campaign in September 2000. The Permanent Observer noted that the Palestinians had accepted the Mitchell Committee's report and had called for the implementation of its recommendations. For its part, the Israeli Government, though it finally accepted the report, had come up with the notion of a seven-day cooling-off period as a condition for implementing the recommendations. The Palestinians viewed Israel's position as unrealistic and impractical.

Israel stated that it had accepted the Mitchell report as a road map leading back to the negotiating table. Even before the Tenet ceasefire took effect in June 2001, Israel had implemented its own unilateral ceasefire. Those actions were met with no reciprocal gestures from the Palestinian side. Consequently, 36 Israelis had been killed and 292 injured in over 1,300 separate attacks since the Tenet plan took effect. Thus, the Council's meeting was taking place not only against the backdrop that the Palestinians had depicted, but also against the backdrop of ongoing Palestinian terrorism. It appeared that despite the 9 August bombing in Jerusalem (see above), the Palestinians had no scruples about convening a Council meeting to discuss Israeli actions. That unprecedented escalation of Palestinian terror was not in itself a new phenomenon, since Israel had faced a calculated campaign of Palestinian terror for more than 10 months. What had changed was the frequency, intensity and horror of the attacks. Israel was obliged, under every norm of international law, to take action in defence of its citizens. In that regard, it should be treated like any other nation that faced armed aggression. The use of human beings as bombs was an alarming phenomenon that presented no obvious response, as individuals who were willing to sacrifice their lives in such a manner would not be deterred by ordinary means. Israel's response, therefore, had to be geared towards cutting off terror at its source, since, once it was unleashed, it was virtually impossible to stop. Chairman Arafat had himself become a party to terrorism, as he released terrorists from jail, used the official Palestinian media to incite them to violence, refused to re-arrest them even when they were about to commit murder, and invited the Hamas and Islamic Jihad organizations to join him in a unity coalition. As long as the Palestinians maintained that policy, Israel would continue to take the steps it deemed necessary to keep the Palestinians' killing machinery off its streets. Israel's seizure of Orient House was not a takeover, an occupation or an act of revenge, but an act of self-defence. Israel took temporary control of buildings that were being used by official Palestinian forces to assist terrorists in carrying out their attacks, and intelligence reports and illegal weapons had been recovered from Orient House that constituted irrefutable proof that the site was being used for political and military purposes. Israel regarded the draft resolution before the Council (an informal text that was not tabled) as a biased and one-sided document that sought to place the onus of the current situation squarely on one party. Since the Mitchell report referred to a direct, face-to-face approach, there appeared to be no justification for further complicating matters by subjecting implementation to international supervision and scrutiny or by imposing any kind of monitoring mechanism that had not been negotiated and agreed to by both parties. Israel therefore remained opposed to an international presence in the region, as that would contravene both the spirit and the letter of direct bilateral negotiations.

Communications (21 August–13 December). In letters dated between 21 August and 10 December [A/ES-10/104-S/2001/812, A/ES-10/105-S/2001/814, A/ES-10/107-S/2001/821, A/ES-10/108-S/2001/826, A/ES-10/111-S/2001/880, A/ES-10/112-S/2001/918, A/ES-10/114-S/2001/928, A/ES-10/115-S/2001/932, A/ES-10/116-S/2001/941, A/ES-10/117-S/2001/971, A/ES-10/118-S/2001/989, A/ES-10/119-S/2001/991, A/ES-10/121-S/2001/1007, A/ES-10/122-S/2001/1024, A/ES-10/123-S/2001/1036, A/ES-10/124-S/2001/1084, A/ES-10/125-S/2001/1092, A/ES-10/126-S/2001/1118, A/ES-10/128-S/2001/1149, A/ES-10/129-S/2001/1166], the Permanent Observer of Palestine informed the Secretary-General and the Council President that Israeli forces continued to kill and injure Palestinian civilians and had used, among other weapons, helicopter gunships to fire missiles against Palestinian security posts while bulldozers had destroyed Palestinian farmlands and buildings; he submitted lists of the names of those killed. On 4 December, Israeli forces fired missiles at PA buildings in Ramallah, in the vicinity of President Arafat's headquarters.

In a series of communications dated between 27 August and 13 December [A/56/324-S/2001/825, A/56/325-S/2001/834, A/56/346-S/2001/858, A/56/367-S/2001/875, A/56/386-S/2001/892, A/56/406-S/2001/907, A/56/438-S/2001/938, A/56/443-S/2001/942, A/56/444-S/2001/943, A/56/450-S/2001/948, A/56/483-S/2001/975, A/56/492-S/2001/990, A/56/506-S/2001/1011, A/56/514-S/2001/1023, A/56/604-S/2001/1048, A/56/617-S/2001/1071, A/56/663-S/2001/1121, A/56/668-S/2001/1133, A/56/670-S/2001/1141, A/56/678-S/2001/1150, A/56/706-S/2001/1198], Israel detailed acts of terrorism committed by Palestinians against Israeli targets and civil-

ians. On 17 October, Israel's Minister of Tourism, Rehavam Zeevi, was killed by Palestinian gunmen. On 1 and 2 December, Palestinian suicide bombers killed 26 Israelis and injured over 200 more in attacks carried out in Jerusalem and Haifa.

On 27 August [A/ES-10/109-S/2001/830], the Sudan, as Chairman of the Arab Group, transmitted to the Secretary-General the texts of two resolutions adopted by the LAS Council at an emergency meeting on 22 August, held at the level of ministers for foreign affairs. The resolutions were entitled "The recent Israeli aggression against the City of Jerusalem" and "World Conference against Racism, Racial Discrimination, Xenophobia and Related Intolerance".

By a 6 September letter [A/ES-10/110-S/2001/855], the PLO Chairman and PA President, Yasser Arafat, informed the Secretary-General that, on 6 September, Israeli forces started to seal off Al-Quds from the surrounding areas of Palestine and had strengthened their presence throughout the city and deployed large numbers of soldiers and policemen.

On 15 October [S/2001/977], Belgium transmitted a 9 October statement by the Presidency of the EU, which welcomed a declaration made by United States President George W. Bush acknowledging the right of the Palestinians to a viable State provided that Israel's right to exist was guaranteed.

On 22 October [S/2001/997], Mali and Qatar informed the Council President that an urgent meeting of the Islamic Group was held on that same day at the ambassadorial level to consider the deteriorating situation in the Occupied Palestinian Territory as a result of Israel's escalation of military action against the Palestinian people. The Islamic Group requested the convening of a meeting of the Council in order to ensure immediate Israeli withdrawal from the areas that it had reoccupied in the preceding few weeks.

On 26 October [S/2001/1019], the Libyan Arab Jamahiriya, as Chairman of the Arab Group, said that it was regrettable that the Council had not taken immediate measures as requested by the Islamic Group on 22 October. The Arab Group called on the Council to consider the situation and adopt a resolution on the matter, particularly with regard to the immediate withdrawal of the Israeli occupation forces.

By a 16 November letter [A/56/636-S/2001/1090], Chile transmitted to the Secretary-General the statement issued on 14 November by the Ministers for Foreign Affairs of the Rio Group (an organization of Latin American States) on the crisis in the Middle East. The Rio Group condemned the acts of violence and reaffirmed their adherence to the UN resolutions which had created a legal framework for the settlement of the Arab-Israeli conflict.

By letters of 26 November [A/56/650-S/2001/1112] and 6 December [A/56/683-S/2001/1160] to the Secretary-General, Qatar condemned the inhuman acts committed by Israel against Palestinian citizens, and protested Israel's policy of assassinating Palestinian representative leaders.

In two separate letters of 7 December to the Secretary-General [A/56/696] and the Council President [S/2001/1170], Chile, on behalf of the Rio Group, called on Israel and the PA to bring to an immediate halt all acts of violence so as to restore the minimum conditions of confidence necessary to prevent a further deterioration in the situation.

By a 12 December letter [A/56/703-S/2001/1192], Qatar transmitted to the Secretary-General the text of a statement made by Qatar's Emir at the opening session of the Ninth Islamic Summit Conference (Doha, 10 December), and the text of the Conference's final communiqué, which called on the Council to dispatch international observers to the region to ensure the necessary protection for the Palestinian people.

Security Council consideration (14 December). At the request of Egypt on behalf of LAS [S/2001/1191], the Security Council, on 14 December [meeting 4438], discussed the situation in the Middle East, including the Palestinian question. With the Council's consent, the President invited, among others, Egypt and Israel, at their request, to participate in the discussion without the right to vote. The President also invited the Permanent Observer of Palestine to participate, at his own request [S/2001/1205], as well as the Chairman of the Committee on Palestinian Rights, also at his own request. The Council considered the text of a draft resolution [S/2001/1199] submitted by Egypt and Tunisia. By that draft, the Council would have encouraged all concerned to establish a monitoring mechanism to help the parties implement the Mitchell Committee's recommendations and called for resumed negotiations between the two sides.

Speaking before the vote, the Permanent Observer of Palestine said that Israel had announced earlier that week that it would sever all contact with PA President Arafat. That decision meant the abandonment of the negotiation process and the prelude to abandoning all existing arrangements between the two sides. On the question of terrorism, the Palestinian side rejected suicide bombings carried out in Israel targeting Israeli civilians. As to acts of violence carried out in the Occupied Palestinian Territory, including Jerusalem, the Palestinian side did not condone them but did not accept any attempt to label them as terrorist acts. Resistance to foreign occupation had been, and remained, a legitimate right under international law. Israel's violence against the Palestinians and widespread destruction of their property represented serious breaches of the Fourth Geneva Convention. The Permanent Observer charged Israel with, among other things, carrying out State terrorism against the Palestinians.

Israel said that there had been a recent incredible escalation of Palestinian terrorism against Israel, which was unparalleled in more than 14 months of violence. Israel had repeatedly expressed its sympathy for the unfortunate deaths of Palestinian civilians and for the Palestinian population that had to endure the precautionary security measures foisted upon Israel by the inaction of the Palestinian leadership. But while Israel considered the death of any civilian, whether Israeli or Palestinian, to be tragic, for the Palestinian terrorists those deaths were deliberate, premeditated and desired. The obstacle to peace in the region was not occupation, but the continuing murder of civilians and the Palestinian leadership's attempts to justify those murders. Mr. Arafat had no intention of ending the violence by taking action against the terrorists.

Egypt said that the destruction of the PA's installations by Israeli forces would not end the crisis or reduce the level of violence between the two parties. The Israeli decision to cut off contacts with Palestinian leaders only signified a desire to prolong the conflict and, perhaps, represented a complete renunciation of all agreements signed by the two parties and a prelude to a new phase in the conflict.

The United States said that the draft resolution under consideration failed to address the dynamic at work in the region. Instead, its purpose was to isolate politically one of the parties to the conflict by throwing the weight of the Council behind the other party. A major flaw of the draft resolution was that it never mentioned the acts of terrorism against Israel or those responsible for them. Terrorist organizations such as Hamas and the Palestinian Islamic Jihad were deliberately seeking to sabotage any potential peace negotiation between the two parties. It was President Arafat's responsibility to take a strategic stand against terrorism. The PA had to arrest those responsible for planning and carrying out terrorist attacks and destroy the structures that perpetuated terrorism. Israel, for its part, had to focus very carefully on the repercussions of any actions it took. Neither party could lose sight of the need to resume progress towards the resumption of a dialogue. The United States believed that the

Council should not take an action that would turn the parties away from the efforts needed to improve an already tense situation. Consequently, the United States had decided to make use of its veto to block the draft resolution.

The draft resolution was not adopted (12-1-2), owing to the negative vote of a permanent member of the Council.

Emergency special session

In accordance with General Assembly resolution ES-10/7 [YUN 2000, p. 421] and at the request of Egypt [A/ES-10/130], on behalf of LAS, and South Africa, in its capacity as Chairman of the Movement of Non-Aligned Countries [A/ES-10/131], the tenth emergency special session of the Assembly resumed on 20 December to discuss "Illegal Israeli actions in Occupied East Jerusalem and the rest of the Occupied Palestinian Territory". The session was first convened in April 1997 [YUN 1997, p. 394] and resumed in July and November of that year, as well as in March 1998 [YUN 1998, p. 425], February 1999 [YUN 1999, p. 402] and October 2000 [YUN 2000, p. 421].

The Assembly had before it two draft resolutions. By the first draft, the Assembly demanded the immediate cessation of all acts of violence and, among other things, encouraged all concerned to establish a monitoring mechanism to help the parties implement the Mitchell Committee's recommendations. By the second, it reiterated the applicability of the Fourth Geneva Convention to the Occupied Palestinian Territory, including East Jerusalem, and expressed support for the declaration adopted by the 5 December Conference of High Contracting Parties to the Convention (see p. 425).

On 20 December [meeting 15], the General Assembly adopted **resolution ES-10/8** [draft: A/ES-10/L.7] by recorded vote (124-6-25) [agenda item 5].

Illegal Israeli actions in Occupied East Jerusalem and the rest of the Occupied Palestinian Territory

The General Assembly,

Recalling its relevant resolutions,

Recalling also relevant Security Council resolutions, including resolution 1322(2000) of 7 October 2000,

Emphasizing the need for a just, lasting and comprehensive peace in the Middle East based on Security Council resolutions 242(1967) of 22 November 1967 and 338(1973) of 22 October 1973 and the principle of land for peace,

Emphasizing also in that regard the essential role of the Palestinian Authority, which remains the indispensable and legitimate party for peace and needs to be preserved fully,

Expressing its grave concern at the continuation of the tragic and violent events that have taken place since September 2000,

Expressing also its grave concern at the recent dangerous deterioration of the situation and its possible impact on the region,

Emphasizing further the importance of the safety and well-being of all civilians in the whole Middle East region, and condemning in particular all acts of violence and terror resulting in the deaths and injuries among Palestinian and Israeli civilians,

Expressing its determination to contribute to ending the violence and to promoting dialogue between the Israeli and Palestinian sides,

Reiterating the need for the two sides to comply with their obligations under the existing agreements,

Also reiterating the need for Israel, the occupying Power, to abide scrupulously by its legal obligations and responsibilities under the Fourth Geneva Convention relative to the Protection of Civilian Persons in Time of War of 12 August 1949,

1. *Demands* the immediate cessation of all acts of violence, provocation and destruction, as well as the return to the positions and arrangements that existed prior to September 2000;

2. *Condemns* all acts of terror, in particular those targeting civilians;

3. *Also condemns* all acts of extrajudiciary executions, excessive use of force and wide destruction of properties;

4. *Calls upon* the two sides to start the comprehensive and immediate implementation of the recommendations made in the report of the Sharm el-Sheikh Fact-Finding Committee (Mitchell report) in a speedy manner;

5. *Encourages* all concerned to establish a monitoring mechanism to help the parties implement the recommendations of the report of the Fact-Finding Committee and to help to create a better situation in the Occupied Palestinian Territory;

6. *Calls* for the resumption of negotiations between the two sides within the Middle East peace process on its agreed basis, taking into consideration developments in previous discussions between the two sides, and urges them to reach a final agreement on all issues, on the basis of their previous agreements, with the objective of implementing Security Council resolutions 242(1967) and 338(1973);

7. *Decides* to remain seized of the matter.

RECORDED VOTE ON RESOLUTION ES-10/8:

In favour: Afghanistan, Algeria, Andorra, Antigua and Barbuda, Argentina, Armenia, Austria, Azerbaijan, Bahrain, Bangladesh, Belarus, Belgium, Belize, Benin, Bhutan, Bolivia, Brazil, Brunei Darussalam, Burkina Faso, Burundi, Cambodia, Cape Verde, Chile, China, Colombia, Congo, Costa Rica, Côte d'Ivoire, Cuba, Cyprus, Czech Republic, Democratic People's Republic of Korea, Denmark, Djibouti, Ecuador, Egypt, El Salvador, Equatorial Guinea, Eritrea, Ethiopia, Finland, France, Gabon, Germany, Ghana, Greece, Grenada, Guatemala, Guinea, Guyana, Haiti, Honduras, Hungary, India, Indonesia, Iran, Ireland, Italy, Jamaica, Jordan, Kenya, Kuwait, Lao People's Democratic Republic, Lebanon, Libyan Arab Jamahiriya, Liechtenstein, Luxembourg, Madagascar, Malaysia, Maldives, Mali, Malta, Mauritania, Mauritius, Mexico, Monaco, Mongolia, Morocco, Mozambique, Myanmar, Namibia, Nepal, Netherlands, New Zealand, Nigeria, Oman, Pakistan, Panama, Peru, Philippines, Poland, Portugal, Qatar, Republic of Korea, Russian Federation, Saint Lucia, San Marino, Saudi Arabia, Senegal, Sierra Leone, Singapore, Slovakia, South Africa, Spain, Sri Lanka, Sudan, Swaziland, Sweden, Syrian Arab Republic, Thailand, Togo, Tunisia, Turkey, Uganda, Ukraine, United Arab Emirates, United Republic of Tanzania, Uruguay, Venezuela, Viet Nam, Yemen, Yugoslavia, Zambia, Zimbabwe.

Against: Israel, Marshall Islands, Micronesia, Nauru, Tuvalu, United States.

Abstaining: Albania, Australia, Bosnia and Herzegovina, Bulgaria, Cameroon, Canada, Croatia, Dominican Republic, Estonia, Georgia, Iceland, Japan, Latvia, Lithuania, Nicaragua, Norway, Papua New Guinea, Paraguay, Romania, Samoa, Slovenia, Solomon Islands, Tonga, United Kingdom, Vanuatu.

On the same day [meeting 15], the Assembly adopted **resolution ES-10/9** [draft: A/ES-10/L.8] by recorded vote (133-4-16) [agenda item 5].

Illegal Israeli actions in Occupied East Jerusalem and the rest of the Occupied Palestinian Territory

The General Assembly,

Recalling its relevant resolutions, including resolutions of the tenth emergency special session on the situation in Occupied East Jerusalem and the rest of the Occupied Palestinian Territory,

Recalling also relevant Security Council resolutions, including resolutions 237(1967) of 14 June 1967, 242(1967) of 22 November 1967, 259(1968) of 27 September 1968, 271(1969) of 15 September 1969, 338 (1973) of 22 October 1973, 446(1979) of 22 March 1979, 452(1979) of 20 July 1979, 465(1980) of 1 March 1980, 468(1980) of 8 May 1980, 469(1980) of 20 May 1980, 471(1980) of 5 June 1980, 476(1980) of 30 June 1980, 478(1980) of 20 August 1980, 484(1980) of 19 December 1980, 592(1986) of 8 December 1986, 605(1987) of 22 December 1987, 607(1988) of 5 January 1988, 608 (1988) of 14 January 1988, 636(1989) of 6 July 1989, 641(1989) of 30 August 1989, 672(1990) of 12 October 1990, 673(1990) of 24 October 1990, 681(1990) of 20 December 1990, 694(1991) of 24 May 1991, 726(1992) of 6 January 1992, 799(1992) of 18 December 1992, 904(1994) of 18 March 1994 and 1322(2000) of 7 October 2000,

Taking note with appreciation of the convening of the Conference of High Contracting Parties to the Fourth Geneva Convention, on 15 July 1999, as recommended by the General Assembly in its resolution ES-10/6 of 9 February 1999, and the statement adopted by the Conference,

Taking note with appreciation also of the reconvening of the above-mentioned Conference, on 5 December 2001, and the important declaration adopted by the Conference,

Recalling relevant provisions of the Rome Statute of the International Criminal Court,

Reaffirming the position of the international community on Israeli settlements in the Occupied Palestinian Territory, including East Jerusalem, as illegal and as an obstacle to peace,

Expressing its concern at Israeli actions taken recently against the Orient House and other Palestinian institutions in Occupied East Jerusalem as well as other illegal Israeli actions aimed at altering the status of the city and its demographic composition,

Reiterating the applicability of the Fourth Geneva Convention relative to the Protection of Civilian Persons in Time of War of 12 August 1949 to the Occupied Palestinian Territory, including East Jerusalem,

Stressing that the Fourth Geneva Convention, which takes fully into account imperative military necessity, has to be respected in all circumstances,

Bearing in mind the relevant provisions of the Charter of the United Nations, including Article 96 thereof,

1. *Expresses its full support* for the declaration adopted by the Conference of High Contracting Parties to the Fourth Geneva Convention, convened on 5 December 2001 at Geneva;

2. *Calls upon* all members and observers of the United Nations as well as the Organization and its agencies to observe the above-mentioned declaration;

3. *Decides* to adjourn the tenth emergency special session temporarily and to authorize the President of the General Assembly at its most recent session to resume its meeting upon request from Member States.

RECORDED VOTE ON RESOLUTION ES-10/9:

In favour: Afghanistan, Albania, Algeria, Andorra, Antigua and Barbuda, Argentina, Armenia, Austria, Azerbaijan, Bahrain, Bangladesh, Belarus, Belgium, Belize, Benin, Bhutan, Bolivia, Bosnia and Herzegovina, Brazil, Brunei Darussalam, Bulgaria, Burkina Faso, Burundi, Cambodia, Cape Verde, Chile, China, Colombia, Congo, Côte d'Ivoire, Croatia, Cuba, Cyprus, Czech Republic, Democratic People's Republic of Korea, Denmark, Djibouti, Ecuador, Egypt, Equatorial Guinea, Eritrea, Estonia, Ethiopia, Finland, France, Gabon, Germany, Ghana, Greece, Grenada, Guinea, Guyana, Haiti, Hungary, Iceland, India, Indonesia, Iran, Ireland, Italy, Jamaica, Japan, Jordan, Kenya, Kuwait, Lao People's Democratic Republic, Latvia, Lebanon, Libyan Arab Jamahiriya, Liechtenstein, Lithuania, Luxembourg, Madagascar, Malaysia, Maldives, Mali, Malta, Mauritania, Mauritius, Mexico, Mongolia, Morocco, Mozambique, Myanmar, Namibia, Nepal, Netherlands, New Zealand, Nigeria, Norway, Oman, Pakistan, Panama, Peru, Philippines, Poland, Portugal, Qatar, Republic of Korea, Romania, Russian Federation, Saint Lucia, San Marino, Saudi Arabia, Senegal, Sierra Leone, Singapore, Slovakia, Slovenia, South Africa, Spain, Sri Lanka, Sudan, Suriname, Swaziland, Sweden, Syrian Arab Republic, Thailand, Togo, Tunisia, Turkey, Uganda, Ukraine, United Arab Emirates, United Kingdom, United Republic of Tanzania, Uruguay, Venezuela, Viet Nam, Yemen, Yugoslavia, Zambia, Zimbabwe.

Against: Israel, Marshall Islands, Micronesia, United States.

Abstaining: Australia, Cameroon, Canada, Costa Rica, Dominican Republic, Georgia, Guatemala, Nauru, Nicaragua, Papua New Guinea, Paraguay, Samoa, Solomon Islands, Tonga, Tuvalu, Vanuatu.

Speaking before the votes on the two resolutions [A/ES-10/PV.15], the Assembly President said that one of the most daunting tasks before the United Nations was to bring lasting peace to the Middle East, an issue that not only involved the region, but was a global concern, constituting a serious threat to world peace and security. He urged both parties directly concerned to return to dialogue and negotiation.

The Permanent Observer of Palestine said that the resumption of the emergency special session was the result of the Security Council's failure to fulfil its primary responsibility due to the exercise by one of its permanent members of the veto during the vote on the draft resolution on 15 December (see p. 414). He called on Member States to adopt the same text of the draft resolution that had been before the Council and another draft concerning the Fourth Geneva Convention and the declaration adopted by the Conference of High Contracting Parties on 5 December. With regard to the situation in the Security Council, the question was whether the Council was used by some only when it suited them or whether it represented and acted on behalf of all members of the international community. The Palestinians would continue to work with the Council in the hope of overcoming the existing crisis. On 16 December, President Arafat had called for an immediate ceasefire in an attempt to stop the violence on the ground. On the other hand, the Israeli Government had adopted policies undermining the peace efforts; it had evaded the implementation of the Mitchell Committee's report by insisting on the precondition of seven quiet days and had then made a new demand, namely, that the PA had to first combat and end terrorism before peace negotiations could begin. Meanwhile, Israel continued to assault the PA and its institutions, disabling its security apparatus and preventing it from functioning. Finally, the Israeli Government had announced a boycott of the PA, which was tantamount to abandoning the peace process. The Permanent Observer charged the Israeli occupation with committing war crimes against the Palestinian people. The only solution to the crisis was to end the Israeli occupation and to ensure the rights of the Palestinians, including their right to establish their own independent State with Jerusalem as its capital.

Israel said that Chairman Arafat, a few days after calling for a stop to violent attacks against Israelis, had called for a continuation of the fighting during a rally in Ramallah. The PA had failed to take the steps necessary to end the violence and terrorism, steps that were a precondition for resuming political negotiations. The Assembly's emergency special session represented the continuance of the Palestinians' drive to win international sanction for their intransigence. After failing to prevail in the Security Council on 15 December, the Palestinians had turned to the Assembly, where numerous one-sided resolutions were adopted every year. The United Nations expended copious scarce resources each year to publicize the Palestinian cause, and an entire division of the Secretariat was devoted exclusively to advancing Palestinian rights. However, the root of the conflict in the region was terrorism and not the Israeli occupation. Only in UN resolutions was the basic reality of the conflict so grossly misinterpreted. The draft resolutions under consideration served merely to divert the attention and the resources of the international community, and to relieve the mounting pressure on the Palestinian leadership to exert its authority to bring an end to violence and terrorism. Furthermore, the texts made assertions that sought to prejudice the outcome of the negotiations and to establish a false correlation between those who perpetrated terror and those who fought it.

The United States said that it opposed the draft resolution [A/ES-10/L.7] because, among other things, it called for a monitoring mechanism regardless of whether the parties agreed to it. In addition, the text did not demand a cessation of terrorism. The United States was committed to achieving implementation of the Mitchell Committee's recommendations through the establishment of a durable ceasefire between the Israelis and the Palestinians. As the Palestinians assumed their responsibilities to confront terrorist groups, Israel needed to do its part to create an environment in which Palestinians could sustain and expand their efforts. Moreover, the daily plight of the Palestinian people had to be eased. The proper role of the United Nations was to facilitate and strengthen the agreements that the two parties had reached with each other. One-sided resolutions did not further that goal.

Qatar said that while Israel was committing atrocities in the occupied territories, it expected the PA to shoulder its responsibilities for security, something that was patently impossible. Israeli military actions had escalated tensions, sharpened hatred and increased violence, the proof being that while President Arafat, on 16 December, called for an end to military attacks by both sides, Israeli forces continued to invade entire areas in the West Bank and Gaza Strip. The Israeli Government had broken off all contacts with the PA and President Arafat was almost under house arrest. However, he could not be marginalized, as he remained the main interlocutor and participant in the peace process.

Switzerland, as depositary of the Geneva Conventions, said that on 5 December, 115 States parties to the Fourth Geneva Convention met in Geneva and issued a declaration by which they reaffirmed the applicability of the Convention to the Occupied Palestinian Territory, including East Jerusalem (see p. 425). Switzerland stressed the need for all States to ensure a follow-up to the declaration's implementation.

Communications (21-26 December). In identical letters of 21 December to the Secretary-General and the Council President [A/ES-10/133-S/2001/1239], the Permanent Observer of Palestine said that Israel continued its military campaign against the Palestinian people; he submitted lists of the names of those killed.

On 26 December [A/ES-10/134-S/2001/1261], the Permanent Observer said that Israel, on Christmas Eve, had used military measures to prevent President Arafat from attending religious observances in Bethlehem. That step represented a severe violation of the agreements reached between the two sides and of the principle of freedom of movement and freedom of access to holy places.

Special Committee on Israeli Practices. In its thirty-third report [A/56/491], the Special Committee to Investigate Israeli Practices Affecting the Human Rights of the Palestinian People and Other Arabs of the Occupied Territories (Special

Committee on Israeli Practices) stated that relations between settlers in the West Bank and Gaza and the Palestinians were reaching, at times, high levels of intensity and violence. Approximately 190 settlements inhabited by about 360,000 settlers had been established in the West Bank and Gaza. The settlements were scattered throughout the occupied territories, but as in the case of the city of Hebron, they were often located close to Palestinian areas of residence. The system of by-pass roads, enabling settlers to move quickly and safely through the West Bank, extended to almost 400 kilometres of roads and prevented the expansion of Palestinian villages and the movement of commerce and workers from one Palestinian area to another. The construction of such roads required the taking of Palestinian land, often land under cultivation, and the demolition of homes. Settlements and settlers were seen as being in a privileged position, to the disadvantage of the Palestinians with respect to the location of the settlements; the effects of settlements on surrounding lands; access to water; travel on bypass roads; and protection by Israeli security forces.

Report of Secretary-General. On 25 July [A/56/216], the Secretary-General informed the Assembly that Israel had not replied to his May request for information on steps taken or envisaged to implement the relevant provisions of resolution 55/132 [YUN 2000, p. 428], demanding that Israel, among other things, cease all construction of new settlements in the Occupied Palestinian Territory, including Jerusalem.

GENERAL ASSEMBLY ACTION

On 10 December [meeting 82], the General Assembly, on the recommendation of the Fourth (Special Political and Decolonization) Committee [A/56/550], adopted **resolution 56/61** by recorded vote (145-4-3) [agenda item 88].

Israeli settlements in the Occupied Palestinian Territory, including Jerusalem, and the occupied Syrian Golan

The General Assembly,

Guided by the principles of the Charter of the United Nations, and affirming the inadmissibility of the acquisition of territory by force,

Recalling its relevant resolutions, including those adopted at its tenth emergency special session, as well as relevant Security Council resolutions, including resolutions 242(1967) of 22 November 1967, 446(1979) of 22 March 1979, 465(1980) of 1 March 1980 and 497(1981) of 17 December 1981,

Reaffirming the applicability of the Geneva Convention relative to the Protection of Civilian Persons in Time of War, of 12 August 1949, to the Occupied Palestinian Territory, including Jerusalem, and to the occupied Syrian Golan,

Aware of the Middle East peace process started at Madrid and the agreements reached between the parties, in particular the Declaration of Principles on Interim Self-Government Arrangements of 13 September 1993, and the subsequent implementation agreements,

Expressing grave concern about the continuation by Israel of settlement activities, including the ongoing construction of the settlement in Jabal Abu-Ghneim and in Ras Al-Amud in and around Occupied East Jerusalem, in violation of international humanitarian law, relevant United Nations resolutions and the agreements reached between the parties,

Taking into consideration the detrimental impact of Israeli settlement policies, decisions and activities on the Middle East peace process,

Gravely concerned in particular about the dangerous situation resulting from actions taken by the illegal armed Israeli settlers in the occupied territory, as illustrated by the massacre of Palestinian worshippers by an illegal Israeli settler in Al-Khalil on 25 February 1994, and during the past year,

Taking note of the report of the Secretary-General,

1. *Reaffirms* that Israeli settlements in the Palestinian territory, including Jerusalem, and in the occupied Syrian Golan are illegal and an obstacle to peace and economic and social development;

2. *Calls upon* Israel to accept the de jure applicability of the Geneva Convention relative to the Protection of Civilian Persons in Time of War, of 12 August 1949, to the Occupied Palestinian Territory, including Jerusalem, and to the occupied Syrian Golan and to abide scrupulously by the provisions of the Convention, in particular article 49;

3. *Demands* complete cessation of the construction of the settlement in Jabal Abu-Ghneim and of all Israeli settlement activities in the Occupied Palestinian Territory, including Jerusalem, and in the occupied Syrian Golan;

4. *Stresses* the need for full implementation of Security Council resolution 904(1994) of 18 March 1994, in which, among other things, the Council called upon Israel, the occupying Power, to continue to take and implement measures, including confiscation of arms, with the aim of preventing illegal acts of violence by Israeli settlers, and called for measures to be taken to guarantee the safety and protection of the Palestinian civilians in the occupied territory;

5. *Reiterates its call* for the prevention of illegal acts of violence by Israeli settlers, particularly in the light of recent developments;

6. *Requests* the Secretary-General to report to the General Assembly at its fifty-seventh session on the implementation of the present resolution.

RECORDED VOTE ON RESOLUTION 56/61:

In favour: Algeria, Andorra, Angola, Antigua and Barbuda, Argentina, Armenia, Australia, Austria, Azerbaijan, Bahamas, Bahrain, Bangladesh, Barbados, Belarus, Belgium, Belize, Benin, Bhutan, Bolivia, Brazil, Brunei Darussalam, Bulgaria, Burkina Faso, Burundi, Cambodia, Canada, Cape Verde, Chile, China, Colombia, Comoros, Congo, Costa Rica, Côte d'Ivoire, Croatia, Cuba, Cyprus, Czech Republic, Democratic People's Republic of Korea, Denmark, Djibouti, Dominican Republic, Ecuador, Egypt, El Salvador, Equatorial Guinea, Eritrea, Estonia, Ethiopia, Fiji, Finland, France, Gabon, Georgia, Germany, Ghana, Greece, Grenada, Guatemala, Guinea, Guyana, Haiti, Honduras, Hungary, Iceland, India, Indonesia, Iran, Ireland, Italy, Jamaica, Japan, Jordan, Kazakhstan, Kenya, Kuwait, Lao People's Democratic Republic, Latvia, Lebanon, Libyan Arab Jamahiriya, Liechtenstein, Lithuania, Luxembourg, Madagascar, Malaysia, Maldives, Mali, Malta, Mauritania, Mexico, Monaco, Mongolia, Morocco, Mozambique, Myanmar, Namibia, Nepal, Netherlands, New Zealand, Nigeria, Norway, Oman, Pakistan, Panama, Paraguay, Peru, Philippines, Poland, Portugal, Qatar, Republic of Korea, Republic of Moldova, Romania, Russian Federation, Saint Lucia, San Marino, Saudi Arabia, Senegal, Seychelles, Sierra

Leone, Singapore, Slovakia, Slovenia, South Africa, Spain, Sri Lanka, Sudan, Sweden, Syrian Arab Republic, Thailand, The former Yugoslav Republic of Macedonia, Togo, Trinidad and Tobago, Tunisia, Turkey, Ukraine, United Arab Emirates, United Kingdom, United Republic of Tanzania, Uruguay, Venezuela, Viet Nam, Yemen, Yugoslavia, Zambia.
Against: Israel, Marshall Islands, Micronesia, United States.
Abstaining: Nicaragua, Papua New Guinea, Solomon Islands.

Jerusalem

East Jerusalem, where most of the city's Arab inhabitants lived, remained one of the most sensitive issues in the Middle East peace process and a focal point of concern for the United Nations in 2001. The escalation of violence and the occupation by Israeli forces of the PA's building in East Jerusalem, including Orient House (see p. 411), led to the resumption of the General Assembly's tenth emergency special session (see p. 414).

Communication. On 15 May [A/55/943-S/2001/490], the Permanent Observer of Palestine transmitted to the Secretary-General the text of a resolution adopted by the LAS Council at its one hundred and fifteenth regular session (Cairo, 12 March) on the question of Jerusalem. The Council, among other things, affirmed Palestinian sovereignty over East Jerusalem.

Special Committee on Israeli Practices. In its annual report [A/56/491], the Special Committee on Israeli Practices described restrictions imposed by Israeli authorities on Jerusalem's Palestinian population and Israeli violations of their human rights.

The Committee said that Israel had continued to pursue a policy of passive transfer of Palestinian residents of East Jerusalem, in order to establish a demographic balance between Jews and Arabs by capping the Arab population of Jerusalem at 26 per cent. Israel had used various means against Palestinian residents to prevent an increase in the population and had tried to encourage them to leave the city. Under Israeli law, Arab inhabitants were treated as permanent residents of the State of Israel. They did not possess Israeli citizenship but had the right to work in Israel without needing special permits. They could participate in local but not Israeli elections. A "centre of life" policy required Arab inhabitants, in order to retain their residency status, to prove that their centre of life was in Jerusalem by submitting documentary evidence, such as rental contracts or water bills. The policy had resulted in the confiscation of Jerusalem identity cards of those unable to prove that their centre of life was in Jerusalem; refusal by Israeli authorities to register children born to parents, one of whom did not possess a Jerusalem identity card; and refusal to register persons for family reunification, in particular a spouse who did not have an identity card. In 2001, Israeli authorities placed all requests for family reunification on hold. The pro-

ceeds from the *arnona* (municipal tax) were used to fund the provision of services by the Jerusalem Municipality. Even though more than 50 per cent of East Jerusalem was in the highest tax band, there was discrimination between the level of services provided to Palestinian areas and to Jewish areas. Israel was also seeking to prevent territorial contiguity between East Jerusalem and Ramallah to the north, East Jerusalem and Bethlehem to the south, and East Jerusalem and Jericho to the west and to control all the land around Jerusalem. An eastern ring road project envisioned the construction of a network of roads linking all the settlements and encircling Arab East Jerusalem. Lands had been confiscated and houses demolished for that purpose.

Committee on Palestinian Rights. In its annual report [A/56/35 & Corr.1], the Committee on Palestinian Rights said that since April 2001, it had observed with concern what appeared to be an emerging pattern of Israeli incursions into areas under full Palestinian control. On 10 August, Israeli forces occupied Orient House in East Jerusalem, an act that was aimed at accelerating the process of Judaization of the city. There had also been an increase in the demolition of Palestinian property, with some 30 Palestinian houses demolished in East Jerusalem. In addition, throughout the year, tenders had been issued by Israeli authorities for the construction of settler housing in and around Jerusalem.

Transfer of diplomatic missions

Report of Secretary-General. On 17 October [A/56/480], the Secretary-General reported that five Member States, including Israel, had replied to his request for information on steps taken or envisaged to implement General Assembly resolution 55/50 [YUN 2000, p. 429], which addressed the transfer by some States of their diplomatic missions to Jerusalem in violation of Security Council resolution 478(1980) [YUN 1980, p. 426] and called on them to abide by the relevant UN resolutions. Israel said the one-sided approach reflected in those resolutions undermined fundamental agreements reached between the parties, according to which the achievement of a just and lasting peace in the region was possible only through direct bilateral negotiations.

Communications. In a 9 March letter to the Secretary-General [A/55/832-S/2001/210], Qatar expressed concern regarding a statement by United States Secretary of State Colin L. Powell to the effect that Jerusalem was the capital of Israel and that the United States should move its Embassy to that city. On 13 March [A/55/837-S/2001/220], the United Arab Emirates also took exception to Mr. Powell's remarks concerning Jerusalem.

GENERAL ASSEMBLY ACTION

On 3 December [meeting 72], the General Assembly adopted **resolution 56/31** [draft: A/56/L.23 & Add.1] by recorded vote (130-2-10) [agenda item 42].

Jerusalem

The General Assembly,

Recalling its resolutions 36/120 E of 10 December 1981, 37/123 C of 16 December 1982, 38/180 C of 19 December 1983, 39/146 C of 14 December 1984, 40/168 C of 16 December 1985, 41/162 C of 4 December 1986, 42/209 D of 11 December 1987, 43/54 C of 6 December 1988, 44/40 C of 4 December 1989, 45/83 C of 13 December 1990, 46/82 B of 16 December 1991, 47/63 B of 11 December 1992, 48/59 A of 14 December 1993, 49/87 A of 16 December 1994, 50/22 A of 4 December 1995, 51/27 of 4 December 1996, 52/53 of 9 December 1997, 53/37 of 2 December 1998, 54/37 of 1 December 1999 and 55/50 of 1 December 2000, in which it, inter alia, determined that all legislative and administrative measures and actions taken by Israel, the occupying Power, which have altered or purported to alter the character and status of the Holy City of Jerusalem, in particular the so-called "Basic Law" on Jerusalem and the proclamation of Jerusalem as the capital of Israel, were null and void and must be rescinded forthwith,

Recalling also Security Council resolution 478(1980) of 20 August 1980, in which the Council, inter alia, decided not to recognize the "Basic Law" and called upon those States which had established diplomatic missions in Jerusalem to withdraw such missions from the Holy City,

Having considered the report of the Secretary-General,

1. *Determines* that the decision of Israel to impose its laws, jurisdiction and administration on the Holy City of Jerusalem is illegal and therefore null and void and has no validity whatsoever;

2. *Deplores* the transfer by some States of their diplomatic missions to Jerusalem in violation of Security Council resolution 478(1980) and their refusal to comply with the provisions of that resolution;

3. *Calls once more upon* those States to abide by the provisions of the relevant United Nations resolutions, in conformity with the Charter of the United Nations;

4. *Requests* the Secretary-General to report to the General Assembly at its fifty-seventh session on the implementation of the present resolution.

RECORDED VOTE ON RESOLUTION 56/31:

In favour: Algeria, Andorra, Argentina, Armenia, Austria, Azerbaijan, Bahrain, Bangladesh, Barbados, Belarus, Belgium, Belize, Benin, Bolivia, Botswana, Brazil, Bulgaria, Burundi, Cambodia, Canada, Cape Verde, Chad, Chile, China, Colombia, Comoros, Congo, Croatia, Cyprus, Czech Republic, Democratic People's Republic of Korea, Denmark, Djibouti, Dominican Republic, Ecuador, Egypt, Equatorial Guinea, Eritrea, Estonia, Ethiopia, Fiji, Finland, France, Georgia, Germany, Ghana, Greece, Grenada, Guyana, Honduras, Iceland, India, Indonesia, Iran, Ireland, Italy, Jamaica, Japan, Jordan, Kazakhstan, Kenya, Kuwait, Lao People's Democratic Republic, Latvia, Lebanon, Libyan Arab Jamahiriya, Liechtenstein, Luxembourg, Madagascar, Malaysia, Maldives, Mali, Malta, Mauritania, Mauritius, Mexico, Monaco, Mongolia, Morocco, Mozambique, Myanmar, Namibia, Nepal, Netherlands, Nigeria, Norway, Oman, Pakistan, Panama, Paraguay, Peru, Philippines, Poland, Portugal, Qatar, Republic of Korea, Romania, Russian Federation, Saint Lucia, San Marino, Saudi Arabia, Senegal, Seychelles, Sierra Leone, Singapore, Slovakia, Slovenia, Spain, Sri Lanka, Sudan, Suriname, Sweden, Syrian Arab Republic, Thailand, The

former Yugoslav Republic of Macedonia, Togo, Trinidad and Tobago, Tunisia, Turkey, Ukraine, United Arab Emirates, United Kingdom, United Republic of Tanzania, Uruguay, Venezuela, Viet Nam, Yemen, Yugoslavia, Zambia, Zimbabwe.

Against: Israel, Nauru.

Abstaining: Australia, Haiti, Marshall Islands, Micronesia, Nicaragua, Papua New Guinea, Solomon Islands, Tuvalu, United States, Vanuatu.

Economic and social situation

A June report on the economic and social repercussions of the Israeli occupation on the living conditions of Palestinians in the occupied territory, including Jerusalem, and of the Arab population in the occupied Syrian Golan [A/56/90-E/2001/17] was prepared by the Economic and Social Commission for Western Asia (ESCWA), in accordance with Economic and Social Council resolution 2000/31 [YUN 2000, p. 431] and General Assembly resolution 55/209 [ibid., p. 432]; it covered the period since ESCWA's previous report [ibid., p. 430].

The report stated that the delays in the implementation of the agreements reached between Israel and the PLO, together with Israeli practices, particularly the settlement expansion and the closure of passage routes from areas controlled by the PA to Israel, had an adverse effect on the living conditions of the Palestinian people and were among the primary causes of the outbreak of violence. As a consequence of the crisis, restrictions on the mobility of the Palestinians had increased and mobility between the West Bank and Gaza, and between the occupied territory and the rest of the world, had been severely impeded. In addition, imports and exports trans-shipped through Israeli ports had been delayed or blocked completely, while the Gaza International Airport and the border crossings at Rafah and the Allenby/Karameh Bridge had been closed for extended periods. Since September 2000, Israel had engaged in a wide-ranging campaign to construct scores of new roads aimed at ensuring safe passage between the settlements and Israel, while Israeli military bases had been established throughout the West Bank. The geographical distribution of settlements restricted the growth of Palestinian communities. Although settlements themselves directly controlled less than 10 per cent of the West Bank and 5 per cent of Gaza, prospects for Palestinian sovereignty would be compromised by the extensive security measures required to ensure their existence. Israel had declared 290,970 acres of the West Bank (20.2 per cent of its total area) as closed military areas, and had created an additional 29 closed military areas in Gaza (420 acres). Moreover, Israel maintained 71 military bases in the West Bank (9,563 acres). Although most of those areas had low agricultural value, they constituted the major grazing areas in the

West Bank. Since Palestinian pastoralists were denied access to those areas, the remaining grazing areas suffered from severe overgrazing and were under threat of permanent desertification

Water remained a critical issue, with over 150 West Bank villages, home to some 215,000 Palestinians, not connected to a network of running water. Waste produced by Israeli settlements located in the Occupied Palestinian Territory continued to degrade the area's water resources, causing environmental damage that compromised the Palestinians' quality of life. A declaration stating that water and sewage infrastructures had not to be harmed despite the military conflict was signed by Israeli and Palestinian representatives at the Erez Junction on 31 January; the two sides promised to take steps to provide water and treat sewage in the West Bank and Gaza, and to repair quickly malfunctions and damage to the systems. Both sides made it clear in an appeal to their public opinions that the water systems were intertwined and served both populations, and that any harm done to them would cause damage to Israelis and Palestinians alike. However, Palestinians from the village of Hares reported that water had been regularly cut off since the inception of the crisis in September 2000—not by the Israeli water company that provided it, but by Jewish settlers operating under cover of darkness.

The crisis that erupted in September 2000 ended more than three years of limited economic recovery and progress in the PA areas. Private economic losses during the first three weeks of the crisis were estimated at $186.2 million. Lost income-earning opportunities were estimated at about half of the value of domestic production and nearly all of the income earned by Palestinians working in Israel. In addition, the loss of life, injuries and the physical destruction of private and public property had become more widespread. The main impact of mobility restrictions and border closures imposed by Israeli authorities had been the disruption of productive activities and the circulation of goods. The short-term economic losses included a reduction in the income of farmers, workers, merchants and business people who could not reach their places of employment in the occupied territory or who were unable to obtain inputs or sell their goods and services. Loss of employment in Israel plus mobility restrictions and border closures had resulted in an average unemployment rate of 38 per cent (more than 250,000 persons) as compared with 11 per cent (71,000 persons) in the first nine months of 2000. Owing to the high dependency ratio, unemployment directly affected the in-

comes of about 900,000 Palestinians, or 29 per cent of the population. The direct economic losses arising from movement restrictions were estimated at 50 per cent of the gross domestic product for the four-month period from October 2000 to January 2001 and 75 per cent of wage income earned by Palestinian workers in Israel.

Israeli settlement expansion in the Golan Heights continued, while employment opportunities and access to education for the Arab population remained limited. Moreover, Israel's taxation policy enhanced the deterioration of living standards of the Arab population.

ECONOMIC AND SOCIAL COUNCIL ACTION

On 25 July [meeting 42], the Economic and Social Council adopted **resolution 2001/19** [draft: E/2001/L.26] by roll-call vote (42-1-5) [agenda item 11].

Economic and social repercussions of the Israeli occupation on the living conditions of the Palestinian people in the occupied Palestinian territory, including Jerusalem, and the Arab population in the occupied Syrian Golan

The Economic and Social Council,

Recalling General Assembly resolution 54/230 of 22 December 1999,

Also recalling its resolution 2000/31 of 28 July 2000,

Guided by the principles of the Charter of the United Nations affirming the inadmissibility of the acquisition of territory by force, and recalling relevant Security Council resolutions, including resolutions 242 (1967) of 22 November 1967, 465(1980) of 1 March 1980 and 497(1981) of 17 December 1981,

Reaffirming the applicability of the Geneva Convention relative to the Protection of Civilian Persons in Time of War, of 12 August 1949, to the Occupied Palestinian Territory, including Jerusalem, and other Arab territories occupied by Israel since 1967,

Stressing the importance of the revival of the Middle East peace process on the basis of Security Council resolutions 242(1967), 338(1973) of 22 October 1973 and 425(1978) of 19 March 1978 and the principle of land for peace as well as the full and timely implementation of the agreements reached between the Government of Israel and the Palestine Liberation Organization, the representative of the Palestinian people,

Reaffirming the principle of the permanent sovereignty of peoples under foreign occupation over their natural resources,

Convinced that the Israeli occupation impedes efforts to achieve sustainable development and a sound economic environment in the Occupied Palestinian Territory, including Jerusalem, and the occupied Syrian Golan,

Gravely concerned about the deterioration of economic and living conditions of the Palestinian people in the Occupied Palestinian Territory, including Jerusalem, and of the Arab population of the occupied Syrian Golan, and the exploitation by Israel, the occupying Power, of their natural resources,

Expressing grave concern over the continuation of the recent tragic and violent events that have led to many deaths and injuries,

Aware of the important work being done by the United Nations and the specialized agencies in support of the economic and social development of the Palestinian people,

Conscious of the urgent need for the development of the economic and social infrastructure of the Occupied Palestinian Territory, including Jerusalem, and for the improvement of the living conditions of the Palestinian people as a key element of a lasting peace and stability,

1. *Stresses* the need to preserve the territorial integrity of all of the Occupied Palestinian Territory and to guarantee the freedom of movement of persons and goods in the Territory, including the removal of restrictions on going into and from East Jerusalem, and the freedom of movement to and from the outside world;

2. *Also stresses* the vital importance of the construction and operation of the seaport in Gaza and safe passage to the economic and social development of the Palestinian people;

3. *Calls upon* Israel, the occupying Power, to cease its measures against the Palestinian people, in particular the closure of the Occupied Palestinian Territory, the enforced isolation of Palestinian towns, the destruction of homes and the isolation of Jerusalem;

4. *Reaffirms* the inalienable right of the Palestinian people and the Arab population of the occupied Syrian Golan to all their natural and economic resources, and calls upon Israel, the occupying Power, not to exploit, endanger or cause loss or depletion of these resources;

5. *Also reaffirms* that Israeli settlements in the Occupied Palestinian Territory, including Jerusalem, and the occupied Syrian Golan, are illegal and an obstacle to economic and social development;

6. *Stresses* the importance of the work of the organizations and agencies of the United Nations and of the United Nations Special Coordinator for the Middle East Peace Process and Personal Representative of the Secretary-General to the Palestine Liberation Organization and the Palestinian Authority;

7. *Urges* Member States to encourage private foreign investment in the Occupied Palestinian Territory, including Jerusalem, in infrastructure, job-creation projects and social development in order to alleviate the hardship of the Palestinian people and improve living conditions;

8. *Requests* the Secretary-General to submit to the General Assembly at its fifty-seventh session, through the Economic and Social Council, a report on the implementation of the present resolution and to continue to include, in the report of the United Nations Special Coordinator, an update on the living conditions of the Palestinian people, in collaboration with relevant United Nations agencies;

9. *Decides* to include the item entitled "Economic and social repercussions of the Israeli occupation on the living conditions of the Palestinian people in the Occupied Palestinian Territory, including Jerusalem, and the Arab population in the occupied Syrian Golan" in the agenda of its substantive session of 2002.

ROLL-CALL VOTE ON RESOLUTION 2001/19:

In favour: Andorra, Argentina, Austria, Bahrain, Bolivia, Brazil, Bulgaria, Burkina Faso, Canada, China, Croatia, Cuba, Czech Republic, Denmark, Egypt, France, Germany, Indonesia, Iran, Italy, Japan, Malta, Mexico, Morocco, Nepal, Netherlands, Nigeria, Norway, Pakistan, Peru, Portugal,

Republic of Korea, Romania, Russian Federation, Saudi Arabia, South Africa, Sudan, Suriname, Syrian Arab Republic, Uganda, United Kingdom, Venezuela.
Against: United States.
Abstaining: Angola, Cameroon, Costa Rica, Fiji, Honduras.

GENERAL ASSEMBLY ACTION

On 21 December [meeting 90], the General Assembly, on the recommendation of the Second (Economic and Financial) Committee [A/56/564], adopted **resolution 56/204** by recorded vote (148-4-4) [agenda item 101].

Permanent sovereignty of the Palestinian people in the Occupied Palestinian Territory, including Jerusalem, and of the Arab population in the occupied Syrian Golan over their natural resources

The General Assembly,

Recalling its resolution 55/209 of 20 December 2000, and taking note of Economic and Social Council resolution 2001/19 of 25 July 2001,

Reaffirming the principle of the permanent sovereignty of peoples under foreign occupation over their natural resources,

Guided by the principles of the Charter of the United Nations affirming the inadmissibility of the acquisition of territory by force, and recalling relevant Security Council resolutions, including resolutions 242 (1967) of 22 November 1967, 465(1980) of 1 March 1980 and 497(1981) of 17 December 1981,

Reaffirming the applicability of the Geneva Convention relative to the Protection of Civilian Persons in Time of War, of 12 August 1949, to the Occupied Palestinian Territory, including Jerusalem, and other Arab territories occupied by Israel since 1967,

Expressing its concern at the exploitation by Israel, the occupying Power, of the natural resources of the Occupied Palestinian Territory, including Jerusalem, and other Arab territories occupied by Israel since 1967,

Aware of the additional detrimental economic and social impact of the Israeli settlements on Palestinian and other Arab natural resources, especially the confiscation of land and the forced diversion of water resources,

Reaffirming the need for an immediate resumption of negotiations within the Middle East peace process, on the basis of Security Council resolutions 242(1967) of 22 November 1967, 338(1973) of 22 October 1973 and 425(1978) of 19 March 1978 and the principle of land for peace, and for the achievement of a final settlement on all tracks,

1. *Takes note* of the note by the Secretary-General on the economic and social repercussions of the Israeli occupation on the living conditions of the Palestinian people in the Occupied Palestinian Territory, including Jerusalem, and of the Arab population in the occupied Syrian Golan;

2. *Reaffirms* the inalienable rights of the Palestinian people and the population of the occupied Syrian Golan over their natural resources, including land and water;

3. *Calls upon* Israel, the occupying Power, not to exploit, to cause loss or depletion of or to endanger the natural resources in the Occupied Palestinian Territory, including Jerusalem, and in the occupied Syrian Golan;

4. *Recognizes* the right of the Palestinian people to claim restitution as a result of any exploitation, loss or depletion of, or danger to, their natural resources, and expresses the hope that this issue will be dealt with in the framework of the final status negotiations between the Palestinian and Israeli sides;

5. *Requests* the Secretary-General to report to it at its fifty-seventh session on the implementation of the present resolution, and decides to include in the agenda of its fifty-seventh session the item entitled "Permanent sovereignty of the Palestinian people in the Occupied Palestinian Territory, including Jerusalem, and of the Arab population in the occupied Syrian Golan over their natural resources".

RECORDED VOTE ON RESOLUTION 56/204:

In favour: Albania, Algeria, Andorra, Angola, Antigua and Barbuda, Argentina, Armenia, Australia, Austria, Azerbaijan, Bahamas, Bahrain, Bangladesh, Barbados, Belarus, Belgium, Belize, Benin, Bhutan, Bolivia, Bosnia and Herzegovina, Botswana, Brazil, Brunei Darussalam, Bulgaria, Burkina Faso, Burundi, Cambodia, Canada, Cape Verde, Chile, China, Colombia, Congo, Croatia, Cuba, Cyprus, Czech Republic, Democratic People's Republic of Korea, Denmark, Djibouti, Dominica, Dominican Republic, Ecuador, Egypt, Equatorial Guinea, Eritrea, Estonia, Ethiopia, Finland, France, Gabon, Georgia, Germany, Ghana, Greece, Grenada, Guyana, Haiti, Honduras, Hungary, Iceland, India, Indonesia, Iran, Ireland, Italy, Jamaica, Japan, Jordan, Kazakhstan, Kenya, Kuwait, Lao People's Democratic Republic, Latvia, Lebanon, Libyan Arab Jamahiriya, Liechtenstein, Lithuania, Luxembourg, Madagascar, Malaysia, Maldives, Mali, Malta, Mauritania, Mauritius, Mexico, Monaco, Mongolia, Morocco, Mozambique, Myanmar, Namibia, Nepal, Netherlands, New Zealand, Nigeria, Norway, Oman, Pakistan, Panama, Paraguay, Peru, Philippines, Poland, Portugal, Qatar, Republic of Korea, Republic of Moldova, Romania, Russian Federation, Saint Lucia, Saint Vincent and the Grenadines, Samoa, San Marino, Saudi Arabia, Senegal, Sierra Leone, Singapore, Slovakia, Slovenia, Solomon Islands, South Africa, Spain, Sri Lanka, Sudan, Swaziland, Sweden, Syrian Arab Republic, Thailand, The former Yugoslav Republic of Macedonia, Togo, Trinidad and Tobago, Tunisia, Turkey, Uganda, Ukraine, United Arab Emirates, United Kingdom, United Republic of Tanzania, Uruguay, Venezuela, Viet Nam, Yemen, Yugoslavia, Zambia, Zimbabwe.

Against: Israel, Marshall Islands, Micronesia, United States.

Abstaining: Cameroon, Fiji, Nicaragua, Papua New Guinea.

Other aspects

Special Committee on Israeli Practices. On 22 October, the Special Committee on Israeli Practices reported for the thirty-third time to the General Assembly on events in the territories it considered to be occupied—the Golan Heights, the West Bank, including East Jerusalem, and the Gaza Strip [A/56/491].

In addition to the annual report, the Special Committee, in response to a request by the Assembly in resolution 55/130 [YUN 2000, p. 435], submitted two periodic reports in 2001, one covering the period from 1 August 2000 to 30 April 2001 [A/56/428] and the other covering the period from May to August 2001 [A/56/428/Add.1]. The three reports contained information obtained from the Arab and Israeli press; testimony from persons from the occupied territories; and communications and reports from Governments, organizations and individuals. The Committee benefited from the cooperation of Egypt, Jordan, the Syrian Arab Republic, Palestinian representatives, the UN Resident Coordinator for the Syrian Arab Republic, and representatives from the International Labour Organization (ILO). As in the past, the Committee received no response from Israel to its request for cooperation and was unable to obtain access to the occupied territories, which had been the case since 1968, when the Committee was established [YUN 1968, p. 556].

The Committee stated that, since September 2000, tensions in Gaza, the West Bank and East Jerusalem had been greatly heightened. It was informed that the Israeli authorities had enforced their systems of control with intensity and severity and there had been almost daily hostile confrontations between Israeli forces and Palestinians. Conditions on the ground had been exacerbated due to the use of greatly disproportionate force by Israeli authorities. The toll of dead and injured was rising, with the Palestinians suffering the greater casualties. Closures of entry into and out of the West Bank and Gaza, internal closures of borders and numerous checkpoints and restrictions on movement out of towns and villages had resulted in a state of siege. The consequences of such systems of control on Palestinian life as a whole had been catastrophic, with grave consequences for the economic and social, cultural and political life, and other aspects of Palestinian life in the occupied territories.

Since the eruption of violence, the practices of Israeli authorities vis-à-vis the Palestinians on such matters as methods of arrest and interrogation, administrative detention, access to family and lawyers, and conditions of imprisonment had continued to be severe. At the same time, living conditions in the Palestinian refugee camps had deteriorated even further.

The Special Committee visited the Syrian Arab Republic and reported on the Israeli-occupied Syrian Golan Heights (for details, see p. 461).

The Special Committee observed that the extensive controls placed over the Palestinians in the occupied territories by the Israeli authorities, and the severe measures taken by Israel in enforcing such controls, appeared to be generally dismissive of human rights and oppressive.

Report of Secretary-General. On 25 July [A/56/218], the Secretary-General informed the General Assembly that Israel had not replied to his May request for information on steps taken or envisaged to implement Assembly resolution 55/133 [YUN 2000, p. 434], demanding that Israel, among other things, cease all practices and actions that violated the human rights of the Palestinian people and accelerate the release of all remaining Palestinians arbitrarily detained or imprisoned.

Commission on Human Rights. The Human Rights Inquiry Commission to investigate violations of human rights and humanitarian law in the occupied Palestinian territories after 28 September 2000 was established on 2 January 2001, as recommended by the Commission on Human Rights in October 2000 [YUN 2000, p. 776] and endorsed by the Economic and Social Council in decision 2000/311 [ibid.]. The Commission held its first meeting in Geneva (14-16 January) and then visited the occupied Palestinian territories and Israel from 10 to 18 February. By a 16 March report to the Commission on Human Rights [E/CN.4/2001/121], the Inquiry Commission observed that the most worrying aspect of the escalation of violence was that the hopes and expectations created by the peace process were smothered by mutual perceptions ascribing the worst of motives to each other, thus generating intense distrust and destructive emotions. It recommended urgent measures for the protection of the Palestinians' human rights and for the transformation of the climate of hostility into one of dialogue and peace (for details, see p. 735).

On 21 March [E/CN.4/2001/30], the Special Rapporteur submitted to the Commission on Human Rights an update to his October 2000 mission report [YUN 2000, p. 775] on Israel's violations of human rights in the Palestinian territories occupied since 1967 (for details, see p. 736).

GENERAL ASSEMBLY ACTION

On 10 December [meeting 82], following consideration of the Special Committee's annual and periodic reports and six reports of the Secretary-General on specific aspects of the situation in the occupied territories [A/56/214-219], the General Assembly, on the recommendation of the Fourth Committee [A/56/550], adopted **resolution 56/62** by recorded vote (145-4-2) [agenda item 88].

Israeli practices affecting the human rights of the Palestinian people in the Occupied Palestinian Territory, including Jerusalem

The General Assembly,

Recalling its relevant resolutions, including those adopted at its tenth emergency special session, and the resolutions of the Commission on Human Rights,

Bearing in mind the relevant resolutions of the Security Council, the most recent of which are resolutions 904(1994) of 18 March 1994, 1073(1996) of 28 September 1996 and 1322(2000) of 7 October 2000,

Having considered the reports of the Special Committee to Investigate Israeli Practices Affecting the Human Rights of the Palestinian People and Other Arabs of the Occupied Territories and the reports of the Secretary-General,

Taking note of the report of the Human Rights Inquiry Commission established by the Commission on Human Rights and the report of the Special Rapporteur on the situation of human rights in the Palestinian territories occupied by Israel since 1967,

Aware of the responsibility of the international community to promote human rights and ensure respect for international law,

Reaffirming the principle of the inadmissibility of the acquisition of territory by force,

Reaffirming also the applicability of the Geneva Convention relative to the Protection of Civilian Persons in Time of War, of 12 August 1949, to the Occupied Palestinian Territory, including Jerusalem, and other Arab territories occupied by Israel since 1967,

Stressing the need for compliance with the Israeli-Palestinian agreements reached within the context of the Middle East peace process, as well as for the immediate and full implementation of the recommendations of the Sharm El-Sheikh Fact-Finding Committee (Mitchell report),

Noting that during the reporting period, the third agreed-upon phase of redeployment of the Israeli army has not been implemented, and that serious incursions into the areas under the full control of the Palestinian Authority have occurred,

Concerned about the continuing violation of the human rights of the Palestinian people by Israel, the occupying Power, including the use of collective punishment, closure of areas, annexation of land, establishment of settlements and the continuing actions by it designed to change the legal status, geographical nature and demographic composition of the Occupied Palestinian Territory, including Jerusalem,

Deeply concerned by the tragic events that have occurred since 28 September 2000 and that have led to numerous deaths and injuries, mostly among Palestinians, the severe restrictions on the movement of persons and goods, and the widespread destruction, including of agricultural land,

Convinced of the positive impact of a temporary international or foreign presence in the Occupied Palestinian Territory for the safety and protection of the Palestinian people,

Convinced also of the need for third-party monitoring to help the parties to implement the recommendations of the Sharm El-Sheikh Fact-Finding Committee,

Expressing its appreciation to the countries that participated in the Temporary International Presence in Hebron for their positive contribution,

Convinced of the need for the full implementation of Security Council resolutions 904(1994), 1073(1996) and 1322(2000),

1. *Determines* that all measures and actions taken by Israel, the occupying Power, in the Occupied Palestinian Territory, including Jerusalem, in violation of the relevant provisions of the Geneva Convention relative to the Protection of Civilian Persons in Time of War, of 12 August 1949, and contrary to the relevant resolutions of the Security Council, are illegal and have no validity;

2. *Demands* that the measures and actions taken in violation of the Fourth Geneva Convention of 1949 cease immediately, including the practice of extrajudicial killings;

3. *Condemns* acts of violence, especially the excessive use of force by Israeli forces against Palestinian civilians, resulting in extensive loss of life, vast numbers of injuries and massive destruction;

4. *Demands* that Israel, the occupying Power, cease all practices and actions which violate the human rights of the Palestinian people;

5. *Stresses* the need to preserve the territorial integrity of all the Occupied Palestinian Territory and to guarantee the freedom of movement of persons and goods within the Palestinian territory, including the removal of restrictions on movement into and from East Jerusalem, and the freedom of movement to and from the outside world;

6. *Calls* for complete respect by Israel, the occupying Power, of all fundamental freedoms of the Palestinian people;

7. *Requests* the Secretary-General to report to the General Assembly at its fifty-seventh session on the implementation of the present resolution.

RECORDED VOTE ON RESOLUTION 56/62:

In favour: Algeria, Andorra, Angola, Antigua and Barbuda, Argentina, Armenia, Australia, Austria, Azerbaijan, Bahrain, Bangladesh, Barbados, Belarus, Belgium, Belize, Benin, Bhutan, Bolivia, Brazil, Brunei Darussalam, Bulgaria, Burkina Faso, Burundi, Cambodia, Canada, Cape Verde, Chile, China, Colombia, Comoros, Congo, Costa Rica, Côte d'Ivoire, Croatia, Cuba, Cyprus, Czech Republic, Democratic People's Republic of Korea, Denmark, Djibouti, Dominican Republic, Ecuador, Egypt, El Salvador, Equatorial Guinea, Eritrea, Estonia, Ethiopia, Fiji, Finland, France, Gabon, Georgia, Germany, Ghana, Greece, Grenada, Guatemala, Guinea, Guyana, Haiti, Honduras, Hungary, Iceland, India, Indonesia, Iran, Ireland, Italy, Jamaica, Japan, Jordan, Kazakhstan, Kuwait, Lao People's Democratic Republic, Latvia, Lebanon, Libyan Arab Jamahiriya, Liechtenstein, Lithuania, Luxembourg, Madagascar, Malaysia, Maldives, Mali, Malta, Mauritania, Mexico, Monaco, Mongolia, Morocco, Mozambique, Myanmar, Namibia, Nepal, Netherlands, New Zealand, Nigeria, Norway, Oman, Pakistan, Panama, Paraguay, Peru, Philippines, Poland, Portugal, Qatar, Republic of Korea, Republic of Moldova, Romania, Russian Federation, Saint Lucia, San Marino, Saudi Arabia, Senegal, Seychelles, Sierra Leone, Singapore, Slovakia, Slovenia, Solomon Islands, South Africa, Spain, Sri Lanka, Sudan, Swaziland, Sweden, Syrian Arab Republic, Thailand, The former Yugoslav Republic of Macedonia, Togo, Trinidad and Tobago, Tunisia, Turkey, Ukraine, United Arab Emirates, United Kingdom, United Republic of Tanzania, Uruguay, Venezuela, Viet Nam, Yemen, Yugoslavia, Zambia.

Against: Israel, Marshall Islands, Micronesia, United States.

Abstaining: Nicaragua, Papua New Guinea.

By **resolution 56/142** of 19 December, the Assembly reaffirmed the right of the Palestinian people to self-determination, including their right to a State, and urged all States, as well as UN specialized agencies and organizations, to continue to support the Palestinian people in their quest for self-determination (see p. 630).

Work of Special Committee

In a July report [A/56/214], the Secretary-General stated that all necessary facilities were provided to the Special Committee on Israeli Practices, as requested in General Assembly resolution 55/130 [YUN 2000, p. 435]. Arrangements were made for it to meet in March and October, and a field mission was carried out to Egypt, Jordan and the Syrian Arab Republic in May. Two periodic reports [A/55/373 & Add.1] and the thirty-second annual report of the Special Committee [A/55/453] were circulated to Member States. The UN Department of Public Information continued to provide press coverage of Special Committee meetings and to disseminate information materials on its activities.

GENERAL ASSEMBLY ACTION

On 10 December [meeting 82], the General Assembly, on the recommendation of the Fourth Committee [A/56/550], adopted **resolution 56/59** by recorded vote (83-4-58) [agenda item 88].

Work of the Special Committee to Investigate Israeli Practices Affecting the Human Rights of the Palestinian People and Other Arabs of the Occupied Territories

The General Assembly,

Guided by the purposes and principles of the Charter of the United Nations,

Guided also by the principles of international humanitarian law, in particular the Geneva Convention relative to the Protection of Civilian Persons in Time of War, of 12 August 1949, as well as international standards of human rights, in particular the Universal Declaration of Human Rights and the International Covenants on Human Rights,

Recalling its relevant resolutions, including resolution 2443(XXIII) of 19 December 1968, and relevant resolutions of the Commission on Human Rights,

Recalling also relevant resolutions of the Security Council,

Aware of the lasting impact of the uprising (intifada) of the Palestinian people,

Convinced that occupation itself represents a gross violation of human rights,

Gravely concerned about the continuation of the tragic events that have taken place since 28 September 2000, including the excessive use of force by the Israeli occupying forces against Palestinian civilians, resulting in numerous deaths and injuries,

Having considered the reports of the Special Committee to Investigate Israeli Practices Affecting the Human Rights of the Palestinian People and Other Arabs of the Occupied Territories and the relevant reports of the Secretary-General,

Recalling the signing of the Declaration of Principles on Interim Self-Government Arrangements by the Government of Israel and the Palestine Liberation Organization in Washington, D.C., on 13 September 1993, as well as the subsequent implementation agreements, including the Israeli-Palestinian Interim Agreement on the West Bank and the Gaza Strip signed in Washington, D.C., on 28 September 1995,

Expressing the hope that, with the progress of the peace process, the Israeli occupation will be brought to an end and therefore violation of the human rights of the Palestinian people will cease,

1. *Commends* the Special Committee to Investigate Israeli Practices Affecting the Human Rights of the Palestinian People and Other Arabs of the Occupied Territories for its efforts in performing the tasks assigned to it by the General Assembly and for its impartiality;

2. *Demands* that Israel cooperate with the Special Committee in implementing its mandate;

3. *Deplores* those policies and practices of Israel which violate the human rights of the Palestinian people and other Arabs of the occupied territories, as reflected in the reports of the Special Committee covering the reporting period;

4. *Expresses grave concern* about the situation in the Occupied Palestinian Territory, including Jerusalem, as a result of Israeli practices and measures, and espe-

cially condemns the excessive use of force in the past year which has resulted in more than seven hundred Palestinian deaths and tens of thousands of injuries;

5. *Requests* the Special Committee, pending complete termination of the Israeli occupation, to continue to investigate Israeli policies and practices in the Occupied Palestinian Territory, including Jerusalem, and other Arab territories occupied by Israel since 1967, especially Israeli lack of compliance with the provisions of the Geneva Convention relative to the Protection of Civilian Persons in Time of War, of 12 August 1949, and to consult, as appropriate, with the International Committee of the Red Cross according to its regulations in order to ensure that the welfare and human rights of the peoples of the occupied territories are safeguarded and to report to the Secretary-General as soon as possible and whenever the need arises thereafter;

6. *Also requests* the Special Committee to submit regularly to the Secretary-General periodic reports on the current situation in the Occupied Palestinian Territory, including Jerusalem;

7. *Further requests* the Special Committee to continue to investigate the treatment of prisoners in the Occupied Palestinian Territory, including Jerusalem, and other Arab territories occupied by Israel since 1967;

8. *Requests* the Secretary-General:

(a) To provide the Special Committee with all necessary facilities, including those required for its visits to the occupied territories, so that it may investigate the Israeli policies and practices referred to in the present resolution;

(b) To continue to make available such additional staff as may be necessary to assist the Special Committee in the performance of its tasks;

(c) To circulate regularly to Member States the periodic reports mentioned in paragraph 6 above;

(d) To ensure the widest circulation of the reports of the Special Committee and of information regarding its activities and findings, by all means available, through the Department of Public Information of the Secretariat and, where necessary, to reprint those reports of the Special Committee that are no longer available;

(e) To report to the General Assembly at its fifty-seventh session on the tasks entrusted to him in the present resolution;

9. *Decides* to include in the provisional agenda of its fifty-seventh session the item entitled "Report of the Special Committee to Investigate Israeli Practices Affecting the Human Rights of the Palestinian People and Other Arabs of the Occupied Territories".

RECORDED VOTE ON RESOLUTION 56/59:

In favour: Algeria, Antigua and Barbuda, Armenia, Azerbaijan, Bahrain, Bangladesh, Barbados, Belarus, Belize, Benin, Bhutan, Bolivia, Brazil, Brunei Darussalam, Burkina Faso, Cambodia, Chile, China, Colombia, Côte d'Ivoire, Cuba, Cyprus, Democratic People's Republic of Korea, Djibouti, Dominican Republic, Ecuador, Egypt, Equatorial Guinea, Eritrea, Ethiopia, Gabon, Ghana, Guatemala, Guinea, Guyana, Haiti, Honduras, India, Indonesia, Iran, Jordan, Kuwait, Lao People's Democratic Republic, Lebanon, Libyan Arab Jamahiriya, Malaysia, Maldives, Mali, Malta, Mauritania, Mexico, Morocco, Mozambique, Myanmar, Namibia, Nepal, Nigeria, Oman, Pakistan, Panama, Philippines, Qatar, Saint Lucia, Saudi Arabia, Senegal, Sierra Leone, Singapore, South Africa, Sri Lanka, Sudan, Swaziland, Syrian Arab Republic, Thailand, Togo, Trinidad and Tobago, Tunisia, Turkey, United Arab Emirates, United Republic of Tanzania, Venezuela, Viet Nam, Yemen, Zambia.

Against: Israel, Marshall Islands, Micronesia, United States.

Abstaining: Andorra, Angola, Argentina, Australia, Austria, Bahamas, Belgium, Bulgaria, Canada, Croatia, Czech Republic, Denmark, Estonia, Fiji, Finland, France, Georgia, Germany, Greece, Grenada, Hungary, Iceland, Ireland, Italy, Jamaica, Japan, Kazakhstan, Latvia, Liechtenstein, Lithuania, Luxembourg, Monaco, Mongolia, Netherlands, New Zealand, Nicaragua, Norway, Papua New Guinea, Paraguay, Peru, Poland, Portugal, Republic of Korea, Republic of Moldova, Romania, Russian Federation, San Marino, Slovakia, Slovenia, Solomon Islands, Spain, Sweden, The former Yugoslav Republic of Macedonia, Tonga, Ukraine, United Kingdom, Uruguay, Yugoslavia.

Fourth Geneva Convention

Conference of High Contracting Parties

The Conference of High Contracting Parties to the Fourth Geneva Convention on Measures to Enforce the Convention in the Occupied Palestinian Territory, including Jerusalem, reconvened on 5 December in Geneva, under the chairmanship of Switzerland as the depositary of the Geneva Conventions. By resolution ES-10/7 [YUN 2000, p. 421], the General Assembly had invited Switzerland to consult on the development of the humanitarian situation in the field, with the aim of ensuring respect for the Convention in accordance with common article 1 of the four Conventions. Accordingly, Switzerland undertook informal consultations at the bilateral level and held a series of informal meetings of a group of "Friends of the Depository", including States parties from all regions of the world. The first Conference was held in July 1999 [YUN 1999, p. 415], following the recommendation made by the General Assembly in resolution ES-10/6 [ibid., p. 402]. The 1999 Conference adjourned on the understanding that it would convene again in the light of consultations on the development of the humanitarian situation in the field.

The Conference was attended by 115 high contracting parties and eight other participants and observers, including representatives from Palestine, the International Committee of the Red Cross, the United Nations Relief and Works Agency for Palestine Refugees in the Near East (UNRWA) and the Office of the UN High Commissioner for Human Rights. Australia, Israel and the United States announced that they would not participate.

The Conference adopted without vote a declaration by which it reaffirmed the applicability of the Fourth Geneva Convention to the Occupied Palestinian Territory, including Jerusalem, and reiterated the need for full respect for the Convention. The high contracting parties called on the occupying Power to respect the Convention's provisions and not to commit any grave breaches or other violations of the Convention.

Report of Secretary-General. In July [A/56/215], the Secretary-General informed the General Assembly that Israel had not replied to his May request for information on steps taken or envisaged to implement Assembly resolution 55/131 [YUN 2000, p. 437] demanding that Israel accept the de jure applicability of the Fourth Geneva Convention in the Occupied Palestinian Territory, including Jerusalem, and that it comply scrupulously with its provisions. Also in May, the Secretary-General noted, he had drawn the attention of all States parties to the Convention to paragraph 3 of resolution 55/131 calling on them to exert all efforts to ensure respect by Israel for the Convention's provisions.

GENERAL ASSEMBLY ACTION

On 10 December [meeting 82], the General Assembly, on the recommendation of the Fourth Committee [A/56/550], adopted **resolution 56/60** by recorded vote (148-4-2) [agenda item 88].

Applicability of the Geneva Convention relative to the Protection of Civilian Persons in Time of War, of 12 August 1949, to the Occupied Palestinian Territory, including Jerusalem, and the other occupied Arab territories

The General Assembly,

Bearing in mind the relevant resolutions of the Security Council,

Recalling its relevant resolutions,

Having considered the reports of the Special Committee to Investigate Israeli Practices Affecting the Human Rights of the Palestinian People and Other Arabs of the Occupied Territories and the relevant reports of the Secretary-General,

Considering that the promotion of respect for the obligations arising from the Charter of the United Nations and other instruments and rules of international law is among the basic purposes and principles of the United Nations,

Noting the convening of the meeting of experts of the high contracting parties to the Geneva Convention relative to the Protection of Civilian Persons in Time of War, of 12 August 1949, at Geneva from 27 to 29 October 1998, at the initiative of the Government of Switzerland in its capacity as the depositary of the Convention, concerning general problems of application of the Convention in general and, in particular, in occupied territories,

Noting also the convening for the first time, on 15 July 1999, of a Conference of High Contracting Parties to the Fourth Geneva Convention, as recommended by the General Assembly in its resolution ES-10/6 of 9 February 1999, on measures to enforce the Convention in the Occupied Palestinian Territory, including Jerusalem, and to ensure respect thereof in accordance with article 1 common to the four Geneva Conventions, and aware of the statement adopted by the Conference,

Stressing that Israel, the occupying Power, should comply strictly with its obligations under international law,

1. *Reaffirms* that the Geneva Convention relative to the Protection of Civilian Persons in Time of War, of 12 August 1949, is applicable to the Occupied Palestinian Territory, including Jerusalem, and other Arab territories occupied by Israel since 1967;

2. *Demands* that Israel accept the de jure applicability of the Convention in the Occupied Palestinian Territory, including Jerusalem, and other Arab territories occupied by Israel since 1967, and that it comply scrupulously with the provisions of the Convention;

3. *Calls upon* all States parties to the Convention, in accordance with article 1 common to the four Geneva Conventions, to exert all efforts in order to ensure respect for its provisions by Israel, the occupying Power, in the Occupied Palestinian Territory, including Jerusalem, and other Arab territories occupied by Israel since 1967;

4. *Reiterates* the need for speedy implementation of the recommendations contained in its resolutions ES-10/3 of 15 July 1997, ES-10/4 of 13 November 1997, ES-10/5 of 17 March 1998, ES-10/6 of 9 February 1999 and ES-10/7 of 20 October 2000 with regard to ensuring respect by Israel, the occupying Power, for the provisions of the Convention;

5. *Requests* the Secretary-General to report to the General Assembly at its fifty-seventh session on the implementation of the present resolution.

RECORDED VOTE ON RESOLUTION 56/60:

In favour: Algeria, Andorra, Antigua and Barbuda, Argentina, Armenia, Australia, Austria, Azerbaijan, Bahamas, Bahrain, Bangladesh, Barbados, Belarus, Belgium, Belize, Benin, Bhutan, Bolivia, Brazil, Brunei Darussalam, Bulgaria, Burkina Faso, Burundi, Cambodia, Canada, Cape Verde, Chile, China, Colombia, Comoros, Congo, Costa Rica, Côte d'Ivoire, Croatia, Cuba, Cyprus, Czech Republic, Democratic People's Republic of Korea, Denmark, Djibouti, Dominican Republic, Ecuador, Egypt, El Salvador, Equatorial Guinea, Eritrea, Estonia, Ethiopia, Fiji, Finland, France, Gabon, Georgia, Germany, Ghana, Greece, Grenada, Guatemala, Guinea, Guyana, Haiti, Honduras, Hungary, Iceland, India, Indonesia, Iran, Ireland, Italy, Jamaica, Japan, Jordan, Kazakhstan, Kenya, Kuwait, Lao People's Democratic Republic, Latvia, Lebanon, Libyan Arab Jamahiriya, Liechtenstein, Lithuania, Luxembourg, Madagascar, Malaysia, Maldives, Mali, Malta, Mauritania, Mexico, Monaco, Mongolia, Morocco, Mozambique, Myanmar, Namibia, Nepal, Netherlands, New Zealand, Nigeria, Norway, Oman, Pakistan, Panama, Papua New Guinea, Paraguay, Peru, Philippines, Poland, Portugal, Qatar, Republic of Korea, Republic of Moldova, Romania, Russian Federation, Saint Lucia, San Marino, Saudi Arabia, Seychelles, Sierra Leone, Singapore, Slovakia, Slovenia, Solomon Islands, South Africa, Spain, Sri Lanka, Sudan, Swaziland, Sweden, Syrian Arab Republic, Thailand, The former Yugoslav Republic of Macedonia, Togo, Tonga, Trinidad and Tobago, Tunisia, Turkey, Ukraine, United Arab Emirates, United Kingdom, United Republic of Tanzania, Uruguay, Venezuela, Viet Nam, Yemen, Yugoslavia, Zambia.

Against: Israel, Marshall Islands, Micronesia, United States.

Abstaining: Angola, Nicaragua.

Palestinian women

The Secretary-General, in a report [E/CN.6/2001/2] to the Commission on the Status of Women on follow-up to and progress in the implementation of the Beijing Declaration and Platform for Action [YUN 1995, p. 1170], reviewed, in response to Economic and Social Council resolution 2000/23 [YUN 2000, p. 439], the situation of Palestinian women and described assistance provided by UN organizations during the period from September 1999 to September 2000. He stated that women's employment and participation in the labour force grew faster than for men. That could be explained by the rapid expansion in the agriculture and services sectors, where women were present in high numbers. However, women were still found mainly in part-time jobs. The closure policy applied by the Israeli authorities, coupled with border crossing restrictions and the expansion of Israeli settlements, continued to have a detrimental effect on Palestinian economic development, in particular on the living conditions of Palestinian families. In addition, the imprisonment of Palestinian men had forced many women to take on additional burdens and acquire roles other than the ones traditionally performed by them. That situation had the potential of leading to conflicts within the family due to the difficulty in adapting to and accepting change, but it could also provide opportunities for women's empowerment as they gained new decision-making power within the household.

The UN system continued to provide assistance to Palestinian women. ESCWA, among other things, prepared a study on gender and citizenship and the role of non-governmental organizations (NGOs) in the occupied territories, with the aim of increasing gender-sensitivity through action-oriented policy recommendations. UNRWA continued to provide education, health, relief and social services. More than 50 per cent of UNRWA's special hardship case families, who received direct food and material assistance from the Agency, were headed by women. Seventy Women's Programme Centres served as focal points within the refugee community for UNRWA's work with women. During 1999/2000, UNRWA's income-generation programme granted loans valued at $3.1 million to 3,716 women, who supported 20,050 dependants.

ILO carried out a number of activities in gender mainstreaming, the development of women's entrepreneurship and capacity-building on gender, poverty and employment.

The United Nations Children's Fund (UNICEF) promoted society's awareness of the scope and meaning of women's rights, non-discrimination and gender equality, by using information from all its projects and education strategies, including better parenting, gender equality in education and life skills. The UNICEF women's health project included midwife training and workshops for maternal health care professionals and for physicians and nurses in hospital obstetric and neonatal departments. UNICEF also supported an enabling environment that influenced legislation and mobilized resources for Palestinian women.

The Secretary-General observed that the status and living conditions of Palestinian women were linked to the peace process. Towards the end of the reporting period, violence between Israeli security forces and Palestinian civilians erupted in the occupied territories, jeopardizing the peace process and hindering UN assistance efforts. It was particularly important that Palestinian women should continue to receive assistance in such areas as education, health, social services and microcredit. The gender perspective should continue to be fully integrated in international assistance programmes through, among other things, greater gender analysis and the collection of sex-disaggregated data.

ECONOMIC AND SOCIAL COUNCIL ACTION

On 24 July [meeting 39], the Economic and Social Council, on the recommendation of the Commission on the Status of Women [E/2001/27 & Corr.1], adopted **resolution 2001/2** by roll-call vote (39-1-1) [agenda item 14 (a)].

The situation of and assistance to Palestinian women

The Economic and Social Council,

Having considered with appreciation section III.A concerning the situation of Palestinian women and assistance provided by organizations of the United Nations system, contained in the report of the Secretary-General on follow-up to and implementation of the Beijing Declaration and Platform for Action,

Recalling the Nairobi Forward-looking Strategies for the Advancement of Women, in particular paragraph 260 concerning Palestinian women and children, the Beijing Platform for Action adopted at the Fourth World Conference on Women, and the outcome of the twenty-third special session of the General Assembly, entitled "Women 2000: gender equality, development and peace for the twenty-first century",

Recalling also its resolution 2000/23 of 28 July 2000 and other relevant United Nations resolutions,

Recalling further the Declaration on the Elimination of Violence against Women as it concerns the protection of civilian populations,

Stressing the need for compliance with the existing Israeli-Palestinian agreements concluded within the context of the Middle East peace process and the need to resume peace negotiations, as soon as possible, in order to reach a final settlement,

Concerned about the deterioration of the situation of Palestinian women in the Occupied Palestinian Territory, including Jerusalem, and about the severe consequences of continuous illegal Israeli settlements activities as well as the harsh economic conditions and other consequences for the situation of Palestinian women and their families, resulting from the frequent closures and isolation of the occupied territory,

Expressing its condemnation of acts of violence, especially the excessive use of force against Palestinians, resulting in injury and loss of human life,

1. *Calls upon* the concerned parties, as well as the entire international community, to exert all the necessary efforts to ensure the immediate resumption of the peace process on its agreed basis, taking into account the common ground already gained, and calls for measures for tangible improvements in the difficult situation on the ground and living conditions faced by Palestinian women and their families;

2. *Reaffirms* that the Israeli occupation remains a major obstacle for Palestinian women with regard to their advancement, self-reliance and integration into the development planning of their society;

3. *Demands* that Israel, the occupying Power, comply fully with the provisions and principles of the Universal Declaration of Human Rights, the Regulations annexed to the Hague Convention IV, of 18 October 1907, and the Geneva Convention relative to the Protection of Civilian Persons in Time of War, of 12 August 1949, in order to protect the rights of Palestinian women and their families;

4. *Calls upon* Israel to facilitate the return of all refugees and displaced Palestinian women and children to their homes and properties, in compliance with the relevant United Nations resolutions;

5. *Urges* Member States, financial organizations of the United Nations system, non-governmental organizations and other relevant institutions to intensify their efforts to provide financial and technical assistance to Palestinian women, especially during the transitional period;

6. *Requests* the Commission on the Status of Women to continue to monitor and take action with regard to the implementation of the Nairobi Forward-looking Strategies for the Advancement of Women, in particular paragraph 260 concerning Palestinian women and children, the Beijing Platform for Action, and the outcome of the twenty-third special session of the General Assembly, entitled "Women 2000: gender equality, development and peace for the twenty-first century";

7. *Requests* the Secretary-General to continue to review the situation and to assist Palestinian women by all available means, and to submit to the Commission on the Status of Women at its forty-sixth session a report on the progress made in the implementation of the present resolution.

ROLL-CALL VOTE ON RESOLUTION 2001/2:

In favour: Andorra, Angola, Argentina, Austria, Bahrain, Bolivia, Brazil, Burkina Faso, Cameroon, China, Croatia, Cuba, Czech Republic, Denmark, Egypt, Ethiopia, France, Georgia, Honduras, Indonesia, Iran, Japan, Malta, Mexico, Morocco, Nepal, Netherlands, Nigeria, Norway, Pakistan, Peru, Republic of Korea, Saudi Arabia, South Africa, Sudan, Suriname, Uganda, United Kingdom, Venezuela.
Against: United States.
Abstaining: Canada.

Issues related to Palestine

General aspects

The General Assembly continued to consider the question of Palestine in 2001. Having discussed the annual report of the Committee on the Exercise of the Inalienable Rights of the Palestinian People (Committee on Palestinian Rights) [A/56/35 & Corr.1], the Assembly adopted four resolutions, reaffirming, among other things, the necessity of achieving a peaceful settlement of the Palestine question—the core of the Arab-Israeli conflict—and stressing the need for the realization of the inalienable rights of the Palestinians, primarily the right to self-

determination, for Israeli withdrawal from the Palestinian territory occupied since 1967 and for resolving the problem of the Palestine refugees.

The International Day of Solidarity with the Palestinian People, celebrated annually on 29 November, in accordance with Assembly resolution 32/40 B [YUN 1977, p. 304], was observed at UN Headquarters and at the UN Offices at Geneva and Vienna. However, due to the situation in the occupied territory and the enhanced security measures in New York and at Headquarters after 11 September 2001, the traditional Palestinian exhibit could not be organized.

Report of Secretary-General. In a November report on the question of Palestine [A/56/642-S/2001/1100], the Secretary-General made observations on the Middle East peace process (see p. 405). He stated that since the outbreak of the Palestinian intifada at the end of September 2000 [YUN 2000, p. 416] over 900 people had been killed and many thousands had been injured, the vast majority of them Palestinians. Israel's response to the violence had included a disproportionate use of military force and incursions into the area under full Palestinian authority. The Secretary-General condemned the practice of so-called "targeted assassinations" and attacks on civilians by settler groups. He also strongly condemned acts of violence or terror from whatever quarter, especially indiscriminate suicide bombing attacks against Israelis by Palestinian groups, and called on the PLO to control violence. Those developments had increased mutual distrust, hardened the positions of the two sides and strengthened extremist elements. Since the beginning of the intifada, the level of poverty, misery and suffering among Palestinians had increased dramatically.

By notes verbales of 18 and 24 July, the Secretary-General sought the positions of the Governments of Egypt, Israel, Jordan, Lebanon and the Syrian Arab Republic, as well as the PLO, regarding steps taken by them to implement the relevant provisions of resolution 55/55 [YUN 2000, p. 440]. As at 15 November, only Israel and the PLO had responded.

Israel said that it viewed that resolution as unbalanced and an undue interference in the Israeli-Palestinian bilateral negotiations. The ongoing violence in the region was a result of a Palestinian decision to abandon peace negotiations and pursue their goals through violence and terrorism. The one-sided approach reflected in the resolution, which sought to dictate the outcome of the negotiating process, rewarded violence at a time when the Palestinian side should be compelled to renounce all acts of violence and return to the path of peaceful dialogue.

The Permanent Observer of Palestine said that the many principles and components of the resolution remained valid and essential in the search for a just and a lasting solution to the decades-long question of Palestine. The decline of the situation on the ground since 28 September 2000 had been characterized by an excessive and indiscriminate use of force by Israeli occupying forces against Palestinian civilians. Israel, moreover, had not endorsed or accepted the recommendations contained in the Mitchell report (see p. 409).

The Secretary-General observed that only a package solution based on the Mitchell report, including not only security and economic aspects but also a political component, could halt the cycle of violence, restore calm and create the right atmosphere for the resumption of sustainable peace talks. There was no alternative to a return to the negotiating table and to a peaceful settlement. However, the mutual distrust between the parties had reached such a level that there was a need for constant third-party involvement in order to break the impasse. Therefore, it was imperative to accelerate joint efforts with a view to generating new momentum towards a peaceful solution to the crisis.

The Israeli-Palestinian confrontation had had a devastating impact on the humanitarian and economic situation in the Occupied Palestinian Territory. Severe closures and blockades had resulted in large-scale losses to the Palestinian economy, wiping out more than three years of growth and increasing dramatically the level of unemployment and poverty. In addition, the drop in domestic tax revenue and the continued withholding of Palestinian tax revenues by Israeli authorities had led to a significant budget deficit in 2001. Therefore, a well-coordinated and concerted international relief and assistance effort was essential to address the most pressing needs and gradually improve living conditions. Measures were also needed to remove the restrictions placed on the movement of staff and goods related to the delivery of humanitarian assistance.

As the Assembly had underscored on many occasions, achieving a final and peaceful settlement of the question of Palestine was imperative for the attainment of a comprehensive and lasting peace in the Middle East. The Secretary-General hoped that there would also be movement on the Syrian and Lebanese tracks so that peace, security and stability could be achieved on the basis of Security Council resolutions 242(1967) [YUN 1967, p. 257] and 338(1973) [YUN 1973, p. 213].

GENERAL ASSEMBLY ACTION

On 3 December [meeting 72], the General Assembly adopted **resolution 56/36** [draft: A/56/L.22 & Add.1] by recorded vote (131-6-20) [agenda item 41].

Peaceful settlement of the question of Palestine
The General Assembly,

Recalling its relevant resolutions, including resolutions adopted at the tenth emergency special session,

Recalling also the relevant Security Council resolutions, including resolutions 242(1967) of 22 November 1967 and 338(1973) of 22 October 1973,

Aware that it has been more than fifty years since the adoption of resolution 181(II) of 29 November 1947 and thirty-four years since the occupation of Palestinian territory, including Jerusalem, in 1967,

Having considered the report of the Secretary-General submitted pursuant to the request made in its resolution 55/55 of 1 December 2000,

Reaffirming the permanent responsibility of the United Nations with regard to the question of Palestine until the question is resolved in all its aspects,

Convinced that achieving a final and peaceful settlement of the question of Palestine, the core of the Arab-Israeli conflict, is imperative for the attainment of a comprehensive and lasting peace in the Middle East,

Aware that the principle of equal rights and self-determination of peoples is among the purposes and principles embodied in the Charter of the United Nations,

Affirming the principle of the inadmissibility of the acquisition of territory by war,

Affirming also the illegality of the Israeli settlements in the territory occupied since 1967 and of Israeli actions aimed at changing the status of Jerusalem,

Affirming once again the right of all States in the region to live in peace within secure and internationally recognized borders,

Recalling the mutual recognition between the Government of the State of Israel and the Palestine Liberation Organization, the representative of the Palestinian people, and the signing by the two parties of the Declaration of Principles on Interim Self-Government Arrangements in Washington, D.C., on 13 September 1993, as well as the subsequent implementation agreements, including the Israeli-Palestinian Interim Agreement on the West Bank and the Gaza Strip, signed in Washington, D.C., on 28 September 1995,

Recalling also the withdrawal of the Israeli army, which took place in the Gaza Strip and the Jericho area in 1995 in accordance with the agreements reached by the parties, and the initiation of the Palestinian Authority in those areas, as well as the subsequent redeployments of the Israeli army in the rest of the West Bank,

Noting with satisfaction the successful holding of the first Palestinian general elections,

Noting the appointment by the Secretary-General of the United Nations Special Coordinator for the Middle East Peace Process and Personal Representative of the Secretary-General to the Palestine Liberation Organization and the Palestinian Authority, and its positive contribution,

Welcoming the convening of the Conference to Support Middle East Peace in Washington, D.C., on 1 October 1993, as well as all follow-up meetings and the international mechanisms established to provide assistance to the Palestinian people, including the donor meetings held in Lisbon on 7 and 8 June 2000 and in Stockholm on 11 April 2001,

Expressing its deep concern over the tragic events in Occupied East Jerusalem and the Occupied Palestinian Territory since 28 September 2000, which have resulted in a high number of deaths and injuries, mostly among Palestinian civilians, and concerned also about the clashes between the Israeli armed forces and the Palestinian police and the casualties on both sides,

Expressing its deep concern also over the continued imposition of closures and restrictions by Israel on the Occupied Palestinian Territory, including Jerusalem, as well as the serious incursions into Palestinian-controlled areas and actions against Palestinian institutions,

Expressing its grave concern over the serious deterioration of the situation in the Occupied Palestinian Territory, including Jerusalem, and the difficulties facing the Middle East peace process,

Affirming the urgent need for the parties to implement the recommendations of the Sharm el-Sheikh Fact-Finding Committee (Mitchell Committee) and to resume negotiations towards a final peaceful settlement,

1. *Reaffirms* the necessity of achieving a peaceful settlement of the question of Palestine, the core of the Arab-Israeli conflict, in all its aspects;

2. *Expresses its full support* for the peace process, which began in Madrid, and the Declaration of Principles on Interim Self-Government Arrangements of 1993, as well as the subsequent implementation agreements, and expresses the hope that the process will be reinvigorated and will soon lead to the establishment of a comprehensive, just and lasting peace in the Middle East;

3. *Stresses* the necessity for commitment to the principle of land for peace and the implementation of Security Council resolutions 242(1967) and 338(1973), which form the basis of the Middle East peace process;

4. *Calls upon* the concerned parties, the co-sponsors of the peace process and other interested parties, as well as the entire international community to exert all the efforts and initiatives necessary to reverse immediately all measures taken on the ground since 28 September 2000, in implementation of the recommendations of the Sharm el-Sheikh Fact-Finding Committee (Mitchell Committee), and in order to ensure a successful and speedy resumption of negotiations and conclusion of the peace process;

5. *Stresses* the need for:

(a) The realization of the inalienable rights of the Palestinian people, primarily the right to self-determination and the right to establish their independent State;

(b) The withdrawal of Israel from the Palestinian territory occupied since 1967;

6. *Also stresses* the need for resolving the problem of the Palestine refugees in conformity with its resolution 194(III) of 11 December 1948;

7. *Urges* Member States to expedite the provision of economic and technical assistance to the Palestinian people during this critical period;

8. *Emphasizes* the importance for the United Nations to play a more active and expanded role in the current peace process and in the implementation of the Declaration of Principles;

9. *Requests* the Secretary-General to continue his efforts with the parties concerned, and in consultation with the Security Council, for the promotion of peace in the region and to submit progress reports on developments in this matter.

RECORDED VOTE ON RESOLUTION 56/36:

In favour: Afghanistan, Algeria, Andorra, Angola, Argentina, Armenia, Austria, Azerbaijan, Bahrain, Bangladesh, Barbados, Belarus, Belgium, Belize, Benin, Bolivia, Botswana, Brazil, Brunei Darussalam, Bulgaria, Burkina Faso, Burundi, Cambodia, Cameroon, Cape Verde, Chad, Chile, China, Colombia, Comoros, Congo, Costa Rica, Croatia, Cuba, Cyprus, Democratic People's Republic of Korea, Djibouti, Dominican Republic, Ecuador, Egypt, El Salvador, Equatorial Guinea, Eritrea, Ethiopia, Fiji, Finland, France, Ghana, Greece, Grenada, Guatemala, Guinea, Guyana, Haiti, Honduras, India, Indonesia, Ireland, Italy, Jamaica, Japan, Jordan, Kenya, Kuwait, Lao People's Democratic Republic, Lebanon, Libyan Arab Jamahiriya, Liechtenstein, Lithuania, Luxembourg, Madagascar, Malawi, Malaysia, Maldives, Mali, Malta, Mauritania, Mauritius, Mexico, Monaco, Mongolia, Morocco, Mozambique, Myanmar, Namibia, Nepal, New Zealand, Nigeria, Oman, Pakistan, Panama, Peru, Philippines, Portugal, Qatar, Republic of Korea, Republic of Moldova, Russian Federation, Saint Lucia, San Marino, Saudi Arabia, Senegal, Seychelles, Sierra Leone, Singapore, Slovakia, Slovenia, Solomon Islands, South Africa, Spain, Sri Lanka, Sudan, Suriname, Sweden, Syrian Arab Republic, Thailand, Togo, Trinidad and Tobago, Tunisia, Turkey, Uganda, Ukraine, United Arab Emirates, United Republic of Tanzania, Uruguay, Venezuela, Viet Nam, Yemen, Yugoslavia, Zambia, Zimbabwe.

Against: Israel, Marshall Islands, Micronesia, Nauru, Tuvalu, United States.

Abstaining: Australia, Canada, Czech Republic, Denmark, Estonia, Georgia, Germany, Hungary, Iceland, Latvia, Netherlands, Nicaragua, Norway, Papua New Guinea, Paraguay, Poland, Romania, Rwanda, The former Yugoslav Republic of Macedonia, United Kingdom.

Speaking after the vote, the Permanent Observer of Palestine said that the result of the voting showed that there was a clear position regarding the State of Palestine, whose establishment was absolutely essential for achieving overall peace in the region. The Palestinian leadership, on 2 December, had adopted a series of decisions that declared a temporary state of emergency and made it illegal for any Palestinian faction not to comply with a ceasefire. The day after, however, Israeli helicopter gunships had fired missiles in the area of Chairman Arafat's offices. Terrorist attacks had been carried out inside Israel, but that phenomenon had started only a few years earlier and was an outcome of and not the reason for the current situation. The reason was the uprooting of the Palestinian people from their homeland and their denial of their own State for more than 50 years.

Israel stated that the international community was duty-bound to denounce Palestinian terrorist practices without ambiguity or understatement. By recalling the true nature of Palestinian terrorism and denouncing it for what it was, the international community could truly help the Palestinians to become committed to dialogue, coexistence and peace. Justice and peace would be restored to the region through education for peace, through an end to hatred and incitement and through an absolute renunciation of terrorist practices.

By **decision 56/464** of 24 December, the Assembly decided that the agenda items entitled "Question of Palestine" and "The situation in the Middle East" would remain for consideration during its resumed fifty-sixth (2002) session.

Committee on Palestinian Rights

As mandated by General Assembly resolution 55/52 [YUN 2000, p. 444], the Committee on the Exercise of the Inalienable Rights of the Palestinian People continued to review the situation relating to the Palestine question, reported on it and made suggestions to the Assembly or the Security Council.

The Committee continued to encourage cooperation, coordination and networking among civil society organizations. It maintained and developed liaison with national, regional and international coordinating mechanisms accredited to it, in addition to the already-established liaison with NGOs. Consultations between the Committee and NGO representatives were held on 22 February 2001 in Vienna; Palestinian NGOs were unable to participate due to the general closure imposed by Israel on the occupied territory. The Committee asked NGOs to focus their work on mobilizing emergency relief; to lobby their Governments to live up to their responsibilities under the Fourth Geneva Convention; and to support initiatives at the United Nations and elsewhere to establish a protection force to be deployed in the Occupied Palestinian Territory. At the United Nations NGO meeting in solidarity with the Palestinian people (Madrid, Spain, 19 July), participants urged the Security Council to place an international protection force in the Occupied Palestinian Territory and decided to undertake advocacy steps in that regard.

The Committee continued to follow the Palestine-related activities of intergovernmental bodies, such as the Organization of African Unity, the Non-Aligned Movement Committee on Palestine and the Non-Aligned Movement Security Council Caucus, and, through its Chairman, participated in a number of high-level meetings of those bodies. Through its Bureau, the Committee continued to cooperate on the question of Palestine with the EU. A Committee delegation took part in the United Nations Latin American and Caribbean Meeting on the Question of Palestine (Havana, Cuba, 12-14 June). The Havana Declaration, the Meeting's final document, supported the right of the Palestinians to self-determination and the establishment of an independent and sovereign Palestinian State and the right to return to their homeland.

An NGO workshop, organized in Havana on 14 June in connection with the Meeting, focused on action by civil society in Latin America and the Caribbean in solidarity with the Palestinian people.

The Committee, together with the UN Division for Palestinian Rights, organized the United Nations International Meeting on the Question of Palestine: "The Road to Israeli-Palestinian Peace" (Madrid, 17-18 July), which was attended by, among others, international experts, representatives of Governments, intergovernmental organizations, UN system entities, the PA and the media. In the general remarks of the Meeting, participants expressed their conviction that the recommendations contained in the Mitchell report and the subsequent United States–brokered ceasefire agreement should be implemented as a whole; that Israel's excessive use of force, the closures and the economic blockade of Palestinian population centres, the incursions into Palestinian-controlled areas and all other measures of collective punishment against the Palestinian people should be brought to an end; that the high contracting parties to the Fourth Geneva Convention should expedite the reconvening of the Conference of High Contracting Parties; and that an international presence had to be established to protect innocent civilians and to monitor the implementation of agreements and understandings reached.

In its annual report to the Assembly [A/56/35 & Corr.1] covering the period from 11 October 2000 to 10 October 2001, the Committee said that peace talks had been suspended since January 2001, owing to the position on the peace negotiations taken by the new Israeli Government and the continuing violence in the West Bank, the Gaza Strip and East Jerusalem. The Al-Aqsa intifada, as it became known in 2001, had three distinctive characteristics: the rapid escalation of operations of the Israel Defence Forces (IDF) against the Palestinians; the introduction of a policy of targeted extrajudicial assassinations of Palestinian leaders and activists; and the frequent incursions into areas under full Palestinian control.

Since the beginning of the intifada in October 2000, over 660 Palestinians had been killed by IDF, security forces and settlers, while some 20,000 Palestinians had been wounded. IDF, in attacking the Palestinians, continued to rely on heavy and sophisticated weapons, using them in an indiscriminate manner. On 18 May, the Israeli Government changed the nature and scale of the conflict by authorizing the use of fighter aircraft against unprotected Palestinian targets. Since December 2000, more than 50 Palestinians had been killed in targeted attacks that often claimed the lives of innocent bystanders. Israeli incursions into Palestinian-controlled areas constituted a virtual reoccupation of Palestinian lands; they were often accompanied by the destruction of public and private property in Palestinian towns, villages and refugee camps.

During the year, the Israeli authorities had considered unilateral separation schemes aimed at further isolating Palestinian population centres from the settlements and restricting the movement of Palestinians throughout the occupied territory. In late September 2001, Israel established a 30-kilometre-long closed military zone in the northern part of the territory, stretching from Jenin to Tulkarm.

Despite intensive efforts by various international parties to hold violence in check and reach a political solution, the peace process remained at a standstill. A major obstacle to political dialogue and negotiations had been the persistence with which the Israeli authorities had been expanding the illegal settlements and infrastructure in the Occupied Palestinian Territory, including Jerusalem. The number of settlers in the West Bank and Gaza had increased by 17,000 in 2001, reaching nearly 277,000. The scope and intensity of settler violence against the Palestinians also increased in the course of the year. In several parts of the West Bank, settlers had instituted armed patrols.

The Palestinian economy in 2001 showed signs of rapid disintegration as a result of the Israeli military occupation. Protracted closures and restrictions on the movement of goods and the labour force had decimated all sectors of the economy. In contrast to previous years, there had been a noticeable shift to emergency assistance and humanitarian aid. Unemployment rose to the 1996 levels, while the poverty rate reached the 50 per cent mark, meaning that half of the Palestinian population was living on $2 or less a day. In addition, Israeli authorities continued to exercise control over Palestinian water resources, with thousands of families deprived of connection to water networks.

The Committee, in its conclusions and recommendations, said that 34 years after the illegal occupation by Israel of Palestinian land, the Palestinians were yet to see their aspirations for self-determination and the exercise of their inalienable and natural rights realized. The deplorable events since September 2000 had underscored the urgency of pressing forward with efforts to bring calm, stabilize the situation and enable the parties to resume their dialogue. The Committee called for the immediate implementation of the Mitchell Committee recommendations and for the reconvening of the Conference of High Contracting Parties to the Fourth Geneva Convention, in order to ensure respect for the Convention and provide the necessary protection to the Palestinian people.

The Committee reaffirmed its long-standing position that the United Nations should continue to exercise its permanent responsibility with respect to all aspects of the question of Palestine until it was resolved in a satisfactory manner, in conformity with relevant UN resolutions and international legitimacy, and until the inalienable rights of the Palestinian people were fully realized. There was also a need for civil society initiatives, with special emphasis on mobilizing wide support for measures aimed at protecting the Palestinian people. The Committee would continue to review and assess its programme with a view to making it more responsive to the developments on the ground and in the peace process.

GENERAL ASSEMBLY ACTION

On 3 December [meeting 72], the General Assembly adopted **resolution 56/33** [draft: A/56/L.19 & Add.1] by recorded vote (106-5-48) [agenda item 41].

Committee on the Exercise of the Inalienable Rights of the Palestinian People

The General Assembly,

Recalling its resolutions 181 (II) of 29 November 1947, 194 (III) of 11 December 1948, 3236 (XXIX) of 22 November 1974, 3375 (XXX) and 3376 (XXX) of 10 November 1975, 31/20 of 24 November 1976, 32/40 A of 2 December 1977, 33/28 A and B of 7 December 1978, 34/65 A of 29 November 1979 and 34/65 C of 12 December 1979, ES-7/2 of 29 July 1980, 35/169 A and C of 15 December 1980, 36/120 A and C of 10 December 1981, ES-7/4 of 28 April 1982, 37/86 A of 10 December 1982, 38/58 A of 13 December 1983, 39/49 A of 11 December 1984, 40/96 A of 12 December 1985, 41/43 A of 2 December 1986, 42/66 A of 2 December 1987, 43/175 A of 15 December 1988, 44/41 A of 6 December 1989, 45/67 A of 6 December 1990, 46/74 A of 11 December 1991, 47/64 A of 11 December 1992, 48/158 A of 20 December 1993, 49/62 A of 14 December 1994, 50/84 A of 15 December 1995, 51/23 of 4 December 1996, 52/49 of 9 December 1997, 53/39 of 2 December 1998, 54/39 of 1 December 1999 and 55/52 of 1 December 2000,

Having considered the report of the Committee on the Exercise of the Inalienable Rights of the Palestinian People,

Recalling the signing of the Declaration of Principles on Interim Self-Government Arrangements, including its Annexes and Agreed Minutes, by the Government of the State of Israel and the Palestine Liberation Organization, the representative of the Palestinian people, in Washington, D.C., on 13 September 1993, as well as the subsequent implementation agreements, in particular the Israeli-Palestinian Interim Agreement on the West Bank and the Gaza Strip, signed in Washington, D.C., on 28 September 1995,

Reaffirming that the United Nations has a permanent responsibility with respect to the question of Palestine until the question is resolved in all its aspects in a satisfactory manner in accordance with international legitimacy,

1. *Expresses its appreciation* to the Committee on the Exercise of the Inalienable Rights of the Palestinian People for its efforts in performing the tasks assigned to it by the General Assembly;

2. *Considers* that the Committee can continue to make a valuable and positive contribution to international efforts to promote the Middle East peace process and the full implementation of the agreements reached and to mobilize international support for and assistance to the Palestinian people during the transitional period;

3. *Endorses* the conclusions and recommendations of the Committee contained in chapter VII of its report;

4. *Requests* the Committee to continue to keep under review the situation relating to the question of Palestine and to report and make suggestions to the General Assembly or the Security Council, as appropriate;

5. *Authorizes* the Committee to continue to exert all efforts to promote the exercise of the inalienable rights of the Palestinian people, to make such adjustments in its approved programme of work as it may consider appropriate and necessary in the light of developments, to give special emphasis to the need to mobilize support and assistance for the Palestinian people and to report thereon to the General Assembly at its fifty-seventh session and thereafter;

6. *Requests* the Committee to continue to extend its cooperation and support to Palestinian and other civil society organizations in order to mobilize international solidarity and support for the achievement by the Palestinian people of its inalienable rights and for a peaceful settlement of the question of Palestine, and to involve additional civil society organizations in its work;

7. *Requests* the United Nations Conciliation Commission for Palestine, established under General Assembly resolution 194(III), and other United Nations bodies associated with the question of Palestine to continue to cooperate fully with the Committee and to make available to it, at its request, the relevant information and documentation which they have at their disposal;

8. *Requests* the Secretary-General to circulate the report of the Committee to all the competent bodies of the United Nations, and urges them to take the necessary action, as appropriate;

9. *Also requests* the Secretary-General to continue to provide the Committee with all the necessary facilities for the performance of its tasks.

RECORDED VOTE ON RESOLUTION 56/33:

In favour: Afghanistan, Algeria, Angola, Armenia, Azerbaijan, Bahrain, Bangladesh, Barbados, Belarus, Belize, Benin, Bolivia, Botswana, Brazil, Brunei Darussalam, Burkina Faso, Burundi, Cambodia, Cameroon, Cape Verde, Chad, Chile, China, Colombia, Comoros, Costa Rica, Cuba, Cyprus, Democratic People's Republic of Korea, Djibouti, Dominican Republic, Ecuador, Egypt, El Salvador, Equatorial Guinea, Eritrea, Ethiopia, Fiji, Ghana, Grenada, Guatemala, Guinea, Guyana, Haiti, Honduras, India, Indonesia, Iran, Jamaica, Jordan, Kenya, Kuwait, Lao People's Democratic Republic, Lebanon, Libyan Arab Jamahiriya, Madagascar, Malawi, Malaysia, Maldives, Mali, Malta, Mauritania, Mauritius, Mexico, Mongolia, Morocco, Mozambique, Myanmar, Namibia, Nepal, Nigeria, Oman, Pakistan, Panama, Papua New Guinea, Paraguay, Peru, Philippines, Qatar, Republic of Korea, Rwanda, Saint Lucia, Saudi Arabia, Senegal, Sierra Leone, Singapore, Solomon Islands, Sri Lanka, Sudan, Suriname, Syrian Arab Republic, Thailand, Togo, Trinidad and Tobago, Tunisia, Turkey, Uganda, Ukraine, United Arab Emirates, United Republic of Tanzania, Uruguay, Venezuela, Viet Nam, Yemen, Zambia, Zimbabwe.

Against: Israel, Marshall Islands, Micronesia, Tuvalu, United States.

Abstaining: Andorra, Argentina, Australia, Austria, Belgium, Bulgaria, Canada, Croatia, Czech Republic, Denmark, Estonia, Finland, France, Georgia, Germany, Greece, Hungary, Iceland, Ireland, Italy, Japan, Kazakhstan, Latvia, Liechtenstein, Lithuania, Luxembourg, Monaco, Nauru, Netherlands, New Zealand, Nicaragua, Norway, Poland, Portugal, Republic of Moldova, Romania, Russian Federation, San Marino, Slovakia, Slovenia, South Africa, Spain, Sweden, The former Yugoslav Republic of Macedonia, Tonga, United Kingdom, Vanuatu, Yugoslavia.

Division for Palestinian Rights

Under the guidance of the Committee on Palestinian Rights, the Division for Palestinian Rights of the UN Secretariat continued to function as a centre of research, monitoring, preparation of studies, and collection and dissemination of information on all issues related to the Palestine question. The Division responded to requests for information and prepared and disseminated the following publications: a monthly bulletin covering action by the Committee, UN bodies and agencies, and intergovernmental organizations concerned with Palestine; a monthly chronology of events relating to the question of Palestine, based on media reports and other sources; reports of meetings organized under the auspices of the Committee; a special bulletin on the observance of the International Day of Solidarity with the Palestinian People (29 November); an annual compilation of relevant General Assembly and Security Council resolutions, decisions and statements; and an update of a study entitled "Origins and Evolution of the Palestine Problem, 1917-1988".

The Committee, in its annual report [A/56/35 & Corr.1], noted that the Division continued to develop the electronic United Nations Information System on the Question of Palestine (UNISPAL), as mandated by Assembly resolution 46/74 B [YUN 1991, p. 228]. The Division maintained the Internet web site entitled "NGO Network on the Question of Palestine" as a permanent tool of mutual information and cooperation between civil society and the Committee. It also continued the training programme for PA staff and issued its bimonthly newsletter entitled *NGO Action News* covering the activities of civil society on the various aspects of the question of Palestine.

The Committee requested the Division to continue its publications programme and other informational activities, particularly the further development of the UNISPAL documents collection and annual training activities for PA staff.

GENERAL ASSEMBLY ACTION

On 3 December [meeting 72], the General Assembly adopted **resolution 56/34** [draft: A/56/L.20 & Add.1] by recorded vote (107-5-47) [agenda item 41].

Division for Palestinian Rights of the Secretariat

The General Assembly,

Having considered the report of the Committee on the Exercise of the Inalienable Rights of the Palestinian People,

Taking note in particular of the relevant information contained in chapter V.B of that report,

Recalling its resolutions 32/40 B of 2 December 1977, 33/28 C of 7 December 1978, 34/65 D of 12 December 1979, 35/169 D of 15 December 1980, 36/120 B of 10 December 1981, 37/86 B of 10 December 1982, 38/58 B of 13 December 1983, 39/49 B of 11 December 1984, 40/96 B of 12 December 1985, 41/43 B of 2 December 1986, 42/66 B of 2 December 1987, 43/175 B of 15 December 1988, 44/41 B of 6 December 1989, 45/67 B of 6 December 1990, 46/74 B of 11 December 1991, 47/64 B of 11 December 1992, 48/158 B of 20 December 1993, 49/62 B of 14 December 1994, 50/84 B of 15 December 1995, 51/24 of 4 December 1996, 52/50 of 9 December 1997, 53/40 of 2 December 1998, 54/40 of 1 December 1999 and 55/53 of 1 December 2000,

1. *Notes with appreciation* the action taken by the Secretary-General in compliance with its resolution 55/53;

2. *Considers* that the Division for Palestinian Rights of the Secretariat continues to make a useful and constructive contribution;

3. *Requests* the Secretary-General to continue to provide the Division with the necessary resources and to ensure that it continues to carry out its programme of work as detailed in the relevant earlier resolutions, in consultation with the Committee on the Exercise of the Inalienable Rights of the Palestinian People and under its guidance, including, in particular, the organization of meetings in various regions with the participation of all sectors of the international community, the further development and expansion of the documents collection of the United Nations Information System on the Question of Palestine, the preparation and widest possible dissemination of publications and information materials on various aspects of the question of Palestine, and the provision of the annual training programme for staff of the Palestinian Authority;

4. *Also requests* the Secretary-General to ensure the continued cooperation of the Department of Public Information and other units of the Secretariat in enabling the Division to perform its tasks and in covering adequately the various aspects of the question of Palestine;

5. *Invites* all Governments and organizations to extend their cooperation to the Committee and the Division in the performance of their tasks;

6. *Notes with appreciation* the action taken by Member States to observe annually on 29 November the International Day of Solidarity with the Palestinian People, requests them to continue to give the widest possible publicity to the observance, and requests the Committee and the Division to continue to organize, as part of the observance of the Day of Solidarity, an annual exhibit on Palestinian rights in cooperation with the Permanent Observer Mission of Palestine to the United Nations.

RECORDED VOTE ON RESOLUTION 56/34:

In favour: Afghanistan, Algeria, Angola, Armenia, Azerbaijan, Bahrain, Bangladesh, Barbados, Belarus, Belize, Benin, Bolivia, Botswana, Brazil, Brunei Darussalam, Burkina Faso, Burundi, Cambodia, Cameroon, Cape Verde, Chad, Chile, China, Colombia, Comoros, Congo, Costa Rica, Cuba, Cyprus, Democratic People's Republic of Korea, Djibouti, Dominican Republic, Ecuador, Egypt, El Salvador, Equatorial Guinea, Eritrea, Ethiopia, Fiji, Ghana, Grenada, Guatemala, Guinea, Guyana, Haiti, Honduras, India, Indonesia, Iran, Jamaica, Jordan, Kenya, Kuwait, Lao People's Democratic Republic, Lebanon, Libyan Arab Jamahiriya, Madagascar, Malaysia, Maldives, Mali, Malta, Mauritania, Mauritius, Mexico, Mongolia, Morocco, Mozambique, Myanmar, Namibia, Nepal, Nicaragua, Nigeria, Oman, Pakistan, Panama, Papua New Guinea, Paraguay, Peru, Philippines, Qatar, Republic of Korea, Rwanda, Saint Lucia, Saudi Arabia, Senegal, Sierra Leone, Singapore, Solomon Islands, Sri Lanka, Sudan, Suriname, Syrian Arab Republic, Thailand, Togo, Trinidad and Tobago, Tunisia, Turkey, Uganda, Ukraine, United Arab Emirates, United Republic of Tanzania, Uruguay, Venezuela, Viet Nam, Yemen, Zambia, Zimbabwe.

Against: Israel, Marshall Islands, Micronesia, Tuvalu, United States.

Abstaining: Andorra, Argentina, Australia, Austria, Belgium, Bulgaria, Canada, Croatia, Czech Republic, Denmark, Estonia, Finland, France, Georgia, Germany, Greece, Hungary, Iceland, Ireland, Italy, Japan, Kazakhstan, Latvia, Liechtenstein, Lithuania, Luxembourg, Monaco, Nauru, Netherlands, New Zealand, Norway, Poland, Portugal, Republic of Moldova, Romania, Russian Federation, San Marino, Slovakia, Slovenia, South Africa, Spain, Sweden, The former Yugoslav Republic of Macedonia, Tonga, United Kingdom, Vanuatu, Yugoslavia.

Special information programme

As requested in General Assembly resolution 55/54 [YUN 2000, p. 446], the UN Department of Public Information in 2001 continued its special information programme on the question of Palestine, which included the organization of its annual training programme for Palestinian broadcasters and journalists and the organization of an international media encounter on the question of Palestine at the headquarters of the United Nations Educational, Scientific and Cultural Organization (UNESCO) in Paris. The quarterly *UN Chronicle* continued to cover the Palestine question and regularly reported on peacekeeping activities in the Middle East. The Radio News Unit covered aspects of the Palestine question and related issues in its news and current affairs programmes in various languages for regional and worldwide dissemination.

As in previous years, the United Nations information centres (UNICs), information services and other UN offices carried out numerous activities in connection with the International Day of Solidarity with the Palestinian People. Throughout the year, many UNICs dealt with the Palestinian question and organized special outreach activities related to the issue, including the launch by UNIC Harare (Zimbabwe) of the UNESCO Bethlehem 2000 roving photo exhibit in May.

GENERAL ASSEMBLY ACTION

On 3 December [meeting 72], the General Assembly adopted **resolution 56/35** [draft: A/56/L.21 & Add.1] by recorded vote (153-4-3) [agenda item 41].

Special information programme on the question of Palestine of the Department of Public Information of the Secretariat

The General Assembly,

Having considered the report of the Committee on the Exercise of the Inalienable Rights of the Palestinian People,

Taking note in particular of the information contained in chapter VI of that report,

Recalling its resolution 55/54 of 1 December 2000,

Convinced that the worldwide dissemination of accurate and comprehensive information and the role of civil society organizations and institutions remain of vital importance in heightening awareness of and support for the inalienable rights of the Palestinian people,

Aware of the Declaration of Principles on Interim Self-Government Arrangements signed by the Government of the State of Israel and the Palestine Liberation Organization in Washington, D.C., on 13 September 1993, and of the subsequent implementation agreements, in particular the Israeli-Palestinian Interim Agreement on the West Bank and the Gaza Strip signed in Washington, D.C., on 28 September 1995,

Recalling with satisfaction the important contribution made by the United Nations towards the promotion of the Bethlehem 2000 Project,

1. *Notes with appreciation* the action taken by the Department of Public Information of the Secretariat in compliance with resolution 55/54;

2. *Considers* that the special information programme on the question of Palestine of the Department is very useful in raising the awareness of the international community concerning the question of Palestine and the situation in the Middle East in general, including the achievements of the peace process, and that the programme is contributing effectively to an atmosphere conducive to dialogue and supportive of the peace process;

3. *Requests* the Department, in full cooperation and coordination with the Committee on the Exercise of the Inalienable Rights of the Palestinian People, to continue, with the necessary flexibility as may be required by developments affecting the question of Palestine, its special information programme for the biennium 2002-2003, in particular:

(a) To disseminate information on all the activities of the United Nations system relating to the question of Palestine, including reports on the work carried out by the relevant United Nations organizations;

(b) To continue to issue and update publications on the various aspects of the question of Palestine in all fields, including materials concerning the recent developments in that regard, in particular the prospects for peace;

(c) To expand its collection of audio-visual material on the question of Palestine and to continue the production and preservation of such material, and the updating of the exhibit in the Secretariat;

(d) To organize and promote fact-finding news missions for journalists to the area, including the territory under the jurisdiction of the Palestinian Authority and the Occupied Territory;

(e) To organize international, regional and national seminars or encounters for journalists, aiming in particular at sensitizing public opinion to the question of Palestine;

(f) To continue to provide assistance to the Palestinian people in the field of media development, in particular to strengthen the training programme for Palestinian broadcasters and journalists initiated in 1995.

RECORDED VOTE ON RESOLUTION 56/35:

In favour: Afghanistan, Algeria, Andorra, Angola, Argentina, Armenia, Australia, Austria, Azerbaijan, Bahrain, Bangladesh, Barbados, Belarus, Belgium, Belize, Benin, Bolivia, Botswana, Brazil, Brunei Darussalam, Bulgaria, Burkina Faso, Burundi, Cambodia, Cameroon, Canada, Cape Verde, Chad, Chile, China, Colombia, Comoros, Congo, Costa Rica, Croatia, Cuba, Cyprus, Czech Republic, Democratic People's Republic of Korea, Denmark, Djibouti, Dominican Republic, Ecuador, Egypt, El Salvador, Equatorial Guinea, Eritrea, Estonia, Ethiopia, Fiji, Finland, France, Georgia, Germany, Ghana, Greece, Grenada, Guatemala, Guinea, Guyana, Haiti, Honduras, Hungary, Iceland, India, Indonesia, Iran, Ireland, Italy, Jamaica, Japan, Jordan, Kazakhstan, Kenya, Kuwait, Lao People's Democratic Republic, Latvia, Lebanon, Libyan Arab Jamahiriya, Liechtenstein, Lithuania, Luxembourg, Madagascar, Malawi, Malaysia, Maldives, Mali, Malta, Mauritania, Mauritius, Mexico, Monaco, Mongolia, Morocco, Mozambique, Myanmar, Namibia, Nepal, Netherlands, New Zealand, Nicaragua, Nigeria, Norway, Oman, Pakistan, Panama, Papua New Guinea, Paraguay, Peru, Philippines, Poland, Portugal, Qatar, Republic of Korea, Republic of Moldova, Romania, Russian Federation, Rwanda, Saint Lucia, San Marino, Saudi Arabia, Senegal, Seychelles, Sierra Leone, Singapore, Slovakia, Slovenia, Solomon Islands, South Africa, Spain, Sri Lanka, Sudan, Suriname, Sweden, Syrian Arab Republic, Thailand, The former Yugoslav Republic of Macedonia, Togo, Trinidad and Tobago, Tunisia, Turkey, Uganda, Ukraine, United Arab Emirates, United Kingdom, United Republic of Tanzania, Uruguay, Venezuela, Viet Nam, Yemen, Yugoslavia, Zambia, Zimbabwe.

Against: Israel, Marshall Islands, Micronesia, United States.

Abstaining: Nauru, Tuvalu, Vanuatu.

Assistance to Palestinians

UN activities

Report of Secretary-General. In response to General Assembly resolution 55/173 [YUN 2000, p. 448], the Secretary-General submitted a July report [A/56/123-E/2001/97 & Corr.1], in which he described UN assistance to the Palestinian people between June 2000 and May 2001.

During the reporting period, the realities and priorities in the Occupied Palestinian Territory had shifted significantly due to the crisis that began on 28 September 2000, following the visit of then Israeli opposition leader Ariel Sharon to the Temple Mount/Al-Haram al-Sharif in East Jerusalem [YUN 2000, p. 416]. Apart from loss of life and injuries, the crisis was characterized by severe internal and external closures of both the West Bank and Gaza, which resulted in large-scale losses to the Palestinian economy, wiping out more than three years of prior growth. The impact of the closures was monitored by the United Nations Special Coordinator for the Middle East Process and Personal Representative of the Secretary-General to the PLO and the PA, who continued to ensure coordination between the relevant institutions of the PA and UN agencies, and coordinated UN assistance related to the peace process in Jordan, Lebanon and the Syrian Arab Republic.

The Secretary-General said that the ongoing crisis in Israeli-Palestinian relations had been the most difficult and challenging since the United Nations began intensive development assistance to the Occupied Palestinian Territory in 1993 [YUN 1993, p. 534] and was testing the ability of the UN system to respond appropriately and effectively to urgent priority humanitarian needs. A UN emergency coordination mechanism, the

Humanitarian Task Force for Emergency Needs, was established within days of the outbreak of the conflict. The Task Force, initially envisaged to focus on health needs, was extended to address other priority sectors, such as education, water and energy, as soon as the need became evident. In addition, ad hoc sector working groups were formed for job creation and food/social assistance, which were considered to be areas central to an effective emergency response. The UN Office for the Coordination of Humanitarian Affairs was supporting enhanced and strengthened capacities for planning and response to humanitarian needs through a variety of ongoing actions. Although emergency assistance received had contributed to meeting some of the immediate requirements, much work needed to be done to reduce and repair the extensive negative effects of the crisis on the Palestinian economy and society. What seemed initially to be a short-term emergency, warranting limited humanitarian aid, had developed into a protracted conflict necessitating more sustained UN action to address emergency needs and future development. It would be necessary for the UN system to strengthen and fine-tune existing coordination mechanisms, to eliminate potential duplication and to ensure responsiveness to needs identified by the beneficiaries. The various UN organizations and specialized agencies had to continue to reconfigure their work so as to strike the optimal balance between relief and development.

Seminar on assistance to Palestinian people. On 7 March [A/56/59-E/2001/9], the Chairman of the Committee on Palestinian Rights notified the Secretary-General that the four Palestinian officials invited to speak at the seminar on assistance to the Palestinian people (Vienna, 20-21 February) and a number of NGO participants from the Occupied Territory were unable to attend owing to the general closure and travel restrictions imposed by Israel.

By a 19 June letter [A/56/89-E/2001/89], the Committee Chairman transmitted to the Secretary-General the report of the February seminar, which was attended by representatives of Governments, Palestine, intergovernmental organizations, NGOs and UN system organizations and agencies, and by experts. The participants discussed the crisis of 2000-2001, particularly the impact of Israeli policies on the Palestinian economy; the role of the UN system in alleviating hardships; assistance by Arab and Islamic States and intergovernmental organizations to the Palestinian people; and efforts by the international community. In his concluding remarks, the Committee Chairman emphasized that the change of

leadership in Israel at the beginning of February 2001 had undercut the momentum for reaching a final and comprehensive agreement. Since September 2000, the Palestinian people had been reduced to fighting for their survival and for the satisfaction of their day-to-day needs rather than working for long-term development. The Committee called on the donor community to contribute the funds needed to remedy the serious budgetary crisis faced by the PA; Palestinian economic rehabilitation was a prerequisite for peace in the Middle East.

GENERAL ASSEMBLY ACTION

On 14 December [meeting 87], the General Assembly adopted **resolution 56/111** [draft: A/56/L.59 & Add.1] without vote [agenda item 20 (e)].

Assistance to the Palestinian people

The General Assembly,

Recalling its resolution 55/173 of 14 December 2000,

Recalling also previous resolutions on the question,

Welcoming the signing of the Declaration of Principles on Interim Self-Government Arrangements in Washington, D.C., on 13 September 1993, between the Government of the State of Israel and the Palestine Liberation Organization, the representative of the Palestinian people, as well as the signing of the subsequent implementation agreements, including the Israeli-Palestinian Interim Agreement on the West Bank and the Gaza Strip, in Washington, D.C., on 28 September 1995, and the signing of the Sharm el-Sheikh Memorandum on 4 September 1999,

Gravely concerned at the difficult economic and employment conditions facing the Palestinian people throughout the occupied territory,

Conscious of the urgent need for improvement in the economic and social infrastructure of the occupied territory and the living conditions of the Palestinian people,

Aware that development is difficult under occupation and best promoted in circumstances of peace and stability,

Noting the great economic and social challenges facing the Palestinian people and their leadership,

Conscious of the urgent necessity for international assistance to the Palestinian people, taking into account the Palestinian priorities,

Noting the convening of the United Nations seminar on assistance to the Palestinian people, held in Vienna on 20 and 21 February 2001, to review the state of the Palestinian economy,

Stressing the need for the full engagement of the United Nations in the process of building Palestinian institutions and in providing broad assistance to the Palestinian people, including assistance in the fields of elections, police training and public administration,

Noting the appointment by the Secretary-General of the United Nations Special Coordinator for the Middle East Peace Process and Personal Representative of the Secretary-General to the Palestine Liberation Organization and the Palestinian Authority,

Welcoming the results of the Conference to Support Middle East Peace, convened in Washington, D.C., on

1 October 1993, and the establishment of the Ad Hoc Liaison Committee and the work being done by the World Bank as its secretariat, as well as the establishment of the Consultative Group,

Welcoming also the work of the Joint Liaison Committee, which provides a forum in which economic policy and practical matters related to donor assistance are discussed with the Palestinian Authority,

Welcoming further the results of the Ministerial Conference to Support Middle East Peace and Development, held in Washington, D.C., on 30 November 1998, and expressing appreciation for the pledges of the international donor community,

Welcoming the meeting of the Consultative Group in Frankfurt, Germany, on 4 and 5 February 1999, in particular the pledges of the international donor community and the presentation of the Palestinian Development Plan for the years 1999-2003,

Welcoming also the meeting of the Ad Hoc Liaison Committee held in Lisbon on 7 and 8 June 2000,

Having considered the report of the Secretary-General,

Expressing grave concern at the continuation of the recent tragic and violent events that have led to many deaths and injuries,

1. *Takes note* of the report of the Secretary-General;

2. *Expresses its appreciation* to the Secretary-General for his rapid response and efforts regarding assistance to the Palestinian people;

3. *Expresses its appreciation* to the Member States, United Nations bodies and intergovernmental, regional and non-governmental organizations that have provided and continue to provide assistance to the Palestinian people;

4. *Stresses* the importance of the work of the United Nations Special Coordinator for the Middle East Peace Process and Personal Representative of the Secretary-General to the Palestine Liberation Organization and the Palestinian Authority and of the steps taken under the auspices of the Secretary-General to ensure the achievement of a coordinated mechanism for United Nations activities throughout the occupied territories;

5. *Urges* Member States, international financial institutions of the United Nations system, intergovernmental and non-governmental organizations and regional and interregional organizations to extend, as rapidly and as generously as possible, economic and social assistance to the Palestinian people, in close cooperation with the Palestine Liberation Organization and through official Palestinian institutions;

6. *Calls upon* relevant organizations and agencies of the United Nations system to intensify their assistance in response to the urgent needs of the Palestinian people in accordance with Palestinian priorities set forth by the Palestinian Authority, with emphasis on national execution and capacity-building;

7. *Urges* Member States to open their markets to exports of Palestinian products on the most favourable terms, consistent with appropriate trading rules, and to implement fully existing trade and cooperation agreements;

8. *Calls upon* the international donor community to expedite the delivery of pledged assistance to the Palestinian people to meet their urgent needs;

9. *Stresses* in this context the importance of ensuring the free passage of aid to the Palestinian people and the free movement of persons and goods;

10. *Urges* the international donor community, United Nations agencies and organizations and non-governmental organizations to extend as rapidly as possible emergency economic and humanitarian assistance to the Palestinian people to counter the impact of the current crisis;

11. *Stresses* the need to implement the Paris Protocol on Economic Relations of 29 April 1994, fifth annex to the Israeli-Palestinian Interim Agreement on the West Bank and the Gaza Strip, in particular with regard to the full and prompt clearance of Palestinian indirect tax revenues;

12. *Suggests* the convening in 2002 of a United Nations–sponsored seminar on assistance to the Palestinian people;

13. *Requests* the Secretary-General to submit a report to the General Assembly at its fifty-seventh session, through the Economic and Social Council, on the implementation of the present resolution, containing:

(*a*) An assessment of the assistance actually received by the Palestinian people;

(*b*) An assessment of the needs still unmet and specific proposals for responding effectively to them;

14. *Decides* to include in the provisional agenda of its fifty-seventh session the sub-item entitled "Assistance to the Palestinian people".

UNRWA

In 2001, the United Nations Relief and Works Agency for Palestine Refugees in the Near East continued to provide vital education, health and relief and social services to a growing refugee population, despite a severe budget deficit and cash-flow crisis.

On 30 June, 3.87 million refugees were registered with UNRWA, an increase of 3.5 per cent over the 2000 figure of 3.7 million. The largest refugee population was registered in Jordan (42.3 per cent of the Agency-wide total), followed by the Gaza Strip (22 per cent), the West Bank (15.7 per cent), the Syrian Arab Republic (10.1 per cent) and Lebanon (9.9 per cent). Of the registered population, 36.51 per cent were aged 15 or under and about one third lived in 59 refugee camps, while the remainder resided in towns and villages.

In his annual report on the work of the Agency from 1 July 2000 to 30 June 2001 [A/56/13], the UNRWA Commissioner-General said that since the outbreak of strife in the Occupied Palestinian Territory in September 2000 [YUN 2000, p. 416], the Agency had had to develop an emergency programme of humanitarian assistance for the refugees affected by the severe economic decline in Gaza and the West Bank, brought about by closures and other restrictive measures applied by the Israeli authorities. Since October 2000, entry to or exit from Gaza and the West Bank had been severely restricted for Palestinians most of the time. The economic impact of the closures had rendered unemployed large numbers of Palestinians who worked in Israel. To meet immediate needs arising from the severe deterioration in economic conditions, the Agency launched emergency appeals (see p. 439).

Although the international community's response to the emergency appeals showed a clear appreciation of the need for continued assistance for Palestine refugees, the level of support for UNRWA's regular budget did not convey a message of adequate recognition of the serious threat that the funding shortfalls posed to the Agency's services. Major donors had been increasing their annual contributions to the regular budget at a steady rate. However, that growth was offset by the increased number of refugees and by inflation.

Since the crisis erupted in September 2000, UNRWA had been forced to shift its focus from development to emergency humanitarian assistance. In addition, the violence and general closures imposed by Israel created a number of obstacles that impaired the Agency's ability to run its humanitarian operations effectively, staff were frequently delayed or prevented from arriving at their workplaces because of delays at Israeli checkpoints, and the movement of UNRWA trucks between the West Bank and Gaza carrying essential humanitarian cargoes had been suspended because of search procedures imposed by Israeli authorities. UNRWA had introduced an operational support officers programme that was designed to assist in alleviating the adverse effects the restrictions were having on the provision of humanitarian services.

Despite financial constraints, UNRWA had persisted with its long-term reform programme. The current phase focused on improving the efficiency and effectiveness of the management of the Agency's resources; the development of an open management culture; the strengthening of its strategic planning capabilities; expansion and improvement in the Agency's relations with donor countries and UN agencies and programmes; and increased responsiveness, effectiveness and efficiency in the Agency's operations in providing services for the refugees against the background of changing socio-political conditions.

In recognition of the increasing importance of project funding and to establish a more targeted fund-raising approach, UNRWA established Agency-wide project priorities that formed the basis for the projects section of the 2000-2001 biennium budget. The projects budget provided a complete picture of the Agency's financial re-

quirements and linked the project-funded activities directly to programme activities under the regular budget. The 2000-2001 projects budget comprised mainly non-recurrent infrastructure costs.

Advisory Commission. By a 25 September letter to the Commissioner-General, which he included in his report [A/56/13], the Advisory Commission of UNRWA noted with concern the deteriorating political, social and economic situation in the region, which affected the Palestinian refugees in particular, and expressed concern at the difficulties faced by UNRWA resulting from a whole range of restrictions imposed by Israel. It also noted that pledges for the 2000-2001 budget amounted to only $280 million against the $310.4 million approved by the General Assembly. There was therefore a need to raise donor contributions to enable the Agency to rebuild its depleted reserves to meet operational needs. The Commission expressed appreciation for the implementation of management reforms and for the manner in which UNRWA's staff had continued to work despite the often dangerous conditions in which they had to carry out their humanitarian tasks.

Peace Implementation Programme

In its eighth year of operation, UNRWA's Peace Implementation Programme (PIP) remained the foremost channel for extrabudgetary funding of activities carried out within the framework of the Agency's education, health, relief and social services and income-generation programmes. Since its inception in October 1993 [YUN 1993, p. 569], PIP had improved the refugees' overall living conditions, created employment opportunities and developed infrastructure. Following the adoption of the 2000-2001 programme-based biennium budget, which divided the Agency's budget into regular budget and projects budget sections, all new non-core contributions were credited to the projects budget.

Between mid-2000 and mid-2001, UNRWA, with PIP funding, completed the construction of five schools, 20 additional classrooms, one school laboratory, one library, one home economics unit, two health centres, a public health laboratory, a community rehabilitation centre and a women's programme centre. PIP made it possible to complete the rehabilitation of 37 shelters for special hardship case families Agency-wide. In environmental health, a feasibility study was completed for improving water supply in camps and construction of a sewage system in the Syrian Arab Republic. Another major project for construction of sewer and water networks in camps in Lebanon was ongoing, while infrastructure improvements in the Shu'fat camp in the West Bank were completed. Other projects completed during the reporting period included: purchase of educational materials, library reference books and furniture; provision of school desks; integration of visually impaired children; care for destitute aged; provision for hospitalization services; promotion of tolerance, conflict resolution and basic human rights in UNRWA schools; and development of human resources for health staff. PIP also helped to sustain regular Agency programmes through the continued funding of university scholarships for refugee students and the procurement of medical supplies. Further funding went to upgrading facilities and courses at several UNRWA vocational training centres.

Cash expenditures under PIP amounted to $7.6 million during the reporting period. No new funding was received specifically for PIP and the small amount remaining was merged into the Agency's projects budget. As at 30 June 2001, the outstanding amount from donors related to ongoing PIP projects was $13.8 million.

Lebanon appeal

Most of the 380,000 registered Palestine refugees in Lebanon continued to face socio-economic hardship and depended almost entirely on UNRWA for basic services. By mid-2001, the Agency had received $9.2 million of the $11 million sought in additional contributions under the special emergency appeal, launched in 1997 to support essential health, education, relief and social services activities for Palestine refugees in Lebanon. Completed projects included construction, equipping and furnishing of a health centre, the construction and repair of shelters and the purchase of medical supplies.

Emergency appeals

The UNRWA Commissioner-General stated that the strife that broke out in September 2000 in the Occupied Palestinian Territory undermined years of economic progress and infrastructure development, with profound effects on refugees in terms of lives, livelihoods and shelter lost. Of the hundreds of Palestinians killed since the outbreak of the intifada, more than half were UNRWA-registered refugees, with many more injured. Over 1,700 shelters in refugee camps were damaged and many destroyed. Closures imposed by Israel limited mobility, economic activity and access to health and educational services.

Responding to that humanitarian crisis, UNRWA launched a series of emergency appeals that started with a flash emergency appeal in October 2000 and the first consolidated emergency appeal in November 2000, which covered the period from December 2000 to February 2001 [YUN 2000, p. 450]. The second emergency appeal, launched on 22 February 2001, enabled UNRWA to provide short-term emergency employment opportunities for refugees, in addition to food and cash assistance, shelter repairs and health services for the period from March to May 2001. The third appeal, launched on 22 June, provided for continued emergency relief from June to December 2001. UNRWA received $24 million in funding in response to the second emergency appeal, and approximately $63 million in response to the third.

Major service areas

UNRWA continued to provide educational, health, and relief and social services to, and carried out microfinance and microenterprise activities for, Palestine refugees throughout the occupied territories.

During the 2000/01 school year, the 634 UNRWA schools across the region accommodated 474,742 pupils, most of whom were in elementary and preparatory cycles, apart from 2,474 pupils at the five Agency secondary schools in Lebanon. Total enrolment increased by 1.67 per cent, or 7,787 pupils, over the 1999/2000 school year. The Jordan and Gaza fields each accounted for approximately one third of total Agency pupil enrolment, while the other three fields (Lebanon, Syrian Arab Republic, West Bank) together accounted for the remaining third. UNRWA's school system continued to maintain full gender equality, with 50 per cent of pupils being female. The education programme, which was run in cooperation with UNESCO, remained the largest single area of UNRWA activity, with 16,246 education personnel representing 72 per cent of all Agency staff. The policy of operating schools on a double-shift basis (housing two schools in a single building) continued due to financial constraints and steadily rising student enrolment. Also due to financial constraints, the Agency remained unable to extend the basic education cycle in the West Bank and Gaza from 9 to 10 years; however, tenth-grade students were accommodated in PA schools.

A new Palestinian curriculum was introduced in 2000/01, for first and sixth grades, to replace the Jordanian curriculum in the West Bank and the Egyptian curriculum in Gaza. In the Syrian Arab Republic, a new study plan and new curricula and textbooks for the elementary and preparatory cycles were gradually introduced. The Agency continued to provide remedial and special education services for pupils with learning difficulties. In the absence of sustained project funding for special education, UNRWA explored ways to provide assistance to all children with learning difficulties at no additional cost by utilizing the Agency's available resources and expertise. Total enrolment in the eight UNRWA vocational and technical training centres was 4,700 in the 2000/01 school year, a marginal decrease from the previous year. Overall, women accounted for 65.2 per cent of all trainees enrolled in technical/semi-professional courses. The Agency continued with project funding to support some university students with scholarship awards until they graduated and offered placement and career guidance services to Palestine refugee graduates of UNRWA training centres and other educational institutions.

UNRWA's health-care programme remained focused on comprehensive primary health care, including a full range of maternal and child health and family planning services; school health services, health education and promotion activities; outpatient medical care services; prevention and control of communicable diseases and noncommunicable diseases; and specialist care, with emphasis on gynaecology and obstetrics, paediatrics and cardiology. Those services were complemented by dental and basic support services, such as radiology and laboratory facilities. Services were delivered through a network of 122 primary health-care facilities located in and outside refugee camps. UNRWA participated in two rounds of national immunization campaigns for poliomyelitis eradication in the context of a World Health Organization (WHO) regional strategy. The Agency continued to emphasize the development of human resources for health through basic, in-service and postgraduate training as a key element in improving programme efficiency and the quality of care. Approximately 1.2 million Palestine refugees in 59 official camps in the five fields of operation, representing 32 per cent of the total registered population, benefited from environmental health services provided by UNRWA in cooperation with local municipalities, including sewage disposal, the provision of safe drinking water, the collection and disposal of refuse and the control of insect and rodent infestation. The health budget for the 2000-2001 biennium was established at $108 million under the regular programme, representing 18.6 per cent of the Agency's total operating budget.

The relief and social services programme supported those Palestine refugees who were unable to meet the basic needs for food, shelter and other essentials. It also maintained records on Palestine refugees to determine eligibility for UNRWA services. Further strides were made to improve the performance of the field registration system, pending its redesign. The Unified Regis-

tration System Unit completed installation of a new version of the field registration system in all field and area offices and conducted training for all users, and a new system module to consolidate field social study data on special hardship case (SHC) families was installed. The principal means of assistance to SHC families were food support, shelter rehabilitation, selective cash assistance, hospitalization subsidies and preferential access to UNRWA training centres. The number of refugees in households that met the eligibility criteria—no male adult medically fit to earn an income and no other identifiable means of financial support above a defined threshold—increased by 4.7 per cent, from 207,150 on 30 June 2000 to 217,388 on 30 June 2001. The percentage of refugees enrolled in the programme was highest in Lebanon and lowest in Jordan. The modest allocation of $500,000 for selective cash assistance, which was partially reinstated in 2000 following the budget freeze in August 1997, was maintained in 2001. Since then, small grants, at an average of $138.50, had been provided on a case-by-case basis to SHC families facing emergency situations. UNRWA also rehabilitated a total of 358 shelters of SHC families, as compared to 217 in the previous reporting period. The poverty alleviation programme continued to address poverty at the micro level and to promote the income-generating capacity of poor refugees through skills training, apprenticeships, awareness-raising sessions on the cause of poverty, "start your own business" training and/or provision of credit. While the latter often benefited clients from SHC families, it increasingly included loans, ranging in size from $500 to $10,000, to both individuals and groups. UNRWA-sponsored centres within the refugee camps or community-based organizations (CBOs) increased from 131 at mid-2000 to 134 at mid-2001, with a total of 71 women's programme centres, 27 youth activity centres and 36 community rehabilitation centres for the physically and mentally challenged. CBOs offered social development activities, including skills-training opportunities for women and disabled people, technical assistance for refugee-owned and/or -operated income-generation enterprises, and public awareness drives on social issues, such as early marriage, drug addiction, smoking and domestic violence. The relief and social services programme continued to promote participation, self-reliance, organizational network building, revenue generation and project development skills. In accordance with previously established goals, the Agency pursued its commitment to strengthening the organizational capacities of CBOs to enable them to manage and sustain their progress autonomously. The regular budget for the relief and social services programme for the 2001-2002 biennium was $62.4 million, representing 10 per cent of UNRWA's total regular budget.

During the reporting period, UNRWA changed the name of its income-generation programme in the West Bank and Gaza Strip to the microfinance and microenterprise programme in order to draw a clear distinction between the commercial, self-sustaining and market-oriented microfinance services being delivered through it and the various income-generating activities being undertaken through the relief and social services programme. The microfinance and microenterprise programme continued to support the development of the small-scale business sector within the refugee community by providing working capital and capital investment loans. Those products strengthened business activity, created jobs, generated income for participants, helped alleviate poverty and encouraged women's economic participation. From mid-2000 to mid-2001, the programme provided 10,083 loans worth $9.92 million for Palestinian-owned enterprises, of which women entrepreneurs received 37.43 per cent. In the Gaza Strip, UNRWA's microfinance programme activities had made it the largest financial intermediary to small business and the microenterprise sector. In the West Bank, the Agency's microenterprise credit subprogramme was the fastest growing of its credit subprogrammes. As part of its institutional reform process, UNRWA established a microfinance and microenterprise programme advisory board to provide the Commissioner-General with policy guidance and recommendations. The credit operations of the microfinance and microenterprise programme were severely hampered by the economic consequences of the closures and other measures restricting the movement of labour and goods imposed by the Israeli authorities. The continuation of the conflict placed the programme's self-sufficiency at risk amidst the deteriorating business environment and could compel the programme to use up its capital base to survive the crisis.

GENERAL ASSEMBLY ACTION

On 10 December [meeting 82], the General Assembly, on the recommendation of the Fourth Committee [A/56/549], adopted **resolution 56/52** by recorded vote (151-2-2) [agenda item 87].

Assistance to Palestine refugees

The General Assembly,

Recalling its resolution 55/123 of 8 December 2000 and all its previous resolutions on the question, including resolution 194(III) of 11 December 1948,

Taking note of the report of the Commissioner-General of the United Nations Relief and Works Agency for Palestine Refugees in the Near East covering the period from 1 July 2000 to 30 June 2001,

Stressing the importance of the Middle East peace process,

Welcoming the signature in Washington, D.C., on 13 September 1993 by the Government of the State of Israel and the Palestine Liberation Organization, the representative of the people of Palestine, of the Declaration of Principles on Interim Self-Government Arrangements and the subsequent implementation agreements,

Aware that the Multilateral Working Group on Refugees of the Middle East peace process has an important role to play in the peace process,

1. *Notes with regret* that repatriation or compensation of the refugees, as provided for in paragraph 11 of its resolution 194(III), has not yet been effected and that, therefore, the situation of the refugees continues to be a matter of concern;

2. *Also notes with regret* that the United Nations Conciliation Commission for Palestine has been unable to find a means of achieving progress in the implementation of paragraph 11 of General Assembly resolution 194(III), and requests the Commission to exert continued efforts towards the implementation of that paragraph and to report to the Assembly as appropriate, but no later than 1 September 2002;

3. *Expresses its thanks* to the Commissioner-General and to all the staff of the United Nations Relief and Works Agency for Palestine Refugees in the Near East, recognizing that the Agency is doing all it can within the limits of available resources, and also expresses its thanks to the specialized agencies and to private organizations for their valuable work in assisting refugees;

4. *Notes* the significant success of the Peace Implementation Programme of the Agency since the signing of the Declaration of Principles on Interim Self-Government Arrangements, and stresses the importance that contributions to this Programme not be at the expense of the General Fund;

5. *Welcomes* the increased cooperation between the Agency and international and regional organizations, States and relevant agencies and non-governmental organizations, which is essential to enhancing the contributions of the Agency towards improved conditions for the refugees and thereby the social stability of the occupied territory;

6. *Urges* all Member States to extend and expedite aid and assistance with a view to the economic and social development of the Palestinian people and the occupied territory;

7. *Reiterates its deep concern* regarding the persisting critical financial situation of the Agency, as outlined in the report of the Commissioner-General;

8. *Commends* the efforts of the Commissioner-General to move towards budgetary transparency and internal efficiency, and welcomes in this respect the unified budget for the biennium 2002-2003;

9. *Welcomes* the consultative process between the Agency, host Governments, the Palestinian Authority and donors on management reforms;

10. *Notes with profound concern* that the continuing shortfall in the finances of the Agency, in particular at this time of acute crisis, has a significant negative influence on the living conditions of the Palestine refugees

most in need and that it therefore has possible consequences for the peace process;

11. *Expresses deep concern* about the continuing problem of restrictions on the freedom of movement of Agency staff, vehicles and goods in the occupied territory, which has an adverse impact on the operational effectiveness of the Agency's programmes;

12. *Calls upon* all donors, as a matter of urgency, to make the most generous efforts possible to meet the anticipated needs of the Agency, including the remaining costs of moving the headquarters to Gaza, encourages contributing Governments to contribute regularly and to consider increasing their regular contributions, and urges non-contributing Governments to contribute;

13. *Decides* to extend the mandate of the Agency until 30 June 2005, without prejudice to the provisions of paragraph 11 of its resolution 194(III).

RECORDED VOTE ON RESOLUTION 56/52:

In favour: Algeria, Andorra, Angola, Antigua and Barbuda, Argentina, Armenia, Australia, Austria, Azerbaijan, Bahamas, Bahrain, Bangladesh, Barbados, Belarus, Belgium, Belize, Benin, Bhutan, Bolivia, Brazil, Brunei Darussalam, Bulgaria, Burkina Faso, Burundi, Cambodia, Cameroon, Canada, Cape Verde, Chile, China, Colombia, Comoros, Congo, Costa Rica, Côte d'Ivoire, Croatia, Cuba, Cyprus, Czech Republic, Democratic People's Republic of Korea, Denmark, Djibouti, Dominican Republic, Ecuador, Egypt, El Salvador, Equatorial Guinea, Eritrea, Estonia, Ethiopia, Fiji, Finland, France, Gabon, Georgia, Germany, Ghana, Greece, Grenada, Guatemala, Guinea, Guyana, Haiti, Honduras, Hungary, Iceland, India, Indonesia, Iran, Ireland, Italy, Jamaica, Japan, Jordan, Kazakhstan, Kenya, Kuwait, Lao People's Democratic Republic, Latvia, Lebanon, Libyan Arab Jamahiriya, Liechtenstein, Lithuania, Luxembourg, Madagascar, Malaysia, Maldives, Mali, Malta, Mauritania, Mexico, Monaco, Mongolia, Morocco, Mozambique, Myanmar, Namibia, Nepal, Netherlands, New Zealand, Nicaragua, Nigeria, Norway, Oman, Pakistan, Panama, Papua New Guinea, Paraguay, Peru, Philippines, Poland, Portugal, Qatar, Republic of Korea, Republic of Moldova, Romania, Russian Federation, Saint Lucia, San Marino, Saudi Arabia, Senegal, Seychelles, Sierra Leone, Singapore, Slovakia, Slovenia, Solomon Islands, South Africa, Spain, Sri Lanka, Sudan, Swaziland, Sweden, Syrian Arab Republic, Thailand, The former Yugoslav Republic of Macedonia, Togo, Tonga, Trinidad and Tobago, Tunisia, Turkey, Ukraine, United Arab Emirates, United Kingdom, United Republic of Tanzania, Uruguay, Venezuela, Viet Nam, Yemen, Yugoslavia, Zambia.

Against: Israel, Marshall Islands.

Abstaining: Micronesia, United States.

The Assembly, on the same date [meeting 82] and also on the Fourth Committee's recommendation [A/56/549], adopted **resolution 56/56** by recorded vote (151-3-1) [agenda item 87].

Operations of the United Nations Relief and Works Agency for Palestine Refugees in the Near East

The General Assembly,

Recalling its resolutions 194(III) of 11 December 1948, 212(III) of 19 November 1948, 302(IV) of 8 December 1949 and all subsequent related resolutions,

Recalling also the relevant Security Council resolutions,

Having considered the report of the Commissioner-General of the United Nations Relief and Works Agency for Palestine Refugees in the Near East covering the period from 1 July 2000 to 30 June 2001,

Taking note of the letter dated 25 September 2001 from the Chairman of the Advisory Commission of the United Nations Relief and Works Agency for Palestine Refugees in the Near East addressed to the Commissioner-General, contained in the report of the Commissioner-General,

Having considered the reports of the Secretary-General submitted in pursuance of its resolutions

48/40 E, 48/40 H and 48/40 J of 10 December 1993 and 49/35 C of 9 December 1994,

Recalling Articles 100, 104 and 105 of the Charter of the United Nations and the Convention on the Privileges and Immunities of the United Nations,

Affirming the applicability of the Geneva Convention relative to the Protection of Civilian Persons in Time of War, of 12 August 1949, to the Palestinian territory occupied since 1967, including Jerusalem,

Aware of the fact that Palestine refugees have, for over five decades, lost their homes, lands and means of livelihood,

Also aware of the continuing needs of Palestine refugees throughout the Occupied Palestinian Territory and in the other fields of operation, namely, in Lebanon, Jordan and the Syrian Arab Republic,

Further aware of the valuable work done by the refugee affairs officers of the Agency in providing protection to the Palestinian people, in particular Palestine refugees,

Gravely concerned about the increased suffering of the Palestine refugees, including loss of life and injury, during the recent tragic events in the Occupied Palestinian Territory, including Jerusalem,

Gravely concerned also about the policies of closure and severe restrictions on the movement of persons and goods throughout the Occupied Palestinian Territory, including Jerusalem, which have had a grave impact on the socio-economic situation of the Palestine refugees,

Deeply concerned about the negative impact of these closures and restrictions on the staff and services of the Agency,

Deeply concerned also about the continuing critical financial situation of the Agency and its effect on the continuity of provision of necessary Agency services to the Palestine refugees, including the emergency-related programmes,

Aware of the work of the Peace Implementation Programme of the Agency,

Recalling the signing in Washington, D.C., on 13 September 1993 of the Declaration of Principles on Interim Self-Government Arrangements by the Government of the State of Israel and the Palestine Liberation Organization and the subsequent implementation agreements,

Taking note of the agreement reached on 24 June 1994, embodied in an exchange of letters between the Agency and the Palestine Liberation Organization,

Aware of the establishment of a working relationship between the Advisory Commission of the Agency and the Palestine Liberation Organization in accordance with General Assembly decision 48/417 of 10 December 1993,

1. *Expresses its appreciation* to the Commissioner-General of the United Nations Relief and Works Agency for Palestine Refugees in the Near East, as well as to all the staff of the Agency, for their tireless efforts and valuable work, including and particularly during the difficult situation of the past year;

2. *Also expresses its appreciation* to the Advisory Commission of the Agency, and requests it to continue its efforts and to keep the General Assembly informed of its activities, including the full implementation of decision 48/417;

3. *Takes note* of the functioning of the headquarters of the Agency in Gaza City on the basis of the Headquarters Agreement between the Agency and the Palestinian Authority;

4. *Acknowledges* the support of the host Government and the Palestine Liberation Organization for the Agency in the discharge of its duties;

5. *Calls upon* Israel, the occupying Power, to accept the de jure applicability of the Geneva Convention relative to the Protection of Civilian Persons in Time of War, of 12 August 1949, and to abide scrupulously by its provisions;

6. *Also calls upon* Israel to abide by Articles 100, 104 and 105 of the Charter of the United Nations and the Convention on the Privileges and Immunities of the United Nations with regard to the safety of the personnel of the Agency, the protection of its institutions and the safeguarding of the security of the facilities of the Agency in the Occupied Palestinian Territory, including Jerusalem;

7. *Calls once again upon* the Government of Israel to compensate the Agency for damage to its property and facilities resulting from actions by the Israeli side;

8. *Calls upon* Israel particularly to cease obstructing the movement of the personnel, vehicles and supplies of the Agency, which has a detrimental impact on the Agency's operations;

9. *Also calls upon* Israel to cease its policies of closure and of placing restrictions on the movement of persons and goods, which have had a grave impact on the socio-economic situation of the Palestinian population, in particular the Palestine refugees;

10. *Requests* the Commissioner-General to proceed with the issuance of identification cards for Palestine refugees and their descendants in the Occupied Palestinian Territory;

11. *Notes* that the context created by the signing of the Declaration of Principles on Interim Self-Government Arrangements by the Government of the State of Israel and the Palestine Liberation Organization and subsequent implementation agreements has had major consequences for the activities of the Agency, which is henceforth called upon, in close cooperation with the United Nations Special Coordinator for the Middle East Peace Process and Personal Representative of the Secretary-General to the Palestine Liberation Organization and the Palestinian Authority, the specialized agencies and the World Bank, to continue to contribute towards the development of economic and social stability in the occupied territory;

12. *Notes also* that the functioning of the Agency remains essential in all fields of operation;

13. *Notes further* the significant success of the Peace Implementation Programme of the Agency, as well as the microfinance and enterprise programmes;

14. *Expresses concern* about those remaining austerity measures due to the financial crisis, which have affected the quality and level of some of the services of the Agency;

15. *Reiterates its request* to the Commissioner-General to proceed with the modernization of the archives of the Agency;

16. *Urges* all States, specialized agencies and non-governmental organizations to continue and to increase their contributions to the Agency so as to ease the current financial constraints and to support the

Agency in maintaining the provision of the most basic and effective assistance to the Palestine refugees.

RECORDED VOTE ON RESOLUTION 56/56:

In favour: Algeria, Andorra, Angola, Antigua and Barbuda, Argentina, Armenia, Australia, Austria, Azerbaijan, Bahamas, Bahrain, Bangladesh, Barbados, Belarus, Belgium, Belize, Benin, Bhutan, Bolivia, Brazil, Brunei Darussalam, Bulgaria, Burkina Faso, Burundi, Cambodia, Cameroon, Canada, Cape Verde, Chile, China, Colombia, Comoros, Congo, Costa Rica, Côte d'Ivoire, Croatia, Cuba, Cyprus, Czech Republic, Democratic People's Republic of Korea, Denmark, Djibouti, Dominican Republic, Ecuador, Egypt, El Salvador, Equatorial Guinea, Eritrea, Estonia, Ethiopia, Fiji, Finland, France, Gabon, Georgia, Germany, Ghana, Greece, Grenada, Guatemala, Guinea, Guyana, Haiti, Honduras, Hungary, Iceland, India, Indonesia, Iran, Ireland, Italy, Jamaica, Japan, Jordan, Kazakhstan, Kenya, Kuwait, Lao People's Democratic Republic, Latvia, Lebanon, Libyan Arab Jamahiriya, Liechtenstein, Lithuania, Luxembourg, Madagascar, Malaysia, Maldives, Mali, Malta, Mauritania, Mexico, Monaco, Mongolia, Morocco, Mozambique, Myanmar, Namibia, Nepal, Netherlands, New Zealand, Nicaragua, Nigeria, Norway, Oman, Pakistan, Panama, Papua New Guinea, Paraguay, Peru, Philippines, Poland, Portugal, Qatar, Republic of Korea, Republic of Moldova, Romania, Russian Federation, Saint Lucia, San Marino, Saudi Arabia, Senegal, Seychelles, Sierra Leone, Singapore, Slovakia, Slovenia, Solomon Islands, South Africa, Spain, Sri Lanka, Sudan, Swaziland, Sweden, Syrian Arab Republic, Thailand, The former Yugoslav Republic of Macedonia, Togo, Tonga, Trinidad and Tobago, Tunisia, Turkey, Ukraine, United Arab Emirates, United Kingdom, United Republic of Tanzania, Uruguay, Venezuela, Viet Nam, Yemen, Yugoslavia, Zambia.

Against: Israel, Marshall Islands, United States.

Abstaining: Micronesia.

UNRWA financing

In 2001, UNRWA's financial situation continued to be difficult and bleak, characterized by large funding shortfalls in the regular budget, depleted working capital and cash reserves, and cumulative deficits in certain project accounts. The structural deficit emanating from the inability of income to keep pace with needs arising from natural growth in the refugee population and inflation remained a problem. Despite a combination of ad hoc additional donor contributions and prudent financial management, a budget deficit was expected by the end of 2001 unless additional contributions were received.

At mid-2001, the Agency's cash position remained critical, forcing it to live from hand to mouth in terms of balancing incoming funds and outgoing payments. Expected cash expenditure in the regular programme was $311 million, as against expected cash income of $245 million. Working capital, defined as the difference between assets and liabilities in the regular budget for the calendar year, was for all practical purposes non-existent, making UNRWA vulnerable to any change in expected income or expenditure. Estimates indicated that the Agency's regular cash budget for 2001 would face a deficit of $66 million by year's end.

The Commissioner-General said that the Agency's 2002-2003 budget [A/56/13/Add.1] represented another step forward in the Agency's efforts to improve budgetary transparency and usefulness of the budget as a planning, managerial and fund-raising tool. The budget exercise was oriented towards preparing a programme-based budget more structured around UNRWA's service-providing role. The Agency's budget requirements for the 2002-2003 biennium were estimated at $791.7 million.

Working Group. The Working Group on the Financing of UNRWA held two meetings in 2001, on 14 September and 3 October. In its report to the General Assembly [A/56/430], the Working Group said that the critical financial situation of 2000 had continued in 2001. In 2000, UNRWA had an income of $270.9 million, of which $256 million was for the cash portion of the regular budget and $14.9 million for the in-kind portion. Those funds were received against a regular budget of $300.9 million, of which $280.4 million represented the cash portion and $20.5 million the in-kind portion, leaving a deficit of $24.4 million. In cash terms, UNRWA ended the year 2000 with nothing for its General Fund; consequently, it was forced to reduce expenditure to match income and could not allocate any funds towards building up the working capital or salary reserve. By the end of June 2001, UNRWA faced the prospect of a deficit in its regular cash budget of $66 million by the end of the year. However, additional contributions from the Agency's major donors reduced that deficit to $31 million by the end of September. Income for 2001 was expected to be $280 million, against a cash budget of $311 million.

The Working Group noted that UNRWA had made significant progress towards eliminating the structural deficit problem that had plagued the Agency in previous years, in particular through reductions in international staffing and other reforms. However, it expressed concern that eight years of austerity measures had eroded the level and quality of the services provided by UNRWA for some 4 million Palestine refugees.

The Working Group said that UNRWA services had to be viewed as the minimum required to enable the refugees to lead decent lives. Any further reduction in those services not only would deprive the refugees of the minimum level of support to which they were entitled, but could also have a destabilizing effect on the entire region. The Group expressed the hope that the international support for UNRWA embodied in the resolutions adopted each year by the General Assembly, in which the Assembly recognized the importance of UNRWA's work and requested that Governments contribute to it, would be translated into measures to ensure the survival of the Agency on a secure financial basis.

GENERAL ASSEMBLY ACTION

On 10 December [meeting 82], the General Assembly, on the recommendation of the Fourth Committee [A/56/549], adopted **resolution 56/53** without vote [agenda item 87].

Working Group on the Financing of the United Nations Relief and Works Agency for Palestine Refugees in the Near East

The General Assembly,

Recalling its resolutions 2656(XXV) of 7 December 1970, 2728(XXV) of 15 December 1970, 2971(XXVI) of 6 December 1971, 55/124 of 8 December 2000 and the previous resolutions on this question,

Recalling also its decision 36/462 of 16 March 1982, by which it took note of the special report of the Working Group on the Financing of the United Nations Relief and Works Agency for Palestine Refugees in the Near East,

Having considered the report of the Working Group,

Taking into account the report of the Commissioner-General of the United Nations Relief and Works Agency for Palestine Refugees in the Near East covering the period from 1 July 2000 to 30 June 2001,

Deeply concerned about the continuing financial situation of the Agency, which has affected and affects the continuation of the provision of necessary Agency services to Palestine refugees, including the emergency-related and humanitarian programmes,

Emphasizing the continuing need for extraordinary efforts in order to maintain, at least at the current level, the activities of the Agency, as well as to enable the Agency to carry out essential construction,

1. *Commends* the Working Group on the Financing of the United Nations Relief and Works Agency for Palestine Refugees in the Near East for its efforts to assist in ensuring the financial security of the Agency;

2. *Takes note with approval* of the report of the Working Group;

3. *Requests* the Working Group to continue its efforts, in cooperation with the Secretary-General and the Commissioner-General, to find a solution to the financial situation of the Agency;

4. *Welcomes* the new, unified budget structure for the biennium 2002-2003, which can contribute significantly to improved budgetary transparency of the Agency;

5. *Requests* the Secretary-General to provide the necessary services and assistance to the Working Group for the conduct of its work.

Displaced persons

In a September report [A/56/382] on compliance with General Assembly resolution 55/125 [YUN 2000, p. 456], which called for the accelerated return of all persons displaced as a result of the June 1967 and subsequent hostilities to their homes or former places of residence in the territories occupied by Israel since 1967, the Secretary-General said that since UNRWA was not involved in arrangements for the return of either refugees or displaced persons not registered with it, the Agency's information was based on requests by returning registered refugees for the transfer of their entitlements to their areas of return. Displaced refugees known by UNRWA to have returned to the West Bank and Gaza Strip since 1967 numbered 21,632. Records indicated that, between 1 July 2000 and 30 June 2001, 1,320 refugees had returned to the West Bank and 36 to Gaza. Some of the refugees might not have been displaced since 1967, but might be family members of a displaced registered refugee whom they either had accompanied on return or had joined later.

GENERAL ASSEMBLY ACTION

On 10 December [meeting 82], the General Assembly, on the recommendation of the Fourth Committee [A/56/549], adopted **resolution 56/54** by recorded vote (151-3-1) [agenda item 87].

Persons displaced as a result of the June 1967 and subsequent hostilities

The General Assembly,

Recalling its resolutions 2252(ES-V) of 4 July 1967, 2341 B (XXII) of 19 December 1967 and all subsequent related resolutions,

Recalling also Security Council resolutions 237(1967) of 14 June 1967 and 259(1968) of 27 September 1968,

Taking note of the report of the Secretary-General submitted in pursuance of its resolution 55/125 of 8 December 2000,

Taking note also of the report of the Commissioner-General of the United Nations Relief and Works Agency for Palestine Refugees in the Near East covering the period from 1 July 2000 to 30 June 2001,

Concerned about the continuing human suffering resulting from the June 1967 and subsequent hostilities,

Taking note of the relevant provisions of the Declaration of Principles on Interim Self-Government Arrangements, signed in Washington, D.C., on 13 September 1993 by the Government of the State of Israel and the Palestine Liberation Organization, with regard to the modalities for the admission of persons displaced in 1967, and concerned that the process agreed upon has not yet been effected,

1. *Reaffirms* the right of all persons displaced as a result of the June 1967 and subsequent hostilities to return to their homes or former places of residence in the territories occupied by Israel since 1967;

2. *Expresses deep concern* that the mechanism agreed upon by the parties in article XII of the Declaration of Principles on Interim Self-Government Arrangements on the return of displaced persons has not been effected, and expresses the hope for an accelerated return of displaced persons;

3. *Endorses,* in the meanwhile, the efforts of the Commissioner-General of the United Nations Relief and Works Agency for Palestine Refugees in the Near East to continue to provide humanitarian assistance, as far as practicable, on an emergency basis and as a temporary measure, to persons in the area who are currently displaced and in serious need of continued assistance as a result of the June 1967 and subsequent hostilities;

4. *Strongly appeals* to all Governments and to organizations and individuals to contribute generously to the Agency and to the other intergovernmental and non-governmental organizations concerned for the above-mentioned purposes;

5. *Requests* the Secretary-General, after consulting with the Commissioner-General, to report to the General Assembly before its fifty-seventh session on the progress made with regard to the implementation of the present resolution.

RECORDED VOTE ON RESOLUTION 56/54:

In favour: Algeria, Andorra, Angola, Antigua and Barbuda, Argentina, Armenia, Australia, Austria, Azerbaijan, Bahamas, Bahrain, Bangladesh, Barbados, Belarus, Belgium, Belize, Benin, Bhutan, Bolivia, Brazil, Brunei Darussalam, Bulgaria, Burkina Faso, Burundi, Cambodia, Cameroon, Canada, Cape Verde, Chile, China, Colombia, Comoros, Congo, Costa Rica, Côte d'Ivoire, Croatia, Cuba, Cyprus, Czech Republic, Democratic People's Republic of Korea, Denmark, Djibouti, Dominican Republic, Ecuador, Egypt, El Salvador, Equatorial Guinea, Eritrea, Estonia, Ethiopia, Fiji, Finland, France, Gabon, Georgia, Germany, Ghana, Greece, Grenada, Guatemala, Guinea, Guyana, Haiti, Honduras, Hungary, Iceland, India, Indonesia, Iran, Ireland, Italy, Jamaica, Japan, Jordan, Kazakhstan, Kenya, Kuwait, Lao People's Democratic Republic, Latvia, Lebanon, Libyan Arab Jamahiriya, Liechtenstein, Lithuania, Luxembourg, Madagascar, Malaysia, Maldives, Mali, Malta, Mauritania, Mexico, Monaco, Mongolia, Morocco, Mozambique, Myanmar, Namibia, Nepal, Netherlands, New Zealand, Nicaragua, Nigeria, Norway, Oman, Pakistan, Panama, Papua New Guinea, Paraguay, Peru, Philippines, Poland, Portugal, Qatar, Republic of Korea, Republic of Moldova, Romania, Russian Federation, Saint Lucia, San Marino, Saudi Arabia, Senegal, Seychelles, Sierra Leone, Singapore, Slovakia, Slovenia, Solomon Islands, South Africa, Spain, Sri Lanka, Sudan, Swaziland, Sweden, Syrian Arab Republic, Thailand, The former Yugoslav Republic of Macedonia, Togo, Tonga, Trinidad and Tobago, Tunisia, Turkey, Ukraine, United Arab Emirates, United Kingdom, United Republic of Tanzania, Uruguay, Venezuela, Viet Nam, Yemen, Yugoslavia, Zambia.

Against: Israel, Marshall Islands, United States.

Abstaining: Micronesia.

Education, training and scholarships

In a September report [A/56/375], the Secretary-General transmitted responses to the General Assembly's appeal in resolution 55/126 [YUN 2000, p. 457] for States, specialized agencies and NGOs to augment special allocations for scholarships and grants to Palestine refugees, for which UNRWA acted as recipient and trustee.

In the 2001 fiscal year, Japan awarded 12 fellowships to Palestine refugees who were employed by UNRWA as vocational training staff at the eight vocational training centres in the Agency's area of operations. During the 2000/01 academic year, owing to the cancellation in 1999 of the portion of the university scholarship fund for secondary school graduates financed from UNRWA's General Fund budget and the fact that financing was not forthcoming from donors to fund the subprogramme, UNRWA's Education Department used funds already available from the Japanese contribution, as well as from contributions made by Switzerland, to finance the studies of some students until their graduation. UNESCO granted 78 scholarships to Palestinian students in 2000/01, while WHO provided 27 fellowships/study tours for qualified Palestinian candidates. The United World Colleges offered one scholarship for 2000/01. The International Development Research Centre pledged $1,314,607 to UNRWA to finance the scholarship fund for Palestine refugee women in Lebanon, with an implementation period of six years. In

2000/01, 25 students were enrolled in seven specializations at various Lebanese universities.

GENERAL ASSEMBLY ACTION

On 10 December [meeting 82], the General Assembly, on the recommendation of the Fourth Committee [A/56/549], adopted **resolution 56/55** by recorded vote (154-0-1) [agenda item 87].

Offers by Member States of grants and scholarships for higher education, including vocational training, for Palestine refugees

The General Assembly,

Recalling its resolution 212(III) of 19 November 1948 on assistance to Palestine refugees,

Recalling also its resolutions 35/13 B of 3 November 1980, 36/146 H of 16 December 1981, 37/120 D of 16 December 1982, 38/83 D of 15 December 1983, 39/99 D of 14 December 1984, 40/165 D of 16 December 1985, 41/69 D of 3 December 1986, 42/69 D of 2 December 1987, 43/57 D of 6 December 1988, 44/47 D of 8 December 1989, 45/73 D of 11 December 1990, 46/46 D of 9 December 1991, 47/69 D of 14 December 1992, 48/40 D of 10 December 1993, 49/35 D of 9 December 1994, 50/28 D of 6 December 1995, 51/127 of 13 December 1996, 52/60 of 10 December 1997, 53/49 of 3 December 1998, 54/72 of 6 December 1999 and 55/126 of 8 December 2000,

Cognizant of the fact that the Palestine refugees have, for the last five decades, lost their homes, lands and means of livelihood,

Having considered the report of the Secretary-General,

Having also considered the report of the Commissioner-General of the United Nations Relief and Works Agency for Palestine Refugees in the Near East covering the period from 1 July 2000 to 30 June 2001,

1. *Urges* all States to respond to the appeal made in its resolution 32/90 F of 13 December 1977 and reiterated in subsequent relevant resolutions in a manner commensurate with the needs of Palestine refugees for higher education, including vocational training;

2. *Strongly appeals* to all States, specialized agencies and non-governmental organizations to augment the special allocations for grants and scholarships to Palestine refugees, in addition to their contributions to the regular budget of the United Nations Relief and Works Agency for Palestine Refugees in the Near East;

3. *Expresses its appreciation* to all Governments, specialized agencies and non-governmental organizations that responded favourably to its resolutions on this question;

4. *Invites* the relevant specialized agencies and other organizations of the United Nations system to continue, within their respective spheres of competence, to extend assistance for higher education to Palestine refugee students;

5. *Appeals* to all States, specialized agencies and the United Nations University to contribute generously to the Palestinian universities in the Palestinian territory occupied by Israel since 1967, including, in due course, the proposed University of Jerusalem "Al-Quds" for Palestine refugees;

6. *Appeals* to all States, specialized agencies and other international bodies to contribute towards the establishment of vocational training centres for Palestine refugees;

7. *Requests* the Agency to act as the recipient and trustee for the special allocations for grants and scholarships and to award them to qualified Palestine refugee candidates;

8. *Requests* the Secretary-General to report to the General Assembly at its fifty-seventh session on the implementation of the present resolution.

RECORDED VOTE ON RESOLUTION 56/55:

In favour: Algeria, Andorra, Angola, Antigua and Barbuda, Argentina, Armenia, Australia, Austria, Azerbaijan, Bahamas, Bahrain, Bangladesh, Barbados, Belarus, Belgium, Belize, Benin, Bhutan, Bolivia, Brazil, Brunei Darussalam, Bulgaria, Burkina Faso, Burundi, Cambodia, Cameroon, Canada, Cape Verde, Chile, China, Colombia, Comoros, Congo, Costa Rica, Côte d'Ivoire, Croatia, Cuba, Cyprus, Czech Republic, Democratic People's Republic of Korea, Denmark, Djibouti, Dominican Republic, Ecuador, Egypt, El Salvador, Equatorial Guinea, Eritrea, Estonia, Ethiopia, Fiji, Finland, France, Gabon, Georgia, Germany, Ghana, Greece, Grenada, Guatemala, Guinea, Guyana, Haiti, Honduras, Hungary, Iceland, India, Indonesia, Iran, Ireland, Italy, Jamaica, Japan, Jordan, Kazakhstan, Kenya, Kuwait, Lao People's Democratic Republic, Latvia, Lebanon, Libyan Arab Jamahiriya, Liechtenstein, Lithuania, Luxembourg, Madagascar, Malaysia, Maldives, Mali, Malta, Marshall Islands, Mauritania, Mexico, Micronesia, Monaco, Mongolia, Morocco, Mozambique, Myanmar, Namibia, Nepal, Netherlands, New Zealand, Nicaragua, Nigeria, Norway, Oman, Pakistan, Panama, Papua New Guinea, Paraguay, Peru, Philippines, Poland, Portugal, Qatar, Republic of Korea, Republic of Moldova, Romania, Russian Federation, Saint Lucia, San Marino, Saudi Arabia, Senegal, Seychelles, Sierra Leone, Singapore, Slovakia, Slovenia, Solomon Islands, South Africa, Spain, Sri Lanka, Sudan, Swaziland, Sweden, Syrian Arab Republic, Thailand, The former Yugoslav Republic of Macedonia, Togo, Tonga, Trinidad and Tobago, Tunisia, Turkey, Ukraine, United Arab Emirates, United Kingdom, United Republic of Tanzania, United States, Uruguay, Venezuela, Viet Nam, Yemen, Yugoslavia, Zambia.

Against: None.

Abstaining: Israel.

Proposed University of Jerusalem "Al-Quds"

In response to General Assembly resolution 55/129 [YUN 2000, p. 458], the Secretary-General submitted a September report on the proposal to establish a university for Palestine refugees in Jerusalem [A/56/421]. First mentioned by the Assembly in resolution 35/13 B [YUN 1980, p. 443], the issue had been the subject of annual reports by the Secretary-General.

To assist in the preparation of a feasibility study and at the Secretary-General's request, the Rector of the United Nations University again asked expert Mihaly Simai to visit the area and meet with Israeli officials. In response to the Secretary-General's note verbale of 18 July, requesting Israel to facilitate the visit, Israel, in a 17 September reply, stated that it had consistently voted against the resolution on the proposed university and that its position remained unchanged. It charged that the resolution's sponsors sought to exploit higher education for political purposes extraneous to genuine academic pursuits. Accordingly, Israel was of the opinion that the proposed visit would serve no useful purpose. The Secretary-General reported that it had not been possible to complete the study as planned.

On 10 December [meeting 82], the General Assembly, on the recommendation of the Fourth Committee [A/56/549], adopted **resolution 56/58** by recorded vote (151-3-1) [agenda item 87].

University of Jerusalem "Al-Quds" for Palestine refugees

The General Assembly,

Recalling its resolutions 36/146 G of 16 December 1981, 37/120 C of 16 December 1982, 38/83 K of 15 December 1983, 39/99 K of 14 December 1984, 40/165 D and K of 16 December 1985, 41/69 K of 3 December 1986, 42/69 K of 2 December 1987, 43/57 J of 6 December 1988, 44/47 J of 8 December 1989, 45/73 J of 11 December 1990, 46/46 J of 9 December 1991, 47/69 J of 14 December 1992, 48/40 I of 10 December 1993, 49/35 G of 9 December 1994, 50/28 G of 6 December 1995, 51/130 of 13 December 1996, 52/63 of 10 December 1997, 53/52 of 3 December 1998, 54/75 of 6 December 1999 and 55/129 of 8 December 2000,

Having considered the report of the Secretary-General,

Having also considered the report of the Commissioner-General of the United Nations Relief and Works Agency for Palestine Refugees in the Near East covering the period from 1 July 2000 to 30 June 2001,

1. *Emphasizes* the need for strengthening the educational system in the Palestinian territory occupied by Israel since 5 June 1967, including Jerusalem, and specifically the need for the establishment of the proposed university;

2. *Requests* the Secretary-General to continue to take all necessary measures for establishing the University of Jerusalem "Al-Quds", in accordance with General Assembly resolution 35/13 B of 3 November 1980, giving due consideration to the recommendations consistent with the provisions of that resolution;

3. *Calls once again upon* Israel, the occupying Power, to cooperate in the implementation of the present resolution and to remove the hindrances that it has put in the way of establishing the University of Jerusalem "Al-Quds";

4. *Requests* the Secretary-General to report to the General Assembly at its fifty-seventh session on the progress made in the implementation of the present resolution.

RECORDED VOTE ON RESOLUTION 56/58:

In favour: Algeria, Andorra, Angola, Antigua and Barbuda, Argentina, Armenia, Australia, Austria, Azerbaijan, Bahamas, Bahrain, Bangladesh, Barbados, Belarus, Belgium, Belize, Benin, Bhutan, Bolivia, Brazil, Brunei Darussalam, Bulgaria, Burkina Faso, Burundi, Cambodia, Cameroon, Canada, Cape Verde, Chile, China, Colombia, Comoros, Congo, Costa Rica, Côte d'Ivoire, Croatia, Cuba, Cyprus, Czech Republic, Democratic People's Republic of Korea, Denmark, Djibouti, Dominican Republic, Ecuador, Egypt, El Salvador, Equatorial Guinea, Eritrea, Estonia, Ethiopia, Fiji, Finland, France, Gabon, Georgia, Germany, Ghana, Greece, Grenada, Guatemala, Guinea, Guyana, Haiti, Honduras, Hungary, Iceland, India, Indonesia, Iran, Ireland, Italy, Jamaica, Japan, Jordan, Kazakhstan, Kenya, Kuwait, Lao People's Democratic Republic, Latvia, Lebanon, Libyan Arab Jamahiriya, Liechtenstein, Lithuania, Luxembourg, Madagascar, Malaysia, Maldives, Mali, Malta, Mauritania, Mexico, Monaco, Mongolia, Morocco, Mozambique, Myanmar, Namibia, Nepal, Netherlands, New Zealand, Nicaragua, Nigeria, Norway, Oman, Pakistan, Panama, Papua New Guinea, Paraguay, Peru, Philippines, Poland, Portugal, Qatar, Republic of Korea, Republic of Moldova, Romania, Russian Federation, Saint Lucia, San Marino, Saudi Arabia, Senegal, Seychelles, Sierra Leone, Singapore, Slovakia, Slovenia, Solomon Islands, South Africa, Spain, Sri Lanka, Sudan, Swaziland, Sweden, Syrian Arab Republic, Thailand, The former Yugoslav Republic of Macedonia, Togo, Tonga, Trinidad and Tobago, Tunisia, Turkey, Ukraine, United Arab Emirates, United Kingdom, United Republic of Tanzania, Uruguay, Venezuela, Viet Nam, Yemen, Yugoslavia, Zambia.

Against: Israel, Marshall Islands, United States.

Abstaining: Micronesia.

Property rights

In response to General Assembly resolution 55/128 [YUN 2000, p. 459], the Secretary-General submitted a September report [A/56/420] on steps taken to protect and administer Arab property, assets and property rights in Israel, and establish a fund for income derived therefrom, on behalf of the rightful owners. He indicated that he had transmitted the resolution to Israel and all other Member States, requesting information on any steps taken or envisaged with regard to its implementation.

In a 17 September reply, reproduced in the report, Israel stated that its position on the resolutions on Palestine refugees had been set forth in successive annual replies, the latest of which had been included in the Secretary-General's 2000 report on the subject [YUN 2000, p. 458]. Israel regretted that the resolutions regarding UNRWA remained rife with political issues irrelevant to the Agency's work and detached from the reality in the area. While Israel believed that UNRWA could play an important role in promoting the social and economic advancement foreseen in agreements between Israel and the Palestinians, it considered it essential that the Assembly consolidate the resolutions on UNRWA into one directly related to the Agency's humanitarian tasks.

No replies were received from other Member States.

Report of Conciliation Commission. The United Nations Conciliation Commission for Palestine, in its fifty-fifth report covering the period from 1 September 2000 to 31 August 2001 [A/56/290], noted its August 2000 report [YUN 2000, p. 459] and observed that it had nothing new to report since its submission.

On 10 December [meeting 82], the General Assembly, on the recommendation of the Fourth Committee [A/56/459], adopted **resolution 56/57** by recorded vote (150-3-1) [agenda item 87].

Palestine refugees' properties and their revenues

The General Assembly,

Recalling its resolutions 194(III) of 11 December 1948, 36/146 C of 16 December 1981 and all its subsequent resolutions on the question,

Taking note of the report of the Secretary-General submitted in pursuance of resolution 55/128 of 8 December 2000,

Taking note also of the report of the United Nations Conciliation Commission for Palestine for the period from 1 September 2000 to 31 August 2001,

Recalling that the Universal Declaration of Human Rights and the principles of international law uphold the principle that no one shall be arbitrarily deprived of his or her property,

Recalling in particular its resolution 394(V) of 14 December 1950, in which it directed the Conciliation Commission, in consultation with the parties concerned, to prescribe measures for the protection of the rights, property and interests of the Palestine Arab refugees,

Noting the completion of the programme of identification and evaluation of Arab property, as announced by the Conciliation Commission in its twenty-second progress report, and the fact that the Land Office had a schedule of Arab owners and file of documents defining the location, area and other particulars of Arab property,

Recalling that, in the framework of the Middle East peace process, the Palestine Liberation Organization and the Government of Israel agreed, in the Declaration of Principles on Interim Self-Government Arrangements of 13 September 1993, to commence negotiations on permanent status issues, including the important issue of the refugees,

1. *Reaffirms* that the Palestine Arab refugees are entitled to their property and to the income derived therefrom, in conformity with the principles of justice and equity;

2. *Requests* the Secretary-General to take all appropriate steps, in consultation with the United Nations Conciliation Commission for Palestine, for the protection of Arab property, assets and property rights in Israel;

3. *Expresses its appreciation* for the work done to preserve and modernize the existing records of the Conciliation Commission;

4. *Calls once again upon* Israel to render all facilities and assistance to the Secretary-General in the implementation of the present resolution;

5. *Calls upon* all the parties concerned to provide the Secretary-General with any pertinent information in their possession concerning Arab property, assets and property rights in Israel that would assist him in the implementation of the present resolution;

6. *Urges* the Palestinian and Israeli sides, as agreed between them, to deal with the important issue of Palestine refugees' properties and their revenues in the framework of the final status negotiations of the Middle East peace process;

7. *Requests* the Secretary-General to report to the General Assembly at its fifty-seventh session on the implementation of the present resolution.

RECORDED VOTE ON RESOLUTION 56/57:

In favour: Algeria, Andorra, Angola, Antigua and Barbuda, Argentina, Armenia, Australia, Austria, Azerbaijan, Bahamas, Bahrain, Bangladesh, Barbados, Belarus, Belgium, Belize, Benin, Bhutan, Bolivia, Brazil, Brunei Darussalam, Bulgaria, Burkina Faso, Burundi, Cambodia, Cameroon, Canada, Cape Verde, Chile, China, Colombia, Comoros, Congo, Costa Rica, Côte d'Ivoire, Croatia, Cuba, Cyprus, Czech Republic, Democratic People's Republic of Korea, Denmark, Djibouti, Dominican Republic, Ecuador, Egypt, El Salvador, Equatorial Guinea, Eritrea, Estonia, Ethiopia, Fiji, Finland, France, Gabon, Georgia, Germany, Ghana, Greece, Guatemala, Guinea, Guyana, Haiti, Honduras, Hungary, Iceland, India, Indonesia, Iran, Ireland, Italy, Jamaica, Japan, Jordan, Kazakhstan, Kenya, Kuwait, Lao People's Democratic Republic, Latvia, Lebanon, Libyan Arab Jamahiriya, Liechtenstein, Lithuania, Luxembourg, Madagascar, Malaysia, Maldives, Mali, Malta, Mauritania, Mexico, Monaco, Mongolia, Morocco, Mozambique, Myanmar, Namibia, Nepal, Netherlands, New Zealand, Nicaragua, Nigeria, Norway, Oman, Pakistan, Panama, Papua New Guinea, Paraguay, Peru, Philippines, Poland, Portugal, Qatar, Republic of Korea, Republic of Moldova, Romania, Russian Federation, Saint Lucia, San Marino, Saudi Arabia, Senegal, Seychelles, Sierra Leone, Singapore, Slovakia, Slovenia, Solomon Islands, South Africa, Spain, Sri Lanka, Sudan, Swaziland, Sweden, Syrian Arab Republic, Thailand, The former Yugoslav Republic of Macedonia, Togo, Tonga, Trinidad and Tobago, Tunisia, Turkey, Ukraine, United Arab Emirates, United Kingdom, United Republic of Tanzania, Uruguay, Venezuela, Viet Nam, Yemen, Yugoslavia, Zambia.

Against: Israel, Marshall Islands, United States.

Abstaining: Micronesia.

Peacekeeping operations

In 2001, the United Nations Truce Supervision Organization (UNTSO), originally set up to monitor the ceasefire called for by the Security Council in resolution S/801 of 29 May 1948 [YUN 1947-48, p. 427] in newly partitioned Palestine, continued its work. UNTSO's unarmed military observers fulfilled changing mandates—from supervising the original four armistice agreements between Israel and its neighbours (Egypt, Jordan, Lebanon and the Syrian Arab Republic) to observing and monitoring other ceasefires, as well as performing a number of additional tasks. During the year, UNTSO personnel worked with the two remaining UN peacekeeping forces in the Middle East—the United Nations Disengagement Observer Force (UNDOF) in the Golan Heights and the United Nations Interim Force in Lebanon (UNIFIL).

During the year, UNIFIL underwent a gradual reconfiguration and redeployment, having confirmed the withdrawal of Israeli troops in June 2000 from southern Lebanon [YUN 2000, p. 460] and having assisted the Lebanese authorities as they returned to the area vacated by Israel. A line of withdrawal—the so-called Blue Line—was identified by the United Nations on the ground following the withdrawal of Israeli troops in 2000 [ibid., p. 462].

Lebanon

In 2001, serious breaches occurred relating to the farmlands in the Shab'a area on the border; the paramilitary group Hizbullah carried out attacks against targets inside Israel and the Israel Defence Forces (IDF) attacked targets within Lebanon, including Syrian radar installations. The Shab'a farmlands had been a source of contention since the withdrawal of Israeli forces from Lebanon in June 2000. According to the Lebanese Government, Israel's withdrawal from southern Lebanon was incomplete, as Israeli forces continued to occupy the Shab'a farms, while Israel's position was that the area was occupied Syrian territory and thus within the purview of Security Council resolution 242(1967) [YUN 1967, p. 257] on the Israeli-Syrian conflict, and not resolution 425(1978) [YUN 1978, p. 312], which dealt with Israel's withdrawal from Lebanon. However, Lebanon and the Syrian Arab Republic continued to claim that the Shab'a farmlands were inside Lebanese territory.

In January 2001, Staffan de Mistura assumed his position as the Secretary-General's Personal Representative for southern Lebanon, responsible for coordinating UN activities in the area.

In a series of communications received throughout the year [A/55/733-S/2001/43, A/55/736-S/2001/56, A/55/738-S/2001/62, A/55/766-S/2001/110, A/55/802-S/2001/164, A/55/818-S/2001/184, A/55/841-S/2001/243, A/55/868-S/2001/313, A/55/894-S/2001/344, A/55/898-S/2001/355, A/55/923-S/2001/430, A/55/930-S/2001/454, A/55/937-S/2001/476, A/55/938-S/2001/478, A/55/948-S/2001/502, A/55/959-S/2001/531, A/55/991-S/2001/606, A/55/995-S/2001/630, A/56/396-S/2001/901, A/56/503-S/2001/1004, A/56/695-S/2001/1177, A/56/718-S/2001/1206, A/56/762-S/2001/1337], Lebanon detailed Israeli attacks on southern Lebanon and the Western Bekaa, as well as Israeli violations of Lebanese sovereignty.

In communications dated between 6 February and 24 October [A/55/767-S/2001/111, A/55/792-S/2001/142, A/55/901-S/2001/364, A/55/1002-S/2001/643, A/56/507-S/2001/1012], Israel detailed terrorist attempts to infiltrate its northern border from Lebanon, as well as the launching of mortars and anti-tank shells by the paramilitary group Hizbullah against Israeli targets, in violation of the Blue Line.

Throughout 2001, Israel, Lebanon, the Syrian Arab Republic, other countries of the region and several international organizations transmitted communications to the United Nations concerning the situation on the Israel/Lebanon border.

In identical letters of 2 February [S/2001/99] to the Secretary-General and the Security Council President, Lebanon said that Israel had established a gateway complex at the entrance to the village of Ghajar, had excavated a trench there and had set up a 400-metre-long concrete barrier running parallel to the road leading to Ghajar inside Lebanese territory. That action constituted a violation of the Blue Line and an assault on Lebanon's sovereignty.

On 28 February [A/55/817-S/2001/180], Syria informed the Secretary-General that the Israeli authorities had begun to bring pressure to bear on the inhabitants of Ghajar for the construction of a barbed-wire fence that would result in the partitioning of the village. The inhabitants had stated unequivocally that they were born as Syrians and that they would remain Syrian in all circumstances.

On 29 March [A/55/864-S/2001/292], Lebanon said that Israel was threatening to launch new attacks on Lebanese territory based on the allegation that Lebanon had set about diverting the course of the Hasbani river, which would deprive Israel of its water. Lebanon stated that Israel's allegations were untrue and had the objective of obstructing Lebanon's reconstruction efforts in those areas that had been occupied by Israel for 22 years.

On 16 April [S/2001/367], Israel notified the Council President that, on 14 April, Hizbullah gunmen had fired two anti-tank missiles at an IDF tank on patrol on the Israeli side of the Blue Line, killing one Israeli soldier. That act of aggression followed continuous attacks and provocations from Lebanese territory since Israel's withdrawal in 2000.

Also on 16 April [A/55/900-S/2001/362], Syria said that Israeli formations had that day violated Lebanese airspace and bombed a Syrian radar installation in Lebanese territory. Syria regarded that aggression as a serious escalation that could undermine peace and stability in the region.

On 17 April [A/55/902-S/2001/371], Lebanon said that Israel's 16 April attack against Syrian military positions inside Lebanese territory had caused the death of one member of the Syrian Arab Force and the wounding of four others.

The United Arab Emirates, on 18 April [A/55/903-S/2001/375], condemned the aggression committed by Israeli forces against Lebanese territory on 16 April, as did Qatar, in its capacity as Chairman of the Organization of the Islamic Conference [A/55/906-S/2001/383].

Responding on 18 April [A/55/908-S/2001/385], Israel said that Syria, as the main power broker in Lebanon with 35,000 troops stationed there, supported Hizbullah and had directly enhanced the capacity of the organization to launch attacks against Israel. Syria had also allowed Hizbullah to maintain terrorist training facilities in the Syrian-controlled Bekaa Valley. Following the act of aggression perpetrated by Hizbullah on 14 April (see above), Israel was compelled to respond and exercised its legitimate right to self-defence in the 16 April operation, which aimed to prevent the recurrence of aggression from Lebanese soil.

On 23 April [A/55/914-S/2001/407], Yemen condemned and denounced Israel's aggression against Lebanese territory and its bombing of Syrian forces in the Bekaa area.

On the same day [A/55/920-S/2001/426], Sweden, on behalf of the EU, said that Israel's attack on Syrian objectives in Lebanon, the first in many years, as a retaliation for Hizbullah attacks on the

Shab'a farms, was an excessive and disproportionate response.

In identical letters of 2 May [A/55/926-S/2001/438 & Corr.1] to the Secretary-General and the Council President, Syria said that Israel had deliberately misled international public opinion by distorting the facts. The true reasons for the deteriorating situation in the Middle East were essentially attributable to the continuing Israeli policies of occupation, expansion and aggression. Israel was fully aware that Lebanon and Syria had a pact of brotherhood and cooperation that governed the relationship between the two countries. Consequently, Syria supported Lebanon by providing everything that it needed to defend its territory and achieve its security and stability.

On 3 May [A/55/927-S/2001/440], Syria said that on 14 April an Israeli military patrol inside Syrian territory fired several rounds at a Syrian police position in the sector of a UN position.

Lebanon, on 7 May [A/55/929-S/2001/444], said that the Syrian forces stationed inside Lebanese territory were there at the request and with the agreement of the Lebanese Government, and their presence was a necessary, legitimate and temporary one that was not Israel's concern.

On 29 May [A/55/958-S/2001/530], Lebanon said that Israel had installed an observation post 20 metres inside Lebanese territory in the vicinity of Ghajar village, in violation of Lebanese sovereignty and relevant UN resolutions.

On 27 June [A/55/1001-S/2001/642], Lebanon said that on 13 and 14 June Israeli forces deliberately set fire to extensive areas in the occupied Shab'a farmlands.

In two separate letters of 2 July to the Council President and the Secretary-General [S/2001/654, A/55/1006], Lebanon said that, on the previous day, Israeli warplanes had violated Lebanese airspace and attacked a Syrian radar position operating in Lebanon. Two members of the Syrian forces were wounded, as was an enlisted Lebanese soldier.

On the same day [A/55/1007-S/2001/653], Lebanon forwarded to the Secretary-General a statement issued on 30 June following consultations between the Lebanese and Syrian Ministers for Foreign Affairs. Having noted statements made by Israeli officials concerning acts of resistance to the Israeli occupation in the Shab'a farmlands and allegations made about the weapons used against Israeli forces, the Ministers said that the defensive weapons that the resistance possessed could not be compared with the weapons of mass destruction, warplanes, heavy artillery and battle tanks available to the Israeli armed forces. Lebanon affirmed its right under the UN Charter and relevant international covenants to liberate its territory using all legitimate means, and both Lebanon and Syria would hold Israel responsible for the consequences of any new aggression.

In identical letters of 3 July [A/55/1011, S/2001/670] to the Secretary-General and the Council President, Qatar said that the Arab Group at the United Nations had held a meeting that day in New York at the level of ambassadors and permanent representatives to the United Nations. The Arab Group condemned the repeated Israeli attacks on Lebanon and on the Syrian Arab forces operating in Lebanon. It affirmed its support for Lebanon in asserting all of its rights and in taking all legitimate measures to liberate the occupied Shab'a farmlands.

On 6 July [A/56/161-S/2001/673], Israel informed the Secretary-General that on 29 June two Israeli soldiers were wounded by shrapnel when Hizbullah terrorists fired dozens of anti-tank missiles and mortars at two army outposts in the Mount Dov region on the Israeli side of the Blue Line. By their active and tacit support for Hizbullah's activities, both Lebanon and Syria were in violation of basic norms of international law and relevant UN resolutions. Lebanon's failure to assert control in the southern part of the country was due, to a large extent, to the overwhelming degree of control that the Syrian Government exerted over its neighbour.

Responding on 30 July [A/56/226-S/2001/746], Syria said that Israel's letter sought to distract attention from its daily violations of Lebanon's territorial integrity and from the acts of aggression committed by Israeli aircraft against Syrian Arab forces operating in Lebanon. Lebanon had declared that the relevant international covenants gave it the right to take action to free its territory from Israeli occupation. Syria supported Lebanon in seeking the restoration of all of its territory.

On 9 August [A/56/283-S/2001/777], Israel replied that, contrary to Syria's assertions, it was not occupying Lebanese land in the Shab'a farmlands as it had withdrawn its forces from Lebanon in June 2000, as attested by Council resolution 1310(2000) [YUN 2000, p. 470]. Syria's allegations, moreover, had to be viewed within the context of the continued Syrian occupation of Lebanon.

By a 28 August letter to the Security Council President [S/2001/831], Israel noted that on 4 August UNIFIL had evacuated its position at the Abbasiyah checkpoint, which had controlled the northern pathway entering the village of Rajar. The Blue Line cut through Rajar, the northern path being inside Lebanese territory and the southern part inside Israeli territory. Following the evacuation, Hizbullah removed part of the dividing fence and started to construct an outpost at the approach to the village, posing a danger to the security of Israeli soldiers and civilians. Israel called on the United Nations to regain control of the Abbasiyah checkpoint, to establish a new outpost at the northern approach to Rajar and to enable the repair of the northern fence.

Responding on 4 September [S/2001/856], Lebanon said that Israel was attempting to cover up its provocations by land, air and sea, which were combined with a field trip by the Israeli Prime Minister over the whole length of Lebanon's southern border. There had also been a concentration of Israeli troops in that area.

Addressing the situation in the Ghajar/Abbasiyah area in a 5 September letter to the Security Council President [S/2001/848], the Under-Secretary-General for Peacekeeping Operations said that since the Israeli withdrawal from Lebanon, UNIFIL no longer exercised any control over the area of operation and did not maintain checkpoints since the drawing of the Blue Line [YUN 2000, p. 465]. UNIFIL carried out its functions through mobile patrols and observation from fixed positions and through close contacts with the parties to correct violations. The establishment of fixed positions was based on operational considerations and should not be dictated by the parties. In the vicinity of Ghajar, UNIFIL had a position known as 4-28, approximately 1.5 kilometres east of the village. UNIFIL temporarily stored containers about 200 metres away by a gate in the old technical fence on the road leading to the abandoned village of Abbasiyah. At no time did those containers constitute a position or, as asserted by Israel, a checkpoint. The village of Abbasiyah, the road leading to Ghajar and the entire surrounding area were clearly on the Lebanese side of the Blue Line. The United Nations was key to the establishment of the status quo in Ghajar and was endeavouring to maintain it. Initiatives at the political level by the United Nations combined with UNIFIL efforts on the ground, including assertive UNIFIL patrolling by armoured personnel carriers, were able to bring about a decrease in provocative activity resulting in reduced tension. The situation had improved significantly, fostering conditions on the ground that might allow a return to the status quo.

On 10 October [S/2001/957], the League of Arab States (LAS) forwarded to the Council President a resolution entitled "Solidarity with Lebanon", adopted by the LAS Council of Ministers at its one hundred and sixteenth regular session (Cairo, 9-10 September). The Ministers strongly condemned Israel for, among other things, its continued occupation of Lebanese territory, the de-tention of Lebanese prisoners and the refusal to hand over to the United Nations all the maps indicating the location of mines that Israeli forces had laid in southern Lebanon.

In connection with those allegations, Israel, on 6 December [S/2001/1173], said that when it withdrew forces from Lebanon in 2000, IDF transferred to UNIFIL all information pertaining to the location of minefields in southern Lebanon, including detailed maps. Since then, large quantities of mines and other devices had been laid by terrorist groups in southern Lebanon. It was the responsibility of the Lebanese Government to establish effective control and restore peace in the area.

In a 31 December letter [A/56/761-S/2001/1336], Lebanon informed the Secretary-General that on 24 December Israel had dug a trench on the road east of Ghajar, with the intention of erecting a fence along the town boundary in occupied Syrian territory to the heights above Abbasiyah. The work had been suspended following the intervention of UNIFIL's Commander and units of the Lebanese liaison service.

UNIFIL

The Security Council twice extended the mandate of the United Nations Interim Force in Lebanon in 2001, in January and July, each time for a six-month period.

UNIFIL, which was established by Council resolution 425(1978) [YUN 1978, p. 312] following Israel's invasion of Lebanon [ibid., p. 296], was originally entrusted with confirming the withdrawal of Israeli forces, restoring international peace and security, and assisting the Lebanese Government in ensuring the return of its effective authority in southern Lebanon. Following a second Israeli invasion of Lebanon in 1982 [YUN 1982, p. 428], the Council, in resolution 511(1982) [ibid., p. 450], authorized the Force to carry out, in addition to its original mandate, the interim task of providing protection and humanitarian assistance to the local population, while maintaining its positions in the area of deployment. With the withdrawal of IDF from Lebanon in June 2000 [YUN 2000, p. 461], UNIFIL's operational role changed significantly. A phased reinforcement was initiated in order for UNIFIL to carry out its tasks related to confirming Israel's withdrawal, which included extending its operations into those territories that had been occupied by IDF [ibid., p. 465]. In 2001, having fulfilled those responsibilities, UNIFIL started a reconfiguration and redeployment phase.

The Force headquarters, based predominantly in Naqoura, provided command and control, as well as liaison with Lebanon and Israel, UNDOF, UNTSO and a number of NGOs.

Composition and deployment

The reconfiguration and redeployment of UNIFIL proceeded as set out in the Secretary-General's April 2001 report (see p. 453). Following the repatriation of the Nepalese battalion and the Polish engineering company at the end of July, the Finnish and Irish battalions were repatriated in October and November, respectively. UNIFIL closed a number of rear positions and moved troops into closer proximity to the Blue Line.

As at 31 December, as a result of the reconfiguration, UNIFIL comprised 3,494 troops from Fiji (458), France (233), Ghana (811), India (819), Italy (52), Poland (483) and Ukraine (638). The Force was assisted in its tasks by 51 military observers of UNTSO. In addition, UNIFIL employed 448 civilian staff, of whom 135 were recruited internationally and 313 locally. On 6 August [S/2001/767], the Security Council took note of the Secretary-General's intention [S/2001/766] to appoint Major General Lalit Mohan Tewari (India) as Force Commander to replace Major General Seth Kofi Obeng (Ghana), who completed his tour of duty on 15 May.

Since the establishment of UNIFIL, 239 members of the Force had lost their lives: 78 as a result of firings or bomb explosions, 101 in accidents and 60 from other causes. A total of 344 were wounded by firing or mine explosions.

Activities

Report of Secretary-General (January). In a report on developments from 18 July 2000 to 18 January 2001 in the UNIFIL area of operations [S/2001/66], the Secretary-General said that the general situation in south Lebanon had remained stable, despite some minor violations of the Blue Line. As far as the reconfiguration of the UN presence in south Lebanon was concerned, of the three parts of its mandate, UNIFIL had essentially completed two. It had confirmed the withdrawal of Israeli forces and assisted the Lebanese authorities as they returned to the area vacated by Israel. The Force functioned in close cooperation with those authorities and no longer exercised any control over the area of operation. However, the Lebanese Government had yet to deploy its personnel down to the Blue Line and UNIFIL could not, of course, compel it to do so. UNIFIL was focusing on the remaining part of its mandate, the restoration of international peace and security. Pending a comprehensive peace, UNIFIL sought to maintain the ceasefire along the Blue Line through patrols and observation from fixed positions and close contact with the parties, with a view to correcting violations and preventing the escalation of incidents.

The Secretary-General observed that UNIFIL's functions had evolved into those of an observer mission. However, in view of the conditions in the region, he was reluctant to entrust the task to unarmed observers alone and therefore recommended instead a combination of armed infantry and unarmed observers, specifically two infantry battalions, a group of UNTSO observers and support. He also viewed a gradual reconfiguration as the most prudent and appropriate approach. As a possible first stage, UNIFIL's force could be brought back to the strength it had before the June 2000 augmentation—about 4,500 all ranks. In the light of the conditions in the area, he recommended that the Force's mandate be extended for another six months, until 31 July 2001.

Communications. By a 5 January letter [S/2001/14] to the Secretary-General, Lebanon requested that UNIFIL's mandate be extended for a further six-month period, especially in the light of Israel's daily violations of Lebanese sovereignty.

Responding on 17 January [S/2001/55], Israel rejected Lebanon's allegations regarding violations of its territory and drew attention to the regular assaults on Israeli soldiers and civilians emanating from Lebanon. Lebanon had not only failed to prevent those acts of aggression; it had encouraged them and failed to deploy its armed forces along the border with Israel.

SECURITY COUNCIL ACTION (January)

On 30 January [meeting 4267], the Security Council unanimously adopted **resolution 1337 (2001)**. The draft text [S/2001/87] was prepared in consultations among Council members.

The Security Council,

Recalling its resolutions 425(1978) and 426(1978) of 19 March 1978, 501(1982) of 25 February 1982, 508(1982) of 5 June 1982, 509(1982) of 6 June 1982, 520(1982) of 17 September 1982 and 1310(2000) of 27 July 2000, as well as its resolutions and the statements of its President on the situation in Lebanon,

Recalling further its resolution 1308(2000) of 17 July 2000,

Recalling also the Secretary-General's conclusion that, as of 16 June 2000, Israel had withdrawn its forces from Lebanon in accordance with resolution 425(1978) and met the requirements defined in the Secretary-General's report of 22 May 2000,

Emphasizing the interim nature of the United Nations Interim Force in Lebanon,

Recalling the relevant principles contained in the Convention on the Safety of United Nations and Associated Personnel adopted on 9 December 1994,

Responding to the request of the Government of Lebanon as stated in the letter from its Permanent Representative to the United Nations of 5 January 2001 to the Secretary-General,

1. *Welcomes* the report of the Secretary-General on the United Nations Interim Force in Lebanon of 22 January 2001 and endorses his observations and recommendations;

2. *Decides* to extend the present mandate of the Force for a further period of six months, until 31 July 2001;

3. *Decides* to return the military personnel of the Force to the operational level referred to in paragraph 24 of the Secretary-General's report of 22 January 2001 by 31 July, and requests that the Secretary-General take the necessary measures to implement this decision, including taking into account the upcoming rotations of the battalions, in consultation with the Government of Lebanon and the troop-contributing countries;

4. *Reiterates* its strong support for the territorial integrity, sovereignty and political independence of Lebanon within its internationally recognized boundaries;

5. *Calls upon* the Government of Lebanon to ensure the return of its effective authority and presence in the south, and in particular to increase the rate of the deployment of the Lebanese armed forces;

6. *Welcomes* the establishment of checkpoints by the Government of Lebanon in the vacated area, and encourages the Government of Lebanon to ensure a calm environment throughout the south, including through the control of all checkpoints;

7. *Calls upon* the parties to fulfil the commitments they have given to respect fully the withdrawal line identified by the United Nations, as set out in the Secretary-General's report of 16 June 2000, to exercise utmost restraint and to cooperate fully with the United Nations and with the Force;

8. *Condemns* all acts of violence, expresses concern about the serious breaches and violations of the withdrawal line, and urges the parties to put an end to them and to respect the safety of personnel of the Force;

9. *Commends* the Force for having fulfilled its mandate regarding verification of Israeli withdrawal, and supports its continued efforts to maintain the ceasefire along the withdrawal line through patrols and observation from fixed positions and close contacts with the parties, with a view to correcting violations and preventing the escalation of incidents;

10. *Welcomes* the contribution of the Force to operational demining, encourages further assistance in mine action by the United Nations to the Government of Lebanon in support of both the continued development of its national mine action capacity and emergency demining activities in the south, and calls upon donor countries to support these efforts through financial and in-kind contributions;

11. *Requests* the Secretary-General to continue consultations with the Government of Lebanon and other parties directly concerned on the implementation of the present resolution and to report to the Security Council thereon;

12. *Looks forward* to the early fulfilment of the mandate of the Force;

13. *Endorses* the general approach for reconfiguration of the Force, as outlined in paragraph 23 of the report of the Secretary-General of 22 January 2001, and requests the Secretary-General to submit to the Council a detailed report by 30 April 2001 on the Force's reconfiguration plans and on the tasks that could be carried out by the United Nations Truce Supervision Organization;

14. *Decides* to review the situation by early May 2001 and to consider any steps it deems appropriate regarding the Force and the Truce Supervision Organization, on the basis of this report;

15. *Stresses* the importance of, and the need to achieve, a comprehensive, just and lasting peace in the Middle East, based on all its relevant resolutions including its resolutions 242(1967) of 22 November 1967 and 338(1973) of 22 October 1973.

Report of Secretary-General (April). In response to resolution 1337(2001), the Secretary-General submitted to the Security Council on 30 April [S/2001/423] an interim report on the plans for UNIFIL's reconfiguration and on the tasks that could be carried out by UNTSO. He reported that, since the adoption of resolution 1337(2001), serious breaches had occurred relating to the Shab'a farms dispute, with attacks carried out by the paramilitary group Hizbullah against targets inside Israeli territory and retaliatory attacks by IDF against targets in Lebanon. There had also been frequent minor ground violations of the Blue Line and almost daily violations of the Line by Israeli aircraft.

The Secretary-General said that UNIFIL would continue to focus on the Blue Line and the adjacent area. It was envisaged that the area would be divided into two sectors. The bulk of the troops would be deployed in protected positions close to the Blue Line and there would be fewer fixed positions to avoid too many personnel being absorbed by guard and maintenance duties. UNIFIL would be present on the Blue Line primarily through its patrols. Its headquarters would remain at Naqoura and UNIFIL would continue to require full freedom of movement to meet its operational, administrative and logistic requirements. UNTSO's unarmed military observers would be entirely mobile and would no longer maintain static observation posts, which would enable them to undertake daytime patrolling, carry out investigations and perform liaison functions. The strength of the Observer Group Lebanon (51) was deemed sufficient for those tasks. It was envisaged that the demining unit would remain, since mines remained a serious hazard for the Force. The Secretary-General's Personal Representative had been active in generating support for mine clearance and ensuring effective coordination between the Lebanese authorities and UN agencies. Once the reconfiguration was completed, the Force would comprise troops from France (headquarters guard),

Ghana (infantry), India (infantry), Italy (helicopters), Poland (logistics) and Ukraine (engineers/demining). Its overall strength would then be close to 2,000 all ranks.

The Secretary-General stated that the Force's reconfiguration would be achieved through the non-replacement or reduction of units on the occasion of their normal rotations. Ireland had already said that it would not replace its contingent at the time of its rotation in October/November. The Finnish contingent would be reduced by 350 troops by the end of July, and the Secretary-General noted that he would not request a replacement for the remaining Finnish troops at the time of their repatriation in October. The departure of those two contingents would bring the Force's strength to about 3,600. The Secretary-General recommended that the Force maintain that level until January 2002 and noted that the reconfiguration could be completed during the following mandate, ending in July 2002.

Communications. By a 9 May letter to the Secretary-General [A/55/934-S/2001/464], Lebanon said that UNIFIL's reconfiguration, as recommended by the Secretary-General in his April report, would create a climate of instability in the area that could undermine the sense of security and safety created by the Mission's presence.

On 18 May [S/2001/500], the Security Council informed the Secretary-General that it endorsed in general the technical reconfiguration approach for UNIFIL.

On 9 July [S/2001/677], Lebanon requested the Council to extend UNIFIL's mandate, which was due to expire on 31 July, for a further period of six months.

Report of Secretary-General (July). In a report on UNIFIL covering 23 January to 20 July [S/2001/714], the Secretary-General said that the situation had been marked by general stability throughout most of the UNIFIL area of operation, with the exception of tensions and serious breaches of the Blue Line connected to the dispute over the Shab'a farms area, including Hizbullah attacks and Israeli retaliations. Israeli aircraft flew deep into Lebanese airspace almost daily; low-level flights that broke the sound barrier over populated areas caused great anxiety to the civilian population. Civil administration in south Lebanon was somewhat strengthened during the reporting period, with local administration and the central authority in Beirut taking a more active role. Communications, health and welfare systems, as well as postal services, made further slow progress towards integration with the rest of the country. The 1,000-strong contingent of the Lebanese Joint Security Force, comprising army and internal security forces, contin-

ued to operate in the areas vacated by Israel in 2000, carrying out patrolling and policing of local communities. The Lebanese Government continued to maintain the position that as long as there was no comprehensive peace with Israel, the Lebanese armed forces would not be deployed along the Blue Line. Areas along the Blue Line were monitored by Hizbullah through a network of mobile and fixed positions. In some instances, Hizbullah acted as surrogate for the civil administration by extending social, medical and educational services to the local population. On several occasions, Hizbullah personnel restricted UNIFIL's freedom of movement and interfered with its redeployment.

The focus of UNIFIL operations remained on the Blue Line and the adjacent area. A controversy arose between the Israeli authorities and the United Nations over a UNIFIL videotape, filmed on 8 October 2000, of vehicles that might have been used by Hizbullah in the abduction of three Israeli soldiers [YUN 2000, p. 471]. Israel and Lebanon had been offered the opportunity to view the tape, with the identities of non-UN personnel obscured, on UN premises. The Secretary-General initiated an investigation into the internal handling of the matter. In some villages in the south, tensions developed between local residents and former members of the dismantled South Lebanese Army who had returned home after serving their terms in prison for collaboration with Israel. UNIFIL continued to assist the civilian population in the form of medical care, water projects, equipment or services for schools and orphanages, and supplies of social services to the needy. The clearance of mines and unexploded ordnance in southern Lebanon gained momentum. At a high-level workshop on mine clearance, convened on 21 and 22 May by the Lebanese Government with the participation of the United Nations and NGOs, it was announced that the United Arab Emirates had pledged $50 million for mine clearance in the southern part of Lebanon. A Regional Mine Action Coordination Cell in Tyre, Lebanon, continued to coordinate UN mine-clearing activity, while the United Nations Mine Action Service cooperated closely with the National Demining Office of Lebanon.

The Secretary-General observed that, during his visit to the region in June (see p. 406), he had discussed violations of the Blue Line in the Shab'a farms area with the political leadership in Lebanon and Israel. In the light of conditions prevailing in the area, he recommended that UNIFIL's mandate be extended for another six months, until 31 January 2002.

Communication. In a 26 July letter to the Security Council President [S/2001/734], Lebanon said that the request to the Secretary-General to put forward an idea for the reconfiguration of UNIFIL as merely an observer mission should be abandoned. It regarded that request as incompatible with UNIFIL's original mission, as defined by Council resolutions 425(1978) and 426(1978) [YUN 1978, p. 312].

SECURITY COUNCIL ACTION (July)

On 31 July [meeting 4354], the Security Council unanimously adopted **resolution 1365(2001)**. The draft [S/2001/748] was prepared in consultations among Council members.

The Security Council,

Recalling all its previous resolutions on Lebanon, in particular resolutions 425(1978) and 426(1978) of 19 March 1978, 1310(2000) of 27 July 2000 and 1337(2001) of 30 January 2001, as well as the statements of its President on the situation in Lebanon, in particular the statement of 18 June 2000 (S/PRST/2000/21),

Recalling further the letter from its President to the Secretary-General of 18 May 2001,

Recalling also the Secretary-General's conclusion that, as of 16 June 2000, Israel had withdrawn its forces from Lebanon in accordance with resolution 425(1978) and met the requirements defined in the Secretary-General's report of 22 May 2000, as well as the Secretary-General's conclusion that the United Nations Interim Force in Lebanon had essentially completed two of the three parts of its mandate, focusing now on the remaining task of restoring international peace and security,

Emphasizing the interim nature of the Force,

Recalling its resolution 1308(2000) of 17 July 2000,

Recalling further the relevant principles contained in the Convention on the Safety of United Nations and Associated Personnel adopted on 9 December 1994,

Responding to the request of the Government of Lebanon, as stated in the letter from its Permanent Representative to the United Nations of 9 July 2001 to the Secretary-General,

1. *Welcomes* the report of the Secretary-General on the United Nations Interim Force in Lebanon of 20 July 2001, and endorses his observations and recommendations;

2. *Decides* to extend the present mandate of the Force, as recommended by the Secretary-General, for a further period of six months, until 31 January 2002;

3. *Requests* the Secretary-General to continue to take the necessary measures to implement the reconfiguration and redeployment of the Force as outlined in his report and in accordance with the letter of the President of the Security Council of 18 May 2001 in the light of developments on the ground and in consultation with the Government of Lebanon and the troop-contributing countries;

4. *Reiterates* its strong support for the territorial integrity, sovereignty and political independence of Lebanon within its internationally recognized boundaries;

5. *Calls upon* the Government of Lebanon to take more steps to ensure the return of its effective authority throughout the south, including the deployment of Lebanese armed forces;

6. *Calls upon the parties to ensure* the Force is accorded full freedom of movement in the discharge of its mandate throughout its area of operation;

7. *Encourages* the Government of Lebanon to ensure a calm environment throughout the south;

8. *Reiterates its call* on the parties to continue to fulfil the commitments they have given to respect fully the withdrawal line identified by the United Nations, as set out in the Secretary-General's report of 16 June 2000, to exercise utmost restraint and to cooperate fully with the United Nations and the Force;

9. *Condemns* all acts of violence, expresses great concern about the serious breaches and the air, sea and land violations of the withdrawal line, and urges the parties to put an end to them and to respect the safety of the personnel of the Force;

10. *Supports* the continued efforts of the Force to maintain the ceasefire along the withdrawal line through mobile patrols and observation from fixed positions and through close contacts with the parties to correct violations, resolve incidents and prevent the escalation of incidents;

11. *Welcomes* the continued contribution of the Force to operational demining, encourages further assistance in mine action by the United Nations to the Government of Lebanon in support of both the continued development of its national mine action capacity and emergency demining activities in the south, commends donor countries for supporting these efforts through financial and in-kind contributions, and stresses the necessity to provide the Government of Lebanon and the Force with any additional maps and records on the location of mines;

12. *Requests* the Secretary-General to continue consultations with the Government of Lebanon and other parties directly concerned on the implementation of the present resolution;

13. *Looks forward* to the early fulfilment of the mandate of the Force;

14. *Requests* the Secretary-General, following appropriate consultations, including with the Government of Lebanon and the troop-contributing countries, to submit to the Council before the end of the present mandate a comprehensive report on the activities of the Force, taking into account its possible reconfiguration to an observer mission in the light of developments on the ground and on the tasks carried out by the United Nations Truce Supervision Organization;

15. *Stresses* the importance of, and the need to achieve, a comprehensive, just and lasting peace in the Middle East, based on all its relevant resolutions including its resolution 242(1967) of 22 November 1967 and 338(1973) of 22 October 1973.

Further developments. In a report on developments during the second half of 2001 [S/2002/55], the Secretary-General said that the general situation in south Lebanon continued to be stable, with the exception of tensions and breaches of the Blue Line in the Shab'a farms area. There was a decrease in the number of ground violations of the Line, but Israeli air violations continued on an almost daily basis. Local administration in the south was further strengthened, linked in large part to the successful municipal elections held in southern Lebanon in early September, which were marked by high voter turnout. As the Lebanese Government continued to refuse to deploy its troops along the Blue Line, Hizbullah increased its visible presence through its network of mobile and fixed positions. The United Nations facilitated international mine-action assistance to Lebanon under the supervision of the Secretary-General's Personal Representative and in collaboration with the United Nations Development Programme (UNDP). Concern over the number of mines and unexploded ordnance in southern Lebanon took on a new dimension in December when IDF turned over to UNIFIL a substantial amount of information on the presence of additional minefields in the area, most within a short distance of the Blue Line. Progress was achieved in discussions between the United Nations and Israel on issues connected to UNIFIL's videotapes of events related to the abduction by Hizbullah of three Israeli soldiers in October 2000 [YUN 2000, p. 471]. UNDP continued to lead the efforts of the UN system in working with the Lebanese authorities for the development and rehabilitation of the south.

Financing

Reports of Secretary-General and ACABQ (February and April). On 1 February, the Secretary-General submitted the financial performance report of UNIFIL for the period 1 July 1999 to 30 June 2000 [A/55/757]. Expenditures for the period totalled $149,475,700 gross ($146,146,100 net), excluding budgeted voluntary contributions in kind of $135,000, resulting in an overrun of $571,000 gross ($1,270,800 net) against the amount of $148,904,683 gross ($144,875,283 net) appropriated by the General Assembly in resolution 53/227 [YUN 1999, p. 448].

On 20 February [A/55/482/Add.1], the Secretary-General submitted the revised budget for UNIFIL for the period 1 July 2000 to 30 June 2001 in the amount of $207,154,194 gross ($201,981,841 net), exclusive of budgeted voluntary contributions in kind amounting to $180,000. The amount represented a $26,437,900 reduction as compared to the approved gross budget allocated in 2000 by Assembly resolutions 54/267 [YUN 2000, p. 472] and 55/180 A [ibid., p. 474]. The revised budget was based on the fact that the budgeted deployment of two battalions, as envisaged by Assembly resolution 55/180 A, did not take place, and that the Security Council, in resolution 1337(2001) (see p. 452), had called for the

reduction of UNIFIL to its previous strength, before its augmentation to some 4,500 troops in 2000.

The comments and recommendations of ACABQ were contained in a 4 April report [A/55/885] on UNIFIL's financial performance for the period from 1 July 1999 to 30 June 2000, and in a 6 April report [A/55/874] on the financing of UN peacekeeping operations.

On 14 June [meeting 103], the General Assembly, on the recommendation of the Fifth (Administrative and Budgetary) Committee [A/55/681/Add.1], adopted **resolution 55/180 B** by recorded vote (115-3) [agenda item 138 *(b)*].

Financing of the United Nations Interim Force in Lebanon

The General Assembly,

Having considered the reports of the Secretary-General on the financing of the United Nations Interim Force in Lebanon and the related reports of the Advisory Committee on Administrative and Budgetary Questions,

Bearing in mind Security Council resolution 425 (1978) of 19 March 1978, by which the Council established the United Nations Interim Force in Lebanon, and the subsequent resolutions by which the Council extended the mandate of the Force, the latest of which was resolution 1337(2001) of 30 January 2001,

Recalling its resolutions S-8/2 of 21 April 1978 on the financing of the Force and its subsequent resolutions thereon, the latest of which was resolution 55/180 A of 19 December 2000,

Reaffirming its resolutions 51/233 of 13 June 1997, 52/237 of 26 June 1998, 53/227 of 8 June 1999, 54/267 of 15 June 2000 and 55/180 A,

Reaffirming also the general principles underlying the financing of United Nations peacekeeping operations, as stated in General Assembly resolutions 1874 (S-IV) of 27 June 1963, 3101(XXVIII) of 11 December 1973 and 55/235 of 23 December 2000,

Noting with appreciation that voluntary contributions have been made to the Force,

Mindful of the fact that it is essential to provide the Force with the necessary financial resources to enable it to fulfil its responsibilities under the relevant resolutions of the Security Council,

Concerned that the Secretary-General continues to face difficulties in meeting the obligations of the Force on a current basis, including reimbursement to current and former troop-contributing States,

Concerned also that the surplus balances in the Special Account for the United Nations Interim Force in Lebanon have been used to meet expenses of the Force in order to compensate for the lack of income resulting from non-payment and late payment by Member States of their contributions,

1. *Reaffirms* its resolution 49/233 A of 23 December 1994, in particular those paragraphs regarding the peacekeeping budgetary cycles, which should be adhered to in the future budgetary process, where possible;

2. *Expresses its deep concern* that Israel did not comply with its resolutions 51/233, 52/237, 53/227, 54/267 and 55/180 A;

3. *Stresses once again* that Israel should strictly abide by its resolutions 51/233, 52/237, 53/227, 54/267 and 55/180 A;

4. *Takes note* of the status of contributions to the United Nations Interim Force in Lebanon as at 30 April 2001, including the contributions outstanding in the amount of 124.5 million United States dollars, representing 3.9 per cent of the total assessed contributions from the inception of the Force to the period ending 31 January 2001, notes that some 20 per cent of the Member States have paid their assessed contributions in full, and urges all other Member States concerned, in particular those in arrears, to ensure payment of their outstanding assessed contributions;

5. *Expresses its appreciation* to those Member States which have paid their assessed contributions in full;

6. *Expresses concern* about the financial situation with regard to peacekeeping activities, in particular as regards the reimbursements to troop contributors that bear additional burdens owing to overdue payments by Member States of their assessments;

7. *Urges* all other Member States to make every possible effort to ensure payment of their assessed contributions to the Force in full and on time;

8. *Expresses concern* at the delay experienced by the Secretary-General in deploying and providing adequate resources to some recent peacekeeping missions, in particular those in Africa;

9. *Emphasizes* that all future and existing peacekeeping missions shall be given equal and non-discriminatory treatment in respect of financial and administrative arrangements;

10. *Also emphasizes* that all peacekeeping missions shall be provided with adequate resources for the effective and efficient discharge of their respective mandates;

11. *Reiterates its request* to the Secretary-General to make the fullest possible use of facilities and equipment at the United Nations Logistics Base at Brindisi, Italy, in order to minimize the costs of procurement for the Force;

12. *Endorses* the conclusions and recommendations contained in the reports of the Advisory Committee on Administrative and Budgetary Questions, and requests the Secretary-General to ensure full implementation;

13. *Requests* the Secretary-General to take all necessary action to ensure that the Force is administered with a maximum of efficiency and economy;

14. *Also requests* the Secretary-General, in order to reduce the cost of employing General Service staff, to continue efforts to recruit local staff for the Force against General Service posts, commensurate with the requirements of the Force;

15. *Reiterates its request* to the Secretary-General to take the necessary measures to ensure the full implementation of paragraph 8 of General Assembly resolution 51/233, paragraph 5 of its resolution 52/237, paragraph 11 of its resolution 53/227, paragraph 14 of its resolution 54/267 and paragraph 14 of its resolution 55/180 A, stresses once again that Israel shall pay the amount of 1,284,633 dollars resulting from the incident at Qana on 18 April 1996, and requests the

Secretary-General to report on this matter to the Assembly during the main part of its fifty-sixth session;

16. *Decides* to reduce the appropriation provided by the General Assembly in its resolutions 54/267 and 55/180 A from the amount of 233,592,094 dollars gross (228,191,141 dollars net), inclusive of the amount of 6,967,059 dollars gross (5,895,590 dollars net) for the support account for peacekeeping operations and the amount of 1,089,216 dollars gross (969,161 dollars net) for the United Nations Logistics Base for the maintenance and expansion of the Force for the period from 1 July 2000 to 30 June 2001, to the amount of 207,154,194 dollars gross (201,981,841 dollars net), inclusive of the amount of 6,967,059 dollars gross (5,895,590 dollars net) for the support account and the amount of 1,089,216 dollars gross (969,161 dollars net) for the Logistics Base;

17. *Decides also* to reduce the apportionment provided by the General Assembly in its resolutions 54/267 and 55/180 A for the period from 1 February to 30 June 2001 from the amount of 97,330,038 dollars gross (95,079,645 dollars net) to the amount of 70,892,138 dollars gross (68,870,345 dollars net), taking into account the amount of 194,660,080 dollars gross (190,159,283 dollars net) already apportioned for the period from 1 July 2000 to 30 April 2001;

18. *Decides further* that, in accordance with the provisions of its resolution 973(X) of 15 December 1955, there shall be set off against the apportionment among Member States, as provided for in paragraph 17 above, their respective share in the Tax Equalization Fund of the estimated reduced staff assessment income of 2,021,793 dollars approved for the Force for the period from 1 February to 30 June 2001;

19. *Authorizes* the Secretary-General to enter into commitments in the amount of 99,548,960 dollars gross (97,558,500 dollars net) for the maintenance of the Force for the period from 1 July to 31 December 2001, and decides to appropriate the amount of 6,021,721 dollars gross (5,284,652 dollars net) for the support account and the amount of 629,045 dollars gross (564,879 dollars net) for the United Nations Logistics Base, representing the prorated share of the Force in the support account and Logistics Base requirements for the period from 1 July 2001 to 30 June 2002;

20. *Decides* to apportion among Member States the amount of 16,591,493 dollars gross (16,259,750 dollars net) for the period from 1 to 31 July 2001 in accordance with the levels set out in its resolution 55/235, as adjusted by the General Assembly in its resolution 55/236 of 23 December 2000, and taking into account the scale of assessments for the year 2001, as set out in its resolution 55/5 B of 23 December 2000;

21. *Decides also* that, in accordance with the provisions of its resolution 973(X), there shall be set off against the apportionment among Member States, as provided for in paragraph 20 above, their respective share in the Tax Equalization Fund of the estimated staff assessment income of 331,743 dollars approved for the Force for the period from 1 to 31 July 2001;

22. *Decides further* to apportion among Member States the amount of 82,957,467 dollars gross (81,298,750 dollars net) for the period from 1 August to 31 December 2001, at a monthly rate of 16,591,493 dollars gross (16,259,750 dollars net) in accordance with

paragraph 20 above, and taking into account the scale of assessments for the year 2001, as set out in its resolution 55/5 B, subject to the decision of the Security Council to extend the mandate of the Force beyond 31 July 2001;

23. *Decides* that, in accordance with the provisions of its resolution 973(X), there shall be set off against the apportionment among Member States, as provided for in paragraph 22 above, their respective share in the Tax Equalization Fund of the estimated staff assessment income of 1,658,717 dollars approved for the Force for the period from 1 August to 31 December 2001;

24. *Decides also* to apportion among Member States the amount of 6,021,721 dollars gross (5,284,652 dollars net) for the support account and the amount of 629,045 dollars gross (564,879 dollars net) for the United Nations Logistics Base for the period from 1 July 2001 to 30 June 2002 in accordance with paragraph 20 above, and taking into account the scale of assessments for the years 2001 and 2002, as set out in its resolution 55/5 B, the scale of assessments for the year 2001 to be applied against a portion thereof, that is, 3,010,861 dollars gross (2,642,326 dollars net) for the support account and 314,523 dollars gross (282,440 dollars net) for the Logistics Base for the period from 1 July to 31 December 2001, and the scale of assessments for the year 2002 to be applied against the balance, that is, 3,010,860 dollars gross (2,642,326 dollars net) for the support account and 314,522 dollars gross (282,439 dollars net) for the Logistics Base for the period from 1 January to 30 June 2002;

25. *Decides further* that, in accordance with the provisions of its resolution 973(X), there shall be set off against the apportionment among Member States, as provided for in paragraph 24 above, their respective share in the Tax Equalization Fund of the estimated staff assessment income of 737,069 dollars for the support account and 64,166 dollars for the United Nations Logistics Base approved for the period from 1 July 2001 to 30 June 2002, 368,535 dollars for the support account and 32,083 dollars for the Logistics Base being amounts pertaining to the period from 1 July to 31 December 2001 and the balance, that is, 368,534 dollars, for the support account and 32,083 dollars for the Logistics Base pertaining to the period from 1 January to 30 June 2002;

26. *Decides* that, for Member States that have fulfilled their financial obligations to the Force, there shall be set off against the apportionment, as provided for in paragraph 20 above, their respective share of the remaining balance of 186,252 dollars in the reserve account for third-party liability insurance of helicopters for the Force, in accordance with the composition of groups set out in paragraphs 3 and 4 of General Assembly resolution 43/232 of 1 March 1989, as adjusted by the Assembly in subsequent relevant resolutions and decisions, for the ad hoc apportionment of peacekeeping appropriations, the latest of which were its resolution 52/230 of 31 March 1998 and its decisions 54/456 to 54/458 of 23 December 1999 for the period 1998-2000, and taking into account the scale of assessments for the year 2000, as set out in its resolutions 52/215 A of 22 December 1997 and 54/237 A of 23 December 1999;

27. *Decides also* that, for Member States that have not fulfilled their financial obligations to the Force, their share of the remaining balance of 186,252 dollars in the reserve account for third-party liability insurance of helicopters for the Force shall be set off against their outstanding obligations in accordance with the scheme set out in paragraph 26 above;

28. *Takes note* of additional requirements in the amount of 571,000 dollars gross (1,270,800 dollars net) for the operation of the Force for the period ending 30 June 2000, and authorizes the Secretary-General to utilize credits in an equal amount arising from the cancellation of obligations pertaining to the same period to meet the additional requirements;

29. *Emphasizes* that no peacekeeping mission shall be financed by borrowing funds from other active peacekeeping missions;

30. *Encourages* the Secretary-General to continue to take additional measures to ensure the safety and security of all personnel under the auspices of the United Nations participating in the Force;

31. *Invites* voluntary contributions to the Force in cash and in the form of services and supplies acceptable to the Secretary-General, to be administered, as appropriate, in accordance with the procedure and practices established by the General Assembly;

32. *Decides* to include in the provisional agenda of its fifty-sixth session, under the item entitled "Financing of the United Nations peacekeeping forces in the Middle East", the sub-item entitled "United Nations Interim Force in Lebanon".

RECORDED VOTE ON RESOLUTION 55/180 B:

In favour: Algeria, Andorra, Argentina, Armenia, Australia, Austria, Azerbaijan, Bahamas, Bahrain, Bangladesh, Belgium, Belize, Benin, Bolivia, Brazil, Brunei Darussalam, Bulgaria, Burkina Faso, Cambodia, Canada, Cape Verde, Chile, China, Colombia, Comoros, Congo, Côte d'Ivoire, Croatia, Cuba, Cyprus, Czech Republic, Denmark, Dominican Republic, Ecuador, Egypt, Estonia, Ethiopia, Fiji, Finland, France, Gabon, Germany, Ghana, Greece, Guatemala, Guyana, Haiti, Hungary, Iceland, India, Indonesia, Ireland, Italy, Japan, Jordan, Kazakhstan, Kuwait, Lao People's Democratic Republic, Lebanon, Libyan Arab Jamahiriya, Liechtenstein, Lithuania, Luxembourg, Malaysia, Maldives, Malta, Mauritania, Mauritius, Mexico, Monaco, Mongolia, Morocco, Myanmar, Nepal, Netherlands, New Zealand, Nicaragua, Nigeria, Norway, Oman, Pakistan, Panama, Peru, Philippines, Poland, Portugal, Qatar, Republic of Korea, Romania, Russian Federation, San Marino, Saudi Arabia, Senegal, Singapore, Slovakia, Slovenia, South Africa, Spain, Sri Lanka, Sweden, Syrian Arab Republic, Thailand, Tonga, Tunisia, Turkey, Uganda, Ukraine, United Arab Emirates, United Kingdom, United Republic of Tanzania, Uruguay, Venezuela, Viet Nam, Yemen, Zambia.

Against: Israel, Marshall Islands, United States.

The Assembly and the Committee each had adopted the fourth preambular paragraph and operative paragraphs 2, 3 and 15 by a single recorded vote of, respectively, 70 to 3, with 42 abstentions, and 69 to 2, with 40 abstentions.

Speaking after the vote in the Assembly, Israel said that it had voted against the text because of the reference to the April 1996 incident in Qana, Lebanon [YUN 1996, p. 429]. There was no precedent whatsoever for a particular Member State bearing sole financial responsibility for damage sustained by UN forces during peacekeeping operations. Such damages should be absorbed by the general budget for peacekeeping operations, in accordance with the principle of collective responsibility. Israel was also concerned about the political manipulation of the Fifth Committee and called on Member States to drop the annual four paragraphs regarding Qana that were dictated by Lebanon.

Speaking in exercise of the right of reply, Lebanon said that all additional paragraphs to the resolution called for by the Group of 77 developing countries were purely financial and administrative in nature and contained no political wording whatsoever. Israel should not leap into political discourse, but should implement the Assembly's resolutions calling on it to pay compensation for the damages it caused in 1996 to the compound of the international forces in Qana. The Group of 77 was calling for reparations and compensation for the United Nations, not for Lebanon.

Reports of Secretary-General and ACABQ (October). By a 3 October report [A/56/431 & Corr.1], the Secretary-General submitted the budget of UNIFIL for the period 1 July 2001 to 30 June 2002 in the amount of $136,816,100 gross ($132,983,100 net), inclusive of budgeted voluntary contributions in kind amounting to $201,200.

The comments and recommendations of ACABQ were contained in a 29 October report [A/56/510 & Corr.1].

GENERAL ASSEMBLY ACTION (December)

On 21 December [meeting 91], the General Assembly, on the recommendation of the Fifth Committee [A/56/722], adopted **resolution 56/214** by recorded vote (123-2-2) [agenda item 134 (b)].

Financing of the United Nations Interim Force in Lebanon

The General Assembly,

Having considered the report of the Secretary-General on the financing of the United Nations Interim Force in Lebanon for the period from 1 July 2001 to 30 June 2002 and the related report of the Advisory Committee on Administrative and Budgetary Questions,

Bearing in mind Security Council resolution 425 (1978) of 19 March 1978, by which the Council established the United Nations Interim Force in Lebanon, and the subsequent resolutions by which the Council extended the mandate of the Force, the most recent of which was resolution 1365(2001) of 31 July 2001,

Recalling its resolution S-8/2 of 21 April 1978 on the financing of the Force and its subsequent resolutions thereon, the most recent of which was resolution 55/180 B of 14 June 2001,

Reaffirming its resolutions 51/233 of 13 June 1997, 52/237 of 26 June 1998, 53/227 of 8 June 1999, 54/267 of 15 June 2000, 55/180 A of 19 December 2000 and 55/180 B,

Reaffirming also the general principles underlying the financing of United Nations peacekeeping operations, as stated in General Assembly resolutions 1874 (S-IV) of 27 June 1963, 3101(XXVIII) of 11 December 1973 and 55/235 of 23 December 2000,

Noting with appreciation that voluntary contributions have been made to the Force,

Mindful of the fact that it is essential to provide the Force with the necessary financial resources to enable it to fulfil its responsibilities under the relevant resolutions of the Security Council,

Concerned that the Secretary-General continues to face difficulties in meeting the obligations of the Force on a current basis, including reimbursement to current and former troop-contributing States,

Concerned also that the surplus balances in the Special Account for the United Nations Interim Force in Lebanon have been used to meet expenses of the Force in order to compensate for the lack of income resulting from non-payment and late payment by Member States of their contributions,

1. *Takes note* of the status of contributions to the United Nations Interim Force in Lebanon as at 15 November 2001, including the contributions outstanding in the amount of 179.4 million United States dollars, representing 4 per cent of the total assessed contributions from the inception of the Force up to the period ending 31 December 2001, notes that some 15.5 per cent of the Member States have paid their assessed contributions in full, and urges all other Member States concerned, in particular those in arrears, to ensure payment of their outstanding assessed contributions;

2. *Expresses its appreciation* to those Member States that have paid their assessed contributions in full and on time, and urges all other Member States to make every possible effort to ensure payment of their assessed contributions to the Force in full and on time;

3. *Expresses its deep concern* that Israel did not comply with General Assembly resolutions 51/233, 52/237, 53/227, 54/267, 55/180 A and 55/180 B;

4. *Stresses once again* that Israel should strictly abide by General Assembly resolutions 51/233, 52/237, 53/227, 54/267, 55/180 A and 55/180 B;

5. *Expresses concern* about the financial situation with regard to peacekeeping activities, in particular as regards the reimbursements to troop contributors that bear additional burdens owing to overdue payments by Member States of their assessments;

6. *Also expresses concern* at the delay experienced by the Secretary-General in deploying and providing adequate resources to some recent peacekeeping missions, in particular those in Africa;

7. *Emphasizes* that all future and existing peacekeeping missions shall be given equal and non-discriminatory treatment in respect of financial and administrative arrangements;

8. *Also emphasizes* that all peacekeeping missions shall be provided with adequate resources for the effective and efficient discharge of their respective mandates;

9. *Reiterates its request* to the Secretary-General to make the fullest possible use of facilities and equipment at the United Nations Logistics Base at Brindisi, Italy, in order to minimize the costs of procurement for the Force;

10. *Takes note* of paragraph 11 of, and endorses the remaining conclusions and recommendations contained in, the report of the Advisory Committee on Administrative and Budgetary Questions, and requests the Secretary-General to ensure full implementation;

11. *Requests* the Secretary-General to take all necessary action to ensure that the Force is administered with a maximum of efficiency and economy;

12. *Also requests* the Secretary-General, in order to reduce the cost of employing General Service staff, to continue efforts to recruit local staff for the Force against General Service posts, commensurate with the requirements of the Force;

13. *Reiterates its request* to the Secretary-General to take the necessary measures to ensure the full implementation of paragraph 8 of its resolution 51/233, paragraph 5 of its resolution 52/237, paragraph 11 of its resolution 53/227, paragraph 14 of its resolution 54/267, paragraph 14 of its resolution 55/180 A and paragraph 15 of its resolution 55/180 B, stresses once again that Israel shall pay the amount of 1,284,633 dollars resulting from the incident at Qana on 18 April 1996, and requests the Secretary-General to report on this matter to the Assembly at its resumed fifty-sixth session;

14. *Decides* to appropriate the amount of 137,257,440 dollars gross (133,375,991 dollars net) for the maintenance of the Force for the twelve-month period from 1 July 2001 to 30 June 2002, inclusive of the amount of 642,540 dollars gross (594,091 dollars net) for the support account for peacekeeping operations, in addition to the amount of 6,021,721 dollars gross (5,284,652 dollars net) already appropriated for the support account for peacekeeping operations and the amount of 629,045 dollars gross (564,879 dollars net) already appropriated for the United Nations Logistics Base in its resolution 55/180 B, and inclusive of the amount of 99,548,960 dollars gross (97,558,500 dollars net) authorized in its resolution 55/180 B;

15. *Decides also*, taking into account the amount of 99,548,960 dollars gross (97,558,500 dollars net) already apportioned for the period from 1 July to 31 December 2001 and the amount of 6,650,766 dollars gross (5,849,531 dollars net) already apportioned for the period from 1 July 2001 to 30 June 2002 in accordance with the provisions of its resolution 55/180 B, to apportion among Member States the amount of 6,820,197 dollars gross (6,464,658 dollars net) for the period from 1 to 31 January 2002 in accordance with the levels set out in its resolution 55/235, as adjusted in its resolution 55/236 of 23 December 2000, and taking into account the scale of assessments for the year 2002, as set out in its resolution 55/5 B of 23 December 2000;

16. *Decides further* that, in accordance with the provisions of its resolution 973(X) of 15 December 1955, there shall be set off against the apportionment among Member States, as provided for in paragraph 15 above, their respective share in the Tax Equalization Fund of the estimated additional staff assessment income of 355,539 dollars approved for the Force for the period from 1 to 31 January 2002;

17. *Decides* to apportion among Member States the amount of 30,888,283 dollars gross (29,352,833 dollars net) for the period from 1 February to 30 June 2002, at a monthly rate of 6,177,656 dollars gross (5,870,566 dollars net) in accordance with the scheme set out in the present resolution and taking into account the scale of assessments for the year 2002, as set out in its resolution 55/5 B, subject to the decision of the Security Council to extend the mandate of the Force beyond 31 January 2002;

18. *Decides also* that, in accordance with the provisions of its resolution 973(X), there shall be set off against the apportionment among Member States, as provided for in paragraph 17 above, their respective share in the Tax Equalization Fund of the estimated additional staff assessment income of 1,535,450 dollars net approved for the Force for the period from 1 February to 30 June 2002;

19. *Emphasizes* that no peacekeeping mission shall be financed by borrowing funds from other active peacekeeping missions;

20. *Encourages* the Secretary-General to continue to take additional measures to ensure the safety and security of all personnel under the auspices of the United Nations participating in the Force;

21. *Invites* voluntary contributions to the Force in cash and in the form of services and supplies acceptable to the Secretary-General, to be administered, as appropriate, in accordance with the procedure and practices established by the General Assembly;

22. *Decides* to keep under review during its fifty-sixth session, under the item entitled "Financing of the United Nations peacekeeping forces in the Middle East", the sub-item entitled "United Nations Interim Force in Lebanon".

RECORDED VOTE ON RESOLUTION 56/214:

In favour: Albania, Algeria, Andorra, Argentina, Armenia, Australia, Austria, Azerbaijan, Bahamas, Bahrain, Bangladesh, Belgium, Belize, Benin, Bhutan, Bolivia, Bosnia and Herzegovina, Botswana, Brazil, Brunei Darussalam, Bulgaria, Burkina Faso, Cambodia, Canada, Cape Verde, Chile, China, Colombia, Costa Rica, Côte d'Ivoire, Croatia, Cuba, Cyprus, Czech Republic, Democratic People's Republic of Korea, Denmark, Djibouti, Ecuador, Egypt, El Salvador, Equatorial Guinea, Estonia, Ethiopia, Fiji, Finland, France, Gabon, Georgia, Germany, Ghana, Greece, Guatemala, Hungary, Iceland, India, Indonesia, Ireland, Italy, Japan, Jordan, Kazakhstan, Kuwait, Lao People's Democratic Republic, Latvia, Lebanon, Libyan Arab Jamahiriya, Liechtenstein, Lithuania, Luxembourg, Madagascar, Malaysia, Maldives, Malta, Mauritius, Mexico, Monaco, Morocco, Myanmar, Namibia, Nepal, Netherlands, New Zealand, Nicaragua, Nigeria, Norway, Oman, Pakistan, Panama, Paraguay, Peru, Philippines, Poland, Portugal, Qatar, Republic of Korea, Romania, Russian Federation, San Marino, Saudi Arabia, Senegal, Singapore, Slovakia, Slovenia, South Africa, Spain, Sri Lanka, Sudan, Sweden, Syrian Arab Republic, Thailand, The former Yugoslav Republic of Macedonia, Togo, Tunisia, Turkey, Ukraine, United Arab Emirates, United Kingdom, United Republic of Tanzania, Uruguay, Venezuela, Yemen, Yugoslavia, Zambia.

Against: Israel, United States.

Abstaining: Papua New Guinea, Tuvalu.

The Assembly and the Committee each had adopted the fourth preambular paragraph and operative paragraphs 3, 4 and 13 by a single recorded vote of, respectively, 68 to 2, with 54 abstentions, and 69 to 2, with 40 abstentions.

Speaking before the vote in the Assembly, Israel said that the draft resolution violated the principle of collective responsibility, which dictated that costs resulting from peacekeeping operations were to be shared equally among Member States.

Speaking after the vote, Lebanon said that the principle of collective responsibility did not contradict the principle of international responsibility, by which any State that caused damage or harm to another State or to an international organization had to pay reparations.

On 24 December, the Assembly decided that the item on financing of the UN peacekeeping forces in the Middle East would remain for consideration at the resumed fifty-sixth (2002) session (**decision 56/464**) and that the Fifth Committee would continue consideration of UNIFIL's financing at that session (**decision 56/458**).

Syrian Arab Republic

In 2001, the General Assembly again called for Israel's withdrawal from the Golan Heights in the Syrian Arab Republic, which it had occupied since 1967. The area was effectively annexed by Israel when it extended its laws, jurisdiction and administration to the territory towards the end of 1981 [YUN 1981, p. 309].

Israeli policies and measures affecting the human rights of the population in the Golan Heights and other occupied territories were monitored by the Special Committee to Investigate Israeli Practices Affecting the Human Rights of the Palestinian People and Other Arabs of the Occupied Territories (Committee on Israeli Practices) and were the subject of resolutions adopted by the Commission on Human Rights (see PART TWO, Chapter III) and the Assembly.

Committee on Israeli Practices. In its annual report [A/56/491], the Committee on Israeli Practices stated that it had visited Damascus and Quneitra province, which bordered the occupied area, where it received information from persons with personal knowledge of the occupied Syrian Arab Golan. Although the area did not experience the confrontations and violence that Gaza, the West Bank and East Jerusalem had witnessed during 2001, the economic and social conditions of the Arab population did not improve and the human rights situation continued to deteriorate. The problems of preserving the national identity of the Arab population, the expansion and increase in Israeli settlements and the privileged position of the settlers, economic hardships and the personal tragedies that afflicted families divided because of the occupation continued undiminished throughout the year.

Communications. On 18 May [A/56/79], Israel informed the Secretary-General of anti-Semitic statements made by the President of the Syrian Arab Republic, Bashar Al-Assad, at a welcoming ceremony in Damascus for Pope John Paul II and by senior Syrian officials on other occasions. Those allegations were denied by Syria on 14 June [A/56/94].

In a 29 May letter to the Secretary-General [A/55/957-S/2001/527], Syria stated that, on 2 May, two Israeli artillery shells had impacted south of Sayda village in Syrian territory.

On 16 July [A/56/185-S/2001/699], Syria informed the Secretary-General that Prime Minister Sharon, in a 10 July speech, had stated that increasing the Jewish population and bringing new residents into the Golan would transform settlement in that area into an irreversible reality.

Reports of Secretary-General. On 25 July [A/56/219], the Secretary-General reported that no reply had been received from Israel to his May request for information on steps taken or envisaged to implement General Assembly resolution 55/134 [YUN 2000, p. 478], which called on Israel to desist from changing the physical character, demographic composition, institutional structure and legal status of the Golan, and from its repressive measures against the population.

By a 17 October report [A/56/480], the Secretary-General transmitted replies received from five Member States, including Israel, in response to his request for information on steps taken or envisaged to implement Assembly resolution 55/51 [YUN 2000, p. 477], which dealt with Israeli policies in the Syrian territory occupied since 1967, and resolution 55/50 [ibid., p. 429], on the transfer by some States of their diplomatic missions to Jerusalem (see p. 418).

GENERAL ASSEMBLY ACTION

On 3 December [meeting 72], the General Assembly adopted **resolution 56/32** [draft: A/56/L.24 & Add.1] by recorded vote (90-5-54) [agenda item 42].

The Syrian Golan

The General Assembly,

Having considered the item entitled "The situation in the Middle East",

Taking note of the report of the Secretary-General,

Recalling Security Council resolution 497(1981) of 17 December 1981,

Reaffirming the fundamental principle of the inadmissibility of the acquisition of territory by force, in accordance with international law and the Charter of the United Nations,

Reaffirming once more the applicability of the Geneva Convention relative to the Protection of Civilian Persons in Time of War, of 12 August 1949, to the occupied Syrian Golan,

Deeply concerned that Israel has not withdrawn from the Syrian Golan, which has been under occupation since 1967, contrary to the relevant Security Council and General Assembly resolutions,

Stressing the illegality of the Israeli settlement construction and activities in the occupied Syrian Golan since 1967,

Noting with satisfaction the convening in Madrid on 30 October 1991 of the Peace Conference on the Middle East, on the basis of Security Council resolutions 242(1967) of 22 November 1967, 338(1973) of 22 October 1973 and 425(1978) of 19 March 1978 and the formula of land for peace,

Expressing grave concern over the halt in the peace process on the Syrian track, and expressing the hope that peace talks will soon resume from the point they had reached,

1. *Declares* that Israel has failed so far to comply with Security Council resolution 497(1981);

2. *Also declares* that the Israeli decision of 14 December 1981 to impose its laws, jurisdiction and administration on the occupied Syrian Golan is null and void and has no validity whatsoever, as confirmed by the Security Council in its resolution 497(1981), and calls upon Israel to rescind it;

3. *Reaffirms its determination* that all relevant provisions of the Regulations annexed to the Hague Convention of 1907, and the Geneva Convention relative to the Protection of Civilian Persons in Time of War, of 12 August 1949, continue to apply to the Syrian territory occupied by Israel since 1967, and calls upon the parties thereto to respect and ensure respect for their obligations under those instruments in all circumstances;

4. *Determines once more* that the continued occupation of the Syrian Golan and its de facto annexation constitute a stumbling block in the way of achieving a just, comprehensive and lasting peace in the region;

5. *Calls upon* Israel to resume the talks on the Syrian and Lebanese tracks and to respect the commitments and undertakings reached during the previous talks;

6. *Demands once more* that Israel withdraw from all the occupied Syrian Golan to the line of 4 June 1967 in implementation of the relevant Security Council resolutions;

7. *Calls upon* all the parties concerned, the co-sponsors of the peace process and the entire international community to exert all the necessary efforts to ensure the resumption of the peace process and its success by implementing Security Council resolutions 242(1967) and 338(1973);

8. *Requests* the Secretary-General to report to the General Assembly at its fifty-seventh session on the implementation of the present resolution.

RECORDED VOTE ON RESOLUTION 56/32:

In favour: Afghanistan, Algeria, Argentina, Armenia, Azerbaijan, Bahrain, Bangladesh, Barbados, Belarus, Belize, Bolivia, Botswana, Burkina Faso, Burundi, Cambodia, Cape Verde, Chad, Chile, China, Colombia, Comoros, Congo, Costa Rica, Cuba, Cyprus, Democratic People's Republic of Korea, Djibouti, Dominican Republic, Ecuador, Egypt, El Salvador, Equatorial Guinea, Eritrea, Ethiopia, Fiji, Ghana, Guyana, Honduras, India, Indonesia, Iran, Jamaica, Jordan, Kuwait, Lao People's Democratic Republic, Lebanon, Libyan Arab Jamahiriya, Madagascar, Malaysia, Maldives, Mali, Malta, Mauritania, Mauritius, Mexico, Mongolia, Morocco, Mozambique, Myanmar, Namibia, Nepal, Nigeria, Oman, Pakistan, Panama, Papua New Guinea, Philippines, Qatar, Russian Federation, Saint Lucia, Saudi Arabia, Senegal, Sierra Leone, Singapore, Sri Lanka, Sudan, Suriname, Syrian Arab Republic, Thailand, Togo, Trinidad and Tobago, Tunisia, Turkey, United Arab Emirates, United Republic of Tanzania, Venezuela, Viet Nam, Yemen, Zambia, Zimbabwe.

Against: Israel, Marshall Islands, Micronesia, Tuvalu, United States.

Abstaining: Andorra, Australia, Austria, Belgium, Benin, Brazil, Bulgaria, Canada, Croatia, Czech Republic, Denmark, Estonia, Finland, France, Georgia, Germany, Greece, Haiti, Iceland, Ireland, Italy, Japan, Kazakhstan, Kenya, Latvia, Liechtenstein, Lithuania, Luxembourg, Monaco, Nauru, Netherlands, New Zealand, Nicaragua, Norway, Paraguay, Peru, Poland, Portugal, Republic of Korea, Romania, San Marino, Slovakia, Slovenia, Solomon Islands, South Africa, Spain, Sweden, The former Yugoslav Republic of Macedonia, Tonga, Ukraine, United Kingdom, Uruguay, Vanuatu, Yugoslavia.

On 10 December [meeting 82], the Assembly, under the agenda item on the report of the Committee on Israeli Practices and on the Fourth Committee's recommendation [A/56/550], adopted **resolution 56/63** by recorded vote (147-2-3) [agenda item 88].

The occupied Syrian Golan

The General Assembly,

Having considered the reports of the Special Committee to Investigate Israeli Practices Affecting the Human Rights of the Palestinian People and Other Arabs of the Occupied Territories,

Deeply concerned that the Syrian Golan, occupied since 1967, has been under continued Israeli military occupation,

Recalling Security Council resolution 497(1981) of 17 December 1981,

Recalling also its previous relevant resolutions, the last of which was resolution 55/134 of 8 December 2000,

Having considered the report of the Secretary-General submitted in pursuance of resolution 55/134,

Recalling its previous relevant resolutions in which, inter alia, it called upon Israel to put an end to its occupation of the Arab territories,

Reaffirming once more the illegality of the decision of 14 December 1981 taken by Israel to impose its laws, jurisdiction and administration on the occupied Syrian Golan, which has resulted in the effective annexation of that territory,

Reaffirming that the acquisition of territory by force is inadmissible under international law, including the Charter of the United Nations,

Reaffirming also the applicability of the Geneva Convention relative to the Protection of Civilian Persons in Time of War, of 12 August 1949, to the occupied Syrian Golan,

Bearing in mind Security Council resolution 237 (1967) of 14 June 1967,

Welcoming the convening in Madrid of the Peace Conference on the Middle East on the basis of Security Council resolutions 242(1967) of 22 November 1967 and 338(1973) of 22 October 1973 aimed at the realization of a just, comprehensive and lasting peace, and expressing grave concern about the stalling of the peace process on all tracks,

1. *Calls upon* Israel, the occupying Power, to comply with the relevant resolutions on the occupied Syrian Golan, in particular Security Council resolution 497(1981), in which the Council, inter alia, decided that the Israeli decision to impose its laws, jurisdiction and administration on the occupied Syrian Golan was null and void and without international legal effect, and demanded that Israel, the occupying Power, rescind forthwith its decision;

2. *Also calls upon* Israel to desist from changing the physical character, demographic composition, institutional structure and legal status of the occupied Syrian Golan and in particular to desist from the establishment of settlements;

3. *Determines* that all legislative and administrative measures and actions taken or to be taken by Israel, the occupying Power, that purport to alter the character and legal status of the occupied Syrian Golan are null and void, constitute a flagrant violation of international law and of the Geneva Convention relative to the Protection of Civilian Persons in Time of War, of 12 August 1949, and have no legal effect;

4. *Calls upon* Israel to desist from imposing Israeli citizenship and Israeli identity cards on the Syrian citizens in the occupied Syrian Golan and from taking re-

pressive measures against the population of the occupied Syrian Golan;

5. *Deplores* the violations by Israel of the Geneva Convention relative to the Protection of Civilian Persons in Time of War, of 12 August 1949;

6. *Calls once again upon* Member States not to recognize any of the legislative or administrative measures and actions referred to above;

7. *Requests* the Secretary-General to report to the General Assembly at its fifty-seventh session on the implementation of the present resolution.

RECORDED VOTE ON RESOLUTION 56/63:

In favour: Algeria, Andorra, Angola, Antigua and Barbuda, Argentina, Armenia, Australia, Austria, Azerbaijan, Bahamas, Bahrain, Bangladesh, Barbados, Belarus, Belgium, Belize, Benin, Bhutan, Bolivia, Brazil, Brunei Darussalam, Bulgaria, Burkina Faso, Burundi, Cambodia, Canada, Cape Verde, Chile, China, Colombia, Comoros, Congo, Costa Rica, Côte d'Ivoire, Croatia, Cuba, Cyprus, Czech Republic, Democratic People's Republic of Korea, Denmark, Djibouti, Dominican Republic, Ecuador, Egypt, El Salvador, Equatorial Guinea, Eritrea, Estonia, Ethiopia, Fiji, Finland, France, Gabon, Georgia, Germany, Ghana, Greece, Grenada, Guatemala, Guinea, Guyana, Haiti, Honduras, Hungary, Iceland, India, Indonesia, Iran, Ireland, Italy, Jamaica, Japan, Jordan, Kazakhstan, Kuwait, Lao People's Democratic Republic, Latvia, Lebanon, Libyan Arab Jamahiriya, Liechtenstein, Lithuania, Luxembourg, Madagascar, Malaysia, Maldives, Mali, Malta, Mauritania, Mexico, Monaco, Mongolia, Morocco, Mozambique, Myanmar, Namibia, Nepal, Netherlands, New Zealand, Nigeria, Norway, Oman, Pakistan, Panama, Papua New Guinea, Paraguay, Peru, Philippines, Poland, Portugal, Qatar, Republic of Korea, Republic of Moldova, Romania, Russian Federation, Saint Lucia, San Marino, Saudi Arabia, Senegal, Seychelles, Sierra Leone, Singapore, Slovakia, Slovenia, Solomon Islands, South Africa, Spain, Sri Lanka, Sudan, Swaziland, Sweden, Syrian Arab Republic, Thailand, The former Yugoslav Republic of Macedonia, Togo, Trinidad and Tobago, Tunisia, Turkey, Ukraine, United Arab Emirates, United Kingdom, United Republic of Tanzania, Uruguay, Venezuela, Viet Nam, Yemen, Yugoslavia, Zambia.

Against: Israel, Marshall Islands.

Abstaining: Micronesia, Nicaragua, United States.

UNDOF

The mandate of the United Nations Disengagement Observer Force, established by Security Council resolution 350(1974) [YUN 1974, p. 205] to supervise the observance of the ceasefire between Israel and the Syrian Arab Republic in the Golan Heights area and ensure the separation of their forces, was renewed twice in 2001, in May and November, each time for a six-month period.

UNDOF maintained an area of separation, which was some 80 kilometres long and varied in width between approximately 10 kilometres in the centre to less than 1 kilometre in the extreme south. The area of separation was inhabited and policed by the Syrian authorities, and no military forces other than UNDOF were permitted within it.

Composition and deployment

As at 15 November, UNDOF comprised 1,056 troops from Austria (372), Canada (188), Japan (45), Poland (356) and Slovakia (95). It was assisted by 78 UNTSO military observers. Major General Bo Wranker (Sweden) continued as Force Commander. The Force was entirely deployed within and close to the area of separation, with two base camps, 44 permanently manned positions and 11 observation posts. UNDOF's

headquarters was located at Camp Faouar and an office was maintained in Damascus.

The Austrian battalion, which included a Slovak company, was deployed in the northern part of the area of separation, and the Polish battalion was deployed in the southern part. Both battalions conducted mine-clearing operations. The Canadian and Japanese logistic units, based in Camp Ziouani, with a detachment in Camp Faouar, performed second-line general transport, control and management of goods received by the Force and maintained heavy equipment.

Activities

UNDOF continued in 2001 to supervise the area of separation between Israeli and Syrian troops in the Golan Heights, to ensure that no military forces of either party were deployed there, by means of fixed positions and patrols. The Force, accompanied by liaison officers from the party concerned, carried out fortnightly inspections of equipment and force levels in the areas of limitation. As in the past, both sides denied inspection teams access to some of their positions and imposed some restrictions on the Force's freedom of movement. Israel, however, allowed inspections to resume in the Shab'a farms area (Area 6) in the second half of the year (see below).

UNDOF assisted the International Committee of the Red Cross with facilities for mail and the passage of persons through the area of separation. Within the means available, medical treatment was provided to the local population on request.

Reports of Secretary-General. The Secretary-General reported to the Security Council on UNDOF activities between 22 November 2000 and 18 May 2001 [S/2001/499] and between 19 May and 15 November 2001 [S/2001/1079]. Both reports noted that UNDOF continued to perform its functions effectively, with the cooperation of the parties. In general, the ceasefire in the Israel-Syria sector was maintained without serious incident and the UNDOF area of operation remained calm, except in the Shab'a farms area. Mines, especially in the area of separation, continued to pose a threat to UNDOF personnel and local inhabitants. Through the Minefield Security Programme, numerous known as well as previously unidentified minefields in the area of separation were marked.

UNDOF undertook a comprehensive review of its facilities, support structure and deployment and initiated a modernization programme to increase its monitoring and observation effectiveness. Key components of that programme were the full integration of the military and civilian administrative and logistics components of the Force, replacement of outdated facilities, consolidation of some positions in the area of separation and mobility enhancement.

The Secretary-General observed that the situation in the Israel-Syria sector remained generally quiet. However, the situation in the Middle East continued to be potentially dangerous and was likely to remain so unless and until a comprehensive settlement covering all aspects of the Middle East problem could be reached. He hoped that determined efforts would be made by all concerned to tackle the problem in all its aspects, with a view to arriving at a just and durable peace settlement, as called for by Council resolution 338(1973) [YUN 1973, p. 213]. Stating that he considered the Force's continued presence in the area to be essential, the Secretary-General, with the agreement of both Israel and Syria, recommended that UNDOF's mandate be extended for a further six months, until 30 November 2001 in the first instance and 31 May 2002 in the second.

SECURITY COUNCIL ACTION

On 30 May [meeting 4322], the Security Council unanimously adopted **resolution 1351(2001)**. The draft [S/2001/523] was prepared in consultations among Council members.

The Security Council,

Having considered the report of the Secretary-General on the United Nations Disengagement Observer Force of 18 May 2001, and also reaffirming its resolution 1308(2000) of 17 July 2000,

1. *Calls upon* the parties concerned to implement immediately its resolution 338(1973) of 22 October 1973;

2. *Decides* to renew the mandate of the United Nations Disengagement Observer Force for another period of six months, that is, until 30 November 2001;

3. *Requests* the Secretary-General to submit, at the end of this period, a report on the developments in the situation and the measures taken to implement resolution 338(1973).

On 27 November [meeting 4428], the Council unanimously adopted **resolution 1381(2001)**. The draft [S/2001/1110] was prepared during consultations.

The Security Council,

Having considered the report of the Secretary-General on the United Nations Disengagement Observer Force of 15 November 2001, and also reaffirming its resolution 1308(2000) of 17 July 2000,

1. *Calls upon* the parties concerned to implement immediately its resolution 338(1973) of 22 October 1973;

2. *Decides* to renew the mandate of the United Nations Disengagement Observer Force for another period of six months, that is, until 31 May 2002;

3. *Requests* the Secretary-General to submit, at the end of this period, a report on the developments in the situation and the measures taken to implement resolution 338(1973).

After the adoption of each resolution, the President made statements **S/PRST/2001/15** [meeting 4322] and **S/PRST/2001/37** [meeting 4428] on behalf of the Council:

In connection with the resolution just adopted on the renewal of the mandate of the United Nations Disengagement Observer Force, I have been authorized to make the following complementary statement on behalf of the Security Council:

As is known, the report of the Secretary-General on the United Nations Disengagement Observer Force states, in paragraph 11 [12 in the November report]: "... the situation in the Middle East continues to be potentially dangerous and is likely to remain so unless and until a comprehensive settlement covering all aspects of the Middle East problem can be reached". That statement of the Secretary-General reflects the view of the Security Council.

Financing

Reports of Secretary-General and ACABQ. On 26 January, the Secretary-General presented a report on UNDOF's financial performance for the period 1 July 1999 to 30 June 2000 [A/55/747]. Expenditures totalled $35,026,400 gross ($34,320,700 net), resulting in an unencumbered balance of $324,900 gross ($297,700 net). On 9 February, he submitted UNDOF's proposed budget for the period 1 July 2001 to 30 June 2002 [A/55/778] totalling $34,536,300 gross ($33,778,900 net), which reflected a 1.2 per cent decrease in gross terms compared with the resources approved for the preceding 12 months.

ACABQ's comments and recommendations on the two reports were contained in an April report to the Assembly [A/55/874/Add.1].

GENERAL ASSEMBLY ACTION

On 14 June [meeting 103], the General Assembly, on the recommendation of the Fifth Committee [A/55/975], adopted **resolution 55/264** without vote [agenda item 138 *(a)*].

Financing of the United Nations Disengagement Observer Force

The General Assembly,

Having considered the reports of the Secretary-General on the financing of the United Nations Disengagement Observer Force and the related reports of the Advisory Committee on Administrative and Budgetary Questions,

Recalling Security Council resolution 350(1974) of 31 May 1974, by which the Council established the United Nations Disengagement Observer Force, and the subsequent resolutions by which the Council extended the mandate of the Force, the latest of which was resolution 1351(2001) of 30 May 2001,

Recalling also its resolution 3211 B (XXIX) of 29 November 1974 on the financing of the United Nations Emergency Force and of the United Nations Disengagement Observer Force, and its subsequent resolutions thereon, the latest of which was resolution 54/266 of 15 June 2000,

Reaffirming the general principles underlying the financing of United Nations peacekeeping operations, as stated in General Assembly resolutions 1874(S-IV) of 27 June 1963, 3101(XXVIII) of 11 December 1973 and 55/235 of 23 December 2000,

Noting with appreciation that voluntary contributions have been made to the United Nations Disengagement Observer Force,

Mindful of the fact that it is essential to provide the Force with the necessary financial resources to enable it to fulfil its responsibilities under the relevant resolutions of the Security Council,

Concerned that the surplus balances in the Special Account for the United Nations Disengagement Observer Force have been used to meet expenses of the Force in order to compensate for the lack of income resulting from non-payment and late payment by Member States of their contributions,

Bearing in mind the reported hardships incurred by the local staff upon relocation of the headquarters of the Force from Damascus to Camp Faouar, and welcoming the efforts made to address them,

1. *Notes* that some of the concerns regarding the improvement of the working conditions of the local staff in the United Nations Disengagement Observer Force have been addressed;

2. *Reaffirms its request* to the Secretary-General to continue the process of improving the working conditions of the local staff, including by making allowance for difficulties resulting from the relocation of the headquarters of the Force from Damascus to Camp Faouar, through mutual and fruitful dialogue;

3. *Notes* that paragraph 2 of its resolution 54/266 was not fully implemented, in particular with regard to making allowance for the difficulties mentioned in that paragraph, and in this regard requests the Secretary-General to take concrete measures to ensure the full implementation of the matter and to report thereon to the General Assembly during the first part of its resumed fifty-sixth session;

4. *Takes note* of the status of contributions to the Force as at 30 April 2001, including the contributions outstanding in the amount of 22.8 million United States dollars, representing some 1.4 per cent of the total assessed contributions from the inception of the Force to the period ending 31 May 2001, notes that some 19 per cent of the Member States have paid their assessed contributions in full, and urges all other Member States concerned, in particular those in arrears, to ensure payment of their outstanding assessed contributions;

5. *Expresses its appreciation* to those Member States which have paid their assessed contributions in full;

6. *Expresses concern* about the financial situation with regard to peacekeeping activities, in particular as regards the reimbursements to troop contributors that bear additional burdens owing to overdue payments by Member States of their assessments;

7. *Urges* all other Member States to make every possible effort to ensure payment of their assessed contributions to the Force in full and on time;

8. *Expresses concern* at the delay experienced by the Secretary-General in deploying and providing adequate resources to some recent peacekeeping missions, in particular those in Africa;

9. *Emphasizes* that all future and existing peacekeeping missions shall be given equal and non-discriminatory treatment in respect of financial and administrative arrangements;

10. *Also emphasizes* that all peacekeeping missions shall be provided with adequate resources for the effective and efficient discharge of their respective mandates;

11. *Reiterates its request* to the Secretary-General to make the fullest possible use of facilities and equipment at the United Nations Logistics Base at Brindisi, Italy, in order to minimize the costs of procurement for the Force;

12. *Endorses* the recommendations contained in paragraphs 8 and 26 of the report of the Advisory Committee on Administrative and Budgetary Questions, and requests the Secretary-General to ensure their full implementation;

13. *Requests* the Secretary-General to take all necessary action to ensure that the Force is administered with a maximum of efficiency and economy;

14. *Also requests* the Secretary-General, in order to reduce the cost of employing General Service staff, to continue efforts to recruit local staff for the Force against General Service posts, commensurate with the requirements of the Force;

15. *Decides* to appropriate to the Special Account for the United Nations Disengagement Observer Force the amount of 35,689,968 dollars gross (34,793,582 dollars net) for the maintenance of the Force for the period from 1 July 2001 to 30 June 2002, inclusive of the amount of 1,044,551 dollars gross (916,696 dollars net) for the support account for peacekeeping operations and the amount of 109,117 dollars gross (97,986 dollars net) for the United Nations Logistics Base;

16. *Decides also* to apportion among Member States the amount of 35,689,968 dollars gross (34,793,582 dollars net) at a monthly rate of 2,974,164 dollars gross (2,899,465 dollars net), in accordance with the levels set out in General Assembly resolution 55/235 and as adjusted by the Assembly in its resolution 55/236 of 23 December 2000, and taking into account the scale of assessments for the years 2001 and 2002, as set out in its resolution 55/5 B of 23 December 2000, subject to the decision of the Security Council to extend the mandate of the Force;

17. *Decides further* that, in accordance with the provisions of its resolution 973(X) of 15 December 1955, there shall be set off against the apportionment among Member States, as provided for in paragraph 16 above, their respective share in the Tax Equalization Fund of the estimated staff assessment income of 896,386 dollars approved for the Force for the period from 1 July 2001 to 30 June 2002;

18. *Decides* that, for Member States that have fulfilled their financial obligations to the Force, there shall be set off against the apportionment, as provided for in paragraph 16 above, their respective share of the unencumbered balance of 324,900 dollars gross (297,700 dollars net) in respect of the period ending 30 June 2000, in accordance with the composition of groups set out in paragraphs 3 and 4 of General Assembly resolution 43/232 of 1 March 1989, as adjusted by the Assembly in subsequent relevant resolutions and decisions for the ad hoc apportionment of peacekeeping appropriations, the latest of which were resolution 52/230 of 31 March 1998 and decisions 54/456 to 54/458 of 23 December 1999 for the period 1998-2000, and taking into account the scale of assessments for the year 2000, as set out in its resolutions 52/215 A of 22 December 1997 and 54/237 A of 23 December 1999;

19. *Decides also* that, for Member States that have not fulfilled their financial obligations to the Force, their respective share of the unencumbered balance of 324,900 dollars gross (297,700 dollars net) in respect of the period ending 30 June 2000 shall be set off against their outstanding obligations in accordance with the scheme set out in paragraph 18 above;

20. *Decides further,* pursuant to the provisions of paragraph 13 of its resolution 53/226 of 8 June 1999, to credit back to Member States the amount of 4 million dollars during the fifty-fifth session of the General Assembly, representing the remaining net balance held in the suspense account for the Force, according to the procedures set out in paragraphs 16 to 19 above;

21. *Emphasizes* that no peacekeeping mission shall be financed by borrowing funds from other active peacekeeping missions;

22. *Encourages* the Secretary-General to continue to take additional measures to ensure the safety and security of all personnel under the auspices of the United Nations participating in the Force;

23. *Invites* voluntary contributions to the Force in cash and in the form of services and supplies acceptable to the Secretary-General, to be administered, as appropriate, in accordance with the procedure and practices established by the General Assembly;

24. *Decides* to include in the provisional agenda of its fifty-sixth session, under the item entitled "Financing of the United Nations peacekeeping forces in the Middle East", the sub-item entitled "United Nations Disengagement Observer Force".

On 24 December, the Assembly decided that the item on financing of the UN peacekeeping forces in the Middle East would remain for consideration during the resumed fifty-sixth (2002) session (**decision 56/464**) and that the Fifth Committee would continue consideration of the item on the financing of UNDOF at that session (**decision 56/458**).

Chapter VII

Disarmament

The United Nations Conference on the Illicit Trade in Small Arms and Light Weapons in All Its Aspects, considered one of the most important disarmament events in 2001, met in July and adopted a Programme of Action, which was seen as a significant first step towards curbing the illicit trade and proliferation of those weapons. In August, the Security Council called on Member States to implement the Programme.

In 2001, the terrorist attacks of 11 September (see p. 60) and subsequent anthrax incidents in the United States raised further concern among the international community over the threat of bioterrorism and the use of weapons of mass destruction. Despite the increased concern, multilateral efforts to strengthen the 1971 Convention on the Prohibition of the Development, Production and Stockpiling of Bacteriological (Biological) and Toxin Weapons and on Their Destruction suffered setbacks, as the Fifth Review Conference of the States Parties was suspended in December due to divergent positions on key issues. Earlier in the year, the Ad Hoc Group of the States Parties to the Convention failed to conclude negotiation on a compliance protocol. In related action, the General Assembly, in November, recognizing the close connection between international terrorism and illicit arms-trafficking and the illegal movement of nuclear, chemical, biological and other potentially deadly materials, called for multilateral cooperation to deal with the problem.

The Conference on Disarmament once again did not agree on a programme of work and thus remained unable to take action on any of its agenda items during its 2001 session. The Disarmament Commission continued to consider ways and means to achieve nuclear disarmament and practical confidence-building measures in the field of conventional arms.

With regard to anti-personnel mines, the Third Meeting of the States Parties to the 1997 Convention on the Prohibition of the Use, Stockpiling, Production and Transfer of Anti-personnel Mines and on Their Destruction, in September, noted that considerable areas of mined land had been cleared over the past year, casualty rates had been reduced in several of the most affected States and victim assistance had improved. The Second Review Conference of the States Parties to the 1980 Convention on Prohibitions or Restrictions on the Use of Certain Conventional Weapons Which May Be Deemed to Be Excessively Injurious or to Have Indiscriminate Effects, held in December, agreed to amend article I of the Convention in order to expand the scope of its application to non-international armed conflicts. The Third Annual Conference of the States Parties to the 1980 Convention's amended Protocol on the Use of Mines, Booby Traps and Other Devices (Protocol II) reaffirmed the States parties' commitment to restricting the use of, or outlawing, anti-personnel landmines.

In November, the Conference on Facilitating the Entry into Force of the 1996 Comprehensive Nuclear-Test-Ban Treaty called on signatory States to ratify the Treaty as soon as possible.

At the bilateral level, the Russian Federation and the United States conducted the last inspection pursuant to the provisions of the 1987 Treaty on Intermediate-Range Nuclear Forces, under which they agreed to eliminate their intermediate-range and shorter-range missiles no later than three years after the Treaty's entry into force, and to conduct on-site inspections on each other's territory for 13 years. They also completed reductions of their respective nuclear arsenals, in accordance with the terms of the 1991 Treaty on the Reduction and Limitation of Strategic Offensive Arms (START I). During the year, both parties held discussions on additional reductions of their nuclear arsenals and on related strategic issues, including the 1972 Treaty on the Limitation of Anti-Ballistic Missile Systems (ABM Treaty). In December, the United States announced that it had decided to withdraw unilaterally from the ABM Treaty.

UN role in disarmament

UN machinery

Disarmament issues before the United Nations were considered mainly through the General Assembly and its First (Disarmament and International Security) Committee, the Disarmament Commission (a deliberative body) and the Conference on Disarmament (a multilateral negotiating forum, which met in Geneva).

The Department for Disarmament Affairs of the UN Secretariat continued to support the work of Member States and treaty bodies, to service the Advisory Board on Disarmament Matters and to administer the UN disarmament fellowship programme.

Fourth special session on disarmament

Pursuant to General Assembly resolution 55/33 M [YUN 2000, p. 484], the Secretary-General, in a July report [A/56/166], presented the views of seven Member States on the objectives, agenda and timing of the fourth special session of the Assembly devoted to disarmament.

The Assembly had decided, by resolution 51/45 C [YUN 1996, p. 447], to convene the special session in 1999, subject to the emergence of a consensus on its agenda and objectives.

GENERAL ASSEMBLY ACTION

On 29 November [meeting 68], the General Assembly, on the recommendation of the First Committee [A/56/536], adopted **resolution 56/24 D** without vote [agenda item 74 *(m)*].

Convening of the fourth special session of the General Assembly devoted to disarmament

The General Assembly,

Recalling its resolutions 49/75 I of 15 December 1994, 50/70 F of 12 December 1995, 51/45 C of 10 December 1996, 52/38 F of 9 December 1997, 53/77 AA of 4 December 1998, 54/54 U of 1 December 1999 and 55/33 M of 20 November 2000,

Recalling also that, there being a consensus to do so in each case, three special sessions of the General Assembly devoted to disarmament were held, in 1978, 1982 and 1988, respectively,

Bearing in mind the Final Document of the Tenth Special Session of the General Assembly, adopted by consensus at the first special session devoted to disarmament, which included the Declaration, the Programme of Action and the Machinery for disarmament,

Bearing in mind also the objective of general and complete disarmament under effective international control,

Taking note of paragraph 145 of the Final Document of the Twelfth Conference of Heads of State or Government of Non-Aligned Countries, held at Durban, South Africa, from 29 August to 3 September 1998, which supported the convening of the fourth special session of the General Assembly devoted to disarmament, which would offer an opportunity to review, from a perspective more in tune with the current international situation, the most critical aspects of the process of disarmament and to mobilize the international community and public opinion in favour of the elimination of nuclear and other weapons of mass destruction and of the control and reduction of conventional weapons,

Taking note also of the report of the Disarmament Commission on its 1999 substantive session and of the fact that no consensus was reached on the item entitled "Fourth special session of the General Assembly devoted to disarmament",

Desiring to build upon the substantive exchange of views on the fourth special session of the General Assembly devoted to disarmament during the 1999 substantive session of the Disarmament Commission,

Reiterating its conviction that a special session of the General Assembly devoted to disarmament can set the future course of action in the field of disarmament, arms control and related international security matters,

Emphasizing the importance of multilateralism in the process of disarmament, arms control and related international security matters,

Noting that, with the recent accomplishments made by the international community in the field of weapons of mass destruction as well as conventional arms, the following years would be opportune for the international community to start the process of reviewing the state of affairs in the entire field of disarmament and arms control in the post-cold-war era,

Taking note of the United Nations Millennium Declaration, in which heads of State and Government resolved to strive for the elimination of weapons of mass destruction, particularly nuclear weapons, and to keep all options open for achieving that aim, including the possibility of convening an international conference to identify ways of eliminating nuclear dangers,

Taking note also of the report of the Secretary-General regarding the views of Member States on the objectives, agenda and timing of the fourth special session of the General Assembly devoted to disarmament,

1. *Decides*, subject to the emergence of a consensus on its objectives and agenda, to convene the fourth special session of the General Assembly devoted to disarmament;

2. *Requests* the Secretary-General to seek the views of Member States on the objectives, agenda and timing of the special session and to report to the General Assembly at its fifty-seventh session;

3. *Decides* to include in the provisional agenda of its fifty-seventh session the item entitled "Convening of the fourth special session of the General Assembly devoted to disarmament".

Disarmament Commission

The Disarmament Commission, composed of all UN Member States, held seven plenary meetings in 2001 (New York, 9-27 April) [A/56/42] and organizational meetings on 9 April and 2 November.

The Commission continued to consider ways to achieve nuclear disarmament (see p. 473) and practical confidence-building measures in the field of conventional arms (see p. 506). The Commission adopted consensus texts on those items, following consideration of the issues by its working groups.

GENERAL ASSEMBLY ACTION

On 29 November [meeting 68], the General Assembly, on the recommendation of the First Committee [A/56/538], adopted **resolution 56/26 A** without vote [agenda item 76 (*d*)].

Report of the Disarmament Commission

The General Assembly,

Having considered the report of the Disarmament Commission,

Recalling its resolutions 47/54 A of 9 December 1992, 47/54 G of 8 April 1993, 48/77 A of 16 December 1993, 49/77 A of 15 December 1994, 50/72 D of 12 December 1995, 51/47 B of 10 December 1996, 52/40 B of 9 December 1997, 53/79 A of 4 December 1998, 54/56 A of 1 December 1999 and 55/35 C of 20 November 2000,

Considering the role that the Disarmament Commission has been called upon to play and the contribution that it should make in examining and submitting recommendations on various problems in the field of disarmament and in the promotion of the implementation of the relevant decisions adopted by the General Assembly at its tenth special session,

Bearing in mind its decision 52/492 of 8 September 1998,

1. *Takes note* of the report of the Disarmament Commission;

2. *Reaffirms* the importance of further enhancing the dialogue and cooperation among the First Committee, the Disarmament Commission and the Conference on Disarmament;

3. *Also reaffirms* the role of the Disarmament Commission as the specialized, deliberative body within the United Nations multilateral disarmament machinery that allows for in-depth deliberations on specific disarmament issues, leading to the submission of concrete recommendations on those issues;

4. *Requests* the Disarmament Commission to continue its work in accordance with its mandate, as set forth in paragraph 118 of the Final Document of the Tenth Special Session of the General Assembly, and with paragraph 3 of Assembly resolution 37/78 H of 9 December 1982, and to that end to make every effort to achieve specific recommendations on the items of its agenda, taking into account the adopted "Ways and means to enhance the functioning of the Disarmament Commission";

5. *Notes* that the Disarmament Commission, at its 2001 organizational session, adopted the following items for consideration at its 2002 substantive session:

(*a*) Ways and means to achieve nuclear disarmament;

(*b*) Practical confidence-building measures in the field of conventional arms;

6. *Requests* the Disarmament Commission to meet for a period not exceeding three weeks during 2002 and to submit a substantive report to the General Assembly at its fifty-seventh session;

7. *Requests* the Secretary-General to transmit to the Disarmament Commission the annual report of the Conference on Disarmament, together with all the official records of the fifty-sixth session of the General Assembly relating to disarmament matters, and to render all assistance that the Commission may require for implementing the present resolution;

8. *Also requests* the Secretary-General to ensure full provision to the Disarmament Commission and its subsidiary bodies of interpretation and translation facilities in the official languages and to assign, as a matter of priority, all the necessary resources and services, including verbatim records, to that end;

9. *Decides* to include in the provisional agenda of its fifty-seventh session the item entitled "Report of the Disarmament Commission".

Conference on Disarmament

The Conference on Disarmament, a multilateral negotiating body, held a three-part session in Geneva in 2001 (22 January–30 March, 14 May–29 June and 30 July–14 September) [A/56/27].

The Conference continued to consider the cessation of the nuclear arms race and nuclear disarmament; prevention of nuclear war; prevention of an arms race in outer space; effective international arrangements to assure non-nuclear-weapon States against the use or threat of use of nuclear weapons; new types of weapons of mass destruction and new systems of such weapons; radiological weapons; a comprehensive programme of disarmament; and transparency in armaments.

During the session, successive Presidents of the Conference held consultations and put forward informal proposals with a view to reaching consensus on a programme of work, none of which achieved consensus. Thus, the Conference did not agree on a programme of work and did not re-establish or establish any mechanism on any of its substantive agenda items. However, on 14 June [CD/1646], the Conference reaffirmed its commitment to work towards the approval of a programme of work, maintaining the Amorim proposal [YUN 2000, p. 485], which envisaged the establishment of ad hoc committees with non-negotiating mandates on nuclear disarmament and the prevention of an arms race in outer space, as a basis for further consultations, and taking into consideration all relevant proposals. The Conference appointed three Special Coordinators on the review of its agenda (Germany), expansion of its membership (Bulgaria) and its improved and effective functioning (Sri Lanka), all of whom reported on their consultations at the end of the session. The Conference agreed that priority should be given to substantive work and that Special Coordinators on the same issues should be reappointed as early as possible at the 2002 session. The Conference requested its President and the incoming President to hold consultations during the intersessional period, with a view to beginning work early in 2002.

GENERAL ASSEMBLY ACTION

On 29 November [meeting 68], the General Assembly, on the recommendation of the First Committee [A/56/538], adopted **resolution 56/26 B** without vote [agenda item 76 (*c*)].

Report of the Conference on Disarmament

The General Assembly,

Having considered the report of the Conference on Disarmament,

Convinced that the Conference on Disarmament, as the single multilateral disarmament negotiating forum of the international community, has the primary role in substantive negotiations on priority questions of disarmament,

Recognizing the need to conduct multilateral negotiations with the aim of reaching agreement on concrete issues for negotiation,

Recalling, in this respect, that the Conference has a number of urgent and important issues for negotiation,

1. *Reaffirms* the role of the Conference on Disarmament as the single multilateral disarmament negotiating forum of the international community;

2. *Urges* the Conference to fulfil that role in the light of the evolving international situation, with a view to making early substantive progress on priority items on its agenda;

3. *Welcomes* the strong collective interest of the Conference in commencing substantive work as soon as possible during its 2002 session;

4. *Also welcomes* the decision of the Conference to request its President to conduct appropriate consultations with its incoming President during the intersessional period to try to achieve this goal, as expressed in paragraph 40 of its report;

5. *Further welcomes* the recommendation of the Conference, as expressed in paragraph 41 of its report, to reappoint the Special Coordinator on Review of the Agenda of the Conference on Disarmament, the Special Coordinator on Expansion of Membership of the Conference on Disarmament and the Special Coordinator on Improved and Effective Functioning of the Conference on Disarmament as early as possible during its 2002 session;

6. *Requests* the Secretary-General to continue to ensure the provision to the Conference of adequate administrative, substantive and conference support services;

7. *Requests* the Conference to submit a report on its work to the General Assembly at its fifty-seventh session;

8. *Decides* to include in the provisional agenda of its fifty-seventh session the item entitled "Report of the Conference on Disarmament".

Multilateral disarmament agreements

As at 31 December 2001, the following numbers of States had become parties to the multilateral agreements listed below (in chronological order, with the years in which they were initially signed or opened for signature).

(Geneva) Protocol for the Prohibition of the Use in War of Asphyxiating, Poisonous or Other Gases, and of Bacteriological Methods of Warfare (1925): 132 parties

The Antarctic Treaty (1959): 45 parties

Treaty Banning Nuclear Weapon Tests in the Atmosphere, in Outer Space and under Water (1963): 124 parties

Treaty on Principles Governing the Activities of States in the Exploration and Use of Outer Space, including the Moon and Other Celestial Bodies (1967) [YUN 1966, p. 41, GA res. 2222(XXI), annex]: 97 parties

Treaty for the Prohibition of Nuclear Weapons in Latin America and the Caribbean (Treaty of Tlatelolco) (1967): 38 parties

Treaty on the Non-Proliferation of Nuclear Weapons (1968) [YUN 1968, p. 17, GA res. 2373(XXII), annex]: 187 parties

Treaty on the Prohibition of the Emplacement of Nuclear Weapons and Other Weapons of Mass Destruction on the Seabed and the Ocean Floor and in the Subsoil Thereof (1971) [YUN 1970, p. 18, GA res. 2660(XXV), annex]: 92 parties

Convention on the Prohibition of the Development, Production and Stockpiling of Bacteriological (Biological) and Toxin Weapons and on Their Destruction (1972) [YUN 1971, p. 19, GA res. 2826(XXVI), annex]: 144 parties

Convention on the Prohibition of Military or Any Other Hostile Use of Environmental Modification Techniques (1977) [YUN 1976, p. 45, GA res. 31/72, annex]: 66 parties

Agreement Governing the Activities of States on the Moon and Other Celestial Bodies (1979) [YUN 1979, p. 111, GA res. 34/68, annex]: 10 parties

Convention on Prohibitions or Restrictions on the Use of Certain Conventional Weapons Which May Be Deemed to Be Excessively Injurious or to Have Indiscriminate Effects (1981): 88 parties

South Pacific Nuclear-Free Zone Treaty (Treaty of Rarotonga) (1985): 17 parties

Treaty on Conventional Armed Forces in Europe (CFE Treaty) (1990): 30 parties

Treaty on Open Skies (1992): 26 parties

Convention on the Prohibition of the Development, Production, Stockpiling and Use of Chemical Weapons and on Their Destruction (1993): 145 parties

Treaty on the South-East Asia Nuclear-Weapon-Free Zone (Bangkok Treaty) (1995): 10 parties

African Nuclear-Weapon-Free Zone Treaty (Pelindaba Treaty) (1996): 19 parties

Comprehensive Nuclear-Test-Ban Treaty (1996): 89 parties

Inter-American Convention against the Illicit Manufacturing of and Trafficking in Firearms, Ammunition, Explosives, and Other Related Materials (1997): 10 parties

Convention on the Prohibition of the Use, Stockpiling, Production and Transfer of Anti-personnel Mines and on Their Destruction (Mine-Ban Convention, formerly known as Ottawa Convention) (1997): 122 parties

Inter-American Convention on Transparency in Conventional Weapons Acquisitions (1999): 4 parties

Agreement on Adaptation of the CFE Treaty (1999): 1 party

[*United Nations Disarmament Yearbook*, vol. 26: *2001*, Sales No. E.02.IX.1]

Nuclear disarmament

Conference on Disarmament

In 2001, despite the inability of the Conference on Disarmament to establish a subsidiary body on nuclear disarmament (see p. 469), some progress was made on the issue. In an important shift in position, the Russian Federation supported the establishment of a subsidiary body with an exploratory mandate for broad discussions on nuclear disarmament, and, in May [CD/1644], submitted a working paper containing a draft decision to establish an ad hoc committee based in part on the Amorim proposal (see p. 469), but with a vaguer mandate. Also in a change of position, the United States expressed its readiness to agree on a programme of work providing for the establishment of ad hoc committees on nuclear disarmament and on prevention of an arms race in outer space, in the context of ongoing negotiations on the prohibition of the production of fissile material for weapons purposes. Thus, for the first time in 30 years, there was a general willingness in the Conference to establish such a committee to consider nuclear disarmament.

Fissile material

The persistent difficulties in reaching an agreement on a programme of work prevented the Conference on Disarmament from establishing an ad hoc committee on the prohibition of the production of fissile material for nuclear weapons and other nuclear explosive devices, leaving the issue to be addressed in plenary meetings.

While Western and Eastern European countries continued to advocate the immediate re-establishment of an ad hoc committee and the start of negotiations on a fissile material cut-off treaty, China and States of the Movement of Non-Aligned Countries maintained that negotiations on a treaty should be launched within the framework of a comprehensive and balanced programme of work and that the issue of existing stocks of fissile material must be addressed during negotiations.

During the year, the General Assembly returned to the question of the establishment of an ad hoc committee to negotiate a treaty banning the production of fissile material for nuclear weapons and other nuclear explosive devices, which it had previously considered in resolutions 48/75 L [YUN 1993, p. 118], 53/77 I [YUN 1998, p. 493] and 55/33 Y [YUN 2000, p. 488].

GENERAL ASSEMBLY ACTION

On 29 November [meeting 68], the General Assembly, on the recommendation of the First Committee [A/56/536], adopted **resolution 56/24 J** without vote [agenda item 74].

The Conference on Disarmament decision (CD/1547) of 11 August 1998 to establish, under item 1 of its agenda entitled "Cessation of the nuclear arms race and nuclear disarmament", an ad hoc committee to negotiate, on the basis of the report of the Special Coordinator (CD/1299) and the mandate contained therein, a non-discriminatory, multilateral and internationally and effectively verifiable treaty banning the production of fissile material for nuclear weapons or other nuclear explosive devices

The General Assembly,

Recalling its resolutions 48/75 L of 16 December 1993, 53/77 I of 4 December 1998 and 55/33 Y of 20 November 2000,

Convinced that a non-discriminatory, multilateral and internationally and effectively verifiable treaty banning the production of fissile material for nuclear weapons or other nuclear explosive devices would be a significant contribution to nuclear disarmament and nuclear non-proliferation,

Recalling the 1998 report of the Conference on Disarmament, in which, inter alia, the Conference records that, in proceeding to take a decision on this matter, that decision is without prejudice to any further decisions on the establishment of further subsidiary bodies under agenda item 1 and that intensive consultations will be pursued to seek the views of the members of the Conference on Disarmament on appropriate methods and approaches for dealing with agenda item 1, taking into consideration all proposals and views in that respect,

1. *Recalls* the decision of the Conference on Disarmament to establish, under item 1 of its agenda entitled "Cessation of the nuclear arms race and nuclear disarmament", an ad hoc committee which shall negotiate, on the basis of the report of the Special Coordinator and the mandate contained therein, a non-discriminatory, multilateral and internationally and effectively verifiable treaty banning the production of fissile material for nuclear weapons or other nuclear explosive devices;

2. *Urges* the Conference on Disarmament to agree on a programme of work that includes the immediate commencement of negotiations on such a treaty.

Security assurances

The Conference on Disarmament considered the issue of security assurances for non-nuclear-weapon States against the use or threat of use of nuclear weapons in the context of adopting its programme of work. Owing to the stalemate regarding a comprehensive programme of work, the Conference did not re-establish an ad hoc committee. Statements in plenary meetings addressed security assurances and generally reaffirmed members' long-held positions.

The question of security assurances was also addressed within the context of overcoming a deadlock on procedural matters. In that regard, the Special Coordinator appointed to review the agenda reported that there was a general agreement on retaining the item, at least in substance if not in wording.

GENERAL ASSEMBLY ACTION

On 29 November [meeting 68], the General Assembly, on the recommendation of the First Committee [A/56/534], adopted **resolution 56/22** by recorded vote (105-0-54) [agenda item 72].

Conclusion of effective international arrangements to assure non-nuclear-weapon States against the use or threat of use of nuclear weapons

The General Assembly,

Bearing in mind the need to allay the legitimate concern of the States of the world with regard to ensuring lasting security for their peoples,

Convinced that nuclear weapons pose the greatest threat to mankind and to the survival of civilization,

Welcoming the progress achieved in recent years in both nuclear and conventional disarmament,

Noting that, despite recent progress in the field of nuclear disarmament, further efforts are necessary towards the achievement of general and complete disarmament under effective international control,

Convinced that nuclear disarmament and the complete elimination of nuclear weapons are essential to remove the danger of nuclear war,

Determined to abide strictly by the relevant provisions of the Charter of the United Nations on the non-use of force or threat of force,

Recognizing that the independence, territorial integrity and sovereignty of non-nuclear-weapon States need to be safeguarded against the use or threat of use of force, including the use or threat of use of nuclear weapons,

Considering that, until nuclear disarmament is achieved on a universal basis, it is imperative for the international community to develop effective measures and arrangements to ensure the security of non-nuclear-weapon States against the use or threat of use of nuclear weapons from any quarter,

Recognizing that effective measures and arrangements to assure non-nuclear-weapon States against the use or threat of use of nuclear weapons can contribute positively to the prevention of the spread of nuclear weapons,

Bearing in mind paragraph 59 of the Final Document of the Tenth Special Session of the General Assembly, the first special session devoted to disarmament, in which it urged the nuclear-weapon States to pursue efforts to conclude, as appropriate, effective arrangements to assure non-nuclear-weapon States against the use or threat of use of nuclear weapons, and desirous of promoting the implementation of the relevant provisions of the Final Document,

Recalling the relevant parts of the special report of the Committee on Disarmament submitted to the General Assembly at its twelfth special session, the second special session devoted to disarmament, and of the special report of the Conference on Disarmament submitted to the Assembly at its fifteenth special session, the third special session devoted to disarmament, as well as the report of the Conference on its 1992 session,

Recalling also paragraph 12 of the Declaration of the 1980s as the Second Disarmament Decade, contained in the annex to its resolution 35/46 of 3 December 1980, which states, inter alia, that all efforts should be exerted by the Committee on Disarmament urgently to negotiate with a view to reaching agreement on effective international arrangements to assure non-nuclear-weapon States against the use or threat of use of nuclear weapons,

Noting the in-depth negotiations undertaken in the Conference on Disarmament and its Ad Hoc Committee on Effective International Arrangements to Assure Non-Nuclear-Weapon States against the Use or Threat of Use of Nuclear Weapons, with a view to reaching agreement on this question,

Taking note of the proposals submitted under the item in the Conference on Disarmament, including the drafts of an international convention,

Taking note also of the relevant decision of the Twelfth Conference of Heads of State or Government of Non-Aligned Countries, held at Durban, South Africa, from 29 August to 3 September 1998, as well as the relevant recommendations of the Organization of the Islamic Conference,

Taking note further of the unilateral declarations made by all the nuclear-weapon States on their policies of non-use or non-threat of use of nuclear weapons against the non-nuclear-weapon States,

Noting the support expressed in the Conference on Disarmament and in the General Assembly for the elaboration of an international convention to assure non-nuclear-weapon States against the use or threat of use of nuclear weapons, as well as the difficulties pointed out in evolving a common approach acceptable to all,

Taking note of Security Council resolution 984(1995) of 11 April 1995 and the views expressed on it,

Recalling its relevant resolutions adopted in previous years, in particular resolutions 45/54 of 4 December 1990, 46/32 of 6 December 1991, 47/50 of 9 December 1992, 48/73 of 16 December 1993, 49/73 of 15 December 1994, 50/68 of 12 December 1995, 51/43 of 10 December 1996, 52/36 of 9 December 1997, 53/75 of 4 December 1998, 54/52 of 1 December 1999 and 55/31 of 20 November 2000,

1. *Reaffirms* the urgent need to reach an early agreement on effective international arrangements to assure non-nuclear-weapon States against the use or threat of use of nuclear weapons;

2. *Notes with satisfaction* that in the Conference on Disarmament there is no objection, in principle, to the idea of an international convention to assure non-nuclear-weapon States against the use or threat of use

of nuclear weapons, although the difficulties with regard to evolving a common approach acceptable to all have also been pointed out;

3. *Appeals* to all States, especially the nuclear-weapon States, to work actively towards an early agreement on a common approach and, in particular, on a common formula that could be included in an international instrument of a legally binding character;

4. *Recommends* that further intensive efforts be devoted to the search for such a common approach or common formula and that the various alternative approaches, including, in particular, those considered in the Conference on Disarmament, be further explored in order to overcome the difficulties;

5. *Recommends also* that the Conference on Disarmament actively continue intensive negotiations with a view to reaching early agreement and concluding effective international arrangements to assure the non-nuclear-weapon States against the use or threat of use of nuclear weapons, taking into account the widespread support for the conclusion of an international convention and giving consideration to any other proposals designed to secure the same objective;

6. *Decides* to include in the provisional agenda of its fifty-seventh session the item entitled "Conclusion of effective international arrangements to assure non-nuclear-weapon States against the use or threat of use of nuclear weapons".

RECORDED VOTE ON RESOLUTION 56/22:

In favour: Afghanistan, Algeria, Angola, Azerbaijan, Bahamas, Bahrain, Bangladesh, Barbados, Bhutan, Botswana, Brazil, Brunei Darussalam, Burkina Faso, Burundi, Cambodia, Cameroon, Cape Verde, Chile, China, Colombia, Comoros, Costa Rica, Côte d'Ivoire, Cuba, Democratic People's Republic of Korea, Djibouti, Dominican Republic, Ecuador, Egypt, El Salvador, Eritrea, Ethiopia, Fiji, Gabon, Ghana, Grenada, Guatemala, Guinea, Guyana, Haiti, Honduras, India, Indonesia, Iran, Jamaica, Japan, Jordan, Kazakhstan, Kenya, Kuwait, Lao People's Democratic Republic, Lebanon, Lesotho, Libyan Arab Jamahiriya, Madagascar, Malaysia, Maldives, Mali, Mauritania, Mauritius, Mexico, Mongolia, Morocco, Mozambique, Myanmar, Namibia, Nauru, Nepal, Nicaragua, Nigeria, Oman, Pakistan, Panama, Papua New Guinea, Paraguay, Peru, Philippines, Qatar, Saint Lucia, Samoa, Saudi Arabia, Senegal, Seychelles, Sierra Leone, Singapore, Solomon Islands, Sri Lanka, Sudan, Swaziland, Syrian Arab Republic, Thailand, Togo, Tonga, Trinidad and Tobago, Tunisia, Turkmenistan, Uganda, Ukraine, United Arab Emirates, United Republic of Tanzania, Uruguay, Venezuela, Viet Nam, Yemen, Zambia.

Against: None.

Abstaining: Albania, Andorra, Argentina, Armenia, Australia, Austria, Belarus, Belgium, Bolivia, Bosnia and Herzegovina, Bulgaria, Canada, Croatia, Cyprus, Czech Republic, Denmark, Estonia, Finland, France, Georgia, Germany, Greece, Hungary, Iceland, Ireland, Israel, Italy, Latvia, Liechtenstein, Lithuania, Luxembourg, Malta, Micronesia, Monaco, Netherlands, New Zealand, Norway, Poland, Portugal, Republic of Korea, Republic of Moldova, Romania, Russian Federation, San Marino, Slovakia, Slovenia, South Africa, Spain, Sweden, The former Yugoslav Republic of Macedonia, Turkey, United Kingdom, United States, Yugoslavia.

Disarmament Commission

In April [A/56/42], Working Group I of the Disarmament Commission considered its Chairman's working paper on ways and means to achieve nuclear disarmament. Following deliberations, the Group noted that the paper required further discussion, elaboration and refinement. On 26 April, the Group adopted its report by consensus and requested the Chairman to conduct intersessional consultations and to present a revised version of his paper before the Commission's 2002 session. The Chairman's pa-

per, which was annexed to the Commission's report, discussed the interrelationship between nuclear disarmament, international peace, security and stability, achievements and current developments in nuclear disarmament, mechanisms dealing with nuclear disarmament and the role of the United Nations, and ways and means to achieve nuclear disarmament.

START and other bilateral agreements and unilateral measures

The United States and Russian Federation continued to implement the 1991 Treaty on the Reduction and Limitation of Strategic Offensive Arms (START I) [YUN 1991, p. 34], which entered into force on 5 December 1994 [YUN 1994, p. 145], by reducing their nuclear arms stockpiles. However, the START process was seemingly pushed into the background in 2001, overshadowed by proposals for a new strategic framework between the Russian Federation and the United States (see below). START II, which envisaged nuclear reductions to the level of 3,000 to 3,500 warheads, would, in effect, be superseded if the two nuclear Powers succeeded in completing a more far-reaching agreement. As at 5 December, both countries had completed reductions of their respective nuclear arsenals to the levels required under START I. The control mechanisms foreseen under the Treaty would stay in force until the end of 2009.

President George W. Bush of the United States, on 1 May (Washington, D.C.), outlining his views on a new United States defence policy, particularly regarding the establishment of missile defences, highlighted United States views on the need for new concepts of deterrence relying on both offensive and defensive forces, and the need for a new framework allowing for the establishment of missile defences in order for the United States to move beyond the constraints of the 1972 Treaty on the Limitation of Anti-Ballistic Missile Systems (ABM Treaty) and to encourage further cuts in nuclear weapons. There was a pledge to consult closely with allies and other States on the missile defence issue. China reiterated its view that the ABM Treaty remained the cornerstone of strategic stability, emphasizing that United States missile defence plans would spark a new arms race. Although the Russian Federation also stressed the importance of the ABM Treaty, it welcomed the United States proposal for a new strategic dialogue and stated its readiness to hold negotiations on global strategic stability. The UN Secretary-General stated that the new United States defence policy impacted upon global security and strategic stability, and appealed to States to engage in negotiations towards legally binding disarmament agreements that were verifiable and irreversible.

The Foreign Ministers of member States of the North Atlantic Treaty Organization (NATO) (Budapest, Hungary, 29-30 May) welcomed the United States' initiative on the strategic review and stressed that consultations would address the full range of strategic issues affecting NATO's common security. Related issues were taken up during the summit of the Group of Eight (G-8) major industrialized countries (Genoa, Italy, 20-22 July), following which, on 22 July, Presidents Bush and Vladimir V. Putin of the Russian Federation agreed in a joint statement that major changes in the world warranted concrete discussions on both offensive and defensive systems and that they would begin intensive bilateral consultations shortly thereafter on nuclear cutbacks and missile defences. During a further summit (Washington, D.C., and Crawford, Texas, 13-15 November), both leaders pledged to cut their nuclear arsenals. While President Bush announced that the United States would unilaterally reduce its stockpile of offensive warheads to between 1,700 and 2,200 over the next decade, the Russian Federation later indicated that it was prepared for reductions to a level of 1,500 warheads.

On 13 December, President Bush announced that the United States had decided to withdraw unilaterally from the ABM Treaty, stating that it hindered the Government's ability to develop ways to protect the country from future missile attacks from rogue States or terrorists. At the same time, the United States reiterated its willingness to develop elements of a new strategic relationship with Russia, including deep cuts in nuclear forces.

With the last inspection conducted on 31 May, pursuant to the provisions of the 1987 Treaty on Intermediate-Range Nuclear Forces, Russia and the United States ended the 13-year inspection regime under the Treaty.

Communications. In September [A/56/348], Kazakhstan transmitted the text of the final memorandum of an international conference on "The twenty-first century: towards a nuclear-weapon-free world" (Almaty, Kazakhstan, 29-30 August), which called for humanity to use its scientific and technological capabilities in the service of further peaceful development, progress and prosperity. Kazakhstan also transmitted a September appeal by its parliament [A/C.1/56/5], which called on parliaments and Governments worldwide to take steps to eliminate nuclear weapons.

In October [A/C.1/56/4], South Africa, on behalf of the partner countries of the New Agenda Initiative (Brazil, Egypt, Ireland, Mexico, New Zealand, South Africa, Sweden), transmitted a communiqué on further measures to be taken in pursuit of their joint initiative to achieve a nuclear-weapon-free world.

In November [A/56/609-S/2001/1053], Ukraine announced that it had destroyed, on 30 October, the last SS-24 intercontinental missile silo on its territory, marking the fulfilment of its commitment under START to eliminate in the course of seven years all nuclear arsenals and strategic offensive weapons.

Also in November [A/C.1/56/7], Mexico transmitted a paper, supported by members of the New Agenda Initiative on reductions of non-strategic nuclear weapons, stating that despite progress achieved in both strategic and non-strategic nuclear weapon reductions, the members remained concerned that the total number of nuclear weapons deployed and in stockpile still amounted to many thousands. The United States and Russia were urged to proceed with the reduction of non-strategic nuclear weapons in a transparent and irreversible manner.

Reports of Secretary-General. In August [A/56/309], the Secretary-General described action taken to implement General Assembly resolution 55/33 C [YUN 2000, p. 495] on the need for action to achieve a world free from nuclear weapons.

The Secretary-General stated that in 2000 the elimination of nuclear weapons remained a priority, during the Assembly's Millennium Summit, which adopted the Millennium Declaration [YUN 2000, p. 49], and during the Review Conference [ibid., p. 487] of the Parties to the Treaty on the Non-Proliferation of Nuclear Weapons (NPT), adopted by the Assembly in resolution 2373(XXII) [YUN 1968, p. 17]. However, despite the political commitments made, the level of international cooperation in disarmament remained lower than it could and should be. There was concern about the future of some important arms control and disarmament agreements, including the Comprehensive Nuclear-Test-Ban Treaty (CTBT) (see p. 482). The Secretary-General reiterated his call to States that had not done so to sign and ratify CTBT without delay and conditions.

Pursuant to General Assembly resolution 55/33 N [YUN 2000, p. 497], the Secretary-General, in September [A/56/400], summarized the discussions of the Advisory Board on Disarmament Matters (see p. 519) regarding specific measures that might significantly reduce the risk of nuclear war. The Board concurred that nuclear danger would be eliminated only when nuclear weapons were eliminated and encouraged the Secretary-

General to assign that goal high priority. The Board members reached broad agreement on seven recommendations for reducing nuclear danger, while other measures and approaches received varying degrees of support. Annexed to the report were five discussion papers prepared by Board members.

In response to Assembly resolution 55/33 T [YUN 2000, p. 493] on nuclear disarmament, the Secretary-General, in September [A/56/404], reported on the resolution's implementation. He noted that the pace of implementation of the commitments made towards the elimination of nuclear weapons by world leaders at the Assembly's Millennium Summit [YUN 2000, p. 47] and by States parties to NPT during the 2000 Review Conference remained disappointingly low. Arms control and disarmament agreements played an essential role in the pursuit of nuclear disarmament and strengthening such agreements required action at all levels. Expressing concern at the continuing impasse in the Conference on Disarmament, the Secretary-General called on all members to overcome their differences so as to resolve outstanding issues and ensure the credibility of the Conference as the single multilateral disarmament negotiating body.

GENERAL ASSEMBLY ACTION

On 29 November [meeting 68], the General Assembly, on the recommendation of the First Committee [A/56/536], adopted a series of resolutions and decisions related to nuclear disarmament.

The Assembly adopted **resolution 56/24 N** by recorded vote (139-3-19) [agenda item 74].

A path to the total elimination of nuclear weapons

The General Assembly,

Recalling its resolutions 49/75 H of 15 December 1994, 50/70 C of 12 December 1995, 51/45 G of 10 December 1996, 52/38 K of 9 December 1997, 53/77 U of 4 December 1998, 54/54 D of 1 December 1999 and 55/33 R of 20 November 2000,

Recognizing that the enhancement of international peace and security and the promotion of nuclear disarmament mutually complement and strengthen each other,

Reaffirming the crucial importance of the Treaty on the Non-Proliferation of Nuclear Weapons as the cornerstone of the international regime for nuclear non-proliferation and as an essential foundation for the pursuit of nuclear disarmament,

Recognizing the progress made by the nuclear-weapon States in the reduction of their nuclear weapons unilaterally or through negotiations, including the START process, and the efforts made towards nuclear disarmament and non-proliferation by the international community,

Reaffirming the conviction that further advancement in nuclear disarmament will contribute to consolidating the international regime for nuclear non-proliferation, ensuring international peace and security,

Bearing in mind the recent nuclear tests, as well as the regional situations, which pose a challenge to international efforts to strengthen the global regime for non-proliferation of nuclear weapons,

Taking note of the report of the Tokyo Forum for Nuclear Non-Proliferation and Disarmament, bearing in mind the various views of Member States on the report,

Welcoming the successful adoption of the Final Document of the 2000 Review Conference of the Parties to the Treaty on the Non-Proliferation of Nuclear Weapons, and stressing the importance of implementing its conclusions,

Also welcoming the successful convening of the International Symposium for the Further Reinforcement of International Atomic Energy Agency Safeguards in the Asia-Pacific Region: Towards Universalization of Additional Protocol, recently held in Tokyo, and sharing the hope for continued efforts to hold similar symposiums in other regions for strengthening the International Atomic Energy Agency safeguards system, including universalization of its safeguards agreements, and the additional protocols thereto,

Encouraging the Russian Federation and the United States of America to continue their intensive consultations on the interrelated subjects of offensive and defensive systems and to complete them with a view to enhancing international peace and security,

Calling for efforts towards the success of the Conference on Facilitating the Entry into Force of the Comprehensive Nuclear-Test-Ban Treaty, to be convened in accordance with article XIV of the Treaty,

1. *Reaffirms* the importance of achieving the universality of the Treaty on the Non-Proliferation of Nuclear Weapons, and calls upon States not parties to the Treaty to accede to it as non-nuclear-weapon States without delay and without conditions;

2. *Also reaffirms* the importance for all States parties to the Treaty on the Non-Proliferation of Nuclear Weapons to fulfil their obligations under the Treaty;

3. *Stresses* the central importance of the following practical steps for the systematic and progressive efforts to implement article VI of the Treaty on the Non-Proliferation of Nuclear Weapons, and paragraphs 3 and 4 *(c)* of the decision on principles and objectives for nuclear non-proliferation and disarmament of the 1995 Review and Extension Conference of the Parties to the Treaty:

(a) The importance and urgency of signatures and ratifications, without delay and without conditions and in accordance with constitutional processes, to achieve the early entry into force of the Comprehensive Nuclear-Test-Ban Treaty as well as a moratorium on nuclear-weapon-test explosions or any other nuclear explosions pending the entry into force of that Treaty;

(b) The establishment of an ad hoc committee in the Conference on Disarmament as early as possible during its 2002 session to negotiate a non-discriminatory, multilateral and internationally and effectively verifiable treaty banning the production of fissile material for nuclear weapons or other nuclear explosive devices, in accordance with the report of the Special Coordinator of 1995 and the mandate contained therein, taking into consideration both nuclear

disarmament and non-proliferation objectives, with a view to its conclusion within five years and, pending its entry into force, a moratorium on the production of fissile material for nuclear weapons;

(c) The establishment of an appropriate subsidiary body with a mandate to deal with nuclear disarmament in the Conference on Disarmament as early as possible during its 2002 session in the context of establishing a programme of work;

(d) The inclusion of the principle of irreversibility to apply to nuclear disarmament, nuclear and other related arms control and reduction measures;

(e) An unequivocal undertaking by the nuclear-weapon States, as agreed at the 2000 Review Conference of the Parties to the Treaty on the Non-Proliferation of Nuclear Weapons, to accomplish the total elimination of their nuclear arsenals, leading to nuclear disarmament, to which all States parties to the Treaty are committed under article VI of the Treaty;

(f) Deep reductions by the Russian Federation and the United States of America in their strategic offensive arsenals, while placing great importance on the existing multilateral treaties, with a view to maintaining and strengthening strategic stability and international security;

(g) Steps by all the nuclear-weapon States leading to nuclear disarmament in a way that promotes international stability, and based on the principle of undiminished security for all:

(i) Further efforts by all the nuclear-weapon States to continue to reduce their nuclear arsenals unilaterally;

(ii) Increased transparency by the nuclear-weapon States with regard to their nuclear weapons capabilities and the implementation of agreements pursuant to article VI of the Treaty and as voluntary confidence-building measures to support further progress on nuclear disarmament;

(iii) The further reduction of non-strategic nuclear weapons, based on unilateral initiatives and as an integral part of the nuclear arms reduction and disarmament process;

(iv) Concrete agreed measures to reduce further the operational status of nuclear weapons systems;

(v) A diminishing role for nuclear weapons in security policies to minimize the risk that these weapons will ever be used and to facilitate the process of their total elimination;

(vi) The engagement, as soon as appropriate, of all nuclear-weapon States in the process leading to the total elimination of their nuclear weapons;

(h) Reaffirmation that the ultimate objective of the efforts of States in the disarmament process is general and complete disarmament under effective international control;

4. *Recognizes* that the realization of a world free of nuclear weapons will require further steps, including deeper reductions in nuclear weapons by all nuclear-weapon States in the process of working towards achieving their elimination;

5. *Invites* the nuclear-weapon States to keep the States Members of the United Nations duly informed of the progress or efforts made towards nuclear disarmament;

6. *Emphasizes* the importance of a successful Review Conference of the Parties to the Treaty on the Non-

Proliferation of Nuclear Weapons in 2005 as the first session of the Preparatory Committee is convened in 2002;

7. *Welcomes* the ongoing efforts in the dismantlement of nuclear weapons, notes the importance of the safe and effective management of the resultant fissile materials and calls for arrangements by all the nuclear-weapon States to place, as soon as practicable, the fissile material designated by each of them as no longer required for military purposes under the International Atomic Energy Agency or other relevant international verification and arrangements for the disposition of such material for peaceful purposes in order to ensure that such material remains permanently outside military programmes;

8. *Stresses* the importance of further development of the verification capabilities, including International Atomic Energy Agency safeguards, that will be required to provide assurance of compliance with nuclear disarmament agreements for the achievement and maintenance of a nuclear-weapon-free world;

9. *Calls upon* all States to redouble their efforts to prevent and curb the proliferation of nuclear and other weapons of mass destruction, confirming and strengthening, if necessary, their policies not to transfer equipment, materials or technology that could contribute to the proliferation of those weapons, while ensuring that such policies are consistent with the obligations of States under the Treaty on the Non-Proliferation of Nuclear Weapons;

10. *Also calls upon* all States to maintain the highest possible standards of security, safe custody, effective control and physical protection of all materials that could contribute to the proliferation of nuclear and other weapons of mass destruction in order, inter alia, to prevent those materials from falling into the hands of terrorists;

11. *Welcomes* the adoption and stresses the importance of resolution GC(45)/RES/13, adopted on 21 September 2001 by the General Conference of the International Atomic Energy Agency, in which it is recommended that the Director General of the Agency, its Board of Governors and member States continue to consider implementing the elements of the plan of action outlined in resolution GC(44)/RES/19, adopted on 22 September 2000 by the General Conference of the Agency, to promote and facilitate the conclusion and entry into force of safeguards agreements and additional protocols, and calls for the early and full implementation of that resolution;

12. *Encourages* the constructive role played by civil society in promoting nuclear non-proliferation and nuclear disarmament.

RECORDED VOTE ON RESOLUTION 56/24 N:

In favour: Afghanistan, Albania, Algeria, Andorra, Angola, Argentina, Armenia, Australia, Austria, Azerbaijan, Bahamas, Bahrain, Bangladesh, Barbados, Belgium, Benin, Bolivia, Bosnia and Herzegovina, Botswana, Brunei Darussalam, Bulgaria, Burkina Faso, Burundi, Cambodia, Cameroon, Canada, Cape Verde, Chile, Colombia, Comoros, Costa Rica, Côte d'Ivoire, Croatia, Cyprus, Czech Republic, Denmark, Djibouti, Dominican Republic, Ecuador, El Salvador, Eritrea, Estonia, Ethiopia, Fiji, Finland, France, Gabon, Georgia, Germany, Ghana, Greece, Grenada, Guatemala, Guinea, Guyana, Haiti, Honduras, Hungary, Iceland, Indonesia, Italy, Jamaica, Japan, Jordan, Kazakhstan, Kenya, Kuwait, Lao People's Democratic Republic, Latvia, Lebanon, Lesotho, Libyan Arab Jamahiriya, Liechtenstein, Lithuania, Luxembourg, Madagascar, Malaysia, Maldives, Mali, Malta, Mauritania, Monaco, Mongolia, Morocco, Mozambique, Namibia, Nauru, Nepal, Netherlands, Nicaragua, Nigeria, Norway, Oman, Panama, Papua New Guinea, Paraguay, Peru, Philippines, Poland, Portugal, Qatar, Republic of Korea, Republic of Moldova, Romania, Saint Lucia, Samoa, Saudi Arabia, Senegal, Seychelles, Sierra Leone, Singapore, Slovakia, Slovenia, Solomon Islands, Spain, Sri Lanka, Sudan, Swaziland, Syrian Arab Republic, Thailand, The former Yugoslav Republic of Macedonia, Togo, Tonga, Trinidad and Tobago, Tunisia, Turkey, Turkmenistan, Uganda, Ukraine, United Arab Emirates, United Kingdom, United Republic of Tanzania, Uruguay, Venezuela, Viet Nam, Yemen, Yugoslavia, Zambia, Zimbabwe.

Against: India, Micronesia, United States.

Abstaining: Belarus, Bhutan, Brazil, China, Cuba, Democratic People's Republic of Korea, Egypt, Iran, Ireland, Israel, Mauritius, Mexico, Myanmar, New Zealand, Pakistan, Russian Federation, San Marino, South Africa, Sweden.

The Assembly adopted **resolution 56/24 R** by recorded vote (103-41-17) [agenda item 74 *(r)*].

Nuclear disarmament

The General Assembly,

Recalling its resolution 49/75 E of 15 December 1994 on a step-by-step reduction of the nuclear threat, and its resolutions 50/70 P of 12 December 1995, 51/45 O of 10 December 1996, 52/38 L of 9 December 1997, 53/77 X of 4 December 1998, 54/54 P of 1 December 1999 and 55/33 T of 20 November 2000 on nuclear disarmament,

Reaffirming the commitment of the international community to the goal of the total elimination of nuclear weapons and the establishment of a nuclear-weapon-free world,

Bearing in mind that the Convention on the Prohibition of the Development, Production and Stockpiling of Bacteriological (Biological) and Toxin Weapons and on Their Destruction of 1972 and the Convention on the Prohibition of the Development, Production, Stockpiling and Use of Chemical Weapons and on Their Destruction of 1993 have already established legal regimes on the complete prohibition of biological and chemical weapons, respectively, and determined to achieve a nuclear weapons convention on the prohibition of the development, testing, production, stockpiling, loan transfer, use and threat of use of nuclear weapons and on their destruction, and to conclude such an international convention at an early date,

Recognizing that there now exist conditions for the establishment of a world free of nuclear weapons,

Bearing in mind paragraph 50 of the Final Document of the Tenth Special Session of the General Assembly, the first special session devoted to disarmament, calling for the urgent negotiation of agreements for the cessation of the qualitative improvement and development of nuclear-weapon systems, and for a comprehensive and phased programme with agreed time frames, wherever feasible, for the progressive and balanced reduction of nuclear weapons and their means of delivery, leading to their ultimate and complete elimination at the earliest possible time,

Noting the reiteration by the States parties to the Treaty on the Non-Proliferation of Nuclear Weapons of their conviction that the Treaty is a cornerstone of nuclear non-proliferation and nuclear disarmament and the reaffirmation by the States parties of the importance of the decision on strengthening the review process for the Treaty, the decision on principles and objectives for nuclear non-proliferation and disarmament, the decision on the extension of the Treaty and the resolution on the Middle East, adopted by the 1995 Review and Extension Conference of the Parties to the Treaty on the Non-Proliferation of Nuclear Weapons,

Reiterating the highest priority accorded to nuclear disarmament in the Final Document of the Tenth Special Session of the General Assembly and by the international community,

Recognizing that the Comprehensive Nuclear-Test-Ban Treaty and any proposed treaty on fissile material for nuclear weapons or other nuclear explosive devices must constitute disarmament measures, and not only non-proliferation measures,

Welcoming the entry into force of the Treaty on the Reduction and Limitation of Strategic Offensive Arms (START I), to which Belarus, Kazakhstan, the Russian Federation, Ukraine and the United States of America are States parties,

Welcoming also the ratification of the Treaty on Further Reduction and Limitation of Strategic Offensive Arms (START II) by the Russian Federation, and looking forward to its early entry into force and its full implementation and to an early commencement of START III negotiations,

Noting with appreciation the unilateral measures by the nuclear-weapon States for nuclear arms limitation, and encouraging them to take further such measures,

Recognizing the complementarity of bilateral, plurilateral and multilateral negotiations on nuclear disarmament, and that bilateral negotiations can never replace multilateral negotiations in this respect,

Noting the support expressed in the Conference on Disarmament and in the General Assembly for the elaboration of an international convention to assure non-nuclear-weapon States against the use or threat of use of nuclear weapons, and the multilateral efforts in the Conference on Disarmament to reach agreement on such an international convention at an early date,

Recalling the advisory opinion of the International Court of Justice on the *Legality of the Threat or Use of Nuclear Weapons*, issued on 8 July 1996, and welcoming the unanimous reaffirmation by all Judges of the Court that there exists an obligation for all States to pursue in good faith and bring to a conclusion negotiations leading to nuclear disarmament in all its aspects under strict and effective international control,

Mindful of paragraph 114 and other relevant recommendations in the Final Document of the Twelfth Conference of Heads of State or Government of Non-Aligned Countries, held at Durban, South Africa, from 29 August to 3 September 1998, calling upon the Conference on Disarmament to establish, on a priority basis, an ad hoc committee to commence negotiations in 1998 on a phased programme of nuclear disarmament and for the eventual elimination of nuclear weapons with a specified framework of time,

Recalling paragraph 72 of the Final Document of the Thirteenth Ministerial Conference of the Movement of Non-Aligned Countries, held at Cartagena, Colombia, on 8 and 9 April 2000,

Bearing in mind the principles and guidelines on the establishment of nuclear-weapon-free zones, adopted by the Disarmament Commission at its substantive session of 1999,

Welcoming the United Nations Millennium Declaration, in which heads of State and Government resolve to strive for the elimination of weapons of mass destruction, in particular nuclear weapons, and to keep all options open for achieving this aim, including the possibility of convening an international conference to identify ways of eliminating nuclear dangers,

Seized of the danger of the use of weapons of mass destruction, particularly nuclear weapons, in terrorist acts and the urgent need for concerted international efforts to control and overcome it,

1. *Recognizes* that, in view of recent political developments, the time is now opportune for all the nuclear-weapon States to take effective disarmament measures with a view to the elimination of these weapons;

2. *Also recognizes* that there is a genuine need to diminish the role of nuclear weapons in security policies to minimize the risk that these weapons will ever be used and to facilitate the process of their total elimination;

3. *Urges* the nuclear-weapon States to stop immediately the qualitative improvement, development, production and stockpiling of nuclear warheads and their delivery systems;

4. *Also urges* the nuclear-weapon States, as an interim measure, to de-alert and deactivate immediately their nuclear weapons and to take other concrete measures to reduce further the operational status of their nuclear-weapon systems;

5. *Reiterates its call upon* the nuclear-weapon States to undertake the step-by-step reduction of the nuclear threat and to carry out effective nuclear disarmament measures with a view to the total elimination of these weapons;

6. *Calls upon* the nuclear-weapon States, pending the achievement of the total elimination of nuclear weapons, to agree on an internationally and legally binding instrument on the joint undertaking not to be the first to use nuclear weapons, and calls upon all States to conclude an internationally and legally binding instrument on security assurances of non-use and non-threat of use of nuclear weapons against non-nuclear-weapon States;

7. *Urges* the nuclear-weapon States to commence plurilateral negotiations among themselves at an appropriate stage on further deep reductions of nuclear weapons as an effective measure of nuclear disarmament;

8. *Underlines* the importance of applying the principle of irreversibility to the process of nuclear disarmament, nuclear and other related arms control and reduction measures;

9. *Welcomes* the positive outcome of the 2000 Review Conference of the Parties to the Treaty on the Non-Proliferation of Nuclear Weapons and the unequivocal undertaking by the nuclear-weapon States, in the Final Document of the Review Conference, to accomplish the total elimination of their nuclear arsenals leading to nuclear disarmament, to which all States parties are committed under article VI of the Treaty, and the reaffirmation by the States parties that the total elimination of nuclear weapons is the only absolute guarantee against the use or threat of use of nuclear weapons, and calls for the full and effective implementation of the steps set out in the Final Document;

10. *Calls* for the immediate commencement of negotiations in the Conference on Disarmament on a non-discriminatory, multilateral and internationally and effectively verifiable treaty banning the production of fissile material for nuclear weapons or other nuclear explosive devices on the basis of the report of the Special Coordinator and the mandate contained therein;

11. *Urges* the Conference on Disarmament to agree on a programme of work which includes the immediate commencement of negotiations on such a treaty with a view to their conclusion within five years;

12. *Calls* for the conclusion of an international legal instrument or instruments on adequate security assurances to non-nuclear-weapon States;

13. *Calls also* for the early entry into force and strict observance of the Comprehensive Nuclear-Test-Ban Treaty;

14. *Expresses its regret* that the Conference on Disarmament was unable to establish an ad hoc committee on nuclear disarmament at its 2001 session, as called for in General Assembly resolution 55/33 T;

15. *Reiterates its call upon* the Conference on Disarmament to establish, on a priority basis, an ad hoc committee to deal with nuclear disarmament early in 2002 and to commence negotiations on a phased programme of nuclear disarmament leading to the eventual elimination of nuclear weapons;

16. *Calls* for the convening of an international conference on nuclear disarmament in all its aspects at an early date to identify and deal with concrete measures of nuclear disarmament;

17. *Requests* the Secretary-General to submit to the General Assembly at its fifty-seventh session a report on the implementation of the present resolution;

18. *Decides* to include in the provisional agenda of its fifty-seventh session the item entitled "Nuclear disarmament".

RECORDED VOTE ON RESOLUTION 56/24 R:

In favour: Afghanistan, Algeria, Angola, Armenia, Bahamas, Bahrain, Bangladesh, Barbados, Benin, Bhutan, Bolivia, Botswana, Brazil, Brunei Darussalam, Burkina Faso, Burundi, Cambodia, Cameroon, Cape Verde, Chile, China, Colombia, Comoros, Costa Rica, Côte d'Ivoire, Cuba, Democratic People's Republic of Korea, Djibouti, Dominican Republic, Ecuador, Egypt, El Salvador, Equatorial Guinea, Eritrea, Ethiopia, Fiji, Gabon, Ghana, Grenada, Guatemala, Guinea, Guyana, Haiti, Honduras, Indonesia, Iran, Jamaica, Jordan, Kenya, Kuwait, Lao People's Democratic Republic, Lebanon, Lesotho, Libyan Arab Jamahiriya, Madagascar, Malaysia, Maldives, Mali, Mauritania, Mexico, Mongolia, Morocco, Mozambique, Myanmar, Namibia, Nepal, New Zealand, Nicaragua, Nigeria, Oman, Panama, Papua New Guinea, Paraguay, Peru, Philippines, Qatar, Saint Lucia, Samoa, Saudi Arabia, Senegal, Seychelles, Sierra Leone, Singapore, Solomon Islands, South Africa, Sri Lanka, Sudan, Swaziland, Syrian Arab Republic, Thailand, Togo, Tonga, Trinidad and Tobago, Tunisia, Uganda, United Arab Emirates, United Republic of Tanzania, Uruguay, Venezuela, Viet Nam, Yemen, Zambia, Zimbabwe.

Against: Albania, Andorra, Australia, Austria, Belgium, Bosnia and Herzegovina, Bulgaria, Canada, Croatia, Czech Republic, Denmark, Estonia, Finland, France, Germany, Greece, Hungary, Iceland, Italy, Latvia, Liechtenstein, Lithuania, Luxembourg, Malta, Micronesia, Monaco, Nauru, Netherlands, Norway, Poland, Portugal, Romania, San Marino, Slovakia, Slovenia, Spain, The former Yugoslav Republic of Macedonia, Turkey, United Kingdom, United States, Yugoslavia.

Abstaining: Argentina, Azerbaijan, Belarus, Cyprus, Georgia, India, Ireland, Israel, Japan, Kazakhstan, Mauritius, Pakistan, Republic of Korea, Republic of Moldova, Russian Federation, Sweden, Ukraine.

In the First Committee, paragraph 9 was adopted by a recorded vote of 132 to 3, with 6 abstentions. The Assembly retained the paragraph by a recorded vote of 149 to 3, with 6 abstentions.

The Assembly adopted **resolution 56/24 C** by recorded vote (98-45-14) [agenda item 74 *(n)*].

Reducing nuclear danger

The General Assembly,

Bearing in mind that the use of nuclear weapons poses the most serious threat to mankind and to the survival of civilization,

Reaffirming that any use or threat of use of nuclear weapons would constitute a violation of the Charter of the United Nations,

Convinced that the proliferation of nuclear weapons in all its aspects would seriously enhance the danger of nuclear war,

Convinced also that nuclear disarmament and the complete elimination of nuclear weapons are essential to remove the danger of nuclear war,

Considering that, until nuclear weapons cease to exist, it is imperative on the part of the nuclear-weapon States to adopt measures that assure non-nuclear-weapon States against the use or threat of use of nuclear weapons,

Considering also that the hair-trigger alert of nuclear weapons carries unacceptable risks of unintentional or accidental use of nuclear weapons, which would have catastrophic consequences for all mankind,

Emphasizing the imperative need to adopt measures to avoid accidental, unauthorized or unexplained incidents arising from computer anomaly or other technical malfunctions,

Conscious that limited steps relating to detargeting have been taken by the nuclear-weapon States and that further practical, realistic and mutually reinforcing steps are necessary to contribute to the improvement in the international climate for negotiations leading to the elimination of nuclear weapons,

Mindful that reduction of tensions brought about by a change in nuclear doctrines would positively impact on international peace and security and improve the conditions for the further reduction and the elimination of nuclear weapons,

Reiterating the highest priority accorded to nuclear disarmament in the Final Document of the Tenth Special Session of the General Assembly and by the international community,

Recalling that in the advisory opinion of the International Court of Justice on the *Legality of the Threat or Use of Nuclear Weapons* it is stated that there exists an obligation for all States to pursue in good faith and bring to a conclusion negotiations leading to nuclear disarmament in all its aspects under strict and effective international control,

Welcoming the call in the United Nations Millennium Declaration to seek to eliminate the dangers posed by weapons of mass destruction and the resolve to strive for the elimination of weapons of mass destruction, particularly nuclear weapons, including the possibility of convening an international conference to identify ways of eliminating nuclear dangers,

1. *Calls* for a review of nuclear doctrines and, in this context, immediate and urgent steps to reduce the risks of unintentional and accidental use of nuclear weapons;

2. *Requests* the five nuclear-weapon States to take measures towards the implementation of paragraph 1 of the present resolution;

3. *Calls upon* Member States to take the necessary measures to prevent the proliferation of nuclear weapons in all its aspects and to promote nuclear disarmament, with the objective of eliminating nuclear weapons;

4. *Takes note* of the report prepared by the Advisory Board on Disarmament Matters and submitted by the Secretary-General in pursuance of paragraph 5 of General Assembly resolution 55/33 N of 20 November 2000, in particular the seven recommendations highlighted for further action;

5. *Requests* the Secretary-General to take steps towards the implementation of the seven recommendations identified in the report of the Advisory Board that would significantly reduce the risk of nuclear war, including the proposal contained in the United Nations Millennium Declaration for convening an international conference to identify ways of eliminating nuclear dangers, and to report thereon to the General Assembly at its fifty-seventh session;

6. *Decides* to include in the provisional agenda of its fifty-seventh session the item entitled "Reducing nuclear danger".

RECORDED VOTE ON RESOLUTION 56/24 C:

In favour: Afghanistan, Algeria, Angola, Bahamas, Bahrain, Bangladesh, Barbados, Benin, Bhutan, Bolivia, Botswana, Brunei Darussalam, Burkina Faso, Burundi, Cambodia, Cameroon, Cape Verde, Chile, Colombia, Comoros, Costa Rica, Côte d'Ivoire, Cuba, Democratic People's Republic of Korea, Djibouti, Dominican Republic, Ecuador, Egypt, El Salvador, Eritrea, Ethiopia, Fiji, Gabon, Ghana, Grenada, Guatemala, Guinea, Guyana, Haiti, Honduras, India, Indonesia, Iran, Jordan, Kenya, Kuwait, Lao People's Democratic Republic, Lebanon, Lesotho, Libyan Arab Jamahiriya, Madagascar, Malaysia, Maldives, Mali, Mauritania, Mauritius, Mexico, Mongolia, Morocco, Mozambique, Myanmar, Namibia, Nepal, Nicaragua, Nigeria, Oman, Pakistan, Panama, Papua New Guinea, Peru, Philippines, Qatar, Samoa, Saudi Arabia, Senegal, Sierra Leone, Singapore, Solomon Islands, South Africa, Sri Lanka, Sudan, Swaziland, Syrian Arab Republic, Thailand, Togo, Tonga, Trinidad and Tobago, Tunisia, Turkmenistan, Uganda, United Arab Emirates, United Republic of Tanzania, Uruguay, Venezuela, Viet Nam, Yemen, Zambia.

Against: Albania, Andorra, Australia, Austria, Belgium, Bosnia and Herzegovina, Bulgaria, Canada, Croatia, Cyprus, Czech Republic, Denmark, Estonia, Finland, France, Germany, Greece, Hungary, Iceland, Ireland, Italy, Latvia, Liechtenstein, Lithuania, Luxembourg, Malta, Micronesia, Monaco, Netherlands, New Zealand, Norway, Poland, Portugal, Romania, Russian Federation, San Marino, Slovakia, Slovenia, Spain, Sweden, The former Yugoslav Republic of Macedonia, Turkey, United Kingdom, United States, Yugoslavia.

Abstaining: Argentina, Armenia, Azerbaijan, Belarus, Brazil, China, Georgia, Israel, Japan, Kazakhstan, Paraguay, Republic of Korea, Republic of Moldova, Ukraine.

Decision 56/413 was adopted by recorded vote [agenda item 74].

United Nations conference to identify ways of eliminating nuclear dangers in the context of nuclear disarmament

At its 68th plenary meeting, on 29 November 2001, the General Assembly, by a recorded vote of 115 to 7, with 37 abstentions, and on the recommendation of the First Committee, decided to include in the provisional agenda of its fifty-seventh session an item entitled "United Nations conference to identify ways of eliminating nuclear dangers in the context of nuclear disarmament".

RECORDED VOTE ON DECISION 56/413:

In favour: Afghanistan, Algeria, Angola, Argentina, Armenia, Bahamas, Bahrain, Bangladesh, Barbados, Belarus, Benin, Bhutan, Bolivia, Botswana, Brazil, Brunei Darussalam, Burkina Faso, Burundi, Cambodia, Cameroon, Cape Verde, Chile, China, Colombia, Comoros, Costa Rica, Côte d'Ivoire, Cuba, Cyprus, Democratic People's Republic of Korea, Djibouti, Dominican Republic, Ecuador, Egypt, El Salvador, Equatorial Guinea, Eritrea, Ethiopia, Fiji, Gabon, Ghana, Grenada, Guatemala, Guinea, Guyana, Haiti, Honduras, India, Indonesia, Iran, Ireland, Jamaica, Japan, Jordan, Kazakhstan, Kenya, Kuwait, Lao People's Democratic Republic, Lebanon, Lesotho, Libyan Arab Jamahiriya, Madagascar, Malaysia, Maldives, Mali, Mauritania, Mauritius, Mexico, Mongolia, Morocco, Mozambique, Myanmar, Namibia, Nauru, Nepal, New Zealand, Nicaragua, Nigeria, Oman, Pakistan, Panama, Papua New Guinea, Paraguay, Peru, Philippines, Qatar, Russian Federation, Saint Lucia, Samoa, San Marino, Saudi Arabia, Senegal, Seychelles, Sierra Leone, Singapore, Solomon Islands, South Africa, Sri Lanka, Sudan, Swaziland, Sweden, Syrian Arab Republic, Thai-

land, Togo, Trinidad and Tobago, Tunisia, Uganda, United Arab Emirates, United Republic of Tanzania, Uruguay, Venezuela, Viet Nam, Yemen, Zambia, Zimbabwe.
  Against: France, Germany, Israel, Monaco, Poland, United Kingdom, United States.
  Abstaining: Albania, Andorra, Australia, Austria, Azerbaijan, Belgium, Bosnia and Herzegovina, Canada, Croatia, Czech Republic, Denmark, Estonia, Finland, Georgia, Greece, Hungary, Iceland, Italy, Latvia, Liechtenstein, Lithuania, Luxembourg, Malta, Micronesia, Netherlands, Norway, Portugal, Republic of Korea, Republic of Moldova, Romania, Slovakia, Slovenia, Spain, The former Yugoslav Republic of Macedonia, Turkey, Ukraine, Yugoslavia.

Also on 29 November, the Assembly decided to include in the provisional agenda of its fifty-seventh (2002) session the item "Towards a nuclear-weapon-free world: the need for a new agenda" (**decision 56/411**).

ABM Treaty and other missile issues

In 2001, missile defence issues, particularly regarding the proliferation of long-range ballistic missiles, United States plans to establish a national missile defence system [YUN 1999, p. 469] and the status of the ABM Treaty, continued to be of international concern.

Regarding the ABM Treaty, on 13 December President Bush announced that the United States had decided to withdraw unilaterally from it, effective six months from the announcement, stating that it hindered the Government's ability to develop ways to protect the United States from future missile attacks from rogue States or terrorists; at the same time, he reiterated the United States willingness to develop a new strategic relationship with Russia, including deeper cuts in warheads. On 13 December [A/56/707], President Putin considered that decision a mistake but said it would not pose a threat to the Russian Federation's national security. The Secretary-General expressed concern that the annulment of the Treaty might provoke a new arms race, especially in the missile area, and called on States to explore new binding and irreversible initiatives.

The Russian Federation organized an international expert meeting (Moscow, 15 February) to continue discussions on its proposal for a global control system for the non-proliferation of missiles and missile technology. On 31 May, the Russian Federation and the United States ended the 13-year inspection regime under the 1987 Treaty on Intermediate-Range Nuclear Forces [YUN 1987, p. 47], which had committed the two parties to eliminate their intermediate-range (1,000-5,500 kilometres) and shorter-range (500-1,000 kilometres) missiles no later than three years after the Treaty's entry into force in 1988 [YUN 1988, p. 56], and to conduct on-site inspections on each other's territory for 13 years. The European Union (EU), following a summit (Göteborg, Sweden, 15-16 June), issued a declaration stressing

the need for a common position in the fight against ballistic missile proliferation.

Report of Secretary-General. In response to General Assembly resolution 55/33 A [YUN 2000, p. 499], the Secretary-General, in a July report with later addenda [A/56/136 & Add.1,2], presented the views of eight Member States and the EU on the issue of missiles in all its aspects.

Expert panel. A panel of governmental experts, established by the Secretary-General in accordance with resolution 55/33 A to prepare a report on the issue of missiles for the Assembly's consideration in 2002, held its first session (New York, 30 July–3 August). Further meetings were scheduled for 2002.

GENERAL ASSEMBLY ACTION

On 29 November [68 meeting], the General Assembly, on the recommendation of the First Committee [A/56/536], adopted **resolution 56/24 B** by recorded vote (98-0-58) [agenda item 74 *(d)*].

Missiles
The General Assembly,
Recalling its resolutions 54/54 F of 1 December 1999 and 55/33 A of 20 November 2000,
Reaffirming the role of the United Nations in the field of arms regulation and disarmament and the commitment of Member States to take concrete steps to strengthen that role,
Realizing the need to promote regional and international peace and security in a world free from the scourge of war and the burden of armaments,
Convinced of the need for a comprehensive approach towards missiles, in a balanced and non-discriminatory manner, as a contribution to international peace and security,
Bearing in mind that the security concerns of Member States at the international and regional levels should be taken into consideration in addressing the issue of missiles,
Underlining the complexities involved in considering the issue of missiles in the conventional context,
Expressing its support for the international efforts against the development and proliferation of all weapons of mass destruction,
Considering that the Secretary-General has been requested, with the assistance of a panel of governmental experts, to prepare a report for the consideration of the General Assembly at its fifty-seventh session on the issue of missiles in all its aspects,
  1. *Notes with satisfaction* that the panel of governmental experts established by the Secretary-General held its first session in New York in 2001 and that it intends to convene two more sessions in 2002 in order to complete its mandate;
  2. *Takes note with appreciation* of the report of the Secretary-General submitted pursuant to resolution 55/33 A;
  3. *Requests* the Secretary-General further to seek the views of Member States on the issue of missiles in all its aspects and to submit a report to the General Assembly at its fifty-seventh session;

4. *Decides* to include in the provisional agenda of its fifty-seventh session the item entitled "Missiles".

RECORDED VOTE ON RESOLUTION 56/24 B:

In favour: Afghanistan, Algeria, Angola, Bahamas, Bahrain, Bangladesh, Barbados, Belarus, Benin, Bhutan, Botswana, Brazil, Brunei Darussalam, Burkina Faso, Burundi, Cambodia, Cameroon, Cape Verde, Chile, China, Colombia, Comoros, Costa Rica, Côte d'Ivoire, Cuba, Djibouti, Dominican Republic, Ecuador, Egypt, El Salvador, Eritrea, Ethiopia, Fiji, Gabon, Ghana, Grenada, Guatemala, Guinea, Guyana, Haiti, Honduras, India, Indonesia, Iran, Jamaica, Jordan, Kazakhstan, Kenya, Kuwait, Lao People's Democratic Republic, Lebanon, Lesotho, Libyan Arab Jamahiriya, Madagascar, Malaysia, Maldives, Mali, Mauritius, Mexico, Mongolia, Morocco, Mozambique, Myanmar, Namibia, Nauru, Nepal, Nicaragua, Nigeria, Oman, Pakistan, Panama, Papua New Guinea, Peru, Philippines, Qatar, Russian Federation, Saint Lucia, Saudi Arabia, Senegal, Sierra Leone, South Africa, Sri Lanka, Sudan, Swaziland, Syrian Arab Republic, Thailand, Togo, Tonga, Trinidad and Tobago, Tunisia, Turkmenistan, Uganda, United Arab Emirates, United Republic of Tanzania, Venezuela, Viet Nam, Yemen, Zambia.

Against: None.

Abstaining: Albania, Andorra, Argentina, Armenia, Australia, Austria, Azerbaijan, Belgium, Bolivia, Bosnia and Herzegovina, Bulgaria, Canada, Croatia, Cyprus, Czech Republic, Denmark, Estonia, Finland, France, Georgia, Germany, Greece, Hungary, Iceland, Ireland, Israel, Italy, Japan, Latvia, Liechtenstein, Lithuania, Luxembourg, Malta, Micronesia, Monaco, Netherlands, New Zealand, Norway, Paraguay, Poland, Portugal, Republic of Korea, Republic of Moldova, Romania, Samoa, San Marino, Singapore, Slovakia, Slovenia, Spain, Sweden, The former Yugoslav Republic of Macedonia, Turkey, Ukraine, United Kingdom, United States, Uruguay, Yugoslavia.

Also on 29 November [meeting 68], the Assembly, on the recommendation of the First Committee [A/56/536], adopted **resolution 56/24 A** by recorded vote (82-5-62) [agenda item 74 *(e)*].

Preservation of and compliance with the Treaty on the Limitation of Anti-Ballistic Missile Systems

The General Assembly,

Recalling its resolutions 50/60 of 12 December 1995 and 52/30 of 9 December 1997 on compliance with arms limitation and disarmament and non-proliferation agreements and its resolutions 54/54 A of 1 December 1999 and 55/33 B of 20 November 2000 on preservation of and compliance with the Treaty on the Limitation of Anti-Ballistic Missile Systems,

Recognizing the historical role of the Treaty on the Limitation of Anti-Ballistic Missile Systems of 26 May 1972 between the United States of America and the Union of Soviet Socialist Republics as a cornerstone for maintaining global peace and security and strategic stability, and reaffirming its continued validity and relevance, especially in the current international situation,

Stressing the paramount importance of full and strict compliance with the Treaty by the parties,

Recalling that the provisions of the Treaty are intended as a contribution to the creation of more favourable conditions for further negotiations on limiting strategic arms,

Mindful of the obligations of the parties to the Treaty under article VI of the Treaty on the Non-Proliferation of Nuclear Weapons,

Concerned that the implementation of any measures undermining the purposes and provisions of the Treaty affects not only the security interests of the parties, but also those of the whole international community,

Recalling the widespread concern about the proliferation of weapons of mass destruction and their means of delivery,

1. *Calls* for continued efforts to strengthen the Treaty on the Limitation of Anti-Ballistic Missile Systems and to preserve its integrity and validity so that it remains a cornerstone in maintaining global strategic stability and world peace and in promoting further strategic nuclear arms reductions;

2. *Calls also* for renewed efforts by each of the States parties to preserve and strengthen the Treaty through full and strict compliance;

3. *Calls upon* the parties to the Treaty, in accordance with their obligations under the Treaty, to limit the deployment of anti-ballistic missile systems, to refrain from the deployment of anti-ballistic missile systems for the defence of the territory of their country, not to provide a base for such a defence and not to transfer to other States or deploy outside their national territory anti-ballistic missile systems or their components limited by the Treaty;

4. *Considers* that the implementation of any measure undermining the purposes and the provisions of the Treaty also undermines global strategic stability and world peace and the promotion of further strategic nuclear arms reductions;

5. *Urges* all Member States to support efforts aimed at stemming the proliferation of weapons of mass destruction and their means of delivery;

6. *Supports* further efforts by the international community, in the light of emerging developments, towards safeguarding the inviolability and integrity of the Treaty, which is in the strongest interest of the international community;

7. *Welcomes* the ongoing dialogue between the Russian Federation and the United States of America on a new strategic framework premised on openness, mutual confidence and real opportunities for cooperation, which is of paramount importance, especially in a changing security environment, and hopes that this dialogue will successfully lead to substantial reductions in offensive nuclear forces and contribute to the maintenance of international stability;

8. *Decides* to include in the provisional agenda of its fifty-seventh session the item entitled "Preservation of and compliance with the Treaty on the Limitation of Anti-Ballistic Missile Systems".

RECORDED VOTE ON RESOLUTION 56/24 A:

In favour: Afghanistan, Algeria, Angola, Armenia, Barbados, Belarus, Bhutan, Botswana, Brunei Darussalam, Burkina Faso, Burundi, Cambodia, Cameroon, Cape Verde, China, Colombia, Comoros, Costa Rica, Côte d'Ivoire, Cuba, Cyprus, Democratic People's Republic of Korea, Djibouti, Ecuador, Egypt, Eritrea, Ethiopia, Fiji, Gabon, Guinea, Guyana, Haiti, Honduras, India, Indonesia, Iran, Ireland, Jamaica, Jordan, Kazakhstan, Kenya, Lao People's Democratic Republic, Lebanon, Lesotho, Libyan Arab Jamahiriya, Madagascar, Malaysia, Mali, Mauritania, Mexico, Mongolia, Mozambique, Myanmar, Namibia, Nauru, Nepal, Nigeria, Oman, Pakistan, Panama, Papua New Guinea, Republic of Moldova, Russian Federation, Saint Lucia, Senegal, Sierra Leone, Singapore, South Africa, Sri Lanka, Sudan, Swaziland, Syrian Arab Republic, Thailand, Togo, Tonga, Turkmenistan, Uganda, United Republic of Tanzania, Venezuela, Viet Nam, Yemen, Zambia.

Against: Albania, Benin, Israel, Micronesia, United States.

Abstaining: Andorra, Argentina, Australia, Austria, Bahamas, Bahrain, Bangladesh, Belgium, Bolivia, Brazil, Bulgaria, Canada, Chile, Croatia, Czech Republic, Denmark, Dominican Republic, Estonia, Finland, France, Georgia, Germany, Ghana, Greece, Grenada, Guatemala, Hungary, Iceland, Italy, Japan, Latvia, Liechtenstein, Lithuania, Luxembourg, Malta, Mauritius, Monaco, Morocco, Netherlands, New Zealand, Nicaragua, Norway, Paraguay, Peru, Philippines, Poland, Portugal, Republic of Korea, Romania, Samoa, San Marino, Slovakia, Slovenia, Spain, Sweden, The former Yugoslav Republic of Macedonia, Trinidad and Tobago, Turkey, Ukraine, United Kingdom, Uruguay, Yugoslavia.

Comprehensive Nuclear-Test-Ban Treaty

Status

As at 31 December, 165 States had signed the 1996 Comprehensive Nuclear-Test-Ban Treaty (CTBT), adopted by General Assembly resolution 50/245 [YUN 1996, p. 454], and 89 had ratified it. During the year, instruments of ratification were deposited by Benin, Costa Rica, Croatia, Ecuador, Guyana, the Holy See, Jamaica, Latvia, Malta, Namibia, Nauru, Nigeria, Paraguay, the Philippines, Saint Lucia, Sierra Leone, Singapore, Uganda, Ukraine and Uruguay. In accordance with article XIV, CTBT was to enter into force 180 days after the 44 States possessing nuclear reactors, listed in annex 2 to the Treaty, had deposited their instruments of ratification. By year's end, 31 of those States had ratified the Treaty.

Conference on facilitating entry into force

The second Conference on Facilitating the Entry into Force of CTBT (New York, 11-13 November) was convened in accordance with article XIV of the Treaty, which stipulated that if the Treaty had not entered into force three years from the date it opened for signature (September 1996) [YUN 1996, p. 452], the depositary should convene a conference at the request of a majority of ratifying States to consider and decide by consensus measures to facilitate early entry into force. In February, the Secretary-General, as depositary, following a request from the majority of States [YUN 2000, p. 500], informed all States of his intention to convene the conference. The first conference took place in 1999 [YUN 1999, p. 471].

On 13 November [CTBT-ART.XIV/2001/6], the Conference, which was attended by 109 ratifying and signatory States, nine non-signatory States and a number of specialized agencies and intergovernmental and non-governmental organizations (NGOs), adopted a Final Declaration, by which it reaffirmed strong support for CTBT and called on signatory States to ratify the Treaty as soon as possible, especially those whose ratification was needed for the Treaty's entry into force. It urged the three States (Democratic People's Republic of Korea, India, Pakistan) whose ratification was required for the Treaty's entry into force, but which had not yet signed, to do so, and called on the remaining two nuclear-weapon States (China, United States) to accelerate their ratification process. States were called on to maintain a moratorium on nuclear-weapon-test explosions or any other nuclear explosions.

In accordance with the Final Declaration, Mexico, which held the Presidency of the Conference, was entrusted with coordinating informal consultations with interested States to promote the Treaty's early entry into force and to encourage regional and multilateral initiatives aimed at promoting further signatures and ratifications.

GENERAL ASSEMBLY ACTION

On 29 November, the General Assembly, on the recommendation of the First Committee [A/56/544], adopted **decision 56/415** by recorded vote [agenda item 82].

Comprehensive Nuclear-Test-Ban Treaty

At its 68th plenary meeting, on 29 November 2001, the General Assembly, by a recorded vote of 161 to 1, with no abstentions, and noting the holding of the Conference on Facilitating the Entry into Force of the Comprehensive Nuclear-Test-Ban Treaty in New York from 11 to 13 November 2001, decided, on the recommendation of the First Committee, to include in the provisional agenda of its fifty-seventh session the item entitled "Comprehensive Nuclear-Test-Ban Treaty".

RECORDED VOTE ON DECISION 56/415:

In favour: Afghanistan, Albania, Algeria, Andorra, Angola, Argentina, Armenia, Australia, Austria, Azerbaijan, Bahamas, Bahrain, Bangladesh, Barbados, Belarus, Belgium, Benin, Bhutan, Bolivia, Bosnia and Herzegovina, Botswana, Brazil, Brunei Darussalam, Bulgaria, Burkina Faso, Burundi, Cambodia, Cameroon, Canada, Cape Verde, Chile, China, Colombia, Comoros, Congo, Costa Rica, Côte d'Ivoire, Croatia, Cuba, Cyprus, Czech Republic, Denmark, Djibouti, Dominican Republic, Ecuador, Egypt, El Salvador, Equatorial Guinea, Eritrea, Estonia, Ethiopia, Fiji, Finland, France, Gabon, Georgia, Germany, Ghana, Greece, Grenada, Guatemala, Guinea, Guyana, Haiti, Honduras, Hungary, Iceland, India, Indonesia, Iran, Ireland, Israel, Italy, Jamaica, Japan, Jordan, Kazakhstan, Kenya, Kuwait, Lao People's Democratic Republic, Latvia, Lebanon, Lesotho, Libyan Arab Jamahiriya, Liechtenstein, Lithuania, Luxembourg, Madagascar, Malaysia, Maldives, Mali, Malta, Mauritania, Mauritius, Mexico, Micronesia, Monaco, Mongolia, Morocco, Mozambique, Myanmar, Namibia, Nauru, Nepal, Netherlands, New Zealand, Nicaragua, Nigeria, Norway, Oman, Pakistan, Panama, Papua New Guinea, Paraguay, Peru, Philippines, Poland, Portugal, Qatar, Republic of Korea, Republic of Moldova, Romania, Russian Federation, Saint Lucia, Samoa, San Marino, Saudi Arabia, Senegal, Seychelles, Sierra Leone, Singapore, Slovakia, Slovenia, Solomon Islands, South Africa, Spain, Sri Lanka, Sudan, Swaziland, Sweden, Syrian Arab Republic, Thailand, The former Yugoslav Republic of Macedonia, Togo, Tonga, Trinidad and Tobago, Tunisia, Turkey, Turkmenistan, Uganda, Ukraine, United Arab Emirates, United Kingdom, United Republic of Tanzania, Uruguay, Venezuela, Viet Nam, Yemen, Yugoslavia, Zambia, Zimbabwe.
Against: United States.

Preparatory Commission for CTBT Organization

The Preparatory Commission for the Comprehensive Nuclear-Test-Ban Treaty Organization, established in 1996 [YUN 1996, p. 452], continued efforts towards developing the global verification regime to monitor Treaty compliance, the options for enhanced cooperation under the relationship agreement between the United Nations and the Commission, adopted in General Assembly resolution 54/280 [YUN 2000, p. 501], and the level and pace of signatures and ratifications of CTBT as indicators of the international community's support for the Treaty. Progress was made in building the International Monitoring System (IMS) [YUN 1999, p. 472], the global network of 337 facilities in 90 countries, designed to track and detect nuclear explosions prohibited by CTBT via a global satellite communication system and transmit the data to the International Data Centre (IDC) in Vienna. By year's end, 121 stations had been completed and another 90 were either under construction or in contract negotiation. IDC and the verification system as a whole also continued to be developed and refined.

The Preparatory Commission held its fourteenth (24-26 April) [CTBT/PC-14/1], fifteenth (21-23 August) [CTBT/PC-15/1] and sixteenth (19-24 November) [CTBT/PC-16/1] sessions, all in Vienna, to consider the reports of its working groups and to discuss organizational, budgetary and other matters. The Commission adopted its 2002 programme and budget, totalling $85.1 million, of which approximately half was earmarked for IMS. The remainder would be used to develop IDC, the global communications infrastructure, and procedures and guidelines to support on-site inspection once the Treaty entered into force.

Note of Secretary-General. In August [A/56/317], the Secretary-General informed the General Assembly of the availability of the report of the Commission's Executive Secretary covering 2000.

GENERAL ASSEMBLY ACTION

On 7 December [meeting 80], the General Assembly adopted **resolution 56/49** [draft: A/56/L.38 & Add.1] by recorded vote (134-1-2) [agenda item 21 (k)].

Cooperation between the United Nations and the Preparatory Commission for the Comprehensive Nuclear-Test-Ban Treaty Organization

The General Assembly,

Taking note of the note by the Secretary-General on cooperation between the United Nations and the Preparatory Commission for the Comprehensive Nuclear-Test-Ban Treaty Organization,

Taking note also of the report of the Executive Secretary of the Preparatory Commission for the Comprehensive Nuclear-Test-Ban Treaty Organization,

Decides to include in the provisional agenda of its fifty-seventh session the sub-item entitled "Cooperation between the United Nations and the Preparatory Commission for the Comprehensive Nuclear-Test-Ban Treaty Organization".

RECORDED VOTE ON RESOLUTION 56/49:

In favour: Algeria, Andorra, Angola, Argentina, Armenia, Australia, Austria, Azerbaijan, Bahamas, Bahrain, Bangladesh, Barbados, Belarus, Belgium, Benin, Bolivia, Bosnia and Herzegovina, Botswana, Brazil, Brunei Darussalam, Bulgaria, Burkina Faso, Burundi, Cambodia, Canada, Cape Verde, Chad, Chile, China, Colombia, Congo, Costa Rica, Côte d'Ivoire, Croatia, Cuba, Cyprus, Czech Republic, Denmark, Djibouti, Dominican Republic, Ecuador, Egypt, El Salvador, Equatorial Guinea, Eritrea, Ethiopia, Fiji, Finland, France, Gabon, Georgia, Germany, Ghana, Greece, Guatemala, Guyana, Haiti, Hungary, Iceland, Indonesia, Iran, Ireland, Israel, Italy, Japan, Jordan, Kazakhstan, Kenya, Kuwait, Lao People's Democratic Republic, Latvia, Lebanon, Libyan Arab Jamahiriya, Liechtenstein, Lithuania, Luxembourg, Madagascar, Malaysia, Maldives, Mali, Malta, Mauritius, Mexico, Monaco, Mongolia, Morocco, Myanmar, Namibia, Nauru, Nepal, Netherlands, New Zealand, Nigeria, Norway, Oman, Panama, Papua New Guinea, Paraguay, Peru, Philippines, Poland, Portugal, Qatar, Republic of Korea, Republic of Moldova, Romania, Russian Federation, San Marino, Senegal, Singapore, Slovakia, Slovenia, South Africa, Spain, Sri Lanka, Sudan, Swaziland, Sweden, Syrian Arab Republic, Thailand, The former Yugoslav Republic of Macedonia, Togo, Tonga, Tunisia, Turkey, Ukraine, United Arab Emirates, United Kingdom, United Republic of Tanzania, Uruguay, Venezuela, Viet Nam, Yugoslavia, Zambia.
Against: United States.
Abstaining: India, Pakistan.

Non-Proliferation Treaty

Status

In 2001, the number of States party to the 1968 Treaty on the Non-Proliferation of Nuclear Weapons (NPT), adopted by the General Assembly in resolution 2373(XXII) [YUN 1968, p. 17], remained at 187. NPT entered into force on 5 March 1970.

2005 review conference

The parties to NPT decided that the first session of the Preparatory Committee for the 2005 Review Conference of the Parties would take place in New York from 8 to 19 April 2002.

Quinquennial review conferences, as called for under article VIII, paragraph 3, of the Treaty, were held in 1975 [YUN 1975, p. 27], 1980 [YUN 1980, p. 51], 1985 [YUN 1985, p. 56], 1990 [YUN 1990, p. 50], 1995 [YUN 1995, p. 189] and 2000 [YUN 2000, p. 487].

GENERAL ASSEMBLY ACTION

On 29 November [meeting 68], the General Assembly, on the recommendation of the First Committee [A/56/536], adopted **resolution 56/24 O** by recorded vote (156-1-3) [agenda item 74].

2005 Review Conference of the Parties to the Treaty on the Non-Proliferation of Nuclear Weapons and its Preparatory Committee

The General Assembly,

Recalling its resolution 2373(XXII) of 12 June 1968, the annex to which contains the Treaty on the Non-Proliferation of Nuclear Weapons,

Noting the provisions of article VIII, paragraph 3, of the Treaty regarding the convening of review conferences at five-year intervals,

Recalling the decision of the 2000 Review Conference of the Parties to the Treaty on improving the effectiveness of the strengthened review process for the Treaty, which reaffirmed the provisions in the decision on strengthening the review process for the Treaty, adopted by the 1995 Review and Extension Conference of the Parties to the Treaty,

Noting the decision on strengthening the review process for the Treaty in which it was agreed that Review Conferences should continue to be held every five years, and noting that, accordingly, the next Review Conference should be held in 2005,

Recalling the decision of the 2000 Review Conference that three sessions of the Preparatory Committee should be held in the years prior to the Review Conference,

Recalling also its resolution 55/33 D of 20 November 2000, in which it welcomed the adoption by consensus of the Final Document of the 2000 Review Conference of the Parties to the Treaty on the Non-Proliferation of Nuclear Weapons,

1. *Takes note* of the decision of the parties to the Treaty on the Non-Proliferation of Nuclear Weapons, following appropriate consultations, to hold the first session of the Preparatory Committee in New York from 8 to 19 April 2002;

2. *Requests* the Secretary-General to render the necessary assistance and to provide such services, including summary records, as may be required for the 2005 Review Conference of the Parties to the Treaty on the Non-Proliferation of Nuclear Weapons and its Preparatory Committee.

RECORDED VOTE ON RESOLUTION 56/24 O:

In favour: Afghanistan, Albania, Algeria, Andorra, Angola, Argentina, Armenia, Australia, Austria, Azerbaijan, Bahamas, Bahrain, Bangladesh, Barbados, Belarus, Belgium, Benin, Bhutan, Bolivia, Bosnia and Herzegovina, Botswana, Brazil, Brunei Darussalam, Bulgaria, Burkina Faso, Burundi, Cambodia, Cameroon, Canada, Cape Verde, Chile, China, Colombia, Comoros, Costa Rica, Côte d'Ivoire, Croatia, Cyprus, Czech Republic, Denmark, Djibouti, Dominican Republic, Ecuador, Egypt, El Salvador, Eritrea, Estonia, Ethiopia, Fiji, Finland, France, Gabon, Georgia, Germany, Ghana, Greece, Grenada, Guatemala, Guinea, Guyana, Haiti, Honduras, Hungary, Iceland, Indonesia, Iran, Ireland, Italy, Jamaica, Japan, Jordan, Kazakhstan, Kenya, Kuwait, Lao People's Democratic Republic, Latvia, Lebanon, Lesotho, Libyan Arab Jamahiriya, Liechtenstein, Lithuania, Luxembourg, Madagascar, Malaysia, Maldives, Mali, Malta, Mauritania, Mauritius, Mexico, Micronesia, Monaco, Mongolia, Morocco, Mozambique, Myanmar, Namibia, Nauru, Nepal, Netherlands, New Zealand, Nicaragua, Nigeria, Norway, Oman, Panama, Papua New Guinea, Paraguay, Peru, Philippines, Poland, Portugal, Qatar, Republic of Korea, Republic of Moldova, Romania, Russian Federation, Saint Lucia, Samoa, San Marino, Saudi Arabia, Senegal, Seychelles, Sierra Leone, Singapore, Slovakia, Slovenia, Solomon Islands, South Africa, Spain, Sri Lanka, Sudan, Swaziland, Sweden, Syrian Arab Republic, Thailand, The former Yugoslav Republic of Macedonia, Togo, Tonga, Trinidad and Tobago, Tunisia, Turkey, Turkmenistan, Uganda, Ukraine, United Arab Emirates, United Kingdom, United Republic of Tanzania, United States, Uruguay, Venezuela, Viet Nam, Yemen, Yugoslavia, Zambia, Zimbabwe.

Against: India.

Abstaining: Cuba, Israel, Pakistan.

IAEA safeguards

As at 31 December, the Model Protocol Additional to Safeguards Agreements strengthening the safeguards regime of the International Atomic Energy Agency (IAEA), approved by the IAEA Board of Governors in 1997 [YUN 1997, p. 486], had been signed by 61 States, including the five nuclear-weapon States, and was in force or being provisionally applied in 25 States.

The IAEA General Conference [GC(45)/RES/13], as in previous years, requested all concerned States and other parties to safeguards agreements that had not done so to sign additional protocols promptly. Asking those that had signed the protocols to bring them into force, the Conference recommended that the Director General, the Board of Governors and member States continue to consider implementing elements of a plan of action outlined in a 2000 resolution of the Conference [YUN 2000, p. 504], in order to facilitate the entry into force of safeguards agreements and additional protocols.

For nearly three years, IAEA was unable to implement its mandate with regard to Iraq under the relevant Security Council resolutions (see p. 437). Thus, the Agency was not in a position to provide any assurances that Iraq was in compliance with its obligations under those resolutions. However, IAEA conducted, in January, a physical inventory verification under the safeguards agreement between Iraq and IAEA pursuant to NPT, during which Agency inspectors verified the presence of nuclear materials under safeguards. The General Conference [GC(45)/RES/17], noting that the physical inventory verification could not serve as a substitute for IAEA's Security Council–mandated activities, again called on Iraq to cooperate fully and provide the necessary access to enable IAEA to carry out its mandate.

Concerning the implementation of the agreement between IAEA and the Democratic People's Republic of Korea (DPRK) for the application of safeguards under NPT, the Director General stated in September that, since 1993, the Agency had not been able to verify fully that all nuclear material subject to safeguards in the DPRK had been declared to IAEA (see p. 464). In May, IAEA proposed practical steps to move the verification process forward, which the DPRK declined to accept unconditionally. On 21 September [GC(45)/RES/16], the General Conference, expressing deep concern over the continuing non-compliance of the DPRK with its safeguards agreement with IAEA, encouraged the DPRK to respond positively to the Agency's proposals.

Middle East

In 2001, the General Assembly (see below) and the IAEA General Conference [GC(45)/RES/18] took action regarding the risk of nuclear proliferation in the Middle East. While the Assembly called on the non-party in the region to accede to NPT and to place all its nuclear facilities under IAEA safeguards, IAEA emphasized the need for States in the region to accept the application of full-scope Agency safeguards to all their nuclear activities as an important confidence-building measure.

Pursuant to Assembly resolution 55/36 [YUN 2000, p. 505], the Secretary-General reported, in October [A/56/425], that apart from the IAEA resolution on the application of IAEA safeguards in the Middle East, he had not received any additional information since his 2000 report on the subject [YUN 2000, p. 505]. The IAEA resolution was annexed to the Secretary-General's report.

GENERAL ASSEMBLY ACTION

On 29 November [meeting 68], the General Assembly, on the recommendation of the First Committee [A/56/539], adopted **resolution 56/27** by recorded vote (153-3-6) [agenda item 77].

The risk of nuclear proliferation
in the Middle East

The General Assembly,

Bearing in mind its relevant resolutions,

Taking note of the relevant resolutions adopted by the General Conference of the International Atomic Energy Agency, the latest of which is resolution GC(45)/RES/18, adopted on 21 September 2001,

Cognizant that the proliferation of nuclear weapons in the region of the Middle East would pose a serious threat to international peace and security,

Mindful of the immediate need for placing all nuclear facilities in the region of the Middle East under full-scope safeguards of the International Atomic Energy Agency,

Recalling the decision on principles and objectives for nuclear non-proliferation and disarmament adopted by the 1995 Review and Extension Conference of the Parties to the Treaty on the Non-Proliferation of Nuclear Weapons on 11 May 1995, in which the Conference urged universal adherence to the Treaty as an urgent priority and called upon all States not yet parties to the Treaty to accede to it at the earliest date, particularly those States that operate unsafeguarded nuclear facilities,

Recognizing with satisfaction that, in the Final Document of the 2000 Review Conference of the Parties to the Treaty on the Non-Proliferation of Nuclear Weapons, the Conference undertook to make determined efforts towards the achievement of the goal of universality of the Treaty on the Non-Proliferation of Nuclear Weapons, and called upon those remaining States not parties to the Treaty to accede to it, thereby accepting an international legally binding commitment not to acquire nuclear weapons or nuclear explosive devices and to accept International Atomic Energy Agency safeguards on all their nuclear activities, and underlined the necessity of universal adherence to the Treaty and of strict compliance by all parties with their obligations under the Treaty,

Recalling the resolution on the Middle East adopted by the 1995 Review and Extension Conference of the Parties to the Treaty on the Non-Proliferation of Nuclear Weapons on 11 May 1995, in which the Conference noted with concern the continued existence in the Middle East of unsafeguarded nuclear facilities, reaffirmed the importance of the early realization of universal adherence to the Treaty and called upon all States in the Middle East that had not yet done so, without exception, to accede to the Treaty as soon as possible and to place all their nuclear facilities under full-scope International Atomic Energy Agency safeguards,

Noting that Israel remains the only State in the Middle East that has not yet become party to the Treaty on the Non-Proliferation of Nuclear Weapons,

Concerned about the threats posed by the proliferation of nuclear weapons to the security and stability of the Middle East region,

Stressing the importance of taking confidence-building measures, in particular the establishment of a nuclear-weapon-free zone in the Middle East, in order to enhance peace and security in the region and to consolidate the global non-proliferation regime,

Emphasizing the need for all parties directly concerned to consider seriously taking the practical and urgent steps required for the implementation of the proposal to establish a nuclear-weapon-free zone in the region of the Middle East in accordance with the relevant resolutions of the General Assembly and, as a means of promoting this objective, inviting the countries concerned to adhere to the Treaty on the Non-Proliferation of Nuclear Weapons and, pending the establishment of the zone, to agree to place all their nuclear activities under International Atomic Energy Agency safeguards,

Noting that one hundred and sixty-one States have signed the Comprehensive Nuclear-Test-Ban Treaty, including a number of States in the region,

1. *Welcomes* the conclusions on the Middle East of the 2000 Review Conference of the Parties to the Treaty on the Non-Proliferation of Nuclear Weapons;

2. *Reaffirms* the importance of Israel's accession to the Treaty on the Non-Proliferation of Nuclear Weapons and placement of all its nuclear facilities under comprehensive International Atomic Energy Agency safeguards, in realizing the goal of universal adherence to the Treaty in the Middle East;

3. *Calls upon* that State to accede to the Treaty on the Non-Proliferation of Nuclear Weapons without further delay and not to develop, produce, test or otherwise acquire nuclear weapons, and to renounce possession of nuclear weapons, and to place all its unsafeguarded nuclear facilities under full-scope International Atomic Energy Agency safeguards as an important confidence-building measure among all States of the region and as a step towards enhancing peace and security;

4. *Requests* the Secretary-General to report to the General Assembly at its fifty-seventh session on the implementation of the present resolution;

5. *Decides* to include in the provisional agenda of its fifty-seventh session the item entitled "The risk of nuclear proliferation in the Middle East".

RECORDED VOTE ON RESOLUTION 56/27:

In favour: Afghanistan, Albania, Algeria, Andorra, Angola, Argentina, Armenia, Austria, Azerbaijan, Bahamas, Bahrain, Bangladesh, Barbados, Belarus, Belgium, Benin, Bhutan, Bolivia, Bosnia and Herzegovina, Botswana, Brazil, Brunei Darussalam, Bulgaria, Burkina Faso, Burundi, Cambodia, Cape Verde, Chile, China, Colombia, Comoros, Congo, Costa Rica, Côte d'Ivoire, Croatia, Cuba, Cyprus, Czech Republic, Democratic People's Republic of Korea, Denmark, Djibouti, Dominican Republic, Ecuador, Egypt, El Salvador, Equatorial Guinea, Eritrea, Estonia, Fiji, Finland, France, Gabon, Georgia, Germany, Ghana, Greece, Grenada, Guatemala, Guinea, Guyana, Haiti, Honduras, Hungary, Iceland, Indonesia, Iran, Ireland, Italy, Jamaica, Japan, Jordan, Kazakhstan, Kenya, Kuwait, Lao People's Democratic Republic, Latvia, Lebanon, Lesotho, Libyan Arab Jamahiriya, Liechtenstein, Lithuania, Luxembourg, Madagascar, Malaysia, Maldives, Mali, Malta, Mauritania, Mauritius, Mexico, Monaco, Mongolia, Morocco, Mozambique, Myanmar, Namibia, Nauru, Nepal, Netherlands, New Zealand, Nicaragua, Nigeria, Norway, Oman, Pakistan, Panama, Papua New Guinea, Paraguay, Peru, Philippines, Poland, Portugal, Qatar, Republic of Korea, Republic of Moldova, Romania, Russian Federation, Saint Lucia, Samoa, San Marino, Saudi Arabia, Senegal, Seychelles, Sierra Leone, Singapore, Slovakia, Slovenia, Solomon Islands, South Africa, Spain, Sri Lanka, Sudan, Swaziland, Sweden, Syrian Arab Republic, Thailand, The former Yugoslav Republic of Macedonia, Togo, Tunisia, Turkey, Turkmenistan, Uganda, Ukraine, United Arab Emirates, United Kingdom, United Republic of Tanzania, Uruguay, Venezuela, Viet Nam, Yemen, Yugoslavia, Zambia, Zimbabwe.

Against: Israel, Micronesia, United States.

Abstaining: Australia, Canada, Ethiopia, India, Tonga, Trinidad and Tobago.

The First Committee adopted the sixth preambular paragraph by a recorded vote of 139 to 2, with 6 abstentions. The Assembly retained the paragraph by a recorded vote of 153 to 2, with 4 abstentions.

Prohibition of use of nuclear weapons

In 2001, the Conference on Disarmament was unable to undertake negotiations on a convention on the prohibition of the use of nuclear weapons, as called for in General Assembly resolution 55/34 G [YUN 2000, p. 506].

On 29 November [meeting 68], the General Assembly, on the recommendation of the First Committee [A/56/537], adopted **resolution 56/25 B** by recorded vote (104-46-11) [agenda item 75 *(e)*].

Convention on the Prohibition of the Use of Nuclear Weapons

The General Assembly,

Convinced that the use of nuclear weapons poses the most serious threat to the survival of mankind,

Bearing in mind the advisory opinion of the International Court of Justice of 8 July 1996 on the *Legality of the Threat or Use of Nuclear Weapons,*

Convinced that a multilateral, universal and binding agreement prohibiting the use or threat of use of nuclear weapons would contribute to the elimination of the nuclear threat and to the climate for negotiations leading to the ultimate elimination of nuclear weapons, thereby strengthening international peace and security,

Conscious that some steps taken by the Russian Federation and the United States of America towards a reduction of their nuclear weapons and the improvement in the international climate can contribute towards the goal of the complete elimination of nuclear weapons,

Recalling that, in paragraph 58 of the Final Document of the Tenth Special Session of the General Assembly, it is stated that all States should actively participate in efforts to bring about conditions in international relations among States in which a code of peaceful conduct of nations in international affairs could be agreed upon and that would preclude the use or threat of use of nuclear weapons,

Reaffirming that any use of nuclear weapons would be a violation of the Charter of the United Nations and a crime against humanity, as declared in its resolutions 1653(XVI) of 24 November 1961, 33/71 B of 14 December 1978, 34/83 G of 11 December 1979, 35/152 D of 12 December 1980 and 36/92 I of 9 December 1981,

Determined to achieve an international convention prohibiting the development, production, stockpiling and use of nuclear weapons, leading to their ultimate destruction,

Stressing that an international convention on the prohibition of the use of nuclear weapons would be an important step in a phased programme towards the complete elimination of nuclear weapons, with a specified framework of time,

Noting with regret that the Conference on Disarmament, during its 2001 session, was unable to undertake negotiations on this subject as called for in General Assembly resolution 55/34 G of 20 November 2000,

1. *Reiterates its request* to the Conference on Disarmament to commence negotiations in order to reach agreement on an international convention prohibiting the use or threat of use of nuclear weapons under any circumstances;

2. *Requests* the Conference on Disarmament to report to the General Assembly on the results of those negotiations.

RECORDED VOTE ON RESOLUTION 56/25 B:

In favour: Afghanistan, Algeria, Angola, Bahamas, Bahrain, Bangladesh, Barbados, Belarus, Benin, Bhutan, Bolivia, Botswana, Brazil, Brunei Darussalam, Burkina Faso, Burundi, Cambodia, Cameroon, Cape Verde, Chile, Colombia, Comoros, Congo, Costa Rica, Côte d'Ivoire, Cuba, Democratic People's Republic of Korea, Djibouti, Dominican Republic, Ecuador, Egypt, El Salvador, Equatorial Guinea, Eritrea, Ethiopia, Fiji, Gabon, Ghana, Grenada, Guinea, Guyana, Haiti, Honduras, India, Indonesia, Iran, Jamaica, Jordan, Kenya, Kuwait, Lao People's Democratic Republic, Lebanon, Lesotho, Libyan Arab Jamahiriya, Madagascar, Malaysia, Maldives, Mali, Mauritania, Mauritius, Mexico, Mongolia, Morocco, Mozambique, Myanmar, Namibia, Nauru, Nepal, Nicaragua, Nigeria, Oman, Pakistan, Panama, Papua New Guinea, Paraguay, Peru, Philippines, Qatar, Saint Lucia, Samoa, Saudi Arabia, Senegal, Sierra Leone, Singapore, Solomon Islands, South Africa, Sri Lanka, Sudan, Swaziland, Syrian Arab Republic, Thailand, Togo, Tonga, Trinidad and Tobago, Tunisia, Uganda, United Arab Emirates, United Republic of Tanzania, Uruguay, Venezuela, Viet Nam, Yemen, Zambia, Zimbabwe.

Against: Albania, Andorra, Australia, Austria, Belgium, Bosnia and Herzegovina, Bulgaria, Canada, Croatia, Cyprus, Czech Republic, Denmark, Estonia, Finland, France, Germany, Greece, Hungary, Iceland, Ireland, Israel, Italy, Latvia, Liechtenstein, Lithuania, Luxembourg, Malta, Micronesia, Monaco, Netherlands, New Zealand, Norway, Poland, Portugal, Republic of Moldova, Romania, San Marino, Slovakia, Slovenia, Spain, Sweden, The former Yugoslav Republic of Macedonia, Turkey, United Kingdom, United States, Yugoslavia.

Abstaining: Argentina, Armenia, Azerbaijan, China, Georgia, Japan, Kazakhstan, Republic of Korea, Russian Federation, Turkmenistan, Ukraine.

Advisory opinion of International Court of Justice

Pursuant to General Assembly resolution 55/33 X [YUN 2000, p. 507] on the advisory opinion of the International Court of Justice that the threat or use of nuclear weapons was contrary to the UN Charter [YUN 1996, p. 461], the Secretary-General presented information received from five States (Jordan, Malaysia, Mexico, Philippines, Syrian Arab Republic) on measures they had taken to implement the resolution and nuclear disarmament [A/56/130 & Add.1].

On 29 November [meeting 68], the General Assembly, on the recommendation of the First Committee [A/56/536], adopted **resolution 56/24 S** by recorded vote (111-29-21) [agenda item 74 *(v)*].

Follow-up to the advisory opinion of the International Court of Justice on the *Legality of the Threat or Use of Nuclear Weapons*

The General Assembly,

Recalling its resolutions 49/75 K of 15 December 1994, 51/45 M of 10 December 1996, 52/38 O of 9 December 1997, 53/77 W of 4 December 1998, 54/54 Q of 1 December 1999 and 55/33 X of 20 November 2000,

Convinced that the continuing existence of nuclear weapons poses a threat to all humanity and that their use would have catastrophic consequences for all life on Earth, and recognizing that the only defence against a nuclear catastrophe is the total elimination of nuclear weapons and the certainty that they will never be produced again,

Reaffirming the commitment of the international community to the goal of the total elimination of nuclear weapons and the creation of a nuclear-weapon-free world,

Mindful of the solemn obligations of States parties, undertaken in article VI of the Treaty on the Non-Proliferation of Nuclear Weapons, particularly to pursue negotiations in good faith on effective measures relating to cessation of the nuclear-arms race at an early date and to nuclear disarmament,

Recalling the principles and objectives for nuclear non-proliferation and disarmament adopted at the 1995 Review and Extension Conference of the Parties to the Treaty on the Non-Proliferation of Nuclear Weapons,

Welcoming the unequivocal undertaking by the nuclear-weapon States to accomplish the total elimination of their nuclear arsenals leading to nuclear disarmament, adopted at the 2000 Review Conference of the Parties to the Treaty on the Non-Proliferation of Nuclear Weapons,

Recalling the adoption of the Comprehensive Nuclear-Test-Ban Treaty in its resolution 50/245 of 10 September 1996, and expressing its satisfaction at the increasing number of States that have signed and ratified the Treaty,

Recognizing with satisfaction that the Antarctic Treaty and the treaties of Tlatelolco, Rarotonga, Bangkok and Pelindaba are gradually freeing the entire southern hemisphere and adjacent areas covered by those treaties from nuclear weapons,

Noting the efforts by the States possessing the largest inventories of nuclear weapons to reduce their stockpiles of such weapons through bilateral agreements or arrangements and unilateral decisions, and calling for the intensification of such efforts to accelerate the significant reduction of nuclear-weapon arsenals,

Stressing the importance of strengthening all existing nuclear-related disarmament, arms control and reduction measures,

Recognizing the need for a multilaterally negotiated and legally binding instrument to assure non-nuclear-weapon States against the threat or use of nuclear weapons,

Reaffirming the central role of the Conference on Disarmament as the single multilateral disarmament negotiating forum, and regretting the lack of progress in disarmament negotiations, particularly nuclear disarmament, in the Conference during its 2001 session,

Emphasizing the need for the Conference on Disarmament to commence negotiations on a phased programme for the complete elimination of nuclear weapons with a specified framework of time,

Desiring to achieve the objective of a legally binding prohibition of the development, production, testing, deployment, stockpiling, threat or use of nuclear weapons and their destruction under effective international control,

Recalling the advisory opinion of the International Court of Justice on the *Legality of the Threat or Use of Nuclear Weapons*, issued on 8 July 1996,

Taking note of the relevant portions of the note by the Secretary-General relating to the implementation of resolution 55/33 X,

1. *Underlines once again* the unanimous conclusion of the International Court of Justice that there exists an obligation to pursue in good faith and bring to a conclusion negotiations leading to nuclear disarmament in all its aspects under strict and effective international control;

2. *Calls once again upon* all States immediately to fulfil that obligation by commencing multilateral negotiations in 2002 leading to an early conclusion of a nuclear weapons convention prohibiting the development, production, testing, deployment, stockpiling, transfer, threat or use of nuclear weapons and providing for their elimination;

3. *Requests* all States to inform the Secretary-General of the efforts and measures they have taken on the implementation of the present resolution and nuclear disarmament, and requests the Secretary-General to apprise the General Assembly of that information at its fifty-seventh session;

4. *Decides* to include in the provisional agenda of its fifty-seventh session the item entitled "Follow-up to the advisory opinion of the International Court of Justice on the *Legality of the Threat or Use of Nuclear Weapons*".

RECORDED VOTE ON RESOLUTION 56/24 S:

In favour: Afghanistan, Algeria, Angola, Argentina, Bahamas, Bahrain, Bangladesh, Barbados, Benin, Bhutan, Bolivia, Botswana, Brazil, Brunei Darussalam, Burkina Faso, Burundi, Cambodia, Cameroon, Cape Verde, Chile, China, Colombia, Comoros, Costa Rica, Côte d'Ivoire, Cuba, Democratic People's Republic of Korea, Djibouti, Dominican Republic, Ecuador, Egypt, El Salvador, Equatorial Guinea, Eritrea, Ethiopia, Fiji, Gabon, Ghana, Grenada, Guatemala, Guyana, Haiti, Honduras, India, Indonesia, Iran, Ireland, Jamaica, Jordan, Kenya, Kuwait, Lao People's Democratic Republic, Lebanon, Lesotho, Libyan Arab Jamahiriya, Madagascar, Malaysia, Maldives, Mali, Malta, Mauritania, Mauritius, Mexico, Mongolia, Morocco, Mozambique, Myanmar, Namibia, Nauru, Nepal, New Zealand, Nicaragua, Nigeria, Oman, Pakistan, Panama, Papua New Guinea, Paraguay, Peru, Philippines, Qatar, Saint Lucia, Samoa, San Marino, Saudi Arabia, Senegal, Seychelles, Sierra Leone, Singapore, Solomon Islands, South Africa, Sri Lanka, Sudan, Swaziland, Sweden, Syrian Arab Republic, Thailand, Togo, Tonga, Trinidad and Tobago, Tunisia, Uganda, Ukraine, United Arab Emirates, United Republic of Tanzania, Uruguay, Venezuela, Viet Nam, Yemen, Zambia, Zimbabwe.

Against: Albania, Andorra, Belgium, Bulgaria, Czech Republic, Denmark, France, Germany, Greece, Hungary, Iceland, Israel, Italy, Latvia, Lithuania, Luxembourg, Monaco, Netherlands, Norway, Poland, Portugal, Romania, Russian Federation, Slovakia, Slovenia, Spain, Turkey, United Kingdom, United States.

Abstaining: Armenia, Australia, Austria, Azerbaijan, Belarus, Bosnia and Herzegovina, Canada, Croatia, Cyprus, Estonia, Finland, Georgia, Japan, Kazakhstan, Liechtenstein, Micronesia, Republic of Korea, Republic of Moldova, The former Yugoslav Republic of Macedonia, Turkmenistan, Yugoslavia.

The First Committee adopted paragraph 1 by a recorded vote of 139 to 4, with 2 abstentions. The Assembly retained the paragraph by a recorded vote of 153 to 4, with 2 abstentions.

Radioactive waste

On 18 June, the Joint Convention on the Safety of Spent Fuel Management and on the Safety of Radioactive Waste Management [YUN 1997, p. 487] entered into force, 90 days following the deposit of the twenty-fifth instrument of ratification, acceptance or approval.

The IAEA General Conference, in September [GC(45)/RES/10], recalled its previous requests to States shipping radioactive materials to assure concerned States that the Agency's regulations regarding the transportation of such materials had been honoured, and called for further efforts to improve measures relating to international maritime transport in that respect.

Communication. In September [A/56/360], Chile transmitted a communiqué on the transport of radioactive material and hazardous wastes, adopted by the Ministers for Foreign Affairs of countries of the Rio Group (Santiago, 27 March), which expressed concern about the transit of radioactive material and hazardous wastes along the coasts of member States, in view of the risks of harmful effects on the health of coastal populations and on the marine environment.

GENERAL ASSEMBLY ACTION

On 29 November [meeting 68], the General Assembly, on the recommendation of the First Committee [A/56/536], adopted **resolution 56/24 L** without vote [agenda item 74 (c)].

Prohibition of the dumping of radioactive wastes

The General Assembly,

Bearing in mind resolutions CM/Res.1153(XLVIII) of 1988 and CM/Res.1225(L) of 1989, adopted by the Council of Ministers of the Organization of African Unity, concerning the dumping of nuclear and industrial wastes in Africa,

Welcoming resolution GC(XXXIV)/RES/530 establishing a Code of Practice on the International Transboundary Movement of Radioactive Waste, adopted on 21 September 1990 by the General Conference of the International Atomic Energy Agency at its thirty-fourth regular session,

Taking note of the commitment by the participants in the Summit on Nuclear Safety and Security, held in Moscow on 19 and 20 April 1996, to ban the dumping at sea of radioactive wastes,

Considering its resolution 2602 C (XXIV) of 16 December 1969, in which it requested the Conference of the Committee on Disarmament,[a] inter alia, to consider effective methods of control against the use of radiological methods of warfare,

Aware of the potential hazards underlying any use of radioactive wastes that would constitute radiological warfare and its implications for regional and international security, in particular for the security of developing countries,

Recalling all its resolutions on the matter since its forty-third session in, 1988, including its resolution 51/45 J of 10 December 1996,

Also recalling resolution GC(45)/RES/10 adopted by consensus on 21 September 2001 by the General Conference of the International Atomic Energy Agency at its forty-fifth regular session, in which States shipping radioactive materials are invited to provide, as appropriate, assurances to concerned States, upon their request, that the national regulations of the shipping State take into account the Agency's transport regula-

tions and to provide them with relevant information relating to the shipment of such materials; the information provided should in no case be contradictory to the measures of physical security and safety,

Welcoming the adoption at Vienna, on 5 September 1997, of the Joint Convention on the Safety of Spent Fuel Management and on the Safety of Radioactive Waste Management, as recommended by the participants at the Summit on Nuclear Safety and Security,

Noting with satisfaction that the Joint Convention on the Safety of Spent Fuel Management and on the Safety of Radioactive Waste Management entered into force on 18 June 2001, and noting also that the Secretariat has convened a preparatory meeting of the Contracting Parties, to be held from 10 to 14 December 2001, to prepare for the first Review Meeting of the Contracting Parties,

Desirous of promoting the implementation of paragraph 76 of the Final Document of the Tenth Special Session of the General Assembly, the first special session devoted to disarmament,

1. *Takes note* of the part of the report of the Conference on Disarmament relating to a future convention on the prohibition of radiological weapons;

2. *Expresses grave concern* regarding any use of nuclear wastes that would constitute radiological warfare and have grave implications for the national security of all States;

3. *Calls upon* all States to take appropriate measures with a view to preventing any dumping of nuclear or radioactive wastes that would infringe upon the sovereignty of States;

4. *Requests* the Conference on Disarmament to take into account, in the negotiations for a convention on the prohibition of radiological weapons, radioactive wastes as part of the scope of such a convention;

5. *Also requests* the Conference on Disarmament to intensify efforts towards an early conclusion of such a convention and to include in its report to the General Assembly at its fifty-eighth session the progress recorded in the negotiations on this subject;

6. *Takes note* of resolution CM/Res.1356(LIV) of 1991, adopted by the Council of Ministers of the Organization of African Unity, on the Bamako Convention on the Ban on the Import of Hazardous Wastes into Africa and on the Control of Their Transboundary Movements within Africa;

7. *Expresses the hope* that the effective implementation of the International Atomic Energy Agency Code of Practice on the International Transboundary Movement of Radioactive Waste will enhance the protection of all States from the dumping of radioactive wastes on their territories;

8. *Appeals* to all Member States that have not yet taken the necessary steps to become party to the Joint Convention on the Safety of Spent Fuel Management and on the Safety of Radioactive Waste Management to do so in time to attend the first Review Meeting of the Contracting Parties;

9. *Decides* to include in the provisional agenda of its fifty-eighth session the item entitled "Prohibition of the dumping of radioactive wastes".

---

[a]The Conference of the Committee on Disarmament became the Committee on Disarmament as from the tenth special session of the General Assembly. The Committee on Disarmament was redesignated the Conference on Disarmament as from 7 February 1984.

Nuclear-weapon-free zones

Africa

As at 31 December, 19 States had ratified the African Nuclear-Weapon-Free Zone Treaty (Treaty of Pelindaba) [YUN 1995, p. 203], which was opened for signature in 1996 [YUN 1996, p. 486]. China, France and the United Kingdom had ratified Protocols I and II thereto, and France had also ratified Protocol III. The Russian Federation and the United States had signed Protocols I and II. The Treaty had 55 signatories.

GENERAL ASSEMBLY ACTION

On 29 November [meeting 68], the General Assembly, on the recommendation of the First Committee [A/56/529], adopted **resolution 56/17** without vote [agenda item 67].

African Nuclear-Weapon-Free Zone Treaty (Treaty of Pelindaba)

The General Assembly,

Recalling its resolution 54/48 of 1 December 1999 and all its other relevant resolutions, as well as those of the Organization of African Unity,

Recalling also the successful conclusion of the signing ceremony of the African Nuclear-Weapon-Free Zone Treaty (Treaty of Pelindaba) that was held at Cairo on 11 April 1996,

Recalling further the Cairo Declaration adopted on that occasion, which emphasized that nuclear-weapon-free zones, especially in regions of tension, such as the Middle East, enhance global and regional peace and security,

Noting the statement made by the President of the Security Council on behalf of the members of the Council on 12 April 1996, in which it was stated that the signature of the African Nuclear-Weapon-Free Zone Treaty constituted an important contribution by the African countries to the maintenance of international peace and security,

Considering that the establishment of nuclear-weapon-free zones, especially in the Middle East, would enhance the security of Africa and the viability of the African nuclear-weapon-free zone,

1. *Calls upon* African States that have not yet done so to sign and ratify the African Nuclear-Weapon-Free Zone Treaty (Treaty of Pelindaba) as soon as possible so that it may enter into force without delay;

2. *Expresses its appreciation* to the nuclear-weapon States that have signed the Protocols that concern them, and calls upon those that have not yet ratified the Protocols concerning them to do so as soon as possible;

3. *Calls upon* the States contemplated in Protocol III to the Treaty that have not yet done so to take all necessary measures to ensure the speedy application of the Treaty to territories for which they are, de jure or de facto, internationally responsible and which lie within the limits of the geographical zone established in the Treaty;

4. *Calls upon* the African States parties to the Treaty on the Non-Proliferation of Nuclear Weapons that have not yet done so to conclude comprehensive safeguards agreements with the International Atomic Energy Agency pursuant to the Treaty, thereby satisfying the requirements of article 9 *(b)* of and annex II to the Treaty of Pelindaba when it enters into force, and to conclude additional protocols to their safeguards agreements on the basis of the Model Protocol approved by the Board of Governors of the Agency on 15 May 1997;

5. *Expresses its gratitude* to the Secretary-General of the United Nations, the Secretary-General of the Organization of African Unity and the Director General of the International Atomic Energy Agency for the diligence with which they have rendered effective assistance to the signatories to the Treaty;

6. *Decides* to include in the provisional agenda of its fifty-eighth session the item entitled "African Nuclear-Weapon-Free Zone Treaty".

Asia

Central Asia

In 2001, negotiations continued on drafting the text of a treaty for a nuclear-weapon-free zone in Central Asia. Although the UN-sponsored expert group, consisting of experts from each of the five States of the region (Kazakhstan, Kyrgyzstan, Tajikistan, Turkmenistan, Uzbekistan), had met in 2000 and accepted almost all the draft provisions on an *ad credendum* basis (as an article of faith) [YUN 2000, p. 508], outstanding issues remained.

On 29 November, the General Assembly decided to include in the provisional agenda of its fifty-seventh (2002) session the item "Establishment of a nuclear-weapon-free zone in Central Asia" (**decision 56/412**).

Mongolia

In accordance with General Assembly resolution 55/33 S [YUN 2000, p. 509], a UN-sponsored expert group meeting (Sapporo, Japan, 5-6 September), held under the auspices of the UN Regional Centre for Peace and Disarmament in Asia and the Pacific (see p. 521), examined ways and means of strengthening Mongolia's international security and nuclear-weapon-free status. The Foreign Ministers of the Movement of Non-Aligned Countries (New York, 14 November) [A/56/682-S/2001/1159] reaffirmed support for Mongolia's nuclear-weapon-free status and considered that the institutionalization of that status would be an important measure towards strengthening the non-proliferation regime in the region.

South-East Asia

Regarding the Treaty on the South-East Asia Nuclear-Weapon-Free Zone (Bangkok Treaty), which opened for signature in 1995 [YUN 1995, p. 207] and entered into force in 1997 [YUN 1997, p. 495], States parties continued negotiations with nuclear-weapon States regarding the accession of the latter to the Treaty's Protocol. The implementing organs of the Treaty—a Commission and an Executive Committee—had begun their work and undertaken consultations with IAEA. Ratification by the Philippines in 2001 raised the number of ratifying States to 10.

Latin America and the Caribbean

On 29 November [meeting 68], the General Assembly, on the recommendation of the First Committee [A/56/542], adopted **resolution 56/30** without vote [agenda item 80].

Consolidation of the regime established by the Treaty for the Prohibition of Nuclear Weapons in Latin America and the Caribbean (Treaty of Tlatelolco)

The General Assembly,

Recalling that, in its resolution 1911(XVIII) of 27 November 1963, it expressed the hope that the States of Latin America would take appropriate measures to conclude a treaty that would prohibit nuclear weapons in Latin America,

Recalling also that, in the same resolution, it voiced its confidence that, once such a treaty was concluded, all States, and in particular the nuclear-weapon States, would lend it their full cooperation for the effective realization of its peaceful aims,

Considering that, in its resolution 2028(XX) of 19 November 1965, it established the principle of an acceptable balance of mutual responsibilities and obligations between nuclear-weapon States and those that do not possess such weapons,

Recalling that the Treaty for the Prohibition of Nuclear Weapons in Latin America and the Caribbean (Treaty of Tlatelolco) was opened for signature at Mexico City on 14 February 1967,

Noting with satisfaction the holding on 14 February 1997 of the eleventh special session of the General Conference of the Agency for the Prohibition of Nuclear Weapons in Latin America and the Caribbean in commemoration of the thirtieth anniversary of the opening for signature of the Treaty of Tlatelolco,

Recalling that, in its preamble, the Treaty of Tlatelolco states that military denuclearized zones are not an end in themselves but rather a means for achieving general and complete disarmament at a later stage,

Recalling also that, in its resolution 2286(XXII) of 5 December 1967, it welcomed with special satisfaction the Treaty of Tlatelolco as an event of historic significance in the efforts to prevent the proliferation of nuclear weapons and to promote international peace and security,

Recalling further that in 1990, 1991 and 1992 the General Conference of the Agency for the Prohibition of Nuclear Weapons in Latin America and the Caribbean approved and opened for signature a set of amendments to the Treaty of Tlatelolco, with the aim of enabling the full entry into force of that instrument,

Recalling resolution C/E/RES.27 of the Council of the Agency for the Prohibition of Nuclear Weapons in Latin America and the Caribbean, in which the Council called for the promotion of cooperation and consultations with other nuclear-weapon-free zones,

Noting with satisfaction that the Treaty of Tlatelolco is now in force for thirty-two sovereign States of the region,

Also noting with satisfaction that the amended Treaty of Tlatelolco is fully in force for Argentina, Barbados, Brazil, Chile, Colombia, Costa Rica, Ecuador, Guyana, Jamaica, Mexico, Panama, Paraguay, Peru, Suriname, Uruguay and Venezuela,

1. *Welcomes* the concrete steps taken by some countries of the region during recent years for the consolidation of the regime of military denuclearization established by the Treaty for the Prohibition of Nuclear Weapons in Latin America and the Caribbean (Treaty of Tlatelolco);

2. *Urges* the countries of the region that have not yet done so to deposit their instruments of ratification of the amendments to the Treaty of Tlatelolco approved by the General Conference of the Agency for the Prohibition of Nuclear Weapons in Latin America and the Caribbean in its resolutions 267(E-V), 268(XII) and 290(E-VII);

3. *Decides* to include in the provisional agenda of its fifty-eighth session the item entitled "Consolidation of the regime established by the Treaty for the Prohibition of Nuclear Weapons in Latin America and the Caribbean (Treaty of Tlatelolco)".

Middle East

In response to General Assembly resolution 55/30 on the establishment of a nuclear-weapon-free zone in the Middle East [YUN 2000, p. 511], the Secretary-General, in July [A/56/187], reported on the implementation of the resolution. He carried out consultations with concerned parties within and outside the region to explore further ways to promote the establishment of a nuclear-weapon-free zone. He believed that the multilateral Working Group on Arms Control and Regional Security, which functioned under the auspices of the Middle East multilateral peace process, could act as a forum for discussing the issue and stressed the importance of reaching early agreement on a comprehensive agenda for the Group. The report included the views of Belgium (on behalf of the EU), Egypt, Mexico and the Syrian Arab Republic.

In September, the IAEA General Conference, in a resolution on the Middle East [GC(45)/RES/18], called on all parties directly concerned to take steps required for the implementation of the proposal to establish a mutually and effectively verifiable nuclear-weapon-free zone in the region.

GENERAL ASSEMBLY ACTION

On 29 November [meeting 68], the General Assembly, on the recommendation of the First Committee [A/56/532], adopted **resolution 56/21** without vote [agenda item 71].

Establishment of a nuclear-weapon-free zone in the region of the Middle East

The General Assembly,

Recalling its resolutions 3263 (XXIX) of 9 December 1974, 3474(XXX) of 11 December 1975, 31/71 of 10 December 1976, 32/82 of 12 December 1977, 33/64 of 14 December 1978, 34/77 of 11 December 1979, 35/147 of 12 December 1980, 36/87 A and B of 9 December 1981, 37/75 of 9 December 1982, 38/64 of 15 December 1983, 39/54 of 12 December 1984, 40/82 of 12 December 1985, 41/48 of 3 December 1986, 42/28 of 30 November 1987, 43/65 of 7 December 1988, 44/108 of 15 December 1989, 45/52 of 4 December 1990, 46/30 of 6 December 1991, 47/48 of 9 December 1992, 48/71 of 16 December 1993, 49/71 of 15 December 1994, 50/66 of 12 December 1995, 51/41 of 10 December 1996, 52/34 of 9 December 1997, 53/74 of 4 December 1998, 54/51 of 1 December 1999 and 55/30 of 20 November 2000 on the establishment of a nuclear-weapon-free zone in the region of the Middle East,

Recalling also the recommendations for the establishment of such a zone in the Middle East consistent with paragraphs 60 to 63, and in particular paragraph 63 *(d)*, of the Final Document of the Tenth Special Session of the General Assembly,

Emphasizing the basic provisions of the above-mentioned resolutions, which call upon all parties directly concerned to consider taking the practical and urgent steps required for the implementation of the proposal to establish a nuclear-weapon-free zone in the region of the Middle East and, pending and during the establishment of such a zone, to declare solemnly that they will refrain, on a reciprocal basis, from producing, acquiring or in any other way possessing nuclear weapons and nuclear explosive devices and from permitting the stationing of nuclear weapons on their territory by any third party, to agree to place their nuclear facilities under International Atomic Energy Agency safeguards and to declare their support for the establishment of the zone and to deposit such declarations with the Security Council for consideration, as appropriate,

Reaffirming the inalienable right of all States to acquire and develop nuclear energy for peaceful purposes,

Emphasizing the need for appropriate measures on the question of the prohibition of military attacks on nuclear facilities,

Bearing in mind the consensus reached by the General Assembly since its thirty-fifth session that the establishment of a nuclear-weapon-free zone in the Middle East would greatly enhance international peace and security,

Desirous of building on that consensus so that substantial progress can be made towards establishing a nuclear-weapon-free zone in the Middle East,

Welcoming all initiatives leading to general and complete disarmament, including in the region of the Middle East, and in particular on the establishment therein of a zone free of weapons of mass destruction, including nuclear weapons,

Noting the peace negotiations in the Middle East, which should be of a comprehensive nature and represent an appropriate framework for the peaceful settlement of contentious issues in the region,

Recognizing the importance of credible regional security, including the establishment of a mutually verifiable nuclear-weapon-free zone,

Emphasizing the essential role of the United Nations in the establishment of a mutually verifiable nuclear-weapon-free zone,

Having examined the report of the Secretary-General on the implementation of General Assembly resolution 55/30,

1. *Urges* all parties directly concerned to consider seriously taking the practical and urgent steps required for the implementation of the proposal to establish a nuclear-weapon-free zone in the region of the Middle East in accordance with the relevant resolutions of the General Assembly, and, as a means of promoting this objective, invites the countries concerned to adhere to the Treaty on the Non-Proliferation of Nuclear Weapons;

2. *Calls upon* all countries of the region that have not done so, pending the establishment of the zone, to agree to place all their nuclear activities under International Atomic Energy Agency safeguards;

3. *Takes note* of resolution GC(45)/RES/18, adopted on 21 September 2001 by the General Conference of the International Atomic Energy Agency at its forty-fifth regular session, concerning the application of Agency safeguards in the Middle East;

4. *Notes* the importance of the ongoing bilateral Middle East peace negotiations and the activities of the multilateral Working Group on Arms Control and Regional Security in promoting mutual confidence and security in the Middle East, including the establishment of a nuclear-weapon-free zone;

5. *Invites* all countries of the region, pending the establishment of a nuclear-weapon-free zone in the region of the Middle East, to declare their support for establishing such a zone, consistent with paragraph 63 *(d)* of the Final Document of the Tenth Special Session of the General Assembly, and to deposit those declarations with the Security Council;

6. *Also invites* those countries, pending the establishment of the zone, not to develop, produce, test or otherwise acquire nuclear weapons or permit the stationing on their territories, or territories under their control, of nuclear weapons or nuclear explosive devices;

7. *Invites* the nuclear-weapon States and all other States to render their assistance in the establishment of the zone and at the same time to refrain from any action that runs counter to both the letter and the spirit of the present resolution;

8. *Takes note* of the report of the Secretary-General;

9. *Invites* all parties to consider the appropriate means that may contribute towards the goal of general and complete disarmament and the establishment of a zone free of weapons of mass destruction in the region of the Middle East;

10. *Requests* the Secretary-General to continue to pursue consultations with the States of the region and other concerned States, in accordance with paragraph 7 of resolution 46/30 and taking into account the evolving situation in the region, and to seek from those States their views on the measures outlined in chapters III and IV of the study annexed to his report of 10 October 1990 or other relevant measures, in order to move

towards the establishment of a nuclear-weapon-free zone in the Middle East;

11. *Also requests* the Secretary-General to submit to the General Assembly at its fifty-seventh session a report on the implementation of the present resolution;

12. *Decides* to include in the provisional agenda of its fifty-seventh session the item entitled "Establishment of a nuclear-weapon-free zone in the region of the Middle East".

South Pacific

In 2001, the number of States that had ratified the 1985 South Pacific Nuclear-Free Zone Treaty (Treaty of Rarotonga) [YUN 1985, p. 58] remained at 17. China and the Russian Federation had ratified Protocols 2 and 3, and France and the United Kingdom had ratified all three Protocols.

Under Protocol 1, the States internationally responsible for territories situated within the zone would undertake to apply the relevant prohibitions of the Treaty to those territories; under Protocol 2, the five nuclear-weapon States would provide security assurances to parties or to territories within the same zone; and under Protocol 3, the five would not carry out nuclear tests in the zone.

Southern hemisphere and adjacent areas

On 29 November [meeting 68], the General Assembly, on the recommendation of the First Committee [A/56/536], adopted **resolution 56/24 G** by recorded vote (148-4-4) [agenda item 74 *(j)*].

Nuclear-weapon-free southern hemisphere and adjacent areas

The General Assembly,

Recalling its resolutions 51/45 B of 10 December 1996, 52/38 N of 9 December 1997, 53/77 Q of 4 December 1998, 54/54 L of 1 December 1999 and 55/33 I of 20 November 2000,

Welcoming the adoption by the Disarmament Commission at its 1999 substantive session of a text entitled "Establishment of nuclear-weapon-free zones on the basis of arrangements freely arrived at among the States of the region concerned",

Determined to pursue the total elimination of nuclear weapons,

Determined also to continue to contribute to the prevention of the proliferation of nuclear weapons in all its aspects and to the process of general and complete disarmament under strict and effective international control, in particular in the field of nuclear weapons and other weapons of mass destruction, with a view to strengthening international peace and security, in accordance with the purposes and principles of the Charter of the United Nations,

Recalling the provisions on nuclear-weapon-free zones of the Final Document of the Tenth Special Session of the General Assembly, the first special session devoted to disarmament,

Stressing the importance of the treaties of Tlatelolco, Rarotonga, Bangkok and Pelindaba, establishing nuclear-weapon-free zones, as well as the Antarctic Treaty, to, inter alia, achieve a world entirely free of nuclear weapons,

Underlining the value of enhancing cooperation among the nuclear-weapon-free zone treaty members by means of mechanisms such as joint meetings of States parties, signatories and observers to those treaties,

Recalling the applicable principles and rules of international law relating to the freedom of the high seas and the rights of passage through maritime space, including those of the United Nations Convention on the Law of the Sea,

1. *Welcomes* the continued contribution that the Antarctic Treaty and the treaties of Tlatelolco, Rarotonga, Bangkok and Pelindaba are making towards freeing the southern hemisphere and adjacent areas covered by those treaties from nuclear weapons;

2. *Calls* for the ratification of the treaties of Tlatelolco, Rarotonga, Bangkok and Pelindaba by all States of the region, and calls upon all concerned States to continue to work together in order to facilitate adherence to the protocols to nuclear-weapon-free zone treaties by all relevant States that have not yet done so;

3. *Welcomes* the steps taken to conclude further nuclear-weapon-free zone treaties on the basis of arrangements freely arrived at among the States of the region concerned, and calls upon all States to consider all relevant proposals, including those reflected in its resolutions on the establishment of nuclear-weapon-free zones in the Middle East and South Asia;

4. *Convinced* of the important role of nuclear-weapon-free zones in strengthening the nuclear non-proliferation regime and in extending the areas of the world that are nuclear-weapon-free, and, with particular reference to the responsibilities of the nuclear-weapon States, calls upon all States to support the process of nuclear disarmament and to work for the total elimination of all nuclear weapons;

5. *Calls upon* the States parties and signatories to the treaties of Tlatelolco, Rarotonga, Bangkok and Pelindaba, in order to pursue the common goals envisaged in those treaties and to promote the nuclear-weapon-free status of the southern hemisphere and adjacent areas, to explore and implement further ways and means of cooperation among themselves and their treaty agencies;

6. *Welcomes* the vigorous efforts being made among States parties and signatories to those treaties to promote their common objectives, and considers that an international conference of States parties and signatories to the nuclear-weapon-free zone treaties might be held to support the common goals envisaged in those treaties;

7. *Encourages* the competent authorities of the nuclear-weapon-free-zone treaties to provide assistance to the States parties and signatories to those treaties so as to facilitate the accomplishment of these goals;

8. *Decides* to include in the provisional agenda of its fifty-seventh session the item entitled "Nuclear-weapon-free southern hemisphere and adjacent areas".

RECORDED VOTE ON RESOLUTION 56/24 G:

In favour: Afghanistan, Albania, Algeria, Andorra, Angola, Argentina, Armenia, Australia, Austria, Azerbaijan, Bahamas, Bahrain, Bangladesh, Barbados, Belarus, Belgium, Benin, Bhutan, Bolivia, Bosnia and Herzegovina, Botswana, Brazil, Brunei Darussalam, Bulgaria, Burkina Faso, Burundi, Cambodia, Cameroon, Canada, Cape Verde, Chile, China, Colombia,

Comoros, Costa Rica, Côte d'Ivoire, Croatia, Cuba, Cyprus, Czech Republic, Denmark, Djibouti, Dominican Republic, Ecuador, Egypt, El Salvador, Eritrea, Estonia, Ethiopia, Fiji, Finland, Gabon, Georgia, Germany, Ghana, Greece, Grenada, Guatemala, Guinea, Guyana, Haiti, Honduras, Hungary, Iceland, Indonesia, Iran, Ireland, Jamaica, Japan, Jordan, Kazakhstan, Kenya, Kuwait, Lao People's Democratic Republic, Latvia, Lebanon, Lesotho, Libyan Arab Jamahiriya, Liechtenstein, Lithuania, Luxembourg, Madagascar, Malaysia, Maldives, Mali, Malta, Mauritania, Mauritius, Mexico, Mongolia, Morocco, Mozambique, Myanmar, Namibia, Nauru, Nepal, Netherlands, New Zealand, Nicaragua, Nigeria, Norway, Oman, Pakistan, Panama, Papua New Guinea, Paraguay, Peru, Philippines, Poland, Portugal, Qatar, Republic of Korea, Republic of Moldova, Romania, Saint Lucia, Samoa, San Marino, Saudi Arabia, Seychelles, Sierra Leone, Singapore, Slovakia, Slovenia, Solomon Islands, South Africa, Sri Lanka, Sudan, Swaziland, Sweden, Syrian Arab Republic, Thailand, The former Yugoslav Republic of Macedonia, Togo, Tonga, Trinidad and Tobago, Tunisia, Turkey, Turkmenistan, Uganda, Ukraine, United Arab Emirates, United Republic of Tanzania, Uruguay, Venezuela, Viet Nam, Yemen, Yugoslavia, Zambia.

Against: France, Monaco, United Kingdom, United States.

Abstaining: India, Israel, Russian Federation, Spain.

The First Committee adopted paragraph 3 and its last three words, "and South Asia", by two separate recorded votes of 136 to 2, with 8 abstentions, and 132 to 3, with 8 abstentions, respectively. The Assembly also retained paragraph 3 and the last three words by recorded votes of 145 to 1, with 7 abstentions, and 140 to 2, with 8 abstentions, respectively.

Bacteriological (biological) and chemical weapons

Bacteriological (biological) weapons

In 2001, the terrorist attacks of 11 September (see p. 60) and subsequent anthrax incidents in the United States again raised concern among the international community over the threat of bioterrorism and the use of weapons of mass destruction. Despite the increased concern, multilateral efforts to strengthen the Convention on the Prohibition of the Development, Production and Stockpiling of Bacteriological (Biological) and Toxin Weapons and on Their Destruction (BWC), adopted by the General Assembly in resolution 2826(XXVI) [YUN 1971, p. 19], suffered setbacks, as the Ad Hoc Group of the States Parties to the Convention failed to conclude negotiation on a compliance protocol and the Fifth Review Conference of the States parties (see below) was suspended.

Ad Hoc Group

The Ad Hoc Group of the States Parties to BWC held its twenty-second (12-23 February) [BWC/AD HOC GROUP/55-1], twenty-third (23 April–11 May) [BWC/AD HOC GROUP/56-1] and twenty-fourth (23 July–17 August) sessions in 2001, all in Geneva.

The Group continued to consider elements of the rolling text of a future draft protocol on verification and confidence-building relating to the preamble; general provisions; definitions of terms and objective criteria; measures to promote compliance; investigations; confidentiality issues; legal issues, measures related to article X of the Convention (scientific and technological exchange and technical cooperation); declaration formats; and seat of the organization. Work continued to be conducted under the guidance of the Chairman and Friends of the Chair.

At the twenty-third session, the Chairman consolidated "written elements" of the rolling text into a single document (the composite text) containing compromise proposals on all outstanding issues. Discussions explored solutions on a limited number of specific issues, as identified by the Chairman, in the following areas: definitions; declarations; follow-up after submission of declarations; measures to strengthen implementation of article III of the Convention; investigations; and legal issues. The Ad Hoc Group was not able to continue negotiations on the draft protocol because the composite text was not acceptable to all States parties.

Fifth Review Conference

The Fifth Review Conference of the States Parties to BWC (Geneva, 19 November–7 December) [BWC/CONF.V/12] was held to review the provisions and operation of the Convention. Previous review conferences were held in 1980 [YUN 1980, p. 70], 1986 [YUN 1986, p. 64], 1991 [YUN 1991, p. 52] and 1996 [YUN 1996, p. 477].

The Conference established a General Committee, a Committee of the Whole, a Drafting Committee and a Credentials Committee. Substantive issues relating to the provisions and operation of the Convention were discussed largely by the Committee of the Whole. On 30 November, the Conference took note of the draft report of the Committee. Due to persisting divergent views on certain key issues regarding several of the Convention's articles, the Conference, on 7 December, decided by consensus to adjourn and reconvene in November 2002.

The General Assembly, by **decision 56/414** of 29 November, requested the Secretary-General to continue to assist the depositary Governments, to provide such services as might be required to implement the decisions and recommendations of the Review Conferences as well as the decisions contained in the final report of the 1994 Special Conference of the States Parties to the Convention [YUN 1994, p. 138], and to assist and provide such services as might be required to hold the Fifth Review Conference. The Assembly decided to include in the provisional agenda of its fifty-seventh (2002) session the item on BWC.

Preparatory process

The Preparatory Committee for the Fifth Review Conference (Geneva, 25-27 April) [BWC/CONF.V/PC/1] agreed on, among other things, the date, venue, provisional agenda, draft rules of procedure, background documentation and final documents of the Conference.

Chemical weapons

Chemical weapons convention

In 2001, Dominica, Nauru, Uganda and Zambia ratified the Convention on the Prohibition of the Development, Production, Stockpiling and Use of Chemical Weapons and on Their Destruction, bringing the total number of States parties to 145. The number of signatories stood at 165. The Convention was adopted by the Conference on Disarmament in 1992 [YUN 1992, p. 65] and entered into force in 1997 [YUN 1997, p. 499].

The sixth session of the Conference of the States Parties to the Convention (The Hague, Netherlands, 14-19 May) [OPCW, C-VI/6 & Corr.1] considered, among other issues, the status of the Convention's implementation, fostering international cooperation for peaceful purposes in the area of chemical activities, ensuring universality of the Convention and administrative and budgetary matters. Based on recommendations of the Executive Council of the Organization for the Prohibition of Chemical Weapons (OPCW), the Conference adopted decisions on the OPCW analytical database and on-site databases, agreements on privileges and immunities of OPCW, and administrative and budgetary matters, including approval of the 2002 OPCW programme and budget. It approved the relationship agreement between the United Nations and OPCW (see p. 495) and a request of the Russian Federation to use a chemical weapons production facility for purposes not prohibited under the Convention. The seventh session of the Conference of the States Parties was scheduled to take place in October 2002.

The first review conference of the Convention was planned to begin on 28 April 2003 in The Hague. Preparations were under way by OPCW (see p. 495).

GENERAL ASSEMBLY ACTION

On 29 November [meeting 68], the General Assembly, on the recommendation of the First Committee [A/56/536], adopted **resolution 56/24 K** without vote [agenda item 74 (i)].

Implementation of the Convention on the Prohibition of the Development, Production, Stockpiling and Use of Chemical Weapons and on Their Destruction

The General Assembly,

Recalling its previous resolutions on the subject of chemical weapons, in particular resolution 55/33 H of 20 November 2000, adopted without a vote, in which it noted with appreciation the ongoing work to achieve the objective and purpose of the Convention on the Prohibition of the Development, Production, Stockpiling and Use of Chemical Weapons and on Their Destruction,

Determined to achieve the effective prohibition of the development, production, acquisition, transfer, stockpiling and use of chemical weapons and their destruction,

Noting with satisfaction that since the adoption of resolution 55/33 H, three additional States have ratified or acceded to the Convention, bringing the total number of States parties to the Convention to one hundred and forty-three,

1. *Emphasizes* the necessity of universal adherence to the Convention on the Prohibition of the Development, Production, Stockpiling and Use of Chemical Weapons and on Their Destruction, and calls upon all States that have not yet done so to become parties to the Convention without delay;

2. *Notes with appreciation* the ongoing work of the Organization for the Prohibition of Chemical Weapons to achieve the objective and purpose of the Convention, to ensure the full implementation of its provisions, including those for international verification of compliance with it, and to provide a forum for consultation and cooperation among States parties;

3. *Stresses* the importance of the Organization for the Prohibition of Chemical Weapons in verifying compliance with the provisions of the Convention as well as in promoting the timely and efficient accomplishment of all its objectives;

4. *Also stresses* the vital importance of full and effective implementation of and compliance with all provisions of the Convention;

5. *Urges* all States parties to the Convention to meet in full and on time their obligations under the Convention and to support the Organization for the Prohibition of Chemical Weapons in its implementation activities;

6. *Stresses* the importance to the Convention that all possessors of chemical weapons, chemical weapons production facilities or chemical weapons development facilities, including previously declared possessor States, should be among the States parties to the Convention, and welcomes progress to that end;

7. *Welcomes* the cooperation between the United Nations and the Organization for the Prohibition of Chemical Weapons and the signature of the Relationship Agreement between the United Nations and the Organization, in accordance with the provisions of the Convention;

8. *Decides* to include in the provisional agenda of its fifty-seventh session the item entitled "Implementation of the Convention on the Prohibition of the Development, Production, Stockpiling and Use of Chemical Weapons and on Their Destruction".

Organization for the Prohibition of Chemical Weapons

In 2001, OPCW conducted some 1,100 inspections at chemical weapons facilities in 49 States parties. All 8.6 million chemical weapons declared by the four States parties possessing chemical weapons were inventoried by OPCW inspectors and regularly re-inspected to ensure non-diversion. Since the entry into force of the Convention, one fifth of those chemical munitions and containers had been destroyed, and all 61 former chemical weapons production facilities declared by 11 States parties had been deactivated and shut down.

In preparation for the first review conference of the Convention, OPCW was conducting a review process of the Convention and its implementation. The review process would focus on scientific and technological developments and their impact on the Convention, the verification regime, the scope of the Convention's schedules of chemicals, the need for universal adherence and programmes to coordinate international cooperation and assistance. The review was being directed by a working group of the OPCW Executive Council.

The OPCW Executive Council addressed a wide range of issues at its twenty-third (20-23 February), twenty-fourth (3-6 April), twenty-fifth (27-28 June), twenty-sixth (25-28 September) and twenty-seventh (4-7 December) sessions. In the light of the terrorist attacks of 11 September (see p. 60), the Executive Council considered the implementation of the Convention within the context of global efforts to combat all forms of terrorism, including those involving chemical weapons. In that regard, it established a working group to develop recommendations for OPCW's contribution to the global anti-terrorism effort.

Cooperation between United Nations and OPCW

The Agreement concerning the Relationship between the United Nations and OPCW, signed in 2000 [YUN 2000, p. 516] and approved by the Conference of the States Parties (see p. 494) and the General Assembly in 2001 (see below), entered into force on 24 September.

Notes by Secretary-General. By a June note [A/55/988], the Secretary-General submitted the text of the Agreement for approval by the General Assembly.

In October [A/56/490], the Secretary-General submitted to the Assembly the 2000 report of OPCW, in accordance with the Agreement.

GENERAL ASSEMBLY ACTION

On 7 September [meeting 111], the General Assembly adopted **resolution 55/283** [draft: A/55/L.92 & Add.1] without vote [agenda item 181].

Cooperation between the United Nations and the Organization for the Prohibition of Chemical Weapons

The General Assembly,

Recalling its resolution 51/230 of 22 May 1997, by which it invited the Secretary-General to take steps to conclude with the Director-General of the Technical Secretariat of the Organization for the Prohibition of Chemical Weapons an agreement between the United Nations and the organization to regulate the relationship between the two organizations, and to present the negotiated draft relationship agreement to the General Assembly for its approval,

Noting the decision of the Conference of the States Parties to the Chemical Weapons Convention of 17 May 2001 to approve the Agreement concerning the Relationship between the United Nations and the Organization for the Prohibition of Chemical Weapons,

Having considered the Agreement concerning the Relationship between the United Nations and the Organization for the Prohibition of Chemical Weapons,

1. *Approves* the Agreement concerning the Relationship between the United Nations and the Organization for the Prohibition of Chemical Weapons, the text of which is annexed to the present resolution;

2. *Decides* to include in the provisional agenda of its fifty-sixth and subsequent sessions the item entitled "Cooperation between the United Nations and the Organization for the Prohibition of Chemical Weapons".

ANNEX
Agreement concerning the Relationship between the United Nations and the Organization for the Prohibition of Chemical Weapons

The United Nations and the Organization for the Prohibition of Chemical Weapons,

Bearing in mind the relevant provisions of the Charter of the United Nations (hereinafter the "Charter") and of the Convention on the Prohibition of the Development, Production, Stockpiling and Use of Chemical Weapons and on Their Destruction (hereinafter the "Convention"),

Bearing in mind that, in accordance with the Charter, the United Nations is the principal organization dealing with matters relating to the maintenance of international peace and security, and acts as a centre for harmonizing the actions of nations in the attainment of the goals set out in the Charter,

Considering that the Organization for the Prohibition of Chemical Weapons (hereinafter "OPCW") shares the purposes and principles of the Charter, and that its activities performed pursuant to the provisions of the Convention contribute to the realization of the purposes and principles of the Charter,

Desiring to make provision for a mutually beneficial relationship, to avoid unnecessary duplication of their activities and services and to facilitate the discharge of the respective responsibilities of both organizations,

Noting General Assembly resolution 51/230 of 22 May 1997 and the relevant decision of the Conference of the States Parties at its fourth session (C-IV/DEC.4, dated 2 July 1999) calling for the conclusion of a relationship agreement between the United Nations and OPCW,

Have agreed as follows:

Article I
General

1. The United Nations recognizes OPCW as the organization, in relationship to the United Nations as specified in this Agreement, responsible for activities to achieve the comprehensive prohibition of chemical weapons in accordance with the Convention.

2. The United Nations recognizes that OPCW, by virtue of the Convention, shall function as an independent, autonomous international organization in the working relationship with the United Nations established by this Agreement.

3. OPCW recognizes the responsibilities of the United Nations, in accordance with its Charter, in particular in the fields of international peace and security and economic, social, cultural and humanitarian development, protection and preservation of the environment and peaceful settlement of disputes.

4. OPCW undertakes to conduct its activities in accordance with the purposes and principles of the Charter to promote peace, disarmament and international cooperation and with due regard to the policies of the United Nations furthering safeguarded worldwide disarmament.

Article II
Cooperation

1. The United Nations and OPCW, recognizing the need to work jointly to achieve mutual objectives, and with a view to facilitating the effective exercise of their responsibilities, agree to cooperate closely within their respective mandates and to consult on matters of mutual interest and concern. To that end, the United Nations and OPCW shall cooperate with each other in accordance with the provisions of their respective constituent instruments.

2. Cooperation between the United Nations and OPCW, in particular, shall require that:

(a) Cases of particular gravity and urgency which, in accordance with paragraph 36 of article VIII of the Convention, shall, including relevant information and conclusions, be brought directly to the attention of the General Assembly and the Security Council by the Executive Council, through the Secretary-General, in accordance with the existing United Nations procedures;

(b) Cases of particular gravity which, in accordance with paragraph 4 of article XII of the Convention, shall, including relevant information and conclusions, be brought to the attention of the General Assembly and the Security Council by the Conference of the States Parties, through the Secretary-General, in accordance with the existing United Nations procedures;

(c) OPCW shall, in accordance with paragraph 27 of Part XI of the Verification Annex, closely cooperate with the Secretary-General in cases of the alleged use of chemical weapons involving a State not party to the Convention or in a territory not controlled by a State Party to the Convention and, if so requested, shall in such cases place its resources at the disposal of the Secretary-General;

(d) OPCW and the United Nations shall, in accordance with their respective mandates, explore possibilities for cooperation in the provision of assistance to States concerned in cases of the use or serious threat of use of chemical weapons, as provided for in paragraph 10 of article X of the Convention;

(e) OPCW and the United Nations shall, insofar as covered by their respective mandates, in the context of economic and technological development in their member States, cooperate to foster international cooperation for peaceful purposes in the field of chemical activities and facilitating the exchange of chemicals, equipment and scientific and technical information relating to the development and application of chemistry for purposes not prohibited under the Convention; and

(f) The United Nations and OPCW shall cooperate on any matter that may relate to the object and purpose of the Convention, or which may arise in connection with its implementation.

3. OPCW, within its competence and in accordance with the provisions of the Convention, shall cooperate with the General Assembly and the Security Council by furnishing them, at the request of either, such information and assistance as may be required in the exercise of their respective responsibilities under the Charter of the United Nations.

4. The United Nations and OPCW shall cooperate in the field of public information and shall arrange, upon request, for the exchange of information, publications and reports of mutual interest and for the furnishing of special reports and studies and information.

5. The Secretariat of the United Nations and the Technical Secretariat of OPCW shall maintain a close working relationship in accordance with such arrangements as may be agreed between the Secretary-General and the Director-General.

Article III
Coordination

The United Nations and OPCW recognize the necessity of achieving, where applicable, effective coordination of the activities and services of OPCW and of the United Nations, and of avoiding unnecessary duplication of their activities and services.

Article IV
Reporting

1. The Director-General will keep the United Nations informed of the routine activities of OPCW, and will report on a regular basis, as appropriate and as duly mandated by the Executive Council, through the Secretary-General to the General Assembly and the Security Council.

2. If the Executive Council takes a decision to provide, pursuant to article X of the Convention, supplementary assistance to a State Party to the Convention requesting such assistance in connection with the use or threat of use of chemical weapons, the Director-General (representing OPCW, as specified in this Agreement) shall transmit to the Secretary-General (representing the United Nations, as specified in this Agreement) the above-mentioned decision of the Executive Council, together with the investigation report prepared by the Technical Secretariat in connection with the request for such assistance.

3. Whenever decisions are taken by the Conference of the States Parties, pursuant to article XII of the Convention, on measures, including collective measures recommended to States Parties, to ensure compliance with the Convention and to redress and remedy any situation which contravenes the provisions of the Convention, the Director-General, upon instructions from

the Conference, shall inform the General Assembly and the Security Council accordingly, through the Secretary-General.

4. Should the Secretary-General report to the United Nations on the common activities of the United Nations and OPCW or on the development of relations between them, any such report shall be promptly transmitted by the Secretary-General to OPCW.

5. Should the Director-General report to OPCW on the common activities of OPCW and the United Nations or on the development of relations between them, any such report shall be promptly transmitted by the Director-General to the United Nations.

Article V
Reciprocal representation

1. The Secretary-General shall be entitled to attend and to participate in relation to matters of common interest, without vote and in accordance with the relevant rules of procedure, in sessions of the Conference of the States Parties and in sessions of the Executive Council of OPCW. The Secretary-General shall also be invited, as appropriate, to attend and to participate without vote in such other meetings as OPCW may convene at which matters of interest to the United Nations are under consideration. The Secretary-General may, for the purposes of this paragraph, designate any person as his/her representative.

2. The Director-General shall be entitled to attend plenary meetings of the General Assembly of the United Nations for the purpose of consultations. The Director-General shall be entitled to attend and to participate without vote in the meetings of the Committees of the General Assembly and in meetings of the Economic and Social Council and, as appropriate, of any subsidiary organs of these bodies and the General Assembly. The Director-General may, at the invitation of the Security Council, attend its meetings to supply the Council, as duly mandated by the Executive Council, with information or give other assistance with regard to matters within the competence of OPCW. The Director-General may, for the purposes of this paragraph, designate any person as his/her representative.

3. Written statements presented by the United Nations to OPCW for distribution shall be distributed by the Technical Secretariat of OPCW to all members of the appropriate organ(s) or subsidiary organ(s) of OPCW. Written statements presented by OPCW to the United Nations for distribution shall be distributed by the Secretariat of the United Nations to all members of the appropriate organ(s) or subsidiary organ(s) of the United Nations.

Article VI
Agenda items

1. The United Nations may propose agenda items for consideration by OPCW. In such cases, the United Nations shall notify the Director-General of the agenda item or items concerned, and the Director-General shall, in accordance with his/her authority and the relevant rules of procedure, bring any such agenda item or items to the attention of the Conference of the States Parties, the Executive Council or such other organ(s) of OPCW as may be appropriate.

2. OPCW may propose agenda items for consideration by the United Nations. In such cases, OPCW shall notify the Secretary-General of the agenda item or items concerned, and the Secretary-General shall, in accordance with his/her authority, bring any such item or items to the attention of the General Assembly, the Security Council, the Economic and Social Council or such other organ(s) of the United Nations as may be appropriate.

Article VII
International Court of Justice

1. The United Nations takes note of article XIV, paragraph 5, of the Convention, which empowers the Conference of the States Parties or the Executive Council of OPCW, subject to authorization from the General Assembly of the United Nations, to request the International Court of Justice to give an advisory opinion on any legal question(s) arising from within the scope of activities of OPCW, apart from any question(s) concerning the mutual relationship between OPCW and the United Nations.

2. The United Nations and OPCW agree that each such request for an advisory opinion shall first be submitted to the General Assembly, which will decide upon the request in accordance with Article 96 of the Charter.

3. When seeking an advisory opinion, as referred to in paragraph 1 of this article, OPCW agrees to furnish, in accordance with the Confidentiality Annex to the Convention and the OPCW Policy on Confidentiality, any such information as may be required by the International Court of Justice in accordance with the Statute of the International Court of Justice.

Article VIII
Resolutions of the United Nations

The Secretary-General shall transmit to the Director-General resolutions of the General Assembly or the Security Council pertaining to issues relevant to the Convention. Upon receipt thereof, the Director-General will bring the resolutions concerned to the attention of the relevant organs of OPCW and will report back to the Secretary-General on any action taken by OPCW, as appropriate.

Article IX
United Nations laissez-passer

Officials of OPCW shall be entitled, in accordance with such administrative arrangements as may be concluded between the Secretary-General and the Director-General, to use the laissez-passer of the United Nations as a valid travel document where such use is recognized by States Parties in the applicable instruments defining the privileges and immunities of OPCW and its officials. The administrative arrangements will take into account, to the extent possible, the special requirements of OPCW arising from its verification activities under the Convention.

Article X
Personnel arrangements

1. The United Nations and OPCW agree to consult whenever necessary concerning matters of common interest relating to the terms and conditions of employment of staff.

2. The United Nations and OPCW agree to cooperate regarding the exchange of personnel, bearing in mind the nationality of States members of OPCW, and to determine conditions of such cooperation in supple-

mentary arrangements to be concluded for that purpose in accordance with article XIV of this Agreement.

Article XI
Budgetary and financial matters

1. OPCW recognizes the desirability of establishing budgetary and financial cooperation with the United Nations in order that OPCW may benefit from the experience of the United Nations in this field and in order to ensure, as far as may be practicable, the consistency of the administrative operations of the two organizations in this field.

2. The United Nations may arrange for studies to be undertaken concerning budgetary and financial matters of interest to OPCW with a view, as far as may be practicable, to achieving coordination and securing consistency in such matters.

3. OPCW agrees to follow, as far as may be practicable, the standard budgetary and financial practices and forms used by the United Nations.

Article XII
Expenses

Expenses resulting from any cooperation or provision of services pursuant to this Agreement shall be subject to separate arrangements between OPCW and the United Nations.

Article XIII
Protection of confidentiality

1. Subject to paragraphs 1 and 3 of article II, nothing in this Agreement shall be so construed as to require either the United Nations or OPCW to furnish any material, data and information whose disclosure could, in its judgement, require it to violate its obligation, under its constituent instrument or policy on confidentiality, to protect such information.

2. The United Nations and OPCW shall ensure the appropriate protection, in accordance with their constituent instruments and policies on confidentiality, in respect to such information.

Article XIV
Implementation of the Agreement

The Secretary-General and the Director-General may enter into such supplementary arrangements and develop such practical measures for the implementation of this Agreement as may be found desirable.

Article XV
Amendments

This Agreement may be amended by mutual consent between the United Nations and OPCW. Any such amendment, once agreed upon, shall enter into force on the date on which the United Nations and OPCW have exchanged written notifications that their internal requirements for entry into force have been met.

Article XVI
Entry into force

1. This Agreement shall enter into force on the date on which the United Nations and OPCW have exchanged written notifications that their internal requirements for entry into force have been met.

2. This Agreement shall be applied provisionally by the United Nations and OPCW upon signature.

IN WITNESS WHEREOF, the undersigned, being duly authorized representatives of the United Nations and OPCW, have signed the present Agreement.

SIGNED this 17th day of October 2000 at New York in two originals in the English language.

For the United Nations
(*Signed*) Louise FRÉCHETTE
Deputy Secretary-General

For the Organization for the Prohibition
of Chemical Weapons
(*Signed*) José M. BUSTANI
Director-General

On 7 December [meeting 80], the Assembly adopted **resolution 56/42** [draft: A/56/L.30] without vote [agenda item 21 *(l)*].

Cooperation between the United Nations and the Organization for the Prohibition of Chemical Weapons
The General Assembly,

Recalling its resolution 55/283 of 7 September 2001, in which it approved the Agreement concerning the Relationship between the United Nations and the Organization for the Prohibition of Chemical Weapons, and the decision of 17 May 2001 of the Conference of the States Parties to the Convention on the Prohibition of the Development, Production, Stockpiling and Use of Chemical Weapons and on Their Destruction to approve the Agreement,

Having received the annual report for 2000 of the Organization for the Prohibition of Chemical Weapons on the implementation of the Convention,

1. *Welcomes* the entry into force of the Agreement concerning the Relationship between the United Nations and the Organization for the Prohibition of Chemical Weapons;

2. *Takes note* of the annual report for 2000 of the Organization for the Prohibition of Chemical Weapons submitted by its Director-General on its behalf;

3. *Decides* to include in the provisional agenda of its fifty-seventh session the sub-item entitled "Cooperation between the United Nations and the Organization for the Prohibition of Chemical Weapons".

Conventional weapons

The United Nations Conference on the Illicit Trade in Small Arms and Light Weapons in All its Aspects was one of the major disarmament events in 2001. The Programme of Action adopted by the Conference was seen as a significant first step towards curbing the illicit trade and proliferation of those weapons. However, several important issues were not included in the document; no agreement was reached on restricting the supply of small arms and light weapons to Governments; the issue of prohibition of unrestricted trade and private ownership of small arms and light weapons designed for military purposes remained outside the document; and it contained no commitment to negotiate international legal instruments on marking and tracing small arms and light weapons or on regulating brokering activities in their transfers. In related action, the General Assembly, prior to the Conference, had adopted a Protocol against the Illicit Manufacturing of and Trafficking in Firearms, Their Parts and Components and Ammunition (**resolution 55/255**) (see p. 1036), which was designed to strengthen cooperation among States in order to prevent, combat and eradicate illicit activities involving firearms and ammunition, and supplemented the United Nations Convention against Transnational Organized Crime.

Other major activities relating to certain conventional weapons were carried out within the framework of preparations for the Second Review Conference of the States Parties to the 1980 Convention on Prohibitions or Restrictions on the Use of Certain Conventional Weapons Which May Be Deemed to Be Excessively Injurious or to Have Indiscriminate Effects [YUN 1980, p. 76] and at the Review Conference itself, held in December. Regarding anti-personnel mines, the Third Annual Conference of the States Parties to Amended Protocol II to the 1980 Convention took place, as did the Third Meeting of the States Parties to the 1997 Convention on the Prohibition of the Use, Stockpiling, Production and Transfer of Anti-personnel Mines and on Their Destruction [YUN 1997, p. 503].

During the year, a number of activities contributed to a wider acceptance by Governments of the UN Register of Conventional Arms, which remained the most well-known instrument of transparency for conventional weapons. However, differences persisted among Member States regarding the Register's future development, especially on expanding its scope to include data on military holdings and procurement through national production, on the same basis as data on transfers. The question of the inclusion of weapons of mass destruction continued to be controversial.

Small arms

Expert meetings. The Group of Governmental Experts on Small Arms, established pursuant to General Assembly resolution 54/54 V [YUN 1999, p. 487], completed its study on the feasibility of restricting the manufacture and trade of small arms and light weapons to manufacturers and dealers authorized by States (third and final session, New York, 5-9 February). It also held informal meetings (Ottawa, Canada, 29 January–2 February) [A/CONF.192/PC/33 & A/CONF.192/2]. The Group identified and evaluated options and approaches at the national, regional and global

levels related to manufacturing, stockpiles and surplus weapons, and trade, including brokering and related activities.

Illicit traffic

Reports of Secretary-General. Pursuant to General Assembly resolution 55/33 F [YUN 2000, p. 520], the Secretary-General, in a July report [A/56/182], described UN initiatives and regional and subregional efforts to assist States to curb the illicit traffic in small arms and to collect them. He described requests for assistance received from Albania, Cambodia, the Congo, Kenya, Niger and Papua New Guinea, and the UN response thereto.

In response to Assembly resolution 55/33 Q [YUN 2000, p. 519], the Secretary-General, in an August report [A/56/296], provided an overview of his ongoing consultations on illicit trafficking in small arms and light weapons. He presented the outcome of meetings convened under UN auspices, by regional and subregional organizations and by States or groups of States (see pp. 511-14). Annexed to the report were the views of 12 Member States on the types and quantities of surplus, confiscated or collected small arms and light weapons that had been destroyed, and on their methods of destruction.

UN Conference

The United Nations Conference on the Illicit Trade in Small Arms and Light Weapons in All Its Aspects (New York, 9-20 July 2001) [A/CONF.192/15] adopted the Programme of Action to Prevent, Combat and Eradicate the Illicit Trade in Small Arms and Light Weapons in All Its Aspects. States participating at the Conference numbered 169. UN bodies, other international and regional organizations and NGOs also participated.

The Programme of Action contained commitments at the national, regional and global levels for combating the illicit trade in small arms and light weapons, measures for enhancing cooperation among States and for assisting those affected, as well as a follow-up mechanism to oversee implementation and further development.

States were committed to develop, strengthen and implement agreed norms and measures to prevent, combat and eradicate illicit manufacture and trade. The Programme emphasized post-conflict regions and promoting responsible action by States regarding small weapons' export, import, transit and retransfer. States were also committed to developing or strengthening national legislation and administrative measures and to criminalizing illicit activities; to applying unique markings on and accurate record-keeping of each weapon; to destroying illicit or surplus weapons as necessary; and to enhancing transparency. They agreed to support national disarmament, demobilization and reintegration programmes; to further enhance cooperation among themselves in tracing and identifying illicit arms; and to assist affected States. The Programme of Action encouraged the United Nations and other international organizations to undertake initiatives to promote its implementation. It requested the Secretary-General, through the Department for Disarmament Affairs (DDA), to collate and circulate data and information on the Programme's implementation, provided by States on a voluntary basis. A conference would be convened no later than 2006 to review progress made in implementing the Programme. In the interim, biennial meetings would be held for that purpose, and a UN study would be undertaken to examine the feasibility of developing an international instrument to identify and trace small arms and light weapons.

A statement by the Conference President, annexed to the report, while noting that the Conference had taken a significant step forward, expressed disappointment that agreement could not be reached on the need to establish and maintain controls over private ownership of small arms and light weapons and the need to prevent the sales of those weapons to non-State groups.

Preparatory Committee

The Preparatory Committee for the Conference held its second (8-19 January) and third (19-30 March) sessions, both in New York [A/CONF.192/1]. At those sessions, the Committee considered a large number of proposals by Member States on the draft programme of action and documents transmitted by them, including a statement by South Africa [A/CONF.192/PC/31], on its unilateral destruction of surplus small arms; by Bulgaria [A/CONF.192/PC/37], views and suggestions on regional and subregional activities; by France [A/CONF.192/PC/38], a summary of the Franco-Swiss Seminar on the Traceability of Small Arms and Light Weapons (Geneva, 12-13 March); and by Namibia [A/CONF.192/PC/35], the text of the Declaration concerning Firearms, Ammunition and Other Related Materials in the Southern African Development Community (see p. 511).

The Committee adopted a decision, based on a joint proposal by Brazil, Mali, the Netherlands and the United Kingdom [A/CONF.192/PC/57], to proclaim the first day of the Conference "Small Arms Destruction Day", and to call on States to organize voluntarily on that day the public destruction of small arms and light weapons. It also recommended that the draft programme of action, drawn up on the basis of the Chairman's working paper, be forwarded to the Conference for further consideration and that the Conference be held at the ministerial level. The Committee adopted several procedural decisions.

Communication. On 9 July [S/2001/732], Colombia proposed an open debate on the question of small arms in the Security Council in August, under its Presidency. Among the proposed issues for consideration was the outcome of the Conference.

SECURITY COUNCIL ACTION

On 31 August [meeting 4362], the Security Council President made statement **S/PRST/2001/21** on behalf of the Council:

The Security Council reaffirms the statement of its President of 24 September 1999 (S/PRST/1999/28) and its resolution 1209(1998) of 19 November 1998, and notes with grave concern that the destabilizing accumulation and uncontrolled spread of small arms and light weapons in many regions of the world increases the intensity and duration of armed conflicts, undermines the sustainability of peace agreements, impedes the success of peace-building, frustrates efforts aimed at the prevention of armed conflict, hinders considerably the provision of humanitarian assistance, and compromises the effectiveness of the Security Council in discharging its primary responsibility for the maintenance of international peace and security. The Council expressed grave concern at the harmful impact of small arms and light weapons on civilians in situations of armed conflict, particularly on vulnerable groups such as women and children, and recalls in this regard its resolutions 1296(2000) of 19 April 2000 and 1314 (2000) of 11 August 2000.

The Council further notes with satisfaction the growing awareness within the international community of the problem of the illicit trade in small arms and light weapons as a challenge that involves security, humanitarian and development dimensions. In this regard the Council welcomes recent global and regional initiatives such as the Programme of Action to Prevent, Combat and Eradicate the Illicit Trade in Small Arms and Light Weapons in All Its Aspects; the Protocol against the Illicit Manufacturing of and Trafficking in Firearms, Their Parts and Components and Ammunition, supplementing the United Nations Convention against Transnational Organized Crime; the Document on Small Arms and Light Weapons adopted by the Organization for Security and Cooperation in Europe; the resolution on small arms of the Council of Ministers of the European Union; the Bamako Declaration on an African Common Position on the Illicit Proliferation, Circulation and Trafficking of Small Arms and Light Weapons; and the extension of the Economic Community of West African States Moratorium on the Production and Trade in Small Arms and Light Weapons.

The Council welcomes the adoption of the Programme of Action of the United Nations Conference in the Illicit Trade in Small Arms and Light Weapons in All Its Aspects, and calls on all Member States to take the required measures to promptly implement the recommendations contained therein. The Council recognizes its responsibility in assisting in the implementation of this Programme of Action, and stresses that the success of this Programme depends on the political will and efforts of Member States to implement its measures at the national, regional and global levels, as well as on the provision of international cooperation and assistance and on the follow-up agreed by the Conference, including the convening of a review conference no later than 2006.

The Council reaffirms the inherent right of individual or collective self-defence in accordance with Article 51 of the Charter of the United Nations and, subject to the Charter, the right of each State to import, produce and retain small arms and light weapons for its self-defence and security needs. Bearing in mind the considerable volume of licit trade in small arms and light weapons, the Council underlines the vital importance of effective national regulations and controls for this trade. In this regard, arms-exporting countries should exercise the highest degree of responsibility in small arms and light weapons transactions, and all countries have the responsibility to prevent their illegal diversion and re-export, so as to stem the leakage of legal weapons to illegal markets. The Council also stresses the importance of international cooperation to enable States to identify and trace in a timely and reliable manner illicit small arms and light weapons.

The Council underlines the importance of practical disarmament measures in averting armed conflicts and encourages States and relevant international and regional organizations to facilitate the appropriate cooperation of civil society actors in activities related to the prevention and combating of the excessive and destabilizing accumulation of and illicit trafficking in small arms and light weapons, including facilitating greater awareness and better understanding of the nature and scope of this problem.

The Council recognizes the important role of regional and subregional organizations in providing useful information and perspectives on the regional and subregional dimensions that characterize arms flows to conflicts, and underscores the importance of regional agreements and cooperation in this regard.

The Council emphasizes the importance of the effective collection and control of small arms and light weapons, and of their storage and destruction, as appropriate, in the context of disarmament, demobilization and reintegration programmes, as well as other measures that may contribute to the effective disposal of small arms and light weapons, and to prevention of the spread of these weapons to other regions. To this end, the Council welcomes the publication by the Secretary-General of the Handbook on Environmentally Sound Methods of Destruction of Small Arms, Light Weapons, Ammunition and Explosives. The Council stresses the importance of incorporating, on a case-by-case basis, in the negotiation, consolidation and implementation of peace agreements, as well as in the mandates of United Nations peacekeeping operations, appropriate provisions for the disarmament, demobilization and reintegration of ex-combatants, taking into account the special needs of child soldiers.

The Council reiterates its call for the effective implementation of arms embargoes imposed by the Council in its relevant resolutions, and encourages Member States to provide the Sanctions Committees with available information on alleged violations of arms embargoes. The Council expresses its determination to continue to improve the efficiency of the arms embargoes imposed by the Council on a case-by-case basis, including through the establishment of specific monitoring mechanisms or similar arrangements as appropriate. The Council stresses the need to engage the relevant international organizations, non-governmental organizations, business and financial institutions and other actors at the international, regional and local levels to contribute to the implementation of arms embargoes.

The Council stresses the need for cooperation and sharing of information among the Member States, and among the different Sanctions Committees on arms traffickers that have violated arms embargoes established by the Council. This information could also be provided to Interpol's International Weapons and Explosives Tracking System database or any other relevant database that may be developed for this purpose.

The Council stresses the need for innovative strategies to address the relationship between the illicit exploitation of natural and other resources and the purchase and trade in illegal weapons in those situations under its consideration. The Council expresses its intention to continue to consider employing effective measures to prevent the illicit exploitation of natural and other resources from fuelling those conflicts. In this regard, information on financial or other transactions fuelling the illicit flow of arms to those conflicts should be made available to the Council.

The Council requests the Secretary-General to include in his reports regarding relevant situations under consideration in the Council analytical assessments on the illicit trade in small arms and light weapons including, to the extent possible and within available resources, availability, stockpiling, lines of supply, brokering, transportation arrangements and financial networks for these weapons, as well as their humanitarian impact, especially on children.

The Council recognizes the role of the Secretary-General in supporting the coordination of all United Nations activities to combat the illicit trade in small arms and light weapons. In this connection, the Council requests the Secretary-General to submit a report to the Council by September 2002 containing specific recommendations on ways and means in which the Council may contribute to deal with the question of illicit trade in small arms and light weapons in situations under its consideration, taking into account the views of Member States, recent experiences in the field and the contents of this statement.

On 29 November [meeting 68], the General Assembly, on the recommendation of the First Committee [A/56/536], adopted **resolution 56/24 U** without vote [agenda item 74 *(g)*].

Assistance to States for curbing the illicit traffic in small arms and collecting them

The General Assembly,

Considering that the proliferation and illicit circulation of and traffic in small arms impede development, constitute a threat to populations and to national and regional security and are a factor contributing to the destabilization of States,

Deeply disturbed by the magnitude of the proliferation, illicit circulation and traffic of small arms in the States of the Sahelo-Saharan subregion,

Noting with satisfaction the conclusions of the United Nations advisory missions dispatched by the Secretary-General to the affected countries of the subregion to study the most appropriate way of halting the illicit circulation of small arms and collecting them,

Welcoming the designation of the Department for Disarmament Affairs of the Secretariat as a centre for the coordination of all activities of United Nations bodies concerned with small arms,

Thanking the Secretary-General for his report on the causes of conflict and the promotion of durable peace and sustainable development in Africa, and bearing in mind the statement on small arms made by the President of the Security Council on 24 September 1999,

Welcoming the recommendations resulting from the meetings of the States of the subregion held at Banjul, Algiers, Bamako, Yamoussoukro and Niamey to establish close regional cooperation with a view to strengthening security,

Welcoming also the initiative taken by the Economic Community of West African States concerning the declaration of a moratorium on the importation, exportation and manufacture of small arms and light weapons in West Africa,

Recalling the Algiers Declaration adopted by the Assembly of Heads of State and Government of the Organization of African Unity at its thirty-fifth ordinary session, held at Algiers from 12 to 14 July 1999,

Emphasizing the need to advance efforts towards wider cooperation and better coordination in the struggle against the accumulation, proliferation and widespread use of small arms through the common understanding reached at the meeting on small arms held at Oslo on 13 and 14 July 1998 and the Brussels Call for Action adopted by the International Conference on Sustainable Disarmament for Sustainable Development, held at Brussels on 12 and 13 October 1998,

Bearing in mind the Bamako Declaration on an African Common Position on the Illicit Proliferation, Circulation and Trafficking of Small Arms and Light Weapons, adopted at Bamako on 1 December 2000,

Taking note of the millennium report of the Secretary-General,

Welcoming the Programme of Action of the first United Nations Conference on the Illicit Trade in Small Arms and Light Weapons in All Its Aspects, held in New York from 9 to 20 July 2001,

Recognizing the important role that the organizations of civil society play in detection, prevention and arousing public awareness in efforts to curb the illicit traffic in small arms,

1. *Notes with satisfaction* the Declaration of the Ministerial Conference on Security, Stability, Development and Cooperation in Africa, held in Abuja on 8 and 9 May 2000, encourages the Secretary-General to pursue his action in the context of the implementation of resolution 49/75 G of 15 December 1994 and of the recommendations of the United Nations advisory missions, aimed at curbing the illicit circulation of small arms and collecting such arms in the affected States that so request, with the support of the United Nations Regional Centre for Peace and Disarmament in Africa and in close cooperation with the Organization of African Unity;

2. *Encourages* the establishment in the countries of the Sahelo-Saharan subregion of national commissions to combat the proliferation of small arms, and invites the international community to lend its support wherever possible to ensure the smooth functioning of the said commissions;

3. *Welcomes* the Declaration of a Moratorium on the Importation, Exportation and Manufacture of Small Arms and Light Weapons in West Africa, adopted by the heads of State and Government of the Economic Community of West African States in Abuja on 31 October 1998, and encourages the international community to support the implementation of the said moratorium;

4. *Encourages* the involvement of civil society organizations and associations in the efforts of the national committees to combat the illicit traffic in small arms and their participation in the implementation of the moratorium on the importation, exportation and manufacture of small arms and light weapons in West Africa;

5. *Takes note* of the conclusions of the meeting of Ministers for Foreign Affairs of the Economic Community of West African States, held in Bamako on 24 and 25 March 1999, with respect to the modalities for implementing the Programme for Coordination and Assistance for Security and Development, and welcomes the adoption by the meeting of a plan of action;

6. *Encourages* cooperation between State organs, international organizations and civil society in combating the illicit traffic in small arms and supporting operations to collect the said arms in the subregions;

7. *Invites* the Secretary-General and those States and organizations that are in a position to do so to provide assistance to States for curbing the illicit traffic in small arms and collecting them;

8. *Calls upon* the international community to provide technical and financial support to strengthen the capacity of civil society organizations to take action to combat the illicit trade in small arms;

9. *Requests* the Secretary-General to continue to consider the matter and to report to the General Assembly at its fifty-seventh session on the implementation of the present resolution;

10. *Decides* to include in the provisional agenda of its fifty-seventh session the item entitled "Assistance to States for curbing the illicit traffic in small arms and collecting them".

On 24 December [meeting 92], the Assembly, also on the recommendation of the First Committee

[A/56/536], adopted **resolution 56/24 V** without vote [agenda item 74 *(q)*].

The illicit trade in small arms and light weapons in all its aspects

The General Assembly,

Recalling its resolutions 50/70 B of 12 December 1995, 52/38 J of 9 December 1997, 53/77 E and 53/77 T of 4 December 1998, 54/54 R of 1 December 1999, 54/54 V of 15 December 1999 and 55/33 Q of 20 November 2000,

Recalling also its decision 55/415 of 20 November 2000 to convene the United Nations Conference on the Illicit Trade in Small Arms and Light Weapons in All Its Aspects in New York from 9 to 20 July 2001,

Welcoming the adoption by consensus of the Programme of Action to Prevent, Combat and Eradicate the Illicit Trade in Small Arms and Light Weapons in All Its Aspects by the Conference, held in New York from 9 to 20 July 2001,

1. *Decides* to convene a conference, no later than 2006, to review progress made in the implementation of the Programme of Action to Prevent, Combat and Eradicate the Illicit Trade in Small Arms and Light Weapons in All Its Aspects, the date and venue to be decided by the General Assembly at its fifty-eighth session;

2. *Also decides* to convene a meeting of States on a biennial basis, commencing in 2003, to consider the national, regional and global implementation of the Programme of Action;

3. *Calls upon* all States to implement the Programme of Action;

4. *Encourages* the United Nations and other appropriate international and regional organizations to undertake initiatives to promote the implementation of the Programme of Action;

5. *Encourages* non-governmental organizations and civil society to engage, as appropriate, in all aspects of international, regional, subregional and national efforts to implement the Programme of Action;

6. *Encourages* all States to promote and strengthen regional and subregional initiatives to prevent, combat and eradicate the illicit trade in small arms and light weapons in all its aspects;

7. *Continues to encourage* States to take appropriate national measures to destroy surplus, confiscated or collected small arms and light weapons, subject to any legal constraint associated with the preparation of criminal prosecutions, unless another form of disposition or use has been officially authorized and provided that such weapons have been duly marked and registered, and to submit, on a voluntary basis, information to the Secretary-General on types and quantities destroyed as well as the methods of their destruction or disposition;

8. *Requests* the Secretary-General to ensure that resources and expertise are made available to the Secretariat to promote the implementation of the Programme of Action;

9. *Encourages* all initiatives to mobilize resources and expertise to promote the implementation of the Programme of Action and to provide assistance to States in their implementation of the Programme of Action;

10. *Requests* the Secretary-General to undertake a United Nations study, commencing during the fifty-sixth session of the General Assembly, within available financial resources and with any other assistance provided by States in a position to do so, and with the assistance of governmental experts appointed by him on the basis of equitable geographical representation, while seeking the views of States, to examine the feasibility of developing an international instrument to enable States to identify and trace, in a timely and reliable manner, illicit small arms and light weapons and to submit the study to the General Assembly at its fifty-eighth session;

11. *Decides* to consider at its fifty-seventh session further steps to enhance international cooperation in preventing, combating and eradicating illicit brokering in small arms and light weapons;

12. *Requests* the Secretary-General, within existing resources, through the Department for Disarmament Affairs of the Secretariat, to collate and circulate data and information provided by States on a voluntary basis, including national reports, on the implementation by those States of the Programme of Action;

13. *Also requests* the Secretary-General to report to the General Assembly at its fifty-seventh session on the implementation of the present resolution;

14. *Decides* to include in the provisional agenda of its fifty-seventh session an item entitled "The illicit trade in small arms and light weapons in all its aspects".

Convention on excessively injurious conventional weapons and Protocols

In response to General Assembly resolution 55/37 [YUN 2000, p. 522], the Secretary-General reported on the status, as at 31 May [A/56/163], of the 1980 Convention on Prohibitions or Restrictions on the Use of Certain Conventional Weapons Which May Be Deemed to Be Excessively Injurious or to Have Indiscriminate Effects and its three annexed Protocols [YUN 1980, p. 76]: on Non-Detectable Fragments (Protocol I); on Prohibitions or Restrictions on the Use of Mines, Booby Traps and Other Devices, as amended on 3 May 1996 (Protocol II) [YUN 1996, p. 484]; and on Prohibitions or Restrictions on the Use of Incendiary Weapons (Protocol III); as well as the 1995 Protocol on Blinding Laser Weapons (Protocol IV) [YUN 1995, p. 221], which had taken effect on 30 July 1998 [YUN 1998, p. 530].

The accession of Bolivia, Mali, Nauru and the Republic of Korea and the succession of Yugoslavia brought the number of States parties to the Convention to 88 as at 31 December.

As decided by the Second Annual Conference of the States Parties to Amended Protocol II in 2000 [YUN 2000, p. 521], the Third Annual Conference was held in Geneva on 10 December [CCW/AP.II/CONF.3/4 (Parts I and II) & Corr.1,2]. The Conference reviewed the operation and status of amended Protocol II and examined 38 national reports received from 36 States parties, containing information on dissemination of information on the Protocol to armed forces and civilians; mine clearance and rehabilitation programmes; steps taken to meet technical requirements of the Protocol and other relevant information; legislation related to the Protocol; measures taken on international technical information exchange, on international cooperation on mine clearance, and on technical cooperation and assistance; and other relevant matters. The Conference adopted a final document, containing conclusions and recommendations and an appeal to States that had not done so to accede to amended Protocol II as soon as possible. The Conference recommended that the Secretary-General, as depositary, and the President of the Conference exercise their authority to achieve the goal of universality of the Protocol and called on States parties to promote wider adherence. In accordance with General Assembly resolution 56/28 (see below), the Conference decided to convene the Fourth Annual Conference in December 2002.

Second Review Conference

Pursuant to General Assembly resolution 55/37 [YUN 2000, p. 522] and based on the decisions of the First Review Conference in 1995-1996 [YUN 1996, p. 484], the Second Review Conference of the States Parties to the Convention met (Geneva, 11-21 December) [CCW/CONF.II/2] to review the scope and operation of the Convention and its annexed Protocols, and to consider proposals for amending them, as well as proposals for additional protocols relating to other categories of conventional weapons. The Preparatory Committee for the Conference held its second (2-6 April) [CCW/CONF.II/PC.2/1] and third (24-28 September) [CCW/CONF.II/PC.3/1] sessions, as well as informal intersessional consultations, all in Geneva.

The Conference, which was attended by 65 States parties, a number of signatory States and non-parties, the International Committee of the Red Cross, the United Nations Children's Fund and NGOs, adopted by consensus its report and Final Declaration. The Declaration contained a decision to amend article I of the Convention by extending its scope of application to situations referred to in article 3 common to the Geneva Conventions of 12 August 1949, while excluding situations of internal disturbances and tensions— riots and isolated and sporadic acts of violence— as not being armed conflicts. Other parts of that decision contained some restrictions and explanations relating to the amendment.

The Final Declaration contained procedural decisions relating to: follow-up work on decisions of the Conference, to be overseen by a chairman-designate at a meeting of the States parties in December 2002; the establishment of a group of governmental experts to meet in 2002 to consider the issue of explosive remnants of war and to further explore the issue of mines other than anti-personnel mines; promotion of compliance with the Convention and its annexed Protocols; and consideration of issues concerning small-calibre weapons and ammunition. The Conference decided to convene the next review conference five years following the entry into force of any amendments adopted, but not later than 2006. The Conference proposed that the next review conference consider further measures in relation to other conventional weapons, which may be deemed to cause unnecessary suffering or to have indiscriminate effects.

GENERAL ASSEMBLY ACTION

On 29 November [meeting 68], the General Assembly, on the recommendation of the First Committee [A/56/540], adopted **resolution 56/28** without vote [agenda item 78].

Convention on Prohibitions or Restrictions on the Use of Certain Conventional Weapons Which May Be Deemed to Be Excessively Injurious or to Have Indiscriminate Effects

The General Assembly,

Recalling its resolution 55/37 of 20 November 2000 and previous resolutions referring to the Convention on Prohibitions or Restrictions on the Use of Certain Conventional Weapons Which May Be Deemed to Be Excessively Injurious or to Have Indiscriminate Effects,

Recalling with satisfaction the adoption, on 10 October 1980, of the Convention, together with the Protocol on Non-Detectable Fragments (Protocol I), the Protocol on Prohibitions or Restrictions on the Use of Mines, Booby Traps and Other Devices (Protocol II) and the Protocol on Prohibitions or Restrictions on the Use of Incendiary Weapons (Protocol III), which entered into force on 2 December 1983,

Also recalling with satisfaction the adoption by the Review Conference of the States Parties to the Convention on Prohibitions or Restrictions on the Use of Certain Conventional Weapons Which May Be Deemed to Be Excessively Injurious or to Have Indiscriminate Effects, on 13 October 1995, of the Protocol on Blinding Laser Weapons (Protocol IV), and on 3 May 1996 of the amended Protocol on Prohibitions or Restrictions on the Use of Mines, Booby Traps and Other Devices (Protocol II), which entered into force on 30 July 1998 and 3 December 1998, respectively,

Welcoming the additional ratifications and acceptances of or accessions to the Convention, as well as the ratifications and acceptances of or accessions to amended Protocol II and Protocol IV,

Recalling the role played by the International Committee of the Red Cross in the elaboration of the Convention and the Protocols thereto,

Recalling also that the States parties at the Review Conference declared their commitment to keeping the provisions of Protocol II under review in order to ensure that the concerns regarding the weapons it covers are addressed, and that they would encourage the efforts of the United Nations and other organizations to address all problems of landmines,

Commending the efforts of the Secretary-General and the President of the First Annual Conference of States Parties to Amended Protocol II towards the promotion of the goal of universality of amended Protocol II,

Noting that, in conformity with article 8 of the Convention, conferences may be convened to examine amendments to the Convention or to any of the Protocols thereto, to examine additional protocols concerning other categories of conventional weapons not covered by existing Protocols or to review the scope and application of the Convention and the Protocols thereto and to examine any proposed amendments or additional protocols,

Noting also that, in accordance with article 13 of amended Protocol II, a conference of States parties to that Protocol shall be held annually for the purpose of consultations and cooperation on all issues in relation to the Protocol,

Noting further that the rules of procedure of the First Annual Conference of States Parties to Amended Protocol II provide for the invitation of States not parties to the Protocol, the International Committee of the Red Cross and interested non-governmental organizations to take part in the Conference,

Welcoming the particular efforts of the International Committee of the Red Cross in raising awareness of the humanitarian consequences of explosive remnants of war,

Welcoming also the results of the Second Annual Conference of States Parties to Amended Protocol II, held at Geneva from 11 to 13 December 2000,

Recalling the decision of States parties to the Convention to convene the next review conference from 11 to 21 December 2001, preceded by three sessions of the preparatory committee for the review conference, on 14 December 2000, from 2 to 6 April 2001 and from 24 to 28 September 2001, respectively,

Welcoming the convening, in the context of the preparatory process, of the informal open-ended consultations of the States parties to the Convention and other interested States at Geneva from 27 to 31 August 2001, which provided for structured discussions, building on work by the respective Friends of Chair on several issues pertaining to the Second Review Conference of the States Parties to the Convention and the Preparatory Committee for the Second Review Conference,

1. *Calls upon* all States that have not yet done so to take all measures to become parties, as soon as possible, to the Convention on Prohibitions or Restrictions on the Use of Certain Conventional Weapons Which May Be Deemed to Be Excessively Injurious or to Have Indiscriminate Effects and the Protocols thereto, in particular the amended Protocol on Prohibitions or Restrictions on the Use of Mines, Booby Traps and Other Devices (Protocol II), with a view to achieving the widest possible adherence to this instrument at an early date, and calls upon successor States to take appropriate measures so that ultimately adherence to these instruments will be universal;

2. *Calls upon* all States parties to the Convention that have not yet done so to express their consent to be bound by the Protocols to the Convention;

3. *Welcomes* the convening, on 10 December 2001, of the Third Annual Conference of States Parties to Amended Protocol II, in accordance with article 13 thereof, and calls upon all States parties to amended Protocol II to address at that meeting, inter alia, the question of holding the fourth annual conference in 2002;

4. *Welcomes also* the proposal contained in the Final Declaration of the Review Conference of the States Parties to the Convention, adopted by consensus on 3 May 1996, that the next review conference consider the question of eventual further measures in relation to other conventional weapons which may be deemed to cause unnecessary suffering or to have indiscriminate effects;

5. *Notes*, therefore, the proposals put forward by States parties and the International Committee of the Red Cross for consideration by the 2001 Review Conference, concerning, inter alia, the following issues:

   (a) Compliance procedures and mechanisms;

   (b) Explosive remnants of war;

   (c) Extension of the scope of application of the Convention and the Protocols thereto to non-international armed conflicts;

   (d) Landmines other than anti-personnel mines;

   (e) Small-calibre ammunitions;

6. *Requests* the Secretary-General to render the necessary assistance and to provide such services, including summary records, as may be required for the Second Review Conference of the States Parties to the Convention as well as for any possible continuation of work after the Conference, should the States parties deem it appropriate;

7. *Also requests* the Secretary-General, in his capacity as depositary of the Convention and the Protocols thereto, to continue to inform the General Assembly periodically of ratifications and acceptances of and accessions to the Convention and the Protocols thereto;

8. *Decides* to include in the provisional agenda of its fifty-seventh session the item entitled "Convention on Prohibitions or Restrictions on the Use of Certain Conventional Weapons Which May Be Deemed to Be Excessively Injurious or to Have Indiscriminate Effects".

Practical disarmament

The group of interested States, established in 1998 [YUN 1998, p. 531] to examine and support concrete projects of practical disarmament, met four times in 2001 (27 March, 17 May, 10 October and 13 December) to discuss practical disarmament measures in Cambodia, Kenya and Niger. The group continued to consider the provision of political and technical advice to several institutions involved in practical disarmament measures. Discussions in that regard focused on the Programme of Action adopted at the 2001 Conference on the Illicit Trade in Small Arms and Light Weapons in All Its Aspects (see p. 499) and its relevance to other practical disarmament measures under consideration.

Disarmament Commission action. In 2001 [A/56/42], the Disarmament Commission allocated to Working Group II the item entitled "Practical confidence-building measures in the field of conventional arms". The Group took note of a non-paper presented by the Chair, which was seen as a contribution to the Group's future work but required further discussion, elaboration and refinement. The non-paper was annexed to the Commission's report. On 26 April, the Working Group adopted its report by consensus.

GENERAL ASSEMBLY ACTION

On 29 November [meeting 68], the General Assembly, on the recommendation of the First Committee [A/56/536], adopted **resolution 56/24 P** without vote [agenda item 74 (h)].

Consolidation of peace through practical disarmament measures

The General Assembly,

Recalling its resolutions 51/45 N of 10 December 1996, 52/38 G of 9 December 1997, 53/77 M of 4 December 1998, 54/54 H of 1 December 1999 and 55/33 G of 20 November 2000,

Convinced that a comprehensive and integrated approach towards certain practical disarmament measures often is a prerequisite to maintaining and consolidating peace and security and thus provides a basis for effective post-conflict peace-building, namely the rehabilitation and social and economic development in areas that have suffered from conflict; such measures are, inter alia, collection and responsible disposal, preferably through destruction, of weapons obtained through illicit trafficking or illicit manufacture as well as of weapons and ammunition declared by competent national authorities to be surplus to requirements, particularly with regard to small arms and light weapons, unless another form of disposition or use has been officially authorized and provided that such weapons have been duly marked and registered; confidence-building measures; disarmament, demobilization and reintegration of former combatants; demining; and conversion,

Noting with satisfaction that the international community is more than ever aware of the importance of such practical disarmament measures, especially with regard to the growing problems arising from the excessive accumulation and uncontrolled spread of small arms and light weapons, which pose a threat to peace and security and reduce the prospects for economic development in many regions, particularly in post-conflict situations,

Stressing that further efforts are needed in order to develop and effectively implement programmes of practical disarmament in affected areas so as to complement, on a case-by-case basis, peacekeeping and peace-building efforts,

Taking note of the report of the Secretary-General prepared with the assistance of the Group of Governmental Experts on Small Arms, and in particular the recommendations contained therein, as an important contribution to the consolidation of the peace process through practical disarmament measures,

Taking into account the deliberations at the 2001 substantive session of the Disarmament Commission in Working Group II on agenda item 5, entitled "Practical confidence-building measures in the field of conventional arms", and encouraging the Disarmament Commission to continue its efforts aimed at the identification of such measures,

Welcoming the Programme of Action adopted by the United Nations Conference on the Illicit Trade in Small Arms and Light Weapons in All Its Aspects, which should be implemented expeditiously,

1. *Stresses*, in the context of the present resolution, the particular relevance of the "Guidelines on conventional arms control/limitation and disarmament, with particular emphasis on consolidation of peace in the context of General Assembly resolution 51/45 N", adopted by the Disarmament Commission by consensus at its 1999 substantive session;

2. *Takes note* of the report of the Secretary-General on the consolidation of peace through practical disarmament measures, submitted pursuant to resolution 51/45 N, and once again encourages Member States, as well as regional arrangements and agencies, to lend their support to the implementation of recommendations contained therein;

3. *Welcomes* the activities undertaken by the group of interested States that was formed in New York in March 1998, and invites the group to continue to analyse lessons learned from previous disarmament and peace-building projects, as well as to promote new practical disarmament measures to consolidate peace, especially as undertaken or designed by affected States themselves;

4. *Encourages* Member States, including the group of interested States, to lend their support to the Secretary-General in responding to requests by Member States to collect and destroy small arms and light weapons in post-conflict situations;

5. *Requests* the Secretary-General to submit to the General Assembly at its fifty-seventh session a report on the implementation of the present resolution, taking into consideration the activities of the group of interested States in this regard;

6. *Decides* to include in the provisional agenda of its fifty-seventh session the item entitled "Consolidation of peace through practical disarmament measures".

Transparency

Conference on Disarmament. In 2001, the issue of transparency in armaments was considered during plenary meetings of the Conference on Disarmament [A/56/27] in connection with efforts to reach a comprehensive agreement on the establishment of subsidiary bodies on agenda items. Although the Conference did not establish or re-establish any mechanism to deal with transparency in armaments because it did not achieve consensus on a programme of work, the Special Coordinator for the review of the agenda of the Conference (see p. 469) stated that there was general agreement on retaining the item.

UN Register of Conventional Arms

In response to General Assembly resolution 55/33 U [YUN 2000, p. 524], the Secretary-General submitted the ninth annual report on the United Nations Register of Conventional Arms [A/56/257 & Add.1,2], which was established in 1992 [YUN 1992, p. 75] to promote enhanced levels of transparency on arms transfers.

The report presented information provided by 117 Governments on imports and exports during 2000 in the seven categories of conventional arms (battle tanks, armoured combat vehicles, large-calibre artillery systems, attack helicopters, combat aircraft, warships, and missiles and missile launchers). Governments also provided information on procurement from national production and military holdings. The report indicated a substantial increase in the number of submissions.

In response to the Assembly's request in resolution 55/33 U that the Secretary-General implement the recommendations contained in the 2000 report of the Group of Governmental Experts on the continuing operation and further development of the Register [YUN 2000, p. 524], the report outlined regional activities undertaken by the Secretariat during the year, through DDA, in collaboration with Governments and regional organizations, to enhance familiarity with and greater participation in the Register.

GENERAL ASSEMBLY ACTION

On 29 November [meeting 68], the General Assembly, on the recommendation of the First Committee [A/56/536], adopted **resolution 56/24 Q** by recorded vote (135-0-23) [agenda item 74 (s)].

Transparency in armaments

The General Assembly,

Recalling its resolutions 46/36 L of 9 December 1991, 47/52 L of 15 December 1992, 48/75 E of 16 December 1993, 49/75 C of 15 December 1994, 50/70 D of 12 December 1995, 51/45 H of 10 December 1996, 52/38 R of 9 December 1997, 53/77 V of 4 December 1998, 54/54 O of 1 December 1999 and 55/33 U of 20 November 2000 entitled "Transparency in armaments",

Continuing to take the view that an enhanced level of transparency in armaments contributes greatly to confidence-building and security among States and that the establishment of the United Nations Register of Conventional Arms constitutes an important step forward in the promotion of transparency in military matters,

Welcoming the consolidated report of the Secretary-General on the Register, which includes the returns of Member States for 2000,

Welcoming also the response of Member States to the request contained in paragraphs 9 and 10 of resolution 46/36 L to provide data on their imports and exports of arms, as well as available background information

regarding their military holdings, procurement through national production and relevant policies,

Stressing that the continuing operation of the Register and its further development should be reviewed in order to secure a Register that is capable of attracting the widest possible participation,

1. *Reaffirms* its determination to ensure the effective operation of the United Nations Register of Conventional Arms, as provided for in paragraphs 7 to 10 of resolution 46/36 L;

2. *Calls upon* Member States, with a view to achieving universal participation, to provide the Secretary-General by 31 May annually with the requested data and information for the Register, including nil reports if appropriate, on the basis of resolutions 46/36 L and 47/52 L, the recommendations contained in paragraph 64 of the 1997 report of the Secretary-General on the continuing operation of the Register and its further development and the recommendations contained in paragraph 94 of the 2000 report of the Secretary-General and the appendices and annexes thereto;

3. *Invites* Member States in a position to do so, pending further development of the Register, to provide additional information on procurement from national production and military holdings and to make use of the "Remarks" column in the standardized reporting form to provide additional information such as types or models;

4. *Reaffirms* its decision, with a view to further development of the Register, to keep the scope of and participation in the Register under review and, to that end:

(a) *Recalls* its request to Member States to provide the Secretary-General with their views on the continuing operation of the Register and its further development and on transparency measures related to weapons of mass destruction;

(b) *Requests* the Secretary-General, with the assistance of a group of governmental experts to be convened in 2003, on the basis of equitable geographical representation, to prepare a report on the continuing operation of the Register and its further development, taking into account the work of the Conference on Disarmament, the views expressed by Member States and the reports of the Secretary-General on the continuing operation of the Register and its further development, with a view to a decision at its fifty-eighth session;

5. *Also requests* the Secretary-General to implement the recommendations contained in his 2000 report on the continuing operation of the Register and its further development and to ensure that sufficient resources are made available for the Secretariat to operate and maintain the Register;

6. *Invites* the Conference on Disarmament to consider continuing its work undertaken in the field of transparency in armaments;

7. *Reiterates its call upon* all Member States to cooperate at the regional and subregional levels, taking fully into account the specific conditions prevailing in the region or subregion, with a view to enhancing and coordinating international efforts aimed at increased openness and transparency in armaments;

8. *Requests* the Secretary-General to report to the General Assembly at its fifty-seventh session on progress made in implementing the present resolution;

9. *Decides* to include in the provisional agenda of its fifty-seventh session the item entitled "Transparency in armaments".

RECORDED VOTE ON RESOLUTION 56/24 Q:

In favour: Afghanistan, Albania, Andorra, Angola, Argentina, Armenia, Australia, Austria, Azerbaijan, Bahamas, Bangladesh, Barbados, Belarus, Belgium, Benin, Bhutan, Bolivia, Bosnia and Herzegovina, Botswana, Brazil, Brunei Darussalam, Bulgaria, Burkina Faso, Burundi, Cambodia, Cameroon, Canada, Cape Verde, Chile, Colombia, Costa Rica, Côte d'Ivoire, Croatia, Cuba, Cyprus, Czech Republic, Denmark, Dominican Republic, Ecuador, El Salvador, Equatorial Guinea, Eritrea, Estonia, Ethiopia, Fiji, Finland, France, Gabon, Georgia, Germany, Ghana, Greece, Grenada, Guatemala, Guinea, Guyana, Haiti, Honduras, Hungary, Iceland, India, Indonesia, Ireland, Israel, Italy, Jamaica, Japan, Kazakhstan, Kenya, Latvia, Lesotho, Liechtenstein, Lithuania, Luxembourg, Madagascar, Malaysia, Maldives, Mali, Malta, Mauritius, Micronesia, Monaco, Mongolia, Mozambique, Namibia, Nauru, Nepal, Netherlands, New Zealand, Nicaragua, Nigeria, Norway, Panama, Papua New Guinea, Paraguay, Peru, Philippines, Poland, Portugal, Republic of Korea, Republic of Moldova, Romania, Russian Federation, Saint Lucia, Samoa, San Marino, Senegal, Seychelles, Sierra Leone, Singapore, Slovakia, Slovenia, Solomon Islands, South Africa, Spain, Sri Lanka, Swaziland, Sweden, Thailand, The former Yugoslav Republic of Macedonia, Togo, Tonga, Trinidad and Tobago, Turkey, Turkmenistan, Uganda, Ukraine, United Kingdom, United Republic of Tanzania, United States, Uruguay, Venezuela, Yugoslavia, Zambia, Zimbabwe.

Against: None.

Abstaining: Algeria, Bahrain, China, Comoros, Democratic People's Republic of Korea, Djibouti, Egypt, Iran, Jordan, Kuwait, Lebanon, Libyan Arab Jamahiriya, Mauritania, Mexico, Morocco, Myanmar, Pakistan, Qatar, Saudi Arabia, Sudan, Syrian Arab Republic, Tunisia, Yemen.

The First Committee adopted paragraphs 4 *(b)* and 6 by separate recorded votes of 123 to 4, with 13 abstentions, and 123 to none, with 17 abstentions, respectively. The Assembly retained the paragraphs by 133 to 4, with 12 abstentions, and 133 to none, with 17 abstentions, respectively.

Transparency of military expenditures

In response to General Assembly resolution 54/43 [YUN 1999, p. 497], the Secretary-General, in August [A/56/267], presented reports received from 59 Member States on military expenditures for the latest fiscal year for which data were available. The reporting instrument was that recommended by the Assembly in resolution 35/142 B [YUN 1980, p. 88].

Also in accordance with resolution 54/43, DDA facilitated and participated in a meeting of the Committee on Hemispheric Security of the Organization of American States (Washington, D.C., 4 May), which was devoted to arms transparency issues at the regional level.

GENERAL ASSEMBLY ACTION

On 29 November [meeting 68], the General Assembly, on the recommendation of the First Committee [A/56/526], adopted **resolution 56/14** without vote [agenda item 64 *(b)*].

Objective information on military matters, including transparency of military expenditures

The General Assembly,

Recalling its resolutions 53/72 of 4 December 1998 and 54/43 of 1 December 1999 on objective information on military matters, including transparency of military expenditures,

Also recalling its resolution 35/142 B of 12 December 1980, which introduced the United Nations system for the standardized reporting of military expenditures, and its resolutions 48/62 of 16 December 1993, 49/66 of 15 December 1994, 51/38 of 10 December 1996 and 52/32 of 9 December 1997, calling upon all Member States to participate in it, and its resolution 47/54 B of 9 December 1992, endorsing the guidelines and recommendations for objective information on military matters and inviting Member States to provide the Secretary-General with relevant information regarding their implementation,

Noting that since then national reports on military expenditures and on the guidelines and recommendations for objective information on military matters have been submitted by a number of Member States belonging to different geographic regions,

Convinced that the improvement of international relations forms a sound basis for promoting further openness and transparency in all military matters,

Also convinced that transparency in military matters is an essential element for building a climate of trust and confidence between States worldwide and that a better flow of objective information on military matters can help relieve international tension and is therefore an important contribution to conflict prevention,

Noting the role of the standardized reporting system, as instituted through its resolution 35/142 B, as an important instrument to enhance transparency in military matters,

Conscious that the value of the standardized reporting system would be enhanced by a broader participation of Member States,

Welcoming, therefore, the report of the Secretary-General on ways and means to implement the guidelines and recommendations for objective information on military matters, including, in particular, how to strengthen and broaden participation in the standardized reporting system,

Recalling that the guidelines and recommendations for objective information on military matters recommended certain areas for further consideration, such as the improvement of the standardized reporting system,

Noting the efforts of several regional organizations to promote transparency of military expenditures, including standardized annual exchanges of relevant information among their member States,

1. *Calls upon* Member States to report annually, by 30 April, to the Secretary-General their military expenditures for the latest fiscal year for which data are available, using, preferably and to the extent possible, the reporting instrument as recommended in its resolution 35/142 B or, as appropriate, any other format developed in conjunction with similar reporting on military expenditures to other international or regional organizations, and, in the same context, encourages Member States that have no information to provide to submit nil returns;

2. *Recommends* the guidelines and recommendations for objective information on military matters to all Member States for implementation, fully taking into account specific political, military and other conditions prevailing in a region, on the basis of initiatives and with the agreement of the States of the region concerned;

3. *Encourages* relevant international bodies and regional organizations to promote transparency of military expenditures and to enhance complementarity among reporting systems, taking into account the particular characteristics of each region, and to consider the possibility of an exchange of information with the United Nations;

4. *Takes note* of the report of the Secretary-General on objective information on military matters, including transparency of military expenditures;

5. *Requests* the Secretary-General, within available resources:

(a) To continue the practice of sending an annual note verbale to Member States requesting the submission of data to the standardized reporting system, together with the reporting format and related instructions, and to publish in a timely fashion in appropriate United Nations media the due date for transmitting data on military expenditures;

(b) To circulate annually the reports on military expenditures as received from Member States;

(c) To continue consultations with relevant international bodies with a view to ascertaining requirements for adjusting the present instrument, with a view to encouraging wider participation, and to make recommendations, based on the outcome of those consultations and taking into account the views of Member States, on necessary changes to the content and structure of the standardized reporting system;

(d) To encourage relevant international bodies and organizations to promote transparency of military expenditures and to consult with those bodies and organizations with emphasis on examining possibilities for enhancing complementarity among international and regional reporting systems and for exchanging related information between those bodies and the United Nations;

(e) To encourage the United Nations regional centres for peace and disarmament in Africa, in Asia and the Pacific, and in Latin America and the Caribbean to assist Member States in their regions in enhancing their knowledge of the standardized reporting system;

(f) To promote international and regional/subregional symposia and training seminars to explain the purpose of the standardized reporting system and to give relevant technical instructions;

(g) To report on experiences gained during such symposia and training seminars;

6. *Encourages* Member States:

(a) To inform the Secretary-General about possible problems with the standardized reporting system and their reasons for not submitting the requested data;

(b) To provide the Secretary-General, in time for deliberation by the General Assembly at its fifty-eighth session, with their views and suggestions on ways and means to strengthen and broaden participation in the standardized reporting system, including necessary changes to its content and structure;

7. *Decides* to include in the provisional agenda of its fifty-eighth session the item entitled "Objective information on military matters, including transparency of military expenditures".

Verification

In response to General Assembly resolution 54/46 [YUN 1999, p. 498], the Secretary-General submitted a September report [A/56/347] updating developments since 1999 on the verification of treaties. The report contained the views of one Member State (Qatar) on the recommendations contained in the expert study on verification in all its aspects, including the UN role in verification [YUN 1995, p. 233].

GENERAL ASSEMBLY ACTION

On 29 November [meeting 68], the General Assembly, on the recommendation of the First Committee [A/56/527], adopted **resolution 56/15** without vote [agenda item 65].

Verification in all its aspects, including the role of the United Nations in the field of verification

The General Assembly,

Noting the critical importance of, and the vital contribution that has been made by, effective verification measures in arms limitation and disarmament agreements and other similar obligations,

Reaffirming its support for the sixteen principles of verification drawn up by the Disarmament Commission,

Recalling its resolutions 40/152 O of 16 December 1985, 41/86 Q of 4 December 1986, 42/42 F of 30 November 1987, 43/81 B of 7 December 1988, 45/65 of 4 December 1990, 47/45 of 9 December 1992, 48/68 of 16 December 1993, 50/61 of 12 December 1995, 52/31 of 9 December 1997 and 54/46 of 1 December 1999,

Recalling also the reports of the Secretary-General of 11 July 1986, 28 August 1990, 16 September 1992, 26 July 1993, 22 September 1995, 6 August 1997, 9 July 1999 and 10 September 2001, and the addenda thereto,

1. *Reaffirms* the critical importance of, and the vital contribution that has been made by, effective verification measures in arms limitation and disarmament agreements and other similar obligations;

2. *Requests* the Secretary-General to report to the General Assembly at its fifty-eighth session on further views received from Member States pursuant to resolutions 50/61, 52/31 and 54/46;

3. *Decides* to include in the provisional agenda of its fifty-eighth session the item entitled "Verification in all its aspects, including the role of the United Nations in the field of verification".

Anti-personnel mines

1997 Convention

The number of States parties to the Convention on the Prohibition of the Use, Stockpiling, Production and Transfer of Anti-personnel Mines and on Their Destruction (Mine-Ban Convention), which was adopted in 1997 [YUN 1997, p. 503] and entered into force in 1999 [YUN 1999, p. 498], totalled 122 as at 31 December. During the year, 13 States ratified or acceded to the Convention.

The Third Meeting of the States Parties to the Convention (Managua, Nicaragua, 18-21 September) [APLC/MSP.3/2001/1], convened pursuant to General Assembly resolution 55/33 V [YUN 2000, p. 526], reviewed the general status and operation of the Convention. It noted that 30 countries had destroyed their stockpile of anti-personnel mines completely, while 17 others were in the process of doing so, and that considerable areas of mined land had been cleared over the past year, casualty rates had been reduced in several of the world's most affected States and victim assistance had improved. On 21 September, the States parties adopted the President's Action Programme, which outlined specific initiatives and activities envisaged for the intersessional period and identified priorities for the coming year. They also adopted a Declaration, in which the States parties, reaffirming their commitment to the total eradication of anti-personnel mines and to addressing the inhumane effects of those weapons, called on all Governments and people to join in the common task to meet the challenges of mine action.

The Standing Committee on the general status and operation of the Convention noted that 34 States parties had reported that they had retained anti-personnel mines for training and development purposes. In 2001, the Standing Committee on mine clearance and related technologies became the Standing Committee on mine clearance, mine awareness and mine action technologies and the Standing Committee on victim assistance, socio-economic reintegration and mine awareness became the Standing Committee on victim assistance and socio-economic reintegration.

The Fourth Meeting of the States Parties was planned for September 2002 in Geneva.

GENERAL ASSEMBLY ACTION

On 29 November [meeting 68], the General Assembly, on the recommendation of the First Committee [A/56/536], adopted **resolution 56/24 M** by recorded vote (138-0-19) [agenda item 74 (*t*)].

Implementation of the Convention on the Prohibition of the Use, Stockpiling, Production and Transfer of Anti-personnel Mines and on Their Destruction

The General Assembly,

Recalling its resolutions 54/54 B of 1 December 1999 and 55/33 V of 20 November 2000,

Reaffirming its determination to put an end to the suffering and casualties caused by anti-personnel mines, which kill or maim hundreds of people every week, mostly innocent and defenceless civilians and especially children, obstruct economic development and reconstruction, inhibit the repatriation of refugees and internally displaced persons, and have other severe consequences for years after emplacement,

Believing it necessary to do the utmost to contribute in an efficient and coordinated manner to facing the challenge of removing anti-personnel mines placed throughout the world, and to ensure their destruction,

Wishing to do the utmost in ensuring assistance for the care and rehabilitation, including the social and economic reintegration, of mine victims,

Welcoming the entry into force on 1 March 1999 of the Convention on the Prohibition of the Use, Stockpiling, Production and Transfer of Anti-personnel Mines and on Their Destruction, and noting with satisfaction the work undertaken to implement the Convention and the substantial progress made towards addressing the global landmine problem,

Recalling the First Meeting of States Parties to the Convention, held at Maputo from 3 to 7 May 1999, and the reaffirmation made in the Maputo Declaration of a commitment to the total eradication of anti-personnel mines,

Recalling also the Second Meeting of States Parties to the Convention, held at Geneva from 11 to 15 September 2000, and the Declaration of the Second Meeting of States Parties reaffirming the commitment to implement completely and fully all provisions of the Convention,

Recalling further the Third Meeting of States Parties to the Convention, held at Managua from 18 to 21 September 2001, and the Declaration of the Third Meeting of States Parties reaffirming the unwavering commitment both to the total eradication of anti-personnel mines and to addressing the insidious and inhumane effects of those weapons,

Noting with satisfaction that additional States have ratified or acceded to the Convention, bringing the total number of States that have formally accepted the obligations of the Convention to one hundred and twenty-two,

Emphasizing the desirability of attracting the adherence of all States to the Convention, and determined to work strenuously towards the promotion of its universalization,

Noting with regret that anti-personnel mines continue to be used in conflicts around the world, causing human suffering and impeding post-conflict development,

1. *Invites* all States that have not signed the Convention on the Prohibition of the Use, Stockpiling, Production and Transfer of Anti-personnel Mines and on Their Destruction to accede to it without delay;

2. *Urges* all States that have signed but not ratified the Convention to ratify it without delay;

3. *Stresses* the importance of the full and effective implementation of, and compliance with, the Convention;

4. *Urges* all States parties to provide the Secretary-General with complete and timely information, as required under article 7 of the Convention, in order to promote transparency and compliance with the Convention;

5. *Invites* all States that have not ratified the Convention or acceded to it to provide, on a voluntary basis, information to make global mine action efforts more effective;

6. *Renews its call upon* all States and other relevant parties to work together to promote, support and advance the care, rehabilitation and social and economic reintegration of mine victims, mine awareness pro-

grammes, and the removal of anti-personnel mines placed throughout the world and the assurance of their destruction;

7. *Invites and encourages* all interested States, the United Nations, other relevant international organizations or institutions, regional organizations, the International Committee of the Red Cross and relevant non-governmental organizations to participate in the programme of intersessional work established at the First Meeting of States Parties to the Convention and further developed at the Second and Third Meetings of States Parties to the Convention;

8. *Requests* the Secretary-General, in accordance with article 11, paragraph 2, of the Convention, to undertake the preparations necessary to convene the Fourth Meeting of States Parties to the Convention at Geneva from 16 to 20 September 2002, and, on behalf of States parties and in accordance with article 11, paragraph 4, of the Convention, to invite States not parties to the Convention, as well as the United Nations, other relevant international organizations or institutions, regional organizations, the International Committee of the Red Cross and relevant non-governmental organizations to attend the Meeting as observers;

9. *Decides* to include in the provisional agenda of its fifty-seventh session the item entitled "Implementation of the Convention on the Prohibition of the Use, Stockpiling, Production and Transfer of Anti-personnel Mines and on Their Destruction".

RECORDED VOTE ON RESOLUTION 56/24 M:

In favour: Afghanistan, Albania, Algeria, Andorra, Angola, Argentina, Armenia, Australia, Austria, Bahamas, Bahrain, Bangladesh, Barbados, Belarus, Belgium, Benin, Bhutan, Bolivia, Bosnia and Herzegovina, Botswana, Brazil, Brunei Darussalam, Bulgaria, Burkina Faso, Burundi, Cambodia, Cameroon, Canada, Cape Verde, Chile, Colombia, Comoros, Costa Rica, Côte d'Ivoire, Croatia, Cyprus, Czech Republic, Denmark, Djibouti, Dominican Republic, Ecuador, El Salvador, Eritrea, Estonia, Ethiopia, Fiji, Finland, France, Gabon, Georgia, Germany, Ghana, Greece, Grenada, Guatemala, Guinea, Guyana, Haiti, Honduras, Hungary, Iceland, Indonesia, Ireland, Italy, Jamaica, Japan, Jordan, Kenya, Latvia, Lesotho, Liechtenstein, Lithuania, Luxembourg, Madagascar, Malaysia, Maldives, Mali, Malta, Mauritania, Mauritius, Mexico, Monaco, Mongolia, Mozambique, Namibia, Nauru, Nepal, Netherlands, New Zealand, Nicaragua, Nigeria, Norway, Oman, Panama, Papua New Guinea, Paraguay, Peru, Philippines, Poland, Portugal, Qatar, Republic of Moldova, Romania, Saint Lucia, Samoa, San Marino, Senegal, Seychelles, Sierra Leone, Singapore, Slovakia, Slovenia, Solomon Islands, South Africa, Spain, Sri Lanka, Sudan, Swaziland, Sweden, Thailand, The former Yugoslav Republic of Macedonia, Togo, Tonga, Trinidad and Tobago, Tunisia, Turkey, Turkmenistan, Uganda, Ukraine, United Arab Emirates, United Kingdom, United Republic of Tanzania, Uruguay, Venezuela, Yemen, Yugoslavia, Zambia, Zimbabwe.

Against: None.

Abstaining: Azerbaijan, China, Cuba, Egypt, India, Iran, Israel, Kazakhstan, Lebanon, Libyan Arab Jamahiriya, Micronesia, Morocco, Myanmar, Pakistan, Republic of Korea, Russian Federation, Syrian Arab Republic, United States, Viet Nam.

Regional and other approaches to disarmament

Africa

In 2001, the Organization of African Unity (OAU) Council of Ministers, at its seventy-fourth ordinary session from 5 to 8 July, and the OAU Assembly of Heads of State and Government, at its thirty-seventh ordinary session from 9 to 11 July,

both held in Lusaka, Zambia [A/56/457], requested assistance from the international community to eradicate small arms and light weapons from Africa.

At the subregional level, the heads of State and Government of the Economic Community of West African States (ECOWAS) (Lusaka, July) [S/2001/700] renewed for a second three-year period the 1998 ECOWAS Moratorium on the Importation, Exportation and Manufacture of Light Weapons in West Africa [YUN 1998, p. 537] as from 5 July 2001.

On 9 March [A/CONF.192/PC/35], member States of the Southern African Development Community, meeting in Windhoek, Namibia, adopted a Declaration concerning Firearms, Ammunition and Other Related Materials in the subregion.

Standing Advisory Committee

In response to General Assembly resolution 55/34 B [YUN 2000, p. 528], the Secretary-General, in August [A/56/285], described the activities of the United Nations Standing Advisory Committee on Security Questions in Central Africa. At its fifteenth ministerial meeting (Bujumbura, Burundi, 16-20 April), the Standing Committee reviewed the geopolitical and security situation of its member States, examined cooperation on security matters among them and evaluated the implementation of its previous decisions.

In September, the Democratic Republic of the Congo (DRC) transmitted the report of the Committee's sixteenth ministerial meeting (Kinshasa, DRC, 13-17 August) [A/56/378-S/2001/890]. The Committee reviewed the geopolitical and security situation in Central Africa and intergovernmental cooperation in security matters there, and adopted its 2001-2002 work programme.

In December, the DRC transmitted the report of the subregional conference on the protection of women and children in armed conflict in Central Africa (Kinshasa, 14-16 November) [A/56/680-S/2001/1155], organized by the Standing Committee. The conference adopted a plan of action for implementation at the national, subregional and international levels.

GENERAL ASSEMBLY ACTION

On 29 November [meeting 68], the General Assembly, on the recommendation of the First Committee [A/56/537], adopted **resolution 56/25 A** without vote [agenda item 75 (a)].

Regional confidence-building measures: activities of the United Nations Standing Advisory Committee on Security Questions in Central Africa

The General Assembly,

Bearing in mind the purposes and principles of the United Nations and its primary responsibility for the maintenance of international peace and security in accordance with the Charter of the United Nations,

Recalling its resolutions 43/78 H and 43/85 of 7 December 1988, 44/21 of 15 November 1989, 45/58 M of 4 December 1990, 46/37 B of 6 December 1991, 47/53 F of 15 December 1992, 48/76 A of 16 December 1993, 49/76 C of 15 December 1994, 50/71 B of 12 December 1995, 51/46 C of 10 December 1996, 52/39 B of 9 December 1997, 53/78 A of 4 December 1998, 54/55 A of 1 December 1999 and 55/34 B of 20 November 2000,

Considering the importance and effectiveness of confidence-building measures taken at the initiative and with the participation of all States concerned and taking into account the specific characteristics of each region, since such measures can contribute to regional stability and to international peace and security,

Convinced that the resources released by disarmament, including regional disarmament, can be devoted to economic and social development and to the protection of the environment for the benefit of all peoples, in particular those of the developing countries,

Recalling the guidelines for general and complete disarmament adopted at its tenth special session, the first special session devoted to disarmament,

Convinced that development can be achieved only in a climate of peace, security and mutual confidence both within and among States,

Bearing in mind the establishment by the Secretary-General on 28 May 1992 of the United Nations Standing Advisory Committee on Security Questions in Central Africa, the purpose of which is to encourage arms limitation, disarmament, non-proliferation and development in the subregion,

Recalling the Brazzaville Declaration on Cooperation for Peace and Security in Central Africa, the Bata Declaration for the Promotion of Lasting Democracy, Peace and Development in Central Africa, and the Yaoundé Declaration on Peace, Security and Stability in Central Africa,

Bearing in mind resolutions 1196(1998) and 1197(1998), adopted by the Security Council on 16 and 18 September 1998 respectively, following its consideration of the report of the Secretary-General on the causes of conflict and the promotion of durable peace and sustainable development in Africa,

Emphasizing the need to strengthen the capacity for conflict prevention and peacekeeping in Africa,

Recalling the decision of the fourth ministerial meeting of the Standing Advisory Committee in favour of establishing, under the auspices of the United Nations High Commissioner for Human Rights, a subregional centre for human rights and democracy in Central Africa at Yaoundé,

1. *Takes note* of the report of the Secretary-General on regional confidence-building measures, which deals with the activities of the United Nations Standing Advisory Committee on Security Questions in Central Africa in the period since the adoption by the General Assembly of resolution 55/34 B;

2. *Reaffirms its support* for efforts aimed at promoting confidence-building measures at regional and subregional levels in order to ease tensions and conflicts in Central Africa and to further peace, stability and sustainable development in the subregion;

3. *Also reaffirms its support* for the programme of work of the Standing Advisory Committee adopted at the organizational meeting of the Committee, held at Yaoundé from 27 to 31 July 1992;

4. *Notes with satisfaction* the progress made by the States members of the Standing Advisory Committee in implementing the programme of activities for the period 2000-2001, in particular by:

(*a*) Holding the Subregional Conference on the Question of Refugees and Displaced Persons in Central Africa at Bujumbura from 14 to 16 August 2000;

(*b*) Holding the fourteenth ministerial meeting of the Standing Advisory Committee at Bujumbura on 17 and 18 August 2000;

(*c*) Holding the fifteenth ministerial meeting of the Standing Advisory Committee at Bujumbura from 16 to 20 April 2001;

(*d*) Holding the meeting of experts on the texts governing the Subregional Centre for Human Rights and Democracy in Central Africa at Libreville from 2 to 5 July 2001;

(*e*) Holding the sixteenth ministerial meeting of the Standing Advisory Committee at Kinshasa from 13 to 17 August 2001;

5. *Emphasizes* the importance of providing the States members of the Standing Advisory Committee with the essential support they need to carry out the full programme of activities which they adopted at their ministerial meetings;

6. *Welcomes* the creation of a mechanism for the promotion, maintenance and consolidation of peace and security in Central Africa, to be known as the Council for Peace and Security in Central Africa, by the Conference of Heads of State and Government of the member countries of the Economic Community of Central African States, held at Yaoundé on 25 February 1999, and requests the Secretary-General to give his full support to the effective realization of that important mechanism;

7. *Emphasizes* the need to make the early warning mechanism in Central Africa operational so that it will serve, on the one hand, as an instrument for analysing and monitoring political situations in the States members of the Standing Advisory Committee with a view to preventing the outbreak of future armed conflicts and, on the other hand, as a technical body through which the member States will carry out the programme of work of the Committee, adopted at its organizational meeting held at Yaoundé in 1992, and requests the Secretary-General to provide it with the assistance necessary for it to function properly;

8. *Requests* the Secretary-General, pursuant to Security Council resolution 1197(1998), to provide the States members of the Standing Advisory Committee with the necessary support for the implementation and smooth functioning of the Council for Peace and Security in Central Africa and the early warning mechanism;

9. *Also requests* the Secretary-General to support the establishment of a network of parliamentarians with a view to the creation of a subregional parliament in Central Africa;

10. *Requests* the Secretary-General and the United Nations High Commissioner for Refugees to continue to provide increased assistance to the countries of Central Africa for coping with the problems of refugees and displaced persons in their territories;

11. *Welcomes with satisfaction* the decision taken at the fourteenth ministerial meeting to organize a sub-

regional conference on the protection of women and children in armed conflict, and requests the Secretary-General to lend all the necessary support for the holding of the conference;

12. *Thanks* the Secretary-General for having established the Trust Fund for the United Nations Standing Advisory Committee on Security Questions in Central Africa;

13. *Appeals* to Member States and to governmental and non-governmental organizations to make additional voluntary contributions to the Trust Fund for the implementation of the programme of work of the Standing Advisory Committee;

14. *Requests* the Secretary-General to continue to provide the States members of the Standing Advisory Committee with assistance to ensure that they are able to carry on their efforts;

15. *Also requests* the Secretary-General to submit to the General Assembly at its fifty-seventh session a report on the implementation of the present resolution;

16. *Decides* to include in the provisional agenda of its fifty-seventh session the item entitled "Regional confidence-building measures: activities of the United Nations Standing Advisory Committee on Security Questions in Central Africa".

Asia and the Pacific

In 2001, the Association of South-East Asian Nations (ASEAN), its Regional Forum (ARF) and the Council for Security and Cooperation in Asia and the Pacific continued to address issues related to security and stability in the region. The UN Regional Centre for Peace and Disarmament in Asia and the Pacific also contributed to confidence-building and stability in the region through its activities (see p. 521).

The ministers participating in the thirty-fourth ASEAN Ministerial Meeting (23-24 July) and the eight meeting of ARF (25 July), both held in Hanoi, Viet Nam, emphasized the importance of confidence-building, acknowledging that it remained the foundation and main thrust of the ARF process.

The Department for Disarmament Affairs, together with the Institute of Security and International Studies, Chulalongkorn University and the Embassy of Sri Lanka, all based in Thailand, co-sponsored a regional seminar on "International security issues: a call for regional cooperation" (Bangkok, 14 December). Discussions centred on the challenges posed by the illicit trafficking of small arms and light weapons in the region and how to tackle the issue within the context of the Programme of Action adopted by the 2001 UN Conference on small arms (see p. 499).

Europe

During the year, the North Atlantic Treaty Organization (NATO) continued its activities mainly through the Euro-Atlantic Partnership Council and the NATO-Russian Permanent Joint Council, both established in 1997 [YUN 1997, pp. 518-19], as well as through the Partnership for Peace initiative, established in 1994 to promote bilateral cooperation between NATO and individual partner countries in the Euro-Atlantic area. In August/September, NATO collected weapons voluntarily handed over by Albanian militias in the former Yugoslav Republic of Macedonia.

The EU continued to implement its 1998 Joint Action on small arms [YUN 1998, p. 540] and published, in January, its second annual report on the implementation of the EU Code of Conduct for Arms Exports [ibid.]. States parties to the 1990 Treaty on Conventional Armed Forces in Europe (CFE Treaty) [YUN 1990, p. 79], at their Second Review Conference (Vienna, 28 May–1 June), reaffirmed the fundamental role of the Treaty as a cornerstone of European security.

On 18 June, negotiations were finalized on regional stability in Southern Europe, within the context of the 1995 General Framework Agreement for Peace in Bosnia and Herzegovina (the Peace Agreement) [YUN 1995, p. 544]. The 20 participating States had achieved consensus on a concluding document containing a number of confidence- and security-building measures. The States parties to the 1996 Agreement on Subregional Arms Control [YUN 1996, p. 493], signed by Bosnia and Herzegovina, the Federation of Bosnia and Herzegovina and Republika Srpska, Croatia and the Federal Republic of Yugoslavia, continued to implement the Agreement and considered proposals for voluntary measures to increase confidence and transparency.

The European Council, in July, adopted two regulations that provided the basis for a coherent and effective approach for EU action on antipersonnel landmines in third countries. The Council, in a 15 November resolution, welcomed the results of the UN Conference on small arms and called for negotiations on a legally binding international instrument regulating arms brokering.

In November, the 1999 Stability Pact for South-Eastern Europe [YUN 1999, p. 397] launched a regional plan to combat the proliferation of small arms and light weapons, which was modelled after the Programme of Action adopted by the UN Conference on small arms (see p. 499).

The Organization for Security and Cooperation in Europe, in addition to efforts to promote conflict prevention and confidence-building measures, continued to play a leading role in the region regarding the issue of small arms and light weapons.

Latin America

The General Assembly of the Organization of American States (OAS) (San José, Costa Rica, 3-5 June) adopted a number of resolutions relating to peace, security and disarmament in the hemisphere, particularly regarding combating the illicit trafficking of firearms, confidence- and security-building measures, transparency in conventional weapons and anti-personnel mines. Regarding anti-personnel mines, OAS member States reaffirmed their goal of global elimination of those weapons, and of the advent of the western hemisphere as an anti-personnel-mine-free zone. At their eleventh summit (Lima, Peru, 23-24 November) [CD/1659], the heads of State and Government of Latin American countries and of Spain and Portugal (the Ibero-American Community) adopted the "Lima Declaration: United for Tomorrow", by which they condemned terrorism and reaffirmed support for the non-proliferation of weapons of mass destruction, the Treaty for the Prohibition of Nuclear Weapons in Latin America and the Caribbean (Treaty of Tlatelolco) [YUN 1967, p. 13] and the Managua Declaration adopted by the Third Meeting of the States Parties to the Mine-Ban Convention (see p. 509).

GENERAL ASSEMBLY ACTION

On 29 November [meeting 68], the General Assembly, on the recommendation of the First Committee [A/56/536], adopted **resolution 56/24 H** without vote [agenda item 74 (*o*)].

Regional disarmament

The General Assembly,

Recalling its resolutions 45/58 P of 4 December 1990, 46/36 I of 6 December 1991, 47/52 J of 9 December 1992, 48/75 I of 16 December 1993, 49/75 N of 15 December 1994, 50/70 K of 12 December 1995, 51/45 K of 10 December 1996, 52/38 P of 9 December 1997, 53/77 O of 4 December 1998, 54/54 N of 1 December 1999 and 55/33 O of 20 November 2000 on regional disarmament,

Believing that the efforts of the international community to move towards the ideal of general and complete disarmament are guided by the inherent human desire for genuine peace and security, the elimination of the danger of war and the release of economic, intellectual and other resources for peaceful pursuits,

Affirming the abiding commitment of all States to the purposes and principles enshrined in the Charter of the United Nations in the conduct of their international relations,

Noting that essential guidelines for progress towards general and complete disarmament were adopted at the tenth special session of the General Assembly,

Taking note of the guidelines and recommendations for regional approaches to disarmament within the context of global security adopted by the Disarmament Commission at its 1993 substantive session,

Welcoming the prospects of genuine progress in the field of disarmament engendered in recent years as a result of negotiations between the two super-Powers,

Taking note of the recent proposals for disarmament at the regional and subregional levels,

Recognizing the importance of confidence-building measures for regional and international peace and security,

Convinced that endeavours by countries to promote regional disarmament, taking into account the specific characteristics of each region and in accordance with the principle of undiminished security at the lowest level of armaments, would enhance the security of all States and would thus contribute to international peace and security by reducing the risk of regional conflicts,

1. *Stresses* that sustained efforts are needed, within the framework of the Conference on Disarmament and under the umbrella of the United Nations, to make progress on the entire range of disarmament issues;

2. *Affirms* that global and regional approaches to disarmament complement each other and should therefore be pursued simultaneously to promote regional and international peace and security;

3. *Calls upon* States to conclude agreements, wherever possible, for nuclear non-proliferation, disarmament and confidence-building measures at the regional and subregional levels;

4. *Welcomes* the initiatives towards disarmament, nuclear non-proliferation and security undertaken by some countries at the regional and subregional levels;

5. *Supports and encourages* efforts aimed at promoting confidence-building measures at the regional and subregional levels to ease regional tensions and to further disarmament and nuclear non-proliferation measures at the regional and subregional levels;

6. *Decides* to include in the provisional agenda of its fifty-seventh session the item entitled "Regional disarmament".

Also on 29 November [meeting 68], on the recommendation of the First Committee [A/56/536], the Assembly adopted **resolution 56/24 I** by recorded vote (151-1-1) [agenda item 74 (*p*)].

Conventional arms control at the regional and subregional levels

The General Assembly,

Recalling its resolutions 48/75 J of 16 December 1993, 49/75 O of 15 December 1994, 50/70 L of 12 December 1995, 51/45 Q of 10 December 1996, 52/38 Q of 9 December 1997, 53/77 P of 4 December 1998, 54/54 M of 1 December 1999 and 55/33 P of 20 November 2000,

Recognizing the crucial role of conventional arms control in promoting regional and international peace and security,

Convinced that conventional arms control needs to be pursued primarily in the regional and subregional contexts since most threats to peace and security in the post-cold-war era arise mainly among States located in the same region or subregion,

Aware that the preservation of a balance in the defence capabilities of States at the lowest level of armaments would contribute to peace and stability and should be a prime objective of conventional arms control,

Desirous of promoting agreements to strengthen regional peace and security at the lowest possible level of armaments and military forces,

Noting with particular interest the initiatives taken in this regard in different regions of the world, in particular the commencement of consultations among a number of Latin American countries and the proposals for conventional arms control made in the context of South Asia, and recognizing, in the context of this subject, the relevance and value of the Treaty on Conventional Armed Forces in Europe, which is a cornerstone of European security,

Believing that militarily significant States and States with larger military capabilities have a special responsibility in promoting such agreements for regional security,

Believing also that an important objective of conventional arms control in regions of tension should be to prevent the possibility of military attack launched by surprise and to avoid aggression,

1. *Decides* to give urgent consideration to the issues involved in conventional arms control at the regional and subregional levels;

2. *Requests* the Conference on Disarmament to consider the formulation of principles that can serve as a framework for regional agreements on conventional arms control, and looks forward to a report of the Conference on this subject;

3. *Requests* the Secretary-General, in the meantime, to seek the views of Member States on the subject and to submit a report to the General Assembly at its fifty-seventh session;

4. *Decides* to include in the provisional agenda of its fifty-seventh session the item entitled "Conventional arms control at the regional and subregional levels".

RECORDED VOTE ON RESOLUTION 56/24 I:

In favour: Afghanistan, Albania, Algeria, Andorra, Angola, Argentina, Armenia, Australia, Austria, Azerbaijan, Bahamas, Bahrain, Bangladesh, Barbados, Belarus, Belgium, Benin, Bolivia, Bosnia and Herzegovina, Botswana, Brazil, Brunei Darussalam, Bulgaria, Burkina Faso, Burundi, Cameroon, Canada, Cape Verde, Chile, China, Colombia, Comoros, Costa Rica, Côte d'Ivoire, Croatia, Cyprus, Czech Republic, Denmark, Djibouti, Dominican Republic, Ecuador, Egypt, El Salvador, Eritrea, Estonia, Ethiopia, Finland, France, Gabon, Georgia, Germany, Ghana, Greece, Grenada, Guatemala, Guinea, Guyana, Haiti, Honduras, Hungary, Iceland, Indonesia, Iran, Ireland, Israel, Italy, Jamaica, Japan, Jordan, Kazakhstan, Kenya, Kuwait, Latvia, Lebanon, Lesotho, Libyan Arab Jamahiriya, Liechtenstein, Lithuania, Luxembourg, Madagascar, Malaysia, Maldives, Mali, Malta, Mauritania, Mauritius, Mexico, Monaco, Mongolia, Morocco, Mozambique, Myanmar, Namibia, Nauru, Nepal, Netherlands, New Zealand, Nicaragua, Nigeria, Norway, Oman, Pakistan, Panama, Papua New Guinea, Paraguay, Peru, Philippines, Poland, Portugal, Republic of Korea, Republic of Moldova, Romania, Russian Federation, Saint Lucia, Samoa, San Marino, Saudi Arabia, Senegal, Seychelles, Sierra Leone, Singapore, Slovakia, Slovenia, Solomon Islands, South Africa, Spain, Sri Lanka, Sudan, Swaziland, Sweden, Syrian Arab Republic, Thailand, The former Yugoslav Republic of Macedonia, Togo, Tonga, Trinidad and Tobago, Tunisia, Turkey, Turkmenistan, Uganda, Ukraine, United Arab Emirates, United Kingdom, United Republic of Tanzania, United States, Uruguay, Venezuela, Yemen, Yugoslavia, Zambia, Zimbabwe.

Against: India.

Abstaining: Bhutan.

Other disarmament issues

Terrorism

Following the terrorist attacks of 11 September on the United States, the Security Council (see p. 61) and the General Assembly (see below) noted the close connection between international terrorism and illicit arms-trafficking and the illegal movement of nuclear, chemical, biological and other potentially deadly materials, and called for multilateral cooperation in dealing with the problem.

In October, the Department for Disarmament Affairs (DDA) sponsored a symposium at which high-level experts discussed terrorism and its relationship to disarmament, as well as the contributions that disarmament multilateral treaties and institutions could make in addressing related threats. The experts considered an overview of the terrorist threat to international peace and security, focusing on aspects relating to nuclear, chemical and biological weapons and small arms and light weapons. It also discussed the question of financing weapons acquisitions by terrorists.

(See also p. 63.)

GENERAL ASSEMBLY ACTION

On 29 November [meeting 68], the General Assembly, on the recommendation of the First Committee [A/56/536], adopted **resolution 56/24 T** without vote [agenda item 74].

Multilateral cooperation in the area of disarmament and non-proliferation and global efforts against terrorism

The General Assembly,

Guided by the purposes and principles of the Charter of the United Nations,

Recalling that the United Nations Millennium Declaration stated that the responsibility for managing threats to international peace and security must be shared among the nations of the world,

Recognizing that disarmament and non-proliferation are essential for the maintenance of international peace and security,

Emphasizing that all General Assembly and Security Council resolutions relating to terrorism, in particular General Assembly resolutions 49/60 of 9 December 1994 and 56/1 of 12 September 2001 and Security Council resolutions 1368(2001) of 12 September 2001 and 1373(2001) of 28 September 2001, demonstrate the unity and solidarity of the international community in the face of the common threat of terrorism and its determination to combat it,

Recognizing the close connection between international terrorism and illicit arms-trafficking and the illegal movement of nuclear, chemical, biological and other potentially deadly materials,

Reaffirming the importance of taking all necessary steps to combat terrorism in all its forms and manifestations,

Noting with concern the lack of sufficient progress in multilateral disarmament diplomacy,

Determined to build a common response to global threats in the area of disarmament and non-proliferation,

1. *Reaffirms* multilateralism as a core principle in negotiations in the area of disarmament and non-

proliferation with a view to maintaining and strengthening universal norms and enlarging their scope;

2. *Emphasizes* that progress is urgently needed in the area of disarmament and non-proliferation in order to help maintain international peace and security and to contribute to global efforts against terrorism;

3. *Calls upon* all Member States to renew and fulfil their individual and collective commitments to multilateral cooperation as an important means of pursuing and achieving their common objectives in the area of disarmament and non-proliferation.

Prevention of an arms race in outer space

In 2001, the Conference on Disarmament did not establish an ad hoc committee on the prevention of an arms race in outer space. Nonetheless, many delegations continued to raise the issue of the militarization of outer space, particularly in connection with ongoing plans by the United States to develop a national missile defence system (see p. 480).

(see p. 480).

GENERAL ASSEMBLY ACTION

On 29 November [meeting 68], the General Assembly, on the recommendation of the First Committee [A/56/535], adopted **resolution 56/23** by recorded vote (156-0-4) [agenda item 73].

Prevention of an arms race in outer space

The General Assembly,

Recognizing the common interest of all mankind in the exploration and use of outer space for peaceful purposes,

Reaffirming the will of all States that the exploration and use of outer space, including the Moon and other celestial bodies, shall be for peaceful purposes and shall be carried out for the benefit and in the interest of all countries, irrespective of their degree of economic or scientific development,

Reaffirming also the provisions of articles III and IV of the Treaty on Principles Governing the Activities of States in the Exploration and Use of Outer Space, including the Moon and Other Celestial Bodies,

Recalling the obligation of all States to observe the provisions of the Charter of the United Nations regarding the use or threat of use of force in their international relations, including in their space activities,

Reaffirming paragraph 80 of the Final Document of the Tenth Special Session of the General Assembly, in which it is stated that in order to prevent an arms race in outer space further measures should be taken and appropriate international negotiations held in accordance with the spirit of the Treaty,

Recalling its previous resolutions on this issue, and taking note of the proposals submitted to the General Assembly at its tenth special session and at its regular sessions, and of the recommendations made to the competent organs of the United Nations and to the Conference on Disarmament,

Recognizing that prevention of an arms race in outer space would avert a grave danger for international peace and security,

Emphasizing the paramount importance of strict compliance with existing arms limitation and disarmament agreements relevant to outer space, including bilateral agreements, and with the existing legal regime concerning the use of outer space,

Considering that wide participation in the legal regime applicable to outer space could contribute to enhancing its effectiveness,

Noting that the Ad Hoc Committee on the Prevention of an Arms Race in Outer Space, taking into account its previous efforts since its establishment in 1985 and seeking to enhance its functioning in qualitative terms, continued the examination and identification of various issues, existing agreements and existing proposals, as well as future initiatives relevant to the prevention of an arms race in outer space, and that this contributed to a better understanding of a number of problems and to a clearer perception of the various positions,

Noting also that there were no objections in principle in the Conference on Disarmament to the re-establishment of the Ad Hoc Committee, subject to re-examination of the mandate contained in the decision of the Conference on Disarmament of 13 February 1992,

Emphasizing the mutually complementary nature of bilateral and multilateral efforts in the field of preventing an arms race in outer space, and hoping that concrete results will emerge from those efforts as soon as possible,

Convinced that further measures should be examined in the search for effective and verifiable bilateral and multilateral agreements in order to prevent an arms race in outer space, including the weaponization of outer space,

Stressing that the growing use of outer space increases the need for greater transparency and better information on the part of the international community,

Recalling in this context its previous resolutions, in particular resolutions 45/55 B of 4 December 1990, 47/51 of 9 December 1992 and 48/74 A of 16 December 1993, in which, inter alia, it reaffirmed the importance of confidence-building measures as means conducive to ensuring the attainment of the objective of the prevention of an arms race in outer space,

Conscious of the benefits of confidence- and security-building measures in the military field,

Recognizing that negotiations for the conclusion of an international agreement or agreements to prevent an arms race in outer space remain a priority task of the Ad Hoc Committee and that the concrete proposals on confidence-building measures could form an integral part of such agreements,

1. *Reaffirms* the importance and urgency of preventing an arms race in outer space and the readiness of all States to contribute to that common objective, in conformity with the provisions of the Treaty on Principles Governing the Activities of States in the Exploration and Use of Outer Space, including the Moon and Other Celestial Bodies;

2. *Reaffirms its recognition*, as stated in the report of the Ad Hoc Committee on the Prevention of an Arms Race in Outer Space, that the legal regime applicable to outer space does not in and of itself guarantee the prevention of an arms race in outer space, that the regime plays a significant role in the prevention of an arms race in that environment, that there is a need to

consolidate and reinforce that regime and enhance its effectiveness and that it is important to comply strictly with existing agreements, both bilateral and multilateral;

3. *Emphasizes* the necessity of further measures with appropriate and effective provisions for verification to prevent an arms race in outer space;

4. *Calls upon* all States, in particular those with major space capabilities, to contribute actively to the objective of the peaceful use of outer space and of the prevention of an arms race in outer space and to refrain from actions contrary to that objective and to the relevant existing treaties in the interest of maintaining international peace and security and promoting international cooperation;

5. *Reiterates* that the Conference on Disarmament, as the single multilateral disarmament negotiating forum, has the primary role in the negotiation of a multilateral agreement or agreements, as appropriate, on the prevention of an arms race in outer space in all its aspects;

6. *Invites* the Conference on Disarmament to complete the examination and updating of the mandate contained in its decision of 13 February 1992 and to establish an ad hoc committee as early as possible during its 2002 session;

7. *Recognizes*, in this respect, the growing convergence of views on the elaboration of measures designed to strengthen transparency, confidence and security in the peaceful uses of outer space;

8. *Urges* States conducting activities in outer space, as well as States interested in conducting such activities, to keep the Conference on Disarmament informed of the progress of bilateral and multilateral negotiations on the matter, if any, so as to facilitate its work;

9. *Decides* to include in the provisional agenda of its fifty-seventh session the item entitled "Prevention of an arms race in outer space".

RECORDED VOTE ON RESOLUTION 56/23:

In favour: Afghanistan, Albania, Algeria, Andorra, Angola, Argentina, Armenia, Australia, Austria, Azerbaijan, Bahamas, Bahrain, Bangladesh, Barbados, Belarus, Belgium, Benin, Bhutan, Bolivia, Bosnia and Herzegovina, Botswana, Brazil, Brunei Darussalam, Bulgaria, Burkina Faso, Burundi, Cambodia, Cameroon, Canada, Cape Verde, Chile, China, Colombia, Comoros, Costa Rica, Côte d'Ivoire, Croatia, Cuba, Cyprus, Czech Republic, Democratic People's Republic of Korea, Denmark, Djibouti, Dominican Republic, Ecuador, Egypt, El Salvador, Eritrea, Estonia, Ethiopia, Fiji, Finland, France, Gabon, Germany, Ghana, Greece, Grenada, Guatemala, Guinea, Guyana, Haiti, Honduras, Hungary, Iceland, India, Indonesia, Iran, Ireland, Italy, Jamaica, Japan, Jordan, Kazakhstan, Kenya, Kuwait, Lao People's Democratic Republic, Latvia, Lebanon, Lesotho, Libyan Arab Jamahiriya, Liechtenstein, Lithuania, Luxembourg, Madagascar, Malaysia, Maldives, Mali, Malta, Mauritania, Mauritius, Mexico, Monaco, Mongolia, Morocco, Mozambique, Myanmar, Namibia, Nauru, Nepal, Netherlands, New Zealand, Nicaragua, Nigeria, Norway, Oman, Pakistan, Panama, Papua New Guinea, Paraguay, Peru, Philippines, Poland, Portugal, Qatar, Republic of Korea, Republic of Moldova, Romania, Russian Federation, Saint Lucia, Samoa, San Marino, Saudi Arabia, Senegal, Seychelles, Sierra Leone, Singapore, Slovakia, Slovenia, Solomon Islands, South Africa, Spain, Sri Lanka, Sudan, Swaziland, Sweden, Syrian Arab Republic, Thailand, The former Yugoslav Republic of Macedonia, Togo, Tonga, Trinidad and Tobago, Tunisia, Turkey, Turkmenistan, Uganda, Ukraine, United Arab Emirates, United Kingdom, United Republic of Tanzania, Uruguay, Venezuela, Viet Nam, Yemen, Yugoslavia, Zambia.

Against: None.

Abstaining: Georgia, Israel, Micronesia, United States.

Seabed treaty

Pursuant to General Assembly resolution 44/116 O [YUN 1989, p. 81], the Secretary-General,

in a July report [A/56/172], presented the replies of three Governments in response to his request for information on technological developments relevant to the Treaty on the Prohibition of the Emplacement of Nuclear Weapons and Other Weapons of Mass Destruction on the Seabed and the Ocean Floor and in the Subsoil Thereof, adopted by the Assembly in resolution 2660 (XXV) [YUN 1970, p. 18], and to the verification of compliance with the Treaty.

Disarmament and development

In response to General Assembly resolution 55/33 L [YUN 2000, p. 533], the Secretary-General, in July [A/56/183], described activities undertaken to implement the action programme adopted at the 1987 International Conference on the Relationship between Disarmament and Development [YUN 1987, p. 83]. In that context, the Secretary-General noted that DDA, in collaboration with the UN Department of Economic and Social Affairs, organized on 26 April in New York a symposium to examine the interrelationship between armed conflicts, military expenditures and development. DDA continued to seek the views of independent experts on the changing paradigm of disarmament and development.

The report contained information submitted by Sweden, on behalf of the EU, on the implementation of the action programme, pursuant to resolution 55/33 L.

GENERAL ASSEMBLY ACTION

On 29 November [meeting 68], the General Assembly, on the recommendation of the First Committee [A/56/536], adopted **resolution 56/24 E** without vote [agenda item 74 (*l*)].

Relationship between disarmament and development

The General Assembly,

Recalling the provisions of the Final Document of the Tenth Special Session of the General Assembly concerning the relationship between disarmament and development,

Recalling also the adoption on 11 September 1987 of the Final Document of the International Conference on the Relationship between Disarmament and Development,

Recalling further its resolutions 49/75 J of 15 December 1994, 50/70 G of 12 December 1995, 51/45 D of 10 December 1996, 52/38 D of 9 December 1997, 53/77 K of 4 December 1998, 54/54 T of 1 December 1999 and 55/33 L of 20 November 2000,

Bearing in mind the Final Document of the Twelfth Conference of Heads of State or Government of Non-Aligned Countries, held at Durban, South Africa, from 29 August to 3 September 1998, and the Final Document of the Thirteenth Ministerial Conference of the Movement of Non-Aligned Countries, held at Cartagena, Colombia, on 8 and 9 April 2000,

Welcoming the different activities organized by the high-level Steering Group on Disarmament and Development, as described in the report of the Secretary-General,

Stressing the growing importance of the symbiotic relationship between disarmament and development in current international relations,

1. *Calls upon* the high-level Steering Group on Disarmament and Development to strengthen and enhance its programme of activities, in accordance with the mandate set out in the action programme adopted at the International Conference on the Relationship between Disarmament and Development;

2. *Urges* the international community to devote part of the resources made available by the implementation of disarmament and arms limitation agreements to economic and social development, with a view to reducing the ever-widening gap between developed and developing countries;

3. *Invites* all Member States to communicate to the Secretary-General, by 15 April 2002, their views and proposals for the implementation of the action programme adopted at the International Conference on the Relationship between Disarmament and Development, as well as any other views and proposals with a view to achieving the goals of the action programme, within the framework of current international relations;

4. *Requests* the Secretary-General to continue to take action, through appropriate organs and within available resources, for the implementation of the action programme adopted at the International Conference on the Relationship between Disarmament and Development;

5. *Also requests* the Secretary-General to submit a report to the General Assembly at its fifty-seventh session;

6. *Decides* to include in the provisional agenda of its fifty-seventh session the item entitled "Relationship between disarmament and development".

Arms limitation and disarmament agreements

Pursuant to General Assembly resolution 55/33 K [YUN 2000, p. 534], the Secretary-General submitted a July report with later addendum [A/56/165 & Add.1] containing information from seven Member States on measures they had taken to ensure the application of scientific and technological progress in the context of international security, disarmament and related areas, without detriment to the environment or to its effective contribution to attaining sustainable development.

GENERAL ASSEMBLY ACTION

By **decision 56/416** of 29 November, the General Assembly took note of the report of the First Committee [A/56/545] on compliance with arms limitation and disarmament and non-proliferation agreements.

Also on 29 November [meeting 68], the Assembly, on the recommendation of the First Committee [A/56/536], adopted **resolution 56/24 F** by recorded vote (154-0-5) [agenda item 74 (k)].

Observance of environmental norms in the drafting and implementation of agreements on disarmament and arms control

The General Assembly,

Recalling its resolutions 50/70 M of 12 December 1995, 51/45 E of 10 December 1996, 52/38 E of 9 December 1997, 53/77 J of 4 December 1998, 54/54 S of 1 December 1999 and 55/33 K of 20 November 2000,

Emphasizing the importance of the observance of environmental norms in the preparation and implementation of disarmament and arms limitation agreements,

Recognizing that it is necessary to take duly into account the agreements adopted at the United Nations Conference on Environment and Development, as well as prior relevant agreements, in the drafting and implementation of agreements on disarmament and arms limitation,

Taking note of the report of the Secretary-General,

Mindful of the detrimental environment effects of the use of nuclear weapons,

1. *Reaffirms* that international disarmament forums should take fully into account the relevant environmental norms in negotiating treaties and agreements on disarmament and arms limitation and that all States, through their actions, should fully contribute to ensuring compliance with the aforementioned norms in the implementation of treaties and conventions to which they are parties;

2. *Calls upon* States to adopt unilateral, bilateral, regional and multilateral measures so as to contribute to ensuring the application of scientific and technological progress in the framework of international security, disarmament and other related spheres, without detriment to the environment or to its effective contribution to attaining sustainable development;

3. *Welcomes* the information provided by Member States on the implementation of the measures they have adopted to promote the objectives envisaged in the present resolution;

4. *Invites* all Member States to communicate to the Secretary-General information on the measures they have adopted to promote the objectives envisaged in the present resolution, and requests the Secretary-General to submit a report containing this information to the General Assembly at its fifty-seventh session;

5. *Decides* to include in the provisional agenda of its fifty-seventh session the item entitled "Observance of environmental norms in the drafting and implementation of agreements on disarmament and arms control".

RECORDED VOTE ON RESOLUTION 56/24 F:

In favour: Afghanistan, Albania, Algeria, Andorra, Angola, Argentina, Armenia, Australia, Austria, Azerbaijan, Bahamas, Bahrain, Bangladesh, Barbados, Belarus, Belgium, Benin, Bhutan, Bolivia, Bosnia and Herzegovina, Botswana, Brazil, Brunei Darussalam, Bulgaria, Burkina Faso, Burundi, Cambodia, Cameroon, Canada, Cape Verde, Chile, China, Colombia, Comoros, Costa Rica, Côte d'Ivoire, Croatia, Cuba, Cyprus, Czech Republic, Democratic People's Republic of Korea, Denmark, Djibouti, Dominican Republic, Ecuador, Egypt, El Salvador, Eritrea, Estonia, Ethiopia, Fiji, Finland, Gabon, Georgia, Germany, Ghana, Greece, Grenada, Guatemala, Guinea, Guyana, Haiti, Honduras, Hungary, Iceland, India, Indonesia, Iran, Ireland, Jamaica, Japan, Jordan, Kazakhstan, Kenya, Kuwait, Lao People's Democratic Republic, Latvia, Lebanon, Lesotho, Libyan Arab Jamahiriya,

Liechtenstein, Lithuania, Luxembourg, Madagascar, Malaysia, Maldives, Mali, Malta, Mauritania, Mauritius, Mexico, Monaco, Mongolia, Morocco, Mozambique, Myanmar, Namibia, Nauru, Nepal, Netherlands, New Zealand, Nicaragua, Nigeria, Norway, Oman, Pakistan, Panama, Papua New Guinea, Paraguay, Peru, Philippines, Poland, Portugal, Qatar, Republic of Korea, Republic of Moldova, Romania, Russian Federation, Saint Lucia, Samoa, San Marino, Saudi Arabia, Senegal, Seychelles, Sierra Leone, Singapore, Slovakia, Slovenia, Solomon Islands, South Africa, Spain, Sri Lanka, Sudan, Swaziland, Sweden, Syrian Arab Republic, Thailand, The former Yugoslav Republic of Macedonia, Togo, Tonga, Trinidad and Tobago, Tunisia, Turkey, Turkmenistan, Uganda, Ukraine, United Arab Emirates, United Republic of Tanzania, Uruguay, Venezuela, Viet Nam, Yemen, Yugoslavia, Zambia.

Against: None.

Abstaining: France, Israel, Micronesia, United Kingdom, United States.

Studies, information and training

Disarmament studies programme

The Group of Governmental Experts on restricting the manufacture and trade in small arms and light weapons to manufacturers and dealers authorized by Governments, appointed by the Secretary-General pursuant to General Assembly resolution 54/54 V [YUN 1999, p. 487], completed its study in February. Its report [A/CONF.192/2] was submitted to the 2001 UN Conference on small arms (see p. 499). The Panel of Governmental Experts on the issue of missiles in all its aspects, appointed by the Secretary-General in response to Assembly resolution 55/33 A [YUN 2000, p. 499], also met during the year, as did the Group of Governmental Experts on disarmament and non-proliferation education, appointed by the Secretary-General pursuant to Assembly resolution 55/33 E [YUN 2000, p. 535].

In 2001, the Assembly, in **resolution 56/24 Q**, requested the Secretary-General to prepare, with the assistance of governmental experts, a report on the continuing operation and future development of the UN Register of Conventional Arms (see p. 507), for consideration in 2003. By **resolution 56/24 V**, the Assembly requested the Secretary-General to prepare, with the assistance of governmental experts, a study on the feasibility of developing an international instrument to enable States to identify and trace illicit small arms and light weapons, also to be considered in 2003.

Disarmament Information Programme

During the year, a major focus of the Disarmament Information Programme was the information campaign on the 2001 UN Conference on small arms, launched by DDA in collaboration with the UN Department of Public Information. Other activities, carried out through DDA publications, web-site access, symposiums and exhibits, focused on multilateral disarmament agreements relating to weapons of mass destruction and conventional weapons. DDA hosted a panel seminar on the implications for disarmament and the United Nations of the revolution in military affairs, and, in collaboration with the Global Security Institute, a symposium on lessons for today from the Cuban missile crises. In the wake of the terrorist attacks of 11 September, the Department sponsored a symposium on terrorism and disarmament (New York, 25 October). Efforts were made to raise awareness about the links between gender and disarmament, and to support weapons collection projects in communities that had suffered from conflicts or civil strife.

Advisory Board on Disarmament Matters

The Advisory Board on Disarmament Matters, which advised the Secretary-General on the disarmament studies programme and implementation of the Disarmament Information Programme and served as the Board of Trustees of the United Nations Institute for Disarmament Research (UNIDIR) (see below), held its thirty-sixth and thirty-seventh sessions (New York, 31 January–2 February; Geneva, 25-27 July) [A/56/418]. At its thirty-sixth session, the Board deliberated on the "revolution in military affairs", the illicit trade in small arms, reducing nuclear danger and non-proliferation regimes. In July, it continued discussions on some of those items and also addressed nuclear-weapon-free zones as instruments of disarmament.

The Board agreed that, among other things, there existed a crisis of multilateral disarmament diplomacy and that the United Nations had important roles to play in addressing the crisis; the proposal contained in the Millennium Declaration, adopted by the General Assembly in resolution 55/2 [YUN 2000, p. 49], for convening a major international conference on eliminating nuclear dangers would best be pursued through an incremental process given the lack of global consensus to convene the conference; and disarmament and non-proliferation regimes were inseparable and mutually dependent on the wider international strategic environment. In response to Assembly resolution 55/33 N [ibid., p. 497], the Board forwarded to the Secretary-General specific measures to reduce nuclear danger (see p. 474).

UN Institute for Disarmament Research

The Secretary-General transmitted to the General Assembly the report of the UNIDIR Director covering the period from July 2000 to July 2001, as well as the report of the UNIDIR Board of Trustees on the proposed 2001-2002 programme of work and budget [A/56/359].

The Institute's research activities continued to focus on global security, regional security and human security. The report highlighted UNIDIR's networking initiatives with other research institutes, as well as disarmament entities in the UN system, and contained a list of publications issued during the reporting period.

The Board of Trustees recommended a subvention of $213,000 from the UN regular budget for 2002, which the Assembly approved on 24 December (**resolution 56/255, section I**).

Disarmament fellowship, training and advisory services

In 2001, 28 fellows participated in the UN disarmament fellowship, training and advisory services programme, which began in Geneva on 3 September and ended in New York on 8 November. The programme included a study session in Geneva; study trips to Austria, The Hague (Netherlands), Germany and Japan; and a study session at UN Headquarters.

Regional centres for peace and disarmament

On 29 November [meeting 68], the General Assembly, on the recommendation of the First Committee [A/56/537], adopted **resolution 56/25 C** without vote [agenda item 75 (d)].

United Nations regional centres for peace and disarmament

The General Assembly,

Recalling its resolution 55/34 F of 20 November 2000 regarding the maintenance and revitalization of the three United Nations regional centres for peace and disarmament,

Recalling also the reports of the Secretary-General on the United Nations Regional Centre for Peace and Disarmament in Africa, the United Nations Regional Centre for Peace and Disarmament in Asia and the Pacific and the United Nations Regional Centre for Peace, Disarmament and Development in Latin America and the Caribbean,

Reaffirming its decision, taken in 1982 at its twelfth special session, to establish the United Nations Disarmament Information Programme, the purpose of which is to inform, educate and generate public understanding and support for the objectives of the United Nations in the field of arms control and disarmament,

Bearing in mind its resolutions 40/151 G of 16 December 1985, 41/60 J of 3 December 1986, 42/39 D of 30 November 1987 and 44/117 F of 15 December 1989 on the regional centres for peace and disarmament in Nepal, Peru and Togo,

Recognizing that the changes that have taken place in the world have created new opportunities as well as posed new challenges for the pursuit of disarmament and, in this regard, bearing in mind that the regional centres for peace and disarmament can contribute substantially to understanding and cooperation among States in each particular region in the areas of peace, disarmament and development,

Noting that in paragraph 146 of the Final Document of the Twelfth Conference of Heads of State or Government of the Non-Aligned Countries, held at Durban, South Africa, from 29 August to 3 September 1998, the heads of State or Government welcomed the decision adopted by the General Assembly on maintaining and revitalizing the three regional centres for peace and disarmament in Nepal, Peru and Togo,

1. *Reiterates* the importance of the United Nations activities at the regional level to increase the stability and security of its Member States, which could be promoted in a substantive manner by the maintenance and revitalization of the three regional centres for peace and disarmament;

2. *Reaffirms* that, in order to achieve positive results, it is useful for the three regional centres to carry out dissemination and educational programmes that promote regional peace and security aimed at changing basic attitudes with respect to peace and security and disarmament so as to support the achievement of the principles and purposes of the United Nations;

3. *Appeals* to Member States in each region and those that are able to do so, as well as to international governmental and non-governmental organizations and foundations, to make voluntary contributions to the regional centres in their respective regions to strengthen their programmes of activities and implementation;

4. *Requests* the Secretary-General to provide all necessary support, within existing resources, to the regional centres in carrying out their programmes of activities;

5. *Decides* to include in the provisional agenda of its fifty-seventh session the item entitled "United Nations regional centres for peace and disarmament".

Africa

Pursuant to General Assembly resolution 55/34 D [YUN 2000, p. 539], the Secretary-General described the activities of the United Nations Regional Centre for Peace and Disarmament in Africa [A/56/137], covering the period from July 2000 to June 2001. The Centre was established in Lomé, Togo, in 1986 [YUN 1986, p. 85].

During the reporting period, the Centre provided substantive and political support to the Programme for Coordination and Assistance for Security and Development, to ensure the effective implementation of the ECOWAS Moratorium on the Importation, Exportation and Manufacture of Small Arms and Light Weapons in West Africa [YUN 1998, p. 537]. As part of its advocacy and outreach programme, the Centre in January, inaugurated the disarmament forum—a monthly briefing on disarmament, peace and security issues in Africa. In May, the Centre, with the support of the Government of Germany, launched the fellowship programme on peace, security and disarmament in Africa, which permitted three research fellows each year to conduct research on a topic related to peace, security and disarmament in the region.

In the course of the year, the Centre assisted a number of African countries, including Togo, Kenya and Guinea-Bissau, to address problems related to small arms and light weapons, and, in addition, organized or assisted in organizing conferences, seminars and training programmes on disarmament and security-related issues. Working with civil society organizations, the Centre provided assistance and technical support to the launching of a continent-wide campaign for peace.

GENERAL ASSEMBLY ACTION

On 29 November [meeting 68], the General Assembly, on the recommendation of the First Committee [A/56/537], adopted **resolution 56/25 D** without vote [agenda item 75 (b)].

United Nations Regional Centre for Peace and Disarmament in Africa

The General Assembly,

Mindful of the provisions of Article 11, paragraph 1, of the Charter of the United Nations stipulating that a function of the General Assembly is to consider the general principles of cooperation in the maintenance of international peace and security, including the principles governing disarmament and arms limitation,

Recalling its resolutions 40/151 G of 16 December 1985, 41/60 D of 3 December 1986, 42/39 J of 30 November 1987 and 43/76 D of 7 December 1988 on the United Nations Regional Centre for Peace and Disarmament in Africa, and its resolutions 46/36 F of 6 December 1991 and 47/52 G of 9 December 1992 on regional disarmament, including confidence-building measures,

Recalling also its resolutions 48/76 E of 16 December 1993, 49/76 D of 15 December 1994, 50/71 C of 12 December 1995, 51/46 E of 10 December 1996, 52/220 of 22 December 1997, 53/78 C of 4 December 1998, 54/55 B of 1 December 1999 and 55/34 D of 20 November 2000,

Aware of the widespread support for the revitalization of the Regional Centre and the important role that the Centre can play in the present context in promoting confidence-building and arms-limitation measures at the regional level, thereby promoting progress in the area of sustainable development,

Taking into account the report of the Secretary-General on the causes of conflict and the promotion of durable peace and sustainable development in Africa,

Bearing in mind the efforts undertaken in the framework of the revitalization of the activities of the Regional Centre for the mobilization of the resources necessary for its operational costs,

Taking into account the need to establish close cooperation between the Regional Centre and the Mechanism for Conflict Prevention, Management and Resolution of the Organization of African Unity, in conformity with the relevant decision adopted by the Assembly of Heads of State and Government of the Organization of African Unity at its thirty-fifth ordinary session, held at Algiers from 12 to 14 July 1999,

Welcoming the adoption by the United Nations Conference on the Illicit Trade in Small Arms and Light Weapons in All Its Aspects, held in New York from 9 to 20 July 2001, of the Programme of Action to Prevent, Combat and Eradicate the Illicit Trade in Small Arms and Light Weapons in All Its Aspects, and emphasizing the need for the appropriate implementation of the Programme of Action by all States,

1. *Takes note* of the report of the Secretary-General, and commends the activities which the United Nations Regional Centre for Peace and Disarmament in Africa is continuing to carry out, in particular in support of the efforts made by the African States in the areas of peace and security;

2. *Reaffirms* its strong support for the revitalization of the Regional Centre, and emphasizes the need to provide it with the necessary resources to enable it to strengthen its activities and carry out its programmes;

3. *Appeals once again* to all States, as well as to international governmental and non-governmental organizations and the foundations, to make voluntary contributions in order to strengthen the programmes and activities of the Regional Centre and facilitate their implementation;

4. *Requests* the Secretary-General to continue to provide the necessary support to the Regional Centre for better achievements and results;

5. *Also requests* the Secretary-General to facilitate the establishment of close cooperation between the Regional Centre and the Organization of African Unity, in particular in the area of peace, security and development, and to continue to assist the Director of the Regional Centre in his efforts to stabilize the financial situation of the Centre and revitalize its activities;

6. *Appeals in particular* to the Regional Centre, in cooperation with the Organization of African Unity, regional and subregional organizations and the African States, to take steps to promote the consistent implementation of the Programme of Action to Prevent, Combat and Eradicate the Illicit Trade in Small Arms and Light Weapons in All Its Aspects;

7. *Requests* the Secretary-General to report to the General Assembly at its fifty-seventh session on the implementation of the present resolution;

8. *Decides* to include in the provisional agenda of its fifty-seventh session the item entitled "United Nations Regional Centre for Peace and Disarmament in Africa".

Asia and the Pacific

As requested by the General Assembly in resolution 55/34 H [YUN 2000, p. 540], the Secretary-General described the activities of the United Nations Regional Centre for Peace and Disarmament in Asia and the Pacific from August 2000 to July 2001 [A/56/266]. The Centre was inaugurated in Kathmandu, Nepal, in 1989 [YUN 1989, p. 88].

During the period under review, the Centre organized the thirteenth regional disarmament meeting in Asia and the Pacific on prospects for further confidence-building (Kathmandu, 9-11 March), which focused on issues relating to the Korean peninsula, denuclearization and non-proliferation, organized crime, terrorism, information technology and national security, and disarmament and the environment. The Centre organized a meeting on disarmament and the Pacific (Wellington, New Zealand, 27-30 March), which examined the region's security and disarmament concerns. The Centre organized a conference (Kanazawa, Japan, 28-31 August 2001) on "The Asia-Pacific region: evolution of the scope of security and disarmament in the twenty-first century", which discussed, among other things, stability and prosperity in North-East Asia, human security, disarmament and non-proliferation, and issues relating to the illicit trade in small arms.

The Centre continued to assist the five Central Asian States (Kazakhstan, Kyrgyzstan, Tajikistan, Turkmenistan, Uzbekistan) in the drafting of a treaty on the establishment of a nuclear-weapon-free zone in Central Asia (see p. 489), as well as Mongolia, to consolidate its nuclear-weapon-free status (see p. 489).

During the year, progress was made towards relocating the Centre to Kathmandu, which, for lack of sufficient extrabudgetary resources, continued to operate from Headquarters.

GENERAL ASSEMBLY ACTION

On 29 November [meeting 68], the General Assembly, on the recommendation of the First Committee [A/56/537], adopted **resolution 56/25 F** without vote [agenda item 75 (*f*)].

United Nations Regional Centre for Peace and Disarmament in Asia and the Pacific

The General Assembly,

Recalling its resolutions 42/39 D of 30 November 1987 and 44/117 F of 15 December 1989, by which it established the United Nations Regional Centre for Peace and Disarmament in Asia and renamed it the United Nations Regional Centre for Peace and Disarmament in Asia and the Pacific, with headquarters in Kathmandu and with the mandate of providing, on request, substantive support for the initiatives and other activities mutually agreed upon by the Member States of the Asia-Pacific region for the implementation of measures for peace and disarmament, through appropriate utilization of available resources,

Welcoming the report of the Secretary-General, in which he expresses his belief that the mandate of the Regional Centre remains valid and that the Centre could be a useful instrument for fostering a climate of cooperation in the post-cold-war era,

Noting that trends in the post-cold-war era have emphasized the function of the Regional Centre in assisting Member States as they deal with new security concerns and disarmament issues emerging in the region,

Commending the useful activities carried out by the Regional Centre in encouraging regional and sub-regional dialogue for the enhancement of openness, transparency and confidence-building, as well as the promotion of disarmament and security through the organization of regional meetings, which has come to be widely known within the Asia-Pacific region as the "Kathmandu process",

Expressing its appreciation to the Regional Centre for its organization of the thirteenth regional disarmament meeting in Asia and the Pacific, held at Kathmandu from 9 to 11 March 2001, the United Nations regional disarmament meeting on the theme "A Pacific Way to Disarmament", held at Wellington from 27 to 30 March 2001, and the meeting of the United Nations Conference on Disarmament Issues on the theme "The Asia-Pacific region: evolution of the scope of security and disarmament in the twenty-first century", held at Kanazawa, Japan, from 28 to 31 August 2001,

Welcoming the idea of the possible creation of an educational and training programme for peace and disarmament in Asia and the Pacific for young people with different backgrounds, to be financed from voluntary contributions,

Noting the important role of the Regional Centre in assisting region-specific initiatives of Member States, including its assistance in the work related to the establishment of a nuclear-weapon-free zone in Central Asia, as well as to Mongolia's international security and nuclear-weapon-free status, including the organization of a United Nations–sponsored non-governmental expert group meeting on the theme "Ways and means of strengthening Mongolia's international security and nuclear-weapon-free status", held at Sapporo, Japan, on 5 and 6 September 2001,

Appreciating highly the important role that Nepal has played as the host nation of the headquarters of the Regional Centre,

1. *Reaffirms* its strong support for the forthcoming operation and further strengthening of the United Nations Regional Centre for Peace and Disarmament in Asia and the Pacific;

2. *Underlines* the importance of the Kathmandu process as a powerful vehicle for the development of the practice of region-wide security and disarmament dialogue;

3. *Expresses its appreciation* for the continuing political support and voluntary financial contributions to the Regional Centre, which are essential for its continued operation;

4. *Appeals* to Member States, in particular those within the Asia-Pacific region, as well as to international governmental and non-governmental organizations and foundations, to make voluntary contributions, the only resources of the Regional Centre, to strengthen the programme of activities of the Centre and the implementation thereof;

5. *Requests* the Secretary-General, taking note of paragraph 6 of General Assembly resolution 49/76 D of 15 December 1994, to provide the Regional Centre with the necessary support, within existing resources, in carrying out its programme of activities;

6. *Urges* the Secretary-General to ensure the physical operation of the Regional Centre from Kathmandu within six months of the date of signature of the host country agreement and to enable the Centre to function effectively;

7. *Requests* the Secretary-General to report to the General Assembly at its fifty-seventh session on the implementation of the present resolution;

8. *Decides* to include in the provisional agenda of its fifty-seventh session the item entitled "United Nations Regional Centre for Peace and Disarmament in Asia and the Pacific".

Latin America and the Caribbean

As requested by the General Assembly in resolution 55/34 E [YUN 2000, p. 541], the Secretary-General reported on the activities of the United Nations Regional Centre for Peace, Disarmament and Development in Latin America and the Caribbean from August 2000 to June 2001 [A/56/154]. The Centre was inaugurated in Lima, Peru, in 1987 [YUN 1987, p. 88].

The activities of the Centre related to firearms, ammunition and explosives; anti-personnel mines; nuclear issues; disarmament and development; civil-military relations; and information and public events.

A number of activities were carried out under a project on the regional clearing house on firearms, ammunition and explosives, an initiative designed to nurture national and regional expertise in the area of practical disarmament. In January, the Centre and the Inter-American Drug Abuse Control Commission were designated the implementing institutions for projects on illicit trafficking in firearms, ammunition and explosives, under a memorandum of understanding between DDA and OAS. A workshop organized by the Centre in February on civil-military relations in the region addressed such issues as democratic society's influence on armed forces and highlighted the need for greater participation of civil society in security-related matters. The Centre held a workshop (Lima, 28 March) on preparations for the third meeting of the States parties to the Mine-Ban Convention (see p. 509). On 30 May, it acted as an observer in the destruction of 33,421 anti-personnel mines in northern Peru, a first step to the destruction of 310,000 landmines. The Centre collaborated with, among others, the UN Mine Action Service to organize a workshop (Lima, 31 May–1 June) on international mine action standards, intended to assist in the development and amendment of national mine action standards in the region.

The Centre also undertook activities relating to the 2001 UN Conference on small arms and participated in information and training events within and outside the region, including seminars, conferences, workshops and symposiums.

As at 31 December 2000, the balance of the Trust Fund for the Centre totalled $61,608.

GENERAL ASSEMBLY ACTION

On 29 November [meeting 68], the General Assembly, on the recommendation of the First Committee [A/56/537], adopted **resolution 56/25 E** without vote [agenda item 75 *(c)*].

United Nations Regional Centre for Peace,
Disarmament and Development
in Latin America and the Caribbean

The General Assembly,

Recalling its resolutions 41/60 J of 3 December 1986, 42/39 K of 30 November 1987 and 43/76 H of 7 December 1988 on the United Nations Regional Centre for Peace, Disarmament and Development in Latin America and the Caribbean, with headquarters in Lima,

Recalling also its resolutions 46/37 F of 9 December 1991, 48/76 E of 16 December 1993, 49/76 D of 15 December 1994, 50/71 C of 12 December 1995, 52/220 of 22 December 1997, 53/78 F of 4 December 1998, 54/55 F of 1 December 1999 and 55/34 E of 20 November 2000,

Underlining the revitalization of the Regional Centre, the efforts made by the Government of Peru to that end and the appointment of the Director of the Centre by the Secretary-General,

Welcoming the report of the Secretary-General, which concludes that the Regional Centre has launched projects aimed at furthering the understanding of the relationship between security and development, enhanced the role of the United Nations as a regional catalyst for activities on peace and disarmament and acted as a politically neutral platform for discussions on security and development issues,

Noting the agreement between the Regional Centre and the Inter-American Drug Abuse Control Commission to strengthen their cooperation with respect to their mutual interest in reducing firearms trafficking and related activities among States under their respective mandates, as well as to strengthen the capacity of those countries to deal with those problems,

Noting also that security and disarmament issues have always been recognized as significant topics in Latin America and the Caribbean, the first inhabited region in the world to be declared a nuclear-weapon-free zone,

Bearing in mind the important role that the Regional Centre can play in promoting confidence-building measures, arms control and limitation, disarmament and development at the regional level,

Also bearing in mind the importance of information, research, education and training for peace, disarmament and development in order to achieve understanding and cooperation among States,

Recognizing the need to provide the three United Nations regional centres for peace and disarmament with sufficient financial resources for the planning and implementation of their programmes of activities,

1. *Reiterates* its strong support for the role of the United Nations Regional Centre for Peace, Disarmament and Development in Latin America and the Caribbean in the promotion of United Nations activities at the regional level to strengthen peace, stability, security and development among its member States;

2. *Expresses its satisfaction* and congratulates the Regional Centre for the vast range of activities carried out last year;

3. *Encourages* the Regional Centre to continue to provide assistance for the States of the region in all issues related to disarmament, including the effective

implementation of the Programme of Action to Prevent, Combat and Eradicate the Illicit Trade in Small Arms and Light Weapons in All Its Aspects and, in this connection, welcomes the holding of a regional seminar in Santiago, from 19 to 21 November 2001;

4. *Expresses its appreciation* for the political support and financial contributions to the Regional Centre, which are essential for its continued operation;

5. *Invites* all States of the region to take part in the activities of the Regional Centre, proposing items for inclusion in its agenda, making greater and better use of the Centre's potential to meet the current challenges facing the international community and with a view to fulfilling the aims of the Charter of the United Nations in the fields of peace, disarmament and development;

6. *Welcomes* the report of the Secretary-General on the relationship between disarmament and development, and supports the role that the Regional Centre plays to promote those issues in the region in pursuit of its mandate to promote economic and social development related to peace and disarmament;

7. *Appeals* to Member States, in particular the States of the Latin American and Caribbean region, and to international governmental and non-governmental organizations and to foundations, to make voluntary contributions to strengthen the Regional Centre, its programme of activities and the implementation thereof;

8. *Requests* the Secretary-General to provide the Regional Centre with all necessary support, within existing resources, so that it may carry out its programme of activities in accordance with its mandate;

9. *Also requests* the Secretary-General to report to the General Assembly at its fifty-seventh session on the implementation of the present resolution;

10. *Decides* to include in the provisional agenda of its fifty-seventh session the item entitled "United Nations Regional Centre for Peace, Disarmament and Development in Latin America and the Caribbean".

Chapter VIII

Other political and security questions

United Nations consideration of other political and security questions in 2001 included the Organization's efforts to support and consolidate democratization worldwide, the promotion of decolonization, public information activities and the peaceful uses of outer space.

The first meeting of the follow-up mechanism to the Fourth (2000) International Conference of New or Restored Democracies agreed to draw up a comprehensive plan to implement the Cotonou Declaration on peace, security, democracy and development adopted at that Conference. Plans were under way for convening the Fifth International Conference in 2003.

The Secretary-General submitted an updated plan of action for the Second International Decade for the Eradication of Colonialism (2001-2010), setting out action to be taken by the administering Powers, other Member States, the UN system and non-governmental organizations to support the process.

The Department of Public Information made considerable progress in reorienting the Organization's information and communications policies. The adoption of new technologies allowed for a wider dissemination of accurate information on the work of the Organization. A notable achievement in the reorientation process was the highly successful pilot project for direct international radio broadcasting from UN Headquarters.

In December, the General Assembly noted the establishment of action teams to implement the recommendations of the Third (1999) United Nations Conference on the Exploration and Peaceful Uses of Outer Space and requested the Secretary-General to report on the implementation process.

The Assembly further adopted a resolution on the role of science and technology in the context of international security and disarmament, which encouraged the use of science and technology for peaceful purposes, and another on developments in information and telecommunications, calling on States to promote information security.

In September, the Assembly adopted a resolution declaring 21 September of each year as the International Day of Peace, to be observed as a day of global ceasefire and non-violence.

General aspects of international security

Support for democracies

Report of Secretary-General. In response to General Assembly resolution 55/43 [YUN 2000, p. 543], the Secretary-General, in an October report [A/56/499], reviewed the results of the Fourth (2000) International Conference of New or Restored Democracies and the Cotonou Declaration on peace, security, democracy and development adopted by the Conference [YUN 2000, p. 544], and reported on the activities of the Conference's follow-up mechanism. The report also offered perspectives and suggestions on how the United Nations could promote and consolidate democratic development worldwide.

At the first meeting of the follow-up mechanism to the Conference (Benin, 20 September), participants agreed to draw up a comprehensive plan to implement the provisions of the Cotonou Declaration. Member States accepted Mongolia's invitation to hold the Fifth International Conference in 2003 in Ulaanbaatar.

The Secretary-General stated that, because of the biennialization of consideration of the item (**resolution 55/285**), the next report on new or restored democracies, containing an updated inventory of UN activities in that field, would be submitted to the Assembly's fifty-eighth (2003) session. Towards that end, all UN departments, offices, funds and programmes would be informed of the contents of the Cotonou Declaration and asked to reflect on the activities within their mandates that would contribute to its implementation.

The Secretary-General observed that the near doubling of the number of democracies worldwide was one of the most remarkable achievements of the 1990s, and the United Nations had played an important supporting role. There could be no one prescribed form of democracy, but it had to be authentic, reflecting the culture, history and experience of its citizens, and based on the rule of law. The benchmark for sustainable democracy was the extent to which a State acted in accordance with civil, political, economic, social and cultural rights. The status of human rights was therefore a barometer of a healthy democracy. Democracy was also a fundamental right of all citizens. It was intrinsically linked to sustainable development, contributing to poverty eradication and development, and should be seen as the most promising long-term strategy for preventing armed conflict. Peace and security were essential preconditions for a healthy and vibrant democracy and, once established, democratic culture was the best safeguard against war, destruction and terrorism.

The Secretary-General stated that international forums, such as the International Conference of New or Restored Democracies and the Community of Democracies, played an important role in advancing the democratization process, and they should consider further steps towards that end. Activities of Governments, the UN system and non-governmental organizations (NGOs) to assist the democratization process had dramatically increased, and it was important to continue those efforts. The Secretary-General called on States to explore the lessons learned in the practice of democracy and share them with civil society and the international community. He declared that he stood ready to work together with new or restored democracies and all Member States to achieve the goals of the Cotonou Declaration.

GENERAL ASSEMBLY ACTION

On 14 December [meeting 86], the General Assembly adopted **resolution 56/96** [draft: A/56/L.46 & Add.1] without vote [agenda item 35].

Support by the United Nations system of the efforts of Governments to promote and consolidate new or restored democracies

The General Assembly,

Bearing in mind the indissoluble links between the principles enshrined in the Universal Declaration of Human Rights and the foundations of any democratic society,

Recalling its resolution 49/30 of 7 December 1994, in which it recognized the importance of the Managua Declaration and Plan of Action adopted by the Second International Conference of New or Restored Democracies in July 1994, as well as its resolutions 50/133 of 20 December 1995, 51/31 of 6 December 1996, 52/18 of 21 November 1997, 53/31 of 23 November 1998, 54/36 of 29 November 1999 and 55/43 of 27 November 2000,

Recalling also the United Nations Millennium Declaration adopted by heads of State and Government on 8 September 2000, in particular paragraphs 6 and 24 thereof,

Recalling further the declarations and plans of action of the four international conferences of new or restored democracies adopted in Manila in 1988, Managua in 1994, Bucharest in 1997 and Cotonou in 2000,

Recalling that the Fourth International Conference of New or Restored Democracies focused on peace, security, democracy and development,

Considering the major changes taking place on the international scene and the aspirations of all peoples for an international order based on the principles enshrined in the Charter of the United Nations, including the promotion and encouragement of respect for human rights and fundamental freedoms for all and other important principles, such as respect for the equal rights and self-determination of peoples, peace, democracy, justice, equality, the rule of law, pluralism, development, better standards of living and solidarity,

Expressing its deep appreciation to the Government of Benin for the generous manner in which it hosted and provided facilities for the Fourth International Conference of New or Restored Democracies,

Bearing in mind that the activities of the United Nations carried out in support of the efforts of Governments to promote and consolidate democracy are undertaken in accordance with the Charter and only at the specific request of the Member States concerned,

Taking note with satisfaction of the seminars, workshops and conferences on democratization and good governance convened in 2001, as well as those held under the auspices of the International Conference of New or Restored Democracies,

Taking note of the views expressed by Member States in the debate on this question at its forty-ninth to fifty-sixth sessions,

Bearing in mind that democracy, development and respect for all human rights and fundamental freedoms are interdependent and mutually reinforcing and that democracy is based on the freely expressed will of the people to determine their own political, economic, social and cultural systems and on their full participation in all aspects of their lives,

Noting that a considerable number of societies have recently undertaken significant efforts to achieve their social, political and economic goals through democratization and the reform of their economies, pursuits that are deserving of the support and recognition of the international community,

Expressing its deep appreciation for the support provided by Member States, the United Nations system, including the specialized agencies, and other intergovernmental organizations to the Government of Benin for the holding of the Fourth International Conference of New or Restored Democracies,

Having considered the report of the Secretary-General, and its focus on the Cotonou Declaration, and the final report adopted by the Fourth International Conference of New or Restored Democracies in Cotonou on 6 December 2000,

1. *Takes note with appreciation* of the report of the Secretary-General;

2. *Encourages* Member States to promote democratization and to make additional efforts to identify possible steps to support the efforts of Governments to promote and consolidate new or restored democracies;

3. *Welcomes* the work carried out by the intergovernmental follow-up mechanism to the Fourth International Conference of New or Restored Democracies;

4. *Invites* Member States, the relevant specialized agencies and bodies of the United Nations system, and other intergovernmental and non-governmental or-

ganizations to continue to contribute actively to the follow-up to the Fourth International Conference of New or Restored Democracies;

5. *Recognizes* that the United Nations has an important role to play in providing timely, appropriate and coherent support to the efforts of Governments to achieve democratization within the context of their development efforts;

6. *Encourages* the Secretary-General to continue to improve the capacity of the Organization to respond effectively to the requests of Member States by providing coherent and adequate support for their efforts to achieve the goals of good governance and democratization;

7. *Stresses* that the activities of the Organization must be undertaken in accordance with the Charter of the United Nations;

8. *Commends* the Secretary-General, and through him the United Nations system, for the activities undertaken at the request of Governments to support efforts to consolidate democracy;

9. *Requests* the Secretary-General to examine options for strengthening the support provided by the United Nations system for the efforts of Member States to consolidate democracy, including the designation of a focal point;

10. *Welcomes* the decision of the Government of Mongolia to host the Fifth International Conference of New or Restored Democracies in 2003;

11. *Requests* the Secretary-General to submit a report to the General Assembly at its fifty-eighth session on the implementation of the present resolution;

12. *Decides* to include in the provisional agenda of its fifty-eighth session the item entitled "Support by the United Nations system of the efforts of Governments to promote and consolidate new or restored democracies".

Regional aspects of international peace and security

South Atlantic

As requested in General Assembly resolution 55/49 [YUN 2000, p. 545], the Secretary-General submitted an October report on the zone of peace and cooperation of the South Atlantic [A/56/454], declared in 1986 to promote cooperation among States of the region in the political, economic, scientific, technical, cultural and other fields [YUN 1986, p. 369]. The Secretary-General stated that, as at 30 September, four Governments (Argentina, Dominican Republic, Gambia, South Africa) had responded to his request for views on the implementation of the declaration's objectives; a fifth response, from Brazil, was submitted later [A/56/454/Add.1]. Five UN bodies had also responded.

GENERAL ASSEMBLY ACTION

On 21 November [meeting 61], the General Assembly adopted **resolution 56/7** [draft: A/56/L.12 & Add.1] by recorded vote (93-0-1) [agenda item 36].

Zone of peace and cooperation of the South Atlantic

The General Assembly,

Recalling its resolution 41/11 of 27 October 1986, in which it solemnly declared the Atlantic Ocean, in the region between Africa and South America, a zone of peace and cooperation of the South Atlantic,

Recalling also its subsequent resolutions on the matter, including resolution 45/36 of 27 November 1990, in which it reaffirmed the determination of the States of the zone to enhance and accelerate their cooperation in the political, economic, scientific, cultural and other spheres,

Reaffirming the importance of the purposes and objectives of the zone of peace and cooperation of the South Atlantic as a basis for the promotion of cooperation among the countries of the region,

Reaffirming also that the questions of peace and security and those of development are interrelated and inseparable and that cooperation for peace and development among States of the region will promote the objectives of the zone of peace and cooperation of the South Atlantic,

Recalling the agreement reached at the third meeting of the States members of the zone, held in Brasilia in 1994, to encourage democracy and political pluralism and, in accordance with the Vienna Declaration and Programme of Action adopted by the World Conference on Human Rights on 25 June 1993, to promote and defend all human rights and fundamental freedoms and to cooperate towards the achievement of these goals,

Aware of the importance that the States of the zone attach to the protection of the environment of the region, and recognizing the threat that pollution from any source poses to the marine and coastal environment, its ecological balance and its resources,

Welcoming the adoption of the Programme of Action to Prevent, Combat and Eradicate the Illicit Trade in Small Arms and Light Weapons in All Its Aspects at the United Nations Conference on the Illicit Trade in Small Arms and Light Weapons in All Its Aspects, held in New York from 9 to 20 July 2001,

Taking note with appreciation of the report of the Secretary-General, submitted in accordance with General Assembly resolution 55/49 of 29 November 2000,

1. *Calls upon* all States to cooperate in the promotion of the objectives established in the declaration of the zone of peace and cooperation of the South Atlantic and to refrain from any action inconsistent with those objectives and with the Charter of the United Nations and relevant resolutions of the Organization, in particular actions that may create or aggravate situations of tension and potential conflict in the region;

2. *Welcomes* the progress towards the full entry into force of the Treaty for the Prohibition of Nuclear Weapons in Latin America and the Caribbean (Treaty of Tlatelolco) and of the African Nuclear-Weapon-Free Zone Treaty (Treaty of Pelindaba);

3. *Encourages* all States, in particular the members of the zone of peace and cooperation of the South Atlantic, to cooperate in promoting and strengthening global, regional, subregional and national initiatives to prevent, combat and eradicate the illicit trade in small arms and light weapons;

4. *Welcomes* in this regard the entry into force of the Inter-American Convention against the Illicit Manufacturing of and Trafficking in Firearms, Ammunition, Explosives and Other Related Materials, adopted in November 1997, and the adoption of the Inter-American Convention on Transparency in Conventional Weapons Acquisitions by the Organization of American States in June 1999;

5. *Also welcomes* the Bamako Declaration on an African Common Position on the Illicit Proliferation, Circulation and Trafficking of Small Arms and Light Weapons, adopted by the Ministers of the States members of the Organization of African Unity on 1 December 2000, the Declaration concerning Firearms, Ammunition and Other Related Materials in the Southern African Development Community, adopted by the heads of State or Government of the States members of the Community at Windhoek on 9 March 2001, as well as the Protocol on the Control of Firearms, Ammunition and Other Related Materials in the Southern African Development Community Region, adopted by the heads of State and Government of the States members of the Community at Blantyre, Malawi, in August 2001, and the initiatives taken by States members of the Economic Community of West African States to further extend their agreement on a moratorium on the import, export and manufacture of light weapons;

6. *Reaffirms* the importance for Member States to contribute by all means at their disposal to an effective and lasting peace in Angola, and in that context reiterates that the primary cause of the present situation in Angola is the failure of the National Union for the Total Independence of Angola, under the leadership of Jonas Savimbi, to comply with its obligations under the Peace Accords, the Lusaka Protocol and relevant Security Council resolutions;

7. *Affirms* the importance of the South Atlantic to global maritime and commercial transactions and its determination to preserve the region for all peaceful purposes and activities protected by international law, in particular the United Nations Convention on the Law of the Sea;

8. *Calls upon* Member States to continue their efforts towards the achievement of appropriate regulation of maritime transport of radioactive and toxic wastes, taking into account the interests of coastal States and in accordance with the United Nations Convention on the Law of the Sea and the regulations of the International Maritime Organization and the International Atomic Energy Agency;

9. *Views with concern* the increase in drug trafficking and related crimes, including drug abuse, and calls upon the international community and the States members of the zone to promote regional and international cooperation to combat all aspects of the problem of drugs and related offences;

10. *Recognizes*, in the light of the number, magnitude and complexity of natural disasters and other emergencies, the need to continue to strengthen the co-ordination of humanitarian assistance by States members of the zone, so as to ensure a timely and effective response;

11. *Welcomes* the offer by Benin to host the sixth meeting of the States members of the zone;

12. *Requests* the relevant organizations, organs and bodies of the United Nations system to render all appropriate assistance that States members of the zone may seek in their joint efforts to implement the declaration of the zone of peace and cooperation of the South Atlantic;

13. *Requests* the Secretary-General to keep the implementation of resolution 41/11 and subsequent resolutions on the matter under review and to submit a report to the General Assembly at its fifty-eighth session, taking into account, inter alia, the views expressed by Member States;

14. *Decides* to include in the provisional agenda of its fifty-eighth session the item entitled "Zone of peace and cooperation of the South Atlantic".

RECORDED VOTE ON RESOLUTION 56/7:

In favour: Algeria, Andorra, Angola, Argentina, Armenia, Australia, Austria, Bahrain, Bangladesh, Belarus, Belgium, Bolivia, Brazil, Brunei Darussalam, Burkina Faso, Cambodia, Canada, Chile, China, Colombia, Croatia, Cuba, Cyprus, Czech Republic, Denmark, Egypt, Equatorial Guinea, Finland, France, Gambia, Germany, Ghana, Greece, Grenada, Guatemala, Iceland, Indonesia, Iran, Ireland, Italy, Jamaica, Japan, Jordan, Kazakhstan, Kenya, Kuwait, Lebanon, Libyan Arab Jamahiriya, Liechtenstein, Luxembourg, Madagascar, Malaysia, Maldives, Mexico, Monaco, Mongolia, Morocco, Myanmar, Netherlands, Nigeria, Norway, Oman, Pakistan, Paraguay, Peru, Philippines, Poland, Portugal, Qatar, Republic of Moldova, Romania, San Marino, Senegal, Sierra Leone, Singapore, Slovakia, Slovenia, South Africa, Spain, Sri Lanka, Sweden, Syrian Arab Republic, Thailand, The former Yugoslav Republic of Macedonia, Togo, Tunisia, Turkey, Ukraine, United Kingdom, Uruguay, Venezuela, Yugoslavia, Zambia.

Against: None.

Abstaining: United States.

Indian Ocean

In 2001, the Ad Hoc Committee on the Indian Ocean (New York, 5 July) [A/56/29] continued to consider approaches for achieving the goals of the 1971 Declaration of the Indian Ocean as a Zone of Peace, adopted by the General Assembly in resolution 2832(XXVI) [YUN 1971, p. 34].

Pursuant to resolution 54/47 [YUN 1999, p. 519], the Chairman of the Committee, following informal consultations with Committee members, concluded that implementation of the Declaration gave rise to a number of difficulties, making progress in that regard elusive. It was generally felt that the time was not yet opportune for a focused discussion on practical measures to ensure conditions of peace, security and stability in the Indian Ocean region, and the General Assembly should allow further time for consultations on how that could be achieved. Three permanent members of the Security Council (France, United Kingdom, United States) continued their non-participation in the Committee's work.

The Ad Hoc Committee reaffirmed the conclusions of its 1994 [YUN 1994, p. 155], 1995 [YUN 1995, p. 182] and 1996 [YUN 1996, p. 512] sessions and re-emphasized the need to foster consensual, step-by-step approaches. It reiterated its conviction that the participation of all permanent Security Council members and the major maritime users of the Indian Ocean in the Committee's work would assist the progress of a mutually beneficial dialogue to develop conditions of peace, security and stability in the region. The Chairman was requested to continue informal consultations and to report to the Assembly in 2003.

GENERAL ASSEMBLY ACTION

On 29 November [meeting 68], the General Assembly, on the recommendation of the First (Disarmament and International Security) Committee [A/56/528], adopted **resolution 56/16** by recorded vote (110-3-41) [agenda item 66].

Implementation of the Declaration of the Indian Ocean as a Zone of Peace

The General Assembly,

Recalling the Declaration of the Indian Ocean as a Zone of Peace, contained in its resolution 2832(XXVI) of 16 December 1971, and recalling also its resolution 54/47 of 1 December 1999 and other relevant resolutions,

Recalling also the report of the Meeting of the Littoral and Hinterland States of the Indian Ocean held in July 1979,

Recalling further paragraph 148 of the Final Document of the Twelfth Conference of Heads of State or Government of Non-Aligned Countries, held at Durban, South Africa, from 29 August to 3 September 1998, in which it was noted, inter alia, that the Chairperson of the Ad Hoc Committee on the Indian Ocean would continue his informal consultations on the future work of the Committee,

Emphasizing the need to foster consensual approaches that are conducive to the pursuit of such endeavours,

Noting the initiatives taken by countries of the region to promote cooperation, in particular economic cooperation, in the Indian Ocean area and the possible contribution of such initiatives to overall objectives of a zone of peace,

Convinced that the participation of all permanent members of the Security Council and the major maritime users of the Indian Ocean in the work of the Ad Hoc Committee is important and would assist the progress of a mutually beneficial dialogue to develop conditions of peace, security and stability in the Indian Ocean region,

Considering that greater efforts and more time are required to develop a focused discussion on practical measures to ensure conditions of peace, security and stability in the Indian Ocean region,

Having considered the report of the Ad Hoc Committee on the Indian Ocean,

1. *Takes note* of the report of the Ad Hoc Committee on the Indian Ocean;

2. *Reiterates its conviction* that the participation of all permanent members of the Security Council and the major maritime users of the Indian Ocean in the work

of the Ad Hoc Committee is important and would greatly facilitate the development of a mutually beneficial dialogue to advance peace, security and stability in the Indian Ocean region;

3. *Requests* the Chairman of the Ad Hoc Committee to continue his informal consultations with the members of the Committee and to report through the Committee to the General Assembly at its fifty-eighth session;

4. *Requests* the Secretary-General to continue to render, within existing resources, all necessary assistance to the Ad Hoc Committee, including the provision of summary records;

5. *Decides* to include in the provisional agenda of its fifty-eighth session the item entitled "Implementation of the Declaration of the Indian Ocean as a Zone of Peace".

RECORDED VOTE ON RESOLUTION 56/16:

In favour: Afghanistan, Algeria, Argentina, Armenia, Australia, Azerbaijan, Bahamas, Bahrain, Bangladesh, Barbados, Belarus, Bhutan, Bolivia, Botswana, Brazil, Brunei Darussalam, Burkina Faso, Burundi, Cambodia, Cameroon, Cape Verde, Chile, China, Colombia, Comoros, Costa Rica, Côte d'Ivoire, Cuba, Democratic People's Republic of Korea, Djibouti, Dominican Republic, Ecuador, Egypt, El Salvador, Eritrea, Ethiopia, Fiji, Gabon, Ghana, Grenada, Guatemala, Guinea, Guyana, Haiti, Honduras, India, Indonesia, Iran, Jamaica, Japan, Jordan, Kazakhstan, Kenya, Lao People's Democratic Republic, Lebanon, Lesotho, Libyan Arab Jamahiriya, Madagascar, Malaysia, Maldives, Mali, Mauritania, Mauritius, Mexico, Mongolia, Morocco, Mozambique, Myanmar, Namibia, Nauru, Nepal, New Zealand, Nicaragua, Nigeria, Oman, Pakistan, Panama, Papua New Guinea, Peru, Philippines, Qatar, Republic of Korea, Russian Federation, Samoa, Saudi Arabia, Senegal, Seychelles, Sierra Leone, Singapore, Solomon Islands, South Africa, Sri Lanka, Sudan, Swaziland, Syrian Arab Republic, Thailand, Togo, Tonga, Trinidad and Tobago, Tunisia, Turkmenistan, Uganda, Ukraine, United Arab Emirates, United Republic of Tanzania, Uruguay, Venezuela, Viet Nam, Yemen, Zambia.

Against: France, United Kingdom, United States.

Abstaining: Albania, Andorra, Austria, Belgium, Bosnia and Herzegovina, Bulgaria, Canada, Croatia, Cyprus, Czech Republic, Denmark, Estonia, Finland, Georgia, Germany, Greece, Hungary, Iceland, Ireland, Israel, Italy, Latvia, Liechtenstein, Lithuania, Luxembourg, Malta, Micronesia, Netherlands, Norway, Poland, Portugal, Republic of Moldova, Romania, San Marino, Slovakia, Slovenia, Spain, Sweden, The former Yugoslav Republic of Macedonia, Turkey, Yugoslavia.

Decolonization

The General Assembly's Special Committee on the Situation with regard to the Implementation of the Declaration on the Granting of Independence to Colonial Countries and Peoples (Special Committee on decolonization) held its annual session in New York in two parts—21 February and 12 March (first part); and 18-19, 21 and 28-29 June and 2-3 July (second part). It considered various aspects of the implementation of the 1960 Declaration, adopted by the Assembly in resolution 1514(XV) [YUN 1960, p. 49], including general decolonization issues and the situation of individual Non-Self-Governing Territories (NSGTs). Pursuant to Assembly resolution 55/147 [YUN 2000, p. 549], the Special Committee transmitted to the Assembly the report on its 2001 activities [A/56/23].

Decade for the Eradication of Colonialism

Plan of Action for the Second Decade

The Secretary-General, as requested in General Assembly resolution 55/146 [YUN 2000, p. 548], submitted a March report [A/56/61], the annex to which contained the plan of action for the Second International Decade for the Eradication of Colonialism (2001-2010). The Secretary-General explained that, since the views and suggestions of Member States contained in the plan of action for the first Decade [YUN 1991, p. 777], and approved by the Assembly in resolution 46/181 [ibid.], remained largely relevant for the Second Decade, that plan had been updated accordingly.

The plan of action set out steps to be taken at the international level, areas in which the United Nations, in cooperation with the administering Powers, should take action as a matter of priority, and areas in which the administering Powers should take action; identified the role of the specialized agencies and other organizations of the UN system and NGOs; and indicated action the Special Committee on decolonization should take. The plan also provided for coordination, review, appraisal and reporting.

Caribbean regional seminar

As part of its activities to implement the plan of action for the Second International Decade, the Special Committee on decolonization [A/56/23] organized a Caribbean regional seminar (Havana, Cuba, 23-25 May) to review political, economic and social developments in the small island NSGTs.

The seminar welcomed the proclamation of the Second International Decade as a political framework for supporting the decolonization process and the UN role in that regard, and called for the full implementation of the Decade's plan of action. The regional seminars served as effective forums for discussing the concerns of NSGTs and for presenting their views and recommendations to the Special Committee.

In addition to recommending measures to move NSGTs closer to self-determination and restating earlier recommendations [YUN 2000, p. 549], the seminar called for the regular update of the decolonization web page by the Secretariat's Departments of Political Affairs (DPA) and of Public Information (DPI) to raise awareness of the political rights of NSGTs and the options for determining their political status. Participants urged the Special Committee to implement its programme of work regarding the situation in NSGTs and called for their increased involvement in UN system programmes and activities for furthering the decolonization process. The seminar

encouraged UN information assistance to those NSGTs with observer status in UN world conferences and General Assembly special sessions. It requested those Special Committee members that were members of the Economic and Social Council to support the inclusion as observers in the Council of those NSGTs that were associate members of UN regional commissions.

Participants welcomed as an observer at the seminar, for the first time, the representative of the United Kingdom and a statement regarding the United Kingdom's intention to engage with the Special Committee with a view to enhancing cooperation.

GENERAL ASSEMBLY ACTION

On 10 December [meeting 82], the General Assembly adopted **resolution 56/74** [draft: A/56/L.40] by recorded vote (132-2-21) [agenda item 18].

Implementation of the Declaration on the Granting of Independence to Colonial Countries and Peoples

The General Assembly,

Having examined the report of the Special Committee on the Situation with regard to the Implementation of the Declaration on the Granting of Independence to Colonial Countries and Peoples,

Recalling its resolution 1514(XV) of 14 December 1960, containing the Declaration on the Granting of Independence to Colonial Countries and Peoples, and all its subsequent resolutions concerning the implementation of the Declaration, most recently resolution 55/147 of 8 December 2000, as well as the relevant resolutions of the Security Council,

Bearing in mind the declaration of the period 2001-2010 as the Second International Decade for the Eradication of Colonialism, and the need to examine ways to ascertain the wishes of the peoples of the Non-Self-Governing Territories on the basis of resolution 1514(XV) and other relevant resolutions on decolonization,

Recognizing that the eradication of colonialism has been one of the priorities of the Organization and continues to be one of its priorities for the decade that began in 2001,

Reconfirming the need to take measures to eliminate colonialism before 2010, as called for in its resolution 55/146 of 8 December 2000,

Reiterating its conviction of the need for the eradication of colonialism, as well as of racial discrimination and violations of basic human rights,

Noting with satisfaction the achievements of the Special Committee in contributing to the effective and complete implementation of the Declaration and other relevant resolutions of the United Nations on decolonization,

Stressing the importance of the participation of the administering Powers in the work of the Special Committee,

Noting with concern that the non-participation of certain administering Powers has adversely affected the implementation of the mandate and work of the Special Committee,

Noting with satisfaction the cooperation and active participation of some administering Powers in the work of the Special Committee,

Noting that the other administering Powers have now agreed to work informally with the Special Committee,

Taking note of the consultations and agreements between the parties concerned in some Non-Self-Governing Territories and the action taken by the Secretary-General in relation to certain Non-Self-Governing Territories,

Aware of the pressing need of newly independent and emerging States for assistance from the United Nations and its system of organizations in the economic, social and other fields,

Aware also of the pressing need of many of the remaining Non-Self-Governing Territories, including in particular small island Territories, for economic, social and other assistance from the United Nations and the organizations of its system,

Taking special note of the fact that the Special Committee held a Caribbean regional seminar to review the situation in the small island Non-Self-Governing Territories, particularly their political evolution towards self-determination for the year 2001 and beyond, in Havana from 23 to 25 May 2001,

1. *Reaffirms* its resolution 1514(XV) and all other resolutions and decisions on decolonization, including its resolution 55/146, in which it declares the period 2001-2010 the Second International Decade for the Eradication of Colonialism, and calls upon the administering Powers, in accordance with those resolutions, to take all necessary steps to enable the peoples of the Non-Self-Governing Territories concerned to exercise fully as soon as possible their right to self-determination, including independence;

2. *Reaffirms once again* that the existence of colonialism in any form or manifestation, including economic exploitation, is incompatible with the Charter of the United Nations, the Declaration on the Granting of Independence to Colonial Countries and Peoples and the Universal Declaration of Human Rights;

3. *Reaffirms its determination* to continue to take all steps necessary to bring about the complete and speedy eradication of colonialism and the faithful observance by all States of the relevant provisions of the Charter, the Declaration on the Granting of Independence to Colonial Countries and Peoples and the Universal Declaration of Human Rights;

4. *Affirms once again its support* for the aspirations of the peoples under colonial rule to exercise their right to self-determination, including independence, in accordance with relevant resolutions of the United Nations on decolonization;

5. *Approves* the report of the Special Committee on the Situation with regard to the Implementation of the Declaration on the Granting of Independence to Colonial Countries and Peoples covering its work during 2001, including the programme of work envisaged for 2002;

6. *Calls upon* the administering Powers to cooperate fully with the Special Committee to finalize before the end of 2002 a constructive programme of work on a case-by-case basis for the Non-Self-Governing Territories to facilitate the implementation of the mandate of the Special Committee and the relevant resolutions on

decolonization, including resolutions on specific Territories;

7. *Welcomes* the ongoing consultations between the Special Committee and New Zealand, as administering Power for Tokelau, with the participation of representatives of the people of Tokelau, with a view to formulating a programme of work on the question of Tokelau;

8. *Requests* the Special Committee to continue to seek suitable means for the immediate and full implementation of the Declaration and to carry out those actions approved by the General Assembly regarding the International Decade for the Eradication of Colonialism and the Second International Decade in all Territories that have not yet exercised their right to self-determination, including independence, and in particular:

(*a*) To formulate specific proposals to bring about an end to colonialism and to report thereon to the General Assembly at its fifty-seventh session;

(*b*) To continue to examine the implementation by Member States of resolution 1514(XV) and other relevant resolutions on decolonization;

(*c*) To continue to pay special attention to the small Territories, including through the dispatch of visiting missions, and to recommend to the General Assembly the most suitable steps to be taken to enable the populations of those Territories to exercise their right to self-determination, including independence;

(*d*) To finalize before the end of 2002 a constructive programme of work on a case-by-case basis for the Non-Self-Governing Territories to facilitate the implementation of the mandate of the Special Committee and the relevant resolutions on decolonization, including resolutions on specific Territories;

(*e*) To take all necessary steps to enlist worldwide support among Governments, as well as national and international organizations, for the achievement of the objectives of the Declaration and the implementation of the relevant resolutions of the United Nations;

(*f*) To conduct seminars, as appropriate, for the purpose of receiving and disseminating information on the work of the Special Committee, and to facilitate participation by the peoples of the Non-Self-Governing Territories in those seminars;

(*g*) To observe annually the Week of Solidarity with the Peoples of Non-Self-Governing Territories;

9. *Calls upon* all States, in particular the administering Powers, as well as the specialized agencies and other organizations of the United Nations system, to give effect within their respective spheres of competence to the recommendations of the Special Committee for the implementation of the Declaration and other relevant resolutions of the United Nations;

10. *Calls upon* the administering Powers to ensure that the economic activities in the Non-Self-Governing Territories under their administration do not adversely affect the interests of the peoples but instead promote development, and to assist them in the exercise of their right to self-determination;

11. *Urges* the administering Powers concerned to take effective measures to safeguard and guarantee the inalienable rights of the peoples of the Non-Self-Governing Territories to their natural resources, including land, and to establish and maintain control over the future development of those resources, and

requests the administering Powers to take all necessary steps to protect the property rights of the peoples of those Territories;

12. *Reiterates* that military activities and arrangements by administering Powers in the Non-Self-Governing Territories under their administration should not run counter to the rights and interests of the peoples of the Territories concerned, especially their right to self-determination, including independence, calls upon the administering Powers concerned to terminate such activities and to eliminate the remaining military bases in compliance with the relevant resolutions of the General Assembly, and also calls upon the administering Powers to promote alternative sources of livelihood for the peoples of the Territories concerned;

13. *Urges* all States, directly and through their action in the specialized agencies and other organizations of the United Nations system, to provide moral and material assistance to the peoples of the Non-Self-Governing Territories, and requests that the administering Powers take steps to enlist and make effective use of all possible assistance, on both a bilateral and a multilateral basis, in the strengthening of the economies of those Territories;

14. *Reaffirms* that the United Nations visiting missions to the Territories are an effective means of ascertaining the situation in the Territories, as well as the wishes and aspirations of their inhabitants, and calls upon the administering Powers to continue to cooperate with the Special Committee in the discharge of its mandate and to facilitate visiting missions to the Territories;

15. *Calls upon* the administering Powers that have not participated formally in the work of the Special Committee to do so at its session in 2002;

16. *Requests* the Secretary-General, the specialized agencies and other organizations of the United Nations system to provide economic, social and other assistance to the Non-Self-Governing Territories and to continue to do so, as appropriate, after they exercise their right to self-determination, including independence;

17. *Requests* the Secretary-General to provide the Special Committee with the facilities and services required for the implementation of the present resolution, as well as of the other resolutions and decisions on decolonization adopted by the General Assembly and the Special Committee.

RECORDED VOTE ON RESOLUTION 56/74:

In favour: Algeria, Andorra, Angola, Antigua and Barbuda, Argentina, Armenia, Australia, Austria, Azerbaijan, Bahamas, Bahraïn, Bangladesh, Barbados, Belarus, Belize, Benin, Bhutan, Bolivia, Botswana, Brazil, Brunei Darussalam, Burkina Faso, Burundi, Cambodia, Canada, Cape Verde, Chile, China, Colombia, Comoros, Congo, Costa Rica, Côte d'Ivoire, Croatia, Cuba, Cyprus, Czech Republic, Democratic People's Republic of Korea, Denmark, Djibouti, Dominican Republic, Ecuador, Egypt, El Salvador, Equatorial Guinea, Eritrea, Ethiopia, Fiji, Gabon, Ghana, Grenada, Guatemala, Guinea, Guyana, Haiti, Honduras, Iceland, India , Indonesia, Iran, Ireland, Jamaica, Japan, Jordan, Kazakhstan, Kenya, Kuwait, Lao People's Democratic Republic, Lebanon, Libyan Arab Jamahiriya, Liechtenstein, Madagascar, Malaysia, Maldives, Mali, Malta, Mauritania, Mexico, Mongolia, Morocco, Mozambique, Myanmar, Namibia, Nepal, New Zealand, Nicaragua, Nigeria, Norway, Oman, Pakistan, Panama , Papua New Guinea, Paraguay, Peru, Philippines, Poland, Portugal, Qatar, Republic of Moldova, Romania, Russian Federation, Saint Lucia, San Marino, Saudi Arabia, Senegal, Seychelles, Sierra Leone, Singapore, Slovakia, Solomon Islands, South Africa, Spain, Sri Lanka, Sudan, Swaziland, Sweden, Syrian Arab Republic, Thailand, Togo, Tonga, Trinidad and Tobago, Tunisia, Ukraine, United Arab Emirates, United Republic of Tanzania, Uruguay, Venezuela, Viet Nam, Yemen, Yugoslavia, Zambia, Zimbabwe.

Against: United Kingdom, United States.

Abstaining: Belgium, Bulgaria, Estonia, Finland, France, Georgia, Germany, Greece, Hungary, Israel, Italy, Latvia, Lithuania, Luxembourg, Marshall Islands, Micronesia, Netherlands, Republic of Korea, Slovenia, The former Yugoslav Republic of Macedonia, Turkey.

Speaking after the vote, the United Kingdom said that it continued to find some elements of the text unacceptable, including, but not limited to, operative paragraph 12, which called on the administering Powers to eliminate the remaining military bases in NSGTs. However, it remained sincerely committed to furthering the process of informal dialogue with the Special Committee on decolonization.

By **decision 56/464** of 24 December, the Assembly decided that the agenda item on the implementation of the Declaration on the Granting of Independence to Colonial Countries and Peoples would remain for consideration during its resumed fifty-sixth (2002) session.

Implementation by international organizations

In May [A/56/65], the Secretary-General reported that he had brought General Assembly resolution 55/139 [YUN 2000, p. 553] on the implementation of the 1960 Declaration on decolonization to the attention of the specialized agencies and international institutions associated with the United Nations and invited them to submit information regarding their implementation activities in support of NSGTs. Replies received from 13 departments, agencies and institutions were summarized in a May report of the President of the Economic and Social Council [E/2001/57]. According to the information provided, a number of specialized agencies and organizations continued to extend assistance to NSGTs through programmes from within their own budgetary resources, in addition to their respective contributions as executing agencies of projects funded by the United Nations Development Programme (UNDP). UNDP itself continued to fund assistance projects in close collaboration with other agencies and organizations.

ECONOMIC AND SOCIAL COUNCIL ACTION

On 26 July [meeting 43], the Economic and Social Council adopted **resolution 2001/28** [draft: E/2001/L.22, orally revised] by roll-call vote (30-0-19) [agenda item 9].

Implementation of the Declaration on the Granting of Independence to Colonial Countries and Peoples by the specialized agencies and the international institutions associated with the United Nations

The Economic and Social Council,

Having examined the report of the Secretary-General and the report of the President of the Economic and Social Council containing the information submitted by the specialized agencies and other organizations of the United Nations system on their activities with regard to the implementation of the Declaration on the Granting of Independence to Colonial Countries and Peoples,

Having heard the statement by the representative of the Special Committee on the Situation with regard to the Implementation of the Declaration on the Granting of Independence to Colonial Countries and Peoples,

Recalling General Assembly resolutions 1514(XV) of 14 December 1960 and 1541(XV) of 15 December 1960, the resolutions of the Special Committee and other relevant resolutions and decisions, including in particular Economic and Social Council resolution 2000/30 of 28 July 2000,

Bearing in mind the relevant provisions of the final documents of the successive Conferences of Heads of State or Government of Non-Aligned Countries and of the resolutions adopted by the Assembly of Heads of State and Government of the Organization of African Unity, the Pacific Islands Forum and the Caribbean Community,

Conscious of the need to facilitate the implementation of the Declaration,

Welcoming the current participation in their capacity as observers of those Non-Self-Governing Territories that are associate members of the regional commissions in United Nations world conferences in the economic and social sphere, subject to the rules of procedure of the General Assembly and in accordance with relevant United Nations resolutions and decisions, including resolutions and decisions of the Assembly and the Special Committee on specific Territories, and in the special session of the Assembly for an overall review and appraisal of the implementation of the outcome of the United Nations Conference on Human Settlements (Habitat II), held in New York from 6 to 9 June 2001,

Noting that the large majority of the remaining Non-Self-Governing Territories are small island Territories,

Welcoming the assistance extended to Non-Self-Governing Territories by certain specialized agencies and other organizations of the United Nations system, in particular the United Nations Development Programme,

Stressing that, because the development options of the small island Non-Self-Governing Territories are limited, there are special challenges to planning for and implementing sustainable development and that those Territories will be constrained in meeting the challenges without the continued cooperation and assistance of the specialized agencies and other organizations of the United Nations system,

Stressing also the importance of securing the necessary resources for funding expanded assistance programmes for the peoples concerned and the need to enlist the support of all major funding institutions within the United Nations system in that regard,

Reaffirming the mandates of the specialized agencies and other organizations of the United Nations system to take all the appropriate measures, within their respective spheres of competence, to ensure the full implementation of resolution 1514(XV) and other relevant resolutions,

Expressing its appreciation to the Organization of African Unity, the Pacific Islands Forum, the Caribbean Community and other regional organizations for the continued cooperation and assistance they have extended to the specialized agencies and other organizations of the United Nations system in this regard,

Expressing its conviction that closer contacts and consultations between and among the specialized agencies and other organizations of the United Nations system and regional organizations help to facilitate the effective formulation of assistance programmes to the peoples concerned,

Mindful of the imperative need to keep under continuous review the activities of the specialized agencies and other organizations of the United Nations system in the implementation of the various relevant United Nations decisions,

Bearing in mind the extremely fragile economies of the small island Non-Self-Governing Territories and their vulnerability to natural disasters, such as hurricanes, cyclones and sea-level rise, and recalling the relevant resolutions of the General Assembly,

Recalling General Assembly resolution 55/139 of 8 December 2000, entitled "Implementation of the Declaration on the Granting of Independence to Colonial Countries and Peoples by the specialized agencies and the international institutions associated with the United Nations",

1. *Takes note* of the report of the President of the Economic and Social Council containing the information submitted by the specialized agencies and other organizations of the United Nations system on their activities with regard to the implementation of the Declaration on the Granting of Independence to Colonial Countries and Peoples, and endorses the observations and suggestions arising therefrom;

2. *Also takes note* of the report of the Secretary-General;

3. *Recommends* that all States intensify their efforts in the specialized agencies and other organizations of the United Nations system to ensure the full and effective implementation of the Declaration, contained in resolution 1514(XV), and other relevant resolutions of the United Nations;

4. *Reaffirms* that the specialized agencies and other organizations and institutions of the United Nations system should continue to be guided by the relevant resolutions of the United Nations in their efforts to contribute to the implementation of the Declaration and all other relevant General Assembly resolutions;

5. *Also reaffirms* that the recognition by the General Assembly, the Security Council and other United Nations organs of the legitimacy of the aspirations of the peoples of the Non-Self-Governing Territories to exercise their right to self-determination entails, as a corollary, the extension of all appropriate assistance to those peoples;

6. *Expresses its appreciation* to those specialized agencies and other organizations of the United Nations system that have continued to cooperate with the United Nations and the regional and subregional organizations in the implementation of resolution 1514(XV) and other relevant resolutions of the United Nations, and requests all the specialized agencies and other organizations of the United Nations system to implement the relevant provisions of those resolutions;

7. *Requests* the specialized agencies and other organizations of the United Nations system and international and regional organizations to examine and review conditions in each Territory so as to take appropriate measures to accelerate progress in the economic and social sectors of the Territories;

8. *Requests* the specialized agencies and the international institutions associated with the United Nations and regional organizations to strengthen existing measures of support and formulate appropriate programmes of assistance to the remaining Non-Self-Governing Territories, within the framework of their respective mandates, in order to accelerate progress in the economic and social sectors of those Territories;

9. *Recommends* that the executive heads of the specialized agencies and other organizations of the United Nations system formulate, with the active cooperation of the regional organizations concerned, concrete proposals for the full implementation of the relevant resolutions of the United Nations and submit the proposals to their governing and legislative organs;

10. *Also recommends* that the specialized agencies and other organizations of the United Nations system continue to review, at the regular meetings of their governing bodies, the implementation of resolution 1514(XV) and other relevant resolutions of the United Nations;

11. *Welcomes* the continuing initiative exercised by the United Nations Development Programme in maintaining close liaison among the specialized agencies and other organizations of the United Nations system and in providing assistance to the peoples of the Non-Self-Governing Territories;

12. *Encourages* Non-Self-Governing Territories to take steps to establish and/or strengthen disaster preparedness and management institutions and policies;

13. *Requests* the administering Powers concerned to facilitate, when appropriate, the participation of appointed and elected representatives of Non-Self-Governing Territories in the relevant meetings and conferences of the specialized agencies and other organizations of the United Nations system, in accordance with relevant United Nations resolutions and decisions, including resolutions and decisions of the General Assembly and the Special Committee, on specific Territories, so that the Territories may benefit from the related activities of those agencies and organizations;

14. *Recommends* that all Governments intensify their efforts in the specialized agencies and other organizations of the United Nations system of which they are members to accord priority to the question of providing assistance to the peoples of the Non-Self-Governing Territories;

15. *Draws the attention* of the Special Committee to the present resolution and to the discussion held on the subject at the substantive session of 2001 of the Economic and Social Council;

16. *Welcomes* the adoption by the Economic Commission for Latin America and the Caribbean of resolution 574(XXVII) of 16 May 1998 calling for the necessary mechanisms for its associate members, including small island Non-Self-Governing Territories, to participate in the special sessions of the General Assembly, subject to the rules of procedure of the Assembly, to review and assess the implementation of the plans of action of those United Nations world conferences in which the Territories originally participated in the capacity of observer, and in the work of the Economic and Social Council and its subsidiary bodies;

17. *Requests* the President of the Council to continue to maintain close contact on these matters with the Chairman of the Special Committee, and to report thereon to the Council;

18. *Requests* the Secretary-General to follow the implementation of the present resolution, paying particular attention to cooperation and integration arrangements for maximizing the efficiency of the assistance activities undertaken by various organizations of the United Nations system, and to report thereon to the Council at its substantive session of 2002;

19. *Decides* to keep these questions under continuous review.

ROLL-CALL VOTE ON RESOLUTION 2001/28:

In favour: Angola, Argentina, Bahrain, Bolivia, Brazil, Burkina Faso, Cameroon, China, Costa Rica, Cuba, Egypt, Ethiopia, Fiji, Honduras, Indonesia, Iran, Mexico, Morocco, Nepal, Nigeria, Pakistan, Peru, Republic of Korea, Saudi Arabia, South Africa, Sudan, Suriname, Syrian Arab Republic, Uganda, Venezuela.

Against: None.

Abstaining: Andorra, Austria, Bulgaria, Canada, Croatia, Czech Republic, Denmark, France, Germany, Italy, Japan, Malta, Netherlands, Norway, Portugal, Romania, Russian Federation, United Kingdom, United States.

GENERAL ASSEMBLY ACTION

On 10 December [meeting 82], the General Assembly, on the recommendation of the Fourth (Special Political and Decolonization) Committee [A/56/555], adopted **resolution 56/67** by recorded vote (106-0-50) [agenda items 93 & 12].

Implementation of the Declaration on the Granting of Independence to Colonial Countries and Peoples by the specialized agencies and the international institutions associated with the United Nations

The General Assembly,

Having considered the item entitled "Implementation of the Declaration on the Granting of Independence to Colonial Countries and Peoples by the specialized agencies and the international institutions associated with the United Nations",

Having also considered the report of the Secretary-General on the item,

Having examined the chapter of the report of the Special Committee on the Situation with regard to the Implementation of the Declaration on the Granting of Independence to Colonial Countries and Peoples relating to the item,

Recalling its resolutions 1514(XV) of 14 December 1960 and 1541(XV) of 15 December 1960 and the resolutions of the Special Committee, as well as other relevant resolutions and decisions, including in particular Economic and Social Council resolution 2000/30 of 28 July 2000,

Bearing in mind the relevant provisions of the final documents of the successive Conferences of Heads of State or Government of Non-Aligned Countries and of the resolutions adopted by the Assembly of Heads of State and Government of the Organization of African Unity, the Pacific Islands Forum and the Caribbean Community,

Conscious of the need to facilitate the implementation of the Declaration on the Granting of Independence to Colonial Countries and Peoples, contained in resolution 1514(XV),

Noting that the large majority of the remaining Non-Self-Governing Territories are small island Territories,

Welcoming the assistance extended to Non-Self-Governing Territories by certain specialized agencies and other organizations of the United Nations system, in particular the United Nations Development Programme,

Also welcoming the current participation in the capacity of observers of those Non-Self-Governing Territories which are associate members of regional commissions in the world conferences in the economic and social sphere, subject to the rules of procedure of the General Assembly and in accordance with relevant United Nations resolutions and decisions, including resolutions and decisions of the Assembly and the Special Committee on specific Territories, and in the special session of the General Assembly on the review and appraisal of the implementation of the Programme of Action of the International Conference on Population and Development, held at Headquarters from 30 June to 2 July 1999,

Noting that only some specialized agencies and other organizations of the United Nations system have been involved in providing assistance for Non-Self-Governing Territories,

Stressing that, because the development options of the small island Non-Self-Governing Territories are limited, there are special challenges to planning for and implementing sustainable development and that those Territories will be constrained in meeting the challenges without the continued cooperation and assistance of the specialized agencies and other organizations of the United Nations system,

Stressing also the importance of securing the necessary resources for funding expanded assistance programmes for the peoples concerned and the need to enlist the support of all major funding institutions within the United Nations system in that regard,

Reaffirming the mandates of the specialized agencies and other organizations of the United Nations system to take all appropriate measures, within their respective spheres of competence, to ensure the full implementation of General Assembly resolution 1514(XV) and other relevant resolutions,

Expressing its appreciation to the Organization of African Unity, the Pacific Islands Forum, the Caribbean Community and other regional organizations for the continued cooperation and assistance they have extended to the specialized agencies and other organizations of the United Nations system in this regard,

Expressing its conviction that closer contacts and consultations between and among the specialized agencies and other organizations of the United Nations system and regional organizations help to facilitate the effective formulation of assistance programmes to the peoples concerned,

Mindful of the imperative need to keep under continuous review the activities of the specialized agencies and other organizations of the United Nations system in the implementation of the various United Nations decisions relating to decolonization,

Bearing in mind the extremely fragile economies of the small island Non-Self-Governing Territories and their vulnerability to natural disasters, such as hurricanes, cyclones and sea-level rise, and recalling the relevant resolutions of the General Assembly,

Recalling its resolution 55/139 of 8 December 2000 on the implementation of the Declaration by the specialized agencies and the international institutions associated with the United Nations,

1. *Takes note* of the report of the Secretary-General;

2. *Recommends* that all States intensify their efforts in the specialized agencies and other organizations of the United Nations system to ensure the full and effective implementation of the Declaration on the Granting of Independence to Colonial Countries and Peoples, contained in General Assembly resolution 1514(XV), and other relevant resolutions of the United Nations;

3. *Reaffirms* that the specialized agencies and other organizations and institutions of the United Nations system should continue to be guided by the relevant resolutions of the United Nations in their efforts to contribute to the implementation of the Declaration and all other relevant General Assembly resolutions;

4. *Reaffirms also* that the recognition by the General Assembly, the Security Council and other United Nations organs of the legitimacy of the aspirations of the peoples of the Non-Self-Governing Territories to exercise their right to self-determination entails, as a corollary, the extension of all appropriate assistance to those peoples;

5. *Expresses its appreciation* to those specialized agencies and other organizations of the United Nations system that have continued to cooperate with the United Nations and the regional and subregional organizations in the implementation of General Assembly resolution 1514(XV) and other relevant resolutions of the United Nations, and requests all the specialized agencies and other organizations of the United Nations system to implement the relevant provisions of those resolutions;

6. *Requests* the specialized agencies and other organizations of the United Nations system and international and regional organizations to examine and review conditions in each Territory so as to take appropriate measures to accelerate progress in the economic and social sectors of the Territories;

7. *Urges* those specialized agencies and organizations of the United Nations system that have not yet provided assistance for Non-Self-Governing Territories to do so as soon as possible;

8. *Requests* the specialized agencies and other organizations and institutions of the United Nations system and regional organizations to strengthen existing measures of support and formulate appropriate programmes of assistance to the remaining Non-Self-Governing Territories, within the framework of their respective mandates, in order to accelerate progress in the economic and social sectors of those Territories;

9. *Requests* the specialized agencies and other organizations of the United Nations system concerned to provide information on:

(a) Environmental problems facing the Non-Self-Governing Territories;

(b) The impact of natural disasters, such as hurricanes and volcanic eruptions, and other environmental problems, such as beach and coastal erosion and droughts, on those Territories;

(c) Ways and means to assist the Territories to fight drug trafficking, money-laundering and other illegal and criminal activities;

(d) The illegal exploitation of the marine resources of the Territories and the need to utilize those resources for the benefit of the peoples of the Territories;

10. *Recommends* that the executive heads of the specialized agencies and other organizations of the United Nations system formulate, with the active cooperation of the regional organizations concerned, concrete proposals for the full implementation of the relevant resolutions of the United Nations and submit the proposals to their governing and legislative organs;

11. *Also recommends* that the specialized agencies and other organizations of the United Nations system continue to review at the regular meetings of their governing bodies the implementation of General Assembly resolution 1514(XV) and other relevant resolutions of the United Nations;

12. *Welcomes* the continuing initiative exercised by the United Nations Development Programme in maintaining close liaison among the specialized agencies and other organizations of the United Nations system and in providing assistance for the peoples of the Non-Self-Governing Territories;

13. *Encourages* Non-Self-Governing Territories to take steps to establish and/or strengthen disaster preparedness and management institutions and policies;

14. *Requests* the administering Powers concerned to facilitate, when appropriate, the participation of appointed and elected representatives of Non-Self-Governing Territories in the relevant meetings and conferences of the specialized agencies and other organizations of the United Nations system, in accordance with relevant United Nations resolutions and decisions, including resolutions and decisions of the General Assembly and the Special Committee on the Situation with regard to the Implementation of the Declaration on the Granting of Independence to Colonial Countries and Peoples on specific Territories, so that the Territories may benefit from the related activities of those agencies and organizations;

15. *Recommends* that all Governments intensify their efforts in the specialized agencies and other organizations of the United Nations system of which they are members to accord priority to the question of providing assistance for the peoples of the Non-Self-Governing Territories;

16. *Requests* the Secretary-General to continue to assist the specialized agencies and other organizations of the United Nations system in working out appropriate measures for implementing the relevant resolutions of the United Nations and to prepare for submission to the relevant bodies, with the assistance of those agencies and organizations, a report on the action taken in implementation of the relevant resolutions, including the present resolution, since the circulation of his previous report;

17. *Commends* the Economic and Social Council for its debate and resolution on this question, and requests it to continue to consider, in consultation with the Special Committee, appropriate measures for coordination of the policies and activities of the specialized agencies and other organizations of the United Nations system in implementing the relevant resolutions of the General Assembly;

18. *Requests* the specialized agencies to report periodically to the Secretary-General on the implementation of the present resolution;

19. *Requests* the Secretary-General to transmit the present resolution to the governing bodies of the appropriate specialized agencies and international institutions associated with the United Nations so that those bodies may take the necessary measures to implement the resolution, and also requests the Secretary-General to report to the General Assembly at its fifty-seventh session on the implementation of the present resolution;

20. *Requests* the Special Committee to continue to examine the question and to report thereon to the General Assembly at its fifty-seventh session.

RECORDED VOTE ON RESOLUTION 56/67:

In favour: Algeria, Angola, Antigua and Barbuda, Argentina, Australia, Azerbaijan, Bahamas, Bahrain, Bangladesh, Barbados, Belarus, Belize, Benin, Bhutan, Bolivia, Botswana, Brazil, Brunei Darussalam, Burkina Faso, Burundi, Cambodia, Cameroon, Cape Verde, Chile, China, Colombia, Comoros, Congo, Costa Rica, Côte d'Ivoire, Cuba, Democratic People's Republic of Korea, Djibouti, Dominican Republic, Ecuador, Egypt, El Salvador, Equatorial Guinea, Eritrea, Ethiopia, Fiji, Gabon, Ghana, Grenada, Guatemala, Guinea, Guyana, Haiti, Honduras, India, Indonesia, Iran, Jamaica, Jordan, Kenya, Kuwait, Lao People's Democratic Republic, Lebanon, Libyan Arab Jamahiriya, Madagascar, Malaysia, Maldives, Mali, Mauritania, Mexico, Mongolia, Morocco, Mozambique, Myanmar, Namibia, Nepal, New Zealand, Nicaragua, Nigeria, Oman, Pakistan, Panama, Papua New Guinea, Paraguay, Peru, Philippines, Qatar, Saint Lucia, Saudi Arabia, Senegal, Seychelles, Sierra Leone, Singapore, Solomon Islands, South Africa, Sri Lanka, Sudan, Swaziland, Syrian Arab Republic, Thailand, Togo, Trinidad and Tobago, Tunisia, United Arab Emirates, United Republic of Tanzania, Uruguay, Venezuela, Viet Nam, Yemen, Zambia, Zimbabwe.

Against: None.

Abstaining: Andorra, Armenia, Austria, Belgium, Bulgaria, Canada, Croatia, Cyprus, Czech Republic, Denmark, Estonia, Finland, France, Georgia, Germany, Greece, Hungary, Iceland, Ireland, Israel, Italy, Japan, Latvia, Liechtenstein, Lithuania, Luxembourg, Malta, Marshall Islands, Micronesia, Monaco, Netherlands, Norway, Poland, Portugal, Republic of Korea, Republic of Moldova, Romania, Russian Federation, San Marino, Slovakia, Slovenia, Spain, Sweden, The former Yugoslav Republic of Macedonia, Tonga, Turkey, Ukraine, United Kingdom, United States, Yugoslavia.

Military activities and arrangements in colonial countries

The Special Committee on decolonization considered military activities and arrangements by colonial Powers in Territories under their administration. It had before it Secretariat working papers containing information on, among other subjects, military activities and arrangements in Bermuda [A/AC.109/2001/9], Guam [A/AC.109/2001/4] and the United States Virgin Islands [A/AC.109/2001/3]. On 3 July, it recommended a draft decision for adoption by the General Assembly (see below).

GENERAL ASSEMBLY ACTION

In December, the General Assembly, on the recommendation of the Fourth Committee [A/56/554], adopted **decision 56/420** by recorded vote (92-51) [agenda items 92 & 18].

Military activities and arrangements by colonial Powers in Territories under their administration

At its 82nd plenary meeting, on 10 December 2001, the General Assembly, by a recorded vote of 92 to 51, with no abstentions, and on the recommendation of the Special Political and Decolonization Committee (Fourth Committee), adopted the following text:

"1. The General Assembly, having considered the chapter of the report of the Special Committee on the Situation with regard to the Implementation of the Declaration on the Granting of Independence to Colonial Countries and Peoples relating to an item on the agenda of the Special Committee entitled 'Military activities and arrangements by colonial Powers in Territories under their administration', and recalling its resolution 1514(XV) of 14 December 1960 and all other relevant resolutions and decisions of the United Nations relating to military activities in colonial and Non-Self-Governing Territories, reaffirms its strong conviction that military bases and installations in the Territories concerned could constitute an obstacle to the exercise by the people of those Territories of their right to self-determination, and reiterates its strong views that existing bases and installations, which are impeding the implementation of the Declaration on the Granting of Independence to Colonial Countries and Peoples, should be withdrawn.

"2. Aware of the presence of such bases and installations in some of those Territories, the General Assembly urges the administering Powers concerned to continue to take all necessary measures not to involve those Territories in any offensive acts or interference against other States.

"3. The General Assembly reiterates its concern that military activities and arrangements by colonial Powers in Territories under their administration might run counter to the rights and interests of the colonial peoples concerned, especially their right to self-determination and independence. The Assembly once again calls upon the administering Powers concerned to terminate such activities and to eliminate such military bases in compliance with its relevant resolutions. Alternative sources of livelihood for the peoples of the Non-Self-Governing Territories should be provided.

"4. The General Assembly reiterates that the colonial and Non-Self-Governing Territories and areas adjacent thereto should not be used for nuclear testing, dumping of nuclear wastes or deployment of nuclear and other weapons of mass destruction.

"5. The General Assembly deplores the continued alienation of land in colonial and Non-Self-Governing Territories, particularly in the small island Territories of the Pacific and Caribbean regions, for military installations. The large-scale utilization of the local resources for this purpose could adversely affect the economic development of the Territories concerned.

"6. The General Assembly takes note of the decision of some of the administering Powers to close or downsize some of those military bases in the Non-Self-Governing Territories.

"7. The General Assembly requests the Secretary-General to continue to inform world public opinion of those military activities and arrangements in colonial and Non-Self-Governing Territories which constitute an obstacle to the implementation of the Declaration on the Granting of Independence to Colonial Countries and Peoples.

"8. The General Assembly requests the Special Committee on the Situation with regard to the Implementation of the Declaration on the Granting of Independence to Colonial Countries and Peoples to continue to examine this question and to report thereon to the Assembly at its fifty-seventh session."

RECORDED VOTE ON DECISION 56/420:

In favour: Algeria, Angola, Antigua and Barbuda, Argentina, Bahrain, Bangladesh, Barbados, Belarus, Belize, Benin, Bhutan, Bolivia, Brazil, Brunei Darussalam, Burkina Faso, Burundi, Cambodia, Cameroon, Cape Verde, Chile, China, Colombia, Congo, Costa Rica, Côte d'Ivoire, Cuba, Cyprus, Djibouti, Dominican Republic, Ecuador, Egypt, El Salvador, Eritrea, Ethiopia, Fiji, Gabon, Ghana, Guatemala, Guinea, Guyana, Haiti, Honduras, India, Indonesia, Iran, Jamaica, Jordan, Kuwait, Lao People's Democratic Republic, Lebanon, Libyan Arab Jamahiriya, Madagascar, Malaysia, Maldives, Mali, Mauritania, Mexico, Mongolia, Mozambique, Myanmar, Namibia, Nepal, Nicaragua, Nigeria, Oman, Pakistan, Panama, Papua New Guinea, Philippines, Qatar, Saint Lucia, Saudi Arabia, Senegal, Sierra Leone, Singapore, South Africa, Sri Lanka, Sudan, Swaziland, Syrian Arab Republic, Thailand, Togo, Trinidad and Tobago, Tunisia, United Arab Emirates, United Republic of Tanzania, Uruguay, Venezuela, Viet Nam, Yemen, Zambia, Zimbabwe.

Against: Andorra, Armenia, Australia, Austria, Belgium, Bulgaria, Canada, Croatia, Czech Republic, Denmark, Estonia, Finland, France, Georgia, Germany, Greece, Hungary, Iceland, Ireland, Israel, Italy, Japan, Latvia, Liechtenstein, Lithuania, Luxembourg, Malta, Marshall Islands, Micronesia, Monaco, Netherlands, New Zealand, Norway, Paraguay, Poland, Portugal, Republic of Korea, Republic of Moldova, Russian Federation, San Marino, Slovakia, Slovenia, Spain, Sweden, The former Yugoslav Republic of Macedonia, Turkey, Ukraine, United Kingdom, United States, Yugoslavia.

Economic and other activities affecting the interests of NSGTs

The Special Committee on decolonization continued consideration of economic and other activities affecting the interests of the peoples of NSGTs. It had before it Secretariat working papers containing information on, among other things, economic conditions, with particular reference to foreign economic activities in Anguilla, American Samoa, Bermuda, the British Virgin Islands, the Cayman Islands, Guam, Montserrat, the Turks and Caicos Islands and the United States Virgin Islands [A/AC.109/2001/13, A/AC.109/2001/17, A/AC.109/2001/9, A/AC.109/2001/8, A/AC.109/2001/15, A/AC.109/2001/4, A/AC.109/2001/6, A/AC.109/2001/7, A/AC.109/2001/3].

GENERAL ASSEMBLY ACTION

On 10 December [meeting 82], the General Assembly, on the recommendation of the Fourth Committee [A/56/554], adopted **resolution 56/66** by recorded vote (147-2-5) [agenda items 92 & 18].

Economic and other activities which affect the interests of the peoples of the Non-Self-Governing Territories

The General Assembly,

Having considered the item entitled "Economic and other activities which affect the interests of the peoples of the Non-Self-Governing Territories",

Having examined the chapter of the report of the Special Committee on the Situation with regard to the Implementation of the Declaration on the Granting of Independence to Colonial Countries and Peoples relating to the item,

Recalling its resolution 1514(XV) of 14 December 1960, as well as all other relevant General Assembly resolutions, including, in particular, resolutions 46/181 of 19 December 1991 and 55/146 of 8 December 2000,

Reaffirming the solemn obligation of the administering Powers under the Charter of the United Nations to promote the political, economic, social and educational advancement of the inhabitants of the Territories under their administration and to protect the human and natural resources of those Territories against abuses,

Reaffirming also that any economic or other activity that has a negative impact on the interests of the peoples of the Non-Self-Governing Territories and on the exercise of their right to self-determination in conformity with the Charter and General Assembly resolution 1514(XV) is contrary to the purposes and principles of the Charter,

Reaffirming further that the natural resources are the heritage of the peoples of the Non-Self-Governing Territories, including the indigenous populations,

Aware of the special circumstances of the geographical location, size and economic conditions of each Territory, and bearing in mind the need to promote the economic stability, diversification and strengthening of the economy of each Territory,

Conscious of the particular vulnerability of the small Territories to natural disasters and environmental degradation,

Conscious also that foreign economic investment, when done in collaboration with the peoples of the Non-Self-Governing Territories and in accordance with their wishes, could make a valid contribution to the socio-economic development of the Territories and could also make a valid contribution to the exercise of their right to self-determination,

Concerned about any activities aimed at exploiting the natural and human resources of the Non-Self-Governing Territories to the detriment of the interests of the inhabitants of those Territories,

Bearing in mind the relevant provisions of the final documents of the successive Conferences of Heads of State or Government of Non-Aligned Countries and of the resolutions adopted by the Assembly of Heads of State and Government of the Organization of African Unity, the Pacific Islands Forum and the Caribbean Community,

1. *Reaffirms* the right of peoples of Non-Self-Governing Territories to self-determination in conformity with the Charter of the United Nations and with General Assembly resolution 1514(XV), containing the Declaration on the Granting of Independence to Colonial Countries and Peoples, as well as their right to the enjoyment of their natural resources and their right to dispose of those resources in their best interest;

2. *Affirms* the value of foreign economic investment undertaken in collaboration with the peoples of the Non-Self-Governing Territories and in accordance with their wishes in order to make a valid contribution to the socio-economic development of the Territories;

3. *Reaffirms* the responsibility of the administering Powers under the Charter to promote the political, eco-

nomic, social and educational advancement of the Non-Self-Governing Territories, and reaffirms the legitimate rights of their peoples over their natural resources;

4. *Reaffirms its concern* about any activities aimed at the exploitation of the natural resources that are the heritage of the peoples of the Non-Self-Governing Territories, including the indigenous populations, in the Caribbean, the Pacific and other regions, as well as their human resources, to the detriment of their interests, and in such a way as to deprive them of their right to dispose of those resources;

5. *Affirms* the need to avoid any economic and other activities which adversely affect the interests of the peoples of the Non-Self-Governing Territories;

6. *Calls once again upon* all Governments that have not yet done so to take, in accordance with the relevant provisions of General Assembly resolution 2621(XXV) of 12 October 1970, legislative, administrative or other measures in respect of their nationals and the bodies corporate under their jurisdiction that own and operate enterprises in the Non-Self-Governing Territories that are detrimental to the interests of the inhabitants of those Territories, in order to put an end to such enterprises;

7. *Reiterates* that the damaging exploitation and plundering of the marine and other natural resources of the Non-Self-Governing Territories, in violation of the relevant resolutions of the United Nations, is a threat to the integrity and prosperity of those Territories;

8. *Invites* all Governments and organizations of the United Nations system to take all possible measures to ensure that the permanent sovereignty of the peoples of the Non-Self-Governing Territories over their natural resources is fully respected and safeguarded;

9. *Urges* the administering Powers concerned to take effective measures to safeguard and guarantee the inalienable right of the peoples of the Non-Self-Governing Territories to their natural resources and to establish and maintain control over the future development of those resources, and requests the administering Powers to take all necessary steps to protect the property rights of the peoples of those Territories;

10. *Calls upon* the administering Powers concerned to ensure that no discriminatory working conditions prevail in the Territories under their administration and to promote in each Territory a fair system of wages applicable to all the inhabitants without any discrimination;

11. *Requests* the Secretary-General to continue, through all means at his disposal, to inform world public opinion of any activity that affects the exercise of the right of the peoples of the Non-Self-Governing Territories to self-determination in conformity with the Charter and General Assembly resolution 1514(XV);

12. *Appeals* to the mass media, trade unions and non-governmental organizations, as well as individuals, to continue their efforts to promote the economic well-being of the peoples of the Non-Self-Governing Territories;

13. *Decides* to follow the situation in the Non-Self-Governing Territories so as to ensure that all economic activities in those Territories are aimed at strengthening and diversifying their economies in the interest of their peoples, including the indigenous populations,

and at promoting the economic and financial viability of those Territories;

14. *Requests* the Special Committee on the Situation with regard to the Implementation of the Declaration on the Granting of Independence to Colonial Countries and Peoples to continue to examine this question and to report thereon to the General Assembly at its fifty-seventh session.

RECORDED VOTE ON RESOLUTION 56/66:

In favour: Algeria, Andorra, Angola, Antigua and Barbuda, Argentina, Armenia, Australia, Austria, Azerbaijan, Bahamas, Bahrain, Bangladesh, Barbados, Belarus, Belgium, Belize, Benin, Bhutan, Bolivia, Botswana, Brazil, Brunei Darussalam, Bulgaria, Burkina Faso, Burundi, Cambodia, Cameroon, Canada, Cape Verde, Chile, China, Colombia, Comoros, Congo, Costa Rica, Côte d'Ivoire, Croatia, Cuba, Cyprus, Czech Republic, Democratic People's Republic of Korea, Denmark, Djibouti, Dominican Republic, Ecuador, Egypt, El Salvador, Eritrea, Estonia, Ethiopia, Fiji, Finland, Gabon, Germany, Ghana, Greece, Grenada, Guatemala, Guinea, Guyana, Haiti, Honduras, Hungary, Iceland, India, Indonesia, Iran, Ireland, Italy, Jamaica, Japan, Jordan, Kazakhstan, Kenya, Kuwait, Lao People's Democratic Republic, Latvia, Lebanon, Libyan Arab Jamahiriya, Liechtenstein, Lithuania, Luxembourg, Madagascar, Malaysia, Maldives, Mali, Malta, Mauritania, Mexico, Mongolia, Mozambique, Myanmar, Namibia, Nepal, Netherlands, New Zealand, Nicaragua, Nigeria, Norway, Oman, Pakistan, Panama, Papua New Guinea, Paraguay, Peru, Philippines, Poland, Portugal, Qatar, Republic of Korea, Republic of Moldova, Romania, Russian Federation, Saint Lucia, San Marino, Saudi Arabia, Senegal, Seychelles, Sierra Leone, Singapore, Slovakia, Slovenia, Solomon Islands, South Africa, Spain, Sri Lanka, Sudan, Swaziland, Sweden, Syrian Arab Republic, Thailand, The former Yugoslav Republic of Macedonia, Togo, Tonga, Trinidad and Tobago, Tunisia, Turkey, Ukraine, United Arab Emirates, United Republic of Tanzania, Uruguay, Venezuela, Viet Nam, Yemen, Yugoslavia, Zambia, Zimbabwe.

Against: Israel, United States.

Abstaining: France, Georgia, Marshall Islands, Micronesia, United Kingdom.

Dissemination of information

The Special Committee on decolonization held consultations in June with representatives of DPA and DPI on the dissemination of information on decolonization. The Committee also considered a DPI report on the topic [A/AC.109/2001/19].

GENERAL ASSEMBLY ACTION

On 10 December [meeting 82], the General Assembly, on the recommendation of the Special Committee on decolonization [A/56/23], adopted **resolution 56/73** by recorded vote (147-2-4) [agenda item 18].

Dissemination of information on decolonization

The General Assembly,

Having examined the chapter of the report of the Special Committee on the Situation with regard to the Implementation of the Declaration on the Granting of Independence to Colonial Countries and Peoples relating to the dissemination of information on decolonization and publicity for the work of the United Nations in the field of decolonization,

Recalling its resolution 1514(XV) of 14 December 1960, containing the Declaration on the Granting of Independence to Colonial Countries and Peoples, and other resolutions and decisions of the United Nations concerning the dissemination of information on decolonization, in particular General Assembly resolution 55/145 of 8 December 2000,

Recognizing the need for flexible, practical and innovative approaches towards reviewing the options of self-determination for the peoples of Non-Self-Governing Territories with a view to achieving the goals of the Second International Decade for the Eradication of Colonialism,

Reiterating the importance of dissemination of information as an instrument for furthering the aims of the Declaration, and mindful of the role of world public opinion in effectively assisting the peoples of Non-Self-Governing Territories to achieve self-determination,

Recognizing the role played by the administering Powers in transmitting information to the Secretary-General in accordance with the terms of Article 73 *e* of the Charter of the United Nations,

Aware of the role of non-governmental organizations in the dissemination of information on decolonization,

1. *Approves* the activities in the field of dissemination of information on decolonization undertaken by the Department of Public Information and the Department of Political Affairs of the Secretariat;

2. *Considers it important* to continue its efforts to ensure the widest possible dissemination of information on decolonization, with particular emphasis on the options of self-determination available for the peoples of Non-Self-Governing Territories;

3. *Requests* the Department of Political Affairs and the Department of Public Information to take into account the suggestions of the Special Committee on the Situation with regard to the Implementation of the Declaration on the Granting of Independence to Colonial Countries and Peoples to continue their efforts to take measures through all the media available, including publications, radio and television, as well as the Internet, to give publicity to the work of the United Nations in the field of decolonization and, inter alia:

(a) To continue to collect, prepare and disseminate, particularly to the Territories, basic material on the issue of self-determination of the peoples of Non-Self-Governing Territories;

(b) To seek the full cooperation of the administering Powers in the discharge of the tasks referred to above;

(c) To maintain a working relationship with the appropriate regional and intergovernmental organizations, particularly in the Pacific and Caribbean regions, by holding periodic consultations and exchanging information;

(d) To encourage the involvement of non-governmental organizations in the dissemination of information on decolonization;

(e) To report to the Special Committee on measures taken in the implementation of the present resolution;

4. *Requests* all States, including the administering Powers, to continue to extend their cooperation in the dissemination of information referred to in paragraph 2 above;

5. *Requests* the Special Committee to follow the implementation of the present resolution and to report thereon to the General Assembly at its fifty-seventh session.

RECORDED VOTE ON RESOLUTION 56/73:

In favour: Algeria, Andorra, Angola, Argentina, Armenia, Australia, Austria, Azerbaijan, Bahamas, Bahrain, Bangladesh, Barbados, Belarus, Belgium, Belize, Bhutan, Bolivia, Botswana, Brazil, Brunei Darussalam, Bulgaria, Burkina Faso, Burundi, Cambodia, Canada, Cape Verde, Chile, China, Colombia, Comoros, Congo, Costa Rica, Côte d'Ivoire, Croatia, Cuba, Cyprus, Czech Republic, Democratic People's Republic of Korea, Denmark,

Djibouti, Dominican Republic, Ecuador, Egypt, El Salvador, Equatorial Guinea, Eritrea, Estonia, Ethiopia, Fiji, Finland, Gabon, Georgia, Germany, Ghana, Greece, Grenada, Guatemala, Guinea, Guyana, Haiti, Honduras, Hungary, Iceland, India, Indonesia, Iran, Ireland, Italy, Jamaica, Japan, Jordan, Kazakhstan, Kenya, Kuwait, Lao People's Democratic Republic, Latvia, Lebanon, Libyan Arab Jamahiriya, Liechtenstein, Lithuania, Luxembourg, Madagascar, Malaysia, Maldives, Mali, Malta, Mauritania, Mexico, Mongolia, Morocco, Mozambique, Myanmar, Namibia, Nepal, Netherlands, New Zealand, Nicaragua, Nigeria, Norway, Oman, Pakistan, Panama, Papua New Guinea, Paraguay, Peru, Philippines, Poland, Portugal, Qatar, Republic of Korea, Republic of Moldova, Romania, Russian Federation, Saint Lucia, San Marino, Saudi Arabia, Senegal, Seychelles, Sierra Leone, Singapore, Slovakia, Slovenia, Solomon Islands, South Africa, Spain, Sri Lanka, Sudan, Swaziland, Sweden, Syrian Arab Republic, Thailand, The former Yugoslav Republic of Macedonia, Togo, Tonga, Trinidad and Tobago, Tunisia, Turkey, Ukraine, United Arab Emirates, United Republic of Tanzania, Uruguay, Venezuela, Viet Nam, Yemen, Yugoslavia, Zambia, Zimbabwe.

Against: United Kingdom, United States.

Abstaining: France, Israel, Marshall Islands, Micronesia.

Speaking after the vote, the United Kingdom stated that it continued to view the obligation that the text placed on the Secretariat to publicize decolonization issues as an unwarranted drain on scarce UN resources.

Information on Territories

In response to General Assembly resolution 55/137 [YUN 2000, p. 558], the Secretary-General submitted a May report [A/56/67] showing the dates on which information on economic, social and educational conditions in NSGTs was transmitted to him from 1999 to 2001, under Article 73 *e* of the United Nations Charter.

GENERAL ASSEMBLY ACTION

On 10 December [meeting 82], the General Assembly, on the recommendation of the Fourth Committee [A/56/553], adopted **resolution 56/65** by recorded vote (149-0-6) [agenda item 91].

Information from Non-Self-Governing Territories transmitted under Article 73 *e* of the Charter of the United Nations

The General Assembly,

Having examined the chapter of the report of the Special Committee on the Situation with regard to the Implementation of the Declaration on the Granting of Independence to Colonial Countries and Peoples relating to the information from Non-Self-Governing Territories transmitted under Article 73 *e* of the Charter of the United Nations and the action taken by the Special Committee in respect of that information,

Having also examined the report of the Secretary-General,

Recalling its resolution 1970(XVIII) of 16 December 1963, in which it requested the Special Committee to study the information transmitted to the Secretary-General in accordance with Article 73 *e* of the Charter and to take such information fully into account in examining the situation with regard to the implementation of the Declaration on the Granting of Independence to Colonial Countries and Peoples, contained in General Assembly resolution 1514(XV) of 14 December 1960,

Recalling also its resolution 55/137 of 8 December 2000, in which it requested the Special Committee to

continue to discharge the functions entrusted to it under resolution 1970(XVIII),

Stressing the importance of timely transmission by the administering Powers of adequate information under Article 73 *e* of the Charter, in particular in relation to the preparation by the Secretariat of the working papers on the Territories concerned,

1. *Approves* the chapter of the report of the Special Committee on the Situation with regard to the Implementation of the Declaration on the Granting of Independence to Colonial Countries and Peoples relating to the information from Non-Self-Governing Territories transmitted under Article 73 *e* of the Charter of the United Nations;

2. *Reaffirms* that, in the absence of a decision by the General Assembly itself that a Non-Self-Governing Territory has attained a full measure of self-government in terms of Chapter XI of the Charter, the administering Power concerned should continue to transmit information under Article 73 *e* of the Charter with respect to that Territory;

3. *Requests* the administering Powers concerned to transmit or continue to transmit to the Secretary-General the information prescribed in Article 73 *e* of the Charter, as well as the fullest possible information on political and constitutional developments in the Territories concerned, within a maximum period of six months following the expiration of the administrative year in those Territories;

4. *Requests* the Secretary-General to continue to ensure that adequate information is drawn from all available published sources in connection with the preparation of the working papers relating to the Territories concerned;

5. *Requests* the Special Committee to continue to discharge the functions entrusted to it under General Assembly resolution 1970(XVIII), in accordance with established procedures.

RECORDED VOTE ON RESOLUTION 56/65:

In favour: Algeria, Andorra, Angola, Antigua and Barbuda, Argentina, Armenia, Australia, Austria, Azerbaijan, Bahamas, Bahrain, Bangladesh, Barbados, Belarus, Belgium, Belize, Benin, Bhutan, Bolivia, Botswana, Brazil, Brunei Darussalam, Bulgaria, Burkina Faso, Burundi, Cambodia, Cameroon, Canada, Cape Verde, Chile, China, Colombia, Congo, Costa Rica, Côte d'Ivoire, Croatia, Cuba, Cyprus, Czech Republic, Democratic People's Republic of Korea, Denmark, Djibouti, Dominican Republic, Ecuador, Egypt, El Salvador, Equatorial Guinea, Eritrea, Estonia, Ethiopia, Fiji, Finland, Gabon, Georgia, Germany, Ghana, Greece, Grenada, Guatemala, Guinea, Guyana, Haiti, Honduras, Hungary, Iceland, India, Indonesia, Iran, Ireland, Italy, Jamaica, Japan, Jordan, Kazakhstan, Kenya, Kuwait, Lao People's Democratic Republic, Latvia, Lebanon, Libyan Arab Jamahiriya, Liechtenstein, Lithuania, Luxembourg, Madagascar, Malaysia, Maldives, Mali, Malta, Mauritania, Mexico, Mongolia, Morocco, Mozambique, Myanmar, Namibia, Nepal, Netherlands, New Zealand, Nicaragua, Nigeria, Norway, Oman, Pakistan, Panama, Papua New Guinea, Paraguay, Peru, Philippines, Poland, Portugal, Qatar, Republic of Korea, Republic of Moldova, Romania, Russian Federation, Saint Lucia, San Marino, Saudi Arabia, Senegal, Seychelles, Sierra Leone, Singapore, Slovakia, Slovenia, Solomon Islands, South Africa, Spain, Sri Lanka, Sudan, Swaziland, Sweden, Syrian Arab Republic, Thailand, The former Yugoslav Republic of Macedonia, Togo, Tonga, Trinidad and Tobago, Tunisia, Turkey, Ukraine, United Arab Emirates, United Republic of Tanzania, Uruguay, Venezuela, Viet Nam, Yemen, Yugoslavia, Zambia, Zimbabwe.

Against: None.

Abstaining: France, Israel, Marshall Islands, Micronesia, United Kingdom, United States.

Study and training

In response to General Assembly resolution 55/140 [YUN 2000, p. 559], the Secretary-General reported on offers of study and training scholarships for inhabitants of NSGTs during the period 1 June 2000 to 7 June 2001 by seven Member States (Antigua and Barbuda, Argentina, Canada, Colombia, Mexico, Norway, Qatar) and one non-member State (Holy See) [A/56/88]. Fifty-three Member States and two non-member States had made such offers over the years.

GENERAL ASSEMBLY ACTION

On 10 December [meeting 82], the General Assembly, on the recommendation of the Fourth Committee [A/56/556], adopted **resolution 56/68** without vote [agenda item 94].

Offers by Member States of study and training facilities for inhabitants of Non-Self-Governing Territories

The General Assembly,

Recalling its resolution 55/140 of 8 December 2000,

Having examined the report of the Secretary-General on offers by Member States of study and training facilities for inhabitants of Non-Self-Governing Territories, prepared pursuant to its resolution 845(IX) of 22 November 1954,

Conscious of the importance of promoting the educational advancement of the inhabitants of Non-Self-Governing Territories,

Strongly convinced that the continuation and expansion of offers of scholarships is essential in order to meet the increasing need of students from Non-Self-Governing Territories for educational and training assistance, and considering that students in those Territories should be encouraged to avail themselves of such offers,

1. *Takes note* of the report of the Secretary-General;

2. *Expresses its appreciation* to those Member States that have made scholarships available to the inhabitants of Non-Self-Governing Territories;

3. *Invites* all States to make or continue to make generous offers of study and training facilities to the inhabitants of those Territories that have not yet attained self-government or independence and, wherever possible, to provide travel funds to prospective students;

4. *Urges* the administering Powers to take effective measures to ensure the widespread and continuous dissemination in the Territories under their administration of information relating to offers of study and training facilities made by States and to provide all the necessary facilities to enable students to avail themselves of such offers;

5. *Requests* the Secretary-General to report to the General Assembly at its fifty-seventh session on the implementation of the present resolution;

6. *Draws the attention* of the Special Committee on the Situation with regard to the Implementation of the Declaration on the Granting of Independence to Colonial Countries and Peoples to the present resolution.

Visiting missions

In June, the Special Committee on decolonization considered the question of sending visiting missions to NSGTs [A/56/23]. It adopted a resolution stressing the need to dispatch periodic visiting missions to facilitate the full implementation of the 1960 Declaration on decolonization, called on administering Powers to receive those missions in the Territories under their administration, and asked its Chairman to enter into consultations with the administering Power of Guam to facilitate a mission to that Territory to coincide with a proposed plebiscite scheduled for September 2002.

In draft resolutions on 11 small NSGTs (see p. 547) and on Tokelau (see p. 546), which it recommended to the General Assembly for adoption, the Committee endorsed a number of conclusions and recommendations concerning the sending of visiting missions to Territories.

Puerto Rico

In accordance with the Special Committee's 2000 resolution concerning the self-determination and independence of Puerto Rico [YUN 2000, p. 560], the Committee's Rapporteur, in a May report [A/AC.109/2001/L.3], described recent political developments, United States military and crime prevention activities in Puerto Rico, UN action and the views of the parties concerned on Puerto Rico's political status.

On the basis of its usual practice, the Committee acceded to requests for hearings from representatives of a number of organizations, who presented their views on 21 June [A/56/23]. The Committee adopted a resolution without vote by which it reaffirmed the inalienable right of the people of Puerto Rico to self-determination and independence; called on the United States to assume its responsibility to expedite a process to allow the Puerto Rican people to exercise that right; urged the United States to halt all military drills and manoeuvres on the island of Vieques and to return it to the people of Puerto Rico; and requested the Rapporteur to report in 2002 on the resolution's implementation.

Territories under review

East Timor

The Secretariat, in a working paper submitted in May [A/AC.109/2001/18], updated the Special Committee on decolonization on East Timor's transition to independence. The paper drew attention to the Secretary-General's report to the Security Council on 16 January [S/2001/42], in which he noted that a consensus had emerged among East Timorese leaders to seek independence by the end of 2001. Broad public consultations that began in 2000 had led to an agreement on a two-phased approach: a nationwide consultation and decisions regarding the electoral modalities and composition of the Constituent Assembly; and the drafting of a constitution by the Constituent Assembly. The modalities for the adoption of the constitution, whether by the Assembly or by referendum, were still under discussion. On 16 March, the regulation on the election of the Constituent Assembly was promulgated and the civil registration of all residents began. Those elections were held on 30 August.

(For further information on political and security developments and human rights issues relating to East Timor, see PART ONE, Chapter IV, and PART TWO, Chapter III, respectively.)

Falkland Islands (Malvinas)

The Special Committee on decolonization considered the question of the Falkland Islands (Malvinas) on 29 June [A/56/23], when it examined a Secretariat working paper on constitutional and political developments, mine clearance, and economic and social conditions in that Territory [A/AC.109/2001/11].

In a 3 January letter to the Secretary-General [A/55/729], Argentina transmitted a press communiqué reiterating its determination to recover sovereignty over the Malvinas and surrounding islands and maritime areas by peaceful means, and reaffirming its conviction that the resumption of negotiations with the United Kingdom on the sovereignty question would help create a framework for achieving a fair and lasting solution to the dispute. In response, the United Kingdom, on 19 March [A/55/843], restated that it had no doubt about its sovereignty over the Falkland Islands and the other Territories in question and rejected as unfounded any sovereignty claims by Argentina.

On 29 October [A/56/515], Argentina rejected a 1999 United Kingdom "White Paper on Partnership for Peace and Prosperity: Britain and the Overseas Territories" insofar as it referred to the Malvinas, South Georgia and South Sandwich Islands. It rejected their designation as Overseas Territories of the United Kingdom, as well as any attempt to introduce unilateral changes in that situation while the sovereignty dispute was still unresolved. The letter recalled several General Assembly resolutions recognizing the existence of a sovereignty dispute over those Territories.

On 10 November [A/56/PV.44], President Fernando de la Rúa of Argentina, in remarks before the General Assembly, recalled the repeated United Nations requests for Argentina and the United Kingdom to resume negotiations on a just and lasting solution to the sovereignty dispute. He reiterated Argentina's readiness to resume those bilateral negotiations and to support the Secretary-General's good offices mission to that end.

In exercise of its right of reply, the United Kingdom, in a 10 November letter to the Assembly President [A/56/616], welcomed the Argentine President's resolve to continue that bilateral dialogue, which would build on the positive exchanges between the two countries. The United Kingdom pointed out that the joint statement signed in 1999 [YUN 1999, p. 536] demonstrated clearly that the two countries could manage their differences over sovereignty, while making progress on matters of common interest in the South Atlantic but that did not compromise the United Kingdom's position on sovereignty. It had a duty to respect the right to self-determination of the people of the Falkland Islands, whose representatives had expressed to the Special Committee on 29 June the wish to exercise that right. The British Government remained committed to the joint statement and, despite their differences, was confident that the two countries could build on it and that their relations would continue to flourish in the spirit of cooperation and mutual interest.

In that context, Argentina and the United Kingdom conveyed to the Secretary-General, in a joint letter of 19 November [A/56/639], the text of an exchange of notes on an understanding between the two Governments to carry out a feasibility study on the clearance of landmines in the Falkland Islands (Malvinas).

By **decision 56/410** of 26 November, the Assembly deferred consideration of the item on the Falkland Islands (Malvinas) and included it in the provisional agenda of its fifty-seventh (2002) session.

Gibraltar

The Special Committee on decolonization considered the question of Gibraltar on 19 and 29 June [A/56/23]. Before it was a working paper describing political developments and economic and social conditions in the Territory, and setting forth the positions of the United Kingdom (the administering Power), Gibraltar and Spain concerning Gibraltar's future status [A/AC.109/2001/10].

In statements made to the Foreign Affairs Committees of the Spanish Senate and the Spanish Congress on 8 February and 14 March, respectively, the Minister for Foreign Affairs reaffirmed Spain's long-standing goal of regaining sovereignty over Gibraltar, while on 15 March, the Spanish President, according to press reports, cautioned that any change in the status of the Territory would be considered a serious violation of the 1713 Treaty of Utrecht and a very grave act.

Regular discussions continued between Gibraltar and United Kingdom officials, including talks on modernizing Gibraltar's Constitution. According to the Government of Gibraltar, its Select Committee on Constitutional Reform aimed to propose to the United Kingdom reforms that would end the Territory's colonial status through self-determination. According to British and Spanish press reports, the United Kingdom reiterated that it would consider only constitutional reform proposals by Gibraltar that were in line with international obligations, including the Treaty of Utrecht. A further statement issued by the United Kingdom on 11 April reiterated its defence of Gibraltar's interests and its intention to continue regular meetings and ongoing discussions with officials in Gibraltar on key matters of mutual interest.

After hearing statements by Spain, the Chief Minister of Gibraltar and the Leader of the Opposition, the Special Committee decided to continue consideration of the question in 2002.

GENERAL ASSEMBLY ACTION

In December, the General Assembly, on the recommendation of the Fourth Committee [A/56/557], adopted **decision 56/421** without vote [agenda item 18].

Question of Gibraltar

At its 82nd plenary meeting, on 10 December 2001, the General Assembly, on the recommendation of the Special Political and Decolonization Committee (Fourth Committee), adopted the following text:

"The General Assembly, recalling its decision 55/427 of 8 December 2000, and recalling at the same time that the statement agreed to by the Governments of Spain and the United Kingdom of Great Britain and Northern Ireland at Brussels on 27 November 1984 stipulated, inter alia, the following:

'The establishment of a negotiating process aimed at overcoming all the differences between them over Gibraltar and at promoting cooperation on a mutually beneficial basis on economic, cultural, touristic, aviation, military and environmental matters. Both sides accept that the issues of sovereignty will be discussed in that process. The British Government will fully maintain its commitment to honour the wishes of the people of Gibraltar as set out in the preamble of the 1969 Constitution',

takes note of the fact that, as part of this process, the Ministers for Foreign Affairs of Spain and of the United Kingdom of Great Britain and Northern Ireland hold annual meetings alternately in each capital, the most recent of which was held in London on 26 July 2001, and urges both Governments to continue their negotiations with the object of reaching a definitive solution to the problem of Gibraltar

in the light of relevant resolutions of the General Assembly and in the spirit of the Charter of the United Nations."

In a 7 May letter [S/2001/453], Spain drew attention to the final report of the Monitoring Mechanism on Sanctions with regard to Angola [S/2000/1225 & Corr.1,2], which contained a reference to Gibraltar that it felt implied that Gibraltar was a country. Spain wished to make clear that Gibraltar was an NSGT administered by the United Kingdom, subject to the decolonization process and over which Spain maintained a claim of sovereignty.

New Caledonia

The Special Committee on decolonization considered the question of New Caledonia on 29 June and 2 and 3 July [A/56/23]. Before it was a Secretariat working paper describing the political situation and economic developments in the Territory [A/AC.109/2001/14].

In accordance with the 1998 Nouméa Accord on the Territory's future status [YUN 1998, p. 574], the transfer of power from France (the administering Power) continued in 2001. Several services and jurisdictions were transferred to the Government of New Caledonia, and measures were under way to transfer the Institut de Formation des Personnels Administratifs and the Office des Postes et Télécommunications. A later Secretariat working paper [A/AC.109/2002/13] reported that, according to the French Government, the new institutions remained steady throughout 2001, in spite of uncertainties in the political sphere, and there was progress in redressing the Territory's economic imbalance and intensifying regional ties. Seven new "laws of the country", mainly related to labour conditions, were enacted.

The first municipal elections after the signing of the Nouméa Accord were held from 11 to 18 March, with the integrationist Rassemblement pour la Calédonie dans la République (RPCR) receiving 58 per cent of the vote and the pro-independence Front de libération nationale kanak socialiste (FLNKS), 37 per cent. In new elections held on 5 April, following the resignation of President Jean Lècques, Pierre Frogier of RPCR was elected New Caledonia's second President and Déwé Gorodey of FLNKS, Vice-President. RPCR held six portfolios in the new Cabinet and its ally, the Fédération des comités de coopération indépendantistes, one. FLNKS held three portfolios, and one of its components, Union Calédonienne, held one. Rotation of the presidency of the Customary Senate proceeded according to plan. The Senate currently focused on land tenure and on making French law and customary law compatible.

However, progress continued to be hindered by the friction between RPCR and FLNKS, owing to their differing interpretations of "collegiality" in government matters. Those opposing positions remained acute throughout 2001, particularly over the FLNKS insistence on participation in the Government's decision-making process. That disagreement was heightened in September when the French State Council invalidated the appointment of an FLNKS government member because of irregularities in the April congressional elections, weakening the FLNKS position in the Government. In October, FLNKS expressed its disagreement over that decision and announced that its two remaining Cabinet members would not take part in government affairs until it had reviewed its position at a party Congress. That was further complicated by internal divisions within FLNKS over the issue of leadership.

The French Secretary of State for Overseas Territories visited New Caledonia in November, after which both FLNKS and RPCR agreed to hold a second meeting of signatories of the Nouméa Accord in January 2002. Meanwhile, tensions arising from the increasing arrivals of settlers from the French Territory of Wallis and Futuna led to violent confrontations in December with the local Kanak community, which demanded that all Wallisians leave Kanak tribal land.

The issue of voter eligibility [YUN 1999, p. 538] remained unsettled, as ratification of a constitutional amendment by a joint session of the French National Assembly and the Senate was indefinitely postponed.

At its 3 July meeting, the Special Committee adopted a resolution on the question of New Caledonia [A/AC.109/2001/28], deciding to keep under continuous review the Nouméa Accord process and to report to the General Assembly in 2002.

GENERAL ASSEMBLY ACTION

On 10 December [meeting 82], the General Assembly, on the recommendation of the Fourth Committee [A/56/557], adopted **resolution 56/70** without vote [agenda item 18].

Question of New Caledonia

The General Assembly,

Having considered the question of New Caledonia,

Having examined the chapter of the report of the Special Committee on the Situation with regard to the Implementation of the Declaration on the Granting of Independence to Colonial Countries and Peoples relating to New Caledonia,

Reaffirming the right of peoples to self-determination as enshrined in the Charter of the United Nations,

Recalling its resolutions 1514(XV) of 14 December 1960 and 1541(XV) of 15 December 1960,

Noting the importance of the positive measures being pursued in New Caledonia by the French authorities, in cooperation with all sectors of the population, to promote political, economic and social development in the Territory, including measures in the area of environmental protection and action with respect to drug abuse and trafficking, in order to provide a framework for its peaceful progress to self-determination,

Noting also, in this context, the importance of equitable economic and social development, as well as continued dialogue among the parties involved in New Caledonia in the preparation of the act of self-determination of New Caledonia,

Noting with satisfaction the intensification of contacts between New Caledonia and neighbouring countries of the South Pacific region,

1. *Welcomes* the significant developments that have taken place in New Caledonia as exemplified by the signing of the Nouméa Accord of 5 May 1998 between the representatives of New Caledonia and the Government of France;

2. *Urges* all parties involved, in the interest of all of the people of New Caledonia, to maintain, in the framework of the Nouméa Accord, their dialogue in a spirit of harmony;

3. *Notes* the relevant provisions of the Nouméa Accord aimed at taking more broadly into account the Kanak identity in the political and social organization of New Caledonia, and also those provisions of the Accord relating to control of immigration and protection of local employment;

4. *Also notes* the relevant provisions of the Nouméa Accord to the effect that New Caledonia may become a member or an associate member of certain international organizations, such as international organizations in the Pacific region, the United Nations, the United Nations Educational, Scientific and Cultural Organization and the International Labour Organization, in accordance with their regulations;

5. *Further notes* the agreement between the signatories of the Nouméa Accord that the progress made in the emancipation process shall be brought to the attention of the United Nations;

6. *Welcomes* the fact that the administering Power invited to New Caledonia, at the time the new institutions were established, a mission of information which comprised representatives of countries of the Pacific region;

7. *Calls upon* the administering Power to transmit information regarding the political, economic and social situation of New Caledonia to the Secretary-General;

8. *Invites* all parties involved to continue to promote a framework for the peaceful progress of the Territory towards an act of self-determination in which all options are open and which would safeguard the rights of all New Caledonians according to the letter and the spirit of the Nouméa Accord, which is based on the principle that it is for the populations of New Caledonia to choose how to control their destiny;

9. *Welcomes* measures that have been taken to strengthen and diversify the New Caledonian economy

in all fields, and encourages further such measures in accordance with the spirit of the Matignon and Nouméa Accords;

10. *Also welcomes* the importance attached by the parties to the Matignon and Nouméa Accords to greater progress in housing, employment, training, education and health care in New Caledonia;

11. *Acknowledges* the contribution of the Melanesian Cultural Centre to the protection of the indigenous culture of New Caledonia;

12. *Notes* the positive initiatives aimed at protecting the natural environment of New Caledonia, notably the "Zonéco" operation designed to map and evaluate marine resources within the economic zone of New Caledonia;

13. *Acknowledges* the close links between New Caledonia and the peoples of the South Pacific and the positive actions being taken by the French and territorial authorities to facilitate the further development of those links, including the development of closer relations with the countries members of the Pacific Islands Forum;

14. *Welcomes,* in this regard, the accession by New Caledonia to the status of observer in the Pacific Islands Forum, continuing high-level visits to New Caledonia by delegations from countries of the Pacific region and high-level visits by delegations from New Caledonia to countries members of the Pacific Islands Forum;

15. *Decides* to keep under continuous review the process unfolding in New Caledonia as a result of the signing of the Nouméa Accord;

16. *Requests* the Special Committee on the Situation with regard to the Implementation of the Declaration on the Granting of Independence to Colonial Countries and Peoples to continue to examine the question of the Non-Self-Governing Territory of New Caledonia and to report thereon to the General Assembly at its fifty-seventh session.

Tokelau

The Special Committee on decolonization considered, on 28 June, the question of Tokelau (the three small atolls of Nukunonu, Fakaofo and Atafu in the South Pacific), administered by New Zealand [A/56/23]. Before it was a Secretariat working paper detailing constitutional and political developments, as well as economic and social conditions in the Territory, and setting out the positions of New Zealand and Tokelau on the Territory's future status [A/AC.109/2001/5].

According to New Zealand, Tokelau had advanced its governance project, enabling the gradual implementation of the Modern House of Tokelau project [YUN 1998, p. 575]. Starting in January, a transition team [YUN 2000, p. 563] spent two weeks on each atoll to consult on good governance, conduct workshops, review national and village administration, complete training needs identification and inform people about the project. On 8 March, a Joint Committee [ibid.] charged with Modern House project oversight met to review

progress. The Joint Committee noted the Taupulega's (each village's Council of Elders) agreement to a village governance structure for Nukunonu and the appointment of a village General Manager; approved a capacity-building programme and the appointment of a 12-month National Project Manager and part-time village coordinators; and decided to develop a Modern House web site. It agreed that the Taupulega was the basis of government and decision-making; that new structures should promote public service, incorporating both national and village services; and that Tokelau's limited resources and skills should be maximized through the coordination, integration and sharing of services.

On 10 February, the General Fono (Tokelau's national representative body) adopted the Tokelau Public Service Rules 2001, establishing a three-member Tokelau Employment Commission to succeed the State Services Commissioner in New Zealand. A later working paper [A/AC.109/2002/6] reported that Tokelau officially took over local public services as scheduled on 1 July. In November, the General Fono approved a Tokelau Public Service manual, setting down principles governing service, terms and conditions of work, as well as guidance for public servants.

The General Fono also changed the basis for its membership from the current system of equal representation (six members for each of the three atolls) to a new system of proportional representation based on the 2001 census. Under the new structure, seats in the new 21-member Fono would be determined by each atoll's population size (8 from Atafu, 7 from Fakaofo and 6 from Nukunonu).

Meetings were held in New York in June between the *Ulu-o-Tokelau* (titular head of the Territory), his delegation, the Administrator and the Special Committee's Working Group for the Pacific Region, to develop a programme of work defining key activities and to assist in assessing Tokelau's progress towards self-determination. It was agreed that the programme of work would be revised and expanded as the situation evolved.

On 8 October, New Zealand, in a statement to the Fourth Committee, said that Tokelau and New Zealand saw self-determination as a dynamic and evolving process. New Zealand's withdrawal of its State Services Commissioner as employer of the Tokelau Public Service was a major step towards self-government, and Tokelau's international identity was developing with its admission as an associate member of the United Nations Educational, Scientific and Cultural Organization (UNESCO) on 15 October. At issue in Tokelau was not the elimination of colonialism but a resolution of issues of governance; New

Zealand continued to respect Tokelau's wish to move at its own pace towards self-determination.

On 28 June, the *Ulu-o-Tokelau* told the Special Committee that the act of self-determination would not be a sudden vote on the options available but was a long process of elimination and negotiation with the administering Power on the merits and demerits of the free association and integration options.

Governance and capacity-building were two important areas that would continue to be consolidated through the Modern House project, and much energy would be required to support the equal development of all three villages, especially the councils of elders, which would be a major focus in the coming months. Of equal importance was the attention paid to the economic sector. New Zealand had demonstrated its commitment to the Tokelau process with extra resources and material support for the Modern House project and the Tokelau Trust Fund, and the depth of understanding of the Administrator had contributed immensely to the success of the Tokelau process.

GENERAL ASSEMBLY ACTION

On 10 December [meeting 82], the General Assembly, on the recommendation of the Fourth Committee [A/56/557], adopted **resolution 56/71** without vote [agenda item 18].

Question of Tokelau

The General Assembly,

Having considered the question of Tokelau,

Having examined the chapter of the report of the Special Committee on the Situation with regard to the Implementation of the Declaration on the Granting of Independence to Colonial Countries and Peoples relating to the question of Tokelau,

Recalling the solemn declaration on the future status of Tokelau, delivered by the *Ulu-o-Tokelau* (the highest authority on Tokelau) on 30 July 1994, which states that an act of self-determination in Tokelau is now under active consideration, together with the constitution of a self-governing Tokelau, and that the present preference of Tokelau is for a status of free association with New Zealand,

Recalling also its resolution 1514(XV) of 14 December 1960, containing the Declaration on the Granting of Independence to Colonial Countries and Peoples, and all resolutions and decisions of the United Nations relating to Non-Self-Governing Territories, in particular General Assembly resolution 55/143 of 8 December 2000,

Recalling further the emphasis placed in the solemn declaration on the terms of Tokelau's special relationship with New Zealand, including the expectation that the form of help that Tokelau could continue to expect from New Zealand in promoting the well-being of its people, besides its external interests, would be clearly established within the framework of that relationship,

Noting with appreciation the continuing exemplary cooperation of New Zealand as the administering Power with regard to the work of the Special Committee relating to Tokelau and its readiness to permit access by United Nations visiting missions to the Territory,

Noting also with appreciation the collaborative contribution to the development of Tokelau by New Zealand and the specialized agencies and other organizations of the United Nations system, in particular the United Nations Development Programme and the World Health Organization,

Recalling the dispatch in 1994 of a United Nations visiting mission to Tokelau,

Noting that, as a small island Territory, Tokelau exemplifies the situation of most remaining Non-Self-Governing Territories,

Noting also that, as a case study pointing to successful decolonization, Tokelau has wider significance for the United Nations as it seeks to complete its work in decolonization,

1. *Notes* that Tokelau remains firmly committed to the development of self-government and to an act of self-determination that would result in Tokelau assuming a status in accordance with the options on future status for Non-Self-Governing Territories contained in principle VI of the annex to General Assembly resolution 1541(XV) of 15 December 1960;

2. *Also notes* the desire of Tokelau to move at its own pace towards an act of self-determination;

3. *Further notes* the inauguration in 1999 of a national Government based on village elections by universal adult suffrage;

4. *Acknowledges* Tokelau's goal to return authority to its traditional leadership, and its wish to provide that leadership with the necessary support to carry out its functions in the contemporary world;

5. *Also acknowledges* the progress made towards that goal under the Modern House of Tokelau project, and Tokelau's view that that project, in its governance and economic development dimensions, is seen by its people as the means to achieving their act of self-determination;

6. *Notes* that, consistent with the expressed desires of past traditional leaders and the principles of the Modern House of Tokelau, Tokelau has established a local public service employer which enabled the New Zealand State Services Commissioner to withdraw from his role as employer of the Tokelau Public Service as from 30 June 2001;

7. *Also notes* the positive outcomes of the visit by the elected village and national leaders to New Zealand in May 2001;

8. *Welcomes* the initiation of the dialogue with the administering Power and the Territory in June 2001 with a view to the development of a programme of work for Tokelau in accordance with General Assembly resolution 55/147 of 8 December 2000;

9. *Acknowledges* the continuing support which New Zealand has committed to the Modern House of Tokelau project in the period 2001-2002, and the cooperation of the United Nations Development Programme in aligning its programmes under the project;

10. *Notes* that the Constitution of a self-governing Tokelau will continue to develop as a part and as a consequence of the building of the Modern House of To-

kelau, and that both have national and international importance for Tokelau;

11. *Acknowledges* Tokelau's need for continued reassurance given the cultural adjustments that are taking place with the strengthening of its capacity for self-government and, given that local resources cannot adequately cover the material side of self-determination, the ongoing responsibility of Tokelau's external partners to assist Tokelau in balancing its desire to be self-reliant to the greatest extent possible with its need for external assistance;

12. *Notes* the special challenge inherent in the situation of Tokelau, among the smallest of the small Territories, and how a Territory's exercise of its inalienable right to self-determination may be brought closer, as in the case of Tokelau, by the meeting of that challenge in innovative ways;

13. *Welcomes* the assurance of the Government of New Zealand that it will meet its obligations to the United Nations with respect to Tokelau and abide by the freely expressed wishes of the people of Tokelau with regard to their future status;

14. *Also welcomes* the application by Tokelau, with the full support of New Zealand, for associate membership in the United Nations Educational, Scientific and Cultural Organization, and its application for full membership in the Forum Fisheries Agency;

15. *Calls upon* the administering Power and United Nations agencies to continue to provide assistance to Tokelau as it further develops its economy and governance structures in the context of its ongoing constitutional evolution;

16. *Requests* the Special Committee on the Situation with regard to the Implementation of the Declaration on the Granting of Independence to Colonial Countries and Peoples to continue to examine the question of the Non-Self-Governing Territory of Tokelau and to report thereon to the General Assembly at its fifty-seventh session.

Western Sahara

The Special Committee on decolonization considered the question of Western Sahara on 21 June [A/56/23]. A Secretariat working paper [A/AC.109/2001/12] provided details of the Secretary-General's good offices with the parties concerned and action taken by the General Assembly and the Security Council (see p. 213). The Special Committee transmitted the relevant documentation to the Assembly's fifty-sixth (2001) session to facilitate the Fourth Committee's consideration of the question. The Secretary-General's report was submitted to the Assembly in July [A/56/159].

Island Territories

The Special Committee on decolonization [A/56/23] considered working papers prepared by the Secretariat on American Samoa [A/AC.109/2001/17], Anguilla [A/AC.109/2001/13], Bermuda [A/AC.109/2001/9], the British Virgin Islands [A/AC.109/2001/8], the Cayman Islands [A/AC.109/2001/15], Guam [A/AC.109/2001/4], Montserrat

[A/AC.109/2001/6], Pitcairn [A/AC.109/2001/2], St. Helena [A/AC.109/2001/16], the Turks and Caicos Islands [A/AC.109/2001/7] and the United States Virgin Islands [A/AC.109/2001/3], describing political developments and economic and social conditions in each of those 11 island Territories. On 28 June, the Committee approved a two-part consolidated draft resolution for adoption by the General Assembly (see below).

GENERAL ASSEMBLY ACTION

On 10 December [meeting 82], the General Assembly, on the recommendation of the Fourth Committee [A/56/557], adopted **resolutions 56/72 A** and **B** without vote [agenda item 18].

Questions of American Samoa, Anguilla, Bermuda, the British Virgin Islands, the Cayman Islands, Guam, Montserrat, Pitcairn, St. Helena, the Turks and Caicos Islands and the United States Virgin Islands

A
General

The General Assembly,

Having considered the questions of American Samoa, Anguilla, Bermuda, the British Virgin Islands, the Cayman Islands, Guam, Montserrat, Pitcairn, St. Helena, the Turks and Caicos Islands and the United States Virgin Islands, hereinafter referred to as "the Territories",

Having examined the relevant chapter of the report of the Special Committee on the Situation with regard to the Implementation of the Declaration on the Granting of Independence to Colonial Countries and Peoples,

Recalling its resolution 1514(XV) of 14 December 1960, containing the Declaration on the Granting of Independence to Colonial Countries and Peoples, and all resolutions and decisions of the United Nations relating to those Territories, including, in particular, the resolutions adopted by the General Assembly at its fifty-fifth session on the individual Territories covered by the present resolution,

Recognizing that the specific characteristics and the sentiments of the peoples of the Territories require flexible, practical and innovative approaches to the options for self-determination, without any prejudice to territorial size, geographical location, size of population or natural resources,

Recalling its resolution 1541(XV) of 15 December 1960, containing the principles that should guide Member States in determining whether or not an obligation exists to transmit the information called for under Article 73 *e* of the Charter of the United Nations,

Expressing its concern that, even forty-one years after the adoption of the Declaration, there still remain a number of Non-Self-Governing Territories,

Acknowledging the significant achievements by the international community towards the eradication of colonialism in accordance with the Declaration, and conscious of the importance of continuing effective implementation of the Declaration, taking into account the target set by the United Nations to eradicate colonialism by 2010 and the plan of action for the Second International Decade for the Eradication of Colonialism,

Noting the positive constitutional developments in some Non-Self-Governing Territories about which the Special Committee has received information, while also acknowledging the need for recognition to be given to expressions of self-determination by the peoples of the Territories consistent with practice under the Charter,

Recognizing that in the decolonization process there is no alternative to the principle of self-determination as enunciated by the General Assembly in its resolutions 1514(XV), 1541(XV) and other resolutions,

Welcoming the stated position of the Government of the United Kingdom of Great Britain and Northern Ireland that it continues to take seriously its obligations under the Charter to develop self-government in the dependent Territories and, in cooperation with the locally elected Governments, to ensure that their constitutional frameworks continue to meet the wishes of the people, and the emphasis that it is ultimately for the peoples of the Territories to decide their future status,

Welcoming also the stated position of the Government of the United States of America that it supports fully the principles of decolonization and takes seriously its obligations under the Charter to promote to the utmost the well-being of the inhabitants of the Territories under United States administration,

Aware of the special circumstances of the geographical location and economic conditions of each Territory, and bearing in mind the necessity of promoting economic stability and diversifying and strengthening further the economies of the respective Territories as a matter of priority,

Conscious of the particular vulnerability of the Territories to natural disasters and environmental degradation and, in this connection, bearing in mind the programmes of action of the United Nations Conference on Environment and Development, the World Conference on Natural Disaster Reduction, the Global Conference on the Sustainable Development of Small Island Developing States and other relevant world conferences,

Aware of the usefulness both to the Territories and to the Special Committee of the participation of appointed and elected representatives of the Territories in the work of the Special Committee,

Convinced that the wishes and aspirations of the peoples of the Territories should continue to guide the development of their future political status and that referendums, free and fair elections and other forms of popular consultation play an important role in ascertaining the wishes and aspirations of the people,

Convinced also that any negotiations to determine the status of a Territory must not take place without the active involvement and participation of the people of that Territory,

Recognizing that all available options for self-determination of the Territories are valid as long as they are in accordance with the freely expressed wishes of the peoples concerned and in conformity with the clearly defined principles contained in resolutions 1514(XV), 1541(XV) and other resolutions of the General Assembly,

Mindful that United Nations visiting missions provide an effective means of ascertaining the situation in the Territories, and considering that the possibility of sending further visiting missions to the Territories at an appropriate time and in consultation with the administering Powers should be kept under review,

Mindful also that, by holding a Caribbean regional seminar at Havana from 23 to 25 May 2001, the Special Committee was able to hear the views of the representatives of the Territories, as well as Governments and organizations in the region, in order to review the political, economic and social conditions in the Territories,

Mindful further that, in order for it to enhance its understanding of the political status of the peoples of the Territories and to fulfil its mandate effectively, it is important for the Special Committee to be apprised by the administering Powers and to receive information from other appropriate sources, including the representatives of the Territories, concerning the wishes and aspirations of the peoples of the Territories,

Mindful, in this connection, that the holding of regional seminars in the Caribbean and Pacific regions and at Headquarters and other venues, with the active participation of representatives of the Non-Self-Governing Territories, provides a helpful means for the Special Committee to fulfil its mandate, while recognizing the need for reviewing the role of those seminars in the context of a United Nations programme for ascertaining the political status of the Territories,

Mindful also that some Territories have not received a United Nations visiting mission for a long period of time and that no visiting missions have been sent to some of the Territories,

Noting with appreciation the contribution to the development of some Territories by specialized agencies and other organizations of the United Nations system, in particular the United Nations Development Programme, and regional institutions such as the Caribbean Development Bank,

Noting that some territorial Governments have made efforts towards achieving the highest standards of financial supervision, but that some others have been listed by the Organisation for Economic Cooperation and Development as having met the criteria of a tax haven according to its definition, and noting also that some territorial Governments have expressed concern about insufficient dialogue between them and the Organisation,

Recalling the ongoing efforts of the Special Committee in carrying out a critical review of its work with the aim of making appropriate and constructive recommendations and decisions to attain its objectives in accordance with its mandate,

1. *Reaffirms* the inalienable right of the peoples of the Territories to self-determination, including, if they so wish, independence, in conformity with the Charter of the United Nations and with General Assembly resolution 1514(XV), containing the Declaration on the Granting of Independence to Colonial Countries and Peoples;

2. *Reaffirms also* that it is ultimately for the peoples of the Territories themselves to determine freely their future political status in accordance with the relevant provisions of the Charter, the Declaration and the relevant resolutions of the General Assembly, and in that connection calls upon the administering Powers, in cooperation with the territorial Governments, to facili-

tate programmes of political education in the Territories in order to foster an awareness among the people of their right to self-determination in conformity with the legitimate political status options, based on the principles clearly defined in General Assembly resolution 1541(XV);

3. *Requests* the administering Powers to transmit to the Secretary-General information called for under Article 73 *e* of the Charter and other updated information and reports, including reports on the wishes and aspirations of the peoples of the Territories regarding their future political status as expressed in fair and free referendums and other forms of popular consultation, as well as the results of any informed and democratic processes consistent with practice under the Charter that indicate the clear and freely expressed wish of the people to change the existing status of the Territories;

4. *Stresses* the importance for it to be apprised of the views and wishes of the peoples of the Territories and to enhance its understanding of their conditions;

5. *Reaffirms* that United Nations visiting missions to the Territories at an appropriate time and in consultation with the administering Powers are an effective means of ascertaining the situation in the Territories, and requests the administering Powers and the elected representatives of the peoples of the Territories to assist the Special Committee on the Situation with regard to the Implementation of the Declaration on the Granting of Independence to Colonial Countries and Peoples in this regard;

6. *Reaffirms also* the responsibility of the administering Powers under the Charter to promote the economic and social development and to preserve the cultural identity of the Territories, and recommends that priority continue to be given, in consultation with the territorial Governments concerned, to the strengthening and diversification of their respective economies;

7. *Requests* the administering Powers, in consultation with the peoples of the Territories, to take all necessary measures to protect and conserve the environment of the Territories under their administration against any environmental degradation, and requests the specialized agencies concerned to continue to monitor environmental conditions in those Territories;

8. *Calls upon* the administering Powers, in cooperation with the respective territorial Governments, to continue to take all necessary measures to counter problems related to drug trafficking, money-laundering and other offences;

9. *Calls upon* the administering Powers to enter into constructive dialogue with the Special Committee before the fifty-sixth session of the General Assembly to develop a framework for the implementation of provisions of Article 73 *e* of the Charter and the Declaration on the Granting of Independence to the Colonial Countries and Peoples for the period 2001-2010;

10. *Notes* the particular circumstances that prevail in the Territories concerned, and encourages the political evolution in them towards self-determination;

11. *Urges* Member States to contribute to the efforts of the United Nations to usher in the twenty-first century in a world free of colonialism, and calls upon them to continue to give their full support to the Special Committee in its endeavours towards that noble goal;

12. *Invites* the specialized agencies and other organizations of the United Nations system to initiate or to continue to take all necessary measures to accelerate progress in the social and economic life of the Territories, and calls for closer cooperation between the Special Committee and the Economic and Social Council in furtherance of the provision of assistance to the Territories;

13. *Takes note* of statements made by the elected representatives of the Territories concerned emphasizing their willingness to cooperate with all international efforts aimed at preventing abuse of the international financial system and to promote regulatory environments with highly selective licensing procedures, robust supervisory practices and well-established anti-money-laundering regimes;

14. *Calls* for an enhanced and constructive dialogue between the Organisation for Economic Cooperation and Development and the concerned territorial Governments with a view to bringing about the changes needed to meet the highest standards of transparency and information exchange in order to facilitate the removal of those Non-Self-Governing Territories from the list of jurisdictions classified as tax havens, and requests the administering Powers to assist those Territories in resolving the matter;

15. *Requests* the Secretary-General to report to the General Assembly on the implementation of decolonization resolutions since the declaration of the International Decade for the Eradication of Colonialism;

16. *Requests* the Special Committee to continue its examination of the question of the small Territories and to report thereon to the General Assembly at its fifty-seventh session with recommendations on appropriate ways to assist the peoples of the Territories in exercising their right to self-determination.

B
Individual territories
The General Assembly,
Referring to resolution A above,

I
American Samoa

Taking note of the report by the administering Power that most American Samoan leaders express satisfaction with the Territory's present relationship with the United States of America,

Taking note with interest of the statement made and the information on the political and economic situation in American Samoa provided by the Governor of American Samoa and the delegate of American Samoa to the United States Congress to the Caribbean regional seminar, held at Havana from 23 to 25 May 2001,

Noting that the Government of the Territory continues to have significant financial, budgetary and internal control problems and that the Territory's deficit and financial condition are compounded by the high demand for governmental services from the rapidly growing population, a limited economic and tax base and recent natural disasters,

Noting also that the Territory, similar to isolated communities with limited funds, continues to experience a lack of adequate medical facilities and other infrastructural requirements,

Aware of the efforts of the Government of the Territory to control and reduce expenditures, while continuing its programme of expanding and diversifying the local economy,

1. *Requests* the administering Power, bearing in mind the views of the people of the Territory ascertained through a democratic process, to keep the Secretary-General informed of the wishes and aspirations of the people regarding their future political status;

2. *Calls upon* the administering Power to continue to assist the territorial Government in the economic and social development of the Territory, including measures to rebuild financial management capabilities and strengthen other governmental functions of the Government of the Territory;

3. *Welcomes* the invitation extended to the Special Committee on the Situation with regard to the Implementation of the Declaration on the Granting of Independence to Colonial Countries and Peoples by the Governor of American Samoa to send a visiting mission to the Territory;

II
Anguilla

Conscious of the commitment of both the Government of Anguilla and the administering Power to a new and closer policy of dialogue and partnership through the Strategic Country Programme 2000-2003,

Aware of the efforts of the Government of Anguilla to continue to develop the Territory as a viable offshore centre and well-regulated financial centre for investors, by enacting modern company and trust laws, as well as partnership and insurance legislation, and computerizing the company registry system,

Noting the need for continued cooperation between the administering Power and the territorial Government in tackling the problems of drug trafficking and money-laundering,

Noting also that general elections were held on 3 March 2000, resulting in a new coalition government in the House of Assembly,

1. *Requests* the administering Power, bearing in mind the views of the people of the Territory ascertained through a democratic process, to keep the Secretary-General informed of the wishes and aspirations of the people regarding their future political status;

2. *Calls upon* the administering Power and all States, organizations and United Nations agencies to continue to assist the Territory in social and economic development;

3. *Welcomes* the Country Cooperation Framework of the United Nations Development Programme for the period 1997-1999 currently being implemented following consultations with the territorial Government and key development partners in the United Nations system and the donor community;

4. *Also welcomes* the assessment by the United Nations Development Programme that the Territory has made considerable progress in the domain of sustainable human development and in its sound management and preservation of the environment, which has been incorporated into the National Tourism Plan;

5. *Further welcomes* the assessment by the Caribbean Development Bank in its 1999 report on the Territory that, despite economic contraction in the first quarter,

the economy rebounded to reach 6 per cent growth during 1999;

III
Bermuda

Noting the results of the independence referendum held on 16 August 1995, and conscious of the different viewpoints of the political parties of the Territory on the future status of the Territory,

Noting also the functioning of the democratic process and the smooth transition of government in November 1998,

Noting further the comments made by the administering Power in its White Paper entitled "Partnership for Progress and Prosperity: Britain and the Overseas Territories",

1. *Requests* the administering Power, bearing in mind the views of the people of the Territory ascertained through a democratic process, to keep the Secretary-General informed of the wishes and aspirations of the people regarding their future political status;

2. *Calls upon* the administering Power to continue to work with the Territory for its socio-economic development;

3. *Requests* the administering Power to elaborate, in consultation with the territorial Government, programmes specifically intended to alleviate the economic, social and environmental consequences of the closure of the military bases and installations of the United States of America in the Territory;

IV
British Virgin Islands

Noting the completion of the constitutional review in the Territory and the coming into force of the amended Constitution, and noting also the results of the general elections held on 17 May 1999,

Noting also the results of the constitutional review of 1993-1994, which made it clear that a prerequisite to independence must be a constitutionally expressed wish by the people as a result of a referendum,

Taking note of the statement made in 1995 by the Chief Minister of the British Virgin Islands that the Territory was ready for constitutional and political advancement towards full internal self-government and that the administering Power should assist through the gradual transfer of power to elected territorial representatives,

Noting that the Territory is emerging as one of the world's leading offshore financial centres,

Noting also the need for continued cooperation between the administering Power and the territorial Government in countering drug trafficking and money-laundering,

Noting further that the Territory commemorated its annual British Virgin Islands–United States Virgin Islands Friendship Day on 27 May 2000 in official ceremonies on Tortola,

1. *Requests* the administering Power, bearing in mind the views of the people of the Territory ascertained through a democratic process, to keep the Secretary-General informed of the wishes and aspirations of the people regarding their future political status;

2. *Requests* the administering Power, the specialized agencies and other organizations of the United Na-

tions system and all financial institutions to continue to provide assistance to the Territory for socio-economic development and the development of human resources, bearing in mind the vulnerability of the Territory to external factors;

V
Cayman Islands

Noting the constitutional review of 1992-1993, according to which the population of the Cayman Islands expressed the sentiment that the existing relations with the United Kingdom of Great Britain and Northern Ireland should be maintained and that the current status of the Territory should not be altered,

Aware that the Territory has one of the highest per capita incomes in the region, a stable political climate and virtually no unemployment,

Noting the actions taken by the territorial Government to implement its localization programme to promote increased participation by the local population in the decision-making process in the Cayman Islands,

Noting with concern the vulnerability of the Territory to drug trafficking, money-laundering and related activities,

Noting the measures taken by the authorities to deal with those problems,

Noting also that the Territory has emerged as one of the world's leading offshore financial centres,

Noting further the approval by the Cayman Islands Legislative Assembly of the Territory's Vision 2008 Development Plan, which aims to promote development that is consistent with the aims and values of Caymanian society,

1. *Requests* the administering Power, bearing in mind the views of the people of the Territory ascertained through a democratic process, to keep the Secretary-General informed of the wishes and aspirations of the people regarding their future political status;

2. *Requests* the administering Power, the specialized agencies and other organizations of the United Nations system to continue to provide the territorial Government with all required expertise to enable it to achieve its socio-economic aims;

3. *Calls upon* the administering Power and the territorial Government to continue to cooperate to counter problems related to money-laundering, smuggling of funds and other related crimes, as well as drug trafficking;

4. *Requests* the administering Power, in consultation with the territorial Government, to continue to facilitate the expansion of the current programme of securing employment for the local population, in particular at the decision-making level;

5. *Welcomes* the implementation of the Country Cooperation Framework of the United Nations Development Programme for the Territory, which is designed to ascertain national development priorities and United Nations assistance needs;

VI
Guam

Recalling that, in a referendum held in 1987, the registered and eligible voters of Guam endorsed a draft Guam Commonwealth Act that would establish a new framework for relations between the Territory and the administering Power, providing for a greater measure of internal self-government for Guam and recognition of the right of the Chamorro people of Guam to self-determination for the Territory,

Recalling also its resolution 1514(XV) of 14 December 1960, containing the Declaration on the Granting of Independence to Colonial Countries and Peoples, and all resolutions and decisions of the United Nations relating to the Non-Self-Governing Territories, in particular, General Assembly resolutions 55/144 A and B of 8 December 2000,

Recalling further the requests by the elected representatives and non-governmental organizations of the Territory that Guam not be removed from the list of the Non-Self-Governing Territories with which the Special Committee is concerned, pending the self-determination of the Chamorro people and taking into account their legitimate rights and interests,

Aware that negotiations between the administering Power and the territorial Government on the draft Guam Commonwealth Act are no longer continuing and that Guam had established the process for a self-determination vote by the eligible Chamorro voters,

Cognizant that the administering Power continues to implement its programme of transferring surplus federal land to the Government of Guam,

Noting that the people of the Territory have called for reform in the programme of the administering Power with respect to the thorough, unconditional and expeditious transfer of land property to the people of Guam,

Conscious that immigration into Guam has resulted in the indigenous Chamorros becoming a minority in their homeland,

Aware of the potential for diversifying and developing the economy of Guam through commercial fishing and agriculture and other viable activities,

Noting the proposed closing and realigning of four United States Navy installations on Guam and the request for the establishment of a transition period to develop some of the closed facilities as commercial enterprises,

Recalling the dispatch in 1979 of a United Nations visiting mission to the Territory, and noting the recommendation of the 1996 Pacific regional seminar for sending a visiting mission to Guam,

Noting with interest the statements made and the information on the political and economic situation in Guam provided by the representatives of the Territory to the Caribbean regional seminar, held at Havana from 23 to 25 May 2001,

1. *Requests* the administering Power to work with Guam's Commission on Decolonization for the Implementation and Exercise of Chamorro Self-Determination with a view to facilitating Guam's decolonization and to keep the Secretary-General informed of the progress to that end;

2. *Calls upon* the administering Power to take into consideration the expressed will of the Chamorro people as supported by Guam voters in the plebiscite of 1987 and as provided for in Guam law, encourages the administering Power and the territorial Government of Guam to enter into negotiations on the matter, and requests the administering Power to inform the Secretary-General of progress to that end;

3. *Requests* the administering Power to continue to assist the elected territorial Government in achieving its political, economic and social goals;

4. *Also requests* the administering Power, in co-operation with the territorial Government, to continue to transfer land to the original landowners of the Territory;

5. *Further requests* the administering Power to continue to recognize and respect the political rights and the cultural and ethnic identity of the Chamorro people of Guam, and to take all necessary measures to respond to the concerns of the territorial Government with regard to the question of immigration;

6. *Requests* the administering Power to cooperate in establishing programmes specifically intended to promote the sustainable development of economic activities and enterprises, noting the special role of the Chamorro people in the development of Guam;

7. *Also requests* the administering Power to continue to support appropriate measures by the territorial Government aimed at promoting growth in commercial fishing and agricultural and other viable activities;

VII
Montserrat

Taking note with interest of the statements made and the information on the political and economic situation in Montserrat provided by the elected representative of the Territory to the Caribbean regional seminar, held at Havana from 23 to 25 May 2001,

Taking note of the statement made by the Chief Minister of Montserrat on 22 May 1998 on the occasion of the observance of the Week of Solidarity with the Peoples of All Colonial Territories Fighting for Freedom, Independence and Human Rights,

Noting that the last visiting mission to the Territory took place in 1982,

Noting also the functioning of a democratic process in Montserrat and that general elections were held in the Territory in November 1996,

Taking note of the reported statement of the Chief Minister that his preference was for independence within a political union with the Organization of Eastern Caribbean States and that self-reliance was more of a priority than independence,

Noting with concern the dire consequences of a volcanic eruption, which led to the evacuation of three quarters of the Territory's population to safe areas of the island and to areas outside the Territory, in particular Antigua and Barbuda and the United Kingdom of Great Britain and Northern Ireland, and which continues to have a negative impact upon the economy of the island,

Noting the efforts of the administering Power and the Government of the Territory to meet the emergency situation caused by the volcanic eruption, including the implementation of a wide range of contingency measures for both the private and the public sectors in Montserrat,

Noting also the coordinated response measures taken by the United Nations Development Programme and the assistance of the United Nations Disaster Management Team,

Noting with concern that a number of the inhabitants of the Territory continue to live in shelters because of volcanic activity,

1. *Requests* the administering Power, bearing in mind the views of the people of the Territory ascertained through a democratic process, to keep the Secretary-General informed of the wishes and aspirations of the people regarding their future political status;

2. *Calls upon* the administering Power, the specialized agencies and other organizations of the United Nations system as well as regional and other organizations to continue to provide urgent emergency assistance to the Territory in alleviating the consequences of the volcanic eruption;

3. *Welcomes* the support of the Caribbean Community in the construction of housing in the safe zone to alleviate a shortage caused by the environmental and human crisis of the eruption of the Montsoufriere volcano, as well as the material and financial support from the international community to help alleviate the suffering caused by the crisis;

VIII
Pitcairn

Taking into account the unique nature of Pitcairn in terms of population and area,

Expressing its satisfaction with the continued economic and social advancement of the Territory, as well as with the improvement of its communications with the outside world and its management plan to address conservation issues,

1. *Requests* the administering Power, bearing in mind the views of the people of the Territory ascertained through a democratic process, to keep the Secretary-General informed of the wishes and aspirations of the people regarding their future political status;

2. *Also requests* the administering Power to continue its assistance for the improvement of the economic, social, educational and other conditions of the population of the Territory;

3. *Calls upon* the administering Power to continue its discussions with the representatives of Pitcairn on how best to support their economic security;

IX
St. Helena

Taking into account the unique character of St. Helena, its population and its natural resources,

Noting that a Commission of Inquiry into the Constitution appointed at the request of the Legislative Council of St. Helena reported its recommendations in March 1999, and that the Legislative Councillors are currently considering its recommendations,

Also noting the administering Power's commitment to consider carefully suggestions for specific proposals for constitutional change from territorial Governments as stated in its White Paper entitled "Partnership for Progress and Prosperity: Britain and the Overseas Territories",

Welcoming the participation of an expert from the St. Helena Legislative Council for the first time in the Pacific regional seminar held at Majuro, from 16 to 18 May 2000,

Aware of the establishment by the Government of the Territory of the Development Agency in 1995 to encourage private sector commercial development on the island,

Also aware of the efforts of the administering Power and the territorial authorities to improve the socio-economic conditions of the population of St. Helena, in particular with regard to food production, continuing high unemployment and limited transport and communications, and calls for continuing negotiations to allow access to Ascension Island by civilian charter flights,

Noting with concern the problem of unemployment on the island and the joint action of the administering Power and the territorial Government to deal with it,

1. *Notes* that the administering Power has taken note of various statements made by members of the Legislative Council of St. Helena about the Constitution and that it is prepared to discuss them further with the people of St. Helena;

2. *Requests* the administering Power, bearing in mind the views of the people of the Territory ascertained through a democratic process, to keep the Secretary-General informed of the wishes and aspirations of the people regarding their future political status;

3. *Requests* the administering Power and relevant regional and international organizations to continue to support the efforts of the territorial Government to address the socio-economic development challenges, including the high unemployment and the limited transport and communications problems;

X
Turks and Caicos Islands

Taking note with interest of the statements made and the information on the political and economic situation in the Turks and Caicos Islands provided by the Cabinet Minister as well as a member of the legislature from the opposition of the Territory to the Caribbean regional seminar, held at St. John's from 21 to 23 May 1997,

Noting that the People's Democratic Movement was elected to power in the Legislative Council elections held in March 1999,

Also noting the efforts by the Government of the Territory to strengthen financial management in the public sector, including efforts to increase revenue,

Noting with concern the vulnerability of the Territory to drug trafficking and related activities, as well as its problems caused by illegal immigration,

Noting the need for continued cooperation between the administering Power and the territorial Government in countering drug trafficking and money-laundering,

Welcoming the assessment by the Caribbean Development Bank in its 1999 report that the economic performance of the Territory remained strong, with an increase in gross domestic product estimated at 8.7 per cent, reflecting strong growth in the tourism and construction sectors,

1. *Requests* the administering Power, bearing in mind the views of the people of the Territory ascertained through a democratic process, to keep the Secretary-General informed of the wishes and aspirations of the people regarding their future political status;

2. *Invites* the administering Power to take fully into account the wishes and interests of the Government

and the people of the Turks and Caicos Islands in the governance of the Territory;

3. *Calls upon* the administering Power and the relevant regional and international organizations to continue to provide assistance for the improvement of the economic, social, educational and other conditions of the population of the Territory;

4. *Calls upon* the administering Power and the territorial Government to continue to cooperate in order to counter problems related to money-laundering, smuggling of funds and other related crimes, as well as drug trafficking;

5. *Welcomes* the assessment by the Caribbean Development Bank in its 1999 report that the economy continued to expand with considerable output and low inflation;

6. *Also welcomes* the first Country Cooperation Framework approved by the United Nations Development Programme for the period 1998-2002, which should, inter alia, assist in the development of a national integrated development plan that will put into place procedures for determining the national development priorities over ten years, with the focus of attention on health, population, education, tourism and economic and social development;

7. *Takes note* of the statement made by the elected Chief Minister in May 2000 that the Territory is in the process of developing diversified resource mobilization strategies, including joint ventures with the private sector, and that external assistance would be welcomed as part of that process;

XI
United States Virgin Islands

Taking note with interest of the statements made and the information provided by the representative of the Governor of the United States Virgin Islands to the Caribbean regional seminar, held at Havana from 23 to 25 May 2001,

Noting that although 80.4 per cent of the 27.5 per cent of the electorate that voted in the referendum on the political status of the Territory held on 11 October 1993 supported the existing territorial status arrangements with the administering Power, the law required the participation of 50 per cent of the registered voters for the results to be declared legally binding and therefore the status was left undecided,

Noting also the continuing interest of the territorial Government in seeking associate membership in the Organization of Eastern Caribbean States and observer status in the Caribbean Community and the Association of Caribbean States,

Noting further the necessity of further diversifying the economy of the Territory,

Noting the efforts of the Government of the Territory to promote the Territory as an offshore financial services centre,

Noting with satisfaction the interest of the Territory in joining the United Nations International Drug Control Programme as a full participant,

Recalling the dispatch in 1977 of a United Nations visiting mission to the Territory,

Noting that the Territory commemorated its annual British Virgin Islands–United States Virgin Islands Friendship Day on 27 May 2000 in official ceremonies on Tortola,

1. *Requests* the administering Power, bearing in mind the views of the people of the Territory ascertained through a democratic process, to keep the Secretary-General informed of the wishes and aspirations of the people regarding their future political status;

2. *Also requests* the administering Power to continue to assist the territorial Government in achieving its political, economic and social goals;

3. *Further requests* the administering Power to facilitate the participation of the Territory, as appropriate, in various organizations, in particular the Organization of Eastern Caribbean States, the Caribbean Community and the Association of Caribbean States;

4. *Expresses concern* that the Territory, which is already heavily indebted, had to borrow 21 million United States dollars from a commercial bank to carry out its year 2000 computer compliance programme, and calls for the United Nations year 2000 programme to be made available to the Non-Self-Governing Territories;

5. *Notes* that the general elections held in the Territory in November 1998 resulted in the orderly transfer of power;

6. *Expresses concern* that the territorial Government is facing severe fiscal problems, which has resulted in an accumulated debt of more than 1 billion dollars;

7. *Welcomes* the measures being taken by the newly elected territorial Government in addressing the crisis, including the adoption of a five-year operating and strategic financial plan, and calls upon the administering Power to provide every assistance required by the Territory to alleviate the fiscal crisis, including, inter alia, the provision of debt relief and loans;

8. *Notes* that the 1994 report of the United States Virgin Islands Commission on Status and Federal Relations concluded that, owing to the insufficient level of voter participation, the results of the 1993 referendum were declared legally null and void.

Information

UN public information

The General Assembly's 96-member Committee on Information, at its twenty-third session held in New York from 30 April to 11 May 2001 (first part) and from 5 to 7 September (resumed) [A/56/21 & Add.1], continued to consider UN information policies and activities and to evaluate and follow up efforts made and progress achieved in information and communications. The Committee had before it reports on the reorientation of UN activities in public information and communications, public information activities for the United Nations Year of Dialogue among Civilizations (2001) (see p. 1013), and the implementation of the views of host Governments on the integration of UN information centres with UNDP field offices. It also considered the equitable disburse-

ment of resources to UN information centres, cooperation between the Department of Public Information (DPI) and the University for Peace in Costa Rica [A/AC.198/2001/6], a progress report on the pilot project on the development of an international radio broadcasting capacity for the United Nations, the continued multilingual development, maintenance and enrichment of the UN web site, and the 2000 activities of the Joint United Nations Information Committee (see below).

By **decision 56/419** of 10 December, the Assembly increased the Committee's membership from 96 to 98.

Reorientation of information and communications activities

Pursuant to General Assembly resolution 55/136 B [YUN 2000, p. 578], the Secretary-General submitted to the Committee on Information a March report [A/AC.198/2001/2] highlighting recent measures to develop further the conceptual framework and operational priorities for the reorientation of the Organization's information and communications policies, as detailed to the Committee in 1998 [YUN 1998, p. 583]. DPI had made considerable progress in the core areas of policy and strategic direction, the use of new technology, media access, radio and television programming, the development of thematic information programmes, building global partnerships, information activities in the field, publications and library services.

Building on worldwide public interest in the United Nations generated by the Millennium Summit [YUN 2000, p. 47], innovations were made to increase support for DPI activities, including the optimization of information technology to bring UN goals and activities to all regions of the world, particularly to news desks; strengthening the UN web site; creation of a 24-hour UN news service; introduction of live, 15-minute UN radio broadcasts in the six official languages to radio stations worldwide; implementation of "The United Nations Works" programme [ibid., p. 572]; and new ways of building partnerships within the UN system and with NGOs, academic institutions, the business community and the media.

Underlying DPI's initiatives was the commitment to embrace new communications technology to strengthen programmes and allow for the instantaneous transmission of text, image and voice messages. Guidelines for Internet publishing were issued and new web pages launched. Based on the recommendation of an expert consultant, DPI was proposing a 5-year technology strategy to overhaul its 30-year-old radio and television broadcast facilities to meet the requirements of the new media production and dissemination environment.

Use of the Internet-based United Nations News Centre increased, and its new design included a "ticker tape" for breaking news and headline summaries, improved audio links and regular feature and interview sections. Integrated digital photo management was also being deployed, while an electronic mail–based news alert service for news desks worldwide was to be launched in 2002.

DPI continued to enhance its services to the media through an increased flow of information from the Office of the Spokesman for the Secretary-General, briefings for journalists in various world regions through teleconferencing, along with high-level briefings to senior journalists, and the continued global placement of op-ed articles by the Secretary-General and other senior officials.

A successful example of DPI's reorientation was the pilot project for direct international radio broadcasting from UN Headquarters (see below). DPI also increased the flow of live television feeds and other readily usable video materials for use by international news syndicators and national broadcasters.

DPI continued to help Secretariat departments and other entities to develop information programmes and products to advocate their work on priority issues. It was implementing communications strategies, similar to the one developed for the Millennium Summit, to publicize the forthcoming series of follow-up conferences and Assembly special sessions, utilizing, among other methods, the creative techniques and expertise of modern global public relations companies on a pro bono basis. In cooperation with the Department of Peacekeeping Operations (DPKO), it continued to provide operational planning and support to field information offices to strengthen the public information capacity of peacekeeping and other missions.

In addition, DPI strongly encouraged learning and teaching about the United Nations through visits and programmes at Headquarters, model UN conferences and related products, and distance learning.

UN information centres were working extensively with educational institutions and youth organizations to stimulate interest in the Organization. Through investment in new technology, significant improvements were made in the transmission of information material to those centres and in their ability to disseminate it locally.

Technological innovation also enhanced the production, range and circulation of UN publications in both print and electronic formats. The *UN Chronicle* continued its large hard-copy subscriber base, while online editions made spontaneous readership and response possible. *Africa Recovery* continued to work with key African dailies to reproduce UN stories locally, and an electronic mail service was being planned to provide journalists in Africa with more timely information. The first half-century of the editions of the *Yearbook of the United Nations* were being compiled on CD-ROM. *UN Development Business* continued to provide procurement and bidding information on development projects worldwide, and its web site allowed for faster, more efficient dissemination of information.

The Dag Hammarskjöld Library's new web page on technical assistance to small and field libraries, aimed at preventing the duplication of work, facilitating resource sharing and encouraging the exchange of training, standards and best practices, was being further developed into a comprehensive UN system library network. The Library was also translating into all official languages the *United Nations Documentation: Research Guide* and its *Bibliographic Information System Thesaurus*, as well as other documentation databases, and was posting more pre-1993 parliamentary documents on the optical disk system. The Library also continued to expand its Secretariat partnerships and its inter-agency cooperative efforts.

UN international radio broadcasting capacity

The Committee on Information considered a March progress report by the Secretary-General, submitted pursuant to General Assembly resolution 55/136 B [YUN 2000, p. 578], on the implementation of the pilot project for the development of an international radio broadcasting capacity for the United Nations [A/AC.198/2001/7]. Launched in August 2000 [YUN 2000, p. 574], the project, through its live, 15-minute radio programmes, continued to provide information daily in the six official UN languages on events throughout the world from a UN perspective. The programme also included interviews, background reports, features, updates from peacekeeping missions and coverage of activities related to development. It also served as a public service mechanism and covered issues of priority to Member States, such as the HIV/AIDS epidemic. The Secretary-General's reaction to breaking news was featured on a regular basis. To meet the needs of specific markets, broadcasts were received worldwide through a range of transmission vehicles, including satellite communication providers, short-wave transmitters, telephone transmissions from DPI's International Broadcasting Centre and the Internet.

DPI continued to expand partnerships with local, regional and national broadcasting organizations in the different languages of transmission. It also enhanced cooperation with the UN common system and would continue to develop its field network of contributors and pursue more frequent access by United Nations Radio staff to delegations and field staff.

In a final report on the implementation of the pilot project submitted in July [A/AC.198/2001/10], the Secretary-General said that United Nations Radio had succeeded in establishing itself as an important international broadcaster and had contributed to the overall goal of generating understanding about the United Nations among millions of listeners across the globe. It had proved useful to media outlets, mainly in the developing world, and even broadcasters with correspondents in New York had picked up the feed, thereby further amplifying the international coverage of the United Nations. The project also constituted a striking example of DPI's commitment to multilingualism, and the partnerships it had generated demonstrated the high regard in which its programming was held.

Positive feedback had been received from both partner stations and individual listeners. During the first part of the twenty-third session of the Committee on Information, Member States expressed widespread support for the development of the project and its role in enabling developing nations to meet their information and communications needs.

In terms of the project's future, the production and distribution of relevant and timely radio products would be reinforced by cost-effective production techniques. As part of the upgrading of its radio and television facilities, DPI was acquiring an electronic news production system that would permit easy news gathering and radio editing. Promotion activities in support of the live radio broadcast would continue, and the database developed for the Russian-language radio stations would be replicated in other official languages.

The cost of the project, estimated to amount to $1.9 million by 31 December 2001, was absorbed within the approved 2000-2001 programme budget. Without a legislative mandate for continuing the project beyond the pilot phase, resource provisions were not included in the proposed 2002- 2003 programme budget. However, an estimated $3.5 million would be required if the Assembly should decide to continue the project.

DPI activities

The Secretary-General's September report on questions related to information [A/56/411] noted that DPI had reoriented its activities to ensure that communication was at the heart of the strategic management of the Organization. It was responding to the General Assembly's call to maintain and improve its activities in areas of special need in developing countries through the outreach of UN information centres in the field, training programmes at Headquarters for media practitioners from developing countries, and special communication strategies for the current cycle of conferences and special sessions of the Assembly on economic and social issues.

Through use of the latest technologies, DPI was retooling its capabilities to widen the Organization's outreach in a fast-moving and competitive communications environment. It was developing an electronic mail–based United Nations News Service to provide instantaneously specially targeted information to influential journalists in every region, and had successfully developed an in-house capability for live webcasting. As part of its efforts to strengthen the UN web site, all parliamentary documents were to be made available in the six official languages through the Official Document System (ODS) in early 2002, and the United Nations CyberSchoolBus, the site for young people and teachers, was redesigned and a uniform database-driven navigational system implemented. As part of continuing efforts to bridge the digital divide, DPI organized training seminars in Beirut, Lebanon, and New York on the use of the Internet as a tool for development.

The Office of the Spokesman for the Secretary-General added a new section to its web page containing the Secretary-General's latest statements, including a quote of the day. DPI, with the assistance of its information centres, continued to build and expand its network of United Nations Radio rebroadcasting partners. It continued to enhance the electronic delivery of news on UN system activities through a redesigned News Centre web site, featuring an improved search function. The Department was also developing the ability of UN offices around the world to post news directly onto the central News Centre. In addition to its weekly and annual television programmes, DPI also produced special documentaries on the worldwide proliferation of small arms and on the problems of people emerging from conflict, both of which won international film festival awards. In cooperation with Synergy Films, it produced a film on AIDS in South Africa entitled "Together We Can".

DPI improved its working relationships with the 1,600 associated NGOs, focusing on a new system to monitor compliance with the criteria for association and on increased outreach.

In cooperation with other UN departments, DPI implemented its thematic information programmes, which included communication strategies to promote global conferences and special sessions of the General Assembly. It also organized a number of activities in support of the United Nations Year of Dialogue among Civilizations (see p. 1013), proclaimed by the General Assembly in resolution 53/22 [YUN 1998, p. 1031]. Those activities were detailed in a March report of the Secretary-General [A/AC.198/2001/3].

Library services

The Dag Hammarskjöld Library continued to reinforce its commitment to bridging the digital divide by placing major emphasis on web-related activities, the digitization of UN documents, inter-agency resource sharing, the provision of extensive training programmes and multilingual access to written information, and forging strategic partnerships throughout the UN system. It launched the Arabic, Chinese and Russian versions of its own web page in July. The page entitled "United Nations documentation: research guide", already available in Arabic and French, was being translated into the other three official languages. With the upcoming web availability of the *United Nations Bibliographic Information System Thesaurus* in Arabic, Chinese and Russian, multilingual subject access to the ODS and other UN documentation databases would be achieved.

Inter-agency cooperative efforts continued through the United Nations System Electronic Information Acquisition Consortium, which centralized the purchasing of online information products and services for more than 50 entities throughout the UN system. The Consortium continued to effect significant cost savings, thus providing permanent missions and UN offices worldwide with previously unaffordable access to electronic databases and services.

The number of UN depository libraries continued to grow, with 394 as at 30 June. Since January, 35 depository libraries had converted their hardcopy entitlements of official records and documents into ODS access. DPI continued to expand its cartographic and geographic services with revised peacekeeping and general maps and new maps posted on the cartographic web site for free access by Member States and the Secretariat. In August, DPI began development of a common UN geographic database in cooperation with the Department of Political Affairs, DPKO and the Office for the Coordination of Humanitarian Affairs.

UN information centres

The United Nations information centres (UNICs) continued to disseminate information on the work and priority themes of the Organization to the general public, as well as to key partners, including the private sector, NGOs, the media, academics and students. Their public outreach activities, such as seminars, round tables, media briefings, press conferences, film screenings, exhibits, workshops and conferences, helped to raise awareness and understanding of the United Nations among local communities. The centres were resourceful in highlighting significant UN events during the year, particularly activities in support of the General Assembly's special session on HIV/AIDS (see p. 1125). DPI strengthened the centres' technological capacity, allowing them to produce better and timely information materials locally. A growing number of centres had developed their own web sites, providing news and other information materials on UN themes and events, including local-language versions of major reports.

At its 2001 session, the Committee on Information considered the Secretary-General's report on the implementation of the views of host Governments on the integration of UNICs with field offices of UNDP [A/AC.198/2001/4], prepared in response to General Assembly resolution 55/136 B [YUN 2000, p. 578]. Seven of 14 host Governments had responded to a survey questionnaire inviting comments and suggestions on the integration experience. Of those, five Governments made specific recommendations on enhancing the effectiveness of the centres located in their capitals. Subsequent efforts were made to address those issues.

In March [A/AC.198/2001/5], the Secretary-General reported on the equitable disbursement of resources to UNICs along with a breakdown of host government assistance.

Development of UN web sites

In response to General Assembly resolution 55/136 B [YUN 2000, p. 578], the Secretary-General reported in March on the continued multilingual development, maintenance and enrichment of the UN web sites [A/AC.198/2001/8]. He said that progress had been slower than expected due to a lack of in-house expertise and resources in the non-working languages of the Secretariat. Moreover, achieving a truly equal multilingual web site would remain elusive if the issues of public information content creation and ongoing maintenance, coordination and management were not dealt with separately. Regular maintenance and enhancement of the web site required a sound staffing and resource foundation, and thus the need for additional allocations. Accordingly, DPI believed that the feasibility study called for in an earlier report [YUN 2000, p. 576] was still necessary.

To date, six proposals for the further development of the UN web site had been presented to the Committee on Information for its consideration, each involving additional funding. However, given the constraints imposed by a zero-growth budget, future development and enhancement of the web site would depend on policy decisions by the Assembly with regard to making official documents available online in all languages free of charge. Decisions would also have to be made regarding the gradual development of the various language components. Furthermore, the gap between the English and other language sites continued to grow, ensuring that total language parity would become increasingly challenging and resource-intensive. Therefore, the proposal presented in 2000 [YUN 2000, p. 576] continued to represent the minimum resource requirement for establishing a sound footing for regular web-site maintenance and enhancement.

Meanwhile, the Information Technology Section had been restructured to focus on the development of the language sites with a team for each language. DPI would continue to develop special web pages for specific UN events and all efforts would be made to present such sites in the six official languages. DPI had also started identifying portions of the main English language site for rendition in each of the other official languages. Each language site was scheduled to be enhanced in small modules. The policy issues related to making all public information available in all official languages were to be examined through an interdepartmental working group.

The General Assembly, in **resolution 56/253** of 24 December (see p. 1297), requested the Secretary-General to report to the Assembly's fifty-seventh (2002) session on the financial implications of redressing the imbalance among the six official languages of the United Nations on the UN web site.

JUNIC

At its twenty-seventh session (Geneva, 10-12 July) [ACC/2001/13], the Joint United Nations Information Committee (JUNIC), the inter-agency Administrative Committee on Coordination (ACC) body on information activities within the UN system, proposed that its secretariat look further into the possibility of creating a .un domain name, in order to create a powerful branding for the UN system and restrict the possible misuse of the United Nations name. JUNIC supported the call by ACC and the Committee on Information for the establishment of a central UN Internet portal, coordinated by DPI, encompassing all web sites of UN system organizations.

JUNIC examined the issue of web journalism and the effect of the availability of online publications on hard-copy sales. Nearly all members of JUNIC reported that online availability of sales publications either kept sales stable or led to small increases, and several members reported that the outsourcing of translation work combined with in-house quality control produced satisfactory results and led to considerable savings. JUNIC requested DPI to conduct a survey of photographic materials available within UN system organizations, providing online links among the libraries and, resources permitting, filling the thematic gaps.

JUNIC considered communications and public information challenges in preparing for the 2002 World Summit on Sustainable Development (see p. 749) and in follow-up to the June General Assembly special session on HIV/AIDS (see p. 1125), and decided that an open-ended steering group would be developed for the Summit, based on a similar group established for the special session on HIV/AIDS.

JUNIC noted that although many UN system organizations were implementing programmes in support of the global campaign for poverty eradication, additional efforts were needed to communicate with one voice. It agreed that inter-agency public information cooperation should be re-energized, making it more dynamic, issues-oriented, results-based, flexible and modern. To those ends, JUNIC agreed to retain its fixed annual session to promote a common sense of purpose within the UN information community and to facilitate networking, and to establish a direct link to the weekly Communications Group meeting held at Headquarters so that its members could be better informed. Committee members should establish steering groups to develop and implement joint communications strategies for priority issues or major conferences. JUNIC also agreed to retain its rotating two-year chairmanship and to keep its secretariat within DPI. It decided to evaluate its functioning periodically.

JUNIC agreed on the importance of its continued close relationship with the Non-Governmental Liaison Service, to maintain the current reporting arrangements through the annual programme and coordination meetings, and to discuss in-depth public information and communications aspects of the Liaison Service's work during its annual sessions.

JUNIC agreed to consider holding an in-depth discussion on cooperation in the field of television at its next session.

The Secretary-General's report on the 2000 activities of JUNIC [A/AC.198/2001/9] was submitted to the twenty-third session of the Committee on Information.

GENERAL ASSEMBLY ACTION

On 10 December [meeting 82], the General Assembly, on the recommendation of the Fourth Committee [A/56/522], adopted **resolution 56/64 A** without vote [agenda item 90].

Information in the service of humanity

The General Assembly,

Taking note of the comprehensive and important report of the Committee on Information,

Also taking note of the report of the Secretary-General on questions relating to information,

Urges all countries, organizations of the United Nations system as a whole and all others concerned, reaffirming their commitment to the principles of the Charter of the United Nations and to the principles of freedom of the press and freedom of information, as well as to those of the independence, pluralism and diversity of the media, deeply concerned by the disparities existing between developed and developing countries and the consequences of every kind arising from those disparities that affect the capability of the public, private or other media and individuals in developing countries to disseminate information and communicate their views and their cultural and ethical values through endogenous cultural production, as well as to ensure the diversity of sources and their free access to information, and recognizing the call in this context for what in the United Nations and at various international forums has been termed "a new world information and communication order, seen as an evolving and continuous process":

(*a*) To cooperate and interact with a view to reducing existing disparities in information flows at all levels by increasing assistance for the development of communication infrastructures and capabilities in developing countries, with due regard for their needs and the priorities attached to such areas by those countries, and in order to enable them and the public, private or other media in developing countries to develop their own information and communication policies freely and independently and increase the participation of media and individuals in the communication process, and to ensure a free flow of information at all levels;

(*b*) To ensure for journalists the free and effective performance of their professional tasks and condemn resolutely all attacks against them;

(*c*) To provide support for the continuation and strengthening of practical training programmes for broadcasters and journalists from public, private and other media in developing countries;

(*d*) To enhance regional efforts and cooperation among developing countries, as well as cooperation between developed and developing countries, to strengthen communication capacities and to improve the media infrastructure and communication technology in the developing countries, especially in the areas of training and dissemination of information;

(*e*) To aim at, in addition to bilateral cooperation, providing all possible support and assistance to the developing countries and their media, public, private or other, with due regard to their interests and needs in the field of information and to action already adopted within the United Nations system, including:

(i) The development of the human and technical resources that are indispensable for the improvement of information and communication systems in developing countries and support for the continuation and strengthening of practical training programmes, such as those already operating under both public and private auspices throughout the developing world;

(ii) The creation of conditions that will enable developing countries and their media, public, private or other, to have, by using their national and regional resources, the communication technology suited to their national needs, as well as the necessary programme material, especially for radio and television broadcasting;

(iii) Assistance in establishing and promoting telecommunication links at the subregional, regional and interregional levels, especially among developing countries;

(iv) The facilitation, as appropriate, of access by the developing countries to advanced communication technology available on the open market;

(*f*) To provide full support for the International Programme for the Development of Communication of the United Nations Educational, Scientific and Cultural Organization, which should support both public and private media.

On 24 December [meeting 92], the Assembly, on the recommendation of the Fourth Committee [A/56/552], adopted **resolution 56/64 B** without vote [agenda item 90].

United Nations public information policies and activities

The General Assembly,

Reiterating its decision to consolidate the role of the Committee on Information as its main subsidiary body mandated to make recommendations to it relating to the work of the Department of Public Information of the Secretariat,

Concurring with the view of the Secretary-General that public information and communications should be placed at the heart of the strategic management of the United Nations, and that a culture of communications should permeate all levels of the Organization, as a means of fully informing the peoples of the world of the aims and activities of the United Nations, in accordance with the principles and purposes enshrined in the Charter of the United Nations, in order to create broad-based global support for the United Nations,

Stressing that the primary mission of the Department of Public Information is to provide, through its outreach activities, accurate, impartial, comprehensive and timely information to the public on the tasks and responsibilities of the United Nations in order to strengthen international support for the activities of the Organization with the greatest transparency,

Expressing its concern that the gap in the information and communication technologies between the developed and the developing countries has continued to widen and that vast segments of the population in developing countries are not benefiting from the present information and technology revolution and, in this regard, underlining the necessity of rectifying the imbalances of the global information and technology revolution in order to make it more just, equitable and effective,

Recognizing that developments in the information and communication technology revolution open vast new opportunities for economic growth and social development and can play an important role in the eradication of poverty in developing countries and, at the same time, emphasizing that it also poses challenges and risks and could lead to further widening of disparities between and within countries,

Stating that the present developments and rapid changes in the field of information and communication technology have a tremendous impact on the functioning of the United Nations and the Department of Public Information in particular, which may necessitate suitable adjustments in the manner in which the mandate of the Department is implemented,

Noting other initiatives aimed at bridging the digital divide, including those by the World Bank, the International Telecommunication Union, the United Nations Conference on Trade and Development, the United Nations Development Programme, the Digital Opportunity Task Force of the Group of Eight Nations and the Group of 77 South Summit,

Recalling its resolutions 50/11 of 2 November 1995, 52/23 of 25 November 1997 and 54/64 of 6 December 1999 on multilingualism, and emphasizing the importance of making appropriate use of the official languages in the activities of the Department of Public Information, seeking to reduce the gap between the use of English and the other five official languages,

Stating that the Secretary-General should continue to enhance the effectiveness of the activities of the Department of Public Information,

Welcoming Armenia and the Libyan Arab Jamahiriya to membership in the Committee on Information,

I
Introduction

1. *Reaffirms* its resolution 13(I) of 13 February 1946, in which it established the Department of Public Information of the Secretariat, and all other relevant General Assembly resolutions related to the activities of the Department;

2. *Calls upon* the Secretary-General, in respect of the public information policies and activities of the United Nations, to continue to implement fully the recommendations contained in paragraph 2 of its resolution 48/44 B of 10 December 1993 and other mandates as established by the General Assembly;

3. *Emphasizes* the importance of the medium-term plan for the period 2002-2005, as approved by the General Assembly in its resolution 55/234 of 23 December 2000, as a guideline that sets out the overall orientation of the public information programme for the Organization's goals through effective communication;

4. *Welcomes* the United Nations Millennium Declaration, the ministerial declaration adopted by the Economic and Social Council at the high-level segment of its substantive session of 2000 and the Secretary-General's millennium report, which indicate clearly that there is a great amount of hope and concern in the field of information and communications;

5. *Calls upon* States, in accordance with their laws, to make every effort to prevent the use of the traditional media and new information and communication technologies that undermine legitimate Governments and democracy, fan ethnic strife and xenophobia, incite hatred and violence and contribute to any manifestations of extremism;

6. *Acknowledges* the important work carried out by the United Nations Educational, Scientific and Cultural Organization and its collaboration with news agencies and broadcasting organizations in developing countries in disseminating information on priority issues;

II
General activities of the Department of Public Information

7. *Reaffirms* that the Department of Public Information is the focal point for information policies of the United Nations and the primary news centre for information about the United Nations and its activities and those of the Secretary-General;

8. *Welcomes* the development of the United Nations News Service by the Department of Public Information, and requests the Secretary-General to continue to exert all efforts to ensure that publications and other information services of the Secretariat, including the United Nations web site and the United Nations News Service, contain comprehensive, objective and equitable information about the issues before the Organization and that they maintain editorial independence, impartiality, accuracy and full consistency with resolutions and decisions of the General Assembly;

9. *Takes note* of the report of the Secretary-General on the reorientation of United Nations activities in the field of public information and communications, encourages him to continue the reorientation exercise, while stressing the need to take into account the views of Member States, and requests him to report thereon to the Committee on Information at its twenty-fourth session;

10. *Emphasizes* that, through its reorientation, the Department of Public Information should maintain and improve its activities in the areas of special interest to developing countries and, where appropriate, other countries with special needs, including countries in transition, and that such reorientation contributes to bridging the existing gap between the developing and the developed countries in the crucial field of public information and communications;

11. *Concurs* with the view of the Secretary-General that the development of a strategic vision linking all the components of the Secretariat with emphasis on planning cooperation within the Organization constitutes the central element for continuing reorientation, and encourages the Department of Public Information to maintain, improve and expand its activities in the areas of special interest to developing countries;

12. *Encourages* the Secretary-General to strengthen the cooperation between the Department of Public Information and other departments of the Secretariat, in particular those dealing with priority issues;

13. *Welcomes* the initiatives that have been taken by the Department of Public Information to strengthen the public information system of the United Nations, and, in this regard, stresses the importance of a coher-

ent and results-oriented approach being undertaken by the United Nations, the specialized agencies and the programmes and funds of the United Nations system involved in public information activities and the provision of resources for their implementation, and that this be done taking into account feedback from Member States on the relevance and effectiveness of its programme delivery;

14. *Requests* the Department of Public Information to continue to ensure the greatest possible access for United Nations guided tours and to ensure that displays in public areas are kept as informative, up-to-date, relevant and as technologically innovative as possible;

15. *Recognizes* the need for the Department of Public Information to increase its outreach activities in all regions, requests the Secretary-General to include, in his next report on the reorientation of United Nations activities in the field of public information and communications, an analysis of the present reach and scope of the Department's activities, identifying the widest possible spectrum of audiences and geographical areas which are not covered adequately and which may require special attention, including the appropriate means of communication, and bearing in mind local language requirements;

III
Multilingualism and public information

16. *Emphasizes* the importance of ensuring the full, equitable treatment of all the official languages of the United Nations in all activities of the Department of Public Information, and stresses the importance of fully implementing its resolution 52/214 of 22 December 1997, in section C of which it requested the Secretary-General to ensure that the texts of all new public documents in all six official languages, and information materials of the United Nations, are made available through the United Nations web site daily and are accessible to Member States without delay;

17. *Requests* the Secretary-General to submit updated figures on the use and command of all six official languages by the staff of the Department of Public Information to the Committee on Information at its twenty-fourth session;

18. *Also requests* the Secretary-General to ensure that the Department of Public Information has appropriate staffing capacity in all official languages of the United Nations to undertake all its activities;

19. *Reminds* the Secretary-General of the need to include in future programme budget proposals for the Department of Public Information the importance of using all six official languages in its activities;

20. *Takes note* of the Internet Publishing Guidelines, and in this regard requests the Department of Public Information and the Working Group on Internet Matters to include in these guidelines specific recommendations towards achieving the goal of making all documentation on the web sites available in all six official languages of the Organization;

IV
Promotional campaigns

21. *Recalls* its resolutions 53/202 of 17 December 1998 and 54/254 of 15 March 2000, concerning the designation of the fifty-fifth session of the General Assembly as the Millennium Assembly of the United Na-

tions and the convening, as an integral part of the Millennium Assembly, of the Millennium Summit of the United Nations, takes note of the report of the Secretary-General on the millennium promotional campaign, and commends the Department of Public Information for the important role that it played in implementing the promotional campaign;

22. *Appreciates* the Secretary-General's initiatives in promoting 2001 as the United Nations Year of Dialogue among Civilizations and, mindful of the importance of drawing international attention to the impact that dialogue among civilizations could have on promoting mutual understanding, tolerance and peaceful coexistence, encourages the Secretary-General to intensify the promotional campaign through the use of as many broadcasters and languages, in addition to the official languages, as possible, to spread coverage, with special emphasis on publicizing the findings of the Group of Eminent Persons for the United Nations Year of Dialogue among Civilizations, and requests the Secretary-General to report thereon to the Committee on Information at its twenty-fourth session;

23. *Recalls* paragraph 10 of General Assembly resolution 55/47 of 29 November 2000, entitled "International Decade for a Culture of Peace and Non-Violence for the Children of the World, 2001-2010", and, in this context, encourages the Department of Public Information to undertake specific dissemination of information on a culture of peace, keeping in mind the ongoing Decade;

24. *Recognizes* the need for enhanced publicity through a targeted strategy to be developed by the Department of Public Information on the special sessions and conferences, including on the least developed countries, children, illicit trade in small arms and light weapons, the human immunodeficiency virus/acquired immunodeficiency syndrome (HIV/AIDS), racism, the environment, financing for development, sustainable development, and ageing, which will address issues crucial to the international community, particularly the developing countries, as well as on the ongoing Second International Decade for the Eradication of Colonialism, and requests the Secretary-General to take the necessary action in this regard and report to the Committee on Information at its twenty-fourth session in the context of his report on the reorientation of United Nations activities in the field of public information and communications;

25. *Recalls* its resolutions 53/59 B of 3 December 1998 and 54/82 B of 6 December 1999, and urges the Department of Public Information to take the necessary measures, through the provision of relevant and objective information, towards achieving the major objectives set forth in the report of the Secretary-General on the causes of conflict and the promotion of durable peace and sustainable development in Africa, and to publicize the activities of the open-ended working group established for that purpose;

26. *Also recalls* its resolutions concerning the consequences of the Chernobyl disaster, in particular resolutions 51/138 B of 13 December 1996 and 52/172 of 16 December 1997, and encourages the Department of Public Information, in cooperation with the countries concerned and with the relevant organizations and bodies of the United Nations system, to continue to

take appropriate measures to enhance world public awareness of the consequences of that disaster;

27. *Further recalls* its resolution 55/44 of 27 November 2000, concerning international cooperation and coordination for the human and ecological rehabilitation of the Semipalatinsk region of Kazakhstan, which has been affected by nuclear tests, and encourages the Department of Public Information, in cooperation with relevant organizations and bodies of the United Nations system, to take appropriate measures to enhance world public awareness of the problems and needs of the Semipalatinsk region;

V
Bridging the digital divide

28. *Commends* the Secretary-General for the establishment of the United Nations Information Technology Service, the Health InterNetwork and the Information and Communications Technology Task Force with a view to bridging the digital divide and as a response to the continuing gulf between developed and developing countries, welcomes the contribution of the Department of Public Information in publicizing the efforts of the Secretary-General in closing the digital divide as a means of spurring economic growth and as a response to the continuing gulf between developed and developing countries, and, in this context, requests the Department further to enhance its role;

VI
United Nations information centres

29. *Stresses* that the United Nations information centres and information components should continue to play a significant role in disseminating information about the work of the Organization to the peoples of the world, in particular in the areas of economic and social development;

30. *Takes note* of the report of the Secretary-General entitled "Integration of United Nations information centres with field offices of the United Nations Development Programme: implementation of the views of host Governments", welcomes the action taken by the Department of Public Information to implement the views of those host Governments as expressed in their replies to the questionnaire provided by the Secretariat, and requests the Secretary-General to take the necessary steps for the continued implementation of those views and to report thereon to the Committee on Information at its twenty-fourth session;

31. *Requests* the Secretary-General to report to the Committee on Information at its twenty-fourth session on any possible proposal to continue, if feasible and on a case-by-case basis, the integration policy in a cost-effective manner, while maintaining the operational and functional independence of United Nations information centres, taking into account the views of the host countries to ensure that the information functions and the autonomy of United Nations information centres are not adversely affected, to meet the policy's stated objective of improving the provision of information by the United Nations;

32. *Also requests* the Secretary-General to include in his report on the reorientation of United Nations activities in the field of public information and communications, to be submitted to the Committee on Information at its twenty-fourth session, information on the involvement of the Department of Public Information in the context of the implementation of his recommendations on the establishment of United Nations houses;

33. *Takes note* of the report of the Secretary-General on the equitable disbursement of resources to United Nations information centres, emphasizes that further efforts are needed to ensure the most equitable disbursement possible of resources to United Nations information centres, and stresses that particular attention should be paid to the concerns of developing countries and, where appropriate, other countries with special needs, including countries in transition;

34. *Emphasizes* that the United Nations information centres, as the "field voice" of the Department of Public Information, should promote public awareness and mobilize support for the work of the United Nations at the local level, and recognizes the appeal made by the Secretary-General to the host Governments of United Nations information centres to facilitate the work of the centres in their countries by providing rent-free or rent-subsidized office space, while taking into account the economic condition of the host Governments and bearing in mind that such support should not be a substitute for the full allocation of financial requirements for the United Nations information centres in the context of the programme budget of the United Nations;

35. *Reaffirms* that the United Nations information centres should continue to publicize United Nations activities and accomplishments in the areas of economic and social development, poverty eradication, debt relief, health, education, the elimination of illiteracy, women's rights, children's rights, the plight of children in armed conflict, the sexual exploitation of children, the eradication of drug trafficking, environmental issues, peace and security, and other relevant issues;

36. *Also reaffirms* the role of the General Assembly in relation to the opening of new United Nations information centres, invites the Secretary-General to make such recommendations as he may consider necessary regarding the establishment and location of such centres, and, in this regard, welcomes the requests by the Governments of Croatia, Gabon, Guinea, Haiti, Jamaica and Kyrgyzstan for information centres or information components;

37. *Takes note* of the efforts by some United Nations information centres to develop their own web pages in local languages, and, in this respect, encourages the Department of Public Information to provide resources and technical facilities, in particular to United Nations information centres whose web pages are not yet operational, to develop web pages in the respective local languages of their host countries, and encourages host Governments to respond to the needs of United Nations information centres;

VII
Role of the Department of Public Information in United Nations peacekeeping

38. *Takes note with appreciation* of the efforts of the Secretary-General to strengthen the public information capacity of the Department of Public Information for the establishment and day-to-day functioning of the information components of peacekeeping and other field operations of the United Nations, and re-

quests the Secretariat to continue to ensure the involvement of the Department from the planning stage of such future operations through interdepartmental consultations and coordination with other departments of the Secretariat, in particular with the Department of Peacekeeping Operations, and to report thereon to the Committee on Information at its twenty-fourth session, including any possible proposals for enhancing the role of the Department of Public Information in this regard;

39. *Notes* the ongoing discussion on the report of the Secretary-General on resource requirements for implementation of the report of the Panel on United Nations Peace Operations, and, in this regard, stresses that the Department of Public Information should continue its efforts to strengthen its capacity to contribute significantly to the functioning of information components in United Nations peacekeeping operations, and requests the Secretary-General to report to the Committee on Information at its twenty-fourth session in the report requested in paragraph 38 above;

40. *Stresses* the importance of enhancing the public information capacity of the Department of Public Information in the field of peacekeeping operations and its role in the selection process of spokespersons for United Nations peacekeeping operations or missions, and, in this regard, encourages the Department to second spokespersons who have the necessary skills to fulfil the tasks of the operations or missions, and to consider views expressed, especially by host countries, when appropriate, in this regard;

VIII
Dag Hammarskjöld Library

41. *Takes note* of the continuing efforts of the Secretary-General to make the Dag Hammarskjöld Library a virtual library with world outreach, making United Nations information and other acquired materials accessible electronically to a growing number of readers and users, and, at the same time, requests the Secretary-General to enrich on a multilingual basis the stock of books and journals in the Library, including publications on peace and security and development-related issues, to ensure that the Library continues to be a broadly accessible resource for information about the United Nations and its activities;

42. *Encourages* the Dag Hammarskjöld Library to alert its clientele, including Member States through their missions, for example, via electronic mail, of any new publications and collections;

43. *Welcomes* the training courses conducted by the Dag Hammarskjöld Library for the representatives of Member States and Secretariat staff on Cyberseek, web search, the Intranet, United Nations documentation, UN-I-QUE and the Official Document System of the United Nations, and, in that regard, encourages the Library to further develop such courses;

44. *Also welcomes* the role of the Department of Public Information in fostering increased collaboration among libraries of the United Nations system, particularly in establishing one central system-wide online catalogue that will allow for the searching of the bibliographic records of all print holdings of all United Nations system libraries and the searching of all electronic holdings and electronic databases maintained by all United Nations system libraries, and requests the

Secretary-General to report thereon to the Committee on Information at its twenty-fourth session in the context of his report on the reorientation of United Nations activities in the field of public information and communications;

45. *Requests* the Department of Public Information to ensure the continued development of the integrated library system in the Dag Hammarskjöld Library, and requests the Secretary-General to report thereon to the Committee on Information at its twenty-fourth session in the context of his report on the reorientation of United Nations activities in the field of public information and communications;

IX
Traditional means of communication: radio, television and publications

46. *Welcomes* the progress report and the final report of the Secretary-General on the implementation of the pilot project on the development of an international radio broadcasting capacity for the United Nations, and also welcomes the extensive network of partnerships established with local, national and regional broadcasters in Member States, and concurs with the Secretary-General that the project has contributed to the overall goal of the Department of Public Information of generating understanding about the United Nations among millions of listeners across the globe and has been one of the more successful examples of the reorientation of the Department;

47. *Decides*, building upon the success of the pilot project as well as the scope of its programme distribution and established partnerships, to expand the international radio broadcasting capacity of the United Nations in all six official languages;

48. *Requests* the Secretary-General to convey the necessary justification of the resource requirements, including information on the possibility of extrabudgetary financing and/or the redeployment of resources, concerning the expansion of the international radio broadcasting capacity for the biennium 2002-2003 for consideration by the relevant committees of the General Assembly;

49. *Also requests* the Secretary-General to submit a report on the implementation of the United Nations international radio broadcasting capacity to the Committee on Information at its twenty-fifth session, including information that can be obtained from the local, national and regional radio partners about the estimated number of listeners reached, in order for the Committee to decide on the future of this capacity;

50. *Stresses* that radio remains one of the most cost-effective and far-reaching traditional media available to the Department of Public Information and an important instrument in United Nations activities, such as development and peacekeeping, in accordance with General Assembly resolution 48/44 B;

51. *Takes note* of the efforts under way by the Department of Public Information to disseminate programmes directly to broadcasting stations all over the world in the six official languages as well as in other languages, and, in that regard, stresses the need for impartiality and objectivity concerning information activities of the United Nations;

52. *Requests* the Department of Public Information, in view of the need for efficiency and for a wider dis-

semination of information services of the United Nations Radio, to enhance where necessary the use of non-official languages to meet the information needs of its audiences;

53. *Encourages* the Department of Public Information to continue to include in its radio and television programming specific programmes addressing the needs of developing nations;

54. *Expresses its appreciation* to the Department of Public Information for the ongoing programme for broadcasters and journalists from developing countries and countries in transition, and calls for its further continuation along the lines of its current implementation, while including a larger number of trainees from those countries;

55. *Emphasizes* that all publications of the Department of Public Information, in accordance with existing mandates, should fulfil an identifiable need, should not duplicate other publications of the United Nations system and should be produced in a cost-effective manner;

X
United Nations web site

56. *Notes*, while appreciating current efforts, that there is a need for the Secretary-General to continue to develop proposals for the multilingual development, maintenance and enrichment of the United Nations web site in order to lead ultimately to achieving full parity among the official languages of the United Nations, and requests the Secretary-General to report thereon to the Committee on Information at its twenty-fourth session;

57. *Requests* the Secretary-General in the meantime and until a decision has been taken on the proposals to be submitted for the multilingual development, maintenance and enrichment of the United Nations web site, to ensure, to the extent possible, while maintaining an up-to-date and accurate web site, the equitable distribution of financial and human resources within the Department of Public Information allocated to the United Nations web site among all official languages on a continuous basis;

58. *Requests* the Department of Public Information, as the manager of the Organization's web site, to take the lead in developing a proposal for the establishment of one central Internet portal that will encompass all web sites of the United Nations system, preferably through system-wide cooperation, and that will allow for the search and retrieval of information from all web sites in the United Nations system from one central search facility, and requests the Secretary-General to report thereon to the Committee on Information at its twenty-fourth session in the context of his report on the reorientation of United Nations activities in the field of public information and communications;

59. *Stresses* the importance of access to United Nations Treaty Collection and United Nations parliamentary documentation for the public;

60. *Commends* the efforts of the Information Technology Services Division of the Office of Central Support Services in ensuring that the required technological infrastructure is in place to accommodate the imminent linkage of the Official Document System to the United Nations web site;

61. *Recognizes* the far-reaching impact that the linking of the Official Document System with the United Nations web site will have in furthering the goals of the Organization by making all parliamentary documents in the six official languages publicly available, and stresses that the integration of the Official Document System with the United Nations web site will represent one of the steps towards significantly enhancing the multilingual nature of the United Nations web site and will lead to efficiencies in all Secretariat departments;

62. *Takes note with interest* of the electronic mail-based news alert service distributed worldwide by the Department of Public Information, and emphasizes that extra care needs to be taken to ensure that news-breaking stories and news alerts are accurate, impartial and free of any bias;

63. *Encourages* the Secretary-General, through the Department of Public Information, to continue to take full advantage of recent developments in information technology, including the Internet, in order to improve, in a cost-effective manner, the expeditious dissemination of information on the United Nations, in accordance with the priorities established by the General Assembly and taking into account the linguistic diversity of the Organization;

64. *Encourages* an increase in the number of programmes of United Nations Radio, in all available languages, on the United Nations web site;

XI
Final remarks

65. *Recognizes* the need for constructive interaction between the management of the Department of Public Information and members of the Committee on Information, and requests the Department to arrange, in consultation with the Chairman, informal meetings with the members of the Committee every three months to discuss the ongoing work of the Department, and in this regard requests the Department, in preparation for these meetings, to invite members of the Committee, no later than two weeks prior to their convening, to propose topics for discussion;

66. *Requests* the Secretary-General to report to the Committee on Information at its twenty-fourth session and to the General Assembly at its fifty-seventh session on the activities of the Department of Public Information and on the implementation of the recommendations contained in the present resolution;

67. *Requests* the Committee on Information to report to the General Assembly at its fifty-seventh session;

68. *Decides* to include in the provisional agenda of its fifty-seventh session the item entitled "Questions relating to information".

Also on 24 December, the Assembly, in **resolution 56/253** on questions relating to the proposed 2002-2003 programme budget (Part VII) (see p. 1304), requested the Secretary-General to conduct a comprehensive review of DPI's management and operations and to report to the Assembly's fifty-seventh (2002) session.

Other public information activities

The Advisory Committee on Administrative and Budgetary Questions, in reviewing Section 26, Public information, in its first report on the proposed 2002-2003 programme budget [A/56/7], recommended that DPI further clarify and define what constituted outputs for public information and for programme implementation in substantive departments and offices throughout the Secretariat, since the difference between them had become blurred, and report its conclusions to the General Assembly's fifty-sixth session.

In response to that request, the Secretary-General submitted in November [A/C.5/56/17] a report reviewing public information activities in the Secretariat outside DPI, particularly those of the Departments of Economic and Social Affairs, of Political Affairs and for Disarmament Affairs, the Offices of Legal Affairs and for the Coordination of Humanitarian Affairs, and the regional commissions.

The review revealed that DPI regularly assisted Secretariat departments and offices in formulating communication strategies and provided departments and other organizational units with expertise and influential communication tools, including through UNICs and the UN web site. Substantive departments and offices turned to DPI for assistance in tailoring their messages and in developing focused information strategies. Any public information materials they produced without DPI's assistance were generally in response to a specific mandate and for a limited audience. DPI might then assist in disseminating those materials to a wider, more general public.

The Secretary-General had spearheaded a drive to promote a culture of communication and a spirit of cooperation at all levels of the Organization, establishing the Communications Group as a mechanism for high-level coordination on communication issues by senior New York–based information officials. Coordination was also achieved through JUNIC, especially in convening system-wide task forces to coordinate communication efforts for specific global conferences and campaigns. Coordination and cooperation had been enhanced as DPI increasingly worked closely with other departments and offices on a daily basis to formulate and disseminate their messages (see p. 555).

The Secretary-General observed that information received from other Secretariat organizational units indicated that their public information activities complemented those of DPI, and the Department's ongoing working relationships and coordination within them helped to mini-mize duplication and overlap. Those efforts could be more successful if DPI was included from the beginning in preparations for major activities and if its information centres were involved at all stages of joint activities so as to enhance field connectivity and coverage.

DPI provided its expertise to other departments and to the UN system within its limited resources. Public information priorities should therefore be part of joint strategic planning among Secretariat organizational units and discussed prior to the submission of future programme budget proposals.

Information and communications in the context of international security

Pursuant to General Assembly resolution 55/28 [YUN 2000, p. 582], the Secretary-General, in a July report with later addendum [A/56/164 & Add.1], transmitted the views of five Member States, including Sweden on behalf of the States of the European Union that were Members of the United Nations, on the general appreciation of the issues of information security; the definition of basic notions related to information security, including unauthorized interference with or misuse of information and telecommunication systems and information resources; and the content of relevant international concepts aimed at strengthening the security of global information and telecommunication systems.

GENERAL ASSEMBLY ACTION

On 29 November [meeting 68], the General Assembly, on the recommendation of the First Committee [A/56/533], adopted **resolution 56/19** without vote [agenda item 69].

Developments in the field of information and telecommunications in the context of international security

The General Assembly,

Recalling its resolutions 53/70 of 4 December 1998, 54/49 of 1 December 1999 and 55/28 of 20 November 2000,

Recalling also its resolutions on the role of science and technology in the context of international security, in which, inter alia, it recognized that scientific and technological developments could have both civilian and military applications and that progress in science and technology for civilian applications needed to be maintained and encouraged,

Noting that considerable progress has been achieved in developing and applying the latest information technologies and means of telecommunication,

Affirming that it sees in this process the broadest positive opportunities for the further development of civilization, the expansion of opportunities for co-operation for the common good of all States, the enhancement of the creative potential of mankind and additional improvements in the circulation of information in the global community,

Recalling, in this connection, the approaches and principles outlined at the Information Society and Development Conference, held at Midrand, South Africa, from 13 to 15 May 1996,

Bearing in mind the results of the Ministerial Conference on Terrorism, held in Paris on 30 July 1996, and the recommendations that it made,

Noting that the dissemination and use of information technologies and means affect the interests of the entire international community and that optimum effectiveness is enhanced by broad international cooperation,

Expressing concern that these technologies and means can potentially be used for purposes that are inconsistent with the objectives of maintaining international stability and security and may adversely affect the security of States in both civil and military fields,

Considering that it is necessary to prevent the use of information resources or technologies for criminal or terrorist purposes,

Noting the contribution of those Member States that have submitted their assessments on issues of information security to the Secretary-General pursuant to paragraphs 1 to 3 of resolutions 53/70, 54/49 and 55/28,

Taking note of the reports of the Secretary-General containing those assessments,

Welcoming the initiative taken by the Secretariat and the United Nations Institute for Disarmament Research in convening an international meeting of experts at Geneva in August 1999 on developments in the field of information and telecommunications in the context of international security, as well as its results,

Considering that the assessments of the Member States contained in the reports of the Secretary-General and the international meeting of experts have contributed to a better understanding of the substance of issues of international information security and related notions,

1. *Calls upon* Member States to promote further at multilateral levels the consideration of existing and potential threats in the field of information security, as well as possible measures to limit the threats emerging in this field, consistent with the need to preserve the free flow of information;

2. *Considers* that the purpose of such measures could be served through the examination of relevant international concepts aimed at strengthening the security of global information and telecommunications systems;

3. *Invites* all Member States to continue to inform the Secretary-General of their views and assessments on the following questions:

(*a*) General appreciation of the issues of information security;

(*b*) Definition of basic notions related to information security, including unauthorized interference with or misuse of information and telecommunications systems and information resources;

(*c*) The content of the concepts mentioned in paragraph 2 of the present resolution;

4. *Requests* the Secretary-General to consider existing and potential threats in the sphere of information security and possible cooperative measures to address them, and to conduct a study on the concepts referred to in paragraph 2 of the present resolution, with the assistance of a group of governmental experts, to be established in 2004, appointed by him on the basis of equitable geographical distribution and with the help of Member States in a position to render such assistance, and to submit a report on the outcome of the study to the General Assembly at its sixtieth session;

5. *Decides* to include in the provisional agenda of its fifty-seventh session the item entitled "Developments in the field of information and telecommunications in the context of international security".

Role of science and technology in the context of international security and disarmament

On 29 November [meeting 68], the General Assembly, on the recommendation of the First Committee [A/56/531], adopted **resolution 56/20** by recorded vote (92-46-17) [agenda item 70].

Role of science and technology in the context of international security and disarmament

The General Assembly,

Recognizing that scientific and technological developments can have both civilian and military applications and that progress in science and technology for civilian applications needs to be maintained and encouraged,

Concerned that military applications of scientific and technological developments can contribute significantly to the improvement and upgrading of advanced weapons systems and, in particular, weapons of mass destruction,

Aware of the need to follow closely the scientific and technological developments that may have a negative impact on international security and disarmament, and to channel scientific and technological developments for beneficial purposes,

Cognizant that the international transfers of dual-use as well as high-technology products, services and know-how for peaceful purposes are important for the economic and social development of States,

Also cognizant of the need to regulate such transfers of dual-use goods and technologies and high technology with military applications through multilaterally negotiated, universally applicable, non-discriminatory guidelines,

Expressing concern about the growing proliferation of ad hoc and exclusive export control regimes and arrangements for dual-use goods and technologies, which tend to impede the economic and social development of developing countries,

Recalling that in the Final Document of the Twelfth Conference of Heads of State or Government of Non-Aligned Countries, held at Durban, South Africa, from 29 August to 3 September 1998, it was noted with concern that undue restrictions on exports to developing countries of material, equipment and technology for peaceful purposes persist,

Emphasizing that internationally negotiated guidelines for the transfer of high technology with military applications should take into account the legitimate defence requirements of all States and the requirements for the maintenance of international peace and security, while ensuring that access to high-technology products and services and know-how for peaceful purposes is not denied,

1. *Affirms* that scientific and technological progress should be used for the benefit of all mankind to promote the sustainable economic and social development of all States and to safeguard international security and that international cooperation in the use of science and technology through the transfer and exchange of technological know-how for peaceful purposes should be promoted;

2. *Invites* Member States to undertake additional efforts to apply science and technology for disarmament-related purposes and to make disarmament-related technologies available to interested States;

3. *Urges* Member States to undertake multilateral negotiations with the participation of all interested States in order to establish universally acceptable, non-discriminatory guidelines for international transfers of dual-use goods and technologies and high technology with military applications;

4. *Encourages* United Nations bodies to contribute, within existing mandates, to promoting the application of science and technology for peaceful purposes;

5. *Decides* to include in the provisional agenda of its fifty-seventh session the item entitled "Role of science and technology in the context of international security and disarmament".

RECORDED VOTE ON RESOLUTION 56/20:

In favour: Afghanistan, Algeria, Bahamas, Bahrain, Bangladesh, Barbados, Bhutan, Bolivia, Botswana, Brunei Darussalam, Burkina Faso, Burundi, Cambodia, Cameroon, Cape Verde, Chile, China, Colombia, Costa Rica, Côte d'Ivoire, Cuba, Democratic People's Republic of Korea, Djibouti, Dominican Republic, Ecuador, Egypt, El Salvador, Eritrea, Ethiopia, Fiji, Gabon, Ghana, Grenada, Guatemala, Guinea, Guyana, Haiti, Honduras, India, Indonesia, Iran, Jamaica, Jordan, Kenya, Kuwait, Lao People's Democratic Republic, Lebanon, Lesotho, Libyan Arab Jamahiriya, Madagascar, Malaysia, Maldives, Mali, Mauritania, Mauritius, Mexico, Mongolia, Morocco, Mozambique, Myanmar, Namibia, Nauru, Nepal, Nicaragua, Nigeria, Oman, Pakistan, Panama, Papua New Guinea, Peru, Philippines, Qatar, Saint Lucia, Saudi Arabia, Senegal, Sierra Leone, Singapore, Sri Lanka, Sudan, Swaziland, Syrian Arab Republic, Thailand, Togo, Trinidad and Tobago, Tunisia, Uganda, United Arab Emirates, United Republic of Tanzania, Venezuela, Viet Nam, Yemen, Zambia.

Against: Albania, Andorra, Australia, Austria, Belgium, Bosnia and Herzegovina, Bulgaria, Canada, Croatia, Cyprus, Czech Republic, Denmark, Estonia, Finland, France, Germany, Greece, Hungary, Iceland, Ireland, Israel, Italy, Latvia, Liechtenstein, Lithuania, Luxembourg, Malta, Micronesia, Monaco, Netherlands, New Zealand, Norway, Poland, Portugal, Republic of Moldova, Romania, San Marino, Slovakia, Slovenia, Spain, Sweden, The former Yugoslav Republic of Macedonia, Turkey, United Kingdom, United States, Yugoslavia.

Abstaining: Argentina, Armenia, Azerbaijan, Belarus, Brazil, Georgia, Japan, Kazakhstan, Paraguay, Republic of Korea, Russian Federation, Samoa, South Africa, Tonga, Turkmenistan, Ukraine, Uruguay.

Peaceful uses of outer space

The Committee on the Peaceful Uses of Outer Space (Committee on Outer Space), at its forty-fourth session (Vienna, 6-15 June) [A/56/20 & Corr.1], discussed ways to maintain outer space for peaceful purposes and the spin-off benefits of space technology. It examined the implementation of the recommendations of the Third (1999)

United Nations Conference on the Exploration and Peaceful Uses of Outer Space (UNISPACE III) [YUN 1999, p. 556] and reviewed the work of its two subcommittees, one concerned with scientific and technical issues and the other with legal questions. The Committee also considered the enlargement of its membership. In December, the General Assembly endorsed the Committee's recommendations for its future work, including those made by its subcommittees.

Implementation of UNISPACE III recommendations

Responding to General Assembly resolution 55/122 [YUN 2000, p. 587], the Scientific and Technical Subcommittee, at its thirty-eighth session (Vienna, 12-23 February) [A/AC.105/761], convened the Working Group of the Whole to consider, among other subjects, the implementation of UNISPACE III recommendations.

The Working Group recommended a mechanism for assessing and implementing those recommendations through the voluntary leadership of individual member States and their appropriate governmental institutions on particular actions. As team leaders, those States would seek the widest possible participation of non-governmental entities and report to the Scientific and Technical Subcommittee, which would act as coordinator. The Working Group also recommended that a survey be conducted to identify Member States' interest and priority for each action constituting the nucleus of a strategy contained in "The Space Millennium: Vienna Declaration on Space and Human Development", adopted by UNISPACE III [YUN 1999, p. 556]. The survey would also allow Member States to indicate their interest in being the leader or member of particular teams. The results of the survey were to be submitted to the forty-fourth session of the Committee on Outer Space (see below).

The Working Group also recommended that expert groups be established to conduct research, analyse and make recommendations on particular actions. In that regard, it established an expert group to propose a plan for a global disaster mitigation management system.

The Working Group stressed the importance of the full implementation of the plan of action of the Office for Outer Space Affairs for implementing UNISPACE III recommendations [YUN 2000, p. 583] with the necessary resources in 2002 and hoped the General Assembly would take that fully into account.

The Committee on Outer Space, at its June session [A/56/20 & Corr.1], endorsed the Working Group's recommendations. It also considered the results of the survey requested by the Working Group (see p. 567), contained in a May note by the Secretariat [A/AC.105/L.234] and later conference room papers. Attached to the note were tables setting out the UNISPACE III recommendations into three groups, and indicating States that had offered to be team leaders and a list of members of each group.

The Committee on Outer Space noted the comprehensive response to the survey and agreed that implementation of UNISPACE III recommendations could proceed in stages. The first stage would involve recommendations in Group 1, considered by Member States as being of highest priority, and those in Group 2, where States had offered to be coordinators of action teams. For each recommendation, there would be an assessment phase and an implementation phase. During the assessment phase, third parties, including intergovernmental organizations within the UN system, with strong interest in participating in the implementation of the recommendation, would be identified. The Committee identified as the recommendations that had been assigned the highest priority the development of a comprehensive, worldwide environmental strategy (recommendation 1), improving the management of the Earth's natural resources (2), implementing an integrated, global system to manage natural disaster mitigation, relief and prevention efforts (7), improving universal access to and compatibility of space-based navigation and positioning systems (10), promoting sustainable development (11), and increasing awareness among decision makers and the public of the importance of space activities (18).

The Committee agreed that India, Nigeria, for the African States, and the United States with Austria would act as interim coordinators for recommendations 2, 11 and 18, respectively, prior to the 2002 session of the Scientific and Technical Subcommittee. The Committee also agreed that Canada, China, France, Japan, Portugal and the United Kingdom would act as interim coordinators for the recommendations for which they had offered to be leaders, and that the work of the action teams would begin as proposed by the respective countries. The Committee noted the list of experts nominated by Member States for the expert group on the implementation of an integrated, space-based global natural disaster management system [A/AC.105/L.233 & Add.1-3] and agreed that the expert group be merged into the action team on recommendation 7. The Committee requested the interim coordinators to report on their work and to submit work plans to the Scientific and Technical Subcommittee in 2002 for

approval. The Subcommittee would agree at that time on the principal participants in the teams, identify any other recommendations for which urgent actions were required and agree on interim coordinators of teams to be responsible for those recommendations.

The Committee urged all Member States that had not done so to contribute to the Trust Fund for the United Nations Programme on Space Applications, which had been modified to include implementation of UNISPACE III recommendations, in particular to support the projects and activities recommended by the Committee at its 2000 session.

The Chairman of the Committee expressed concern that, while the United Nations had organized global conferences to identify priorities for the twenty-first century to promote human development, none of those conferences had taken the contribution of space science and technology into account. The Committee agreed that its Chairman should bring to the Secretary-General's attention the need to consider that contribution to a greater extent in major UN conferences, taking particular account of the needs of developing countries. That request was conveyed to the Secretary-General by the Committee Chairman in a 19 July letter [A/56/306], in which attention was also drawn to the mechanism set up for implementing UNISPACE III recommendations, including the list of open-ended action teams that were to begin implementing those recommendations in 2001.

Report of Secretary-General. In response to General Assembly resolution 55/122 [YUN 2000, p. 587], the Secretary-General reported in September [A/56/394 & Corr.1] on action taken by the Committee on Outer Space at its June session to implement the UNISPACE III recommendations and the plan of action of the Office for Outer Space Affairs, and to further enhance inter-agency coordination and cooperation.

Scientific and Technical Subcommittee

The Scientific and Technical Subcommittee of the Committee on Outer Space, at its thirty-eighth session [A/AC.105/761], considered the United Nations Programme on Space Applications following UNISPACE III.

The Subcommittee also dealt with matters related to remote sensing of the Earth by satellite, including applications for developing countries and the monitoring of the Earth's environment; the use of nuclear power sources in outer space; mechanisms for strengthening inter-agency cooperation and increasing the use of space applications and services within and among UN system entities; the implementation of an integrated, space-based global natural disaster management system; space debris; the examination of the physical nature and technical attributes of the geostationary orbit and of its utilization and applications; and government and private activities to promote education in space science and engineering.

UN Programme on Space Applications

The United Nations Programme on Space Applications, as mandated by General Assembly resolution 37/90 [YUN 1982, p. 163], continued to focus on developing indigenous capability at the local level in space science and technology through long-range training fellowships, technical advisory services, regional and international training courses and conferences; acquiring and disseminating space-related information; and promoting cooperation between developed and developing countries.

According to the United Nations Expert on Space Applications, in his report to the Subcommittee [A/AC.105/773], pursuant to Assembly resolution 45/72 [YUN 1990, p. 99], regional workshops continued to be organized on the use of space technology in disaster management, particularly for the benefit of developing countries. The workshops would support the Committee's action team on disaster management. Efforts in developing indigenous capability continued to focus largely on establishing regional centres for space science and technology education in developing countries and a Network of Space Science and Technology Education and Research Institutions for Central, Eastern and South-Eastern Europe.

The Programme held nine training courses, workshops and conferences in 2001, including its long-term fellowships for in-depth training. Various technical advisory services and activities promoting regional cooperation continued to be provided.

In considering the January 2001 report of the Expert on Space Applications [A/AC.105/750], the Subcommittee continued to express its concern over the Programme's limited financial resources and appealed to Member States for voluntary contributions. It also noted the Programme's assistance to developing countries and countries with economies in transition, as proposed in the UNISPACE III recommendations, particularly those contained in the Vienna Declaration on Space and Human Development.

The Assembly, in **resolution 56/51** (see p. 847), endorsed the United Nations Programme on Space Applications, as proposed by the Expert.

Cooperation

The Inter-Agency Meeting on Outer Space Activities, at its twenty-first session (Vienna, 22-24 January) [A/AC.105/756], discussed the coordination of plans and programmes in the practical application of space technology and the enhancement of coordination among UN system organizations through the use of information technologies. It also reviewed cooperation within the UN system in remote sensing and related geographic information systems, and the UNISPACE III action plan and implementation of follow-up activities.

The Meeting reaffirmed its commitment to strengthening existing coordination mechanisms both within and outside the UN system and considered a proposal by the Office for Outer Space Affairs on its joint initiative with the United Nations International Strategy for Disaster Reduction on the use of space technologies in disaster management. It agreed that the Office for Outer Space Affairs should make a presentation to the Subcommittee highlighting examples of inter-agency collaboration in space-related areas, and should more actively bring to the attention of other UN intergovernmental bodies the benefits of space applications and related activities being carried out by UN system organizations. The Secretary-General's report on the coordination of outer space activities within the UN system: programme of work for 2001 and 2002 and future years [A/AC.105/757] should be summarized, highlighting inter-agency collaboration, and widely circulated.

The Meeting reaffirmed the importance of linking UN system institutions concerned with space applications and those concerned with development. It stressed the importance of strengthening its interaction with the Commission on Sustainable Development, and encouraged participating organizations involved in outer space activities to promote the use of space technology for sustainable development at the Commission's ninth (2001) session (see p. 747) and at the 2002 World Summit on Sustainable Development (see p. 749). The Meeting agreed that discussion on UN system cooperation in remote sensing and related geographic information system activities and Agenda 21, adopted by the 1992 United Nations Conference on Environment and Development [YUN 1992, p. 672], should include the promotion of relevant space-related technologies in sustainable development.

The Committee on Outer Space [A/56/20 & Corr.1] noted the report of the Inter-Agency Meeting and the Secretary-General's report on coordination of outer space activities within the UN system.

Other related documents submitted to the Subcommittee were Secretariat notes [A/AC.105/ C.1/L.241 & Corr.1 & Add.1] containing the views of UN system organizations on the strengthening of inter-agency cooperation and increasing the use of space applications and services within and among UN system entities.

Scientific and technical issues

In 2001, the Scientific and Technical Subcommittee [A/AC.105/761] continued to emphasize the importance of providing non-discriminatory access to state-of-the-art remote sensing data and to derived information at reasonable cost, and of capacity-building in the adoption and use of remote sensing technology, particularly to meet the needs of developing countries. It also emphasized the importance of remote sensing systems for advancing sustainable development. It agreed that revision of the Principles Relevant to the Use of Nuclear Power Sources in Outer Space [YUN 1992, p. 116] was currently not warranted, and, until a firm scientific and technical consensus had been reached, it would be inappropriate to refer the topic to the Legal Subcommittee.

The Subcommittee noted examples of existing use of space technology for disaster management, the obstacles to further such use, and efforts to improve space-based services for disaster management and to develop the expertise of potential users of space-based information for disaster management.

The Subcommittee examined the costs and benefits of space debris mitigation measures. As requested by the Committee on Outer Space [YUN 2000, p. 586], the Secretariat had prepared a sample index to the United Nations Register of Objects Launched into Outer Space. The Subcommittee noted that a process of controlled de-orbiting for large artificial space objects was being gradually introduced by national space agencies.

The Subcommittee agreed that: international cooperation was needed to minimize the potential impact of space debris on future space missions; Member States should pay more attention to the problem of collisions of space objects, including those with nuclear power sources on board, with space debris and to other aspects of space debris; and Member States and international organizations should make available the results of national research on space debris, including information on minimizing its creation. The Subcommittee also agreed that a work plan should be established to expedite international adoption of voluntary debris mitigation measures.

The Committee on Outer Space [A/56/20 & Corr.1] agreed with the Subcommittee concerning the revision of the 1992 Principles, and that States making use of nuclear power sources should conduct their activities in full accordance with those Principles. Member States should be invited to report to the Secretary-General annually on national and international research on the subject, and further studies should be conducted on the issue of collision between space debris and orbiting space objects with nuclear power sources.

The Committee agreed that, starting in 2002, the Subcommittee should consider space debris according to the multi-year work plan adopted at its thirty-eighth (2001) session. It noted that the recommended practice of re-orbiting satellites before the end of their operational life had not been universally applied and requested the European Space Operations Centre of the European Space Agency to provide updates on the state of application of that practice in 2002.

In response to the Committee's request that Member States report on national and international research concerning the safety of space objects with nuclear power sources, the Secretariat, in November [A/AC.105/770], submitted replies received from six Member States and two international organizations on the subject.

Legal Subcommittee

The Legal Subcommittee, at its fortieth session (Vienna, 2-12 April) [A/AC.105/763 & Corr.1], considered the draft convention of the International Institute for the Unification of Private Law (Unidroit) on international interests in mobile equipment and the preliminary draft protocol thereto on matters specific to space property. The issue was raised of potential overlap between the legal regimes to be established under the Unidroit draft convention and that being prepared by the United Nations Commission on International Trade Law on assignment of receivables. The Subcommittee established an ad hoc consultative mechanism to review those and other related issues. A working meeting of the mechanism was held in Paris (10-11 September) and the results of consultations undertaken through the mechanism would be reported to the Subcommittee in 2002. The Convention was adopted at the Diplomatic Conference to Adopt a Mobile Equipment Convention and an Aircraft Protocol (Cape Town, South Africa, 29 October–16 November) and was opened for signature on 16 November.

The Subcommittee discussed the status and application of the five UN treaties on outer space, including a review of their implementation and obstacles to their universal acceptance. The treaties in question were: the 1966 Treaty on Principles Governing the Activities of States in the Exploration and Use of Outer Space, including the Moon and Other Celestial Bodies, adopted by the General Assembly in resolution 2222(XXI) [YUN 1966, p. 41]; the 1967 Agreement on the Rescue of Astronauts, the Return of Astronauts and the Return of Objects Launched into Outer Space, adopted in resolution 2345(XXII) [YUN 1967, p. 33]; the 1971 Convention on International Liability for Damage Caused by Space Objects, contained in resolution 2777(XXVI) [YUN 1971, p. 52]; the 1974 Convention on Registration of Objects Launched into Outer Space, contained in resolution 3235(XXIX) [YUN 1974, p. 63]; and the 1979 Agreement Governing the Activities of States on the Moon and Other Celestial Bodies, contained in resolution 34/68 [YUN 1979, p. 111].

The Subcommittee re-established its Working Group on the definition and delimitation of outer space, which agreed that, as few replies had been received to the questionnaire on aerospace objects, Member States should consider submitting or updating their replies in the interest of making progress on the subject. The Secretariat should prepare a summary of the question, indicating points of consensus that had emerged over the years.

The Legal Subcommittee noted the work of the Scientific and Technical Subcommittee at its 2001 session on the use of nuclear power sources in outer space under a four-year work plan, the second year of which reviewed national and international processes, proposals and standards, and national working papers relevant to the launch and peaceful use of nuclear power sources in outer space. The Scientific and Technical Subcommittee's Working Group on the issue would submit an information report in 2002.

The Legal Subcommittee also reviewed the concept of the "launching State" through its Working Group on the subject.

GENERAL ASSEMBLY ACTION

On 10 December [meeting 82], the General Assembly, on the recommendation of the Fourth Committee [A/56/548], adopted **resolution 56/51** without vote [agenda item 86].

International cooperation in the peaceful uses of outer space

The General Assembly,

Recalling its resolutions 51/122 of 13 December 1996, 54/68 of 6 December 1999 and 55/122 of 8 December 2000,

Deeply convinced of the common interest of mankind in promoting and expanding the exploration and use of outer space, as the province of all mankind, for peaceful purposes and in continuing efforts to extend to all States the benefits derived therefrom, and also of the importance of international cooperation in this field, for which the United Nations should continue to provide a focal point,

Reaffirming the importance of international cooperation in developing the rule of law, including the relevant norms of space law and their important role in international cooperation for the exploration and use of outer space for peaceful purposes, and of the widest possible adherence to international treaties that promote the peaceful uses of outer space in order to meet emerging new challenges,

Seriously concerned about the possibility of an arms race in outer space,

Recognizing that all States, in particular those with major space capabilities, should contribute actively to the goal of preventing an arms race in outer space as an essential condition for the promotion and strengthening of international cooperation in the exploration and use of outer space for peaceful purposes,

Considering that space debris is an issue of concern to all nations,

Noting the progress achieved in the further development of peaceful space exploration and applications as well as in various national and cooperative space projects, which contributes to international cooperation, and the importance of further developing the legal framework to strengthen international cooperation in this field,

Convinced of the importance of the recommendations in the resolution entitled "The Space Millennium: Vienna Declaration on Space and Human Development", adopted by the Third United Nations Conference on the Exploration and Peaceful Uses of Outer Space (UNISPACE III), held at Vienna from 19 to 30 July 1999,

Taking note of the report of the Secretary-General on the implementation of the recommendations of UNISPACE III,

Convinced that the use of space science and technology and their applications, in such areas as telemedicine, tele-education and Earth observation, contribute to achieving the objectives of the global conferences of the United Nations that address various aspects of economic, social and cultural development, inter alia, poverty eradication,

Having considered the report of the Committee on the Peaceful Uses of Outer Space on the work of its forty-fourth session,

1. *Endorses* the report of the Committee on the Peaceful Uses of Outer Space on the work of its forty-fourth session;

2. *Urges* States that have not yet become parties to the international treaties governing the uses of outer space to give consideration to ratifying or acceding to those treaties;

3. *Notes* that, at its fortieth session, the Legal Subcommittee of the Committee on the Peaceful Uses of Outer Space continued its work, as mandated by the General Assembly in its resolution 55/122;

4. *Notes with satisfaction* the agreement reached by the Legal Subcommittee on the question of the character and utilization of the geostationary orbit and the subsequent endorsement of that agreement by the Committee;

5. *Endorses* the recommendation of the Committee that the Legal Subcommittee, at its forty-first session, taking into account the concerns of all countries, in particular those of developing countries:

(a) Consider the following as regular agenda items:

(i) General exchange of views;

(ii) Status and application of the five United Nations treaties on outer space;

(iii) Information on the activities of international organizations relating to space law;

(iv) Matters relating to:

a. The definition and delimitation of outer space;

b. The character and utilization of the geostationary orbit, including consideration of ways and means to ensure the rational and equitable use of the geostationary orbit without prejudice to the role of the International Telecommunication Union;

(b) Consider the following single issues/items for discussion:

(i) Review and possible revision of the Principles Relevant to the Use of Nuclear Power Sources in Outer Space;

(ii) Consideration of the Convention on International Interests in Mobile Equipment, which was opened for signature at Cape Town, South Africa, on 16 November 2001, and the preliminary draft protocol on matters specific to space property;

(c) Continue its review of the concept of the "launching State", in accordance with the work plan adopted by the Committee;

6. *Notes* that the Legal Subcommittee, at its forty-first session, will submit its proposals to the Committee for new items to be considered by the Subcommittee at its forty-second session, in 2003;

7. *Agrees* that, in the context of paragraph 5 (a) (ii) above, the Legal Subcommittee should establish a working group with the terms of reference as agreed upon by the Legal Subcommittee at its fortieth session, to be convened for three years, from 2002 to 2004;

8. *Notes* that the Committee would invite interested member States to designate experts to identify which aspects of the report on the ethics of space policy of the World Commission on the Ethics of Scientific Knowledge and Technology of the United Nations Educational, Scientific and Cultural Organization might need to be studied by the Committee and to draft a report, in consultation with other international organizations and in close liaison with the World Commission, with a view to making a presentation on the matter at the forty-second session of the Legal Subcommittee, under the agenda item entitled "Information on the activities of international organizations relating to space law";

9. *Notes also* that, in the context of paragraph 5 (a) (iv) above and in accordance with the agreement referred to in paragraph 4 above, the Legal Subcommittee will reconvene its working group on the item only to consider matters relating to the definition and delimitation of outer space;

10. *Endorses* the agreement of the Legal Subcommittee, in the context of paragraph 5 (b) (ii) above, concerning the establishment of an ad hoc consultative mechanism to review the relevant issues;

11. *Notes* that, in the context of paragraph 5 (c) above, the Legal Subcommittee will reconvene its working group to consider the item;

12. *Agrees* that, in accordance with the measures relating to the working methods of the Committee and its subsidiary bodies, which were endorsed by the General Assembly in paragraph 11 of its resolution 52/56 of 10 December 1997, the Committee should reach consensus agreement at its forty-fifth session, in 2002, on the composition of the bureaux of the Committee and its subsidiary bodies for the third term, starting in 2003;

13. *Notes* that the Scientific and Technical Subcommittee, at its thirty-eighth session, continued its work as mandated by the General Assembly in its resolution 55/122;

14. *Notes with satisfaction* that the Scientific and Technical Subcommittee at its thirty-eighth session continued to consider, on a priority basis, the agenda item on space debris;

15. *Endorses* the recommendation of the Committee that the Scientific and Technical Subcommittee, at its thirty-ninth session, taking into account the concerns of all countries, in particular those of developing countries:

(a) Consider the following items:

(i) General exchange of views and introduction to reports submitted on national activities;

(ii) United Nations Programme on Space Applications;

(iii) Implementation of the recommendations of the Third United Nations Conference on the Exploration and Peaceful Uses of Outer Space (UNISPACE III);

(iv) Matters relating to remote sensing of the Earth by satellite, including applications for developing countries and monitoring of the Earth's environment;

(b) Consider the following items in accordance with the work plans adopted by the Committee;

(i) Use of nuclear power sources in outer space;

(ii) Means and mechanisms for strengthening inter-agency cooperation and increasing the use of space applications and services within and among entities of the United Nations system;

(iii) Implementation of an integrated, space-based global natural disaster management system;

(iv) Space debris;

(c) Consider the following single issues/items for discussion:

(i) Examination of the physical nature and technical attributes of the geostationary orbit and its utilization and applications, including, inter alia, in the field of space communications, as well as other questions relating to developments in space communications, taking particular account of the needs and interests of developing countries;

(ii) International cooperation in limiting obtrusive space advertising that could interfere with astronomical observations;

(iii) Mobilization of financial resources to develop capacity in space science and technology applications;

16. *Notes* that the Scientific and Technical Subcommittee at its thirty-ninth session will submit its proposal

to the Committee for a draft provisional agenda for the fortieth session of the Subcommittee, in 2003;

17. *Endorses* the recommendation of the Committee that the Committee on Space Research and the International Astronautical Federation, in liaison with member States, be invited to arrange a symposium on the theme "Remote sensing for water management in arid and semi-arid countries", with as wide a participation as possible, to be held during the first week of the thirty-ninth session of the Scientific and Technical Subcommittee;

18. *Notes with satisfaction* that an industry symposium, with the participation of member States, will be organized during the thirty-ninth session of the Scientific and Technical Subcommittee, focusing on the promising area of very high resolution remote sensing and its impact on operational applications and also discussing the new space market situation;

19. *Agrees* that, in the context of paragraphs 15 *(a)* (ii) and (iii) and 16 above, the Scientific and Technical Subcommittee at its thirty-ninth session should reconvene the Working Group of the Whole;

20. *Also agrees* that, in the context of paragraph 15 *(b)* (i) above, the Scientific and Technical Subcommittee at its thirty-ninth session should reconvene its Working Group on the Use of Nuclear Power Sources in Outer Space;

21. *Invites* the Inter-Agency Meeting on Outer Space Activities to contribute to the work of the Scientific and Technical Subcommittee in the context of paragraph 15 *(b)* (ii) above by, inter alia, considering the barriers to greater use of space applications and services within the United Nations system and suggesting means and mechanisms to eliminate those barriers;

22. *Endorses* the United Nations Programme on Space Applications for 2002, as proposed to the Committee by the Expert on Space Applications;

23. *Notes with satisfaction* that, in accordance with paragraph 30 of General Assembly resolution 50/27 of 6 December 1995, the African regional centres for space science and technology education, in the French language and in the English language, located in Morocco and Nigeria, respectively, and the Centre for Space Science and Technology Education in Asia and the Pacific continued their education programmes in 2001 and that progress has been achieved in furthering the goals of the Network of Space Science and Technology Education and Research Institutions of Central, Eastern and South-Eastern Europe and in establishing regional centres for space science and technology education in the other regions;

24. *Notes* that Member States concerned in Asia and the Pacific continued to hold further consultations, with the assistance of the Office for Outer Space Affairs, with a view to making the Centre for Space Science and Technology Education in Asia and the Pacific grow into a network of nodes;

25. *Recognizes* the usefulness and significance of the Space Conferences of the Americas for the Latin American countries, notes with satisfaction that Colombia offered to host a Fourth Space Conference of the Americas in 2003, for which a Preparatory Conference will be convened during the International Air and Space Fair, known as FIDAE, to be held in Santiago in April 2002, and encourages other regions to convene periodically regional conferences with a view to achieving convergence of positions on issues of common concern in the field of the peaceful uses of outer space among States Members of the United Nations;

26. *Urges* all Governments, organs, organizations and programmes within the United Nations system as well as intergovernmental and non-governmental entities conducting space-related activities to take the necessary action for the effective implementation of the recommendations of UNISPACE III, in particular its resolution entitled "The Space Millennium: Vienna Declaration on Space and Human Development", and requests the Secretary-General to report to the General Assembly at its fifty-seventh session on the implementation of the recommendations of UNISPACE III;

27. *Notes with satisfaction* that the Committee at its forty-fourth session established action teams under the voluntary leadership of Member States to implement the recommendations of UNISPACE III, which had been assigned highest priority by Member States and for which Member States had offered to lead activities, and that those action teams would report on the work conducted and submit work plans to the Scientific and Technical Subcommittee at its thirty-ninth session for approval;

28. *Notes* that, in accordance with paragraph 29 of General Assembly resolution 55/122, the resources necessary to carry out measures and activities contained in the plan of action submitted by the Office for Outer Space Affairs to implement recommendations of UNISPACE III had been included in the proposed programme budget for the biennium 2002-2003 and that the Committee stressed the importance of the full implementation of the plan of action with the necessary resources in 2002;

29. *Agrees* that, in accordance with paragraph 30 of General Assembly resolution 55/122, the Committee should include in the agendas of its forty-fifth to forty-seventh sessions an item on the implementation of the recommendations of UNISPACE III;

30. *Requests* the Committee to prepare a report under the agenda item on the implementation of the recommendations of UNISPACE III for submission to the General Assembly, in order for the Assembly to review and appraise, at its fifty-ninth session, in 2004, in accordance with paragraph 16 of General Assembly resolution 54/68, the implementation of the outcome of UNISPACE III and to consider further actions and initiatives, and agrees that in this context, it would be advisable to establish a working group of the Committee which would take into account the work of the Scientific and Technical Subcommittee on the matter;

31. *Also requests* the Committee to submit for consideration by the General Assembly at its fifty-seventh session recommendations on the format, scope and organizational aspects of the above-mentioned review by the Assembly;

32. *Urges* all Member States to contribute to the Trust Fund for the United Nations Programme on Space Applications to support activities to implement the recommendations of UNISPACE III, in particular the priority project proposals as recommended by the Committee at its forty-third session;

33. *Recommends* that more attention be paid and political support be provided to all matters relating to the protection and the preservation of the outer space

environment, especially those potentially affecting the Earth's environment;

34. *Considers* that it is essential that Member States pay more attention to the problem of collisions of space objects, including those with nuclear power sources, with space debris, and other aspects of space debris, calls for the continuation of national research on this question, for the development of improved technology for the monitoring of space debris and for the compilation and dissemination of data on space debris, also considers that, to the extent possible, information thereon should be provided to the Scientific and Technical Subcommittee, and agrees that international cooperation is needed to expand appropriate and affordable strategies to minimize the impact of space debris on future space missions;

35. *Urges* all States, in particular those with major space capabilities, to contribute actively to the goal of preventing an arms race in outer space as an essential condition for the promotion of international cooperation in the exploration and use of outer space for peaceful purposes;

36. *Emphasizes* the need to increase the benefits of space technology and its applications and to contribute to an orderly growth of space activities favourable to sustained economic growth and sustainable development in all countries, including mitigation of the consequences of disasters, in particular in the developing countries;

37. *Agrees* that the benefits of space technology and its applications should be prominently brought to the attention of conferences organized within the United Nations system to address global issues relating to social, economic and cultural development and that the use of space technology should be promoted towards achieving the objectives of those conferences and implementing the United Nations Millennium Declaration;

38. *Notes* that the Chairman of the Committee on the Peaceful Uses of Outer Space submitted a letter to the Secretary-General, as requested by the Committee at its forty-fourth session, bringing to his attention the need to consider the contributions of space science and technology to a greater extent in achieving the objectives of major United Nations conferences, taking particular account of the needs of developing countries;

39. *Invites* all the organs, organizations and programmes of the United Nations system, particularly those that participate in the Inter-Agency Meeting on Outer Space Activities, to identify recommendations of major United Nations conferences that could be implemented with the use of space science and technology;

40. *Decides* that the practice of sharing seats on a rotating basis between Cuba and Peru as well as Malaysia and the Republic of Korea shall be terminated, that those four countries shall become full members of the Committee, and that Saudi Arabia and Slovakia shall become members of the Committee;

41. *Agrees* that, after the current enlargement of the membership of the Committee, there would be no need to expand its membership further for the next seven years, except in special circumstances meriting consideration before that period has elapsed;

42. *Also agrees* that each regional group should hold consultations among its members that are also members of the Committee, for the purpose of urging them to participate in the work of the Committee and its two subcommittees, and that the regional groups would report to the Committee at its forty-fifth session on the results of their consultations;

43. *Endorses* the decision of the Committee to grant permanent observer status to the European Association for the International Space Year, the National Space Society and the Space Generation Advisory Council;

44. *Requests* the Committee to continue to consider, as a matter of priority, ways and means of maintaining outer space for peaceful purposes and to report thereon to the Assembly at its fifty-seventh session;

45. *Also requests* the Committee to continue to consider, at its forty-fifth session, its agenda item entitled "Spin-off benefits of space technology: review of current status";

46. *Agrees* that a new item entitled "Space and society" should be included in the agenda of the Committee at its forty-fifth and forty-sixth sessions;

47. *Also agrees* that the Committee should consider a report on the activities of the International Satellite System for Search and Rescue as a part of its consideration of the United Nations Programme on Space Applications under the agenda item entitled "Report of the Scientific and Technical Subcommittee", and invites Member States to report on their activities regarding the System;

48. *Invites* the Committee to expand the scope of international cooperation relating to the social, economic, ethical and human dimension in space science and technology applications;

49. *Requests* the specialized agencies and other international organizations to continue and, where appropriate, enhance their cooperation with the Committee and to provide it with progress reports on their work relating to the peaceful uses of outer space;

50. *Requests* the Committee to continue its work, in accordance with the present resolution, to consider, as appropriate, new projects in outer space activities and to submit a report to the General Assembly at its fifty-seventh session, including its views on which subjects should be studied in the future;

51. *Also requests* the Committee to consider and identify new mechanisms of international cooperation in the peaceful uses of outer space, in accordance with the preamble to the present resolution.

Effects of atomic radiation

At its fiftieth session (Vienna, 23-27 April) [A/56/46], the United Nations Scientific Committee on the Effects of Atomic Radiation decided on its new programme of work, which would comprise gathering new data on radiation exposures from natural, man-made and occupational sources; extending its evaluation of medical exposures, especially in relation to new diagnostic procedures that could result in high doses; performing a comprehensive assessment of radon in homes and workplaces; and examining the effects of radiation on the environment as part of a study on radioecology. The Committee also planned to address radiation effects at the level of tissues and organs; examine the potential consequences for development of cancer risk from radiation of newly identified cellular responses to radiation; continue to perform epidemiological evaluation of cancer and of diseases other than cancer that might be increased by radiation; and continue its studies on the radiological health effects from the Chernobyl accident [YUN 1986, p. 584], which were expected to be completed and published in 2005. The Committee also completed a comprehensive review of hereditary risks following parental exposure to radiation and concluded that a sounder basis currently existed for estimating that risk.

GENERAL ASSEMBLY ACTION

On 10 December [meeting 82], the General Assembly, on the recommendation of the Fourth Committee [A/56/547], adopted **resolution 56/50** without vote [agenda item 85].

Effects of atomic radiation

The General Assembly,

Recalling its resolution 913(X) of 3 December 1955, by which it established the United Nations Scientific Committee on the Effects of Atomic Radiation, and its subsequent resolutions on the subject, including resolution 55/121 of 8 December 2000, in which, inter alia, it requested the Scientific Committee to continue its work,

Taking note with appreciation of the work of the Scientific Committee and of the release of its extensive report, entitled *Hereditary Effects of Radiation: United Nations Scientific Committee on the Effects of Atomic Radiation 2001 Report to the General Assembly, with Scientific Annex,*[a]

Reaffirming the desirability of the Scientific Committee continuing its work,

Concerned about the potentially harmful effects on present and future generations resulting from the levels of radiation to which mankind and the environment are exposed,

Noting the views expressed by Member States at its fifty-sixth session with regard to the work of the Scientific Committee,

Conscious of the continuing need to examine and compile information about atomic and ionizing radiation and to analyse its effects on mankind and the environment,

1. *Commends* the United Nations Scientific Committee on the Effects of Atomic Radiation for the valuable contribution it has been making in the course of the past forty-six years, since its inception, to wider knowledge and understanding of the levels, effects and risks of ionizing radiation, and for fulfilling its original mandate with scientific authority and independence of judgement;

2. *Takes note with appreciation* of the work of the Scientific Committee and of the release of its extensive report, which provides the scientific and world community with the Committee's latest evaluations of the hereditary effects of radiation;

3. *Reaffirms* the decision to maintain the present functions and independent role of the Scientific Committee, including its present reporting arrangements;

4. *Requests* the Scientific Committee to continue its work, including its important activities to increase knowledge of the levels, effects and risks of ionizing radiation from all sources, and invites the Scientific Committee to submit its programme of work to the General Assembly;

5. *Endorses* the intentions and plans of the Scientific Committee for its future activities of scientific review and assessment on behalf of the General Assembly;

6. *Requests* the Scientific Committee to continue at its next session the review of the important problems in the field of ionizing radiation and to report thereon to the General Assembly at its fifty-seventh session;

7. *Requests* the United Nations Environment Programme to continue providing support for the effective conduct of the work of the Scientific Committee and for the dissemination of its findings to the General Assembly, the scientific community and the public;

8. *Expresses its appreciation* for the assistance rendered to the Scientific Committee by Member States, the specialized agencies, the International Atomic Energy Agency and non-governmental organizations, and invites them to increase their cooperation in this field;

9. *Invites* the Scientific Committee to continue its consultations with scientists and experts from interested Member States in the process of preparing its future scientific reports;

10. *Welcomes,* in this context, the readiness of Member States to provide the Scientific Committee with relevant information on the effects of ionizing radiation in affected areas, and invites the Scientific Committee to analyse and give due consideration to such information, particularly in the light of its own findings;

11. *Invites* Member States, the organizations of the United Nations system and non-governmental organizations concerned to provide further relevant data about doses, effects and risks from various sources of radiation, which would greatly help in the preparation of future reports of the Scientific Committee to the General Assembly.

[a]Sales No. E.01.IX.2.

International Day of Peace

On 7 September [meeting 111], the General Assembly adopted **resolution 55/282** [draft: A/55/L.95 & Add.1] without vote [agenda item 33].

International Day of Peace

The General Assembly,

Recalling its resolution 36/67 of 30 November 1981, by which it declared that the third Tuesday of September, the opening day of the regular sessions of the General Assembly, shall be officially proclaimed and observed as International Day of Peace and shall be devoted to commemorating and strengthening the ideals of peace both within and among all nations and peoples,

Recalling also its other relevant resolutions, including resolution 55/14 of 3 November 2000,

Reaffirming the contribution that the observance and celebration of the International Day of Peace makes in strengthening the ideals of peace and alleviating tensions and causes of conflict,

Considering the unique opportunity it offers for a cessation of violence and conflict throughout the world, and the related importance of achieving the broadest possible awareness and observance of the International Day of Peace among the global community,

Desiring to draw attention to the objectives of the International Day of Peace, and therefore to fix a date for its observance each year that is separate from the opening day of the regular sessions of the General Assembly,

1. *Decides* that, with effect from the fifty-seventh session of the General Assembly, the International Day of Peace shall be observed on 21 September each year, with this date to be brought to the attention of all people for the celebration and observance of peace;

2. *Declares* that the International Day of Peace shall henceforth be observed as a day of global ceasefire and non-violence, an invitation to all nations and people to honour a cessation of hostilities for the duration of the Day;

3. *Invites* all Member States, organizations of the United Nations system, regional and non-governmental organizations and individuals to commemorate, in an appropriate manner, the International Day of Peace, including through education and public awareness, and to cooperate with the United Nations in the establishment of the global ceasefire.

PART TWO

Human rights

Chapter I

Promotion of human rights

United Nations efforts to promote human rights continued in 2001 through the Commission on Human Rights and its subsidiary body, the Subcommission on the Promotion and Protection of Human Rights. The Office of the United Nations High Commissioner for Human Rights (OHCHR) continued its human rights coordination and implementation activities, and the provision of advisory services and technical cooperation.

Human rights instruments and their monitoring bodies promoted civil, political, economic, social and cultural rights, and aimed to eliminate racial discrimination and discrimination against women, to protect children and to end the practice of torture and other cruel, inhuman or degrading treatment or punishment.

The Subregional Centre for Human Rights and Democracy in Central Africa in Yaoundé, Cameroon, established as a subregional office of OHCHR in cooperation with the Economic Community of Central African States and the UN Department of Political Affairs, became operational in March.

UN machinery

Commission on Human Rights

The Commission on Human Rights held its fifty-seventh session in Geneva from 19 March to 27 April [E/2001/23], during which it adopted 82 resolutions and 19 decisions. The Commission recommended 51 draft decisions for adoption by the Economic and Social Council. On 26 July, the Council took note of the Commission's report (**decision 2001/317**).

The Commission held an informal one-day meeting on 25 September [E/CN.4/IM/2001/1], pursuant to a 2000 Commission decision [YUN 2000, p. 595], to facilitate exchange of information in advance of the fifty-sixth (2001) session of the General Assembly.

Presentations were made on the human rights items allocated by the Assembly to the Third (Social, Humanitatian and Cultural) Committee.

From May to August 2001, the Bureau of the Commission's 2001 session held a series of post-sessional meetings and consultations, which were summarized in a September note of the Secretariat [E/CN.4/IM/2001/2].

Regarding the procedure for dealing with communications concerning violations of human rights and fundamental freedoms, established by Economic and Social Council resolution 1503(XLVIII) [YUN 1970, p. 530] (the 1503 procedure), concern was expressed about the Secretariat practice of sharing details of 1503 communications with the UN Division for the Advancement of Women, to be dealt with by the Commission on the Status of Women. While procedures of the Commission on the Status of Women and the Commission on Human Rights were confidential, their memberships were not identical, and a question had been raised as to whether sharing the information involved a breach of the confidentiality mandated by the 1503 procedure. On 26 July, the Council, pursuant to its resolution 2000/3 [YUN 2000, p. 595], asked the Commission on Human Rights to consider the issue in 2002 and to provide the Council with recommendations, and decided to consider the issue in 2002 (**decision 2001/304**).

Organization of work in 2002

On 27 April [dec. 2001/117], the Commission decided that its fifty-eighth session would be held from 18 March to 26 April 2002. On 24 July, the Economic and Social Council approved the decision (**decision 2001/286**).

Also on 27 April [dec. 2001/118], the Commission recommended that the Council authorize 35 fully serviced additional meetings of the Commission's 2002 session, and requested the Chairperson of the session to organize its work within the times normally allotted so that the additional meetings would be used only if necessary. By **decision 2001/287** of 24 July, the Council authorized the additional meetings and approved the Commission's request to its Chairperson.

Thematic procedures

In accordance with a 2000 Commission decision [YUN 2000, p. 598], the Secretary-General presented, in January [E/CN.4/2001/1/Add.1], a list of all persons currently constituting the thematic and country procedures.

Pursuant to a 2000 Commission request [YUN 2000, p. 598], the Secretariat issued a February note [E/CN.4/2001/101] containing references to the conclusions and recommendations of thematic special rapporteurs and working groups.

A meeting of the special rapporteurs/representatives, experts and chairpersons of working groups of the special procedures and advisory services programme of the Commission was held in 2001 (see p. 598).

Commission action. On 25 April [dec. 2001/116], the Commission postponed consideration of a draft resolution on human rights and thematic procedures and the proposed amendments thereto until 2002.

Subcommission on the Promotion and Protection of Human Rights

2001 session

The Subcommission on the Promotion and Protection of Human Rights, at its fifty-third session (Geneva, 30 July–17 August) [E/CN.4/2002/2], adopted 24 resolutions and 22 decisions, and recommended nine draft decisions for adoption by the Commission.

The Subcommission approved the composition of its working groups for 2002 [dec. 2001/118], asked the Commission to restore its annual session to four weeks' duration [dec. 2001/117] and adjourned the debate on State cooperation with UN human rights mechanisms [dec. 2001/121]. It submitted a draft text for adoption by the Commission regarding proposals on measures to improve the Subcommission's functioning [dec. 2001/116].

A June note by the Secretary-General [E/CN.4/Sub.2/2001/23] reviewed developments between 1 June 2000 and 1 June 2001 in areas with which the Subcommission had been previously concerned.

Report of Subcommission Chairperson. The Commission considered a February report [E/CN.4/2001/86] of the Subcommission's 2000 Chairperson, Iulia-Antoanella Motoc (Romania), which mostly dealt with the Subcommission's working methods in 2000, including the report of the Working Group on Enhancing the Effectiveness of the Mechanisms of the Commission [YUN 2000, p. 595], and Subcommission reports, studies and new subject areas.

Commission action. On 24 April [res. 2001/60], the Commission recommended that the Subcommission improve its methods of work by focusing on its role as an advisory body, giving attention to the studies recommended by the Commission, respecting the highest standards of impartiality and expertise, facilitating the participation of non-governmental organizations (NGOs), fully considering studies and working papers before sending them to the Commission, focusing on human rights issues under its mandate and avoiding duplication of work carried out by other bodies. The Commission presented guidelines for States when nominating and electing Subcommission members.

The Commission invited the Secretary-General to assist the Subcommission with regard to requests for information from Governments, intergovernmental organizations and NGOs, but to consider the requests only after they had been approved by the Commission.

In view of the Commission's decision that the Subcommission should not adopt country-specific resolutions and, in negotiating and adopting thematic resolutions, should refrain from referring to specific countries, the Secretariat, by a May note [E/CN.4/Sub.2/2001/5], provided the Subcommission with a list of countries whose human rights situations the Commission was considering under public procedures for dealing with human rights violations.

Office of the High Commissioner for Human Rights

Reports of High Commissioner. In her annual report to the Commission [E/CN.4/2001/16], the United Nations High Commissioner for Human Rights, Mary Robinson (Ireland), addressed State responsibility to eliminate racial discrimination, contemporary trends in racism, gender and racism, and youth and racism, which were some of the challenges to be considered at the World Conference against Racism, Racial Discrimination, Xenophobia and Related Intolerance (see p. 615). All States needed to ratify the International Convention on the Elimination of All Forms of Racial Discrimination, adopted by the General Assembly in resolution 2106 A (XX) [YUN 1965, p. 440] (see p. 593), and participate regularly in its reporting procedures. Mechanisms such as laws, policies, and national and independent institutions were needed. Attention should be given to education and the promotion of diversity and respect for each other. The report described country missions made by the High Commissioner to China, Colombia, the Democratic Republic of the Congo (DRC), Mexico and Venezuela.

In a May report [E/2001/64], the High Commissioner focused on the rights of some vulnerable groups, in the light of the Third United Nations Conference on the Least Developed Countries (see p. 770), the special session of the General Assembly on HIV/AIDS (see p. 1125) and the World Conference against Racism, Racial Discrimination, Xenophobia and Related Intolerance. She described recent action to advance the rights of indigenous peoples, persons living with HIV/AIDS and persons with disabilities, and addressed the situation in the least developed countries, as a group of particularly vulnerable countries. She also presented an overview of the Commission's 2001 session.

On 26 July, the Economic and Social Council took note of the High Commissioner's May report (**decision 2001/317**).

In a September report to the General Assembly [A/56/36 & Corr.1], the High Commissioner stated that the right to equality and efforts to combat discrimination were themes that characterized OHCHR's work in 2001. She reviewed how OHCHR addressed human rights and conflict; the rights of indigenous peoples; the human rights approach to HIV/AIDS; human rights, development and poverty reduction; trafficking in human beings; corporate responsibility and human rights; human rights and bioethics; and enhancing the rights of the child. In tackling the issues placed before it, OHCHR focused on legal frameworks and concrete national policies, plans, programmes and institutions. OHCHR assisted in the promotion and protection of human rights, including in Afghanistan, the DRC, Haiti, Indonesia (East Timor), the Russian Federation (Chechnya) and the former Yugoslav Republic of Macedonia (FYROM). Commenting on the terrorist attacks in the United States (see p. 60), the High Commissioner called for an approach that eliminated discrimination and built a just and tolerant world, encouraged States to cooperate against terrorism and strengthened the collective commitment to justice and the rule of law. In a November addendum to her report [A/56/36/Add.1], the High Commissioner described the activities of the newly created Subregional Centre for Human Rights and Democracy in Central Africa from September 2000 to July 2001 (see p. 612).

On 19 December, the Assembly took note of the High Commissioner's September report (**decision 56/429**) and the report of the Third Committee [A/56/583/Add.5] pertaining to it (**decision 56/431**).

Appointment. On 31 May, the General Assembly extended the High Commissioner's term of office for a one-year period, beginning on 12 September 2001 and ending on 11 September 2002 (**decision 55/322**), as proposed by the Secretary-General [A/55/110].

Commission action. On 27 April [dec. 2001/119], the Commission renewed its appeal to the Eco-

nomic and Social Council and the General Assembly to allocate additional resources to OHCHR. The Council endorsed that action on 24 July (**decision 2001/288**).

Annual Appeal 2001

The overall target of the Annual Appeal 2001 amounted to $53.8 million, slightly higher than in 2000. Total pledges decreased from $41.8 million in 2000 to $34.7 million in 2001. Payments actually received in 2001 amounted to $31.4 million. During the year, OHCHR substantially increased its rate of implementation compared to previous years, with total expenditure from extrabudgetary funds as at 31 December 2001 amounting to $48.8 million. The high implementation rate was possible only because of the balance ($36.8 million) carried over from 2000 to 2001. The carry-over into 2002 amounted to $32.9 million ($26.9 million net).

Composition of staff

Report of High Commissioner. Pursuant to a 2000 Commission request [YUN 2000, p. 600], the High Commissioner submitted a report [E/CN.4/2001/100] on the composition of OHCHR staff reflecting grade, nationality and gender as at 1 November 2000. The report described measures taken by OHCHR regarding personnel matters.

Commission action. On 25 April [res. 2001/78], by a roll-call vote of 34 to 16, with 2 abstentions, the Commission considered it necessary to change the geographical distribution of staff to a more equitable distribution of posts, particularly by recruiting personnel from developing countries. It invited the High Commissioner to consider establishing a task force to recruit and train qualified personnel from developing countries for OHCHR. The Secretary-General was requested to ensure that attention was paid to recruiting personnel from developing countries to ensure an equitable geographical distribution, giving priority to high-level and Professional posts and the recruitment of women. The Commission asked the High Commissioner to report in 2002. Annexed to the Commission's decision were tables indicating the geographical distribution by region of OHCHR staff.

Strengthening action to promote human rights

Report of Secretary-General. As requested in General Assembly resolution 55/104 [YUN 2000, p. 600], the Secretary-General, in an August report with later addendum [A/56/292 & Add.1], summarized the proposals received from five Member States to strengthen UN action in human rights, through the promotion of international cooperation based on the principles of non-selectivity, impartiality and objectivity.

GENERAL ASSEMBLY ACTION

On 19 December [meeting 88], the General Assembly, on the recommendation of the Third Committee [A/56/583/Add.2], adopted **resolution 56/153** without vote [agenda item 119 (b)].

Strengthening United Nations action in the field of human rights through the promotion of international cooperation and the importance of non-selectivity, impartiality and objectivity

The General Assembly,

Bearing in mind that among the purposes of the United Nations are those of developing friendly relations among nations based on respect for the principle of equal rights and self-determination of peoples and taking other appropriate measures to strengthen universal peace, as well as achieving international cooperation in solving international problems of an economic, social, cultural or humanitarian character and in promoting and encouraging respect for human rights and fundamental freedoms for all without distinction as to race, sex, language or religion,

Desirous of achieving further progress in international cooperation in promoting and encouraging respect for human rights and fundamental freedoms,

Considering that such international cooperation should be based on the principles embodied in international law, especially the Charter of the United Nations, as well as the Universal Declaration of Human Rights, the International Covenants on Human Rights and other relevant instruments,

Deeply convinced that United Nations action in this field should be based not only on a profound understanding of the broad range of problems existing in all societies but also on full respect for the political, economic and social realities of each of them, in strict compliance with the purposes and principles of the Charter and for the basic purpose of promoting and encouraging respect for human rights and fundamental freedoms through international cooperation,

Recalling its previous resolutions in this regard,

Reaffirming the importance of ensuring the universality, objectivity and non-selectivity of the consideration of human rights issues, as affirmed in the Vienna Declaration and Programme of Action adopted by the World Conference on Human Rights on 25 June 1993,

Affirming the importance of the objectivity, independence and discretion of the special rapporteurs and representatives on thematic issues and on countries, as well as of the members of the working groups, in carrying out their mandates,

Underlining the obligation that Governments have to promote and protect human rights and to carry out the responsibilities that they have undertaken under international law, especially the Charter, as well as various international instruments in the field of human rights,

1. *Reiterates* that, by virtue of the principle of equal rights and self-determination of peoples enshrined in the Charter of the United Nations, all peoples have the right freely to determine, without external interference, their political status and to pursue their eco-

nomic, social and cultural development, and that every State has the duty to respect that right within the provisions of the Charter, including respect for territorial integrity;

2. *Reaffirms* that it is a purpose of the United Nations and the task of all Member States, in cooperation with the Organization, to promote and encourage respect for human rights and fundamental freedoms and to remain vigilant with regard to violations of human rights wherever they occur;

3. *Calls upon* all Member States to base their activities for the promotion and protection of human rights, including the development of further international cooperation in this field, on the Charter of the United Nations, the Universal Declaration of Human Rights, the International Covenant on Economic, Social and Cultural Rights, the International Covenant on Civil and Political Rights and other relevant international instruments, and to refrain from activities that are inconsistent with that international framework;

4. *Considers* that international cooperation in this field should make an effective and practical contribution to the urgent task of preventing mass and flagrant violations of human rights and fundamental freedoms for all and to the strengthening of international peace and security;

5. *Reaffirms* that the promotion, protection and full realization of all human rights and fundamental freedoms, as a legitimate concern of the world community, should be guided by the principles of non-selectivity, impartiality and objectivity and should not be used for political ends;

6. *Requests* all human rights bodies within the United Nations system, as well as the special rapporteurs and representatives, independent experts and working groups, to take duly into account the contents of the present resolution in carrying out their mandates;

7. *Expresses its conviction* that an unbiased and fair approach to human rights issues contributes to the promotion of international cooperation as well as to the effective promotion, protection and realization of human rights and fundamental freedoms;

8. *Stresses*, in this context, the continuing need for impartial and objective information on the political, economic and social situations and events of all countries;

9. *Invites* Member States to consider adopting, as appropriate, within the framework of their respective legal systems and in accordance with their obligations under international law, especially the Charter, and international human rights instruments, the measures that they may deem appropriate to achieve further progress in international cooperation in promoting and encouraging respect for human rights and fundamental freedoms;

10. *Requests* the Commission on Human Rights to take duly into account the present resolution and to consider further proposals for the strengthening of United Nations action in the field of human rights through the promotion of international cooperation and the importance of non-selectivity, impartiality and objectivity;

11. *Takes note* of the report of the Secretary-General, and requests the Secretary-General to invite Member States to present practical proposals and ideas that

would contribute to the strengthening of United Nations action in the field of human rights, through the promotion of international cooperation based on the principles of non-selectivity, impartiality and objectivity, and to submit a comprehensive report on this question to the General Assembly at its fifty-seventh session;

12. *Decides* to consider this matter at its fifty-seventh session under the item entitled "Human rights questions".

By **decision 56/464** of 24 December, the Assembly decided that human rights questions would remain for consideration during its resumed fifty-sixth (2002) session.

International cooperation and promotion of dialogue

Report of High Commissioner. Pursuant to a 1999 Commission request [YUN 1999, p. 572], the High Commissioner, in a January report [E/CN.4/2001/95], outlined ways of enhancing international human rights cooperation, including through States' fulfilment of their reporting obligations under various human rights instruments, international decades proclaimed by the United Nations, the establishment of the International Criminal Court (see p. 1213) to reinforce UN human rights machinery, and activities to strengthen regional cooperation to promote and protect human rights.

Commission action. On 25 April [res. 2001/67], the Commission called on Member States, specialized agencies and intergovernmental organizations to carry out a constructive dialogue and consultations to enhance human rights promotion and protection, and encouraged NGOs to participate. States and relevant UN human rights mechanisms and procedures were invited to pay attention to the importance of mutual cooperation, understanding and dialogue in ensuring the promotion and protection of all human rights.

GENERAL ASSEMBLY ACTION

On 19 December [meeting 88], the General Assembly, on the recommendation of the Third Committee [A/56/583/Add.2], adopted **resolution 56/149** without vote [agenda item 119 *(b)*].

Enhancement of international cooperation in the field of human rights

The General Assembly,

Reaffirming its commitment to promoting international cooperation, as set forth in the Charter of the United Nations, in particular Article 1, paragraph 3, as well as relevant provisions of the Vienna Declaration and Programme of Action adopted by the World Conference on Human Rights on 25 June 1993, for enhanc-

ing genuine cooperation among Member States in the field of human rights,

Recalling its adoption of the United Nations Millennium Declaration on 8 September 2000 and its resolution 55/109 of 4 December 2000, and taking note of Commission on Human Rights resolution 2001/67 of 25 April 2001 on the enhancement of international cooperation in the field of human rights,

Recalling also the World Conference against Racism, Racial Discrimination, Xenophobia and Related Intolerance, held at Durban, South Africa, from 31 August to 8 September 2001, and its role in the enhancement of international cooperation in the field of human rights,

Recognizing that the enhancement of international cooperation in the field of human rights is essential for the full achievement of the purposes of the United Nations, including the effective promotion and protection of all human rights,

Reaffirming that dialogue among religions, cultures and civilizations in the field of human rights could contribute greatly to the enhancement of international cooperation in this field, and recalling its decision to proclaim the year 2001 as the United Nations Year of Dialogue among Civilizations, as well as its resolution 55/23 of 13 November 2000 and its resolution 56/6 of 9 November 2001 entitled "Global Agenda for Dialogue among Civilizations",

Emphasizing the need for further progress in the promotion and encouragement of respect for human rights and fundamental freedoms through, inter alia, international cooperation,

Underlining the fact that mutual understanding, dialogue, cooperation, transparency and confidence-building are important elements in all the activities for the promotion and protection of human rights,

Recalling the adoption of resolution 2000/22 of 18 August 2000, entitled "Promotion of dialogue on human rights issues", by the Subcommission on the Promotion and Protection of Human Rights at its fifty-second session,

1. *Reaffirms* that it is one of the purposes of the United Nations and the responsibility of all Member States to promote, protect and encourage respect for human rights and fundamental freedoms through, inter alia, international cooperation;

2. *Also reaffirms* that dialogue among cultures and civilizations facilitates the promotion of a culture of tolerance and respect for diversity, and welcomes in this regard the holding of several conferences and meetings at the national, regional and international levels on dialogue among civilizations, as well as the meetings of the General Assembly under the agenda item entitled "United Nations Year of Dialogue among Civilizations", held on 8 and 9 November 2001;

3. *Considers* that international cooperation in this field, in conformity with the purposes and principles set out in the Charter of the United Nations and international law, should make an effective and practical contribution to the urgent task of preventing violations of human rights and of fundamental freedoms for all;

4. *Reaffirms* that the promotion, protection and full realization of all human rights and fundamental freedoms should be guided by the principles of universality, non-selectivity, objectivity and transparency, in a manner consistent with the purposes and principles set out in the Charter;

5. *Calls upon* Member States, specialized agencies and intergovernmental organizations to continue to carry out a constructive dialogue and consultations for the enhancement of understanding and the promotion and protection of all human rights and fundamental freedoms, and encourages non-governmental organizations to contribute actively to this endeavour;

6. *Invites* States and relevant United Nations human rights mechanisms and procedures to continue to pay attention to the importance of mutual cooperation, understanding and dialogue in ensuring the promotion and protection of all human rights;

7. *Decides* to continue its consideration of this question at its fifty-seventh session.

On the same date, the Assembly, also on the recommendation of the Third Committee [A/56/583/Add.2], adopted **resolution 56/152** by recorded vote (100-54-15) [agenda item 119 (b)].

Respect for the purposes and principles contained in the Charter of the United Nations to achieve international cooperation in promoting and encouraging respect for human rights and for fundamental freedoms and in solving international problems of a humanitarian character

The General Assembly,

Recalling that, in accordance with Article 56 of the Charter of the United Nations, all Member States have pledged themselves to take joint and separate action in cooperation with the Organization for the achievement of the purposes set forth in Article 55, including universal respect for and observance of human rights and fundamental freedoms for all without distinction as to race, sex, language or religion,

Recalling also the Preamble to the Charter, in particular the determination to reaffirm faith in fundamental human rights, in the dignity and worth of the human person and in the equal rights of men and women and of nations large and small,

Reaffirming that the promotion and protection of all human rights and fundamental freedoms must be considered a priority objective of the United Nations in accordance with its purposes and principles, in particular the purpose of international cooperation, and that, within the framework of these purposes and principles, the promotion and protection of all human rights are a legitimate concern of the international community,

Considering the major changes taking place on the international scene and the aspirations of all peoples to an international order based on the principles enshrined in the Charter, including promoting and encouraging respect for human rights and fundamental freedoms for all and respect for the principle of equal rights and self-determination of peoples, peace, democracy, justice, equality, the rule of law, pluralism, development, better standards of living and solidarity,

Recognizing that the international community should devise ways and means to remove current obstacles and meet the challenges to the full realization of all human rights and to prevent the continuation of human rights violations resulting therefrom throughout the world, as well as continue to pay attention to the importance of mutual cooperation, understanding and dialogue in ensuring the promotion and protection of all human rights,

Reaffirming that the enhancement of international cooperation in the field of human rights is essential for the full achievement of the purposes of the United Nations and that human rights and fundamental freedoms are the birthright of all human beings, the promotion and protection of such rights and freedoms being the first responsibility of Governments,

Reaffirming also that all human rights are universal, indivisible, interdependent and interrelated and that the international community must treat human rights globally in a fair and equal manner, on the same footing and with the same emphasis,

Reaffirming further the various articles of the Charter setting out the respective powers and functions of the General Assembly, the Security Council and the Economic and Social Council, as the paramount framework for the achievement of the purposes of the United Nations,

Reaffirming the commitment of all States to fulfil their obligations under other important instruments of international law, in particular those of international human rights and humanitarian law,

Taking into account that, in accordance with Article 103 of the Charter, in the event of a conflict between the obligations of the Members of the United Nations under the Charter and their obligations under any other international agreement, their obligations under the Charter shall prevail,

1. *Affirms* the solemn commitment of all States to enhance international cooperation in the field of human rights and in the solution to international problems of a humanitarian character in full compliance with the Charter of the United Nations, inter alia, by the strict observance of all the purposes and principles set forth in Articles 1 and 2 thereof;

2. *Stresses* the vital role of the work of United Nations and regional arrangements, acting consistently with the purposes and principles enshrined in the Charter, in promoting and encouraging respect for human rights and fundamental freedoms, as well as in solving international problems of a humanitarian character, and affirms that all States, in these activities, must fully comply with the principles set forth in Article 2 of the Charter, in particular respecting the sovereign equality of all States and refraining from the threat or use of force against the territorial integrity or political independence of any State, or acting in any other manner inconsistent with the purposes of the United Nations;

3. *Reaffirms* that the United Nations shall promote universal respect for and observance of human rights and fundamental freedoms for all without distinction as to race, sex, language or religion;

4. *Calls upon* all States to cooperate fully, through constructive dialogue, in order to ensure the promotion and protection of all human rights for all and in promoting peaceful solutions to international problems of a humanitarian character and, in their actions towards that purpose, to comply strictly with the principles and norms of international law, inter alia, by fully respecting international human rights and humanitarian law;

5. *Requests* the Secretary-General to bring the present resolution to the attention of Member States, organs, bodies and other components of the United Nations system, and intergovernmental and non-

governmental organizations, and to disseminate it on the widest possible basis;

6. *Decides* to consider this question at its fifty-seventh session under the item entitled "Human rights questions".

RECORDED VOTE ON RESOLUTION 56/152:

In favour: Afghanistan, Algeria, Angola, Antigua and Barbuda, Azerbaijan, Bahamas, Bahrain, Bangladesh, Barbados, Belarus, Belize, Benin, Bhutan, Bolivia, Botswana, Brunei Darussalam, Burkina Faso, Burundi, Cambodia, Cameroon, Cape Verde, Chad, China, Colombia, Comoros, Congo, Costa Rica, Côte d'Ivoire, Cuba, Democratic People's Republic of Korea, Democratic Republic of the Congo, Djibouti, Dominica, Dominican Republic, Ecuador, Egypt, El Salvador, Equatorial Guinea, Eritrea, Ethiopia, Fiji, Gabon, Gambia, Ghana, Grenada, Guyana, Haiti, Honduras, India, Indonesia, Iran, Jamaica, Jordan, Kazakhstan, Kenya, Kuwait, Lao People's Democratic Republic, Lebanon, Libyan Arab Jamahiriya, Malaysia, Maldives, Mali, Mauritania, Mauritius, Mexico, Mongolia, Morocco, Mozambique, Myanmar, Namibia, Nepal, Nigeria, Oman, Pakistan, Panama, Papua New Guinea, Qatar, Russian Federation, Rwanda, Saint Kitts and Nevis, Saint Lucia, Saudi Arabia, Senegal, Sierra Leone, Solomon Islands, Sri Lanka, Sudan, Suriname, Syrian Arab Republic, Togo, Trinidad and Tobago, Tunisia, Uganda, United Arab Emirates, United Republic of Tanzania, Vanuatu, Venezuela, Viet Nam, Yemen, Zambia.

Against: Albania, Andorra, Armenia, Australia, Austria, Belgium, Bosnia and Herzegovina, Bulgaria, Canada, Croatia, Cyprus, Czech Republic, Denmark, Estonia, Finland, France, Georgia, Germany, Greece, Hungary, Iceland, Ireland, Israel, Italy, Japan, Latvia, Liechtenstein, Lithuania, Luxembourg, Malta, Marshall Islands, Micronesia, Monaco, Netherlands, New Zealand, Norway, Poland, Portugal, Republic of Korea, Republic of Moldova, Romania, Samoa, San Marino, Slovakia, Slovenia, Spain, Sweden, The former Yugoslav Republic of Macedonia, Turkey, Tuvalu, Ukraine, United Kingdom, United States, Yugoslavia.

Abstaining: Argentina, Brazil, Chile, Guatemala, Guinea, Madagascar, Malawi, Nicaragua, Paraguay, Peru, Philippines, Singapore, South Africa, Thailand, Uruguay.

Right to promote and protect human rights

Human rights defenders

Reports of Special Representative. A January report [E/CN.4/2001/94] of the Secretary-General's Special Representative on human rights defenders, Hina Jilani (Pakistan), summarized urgent appeals and communications sent to and received from Governments in 2000 regarding alleged human rights violations targeting human rights defenders. Seven urgent appeals were sent to four countries and four communications to three countries, of which five were transmitted jointly with other thematic mechanisms. The Special Representative expressed concern that a variety of repressive trends, measures and practices, including State apparatus, oppressive laws and other tools, persisted, threatening the freedom of action of human rights defenders, despite some advances in legal and normative frameworks for the protection of human rights defenders in many parts of the world. Areas requiring her special attention included the activities of armed groups, the rights to freedom of association and movement, repressive measures faced by defenders, and strategies to implement the 1998 Declaration on the Right and Responsibility of Individuals, Groups and Organs of Society to Promote and Protect Universally Recognized Human Rights and Fundamental Freedoms, adopted by the General Assembly in resolution 53/144 [YUN 1998, p. 608]. She would also focus on the compilation of relevant legislation or regulatory frameworks; remedial measures for defenders sentenced after unfair trials, including compensation; measures to enhance the protection of defenders; and states of emergency and the ensuing occurrence of impunity insofar as they affected the activities of human rights defenders.

In a September report [A/56/341], the Special Representative stated that from October 2000 to August 2001 she had transmitted 83 urgent appeals to Governments as well as nine allegation letters. Issues of special concern were impunity in cases of threats and attacks against human rights defenders, legal action against defenders, and intelligence activities and propaganda campaigns against them. As to the implementation of the 1998 Declaration, the Special Representative drew attention to the connection between militarism and the severity of human rights violations, and asserted that numerous laws existed that were incompatible with international standards and had become tools for giving legitimacy to State actions that violated human rights. She regretted the lack of progress in creating an enabling environment for the promotion of human rights and the protection of defenders and, as a major reason, pointed to the level of tension between the State and civil society.

In later reports, the Special Representative described her visits to Kyrgyzstan (30 July–4 August) [E/CN.4/2002/106/Add.1] and Colombia (23-31 October) [E/CN.4/2002/106/Add.2].

The Special Representative observed that Kyrgyzstan, like other countries in transition to democratic rule and a market economy, was undergoing a difficult period of political and economic change. She expressed distress that the freedom of human rights defenders had been curtailed by violations of their rights to life, personal security, liberty, privacy, integrity and reputation, and was concerned about mistrust between the Government and civil society, repression of the right to protest human rights violations, the Government's policy of restraint regarding the right to information, the lack of freedom of expression and of the press, and the lack of confidence in the independence of judicial or other authorities, which discouraged action to seek remedies in cases of human rights violations. On the positive side, the Government had taken initiatives on human rights education and progress had been made in establishing national human rights institutions. The Special Representative urged the Government to review legal restrictions on the freedoms of assembly, association and expression; guarantee the protection of human rights and establish mechanisms for that purpose; initiate a dialogue with civil society to build mutual trust; investigate violations committed against human rights defenders and bring those responsible to justice; respect citizens' rights to hold peaceful demonstrations and assemblies; strengthen governmental institutions and train persons involved in the administration of justice; and ensure observance of the 1998 Declaration.

The Special Representative visited Colombia to study and evaluate the situation of human rights defenders and the security conditions under which they pursued their activities in the context of the conflict in the country. She regretted the Government's lack of commitment to deal seriously with violence against human rights defenders, and observed limited consistency in the State's policy of defending human rights, particularly human rights defenders. The Special Representative noted that the main perpetrators of violations of the rights of human rights defenders were the paramilitary groups, and she also deplored the serious violations of international humanitarian law perpetrated by guerrillas against civilians and human rights defenders. She expressed concern at certain practices used by the police and the army against human rights defenders, in particular the keeping of intelligence files containing false information and telephone tapping at NGO offices. She recommended that the Government, among other measures, adopt a comprehensive policy on human rights and international human rights law, strengthen protection mechanisms for judges, prosecutors, investigators, victims, witnesses and threatened persons, combat paramilitarism and dismantle paramilitary groups, disseminate and ensure full observance of the 1998 Declaration, respond to enforced disappearances and adopt a strategy to prevent attacks against human rights defenders. Further recommendations were made regarding the most targeted and vulnerable groups—trade unionists, indigenous and Afro-Colombian communities, internally displaced persons, women, journalists and media representatives. The Special Representative urged the Government to cooperate fully with OHCHR in Colombia (see p. 710).

Commission action. On 25 April [res. 2001/64], the Commission called on States to promote and give effect to the Declaration and to ensure the protection of human rights defenders. Governments were urged to cooperate with the Special Representative, and UN agencies and organizations were asked to assist her.

GENERAL ASSEMBLY ACTION

On 19 December [meeting 88], the General Assembly, on the recommendation of the Third Committee [A/56/583/Add.2], adopted **resolution 56/163** without vote [agenda item 119 (b)].

Declaration on the Right and Responsibility of Individuals, Groups and Organs of Society to Promote and Protect Universally Recognized Human Rights and Fundamental Freedoms

The General Assembly,

Recalling its resolution 53/144 of 9 December 1998, by which it adopted by consensus the Declaration on the Right and Responsibility of Individuals, Groups and Organs of Society to Promote and Protect Universally Recognized Human Rights and Fundamental Freedoms,

Reiterating the importance of the Declaration and its promotion and implementation,

Noting with deep concern that, in many countries, persons and organizations engaged in promoting and defending human rights and fundamental freedoms are facing threats, harassment and insecurity as a result of those activities,

Noting also with deep concern the considerable number of communications received by the Special Representative of the Secretary-General on human rights defenders that, together with the reports submitted by some of the special procedure mechanisms, indicate the serious nature of the risks faced by human rights defenders,

Noting further with deep concern that, in a number of countries in all regions of the world, impunity for threats, attacks and acts of intimidation against human rights defenders persists and that this has a negative impact on the work and safety of human rights defenders,

Emphasizing the important role that individuals, non-governmental organizations and groups play in the promotion and protection of human rights and fundamental freedoms, including in combating impunity,

Welcoming the cooperation between the Special Representative and other special procedures of the Commission on Human Rights,

Recalling that the primary responsibility for promoting and protecting human rights rests with the State, and noting with deep concern that the activities of non-State actors pose a major threat to the security of human rights defenders,

Emphasizing the need for strong and effective measures for the protection of human rights defenders,

1. *Calls upon* all States to promote and give full effect to the Declaration on the Right and Responsibility of Individuals, Groups and Organs of Society to Promote and Protect Universally Recognized Human Rights and Fundamental Freedoms;

2. *Takes note with appreciation* of the reports of the Special Representative of the Secretary-General on human rights defenders;

3. *Emphasizes* the importance of combating impunity, and in this regard urges States to take appropriate measures to address the question of impunity for threats, attacks and acts of intimidation against human rights defenders;

4. *Urges* all Governments to cooperate with and assist the Special Representative in the performance of her tasks and to furnish upon request all information in the fulfilment of her mandate;

5. *Requests* all concerned United Nations agencies and organizations, within their mandates, to provide all possible assistance and support to the Special Representative in the implementation of her programme of activities;

6. *Calls upon* all States to take all necessary measures to ensure the protection of human rights defenders;

7. *Decides* to consider this question at its fifty-seventh session under the item entitled "Human rights questions".

Human rights and human responsibilities

Note by Special Rapporteur. A March note [E/CN.4/2001/96] by the Special Rapporteur appointed by the Subcommission to undertake a study on human rights and human responsibilities, Miguel Alfonso Martínez (Cuba), raised a number of operational and practical points, should the Commission and the Economic and Social Council authorize him to undertake the study.

Commission action. Recalling a 2000 Subcommission decision [YUN 2000, p. 605] regarding the appointment of a Subcommission member to undertake a study on human rights and human responsibilities, the Commission, on 25 April [dec. 2001/115], by a roll-call vote of 34 to 14, with 4 abstentions, recommended a decision for adoption by the Economic and Social Council.

The Council, on 24 July, authorized the Subcommission to appoint Mr. Martínez to undertake the study and to submit a preliminary report to the Commission in 2002 and a final report in 2003 (**decision 2001/285**).

Other aspects

Good governance

Commission action. On 25 April [dec. 2001/72], the Commission asked the High Commissioner to reiterate her invitation to States to provide examples of effective activities in strengthening good governance practices for promoting human rights at the national level, including activities in the context of development cooperation between States, and to extend it to UN and other relevant international bodies, for inclusion in a compilation of practices that could be consulted by interested States. It asked her to inform the Commission of the utility of the material provided in the responses.

Note by Secretariat. A note by the Secretariat [E/CN.4/2002/105 & Corr.1] reported that, as at 15 November, eight States, one specialized agency and two non-governmental entities had provided practical examples of activities that had been effective in strengthening good governance at the national level. Ten replies had been received in 2000 [YUN 2000, p. 605].

The High Commissioner informed the Commission that, given the comprehensiveness of the material received so far, OHCHR had determined that a dedicated effort would be necessary to process and condense the responses into a manageable and user-friendly compilation and had requested extrabudgetary resources to do so.

Human rights instruments

General aspects

In 2001, six main UN human rights instruments were in force that required monitoring of their implementation by treaty bodies. The instruments and their treaty bodies were: the 1965 International Convention on the Elimination of All Forms of Racial Discrimination [YUN 1965, p. 440, GA res. 2106 A (XX)] (Committee on the Elimination of Racial Discrimination); the 1966 International Covenant on Civil and Political Rights [YUN 1966, p. 423, GA res. 2200 A (XXI)] (Human Rights Committee); the 1966 International Covenant on Economic, Social and Cultural Rights [ibid., p. 419, GA res. 2200 A (XXI)] (Committee on Economic, Social and Cultural Rights); the 1979 Convention on the Elimination of All Forms of Discrimination against Women [YUN 1979, p. 895, GA res. 34/180] (Committee on the Elimination of Discrimination against Women); the 1984 Convention against Torture and Other Cruel, Inhuman or Degrading Treatment or Punishment [YUN 1984, p. 813, GA res. 39/46] (Committee against Torture); and the 1989 Convention on the Rights of the Child [YUN 1989, p. 560, GA res. 44/25] (Committee on the Rights of the Child).

An April note by the Secretariat [HRI/GEN/1/Rev.5 & Add.1] contained a compilation of the general comments or general recommendations adopted by the treaty bodies of the UN human rights instruments in force.

Human rights treaty bodies

Pursuant to General Assembly resolution 55/90 [YUN 2000, p. 606], the Secretary-General transmitted the report of the persons chairing the human rights treaty bodies on their thirteenth session (Geneva, 18-22 June) [A/57/56]. The chairpersons reviewed recent developments relating to the work of the treaty bodies, as well as cooperation of the treaty bodies with specialized agencies, UN departments, funds, programmes and mechanisms, and NGOs. They held an informal meeting with representatives of States, at which they exchanged views on topics relating to the treaty bodies, including some of the difficulties they encountered. On 21 June, a joint meeting was held between the chairpersons and the special rapporteurs and representatives, experts and chairpersons of working groups of the special procedures system of the Commission and of the OHCHR advisory services programme. At the meeting, suggestions were made to improve collaboration among the treaty bodies and special procedures.

In a report of 8 June [HRI/MC/2001/2], the Secretariat updated the chairpersons on the implementation of the recommendations adopted at their twelfth meeting [YUN 2000, p. 606], including the status of the three Plans of Action for the Geneva-based treaty bodies. The Plans of Action, which had been incorporated into a global project included in the consolidated annual appeals of the High Commissioner, would be continued through 2004. The chairpersons decided to hold, in 2002, a meeting among members of all the treaty bodies to develop a common approach to specific common issues, which should address the methods of work of the treaty bodies.

Commission action. On 25 April [res. 2001/76], the Commission, by a roll-call vote of 35 to 15, with 2 abstentions, recommended that the General Assembly encourage States parties to UN human rights instruments to establish quota distribution systems by geographical region for the election of treaty body members. The Commission's recommendation was endorsed by the Economic and Social Council on 24 July (**decision 2001/275**). The Commission also recommended adopting flexible procedures when establishing the quotas and presented criteria for doing so, which were incorporated into the Assembly's resolution on the subject (below).

GENERAL ASSEMBLY ACTION

On 19 December [meeting 88], the General Assembly, on the recommendation of the Third Committee [A/56/583/Add.1], adopted **resolution 56/146** by recorded vote (113-47-5) [agenda item 119 (a)].

Equitable geographical distribution in the membership of the human rights treaty bodies

The General Assembly,

Taking note of Commission on Human Rights resolution 2001/76 of 25 April 2001 and Economic and Social Council decision 2001/275 of 24 July 2001,

Reaffirming the importance of the goal of universal ratification of the United Nations human rights instruments,

Welcoming the significant increase in the number of ratifications of United Nations human rights instru-

ments, which has especially contributed to their universality,

Reiterating the importance of the effective functioning of treaty bodies established pursuant to United Nations human rights instruments for the full and effective implementation of those instruments,

Recalling that, with regard to the election of the members of the human rights treaty bodies, the Commission on Human Rights has recognized the importance of giving consideration in their membership to equitable geographical distribution, gender balance and representation of the principal legal systems, and of bearing in mind that the members shall be elected and shall serve in their personal capacity, and shall be of high moral character, acknowledged impartiality and recognized competence in the field of human rights,

Recalling also that the Commission on Human Rights has encouraged States parties to United Nations human rights treaties, individually and through meetings of States parties, to consider how to give better effect, inter alia, to the principle of equitable geographical distribution in the membership of treaty bodies,

Expressing concern at the clear regional imbalance in the current composition of the membership of the human rights treaty bodies, with the exception of the Committee on Economic, Social and Cultural Rights, which is applying a quota system in the distribution of its seats by regional groups,

Noting in particular that the status quo tends to be particularly detrimental to the election of experts from some regional groups,

Convinced that the goal of equitable geographical distribution in the membership of human rights treaty bodies is perfectly compatible and can be fully realized and achieved in harmony with the need to ensure gender balance and the representation of the principal legal systems in those bodies and the high moral character, acknowledged impartiality and recognized competence in the field of human rights of their members,

1. *Encourages* States parties to the United Nations human rights instruments to establish quota distribution systems by geographical region for the election of the members of the treaty bodies;

2. *Calls upon* the States parties to the United Nations human rights instruments to include, as an agenda item at their forthcoming meetings, the establishment of equitable geographical distribution in the membership of the human rights treaty bodies, based on the recommendations of the Commission on Human Rights and the Economic and Social Council and the provisions of the present resolution;

3. *Recommends*, when establishing the quota for each geographical region in each treaty body, the introduction of flexible procedures that encompass the following criteria:

(a) Each of the five regional groups established by the General Assembly must be assigned a quota of the membership of each treaty body in equivalent proportion to the number of States parties to the instrument that it represents;

(b) There must be provision for periodic revisions that reflect the relative changes in the geographical distribution of States parties;

(c) Automatic periodic revisions should be envisaged in order to avoid amending the text of the instrument when the quotas are revised;

4. *Stresses* that the process needed to achieve the goal of equitable geographical distribution in the membership of human rights treaty bodies can contribute to raising awareness of the importance of gender balance, the representation of the principal legal systems and the principle that the members of the treaty bodies shall be elected and shall serve in their personal capacity, and shall be of high moral character, acknowledged impartiality and recognized competence in the field of human rights.

RECORDED VOTE ON RESOLUTION 56/146:

In favour: Afghanistan, Algeria, Angola, Antigua and Barbuda, Azerbaijan, Bahamas, Bahrain, Bangladesh, Barbados, Belarus, Belize, Benin, Bhutan, Bolivia, Botswana, Brunei Darussalam, Burkina Faso, Burundi, Cambodia, Cameroon, Cape Verde, Chad, China, Colombia, Comoros, Congo, Costa Rica, Côte d'Ivoire, Croatia, Cuba, Democratic People's Republic of Korea, Democratic Republic of the Congo, Djibouti, Dominica, Dominican Republic, Ecuador, Egypt, El Salvador, Equatorial Guinea, Eritrea, Ethiopia, Fiji, Gabon, Georgia, Ghana, Grenada, Guatemala, Guyana, Haiti, Honduras, India, Indonesia, Iran, Jamaica, Jordan, Kazakhstan, Kenya, Kuwait, Lao People's Democratic Republic, Lebanon, Libyan Arab Jamahiriya, Madagascar, Malawi, Malaysia, Maldives, Mali, Mauritania, Mauritius, Mexico, Mongolia, Morocco, Mozambique, Myanmar, Namibia, Nepal, Nicaragua, Nigeria, Oman, Pakistan, Papua New Guinea, Paraguay, Peru, Philippines, Qatar, Russian Federation, Rwanda, Saint Kitts and Nevis, Saint Lucia, Samoa, Saudi Arabia, Senegal, Sierra Leone, Singapore, Solomon Islands, South Africa, Sri Lanka, Sudan, Suriname, Syrian Arab Republic, Thailand, Togo, Trinidad and Tobago, Tunisia, Turkmenistan, Uganda, Ukraine, United Arab Emirates, United Republic of Tanzania, Uruguay, Venezuela, Viet Nam, Yemen, Zambia.

Against: Albania, Andorra, Armenia, Australia, Austria, Belgium, Bulgaria, Canada, Chile, Cyprus, Czech Republic, Denmark, Estonia, Finland, France, Germany, Greece, Hungary, Iceland, Ireland, Israel, Italy, Japan, Latvia, Liechtenstein, Lithuania, Luxembourg, Malta, Marshall Islands, Micronesia, Monaco, Netherlands, New Zealand, Norway, Panama, Poland, Portugal, Republic of Korea, Republic of Moldova, Romania, San Marino, Slovenia, Spain, Sweden, United Kingdom, United States, Yugoslavia.

Abstaining: Argentina, Brazil, Gambia, Slovakia, The former Yugoslav Republic of Macedonia.

Reservations to human rights treaties

Commission action. On 25 April [dec. 2001/113], the Commission, taking note of a 2000 resolution of the Subcommission [YUN 2000, p. 609] appointing Françoise Hampson (United Kingdom) as Special Rapporteur to prepare a comprehensive study on reservations to human rights treaties, and of its own decision in 2000 [ibid.] requesting the Subcommission to clarify how the study would complement the work already under way by the International Law Commission (ILC), asked the Subcommission to reconsider its request in the light of the work of ILC.

Subcommission action. On 16 August [res. 2001/17], the Subcommission entrusted Ms. Hampson with preparing an expanded working paper on reservations to human rights treaties based on her 1999 working paper [YUN 1999, p. 574] and discussions by the Subcommission. The Subcommission stated that the study would not duplicate the work of ILC, which dealt with the legal regime applicable to reservations and interpretative declarations in general, as the proposed study involved the examination of the actual reservations and interpretative declarations made to human rights treaties in the light of the legal regime applicable to reservations and interpretative declarations, as set out in the 1999 working paper. It called for submission of the extended working paper in 2002.

States not parties to 1966 Covenants

On 25 April [dec. 2001/114], the Commission, taking note of a 2000 Subcommission resolution [YUN 2000, p. 609] requesting the High Commissioner to convene a seminar of States not parties to the 1966 International Covenants on Human Rights (below), asked the Subcommission to reconsider its request in the light of the developments in its work.

Covenant on Civil and Political Rights and Optional Protocols

Accessions and ratifications

As at 31 December 2001, the numbers of parties to the International Covenant on Civil and Political Rights and the Optional Protocol thereto, adopted by the General Assembly in resolution 2200 A (XXI) [YUN 1966, p. 423], stood at 147 and 101, respectively. While no new parties ratified the Covenant in 2001, the Federal Republic of Yugoslavia (FRY) succeeded to it, replacing the former Socialist Federal Republic of Yugoslavia. FRY ratified the Optional Protocol and Azerbaijan and Mali acceded to it.

The Second Optional Protocol, aiming at the abolition of the death penalty, adopted by the Assembly in resolution 44/128 [YUN 1989, p. 484], was ratified by Bosnia and Herzegovina and acceded to by FRY, bringing the total number of States parties to 46 at year's end.

The Secretary-General reported on the status of the Covenant and its Optional Protocols as at 1 July [A/56/178] and 1 November [E/CN.4/2002/101].

Implementation

Monitoring body. The Human Rights Committee, established under article 28 of the Covenant, held three sessions in 2001: its seventy-first from 19 March to 6 April in New York, and its seventy-second from 9 to 27 July [A/56/40, vol. 1] and its seventy-third from 15 October to 2 November [A/57/40, vol. 1], both in Geneva. A working group met before each session to make recommendations regarding communications received under the Optional Protocol and to prepare lists of issues concerning the reports scheduled for the Committee's consideration. On 26 March, the Committee held a commemorative meeting to mark the twenty-fifth anniversary of the entry into force of the Covenant.

In 2001, the Committee considered reports from 15 States—Afghanistan, Azerbaijan, Croatia, Czech Republic, Democratic People's Republic of Korea, Dominican Republic, Guatemala, Monaco, Netherlands (Netherlands, Netherlands Antilles, Aruba), Switzerland, Syrian Arab Republic, Ukraine, United Kingdom (and Overseas Territories), Uzbekistan, Venezuela—under article 40 of the Covenant. It adopted views on communications from individuals claiming that their rights under the Covenant had been violated, and decided that other such communications were inadmissible. Those views and decisions were annexed to the Committee's reports [A/56/40, vol. II; A/57/40, vol. II].

On 24 July, the Committee adopted General Comment No. 29 on article 4 concerning derogations from the provisions of the Covenant during a state of emergency.

The Government of the Sudan notified other States parties, through the intermediary of the Secretary-General, that a presidential decree adopted in January 2001 pursuant to its Constitution had extended a state of emergency in the Sudan to 31 December 2001. Similarly, Argentina notified other States parties that a state of siege had been declared from 19 to 21 December on all its territory, and from 21 to 31 December in the provinces of Buenos Aires, Entre Rios and San Juan.

The Committee, on 24 October, recommended that the General Assembly endorse the Committee's request to hold an additional week of meetings following its seventy-fifth (July 2002) session in Geneva.

Annexed to the Committee's report [A/56/40 & Add.1] were excerpts from its contribution to the World Conference against Racism, Racial Discrimination, Xenophobia and Related Intolerance [A/CONF.189/PC.2/14] (see p. 615).

Covenant on Economic, Social and Cultural Rights

Accessions and ratifications

As at 31 December 2001, the number of States parties to the International Covenant on Economic, Social and Cultural Rights, adopted by the General Assembly in resolution 2200 A (XXI) [YUN 1966, p. 419], rose to 145, with ratification during the year by China, accession by Eritrea and succession by FRY, which replaced the former Socialist Federal Republic of Yugoslavia.

On 20 April [res. 2001/30], the Commission called on States to consider signing and ratifying,

and the States parties to implement, the Covenant. States parties were called on to withdraw reservations and to ensure that the Covenant was taken into account in their national and international policy-making processes.

The Secretary-General reported on the status of the Covenant and its Optional Protocols as at 1 July [A/56/178] and 1 November [E/CN.4/2002/101].

Draft optional protocol

Report of High Commissioner. The Commission had before it a report of the High Commissioner [E/CN.4/2001/62 & Add.1] presenting the views of five States, three specialized agencies and six NGOs on the draft optional protocol that would allow the consideration of communications in relation to the Covenant. The report contained comments received from one State and three NGOs on options regarding the optional protocol proposed by the High Commissioner in 2000 [YUN 2000, p. 610].

A March addendum to the High Commissioner's report [E/CN.4/2001/62/Add.2] contained the conclusions, recommendations and options regarding progress towards the adoption of the protocol, made by the workshop on the justiciability of economic, social and cultural rights (Geneva, 5-6 February). The workshop, which was organized in cooperation with the International Commission of Jurists and supported by Finland, expressed support for the draft being designed to respond to violations of the rights of individuals and groups, rather than to a lesser standard of unsatisfactory application. Decisions of the Committee on Economic, Social and Cultural Rights under the protocol should include a legal finding, as well as recommendations for remedial action and changes in law, policy and practice. Most participants agreed that the most suitable next step was for the Commission on Human Rights to establish an open-ended working group to work towards the adoption of the optional protocol.

Commission action. On 20 April [res. 2001/30], the Commission decided to appoint an independent expert to examine the question of a draft optional protocol and to report in 2002 with a view to its consideration of possible further action, including the establishment of an open-ended working group. The Secretary-General was asked to report in 2002.

On 4 June, the Economic and Social Council endorsed the Commission's decision regarding the expert's appointment and submission of a report (**decision 2001/220**).

Pursuant to the Commission's resolution, Hatem Kotrane (Tunisia) was appointed independent expert in June.

Activities of independent expert. The independent expert held a series of meetings (20-24 August) with members and officials of the Committee on Economic, Social and Cultural Rights, the Human Rights Committee, the Committee on the Rights of the Child and the International Labour Organization. He held a second series of consultations (27 November–7 December) to hear first-hand the views of States on the draft optional protocol. He also attended a round table on the optional protocol (Geneva, 30 November) [E/CN.4/2002/161], hosted by the International Commission of Jurists, which was held for the exchange of views between States, organizations and experts in the area of economic, social and cultural rights.

Subcommission action. On 15 August [res. 2001/6], the Subcommission urged the Commission to give high priority to the consideration of a draft optional protocol and reiterated its suggestion that the Commission establish an open-ended working group for further study.

Implementation

Monitoring body. The Committee on Economic, Social and Cultural Rights held its twenty-fifth (23 April–11 May), twenty-sixth (extraordinary) (13-31 August) and twenty-seventh (12-30 November) sessions, all in Geneva [E/2002/22]. The Committee's extraordinary session was used entirely for the consideration of States parties' reports in order to reduce the backlog. The Committee's five-member working group met in Geneva prior to each session to identify issues to be discussed with reporting States.

On 26 July, the Economic and Social Council took note of the Committee's report on its twenty-second, twenty-third and twenty-fourth sessions, held in 2000 [YUN 2000, p. 610] (**decision 2001/317**).

During its 2001 sessions, the Committee examined reports prepared under articles 16 and 17 of the Covenant submitted by Algeria, Bolivia, China (Hong Kong, Special Administrative Region), Colombia, Croatia, France, Germany, Honduras, Israel, Jamaica, Japan, Nepal, Panama, the Republic of Korea, Senegal, Sweden, the Syrian Arab Republic, Togo, Ukraine and Venezuela.

The Committee adopted, on 4 May, a statement on the eradication of poverty.

On 7 May, the Committee held an international consultation, organized in cooperation with the Haut conseil de la coopération internationale, on economic, social and cultural rights in relation to the development activities of international institutions. Panel discussions were held on international institutions and the Covenant and on possible advances in economic, social and cultural rights. One of the issues raised at the consultation was the desirability of assisting States that might wish to integrate human rights into their poverty reduction strategies. OHCHR agreed to undertake a project to prepare guidelines setting out how States could do so.

By a letter of 11 May [E/2001/77], the Committee Chairperson drew the Council's attention to a letter from the Committee to Israel expressing grave concern over accounts of violations of the economic, social and cultural rights of Palestinians. The Chairperson stated that the Committee was limited in enforcement means required to uphold the Covenant in such a situation; the international measures likely to contribute to the progressive implementation of the Covenant therefore fell within the purview of other UN bodies; and the Committee would be remiss if it did not underscore the need for protection measures for the population of the occupied territories.

Commission action. On 20 April [res. 2001/30], the Commission encouraged the Committee to continue efforts to promote, protect and fully realize the rights enshrined in the Covenant. It also encouraged the High Commissioner to continue to ensure better support for the Committee, to strengthen the research and analytical capacities of her Office in economic, social and cultural rights and to share her expertise through the holding of expert meetings.

GENERAL ASSEMBLY ACTION

On 19 December [meeting 88], the General Assembly, on the recommendation of the Third Committee [A/56/583/Add.1], adopted **resolution 56/144** without vote [agenda item 119 (a)].

International Covenants on Human Rights

The General Assembly,

Recalling its resolutions 54/157 of 17 December 1999 and 55/90 of 4 December 2000 and Commission on Human Rights resolution 2000/67 of 26 April 2000,

Mindful that the International Covenants on Human Rights constitute the first all-embracing and legally binding international treaties in the field of human rights and, together with the Universal Declaration of Human Rights, form the core of the International Bill of Human Rights,

Taking note of the report of the Secretary-General on the status of the International Covenant on Economic, Social and Cultural Rights, the International Covenant on Civil and Political Rights and the Optional Protocols to the International Covenant on Civil and Political Rights,

Recalling the International Covenant on Economic, Social and Cultural Rights and the International Covenant on Civil and Political Rights, and reaffirming that all human rights and fundamental freedoms are universal, indivisible, interdependent and interrelated and that the promotion and protection of one category of rights should never exempt or excuse States from the promotion and protection of the other rights,

Recognizing the important role of the Human Rights Committee and the Committee on Economic, Social and Cultural Rights in examining the progress made by States parties in fulfilling the obligations undertaken in the International Covenants on Human Rights and the Optional Protocols to the International Covenant on Civil and Political Rights and in providing recommendations to States parties on their implementation,

Considering that the effective functioning of the Human Rights Committee and the Committee on Economic, Social and Cultural Rights is indispensable for the full and effective implementation of the International Covenants on Human Rights,

Recognizing the importance of regional human rights instruments and monitoring mechanisms in complementing the universal system of promotion and protection of human rights,

1. *Reaffirms* the importance of the International Covenants on Human Rights as major components of international efforts to promote universal respect for and observance of human rights and fundamental freedoms;

2. *Welcomes* the initiative of the Secretary-General at the Millennium Assembly of the United Nations to invite heads of State and Government to sign, ratify or accede to the International Covenants on Human Rights, and expresses its appreciation to those States that have done so;

3. *Strongly appeals* to all States that have not yet done so to become parties to the International Covenant on Economic, Social and Cultural Rights and the International Covenant on Civil and Political Rights, as well as to accede to the Optional Protocols to the International Covenant on Civil and Political Rights and to make the declaration provided for in article 41 of the Covenant;

4. *Invites* the United Nations High Commissioner for Human Rights to intensify systematic efforts to encourage States to become parties to the International Covenants on Human Rights and, through the programme of advisory services in the field of human rights, to assist such States, at their request, in ratifying or acceding to the Covenants and to the Optional Protocols to the International Covenant on Civil and Political Rights with a view to achieving universal adherence;

5. *Emphasizes* the importance of the strictest compliance by States parties with their obligations under the International Covenant on Economic, Social and Cultural Rights and the International Covenant on Civil and Political Rights and, where applicable, the Optional Protocols to the International Covenant on Civil and Political Rights;

6. *Stresses* the importance of avoiding the erosion of human rights by derogation, and underlines the necessity of strict observance of the agreed conditions and procedures for derogation under article 4 of the International Covenant on Civil and Political Rights, bearing in mind the need for States parties to provide the fullest possible information during states of emergency so that the justification for the appropriateness of measures taken in those circumstances can be assessed, and in this regard takes note of General Comment No. 29 adopted by the Human Rights Committee;

7. *Encourages* States parties to consider limiting the extent of any reservations that they lodge to the International Covenants on Human Rights, to formulate any reservations as precisely and narrowly as possible and to ensure that no reservation is incompatible with the object and purpose of the relevant treaty;

8. *Also encourages* States parties to review regularly any reservations made in respect of the provisions of the International Covenants on Human Rights and the Optional Protocols to the International Covenant on Civil and Political Rights with a view to withdrawing them;

9. *Takes note with appreciation* of the annual reports of the Human Rights Committee submitted to the General Assembly at its fifty-fifth and fifty-sixth sessions, and takes note of General Comments Nos. 27, 28 and 29 adopted by the Committee;

10. *Welcomes* the reports of the Committee on Economic, Social and Cultural Rights on its twentieth and twenty-first sessions and on its twenty-second, twenty-third and twenty-fourth sessions, and takes note of General Comments Nos. 11, 12, 13 and 14 adopted by the Committee;

11. *Urges* States parties to fulfil in good time such reporting obligations under the International Covenants on Human Rights as may be requested and to make use in their reports of gender-disaggregated data, and stresses the importance of taking fully into account a gender perspective in the implementation of the Covenants at the national level, including in the national reports of States parties and in the work of the Human Rights Committee and the Committee on Economic, Social and Cultural Rights;

12. *Calls upon* States parties that have not yet submitted core documents to the Office of the United Nations High Commissioner for Human Rights to do so, and invites all States parties regularly to review and update their core documents;

13. *Urges* States parties to take duly into account, in implementing the provisions of the International Covenants on Human Rights, the recommendations and observations made during the consideration of their reports by the Human Rights Committee and by the Committee on Economic, Social and Cultural Rights, as well as the views adopted by the Human Rights Committee under the first Optional Protocol to the International Covenant on Civil and Political Rights;

14. *Invites* States parties to give particular attention to the dissemination at the national level of their reports submitted to the Human Rights Committee and the Committee on Economic, Social and Cultural Rights, the summary records relating to the examination of those reports by the Committees and the recommendations and observations made by the Committees after the examination of those reports;

15. *Urges* all States to publish the texts of the International Covenant on Economic, Social and Cultural Rights, the International Covenant on Civil and Political Rights and the Optional Protocols to the International Covenant on Civil and Political Rights in as many local languages as possible and to distribute them and

make them known as widely as possible in their territories;

16. *Urges* each State party to translate, publish and make widely available in its territory by appropriate means the full text of the concluding observations on its reports to the Human Rights Committee and the Committee on Economic, Social and Cultural Rights;

17. *Reiterates* that States parties should take into account, in their nomination of members to the Human Rights Committee and the Committee on Economic, Social and Cultural Rights, that the Committees shall be composed of persons of high moral character and recognized competence in the field of human rights, consideration being given to the usefulness of the participation of some persons having legal experience, and that members serve in their personal capacity, and also reiterates that, in the elections of the Committees, consideration shall be given to equitable geographical distribution of membership and to the representation of the different forms of civilization and of the principal legal systems;

18. *Invites* the Human Rights Committee and the Committee on Economic, Social and Cultural Rights, when considering the reports of States parties, to continue to identify specific needs that might be addressed by United Nations departments, funds and programmes and the specialized agencies, including through the advisory services and technical assistance programme of the Office of the United Nations High Commissioner for Human Rights;

19. *Stresses* the need for improved coordination among relevant United Nations mechanisms and bodies in supporting States parties, upon their request, in implementing the International Covenants on Human Rights and the Optional Protocols to the International Covenant on Civil and Political Rights, and encourages continued efforts in this direction;

20. *Takes note* of the adoption by the Human Rights Committee of its revised rules of procedure, and welcomes the efforts of the Human Rights Committee and the Committee on Economic, Social and Cultural Rights regularly to review their working methods in order to increase their efficiency and effectiveness;

21. *Welcomes* the meeting between the Human Rights Committee and States parties, held on 30 October 2000, to exchange ideas on how to render the working methods of the Committee more efficient, expresses appreciation for the decision of the Committee to organize similar consultations in 2002, and encourages all States parties to continue to contribute to the dialogue with practical and concrete proposals and ideas on ways to improve the effective functioning of the Human Rights Committee and the Committee on Economic, Social and Cultural Rights;

22. *Also welcomes* the continuing efforts of the Human Rights Committee and the Committee on Economic, Social and Cultural Rights to strive for uniform standards in the implementation of the provisions of the International Covenants on Human Rights, and appeals to other bodies dealing with similar human rights questions to respect those uniform standards, as expressed in the general comments of the Committees;

23. *Stresses* the need for further efforts towards developing indicators and benchmarks to measure progress in the national implementation by States parties of the rights protected by the International Covenant on Economic, Social and Cultural Rights;

24. *Welcomes* Economic and Social Council decision 2001/220 of 4 June 2001, in which the Council authorized the appointment by the Commission on Human Rights of an independent expert to examine the question of a draft optional protocol to the International Covenant on Economic, Social and Cultural Rights, and invites the Committee on Economic, Social and Cultural Rights to consider contributing to the work of the independent expert;

25. *Encourages* the Secretary-General to continue to assist States parties to the International Covenants on Human Rights in the preparation of their reports, including by convening seminars or workshops at the national level for the training of government officials engaged in the preparation of such reports and by exploring other possibilities available under the programme of advisory services in the field of human rights;

26. *Requests* the Secretary-General to ensure that the Office of the United Nations High Commissioner for Human Rights effectively assists the Human Rights Committee and the Committee on Economic, Social and Cultural Rights in the implementation of their respective mandates by providing, inter alia, adequate Secretariat staff resources and conference and other relevant support services;

27. *Decides* to endorse the request by the Human Rights Committee to hold an additional week of meetings at Geneva in 2002 in order to reduce further the existing backlog;

28. *Welcomes* the initiative of the Secretary-General, taking into account the suggestions of the Human Rights Committee, to take determined steps, in particular through the Department of Public Information of the Secretariat, to give more publicity to the work of that Committee and, similarly, to the work of the Committee on Economic, Social and Cultural Rights;

29. *Requests* the Secretary-General to submit to the General Assembly at its fifty-eighth session, under the item entitled "Human rights questions", a report on the status of the International Covenant on Economic, Social and Cultural Rights, the International Covenant on Civil and Political Rights and the Optional Protocols to the International Covenant on Civil and Political Rights, including all reservations and declarations.

Convention against racial discrimination

Accessions and ratifications

As at 31 December 2001, there were 161 parties to the International Convention on the Elimination of All Forms of Racial Discrimination, adopted by the General Assembly in resolution 2106 A (XX) [YUN 1965, p. 440]. During the year, Belize, Benin, Eritrea and Kenya became parties, and FRY succeeded to the Convention, replacing the former Socialist Federal Republic of Yugoslavia.

On 18 April [res. 2001/5], the Commission appealed to States that had not done so to consider ratifying or acceding to the Convention and called on States that had done so to implement it. States parties were urged to consider making the declaration provided for in article 14 of the Convention (below) and to adopt measures aimed at eliminating all forms of discrimination, xenophobia and related intolerance.

Implementation

Monitoring body. The Committee on the Elimination of Racial Discrimination (CERD), established under article 8 of the Convention, held its fifty-eighth and fifty-ninth sessions, both in Geneva, from 6 to 23 March and from 30 July to 17 August, respectively [A/56/18].

The Committee considered reports, comments and information submitted by 23 States parties—Algeria, Argentina, Bangladesh, China, Cyprus, Egypt, Gambia, Georgia, Germany, Greece, Iceland, Italy, Japan, Liberia, Portugal, Sierra Leone, Sri Lanka, Sudan, Togo, Trinidad and Tobago, Ukraine, United States, Viet Nam—on measures they had taken to implement the Convention and summarized its members' views on each country report and the statements made by the States parties concerned.

Under article 14 of the Convention, CERD considered communications from individuals or groups of individuals claiming violation of their rights enumerated in the Convention by a State party recognizing the Committee's competence to receive and consider such communications. Thirty-four States parties had declared such recognition (Algeria, Australia, Belgium, Bulgaria, Chile, Costa Rica, Cyprus, Czech Republic, Denmark, Ecuador, Finland, France, Hungary, Iceland, Ireland, Italy, Luxembourg, Malta, Netherlands, Norway, Peru, Poland, Portugal, Republic of Korea, Russian Federation, Senegal, Slovakia, South Africa, Spain, Sweden, FYROM, Ukraine, Uruguay, FRY).

In accordance with article 15, the Committee was empowered to consider copies of petitions, reports and other information relating to Trust and Non-Self-Governing Territories. CERD noted, as it had in the past, that it was difficult to fulfil its functions under the article as the documents did not include copies of petitions and contained scant information directly related to the Convention's principles and objectives. The Committee requested the submission of the appropriate information.

In its decisions, CERD considered the situation in Liberia to be extremely grave with respect to implementation of the Convention and urged the country to fulfil its obligations under it; reaffirmed the importance of ending the foreign occupation of Cyprus (see p. 390); and requested

the High Commissioner to provide funding for certain meetings.

The Committee finalized its written contribution [A/CONF.189/PC.2/13] to the preparatory process of the World Conference against Racism, Racial Discrimination, Xenophobia and Related Intolerance (see p. 615) and the Third Decade to Combat Racism and Racial Discrimination (see p. 614).

As at 31 December, 32 States parties had accepted an amendment to the Convention regarding the financing of CERD [YUN 1992, p. 714]. The amendment was to enter into force when accepted by a two-thirds majority of States parties.

Convention against torture

Accessions and ratifications

As at 31 December 2001, 127 States were parties to the 1984 Convention against Torture and Other Cruel, Inhuman or Degrading Treatment or Punishment, adopted by the General Assembly in resolution 39/46 [YUN 1984, p. 813]. Lesotho, Nigeria, Saint Vincent and the Grenadines and Sierra Leone became parties to the Convention in 2001, and FRY succeeded to it, replacing the former Socialist Federal Republic of Yugoslavia. Forty-five parties had made the required declarations under articles 21 and 22 (under which a party recognized the competence of the Committee against Torture to receive and consider communications from a party claiming that another was not fulfilling its obligations under the Convention, and to receive communications from or on behalf of individuals who claimed to be victims of a violation of the Convention by a State party) and three had made the declaration only under article 21 and one under article 22. Amendments to articles 17 and 18, adopted in 1992 [YUN 1992, p. 735], had been accepted by 23 States parties as at year's end.

On 25 April [res. 2001/62], the Commission urged States to become parties to the Convention and invited all ratifying or acceding States that had not done so to make the declaration provided for in articles 21 and 22 and to consider withdrawing their reservations to article 20. It asked the Secretary-General to continue to report annually on the status of the Convention.

The Secretary-General reported on the status of the Convention as at 11 June [A/56/603] and 13 December [E/CN.4/2002/65].

The Assembly, by **resolution 56/143**, urged States that had not become parties to do so. States parties were urged to comply with their obligations under the Convention, and those becoming parties and those that were parties but had not done so were invited to make the declarations provided for in articles 21 and 22 and to consider withdrawing reservations to article 20.

Draft optional protocol

Working group activities. The open-ended working group on a draft optional protocol to the Convention intended to establish a system of regular visits to places of detention, at its ninth session (Geneva, 12-23 February) [E/CN.4/2001/67], held a general debate on an alternative text presented by Mexico with the support of the group of Latin American countries and on the role of national and international mechanisms in the framework of the optional protocol, and the relationship between them. It discussed the scope of prevention activities to be conducted by national and international mechanisms. Annexed to the report were the draft alternative text and proposed new and revised articles submitted by Sweden on behalf of the European Union (EU).

Commission action. On 23 April [res. 2001/44], the Commission asked the working group on the draft optional protocol to the Convention to meet prior to the Commission's 2002 session to complete the final and substantive text. The Secretary-General was asked to transmit the working group's report to Governments, specialized agencies, chairpersons of human rights treaty bodies, intergovernmental organizations and NGOs and to invite them to submit their comments to the group. He was also asked to invite them, as well as the Chairperson of the Committee against Torture and the Special Rapporteur on the question of torture, to participate in working group activities.

On 24 July, the Economic and Social Council authorized the group to meet for two weeks and encouraged the group's Chairperson-Rapporteur to facilitate the completion of a consolidated text (**decision 2001/265**).

Implementation

Monitoring body. The Committee against Torture, established as a monitoring body under the Convention, held its twenty-sixth and twenty-seventh sessions in Geneva from 30 April to 18 May [A/56/44] and from 12 to 23 November [A/57/44], respectively. Under article 19, it considered reports submitted by Benin, Bolivia, Brazil, Costa Rica, the Czech Republic, Georgia, Greece, Indonesia, Israel, Kazakhstan, Slovakia, Ukraine and Zambia.

The Committee held closed meetings in May and in November, during which, in accordance with article 20, it studied confidential information that contained indications that torture was systematically practised in a State party to the Convention. Under article 22, the Committee considered communications submitted by individuals who claimed that their rights, as enumerated in the Convention, had been violated by a State party and that they had exhausted all available domestic remedies.

The Committee decided to request an opinion from the United Nations Legal Counsel on the question of the applicability of the Convention in the Occupied Palestinian Territory.

The Committee's contribution to the preparatory process for the World Conference against Racism, Racial Discrimination, Xenophobia and Related Intolerance (see p. 615) was annexed to its report [A/56/44], as was a joint declaration on the UN International Day in Support of Victims of Torture (26 June) by the Committee, the Board of Trustees of the United Nations Voluntary Fund for Victims of Torture, the Special Rapporteur on the question of torture (see p. 644) and the High Commissioner.

The eighth meeting of States parties (Geneva, 28 November) [CAT/SP/24] elected five Committee members to replace those whose terms were to expire on 31 December 2001.

Convention on elimination of discrimination against women and optional protocol

On 24 December, the General Assembly, in **resolution 56/229**, expressing disappointment that universal ratification of the 1979 Convention on the Elimination of All Forms of Discrimination against Women was not achieved by 2000, urged States that had not ratified or acceded to it to do so. It urged Governments, UN system agencies and organizations and NGOs to disseminate the Convention and the Optional Protocol.

(For details on the status of the Convention and on the Optional Protocol, see p. 1074.)

Convention on the Rights of the Child

Accessions and ratifications

As at 31 December 2001, there continued to be 191 States parties to the 1989 Convention on the Rights of the Child, adopted by the General Assembly in resolution 44/25 [YUN 1989, p. 560]. The Optional Protocols to the Convention on involvement of children in armed conflict and on the sale of children, child prostitution and child pornography, adopted by the Assembly in resolution 54/263 [YUN 2000, p. 615], were signed by 93 and 89 States parties to the Convention, respectively, and ratified or acceded to by 13 and 16 States parties, respectively.

The Secretary-General reported on the status of the Convention as at 20 November [E/CN.4/2002/84].

An amendment to the Convention to expand the membership of the Committee on the Rights of the Child (CRC) from 10 to 18, approved by the Assembly in resolution 50/155 [YUN 1995, p. 706], had been accepted by 113 States parties as at 31 December 2001. The amendment required acceptance by a two-thirds majority to enter into force.

On 25 April [res. 2001/75], the Commission urged States that had not done so to sign and ratify or accede to the Convention and to consider signing and ratifying the Optional Protocols. It called on States parties to implement the Convention and to accept the amendment on expanding CRC membership.

Implementation

Monitoring body. In 2001, CRC held its twenty-sixth (8-26 January) [CRC/C/103], twenty-seventh (21 May-8 June) [CRC/C/108] and twenty-eighth (24 September–12 October) [CRC/C/111] sessions, all in Geneva. Each session was preceded by a meeting of a working group, which facilitated the Committee's work by reviewing State party reports and identifying the main questions that would need to be discussed with the representatives of the reporting States. The meetings also provided an opportunity to consider technical assistance and international cooperation.

Under article 44 of the Convention, CRC considered initial or periodic reports from the following States parties: Bhutan, Cameroon, Cape Verde, Côte d'Ivoire, DRC, Denmark, Dominican Republic, Egypt, Ethiopia, Gambia, Guatemala, Kenya, Latvia, Lesotho, Liechtenstein, Lithuania, Mauritania, Monaco, Oman, Palau, Paraguay, Portugal, Qatar, Saudi Arabia, Turkey, United Republic of Tanzania, Uzbekistan.

On 25 January, the Committee adopted general comment no. 1 (aims of education) on article 29, paragraph 1, of the Convention; the comment dealt with the significance and functions of the article, human rights education, and implementation, monitoring and review of the article.

In September, the Committee devoted its day of general discussion to violence against children within the family and at school.

Commission action. On 25 April [res. 2001/75], the Commission welcomed the Committee's recommendation [CRC/C/111] that the Secretary-General conduct a study on violence against children, including the different types of violent treatment of which children were victims, to identify their causes, the extent of such violence and its impact on children, and to make recommendations, including remedies and preventive and rehabilitative measures.

Note by Secretary-General. An October note by the Secretary-General [A/56/488] transmitted a letter of the CRC Chairperson containing the recommendation for an in-depth study on violence against children.

Convention on migrant workers

Accessions and ratifications

As at 31 December 2001, the International Convention on the Protection of the Rights of All Migrant Workers and Members of Their Families, adopted by the General Assembly in resolution 45/158 [YUN 1990, p. 594], had been ratified or acceded to by Azerbaijan, Belize, Bolivia, Bosnia and Herzegovina, Cape Verde, Colombia, Egypt, Ghana, Guinea, Mexico, Morocco, the Philippines, Senegal, Seychelles, Sri Lanka, Uganda and Uruguay, and signed by Bangladesh, Burkina Faso, Chile, the Comoros, Guatemala, Guinea-Bissau, Paraguay, Sao Tome and Principe, Sierra Leone, Tajikistan, Togo and Turkey. The Convention was to enter into force three months following the date of deposit of the twentieth instrument of ratification or accession.

The Secretary-General reported on the status of the Convention as at 1 June [A/56/179] and 6 December [E/CN.4/2002/89].

Commission action. On 24 April [res. 2001/53], the Commission, welcoming the activities of the global campaign for the Convention's entry into force, called on all Member States to sign and ratify or accede to the Convention as a matter of priority. It asked the Secretary-General to assist in promoting the Convention through the World Public Information Campaign for Human Rights, launched by the General Assembly in resolution 43/128 [YUN 1988, p. 539] (see p. 604), and the programme of advisory services in human rights. He was requested to report in 2002 on the Convention's status and on Secretariat efforts to promote it, as well as on the protection of migrant workers' rights.

(For further information on migrant workers, see p. 618.)

GENERAL ASSEMBLY ACTION

On 19 December [meeting 88], the General Assembly, on the recommendation of the Third Committee [A/56/583/Add.1], adopted **resolution 56/145** without vote [agenda item 119 (a)].

International Convention on the Protection of the Rights of All Migrant Workers and Members of Their Families

The General Assembly,

Reaffirming once more the permanent validity of the principles and norms set forth in the basic instruments regarding the international protection of human rights, in particular the Universal Declaration of Human Rights, the International Covenants on Human Rights, the International Convention on the Elimination of All Forms of Racial Discrimination, the Convention on the Elimination of All Forms of Discrimination against Women and the Convention on the Rights of the Child,

Bearing in mind the principles and norms established within the framework of the International Labour Organization and the importance of the work done in connection with migrant workers and members of their families in other specialized agencies and in various organs of the United Nations,

Reiterating that, despite the existence of an already established body of principles and norms, there is a need to make further efforts to improve the situation and to guarantee respect for the human rights and dignity of all migrant workers and members of their families,

Aware of the situation of migrant workers and members of their families and the marked increase in migratory movements that has occurred, especially in certain parts of the world,

Considering that, in the Vienna Declaration and Programme of Action adopted by the World Conference on Human Rights on 25 June 1993, all States are urged to guarantee the protection of the human rights of all migrant workers and members of their families,

Underlining the importance of the creation and promotion of conditions to foster greater harmony and tolerance between migrant workers and the rest of the society of the State in which they reside, with the aim of eliminating the growing manifestations of racism and xenophobia perpetrated in segments of many societies by individuals or groups against migrant workers,

Recalling its resolution 45/158 of 18 December 1990, by which it adopted and opened for signature, ratification and accession the International Convention on the Protection of the Rights of All Migrant Workers and Members of Their Families,

Bearing in mind that, in the Vienna Declaration and Programme of Action, States are invited to consider the possibility of signing and ratifying the Convention at the earliest possible time,

1. *Expresses its deep concern* at the growing manifestations of racism, xenophobia and other forms of discrimination and inhuman or degrading treatment directed against migrant workers in various parts of the world;

2. *Welcomes* the signature or ratification of or accession to the International Convention on the Protection of the Rights of All Migrant Workers and Members of Their Families by some Member States;

3. *Calls upon* all Member States to consider signing and ratifying or acceding to the Convention as a matter of priority, expresses the hope that it will enter into force at an early date, and notes that, pursuant to article 87 of the Convention, only four more ratifications or accessions are needed for it to enter into force;

4. *Requests* the Secretary-General to provide all the facilities and assistance necessary for the promotion of the Convention through the World Public Information Campaign on Human Rights and the programme of advisory services in the field of human rights;

5. *Welcomes* the global campaign for the entry into force of the Convention, and invites the organizations and agencies of the United Nations system and intergovernmental and non-governmental organizations to intensify further their efforts with a view to disseminating information on and promoting understanding of the importance of the Convention;

6. *Also welcomes* the work of the Special Rapporteur of the Commission on Human Rights on the human rights of migrants in relation to the Convention, and encourages her to continue in this endeavour;

7. *Takes note* of the report of the Secretary-General, and requests him to submit an updated report on the status of the Convention to the General Assembly at its fifty-seventh session;

8. *Decides* to consider the report of the Secretary-General at its fifty-seventh session under the sub-item entitled "Implementation of human rights instruments".

Convention on genocide

As at 31 December 2001, 133 States were parties to the 1948 Convention on the Prevention and Punishment of the Crime of Genocide, adopted by the General Assembly in resolution 260 A (III) [YUN 1948-49, p. 959]. In 2001, Paraguay ratified the Convention.

The Secretary-General reported on the status of the Convention as at 1 June [A/56/177]. On 19 December, the Assembly took note of the report (**decision 56/429**).

On 25 April [res. 2001/66], the Commission, reaffirming the significance of the Convention as an effective international instrument for the punishment of the crime of genocide, invited States that had not ratified or acceded to the Convention to do so and to enact legislation giving effect to its provisions.

Other activities

Follow-up to 1993 World Conference

Report of High Commissioner. The Commission on Human Rights considered a February report of the High Commissioner [E/CN.4/2001/16] on follow-up to the World Conference on Human Rights [YUN 1993, p. 908]. In view of the forthcoming World Conference against Racism, Racial Discrimination, Xenophobia and Related Intolerance (see p. 615), the report focused on racism and racial discrimination and State responsibility to combat them. Annexed to the report was a description of country missions made by the High Commissioner to China, Colombia, the DRC, Mexico and Venezuela.

Annual meeting. The High Commissioner transmitted the report of the meeting of special rapporteurs/representatives, experts and chairpersons of working groups of the special procedures and advisory services programme of the Commission (Geneva, 18-22 June) [E/CN.4/2002/14], as called for in the Vienna Declaration and Programme of Action, adopted at the 1993 World Conference. The meeting adopted conclusions and recommendations regarding OHCHR resources and staff support; enhancing the effectiveness of the special procedures system; noncooperation and non-compliance on the part of Governments; OHCHR support services; participation in the work of other UN bodies, including the Security Council; human rights and corporate responsibility; monitoring activities and technical cooperation; the World Conference against Racism, Racial Discrimination, Xenophobia and Related Intolerance (see p. 615); and cooperation with the Bureau of the Commission, NGOs and human rights treaty bodies.

On 19 December, the General Assembly took note of the Third Committee's report [A/56/583/Add.4] on implementation of and follow-up to the Vienna Declaration and Programme of Action (**decision 56/430**).

Advisory services and technical cooperation

In 2001 [E/CN.4/2002/116], the OHCHR technical cooperation programme supported countries in promoting and protecting all human rights, at their request, by incorporating international human rights standards in national laws, policies and practices, and by building sustainable national capacities to implement the standards and ensure respect for human rights. Among the key result areas defined by OHCHR for 1999-2001 were national capacity-building to develop human rights strategies and structures; human rights education; the implementation of economic, social and cultural rights and the right to development; racism; the rights of indigenous people; trafficking of women and children, gender issues and women's human rights; the rights of the child; humanitarian law and human rights; and developing a policy for future human rights field activities and consolidating existing activities. Assistance was provided through expertise, advisory services, training courses, workshops and seminars, fellowships, grants and the provision of information and documentation.

During the year, 41 projects were completed, 37 were under way or approved, and new requests were received from 17 countries. National technical cooperation field presences were operational in Chad, Ecuador, Madagascar, Mexico, Somalia, South Africa, the Sudan, Yemen and Palestine. The subregional office in Pretoria, South Africa, continued to implement and facilitate activities at the regional level, as well as in various Southern African countries. The new Subregional Centre for Human Rights and Democracy in Central Africa became operational (see p. 612). The following OHCHR field presences combined monitoring and technical cooperation mandates: Bosnia and Herzegovina, Burundi, Cambodia, Colombia, Croatia, the DRC and FRY.

The programme cooperated with the United Nations Development Programme (UNDP) through the joint programme on Human Rights Strengthening (HURIST), supporting the implementation of UNDP's policy on human rights as presented in a policy document. HURIST, which tested guidelines and methodologies and identified best practices and learning opportunities in the development of national capacities to promote and protect human rights and in the application of a human rights approach to development programming, was active in 30 countries in 2001. The Assisting Communities Together (ACT) project, also a joint OHCHR-UNDP project, aimed at financially supporting, through micro-grants, human rights initiatives carried out by individuals/NGOs at the grass-roots level. Under the second phase of the ACT project, launched in November 1999, 97 activities were selected for funding, of which 90 were fully implemented during 2001. OHCHR also cooperated with other UN agencies and programmes, as well as non-UN partners.

Activities were funded mainly by the United Nations Voluntary Fund for Technical Cooperation in the Field of Human Rights and partly by the UN regular budget. At its fifteenth and sixteenth sessions (5-7 June, 13-15 November), the Fund's Board reviewed 35 new project proposals; discussed 10 completed and evaluated projects; discussed thematic issues, methodologies and procedures of the programme; and examined financial and administrative matters. As at 30 November, the Fund's income amounted to $22.1 million; commitments totalled $11.7 million, leaving a balance of $8.2 million in available funds and $2.2 million in reserves.

Cambodia

Commission action. On 25 April [res. 2001/82], the Commission, expressing grave concern about human rights violations in Cambodia, noted some progress made by the Government. It welcomed the Governance Action Plan, the enactment of the Law on the Administration and Management of Communes/Sangkat and the Law on the Election of Commune/Sangkat Councils, and progress towards the adoption by Parliament of a draft law on the establishment of extraordinary chambers to prosecute crimes committed during the period of Democratic Kampuchea (see p. 314).

Regretting the delays encountered in extending the agreement to implement the mandate of OHCHR/Cambodia after 2000, the Commission requested the Government and OHCHR to sign the relevant memorandum of understanding (MOU). The Secretary-General was asked, through his Special Representative for human rights in Cambodia, in collaboration with OHCHR/Cambodia, to assist the Government in ensuring the protection of the Cambodian people's human rights and to ensure adequate resources for the continued functioning of OHCHR/Cambodia; that request was approved by the Economic and Social Council on 24 July (**decision 2001/278**). The Secretary-General was asked to report in 2002.

Reports of Special Representative. In July [A/56/209], the Secretary-General transmitted a report of his Special Representative for human rights in Cambodia, Peter Leuprecht (Austria), pursuant to General Assembly resolution 55/95 [YUN 2000, p. 625], following his visits to the country (16-23 February, 22-28 June). The report focused on land rights, natural resources, demobilization of armed forces, the judiciary, prison conditions, mob killings, commune elections, human trafficking, Vietnamese refugees, the Khmer Rouge tribunal and labour issues.

Land grabbing and illegal evictions had become major problems. The absence of clear land titles and a proper system for title registration was serious cause for concern. Natural resources were in high demand. Forestry concessions and commercial fishing lots were allocated to companies without regard for the traditional use of such lands and waters by villagers or the negative effects on the environment. The Special Representative expressed concern about the slow implementation of existing laws, the prevalence of corruption and impunity, and the lack of independence of the judiciary. Prison conditions continued to raise serious concern, as did corruption in the prison system. The trafficking of women and children for sexual or labour exploitation was another serious issue. Since February, hundreds had fled Viet Nam, reportedly because of fear of persecution. Cambodia agreed that those granted refugee status by the United Nations High Commissioner for Refugees could remain in the country temporarily. The Special Representative welcomed Cambodia's demobili-

zation programme and its fight against poverty. He also welcomed the adoption of laws on commune elections and commune administration, but raised concern regarding the composition of the National Election Committee and the political climate leading up to the first elections at the communal level.

The Special Representative recommended the creation of an efficient and transparent land registration system; the sustainable use of natural resources, compliance with environmental laws and measures to preserve forestry and family-scale fishing; implementation of the demobilization programme; reform of the judicial system to ensure its independence; adoption and implementation of a juvenile justice system; and improved conditions of detention. The Special Representative noted that mob killings had increased and appealed to the authorities to prevent such incidents. He called for the guarantee of commune elections that were fair, transparent and free from violence.

On 11 December [A/56/697], Cambodia stated that the Special Representative's report was misleading and that the depiction of Cambodian society was unacceptable.

A subsequent visit to Cambodia by the Special Representative (18-28 November) [E/CN.4/2002/118] focused on Commune Council elections scheduled for 3 February 2002 and on judicial reform. The Special Representative had a favourable impression of preparations for the Commune Council elections, which would result in the replacement of current and long-standing commune chiefs by elected Commune Councils, representing an important step towards democratization and decentralization in Cambodia. However, he noted the killing of seven candidates or prospective candidates and two political activists in 2001 as an instance of pre-election violence and intimidation. In the period from 1 June to 30 November, OHCHR/Cambodia and local human rights organizations received 198 allegations of election-related instances of violence and intimidation. Of those, 93 were determined to be politically related, and most were committed by village and commune officials. The Special Representative welcomed the establishment, on 3 August, of the Central Security Office for the Defence of the Commune/Sangkat Elections to deal with election-related violence. The judicial sector suffered from a lack of resources, interference regarding judgements and their execution, politicization and a lack of lawyers. The need for a juvenile justice system was becoming increasingly acute as the number of children in contact with the justice system and being detained was on the rise. Although the Constitution guaranteed free primary and secondary education to all citizens, many were unable to pay the extra fees that were often requested. Poverty was the cause and the effect of the dire situation of education. Discrimination related to access to education was practised on the grounds of gender, geography, ethnicity, disability and wealth. Among other recommendations, the Special Representative called for the establishment of an independent national election body to administer elections free of influence, interference or intimidation and the investigation of all allegations of violence or intimidation.

OHCHR/Cambodia

In a December report [E/CN.4/2002/117] covering the period July to November 2001, the Secretary-General reported on the activities of OHCHR/Cambodia, noting that the MOU between OHCHR and Cambodia had expired on 28 February 2000. Although the Government had agreed verbally to its extension to March 2002 [YUN 2000, p. 625], the new MOU had not yet been signed.

During the period under review, the office assisted in drafting and implementing legislation to promote and protect human rights. It continued activities to enhance the capacity of governmental institutions through increased application of human rights standards. OHCHR-trained police instructors trained some 2,155 police officials and continued to implement the interagency project on law enforcement against sexual exploitation of children. The investigation team of the Ministry of the Interior, which was established under the project, reported 27 arrests for trafficking, sale, debauchery, illegal confinement and rape. A total of 113 victims were rescued, of whom 47 were under 18 years of age. Training sessions were held on labour rights, the legal aspects of trafficking in human beings and sexual exploitation, and for women and children in difficult situations. OHCHR/Cambodia continued to implement a mentor programme that provided practical assistance to the judiciary and other court personnel, as well as to police and prison officials. Training, legal advice and other forms of technical and financial assistance were provided to strengthen the capacity of local NGOs and other civil society organizations to carry out activities to promote and protect human rights.

GENERAL ASSEMBLY ACTION

On 19 December [meeting 88], the General Assembly, on the recommendation of the Third Committee [A/56/583/Add.2], adopted **resolution 56/169** without vote [agenda item 119 (b)].

Situation of human rights in Cambodia

The General Assembly,

Guided by the purposes and principles embodied in the Charter of the United Nations, the Universal Declaration of Human Rights and the International Covenants on Human Rights,

Recalling the Agreement on a Comprehensive Political Settlement of the Cambodia Conflict, signed in Paris on 23 October 1991, including part III thereof, relating to human rights,

Recalling also its resolution 55/95 of 4 December 2000, taking note of Commission on Human Rights resolution 2001/82 of 25 April 2001, and recalling further previous relevant resolutions,

Recognizing that the tragic history of Cambodia requires special measures to ensure the protection of the human rights of all people in Cambodia and the non-return to the policies and practices of the past, as stipulated in the Agreement signed in Paris on 23 October 1991,

Desiring that the international community continue to respond positively to assisting efforts to investigate the tragic history of Cambodia, including responsibility for past international crimes, such as acts of genocide and crimes against humanity committed during the regime of Democratic Kampuchea from 1975 to 1979,

Bearing in mind the request made in June 1997 by the Cambodian authorities for assistance in responding to past serious violations of Cambodian and international law, the letter dated 15 March 1999 from the Secretary-General to the President of the General Assembly and the President of the Security Council and the report of the Group of Experts appointed by the Secretary-General annexed thereto, and the discussions held between the Government of Cambodia and the United Nations Secretariat on standards and procedures for bringing to justice the Khmer Rouge leaders most responsible for the most serious violations of human rights in the years 1975 to 1979,

Recognizing the legitimate concern of the Government and people of Cambodia in the pursuit of internationally accepted principles of justice and of national reconciliation,

Recognizing also that the accountability of individual perpetrators of grave human rights violations is one of the central elements of any effective remedy for victims of human rights violations and a key factor in ensuring a fair and equitable justice system and, ultimately, reconciliation and stability within a State,

Welcoming the continuing role of the United Nations High Commissioner for Human Rights in the promotion and protection of human rights in Cambodia,

I

Support of and cooperation with the United Nations

1. *Requests* the Secretary-General, through his Special Representative for human rights in Cambodia, in collaboration with the office in Cambodia of the United Nations High Commissioner for Human Rights, to assist the Government of Cambodia in ensuring the protection of the human rights of all people in Cambodia and to ensure adequate resources for the continued functioning of the operational presence in Cambodia of the Office of the United Nations High Commissioner for Human Rights and to enable the

Special Representative to continue to fulfil his tasks expeditiously;

2. *Welcomes* the report of the Secretary-General on the role and achievements of the Office of the High Commissioner in assisting the Government and people of Cambodia in the promotion and protection of human rights;

3. *Also welcomes* the report of the Special Representative, commends the Government of Cambodia on its openness and spirit of cooperation during the visits of the Special Representative, encourages the Government to continue its cooperation at all levels of government, supports the appeals of the Government and the Special Representative to increase international assistance to Cambodia and to continue working towards the reduction of poverty, commends the international community for the interest and support demonstrated at the Consultative Group Meeting on Cambodia, held in Tokyo on 12 and 13 June 2001, and encourages donor countries and other relevant parties to follow up their pledges of assistance and commitments;

4. *Requests* the Government of Cambodia to continue to cooperate with the Office of the High Commissioner to resolve outstanding issues in accordance with international standards so that both parties, without further delay, can sign the memorandum of understanding for the extension of the mandate of the office in Cambodia of the High Commissioner, notes with regret the delays encountered in the process thus far, and encourages the Government to continue to cooperate with the office;

5. *Notes with appreciation* the use by the Secretary-General of the United Nations Trust Fund for a Human Rights Education Programme in Cambodia to finance the programme of activities of the office in Cambodia of the High Commissioner, as defined in resolutions of the General Assembly and the Commission on Human Rights, and invites Governments, intergovernmental and non-governmental organizations, foundations and individuals to consider contributing to the Trust Fund;

II
Administrative, legislative and judicial reform

1. *Notes with concern* the continued problems related to the rule of law and the functioning of the judiciary resulting from, inter alia, corruption, including interference by the executive with the independence of the judiciary, welcomes the continued commitment of the Government of Cambodia to reforming the judiciary, and urges the Government to continue to take the necessary measures to promote the independence, impartiality and effectiveness of the Supreme Council of the Magistracy and the judicial system as a whole and to increase its budgetary allocation to the judiciary, which is expected to result, inter alia, in a decrease in the number of excessive pre-trial detentions;

2. *Urges* the Government of Cambodia to continue its efforts towards the early adoption of the laws and codes that are essential components of the basic legal framework, including the draft statute on magistrates, a penal code, a code of criminal procedures, a new civil code and a code of civil procedure, as well as its efforts to reform the administration of justice and to enhance the training of judges and lawyers, appeals to the international community to assist the Government to this end, and welcomes, inter alia, the drafting of the forestry and fishery laws;

3. *Welcomes* the enactment of the Land Law, notes with concern the problems related to land, inter alia, land grabbing, forced evictions and further displacement, and urges the Government of Cambodia to continue its efforts to implement an effective, efficient and transparent land registration system, as envisaged in the Law, to solve these problems;

4. *Also welcomes* the efforts of the Government of Cambodia to implement its reform programme, including the adoption of the Governance Action Plan, encourages the timely and effective implementation of the Plan, and appeals to the international community to assist the Government in its efforts towards that end;

5. *Expresses serious concern* that the situation of impunity still exists in Cambodia, recognizes the commitment and efforts of the Government of Cambodia to respond to this problem, calls upon the Government, as a matter of critical priority, to take further measures to investigate urgently and to prosecute, in accordance with due process of law and international human rights standards, all of those who have perpetrated serious crimes, including violations of human rights, and encourages the international community to provide means, such as technical assistance or expertise, to help the Government to meet its own commitments to bring perpetrators to justice more effectively;

6. *Welcomes* the efforts of the Government of Cambodia to demobilize its armed forces, including the launching of the first part of the demobilization programme, encourages the Government to implement the contents of the White Paper on National Defence and to continue to carry out effective reform, including the implementation of a full-scale demobilization programme that includes the disarming of demobilized soldiers based on the experience gained from a pilot project, aimed at professional and impartial police and military forces, and invites the international community to continue to assist the Government to this end;

7. *Also welcomes* the enactment of the Law on the Administration and Management of Communes/Sangkat and the Law on the Election of Commune/Sangkat Councils and the elections scheduled for 3 February 2002, strongly urges the Government of Cambodia, including at local and provincial levels, to conduct free and fair elections without violence to any party and encourages the international community to assist the Government to this end, strongly urges all political parties to participate in the elections in a democratic and peaceful manner, and in this regard welcomes the agreement of the two parties in power to abstain from violence, urges the Government to investigate thoroughly any instances of violence and intimidation that occur, and stresses the importance of independent and transparent national, provincial and commune election committees;

8. *Notes with serious concern* the prison conditions in Cambodia, notes with interest some important efforts to improve the prison system, recommends the continuation of international assistance to improve the material conditions of detention, and calls upon the Government of Cambodia to take further measures to improve the conditions of detention, to provide proper health care to detainees, including by strengthening the coordinating role of the Prison Health Department

with the Ministry of Health, provincial authorities and non-governmental organizations working in this field, and to prevent any form of torture;

III
Human rights violations and violence

1. *Expresses grave concern* about the continued violations of human rights, including torture, excessive pre-trial detention, violation of labour rights and forced evictions, as well as political violence, police involvement in violence and the apparent lack of protection from mob killings, as detailed in the reports of the Special Representative, notes some progress made by the Government of Cambodia in addressing these issues, and urges the Government to take all necessary measures to prevent such violations;

2. *Urges* an end to racial violence against and vilification of ethnic minorities, and urges the Government of Cambodia to take all steps to prevent such violence, as well as to meet its obligations as a party to the International Convention on the Elimination of All Forms of Racial Discrimination, inter alia, by seeking technical assistance;

IV
Khmer Rouge tribunal

1. *Reaffirms* that the most serious human rights violations in Cambodia in recent history have been committed by the Khmer Rouge, and acknowledges that the final collapse of the Khmer Rouge and the continued efforts of the Government of Cambodia have paved the way for the restoration of peace, stability and national reconciliation in Cambodia and the investigation and prosecution of the leaders of the Khmer Rouge;

2. *Welcomes* the promulgation of the Law on the Establishment of Extraordinary Chambers in the Courts of Cambodia for the Prosecution of Crimes Committed during the Period of Democratic Kampuchea, noting with appreciation the general provisions and competence of the Law and its provision for a role for the United Nations, appeals to the Government of Cambodia to ensure that the senior leaders of Democratic Kampuchea and those who were most responsible for the crimes and serious violations of Cambodian penal law, international humanitarian law and custom and international conventions recognized by Cambodia are brought to trial in accordance with international standards of justice, fairness and due process of law, encourages the Government to continue to cooperate with the United Nations on this issue, welcomes the efforts of the Secretariat and the international community in assisting the Government to this end, urges the Government and the United Nations to conclude an agreement without delay so that the Extraordinary Chambers can start to function promptly, and appeals to the international community to provide assistance in this regard, including financial and personnel support to the Chambers;

V
Protection of women and children

1. *Welcomes* the progress made in improving the status of women, and urges the Government of Cambodia to take appropriate measures to eliminate all forms of discrimination against women, to combat violence against women in all its forms and to take all steps to meet its obligations as a party to the Convention on the Elimination of All Forms of Discrimination against Women, including by seeking technical assistance;

2. *Notes with grave concern* the continued and growing phenomenon of trafficking in and sexual exploitation of women and children and the increasing incidence of the human immunodeficiency virus/acquired immunodeficiency syndrome (HIV/AIDS), and requests the Government of Cambodia comprehensively to address these problems and their underlying causes;

3. *Urges* the Government of Cambodia to improve further the health conditions of children and their access to education, to provide and promote free and accessible birth registration and to establish an effective juvenile justice system that is consistent with international human rights standards, and invites the international community to continue to assist the Government to this end;

4. *Notes with serious concern* the problem of child labour in its worst forms, calls upon the Government of Cambodia to take immediate and effective measures to protect children from economic exploitation and from performing any work that is likely to be hazardous, to interfere with their education or to be harmful to their health, safety or morals, inter alia, by enforcing Cambodian laws on child labour, the existing Labour Law and anti-trafficking law provisions on behalf of children and prosecuting those who violate these laws, invites the International Labour Organization to continue to extend the necessary assistance in this regard, and encourages the Government to consider ratifying the International Labour Organization Convention concerning the Prohibition and Immediate Action for the Elimination of the Worst Forms of Child Labour (Convention No. 182) adopted in 1999;

VI
Enhancement of human rights

1. *Recognizes* the importance of human rights education and training in Cambodia, commends the efforts of the Government of Cambodia, the Office of the High Commissioner and civil society in this field, encourages further strengthening and wider dissemination of these programmes, and invites the international community to continue to assist these efforts;

2. *Commends* the vital and valuable role played by non-governmental organizations in Cambodia, inter alia, in the development of civil society, and encourages the Government of Cambodia to ensure the protection of those human rights organizations and their members and to continue to work closely and cooperatively with non-governmental organizations in efforts to strengthen and uphold human rights in Cambodia, in particular in the lead-up to the communal elections;

3. *Notes with interest* the activities undertaken by the governmental Cambodian Human Rights Committee, the National Assembly Commission on Human Rights and Reception of Complaints and the Senate Commission on Human Rights and Reception of Complaints, stresses the importance of further promoting trust in those institutions and enhancing their activities, and invites the international community to extend its technical assistance to this end;

4. *Encourages* the Government of Cambodia in its efforts to establish an independent national mechanism for the promotion and protection of human

rights which should be based on the principles relating to the status of national institutions for the promotion and protection of human rights known as the Paris Principles, working in close cooperation with civil society, and requests the Office of the High Commissioner to continue to provide advice and technical assistance in these efforts;

5. *Requests* the Government of Cambodia to follow up the recommendations made by the international human rights treaty bodies regarding the reports submitted by the Government, calls upon the Government to meet its reporting obligations under all international human rights instruments to which Cambodia is a party, and requests the office in Cambodia of the High Commissioner to continue to provide assistance in this regard;

VII
Landmines and small arms

1. *Expresses grave concern* at the devastating consequences and destabilizing effects of anti-personnel landmines on Cambodian society, welcomes the progress made by the Government of Cambodia in the removal of these mines and for victim assistance and mine-awareness programmes, encourages the Government to continue its efforts in this regard, and commends donor countries and other actors of the international community for their contributions and assistance to mine action;

2. *Expresses concern* at the substantial number of small arms still existing in society, commends the progress made by the Government of Cambodia and the cooperation of the international community in dealing with issues of small arms, and encourages the Government to cooperate in regional and international efforts to reduce the number of illicit small arms, including implementation of the existing programmes;

VIII
Conclusion

1. *Requests* the Secretary-General to report to the General Assembly at its fifty-seventh session on the role and achievements of the Office of the High Commissioner in assisting the Government and the people of Cambodia in the promotion and protection of human rights and on the recommendations made by the Special Representative on matters within his mandate;

2. *Decides* to continue its consideration of the situation of human rights in Cambodia at its fifty-seventh session under the item entitled "Human rights questions".

Equatorial Guinea

For information on assistance to Equatorial Guinea and the human rights situation in the country, see p. 703.

Haïti

On 1 March, Adama Dieng (Senegal), independent expert on the situation of human rights in Haiti, submitted his resignation.

In a statement of 25 April [E/2001/23] on behalf of the Commission, agreed on by consensus, the Chairperson stated that the Commission recog-

nized that, while there had been some progress in human rights in Haiti, problems persisted with regard to the administration of justice, impunity, prolonged detention and prison conditions. It called on the Government to eliminate human rights violations and investigate politically motivated crimes, and expressed concern over Haiti's *restaveks*, children who were placed in domestic service, sometimes against their will and in deplorable conditions. The Commission pledged to give serious consideration to the Government's request for assistance to improve human rights, while recognizing that primary responsibility remained with the people of Haiti. The Commission requested a new independent expert to report to the General Assembly in 2001 and to the Commission in 2002. Those requests were approved by the Economic and Social Council on 24 July (**decision 2001/290**).

Note by Secretariat. A note by the Secretariat [E/CN.4/2002/120] stated that, because a new independent expert had not been appointed, no report was submitted to the Commission in 2001.

(See also p. 248.)

Somalia

Commission action. On 25 April [res. 2001/81], the Commission, condemning widespread violations and abuses of human rights and humanitarian law, urged the transitional national Government, the Transitional National Assembly, and all parties and administrations in Somalia to create an environment that would bring into the reconciliation process those who did not participate in the Somalia National Peace Conference [YUN 2000, p. 215]. They were also urged to respect human rights and international humanitarian standards as set out in international instruments, to support the re-establishment of the rule of law and to protect UN personnel, humanitarian relief workers and others.

The High Commissioner was asked to provide for the translation of the Commission's resolution into the local language for dissemination within Somalia. Following the resignation of the independent expert in 2000 [YUN 2000, p. 631], the Commission invited the Secretary-General to appoint a new one. The Commission asked that the future expert report in 2002 and requested the Secretary-General to assist him. On 24 July, the Economic and Social Council endorsed the extension of the future expert's mandate for an additional year, the Commission's request that he report in 2002 and its request to the High Commissioner (**decision 2001/277**).

The new independent expert, Ghanim Al-najjar (Kuwait), was appointed by the Secretary-General, effective 3 June 2001.

Report of independent expert. Independent expert Ghanim Alnajjar visited the three main regions of Somalia—Baidoa, Mogadishu and Hrageisa (28 August–7 September) [E/CN.4/2002/119]. Although the expert did not visit Puntland, given the absence of authorities there with whom to meet, he presented information from accounts that had reached him. He also travelled to Nairobi, Kenya, where he met with representatives of the international community.

During the mission, concerns were raised regarding the establishment of human rights commissions, the inclusion of human rights in school curricula, investigation into specific cases of human rights violations, the deteriorating conditions in prisons, the development of the judicial system, the status of women, the development of law enforcement, the separation of juveniles from adults in prison and the ratification of international human rights treaties. The expert also noted the presence of many child soldiers. Given the widespread support for investigation into past atrocities, the expert urged the Security Council to consider establishing a committee of experts to do so. On the positive side, he observed a civil society that was paving the way for a more reconciliatory atmosphere, which might benefit political reconciliation, and noted wide-ranging freedom of expression in certain regions. The expert offered a series of recommendations for future human rights advisory services.

Among the advisory services implemented in 2001 was a project to mainstream human rights in the work of UN agencies in Somalia, particularly the governance and rule-of-law activities of UNDP. In June, UNDP and OHCHR jointly drafted a paper on considerations for investigating alleged past human rights atrocities in Somalia, components of which were included in the Secretary-General's October report to the Security Council (see p. 209).

Public information and human rights education

Public information

Report of Secretary-General. In a January report [E/CN.4/2001/92], the Secretary-General described public information activities in the area of human rights, including the World Public Information Campaign for Human Rights, launched by the General Assembly in resolution 43/128 [YUN 1988, p. 539] and carried out by the High Commissioner and the UN Department of Public Information (DPI).

Following an external review, the OHCHR publications programme was revised, focusing on basic publications such as fact sheets, key documents, training and education materials, issue papers and promotional materials with improved quality and multi-language availability. The programme would be managed in parallel with the OHCHR web site as part of a comprehensive public information strategy. OHCHR organized briefings for students, diplomats, journalists, public officials, academics, professors and NGOs, provided lecturers for DPI briefings and organized exhibits. It carried out the human rights fellowship programme, offered internships to graduate students and conducted training courses, seminars and workshops. The Office prepared information materials, held meetings and organized special events for the World Conference against Racism, Racial Discrimination, Xenophobia and Related Intolerance (see p. 615).

DPI continued to initiate and coordinate activities within the context of the World Public Information Campaign and the United Nations Decade for Human Rights Education (1995-2004) (see p. 605). Activities were also carried out under the Third Decade to Combat Racism and Racial Discrimination (1993-2003) (see p. 614), the International Decade of the World's Indigenous People (1995-2004) (see p. 689) and the United Nations Decade for the Eradication of Poverty (1997-2006) (see p. 753). DPI covered UN human rights activities, as well as distributed relevant human rights materials, through a multimedia approach, which included the production of printed materials; making material available to the UN web site, radio and television broadcasts, press conferences, press briefings and special events; exhibits; special media outreach activities and activities with educational organizations and NGOs; and services for visitors and public enquiries. The report presented an overview of the activities of the United Nations Information Service at Geneva, as well as those of the United Nations information centres and services and UN offices.

Commission action. On 25 April [res. 2001/63], the Commission urged Member States to develop a national plan of action for human rights education and public information, and called on DPI and relevant UN agencies and bodies further to develop mass media strategies to promote human rights. The Secretary-General was requested to take advantage of the collaboration of other international and regional organizations and NGOs in implementing the World Public Information Campaign and in activities relating to the Decade for Human Rights Education and the World Conference against Racism, Racial Discrimination, Xenophobia and Related Intolerance. He was also asked to make available resources from the

UN regular budget to allow OHCHR and DPI to implement their respective programmes and to report in 2003.

Report of High Commissioner. By an August note [A/56/271], the Secretary-General transmitted a report of the High Commissioner on the Decade for Human Rights Education (below) and public information activities in human rights. The report supplemented information in his January report (see p. 604). During the reporting period (December 2000–mid-July 2001), the Office had distributed more than 40,000 copies of human rights publications, in addition to the 5,000 copies of each publication that were regularly distributed by the United Nations Office at Geneva. OHCHR increased the electronic dissemination of its publications, and expanded the live Internet audio broadcast of human rights events.

Human rights education

Commission action. On 25 April [res. 2001/61], the Commission, taking note of the report containing the midterm global evaluation [YUN 2000, p. 631] of progress made towards the achievement of the objectives of the United Nations Decade for Human Rights Education (1995-2004), proclaimed by the General Assembly in resolution 49/184 [YUN 1994, p. 1039], asked the High Commissioner to bring the report's recommendations and the Commission's current resolution to the attention of the international community, intergovernmental organizations and NGOs. Governments and other Decade actors were asked to consider disseminating the recommendations, which were annexed to the Commission's resolution.

ECONOMIC AND SOCIAL COUNCIL ACTION

On 26 July [meeting 43], the Economic and Social Council adopted **resolution 2001/38** [draft: E/2001/L.33, orally revised] without vote [agenda item 14 (g)].

Human rights education

The Economic and Social Council,

Taking into account Commission on Human Rights resolutions 1993/56 of 9 March 1993 and 2001/61 of 25 April 2001 regarding the importance of human rights education as a priority in education policies,

Convinced that human rights education and information contribute to a concept of development consistent with the dignity of women and men of all ages, which takes into account particularly vulnerable segments of society, such as children, youth, older persons, indigenous people, minorities, rural and urban poor, migrant workers, refugees, persons with human immunodeficiency virus/acquired immunodeficiency syndrome (HIV/AIDS) and disabled persons,

Taking note with appreciation of the midterm global evaluation of the United Nations Decade for Human Rights Education, 1995-2004, by the Office of the United Nations High Commissioner for Human Rights, contained in the report of the High Commissioner,

Taking into account the recommendations of the midterm global evaluation of the Decade,

1. *Invites* all Governments to promote the development of national strategies for human rights education that are comprehensive, participatory and effective and can be embodied in a national plan of action for human rights education as part of a national development plan;

2. *Also invites* the United Nations agencies, in particular the United Nations Educational, Scientific and Cultural Organization, and the relevant intergovernmental organizations, to develop a system-wide approach to the United Nations Decade for Human Rights Education (1995-2004);

3. *Further invites* regional and national human rights organizations, agencies and networks (such as those of women, the media and trade unions), to develop human rights education programmes and strategies for the wider distribution of materials on human rights education in all possible languages;

4. *Requests* non-governmental organizations to develop and implement strategies to encourage and assist Governments, upon request, in integrating human rights education into all levels of education, and to help in the assessment of those strategies.

Report of High Commissioner. In accordance with General Assembly resolution 55/94 [YUN 2000, p. 632], the Secretary-General, by an August note [A/56/271], transmitted a report of the High Commissioner summarizing human rights education and public information activities undertaken by OHCHR between December 2000 and mid-July 2001 and communications received thereon from Governments, intergovernmental organizations and NGOs. The report highlighted the advancements made in implementing some of the components of the Plan of Action for the Decade, including assessing needs and formulating strategies; strengthening international and regional programmes and capacities; coordinated development of materials for human rights education; and global dissemination of the Universal Declaration of Human Rights, adopted by the Assembly in resolution 217 A (III) [YUN 1948-49, p. 535].

GENERAL ASSEMBLY ACTION

On 19 December [meeting 88], the General Assembly, on the recommendation of the Third Committee [A/56/583/Add.2], adopted **resolution 56/147** without vote [agenda item 119 (b)].

Human rights education

The General Assembly,

Taking into account Commission on Human Rights resolution 2001/61 of 25 April 2001 regarding the importance of human rights education as a priority in education policies,

Considering Economic and Social Council resolution 2001/38 of 26 July 2001 on human rights education,

Convinced that human rights education and information contribute to the concept of development consistent with the dignity of women and men of all ages, which takes into account particularly vulnerable segments of society of all ages, such as children, youth, older persons, indigenous people, minorities, rural and urban poor, migrant workers, refugees, persons with the human immunodeficiency virus/acquired immunodeficiency syndrome (HIV/AIDS) and disabled persons,

Considering the importance of human rights education,

Convinced that human rights education is a key to development,

Taking note with appreciation of the midterm global evaluation of the progress made towards the achievement of the objectives of the United Nations Decade for Human Rights Education, 1995-2004, contained in the report of the United Nations High Commissioner for Human Rights,

Taking into account the recommendations of the midterm global evaluation of the progress made towards the achievement of the objectives of the United Nations Decade for Human Rights Education, 1995-2004,

1. *Invites* all Governments to reaffirm their commitments and obligations to develop national strategies for human rights education which are comprehensive, participatory and effective and which can be embodied in a national plan of action for human rights education as part of their national development plan;

2. *Invites* the United Nations, intergovernmental organizations, the United Nations Educational, Scientific and Cultural Organization and other relevant intergovernmental organizations, to adopt a system-wide approach to the United Nations Decade for Human Rights Education, 1995-2004;

3. *Invites* relevant regional human rights organizations, agencies and networks to develop human rights education programmes and human rights training programmes and strategies for wider distribution of material on human rights education in all possible languages;

4. *Recognizes* the role that non-governmental organizations play in developing and implementing strategies to assist Governments to integrate human rights education into all levels of education for children, youth and adults.

On the same date [meeting 88], the Assembly, also on the recommendation of the Third Committee [A/56/583/Add.2], adopted **resolution 56/167** without vote [agenda item 119 *(b)*].

United Nations Decade for Human Rights Education

The General Assembly,

Guided by the fundamental and universal principles enshrined in the Charter of the United Nations and the Universal Declaration of Human Rights,

Reaffirming article 26 of the Declaration, which states that "education shall be directed to the full development of the human personality and to the strengthening of respect for human rights and fundamental freedoms", and recalling the provisions of other relevant international human rights instruments that reflect the aims of this article,

Recalling the high importance attached to human rights education by the World Conference on Human Rights, held in Vienna from 14 to 25 June 1993,

Recalling also the relevant resolutions adopted by the General Assembly and the Commission on Human Rights concerning the United Nations Decade for Human Rights Education, 1995-2004,

Believing that human rights education constitutes an important vehicle for the elimination of gender-based discrimination and for ensuring equal opportunities through the promotion and protection of the human rights of women,

Convinced that every woman, man and child, in order to realize their full human potential, must be made aware of all their human rights and fundamental freedoms,

Convinced also that human rights education should involve more than the provision of information and should constitute a comprehensive, lifelong process by which people at all levels of development and in all societies learn respect for the dignity of others and the means and methods of ensuring that respect in all societies,

Recognizing that human rights education is essential to the realization of human rights and fundamental freedoms and that carefully designed training, dissemination and information programmes can have a catalytic effect on national, regional and international initiatives to promote and protect human rights and prevent human rights violations,

Convinced that human rights education contributes to a holistic concept of development consistent with the dignity of women and men of all ages, which takes into account particularly vulnerable segments of society, such as children, young persons, older persons, indigenous people, minorities, the rural and urban poor, migrant workers, refugees, persons with the human immunodeficiency virus/acquired immunodeficiency syndrome (HIV/AIDS) and disabled persons,

Affirming that human rights education is a key to changing attitudes and behaviour based on racism, racial discrimination, xenophobia and related intolerance and to promoting tolerance and respect for diversity in societies, and that such education is a determining factor in the promotion, dissemination and protection of the democratic values of justice and equity, which are essential to prevent and combat the spread of racism, racial discrimination, xenophobia and related intolerance, as was recognized at the World Conference against Racism, Racial Discrimination, Xenophobia and Related Intolerance, held in Durban, South Africa, from 31 August to 8 September 2001,

Welcoming the holding of the International Consultative Conference on School Education in Relation to Freedom of Religion and Belief, Tolerance and Non-discrimination in Madrid from 23 to 25 November 2001,

Welcoming also the efforts to promote human rights education made by educators and non-governmental organizations in all parts of the world, as well as by intergovernmental organizations, including the Office of the United Nations High Commissioner for Human Rights, the United Nations Educational, Scientific and Cultural Organization, the International Labour Organization, the United Nations Children's Fund and the United Nations Development Programme,

Recognizing the invaluable and creative role that non-governmental and community-based organizations play in the promotion and protection of human rights by disseminating public information and engaging in human rights education, especially at the grassroots level and in remote and rural communities,

Aware of the potential role of the private sector in implementing at all levels of society the Plan of Action for the United Nations Decade for Human Rights Education, 1995-2004, and the World Public Information Campaign on Human Rights through financial support for governmental and non-governmental activities as well as their own creative initiatives,

Convinced that the effectiveness of existing human rights education and public information activities would be enhanced by better coordination and cooperation at the national, regional and international levels,

Recalling that it is within the responsibility of the United Nations High Commissioner for Human Rights to coordinate relevant United Nations education and public information programmes in the field of human rights,

Noting with appreciation the efforts undertaken so far by the Office of the High Commissioner to increase information-sharing in the area of human rights education through the development of a database and resource collection on the human rights education and to disseminate human rights information through its web site and its publications and external relations programmes,

Welcoming the initiative of the Office of the High Commissioner to develop further the project entitled "Assisting Communities Together", launched in 1998, supported by voluntary funds and designed to provide small grants to grass-roots and local organizations carrying out practical human rights activities,

Welcoming also other United Nations public information activities in the field of human rights, including the World Public Information Campaign on Human Rights and the implementation of and follow-up to the Vienna Declaration and Programme of Action, the project of the United Nations Educational, Scientific and Cultural Organization entitled "Towards a culture of peace", and the Dakar Framework for Action adopted at the World Education Forum, which, inter alia, reconfirmed the mandated role of the United Nations Educational, Scientific and Cultural Organization in coordinating Education for All partners and maintaining their collective momentum within the process of securing quality basic education,

Recognizing the value of information and communications technologies in human rights education to promote dialogue and understanding of human rights, and in that context welcoming, inter alia, the "Cyber-SchoolBus" and the United Nations Children's Fund "Voices of Youth" initiatives,

Recalling the midterm global evaluation of progress made towards the achievement of the objectives of the Decade undertaken by the Office of the High Commissioner, in cooperation with all other principal actors in the Decade, which was presented in the relevant report of the High Commissioner to the General Assembly at its fifty-fifth session,

1. *Takes note with appreciation* of the report of the United Nations High Commissioner for Human Rights on the United Nations Decade for Human Rights Education, 1995-2004, and public information activities in the field of human rights;

2. *Urges* all Governments to promote the development of comprehensive, participatory and sustainable national strategies for human rights education and to establish and strengthen, as a priority in education policies, knowledge of human rights in both its theoretical dimension and its practical application;

3. *Welcomes* the steps taken by Governments and intergovernmental and non-governmental organizations to implement the Plan of Action for the United Nations Decade for Human Rights Education, 1995-2004, and to develop public information activities in the field of human rights, as indicated in the report of the High Commissioner;

4. *Urges* all Governments to contribute further to the implementation of the Plan of Action, in particular by:

(*a*) Encouraging the establishment, in accordance with national conditions, of broadly representative national committees for human rights education responsible for the development of comprehensive, effective and sustainable national plans of action for human rights education and information, taking into consideration the recommendations of the midterm global evaluation of the Decade and the guidelines for national plans of action for human rights education developed by the Office of the United Nations High Commissioner for Human Rights;

(*b*) Encouraging, supporting and involving national and local non-governmental and community-based organizations in the implementation of their national plans of action;

(*c*) Initiating and developing cultural and educational programmes aimed at countering racism, racial discrimination, xenophobia and related intolerance, and supporting and implementing public information campaigns and specific training programmes in the field of human rights, as emphasized at the World Conference against Racism, Racial Discrimination, Xenophobia and Related Intolerance;

5. *Encourages* Governments to consider, within their national plans of action for human rights education:

(*a*) The establishment of public access human rights resource and training centres capable of engaging in research, including the gender-sensitive training of trainers;

(*b*) The preparation, collection, translation and dissemination of human rights education and training materials;

(*c*) The organization of courses, conferences, workshops and public information campaigns and assistance in the implementation of internationally sponsored technical cooperation projects for human rights education and public information;

6. *Encourages* States, where such national public access human rights resource and training centres exist, to strengthen their capacity to support human rights education and public information programmes at the international, regional, national and local levels;

7. *Calls upon* Governments, in accordance with national conditions, to accord priority to the dissemination, in the relevant national local and indigenous languages, of the Universal Declaration of Human Rights,

the International Covenants on Human Rights and other human rights instruments, human rights materials and training manuals, including information on human rights mechanisms and complaint procedures and reports of States parties submitted under international human rights treaties, and to provide information and education in those languages on the practical ways in which national and international institutions and procedures may be utilized to ensure the effective implementation of those instruments;

8. *Encourages* Governments to support further, through voluntary contributions, the education and public information efforts undertaken by the Office of the High Commissioner within the framework of the Plan of Action;

9. *Requests* the High Commissioner to continue to coordinate and harmonize human rights education and information strategies within the United Nations system, including the implementation of the Plan of Action, in cooperation, inter alia, with the United Nations Educational, Scientific and Cultural Organization, and to ensure maximum effectiveness and efficiency in the collection, use, processing, management and distribution of human rights information and educational materials, including through electronic means;

10. *Encourages* Governments to contribute to the further development of the web site of the Office of the High Commissioner, in particular with respect to the dissemination of human rights education materials and tools, and to continue and expand the publications and external relations programmes of the Office;

11. *Encourages* the Office of the High Commissioner to continue to support national capacities for human rights education and information through its technical cooperation programme in the field of human rights, including the organization of training courses and peer education initiatives and the development of targeted training materials for professional audiences, as well as the dissemination of human rights information materials as a component of technical cooperation projects, to develop further its databases and resource collection on human rights education and to continue to monitor developments in human rights education;

12. *Urges* the Department of Public Information of the Secretariat to continue to utilize United Nations information centres for the timely dissemination, within their designated areas of activity, of basic information, reference and audio-visual materials on human rights and fundamental freedoms, including the reports of States parties submitted under international human rights instruments, and, to that end, to ensure that the information centres are supplied with adequate quantities of those materials;

13. *Stresses* the need for close collaboration between the Office of the High Commissioner and the Department of Public Information in the implementation of the Plan of Action and the World Public Information Campaign on Human Rights, and the need to harmonize their activities with those of other international organizations, such as the United Nations Educational, Scientific and Cultural Organization with regard to its project entitled "Towards a culture of peace" and the International Committee of the Red Cross, and relevant non-governmental organizations with regard to the dissemination of information on international humanitarian law;

14. *Invites* the specialized agencies and relevant United Nations programmes and funds to continue to contribute, within their respective spheres of competence, to the implementation of the Plan of Action and the World Public Information Campaign and to cooperate and coordinate with each other and with the Office of the High Commissioner in that regard;

15. *Encourages* the relevant organs, bodies and agencies of the United Nations system, all human rights bodies of the United Nations system, including the Office of the United Nations High Commissioner for Human Rights and the Office of the United Nations High Commissioner for Refugees, to provide training in human rights for all United Nations personnel and officials;

16. *Encourages* the human rights treaty bodies, when examining reports of States parties, to place emphasis on the obligations of States parties in the area of human rights education and to reflect that emphasis in their concluding observations;

17. *Calls upon* international, regional and national non-governmental organizations and intergovernmental organizations, in particular those concerned with children and youth, women, labour, development, food, housing, education, health care and the environment, as well as all other social justice groups, human rights advocates, educators, religious organizations, the private sector and the media, to undertake specific activities of formal, non-formal and informal education, including cultural events, alone and in cooperation with the Office of the United Nations High Commissioner for Human Rights, in implementing the Plan of Action;

18. *Welcomes*, in that context, initiatives to include civil society, non-governmental organizations, children and youth in national delegations to world conferences, summits and other meetings, as well as the work of non-governmental organizations and intergovernmental agencies in organizing parallel non-governmental organization and youth satellite meetings, as an important component of human rights education;

19. *Encourages* Governments, regional organizations and intergovernmental and non-governmental organizations to explore the potential support and contribution to human rights education of all relevant partners, including the private sector, development, trade and financial institutions and the media, and to seek their cooperation in the development of human rights education strategies;

20. *Encourages* regional organizations to develop strategies for the wider distribution of materials on human rights education through regional networks and to develop region-specific programmes to maximize the participation of national entities, whether governmental or non-governmental, in programmes on human rights education;

21. *Encourages* intergovernmental organizations to assist, upon request, collaboration between governmental institutions and non-governmental organizations at the national level;

22. *Requests* the Office of the High Commissioner to continue the implementation of and to expand the "Assisting Communities Together" project and to con-

sider other appropriate ways and means to support human rights education activities, including those undertaken by non-governmental organizations;

23. *Requests* the High Commissioner to bring the present resolution to the attention of all members of the international community and of intergovernmental and non-governmental organizations concerned with human rights education and public information, and to report to the General Assembly at its fifty-seventh session on the progress made towards the achievement of the objectives of the Decade under the item entitled "Human rights questions".

Children and a culture of peace

In response to General Assembly resolution 55/47 [YUN 2000, p. 635] on the International Decade for a Culture of Peace and Non-Violence for the Children of the World, 2001-2010, proclaimed by the Assembly in resolution 53/25 [YUN 1998, p. 639], the Secretary-General, in September [A/56/349], reported on progress made by the United Nations Educational, Scientific and Cultural Organization (UNESCO) to implement the Programme of Action on a Culture of Peace, adopted in Assembly resolution 53/243 B [YUN 1999, p. 594]. The report, based on a report of the UNESCO Director-General, also described cooperation with the UN system.

The report reviewed the engagement of Member States, the UN system and civil society during the International Year for the Culture of Peace in 2000, proclaimed by the Assembly in resolution 52/15 [YUN 1997, p. 622], the engagement of Member States during the Decade and UNESCO's responsibility as lead agency for the Decade. It described the roles played by relevant UN bodies, particularly the United Nations Children's Fund and the University for Peace, by civil society and by the media, including new information and communication technology, to promote a culture of peace and non-violence.

GENERAL ASSEMBLY ACTION

On 5 November [meeting 37], the General Assembly adopted **resolution 56/5** [draft: A/56/L.5 & Add.1] without vote [agenda item 28].

International Decade for a Culture of Peace and Non-Violence for the Children of the World, 2001-2010

The General Assembly,

Bearing in mind the Charter of the United Nations, including the purposes and principles contained therein, and especially the dedication to saving succeeding generations from the scourge of war,

Recalling the Constitution of the United Nations Educational, Scientific and Cultural Organization, which states that, since wars begin in the minds of men, it is in the minds of men that the defences of peace must be constructed,

Recalling also its previous resolutions on a culture of peace, in particular resolution 52/15 of 20 November 1997 proclaiming 2000 as the International Year for the Culture of Peace, resolution 53/25 of 10 November 1998 proclaiming the period 2001-2010 as the International Decade for a Culture of Peace and Non-Violence for the Children of the World, and resolution 55/47 of 29 November 2000,

Reaffirming the Declaration and Programme of Action on a Culture of Peace, recognizing that they serve, inter alia, as the basis for the observance of the Decade, and convinced that effective and successful observance of the Decade throughout the world will promote a culture of peace and non-violence that benefits humanity, in particular future generations,

Recalling the United Nations Millennium Declaration which calls for the active promotion of a culture of peace,

Taking note of the report of the Secretary-General on the International Decade for a Culture of Peace and Non-Violence for the Children of the World, including paragraph 28 thereof which indicates that each of the ten years of the Decade will be marked with a different priority theme related to the Programme of Action,

Taking note also of Commission on Human Rights resolution 2000/66 of 26 April 2000, entitled "Towards a culture of peace",

Emphasizing the particular relevance of the special session of the General Assembly on children, to be held in New York during the fifty-sixth session of the General Assembly, the World Conference against Racism, Racial Discrimination, Xenophobia and Related Intolerance, held in Durban, South Africa, from 31 August to 8 September 2001, and the United Nations Decade for Human Rights Education, 1995-2004, for the International Decade for a Culture of Peace and Non-Violence for the Children of the World, 2001-2010,

Taking into account the "Manifesto 2000" initiative of the United Nations Educational, Scientific and Cultural Organization promoting a culture of peace, which has so far received over seventy-four million signatures of endorsement throughout the world,

1. *Reiterates* that the objective of the International Decade for a Culture of Peace and Non-Violence for the Children of the World is to further strengthen the global movement for a culture of peace following the observance of the International Year for the Culture of Peace in 2000;

2. *Invites* Member States to place greater emphasis on and expand their activities promoting a culture of peace and non-violence, in particular during the Decade, at the national, regional and international levels and to ensure that peace and non-violence are fostered at all levels;

3. *Commends* the United Nations Educational, Scientific and Cultural Organization for recognizing the promotion of a culture of peace as the expression of its fundamental mandate, and requests it, as the lead agency for the Decade, to further strengthen the activities it has undertaken for promoting a culture of peace;

4. *Also commends* the relevant United Nations bodies, in particular the United Nations Children's Fund and the University for Peace, for their activities in further promoting a culture of peace and non-violence, including promotion of peace education and activities

related to specific areas identified in the Programme of Action on a Culture of Peace;

5. *Requests* the United Nations Educational, Scientific and Cultural Organization to continue its efforts to disseminate in various languages, inter alia, through its national commissions, the Declaration on a Culture of Peace and the Programme of Action and related materials, in particular throughout the Decade;

6. *Calls upon* the relevant United Nations bodies, in particular the United Nations Educational, Scientific and Cultural Organization and the United Nations Children's Fund, to continue to promote both formal and non-formal education at all levels that foster a culture of peace and non-violence;

7. *Encourages* civil society, including non-governmental organizations, to continue and strengthen its efforts in furtherance of the objectives of the Decade, inter alia, by adopting its own programme of activities to complement the initiatives of Member States, the organizations of the United Nations system and other global and regional organizations;

8. *Also encourages* the involvement of the mass media in education for a culture of peace and non-violence, with particular regard to children and young people, including through the planned expansion of the Culture of Peace News Network as a global network of Internet sites in many languages;

9. *Welcomes* the efforts made by the United Nations Educational, Scientific and Cultural Organization to continue the communication and networking arrangements established during the International Year for providing an instant update of developments related to the observance of the Decade;

10. *Invites* Member States as well as civil society, including non-governmental organizations, to provide information to the Secretary-General on the observance of the Decade and the activities undertaken to promote a culture of peace and non-violence;

11. *Requests* the Secretary-General to submit to the General Assembly at its fifty-seventh session a report on the implementation of the present resolution;

12. *Decides* to include in the provisional agenda of its fifty-seventh session the item entitled "Culture of peace".

National institutions and regional arrangements

National institutions for human rights promotion and protection

Commission action. Welcoming the role of the International Coordinating Committee of National Institutions, in cooperation with OHCHR, in assessing conformity with the Principles relating to the status of national institutions for the promotion and protection of human rights, adopted by the General Assembly in resolution 48/134 [YUN 1993, p. 899], the Commission, on 25 April [res. 2001/80], requested the Secretary-General to continue to provide assistance to Coordinating Committee meetings and, from within existing resources and the UN Voluntary Fund

for Technical Cooperation in the Field of Human Rights (see p. 598), assistance for international and regional meetings of national institutions; the Commission's requests were approved by the Economic and Social Council on 24 July (**decision 2001/276**). The Commission also asked the Secretary-General to report in 2002.

Reports of Secretary-General. In an August report [A/56/255], the Secretary-General described OHCHR activities to establish and strengthen national human rights institutions and related measures taken by Governments, as well as consultations by UN human rights treaty bodies and Commission mechanisms with national human rights institutions. The report covered the period from 9 September 1999 to 1 July 2001.

During the reporting period, at the request of Governments or entities in the process of establishing, or considering establishment of, national human rights institutions, OHCHR provided information, advice or assistance to Azerbaijan, Bangladesh, Burundi, Cambodia, Côte d'Ivoire, East Timor, Fiji, Germany, Ireland, Kazakhstan, Kenya, Kyrgyzstan, Malaysia, Mauritius, Mongolia, Nepal, Nigeria, Palestine, the Republic of Korea, the Republic of Moldova, Rwanda, Sierra Leone, Thailand, the United Kingdom and FRY. The High Commissioner's Special Adviser on National Institutions and the National Institutions Team conducted missions to assist Governments and/or institutions in Australia, Cambodia, Canada, Ecuador, France, Georgia, Germany, Indonesia, Ireland, Jordan, Kenya, Kosovo (FRY), Latvia, Malaysia, Mexico, Mongolia, Morocco, Nepal, New Zealand, Nigeria, the Philippines, the Republic of Moldova, Rwanda, Sierra Leone, Sweden, Thailand, Togo, Uganda, Ukraine, the United Kingdom and FRY. The report described the advisory services and technical cooperation activities of OHCHR in Africa; Asia and the Pacific; Europe, Central Asia and North America; and Latin America and the Caribbean.

At the international and regional levels, OHCHR supported the third Regional Conference of African Institutions for the Promotion and Protection of Human Rights (Lomé, Togo, 14-16 March), at which participants discussed independence, pluralism and the effectiveness of national institutions; cooperation between national institutions; OHCHR and NGOs; human rights, development and HIV/AIDS; child exploitation and trafficking; and the World Conference against Racism, Racial Discrimination, Xenophobia and Related Intolerance (see p. 615). In preparation for the World Conference, support provided by OHCHR by way of grants from the

Rockefeller and Carnegie Foundations enabled some 17 national institutions to receive funding to undertake educational and promotional activities at the national level. The EU provided funding to allow the participation of up to 36 national institutions in the Conference.

The International Coordinating Committee of National Institutions held its eighth and ninth sessions from 17 to 19 March 2000 and from 18 to 20 April 2001, both in Geneva.

In a later report [E/CN.4/2002/114], the Secretary-General stated that OHCHR supported and participated in the sixth annual meeting of the Asia-Pacific Forum of National Human Rights Institutions (Sri Lanka, September) and in the Organization for Security and Co-operation in Europe Human Dimension Implementation Meeting (Poland, September). It participated in the meeting of Euro-Mediterranean national institutions for the promotion and protection of human rights (Greece, November).

GENERAL ASSEMBLY ACTION

On 19 December [meeting 88], the General Assembly, on the recommendation of the Third Committee [A/56/583/Add.2], adopted **resolution 56/158** without vote [agenda item 119 *(b)*].

National institutions for the promotion and protection of human rights

The General Assembly,

Recalling its resolutions and those of the Commission on Human Rights concerning national institutions for the promotion and protection of human rights,

Welcoming the rapidly growing interest throughout the world in the creation and strengthening of independent, pluralistic national institutions for the promotion and protection of human rights,

Convinced of the important role that such national institutions play and will continue to play in promoting and protecting human rights and fundamental freedoms and in developing and enhancing public awareness of those rights and freedoms,

Recognizing that the United Nations has played an important role and should continue to play a more important role in assisting the development of national institutions,

Recalling the Vienna Declaration and Programme of Action adopted by the World Conference on Human Rights on 25 June 1993, which reaffirmed the important and constructive role played by national human rights institutions, in particular in their advisory capacity to the competent authorities and their role in remedying human rights violations, in disseminating information on human rights and in education in human rights,

Recalling also the Beijing Platform for Action, in which Governments were urged to create or strengthen independent national institutions for the promotion and protection of human rights, including the human rights of women,

Noting the diverse approaches adopted throughout the world for the promotion and protection of human rights at the national level, emphasizing the universality, indivisibility and interdependence of all human rights, and emphasizing and recognizing the value of such approaches in promoting universal respect for and observance of human rights and fundamental freedoms,

Noting with satisfaction the constructive participation of representatives of national institutions for the promotion and protection of human rights in, and their positive contribution to, the deliberations of the World Conference on Human Rights, the World Conference against Racism, Racial Discrimination, Xenophobia and Related Intolerance and the Commission on Human Rights, as well as international seminars and workshops on human rights organized or sponsored by the United Nations,

Welcoming the strengthening in all regions of regional cooperation among national human rights institutions and between national human rights institutions and other regional human rights forums,

Welcoming also the strengthening of international cooperation among national human rights institutions, including through the International Coordinating Committee of National Institutions,

1. *Welcomes* the report of the Secretary-General;

2. *Reaffirms* the importance of the development of effective, independent and pluralistic national institutions for the promotion and protection of human rights, in keeping with the principles relating to the status of national institutions for the promotion and protection of human rights contained in the annex to General Assembly resolution 48/134 of 20 December 1993;

3. *Recognizes* that, in accordance with the Vienna Declaration and Programme of Action, it is the right of each State to choose the framework for the national institutions that is best suited to its particular needs at the national level in order to promote human rights in accordance with international human rights standards;

4. *Encourages* Member States to establish or, where they already exist, to strengthen national institutions for the promotion and protection of human rights, as outlined in the Vienna Declaration and Programme of Action;

5. *Welcomes* the growing number of States establishing or considering the establishment of national institutions for the promotion and protection of human rights;

6. *Encourages* national institutions for the promotion and protection of human rights established by Member States to continue to play an active role in preventing and combating all violations of human rights as enumerated in the Vienna Declaration and Programme of Action and relevant international instruments;

7. *Notes with satisfaction* the efforts of those States that have provided their national institutions with more autonomy and independence, including by giving them an investigative role or enhancing such a role, and encourages other Governments to consider taking similar steps;

8. *Reaffirms* the role of national institutions, where they exist, as appropriate agencies, inter alia, for the dissemination of human rights materials and other public information activities, including those of the United Nations, in particular in the context of the

United Nations Decade for Human Rights Education, 1995-2004;

9. *Urges* the Secretary-General to continue to give high priority to requests from Member States for assistance in the establishment and strengthening of national human rights institutions as part of the United Nations Programme of Advisory Services and Technical Assistance in the Field of Human Rights;

10. *Commends* the high priority given by the Office of the United Nations High Commissioner for Human Rights to work on national institutions, and, in view of the expanded activities relating to national institutions, encourages the High Commissioner to ensure that appropriate arrangements are made and budgetary resources provided to continue and further extend activities in support of national human rights institutions, and invites Governments to contribute additional, earmarked funds to the United Nations Voluntary Fund for Technical Cooperation in the Field of Human Rights for that purpose;

11. *Notes with appreciation* the increasingly active and important role of the International Coordinating Committee of National Institutions, as recognized in Commission on Human Rights resolution 1994/54 of 4 March 1994, in close cooperation with the Office of the High Commissioner, in assisting Governments and national institutions, when requested, to follow up on relevant resolutions and recommendations concerning the strengthening of national institutions;

12. *Also notes with appreciation* the holding of regular meetings of the International Coordinating Committee of National Institutions and the arrangements for the participation of national human rights institutions in the annual sessions of the Commission on Human Rights;

13. *Requests* the Secretary-General to continue to provide the necessary assistance for holding meetings of the International Coordinating Committee of National Institutions during the sessions of the Commission on Human Rights, in cooperation with the Office of the High Commissioner;

14. *Welcomes* the continuation of the practice of national institutions convening regional meetings in some regions, and its initiation in others, and encourages national institutions, in cooperation with the United Nations High Commissioner for Human Rights, to organize similar events with Governments and non-governmental organizations in their own regions;

15. *Requests* the Secretary-General to continue to provide, including from the United Nations Voluntary Fund for Technical Cooperation in the Field of Human Rights, the necessary assistance for holding international and regional meetings of national institutions;

16. *Recognizes* the important and constructive role that non-governmental organizations may play, in cooperation with national institutions, for better promotion and protection of human rights;

17. *Encourages* all Member States to take appropriate steps to promote the exchange of information and experience concerning the establishment and effective operation of national institutions;

18. *Encourages* all United Nations entities, funds and agencies to work in close cooperation with national institutions in the promotion and protection of human rights;

19. *Requests* the Secretary-General to report to the General Assembly at its fifty-eighth session on the implementation of the present resolution.

Regional arrangements

Commission action. On 25 April [res. 2001/79], the Commission welcomed the High Commissioner's appointment of four human rights personalities to serve as regional advisers, who would promote human rights and human rights advocacy through the design of strategies and human rights partnerships and facilitate human rights regional technical cooperation. It asked the Secretary-General to strengthen exchanges between the United Nations and regional human rights intergovernmental organizations and to provide resources to promote regional arrangements. OHCHR was requested to pay attention to the most appropriate ways of assisting countries, at their request, under the technical cooperation programme and to make relevant recommendations. The Secretary-General was invited, in his report requested in General Assembly resolution 55/105 [YUN 2000, p. 638], to provide information about the progress made since the adoption of the Vienna Declaration and Programme of Action (see p. 598) on exchanging information and extending collaboration between UN human rights bodies and regional organizations working to promote and protect human rights. He was also asked to report in 2003.

Africa

A November report of the High Commissioner [A/56/36/Add.1] presented the activities of the Subregional Centre for Human Rights and Democracy in Central Africa, established as a subregional office of OHCHR in cooperation with the Economic Community of Central African States and the UN Department of Political Affairs. The Centre, located in Yaoundé, Cameroon, became operational in March. Based on the recommendations contained in a declaration by a subregional workshop on human rights education in Central Africa (Yaoundé, 15-16 March), a programme of priority action for 2001 and 2002 was adopted and approved by the High Commissioner. Under training activities, two workshops were scheduled: one on the development of national human rights action plans and another on respect for human rights by security forces. The Centre published the first issue of its trimestral bulletin on human rights and democracy covering the period from March to June.

GENERAL ASSEMBLY ACTION

On 24 December [meeting 92], the General Assembly, on the recommendation of the Third

Committee [A/56/583/Add.2], adopted **resolution 56/230** without vote [agenda item 119 (*b*)].

Subregional Centre for Human Rights and Democracy in Central Africa

The General Assembly,

Recalling its resolution 55/105 of 4 December 2000 concerning regional arrangements for the promotion and protection of human rights,

Recalling also its resolutions 55/34 B of 20 November 2000 and 55/233 of 23 December 2000 and section III of its resolution 55/234 of 23 December 2000,

Recalling further the report of the United Nations High Commissioner for Human Rights,

1. *Welcomes* the creation of the Subregional Centre for Human Rights and Democracy in Central Africa at Yaoundé;

2. *Notes with satisfaction* the support given to the establishment of the Centre by the host country;

3. *Invites* the Office of the United Nations High Commissioner for Human Rights, under the direction of the Secretary-General, to provide appropriate assistance to the Centre to ensure its efficiency and smooth functioning in accordance with section III of General Assembly resolution 55/234;

4. *Requests* the Secretary-General to submit to the General Assembly at its fifty-seventh session a report on the implementation of the present resolution.

Asia and the Pacific

Commission action. On 25 April [res. 2001/77], the Commission endorsed the conclusions of the ninth workshop on regional cooperation for the promotion and protection of human rights in the Asia and Pacific region (below) and asked the Secretary-General to submit in 2002 a report containing the conclusions of the tenth workshop.

Reports of Secretary-General. In March [E/CN.4/2001/98], the Secretary-General presented the conclusions of the ninth workshop on regional cooperation for the promotion and protection of human rights in the Asia and Pacific region (Bangkok, Thailand, 28 February–2 March), organized by OHCHR, which reviewed progress made since the last workshop, held in 2000 [YUN 2000, p. 639], in the four areas of the framework for regional technical cooperation (national plans of action for human rights promotion and protection and the strengthening of national capacities; human rights education; national institutions for the promotion and protection of human rights; and strategies for the realization of the right to development and economic, social and cultural rights). The workshop also aimed at enhancing partnerships to implement the framework. The

conclusions adopted by the workshop were annexed to the report.

A later report of the Secretary-General [E/CN.4/2002/113] described other meetings held in the region. In April, OHCHR sponsored the Asian Human Rights Education Trainers' Colloquium (Chiengmai, Thailand, 1-6 April). A subregional workshop for judges on the justiciability of economic, social and cultural rights in South Asia (New Delhi, India, 17-18 November) was jointly organized by OHCHR, the International Commission of Jurists and the International Bar Association (IBA). OHCHR had collaborated with IBA in the organization of a workshop focusing on human rights in the administration of justice (March). The Office supported and participated in the sixth annual meeting of the Asia-Pacific Forum of National Human Rights Institutions (Sri Lanka, September) and conducted a workshop on the role of national human rights institutions and other mechanisms in promoting and protecting economic, social and cultural rights (Hong Kong, China, July).

Cooperation with UN human rights bodies

A January report of the Secretary-General [E/CN.4/2001/34] summarized allegations of intimidation and reprisals against private individuals and groups who sought to cooperate with the United Nations and with representatives of its human rights bodies.

Commission action. On 18 April [res. 2001/11], the Commission urged Governments to refrain from acts of intimidation or reprisal against persons who sought to cooperate or had cooperated with representatives of UN human rights bodies, or who had provided testimony or information to them; individuals who availed themselves of UN procedures and those who had provided legal assistance to them for that purpose; those who submitted communications under procedures established by human rights instruments; and relatives of victims of human rights violations. Representatives of UN human rights bodies and treaty bodies monitoring human rights were requested to help prevent the hampering of access to UN human rights procedures, to take steps to prevent intimidation or reprisal, and to include in their reports allegations of intimidation or reprisal, as well as action taken. The Secretary-General was asked to draw the Commission's resolution to the attention of UN human rights and treaty bodies and to report in 2002.

Chapter II

Protection of human rights

In 2001, the protection of human rights—civil and political, as well as economic, social and cultural—continued to be a major focus of UN activities.

The World Conference against Racism, Racial Discrimination, Xenophobia and Related Intolerance (Durban, South Africa, 31 August–8 September) adopted the Durban Declaration and Programme of Action, which pronounced slavery and the slave trade a crime against humanity, condemned racism and related practices, and committed the international community to combating the phenomena.

The International Convention against the Recruitment, Use, Financing and Training of Mercenaries, adopted by the General Assembly in 1989, entered into force on 20 October. As at 31 December, 22 States were party to the Convention.

In November, the Security Council, expressing its determination to give the fullest attention to the protection of children in armed conflict, made a series of recommendations to parties to armed conflict and to Member States, as well as requests to the Secretary-General.

During the year, the Commission on Human Rights appointed a Special Rapporteur on the situation of indigenous peoples' human rights and fundamental freedoms. It appointed an independent expert to examine the existing international criminal and human rights framework to protect persons from involuntary disappearance and decided to establish a working group to develop a legally binding instrument for the protection of all persons from enforced disappearance.

Special rapporteurs, special representatives and independent experts of the Commission and its subsidiary body, the Subcommission on the Promotion and Protection of Human Rights, examined, among other issues, allegations of torture; extralegal executions; impunity; mercenary activity; affirmative action; the rights of migrants; the independence of the judiciary; freedom of opinion and expression; freedom of religion or belief; human rights and terrorism; internally displaced persons; globalization and its impact on human rights; extreme poverty; illicit practices related to toxic and dangerous products and wastes; bioethics; sexual violence

during armed conflict; violence against women; the sale of children, child prostitution and child pornography; the situation of children affected by armed conflict; persons with HIV/AIDS; and persons with disabilities.

Working groups considered arbitrary detention, enforced or involuntary disappearances, discrimination against minorities, the right to development, contemporary forms of slavery and the rights of indigenous peoples.

Racism and racial discrimination

Third Decade against racism

The General Assembly, in resolution 48/91 [YUN 1993, p. 853], had proclaimed the Third Decade to Combat Racism and Racial Discrimination (1993-2003) and adopted the Decade's Programme of Action; the Third Decade's goals and objectives were the same as those of the first Decade, which the Assembly had adopted in resolution 3057(XXVIII) [YUN 1973, p. 523]. The revised Programme of Action for the Third Decade was adopted by the Assembly in resolution 49/146 [YUN 1994, p. 988]. However, in accordance with a 1998 resolution of the Commission on Human Rights [YUN 1998, p. 645], the United Nations High Commissioner for Human Rights reorganized the activities of the Third Decade to focus on the World Conference against Racism, Racial Discrimination, Xenophobia and Related Intolerance (see p. 615).

Implementation of Programme of Action

Commission action. On 18 April [E/2001/23 (res. 2001/5)], the Commission on Human Rights, regretting the lack of interest, support and financial resources for the Decade and Programme of Action and that the activities planned for the Decade had not been fully implemented, recommended that the General Assembly ask the Secretary-General to assign high priority to the Programme's activities and earmark adequate resources to finance them; the Economic and Social Council approved the recommendation on 24 July (**decision 2001/245**). The Commission appealed to Governments, intergovernmental organizations, non-governmental organizations (NGOs) and individuals to contribute to the Trust Fund for the Decade's Programme of Action, and asked the Secretary-General to continue to encourage contributions. It also asked States to encourage the reporting of acts motivated by racism, racial discrimination, xenophobia or ethnic reasons and to give priority to education as the main means of preventing racism and racial discrimination.

Reports of Secretary-General. In response to a 2000 Commission request [YUN 2000, p. 640], the Secretary-General, in a February report [E/CN.4/2001/20], described activities to implement the Programme of Action for the Third Decade, including preparations for the World Conference against racism (see below), the activities of the Special Rapporteur on contemporary forms of racism, racial discrimination, xenophobia and related intolerance (see p. 617), and action taken by the Committee on the Elimination of Racial Discrimination (CERD) in 2000 [YUN 2000, p. 611].

Pursuant to General Assembly resolution 54/154 [YUN 1999, p. 605], the Secretary-General submitted to the Economic and Social Council in May his annual report on implementation of the Programme of Action [E/2001/74]. The report described the activities, taken as at 15 May, by UN bodies and specialized agencies to combat racism and racial discrimination, and presented an overview of the preparatory process for the World Conference against racism. Annexed to the report was a list of contributions made by Governments to the Trust Fund for the Programme of Action for the period 1999 to 2001. On 26 July, the Council took note of the May report (**decision 2001/317**).

In an October report [A/56/481] submitted pursuant to Assembly resolution 53/153 [YUN 1998, p. 636], the Secretary-General presented proposals to supplement the Programme of Action during the remaining two years of the Third Decade. The proposals, which were based on the Programme of Action adopted by the World Conference (see below), included action towards universal ratification by 2005 of the 1965 International Convention on the Elimination of All Forms of Racial Discrimination, adopted by the Assembly in resolution 2106 A (XX) [YUN 1965, p. 440] (see p. 593), capacity-building programmes for Africans and people of African descent and promotion of the Guiding Principles on Internal Displacement [YUN 1998, p. 675]. Other areas for possible action focused on combating discrimination against migrants, a UN year or decade against the trafficking of persons, aspects of globalization that might lead to racism, racial discrimination, xenophobia and related intolerance, and an evaluation of the International Decade of the World's Indigenous People (1995-2004) (see p. 689). Activities recommended for the Office of the High Commissioner for Human Rights (OHCHR) included technical cooperation projects, the establishment of an anti-discrimination unit and the creation of a database containing information on practical means to address racism, racial discrimination, xenophobia and related intolerance, remedies available through international mechanisms, opportunities for technical cooperation and academic studies, and specialized documentation. The report described the preparatory process for the World Conference, Conference activities and follow-up. It provided information on the situation of migrant workers and their families, as requested in Assembly resolution 55/84 [YUN 2000, p. 643], and, pursuant to Assembly resolution 55/162 [ibid., p. 62], highlighted the contribution of the Conference to the implementation of the United Nations Millennium Declaration [ibid., p. 49].

Subcommission action. On 15 August [E/CN.4/2002/2 (res. 2001/11)], the Subcommission on the Promotion and Protection of Human Rights, regretting the lack of interest, support and resources for the Decade and Programme of Action, called on Governments, UN bodies and interested NGOs to contribute to the Programme's implementation.

World Conference

As decided by the General Assembly in resolution 52/111 [YUN 1997, p. 629], the World Conference against Racism, Racial Discrimination, Xenophobia and Related Intolerance (Durban, South Africa, 31 August–8 September) [A/CONF.189/12 & Corr.1 & Parts II & III] focused on practical measures to eradicate racism and racial discrimination, including measures of prevention, education and protection, and the provision of effective remedies.

On 8 September, the Conference adopted the Durban Declaration and Programme of Action, which committed States to undertake a wide range of measures to combat racism, racial discrimination, xenophobia and related intolerance at the international, national and regional levels. Among other things, the Declaration acknowledged that slavery and the slave trade were a crime against humanity and were among the major sources and manifestations of racism, racial discrimination, xenophobia and related intolerance. A large part of the Programme of Action was devoted to prevention, education and protection measures, including the establishment of a follow-up observatory composed of five eminent persons from the various regions to work with the High Commissioner and UN bodies to help in implementing the Declaration and Programme of Action. It contained recommendations regarding Africans and people of African descent, indigenous people, migrants, refugees and other groups, including the Roma, Gypsies, Sinti and Travellers, and proposed that the Assembly develop an international convention to address discriminatory practices affecting persons with disabilities and declare a UN year or decade against trafficking in persons. A number of proposals contained in the Programme of Action were being considered to supplement the Programme of Action for the Third Decade to Combat Racism and Racial Discrimination (see p. 615). The Commission on Human Rights was asked to consider, among other things, establishing a working group or other mechanism to study the problems of racial discrimination affecting people of African descent in the African diaspora.

The Conference had before it the report of its Credentials Committee [A/CONF.189/11] and a contribution of the Special Rapporteur on adequate housing as a component of an adequate standard of living [A/CONF.189/9] (see p. 671), as well as contributions submitted by NGOs [A/CONF. 189/10 & Add.1-9] and national human rights institutions [A/CONF.189/Misc.1].

On 24 December, the General Assembly decided that the item on the elimination of racism and racial discrimination remained for consideration during its resumed fifty-sixth (2002) session (**decision 56/464**).

Preparatory process

The Preparatory Committee for the Conference held its second (21 May–1 June) [A/CONF.189/PC.2/30] and third (30 July–10 August) [A/CONF.189/PC.3/11] sessions, both in Geneva, to conclude its consideration of the agenda, organization and outcome of the Conference. The Committee's first session took place in 2000 [YUN 2000, p. 641].

Contributions to the preparatory process were received from the Secretariat [A/CONF.189/PC.2/29], CERD [A/CONF.189/PC.2/13] and various UN human rights mechanisms, among them reports of the High Commissioner for Human Rights on Internet use to incite racial hatred, racist propaganda and xenophobia [A/CONF.189/PC.2/12], the Subcommission on the Promotion and Protection of Human Rights [A/CONF.189/PC.2/19 & Add.1] and its Working Group on Indigenous Populations [A/CONF.189/PC.3/4], and the Special Rapporteurs on contemporary forms of racism, racial discrimination, xenophobia and related intolerance [A/CONF.189/PC.2/21 & Corr.1], on religious intoler-

ance [A/CONF.189/PC.2/22], on the human rights of migrants [A/CONF.189/PC.2/23], on the right to freedom of opinion and expression [A/CONF.189/PC.2/24] and on violence against women [A/CONF.189/PC.3/5]. (For details of the reports, see under the specific subject item.)

Regional activities included the Regional Conference for Africa (Dakar, Senegal, 22-24 January) [A/CONF.189/PC.2/8] and the Asian Preparatory Meeting (Tehran, Iran, 19-21 February) [A/CONF.189/PC.2/9], an expert round table on the protection of human rights in migrant flows (Segovia, Spain, 16-17 February) [A/CONF.189/PC.2/Misc.4] and a meeting of indigenous peoples (Sydney, Australia, 20-22 February) [A/CONF.189/PC.2/Misc.5].

Commission action. On 18 April [res. 2001/5], the Commission adopted recommendations relating to the Conference and preparatory process, which it submitted to the Economic and Social Council for approval.

ECONOMIC AND SOCIAL COUNCIL ACTION

On 24 July, the Economic and Social Council, on the recommendation of the Commission on Human Rights [E/2001/23], adopted **decision 2001/245** without vote [agenda item 14 *(g)*].

Racism, racial discrimination, xenophobia and related intolerance

At its 40th plenary meeting, on 24 July 2001, the Economic and Social Council, taking note of Commission on Human Rights resolution 2001/5 of 18 April 2001, approved the Commission's recommendation that the General Assembly request the Secretary-General to assign high priority to the activities of the revised Programme of Action for the Third Decade to Combat Racism and Racial Discrimination (1993-2003) and to earmark adequate resources to finance the activities of the Programme.

The Council also approved the Commission's requests to the United Nations High Commissioner for Human Rights:

(a) To continue to undertake research and consultations on the use of the Internet for the purposes of incitement to racial hatred, racist propaganda and xenophobia, to study ways of promoting international cooperation in this area, and to draw up a programme of human rights education and exchanges over the Internet on experience in the struggle against racism, xenophobia and anti-Semitism;

(b) To provide, insofar as possible, non-governmental organizations with technical assistance for the holding of a forum before and partly during the World Conference against Racism, Racial Discrimination, Xenophobia and Related Intolerance;

(c) To explore ways and means of effectively involving all parliaments to participate actively in the preparation of the World Conference through the relevant international organizations.

The Council further approved the Commission's recommendations that:

(*a*) The issue of universal ratification of the International Convention on the Elimination of All Forms of Racial Discrimination, as well as the reservations thereto, and the question of recognition of the competence of the Committee on the Elimination of Racial Discrimination to receive individual complaints, be considered at the World Conference against Racism, Racial Discrimination, Xenophobia and Related Intolerance;

(*b*) A gender-based approach be systematically adopted throughout the preparations for and in the outcome of the World Conference;

(*c*) The particular situation of children and young people receive special attention during the preparations for and during the World Conference itself, and especially in its outcome;

(*d*) The particular situation of indigenous people receive special attention during the preparations for and during the World Conference, and especially in its outcome;

(*e*) Special attention be accorded during the preparations for and during the World Conference, especially in its outcome, to the particular situation of migrants.

Subcommission action. On 15 August [res. 2001/11], the Subcommission suggested topics for discussion at the Conference and recommended that the Conference define a global and system-wide strategy to combat racism and racial discrimination and adopt effective follow-up procedures and mechanisms.

Contemporary forms of racism

Reports of Special Rapporteur. In February [E/CN.4/2001/21 & Corr.1], the Special Rapporteur on contemporary forms of racism, racial discrimination, xenophobia and related intolerance, Maurice Glèlè-Ahanhanzo (Benin), summarized information he had received regarding racial discrimination in the application of the death penalty and in efforts to combat drug trafficking in the United States, racist activities by far-right, neo-Nazi and skinhead organizations in Norway, violence and atrocities against the Dalits in India, and incidents of anti-Semitism in many parts of the world. The report contained replies to allegations of racism, racial discrimination and xenophobia transmitted to four Governments by the Special Rapporteur, legislative, judicial or other measures taken or envisaged by Governments against racist propaganda, and action by civil society.

The Special Rapporteur observed that significant progress had been made to raise awareness about the negative effects of racism, racial discrimination and xenophobia, but that measures adopted by Governments were not always implemented. He made a series of recommendations for States, including the ratification by those that had not done so of the 1965 International Convention on the Elimination of All Forms of Racial Discrimination (see p. 593) and the establishment of national institutions promoting and protecting human rights, with a particular focus on combating racism. In his view, the reform of the UN system had in recent years resulted in a gradual downgrading of efforts to combat racism. Thus, the Special Rapporteur recommended that the Commission establish a major programme or service within OHCHR devoted entirely to combating racism, racial discrimination and related intolerance.

On 15 October [E/CN.4/2002/138], the Libyan Arab Jamahiriya claimed that the Special Rapporteur's references in his report to racist and xenophobic incidents in the country were based on biased media reports.

In an April report [A/CONF.189/PC.2/21 & Corr.1,2] on the main features of extreme-right parties and organizations (ultra-nationalists, neo-Nazis, neo-Fascists, skinheads), the Special Rapporteur concluded that the ideology and violence promoted by them against minorities and immigrants were incompatible with the trend towards global integration and violated the basic principles of equality and non-discrimination enshrined in human rights instruments. He recommended that the Preparatory Committee request Governments concerned to provide the World Conference against racism with a national study on measures adopted to prohibit the activities of extreme-right organizations.

The Special Rapporteur described his visit to Australia (22 April–10 May) [E/CN.4/2002/24/Add.1 & Corr.1], where he evaluated the impact of legislation and government policy in combating racism, racial discrimination and xenophobia on the various components of the population, particularly regarding the situation of the Aboriginal peoples and the Torres Strait Islanders. Information had reached the Special Rapporteur relating to the difficulties in the reconciliation process between indigenous and non-indigenous inhabitants, and discriminatory laws on mandatory sentencing enforced in Western Australia and the Northern Territory, which had led to an excessive percentage of Aboriginals among the prison population. He also examined the policy of multiculturalism underlying Australia's immigration policy and the social cohesion of the country.

The Special Rapporteur concluded that the Government had made substantial efforts to end racism and racial discrimination, and programmes to improve the living conditions of indigenous peoples existed, even if they had not yet succeeded in producing the desired results. The question of reconciliation with the Aboriginal peoples remained outstanding, as their land rights were restricted, no reparation or apology had been made regarding the "stolen generations"—the forcible removal of indigenous children from their families for adoption by white families as a policy of assimilation—cultural clashes occurred and highly precarious living conditions existed outside the wealth of the majority of Australians. The Special Rapporteur recommended, among other things, basing the multiculturalism policy on the recognition of the right to difference and to cultural identity, with broad communication between one culture and another; a humane solution to the question of the stolen generations; and acceleration of compensation to Aboriginals and Torres Strait Islanders whose wages had been withheld since 1897, through the implementation of protection measures.

Report of High Commissioner. An April report of the High Commissioner [A/CONF.189/PC.2/12] described the degree of Internet use worldwide. Racist individuals and groups had availed themselves of technology to establish and strengthen ties among themselves and to make their racist materials available online. She reviewed individual governmental responses to Internet-based racist speech in national court cases and through regulatory efforts, coordinated governmental responses and approaches by industry and other private organizations such as hotlines, codes of conduct and other voluntary restraints, products to block access to sites and rating systems for web sites. The High Commissioner pointed out that some of the measures to combat the phenomenon were legal, while many were of a non-legal nature. She concluded that approaches to combating Internet-based racism were still evolving.

Commission action. On 18 April [res. 2001/5], the Commission invited Governments thus far visited by the Special Rapporteur to consider ways to implement the recommendations contained in his reports and requested him to include in his 2002 report information on measures to implement the recommendations, and to undertake follow-up visits, if necessary. The High Commissioner was urged to provide the countries visited, at their request, with advisory services and technical assistance. She was asked to conduct research and hold consultations on Internet use to incite racial hatred, racist propaganda and xenophobia, to study ways of promoting international cooperation in that area and to draw up a programme of human rights education and exchanges over the Internet on the struggle against racism, xenophobia and anti-Semitism; the Economic and Social Council approved that request on 24 July (**decision 2001/245**).

Racism and democracy

Report of High Commissioner. In response to a 2000 Commission request [YUN 2000, p. 648], the High Commissioner, in a January report [E/CN.4/2001/60], described the activities undertaken by States, Commission mechanisms and human rights treaty bodies to promote tolerance and fight against racism, racial discrimination, xenophobia and related intolerance, as a way to strengthen democracy. In that regard, the report highlighted regional meetings and seminars organized to discuss that item as part of preparations for the World Conference against racism (see p. 616). It also described related activities of the treaty bodies, including the Human Rights Committee, the Committee against Torture and CERD, as well as the work of the Working Group on Indigenous Populations and of the Special Rapporteurs on the right to education, on contemporary forms of racism and on migrants' human rights.

Commission action. On 23 April [res. 2001/43], the Commission, condemning legislation and practices based on racism, racial discrimination, xenophobia and related intolerance as incompatible with democracy, urged States to reinforce their commitment to promote tolerance and to fight racism as a way to strengthen democracy and transparent and accountable governance. It invited the treaty bodies and the Commission's mechanisms, particularly the Special Rapporteur on contemporary forms of racism, racial discrimination, xenophobia and related intolerance, to give attention to human rights violations stemming from the rise of racism and xenophobia in political circles and society at large. The High Commissioner was asked to report in 2002.

Migrant workers

Reports of Special Rapporteur. The Special Rapporteur on the human rights of migrants, Gabriela Rodríguez Pizarro (Costa Rica), in a January report [E/CN.4/2001/83] covering 6 January to 15 December 2000, stated that during the period under review she had sent urgent appeals to five Governments regarding alleged violations of migrants' human rights and communications to two Governments requesting information on migrants' working conditions. The Special Rapporteur discussed matters of concern to her, including irregular migration—trafficking in persons and smuggling of migrants—the sale of fraudulent documents, the situation of migrant women (see p. 1058) and unaccompanied minors, undocumented minors without access to health care and education, broken families and acts of racism, xenophobia and racial discrimination.

The Special Rapporteur stated that incidents of racism, xenophobia and discrimination occurred with greater intensity every day, particularly against migrants. She regretted that during the period under review some incidents resulted in the deaths of many migrants inside trucks, in the holds of ships, on board rafts or in detention centres. She welcomed the signing of the 2000 United Nations Convention against Transnational Organized Crime and its Protocols to Prevent, Suppress and Punish Trafficking in Persons, Especially Women and Children, and against the Smuggling of Migrants by Land, Sea and Air, adopted by the General Assembly in resolution 55/25 [YUN 2000, p. 1048]. The Special Rapporteur recommended measures to protect migrants' human rights and prevent violations. States were urged to hold information campaigns, train border officials and guarantee health services for migrants. Governments were urged to strengthen and encourage civil society and academic institutions to study migration, activate forums and intersectoral round tables, improve the situation of migrants in detention through human rights training for immigration officials and facilitate the return of migrants to their countries of origin.

An April report [A/CONF.189/PC.2/23] of the Special Rapporteur contained suggestions to improve the channels by which discrimination and violence against migrants could be corrected. She recommended information campaigns, educational forums aimed at avoiding racial discrimination, xenophobia and intolerance towards migrants, ratification by States that had not done so of the 1990 International Convention on the Protection of the Rights of All Migrant Workers and Members of Their Families, adopted by the Assembly in resolution 45/158 [YUN 1990, p. 594] (see p. 596), programmes to facilitate migrants' access to basic social services, removing barriers that prevented migrants from equality before the law, ensuring that violations of migrants' human rights were reported and legal proceedings instituted against those responsible, policies to integrate migrant women into all sectors, training for police officers and border guards at ports and airports, and media investigation into the causes of migration.

During her visit to Ecuador (5-16 November) [E/CN.4/2002/94/Add.1], the Special Rapporteur focused on illegal migration and the smuggling of migrants, the situation of families in the places of origin of migration and immigration into Ecuador. She noted that a large-scale flow of Ecuadorians abroad resulted from the lack of opportunities to provide adequately for their families and that extreme poverty, poor knowledge of legal emigration and the lack of proper papers rendered them vulnerable to smugglers and traffickers. The Special Rapporteur recommended campaigns to inform the population of legal means of migration and the risks of illegal routes, assistance to migrants' families, including through psychosocial programmes, and advice on productive investment of migrants' remittances. The Special Rapporteur proposed legislative reforms, guaranteeing migrants without papers basic non-discriminatory health and educational services, the application of protection measures for Ecuadorian migrants abroad who were victims of abuse and advocacy measures by civil society and indigenous, social and peasant organizations.

Report of Secretary-General. In response to General Assembly resolution 55/92 [YUN 2000, p. 652], the Secretary-General, in an August report [A/56/310], summarized action taken by Governments to protect migrants' rights and the Special Rapporteur's activities.

Commission action. On 24 April [res. 2001/52], the Commission asked the Special Rapporteur to request, receive and exchange information on violations of migrants' human rights from Governments, treaty bodies, specialized agencies, special rapporteurs, intergovernmental organizations and NGOs, and to respond to such information. She was also asked to continue her programme of country visits, to take into account bilateral and regional negotiations aimed at addressing the return and reinsertion of nondocumented migrants or those in an irregular situation, and to report in 2002. The Secretary-General was asked to assist her.

Also on 24 April [res. 2001/56], the Commission requested States to adopt measures to prevent the violation of migrants' human rights while in transit, including at ports and airports and at borders and migration checkpoints, and to prosecute those who violated their rights while in transit. States were asked to prosecute labour law violations with regard to migrant workers and to consider acceding to the 1990 Convention.

GENERAL ASSEMBLY ACTION

On 19 December [meeting 88], the General Assembly, on the recommendation of the Third (Social, Humanitarian and Cultural) Committee [A/56/583/Add.2], adopted **resolution 56/170** without vote [agenda item 119 (b)].

Protection of migrants

The General Assembly,

Recalling its resolution 55/92 of 4 December 2000,

Considering that the Universal Declaration of Human Rights proclaims that all human beings are born free and equal in dignity and rights and that everyone is entitled to all the rights and freedoms set out therein, without distinction of any kind, in particular as to race, colour or national origin,

Reaffirming the provisions concerning migrants adopted by the World Conference on Human Rights, the International Conference on Population and Development, the World Summit for Social Development and the Fourth World Conference on Women,

Taking note of the positive treatment of the issue of migrants at the World Conference against Racism, Racial Discrimination, Xenophobia and Related Intolerance, and recognizing the economic, social and cultural contributions of migrants to the countries of destination and origin,

Bearing in mind the report of the Special Rapporteur of the Commission on Human Rights on the human rights of migrants,

Taking note of Commission on Human Rights resolutions 2001/52 on the human rights of migrants and 2001/56 on the protection of migrants and their families, of 24 April 2001,

Recalling its resolution 40/144 of 13 December 1985, by which it approved the Declaration on the Human Rights of Individuals Who are not Nationals of the Country in which They Live,

Recognizing the positive contributions that migrants frequently make, including through their eventual integration into their host society,

Bearing in mind the situation of vulnerability in which migrants frequently find themselves, owing, inter alia, to their absence from their States of origin and to the difficulties they encounter because of differences of language, custom and culture, as well as the economic and social difficulties and obstacles to the return to their States of origin of migrants who are nondocumented or in an irregular situation,

Bearing in mind also the need for a focused and consistent approach towards migrants as a specific vulnerable group, in particular migrant women and children,

Deeply concerned at the manifestations of violence, racism, xenophobia and other forms of discrimination and inhuman and degrading treatment against migrants, especially women and children, in different parts of the world,

Underlining the importance of the creation of conditions that foster greater harmony between migrant workers and the rest of the society of the States in which they reside, with the aim of eliminating the growing manifestations of racism and xenophobia perpetrated in segments of many societies by individuals or groups against migrants,

Encouraged by the increasing interest of the international community in the effective and full protection of the human rights of all migrants, and underlining the need to make further efforts to ensure respect for the human rights and fundamental freedoms of all migrants,

Noting the efforts made by States to penalize the international trafficking of migrants and to protect the victims of this illegal activity,

Taking note of Advisory Opinion OC-16/99, issued by the Inter-American Court of Human Rights on 1 October 1999, on The Right to Information on Consular Assistance in the Framework of the Guarantees of the Due Process of Law, in the case of foreign nationals detained by the authorities of a receiving State,

1. *Welcomes* the renewed commitment made in the United Nations Millennium Declaration to take measures to ensure respect for and protection of the human rights of migrants, migrant workers and their families, to eliminate the increasing acts of racism and xenophobia in many societies and to promote greater harmony and tolerance in all societies;

2. *Requests* all Member States, in conformity with their respective constitutional systems, effectively to promote and protect the human rights of all migrants, in conformity with the Universal Declaration of Human Rights and the international instruments to which they are party, which may include the International Covenants on Human Rights, the Convention against Torture and Other Cruel, Inhuman or Degrading Treatment or Punishment, the International Convention on the Elimination of All Forms of Racial Discrimination, the International Convention on the Protection of the Rights of All Migrant Workers and Members of Their Families, the Convention on the Elimination of All Forms of Discrimination against Women, the Convention on the Rights of the Child and other applicable international human rights instruments;

3. *Strongly condemns* all forms of racial discrimination and xenophobia with regard to access to employment, vocational training, housing, schooling, health services and social services, as well as services intended for use by the public, and welcomes the active role played by governmental and non-governmental organizations in combating racism and assisting individual victims of racist acts, including migrant victims;

4. *Calls upon* all States to review and, where necessary, revise immigration policies with a view to eliminating all discriminatory practices against migrants and to provide specialized training for government policy-making and law enforcement, immigration and other concerned officials, thus underlining the importance of effective action to create conditions that foster greater harmony and tolerance within societies;

5. *Reiterates* the need for all States parties to protect fully the universally recognized human rights of migrants, especially women and children, regardless of their legal status, and to treat them humanely, in particular with regard to assistance and protection;

6. *Reaffirms emphatically* the duty of States parties to ensure full respect for and observance of the Vienna Convention on Consular Relations of 1963, in particular with regard to the right of foreign nationals, regardless of their immigration status, to communicate with a consular official of their own State in the case of detention, and the obligation of the State in whose territory the detention occurs to inform the foreign national of that right;

7. *Reaffirms* the responsibility of Governments to safeguard and protect the rights of migrants against illegal or violent acts, in particular acts of racial discrimination and crimes perpetrated with racist or xenophobic motivation by individuals or groups, and urges them to reinforce measures in this regard;

8. *Urges* all States to adopt effective measures to put an end to the arbitrary arrest and detention of migrants, including by individuals or groups;

9. *Expresses its support* for the work of the Special Rapporteur of the Commission on Human Rights on the human rights of migrants, and requests her to take into account the recommendations contained in the

Durban Declaration and Programme of Action in the performance of her mandate, tasks and duties;

10. *Encourages* Member States that have not yet done so to enact domestic criminal legislation to combat the international trafficking of migrants, which should take into account, in particular, trafficking that endangers the lives of migrants or includes different forms of servitude or exploitation, such as any form of debt bondage or sexual or labour exploitation, and to strengthen international cooperation to combat such trafficking;

11. *Encourages* all Governments to remove obstacles that may prevent the safe, unrestricted and expeditious transfer of earnings, assets and pensions of migrants to their country of origin or to any other countries, in conformity with applicable legislation, and to consider, as appropriate, measures to solve other problems that may impede such transfers;

12. *Welcomes* immigration programmes, adopted by some countries, that allow migrants to integrate fully into the host countries, facilitate family reunification and promote a harmonious and tolerant environment, and encourages States to consider the possibility of adopting these types of programmes;

13. *Calls upon* all States to protect the human rights of migrant children, in particular unaccompanied migrant children, ensuring that the best interests of the children and the importance of reuniting them with their parents, when possible and appropriate, are the paramount consideration, and encourages the relevant United Nations bodies, within the framework of their respective mandates, to pay special attention to the conditions of migrant children in all States and, where necessary, to put forward recommendations for strengthening their protection;

14. *Welcomes* the proclamation of 18 December as International Migrants Day and the invitation to Member States and intergovernmental and nongovernmental organizations to observe it through, inter alia, the dissemination of information on the human rights and fundamental freedoms of migrants and on their economic, social and cultural contributions to their host and home countries, the sharing of experience and the design of actions to ensure their protection;

15. *Encourages* States to participate in regional dialogues on problems of migration, and invites them to design and implement programmes with States of other regions in order to protect the rights of migrants;

16. *Requests* the Secretary-General to submit to the General Assembly at its fifty-seventh session a report on the implementation of the present resolution under the sub-item entitled "Human rights questions, including alternative approaches for improving the effective enjoyment of human rights and fundamental freedoms".

Other forms of intolerance

Cultural prejudice

In response to General Assembly resolution 55/91 [YUN 2000, p. 655], the Secretary-General, in a July report with later addendum [A/56/204 &

Add.1], summarized the views expressed by Governments, UN agencies and NGOs on human rights and cultural diversity.

GENERAL ASSEMBLY ACTION

On 19 December [meeting 88], the General Assembly, on the recommendation of the Third Committee [A/56/583/Add.2], adopted **resolution 56/156** without vote [agenda item 119 *(b)*].

Human rights and cultural diversity

The General Assembly,

Recalling the Universal Declaration of Human Rights, the International Covenant on Economic, Social and Cultural Rights and the International Covenant on Civil and Political Rights, as well as other pertinent human rights instruments,

Recalling also its resolutions 54/160 of 17 December 1999 and 55/91 of 4 December 2000, and recalling further its resolutions 54/113 of 10 December 1999 and 55/23 of 13 November 2000 on the United Nations Year of Dialogue among Civilizations,

Noting that numerous instruments within the United Nations system promote cultural diversity, as well as the conservation and development of culture, in particular the Declaration of the Principles of International Culture Cooperation proclaimed on 4 November 1966 by the General Conference of the United Nations Educational, Scientific and Cultural Organization at its fourteenth session,

Taking note of the report of the Secretary-General,

Welcoming the adoption of the Global Agenda for Dialogue among Civilizations by its resolution 56/6 of 9 November 2001,

Welcoming also the contribution made through the World Conference against Racism, Racial Discrimination, Xenophobia and Related Intolerance, held at Durban, South Africa, from 31 August to 8 September 2001, to the promotion of respect for cultural diversity,

Welcoming further the Universal Declaration on Cultural Diversity of the United Nations Educational, Scientific and Cultural Organization, together with its Action Plan, adopted on 2 November 2001 by the General Conference of the United Nations Educational, Scientific and Cultural Organization at its thirty-first session, in which member States invited the United Nations system and other intergovernmental and nongovernmental organizations concerned to cooperate with the United Nations Educational, Scientific and Cultural Organization in the promotion of the principles set forth in the Declaration and its Action Plan with a view to enhancing the synergy of actions in favour of cultural diversity,

Reaffirming that all human rights are universal, indivisible, interdependent and interrelated and that the international community must treat human rights globally in a fair and equal manner, on the same footing and with the same emphasis, and that, while the significance of national and regional particularities and various historical, cultural and religious backgrounds must be borne in mind, it is the duty of States, regardless of their political, economic and cultural systems, to promote and protect all human rights and fundamental freedoms,

Recognizing that cultural diversity and the pursuit of cultural development by all peoples and nations are a source of mutual enrichment for the cultural life of humankind,

Taking into account that a culture of peace actively fosters non-violence and respect for human rights and strengthens solidarity among peoples and nations and dialogue between cultures,

Recognizing that all cultures and civilizations share a common set of universal values,

Considering that tolerance of cultural, ethnic, religious and linguistic diversities, as well as dialogue among and within civilizations, is essential for peace, understanding and friendship among individuals and people of different cultures and nations of the world, while manifestations of cultural prejudice, intolerance and xenophobia towards different cultures and religions generate hatred and violence among peoples and nations throughout the world,

Recognizing in each culture a dignity and value that deserves recognition, respect and preservation, and convinced that, in their rich variety and diversity, and in the reciprocal influences that they exert on one another, all cultures form part of the common heritage belonging to all humankind,

Convinced that the promotion of cultural pluralism and tolerance towards and dialogue among various cultures and civilizations would contribute to the efforts of all peoples and nations to enrich their cultures and traditions by engaging in a mutually beneficial exchange of knowledge and intellectual, moral and material achievements,

1. *Affirms* the importance for all peoples and nations to hold, develop and preserve their cultural heritage and traditions in a national and international atmosphere of peace, tolerance and mutual respect;

2. *Welcomes* the United Nations Millennium Declaration of 8 September 2000, which considers, inter alia, that tolerance is one of the fundamental values essential to international relations in the twenty-first century and that it should include the active promotion of a culture of peace and dialogue among civilizations, with human beings respecting one another in all their diversity of belief, culture and language, neither fearing nor repressing differences within and between societies but cherishing them as a precious asset of humanity;

3. *Recognizes* the right of everyone to take part in cultural life and to enjoy the benefits of scientific progress and its applications;

4. *Affirms* that the international community should strive to respond to the challenges and opportunities posed by globalization in a manner that ensures respect for the cultural diversity of all;

5. *Also affirms* that intercultural dialogue essentially enriches the common understanding of human rights and that the benefits to be derived from the encouragement and development of international contacts and cooperation in the cultural fields are important;

6. *Welcomes* the recognition at the World Conference against Racism, Racial Discrimination, Xenophobia and Related Intolerance of the necessity of respecting and maximizing the benefits of diversity within and among all nations in working together to build a harmonious and productive future by putting into practice and promoting values and principles such as justice, equality and non-discrimination, democracy,

fairness and friendship, tolerance and respect within and between communities and nations, in particular through public information and education programmes to raise awareness and understanding of the benefits of cultural diversity, including programmes where the public authorities work in partnership with international and non-governmental organizations and other sectors of civil society;

7. *Recognizes* that respect for cultural diversity and the cultural rights of all enhances cultural pluralism, contributing to a wider exchange of knowledge and understanding of cultural background, advancing the application and enjoyment of universally accepted human rights throughout the world and fostering stable friendly relations among peoples and nations worldwide;

8. *Emphasizes* that the promotion of cultural pluralism and tolerance at the national, regional and international levels is important for enhancing respect for cultural rights and cultural diversity;

9. *Also emphasizes* the fact that tolerance and respect for diversity facilitate the universal promotion and protection of human rights, including gender equality and the enjoyment of all human rights by all;

10. *Urges* all actors on the international scene to build an international order based on inclusion, justice, equality and equity, human dignity, mutual understanding and promotion of and respect for cultural diversity and universal human rights, and to reject all doctrines of exclusion based on racism, racial discrimination, xenophobia and related intolerance;

11. *Urges* States to work to ensure that their political and legal systems reflect the multicultural diversity within their societies and, where necessary, to improve democratic institutions so that they are more fully participatory and avoid marginalization and exclusion of, and discrimination against, specific sectors of society;

12. *Calls upon* States, international organizations and United Nations agencies, and invites civil society, including non-governmental organizations, to recognize and promote respect for cultural diversity for the purpose of advancing the objectives of peace, development and universally accepted human rights;

13. *Requests* the Secretary-General, in the light of the present resolution, to prepare a report on human rights and cultural diversity, taking into account the views of Member States, relevant United Nations agencies and non-governmental organizations, as well as the considerations in the present resolution regarding the recognition and importance of cultural diversity among all peoples and nations in the world, and to submit it to the General Assembly at its fifty-seventh session;

14. *Decides* to continue consideration of this question at its fifty-seventh session under the sub-item entitled "Human rights questions, including alternative approaches for improving the effective enjoyment of human rights and fundamental freedoms".

Discrimination against minorities

Commission action. On 24 April [res. 2001/55], the Commission, expressing concern at the frequency and severity of disputes and conflicts regarding minorities, urged States and the international community to promote and protect the rights of persons belonging to national or ethnic, religious and linguistic minorities, as set out in the 1992 Declaration on the Rights of Persons Belonging to National or Ethnic, Religious and Linguistic Minorities, adopted by the General Assembly in resolution 47/135 [YUN 1992, p. 722]. The Secretary-General was asked to provide, at the request of Governments, qualified expertise on minority issues and to report in 2002. The High Commissioner was called on to promote the Declaration's implementation, improve the coordination and cooperation of UN programmes and agencies dealing with minority issues, and invite Governments and relevant intergovernmental organizations and NGOs to submit their views on how best to protect the rights of minorities.

Working Group activities. The five-member Working Group on Minorities, at its seventh session (Geneva, 14-18 May) [E/CN.4/Sub.2/2001/22], reviewed the promotion of the 1992 Declaration, examined possible solutions to problems involving minorities, including the promotion of mutual understanding between and among minorities and Governments, and recommended further measures to promote and protect minority rights. It also discussed its future role.

The Group considered the final text of the commentary on the Declaration [E/CN.4/Sub.2/AC.5/2001/2], prepared by its Chairperson, Asbjørn Eide (Norway), which was intended to serve as a guide to the understanding and application of the Declaration. It also had before it the report of the second workshop on multiculturalism in Africa: peaceful and constructive group accommodation in situations involving minorities and indigenous peoples (Kidal, Mali, 8-13 January) [E/CN.4/Sub.2/AC.5/2001/3]. The workshop was a continuation of discussions at a seminar held in 2000 [YUN 2000, p. 656].

The Group adopted recommendations for Governments, regional and subregional organizations, human rights treaty bodies and NGOs. The High Commissioner was asked to request the views of intergovernmental organizations and NGOs on the drafting of a convention on the rights of minorities. The Commission was requested to consider appointing a special representative on minorities and to recommend the establishment of a voluntary trust fund to facilitate participation in the Group of minority representatives and experts from developing countries, and other relevant activities.

At the invitation of the Government, the Working Group visited Mauritius from 7 to 10 September [E/CN.4/Sub.2/AC.5/2002/2], where it focused on the constructive accommodation of the various ethnic groups on the main island of Mauri-

tius and plans for the autonomy of Rodrigues Island. On the positive side, the Group observed a spirit of tolerance and respect among various ethnic communities, comprehensive legislation to protect all citizens from discrimination, the establishment and activities of the National Commission on Human Rights and a proposal to guarantee autonomous status to Rodrigues Island. Subjects of concern were the lack of statistical data on the participation of various ethnic communities in economic and social life, the low level of educational attainment among the Creole community and the social and economic difficulties faced by the Chagossian/Ilois community while awaiting and campaigning for their return to Chagos Island. The Group proposed the collection of disaggregated data on disadvantaged communities, improvement of primary school facilities in marginalized regions, strengthening the National Commission on Human Rights and minority rights training for adjudication, law enforcement, and public administration personnel. Regarding Rodrigues Island, the Group cautioned the future Government against promoting tourism and other development projects involving the exploitation of natural resources.

Reports of Secretary-General. The Commission considered a report of the Secretary-General [E/CN.4/2001/81], submitted pursuant to its 2000 request [YUN 2000, p. 656], on measures to advance the situation of minorities taken by the High Commissioner, the Working Group on Minorities and the World Conference against racism. He also described activities to promote the 1992 Declaration.

In response to General Assembly resolution 54/162 [YUN 1999, p. 617], the Secretary-General, in an August report [A/56/258], described efforts made to promote minority rights and to establish more effective and long-term responses to prevent ethnic conflict. The report also provided information regarding cooperation among UN programmes and agencies, the participation of NGOs and minorities in the Working Group, intercultural and multicultural education, and the participation of minorities in decisions affecting them. The Secretary-General concluded that there was increasing awareness that protecting and promoting the rights of minorities could lead to stable societies.

Subcommission action. On 15 August [res. 2001/9], the Subcommission, noting the tenth anniversary of the Declaration's adoption in 2002, recommended the designation of an international year for minorities, the appointment of a special rapporteur on minority issues and the establishment of a voluntary trust fund to facilitate the participation in the Working Group of minority representatives and experts from developing countries. It recommended that the High Commissioner, when inviting Governments to submit views on how best to protect minorities' rights, also request their views on drafting a convention on the rights of minorities. OHCHR was asked to provide the Group with additional expertise and services; the Secretary-General, to invite UN funds and programmes to provide information on their policies regarding the protection of minority rights and the incorporation of the matter in their country programmes; and Mr. Eide, to update his 1993 study on peaceful and constructive approaches to situations involving minorities [YUN 1993, p. 869] and to submit a progress report in 2002 and a final report in 2003.

International seminar. Pursuant to Economic and Social Council decision 2000/269 [YUN 2000, p. 656], OHCHR organized the International Seminar on Cooperation for the Better Protection of the Rights of Minorities (Durban, South Africa, 1, 2 and 5 September) [E/CN.4/2002/92]. The seminar considered the relationship between the prevention of racial discrimination and the protection of minorities; facilitating cooperation between international, regional and national bodies and human rights mechanisms to better protect the rights of minorities; and mainstreaming minority rights in development assistance and cooperation as a means of preventing conflict. Participants made recommendations to strengthen the role of various entities to protect the rights of minority communities and groups, including by UN treaty bodies and special procedures, the Working Group on Minorities, OHCHR, multilateral trade, finance and bilateral development actors, Governments, regional and national human rights mechanisms, and institutions, the media and NGOs.

GENERAL ASSEMBLY ACTION

On 19 December [meeting 88], the General Assembly, on the recommendation of the Third Committee [A/56/583/Add.2], adopted **resolution 56/162** without vote [agenda item 119 *(b)*].

Effective promotion of the Declaration on the Rights of Persons Belonging to National or Ethnic, Religious and Linguistic Minorities

The General Assembly,

Recalling its resolution 47/135 of 18 December 1992, as well as its subsequent resolutions on the Declaration on the Rights of Persons Belonging to National or Ethnic, Religious and Linguistic Minorities,

Considering that the promotion and protection of the rights of persons belonging to national or ethnic, religious and linguistic minorities contribute to political and social stability and peace and enrich the cultural diversity and heritage of society as a whole in the States in which such persons live,

Concerned by the frequency and severity of disputes and conflicts concerning minorities in many countries and their often tragic consequences, and concerned also that persons belonging to minorities are particularly vulnerable to displacement through, inter alia, population transfers, refugee flows and forced relocation,

Recognizing that the effective promotion and protection of the rights of persons belonging to minorities is a fundamental part of the promotion and protection of human rights, and acknowledging that measures in this area can also contribute significantly to conflict prevention,

Emphasizing the importance of human rights education as an effective tool to promote an inclusive society and understanding of and tolerance towards and among persons belonging to minorities,

Acknowledging that the United Nations has an important role to play regarding the protection of minorities by, inter alia, taking due account of and giving effect to the Declaration,

Noting that the Working Group on Minorities of the Subcommission on the Promotion and Protection of Human Rights held its sixth and seventh sessions from 22 to 26 May 2000 and 14 to 18 May 2001, respectively,

1. *Takes note* of the report of the Secretary-General;

2. *Recognizes* that respect for human rights and the promotion of understanding and tolerance by Governments as well as between and among minorities are central to the promotion and protection of the rights of persons belonging to minorities;

3. *Reaffirms* the obligation of States to ensure that persons belonging to minorities may exercise fully and effectively all human rights and fundamental freedoms without any discrimination and in full equality before the law, in accordance with the Declaration on the Rights of Persons Belonging to National or Ethnic, Religious and Linguistic Minorities, and as emphasized at the World Conference against Racism, Racial Discrimination, Xenophobia and Related Intolerance, held at Durban, South Africa, from 31 August to 8 September 2001;

4. *Urges* States and the international community to promote and protect the rights of persons belonging to national or ethnic, religious and linguistic minorities, as set out in the Declaration, including through the provision of adequate education and the facilitation of their participation in all aspects of the political, economic, social, religious and cultural life of society and in the economic progress and development of their country, and to apply a gender perspective while doing so;

5. *Calls upon* States to give special attention to the promotion and protection of the human rights of children, girls as well as boys, belonging to minorities;

6. *Urges* States to take, as appropriate, all necessary constitutional, legislative, administrative and other measures to promote and give effect to the Declaration, and appeals to States to cooperate bilaterally and multilaterally, in accordance with the Declaration, in order to promote and protect the rights of persons belonging to national or ethnic, religious and linguistic minorities;

7. *Calls upon* States to take all appropriate measures to protect the cultural and religious sites of national or ethnic, religious and linguistic minorities;

8. *Calls upon* the Secretary-General to make available, at the request of Governments concerned, qualified expertise on minority issues, including the prevention and resolution of disputes, to assist in existing or potential situations involving minorities;

9. *Calls upon* the United Nations High Commissioner for Human Rights to promote, within her mandate, the implementation of the Declaration and to continue to engage in a dialogue with Governments for that purpose, and in this regard draws attention to the work on the United Nations Guide for Minorities;

10. *Requests* the High Commissioner to continue her efforts to improve the coordination and cooperation among United Nations programmes and agencies on activities related to the promotion and protection of the rights of persons belonging to minorities and to take the work of relevant regional organizations active in the field of human rights into account in her endeavours;

11. *Welcomes* the inter-agency consultation of the High Commissioner with United Nations programmes and agencies on minority issues, and calls upon those programmes and agencies to contribute actively to this process;

12. *Invites* the human rights treaty bodies, when considering reports submitted by States parties, as well as the reports of special representatives, special rapporteurs and working groups of the Commission on Human Rights, to continue to give attention, within their respective mandates, to situations and rights of persons belonging to national or ethnic, religious and linguistic minorities;

13. *Encourages* intergovernmental and nongovernmental organizations to continue to contribute to the promotion and protection of the rights of persons belonging to national or ethnic, religious and linguistic minorities;

14. *Calls upon* the Working Group on Minorities of the Subcommission on the Promotion and Protection of Human Rights to implement further its mandate with the involvement of a wide range of participants;

15. *Invites* the High Commissioner to seek voluntary contributions to facilitate the effective participation, including through training seminars, in the work of the Working Group on Minorities of representatives of non-governmental organizations and persons belonging to minorities, in particular those from developing countries;

16. *Requests* the Secretary-General to report to the General Assembly at its fifty-eighth session on the implementation of the present resolution, and to continue to include examples of good practices in the field of education and of the effective participation of minorities in decision-making processes;

17. *Decides* to continue consideration of this question at its fifty-eighth session under the item entitled "Human rights questions".

Discrimination based on work and descent

In response to a 2000 Subcommission request [YUN 2000, p. 657], Rajendra Kalidas Wimala Goonesekere (Sri Lanka) submitted, in June [E/CN.4/Sub.2/2001/16], a working paper on discrimination based on work and descent. He re-

viewed the situation in several Asian countries influenced by the caste system, which comprised some 250 million individuals. Although he had focused on Asia, the problem also existed in parts of Africa and possibly South America. He hoped that the paper demonstrated that there was a serious problem of human rights violations based on work and descent and believed that complaints of discrimination voiced through UN mechanisms merited further study.

Subcommission action. On 15 August [dec. 2001/110], the Subcommission entrusted Mr. Goonesekere with preparing, without financial implications, an expanded paper in 2002.

Affirmative action

Report of Special Rapporteur. In accordance with a 2000 Subcommission decision [YUN 2000, p. 657], the Special Rapporteur on the concept and practice of affirmative action, Marc Bossuyt (Belgium), presented a June progress report [E/CN.4/Sub.2/2001/15] describing the concept of affirmative action, the target groups that should benefit from such action, the justification for it and the forms it might take. The Special Rapporteur stated that he had received replies from Governments and specialized agencies to a questionnaire on national documentation on affirmative action but would wait to receive more responses so that his next report would be based on the widest possible information. A copy of the questionnaire was annexed to the report.

Subcommission action. On 15 August [dec. 2001/107], the Subcommission asked the Secretary-General to invite Governments, international organizations, human rights treaty bodies, particularly the Committee on the Elimination of Racial Discrimination (CERD), and NGOs to transmit their comments on the Special Rapporteur's preliminary [YUN 2000, p. 657] and progress (see above) reports and to remind them to submit their responses to the questionnaire before 1 February 2002.

Rights of non-citizens

In accordance with a 2000 Subcommission decision [YUN 2000, p. 657], the Special Rapporteur on the rights of non-citizens, David Weissbrodt (United States), submitted in June a preliminary report [E/CN.4/Sub.2/2001/20] on a comprehensive study of the rights of non-citizens. The report examined non-citizens' rights, as provided in the 1965 International Convention on the Elimination of All Forms of Racial Discrimination (see p. 593) and the jurisprudence of CERD, other international standards relating to non-citizens, regional developments, particularly in Europe, and other related issues, including distinctions among non-citizens, the situation of the Roma, trafficking in women and children, and the right to freedom of movement. The Special Rapporteur observed that continued discrimination against non-citizens indicated a lack of standards adopted and implemented by States. He recommended that States should be encouraged to abide by the 1985 Declaration on the Human Rights of Individuals Who are not Nationals of the Country in which They Live, adopted by the General Assembly in resolution 40/144 [YUN 1985, p. 850], and those States that had not done so encouraged to sign and ratify the 1990 International Convention on the Protection of the Rights of All Migrant Workers and Members of Their Families (see p. 596). He proposed that treaty bodies prepare general comments and recommendations to establish a consistent, structured approach on the issue. States should incorporate international standards in developing national legislation, policies and practices.

An addendum to the report [E/CN.4/Sub.2/2001/20/Add.1] summarized the various jurisprudence and concluding observations on which the preliminary report was based.

Subcommission action. On 15 August [dec. 2001/108], the Subcommission requested the Secretary-General to transmit a questionnaire of the Special Rapporteur to Governments, intergovernmental organizations, treaty bodies, particularly CERD, and NGOs to solicit information in connection with the study, which would be taken into account by the Special Rapporteur in preparing his 2002 progress report.

Non-discrimination

On 16 August [res. 2001/23], the Subcommission entrusted Fried van Hoof (Netherlands) with preparing for 2002, without financial implications, a working paper on non-discrimination as enshrined in article 2, paragraph 2, of the 1966 International Covenant on Economic, Social and Cultural Rights, adopted by the General Assembly in resolution 2200 A (XXI) [YUN 1966, p. 419] (see p. 590), regarding the exercise of the rights enunciated in the Covenant without discrimination as to race, colour, sex, language, religion, political or other opinion, national or social origin, property, birth or other status.

Religious intolerance

Report of Special Rapporteur. In a February report [E/CN.4/2001/63], the Special Rapporteur on religious intolerance, Abdelfattah Amor (Tunisia), summarized 85 communications, including one urgent appeal, sent by him to 52 States, as well as 17 replies received, regarding incidents and governmental action inconsistent with the provisions of the 1981 Declaration on the Elimination of All Forms of Intolerance and of Discrimination Based on Religion or Belief, adopted in General Assembly resolution 36/55 [YUN 1981, p. 881]. The Special Rapporteur discussed three studies he had prepared, which focused on minorities and women. He summarized the work of the preparatory committee for the international consultative conference on school education in relation to freedom of religion or belief (see p. 627) and reported on follow-up to his visits to Turkey [YUN 1999, p. 619] and Bangladesh [YUN 2000, p. 658]. The Special Rapporteur noted a worldwide trend towards increased religious intolerance and discrimination against minorities. State institutions in many parts of the world had adopted discriminatory, intolerant or indifferent policies, legislation or practices, which threatened the very existence of minorities as a specific community. Minorities were also victims of the intolerance of non-State entities, especially religious communities, extremist organizations and the media. Certain media outlets played a particularly damaging role in helping to foment the fear of Islam and Christianity.

Commission action. On 18 April [res. 2001/4], by a roll-call vote of 28 to 15, with 9 abstentions, the Commission, expressing concern at negative stereotyping of religions and that Islam was associated with human rights violations and terrorism, encouraged States to provide adequate protection against human rights violations resulting from defamation of religions and to promote tolerance and respect for religions. The High Commissioner was called on to integrate human rights aspects into topical seminars and special debates on the positive contributions of cultures, as well as religious and cultural diversity; and to hold joint conferences with other international organizations to promote understanding of the universality of human rights and their implementation. She was asked to report in 2002.

On 23 April [res. 2001/42], the Commission condemned all forms of intolerance and discrimination based on religion or belief and urged States to: provide adequate and effective guarantees of freedom of thought, conscience, religion and belief; ensure that no one, because of religion or belief, was deprived of the right to life, liberty or security of person or tortured or arbitrarily detained; combat hatred, intolerance, violence, intimidation and coercion motivated by religious intolerance; recognize the right to worship or assemble in connection with a religion or belief and to establish and maintain places for those purposes; ensure that religious places were respected and protected; ensure that public officials respected different religions and beliefs; and promote tolerance through education and other means. The Commission decided to extend for three years the Special Rapporteur's mandate under the new title of Special Rapporteur on freedom of religion or belief, as decided in 2000 [YUN 2000, p. 658]. The Special Rapporteur was asked to submit an interim report to the General Assembly in 2001 (see below) and to report to the Commission in 2002.

The Economic and Social Council, on 24 July, endorsed the Commission's decision to extend the Special Rapporteur's mandate and its requests to him to report in 2001 and 2002 (**decision 2001/264**).

Further reports of Special Rapporteur. At the invitation of the Government, the Special Rapporteur visited Argentina (23-30 April) [E/CN.4/2002/73/Add.1], where he focused on the legal aspects of freedom of religion and belief and on policy. According to NGO statistics, the proportion of Catholics was estimated at 88 per cent of the population; Protestants, 7 per cent; Muslims, 1.5 per cent; Jews, 1 per cent; and others, 2.5 per cent. Following an examination of the legal aspects and policy regarding freedom of religion and belief in Argentina, as well as the situation of religious communities and indigenous peoples, the Special Rapporteur noted that constitutional provisions guaranteed the freedom, legislation enshrined the principles of the 1981 Declaration, policy embodied respect for freedom of religion and belief and all religious communities consulted agreed that the situation was satisfactory. However, the Protestant and Russian Orthodox communities considered themselves subjected to unequal treatment by the State and State institutions, and society as a whole had been traumatized by attacks in 1992 and 1994 against the Embassy of Israel and in 1994 against the Israeli Mutual Association in Argentina. The Special Rapporteur noted some Islamophobia accompanied by Arabophobia fostered by the media. The major problem facing the indigenous peoples was their marginalization from society. He recommended that the authorities ensure that manifestations of Catholicism in State institutions did not lead to discrimination. Investigations into the attacks on the Jewish community should continue, and the media should be targeted with an educational campaign regarding Islamophobia and Arabophobia.

A May report [A/CONF.189/PC.2/22] of the Special Rapporteur discussed the factors that negatively influenced education in relation to racial discrimination and religious intolerance, including historical circumstances, the social and economic conditions of groups and minorities, their demographic distribution in an area, their cultural impoverishment, prejudices of dominant groups, the status of the majority and minority languages, the political will of the Government and of the groups themselves, the shortage of resources and the lack of intercultural dialogue. He presented recommendations for States regarding the supervision of the educational system, non-discriminatory access to education, teacher training, linguistic diversity, the content of textbooks, the development of multicultural and intercultural education, human rights education and improving the intercommunity environment of the educational system. International measures proposed were standard-setting efforts, follow-up and monitoring of States' obligations, information gathering on the implications of racial discrimination and religious intolerance, and involving the media in campaigns to raise awareness of the problem.

Pursuant to General Assembly resolution 55/97 [YUN 2000, p. 659], the Secretary-General, in July [A/56/253], transmitted the Special Rapporteur's interim report, covering 49 communications, including two urgent appeals, sent to 24 States, and containing the summaries of 21 replies. The Special Rapporteur characterized the world situation regarding freedom of religion and belief as distressing. However, an analysis of general and mission reports since 1988 showed that improvements had been made through a decline in anti-religious policies and progress in interreligious dialogue, with a view to conflict prevention, management and reconciliation. Nonetheless, he noted that some States had maintained a policy of subtle hostility to religion and anti-religious secularism. There was also a rise in extremism, as well as persisting discrimination and intolerance against women, based on religion or traditions. The Special Rapporteur recommended that the international community develop and adopt commonly accepted rules and principles of conduct and behaviour towards religious extremism, and also support a plan of action against discrimination and intolerance against women based on religion or tradition.

International Conference. The International Consultative Conference on School Education in relation to Freedom of Religion and Belief, Tolerance and Non-discrimination (Madrid, 23-25 November), organized by the Special Rapporteur and the Government of Spain and held on the occasion of the twentieth anniversary of the 1981 Declaration, adopted a final document, which constituted an international strategy on the right to freedom of religion and belief among primary and secondary school students [E/CN.4/2002/73].

Communications. On 29 June [E/CN.4/2002/8], Turkey transmitted its comments on the Special Rapporteur's report on his visit to the country in 1999 [YUN 1999, p. 619]. Turkey disputed his conclusions, particularly the allegations pertaining to the interpretation in Turkey of the principles of secularism and nationalism.

On 5 November [A/56/608], the Netherlands transmitted to the Secretary-General the conclusions of an international seminar on freedom of religion or belief in the region of the Organization for Security and Cooperation in Europe (OSCE): challenges to law and practice (The Hague, 26 June).

GENERAL ASSEMBLY ACTION

On 19 December [meeting 88], the General Assembly, on the recommendation of the Third Committee [A/56/583/Add.2], adopted **resolution 56/157** without vote [agenda item 119 (b)].

Elimination of all forms of religious intolerance

The General Assembly,

Recalling that all States have pledged themselves, under the Charter of the United Nations, to promote and encourage universal respect for and observance of human rights and fundamental freedoms for all without distinction as to race, sex, language or religion,

Reaffirming that discrimination against human beings on the grounds of religion or belief constitutes an affront to human dignity and a disavowal of the principles of the Charter,

Recalling article 18 of the Universal Declaration of Human Rights, article 18 of the International Covenant on Civil and Political Rights and paragraph 4 of the United Nations Millennium Declaration,

Reaffirming its resolution 36/55 of 25 November 1981, by which it proclaimed the Declaration on the Elimination of All Forms of Intolerance and of Discrimination Based on Religion or Belief, and noting that 2001 marks the twentieth anniversary of the adoption of the Declaration,

Emphasizing that the right to freedom of thought, conscience, religion and belief is far-reaching and profound and that it encompasses freedom of thought on all matters, personal conviction and the commitment to religion or belief, whether manifested individually or in community with others, and in public or in private,

Reaffirming the call of the World Conference on Human Rights, held at Vienna from 14 to 25 June 1993, for all Governments to take all appropriate measures in compliance with their international obligations and with due regard to their respective legal systems to counter intolerance and related violence based on religion or belief, including practices of discrimination against women and the desecration of religious sites, recognizing that every individual has the right to freedom of thought, conscience, expression and religion,

Underlining the important role of education in the promotion of tolerance and the elimination of discrimination based on religion or belief,

Calling upon all States to cooperate with the Special Rapporteur of the Commission on Human Rights on freedom of religion or belief to enable him to carry out his mandate fully,

Alarmed that serious instances of intolerance and discrimination on the grounds of religion or belief, including acts of violence, intimidation and coercion motivated by religious intolerance, occur in many parts of the world and threaten the enjoyment of human rights and fundamental freedoms,

Deeply concerned that, as reported by the Special Rapporteur, the rights violated on religious grounds include the right to life, the right to physical integrity and to liberty and security of person, the right to freedom of expression, the right not to be subjected to torture or other cruel, inhuman or degrading treatment or punishment and the right not to be arbitrarily arrested or detained,

Believing that intensified efforts are therefore required to promote and protect the right to freedom of thought, conscience, religion and belief and to eliminate all forms of hatred, intolerance and discrimination based on religion or belief, as also emphasized at the World Conference against Racism, Racial Discrimination, Xenophobia and Related Intolerance, held at Durban, South Africa, from 31 August to 8 September 2001,

1. *Reaffirms* that freedom of thought, conscience, religion and belief is a human right derived from the inherent dignity of the human person and guaranteed to all without discrimination;

2. *Urges* States to ensure that their constitutional and legal systems provide effective guarantees of freedom of thought, conscience, religion and belief, including the provision of effective remedies in cases in which the right to freedom of thought, conscience, religion or belief is violated;

3. *Also urges* States to ensure, in particular, that no one within their jurisdiction is, because of their religion or belief, deprived of the right to life or the right to liberty and security of person or subjected to torture or arbitrary arrest or detention;

4. *Further urges* States, in conformity with international standards of human rights, to take all necessary action to combat hatred, intolerance and acts of violence, intimidation and coercion motivated by intolerance based on religion or belief, with particular regard to persons belonging to religious minorities, and to devote particular attention to practices which violate the human rights of women and discriminate against women;

5. *Emphasizes* that, as underlined by the Human Rights Committee, restrictions on the freedom to manifest religion or belief are permitted only if those limitations that are prescribed by law are necessary to protect public safety, order, health or morals, or the fundamental rights and freedoms of others, and are applied in a manner that does not vitiate the right to freedom of thought, conscience and religion;

6. *Urges* States to ensure that, in the course of their official duties, members of law enforcement bodies and the military, civil servants, educators and other public officials respect different religions and beliefs and do not discriminate against persons professing other religions or beliefs, and that any necessary and appropriate education or training is provided;

7. *Calls upon* all States to recognize, as provided for in the Declaration on the Elimination of All Forms

of Intolerance and of Discrimination Based on Religion or Belief, the right of all persons to worship or assemble in connection with a religion or belief and to establish and maintain places for those purposes;

8. *Expresses its grave concern* at any attack upon religious places, sites and shrines, and calls upon all States, in accordance with their national legislation and in conformity with international human rights standards, to exert their utmost efforts to ensure that such places, sites and shrines are fully respected and protected and to take additional measures in cases where they are vulnerable to desecration or destruction;

9. *Recognizes* that legislation alone is not enough to prevent violations of human rights, including the right to freedom of religion or belief, and that the exercise of tolerance and non-discrimination by persons and groups is necessary for the full realization of the aims of the Declaration, and in this regard invites States, religious bodies and civil society to undertake dialogue at all levels to promote greater tolerance, respect and understanding of freedom of religion or belief and to encourage and promote, through the education system and by other means, understanding, tolerance and respect in matters relating to freedom of religion or belief;

10. *Takes note with appreciation* of the interim report of the Special Rapporteur of the Commission on Human Rights on freedom of religion or belief, and encourages his continued efforts to examine incidents and governmental actions in all parts of the world that are incompatible with the provisions of the Declaration and to recommend remedial measures, as appropriate;

11. *Encourages* Governments to give serious consideration to inviting the Special Rapporteur to visit their countries so as to enable him to fulfil his mandate even more effectively;

12. *Welcomes* the initiatives of Governments and non-governmental organizations to collaborate with the Special Rapporteur, including the convening of the International Consultative Conference on School Education in relation to Freedom of Religion and Belief, Tolerance and Non-discrimination in Madrid from 23 to 25 November 2001, in which Governments, non-governmental organizations and other interested parties were encouraged to participate actively;

13. *Encourages* Governments, when seeking the assistance of the United Nations Programme of Advisory Services and Technical Assistance in the Field of Human Rights, to consider, where appropriate, including requests for assistance in the field of the promotion and protection of the right to freedom of thought, conscience and religion;

14. *Welcomes and encourages* the continuing efforts of non-governmental organizations and religious bodies and groups to promote the implementation and dissemination of the Declaration, and further encourages their work in relation to promoting freedom of religion or belief and in highlighting cases of religious intolerance, discrimination and persecution;

15. *Requests* the Commission on Human Rights to continue its consideration of measures to implement the Declaration;

16. *Requests* the Secretary-General to ensure that the Special Rapporteur receives the necessary resources to enable him to discharge his mandate;

17. *Decides* to consider the question of the elimination of all forms of religious intolerance at its fifty-seventh session under the item entitled "Human rights questions", and requests the Special Rapporteur to submit an interim report to the General Assembly on the question.

Civil and political rights

Right to self-determination

In response to General Assembly resolution 55/85 [YUN 2000, p. 661], the Secretary-General, in August [A/56/295], summarized the views of three Member States on the right of peoples to self-determination.

GENERAL ASSEMBLY ACTION

On 19 December [meeting 88], the General Assembly, on the recommendation of the Third Committee [A/56/582], adopted **resolution 56/141** without vote [agenda item 118].

Universal realization of the right of peoples to self-determination

The General Assembly,

Reaffirming the importance, for the effective guarantee and observance of human rights, of the universal realization of the right of peoples to self-determination enshrined in the Charter of the United Nations and embodied in the International Covenants on Human Rights, as well as in the Declaration on the Granting of Independence to Colonial Countries and Peoples contained in General Assembly resolution 1514 (XV) of 14 December 1960,

Welcoming the progressive exercise of the right to self-determination by peoples under colonial, foreign or alien occupation and their emergence into sovereign statehood and independence,

Deeply concerned at the continuation of acts or threats of foreign military intervention and occupation that are threatening to suppress, or have already suppressed, the right to self-determination of sovereign peoples and nations,

Expressing grave concern that, as a consequence of the persistence of such actions, millions of people have been and are being uprooted from their homes as refugees and displaced persons, and emphasizing the urgent need for concerted international action to alleviate their condition,

Recalling the relevant resolutions regarding the violation of the right of peoples to self-determination and other human rights as a result of foreign military intervention, aggression and occupation adopted by the Commission on Human Rights at its fifty-seventh and previous sessions,

Reaffirming its previous resolutions on the universal realization of the right of peoples to self-determination, including resolution 55/85 of 4 December 2000,

Reaffirming also its resolution 55/2 of 8 September 2000, containing the United Nations Millennium Declaration, which, inter alia, upholds the right to self-determination of peoples under colonial domination and foreign occupation,

Taking note of the report of the Secretary-General on the right of peoples to self-determination,

1. *Reaffirms* that the universal realization of the right of all peoples, including those under colonial, foreign and alien domination, to self-determination is a fundamental condition for the effective guarantee and observance of human rights and for the preservation and promotion of such rights;

2. *Declares its firm opposition* to acts of foreign military intervention, aggression and occupation, since these have resulted in the suppression of the right of peoples to self-determination and other human rights in certain parts of the world;

3. *Calls upon* those States responsible to cease immediately their military intervention in and occupation of foreign countries and territories and all acts of repression, discrimination, exploitation and maltreatment, in particular the brutal and inhuman methods reportedly employed for the execution of those acts against the peoples concerned;

4. *Deplores* the plight of millions of refugees and displaced persons who have been uprooted as a result of the aforementioned acts, and reaffirms their right to return to their homes voluntarily in safety and honour;

5. *Requests* the Commission on Human Rights to continue to give special attention to the violation of human rights, especially the right to self-determination, resulting from foreign military intervention, aggression or occupation;

6. *Requests* the Secretary-General to report on this question to the General Assembly at its fifty-seventh session under the item entitled "Right of peoples to self-determination".

Rights of Palestinians

On 6 April [res. 2001/2], the Commission, by a roll-call vote of 48 to 2, with 2 abstentions, reaffirmed the permanent and unqualified right of the Palestinian people to self-determination, including the right to establish a sovereign and independent Palestinian State. It requested the Secretary-General to transmit its resolution to Israel and all other Governments, to disseminate it as widely as possible and to make available to the Commission, before its 2002 session, information pertaining to its implementation by the Government of Israel.

The Commission had before it a report of the Secretary-General [E/CN.4/2001/17], stating that he had received no reply to his request to Israel for information regarding the implementation of its 2000 resolution on the situation in occupied Palestine [YUN 2000, p. 662].

GENERAL ASSEMBLY ACTION

On 19 December [meeting 88], the General Assembly, on the recommendation of the Third Committee [A/56/582], adopted **resolution 56/142** by recorded vote (161-3-1) [agenda item 118].

The right of the Palestinian people to self-determination

The General Assembly,

Aware that the development of friendly relations among nations, based on respect for the principle of equal rights and self-determination of peoples, is among the purposes and principles of the United Nations, as defined in the Charter,

Recalling the International Covenants on Human Rights, the Universal Declaration of Human Rights, the Declaration on the Granting of Independence to Colonial Countries and Peoples and the Vienna Declaration and Programme of Action adopted at the World Conference on Human Rights on 25 June 1993,

Recalling also the Declaration on the Occasion of the Fiftieth Anniversary of the United Nations,

Recalling further the United Nations Millennium Declaration,

Expressing hope for an immediate resumption of negotiations within the Middle East peace process on its agreed basis and for the speedy achievement of a final settlement between the Palestinian and Israeli sides,

Affirming the right of all States in the region to live in peace within secure and internationally recognized borders,

1. *Reaffirms* the right of the Palestinian people to self-determination, including the right to their independent State;

2. *Expresses the hope* that the Palestinian people will soon be exercising their right to self-determination, which is not subject to any veto, in the current peace process;

3. *Urges* all States and the specialized agencies and the organizations of the United Nations system to continue to support and assist the Palestinian people in their quest for self-determination.

RECORDED VOTE ON RESOLUTION 56/142:

In favour: Afghanistan, Albania, Algeria, Andorra, Angola, Antigua and Barbuda, Argentina, Armenia, Australia, Austria, Azerbaijan, Bahamas, Bahrain, Bangladesh, Barbados, Belarus, Belgium, Belize, Benin, Bhutan, Bolivia, Botswana, Brazil, Brunei Darussalam, Bulgaria, Burkina Faso, Burundi, Cambodia, Cameroon, Canada, Cape Verde, Chad, Chile, China, Colombia, Comoros, Congo, Costa Rica, Côte d'Ivoire, Croatia, Cuba, Cyprus, Czech Republic, Democratic People's Republic of Korea, Democratic Republic of the Congo, Denmark, Djibouti, Dominica, Dominican Republic, Ecuador, Egypt, El Salvador, Equatorial Guinea, Eritrea, Estonia, Ethiopia, Fiji, Finland, France, Gabon, Gambia, Georgia, Germany, Ghana, Greece, Grenada, Guyana, Haiti, Honduras, Hungary, Iceland, India, Indonesia, Iran, Ireland, Italy, Jamaica, Japan, Jordan, Kazakhstan, Kenya, Kuwait, Lao People's Democratic Republic, Latvia, Lebanon, Libyan Arab Jamahiriya, Liechtenstein, Lithuania, Luxembourg, Madagascar, Malawi, Malaysia, Maldives, Mali, Malta, Mauritania, Mauritius, Mexico, Monaco, Mongolia, Morocco, Mozambique, Myanmar, Namibia, Nepal, Netherlands, New Zealand, Nicaragua, Nigeria, Norway, Oman, Pakistan, Panama, Papua New Guinea, Paraguay, Peru, Philippines, Poland, Portugal, Qatar, Republic of Korea, Republic of Moldova, Romania, Russian Federation, Rwanda, Saint Lucia, Samoa, San Marino, Saudi Arabia, Senegal, Seychelles, Sierra Leone, Singapore, Slovakia, Slovenia, Solomon Islands, South Africa, Spain, Sri Lanka, Sudan, Suriname, Sweden, Syrian Arab Republic, Thailand, The former Yugoslav Republic of Macedonia, Togo, Trinidad and Tobago, Tunisia, Turkey, Uganda, Ukraine, United Arab Emirates, United Kingdom, United Republic of Tanzania, Uruguay, Vanuatu, Venezuela, Viet Nam, Yemen, Yugoslavia, Zambia.

Against: Israel, Marshall Islands, United States.

Abstaining: Micronesia.

Western Sahara

On 6 April [res. 2001/1], the Commission called on Morocco and the Frente Popular para la Liberación de Saguia el-Hamra y de Río de Oro to continue to cooperate with the Secretary-

General, his Personal Envoy and his Special Representative in implementing the various stages of the settlement plan. It urged the two parties to implement the measures relating to the identification of voters and the appeals process and reaffirmed support for further efforts of the Secretary-General, in cooperation with the Organization of African Unity, for a UN-supervised referendum on self-determination of the people of Western Sahara (see p. 213).

Mercenaries

Expert meeting. In accordance with its 2000 decision [YUN 2000, p. 662], the Commission held a meeting of experts on the traditional and new forms of mercenary activities as a means of violating human rights and impeding the exercise of the right of peoples to self-determination (Geneva, 29 January–2 February) [E/CN.4/2001/18]. Participants noted that mercenary activities had become more extensive and diversified, and included modern multi-purpose security corporations that might provide forms of military service carried out by mercenaries. UN treatment of the phenomenon should take into account the criminal responsibility of individuals who sold their military services knowing they would be carrying out criminal acts. In addition, there should be criminal responsibility of those recruiting, training, financing, organizing and deploying mercenaries, when those acts led to breaches of international humanitarian law and human rights. Participants called on the United Nations to recognize the existence of new kinds of mercenaries, which demanded additional action and measures. They recommended a systematic and comprehensive review of the legal definition of mercenary, which should include the elements of motive, purpose, payment, type of action and nationality. They urged States to ratify the 1989 International Convention against the Recruitment, Use, Financing and Training of Mercenaries, adopted by the General Assembly in resolution 44/34 [YUN 1989, p. 825], and proposed the establishment of a monitoring body for the Convention. States were urged to prohibit private entities from participating in armed conflicts, creating private armies, engaging in illicit arms trafficking, recruiting mercenaries and being involved in the illegal extraction of natural resources. The group proposed broadening the Special Rapporteur's mandate to include private security and military companies and all other new forms of mercenary activities and more explicit reference to the human rights problems associated with their use.

Commission action. On 6 April [res. 2001/3], the Commission, by a roll-call vote of 35 to 11, with 6 abstentions, welcoming the convening of the expert meeting (see above), requested OHCHR to publicize the adverse effects of mercenary activities and to render advisory services to affected States when requested. States that had not done so were called on to sign or ratify the 1989 Convention. The Commission, in accordance with Assembly resolution 55/86 [YUN 2000, p. 663], decided to renew the Special Rapporteur's mandate for a period of three years, and asked him to take into account new forms, manifestations and modalities of mercenary activities and to report in 2002.

On 24 July, the Economic and Social Council endorsed the Commission's decision to renew the Special Rapporteur's mandate (**decision 2001/244**).

Reports of Special Rapporteur. In response to a 2000 Commission request [YUN 2000, p. 663], the Special Rapporteur on the question of the use of mercenaries, Enrique Bernales Ballesteros (Peru), submitted a January report [E/CN.4/2001/19]. He stated that mercenary activities were continuing, particularly in the context of armed conflicts. Private security and military assistance companies were investing increasingly in information technology, financial investigation services, military communication detection systems and electronic security systems. They continued to employ mercenaries, and, more recently, pilots, aircrews and air bombardment specialists were being hired by air transport companies which, in third countries, were involved in illegal trafficking in arms and munitions, drugs, diamonds and troops. The Special Rapporteur proposed actions for adoption by the Commission, including measures to strengthen national, regional and international mechanisms that could help end armed conflicts and the presence of mercenaries in Africa. The Commission should promote consultations and working meetings, solicit expert opinions to obtain proposals for a better legal definition of mercenarism and to update international instruments, establish international machinery to monitor the diamond trade, promote accession to the 1989 Convention and convene expert meetings to analyse traditional and new forms of mercenary activities and the problems posed by gaps in the existing legal definition. The Commission should be provided with studies on the extent of private offers by military security services, on the recruitment and use of mercenaries by the companies and on the human rights implications resulting therefrom.

In response to General Assembly resolution 55/86 [YUN 2000, p. 663], the Secretary-General, in July [A/56/224], transmitted a report by the Special Rapporteur presenting replies he had received from Member States regarding mercenary activities, and information on private security and military assistance companies, the legal definition of mercenary and the status of the 1989 Convention. The Special Rapporteur, in view of the change in his mandate (see p. 631), requested the Assembly to instruct him, with the support of a second expert meeting, to propose a new definition of mercenary.

1989 International Convention

The 1989 International Convention against the Recruitment, Use, Financing and Training of Mercenaries, adopted by the General Assembly in resolution 44/34 [YUN 1989, p. 825], entered into force on 20 October. As at 31 December, 22 States were party to the Convention.

GENERAL ASSEMBLY ACTION

On 24 December [meeting 92], the General Assembly, on the recommendation of the Third Committee [A/56/582], adopted **resolution 56/232** by recorded vote (77-20-20) [agenda item 118].

Use of mercenaries as a means of violating human rights and impeding the exercise of the right of peoples to self-determination

The General Assembly,

Recalling its resolution 55/86 of 4 December 2000, and taking note of Commission on Human Rights resolution 2001/3 of 6 April 2001,

Recalling also all of its relevant resolutions, in which, inter alia, it condemned any State that permitted or tolerated the recruitment, financing, training, assembly, transit and use of mercenaries with the objective of overthrowing the Governments of States Members of the United Nations, especially those of developing countries, or of fighting against national liberation movements, and recalling further the relevant resolutions and international instruments adopted by the Security Council, the Economic and Social Council and the Organization of African Unity, inter alia, the Convention of the Organization of African Unity on the Elimination of Mercenarism in Africa,

Reaffirming the purposes and principles enshrined in the Charter of the United Nations concerning the strict observance of the principles of sovereign equality, political independence, the territorial integrity of States, the self-determination of peoples, the non-use of force or of the threat of use of force in international relations and non-interference in affairs within the domestic jurisdiction of States,

Reaffirming also that, by virtue of the principle of self-determination, all peoples have the right freely to determine their political status and to pursue their economic, social and cultural development, and that every State has the duty to respect this right in accordance with the provisions of the Charter,

Reaffirming further the Declaration on Principles of International Law concerning Friendly Relations and Cooperation among States in accordance with the Charter of the United Nations,

Alarmed and concerned at the danger that the activities of mercenaries constitute to peace and security in developing countries, in particular in Africa and in small States,

Deeply concerned at the loss of life, the substantial damage to property and the negative effects on the policy and economies of affected countries resulting from criminal mercenary activities,

Convinced that, notwithstanding the way in which they are used or the form they take to acquire some semblance of legitimacy, mercenaries or mercenary-related activities are a threat to peace, security and the self-determination of peoples and an obstacle to the enjoyment of human rights by peoples,

1. *Welcomes* the report of the Special Rapporteur of the Commission on Human Rights on the use of mercenaries as a means of violating human rights and impeding the exercise of the right of peoples to self-determination;

2. *Reaffirms* that the use of mercenaries and their recruitment, financing and training are causes for grave concern to all States and violate the purposes and principles enshrined in the Charter of the United Nations;

3. *Recognizes* that armed conflict, terrorism, arms trafficking and covert operations by third Powers, inter alia, encourage the demand for mercenaries on the global market;

4. *Urges* all States to take the necessary steps and to exercise the utmost vigilance against the menace posed by the activities of mercenaries and to take legislative measures to ensure that their territories and other territories under their control, as well as their nationals, are not used for the recruitment, assembly, financing, training and transit of mercenaries for the planning of activities designed to impede the right of peoples to self-determination, to destabilize or overthrow the Government of any State or to dismember or impair, totally or in part, the territorial integrity or political unity of sovereign and independent States conducting themselves in compliance with the right of peoples to self-determination;

5. *Welcomes* the recent entry into force of the International Convention against the Recruitment, Use, Financing and Training of Mercenaries, and calls upon all States that have not yet done so to consider taking the necessary action to sign or ratify it, as a matter of priority;

6. *Welcomes also* the cooperation extended by those countries that have received visits from the Special Rapporteur;

7. *Welcomes further* the adoption by some States of national legislation that restricts the recruitment, assembly, financing, training and transit of mercenaries;

8. *Calls upon* States to investigate the possibility of mercenary involvement whenever and wherever criminal acts of a terrorist nature occur and to bring to trial those found responsible or to consider their extradition, if so requested, in accordance with domestic law and applicable bilateral or international treaties;

9. *Welcomes* the convening by the Office of the United Nations High Commissioner for Human Rights of a meeting of experts on the question of traditional and new forms of mercenary activities as a means of violating human rights and impeding the exercise of the right of peoples to self-determination, and

takes note of its report, as a valuable contribution to the process of formulating a clearer legal definition of mercenaries that would make more efficient the prevention and punishment of mercenary activities;

10. *Requests* the United Nations High Commissioner for Human Rights to convene, before the fifty-ninth session of the Commission on Human Rights, a second meeting of experts, pursuant to General Assembly resolution 54/151 of 17 December 1999, to continue studying and updating the international legislation and to make recommendations for a clearer legal definition of mercenaries that would make more efficient the prevention and punishment of mercenary activities;

11. *Requests* the Special Rapporteur to propose a clearer definition of mercenaries, including clear nationality criteria, based on his findings, the proposals of States and the outcomes of the meetings of experts, and to make suggestions on the procedure to be followed for international adoption of a new definition;

12. *Requests* the Office of the High Commissioner, as a matter of priority, to publicize the adverse effects of the activities of mercenaries on the right of peoples to self-determination and, when requested and where necessary, to render advisory services to States that are affected by the activities of mercenaries;

13. *Requests* the Special Rapporteur to continue taking into account in the discharge of his mandate the fact that mercenary activities continue to occur in many parts of the world and are taking on new forms, manifestations and modalities;

14. *Urges* all States to cooperate fully with the Special Rapporteur in the fulfilment of his mandate;

15. *Requests* the Secretary-General and the High Commissioner to provide the Special Rapporteur with all the necessary assistance and support for the fulfilment of his mandate, both professional and financial, including through the promotion of cooperation between the Special Rapporteur and other components of the United Nations system that deal with countering mercenary-related activities;

16. *Requests* the Special Rapporteur to consult States and intergovernmental and non-governmental organizations in the implementation of the present resolution and to report, with specific recommendations, to the General Assembly at its fifty-seventh session his findings on the use of mercenaries to undermine the right of peoples to self-determination;

17. *Decides* to consider at its fifty-seventh session the question of the use of mercenaries as a means of violating human rights and impeding the exercise of the right of peoples to self-determination under the item entitled "Right of peoples to self-determination".

RECORDED VOTE ON RESOLUTION 56/232:

In favour: Algeria, Argentina, Armenia, Azerbaijan, Bahamas, Bahrain, Bangladesh, Benin, Bolivia, Botswana, Brazil, Brunei Darussalam, Burkina Faso, Cambodia, Cameroon, Cape Verde, China, Colombia, Congo, Costa Rica, Côte d'Ivoire, Cuba, Democratic People's Republic of Korea, Djibouti, Dominican Republic, Ecuador, Egypt, Equatorial Guinea, Eritrea, Ethiopia, Ghana, Grenada, Guatemala, Guinea, Guyana, Haiti, India, Indonesia, Iran, Jamaica, Jordan, Kenya, Kuwait, Lao People's Democratic Republic, Lebanon, Libyan Arab Jamahiriya, Malaysia, Maldives, Mali, Mauritania, Mauritius, Mexico, Morocco, Mozambique, Myanmar, Nepal, Nigeria, Oman, Pakistan, Peru, Philippines, Russian Federation, Saudi Arabia, Senegal, Singapore, Sri Lanka, Sudan, Syrian Arab Republic, Thailand, Togo, Tunisia, United Republic of Tanzania, Uruguay, Venezuela, Viet Nam, Yemen, Zambia.

Against: Belgium, Canada, Chile, Czech Republic, Denmark, Finland, Germany, Hungary, Iceland, Israel, Japan, Luxembourg, Netherlands, Norway, Poland, Sweden, The former Yugoslav Republic of Macedonia, Ukraine, United Kingdom, United States.

Abstaining: Andorra, Australia, Austria, Bulgaria, Cyprus, France, Greece, Ireland, Italy, Latvia, Lithuania, Malta, Monaco, New Zealand, Portugal, Republic of Korea, San Marino, Slovakia, Spain, Yugoslavia.

Administration of justice

Commission action. On 24 April [dec. 2001/106], the Commission, taking note of a 2000 Subcommission resolution [YUN 2000, p. 598], authorized the Subcommission to convene a working group on the administration of justice.

Subcommission action. On 31 July [dec. 2001/102], the Subcommission established a five-member sessional working group on the administration of justice.

At its meetings on 5, 9 and 10 August [E/CN.4/Sub.2/2001/7], the working group discussed the imposition of the death penalty; summary, arbitrary and extrajudicial executions; privatization of prisons; improvement and efficiency of the judicial instruments for the protection of human rights at the national level and their impact at the international level; administration of justice through military tribunals and other exceptional jurisdictions; the domestic implementation in practice of the obligation to provide domestic remedies; functioning and accountability of UN peace support operations; and discrimination in the criminal justice system. It considered working papers prepared by group members Leïla Zerrougui (Algeria) on discrimination in the criminal justice system, Louis Joinet (France) on the evolution of the administration of justice through military tribunals, and Héctor Fix-Zamudio (Mexico) on the improvement and efficiency of the judicial instruments for the protection of human rights at the national level and their impact at the international level.

On 10 August, the Subcommission requested Mr. Joinet to update, without financial implications, his report and to report in 2002 [dec. 2001/103]; Ms. Zerrougui was asked to pursue her research on the evolution of the administration of justice, also without financial implications, and to submit a final working paper in 2002 [dec. 2001/104].

GENERAL ASSEMBLY ACTION

On 19 December [meeting 88], the General Assembly, on the recommendation of the Third Committee [A/56/583/Add.2], adopted **resolution 56/161** without vote [agenda item 119 (*b*)].

Human rights in the administration of justice

The General Assembly,

Bearing in mind the principles embodied in articles 3, 5, 8, 9 and 10 of the Universal Declaration of Human Rights and the relevant provisions of the International Covenant on Civil and Political Rights and the Optional Protocols thereto, in particular article 6 of the Covenant, which states, inter alia, that no one shall be arbitrarily deprived of his life and prohibits the imposition of the death penalty for crimes committed by persons below 18 years of age, and article 10, which provides that all persons deprived of their liberty shall be treated with humanity and with respect for the inherent dignity of the human person,

Bearing in mind also the relevant provisions of the Convention against Torture and Other Cruel, Inhuman or Degrading Treatment or Punishment, the International Convention on the Elimination of All Forms of Racial Discrimination, in particular the right to equal treatment before the tribunals and all other organs administering justice, the Convention on the Rights of the Child, in particular article 37, according to which every child deprived of liberty shall be treated in a manner which takes into account the needs of persons of his or her age, and the Convention on the Elimination of All Forms of Discrimination against Women, in particular the obligation to treat men and women equally in all stages of procedures in courts and tribunals,

Calling attention to the numerous international standards in the field of the administration of justice,

Emphasizing that the right to access to justice as contained in applicable international human rights instruments forms an important basis for strengthening the rule of law through the administration of justice,

Mindful of the importance of ensuring respect for the rule of law and human rights in the administration of justice, in particular in post-conflict situations, as a crucial contribution to building peace and justice and ending impunity,

Recalling the Guidelines for Action on Children in the Criminal Justice System and the establishment and subsequent meetings of the coordination panel on technical advice and assistance in juvenile justice,

Calling attention to the relevant provisions of the Vienna Declaration on Crime and Justice: Meeting the Challenges of the Twenty-first Century, and of the plans of action for its implementation and follow-up,

Recalling its resolution 54/163 of 17 December 1999, as well as Commission on Human Rights resolution 2000/39 of 20 April 2000 and Economic and Social Council resolution 1999/28 of 28 July 1999,

1. *Reaffirms* the importance of the full and effective implementation of all United Nations standards on human rights in the administration of justice;

2. *Reiterates its call* to all Member States to spare no effort in providing for effective legislative and other mechanisms and procedures, as well as adequate resources, to ensure the full implementation of those standards;

3. *Invites* Governments to provide training, including gender-sensitive training, in human rights in the administration of justice, including juvenile justice, to all judges, lawyers, prosecutors, social workers, immigration and police officers, and other professionals concerned, including personnel deployed in international field presences;

4. *Invites* States to make use of technical assistance offered by the relevant United Nations programmes in order to strengthen national capacities and infrastructures in the field of the administration of justice;

5. *Appeals* to Governments to include in their national development plans the administration of justice as an integral part of the development process and to allocate adequate resources for the provision of legal-aid services with a view to promoting and protecting human rights, and invites the international community to respond favourably to requests for financial and technical assistance for the enhancement and strengthening of the administration of justice;

6. *Encourages* the regional commissions, the specialized agencies and United Nations institutes in the areas of human rights and crime prevention and criminal justice, and other relevant parts of the United Nations system, as well as intergovernmental and non-governmental organizations, including national professional associations concerned with promoting United Nations standards in this field, and other segments of civil society, including the media, to continue to develop their activities in promoting human rights in the administration of justice;

7. *Invites* the Commission on Human Rights and the Commission on Crime Prevention and Criminal Justice, as well as the Office of the United Nations High Commissioner for Human Rights and the Centre for International Crime Prevention of the Office for Drug Control and Crime Prevention of the Secretariat, to coordinate closely their activities relating to the administration of justice;

8. *Calls upon* mechanisms of the Commission on Human Rights and its subsidiary bodies, including special rapporteurs, special representatives and working groups, to continue to give special attention to questions relating to the effective promotion and protection of human rights in the administration of justice, including juvenile justice, and to provide, where appropriate, specific recommendations in this regard, including proposals for advisory services and technical assistance measures;

9. *Calls upon* the United Nations High Commissioner for Human Rights to reinforce, within her mandate, her activities relating to national capacity-building in the field of the administration of justice, in particular in post-conflict situations;

10. *Encourages* the Office of the High Commissioner to continue organizing training courses and other relevant activities aimed at enhancing the promotion and protection of human rights in the field of the administration of justice, and commends the Office for its work on the development of a human rights manual for judges, prosecutors and lawyers within the framework of the United Nations Decade for Human Rights Education, 1995-2004;

11. *Welcomes* the increased attention paid to the issue of juvenile justice by the High Commissioner, in particular through technical assistance activities, and, taking into account that international cooperation to promote juvenile justice reform has become a priority within the United Nations system, encourages further activities, within her mandate, in this regard;

12. *Calls upon* the coordination panel on technical advice and assistance in juvenile justice further to increase cooperation among the partners involved, to share information and to pool their capacities and interests in order to increase the effectiveness of programme implementation;

13. *Underlines* the importance of rebuilding and strengthening structures for the administration of justice and respect for the rule of law and human rights in

post-conflict situations, and requests the Secretary-General to ensure system-wide coordination and coherence of programmes and activities of the relevant parts of the United Nations system in the field of the administration of justice in post-conflict situations, including assistance provided through United Nations field presences;

14. *Stresses* the special need for national capacity-building in the field of the administration of justice, in particular through reform of the judiciary, the police and the penal system, as well as juvenile justice reform, in order to establish and maintain stable societies and the rule of law in post-conflict situations, and in this context welcomes the role of the Office of the High Commissioner in supporting the establishment and functioning of transitional justice mechanisms in post-conflict situations;

15. *Decides* to consider the question of human rights in the administration of justice at its fifty-eighth session under the item entitled "Human rights questions".

Compensation for victims

Commission action. On 23 April [dec. 2001/105], the Commission decided to request the High Commissioner to hold a consultative meeting in Geneva for interested Governments, intergovernmental organizations and NGOs, with a view to finalizing the basic principles and guidelines on the right to a remedy and reparation for victims of violations of international human rights and humanitarian law, based on the revised version prepared in 2000 [YUN 2000, p. 665], and to transmit the outcome in 2002.

The Economic and Social Council, on 24 July, endorsed the Commission's request (**decision 2001/279**).

Note by Secretary-General. In response to a 2000 Subcommission request [YUN 2000, p. 734], the Secretary-General, in June [E/CN.4/Sub.2/2001/8 & Corr.1], presented a working document on mass and flagrant human rights violations which constituted crimes against humanity during the colonial period, wars of conquest and slavery, including proposals to provide reparation to victims and to honour their memory. The Secretary-General examined contemporary definitions of crimes against humanity, stating that the Rome Statute of the International Criminal Court [YUN 1998, p. 1209] constituted to date the most comprehensive definition. He referred to work by the General Assembly, the International Law Commission, the Commission on Human Rights and the Subcommission relating to crimes against humanity and reparation for victims of past violations. The Secretary-General suggested that the Subcommission might wish to take note of the latest formulation in the development of the draft basic principles and guidelines regarding such reparation [YUN 2000, p. 665], and then consider whether, and how, the issue of historical violations and reparations could be addressed in a manner that would generate international consensus.

Subcommission action. On 6 August [res. 2001/1], the Subcommission, convinced that recognition and reparation for mass and flagrant human rights violations constituting crimes against humanity during the period of slavery, colonialism and wars of conquest would constitute the beginning of a dialogue between those whom history had put in conflict for the achievement of a world of understanding, tolerance and peace, requested the countries concerned to take initiatives to raise public awareness of the consequences of those events and initiate a process of reflection on procedures to guarantee the implementation of the current resolution.

State of siege or emergency

As requested by the Commission in 1998 [YUN 1998, p. 664], OHCHR submitted in June [E/CN.4/Sub.2/2001/6 & Corr.1] a list of States in which a state of emergency had been proclaimed before July 1999 and continued thereafter, as well as states of emergencies proclaimed between July 1999 and May 2001.

Humanitarian standards

Report of Secretary-General. The Commission considered a report of the Secretary-General, prepared with the assistance of the International Committee of the Red Cross (ICRC) [E/CN.4/2001/91] and submitted in response to its 2000 request [YUN 2000, p. 666], which presented developments on fundamental standards of humanity applicable in all situations and consistent with international law. The report highlighted developments relating to the jurisprudence of the International Criminal Tribunals for the former Yugoslavia (ICTY) and for Rwanda (ICTR); individual criminal responsibility; crimes under international law, including genocide, crimes against humanity and war crimes; and ratification and implementation of international humanitarian law and human rights instruments. It gave an overview of agreements concluded at the field level, including ground rules, codes of conduct and memorandums of understanding, and noted the identification of customary rules of international humanitarian law in a forthcoming ICRC study. The report concluded that recent developments, particularly the jurisprudence of ICTY and ICTR, indicated that progress had been made towards clarifying uncertainties with regard to fundamental standards of humanity. However, important issues remained unresolved and would require further consideration.

Commission action. On 25 April [dec. 2001/112], the Commission requested the Secretary-General, in consultation with ICRC, to submit a further report in 2002.

Civilians in armed conflict

Report of Secretary-General. In response to Security Council resolution 1296(2000) [YUN 2000, p. 667], the Secretary-General, in a March report [S/2001/331], outlined steps for Member States to strengthen their capacity to protect civilian victims of war and initiatives that the Council and other UN organs could take to complement those efforts. He observed that there was an urgent need to update political and legal instruments to protect civilians in armed conflict, which were developed when State actors were dominant. New mechanisms and strategies were required to deal with changed circumstances, such as the global reach of the media and of new information technologies, the growing influence of civil society organizations and NGOs, the interdependence of the global economy and the reach of international commerce. The Secretary-General made recommendations regarding the need to prosecute violations of international criminal law, particularly impunity; ensure standards for negotiating meaningful access to vulnerable populations; engage armed groups in a dialogue aimed at facilitating the provision of humanitarian assistance and protection; identify and separate armed elements in situations of massive population displacement; develop a regional approach to conflict situations to avoid destabilizing entire regions or subregions; enhance informed decision-making by the Council by utilizing the comparative advantages of other relevant actors within and outside the UN system; develop stronger and more coordinated media and information mechanisms in conflict areas; and engage the private sector by building creative partnerships. Annexed to the report was a summary of initiatives taken to implement the Secretary-General's 1999 recommendations [YUN 1999, p. 648].

(For Security Council action regarding the situation of children in armed conflict, see p. 684.)

Arbitrary detention

Commission action. On 23 April [res. 2001/40], the Commission requested the Governments concerned to take account of the views of the Working Group on Arbitrary Detention, to remedy the situation of persons arbitrarily deprived of their liberty and to pay attention to the Group's urgent appeals. It encouraged them to implement the recommendations of the Group concerning persons who had been detained, ensure that their legislation conformed with the relevant international standards and instruments applicable to them and not extend states of emergency beyond what was strictly required. The Secretary-General was requested to assist Governments, special rapporteurs and working groups to ensure promotion and observance of guarantees relating to states of emergency embodied in international instruments. The Group was asked to report in 2002.

Working Group activities. The Working Group on Arbitrary Detention held its thirtieth (14-18 May), thirty-first (10-14 September) and thirty-second (26 November–5 December) sessions in 2001 in Geneva [E/CN.4/2002/77]. During the year, the Working Group transmitted 36 communications concerning 167 new cases of alleged arbitrary detention to 24 Governments and Palestine, of which 22 provided information. Of the 167 individual alleged cases, 63 were based on information communicated by local or regional NGOs, 78 on information provided by international NGOs and 26 by private sources. The Group also adopted 31 opinions concerning 94 persons in 22 countries and Palestine. A description of the cases transmitted, the contents of Governments' replies and the text of 29 opinions were presented in a separate report [E/CN.4/2002/77/Add.1]. The Group transmitted 79 urgent appeals concerning 897 individuals to 39 Governments and the Palestinian Authority, of which 46 were issued jointly by the Working Group and thematic or geographical special rapporteurs. In 27 cases, the Governments concerned informed the Group that they had taken steps to remedy a detainee's situation.

The Group requested Governments to reduce, to the extent possible, cases of detention caused by extreme poverty, and recommended the repeal of enactments providing for imprisonment for contractual debt, as prohibited under the 1966 International Covenant on Civil and Political Rights, adopted by the General Assembly in resolution 2200 A (XXI) [YUN 1966, p. 423] (see p. 589); measures to ensure that judges took the greatest possible account of the level of income of persons released on bail, in order to give full effect to the principle that release must be the rule and detention the exception; and fines—intended to limit penalties of imprisonment—not disproportionate to the income of the convicted persons concerned. It also recommended that recourse to deprivation of liberty in order to protect victims be reconsidered and supervised by a judicial authority.

Two Working Group members visited Bahrain (19-24 October) [E/CN.4/2002/77/Add.2], where they were granted unrestricted access to all prisons and rehabilitation centres for minors, and spoke freely and without witnesses to prisoners selected at random. The Group members reviewed the development of the rule of law since 1999, which comprised institutional reforms, repeal of emergency legislation and abolition of the State Security Court, reforms of the administration of justice and of the administration of criminal justice, and the organization and operation of the prison administration. The Group recommended that the Government bring into line with international standards the remedies against decisions handed down by courts martial; ensure respect for foreigners' rights; take account of insolvent debtors' good faith in cases of people detained for failure to post bond or pay a fine; bring into line with international standards the legal rules applicable to minors aged 15 to 18; appoint women to responsible positions and allow them to become judicial officers; adopt laws to prevent and punish violence against women; further encourage cooperation between the Government and civil society; and facilitate contact between incarcerated foreigners and the appropriate consular services. The Group considered the visit a success, as the Government subsequently released all prisoners.

Impunity

Report of Secretary-General. In response to a 2000 Commission request [YUN 2000, p. 670], the Secretary-General summarized replies received from Governments, intergovernmental organizations and NGOs regarding steps they had taken to combat impunity for human rights violations and on the appointment of an independent expert to examine the issue [E/CN.4/2001/88 & Corr.1].

Commission action. On 25 April [res. 2001/70], the Commission, by a roll-call vote of 39 to none, with 13 abstentions, stressing the importance of holding accountable perpetrators of violations of international human rights and humanitarian law, urged States to take steps to address the issue. It also urged them to provide a fair and equitable process through which human rights violations could be investigated and made public, and to encourage victims' participation in the process. The Secretary-General was asked to seek the views of Governments, intergovernmental organizations and NGOs on the appointment of an independent expert to examine the issue of impunity, to invite States to provide information on steps they had taken to combat impunity and on remedies available to victims, and to report thereon in 2002.

Subcommission action. On 10 August [dec. 2001/105], the Subcommission, expressing concern at allegations of serious human rights violations on the part of personnel serving in peace support operations, decided to entrust Françoise Hampson (United Kingdom) with preparing, without financial implications, a working paper for submission in 2002 on the scope of the activities and the accountability of armed forces, UN civilian police, international civil servants and experts taking part in peace support operations.

On 16 August [res. 2001/22], the Subcommission urged Governments to implement the relevant resolutions of the General Assembly and other UN bodies and to take measures in accordance with international law to end and prevent war crimes and crimes against humanity and to ensure the punishment of persons found guilty, or their extradition to countries where they had committed the crimes, even when no treaty existed to facilitate that task.

Independence of the judicial system

Reports of Special Rapporteur. In February, the Special Rapporteur on the independence of judges and lawyers, Dato' Param Cumaraswamy (Malaysia), submitted a report covering his activities in 2000 [E/CN.4/2001/65].

The Special Rapporteur transmitted 42 communications to 26 Governments and Palestine and five urgent appeals to four States. Replies to communications were received from 21 countries and Palestine, while eight responded to urgent appeals. In order to avoid duplication of work, the Special Rapporteur joined other special rapporteurs and working groups to transmit seven urgent appeals to six countries and two communications to two countries through normal channels. The report summarized the communications, urgent appeals and replies received from Governments. The Special Rapporteur appealed to Governments to respond promptly and positively to his interventions and requests to field missions. He called on Governments, national judiciaries, bar associations and NGOs to submit court judgements and legislation affecting the independence of the judiciary and the legal profession.

The Special Rapporteur visited Guatemala (10-12 May) [E/CN.4/2002/72/Add.2], at the request of the Government and NGOs, to evaluate the implementation of recommendations he had made in 1999 [YUN 1999, p. 627]. Following consideration of the legal and political developments since his 1999 visit, the Special Rapporteur noted that many of the recommendations had not been implemented. Progress had been piecemeal and isolated and was mainly seen in the professionalization of the judiciary. Reiterating his 1999 recommendations, relating to impunity, lynchings, threats, harassment and intimidation against the judiciary, training, security of tenure and disciplinary procedures for judges, and women and children, the Special Rapporteur called on the Government to implement them in their entirety.

The Special Rapporteur visited Mexico (13-23 May) [E/CN.4/2002/72/Add.1] to investigate allegations of widespread corruption among judges, lawyers and prosecutors, as well as a high level of impunity. He examined the Constitution in the context of the administration of justice and issues relating to the judiciary, including security of tenure, training, disciplinary measures, judicial corruption, relations between the state and the federal judiciary, and the Federal Electoral Tribunal. The Special Rapporteur reviewed the function of the military courts and of the Public Prosecutor's Office and the Attorney-General, and considered the role of public defenders, the legal profession and human rights defenders. He concluded that progress begun in 1994 towards the establishment of a culture of judicial independence had been slow. Impunity and corruption appeared to have continued unabated. Although each segment in the administration of justice appeared to be undertaking reforms, the reforms were not coordinated. Noting that hardly any judicial officer had been disciplined for judicial corruption, the Special Rapporteur welcomed an initiative to develop a database to ensure that officers dismissed for corruption or human rights violations were not recruited elsewhere in the public administration. He expressed concern over the lack of impartiality of the military courts and the reluctance or unwillingness of witnesses to present evidence against military personnel. Harassment and intimidation of lawyers were a matter of grave concern, as were the problems faced by lawyers in gaining access to clients detained by the police and in prison. No specialized tribunals had been created for minors, and indigenous people lacked access to justice.

The Special Rapporteur made recommendations to amend the Constitution to provide security of tenure for judges, establish judicial councils, allocate resources to the judiciary, and make binding on all authorities the recommendations of national and state human rights commissions. Regarding the judiciary, he proposed an evaluation to determine the number of additional courts needed to meet the need for access to justice, bringing new legislation to the attention of the judiciary, the legal profession and the general public, and producing a uniform code of ethics for magistrates and judges. Other recommenda-

tions related to the Judicial Council, military courts, the Public Prosecutor's Office, the legal profession, impunity, harassment of lawyers and human rights defenders, fair trial procedures, indigenous communities and the status of women. The Special Rapporteur proposed a pilot project in two States, aimed at training judges and lawyers on how to apply human rights norms in the daily practice of the administration of justice and at raising awareness about the independence of the judiciary.

Commission action. On 23 April [res. 2001/39], the Commission encouraged Governments that faced difficulties in guaranteeing the independence of judges and lawyers to consult and consider the Special Rapporteur's services by inviting him to visit their country. The High Commissioner was asked to continue to provide technical assistance to train judges and lawyers and to associate the Special Rapporteur in the development of a manual on the human rights training of judges and lawyers. The Special Rapporteur was requested to report in 2002, and the Secretary-General was asked to assist him.

Capital punishment

Report of Secretary-General. By a February note [E/CN.4/2001/89 & Corr.1], the Secretary-General informed the Commission that the revised version of his sixth quinquennial report on capital punishment and implementation of the safeguards guaranteeing the rights of those facing the death penalty, as called for in 2000 [YUN 2000, p. 672], would be prepared and submitted by the UN Centre for International Crime Prevention. The report had covered the period 1994-1998.

In March [E/CN.15/2001/10 & Corr.1], the Secretary-General submitted the revised and updated report, covering the period 1994-2000, which contained 18 additional replies to the Secretary-General's questionnaire, bringing the total number of responses to 63. Of the responding countries, almost two thirds (41) were totally abolitionist (34) or abolitionist for all ordinary crimes (7); some 14 per cent (9) were de facto abolitionist and 21 per cent were retentionist (13). However, only 47 per cent of all abolitionist countries replied.

Regarding changes in the status of the death penalty within the reporting period, all but one of 55 countries and territories that had abolished the death penalty completely for all offences at the beginning of 1994 maintained that status at the end of 2000. Of 14 countries that were abolitionist for ordinary offences, 6 had joined the abolitionists for all offences category, leaving 8 in the group of those that did not change their status. Of the 30 countries considered to be de facto abolitionist at the beginning of the reporting period, 5 became abolitionist, while 8 resumed executions, thereby becoming retentionist. From various sources, it was ascertained that at the beginning of 1994 some 94 countries and territories retained the death penalty, of which 12 became abolitionist for all crimes and 2 for ordinary crimes. The report noted that 17 countries that were retentionist had become de facto abolitionist. Although five retentionist States continued to pass death sentences, no executions were believed to have been carried out within the reporting period. However, executions were carried out by 55 retentionist countries that had given no indication that they intended in the near future to abolish the death penalty. Limited information available suggested that from 1994 to 1999, an estimated 26,800 persons were sentenced to death, while some 15,300 were judicially executed.

The report included information on the implementation of the safeguards guaranteeing protection of the rights of those facing the death penalty, adopted by the Economic and Social Council in resolution 1984/50 [YUN 1984, p. 709].

The Secretary-General concluded that the continued movement towards abolition had been impressive, with 25 countries abolishing the death penalty between 1994 and 2000.

Commission action. By a roll-call vote of 27 to 18, with 7 abstentions, the Commission, on 25 April [res. 2001/68], called on States parties to the International Covenant on Civil and Political Rights that had not done so to consider acceding to or ratifying the 1989 Second Optional Protocol thereto on the death penalty, adopted by the General Assembly in resolution 44/128 [YUN 1989, p. 484]. States that maintained the death penalty were called on to restrict the number of offences for which that penalty might be imposed, to establish a moratorium on executions, with a view to abolishing the death penalty completely, and to provide the public with information regarding the imposition of the death penalty. States that had received an extradition request on a capital charge were asked to reserve the right to refuse extradition in the absence of assurances from the requesting State that capital punishment would not be carried out. The Secretary-General was asked to submit in 2002 a supplement to his quinquennial report, paying special attention to the imposition of the death penalty against persons under 18 years at the time of the offence.

Communication. On 27 April [E/CN.4/2001/161 & Corr.1], Saudi Arabia, also on behalf of 60 other States, dissociated itself from the Commission's resolution.

Juveniles

Report of Secretary-General. The revised version of the Secretary-General's sixth quinquennial report on capital punishment and implementation of the safeguards guaranteeing protection of the rights of those facing the death penalty [E/CN.15/2001/10 & Corr.1] (see p. 638) stated that since 1994 several countries had brought themselves into line with the safeguard concerning persons under 18 years of age. However, during the period under review, 13 persons within that age group were executed.

Right to democracy

Commission action. By a roll-call vote of 44 to none, with 9 abstentions, the Commission, on 23 April [res. 2001/41], called for information sharing and improved coordination in the UN system to facilitate the exchange of lessons learned and best practices in promoting and consolidating democracy. The Commission asked Governments, intergovernmental organizations and NGOs to deepen debates aimed at identifying ways and means to promote and consolidate democracy. OHCHR was requested to build on the initiatives and contributions of Member States, to organize an expert seminar to examine the interdependence between democracy and human rights, and to report on the seminar's conclusions in 2003. The Secretary-General and the High Commissioner were asked to bring the Commission's resolution to the attention of Member States, UN organs, intergovernmental organizations and NGOs and to disseminate it widely.

On 24 July, the Economic and Social Council approved the Commission's request to OHCHR (**decision 2001/263**).

Working paper. Pursuant to a 2000 Subcommission request [YUN 2000, p. 674], Manuel Rodríguez-Cuadros (Peru), in July, submitted a working paper [E/CN.4/Sub.2/2001/32], which considered the measures provided in various international human rights instruments for the promotion and consolidation of democracy. The paper identified threats to democratic stability and good governance such as persistent poverty, corruption, problems of democratic Governments relating to their functioning, representativeness and legitimacy, and the lack or weakness of mechanisms for dialogue that would enable civil society to participate in policy decisions. It concluded that globalization, regardless of its ambivalent effects on peoples' economic and social life, also promoted the values of democracy and human rights. It was essential to adopt a holistic approach that recognized the links between democracy, human rights, the rule of law, good governance and the integrity of public authorities, as well as structural supports for democracy such as the fight against poverty, development, social cohesion, inclusive social policies and the integration of women in the political process and other activities.

Subcommission action. On 16 August [dec. 2001/114], the Subcommission asked Mr. Rodríguez-Cuadros to prepare, without financial implications, an expanded working paper in 2002.

Report of Secretary-General. In a September report [A/56/326], the Secretary-General outlined strategies for meeting the goals and commitments contained in the UN Millennium Declaration [YUN 2000, p. 49]. Regarding human rights, democracy and good governance, the Secretary-General described the current situation and proposed strategies to move forward, such as fostering national human rights institutions; supporting the practical application of a rights-based approach to development; providing electoral assistance to help consolidate new and restored democracies and implementing democratic principles through institutional reform programmes; encouraging the further ratification and implementation of the 1979 Convention on the Elimination of All Forms of Discrimination against Women, adopted by the General Assembly in resolution 34/180 [YUN 1979, p. 895] (see p. 1074); protecting the rights of migrants and their families; and ensuring the freedom and independence of the media.

Electoral processes

Commission action. By a roll-call vote of 28 to 4, with 21 abstentions, the Commission, on 23 April [res. 2001/36], declaring that full popular participation was feasible only if societies had democratic political and electoral systems that guaranteed all citizens participation in government, urged States to foster a democracy that did so. The Secretary-General and the High Commissioner were asked to bring the Commission's resolution to the attention of Member States, UN organs, intergovernmental organizations and NGOs and to disseminate it widely.

Report of Secretary-General. In response to General Assembly resolution 54/173 [YUN 1999, p. 630], the Secretary-General, in October [A/56/344], presented information on UN electoral assistance activities between 1 October 1999 and 31 July 2001. During the reporting period, 47 requests for electoral assistance were received from 37 Member States (see p. 274 for electoral assistance to East Timor). The Electoral Assistance Division of the UN Department of Political Affairs continued to assist the UN focal point in responding to requests. As the number of requests from

Member States continued to be high, the Division developed assistance modalities to cover a comprehensive range of services that could be provided by the UN system, relating to expert advisory services, needs-assessment missions, observation and monitoring of elections, process assistance, which focused on providing expert advice to introduce new systems or upgrade existing ones, capacity-building, institution-building, and system architecture, involving the analysis and design of electoral systems.

Annexed to the report were summaries of Member States' requests for assistance and action taken thereon.

On 19 December [meeting 88], the General Assembly, on the recommendation of the Third Committee [A/56/583/Add.2], adopted **resolution 56/159** by recorded vote (162-0-8) [agenda item 119 (b)].

Strengthening the role of the United Nations in enhancing the effectiveness of the principle of periodic and genuine elections and the promotion of democratization

The General Assembly,

Recalling its previous resolutions on the subject, in particular resolution 54/173 of 17 December 1999,

Reaffirming that United Nations electoral assistance and support for the promotion of democratization are provided only at the specific request of the Member State concerned,

Noting with satisfaction that increasing numbers of Member States are using elections as peaceful means of discerning the will of the people and of confidence-building, thereby contributing to greater national peace and stability,

Recalling the Universal Declaration of Human Rights adopted on 10 December 1948, in particular the principle that the will of the people as expressed through periodic and genuine elections shall be the basis of government authority, as well as the right freely to choose representatives through periodic and genuine elections which shall be by universal and equal suffrage and shall be held by secret vote or by equivalent free voting procedures,

Taking note with interest of Commission on Human Rights resolutions 2001/41 of 23 April 2001 and 2001/72 of 25 April 2001,

Recognizing the need for strengthening democratic processes, electoral institutions and national capacity-building, including the capacity to administer fair elections, increase citizen participation and provide civic education, in requesting countries in order to consolidate and regularize the achievements of previous elections and support subsequent elections,

Welcoming the support provided by States to the electoral assistance activities of the United Nations, inter alia, through the provision of electoral experts, including electoral commission staff, and observers, as well as through contributions to the United Nations Trust Fund for Electoral Observation,

Welcoming also the contributions made by international and regional organizations and also by non-governmental organizations to enhancing the effectiveness of the principle of periodic and genuine elections and the promotion of democratization,

Having considered the report of the Secretary-General on United Nations activities aimed at enhancing the effectiveness of the principle of periodic and genuine elections,

1. *Welcomes* the report of the Secretary-General;

2. *Commends* the electoral assistance provided upon request to Member States by the United Nations, and requests that such assistance continue on a case-by-case basis in accordance with the evolving needs of requesting countries to develop, improve and refine their electoral institutions and processes, recognizing that the fundamental responsibility of organizing free and fair elections lies with Governments;

3. *Requests* the Electoral Assistance Division of the Department of Political Affairs of the Secretariat, in its role as coordinator of United Nations electoral assistance, to continue to inform Member States regularly about the requests received and the nature of any assistance provided;

4. *Requests* that the United Nations continue its efforts to ensure, before undertaking to provide electoral assistance to a requesting State, that there is adequate time to organize and carry out an effective mission for providing such assistance, including the provision of long-term technical cooperation, that conditions exist to allow free and fair elections and that the results of the mission will be reported comprehensively and consistently;

5. *Recommends* that, throughout the entire electoral process time-span, including before and after elections, as appropriate, based on needs assessment missions, the United Nations continue to provide technical advice and other assistance to requesting States and electoral institutions in order to help to strengthen their democratic processes;

6. *Notes with satisfaction* the comprehensive coordination between the Electoral Assistance Division and the United Nations Development Programme, and encourages further engagement of the Office of the United Nations High Commissioner for Human Rights in this context;

7. *Requests* the United Nations Development Programme to continue its governance assistance programmes in cooperation with other relevant organizations, in particular those that strengthen democratic institutions and linkages between civil society and Governments;

8. *Reiterates* the importance of reinforced coordination within and outside the United Nations system in this regard;

9. *Notes with appreciation* additional efforts being made to enhance cooperation with other international, governmental and non-governmental organizations in order to facilitate more comprehensive and needs-specific responses to requests for electoral assistance, and expresses its appreciation to those Member States, regional organizations and non-governmental organizations that have provided observers or technical experts in support of United Nations electoral assistance efforts;

10. *Recalls* the establishment by the Secretary-General of the United Nations Trust Fund for Electoral Observation, and calls upon Member States to consider contributing to the Fund;

11. *Encourages* the Secretary-General, through the Electoral Assistance Division, to continue responding to the evolving nature of requests for assistance and the growing need for specific types of medium-term expert assistance aimed at supporting and strengthening the existing capacity of the requesting Government, in particular by enhancing the capacity of national electoral institutions;

12. *Requests* the Secretary-General to provide the Electoral Assistance Division with adequate human and financial resources to allow it to carry out its mandate and to continue to ensure that the Office of the United Nations High Commissioner for Human Rights is able to respond, within its mandate and in close coordination with the Division, to the numerous and increasingly complex and comprehensive requests from Member States for advisory services;

13. *Also requests* the Secretary-General to report to the General Assembly at its fifty-eighth session on the implementation of the present resolution, in particular on the status of requests from Member States for electoral assistance, and on his efforts to enhance the support by the Organization for the democratization process in Member States.

RECORDED VOTE ON RESOLUTION 56/159:

In favour: Afghanistan, Albania, Algeria, Andorra, Angola, Antigua and Barbuda, Argentina, Armenia, Australia, Austria, Azerbaijan, Bahamas, Bahrain, Bangladesh, Barbados, Belarus, Belgium, Belize, Benin, Bhutan, Bolivia, Bosnia and Herzegovina, Botswana, Brazil, Bulgaria, Burkina Faso, Burundi, Cambodia, Cameroon, Canada, Cape Verde, Chad, Chile, Colombia, Comoros, Congo, Costa Rica, Côte d'Ivoire, Croatia, Cyprus, Czech Republic, Democratic Republic of the Congo, Denmark, Djibouti, Dominica, Dominican Republic, Ecuador, Egypt, El Salvador, Equatorial Guinea, Eritrea, Estonia, Ethiopia, Fiji, Finland, France, Gabon, Gambia, Georgia, Germany, Ghana, Greece, Grenada, Guatemala, Guinea, Guyana, Haiti, Honduras, Hungary, Iceland, India, Indonesia, Iran, Ireland, Israel, Italy, Jamaica, Japan, Jordan, Kazakhstan, Kenya, Kuwait, Latvia, Lebanon, Liechtenstein, Lithuania, Luxembourg, Madagascar, Malawi, Malaysia, Maldives, Mali, Malta, Marshall Islands, Mauritania, Mauritius, Mexico, Micronesia, Monaco, Mongolia, Morocco, Mozambique, Namibia, Nauru, Nepal, Netherlands, New Zealand, Nicaragua, Nigeria, Norway, Oman, Pakistan, Palau, Panama, Papua New Guinea, Paraguay, Peru, Philippines, Poland, Portugal, Qatar, Republic of Korea, Republic of Moldova, Romania, Russian Federation, Rwanda, Saint Kitts and Nevis, Saint Lucia, Samoa, San Marino, Senegal, Seychelles, Sierra Leone, Singapore, Slovakia, Slovenia, Solomon Islands, South Africa, Spain, Sri Lanka, Sudan, Suriname, Sweden, Thailand, The former Yugoslav Republic of Macedonia, Togo, Trinidad and Tobago, Tunisia, Turkey, Tuvalu, Uganda, Ukraine, United Arab Emirates, United Kingdom, United Republic of Tanzania, United States, Uruguay, Vanuatu, Venezuela, Yemen, Yugoslavia, Zambia.

Against: None.

Abstaining: Brunei Darussalam, China, Cuba, Democratic People's Republic of Korea, Libyan Arab Jamahiriya, Myanmar, Syrian Arab Republic, Viet Nam.

Also on 19 December [meeting 88], the Assembly, on the recommendation of the Third Committee [A/56/583/Add.2], adopted **resolution 56/154** by recorded vote (99-10-59) [agenda item 119 *(b)*].

Respect for the principles of national sovereignty and non-interference in the internal affairs of States in electoral processes as an important element for the promotion and protection of human rights

The General Assembly,

Reaffirming the purpose of the United Nations to develop friendly relations among nations based on respect for the principle of equal rights and self-determination of peoples and to take other appropriate measures to strengthen universal peace,

Recalling its resolution 1514(XV) of 14 December 1960, containing the Declaration on the Granting of Independence to Colonial Countries and Peoples,

Recalling also its resolution 2625(XXV) of 24 October 1970, by which it approved the Declaration on Principles of International Law concerning Friendly Relations and Cooperation among States in accordance with the Charter of the United Nations,

Reaffirming the right to self-determination, by virtue of which all peoples can freely determine their political status and freely pursue their economic, social and cultural development,

Recognizing that the principles enshrined in Article 2 of the Charter of the United Nations, in particular respect for national sovereignty and non-interference in the internal affairs of any State, should be respected in the holding of elections,

Recognizing also the richness and diversity of democratic political systems and models of free and fair electoral processes in the world, based on national and regional particularities and various backgrounds,

Stressing the responsibility of States in ensuring ways and means to facilitate full and effective popular participation in their electoral processes,

Recognizing the contribution made by the United Nations of electoral assistance provided to numerous States upon their request,

Reaffirming the solemn commitment of all States to fulfil their obligations to promote universal respect for, and observance and protection of, all human rights and fundamental freedoms for all in accordance with the Charter, other instruments relating to human rights, and international law,

Welcoming the commitment of all Member States, expressed in the United Nations Millennium Declaration, to work collectively for more inclusive political processes allowing genuine participation by all citizens in all countries,

1. *Reaffirms* that all peoples have the right to self-determination, by virtue of which they freely determine their political status and freely pursue their economic, social and cultural development, and that every State has the duty to respect that right, in accordance with the provisions of the Charter of the United Nations;

2. *Reiterates* that periodic, fair and free elections are important elements for the promotion and protection of human rights;

3. *Reaffirms* the right of peoples to determine methods and to establish institutions regarding electoral processes and that, consequently, States should ensure the necessary mechanisms and means to facilitate full and effective popular participation in those processes;

4. *Also reaffirms* that free development of the national electoral process in each State should be fully honoured in a manner that fully respects the principles established in the Charter and in the Declaration on Principles of International Law concerning Friendly Relations and Cooperation among States in accordance with the Charter of the United Nations;

5. *Further reaffirms* that United Nations electoral assistance is provided at the specific request of the Member State concerned;

6. *Calls upon* all States to refrain from financing political parties or other organizations in any other State in a way that is contrary to the principles of the Charter and that undermines the legitimacy of its electoral processes;

7. *Condemns* any act of armed aggression or threat or use of force against peoples, their elected Governments or their legitimate leaders;

8. *Reaffirms* that the will of the people shall be the basis of the authority of government and that this will shall be expressed in periodic and genuine elections, which shall be by universal and equal suffrage and shall be held by secret vote or by equivalent free voting procedures.

RECORDED VOTE ON RESOLUTION 56/154:

In favour: Afghanistan, Algeria, Angola, Antigua and Barbuda, Bahamas, Bahrain, Bangladesh, Barbados, Belize, Benin, Bhutan, Bolivia, Botswana, Brazil, Brunei Darussalam, Burkina Faso, Burundi, Cambodia, Cameroon, Cape Verde, Chad, China, Colombia, Comoros, Congo, Côte d'Ivoire, Cuba, Democratic People's Republic of Korea, Democratic Republic of the Congo, Djibouti, Dominica, Dominican Republic, Ecuador, Egypt, El Salvador, Equatorial Guinea, Eritrea, Ethiopia, Fiji, Gabon, Gambia, Ghana, Grenada, Guyana, Haiti, India, Indonesia, Iran, Jamaica, Japan, Jordan, Kazakhstan, Kenya, Kuwait, Lao People's Democratic Republic, Lebanon, Libyan Arab Jamahiriya, Madagascar, Malawi, Malaysia, Maldives, Mali, Mauritania, Mauritius, Mexico, Mongolia, Morocco, Mozambique, Myanmar, Namibia, Nepal, Nigeria, Oman, Pakistan, Panama, Paraguay, Peru, Philippines, Qatar, Rwanda, Saint Kitts and Nevis, Saint Lucia, Saudi Arabia, Seychelles, Singapore, Sri Lanka, Sudan, Suriname, Syrian Arab Republic, Thailand, Togo, Trinidad and Tobago, Tunisia, United Arab Emirates, United Republic of Tanzania, Venezuela, Viet Nam, Yemen, Zambia.

Against: Argentina, Australia, Canada, Chile, Israel, New Zealand, Norway, Samoa, Tuvalu, United States.

Abstaining: Albania, Andorra, Armenia, Austria, Belarus, Belgium, Bosnia and Herzegovina, Bulgaria, Costa Rica, Croatia, Cyprus, Czech Republic, Denmark, Estonia, Finland, France, Georgia, Germany, Greece, Guatemala, Guinea, Honduras, Hungary, Iceland, Ireland, Italy, Latvia, Liechtenstein, Lithuania, Luxembourg, Malta, Marshall Islands, Micronesia, Monaco, Netherlands, Nicaragua, Papua New Guinea, Poland, Portugal, Republic of Korea, Republic of Moldova, Romania, Russian Federation, San Marino, Senegal, Sierra Leone, Slovakia, Slovenia, South Africa, Spain, Sweden, The former Yugoslav Republic of Macedonia, Turkey, Uganda, Ukraine, United Kingdom, Uruguay, Vanuatu, Yugoslavia.

Other issues

Extralegal executions

Reports of Special Rapporteur. In January [E/CN.4/2001/9 & Corr.1 & Add.1], the Special Rapporteur on extrajudicial, summary or arbitrary executions, Asma Jahangir (Pakistan), updated activities since the submission of her last report [YUN 2000, p. 676]. Between 16 December 1999 and 10 December 2000, she transmitted communications containing allegations regarding violations of the right to life of more than 700 individuals to 37 Governments and the Palestinian Authority, as well as 117 urgent appeals regarding 339 individuals and specific groups of persons to prevent imminent loss of life. The report summarized the cases transmitted to Governments and the replies received. The Special Rapporteur was disturbed at the increasing number of reports of indiscriminate killings of unarmed civilians by government-controlled agents in situations of armed conflict and internal unrest. She noted with concern that steps taken to combat ongoing human rights abuses were seldom effective in curbing violence and ending extrajudicial, summary or arbitrary executions, and regretted that some Governments continued to ignore her urgent appeals and failed to respond to her requests for information. She recommended a series of actions for Governments that related to genocide, excessive use of force by law enforcement officials, deaths in custody, death threats, imminent expulsion of persons to countries where their lives were in danger, failure by officials to prevent violations of the right to life, impunity, children, traditional practices affecting the right to life ("honour" killings), sexual orientation and capital punishment.

The Special Rapporteur visited Turkey (19 February–1 March) [E/CN.4/2002/74/Add.1 & Corr.1] to investigate allegations of violations of the right to life, including deaths in custody, deaths due to excessive use of force by police or military forces and killings connected with abductions and "disappearances". At the time of the Special Rapporteur's visit, incidents of extrajudicial killings had dramatically reduced. However, there was apprehension that the situation could deteriorate, as underlying grievances, tensions and attitudes had not been addressed. The Special Rapporteur recommended that the Government establish a high-level commission to investigate allegations of killings by security forces, set up an independent national human rights commission, reform the justice system, investigate custodial deaths and prosecute and punish those responsible, grant amnesty to prisoners arrested for their political beliefs and abolish the death penalty.

Commission action. On 23 April [res. 2001/45], the Commission, strongly condemning all extrajudicial, summary or arbitrary executions, demanded that Governments end the practice in all its forms. It expressed concern that Governments had not replied to specific allegations and reports of summary or arbitrary executions transmitted by the Special Rapporteur.

The Commission decided to extend the Special Rapporteur's mandate for three years and asked her to continue to examine the problem, to report annually, to respond to information addressed to her, to enhance dialogue with Governments and follow up on her recommendations made after country visits, to pay special attention to cases involving children, peaceful demonstrators and minorities, to continue monitoring the implementation of international standards on safeguards and restrictions relating to capital punishment and to apply a gender perspective in her work. The Secretary-General was asked to assist the Special Rapporteur, continue to use his best endeavours in cases where the minimum

standard of legal safeguards provided for by the International Covenant on Civil and Political Rights (see p. 589) appeared not to be respected and ensure that personnel specialized in human rights and humanitarian law issues formed part of UN missions.

On 24 July, the Economic and Social Council endorsed the Commission's decision to extend the Special Rapporteur's mandate and approved its request to the Secretary-General to assist her (**decision 2001/266**).

Disappearance of persons

Working Group on Enforced or Involuntary Disappearances

Commission action. On 23 April [res. 2001/46], the Commission, deeply concerned by the increase in enforced or involuntary disappearances and reports concerning harassment, ill-treatment and intimidation of witnesses of disappearances or relatives of disappeared persons, urged Governments to cooperate with the Working Group on Enforced or Involuntary Disappearances. States were asked to provide the Group with information on measures taken and the obstacles encountered in preventing such disappearances and in giving effect to the 1992 Declaration on the Protection of All Persons from Enforced Disappearance, adopted by the General Assembly in resolution 47/133 [YUN 1992, p. 744]. The Commission decided to renew the Group's mandate for a three-year period and asked it to report in 2002. The Commission Chairperson was asked to appoint an independent expert to examine the existing international criminal and human rights framework to protect persons from enforced or involuntary disappearance and to report in 2002. The Secretary-General was asked to assist the Group, to provide resources to update the database on cases of enforced disappearance and to inform the Commission and the Group of steps taken to disseminate and promote the Declaration.

The Commission decided to establish in 2002 an intersessional open-ended working group to develop, in the light of the findings of the independent expert, the draft legally binding instrument for the protection of all persons from enforced disappearance [YUN 1998, p. 662].

On 4 June, the Economic and Social Council endorsed the Commission's decision to renew the Group's mandate, appoint an independent expert and establish the intersessional working group (**decision 2001/221**).

In June, Manfred Nowak (Austria) was appointed independent expert.

Note by Secretariat. A March note by the Secretariat [E/CN.4/2001/69/Add.1] contained the views of four States and one specialized agency on the draft convention on the protection of all persons from enforced disappearance, pursuant to a 2000 Commission request [YUN 2000, p. 679].

Working Group activities. The five-member Working Group on Enforced or Involuntary Disappearances held three sessions in 2001: its sixty-third in New York (30 April–4 May) and its sixty-fourth and sixty-fifth in Geneva (13-17 August and 14-21 November) [E/CN.4/2002/79]. In addition to its original mandate, which was to act as a channel of communication between families of disappeared persons and the Governments concerned, with a view to ensuring that sufficiently documented individual cases were investigated, the Working Group monitored States' compliance with the 1992 Declaration.

Cases under active consideration by the Group totalled 41,859, while countries with outstanding cases of alleged disappearance numbered 74. During the period under review, up to 21 November, the last day of the sixty-fifth session, the Group transmitted 243 new cases of enforced or involuntary disappearance to 25 countries, 50 of which allegedly occurred in 2001. The Group sent urgent action appeals to 14 countries and the Palestinian Authority in respect of 58 cases and clarified 4,419 cases in nine countries. The Group noted that although the number of disappearances reported had declined, the attitude of most Governments towards investigating and clarifying cases outstanding had not improved. The Group continued to draw the attention of Governments to the relevant provisions of the 1992 Declaration, emphasizing that its full implementation was crucial for the prevention and termination of enforced disappearances. Since impunity was a major reason for the practice, it was important that the perpetrators be brought to justice.

The Group stated that its reports covering 1999 [YUN 1999, p. 634] and 2000 [YUN 2000, p. 679] had been limited to 32 pages, as requested by the General Assembly in resolution 47/202 B [YUN 1992, p. 1083]. However, since those reports did not properly reflect the Group's work, it had decided to return to the earlier format. The report contained a separate opinion by a Group member objecting to the fact that the report was not in conformity with the Assembly's request.

Torture and cruel treatment

Report of Special Rapporteur. In January [E/CN.4/2001/66], the Special Rapporteur on torture, Sir Nigel S. Rodley (United Kingdom), summarized his activities in 2000. He sent 66 let-

ters to 60 countries on behalf of some 650 individuals and 28 groups involving about 2,250 persons. He also transmitted 164 urgent appeals to 56 Governments on behalf of some 470 individuals (40 known to be women and 35 known to be minors), as well as to 11 groups involving about 1,000 persons, feared to have been subjected to torture and other forms of ill-treatment. Replies were received from 37 Governments regarding some 300 cases submitted during the reporting period, whereas 25 did so regarding some 400 cases submitted in previous years. The report contained summaries of general allegations and individual cases, as well as of the urgent appeals and government replies, and presented the Special Rapporteur's observations where applicable. The Special Rapporteur said that available information suggested that incidents of torture and ill-treatment of persons were increasing, although the increase in information might be attributable to heightened attention to the issue. He was encouraged by recognition of the problem of impunity and of measures aimed at countering it. The Special Rapporteur recommended transparency measures that could help prevent torture and ill-treatment and made proposals to end de facto or de jure impunity.

Commission action. On 25 April [res. 2001/62], the Commission, condemning all forms of torture as described in the 1984 Convention against Torture and Other Cruel, Inhuman or Degrading Treatment or Punishment, contained in General Assembly resolution 39/46 [YUN 1984, p. 813] (see p. 594), called on Governments to become parties to the Convention as a matter of priority and to prohibit the practice. The Commission decided to extend the Special Rapporteur's mandate for three years and asked him to submit an interim report to the Assembly in 2001 and a full report to the Commission in 2002.

The Economic and Social Council, on 24 July, endorsed the Commission's decision to renew the Special Rapporteur's mandate, as well as its request to him to submit reports (**decision 2001/272**).

Following the Special Rapporteur's resignation in November, the Commission appointed, on 28 November, Theo C. van Boven (Netherlands).

Interim reports. In July [A/56/156], the Secretary-General transmitted an interim report of the Special Rapporteur, pursuant to General Assembly resolution 55/89 [YUN 2000, p. 683], covering issues of special concern to the Special Rapporteur, which related to intimidation as a form of torture, enforced or involuntary disappearance, torture and discrimination against sexual minorities, torture and impunity, and prevention and transparency. He recommended abolishing administrative detention, incommunicado detention and secret places of detention, the prevention of prisoner-on-prisoner violence, regular inspection of places of detention, training for police and security personnel, the public condemnation of torture by the highest authorities and instructing health personnel on the 1982 Principles of Medical Ethics relevant to the role of health personnel, particularly physicians, in the protection of detainees and prisoners against torture and other cruel, inhuman or degrading treatment or punishment, contained in Assembly resolution 37/194 [YUN 1982, p. 1081].

In a statement to the Third Committee on 8 November [E/CN.4/2002/76], the Special Rapporteur discussed issues of special concern (see p. 644) and updated information on possible missions.

Communication. On 26 April [E/CN.4/2001/164], Brazil transmitted comments on the Special Rapporteur's recommendations made following his visit to the country in 2000 [YUN 2000, p. 681].

Voluntary fund for torture victims

Commission action. On 25 April [res. 2001/62], the Commission appealed to Governments, organizations and individuals to contribute annually to the Voluntary Fund for Victims of Torture. Stressing the increasing need to assist rehabilitation services for torture victims, it called on the Fund's Board of Trustees to present in 2002 an updated assessment of the need for international funding of those services and of lessons learned from the Fund's activities. The Secretary-General was asked to continue to include the Fund among the programmes receiving donations at the annual UN Pledging Conference for Development Activities, and to ensure adequate staffing and technical facilities for UN bodies and mechanisms dealing with torture. He was also asked to inform the Commission of the Fund's operations.

Reports of Secretary-General. In his annual report on the status of the Fund, submitted in July [A/56/181], the Secretary-General stated that contributions received between 15 May 2000 and 17 May 2001 totalled $7,809,965 from 38 countries. Contributions from two private individuals, staff of the UN Office in Geneva and one NGO totalled $16,386.

The Board of Trustees held its twentieth session in Geneva (18 May–1 June). The total then available for grants to assist victims of torture amounted to some $8 million. Of that sum, some $35,000 was reserved for emergency grants before the Board's next annual session, in addition to a reserve of $140,000 unused since May 2000,

to respond to requests from victims of torture and for emergency care in areas where there was no project financed by the Fund and for organizations already financed by the Fund that were in financial difficulties. During the year, new grants were allocated to 187 assistance projects in 70 countries. Annexed to the report was a declaration on the International Day in Support of Victims of Torture, 26 June 2001, issued jointly by the Board, the Committee against Torture, the Special Rapporteur on torture and the High Commissioner.

On 19 December, the Assembly took note of the Secretary-General's report (**decision 56/429**).

In a later report [A/57/268], the Secretary-General stated that additional contributions received between 18 May and 31 December 2001 amounted to $592,994.

On 19 December [meeting 88], the General Assembly, on the recommendation of the Third Committee [A/56/583/Add.1], adopted **resolution 56/143** without vote [agenda item 119 (a)].

Torture and other cruel, inhuman or degrading treatment or punishment

The General Assembly,

Recalling article 5 of the Universal Declaration of Human Rights, article 7 of the International Covenant on Civil and Political Rights, the Declaration on the Protection of All Persons from Being Subjected to Torture and Other Cruel, Inhuman or Degrading Treatment or Punishment and its resolution 39/46 of 10 December 1984, by which it adopted and opened for signature, ratification and accession the Convention against Torture and Other Cruel, Inhuman or Degrading Treatment or Punishment, and all its subsequent relevant resolutions,

Recalling also that freedom from torture is a right that must be protected under all circumstances, including in times of internal or international disturbance or armed conflict,

Recalling further that the World Conference on Human Rights, held at Vienna from 14 to 25 June 1993, firmly declared that efforts to eradicate torture should, first and foremost, be concentrated on prevention and called for the early adoption of an optional protocol to the Convention against Torture and Other Cruel, Inhuman or Degrading Treatment or Punishment, which is intended to establish a preventive system of regular visits to places of detention,

Urging all Governments to promote the speedy and full implementation of the Vienna Declaration and Programme of Action adopted by the World Conference on Human Rights on 25 June 1993, in particular the section relating to freedom from torture, in which it is stated that States should abrogate legislation leading to impunity for those responsible for grave violations of human rights, such as torture, and prosecute such violations, thereby providing a firm basis for the rule of law,

Recalling its resolution 36/151 of 16 December 1981, in which it noted with deep concern that acts of torture took place in various countries, recognized the need to provide assistance to the victims in a purely humanitarian spirit and established the United Nations Voluntary Fund for Victims of Torture,

Recalling also the recommendation contained in the Vienna Declaration and Programme of Action that high priority should be given to providing the necessary resources to assist victims of torture and effective remedies for their physical, psychological and social rehabilitation, inter alia, through additional contributions to the Fund,

Noting with satisfaction the existence of a considerable international network of centres for the rehabilitation of victims of torture, which plays an important role in providing assistance to victims of torture, and the collaboration of the Fund with the centres,

Commending the persistent efforts by non-governmental organizations to combat torture and to alleviate the suffering of victims of torture,

Mindful of its proclamation, in its resolution 52/149 of 12 December 1997, of 26 June as the United Nations International Day in Support of Victims of Torture,

1. *Condemns* all forms of torture, including through intimidation, as described in article 1 of the Convention against Torture and Other Cruel, Inhuman or Degrading Treatment or Punishment;

2. *Stresses* that all allegations of torture or other cruel, inhuman or degrading treatment or punishment should be promptly and impartially examined by the competent national authority, that those who encourage, order, tolerate or perpetrate acts of torture must be held responsible and severely punished, including the officials in charge of the place of detention at which the prohibited act is found to have taken place, and that national legal systems should ensure that the victims of such acts obtain redress, are awarded fair and adequate compensation and receive appropriate social and medical rehabilitation;

3. *Recalls* the Principles on the Effective Investigation and Documentation of Torture and Other Cruel, Inhuman or Degrading Treatment or Punishment, and strongly encourages Governments to reflect upon the Principles as a useful tool in efforts to combat torture;

4. *Notes with appreciation* that one hundred and twenty-six States have become parties to the Convention;

5. *Urges* all States that have not yet done so to become parties to the Convention as a matter of priority;

6. *Invites* all States ratifying or acceding to the Convention and those States that are parties to the Convention and have not yet done so to consider joining the States parties that have made the declarations provided for in articles 21 and 22 of the Convention and to consider the possibility of withdrawing their reservations to article 20;

7. *Urges* all States parties to the Convention to notify the Secretary-General of their acceptance of the amendments to articles 17 and 18 of the Convention as soon as possible;

8. *Urges* States parties to comply strictly with their obligations under the Convention, including, in view of the high number of reports not submitted, their obligation to submit reports in accordance with article 19 of the Convention, and invites States parties to incorporate a gender perspective and information concerning children and juveniles when submitting reports to the Committee against Torture;

9. *Emphasizes* the obligation of States parties under article 10 of the Convention to ensure education and training for personnel who may be involved in the custody, interrogation or treatment of any individual subjected to any form of arrest, detention or imprisonment;

10. *Stresses*, in this context, that States must not punish personnel referred to in paragraph 9 above for not obeying orders to commit or conceal acts amounting to torture or other cruel, inhuman or degrading treatment or punishment;

11. *Calls upon* all Governments to take appropriate effective legislative, administrative, judicial or other measures to prevent and prohibit the production, trade, export and use of equipment that is specifically designed to inflict torture or other cruel, inhuman or degrading treatment;

12. *Welcomes* the work of the Committee, and takes note of the report of the Committee, submitted in accordance with article 24 of the Convention;

13. *Acknowledges* the number of reports and communications awaiting consideration by the Committee, and in this regard decides to authorize the Committee to establish a pre-sessional working group composed of four of its members to meet for a five-day session during the week preceding each session of the Committee, and invites the Committee to continue to enhance its methods of work;

14. *Calls upon* the United Nations High Commissioner for Human Rights, in conformity with her mandate established in General Assembly resolution 48/141 of 20 December 1993, to continue to provide, at the request of Governments, advisory services for the preparation of national reports to the Committee and for the prevention of torture, as well as technical assistance in the development, production and distribution of teaching material for these purposes;

15. *Urges* States parties to take fully into account the conclusions and recommendations made by the Committee after its consideration of their reports;

16. *Welcomes* the progress made by the open-ended working group of the Commission on Human Rights on a draft optional protocol to the Convention against Torture and Other Cruel, Inhuman or Degrading Treatment or Punishment, and urges the working group to complete as soon as possible a final text for submission to the General Assembly, through the Economic and Social Council, for consideration and adoption;

17. *Takes note with appreciation* of the interim report of the Special Rapporteur of the Commission on Human Rights on the question of torture, describing the overall trends and developments with regard to his mandate, and encourages the Special Rapporteur to continue to include in his recommendations proposals on the prevention and investigation of torture;

18. *Invites* the Special Rapporteur to continue to examine questions of torture and other cruel, inhuman or degrading treatment or punishment directed against women, and conditions conducive to such torture, and to make appropriate recommendations for the prevention and redress of gender-specific forms of

torture, including rape or any other form of sexual violence, and to exchange views with the Special Rapporteur of the Commission on Human Rights on violence against women, its causes and consequences, with the aim of enhancing further their effectiveness and mutual cooperation;

19. *Also invites* the Special Rapporteur to continue to consider questions relating to the torture of children and conditions conducive to such torture and other cruel, inhuman or degrading treatment or punishment and to make appropriate recommendations for the prevention of such torture;

20. *Calls upon* Governments to cooperate with and assist the Special Rapporteur in the performance of his or her task, to provide all necessary information requested by the Special Rapporteur, to respond appropriately and expeditiously to the urgent appeals of the Special Rapporteur and to give serious consideration to requests by the Special Rapporteur to visit their countries, and urges them to enter into a constructive dialogue with the Special Rapporteur in following up his or her recommendations;

21. *Reiterates* the need for the Special Rapporteur to be able to respond effectively, in particular to urgent appeals, to credible and reliable information that comes before him or her, and invites the Special Rapporteur to continue to seek the views and comments of all concerned, in particular Member States;

22. *Requests* the Special Rapporteur to continue to consider including in his or her reports information on the follow-up by Governments to his or her recommendations, visits and communications, including progress made and problems encountered;

23. *Stresses* the need for the continued regular exchange of views among the Committee, the Special Rapporteur and other relevant United Nations mechanisms and bodies, as well as for the pursuance of cooperation with relevant United Nations programmes, notably the United Nations Crime Prevention and Criminal Justice Programme, with a view to enhancing further their effectiveness and cooperation on issues relating to torture, inter alia, by improving their coordination;

24. *Expresses its gratitude and appreciation* to the Governments, organizations and individuals that have contributed to the United Nations Voluntary Fund for Victims of Torture;

25. *Stresses* the importance of the work of the Board of Trustees of the Fund, and appeals to all Governments and organizations to contribute annually to the Fund, preferably by 1 March prior to the annual meeting of the Board, if possible with a substantial increase in the level of contributions, so that consideration may be given to the ever-increasing demand for assistance;

26. *Requests* the Secretary-General to transmit to all Governments the appeals of the General Assembly for contributions to the Fund and to continue to include the Fund on an annual basis among the programmes for which funds are pledged at the United Nations Pledging Conference for Development Activities;

27. *Also requests* the Secretary-General to assist the Board of Trustees of the Fund in its appeal for contributions and in its efforts to make better known the existence of the Fund and the financial means currently available to it, as well as in its assessment of the global need for international funding of rehabilitation services for victims of torture and, in this effort, to make use of all existing possibilities, including the preparation, production and dissemination of information materials;

28. *Further requests* the Secretary-General to ensure the provision of adequate staff and facilities for the bodies and mechanisms involved in combating torture and assisting victims of torture, commensurate with the strong support expressed by Member States for combating torture and assisting victims of torture;

29. *Invites* donor countries and recipient countries to consider including in their bilateral programmes and projects relating to the training of armed forces, security forces, prison and police personnel and health-care personnel matters relating to the protection of human rights and the prevention of torture, while bearing in mind a gender perspective;

30. *Calls upon* all Governments, the Office of the United Nations High Commissioner for Human Rights and other United Nations bodies and agencies, as well as relevant intergovernmental and nongovernmental organizations, to commemorate, on 26 June, the United Nations International Day in Support of Victims of Torture;

31. *Requests* the Secretary-General to submit to the Commission on Human Rights at its fifty-eighth session and to the General Assembly at its fifty-seventh session a report on the status of the Convention and a report on the operations of the Fund;

32. *Decides* to consider at its fifty-seventh session the reports of the Secretary-General, including the report on the United Nations Voluntary Fund for Victims of Torture, the report of the Committee against Torture and the interim report of the Special Rapporteur of the Commission on Human Rights on the question of torture.

Freedom of opinion and expression

Reports of Special Rapporteur. In February [E/CN.4/2001/64], the Special Rapporteur on the promotion and protection of the right to freedom of opinion and expression, Abid Hussain (India), described his 2000 activities and summarized the texts of communications he had sent to 59 States and the Palestinian Authority and the replies thereto. During the reporting period, he had sent 16 allegations and 101 urgent appeals regarding violations of the right. An additional 89 urgent appeals and one allegation were sent jointly with other mechanisms of the Commission.

The Special Rapporteur stated that, based on the communications received, it was clear that the rights to freedom of opinion, expression and information were violated almost routinely in States with widely different political systems and institutional frameworks for governance. In the light of the large number of allegations received relating to the abuse of libel and defamation laws, he urged Governments to ensure that the fines for offences such as "defamation", "libel", "insults" and publication of "false" or "alarmist" information were not out of proportion to the harm done to victims and were not used to limit the free flow of information and ideas. He encouraged Governments to guarantee access to information by democratizing new information technologies, such as the Internet, and to remove obstacles to women's exercise of the right to freedom of expression. Recalling the Commission's 1999 request to integrate the protection of HIV-related human rights and access to information within his mandate [YUN 1999, p. 687], the Special Rapporteur called on Governments, NGOs and other specialized organizations to provide him with information.

A March report of the Special Rapporteur [A/CONF.189/PC.2/24] highlighted the exercise of the right as a positive contribution to combating racism, discrimination, xenophobia and related intolerance, hate speech as an area of conflict between the right to freedom of expression and the principle of non-discrimination, and the use of new technologies, such as the Internet, to fight racism. Annexed to the report was a joint statement on racism and the media issued by the Special Rapporteur, the OSCE representative on freedom and the media and the Organization of American States Special Rapporteur on freedom of expression.

The Special Rapporteur visited Argentina (25 June–2 July) [E/CN.4/2002/75/Add.1]. Although he observed that the right to freedom of opinion and expression was widely respected, he remained concerned about attacks, harassment and threats against journalists and human rights defenders and the deteriorating economic and social situation, which had an impact on exercising the right. Freedom of the media was sometimes restricted by indirect methods, particularly the unequal allocation of publicity spots or advertising. The Special Rapporteur regretted that minorities continued to be discriminated against in terms of their integration into the media. He recommended that the authorities investigate complaints of attacks, death threats and harassment against the media and that more talk shows and debates on rights issues be broadcast on national channels, with more journalists and academics involved. He encouraged the Government to ensure that future legislation that might affect freedom of opinion and expression and the freedom of the media was transparent and participatory. While noting measures taken by Argentina to reduce prejudices against some religious and ethnic minorities, the Special Rapporteur recommended awareness-raising and education to redress cultural stereotyping. He proposed that the technical cooperation programme initiated by OHCHR in Argentina include a focus on the promotion and protection of the right.

Commission action. On 23 April [res. 2001/47], by a roll-call vote of 44 to none, with 8 abstentions, the Commission expressed concern at the detention, extrajudicial killing, persecution, harassment, threats, violence and discrimination directed at persons who exercised the right to freedom of opinion and expression, as well as the right to freedom of thought, conscience and religion, peaceful assembly and association, and participation in public affairs. It appealed to States to ensure respect and support for all persons who exercised those rights, to ensure that they were not discriminated against, to promote and protect the freedom of opinion and expression, and to cooperate with the Special Rapporteur. The Special Rapporteur was asked to: draw the High Commissioner's attention to situations of particularly serious concern to him; pay particular attention, in cooperation with the Special Rapporteur on violence against women, to the situation of women; consider approaches taken to improve access to information, with a view to sharing best practices; provide his views on the advantages and challenges of new information technologies; seek the views of Governments and others concerned; and report in 2002. The Secretary-General was asked to assist him.

Terrorism

Commission action. By a roll-call vote of 33 to 14, with 6 abstentions, the Commission, on 23 April [res. 2001/37], condemning all acts, methods and practices of terrorism, urged States, in conformity with international law, to prevent, combat and eliminate terrorism. States were called on to enhance their cooperation with a view to bringing terrorists to justice and to take appropriate measures before granting refugee status to ensure that an asylum-seeker had not participated in terrorist acts. Relevant human rights mechanisms were urged to address the consequences of the acts, methods and practices of terrorist groups. The Secretary-General was asked to collect information, including a compilation of studies and publications, on the implications of terrorism, as well as the effects of the fight against terrorism on the full enjoyment of human rights, and to make that information available to concerned special rapporteurs and working groups. The Commission endorsed the Subcommission's 2000 request [YUN 2000, p. 688] to the Secretary-General to assist the Special Rapporteur.

Report of Special Rapporteur. In response to a 2000 Subcommission request [YUN 2000, p. 688], the Special Rapporteur on terrorism and human rights, Kalliopi K. Koufa (Greece), in June [E/CN.4/Sub.2/2001/31], updated international action taken against terrorism, considered the criteria for the definition of terrorist acts, described contemporary forms of terrorism and reviewed the impact of terrorism on human rights. She concluded that violations of human rights, humanitarian law and the basic principles of the UN Charter were among the major causes of terrorism; study of those causes should be an essential component of any plan to reduce terrorism. Efforts should be made towards improvement of relations between States, which was essential to the global realization of human rights. The Special Rapporteur stated that much more needed to be assessed regarding extradition in the context of terrorism and that she would like to complete her consideration of sub-State or individual terrorism and the accountability of non-State actors. Thus, she recommended that the Subcommission authorize her to submit a further report.

Report of Secretary-General. In July [A/56/190], the Secretary-General, in response to General Assembly resolution 54/164 [YUN 1999, p. 642], summarized the views of eight Member States on the implications of terrorism for the enjoyment of human rights and fundamental freedoms.

Subcommission action. On 16 August [res. 2001/18], the Subcommission asked the Special Rapporteur to continue her work and to visit the UN offices in New York and Vienna in order to expand, update and expedite her work. The Secretary-General was asked to transmit her progress report (see p. 648) to Governments, specialized agencies and concerned intergovernmental organizations and NGOs for comments and information, to collect information, including the compilation of relevant studies and publications, and make it available to the Special Rapporteur, and to assist her in consulting competent services and bodies of the UN system. The Special Rapporteur was asked to submit another progress report in 2002.

Communication. Iraq, on 10 August [E/CN.4/Sub.2/2001/37], transmitted a statement on terrorism and human rights, claiming that it was being targeted by terrorist groups.

GENERAL ASSEMBLY ACTION

On 19 December [meeting 88], the General Assembly, on the recommendation of the Third Committee [A/56/583/Add.2], adopted **resolution 56/160** by recorded vote (102-0-69) [agenda item 119 (b)].

Human rights and terrorism

The General Assembly,

Guided by the Charter of the United Nations, the Universal Declaration of Human Rights, the Declaration on Principles of International Law concerning Friendly Relations and Cooperation among States in accordance with the Charter of the United Nations and the International Covenants on Human Rights,

Recalling the Declaration on the Occasion of the Fiftieth Anniversary of the United Nations, as well as the Declaration on Measures to Eliminate International Terrorism,

Recalling also the Vienna Declaration and Programme of Action adopted by the World Conference on Human Rights on 25 June 1993, in which the Conference reaffirmed that the acts, methods and practices of terrorism in all its forms and manifestations, as well as its linkage in some countries to drug trafficking, are activities aimed at the destruction of human rights, fundamental freedoms and democracy, threatening territorial integrity and the security of States and destabilizing legitimately constituted Governments, and that the international community should take the necessary steps to enhance cooperation to prevent and combat terrorism,

Recalling further the United Nations Millennium Declaration adopted by the General Assembly,

Recalling its resolutions 48/122 of 20 December 1993, 49/185 of 23 December 1994, 50/186 of 22 December 1995, 52/133 of 12 December 1997 and 54/164 of 17 December 1999,

Recalling in particular that, in its resolution 52/133, it requested the Secretary-General to seek the views of Member States on the implications of terrorism in all its forms and manifestations for the full enjoyment of human rights and fundamental freedoms,

Recalling previous resolutions of the Commission on Human Rights, and taking note in particular of Commission resolution 2001/37 of 23 April 2001, as well as the relevant resolutions of the Subcommission on the Promotion and Protection of Human Rights, in particular its resolution 2001/18, adopted unanimously on 16 August 2001,

Bearing in mind all other relevant General Assembly resolutions,

Bearing in mind also relevant Security Council resolutions,

Aware that, at the dawn of the twenty-first century, the world is witness to historic and far-reaching transformations, in the course of which forces of aggressive nationalism and religious and ethnic extremism continue to produce fresh challenges,

Alarmed that acts of terrorism in all its forms and manifestations aimed at the destruction of human rights have continued despite national and international efforts,

Bearing in mind that the right to life is the basic human right, without which a human being can exercise no other right,

Bearing in mind also that terrorism creates an environment that destroys the right of people to live in freedom from fear,

Reiterating that all States have an obligation to promote and protect all human rights and fundamental freedoms and that every individual should strive to secure their universal and effective recognition and observance,

Seriously concerned about the gross violations of human rights perpetrated by terrorist groups,

Profoundly deploring the increasing number of innocent persons, including women, children and the elderly, killed, massacred and maimed by terrorists in indiscriminate and random acts of violence and terror, which cannot be justified under any circumstances,

Expressing its deepest sympathy and condolences to all the victims of terrorism and their families,

Noting with great concern the growing connection between terrorist groups and other criminal organizations engaged in the illegal traffic in arms and drugs at the national and international levels, as well as the consequent commission of serious crimes such as murder, extortion, kidnapping, assault, the taking of hostages and robbery,

Alarmed in particular at the possibility that terrorist groups may exploit new technologies to facilitate acts of terrorism, which may cause massive damage, including huge loss of human life,

Emphasizing the need to intensify the fight against terrorism at the national level, to enhance effective international cooperation in combating terrorism in conformity with international law and to strengthen the role of the United Nations in this respect,

Emphasizing also the importance of Member States taking appropriate steps to deny safe haven to those who plan, finance or commit terrorist acts by ensuring their apprehension and prosecution or extradition,

Reaffirming that all measures to counter terrorism must be in strict conformity with the relevant provisions of international law, including international human rights standards,

Mindful of the need to protect the human rights of and guarantees for the individual in accordance with the relevant human rights principles and instruments, in particular the right to life,

Noting the growing consciousness within the international community of the negative effects of terrorism in all its forms and manifestations on the full enjoyment of human rights and fundamental freedoms and on the establishment of the rule of law and democratic freedoms as enshrined in the Charter of the United Nations and the International Covenants on Human Rights,

1. *Expresses its solidarity* with the victims of terrorism;

2. *Strongly condemns* the violations of the right to live free from fear and of the right to life, liberty and security;

3. *Reiterates its unequivocal condemnation* of the acts, methods and practices of terrorism in all its forms and manifestations as activities aimed at the destruction of human rights, fundamental freedoms and democracy, threatening the territorial integrity and security of States, destabilizing legitimately constituted Governments, undermining pluralistic civil society and having adverse consequences for the economic and social development of States;

4. *Reaffirms* the decision of the heads of State and Government, as contained in the United Nations Millennium Declaration, to take concerted action against international terrorism and to accede as soon as possible to all the relevant regional and international conventions;

5. *Urges* the international community to enhance cooperation at the regional and international levels in the fight against terrorism, in accordance with relevant international instruments, including those relating to human rights, with the aim of its eradication;

6. *Calls upon* States to take all necessary and effective measures, in accordance with relevant provisions of international law, including international human rights standards, to prevent, combat and eliminate terrorism in all its forms and manifestations, wherever and by whomever it is committed, and also calls upon States to strengthen, where appropriate, their legislation to combat terrorism in all its forms and manifestations;

7. *Urges* all States to deny safe haven to terrorists;

8. *Calls upon* States to take appropriate measures, in conformity with relevant provisions of national and international law, including international human rights standards, before granting refugee status, for the purpose of ensuring that an asylum-seeker has not planned, facilitated or participated in the commission of terrorist acts, including assassinations, and in this context urges those States that have granted refugee status or asylum to persons involved in or claiming to have committed acts of terrorism to review these situations;

9. *Condemns* the incitement to ethnic hatred, violence and terrorism;

10. *Commends* those Governments that have communicated their views on the implications of terrorism in response to the notes verbales by the Secretary-General dated 16 August 1999 and 4 September 2000;

11. *Welcomes* the report of the Secretary-General, and requests him to continue to seek the views of Member States on the implications of terrorism in all its forms and manifestations for the full enjoyment of all human rights and fundamental freedoms and on the possible establishment of a voluntary fund for the victims of terrorism, as well as on ways and means to rehabilitate the victims of terrorism and to reintegrate them into society, with a view to incorporating his findings in his report to the General Assembly;

12. *Decides* to consider this question at its fifty-eighth session under the item entitled "Human rights questions".

RECORDED VOTE ON RESOLUTION 56/160:

In favour: Afghanistan, Algeria, Angola, Antigua and Barbuda, Azerbaijan, Bahamas, Bahrain, Bangladesh, Barbados, Belarus, Belize, Benin, Bhutan, Bolivia, Botswana, Brazil, Brunei Darussalam, Burkina Faso, Cambodia, Cameroon, Cape Verde, Chad, China, Colombia, Comoros, Congo, Costa Rica, Côte d'Ivoire, Cuba, Democratic People's Republic of Korea, Democratic Republic of the Congo, Djibouti, Dominica, Dominican Republic, Ecuador, Egypt, El Salvador, Equatorial Guinea, Ethiopia, Gabon, Gambia, Georgia, Ghana, Grenada, Guatemala, Guinea, Guyana, Haiti, Honduras, India, Indonesia, Iran, Jamaica, Jordan, Kazakhstan, Kenya, Kuwait, Lao People's Democratic Republic, Lebanon, Libyan Arab Jamahiriya, Madagascar, Malaysia, Maldives, Mali, Mauritania, Mauritius, Mexico, Mongolia, Morocco, Mozambique, Myanmar, Namibia, Nepal, Oman, Pakistan, Panama, Paraguay, Peru, Philippines, Qatar, Russian Federation, Rwanda, Saint Kitts and Nevis, Saint Lucia, Saudi Arabia, Senegal, Singapore, Sri Lanka, Sudan, Suriname, Thailand, Togo, Trinidad and Tobago, Tunisia, Turkey, Turkmenistan, Ukraine, United Arab Emirates, United Republic of Tanzania, Uruguay, Viet Nam, Yemen.

Against: None.

Abstaining: Albania, Andorra, Argentina, Armenia, Australia, Austria, Belgium, Bosnia and Herzegovina, Bulgaria, Canada, Chile, Croatia, Cyprus, Czech Republic, Denmark, Eritrea, Estonia, Fiji, Finland, France, Germany, Greece, Hungary, Iceland, Ireland, Israel, Italy, Japan, Latvia, Liechtenstein, Lithuania, Luxembourg, Malawi, Malta, Marshall Islands, Micronesia, Monaco, Netherlands, New Zealand, Nicaragua, Nigeria, Norway, Palau, Papua New Guinea, Poland, Portugal, Republic of Korea, Republic of Moldova, Romania, Samoa, San Marino, Sierra Leone, Slovakia, Slovenia, Solomon Islands, South Africa, Spain, Sweden, Syrian Arab Republic, The former Yugoslav Republic of Macedonia, Tonga, Tuvalu, Uganda, United Kingdom, United States, Vanuatu, Venezuela, Yugoslavia, Zambia.

(For Security Council action regarding terrorism, see p. 61.)

Hostage-taking

On 23 April [res. 2001/38], the Commission, reaffirming that hostage-taking was illegal and unjustifiable under any circumstances, condemned all such acts and demanded the immediate and unconditional release of all hostages. It called on States to prevent, combat and punish hostage-taking and urged thematic rapporteurs and working groups to address the consequences of such acts in their reports.

Freedom of movement

Mass exoduses

Pursuant to General Assembly resolution 54/180 [YUN 1999, p. 644], the Secretary-General, in September [A/56/334], reported on human rights and mass exoduses, including efforts made by the United Nations and other institutions to enhance preventive capacities and steps taken towards more effective coordination to improve emergency responses. The Secretary-General stated that, although greater awareness of the link between racism, ethnic conflicts and human rights violations as the causes of mass exoduses had led to a better response by the international community during humanitarian crises and progress had been made towards more effective coordination of UN activities, more needed to be done. The Secretary-General restated the recommendations made in his 1999 report [YUN 1999, p. 643].

GENERAL ASSEMBLY ACTION

On 19 December [meeting 88], the General Assembly, on the recommendation of the Third Committee [A/56/583/Add.2], adopted **resolution 56/166** without vote [agenda item 119 (b)].

Human rights and mass exoduses

The General Assembly,

Deeply disturbed by the scale and magnitude of exoduses and displacements of people in many regions of the world and by the human suffering of refugees and displaced persons, a high proportion of whom are women and children,

Recalling its previous resolutions on this subject, as well as those of the Commission on Human Rights, and the conclusions of the World Conference on Human Rights, held at Vienna from 14 to 25 June 1993, which recognized, inter alia, that gross violations of human rights, persecution, political and ethnic conflicts, famine and economic insecurity, poverty and generalized violence were among the root causes leading to mass exoduses and displacements of people,

Mindful of the three open debates that have taken place within the Security Council on the protection of civilians in armed conflict and the two reports of the Secretary-General on that subject,

Welcoming the fiftieth anniversary of the 1951 Convention relating to the Status of Refugees, and noting the continuing relevance of the provisions of the Convention to the situation of people in mass exoduses,

Welcoming also the process of the Global Consultations on International Protection launched by the Office of the United Nations High Commissioner for Refugees, and in particular the discussions that took place in March 2001 on the protection of refugees in mass influx situations,

Welcoming further the increased attention being given by the United Nations, including the Office of the High Commissioner, to the problem of camp security, including through the development of operational guidelines on the separation of armed elements from refugee populations,

Stressing the importance of adherence to international humanitarian, human rights and refugee law in order to avert mass exoduses and to protect refugees and internally displaced persons, and expressing its deep concern at the lack of respect for those laws and principles, especially during armed conflict, including the denial of safe and unimpeded access to the displaced,

Reaffirming the primary responsibility of States to ensure the protection of refugees and internally displaced persons,

Noting with satisfaction the efforts by the United Nations system to develop a comprehensive approach to addressing the root causes and effects of movements of refugees and other displaced persons and strengthening emergency preparedness and response mechanisms,

Recognizing that the human rights machinery of the United Nations, including the mechanisms of the Commission on Human Rights and the human rights treaty bodies, has important capabilities to address human rights violations that cause movements of refugees and displaced persons or prevent durable solutions to their plight,

Recognizing also the complementarity between the systems for the protection of human rights and for humanitarian action, in particular the mandates of the United Nations High Commissioner for Human Rights and the United Nations High Commissioner for Refugees, as well as the work of the Representative of the Secretary-General on internally displaced persons and the Special Representative of the Secretary-General for Children and Armed Conflict, and that cooperation between them, in accordance with their respective mandates, as well as coordination between the human rights, political and security components of United Nations operations, make important contributions to the promotion and protection of the human rights of persons forced into mass exodus and displacement,

Acknowledging with appreciation the coordination within, as well as the independent work of, the International Red Cross and Red Crescent Movement in protecting and assisting refugees and internally displaced persons, in cooperation with relevant United Nations bodies,

1. *Takes note* of the report of the Secretary-General;

2. *Strongly deplores* ethnic and other forms of intolerance as one of the major causes of forced migratory movements, and urges States to take all necessary steps to ensure respect for human rights, especially the rights of persons belonging to minorities;

3. *Reaffirms* the need for all Governments, intergovernmental bodies and relevant international organizations to intensify their cooperation and assistance in worldwide efforts to address human rights situations that lead to, as well as the serious problems that result from, mass exoduses of refugees and displaced persons;

4. *Urges* the Secretary-General to continue to give high priority to the consolidation and strengthening of emergency preparedness and response mechanisms, including early warning activities in the humanitarian area, so that, inter alia, effective action is taken to identify all human rights abuses that contribute to mass exoduses of persons;

5. *Encourages* States that have not already done so to consider acceding to the 1951 Convention and the 1967 Protocol relating to the Status of Refugees and to other regional instruments concerning refugees, as applicable, and relevant international instruments of human rights and humanitarian law, and to take appropriate measures to disseminate and implement those instruments domestically to encourage compliance with provisions against arbitrary and forcible displacement and greater respect for the rights of those who flee;

6. *Emphasizes* the responsibility of all States and international organizations to cooperate with those countries affected by mass exoduses of refugees and displaced persons, in particular developing countries;

7. *Calls upon* Governments, the United Nations High Commissioner for Human Rights, the United Nations High Commissioner for Refugees and other relevant parts of the United Nations system, as well as relevant international and non-governmental organizations, to continue to respond to the assistance and protection needs of refugees and other displaced persons worldwide, including to promote durable solutions to their plight;

8. *Urges* States to uphold the civilian and humanitarian character of refugee camps and settlements, consistent with international law, inter alia, through effective measures to prevent the infiltration of armed elements, to identify and separate any such armed elements from refugee populations, to settle refugees at safe locations, where possible away from the border, and to ensure prompt and unhindered access to them by humanitarian personnel;

9. *Encourages* the special rapporteurs, special representatives and working groups of the Commission on Human Rights and the United Nations human rights treaty bodies, acting within their mandates, to seek information, where appropriate, on human rights problems that may result in mass exoduses of populations or impede their voluntary return home and, where appropriate, to include such information, together with recommendations thereon, in their reports and to bring such information to the attention of the United Nations High Commissioner for Human Rights for appropriate action in fulfilment of her mandate, in consultation with the United Nations High Commissioner for Refugees;

10. *Requests* all United Nations bodies, acting within their mandates, the specialized agencies and governmental, intergovernmental and non-governmental organizations to cooperate fully with all mechanisms of the Commission on Human Rights and, in particular, to provide them with all relevant information in their possession on the human rights situations creating or affecting refugees and displaced persons;

11. *Requests* the United Nations High Commissioner for Human Rights, in the exercise of her mandate, as set out in General Assembly resolution 48/141 of 20 December 1993, to coordinate human rights activities throughout the United Nations system and, in cooperation with the United Nations High Commissioner for Refugees, to pay particular attention to situations that cause or threaten to cause mass exoduses or displacements and to contribute to efforts to address such situations effectively and promote sustainable returns through promotion and protection measures, including human rights monitoring in respect of those who fled or have returned as part of mass exoduses, emergency preparedness and response mechanisms, early warning and information-sharing, technical advice, expertise and cooperation in countries of origin as well as host countries;

12. *Welcomes* the efforts of the United Nations High Commissioner for Human Rights to contribute to the creation of an environment viable for return in post-conflict societies through initiatives such as the rehabilitation of the justice system, the creation of national institutions capable of defending human rights and broad-based programmes of human rights education and the strengthening of local non-governmental organizations through field presences and programmes of advisory services and technical cooperation;

13. *Requests* the Secretary-General to prepare and submit to the General Assembly at its fifty-eighth session a report on the implementation of the present resolution as it pertains to all aspects of human rights and mass exoduses, with particular emphasis on efforts by the United Nations system to enhance the protection of those who become displaced during mass exoduses and to facilitate their return and reintegration, as well as information on efforts to continue to enhance the capacity of the United Nations to avert new flows of refugees and other displaced persons and to tackle the root causes of such flows;

14. *Decides* to continue its consideration of this question at its fifty-eighth session.

Internally displaced persons

Reports of Secretary-General's Representative. In January [E/CN.4/2001/5], the Secretary-General's Representative on internally displaced persons, Francis M. Deng (Sudan), updated developments regarding the promotion, dissemination and application of the Guiding Principles on Internal Displacement [YUN 1998, p. 675] and efforts to develop an institutional framework for internally displaced persons. He discussed country visits as a way to focus on specific situations of internal displacement and presented areas where further research was required, including addressing the protection and assistance needs of internally displaced persons living in areas not under government control, donor policies, the mental health of displaced populations and developing a more comprehensive protection regime for refugees and internally displaced persons.

In an August report [A/56/168], submitted pursuant to General Assembly resolution 54/167 [YUN 1999, p. 646], the Representative updated developments since his January report. He said that although some progress had been made in developing institutional arrangements for an effective response to the problems of internally displaced persons worldwide, the global crisis remained acute, affecting 20 million to 25 million persons in at least 40 countries. He pointed out that as an understanding of the issues had increased and deepened, so had the challenge of responding.

The Representative visited the Sudan (11-18 September) [E/CN.4/2002/95/Add.1], where he focused on dialogue with the Government and representatives of the international community in Khartoum, with a view to enhancing national response to internal displacement in the Sudan. Some 4 million Sudanese were internally displaced, representing the largest number of displaced persons worldwide, and an estimated 420,000 had sought refuge elsewhere in Africa and Europe. While natural disasters had resulted in significant displacement, the primary cause was the ongoing civil war. The Representative discussed with the Government the need to develop a national policy and strategy on internal displacement, including the establishment of a national focal point and institution. Several agreements were reached with the Government, including the preparation of a study on the displacement crisis and the ongoing programmes with a view to developing cooperative strategies in the light of the Guiding Principles and the convening of a national seminar, which would provide a forum for discussions with UN agencies, NGOs, donors and internally displaced persons on ways to enhance the national response to internal displacement.

The Representative visited Indonesia (24-29 September) [E/CN.4/2002/95/Add.2] to obtain firsthand information on displacement in the country and to initiate dialogue with the authorities responsible for adopting and implementing policies and programmes to assist and protect internally displaced persons. Some 1.3 million people were internally displaced, owing mostly to conflicts between the Government and local separatist groups and those between religious or ethnic groups. About 750,000 of the internally displaced persons were estimated to be under 18 years, and a great majority were women and children. Their condition was generally reported to be poor. The Representative stated that it was critical for national military and police forces to provide protection for all civilians. Protection and assistance called for collaboration among many actors. Thus, it was important to maintain close partnerships with NGOs and expand the role of the international community beyond humanitarian assistance. Referring to the seminar on internal displacement (see below), the Representative advocated recommendations on the creation of a national commission on internally displaced persons and community recovery, the development of guidelines on data collection, compilation and verification regarding internally displaced persons, and the designation of information focal points.

Commission action. On 24 April [res. 2001/54], the Commission, stressing the need to strengthen inter-agency arrangements and the capacities of relevant UN agencies to meet the immense humanitarian challenge of internal displacement, called on States to provide adequate resources for programmes to assist and protect internally displaced persons. It called on the High Commissioner to develop projects, in cooperation with Governments, international organizations and the Representative, to promote the human rights of internally displaced persons, as part of the programme of advisory services and technical cooperation (see p. 598), and to include in her annual report information on their implementation. The Commission decided to extend the Representative's mandate for a further three years and asked him to continue to report to the General Assembly and the Commission. The Secretary-General was asked to assist him.

The Economic and Social Council, on 24 July, endorsed the Commission's decision to extend the Representative's mandate and its request to him to submit reports (**decision 2001/269**).

Seminar. The Representative transmitted to the Commission the report of the Seminar on Internal Displacement in Indonesia (Jakarta, 26-27 June) [E/CN.4/2002/95/Add.3], organized by the Brookings Institution–City University of New York Project on Internal Displacement, the University of Indonesia, the National Commission on Human Rights of Indonesia, the UN Office for the Coordination of Humanitarian Affairs, the United Nations Development Programme (UNDP) and the Office of the United Nations High Commissioner for Refugees (UNHCR). Participants called for more concerted efforts at the national, provincial and district levels, better emergency needs assessment, and the creation of an effective information system to enable different actors to understand better the needs of internally displaced persons. Other proposals related to safety and protection, coordination, economic empowerment, education, and women and children.

Subcommission action. On 16 August [dec. 2001/122], the Subcommission asked Paulo Sérgio Pinheiro (Brazil) to prepare in 2002, without financial implications, a working paper on the return of refugees' or displaced persons' property.

On 19 December [meeting 88], the General Assembly, on the recommendation of the Third Committee [A/56/583/Add.2], adopted **resolution 56/164** without vote [agenda item 119 *(b)*].

Protection of and assistance to internally displaced persons

The General Assembly,

Deeply disturbed by the alarmingly high numbers of internally displaced persons throughout the world who receive inadequate protection and assistance, and conscious of the serious problem that this is creating for the international community,

Conscious of the human rights and the humanitarian dimensions of the problem of internally displaced persons and the responsibilities that this poses for States and the international community to explore methods and means better to address the protection and assistance needs of those persons,

Noting the growing awareness of the international community of the issue of internally displaced persons worldwide and the urgency of addressing the root causes of their displacement and finding durable solutions, including voluntary return in safety and with dignity or local integration,

Emphasizing that national authorities have the primary responsibility to provide protection and assistance to internally displaced persons within their jurisdiction as well as to address the root causes for the displacement problem in cooperation with the international community,

Recalling the relevant norms of international human rights law, international humanitarian law and analogous refugee law, and recognizing that the protection of internally displaced persons has been strengthened by identifying, reaffirming and consolidating specific standards for their protection, in particular through the Guiding Principles on Internal Displacement,

Taking note of Commission on Human Rights resolution 2001/54 of 24 April 2001, and recalling the Vienna Declaration and Programme of Action adopted by the World Conference on Human Rights on 25 June 1993, regarding the need to develop global strategies to address the problem of internal displacement,

Deploring practices of forced displacement and their negative consequences for the enjoyment of fundamental human rights by large groups of populations,

Noting with appreciation the work of the Representative of the Secretary-General on internally displaced persons in developing a normative framework, in particular a compilation and analysis of legal norms and the development of guiding principles, analysing institutional arrangements, undertaking dialogue with Governments and issuing a series of reports on particular country situations together with proposals for remedial measures,

Welcoming the cooperation established between the Representative of the Secretary-General and the United Nations and other international and regional organizations, in particular the participation of the Representative of the Secretary-General in the meetings of the Inter-Agency Standing Committee and its subsidiary bodies, and encouraging further strengthening of this collaboration in order to promote better protection, assistance and development strategies for internally displaced persons,

Recognizing the central role of the Emergency Relief Coordinator for the inter-agency coordination of protection of and assistance to internally displaced persons, and in this regard welcoming the establishment of the Senior Inter-Agency Network on Internal Displacement and the decision to set up within the Office for the Coordination of Humanitarian Affairs of the Secretariat a unit for coordinating activities regarding internally displaced persons in order to promote better protection, assistance and development strategies for internally displaced persons, as well as to enhance further accountability by the United Nations system,

Acknowledging with appreciation the independent coordination within, as well as the independent work of, the International Red Cross and Red Crescent Movement and other humanitarian agencies in protecting and assisting internally displaced persons in cooperation with relevant international bodies,

Recalling its resolution 54/167 of 17 December 1999,

1. *Welcomes* the report of the Representative of the Secretary-General on internally displaced persons;

2. *Commends* the Representative of the Secretary-General for the activities undertaken so far, for the catalytic role that he continues to play in raising the level of consciousness about the plight of internally displaced persons and for his efforts to promote a comprehensive strategy that focuses on prevention as well as better protection, assistance and development for internally displaced persons;

3. *Expresses its appreciation* to those Governments and intergovernmental and non-governmental organizations that have provided protection and assistance to internally displaced persons and have supported the work of the Representative of the Secretary-General;

4. *Encourages* the Representative of the Secretary-General, through continuous dialogue with Governments and all intergovernmental and non-governmental organizations concerned, to continue his analysis of the causes of internal displacement, the needs and rights of those displaced, measures of prevention and ways to strengthen protection, assistance and solutions for internally displaced persons, taking into account specific situations, and to include information thereon in his reports to the Commission on Human Rights and the General Assembly;

5. *Welcomes* the specific attention paid by the Representative of the Secretary-General to the special protection, assistance and development needs of internally displaced women, children and other groups with specific needs and his commitment to pay more systematic and in-depth attention to their needs;

6. *Also welcomes* the fact that the Representative of the Secretary-General has made use of the Guiding

Principles on Internal Displacement in his dialogue with Governments and intergovernmental and non-governmental organizations, and requests him to continue his efforts in that regard, including considering strategies for addressing such concerns;

7. *Notes with appreciation* that an increasing number of States, United Nations agencies and regional and non-governmental organizations are making use of the Guiding Principles, encourages the further dissemination and application of the Guiding Principles, expresses its appreciation for the dissemination and promotion of the Guiding Principles at regional and other seminars on displacement, and encourages the Representative of the Secretary-General to continue to initiate or support such seminars in consultation with regional organizations, intergovernmental and nongovernmental organizations and other relevant institutions, and to provide support for efforts to promote capacity-building and use of the Guiding Principles;

8. *Calls upon* all Governments to continue to facilitate the activities of the Representative of the Secretary-General, in particular Governments with situations of internal displacement, encourages them to give serious consideration to inviting the Representative to visit their countries so as to enable him to study and analyse more fully the issues involved, and thanks those Governments that have already done so;

9. *Invites* Governments to give due consideration, in dialogue with the Representative of the Secretary-General, to the recommendations and suggestions addressed to them, in accordance with his mandate, and to inform him of measures taken thereon;

10. *Calls upon* Governments to provide protection and assistance, including reintegration and development assistance, to internally displaced persons, and to facilitate the efforts of relevant United Nations agencies and humanitarian organizations in these respects, including by further improving access to internally displaced persons;

11. *Notes with appreciation* the increased attention paid to the issue of internally displaced persons in the consolidated inter-agency appeals process, and encourages further efforts to improve the integration of the protection and assistance needs of internally displaced persons in consolidated appeals;

12. *Emphasizes* the central role of the Emergency Relief Coordinator for the inter-agency coordination of protection of and assistance to internally displaced persons, and in this regard urges the Senior Inter-Agency Network on Internal Displacement and all relevant United Nations humanitarian assistance, human rights and development organizations concerned to enhance further their collaboration and coordination, especially through the Inter-Agency Standing Committee, in order to promote and better carry out protection, assistance and development activities for internally displaced persons and to enhance further their accountability, as well as to provide all possible assistance and support to the Representative of the Secretary-General, and invites the Network better to inform Member States of its activities;

13. *Welcomes* the initiatives undertaken by regional organizations, such as the Organization of African Unity, the Organization of American States, the Organization for Security and Cooperation in Europe, the Council of Europe and the Economic Community of West African States, to address the protection, assistance and development needs of internally displaced persons, and encourages them and other regional organizations to strengthen their activities and their cooperation with the Representative of the Secretary-General;

14. *Notes* the establishment of the global internally displaced persons database, as advocated by the Representative of the Secretary-General, and encourages the members of the Inter-Agency Standing Committee and Governments to continue to collaborate on and support this effort, including by providing financial resources;

15. *Requests* the Secretary-General to provide his Representative, from within existing resources, with all necessary assistance to carry out his mandate effectively, and encourages the Representative to continue to seek the contribution of States, relevant organizations and institutions in order to put the work of the Representative on a more stable basis;

16. *Requests* the Representative of the Secretary-General to prepare, for consideration by the General Assembly at its fifty-eighth session, a report on the implementation of the present resolution;

17. *Decides* to continue its consideration of the question of protection of and assistance to internally displaced persons at its fifty-eighth session.

Vulnerable groups

In a September report [A/56/326] on strategies for realizing the goals contained in the UN Millennium Declaration [YUN 2000, p. 49], the Secretary-General identified measures to protect vulnerable groups, particularly women and children, forced into situations of displacement and abuse owing to complex humanitarian emergencies. The measures included prosecuting violations of international criminal law, gaining access to vulnerable populations, separating civilians and armed elements in situations of forced displacement, fostering a culture of protection for refugees and internally displaced persons, and disseminating the Guiding Principles. The report proposed strengthening international cooperation and helping refugees and displaced persons return voluntarily to their homes and reintegrate into their societies. States were encouraged to ratify and implement the 1989 Convention on the Rights of the Child, adopted by General Assembly resolution 44/25 [YUN 1989, p. 561], and its 2000 Optional Protocols on the involvement of children in armed conflict and on the sale of children, child prostitution and child pornography, adopted by Assembly resolution 54/263 [YUN 2000, p. 615] (see p. 595).

Right to asylum

On 16 August [res. 2001/16], the Subcommission, expressing concern over the fate of persons who had risked their lives fleeing from their homes to escape persecution, starvation or destitution, reaffirmed that their human rights should be protected in accordance with international human rights instruments. It urged the UN High Commissioners for Human Rights and for Refugees to intensify efforts to provide women and girl refugees with adequate protection. The Subcommission recommended that States disputing the refugee status of a particular population cooperate with UNHCR and other interested parties to facilitate verification of the status of those who asserted they were refugees, through an impartial and fair process.

Smuggling and trafficking in persons

A July note [E/CN.4/Sub.2/2001/26] by the Secretary-General, submitted in accordance with a 2000 Subcommission decision [YUN 2000, p. 690], defined trafficked persons as victims of serious and systematic human rights violations, particularly vulnerable to further abuse, and stated that a growing number of migrants were being trafficked or smuggled across national borders. The report described international and regional initiatives on trafficking and migrant smuggling and outlined priority areas for action, such as preventive strategies and addressing the reality of increasing diversity.

Peace and security

By a roll-call vote of 29 to 16, with 7 abstentions, the Commission, on 25 April [res. 2001/69], affirming that States should promote international peace and security, urged them to refrain from using weapons with indiscriminate effects on human health, the environment and economic and social well-being and from measures which encouraged the resurgence of a new arms race.

Weapons of mass destruction

By a vote of 21 to 2, the Subcommission, on 16 August [dec. 2001/119], decided to authorize Yeung Kam Yeung Sik Yuen (Mauritius) to prepare for 2002, without financial implications, a working paper assessing the utility, scope and structure of a study on the enjoyment of human rights posed by the testing, production, storage, transfer, trafficking or use of weapons of mass destruction or with indiscriminate effect, or of a nature to cause superfluous injury or unnecessary suffering, including the use of weaponry containing depleted uranium. The working paper originally was assigned to former Subcommission member Clemencia Forero Ucros (Colombia) in 1997 [YUN 1997, p. 668].

Small arms

On 16 August [dec. 2001/120], the Subcommission, noting issues raised at the United Nations Conference on the Illicit Trade in Small Arms and Light Weapons in All Its Aspects (see p. 499), decided to entrust Barbara Frey (United States) with the task of preparing, without financial implications, a working paper on small arms and light weapons and their use, for submission in 2002.

Economic, social and cultural rights

Right to development

Reports of Secretary-General. As requested by the Commission on Human Rights in 2000 [YUN 2000, p. 691], the Secretary-General presented information received from six Governments and one specialized agency [E/CN.4/2001/24] on follow-up to the 1986 Declaration on the Right to Development, contained in General Assembly resolution 41/128 [YUN 1986, p. 717].

Pursuant to a 1999 Subcommission request [YUN 1999, p. 652], the Secretary-General, in a June report with later addendum [E/CN.4/Sub.2/2001/11 & Add.1], described steps taken by UN bodies and agencies to promote international cooperation for the realization of the right to development in the context of the United Nations Decade for the Eradication of Poverty (1997-2006) (see p. 753).

In accordance with Assembly resolution 55/108 [YUN 2000, p. 692] the Secretary-General submitted, in July [A/56/256], a report on the right to development based on information received from five Governments. On 19 December, the Assembly took note of the report (**decision 56/429**).

Report of High Commissioner. In response to a 2000 Commission request [YUN 2000, p. 691], the United Nations High Commissioner for Human Rights described activities undertaken by her Office to implement the right to development [E/CN.4/2001/25], particularly regarding poverty alleviation, the international financial architecture, corporate responsibility, gender mainstreaming, education, health, food, racial discrimination, indigenous people, good governance, and migrants and trafficked persons. She also provided information related to the implementation of General Assembly and Commission resolutions, and on inter-agency coordination within the UN system to implement Commission resolutions.

Reports of independent expert. In accordance with a 2000 Commission resolution [YUN 2000,

p. 691], the independent expert on the right to development, Arjun Sengupta (India), submitted, in January [E/CN.4/2001/WG.18/2], a report aimed at clarifying issues raised by the Commission's Open-ended Working Group on the Right to Development in 2000 [YUN 2000, p. 691] and at assisting the Group in finalizing its report and recommendations to the Commission. The expert made recommendations regarding international cooperation, stating that a development compact was only one model of the cooperation; the feasibility of that approach, as well as other alternatives, would have to be examined further. The expert proposed that countries that wished to implement the right through development compacts establish national human rights commissions to monitor the fulfilment of their obligations. Once an approach was developed, it might be useful to establish a forum under the auspices of the Commission to discuss the problems encountered in the process of realizing the right to development and measures to overcome them.

In a later report [E/CN.4/2002/WG.18/2/Add.1], the expert summarized his November mission, aimed at further developing and gathering support for the development compact, to the Organisation for Economic Cooperation and Development (OECD) (Paris), the United Kingdom Department for International Development (DFID), the International Monetary Fund (IMF), the World Bank and the United States Department of State (Washington, D.C.), and the Netherlands Ministry of Foreign Affairs.

Regarding the interaction of the development compact in the Poverty Reduction Strategy Papers (PRSPs), the expert noted that the World Bank emphasized a positive connection between the PRSP process and a rights-based approach to development. DFID warned against the development compact being weaker than the PRSP process. The issue of international cooperation as an obligation raised problems for many participants. Thus, the expert believed it would be interesting to make a case study of DFID programmes that used human rights–based approaches. The expert stated that his choice of the Development Assistance Committee of OECD to coordinate a support group composed of the World Health Organization (WHO), the Food and Agriculture Organization of the United Nations (FAO), the United Nations Children's Fund (UNICEF), the United Nations Educational, Scientific and Cultural Organization (UNESCO), OHCHR, UNDP, international financial agencies such as IMF, the World Bank and the regional development banks, and interested donor countries raised many questions; he welcomed input on the issue. Although most of the institutions did not commit

themselves to the compact, they respected the expert's proposition to explore it through the appointment of an expert group.

Working group activities. The Open-ended Working Group on the Right to Development held its second session in Geneva from 29 January to 2 February [E/CN.4/2001/26]; it held a resumed session on 26 and 27 February and met on 2 March for the submission of the Chairperson's conclusions.

Participants discussed the independent expert's proposals regarding a development compact and the possibility of using national human rights institutions as monitoring bodies (see above). UN agencies and international organizations presented information on strategies to realize the right and a general discussion took place on national and international action for the realization of the right to development. The Chairperson prepared draft elements for an agreed outcome of the session, which had been accepted by the majority of delegations. However, five States (Australia, Canada, Japan, New Zealand, United States) raised objections to some elements of the text, which were annexed to the report.

The expert was asked to clarify the development compact further and to prepare a preliminary study on the impact of international economic issues on the enjoyment of human rights. The Group recommended the expansion of its 2002 session to 10 days and the extension of the expert's mandate for a further year.

Commission action. By a roll-call vote of 48 to 2, with 3 abstentions, the Commission, on 18 April [res. 2001/9], asked the independent expert to clarify further the proposed development compact and to prepare, in consultation with relevant UN agencies and the Bretton Woods institutions, a preliminary study on the impact of international economic and financial issues, for consideration by the Working Group. The Group and the independent expert were asked to consider the outcomes of international conferences, such as the South Summit of the Group of 77 [YUN 2000, p. 782] and the follow-up thereto, in elaborating recommendations for implementing the right to development. OHCHR, UN specialized agencies, funds and programmes, the international financial institutions and other actors were asked to collaborate with the independent expert. The Commission recommended that the Economic and Social Council extend the Group's mandate for a further year and that of the independent expert for another three years.

On 24 July, the Council approved the Commission's recommendations and its requests to the independent expert, the Working Group, OHCHR and the specialized agencies, funds and programmes and financial institutions (**decision 2001/247**).

On 20 April [res. 2001/30], the Commission called on States to guarantee economic, social and cultural rights without discrimination of any kind; to secure through national development policies, and with international assistance, full realization of those rights, giving particular attention to the most vulnerable and disadvantaged, most often women and children, especially girls, and communities living in extreme poverty; and to promote the effective participation of civil society in decision-making processes related to those rights.

By a roll-call vote of 36 to 16, on 25 April [res. 2001/73], the Commission, recognizing that insufficient attention was paid to international solidarity as a component of efforts of developing countries to realize the right to development, urged the international community to consider ways to promote and consolidate assistance to those countries.

Workshop. OHCHR and Argentina organized a regional workshop (Buenos Aires, 24-27 October) [A/C.3/56/5], aimed at providing a forum where Latin American and Caribbean States could study and discuss strategies to develop policies designed to promote economic, social and cultural rights.

GENERAL ASSEMBLY ACTION

On 19 December [meeting 88], the General Assembly, on the recommendation of the Third Committee [A/56/583/Add.2], adopted **resolution 56/150** by recorded vote (123-4-44) [agenda item 119 (b)].

The right to development

The General Assembly,

Guided by the Charter of the United Nations, which expresses, in particular, the determination to promote social progress and better standards of life in larger freedom as well as to employ international mechanisms for the promotion of the economic and social advancement of all peoples,

Recalling that the Declaration on the Right to Development, adopted by the General Assembly in its resolution 41/128 of 4 December 1986, confirmed that the right to development is an inalienable human right and that equality of opportunity for development is a prerogative both of nations and of individuals who make up nations,

Recalling also that the outcome of the World Conference on Human Rights, held in Vienna from 14 to 25 June 1993, namely the Vienna Declaration and Programme of Action, reaffirmed the right to development as a universal and inalienable right and an integral part of all fundamental human rights,

Recalling further the outcomes of the World Summit for Social Development, and the twenty-fourth special session of the General Assembly entitled "World Sum-

mit for Social Development and beyond: achieving social development for all in a globalizing world", held in Geneva from 26 June to 1 July 2000, especially as they relate to the realization of the right to development,

Recalling its resolution 55/279 of 12 July 2001, in which it endorsed the Brussels Declaration and the Programme of Action for the Least Developed Countries for the Decade 2001-2010 adopted by the Third United Nations Conference on the Least Developed Countries, held in Brussels from 14 to 20 May 2001, and in this regard emphasizing the importance of implementation and follow-up to the Brussels commitments,

Welcoming the report of the Secretary-General, in preparation for the International Conference on Financing for Development to be held in Monterrey, Mexico, from 18 to 22 March 2002, and expressing its hope that the Conference will set a new partnership for financing sustainable development and for the implementation of the goals set out in the United Nations Millennium Declaration and other internationally agreed development targets,

Taking note of the three studies prepared by the independent expert on the right to development and his proposed possible approaches to the operationalization of the right to development,

Taking note also of the report of the Open-ended Working Group on the Right to Development established to monitor and review progress made in the promotion and implementation of the right to development and of the Chairperson's conclusions on the issue, as well as the comments submitted thereon,

Welcoming the commitment made by the heads of State and Government in the United Nations Millennium Declaration to make the right to development a reality for everyone and their resolve to create an environment, at the national and global levels alike, which is conducive to development and to the elimination of poverty, and their commitment to spare no effort to promote good governance and democracy and to strengthen the rule of law as well as respect for all universally recognized human rights and fundamental freedoms, including the right to development,

Underlining the fact that meeting the objectives of good governance also depends on good governance at the international level and on transparency in the financial, monetary and trading systems and an open, equitable, rules-based, predictable and non-discriminatory multilateral trading and financial system,

Underlining also the fact that the realization of the right to development requires effective development policies at the national level as well as equitable economic relations and a favourable economic environment at the international level,

Underlining further the important role of the United Nations High Commissioner for Human Rights in the promotion and protection of the right to development,

Recalling the need for coordination and cooperation throughout the United Nations system for a more effective promotion and realization of the right to development,

Taking note of the outcome of the South Summit of the Group of Seventy-seven, held in Havana from 10 to 14 April 2000, relating to the realization of the right to development,

1. *Welcomes* the holding of two sessions of the Open-ended Working Group on the Right to Development from 18 to 22 September 2000 and from 29 January to 2 February 2001, which focused on certain issues, as reflected in the report of the Working Group, and emphasizes the need to continue deliberations on the right to development in all its aspects, inter alia, on the basis of the report of the Working Group and the Chairperson's conclusions, as well as comments submitted thereon;

2. *Emphasizes* that, on the basis of the text of the Declaration on the Right to Development, several resolutions and declarations adopted by consensus at subsequent international conferences and the Vienna Declaration and Programme of Action, it should now be possible to reach consensus on the full implementation of the right to development;

3. *Expresses its appreciation* for the reports of the independent expert on the right to development and his additional work on and clarifications of the "development compact" proposal, which contributed to a better understanding of that proposal, while recognizing that further clarification is still needed;

4. *Recognizes* that any development compact would be of a voluntary nature for all parties involved and that its content would be defined on a case-by-case basis and be adapted to the priorities and realities of any country willing to conclude such a compact, which would need the adherence and the support of all international actors involved in its implementation;

5. *Notes* the request by the Commission on Human Rights that the independent expert clarify further the proposed development compact, taking into consideration views expressed during the two sessions of the Working Group and in broad consultation with the Office of the United Nations High Commissioner for Human Rights and United Nations funds and programmes, as well as the specialized agencies, relevant international and regional organizations, nongovernmental organizations and, in particular, those actors and States interested in developing pilot projects in this regard, keeping in mind:

(*a*) The ongoing bilateral, regional and multilateral development cooperation programmes;

(*b*) The formulation of an operational model for a development compact;

(*c*) The views of concerned international organizations and agencies and relevant regional institutions and actors;

(*d*) The need to ensure the added value of a development compact to and its complementarity with the relevant existing mechanisms;

(*e*) The need to address and remedy the national and international dimensions of corruption;

(*f*) The need for country-specific studies from both a national and an international perspective;

6. *Reaffirms* that States have the primary responsibility for the creation of national and international conditions favourable to the realization of the right to development and that they are committed to cooperating with each other to that end;

7. *Also reaffirms* that the realization of the right to development is essential to the implementation of the Vienna Declaration and Programme of Action, which regards all human rights as universal, indivisible, interdependent and interrelated, and which also places the human person at the centre of development and recognizes that, while development facilitates the enjoyment of all human rights, the lack of development may not be invoked to justify the abridgement of internationally recognized human rights;

8. *Recognizes* that, in order to realize the right to development, national action and international cooperation must reinforce each other in a manner that goes beyond the measures for realizing each individual right, and also recognizes that international cooperation for the realization of the right to development should be conducted in the spirit of a partnership, in full respect for all human rights, which are universal, indivisible, interdependent and interrelated;

9. *Also recognizes* that, for many developing countries, the realization of the rights to, inter alia, food, health and education may be important development entry points to the realization of the right to development and that, in this context, the concept of a development compact proposed by the independent expert intends to give expression to some basic tenets of the interdependence of all human rights and national ownership of development strategies and programmes, as well as the importance of international cooperation;

10. *Notes* the ongoing discussion on the question of a suitable permanent follow-up mechanism and the different views expressed thereon in the Working Group, and recognizes the need for a discussion on this issue;

11. *Stresses* the necessity of establishing, at the national level, an enabling legal, political, economic and social environment for the realization of the right to development, and emphasizes the importance of democratic, participatory, transparent and accountable governance, as well as the need for efficient national mechanisms, such as national human rights commissions, to ensure respect for civil, economic, cultural, political and social rights, without any distinction;

12. *Also stresses* the need to prevent, address and take effective action against corruption, at both the national and international levels, including by establishing a firm legal structure for eradicating corruption, and urges States to take all necessary measures to that end;

13. *Recognizes* the importance of the role of the State, civil society, free and independent media, national institutions, the private sector and other relevant institutions in the realization of the right to development, and also recognizes the need to continue discussion on this subject;

14. *Affirms* the role of women in the process of the realization of the right to development, including their role as active participants in and beneficiaries of development, and the need for further actions in this context to ensure the participation of women on equal terms with men in all fields in the realization of the right to development;

15. *Also affirms* the promotion of gender equality and the empowerment of women as effective means to combat poverty, hunger and disease and to stimulate sustainable development, as well as the importance of equal rights and opportunities for women and men, including property rights for women and their access to bank loans, mortgages and other forms of financial

credit, taking into account the best practices of micro-credit in different parts of the world;

16. *Underlines* the fact that, in the process of the realization of the right to development, special attention should be given to persons belonging to minorities, whether national, ethnic, religious or linguistic, as well as to persons belonging to vulnerable groups, such as elderly people, indigenous people, persons facing discrimination on multiple grounds, Roma, migrants, persons with disabilities and children and persons infected with the human immunodeficiency virus/acquired immunodeficiency syndrome (HIV/AIDS), and that such attention should have a gender perspective;

17. *Affirms* in this context that attention should also be given to the right to development of children, with special attention to the rights of the girl child;

18. *Acknowledges* the need to continue discussion on the role of civil society in the realization of the right to development and the role of national institutions in this respect;

19. *Reaffirms* the need for States to cooperate with each other in ensuring development and eliminating obstacles to development, recognizes the importance of the international community in promoting effective international cooperation for the realization of the right to development, and also recognizes that lasting progress towards the implementation of the right to development requires effective development policies at the national level, as well as equitable economic relations and a favourable economic environment at the international level;

20. *Reiterates* that the gap between developed and developing countries remains unacceptably wide, that developing countries continue to face difficulties in participating in the globalization process, and that many risk being marginalized and effectively excluded from its benefits;

21. *Recognizes*, while bearing in mind the existing efforts in this respect, that it is necessary to enhance efforts to consider and evaluate the impact on the enjoyment of human rights of international economic and financial issues, such as:

(*a*) International trade issues;

(*b*) Access to technology;

(*c*) Good governance and equity at the international level;

(*d*) Debt burden;

22. *Notes* the request by the Commission on Human Rights that the independent expert prepare, in consultation with all relevant United Nations agencies and the Bretton Woods institutions, a preliminary study on the impact of those issues on the enjoyment of human rights, starting with an analysis of the existing efforts and means of assessing and evaluating that impact, for consideration by the Working Group at its future sessions;

23. *Also notes* the request by the Commission on Human Rights that the Office of the United Nations High Commissioner for Human Rights, the specialized agencies, funds and programmes, the international financial institutions and other relevant actors collaborate with the independent expert in the fulfilment of his mandate, and encourages further cooperation;

24. *Further notes* the request by the Commission on Human Rights that the Working Group and the independent expert consider, as appropriate, the relevant economic and development outcomes of the international conferences, inter alia, the South Summit of the Group of Seventy-seven, and the follow-up thereto, in elaborating their recommendations for the implementation of the right to development;

25. *Decides* to continue consideration of the issue of the right to development, as a matter of priority, at its fifty-seventh session.

RECORDED VOTE ON RESOLUTION 56/150:

In favour: Afghanistan, Algeria, Angola, Antigua and Barbuda, Argentina, Armenia, Azerbaijan, Bahamas, Bahrain, Bangladesh, Barbados, Belarus, Belize, Benin, Bhutan, Bolivia, Botswana, Brazil, Brunei Darussalam, Burkina Faso, Burundi, Cambodia, Cameroon, Cape Verde, Chad, Chile, China, Colombia, Comoros, Congo, Costa Rica, Côte d'Ivoire, Croatia, Cuba, Democratic People's Republic of Korea, Democratic Republic of the Congo, Djibouti, Dominica, Dominican Republic, Ecuador, Egypt, El Salvador, Equatorial Guinea, Eritrea, Ethiopia, Fiji, Gabon, Gambia, Ghana, Grenada, Guatemala, Guinea, Guyana, Haiti, Honduras, India, Indonesia, Iran, Jamaica, Jordan, Kazakhstan, Kenya, Kuwait, Lao People's Democratic Republic, Lebanon, Libyan Arab Jamahiriya, Madagascar, Malawi, Malaysia, Maldives, Mali, Mauritania, Mauritius, Mexico, Mongolia, Morocco, Mozambique, Myanmar, Namibia, Nepal, Nicaragua, Nigeria, Oman, Pakistan, Panama, Papua New Guinea, Paraguay, Peru, Philippines, Qatar, Russian Federation, Rwanda, Saint Kitts and Nevis, Saint Lucia, Samoa, Saudi Arabia, Senegal, Seychelles, Sierra Leone, Singapore, Solomon Islands, South Africa, Sri Lanka, Sudan, Suriname, Syrian Arab Republic, Thailand, Togo, Tonga, Trinidad and Tobago, Tunisia, Turkey, Turkmenistan, Uganda, Ukraine, United Arab Emirates, United Republic of Tanzania, Uruguay, Vanuatu, Venezuela, Viet Nam, Yemen, Zambia.

Against: Denmark, Israel, Japan, United States.

Abstaining: Albania, Andorra, Australia, Austria, Belgium, Bosnia and Herzegovina, Bulgaria, Canada, Cyprus, Czech Republic, Estonia, Finland, France, Georgia, Germany, Greece, Hungary, Iceland, Ireland, Italy, Latvia, Liechtenstein, Lithuania, Luxembourg, Malta, Marshall Islands, Micronesia, Monaco, Netherlands, New Zealand, Norway, Poland, Portugal, Republic of Korea, Republic of Moldova, Romania, San Marino, Slovakia, Slovenia, Spain, Sweden, The former Yugoslav Republic of Macedonia, United Kingdom, Yugoslavia.

Democratic and equitable international order

By a roll-call vote of 32 to 16, with 4 abstentions, the Commission, on 25 April [res. 2001/65], affirming that a democratic and equitable international order fostered the full realization of human rights, urged States to continue efforts to promote the international order. The Commission asked human rights treaty bodies, OHCHR and Commission and Subcommission mechanisms to contribute to the implementation of its resolution. The Secretary-General was asked to bring the resolution to the attention of Member States, UN organs and bodies, intergovernmental organizations and NGOs and to disseminate it widely. OHCHR was called on to build upon the promotion of a democratic and equitable order and to take the resolution into account when convening any seminar, workshop or other activity relating to democracy.

GENERAL ASSEMBLY ACTION

On 19 December [meeting 88], the General Assembly, on the recommendation of the Third Committee [A/56/583/Add.2], adopted **resolution 56/151** by recorded vote (109-53-6) [agenda item 119 (*b*)].

Promotion of a democratic and equitable international order

The General Assembly,

Recalling its resolution 55/107 of 4 December 2000, and taking note of Commission on Human Rights resolution 2001/65 of 25 April 2001,

Reaffirming the commitment of all States to fulfil their obligations to promote universal respect for, and observance and protection of, all human rights and fundamental freedoms for all, in accordance with the Charter of the United Nations, other instruments relating to human rights and international law,

Affirming that the enhancement of international cooperation for the promotion and protection of all human rights should continue to be carried out in full conformity with the purposes and principles of the Charter and international law as set forth in Articles 1 and 2 of the Charter and, inter alia, with full respect for sovereignty, territorial integrity, political independence, the non-use of force or the threat of force in international relations and non-intervention in matters that are essentially within the domestic jurisdiction of any State,

Recalling the Preamble to the Charter, in particular the determination to reaffirm faith in fundamental human rights, in the dignity and worth of the human person and in the equal rights of men and women and of nations large and small,

Reaffirming that everyone is entitled to a social and international order in which the rights and freedoms set forth in the Universal Declaration of Human Rights can be fully realized,

Reaffirming also the determination expressed in the Preamble to the Charter to save succeeding generations from the scourge of war, to establish conditions under which justice and respect for the obligations arising from treaties and other sources of international law can be maintained, to promote social progress and better standards of life in larger freedom, to practise tolerance and good-neighbourliness, and to employ international machinery for the promotion of the economic and social advancement of all peoples,

Considering the major changes taking place on the international scene and the aspirations of all peoples for an international order based on the principles enshrined in the Charter, including promoting and encouraging respect for human rights and fundamental freedoms for all and respect for the principle of equal rights and self-determination of peoples, peace, democracy, justice, equality, the rule of law, pluralism, development, better standards of living and solidarity,

Considering also that the Universal Declaration of Human Rights proclaims that all human beings are born free and equal in dignity and rights and that everyone is entitled to all the rights and freedoms set out therein, without distinction of any kind, such as race, colour, sex, language, religion, political or other opinion, national or social origin, property, birth or other status,

Reaffirming that democracy, development and respect for human rights and fundamental freedoms are interdependent and mutually reinforcing, and that democracy is based on the freely expressed will of the people to determine their own political, economic, social and cultural systems and their full participation in all aspects of their lives,

Emphasizing that democracy is not only a political concept but that it also has economic and social dimensions,

Recognizing that democracy, respect for all human rights, including the right to development, transparent and accountable governance and administration in all sectors of society, and effective participation by civil society are an essential part of the necessary foundations for the realization of social and people-centred sustainable development,

Underlining the fact that it is imperative for the international community to ensure that globalization becomes a positive force for all the world's people, and that only through broad and sustained efforts, based on common humanity in all its diversity, can globalization be made fully inclusive and equitable,

Stressing that efforts to make globalization fully inclusive and equitable must include policies and measures, at the global level, that correspond to the needs of developing countries and countries with economies in transition and are formulated and implemented with their effective participation,

Resolved, at the beginning of a new century and millennium, to take all measures within its power to secure a democratic and equitable international order,

1. *Affirms* that everyone is entitled to a democratic and equitable international order;

2. *Also affirms* that a democratic and equitable international order fosters the full realization of all human rights for all;

3. *Further affirms* that a democratic and equitable international order requires, inter alia, the realization of the following:

(a) The right of all peoples to self-determination, by virtue of which they can freely determine their political status and freely pursue their economic, social and cultural development;

(b) The right of peoples and nations to permanent sovereignty over their natural wealth and resources;

(c) The right of every human person and all peoples to development;

(d) The right of all peoples to peace;

(e) The promotion of an international economic order based on equal participation in the decision-making process, interdependence, mutual interest, solidarity and cooperation among all States;

(f) Solidarity, as a fundamental value, by virtue of which global challenges must be managed in a way that distributes costs and burdens fairly in accordance with basic principles of equity and social justice and ensures that those who suffer or who benefit the least receive help from those who benefit the most;

(g) The promotion and consolidation of transparent, democratic, just and accountable international institutions in all areas of cooperation, in particular through the implementation of the principles of full and equal participation in their respective decision-making mechanisms;

(h) The principle of equitable regional and gender-balanced representation in the composition of the staff of the United Nations system;

(i) The promotion of a free, just, effective and balanced international information and communications order, based on international cooperation for the establishment of a new equilibrium and greater reciprocity in the international flow of information, in particular, correcting the inequalities in the flow of information to and from developing countries;

(j) Respect for cultural diversity and the cultural rights of all, since this enhances cultural pluralism, contributes to a wider exchange of knowledge and understanding of cultural backgrounds, advances the application and enjoyment of universally accepted human rights across the world and fosters stable, friendly relations among peoples and nations worldwide;

(k) The entitlement of every person and all peoples to a healthy environment;

(l) The promotion of equitable access to benefits from the international distribution of wealth through enhanced international cooperation, in particular in economic, commercial and financial international relations;

(m) The enjoyment by everyone of ownership of the common heritage of mankind;

(n) The shared responsibility of the nations of the world for managing worldwide economic and social development, as well as threats to international peace and security that should be exercised multilaterally;

4. *Stresses* the importance of preserving the rich and diverse nature of the international community of nations and peoples, as well as respect for national and regional particularities and various historical, cultural and religious backgrounds in the enhancement of international cooperation in the field of human rights;

5. *Also stresses* that all human rights are universal, indivisible, interdependent and interrelated and that the international community must treat human rights globally in a fair and equal manner, on the same footing and with the same emphasis, and reaffirms that, while the significance of national and regional particularities and various historical, cultural and religious backgrounds must be borne in mind, it is the duty of States, regardless of their political, economic and cultural systems, to promote and protect all human rights and fundamental freedoms;

6. *Reaffirms* that all States should promote the establishment, maintenance and strengthening of international peace and security and, to that end, should do their utmost to achieve general and complete disarmament under effective international control, as well as to ensure that the resources released by effective disarmament measures are used for comprehensive development, in particular that of the developing countries;

7. *Recalls* the proclamation by the General Assembly of its determination to work urgently for the establishment of an international economic order based on equity, sovereign equality, interdependence, common interest and cooperation among all States, irrespective of their economic and social systems, which shall correct inequalities and redress existing injustices, make it possible to eliminate the widening gap between the developed and the developing countries and ensure steadily accelerating economic and social development and peace and justice for present and future generations;

8. *Reaffirms* that the international community should devise ways and means to remove the current obstacles and meet the challenges to the full realization of all human rights and to prevent the continuation of human rights violations resulting therefrom throughout the world;

9. *Urges* States to continue their efforts, through enhanced international cooperation, towards the promotion of a democratic and equitable international order;

10. *Requests* the Commission on Human Rights, the human rights treaty bodies, the Office of the United Nations High Commissioner for Human Rights and the mechanisms of the Commission on Human Rights and the Subcommission on the Promotion and Protection of Human Rights to pay due attention, within their respective mandates, to the present resolution and to make contributions towards its implementation;

11. *Calls upon* the Office of the United Nations High Commissioner for Human Rights to build upon the issue of the promotion of a democratic and equitable international order and to take into account the present resolution when convening any seminar, workshop or any other activity in relation to the issue of democracy;

12. *Requests* the Secretary-General to bring the present resolution to the attention of Member States, United Nations organs, bodies and components, intergovernmental organizations, in particular the Bretton Woods institutions, and non-governmental organizations and to disseminate it on the widest possible basis;

13. *Decides* to continue consideration of the matter at its fifty-seventh session under the agenda item entitled "Human rights questions".

RECORDED VOTE ON RESOLUTION 56/151:

In favour: Afghanistan, Algeria, Angola, Antigua and Barbuda, Armenia, Azerbaijan, Bahamas, Bahrain, Bangladesh, Barbados, Belarus, Belize, Benin, Bhutan, Bolivia, Botswana, Brazil, Brunei Darussalam, Burkina Faso, Burundi, Cambodia, Cameroon, Cape Verde, Chad, China, Colombia, Comoros, Congo, Costa Rica, Côte d'Ivoire, Cuba, Democratic People's Republic of Korea, Democratic Republic of the Congo, Djibouti, Dominica, Dominican Republic, Ecuador, Egypt, El Salvador, Equatorial Guinea, Eritrea, Ethiopia, Fiji, Gabon, Gambia, Ghana, Grenada, Guinea, Guyana, Haiti, Honduras, India, Indonesia, Iran, Jamaica, Jordan, Kazakhstan, Kenya, Kuwait, Lao People's Democratic Republic, Lebanon, Libyan Arab Jamahiriya, Madagascar, Malawi, Malaysia, Maldives, Mali, Mauritania, Mauritius, Mexico, Mongolia, Morocco, Mozambique, Myanmar, Namibia, Nepal, Nigeria, Oman, Pakistan, Panama, Papua New Guinea, Philippines, Qatar, Russian Federation, Rwanda, Saint Kitts and Nevis, Saint Lucia, Saudi Arabia, Senegal, Seychelles, Sierra Leone, Singapore, Solomon Islands, Sri Lanka, Sudan, Suriname, Syrian Arab Republic, Thailand, Togo, Trinidad and Tobago, Tunisia, Uganda, United Arab Emirates, United Republic of Tanzania, Uruguay, Venezuela, Viet Nam, Yemen, Zambia.

Against: Albania, Andorra, Australia, Austria, Belgium, Bosnia and Herzegovina, Bulgaria, Canada, Chile, Croatia, Cyprus, Czech Republic, Denmark, Estonia, Finland, France, Georgia, Germany, Greece, Hungary, Iceland, Ireland, Israel, Italy, Japan, Latvia, Liechtenstein, Lithuania, Luxembourg, Malta, Marshall Islands, Micronesia, Monaco, Netherlands, New Zealand, Norway, Poland, Portugal, Republic of Korea, Republic of Moldova, Romania, Samoa, San Marino, Slovakia, Slovenia, Spain, Sweden, The former Yugoslav Republic of Macedonia, Tuvalu, Ukraine, United Kingdom, United States, Yugoslavia.

Abstaining: Argentina, Guatemala, Nicaragua, Paraguay, Peru, South Africa.

Globalization

Commission action. By a roll-call vote of 37 to 15, with 1 abstention, the Commission, on 23 April [res. 2001/32], reaffirmed that efforts to make globalization fully inclusive and equitable must include policies and measures at the global level, and asked international economic governance institutions to promote broad-based decision-making. It underlined the need for treaty bodies, special rapporteurs/representatives, independent experts and working groups to take into consideration in their reports the impact of globalization on human rights. The Commission encouraged the Special Rapporteurs on globalization to take into account its resolution in finalizing their study on globalization and its impact on human rights [YUN 2000, p. 696] for consideration in 2003. The High Commissioner, in cooperation with the United Nations Conference on Trade and Development (UNCTAD), was asked to submit a comprehensive report for the Commission's consideration, taking into account the provisions of the resolution.

Report of Secretary-General. In response to General Assembly resolution 55/102 [YUN 2000, p. 696], the Secretary-General submitted a July report with later addendum [A/56/254 & Add.1], presenting the views of seven Governments on globalization and its impact on human rights.

Report of Special Rapporteurs. In an August progress report [E/CN.4/Sub.2/2001/10], the Special Rapporteurs on globalization and its impact on human rights, Joseph Oloka-Onyango (Uganda) and Deepika Udagama (Sri Lanka), updated developments since the submission of their 2000 report [YUN 2000, p. 696]. The report focused on globalization and intellectual property rights, the dispute settlement system of the World Trade Organization (WTO), the poverty eradication strategies of multilateral institutions and international human rights law and its applicability to those institutions. The Special Rapporteurs pointed to the need to strengthen the provisions of the WTO Agreement on Trade-Related Aspects of Intellectual Property Rights (TRIPS), noting that it would be helpful if no provision prohibited WTO members from taking measures to provide access to medicines at affordable prices and to promote public health and nutrition. The obligations within TRIPS and those in various human rights instruments relating to international cooperation and assistance should be given more attention, together with issues such as intellectual property rights and indigenous knowledge or the right to food. As to multilateral institutions, the Special Rapporteurs stated that it was critical to develop minimum guidelines, or a restatement, to serve as a human rights benchmark of acceptable conduct in pursuing the ends of globalization.

Subcommission action. On 15 August [res. 2001/5], the Subcommission encouraged the Special Rapporteurs to examine further the relationship between international human rights law and international economic law, to focus on guidelines and mechanisms to deal effectively with globalization and its impact on human rights, and to propose measures to ensure that the UN human rights regime was strengthened to ad-

dress the challenges of globalization. The Special Rapporteur on the right to food was encouraged to explore the implications for the realization of that right of liberalization of the international trade in agricultural products. The Subcommission recommended that government PRSPs refer to applicable human rights obligations. It further recommended that the Commission request the convening of an expert consultation on economic globalization and human rights, involving the Special Rapporteurs, the Subcommission, UN agencies and other relevant organizations and institutions.

Also on 15 August [dec. 2001/106], the Subcommission appointed Fried van Hoof (Netherlands) as commentator on the minimum guidelines, which would comprise part of the Special Rapporteurs' final 2002 report on globalization.

GENERAL ASSEMBLY ACTION

On 19 December [meeting 88], the General Assembly, on the recommendation of the Third Committee [A/56/583/Add.2], adopted **resolution 56/165** by recorded vote (116-46-9) [agenda item 119 (b)].

Globalization and its impact on the full enjoyment of all human rights

The General Assembly,

Guided by the purposes and principles of the Charter of the United Nations, and expressing in particular the need to achieve international cooperation in promoting and encouraging respect for human rights and fundamental freedoms for all without distinction,

Recalling the Universal Declaration of Human Rights, as well as the Vienna Declaration and Programme of Action adopted by the World Conference on Human Rights on 25 June 1993,

Recalling also the International Covenant on Civil and Political Rights and the International Covenant on Economic, Social and Cultural Rights,

Recalling further the Declaration on the Right to Development adopted by the General Assembly in its resolution 41/128 of 4 December 1986,

Recalling the United Nations Millennium Declaration and the outcome documents of the twenty-third and twenty-fourth special sessions of the General Assembly, held, respectively, in New York from 5 to 10 June 2000 and Geneva from 26 June to 1 July 2000,

Recalling also its resolution 55/102 of 4 December 2000,

Recognizing that all human rights are universal, indivisible, interdependent and interrelated and that the international community must treat human rights globally in a fair and equal manner, on the same footing and with the same emphasis,

Realizing that globalization affects all countries differently and makes them more exposed to external developments, positive as well as negative, including in the field of human rights,

Realizing also that globalization is not merely an economic process but that it also has social, political, environmental, cultural and legal dimensions which have an impact on the full enjoyment of all human rights,

Recognizing that multilateral mechanisms have a unique role to play in meeting the challenges and opportunities presented by globalization,

Expressing concern at the negative impact of international financial turbulence on social and economic development and on the full enjoyment of all human rights,

Deeply concerned that the widening gap between the developed and the developing countries, and within countries, has contributed, inter alia, to deepening poverty and has adversely affected the full enjoyment of all human rights, in particular in developing countries,

Noting that human beings strive for a world that is respectful of human rights and cultural diversity and that, in this regard, they work to ensure that all activities, including those affected by globalization, are consistent with those aims,

1. *Recognizes* that, while globalization, by its impact on, inter alia, the role of the State, may affect human rights, the promotion and protection of all human rights is first and foremost the responsibility of the State;

2. *Reaffirms* that narrowing the gap between rich and poor, both within and between countries, is an explicit goal at the national and international levels, as part of the effort to create an enabling environment for the full enjoyment of all human rights;

3. *Also reaffirms* the commitment to create an environment at both the national and the global level that is conducive to development and to the elimination of poverty through, inter alia, good governance within each country and at the international level, transparency in the financial, monetary and trading systems and commitment to an open, equitable, rule-based, predictable and non-discriminatory multilateral trading and financial system;

4. *Recognizes* that, while globalization offers great opportunities, its benefits are very unevenly shared and its costs are unevenly distributed, an aspect of the process that affects the full enjoyment of all human rights, in particular in developing countries;

5. *Also recognizes* that only through broad and sustained efforts, including policies and measures at the global level to create a shared future based upon our common humanity in all its diversity, can globalization be made fully inclusive and equitable and have a human face, thus contributing to the full enjoyment of all human rights;

6. *Affirms* that globalization is a complex process of structural transformation, with numerous interdisciplinary aspects, which has an impact on the enjoyment of civil, political, economic, social and cultural rights, including the right to development;

7. *Also affirms* that the international community should strive to respond to the challenges and opportunities posed by globalization in a manner that ensures respect for the cultural diversity of all;

8. *Underlines,* therefore, the need to continue to analyse the consequences of globalization for the full enjoyment of all human rights;

9. *Takes note* of the report of the Secretary-General, and requests the Secretary-General to seek further the views of Member States and to submit a comprehensive report on this subject to the General Assembly at its fifty-seventh session.

RECORDED VOTE ON RESOLUTION 56/165:

In favour: Afghanistan, Algeria, Angola, Antigua and Barbuda, Argentina, Armenia, Azerbaijan, Bahamas, Bahrain, Bangladesh, Barbados, Belarus, Belize, Benin, Bhutan, Bolivia, Botswana, Brazil, Brunei Darussalam, Burkina Faso, Burundi, Cambodia, Cameroon, Cape Verde, Chad, China, Comoros, Congo, Costa Rica, Côte d'Ivoire, Cuba, Democratic People's Republic of Korea, Democratic Republic of the Congo, Djibouti, Dominica, Dominican Republic, Ecuador, Egypt, El Salvador, Equatorial Guinea, Eritrea, Ethiopia, Fiji, Gabon, Gambia, Ghana, Grenada, Guinea, Guyana, Haiti, Honduras, India, Indonesia, Iran, Jamaica, Jordan, Kazakhstan, Kenya, Kuwait, Lao People's Democratic Republic, Lebanon, Libyan Arab Jamahiriya, Madagascar, Malawi, Malaysia, Maldives, Mali, Mauritania, Mauritius, Mexico, Mongolia, Morocco, Mozambique, Myanmar, Namibia, Nepal, Nicaragua, Nigeria, Oman, Pakistan, Palau, Panama, Papua New Guinea, Paraguay, Philippines, Qatar, Russian Federation, Rwanda, Saint Kitts and Nevis, Saint Lucia, Samoa, Saudi Arabia, Senegal, Seychelles, Sierra Leone, Solomon Islands, South Africa, Sri Lanka, Sudan, Suriname, Syrian Arab Republic, Thailand, Togo, Trinidad and Tobago, Tunisia, Turkey, Tuvalu, Uganda, United Arab Emirates, United Republic of Tanzania, Uruguay, Vanuatu, Venezuela, Viet Nam, Yemen, Zambia.

Against: Albania, Andorra, Australia, Austria, Belgium, Bosnia and Herzegovina, Bulgaria, Canada, Cyprus, Czech Republic, Denmark, Estonia, Finland, France, Georgia, Germany, Greece, Hungary, Iceland, Ireland, Israel, Italy, Japan, Latvia, Liechtenstein, Lithuania, Luxembourg, Malta, Marshall Islands, Monaco, Netherlands, New Zealand, Norway, Poland, Portugal, Republic of Moldova, Romania, San Marino, Slovakia, Slovenia, Spain, Sweden, Ukraine, United Kingdom, United States, Yugoslavia.

Abstaining: Chile, Colombia, Croatia, Guatemala, Micronesia, Peru, Republic of Korea, Singapore, The former Yugoslav Republic of Macedonia.

Intellectual property rights

Report of Secretary-General. Pursuant to a 2000 Subcommission request [YUN 2000, p. 697], the Secretary-General, in a June report with later addendum [E/CN.4/Sub.2/2001/12 & Add.1], transmitted the views of four States, one UN body, two specialized agencies and 10 NGOs on intellectual property rights and human rights.

Report of High Commissioner. As requested by the Subcommission in 2000 [YUN 2000, p. 697], the High Commissioner, in a June report [E/CN.4/Sub.2/2001/13] on the human rights impact of the TRIPS Agreement, focused on the right to health. She decided to focus on the TRIPS Agreement and the right to health in order to expand on work done by other international organizations in that area and, as the issue of trade agreements and health had been raised at world conferences, the report could be situated within an identifiable international policy context.

The High Commissioner believed that implementation of the Agreement should be characterized by a series of objectives. In that regard, she encouraged States to monitor the implementation of the Agreement to ensure that its minimum standards achieved a balance between the interests of the general public and those of the authors; develop competition laws to prevent abuses of intellectual property rights that led to violations of the right to health, particularly restrictive licensing practices or setting high prices for essential drugs; and implement in national legislation several provisions of the Agreement that offered flexibility in promoting access to affordable essential drugs. Developing countries were encouraged to establish incentives to promote technology transfer and the supply of affordable drugs to them. The High Commissioner supported a call of WHO that countries, when establishing standards of patentability for pharmaceuticals, should consider the implications for health of those standards. She urged the adaptation of intellectual property systems to take account of the rights of indigenous and local communities. The High Commissioner recommended that the Subcommission request further reports on the impact of the Agreement on other specific human rights and recommend that the Commission convoke an expert seminar to consider the human rights dimensions of the Agreement.

Subcommission action. On 16 August [res. 2001/21], the Subcommission requested the High Commissioner to seek observer status with WTO for the ongoing review of the TRIPS Agreement; examine and, if necessary, investigate whether the patent, as a legal instrument, was compatible with human rights promotion and protection; and analyse the impact of the Agreement on the rights of indigenous peoples. It called on her to convene an expert seminar to consider the human rights dimension of the Agreement and to report thereon to the Commission in 2003. The Special Rapporteurs on the right to food, on education and on adequate housing were encouraged to include in their reports a review of the implication of the Agreement for the realization of the rights falling within their mandates.

Liberalization of trade in services

On 15 August [res. 2001/4], the Subcommission requested the High Commissioner to submit in 2002 a report on the human rights implications of liberalization of trade in services. UN agencies, particularly WHO and UNESCO, were encouraged to analyse the implementation of the General Agreement on Trade in Services (GATS) on health and education services. The Subcommission recommended that WTO, in assessing the impact of GATS in its current and future forms, consider the human rights implications of international trade in basic services, such as affordable and accessible health and education services, and the further liberalization thereof. It also recommended that WTO, in the assessment, take into account the report to be prepared by the High Commissioner and any analysis prepared by UN agencies. The High Commissioner and UN agencies that had not already done so were encouraged to request observer status with the the WTO Council for Trade in Services.

Structural adjustment policies

Report of independent expert. In a January report [E/CN.4/2001/56], the independent expert on the effects of structural adjustment policies and foreign debt on human rights, Fantu Cheru (United States), analysed the steps taken since 1999 to grant debt relief to qualifying countries. The report was based on the interim PRSPs of nine States, which were annexed to the report. It focused mainly on the Heavily Indebted Poor Countries (HIPC) Initiative, designed to reduce debts to sustainable levels for poor countries that pursued economic and social policy reforms.

The expert made recommendations to expedite the process of granting immediate relief to eligible HIPC countries, including unlinking the HIPC debt relief from the PRSP process, as their association removed the autonomy of countries to develop a framework that made a connection between macroeconomic policies and poverty reduction goals. He also proposed including UN entities other than the World Bank and IMF in the process; initiating new talks aimed at resolving the debt burden of poor countries; abolishing the IMF poverty reduction and growth facility; and beginning a dialogue on integrating macroeconomic policy issues with broader social development goals.

Note by Secretariat. A February note by the Secretariat [E/CN.4/2001/57] stated that the session of the working group on structural adjustment programmes and economic, social and cultural rights, scheduled to take place prior to the Commission's 2001 session, was postponed. The group last met in 2000 [YUN 2000, p. 698].

Commission action. By a roll-call vote of 31 to 15, with 7 abstentions, the Commission, on 20 April [res. 2001/27], called on Governments, international financial institutions and the private sector to consider cancelling or reducing the debt of heavily indebted poor countries. It requested the independent expert to report annually and the Secretary-General to assist him.

The Commission asked the Economic and Social Council to authorize the working group on structural adjustment to meet for two weeks prior to the Commission's 2002 session to continue elaborating policy guidelines on structural adjustment programmes and economic, social and cultural rights and to report in 2002. On 24 July, the Council authorized the Commission's request (**decision 2001/260**).

Following the expert's resignation in September, the Commission appointed Bernards Andrew Nyamwaya Mudho (Kenya).

Social Forum

Commission action. On 23 April [dec. 2001/103], the Commission, taking note of a 2000 Subcommission resolution [YUN 2000, p. 699], authorized the Subcommission to hold in 2001 a Social Forum, which would focus on economic, social and cultural rights.

Subcommission action. On 16 August [res. 2001/24], the Subcommission, welcoming a preparatory panel meeting on the Social Forum, which recognized the need for a new process within the UN system with broad participation, reflecting the current structure of international society, decided that the Social Forum would meet every year to exchange information on the enjoyment of economic, social and cultural rights and their relationship with the process of globalization, follow up on situations of poverty and destitution and on agreements reached at major world conferences, and propose juridical standards and initiatives, as well as guidelines and recommendations for consideration by the Commission, the Working Group on the Right to Development (see p. 657), the Committee on Economic, Social and Cultural Rights, the specialized agencies and UN bodies. The Subcommission recommended that the Forum address themes relating to civil and political and economic, social and cultural rights; the relationship between poverty, extreme poverty and human rights; income distribution; basic resources; the impact of trade, finance and economic policies on vulnerable groups; multilateral and bilateral international development cooperation; follow-up to world conferences and summits; and social and economic indicators. It decided that the Forum's theme in 2002 would be the relationship between poverty reduction and the realization of the right to food, and asked the High Commissioner to ensure consultation on the theme with those most vulnerable. Subcommission member José Bengoa (Chile) was requested to prepare a preliminary working paper on the methodology and work of the Forum.

The Subcommission invited UN bodies and specialized agencies, functional commissions of the Economic and Social Council, the regional commissions, international financial institutions, the Committee on Economic, Social and Cultural Rights, special rapporteurs and independent experts, NGOs, scholars, trade unions and associations of workers to participate in and to submit studies to the Forum. The Subcommission asked the Forum to submit a report and recommendations in 2002, the Commission and the Council to endorse the holding of the Forum and authorize facilities to prepare and service the event, and the Commission to establish a voluntary fund to facilitate the participation of grass-roots groups and similar organizations for the disadvantaged.

Transnational corporations

The sessional working group on the working methods and activities of transnational corporations (TNCs), at its third session (Geneva, 31 July, 2 and 8 August) [E/CN.4/Sub.2/2001/9], discussed draft guidelines relating to the human rights conduct of companies, which would be legally binding. The group considered a working paper on the topic and papers on economic, social and cultural rights and TNCs, and human rights responsibilities and procedures for implementation and compliance by States and corporations.

Subcommission action. On 31 July [dec. 2001/101], the Subcommission decided to establish a five-member sessional working group to examine the working methods and activities of TNCs.

On 15 August [res. 2001/3], the Subcommission extended for a three-year period the mandate of the group and asked it to report on its 2002 session.

Coercive economic measures

Commission action. By a roll-call vote of 37 to 8, with 8 abstentions, the Commission, on 20 April [res. 2001/26], called on States to avoid the unilateral imposition of coercive economic measures and the extraterritorial application of domestic laws that ran counter to the principles of free trade and hampered the development of developing countries. It decided to consider the negative impact of the measures in its work regarding the implementation of the right to development. The Commission asked the High Commissioner to give urgent consideration to its resolution. The Secretary-General was asked to bring the resolution to the attention of all States, to seek their views on the implications and negative effects of the measures and to report thereon in 2002.

Reports of Secretary-General. Pursuant to a 2000 Commission request [YUN 2000, p. 699], the Secretary-General submitted information received from one State on the implications and negative effects of unilateral coercive measures [E/CN.4/2001/50].

Pursuant to General Assembly resolution 55/110 [YUN 2000, p. 700], the Secretary-General, in a July report with later addendum [A/56/207 & Add.1], presented further information received from five States regarding the effects of unilateral coercive measures.

On 19 December [meeting 88], the General Assembly, on the recommendation of the Third Committee [A/56/583/Add.2], adopted **resolution 56/148** by recorded vote (114-51-2) [agenda item 119 *(b)*].

Human rights and unilateral coercive measures

The General Assembly,

Recalling its resolutions 51/103 of 12 December 1996, 52/120 of 12 December 1997, 53/141 of 9 December 1998, 54/172 of 17 December 1999 and 55/110 of 4 December 2000, as well as Commission on Human Rights resolutions 1998/11 of 9 April 1998 and 2000/11 of 17 April 2000, and taking note of Commission resolution 2001/26 of 20 April 2001,

Reaffirming the pertinent principles and provisions contained in the Charter of Economic Rights and Duties of States proclaimed by the General Assembly in its resolution 3281(XXIX) of 12 December 1974, in particular article 32 thereof, in which it declared that no State may use or encourage the use of economic, political or any other type of measures to coerce another State in order to obtain from it the subordination of the exercise of its sovereign rights,

Taking note of the report submitted by the Secretary-General pursuant to Commission on Human Rights resolution 1999/21 of 23 April 1999, and the report of the Secretary-General on the implementation of resolutions 52/120 and 55/110,

Recognizing the universal, indivisible, interdependent and interrelated character of all human rights, and in this regard reaffirming the right to development as an integral part of all human rights,

Recalling that the World Conference on Human Rights, held at Vienna from 14 to 25 June 1993, called upon States to refrain from any unilateral coercive measure not in accordance with international law and the Charter of the United Nations that creates obstacles to trade relations among States and impedes the full realization of all human rights,

Bearing in mind all the references to this question in the Copenhagen Declaration on Social Development adopted by the World Summit for Social Development on 12 March 1995, the Beijing Declaration and Platform for Action adopted by the Fourth World Conference on Women on 15 September 1995, the Istanbul Declaration on Human Settlements and the Habitat Agenda adopted by the second United Nations Conference on Human Settlements (Habitat II) on 14 June 1996 and their five-year reviews,

Expressing its concern about the negative impact of unilateral coercive measures in the field of international relations, trade, investment and cooperation,

Deeply concerned that, despite the recommendations adopted on this question by the General Assembly and recent major United Nations conferences and contrary to general international law and the Charter of the United Nations, unilateral coercive measures continue to be promulgated and implemented with all their negative implications for the social-humanitarian activities and economic and social development of developing countries, including their extraterritorial effects, thereby creating additional obstacles to the full enjoyment of all human rights by peoples and individuals under the jurisdiction of other States,

Bearing in mind all the extraterritorial effects of any unilateral legislative, administrative and economic measures, policies and practices of a coercive nature against the development process and the enhancement of human rights in developing countries, which create obstacles to the full realization of all human rights,

Noting the continuing efforts of the Open-ended Working Group on the Right to Development of the Commission on Human Rights, and reaffirming in particular its criteria according to which coercive measures are one of the obstacles to the implementation of the Declaration on the Right to Development,

1. *Urges* all States to refrain from adopting or implementing any unilateral measures not in accordance with international law and the Charter of the United Nations, in particular those of a coercive nature with all their extraterritorial effects, which create obstacles to trade relations among States, thus impeding the full realization of the rights set forth in the Universal Declaration of Human Rights and other international human rights instruments, in particular the right of individuals and peoples to development;

2. *Invites* all States to consider adopting administrative or legislative measures, as appropriate, to counteract the extraterritorial application or effects of unilateral coercive measures;

3. *Rejects* unilateral coercive measures with all their extraterritorial effects as tools for political or economic pressure against any country, in particular against developing countries, because of their negative effects on the realization of all the human rights of vast sectors of their populations, in particular children, women and the elderly;

4. *Calls upon* Member States that have initiated such measures to commit themselves to their obligations and responsibilities arising from the international human rights instruments to which they are party by revoking such measures at the earliest possible time;

5. *Reaffirms* in this context the right of all peoples to self-determination, by virtue of which they freely determine their political status and freely pursue their economic, social and cultural development;

6. *Urges* the Commission on Human Rights to take fully into account the negative impact of unilateral coercive measures, including the enactment of national laws and their extraterritorial application, in its task concerning the implementation of the right to development;

7. *Requests* the United Nations High Commissioner for Human Rights, in discharging her functions relating to the promotion, realization and protection of the right to development and bearing in mind the continuing impact of unilateral coercive measures on the population of developing countries, to give priority to the present resolution in her annual report to the General Assembly;

8. *Requests* the Secretary-General to bring the present resolution to the attention of all Member States, to continue to collect their views and information on the implications and negative effects of unilateral coercive measures on their populations and to submit an analytical report thereon to the General Assembly at its fifty-seventh session, highlighting the practical and preventive measures in this respect;

9. *Decides* to examine this question on a priority basis at its fifty-seventh session under the sub-item en-

titled "Human rights questions, including alternative approaches for improving the effective enjoyment of human rights and fundamental freedoms".

RECORDED VOTE ON RESOLUTION 56/148:

In favour: Afghanistan, Algeria, Angola, Antigua and Barbuda, Argentina, Armenia, Bahamas, Bahrain, Bangladesh, Barbados, Belarus, Belize, Benin, Bhutan, Bolivia, Botswana, Brazil, Brunei Darussalam, Burkina Faso, Burundi, Cambodia, Cameroon, Cape Verde, Chile, China, Colombia, Comoros, Congo, Costa Rica, Côte d'Ivoire, Cuba, Democratic People's Republic of Korea, Democratic Republic of the Congo, Djibouti, Dominica, Dominican Republic, Ecuador, Egypt, El Salvador, Equatorial Guinea, Eritrea, Ethiopia, Fiji, Gabon, Gambia, Ghana, Grenada, Guatemala, Guinea, Guyana, Haiti, Honduras, India, Indonesia, Iran, Jamaica, Jordan, Kenya, Kuwait, Lao People's Democratic Republic, Lebanon, Libyan Arab Jamahiriya, Madagascar, Malawi, Malaysia, Mali, Mauritania, Mauritius, Mexico, Mongolia, Morocco, Mozambique, Myanmar, Namibia, Nepal, Nicaragua, Nigeria, Oman, Pakistan, Panama, Papua New Guinea, Paraguay, Peru, Philippines, Qatar, Russian Federation, Rwanda, Saint Kitts and Nevis, Saint Lucia, Samoa, Saudi Arabia, Senegal, Seychelles, Sierra Leone, Singapore, Solomon Islands, South Africa, Sri Lanka, Sudan, Suriname, Syrian Arab Republic, Thailand, Togo, Trinidad and Tobago, Tunisia, Uganda, United Arab Emirates, United Republic of Tanzania, Uruguay, Vanuatu, Venezuela, Viet Nam, Yemen, Zambia.

Against: Albania, Andorra, Australia, Austria, Belgium, Bosnia and Herzegovina, Bulgaria, Canada, Croatia, Cyprus, Czech Republic, Denmark, Estonia, Finland, France, Georgia, Germany, Greece, Hungary, Iceland, Ireland, Israel, Italy, Japan, Latvia, Liechtenstein, Lithuania, Luxembourg, Malta, Marshall Islands, Micronesia, Monaco, Netherlands, New Zealand, Norway, Poland, Portugal, Republic of Korea, Republic of Moldova, Romania, San Marino, Slovakia, Slovenia, Spain, Sweden, The former Yugoslav Republic of Macedonia, Turkey, Ukraine, United Kingdom, United States, Yugoslavia.

Abstaining: Azerbaijan, Kazakhstan.

Extreme poverty

Report of independent expert. Pursuant to a 2000 Commission request [YUN 2000, p. 702], the independent expert on the question of human rights and extreme poverty, Anne-Marie Lizin (Belgium), in a February report [E/CN.4/2001/54 & Corr.1], stated that extreme poverty was worsening in several parts of the world. She noted that migration to escape extreme poverty had expanded. On the positive side, there was a greater commitment on the part of the United Nations, increased awareness of the problem among Governments and NGOs, and changes in the attitudes of international financial institutions, particularly by IMF, which was endeavouring to create conditions for equitable and sustainable growth—the largest contributory factor to poverty reduction. The expert described her interviews with IMF representatives, which brought to light the progress it had made during the past two years, and made recommendations regarding IMF operations. She proposed a four-stage strategy, which aimed to establish knowledge of their rights among the poor themselves, training programmes to fight poverty, a campaign against the condition of poverty and mobilization through a world alliance against poverty. The report contained an analysis of comments on her first report [YUN 2000, p. 701] submitted by Governments, UN bodies and NGOs. Annexed to the report were questionnaires on extreme poverty and human rights sent to Governments, national human

rights bodies and NGOs, as well as one used by the expert during her interviews with the poorest people.

Expert seminar. In response to a 2000 Commission request [YUN 2000, p. 702], OHCHR organized an expert seminar, attended by government, UN and NGO representatives (Geneva, 7-9 February) [E/CN.4/2001/54/Add.1 & Corr.1], to consider the need to develop a draft declaration on extreme poverty and, if appropriate, identify its specific points. As the majority of participants were in favour of a new document, they discussed the possible forms of a text. They expressed the opinion that a human rights–based approach to poverty eradication was an integral part of a human rights–based approach to development and that the text would serve as an interpretative instrument for development work in general and poverty eradication more specifically.

Commission action. On 23 April [res. 2001/31], the Commission called on the General Assembly, specialized agencies, UN bodies and intergovernmental organizations to take into account the contradiction between the existence of extreme poverty and exclusion from society and the duty to guarantee the enjoyment of human rights. States, intergovernmental organizations and NGOs were urged to take into account the links between human rights and extreme poverty, as well as efforts to empower people living in poverty to participate in decision-making processes; they were asked to submit their comments on the independent expert's report in time for the Commission's 2002 session. The United Nations was urged to strengthen poverty eradication as a priority throughout the system. Taking note of the expert seminar, the Commission asked the Subcommission to consider the need to develop guiding principles on the implementation of existing human rights norms and standards in the fight against extreme poverty and to report in 2003. States, UN bodies, specialized agencies, funds and programmes, the functional commissions of the Economic and Social Council, regional commissions and international financial institutions were invited to submit their views on the subject.

Report of Secretary-General. In response to a 1999 Subcommission request [YUN 1999, p. 652], the Secretary-General, in a June report with later addendum [E/CN.4/Sub.2/2001/11 & Add.1], submitted information on the activities taken by UN bodies and the specialized agencies to enhance international cooperation on the right to development in the context of the United Nations Decade for the Eradication of Poverty (1997-2006) (see p. 753).

Subcommission action. On 15 August [res. 2001/8], the Subcommission requested Paulo Sérgio Pinheiro (Brazil), Yozo Yokota (Japan),

El Hadji Guissé (Senegal) and José Bengoa (Chile) to prepare for consideration in 2002 a joint working paper, without financial implications, on the need to develop guiding principles on the implementation of existing human rights norms and standards in the context of the fight against extreme poverty. They were also asked to consider the situations of poverty in Asia, Africa and Latin America, as well as the policies of the World Bank, IMF, WTO and other international bodies to fight poverty, and to present conclusions and recommendations in order to contribute to work on a draft declaration on extreme poverty and human rights and other international and regional initiatives. The Secretariat was asked to assist in the study, while Governments and regional specialized agencies in Asia, Africa and Latin America were asked to provide information.

Right to food

Report of Special Rapporteur. Pursuant to a 2000 Commission request [YUN 2000, p. 704], the Special Rapporteur on the right to food, Jean Ziegler (Switzerland), in a February report [E/CN.4/2001/53], considered the legal definition of the right, relevant international instruments, steps to encourage countries to introduce the right to food in their legislation and the obstacles to the realization of the right, such as developments in world trade, external debt servicing, biotechnology and genetically modified plants, wars, corruption, access to land and credit, and discrimination against women. The Special Rapporteur recommended the provision of local seed and land to families, the extension of daily school meals to all needy children and the introduction of school meal vouchers, and basic food subsidies and food tickets for the most deprived. He asked the Commission to grant him the financial means to convene an international expert seminar to lay the foundation for a handbook on the right to food, confirm his mandate to respond to reliable information on violations of the right to food, entitling him to address urgent appeals to Governments responsible for serious violations, and clarify that the term "food" covered not only solid food but also the nutritional aspects of drinking water.

Expert consultation. As requested by the Commission in 2000 [YUN 2000, p. 704], OHCHR organized an expert consultation on the right to food (Bonn, Germany, 12-14 March) [E/CN.4/2001/148], which focused on implementation mechanisms and on the monitoring role of national human rights commissions, ombudsmen and related institutions. The participants, who represented all regions, explored rights-based policy formulation and programming for food and nutrition security, national legal instruments and institutions, and the justiciability of the right to food and related rights. Presentations reviewed the situation and prospects concerning the national implementation of the right to food in 14 countries.

The consultation recommended new and stronger measures at the national level to increase the accountability of States through a multi-pronged strategy for national implementation, as set out in General Comment No. 12, adopted by the Committee on Economic, Social and Cultural Rights in 1999 [YUN 1999, p. 575]. As to international implementation, it proposed that the Committee reformulate its current guidelines for States reporting on article 11 (the right to adequate food) of the International Covenant on Economic, Social and Cultural Rights (see p. 590), taking into account General Comment No. 12. Further expert consultations were recommended on international obligations and implementation under the International Covenant, particularly the right to food; ways to integrate the right into poverty-related policies, strategies and programmes; and the role of national institutions in monitoring the implementation and realization of the right.

Commission action. By a roll-call vote of 52 to 1, the Commission, on 20 April [res. 2001/25], reaffirming that hunger constituted a violation of human dignity, considered it intolerable that 826 million people did not have enough food to meet their basic nutritional needs. The Special Rapporteur was requested to seek, receive and respond to information on the right to food, including the urgent necessity of eradicating hunger; cooperate with Governments, intergovernmental organizations, particularly FAO, and NGOs; identify emerging issues related to that right worldwide; pay attention to the issue of drinking water; mainstream a gender perspective in his activities; and submit a preliminary report to the General Assembly in 2001 and a final report to the Commission in 2002. He was also asked to contribute to the medium-term review of the 1996 Rome Declaration on World Food Security and the Plan of Action of the World Food Summit [YUN 1996, p. 1129] by submitting his recommendations on the right to food to the High Commissioner. The High Commissioner was asked to assist him. Governments, UN agencies, funds and programmes, treaty bodies and NGOs were invited to cooperate with the Special Rapporteur by submitting suggestions on ways to realize the right to food.

The Commission recommended that the High Commissioner organize a further consultation on the right to food, focusing on the realization of the right as part of strategies and policies for the eradication of poverty.

On 24 July, the Economic and Social Council approved the Commission's requests to the Special Rapporteur and to the High Commissioner to organize an expert consultation (**decision 2001/259**).

Preliminary report of Special Rapporteur. In July [A/56/210], the Secretary-General transmitted the Special Rapporteur's preliminary report on the right to food. The Special Rapporteur reviewed the legal basis for the right to food and examined the right in situations of armed conflict. He also discussed clean drinking water as a component of healthy nutrition and international trade rules and food security. He proposed steps to implement national legislation and for local food security.

The Special Rapporteur called on the General Assembly to reiterate the urgency of eliminating hunger and malnutrition. He made a series of recommendations relating to food security, the nutritional aspects of water and national legislation, and proposed that States adopt an international code of conduct on the right to food, as voluntary guidelines aimed at achieving food security for all.

Subcommission action. On 15 August [res. 2001/7], the Subcommission appealed to world leaders attending the five-year review of the 1996 World Food Summit [YUN 1996, p. 1129] (see p. 1141) to call on States to develop a national strategy to implement that right; promote the incorporation of the right in poverty reduction strategies; encourage further clarification of States' international responsibilities in implementing the right to food; and mobilize and optimize the allocation and utilization of resources to implement sustainable food security policies.

GENERAL ASSEMBLY ACTION

On 19 December [meeting 88], the General Assembly, on the recommendation of the Third Committee [A/56/583/Add.2], adopted **resolution 56/155** by recorded vote (169-2-2) [agenda item 119 *(b)*].

The right to food

The General Assembly,

Recalling all Commission on Human Rights resolutions in this regard, in particular resolution 2000/10 of 17 April 2000, and taking note of Commission resolution 2001/25 of 20 April 2001,

Recalling also the Universal Declaration of Human Rights, which provides that everyone has the right to a standard of living adequate for her/his health and well-being, including food,

Recalling further the provisions of the International Covenant on Economic, Social and Cultural Rights, in which the fundamental right of every person to be free from hunger is recognized,

Recalling the Universal Declaration on the Eradication of Hunger and Malnutrition,

Bearing in mind the Rome Declaration on World Food Security and the Plan of Action of the World Food Summit,

Reaffirming that all human rights are universal, indivisible, interdependent and interrelated,

Recognizing that the problems of hunger and food insecurity have global dimensions and that they are likely to persist and even to increase dramatically in some regions unless urgent, determined and concerted action is taken, given the anticipated increase in the world's population and the stress on natural resources,

Reaffirming that a peaceful, stable and enabling political, social and economic environment, at both the national and the international level, is the essential foundation which will enable States to give adequate priority to food security and poverty eradication,

Reiterating, as did the Rome Declaration, that food should not be used as an instrument of political or economic pressure, and reaffirming in this regard the importance of international cooperation and solidarity, as well as the necessity of refraining from unilateral measures that are not in accordance with international law and the Charter of the United Nations and that endanger food security,

Convinced that each State must adopt a strategy consistent with its resources and capacities to achieve its individual goals in implementing the recommendations contained in the Rome Declaration and Plan of Action of the World Food Summit and, at the same time, cooperate regionally and internationally in order to organize collective solutions to global issues of food security in a world of increasingly interlinked institutions, societies and economies where coordinated efforts and shared responsibilities are essential,

Stressing the importance of reversing the continuing decline of official development assistance devoted to agriculture, both in real terms and as a share of total official development assistance,

1. *Reaffirms* that hunger constitutes an outrage and a violation of human dignity and therefore requires the adoption of urgent measures at the national, regional and international levels for its elimination;

2. *Also reaffirms* the right of everyone to have access to safe and nutritious food, consistent with the right to adequate food and the fundamental right of everyone to be free from hunger so as to be able fully to develop and maintain their physical and mental capacities;

3. *Considers* it intolerable that 826 million people, most of them women and children, throughout the world and particularly in developing countries, do not have enough food to meet their basic nutritional needs, which infringes upon their fundamental human rights and at the same time can generate additional pressures on the environment in ecologically fragile areas;

4. *Encourages* all States to take steps with a view to achieving progressively the full realization of the right to food, including steps to promote the conditions for everyone to be free from hunger and, as soon as possible, to enjoy fully the right to food, and to elaborate and adopt national plans to combat hunger;

5. *Stresses* the need to make efforts to mobilize and optimize the allocation and utilization of technical and financial resources from all sources, including external debt relief for developing countries, and to reinforce national actions to implement sustainable food security policies;

6. *Urges* States to give adequate priority in their development strategies and expenditures to the realization of the right to food;

7. *Takes note* of the report of the United Nations Children's Fund on early childhood entitled *The State of the World's Children, 2001*, and in this context recalls that the nurturing of young children merits the highest priority;

8. *Takes note with appreciation* of the preliminary report of the Special Rapporteur of the Commission on Human Rights on the right to food, submitted in accordance with Commission resolution 2001/25, and commends the Special Rapporteur for his valuable work in the promotion of the right to food;

9. *Supports* the realization of the mandate of the Special Rapporteur as established by the Commission on Human Rights in its resolutions 2000/10 and 2001/25;

10. *Emphasizes* the request of the Commission on Human Rights to the Special Rapporteur to contribute effectively to the medium-term review of the implementation of the Rome Declaration on World Food Security and the Plan of Action of the World Food Summit by submitting to the United Nations High Commissioner for Human Rights his recommendations on all aspects of the right to food;

11. *Encourages* the Special Rapporteur to mainstream a gender perspective in the activities relating to his mandate;

12. *Requests* the Secretary-General and the High Commissioner to provide all the necessary human and financial resources for the effective fulfilment of the mandate of the Special Rapporteur;

13. *Welcomes* the work already done by the Committee on Economic, Social and Cultural Rights in promoting the right to adequate food, in particular its General Comment No. 12 (1999) on the right to adequate food (article 11 of the International Covenant on Economic, Social and Cultural Rights), in which the Committee affirmed, inter alia, that the right to adequate food is indivisibly linked to the inherent dignity of the human person and is indispensable for the fulfilment of other human rights enshrined in the International Bill of Human Rights, and is also inseparable from social justice, requiring the adoption of appropriate economic, environmental and social policies, at both the national and international levels, oriented to the eradication of poverty and the fulfilment of all human rights for all;

14. *Also welcomes* the convening by the High Commissioner at Bonn, from 12 to 14 March 2001, of the Third Expert Consultation on the Right to Food, with a focus on implementation mechanisms at the country level, hosted by the Government of Germany, and takes note with interest of the report of this meeting;

15. *Supports* the recommendation that the High Commissioner organize a fourth expert consultation on the right to food, with a focus on the realization of this right as part of strategies and policies for the eradication of poverty, inviting experts from all regions;

16. *Requests* the Special Rapporteur to submit a comprehensive report to the Commission on Human Rights at its fifty-eighth session and an interim report to the General Assembly at its fifty-seventh session on the implementation of the present resolution;

17. *Invites* Governments, relevant United Nations agencies, funds and programmes, treaty bodies and non-governmental organizations to cooperate fully with the Special Rapporteur in the fulfilment of his mandate, inter alia, through the submission of comments and suggestions on ways and means of realizing the right to food;

18. *Decides* to continue the consideration of this matter at its fifty-seventh session under the agenda item entitled "Human rights questions".

RECORDED VOTE ON RESOLUTION 56/155:

In favour: Afghanistan, Albania, Algeria, Andorra, Angola, Antigua and Barbuda, Argentina, Armenia, Austria, Azerbaijan, Bahamas, Bahrain, Bangladesh, Barbados, Belarus, Belgium, Belize, Benin, Bhutan, Bolivia, Bosnia and Herzegovina, Botswana, Brazil, Brunei Darussalam, Bulgaria, Burkina Faso, Burundi, Cambodia, Cameroon, Canada, Cape Verde, Chad, Chile, China, Colombia, Comoros, Congo, Costa Rica, Côte d'Ivoire, Croatia, Cuba, Cyprus, Czech Republic, Democratic People's Republic of Korea, Democratic Republic of the Congo, Denmark, Djibouti, Dominica, Dominican Republic, Ecuador, Egypt, El Salvador, Equatorial Guinea, Eritrea, Estonia, Ethiopia, Fiji, Finland, France, Gabon, Gambia, Georgia, Germany, Ghana, Greece, Grenada, Guatemala, Guinea, Guyana, Haiti, Honduras, Hungary, Iceland, India, Indonesia, Iran, Ireland, Italy, Jamaica, Japan, Jordan, Kazakhstan, Kenya, Kuwait, Lao People's Democratic Republic, Latvia, Lebanon, Libyan Arab Jamahiriya, Liechtenstein, Lithuania, Luxembourg, Madagascar, Malawi, Malaysia, Maldives, Mali, Malta, Marshall Islands, Mauritania, Mauritius, Mexico, Micronesia, Monaco, Mongolia, Morocco, Mozambique, Myanmar, Namibia, Nauru, Nepal, Netherlands, Nicaragua, Nigeria, Norway, Oman, Pakistan, Palau, Panama, Papua New Guinea, Paraguay, Peru, Philippines, Poland, Portugal, Qatar, Republic of Korea, Republic of Moldova, Romania, Russian Federation, Rwanda, Saint Kitts and Nevis, Saint Lucia, Samoa, San Marino, Saudi Arabia, Senegal, Seychelles, Sierra Leone, Singapore, Slovakia, Slovenia, Solomon Islands, South Africa, Spain, Sri Lanka, Sudan, Suriname, Sweden, Syrian Arab Republic, Thailand, The former Yugoslav Republic of Macedonia, Togo, Trinidad and Tobago, Tunisia, Turkey, Turkmenistan, Tuvalu, Uganda, Ukraine, United Arab Emirates, United Kingdom, United Republic of Tanzania, Uruguay, Vanuatu, Venezuela, Viet Nam, Yemen, Yugoslavia, Zambia.

Against: Israel, United States.

Abstaining: Australia, New Zealand.

Right to adequate housing

Reports of Special Rapporteur. The Special Rapporteur on adequate housing, Miloon Kothari (India), in a January report [E/CN.4/2001/51], stated that housing and living conditions were deteriorating worldwide. No fewer than 100 million people were homeless, of whom between 30 million and 70 million were children. The situation was exacerbated by the trend of rapid urbanization, particularly in Africa and South-East Asia, as well as by growing poverty in countries with a predominantly rural population. The process of globalization was an impediment to the realization of the right to adequate housing, as were limited access to safe drinking water and sanitation, poverty, and discrimination, particularly against women. He recommended that the Commission permit him to report annually to it, to the General Assembly and to the Commission on the Status of Women; request him to convene an expert seminar, in collaboration with relevant UN agencies, to further study the impact of globalization; mandate him to seek, receive and respond to information on all aspects of the realization of the right to adequate housing, particularly urgent action in cases of serious violations of the right; and permit him to submit periodic thematic reports.

In August [A/CONF.189/9], the Special Rapporteur reported on discrimination and segregation in housing. He noted that more research was needed on the extent to which discrimination in housing and land contributed to discrimination and segregation regarding particular people and communities. The specific short- and long-term impact of residential segregation and of globalization policies needed further study.

Commission action. On 20 April [res. 2001/28], the Commission requested the Special Rapporteur to emphasize practical solutions regarding the implementation of the right to adequate housing as a component of the right to an adequate standard of living, based on information on best practices from Governments, UN agencies and NGOs. He was also asked to facilitate technical assistance in that field, to further review the interrelatedness of adequate housing with other human rights and to report in 2002. The High Commissioner was asked to support cooperation between the Special Rapporteur and other Commission mechanisms and UN bodies relevant to his mandate. The Secretary-General was asked to assist him.

The Commission requested OHCHR and the UN Centre for Human Settlements (UNCHS) (see p. 985) to strengthen cooperation and consider developing a joint housing rights programme, and to support the Special Rapporteur. It called on States to give full effect to housing rights, paying particular attention to individuals, often women and children, living in extreme poverty; to ensure indigenous peoples and other minorities non-discriminatory access to adequate housing; and to cooperate with the Special Rapporteur and submit to him information on various experiences, notably on best practices.

During the year, the United Nations Housing Rights Programme was established as a joint initiative of UNCHS and OHCHR. The first phase of the Programme focused on advocacy and outreach; monitoring and evaluation of the realization of housing rights; research and analysis on housing rights; and capacity-building and technical cooperation.

Women's right to property and adequate housing

On 23 April [res. 2001/34], the Commission encouraged Governments to take measures to increase access to land and housing for women living in poverty. OHCHR, UNHCR and other relevant international organizations were asked to address discrimination against women with respect to land, property and adequate housing. The Secretary-General, as Chairman of the Administrative Committee on Coordination, was invited to encourage UN entities to take further initiatives that promoted women's equal ownership of, access to and control over land and the equal rights to own property and to adequate housing, and to allocate further resources to study the impact of complex emergency situations. The Secretary-General was asked to report in 2002.

Right to education

Report of Secretary-General. In response to a 2000 request of the Commission [YUN 2000, p. 705], the Secretary-General, in a January report [E/CN.4/2001/49], summarized the activities in 2000 of the Special Rapporteur on the right to education and the Commission's action regarding the right.

Reports of Special Rapporteur. The Special Rapporteur on the right to education, Katarina Tomasevski (Croatia), in a January report [E/CN.4/2001/52], summarized her correspondence with Governments regarding violations of the right, identified obstacles to the right and discussed the integration of human rights in international education strategies. During her discussions with the World Bank, the major provider of international funding for education, the Special Rapporteur focused on the issue of charging school fees for primary education. Her prior research had indicated that the majority of countries had constitutional guarantees of free and compulsory education for all children. Thus, she recommended that the Bank review its education lending to identify instances where such fees applied, with a view to immediate measures to abolish them. She drew the Commission's attention to the neglect of higher education in international strategies, which could jeopardize prospects for developing countries, and the need for teachers to be educated at the level of secondary and tertiary education, lest primary education be doomed to unqualified staff. The Special Rapporteur suggested that the Commission not renew her mandate due to difficulties she had faced in carrying it out.

The Special Rapporteur visited the United States (Washington, D.C.; Mississippi; Kansas; New York) (24 September–10 October) [E/CN.4/2002/60/Add.1]. She noted that the United States had a long history of free public education, expected to be all-inclusive. However, opportunities for such education had not been open evenly to the whole population owing to racial and/or economic exclusion over the years. She noted that the priorities in efforts to reform the system had tended to change, along with changes in leadership, targeting at different times inequalities in education, improving the performance of individual schools and students, and finding alternatives to public schools instead of improving them. Concerns about economic decline and political crisis had also altered priorities. Under the current Administration, proposals for reforms that would have increased education funding substantially were undermined by the war on terrorism following the 11 September terrorist attacks. Another means through which educational reforms could be realized—enforcement of constitutional and legal human rights guarantees—did not seem to constitute a priority. Many violations of the right to education were being exposed and opposed, and since court cases were time-consuming and expensive, rapid and free remedies in the form of human rights commissions or ombudsmen could facilitate accountability. The fragmentation of decision-making had created a complex educational bureaucracy, with non-teachers in the public school system outnumbering teachers, and teachers earning the lowest salaries. Accountability for student performance required simplifying and streamlining the system, as well as channelling inputs towards teaching and learning.

Commission action. On 20 April [res. 2001/29], the Commission called on States to guarantee that the right to education was recognized and exercised without discrimination; eliminate obstacles limiting access to education; ensure that primary education was compulsory, accessible, free and available to all; close the gap between the school-leaving age and the minimum employment age; reduce dropout rates; ensure quality education and improved enrolment and retention rates; eliminate gender discrimination; and submit information on best practices to eliminate discrimination in access to education. It decided to renew the Special Rapporteur's mandate for three years and asked her to report in 2002. The Secretary-General was requested to assist her.

On 24 July, the Economic and Social Council endorsed the Commission's decision to renew the Special Rapporteur's mandate and its request to the Secretary-General to assist her (**decision 2001/261**).

Environmental and scientific concerns

Reports of Special Rapporteur. In January [E/CN.4/2001/55], the Special Rapporteur on the adverse effects of the illicit movement and dump-ing of toxic and dangerous products and wastes on the enjoyment of human rights, Fatma-Zohra Ouhachi-Vesely (Algeria), described her activities and discussed relevant instruments and standards, the trends in and characteristics of illicit traffic, the role of TNCs and the human rights impact of the problem. She reported that trends indicated an increase in exports of dangerous products and wastes from industrialized countries to developing countries via recycling programmes, which enabled producers to circumvent the ban imposed by the 1989 Basel Convention on the Control of Transboundary Movements of Hazardous Wastes and their Disposal [YUN 1989, p. 420]. The transfer of "dirty" industrial operations from OECD member States to non-member States increased, with the most alarming cases involving the intensive and uncontrolled use of chemicals, toxic agricultural products and persistent organic pollutants. The stockpiling of obsolete chemicals in developing countries was a major cause for concern. Traffickers resorted to fraudulent practices, with corporations making use of front companies; in some cases, transfers were linked to trafficking in weapons, nuclear material or drugs. Cases brought to the Special Rapporteur's attention constituted violations of the right of peoples to self-determination and permanent sovereignty over national resources; the right to development; the rights to life, health, an adequate standard of living and sufficient food, safe and healthy working conditions, housing, information, participation and freedom of association; the right to enjoy the benefits of scientific progress; trade union rights; the right to strike; the right to bargain collectively; and the right to social security. The Special Rapporteur recommended that Governments enact legislation preventing illicit trafficking, TNCs comply with the laws of the importing country and victims be granted access to administrative and judicial proceedings in the exporting States. She called for an international code of conduct for TNCs and the establishment of national commissions of inquiry endowed with judicial or quasi-judicial powers.

A separate report [E/CN.4/2001/55/Add.1] of the Special Rapporteur summarized communications she had received from Governments describing specific incidents.

Commission action. By a roll-call vote of 38 to 15, the Commission, on 23 April [res. 2001/35], urged Governments to take measures to prevent illegal trafficking and the transfer of toxic and hazardous products, and polluting industries and technologies to developing countries. The Commission decided to renew the Special Rapporteur's mandate for three years. It asked her to study existing problems of and solutions to illicit trafficking, particularly in developing countries, and to include in her 2002 report information on persons killed or injured through the illicit movement and dumping of toxic wastes; impunity; rehabilitation of and assistance to victims; the scope of national legislation in relation to transboundary movement and dumping of such products; and the question of fraudulent waste recycling programmes, the transfer of polluting industries, industrial activities and technologies from developed to developing countries, ambiguities in international instruments and gaps in the effectiveness of international regulatory mechanisms. The Secretary-General was asked to assist her.

On 24 July, the Economic and Social Council endorsed the Commission's decision to renew the Special Rapporteur's mandate (**decision 2001/262**).

Follow-up to UNCED

On 25 April [dec. 2001/111], the Commission, noting the World Summit on Sustainable Development in 2002 (see p. 749) for the 10-year review of the implementation of Agenda 21, a programme of action for sustainable development worldwide, which was adopted by the United Nations Conference on Environment and Development (UNCED) [YUN 1992, p. 672], decided to invite the High Commissioner and the Executive Director of the United Nations Environment Programme to organize a joint seminar to review and assess progress achieved since UNCED in promoting and protecting human rights in relation to environmental questions and in the framework of Agenda 21.

On 24 July, the Economic and Social Council endorsed the Commission's decision (decision **2001/284**).

Water and sanitation services

Commission action. On 23 April [dec. 2001/104], the Commission, taking note of a 2000 Subcommission resolution [YUN 2000, p. 706], asked the Subcommission to review the terms of reference for a proposed study on the relationship between the enjoyment of economic, social and cultural rights and the promotion of the right to drinking water supply and sanitation, and to review the level of UN support requested for the study.

Subcommission action. On 10 August [res. 2001/2], the Subcommission recommended that the Commission authorize it to appoint El Hadji Guissé (Senegal) as Special Rapporteur to conduct a study on the relationship between the en-

joyment of economic, social and cultural rights and the right to drinking water supply and sanitation. He was asked to submit a preliminary report in 2002, a progress report in 2003 and a final report in 2004. The Secretary-General was asked to assist him and to invite Governments, UN bodies, specialized agencies and interested NGOs to provide the Special Rapporteur with information.

Bioethics

On 25 April [res. 2001/71], the Commission invited Governments to consider establishing ethics committees, in conjunction with UNESCO's International Bioethics Committee, to assess the ethical, social and human rights questions raised by biomedical research regarding humans and to inform the Secretary-General of action taken. It asked UNESCO, WHO, OHCHR and other UN bodies and specialized agencies to report to the Secretary-General on activities conducted in their respective areas to ensure that the principles set forth in the 1997 Universal Declaration on the Human Genome and Human Rights [YUN 1997, p. 1530], adopted by UNESCO, were taken into account; based on the information received, the Secretary-General was to draw up proposals for the General Assembly's consideration (see below) on ways to coordinate activities on bioethics in the UN system and to consider establishing a working group of independent experts to report to him on possible follow-up to the 1997 Declaration. The Subcommission was asked to consider the contribution it could make to follow-up to the Declaration and to report in 2003. The Secretary-General was asked to report in 2003 and the High Commissioner to pay due attention to the subject.

On 24 July, the Economic and Social Council approved the Commission's requests to the Secretary-General (**decision 2001/273**).

Subcommission action. On 15 August [dec. 2001/113], the Subcommission entrusted Antoanella Iulia Motoc (Romania) with preparing, without financial implications, a working paper on the 1997 Declaration for consideration in 2002 and to transmit it to the Commission in 2003.

Reports of the Secretary-General. In response to a 1999 Commission request [YUN 1999, p. 664], the Secretary-General submitted the replies of 11 Member States and one observer in response to his request for their views on establishing ethics committees and on other activities relating to bioethics [E/CN.4/2001/93 & Add.1].

Pursuant to Commission resolution 2001/71 (see above), the Secretary-General, in a November report [A/56/643], summarized information received from six Governments, three specialized agencies and OHCHR regarding the coordination of bioethics activities. The High Commissioner intended to organize a consultation of high-level experts to discuss the implementation of the 1997 Declaration. Referring to the wide range of activities carried out by the specialized agencies, the Secretary-General realized that there was an enormous potential for and need to consolidate coordination and cooperation between OHCHR, various UN human rights bodies and other specialized agencies within the UN system. In that context, it would be necessary to assess whether a working group of independent experts, as suggested by the Commission, or a high-level group of policy makers, as proposed by UNESCO, was the best way to ensure cooperation and coordination of activities and follow-up on the implementation of the 1997 Declaration. The Secretary-General recommended that UNESCO and WHO, in cooperation with OHCHR, be requested to consult further with other UN bodies and specialized agencies. (See also p. 1254.)

Genetic privacy

On 3 May, the Economic and Social Council, acting on a request of Argentina [E/2001/43], included in its provisional agenda for the substantive session, as a supplementary sub-item under social and human rights questions, "Discrimination and genetic privacy" (**decision 2001/213**).

On 26 July [meeting 43], the Council adopted **resolution 2001/39** [draft: E/2001/L.24/Rev.1] without vote [agenda item 14 (*h*)].

Genetic privacy and non-discrimination

The Economic and Social Council,

Guided by the purposes and principles set forth in the Charter of the United Nations and also by the Universal Declaration of Human Rights, the International Covenants on Human Rights and the other relevant international human rights instruments,

Referring to the Universal Declaration on the Human Genome and Human Rights, adopted on 11 November 1997 by the General Conference of the United Nations Educational, Scientific and Cultural Organization, and to General Assembly resolution 53/152 of 9 December 1998, endorsing the Declaration,

Recalling Commission on Human Rights resolution 2001/71 of 25 April 2001 on the question of human rights and bioethics,

Recalling also the decision taken on 7 May 1998 whereby the Executive Board of the United Nations Educational, Scientific and Cultural Organization established the International Bioethics Committee, which is carrying out work on confidentiality and genetic data,

Recalling further that the life and health of individuals are inevitably related to developments in life sciences and social areas,

Acknowledging the importance of advances in genetic research, which have led to the identification of strategies for early detection, prevention and treatment of diseases,

Bearing in mind that the genetic revolution has far-reaching implications and consequences for all humankind, and that its evaluation and applications should thus be conducted in an open, ethical and participatory manner,

Recognizing the contribution that relevant actors in civil society can make to the protection of genetic privacy and the fight against discrimination based on genetic characteristics,

Reaffirming that the information obtained from genetic tests, which is personal, should be held confidential, based on the conditions set by law,

Recognizing that genetic data associated with an identifiable person can in some instances be specific to other members of the individual's family or to other persons and that the rights and interests of such persons must also be taken into account in the handling of such data,

Stressing the fact that revealing genetic information belonging to individuals without their consent may cause harm and discrimination against them in such areas as employment, education, social issues and medical insurance,

Recalling that, in order to protect human rights and fundamental freedoms, the limitations to the principles of consent and confidentiality may only be prescribed by law, for compelling reasons within the bounds of public international law and the international law of human rights,

1. *Urges* States to ensure that no one shall be subjected to discrimination based on genetic characteristics;

2. *Also urges* States to protect the privacy of those subject to genetic testing and to ensure that genetic testing is done with the prior, free, informed and express consent of the individual or authorization obtained in the manner prescribed by law and in accordance with public international law and the international law of human rights;

3. *Invites* States to take appropriate specific measures, including through legislation, to prevent the use of genetic information and testing leading to discrimination or exclusion against individuals or members of their families or other persons with whom they may share certain genetic characteristics, in all areas, in particular in social, medical or employment-related areas, whether in the public or private sector;

4. *Calls upon* States to promote, as appropriate, the development and implementation of standards providing greater protection with regard to the collection, storage, disclosure and use of genetic information taken from genetic tests that might lead to discrimination or invasion of privacy;

5. *Urges* States to continue to support research in the area of human genetics and biotechnology, subject to accepted scientific and ethical standards and to the potential benefit of all, especially the poor, emphasizing that such research and its applications should fully respect human dignity, freedom and human rights, as well as the prohibition of all forms of discrimination based on genetic characteristics;

6. *Requests* the Secretary-General to bring the present resolution to the attention of all Governments and relevant international organizations and functional

commissions in order to collect the information and comments received pursuant to it, and to submit a report thereon to the Council at its substantive session of 2003.

Slavery and related issues

Working group activities. The five-member Working Group on Contemporary Forms of Slavery, at its twenty-sixth session (Geneva, 11-15 June) [E/CN.4/Sub.2/2001/30], reviewed developments in contemporary forms of slavery and measures to prevent and repress all its forms, including consideration of corruption and international debt as promoting factors of the phenomenon. It considered as a matter of priority the questions of trafficking in persons, particularly women and children, illegal migration, smuggling and prostitution. Other forms of exploitation examined were bonded labour and debt bondage, child labour, sexual exploitation, especially of children, incest, the status of the slavery conventions (see below) and the activities of the United Nations Voluntary Trust Fund on Contemporary Forms of Slavery (see p. 677). The Group concluded that despite progress made in human rights protection and the preservation of human dignity, various forms of slavery still existed and new insidious forms were emerging. It made a series of recommendations on the issues it considered during the session.

Documents considered by the Group included April notes by the Secretary-General [E/CN.4/Sub.2/AC.2/2001/2, E/CN.4/Sub.2/AC.2/2001/3] updating the status of the slavery conventions (1956 Supplementary Convention on the Abolition of Slavery, the Slave Trade and Institutions and Practices Similar to Slavery [YUN 1956, p. 228] and 1949 Convention for the Suppression of the Traffic in Persons and of the Exploitation of the Prostitution of Others, adopted by the General Assembly in resolution 317(IV) [YUN 1948-49, p. 613]) and a May report of the Secretary-General [E/CN.4/Sub.2/AC.2/2001/4], containing information submitted by Governments, UN bodies and NGOs on measures they had taken to prevent and repress all forms of slavery.

Commission action. On 24 April [dec. 2001/109], the Commission, referring to the 1966 *Report on Slavery* [Sales No. E.67.XIV.2], revised in 1984 [Sales No. E.84.XIV.1], decided to recommend to the Economic and Social Council that the 2000 report of existing treaty and customary law covering slavery-related practices and monitoring [YUN 2000, p. 707] be printed in the UN official languages and widely distributed.

On 24 July, the Council approved the Commission's recommendation (**decision 2001/282**).

Subcommission action. On 15 August [res. 2001/14], the Subcommission addressed the traffic in persons and exploitation of the prostitution of others; prevention of trans-border trafficking in children; corruption in the perpetuation of slavery and slavery-like practices; misuse of the Internet for sexual exploitation; migrant workers and domestic migrant workers; eradication of bonded labour and elimination of child labour; and the sale of children, child prostitution and child pornography.

The Subcommission asked the Commission to authorize the High Commissioner to organize in 2002, in cooperation with UNHCR, the International Organization for Migration and other intergovernmental organizations concerned, a workshop to consider all aspects of the smuggling and trafficking in persons and the protection of their human rights. It invited the International Labour Organization, together with other UN organs and specialized agencies, to consider holding a seminar or workshop to determine best practices for the eradication of debt bondage. The Secretary-General was requested to invite all States to inform the Working Group of measures adopted to implement the Programme of Action for the Elimination of the Exploitation of Child Labour [YUN 1993, p. 965] and to report thereon to the Subcommission and Commission in 2002. The Subcommission, in the context of the tenth anniversary of the adoption of the Programme of Action for the Prevention of the Sale of Children, Child Prostitution and Child Pornography (see below), decided to request an NGO to prepare and submit to the Working Group in 2002 an assessment of the implementation of the Programme of Action. It asked the Working Group to examine, as a matter of priority in 2002, the issue of the exploitation of children, particularly in the context of prostitution and domestic servitude.

1992 Programme of Action

A May report of the Secretary-General [E/CN.4/Sub.2/2001/4] on the implementation of the 1992 Programme of Action for the Prevention of the Sale of Children, Child Prostitution and Child Pornography [YUN 1992, p. 814] described the activities taken by three Governments to do so, as well as action they had taken to implement the Stockholm Declaration on Commercial Exploitation of Children, adopted in 1996 by the World Congress against Commercial Sexual Exploitation of Children [YUN 1996, p. 660], and the Optional Protocol to the Convention on the Rights of the Child on the sale of children, child prostitution and child pornography, adopted in General Assembly resolution 54/263 [YUN 2000, p. 618].

The Secretary-General, in a November note [E/CN.4/2002/87], drew the Commission's attention to the report.

Sexual exploitation during armed conflict

Report of High Commissioner. A June report of the High Commissioner [E/CN.4/Sub.2/2001/29] updated information contained in her previous report [YUN 2000, p. 708] regarding steps taken by human rights mechanisms, the Commission, ICTY and ICTR to address the issue of systematic rape, sexual slavery and slavery-like practices during armed conflict. She stated that conventional and extra-conventional human rights mechanisms should continue and strengthen their consideration of gender-based human rights violations. The gender aspect of those crimes should be taken into account in legal and extralegal responses, including prevention, investigation, prosecution, compensation and rehabilitation.

Commission action. On 24 April [dec. 2001/108], the Commission recommended that the Economic and Social Council request the Secretary-General to publish, in the official languages, the report [YUN 1998, p. 698] and updated report [YUN 2000, p. 707] of the Special Rapporteur on systematic rape, sexual slavery and slavery-like practices during armed conflict, including internal armed conflict, and to transmit them to Governments, competent UN bodies, specialized agencies, regional and intergovernmental organizations, the established international tribunals and the Assembly of the States Parties to the Rome Statute of the International Criminal Court [YUN 1998, p. 1209], in order to ensure their wide distribution.

On 24 July, the Council endorsed the Commission's recommendation (**decision 2001/281**).

Subcommission action. On 16 August [res. 2001/20], the Subcommission called on States to provide effective criminal penalties and compensation for unremedied violations in order to end the cycle of impunity regarding sexual violence committed during armed conflicts and encouraged them to promote human rights education on the subject. The High Commissioner was called on to monitor the implementation of the resolution and to report in 2002.

Fund on slavery

Reports of Secretary-General. In February [E/CN.4/2001/82/Add.1], July [A/56/205] and December [E/CN.4/2002/93], the Secretary-General reported on the status of the United Nations Voluntary Trust Fund on Contemporary Forms of Slavery.

The Fund's Board of Trustees, at its sixth session (Geneva, 22-26 January) [E/CN.4/2002/93], recommended 18 project grants amounting to $174,415 and 13 travel grants amounting to $25,715 to enable NGO representatives to participate in the deliberations of the 2001 session of the Working Group on Contemporary Forms of Slavery (see p. 676). The Board estimated that, in order to fulfil its mandate satisfactorily, the Fund would need $400,000 annually. The Secretary-General reported that contributions available to the Board as at 30 November 2001 stood at $69,545, while pledges amounted to $15,000.

On 19 December, the General Assembly took note of the Secretary-General's July report (**decision 56/429**).

Subcommission action. On 16 August [res. 2001/19], the Subcommission invited the Fund's Board of Trustees to promote the participation at the annual sessions of the Working Group of individuals and organizations from as large a number of countries as possible. It urged Governments, NGOs and other private or public entities to contribute to the Fund.

Vulnerable groups

Women

Violence against women

Report of Secretary-General. Pursuant to General Assembly resolution 50/166 [YUN 1995, p. 1188], the Secretary-General, in January [E/CN.4/2001/126-E/CN.6/2001/6], transmitted to the Commission on Human Rights and the Commission on the Status of Women the report of the United Nations Development Fund for Women on activities of the Fund to eliminate violence against women (see p. 1058).

Reports of Special Rapporteur. In January [E/CN.4/2001/73], the Special Rapporteur on violence against women, its causes and consequences, Radhika Coomaraswamy (Sri Lanka), highlighted violence against women perpetrated and/or condoned by the State during times of armed conflict between 1997 and 2000, within the context of the recommendations contained in her 1998 report [YUN 1998, p. 698].

The Special Rapporteur emphasized risks faced by girl children and the gaps in protection and assistance to internally displaced women. She expressed concern about the growing incidents of rape and other sexual abuse committed by UN peacekeeping forces and staff, and by soldiers and staff associated with military bases. Also of concern were the ongoing violence and discrimination in the rehabilitation and reconstruction processes. Regarding emerging legal standards, positive developments had taken place with the development by the international community of precise legal standards clarifying that rape and gender-based violence constituted war crimes, crimes against humanity and components of the crime of genocide. The Special Rapporteur reviewed the work of ICTY and ICTR, as well as the provisions of the Rome Statute [YUN 1998, p. 1209], which defined rape and other gender-based violence as constituent acts of crimes against humanity and war crimes. She made a series of recommendations, among them the development of effective UN policies to protect and assist women and girls during and after armed conflict, according women a greater role in the peace process and involving women in society's efforts to address the past.

In an addendum to her report [E/CN.4/2001/73/Add.1], the Special Rapporteur summarized the texts of communications she had transmitted to 14 States regarding alleged violence against women, and the replies thereon from 10 States.

In a July report [A/CONF.189/PC.3/5], the Special Rapporteur reviewed gender-based discrimination as it intersected with other forms of discrimination based on race, ethnicity, religion and economic status, thus forcing the majority of the world's women into situations of extreme marginalization. She observed that although advances had been made in addressing gender-related problems, a more structured approach was needed to eliminate the multiple forms of discrimination experienced by women. Urgent action was needed to raise awareness of the problem and to mainstream a more holistic approach to the question of racial and gender discrimination.

The Special Rapporteur visited Sierra Leone (21-29 August) [E/CN.4/2001/83/Add.2] to study the widespread violence against women committed during the 10-year conflict in the country and to identify key measures and initiatives to address the rights of women in the aftermath of the conflict. Based on the testimonies of 733 women and girls, documented by the human rights section of the United Nations Mission in Sierra Leone (UN-AMSIL), human rights NGOs and academics, gender-specific abuses included rape, sexual slavery and forced marriages to members of various factions. All victims suffered trauma and almost all required medical treatment. Regarding social support for victims, the Special Rapporteur noted shortcomings in government programmes and described the human rights activities of UNAMSIL and NGOs. The Special Rapporteur observed that failure to investigate,

prosecute and punish those responsible for rape and other forms of gender-based violence had contributed to an environment of impunity, which perpetuated the violence. She proposed recommendations regarding the criminal justice system, international instruments, HIV/AIDS, access to basic health care, basic services for internally displaced persons, illiteracy and technical assistance. The international community should ensure that all reports of rape and other forms of gender-based violence were fully investigated and those responsible brought to justice, and should, in addition, increase funding for programmes addressing the needs of the victims, including medical care, trauma counselling, education, vocational training and income-generating schemes. The human rights section of UNAMSIL should recruit a gender specialist to monitor and report on gender-based violence and ensure that UN peacekeepers fulfilled their mandate to protect civilians from physical violence, including women and girls at risk of abduction, rape and other forms of sexual violence.

The Special Rapporteur visited Colombia (1-7 November) [E/CN.4/2002/83/Add.3] to investigate allegations of gender-based violence, including rape and sexual slavery, by all armed groups involved in the country's protracted conflict and to report on the impact of that conflict on the human rights of women. Violence against women, particularly sexual violence by armed groups, was common practice, sometimes committed at the same time as massacres or as a way of terrorizing or threatening women and communities, and was widespread and systematic. The Special Rapporteur presented the testimonies of victims, some of whom were female combatants. She had heard reports that women and young girls who were internally displaced were being trafficked into forced prostitution in tourist centres in Colombia and abroad. Impunity was one of the factors contributing to the continued violation of women's rights and to the general increase in violence, including domestic violence. Rape cases were hardly addressed, and violence against women continued to occur at alarming levels owing to the armed conflict. There was a lack of interest in the issue by all involved in the conflict, the wider community and the media. The Special Rapporteur stated that training was urgently needed in the criminal justice system and the military. Her recommendations to the State included the appointment of a high-ranking legal adviser on sexual and gender-based violence, full implementation of relevant domestic legislation, steps to combat impunity, efforts to combat paramilitary groups, support for human rights organizations and effective enforcement of the principle of equality and non-discrimination. All parties to the conflict were urged to protect women and girls from gender-based violence, support women's participation in the peace process and subscribe to a global accord on human rights and international humanitarian law. The OHCHR Office in Colombia (see p. 710) should incorporate a gender perspective into all areas of its work and should continue to monitor and report on issues of gender-based violence. She emphasized the need for the international community to increase funding for programmes to assist victims.

Commission action. On 24 April [res. 2001/49], the Commission, condemning all acts of gender-based violence against women, violence occurring in the family and violence against women in situations of armed conflict, asked special rapporteurs, UN bodies, specialized agencies and intergovernmental organizations to consider violence against women in their respective mandates and to cooperate with the Special Rapporteur. It called on all parties to armed conflict to respect the civilian and humanitarian character of camps and settlements for refugees and internally displaced persons, and to improve and strengthen the capacity of women affected by situations of armed conflict by involving them in humanitarian activities. States were urged to provide gender-sensitive training to all actors in peacekeeping missions in dealing with victims of violence, particularly women and girls, and to include women in all peace, reconciliation and reconstruction activities. The Commission further urged that States integrate a gender perspective into commissions of inquiry and for achieving truth and reconciliation, and asked the Special Rapporteur to report, as appropriate, on those mechanisms. The Secretary-General was asked to assist the Special Rapporteur and ensure that her reports were brought to the attention of the Commission on the Status of Women and the Committee on the Elimination of Discrimination against Women.

(For information on violence against women migrant workers, see also p. 1058.)

Traditional practices affecting the health of women and girls

Commission action. On 24 April [dec. 2001/107], the Commission, taking note of a 2000 Subcommission resolution [YUN 2000, p. 711], decided to approve the Subcommission's decision to extend the mandate of the Special Rapporteur on traditional practices affecting the health of women and the girl child for two years, as well as its request to her to report in 2001 and 2002. On 24 July, the Economic and Social Council endorsed the decision (**decision 2001/280**).

Report of Special Rapporteur. In response to a 2000 Subcommission request [YUN 2000, p. 711], Special Rapporteur Halima Embarek Warzazi (Morocco), in a July report [E/CN.4/Sub.2/2001/27], reviewed recent initiatives against the practice of female genital mutilation and other traditional practices.

Subcommission action. On 15 August [res. 2001/13], the Subcommission called on Governments to give attention to the implementation of the 1994 Plan of Action for the Elimination of Harmful Traditional Practices [YUN 1994, p. 1123], and requested the Secretary-General to invite them to submit information on the situation regarding harmful practices in their country. Noting that one of the most effective means of developing government awareness of the problems and solutions would be to organize regional seminars, the Subcommission proposed that three seminars be held, in Africa, Asia and Europe. The High Commissioner was asked to raise funds to organize the seminars. The Special Rapporteur was asked to report in 2002.

(See also p. 1062.)

Traffic in women and girls

Report of Secretary-General. As requested by the Commission in 2000 [YUN 2000, p. 711], the Secretary-General, in January [E/CN.4/2001/72 & Corr.1], described action taken by the UN system and other international organizations to combat trafficking in women and girls. The Secretary-General stated that the trafficking was widespread and growing, rooted in the social and economic conditions of the victims and facilitated by practices which discriminated against women. He urged Member States to ratify the 2000 Protocol to Prevent, Suppress and Punish Trafficking in Persons, Especially Women and Children [YUN 2000, p. 1063], and called on the international human rights community to address the issue.

Commission action. On 24 April [res. 2001/48], the Commission invited Governments, donor countries, OHCHR, international and regional organizations and NGOs to consider the recommendations of the Special Rapporteur on violence against women, notably on trafficking in women and girls, particularly on the need for greater allocation of resources and better coordination of programmes and activities in tackling the problem. Governments were urged to address the root factors, including external factors encouraging trafficking in women and children, particularly girls, for prostitution and other forms of commercialized sex, forced marriages and forced labour; ensure victims' human rights and fundamental freedoms; criminalize trafficking and condemn and penalize traffickers and intermediaries; and provide rehabilitation programmes to victims, through job training, legal assistance and health care. The Secretary-General was asked to report in 2002.

Mainstreaming women's rights

Reports of Secretary-General. Pursuant to a 2000 Commission request [YUN 2000, p. 712], the Secretary-General, in January [E/CN.4/2001/71], described measures to integrate gender perspectives into the UN human rights system, taken by OHCHR and human rights treaty bodies and mechanisms, including the Commission. The Secretary-General stated that progress had been made in implementing the recommendations of the expert group meeting on the development of guidelines for the integration of gender perspectives into human rights activities and programmes [YUN 1995, p. 767]. He recommended that Governments ratify the 1979 Convention on the Elimination of All Forms of Discrimination against Women, adopted by the General Assembly in resolution 34/180 [YUN 1979, p. 895], and the 1989 Convention on the Rights of the Child, adopted by the Assembly in resolution 44/25 [YUN 1989, p. 561]. Action should be taken to change existing or introduce new legislation to protect women's human rights. The obligations of States to prevent and redress violations of women's rights needed further clarification.

In February [E/CN.4/2001/70-E/CN.6/2001/3], the Secretary-General presented the joint work plan of the UN Division for the Advancement of Women and OHCHR for 2001, which emphasized support for the work of treaty bodies and selected special mechanisms and cooperation between national machinery for the advancement of women and national human rights institutions. OHCHR and the Division would facilitate interaction between the Committee on the Elimination of Discrimination against Women (see p. 1074) and other treaty bodies, with a view to enhancing the integration of a gender perspective into their work. In that regard, the Division would provide a gender-specific input and update the 1998 study on integrating a gender perspective into the work of the human rights treaty bodies [YUN 1998, p. 611]. They would cooperate to organize workshops on gender issues; exchange information regarding communications submitted to the Commission on the Status of Women and OHCHR's review of the communications procedures of the Commission on Human Rights (see p. 579); prepare reports to intergovernmental bodies dealing with issues affecting women; and advocate a gender perspective in the preparations and outcome of the World Conference against

Racism, Racial Discrimination, Xenophobia and Related Intolerance (see p. 615). In addition, they would attend each other's meetings, as well as those of other relevant UN bodies and agencies, review the integration of gender issues in reports presented to the Commission on Human Rights by thematic mechanisms and facilitate cooperation between the Commission on the Status of Women and the Commission on Human Rights.

Commission action. On 24 April [res. 2001/50], the Commission, emphasizing the need for further UN system activities to strengthen expertise concerning the equal status and human rights of women, requested special procedures and other human rights mechanisms of the Commission and Subcommission, as well as human rights treaty bodies, to take a gender perspective into account in implementing their mandates and to include in their reports information on and qualitative analysis of women's and girls' human rights. The Commission asked the Secretary-General to report in 2002 and decided to integrate a gender perspective into all of its agenda items.

On 24 July, the Economic and Social Council approved the Commission's request to special procedures and other human rights mechanisms and endorsed its decision to integrate a gender perspective into all agenda items (**decision 2001/267**).

The girl child

On 25 April [res. 2001/75], the Commission called on States to take measures, including legal reforms, to ensure girls' enjoyment of human rights and fundamental freedoms and eliminate discrimination against them, including all forms of violence, harmful traditional practices, the root causes of son preference and forced and early marriages.

(See also p. 1060.)

Women in Afghanistan

Commission action. On 18 April [res. 2001/13], the Commission, condemning the continuing grave human rights violations of women and girls in Afghanistan, particularly in Taliban-controlled areas, urged all Afghan parties to end those violations and to ensure for women and girls: the repeal of discriminatory legislative and other measures; effective participation in civil, cultural, economic, political and social life; respect for their right to work; the right to education without discrimination, the reopening of schools and their admission to all levels of education; respect for their right to security of person;

respect for their freedom of movement; and equal access to facilities of physical and mental health. The Secretary-General was requested to ensure a gender perspective in the selection of the staff of the United Nations Special Mission to Afghanistan.

Report of Secretary-General. The Secretary-General, in an August report [E/CN.4/Sub.2/2001/28], stated that the policy and practices of the Taliban, which exacerbated the discrimination already suffered by Afghan women, continued to be a major concern. The Senior Inter-Agency Network on Internal Displacement, led by the UN Special Coordinator on Internal Displacement, together with representatives of FAO, UNHCR, UNDP, UNICEF, WHO and the NGO community, visited Afghanistan (18-25 April), where they confirmed that the Taliban had pursued a policy of marginalization of women and girls, including by placing a ban on education, prohibiting women from working outside the home and restricting their freedom of movement. The application of those restrictions was inconsistent, which allowed the humanitarian community to devise various entry points to reach some women and girls in need. The mission made recommendations regarding a better response by humanitarian agencies to the needs of the female population, an assessment of the impact of displacement on women and children, and child protection programmes. The Secretary-General called on all Afghan parties to end violations of women's and girls' rights, repeal discriminatory legislation and other measures and ensure women's participation in civil, cultural, economic, political and social life. The international community was urged to support the efforts of the aid community to improve the protection of civilians, particularly women and children, including the allocation of more resources. He encouraged support for the United Nations and its partners to ensure that all UN-assisted programmes were formulated and coordinated to promote and ensure the participation of women, and that women benefited equally with men.

Subcommission action. On 15 August [res. 2001/15], the Subcommission, condemning all forms of discrimination and violation affecting women and girls in territories controlled by Afghan armed groups and official policies discriminating against women, requested the Commission to insist that armed groups abide by international human rights standards in relation to women, which entailed the repeal of all forms of discrimination based on sex. The Secretary-General was asked to make available all information compiled on the situation.

(See also p. 1065.)

Children

On 25 April, the Commission, in its resolution on the rights of the child [res. 2001/75], called on States to ensure the registration of all children immediately after birth, and to respect the right of the child to preserve his or her identity, and to ensure that a child would not be separated from his or her parents against their will, except when determined by competent authorities that such separation was in the best interests of the child. Among other things, States were called on to develop sustainable health systems and social services; support children and their families affected by HIV/AIDS and ensure prevention of HIV infections; promote children's right to education; prevent violence against children; ensure that children were not deprived of their liberty, except as a last resort; and protect refugee and internally displaced children. The Commission requested that, within their mandates, relevant human rights mechanisms and entities of the UN system include a child rights perspective. The Commission's request was approved by the Economic and Social Council on 24 July (**decision 2001/274**). The Secretary-General was asked to assist the Committee on the Rights of the Child (see p. 596) and to report in 2002.

Other aspects of the Commission's resolution— child labour, the prevention and eradication of the sale of children, child prostitution and child pornography, and protection of children affected by armed conflict—are covered below.

GENERAL ASSEMBLY ACTION

On 19 December [meeting 88], the General Assembly, on the recommendation of the Third Committee [A/56/579], adopted **resolution 56/138** without vote [agenda item 115].

The rights of the child

The General Assembly,

Reaffirming all of its resolutions on the rights of the child, in particular resolutions 55/78 and 55/79 of 4 December 2000, and taking note with appreciation of Commission on Human Rights resolution 2001/75 of 25 April 2001,

Considering the postponement of the special session of the General Assembly on children due to exceptional circumstances,

Welcoming the progress made so far in the preparation of the special session of the General Assembly on children, including its outcome document, and reaffirming that the Assembly, at its special session, while reviewing the achievements in the implementation and results of the World Declaration on the Survival, Protection and Development of Children and Plan of Action for Implementing the World Declaration on the Survival, Protection and Development of Children in the 1990s adopted by the World Summit for Children, held in New York on 29 and 30 September 1990, will make a renewed commitment and consider future action for children in the forthcoming decade,

1. *Takes note with appreciation* of the report of the Secretary-General entitled "We the children: end-decade review of the follow-up to the World Summit for Children" and the reports of the Secretary-General on the status of the Convention on the Rights of the Child and on children and armed conflict, as well as the report of the Special Representative of the Secretary-General for Children and Armed Conflict;

2. *Welcomes* the fact that, as at 18 October 2001, ten States had become parties to the Optional Protocol to the Convention on the Rights of the Child on the sale of children, child prostitution and child pornography, thereby allowing it to enter into force on 18 January 2002, and that, as at 12 November 2001, ten States had become parties to the Optional Protocol to the Convention on the Rights of the Child on the involvement of children in armed conflict, thereby allowing it to enter into force on 12 February 2002;

3. *Welcomes also* the adoption of the Protocol to Prevent, Suppress and Punish Trafficking in Persons, Especially Women and Children, supplementing the United Nations Convention against Transnational Organized Crime, as well as the large number of ratifications of International Labour Organization Convention No. 138, concerning the Minimum Age for Admission to Employment and Convention No. 182, concerning the Prohibition and Immediate Action for the Elimination of the Worst Forms of Child Labour;

4. *Welcomes* the convening of the Second World Congress against Commercial Sexual Exploitation of Children at Yokohama, Japan, from 17 to 20 December 2001, and the regional consultative meetings for its preparation, and invites Member States and observers to ensure their participation in the Congress at a high political level;

5. *Decides*:

(*a*) To request the Secretary-General to submit to the General Assembly at its fifty-seventh session a report on the rights of the child, containing information on the status of the Convention on the Rights of the Child and the Optional Protocols thereto;

(*b*) To request the Special Representative of the Secretary-General for Children and Armed Conflict to submit to the General Assembly and the Commission on Human Rights reports containing relevant information on the situation of children affected by armed conflict, bearing in mind the existing mandates and reports of relevant bodies;

(*c*) To request the Secretary-General to conduct an in-depth study on the question of violence against children, taking into account the outcome of the special session of the General Assembly on children, and to put forward recommendations for consideration by Member States for appropriate action, including effective remedies and preventive and rehabilitative measures;

(*d*) To revert to its comprehensive consideration of this question at its fifty-seventh session under the item entitled "Promotion and protection of the rights of children".

Sale of children, child prostitution and child pornography

Report of Special Rapporteur. In response to a 2000 Commission request [YUN 2000, p. 722], the Special Rapporteur on the sale of children, child prostitution and child pornography, Ofelia Calcetas-Santos (Philippines), in January [E/CN.4/2001/78], described international, regional and country-specific developments and focused on the responsibility of the private sector to prevent child abuse. In the light of information received from international chambers of commerce and NGOs, the Special Rapporteur examined the use of child labour and its implications for sexual abuse; press reports of sexual offences that blamed the victim or were over-sensationalized; Internet service providers and the dissemination of child pornography; images of children as sexual objects in advertisements; and the link between tourism, transport and child sexual abuse. She noted that certain elements of the private sector had recognized that their activities could affect children and had started to respond accordingly. She observed an overlap between companies that promoted child development and those providing care and protection.

Commission action. On 25 April [res. 2001/75], the Commission called on States to ensure the implementation of international instruments to prevent and combat the trafficking and the sale of children, increase cooperation to prevent and dismantle networks trafficking in children, criminalize and penalize all forms of sexual exploitation and abuse of children, child pornography and child prostitution, child sex tourism and the use of the Internet for those purposes, and combat markets that encouraged the criminal practices. It decided to renew the Special Rapporteur's mandate for a further three years and asked her to report in 2002.

The Economic and Social Council endorsed the Commission's decision on 24 July (**decision 2001/274**).

Following the Special Rapporteur's resignation, the Commission appointed Juan Miguel Petit (Uruguay) in June.

Child labour

On 25 April [res. 2001/75], the Commission called on States to eliminate child labour that was hazardous, interfered with a child's education or was harmful to the child's health, and to promote education as a key strategy. States that had not done so were called on to consider ratifying ILO Convention No. 182, concerning the Prohibition and Immediate Action for the Elimination of the

Worst Forms of Child Labour, adopted in 1999 [YUN 1999, p. 1388].

Children and armed conflict

Report of Special Representative. In response to General Assembly resolution 55/79 [YUN 2000, p. 714], the Secretary-General's Special Representative for Children and Armed Conflict, Olara A. Otunnu (Côte d'Ivoire), in a January report [E/CN.4/2001/76], covered progress achieved at the end of his three-year mandate. He drew attention to the plight of particularly vulnerable groups of war-affected children, including girls, internally displaced children, children affected by HIV/AIDS and abducted children. In addressing the issue of impunity, the Representative noted that much of the debate about the Special Court for Sierra Leone (see p. 179) focused on the accountability for those who were between 15 and 18 years of age at the time they allegedly committed serious crimes. As they were forcibly recruited as combatants, the Representative considered them victims. However, some young people joined without restraint. The Representative had worked to ensure that the Court would prosecute those who abducted, recruited and used children as combatants. Children's concerns were being integrated into UN peace operations, peace agreements and post-conflict peace-building. International standards in that regard were strengthened by the 2000 Optional Protocol to the Convention on the Rights of the Child on the involvement of children in armed conflict, adopted in General Assembly resolution 54/263 [YUN 2000, p. 616], and the Rome Statute of the International Criminal Court [YUN 1998, p. 1209], which defined as a war crime the conscription of children into the armed forces or groups, or their use in hostilities. Yet, much remained to be done. In the period ahead, his Office would emphasize activities to consolidate and deepen progress already made.

Commission action. On 25 April [res 2001/75], the Commission called on States to end child soldiering and together with parties to armed conflict to respect international humanitarian law. States, UN bodies and agencies and regional organizations were asked to integrate the rights of the child into all activities in conflict and post-conflict situations and to support national and international mine action efforts.

Report of Secretary-General. Pursuant to Security Council resolution 1314(2000) [YUN 2000, p. 723], the Secretary-General, in a September report [A/56/342-S/2001/852], informed the Council and the General Assembly of progress made in implementing his earlier recommendations and relevant Council resolutions. The Secretary-General stated that existing standards, including Council resolutions, had helped define the parameters of acceptable conduct for parties in armed conflict regarding children and other civilians. He stipulated measures intended to protect children during and after armed conflict. States were urged to sign and ratify the Optional Protocol to the Convention on the Rights of the Child on the involvement of children in armed conflict, and to review their national legislation with a view to defining the crimes within the jurisdiction of the International Criminal Court as national crimes and to ensure that national courts had jurisdiction over them and prosecuted violations of children's rights. Other recommendations related to compliance with child protection obligations by parties to armed conflicts and monitoring compliance; child protection training for UN peacekeeping personnel; support for the international research network on children and armed conflict, proposed by the Representative and launched in July, in collaboration with UNICEF, research institutions and NGOs; the exploitation of natural resources in zones of conflict; the prevention of child abduction; the demobilization and reintegration of child soldiers; the impact of HIV/AIDS on children in conflict situations; truth- and justice-seeking processes; the rehabilitation of children affected by armed conflict; and technical support to regional organizations to protect children.

Interim report of Special Representative. In response to General Assembly resolution 54/149 [YUN 1999, p. 676], the Special Representative, in an October report [A/56/453], described his activities covering October 2000 to September 2001, including country visits made by him or by representatives of his Office.

The Office of the Special Representative participated in a mission to Uganda, the Sudan and Kenya (17 March–6 April), led by OHCHR (see p. 686).

The Special Representative visited the Democratic Republic of the Congo (24 May–3 June), where 50 per cent of the estimated population of 50 million were under 16 years, to determine first-hand the conditions of children affected by the ongoing conflict in the country. He observed that hundreds of thousands of children had suffered or died of malnutrition and preventable diseases, more than half of school-age children were not in school and the use of child labour had increased. There was massive recruitment of child soldiers. Girls were forced by soldiers to serve as concubines and exposed to sexual abuse and HIV/AIDS. The Special Representative, in an action plan, recommended placing child protection on the agendas for dialogue and peace, expanding the presence and humanitarian activities of the United Nations Organization Mission in the Democratic Republic of the Congo (see p. 126), providing adequate and sustained resources for protection and curbing child soldiering. He proposed efforts to improve the monitoring of commitments made by parties; foster a subregional approach to child protection; improve data collection and research; ensure attention to the special needs of girls; build local capacity for child protection and advocacy; reinforce traditional values; and end the plunder of natural resources.

The Special Representative described follow-up developments to his 2000 visit to Northern Ireland [YUN 2000, p. 725] and 1998 [YUN 1998, p. 710] and 1999 [YUN 1999, p. 675] visits to Sierra Leone, as well as other activities taken to protect war-affected children.

Children from Colombia, Kosovo and Sierra Leone shared their experiences of war at a symposium (New York, 5 June), organized by the Office of the Special Representative, in collaboration with the Holy See. The Office, in collaboration with the Italian National Childhood and Adolescence Documentation and Analysis Centre and the Social Science Research Council, convened a workshop (Florence, July) to discuss the ways that a stronger knowledge base could help alleviate the plight of war-affected children. In August, the Special Representative participated in the World Conference against Racism, Racial Discrimination, Xenophobia and Related Intolerance (see p. 615) and highlighted the linkage between racism and the victimization of children during armed conflicts.

The report also described efforts made by the Special Representative and his Office to contribute to the work of UN bodies and agencies, regional organizations and NGOs.

SECURITY COUNCIL ACTION

On 20 November [meeting 4423], the Security Council unanimously adopted **resolution 1379 (2001)**. The draft [S/2001/1093] was prepared during consultations among Council members.

The Security Council,

Recalling its resolution 1314(2000) of 11 August 2000,

Further recalling its resolutions 1261(1999) of 28 August 1999, 1265(1999) of 17 September 1999, 1296 (2000) of 19 April 2000, 1306(2000) of 5 July 2000, 1308(2000) of 17 July 2000 and 1325(2000) of 31 October 2000 and the statements of its President of 29 June 1998 (S/PRST/1998/18), 12 February 1999 (S/PRST/1999/6), 8 July 1999 (S/PRST/1999/21), 30 November 1999 (S/PRST/1999/34), 20 July 2000 (S/PRST 2000/25) and of 31 August 2001 (S/PRST/2001/21),

Recognizing the harmful and widespread impact of armed conflict on children and the long-term conse-

quences this has for durable peace, security and development,

Bearing in mind the purposes and principles of the Charter of the United Nations and recalling the primary responsibility of the Security Council for the maintenance of international peace and security and, in this connection, its commitment to address the impact of armed conflict on children,

Underlining the need for all parties concerned to comply with the provisions of the Charter of the United Nations and with international law, in particular those regarding children,

Having considered the report of the Secretary-General of 7 September 2001 on the implementation of resolution 1314(2000) on children and armed conflict,

1. *Expresses its determination,* accordingly, to give the fullest attention to the question of the protection of children in armed conflict when considering the matters of which it is seized;

2. *Expresses its readiness* explicitly to include provisions for the protection of children, when considering the mandates of peacekeeping operations, and reaffirms, in this regard, its readiness to continue to include, where appropriate, child protection advisers in peacekeeping operations;

3. *Supports* the ongoing work of the Secretary-General, the Special Representative of the Secretary-General for Children and Armed Conflict, the United Nations Children's Fund, the Office of the United Nations High Commissioner for Refugees, the Office of the United Nations High Commissioner for Human Rights, other agencies of the United Nations system and other international organizations dealing with children affected by armed conflict;

4. *Expresses its intention,* where appropriate, to call upon the parties to a conflict to make special arrangements to meet the protection and assistance requirements of women, children and other vulnerable groups, including through the promotion of "days of immunization" and other opportunities for the safe and unhindered delivery of basic necessary services;

5. *Underlines* the importance of the full, safe and unhindered access of humanitarian personnel and goods and the delivery of humanitarian assistance to all children affected by armed conflict;

6. *Expresses its intention* to consider taking appropriate steps, in accordance with the Charter of the United Nations, to address the linkages between armed conflict and terrorism, the illicit trade in precious minerals, the illicit trafficking in small arms and light weapons, and other criminal activities, which can prolong armed conflict or intensify its impact on civilian populations, including children;

7. *Undertakes* to consider, as appropriate when imposing measures under Article 41 of the Charter of the United Nations, the economic and social impact of sanctions on children, with a view to providing appropriate humanitarian exemptions that take account of their specific needs and their vulnerability and to minimize such impact;

8. *Calls upon* all parties to armed conflict to:

(a) Respect fully the relevant provisions of applicable international law relating to the rights and protection of children in armed conflict, in particular the Geneva Conventions of 1949 and the obligations applicable to them under the Additional Protocols thereto

of 1977, the United Nations Convention on the Rights of the Child of 1989, the Optional Protocol thereto of 25 May 2000, and the amended Protocol II to the Convention on Prohibition or Restriction on the Use of Certain Conventional Weapons Which May Be Deemed to Be Excessively Injurious or to Have Indiscriminate Effects, the International Labour Organization Convention No. 182 on the Elimination of the Worst Forms of Child Labour and the Ottawa Convention on the Prohibition of the Use, Stockpiling, Production and Transfer of Anti-Personnel Mines and on Their Destruction, and notes the inclusion as a war crime in the Rome Statute of the conscription or enlistment of children under the age of fifteen years into the national armed forces or using them to participate actively in hostilities;

(b) Provide protection and assistance to refugees and internally displaced persons, the majority of whom are women and children, in accordance with applicable international norms and standards;

(c) Take special measures to promote and protect the rights and meet the special needs of girls affected by armed conflict, and to put an end to all forms of violence and exploitation, including sexual violence, particularly rape;

(d) Abide by the concrete commitments they have made to the Special Representative of the Secretary-General for Children and Armed Conflict, as well as relevant United Nations bodies, to ensure the protection of children in situations of armed conflict;

(e) Provide protection of children in peace agreements, including, where appropriate, provisions relating to the disarmament, demobilization, reintegration and rehabilitation of child soldiers and the reunification of families, and to consider, when possible, the views of children in those processes;

9. *Urges* Member States to:

(a) Put an end to impunity, prosecute those responsible for genocide, crimes against humanity, war crimes, and other egregious crimes perpetrated against children and exclude, where feasible, these crimes from amnesty provisions and relevant legislation, and ensure that post-conflict truth-and-reconciliation processes address serious abuses involving children;

(b) Consider appropriate legal, political, diplomatic, financial and material measures, in accordance with the Charter of the United Nations, in order to ensure that parties to armed conflict respect international norms for the protection of children;

(c) Consider, where appropriate, measures that may be taken to discourage corporate actors, within their jurisdiction, from maintaining commercial relations with parties to armed conflicts that are on the Security Council's agenda, when those parties are violating applicable international law on the protection of children in armed conflict;

(d) Consider measures against corporate actors, individuals and entities under their jurisdiction that engage in illicit trade in natural resources and small arms, in violation of relevant Security Council resolutions and the Charter of the United Nations;

(e) Consider ratifying the Optional Protocol to the Convention on the Rights of the Child on involvement of children in armed conflict and the International Labour Organization Convention No. 182 on the Elimination of the Worst Forms of Child Labour;

(f) Consider further steps for the protection of children, especially in the context of the International Decade for a Culture of Peace and Non-violence for the Children of the World (2001-2010);

10. *Requests* the Secretary-General to:

(a) Take the protection of children into account in peacekeeping plans submitted to the Security Council, inter alia, by including, on a case-by-case basis, child protection staff in peacekeeping and, as appropriate, peace-building operations and strengthening expertise and capacity in the area of human rights, where necessary;

(b) Ensure that all peacekeeping personnel receive and follow appropriate guidance on HIV/AIDS and training in international human rights, humanitarian and refugee law relevant to children;

(c) Continue and intensify, on a case-by-case basis, monitoring and reporting activities by peacekeeping and peace-building support operations on the situation of children in armed conflict;

11. *Requests* the agencies, funds and programmes of the United Nations to:

(a) Coordinate their support and assistance to parties to armed conflict in fulfilling their obligations and commitments to children;

(b) Take account of ways of reducing child recruitment that is contrary to accepted international standards when formulating development assistance programmes;

(c) Devote particular attention and adequate resources to the rehabilitation of children affected by armed conflict, particularly their counselling, education and appropriate vocational opportunities, as a preventive measure and as a means of reintegrating them into society;

(d) Ensure that the special needs and particular vulnerabilities of girls affected by armed conflict, including those heading households, orphaned, sexually exploited and used as combatants, are duly taken into account in the design of development assistance programmes, and that adequate resources are allocated to such programmes;

(e) Integrate HIV/AIDS awareness, prevention, care and support into emergency, humanitarian and post-conflict programmes;

(f) Support the development of local capacity to address post-conflict child rehabilitation and reintegration concerns;

(g) Promote a culture of peace, including through support for peace education programmes and other non-violent approaches to conflict prevention and resolution, in peace-building activities;

12. *Encourages* the international financial institutions and regional financial and development institutions to:

(a) Devote part of their assistance to rehabilitation and reintegration programmes conducted jointly by agencies, funds, programmes and State parties to conflicts that have taken effective measures to comply with their obligations to protect children in situations of armed conflict, including the demobilization and reintegration of child soldiers, in particular those who have been used in armed conflicts contrary to international law;

(*b*) Contribute resources for quick-impact projects in conflict zones where peacekeeping operations are deployed or are in the process of deployment;

(*c*) Support the efforts of the regional organizations engaged in activities for the benefit of children affected by armed conflict, by providing them with financial and technical assistance, as appropriate;

13. *Urges* regional and subregional organizations and arrangements to:

(*a*) Consider establishing, within their secretariats, child protection mechanisms for the development and implementation of policies, activities and advocacy for the benefit of children affected by armed conflict, and consider the views of children in the design and implementation of such policies and programmes where possible;

(*b*) Consider including child protection staff in their peacekeeping and field operations and provide training to members of such operations on the rights and protection of children;

(*c*) Take steps leading to the elimination of cross-border activities deleterious to children in times of armed conflict, such as the cross-border recruitment and abduction of children, the sale of or traffic in children, attacks on camps and settlements of refugees and internally displaced persons, the illicit trade in precious minerals, the illicit trafficking in small arms and light weapons, and other criminal activities;

(*d*) Develop and expand regional initiatives to prevent the use of child soldiers in violation of international law and to take appropriate measures to ensure the compliance by parties to armed conflict with obligations to protect children in armed conflict situations;

14. *Requests* the Secretary-General to continue to include in his written reports to the Council on conflict situations his observations concerning the protection of children and recommendations in this regard;

15. *Requests* the Secretary-General to submit a report to the Council by 31 October 2002 on the implementation of the present resolution and of resolutions 1261(1999) and 1314(2000);

16. *Requests* the Secretary-General to attach to his report a list of parties to armed conflict that recruit or use children in violation of the international obligations applicable to them, in situations that are on the Security Council's agenda or that may be brought to the attention of the Security Council by the Secretary-General, in accordance with Article 99 of the Charter of the United Nations, which in his opinion may threaten the maintenance of international peace and security;

17. *Decides* to remain actively seized of this matter.

Abduction of children in northern Uganda

Commission action. On 25 April [res. 2001/74], the Commission, condemning the Lord's Resistance Army (LRA), an armed opposition group in the Sudan, for the continued abduction, torture, killing, rape, enslavement and forcible recruitment of children in northern Uganda, demanded an end to the abductions and called for the children's release and safe return. It urged Member States, international organizations, humanitarian bodies and all other concerned par-

ties to exert pressure on LRA to release all children abducted from northern Uganda. The United Nations Voluntary Fund for Victims of Torture was asked to continue to assist the victims and their families.

Report of High Commissioner. In response to a 2000 Commission request [YUN 2000, p. 725], the High Commissioner reported on a mission to northern Uganda, the Sudan and Kenya (17 March–6 April) [E/CN.4/2002/86], composed of three OHCHR staff members, a UNICEF staff member and a representative of the Office of the Special Representative for Children and Armed Conflict, to assess the situation of children abducted from northern Uganda by LRA. It was estimated that over 10,000 children had been abducted since 1986, most of whom were taken to LRA camps in southern Sudan, where they were severely maltreated and initially used for slave labour to carry heavy loads looted by their captors. The children were forced to take part in beatings and killings of those children who collapsed under the burden of the workload or who had attempted to escape. As for young girls, most were raped and given to LRA soldiers and commanders as wives. An estimated 200 girls lived in the camps with their children who were born there. The death rate of children in the camps was reportedly high, as those who were not killed by other LRA members or during conflict died from starvation or dehydration. An estimated 6,000 of those abducted over the years remained unaccounted for, many of whom were presumed dead. In addition to the conclusion of a number of bilateral agreements between the Sudan and Uganda, various efforts were under way to improve the situation and to meet the victims' needs—in the Sudan, by the Humanitarian Aid Commission and transit centres outside Khartoum, and in Uganda, through the Amnesty Act and Amnesty Commission, and through local authorities, NGOs and community organizations. The mission recommended the implementation of international agreements relevant to the conflict, further support for amnesty and reconciliation, security measures for the local population and assistance to abducted children and the affected population.

Indigenous people

Commission action. On 24 April [res. 2001/59], the Commission recommended that the Economic and Social Council authorize the Subcommission's Working Group on Indigenous Populations to meet for five working days prior to the Subcommission's 2001 session. It welcomed the Group's proposal to highlight specific themes of the International Decade of the World's Indigenous People (1995-2004) (see p. 689), proclaimed by the General Assembly in resolution 48/163 [YUN 1993, p. 865], in its future sessions, noting that in 2001 the Group would focus on the theme of indigenous peoples and their right to development, including their right to participate in development affecting them. The Group was invited to continue its consideration of ways in which the expertise of indigenous people could contribute to its work. The Secretary-General was asked to assist the Group and to transmit its reports to Governments, organizations of indigenous people, intergovernmental organizations and NGOs for comments and suggestions.

On 24 July, the Council authorized the Working Group to meet for five days prior to the Subcommission's 2001 session and approved the Commission's request to the Secretary-General (**decision 2001/271**).

On 24 April [dec. 2001/110], the Commission, taking note of a 2000 Subcommission request [YUN 2000, p. 726], recommended that the Economic and Social Council authorize the Group's former Chairperson-Rapporteur, Erica-Irene Daes (Greece), to continue to participate in preparatory meetings for the World Conference against Racism, Racial Discrimination, Xenophobia and Related Intolerance and in the Conference itself (see p. 615), and to authorize the Chairperson-Rapporteur of the Group's 2000 session, Miguel Alfonso Martínez (Cuba), to participate in the World Conference.

On 24 July, the Council authorized the Commission's recommendation (**decision 2001/283**).

On 24 April [res. 2001/57], the Commission decided to appoint, for a three-year period, a Special Rapporteur on the situation of human rights and fundamental freedoms of indigenous people. It requested the Secretary-General and the High Commissioner to assist the Special Rapporteur, and asked the Special Rapporteur to report in 2002. The Council endorsed the Commission's decision and approved its requests (see below).

ECONOMIC AND SOCIAL COUNCIL ACTION

On 4 June, the Economic and Social Council, on the recommendation of the Commission on Human Rights [E/2001/L.7], adopted **decision 2001/222** without vote [agenda item 14 (*g*)].

Human rights and indigenous issues

At its 9th plenary meeting, on 4 June 2001, the Economic and Social Council, having taken note of Commission on Human Rights resolution 2001/57 of 24 April 2001, endorsed the decision of the Commission:

(*a*) To appoint, for a three-year period, a special rapporteur on the situation of human rights and fun-

damental freedoms of indigenous people, with the following functions:

(i) To gather, request, receive and exchange information and communications from all relevant sources, including Governments, indigenous people themselves and their communities and organizations, on violations of their human rights and fundamental freedoms;

(ii) To formulate recommendations and proposals on appropriate measures and activities to prevent and remedy violations of the human rights and fundamental freedoms of indigenous people;

(iii) To work in close relation with other special rapporteurs, special representatives, working groups and independent experts of the Commission on Human Rights and of the Subcommission on the Promotion and Protection of Human Rights, taking into account the request of the Commission contained in its resolution 1993/30 of 5 March 1993;

(*b*) To invite the Special Rapporteur:

(i) To take into account a gender perspective while carrying out her/his mandate, paying special attention to discrimination against indigenous women;

(ii) To pay special attention to violations of the human rights and fundamental freedoms of indigenous children;

(iii) To take into account, in carrying out his/her task, all the recommendations of the Working Group on Indigenous Populations of the Subcommission on the Promotion and Protection of Human Rights and of the Permanent Forum on Indigenous Issues relevant to his/her mandate;

(iv) To consider, in performing her/his work, the recommendations of the World Conference against Racism, Racial Discrimination, Xenophobia and Related Intolerance on matters concerning his/her mandate;

(*c*) To request the Chairperson of the Commission of Human Rights, following formal consultations with the Bureau and the regional groups through the regional coordinators, to appoint as Special Rapporteur an individual of recognized international standing and experience;

(*d*) To request the Special Rapporteur to submit annual reports on her/his activities to the Commission on Human Rights, starting at its fifty-eighth session;

(*e*) To request the Secretary-General and the United Nations High Commissioner for Human Rights to provide all the necessary human, technical and financial assistance to the Special Rapporteur for the fulfilment of her/his mandate.

On 22 June, the Commission appointed Rodolfo Stavenhagen (Mexico) as the Special Rapporteur.

Working Group activities. The Working Group on Indigenous Populations held its nineteenth session (Geneva, 23-27 July) [E/CN.4/Sub.2/2001/17] to review developments pertaining to the promotion and protection of human rights and fundamental freedoms of indigenous populations, and to give attention to the evolution of standards concerning their rights. In annotations to the provisional agenda [E/CN.4/Sub.2/AC.4/2001/1/Add.1], the Secretary-General presented background information on land issues, education and health; the International Decade of the World's Indigenous People (1995-2004) (see p. 689); the World Conference against Racism, Racial Discrimination, Xenophobia and Related Intolerance (see p. 615); and standard-setting activities, including a review of indigenous peoples' relationship with natural resource, energy and mining companies. Information was received from indigenous organizations regarding extreme poverty and the right to development [E/CN.4/Sub.2/AC.4/2001/6], the Decade [E/CN.4/Sub.2/AC.4/2001/7] and the World Conference [E/CN.4/Sub.2/AC.4/2001/8].

Regarding the session's principal theme—indigenous peoples and their right to development, including their right to participate in development affecting them—the Group considered a note by the Secretariat [E/CN.4/Sub.2/AC.4/2001/2], highlighting some of the possible themes related to indigenous peoples and their right to development. The Group encouraged OHCHR to organize regional seminars and workshops to afford indigenous peoples from all areas the opportunity to participate in activities regarding the Decade. The Group recommended that OHCHR organize a preparatory workshop on the implementation of the recommendations relating to indigenous peoples contained in Agenda 21, adopted in 1992 by UNCED [YUN 1992, p. 672]. Noting OHCHR's efforts to include indigenous components in country programmes, the Group welcomed the organization by the Office of a training workshop on human rights for indigenous peoples (Oaxaca, Mexico, 13-17 August) and expressed appreciation to the organizers of the second NGO workshop on indigenous children and youth (Geneva, 19-20 July). Regarding standard-setting activities during its 2002 session, the Group urged Mr. Alfonso Martínez to submit a working paper on indigenous peoples' relationship with natural resource, energy and mining companies, asked Antoanella-Iulia Motoc (Romania) to prepare working papers on possible future standard-setting that might be undertaken and on the consequences of biotechnology on indigenous peoples, invited UNDP and the World Bank to present their new policy guidelines on indigenous peoples, and asked Ms. Daes to present a working paper on indigenous peoples' permanent sovereignty over natural resources. In other action related to the Group's session in 2002, El Hadji Guissé (Senegal) was asked to prepare a working paper on indigenous peoples' right to development and globalization. The Group decided that in 2002 it would continue as its principal theme "Indigenous peoples and their right to development, including their right to participate in development affecting them". Considering that the year 2002 would mark its twentieth anniversary, the Group decided to highlight the theme "The Working Group on Indigenous Populations: achievements at the United Nations system and a vision for the future". In that context, it invited Ms. Daes to prepare a working paper on the achievements of indigenous peoples at the United Nations. OHCHR was invited to consider how it could organize special events to observe the Group's anniversary.

Workshop. In accordance with a 2000 Subcommission resolution [YUN 2000, p. 728], OHCHR, in collaboration with UNCTAD, ILO, WTO and other organizations, organized a workshop on indigenous peoples, private sector natural resource, energy and mining companies and human rights, including existing international legal frameworks (Geneva, 5-7 December) [E/CN.4/Sub.2/AC.4/2002/3]. The workshop focused on consulting with indigenous communities prior, during and following the development of private sector projects; benefit-sharing by indigenous communities in private sector activities; and solving disputes.

The workshop acknowledged that the recognition of indigenous peoples' rights to their lands and resources was a precondition for equitable relationships between them, States and the private sector. It underscored the importance of economic and sustainable development for indigenous peoples' survival and future. The workshop recommended that States, UN system organizations, indigenous peoples and the private sector continue to review issues relating to private sector natural resource development, best practices and indigenous peoples' land rights, and develop a framework for consultation, benefit-sharing and dispute resolution in private sector projects affecting indigenous peoples. It also recommended, among other measures, a study on existing and emerging human rights standards and industry guidelines relevant to indigenous peoples and private sector resource development on their lands. It was proposed that OHCHR: organize a second workshop to develop a draft framework for dialogue and implementation on consultation, benefit-sharing and dispute resolution in private sector projects affecting indigenous peoples; request from industry and indigenous peoples existing agreements of consultative processes and benefit-sharing between them, facilitate the development of model best practices and consider making available model arrangements on the OHCHR web site; and organize, at the request of industry, human rights training on indigenous peoples for interested industry employees. Other recommendations were made to private sector resource companies and the World Bank.

Subcommission action. On 15 August [res. 2001/10], the Subcommission asked the Secretary-General to submit the Working Group's report on its 2001 session to the High Commissioner, indigenous organizations, Governments, intergovernmental organizations and NGOs concerned, as well as to thematic rapporteurs, special representatives, independent experts and working groups, and asked that it be made available to the Commission in 2002. It recommended that the Group, upon request, assist the open-ended intersessional working group to elaborate further the draft UN declaration on the rights of indigenous people (see p. 691) and adopt for its 2002 session the principal theme "Indigenous peoples and their right to development, including their right to participate in development affecting them". The Subcommission asked the Commission to invite Governments, intergovernmental and indigenous organizations and NGOs to provide information, particularly on the theme, request the Economic and Social Council to authorize the Working Group to meet for five working days prior to the Subcommission's 2002 session, and invite UNDP and the World Bank to present their new policy guidelines on indigenous peoples at that session. The Secretary-General was asked to prepare an annotated agenda for the Group's 2002 session. The Subcommission invited Ms. Motoc to prepare working papers on possible future standard-setting activities and on the consequences of biotechnology on indigenous peoples, and asked Ms. Daes to prepare a working paper on indigenous peoples' permanent sovereignty over natural resources. The High Commissioner was requested, in consultation with interested Governments, to continue to organize meetings on indigenous issues, to encourage studies on the rights to food and adequate nutrition of indigenous peoples and to organize a workshop for indigenous peoples in the context of the International Year of Ecotourism in 2002. Regarding the World Conference against Racism, Racial Discrimination, Xenophobia and Related Intolerance (see p. 615), the Subcommission made recommendations regarding the plenary, the dedication of a chapter to indigenous peoples in the declaration and programme of action, and the participation of indigenous peoples.

Also on 15 August [dec. 2001/111], the Subcommission recommended that OHCHR organize a preparatory workshop on implementation of the recommendations relating to indigenous peoples contained in Agenda 21.

On the same date [dec. 2001/112], the Subcommission requested the Commission to recommend that the Economic and Social Council invite the Working Group's Chairperson-Rapporteur, Ms. Daes, to attend the first meeting of the Permanent Forum on Indigenous Issues in 2002, and to present to it the Group's report on its 2001 session.

Voluntary Fund for Indigenous Populations

A May note by the Secretariat [E/CN.4/Sub.2/AC.4/2001/4] contained the recommendations adopted by the Board of Trustees of the United Nations Voluntary Fund for Indigenous Populations at its fourteenth session (Geneva, 28-30 March and 2 April). The Board recommended travel grants for 79 representatives of indigenous communities and organizations to allow them to attend the Working Group on Indigenous Populations, for a total of about $321,700; travel grants to allow 23 representatives to attend the working group on the draft UN declaration on the rights of indigenous peoples, totalling some $110,200; and sufficient funds, amounting to about $38,000, to allow indigenous representatives to attend, as observers, a possible meeting of the Permanent Forum on Indigenous Peoples in 2002 (see p. 692). The recommendations were approved by the High Commissioner on behalf of the Secretary-General on 7 April. Annexed to the report was a list of beneficiaries.

Subcommission action. On 15 August [res. 2001/10], the Subcommission appealed to Governments, organizations and individuals in a position to do so to contribute to the Fund.

International Decade of the World's Indigenous People

Commission action. On 24 April [res. 2001/59], the Commission invited the Working Group to continue its review of activities undertaken during the International Decade of the World's Indigenous People (1995-2004). The High Commissioner, in her capacity as coordinator of the Decade, was asked to update her annual report on activities within the UN system under the Decade's programme of activities, to ensure that OHCHR's indigenous peoples unit was adequately staffed and resourced, and to give due regard to developing human rights training for indigenous people. The Commission recommended that the situation of indigenous people be taken into account in forthcoming relevant UN conferences. It suggested that the Subcommission's proposal to hold an international conference to evaluate the Decade [YUN 2000, p. 728] be considered in the context of the Economic and Social Council's review of existing mechanisms, procedures and programmes regarding indigenous issues; the conference would take place once the Permanent Forum on Indigenous Issues had been established and had held its first annual session.

UN financial and development institutions, operational programmes and specialized agencies were asked to give increased priority and resources to improve the conditions of indigenous people; launch special projects to strengthen their community-level initiatives and facilitate information exchange and expertise among indigenous people and other relevant experts; and designate focal points or other mechanisms to coordinate with the High Commissioner activities relating to the Decade.

Report of Secretary-General. In July [A/56/206], the Secretary-General summarized implementation of the programme of activities for the Decade undertaken by OHCHR from autumn 2000 to June 2001. OHCHR helped organize the second workshop on multiculturalism in Africa (Kidal, Mali, 8-13 January) (see p. 623) and, as lead agency for the Permanent Forum on Indigenous Issues (see p. 692), held meetings with indigenous peoples, Governments and UN agencies. Technical cooperation projects benefiting indigenous people were under way in Bolivia, Ecuador and Guatemala. Other activities described in the report were updated by the High Commissioner (see below).

Subcommission action. On 15 August [res. 2001/12], the Subcommission, welcoming the observance in 2001 of the International Day of the World's Indigenous People (26 July), recommended that it be held on the fourth day of the Working Group's session in 2002 to ensure as large a participation of indigenous peoples as possible. It recommended that the Decade's coordinator consider holding a fund-raising meeting to encourage financial contributions to the Voluntary Fund for the Decade (see p. 691) and the UN Voluntary Fund for Indigenous Populations (see p. 689), and that qualified staff, including indigenous persons, be appointed to assist OHCHR in the indigenous programme and that she report thereon to the Subcommission and the Working Group in 2002. Governments, intergovernmental organizations, NGOs, individuals and indigenous organizations were urged to contribute to the Voluntary Fund for the Decade. The Subcommission recommended that the High Commissioner organize meetings and activities within the framework of the Decade to raise public awareness about indigenous issues; organize not later than 2002, in collaboration with relevant organizations, a workshop on indigenous peoples, private sector natural resource, energy and mining companies and human rights to contribute to ongoing work in that field; take action to promote the establishment, within the UN Office of Legal Affairs, of a database on national legislation on matters of relevance to indigenous peoples, and a compilation of treaties and agreements between States and indigenous peoples, as well as establish, in coordination with the UN Department of Public Information, a global public awareness programme on indigenous issues; organize a seminar on legal instruments between States and indigenous peoples to discuss possible follow-up to a 1999 study [YUN 1999, p. 686]; and authorize the convening of a conference on indigenous peoples' issues, with the theme "Rio+10", referring to the 10-year review of the implementation of Agenda 21 (see p. 749). The Subcommission invited the Commission to recommend that the Economic and Social Council authorize the convening of an international conference on indigenous issues during the last year of the Decade (2004), with a view to evaluating the Decade and considering policies and programmes that would contribute to action by States to promote better relations between the indigenous and non-indigenous segments of their population.

Report of High Commissioner. A report of the High Commissioner [E/CN.4/2002/96] reviewed UN activities under the programme for the Decade. OHCHR implemented the Indigenous Fellowship Programme (25 June-23 November) for five fellows from Australia, Botswana, Ecuador, Namibia and Thailand and, in cooperation with the University of Deusto (Bilbao, Spain), provided training for five indigenous candidates from Chile, Ecuador, Guatemala, Honduras and Peru. OHCHR organized indigenous parallel events relating to the World Conference against Racism, Racial Discrimination, Xenophobia and Related Intolerance (see p. 615), including an indigenous media dialogue focusing on the media's role in combating discrimination against indigenous peoples, a forum on indigenous women and a round table on current issues and new developments. Regarding other activities, the High Commissioner highlighted OHCHR efforts to prepare for the first (2002) session of the Permanent Forum on Indigenous Issues and to mainstream indigenous issues into its technical cooperation programme. She described the activities of the Voluntary Fund for the Decade (see below) and the Voluntary Fund for Indigenous Populations (see p. 689).

Voluntary Fund for International Decade

A May note by the Secretariat contained the report of the Advisory Group of the United Nations Voluntary Fund for the International Decade of the World's Indigenous People on its sixth session (Geneva, 2-5 April), including its recommendations for grants from the Fund that had been approved by the coordinator of the Decade [E/CN.4/Sub.2/AC.4/2001/5]. Contributions available to the Group as at 23 March totalled some $577,000. The Group recommended 30 project grants, which were approved for a total of some $252,000. Other activities proposed included the workshop on indigenous peoples, the private sector, natural resource, energy and mining companies and human rights (see p. 688) for $47,000; a round table on indigenous peoples, racism and the media for $50,400; a human rights training seminar in Mexico for $40,000; and human rights training for indigenous communities in a single country for $12,000. It approved a new guideline concerning emergency assistance for projects in the intersessional period, under which, in exceptional cases, organizations could request up to $5,000 for programmes that had already been subsidized by the Fund but had encountered financial difficulties. Based on requests received and activities financed, the Advisory Group recommended that a total of $1 million be requested for the Fund in OHCHR's annual appeal for 2002.

Draft declaration

Commission action. On 24 April [res. 2001/58], the Commission, taking note of the report of the working group to elaborate a draft UN declaration on the rights of indigenous peoples on its session in 2000 [YUN 2000, p. 729], recommended that the group meet for 10 working days prior to the Commission's 2002 session and asked the group to submit a progress report.

On 24 July, the Economic and Social Council authorized the group to meet (**decision 2001/270**).

Subcommission action. On 15 August [res. 2001/12], the Subcommission recommended the adoption of the draft declaration as early as possible and not later than the end of the Decade, in accordance with General Assembly resolution 50/157 [YUN 1995, p. 772].

GENERAL ASSEMBLY ACTION

On 19 December [meeting 88], the General Assembly, on the recommendation of the Third Committee [A/56/580], adopted **resolution 56/140** without vote [agenda item 116].

International Decade of the World's Indigenous People

The General Assembly,

Recalling its resolution 55/80 of 4 December 2000 and previous resolutions on the International Decade of the World's Indigenous People,

Recalling also its resolution 40/131 of 13 December 1985, by which it established the United Nations Voluntary Fund for Indigenous Populations,

Recalling further that the goal of the Decade is to strengthen international cooperation for the solution of problems faced by indigenous people in such areas as human rights, the environment, development, education and health, and that the theme of the Decade is "Indigenous people: partnership in action",

Welcoming, in this respect, the contribution made through the World Conference against Racism, Racial Discrimination, Xenophobia and Related Intolerance, held at Durban, South Africa, from 31 August to 8 September 2001, to the realization of the goals of the Decade,

Welcoming also the appointment of a special rapporteur of the Commission on Human Rights on the situation of human rights and fundamental freedoms of indigenous people, with the mandate spelled out in Commission resolution 2001/57 of 24 April 2001,

Recognizing the importance of consultation and cooperation with indigenous people in planning and implementing the programme of activities for the International Decade of the World's Indigenous People, the need for adequate financial support from the international community, including support from within the United Nations system, and the need for adequate coordination and communication channels,

Urging all parties to continue to intensify their efforts to achieve the goals of the Decade,

1. *Takes note* of the report of the Secretary-General on the implementation of the programme of activities for the International Decade of the World's Indigenous People;

2. *Affirms its conviction* of the value and diversity of the cultures and forms of social organization of indigenous people and its conviction that the development of indigenous people within their countries will contribute to the socio-economic, cultural and environmental advancement of all the countries of the world;

3. *Emphasizes* the importance of strengthening the human and institutional capacity of indigenous people to develop their own solutions to their problems;

4. *Requests* the United Nations High Commissioner for Human Rights, as coordinator for the Decade:

(*a*) To continue to promote the objectives of the Decade, taking into account, in the fulfilment of her functions, the special concerns of indigenous people;

(*b*) To give due regard to the dissemination, from within existing resources and voluntary contributions, of information on the situation, cultures, languages, rights and aspirations of indigenous people and, in that context, to consider the possibility of organizing projects, special events, exhibitions and other activities addressed to the public, in particular to young people;

(*c*) To submit, through the Secretary-General, an annual report to the General Assembly on the implementation of the programme of activities for the Decade;

5. *Reaffirms* the adoption of a declaration on the rights of indigenous people as a major objective of the Decade, and underlines the importance of effective participation by indigenous representatives in the open-ended intersessional working group of the Commission on Human Rights charged with developing a draft declaration on the rights of indigenous people, established pursuant to Commission resolution 1995/32 of 3 March 1995;

6. *Welcomes* Economic and Social Council decision 2001/316 of 26 July 2001 concerning the Permanent Forum on Indigenous Issues;

7. *Encourages* Governments to support the Decade by:

(*a*) Preparing relevant programmes, plans and reports in relation to the Decade, in consultation with indigenous people;

(*b*) Seeking means, in consultation with indigenous people, of giving indigenous people greater responsibility for their own affairs and an effective voice in decisions on matters that affect them;

(*c*) Establishing national committees or other mechanisms involving indigenous people to ensure that the objectives and activities of the Decade are planned and implemented on the basis of full partnership with indigenous people;

(*d*) Contributing to the United Nations Trust Fund for the International Decade of the World's Indigenous People;

(*e*) Contributing, together with other donors, to the United Nations Voluntary Fund for Indigenous Populations in order to assist indigenous representatives in participating in the Working Group on Indigenous Populations of the Subcommission on the Promotion and Protection of Human Rights and the open-ended intersessional working group of the Commission on Human Rights charged with elaborating a draft declaration on the rights of indigenous people;

(*f*) Considering contributing, as appropriate, to the Fund for the Development of Indigenous Peoples in Latin America and the Caribbean, in support of the goals of the Decade;

(*g*) Identifying resources for activities designed to implement the goals of the Decade, in cooperation with indigenous people and intergovernmental and non-governmental organizations;

8. *Invites* United Nations financial and development institutions, operational programmes and the specialized agencies and secretariats, as well as other regional and international organizations, in accordance with the existing procedures of their governing bodies:

(*a*) To give increased priority and resources to improving the conditions of indigenous people, with particular emphasis on the needs of those people in developing countries, including through the preparation of specific programmes of action for the implementation of the goals of the Decade, within their areas of competence;

(*b*) To launch special projects, through appropriate channels and in cooperation with indigenous people, to strengthen their community-level initiatives and to facilitate the exchange of information and expertise among indigenous people and other relevant experts;

(*c*) To designate focal points for the coordination of activities related to the Decade with the Office of the United Nations High Commissioner for Human Rights;

and commends those institutions, programmes, agencies and regional and international organizations that have already done so;

9. *Decides* that the United Nations Voluntary Fund for Indigenous Populations should also be used to assist representatives of indigenous communities and organizations in attending, as observers, the sessions of the Permanent Forum on Indigenous Issues;

10. *Appeals* to all Governments and organizations to consider contributing to the United Nations Voluntary Fund for Indigenous Populations, if possible with a substantial increase in the level of contributions;

11. *Recommends* that the Secretary-General ensure coordinated follow-up to the recommendations concerning indigenous people of relevant United Nations conferences, namely, the World Conference on Human Rights, held at Vienna from 14 to 25 June 1993, the United Nations Conference on Environment and Development, held at Rio de Janeiro, Brazil, from 3 to 14 June 1992, the International Conference on Population and Development, held at Cairo from 5 to 13 September 1994, the Fourth World Conference on Women, held at Beijing from 4 to 15 September 1995, the World Summit for Social Development, held at Copenhagen from 6 to 12 March 1995, the second United Nations Conference on Human Settlements (Habitat II), held at Istanbul, Turkey, from 3 to 14 June 1996, and the World Food Summit, held at Rome from 13 to 17 November 1996, and other relevant international conferences;

12. *Requests* the United Nations High Commissioner for Human Rights to submit, through the Secretary-General, a report on the implementation of the programme of activities for the Decade to the General Assembly at its fifty-seventh session;

13. *Decides* to include in the provisional agenda of its fifty-seventh session the item entitled "Programme of activities of the International Decade of the World's Indigenous People".

Permanent Forum on Indigenous Issues

Report of High Commissioner. In May [E/2001/64], the High Commissioner, noting that OHCHR had been designated the lead agency for implementing Economic and Social Council resolution 2000/22 [YUN 2000, p. 731], which established the Permanent Forum on Indigenous Issues, stated that the Office, in February, invited indigenous organizations to hold consultations and to nominate, by 1 October, indigenous candidates for the Forum. OHCHR also undertook consultations with UN departments, organizations and agencies on how the UN system could work together for the success of the Forum. In that context, 10 UN organizations provided information about their activities, appointed focal points for the Forum and expressed willingness to cooperate. Information provided by the UN organizations lacked global statistical data relating to indigenous peoples; thus, the High Commissioner proposed that they prepare a consolidated paper identifying options and approaches for the Forum's interaction with pertinent UN organizations and agencies. She had considered establishing a secretariat to service the Forum, which could draw from the experience, knowledge and support of key UN partners.

ECONOMIC AND SOCIAL COUNCIL ACTION

On 2 July, the Economic and Social Council, acting on a May request of Mexico [E/2001/60], decided to include in the provisional agenda of its 2001 substantive session the supplementary subitem entitled "Permanent Forum on Indigenous Issues", under the item on social and human rights questions (**decision 2001/224**).

On 26 July, the Council adopted **decision 2001/316** [draft: E/2001/L.27] without vote [agenda item 14 (*i*)].

Permanent Forum on Indigenous Issues

At its 43rd plenary meeting, on 26 July 2001, the Economic and Social Council, recalling its resolution 2000/22 of 28 July 2000, in which it established the Permanent Forum on Indigenous Issues, decided:

(*a*) To convene the first annual session of the Forum at United Nations Headquarters from 6 to 17 May 2002, without prejudice to any future venue of the Forum;

(*b*) That the election of the eight government expert members of the Forum would reflect the distribution of seats among the regional groups, as follows, with due regard for the distribution of indigenous people among the countries of each of the regional groups:

(i) One seat for African States;

(ii) One seat for Asian States;

(iii) One seat for Eastern European States;

(iv) One seat for Latin American and Caribbean States;

(v) One seat for Western European and other States;

(vi) Three seats to rotate among the five regional groups in accordance with the following pattern:

Election 1	*Election 2*	*Election 3*	*Election 4*	*Election 5*
Latin America and Caribbean	Africa	Western Europe and other	Eastern Europe	Asia
Western Europe and other	Eastern Europe	Asia	Latin America and Caribbean	Africa
Asia	Latin America and Caribbean	Africa	Western Europe and other	Eastern Europe

This election method is without prejudice to the evaluation of the functioning of the Forum five years after its establishment, as foreseen in Council resolution 2000/22;

(*c*) To hold the first elections and appointments to the Forum at an appropriate time to be announced by the President of the Council but not later than 15 December 2001;

(*d*) To urge the General Assembly at its fifty-sixth session to take action on the proposed programme budget for 2002-2003 in order to secure, within existing resources, an adequately funded and well-functioning Forum that reflects its broad mandate, and in this context recalls paragraph 6 of Council resolution 2000/22;

(*e*) To request the Secretary-General to seek information from Governments, non-governmental organizations, indigenous people's organizations, the Permanent Forum on Indigenous Issues and all existing mechanisms, procedures and programmes within the United Nations concerning indigenous issues, including the Working Group on Indigenous Populations, as a basis for holding the review mandated in paragraph 8 of Council resolution 2000/22 as soon as possible and not later than the substantive session of 2003 of the Council.

Indigenous land rights

Working paper of Special Rapporteur. In June [E/CN.4/Sub.2/2001/21], the Special Rapporteur on indigenous peoples and their relationship to land, Erica Irene A. Daes (Greece), in her final working paper, stated that one of the most widespread contemporary problems was the failure of States to recognize the existence of, and to accord legal status and legal rights to protect, indigenous land use, occupancy and ownership. In countries with laws concerning indigenous peoples, the most significant problems arose because of discriminatory laws and legal doctrines stipulating that indigenous land title could be terminated without due process or compensation and the doctrine that treaties with indigenous peoples could be violated or abrogated without any remedy; the failure of States to demarcate indigenous lands and to implement existing laws to protect indigenous lands and resources; improper, unfair and fraudulent claims processes; and the relocation of indigenous peoples and expropriation of their lands for national development. Additional problems included the allotment of indigenous lands to individuals; settlement programmes on indigenous lands; the practice of requiring that indigenous lands be held in trust by the State; programmes that used indigenous lands as collateral for loans; adverse management of sacred and cultural sites by States; the failure of States to protect the environmental integrity of indigenous lands and resources; and the failure to accord indigenous peoples the right to manage and control the development of their lands and resources.

The Special Rapporteur identified principles that might be helpful in evaluating and guiding State and international measures, and recommended that States enact legislation to recognize, demarcate and protect indigenous lands, territories and resources. Governments should formally renounce discriminatory legal doctrines and policies, and adopt corrective legislation or policies and constitutional reforms. In addition, they should provide measures to implement, amend and enforce land settlements and agreements, and for dispute resolution. In consultation with indigenous peoples, States should create a permanent capital fund to compensate indigenous peoples whose lands and resources were taken. Indigenous peoples should participate in decision-making regarding land, resources and development at the international, regional, national and local levels. The Permanent Forum should consider creating: a fact-finding body to visit sites and report on particular indigenous land and resource issues; a complaint mechanism or procedure for human rights violations pertaining to indigenous land and resources; and a procedure whereby countries could be called upon to report periodically regarding progress in protecting indigenous land and resource rights. It should also consider providing the Special Rapporteur with "peace-seeking" powers to investigate, recommend solutions, conciliate, mediate and assist in preventing or ending violence regarding indigenous land rights. The United Nations, its specialized agencies and other intergovernmental organizations should ensure that indigenous peoples' cultural diversity, traditional values and way of life were protected in the implementation of Agenda 21 [YUN 1992, p. 672].

Subcommission action. On 15 August [dec. 2001/109], the Subcommission decided to submit to the Commission in 2002 the Special Rapporteur's working paper and asked it to invite her to present the paper during the Commission's discussion of indigenous issues. The Secretary-General was asked to assist the Special Rapporteur to enable her to attend the Commission's meetings. It requested that the paper be translated into the UN official languages, published and disseminated widely. The Commission was requested to consider establishing in 2002 a pre-sessional working group, in which the Special Rapporteur should be invited to participate, particularly to discuss the fundamental guiding principles and recommendations proposed in the working paper.

Persons with disabilities

Report of High Commissioner. In May [E/2001/64], the High Commissioner stated that no fewer than 600 million persons, constituting about 10 per cent of the world's total population, suffered from some type of disability, some 80 per cent of whom lived in developing countries.

In the majority of countries, at least 1 of every 10 persons had a physical, mental or sensory impairment, and at least 25 per cent of the entire population of those countries were adversely affected. Persons with functional limitations or disabilities were particularly vulnerable to exclusion, marginalization and abuse. OHCHR had reinforced its support for the work of the Special Rapporteur on disability of the Commission for Social Development and had decided to further encourage UN human rights mechanisms to pay greater attention to the rights of persons with disabilities. OHCHR held a consultation on 17 April with Governments, intergovernmental organizations, NGOs, specialized agencies, UN bodies and national institutions, which reaffirmed the human rights dimension of issues related to disability and strengthened the link between OHCHR, the Special Rapporteur of the Commission for Social Development and the Commission on Human Rights.

Report of Secretary-General. In response to a 2000 Commission request [YUN 2000, p. 733], the Secretary-General, in August [A/56/263], reported on progress made regarding efforts to ensure the full recognition and enjoyment of the human rights of persons with disabilities. In that regard, the report described activities of UN human rights treaty bodies, the Commission and OHCHR (see above).

On 19 December, the General Assembly took note of the Secretary-General's report (**decision 56/429**).

(See also p. 1010.)

People with HIV/AIDS

Report of Secretary-General. In accordance with its 1999 request [YUN 1999, p. 687], the Commission considered a report of the Secretary-General [E/CN.4/2001/80], summarizing comments received from Governments, UN organs, programmes and specialized agencies, as well as from intergovernmental organizations and NGOs, regarding steps they had taken to promote and implement the Guidelines on HIV/AIDS and human rights, recommended by the experts participating in the Second International Consultation on HIV/AIDS and Human Rights [YUN 1996, p. 617]. The report provided information on policies and activities of the United Nations and regional organizations, relating to the promotion and protection of HIV/AIDS-related human rights.

Commission action. By a roll-call vote of 52 to none, with 1 abstention, the Commission, on 23 April [res. 2001/33], called on States to promote the availability in sufficient quantities of pharmaceuticals and medical technologies for treating

HIV/AIDS, and to ensure that they were medically appropriate and accessible to all without discrimination. It called on the international community, particularly developed countries, to continue assistance to developing countries in their fight against HIV/AIDS. The Commission asked the Committee on Economic, Social and Cultural Rights, when considering the human rights dimension of combating pandemics such as HIV/AIDS, to give attention to the issue of medication, and invited States to include appropriate information thereon in their reports to the Committee. The Secretary-General was asked to solicit comments from Governments, UN organs, programmes and specialized agencies, international organizations and NGOs on steps they had taken to promote and implement the resolution and to report in 2002.

On 24 April [res. 2001/51], the Commission asked States to establish coordinated, participatory, gender-sensitive, transparent and accountable national policies and programmes to respond to HIV/AIDS, and translate those policies to district-level and local action; develop and support services, including legal aid, to educate people infected and affected by HIV/AIDS about their rights and to assist them in realizing those rights; combat discrimination, prejudice and stigma, and ensure full enjoyment of all human rights by people infected and affected by HIV/AIDS; ensure that codes of professional conduct, responsibility and practice respected human rights and dignity, including access to care for people with and affected by HIV/AIDS; and develop and support mechanisms to monitor and enforce HIV/AIDS-related human rights. The Commission asked its special representatives, special rapporteurs and working groups, including the special rapporteurs on the right to education, on the promotion and protection of freedom of opinion and expression, on violence against women and on the sale of children, child prostitution and child pornography, to integrate the protection of HIV-related human rights within their respective mandates. The Secretary-General was asked to invite UN bodies and Member States to integrate HIV-related human rights into their policies, programmes and activities, and to involve NGOs and community-based organizations in all phases of development and implementation, in order to help ensure a system-wide approach, stressing the coordinating and catalytic role of the Joint United Nations Programme on HIV/AIDS (see p. 1136). He was also asked to solicit comments from Governments, UN organs, programmes and specialized agencies, international organizations and NGOs on steps taken to promote and implement the Guidelines on HIV/AIDS and human rights, and to report in 2003.

On 24 July, the Economic and Social Council approved the Commission's request to its special representatives, special rapporteurs and working groups (**decision 2001/268**).

Chapter III

Human rights violations

Alleged violations of human rights and international humanitarian law in a number of countries were examined in 2001 by the General Assembly, the Economic and Social Council, the Commission on Human Rights and its Subcommission on the Promotion and Protection of Human Rights, as well as by special rapporteurs, special representatives of the Secretary-General and independent experts appointed to examine the allegations.

General aspects

Under a procedure established by Economic and Social Council resolution 1503(XLVIII) [YUN 1970, p. 530] to deal with communications alleging denial or violation of human rights, the Working Group on Situations of the Commission on Human Rights, established by Council resolution 1990/41 [YUN 1990, p. 648], in closed session on 28 and 30 March, considered the human rights situations in Maldives, the Republic of the Congo, Togo and Uganda. The Commission discontinued consideration of the situations in Maldives, the Republic of the Congo and Uganda.

(For information regarding the right to restitution, compensation and rehabilitation for victims of grave violations of human rights and fundamental freedoms, see p. 635.)

Africa

Burundi

Commission action. On 20 April [E/2001/23 (res. 2001/21)], the Commission on Human Rights, expressing deep concern at the continuing violations of human rights and international humanitarian law in Burundi, urged all parties to the conflict to end the violence, especially against civilians. It noted government efforts to ensure the full respect for established legal safeguards for human rights and international human rights standards and the establishment of a government commission on human rights, and welcomed the dismantling of regroupment camps, the political compact between the Government and the National Assembly and the dialogue among Burundians taking place under the Arusha peace process (see p. 145). The Commission asked the Government to take further measures to end impunity, to continue to carry out judicial reforms and to establish a security environment conducive to the work of aid organizations. The United Nations and the donor community were asked to augment the flow of humanitarian assistance.

The Commission decided to extend the Special Rapporteur's mandate for an additional year and asked her to submit an interim report to the General Assembly in 2001 and a report to the Commission in 2002, giving her work a gender-specific dimension. The Economic and Social Council endorsed the Commission's decision and its requests to the Special Rapporteur on 24 July (**decision 2001/256**).

Reports of Special Rapporteur. In March, Special Rapporteur Marie-Thérèse A. Keita-Bocoum (Côte d'Ivoire) reported on the human rights situation in Burundi during the period from 1 August 2000 to 31 January 2001 [YUN 2000, p. 735], based on her third mission to the country (18-26 January). As she was finishing her report, she learned that violent clashes begun by rebels belonging to the Forces nationales pour la libération (FNL) in February in a primarily Hutu area in northern Bujumbura had caused the displacement of some 20,000 persons. Attacks by Forces pour la défense de la démocratie (FDD) rebels near Rutovu had also caused mass exoduses.

In an interim report covering the period from 1 February to 31 August, which the Secretary-General transmitted to the General Assembly in October [A/56/479], the Special Rapporteur described the political and economic and social situation in Burundi and developments in the peace process (see p. 145), based on her fourth mission to Burundi (5-14 July). She observed that the human rights situation had not improved a great deal since January. The main violations related to the right to life—mostly massacres of civilians carried out by State agents and armed groups—to physical integrity and to personal freedom and security. Violations of the right to freedom of movement and to the freedom to choose one's residence also continued, particularly in the southern and south-eastern provinces, where a portion of the population was seeking refuge in the United Republic of Tanzania. The freedoms of opinion and of expression were restricted. In the majority of secondary detention centres, overcrowding, ill-treatment and illegal arrest and detention were increasingly common. Respect for the rights of women and of the most vulnerable groups, including children, was considered of secondary importance; the same was true of economic, social and cultural rights. The justice system had made little progress due to the political climate, which was influenced by developments in the peace process, and also because of a desperate lack of resources in the courts; in some areas, there had been a marked slowdown, if not a regression. The Governmental Commission on Human Rights, which officially began functioning on 25 April, did not meet the basic requirements demanded of national human rights institutes and appeared to have operational and/or resource difficulties. It was, however, encouraging to note a greater awareness of the need to respect and promote human rights. Seminars, training sessions and days of reflection had been organized with the support of the Burundi office of the United Nations High Commissioner for Human Rights, other UN agencies, the Ministry of Human Rights and human rights associations.

The Special Rapporteur asked parties to the conflict to do all they could to achieve peace through negotiations and urged them to respect the right to life. She recommended implementation of the ban on recruitment into the army of those under the age of 18 and its application to the police force. The Government was invited to adopt more determined action against torture and unlawful detention, especially in military camps, and to devise and promote land management strategies to prevent land disputes. The international community was called on to persuade the belligerents to abandon their attempts to resolve matters through force of arms and to sit down at the negotiating table. The Special Rapporteur supported the convening of a conference in the Great Lakes region.

The General Assembly took note of the report on 19 December (**decision 56/429**).

In a later report covering the period from 1 September to 15 December [E/CN.4/2002/49], based on her fifth mission to Burundi (28 November–14 December), the Special Rapporteur updated the political, economic and social situation, particularly developments in the peace process since the inauguration of the Transitional Government on 1 November (see p. 151). The human rights situation was still marked by continued fighting between government forces and armed groups in various provinces, Bujumbura-rural, Bururi, Rutana, Makamba, Ruyigi and Muramvya provinces being the most affected. The rights to life, security and physical integrity were those most frequently violated. The rights to personal freedom and physical integrity were constantly violated, with numerous reports of illegal arrests and detention in the *cachots* (communal detention centres) of the police and gendarmerie or the military, where torture was practised. The right to freedom of movement and choice of residence was utopic in provinces such as Bujumbura-rural and Bubanza. The security situation had deteriorated as a result of an increase in murders and other crime.

The adoption of a new constitution and the establishment of transitional institutions, such as the National Assembly and the Senate, constituted steps forward in the peace process. However, many Burundians were disappointed by the period following the establishment of the new Government; they considered that the language of the authorities did not reflect reality. The Special Rapporteur observed that some believed the legitimacy of the new Government could be compromised by the fact that its membership was not the outcome of a democratic process. Regarding human rights promotion and strengthening the rule of law, in addition to monitoring, training and seminars, a framework was established for coordination among human rights associations and non-governmental organizations (NGOs). In addition to previous recommendations, the Special Rapporteur urged the mediators to continue efforts to achieve a negotiated solution to the conflict; appealed to the armed groups and the Government to end all violence against civilians; recommended that the Government cease recruiting militias and abandon the programme instituted by the new Government to train civilians to defend themselves against rebel attacks; and called on the Government and the international community to ensure the implementation of the Arusha Agreement on Peace and Reconciliation in Burundi [YUN 2000, p. 146] and to prepare the way for the return of refugees.

Democratic Republic of the Congo

Commission action. On 20 April [res. 2001/19], the Commission, welcoming a number of positive developments regarding the Democratic Republic of the Congo (DRC), including commitments made in Lusaka, Zambia, in February and at the meeting between members of the Political Committee for the Implementation of the Lusaka

Ceasefire Agreement and the Security Council on 21 and 22 February (see p. 119), called on the Government to promote and protect human rights, reform and restore the judicial system, end impunity, create conditions for democratization, ensure respect for freedom of opinion and expression, remove remaining restrictions on the activities of NGOs, facilitate and strengthen cooperation with the UN human rights field office in the DRC, cooperate with the International Criminal Tribunal for Rwanda (ICTR) (see p. 1207) and ensure the security and freedom of movement of personnel of the United Nations Organization Mission in the DRC (MONUC) (see p. 125) and other associated personnel. Parties to the conflict were urged to implement the Lusaka Ceasefire Agreement [YUN 1999, p. 87], protect human rights and respect international law, ensure the safety and freedom of movement of UN and associated personnel, end the recruitment and use of child soldiers, cease military activity, create conditions for the return of refugees and displaced persons and cooperate with the National Commission of Inquiry on alleged massacres of a large number of refugees and also with the Secretary-General and the UN High Commissioner for Human Rights, with a view to the submission of a further report by the National Commission of Inquiry to the Secretary-General on progress made in investigating the massacres. It expressed concern at the adverse impact of the conflict on the human rights situation; the situation of human rights, particularly in the east of the country, and the continuing violations of human rights and international law; conflicts between the Hema and the Lendu ethnic groups in Orientale province; the excessive accumulation and spread of small arms and light weapons and their illicit distribution; violations of the freedoms of expression, opinion, association and assembly; the harassment and persecution of human rights defenders and their organizations; the intimidation of church representatives in the east; the severe insecurity, which impaired the ability of humanitarian organizations to access affected populations; and reports of illegal exploitation of natural resources and other forms of wealth in the country.

The Commission decided to extend the Special Rapporteur's mandate for an additional year and asked him to submit an interim report to the General Assembly in 2001, to report to the Commission in 2002 and to maintain a gender perspective in seeking and analysing information. It requested the Special Rapporteurs on the human rights situation in the DRC and on extrajudicial, summary or arbitrary executions and a member of the Working Group on Enforced or Involuntary Disappearances to carry out, as soon as security considerations permitted, in cooperation with the National Commission of Inquiry to investigate alleged human rights violations and breaches of international humanitarian law in the DRC between 1996 and 1997, a joint mission to investigate all massacres carried out in the DRC, with a view to bringing to justice those responsible and to report to the Assembly in 2001 and to the Commission in 2002. The Commission asked the Secretary-General to assist the Special Rapporteur on the situation of human rights in the DRC and the joint mission, the High Commissioner to provide technical expertise to the joint mission, and the international community to support the DRC human rights field office.

The Economic and Social Council endorsed the Commission's decisions and its requests to the Special Rapporteurs and Working Group member on 24 July (**decision 2001/254**).

Following the resignation of the Special Rapporteur, Roberto Garretón (Chile), the Commission appointed Iulia-Antoanella Motoc (Romania) in November.

Joint mission. In July [A/56/220], the Secretary-General informed the General Assembly that the Special Rapporteur on the human rights situation in the DRC would visit the DRC from 19 July to 2 August. He would pay particular attention to security conditions in order to assess the feasibility of the joint mission and the extent to which the Government and the rebel groups would support its work. The details would be reflected in an interim report to the Assembly (see p. 699).

Reports of Special Rapporteur. In a March addendum [E/CN.4/2001/40/Add.1] to a previous report [YUN 2000, p. 737], Special Rapporteur Roberto Garretón described developments in the DRC, based on his mission to the country (11-21 March). His visit was prompted by the seriousness of the internal armed conflict between the Bahema and the Balendu in Ituri, which had led to the premeditated murder of six International Committee of the Red Cross (ICRC) humanitarian workers. The Special Rapporteur described the various armed conflicts in the DRC (see p. 117) and noted that the situation of child soldiers had deteriorated.

The Special Rapporteur stated that following the assassination, in January, of President Laurent-Désiré Kabila, his son, Joseph was made temporary head of State (see p. 117). In February, President Kabila established an international commission to investigate the assassination, which was given widespread powers—to arrest and detain, to search premises and public and private documents—in exercise of which it committed serious human rights violations.

By an August note [A/56/327], the Secretary-General transmitted to the General Assembly a report of the Special Rapporteur following his visit to the DRC (20 July–1 August). The Special Rapporteur stated that, according to the reports of the NGO International Rescue Committee, 2 million people had died as a result of the war, of whom 200,000 were killed in violent acts. Beyond those figures, the population was enduring tremendous hardships. In areas controlled by the Rassemblement congolais pour la démocratie (RCD) and Rwanda and by the Front de libération du Congo (FLC) and Uganda, the most serious violations were reprisals against civilians, and the systematic, illegal looting of the natural wealth and resources belonging to the Congolese people; there was no freedom of expression and a one-party system was in effect: RCD in the east and FLC in the north-east. A negative aspect of Uganda's involvement was its strong support for the Bahema in the conflict with the Balendu, which had destabilized the region and paved the way for killings and abuses. No improvement was seen in the situation of women and children, and children continued to be recruited by the various national armies and foreign guerrilla movements involved in the war. On the positive side, political prisoners had been released, prison conditions improved, a law on political parties was adopted and interpreted rationally, and organizations that had been shut down resumed operations. The Special Rapporteur noted that the new President had announced measures, some of which had been implemented, including a moratorium on the death penalty, greater freedom of action for political parties, a National Human Rights Conference (June), and authorization for the resumption of a prominent NGO that his father had closed down. In addition, he had pledged to comply with the agreements concluded by his father in Lusaka [YUN 1999, p. 87], especially on supporting MONUC and the Facilitator of the Inter-Congolese Dialogue. However, the most serious human rights situation, the continuing abuses by the Military Court, had not been addressed, nor had the arbitrary actions of the international commission to investigate the assassination of the President. While daily newspapers operated, journalists had been detained and two private radio and television channels remained confiscated.

In addition to previous recommendations, the Special Rapporteur urged all parties to commit themselves to the Inter-Congolese Dialogue, cooperate with MONUC, begin to demobilize, disarm and reintegrate child soldiers and respect international humanitarian law. He recommended that the Government and other public authori-

ties restore the rule of law, draft laws to give effect to agreements reached at the National Human Rights Conference and give precedence to international human rights norms over domestic law. Countries that had violated the sovereignty and territorial integrity of the DRC were asked to comply with Security Council resolutions on withdrawal from the country and the demilitarization of Kisangi and refrain from exploiting Congolese natural wealth and resources and return the goods exploited illegally. RCD and FLC were urged to end their terror against civilians, end relations with the armies that had violated the DRC's sovereignty and suspend action that presupposed the country's partition. The Special Rapporteur proposed that the Office of the United Nations High Commissioner for Human Rights (OHCHR) open new offices in the country's main cities.

(For political details, see p. 116.)

GENERAL ASSEMBLY ACTION

On 19 December [meeting 88], the General Assembly, on the recommendation of the Third (Social, Humanitarian and Cultural) Committee [A/56/583/Add.3], adopted **resolution 56/173** by recorded vote (90-3-69) [agenda item 119 (c)].

Situation of human rights in the Democratic Republic of the Congo

The General Assembly,

Reaffirming that all Member States are required to promote and protect human rights and fundamental freedoms as stated in the Charter of the United Nations, the Universal Declaration of Human Rights, the International Covenants on Human Rights and other applicable human rights instruments,

Aware that the Democratic Republic of the Congo is a party to the International Covenant on Civil and Political Rights, the International Covenant on Economic, Social and Cultural Rights, the Convention against Torture and Other Cruel, Inhuman or Degrading Treatment or Punishment, the Convention on the Elimination of All Forms of Discrimination against Women, the International Convention on the Elimination of All Forms of Racial Discrimination, the Convention on the Rights of the Child, the Geneva Conventions of 12 August 1949 for the protection of victims of war and the first Additional Protocol thereto, of 1977, as well as the African Charter on Human and Peoples' Rights,

Recalling its previous resolutions on the subject, the most recent of which is resolution 55/117 of 4 December 2000, and those of the Commission on Human Rights, as well as Security Council resolutions 1304 (2000) of 16 June 2000, 1332(2000) of 14 December 2000, 1341(2001) of 22 February 2001, 1355(2001) of 15 June 2001 and 1376(2001) of 9 November 2001,

Recalling also the Ceasefire Agreement signed at Lusaka, as well as the Kampala disengagement plan and the Harare sub-plans for disengagement and redeployment, and welcoming the decision of the Security Council to authorize the start-up of phase III of the

United Nations Organization Mission in the Democratic Republic of the Congo,

Concerned at all violations of human rights and international humanitarian law in the territory of the Democratic Republic of the Congo by parties to the conflict, including acts of and incitement to ethnic hatred and violence, as noted in the reports of the Special Rapporteur of the Commission on Human Rights on the situation of human rights in the Democratic Republic of the Congo,

Noting that the promotion and the protection of human rights for all are essential for achieving stability and security in the region and will contribute to the creation of the environment necessary for cooperation among States in the region,

Reiterating its support for the continuation of the Inter-Congolese Dialogue, which, requiring the cooperation and full participation of all the Congolese parties, is an essential process for the future of the Democratic Republic of the Congo and the entire region,

Acknowledging the need to expand the presence and full participation of women in the peace process,

Recalling its decision to request the Special Rapporteurs of the Commission on Human Rights on the situation of human rights in the Democratic Republic of the Congo and on extrajudicial, summary or arbitrary executions and a member of the Working Group on Enforced or Involuntary Disappearances to carry out a joint mission of investigation in the Democratic Republic of the Congo, while regretting that the security situation in the country is still preventing such a mission,

Encouraging the Government of the Democratic Republic of the Congo to give effect to its earlier commitment, including to the United Nations High Commissioner for Human Rights, to restore and reform its judicial system, in accordance with the relevant international conventions, and to put an end to the trying of civilians by the Military Court,

1. *Welcomes:*

(a) The meeting between the Political Committee for the Implementation of the Lusaka Ceasefire Agreement and the Security Council on 9 November 2001, and urges all parties to take the necessary measures to implement phase III of the deployment of the United Nations Organization Mission in the Democratic Republic of the Congo;

(b) The reports of the Special Rapporteur of the Commission on Human Rights on the situation of human rights in the Democratic Republic of the Congo;

(c) The visits made by the Special Rapporteur to the Democratic Republic of the Congo from 11 to 21 March 2001 and from 20 July to 1 August 2001 for the purpose of evaluating the existing situation in the country;

(d) The holding in Gaborone from 20 to 24 August 2001 of the preparatory meeting for the Inter-Congolese Dialogue and the signature by all the parties concerned of a declaration of commitment providing for the release of all prisoners of conscience, the free movement of goods and persons and the protection of the civilian populations;

(e) The effective release by the Government of the Democratic Republic of the Congo of several human rights defenders;

(f) The adoption by the Government of the Democratic Republic of the Congo of Law No. 001 of 17 May 2001, on political parties, and the promise of openness and tolerance which it offers, inviting the Government to continue on that path and to enforce the law fully for the benefit of all political tendencies in the Democratic Republic of the Congo;

(g) The action undertaken by the human rights field office in the Democratic Republic of the Congo, while encouraging the Government to collaborate and further strengthen its cooperation with the office;

(h) The statements by the President of the Democratic Republic of the Congo to the effect that child soldiers would in future no longer be recruited and, in that context, the ratification by the Democratic Republic of the Congo of the Optional Protocol to the Convention on the Rights of the Child on the involvement of children in armed conflict, and the commitment made by the Government of the Democratic Republic of the Congo to cooperate with United Nations organs and non-governmental organizations in order to ensure the demobilization and reintegration of child soldiers, as well as the measures taken by the Government of the Democratic Republic of the Congo to that end, while urging other parties to the conflict to do the same;

(i) The release and repatriation carried out under the auspices of the International Committee of the Red Cross in the Democratic Republic of the Congo, in conformity with international humanitarian law, of persons at risk because of their ethnic origin, and of prisoners of war;

(j) The continuing presence and wider deployment of the United Nations Organization Mission in the Democratic Republic of the Congo in support of the implementation of the Lusaka Ceasefire Agreement;

(k) The commitments made by the President of the Democratic Republic of the Congo to improve the human rights situation, particularly those given when he attended the fifty-seventh session of the Commission on Human Rights, while encouraging him to give concrete effect to those commitments;

(l) The organization of the National Human Rights Conference, held in June 2001, while expressing the hope that its results will lead to an improvement of the situation of human rights in the Democratic Republic of the Congo;

(m) The consent of the President of the Democratic Republic of the Congo to the Special Rapporteur's plan to undertake, within the framework of his mandate and in the coming months, an initial joint mission to investigate the massacres in the province of South Kivu and other atrocities referred to by the Special Rapporteur in his latest and previous reports, with a view to bringing to justice those responsible and reporting thereon to the General Assembly and the Commission on Human Rights, and the agreement given by the rebel groups to that mission of investigation;

2. *Expresses its concern* at:

(a) The resumption of fighting in the eastern part of the country and the adverse impact of the conflict on the situation of human rights and its severe consequences for the security and well-being of the civilian population throughout the territory of the Democratic Republic of the Congo, including the increase in the number of refugees and internally displaced persons, particularly in the eastern part of the country;

(b) The missed opportunity for the implementation of the Inter-Congolese Dialogue at the meeting which was held for that purpose in Addis Ababa on 15 October 2001, while welcoming the scheduled resumption of the process in South Africa;

(c) The situation of human rights in the Democratic Republic of the Congo, particularly in the zones held by the rebel groups and under foreign occupation, and the persistent violations of human rights and international humanitarian law, including the atrocities against the civilian populations, usually committed with complete impunity, while emphasizing in this regard that the occupying forces should be held accountable for the violations of human rights in the territories under their control. It condemns in particular:

(i) All the massacres and atrocities still being committed throughout the territory of the Democratic Republic of the Congo, in particular in the zones held by the armed rebels and under foreign occupation, including Bugobe, Nyatende, Kamisimbi, Lurhala, Nyangesi, Biambwe, Nbingi, Bunyatenge, Kaghumo, Banyuke, and Kirima, Kalemié, Pweto, Rutshuru, Kibumba, Kimia Kimia, Dungo Mulunga and Kasese Bolanga;

(ii) The occurrence of cases of summary and arbitrary execution, disappearance, torture, arbitrary arrest and detention without trial of, among others, journalists, opposition politicians, human rights defenders and people who have co-operated with the United Nations mechanisms;

(iii) The numerous instances of rape and sexual violence against women and children, including as a means of warfare;

(iv) The continuing recruitment and use of child soldiers by armed forces and groups, including the enlistment and kidnapping of children throughout the territory of the Democratic Republic of the Congo, in particular in North and South Kivu and in the eastern province;

(v) The sentencing to death of civilians tried before the Military Court, in violation of the obligations assumed by the Democratic Republic of the Congo under the International Covenant on Civil and Political Rights, as well as the prolonged and arbitrary detentions ordered by the Court;

(vi) The death sentences and summary executions by the Congolese Rally for Democracy-Goma;

(vii) The indiscriminate attacks against civilian populations, including against hospitals in the zones held by rebel forces and the zones held by foreign forces;

(d) The conflicts between the Hema and Lendu ethnic groups in the eastern province, where thousands of Congolese have already been killed and where Uganda, which controls the zone de facto, is responsible for ensuring respect for human rights;

(e) The excessive accumulation and spread of small arms and the distribution, circulation and illicit trafficking of arms in the region and their negative impact on human rights;

(f) The breaches of freedom of expression, opinion, association and assembly throughout the territory of the Democratic Republic of the Congo, in particular in the eastern part of the country;

(g) The harassment and persecution of human rights defenders and other members of civil society;

(h) The acts of intimidation and persecution against representatives of the Churches, as well as the killings of those persons in the eastern part of the country;

(i) The severe insecurity, which seriously hampers the ability of humanitarian organizations to secure access to affected populations, particularly in the zones held by armed rebels and under the control of foreign forces, and condemns the killing of six humanitarian workers of the International Committee of the Red Cross on 26 April 2001 in Ituri Province, for which those responsible must be brought to justice;

(j) The illegal exploitation of the natural resources of the Democratic Republic of the Congo, demands that such exploitation cease, and emphasizes that the natural resources of the country should not be used to finance the conflict there;

3. *Urges* all parties to the conflict in the Democratic Republic of the Congo:

(a) To permit the restoration without delay of the sovereignty and territorial integrity of the Democratic Republic of the Congo, in accordance with the Lusaka Ceasefire Agreement and the relevant resolutions of the Security Council;

(b) To implement fully the Lusaka Ceasefire Agreement;

(c) To cease all military and logistic support as well as all strategic collaboration with the armed groups, particularly those operating in the eastern part of the Democratic Republic of the Congo;

(d) To do everything possible to create the prerequisites for further meetings with a view to advancing the Inter-Congolese Dialogue, with emphasis on ensuring the full participation of women in this process;

(e) To protect human rights and respect international humanitarian law, in particular, as applicable to them, the Geneva Conventions of 12 August 1949 for the protection of victims of war and the Additional Protocols thereto, of 1977, the Hague Convention respecting the Laws and Customs of War on Land of 18 October 1907, the Convention on the Prevention and Punishment of the Crime of Genocide and other relevant provisions of international humanitarian, human rights and refugee law, and in particular to respect the rights of women and children and to ensure the safety of all civilians, including refugees and internally displaced persons, regardless of their origin;

(f) To ensure the safety and freedom of movement of United Nations and associated personnel and to ensure full, safe and unhindered access of humanitarian personnel to all affected populations throughout the territory of the Democratic Republic of the Congo;

(g) To cease all military activity in the Democratic Republic of the Congo which breaches the ceasefire provided for in the Lusaka Ceasefire Agreement and the Kampala disengagement plan, including the Harare sub-plans, and the relevant resolutions of the Security Council, and urges all foreign forces to withdraw without delay from the territory of the Democratic Republic of the Congo;

(h) To put an immediate end to the recruitment and use of child soldiers, which are in contravention of the

international human rights standards, and to extend
unreserved cooperation to the United Nations Organization Mission in the Democratic Republic of the
Congo, the United Nations Children's Fund, the Special Representative of the Secretary-General for Children and Armed Conflict and humanitarian organizations in order to ensure the rapid demobilization of
child soldiers, their return home and their rehabilitation;

(*i*) To define and implement all measures necessary
to create conditions conducive to the voluntary return,
in safety and with dignity, of all refugees and displaced
persons and to ensure their fair and lawful treatment;

(*j*) To authorize access, in complete freedom and security, to the zones which they control in order to permit investigations into violations of human rights and
international human rights law;

(*k*) To cooperate fully with the National Commission responsible for investigating allegations concerning the massacre of a large number of refugees and displaced persons in the Democratic Republic of the
Congo, as well as with the Secretary-General and the
United Nations High Commissioner for Human
Rights, in considering the allegations in question, with
a view to submitting to the Secretary-General, through
the National Commission, a further progress report on
the investigations concerning this matter;

4. *Calls upon* the Government of the Democratic Republic of the Congo to take specific measures in order:

(*a*) To comply fully with its obligations under international human rights law and to promote and protect
human rights and fundamental freedoms, to fulfil its
responsibility to protect the human rights of the population in its territory, as well as to take a leading part in
efforts to prevent conditions that might lead to further
flows of internally displaced persons and refugees
within the Democratic Republic of the Congo and at its
borders;

(*b*) To fulfil its commitment to reform and restore
the judicial system and, in particular, its declared intention progressively to abolish the death penalty, as
well as to reform military justice, in conformity with
the provisions of the International Covenant on Civil
and Political Rights, while encouraging the continuation of the moratorium on executions in force;

(*c*) To put an end to impunity and to fulfil its responsibility to ensure that those responsible for human
rights violations and grave breaches of international
humanitarian law are brought to justice;

(*d*) To create, in accordance with its undertakings
as stipulated in the Lusaka Ceasefire Agreement, and
particularly the articles concerning the Inter-
Congolese Dialogue, conditions that would allow for a
democratization process that is genuine and all-
inclusive and that fully responds to the aspirations of
all people in the country, and to complete the administrative procedures required to permit activities by political parties and prepare for the holding of democratic, free and transparent elections;

(*e*) To ensure full respect for freedom of opinion
and expression, including freedom of the press in relation to all types of mass media, as well as freedom of association and assembly;

(*f*) To remove the restrictions that still affect
the work of non-governmental organizations and to
promote human rights awareness, particularly by

strengthening cooperation with civil society, including
all human rights organizations;

(*g*) To continue to facilitate and strengthen further
its cooperation with the human rights field office in
the Democratic Republic of the Congo;

(*h*) To cooperate fully with the International Criminal Tribunal for the Prosecution of Persons Responsible for Genocide and Other Serious Violations of International Humanitarian Law Committed in the
Territory of Rwanda and Rwandan Citizens Responsible for Genocide and Other Such Violations Committed in the Territory of Neighbouring States between 1 January and 31 December 1994 in ensuring
that all those responsible for the crime of genocide,
crimes against humanity and other violations of article
3 common to the Geneva Conventions of 12 August
1949 and Additional Protocol II thereto, are brought to
justice in accordance with international principles of
due process;

(*i*) To continue to facilitate the creation of the necessary prerequisites for the deployment, in conditions
of security, of the United Nations Organization Mission in the Democratic Republic of the Congo and to
guarantee the safety and freedom of movement of its
personnel and associated personnel;

5. *Decides*:

(*a*) To continue to examine the situation of human
rights in the Democratic Republic of the Congo and to
request the Special Rapporteur to report to the General Assembly at its fifty-seventh session, incorporating
a gender perspective;

(*b*) To request the Special Rapporteurs on the situation of human rights in the Democratic Republic of the
Congo and on extrajudicial, summary or arbitrary executions and a member of the Working Group on Enforced or Involuntary Disappearances to undertake, if
appropriate in cooperation with the National Commission responsible for investigating violations of human
rights and breaches of international humanitarian law
in the Democratic Republic of the Congo (ex-Zaire) between 1996 and 1997, a joint mission to investigate all
the massacres perpetrated in the territory of the Democratic Republic of the Congo, particularly the massacres committed in the province of South Kivu and
other atrocities referred to by the Special Rapporteur
in his latest and previous reports on the situation of human rights in the Democratic Republic of the Congo,
with a view to bringing to justice those responsible, and
to report on this matter to the Commission on Human
Rights at its fifty-eighth session and to the General Assembly at its fifty-seventh session;

(*c*) To request the Secretary-General to give the
Special Rapporteurs and the joint mission all necessary
assistance to enable them fully to discharge their mandate;

(*d*) To request the United Nations High Commissioner for Human Rights to provide the technical skills
needed by the joint mission in order to discharge its
mandate;

(*e*) To request the international community to extend support to the human rights field office in the
Democratic Republic of the Congo, in particular to
enable it:

(i) To expand its participation in technical
    cooperation programmes, advisory services and
    activities to increase awareness of human rights,

in particular by supporting the efforts made by the Government of the Democratic Republic of the Congo to strengthen the judicial system;

(ii) To increase its support to non-governmental organizations defending human rights in the Democratic Republic of the Congo, continue and develop cooperation with them and facilitate the activities of the joint mission, particularly through financial support.

RECORDED VOTE ON RESOLUTION 56/173:

In favour: Albania, Andorra, Argentina, Armenia, Australia, Austria, Bahamas, Barbados, Belarus, Belgium, Belize, Bolivia, Bosnia and Herzegovina, Brazil, Bulgaria, Canada, Chile, Colombia, Costa Rica, Croatia, Cyprus, Czech Republic, Denmark, Dominica, Dominican Republic, Ecuador, El Salvador, Estonia, Fiji, Finland, France, Georgia, Germany, Greece, Grenada, Guatemala, Guyana, Honduras, Hungary, Iceland, Ireland, Israel, Italy, Jamaica, Japan, Kazakhstan, Latvia, Liechtenstein, Lithuania, Luxembourg, Maldives, Malta, Marshall Islands, Mauritius, Mexico, Micronesia, Monaco, Mongolia, Netherlands, New Zealand, Nicaragua, Norway, Panama, Papua New Guinea, Paraguay, Peru, Poland, Portugal, Republic of Korea, Republic of Moldova, Romania, Russian Federation, Samoa, San Marino, Slovakia, Slovenia, Solomon Islands, Spain, Suriname, Sweden, The former Yugoslav Republic of Macedonia, Trinidad and Tobago, Turkey, Tuvalu, Ukraine, United Kingdom, United States, Uruguay, Venezuela, Yugoslavia.

Against: Iran, Rwanda, Uganda.

Abstaining: Afghanistan, Algeria, Angola, Antigua and Barbuda, Bahrain, Bangladesh, Benin, Bhutan, Botswana, Brunei Darussalam, Burkina Faso, Burundi, Cambodia, Cameroon, Cape Verde, Chad, China, Comoros, Congo, Côte d'Ivoire, Cuba, Democratic People's Republic of Korea, Democratic Republic of the Congo, Djibouti, Egypt, Equatorial Guinea, Eritrea, Ethiopia, Gambia, Ghana, Guinea, Haiti, India, Indonesia, Jordan, Kenya, Kuwait, Lao People's Democratic Republic, Lebanon, Libyan Arab Jamahiriya, Madagascar, Malawi, Malaysia, Mali, Mauritania, Morocco, Mozambique, Myanmar, Namibia, Nepal, Nigeria, Pakistan, Philippines, Qatar, Saint Lucia, Senegal, Sierra Leone, Singapore, South Africa, Sri Lanka, Sudan, Syrian Arab Republic, Thailand, Togo, Tunisia, United Arab Emirates, United Republic of Tanzania, Vanuatu, Zambia.

Equatorial Guinea

Commission action. On 20 April [res. 2001/22], the Commission encouraged the Government of Equatorial Guinea to comply with its previous recommendations and those of the Special Representative [YUN 2000, p. 741], and to discuss and agree on the implementation of a national human rights action plan, together with a comprehensive technical assistance programme, with OHCHR. It called on the Government to ensure the independence of the National Commission on Human Rights and to continue to authorize the public registration and freedom of activity of human rights NGOs.

The Commission decided to renew the Special Representative's mandate for an additional year and asked him to assist OHCHR and the Government to establish a human rights technical assistance programme, to verify on behalf of the Commission that the assistance provided supported Equatorial Guinea's national human rights action plan and to report in 2002. The Secretary-General was asked to assist him.

The Economic and Social Council endorsed the Commission's decision and its requests to the Special Representative and the Secretary-General on 24 July (**decision 2001/257**).

Report of Special Representative. Special Representative Gustavo Gallón (Colombia), entrusted with the dual mandate to monitor the human rights situation and the technical assistance provided to Equatorial Guinea, submitted a report based on his visit to the country (4-18 November) [E/CN.4/2002/40]. During his visit, he met with the Inter-Ministerial Commission on Human Rights, a body established by the Government in 2001 to deal specifically with human rights and high-level government representatives, representatives of political groups, members of civil society and detained persons.

The Special Representative characterized the human rights situation in Equatorial Guinea as being absent of any genuine rule of law under a single-party regime, functioning with the support of a military whose powers were not different from those of the police and which even exercised jurisdiction over civilians. He described violations of the right to physical freedom and integrity of the person, the right to due process, the right to vote and be elected, the rights to freedom of movement and of association, the rights to equality and self-determination, freedom of the press, the rights to health and to work, children's and women's rights and the right to education, and noted the lack of independence of the judiciary. During his visit, the authorities justified many human rights restrictions and violations by the need to deal with terrorism, as other countries had done since the terrorist acts of 11 September in the United States (see p. 60).

The Special Representative noted that Equatorial Guinea had implemented some of the Commission's recommendations that did not require technical assistance, such as improving sanitary conditions and the physical premises in some detention centres, making arrangements for the publication of legislation and not prosecuting persons possessing foreign newspapers. The Government informed him that it had decided to accede by March 2002 to the 1965 International Convention on the Elimination of All Forms of Racial Discrimination and the 1984 Convention against Torture and Other Cruel, Inhuman or Degrading Treatment or Punishment, adopted by the General Assembly in resolutions 2106 A (XX) [YUN 1965, p. 440] and 39/46 [YUN 1984, p. 813], respectively. It also expressed its willingness to strengthen mechanisms to enforce the prohibition on arbitrary detentions and prevent women or their family members from being deprived of their liberty for not returning a dowry in the event of divorce, and to submit to Congress a bill to ensure that civilians were not tried by military courts.

Several technical assistance projects had been agreed with Equatorial Guinea and some of them were being implemented by France and Spain and by private companies from Spain and the United States, while others were planned by the United Nations Development Programme and the European Commission.

In November, the Special Representative recommended to OHCHR that a team of experts on the Convention against torture, on judicial investigation techniques that did not involve torture and on military systems of criminal justice should be sent on a mission to support and help the Government. He hoped that the mission would take place in 2002. The Special Representative recommended measures to solve the problem of women's imprisonment, criminal investigations conducted by military courts, trials held in Congress, child prostitution and xenophobia against immigrants from neighbouring countries. He reiterated his appeal that account should be taken of the invitation by the Equatorial Guinean opposition in exile to hold a political dialogue aimed at finding ways of guaranteeing democracy and human rights.

Rwanda

By a 20 April resolution [res. 2001/23], adopted by a roll-call vote of 28 to 16, with 9 abstentions, the Commission, taking note of the Special Representative's report [YUN 2000, p. 742] and an agreement signed by the High Commissioner for Human Rights and the National Commission for Human Rights of Rwanda, called on OHCHR to respond to the Government's requests for human rights technical assistance and advisory services. It decided to end the Special Representative's mandate and its consideration of the situation of human rights in Rwanda.

Sierra Leone

Commission action. On 20 April [res. 2001/20], the Commission, expressing grave concern at the abuses of human rights and humanitarian law committed in Sierra Leone, called on the Government to investigate reports of such abuses and to end impunity; it requested the Secretary-General and the High Commissioner for Human Rights to respond favourably to requests for assistance with the investigations.

The Commission requested: the High Commissioner and the international community to assist the Government to establish and maintain an effective functioning of the Truth and Reconciliation Commission (see p. 180); the international community to participate in strengthening

courts and the judicial system, and support the Secretary-General's appeal for resources to establish and maintain an independent Special Court; the High Commissioner and the international community to render technical assistance to personnel of the Court; the Secretary-General, the High Commissioner and the international community to assist the human rights section of the United Nations Mission in Sierra Leone (UNAMSIL); and the High Commissioner to report to the General Assembly in 2001 and to the Commission in 2002.

The Economic and Social Council, on 24 July, endorsed the Commission's requests to the High Commissioner, the Secretary-General and the international community (**decision 2001/255**).

Report of High Commissioner. In response to the Commission's April request, the High Commissioner submitted an August report [A/56/281] to the General Assembly. She stated that the beginning of 2001 had witnessed a significant momentum in the implementation of the peace process in Sierra Leone (see p. 163). From the beginning of the year until 25 July, about 11,291 combatants, including 1,559 children, were registered by UNAMSIL in a disarmament, demobilization and reintegration programme. Although the Revolutionary United Front (RUF) and the government-allied militia, the Civilian Defence Force (CDF), had agreed to release all child combatants and abductees, concern remained that few women and girls had been released. The High Commissioner, describing gender-specific abuses committed against women, noted that programmes were insufficient to address women's needs (see p. 678 for details of the visit to Sierra Leone by the Special Rapporteur on violence against women). In June, UNAMSIL received information of wanton attacks against civilians, allegedly by CDF, in Kono and Koinadugu Districts, as well as allegations of summary executions by RUF in Koidu town.

With improvements in the security situation, the human rights section of UNAMSIL began to establish satellite offices in provincial locations and its human rights training programme had introduced courses for ex-combatants. UNAMSIL also assisted in the restoration of local courts that applied customary law, provided training in international human rights standards regarding the judicial guarantees of a fair trial and due process of law, and facilitated a conference on the rule of law. OHCHR, in consultation with UNAMSIL, revised and updated its project of support to the establishment of the Truth and Reconciliation Commission. Preparations for the establishment of the Commission were given impetus by a seminar on the Commission's operational and managerial aspects (Freetown, 29 May–1 June). OHCHR was liaising with the United Nations Office of Legal Affairs with regard to establishing an independent special court to try persons who committed or authorized serious violations of international humanitarian law (see p. 179).

The General Assembly took note of the High Commissioner's report on 19 December (**decision 56/429**).

Sudan

Commission action. On 20 April [res. 2001/18], by a vote of 28 to none, with 25 abstentions, the Commission welcomed a number of positive initiatives regarding the human rights situation in the Sudan, among them the Government's commitment to respect and promote human rights and the rule of law, efforts to implement the right to education, shelter given by the Sudan to refugees and initiatives towards national reconciliation. However, it expressed concern at the impact of the ongoing armed conflict and the continuing serious violations of human rights, fundamental freedoms and international humanitarian law by all parties to the conflict and in areas under government control. The parties were urged to respect and protect human rights, fundamental freedoms and humanitarian law; establish a monitored ceasefire; stop the use of weapons against civilians; grant safe and unhindered access to civilians by international agencies and humanitarian organizations; engage in peace negotiations under the auspices of the Intergovernmental Authority on Development; and cease the recruitment of children under the age of 18 as soldiers and fulfil its commitments concerning the protection of children affected by war. The Commission called on the Government to comply with its obligations under international human rights instruments to which it was a party; ratify the 1984 Convention against torture [YUN 1984, p. 813]; lift the state of emergency; ensure respect for freedom of religion; implement existing legislation that safeguarded human rights and democracy; raise the age of criminal responsibility for children; implement the Standard Minimum Rules for the Treatment of Prisoners [YUN 1955, p. 209]; end and prevent acts of torture and cruel, inhuman or degrading treatment; prevent or stop abductions of women and children in southern Sudan; address the problem of internally displaced persons; ensure respect for freedom of expression, opinion, thought, conscience and religion, as well as freedom of association and assembly; and not recruit children under the age of 18 as soldiers.

The Commission decided to extend the Special Rapporteur's mandate for an additional year and asked him to submit an interim report to the General Assembly in 2001 and to report to the Commission in 2002, applying a gender perspective.

The Economic and Social Council endorsed the Commission's decision and its request to the Special Rapporteur on 24 July (**decision 2001/253**).

Reports of Special Rapporteur. In response to the Commission's April request, Special Rapporteur Gerhart Baum (Germany), in a September report to the General Assembly [A/56/336], described the human rights situation in the Sudan, based on his visit to the country (9-14 March). At the end of his mission, he visited Nairobi, Kenya (14-17 March), where he collected information on the human rights situation in areas under the control of the Sudan People's Liberation Movement Army (SPLM/A).

The Special Rapporteur observed that the human rights situation in the Sudan had worsened, as manifested in the renewal of a state of emergency until year's end by the National Assembly, the provisions of the Security Act as endorsed by the Parliament and the tightening of press censorship, and the reduced room for political activities by opposition parties. Deploring the recurrence of human rights violations and lack of official action to investigate the abuses, the Special Rapporteur stressed the need to bring the security police under the rule of law and to fight impunity in a determined manner. He also urged SPLM/A to stop abusing human rights and to allow and develop genuine democratic structures. Stressing the appalling conditions of civilians, who continued to be at the receiving end of violations committed in the framework of the war, the Special Rapporteur said he was particularly struck by the plight of internally displaced persons. The Special Rapporteur recommended that everything be done to improve the social and economic situation of the population; according to reliable sources, oil revenue was insufficiently used to that end and oil exploitation had led to a worsening of the conflict. While positive steps had been taken regarding abductions, there continued to be a need for a massive advocacy campaign.

During a further visit (2-14 October) [E/CN.4/2002/46], the Special Rapporteur continued to receive information to the effect that the overall situation in the Sudan had not improved. No institutional or legal reform had occurred, particularly relating to the extension of the powers of the security organs and the absence of judicial control over them. Censorship had increased since

December 2000, and cases of suppression of political freedoms occurred, targeting journalists as well as human rights activists. Regarding the plight of internally displaced persons, the Special Rapporteur welcomed the September visit of the Secretary-General's Special Representative on internally displaced persons (see p. 653), as well as the Government's commitment to address the problem and follow up the visit, including through holding a conference on the subject in the near future. Islam reportedly had a predominant place in school curricula to the point that teaching Christianity was allegedly forbidden, except outside the school. In that connection, the Government had made a commitment to establish an Advisory Council for Christians and to appoint Christians to senior positions within the Ministry for Religious Affairs. The Special Rapporteur noted irregularities in the Constitutional Court regarding political detainees, and remained concerned at the lack of transparency in the use of oil revenues. He condemned SPLM/A practices such as the use of civilian installations for military purposes and the setting up of military installations in close proximity to civilian ones, and encouraged SPLM to develop genuinely democratic structures, demilitarized and independent from the SPLM hierarchy. Regretting that military developments continued to impact adversely the human rights situation of civilians, the Special Rapporteur appealed to the Government to halt the bombing of civilian targets, particularly when civilians gathered to collect food. He appealed to donors to continue to invest in peace in the Sudan and to view the phases of peace, reconstruction and development in a more integrated manner.

GENERAL ASSEMBLY ACTION

On 19 December [meeting 88], the General Assembly, on the recommendation of the Third Committee [A/56/583/Add.3], adopted **resolution 56/175** by recorded vote (79-37-48) [agenda item 119 (c)].

Situation of human rights in the Sudan

The General Assembly,

Reaffirming that all Member States have an obligation to promote and protect human rights and fundamental freedoms as stated in the Charter of the United Nations, the Universal Declaration of Human Rights, the International Covenants on Human Rights and other applicable human rights instruments and the duty to fulfil the obligations that they have undertaken under the various international instruments in this field,

Mindful that the Sudan is a party to the International Covenant on Civil and Political Rights, the International Covenant on Economic, Social and Cultural Rights, the Convention on the Rights of the Child, the African Charter on Human and Peoples' Rights and the Geneva Conventions of 12 August 1949 for the protection of victims of war,

Recalling its previous resolutions on the situation of human rights in the Sudan, and taking note of Commission on Human Rights resolution 2001/18 of 20 April 2001,

Deeply concerned at the impact of the continuing conflict in the Sudan between the Government of the Sudan and the Sudan People's Liberation Army/Movement on the situation of human rights and at the disregard by all parties to the conflict of relevant rules of international humanitarian law, while welcoming the repeated declarations by the Government of the Sudan of a comprehensive ceasefire,

Deeply concerned also at the lack of progress in the peace process, the repeated offensives of the Sudanese army and the Sudan People's Liberation Army/Movement, the general upsurge in fighting and the continued aerial bombings by the Government of the Sudan,

Aware of the urgent need for the Government of the Sudan to implement effective additional measures in the field of human rights and humanitarian relief in order to protect the civilian population from the effects of armed conflict,

Expressing its firm belief that progress towards a peaceful settlement of the conflict in southern Sudan within the context of the peace initiative of the Intergovernmental Authority on Development will contribute greatly to the creation of a better environment for the respect of human rights in the Sudan,

Taking note of the initiative by Egypt and the Libyan Arab Jamahiriya aiming at a negotiated and lasting peace in the country, and encouraging close coordination with the Intergovernmental Authority on Development,

Condemning the murder of four Sudanese relief workers in April 1999 while in the custody of the Sudan People's Liberation Army/Movement,

1. *Welcomes:*

(a) The appointment of a new Special Rapporteur of the Commission on Human Rights on the situation of human rights in the Sudan and his interim report;

(b) The good cooperation extended by the Government of the Sudan to the former Special Rapporteur and to the new Special Rapporteur during his visits to the Sudan in March and October 2001 and the cooperation extended to other United Nations mandate-holders in the field of human rights, as well as the stated willingness of the Government of the Sudan to continue to cooperate with the Special Rapporteur;

(c) The expressed commitment of the Government of the Sudan to respect and promote human rights and the rule of law and its expressed commitment to a process of democratization with a view to establishing a representative and accountable Government, reflecting the aspirations of the people of the Sudan;

(d) The activities of the Committee for the Eradication of Abduction of Women and Children as a constructive response on the part of the Government of the Sudan, the cooperation extended to the Committee by the local communities and the support of the international community and non-governmental organizations;

(e) The stipulation of basic human rights and freedoms in the Constitution of the Sudan and the establishment of the Constitutional Court, which has been in operation since April 1999;

(f) The repeated statements by the Government of the Sudan in favour of a comprehensive, lasting and effectively monitored ceasefire in southern Sudan;

(g) The proposal to create a broad-based national council to evaluate foreign peace initiatives to end the conflict and make relevant recommendations;

(h) Recent additional efforts by the Government of the Sudan to improve freedom of association and assembly, in particular the adoption of the Associations and Political Parties Act of 2000 and the announcement relating to the creation of a high commission to review the law on public order;

(i) The recent visit, upon the invitation of the Government of the Sudan, of the Representative of the Secretary-General on internally displaced persons, as well as the commitment of the Government to continue its efforts to address the problem of internally displaced persons and to follow up effectively the visit of the Representative, including by holding a conference on the subject of internal displacement in the near future;

(j) The people-to-people peace process at the grass-roots level, including the Nuer conference, held at Kisumu, Kenya, from 16 to 22 June 2001, which led to the Kisumu Declaration for Nuer Unity and Peace, and which, like other conferences held at the local level, should contribute to a comprehensive peace settlement in the context of the existing peace initiatives;

(k) Recent measures to drop lawsuits against some political detainees as well as the liberation of some political detainees, while expressing its deep concern at the fact that at least some of the detainees were re-arrested shortly thereafter on the basis of the National Security Forces Act, thereby perpetuating their detention;

(l) The steps taken by the Government of the Sudan towards the ratification of the International Labour Organization Convention concerning the Prohibition and Immediate Action for the Elimination of the Worst Forms of Child Labour (Convention No. 182);

(m) The reconvening of the National Assembly in April 2001;

(n) The improved role of the National Press Council in monitoring complaints about the press;

(o) The technical cooperation agreement signed by the Government of the Sudan and the Office of the United Nations High Commissioner for Human Rights on 29 March 2000 and the posting of an expert from the Office to the Sudan with the task of advising the Government on the development of national capacity to promote and protect human rights;

(p) The demobilization and repatriation of more than 3,500 child soldiers in close cooperation between the Sudan People's Liberation Army/Movement and the United Nations Children's Fund;

(q) The recent signature by the Sudan People's Liberation Army/Movement of an agreement to prohibit the use, production, stockpiling and transfer of anti-personnel mines throughout the territories under its control, and at the same time encourages the Sudan People's Liberation Army/Movement to implement the agreement swiftly;

(r) The efforts to implement the right to education;

2. *Expresses its deep concern* at:

(a) The impact of the ongoing armed conflict on the situation of human rights and its adverse effects on the civilian population, in particular women and children, and at the continuing serious violations of human rights, fundamental freedoms and international humanitarian law by all parties to the conflict, in particular:

(i) The occurrence of cases of extrajudicial summary or arbitrary execution resulting from armed conflicts between members of the armed forces and their allies and armed insurgent groups within the country, including the Sudan People's Liberation Army/Movement;

(ii) The retention of the state of emergency until the end of 2001;

(iii) The occurrence, within the framework of the conflict in southern Sudan, of the use of children as soldiers and combatants, forced conscription, forced displacement, arbitrary detention, torture and ill-treatment of civilians as well as the still unresolved cases of enforced or involuntary disappearances;

(iv) The plight of internally displaced persons in the Sudan, whose numbers are among the highest in the world, in particular with regard to women and children, and the harassment of these groups;

(v) The forced displacement of populations, in particular in areas surrounding the oilfields, and notes the invitation extended by the Government of the Sudan to the Special Rapporteur to visit the oil-producing areas;

(vi) The continued abduction of women and children by Murahaleen groups and other government militias and their subjection to forced labour or similar conditions;

(vii) The lack of efforts to restrain the establishment by certain groups directly sponsored by the Government, including the Murahaleen, of militias that commit serious human rights abuses such as killings, torture, rape, abduction and the destruction of shelter and livelihood;

(viii) The negative role of undisciplined southern militias, armed by the Sudanese army and the Sudan People's Liberation Army/Movement, which are responsible for killings, torture, rape, the burning of villages, the destruction of crops and the stealing of cattle;

(ix) The continuation of indiscriminate aerial bombardment of civilian targets by the Government of the Sudan, in particular the bombing of schools, hospitals, churches, food distribution areas and market places, which seriously and repeatedly affects the civilian population and civilian installations;

(x) The use by both the Sudanese army and the Sudan People's Liberation Army/Movement of civilian premises for military purposes;

(xi) The use of weapons, including landmines, and indiscriminate artillery shelling against the civilian population;

(xii) The conditions, in contravention of humanitarian principles, imposed by both the Government of the Sudan and the Sudan People's Liberation Army/Movement on humanitarian organizations working in the Sudan, especially the denial of access to them, which have seriously affected their safety and led to the withdrawal of many such organizations, with grave consequences for the already dangerous situation of thousands of people living in areas under their control;

(xiii) The difficulties encountered by United Nations and humanitarian staff in carrying out their mandate because of abductions and harassment by both parties to the conflict, indiscriminate aerial bombings and the reopening of hostilities;

(xiv) The attacks on and use of force against United Nations as well as humanitarian personnel by the Sudan People's Liberation Army/Movement;

(xv) The measures taken by the leadership of the Sudan People's Liberation Army/Movement to prevent tribal elders, women and youths from participating in civil society gatherings such as the Nuer conference;

(b) Continuing violations of human rights in areas under the control of the Government of the Sudan, in particular:

(i) Restrictions on freedom of religion, as well as restrictions on freedom of expression, in particular the significant censorship of the press;

(ii) The restriction of political freedom, in spite of the replacement, in March 2000, of the Political Associations Act of 1998 by the Associations and Political Parties Act and the increased activity by some opposition parties;

(iii) The arbitrary arrest and detention without trial of political opponents, human rights defenders and journalists, in particular, as well as acts of intimidation and harassment against the population by the security organs;

(iv) The new amendment to the National Security Forces Act, approved by Parliament and endorsed by the President, which allows the security forces to arrest and detain individuals for a period of up to six months and three days without proper judicial review and to renew the detention as a preventive measure, practically without limits;

(v) Detention in precarious conditions, the use of torture and violations of human rights by security organs, intelligence agencies and the police, while encouraging the judiciary to exercise more control over such agencies;

(vi) The use of the cruelest forms of corporal punishment in contravention of human rights norms and standards;

(vii) The use of the death penalty in disregard of the provisions of the International Covenant on Civil and Political Rights and United Nations safeguards;

3. *Urges* all parties to the continuing conflict in the Sudan:

(a) To respect and protect human rights and fundamental freedoms, to respect fully international humanitarian law, in particular the need to ensure the protection of civilians and civilian premises, thereby facilitating the voluntary return, repatriation and reinte-

gration of refugees and internally displaced persons to their homes, and to ensure that those responsible for violations of human rights and international humanitarian law are brought to justice;

(b) To work immediately to put in place a global, lasting and effectively monitored ceasefire as a necessary first step to a negotiated settlement to the conflict, and to commit themselves to a permanent ceasefire;

(c) To take immediate steps to implement the 1994 Declaration of Principles, in particular to take all necessary steps towards the negotiation of a ceasefire agreement as agreed upon in point 6 of the Declaration of Principles;

(d) To resume the peace talks immediately and to continue to cooperate fully with the peace efforts of the Intergovernmental Authority on Development;

(e) To stop immediately the use of weapons, including landmines and indiscriminate artillery shelling, against the civilian population, which runs counter to principles of international humanitarian law;

(f) To stop the use of tribal militias that commit serious human rights abuses;

(g) In particular the Government of the Sudan, to cease immediately and unconditionally all indiscriminate aerial bombardment of the civilian population and civilian installations, including schools, hospitals, churches, food distribution areas and market places, which runs counter to fundamental principles of human rights and humanitarian law;

(h) In particular the Sudan People's Liberation Army/Movement, to stop using civilian premises for military purposes, misappropriating humanitarian assistance and diverting relief supplies, including food, from their civilian recipients;

(i) To grant full, safe and unhindered access to all international agencies and humanitarian organizations in order to facilitate by all possible means the delivery of humanitarian assistance, in conformity with international humanitarian law, to all civilians in need of protection and assistance, in particular in the Nuba Mountains, the Western Upper Nile, Blue Nile State, Bahr-el-Ghazal and other areas in need throughout the country, to continue to cooperate with the Office for the Coordination of Humanitarian Affairs of the Secretariat and Operation Lifeline Sudan to deliver such assistance, to take measures against those who are responsible for abductions of United Nations and humanitarian staff, urges in particular the Sudan People's Liberation Army/Movement to lift as soon as possible the conditions it has imposed on the work of international agencies and humanitarian organizations, and also urges in particular the Government of the Sudan to end the use of the denial of humanitarian assistance flights for political purposes;

(j) Not to use or recruit children under the age of 18 as soldiers, encourages the continuation of the process of demobilization of child soldiers currently being undertaken by the United Nations Children's Fund, with the cooperation of the Sudan People's Liberation Army/Movement, and urges both parties to the conflict not to use or recruit children under the age of 18 as soldiers and to refrain from the practice of forced conscription;

(k) To fulfil their commitments concerning the protection of children affected by the conflict, such as to cease the use of anti-personnel landmines and attacks on sites where there is usually a significant presence of children as well as the abduction and exploitation of children and the recruitment of children as soldiers, to advance the demobilization and reintegration of child soldiers and to ensure access to displaced and unaccompanied minors and reunite them with their families;

(*l*) To allow an independent investigation of the case of the four Sudanese nationals who were abducted on 18 February 1999 while travelling with a team from the International Committee of the Red Cross on a humanitarian mission and subsequently killed while in custody of the Sudan People's Liberation Army/Movement, and urges the Sudan People's Liberation Army/Movement to return the bodies to their families;

4. *Calls upon* the Government of the Sudan:

(*a*) To comply fully with its obligations under international human rights instruments to which the Sudan is a party and to promote and protect human rights and fundamental freedoms, as well as to respect its obligations under international humanitarian law;

(*b*) To ratify the Convention against Torture and Other Cruel, Inhuman or Degrading Treatment or Punishment;

(*c*) To sign and ratify the Convention on the Elimination of All Forms of Discrimination against Women;

(*d*) To ratify the Convention on the Prohibition of the Use, Stockpiling, Production and Transfer of Anti-personnel Mines and on Their Destruction;

(*e*) To undertake efforts towards promoting an environment that is more conducive to democratization and to improvements in the field of human rights;

(*f*) To continue to strengthen its efforts to ensure the rule of law by bringing legislation more into line with the Constitution and into conformity with the applicable international human rights instruments to which the Sudan is a party, and to ensure that all individuals in its territory enjoy fully the rights recognized in those instruments;

(*g*) To liberalize the legal provisions on public order and to continue assimilation into a regular criminal justice system;

(*h*) To ensure full respect for freedom of religion and, in this respect, to consult fully with religious leaders and other parties concerned when considering any new legislation on religious activities, to remove obstacles to obtaining permission to construct religious buildings, to respect the sanctity of religious buildings and to resolve church property issues;

(*i*) To implement fully existing legislation, including the appeals procedures, that safeguards human rights and democracy, in particular the Associations and Political Parties Act;

(*j*) To raise the age of criminal responsibility for children in order to take into account the observations of the Committee on the Rights of the Child;

(*k*) To implement the Standard Minimum Rules for the Treatment of Prisoners and to continue to give special consideration to imprisoned women and juveniles;

(*l*) To take all effective measures to end and to prevent all acts of torture and cruel, inhuman or degrading treatment, to take into account extenuating circumstances to the maximum extent possible, to ensure that all accused persons are held in ordinary custody and receive prompt, just and fair trials under internationally recognized standards, to investigate all reported human rights violations, including acts of torture, brought to its attention and to bring to justice those responsible for such violations;

(*m*) To ensure that capital punishment will not be imposed for crimes other than the most serious and will not be pronounced in disregard of the obligations assumed under the International Covenant on Civil and Political Rights and the provisions of United Nations safeguards;

(*n*) To take concrete measures to prevent and stop the abductions of women and children taking place within the framework of the conflict in southern Sudan, to bring to trial any persons suspected of supporting or participating in such activities, to support more strongly and more effectively the Committee for the Eradication of Abduction of Women and Children and to facilitate the safe return of affected children to their families as a matter of priority, in particular through the Committee for the Eradication of Abduction of Women and Children, with which all concerned have the responsibility and the duty to cooperate;

(*o*) To make concerted efforts to restrain the activities of the Murahaleen and to end the grave human rights abuses against civilians associated with their activities, to refrain from integrating them in the Sudanese army's military action and to stop financing and equipping them;

(*p*) To ensure full respect for the freedom of expression, opinion, thought, conscience and religion, as well as the freedom of association and assembly, throughout the territory of the Sudan;

(*q*) To continue to implement fully its commitment to the democratization process and the rule of law and to create, in this context, conditions that would allow for a democratization process that is genuine and that wholly reflects the aspirations of the people of the country and ensures their full participation;

(*r*) To make further efforts to implement the commitment made to the Special Representative of the Secretary-General for Children and Armed Conflict not to recruit children under the age of 18 as soldiers;

(*s*) To make further efforts to address effectively the problem of internally displaced persons, including ensuring their access to effective protection and assistance;

(*t*) To consider the establishment of an independent national institution on human rights;

5. *Encourages*:

(*a*) The Government of the Sudan to continue its cooperation with the United Nations in the field of human rights through the Special Rapporteur and the Office of the United Nations High Commissioner for Human Rights and its expert in Khartoum entrusted with the task of advising the Government on the development of national capacity to promote and protect human rights, and to consider how to strengthen the role of the Office;

(*b*) The Sudan People's Liberation Army/Movement to allow the people-to-people peace process to develop freely and unhindered, and to consider it an important contribution to the peace process;

6. *Calls upon* the international community to expand its support for activities aimed at improving respect for human rights and humanitarian law, in particular those of the Committee for the Eradication of Abduction of Women and Children, and to consider

how to expand the Office of the High Commissioner to include a monitoring role;

7. *Decides* to continue its consideration of the situation of human rights in the Sudan at its fifty-seventh session, under the item entitled "Human rights questions", in the light of further elements provided by the Commission on Human Rights.

RECORDED VOTE ON RESOLUTION 56/175:

In favour: Albania, Andorra, Argentina, Armenia, Australia, Austria, Bahamas, Barbados, Belgium, Belize, Bolivia, Bosnia and Herzegovina, Brazil, Bulgaria, Canada, Chile, Colombia, Croatia, Cyprus, Czech Republic, Denmark, Dominican Republic, Ecuador, El Salvador, Estonia, Fiji, Finland, France, Georgia, Germany, Greece, Guatemala, Guyana, Honduras, Hungary, Iceland, Ireland, Israel, Italy, Japan, Kazakhstan, Latvia, Liechtenstein, Lithuania, Luxembourg, Malta, Marshall Islands, Mauritius, Mexico, Micronesia, Monaco, Mongolia, Namibia, Netherlands, New Zealand, Nicaragua, Norway, Panama, Papua New Guinea, Paraguay, Peru, Poland, Portugal, Republic of Korea, Republic of Moldova, Romania, Samoa, San Marino, Slovakia, Slovenia, Solomon Islands, Spain, Sweden, The former Yugoslav Republic of Macedonia, Trinidad and Tobago, United Kingdom, Uruguay, Venezuela, Yugoslavia.

Against: Algeria, Azerbaijan, Bahrain, Benin, Burkina Faso, Chad, China, Comoros, Cuba, Democratic People's Republic of Korea, Democratic Republic of the Congo, Djibouti, Egypt, Gambia, India, Indonesia, Iran, Jordan, Kuwait, Lao People's Democratic Republic, Lebanon, Libyan Arab Jamahiriya, Malaysia, Mauritania, Morocco, Myanmar, Oman, Pakistan, Qatar, Saudi Arabia, Sierra Leone, Sudan, Syrian Arab Republic, Togo, Tunisia, United Arab Emirates, Viet Nam.

Abstaining: Angola, Antigua and Barbuda, Bangladesh, Belarus, Bhutan, Botswana, Brunei Darussalam, Burundi, Cambodia, Cameroon, Cape Verde, Congo, Côte d'Ivoire, Dominica, Equatorial Guinea, Eritrea, Ethiopia, Gabon, Ghana, Grenada, Guinea, Haiti, Jamaica, Kenya, Madagascar, Malawi, Maldives, Mali, Mozambique, Nepal, Nigeria, Philippines, Russian Federation, Rwanda, Saint Lucia, Senegal, Singapore, South Africa, Sri Lanka, Suriname, Thailand, Tuvalu, Uganda, Ukraine, United Republic of Tanzania, United States, Vanuatu, Zambia.

Togo

In 2001, the Secretary-General and the High Commissioner for Human Rights received communications regarding an Amnesty International report alleging that hundreds of extrajudicial executions and other human rights violations had taken place in Togo in 1998 [YUN 1999, p. 702], and the findings in 2000 [YUN 2000, p. 748] of the International Commission of Inquiry for Togo, which concluded that the allegations should be given due consideration.

On 22 January [E/CN.4/2001/134/Add.1-E/CN.4/Sub.2/2001/3/Add.1], Togo, in a letter to the High Commissioner, stated that the report of the International Commission of Inquiry was partial and exceeded its mandate and that some Commission members were known to have links to Amnesty International. The allegations were without foundation and the report was a political fabrication to discredit the Government and people of Togo. Togo alleged that the Secretary-General of Amnesty International had received bribes in 1999 from the leader of an opposition faction.

On 6 February [E/CN.4/2001/134/Add.2-E/CN.4/Sub.2/2001/3/Add.2], Amnesty International submitted to the High Commissioner its comments on the Commission's report and asserted that Togo's allegations of bribery were a fabrication.

On 22 February [A/55/804], Togo stated that at no time did the International Commission of Inquiry support the allegations against it. It noted that in order to conceal Amnesty International's errors, the Commission, at the initiative of its Chairman, who, Togo said, had links to Amnesty International, attempted to confuse the issue by exceeding its mandate and taking up libellous allegations against the Togo Government.

Americas

Colombia

Commission action. The Commission Chairperson, in a 27 April statement [E/2001/23], urged the Government of Colombia to actively cooperate with the OHCHR Office in Bogotá, and encouraged the opening of field offices. Deploring serious and frequent violations of human rights and international law, particularly the massive and systematic abuses perpetrated by paramilitary and guerrilla groups, the Commission called on the parties to the conflict to reach a comprehensive human rights and humanitarian agreement. It noted the January announcement of a six-point government plan to tackle paramilitary groups. While noting improvements in the human rights performance of the armed forces, the Commission expressed concern at continued reports of human rights violations attributed to the armed and security forces. The Commission remained deeply concerned about the deterioration of the situation of internally displaced persons, poor prison conditions and reports of abuses of detainees' human rights. It noted with concern that the climate of violence in the country had led to systematic violations of the rights of the child. It asked the High Commissioner to report in 2002.

Report of High Commissioner. A report of the High Commissioner, based on information collected by OHCHR/Bogotá, described the human rights situation in Colombia in 2001 [E/CN.4/2002/17].

During the year, the Office received 1,414 complaints, of which 1,052 were accepted. It sent 194 communications to the authorities and made 164 field visits to various parts of the country that were of special concern. OHCHR published one compilation of international human rights, international humanitarian law and international criminal law and another on national and international doctrine and jurisprudence. It also released a collection of recommendations made to

Colombia by international human rights bodies between 1980 and 2000.

The Office continued to provide a broad spectrum of technical assistance and advisory services to the Government. The agreement between the Office and the Government was extended to April 2003.

Progress was seen in constitutional and legislative reform during 2001, with decisions by the Constitutional Court to interpret human rights legislation so as to guarantee its conformity with international instruments, and cooperation with OHCHR/Bogotá by the offices of the Ombudsman, the Procurator-General and the Attorney-General. However, OHCHR/Bogotá continued to observe a marked deterioration in the human rights situation, including grave, massive and systematic violations of the rights to life, integrity, liberty, security of person and due process. Many of the violations, principally committed by different paramilitary and military groups, were part of a widespread attack on civilians. Although only a small percentage of violations were directly attributed to the security forces, the State bore responsibility for actions committed by other people because of its failure to protect, prevent and enforce humanitarian norms. The increased weakness of the State and its institutions seriously endangered the future of the rule of law. The High Commissioner expressed concern about impunity, enforced displacement and prison conditions. With regard to the administration of justice, difficulties persisted in terms of access to justice; the safety of officials, victims and witnesses in criminal trials; judicial delays; adequate defence; and the intervention of oversight bodies. The situation of human rights defenders continued to be critical, and trade union members were the victims of killings, threats and attempted murder. The rights of the child had declined significantly, women continued to be victims of discrimination and the indigenous Afro-Colombian communities experienced an increase in violations of their fundamental rights, in particular as the victims of killings, threats, enforced disappearance, displacement and failure to respect specific rights. Other groups continued to suffer extreme vulnerability, which affected their rights, including the right to life, among them, journalists and social communicators, university professors and students, members of political organizations, former rebels, people with HIV/AIDS and sexual minorities. The State had made noteworthy efforts to assist groups at risk through protection programmes. However, the programmes continued to be affected by financial, administrative and structural shortcomings.

The High Commissioner stated that the terrorist events of 11 September (see p. 60) had two significant outcomes for Colombia: the adoption of Security Council resolution 1373(2001) against terrorism (see p. 61) and the inclusion of the paramilitary groups in the list of terrorist organizations issued by the United States. Those developments resulted in the questioning of armed action by illegal groups and the formulation of government strategies in the framework of the National Security Act, which contained provisions that contravened international standards and democratic principles.

The High Commissioner recommended that the Government increase its cooperation with OHCHR; guarantee the rule of law; strengthen its human rights and international humanitarian law programmes, policies and mechanisms; guarantee effective justice and the right to defence; institute a democratic and rights-based policy on crime; combat paramilitarism; protect human rights defenders; guarantee workers' human rights and the exercise of trade union rights; guarantee the rights of ethnic groups; prevent displacement; protect the rights of vulnerable groups; focus its economic and social policies on the most disadvantaged groups; implement a comprehensive gender policy; eliminate widespread violence against children; guarantee human rights education; and ratify international human rights instruments. The Government, the armed factions and Colombian society were encouraged to continue efforts to reach a negotiated solution to the armed conflict. Parties to the conflict were called on to abide strictly and unconditionally by the principles and standards of international humanitarian law.

Communication. Colombia, responding to the High Commissioner's report [E/CN.4/2002/172], stated, among other things, that it did not deny or conceal the serious human rights situation, but equally did not accept institutional responsibility, since such accusations in the report ignored the harmful humanitarian and social effects of a guerrilla war that had been continuing for more than 40 years, added to the problems of paramilitarism and drug trafficking. Other comments concerned the cases of human rights defenders and social leaders, indigenous groups, economic, social and cultural rights, prison conditions and population displacement.

(For details of the visits to Colombia by the Special Representative of the Secretary-General on the situation of human rights defenders, see p. 586; and by the Special Rapporteur on violence against women, see p. 678.)

Cuba

On 18 April [res. 2001/16], by a roll-call vote of 22 to 20, with 10 abstentions, the Commission called on the Government of Cuba to ensure respect for human rights and fundamental freedoms and called on the authorities to continue to take measures to enhance freedom of religion. While noting the conditional release of three members of the Internal Dissidence Working Group, the Commission stressed its concern about the continued repression of political opposition members and about the detention of dissidents. It called on the Government to release those imprisoned for peacefully expressing their political, religious and social views and for exercising their rights to full and equal participation in public affairs. Cuba was called on to consider acceding to human rights instruments to which it was not a party, to initiate a dialogue with the political opposition, to open contact with other countries, to cooperate with other mechanisms of the Commission and to invite the Commission's thematic mechanisms to visit the country. It recommended that the Government take advantage of OHCHR's technical cooperation programmes.

Asia and the Pacific

Afghanistan

Commission action. On 18 April [res. 2001/13], the Commission condemned the mass killings and systematic human rights violations in Afghanistan against civilians and persons deprived of their liberty for reasons related to the armed conflict. It also condemned interference with the delivery of humanitarian relief supplies and restrictions introduced by the Taliban on UN and NGO operations. Noting with deep concern the widespread human rights violations in Afghanistan, the Commission condemned them and the abuses of humanitarian law. It also condemned the continuing grave violations of the human rights of women and girls; the frequent practice of arbitrary arrest and detention and of summary trials, which had resulted in summary executions; violations by the Taliban in Kandahar of UN immunity; and the delay in the trial of the alleged murderers of UN officials killed in Afghanistan in 1998 [YUN 1998, p. 295]. It urged all Afghan parties to respect the human rights and fundamental freedoms of all; cease hostilities; reaffirm publicly their commitment to international human rights and principles; protect civilians; prohibit child conscription or enlistment; provide effective remedies to victims of grave vio-

lations of human rights and humanitarian rules and bring perpetrators to trial; fulfil their obligations regarding the safety of all personnel of diplomatic missions, the United Nations and other international organizations and NGOs; and treat suspects and convicted and detained persons in accordance with international instruments and refrain from arbitrary detention. The Taliban was urged to avoid discrimination based on ethnicity against people who wished to leave the country and seek asylum abroad. All Afghan parties, particularly the Taliban, were urged to cease human rights violations against women. The United Front and the Taliban were called on to fulfil their commitment to cooperate with investigations of reports of mass killings related to the armed conflict and of rape and cruel treatment. The Taliban was called on to abide by its commitments to protect Afghanistan's cultural heritage.

The Commission asked the High Commissioner to provide advice and human rights training to all Afghan parties, as well as to intergovernmental organizations and NGOs active in the field. It decided to extend the Special Rapporteur's mandate for one year and asked him to report to the General Assembly in 2001 and to the Commission in 2002, applying a gender perspective in the latter report. The Secretary-General was asked to assist him and to consider his recommendations in developing UN activities in Afghanistan.

On 24 July, the Economic and Social Council approved the Commission's requests to the Secretary-General and the High Commissioner and endorsed the extension of the Special Rapporteur's mandate and the Commission's request to him (**decision 2001/249**).

Reports of Special Rapporteur. In a March addendum [E/CN.4/2001/43/Add.1] to his previous report [YUN 2000, p. 751], Special Rapporteur Kamal Hossain (Bangladesh) presented information received regarding summary executions and massacres in Bamian and Takhar provinces in January and February. Reports supported by reliable eyewitnesses in Yakawlang indicated that, in the taking (by the United Front forces, Hezb-e Wahdat and Harakat Islami, in December 2000) and retaking (by the Taliban in January 2001) of Yakawlang district in Bamian, breaches of humanitarian law were committed by both parties as they violated the neutrality of medical facilities in the district and disregarded the rights of civilians to be treated as non-combatants. It was estimated that over 100 civilians were summarily executed by the Taliban; a number of mass graves had been identified. The Special Rapporteur noted that, in the preceding few months, the flow of new refugees into Pakistan and Iran had increased significantly and the humanitarian crisis had deepened.

In response to the Commission's April request, the Special Rapporteur submitted a September report to the General Assembly [A/56/409]. He said that he had visited Pakistan in March on an emergency basis, following reports of gross violations of human rights and breaches of international humanitarian law in Afghanistan, including summary executions of civilians, allegedly committed in the course of resumed conflict, particularly in Hazarajat. While the follow-up investigation into the summary executions committed in Yakawlang in January (see p. 712) was being carried out, reports were received of further summary executions and abuses between 5 May and 3 June when the area was reoccupied by Taliban forces. Preliminary reports indicated that 60 persons were taken to central Bamian to be executed, some 50 were rounded up and taken from Shah-e Dan and some 42 were taken from Shibatoo to Khourghanatoo and from Band-e Amir, Sar-e Qol and Dahani Khanak. In addition, in Nayak, the Taliban engaged in large-scale destruction, burning down much of the town. Other villages were also raided and burnt.

The flow of new refugees (some 150,000 to Pakistan and 200,000 to Iran) had encountered resistance in both countries, given the fact that each of them had existing refugee populations of around 2 million, many of whom had been there for over two decades. On 2 August, Pakistan and the Office of the United Nations High Commissioner for Refugees (UNHCR) concluded a screening agreement to allow thousands of Afghans to be given temporary protection by Pakistan.

In pursuit of the Taliban's declared policy of Islamization, the curriculum for the new school year reflected an increase in Islamic-related subjects. In July, the Taliban banned the use of the Internet and the importation of 30 items, including musical instruments, chessboards, playing cards, tapes, nail polish and neckties. Also of concern was the Taliban order to destroy all non-Islamic statues, including the two historic statues and shrines of Buddha in Bamian province (see p. 1019).

In a November addendum to his report [A/56/409/Add.1], the Special Rapporteur stated that, on an emergency basis, he visited Pakistan and Iran from 22 to 30 October to assess the impact of the military operations launched on 7 October (see p. 259) in the wake of the terrorist attacks of 11 September (see p. 60). The intensity of the aerial bombardment and the targeting of cities led to large-scale evacuation from urban areas and to the loss of civilian life. The humanitarian crisis had been deepening before those operations but it was

feared that the situation could develop into a catastrophe. The Special Rapporteur recommended a durable political settlement to restore a unified Afghanistan, pursued through an inclusive and participatory process that would enable all segments of the Afghan people to establish a broad-based, multi-ethnic and representative government. He proposed measures to meet the human rights imperatives, including a review by the international coalition of the conduct of its military operations so as to comply with international humanitarian law, the redeployment of UN staff inside Afghanistan, on a voluntary basis, so that they could be seen to be standing by the Afghan people, internal security arrangements aimed at preventing massacres and protecting lives and property, urgent measures under the UN umbrella, including internal security arrangements to protect civilians inside the country and refugees from threats posed to their right to life, and providing access to the media, including the establishment of a UN-sponsored radio station to allow the Afghan people to be heard.

In a later report [E/CN.4/2002/43], the Special Rapporteur noted that the Taliban forces had concentrated mainly in Kunduz province in northern Afghanistan, having failed in their attempt to withdraw to southern Afghanistan. On 13 November, the United Front entered Kabul without a battle, since the Taliban had already abandoned the city. The Special Rapporteur appealed for compliance with international humanitarian law, particularly with regard to the treatment of prisoners. He called for an investigation into an eruption of violence, which was sparked on 25 November at the Qala-Jangi detention site during the questioning of some prisoners by two United States Central Intelligence Agency (CIA) agents. A series of violent events involving the shooting of prisoners and the killing of one CIA agent escalated into widespread violence. Reports spoke of a prisoner uprising and military operations involving massive use of force by coalition forces.

(For political details, see p. 255.)

GENERAL ASSEMBLY ACTION

On 19 December [meeting 88], the General Assembly, on the recommendation of the Third Committee [A/56/583/Add.3], adopted **resolution 56/176** without vote [agenda item 119 (c)].

Question of human rights in Afghanistan

The General Assembly,

Guided by the Charter of the United Nations, the Universal Declaration of Human Rights, the International Covenants on Human Rights and accepted humanitarian rules, as set out in the Geneva Conventions of 12 August 1949 and the Additional Protocols thereto, of 1977,

Reaffirming that all Member States have an obligation to promote and protect human rights and fundamental freedoms and to fulfil the obligations they have freely undertaken under the various international instruments,

Recalling that Afghanistan is a party to the Convention on the Prevention and Punishment of the Crime of Genocide, the International Covenant on Civil and Political Rights, the International Covenant on Economic, Social and Cultural Rights, the Convention against Torture and Other Cruel, Inhuman or Degrading Treatment or Punishment, the Convention on the Rights of the Child, the Geneva Convention relative to the Protection of Civilian Persons in Time of War and the conventions of the International Labour Organization on equal remuneration (Convention No. 100) and on the abolition of forced labour (Convention No. 105), and recalling that it has signed the Convention on the Elimination of All Forms of Discrimination against Women,

Recalling also all its relevant resolutions, as well as the resolutions and presidential statements of the Security Council, the decisions of the Economic and Social Council, the resolutions and decisions of the Commission on Human Rights and the resolutions of the Commission on the Status of Women,

Recalling further Security Council resolutions 1333 (2000) of 19 December 2000 and 1378(2001) of 14 November 2001 on the situation in Afghanistan,

Recalling Security Council resolutions 1296(2000) of 19 April 2000 on the protection of civilians, 1379(2001) of 20 November 2001 on children and armed conflict and 1325(2000) of 31 October 2000 and the statement by the President of the Council of 31 October 2001, on women, peace and security,

Expressing grave concern about the appalling proportions of the humanitarian crisis affecting the country,

Warmly welcoming the appointment by the Secretary-General of a Special Representative for Afghanistan, and endorsing the approach outlined by the Special Representative at the meeting of the Security Council on 13 November 2001,

Affirming the essential role of the United Nations in supporting the efforts of the Afghan people to establish a new transitional administration leading to the formation of a Government, both of which:

(*a*) Should be broad-based, multi-ethnic and fully representative of all the Afghan people and committed to peace with the neighbours of Afghanistan,

(*b*) Should respect the human rights of all Afghan people, regardless of gender, ethnicity or religion,

(*c*) Should respect Afghanistan's international obligations, including by cooperating fully in international efforts to combat terrorism and illicit drug trafficking within and from Afghanistan,

(*d*) Should facilitate the urgent delivery of humanitarian assistance and the orderly return of refugees and internally displaced persons, when the situation permits,

Recognizing that the accountability of perpetrators, including their accomplices, of grave human rights violations is one of the central elements of any effective remedy for victims of human rights violations and a key factor in ensuring a fair and equitable justice system

and, ultimately, reconciliation and stability within a State,

Stressing the importance of ensuring.the full and effective participation of women in all decision-making processes regarding the future of Afghanistan,

1. *Welcomes* the interim report of the Special Rapporteur of the Commission on Human Rights on the situation of human rights in Afghanistan and the report of the Special Rapporteur of the Commission on Human Rights on violence against women, its causes and consequences on her mission to Afghanistan and the conclusions and recommendations contained therein;

2. *Strongly condemns*:

(*a*) The cases of summary execution committed by the Taliban at Yakawlang in January, May and June 2001;

(*b*) The widespread violations and abuses of human rights and international humanitarian law in Afghanistan, mainly by the Taliban, including the right to life, liberty and security of person, freedom from torture and from other forms of cruel, inhuman or degrading treatment or punishment, freedom of opinion, expression, religion, association and movement, and the recruitment and use of children in hostilities, contrary to international standards;

(*c*) The civilian massacres involving reprisal killings and summary executions following, in recent years, the taking and retaking of particular areas by warring parties;

(*d*) The frequent Taliban practice of arbitrary arrest and detention and of summary trials, which have resulted in summary executions throughout the country;

(*e*) The gross violations of the human rights of women and girls, including all forms of discrimination against them, notably in areas under the control of the Taliban where findings of further gross violations of the human rights of women and girls include abductions and kidnappings, as well as accounts of many instances of forced marriage and of trafficking;

3. *Strongly condemns also* the killing of foreign correspondents which occurred in Afghanistan in November 2001, reiterates its firm condemnation of the killing of Iranian diplomats and the correspondents of the Islamic Republic News Agency by the Taliban, as well as the attacks on and the killing of United Nations personnel in territories of Afghanistan at that moment under Taliban control, and calls upon all Afghan parties to cooperate in urgent investigations of those heinous crimes with a view to bringing to justice those responsible;

4. *Condemns* the Taliban authorities for allowing the continued use of Afghan territory for terrorist activities;

5. *Notes with deep concern* the existence of millions of Afghan refugees and their increased flow, while recognizing the huge burden shouldered by neighbouring countries, especially the Islamic Republic of Iran and Pakistan, and appreciating the efforts undertaken in these host countries to ease the plight of Afghan refugees;

6. *Underlines* the importance of the fulfilment of obligations under international law, including human rights law, with regard to asylum-seekers;

7. *Expresses its concern* at the large number of internally displaced persons in Afghanistan and their situation, and encourages efforts to meet their protection and assistance needs in Afghanistan;

8. *Supports* the early development of a comprehensive strategy aimed at ensuring respect for human rights and humanitarian law, which would, inter alia, provide for a smooth transition from humanitarian assistance to rehabilitation and long-term sustainable development as well as for a durable solution for refugees and internally displaced persons, including their voluntary return in safety and with dignity, and calls upon the international community to provide additional assistance in this regard;

9. *Urges* all parties to work and cooperate fully with the Special Representative of the Secretary-General for Afghanistan and the United Nations Special Mission to Afghanistan;

10. *Stresses* the need for national reconciliation and for the establishment of the rule of law, good governance and democracy in Afghanistan and, concurrently, the need for extensive rehabilitation and reconstruction;

11. *Strongly condemns* all acts of violence and intimidation against humanitarian personnel, and urges all Afghan parties to ensure the safety, security and free movement of all United Nations and associated personnel, as well as of the personnel of humanitarian organizations, to ensure their safe and unimpeded access to all affected populations and to guarantee the access of all Afghans to aid and to education and health facilities without discrimination on any grounds, including gender, ethnicity or religion;

12. *Calls upon* all Afghan parties:

(a) To respect fully all human rights and fundamental freedoms without discrimination on any grounds, including gender, ethnicity or religion, in accordance with international law;

(b) To refrain from summary and arbitrary executions and from acts of reprisal and to adhere strictly to their obligations under human rights instruments and international humanitarian law;

(c) To reaffirm publicly their commitment to respect fully humanitarian law and international human rights standards and to take all measures to protect the civilian population;

(d) To refrain from the recruitment or use of children in hostilities contrary to international standards and to take all necessary measures for the demobilization and social reintegration of war-affected children;

(e) To facilitate the provision of efficient and effective remedies to the victims of grave violations and abuses of human rights and of international humanitarian law and to bring the perpetrators to justice in accordance with international standards;

(f) To fulfil their obligations and commitments regarding the safety and security of all personnel and premises of diplomatic missions, the United Nations and other international organizations and non-governmental organizations, as well as all humanitarian supplies in Afghanistan, and to cooperate, fully and without discrimination on any grounds, including gender, nationality or religion, with the personnel of United Nations and associated bodies, as well as with those of other humanitarian organizations, agencies and non-governmental organizations;

(g) To treat all suspects and convicted or detained persons in accordance with relevant international law and to refrain from arbitrary detention in violation of international law;

13. *Also calls upon* all Afghan parties to respect fully the equal human rights and fundamental freedoms of women and girls in accordance with international human rights law and, in particular, consistent with the Convention on the Elimination of All Forms of Discrimination against Women, to bring to an end, without delay, all violations of the human rights of women and girls and to take urgent measures to ensure:

(a) The repeal of any legislative and other measures in place that discriminate against women and girls and those that impede the realization of all their human rights;

(b) The full, equal and effective participation of women in civil, cultural, economic, political and social life throughout the country at all levels;

(c) Respect for the right of women to work and their reintegration into employment, including in the United Nations system and human rights organizations;

(d) The equal right of women and girls to education without discrimination, the reopening of schools and the admission of women and girls to all levels of education;

(e) Respect for the equal right of women and girls to security of person, and ensure that those responsible for physical attacks on women are brought to justice;

(f) Respect for the freedom of movement of women and girls;

(g) Respect for the effective and equal access of women and girls to the facilities necessary to protect their right to the highest attainable standard of physical and mental health;

14. *Notes with appreciation* the activities carried out by the United Nations system, international and non-governmental organizations and the International Committee of the Red Cross throughout the territory of Afghanistan;

15. *Recalls* its invitation extended to the Secretary-General and the United Nations High Commissioner for Human Rights to proceed without delay to investigate fully reports of summary executions and of rape and cruel treatment in Afghanistan, expresses deep regret for the lack of cooperation by Afghan parties which prevented effective investigations, and calls upon all parties to fulfil their stated commitment to cooperate with United Nations investigations;

16. *Invites* the relevant bodies of the United Nations to offer, as appropriate, advisory services and technical assistance in the area of human rights;

17. *Appeals* to Member States, organizations and programmes of the United Nations system, specialized agencies and other international organizations:

(a) To ensure that all United Nations operations integrate a gender perspective, including in the selection of personnel for their management, and that women will benefit equally with men from such programmes;

(b) To implement the recommendations of the inter-agency gender mission to Afghanistan under the leadership of the Special Adviser to the Secretary-General on Gender Issues and Advancement of Women and to provide specific programmes for all Afghan women and girls to address their special needs and promote their human rights;

(*c*) To support the elements of civil society active in the field of human rights, in particular women's rights;

18. *Calls upon* the Afghan parties to cooperate fully with the Special Rapporteur of the Commission on Human Rights on the situation of human rights in Afghanistan and all other special rapporteurs who request invitations to visit Afghanistan, and to facilitate their access to all sectors of society and to all parts of the country;

19. *Requests* the Secretary-General:

(*a*) To give all necessary assistance to the Special Rapporteur;

(*b*) To ensure, in consultation with the United Nations High Commissioner for Human Rights, the integration of a human rights capacity in the context of United Nations activities in Afghanistan;

20. *Invites* the Special Rapporteur to provide updates, as appropriate, of his reports on the situation of human rights in Afghanistan to the General Assembly and the Commission on Human Rights;

21. *Decides* to keep the situation of human rights in Afghanistan under consideration at its fifty-seventh session, in the light of additional elements provided by the Commission on Human Rights and the Economic and Social Council.

Cambodia

For information on the human rights situation in Cambodia, see p. 598.

China

On 18 April [E/2001/23], China made a motion that no action be taken on a draft text introduced in the Commission by the United States, which, among other things, called on China to ensure the observance of all human rights; improve the administration of justice and the rule of law; accelerate reform efforts; release political prisoners; permit the peaceful exercise of the rights of freedom of religion or belief and of peaceful assembly; preserve and protect the cultural, ethnic, linguistic and religious identity of Tibetans and others; develop productive bilateral dialogues; and cooperate with the Commission's thematic special rapporteurs and working groups. China's motion was carried by a roll-call vote of 23 to 17, with 12 abstentions.

East Timor

Commission action. In a statement by its Chairperson, the Commission, on 20 April [E/2001/23], emphasizing the importance of the ongoing reconciliation process and human rights promotion and protection, aimed at ensuring future social and political stability in East Timor, welcomed the forthcoming establishment of a

reception, truth and reconciliation commission. The Commission called on the Government of Indonesia to establish without delay an ad hoc human rights court in order to bring to justice those responsible for human rights violations and abuses of humanitarian law in East Timor in 1999 [YUN 1999, p. 707]. Concerned at the large numbers of East Timorese refugees still in camps in West Timor, the Commission encouraged Indonesia to resolve that problem and urged it to ensure full and secure humanitarian access to refugee camps. Efforts should be made to complete the refugee repatriation programme in accordance with international standards, including the need for an impartial and transparent process of registration of refugees in order to enable them to register to vote in the East Timor general elections to be held on 30 August (see p. 278). The Commission asked the High Commissioner to report to the General Assembly in 2001 and to the Commission in 2002.

The Economic and Social Council approved the Commission's request to the High Commissioner on 24 July (**decision 2001/289**).

Reports of High Commissioner. In response to the Commission's April request, the Secretary-General, by a September note [A/56/337], transmitted the High Commissioner's report to the General Assembly. The High Commissioner described OHCHR activities and, based on information provided by the United Nations Transitional Administration in East Timor (UN-TAET), summarized the human rights situation in East Timor.

In April, an agreement on a technical cooperation project to strengthen national infrastructure for the promotion and protection of human rights in East Timor was signed by the High Commissioner and the Secretary-General's Special Representative for East Timor. An OHCHR expert provided training in May on monitoring, investigation and protection to East Timorese district human rights officer interns recruited by the UNTAET Human Rights Unit. In June, OHCHR, the Human Rights Unit, the East Timorese Police Service and the Civilian Police organized two training courses on human rights in law enforcement.

Regarding the human rights situation in East Timor, there was a dire shortage of qualified judicial and legal personnel, the future of minorities was uncertain as there were no regulations governing their status, progress in investigating and prosecuting suspects for the crimes committed in East Timor in 1999 had been slow, and gender bias in court proceedings resulted in the unfair administration of justice for women victims of violence. The High Commissioner reported that the President of Indonesia, on 23 April, had signed a decree establishing an ad hoc tribunal to hear cases of human rights violations committed in East Timor. However, the decree provided only for prosecution of alleged violations that took place after the popular consultation on 30 August 1999 and not of cases that occurred prior to the vote. Indonesia agreed to review the court's jurisdiction, but had not done so, and the ad hoc tribunal had not been established. On 20 June, the East Timorese National Council unanimously adopted a regulation establishing the Commission for Reception, Truth and Reconciliation in East Timor, with a two-year mandate to inquire into and establish the truth about human rights violations committed in East Timor between April 1974 and October 1999; to support the reintegration of those who had committed minor criminal offences or harmful acts in the past, through a community-based reconciliation process; and to submit a report to the Government on its findings and to recommend how to prevent future recurrences of human rights violations. While perpetrators of serious crimes would be dealt with by the courts, those implicated in lesser crimes would be dealt with by the Commission. The High Commissioner recommended developing strong mechanisms to protect human rights, mechanisms for monitoring, investigating and preventing abuses within the police, and independent human rights monitoring. Calling for justice for grave violations of human rights and international law, she recommended that UNTAET, the East Timorese Transitional Administration (ETTA) and OHCHR draw up plans to ensure the unhampered continuation of the tasks of the ETTA Serious Crimes Unit (SCU) during the winding-down phase of UNTAET and following the end of the mission; the UNTAET mandate would expire on 31 January 2002. The High Commissioner encouraged the creation of an independent national human rights institution.

On 19 December, the General Assembly took note of the Secretary-General's note transmitting the High Commissioner's report (**decision 56/429**).

In a later report [E/CN.4/2002/39], the High Commissioner reported that a technical cooperation project between OHCHR and the Government of Indonesia, scheduled to begin midyear, was put on hold pending the revision of a presidential decree establishing the ad hoc human rights court to try cases arising from violence that took place in 1999 in East Timor, which was seen as having limited jurisdiction (see above). The project of technical cooperation between OHCHR and UNTAET to strengthen national infrastructure to promote and protect human rights in East Timor continued with human rights training programmes for judges, prosecutors, public defenders and legal aid lawyers. Assistance was provided to ensure that draft legislation was in accordance with international human rights standards and to establish and develop the Commission for Reception, Truth and Reconciliation.

The East Timorese Prosecutor General had issued 33 indictments for serious crimes committed in 1999, but almost half of the 83 persons indicted, whether members of the Indonesian military or East Timorese militia, were on Indonesian territory. Neither SCU prosecutors nor Special Panel judges had the authority to compel those outside East Timorese territory to submit to its jurisdiction. In December, the Special Panel for Serious Crimes of the East Timorese Court convicted 10 defendants for committing crimes against humanity in East Timor.

The UNTAET Regulation on the Establishment of a Commission for Reception, Truth and Reconciliation in East Timor was promulgated by the Transitional Administrator on 13 July. In August, the UNTAET Human Rights Unit, in cooperation with the Commission's Steering Committee, set up an Interim Office of the Commission in Dili to disseminate information about the Commission; mobilize donor funding; and engage in outreach activities. The shortage of qualified judicial and legal personnel persisted and the status of religious and ethnic minorities continued to cause concern. The East Timorese judiciary was unable to address civil issues as it was struggling to deal with criminal law matters; that had serious implications for women's human rights.

According to UNHCR, as at 31 December, 192,592 refugees had returned from West Timor to East Timor since October 1999. An estimated 60,000 refugees remained in West Timor; many of them remained fearful to return because of misinformation that fighting continued in East Timor and it was not safe. The Government of Indonesia ceased providing food aid and distributing money on 31 December, leaving the refugees to be looked after by a few local and international West Timorese NGOs.

UNTAET was receiving increasing reports about persons suffering from acute psychiatric stress who, in the absence of institutional support, were being arbitrarily detained by their neighbours or relatives. Alleged human rights abuses by extralegal security groups in East Timor continued to be reported. The High Commissioner proposed a series of recommendations relating to the status of investigations and prosecutions of serious crimes committed in 1999; legal and judicial capacity-building; the reception, truth and reconciliation process; and the protection of ethnic and religious minorities and other vulnerable groups.

Iran

Commission action. On 20 April [res. 2001/17], the Commission, by a roll-call vote of 21 to 17, with 15 abstentions, while welcoming a series of positive human rights developments in Iran relating to women's education, democracy and health, children's education and health, juvenile justice, follow-up to judicial cases with a political background, the Baha'is and the conviction of government agents involved in the deaths of intellectuals and political activists, called on the country to continue efforts to consolidate respect for human rights and the rule of law and to abide by its obligations under international human rights instruments. The Commission deplored the continuing executions, particularly public and especially cruel executions, and urged the Government to ensure that capital punishment would not be imposed for other than the most serious crimes. The Government was called on to end the use of torture, expedite judicial reform, give effect to its invitation to the Working Group on Enforced or Involuntary Disappearances to visit the country and to consider extending invitations to other relevant thematic mechanisms to visit Iran.

The Commission decided to extend the Special Representative's mandate for a further year and asked him to submit an interim report to the General Assembly in 2001 and to report to the Commission in 2002, keeping in mind a gender perspective; the Economic and Social Council endorsed the Commission's decision on 24 July (**decision 2001/252**).

Reports of Special Representative. In response to the Commission's April request, Special Representative Maurice Copithorne (Canada) submitted to the General Assembly a report covering the first six months of 2001 [A/56/278]. He believed that progress was being made in the incorporation of human rights values into Iranian society. However, in some respects, the Government seemed to be lagging behind the people, who had made clear their desire for change. The overall picture, he stated, was a mixed one.

The number of executions continued to be high, with some 60 taking place during the period under review, some of which were especially barbaric and unusual. The Special Representative continued to receive reports of torture in the legal system, particularly in pre-trial detention, violations of freedom of the press, violations of women's rights, overcrowding in prisons and the

existence of detention centres outside the control of the National Prisons Organization. Religious and ethnic minorities continued to face varying degrees of official and societal discrimination. A stalemate between the branches of the Government over important policy and legislative decisions had led to a significant degree of paralysis in implementing human rights improvements. With regard to the legal process, the Special Representative received from the Government a list of legal reforms that were being implemented, the most pressing of which was the re-establishment of the procuracy, which could reduce the discretion that judges had in the courtroom, including in most cases being judge and prosecutor and, in some cases, jury and defence counsel as well. Annexed to the report were information on the situation of the Baha'is, a list of supporters of the religious/nationalist movement believed to be held in detention as at 15 July and correspondence between the Special Representative and the Government between December 2000 and June 2001.

In a later report [E/CN.4/2002/42], the Special Representative stated that change in the legal system remained excruciatingly slow. The long-awaited bill on the reform of the judiciary had reached the Majilis (consultative parliament). According to press reports, the bill stipulated that exceptional tribunals like the revolutionary courts would be able to deal only with cases explicitly referred to them by law. Prison conditions continued to be a subject of concern. Towards mid-September, the use of public floggings in Tehran appeared to die down somewhat but incidences in the provinces continued at least until the end of October. Some judges continued to violate detainees' human rights, particularly in the pre-trial stage. With regard to torture in the prison system, a step forward, in late November, was a petition identifying a number of acts of torture carried out during the interrogation of prisoners, signed by a substantial majority of Majilis members and calling for the creation of a council of representatives of the judiciary, the legislature and the executive to supervise the treatment of prisoners. Tensions between the elected and unelected branches of government increased. Violations of the right to freedom of expression continued and, with regard to other sources of information, it was reported that 1,000 satellite dishes were seized in October. There continued to be positive developments in the area of juvenile justice, but child harassment within the family was on the rise and children worked illegally in workshops and factories. The Special Representative expressed concern at the Government's modest efforts to address the high rate of unemployment. Noting the establishment of the National Committee for the Promotion of the Rights of Religious Minorities, he stated that the Committee needed to address many issues, such as that of *diyah* (the Shariah compensation for death and personal injury) and the refusal to accept the devolution of property by inheritance to non-Muslims, where there were Muslim beneficiaries. Annexed to the report were information on the concept of *diyah* and on the situation of the Baha'is, complaints concerning the status of the Azeris (the Azerbaijan Turkic-speaking community, which was possibly the largest ethnic minority in Iran) and of the Kurds, a list of students arrested in July 1999 [YUN 1999, p. 713] and correspondence between the Special Representative and the Government.

GENERAL ASSEMBLY ACTION

On 19 December [meeting 88], the General Assembly, on the recommendation of the Third Committee [A/56/583/Add.3], adopted **resolution 56/171** by recorded vote (72-49-46) [agenda item 119 (c)].

Situation of human rights in the Islamic Republic of Iran

The General Assembly,

Guided by the Charter of the United Nations, the Universal Declaration of Human Rights, the International Covenants on Human Rights and other international human rights instruments,

Reaffirming that all Member States have an obligation to promote and protect human rights and fundamental freedoms and to fulfil the obligations they have undertaken under the various international instruments in this field,

Mindful that the Islamic Republic of Iran is a party to the International Covenant on Civil and Political Rights, the International Covenant on Economic, Social and Cultural Rights, the International Convention on the Elimination of All Forms of Racial Discrimination and the Convention on the Rights of the Child,

Recalling its previous resolutions on the subject, the most recent of which is resolution 55/114 of 4 December 2000, and taking note of Commission on Human Rights resolution 2001/17 of 20 April 2001,

1. *Welcomes:*

(a) The interim report of the Special Representative of the Commission on Human Rights on the situation of human rights in the Islamic Republic of Iran;

(b) The broad participation of the electorate in the presidential elections held in June 2001, which expressed the true commitment of the Iranian people to the democratic process in the Islamic Republic of Iran;

(c) The reports that religion will no longer be requested in the registration of births, marriages, divorces or deaths;

(d) The positive developments regarding the situation of Iranian children in the fields of education, health and juvenile justice, as reported by the United Nations Children's Fund and the Special Representative;

(e) The process of legal reform under way in the Islamic Republic of Iran, and encourages the Government of the Islamic Republic of Iran to continue this process;

(f) The re-establishment of the Majilis Human Rights Commission, and expresses the hope that it will complement the work carried out by the Islamic Human Rights Commission to enhance the human rights situation in the Islamic Republic of Iran;

(g) The public and serious debate, which is taking place within society and in the media, on the validity and utility of the imposition of public flogging and other harsh punishments;

(h) The efforts of the Government of the Islamic Republic of Iran in accepting and caring for large numbers of Afghan refugees;

2. *Notes:*

(a) The commitment made by the Government of the Islamic Republic of Iran to strengthen respect for human rights in the country and to promote the rule of law;

(b) The assessment of the Special Representative that some improvements have taken place, inter alia, in such areas as women's education;

(c) The establishment of the National Committee for the Promotion of the Rights of Religious Minorities, and encourages the Government of the Islamic Republic of Iran to expedite its launching;

3. *Expresses its concern* at:

(a) The continuing violations of human rights in the Islamic Republic of Iran;

(b) The fact that, since 1996, no invitation has been extended by the Government of the Islamic Republic of Iran to the Special Representative to visit the country;

(c) The continued deterioration of the situation with regard to freedom of opinion and expression, especially attacks against the freedom of the press, the imprisonment of journalists and members of Parliament, the harsh sentences imposed on those who participated in the Berlin conference or its preparation, and the harsh reactions to student demonstrations, including the imprisonment and mistreatment of those who participated;

(d) The growing number of executions in the absence of respect for internationally recognized safeguards, and in particular deplores public and especially cruel executions, such as stoning;

(e) The still unsatisfactory compliance with international standards in the administration of justice, the absence of due process of law and the use of national security laws to deny the rights of the individual;

(f) The use of torture and other forms of cruel, inhuman and degrading punishment, in particular the practice of amputation and the growing number of cases of public flogging;

(g) The systemic discrimination against women and girls in law and in practice, and at the recent rejection of legislation to raise the age of marriage for women;

(h) The continuing discrimination against persons belonging to minorities, in particular against Baha'is, Christians, Jews and Sunnis;

(i) The ongoing lack of clarity concerning all the circumstances surrounding the suspicious deaths and killings of intellectuals and political activists in late 1998 and early 1999;

4. *Calls upon* the Government of the Islamic Republic of Iran:

(*a*) To abide by its obligations freely undertaken under the International Covenants on Human Rights and other international instruments on human rights and to continue its efforts to consolidate respect for human rights and the rule of law;

(*b*) To take further measures to promote full and equal enjoyment by women and girls of their human rights and to undertake major educational programmes to promote women's rights;

(*c*) To implement the recommendations made by the Committee on the Rights of the Child as a matter of priority, as well as to consider ratifying the International Labour Organization Convention concerning the Prohibition and Immediate Action for the Elimination of the Worst Forms of Child Labour (Convention No. 182);

(*d*) To eliminate all forms of discrimination based on religious grounds or against persons belonging to minorities and to address this matter in an open manner, with the full participation of the minorities themselves, as well as to implement fully the conclusions and recommendations of the Special Rapporteur of the Commission on Human Rights on the question of religious intolerance relating to the Baha'is and other minority groups until they are completely emancipated;

(*e*) To ensure full respect for freedom of expression;

(*f*) To end the imposition of the death penalty for crimes committed by persons under the age of 18, and to ensure that capital punishment will not be imposed for crimes other than the most serious and will not be pronounced in disregard of the obligations it has assumed under the International Covenant on Civil and Political Rights and the provisions of United Nations safeguards, and to provide the Special Representative with relevant statistics on this matter;

(*g*) To take all necessary measures to end the use of torture and other forms of cruel, inhuman and degrading treatment and punishment, in particular the practices of amputation and public flogging, and to pursue vigorously penitentiary reform;

(*h*) To implement judicial reform speedily and completely, to guarantee the dignity of the individual and to ensure the full application of due process of law and fair and transparent procedures by an independent and impartial judiciary, and in this context to ensure respect for the rights of the defence and the equity of verdicts in all instances, including for members of religious minority groups;

(*i*) To enact as soon as possible legislation to ensure that people are not punished for exercising their political freedoms;

(*j*) To invite the Special Representative to visit the country and cooperate fully with him, in particular so that he can, through direct contacts with all sectors of society, observe the evolution of the human rights situation in the country and assess future needs, including in the area of technical cooperation in the field of human rights;

(*k*) To give effect, in the near future, to its invitation to the Working Group on Enforced or Involuntary Disappearances to visit the Islamic Republic of Iran, as well as to consider extending invitations to other relevant thematic mechanisms to visit the country;

5. *Decides* to continue the examination of the situation of human rights in the Islamic Republic of Iran, paying particular attention to further developments, including the situation of the Baha'is and other minority groups, at its fifty-seventh session, under the agenda item entitled "Human rights questions", in the light of additional elements provided by the Commission on Human Rights.

RECORDED VOTE ON RESOLUTION 56/171:

In favour: Albania, Andorra, Australia, Austria, Bahamas, Barbados, Belgium, Belize, Botswana, Bulgaria, Canada, Costa Rica, Croatia, Czech Republic, Denmark, Dominica, Ecuador, El Salvador, Estonia, Fiji, Finland, France, Germany, Greece, Grenada, Guatemala, Haiti, Honduras, Hungary, Iceland, Ireland, Israel, Italy, Japan, Kiribati, Latvia, Liechtenstein, Lithuania, Luxembourg, Malta, Marshall Islands, Mauritius, Micronesia, Monaco, Nauru, Netherlands, New Zealand, Nicaragua, Norway, Palau, Panama, Papua New Guinea, Paraguay, Peru, Poland, Portugal, Republic of Moldova, Romania, Saint Kitts and Nevis, Samoa, San Marino, Slovakia, Slovenia, Solomon Islands, Spain, Suriname, Sweden, Trinidad and Tobago, Tuvalu, United Kingdom, United States, Yugoslavia.

Against: Afghanistan, Algeria, Armenia, Azerbaijan, Bahrain, Bangladesh, Belarus, Benin, Bhutan, Brunei Darussalam, Chad, China, Comoros, Congo, Cuba, Democratic People's Republic of Korea, Democratic Republic of the Congo, Djibouti, Egypt, Gambia, Guyana, India, Indonesia, Iran, Jordan, Kazakhstan, Lao People's Democratic Republic, Lebanon, Libyan Arab Jamahiriya, Malaysia, Maldives, Mali, Mauritania, Morocco, Myanmar, Oman, Pakistan, Qatar, Russian Federation, Saudi Arabia, Senegal, Sri Lanka, Sudan, Syrian Arab Republic, Tunisia, Turkmenistan, United Republic of Tanzania, Venezuela, Viet Nam.

Abstaining: Angola, Antigua and Barbuda, Argentina, Bolivia, Brazil, Burkina Faso, Burundi, Cameroon, Cape Verde, Chile, Colombia, Côte d'Ivoire, Cyprus, Dominican Republic, Equatorial Guinea, Eritrea, Ethiopia, Gabon, Georgia, Ghana, Guinea, Jamaica, Kenya, Madagascar, Malawi, Mexico, Mozambique, Namibia, Nepal, Nigeria, Philippines, Republic of Korea, Rwanda, Saint Lucia, Sierra Leone, Singapore, South Africa, Thailand, The former Yugoslav Republic of Macedonia, Togo, Uganda, Ukraine, United Arab Emirates, Uruguay, Vanuatu, Zambia.

Iraq

Commission action. On 18 April [res. 2001/14], by a roll-call vote of 30 to 3, with 19 abstentions, the Commission, noting that there had been no improvement in the human rights situation in Iraq, strongly condemned the systematic, widespread and extremely grave violations of human rights and international humanitarian law by the Government; its suppression of freedom of thought, expression, information, association, assembly and movement; the repression of the opposition; widespread use of the death penalty; summary and arbitrary executions; and the widespread, systematic practice of torture. It called on the Government to abide by its obligations under international human rights treaties and international humanitarian law; end summary and arbitrary executions and ensure that capital punishment would not be imposed other than for the most serious crimes; bring its military and security forces in conformity with standards of international law; cooperate with UN human rights mechanisms; establish the independence of the judiciary and abrogate laws granting impunity; abrogate decrees that prescribed cruel and inhuman punishment or treatment; abrogate laws and procedures that penalized free expression; ensure free exercise of political opposition; cease repressive practices aimed at ethnic and religious groups; cooperate to resolve the fate of missing persons; cooperate with aid agencies and NGOs to provide humanitarian assistance; ensure equitable distribution of humanitarian supplies purchased with the proceeds of Iraqi oil; and cooperate in identifying minefields in the country.

The Commission decided to extend the Special Rapporteur's mandate for a further year and asked him to submit an interim report to the General Assembly in 2001 and to report to the Commission in 2002, applying a gender perspective. The Secretary-General was asked to assist the Special Rapporteur and to approve the allocation of resources to send human rights monitors to locations that would facilitate improved information on the human rights situation in Iraq. The Economic and Social Council approved the Commission's decision on 24 July (**decision 2001/250**).

Communications. The Commission had before it notes verbales from Iraq on Iraqi missing persons [E/CN.4/2001/122] and on Kuwaiti missing persons [E/CN.4/2001/124]. Iraq also submitted a document on the sanctions imposed on it [E/CN.4/2001/127] (see p. 298), which, it stated, constituted a violation of international law.

Iraq, in a 31 May note verbale [E/CN.4/2002/4], asserted that Commission resolution 2001/14 lacked objectivity and contained fallacies designed to distort the facts and mislead Commission members.

Subcommission action. On 16 August [E/CN.4/2002/2 (dec. 2001/115)], the Subcommission on the Promotion and Protection of Human Rights appealed to the international community and to the Security Council for the embargo provisions affecting the humanitarian situation of the Iraqi population to be lifted and urged the international community and all Governments, including Iraq, to alleviate the suffering of Iraqis, particularly by facilitating the delivery of food, medical supplies and the wherewithal to meet their basic needs.

Report of Special Rapporteur. In response to General Assembly resolution 55/115 [YUN 2000, p. 761] and the Commission's April request, Special Rapporteur Andreas Mavrommatis (Cyprus) submitted to the Assembly a September report [A/56/340] covering the period from 1 December 2000 to 15 July 2001. He stated that he continued to receive written allegations, reports and communications claiming human rights violations by the Government of Iraq. The allegations related to torture or cruel, inhuman or degrading treatment or punishment; extrajudicial killings and arbitrary executions; the imposition of the death sentence for crimes that were not serious enough

to justify it; persecution on account of political affiliation, ethnicity and religious affiliation; forced population transfers (Arabization); arbitrary arrest and detention; and the lack of fair trial and due process of law. He also received information regarding the humanitarian situation in Iraq as a result of the sanctions regime imposed on the country, the violation of women's rights, and Kuwaitis unaccounted for since Iraq's occupation of Kuwait.

The Special Rapporteur urged the Government to continue its dialogue with the United Nations, remove restrictions on the exercise of religious freedom, revise laws regarding the death penalty and consider a moratorium on executions, ensure that no person was relocated against his or her will, investigate the fate of all missing persons, join the work of the Tripartite Commission and its Technical Subcommittee, established to facilitate work on the issue of missing Kuwaitis (see p. 293), pay attention to allegations of human rights violations against women and examine all allegations of human rights violations. Annexed to the report were a list of letters from the Special Rapporteur to the Government and replies thereto received as at 22 July and sample correspondence between the Special Rapporteur and the Government regarding religious persecution.

(For political details, see p. 290.)

GENERAL ASSEMBLY ACTION

On 19 December [meeting 88], the General Assembly, on the recommendation of the Third Committee [A/56/583/Add.3], adopted **resolution 56/174** by recorded vote (100-2-63) [agenda item 119 *(c)*].

Situation of human rights in Iraq

The General Assembly,

Guided by the Charter of the United Nations, the Universal Declaration of Human Rights, the International Covenants on Human Rights and other human rights instruments,

Reaffirming that all Member States have an obligation to promote and protect human rights and fundamental freedoms and to fulfil the obligations they have undertaken under the various international instruments in this field,

Mindful that Iraq is a party to the International Covenants on Human Rights, other international human rights instruments and the Geneva Conventions of 12 August 1949 for the protection of victims of war,

Recalling its previous resolutions and those of the Commission on Human Rights on the subject, and taking note of the most recent, Commission resolution 2001/14 of 18 April 2001,

Recalling also Security Council resolution 686(1991) of 2 March 1991, in which the Council called upon Iraq to release all Kuwaitis and nationals of other States who might still be held in detention, Council resolution

687(1991) of 3 April 1991, Council resolution 688(1991) of 5 April 1991, in which the Council demanded an end to repression of the Iraqi civilian population and insisted that Iraq cooperate with humanitarian organizations and that the human rights of all Iraqi citizens be respected, Council resolutions 986(1995) of 14 April 1995, 1111(1997) of 4 June 1997, 1129(1997) of 12 September 1997, 1143(1997) of 4 December 1997, 1153(1998) of 20 February 1998, 1175(1998) of 19 June 1998, 1210 (1998) of 24 November 1998, 1242(1999) of 21 May 1999, 1266(1999) of 4 October 1999, 1281(1999) of 10 December 1999, 1302(2000) of 8 June 2000, 1330(2000) of 5 December 2000, 1352(2001) of 1 June 2001 and 1360(2001) of 3 July 2001, in which the Council authorized States to permit imports of Iraqi oil in order to allow Iraq to purchase humanitarian supplies, and Council resolution 1284(1999) of 17 December 1999, in which the Council, by means of a comprehensive approach to the situation in Iraq, inter alia, removed the ceiling for the allowable import of Iraqi oil in order to increase the amount of revenue available for the purchase of humanitarian supplies, laid down new provisions and procedures designed to improve the implementation of the humanitarian programme and to further achievement in meeting the humanitarian needs of the Iraqi population and reiterated the obligation of Iraq to facilitate the repatriation of all Kuwaiti and third-country nationals referred to in paragraph 30 of Council resolution 687(1991),

Taking note of the concluding observations of the Human Rights Committee, the Committee on the Elimination of Racial Discrimination, the Committee on Economic, Social and Cultural Rights, the Committee on the Rights of the Child and the Committee on the Elimination of Discrimination against Women on the recent reports submitted to them by Iraq, in which these treaty-monitoring bodies point to a wide range of human rights problems and express the view that the Government of Iraq remains bound by its treaty obligations, while pointing to the adverse effect of sanctions on the daily life of the population, in particular women and children,

Reaffirming that it is the responsibility of the Government of Iraq to ensure the well-being of its entire population and the full enjoyment of all human rights and fundamental freedoms, concerned about the dire situation in Iraq, which affects the population, in particular children, as stated in the reports of several United Nations human rights treaty bodies, and appealing to all concerned to fulfil their mutual obligations in the management of the humanitarian programme established by the Security Council in its resolution 986(1995),

1. *Welcomes* the report of the Special Rapporteur of the Commission on Human Rights on the situation of human rights in Iraq and the observations, conclusions and recommendations contained therein;

2. *Notes with dismay* that there has been no improvement in the situation of human rights in the country;

3. *Strongly condemns:*

(a) The systematic, widespread and extremely grave violations of human rights and of international humanitarian law by the Government of Iraq, resulting in all-pervasive repression and oppression sustained by broad-based discrimination and widespread terror;

(b) The suppression of freedom of thought, expression, information, association, assembly and movement through fear of arrest, imprisonment, execution, expulsion, house demolition and other sanctions;

(c) The repression faced by any kind of opposition, in particular the harassment and intimidation of and threats against Iraqi opponents living abroad and members of their families;

(d) The widespread use of the death penalty in disregard of the provisions of the International Covenant on Civil and Political Rights and the United Nations safeguards;

(e) Summary and arbitrary executions, including political killings and the continued so-called clean-out of prisons, the use of rape as a political tool, as well as enforced or involuntary disappearances, routinely practised arbitrary arrests and detention and consistent and routine failure to respect due process and the rule of law;

(f) Widespread, systematic torture and the maintaining of decrees prescribing cruel and inhuman punishment as a penalty for offences;

4. *Calls upon* the Government of Iraq:

(a) To abide by its freely undertaken obligations under international human rights treaties and international humanitarian law to respect and ensure the rights of all individuals, irrespective of their origin, ethnicity, gender or religion, within its territory and subject to its jurisdiction;

(b) To put an end to all summary and arbitrary executions and to ensure that capital punishment will not be imposed for crimes other than the most serious and will not be pronounced in disregard of the obligations assumed under the International Covenant on Civil and Political Rights and the provisions of United Nations safeguards;

(c) To bring the actions of its military and security forces into conformity with the standards of international law, in particular those of the International Covenant on Civil and Political Rights;

(d) To cooperate with United Nations human rights mechanisms, in particular by inviting the Special Rapporteur to visit the country and allowing the stationing of human rights monitors throughout Iraq pursuant to the relevant resolutions of the General Assembly and the Commission on Human Rights;

(e) To establish the independence of the judiciary and abrogate all laws granting impunity to specified forces or persons killing or injuring individuals for any purpose beyond the administration of justice under the rule of law as prescribed by international standards;

(f) To abrogate all decrees that prescribe cruel and inhuman punishment or treatment, including mutilation, and to ensure that torture and cruel punishment and treatment no longer occur;

(g) To abrogate all laws and procedures, including Revolution Command Council Decree No. 840 of 4 November 1986, that penalize free expression, and to ensure that the genuine will of the people shall be the basis of authority of the State;

(h) To ensure free exercise of political opposition and to prevent intimidation and repression of political opponents and their families;

(i) To respect the rights of all ethnic and religious groups and to cease immediately its continued repressive practices aimed at the Iraqi Kurds, Assyrians and Turkmen, including the practice of forced deportation and relocation, and to ensure the personal integrity and freedoms of all citizens, including the Shi'a population;

(*j*) To cooperate with the Tripartite Commission and its Technical Subcommittee to establish the whereabouts and resolve the fate of the remaining several hundred missing persons, including prisoners of war, Kuwaiti nationals and third-country nationals, victims of the illegal Iraqi occupation of Kuwait, to cooperate with the Working Group on Enforced or Involuntary Disappearances of the Commission on Human Rights for that purpose, to cooperate with the high-level coordinator of the Secretary-General for Kuwaitis and third-country nationals and Kuwaiti property, to pay compensation to the families of those who died or disappeared in the custody of the Iraqi authorities, through the mechanism established by the Security Council in resolution 692(1991) of 20 May 1991, to release immediately all Kuwaitis and nationals of other States who may still be held in detention and inform families about the whereabouts of arrested persons, to provide information about death sentences imposed on prisoners of war and civilian detainees and to issue death certificates for deceased prisoners of war and civilian detainees;

(*k*) To cooperate further with international aid agencies and non-governmental organizations to provide humanitarian assistance and monitoring in the northern and southern areas of the country;

(*l*) To continue to cooperate in the implementation of Security Council resolutions 986(1995), 1111(1997), 1143(1997), 1153(1998), 1210(1998), 1242(1999), 1266 (1999), 1281(1999), 1302(2000), 1330(2000), 1352(2001) and 1360(2001), as well as to cooperate, together with all concerned, in the implementation of the humanitarian sections of Security Council resolution 1284 (1999), to continue its efforts to ensure fully the timely and equitable distribution, without discrimination, to the Iraqi population, including in remote areas, of all humanitarian supplies purchased under the oil-for-food programme, to address effectively the needs of persons requiring special attention, such as children, pregnant women, the disabled, the elderly and the mentally ill, among others, further to facilitate the work of United Nations humanitarian personnel in Iraq by ensuring the free and unobstructed movement of observers throughout the country, as well as their free access, without any discrimination, to all the population, and to ensure that involuntarily displaced persons receive humanitarian assistance without the need to demonstrate that they have resided for six months at their places of temporary residence;

(*m*) To cooperate in the identification of the minefields existing throughout Iraq, with a view to facilitating their marking and eventual clearing;

5. *Requests* the Secretary-General to provide the Special Rapporteur with all necessary assistance in carrying out his mandate, and decides to continue the examination of the situation of human rights in Iraq at its fifty-seventh session, under the item entitled "Human rights questions", in the light of additional elements provided by the Commission on Human Rights.

RECORDED VOTE ON RESOLUTION 56/174:

In favour: Albania, Andorra, Angola, Argentina, Armenia, Australia, Austria, Bahamas, Barbados, Belgium, Belize, Bhutan, Bolivia, Bosnia and Herzegovina, Botswana, Brazil, Bulgaria, Canada, Chile, Colombia, Comoros, Costa Rica, Côte d'Ivoire, Croatia, Cyprus, Czech Republic, Denmark, Dominican Republic, Ecuador, El Salvador, Estonia, Ethiopia, Fiji, Finland, France, Gabon, Georgia, Germany, Greece, Grenada, Guatemala, Guyana, Honduras, Hungary, Iceland, Ireland, Israel, Italy, Jamaica, Japan, Kazakhstan, Kuwait, Latvia, Liechtenstein, Lithuania, Luxembourg, Malawi, Maldives, Malta, Marshall Islands, Mauritius, Mexico, Micronesia, Monaco, Mongolia, Nauru, Netherlands, New Zealand, Nicaragua, Norway, Palau, Panama, Papua New Guinea, Paraguay, Peru, Poland, Portugal, Republic of Korea, Republic of Moldova, Romania, Samoa, San Marino, Saudi Arabia, Senegal, Seychelles, Slovakia, Slovenia, Solomon Islands, Spain, Suriname, Sweden, The former Yugoslav Republic of Macedonia, Trinidad and Tobago, Turkey, Tuvalu, Ukraine, United Kingdom, United States, Uruguay, Yugoslavia.

Against: Libyan Arab Jamahiriya, Sudan.

Abstaining: Algeria, Antigua and Barbuda, Azerbaijan, Bahrain, Bangladesh, Belarus, Benin, Brunei Darussalam, Burkina Faso, Burundi, Cambodia, Cameroon, Cape Verde, China, Congo, Cuba, Democratic People's Republic of Korea, Democratic Republic of the Congo, Djibouti, Dominica, Egypt, Equatorial Guinea, Eritrea, Gambia, Ghana, Guinea, Haiti, India, Indonesia, Jordan, Kenya, Lao People's Democratic Republic, Lebanon, Madagascar, Malaysia, Mali, Mauritania, Mozambique, Myanmar, Namibia, Nepal, Nigeria, Pakistan, Philippines, Qatar, Russian Federation, Rwanda, Saint Lucia, Sierra Leone, Singapore, South Africa, Sri Lanka, Syrian Arab Republic, Thailand, Togo, Tunisia, Uganda, United Arab Emirates, United Republic of Tanzania, Vanuatu, Venezuela, Viet Nam, Zambia.

Myanmar

Reports of Secretary-General. In response to General Assembly resolution 55/112 [YUN 2000, p. 764], the Secretary-General, in March [E/CN.4/ 2001/33], reported on consultations (5-9 January) held by his Special Envoy, Razali Ismail, with the Government of Myanmar on the situation of human rights in that country. The Secretary-General welcomed the ongoing dialogue between the Government and opposition leaders, including Aung San Suu Kyi, the General-Secretary of the National League for Democracy (NLD), and called on both parties to work towards national reconciliation.

In October [A/56/505], the Secretary-General updated information regarding consultations (1-4 June, 27-30 August) held by his Special Envoy. He was encouraged by the growing indications that a climate of understanding between the Government and Aung San Suu Kyi and NLD was taking root. However, the process was still at the confidence-building stage and much more needed to be done to make it irreversible. The Secretary-General urged the Government to continue releasing the remaining political detainees and to further restore freedom of activity for legitimate political parties. Further consultations were held during the year (27 November–3 December).

Commission action. On 18 April [res. 2001/15], the Commission, welcoming the Myanmar Government's release of democratic political activists, the partial reopening of the university, cooperation with ICRC and the Government's establishment of a preparatory process for a human rights committee, deplored the continuing pattern of gross and systematic human rights violations in the country; the lack of independence of the judiciary; widespread discrimination against minorities; violation of women's and children's human rights; and severe restrictions on the freedoms of opinion, expression, assembly and association, and on freedom of movement. It called on Myanmar to establish a constructive dialogue with the UN system; continue to cooperate with the Secretary-General or his representative and with all UN representatives; and consider becoming a party to human rights instruments. The Government was urged to implement the Special Rapporteur's recommendations; ensure full respect for human rights and fundamental freedoms; establish democracy; allow all citizens to participate freely in the political process; release political detainees; improve conditions of detention; ensure the well-being of all political leaders; fulfil its obligations under the Convention on the Rights of the Child, contained in General Assembly resolution 44/25 [YUN 1989, p. 560], and under the 1979 Convention on the Elimination of All Forms of Discrimination against Women, adopted by the Assembly in resolution 34/180 [YUN 1979, p. 895]; prosecute and punish those who violated women's human rights and carry out human rights education and gender-sensitization training; halt the use of weapons against civilians; end forced labour; cease laying landmines; end enforced displacement of persons; and restore the independence of the judiciary and end impunity.

The Commission asked the High Commissioner to cooperate with the Director-General of the International Labour Organization (ILO) with a view to identifying ways in which their offices might collaborate to improve the human rights situation in Myanmar and requested the Secretary-General to bring its resolution to the attention of the UN system.

The Commission decided to extend the Special Rapporteur's mandate for a further year and asked him to report to the Assembly in 2001 and to the Commission in 2002, keeping a gender perspective in mind. It asked the Secretary-General to assist the Special Rapporteur and to continue his discussions with the Government and with anyone he might consider appropriate to assist in implementing Assembly resolution 55/112 [YUN 2000, p. 764], as well as the Commission's current resolution. The Economic and Social Council, on 24 July, endorsed the Commission's decisions regarding the Special Rapporteur's mandate and submission of reports, the continuation of the Secretary-General's discussions and its request to the High Commissioner (**decision 2001/251**).

Reports of Special Rapporteur. In response to the Commission's April request, Special Rapporteur Paulo Sergio Pinheiro (Brazil) submitted to the General Assembly an August report on the human rights situation in Myanmar [A/56/312], covering developments between 1 January and 14 August. During that period, he visited the country briefly (3-5 April) to establish direct contact with the Government and the people of Myanmar, including their political and civil society leaders. In preparation for the visit, he had travelled to Japan, Malaysia and Thailand to understand the perspectives of those countries on the human rights and humanitarian situation in Myanmar and their corresponding national policies.

The Special Rapporteur observed some positive movement in the area of civil and political rights, but was aware that problems remained. The Government had disseminated human rights standards for public officials through a series of workshops, established a governmental Committee on Human Rights, released political detainees, reopened NLD branches, continued international monitoring of prison conditions and carried on its dialogue with the Commission on Human Rights. While he welcomed the release of more than 160 prisoners from jails and guest houses, the Special Rapporteur stated that there were many other unresolved cases. Noting the reopening of NLD offices, the Special Rapporteur called for further steps in that direction to achieve national reconciliation, including through full respect for the rights to association, participation and free expression.

The Special Rapporteur received reports about the situation of ethnic minorities, particularly those living in zones of counter-insurgency operations (Shan, Mon, Kayah and Kayin States), where the impact of armed conflict, human rights abuses—torture, arbitrary executions, deliberate killings, indiscriminate use of landmines, pressure to join military force—and the combined effects of poverty, lack of basic social infrastructure and practices of local authorities had instilled people with fear. With regard to children, the problem of child soldiers, low levels of primary school enrolment and tuberculosis and malaria remained major concerns. The Special Rapporteur was convinced that humanitarian aid was essential; however, the Government was responsible for creating a positive environment whereby aid could be given and effectively reach the most vulnerable members of the population.

In a later report [E/CN.4/2002/45], the Special Rapporteur described his fact-finding mission to Myanmar (9-20 October) and presented information received by him up to 15 December. While welcoming several positive developments in the country, the Special Rapporteur observed that progress was fragile given the fact that human rights violations occurred within the context of long-standing insurgencies, ethnic and otherwise, and the suppression of the re-emerging democracy movement since 1988. Serious human rights violations still occurred, especially in areas of conflict between the army and armed groups, but on a different scale than before. The Special Rapporteur called for enhancing the country's human rights capacity to an extent that corresponded to the need for the prevention and monitoring of human rights violations and for the State agents involved to be held accountable; the unconditional release of all political prisoners; non-discriminatory conditions for the exercise of basic political freedoms; minimum standards for the treatment of prisoners; reform of the education sector; prevention of and curative action for HIV/AIDS; action to combat violence against women; maximum restraint in military activities; and more adequate attention to the humanitarian situation. Annexed to the report were a description of humanitarian cases and a list of persons who reportedly received prison terms for communicating human rights information to the United Nations.

Communication. By a 5 November letter [A/C.3/56/7], Myanmar transmitted to the Secretary-General a memorandum that detailed steps taken by the Government to improve human rights and to cooperate with UN mechanisms.

GENERAL ASSEMBLY ACTION

On 24 December [meeting 92], the General Assembly, on the recommendation of the Third Committee [A/56/583/Add.3], adopted **resolution 56/231** without vote [agenda item 119 (c)].

Situation of human rights in Myanmar

The General Assembly,

Reaffirming that all Member States have an obligation to promote and protect human rights and fundamental freedoms, as stated in the Charter of the United Nations and elaborated in the Universal Declaration of Human Rights, the International Covenants on Human Rights and other applicable human rights instruments,

Aware that, in accordance with the Charter, the United Nations promotes and encourages respect for human rights and fundamental freedoms for all and that the Universal Declaration of Human Rights states that the will of the people shall be the basis of the authority of government, and therefore expressing its grave concern that the Government of Myanmar has still not implemented its commitment to take all necessary steps towards democracy in the light of the results of the elections held in 1990,

Recalling its resolution 55/112 of 4 December 2000 and Commission on Human Rights resolution 1992/58 of 3 March 1992, in which the Commission, inter alia,

decided to nominate a special rapporteur with a given mandate, and taking note of Commission resolution 2001/15 of 18 April 2001, in which the Commission decided to extend for one year the mandate of its Special Rapporteur on the situation of human rights in Myanmar,

Recalling also the observation made by the former Special Rapporteur that the absence of respect for the rights pertaining to democratic governance is at the root of all major violations of human rights in Myanmar,

Still gravely concerned about the human rights situation in Myanmar, especially the suppression of the exercise of political rights and freedom of thought, expression, association and movement in Myanmar, and about restrictions placed on Aung San Suu Kyi and other members of the National League for Democracy, inter alia, on their freedom to function and to communicate with the outside world,

Gravely concerned that the legal system is effectively used as an instrument of oppression, inter alia, through the intimidation and detention of lawyers,

Recognizing that the systematic violations of civil, political, economic, social and cultural rights by the Government of Myanmar have had a significant adverse effect on the health and welfare of the people of Myanmar,

Welcoming the three visits to Myanmar by the Special Envoy of the Secretary-General during the past year, and the visits by the Special Rapporteur, as well as by the high-level team of the International Labour Organization, and the cooperation extended to them by the Government of Myanmar,

Cautiously encouraged by signs of progress in the ongoing political process in Myanmar, as reported by the Special Rapporteur, especially the release of political prisoners and the relaxation of some of the constraints governing the operation of legal political parties, but still concerned at the slow speed of the process,

1. *Expresses its appreciation* to the Special Rapporteur of the Commission on Human Rights on the situation of human rights in Myanmar for his interim report as well as his oral presentation;

2. *Welcomes* the assistance extended to the Special Rapporteur by the Government of Myanmar during his exploratory visit in April 2001 and his first fact-finding mission in October 2001, which enabled him to establish direct contacts with the Government and all other relevant sectors of society, and calls upon the Government to continue to cooperate with the Special Rapporteur, to allow him to conduct further field missions, without preconditions, and to implement fully his recommendations;

3. *Also welcomes* the report of the Secretary-General on the visits to the country of his Special Envoy for Myanmar, strongly endorses his efforts to help facilitate the national reconciliation process among all interested parties in Myanmar, and encourages the Government of Myanmar to establish a constructive and regular dialogue with the Secretary-General in order to make better use of his good offices;

4. *Deplores* the continued violations of human rights in Myanmar, including extrajudicial, summary or arbitrary executions, enforced disappearances, rape, torture, inhuman treatment, forced labour, including the use of children, forced relocation and denial of free-

dom of assembly, association, expression, religion and movement;

5. *Welcomes* the initiation of confidence-building contacts between the Government and Aung San Suu Kyi, General-Secretary of the National League for Democracy, and hopes that such talks will be extended at an appropriate time to include, among others, representatives of ethnic minorities, thereby facilitating broad-based and inclusive national reconciliation and the restoration of democracy;

6. *Expresses its concern* at the slow progress in the talks between the Government of Myanmar and Aung San Suu Kyi, General-Secretary of the National League for Democracy, and urges that the increasing development and progress of the confidence-building measures ensure the irreversibility of the process towards democracy;

7. *Recognizes* the steps taken by the Government of Myanmar to allow some political functions to be resumed by the opposition, including the reopening of some branch offices of political parties and the cessation of the negative media campaign, but expresses deep concern at the unnecessary and discriminatory stringent restrictions that continue to hamper political parties' freedom of assembly, association, expression, information and movement, as noted by the Special Rapporteur, as well as at the use by the Government of intimidatory methods such as arbitrary detention and abuse of the legal system, and calls for an early restoration of political rights and freedoms;

8. *Notes* the dissemination of human rights standards for public officials through a series of human rights workshops, and encourages the Government of Myanmar to widen participation in these workshops to ensure that this information, and its practical implementation, can benefit all citizens of Myanmar;

9. *Also notes* the establishment by the Government of Myanmar of a national human rights committee, and encourages it to bring this committee into conformity with the Principles relating to the status of national institutions for the promotion and protection of human rights annexed to General Assembly resolution 48/134 of 20 December 1993 (the Paris Principles);

10. *Welcomes* the release from detention of a number of democratic political activists, and strongly urges the Government of Myanmar to release all remaining detained political leaders and all political prisoners, including journalists, to ensure their physical integrity and to permit them to participate in the process of national reconciliation;

11. *Notes with satisfaction* the continued cooperation with the International Committee of the Red Cross, allowing the Committee to communicate with and visit detainees in accordance with its modalities of work, and hopes that the programme will be pursued further;

12. *Welcomes* the reopening of most university courses, but remains concerned that enjoyment of the right to education continues to be limited, often for political reasons, by the reduction in the length of the academic year, the division of the student population and its dispersal to distant campuses and the inadequate allocation of resources;

13. *Strongly urges* the Government of Myanmar to take urgent and concrete measures to ensure the establishment of democracy in accordance with the will of the people as expressed in the democratic elections held in 1990 and, to this end, to extend the talks initiated with Aung San Suu Kyi, General-Secretary of the National League for Democracy, to encompass a genuine and substantive dialogue with all the leaders of political parties and of ethnic minorities, with the aim of achieving national reconciliation and the restoration of democracy, and to ensure that political parties and non-governmental organizations can function freely, and in this context notes the existence of the committee representing the People's Parliament;

14. *Recalls* the resolution adopted by the International Labour Conference at its eighty-eighth session, held from 30 May to 15 June 2000, recommending that international organizations reconsider any cooperation with Myanmar and that Governments, employers and workers take appropriate measures to ensure that the Government of Myanmar could not take advantage of such relations to perpetuate or extend the system of forced or compulsory labour referred to by the Commission of Inquiry established to examine the observance by Myanmar of the International Labour Organization Convention concerning forced or compulsory labour (Convention No. 29) of 1930;

15. *Welcomes* the recent visit to Myanmar undertaken by the high-level team of the International Labour Organization, with the objective of assessing the practical implications and impact of measures taken by the Government to eradicate the practice of forced labour and the cooperation that was extended to the team by the Government of Myanmar;

16. *Notes with regret* that the conclusion of the high-level team was that there was only moderately positive evolution in the situation, since there have been only uneven efforts to disseminate the orders, since the orders have not been observed by the military at the local level and since, despite widespread instances of forced labour, there have been no criminal prosecutions, and that much more will have to be done to address adequately the situation, including movement towards national reconciliation;

17. *Strongly urges* the Government of Myanmar to implement, in close cooperation with the International Labour Organization, concrete legislative, executive and administrative measures to eradicate the practice of forced labour, in conformity with the relevant recommendations of the Commission of Inquiry, and in this context endorses the recommendations of the high-level team, including the establishment of a long-term representation of the International Labour Organization in Myanmar and the creation of an ombudsman, and encourages the Government of Myanmar to pursue the dialogue with the Director-General of the International Labour Organization to this end;

18. *Deplores* the continued violations of human rights, in particular those directed against persons belonging to ethnic and religious minorities, including summary executions, rape, torture, forced labour, forced porterage, forced relocations, use of anti-personnel landmines, destruction of crops and fields and dispossession of land and property, which deprives those persons of all means of subsistence and results in large-scale displacement of persons and flows of refugees to neighbouring countries, with negative effects for those countries, and an increasing number of internally displaced persons;

19. *Urges* the Government of Myanmar to end the systematic enforced displacement of persons and other causes of refugee flows to neighbouring countries and to create conditions conducive to their voluntary return and full reintegration in conditions of safety and dignity and to allow the safe and unhindered access of humanitarian personnel to assist in the return and reintegration process;

20. *Deplores* the continued violations of the human rights of women, especially women who are internally displaced or belong to ethnic minorities or the political opposition, in particular forced labour, trafficking, sexual violence and exploitation, including rape;

21. *Strongly urges* the Government of Myanmar to implement fully the recommendations made by the Committee on the Elimination of Discrimination against Women, in particular the request to prosecute and punish those who violate the human rights of women, and to carry out human rights education and gender-sensitization training, in particular for military personnel;

22. *Deplores* the recruitment of children as soldiers, in particular children belonging to ethnic minorities, and strongly urges the Government of Myanmar and all other parties to the hostilities in Myanmar to end the use of children as soldiers;

23. *Notes* that the Government of Myanmar is starting to address the growing incidence of infection with the human immunodeficiency virus/acquired immunodeficiency syndrome (HIV/AIDS), while recognizing that much still needs to be done, particularly in the area of HIV/AIDS prevention, and urges the Government of Myanmar to recognize fully the severity of the situation and the need to take necessary action against the disease, in cooperation with all relevant political and ethnic groups, and through the development of the United Nations joint plan of action on HIV/AIDS, to be delivered through non-governmental organizations or international agencies with a view to reaching the communities most affected and most vulnerable to HIV/AIDS infection;

24. *Urges* the Government of Myanmar to promote and protect the human rights of people living with HIV/AIDS and guard against the marginalization and discrimination that they may experience and to ensure that the health-care system receives sufficient funding to enable health workers to provide the highest possible standard of health care;

25. *Expresses its grave concern* at the high rates of malnutrition among pre-school-aged children, which constitutes serious violations of their rights to adequate food and the highest attainable standard of health and may have serious repercussions for the health and development of the affected children;

26. *Strongly urges* the Government of Myanmar to ensure full respect for all human rights and fundamental freedoms, including economic and social rights, and to fulfil its obligation to restore the independence of the judiciary and due process and to end the impunity of and bring to justice any perpetrators of human rights violations, including members of the military, and to investigate and prosecute alleged violations committed by government agents in all circumstances;

27. *Requests* the Secretary-General to continue his discussions on the situation of human rights and the restoration of democracy with the Government of Myanmar, to submit additional reports to the General Assembly during its fifty-sixth session on the progress of those discussions, and to report to the Assembly at its fifty-seventh session and to the Commission on Human Rights at its fifty-eighth session on the progress made in the implementation of the present resolution;

28. *Decides* to continue its consideration of this question at its fifty-seventh session.

Forced labour

ECONOMIC AND SOCIAL COUNCIL ACTION

On 3 May, the Economic and Social Council deferred consideration of an April request by ILO [E/2001/48] to include an additional agenda item entitled "Measures to be taken for the implementation by Myanmar of the recommendations of the International Labour Organization Commission of Inquiry on forced labour" (**decision 2001/216**).

On 25 July [meeting 42], the Council adopted **resolution 2001/20** [draft: E/2001/L.21] without vote [agenda item 14 *(b)*].

Developments concerning the question of the observance by the Government of Myanmar of the International Labour Organization Forced Labour Convention, 1930 (No. 29)

The Economic and Social Council,

Recalling the resolution adopted by the International Labour Conference at its eighty-eighth session, held in June 2000, on action to secure compliance with the recommendations of the Commission of Inquiry to examine the observance by Myanmar of its obligations in respect to the Forced Labour Convention, 1930 (No. 29), in which the Conference recommended the inclusion of the item on the agenda of the Economic and Social Council,

Taking note of the conclusions adopted by consensus by the International Labour Conference at its eighty-ninth session, held in June 2001,

1. *Takes note* of the outcome of the discussion of the Committee on the Application of Standards during the eighty-ninth session of the International Labour Conference, held in June 2001;

2. *Also takes note* of the understanding concluded between the International Labour Office and the authorities of Myanmar regarding an objective assessment to be carried out by an International Labour Organization high-level mission with respect to the practical implementation and actual impact of the framework of legislative, executive and administrative measures reported by Myanmar within the overall objective of the complete elimination of forced labour in law and practice;

3. *Further takes note* of the fact that the International Labour Organization Governing Body will examine the report of this mission at its two hundred and eighty-second session, to be held in November 2001;

4. *Requests* the Secretary-General to keep the Economic and Social Council informed of further developments in this matter.

Report of ILO high-level team. In May, the Government of Myanmar agreed to receive an ILO high-level team to assess the implementation of measures that took effect in 2000 [YUN 2000, p. 764] to ensure its compliance with the ILO Forced Labour Convention, 1930 (No. 29). The team visited the country for three weeks beginning on 17 September, when it conducted investigations, met with various NGOs and carried out interviews. Its work was complemented by meetings and interviews in Thailand and by information received from two researchers stationed in Bangladesh.

The team noted that orders prohibiting forced labour had been issued in November 2000. However, they did not specify either the kinds of tasks for which the requisition of labour was prohibited or the manner in which the same tasks would henceforth be performed. Although a procedure existed for prosecuting cases of forced labour, the team noted that there had been widespread instances of forced labour of all kinds, but no prosecutions. The team received accounts of serious reprisals taken by the military against those who complained about forced labour. There were no indications of the current use of forced labour on civil infrastructure projects but it was apparent that there was a strong correlation between the presence of military camps and the practice, whether or not the troops were engaged in military activities.

In November, the ILO Governing Body considered that efforts by the Myanmar authorities to disseminate the orders against forced labour should be strengthened and expressed concern regarding the limited impact of the new legislation, particularly the persistent impunity with regard to criminal prosecution of those who had committed violations. It urged Myanmar to undertake urgent efforts to rectify the situation. The ILO Director-General was requested to continue the dialogue with Myanmar, assist the Government with a view to giving effect to recommendations of the team, including establishing a form of ombudsman, and to report to the Governing Body in 2002.

Europe

Cyprus

In response to a 2000 Commission request [YUN 2000, p. 766], the Secretary-General, in a February report on the human rights situation in Cyprus [E/CN.4/2001/31], described activities carried out under his good offices mission (see

p. 391) and by the United Nations Peacekeeping Force in Cyprus (see p. 393) and the Committee on Missing Persons in Cyprus.

On 20 April [dec. 2001/102], the Commission decided to retain the item on its agenda, on the understanding that action required by previous resolutions would continue to remain operative, including its request to the Secretary-General to report on their implementation.

The former Yugoslavia

Commission action. On 18 April [res. 2001/12], by a roll-call vote of 41 to none, with 11 abstentions, the Commission noted that while varying degrees of progress had been made in the human rights situation in all States and by all parties to the General Framework Agreement for Peace in Bosnia and Herzegovina [YUN 1995, p. 544]—Bosnia and Herzegovina (composed of the Federation of Bosnia and Herzegovina and Republika Srpska), Croatia and the Federal Republic of Yugoslavia (FRY)—additional efforts were required in several areas. All States and parties to the 1995 Agreement were urged to cooperate with the International Tribunal for the Prosecution of Persons Responsible for Serious Violations of International Humanitarian Law Committed in the Territory of the Former Yugoslavia since 1991 (ICTY) (see p. 1198), established by the Security Council in 1993 [YUN 1993, p. 440].

The Commission welcomed the establishment in Bosnia and Herzegovina of the State-level and Federation Governments comprised of non-nationalist parties, but strongly condemned the attempt by the Croatian Democratic Union of Bosnia and Herzegovina extremists to undermine legitimately elected and constitutional bodies, as well as violent attacks by Bosnian Croat extremists in Mostar and other places against representatives of the international community. Noting progress on refugee returns in Bosnia and Herzegovina, the Commission condemned the continued harassment of returning minority refugees and internally displaced persons and recurrent instances of religious discrimination. It called on the authorities to establish a fully staffed and funded judiciary that protected the rights and fundamental freedoms of all citizens, adopt an effective and fair election law, cooperate fully with ICTY, promote an independent media, expand and improve the State Border Service to stem illegal immigration and trafficking in persons and implement the actions mandated by the Peace Implementation Council in 2000 [YUN 2000, p. 338].

Welcoming political changes in FRY and the commitment of the Government to investigate past human rights abuses, the Commission called on the authorities to respect the rights of all persons belonging to any of its national or ethnic, religious and linguistic minorities. It expressed concern at the continued detention in Serbia of political prisoners of Kosovar Albanian and other origins.

The Commission condemned human rights violations in the FRY province of Kosovo that had affected all ethnic groups and urged ethnic leaders in Kosovo to take action at the community level to prevent ethnic violence and to engage in and support efforts to create conditions for the safe, sustainable and dignified return of displaced minority communities.

The Chairperson of the Commission was requested to appoint for one year a special representative to examine the human rights situation in Bosnia and Herzegovina and FRY. The Commission's requests to the special representative regarding reporting methods were approved by Economic and Social Council **decision 2001/219**.

José Cutileiro (Portugal) was appointed Special Representative of the Commission on the situation of human rights in Bosnia and Herzegovina and FRY and assumed his functions in June.

ECONOMIC AND SOCIAL COUNCIL ACTION

In June, the Economic and Social Council adopted **decision 2001/219** [draft: E/2001/L.7, orally corrected] by recorded vote (28-0-10) [agenda item 2].

The situation of human rights in parts of South-Eastern Europe

At its 9th plenary meeting, on 4 June 2001, the Economic and Social Council, having taken note of Commission on Human Rights resolution 2001/12 of 18 April 2001, approved the decision of the Commission:

(a) To request the Chairperson of the Commission on Human Rights to appoint for one year a special representative of the Commission with a mandate to examine the situation of human rights in Bosnia and Herzegovina and the Federal Republic of Yugoslavia; in reporting on the human rights situation in Kosovo, the Special Representative should:

(i) Consult closely with the international civilian presence, particularly representatives of the Organization for Security and Cooperation in Europe;

(ii) Closely monitor the situation, paying particular attention to those areas that remain a source of concern, including cooperation with the International Tribunal for the Prosecution of Persons Responsible for Serious Violations of International Humanitarian Law Committed in the Territory of the Former Yugoslavia since 1991, the release of unjustly detained prisoners, including Kosovar Albanians, the identification of persons missing as a result of conflict, the protection of minorities, trafficking in persons and the right of return of refugees and internally displaced persons;

(iii) Cooperate closely with the offices of the United Nations High Commissioner for Human Rights in Belgrade and Sarajevo and with her Special Envoy on persons deprived of liberty in connection with the Kosovo crisis in the Federal Republic of Yugoslavia so as to avoid duplication of effort;

(b) To request the Special Representative to submit an interim report on her/his findings to the General Assembly at its fifty-sixth session and a report to the Commission on Human Rights at its fifty-eighth session.

RECORDED VOTE ON DECISION 2001/219:

In favour: Andorra, Argentina, Austria, Bolivia, Brazil, Bulgaria, Canada, Costa Rica, Croatia, Czech Republic, Democratic Republic of the Congo, Denmark, France, Georgia, Germany, Indonesia, Italy, Japan, Malta, Mexico, Norway, Portugal, Republic of Korea, Saudi Arabia, Uganda, United Kingdom, United States, Venezuela.

Against: None.

Abstaining: Angola, Benin, Cameroon, China, Cuba, Egypt, Nepal, Russian Federation, Sudan, Syrian Arab Republic.

Report of Special Rapporteur. In an addendum [E/CN.4/2001/47/Add.1] to a previous report [YUN 2000, p. 768], Special Rapporteur Jiri Dienstbier (Czech Republic) described developments from December 2000 to March 2001 in Bosnia and Herzegovina, Croatia and FRY.

An issue that had emerged recently in Bosnia and Herzegovina concerned irregular migration and related human rights matters. The number of irregular migrants apprehended was increasing, with some 28,000 migrants, mostly from Asia and the Middle East, entering the country in 2000, while only 5,000 left legally. Bosnia and Herzegovina appeared to be a main trafficking route to Western Europe. There was a legal vacuum with respect to migration and asylum issues, despite a law that established a legal framework for the admission and stay of aliens, as well as criteria and procedures for determining refugee status and the granting of asylum. The Special Rapporteur emphasized the need for regional cooperation in finding solutions that respected the rights of refugees and migrants.

During his mission to Croatia (26 February–1 March), the Special Rapporteur expressed concern that some serious problems continued, especially regarding discrimination in property restitution and the provision of alternative housing. He also expressed concern over the fairness of trials of ethnic Serbs for war crimes. Referring to mass demonstrations in support of Mirko Norac, a former Croatian Army General charged with war crimes committed in the Gospic area, the Special Rapporteur strongly condemned the rise of nationalism and right-wing extremism. He also condemned attacks on journalists and called for an investigation into a 1 March assault of two reporters and for the prosecution of those responsible.

During a visit to FRY (7-18 March), the Special Rapporteur observed dramatic political changes in Serbia following the ousting of President Slobodan Milosevic in 2000. However, he remained deeply concerned about the continuing violence in the Presevo valley region of southern Serbia. He also expressed concern at the slowness with which the new FRY and Serbian authorities were moving to release political prisoners remaining from the Milosevic era. Although the FRY Parliament adopted an amnesty act in February, affecting some 28,000 Serbs charged with crimes related to the evasion of military service and 100 to 200 of 500 Kosovar Albanian detainees convicted in unfair trials, further steps were needed to release the remaining Kosovar Albanian detainees.

During the brief reporting period, ethnic violence in Kosovo—organized Kosovar Albanian attacks on Kosovo Serbs and other minorities—had intensified to an alarming degree. The divided city of Mitrovica continued to be a flashpoint for ethnic violence against ethnic Serbs and Albanians. One reason violence persisted was the continued struggle of the United Nations Administration Mission in Kosovo (UNMIK) to establish the rule of law. Longstanding efforts to bring judicial norms in Kosovo in conformity with international human rights standards had still not borne fruit. The Special Rapporteur called for an urgent review of security procedures for minorities in Kosovo and a much more aggressive approach by the International Security Force in Kosovo (KFOR) and UNMIK.

In February, the Montenegrin legislature adopted a new referendum law, amendments to the election law and rules for election campaign coverage by State-run media, in anticipation of parliamentary elections scheduled for April, as well as for a possible subsequent referendum. Although the Special Rapporteur welcomed the timely creation of a legal framework, he expressed concern at the politicizing of public discussion on basic human rights issues, such as provisions on the right to vote and the applicable majority in the referendum law, which had led to the polarization of public opinion along political lines instead of focusing on the compliance of the drafted norms with international standards. Although efforts had been made to address the problem of trafficking, there was no adequate overall government policy to combat the phenomenon or to provide republic-wide protection for trafficking victims. The Special Rapporteur welcomed the establishment of the Human Rights Centre at the University of Montenegro.

Reports of Special Representative. In response to the Commission's April request, Special Representative José Cutileiro submitted to the General Assembly an October report [A/56/460] describing his visits to the Federation of Bosnia and Herzegovina (24-27 July) and FRY (27 August–4 September).

The Special Representative observed that in Bosnia and Herzegovina some persons in positions of power were associated with ethnic cleansing, elements of which had been adjudicated as constituting war crimes and crimes against humanity. He called for the arrest and transfer to The Hague of those indicted by ICTY. Regarding reconciliation, a truth and reconciliation commission, to draw conclusions on the nature of the circumstances that produced ethnic mistrust and misunderstandings, was being discussed. The absence of a multi-ethnic, professional police force and an independent judiciary had led to numerous incidents of impunity and disregard for the rule of law. Endemic corruption within governmental structures was of grave concern and militated against progress. Allegations of differential access to employment, social welfare, health services, public utilities and education continued. Bosnia and Herzegovina was predominantly a country of destination in terms of the trafficking of people, although there was increasing evidence that it was becoming a country of origin. The majority of those trafficked were from the Republic of Moldova, Romania and Ukraine and were mostly women and children. The Special Representative called for the development of an integrated and multisectoral approach to irregular migration, engaging the expertise of all of the international agencies that were involved, in close partnership with the State.

Although progress had been made in FRY to address a number of historical human rights violations, the pace of institutional reform remained slow and ad hoc. The Special Representative believed that institutional reform should consist of an effective separation of legislative, executive and judicial powers, with human rights and the rule of law as its foundation. In Serbia (excluding Kosovo), the low salaries of judges left the judicial process susceptible to corruption and abuse. Political appointments affected the quality of justice and the integrity of an independent judiciary. On 11 May, FRY acceded to the 1995 European Framework Convention for the Protection of National Minorities. Ethnic Albanian Kosovars in detention in Serbia were released under the amnesty act; the Special Representative, however, believed that the convictions of a very large number of those held in detention were based on evidence and trials that did not comply with minimum standards of due process. He was deeply concerned by the slow progress in carrying out exhumations and forensic analysis of remains discovered in Kosovo and other parts of Serbia, and urged authorities to cooperate on the issue. For many of the estimated 400,000 refugees and 200,000 internally displaced persons living in FRY, prospects of immediate or longer-term return to their places of former residence remained bleak. The Special Representative welcomed steps to amend the Citizenship Act of 1997 to allow refugees to obtain dual citizenship. Regarding the situation of displaced persons from Kosovo, he expressed deep concern that the current climate of violence and insecurity for ethnic Serbs and other minorities in Kosovo meant that few people were able to return to their homes. The Special Representative welcomed efforts to develop national ombudsman offices and independent and functional national human rights institutions, but cautioned against the creation of a multiplicity of national and municipality structures that were not adequately funded and were autonomous. Regarding southern Serbia, the Special Representative was encouraged by an agreement reached in May between Yugoslav and Serb authorities, the North Atlantic Treaty Organization (NATO) and representatives of the ethnic Albanian community that led to the end of most of the violence in the Presevo valley region and the municipality of Medvedja in the border area with Kosovo. Since June, complaints of ill-treatment by police of ethnic Albanians in southern Serbia had been infrequent. Nevertheless, the Special Representative was concerned that more visible progress needed to be made in fulfilling commitments under the Covic Plan— the core of an agreement on a peaceful solution to the conflict presented by the Government comprising a series of measures to improve the social, economic and political rights of ethnic Albanians in southern Serbia (see also p. 346)— relating to the reintegration of ethnic Albanians into employment in the public service sector and the local economy and the more effective representation of ethnic Albanians in municipal executive bodies.

The most pressing human rights concerns in Kosovo remained those faced by ethnic Serb and other minority communities. Many did not enjoy effective and safe access to health and social services, schools or employment opportunities. Kosovo's judicial system faced major challenges in building a post-conflict legal system. UNMIK had created a functional court system, which still needed substantial changes, and had improved the legal basis upon which executive orders to detain were made, including the commission of an independent detention review committee. The Special Representative was concerned by the lack of adequate consultation and transparency regarding legislation governing pre-trial detention, supervision of the media, terrorism, border control, the rights of detainees and restrictions on the sale of private property in minority areas.

In Montenegro, the continued uncertainty as to its future constitutional status hampered efforts to reform government institutions. Noting cases of accused persons held in pre-trial detention beyond the maximum period prescribed by national law and international standards, the Special Representative urged the authorities to bring the protracted cases to a conclusion in accordance with due process of law. He recommended abolishing criminal custodial sanctions for expression-related matters and special criminal law protection accorded to public figures and symbols. The Special Representative noted that there was some discrepancy between the formal legal guarantees and the actual situation for minorities. Ethnic Albanians and Muslims/Bosniaks were underrepresented in the civil service and in the police force and there were virtually no ethnic Albanian employees in the judicial or internal affairs bodies. The national educational curriculum had not been fully adapted to reflect the needs and cultural values of the different ethnic communities. As to the trafficking in human beings, the victim protection programme adopted earlier in the year, as well as the activities of the National Coordinator against Trafficking, had brought concrete results. The Special Representative urged the authorities to strengthen law enforcement measures and increase criminal sanctions for those involved in trafficking people.

In a later report covering developments until mid-December [E/CN.4/2002/41], the Special Representative expressed the hope that amendments to the property laws in Bosnia and Herzegovina would rectify the uneven implementation of property restitution. The reduction in the number of persons de-authorized to act as police officers because of improper activities was a positive sign; however, the persistent lack of a multiethnic and professional police force and an independent judiciary undermined the rule of law. Nationalism—Bosniak, Serb and Croat biases— and corruption continued to undermine the political and legal systems. The Government had adopted a national plan of action to combat trafficking in persons, which remained a serious problem. Overall, the extent to which corruption featured in the economy and in society remained an obstacle to building a country where human rights were respected and violations redressed by State and Entity agents.

FRY was still in a state of transition, with many institutional changes made but with much still to be done to consolidate those efforts. Institutional reforms necessary to establish the rule of law, reform the judiciary and police, combat organized crime and establish the basis for a free media had moved slowly. While a package of laws on judicial reform had been adopted, legislation governing labour, local self-government, a national human rights institution and the media was still pending. Of equal concern was the process by which legislation for reform was drafted and adopted. The Special Rapporteur remained concerned about specific allegations of human rights violations by members of the police force, including allegations of police ill-treatment and brutality. Progress had been made in strengthening the legislative framework to promote and protect ethnic minorities and creating greater public awareness of minority rights through a tolerance campaign launched in November. The Special Representative welcomed the release from detention of ethnic Kosovo Albanians under the amnesty act passed earlier in the year. He expressed deep concern that the current climate of violence and insecurity for ethnic Serbs and other ethnic minorities in Kosovo meant that few people were able to return to their homes. In the print media, the Special Representative welcomed the repeal by the Serbian Parliament in February of the oppressive information law of 1998 and the payment of compensation to the owners and editors of the print media who had been fined under the law. In the electronic media, the draft law on public broadcasting had not yet been adopted. In May, an agreement was reached between the Federal and Serbian authorities that ended most of the violence in the Presevo valley region of southern Serbia. Respect for human rights in terms of police behaviour had improved substantially in southern Serbia, but a number of complaints of human rights violations by police were recorded during the last months of the year.

Significant developments in self-governance were noted in Kosovo following the election of a Kosovo-wide legislative assembly on 17 November. The first organized return to Kosovo of internally displaced ethnic Serbs, comprising 54 individuals to an isolated Serb village, took place in August, but the current situation did not permit any larger-scale return programmes. The Special Representative noted the establishment of an Office of Returns and Communities with its director under the direct supervision of the Secretary-General's Representative. The Kosovo Ombudsperson had become active in addressing human rights problems that fell under his mandate. Generally, the Special Representative remained concerned by the slow progress in the human rights situation and physical protection of ethnic minorities in Kosovo; the quality of the rule of law; and the extent to which human rights standards and practices were integrated into the work of UNMIK and KFOR.

Uncertainty about the future constitutional status of Montenegro continued to hamper any real progress to reform government institutions, including reforms to improve human rights promotion and protection. Specific areas requiring attention were the right to life, the right to a trial within a reasonable time or release pending trial, freedom of the media and the right to freedom of expression, underrepresentation of minorities in the civil service and media-incited animosity against minority groups. Although trafficking in persons continued, positive developments were the adoption of a national plan of action against trafficking, the appointment of a national governmental coordinator in charge of trafficking issues and the creation of a government interagency task force to combat the problem.

GENERAL ASSEMBLY ACTION

On 19 December [meeting 88], the General Assembly, on the recommendation of the Third Committee [A/56/583/Add.3], adopted **resolution 56/172** without vote [agenda item 119 (c)].

Situation of human rights in parts of South-Eastern Europe

The General Assembly,

Guided by the purposes and principles of the Charter of the United Nations, the Universal Declaration of Human Rights, the International Covenants on Human Rights, the 1951 Convention relating to the Status of Refugees and the 1967 Protocol thereto, the Convention on the Prevention and Punishment of the Crime of Genocide, the Declaration on the Rights of Persons Belonging to National or Ethnic, Religious and Linguistic Minorities, the Declaration on the Elimination of All Forms of Intolerance and of Discrimination Based on Religion or Belief, the Guiding Principles on Internal Displacement, accepted humanitarian rules, as set out in the Geneva Conventions of 12 August 1949, and, for participating States of the Organization for Security and Cooperation in Europe, the Helsinki Final Act of 1 August 1975,

Bearing in mind all resolutions on this subject, in particular Commission on Human Rights resolution 2001/12 of 18 April 2001 and General Assembly resolution 55/113 of 4 December 2000, as well as all Security Council resolutions and presidential statements,

Recalling Security Council resolutions 1160(1998) of 31 March 1998, 1199(1998) of 23 September 1998, 1203(1998) of 24 October 1998, 1239(1999) of 14 May 1999, 1244(1999) of 10 June 1999 and the general principles annexed thereto, 1345(2001) of 21 March 2001, 1367(2001) of 10 September 2001, all previous General Assembly resolutions on the subject, as well as the statement made on 24 March 1998 by the Chairman of the Commission on Human Rights at the fifty-fourth session of the Commission, Commission on Human Rights resolutions 1998/79 of 22 April 1998, 1999/2 of 13 April 1999 and 2000/26 of 18 April 2000 and the report of the United Nations High Commissioner for Human Rights of 27 September 1999 on the situation of human rights in Kosovo, and taking note of the periodic report of 11 October 2001 of the Special Representative of the Commission on Human Rights on the situation of human rights in Bosnia and Herzegovina and the Federal Republic of Yugoslavia,

Underlining the obligation of all authorities in the Federal Republic of Yugoslavia and all parties in Kosovo to cooperate fully in the implementation of Security Council resolution 1244(1999) and the general principles on a political solution to the Kosovo crisis adopted on 6 May 1999, annexed to that resolution, and welcoming the Common Document signed on 5 November 2001 by the United Nations Interim Administration Mission in Kosovo and the Government of the Federal Republic of Yugoslavia,

Expressing its full support for and encouraging efforts towards the full implementation of commitments contained in the General Framework Agreement for Peace in Bosnia and Herzegovina and the annexes thereto (collectively the "Peace Agreement"),

1. *Emphasizes* the need to ensure respect for all human rights and fundamental freedoms and to do everything possible to further the process of reconciliation and regional cooperation;

2. *Welcomes* all efforts by countries of the region to overcome the effects of past conflicts, and also the efforts of the international community, which have helped the countries of the region to make great strides towards peace and stability;

3. *Also welcomes* moves by all parties in the region to establish and maintain a constructive dialogue with their neighbours, an essential element of regional stability, and urges them to continue these efforts;

4. *Notes* that varying degrees of progress have been made in the human rights situation in all States, but that further efforts are required in several areas;

5. *Also notes* the progress in the region, and encourages further free, fair, inclusive and democratic elections throughout the region as an important element of the rule of law and the promotion and protection of human rights;

6. *Urges* all parties to condemn ethnic violence and intolerance and to oppose actively, in a manner consistent with internationally recognized human rights standards, advocates or perpetrators of any form of violence as a means to secure peace and the protection of human rights and fundamental freedoms, and encourages parties to use dialogue to address their differences;

7. *Urges* all authorities in the region to cooperate fully with the International Tribunal for the Prosecution of Persons Responsible for Serious Violations of International Humanitarian Law Committed in the Territory of the Former Yugoslavia since 1991, and in particular to comply with their obligation to arrest immediately and transfer to the custody of the Tribunal all indicted persons, as well as to comply with requests by the Tribunal for access to information and witnesses;

8. *Emphasizes* the need to prevent and end violations of human rights, including cases of arbitrary detention, as well as the continued detention of political prisoners and cases of discrimination on the basis of ethnic origin, nationality, language or religion;

9. *Also emphasizes* the need for sustained progress on all issues that have an impact on the enjoyment of human rights, in particular, legal reform, impunity, protection of all persons belonging to minorities and the fight against organized crime and trafficking in persons;

10. *Stresses* the need for enhanced efforts to foster and effect the prompt and voluntary return and integration of displaced persons and refugees in safety and with dignity;

11. *Underlines* the importance of consistent efforts to establish the fate of missing persons, and encourages all States and parties to provide information to organizations involved in this effort, including through the tracing mechanisms of the International Committee of the Red Cross, and to cooperate fully with organizations such as the International Committee of the Red Cross and the International Commission on Missing Persons that are involved in the effort to determine the identities, whereabouts and fate of missing persons;

12. *Encourages* the United Nations High Commissioner for Human Rights, the United Nations High Commissioner for Refugees, the Organization for Security and Cooperation in Europe and the Council of Europe to enhance their cooperation in the region, including within the Stability Pact for South-Eastern Europe;

13. *Encourages* the international community to continue providing voluntary contributions to meet the pressing human rights and humanitarian needs of the region;

14. *Welcomes* the appointment of the Special Representative of the Commission on Human Rights on the situation of human rights in Bosnia and Herzegovina and the Federal Republic of Yugoslavia, and calls upon all authorities and all concerned parties to cooperate fully with the Special Representative as he carries out his work.

Russian Federation

Republic of Chechnya

Report of High Commissioner. In February [E/CN.4/2001/36], the High Commissioner reported on the implementation of a resolution adopted by the Commission in 2000 [YUN 2000, p. 773] on the situation in Chechnya.

The report summarized information received from the Government regarding criminal cases and charges filed by the military procuracy for alleged crimes by the military against civilians in Chechnya. No similar information was received regarding alleged violations by Ministry of Interior troops and militia, who were under the responsibility of the civilian procuracy. The High Commissioner stated that the reports, which came from a variety of sources, including intergovernmental organizations, Russian and international NGOs and members of the State Duma, indicated that further efforts were needed before adequate conditions for the respect of human rights existed in Chechnya.

The High Commissioner continued to receive reports of serious human rights violations carried out by Chechen fighters against federal and local authorities and against civilians, and urged those responsible to cease such attacks. Other areas of concern were the major gap between the large number of complaints submitted to various government agencies and bodies and the relatively small number of court proceedings, and the economic, social and cultural rights of the Chechen people.

Commission action. On 20 April [res. 2001/24], by a roll-call vote of 22 to 12, with 19 abstentions, the Commission, strongly condemning the continued use of indiscriminate force against civilians by Russian military forces, federal servicemen and State agents, called on the Government of the Russian Federation to comply with its international human rights and humanitarian law obligations in its operations against Chechen fighters and to protect civilians. It also condemned terrorist activities, attacks and breaches of international humanitarian law perpetrated by Chechen fighters and called for the release of all hostages. All parties to the conflict were called on to halt the fighting and indiscriminate use of force and to seek a political solution with the aim of achieving a peaceful outcome. The Russian Federation was called on to establish urgently a national broad-based and independent commission of inquiry to investigate alleged human rights violations and breaches of international humanitarian law committed in Chechnya; ensure criminal investigations and prosecutions of all violations of international humanitarian law and human rights; ensure the return of the Assistance Group of the Organization for Security and Cooperation in Europe to Chechnya; protect internally displaced persons; allow unimpeded access of humanitarian personnel to Chechnya and neighbouring republics; and disseminate, and ensure that the military had knowledge of, the basic principles of human rights and international humanitarian law. The Commission asked the Special Rapporteurs on the question of torture, on extrajudicial, summary or arbitrary executions, and on internally displaced persons to carry out missions to Chechnya. The High Commissioner was asked to report to the Commission in 2002 and to keep it and the General Assembly informed of further developments.

ECONOMIC AND SOCIAL COUNCIL ACTION

In July, the Economic and Social Council, on the recommendation of the Commission on Human Rights [E/2001/23], adopted **decision**

2001/258 by recorded vote (24-4-20) [agenda item 14 (*g*)].

Situation in the Republic of Chechnya of the Russian Federation

At its 40th plenary meeting, on 24 July 2001, the Economic and Social Council, taking note of Commission on Human Rights resolution 2001/24 of 20 April 2001, approved the Commission's request to the United Nations High Commissioner for Human Rights to report to the Commission at its fifty-eighth session on the implementation of Commission resolution 2001/24 and to keep the General Assembly informed of further developments as appropriate.

RECORDED VOTE ON DECISION 2001/258:

In favour: Andorra, Austria, Bulgaria, Canada, Croatia, Czech Republic, Denmark, Fiji, France, Germany, Honduras, Italy, Malta, Mexico, Netherlands, Norway, Pakistan, Portugal, Romania, Saudi Arabia, South Africa, Suriname, United Kingdom, United States.
Against: China, Cuba, Russian Federation, Venezuela.
Abstaining: Angola, Argentina, Bahrain, Bolivia, Brazil, Burkina Faso, Cameroon, Costa Rica, Egypt, Ethiopia, Indonesia, Japan, Nepal, Nigeria, Peru, Republic of Korea, Rwanda, Sudan, Syrian Arab Republic, Uganda.

Middle East

Lebanon

Commission action. On 18 April [res. 2001/10], by a roll-call vote of 33 to 1, with 19 abstentions, the Commission called on Israel to release Lebanese civilians who had been imprisoned and held as hostages for bargaining purposes and to comply with the Geneva Conventions of 12 August 1949 for the protection of war victims, particularly the Geneva Convention relative to the Protection of Civilian Persons in Time of War (Fourth Geneva Convention). Israel was also called on to submit to the United Nations Interim Force in Lebanon all the maps of the landmine fields laid throughout areas occupied by civilians. The Commission asked the Secretary-General to bring its resolution to Israel's attention and to call on Israel to comply with its provisions. He was asked to report to the General Assembly in 2001 and to the Commission in 2002.

The Economic and Social Council approved the Commission's requests to the Secretary-General on 24 July (**decision 2001/248**).

Communication. On 5 April [E/CN.4/2001/54], Israel refuted Lebanon's allegations that it had failed to disclose information regarding the location of mines in southern Lebanon and hand over maps of the minefields.

Reports of Secretary-General. In response to a 2000 Commission request [YUN 2000, p. 773], the Secretary-General stated that he had asked Israel for information on the extent of the implementation of the Commission's 2000 resolution on the human rights situation in southern Lebanon and western Bekaa, but had received no reply [E/CN.4/2001/32].

In July [A/56/217], the Secretary-General reported that he had asked Israel for information on the implementation of the Commission's resolution regarding Lebanese detainees in Israel (see p. 734) and had received no reply.

Territories occupied by Israel

During 2001, the question of human rights violations in the territories occupied by Israel as a result of the 1967 hostilities in the Middle East was again considered by the Commission on Human Rights and by the Human Rights Inquiry Commission, established by the Commission (see below). Political and other aspects were considered by the General Assembly, its Special Committee to Investigate Israeli Practices Affecting the Human Rights of the Palestinian People and Other Arabs of the Occupied Territories (Committee on Israeli Practices) and other bodies (see PART ONE, Chapter VI).

Reports of Secretary-General. Pursuant to a 2000 Commission resolution [YUN 2000, p. 775], the Secretary-General reported that he had brought that resolution, which concerned the occupied Syrian Golan, to the attention of all Governments, the Committee on Israeli Practices, the Committee on the Exercise of the Inalienable Rights of the Palestinian People, the United Nations Relief and Works Agency for Palestine Refugees in the Near East (UNRWA), the specialized agencies, regional intergovernmental organizations and international humanitarian organizations [E/CN.4/2001/28]. The UN Department of Public Information provided press coverage for all meetings of the Committee on Israeli Practices, and distributed information through documents, press releases, briefings and UN information centres and services.

In response to a further 2000 Commission resolution [YUN 2000, p. 774], the Secretary-General stated that he had brought the Commission's resolution on the violation of human rights in the occupied Arab territories to the attention of the Government of Israel and all other Governments, the Committee on Israeli Practices and the Committee on the Exercise of the Inalienable Rights of the Palestinian People, as well as to the specialized agencies, UNRWA, regional intergovernmental organizations and international humanitarian organizations, requesting information pertaining to Israel's implementation of the resolution. He had received no reply from Israel [E/CN.4/2001/27].

The Secretary-General submitted to the Commission in January a list of all United Nations reports issued since 28 April 2000 on the situation of the population living in the occupied Arab territories [E/CN.4/2001/29].

Inquiry Commission. The Human Rights Inquiry Commission, which was established on 2 January in response to a 2000 resolution [YUN 2000, p. 776] adopted by the fifth special session of the Commission on Human Rights, submitted its report [E/CN.4/2001/121] to the Commission in March. Following its first meeting (Geneva, 14-16 January), at which it considered organizational matters, the three-member Inquiry Commission visited the occupied Palestinian territories and Israel from 10 to 18 February. It concluded that the Israeli Defence Force (IDF) had engaged in the excessive use of force at the expense of life and property in Palestine. Although IDF carried out only a small number of extrajudicial executions (estimated at 11 at least) or targeted political assassinations, the Commission accorded special attention to them because they had been officially acknowledged, promoted and condoned. Having considered the implications of Jewish settlements in the West Bank (including East Jerusalem) and Gaza on human rights and humanitarian law, the Commission reaffirmed that the settlements constituted a major violation of international humanitarian law and identified the presence of settlements and settlers as a primary cause of many human rights violations in the occupied territories. Measures of closure, curfew or destruction of property in the territories constituted violations of the Fourth Geneva Convention and human rights obligations binding on Israel. The Palestinian refugees within the territories seemed worse off than the Palestinian refugee diaspora in neighbouring countries. Further, the deterioration of their circumstances throughout the West Bank and Gaza had been accentuated by the recent heightened tensions and violence (see p. 406).

The Inquiry Commission made a series of recommendations to address the root causes of the situation, deter further violence, end the destruction of lives, property and livelihoods and establish a climate conducive to the emergence of a just and durable peace for the peoples of Israel and Palestine. It listed safeguards and procedures that needed to be observed while negotiations aimed at a comprehensive, just and durable peace were pursued.

On 23 March [E/CN.4/2001/145], Egypt, as Chairman of the Council of Arab Permanent Representatives in Geneva Members of the League of Arab States, stated that the Council found unacceptable a paragraph of the Inquiry Commission's report that recommended the application of article 1 D of the 1951 Convention relating to the Status of Refugees [YUN 1951, p. 520] to ensure that a regime of protection under UNHCR authority was extended to Palestinian refugees. The Council asserted that the Palestinian refugee issue was governed by relevant UN resolutions, that UNRWA was responsible for carrying out relief and work programmes for Palestinian refugees and that the Convention's article did not apply to persons who were receiving protection or assistance from the UN system other than UNHCR.

Report of Special Rapporteur. In March [E/CN.4/2001/30], Special Rapporteur Giorgio Giacomelli (Italy) updated information contained in his report following his mission to the region in 2000 [YUN 2000, p. 775]. He stated that certain human rights violations had graduated from sporadic or incidental occurrences to a level of regularity. Radio and print media had reported Israeli military officers admitting that the army had operationalized a policy of extrajudicial executions against Palestinians it suspected of committing attacks against Jewish settlers or Israeli soldiers in the occupied Palestinian territories. Housing and property demolition had emerged as a consistent pattern, with some 773 family homes destroyed by Israeli forces between September 2000 and February 2001. Israel's alleged use of torture and prison conditions in general remained of concern to the human rights community. The Special Rapporteur also cited violations of the rights to food and press freedom. Consequences of ongoing violations resulted in losses for the Palestinian economy, violations of children's human rights, damage and destruction of health facilities and territorial and social fragmentation of the occupied Palestinian territories. As to the use of force, the Special Rapporteur noted that the roles and responsibilities on the Palestinian side, while outside his mandate, remained unclear and difficult to ascertain. He urged international protection for the Palestinians in the occupied territories, measures to restore confidence and rekindle hope in a durable peace, and respect for international law.

In March, the Special Rapporteur resigned and John Dugard (South Africa), who had served as the Chairperson of the Human Rights Inquiry Commission (see p. 735), was appointed to replace him in July.

Commission action. On 18 April [res. 2001/6], by a roll-call vote of 29 to 2, with 21 abstentions, the Commission called on Israel to comply with UN resolutions on the occupied Syrian Golan and demanded that it rescind its decision to impose its laws, jurisdiction and administration on that occupied territory. It also called on Israel to desist from changing the physical character, demo-

graphic composition, institutional structure and legal status of the occupied Syrian Golan and to desist from imposing Israeli citizenship and identity cards on citizens of the Syrian Golan and from its repressive measures against them. The Secretary-General was requested to bring the Commission's resolution to the attention of all Governments, UN organs, specialized agencies, regional intergovernmental organizations and international humanitarian organizations, to give the resolution wide publicity and to report in 2002.

Also on 18 April [res. 2001/7], by a roll-call vote of 28 to 2, with 22 abstentions, the Commission condemned Israel's recourse to force and urged the Government to ensure that its security forces observed international standards regarding the use of force. Deploring the practice of extrajudicial killings of certain Palestinians carried out by Israeli security forces, the Commission urged the Government to respect international law and cease that practice. It also called on Israel to end the expropriation of Palestinian homes in Jerusalem, end the practice of torture against Palestinians during interrogation, desist from all human rights violations in the Palestinian and other occupied Arab territories, respect the bases of international law, the principles of international humanitarian law and its international commitments and agreements, and withdraw from the Palestinian territories. Israel was also urged to implement the recommendations of the Human Rights Inquiry Commission (see p. 735). The Commission requested the Special Rapporteur, acting as a monitoring mechanism, to follow up on the implementation of its recommendations and to report thereon to the General Assembly in 2001 (see p. 737) and to the Commission in 2002; the Economic and Social Council approved the Commission's request on 24 July (**decision 2001/246**). The Secretary-General was asked to bring the Commission's resolution to the attention of the Government of Israel and all other Governments, competent UN organs, the specialized agencies, regional intergovernmental organizations and international humanitarian organizations, to disseminate it as widely as possible and to report in 2002 on its implementation by Israel. He was also asked to provide the Commission with all UN reports issued between its sessions that dealt with conditions in which the Palestinians were living under Israeli occupation.

On the same date [res. 2001/8], by a roll-call vote of 50 to 1, with 1 abstention, the Commission, expressing grave concern at the continuing Israeli settlement activities in the occupied Arab territories, including East Jerusalem, and at closures of and within the Palestinian territories, and condemning all acts of terrorism, urged Israel to comply with the Commission's previous resolutions; to cease its policy of expanding the settlements and related activities in the occupied territories; to forgo and prevent any new installation of settlers; and to ensure that the Israeli security forces protected Palestinians from violence perpetrated by Israeli settlers. All parties were urged to create conditions to allow the resumption of the peace process.

Communications. During the year, the Commission received communications regarding the situation in the occupied Palestinian territories, including from Palestine describing Israeli violence against Palestinian civilians [E/CN.4/2001/3, E/CN.4/2001/136, E/CN.4/2001/142, E/CN.4/2002/11, E/CN.4/2002/126-128, E/CN.4/2002/131], from the Libyan Arab Jamahiriya transmitting a resolution on the humanitarian situation in the occupied territories, adopted by the joint meeting of the Red Crescent/Red Cross National Societies in the Member States of the Organization of the Islamic Conference (Jeddah, Saudi Arabia, 21-22 April) [E/CN.4/2001/166], and from Israel regarding information pertaining to a gunshot fired at the vehicle of the High Commissioner during her visit in 2000 [E/CN.4/2002/6].

Report of Special Rapporteur. By an October note [A/56/440], the Secretary-General transmitted the report of Special Rapporteur John Dugard on the violation of human rights in the occupied Arab territories, including Palestine. During his mission to the occupied Palestinian territories in August, the Special Rapporteur had met with Palestinian and Israeli NGOs, international agencies and the Palestinian Authority (PA). He did not meet with Israeli authorities as the Government had made it clear that it would not cooperate because of objections to his mandate. Since the Special Rapporteur's mandate required him to investigate human rights violations in the occupied Palestinian territories within the context of military occupation, the report focused on military occupation as the root cause of the conflict in the occupied Palestinian territories and Israel, as the cause of the violation of human rights and humanitarian law in the region. The Special Rapporteur described the violence and loss of life since the start of the second intifada in September 2000, during which over 530 Palestinians had been killed and over 15,000 injured and more than 150 Israelis had been killed. He observed that both Israelis and Palestinians had violated important norms of humanitarian law and international law, and asserted that the failed attempts to end the violence (see p. 405) suggested that the time had come for an international monitoring presence. In his view, the principal cause of the second intifada and of the escalating violence was the continuing occupation, the signs of which had intensified. The Special Rapporteur described expanded settlement activity, the demolition of Palestinian houses, restrictions on freedom of movement in the occupied territories imposed by Israel through closures and checkpoints and the Israeli occupation of Orient House, the political headquarters of the Palestinians in East Jerusalem (see p. 411). The Special Rapporteur concluded that it was incumbent on the international community to ensure that Israel and the PA agreed to an international presence to ensure that a ceasefire held. In view of Israel's continued refusal to accept the Fourth Geneva Convention as the governing law, he recommended that the high contracting parties to the Convention convene to consider the applicability of the Convention (see p. 425). The Special Rapporteur called for the dismantling of settlements and attention to Israel's violation of freedom of movement in the occupied Palestinian territories. There was a need to rebuild confidence on both sides, he stated. However, until Israel indicated a willingness to terminate the occupation, it was unlikely that the Palestinians would accept its good faith in negotiations aimed at a permanent settlement.

The General Assembly, on 19 December, took note of the Secretary-General's note transmitting the Special Rapporteur's report (**decision 56/429**).

Communication. In December comments on the Special Rapporteur's report [E/CN.4/2002/129 & Corr.1], Israel stated that he had disregarded its attempts to end the current situation. Israel reiterated its objections to the Special Rapporteur's mandate, refuted his assertion that occupation was the root cause of the conflict, and disagreed with his examination of human rights violations and with his description of the occupation. Israel also claimed biases in the presentation of the facts, legal conclusions and recommendations.

PART THREE

Economic and social questions

Chapter I

Development policy and international economic cooperation

In 2001, the world economy took an unexpectedly severe and widespread downturn. Following an unprecedented period of growth, the slowdown began in the developed economies, particularly North America, but quickly spread around the world through global trade, finance and investment links. The pervasive slowdown, aggravated by the terrorist attacks against the United States in September, led to a substantial decline in global growth from 4 per cent in 2000 to about 1.4 per cent in 2001. Growth in the developed economies was the lowest in a decade, as was annual average growth in the developing countries, with the exception of the year following the Asian crisis. The economies in transition exhibited greater resilience but their average growth also declined during the year.

The global decline took on a particular significance in the context of increasing economic globalization and interdependence, which were important themes of deliberations within the major UN organs in 2001. The General Assembly's second high-level dialogue on strengthening international economic cooperation for development through partnership, which took place in September, focused on responding to globalization by promoting the integration of developing countries into the world economy and enhancing their integration into the emerging global information network. The Assembly also addressed the role of the United Nations in the context of globalization, as well as the importance of promoting global partnerships, particularly with the private sector. The Economic and Social Council adopted agreed conclusions on the role of the United Nations and the importance of relevant partnerships in promoting development, particularly through access to and transfer of information technologies. In April, the Commission on Sustainable Development examined the impact of economic globalization on sustainable development, with particular reference to developing countries. Also in April, the Committee for Development Policy considered economic governance responsibilities in the context of a globalizing world.

In May, the Third United Nations Conference on the Least Developed Countries (LDCs) adopted the Brussels Declaration and the Programme of Action for the Least Developed Countries for the Decade 2001-2010, an updated set of commitments and measures for improving the lives of the 600 million people living in 49 LDCs worldwide.

International economic relations

Development and international economic cooperation

A number of UN bodies addressed development and international economic cooperation issues during 2001, including the General Assembly and the Economic and Social Council.

The Assembly, by **decision 56/453** of 21 December, deferred consideration of the launching of global negotiations on international economic cooperation for development and included the item in the provisional agenda of its fifty-seventh (2002) session.

Also on 21 December, the Assembly took note of the reports of the Second (Economic and Financial) Committee on its discussion of macroeconomic policy questions [A/56/558] (**decision 56/435**) and of sustainable development and international economic cooperation [A/56/560] (**decision 56/436**).

Economic and Social Council consideration. On 1 May, the Economic and Social Council held its fourth special high-level meeting with the Bretton Woods institutions (the World Bank Group and the International Monetary Fund) [E/2001/72]. It had before it a note by the Secretary-General containing background information on selected aspects of international cooperation in strengthening financing for development [E/2001/45] (see p. 882).

Globalization and interdependence

In response to General Assembly resolution 55/212 [YUN 2000, p. 783], the Secretary-General submitted an October report on the role of the United Nations in promoting development in the context of globalization and interdependence

[A/56/445]. The report analysed the increasing linkages and interdependencies among trade, finance, knowledge, technology and investment and their effect on growth and development and explored policy responses. Prepared in collaboration with the United Nations Conference on Trade and Development (UNCTAD) and other organizations of the UN system, the report also addressed policy coherence and consistency for the prevention and management of financial crises.

The Secretary-General observed that the report's conclusions and recommendations should be seen in the context of the preparatory processes for two major conferences: the November ministerial meeting of the World Trade Organization (WTO) (see p. 1432) and the 2002 International Conference on Financing for Development (see p. 882). The key challenge to be met in those and other international policy forums was to place development at the centre in considering how globalization was managed. Development goals should shape the framework of globalization rather than allowing the blind forces of globalization to define the development outcome.

That would require not only ensuring greater policy coherence at the global and national levels, but also making the international trade, finance and technology regimes much more responsive to development. The United Nations had an important role to play in promoting policy coherence and strengthening coordination at the international level. In that regard, the Economic and Social Council could be encouraged to deepen its dialogue with the Bretton Woods institutions and WTO and could encourage the UN system to develop integrated policy responses and a set of mutually reinforcing actions to address globalization, with a view to strengthening efforts to achieve the outcomes of the major UN conferences of the 1990s and the goals set during the Millennium Assembly in 2000 [YUN 2000, p. 47]. To build the capacity in developing countries and economies in transition to deal with the challenges of globalization, additional efforts were called for by the international community in terms of financial resources and technical assistance. Financial support through official development assistance (ODA) should be concentrated on key areas such as physical infrastructure, development of human resources and institutional and managerial capacity-building.

Governments needed to foster an environment to enable the private sector in developing countries and economies in transition to be integrated more effectively into the globalization of economic activities. In that regard, the provision of technical and financial assistance by the international community and the active participation of the private sector were crucial to address structural deficiencies that hindered the ability of developing countries to participate in the knowledge-based global economy.

The report further observed that institutional arrangements for economic governance had fallen far behind the realities of globalization. Global institutional structures could be usefully adapted and evolved in the functioning of financial markets, international capital flows, intellectual property and patent regimes, competition policy and bankruptcy law, taxation and trade policies, and regulation and supervision of banks and financial institutions. Also, given the linkages and interdependence in the driving forces of globalization and its impact on growth and development, Governments needed to cooperate in establishing fair and equitable trade, investment, technology and knowledge regimes.

GENERAL ASSEMBLY ACTION

On 21 December [meeting 90], the General Assembly, on the recommendation of the Second Committee [A/56/568], adopted **resolution 56/209** without vote [agenda item 105].

Role of the United Nations in promoting development in the context of globalization and interdependence

The General Assembly,

Recalling its resolutions 53/169 of 15 December 1998, 54/231 of 22 December 1999 and 55/212 of 20 December 2000 on the role of the United Nations in promoting development in the context of globalization and interdependence,

1. *Takes note* of the report of the Secretary-General;

2. *Takes note also* of the deliberations of the Preparatory Committee for the International Conference on Financing for Development, to be held at Monterrey, Mexico, from 18 to 22 March 2002;

3. *Stresses* the importance of continued substantive consideration of the item on globalization and interdependence;

4. *Requests* the Secretary-General to report to the General Assembly at its fifty-seventh session on globalization and interdependence, bearing in mind, inter alia, the outcome of the International Conference on Financing for Development;

5. *Decides* to include in the provisional agenda of its fifty-seventh session the item entitled "Globalization and interdependence".

Development through partnership

In accordance with resolution 55/193 [YUN 2000, p. 785], the General Assembly held its second high-level dialogue on strengthening international economic cooperation for development through partnership (20-21 September), the first having been held in 1998 [YUN 1998, p. 772]. The dialogue was originally scheduled for 17 and 18 September, as decided by Member States [A/55/955] and agreed to by the Assembly in **decision 55/479** of 31 May. The dialogue was rescheduled and somewhat compressed in format as a result of the 11 September terrorist attacks in the United States.

The theme of the dialogue, "Responding to globalization: facilitating the integration of developing countries into the world economy in the twenty-first century", was considered to be particularly important and timely in the context of the current global economic slowdown. In a report on the dialogue [A/56/482], the Assembly President stated that the two-day discussions, which were held in both plenary meetings and two ministerial round tables/informal panels, could be summarized as follows: globalization was a reality that had to be accepted, but while it could be a formidable multiplier of growth and prosperity, it did not automatically translate into more trade and faster growth for all countries, nor did it protect gains already made; while the international community had done much to promote the integration of developing countries into the world economy, it had to address the legitimate concerns of those that were not yet able to enjoy the benefits of globalization, and give priority to correcting the imbalances in the international economic system that disadvantaged developing countries; in addition to an enabling environment, vulnerable countries needed to be supported through capacity-building in areas such as trade, investment finance and technology, and additional ODA and deeper and wider debt relief were critical for the poorest countries; the benefits of information and communication technologies had to be harnessed and directed towards the long-term, comprehensive development of developing countries to ensure their successful integration into the global economy; globalization was an interactive process that needed to be harnessed and directed, as its benefits were also the results of policy choices; because of their low per capita income and particular vulnerabilities, the least developed, small island developing, landlocked and transit developing countries and African countries should be the focus of attention of the international community; and all countries should be able to engage in a more participatory governance at national, regional and international levels.

On 21 December, the Assembly, by **decision 56/438**, took note of the President's summary of the high-level dialogue.

GENERAL ASSEMBLY ACTION

On 21 December [meeting 90], the General Assembly, on the recommendation of the Second Committee [A/56/560/Add.3], adopted **resolution 56/190** without vote [agenda item 97 *(c)*].

High-level dialogue on strengthening international economic cooperation for development through partnership

The General Assembly,

Recalling its resolutions 48/165 of 21 December 1993, 49/95 of 19 December 1994, 50/122 of 20 December 1995, 51/174 of 16 December 1996, 52/186 of 18 December 1997, 53/181 of 15 December 1998, 54/213 of 22 December 1999 and 55/193 of 20 December 2000,

Reaffirming its resolution 55/2 of 8 September 2000, entitled "United Nations Millennium Declaration",

Recalling the Agenda for Development and the relevant provisions regarding its follow-up and implementation, and the need to give impetus to international economic cooperation for development so as to follow up on the Agenda effectively,

Reaffirming the importance of continuing the dialogue to be conducted in response to the imperative of solidarity, mutual interests and benefits, genuine interdependence, shared responsibility and the partnership in promoting international economic cooperation for development,

Recognizing, in this context, the importance of an enabling environment and sound economic policy at both the national and the international level,

Noting the need to ensure the integrated and coordinated follow-up and implementation by the United Nations system of the outcome of major United Nations conferences and summits,

1. *Reaffirms* the importance of continued constructive dialogue and genuine partnership to promote further international economic cooperation for development;

2. *Requests* the Secretary-General, in close consultation with Governments, all relevant parts of the United Nations system and other relevant stakeholders, to propose the modalities, the nature and the timing of such constructive dialogue and genuine partnership for the promotion of international economic cooperation for development for consideration by the General Assembly at its fifty-seventh session;

3. *Decides* to include in the provisional agenda of its fifty-seventh session, under the item entitled "Sustainable development and international economic cooperation", the sub-item entitled "High-level dialogue on strengthening international economic cooperation for development through partnership", and requests the Secretary-General to submit to it at that session a consolidated report on the implementation of the present resolution.

Private sector partnerships

In accordance with General Assembly resolution 55/215 [YUN 2000, p. 785], the Secretary-General submitted an October report on cooperation between the United Nations and all relevant partners, in particular the private sector [A/56/323]. The comprehensive review, which was based on consultations with Member States, UN entities, business associations and non-governmental organizations (NGOs), observed that, over the preceding 10 years, non-State actors had become engaged to an unprecedented degree in most areas of UN activities, ranging from policy dialogue, standard-setting and normative work to operational activities, advocacy and information work. That engagement offered opportunities for increased effectiveness, but also created some strategic and practical challenges. In particular, cooperation should be viewed as a means of achieving UN goals and enhancing performance, not as an end in itself. The potential private sector contribution to development was multifaceted and needed to be harnessed in a focused and effective manner. Partnerships should focus not only on the mobilization of funds, but also on mobilizing the core competencies, comparative advantages and investment expertise of the private sector.

The report provided examples of the variety of partnerships between the United Nations, the private sector and other non-State actors, particularly a number of cooperative initiatives in support of the goals of the Millennium Declaration, adopted by the General Assembly in 2000 [YUN 2000, p. 49].

The Global Compact, a multi-stakeholder initiative introduced by the Secretary-General in 1999 and officially launched as an operational initiative in 2000 [YUN 2000, p. 989], had emerged as an overall value framework for cooperation between the United Nations and the business community. The Compact, a set of nine universally agreed principles in the areas of environment, labour and human rights, offered a useful point of reference for good corporate citizenship when choosing business partners, stated the report. The Secretariat would establish a working group to consider, among other things, the development of an inter-agency network of private sector focal points, aimed at improving internal learning, information-sharing and outreach capacities for cooperation with non-State actors. Special efforts were needed to ensure that cooperation with the business community and other non-State actors paid particular attention to the needs and priorities of developing countries and countries with economies in transition.

GENERAL ASSEMBLY ACTION

On 11 December [meeting 84], the General Assembly adopted **resolution 56/76** [draft: A/56/L.33 & Add.1] without vote [agenda item 39].

Towards global partnerships

The General Assembly,

Reaffirming the central role of the United Nations, in particular the General Assembly, in the promotion of partnerships in the context of globalization,

Underlining the intergovernmental nature of the United Nations,

Reaffirming its resolve to create an environment, at the national and global levels alike, that is conducive to development and the elimination of poverty,

Recalling the objectives formulated in the United Nations Millennium Declaration, particularly in regard to developing partnerships through the provision of greater opportunities to the private sector, non-governmental organizations and civil society in general so as to enable them to contribute to the realization of the goals and programmes of the Organization, in particular in the pursuit of development and the eradication of poverty,

Stressing that efforts to meet the challenges of globalization could benefit from enhanced cooperation between the United Nations and all relevant partners, in particular the private sector, in order to ensure that globalization becomes a positive force for all,

Encouraging the private sector to accept and implement the principle of good corporate citizenship, that is, bringing sustainable development principles, which are based on the three pillars of economic development, social development and environmental protection, to bear on a conduct and policy that are premised on profit incentives, in conformity with national laws and regulations, and in this context drawing the attention of Member States to multi-stakeholder initiatives, in particular, the Global Compact Initiative of the Secretary-General, the Global Alliance for Vaccines and Immunizations, the multi-stakeholder dialogue process of the Commission on Sustainable Development and the Information and Communication Technologies Task Force,

Recalling the central role and responsibility of Governments in national and international policy-making,

Underlining the fact that cooperation between the United Nations and all relevant partners, in particular the private sector, shall serve the purposes and principles embodied in the Charter of the United Nations and make concrete contributions to the realization of the goals contained in the Millennium Declaration and in the outcomes of major United Nations conferences and summits and their reviews, in particular in the area of development and the eradication of poverty, and shall be undertaken in a manner that maintains the integrity, impartiality and independence of the Organization,

Emphasizing that all relevant partners, in particular the private sector, can contribute in several ways to addressing the obstacles confronted by developing countries in mobilizing the resources needed to finance their sustainable development, and to the realization of the development goals of the United Nations through, inter alia, financial resources, access to technology, management expertise, and support for programmes, including through the reduced pricing of drugs, where appropriate, for the prevention, care and treatment of the human immunodeficiency virus/acquired immunodeficiency syndrome (HIV/AIDS) and other diseases,

Underlining the fact that the resources contributed by the relevant partners, in particular the private sector, should be a complement to, not a substitute for, governmental resources,

Taking into account ideas expressed in the report of the Secretary-General of 27 March 2000, entitled "We the peoples: the role of the United Nations in the twenty-first century", with regard to enhanced cooperation with the private sector,

Recalling its resolution 55/215 of 21 December 2000,

1. *Takes note* of the report of the Secretary-General and its numerous valuable examples of cooperation between the United Nations and all relevant partners, in particular the private sector, which have contributed and should continue to contribute to the realization of the goals and programmes of the Organization, in particular in the pursuit of development and the eradication of poverty;

2. *Stresses* that the principles and approaches that govern such partnerships and arrangements should be built on the firm foundation of United Nations purposes and principles, as set out in the Charter, and invites the United Nations system to continue to adhere to a common approach to partnership which, without imposing undue rigidity in partnership agreements, includes the following principles: common purpose, transparency, bestowing no unfair advantages upon any partner of the United Nations, mutual benefit and mutual respect, accountability, respect for the modalities of the United Nations, striving for balanced representation of relevant partners from developed and developing countries and countries with economies in transition, and not compromising the independence and neutrality of the United Nations system in general and the agencies in particular;

3. *Stresses also* the need for international cooperation to strengthen the participation of enterprises, especially small and medium-sized enterprises, business associations, foundations and non-governmental organizations from developing countries and countries with economies in transition, in particular in partnerships with the United Nations system;

4. *Stresses further* the need for Member States further to discuss partnerships and to consider, in appropriate intergovernmental consultations, ways and means to enhance cooperation between the United Nations and all relevant partners, inter alia, from the developing countries, to give them greater opportunities to contribute to the realization of the goals and programmes of the Organization;

5. *Invites* the Secretary-General to continue to seek the views of relevant partners, in particular the private sector, on how to enhance their cooperation with the United Nations;

6. *Requests* the Secretary-General to submit a report on the implementation of the present resolution, containing proposals of modalities for enhanced cooperation between the United Nations and all relevant partners, in particular the private sector, for consideration by the General Assembly at its fifty-eighth session;

7. *Decides* to include in the agenda of its fifty-eighth session the item entitled "Towards global partnerships".

Business and development

In response to General Assembly resolution 54/204 [YUN 1999, p. 746], the Secretary-General, in October, submitted his fourth biennial report on business and development [A/56/442], in which he reviewed trends in entrepreneurial development, the related issues of property rights, knowledge acquisition and regulatory framework and governance, and the question of socially responsible business behaviour. The report stated that entrepreneurship development had become a priority for many policy makers in both developed and developing countries, in market as well as transition economies. Encouraging entrepreneurship was increasingly perceived as a policy option leading to a higher level of economic development, increased productivity, job creation and promotion of more broad-based participation in productive activities, particularly by the poor and by women. UN efforts to promote entrepreneurship—including those of the International Trade Centre, UNCTAD and the United Nations Industrial Development Organization—focused primarily on problems faced by small and medium-sized enterprises regarding access to markets, finance, business skills and technology. The report noted that the question of business responsibility constituted the core of the Global Compact Initiative, which stressed that pure economic utility and advantage could go hand in hand with business support for human rights, freedom of association and the right to collective bargaining, elimination of compulsory or child labour and discriminatory hiring practices, and environmental protection.

Overall, trends indicated that the structure in which there was one predominant actor (government) and one predominant treasury (public budget) was being replaced with a constellation of actors, public and private, each with its own capacity and treasury, forming ad hoc alliances to solve ad hoc problems. Government organizations, businesses, individuals and formal and informal organizations of civil society could be part of such a constellation.

GENERAL ASSEMBLY ACTION

On 21 December [meeting 90], the General Assembly, on the recommendation of the Second Committee [A/56/559], adopted **resolution 56/185** without vote [agenda item 96 (a)].

Business and development

The General Assembly,

Reaffirming its resolution 54/204 of 22 December 1999,

Welcoming the report of the Secretary-General,

1. *Decides* to include in the provisional agenda of its fifty-seventh session the sub-item entitled "Business and development";

2. *Requests* the Secretary-General, in cooperation with the relevant United Nations organizations, to submit to it at its fifty-seventh session a follow-up report on the continuing implementation of resolution 54/204.

On 24 December, the Assembly decided that the agenda item on sectoral policy questions (dealing with business and development and industrial development cooperation) would remain for consideration at its resumed fifty-sixth (2002) session (**decision 56/464**).

Implementation of the Declaration on International Economic Cooperation and the International Development Strategy

On 21 December [meeting 90], the General Assembly, on the recommendation of the Second Committee [A/56/560/Add.4], adopted **resolution 56/191** without vote [agenda item 97 *(d)*].

Implementation of the Declaration on International Economic Cooperation, in particular the Revitalization of Economic Growth and Development of the Developing Countries, and implementation of the International Development Strategy for the Fourth United Nations Development Decade

The General Assembly,

Reaffirming the importance and continuing validity of the Declaration on International Economic Cooperation, in particular the Revitalization of Economic Growth and Development of the Developing Countries, contained in the annex to its resolution S-18/3 of 1 May 1990, and of the International Development Strategy for the Fourth United Nations Development Decade, contained in the annex to its resolution 45/199 of 21 December 1990,

Recalling its resolutions 45/234 of 21 December 1990, 46/144 of 17 December 1991, 47/152 of 18 December 1992, 48/185 of 21 December 1993, 49/92 of 19 December 1994, 51/173 of 16 December 1996, 53/178 of 15 December 1998, 54/206 of 22 December 1999 and 55/190 of 20 December 2000, and the Agenda for Development,

Recalling also the results of all the major United Nations conferences and summit meetings held since the beginning of the 1990s,

Reaffirming the United Nations Millennium Declaration, in particular the targets and commitments relating to development and poverty eradication,

Recalling the outcomes of the special session of the General Assembly to review and address the problem of human immunodeficiency virus/acquired immunodeficiency syndrome (HIV/AIDS), the Third United Nations Conference on the Least Developed Countries, and the special session of the General Assembly for an overall review and appraisal of the implementation of the Habitat Agenda,

Emphasizing the importance of the other development-oriented meetings to be convened under the auspices of the United Nations in 2002, including the International Conference on Financing for Development, the special session of the General Assembly on children and the World Summit on Sustainable Development,

1. *Expresses regret* that the consultations foreseen in resolution 54/206 could not be held;

2. *Decides* to consider the issue of further development of a new international development strategy during the fifty-seventh session of the General Assembly,

on the basis of the outcomes of the aforementioned meetings and keeping in mind the outcome of the review of the United Nations New Agenda for the Development of Africa in the 1990s;

3. *Requests* the Secretary-General to provide the General Assembly at its fifty-seventh session with an overview of the challenges and constraints as well as progress made towards achieving the major development goals and objectives adopted by the United Nations during the past decade;

4. *Decides* to include in the provisional agenda of its fifty-seventh session, under the item entitled "Sustainable development and international economic cooperation", a sub-item entitled "Implementation of the Declaration on International Economic Cooperation, in particular the Revitalization of Economic Growth and Development of the Developing Countries, and implementation of the International Development Strategy for the Fourth United Nations Development Decade".

Coercive economic measures

In response to General Assembly resolution 54/200 [YUN 1999, p. 748], the Secretary-General submitted an October report on the elimination of economic measures as a means of political and economic coercion [A/56/473], which summarized information on the subject received from 13 Governments.

GENERAL ASSEMBLY ACTION

On 21 December [meeting 90], the General Assembly, on the recommendation of the Second Committee [A/56/558/Add.1], adopted **resolution 56/179** by recorded vote (100-1-46) [agenda item 95 *(a)*].

Unilateral economic measures as a means of political and economic coercion against developing countries

The General Assembly,

Recalling the relevant principles set forth in the Charter of the United Nations,

Reaffirming the Declaration on Principles of International Law concerning Friendly Relations and Cooperation among States in accordance with the Charter of the United Nations, which states, inter alia, that no State may use or encourage the use of unilateral economic, political or any other type of measures to coerce another State in order to obtain from it the subordination of the exercise of its sovereign rights,

Bearing in mind the general principles governing the international trading system and trade policies for development contained in relevant resolutions, rules and provisions of the United Nations and the World Trade Organization,

Recalling its resolutions 44/215 of 22 December 1989, 46/210 of 20 December 1991, 48/168 of 21 December 1993, 50/96 of 20 December 1995, 52/181 of 18 December 1997 and 54/200 of 22 December 1999,

Gravely concerned that the use of unilateral coercive economic measures adversely affects the economy and development efforts of developing countries in particular and has a general negative impact on international economic cooperation and on worldwide efforts to move towards a non-discriminatory and open multilateral trading system,

1. *Takes note* of the report of the Secretary-General;

2. *Urges* the international community to adopt urgent and effective measures to eliminate the use of unilateral coercive economic measures against developing countries that are not authorized by relevant organs of the United Nations or are inconsistent with the principles of international law as set forth in the Charter of the United Nations and that contravene the basic principles of the multilateral trading system;

3. *Requests* the Secretary-General to continue to monitor the imposition of measures of this nature and to study the impact of such measures on the affected countries, including the impact on trade and development;

4. *Also requests* the Secretary-General to submit a report to the General Assembly at its fifty-eighth session on the implementation of the present resolution.

RECORDED VOTE ON RESOLUTION 56/179:

In favour: Algeria, Angola, Antigua and Barbuda, Argentina, Armenia, Azerbaijan, Bahamas, Bahrain, Bangladesh, Barbados, Belarus, Belize, Benin, Bhutan, Bolivia, Botswana, Brazil, Brunei Darussalam, Burkina Faso, Burundi, Cambodia, Cameroon, Cape Verde, China, Colombia, Congo, Costa Rica, Côte d'Ivoire, Cuba, Democratic People's Republic of Korea, Djibouti, Dominica, Dominican Republic, Ecuador, Egypt, Eritrea, Ethiopia, Gabon, Ghana, Grenada, Guatemala, Guyana, Haiti, India, Indonesia, Iran, Jamaica, Jordan, Kazakhstan, Kenya, Kuwait, Lao People's Democratic Republic, Lebanon, Libyan Arab Jamahiriya, Malaysia, Maldives, Mali, Mauritania, Mauritius, Mexico, Mongolia, Morocco, Myanmar, Namibia, Nepal, Nicaragua, Nigeria, Oman, Panama, Papua New Guinea, Paraguay, Peru, Philippines, Qatar, Russian Federation, Saudi Arabia, Senegal, Sierra Leone, Singapore, Solomon Islands, South Africa, Sri Lanka, Sudan, Swaziland, Syrian Arab Republic, Thailand, Togo, Trinidad and Tobago, Tunisia, Turkmenistan, Uganda, United Arab Emirates, United Republic of Tanzania, Uruguay, Vanuatu, Venezuela, Viet Nam, Yemen, Yugoslavia, Zambia.

Against: United States.

Abstaining: Albania, Andorra, Australia, Austria, Belgium, Bulgaria, Canada, Croatia, Cyprus, Czech Republic, Denmark, Estonia, Finland, France, Georgia, Germany, Greece, Hungary, Iceland, Ireland, Israel, Italy, Japan, Latvia, Liechtenstein, Luxembourg, Malta, Marshall Islands, Monaco, Netherlands, New Zealand, Norway, Poland, Portugal, Republic of Korea, Republic of Moldova, Romania, San Marino, Slovakia, Slovenia, Spain, Sweden, The former Yugoslav Republic of Macedonia, Turkey, Ukraine, United Kingdom.

Also on 21 December, the Assembly decided to include in the provisional agenda of its fifty-seventh (2002) session an item on the elimination of unilateral extraterritorial coercive economic measures as a means of political and economic compulsion (last considered in 2000 [YUN 2000, p. 789]) and to continue to consider the item at odd-numbered sessions (**decision 56/455**).

Cuban embargo. On 27 November, the Assembly adopted **resolution 56/9** on the necessity of ending the economic, commercial and financial embargo imposed by the United States against Cuba (see p. 252).

Sustainable development

Commission on Sustainable Development

The Commission on Sustainable Development held the second part of its ninth session in New York from 16 to 27 April [E/2001/29]; an organiza-

tional meeting had been held on 5 May 2000. The session included a multi-stakeholder dialogue on sustainable energy and transport (see p. 933) and a high-level segment on a number of sustainable development issues and preparations for the World Summit on Sustainable Development, to be held in 2002. From 30 April to 2 May, the Commission convened the first organizational session acting as preparatory committee for the Summit (see p. 749).

The Commission adopted decisions on: energy for sustainable development [dec. 9/1] (see p. 932); protection of the atmosphere [dec. 9/2] (see p. 963); transport [dec. 9/3] (see p. 947); information for decision-making and participation [dec. 9/4]; international cooperation for an enabling environment [dec. 9/5] (see p. 748); the draft programme budget for the 2002-2003 biennium for the Division of Sustainable Development of the Department of Economic and Social Affairs [dec. 9/6]; and documents considered by the Commission at its ninth session [dec. 9/7].

By **decision 2001/229** of 19 July, the Economic and Social Council took note of the Commission's report on its ninth session.

International cooperation for an enabling environment

In the context of the call in Agenda 21 [YUN 1992, p. 672], adopted at the 1992 United Nations Conference on Environment and Development (UNCED), for the international community to provide a supportive international climate for achieving environment and development goals, the Secretary-General submitted to the Commission a report on international cooperation for an enabling environment for sustainable development [E/CN.17/2001/5]. The report addressed the impact of globalization on sustainable development and related policy implications, with particular reference to developing countries. Special attention was given to trade and finance, which, supported by technological advances in information and communication, were the areas where globalization manifested itself most profoundly. The report also reviewed approaches and initiatives in international cooperation to facilitate the transition to sustainable development in the context of globalization.

Also before the Commission was the report of the Ad Hoc Intersessional Working Group on Information for Decision-making and Participation and on International Cooperation for an Enabling Environment (New York, 12-16 March) [E/CN.17/2001/17], which contained possible elements for draft decisions by the Commission on the two cross-sectoral themes being considered at the ninth session.

In a 27 April decision [E/2001/29 (dec. 9/5)], the Commission made recommendations for international cooperation and national action, within the framework of Agenda 21, for promoting an enabling environment for sustainable development. Among other things, the Commission called for the urgent fulfilment of all financial commitments of Agenda 21 and for supportive measures to promote access to and transfer of environmentally sound technologies.

Information for decision-making and participation

The Commission on Sustainable Development had before it a report of the Secretary-General on information for decision-making and participation [E/CN.17/2001/4], an issue that cut across all the other issues highlighted in Agenda 21. The report discussed changes in information, particularly technology, since UNCED, identifed issues for discussion and policy recommendations, and reflected the discussions that had taken place in an international expert meeting on information for decision-making and participation (Ottawa, Canada, 25-28 September 2000).

Noting that the revolution in information technology had exploded into the "new knowledge economy", the report observed that there were two main challenges: to create a more level playing field for decision makers in all countries by improving data collection, standardization, access and participation by civil society; and to understand the full potential of new technologies by assembling useful information on sustainable development in more comprehensive integrated frameworks that allowed multiple points of access and responded to the needs of many users. Recommendations for Commission action concerned three key issues: bridging the data gap within and between countries; improving the availability of and access to information; and new information technologies.

In an addendum [E/CN.17/2001/4/Add.1], the Secretary-General reviewed the Commission's work programme on indicators of sustainable development. The Commission also considered a March report of the Secretary-General [E/CN.17/2001/14] on national reporting activities since the Commission's seventh (1999) session and the report of the Ad Hoc Intersessional Working Group on Information for Decision-making and Participation and on International Cooperation for an Enabling Environment [E/CN.17/2001/17] (see p. 747).

In a 27 April decision [E/2001/29 (dec. 9/4)], the Commission called on international organizations to take action to improve the functioning, coherence and coordination of data collection and information on sustainable development, and on countries, particularly developed ones, in cooperation with international organizations, to assist with training and capacity-building on information technology, particularly in developing countries. The need for the Commission to keep under review the full range of indicators of sustainable development was reiterated. The Commission also made recommendations for activities at the national level, including ensuring access to environmental information, public participation in decision-making and access to judicial and administrative proceedings in environmental matters, collecting and providing access to relevant information for decision-making for sustainable development and fostering sustainable development in cooperation with international organizations by providing needed technological infrastructure, particularly to developing countries.

In-depth evaluation

By a March note [E/AC.51/2001/2], the Secretary-General transmitted to the Committee for Progamme and Coordination (CPC) the report of the Office of Internal Oversight Services on the in-depth evaluation of sustainable development. The report proposed that the Department of Economic and Social Affairs (DESA) should promote dialogue between members of the Commission on Sustainable Development and government representatives engaged in other intergovernmental processes. It further recommended that the Secretariat should make proposals to the Commission and other relevant bodies on the format, scope and calendar of reporting on sustainable development issues to intergovernmental bodies so that reporting could more effectively facilitate the preparations of government representatives for the annual or biennial sessions. To reduce the burden placed on countries to report to an increasing number of intergovernmental forums, DESA and members of the Inter-Agency Committee on Sustainable Development should develop procedures to limit requests for national information to that not readily available elsewhere in the UN system. The involvement of UN organizations, in particular those with regional or national offices, in support of implementing national sustainable development strategies needed to be more effectively organized.

At its forty-first session (New York, 11 June–6 July) [A/56/16 & Corr.1], CPC recommended approval of the evaluation's recommendations and emphasized that national monitoring of nationally owned strategies should be encouraged.

Follow-up to UNCED

World Summit on Sustainable Development (2002)

In 2001, the Commission on Sustainable Development acting as the Preparatory Committee for the World Summit on Sustainable Development began preparations for the 10-year review in 2002 of the implementation of Agenda 21—a programme of action for sustainable development worldwide, which was adopted by the United Nations Conference on Environment and Development in 1992 [YUN 1992, p. 672]. The first such review was carried out by the General Assembly at its nineteenth special session in 1997, when it adopted the Programme for the Further Implementation of Agenda 21 [YUN 1997, p. 792].

In accordance with Assembly resolution 55/199 [YUN 2000, p. 793], the Commission, acting as preparatory committee, held its organizational session in New York from 30 April to 2 May [A/56/19] to assess the state of preparations for the World Summit and take action on a number of organizational issues. The Commission had before it reports of the Secretary-General on progress in preparatory activities at the national, regional and international levels [E/CN.17/2001/PC/23] and on suggested arrangements for involving NGOs and other major groups in the Summit and its preparatory process [E/CN.17/2001/PC/22]. It also considered reports of the Secretary-General on issues regarding setting the agenda and determining possible main themes for the Summit, including those on demographic dynamics and sustainability [E/CN.17/2001/PC/2]; information and institutions for decision-making [E/CN.17/2001/PC/3]; the participation of major groups in sustainable development [E/CN.17/2001/PC/4]; combating poverty [E/CN.17/2001/PC/5]; health and sustainable development [E/CN.17/2001/PC/6]; education and public awareness for sustainable development [E/CN.17/2001/PC/7]; changing consumption patterns [E/CN.17/2001/PC/8]; sustainable human settlements development and environmentally sound management of solid wastes [E/CN.17/2001/PC/9]; finance and trade [E/CN.17/2001/PC/10]; transfer of environmentally sound technologies, cooperation and capacity-building and environmentally sound management of biotechnology [E/CN.17/2001/PC/11]; protection of the atmosphere [E/CN.17/2001/PC/12]; agriculture, land and desertification [E/CN.17/2001/PC/13]; sustainable mountain development [E/CN.17/2001/PC/14]; review of progress in forests since UNCED [E/CN.17/2001/PC/15]; oceans and seas [E/CN.17/2001/PC/16]; water as a key resource for sustainable development [E/CN.17/2001/PC/17]; the global status of biodiversity [E/CN.17/2001/PC/18]; management of toxic chemicals and hazardous

and radioactive wastes [E/CN.17/2001/PC/19]; energy and transport [E/CN.17/2001/PC/20]; and sustainable tourism development [E/CN.17/2001/PC/21].

In a 2 May resolution [A/56/19 (res. 2001/PC/1)], the Commission underlined the critical importance of the regional preparations for the World Summit, scheduled to take place from August to November 2001, and invited the Secretary-General, the Secretariat and relevant intergovernmental processes to take specific action in preparation for the Summit. The Commission also recommended to the General Assembly for adoption a draft resoluion containing the draft provisional rules of procedure of the Summit [E/CN.17/2001/PC/24].

In other action, the Commission adopted decisions on specific modalities of future (2002) sessions of the Preparatory Committee [dec. 2001/PC/1] and arrangements for accreditation and participation in the Summit and its preparatory process of NGOs and other major groups [dec. 2001/PC/3].

On 21 December, the Assembly, by **decision 56/441**, took note of the report of the Commission acting as the Preparatory Committee on its organizational session.

Report of Secretary-General. In a September report to the General Assembly on progress in preparations for the World Summit [A/56/379], the Secretary-General stated that a consensus had emerged that the Summit, to take place in Johannesburg, South Africa, from 2 to 11 September 2002, would be a turning point in moving the global society to a sustainable future. The tempo of preparatory activities in recent months had accelerated, with many more events being planned or envisaged by stakeholders at various levels. By August, more than 40 Member States had established national preparatory committees, and national assessment reports had been received from 11 countries, with many more under way. In addition, a number of countries had launched initiatives to help raise awareness, mobilize support and enhance the sense of ownership of the preparatory process, including: 101 ways to promote sustainable development; sustainable development visions for the twenty-first century; children's Agenda 21 posters; and national progression targets.

Regional and subregional preparations focused on stakeholder consultations, intergovernmental preparatory meetings, which would be held from September to November 2001, and eminent persons' round tables, which had been held in all five regions. At the international level, intergovernmental preparations were progressing, mainly within the framework of the United

Nations, while a broad range of international preparatory initiatives had been undertaken by NGOs and other major groups.

Regional meetings. High-level meetings were held in 2001 in each of the regions in preparation for the Summit. The Economic Commission for Europe Regional Ministerial Meeting (Geneva, 24-25 September) adopted a ministerial statement [E/CN.17/2002/PC.2/5/Add.1]; the African Preparatory Conference (Nairobi, Kenya, 17-18 October) adopted the African ministerial statement [E/CN.17/2002/PC.2/5/Add.4]; the Regional Preparatory Conference of Latin America and the Caribbean (Rio de Janeiro, Brazil, 23-24 October) adopted the Rio de Janeiro Platform for Action on the Road to Johannesburg, 2002 [E/CN.17/2002/PC.2/5/Add.2]; the Arab Ministers responsible for development affairs, planning and environment (Cairo, Egypt, 24 October) adopted the Arab Declaration to the World Summit on Sustainable Development [E/CN.17/2002/PC.2/5/Add.3]; and the High-level Regional Meeting for the World Summit on Sustainable Development (Phnom Penh, Cambodia, 28-29 November) adopted the Phnom Penh Regional Platform on Sustainable Development for Asia and the Pacific [E/CN.17/2002/PC.2/8].

GENERAL ASSEMBLY ACTION

On 24 December [meeting 92], the General Assembly, on the recommendation of the Second Committee [A/56/561/Add.1], adopted **resolution 56/226** without vote [agenda item 98 (a)].

World Summit on Sustainable Development

The General Assembly,

Recalling its resolution 55/199 of 20 December 2000 and the decisions adopted by the Commission on Sustainable Development acting as the Preparatory Committee for the World Summit on Sustainable Development at its organizational session,

Encouraging countries and relevant regional and international organizations to support the preparatory processes,

Welcoming national preparations for the Summit, including those at the local level, through the establishment of preparatory committees, with the participation of Governments and other stakeholders, the undertaking of national assessments and the initiation of other preparatory activities, encouraging all countries to intensify that work, and calling upon the United Nations system to support such activities,

Welcoming also the activities of major groups related to the preparations for the Summit, and encouraging them to carry out further preparatory activities,

Welcoming further the valuable contributions from the preparatory activities undertaken at the subregional and the regional level, as well as from other relevant initiatives undertaken at the international level,

Encouraging new initiatives that would contribute to the full implementation of Agenda 21, the Rio Declaration on Environment and Development and other relevant outcomes of the United Nations Conference on Environment and Development by strengthening commitments at all levels, including by reinvigorating, at the highest political level, global commitment and partnerships, especially between Governments of the North and the South, on the one hand, and between Governments and major groups on the other,

Expressing its appreciation for the work undertaken by South Africa and Indonesia as the host Governments, respectively, of the Summit and the fourth session of the Preparatory Committee at the ministerial level,

1. *Takes note* of the report of the Secretary-General on progress in preparatory activities for the World Summit on Sustainable Development;

2. *Approves* the provisional rules of procedure of the World Summit on Sustainable Development, as recommended by the Commission on Sustainable Development acting as the Preparatory Committee for the Summit at its organizational session;

3. *Decides* that the Summit shall be open to all States Members of the United Nations and States members of the specialized agencies, with the participation of observers in accordance with the established practice of the General Assembly and its conferences and with the rules of procedure of the Summit;

4. *Also decides* that the Summit shall be held in Johannesburg, South Africa, from 26 August to 4 September 2002, with the participation of heads of State and Government during the period 2 to 4 September;

5. *Reiterates* that the Summit, including its preparatory process, should ensure a balance between economic development, social development and environmental protection since they are interdependent and mutually reinforcing components of sustainable development;

6. *Invites* countries to be represented at the highest political level at the Summit;

7. *Requests* the Commission on Sustainable Development acting as the Preparatory Committee for the Summit to decide on all remaining issues related to the organization of work of the Summit, including specific details of the series of events to be held in partnership with stakeholders, the short multi-stakeholder event involving the highest level of representation from major groups and Governments, and the round-table meetings to be held at the level of heads of State or Government;

8. *Requests* the Secretary-General to launch a public information campaign to raise global awareness of the Summit, including through reprioritization of the budget of the Department of Public Information of the Secretariat and voluntary contributions;

9. *Invites* donors to continue providing extrabudgetary resources, in particular through voluntary contributions to the Trust Fund, in support of the preparatory activities for the Summit and the Summit itself, and to support the travel and participation of representatives of developing countries, in particular from the least developed countries, and encourages voluntary contributions to support the participation of major groups from developing countries;

10. *Encourages* all countries to complete their national assessment reports, and in that regard calls upon relevant regional and international organizations to

further step up their efforts to assist developing countries in the elaboration of those assessment reports;

11. *Encourages*, at the national level, the active involvement of all Government agencies responsible for economic development, social development and environmental protection, and invites them to provide coordinated inputs and contributions to the preparatory process of the Summit;

12. *Encourages* the active involvement of all relevant regional and international agencies and organizations, and invites them to provide inputs and contributions to the preparatory process of the Summit;

13. *Encourages* effective contributions from and the active participation of all major groups, as identified in Agenda 21, at all stages of the preparatory process, in accordance with the rules and procedures of the Commission on Sustainable Development, as well as its established practices for the participation and engagement of major groups;

14. *Reiterates* the invitation to all intergovernmental processes relevant to the Summit to submit their progress reports to the Commission acting as the Preparatory Committee at its second session, to be held from 28 January to 8 February 2002, and their final results to the Commission acting as the Preparatory Committee at its third session, to be held from 25 March to 5 April 2002, so that they can be fully considered in the preparatory process;

15. *Reiterates* the role of the Commission on Sustainable Development acting as the Preparatory Committee in the global intergovernmental process for the preparations for the Summit, and in that context recalls the mandate and role of its Bureau, as stipulated by the General Assembly in its resolution 55/199 and by the Commission on Sustainable Development acting as the Preparatory Committee in the decisions adopted at its organizational session;

16. *Welcomes* the initiatives undertaken by the Secretary-General to raise international awareness of the Summit;

17. *Requests* the Secretary-General to submit a report on the outcome of the Summit to the General Assembly at its fifty-seventh session, and decides to include in the provisional agenda of its fifty-seventh session the sub-item entitled "Implementation of Agenda 21 and the Programme for the Further Implementation of Agenda 21", taking into account the outcome of the Summit.

Inter-Agency Meeting

An Inter-Agency Meeting on Sustainable Development of the Administrative Committee on Coordination (ACC) (New York, 22-23 March) [ACC/2001/1] was convened in place of the seventeenth meeting of the Inter-Agency Committee on Sustainable Development (IACSD), since 2001 was to be a transition year for ACC, based on a review of its subsidiary machinery (see p. 1365). With a view to strengthening and improving the effectiveness of future inter-agency work in the area of sustainable development, the meeting agreed that IACSD could be transformed from an ACC standing committee into a more flexible

inter-agency group on sustainable development, which would provide for the more direct involvement of organizations that had task manager responsibilities in connection with the implementation of Agenda 21. Meeting once a year, instead of twice, the new group would focus on substantive and policy issues, practical implementation of intergovernmental mandates in the area of sustainable development, and coordination of inter-agency support to the Commission on Sustainable Development. The new flexible approach would allow for a stronger and more direct involvement in the group of those international organizations which were not part of the ACC structure, but whose activities were highly relevant to sustainable development and/or which had been assigned task manager responsibilities (including secretariats of conventions, the World Tourism Organization and regional commissions), and the more substantive involvement of international and regional developmental and financial institutions. The annual meetings would allow a stocktaking of overall progress achieved in sustainable development on the basis of reports of individual task managers/lead organizations, address specific problems and collectively identify future work priorities.

Tourism

By a May note [E/2001/61], the Secretariat transmitted to the Economic and Social Council the text of the Global Code of Ethics for Tourism, which was adopted at the thirteenth session of the General Assembly of the World Tourism Organization (Santiago, Chile, 1 October 1999). In January [E/2001/3], the Secretary-General had proposed that an item on the Code be included in the Council's agenda. A letter and explanatory memorandum from the Secretary-General of the World Tourism Organization were also submitted for the Council's consideration.

ECONOMIC AND SOCIAL COUNCIL ACTION

On 26 July [meeting 43], the Economic and Social Council adopted **resolution 2001/37** [draft: E/2001/L.32] without vote [agenda item 13 *(p)*].

Global Code of Ethics for Tourism

The Economic and Social Council,

Recalling subparagraph *(c)* of its decision 109(LIX) of 23 July 1975, in which the Council decided that the World Tourism Organization might participate, on a continuing basis, in the work of the Council in areas of concern to that organization,

Recalling also article III of the annex to General Assembly resolution 32/156 of 19 December 1977 in which, inter alia, the General Assembly stipulated that the activities of the World Tourism Organization and the activities in respect of or related to tourism of the United Nations and other organizations within the

United Nations system shall be coordinated by the Economic and Social Council through consultations and recommendations,

Having considered the note by the Secretariat bringing to its attention a significant result achieved at the thirteenth session of the General Assembly of the World Tourism Organization, held in Santiago on 1 October 1999, namely, the adoption by consensus of the Global Code of Ethics for Tourism,

Recommends to the General Assembly the adoption of the following draft resolution:

[For text, see General Assembly resolution 56/212 below.]

GENERAL ASSEMBLY ACTION

On 21 December [meeting 90], the General Assembly, on the recommendation of the Second Committee [A/56/571], adopted **resolution 56/212** without vote [agenda item 12].

Global Code of Ethics for Tourism

The General Assembly,

Recalling its resolution 32/156 of 19 December 1977, by which it approved the Agreement on Cooperation and Relationships between the United Nations and the World Tourism Organization,

Reaffirming paragraph 5 of its resolution 36/41 of 19 November 1981, in which it decided that the World Tourism Organization might participate, on a continuing basis, in the work of the General Assembly in areas of concern to that organization,

Recalling the Manila Declaration on World Tourism of 10 October 1980 adopted under the auspices of the World Tourism Organization, the Rio Declaration on Environment and Development and Agenda 21 adopted at the United Nations Conference on Environment and Development on 14 June 1992, and taking note of the Amman Declaration on Peace through Tourism adopted at the Global Summit on Peace through Tourism on 11 November 2000,

Considering that the Commission on Sustainable Development, at its seventh session, held in April 1999, expressed interest in a global code of ethics for tourism and invited the World Tourism Organization to consider the participation of informed major groups in the development, implementation and monitoring of its global code of ethics for tourism,

Recalling its resolution 53/200 of 15 December 1998 on the proclamation of 2002 as the International Year of Ecotourism, in which, inter alia, it reaffirmed Economic and Social Council resolution 1998/40 of 30 July 1998, recognizing the support of the World Tourism Organization for the importance of ecotourism, in particular the designation of the year 2002 as the International Year of Ecotourism, in fostering better understanding among peoples everywhere, in leading to greater awareness of the rich heritage of various civilizations and in bringing about a better appreciation of the inherent values of different cultures, thereby contributing to the strengthening of world peace,

Recognizing the important dimension and role of tourism as a positive instrument towards the alleviation of poverty and the improvement of the quality of life for all people, its potential to make a contribution to economic and social development, especially of the developing countries, and its emergence as a vital force

for the promotion of international understanding, peace and prosperity,

1. *Takes note with interest* of the Global Code of Ethics for Tourism adopted at the thirteenth session of the General Assembly of the World Tourism Organization, which outlines principles to guide tourism development and to serve as a frame of reference for the different stakeholders in the tourism sector, with the objective of minimizing the negative impact of tourism on environment and on cultural heritage while maximizing the benefits of tourism in promoting sustainable development and poverty alleviation as well as understanding among nations;

2. *Emphasizes* the need for the promotion of a responsible and sustainable tourism that could be beneficial to all sectors of society;

3. *Invites* Governments and other stakeholders in the tourism sector to consider introducing, as appropriate, the contents of the Global Code of Ethics for Tourism in relevant laws, regulations and professional practices, and, in this regard, recognizes with appreciation the efforts made and measures already undertaken by some States;

4. *Encourages* the World Tourism Organization to promote effective follow-up to the Global Code of Ethics for Tourism, with the involvement of relevant stakeholders in the tourism sector;

5. *Requests* the Secretary-General to follow up developments related to the implementation of the present resolution based on the reports of the World Tourism Organization and to report thereon to the General Assembly at its fifty-ninth session.

Eradication of poverty

Global campaign

ACC action. The new ACC High-level Committee on Programmes, at its first session (Vienna, 26-27 February) [ACC/2001/6], addressed the role of the UN system in follow-up to the Millennium Summit, convened by the General Assembly in September 2000 [YUN 2000, p. 475]. The High-level Committee recommended that a global campaign on poverty eradication be mounted to mobilize world opinion and engage political leaders in achieving the Millennium Declaration target of halving the proportion of people living in extreme poverty by 2015. It called for broadening the poverty paradigm beyond the numerical target of reducing the number of people living below the level of $1 a day to include social, educational, nutritional, health and cultural dimensions, as well as such qualitative aspects as empowerment. It also recommended that: UN organizations prepare an analysis of their contributions to the Millennium Summit's poverty target; the World Bank and other funding entities collaborate on an annual review of flows of concessional funding for programme elements linked to the global campaign; and a comprehensive review be undertaken of the global funding requirements for reducing poverty by half by 2015. In addition, the UN system's capacity to achieve and monitor progress in poverty eradication should be strengthened through improved data as a common basis for analysis, as well as through closer interactions among officials throughout the system involved in work relevant to poverty eradication.

At its first regular session of 2001 (Nairobi, 2-3 April), ACC endorsed the High-level Committee's proposals [ACC/2001/4].

Note by Secretariat. The Secretariat submitted to the Economic and Social Council a June note on a global campaign for poverty eradication [E/2001/84]. The note outlined approaches and measures being developed within the UN system to lay the groundwork for Council action in relation to the launching of such a campaign, as recommended by the General Assembly in resolution S-24/2 [YUN 2000, p. 1013], adopted at its twenty-fourth special session, which conducted the five-year review of the implementation of the outcome of the 1995 World Summit for Social Development [YUN 1995, p. 1113]. Drawing on the proposals endorsed by ACC in April, the note addressed the importance of improving the effectiveness of UN system activities to help Governments achieve and monitor progress towards the poverty-related goals set out in the outcomes of the twenty-fourth special session and the Millennium Summit. In particular, it was imperative for UN organizations to internalize poverty reduction goals and consolidate their activities in order to enhance the overall coherence of the system's poverty eradication work, including analytical, statistical and programme planning activities. In addition, a major advocacy effort to engage political leaders and mobilize world opinion in achieving the 2015 target embodied in the Millennium Declaration should be a central component of the global campaign. (See also below and p. 1003.)

ECONOMIC AND SOCIAL COUNCIL ACTION.

On 26 July [meeting 43], the Economic and Social Council adopted **resolution 2001/42** [draft: E/2001/L.42] without vote [agenda item 14 (*b*)].

Global campaign for poverty eradication

The Economic and Social Council,

Recalling that the General Assembly invited the Council to consolidate the ongoing initiatives and actions established pursuant to the Copenhagen Declaration on Social Development and the Programme of Action of the World Summit for Social Development, the first United Nations Decade for the Eradication of Poverty (1997-2006) and the recommendations contained in the outcome document of the twenty-fourth special session of the General Assembly, with a view to launching a global campaign to eradicate poverty,

Reaffirming its commitment to promote a coordinated and integrated implementation of and follow-up to the outcomes of the major United Nations conferences and summits,

Having considered the note by the Secretariat on a global campaign for poverty eradication;

1. *Decides* to keep the matter under review in the context of its work on coordinated follow-up to the major United Nations conferences and summits;

2. *Invites* the Secretary-General to report to the Economic and Social Council in 2002 on this matter.

Millennium Declaration road map. In a September report to the General Assembly [A/56/326], the Secretary-General presented a road map towards the implementation of the United Nations Millennium Declaration [YUN 2000, p. 49]. A section of the report on development and poverty eradication: the millennium goals, which focused on sustainable development through poverty eradication, emphasized the importance of halving the number of people currently living on $1 a day or less.

The Assembly took note of the road map in **resolution 56/95** of 14 December (see p. 1279).

UN Decade for Eradication of Poverty

In response to General Assembly resolution 55/210 [YUN 2000, p. 796], the Secretary-General submitted a July report on the first United Nations Decade for the Eradication of Poverty (1997-2006) [A/56/229 & Corr.1]. The report contained a comprehensive review and evaluation of progress towards achieving the goals of the Decade and the Millennium Declaration target of halving by the year 2015 the proportion of the world's people living on less than $1 a day, including resource requirements and possible funding sources. A review of UN system activities in support of national efforts towards achieving those goals was contained in an annex and addendum [A/56/229/Add.1] to the report.

The report found that, despite progress in reducing overall poverty, progress was mixed when examined at the regional and national levels. While it was likely that the 2015 poverty reduction target would be achieved for the world as a whole, many countries, particularly those in sub-Saharan Africa, were not likely to achieve it at the national level. Countries that were not on track to achieve the target and other millennium development goals would need to accelerate economic growth and promote social development, taking into account the multidimensional nature of poverty and the need to achieve pro-poor growth. Despite the best efforts of developing countries to mobilize fully domestic financial resources for poverty eradication, ODA would remain a critically important additional source of development financing for many countries, particularly LDCs, if they were to have a good chance of achieving the 2015 target. The report noted that a global campaign for poverty eradication would provide valuable focus and coordination to efforts at all levels to achieve the Millennium Declaration goal as well as the goal eventually to eradicate poverty within the framework of the Decade.

The report also summarized consultations with 38 Member States and other relevant stakeholders on the proposal to establish a world solidarity fund for poverty eradication. In general, there was broad support for the fund as a mechanism for the international community to contribute, on a voluntary basis, to poverty eradication and promote human resources in the poorest regions of the world, particularly in LDCs.

GENERAL ASSEMBLY ACTION

On 21 December [meeting 90], the General Assembly, on the recommendation of the Second Committee [A/56/566], adopted **resolution 56/207** without vote [agenda item 103].

Implementation of the first United Nations Decade for the Eradication of Poverty (1997-2006), including the proposal to establish a world solidarity fund for poverty eradication

The General Assembly,

Recalling its resolution 47/196 of 22 December 1992, by which it established the International Day for the Eradication of Poverty, as well as its resolution 48/183 of 21 December 1993, by which it proclaimed 1996 the International Year for the Eradication of Poverty,

Recalling also its resolution 50/107 of 20 December 1995 on the observance of the International Year for the Eradication of Poverty and the proclamation of the first United Nations Decade for the Eradication of Poverty (1997-2006), as well as the declarations and programmes of action of the major United Nations conferences and summits, their follow-up and the need for their implementation, as they relate to the eradication of poverty,

Recalling further the United Nations Millennium Declaration, adopted by heads of State and Government on the occasion of the Millennium Summit,

Recalling its resolution 55/210 of 20 December 2000, entitled "Implementation of the first United Nations Decade for the Eradication of Poverty (1997-2006), including the initiative to establish a world solidarity fund for poverty eradication",

Expressing its deep concern that the number of people living in extreme poverty in many countries continues to increase, with women and children constituting the majority and the most affected group, in particular in African countries and the least developed countries,

Recognizing that, while the rate of poverty in some countries has been reduced, some developing countries and disadvantaged groups are being marginalized and others are at risk of being marginalized and effectively excluded from the benefits of globalization, resulting in increased income disparity among and with-

in countries, thereby constraining efforts to eradicate poverty,

Recognizing also that for the poverty eradication strategy to be effective it is imperative for developing countries to be integrated into the world economy and equitably share the benefits of globalization,

Recalling the commitment made by the heads of State and Government at the Millennium Summit to eradicate extreme poverty, in particular the commitment to halve, by 2015, the proportion of the world's people whose income is less than one dollar a day and the proportion of people who suffer from hunger,

Bearing in mind the Copenhagen Declaration on Social Development, the Programme of Action of the World Summit for Social Development and the Political Declaration adopted by the General Assembly at its twenty-fourth special session, entitled "World Summit for Social Development and beyond: achieving social development for all in a globalizing world", held at Geneva from 26 June to 1 July 2000, as well as the objectives of the World Food Summit, held at Rome from 13 to 17 November 1996,

Recognizing that, while it is the primary responsibility of States to attain economic and social development and to achieve the development and poverty eradication goals as set out in the United Nations Millennium Declaration, the international community should support the efforts of the developing countries to eradicate poverty and ensure basic social protection and to promote an enabling international environment,

Expressing concern at the recent economic slowdown, particularly its adverse impact on the economies of developing countries, which could hinder the realization of agreed development goals, in particular the eradication of poverty,

Taking note of the report of the Secretary-General on the first United Nations Decade for the Eradication of Poverty (1997-2006),

1. *Stresses* that the United Nations Decade for the Eradication of Poverty (1997-2006) should contribute to achieving the targets of halving, by 2015, the proportion of the world's people whose income is less than one dollar a day and the proportion of people who suffer from hunger, through decisive national action and strengthened international cooperation;

2. *Reaffirms*, as set out in the United Nations Millennium Declaration, that success in meeting the objectives of development and poverty eradication depends, inter alia, on good governance within each country, and that it also depends on good governance at the international level, on transparency in the financial, monetary and trading systems and on commitment to an open, equitable, rule-based, predictable and non-discriminatory multilateral trading and financial system;

3. *Recognizes* that success in meeting the objective of poverty eradication requires an enabling environment that encourages, inter alia, sustainable development, including economic growth that favours the poor and that upholds human rights, including the right to development, democratic principles and the rule of law, at all levels;

4. *Also recognizes* the responsibility of Governments to adopt policies aimed at preventing and combating corrupt practices at the national and international levels;

5. *Calls upon* all countries to formulate and implement outcome-oriented national strategies and programmes, setting time-bound targets for poverty reduction, including the target of halving, by 2015, the proportion of people living in extreme poverty, which requires the strengthening of national action and international cooperation;

6. *Calls* for strengthened efforts at all levels to implement fully and effectively the United Nations Millennium Declaration, as well as the relevant resolutions and decisions of the United Nations and all agreements and commitments adopted at the major United Nations conferences and summits and their follow-up, as they relate to the eradication of poverty, with a view to achieving tangible results;

7. *Stresses* the importance of tackling the root causes of poverty and the necessity of meeting the basic needs of all, and in this context emphasizes the fundamental role in the eradication of poverty of strong and sustained economic growth that favours the poor, creates substantive expansion in productive opportunities and employment, increases incomes, promotes equitable income distribution and minimizes environmental degradation;

8. *Also stresses* the importance of increasing access to and control over resources, including land, skills, knowledge, capital and social connections, for the poor, in particular women, and of improving access for all to basic social services;

9. *Recognizes* the importance of the adoption of appropriate policy responses to the challenges of globalization at the national level, in particular by pursuing sound and stable domestic policies, including sound macroeconomic and social policies, inter alia, those contributing to increased income of the poor, in order to realize the objective of the eradication of poverty;

10. *Urges* the strengthening of international assistance to developing countries in their efforts to alleviate poverty, inter alia, by creating an enabling environment that would facilitate the integration of developing countries into the world economy, improving their market access, facilitating the flow of financial resources and implementing fully and effectively all initiatives already launched regarding debt relief for developing countries, and emphasizes that the international community should consider further measures that would lead to effective, equitable, development-oriented and durable solutions to the external debt and debt-servicing problems of developing countries so that they can share equally in the benefits of globalization, cope with its negative effects, avoid being marginalized in the process of globalization and achieve full integration into the world economy;

11. *Reaffirms* that, within the context of overall action for the eradication of poverty, special attention should be given to the multidimensional nature of poverty and the national and international conditions and policies that are conducive to its eradication, fostering, inter alia, the social and economic integration of people living in poverty, thus empowering them to participate in decision-making with regard to the policies that affect them, the promotion and protection of all human rights and fundamental freedoms for all, including the right to development, bearing in mind the relationship between all human rights and development,

and an efficient, transparent and accountable public service and administration;

12. *Recognizes* that the eradication of poverty and the achievement and preservation of peace are mutually reinforcing;

13. *Reaffirms* that the causes of poverty should be addressed in an integrated way, taking into account the importance of the need for the empowerment of women and sectoral strategies in such areas as education, development of human resources, health, human settlements, rural development, productive employment, population, environment, freshwater, food security and migration, and the specific needs of disadvantaged and vulnerable groups, and in such a way as to increase opportunities and choices for people living in poverty and to enable them to build and strengthen their assets so as to achieve social and economic development; and in this regard encourages countries to develop their national poverty reduction policies in accordance with their national priorities including, where appropriate, through poverty reduction strategy papers;

14. *Welcomes* the efforts made by the United Nations system to assign priority to the eradication of poverty and to enhance coordination, and in this regard encourages the organizations of the United Nations system, including the Bretton Woods institutions, and other partners in development to continue to support all Member States, members of specialized agencies and United Nations observers in carrying forward their own strategy for the achievement of the objectives of the Decade;

15. *Also welcomes* the holding of the International Conference on Financing for Development at Monterrey, Mexico, from 18 to 22 March 2002, and encourages Governments and stakeholders to take concrete initiatives and actions in support of financing for development;

16. *Further welcomes* the convening of the World Summit on Sustainable Development, to be held at Johannesburg, South Africa, from 26 August to 4 September 2002, as a significant opportunity to renew our commitment to sustainable development, the international development goals, Agenda 21, and the principles contained in the Rio Declaration on Environment and Development;

17. *Notes* the outcome of the Fourth Ministerial Conference of the World Trade Organization, held at Doha from 9 to 13 November 2001;

18. *Recognizes* the importance of the expansion of international trade as an engine of growth and development and, in this context, the need for expeditious and complete integration of developing countries and countries with economies in transition into the international trading system, in full cognizance of the opportunities and challenges of globalization and liberalization and taking into account the circumstances of individual countries, in particular the trade interests and development needs of developing countries;

19. *Also recognizes* the critical need for countries to undertake economic, institutional and regulatory reforms to support wide trade liberalization and to create an enabling environment in which trade can truly serve as an engine for economic growth and development, and in this regard calls upon the international community to continue to support the capacity-building

efforts of developing countries, taking into account their national circumstances;

20. *Reaffirms* that all Governments and the United Nations system should promote an active and visible policy of mainstreaming a gender perspective in all policies and programmes aimed at the eradication of poverty, at both the national and the international level, and encourages the use of gender analysis as a tool for the integration of a gender dimension into planning the implementation of policies, strategies and programmes for the eradication of poverty;

21. *Expresses its appreciation* to the developed countries that have agreed to and have reached the target of 0.7 per cent of their gross national product for overall official development assistance, and calls upon the developed countries that have not yet done so to strengthen their efforts to achieve the agreed target as soon as possible and, where agreed, within that target, to earmark 0.15 to 0.20 per cent of their gross national product for the least developed countries;

22. *Stresses* the important role played by official development assistance in complementing domestic efforts to meet the development needs of developing countries, in particular the least developed countries, and in this regard acknowledges the official development assistance made available to developing countries and the efforts that developing countries have made to eradicate poverty;

23. *Calls* for the full, speedy and effective implementation of the enhanced Heavily Indebted Poor Countries Initiative, and in this regard stresses the need for the donor community to provide the additional resources necessary to fulfil the future financial requirements of the Initiative, welcomes the agreement that financing for heavily indebted poor countries should be reviewed analytically and separately from International Development Association replenishment requirements but immediately after meetings for the thirteenth replenishment of the Association, and calls upon all donors to participate fully in this process;

24. *Calls upon* the heavily indebted poor countries to take, as soon as possible, the policy measures necessary to become eligible for the enhanced Heavily Indebted Poor Countries Initiative and to reach the decision point;

25. *Welcomes* the recognition by the Joint Ministerial Committee of the Boards of Governors of the World Bank and the International Monetary Fund on the Transfer of Real Resources to Developing Countries of the need to take into account worsening global growth prospects and declines in terms of trade, when updating Heavily Indebted Poor Countries Initiative debt sustainability analysis at completion point;

26. *Recognizes* the difficulties faced by heavily indebted middle-income developing countries in meeting their external debt and debt-servicing obligations, and notes the worsening situation in some of them in the context, inter alia, of greater liquidity constraints, which may require debt treatment through various national and international measures designed to assist those countries in making their debt burden sustainable in the long term and in combating poverty effectively;

27. *Calls upon* the developed countries, by means of intensified and effective cooperation with developing countries, to promote capacity-building and facilitate access to and transfer of technologies and corresponding knowledge, in particular to developing countries, on favourable terms, including concessional and preferential terms, as mutually agreed, taking into account the need to protect intellectual property rights, as well as the special needs of developing countries, by identifying and implementing practical steps to ensure the achievement of progress in this regard and to assist developing countries in their efforts to eradicate poverty in an era influenced in large measure by technology;

28. *Stresses* that the goal of halving extreme poverty by 2015 will not be achieved without serious efforts to address the development needs of the least developed countries and to support their efforts in improving the lives of their people, and in this regard welcomes the adoption of the Brussels Declaration and the Programme of Action for the Least Developed Countries for the Decade 2001-2010, at the Third United Nations Conference on the Least Developed Countries, held at Brussels from 14 to 20 May 2001, and calls upon the national Governments of the least developed countries and their development partners to implement fully the commitments undertaken in Brussels;

29. *Emphasizes* the role of microcredit as an important anti-poverty tool that promotes production and self-employment and empowers people living in poverty, especially women, and therefore encourages Governments to adopt policies that support microcredit schemes and the development of microfinance institutions and their capacities, and calls upon the international community, in particular the relevant organs, organizations and bodies of the United Nations system and international and regional financial institutions involved in the eradication of poverty, to support and explore the incorporation of the microcredit approach into their programmes and the further development, as appropriate, of other microfinance instruments;

30. *Welcomes* the New Partnership for Africa's Development launched at Abuja in October 2001, whose objectives are, inter alia, to promote sustained economic growth and development, including human development, so as to eradicate poverty in Africa on the basis of African leadership and enhanced partnership with the international community, and calls upon the developed countries and the United Nations system to support this partnership and complement the efforts undertaken by Africa to overcome the challenges it faces;

31. *Emphasizes* the critical role of both formal and non-formal education, particularly basic education, and training, in particular for girls, in the empowerment of those living in poverty, and in this context welcomes the Dakar Framework for Action adopted at the World Education Forum, as well as the strategy for poverty eradication of the United Nations Educational, Scientific and Cultural Organization, and invites the organs and bodies of the United Nations system, in particular the United Nations Educational, Scientific and Cultural Organization and the United Nations Children's Fund, to continue to promote the inclusion of education in anti-poverty strategies;

32. *Recalls* the commitments of the United Nations conferences and summits to eliminate gender disparity in primary and secondary education by 2005 and to promote universal primary education in all countries

by 2015, and in this regard urges Member States to take immediate measures to remove obstacles to young girls' school attendance and to reduce drop-out rates;

33. *Reaffirms* the role of United Nations funds and programmes, in particular the United Nations Development Programme, in assisting the national efforts of developing countries, inter alia, in the eradication of poverty, and the need for their funding in accordance with relevant United Nations resolutions;

34. *Also reaffirms* the importance of agreeing on a mutual commitment of interested developed and developing country partners to allocate, on average, 20 per cent of official development assistance and 20 per cent of the national budget, respectively, to basic social programmes, and welcomes the efforts made to implement the 20/20 initiative, which emphasizes that promoting access for all to basic social services is essential for sustainable and equitable development and is an integral part of the strategy for the eradication of poverty;

35. *Recognizes* the devastating effect of the human immunodeficiency virus/acquired immunodeficiency syndrome (HIV/AIDS) epidemic on human development, economic growth and poverty reduction efforts in many countries, in particular sub-Saharan African countries, and urges Governments and the international community to give urgent priority to the HIV/AIDS crisis, in particular addressing the special needs of developing countries through strengthened cooperation and assistance as well as through the implementation of commitments undertaken, as agreed in the Declaration of Commitment on HIV/AIDS, adopted by the General Assembly at its twenty-sixth special session in June 2001;

36. *Calls upon* Member States and the international community to support and participate in the global efforts for poverty eradication at the global, regional and country levels in order to ensure that the development and poverty reduction goals, as set out in the United Nations Millennium Declaration, are realized, and also calls upon the international community to support those efforts and to strengthen the resources available to the United Nations in order to enhance its capacity to support and coordinate all relevant initiatives in this regard and play its role of facilitator and advocate;

37. *Encourages* the continuing examination in all relevant intergovernmental forums of ways and means to integrate poverty reduction objectives and strategies into discussions on international financial and development issues;

38. *Welcomes favourably* the proposal to establish a world solidarity fund for poverty eradication and the promotion of human and social development in developing countries, in particular among the poorest segments of their population;

39. *Requests* the Secretary-General, with a view to establishing the fund, to submit to the General Assembly at its fifty-seventh session a report containing his recommendations on mechanisms, modalities, terms of reference, mandates and governance for the operationalization of the fund, bearing in mind the voluntary nature of contributions from Member States, international organizations, the private sector, relevant institutions, foundations and individuals and the need to avoid duplication of existing United Nations funds;

40. *Also requests* the Secretary-General, in the context of the follow-up to the United Nations Millennium Declaration, to submit to the General Assembly at its fifty-seventh session a comprehensive report containing an evaluation of progress made towards achieving the goals of the Decade, including best practices, lessons learned and obstacles, as well as in the achievement of the 2015 targets for poverty reduction, and recommendations for further action to achieve the 2015 targets, including the identification of resource requirements and possible sources of funding;

41. *Decides* to include in the provisional agenda of its fifty-seventh session the item entitled "Implementation of the first United Nations Decade for the Eradication of Poverty (1997-2006)".

Science and technology for development

Commission on Science and Technology for Development

In accordance with Economic and Social Council **decision 2001/209** of 31 January, the Commission on Science and Technology for Development held its fifth session in Geneva from 28 May to 1 June 2001 [E/2001/31]. The session had as its main substantive theme "National capacity-building in biotechnology", with particular attention to agriculture, agro-industry, health and the environment. The Commission also heard country reports on technology and innovation policies presented orally by a number of States, and had before it notes by the Secretariat on activities concerning the coordination of science and technology for development [E/CN.16/2001/5], implementation of and progress made on decisions taken at the Commission's fourth (1999) session [E/CN.16/2001/3] and the budget and intersessional activities [E/CN.16/2001/4]. The Commission recommended three draft resolutions and two draft decisions for adoption by the Economic and Social Council. It brought to the Council's attention a decision [E/2001/31 (dec. 5/1)] by which it decided to include the Chairman's summaries of the discussions at its fifth session in the report of the session.

National capacity-building and biotechnology

The Commission had before it a synthesis report by the Secretary-General [E/CN.16/2001/2], which provided an overview of the outcomes of three panels convened during its intersessional period 1999-2001 in relation to its main substantive theme of national capacity-building in biotechnology. The panels discussed capacity-building in biotechnology (Tehran, Iran, 11-13 April 1999) [E/CN.16/2001/Misc.1], legal and regulatory issues in biotechnology (Geneva, 3-5 July

2000) [E/CN.16/2001/Misc.2] and public awareness and participation in science policy-making in biotechnology (Tunis, Tunisia, 14-16 November 2000) [E/CN.16/2001/Misc.3]. The panels covered issues of human resources development through basic science education and research and development; the transfer, commercialization and diffusion of biotechnology; public awareness and participation in science policy-making; bioethics, biosafety and biodiversity; and legal and regulatory matters. The three panels also proposed a number of recommendations to Governments and the international community in terms of policy options and needed initiatives and strategies for national capacity-building in biotechnology. The Commission also considered a note by the UNCTAD secretariat that reviewed several key issues in biotechnology, especially modern gene technology and its applications in the areas of crop agriculture and medicine [E/CN.16/2001/Misc.7].

ECONOMIC AND SOCIAL COUNCIL ACTION

On 26 July [meeting 43], the Economic and Social Council, on the recommendation of the Commission on Science and Technology for Development [E/2001/31], adopted **resolution 2001/31** without vote [agenda item 13 (*b*)].

Science and technology for development

The Economic and Social Council,

Recognizing the role of the Commission on Science and Technology for Development as a forum for improving the understanding of science and technology issues and for the formulation of recommendations and guidelines on all science and technology matters within the United Nations system,

Reaffirming the need to enhance the capability of United Nations organizations active in science and technology, in particular the United Nations Conference on Trade and Development, to effectively address emerging issues in science and technology,

Recognizing the vital role of new and innovative technologies in raising the productivity and competitiveness of nations and the need, inter alia, for policy guidance and for measures promoting public awareness of science and technology and the transfer and diffusion of such technologies to developing countries,

Taking note with appreciation of the synthesis report of the Secretary-General on the Commission on Science and Technology for Development panels on national capacity-building in biotechnology, the comprehensive note prepared by the secretariat on the implementation of and progress made on decisions taken at the fourth session of the Commission, the note by the secretariat on the budget and intersessional activities of the Commission, the note by the secretariat on activities of the Commission regarding the coordination of science and technology for development and other intersessional activities within the United Nations system, including the outcome of the World Science Conference and other relevant documentation submitted to the Commission for consideration at its fifth session,

Welcoming the establishment by the United Nations Conference on Trade and Development of the Science and Technology for Development Network, which provides information on science and technology activities and programmes within the United Nations system and among intergovernmental and non-governmental organizations and builds awareness of scientific and technological developments that are particularly important for developing countries and countries with economies in transition,

Taking note of the Plan of Action adopted by the United Nations Conference on Trade and Development at its tenth session, held at Bangkok from 12 to 19 February 2000, which noted, inter alia, the widening technology gap between developed and developing countries and stressed the need to promote greater access, transfer and diffusion of technology to developing countries in order to strengthen competitiveness based on the innovative capacities of enterprises in these countries,

Recalling key proposals on science and technology contained in the United Nations Millennium Declaration adopted on 8 September 2000 by the heads of State and Government on the occasion of the Millennium Summit and the declaration adopted at the Summit Conference of the Group of Eight industrialized countries, held in Okinawa, Japan, from 19 to 24 July 2000,

Recalling also the Havana Programme of Action adopted by the Group of 77 and China at the South Summit, held in Havana from 10 to 14 April 2000, which noted with concern the threat of increasing technological marginalization of the South and decided to make science and technology a priority item on the national agenda as well as in the area of South-South cooperation,

Recalling further General Assembly resolution 55/185, which called upon the Secretary-General to strengthen the Commission and its secretariat within the United Nations Conference on Trade and Development by providing it with the necessary resources to enable it to carry out its mandate of assisting the developing countries with their national development efforts in the field of science and technology in an optimal manner,

Activities as follow-up to the earlier work of the Commission on Science and Technology for Development

A. National capacity-building in biotechnology

Recognizing that biotechnology has an outstanding potential to support national efforts towards food security, health, environmental sustainability and increased competitiveness,

Realizing that modern biotechnology may be associated with new risks and unexpected impacts on health and the environment and that it raises a number of socio-economic and ethical concerns with regard to gene manipulation, in particular, human genes, and needs to be used and managed taking into account the precautionary approach contained in principle 15 of the Rio Declaration on Environment and Development,

Realizing also that many developing countries cannot easily access modern biotechnologies and that their transfer, absorption and protection are necessary to ensure the benefits mentioned above,

Bearing in mind that many developing countries cannot adequately protect their traditional knowledge and biological resources and that their protection is also necessary to ensure the benefits mentioned above,

Cognizant that there is a close relationship between the development and transfer of biotechnologies and adequacy of the information and communication technologies infrastructure to facilitate access to information on recent advances,

Taking into account the work of its three panels on biotechnology and the agreed recommendations on the sustainable use of biological resources of the Commission on Trade in Goods and Services and Commodities of the United Nations Conference on Trade and Development,

Aware of the work under the Cartagena Protocol on Biosafety of May 2000, to the Convention on Biological Diversity, and the enabling activities of the United Nations Environment Programme and the Global Environmental Facility,

1. *Decides* to recommend the following actions for consideration by Governments, the international community and the United Nations Conference on Trade and Development in order to assist developing countries, in particular least developed countries, and countries with economies in transition to strengthen their indigenous capacity to produce, promote, monitor, assess, manage and regulate biotechnology:

(a) Governments are encouraged to undertake the following actions in order to establish integrated, consistent policy regimes supporting development in biotechnology:

(i) Coordinate their national policies in education, science and technology, health, environment and agriculture, taking into account biotechnology-driven priorities and needs, also, where appropriate, at the regional level;

(ii) Mobilize and leverage public funding and encourage private sector funding for building scientific capacities and all related infrastructures;

(iii) Create the necessary conditions for the creation and assimilation of scientific and technological know-how;

(iv) Support centres of excellence and networks of key institutions in order to develop and retain national capacity while harnessing the expertise of nationals based overseas;

(v) Ensure that the biotechnology sector is included in the relevant national capacity needs assessments and subsequent strategies and that action plans are developed;

(vi) Ensure that there is a vehicle, such as a focal point or national commission for coordination and enhancement of activities, including national capacity needs assessments and national capacity-building;

(b) The international community is invited to:

(i) Coordinate efforts to assist developing countries and countries with economies in transition to engage in capacity-building, to establish and strengthen the necessary legal and regulatory regimes for biotechnology and to access relevant information and obtain and apply modern biotechnologies suited to their needs;

(ii) Foster information exchange and networking, including through public-private sector partnerships involving government, academia and private enterprise;

(iii) Assist the national authorities of developing countries, including focal points/commissions in formulating frameworks for legal and regulatory regimes for managing and regulating biotechnology, and assist in the implementation of the Cartagena Protocol on Biosafety to the Convention on Biological Diversity;

(iv) Assist the national authorities of developing countries, and institutions within the United Nations system, including the United Nations Conference on Trade and Development, to undertake national capacity needs assessments as well as the above-mentioned tasks;

(c) The United Nations Conference on Trade and Development, within its mandate, as defined in the Plan of Action adopted by the United Nations Conference on Trade and Development at its tenth session, is requested to:

(i) Coordinate and liaise, in its work on biotechnology, with other international organizations working in biotechnology, inter alia, the United Nations regional economic and social commissions;

(ii) Use its newly created electronic network for science and technology to make available information on legal and regulatory frameworks to national authorities, as well as other relevant balanced information on developments in biotechnology to policy makers and diplomats, the public, non-governmental organizations, journalists and the private-business sector;

(iii) Assist the developing countries, in particular least developed countries, to develop strategies and national plans, including through the undertaking of national capacity needs assessments, using extrabudgetary resources;

(iv) Develop special programmes and organize workshops, using extrabudgetary resources, to contribute to ongoing programmes for training scientists, diplomats and journalists in science and technology diplomacy, policy formulation and regulatory matters to assist developing countries, in particular least developed countries, in international negotiations and international norms and standard-setting;

(v) Initiate or contribute to studies on the specific problems faced by developing countries in the areas of technology transfer, capacity-building, regulation and biosafety using extrabudgetary resources;

(vi) Collaborate with the Bureau of the Commission on Science and Technology for Development to ensure the implementation of its recommendations, including mobilization of extrabudgetary funds;

2. *Requests* the Commission on Science and Technology for Development, within its mandate as coordinator of the science and technology activities in the United Nations system, to:

(a) Encourage the national authorities in charge of science and technology, and when appropriate at the regional level, to coordinate their strategies, and to provide substantive support in this regard;

(b) Propose concrete guidelines to facilitate development of, access to and dissemination of information, new technologies and technology-based products on affordable terms, including preferential terms;

(c) Encourage partnerships among interested parties, including through international cooperation;

B. New substantive theme and other activities

Recalling the ministerial declaration adopted by the Economic and Social Council at its substantive session of 2000, in which the Council stressed the central role of information and communication technologies in creating a global knowledge-based economy, in accelerating growth, increasing competitiveness, promoting sustainable development, eradicating poverty and facilitating the effective integration of all countries into the global economy,

Recognizing that information and communication technologies present opportunities and challenges and can lead to a further widening of disparities between and within countries,

Heeding the call of the Council in the above-mentioned ministerial declaration for members of the international community to work cooperatively to bridge the digital divide and to foster "digital opportunity",

Recalling resolution 1/1 of the Commission on Science and Technology for Development,

Also recalling the intersessional programme of work of the Commission for 1997-1999 on information and communication technologies and its publication *Knowledge Societies: Information Technology for Sustainable Development*, as well as its guidelines for national information and communication technology strategies and its conclusions drawn from twenty-nine different coalitions of resources regarding infrastructure and applications of information and communication technologies, remembering its conclusion that, although the cost of using information and communication technologies is still high, the cost of not doing so is likely to be even higher,

Recognizing that the competitiveness of a nation depends on the productivity of its enterprises and that their productivity depends in large measure on investment in new technologies, such as information and communication technologies and access to information available through the Internet,

1. *Decides* to follow up its work on information and communication technologies through its Bureau or, if necessary, through the creation of a subcommittee of the Commission on Science and Technology for Development:

(a) To ensure that its previous findings and recommendations are brought to the attention of the main players in bridging the digital divide, such as the Information and Communication Technologies Task Force, the Digital Opportunity Task Force of the Group of Eight and the task force on information and communication technology of the Group of Fifteen;

(b) To assist in the implementation of the outcome of the review by the Council of the mandates and activities of its subsidiary bodies dealing with information and communication technologies with a view to establishing modalities to provide the United Nations and Governments with comprehensive, practical and action-oriented advice on policies and programmes

and on new developments in the field of information and communication technologies;

(c) To oversee the inclusion of such information in the new Science and Technology for Development Network and strengthen information technology networks at the regional, subregional and interregional levels by linking them with the newly established network;

2. *Calls upon* the Commission and its secretariat to interact closely with the Information and Communication Technologies Task Force in order to promote greater information exchange and coordination of activities in information and communication technologies. Such interaction should include participation of the secretariat in all the meetings of the Task Force and reporting back to the Commission on the outcome of those meetings;

3. *Decides* to choose, as the substantive theme for the intersessional period 2001-2003, the theme "Technology development and capacity-building for competitiveness in a digital society". It is expected that the work of the Commission during the above-mentioned period will be carried out in a multidisciplinary manner, with a synergistic view to scientific and technological, economic and commercial, as well as ethical, social and educational aspects;

C. Coordination of science and technology for development in the United Nations system

Requests the secretariat of the Commission on Science and Technology for Development to continue its efforts to use the newly established Science and Technology for Development Network as a gateway to disseminate information on activities on science and technology for development and to update information on scientific and technological developments that are particularly important for developing countries.

In other action, the Council, by **decision 2001/308** of 26 July, took note of the Commission's report on its fifth session and approved the provisional agenda and documentation for the sixth (2003) session. On the same date, by **decision 2001/309**, the Council extended the mandate of the Gender Advisory Board (an expert group established in 1995 [YUN 1995, p. 850] to facilitate the Commission's discussions on the gender implications of science and technology for developing countries) for a further four years. The Council endorsed the nomination of Brazil and Tunisia for membership on the Board, thus filling the two vacancies on the Board with Commission members in order to ensure continued linkages between the two bodies. It also decided that the Commission should assess, at its sixth session, the desirability of continuing the work of the Board and the potential for obtaining external resources to do so.

Coordination mechanisms

In accordance with General Assembly resolution 55/185 [YUN 2000, p. 801], the Secretary-General submitted to the Assembly and the Economic and Social Council a report on strengthening the coordinating role of the Commission in support of efforts by developing countries to obtain, effectively utilize and benefit from science and technology [A/56/96-E/2001/87]. The Secretary-General presented a number of proposals designed to strengthen the Commission's coordinating role and improve the interaction and coordination on science and technology activities in the UN system. Recommendations for action by the Commission and UN organizations included: establishment of a new trust fund to ensure the provision of adequate resources; creation of an inter-agency network for science and technology; assisting in the formulation of national science and technology policies, strategies, assessments and activities; undertaking joint science and technology studies; coordination of technical cooperation in science and technology; and greater Commission involvement in the follow-up to major UN conferences and increased collaboration with other functional commissions of the Council.

By **decision 2001/310** of 26 July, the Economic and Social Council took note of the report.

Also on 26 July, the Council, by **decision 2001/307**, deferred to its resumed session in 2001 consideration of a draft resolution recommended by the Commission [E/2001/31] containing proposals for strengthening the Commission's work. By the draft, the Council would have recommended that the Commission: meet annually, establish a working group to study ways to improve the Commission's role in the UN policy-making process on science and technology issues, and study the feasibility of establishing an international mechanism for supporting research and development in developing countries, especially in the fields of health, education and agriculture. By **decision 2001/323** of 20 December, the Council again deferred consideration of the draft to its resumed organizational session for 2002.

Trust Fund

On 26 July [meeting 43], the Economic and Social Council, on the recommendation of the Commission on Science and Technology for Development [E/2001/31], adopted **resolution 2001/32** without vote [agenda item 13 (b)].

Special Trust Fund for Activities in the Area of Science and Technology for Development

The Economic and Social Council,

Noting the growing importance of the work on science and technology for development to be implemented within the Commission on Science and Technology for Development,

Recalling General Assembly resolution 55/185 of 20 December 2000, in which the Assembly recognized the need for adequate resources, including the provision of new and additional resources from all sources, to be devoted to fostering science and technology for development,

Taking into account the current situation with resources, in particular extrabudgetary resources, available to implement the mandate received by the secretariat of the United Nations Conference on Trade and Development from the Commission on Science and Technology for Development through the Economic and Social Council, as well as from the Council and the General Assembly,

1. *Recommends* that a special trust fund for activities in the area of science and technology for development be established within the United Nations Conference on Trade and Development with a view to assisting in implementing various mandates received or to be received by the Conference in the area of science and technology for development;

2. *Also recommends* that the Trust Fund for Special Activities on Science and Technology for Development, established by the Secretary-General on 4 April 1985 to disseminate science and technology information, be closed, and resources currently available be transferred to the newly created trust fund referred to in paragraph 1 above;

3. *Invites* contributions to the newly established trust fund.

GENERAL ASSEMBLY ACTION

On 21 December [meeting 90], the General Assembly, on the recommendation of the Second Committee [A/56/558/Add.3], adopted **resolution 56/182** without vote [agenda item 95 (c)].

Science and technology for development

The General Assembly,

Recognizing the role of the Commission on Science and Technology for Development in coordinating the activities of the United Nations system in the area of science and technology for development,

Cognizant of the role of the United Nations Conference on Trade and Development as the secretariat responsible for the substantive servicing of the Commission,

Bearing in mind the cross-cutting nature of science and technology within the United Nations system and the need, inter alia, for effective policy guidance and better coordination,

Recognizing the importance of establishing and strengthening partnership and networking among the public and private sectors and academic institutions of all countries to build, transfer and strengthen the technological capabilities and skills needed, in particular for developing countries,

Stressing that the pace of globalization is influenced in large measure by the development of science and technology and that developing countries and countries with economies in transition need to become well equipped, inter alia, through international assistance, with the knowledge of science and technology and the practical skills and institutional structures associated with technology management, which are among the essential tools for enabling them to benefit from the opportunities offered by globalization and avoid the risk of marginalization in the process of globalization,

Recognizing the need to address the obstacles faced by developing countries in accessing technologies, while taking into account the need to protect intellectual property rights and the special needs of developing countries,

Recognizing also that information and communication technologies are among the critical determinants for creating a global knowledge-based economy, accelerating growth, increasing competitiveness, promoting sustainable development, eradicating poverty and facilitating the effective integration of all countries into the global economy,

Recognizing further the need for dissemination of research knowledge, technologies and expertise in the field of biotechnology, in particular in the areas of agriculture, pharmaceuticals and health care, that could benefit mankind,

Welcoming the establishment of the Information and Communication Technologies Task Force, which will provide overall leadership in the United Nations role in helping to formulate strategies for the development of information and communication technologies, and under whose initiative the United Nations will lend a truly global dimension to efforts to bridge the global digital divide, foster digital opportunity and thus firmly put information and communication technologies in the service of development for all, while bearing in mind the power of information and communication technologies for advancing the internationally agreed development goals of the United Nations Millennium Declaration,

Taking note of the report of the Secretary-General on strengthening the coordinating role of the Commission in support of efforts by developing countries to benefit from science and technology,

1. *Invites* the Economic and Social Council to consider, no later than at its substantive session of 2002, ways and means to strengthen the Commission on Science and Technology for Development, inter alia, through increasing the frequency of its meetings, including their annualization, and through the implementation of the recommendations set out in the report of the Secretary-General, while taking its mandate and budgetary constraints into consideration, and in that regard takes note of the recommendation of the Commission to the Council that the Commission should meet annually;

2. *Also invites* the Economic and Social Council to consider favourably the request of the Commission to establish a working group, to meet during the regular sessions of the Commission, for the purpose of evaluating the work of the Commission, with a view to strengthening the role of the Commission in the United Nations system in the area of science and technology for development and increasing its effectiveness;

3. *Stresses* the importance of facilitating access to and transfer of knowledge and technology on concessional, preferential and favourable terms to the developing countries, as mutually agreed, taking into account the need to protect intellectual property rights and the special needs of developing countries, with the objective of enhancing their technological capacities, capabilities, productivity and competitiveness in the world market;

4. *Also stresses* the need for all Governments to ensure the necessary conditions, including the creation of transparent legal and regulatory frameworks, to facilitate the acquisition and development of technology, to enhance innovation capacity, to improve the absorptive capacity of local enterprises and to build up supply capabilities;

5. *Further stresses* the importance of identifying and tackling barriers to and unjustifiable restrictions on the transfer of technologies, in particular to developing countries, inter alia, with a view to addressing such constraints while creating specific incentives for the transfer of technologies, including new and innovative ones;

6. *Encourages* the United Nations system to take advantage of the coordinating role and expertise of the Commission in the area of science and technology for development, where possible, in the follow-up to and preparation for major international conferences and summits;

7. *Calls upon* the Secretary-General to continue to ensure that the Commission and its secretariat within the United Nations Conference on Trade and Development are provided with the necessary resources to enable it to better carry out its mandate;

8. *Takes note* of the proposal of the Commission for a study regarding the feasibility of establishing an international mechanism for supporting and enhancing research and development within the developing countries and in areas critical to the developing countries, especially in the fields of health, education and agriculture;

9. *Calls upon* the United Nations system and the international community to strengthen South-South cooperation initiatives, as well as subregional and regional cooperation, in the field of science and technology;

10. *Requests* the Secretary-General to submit to the General Assembly, at its fifty-eighth session, a report on the impact of new biotechnologies, with particular attention to sustainable development, including food security, health and economic productivity, with the inclusion of proposals on the aspects of the transfer of such technologies, in particular to developing countries and countries with economies in transition, while taking into account the need to protect intellectual property rights and the special needs of developing countries, as well as on addressing constraints on the adequate utilization of such technologies.

Information and communication technologies

ICT Task Force. In response to the ministerial declaration of the 2000 high-level segment of the substantive session of the Economic and Social Council [YUN 2000, p. 799], in which the Council called for the creation of an information and communication technologies (ICT) task force, the Secretary-General submitted a February report [E/2001/7] in which he described the work of the Group of High-level Advisers on ICT that he had established in 2000, which was composed of representatives of Governments, the private sector, foundations, NGOs and the academic community and chaired by José María Figueres-Olsen, former President of Costa Rica and the Special Representative of the Secretary-General on ICT.

The major conclusion to be drawn from the consultations of the Group was that the initiative to establish an ICT Task Force was considered very timely and enjoyed broad support, including from the private sector. The report summarized a number of elements that the Group had identified as being key to the role that the Task Force should play in harnessing ICT for development. It also outlined the overall objectives and presented a general strategic framework for the Task Force.

With regard to the Task Force's composition, the Secretary-General stated that he would appoint the members following consultations with regional groups. He proposed a membership of 37, comprising 18 representatives of Member States, 8 representatives of the private sector, 4 representatives of the non-profit sector, including academia and NGOs, 6 representatives of UN organizations and the President of the Economic and Social Council (ex officio).

By **decision 2001/210** of 13 March, the Council requested the Secretary-General to undertake the necessary steps to establish the Information and Communication Technologies Task Force and to submit a report on the implementation of its decision to the Council's 2001 substantive session.

At its first meeting (New York, 19-20 November), the ICT Task Force adopted the draft Plan of Action as a framework for guidance for its work. It also set up six working groups on ICT policy and governance; national and regional e-strategies; human resource development and capacity-building; resource mobilization; low-cost connectivity and access; and business enterprise and entrepreneurship. In other action, it approved the setting up of, initially, four regional networks (in Africa, Latin America, Asia and for the Arab countries). Members agreed that the Task Force was not a funding agency but that it could help develop a "matchmaking" function. To that end, it could make proposals available on a web-based platform for consideration by potential partners.

Economic and Social Council consideration. At its coordination segment (2-4 July) [A/56/3/Rev.1], the Council considered the theme "The role of the United Nations in promoting development, particularly with respect to access to and transfer of knowledge and technology, especially information and communication technologies, inter alia, through partnerships with relevant stakeholders, including the private sector". The deliberations further advanced the work started by the Council's ministerial declaration of 2000

and served as an input to the consultations of the General Assembly on enhancing UN cooperation with all relevant partners, in particular the private sector (see p. 743).

In a May report on the theme of the coordination segment [E/2001/59], the Secretary-General explored the issue in an integrated manner, with a view to strengthening the development role of the UN system, the effectiveness of its development activities and its support for national development strategies and programmes by promoting access to and transfer of knowledge and technology, especially ICT, through building partnerships, in particular with the private sector.

Also before the Council was the Secretary-General's progress report [E/2001/91] on the implementation of the Council's 2000 ministerial declaration, which also responded to the Council's March 2001 request for a report on the establishment of the ICT Task Force (see above).

The Council also considered a 1 June letter from Italy [A/56/86-E/2001/79] transmitting the findings and recommendations of the Third Global Forum: Fostering Democracy and Development through E-Government (Naples, 15-17 March) and a 20 July letter from China [A/56/211-E/2001/103] transmitting the findings and recommendations of the International Symposium on Network Economy and Economic Governance (Beijing, 19-20 April), the International Symposium on Government and E-Commerce Development (Ningbo, 23-24 April) and the second High-level Forum on City Informatization in the Asia-Pacific Region (Shanghai, 24-26 May).

In the agreed conclusions of the coordination segment [A/56/3/Rev.1 (agreed conclusions 2001/1)], the Council stated that, while knowledge and technological development were among the critical determinants of economic growth and sustainable development, the majority of the world population still lived in poverty and many had not reaped the full benefits of the ICT revolution. The fact that the potential of ICT and other technologies was not being adequately harnessed threatened to further marginalize the economies and peoples of the majority of developing countries. The Council said that ways and means to provide and improve effective access to and transfer of knowledge and technology to developing countries had to be developed. In that context, it welcomed the forthcoming World Summit on the Information Society (see below) and the establishment of the ICT Task Force (see p. 762) as a major step towards strengthening the UN system's role in bridging the digital divide.

The Council called for strengthening of the UN system's crucial catalytic role in promoting technology transfer and access to knowledge to developing countries and countries with economies in transition, especially through partnerships with the private sector. To that end, the Council recommended that the UN system undertake activities to support national efforts for technological development, to establish ICT infrastructure and to put ICT in the service of development; improve coordination, complementarity and mutual links among knowledge networks of individual organizations of the UN system, especially through the ICT Task Force; ensure that approaches and principles governing partnerships were built on the foundation of UN development goals; assist in the establishment of legal and institutional frameworks to facilitate the acquisition, adaptation and utilization of ICT; strengthen programmes for education, institutional capacity-building and human resources development for ICT; and assist in the building of local, national and regional networks of partnerships, as well as partnerships among chambers of commerce and industry organizations. The private sector should be encouraged towards accepting the principle of good corporate citizenship and the UN system should design special programmes for LDCs and Africa and provide assistance to small and medium-sized enterprises and NGOs in developing countries. In addition, the Council called for the development of mechanisms for monitoring, measuring and evaluating the effectiveness of knowledge and technology transfer partnerships in terms of their performance, especially in relation to achieving socioeconomic goals.

ITU action. The International Telecommunication Union (ITU) Council, at its 2001 session, endorsed the convening of the World Summit on the Information Society in two phases: in Geneva from 10 to 12 December 2003 and in Tunis in 2005. The plan for the Summit resulted from consultations among UN agencies in response to a 1998 resolution of the ITU Plenipotentiary Conference.

At its second regular session (New York, 19-20 October) [ACC/2001/5], ACC was briefed by the ITU Secretary-General on the preparations for the World Summit.

GENERAL ASSEMBLY ACTION

On 21 December [meeting 90], the General Assembly, on the recommendation of the Second Committee [A/56/558/Add.3], adopted **resolution 56/183** without vote [agenda item 95 (c)].

World Summit on the Information Society

The General Assembly,

Recognizing the urgent need to harness the potential of knowledge and technology for promoting the goals of the United Nations Millennium Declaration and to find effective and innovative ways to put this potential at the service of development for all,

Recognizing also the pivotal role of the United Nations system in promoting development, in particular with respect to access to and transfer of technology, especially information and communication technologies and services, inter alia, through partnerships with all relevant stakeholders,

Convinced of the need, at the highest political level, to marshal the global consensus and commitment required to promote the urgently needed access of all countries to information, knowledge and communication technologies for development so as to reap the full benefits of the information and communication technologies revolution, and to address the whole range of relevant issues related to the information society, through the development of a common vision and understanding of the information society and the adoption of a declaration and plan of action for implementation by Governments, international institutions and all sectors of civil society,

Recalling the contributions to international consensus in this field achieved by the Millennium Declaration and the agreements reached at other international conferences and summits in recent years,

Taking note of the action plan presented by the Secretary-General of the International Telecommunication Union to the Administrative Committee on Coordination for the holding of the World Summit on the Information Society and the creation, by the Administrative Committee on Coordination, of a high-level Summit organizing committee, chaired by the Secretary-General of the International Telecommunication Union and consisting of the heads of United Nations bodies and other international organizations interested in participating in the process leading to the Summit,

Considering that the Summit is to be convened under the patronage of the Secretary-General of the United Nations, with the International Telecommunication Union taking the lead role in its preparation, in cooperation with interested United Nations bodies and other international organizations as well as the host countries,

Recalling the ministerial declaration concerning information and communication technologies, adopted by the Economic and Social Council at the high-level segment of its substantive session of 2000, and the subsequent work done in this regard, including the creation of the Information and Communication Technologies Task Force, as well as the welcoming of the forthcoming Summit by the Council in its agreed conclusions 2001/1,

Recognizing the need to harness synergies and to create cooperation among the various information and communication technologies initiatives, at the regional and global levels, currently being undertaken or planned to promote and foster the potential of information and communication technologies for development by other international organizations and civil society,

1. _Welcomes_ the resolution adopted by the Council of the International Telecommunication Union at its 2001 session, in which the Council endorsed the proposal of the Secretary-General of the International Tele-

communication Union to hold the World Summit on the Information Society at the highest possible level in two phases, the first in Geneva from 10 to 12 December 2003 and the second in Tunis in 2005, pursuant to resolution 73 adopted by the Plenipotentiary Conference of the International Telecommunication Union at its 1998 session, held in Minneapolis, United States of America;

2. *Recommends* that the preparations for the Summit take place through an open-ended intergovernmental preparatory committee, which would define the agenda of the Summit, finalize both the draft declaration and the draft plan of action, and decide on the modalities of the participation of other stakeholders in the Summit;

3. *Invites* the International Telecommunication Union to assume the leading managerial role in the executive secretariat of the Summit and its preparatory process;

4. *Invites* Governments to participate actively in the preparatory process of the Summit and to be represented in the Summit at the highest possible level;

5. *Encourages* effective contributions from and the active participation of all relevant United Nations bodies, in particular the Information and Communication Technologies Task Force, and encourages other intergovernmental organizations, including international and regional institutions, non-governmental organizations, civil society and the private sector to contribute to, and actively participate in, the intergovernmental preparatory process of the Summit and the Summit itself;

6. *Invites* the international community to make voluntary contributions to the special trust fund established by the International Telecommunication Union to support the preparations for and the holding of the Summit, as well as to facilitate the effective participation of representatives of developing countries, in particular the least developed countries, in the regional meetings to be held in the second half of 2002, in the preparatory meetings to be held in the first half of 2002 and in 2003, and in the Summit itself;

7. *Invites* the Secretary-General of the United Nations to inform all heads of State and Government of the adoption of the present resolution;

8. *Invites* the Secretary-General of the International Telecommunication Union to submit to the General Assembly, at its fifty-seventh and fifty-eighth sessions, through the Economic and Social Council, for information, a report on the preparations for the Summit.

Economic and social trends

Economic surveys and trends

The *World Economic and Social Survey 2001* [Sales No. E.01.II.C.1], prepared in mid-2001 by the Department of Economic and Social Affairs (DESA), stated that, with recovery from the 1997-1998 international financial crises still incomplete, the world economy was experiencing another set-

back in the form of a significant decline in the growth of global output and trade. While the previous global economic slowdown was set off by financial turmoil in some developing countries and economies in transition, the current one had started with a retrenchment in economic activity in the developed economies, particularly the United States, during the second half of 2000. The downturn had radiated to a large number of countries, both developing and developed, in particular those that relied heavily on the export of high-technology products. Overall, the growth of gross world product (GWP) declined from over 4 per cent in 2000 to about 2.5 per cent in 2001 and the expansion of international trade was expected to decelerate to 5.5 per cent in 2001 from about 12 per cent in 2000. While no major acceleration in inflation was forecast for 2001, global labour markets—which, in many developing countries and economies in transition, were only beginning to recover from the 1997-1998 setback—had weakened as a result of the economic slowdown.

In the developed economies, growth in gross domestic product (GDP) was expected to decelerate to 1.9 per cent in 2001, compared to 3.6 per cent in 2000. Although the slowdown in the United States was the most pronounced in the developed economies, a general weakening became more prominent in many other countries of the group in early 2001. In the United States, growth for 2001 was expected to be only 1.8 per cent, a steep decline from 5 per cent in 2000.

The Japanese economy was also having a dampening effect on the outlook for the developed economies. It grew 1.7 per cent in 2000, but indicators pointed to a slowdown in a broad range of activities and GDP was expected to grow by less than 1 per cent in 2001.

Although remaining initially resilient compared with Japan and the United States, the developed countries of Europe also showed signs of weakening as 2001 progressed. After registering 3.4 per cent in 2000, growth in the euro zone was expected to moderate to 2.7 per cent in 2001, while growth rates in other European economies, including Denmark, Sweden and Switzerland, were also moderating. The impacts of the external slowdown on the United Kingdom and of the appreciation of its currency vis-à-vis the euro were not significant in early 2001, but a broader-based deceleration in growth over the course of the year was unavoidable. There was also a slowdown in Australia and Canada and, to a lesser extent, in New Zealand in early 2001. Declining investment spending in the former two economies led the slowdown.

The outlook for the economies in transition pointed to growth slowing from a remarkable 6.1 per cent in 2000 to about 3.6 per cent in 2001. The deceleration was most marked in the Commonwealth of Independent States (CIS), where growth rates of 7.9 per cent in 2000—the best collective economic performance since transition—fell to 3.7 per cent in 2001. For other transition economies, weakening growth was expected to make the challenges of economic restructuring and addressing macroeconomic imbalances even more difficult to implement.

The outlook for many developing economies also deteriorated in 2001, following a period of dramatic improvement in per capita GDP growth rates in 2000. The slowdown in developed economies was being transmitted to developing countries through several channels, such as reduced exports, weakening commodity prices, stagnant capital inflows and tighter credit conditions in international and local capital markets. For the developing countries as a whole, GDP growth was expected to slow from 5.7 per cent in 2000 to 4.1 per cent in 2001. In spite of the adverse external environment, aggregate GDP growth in Africa was expected to accelerate to 4.25 per cent in 2001 from just over 3 per cent in 2000. However, that growth rate would not be sufficient to reduce poverty by a significant margin in the short term.

In Eastern and Southern Asia, the rapid recovery of many economies in 1999 and most of 2000 was halted abruptly by the sudden slowdown of the United States economy. Combined GDP growth rates for the region (excluding China) were expected to drop from 6.9 per cent in 2000 to 4.1 per cent in 2001. Industrial production in the economies of East Asia, particularly ICT-related production, registered an absolute decline or no growth.

The outlook for China and India was more positive. China's GDP growth was expected to be resilient, though moderating from 8 per cent in 2000 to 7.3 per cent in 2001. India was expected to maintain a 6 per cent growth rate, in spite of serious fiscal imbalances. Elsewhere in the region, including the economies of Bangladesh, Nepal, Pakistan and Sri Lanka, growth in 2001 was expected to moderate by 1 to 2 percentage points.

After recovery in 2000, economic growth in Latin America and the Caribbean was expected to slow from 3.8 per cent in 2000 to 3.1 per cent in 2001. In a number of economies—including Mexico and most countries of Central America and the Caribbean—growth was expected to decelerate sharply because of close trade linkages with the United States. Others, such as Brazil, that had improved their economic fundamentals were less affected; a few, including Ecuador and Vene-

zuela, could even expect their recovery to accelerate. The focus of regional uncertainty remained concentrated on Argentina, where market confidence was low and the economy was hindered by unsustainable public debt and weak domestic private-sector demand.

In Western Asia, GDP was expected to increase by 2.6 per cent, down from 5.7 per cent in 2000, due to decreasing oil revenues. In addition, the escalating conflict between Israel and the Palestinian Authority was causing losses for both the economies directly involved and neighbouring countries.

The *Trade and Development Report, 2001* [Sales No. E.01.II.D.10], published by UNCTAD, examined the principal factors behind the sharp downturn in the world economy and near-term economic prospects. The *Report* noted that expectations remained quite high that a short downturn in the United States could be corrected by appropriate monetary and fiscal action. However, there were doubts that traditional macroeconomic policies would carry the day, given the high level of private indebtedness. In view of its pivotal role in bolstering global demand in recent years, the prospects for the United States economy were a matter of worldwide concern.

According to a report on the world economic situation and prospects [Sales No. E.02.II.C.2], prepared jointly by DESA and UNCTAD, a pervasive slowdown in the world economy during 2001, aggravated by the terrorist attacks against the United States in September, resulted in the lowest growth of GWP in a decade. During the year, GWP grew little more than 1 per cent and the volume of world trade stagnated. The weakness became more widespread as the year progressed, with three quarters of the world's economies registering lower economic growth than in the previous year. Meanwhile, more than a dozen economies, accounting for more than two thirds of the world output and including the world's three largest economies, were falling into recession. The decade-long economic expansion in North America came to an end with declines in GDP in both Canada and the United States. Most Western European economies had joined the global contraction by the end of the year. The deepening slowdown in external demand compounded many domestic structural problems for the Japanese economy, which was not expected to recover soon. The economies in transition, especially the CIS countries, weathered the global slowdown relatively well in 2001, achieving their second best rate of overall growth since transition started. Nonetheless, as export demand faltered and commodity prices dropped, growth decelerated and was expected to slide further.

Growth in the developing countries fell to 2.3 per cent in 2001 from 5.8 per cent in 2000, abruptly halting their recovery from the crises of 1997-1998. In countries accounting for two fifths of the population of the developing world, output per capita increased by less than 3 per cent, compounding the challenge of reducing the number of people living in poverty. In several developing countries, output registered an absolute decline and output per capita fell in West Asia, East Asia and Latin America and the Caribbean when averaged for the regions as a whole. Africa was less adversely affected, with average growth changing little from the previous year. The largest developing countries—China and to a lesser extent India—were among those best able to sustain their growth in the face of the slowdown.

Human Development Report 2001

The *Human Development Report 2001*, prepared by the United Nations Development Programme, addressed the question of how to make new technologies work for human development. It looked specifically at how new technologies affected developing countries and poor people and suggested ways in which technology could be used to empower people, allowing them to harness technology to expand the choices in their daily lives. The *Report* also suggested policies to ensure that the potential benefits of technology were rooted in a pro-poor development strategy. The *Report* pointed out that while many of the high-tech marvels that dazzled the rich North were inappropriate for the poor South, it was also true that research and development addressing specific problems facing poor people—from combating disease to developing distance education—had proved how technology could be not just a reward of successful development but a critical tool for achieving it. The challenge, therefore, was to help identify global and national policies and institutions that could best accelerate the benefits of technological advances while carefully safeguarding against the new risks that inevitably accompanied them.

In addition to providing a critical analysis of a different theme each year, the *Report* assessed the state of human development across the globe. In 2001, it ranked 162 countries in its human development index—12 fewer than in 2000 due to a lack of reliable data—by combining indicators of life expectancy, educational attainment and adjusted per capita income, among other factors. Of the 162 countries listed, 48 were in the high human development category, 78 in the medium category and 36 in the low category.

In 2001, the *Report* introduced a new technology achievement index, which aimed to measure how well a country was creating and diffusing technology and building a human skill base by combining a variety of indicators, including the number of patents granted, technology exports, telephone and electricity use, and levels of schooling, among others. Of the 72 countries covered by the new index, 18 were characterized as leaders, 19 as potential leaders, 26 as dynamic adopters and 9 as marginalized with regard to technological progress.

Development policy and public administration

Committee for Development Policy

The Committee for Development Policy, at its third session (New York, 2-6 April) [E/2001/33], debated the broad theme of improving economic governance at the national, regional and international levels, focusing special attention on the issue of governance responsibilities in a globalizing world. Noting that globalization had redrawn the boundaries of economic activity, making it more difficult to separate national and multilateral interests, the Committee called for bold initiatives in a number of key areas of governance, including the enhanced participation of developing countries in multilateral governance; greater transparency and accountability at all levels of governance; the formulation of "core principles" with regard to governance responsibilities; a greater involvement of people in national and local development; and the development of open and innovative partnerships among various actors and at different levels, such as between donor and recipient Governments and institutions, between the public and the private sectors, and among Governments, social partners and civil society. The Committee recommended better coordination to ensure the maximum efficiency and effectiveness of external assistance, both financial and technical. Developing countries needed to ensure ownership over their development programmes and processes and efficient use of the resources deployed. There was also a need to effectively mobilize national and subnational capabilities and capacities, such as those of the informal sector, whose knowledge and resources should be increasingly incorporated into the formal economy. The Committee further stressed the need to secure adequate resources, especially ODA, and to reduce high debt burdens.

The Committee also examined issues related to its work in the area of LDCs, including methodologies used for addition to or graduation from the LDC list (see p. 769), and the role of the UN system in supporting sustainable development in African countries (see p. 847). With regard to its programme of work, the Committee proposed that the main theme of its next session be "Effectiveness of external assistance", with a special focus on Africa.

On 25 July, the Economic and Social Council deferred to its resumed session of 2001 consideration of the Committee's report on its third session (**decision 2001/291**). In October, the Council, in **resolution 2001/43**, welcomed the Committee's proposals regarding its future work programme (see p. 774).

Public administration

In 2001, the Economic and Social Council renamed the Group of Experts on the United Nations Programme in Public Administration and Finance the Committee of Experts on Public Administration. The Committee did not meet in 2001; its next meeting was scheduled for 2002.

Report of Secretary-General. In July, the Secretary-General, in response to Economic and Social Council decision 1998/220 [YUN 1998, p. 792], submitted to the Council and the General Assembly a five-year assessment of progress made in the implementation of Assembly resolution 50/225 [YUN 1996, p. 750] on public administration and development [A/56/127-E/2001/101 & Add.1]. The report took stock of current trends and challenges affecting public administration, reviewed public administration responses to those challenges and analysed the lessons learned. The analysis was supplemented by a summary of national responses to a questionnaire addressed to government officials responsible for public administration.

Based on the recommendations of the Group of Experts at its fifteenth (2000) meeting [YUN 2000, p. 805], the Secretary-General also presented an agenda for capacity-reinforcement and the role of the United Nations, including: strengthening advocacy, particularly through restructuring and revitalizing the Group of Experts; building common understanding with regard to core issues of public administration; enhanced information-sharing and exchange of experiences; building strategic capacities and essential skills; reinforcing core public service values; providing assistance in institution-building; and improving coordination of development assistance. The report concluded that administrative and

management reform was a continuous and multi-faceted process. It placed special emphasis on the need to assist developing countries and countries with economies in transition in reinforcing their capacity to govern. The capacity to manage continuous reform and change in an orderly fashion should become a key component of capacity-building efforts, stated the report.

ECONOMIC AND SOCIAL COUNCIL ACTION

By **decision 2001/313** of 26 July, the Economic and Social Council deferred consideration of public administration and development to its resumed 2001 session.

On 20 December [meeting 46], the Council adopted **resolution 2001/45** [draft: E/2001/L.46/Rev.2] without vote [agenda item 13 (k)].

Restructuring and revitalization of the Group of Experts on the United Nations Programme in Public Administration and Finance

The Economic and Social Council,

Recalling General Assembly resolutions 50/225 of 19 April 1996 and 53/201 of 15 December 1998 on public administration and development,

Recognizing that efficient, effective and transparent public administration, at both the national and international levels, has a pivotal role to play in the implementation of the key objectives of the United Nations Millennium Declaration, and in that context stressing the need to strengthen national public-sector administrative and managerial capacity-building, in particular in developing countries and countries with economies in transition,

Recalling General Assembly resolutions 50/227 of 24 May 1996 and 52/12 B of 19 December 1997 on the restructuring and revitalization of the United Nations in the economic, social and related fields,

Recalling also its resolutions 1998/46 of 31 July 1998 and 1999/51 of 29 July 1999 on further measures for the restructuring and revitalization of the United Nations in the economic, social and related fields,

Reaffirming its decision 2000/231 of 27 July 2000, by which it endorsed the recommendations contained in the report of the Secretary-General on the work of the Group of Experts on the United Nations Programme in Public Administration and Finance at its fifteenth meeting,

1. *Takes note* of the report of the Secretary-General on the five-year assessment of the progress made in the implementation of resolution 50/225 on public administration and development;

2. *Adopts* the text contained in the annex to the present resolution;

3. *Decides* to consider, at its organizational session for 2002, the nominations for the membership of the Committee of Experts on Public Administration;

4. *Also decides* to bring the present resolution to the attention of the General Assembly at its fifty-sixth session.

ANNEX
**Group of Experts on the United Nations Programme
in Public Administration and Finance**
1. The Group of Experts on the United Nations Programme in Public Administration and Finance shall be renamed the Committee of Experts on Public Administration and shall continue to be a subsidiary body of the Economic and Social Council, without change in its mandate.
2. The Committee shall comprise twenty-four experts, who will serve in their personal capacity. The experts shall be nominated by the Secretary-General, in consultation with member States, and approved by the Economic and Social Council. The membership will be drawn from the interrelated fields of public economics, public administration and public finance, and will reflect an adequate geographical and gender balance. The term of office of members shall be four years.
3. The Committee shall meet biennially for a period not exceeding ten working days.
4. The Economic and Social Council should provide guidance on an appropriate work programme for the Committee. The Committee shall submit its report directly to the Council at its substantive session. The report should include the proposals of the Committee on its work programme, for examination and approval by the Council.
5. In disseminating information on the work of the Committee, the United Nations Online Network in Public Administration and Finance should be fully utilized.
6. In undertaking its responsibilities, the Committee should, in addition to holding its meetings, explore the scope for effective preparations for its deliberations. The Secretariat should provide assistance in that regard.

GENERAL ASSEMBLY ACTION

On 21 December [meeting 90], the General Assembly, on the recommendation of the Second Committee [A/56/571], adopted **resolution 56/213** without vote [agenda item 12].

Public administration and development

The General Assembly,

Recalling its resolution 50/225 of 19 April 1996, adopted at the resumed fiftieth session on the question of public administration and development,

Recognizing that efficient, effective and transparent public administration, at both the national and international levels, has a pivotal role to play in the implementation of the key objectives of the United Nations Millennium Declaration,

1. *Welcomes* the establishment of the United Nations Public Administration Online Network as a powerful tool made available to Member States for the exchange of information and experience in public administration;

2. *Recommends* that the Network be expanded to strengthen the capacity of national ministries and institutions of public administration, to access information, experience and practice in public administration, and to receive online training;

3. *Requests* the Secretary-General to continue to assist Member States, in particular developing countries and countries with economies in transition, upon

their request, in their process of reform, by fostering information-sharing, as appropriate, and the exchange of experience; assisting in building essential capacity and essential skills; providing assistance in institution-building; and improving the coordination of development assistance in this field;

4. *Also requests* the Secretary-General to study the possibility of periodically bringing together high-level policy makers responsible for public administration reform, under the auspices of the United Nations, to discuss issues of common interest and share valuable experience and practice, and to report to the General Assembly at its fifty-seventh session on the results of that study;

5. *Further requests* the Secretary-General to keep under constant review the developments in this field in Member States and to highlight changes and trends as well as successes in this area, with particular emphasis on the role of public administration in the implementation of the United Nations Millennium Declaration, and to summarize his findings in a report to be submitted to the General Assembly at its fifty-seventh session, through the Economic and Social Council.

Also on 21 December, the Assembly took note of the five-year assessment of progress in implementing resolution 50/225 (**decision 56/447**).

Developing countries

Least developed countries

The special problems of the officially designated LDCs were considered in several United Nations forums during 2001 and particularly by the Third UN Conference on LDCs (see below). The Conference culminated in the adoption of the Brussels Declaration and the Programme of Action for the LDCs for the decade 2001-2010. The first such conference had taken place in 1981 [YUN 1981, p. 406] and the second in 1990 [YUN 1990, p. 369].

In December, the General Assembly established the Office of the High Representative for the Least Developed Countries, Landlocked Developing Countries and Small Island Developing States.

The number of officially designated LDCs remained at 49 in 2001.

The full list of LDCs comprised: Afghanistan, Angola, Bangladesh, Benin, Bhutan, Burkina Faso, Burundi, Cambodia, Cape Verde, Central African Republic, Chad, Comoros, Democratic Republic of the Congo, Djibouti, Equatorial Guinea, Eritrea, Ethiopia, Gambia, Guinea, Guinea-Bissau, Haiti, Kiribati, Lao People's Democratic Republic, Lesotho, Liberia, Madagascar, Malawi, Maldives, Mali, Mauritania, Mozambique, Myanmar, Nepal, Niger, Rwanda, Samoa, Sao Tome and Principe, Senegal, Sierra Leone, Solomon Islands, Somalia, Sudan, Togo, Tuvalu, Uganda, United Republic of Tanzania, Vanuatu, Yemen, Zambia.

Third UN Conference on LDCs

As decided by the General Assembly in resolution 52/187 [YUN 1997, p. 839], the Third United Nations Conference on the Least Developed Countries (LDC-III) took place in Brussels, Belgium, from 14 to 20 May [A/CONF.191/13]. With the participation of 159 countries, the high-level Conference reviewed the socio-economic progress in LDCs during the 1990s and progress in international support measures, particularly in the areas of ODA, debt relief, investment and trade. On 20 May, the Conference unanimously adopted the Brussels Declaration, by which the participating Governments reaffirmed their commitment to the development of the 49 LDCs, and the Programme of Action for the Least Developed Countries for the Decade 2001-2010, a set of national and international commitments on policies and measures for accelerating the development process in those countries.

During the Conference general debate, 96 Member States, 25 UN bodies and specialized agencies, 6 intergovernmental organizations and 22 NGOs made statements. A special event on "The challenge of eradicating poverty" was convened on 14 May [A/CONF.191/L.2]. In addition, a series of interactive events were held on: governance, peace and social stability [A/CONF.191/L.1]; enhancing productive capacities: the agricultural sector and food security [A/CONF.191/L.4]; intellectual property and development: an instrument for wealth creation [A/CONF.191/L.6]; enhancing productive capacities: the role of health [A/CONF.191/L.8]; education [A/CONF.191/L.10]; international trade, commodities and services/ tourism [A/CONF.191/L.12]; energy [A/CONF.191/ L.13]; human resources development and employment [A/CONF.191/L.17]; enhancing productive capacities: the role of investment and enterprise development [A/CONF.191/L.21]; infrastructure development [A/CONF.191/L.22]; transport [A/CONF.191/ L.24]; and financing growth and development [A/CONF.191/L.27].

UNCTAD, as the UN focal point for LDCs, was responsible for Conference preparations, follow-up and monitoring, and the UNCTAD Secretary-General served as Secretary-General of the Conference.

In an August report [A/56/297 & Corr.1], the UN Secretary-General provided the General Assembly with an assessment of the Conference outcomes and an account of the preparatory process.

On 21 December, the Assembly, by **decision 56/444**, took note of the report.

Brussels Declaration. In the Brussels Declaration [A/CONF.191/12], Governments expressed their commitment to the eradication of poverty and the improvement of the quality of lives of people in LDCs by improving their abilities to build a better future for themselves and develop their countries. They recognized that the primary responsibility for development in LDCs rested with those countries, but their efforts needed support from Governments and international organizations through genuine partnerships, including with the civil society and the private sector. Particular concern was expressed with regard to the HIV/AIDS pandemic and other communicable diseases, the welfare of people, trade, financing of development, declining ODA flows and external debt. The Governments reaffirmed their commitment to the development of the 49 LDCs and to the improvement of the lives of the more than 600 million people living in those countries.

Programme of Action. The Programme of Action for the Least Developed Countries for the Decade 2001-2010 [A/CONF.191/11] had as its aim the significant improvement of the human conditions of the more than 600 million people in 49 LDCs during the decade. Against the backdrop of lack of progress in socio-economic development in LDCs and in the implementation of the Programme of Action for the 1990s [YUN 1990, p. 370], it provided a framework for a strong global partnership to accelerate sustained economic growth and sustainable development in LDCs, to end marginalization by eradicating poverty, inequality and deprivation in those countries, and to enable them to integrate beneficially into the global economy. Its overarching goal was to make substantial progress towards halving the proportion of people living in extreme poverty and suffering from hunger by 2015 and promoting the sustainable development of LDCs. The Programme of Action included a framework for partnership based on seven mutual commitments by LDCs and their development partners that focused on the following areas: fostering a people-centred policy framework; good governance at national and international levels; building human and institutional capacities; building productive capacities to make globalization work for LDCs; enhancing the role of trade in development; reducing vulnerability and protecting the environment; and mobilizing financial resources. With the support of their development partners, LDCs would strive to attain a GDP growth rate of at least 7 per cent per annum and to increase the ratio of investment to GDP to 25 per cent per annum.

Regarding Conference follow-up, the Programme of Action acknowledged the critical need for an effective mechanism to support implementation, follow-up, monitoring and review at the national, regional and global levels. At the national level, each LDC, with the support of its development partners, would translate actions contained in the Programme of Action into specific measures within their national development framework and poverty eradication strategy. Regarding intergovernmental follow-up at the global level, the General Assembly was invited to continue monitoring implementation of and to consider conducting a comprehensive review of the Programme of Action. The Assembly was also invited, towards the end of the decade, to consider holding a fourth UN Conference on LDCs.

Conference preparations

As decided in General Assembly resolution 53/182 [YUN 1998, p. 794], preparations for LDC-III were undertaken in three sessions of the Intergovernmental Preparatory Committee, all of which were held in New York. The first session took place in 2000 [YUN 2000, p. 808]. At its second session (5-9 February) [A/CONF.191/3], the Committee conducted the first formal reading of the draft Programme of Action and considered other matters relating to preparations for the Conference. At the conclusion of its third and final session (2-6 April) [A/CONF.191/5], the Committee completed its second reading of the draft Programme of Action and transmitted it to the Conference for finalization.

The preparatory process also included a high-level panel for the review of progress in the implementation of the Programme of Action for the LDCs for the 1990s [A/CONF.191/IPC/16], three expert-level regional preparatory meetings, several inter-agency consultations and a number of issue-oriented pre-Conference events. At the country level, preparations focused on the formulation of national action plans, submitted by 46 (out of 49) LDCs, containing commitments to a wide range of policy actions and support of poverty eradication.

GENERAL ASSEMBLY ACTION

On 12 July [meeting 107], the General Assembly adopted **resolution 55/279** [draft: A/55/L.88 & Add.1] without vote [agenda item 102].

Programme of Action for the Least Developed Countries for the Decade 2001-2010

The General Assembly,

Recalling its resolution 52/187 of 18 December 1997, in which it decided to convene the Third United Nations Conference on the Least Developed Countries at a high level in 2001, as well as its resolutions 53/182 of

15 December 1998, 54/235 of 23 December 1999 and 55/214 of 20 December 2000,

1. *Endorses* the Brussels Declaration and the Programme of Action for the Least Developed Countries for the Decade 2001-2010, adopted by the Third United Nations Conference on the Least Developed Countries, held in Brussels from 14 to 20 May 2001;

2. *Decides* to include in the provisional agenda of its fifty-sixth session an item entitled "Implementation of the Programme of Action for the Least Developed Countries for the Decade 2001-2010".

Conference follow-up

Trade and Development Board. The UNCTAD Trade and Development Board, at its forty-eighth session (Geneva, 1-12 October) [A/56/15], had before it a report on progress in the implementation of the elements of the Brussels Declaration and the Programme of Action that fell within the purview of UNCTAD [TD/B/48/16]. The report stated that UNCTAD was developing a "road map" as a general guideline to enable different stakeholders to identify practical ways to implement the various commitments contained in the Programme of Action with properly sequenced priorities and coordinated actions at the national, regional and global levels.

The Board also considered an August report by the UNCTAD secretariat [TD/B/48/14] that reviewed the availability of data and indicators needed to monitor implementation of the Programme of Action. The data available to monitor progress towards the goals were woefully inadequate in terms of the coverage of LDCs, their quality and their timeliness, the report stated. The data problem was particularly acute in relation to the goal of halving the proportion of people living in extreme poverty by 2015. Furthermore, when data were available, it was apparent that the majority of LDCs were off-track in terms of the development goals contained in the Programme of Action.

The Trade and Development Board resolved to consider changing UNCTAD's intergovernmental machinery to increase the focus of its work on LDCs as an important part of implementing the Programme of Action. It recommended that UN agencies and other international organizations be made aware of the need for improvements in the international data available to monitor progress towards implementation of the Conference outcomes, especially in relation to the overarching goal of poverty eradication [A/56/15 (dec. 467(XLVIII))].

ECONOMIC AND SOCIAL COUNCIL ACTION

The Economic and Social Council, by **decision 2001/300** of 26 July, decided to consider creating an annual agenda item on the implementation of the Programme of Action for the LDCs at its resumed (2001) session.

On 24 October, the Council decided to establish, under the regular agenda item entitled "Integrated and coordinated implementation of and follow-up to the major United Nations conferences and summits", a regular sub-item entitled "Review and coordination of the implementation of the Programme of Action for the Least Developed Countries for the Decade 2001-2010". It further decided to consider, at a substantive session before 2005, devoting a high-level segment to the review and coordination of the implementation of the Programme of Action and to consider later in the decade further options for such review and coordination (**decision 2001/320**).

Report of Secretary-General. As requested in the Programme of Action, the Secretary-General submitted to the General Assembly a November report [A/56/645 & Add.1 & Add.1/Corr.1,2] containing his recommendations for a follow-up mechanism for coordinating, monitoring and reviewing implementation of the Programme of Action. The report stated that arrangements for system-wide follow-up to the 1990 Programme of Action for LDCs had not been as effective as envisaged, particularly with regard to monitoring implementation at the national level and throughout the UN system. Follow-up at the global level, which was entrusted to UNCTAD, could not be fully accomplished, mainly because the scope of the Programme of Action was beyond the mandate of any single organization. Taking into account the wider scope of the new Programme of Action, the effectiveness of existing arrangements had to be improved, including through clearer and more rational allocations of responsibility for monitoring and follow-up.

The Secretary-General recommended the establishment of an Office of the High Representative for the Least Developed Countries, Landlocked Developing Countries and Small Island Developing States, to be located at UN Headquarters in New York. The High Representative would be at the Under-Secretary-General level and would report directly to the Secretary-General. The Office would be responsible only for coordination, advocacy and reporting. Analytical and technical cooperation functions would continue to be carried out by other UN organizations, including UNCTAD. The new Office would not replace the UNCTAD Office of the Special Coordinator for the Least Developed, Landlocked and Island Developing Countries, as had been suggested in the Programme of Action, but would involve the transfer of several posts from that Office. Member States were urged to continue contributing to the existing UNCTAD Trust Fund for LDCs, which, the Secretary-General stated, should continue to be an important vehicle for promoting technical cooperation activities and capacity-building.

The key functions of the Office of the High Representative would be: to assist the Secretary-General in ensuring the full mobilization and coordination of all parts of the UN system in the follow-up and monitoring of the Programme of Action at the country, regional and global levels; to provide support to the Economic and Social Council and the General Assembly in assessing progress and in conducting the annual review of the implementation of the Programme of Action; to support implementation of the Global Framework for Transit Transport Cooperation between Landlocked and Transit Developing Countries and the Donor Community [YUN 1995, p. 876] and the Programme of Action for the Sustainable Development of Small Island Developing States (SIDS) [YUN 1994, p. 783]; to support group consultations of and undertake advocacy work on behalf of LDCs, landlocked developing countries and SIDS; and to help mobilize resources for implementation of the Programme of Action for the LDCs and other programmes and initiatives for landlocked developing countries and SIDS. Resource requirements for creating the new Office were presented in the addendum to the report. The programme budget implications of establishing the Office of the High Representative, as contained in a statement by the Secretary-General to the Fifth (Administrative and Budgetary) Committee [A/C.5/56/29], were reviewed by the Advisory Committee on Administrative and Budgetary Questions (ACABQ) in December [A/56/716]. ACABQ stated that net appropriations of up to $1,220,700 would be required in 2002-2003 for the new Office.

Trade issues. The Fourth Ministerial Conference of the World Trade Organization (WTO) (Doha, Qatar, 9-13 November) [A/C.2/56/7] adopted a Ministerial Declaration, which reaffirmed the commitments undertaken at LDC-III and agreed that WTO should take into account, in designing its work programme for LDCs, the trade-related elements of the Brussels Declaration and Programme of Action. WTO Ministers endorsed the Integrated Framework for Trade-related Technical Assistance to LDCs (IF) as a viable model for LDCs' trade development and urged development partners to increase significantly contributions to the IF Trust Fund as well as other trust funds in favour of LDCs.

LDC Ministerial Meeting. By a 20 November letter [A/C.2/56/5], Bangladesh transmitted to the Secretary-General the declaration and decision adopted by the Eleventh Annual Ministerial

Meeting of the LDCs (New York, 15 November). The LDC Ministers, recognizing the importance of strengthened coordination and greater participation of LDCs in the implementation of the LDC-III Programme of Action, decided to establish a coordination mechanism to be called the Coordination Bureau of the LDCs. The new Bureau would begin work on 1 January 2002.

GENERAL ASSEMBLY ACTION

On 24 December [meeting 92], the General Assembly, on the recommendation of the Second Committee [A/56/569], adopted **resolution 56/227** without vote [agenda item 106 (*b*)].

Third United Nations Conference on the Least Developed Countries

The General Assembly,

Recalling its resolution 55/279 of 12 July 2001, in which it endorsed the Brussels Declaration and the Programme of Action for the Least Developed Countries for the Decade 2001-2010,

Emphasizing the importance of a highly visible, efficient and effective follow-up and monitoring arrangement for the implementation of the Programme of Action for the Least Developed Countries for the Decade 2001-2010, as well as of the Programme of Action for the Sustainable Development of Small Island Developing States, the Global Framework for Transit Transport Cooperation between Landlocked and Transit Developing Countries and the Donor Community, and relevant paragraphs of the United Nations Millennium Declaration for those countries,

Taking note with appreciation of the report of the Secretary-General on the follow-up mechanism for coordinating, monitoring and reviewing the implementation of the Programme of Action for the Least Developed Countries for the Decade 2001-2010,

1. *Decides* to establish the Office of the High Representative for the Least Developed Countries, Landlocked Developing Countries and Small Island Developing States, having the functions recommended by the Secretary-General in his report;

2. *Requests* the Secretary-General to take immediate measures to make the Office of the High Representative operational as soon as possible;

3. *Calls upon* the Secretary-General to enhance the operational capacity of the United Nations Conference on Trade and Development as well as that of other organizations and bodies of the United Nations system in their activities aimed at supporting recipient countries, especially developing countries, and in particular the least developed countries, landlocked developing countries and small island developing States;

4. *Reiterates its invitation* to the organizations of the United Nations system and other multilateral organizations to mainstream the implementation of the Brussels Declaration and the Programme of Action for the Least Developed Countries for the Decade 2001-2010 within their programmes of work as well as in their intergovernmental processes;

5. *Requests* the Secretary-General of the United Nations Conference on Trade and Development to review

the title and functions of its current Office of the Special Coordinator;

6. *Invites* Member States to extend all necessary support and cooperation to the Office of the High Representative;

7. *Underlines* the importance of optimal coordination between the Office of the High Representative and the various organizations of the United Nations system and other multilateral organizations;

8. *Invites* the organs, organizations and bodies of the United Nations system, and other relevant multilateral organizations, to provide full support to and cooperation with the Office of the High Representative;

9. *Decides* that the provisions of the present resolution shall be implemented within the approved level of the budget for the biennium 2002-2003, and requests the Secretary-General to seek voluntary contributions for the Office of the High Representative;

10. *Requests* the Secretary-General to submit to the General Assembly at its fifty-seventh session a report on the implementation of the present resolution.

LDC list

Committee for Development Policy. At its third session (New York, 2-6 April) [E/2001/33], the Committee for Development Policy, the body responsible for adding countries to or graduating them from the LDC list, in response to Economic and Social Council resolution 2000/34 [YUN 2000, p. 807], re-examined its 2000 recommendation that Maldives be graduated from the list [ibid.]. Following its review, the Committee confirmed that, on the basis of current criteria, Maldives remained eligible for graduation. However, it recommended that the transition period for Maldives be extended until the next triennial review of the list in 2003 before a decision was taken by the General Assembly on the country's graduation. The extension would make it possible for the Committee to obtain adequate information from development partners and multilateral organizations about the potential impact of post-graduation transition, including an assessment of the implications of graduation for Maldives, as requested by the Council.

Also in resolution 2000/34, the Council had endorsed the Committee's recommendation that Senegal be added to the LDC list.

GENERAL ASSEMBLY ACTION

On 12 April [meeting 98], the General Assembly adopted **resolution 55/253** [draft: A/55/L.80, orally revised] without vote [agenda item 12].

Report of the Committee for Development Policy

The General Assembly,

Recalling its resolutions 46/206 of 20 December 1991 and 52/210 of 18 December 1997,

Recalling also Economic and Social Council resolutions 1998/39 of 30 July 1998 on the status of the least developed countries and 1999/67 of 16 December 1999

on the report of the Committee for Development Policy,

Recognizing that the decision to include any country in the list of the least developed countries should be made with its due consent,

Having considered the recommendations of the Economic and Social Council contained in its resolution 2000/34 of 28 July 2000,

Endorses the recommendation of the Economic and Social Council that Senegal be added to the list of the least developed countries.

Report of Secretary-General. In response to Economic and Social Council resolution 2000/34 [YUN 2000, p. 807], the Secretary-General submitted a report on ensuring a smooth transition of countries graduating from LDC status [E/2001/94 & Corr.1]. The report outlined differences in interpretations of the period of transition from LDC status as well as the benefits, including multilateral trade, finance for development and technical cooperation, associated with LDC status. It also reviewed the case of Botswana, the only country to have graduated from the LDC list.

The report recommended that the three-year pre-graduation transition period be maintained, but also stressed the importance of the post-graduation transition period as crucial to the positive development prospects of the country. In addition, the benefits of LDC status, which varied among donors and were generally related to trade preferences and volume of ODA, should be reduced gradually upon graduation, according to the specific needs of the country.

The report concluded that the Secretariat would be better able to evaluate the potential consequences of graduation more precisely and to identify concrete measures for ensuring a smooth transition once information was received from multilateral organizations and development partners on their likely response to a country's graduation, as suggested by the Committee for Development Policy.

UNCTAD report. In July [E/2001/CRP.5 & Add.1], the Secretary-General transmitted to the Economic and Social Council a note by the UNCTAD secretariat on the benefits associated with LDC status and the question of graduation from the LDC list, including an assessment of the implications of graduation for Maldives and three other potential graduation cases—Cape Verde, Samoa and Vanuatu. The report reviewed the benefits available to countries with LDC status in terms of multilateral trade, finance for development and technical cooperation. It concluded that, although there was strong evidence that the comfort of "smooth transition" was almost always secured because graduality in granting concessions

was generally built into rules and practices, there might be situations in which additional measures were desirable to warrant smoother transition. While the notion of smooth transition connoted the idea of a phasing out of the concessions, concerned LDCs preferred alternative, more differential concessions based on the recognition of the diversity of their problems.

ECONOMIC AND SOCIAL COUNCIL ACTION

On 24 October [meeting 45], the Economic and Social Council adopted **resolution 2001/43** [draft: E/2001/L.49] without vote [agenda item 13 *(a)*].

Report of the Committee for Development Policy

The Economic and Social Council,

Recalling its resolution 1998/46 of 31 July 1998, in which it decided that the Council should decide on an appropriate programme of work for the Committee for Development Policy,

Recalling also its resolution 2000/34 of 28 July 2000 on the report of the Committee on its second session,

Recalling further General Assembly resolution 46/206 of 20 December 1991 on the report of the Committee and criteria for identifying the least developed countries,

Taking note with appreciation of the presentation by the Chairman and other members of the Bureau of the Committee and of the report of the Committee on its third session,

Noting that the Committee had received insufficient information to carry out a thorough re-examination of its recommendation to graduate Maldives from the list of the least developed countries, as requested by the Council in resolution 2000/34,

Taking note of the report of the Secretary-General on ensuring a smooth transition of countries graduating from least developed country status and the note by the secretariat of the United Nations Conference on Trade and Development on the benefits associated with the least developed countries status and the question of graduation,

Having considered the memorandum submitted by the Government of Maldives,

1. *Requests* the Committee for Development Policy to continue its work on the re-examination of its recommendation to graduate Maldives from the list of least developed countries at its fourth and fifth sessions and to submit a progress report to the Economic and Social Council at its next substantive session and the final recommendations to the Council at its 2003 substantive session, taking into account the information referred to in preambular paragraphs 6 and 7 of the present resolution and further information to be provided by relevant development partners and multilateral organizations;

2. *Calls upon* the relevant development partners and multilateral organizations to make available to the Committee the relevant information on their likely response to a country's graduation before the fourth session of the Committee in 2002;

3. *Decides* to extend the transition period of Maldives until the next triennial review of the list of the

least developed countries in 2003, as recommended by the Committee;

4. *Urges* the international organizations, bilateral donors and graduating or near graduating countries to initiate a debate concerning the treatment of graduating countries with a view to ensuring that the graduation of a country from the list of the least developed countries should not result in disruption to its development plans, programmes and projects and the importance of ensuring a smooth transition from least developed country status for countries that become eligible for graduation;

5. *Reiterates* the importance of consulting with relevant Member States in the preparation and use of country vulnerability profiles as well as the continuing need for transparency, objectivity and accuracy in those processes;

6. *Requests* the Committee to continue its work on the methodology to be used for the identification of the least developed countries, where appropriate in association with other international organizations working on environmental and economic vulnerability issues, and to report to the Council in 2002 on the criteria it proposes to use in the triennial review of the list of the least developed countries scheduled for 2003;

7. *Also requests* the Committee, at its fourth session, to examine and make recommendations regarding the theme chosen for the high-level segment of the substantive session of 2002 of the Council;

8. *Welcomes* the proposals made by the Committee regarding its future programme of work;

9. *Invites* the Chairman and, as necessary, other members of the Committee to continue the practice of reporting orally to the Council on the work of the Committee.

Island developing countries

Implementation of Programme of Action

In response to General Assembly resolution 55/202 [YUN 2000, p. 813], the Secretary-General submitted a July report [A/56/170] on progress in implementing the Programme of Action for the Sustainable Development of Small Island Developing States (SIDS), adopted in 1994 at the Global Conference on the subject [YUN 1994, p. 783]. The report summarized the input received from a number of UN organizations on their implementation activities, information on activities at the regional level by non-UN regional intergovernmental bodies and at the national level by a number of Governments. The report also discussed efforts by the UN system to enhance the capacity of SIDS to utilize the benefits of globalization, especially information and communication technologies (ICT) and described work being carried out on the development of a vulnerability index for SIDS. The report stated that a number of UN bodies had been engaged in assisting SIDS in their efforts to deal with globalization and trade liberalization, particularly within the context of WTO

negotiations, but insufficient attention had been paid to the priority area of ICT. While the issue of vulnerability was being addressed by several UN bodies and intergovernmental organizations, it was clear that work had not progressed to a stage where a definitive ruling could be made on the application of a vulnerability index or indices. The report concluded that it would be important for SIDS to undertake impact assessments of all national implementation activities in order to enable an accurate assessment of overall implementation of the Programme of Action.

Alliance of Small Island States

By a 2 February letter [E/CN.17/2001/11], Samoa transmitted to the Secretary-General the report of the third Alliance of Small Island States workshop on climate change, energy and preparations for the ninth (2001) session of the Commission on Sustainable Development (Nicosia, Cyprus, 15-19 January). Concluding that the importance of the energy sector in the SIDS regions had increased significantly in recent years and that energy played a critical role for the sustainable development of SIDS, the workshop proposed strategies and made recommendations concerning a wide range of energy-related issues, including accessibility, rural energy, financing the energy sector, efficiency, advanced fossil and nuclear fuel technologies, renewable energy, transportation and international cooperation.

GENERAL ASSEMBLY ACTION

On 21 December [meeting 90], the General Assembly, on the recommendation of the Second Committee [A/56/561/Add.5], adopted **resolution 56/198** without vote [agenda item 98 (*e*)].

Further implementation of the outcome of the Global Conference on the Sustainable Development of Small Island Developing States

The General Assembly,

Recalling its resolution 49/122 of 19 December 1994 on the Global Conference on the Sustainable Development of Small Island Developing States,

Recalling also its resolutions 51/183 of 16 December 1996, 52/202 of 18 December 1997, 53/189 of 15 December 1998, 54/224 of 22 December 1999 and 55/202 of 20 December 2000,

Recalling further the Declaration of Barbados and the Programme of Action for the Sustainable Development of Small Island Developing States adopted by the Global Conference on the Sustainable Development of Small Island Developing States,

Recalling the Declaration and review document adopted by the General Assembly at its twenty-second special session,

Recalling also the report of the United Nations Conference on Trade and Development on its tenth session,

Recognizing that, within the context of the challenges of development, small island developing States can experience specific problems arising from small size, remoteness, geographical dispersion, vulnerability to natural disasters, fragile ecosystems, constraints on transport and communication, isolation from markets, vulnerability to exogenous economic and financial shocks, limited internal markets, lack of natural resources, limited freshwater supply, heavy dependence on imports and limited commodities, depletion of non-renewable resources and migration,

Recognizing also the efforts of small island developing States to achieve sustainable development and the need to continue to enhance their capacities to participate effectively in the multilateral trading system,

Noting the report of the first workshop of the Alliance of Small Island States on the Cartagena Protocol on Biosafety, held in Saint Kitts and Nevis from 4 to 6 December 2000, and the report of the third workshop of the Alliance of Small Island States on climate change, energy and preparations for the ninth session of the Commission on Sustainable Development, held in Cyprus from 15 to 19 January 2001,

Noting also the significant efforts to implement the Programme of Action at the local, national, regional and international levels and the need for regional and global institutions to continue to supplement the efforts being made at the national level, including through necessary financial support in partnership with the international community,

Acknowledging the efforts of small island developing States to convene, in cooperation with the Small Island Developing States Unit of the Department of Economic and Social Affairs of the Secretariat, a series of capacity-building workshops targeted at issues of specific relevance to small island developing States,

Welcoming the preparatory activities undertaken at the national and regional levels for the World Summit on Sustainable Development,

Expressing its appreciation to the Government of Jamaica for hosting the first workshop of the Alliance of Small Island States on trade, sustainable development and small island developing States from 12 to 15 December 2001,

Noting the current efforts of the Alliance of Small Island States to organize an interregional preparatory meeting of small island developing States for the World Summit on Sustainable Development, to be held in Singapore from 7 to 11 January 2002, and calls upon all relevant international organizations actively to support the meeting,

Emphasizing the continuing need for the financing of projects that were presented within the context of the implementation of the Programme of Action, inter alia, at the meeting of representatives of donor countries and small island developing States, held in New York from 24 to 26 February 1999,

Noting with appreciation the contribution made by some donor countries towards further implementation of the Programme of Action, and underlining the need for those efforts to be intensified and supplemented by other donor countries and agencies,

Emphasizing the need to complete, without delay, the quantitative and analytical work on the vulnerability index mandated in the review document of the twenty-second special session of the General Assembly, taking into account Economic and Social Council resolution 2001/43 of 24 October 2001, in particular paragraph 6 thereof, and emphasizing the relevance of such work to the work of the Committee for Development Policy on criteria for the identification, including designation and graduation, of least developed countries and its importance to relevant small island developing States,

1. *Takes note* of the report of the Secretary-General;

2. *Reiterates* the urgent need for strong and effective implementation of the Programme of Action for the Sustainable Development of Small Island Developing States and of the Declaration and review document adopted by the General Assembly at its twenty-second special session to assist those States in their efforts to enhance their capacities to achieve sustainable development;

3. *Welcomes* efforts made at the national, subregional and regional levels to implement the Programme of Action;

4. *Invites* the relevant organs and agencies of the United Nations system and the regional commissions and organizations, within their respective mandates, to reflect measures for the implementation of the Programme of Action in their programmes;

5. *Invites* donors, as well as all relevant organs and agencies of the United Nations and other regional and international organizations, to provide appropriate support to the interregional preparatory meeting of small island developing States for the World Summit on Sustainable Development;

6. *Invites* all relevant stakeholders, non-governmental organizations and the private sector to participate fully in the activities identified for the further implementation of and effective follow-up to the Programme of Action;

7. *Urges* all relevant organizations to finalize, as a matter of urgency, the work on the development of a vulnerability index, taking into account the particular circumstances and needs of small island developing States;

8. *Welcomes* the strengthened Small Island Developing States Unit, and requests the Secretary-General to consider ways to strengthen the Unit further, inter alia, by establishing the Small Island Developing States Information Network within the Unit and by assisting small island developing States with, inter alia, project implementation advice and assistance in the identification of short- and long-term capacity needs through coordination with regional and international institutions, and to make proposals in that regard;

9. *Calls upon* the Secretary-General to consider further cost-effective ways and means of increasing and improving the United Nations system-wide coordination and dissemination of information on activities in support of small island developing States and the Programme of Action, through the Small Island Developing States Unit, including concrete measures for improving coordination within the United Nations system;

10. *Welcomes* the contributions of donor countries to the strengthening of the Small Island Developing States Unit and the Small Island Developing States Information Network, and encourages other Member States to make contributions, in particular in support of the Network;

11. *Decides* to include in the provisional agenda of its fifty-seventh session, under the item entitled "Environment and sustainable development", the sub-item enti-

tled "Further implementation of the Programme of Action for the Sustainable Development of Small Island Developing States";

12. *Requests* the Secretary-General to submit to the General Assembly at its fifty-seventh session a report on the implementation of the present resolution.

Unit for Landlocked Developing Countries and SIDS

Pursuant to General Assembly resolution 54/249 [YUN 1999, p. 1289], the Secretary-General submitted a July note [A/56/208] transmitting the report of the UNCTAD Secretary-General on the effectiveness of the functioning of the Unit for Landlocked Developing Countries and Small Island Developing States. The report stated that, following the Assembly's decision in resolution 54/249 to re-establish the Unit, the activities of the Office of the Special Coordinator for Least Developed, Landlocked and Island Developing Countries as they related to the needs and problems of 30 landlocked developing countries and 44 SIDS had expanded and intensified, with a view to improving the participation and accelerated integration of the two groups of countries into the global economy, through internationally agreed support measures and special recognition on grounds of vulnerability.

In October [A/56/434], the Secretary-General reported on the resources available to the Office of the Special Coordinator for the biennium 2000-2001. The General Assembly, by **decision 56/444** of 21 December, took note of the two documents.

With regard to the follow-up to the Third UN Conference on LDCs [A/56/645 & Add.1 & Add.1/ Corr.1,2], the Secretary-General recommended that the General Assembly establish an Office of the High Representative for the LDCs, Landlocked Developing Countries and SIDS (see p. 772). The new Office would be responsible for implementation of the Programme of Action, while the UNCTAD Office of the Special Coordinator would continue to provide support to least developed, landlocked and small island developing countries in the areas of its expertise.

Landlocked developing countries

In response to General Assembly resolution 54/199 [YUN 1999, p. 784], the Secretary-General, by an October note [A/56/427], transmitted a progress report of the UNCTAD secretariat on specific actions related to the particular needs and problems of landlocked developing countries. The report presented the conclusions and recommendations of the fifth Meeting of Governmental Experts from Landlocked and Transit Developing Countries and Representatives of Donor Countries and Financial and Development Institutions (New York, 30 July–3 August), which considered problems related to infrastructure and non-physical barriers in lowering transport costs and increasing transit efficiency. It also described UNCTAD activities with regard to the development of transit systems in landlocked and transit developing countries, including assistance in drafting or negotiating bilateral or regional agreements and efforts to improve transport information systems.

Ministerial communiqué. On 19 November [A/C.2/56/4], the Lao People's Democratic Republic transmitted to the Secretary-General the ministerial communiqué adopted at the second annual ministerial meeting of the Group of Landlocked Developing Countries (New York, 14 November).

GENERAL ASSEMBLY ACTION

On 21 December [meeting 90], the General Assembly, on the recommendation of the Second Committee [A/56/558/Add.1], adopted **resolution 56/180** without vote [agenda item 95 (a)].

Specific actions related to the particular needs and problems of landlocked developing countries

The General Assembly,

Recalling the provisions of its resolutions 44/214 of 22 December 1989, 46/212 of 20 December 1991, 48/169 of 21 December 1993, 50/97 of 20 December 1995, 52/183 of 18 December 1997 and 54/199 of 22 December 1999 and the Global Framework for Transit Transport Cooperation between Landlocked and Transit Developing Countries and the Donor Community, as well as the relevant parts of the Agenda for Development,

Recalling also the United Nations Millennium Declaration, in which heads of State and Government recognized the particular needs and problems of the landlocked developing countries and urged both bilateral and multilateral donors to increase financial and technical assistance to this group of countries to meet their particular development needs and to help them to overcome the impediments of geography by improving their transit transport systems, and resolved to create an environment, at the national and global levels alike, that is conducive to development and to the elimination of poverty,

Recognizing that the lack of territorial access to the sea, aggravated by remoteness and isolation from world markets, and prohibitive transit costs and risks impose serious constraints on the overall socio-economic development efforts of the landlocked developing countries,

Recognizing also that sixteen of the landlocked developing countries are also classified by the United Nations as least developed countries and that their geographical situation is an added constraint on their overall ability to cope with the challenges of development,

Recognizing further that most transit countries are themselves developing countries facing serious economic problems, including the lack of adequate infrastructure in the transport sector,

Noting the importance of continuing to strengthen the existing international support measures with a view to addressing further the problems of landlocked developing countries,

Emphasizing the importance of further strengthening effective and close cooperation and collaboration between landlocked developing countries and their transit neighbours, at regional, subregional and bilateral levels, inter alia, through cooperative arrangements in developing efficient transit transport systems in landlocked and transit developing countries, and noting the important role of the activities of the regional commissions in that regard,

Welcoming the holding in New York from 30 July to 3 August 2001 of the fifth Meeting of Governmental Experts from Landlocked and Transit Developing Countries and Representatives of Donor Countries and Financial and Development Institutions,

Expressing its appreciation to donor countries for participating in the fifth Meeting of Governmental Experts and for the generous contribution that facilitated the participation of experts from landlocked and transit developing countries,

Taking note of the Vientiane Plan of Action on measures designed to improve the transit transport systems of the Lao People's Democratic Republic, adopted at the first Specific Consultative Meeting on the Transit Transport Systems of the Lao People's Democratic Republic, held at Vientiane on 14 and 15 December 2000 under the auspices of the United Nations Conference on Trade and Development,

Noting the outcome of the Fourth Ministerial Conference of the World Trade Organization, held at Doha from 9 to 13 November 2001,

1. *Takes note* of the note by the Secretary-General transmitting the progress report of the secretariat of the United Nations Conference on Trade and Development on specific actions related to the particular needs and problems of landlocked developing countries;

2. *Welcomes* the agreed conclusions and recommendations for future action adopted by the fifth Meeting of Governmental Experts from Landlocked and Transit Developing Countries and Representatives of Donor Countries and Financial and Development Institutions;

3. *Reaffirms* the right of access of landlocked countries to and from the sea and freedom of transit through the territory of transit countries by all means of transport, as set forth in article 125 of the United Nations Convention on the Law of the Sea;

4. *Also reaffirms* that transit countries, in the exercise of their full sovereignty over their territory, have the right to take all measures necessary to ensure that the rights and facilities provided for landlocked countries, including landlocked developing countries, in no way infringe upon their legitimate interests;

5. *Calls upon* the landlocked developing countries and their transit neighbours to implement measures to strengthen further their cooperative and collaborative efforts to deal with transit transport issues, including bilateral and, as appropriate, subregional cooperation, inter alia, by improving the physical infrastructure and non-physical aspects of transit transport systems, strengthening and concluding, where appropriate, bi-

lateral and subregional agreements to govern transit transport operations, developing joint ventures in the area of transit transport and strengthening institutions and human resources dealing with transit transport, and, in this respect, notes that South-South cooperation also plays an important role in this field;

6. *Appeals once again* to all States, international organizations and financial institutions to implement, as a matter of urgency and priority, the specific actions related to the particular needs and problems of landlocked developing countries agreed upon in the resolutions adopted by the General Assembly, the outcomes of recent major United Nations conferences relevant to landlocked developing countries and the Global Framework for Transit Transport Cooperation between Landlocked and Transit Developing Countries and the Donor Community and to take fully into account the agreed conclusions and recommendations of the fifth Meeting of Governmental Experts from Landlocked and Transit Developing Countries and Representatives of Donor Countries and Financial and Development Institutions;

7. *Expresses its appreciation* for the financial and technical assistance made available by some donors to landlocked and transit developing countries in the form of grants or concessional loans for the construction, maintenance and improvement of their transport, storage and other transit-related facilities, including alternative routes and improved communications;

8. *Invites* donor countries, the United Nations Development Programme and multilateral financial and development institutions to provide landlocked and transit developing countries with appropriate financial and technical assistance in the form of grants or concessional loans for the construction, maintenance and improvement of their transport, storage and other transit-related facilities, including alternative routes and improved communications, to promote subregional, regional and interregional projects and programmes, and, in this regard, to consider, inter alia, improving the availability and optimal use of different transport modes and intermodal efficiency along transport corridors;

9. *Emphasizes* that assistance for the improvement of transit transport facilities and services should be integrated into the overall economic development strategies of the landlocked and transit developing countries and that donor countries should consequently take into account the requirements for the long-term restructuring of the economies of the landlocked developing countries;

10. *Notes* the important role that the simplification, harmonization and standardization of transit procedures and documentation as well as the application of information technologies have played in enhancing the efficiency of transit systems, and calls upon the United Nations Conference on Trade and Development, in close cooperation with other relevant organizations of the United Nations system, to continue to assist landlocked and transit developing countries in those areas, in accordance with their mandates;

11. *Invites* those countries that have not done so to consider ratifying or acceding to international agreements and conventions related to transit trade and transport, and invites landlocked and transit countries to consider concluding bilateral or subregional inter-

governmental agreements regarding various aspects of transit transport;

12. *Invites* the international community to continue to provide technical and financial support to landlocked and transit developing countries to assist with effective implementation of their cooperation agreements and arrangements on transit transport, taking into account the fact that many landlocked and transit developing countries have concluded bilateral and regional arrangements and are making efforts to implement them;

13. *Requests* the Secretary-General to convene in 2003 an International Ministerial Meeting of Landlocked and Transit Developing Countries and Donor Countries and International Financial and Development Institutions on Transit Transport Cooperation, within the existing resources of the budget for the biennium 2002-2003 and with voluntary contributions, to review the current situation of transit transport systems, including the implementation of the Global Framework for Transit Transport Cooperation of 1995, and to formulate, inter alia, appropriate policy measures and action-oriented programmes aimed at developing efficient transit transport systems, which would be held for two days and would be preceded by a three-day meeting of senior officials to finalize the substantive preparations;

14. *Invites* Member States, members of the specialized agencies and United Nations observers, including landlocked and transit developing countries and donor countries, and international financial and development institutions, including relevant regional and subregional economic organizations and commissions, to participate in the International Ministerial Meeting and its preparatory process;

15. *Requests* the Secretary-General, in close cooperation with and with the full involvement of the secretariat of the United Nations Conference on Trade and Development, as appropriate, to provide substantive and organizational support, within the existing resources of the budget for the biennium 2002-2003 and with voluntary contributions, for the International Ministerial Meeting, and requests that, in this context, the necessary preparations be undertaken at the subregional and regional levels, as appropriate, with the involvement of all major stakeholders, including the private sector;

16. *Decides* to consider the precise timing and venue of the International Ministerial Meeting at its fifty-seventh session, taking into consideration the generous offer made by the Government of Kazakhstan to host the meeting;

17. *Requests* the Secretary-General to convene in 2003, prior to the International Ministerial Meeting and within the existing resources for the biennium 2002-2003, the sixth Meeting of Governmental Experts from Landlocked and Transit Developing Countries and Representatives of Donor Countries and Financial and Development Institutions, including relevant regional and subregional economic organizations and commissions, and decides that that meeting shall serve as a preparatory committee for the International Ministerial Meeting, in both substantive and organizational aspects;

18. *Also requests* the Secretary-General of the United Nations, in close cooperation with the Secretary-General of the United Nations Conference on Trade and Development, as appropriate, to seek voluntary contributions to facilitate the preparations for the International Ministerial Meeting, including the participation of representatives of landlocked and transit developing countries at the meeting;

19. *Notes with appreciation* the contribution of the United Nations Conference on Trade and Development to formulating international policies and measures dealing with the particular problems of landlocked developing countries, inter alia, through technical cooperation programmes, and urges the Conference, inter alia, to keep under constant review the evolution of transit transport infrastructure facilities, institutions and services, to monitor the implementation of agreed measures, inter alia, by means of a case study as necessary, to promote regional and subregional cooperation, to build consensus on cooperative arrangements, to mobilize international support measures, to collaborate in all relevant initiatives, including those of the private sector and nongovernmental organizations, and to serve as a focal point for cross-regional issues of landlocked developing countries;

20. *Invites* the Secretary-General of the United Nations, in consultation with the Secretary-General of the United Nations Conference on Trade and Development, as appropriate, to take appropriate measures, within the existing resources of the budget for the biennium 2002-2003 and with voluntary contributions, for the effective implementation of the activities called for in the present resolution, and to provide the Office of the Special Coordinator for Least Developed, Landlocked and Island Developing Countries of the Conference with adequate resources so as to allow it to continue to support landlocked developing countries, to the extent of its mandate, including in the effective preparations for the International Ministerial Meeting;

21. *Requests* the Secretary-General to prepare a report on the implementation of the present resolution and to submit it to the Trade and Development Board and to the General Assembly at its fifty-seventh session;

22. *Decides* to include in the provisional agenda of its fifty-seventh session, under the item entitled "Macroeconomic policy questions", a sub-item entitled "Preparations for the International Ministerial Meeting on Transit Transport Cooperation";

23. *Also decides* to include in the provisional agenda of its fifty-eighth session, under the item entitled "Macroeconomic policy questions", a sub-item entitled "Specific actions related to the particular needs and problems of landlocked developing countries".

Chapter II

Operational activities for development

In 2001, the United Nations system continued to provide development assistance to developing countries and countries with economies in transition, primarily through the United Nations Development Programme (UNDP), the central United Nations funding body for technical assistance. UNDP's income in 2001 totalled $2,828 million, up from $2,555 million in 2000. That included, for the first time in eight years, a slight increase in regular resources. Total expenditure for all programme activities and support costs reached $2,725 million in 2001 as compared with $2,514 million the previous year. Other technical cooperation, totalling $51.1 million, was provided through the executive programme of the UN Department of Economic and Social Affairs, $105.7 million through the United Nations Fund for International Partnerships and $28.6 million through the UN Capital Development Fund. In addition, some $8.9 million had been spent as at 31 March under the UN Development Account.

In 2001, the United Nations conducted a triennial comprehensive policy review of UN system operational activities for development. The review analysed the advances made in and challenges facing UN development cooperation, particularly in view of new global economic trends, and made recommendations on the role and responsibilities of the UN system for development. The review also provided an opportunity for the United Nations to assess its own progress in fulfilling the goals of the United Nations Millennium Declaration, which included set targets for operational activities for development. In December, the General Assembly adopted a far-reaching outline for future development activities of the UN system.

UNDP and its associated funds and programmes continued to make progress in enhancing their overall development impact. UNDP activities were focused on six major goals—sustainable human development, poverty reduction, the environment, gender equality, special development situations and support of the UN system.

The United Nations Office for Project Services, which continued to operate under the self-financing principle with no assessed budget financing, had a total value of project and loan portfolios of $3.7 billion in 2001, comprising $1.4 billion in project value and $2.3 billion in

loans under its supervision. Total project delivery was $505 million.

The United Nations Volunteers (UNV) programme, administered by UNDP, continued to grow in 2001, with over 5,000 volunteers carrying out some 5,400 assignments. Growth was strongest in the number of volunteers serving in UN peacekeeping operations. The United Nations observed 2001 as the International Year of Volunteers; UNV served as focal point for the related activities. The Assembly, in December, made recommendations on ways Governments and the UN system could support volunteering.

The High-level Committee on the Review of Technical Cooperation among Developing Countries (TCDC), in May/June, reviewed progress made in implementing the 1978 Buenos Aires Plan of Action for Promoting and Implementing TCDC and progress in implementing the new directions strategy for TCDC. In December, the Assembly noted the expanded use of South-South cooperation and urged developing countries to intensify technical and economic cooperation at the regional and interregional levels, particularly in information and communication technologies.

System-wide activities

Operational activities segment of the Economic and Social Council

The Economic and Social Council, at its 2001 substantive session (Geneva, 2-26 July) [A/56/3/Rev.1], considered the question of operational activities of the United Nations for international development cooperation at meetings on 5, 6, 9 and 10 July. As the Council had decided on 31 January (**decision 2001/205**), the theme for the operational activities segment was "Triennial policy review of operational activities for development". A high-level meeting on operational activities was held on 5 and 6 July. On 6 July, the Council held an informal dialogue with the heads of UN funds and programmes. On 5 and 10 July, the Council considered follow-up to policy recommendations of the General Assembly and the Council, and the reports of the Executive

Boards of the United Nations Development Programme (UNDP)/United Nations Population Fund (UNFPA), the United Nations Children's Fund (UNICEF) and the World Food Programme (WFP). The Council, on 10 July, considered the question of economic and technical cooperation among developing countries. On 19 July, it held an informal dialogue with the UN system country teams from China and the United Republic of Tanzania. Among the documents before the Council were the May interim report of the Secretary-General on the triennial comprehensive policy review of operational activities of the UN system for development [E/2001/66]; a report on progress in implementing the multi-year funding frameworks (MYFFs) and evaluating the United Nations Development Assistance Framework (UNDAF) [A/56/70-E/2001/58 & Add.1,2]; and a conference room paper containing a consolidated list of issues on which the funds and programmes sought the Council's guidance.

ECONOMIC AND SOCIAL COUNCIL ACTION

On 10 July [meeting 21], the Economic and Social Council adopted **resolution 2001/1** [draft: E/2001/L.17] without vote [agenda item 3 (a)].

Triennial comprehensive policy review of operational activities for development of the United Nations system

The Economic and Social Council,

Recalling the United Nations Millennium Declaration, which sets out priorities and goals to be reached by the international community up to the year 2015,

Recalling also General Assembly resolutions 47/199 of 22 December 1992, 50/120 of 20 December 1995 and 53/192 of 15 December 1998 on the triennial policy review of operational activities for development of the United Nations system,

Recalling further its resolutions 1999/5 and 1999/6 of 23 July 1999 and 2000/19 and 2000/20 of 28 July 2000,

Having considered the reports of the Secretary-General on the triennial policy review of operational activities for development of the United Nations system and on progress in the implementation of the multi-year funding frameworks and evaluation of the United Nations Development Assistance Framework,

1. *Requests* the Secretary-General, when finalizing his report on the triennial policy review for submission to the General Assembly at its fifty-sixth session, to take into account the views and comments expressed by Member States during the operational activities segment of the substantive session of 2001 of the Economic and Social Council and to make appropriate recommendations;

2. *Also requests* the Secretary-General, when finalizing his report on the triennial policy review, to provide an analysis of the current state of the implementation of resolution 53/192 and other related resolutions on operational activities;

3. *Invites* the Secretary-General, in accordance with the coordination, guidance and oversight roles of the Council in the implementation by the United Nations system of the triennial policy review of operational activities, to make recommendations, when finalizing his report on the triennial policy review, on the possible themes that could be discussed at the substantive sessions of 2002 and 2003 of the Council, taking into account the necessary preparatory work for the following triennial policy review.

Triennial policy review

The Secretary-General, in response to General Assembly resolution 53/192 [YUN 1998, p. 802] and Economic and Social Council resolution 2001/1 (see above), reported, in August [A/56/320], on the triennial comprehensive policy review of operational activities for development of the UN system, summarizing the more detailed analysis of the implementation of resolution 53/192 on the 1998 triennial policy review, which was presented in an addendum to the report [A/56/320/Add.1]. The Secretary-General highlighted the conclusions of that analysis, outlined the challenges facing UN development cooperation, and made recommendations on the UN role and responsibilities for development for consideration by the Assembly. It was supplemented by the Secretary-General's report on progress in the implementation of MYFFs and evaluation of UNDAF [A/56/70-E/2001/58], and reports containing comprehensive statistical data for 1999 [A/56/70/Add.1-E/2001/58/Add.1] and preliminary statistical data for 2000 [A/56/70/Add.2-E/2001/58/Add.2] operational activities for development.

The Secretary-General stated that the review, the first of its kind since the adoption of the United Nations Millennium Declaration [YUN 2000, p. 49], identified time-bound targets and offered a frame of reference for UN system operational activities for development. Recent global conferences and the Millennium Declaration had helped to define and focus the UN development agenda.

The operational activities for development of the UN system needed to respond to a continuously changing global context. The Council, at its 2001 substantive session, had identified globalization, liberalization, technological change and the need for developing countries to integrate into the world economy as the major challenges for development, as well as for the role and content of UN operational activities. The UN development system was called upon to assist developing countries in addressing globalization and in taking advantage of the opportunities it created to reduce poverty. New technologies, such as information and communication technologies, also provided opportunities for economic development and empowerment, and could help countries to overcome or mitigate traditional development gaps. The UN system could play a key role in bridging the digital divide by promoting the transfer of technology to developing countries and accelerating access to information technology knowledge.

Thus, the scope of UN development cooperation continued to expand and included situations of conflict and post-conflict conditions. Demands for support also arose in new areas such as: strengthening capacity-building and enabling developing countries to integrate in the world economy; adapting international development goals to the national context; and responding to new political, humanitarian and socio-economic challenges, including governance, humanitarian assistance, peace-building and conflict prevention. The UN development system was expected to adapt and respond flexibly to the new development challenges and intensify its internal coordination, while ensuring a coherent and integrated response to national development needs. The system needed to challenge itself also by upgrading the capacities of its country teams to make optimal use of resources and the comparative advantages of UN system organizations.

The goals set by the Millennium Declaration and the development process required considerable financial resources, both domestic and international. However, although the UN system was still viewed as a valuable partner, the UN development system would have to play its role in a more intensely competitive environment, with a broader development agenda and with reduced resources.

The reform process launched in 1997 [YUN 1997, p. 1389], aimed at a more effective and efficient use of resources through better management, had begun to have a positive impact on the effectiveness and relevance of UN operational activities. By that process, a more integrated approach to development cooperation was achieved through inter-agency modalities, including the establishment of the United Nations Development Group, the streamlining of the strategic direction of operational activities through collaboration and programmatic coherence, the introduction of processes, such as the common country assessment (CCA) and UNDAF, measures to strengthen the UN resident coordinator system and UN country teams, as well as common premises and integrated information services. The introduction of MYFFs and the reinforcement of results-based management were steps towards more efficient programming, monitoring and evaluation. The availability of resources for operational activities was essential for sustaining those reforms on a predictable and assured basis.

However, resources remained insecure, unstable, stagnant, volatile and vulnerable, and the introduction of MYFFs had not managed to reverse the negative trends in core funding, while financial support for development cooperation still came from a limited number of donors. A renewed commitment to financing UN development cooperation on a more secure and predictable footing was needed. The forthcoming International Conference on Financing for Development (see p. 886) provided an opportunity to achieve a breakthrough in that area.

The report reviewed the impact of management reforms, introduced in recent years to achieve greater coherence and coordination in UN development cooperation, which focused on intergovernmental oversight of operational activities, lessons learned from their impact evaluation, strategic frameworks for programming and field-level coordination.

It concluded that, to become more relevant in facing the global challenges, UN development support should aim at closer integration with national development policies and programmes. Its focus should shift to integration into national efforts, shared programmes within the system and with Governments and other stakeholders, increased attention to the substantive content of development support, capacity-building and greater development impact on recipient countries.

The challenge of integrating development cooperation in national development efforts required the interaction of a variety of interlocutors at the intergovernmental level; the Economic and Social Council could provide the forum for a substantive dialogue among key stakeholders on the overall direction and orientations of development cooperation, and provide guidance to the UN system and the governing bodies of its organizations. Participation in the Council's operational activities segment would have to be at a high level and extended to a wider range of stakeholders. The dialogue on development cooperation at the Council's operational activities segment should encourage a greater harmonization of policies, instruments and procedures of all external partners as a basis for more effective integration of all external assistance into national development.

The review also examined the strategic frameworks developed by the international community to help developing countries define their comprehensive country strategies, in particular CCA and UNDAF. The role and implementation of those two instruments over the past three years were evaluated in an addendum to the report [A/56/320/Add.1] and in more detail in a separate report [A/56/70-E/2001/58]. Experience in a number of countries where CCA and UNDAF had been applied showed that notable advances had been made, the system was working more coherently at the country level and UNDAF could be a major tool for inducing greater coherence and synergy in UN system operational activities at the country level. However, the degree of government involvement in countries where the process was launched had been uneven, and the involvement of other national development partners appeared to be limited. To be relevant in development terms, UNDAF should serve not only as a framework for UN system country programmes, but also as a broader instrument to assist programme countries in achieving their own development goals. That required greater involvement of the Government and other national partners in all stages of formulation and implementation, a better dialogue with all relevant external partners, good quality technical work to accompany those processes, adequate monitoring and the building of national capacities in coordination functions. The review noted the concern over the multiplicity of country-level coordination frameworks and the burden they might place on programme countries, UN system staff and other multilateral and bilateral institutions, resulting in higher transaction costs. Progress could be made by ensuring coherence and consistency among them.

Concerning impact evaluations of UN system support in capacity-building and poverty eradication, the review showed that, while the system could play an important role in poverty reduction, with support to capacity-building being an important element in that process, the resources available for poverty eradication were still inadequate. Although capacity-building was a central objective of operational activities for the entire UN system, it was still seen as an area reserved to UNDP. Moreover, the impact evaluations showed that poverty eradication as a central goal of the UN system could be linked, in a more structural way, to the development role played by each system organization. The absence of a clear link left a certain lack of clarity regarding the way to tackle poverty eradication. Poverty eradication needed to be conceived not as a remedial or compensatory initiative but as the outcome of policies and programmes that promoted inclusive economic growth and overall social development.

The review examined several issues related to field-level coordination. It noted that greater efforts were needed to achieve further progress in the simplification and harmonization of the multiplicity of rules, procedures and modalities specific to each organization. It also noted that,

while the functioning of the resident coordinator system had improved, there was still room for more participation by UN specialized agencies, as well as for the introduction of innovations to enhance the system's capacity to involve and interact with other partners, to encourage a sense of belonging to the UN system as a whole, and to further involve the broader donor community in the work of the resident coordinator system and facilitate closer complementarity in the country work of all external partners. The review noted the progress made over the past three years in enhancing the efficiency of programme delivery through the process of common premises and shared services.

In terms of monitoring and evaluation, the review revealed that, despite the move towards strategic and policy-oriented monitoring, there was little institutional memory within the system on the impact of its operational activities and there was a need to enhance its capacity to learn from past experiences. The involvement of specialized agencies was another area of concern, and the importance of enhancing that involvement in the country-level dialogue between the UN system and the Government and other national partners was underlined. Providing adequate resources, including budgetary support to specialized agencies, was also important in helping those agencies without direct field representation in recipient countries to enable national stakeholders to have access to their services. The potential for greater collaboration between the UN development system and regional development banks should be more fully explored. Considerable scope also existed for tripartite collaboration among the UN development system, the Bretton Woods institutions (the World Bank Group and the International Monetary Fund) and regional development banks.

Other dimensions of operational activities, such as the interrelationships among conflict prevention, relief, rehabilitation and development, needed further clarification, as did the mainstreaming of the gender perspective. In addition, technical and economic cooperation among developing countries, when further integrated into operational activities for development, had a greater impact on development efforts.

GENERAL ASSEMBLY ACTION

On 21 December [meeting 90], the General Assembly, on the recommendation of the Second (Economic and Financial) Committee [A/56/562/Add.1], adopted **resolution 56/201** without vote [agenda item 99 *(a)*].

Triennial policy review of operational activities for development of the United Nations system

The General Assembly,

Recalling its resolutions 44/211 of 22 December 1989, 47/199 of 22 December 1992, 50/120 of 20 December 1995, 52/203 of 18 December 1997, 52/12 B of 19 December 1997 and 53/192 of 15 December 1998, as well as Economic and Social Council resolutions 1999/5 and 1999/6 of 23 July 1999, and 2000/19 and 2000/20 of 28 July 2000, and taking note of agreed conclusions 2001/1 of the Council of 4 July 2001, the ministerial declaration of the high-level segment of the substantive session of the Council of 18 July 2001, Council resolution 2001/41 of 26 July 2001 and other relevant resolutions,

Recalling also the United Nations Millennium Declaration of 8 September 2000 and its importance for international development cooperation, including the operational activities for development of the United Nations system, and in particular the development and poverty eradication goals and targets contained therein,

Reaffirming that the operational activities for development of the United Nations system have an important role to play in enabling developing countries to continue to take a lead role in the management of their own development process in a continuously changing global context,

Reaffirming also that the fundamental characteristics of the operational activities of the United Nations system should be, inter alia, their universal, voluntary and grant nature, their neutrality and their multilateralism, as well as their ability to respond to the development needs of developing countries in a flexible manner, and that the operational activities of the United Nations system are carried out for the benefit of recipient countries, at the request of those countries and in accordance with their own policies and priorities for development,

Stressing that national plans and priorities constitute the only viable frame of reference for the national programming of operational activities for development of the United Nations system and that programmes should be based on such development plans and priorities and should therefore be country-driven,

Bearing in mind that the effectiveness of operational activities should be assessed by their impact on poverty eradication, economic growth and sustainable development of recipient countries as set out in the commitments, goals and targets of the Millennium Declaration and of the major United Nations conferences,

Welcoming the efforts undertaken so far to rationalize and improve the functioning and impact of United Nations funds, programmes and specialized agencies,

Recognizing that globalization, technological change and the need for the integration of the developing countries and other recipient countries into the world economy represent major challenges and, at the same time, opportunities for their development,

Recognizing also that new technologies, including information and communication technologies, present an opportunity to accelerate development, especially in developing countries, but that the access to those technologies is uneven and that a digital divide still prevails,

Noting that, while the scope of operational activities of the organizations of the United Nations system includes situations where a more flexible response capacity of the system is required, the focus of operational activities should be on actions that have a long-term impact on poverty eradication, economic growth and sustainable development,

Recognizing the urgent and specific needs of low-income countries, in particular the least developed countries,

Emphasizing that developing countries are responsible for their development processes, and in this context stressing the responsibility of the international community, in partnership, to assist developing countries in their national development efforts,

Recognizing that the United Nations development system should take into account the specific needs and requirements of the countries with economies in transition and other recipient countries,

Recalling the role of the Economic and Social Council in providing coordination and guidance to the United Nations system to ensure that policies formulated by the General Assembly, in particular during the triennial policy review of operational activities, are implemented on a system-wide basis in accordance with Assembly resolutions 48/162 of 20 December 1993 and 50/227 of 24 May 1996,

Noting with deep concern the failure to provide the United Nations development system with a critical mass of the core resources required to enable long-term development cooperation towards attaining development goals and targets and towards providing a more integrated development support,

1. *Takes note with appreciation* of the reports of the Secretary-General on the triennial comprehensive policy review of operational activities for development of the United Nations system and on progress in the implementation of the multi-year funding frameworks and evaluation of the United Nations Development Assistance Framework;

2. *Reaffirms* its resolutions 47/199, 50/120, 53/192 and the parts relevant to operational activities for development of its resolution 52/12 B, and stresses the need to implement fully, on the basis of lessons learned, all the elements of those resolutions in a coherent and timely manner, keeping in mind their interlinkages;

3. *Stresses* the primary responsibility of national Governments for their countries' development, and recognizes the importance of national ownership of development programmes;

4. *Emphasizes* that recipient Governments have the primary responsibility for coordinating, on the basis of national strategies and priorities, all types of external assistance, including that provided by multilateral organizations, in order to integrate effectively such assistance into their development process;

5. *Emphasizes also* the need for all organizations of the United Nations development system to enhance their coordination in accordance with their mandates, mission statements and the relevant decisions of their governing bodies, in order to avoid overlapping and duplication and to enhance their complementarity;

6. *Emphasizes further* the need to fulfil the commitments, goals and targets set in the United Nations Millennium Declaration and by the major United Nations

conferences, and in that context reiterates the importance of continuously monitoring progress made in that direction;

7. *Stresses* that the United Nations development system, in order to ensure national ownership of its operational activities for development, should integrate its country-level operations with national policies and programmes for development and poverty eradication, including, as appropriate, national poverty reduction strategies, under the leadership of the Government;

8. *Also stresses* that the United Nations development system should assist programme countries in addressing the goals and targets identified in the Millennium Declaration and in the outcomes and commitments of relevant major United Nations conferences, in the context of the current challenges and opportunities of globalization;

9. *Welcomes* the efforts undertaken so far to improve the functioning and the impact of the operational activities for development of the United Nations system, and in this regard encourages the organizations of the United Nations system to continue those efforts, with a view to improving further the effectiveness and increasing the relevance of such activities;

I
Role of operational activities in the context of a globalizing world

10. *Stresses* the need for all organizations of the United Nations development system, in accordance with their respective mandates, to focus their efforts at the field level in accordance with the priorities identified by recipient countries and the goals, targets and commitments set in the Millennium Declaration and by the major United Nations conferences;

11. *Recognizes,* in this context, the need for all organizations of the United Nations system to assist programme countries to respond more effectively to the economic and social impact of globalization and to support their efforts to integrate into the world economy, to accelerate their economic growth and development and to reduce their poverty;

12. *Calls upon* the organizations of the United Nations system to strengthen and adapt their strategies and activities and enhance their coordination and collaboration, in order to enhance their supportive role in meeting the commitments, goals and targets of the Millennium Assembly and major United Nations conferences, in particular the development and poverty eradication goals and targets;

13. *Encourages* the United Nations system to support national efforts to acquire the capacities and infrastructure required to mobilize information and communication technologies and put them at the service of development, and encourages all organizations of the system to collaborate with the recently established Information and Communication Technologies Task Force;

II
Funding for operational activities for development of the United Nations system

14. *Stresses* that core resources, inter alia, because of their untied nature, are the bedrock of the operational activities of the United Nations system, and in this regard notes with serious concern the overall decline or stagnation in core resources available to many United Nations funds and programmes, in particular the United Nations Development Programme;

15. *Strongly reaffirms* that the impact of operational activities for development of the United Nations system must be enhanced by, inter alia, a substantial increase in core or regular resources on a predictable, continuous and sustained basis, commensurate with the increasing needs of developing countries, as well as through the full implementation of resolutions 47/199, 48/162, 50/120, 53/192 and the parts relevant to operational activities for development of resolution 52/12 B;

16. *Notes* the efforts of the executive boards and secretariats of the United Nations Development Programme and United Nations Population Fund and of the United Nations Children's Fund to establish multi-year funding frameworks that integrate programme objectives, resources, budgets and outcomes, with the objective of increasing core resources and enhancing their predictability, and in this regard invites them to continue to develop and refine the frameworks as a strategic resource management tool;

17. *Stresses,* in this regard, the continued need for funds, programmes and agencies of the United Nations development system to continue to report on the overall results achieved to their executive boards or governing bodies and to the Economic and Social Council;

18. *Notes with regret* that, although significant progress has been achieved with regard to the governance and functioning of the United Nations development system, there has not been, as part of that overall process of change, a significant increase in core resources for operational activities for development;

19. *Underlines* the need to avoid over-dependence on a limited number of donors, emphasizes the importance of shared responsibility in a spirit of partnership, taking into account established official development assistance targets, including targets established at the Third United Nations Conference on the Least Developed Countries, and calls upon donors and countries in a position to do so to increase their contributions to the core or regular resources of United Nations funds and programmes;

20. *Appreciates,* in this context, the efforts of countries, including donor and programme countries, that have increased or maintained their high level of contributions to the core resources of United Nations funds and programmes, and of those that have made multi-year pledges to core resources;

21. *Notes* the increase in non-core resources, including cost-sharing, trust funds and non-traditional sources of financing, as a mechanism to supplement the means of operational activities for development, contributing to an increase in total resources, while recognizing that non-core resources are not a substitute for core resources;

22. *Reaffirms* the need for priority allocation of scarce grant resources to programmes and projects in low-income countries, in particular the least developed countries;

23. *Requests* that the establishment of new trust funds by United Nations funds and programmes be done in accordance with their mandates, mission statements and the relevant decisions of their governing

bodies, and that such new trust funds, to the extent possible, be multi-donor in nature and not detrimental to core or regular resources;

24. *Notes*, in this context, the contributions of private sources, which can supplement but cannot substitute for contributions of Governments, to finance or extend programmes implemented within existing guidelines of United Nations funds and programmes;

25. *Stresses* the need for continuous overall improvement in the effectiveness, efficiency, management and impact of the United Nations system in delivering its development assistance, and welcomes steps that have been taken to that end;

26. *Requests* the Secretary-General to submit, for consideration by the General Assembly at its fifty-seventh session, a report presenting options alternative to the current modality of the annual United Nations Pledging Conference for Development Activities, including a regular pledging event, taking into account the funding sessions convened under the multi-year funding frameworks, the needs of other agencies of the United Nations system, appropriate timing and options to enhance public support for operational activities for development of the United Nations system, including through the proposed options;

27. *Requests* the Economic and Social Council to consider, at its substantive session of 2003, the conclusions reached at the present triennial policy review on resources for operational activities for development, reviewing the progress made on the issue of funding of development cooperation activities of the United Nations system;

III
Capacity-building

28. *Stresses* that capacity-building and its sustainability should be explicitly articulated as a goal of technical assistance provided by operational activities of the United Nations system, with the aim of strengthening national capacities, and that the technical skills profiles of country offices should be regularly assessed to ensure effective capacity-building of the recipient countries, and requests United Nations organizations to review their efforts in the field of capacity-building and to report, through the Secretary-General, to the Economic and Social Council, at its substantive session of 2002, on the results achieved in this area;

29. *Also stresses* the importance of disseminating, to the fullest extent possible, the expertise acquired through the technical assistance provided by operational activities for development of the United Nations system in the programme countries;

30. *Reiterates* that the United Nations system should use, to the fullest extent possible and practicable, available national expertise and indigenous technologies in the implementation of operational activities, and also reiterates its call for the development of common guidelines at the field level for the recruitment, remuneration and training of national project personnel, including national consultants, for the formulation and implementation of development projects and programmes supported by the United Nations development system;

31. *Requests* the United Nations system to enhance the capacity of national Governments to coordinate the external assistance received from the international community, including from the United Nations system;

32. *Calls upon* the organizations of the United Nations development system to support the strengthening of the capacity of Governments to establish databanks and carry out poverty assessments at the country level;

IV
Common country assessment and United Nations Development Assistance Framework

33. *Notes* that, while progress has been made since the introduction of the common country assessment and the United Nations Development Assistance Framework in its pilot phase, there still is a need to continue to improve the preparatory process and the quality of those instruments, inter alia, on the basis of the recommendations of the external evaluation of the common country assessment and the Framework, as reflected in the report of the Secretary-General and his recommendations, with a view to ensuring their effectiveness;

34. *Requests* the United Nations system to conduct the common country assessment and the Framework processes as efforts to improve support for national development priorities and policies, and stresses that full governmental participation and leadership is required at all stages of those processes;

35. *Stresses* the need to ensure the full and active participation of the funds, programmes and specialized agencies of the United Nations system in the preparation of the common country assessment and the Framework;

36. *Encourages* the United Nations system to ensure full and active system-wide collaboration and coherence in developing the common country assessment and the Framework processes;

37. *Recognizes* the need to ensure that lessons learned in the elaboration of the common country assessment and the Framework are systematically shared within the United Nations system and with Governments of programme countries as well as other development partners;

38. *Also recognizes* the common country assessment as a common analytical instrument for the United Nations development system which takes into account national priorities and needs as well as the commitments, goals and targets set in the Millennium Declaration and by the major United Nations conferences;

39. *Further recognizes* that the common country assessment can also be used by recipient countries in formulating their own national policies;

40. *Recognizes* that the Framework, where it exists, is the common planning framework for the development operations of the United Nations system at the country level, consisting of common objectives and strategies of cooperation, a programme resource framework and proposals for follow-up, monitoring and evaluation;

41. *Urges* the organizations of the United Nations system to ensure consistency and complementarity of country programmes and other similar instruments used in individual organizations of the system with the approved Framework;

42. *Notes* the role that the Framework should play to facilitate the contribution of the United Nations system to the integrated and coordinated implementation

of the Millennium Declaration and the outcomes of major United Nations conferences and summits at the country level and to provide a more coherent and integrated response by the United Nations system to national development priorities;

43. *Also notes* the importance of closer consultation in the formulation of the common country assessment and the Framework, among national Governments, relevant United Nations development agencies, including specialized agencies, and other relevant stakeholders;

44. *Encourages* greater cooperation among the World Bank, regional development banks and all funds and programmes, taking into account their respective competencies, mandates and comparative advantages, with a view to achieving increased complementarity and better division of labour, as well as enhanced coherence in their sectoral activities, building on the existing arrangements and in full accordance with the priorities of the recipient Government, and in this regard emphasizes the importance of ensuring, under the leadership of national Governments, greater consistency between the strategic frameworks developed by the United Nations funds, programmes and agencies and the Bretton Woods institutions, and the national poverty reduction strategies, including the poverty reduction strategy papers, where they exist;

45. *Urges* the organizations of the United Nations system, when the common country assessment and the Framework are undertaken, to ensure that measures are adopted to simplify and harmonize country assessment procedures and programming so as to reduce transaction costs and avoid additional procedural requirements and workload for recipient countries and United Nations country teams;

46. *Encourages* bilateral donors and the United Nations system to coordinate their efforts more actively at the field level, under the leadership of recipient Governments, inter alia, by using the common country assessment;

47. *Requests* the Secretary-General, in consultation with Member States, to undertake an evaluation of the progress of the common country assessment and Framework processes and their impact on the field of operational activities, as an integral part of the next triennial policy review of operational activities, and to submit a report, through the Economic and Social Council at its substantive session of 2004, on the results of such an evaluation, including lessons learned and recommendations made, for consideration by the General Assembly at its fifty-ninth session;

V
Evaluation of operational activities for development

48. *Emphasizes* the importance of the monitoring and evaluation of operational activities of the United Nations system in order to enhance their effectiveness and impact, and reiterates that the monitoring and evaluation process of operational activities, including, where appropriate, joint evaluations by the United Nations system, should be impartial and independent, under the overall leadership of the Government;

49. *Reiterates* the need to strengthen the capacities of the recipient countries to perform effective programme, project and financial monitoring, as well as impact evaluations of operational activities funded by the United Nations, and underlines the importance of promoting, under the leadership of Governments, greater collaboration on questions relating to evaluation among recipient Governments and the United Nations development system, in particular the members of the United Nations Development Group, at the country level;

50. *Recognizes* that a comprehensive and participatory approach to monitoring and evaluation calls for a closer involvement of national authorities and civil society in the monitoring and evaluation of the effectiveness and impact of operational activities, in order to ensure that the results of those evaluations are utilized to improve operational activities for development and their impact;

51. *Notes* that coordination activities, though beneficial, represent transaction costs that are borne by both recipient countries and the organizations of the United Nations system, and emphasizes the need for their continuous evaluation and for an analysis and assessment of costs compared with the total programme expenditures on operational activities for development in order to ensure maximum efficiency and feasibility;

52. *Takes note* of the impact evaluations of capacity-building and poverty eradication undertaken according to resolution 53/192, and requests the organizations of the United Nations system to review the conclusions of those evaluations and the lessons learned and to incorporate them, in the light of their own experience, into their operational activities for development;

53. *Requests* the Secretary-General to continue to provide, in the context of the triennial comprehensive policy review, an overall assessment of the effectiveness of the operational activities for development of the United Nations system and of the functioning of the United Nations development system at the country level, and to submit to the Economic and Social Council, at its substantive session of 2002, in consultation with Member States and on the basis of the experience acquired with the impact evaluation studies, suggestions on how to strengthen the modalities and enhance the approach for such an assessment, in particular in the areas identified in the present resolution;

54. *Reiterates* the need for recipient Governments concerned to be fully and effectively involved in the assessment of the effectiveness of the operational activities for development of the United Nations system;

55. *Requests* the United Nations system at the country level to support those Governments that intend to undertake capacity-building impact evaluations themselves, as and when required;

56. *Reiterates* the need for the United Nations system to strengthen its efforts, in consultation with recipient countries, to ensure that the lessons learned from both monitoring and evaluation exercises are systematically applied to programming processes at the operational level and that evaluation criteria are built into all projects and programmes at their design stage, requests the Secretary-General to carry out an impartial and independent assessment of the extent to which the United Nations funds, programmes and agencies at the field level learn lessons from their evaluations and to formulate proposals on how to improve the feedback mechanisms at the field level, and requests the Secretary-General to report to the Economic and

Social Council at its substantive session of 2003 in this regard;

VI
Simplification and harmonization of rules and procedures

57. *Reaffirms* that simplification and harmonization of procedures, as well as their decentralization, should support improved organizational efficiency and effectiveness and be responsive to the needs of recipient countries;

58. *Notes* the progress achieved in the harmonization of programming cycles, the harmonization of the programme approval process and the simplification and harmonization of rules and procedures, with the assistance of the United Nations Development Group, and calls upon the funds, programmes and specialized agencies of the United Nations system to continue to improve coordination efforts by taking further steps to enhance and ensure the sustainability of that process;

59. *Emphasizes* that the simplification and harmonization of rules and procedures should aim at reducing, where appropriate, the complexities and diversity of requirements, which still place an enormous burden on the recipient countries through high transaction costs, and that innovations in this area should achieve, in their implementation, the objective of reducing the administrative and financial costs to the recipient country as well as to the United Nations system;

60. *Requests* the funds, programmes and specialized agencies of the United Nations system to examine ways to simplify further their rules and procedures and, in this context, to accord the issue of simplification and harmonization high priority and to take concrete steps in the following areas: the decentralization and delegation of authority; the financial regulations; the procedures for implementing programmes and projects and, in particular, the requirements in terms of monitoring and reporting; the common shared services at country offices; and the recruitment, training and remuneration of national project personnel;

61. *Requests* the funds and programmes of the United Nations system to submit to the Economic and Social Council at its substantive session of 2002 a programme of work for full simplification and harmonization in the above-mentioned areas, to be completed before the end of 2004, including provisions to phase out redundant rules and procedures, benchmarks, responsibilities, as well as a timetable to monitor the progress made towards reaching that target;

62. *Requests* the Executive Committee of the United Nations Development Group to facilitate the definition of the above-mentioned agenda and its implementation;

63. *Requests* the funds and programmes to provide, in their annual reports to the Economic and Social Council, specific information on the progress achieved in reaching the above-mentioned target;

64. *Invites* the executive boards and governing bodies of the funds, programmes and specialized agencies to assess regularly the progress achieved in the area of simplification and harmonization of rules and procedures;

65. *Requests* the United Nations System Chief Executives Board for Coordination to address the requirements for further simplification and harmonization of procedures;

VII
Resident coordinator system

66. *Reaffirms* that the resident coordinator system, within the framework of national ownership, has a key role to play in the effective and efficient functioning of the United Nations system at the country level, including in the formulation of common country assessments and United Nations Development Assistance Frameworks, and is a key instrument for the efficient and effective coordination of the operational activities for development of the United Nations system, and requests the United Nations system, including the funds and programmes, the specialized agencies and the Secretariat, to enhance support to the resident coordinator system;

67. *Appreciates* efforts, including through the United Nations Development Group, to improve further the resident coordinator system and the progress achieved so far in broadening the pool of resident coordinators, improving their gender balance, using competency assessments to select resident coordinator candidates, and implementing improved staff training and annual performance appraisals, and urges the funds, programmes and specialized agencies of the United Nations system to make further efforts in that direction, including through appropriate training and recruitment of qualified staff with the required professional skills and backgrounds;

68. *Encourages* the funds, programmes and specialized agencies to make full use of the United Nations Staff College as an institution for system-wide knowledge management, training and learning;

69. *Encourages* enhanced dialogue, feedback, participation and interaction between the resident coordinator on the one hand, and the specialized agencies, small technical agencies, the regional commissions and organizations of the United Nations system without field level representation on the other, including through a wider use of information and communication technologies;

70. *Encourages* the international financial institutions and other development partners to support the resident coordinator system, including through enhanced dialogue, in addressing national development objectives;

71. *Recognizes* the need for the resident coordinator system to interact more effectively and substantively with the Government of the recipient country, as well as with civil society and other relevant stakeholders, as appropriate;

72. *Requests* the resident coordinator system to assist Governments in their efforts towards implementation of the commitments, goals and targets set in the Millennium Declaration and by the major United Nations conferences, and encourages further work by the country-level theme groups;

73. *Requests* all organizations of the United Nations system, including those with no field-level representation and the regional commissions, to continue to improve and strengthen the resident coordinator system through their support to and active participation in that system, on the basis of their respective mandates

and in close consultation with the national Government;

VIII
United Nations Development Group

74. *Recognizes* the progress achieved towards a more coherent United Nations performance in the development field in the past three years, as reflected by a new culture of shared responsibility, cooperation and coordination among the members of the United Nations Development Group, and in particular the role of the Executive Committee of the Group;

75. *Requests* the member organizations of the United Nations Development Group, in particular the member organizations represented in its Executive Committee, to continue to support and actively participate in the work of the Group;

IX
Planning, programming and implementation

76. *Decides* that, with the agreement of the host country, the United Nations development system should assist national Governments in creating an enabling environment in which the links among national Governments, the United Nations development system, civil society, national non-governmental organizations and the private sector involved in the development process are strengthened, with a view to seeking new and innovative solutions to development problems, in accordance with national policies and priorities;

77. *Encourages* greater cooperation among the World Bank, regional development banks and all funds and programmes with a view to achieving increased complementarity and better division of labour as well as enhanced coherence in their sectoral activities, building on the existing arrangements and in full accordance with the priorities of the recipient Government;

78. *Recognizes* that the diversity of programming procedures of the funds, programmes and specialized agencies of the United Nations system results from the diversity of their mandates and the decisions of their respective governing bodies, and, that notwithstanding, calls upon those organizations to intensify their efforts to utilize all avenues for stronger cooperation and coordination at the headquarters level, which should complement similar coordination efforts at the country level, and urges them to keep countries fully informed of decisions taken at headquarters;

79. *Notes* the progress achieved in the area of common premises and shared services at the country level within the United Nations system, reaffirms the need to take fully into account cost-benefit studies as called for in relevant resolutions, and encourages further implementation of such initiatives, where appropriate, while ensuring that there will be no additional burden imposed on host countries;

80. *Recognizes* that the utilization of advanced information and communication technologies could also provide the necessary platform for more coordination and cohesion at the field level;

81. *Encourages* the use of information technologies as a means to support more effectively the delivery of development cooperation by the United Nations system, and therefore calls for the urgent harmonization of the information technology platforms utilized by the United Nations system, at both the field and headquarters levels;

X
Humanitarian assistance

82. *Reiterates* that the phases of relief, rehabilitation, reconstruction and development are generally not consecutive but often overlap and occur simultaneously, and notes the urgent need to develop, through a strategic framework, when appropriate, a comprehensive approach to countries in crisis, notes that the development of such a comprehensive approach must involve national authorities as well as the United Nations system, donors and intergovernmental and non-governmental organizations, and that national authorities must take a leading role in all aspects of the recovery plan, notes in this context the need for an early application of developmental tools in humanitarian emergencies, and takes note with appreciation of the recommendations included in the report of the Secretary-General in this regard;

83. *Expresses its appreciation* to those countries which have substantially contributed to humanitarian assistance during natural and man-made disasters;

84. *Stresses* that contributions to humanitarian assistance should not be provided at the expense of development assistance and that sufficient resources for humanitarian assistance should be made available by the international community;

XI
Gender

85. *Welcomes* the progress achieved in gender mainstreaming in operational activities, and encourages further work in the areas of equitable access to financial and productive resources to ensure a reversal in the feminization of poverty;

86. *Encourages* the continuing efforts to improve the gender balance on appointments within the United Nations system at the headquarters and the country level in positions that affect operational activities;

87. *Calls* for renewed and accelerated efforts in gender mainstreaming in the framework of the operational activities for development of the United Nations system in all fields, in particular in support of poverty eradication, and encourages the empowerment of women as a priority for operational activities for development;

XII
Regional dimensions of operational activities

88. *Reiterates* the growing need for incorporating the regional and subregional dimensions, where appropriate, in the operational activities for development of the United Nations system, and encourages the resident coordinators, in close consultation with Governments, to secure the greater involvement of the regional commissions, taking into account their agreed mandates and work programmes, in the common country assessment and the United Nations Development Assistance Framework, as appropriate;

XIII
South-South cooperation/economic and technical cooperation among developing countries

89. *Reiterates* that South-South cooperation, including technical and economic cooperation among developing countries, offers viable opportunities for the de-

velopment of developing countries, and in this context requests the executive boards of the funds and programmes to review, with a view to considering an increase, the allocation of resources for activities involving technical cooperation among developing countries;

90. *Requests* the United Nations system to take appropriate measures to improve the effective incorporation of technical cooperation among developing countries into their programmes and projects, and to intensify efforts towards mainstreaming the modality of technical cooperation among developing countries, including through support for the activities of the Special Unit for Technical Cooperation among Developing Countries, and encourages other relevant international institutions to take similar measures;

XIV
Follow-up

91. *Reaffirms* that the governing bodies of the funds, programmes and specialized agencies of the United Nations system should take appropriate action for the full implementation of the present resolution, and requests the executive heads of those funds, programmes and specialized agencies to submit a yearly progress report to their governing bodies on measures taken and envisaged for the implementation of the present resolution, as well as appropriate recommendations;

92. *Invites* the executive boards of the funds and programmes of the United Nations system to ensure that the heads of those funds and programmes include in their annual reports to the Economic and Social Council, prepared in accordance with Council resolution 1994/33 of 28 July 1994, a thorough analysis of problems encountered and lessons learned, with emphasis on issues arising from the implementation of the reform programme of the Secretary-General, the triennial policy review and the follow-up to the Millennium Declaration and major United Nations conferences, so as to allow the Council to fulfil its coordinating role;

93. *Reiterates* the provisions of its resolutions 48/162, 50/227 and 52/12 B which detail the respective functions of the General Assembly, the Economic and Social Council and the executive boards of the funds and programmes of the United Nations system, and encourages the Economic and Social Council, within the context of its institutional role, to provide overall guidance to the United Nations system on operational activities for development;

94. *Requests* the Secretary-General, after consultation with the funds, programmes and specialized agencies of the United Nations system, to submit a progress report to the Economic and Social Council, at its substantive session of 2002, on an appropriate management process, containing clear guidelines, targets, benchmarks and time frames for the full implementation of the present resolution;

95. *Invites* the Economic and Social Council, during the operational activities segment of its substantive sessions of 2002 and 2003, to examine the operational activities of the United Nations system in order to evaluate the implementation of the present resolution with a view to ensuring its full implementation;

96. *Requests* the Secretary-General to submit to the General Assembly at its fifty-ninth session, through the Economic and Social Council, a comprehensive analysis of the implementation of the present resolution in the context of the triennial policy review, and to make appropriate recommendations.

Internal oversight mechanisms

The General Assembly, at its resumed fifty-fifth session, considered the Secretary-General's note [A/C.5/55/23] on enhancing the internal oversight mechanisms in operational funds and programmes, pursuant to General Assembly resolution 54/244 [YUN 1999, p. 1274]. The Secretary-General said that the issuance of the report requested in that resolution, updating his 1997 report [YUN 1997, p. 855] on enhancing the internal oversight mechanisms in operational funds and programmes, had been postponed to March 2001 to allow for consultations with funds and programmes on the 1997 recommendations. However, the preliminary information indicated that improvements in oversight functions had been made since 1997. The Secretary-General noted the establishment by UNDP of the Management Review and Oversight Committee, with the participation of the UN Office of Internal Oversight Services (OIOS), which periodically reviewed UNDP's accountability framework and reported to its Executive Board. The Secretary-General intended to make a number of recommendations in his March report for improving the internal oversight functions, including the establishment by all funds and programmes of similar oversight committees.

The Secretary-General's March report [A/55/826 & Corr.1] on enhancing the internal oversight mechanisms in operational funds and programmes was based on the analysis of responses received from funds and programmes with respect to changes in their oversight mechanisms since the 1997 report relating to auditing, evaluation, monitoring (programme performance), inspection, investigation, coordination of oversight activities, monitoring implementation of recommendations and reporting of allegations.

The new information from the funds and programmes indicated that, overall, their internal oversight mechanisms had improved, especially with regard to intensified cooperation between them and OIOS and the adoption of new oversight procedures. Many of the 1997 recommendations were being implemented through differing but viable organizational arrangements for oversight. However, gaps remained concerning other crucial recommendations, including recommendation 3 [YUN 1997, p. 856] relating to budgetary provisions for investigation services provided by OIOS, which had not been implemented. In addition, most funds and programmes depended on

OIOS for their complex investigations because they did not employ professional investigators, had not established their own independent investigations units and had not developed confidential reporting procedures to protect those who made reports in good faith or were the subject of such reports. Regarding the auditing function, some of the funds and programmes had separate audit units functioning with sufficient operational independence, which enabled them to improve the extent and depth of their coverage.

To further enhance the oversight coverage of those funds and programmes, while guaranteeing OIOS the resources for its services, particularly regarding investigations and audit services, the Secretary-General proposed a new set of recommendations.

Recommendation 1A called for the establishment of a budgetary provision for all aspects of oversight coverage at each existing entity and the creation of new entities to ensure that the responsibility and source of funding for oversight were clearly identified.

Recommendation 1B called for the establishment of a mechanism to reimburse OIOS fully for investigations and audit services and, in special cases, for other services it provided to funds and programmes. That would require each fund and programme to enter into a memorandum of understanding specifying the level of service to be provided, based on a standard cost of service, including indirect costs incurred (travel, equipment and training, among others).

Recommendation 2 called for the establishment of an oversight committee at each entity, with appropriate terms of reference and with OIOS representation, to strengthen information exchange and coordination on internal oversight.

The Assembly, in **resolution 55/259** of 14 June (see p. 1282), deferred until its fifty-sixth session consideration of the Secretary-General's March report and requested him to seek updated views on the report from the funds and programmes.

Financing of operational activities in 2000

Expenditures of the UN system on operational activities, excluding loans and grants through the World Bank Group, totalled $6.5 billion in 2000 [A/56/70/Add.2-E/2001/58/Add.2], the most recent year for which figures were available, as compared with $6 billion in 1999 and $5.3 billion in 1998. Of the 2000 amount, $1,917.6 million was distributed in development grants by UNDP or UNDP-administered funds, $1,553.3 million by specialized agencies and other organizations from extrabudgetary sources, $1,491.1 million by WFP, $885 million by UNICEF, $469.6 million by specialized agencies and other organizations from regular budgets (mostly the World Health Organization (WHO)) and $134.1 million by UNFPA.

By region, $2,156 million of the total development grants, excluding those by the International Fund for Agricultural Development (IFAD) and self-supporting programmes, went to Africa, $1,351 million to Asia and the Pacific, $1,311 million to Latin America and the Caribbean, $301 million to Europe and $838 million to Western Asia. Some $493 million went to interregional and global programmes and other countries not classified elsewhere, including those of the Commonwealth of Independent States (CIS).

Contributions for operational activities from Governments and other sources, excluding contributions to IFAD and government "self-supporting" contributions, reached $7.2 billion in 2000, as compared to $6.9 billion in 1999 and $5.7 billion in 1998.

The UNDP Administrator, in an August report on UN system technical cooperation expenditure in 2000 [DP/2001/30 & Corr.1 & Add.1], stated that the delivery of $6.5 billion in technical cooperation in 2000 was the highest ever, up by 7.4 per cent from 1999, due mainly to the spectacular growth rate of 32.6 per cent recorded by the executing and specialized agencies. As a group, they surpassed the $2 billion mark for the first time and achieved the highest share of expenditures at 31.4 per cent. The significant increase in the delivery figure for that group was generated by WHO, which represented 39 per cent of the total expenditure.

In terms of sector distribution, 26 per cent of the aggregate, or $1.7 billion, was deployed for humanitarian assistance, 21 per cent, or $1.4 billion, for health, and 10 per cent, or $631.1 million, for agriculture.

The UNDP/UNFPA Executive Board, on 14 September [E/2001/35 (dec. 2001/17)], took note of the Administrator's report.

At the 2001 United Nations Pledging Conference for Development Activities (New York, 7 November) [A/CONF.196/3], Governments made pledges to UN programmes and funds concerned with development. The Conference noted that several Governments were not in a position to announce their contributions, but proposed to communicate their announcement of such contributions to the Secretary-General as soon as they were in a position to do so.

The Secretary-General provided a statement of contributions pledged or paid at the 2000 Pledging Conference, as at 30 June, to 29 funds and programmes [A/CONF.193/2]. The total amounted to some $1,067 million, of which $450 million was pledged to UNDP.

Technical cooperation through UNDP

The UNDP Administrator, in his annual report for 2001, which included the results-oriented annual report (ROAR) [DP/2002/15 & Add.1,2], said that UNDP's vision, as outlined by the Administrator in his Business Plans, 2000-2003 [YUN 1999, p. 802], and its contribution to the implementation of the millennium development goals, set out in General Assembly resolution 55/2 [YUN 2000, p. 49], in particular the commitment to halve global poverty by 2015, were translated into concrete results in 2001 throughout UNDP activities, notably in Brazil, Burkina Faso and Gujarat, India.

That new vision was achieved through a worldwide knowledge-management system, comprising nine subregional resource facilities (SURFs) established in Addis Ababa (Ethiopia), Bangkok (Thailand), Beirut (Lebanon), Bratislava (Slovakia), Harare (Zimbabwe), Kathmandu (Nepal), Port of Spain (Trinidad and Tobago), Dakar (Senegal) and Panama. SURFs provided timely, high-quality substantive support to all country offices, including policy advisory services to programme countries, technical backstopping to country offices, access to substantive programme-related information, networking and information-sharing, and identification, documentation and dissemination of best practices in UNDP focus areas. A survey of the performance of SURFs and of the 37 existing knowledge networks on areas from microfinance to community governance showed a growing rate of client satisfaction as country offices had begun to share knowledge and expertise. The expert network had facilitated and extended the organization's expert capacity and outreach. In 2001, over 1,400 referrals were fielded by the SURFs and networks, with an average response time of under three days.

With regard to conflict and post-conflict situations, the Administrator created the Bureau for Crisis Prevention and Recovery in 2001 to respond better to the demands placed on the organization and to allow UNDP to play its role fully in partnership with international and national actors. The Bureau ensured proactive and responsive systems for handling special development situations.

Advocacy was central to UNDP activities through policy advice and the promotion of dialogue on key global and national issues. The *Human Development Report 2001* [Sales No. E.01.III.B.1] (see p. 767) contributed to the international debate on development issues. With UNDP support, national human development reports took the *Report*'s approach to the national level by promoting the mainstreaming of the human development concept in national policy dialogue.

UNDP continued to build strategic partnerships with the UN system, international financial institutions, civil society organizations, foundations and the private sector. One of the most notable partnership developments with the UN system in 2001 was the compact agreed between DESA and UNDP for the mutual reinforcement of their distinct but complementary roles, particularly in pursuing the millennium development goals. Cooperation with the Bretton Woods institutions, in particular the World Bank, developed significantly as the organizations worked together on poverty reduction strategies. UNDP further developed cooperation with regional development banks, especially the African Development Bank and the Asian Development Bank, and also strengthened its partnership with the United Nations Foundation (see p. 810). UNDP focused on promoting South-South cooperation, using information and communication technology (ICT) for development and engaging with civil society and private sector partners. There was a concerted effort in 2001 to develop policy-based partnerships with civil society organizations (CSOs) from both North and South, which were important in building UNDP's profile as a policy and advocacy organization. CSO consultations addressed such issues as globalization, trade, poverty reduction strategies, pro-poor budgeting and the millennium development goals. UNDP stepped up efforts to mobilize and engage the business sector, developing a comprehensive toolkit for collaboration with that sector. It also prepared a strategy for introducing the Secretary-General's Global Compact [YUN 2000, p. 989] at the country level, which included outreach and advocacy, policy dialogue, partnership projects and learning. UNDP facilitated the introduction of the Compact in some 20 countries in 2001. In addition, UNDP developed concrete partnership projects with the business sector, particularly in the Democratic Republic of the Congo, Iran and Malaysia.

In November 2001, the Administrator was called upon to lead the early recovery effort in Afghanistan (see p. 265). UNDP supported the Secretary-General's Special Representative, assisted the Afghan Interim Administration and strengthened the organization's presence in the country. It also assisted the Deputy Special Representative for Relief, Recovery and Reconstruction.

UNDP regular resources experienced an important turnaround in 2001 (see p. 805). In addition to increased pledges, including multi-year pledges, most donors made payments according to schedules communicated to the organization, with major donors making early payments, resulting in a much-improved liquidity position. In 2001, UNDP established the thematic trust funds as a flexible co-financing instrument designed to attract additional funding in the areas of democratic governance, poverty reduction, crisis prevention and recovery, ICT, energy and environment and HIV/AIDS, so as to facilitate greater substantive alignment of UNDP activities around those areas. The facility allowed programmable funds, not readily available either from regular resources or from other multi-bilateral funding at the country level, to be channelled into a consistent set of development interventions across countries and regions, particularly the least developed countries and Africa.

UNDP/UNFPA Executive Board

In 2001, the UNDP/UNFPA Executive Board held two regular sessions (26 January and 29 January–6 February, and 10-14 September) and an annual session (11-22 June), all in New York [E/2001/35].

At the first regular session, the Board adopted seven decisions, including one that gave an overview of the Board's action taken at that session [E/2001/35 (dec. 2001/7)]. Other decisions dealt with UNDP's role in crisis and post-conflict situations (see p. 802); technical cooperation among developing countries (see p. 818); follow-up to the recommendations contained in the reports of the Board of Auditors for 1998-1999 on UNDP, UNFPA and the United Nations Office for Project Services (UNOPS) (see pp. 808, 1000 and 814, respectively); and proposed financial regulations concerning contributions from non-governmental sources (see p. 809).

The Executive Board, at its annual session, adopted five decisions. In addition to an overview decision summarizing the action taken during that session [dec. 2001/12], the Board adopted decisions on the annual report of the UNOPS Executive Director (see p. 812), the UNDP/UNFPA programming process (see p. 799) and the UNFPA information and communication strategy and strategic plan for HIV/AIDS for 2001-2005 (see p. 996).

At its second regular session, the Board adopted five decisions, including an overview decision [dec. 2001/17]. The others concerned UNDP

budget estimates for 2002-2003 (see p. 808), the UNOPS revised budget for 2000-2001 and budget estimates for 2002-2003 (see p. 813), assistance to Myanmar (see p. 794) and UNFPA budget estimates for 2002-2003 (see p. 999).

The Economic and Social Council, by **decision 2001/226** of 10 July, took note of the Board's reports on its first regular and annual sessions.

UNDP/UNFPA reports

In June [dec. 2001/12], the UNDP/UNFPA Executive Board took note of the Administrator's 2000 annual report, including the ROAR for that year [YUN 2000, p. 824].

By **decision 2001/226** of 10 July, the Economic and Social Council took note of the annual reports of the UNDP Administrator and the UNFPA Executive Director to the Council [E/2001/10].

UNDP operational activities

Country programmes

The UNDP/UNFPA Executive Board, at its first regular session in February [dec. 2001/7], took note of the report on assistance to Myanmar [DP/2001/5] and requested the Administrator, taking into account the findings of the independent assessment mission to Myanmar, to submit a proposal for continued UNDP assistance to that country (see p. 794). The Board approved the first country cooperation framework (CCF) for Turkey and the second CCFs for Bangladesh, Belarus, Bosnia and Herzegovina, Cambodia, Croatia, Georgia, Latvia, Lithuania, Mauritius, the Russian Federation, St. Helena, Saudi Arabia and Uganda. It took note of the first extensions of CCFs for Burundi, Kuwait, the Lao People's Democratic Republic, the Libyan Arab Jamahiriya, Rwanda and the Syrian Arab Republic. It approved second CCF extensions for Eritrea, Estonia and the Republic of Moldova; a second extension of the first regional cooperation framework for Europe and CIS; and the second global cooperation framework. The Board took note of country reviews for Lesotho, Lithuania, Nepal and Yemen and the first regional cooperation framework for the Arab States.

At its annual session in June [dec. 2001/12], the Board approved the second CCFs for the former Yugoslav Republic of Macedonia and Tajikistan and the second extension of the first CCF for Ukraine. It took note of the first extensions of CCFs for Algeria, Lesotho and Namibia, and reports on field visits to Honduras [DP/2001/CRP.6] and to Bosnia and Herzegovina [DP/2001/CRP.7].

At its second regular session, the Board, on 14 September [dec. 2001/15], took note of the proposals made in the Administrator's note on future assistance to Myanmar [DP/2001/27] and approved continued funding of UNDP project activities for Myanmar from target for resource assignment from the core (TRAC) funding (approximately $22 million). It authorized the Administrator to approve, on a project-by-project basis, human development index (HDI) project extensions up to $50 million if additional funding from non-core resources became available, and to mobilize non-core resources for HDI activities proposed for the 2002-2004 programme planning period.

On the same date [dec. 2001/17], the Board approved the second regional cooperation framework for Asia and the Pacific, the first sub-regional cooperation framework for the Caribbean and the second extension of the first CCF for Argentina. It approved second CCFs for Bhutan, Brazil, Burkina Faso, Burundi, Chad, Chile, China, the Democratic People's Republic of Korea, the Gambia, Guatemala, Indonesia, Lesotho, Malawi, Mongolia, Mozambique, Nepal, Peru, the Republic of Moldova, Senegal, Sri Lanka, Swaziland, Togo, the United Republic of Tanzania, Uruguay and Zambia, and took note of country review reports for Brazil, the Democratic People's Republic of Korea, Egypt, Ghana, Guyana and the Republic of Moldova, as well as a report on Nauru: earmarkings from TRAC [DP/2001/31]. The Board took note of the first extensions of CCFs for Benin, the Comoros, Côte d'Ivoire, Fiji, Ghana, India, Kiribati, the Marshall Islands, Mauritania, Micronesia, Niue, Palau, Papua New Guinea, Samoa, Solomon Islands, Tonga, Tuvalu and Vanuatu.

UNDP performance analysis by goal

The Administrator reported in the ROAR for 2001 [DP/2002/15 & Add.1,2] on UNDP's performance in its six goals: creating an enabling environment for sustainable human development; reduction of poverty; environmentally sustainable development; advancement of women and gender equality; special development situations; and UNDP support to the United Nations. The report also provided an analysis of three sub-goals: under goal 3, sustainable environmental management and energy development to improve conditions for the poor; under goal 4, advancement of women by implementing global commitments; and under goal 6, increasingly collaborative, efficient and effective operational activities for development.

The Administrator, in his summary of the 2001 ROAR general conclusions, said that the emerging picture from all six goals was that the achievement of sustainable and pro-poor development required UNDP to be more proactive in influencing policies, laws and socio-economic practices. That in turn called for more outcome-oriented and consensual partnerships with civil society and the private sector and with Governments. Integral to that aim was the need to ensure national ownership in order to sustain capacity-development efforts, to prompt policy change and to implement policy commitments.

Policy advice and capacity development currently constituted the main forms of UNDP cooperation, but each had distinct challenges. Obtaining high levels of performance in results through policy advice required national commitment at the highest levels, combined with the ability to sustain such results over an extended period of time. Capacity development, on the other hand, which was central to ownership and sustainability, demanded sustained and relatively costly support over long periods.

Effective partnership management was emphasized in the report. However, there was still a sizeable gap in many cases between good results at the output levels within each goal of the strategic results framework and their contribution to realizing larger development outcomes, reflecting the challenges of marshalling other development partners in order to achieve the envisaged outcomes. Similarly, UN country teams needed to move past coordination of programmes to actual joint efforts to realize mutually reinforcing development results. UNDP should make a concerted effort to cultivate partnerships in the international community that contributed to lasting development outcomes at the country level, rather than simply generating agency-specific outputs.

In 2001, results-based management principles were incorporated throughout UNDP's programming, and guided major initiatives to simplify business practices and reduce transaction costs. The main instruments in UNDP programming had been revised to reflect a results-driven approach, as had evaluation policies and tools. With better strategic planning and assessment of performance, UNDP was better equipped to respond to changing needs and priorities. While results orientation was taking hold in the organization, the potential for informing policy change and managerial supervision had yet to be fully realized. UNDP was receiving increasing requests from Governments and development partners to share its experiences as they initiated their own performance management systems. UNDP should develop its in-house capacity to respond to that demand. Its experience in results-based management could potentially be transformed into distinct support to programme Governments, the UN family and the wider development community. Within the organization, greater attention was paid to realigning resources and activities to influence greater change in policy, laws and socio-economic practices in the context of strengthening the capacities of institutions and societies to manage their own development processes. Serious challenges remained in a number of areas, notably gender, and the organization needed to attach high priority to partnerships if its good performance at the output level was to translate into strong and sustained progress towards outcomes.

Creating an enabling environment for SHD

In 2001, UNDP support for creating an enabling environment for sustainable human development (SHD) confirmed its emphasis on assistance to democratic transition. UNDP supported governance initiatives in 145 countries through the coordination of donor support to electoral processes, the facilitation of national dialogue and the promotion of civil society participation in political reform. However, its mixed performance in achieving lasting change suggested that greater attention was required in such areas as building national commitment to post-election reforms, and emphasized the need for closer partnerships with local actors in civil society and government.

The ROAR 2001 indicated that national human development reports (NHDRs) were being used in a growing number of instances in setting public policy, in orienting public representatives and officials and in school curricula development. Country offices were using NHDRs to advocate changes to policy and laws to make them more pro-poor and pro-women, and there was greater use of gender-disaggregated data in NHDRs and other UNDP publications, particularly in Latin America and the Caribbean where such data had been integrated into 23 NHDRs.

Support to ICT for development had become increasingly sophisticated, while the demand to establish basic connectivity and more conventional uses remained. Innovative application of ICT for democratic governance included increasing people's access to data on financial and productive resources, land registration, tax administration, small business registration and public-resource management.

UNDP cooperation in local governance expanded in 2001, with 42 country offices reporting sharp increases in strategic interventions in decentralization. Interaction with other UN organizations in subnational governance was more evident, particularly with the United Nations

Capital Development Fund (UNCDF) in local development planning to promote accountable fiscal devolution. Regional programmes provided value-added contributions to provincial and municipal governance, notably in Asia and the Pacific.

Despite those achievements, lasting results were sometimes mixed, even when UNDP delivered its own outputs at reasonable levels, due, in part, to a number of constraints in governance, including uneven national commitment. Those constraints pointed to the need to establish and manage productive partnerships, especially in situations where there was a growing volume of activity, as in local governance, and in more nascent and sensitive areas, such as in fighting corruption and in promoting human rights for marginalized or minority communities. Further attention was needed in three areas: human security and youth at risk; the application of performance-based methods of assessment in UNDP support to greater efficiency in public administrations; and interventions supporting globalization, private sector reform and regional development cooperation. Reported results in those areas increased on average by 60 per cent.

Reduction of poverty

UNDP's commitment in 2001 to supporting the preparation of national poverty reduction strategies, including poverty reduction strategy papers (PRSPs), was clearly demonstrated by its collaboration with Governments and other partners to strengthen national poverty reduction strategies in 85 countries. Involvement in the PRSP process increased from 11 countries in 1999 to 36 in 2001, with over half of those in sub-Saharan Africa. Country offices fully or partially achieved 90 per cent of their annual output targets for 2001, which contributed to the achievement of 78 per cent of outcomes.

UNDP enhanced the participation of stakeholders in poverty reduction processes in 25 countries. It chaired or co-chaired national steering committees on reducing poverty, and facilitated the review of interim PRSPs by CSOs and non-governmental organizations (NGOs).

Almost half of the results in poverty monitoring linked monitoring with efforts to promote policy change or inform policy formulation, up from a quarter in 1999, thus reflecting the increasing integration of assessments and monitoring within the policy process and UNDP's commitment to support the assessment of progress towards achieving the millennium development goals. Also within the poverty goal, there was evidence of the impact of UNDP's work on HIV/AIDS in sub-Saharan Africa. The sub-goal addressing national anti-poverty strategies, pro-poor macroeconomic policies, poverty monitoring and HIV/AIDS accounted for 60 per cent of UNDP results in poverty reduction.

The other sub-goal that addressed the human, physical and financial asset base of the poor included activities to promote greater access by the poor to key physical and financial assets, basic social services, systems of risk management, ICT for poverty reduction and support for sustainable livelihoods. The United Nations Volunteers (UNV) programme continued to be an important partner in UNDP's poverty reduction efforts.

UNDP needed to pay more attention to the pro-poor and pro-women focus of HIV/AIDS and ICT interventions because, despite its efforts to mainstream HIV/AIDS issues into strategies for reducing poverty and gender inequities in some countries, it did not systematically address those areas in 2001. The regional variation in UNDP's HIV/AIDS work highlighted the need for greater sharing of experience and knowledge between countries and within UNDP and for greater South-South cooperation. Another cause for concern was the low level and unstructured nature of the organization's engagement in access to assets. Many partnerships in that area were limited to traditional arrangements for resource mobilization and project implementation. Reporting on cross-cutting issues, such as those between poverty reduction and environment, was not strong, and, while UNDP was developing capacity to generate gender-disaggregated data, there was a need to integrate gender analysis much more systematically and purposefully in its support of poverty reduction. Work on basic social services and on strengthening systems of risk management had tapered off, and a major effort was needed to revive UNDP's contribution in those areas and in efforts to support pro-poor economic growth.

Environmentally sustainable development

Country offices reported results in environmentally sustainable development to reduce human poverty in 139 States, reflecting a high demand for UNDP services in energy and environmental management. Overall, country offices fully or partially achieved 81 per cent of their annual output targets for 2001, reflecting a 71 per cent rate of progress against intended outcomes.

The majority of UNDP outputs addressed national policy and regulatory frameworks for environmental management (60 offices), building institutional frameworks (71 offices) and the development of national capacity for participation in global conventions (68 offices). Capacity development was extended beyond central government ministries to local levels, and efforts were made to integrate international environmental obligations into plans and policies for domestic macroeconomic development and poverty reduction. Only eight country offices, however, reported on environmentally sustainable development with explicit reference to promoting gender equality and empowering women. There were only a few upstream efforts to influence national policies to enhance energy access for the poor. On the other hand, positive results were achieved in sustainable energy development, including several interventions in renewable energy, with funding provided by the Global Environment Facility.

Links between UNDP deliverables in the environment goal and larger development results remained weak, with an unclear sharing of roles and responsibilities within partnerships. Activities needed to be intensified in the monitoring of environmental conditions (17 offices) and in regional environmental management initiatives (21 offices).

Gender equality and advancement of women

Most of UNDP's cooperation for advancement in the status of women and gender equality was related to policy-setting, institution-building, advocacy and monitoring, achieving 66 per cent of outcomes and 65 per cent of outputs. The remaining outcomes and outputs focused on the implementation of the Beijing Platform for Action [YUN 1995, p. 1170] and the Convention on the Elimination of All Forms of Discrimination against Women, adopted by the General Assembly in resolution 34/180 [YUN 1979, p. 895], as well as violence against women.

Joint UNDP/United Nations Development Fund for Women (UNIFEM) interventions, which included support to national policy formulation and institution-building, were reported by 51 offices (57 per cent of the total number of offices). Ninety countries in which UNDP supported programmes (58 per cent of the total) reported gender-specific programmes in 2001, as compared to 75 countries in 2000. However, an additional 29 programme countries (19 per cent) reported gender considerations in programmes within other goals, compared to 37 in 2000. Overall, across all other goals of the strategic results framework, activities with actual results reflecting gender considerations were reported in 119 countries, compared with 112 in 2000.

Forty per cent of all programme countries reported support for the collection of gender-disaggregated data to enhance national reporting and capacity for gender analysis in the 2001

ROAR. The trend for more comprehensive support to the empowerment of women and gender equality continued. Gender-auditing mechanisms for improved implementation of gender policies and law enforcement to ensure women's access to economic decision-making were developed. Moreover, there was an increasing trend in the linking of national plans of action, institutional capacity-development, data collection and implementation of the Convention.

Most gender-mainstreaming interventions were reported under goal 1 (governance) and goal 2 (poverty), while goal 3 (environment), goal 5 (special development situations) and goal 6 (UNDP support to the United Nations) lagged behind. However, interventions relating to the empowerment of women and gender equality in special development situations were increasingly reported under goal 4.

UNDP regional programmes focused on enhancing dialogue and advocacy at regional levels and helped to strengthen partnerships with NGOs and regional and subregional organizations.

In general, the quality of reporting on gender mainstreaming remained weak, which might warrant a review by UNDP of its approach to cooperation in that area.

Knowledge networks and electronic communication enabled UNDP to strengthen its capacity-development support on gender equality, particularly through its UNDP gender-knowledge network, Gender Beat, an electronic newsletter, and the gender-mainstreaming electronic discussion. Regional gender-knowledge networks were further developed along with cross-regional linkages. New areas of intervention included gender-sensitive budgeting, the gender dimension of poverty strategies, social policy and monitoring millennium development goals.

Despite the marginal increase in the number of programme countries reporting gender results in other goals, there was little insight into ways to mainstream gender analysis and gender perspectives effectively. The uncertain progress required a reappraisal of available capacity and current tools and methodologies used to mainstream gender considerations. A UNDP/UNIFEM workshop was held in Ecuador to address that concern.

Special development situations

Sixty-three offices reported in 2001 under the goal of reducing the incidence of and recovery and transition from complex emergencies and natural disasters, compared to 54 in 2000. The development dimension of countries going through or emerging from conflict situations was an increasingly prominent feature of UNDP work, especially in disaster management, human security and community-based recovery. Although UNDP continued to work towards greater integration between community-based activities in post-conflict situations, specifically in the generation of livelihood opportunities, sustainable recovery processes and the reintegration of war-affected populations were still limited. It actively coordinated partners, both among UN organizations and bilateral donors and NGOs, in guiding multi-sectoral recovery programmes and in designing transition programmes in the aftermath of a crisis. UNDP was increasingly the lead player in the rapid design of transition programmes. Most of its work under this goal was in capacity development of institutions, strategy-setting and policy options, empowerment and social cohesion, capacity development data and pilot interventions.

UNDP, with UNV inputs, supported UN activities in major peacekeeping operations, notably in East Timor and the Kosovo province of the Federal Republic of Yugoslavia, but also in the Democratic Republic of the Congo, Eritrea and Sierra Leone. It worked closely with bilateral donor countries in demining, disarmament and demobilization. Support was also provided for special development operations, including mine action and/or justice reform, in Angola, Cambodia, the Congo, Croatia, El Salvador, Yemen and other countries. Technical cooperation in strengthening the capacity for sustainable mine-action programmes remained important for poverty reduction. The opening up of productive land for agriculture facilitated the resumption of productive activities by poor rural communities in Cambodia, the Lao People's Democratic Republic and Thailand.

In countries in special development situations, there were relatively few reported examples where UNDP country offices were able to mainstream gender, poverty and environmental concerns. Eleven per cent of country offices that reported mentioned gender as part of their programme and attempted to incorporate gender into at least one of their outcomes. With the wider range of activities in situations of complex emergencies, it was important to reflect gender issues adequately, since women and children were usually the most vulnerable in conflict and disaster situations. The 2001 reports showed that was an area not receiving enough attention, and the Bureau for Conflict Prevention and Recovery was preparing specific guidelines to redress that shortcoming.

Fourteen per cent of country offices reported on improving coordination in the most challenging of environments. Such emergencies called for a quick and more flexible approach than that implied by the normal CCA/UNDAF process, as the UN plan for the coordination of development aid in a complex emergency context drawn up for the Congo had demonstrated.

A coherent and effective UN system

The results reported in 2001 under the goal of a coherent and effective UN system were similar to those in 2000, confirming some progress in reforms and some new initiatives by a few countries. The advances, however, were not widespread or systemic enough to have a major effect on development results at the country level.

Some 129 country offices (87 per cent of the total) reported positive change for about 50 per cent of outcomes, while annual targets were fully or partially achieved for about 80 per cent of outputs. Divergence between the high rate of output-target achievement and the low level of progress towards outcomes might indicate that offices were focusing more on process than on expected results. With greater inter-agency coherence, emphasis was expected to shift from improving processes to strategic results shared by UN country teams and national counterparts. To that end, steps taken to make collaboration beyond CCA/UNDAF more concrete included the establishment by the United Nations Development Group (UNDG) of programme and management groups to focus on harmonization and simplification issues among UNFPA, UNICEF, UNDP and WFP. The UNDP Group, which included the Special Unit for Technical Cooperation among Developing Countries, UNCDF, UNDP, UNIFEM and UNV, undertook a comparative review of current results-oriented approaches as a step towards closer interaction. Piloting of UN common services at the country level was also under way.

Monitoring the implementation of the global agenda for development was the primary focus of UN country teams in 2001. Integrated support for achieving global goals, however, had not become an important component of follow-up actions. It was expected that millennium development goals would provide a framework and impetus for fostering greater cohesion in UN system activities at the country level. The major challenge was relating the pursuit of those goals to in-country needs and priorities for human development.

Programme planning and management

Reform measures

The UNDP Administrator, in a December report [DP/2002/7], addressed the implementation of the Secretary-General's reform programme and the provisions of the comprehensive triennial policy review of operational activities for development of the UN system for 2001 (see p. 781). The areas covered in the report were: structures and mechanisms; funding and resources; the resident coordinator system; implementation of CCA and UNDAF; harmonization of programming periods and procedures; gender mainstreaming within UNDP; evaluation; and cooperation with the World Bank (see below under each topic). The report also included a discussion of follow-up to international conferences and the Millennium Declaration, and to special economic, humanitarian and disaster relief assistance.

The Administrator reported that UNDG had been restructured to mirror the new United Nations System Chief Executives Board for Coordination (formerly the Administrative Committee on Coordination) (see p. 1364), which should strengthen relations between UNDG and UN system organizations that were not members of UNDG. Five United Nations Houses were designated in 2001 (Japan, Kyrgyzstan, Namibia, Paraguay, Trinidad and Tobago), and funding had been secured for a pilot programme to facilitate the implementation of common services at the country level.

The Administrator also reported that the strengthening of the resident coordinator system remained a top priority for UNDP. The selection process introduced in 2000 [YUN 2000, p. 830] had resulted in a wider pool of resident coordinators, with emphasis on increasing candidates from organizations other than UNDP and the number of female candidates. As at June 2001, of 115 resident coordinators, some 22 (19 per cent) were from organizations other than UNDP and 30 (26 per cent) were women. In late 2001, UNDG determined that 50 per cent of the candidates proposed by all organizations for the resident coordinator assessment should be women.

In terms of the implementation of the CCA/UNDAF, an external evaluation of UNDAFs was undertaken in 2001 by DESA in preparation for the formulation of the Secretary-General's report on the comprehensive triennial policy review of operational activities (see p. 781). On 6 July, the UNDG Executive Committee endorsed 22 recommendations as a follow-up to that assessment, and urged all resident coordinators and UN country teams to review them and the implications for their work at the country level. During the year, CCA and UNDAF were further complemented by the adoption of common strategies on poverty reduction and girls' education and by the issuance of guidelines on joint programmes.

UNDP was designated by the Secretary-General to coordinate country-level assistance from the UN system to monitor progress towards development goals set out in the United Nations Millennium Declaration [YUN 2000, p. 49]. UNDP led the UNDG effort to clarify and define the framework of the millennium development goals, targets and indicators. A guidance note on reporting on the millennium development goals at the country level was adopted by UNDG in November. Reports had been piloted in 13 countries, the first of which, in the United Republic of Tanzania, had been submitted to the Economic and Social Council.

In its efforts to link relief, rehabilitation and development in post-conflict situations (see p. 801), UNDP was introducing the transition recovery programme concept, which involved the mobilization of transition recovery teams, with a view to supporting UN country teams in initiating appropriate and timely support for early recovery.

Programming process

The UNDP Administrator and the UNFPA Executive Director, as requested by the Executive Board in 2000 [YUN 2000, p. 1006], submitted an April report on progress and future options in the programming process [DP/2001/12-DP/FPA/2001/7]. The report reflected the common understanding and vision of UNDG organizations on the harmonization of the programme approval process. It established a number of principles to guide the elaboration of a future programme approval process and presented two options for harmonizing that process. The first would begin with a jointly undertaken and finalized CCA to be used as a basis for drafting the UNDAF, which would be approved by the host Government and the UN country team and submitted to UNDG by the end of January of the last year of the programming cycle. Draft country programme outlines would subsequently be prepared by UNDG partner agencies, highlighting the main components of the proposed country programmes, for presentation to the respective Executive Boards; the Boards would approve resource allocation and authorize the finalization of the country programmes. The time frame for completing that process was 17 months. The second option would follow the same steps as the first, but, after approval of the UNDAF by the host Government and the UN country teams, agency-specific strategy notes would be drafted for submission to the individual Executive Boards for review. That would be followed either by finalization and submission of the final country programmes to the January sessions of the Executive Boards

for final approval on a no-objection basis or by the presentation of an omnibus report to the Executive Boards reflecting Board comments on the respective programmes. That report would also contain financial allocations and an intended results matrix for each country programme for Board approval. The time frame for the second option would be 20 months.

UNDP and UNFPA expressed a preference for the first option, as it would meet the principle of simplifying the current process so as to reduce the burden imposed on programme countries and UN country teams. In that regard, the Administrator, in June [DP/2001/CRP.11], presented a number of proposals designed to ensure that the introduction of new instruments and methods of work did not add to the transaction costs faced by programme countries and country offices. Those proposals included elimination of the advisory note in all countries, first introduced in the 1996 programming guidelines [YUN 1996, p. 780], which preceded the preparation of the CCA. In those countries without a CCA or UNDAF, alternative analyses would form the basis of consultations with the Government and other local partners. Assuming that option 1 (above) on the proposed new programming approval process would be adopted by the Executive Board, the Administrator suggested that the programming period of a country would be agreed on by the UN country team and the respective Government; the country programme outline, although similar to a CCF, would be shorter, with cross references and hypertext links; the final country programme document would consist mainly of a results matrix, showing planned outcomes and indicators and key outputs, and would be fully aligned with the strategic results framework and updated annually; and multi-country CCFs for countries that shared similar characteristics and that had relatively small programmes and wished to proceed in that way. He also proposed a standardized format for the notes by the Administrator on which the Board based its decisions regarding countries in special circumstances that were unable to prepare a CCF, and the presentation, together as short summary reports at each session of the Board, of one-year CCF extensions approved by the Administrator and reported to the Board, and those for two or more years submitted to the Board directly for approval.

The UNDP/UNFPA Executive Board, on 22 June [dec. 2001/11], emphasized that the programming process should be country-led and country-driven, based on national priorities and needs. It encouraged programme countries to use the CCA/UNDAF process, on a pilot basis, as a common planning framework for UN operational activities at the country level, from 2002. The Board decided that the common programming process would be based on the existing common planning framework and that national Governments would develop the country outlines of the respective organizations in consultation with relevant UN agencies and other partners. The draft country outlines, highlighting priorities, strategies, outcomes and proposed budget, would be presented to the annual session of the Executive Board, and, where applicable, the CCA/UNDAF would be made available for information. The Executive Board would review the draft country outlines, on which the UNDP Administrator and the UNFPA Executive Director would assist the Government in finalizing the country programmes, which would be posted on the World Wide Web by October of the last year of the country programme, and approved in January of the following year on a no-objection basis, unless at least five members requested the Board's special consideration.

The Board requested the Administrator and the Executive Director to report in 2003 on tools to monitor progress and evaluate outcomes/results of country programmes with a view to further harmonizing and standardizing the programming process, and in 2004 on progress in implementing its decision. UNDG was asked to refine the programming process further, taking into account the comments of the respective Executive Boards.

In December [DP/2002/7], the Administrator and the Executive Director informed all country teams of the new common programming procedures and provided guidance to them on the preparation of country programme outlines and country programmes. With the adoption of a common programming procedure for UNDP and UNFPA, it was expected that the UNICEF and WFP Executive Boards would consider a harmonized programme approval process in 2002.

UNDP Business Plans, 2000-2003

At its January/February session [E/2001/35], the UNDP/UNFPA Executive Board had before it an update of the UNDP Business Plans, 2000-2003 [DP/2001/CRP.2], which presented results achieved in 2000.

Among those results were the restructuring of the Bureau for Development Policy (BDP) to focus on policy advice and its transformation into a service-oriented, decentralized unit, the establishment of a National Human Development Report Unit at headquarters, and the preparation of the strategy on UNDP's role in post-conflict situations (see p. 801). Other significant developments included the creation of the new Bureau

for Resources and Strategic Partnerships and the formulation of a strategy for partnership with the private sector. Partnership surveys were launched to better assess partners' perception of UNDP's role and performance. A headquarters-wide functional review was undertaken, leading to a redefinition of functions and posts, the launch of a 360-degree feedback programme, and the introduction of results and competency assessment as a replacement for the performance appraisal review system.

On 5 February [dec. 2001/7], the Executive Board took note of the update.

A December report [DP/2002/CRP.2], describing results achieved in 2001, indicated that the transformation of BDP proceeded as planned.

One of its core programmes, the Office to Combat Desertification and Drought, was relocated to Nairobi, Kenya, and 13 staff were redeployed to the field and 31 policy specialists were outposted. Headquarters staff was reduced by 39 per cent and further reductions and outpostings were planned. Thematic trust funds were established to attract additional funding in the areas of governance, poverty reduction, crisis prevention and recovery, ICT, energy and environment, and HIV/AIDS, with a view to facilitating greater alignment of UNDP activities around those themes. Thirty-seven knowledge networks were currently active, seven of them representing UNDP's core thematic areas of governance, poverty, environment, information technology, HIV/AIDS, microfinance and NHDRs. UNDP strengthened its partnerships with other UN organizations, in particular through participation in UNDG and its programme and management groups, and maintained its cooperation with the Bretton Woods institutions. A partnership facility was created to develop new partnerships and strengthen existing ones at the country level. UNDP mobilized $450,000 for that purpose. Partnership surveys conducted in 17 countries revealed that UNDP had a positive image at the country level and was seen as a valuable partner. However, organizational effectiveness and responsiveness could be improved. Only 52 per cent of the respondents had a positive assessment of UNDP's operational performance. Responsiveness and client orientation also emerged as a weak area.

UNDP's downsizing and workforce renewal continued in 2001. Through a large-scale voluntary separation package, some 415 agreed separations took place in country offices and an additional 20 were planned. At the same time, a new generation of 19 professionals was hired through the leadership development programme. At headquarters, the net staff reduction was expected by year-end to reach 22 per cent of the targeted 25 per cent reduction. The results and competency assessment was redesigned to strengthen results orientation and better define competencies and development needs. An exercise was conducted in 2001 to interconnect programme, management and performance assessment instruments, with the objective of encouraging country offices to use a single results-based management system to plan, monitor and report on their work. Strategic results frameworks (SRFs) were used to plan for development outcomes, while management results were captured through the scorecard/management-results framework. UNDP finalized an ICT strategy for the period 2002-2005 to strengthen its country offices network through reliable and efficient tools to communicate and share data, experience and knowledge.

Country office performance was a priority for the organization in 2001. The New Horizons initiative, a package of corporate support to country offices, helped to align the structures and capacity of those offices with the transformational agenda set out in the Business Plans. Some $14 million was disbursed for country offices support and over 125 missions were fielded. Country offices were also able to realign their human and financial resources with the service lines of the new UNDP business model: coordination with the UN system; advocacy and advisory services; and development services. The accent put on the need to reduce operational costs resulted in a substantial increase in the cost-recovery scheme in 2001. Staff capacity was strengthened in organizational development, resulting in a strong, internal consulting capacity at headquarters and in country offices.

The report concluded that the first two years of implementation of the Business Plans had focused on the internal reforms necessary to build a new UNDP. Special emphasis was given to downsizing, restructuring and aligning resources and staff capacities with organizational requirements both at headquarters and in country offices. Further work in that area was expected, along with the re-engineering of business processes and the development of a new ICT platform.

UNDP role in crisis and post-conflict situations

In response to the Executive Board's request [YUN 2000, p. 832], UNDP submitted a report on the role of the organization in crisis and post-conflict (CPC) situations [DP/2001/4 & Corr.1]. UNDP found that the increased incidence and risk of violent conflict and natural disaster in programme countries had led to an increase in the demand for its services in CPC environments. Since 1997, funding from TRAC line 1.1.3 had provided a financial backbone for UNDP CPC activities, providing $155 million in assistance for 250 projects across all regions, of which 43 per cent had been allocated to community recovery projects, 25 per cent to disaster mitigation and response, 11 per cent to peace processes, 8 per cent to mine action, 7 per cent to institutional support and 3 per cent to coordination and preparation of strategic frameworks. UNDP was also successful in mobilizing non-core funds estimated at $100 million to $150 million each year. While UNDP had been active in CPC situations for several decades, the environment in which it was operating had changed. Reforms at the United Nations, calls for a shift to a "culture of prevention", a new system-wide approach to peace missions and a growing body of experience on the shortcomings of the current handling of transition processes were some of the forces that required UNDP to update its strategy for dealing with such situations.

The lessons learned and experiences gained posed two challenges. The first was the need for improved coherence in all UNDP activities, particularly within its portfolio of development activities for CPC situations and between its CPC activities and that of the work of the organization in its wider poverty eradication efforts. The second challenge was the issue of an effective UNDP response to challenges in prevention, recovery and coordination of the CPC environment. The role of UNDP in CPC situations was strictly limited to addressing the development dimensions of those situations, within the broader mission of enabling sustainable social and economic development. With its emphasis on local capacity-building, needs identification and management, the work in that area did not differ significantly from activities in the regular work programme. However, the way in which UNDP operated had to differ in such circumstances. Reforms to corporate systems that involved staff competencies, deployment, resource management and mobilization and programming procedures were under way to bolster the operational performance of the organization. Better-integrated headquarters backstopping for country offices and closer oversight by senior managers would ensure greater discipline in regard to corporate policies coupled with incentives to reward staff that performed well in those duty stations. Those reforms complemented the 2001 change management process launched by the Administrator in his Business Plans (see above). The commitment of the Executive Board was also required to support the realignment of such programmes through financial and in-kind resources and political support. With those measures in place, UNDP would be in a position to take a strong leadership role in international aid operations in CPC situations and to support programme countries effectively in their efforts towards building durable peace and sustainable development.

On 5 February [dec. 2001/1], the Executive Board took note of the report on the UNDP role in CPC situations. The Board recognized that crisis prevention and disaster mitigation should be integral parts of sustainable human development strategies and that UNDP had relevant operational experience in CPC situations. The Board reiterated its concern about the low level of UNDP core resources and requested the Administrator to take steps to augment those resources. UNDP was encouraged to promote the importance of a long-term development perspective, and, in its capacity as manager of the resident coordinator system, it was requested to strengthen its coordinating role and its cooperation with other UN entities.

In December [DP/2002/7], the Administrator reported that, in its effort to link relief, rehabilitation and development in post-conflict and natural disaster situations, UNDP was introducing a transition recovery programme concept involving the dispatch of transition recovery teams to support UN country teams in initiating appropriate and timely support for early recovery. Within the UN system, UNDP was responsible for providing capacity-building assistance to mine-affected countries and addressing the socio-economic aspects of landmine contamination. In 2001, UNDP undertook capacity-building activities in 16 countries and raised over $30 million to support them. UNDP continued to strengthen regional, national and local capacities in natural disaster prevention, preparedness, mitigation and recovery. In 2001, that included support to over 50 programmes at the country and regional levels.

UNDP funding

Multi-year funding framework

In August [DP/2001/25], UNDP provided an update on the multi-year funding framework (MYFF) and its revised 2000-2003 integrated resources framework (IRF) [YUN 1999, p. 806], which brought together all funding sources covering programme, programme support, management and administration and support to UN operational activities. The revision took into account actual performance in 2000 and updated projections for 2001-2003. The report presented the revised IRF and highlighted some implications for

UNDP. As agreed in 2000 [YUN 2000, p. 833], the UNDP/UNFPA Executive Board considered the revised IRF in conjunction with the 2002-2003 biennial budget. Based on the levels of voluntary contributions to regular resources in 1999 and 2000, the projections for 2002 and 2003 of $1 billion and $1.1 billion, respectively, were adjusted to $800 million and $900 million, respectively. Those figures would become the revised income projections for 2002-2003, amounting to a regular resource base of $1.7 billion for the biennium, reflecting a two-year delay in achieving the initial voluntary-contribution targets. However, based on recent increases by the majority of donors, the level of voluntary contributions was expected to increase in 2001 following annual declines over eight consecutive years.

Total income projections underlying the IRF for 2000-2003 amounted to $9.4 billion, comprising: $5.6 billion in donor resources, of which $3 billion was projected for voluntary contributions to regular core resources and $2.6 billion for third-party co-financing, and $3.8 billion for programme-country cost-sharing. The net support budget covering all budgetary categories was 21 per cent of total donor resources.

The erosion of regular resources over the past years had impaired UNDP's ability to produce the development outcomes envisioned in the CCFs and in the strategic results framework of the MYFF. The funding shortfall also threatened the organization's ability to sustain a strong global platform and a universal country presence on behalf of the UN system and the wider international community. It was therefore crucial to place UNDP on a stable financial footing in terms of both regular and other resources.

In September [dec. 2001/17], the Executive Board took note of the report on the update on the MYFF and revised IRF.

Programming arrangements

In response to an Executive Board request [YUN 1999, p. 808], the Administrator, in April [DP/2001/CRP.10], issued a conference room paper on issues and principles for possible improvements in the current arrangements for programme financing. The purpose of the paper was to initiate the consultative process leading to a Board decision in 2002 that would confirm or replace the current programming arrangements, as outlined in 1995 [YUN 1995, p. 895], for 2004 and beyond. The current system used the TRAC resource distribution model, with each recipient country allocated a base amount (TRAC line 1.1.1), a possible additional allocation (TRAC line 1.1.2) and a special allocation for countries in special development circumstances to be assigned on the basis of need (TRAC line 1.1.3). The Administrator outlined the principles and issues to be considered in future improvements to current programming arrangements around the themes: a focus on the poorest countries, and performance and flexibility.

In June [dec. 2001/12], the Board took note of the paper.

Evaluation

The UNDP Administrator, in a July report [DP/2001/26], described progress achieved by the organization in three strategic areas of evaluation: aligning monitoring and evaluation practices with results-based management (RBM) principles; strengthening substantive accountability; and promoting organizational learning and partnerships. The report also presented the organization's substantive performance results from evidence on macro-level performance based on project evaluation data, and completed evaluations from UNDP and its associated funds and programmes. The report presented future strategic directions to meet the challenges for the role of evaluation in contributing to organizational and development effectiveness.

UNDP achieved positive results in advancing RBM tools and methodologies across all levels of its operations. It made progress in refining the strategic results framework , in improving the methodology on which the 2000 ROAR was prepared, and in aligning monitoring and evaluation practices with results-oriented approaches designed to achieve a more transparent and verifiable assessment of performance. UNDP drew on the experience and lessons learned through country-office operations in furthering those RBM methodological innovations. Both accountability and organizational learning had contributed to the UNDP culture of performance. UNDP initiated the development of a knowledge-management strategy to serve as a driving force for improved organizational and development effectiveness.

The report pointed out UNDP efforts to understand how organizational effectiveness was translated into development impact. An element of that challenge was investing in partnerships, working with other evaluation agencies and building evaluation capacity in developing countries.

In response to a 1998 Board decision [YUN 1998, p. 824], the Administrator submitted a June note containing an executive summary of the evaluation of UNDP's non-core resources and the Administrator's comments thereon [DP/2001/CRP.12].

The report noted that, while UNDP had experienced a sharp decline in core expenditure over the past decade, its non-core resources (government and third-party cost-sharing, and trust funds) had emerged as a substantial funding source, representing 75 per cent of its total expenditures. Non-core resources were not driven by need, but responded to supply and demand factors: on the supply side, by donors pursuing their respective political mandates and promoting their own projects in the thematic areas of their choice; and on the demand side, by requests of Governments to finance their own programmes and projects. From the evidence, non-core funding would continue to grow and to pressure the traditional institutional aid environment. UNDP would therefore have to change and adapt to a situation that was competitive and focused on results and effectiveness. That left little choice for the organization but to position itself, or the funds would go elsewhere. UNDP's ability to do that was closely linked to the further upgrading of its technical and managerial capacity and the use of performance-driven incentives.

The evaluation recommended strengthening the links between core and non-core funding, particularly in the country-level programming process, addressing the core/non-core funding imbalance, re-examining the relationship between core and non-core funding and devising a more balanced approach to their use. UNDP should have the flexibility to attract additional funding centrally to finance global or regional concerns not adequately covered by core funding and to adopt a competitive positioning strategy to attract and manage those funds. The organization should adopt a differentiated approach to resource mobilization that was specific to and consistent with the social, economic and political conditions in each region, in strong partnerships with key bilateral and multilateral agencies. The organization should also adapt systems to increase its efficiency and accountability, making it an attractive organization with which to do business.

The Administrator, in his general remarks, expressed broad agreement with the recommendations of the evaluation.

Also in June [DP/2001/CRP.13], UNDP submitted to the Executive Board an evaluation of direct execution, which assessed UNDP's experience as an executing agent. Direct execution constituted a very small portion of UNDP business (just 5 per cent of total UNDP project value between 1995 and 2000), but commanded great attention, especially when national execution was the norm. That raised a number of questions, including the ability of direct execution to produce sound project performance with tangible results, to support national ownership and capacity-building, and to allow for greater accountability.

The evaluation found that direct execution projects had generally delivered sound results, as evidenced in Bosnia and Herzegovina and the United Republic of Tanzania. However, sustainability for the most part was limited, owing to the short-term, crisis nature of a number of country programmes that were not linked to a longer-term or development strategy. The strengths of direct execution projects resided in UNDP's capacity for quick response, and their flexibility, especially in crisis and post-conflict situations and other special situations. They created an enabling environment for applying innovative solutions and approaches, reflected clear lines of responsibility, limited the potential for corruption and undue political influence through the transparency of decision-making, and allowed UNDP direct control over project inputs. However, their weakness lay in increased start-up costs, the current inability of the UNDP systems to support the financial management requirements of such projects adequately, and delays and inefficiencies in decision-making caused by current review and approval processes at headquarters.

The findings of the evaluation pointed to important challenges for UNDP in the direct delivery of services and to questions of execution in general. A consensus had emerged that it was time for UNDP to carry out a fundamental rethinking of execution in the broader sense, including using direct delivery to support the service delivery and operational priorities as expressed in the Administrator's Business Plans. The evaluation made a number of recommendations for policy reform and improvement, management and administration and support.

The Administrator, in his remarks on the recommendations, stated that the changes outlined were far-reaching and ambitious, and attention should be paid to the sequencing of measures so that future policies for service delivery were adequately supported by approvals, systems and procedures when launched.

The Board, in September, decided to postpone consideration of the item on evaluation to its first 2002 session.

Information technology for development

In June [DP/2001/CRP.8], UNDP reported on its role in information and communication technology (ICT) for development, highlighting the opportunities and challenges of ICT in development, UNDP's activities and strategy in relation to ICT and its modalities for programme support, monitoring and funding.

The report pointed out that ICT for development was a priority area for UNDP and one of its strategic initiatives in the second global cooperation framework. Since 1993, it had been active in ICT for development and had developed considerable expertise. UNDP had a particular development and organizational niche to assist developing countries with their ICT for development strategies. Its comparative advantage as a policy advisory and operational organization enabled it to assist countries and to bring a development perspective to bear on the formulation of national ICT strategies. As a cross-cutting issue, ICT had a direct impact on all of the critical developmental areas that UNDP supported and promoted, enabling the integration of ICT into such areas as poverty alleviation and democratic governance. Its efforts to help developing countries build strategic cross-sectoral policy frameworks to address broad development goals offered another entry point for introducing ICT as an enabler for development.

UNDP had helped deploy the first Internet nodes in more than 45 countries, trained more than 25,000 organizations and institutions and created awareness about ICT potential. It had also assisted in the formulation of national ICT strategies and the deployment of ICT to enhance, among other areas, democratic governance, gender equity, the creation of jobs and economic opportunities and programmes to extend public access. Through partnerships and global, regional and local programmes, UNDP had promoted the development of infrastructure, connectivity and access, deployment of ICT to increase the effectiveness of government and governance mechanisms, the creation of jobs, commerce, trade exchanges, education and training. It also assisted countries with policy advice.

The UNDP ICT-for-development strategy was undergoing a major shift in direction and scope. Aside from streamlining its activities, a more upstream policy focus and support to national strategies were expected to complement the downstream project focus to enable countries to leverage better the potential of ICT for development. It was also seeking to promote new and innovative mechanisms for financing and partnerships to promote ICT access, deployment and innovative solutions. UNDP had established the ICT for Development Thematic Trust Fund to fund country-level ICT-for-development programmes and critical interventions at the global and regional levels, in support of the services provided at the country level.

On 22 June [dec. 2001/12], the Executive Board took note of the report on UNDP's role in information technology for development.

Contribution to HIV/AIDS plan

In response to Economic and Social Council resolution 1999/36 [YUN 1999, p. 1149], UNDP reported in May [DP/2001/16] on its contribution to the development of the UN system strategic plan for HIV/AIDS for 2001-2005, which was endorsed by the Programme Coordination Board of the Joint United Nations Programme on HIV/AIDS (UNAIDS) in April, and to the implementation of the plan. The report described the UNDP strategy on HIV/AIDS and its actions, particularly in governance and capacity-building, and in the social and economic dimensions of the epidemic. It also addressed the role of the resident coordinator in supporting the UN response at the country level.

In 2000, UNDP made HIV/AIDS one of its organizational priorities. As a co-sponsor of UN-AIDS, UNDP supported countries in addressing the governance challenge of the epidemic, such as mobilizing actors and institutions beyond the health sector; promoting community-led action to reduce vulnerability to and risk of HIV infection; supporting Governments to ensure that the full power of the State was brought to bear on the crisis; raising domestic and international resources; integrating HIV/AIDS priorities in the mainstream of development planning; and ensuring a coordinated response. UNDP's shift towards a more focused strategy on HIV/AIDS was clearly producing results at the country level. It was assisting Governments to formulate national HIV/AIDS strategies, build their capacity to implement such strategies and support the strengthening of decentralized structures to manage local action.

Five areas for related support services were defined. Under advocacy and policy dialogue, UNDP promoted action-oriented advocacy for leadership at all levels, political commitment and mobilization of actors across all sectors, as in Botswana, where it supported the publication of the national human development report focusing on the impact of HIV/AIDS on human development. Its capacity development services included the planning, management, implementation and decentralization of multisectoral, gender-sensitive national HIV/AIDS plans through processes involving all government sectors and non-governmental and private sector stakeholders. In Angola, Botswana, Gabon, Malawi, Namibia and Swaziland, UNDP sponsored policy-oriented studies to provide information to Governments on how to deal with the impact of HIV/AIDS on specific sectors. Under mainstreaming, UNDP supported government efforts to integrate HIV/AIDS priorities into development planning, particularly in Burkina Faso and Cameroon, where HIV/AIDS interventions formed part of the national poverty reduction strategies. In the area of human rights, the aim was to promote human rights as an essential aspect of the response to HIV/AIDS, thereby removing discrimination against those infected. In Angola, the Gambia, Honduras and Rwanda, UNDP supported associations and networks of people living with HIV/AIDS. Information and multimedia technology services provided for awareness-raising interventions and large-scale publicity to increase the visibility of the epidemic and decrease the stigma.

UNDP used a number of modalities and instruments for programme support, monitoring, coordination, partnership and funding. Among them were the global cooperation framework, which was used to align the UNDP response to the crisis at the global, regional and national levels; the resident coordinator to spearhead a cohesive response by the UN system and other donors; modalities and partnerships for active collaboration with a wide range of partners at the global and national levels; UN Volunteers to participate in projects at the community, national and regional levels; monitoring results by the strategic results framework and ROAR; global and regional support activities; and financial assistance.

On 22 June [dec. 2001/12], the Board decided to resume in 2002 consideration of UNDP contributions to the UN strategic plan for HIV/AIDS for 2001-2005.

Financing

The Administrator, in his annual review of the financial situation [DP/2002/25 & Add.1], reported that for the first time in eight years UNDP was able in 2001 to reverse the long downward trend in its regular resources. However, while encouraging, the growth remained modest in relation to the targets set by the Executive Board and what was actually required to maximize the impact of the organization's work, particularly in the least developed countries. The overall level of funding reached $2.6 billion, up by 9 per cent, compared to the 2000 level of $2.4 billion, due primarily to growth in other resources, such as third-party co-financing, which represented 30 per cent of aggregate income, and programme country cost-sharing, which represented 41 per cent of aggregate income, reflecting increased political will and support by UNDP partner countries.

Compared to 2000, total regular resources income increased by 2 per cent to $665 million, while total expenditure remained stable at $703 million. The resource balance, exclusive of operational reserves, was reduced by 41 per cent.

Voluntary contributions to regular resources increased by 3 per cent to $651.8 million. Contributions received from the top 15 non-programme country donors (Belgium, Canada, Denmark, Finland, France, Germany, Italy, Japan, Netherlands, Norway, Spain, Sweden, Switzerland, United Kingdom, United States) totalled $998 million, or 96 per cent of total resources. Improvements were recorded in payment performance, resulting in an increase in UNDP's cash flow and minimizing the organization's need to draw against the regular resources operational reserve.

Total expenditure under regular resources remained at the 2000 level of $703 million. Programme expenditures in 2001 fell by 12.1 per cent to $333 million, compared to $378 million the previous year. In terms of the percentage share of programme expenditure among regions, Latin America and the Caribbean recorded the highest share of programme delivery, accounting for 50 per cent or $1.1 billion of aggregate figures; Africa, $313 million or 14 per cent; Asia and the Pacific, $304 million or 14 per cent; the Arab States, $227 million or 11 per cent; and Europe and CIS, $145 million or 7 per cent.

The percentage share for execution modalities showed that national execution still represented 60 per cent of the overall UNDP figure, followed by UNOPS, 13 per cent, direct execution, 10 per cent, and other agencies, 8 per cent. Programme support to implementing agents decreased to $34 million, compared to $42 million in 2000.

As at 31 December, the balance of unexpended resources for regular resources activities was at its lowest level since 1984 at $45.3 million, a decline of 41 per cent from the 2000 figure of $76 million. At the end of 2001, UNDP held cash and investments for regular resources totalling $278 million, inclusive of the operational reserve of $152 million.

For the other resources activities, which comprised mainly government and third-party cost-sharing, government cash-counterpart contributions, trust funds, management services agreements, the Junior Professional Officer programme and the reserve for field accommodation, representing the bulk of all activities managed by UNDP, overall income increased from $1.8 billion in 2000 to $2.1 billion in 2001. Overall expenditure also increased by 13 per cent ($219 million) to $1.8 billion. Contributions received totalled $1.9 billion, of which 57 per cent accounted for programme country cost-sharing. Third-party co-financing increased by 9 per cent from $712 million in 2000 to $781 million in 2001.

In September [dec. 2001/17], the Executive Board took note of the UNDP annual review report on the financial situation for 2000 [YUN 2000, p. 834].

Regular funding commitments to UNDP

In May [DP/2001/18], UNDP submitted a report on the status of regular funding commitments to the organization and its associated funds and programmes for 2001 and onward. According to provisional data for 2000, total net income for the year was $634 million, some $47 million below the net income figure of $681 million recorded for 1999. Current estimates for gross contributions to regular resources for 2001, using the UN official exchange rate as at 1 May 2001, were just over $670 million, a projected increase of 6 per cent over the level of regular resources in 2000. The shortfall in 2000 came about even though 11 members of the Development Assistance Committee of the Organisation for Economic Cooperation and Development (OECD/DAC) increased their contributions in local currency, 4 of them by 20 per cent, and another 4 announced additional contributions to regular resources for 2000 at or after the Ministerial Meeting on UNDP [YUN 2000, p. 836]. The shortfall was mainly due to the reduction in contribution levels of three OECD/DAC donors and non-payment of 2000 pledges by two donors. The exchange rate was also a significant factor, particularly the continued strength of the United States dollar. On a positive note, 36 programme countries contributed to UNDP regular resources in 2000, including 11 that increased their contribution and 18 that commenced or resumed payments. In 2000, 19 countries provided fixed payment schedules. While 15 major donors announced specific payment schedules for their 2000 voluntary contributions, the cash flow of voluntary contributions from major donors in 2000 was again suboptimal. By the beginning of December 2000, 20 per cent of contributions pledged in 2000 remained unpaid, as compared to 22 per cent in 1999. UNDP was able to engage in hedging for only a relatively small amount of anticipated contributions in non-dollar denominated contributions, owing in part to the lack of definitive information concerning amounts and/or payment schedules early in the year for several contributors. Throughout 2000, UNDP experienced significant cash-flow problems, forcing it to draw some $38 million from the operational reserve at the end of November.

In a June update [DP/2001/CRP.8] to the May report (above), UNDP reported that estimates for the gross contributions to UNDP regular resources for 2001, using the UN official exchange rate as at 1 June 2001, amounted to $660 million, a projected increase of 2.3 per cent over the 2000 level. Although that represented a significant shortfall in relation to agreed targets, it should not obscure the positive increase in commitments to UNDP regular resources made by 25 countries in 2001. Moreover, nine OECD/DAC donors and eight programme countries had made multi-year pledges.

Overall, compliance with payment schedules had improved in the first part of 2001, resulting in a rise in contributions to $164 million in April, compared with $50 million in April 2000. Projections for contributions to regular resources in 2001 indicated that the seven-year downward trend would be halted in 2001, marking a return to growth in the regular resource base. The 2000 Ministerial Meeting on UNDP had resulted in widespread endorsement that the UNDP reform process was on the right track, and subsequent communication with political leaders had provided an impetus to rebuilding political will for the organization. The MYFF/ROAR process had demonstrated clear results, and the Business Plans, 2000-2003, were strengthening UNDP's performance. All those factors provided an important stimulus to resource mobilization, resulting in a large number of countries announcing increases in contributions in 2001. Nevertheless, despite the positive signs of increased political support, the regular resource situation remained critical.

In June [dec. 2001/12], the Executive Board took note of the reports on the status of regular funding commitments.

Follow-up to Ministerial Meeting on UNDP

The Executive Board considered a report [DP/2001/CRP.3] on follow-up to the 2000 Ministerial Meeting on UNDP [YUN 2000, p. 836], which had endorsed the Secretary-General's vision of the role of the United Nations in development and of the part played by UNDP in that context and had expressed concern about UNDP's resource situation and the importance of rebuilding its core resource base.

Building on specific suggestions made by Ministers during the meeting, UNDP proposed follow-up actions to build on the new momentum of political support at the country and regional levels and at the Executive Board level. Foremost among those proposals was the acceleration of national efforts to rebuild regular resources to agreed targets through consultations between Governments and UNDP on the support UNDP could provide to efforts at the country level to rebuild greater political and financial support for UNDP. At regional and international forums, the importance of the United Nations in develop-

ment and of the specific role of UNDP should be highlighted. The Administrator recommended that consideration be given to holding a follow-up Ministerial Meeting in September 2001. In addition, the secretariat should review with the Board the structuring of a dialogue around priority issues in order to promote high-level participation in the Board's sessions. The Administrator should report to the Board on progress in addressing UNDP's performance in the context of the implementation of the Business Plans, 2000-2003. Other recommendations called for Governments to increase contributions to regular resources to achieve a more durable solution to UNDP core funding problems, and to adopt a standard schedule of contributions. They were urged to communicate, as early as possible, their contributions to regular resources for 2001 and following years, and their preferred payment-schedule option. Regarding non-core contributions, the report proposed that the Administrator report to the Board on new initiatives in the development of a non-core strategy, and on the presentation and relationship of regular resources to different types of other resources in the 2002-2003 biennial support budget.

The Board, in February [dec. 2001/7], took note of the report on the follow-up to the Ministerial Meeting.

Audit reports

At its January/February session, the Executive Board considered the Administrator's report [DP/2001/7] on follow-up to the Board of Auditors' report for 1998-1999 [YUN 2000, p. 1316], which contained a summary of the recommendations of the Board of Auditors for the 1998-1999 biennium, listed by area of audit, with the status of follow-up action, including target dates for completion. The Administrator said that progress had been made in many areas and efforts were being made to address outstanding issues.

Also before the Board was another report [DP/2001/CRP.5], which provided information on steps taken by UNDP to address the qualified opinion of the Board of Auditors on the 1998-1999 financial statements relating to national execution and bank reconciliation. In relation to national execution, UNDP reported that, while the audit coverage of nationally executed projects had improved appreciably, a number of aspects remained to be dealt with, including the issues of timing and national capacity constraints, which led to late or non-submission of audit certificates. To increase the level of audit coverage, the Administrator had instructed resident representatives, effective 2000, to ensure that an audit was conducted for all UNDP projects with estimated expenditures over $100,000. Concerning the qualification on UNDP 1998-1999 financial statements of $723 million in national execution expenditure in 30 countries, the Administrator had instructed that resident representatives of those countries ensure, retroactively, an increase of the audit coverage for that period. Country offices were to discuss with government counterparts the need to carry out an interim audit and to complete the final audit once the 12-month expenditure reports were ready in order to meet the 30 April deadline. Those instructions were effective as from 1 February 2001, and government counterparts were to be encouraged to use local private audit firms, if necessary, to meet that deadline.

As to the bank reconciliation, UNDP reported that the $5.8 million of disbursements shown in the bank statement but not in the UNDP accounting records had been reconciled and cleared and only $0.7 million remained to be cleared. UNDP was sure that there was no risk of loss to the organization from that outstanding amount and was continuing efforts to reconcile the items.

On 1 February [dec. 2001/3], the Executive Board noted that considerable progress had been made by UNDP in implementing the recommendations of previous reports of the Board of Auditors and that action was being taken to address all recommendations in the report for 1998-1999. The Executive Board welcomed the measures described in the document [DP/2001/CRP.5] and urged the secretariat to ensure the timely delivery of compliant and accurate financial statements according to UN accounting standards.

In April [DP/2001/13], the Administrator submitted a report on UNDP internal audit and oversight activities for 2000 provided by its Office of Audit and Performance Review (OAPR).

In 2000, the number of internal audit reports declined significantly, to 46 from 76 in 1999, due to extensive recruitment of audit resources for activities of limited duration and the shift from compliance audits to the broader management audits. The number of control self-assessment sessions also declined, from 33 in 1999 to 18 in 2000. However, national execution audit reports increased 14 per cent, from 1,231 in 1999 to 1,401 in 2000, owing to a corresponding increase in the number of national execution projects. The number of investigation cases declined slightly, from 25 new cases in 1999 to 20 in 2000. OAPR conducted an audit of global and regional projects and followed up the principal findings of audits completed in 1999. The Office contracted a public accounting firm to conduct an audit of the Electricity Network Rehabilitation Programme in northern Iraq, funded by the oil-for-food pro-gramme for Iraq (see p. 300). The Office provided internal audit services to 39 country offices. A total of 39 internal audit and 4 special audit reports were issued, containing 1,542 recommendations, of which 94 per cent were accepted by auditees and the remaining 6 per cent were being pursued.

During 2000, OAPR received and reviewed 1,401 project audit reports of national execution expenditures for 1999, covering 113 of the 140 countries with national execution expenditures exceeding $100,000. Of the 113 countries assessed, 55 had offices rated satisfactory, 52 were marginally deficient and 6 were deficient. The 27 countries that did not submit audit reports before the end of 2000 were also rated deficient. In general, the reports revealed recurring issues in the areas of personnel, procurement, finance, project design and implementation, and inventory. Many of the problems were attributed to a lack of awareness of proper procedures. For all countries assessed, OAPR received or requested action plans to address the audit findings. In all, 53 investigation cases remained active during 2000, of which 42 concerned UNDP.

In June [dec. 2001/12], the Executive Board took note of the report on internal audit and oversight activities of UNDP.

Budget estimates for 2002-2003

In June [DP/2001/21], the Administrator submitted budget estimates for the 2002-2003 biennium. He proposed a nominally reduced budget in net terms of $502.6 million for 2002-2003, $15.7 million less than the net approved budget for 2000-2001 [YUN 1999, p. 810]. The proposals resulted in a decrease of the gross budget from $585.4 million for 2000-2001 to $566.9 million for 2002-2003.

The proposals incorporated total net volume reductions of $43.1 million and net cost increases of $24.6 million. The estimates also incorporated a more realistic projection of income that offset the gross support budget of $64.3 million in 2002-2003, down from $67.1 million in 2000-2001.

The Advisory Committee on Administrative and Budgetary Questions (ACABQ) submitted its comments on the budget estimates for 2002-2003 in a June report [DP/2001/24], which the Executive Board noted in September [dec. 2001/17].

The Board took note [dec. 2001/13] of the Administrator's report on the biennial budget estimates for 2002-2003, which was an integral part of the IRF of the MYFF. It also noted the Administrator's proposals on the financial framework and the related UNDP resource plan. The Board approved gross appropriations in the amount of

$566,889,700 for the 2002-2003 biennial support budget and resolved that the income estimates of $64,327,000 should be used to offset the gross appropriations, resulting in estimated net appropriations of $502,562,700. The Administrator was authorized to redeploy resources between appropriation lines up to a maximum of 5 per cent of the appropriation line to which the resources were redeployed.

The Board took note of the Administrator's report on the 2002-2003 budget estimates for the United Nations Capital Development Fund (see p. 822) and the United Nations Development Fund for Women [DP/2001/21], and approved gross appropriations for each of those funds in the amounts of $13,685,500 and $12,337,500, respectively [dec. 2001/13].

Revision of Financial Regulations and Rules

The Executive Board, at its first regular session, had before it two proposals from the UNDP Administrator and the UNFPA Executive Director, as requested by the Board [YUN 2000, p. 1005], concerning common Financial Regulations for both organizations relating to contributions from non-governmental sources [DP/FPA/2001/3-DP/2001/9]. The first proposed common regulation would replace the current UNFPA Financial Regulations 4.1 and 4.9 and UNDP Financial Regulation 5.02, and would expand the sources from which contributions could be received and explicitly require that, for UNDP, such contributions be consistent with UNDP's purposes. The second proposed common regulation and corresponding new rule, replacing UNFPA Financial Regulation 4.11 and UNDP Regulation 5.09, would retain the threshold for reporting those contributions to the Executive Board at $100,000 for both organizations.

On 31 January [dec. 2001/6], the Board approved the proposed changes to the common financial regulations, which were annexed to its decision.

The Administrator, in August [DP/2001/CRP.18], proposed amendments to UNDP Financial Rule 116.04 so that nationally executed projects exceeding an annual expenditure of $100,000 would be audited annually instead of biennially. He also proposed amending Financial Rule 125.11 authorizing the Treasurer to establish guarantee facilities to facilitate UNDP commercial financial operations through measures such as bank-issued guarantees and/or bank-issued commercial letters of credit, with the proviso that there be no borrowing of funds by UNDP in connection with such issuance.

In September [dec. 2001/17], the Board took note of the amendment to the UNDP financial rules.

Other technical cooperation

UN activities

Department of Economic and Social Affairs

The Department of Economic and Social Affairs (DESA), responsible for UN technical cooperation activities, had more than 950 technical cooperation projects under execution in a dozen substantive sectors, with a total project expenditure of some $51.1 million. Projects financed by UNDP represented $21.6 million; those by trust funds, $27.7 million; and those by UNFPA, $1.8 million.

On a geographical basis, DESA's executive programme included expenditures of $25.3 million in interregional and global programmes; $10.1 million in Africa; $6.9 million in Asia and the Pacific; $6.7 million in the Middle East; $1.3 million in the Americas; and $0.8 million in Europe.

Distribution of expenditures by substantive sectors was as follows: Associate Expert programme, $16.6 million; economic policy, $9.4 million; energy, $7.8 million; public administration, $7 million; water, $2.7 million; social policy, $2.2 million; programme support, $2 million; statistics, $1.6 million; infrastructure, $0.8 million; minerals, $0.6 million; population, $0.2 million; public finance and the private sector, $0.1 million; and advancement of women, $0.1 million. Of the total delivery of $51.1 million, the Associate Expert programme comprised 32 per cent; economic policy, 18 per cent; energy, 15 per cent; and public administration, 14 per cent.

On a component basis, DESA delivery in 2001 included $38 million for project personnel, $6.1 million for subcontracts, $2.9 million for training, $3.5 million for equipment and $0.6 million for miscellaneous expenses.

Development Account

The Secretary-General, in response to General Assembly resolutions 53/220 A and B [YUN 1999, pp. 1305 & 1306], reported in April [A/55/913] on implementation of projects financed from the Development Account, financed by savings from budget efficiencies in the regular programme budget. The Secretary-General reviewed the 23 projects approved since the establishment of the Account in 1998 and falling under the first and second tranches with a total value of $26.1 million. The review revealed a number of reporting weaknesses, including a focus on activities rather than outputs; insufficient quantifiable information or other data to gauge progress; insufficient information on proposed new scheduling; lack of information on the institutional environment of projects and the prospects for their sustainability after the completion of Development Account funding; lack of clarity on coordination arrangements; and inadequate compliance with the guidelines established for reporting progress.

In 2000, OIOS conducted an audit of the implementation of projects financed from the Account. OIOS recommended that the programme manager clarify the requirement of low-cost implementation, particularly by proposing a financial ceiling for individual projects; that joint implementation of projects should be encouraged and included in the selection criteria; and that cooperation frameworks created by Account projects should be maintained after activities were completed. Programme support contributed by each entity should be accounted for as efficiency gains. Project proposals would have to include all costs, whether financed from the Development Account or not.

ACABQ, in its first report on the proposed programme budget for 2002-2003 [A/56/7], noted that, of the $26.1 million approved since the establishment of the Development Account, a total of $8.9 million had been spent for projects funded from the 1998-1999 and the 2000-2001 programme budgets as at 31 March 2001, leaving a balance of $17.2 million. It also noted that no proposals had been made for transfer to the Account for 2002-2003. ACABQ requested the Secretary-General, in his next report on the issue, to provide a thematic impact analysis of the projects, and to include in his description of each project the date of commencement, the projected date of completion and the implementing agency.

GENERAL ASSEMBLY ACTION

On 24 December [meeting 92], the General Assembly, on the recommendation of the Fifth (Administrative and Budgetary) Committee [A/56/653], adopted **resolution 56/237** without vote [agenda item 122].

Development Account

The General Assembly,

Recalling its resolutions 52/12 B of 19 December 1997 and 52/220 and 52/221 A of 22 December 1997,

Reaffirming its resolutions 52/235 of 26 June 1998, 53/220 A of 7 April 1999, 53/220 B of 8 June 1999 and 54/15 of 29 October 1999,

Having considered the report of the Secretary-General on the implementation of projects financed from the Development Account, including the observations of the Office of Internal Oversight Services in section V thereof, and the related report of the Advisory Committee on Administrative and Budgetary Questions,

1. *Expresses concern* at the low implementation rate of the projects undertaken through the Development Account;

2. *Urges* a more expeditious and effective rate of implementation of projects, and requests that project proposals include all costs, including support costs, and whether or not they are financed from the Development Account;

3. *Requests* the Secretary-General to include in his next report the date of commencement, the implementing agency and the anticipated dates of completion of all ongoing projects and to provide explanations for any schedule changes in the completion of these projects;

4. *Also requests* the Secretary-General to intensify efforts to enhance efficiency measures that may result in sustainable savings, with a view to augmenting the Development Account, in accordance with the provisions of General Assembly resolution 54/15;

5. *Reaffirms* that projects financed from the Development Account should be implemented in accordance with the provisions of General Assembly resolutions 53/220 A and 53/220 B;

6. *Welcomes* the fact that the implementation of the approved projects financed from the Development Account has a developmental impact on a country, is cost-effective, in particular through the use of information and communication technology, and is jointly designed and carried out by several entities of the United Nations;

7. *Requests* the Secretary-General to monitor the implementation rate of the projects, with a view to identifying those projects that are underperforming and the causes, and to submit proposals to correct this situation or to redeploy funds from such projects to those that are delivering results;

8. *Decides* to continue to keep the implementation of the Development Account under review, and requests the Secretary-General to submit a report on the subject to the General Assembly at its fifty-seventh session.

UN Fund for International Partnerships

ACABQ, in a March report [A/55/7/Add.9], recommended that the General Assembly note the Secretary-General's report [YUN 2000, p. 1328], submitted pursuant to Assembly decision 53/475 [YUN 1999, p. 1318], on the status, as at December 2000, of the United Nations Fund for International Partnerships (UNFIP), established in 1998 [YUN 1998, p. 1297] to manage the process of grant allocations through the United Nations Foundation (UNF), a public charity founded by Robert Edward Turner to channel a gift to the United Nations of 18 million shares of Time Warner stock valued at some $1 billion. ACABQ said that it would provide further comments in the context of additional information provided in the 2002-2003 programme budget.

By **decision 55/471** of 12 April, the Assembly took note of the Secretary-General's report on UNFIP and ACABQ's related comments and recommendations.

In his report on activities as at the end of 2001 [A/57/133], the Secretary-General provided data on the outcome of the ninth and tenth funding cycles, as well as on progress in each programmatic focus area. The UNF Board of Directors approved a total of $105.7 million in the ninth and tenth funding rounds (36 grants totalling $70.6 million during the ninth funding cycle, and 17 grants amounting to $35.1 million during the tenth). Three intersessional requests were also approved, bringing the total for 2001 to $111.9 million. By sector, grants totalling $36.8 million were awarded for projects concerning the environment; $32.2 million for children's health; $19.2 million for peace, security and human rights; $18.4 million for population and women; and $5.2 million for institutional capacity-building. Total funding since the inception of the UNFIP-UNF partnership to the end of 2001 amounted to $423 million.

UNFIP also served as facilitator for partnerships with the private sector and foundations. In 2001, it organized a dialogue between the Secretary-General and leading representatives of companies and foundations on the Secretary-General's "Call to Action for HIV/AIDS" and established an interim facility to receive contributions to the Global Fund to Fight AIDS, Malaria and Tuberculosis. In December, the "Mother-to-Child Transmission, plus care for positive mothers" initiative, a $100 million five-year programme, was launched with the support of a group of nine major foundations. During the year, UNFIP increased its outreach with partners to implement the millennium development goals, identifying 150 foundations to assist the UN system. A particular effort was made to include more African, Asian and European affiliates.

UN Office for Project Services

The United Nations Office for Project Services (UNOPS) continued to respond to requests for project services, operating in accordance with the self-financing principle with no assessed budget financing, and executing programmes on behalf of UN organizations.

2001 activities

The UNOPS Executive Director, in his annual report on UNOPS activities in 2001 [DP/2002/19], provided an overview of performance as compared with financial targets set in the 2000-2001 UNOPS business plan, reviewed UNOPS activities during the year and addressed issues involving services and new client-centred business processes. Information was also given on the status of the organizational reform process initiated in

1995 and measures taken to reduce budget estimates for 2002.

The total value of the UNOPS project and loan portfolios for 2001 amounted to $3.8 billion, comprising $1.4 billion in project value and $2.3 billion in loan value. Project delivery totalled $505 million, compared with the UNOPS business plan target of $616 million. The shortfall stemmed from unexpected changes in the UNOPS business environment, including delay or postponement of a number of large management services agreements, in particular for projects in Argentina, Ecuador, Peru and Turkey. Actual requests for UNOPS services by a few UN entities turned out to be smaller than what was initially agreed to. Disbursements authorized by UNOPS under the IFAD loan portfolio totalled $195.5 million.

Total income was $47.2 million, which was $9.6 million, or 17 per cent, less than the $56.8 million projected. Of that total, $37.9 million was generated from project income, $7 million from delivery of loan administration and other services, and $2.3 million from miscellaneous sources.

Administrative expenditures totalled $52.8 million, which was $2.5 million, or 5 per cent, less than the approved amount of $55.3 million. Of that total, $34.5 million was for staff costs, $11.3 million for equipment, communications, travel and operating expenses, and $7 million in reimbursements to UNDP and the United Nations for support services at the country level. As UNOPS expenditures exceeded income, it had to draw down $5.6 million from its operational reserve. UNOPS took a number of cost-cutting measures to reduce expenditures, including discontinuation of staff recruitment, cutbacks in information technology investments and deferral of various activities and expenses.

In reviewing the Office's operational activities, the Executive Director reported that UNOPS found new ways of working with clients. With the United Nations Environment Programme (UNEP), it helped evaluate the environmental impact of major projects before launching, such as the evaluation of combined heat and power plants in Poland. UNOPS continued to establish "execution partnerships" in projects it implemented for clients, with clear division of labour resulting in cost-effectiveness. The management of financial risks through a range of contracting tools, insurance arrangements and training continued to be part of the UNOPS services offerings. UNOPS expanded the range of potential risks it managed to cover financial risks relating to project inputs and outputs. In that regard, an intellectual property audit of projects was used to assess possible risks associated with third-party rights in works for hire, including software, multimedia presentations and reports.

Among its noteworthy undertakings, UNOPS resumed operations in Afghanistan after a short suspension resulting from the events of 11 September (see p. 60).

On behalf of UNDP and Japan, UNOPS helped the population of the Kosovo province of the Federal Republic of Yugoslavia by employing local contractors to supply housing for 800 families and assisted the United Nations Interim Administration Mission in Kosovo (UNMIK) (see p. 348) in the rehabilitation of a brick factory, two municipal waste-management systems and city parks. Working with the Mine Action Coordination Committee, UNOPS helped in the removal of 25,000 landmines, 8,500 cluster bombs and 14,000 other unexploded devices.

At the request of the Office of the Iraq Programme and UNICEF, UNOPS managed a $150 million fund for improving water and sanitation in urban areas in northern Iraq, and implemented a mine-action programme in the country.

In East Timor, UNOPS, on behalf of the United Nations Transitional Administration for East Timor (see p. 272), awarded construction contracts worth $1.4 million to 28 local companies. On behalf of UNDP and Portugal, it managed three projects in electricity, water and sanitation, as well as six emergency infrastructure projects, funded by Japan.

The UN Office for Drug Control and Crime Prevention sought UNOPS assistance in corruption and human-trafficking prevention projects in Colombia, the Czech Republic, Lebanon, Nigeria, the Philippines, Poland and South Africa. The Intergovernmental Authority on Development, a subregional organization of seven Eastern African countries, selected UNOPS to provide project services for a disaster preparedness initiative, including procurement and the hiring of consultants. UNOPS was also selected to develop, in partnership with the United Nations Institute for Training and Research (UNITAR), a programme to make geographic information, including satellite data, accessible at reduced cost to UN organizations and other agencies involved in humanitarian assistance, crisis response and post-disaster recovery.

During the year, UNOPS worked with the International Labour Organization to introduce local economic development agencies in about 20 countries. Seven new agreements were signed with the Office of the United Nations High Commissioner for Refugees (UNHCR). In Zambia, UNOPS agreed to provide administrative support in recruiting personnel and advising on a strategy for dealing with the refugee situation. It also worked with UNDP in support of national execution in Guatemala.

Within the organization, UNOPS implemented project management training to improve employee tools and skills, and developed a programme to ensure that the staff remained abreast of current management and business techniques. The funds control system was overhauled, with a new Web-based application enabling portfolio managers to input and download information at any time and to provide clients with up-to-date financial reports. The UNOPS web site was improved, allowing UNOPS staff to post invitations to bid, expressions of interest, requests for proposals, contract awards and vacancy announcements.

On 14 June [E/2001/35 (dec. 2001/10)], the UNDP Executive Board took note of the Executive Director's report on UNOPS activities. It also noted the drawdown of $6.8 million from the UNOPS operational reserve in 2000, consisting of $3 million in previously approved non-recurring expenditures and a shortfall in 2000 income of $3.8 million. The Board requested the Executive Director to keep the parameters of the UNOPS financial model under review and report on trends as part of the report on budget estimates for the current and future bienniums (see below).

UNDP/UNOPS relationship

The UNOPS Executive Director and the UNDP Administrator, in June [DP/2001/CRP.15], submitted an evaluation of the relationship between UNDP and UNOPS, specifically the progress achieved in implementing the recommendations made in 2000 [YUN 2000, p. 840].

Concerning the recommendation that overlaps between UNDP and UNOPS in the area of crisis and post-conflict situations be corrected, there was ample opportunity for future collaboration between the organizations in that area, with UNDP ensuring cooperation among UN entities, including in areas of project execution and provision of services. In terms of the delineation of responsibilities, the UNDP-UNOPS Operations Working Group had established a sub–working group to review the functions performed by UNDP on behalf of UNOPS at headquarters and country office levels. Some progress was made on work relating to country office services, but progress was limited on headquarters central services. The recommendation that the Users Advisory Group be maintained and convened at least once a year was not carried out in 2001, pending intended realignment by UNOPS of its organizational structure.

The recommendation that direct execution by UNDP be used as an execution modality only when no other executing agency was capable of doing so was already being followed by UNOPS. Another recommendation was that the respective responsibilities of UNDP and of the executing/implementing entity be clearly defined for each project in a project management matrix. UNOPS reported that the model project management matrix was expected to be finalized shortly and would be forwarded to all resident representatives with the letter outlining the role of the UNOPS resident representative. Financial reporting had improved, enabling UNOPS to provide all partners with financial reports by the end of 2001. Action had been taken also on a number of administrative issues.

On 22 June [dec. 2001/12], the Executive Board decided to postpone consideration of the overall UNDP/UNOPS relationship to its second regular session in September. At that session [dec. 2001/17], the Board stressed its responsibility for providing strategic direction to UNDP and UNOPS on follow-up to the evaluation of their relationship, and requested an OIOS report on the matter, together with the Secretary-General's related comments and those of UNDP and UNOPS, by mid-November 2001.

Budget estimates

In July [DP/2001/28 & Add.1], the UNOPS Executive Director issued the revised budget estimates for the 2000-2001 biennium, based on actual delivery, income and expenditure for 2000 and on projections for 2001.

Actual total income for 2000 amounted to $48.5 million and actual administrative expenses totalled $55.3 million. The 2001 target for project delivery was increased from $590 million to $616 million; the total income target therefore rose from $51.6 million to $56.8 million and administrative budget provisions were increased from $51.6 million to $55.3 million.

The Executive Director also submitted budget estimates for 2002-2003, which envisaged a total project delivery of $1.3 billion, with income estimated at $97.3 million. Total income for the biennium was projected to be $116.2 million and administrative expenses $113 million.

The Executive Director also reviewed the level of the operational reserve, which, currently targeted at 4 per cent of the combined expenditure on administrative and project budgets of the previous year, appeared sufficient to meet requirements originally included in the definition of the reserve. That view was confirmed by the external consultant firm KPMG. However, two issues needed further consideration: the level of funding for medical and dental benefits for retired staff members; and the fluctuations in the level of the reserve that derived from the single-year

basis of the calculation formula. UNOPS was working with the UN Secretariat and UNDP to establish the level of those medical and dental obligations, which the Executive Director proposed to fund, in the meantime, from the UNOPS Account and project accounts, requiring a modification of Financial Regulation 8.3 (a) (iv). Concerning the level of the reserve, KPMG had recommended that the current formula be replaced with one that moved from the existing single-year calculation of the reserve level to a three-year moving average of expenditure on administrative and project budgets. The new proposal would take 4 per cent of the average of the project delivery and administrative expenditures for 1998, 1999 and 2000.

In September [DP/2001/29], ACABQ noted that the 2000-2001 revised estimates and the 2002-2003 projections were affected by the shortfall of project income in 2000, resulting in the cancellation or delay of approved project budgets. ACABQ was of the opinion that the experience should be analysed with a view to refining procedures for adjusting UNOPS fixed assets to take account of such fluctuations. The termination or postponement of project budgets should be managed through consultation of all parties concerned so as to minimize the financial consequences and their impact on UNOPS. ACABQ also suggested that the nature and profile of UNOPS contracts for personal services should be re-examined, as should the structure of its business portfolio. ACABQ urged the UNOPS Executive Director and the UNDP Administrator to review expeditiously the question of the future status of UNDP personnel working with UNOPS and the respective liabilities of both organizations and to keep the Executive Board informed. It requested the Executive Director, in the context of the 2004-2005 estimates, to give his views on presenting future estimates biennially. ACABQ recommended approval of the revised 2000-2001 budget, budget estimates for 2002-2003, the staffing level proposed for 2000-2001 and the proposals regarding the operational reserve.

On 14 September [dec. 2001/17], the Executive Board took note of the ACABQ report.

On 13 September [dec. 2001/14], the Executive Board approved the revised budget estimates for 2000-2001 in the amount of $110.6 million and the budget estimates for 2002-2003 in the amount of $113 million. It also approved the staffing level as proposed for 2000-2001, a modification to UNOPS Financial Regulation 8.3 (a) (iv) on the use of the operational reserve, and the proposal to change the basis for calculating the level of that reserve to 4 per cent of the rolling average of the combined administrative and project expenditures for the three previous years.

Audit reports

The Executive Board had before it an overview [DP/2001/8] of the implementation of the recommendations relating to UNOPS as contained in the first report on the implementation of the recommendations of the Board of Auditors on UN funds and programmes for the biennium ended 31 December 1999 [YUN 2000, p. 1317]. The Executive Director reported that efforts to address both the financial and management issues raised in that report were under way.

On 1 February [dec. 2001/4], the Executive Board took note of the follow-up report to the recommendations of the Board of Auditors and requested the Executive Director to provide in 2002 an updated overview, including follow-up action completed.

In April [DP/2001/15], the Executive Director issued his annual report on UNOPS internal audit and oversight activities, which included an external audit performed by the UN Board of Auditors; an internal audit performed by OAPR; and internal management oversight.

OAPR conducted audits and management reviews of headquarters and field activities. In 2000, a total of 34 audit reports were issued containing 207 recommendations. Of those recommendations, 113 were in finance, 36 in management, 27 in administration (including contracts and procurement), 12 in personnel, 12 in programme and 7 in policy. UNOPS agreed with 107 of the recommendations and provided its response on action taken or contemplated to implement them.

The Executive Director indicated his intention to establish an internal management oversight unit within UNOPS to address control, quality assurance, standards issues and relations with internal and external oversight bodies.

In June [dec. 2001/12], the Executive Board took note of the report on UNOPS internal audit and oversight activities.

UN Volunteers

UNV activities

The UNDP Administrator, in a report to the Executive Board [DP/2002/18], provided information on the United Nations Volunteers (UNV) programme—administered by UNDP—in 2001, the thirtieth year of its operation.

The number of volunteers grew from 4,780 in 2000 to 5,090 in 2001, representing 160 nationalities working in 140 countries. The number of as-

signments carried out in 2001 increased to 5,432, up from 5,181 in 2000. The majority of volunteers (66 per cent) were from developing countries. The number of women serving as volunteers increased from 1,694 in 2000 to 1,833 in 2001.

By programme area, one third of all UNV assignments supported activities in sustainable human development, 20 per cent in poverty reduction, 30 per cent in special development situations and 12 per cent in support to the UN system, while around 3 to 4 per cent were devoted to activities related to the environment and to gender.

In a report on the review of the financial situation in 2001 [DP/2002/25 & Add.1], the Administrator stated that income recorded in 2001 for UNV increased by $5 million, or 27.2 per cent, compared to 2000. Programme expenditure in 2001 decreased marginally by $0.2 million, or 2.5 per cent, as compared to 2000. The balance of the operational reserve as at 31 December 2001 was $1.8 million.

The Secretary-General, as requested by the General Assembly in resolution 54/245 A [YUN 1999, p. 365], reported on the participation of UNVs in peacekeeping operations [A/55/697]. He concluded that the UNV programme had proved capable of expeditiously identifying and deploying qualified UNVs to peacekeeping missions and field operations. During the current period of unprecedented expectations and demands from the United Nations, the Department of Peacekeeping Operations was committed to extending its collaboration with the programme by exploiting the potential for increased use of UNVs wherever feasible, in particular for those functions that were not normally available in the Secretariat.

The General Assembly, on 14 June, deferred consideration of the Secretary-General's report until its fifty-sixth session (**decision 55/480**).

International Year of Volunteers

As proclaimed by the General Assembly in resolution 52/17 [YUN 1997, p. 889], the International Year of Volunteers was observed in 2001 (IYV 2001). UNV served as focal point for the relevant activities [DP/2002/18].

UNV launched an extensive advocacy campaign aimed at promoting greater awareness of the role that volunteers played in social and economic development; stimulating discussion on the concept of volunteerism; and publicizing the Year and its objectives. As focal point, UNV established a team to facilitate coordination of IYV 2001, and mobilized resources to support its activities related to the Year. It established an interactive IYV web site in four languages, to which more than 21,000 organizations and individuals had access to exchange views and experiences on policy issues, supportive legislation and good practice pertaining to volunteering. Drawing on the material posted on the web site, UNV published a monthly electronic newsletter to over 14,000 subscribers. To reach those without access to the Internet, information materials were distributed through UNDP country offices, civil society groups and NGO liaison organizations. In partnership with researchers, UNV launched a comparative study on the volume and value of volunteering in countries of different income levels, and issued a report on volunteering and the United Nations in December.

At the national level, UNV assisted developing countries in their preparations for IYV 2001, including in the formation of national steering committees. By the end of the year, 125 national and 14 city IYV committees had been established. At the global level, UNV supported and participated in a number of important international meetings and workshops, and worked with various intergovernmental bodies to ensure that due recognition was given to the contributions of volunteers in their work programmes and conference decisions. It also involved the private sector in raising awareness of the diverse and significant contributions of volunteers worldwide. The Secretary-General invited a group of eminent persons, representing different regions and facets of volunteer involvement, to support a range of activities undertaken during the Year, thus heightening awareness of volunteers' contributions.

Responding to General Assembly resolution S-24/2 [YUN 2000, p. 1013], the Commission for Social Development, at its thirty-ninth session (13-23 February) [E/2001/26], considered the role of volunteerism in the promotion of social development, on the basis of the Secretary-General's note on the subject [E/CN.5/2001/6]. The Commission [E/2001/26 (res. 39/2)], welcoming the work of UNV as the focal point for the Year in liaising with national committees for the Year, encouraged Governments to support voluntary action for social development by creating a favourable environment.

Support for volunteering

In August [A/56/288], the Secretary-General issued a report on support for volunteering. Noting the economic and social benefits derived from those activities, he described how volunteering could play a role in poverty reduction, environmental protection and regeneration, health, and disaster management and mitigation. He also addressed the role of Governments and the UN system in promoting volunteerism.

GENERAL ASSEMBLY ACTION

On 5 December [meeting 76], the General Assembly adopted **resolution 56/38** [draft: A/56/L.27 & Add.1, orally revised] without vote [agenda item 108].

Recommendations on support for volunteering
The General Assembly,

Recalling its resolution 52/17 of 20 November 1997, in which it proclaimed the year 2001 as the International Year of Volunteers, based on Economic and Social Council resolution 1997/44 of 22 July 1997, and its resolution 55/57 of 4 December 2000, in which it requested the Secretary-General to prepare a report on ways in which Governments and the United Nations system could support volunteering, and bearing in mind Commission for Social Development resolution 39/2 of 23 February 2001,

Recalling also the outcome document of the twenty-fourth special session of the General Assembly entitled "World Summit for Social Development and beyond: achieving social development for all in a globalizing world", in which the General Assembly recommended the promotion of the involvement of volunteers in social development, inter alia, by encouraging Governments, taking into account the views of all actors, to develop comprehensive strategies and programmes by raising public awareness about the value and opportunities of volunteerism and by facilitating an enabling environment for individuals and other actors of civil society to engage in voluntary activities, and the private sector to support such activities,

Recalling further paragraphs 73 and 179 (f) of the Platform for Action adopted by the Fourth World Conference on Women, paragraph 42 of the Declaration on Cities and Other Human Settlements in the New Millennium adopted at the twenty-fifth special session of the General Assembly for an overall review and appraisal of the implementation of the outcome of the United Nations Conference on Human Settlements (Habitat II) in June 2001, and paragraphs 32 (i) (b) and 41 (ii) (a) of the Programme of Action for the Least Developed Countries for the Decade 2001-2010 adopted at the Third United Nations Conference on the Least Developed Countries in May 2001,

Recognizing the valuable contribution of volunteering, including traditional forms of mutual aid and self-help, formal service delivery and other forms of civic participation, to economic and social development, benefiting society at large, communities and the individual volunteer,

Recognizing also that volunteerism is an important component of any strategy aimed at, inter alia, such areas as poverty reduction, sustainable development, health, disaster prevention and management and social integration and, in particular, overcoming social exclusion and discrimination,

Recognizing further the existing contribution of the organizations of the United Nations system to supporting volunteering, including the work of United Nations Volunteers around the world, by promoting volunteerism, including by placing volunteers,

Aware of the need to approach voluntary activities strategically as a means of enhancing resources, addressing global issues and improving the quality of life for everyone,

1. *Welcomes* the report of the Secretary-General on support for volunteering;

2. *Also welcomes* the work of the United Nations Volunteers as the focal point for the International Year of Volunteers in supporting national International Year of Volunteers committees and in collecting and disseminating information on the Year, including through its web site;

3. *Expresses its appreciation* regarding the support to the International Year of Volunteers extended by States, international organizations and civil society, including non-governmental organizations, especially at the local, national and regional levels;

4. *Commends* the ongoing contributions of all volunteers to society, including in extraordinary conditions such as disasters;

5. *Encourages* all people to become more engaged in voluntary activities;

6. *Lays down* in the annex to the present resolution the recommendations on ways in which Governments and the United Nations system could support volunteering;

7. *Requests* the Secretary-General to take specific measures, in particular within the mandates of the United Nations Volunteers and the Department of Public Information of the Secretariat, to disseminate widely the present resolution and the annex;

8. *Calls upon* all Governments and organizations of the United Nations system to give these recommendations due consideration;

9. *Decides* that on 5 December 2002, International Volunteer Day for Economic and Social Development, two plenary meetings at the fifty-seventh session of the General Assembly shall be devoted to the outcome of the International Year of Volunteers and its follow-up under the agenda item entitled "Social development, including questions relating to the world social situation and to youth, ageing, disabled persons and the family";

10. *Requests* the Secretary-General, in his report to the General Assembly at its fifty-seventh session on the outcome of the International Year of Volunteers and its follow-up, to include proposals for an integrated and coordinated follow-up, to be pursued in the relevant parts of the United Nations system, as well as on cross-cutting issues, building on his report to the Assembly at the present session and taking into account the present resolution, the discussions held during the present session and other relevant contributions.

ANNEX
Recommendations on ways in which Governments and the United Nations system could support volunteering

I. General considerations

1. In these recommendations, the terms volunteering, volunteerism and voluntary activities refer to a wide range of activities, including traditional forms of mutual aid and self-help, formal service delivery and other forms of civic participation, undertaken of free will, for the general public good and where monetary reward is not the principal motivating factor.

2. Actions by Governments and the United Nations system are mutually reinforcing but are treated separately below for the sake of clarity.

3. There is not one universal model of best practice, since what works well in one country may not work in another with very different cultures and traditions.

4. Support for voluntary activities does not imply support for government downsizing or for replacing paid employment.

5. It is not just targeted measures that have an impact on volunteering; general social and economic policy measures can also influence citizens' opportunities and willingness to volunteer.

6. Neglecting to factor volunteering into the design and implementation of policies could entail the risk of overlooking a valuable asset and undermine traditions of cooperation that bind communities together.

7. It is important to ensure that opportunities for volunteering in all sectors are open both to women and men, given their different levels of participation in different areas, and recognizing the potential positive effect of volunteering on the empowerment of women.

II. Government support

1. It is recommended that Governments further support voluntary activities by creating a favourable environment, including through the following policies and measures, and taking into account the local cultural context.

(a) *Increasing public awareness of the vital contribution of volunteerism to the social and economic functioning of their communities through, inter alia, public information activities and public events*

(i) Highlight the contribution of volunteering; organize briefings and seminars for policy makers and the media. Official papers on the status of volunteering and the issues that need to be addressed can be published and widely disseminated. High-profile events and campaigns can be organized on national days and on International Volunteer Day for Economic and Social Development on 5 December. Negative stereotyping of volunteers can be challenged. The promotion of volunteering can be achieved through special programmes and public service announcements or by joint initiatives such as award schemes;

(ii) Encourage the media to play a supportive role in public awareness-raising activities;

(iii) Disseminate the results of studies and surveys on the contribution of volunteerism, where they exist, through the media, schools, non-governmental organizations and other channels.

(b) *Taking general measures concerning encouragement and facilitation, preparation, training and recognition of volunteers*

(i) Provide, in a way complementary to the support from other sources, an adequate human and physical infrastructure for volunteering. This could include, inter alia, awareness-raising campaigns, development of a volunteer centre infrastructure, establishment of focal points or the use of pilot schemes and the promotion of online volunteering. Specific campaigns in the area of, for example, mass immunization, literacy, or low-cost housing, could include budgetary provision for the encouragement and facilitation, orientation and training, monitoring and recognition of volunteers;

(ii) Facilitate the establishment and functioning of volunteer centres, which provide a valuable stimulus to formal service volunteering through advocacy, monitoring and encouraging new initiatives. National volunteer centres provide effective leadership in the formal volunteer movement, while regional and local centres ensure linkages with the grass-roots communities and organizations. Legal and fiscal frameworks are important factors in the sustainability of such centres and financial support may also be desirable;

(iii) Provide or facilitate specialized training and the formation of professional volunteer managers and trainers in the area of formal service volunteering, including by introducing formal credentials and standards;

(iv) Encourage public sector workers to volunteer, for instance by facilitating measures, recognition, career enhancement incentives and the establishment of a dedicated special unit. This sets a positive example for society and helps to strengthen the sense of collective responsibility.

(c) *Enabling fiscal, legislative and other frameworks, including for community-based organizations and not-for-profit organizations engaged in volunteering*

(i) Introduce enabling legislation. The goal is to encourage or inspire citizens to volunteer but allow the choice to rest with the individual or organization; it can also facilitate employee volunteering. It can provide tax incentives and subsidies for organizations, as well as coverage and protection against risks, in a way fitting the particular society;

(ii) Facilitate partnership-building around volunteer-based activities of civil society, including arrangements for joint planning, implementation and monitoring. This could incorporate employee volunteer activities of the private sector.

(d) *Encouraging and undertaking research in the various aspects of volunteerism and its impact on society*

(i) Ensure that consideration of the issues regarding volunteering is based on a sound appreciation and analysis of the parameters, profile and trends of volunteering in the particular country context. Studies on volunteering can be undertaken by independent public policy research and/or academic institutions. Governments can also initiate research themselves, in partnership with other stakeholders;

(ii) Establish the economic value of volunteering to help to highlight one important aspect of its overall contribution to society and thereby assist in the development of informed policies which take into account the different levels of participation of women and men, youth and older people in different fields of volunteering.

(e) *Ensuring citizens' access to information on opportunities for volunteering*

(i) Facilitate the establishment of national databases on volunteer opportunities in collaboration with community-based organizations and not-for-profit organizations;

(ii) Disseminate information through the media, schools, and other channels with particular attention given to ensuring that information is accessible also to disadvantaged segments of the population. Encourage media companies to support and expand the concept of pro bono public service announcements on behalf of volunteer-based organizations and activities.

(f) *Addressing the possible impact of general social and economic policy measures upon citizens' opportunities and willingness to volunteer*

(i) Take into account the possible impact of general social and economic policy upon citizens' opportunities to volunteer. Such a "volunteer check" could pertain to measures related to labour, for example, such as the length of the work week and the age of retirement, which have an impact on the profile of volunteering. Legal and fiscal measures could also be reviewed to assess whether they impinge negatively on the status of volunteer-involving organizations, including issues related to juridical status, rights to associational activities, and resource mobilization. Subsequently, legal and administrative hindrances to volunteering, where they exist, can be reduced;

(ii) Give due weight to local ownership and citizen participation, to bring public services closer to communities and to open space for greater citizen engagement expressed through channels such as parental involvement in schools and community involvement in natural resource management;

(iii) Recognize that transport, communication and other infrastructure, such as public spaces, enhance the capacity of people to organize for voluntary activities. This is especially true of geographically dispersed populations and of people living in poverty, as well as older persons and people with disabilities. It is desirable that the impact of such infrastructure on levels of volunteering be factored into the planning process.

(g) *Integrating volunteerism into national development planning, recognizing the potential contribution of volunteerism to the achievement of sustainable development goals*

(i) Extend the notion of volunteerism as an additional valuable component of national development planning to development cooperation policy. Recognizing and building strategically on rich, local traditions of voluntary self-help and mutual aid can open the way to building up a new constituency in support of development efforts. Forging a link in the mind of the general public in countries providing development assistance between domestic volunteering in those countries and volunteering in countries receiving assistance can also help enlist public support for development cooperation.

(h) *Participation of all population groups*

(i) Consider all means available for more people to become involved in voluntary activities and to be drawn from a broader cross-section of society, including youth, older persons and people with disabilities and persons belonging to minorities, targeting opportunities for voluntary activities to facilitate the active participation of those groups which have little or no access to the benefits of engaging in volunteering;

(ii) Promote volunteering within educational establishments and youth services; develop specific programmes to encourage youth volunteering; put in place systems to recognize and accredit volunteering by youth; and work with the media to present an attractive image of volunteering. This can have a significant impact on the level of youth participation and constitute a sound investment in a country's human resources.

III. Support by the United Nations system

1. It is recommended that the relevant organizations and bodies of the United Nations system, including the regional commissions, further support voluntary activities by creating a favourable environment, including through:

(a) *Awareness-raising*

(i) Raise awareness internally and with their partners as regards the role of volunteerism in the various areas in which they are active and can sensitize their constituencies as to the implications in terms of activities undertaken. At the political level, strategically manage and support volunteering and incorporate it into the agenda of their meetings;

(ii) Undertake research and disseminate information about the cross-cutting link between volunteerism and major global concerns, including through technical and popular publications, workshops and Internet sites. This would serve also to extend recognition to volunteers and their organizations, which could be complemented by awards and other measures, including raising the profile of International Volunteer Day.

(b) *Recognition of the contributions of volunteers*

(i) Enhance and expand the current practice of extending special recognition to volunteers and volunteer-involving organizations across the United Nations system.

(c) *Involving volunteers in their programmes, interlinking with national initiatives*

(i) Include volunteers in their activities, supporting, inter alia, the establishment of volunteer schemes to address a range of global concerns. Where they exist, national and local volunteer centres could benefit substantially from the specialized expertise and networks of the United Nations system;

(ii) Actively encourage staff of the United Nations system to volunteer, utilizing their special skills and experiences.

(d) *Long-term planning for the enhancement of social capital by including all segments of society in volunteering*

(i) Make a strategic choice for the involvement of all segments of society, including youth, older persons and people with disabilities and persons belonging to minorities, targeting opportunities for voluntary activities to facilitate the participation of those groups that have little or no access to the benefits of engaging in volunteering. In this way, building on societal norms and net-

works will enhance the social capital of the society concerned, strengthen its capacity for development and have a lasting impact on its well-being.

(e) *Assisting in building national capacities, including in the field of training*

(i) Assist countries, upon request, in building national capacities, including in the field of training, and further support Governments in their actions to promote volunteerism as a strategic tool to enhance economic and social development;

(ii) Recognize the continuing role of the United Nations Volunteers as the volunteer arm of the United Nations system, placing volunteers in development and humanitarian programmes and promoting online volunteering. Build on the acquired experience of the United Nations Volunteers in enhancing the recognition, facilitation, networking and promotion of volunteering, deriving from its role as focal point for the International Year of Volunteers.

Economic and technical cooperation among developing countries

The UNDP/UNFPA Executive Board considered the second cooperation framework for technical cooperation among developing countries (TCDC) (2001-2003) [DP/CF/TCDC/2] at its January/February session. The second framework, which built on lessons learned in implementing the first framework, emphasized the need for developing countries to build and share capacities essential to participation in multilateral processes, to adapt domestic policy and institutional arrangements to the requirements of the new global economic system, and to protect and promote the development interests of the South by acquiring the knowledge and skills to compete in the current socio-economic environment. The second framework focused on the activities of the UNDP Special Unit for TCDC on issues that called for South-South solutions in international development cooperation, including initiatives to mainstream the practical use of the TCDC modality in UNDP and the UN system. Those efforts would be supported by improved online services linking the TCDC information service, WIDE, to other databases in the UN system, including the subregional resource facilities (SURFs).

The total core resources likely to be available for the programme in 2001-2003 were estimated at $5 million. The Special Unit for TCDC planned to mobilize an additional $15 million in non-core resources under the Voluntary Trust Fund for the Promotion of South-South Cooperation.

In February [dec. 2001/7], the Executive Board approved the second TCDC cooperation framework (2001-2003). In another decision [dec. 2001/2], it noted the lessons learned from the first cooperation framework, including the need for synergy between, and complementarity with, other UNDP efforts in that area, and for a more systematic assessment of the impact of TCDC and the need to focus on facilitating South-South capacity-building processes. The Board welcomed the Administrator's efforts to enhance and mainstream TCDC within UNDP and recognized the unique role of the Special Unit for TCDC in those efforts. It appreciated the contribution made to the South-South Trust Fund by donors and encouraged all partners to increase support for TCDC, in particular through innovative models of South-South cooperation. The Board reiterated its concern about the low level of UNDP core resources, which affected the resources allocated to the Special Unit. It requested the Administrator to review the allocation of additional resources for TCDC activities.

High-level Committee on TCDC

The High-level Committee on the Review of Technical Cooperation among Developing Countries, at its twelfth session (New York, 29 May–1 June) [A/56/39], considered a biennial progress report (1999-2000) on the implementation of the Buenos Aires Plan of Action [YUN 1978, p. 467] and its own decisions at previous sessions [TCDC/12/1 & Corr.1], and a progress report on the implementation of the new directions strategy [YUN 1995, p. 902] [TCDC/12/2]. It also held a thematic discussion on the role of TCDC in science and technology for development.

The Committee adopted three substantive decisions. In the first [A/56/39 (dec. 12/1 A)], it encouraged developing countries that had not done so to put in place a national TCDC policy, including a clear delineation of the TCDC focal point's role. It requested the TCDC Special Unit to organize subregional orientation workshops to facilitate greater understanding of TCDC. The Unit, in collaboration with other organizations, should promote the use of southern research and development capacities for increased agricultural productivity, and catalyse TCDC programmes designed to enhance the sharing of knowledge on science and technology. The Committee asked the UNDP Administrator to support the mainstreaming of the TCDC modality through, among other things, the use of national planning mechanisms and regional and international mechanisms, and urged the international community to provide support so that developing countries could respond to the challenges resulting from globalization. It commended the Unit for establishing an Internet-based information source, known as WIDE.

The High-level Committee, in another decision [dec. 12/1 B], noted that more developing countries were initiating and sponsoring technical and economic cooperation among developing countries (ECDC) activities and that developed countries' support to TCDC and ECDC had increased. The Committee requested UN system and other relevant organizations to take additional steps to integrate TCDC and ECDC modalities into their regular cooperation programmes in line with the new directions strategy. It encouraged the Special Unit to document and disseminate innovative and successful TCDC and ECDC practices. The Committee welcomed the strategic orientation and programme focus of the second cooperation framework for TCDC (above) and called for increased support to the Special Unit in implementing the framework. The Special Unit was requested to assist in documenting and disseminating the special problems and needs of developing countries, in particular the least developed countries, small island developing States and landlocked developing countries, through WIDE.

In a decision on the overall framework for promoting and applying TCDC [dec. 12/2], the Committee decided to review in 2003 the revised guidelines for the review of policies and procedures concerning TCDC and the common results framework. The guidelines had been applied on an experimental basis since 1993 and revised in 1997 [YUN 1997, p. 891]. Welcoming the promotion of South-South cooperation in the Administrator's Business Plans, the Committee called on him to promote the effectiveness of the TCDC focal point mechanism, especially at the regional and national levels, and to ensure that the separate identity of the TCDC Special Unit was maintained. The Committee decided to review periodically the impact and functioning of the Special Unit in promoting and coordinating TCDC on a global and system-wide basis.

The Executive Board, in June [dec. 2001/12], took note of the High-level Committee's decisions adopted at its twelfth session.

The Economic and Social Council, by **decision 2001/227** of 10 July, took note of the Committee's report on its twelfth session.

South-South cooperation

The Secretary-General, in response to General Assembly resolution 54/226 [YUN 1999, p. 819], reported in October [A/56/465] on the state of South-South cooperation during the 1998-2000 period, especially in trade, investment and monetary and financial arrangements.

He stated that South-South cooperation was gaining importance in promoting developing countries' participation in the international economic system. It diversified and expanded development partnerships and economic links and generated momentum towards more equitable forms of global interdependence. Developing countries had put forward numerous policy decisions, declarations and plans of action covering various aspects of South-South cooperation, the latest of which, the Tehran Consensus [A/56/358], adopted by the Group of 77 and China in August, proclaimed the following objectives: consolidating the South-South platform; building stronger southern institutions at the global level; bridging the knowledge and information gap; building broad-based partnerships; and mobilizing global support for advancing South-South cooperation. Regional economic groups were being energized and new groups were being formed to promote objectives, such as free trade, investment cooperation, transport integration, harmonized social action and integrated resource use. The World Bank estimated that the number of such cooperation arrangements had increased from 39 in 1970 to 82 by 1997. One third of global trade currently took place among regional trade groups. The formation of growth triangles or cooperative subregions was continuing. China, Mongolia and the Russian Federation were cooperating in a Euro-Asia Continental Land Bridge Programme focused on trade growth and transport integration, and the Malawi-Zambia-Mozambique growth triangle promoted trade and investment.

Preferential trade agreements also increased in number and significance. In 2000, 20 new agreements were added to the 214 already in existence, the most notable of which was the United States Trade and Development Act of 2000, which granted concessional terms to imports from 48 African and 25 Caribbean countries. Three fourths of global trade was currently governed by such agreements, which also focused on investment measures, competition policy and trade in services. Developing countries were making efforts to pool their resources and capacities—institutional, intellectual, technical and financial—to address common issues, as illustrated by the South Centre, an intergovernmental entity, and the Third World Network, which were involved in research and analysis on the implications of globalization for developing countries. Successful South-South partnering was exemplified by the Africa-Asia Business Forum, launched by UNDP and funded primarily by Japan, as a follow-up to the second Tokyo International Conference on African Development (Durban, South Africa, July) (see p. 898) to advance trade and investment cooperation between African and Asian firms.

The Secretary-General concluded that regional arrangements designed to achieve exchange-rate stability and manage crises should incorporate mechanisms to ensure regional surveillance, information-sharing and early warning. Domestic reforms were still needed to provide a sound basis for regional cooperation. While developing countries had advanced economic and technical cooperation among themselves, a more systematic and objective assessment of those frameworks and relevant cooperation arrangements was needed. It was incumbent upon the international community and the donor community to provide the necessary support, including financial resources, to South-South cooperation.

GENERAL ASSEMBLY ACTION

On 21 December [meeting 90], the General Assembly, on the recommendation of the Second Committee [A/56/562/Add.2], adopted **resolution 56/202** without vote [agenda item 99 (b)].

Economic and technical cooperation among developing countries

The General Assembly,

Stressing that South-South cooperation, as an important element of international cooperation for development, offers viable opportunities for developing countries in their individual and collective pursuit of sustained economic growth and sustainable development, in accordance with relevant General Assembly resolutions and recent United Nations conferences, and for ensuring their effective and meaningful participation in the newly emerging global economic system,

Recognizing that developing countries have the primary responsibility for promoting and implementing economic and technical cooperation among themselves, and reiterating the need for the international community to support the efforts of the developing countries to expand South-South cooperation through the modality of economic and technical cooperation among developing countries,

Reaffirming its resolution 33/134 of 19 December 1978, in which it endorsed the Buenos Aires Plan of Action for Promoting and Implementing Technical Cooperation among Developing Countries, resolution 46/159 of 19 December 1991 on technical cooperation among developing countries, resolution 49/96 of 19 December 1994 on a United Nations conference on South-South cooperation and resolutions 50/119 of 20 December 1995, 52/205 of 18 December 1997 and 54/226 of 22 December 1999 on economic and technical cooperation among developing countries, as well as other relevant resolutions of the General Assembly and the Economic and Social Council on economic and technical cooperation among developing countries,

Recalling the principles and objectives embodied in the Caracas Programme of Action, adopted at the High-level Conference on Economic Cooperation among Developing Countries, held at Caracas in May 1981, the San José Declaration and Plan of Action, adopted by the Group of 77 at the South-South Conference on Trade, Investment and Finance, held at San José from 13 to 15 January 1997, the Bali Declaration and the Bali Plan of Action on Regional and Subregional Economic Cooperation of the Developing Countries, adopted by the Group of 77 High-level Conference on Regional and Subregional Economic Cooperation of the Developing Countries, held in Bali, Indonesia, from 2 to 5 December 1998, and the Declaration of the South Summit and the Havana Programme of Action, adopted by the South Summit of the Group of 77, held at Havana from 10 to 14 April 2000, which accorded South-South cooperation high priority in order for developing countries to meet new development challenges, as well as other relevant declarations and plans of action,

Taking note of the Ministerial Declaration adopted by the Ministers for Foreign Affairs of the States members of the Group of 77 at their twenty-fifth annual meeting, held in New York on 16 November 2001, in which the increased importance and relevance of South-South cooperation was emphasized,

Taking note also of the Tehran Consensus, adopted at the Tenth Meeting of the Intergovernmental Follow-up and Coordination Committee on Economic Cooperation among Developing Countries of the Group of 77, held at Tehran from 18 to 22 August 2001, which called for consolidating the South-South platform, building stronger South institutions at the global level, bridging the knowledge and information gap, building broad-based partnerships and mobilizing global support for South-South cooperation,

1. *Endorses* the report of the High-level Committee on the Review of Technical Cooperation among Developing Countries on its twelfth session and the decisions adopted by the High-level Committee at that session;

2. *Takes note with appreciation* of the report of the Secretary-General on the state of South-South cooperation;

3. *Notes with satisfaction* the significant increase and expanded use of South-South cooperation by developing countries as an important and effective instrument of international cooperation, and in this connection urges developing countries in a position to do so to intensify technical and economic cooperation initiatives at the regional and interregional levels in areas such as health, education, training, agriculture, science and new technologies, and in particular information and communication technologies;

4. *Reiterates* that South-South cooperation should be viewed not as a substitute for but rather as a complement to North-South cooperation, and, in that connection, notes with appreciation the increasing number of developed countries and development foundations supporting South-South cooperation activities through a variety of triangular arrangements, including direct support or cost-sharing arrangements, joint research and development projects and third-country training programmes;

5. *Emphasizes* the need for concerted action by developing countries and their development partners, including relevant international organizations, with a view to strengthening cooperation and collaboration among developing countries at the subregional, regional and interregional levels;

6. *Notes with appreciation* the contributions made by a number of countries to the Voluntary Trust Fund for the Promotion of South-South Cooperation and to the Perez-Guerrero Trust Fund for Economic and Technical Cooperation among Developing Countries, and invites all countries to contribute to the trust funds in support of a revitalized South-South platform that is designed to benefit developing countries, especially the least developed, landlocked and small island developing countries;

7. *Recognizes* the need to strengthen institutions of the South, including policy research and development institutions and centres of excellence, especially at the regional and interregional levels, with a view to making more effective use of the institutional capacity of the South through, inter alia, improved South-South knowledge-sharing, networking, capacity-building and flow of information and policy analysis and coordination among developing countries on major development issues of common concern;

8. *Requests* all organizations and agencies of the United Nations development system to make concerted and intensified efforts to effectively mainstream the use of South-South cooperation by giving such cooperation appropriate consideration in the design, formulation and implementation of their regular programmes;

9. *Calls upon* all relevant United Nations organizations and multilateral institutions to consider increasing allocations of human, technical and financial resources for South-South cooperation, and in this context takes note of decision 2001/2 of the Executive Board of the United Nations Development Programme and the United Nations Population Fund, in which the Board requested the Administrator of the United Nations Development Programme to consider reviewing, in the context of the successor programming arrangements, the allocation of additional resources for activities involving technical cooperation among developing countries, taking into account the overall financial situation and the need for appropriate resources for other activities;

10. *Recognizes* the need for raising public awareness of and support for South-South cooperation as a dynamic form of international development cooperation which can give real content to the concept of ownership and partnership, and, for this reason, takes note of the Tehran Consensus proposal to launch the first international decade on South-South cooperation and the United Nations day for South-South cooperation;

11. *Requests* the Secretary-General, through coordination of the Special Unit for Technical Cooperation among Developing Countries of the United Nations Development Programme and in consultation with relevant organizations and agencies of the United Nations system and other relevant institutions in the South, to include in the report to be submitted to the General Assembly at its fifty-seventh session concrete measures for promoting and facilitating South-South cooperation, taking into account all relevant initiatives and proposals in this regard;

12. *Reiterates its request* to the Administrator of the United Nations Development Programme to ensure that the separate identity of the Special Unit for Tech-

nical Cooperation among Developing Countries is maintained and that the Unit is supported so that it may fully implement its mandate and responsibilities as a focal point of the United Nations system for South-South cooperation;

13. *Decides* to include in the provisional agenda of its fifty-eighth session the sub-item entitled "Economic and technical cooperation among developing countries", and requests the Secretary-General, in collaboration with the Special Unit for Technical Cooperation among Developing Countries and the United Nations Conference on Trade and Development, to submit to it at that session a comprehensive report on the state of South-South cooperation and the implementation of the present resolution.

UN Capital Development Fund

Contributions to the United Nations Capital Development Fund (UNCDF) regular resources in 2001 amounted to $24.3 million, a modest increase from the 2000 contributions of $23.9 million [DP/2002/25]. Total resources, including miscellaneous income and other (non-core) resources, amounted to $28.6 million. In applying its funding formula, the Fund reduced its new approvals downwards to $10.6 million from an original target of $20 million. Programme expenditure (including support costs paid to implementing agents) totalled $34.4 million. Total expenditure in 2001 represented an overall project delivery of

70 per cent, compared to $43.2 million or 85 per cent in 2000. UNCDF unexpended resources as at 31 December were $58.9 million, compared with $70.9 million a year earlier, including $33 million in the operational reserve.

UNCDF presented its first results-oriented annual report (ROAR) in 2001 [DP/2001/17], covering activities in 2000. The report presented an analysis of UNCDF performance assessed against its strategic results framework for 2000-2003. Progress in the sub-goals on local governance and microfinance was conclusive, confirming the Fund's comparative advantage in those areas. While the assessment was positive overall, improvement was needed in measuring the organization's performance in natural resources management. Although the number of new donors, including programme countries, increased, core resources were still below target and, because of the shortfall in available resources, the Fund could not meet all the demands from programme countries.

The Executive Board, in June [dec. 2001/12], took note of the ROAR and postponed consideration of the evaluation of the impact of the Fund's programmes to 2004. In September [dec. 2001/13], the Board took note of the Administrator's report on the 2002-2003 biennial budget estimates for UNCDF [DP/2001/21] and approved a gross appropriation of $13.7 million.

Chapter III

Humanitarian and special economic assistance

In 2001, the United Nations, through the Office for the Coordination of Humanitarian Affairs (OCHA), continued to coordinate the response of humanitarian agencies, particularly those of the UN system, to alleviate human suffering in disasters and emergencies, promote preparedness and prevention, and facilitate sustainable solutions. The 2001 consolidated inter-agency appeals process was launched globally under the theme "Women and war". During the year, appeals were launched for Angola, Burundi, the northern Caucasus, the Congo, the Democratic People's Republic of Korea, the Democratic Republic of the Congo, Eritrea, Ethiopia, the Great Lakes region and Central Africa, the Maluku islands of Indonesia, Sierra Leone, Somalia, South-Eastern Europe, the Sudan, Tajikistan, Uganda, the United Republic of Tanzania and West Africa. The total sought amounted to $2,559 million, of which $1,415 million was received, meeting 55.3 per cent of requirements. In addition, an inter-agency appeal covering Afghanistan for 2001, which sought $332.6 million, received contributions of $150 million, or 45.1 per cent of requirements. In September, a donor alert for Afghanistan, appealing for $662 million and covering October 2001 to March 2002, replaced the appeal; it received contributions of $496 million, or 75 per cent of requirements.

OCHA reported contributions to cover assistance in 2001 for natural disasters totalling $332 million, excluding in-kind contributions and services, for 49 situations in 36 countries and two regions. Through the Response Coordination and Emergency Services Branches, OCHA mobilized and coordinated assistance to 67 natural disasters.

The United Nations mine-action policy document, which continued to guide UN agencies and their partners in implementing their mine-action responsibilities, was further developed in 2001. In October, the Secretary-General presented the United Nations mine-action strategy for 2001-2005, intended to turn the policy into concrete action. He also outlined the United Nations policy on information management for mine action.

During the year, preparations were under way for the final review and appraisal in 2002 of the implementation of the United Nations New Agenda for the Development of Africa in the 1990s.

Humanitarian assistance

Coordination

Humanitarian affairs segment of the Economic and Social Council

During the humanitarian affairs segment of the Economic and Social Council, held from 11 to 13 July with the theme "Strengthening the coordination of emergency humanitarian assistance of the United Nations" (**decision 2001/206** of 31 January), the Council held panel discussions on emergency humanitarian assistance for groups with special needs and on natural disaster preparedness and response measures (**decision 2001/225** of 2 July).

The Council had before it a June report of the Secretary-General [A/56/95-E/2001/85] on strengthening the coordination of UN emergency humanitarian assistance, submitted pursuant to requests by the General Assembly in resolutions 46/182 [YUN 1991, p. 421] and 55/164 [YUN 2000, p. 848] and by the Council in resolution 1995/56 [YUN 1995, p. 927]. Noting that the year 2001 marked the tenth anniversary of the adoption of resolution 46/182 with the goal of improving the efficiency and effectiveness of UN humanitarian operations in the field, the Secretary-General presented an overview of the changes in humanitarian environments over the preceding decade and progress and constraints in strengthening humanitarian coordination. With regard to the period 2000-2001, the report discussed the context and challenges of providing humanitarian assistance during that period.

The UN system, in consultation with affected Governments, had conducted lessons-learned exercises to chart the course to better prevention and response. A recurring theme of those evaluations was the need for strong contingency planning, strengthened national disaster management capacity and disaster response coordination mechanisms, which included information management as well as regional cooperation. Inter-agency efforts included a series of initiatives, such as the inter-agency contingency planning guidelines prepared by the

Inter-Agency Standing Committee (IASC) to deal with environmental or natural disasters, civil unrest and conflict, or the related refugee outflows and internal displacement. The Office for the Coordination of Humanitarian Affairs (OCHA) had brought on board three regional disaster response advisers for Latin America, Asia and the Pacific, who provided technical support to UN country teams and, through them, to the regional and national authorities, for the preparation of contingency plans and the coordination of natural disaster response. Two more advisers were foreseen for the Caribbean and Central America and for Southern Africa. Inter-agency response was also effected through joint missions.

Some key issues in the coordination of humanitarian assistance included the protection of civilians in armed conflict, internal displacement, gender and children. Representatives of the Senior Inter-Agency Network on Internal Displacement, while visiting Afghanistan, Angola, Burundi, Eritrea and Ethiopia (October 2000 to May 2001), confirmed serious gaps in the UN humanitarian response to the needs of internally displaced persons. In response, OCHA planned to establish a small, inter-agency, non-operational Internally Displaced Persons Unit to advise the Emergency Relief Coordinator (ERC) on and ensure an improved coordinated response to the needs of internally displaced persons. The Unit would support and complement the advocacy efforts of the Secretary-General's Representative on internally displaced persons (see p. 652). IASC focused on providing support to UN country teams to bring the international community's attention to the needs and problems of women and girls in conflict and post-conflict situations. In 2001, the consolidated appeals process was launched globally under the theme "Women and war". IASC reviewed the guidelines and training tools for the process to ensure that they carried appropriate mainstreamed messages concerning gender; its electronic resource package aimed to assist humanitarian coordinators and field staff in mainstreaming gender into the 2002 consolidated appeals process. In response to the Economic and Social Council's agreed conclusions 1999/1 [YUN 1999, p. 824], steps were taken to reflect the growing political commitment towards child protection. Security Council resolutions 1261 (1999) and 1265(1999) [ibid., pp. 672 & 649], which included the protection of children in the mandates of UN peacekeeping operations for the Democratic Republic of the Congo (DRC) and Sierra Leone, respectively, allowed for the appointment of child protection advisers as an integral part of the missions. Nonetheless, sustained access to all children affected by armed conflict remained elusive, mainly against a background of low funding of child-specific priority projects.

In reviewing progress and constraints in strengthening coordination, the Secretary-General stated that a key task for the ERC remained that of advocating respect for the humanitarian agenda and the principles of humanitarian action, particularly in peacekeeping operations. Other challenges included strengthening his leadership as the inter-agency focal point on internally displaced persons and engaging more actively in negotiations for access to vulnerable populations. IASC needed to be strengthened to maintain its central role as a key coordination and consultative mechanism among its core members and standing invitees. Continuous efforts had been made to improve the consolidated appeals process as a process and a coordination tool. However, a few key challenges remained, such as better prioritizing the needs outlined in consolidated appeal documents. At a retreat on the appeals process and coordination in humanitarian emergencies (Montreux, Switzerland, March), donors expressed support for the process. However, statements of support needed to be accompanied by further coordination among donors, said the Secretary-General. Despite growing donor interest in better coordinated and consolidated plans, there continued to be a tendency to favour bilateral assistance, which, at times, eclipsed multilateral funding, making the coordination of international response more difficult. Contributions to the consolidated appeals had steadily declined from $1.96 billion in 1994 to $1.2 billion in 2000, leaving goals, particularly those relating to rehabilitation, unmet and urgent needs unaddressed. OCHA intended to carry out an analysis of donor funding patterns and the strategic coherence of the appeals process to identify ways to address imbalances. Linkages were needed between the consolidated appeals process and the United Nations Development Assistance Framework (UNDAF) to ensure an integrated strategy in the recovery phase. The UN country team in the Republic of the Congo had devised an innovative approach, combining the essential elements of the consolidated appeals process, the common country assessment and UNDAF into a single "United Nations Plan", which responded to challenges in the transition phase with a single planning document.

Recommendations were made on strengthening the coordination and response role of regional, national and local actors. There was a need to engage the entire community in responding to any disaster and, to strengthen the role of regional bodies and national actors, the international community should promote decentralization of humanitarian assistance management.

International actors should focus on strengthening indigenous preparedness capabilities to facilitate increased responsibility for and ownership of humanitarian response at the regional and national levels. Building partnership and trust with Governments and local authorities was key to providing more effective assistance.

Among the key challenges facing humanitarian operations was access, particularly in complex emergencies. Negotiating access raised problems of its own and was an extremely intricate and time-consuming process, with no certain guarantees. Member States had a vital role to play in supporting access negotiations by providing additional leverage or undertaking complementary diplomatic and political action. Another challenge was the development in humanitarian emergencies of "war economies"—alternative structures that emerged and gained total control of economic assets—which were often the instigators and promoters of violence; that was particularly true if the resources controlled by those structures related to illegal trade, such as narcotics. Other "war economies" could develop, such as arms trafficking or the misappropriation and sale of humanitarian assistance. Other challenges were sanctions regimes, the need to link relief and development, and administrative procedures. Regarding the last, OCHA had recommended changes to address the shortcomings, including enhanced delegation of authority for recruiting personnel and conducting financial transactions and procurement in the field.

The Secretary-General made recommendations to the General Assembly and the Economic and Social Council regarding further strengthening coordination of humanitarian assistance, prevention, preparedness and response mechanisms, and groups with special needs.

Summarizing the debate on the Secretary-General's report, the Council Vice-President stated that the Council reaffirmed the value and significance of the guiding principles laid down in Assembly resolution 46/182 and supported the strengthening of the tools and mechanisms established therein. They highlighted the need to increase national and regional capacities for preparing for and responding to natural disasters and called for greater collaboration and partnership between the UN system and regional, national and local actors. Members placed strong emphasis on the primary responsibility of the State concerned to protect and assist civilian populations, particularly the vulnerable and displaced, and agreed that Governments and parties to conflict should facilitate the access of humanitarian workers to those in need. They also attached the highest importance to strengthening measures to enhance the security of humanitarian personnel.

The Vice President also summarized the panel discussions.

On 13 July, the Council took note of the Secretary-General's report (**decision 2001/228**).

GENERAL ASSEMBLY ACTION

On 14 December [meeting 87], the General Assembly adopted **resolution 56/107** [draft: A/56/L.55 & Add.1] without vote [agenda item 20 (a)].

Strengthening of the coordination of emergency humanitarian assistance of the United Nations
The General Assembly,

Recalling its resolution 46/182 of 19 December 1991 and the guiding principles contained in the annex thereto, other relevant General Assembly and Economic and Social Council resolutions and agreed conclusions of the Council,

Taking note of the report of the Secretary-General,

Taking note also of the note by the Secretary-General on enhancing the functioning and utilization of the Central Emergency Revolving Fund, submitted to the General Assembly at its fifty-fifth session pursuant to its resolution 54/95 of 8 December 1999,

Recognizing the importance of the Revolving Fund as a cash-flow mechanism for a timely, prompt, effective and coordinated response by the organizations of the United Nations system,

Recognizing also that the pattern of utilization has been uneven in recent years and that there is a need to ensure that the Revolving Fund is used where the needs are greatest and most urgent,

1. *Welcomes* the holding of the fourth humanitarian affairs segment of the Economic and Social Council during its substantive session of 2001;

2. *Invites* the Economic and Social Council to continue to consider ways to enhance further the humanitarian affairs segment of future sessions of the Council;

3. *Emphasizes* the importance of discussion of humanitarian policies and activities in the General Assembly and the Economic and Social Council;

4. *Calls upon* relevant organizations of the United Nations system, other relevant international organizations, Governments and non-governmental organizations to cooperate with the Secretary-General and the Emergency Relief Coordinator to ensure timely implementation of and follow-up to agreed conclusions of the humanitarian affairs segment of the substantive session of the Economic and Social Council;

5. *Welcomes* the progress made by the Emergency Relief Coordinator and the Office for the Coordination of Humanitarian Affairs of the Secretariat in strengthening the coordination of humanitarian assistance of the United Nations;

6. *Expresses its deepest appreciation* to those Governments that have contributed to the Central Emergency Revolving Fund;

7. *Encourages* better use of the Revolving Fund, and in that context endorses the proposal of the Secretary-General to expand the utilization of the Fund to include humanitarian assistance for natural disasters, humanitarian assistance for new requirements in pro-

tracted emergencies and emergency staff safety arrangements for United Nations and associated personnel;

8. *Decides* that the expanded utilization of the Revolving Fund shall follow the same procedures and terms of reference that have been established in resolution 46/182 for advances and reimbursement of the resources of the Fund;

9. *Requests* the Secretary-General to inform Governments regularly about the use of the Revolving Fund and to report to the General Assembly at its fifty-seventh session on the utilization of the Fund and on further possible improvements in its terms of reference in order to enhance its functioning and utilization, inter alia, in relation to the great need for urgent assistance in many underfunded, so-called forgotten emergencies;

10. *Also requests* the Secretary-General to report to the General Assembly at its fifty-seventh session, through the 2002 substantive session of the Economic and Social Council, on progress made in strengthening the coordination of emergency humanitarian assistance of the United Nations, including the implementation of and follow-up to relevant agreed conclusions of the Council and progress made in the implementation of the present resolution.

On 24 December, the Assembly decided that the item "Strengthening of the coordination of humanitarian and disaster relief assistance of the United Nations, including special economic assistance" would remain for consideration during its resumed fifty-sixth (2002) session (**decision 56/464**).

UN and other humanitarian personnel

In response to General Assembly resolution 55/175 [YUN 2000, p. 1348], the Secretary-General submitted a September report on the safety and security of humanitarian personnel and protection of UN personnel [A/56/384 & Corr.1] (see p. 1347).

In **resolution 56/217** of 21 December, the Assembly strongly condemned any act or failure to act that obstructed or prevented humanitarian and UN personnel from discharging their humanitarian functions, or which entailed their being subjected to threats, the use of force or physical attack.

Resource mobilization

Central Emergency Revolving Fund

In 2001, the Central Emergency Revolving Fund (CERF), established in 1992 [YUN 1992, p. 584] as a cash-flow mechanism for the initial phase of humanitarian emergencies, granted 24 advances, amounting to $25.7 million.

In December, the General Assembly, having considered a 2000 report of the Secretary-General on enhancing the functioning and utilization of CERF [YUN 2000, p. 850], adopted **resolution 56/107** (see p. 825), in which it requested the Secretary-General to propose further possible improvements to enhance the use of the Fund.

Consolidated appeals

The consolidated appeals process continued to coordinate and facilitate the capacity of the UN system to meet its inter-agency resource requirements. In 2001, the United Nations and its humanitarian partners issued 19 consolidated appeals that sought some $2.8 billion for assistance to Afghanistan, Angola, Burundi, the northern Caucasus, the Congo, the Democratic People's Republic of Korea, the Democratic Republic of the Congo, Eritrea, Ethiopia, the Great Lakes region and Central Africa, the Maluku crisis (Indonesia), Sierra Leone, Somalia, South-Eastern Europe, the Sudan, Tajikistan, Uganda, the United Republic of Tanzania and West Africa.

Contributions to the consolidated appeals process fell from $1.96 billion in 1994 to $1.2 billion in 2000, and the share of requirements met showed a steady downward trend, from 80 per cent in 1994 to 59 per cent in 2000. The 2001 mid-year review placed particular focus on the impact of underfunding. As at 22 May, six months after the 2001 consolidated appeals were launched, only 23 per cent of the $2.8 billion requested had been funded. In addition, some crises were almost ignored and in others emergency food aid received the bulk of contributions, while non-food sectors, such as agriculture, health, education and water and sanitation, remained underfunded. Donors were urged to work more closely together to address the requirements in a more balanced way.

White Helmets

In response to General Assembly resolution 54/98 [YUN 1999, p. 829], the Secretary-General submitted an August report on the "White Helmets" initiative [A/56/308], which was established by Argentina to provide expertise on a standby team basis from various national volunteer corps to support immediate relief, rehabilitation, construction and development activities. The report, which covered the period from July 1999 to July 2001, provided an overview of progress made in collaboration with various partners, particularly the Government of Argentina, through the White Helmets Commission of Argentina. It highlighted programme activities undertaken in the context of the United Nations Volunteers (see p. 814) and White Helmets Commission partnership.

(For information on the International Year of Volunteers, see p. 814.)

(For information on the International Year of Volunteers, see p. 814.)

GENERAL ASSEMBLY ACTION

On 14 December [meeting 87], the General Assembly adopted **resolution 56/102** [draft: A/56/L.50 & Add.1] without vote [agenda item 20 *(d)*].

Participation of volunteers, "White Helmets", in the activities of the United Nations in the field of humanitarian relief, rehabilitation and technical cooperation for development

The General Assembly,

Reaffirming its resolutions 50/19 of 28 November 1995, 52/171 of 16 December 1997 and 54/98 of 8 December 1999,

Reaffirming also its resolutions 46/182 of 19 December 1991, 47/168 of 22 December 1992, 48/57 of 14 December 1993, 49/139 A and B of 20 December 1994, 50/57 of 12 December 1995 and 51/194 of 17 December 1996 and Economic and Social Council resolutions 1995/56 of 28 July 1995 and 1996/33 of 25 July 1996,

Recognizing that recent events emphasize the need for the international community, in addressing the growing magnitude and complexity of natural disasters and other humanitarian emergencies, to rely not only on the formulation of a well-coordinated global response within the framework of the United Nations but also on the promotion of a smooth transition from relief to rehabilitation, reconstruction and development,

Recalling that prevention, preparedness and contingency planning for emergencies at the global level depend, for the most part, on the strengthened local and national response capacities as well as on the availability of financial resources, both domestic and international,

1. *Takes note* of the report of the Secretary-General, prepared in pursuance of its resolution 54/98 on the participation of volunteers, "White Helmets", in activities of the United Nations in the field of humanitarian relief, rehabilitation and technical cooperation for development;

2. *Encourages* voluntary national and regional actions aimed at making available to the United Nations system, through the United Nations Volunteers and other agencies, national volunteer corps such as the White Helmets on a standby basis, in accordance with accepted United Nations procedures and practices, in order to provide specialized human and technical resources for emergency relief and rehabilitation;

3. *Expresses its appreciation* for the commendable progress of the White Helmets initiative as a singular voluntary international effort to provide the United Nations system with voluntary expertise to respond, in a quick and coordinated manner, to humanitarian relief, rehabilitation, reconstruction and development, while preserving the non-political, neutral and impartial character of humanitarian action;

4. *Recognizes* that the White Helmets, in close cooperation with the Office for the Coordination of Humanitarian Affairs of the Secretariat and as an operational partner of the United Nations system, are an efficient and viable mechanism for making pre-identified and trained homogeneous teams available to the United Nations, in support of immediate relief, re-

habilitation, reconstruction and development activities, in the light of the increasing number, growing magnitude and complexity of natural disasters and other emergencies;

5. *Calls upon* Member States to promote the facilitation of cooperative actions between the United Nations system and civil society, through national volunteer corps, in order to strengthen the United Nations capacities for early and effective response to humanitarian emergencies, and invites them to make the commensurate financial resources available through the special financing window of the Special Voluntary Fund of the United Nations Volunteers, or in coordination with it;

6. *Encourages* Member States to identify and support their respective national focal points for the White Helmets in order to continue to provide the United Nations system with an accessible global network of rapid response facilities in case of humanitarian emergencies;

7. *Recognizes with appreciation* the progress made by the States members of the Common Market of the South and associated partners in the strengthening and broadening of the White Helmets humanitarian assistance concept within a regional framework, and encourages Member States in other regional associations to consider implementing that concept in their efforts aimed at extending humanitarian assistance cooperation;

8. *Invites* Member States, international financial institutions, regional organizations and the United Nations system to consider ways and means to ensure the integration of the White Helmets initiative into their programme activities, particularly those related to humanitarian and disaster relief assistance;

9. *Invites* the Secretary-General, on the basis of the experience acquired, to consider further the potential use of White Helmets as a resource for preventing and mitigating the effects of emergencies and post-conflict humanitarian emergencies and, in this context, to maintain an adequate structure for the White Helmets liaison functions, taking into account the outgoing reforms process;

10. *Recommends* that the Secretary-General encourage relevant agencies of the United Nations system to explore opportunities for collaboration with White Helmets, taking into account the success of coordinated actions carried out, inter alia, with the United Nations Children's Fund, the World Food Programme, the Office for the Coordination of Humanitarian Affairs, the United Nations Development Programme and the United Nations Volunteers;

11. *Requests* the Secretary-General to continue the consideration of the possible strengthening and broadening of consultative mechanisms to promote further and operationalize the concept, as referred to in paragraphs 9 and 10 above, and to report to the General Assembly at its fifty-eighth session, under the item entitled "Strengthening of the coordination of humanitarian and disaster relief assistance of the United Nations, including special economic assistance", on the actions taken in conformity with the present resolution.

Mine clearance

In response to General Assembly resolution 55/120 [YUN 2000, p. 851], the Secretary-General, in an October report [A/56/448], presented information on key developments, achievements and challenges encountered by the mine-action community in 2001, with an emphasis on cross-cutting issues of concern to all partners, such as global coordination and resource mobilization; assistance to national and local authorities; emergency assistance; information management; quality control; training and standards; and advocacy. Significant progress was made in mine action over the preceding 12 months, particularly in terms of strategic planning, operational support, coordination and information management. At the same time, new landmines continued to be laid in several countries.

The UN mine-action policy document, "Mine action and effective coordination: the United Nations policy", which continued to guide UN agencies and their partners in implementing their mine-action responsibilities, was further elaborated in 2001, through the development of a five-year strategy for UN mine action covering the period 2001-2005 [A/56/448/Add.1], intended to turn the policy into concrete action, and the completion of the UN policy on information management for mine action, prepared by the Meeting of Mine Action Programme Directors and Advisers and approved by the Inter-Agency Coordination Group on Mine Action [A/56/448/Add.2].

Global coordination for mine-related activities within the UN system was the responsibility of the Mine Action Service, which relied on two mechanisms, the Inter-Agency Coordination Group on Mine Action and the Steering Committee on Mine Action. The former was a UN inter-agency forum, while the latter promoted coordinated UN initiatives with those of other partners and included the International Committee of the Red Cross (ICRC), the Geneva International Centre for Humanitarian Demining, the International Campaign to Ban Landmines and other non-governmental organizations (NGOs), in addition to UN mine-action entities. At May and September meetings, the Steering Committee addressed the landmine problems in Eritrea and Kosovo (Federal Republic of Yugoslavia), the emergency response plan, explosive remnants of war and the possibility of using a universal mine-action logo in support of advocacy initiatives. The Mine Awareness Working Group, composed of mine-awareness practitioners, mainly from the field, but also representing the United Nations, ICRC, NGOs, independent expert bodies and others, held its first meeting in May. During the year, significant changes were made to the annual portfolio of mine-related projects, designed for sharing information and mobilizing resources;

in an attempt to present the country projects in a broader humanitarian and socio-economic context and to define the UN support strategy for each affected region, it included country briefs, intended to help the understanding of the linkages among individual projects, as well as between mine-action projects and other humanitarian and development activities. In 2001, $1.25 million was advanced to the Mine Action Service from CERF to support emergency activities in Eritrea and Kosovo. Through the Adopt-A-Minefield campaign, based on a partnership agreement between the United Nations Development Programme (UNDP) and the United Nations Association of the United States of America, $2.7 million was transferred to UNDP by the end of May for clearance tasks in Afghanistan, Bosnia and Herzegovina, Cambodia, Croatia and Mozambique. The campaign grew to include two new satellite partnerships in Canada and the United Kingdom. The Database of Mine Action Investments, which tracked the flow of resources to mine-action programmes, indicated that funding had regularly increased over the preceding four years. Of an estimated $200 million invested in mine-action assistance by the international community annually, about 40 per cent was channelled through the UN system and used primarily to finance field activities. A total of $151 million had been requested for the 2001 portfolio, of which $74 million was raised by 30 April.

UNDP supported mine-action programmes in 16 countries. During the year, new programmes were launched to assist in Albania, Eritrea, Ethiopia, Guinea-Bissau, Lebanon and Thailand, while assistance continued to more established programmes in Angola, Azerbaijan, Bosnia and Herzegovina, Cambodia, Chad, Croatia, the Lao People's Democratic Republic, Mozambique, Somalia and Yemen. Emergency mine-action assistance for southern Lebanon, the temporary security zone between Eritrea and Ethiopia, Kosovo, Afghanistan and northern Iraq was channelled through the United Nations. Other areas of concern from a humanitarian point of view included Angola, Burundi, the DRC, the Russian Federation (Ingushetia), Sri Lanka and the Sudan.

To handle situations where landmines were an obstacle to humanitarian relief efforts and/or peacekeeping deployment, the United Nations developed a plan for a rapid emergency mine-action response capability, which focused on early reconnaissance, leading to the establishment of an appropriately configured coordination capacity in the early stages of an emergency and a range of mine-action capabilities to address the immediate threat in each situation. In that context, mine-action start-up kits were being developed.

An annex to the report listed contributions by donors to the Voluntary Trust Fund for Assistance in Mine Action as at 31 July, which totalled $79.7 million.

GENERAL ASSEMBLY ACTION

On 21 December [meeting 91], the General Assembly adopted **resolution 56/219** [draft: A/56/L.63/Rev.1 & Add.1] without vote [agenda item 38].

Assistance in mine action

The General Assembly,

Recalling its resolutions 48/7 of 19 October 1993, 49/215 of 23 December 1994, 50/82 of 14 December 1995, 51/149 of 13 December 1996 and 52/173 of 18 December 1997, on assistance in mine clearance, and its resolutions 53/26 of 17 November 1998, 54/191 of 17 December 1999 and 55/120 of 6 December 2000, on assistance in mine action, all adopted without a vote,

Considering mine action to be an important component of United Nations humanitarian and development activities,

Reaffirming its deep concern at the tremendous humanitarian and development problems caused by the presence of mines and other unexploded ordnance that constitute an obstacle to the return of refugees and other displaced persons, to humanitarian aid operations and to reconstruction and economic development, as well as to the restoration of normal social conditions, and that have serious and lasting social and economic consequences for the populations of mine-affected countries,

Bearing in mind the serious threat that mines and other unexploded ordnance pose to the safety, health and lives of local civilian populations, as well as of personnel participating in humanitarian, peacekeeping and rehabilitation programmes and operations,

Reiterating its dismay at the high number of victims of mines, especially among civilian populations, including women and children, and recalling in this context Commission on Human Rights resolutions 1995/79 of 8 March 1995, 1996/85 of 24 April 1996, 1997/78 of 18 April 1997, 1998/76 of 22 April 1998, 1999/80 of 28 April 1999, 2000/85 of 27 April 2000 and 2001/75 of 25 April 2001, on the rights of the child, and resolutions 1996/27 of 19 April 1996, 1998/31 of 17 April 1998, 2000/51 of 25 April 2000 and decision 1997/107 of 11 April 1997, on the human rights of persons with disabilities,

Deeply alarmed by the number of mines that continue to be laid each year, as well as the presence of a large number of mines and other unexploded ordnance as a result of armed conflicts, and thus convinced of the necessity and urgency of a significant increase in mine-clearance efforts by the international community with a view to eliminating the threat of landmines to civilians as soon as possible,

Noting the inclusion in Amended Protocol II to the Convention on Prohibitions or Restrictions on the Use of Certain Conventional Weapons Which May Be Deemed to Be Excessively Injurious or to Have Indiscriminate Effects of a number of provisions of importance for mine-clearance operations, notably the requirement of detectability, and provision of information and technical and material assistance necessary to remove or otherwise render ineffective existing minefields, mines and booby traps, and noting also that Amended Protocol II to the Convention entered into force on 3 December 1998,

Noting also the conclusions and recommendations adopted at the Second Annual Conference of the States Parties to Amended Protocol II to the Convention, held in Geneva from 11 to 13 December 2000,

Recalling that the States parties at the First Review Conference of the States Parties to the Convention declared their commitment to keep the provisions of the Protocol under review in order to ensure that the concerns regarding the weapons it covers are addressed, and that they would encourage the efforts of the United Nations and other organizations to address all problems related to landmines,

Noting that the Convention on the Prohibition of the Use, Stockpiling, Production and Transfer of Anti-personnel Mines and on Their Destruction entered into force on 1 March 1999 and that the Convention has been accepted formally by one hundred and twenty-two States and signed but not yet ratified by an additional twenty States,

Noting also the conclusions of the Third Meeting of the States Parties to the Convention, held in Managua from 18 to 21 September 2001, taking note of the reaffirmed commitments that were made, among other things, to provide assistance for mine clearance and rehabilitation, the social and economic reintegration of mine victims and mine-awareness programmes and to eradicate anti-personnel mines, and taking note also of the work of the intersessional programme established by States parties to the Convention,

Stressing the need to convince mine-affected States to halt new deployments of anti-personnel mines in order to ensure the effectiveness and efficiency of mine-clearance operations,

Recognizing the important role that the international community, in particular States involved in the deployment of mines, can play in assisting mine clearance in mine-affected countries by providing necessary maps and information and appropriate technical and material assistance to remove or otherwise render ineffective existing minefields, mines and booby traps,

Concerned at the limited availability of safe and cost-effective mine-detection and mine-clearance equipment, as well as the need for effective global coordination in research and development to improve the relevant technology, and conscious of the need to promote further and more rapid progress in this field and to foster international technical cooperation to this end,

Concerned also at the limited availability of the technical, material and financial resources needed to meet the cost associated with mine-clearance activities in mine-affected countries,

Recognizing that, in addition to the primary role of States, the United Nations has an important role to play in the field of assistance in mine action,

Reaffirming the need to reinforce international cooperation in the area of mine action and to devote the necessary resources to that end,

Concerned at the critical financial situation of the Mine Action Service of the Department of Peacekeeping Operations of the Secretariat,

Welcoming the mine-action coordination centres already established under the auspices of the United Nations, as well as the creation of international trust funds for mine clearance and other mine-action activities,

Noting with satisfaction the inclusion in the mandates of several peacekeeping operations of provisions relating to mine-action work carried out under the direction of the Department of Peacekeeping Operations, in the context of such operations,

Commending the action already taken by the United Nations system, donor and recipient Governments, the International Committee of the Red Cross and non-governmental organizations to coordinate their efforts and seek solutions to the problems related to the presence of mines and other unexploded ordnance, as well as their assistance to victims of mines,

Welcoming the role of the Secretary-General in increasing public awareness of the problem of landmines,

1. *Takes note with appreciation* of the report of the Secretary-General on assistance in mine action;

2. *Calls*, in particular, for the continuation of the efforts of the United Nations, with the assistance of States and institutions as appropriate, to foster the establishment of mine-action capacities in countries where mines constitute a serious threat to the safety, health and lives of the local population or an impediment to social and economic development efforts at the national and local levels, emphasizes the importance of developing national mine-action capacities, and urges all Member States, in particular those that have the capacity to do so, to assist mine-affected countries in the establishment and development of national capacities in mine clearance, mine awareness and victim assistance;

3. *Invites* Member States to develop and support national programmes, in cooperation with the relevant bodies of the United Nations system where appropriate, to promote awareness of landmines, especially among women and children;

4. *Expresses its appreciation* to Governments, regional organizations and other donors for their financial and in-kind contributions to mine action, including contributions for emergency operations and for national capacity-building programmes;

5. *Appeals* to Governments, regional organizations and other donors to continue, and whenever possible increase, their support to mine action through further contributions, including contributions through the Voluntary Trust Fund for Assistance in Mine Action, to allow for the timely delivery of mine-action assistance in emergency situations;

6. *Encourages* all relevant multilateral and national programmes and bodies to include, in coordination with the United Nations, activities related to mine action in their humanitarian, rehabilitation, reconstruction and development assistance activities, where appropriate, bearing in mind the need to ensure national ownership, sustainability and capacity-building;

7. *Stresses* the importance of international support for emergency assistance to victims of mines and for the care and rehabilitation and social and economic re-integration of the victims, and also stresses that such assistance should be integrated into broader public health and socio-economic strategies;

8. *Encourages* Governments, relevant United Nations bodies and other donors to take further action to promote gender- and age-appropriate mine-awareness programmes, victim assistance and child-centred rehabilitation, thereby reducing the number of child victims and relieving their plight;

9. *Emphasizes again* the important role of the United Nations in the effective coordination of mine-action activities, including those by regional organizations, and especially the role of the Mine Action Service of the Department of Peacekeeping Operations of the Secretariat, and stresses the need for the continuous assessment of this role by the General Assembly;

10. *Emphasizes* in this regard the role of the Mine Action Service as the focal point for mine action within the United Nations system and its ongoing collaboration with and coordination of all the mine-related activities of the United Nations agencies, funds and programmes;

11. *Notes with appreciation* the mine-action strategy covering the period 2001-2005 submitted by the Secretary-General, requests him to optimize it by seeking and taking into account the views of Member States and taking into consideration the impact of the landmine problem on rehabilitation, reconstruction and development, with a view to ensuring the effectiveness of assistance in mine action by the United Nations, emphasizes in this respect the importance of further multisectoral assessments and surveys better to define the nature, scope and impact of the landmine problem in affected countries and to support the establishment of clear priorities and national plans of action, notes with appreciation in this regard the ongoing development by the United Nations of International Mine Action Standards to support the safe and effective conduct of mine-action activities, emphasizes the need for an inclusive process to be followed in the development of such standards, and encourages the Secretary-General to circulate the completed standards as a United Nations document to all Member States;

12. *Takes note with appreciation* of the Information Management Policy for Mine Action submitted by the Secretary-General, and emphasizes in this context the importance of developing a comprehensive information management system for mine action, following an inclusive process, under the overall coordination of the Mine Action Service and with the support of the Geneva International Centre for Humanitarian Demining, in order to facilitate the coordination of field activities and the setting of priorities therein;

13. *Welcomes* in this respect the development of an Electronic Mine Information Network to support the role of the United Nations as a repository of mine-related information and to serve as a gateway to all relevant data made available by Member States and regional, governmental and non-governmental organizations and foundations for mine action;

14. *Also welcomes* recent approaches with regard to the establishment of mine-action coordination centres, encourages the further establishment of such centres, especially in emergency situations, and also encourages States to support the activities of mine-action coordination centres and trust funds established to co-

ordinate assistance in mine action under the auspices of the Mine Action Service;

15. *Encourages* the ongoing development of an emergency response plan by the United Nations to respond to emergency mine-action requirements, and emphasizes the need for such a plan to build upon all existing capacities;

16. *Urges* Member States and regional, governmental and non-governmental organizations and foundations to continue to extend full assistance and cooperation to the Secretary-General and, in particular, to provide him with information and data, as well as other appropriate resources that could be useful in strengthening the coordination role of the United Nations in mine action, in particular in the fields of mine awareness, training, surveying, detection and clearance, scientific research on mine-detection and mine-clearance technology and information on and distribution of medical equipment and supplies;

17. *Emphasizes* in this regard the importance of recording the location of mines, of retaining all such records and making them available to concerned parties upon cessation of hostilities, and welcomes the strengthening of the relevant provisions in international law;

18. *Calls upon* Member States, especially those that have the capacity to do so, to provide the necessary information and technical, financial and material assistance, as appropriate, and to locate, remove, destroy or otherwise render ineffective existing minefields, mines, booby traps and other devices in accordance with international law, as soon as possible;

19. *Urges* Member States and regional, intergovernmental and non-governmental organizations and foundations that have the ability to do so to provide, as appropriate, technological assistance to mine-affected countries and to promote scientific research and development on humanitarian mine-action techniques and technology so that mine-action activities may be carried out more effectively at lower costs and through safer means and to promote international collaboration in this regard;

20. *Encourages* Member States and regional, intergovernmental and non-governmental organizations and foundations to continue to support ongoing activities to promote appropriate technology, as well as international operational and safety standards for humanitarian mine-action activities;

21. *Requests* the Secretary-General to submit to the General Assembly at its fifty-seventh session a report on the progress achieved on all relevant issues outlined both in his previous reports to the Assembly on assistance in mine clearance and mine action and in the present resolution, including the progress made by the International Committee of the Red Cross and other international and regional organizations as well as national programmes, and on the operation of the Voluntary Trust Fund for Assistance in Mine Action and other mine-action programmes;

22. *Invites* the Secretary-General to continue to study how to secure a more sound financial basis for the Mine Action Service and to present options to this effect to the General Assembly;

23. *Also invites* the Secretary-General further to study ways and means of increasing public awareness of the impact of the problem of landmines and other unexploded ordnance on affected countries and to present options to this effect to the General Assembly;

24. *Decides* to include in the provisional agenda of its fifty-seventh session the item entitled "Assistance in mine action".

Humanitarian activities

Africa

Angola

The UN Consolidated Inter-Agency Appeal for Angola, launched in 2000 for a total of $226 million to cover January to December 2001, was revised during the year to $233.2 million. Some 50 per cent ($116.6 million) was met.

The general humanitarian situation in Angola did not improve during 2001. Displacement reached triple projected levels and resettlement stagnated, putting further strain on overstretched emergency programmes. Food security worsened for many vulnerable populations, in terms of both availability and access to food, as a result of factors that included late and irregular rains, lack of suitable land and inputs, and declining living standards. Guerrilla and counter-insurgency warfare had a serious impact on civilians living in militarily contested areas, and widespread insecurity affected the delivery of humanitarian assistance. By year's end, despite numerous widespread emergency interventions, noticeable improvements in humanitarian conditions occurred for only a few population groups. OCHA launched a further consolidated inter-agency appeal covering 2002.

Eritrea

The UN Consolidated Inter-Agency Appeal for Eritrea, which was launched in February, initially sought $157.5 million. That amount was revised to $133.2 million in October. The donor community covered 60 per cent ($79.9 million) of the requirements.

Following the arrival of the peacekeepers of the United Nations Mission in Ethiopia and Eritrea in late 2000 [YUN 2000, p. 174] and the establishment of a Temporary Security Zone along the southern border with Ethiopia (see p. 195), thousands of internally displaced persons began to return to their home areas from camps. During 2001, thousands of Eritrean refugees, some of whom had spent the last 20 to 30 years in neighbouring countries, also returned. Although many parts of the country received good rains, drought continued to affect more than 524,000 persons as at mid-September. Significant progress was made in stabilizing the humanitarian situation of the most vulnerable groups through the implementation of emergency relief interventions to internally displaced persons in camps, returned refugees and other war- and drought-affected communities. A further consolidated appeal was launched to cover assistance requirements for 2002.

Ethiopia

The total funding requirement for the 2001 UN Consolidated Inter-Agency Appeal for Ethiopia, launched in February and totalling $203.3 million, was revised later in the year to $250.8 million. Some 40.8 per cent ($102 million) was received.

In addition to the border conflict with Eritrea (see p. 191), lingering internal localized conflicts in Ethiopia had an overall negative effect on economic and development efforts. Furthermore, Ethiopia, one of the world's poorest countries, was subject to drastic weather patterns, which included cyclical periods of drought and regular onsets of heavy rain. It was also periodically subject to pest infestations and seasonal peaks of communicable diseases. In 2001, a significant portion of the war-affected population in the north returned home, with the exception of those in areas where landmines and property damage hindered a return. However, the drought-affected caseload, notably the assumed 80,000 drought-displaced as well as those dispersed from refugee camps in the Somali region, remained significant and required further assistance. A further appeal was launched to assist the country in 2002.

Great Lakes region and Central Africa

The UN Consolidated Inter-Agency Appeal for the Great Lakes region and Central Africa, launched in 2000 and covering January to December 2001, sought a total of $475.7 million ($28.1 million for the regional appeal itself, and $448 million for Burundi, the Congo, the DRC, Uganda and the United Republic of Tanzania). There was no appeal for Rwanda in 2001. Of the total sought, $248.2 million, or 52.2 per cent, was received as at October.

Despite some positive political developments in the Great Lakes region, the humanitarian situation continued to be of serious concern. In addition to the complex political and military environment (see p. 115), it continued to be plagued by chronic drought and flooding, and the possibility of sudden-onset natural disaster in the form of volcanic or seismic activity in the vicinity of Lake Kivu. Across the region, the needs of vulnerable populations remained acute. Some 1,130,458 people from the region were refugees, and a further 3,012,925 were displaced within their own countries. However, not only those populations were at risk; host communities faced additional demands on their own meagre resources, livelihoods were threatened by insecurity, and access to the most basic social services, such as health and education, was limited. A further appeal was launched to cover humanitarian needs in the region in 2002.

Burundi

The UN Consolidated Inter-Agency Appeal for Burundi, covering January to December 2001, which, when launched in 2000, sought $102 million, was revised in May 2001 to $111.5 million. Some 47.8 per cent ($53.3 million) of that amount was met.

The plight of 432,000 Burundians in internal displacement sites continued to dominate the humanitarian agenda. In addition, assistance was needed for 200,000 displaced persons, surviving under ad hoc arrangements, making the delivery of assistance more difficult. More than 380,000 had sought refuge in neighbouring countries, mainly the United Republic of Tanzania. Following persistent drought since 1998, food insecurity remained high. An unprecedented malaria epidemic, with 1 million cases reported at its height in November 2000, also reached high-altitude regions of the country, where natural resistance was low. Transmission of HIV and other infectious diseases continued to rise. Although the proposed Transitional Government in Burundi, scheduled to take office on 1 November, was a significant step forward (see p. 151), the security situation remained volatile, with a general increase in armed banditry and continued fighting in traditional zones of insecurity, particularly in areas close to the Tanzanian border; humanitarian actors had irregular access to those areas. An appeal was launched for assistance in 2002.

Congo (Republic of the)

Within the UN Consolidated Inter-Agency Appeal for the Great Lakes region and Central Africa covering January to December 2001, an appeal was launched for the Republic of the Congo totalling $32.5 million, of which 37.2 per cent ($12.1 million) was received.

A UN Plan for 2001-2002 assessed the status of development in the Congo and listed the goals that the UN country team had set to respond to the situation. In order to support the population directly and provide capacity-building assistance to consolidate peace and reduce poverty, the goals were to: revive productive and income-generating activities; re-establish basic social services and infrastructure; meet emergency needs and establish early warning systems; and support efforts to promote democracy and human rights. The team also drew up a common humanitarian action plan that comprised scaled-down emergency assistance (should stabilization within the country continue), a continued presence for early warning and potential resurgence of humanitarian needs, and refugee assistance.

Democratic Republic of the Congo

The UN Consolidated Inter-Agency Appeal for the DRC, issued in 2000, which sought $139.5 million to cover January to December 2001, was revised in September to $122.9 million. Assistance covering 66.7 per cent ($82 million) of that amount was received.

Political developments and the military disengagement observed in the DRC since January (see p. 117) did not lead to significant improvements in the dire humanitarian situation. Humanitarian space shrank along the eastern borders as a result of renewed fighting and overwhelming distrust between protagonists of all sides. However, civilians in the relatively peaceful central and western areas awaited economic and institutional reconstruction. In other areas, expanded access as a follow-up to disengagement from the conventional lines brought NGOs and agencies closer to displaced and hosting communities. In eastern DRC, the killing in April of six ICRC relief workers in Ituri and the massive influx of armed forces in May in areas of the Kivu provinces limited the activities of humanitarian agencies and led to an increased recourse to air interventions. A further appeal was launched to cover 2002.

In December (**resolution 56/100**) (see p. 852), the General Assembly requested the Secretary-General to keep under review the economic situation in the DRC with a view to promoting participation in and support for a programme of financial and material assistance to enable the country to meet its urgent needs in terms of economic recovery and reconstruction.

Uganda

The Consolidated Inter-Agency Appeal for Uganda, launched in 2000, which sought $78.7 million for January to December 2001, was revised in September to $80 million. The donor community met 43.2 per cent ($33.5 million) of requirements.

In 2001, several initiatives were under way in Uganda to reconcile internal differences and seek rapprochement with neighbouring countries. Against that backdrop, 717,532 refugees,

displaced persons and drought victims remained in camps, without sufficient land, shelter, income and other basic rights. Some 5,950 abducted children remained missing. In addition to funding shortfalls, planning, implementation and monitoring of emergency and recovery assistance were constrained by the lack of government policy and strategy concerning the status and rights of displaced Ugandan citizens, daily security incidents in Katakwi, Karamoja and other affected areas, heightened security risks to staff, vehicles and equipment due to repeated rebel incursions in Gulu, Kitgum, Adjumani, Yumbe, Moyo, Bundibugyo, Kasesse and Kabarole and attacks by Karamojong warriors on neighbouring districts in Katakwi, Soroti and Kumi, and military escorts for convoys that were irregular due to lack of fuel supplies, armoured vehicles and personnel. A further appeal was launched to cover 2002.

United Republic of Tanzania

The UN Consolidated Inter-Agency Appeal for the United Republic of Tanzania, launched in 2000, which sought $110.4 million for January to December 2001, received funding to cover 82.2 per cent ($91 million) of requirements.

Tanzania continued to receive refugees from Burundi and the DRC, as well as small numbers from Rwanda. However, the overall refugee caseload dropped from 543,145 to 509,655, as a result of a re-registration exercise undertaken in September.

Somalia

In response to General Assembly resolution 55/168 [YUN 2000, p. 860], the Secretary-General, in a September report [A/56/389], reviewed the current situation in Somalia and the humanitarian and rehabilitation assistance provided by the United Nations and its partners over the preceding year.

Somalia's long history of civil strife and economic stratification had resulted in some of the world's highest rates of mortality, morbidity and malnutrition. The socio-political map remained divided between the relatively stable environments in north-west and north-east Somalia and insecurity in the south (see p. 207), where civilians still suffered intermittent violence and the continuing instability restricted aid programming. Over the preceding year, emergency conditions across the country abated significantly, owing to positive environmental conditions and good harvests. However, gains were insufficient to break the seasonal cycle of boom and bust for poor and middle-income households. During the period under review, more than $100 million had been disbursed in aid (some $50 million through the UN system). UN agencies had adopted a humanitarian development strategy to increase access to essential social services and build an enabling environment for peace and reconciliation. However, Somalia remained one of the most difficult operating environments in the world, with restricted and unpredictable access owing to insecurity, the lack of presence of international partners in much of southern and central Somalia, limited or late funding, and community expectations and needs that heavily outweighed the capacity of many agencies. The Secretary-General described activities undertaken by the UN system in the areas of food security and rural development, health services and nutrition, water facilities and sanitation, education, human rights and gender, repatriation and reintegration, economic development and coordination, and UN staff security. The Secretary-General stated that the international community would continue efforts to ensure a coordinated political and aid approach in Somalia allowing for humanitarian access and neutrality.

The UN Consolidated Inter-Agency Appeal for Somalia, launched in 2000, which requested $129.6 million to cover the period January to December 2001, was revised to $140.4 million. Of that amount, 21.7 per cent ($30.5 million) was met. A further consolidated appeal was issued for 2002.

GENERAL ASSEMBLY ACTION

On 14 December [meeting 87], the General Assembly adopted **resolution 56/106** [draft: A/56/L.54 & Add.1] without vote [agenda item 20 *(b)*].

Assistance for humanitarian relief and the economic and social rehabilitation of Somalia

The General Assembly,

Recalling its resolutions 47/160 of 18 December 1992, 48/201 of 21 December 1993, 49/21 L of 20 December 1994, 50/58 G of 20 December 1995, 51/30 G of 13 December 1996, 52/169 L of 16 December 1997, 53/1 M of 8 December 1998, 54/96 D of 8 December 1999 and 55/168 of 14 December 2000 as well as the resolutions and decisions of the Economic and Social Council on emergency assistance to Somalia,

Recalling also Security Council resolution 733(1992) of 23 January 1992 and all subsequent relevant resolutions, in which the Council, inter alia, urged all parties, movements and factions in Somalia to facilitate the efforts of the United Nations, the specialized agencies and humanitarian organizations to provide urgent humanitarian assistance to the affected population in Somalia, and reiterated the call for the full respect of the security and safety of the personnel of those organizations and guarantee of their complete freedom of movement in and around Mogadishu and other parts of Somalia,

Recalling further the statement by the President of the Security Council of 31 October 2001, in which the Security Council reiterated its support for the outcome of the Somalia National Peace Conference, held in Arta, Republic of Djibouti, and the establishment of the Transitional National Assembly and the Transitional National Government, and encouraged the Government to continue, in the spirit of constructive dialogue, the process of engaging all groups in the country, including in the north-eastern and north-western areas, with a view to preparing for the installation of permanent governance arrangements through the democratic process,

Noting the cooperation between the United Nations, the Organization of African Unity, the League of Arab States, the European Union, the Organization of the Islamic Conference, the countries members of the Intergovernmental Authority on Development and its Partners Forum, the Movement of Non-Aligned Countries and others in their efforts to resolve the humanitarian, security and political crisis in Somalia, and bearing in mind the respect for the sovereignty, territorial integrity and unity of Somalia,

Noting with appreciation the continued efforts made by the Secretary-General to assist the Somali people in their efforts to promote peace, stability and national reconciliation,

Commending the initiative of the President of the Republic of Djibouti aimed at restoring peace and stability in Somalia, and noting with appreciation the efforts of the Government and people of Djibouti in hosting and facilitating the Somalia National Peace Conference,

Welcoming the outcome of the Arta peace process, led by Djibouti and sponsored by the Intergovernmental Authority on Development, which provides for the establishment of a transitional national parliament and the formation of a transitional national government,

Noting with appreciation that the mandate provided in the three-year transitional national charter emphasizes priorities, including reconciliation, demobilization of armed militia, restitution of properties to their lawful owners, holding of a national census, formulation of a new constitution, democratization, rehabilitation, recovery and reconstruction,

Welcoming the efforts of the Transitional National Government of Somalia to promote national reconciliation within Somalia, recognizing that progress has been achieved in some regions in re-establishing economic and administrative stability, and urging the Government, political and traditional leaders and factions to make every effort to complete, without preconditions, the peace and reconciliation process through dialogue and the involvement of all parties in a spirit of mutual accommodation and tolerance,

Noting with concern that the lack of effective civil institutions in Somalia continues to impede sustained comprehensive development and that, while the environment has become more conducive to some reconstruction and development-oriented work in certain parts of the country, the humanitarian and security situation has remained fragile in other parts,

Reaffirming its support for the joint strategy for targeted assistance of the United Nations system that is focused on the rehabilitation and reconstruction of infrastructure and on sustainable community-based activities, as well as for the importance it attaches to the need for effective coordination and cooperation among the United Nations agencies and their partners,

Taking note of the report of the Secretary-General,

Deeply appreciative of the humanitarian assistance and rehabilitation support rendered by a number of States and relevant organizations to alleviate the hardship and suffering of the affected Somali population,

Recognizing that, while the humanitarian situation remains fragile in some parts of Somalia, there is a need to continue the ongoing rehabilitation and reconstruction process alongside the national reconciliation process, without prejudice to the provision of emergency relief assistance wherever and whenever required, as security allows,

Noting with appreciation that the prospects for humanitarian, rehabilitation and development activities have been more favourable in some parts of the country, owing to the formation of stronger administrative structures, the commitment shown to re-establishing the rule of law in general and the leadership shown by some regional authorities and by civil society groups in attempting to establish an inclusive alternative to the faction-ridden past of Somalia,

Noting with appreciation also the efforts of the United Nations system aimed at working directly with Somali communities at the local level, whenever possible, and emphasizing the need for coordination with the Transitional National Government and with local and regional authorities,

Welcoming the continued focus of the United Nations, in partnership with Somali elders, other local leaders and skilled local counterparts at the grass-roots level, concerned Somali organizations and professionals in the diaspora and non-governmental organizations, on a programme of assistance, including both humanitarian and developmental approaches, given the varying conditions in different areas,

Re-emphasizing the importance of the further implementation of its resolution 47/160 to rehabilitate basic social and economic services at the local and regional levels throughout the country,

1. *Expresses its gratitude* for the further implementation of its resolution 47/160 to rehabilitate basic social and economic services at the local and regional levels throughout the country;

2. *Expresses its appreciation* to the Secretary-General for his continued and tireless efforts to mobilize assistance to the Somali people;

3. *Welcomes* the ongoing efforts of the United Nations, the Organization of African Unity, the League of Arab States, the European Union, the Organization of the Islamic Conference, the countries members of the Intergovernmental Authority on Development and its Partners Forum, the Movement of Non-Aligned Countries and others to contribute positively to the reconciliation process in Somalia;

4. *Also welcomes* the strategy of the United Nations focusing on the implementation of community-based interventions aimed at rebuilding local infrastructures and increasing the self-reliance of the local population, and the ongoing efforts by the United Nations agencies, their Somali counterparts and their partner organizations to establish and maintain close coordination and cooperation mechanisms available for the implementation of relief, rehabilitation and reconstruction programmes;

5. *Notes with appreciation* the holistic and prioritized approach of the United Nations system to addressing the continuing crisis in some parts of Somalia, while making long-term commitments to rehabilitation, recovery and development activities in more stable parts;

6. *Emphasizes* the principle that the Somali people have the primary responsibility for their own development and for the sustainability of rehabilitation and reconstruction assistance programmes, and reaffirms the importance it attaches to the creation of workable arrangements for collaboration between the United Nations system and its partner organizations and their Somali counterparts for the effective execution of rehabilitation and development activities in those parts of the country in which peace and security prevail;

7. *Urges* all States and intergovernmental and non-governmental organizations concerned to continue to implement further its resolution 47/160 in order to assist the Somali people in embarking on the rehabilitation of basic social and economic services, as well as institution-building aimed at the restoration of civil administration at all levels in all parts of the country in which peace and security prevail;

8. *Strongly urges* all political groups in Somalia, in particular those which have remained outside the Arta peace process, to participate in the ongoing peace process and to establish a constructive dialogue with the Transitional National Government in order to achieve national reconciliation that allows for transition from relief to reconstruction and development and preserves economic and administrative progress achieved in many regions;

9. *Calls upon* all parties, individual political leaders and factions in Somalia to respect fully the security and safety of personnel of the United Nations and the specialized agencies and of non-governmental organizations, and to guarantee their complete freedom of movement and safe access throughout Somalia;

10. *Calls upon* the Secretary-General to continue to mobilize international humanitarian, rehabilitation and reconstruction assistance for Somalia;

11. *Calls upon* the international community to provide continuing and increased assistance in response to the United Nations Consolidated Inter-Agency Appeal for relief, rehabilitation and reconstruction assistance for Somalia;

12. *Requests* the Secretary-General, in view of the critical situation in Somalia, to take all necessary measures for the implementation of the present resolution and to report thereon to the General Assembly at its fifty-seventh session.

Sudan

In response to General Assembly resolution 54/96 J [YUN 1999, p. 836], the Secretary-General, in a September report [A/56/412], reviewed the situation in the Sudan and described humanitarian assistance provided by the United Nations and its partners during the period 15 July 1999 to 15 July 2001.

Ongoing armed conflict between the military forces of the parties to the conflict and their allied militias, both in the south and in the so-called transitional zone between the northern and southern parts of the country, continued to threaten already fragile coping mechanisms among communities. The humanitarian situation for the war-affected and the displaced was compounded by natural disasters in many parts of the country. For the war-affected areas of the south, the principal umbrella and vehicle for the implementation of humanitarian relief activities continued to be the Operation Lifeline Sudan (OLS) access agreements, endorsed by the Government of the Sudan, the rebel Sudan People's Liberation Movement and Liberation Army, and the United Nations. A network of OCHA field coordination offices in key locations throughout the Sudan, staffed by national field officers, provided overall coordination of the humanitarian operation. The Secretary-General's Special Envoy for Humanitarian Affairs for the Sudan visited the country four times during the reporting period to discuss the assistance programme, including OLS. The Secretary-General described the security situation and its effect on humanitarian relief efforts, efforts to gain access to affected populations, assistance to internally displaced persons, relief food assistance and non-food assistance—household food security, nutrition and health, water and environmental sanitation, emergency education, rights, child protection and peace-building, and refugee assistance. He stated that, in view of the situation in the Sudan, increased humanitarian access, safety and protection of civilians, adequate resources and guaranteed security for humanitarian workers remained the core conditions of the assistance programme.

The UN Consolidated Inter-Agency Appeal for the Sudan, launched in 2000 to solicit $194.2 million to cover the period January to December 2001, was revised to $252 million. Some 61.8 per cent ($155.7 million) of that amount was received. OCHA issued a further appeal for 2002.

GENERAL ASSEMBLY ACTION

On 14 December [meeting 87], the General Assembly adopted **resolution 56/112** [draft: A/56/L.60 & Add.1] without vote [agenda item 20 (b)].

Emergency assistance to the Sudan

The General Assembly,

Recalling its resolution 54/96 J of 17 December 1999 and its previous resolutions on emergency assistance to the Sudan,

Reaffirming its resolution 46/182 of 19 December 1991 on strengthening of the coordination of humanitarian emergency assistance of the United Nations,

Bearing in mind its resolution 55/175 of 19 December 2000 on the safety and security of humanitarian personnel and protection of United Nations personnel,

Welcoming agreed conclusions 1998/1 of the Economic and Social Council, adopted by the Council at the humanitarian segment of its substantive session of 1998, in which, among other things, the Council reaffirmed that international cooperation to address emergency situations should be provided in accordance with international law and national laws, and that the affected State has the primary role in the initiation, organization, coordination and implementation of humanitarian assistance within its territory,

Welcoming also agreed conclusions 1999/1 of the Economic and Social Council, in which the Council addressed the theme of "International cooperation and coordinated responses to humanitarian emergencies, in particular in the transition from relief to rehabilitation, reconstruction and development", during its second humanitarian segment,

Taking note of the report of the Secretary-General on humanitarian assistance to the Sudan,

Welcoming the decision of the Government of the Sudan to provide access to the Nuba Mountains and recent efforts towards its implementation, noting in that regard the results of the inter-agency needs-assessment mission undertaken by the United Nations, and calling upon all parties to continue to cooperate with the United Nations in meeting the needs identified in that assessment,

Noting with concern existing obstacles to the delivery of humanitarian assistance, welcoming the agreements reached by the parties to Operation Lifeline Sudan, among them the Rome protocol, and noting the arrangements reached on 15 August 2001 between the Government of the Sudan and the United Nations inter-agency mission on the modalities of access for the Operation, aimed at facilitating delivery of relief assistance to affected populations, as well as the progress made by the Emergency Relief Coordinator and the Office for the Coordination of Humanitarian Affairs of the Secretariat in strengthening the coordination of the Operation,

Urging United Nations agencies, non-governmental organizations and donor countries to continue contributing and channelling their humanitarian assistance to all affected populations in the Sudan through Operation Lifeline Sudan,

Expressing concern at the continued conflict in the Sudan and its negative impact on the humanitarian situation,

Noting the ongoing peace efforts under the auspices of the Intergovernmental Authority on Development, and the initiative of Egypt and the Libyan Arab Jamahiriya for achieving a negotiated and lasting peace in the Sudan,

Noting with appreciation the contributions for the inter-agency appeal for Operation Lifeline Sudan and the progress made in the Operation, and noting also that considerable relief needs still remain to be addressed, including assistance to combat diseases such as malaria and assistance for logistic needs, emergency recovery, rehabilitation and development,

Expressing concern at the damaging consequences of floods and drought that have occurred in various parts of the Sudan in recent years,

Calling for an early resolution to the conflict, and expressing concern that its continuation further increases the suffering of the civilian population and undermines the effectiveness of international, regional and national humanitarian assistance,

Reaffirming the need for all parties to continue to facilitate the work of humanitarian organizations in implementing emergency assistance, in particular the supply of food, medicine, shelter and health care, and to ensure safe and unhindered access to all affected populations,

Recognizing the need in emergency situations to ensure the smooth transition from relief to rehabilitation and development so as to reduce dependence on external food aid and other relief services,

1. *Acknowledges with appreciation* the cooperation by the Government of the Sudan with the United Nations, including the agreements and arrangements achieved to facilitate relief operations with a view to improving the conditions for United Nations assistance to the population in the affected areas, encourages the continuation of that cooperation, and calls upon all parties to the conflict to agree to comprehensive and permanent humanitarian ceasefire arrangements in order to ensure the delivery of relief assistance;

2. *Expresses its appreciation* to the donor community, United Nations agencies and governmental and non-governmental organizations for the contributions so far made to the humanitarian needs of the Sudan, and calls upon them to continue their assistance, in particular by responding to the consolidated appeal and providing support for programmes in the Nuba Mountains;

3. *Stresses* the need for Operation Lifeline Sudan to be operated and managed with a view to ensuring its efficiency, transparency and effectiveness, with the full involvement and cooperation of the Government of the Sudan, taking cognizance of the relevant Operation Lifeline Sudan agreements reached by the parties, as well as consultations in the preparation of the consolidated annual inter-agency appeal for the Operation;

4. *Recognizes* the need for Operation Lifeline Sudan to be conducted in strict adherence to the principles of neutrality and impartiality and within the principles of national sovereignty and territorial integrity of the Sudan, and within the framework of international cooperation, in accordance with the relevant provisions of international law;

5. *Calls upon* the international community to continue to contribute generously to the emergency needs, recovery and development of the Sudan, and urges all parties to the conflict to facilitate the achievement of those objectives;

6. *Urges* the international community to give assistance for the rehabilitation of transportation means and infrastructure vital for the provision of relief supplies in the Sudan and their cost-effectiveness, and in that context stresses the importance of continued cooperation by all the parties involved so as to facilitate and improve the delivery of relief supplies;

7. *Calls upon* the donor community and the organizations of the United Nations system to provide financial, technical and medical assistance, guided by the actions called for by the General Assembly in its relevant resolutions, to combat such diseases as malaria and other epidemics in the Sudan;

8. *Welcomes* the recent visit, upon invitation from the Government of the Sudan, of the Special Representative of the Secretary-General on internally displaced persons, as well as the commitment of the Government to continue its efforts to address the problem of internally displaced persons;

9. *Urges* the international community to continue to support national and international programmes of rehabilitation, voluntary resettlement and reintegration of returnees and internally displaced persons, as well as assistance to refugees;

10. *Stresses* the imperative of ensuring the safety and security of humanitarian personnel, as well as safe and unhindered access for providing relief assistance to all affected populations, and the importance of strict observance of the principles and guidelines of Operation Lifeline Sudan, and of international humanitarian law reaffirming the necessity for humanitarian personnel to respect the national laws of the Sudan;

11. *Recognizes* the need for a peaceful resolution to the conflict, and urges the parties to work towards that end;

12. *Urges* all parties involved to continue to offer all feasible and necessary assistance, including facilitating the movement of relief supplies and personnel, so as to guarantee the success of Operation Lifeline Sudan in all affected parts of the country, with special emphasis on national capacity-building in the humanitarian field for governmental and non-governmental organizations, as well as on meeting emergency relief needs;

13. *Calls upon* all parties to respect international humanitarian law on the protection of civilians during times of war, and in that connection condemns attacks against civilians and attacks against and detention of humanitarian personnel, including the incidents leading to the deaths of fifteen humanitarian workers in the last two years, and calls for appropriate investigations into all allegations surrounding such incidents;

14. *Recalls* the signing by the Government of the Sudan of the Convention on the Prohibition of the Use, Stockpiling, Production and Transfer of Anti-personnel Mines and on Their Destruction, urges all parties to the conflict to desist from using them, calls upon the international community to refrain from supplying mines to the region, and urges the international community and United Nations agencies to provide appropriate assistance related to mine action in the Sudan;

15. *Requests* the Secretary-General to continue to mobilize and coordinate resources and support for Operation Lifeline Sudan, and to report to the General Assembly at its fifty-eighth session on the emergency situation in the affected areas and the recovery, rehabilitation and development of the Sudan.

West Africa

The UN Consolidated Inter-Agency Appeal for West Africa, issued in March to cover January to December 2001 for a total of $65 million to assist Guinea, Liberia and Sierra Leone in particular and the subregion in general, was revised to $62 million. The donor community covered 32 per cent ($19.7 million) of that amount.

In early 2001, the West African subregion, including Côte d'Ivoire, Guinea, Liberia and Sierra Leone, continued to be battered by escalating political and economic instability. Insecurity in the border areas of the Mano River Union States (Guinea, Liberia, Sierra Leone) (see p. 159) caused further displacement of refugees, and their sudden return to already overcrowded host communities and camps for internally displaced persons in Sierra Leone. The emergence of internally displaced persons and vulnerable host communities had compounded Guinea's refugee burden. Ethnic polarization, cross-border insurgency and economic stagnation in Liberia had left the population impoverished and vulnerable. In Côte d'Ivoire, a tense political and ethnic environment continued to trigger the exodus of foreigners, most of them migrant workers from Burkina Faso and Mali. Increasingly complex and massive displacement patterns, related security risks for both the humanitarian actors and beneficiaries, and lack of humanitarian access rendered humanitarian assistance efforts expensive and of limited impact. Although there were a number of positive political movements towards the end of the year, the situation in the subregion remained volatile. OCHA launched a further appeal to cover 2002.

Sierra Leone

The UN Consolidated Inter-Agency Appeal for Sierra Leone, which originally requested $78.1 million to cover January to December 2001, was revised to $74.2 million. Of that amount, 80.2 per cent ($60 million) was received.

The significant progress made in the peace process in Sierra Leone (see p. 163), particularly through the disarmament and demobilization programme, altered the operating environment for humanitarian operations. Increased security enabled the resettlement of some 45,000 internally displaced persons and permitted the delivery of essential humanitarian assistance. However, the deterioration of the situation in neighbouring Guinea and Liberia led to the premature repatriation of Sierra Leonean refugees, who remained displaced within the country. OCHA issued a further appeal for 2002.

Asia

Afghanistan

The UN Consolidated Appeal for Afghanistan, launched in 2000 to cover January to December 2001 in the amount of $229.2 million, was revised to $332.6 million. In September, the Consolidated Appeal was replaced by a Donor

Alert (below). Some $150 million (45.1 per cent) of the Consolidated Appeal's requirements were met.

On 4 September, the United Nations and its partners issued a report entitled "The deepening crisis", which was a plan of action to support critically vulnerable Afghans for the upcoming winter period and beyond. It highlighted the needs of 5 million people who were already affected by three years of drought and many years of fighting, as well as a huge human rights deficit (see p. 712). Assistance included food distribution, shelter assistance in camps for internally displaced persons and assistance to help people to stay in their homes. In view of the rapidly deteriorating humanitarian situation in Afghanistan, following the events of 11 September (see p. 60), the United Nations and its partners developed a Donor Alert to support an inter-agency emergency humanitarian assistance plan for Afghans in Afghanistan and in neighbouring countries, which replaced the 2001 Consolidated Appeal on 27 September. The plan, which presented a new set of requirements linked to recent events and possible future developments in Afghanistan (see p. 255), covered the period from October 2001 to March 2002 and sought $584 million to ensure the delivery of humanitarian assistance and protection programmes for up to 7.5 million Afghans. The Donor Alert was later revised to $662 million, of which 75 per cent, or $496 million, was met.

Report of Secretary-General. In response to General Assembly resolution 55/174 B [YUN 2000, p. 864], the Secretary-General, in a December report [A/56/687], described developments in Afghanistan during the period 1 July 2000 to 30 June 2001 and the assistance provided by the UN system and its partners.

The Secretary-General stated that the humanitarian situation had become increasingly alarming as a result of the effects of a severe drought, significant human rights abuses and the continuing conflict in 17 of the 28 provinces in the country. Relations with the Taliban authorities had been characterized by a series of adverse developments since early 2001, including the arrests of humanitarian staff. The economy continued to be constrained by the war and political crisis. The Secretary-General described efforts by the UN system and its partners to provide assistance for food aid and security, health, water and sanitation, education, mine action, food and agriculture, rural and urban rehabilitation, voluntary repatriation, drug control, and human rights and gender issues. He concluded that the overall situation was very serious and, given the scale and magnitude of the food crisis, there was a need for a concerted international response to avert a catastrophe. Moreover, he said, there were huge rehabilitation and development needs, which were only marginally met by the current assistance.

GENERAL ASSEMBLY ACTION

On 21 December [meeting 91], the General Assembly adopted **resolution 56/220 B** [draft: A/56/L.62 & Add.1] without vote [agenda items 20 (f) and 43].

Emergency international assistance for peace, normalcy and reconstruction of war-stricken Afghanistan

The General Assembly,

Recalling its resolution 55/174 B of 19 December 2000 and all its previous relevant resolutions,

Strongly welcoming the successful conclusion of the agreement reached among various Afghan groups in Bonn, Germany, on 5 December 2001,

Expressing its grave concern at the decades of conflict in Afghanistan, which has caused massive loss of life, extensive human suffering, destruction of property, serious damage to the economic and social infrastructure, refugee flows and other forcible displacements of large numbers of people,

Mindful of the fact that Afghanistan is highly vulnerable to natural disasters and that it is currently affected by the worst drought in living memory,

Remaining deeply concerned at the problem of millions of anti-personnel landmines and unexploded ordnance, which constitutes a great danger for the civilian population and a major obstacle to the return of refugees and displaced populations, to the resumption of agricultural activities, to the provision of humanitarian assistance and to future rehabilitation and reconstruction efforts,

Noting with deep concern that the majority of the Afghan people are still unable to enjoy fully their human rights and fundamental freedoms owing to policies and practices, particularly of the Taliban, aimed at discriminating against or marginalizing parts of the population, in particular women and children, a situation which is exacerbated by the effects of war, poverty and profound underdevelopment,

Expressing its deep concern at widespread violations of international humanitarian and human rights law committed by Afghan groups, and in this regard reminding all Afghan groups of their commitment to respect human rights in the country as contained in the Bonn agreement,

Deeply disturbed by the continuing security threat to humanitarian personnel and United Nations and associated personnel, including locally recruited staff,

Expressing its appreciation to the Afghan staff of the United Nations and other humanitarian organizations, who have continued to provide assistance to vulnerable populations throughout the current crisis,

Noting with grave concern that limited access to certain areas of Afghanistan and inadequate conditions for the delivery of aid threatens the well-being of internally displaced persons and vulnerable sections of the civilian population,

Recognizing that a secure environment is absolutely necessary for the safe and effective delivery and distribution of humanitarian assistance,

Welcoming the timely preparation of operational plans by the United Nations in response to the latest humanitarian crisis, and affirming the urgent need to reinforce international emergency assistance to Afghanistan in order to alleviate the human suffering and restore basic services,

Recognizing the need to develop and implement a comprehensive strategy and process for a seamless connection between humanitarian relief and the rehabilitation and reconstruction of Afghanistan in a timely manner, with particular emphasis on all aspects of sustainable development, including vulnerability reduction and mitigation, and the promotion of human rights and fundamental freedoms,

Stressing the importance of a well-coordinated approach to implementing such a strategy, and welcoming in this respect the appointment of the Special Representative of the Secretary-General for Afghanistan as the coordinator for the United Nations system,

Noting with deep concern that a significant number of Afghan refugees remain in neighbouring countries, as conditions in many parts of Afghanistan are still not conducive to a safe and sustainable return of the majority of refugees, and acknowledging that those refugees constitute a continuing socio-economic burden for the host countries,

Expressing its gratitude to all Governments that have rendered assistance to Afghan refugees, as well as to the Governments of neighbouring countries that continue to host Afghan refugee populations, and at the same time once again calling upon all parties to continue to fulfil their obligations for the protection of refugees and internally displaced persons and to allow international access for their protection and care,

Expressing its appreciation to the United Nations system and to all States and international and non-governmental organizations that have responded positively and continue to respond, where conditions permit, to the humanitarian needs of Afghanistan, as well as to the Secretary-General for his efforts in mobilizing and coordinating the delivery of appropriate humanitarian assistance,

1. *Takes note* of the report of the Secretary-General, and endorses the observations contained therein;

2. *Stresses* that the responsibility for the solution of the humanitarian crisis lies above all with the Afghan people themselves, and urges them to attach the highest priority to national reconciliation;

3. *Urges* all Afghan groups to call a complete halt to the use of landmines and to cooperate fully with the United Nations Mine Action Programme;

4. *Calls upon* all relevant organizations of the United Nations system to continue to coordinate closely their humanitarian assistance to Afghanistan on the basis of the principles laid out in the Strategic Framework for Afghanistan, and appeals to donor countries as well as other humanitarian organizations to cooperate closely with the United Nations, taking into account the priorities and requirements outlined in the donor alert and subsequent appeals;

5. *Stresses* the coordinating role of the Special Representative of the Secretary-General for Afghanistan for the United Nations system in the development and implementation of a strategy and process for a seamless connection between humanitarian relief and the rehabilitation and reconstruction of Afghanistan, in-

cluding the cooperation of the United Nations system with the international community, in particular those countries actively engaged in humanitarian assistance and reconstruction efforts in Afghanistan, as well as the international financial institutions;

6. *Supports* the efforts of the Emergency Relief Coordinator in coordinating humanitarian assistance to Afghanistan, underlines the continuing relevance of coordination structures in place for Afghanistan, encourages agencies to build upon them in response to the current crisis, and also encourages the humanitarian community to strengthen the coordination of their assistance to Afghanistan through existing mechanisms, including donor coordination through the Afghan Support Group;

7. *Welcomes* the designation by the Secretary-General of the Administrator of the United Nations Development Programme to lead the early recovery efforts in Afghanistan, and invites the relevant United Nations organizations and agencies, as well as the World Bank, the International Monetary Fund, the Islamic Development Bank, the Asian Development Bank and relevant non-governmental organizations to develop jointly, in close collaboration with the interim authority and Afghan civil society, a comprehensive strategy and process for the early recovery and reconstruction efforts in Afghanistan, to be implemented where and when conditions permit;

8. *Encourages*, in this regard, all parts of the United Nations system to work together closely on the relief, rehabilitation and reconstruction efforts in order to ensure a smooth transition from relief to development in Afghanistan;

9. *Calls upon* the international community to ensure, within the implementation of such a comprehensive strategy for the reconstruction and rehabilitation of Afghanistan, adequate and effective measures, inter alia, for demining, disaster reduction and the disarmament, demobilization and reintegration of combatants;

10. *Strongly condemns* all acts of violence and intimidation directed against United Nations and other humanitarian personnel, and regrets the loss of life and physical harm suffered among the Afghan staff;

11. *Urges* all Afghan groups to respect international humanitarian law, to ensure the safety, security and free movement of all United Nations and humanitarian personnel, as well as their safe and unimpeded access to all affected populations, and to protect the property of the United Nations and of humanitarian organizations, including non-governmental organizations, against, inter alia, looting and theft, so as to facilitate their work;

12. *Encourages* the Afghan groups to facilitate the operations of the United Nations and other humanitarian organizations, and urges them to cooperate fully and without discrimination on grounds of gender, nationality or religion with the United Nations and associated bodies, as well as with other agencies and humanitarian organizations, to refrain from all interference in the delivery of humanitarian relief supplies and to guarantee the secure and uninterrupted supply of humanitarian aid to all vulnerable populations;

13. *Strongly condemns* discrimination against women and girls as well as ethnic and religious groups, including minorities, which adversely affects, inter alia, international relief, rehabilitation and reconstruction

efforts in Afghanistan, and emphasizes the importance of actively involving all elements of Afghan society, in particular women, in the development and implementation of relief, rehabilitation and reconstruction programmes;

14. *Calls upon* all Afghan groups to respect fully the human rights and fundamental freedoms of all, without discrimination of any kind, including on the basis of gender, ethnicity or religion, and in accordance with their obligations under international law, and to protect and promote the equal rights of women and men;

15. *Urges* all Afghan groups to refrain from the recruitment or use of children in armed conflicts contrary to international standards and to take all necessary measures for the demobilization and social reintegration of war-affected children;

16. *Stresses* the responsibility of all Afghan groups to facilitate the provision of efficient and effective remedies to the victims of grave violations and abuses of human rights and international humanitarian law and to bring the perpetrators to justice in accordance with international standards;

17. *Appeals* to all States and to the international community to ensure that all humanitarian assistance and future rehabilitation and reconstruction programmes integrate a gender perspective, that they actively attempt to promote the participation of both women and men, and that women benefit equally with men from those programmes;

18. *Expresses its appreciation* to those Governments that continue to host Afghan refugees, urges the Governments concerned to fulfil their obligations under international refugee law with respect to the protection of refugees and the right to seek asylum, and calls upon the international community to do likewise;

19. *Recognizes* the large number of refugees in neighbouring countries, and calls upon the international community to consider providing further assistance in support of Afghan refugees;

20. *Expresses its appreciation* to the Governments of neighbouring States hosting United Nations agencies for their cooperation, and calls upon them to continue to facilitate the work of those United Nations humanitarian operations which are temporarily based on their territory in order to ensure an efficient delivery of emergency aid into Afghanistan;

21. *Urgently appeals* to all States, the United Nations system and international and non-governmental organizations to continue to provide, in close collaboration with the interim authority and Afghan civil society, when conditions on the ground permit, all possible humanitarian, financial, technical and material assistance for the Afghan population, especially in the areas most affected by the drought, as well as assistance to promote the voluntary, safe and dignified return of refugees and internally displaced persons;

22. *Calls upon* the international community to respond generously to the donor alert, future consolidated appeals as well as long-term interventions towards rehabilitation and reconstruction, and in this respect invites Member States to participate actively in the ministerial level meeting on reconstruction assistance to be held in Japan in January 2002;

23. *Requests* the Secretary-General to submit to the General Assembly at its fifty-seventh session a report on the actions taken pursuant to the present resolution.

In **resolution 56/220 A** of 21 December, the Assembly called on the international community to provide assistance to alleviate the urgent humanitarian needs of Afghanistan and to support post-conflict rehabilitation and reconstruction.

East Timor

In response to General Assembly resolution 55/172 [YUN 2000, p. 867], the Secretary-General submitted a September report [A/56/338] covering developments in East Timor from January to June 2001.

The humanitarian situation in East Timor continued to improve. Although many people remained vulnerable, it was generally accepted that the humanitarian phase had shifted to a more normalized development situation. Capacity development was the core development challenge facing East Timor, particularly in the areas of human resources development, enhancing the policy and legal framework, managing the changing role of international personnel and managing the linguistic transition. The establishment of a fully functional civil service managed by East Timorese staff had progressed significantly (see p. 272). However, the East Timorese and their development partners faced enormous challenges in transforming an administration that was essentially international in character into a sustainable national administration.

With regard to the health sector, data collected in March indicated that 80 per cent of the population had access to permanent health-care facilities. However, ongoing monitoring suggested that utilization of health services was low and highly variable, with below 40 per cent of facilities properly utilized. The shift from emergency relief to a development phase had allowed the development of non-emergency medical services. Only moderate success had been achieved in education, primarily due to teacher shortages and a lack of school furniture. The central areas of the justice system—the court system, prosecution services, public defender services and prison services—had seen significant progress. The trend towards improvement in public safety had continued. In agriculture, a joint donors' mission (26 March–7 April), with the participation of the World Bank, the United States Agency for International Development, the Australian Agency for International Development, Portugal, the Food and Agriculture Organization of the United Nations (FAO), UNDP, the United Nations Office for Project Services and the Japanese International Cooperation Agency, called for an integrated approach to support the agricultural sector in terms of cross-sectoral rural development. While measures to rehabilitate the infrastructure were advancing at a fast pace, progress towards the development of long-term sustainability had been hampered by a fundamental lack of capacity. In 2001, donors' meetings were held in Canberra, Australia, and Oslo, Norway. In Canberra (June), donors endorsed the second national budget of East Timor.

During the year, an appeal was launched to cover 2002.

GENERAL ASSEMBLY ACTION

On 14 December [meeting 87], the General Assembly adopted **resolution 56/104** [draft: A/56/L.52 & Add.1] without vote [agenda item 20 *(b)*].

Assistance for humanitarian relief, rehabilitation and development for East Timor

The General Assembly,

Recalling all of its relevant resolutions on the situation in East Timor,

Recalling also its resolution 46/182 of 19 December 1991 and the guiding principles contained in the annex to that resolution,

Recalling further all of the relevant Security Council resolutions and decisions on the situation in East Timor, in particular resolutions 1272(1999) of 25 October 1999, 1319(2000) of 8 September 2000 and 1338 (2001) of 31 January 2001,

Recalling the establishment by Security Council resolution 1272(1999) of the United Nations Transitional Administration in East Timor, whose mandate includes the coordination and delivery of humanitarian, rehabilitation and development assistance, support for capacity-building for self-government and assistance in the establishment of conditions for sustainable development,

Welcoming the response of the United Nations, other intergovernmental organizations, Member States and non-governmental organizations, with the coordination of the Transitional Administration since 1 January 2000, and in cooperation with the East Timorese people, in terms of addressing the humanitarian relief, rehabilitation and development needs of East Timor,

Welcoming also the passing of the immediate emergency and humanitarian phase in East Timor, while noting continuing vulnerabilities, including the need to strengthen the preparedness and response capacity for addressing humanitarian emergencies, and the remaining challenges of rehabilitation, reconstruction and development,

Acknowledging the continuing progress made in the transition from relief to development in East Timor and, in this regard, the important role played by the Transitional Administration in supporting the resilient and determined efforts of the East Timorese people themselves,

Emphasizing the need for continued international assistance to East Timor to support the transition from relief and rehabilitation to development, and recognizing the significant challenges that are to be faced in this regard in preparation for independence and in the post-independence period, inter alia, in the sectors of public administration, education, health, agriculture and infrastructure,

Welcoming the efforts of the Government of Indonesia and relevant intergovernmental and non-governmental organizations in providing humanitarian assistance to the East Timorese refugees in the province of East Nusa Tenggara, West Timor, and in facilitating their return to East Timor, and in this respect recognizing the importance of the international community in assisting the efforts of the Government of Indonesia to implement programmes for the resettlement and repatriation of East Timorese refugees,

Welcoming also the initiation by Indonesia of criminal proceedings against the perpetrators of the deplorable killing of three personnel of the Office of the United Nations High Commissioner for Refugees at Atambua on 6 September 2000, bearing in mind the importance of the independence of the national judiciary, and expressing the hope that the final sentences for those found guilty will be commensurate with the serious nature of the crimes,

1. *Takes note* of the report of the Secretary-General;

2. *Encourages* the United Nations, other intergovernmental organizations, Member States and non-governmental organizations, with the coordination of the United Nations Transitional Administration in East Timor, and in close consultation and cooperation with the East Timorese people, to continue to collaborate to address the remaining longer-term vulnerabilities of East Timor, including in the area of preparedness and response capacity for addressing humanitarian emergencies, and to support the transition from relief and rehabilitation to development;

3. *Emphasizes* the importance of continuing close consultation with and participation of East Timorese institutions and civil society, including local non-governmental organizations, in the planning and delivery of rehabilitation, reconstruction and development assistance to East Timor;

4. *Urges* United Nations organizations, the international community and non-governmental organizations to continue their efforts aimed at the enhanced ownership and participation of all East Timorese, including women and vulnerable groups, in the rehabilitation, reconstruction and development of East Timor, and in this regard stresses the need for continued international assistance to support local capacity-building, inter alia, in areas such as education, health, agriculture and rural development, the judiciary, governance and public administration, security and law and order;

5. *Welcomes* the convening of donor meetings for East Timor in Tokyo in December 1999, Lisbon in June 2000, Brussels in December 2000, Canberra in June 2001 and Oslo in December 2001, which focused on the national budget and the transition towards independence in East Timor in four key areas, political, public administration, public finances, and economic and social reconstruction, and urges the international community to fulfil its pledges to meet the external requirements for rehabilitation, reconstruction and development activities for East Timor;

6. *Also welcomes* the official launching of the joint appeal for East Timorese refugees, presented by the Government of Indonesia and the United Nations in Jakarta on 27 November 2001;

7. *Further welcomes* the successful holding, on 30 August 2001, of the elections for the East Timor Constituent Assembly and the appointment, on 20 September 2001, of the all–East Timorese Second Transitional Government;

8. *Acknowledges* that the establishment of an effective and functioning governmental administration is crucial to fostering a stable and secure social, economic and political environment in East Timor, and in this regard urges the international community to continue to support efforts aimed at institution-building and the training of civil servants, in particular in the areas of public finances, the judiciary, senior management and the development and maintenance of the central administrative systems of government;

9. *Welcomes* the continuing response to food aid needs by the international community, and calls upon the United Nations, other intergovernmental organizations, Member States and non-governmental organizations to assist the East Timorese in ensuring sustainable development in the areas of agriculture, livestock and fisheries;

10. *Recommends* that outstanding infrastructure needs remain an essential focus of international assistance in such areas as the reconstruction and rehabilitation of public buildings, educational facilities, roads and public services, including water and sanitation and the supply of electricity;

11. *Commends* the rapid international response in terms of providing health services to the general population, including the early deployment of immunization and disease prevention programmes, and reproductive health care and child nutrition programmes, while recognizing the need for further assistance to rebuild hospitals and train health-care professionals and enhance capacity-building to meet the challenge to public health posed by diseases such as tuberculosis, malaria and the human immunodeficiency virus/acquired immunodeficiency syndrome (HIV/AIDS);

12. *Welcomes* the ongoing reopening of schools, the supply and distribution of educational materials, and teacher training, while emphasizing the need for capacity-building, particularly in the area of secondary and higher education, and for continued attention to the rehabilitation needs, including psychosocial support, of children affected by the violence;

13. *Acknowledges* the efforts of the Government of Indonesia, in cooperation with the Transitional Administration, the Office of the United Nations High Commissioner for Refugees, the International Organization for Migration and other humanitarian organizations, to facilitate organized and spontaneous returns of East Timorese refugees from West Timor, and encourages the Government of Indonesia to continue its efforts to establish effective security in and around the refugee camps in West Timor in order to facilitate safe and voluntary returns of refugees;

14. *Reaffirms* the need to ensure safe and unhindered access of humanitarian personnel and assistance to all those in need, recognizes in this regard the continuing implementation by the Government of Indonesia of Security Council resolution 1319(2000), encour-

ages the Government to continue its efforts in that regard in full cooperation with Member States, the United Nations system and non-governmental organizations, and underscores the importance of continued international assistance to support the efforts of the Government of Indonesia and relevant organizations to meet the needs of East Timorese refugees in West Timor, inter alia, by assisting their voluntary repatriation or resettlement, and by contributing to humanitarian assistance needs in the camps in West Timor;

15. *Urges* the United Nations to continue to address the rehabilitation, reconstruction and development needs of East Timor;

16. *Requests* the Secretary-General to prepare a report on the implementation of the present resolution for consideration by the General Assembly at its fifty-seventh session.

Indonesia

Maluku

The UN Consolidated Inter-Agency Appeal for the crisis in Maluku, Indonesia, amounting to $10.8 million and covering January to December 2001, received 30.8 per cent ($3.3 million) of requirements.

The crisis began in 1999 when violence erupted between Christians and Muslims and, although small-scale interaction between the two groups had increased, segregation remained deep. The military presence had been reduced by half without negative implications. Humanitarian actors had adjusted to the improved environment by decreasing direct assistance, focusing more on capacity-building, and by enabling people to take charge of either food production or generation of income to purchase basic needs. The focus shifted towards rehabilitation, particularly in North Maluku where the security environment was more conducive.

Tajikistan

In response to General Assembly resolution 55/45 [YUN 2000, p. 870], the Secretary-General submitted an October report [A/56/470], covering developments in the humanitarian situation in Tajikistan from 15 July 2000 to 15 July 2001.

Despite significant improvements in peace and security during the reporting period, the humanitarian situation continued to deteriorate owing to the prevailing drought, severe economic conditions and insufficient livelihoods for over half of the Tajik population. Food production continued to follow the declining trend of preceding years. Although efforts had been made to rehabilitate health-care facilities, health care remained sub-standard. Access to other basic social services, such as water, sanitation and education, was limited by the absence of essential supplies

and proper maintenance. Urgent assistance was needed to rehabilitate the collapsing irrigation infrastructure, maintain and renovate agricultural equipment, produce and procure quality cereal seeds and establish an adequate rural finance system.

During the reporting period, 1,835 Tajiks repatriated voluntarily, with the assistance of the Office of the United Nations High Commissioner for Refugees (UNHCR). As a result of continued fighting in Afghanistan, some 10,000 Afghans sought refuge on the border between Tajikistan and Afghanistan; UNHCR and OCHA coordinated inter-agency assistance.

In general, the operating environment for the United Nations and international organizations had improved slightly, although recent insecurity limited the number of accessible areas. Operating in three of Tajikistan's four regions, the UNDP Reconstruction, Rehabilitation and Development Programme made significant contributions to social and economic recovery. At the World Bank–led consultative group meeting (Tokyo, 16 May), donors pledged $439 million in support of economic reform and investment programmes for the 2001-2002 biennium. The Secretary-General observed that the provision of increased humanitarian and development assistance was crucial to maintaining and strengthening the achievements of the UN post-conflict peace-building efforts and to keeping Tajikistan on the road to stabilization, democratic development and economic reform.

The Consolidated Inter-Agency Appeal for Tajikistan, launched in 2000, which initially sought $82 million to cover January to December 2001, was revised to $78 million. Of that amount, 75 per cent ($58.5 million) was received. A further appeal was issued for 2002.

GENERAL ASSEMBLY ACTION

On 27 November [meeting 65], the General Assembly adopted **resolution 56/10** [draft: A/56/L.15 & Add.1] without vote [agenda item 20 *(b)*].

**Emergency international assistance for peace,
normalcy and rehabilitation in Tajikistan**

The General Assembly,

Recalling its resolutions 51/30 J of 25 April 1997, 52/169 I of 16 December 1997, 53/1 K of 7 December 1998, 54/96 A of 8 December 1999 and 55/45 of 27 November 2000,

Having considered the report of the Secretary-General,

Welcoming the progress made by Tajikistan in consolidating peace and stability, and noting the significantly improved security environment in the country,

Recognizing with satisfaction that the United Nations has played a successful and important role in the peace process, and believing that the Organization should continue to provide assistance to Tajikistan in post-conflict peace-building,

Welcoming in this regard the efforts of the United Nations Tajikistan Office for Peace-building aimed at the consolidation of peace, national recovery and reconstruction, promotion of the rule of law and the strengthening of democratic institutions,

Noting with regret that the humanitarian situation has not improved, owing to the severe economic deterioration and the prevailing drought, and that significant humanitarian needs continue to exist throughout Tajikistan,

Recognizing that, until the economy is able to support the Tajik population, humanitarian operations will remain a critical factor in consolidating the achievements of the peace-building process in Tajikistan,

Expressing regret that, despite the widely recognized importance of humanitarian assistance in maintaining and consolidating the achievements of the peace-building efforts, the donor response to the 2001 consolidated inter-agency appeal has not yet reached its target,

Stressing that international funding for humanitarian operations is particularly important since such operations remain the principal means by which hundreds of thousands of Tajiks meet their basic needs,

Noting with concern the lack of support especially for important sectors such as health, education, water and sanitation, which must receive immediate funding if social catastrophe is to be avoided in Tajikistan,

1. *Takes note* of the report of the Secretary-General;

2. *Welcomes* the continued role of the United Nations in post-conflict peace-building in Tajikistan and the efforts of the United Nations Tajikistan Office for Peace-building in this regard;

3. *Stresses* that Tajikistan has entered a new phase of post-conflict peace-building, which requires continued international economic assistance;

4. *Recognizes* that humanitarian and rehabilitation assistance remains crucial, not only to sustain life but also to promote development and prevent renewed conflict;

5. *Welcomes with appreciation* the efforts undertaken by the Secretary-General in drawing the attention of the international community to the acute humanitarian problems of Tajikistan and in mobilizing assistance for the post-conflict rehabilitation, recovery and reconstruction of the country;

6. *Welcomes* the results achieved at the consultative group meeting of donor countries, held in Tokyo on 16 May 2001;

7. *Expresses its appreciation* to the States, the United Nations, the European Union, the World Bank and other intergovernmental organizations and all relevant humanitarian organizations, agencies and non-governmental organizations, including the International Federation of Red Cross and Red Crescent Societies, that have responded and continue to respond positively to the humanitarian needs of Tajikistan;

8. *Encourages* Member States and others concerned to continue to provide assistance to alleviate the urgent humanitarian needs of Tajikistan and to offer support to Tajikistan for the post-conflict rehabilitation and reconstruction of its economy;

9. *Emphasizes* the importance of further co-operation and assistance from the authorities in facilitating the work of humanitarian organizations, including non-governmental organizations, welcomes in this regard the establishment of the National Coordination Committee on Humanitarian Assistance by the Government of Tajikistan, and urges the authorities to simplify and streamline without delay the relevant internal bureaucratic procedures and requirements for the delivery of humanitarian assistance;

10. *Warmly welcomes* the intention of the Secretary-General to continue the United Nations humanitarian programme in Tajikistan by issuing a consolidated inter-agency appeal for humanitarian assistance to Tajikistan for 2002, taking into account current developments in the region, and urges Member States to fund fully programmes included in the appeal;

11. *Calls upon* the Secretary-General to continue to re-evaluate all United Nations humanitarian assistance activities in Tajikistan with a view to preparing a common humanitarian strategy that would support the relief and recovery operations during the transitional period from relief to development, with a major focus on promoting self-reliance and sustainable development;

12. *Stresses* the need to ensure the security and freedom of movement of humanitarian personnel, and of United Nations and associated personnel, as well as the safety and security of their premises, equipment and supplies;

13. *Requests* the Secretary-General to continue to monitor the humanitarian situation in Tajikistan and to report to the General Assembly at its fifty-seventh session on the progress made in the implementation of the present resolution;

14. *Decides* to consider at its fifty-seventh session the question of the situation in Tajikistan under the item entitled "Strengthening of the coordination of humanitarian and disaster relief assistance of the United Nations, including special economic assistance".

Europe

Northern Caucasus (Russian Federation)

The UN Consolidated Inter-Agency Appeal for the Northern Caucasus, issued in 2000, which sought $44.9 million to cover January to December 2001, was revised in June to $42.5 million. The donor community met 89.3 per cent ($38 million) of requirements.

In 2001, the overall situation in the northern Caucasus remained difficult due to the persistent extreme insecurity and high level of poverty in Chechnya. Resource transfers from the federal to the regional level to restore socio-economic life were lower than planned. Insecurity, lack of documents and sufficient shelter, and a dearth of basic services discouraged displaced people from returning to Chechnya. Overall, more people left Chechnya than returned there.

In Ingushetia, there was stability in terms of security and a government structure. However, the social and physical infrastructure was over-burdened by the continued presence of displaced persons. In April, the Government stopped registering new arrivals, thereby hampering their access to the Government's humanitarian assistance. Tension increased between host families and internally displaced persons, and a growing number of internally displaced persons faced eviction from spontaneous settlements and host families. In addition, the flow of people leaving Chechnya to go to Ingushetia reached 8,000 by October. A further appeal was launched for 2002.

South-Eastern Europe
(Albania and the former Yugoslavia)

The UN Consolidated Inter-Agency Appeal for South-Eastern Europe (Albania, Bosnia and Herzegovina, Croatia, the Federal Republic of Yugoslavia (FRY) and the former Yugoslav Republic of Macedonia (FYROM)), issued in 2000, which sought $429.2 million to cover January to December 2001, was revised to $413.2 million. The donor community covered 53.4 per cent ($220.5 million) of that amount.

In 2001, the general trend towards stability and development continued in South-Eastern Europe, allowing UN agencies to make progress on return and local integration programmes for refugees and internally displaced persons, and to support the transition from relief assistance towards development programming. However, violent conflict in FYROM early in the year (see p. 368) led to the displacement of some 140,000 persons both within the country and into neighbouring territories. Conflict between ethnic Albanian armed groups and State security forces also escalated in southern Serbia. The United Nations responded with programmes to address the needs of new caseloads generated by the conflicts. By October, peace processes were under way in both countries, and agencies were assisting returns, addressing the enormous needs in conflict-affected areas and working to rebuild community confidence. Other parts of the region enjoyed relative stability, accompanied by political progress and steps towards recovery of civil society.

Albania was characterized by chronic under-development, which affected all segments of the population. In Bosnia and Herzegovina, minority returns increased by nearly 90 per cent, largely prompted by the implementation of property laws. In contrast to the positive side of the return trend, new humanitarian needs were created by the returns due to limited economic opportunities in the country. Organized and spontaneous returns to Croatia increased, as the

Government removed many legislative barriers, gave return clearance for former habitual residents and simplified the return procedure. However, the returnees faced difficulties related to housing and employment or income-generating opportunities. After seven months of conflict and displacement, the humanitarian situation in FYROM stabilized in the autumn. Significant resources were required to help stabilize the situation further, allow for the return of refugees and displaced persons, care for those unable to return and maintain emergency preparedness. In FRY, excluding Kosovo, high rates of unemployment and inflation placed 2 million people at or below the poverty line. Already facing depleted health, education and social welfare services, a large segment of the population was unable to meet basic needs, especially during the harsh winter months. The conflict in FYROM resulted in the influx of some 10,000 refugees into FRY, mainly into southern Serbia. While the overall humanitarian situation had improved in the Kosovo province of FRY, unemployment remained high. Poor infrastructure, high crime and lack of respect for the rule of law, coupled with the volatility of the region in general, meant that high unemployment and related pressure for labour migration were likely to continue. Much of Kosovo's economy was geared towards and dependent on the presence of the international community and was considered unsustainable. There were still residual humanitarian needs, particularly related to the influx of some 81,000 mainly ethnic Albanian refugees from FYROM, minority returnees and isolated minority communities. A further appeal for the region was launched to cover 2002.

Federal Republic of Yugoslavia

In response to General Assembly resolution 55/169 [YUN 2000, p. 872], the Secretary-General, in a September report [A/56/361], reviewed humanitarian, socio-economic and human rights developments in FRY during the period 1 July 2000 to 15 July 2001. He described assistance provided by the United Nations and its partners relating to coordination, winterization efforts, food aid, shelter, health, water and sanitation, education and child welfare, agriculture, durable solutions, environmental damage, mine action and human rights.

During the period under review, the domestic and international political context of FRY changed dramatically, strengthening the prospects for making real progress in addressing the root causes of large-scale humanitarian needs. However, the process of development was unlikely to be linear and significant obstacles remained regarding durable solutions. Meeting the basic needs of vulnerable groups within the refugee, displaced and resident populations remained a priority for humanitarian agencies, as did the provision of transitional support to essential services such as health, education and social welfare in order to meet immediate needs, maintain services at a minimum and strengthen the reform process. A donors' conference, co-hosted by the World Bank and the European Commission (Brussels, 29 June), proposed a programme for reform and development, which received strong support.

GENERAL ASSEMBLY ACTION

On 14 December [meeting 87], the General Assembly adopted **resolution 56/101** [draft: A/56/L.49 & Add.1] without vote [agenda item 20 (b)].

Humanitarian assistance to the Federal Republic of Yugoslavia

The General Assembly,

Recalling its resolution 46/182 of 19 December 1991, and reaffirming that humanitarian assistance should be provided in accordance with the guiding principles contained in the annex to that resolution,

Recalling also its resolutions 54/96 F of 15 December 1999 and 55/169 of 14 December 2000, concerning humanitarian assistance to the Federal Republic of Yugoslavia,

Deeply appreciative of the humanitarian assistance and the rehabilitation support rendered by a number of States, in particular major contributors, international agencies and organizations and non-governmental organizations to alleviate the humanitarian needs of the affected population in the Federal Republic of Yugoslavia, in particular the emergency assistance provided by the European Union and various countries,

Recognizing the role of the Stability Pact for South-Eastern Europe and the stabilization and association process for the western Balkans in assisting the Federal Republic of Yugoslavia in its efforts in further promoting democratic and economic reforms and in intensifying regional cooperation,

Deeply appreciative of the humanitarian assistance given to the Federal Republic of Yugoslavia through the United Nations consolidated inter-agency appeal for South-Eastern Europe, and the humanitarian assistance provided by many Member States outside the framework of the consolidated appeal, through non-governmental organizations, regional organizations and initiatives and bilateral channels,

Welcoming the fact that, at the donor conference hosted jointly by the World Bank and the European Commission in Brussels on 29 June 2001, the programme for reform and development of the Federal Republic of Yugoslavia received strong support and confirmed that meeting the basic needs of vulnerable groups within the refugee, displaced and resident populations remains a priority for humanitarian agencies,

Deeply concerned at the continuing urgency of the humanitarian situation in the Federal Republic of Yugoslavia, aware of the magnitude of the humanitarian requirements of the country, and recognizing the need to ensure effective links between relief, rehabilitation, reconstruction and development efforts in the Federal Republic of Yugoslavia,

Aware of the weakness of the economy and basic services, which exacerbates further the situation of socially and economically vulnerable segments of the population, including refugees and internally displaced persons, and which is coupled with a continuing decrease in basic social services capacity, especially in the health sector,

Acknowledging that a large number of refugees remain in the Federal Republic of Yugoslavia and that assistance requirements will include, as appropriate, local integration,

Taking note of the report of the Secretary-General,

Taking note also of the biweekly reports on the humanitarian situation in the Federal Republic of Yugoslavia, prepared in Belgrade by the Office for the Coordination of Humanitarian Affairs of the Secretariat,

Recognizing the role of the United Nations in helping the Federal Republic of Yugoslavia to resolve the humanitarian problems that confront it and in coordinating the efforts of the international community to provide humanitarian assistance to the country,

1. *Calls upon* all States, regional organizations, intergovernmental and non-governmental organizations and other relevant bodies to provide humanitarian assistance to alleviate the humanitarian needs of the affected population in the Federal Republic of Yugoslavia, bearing in mind in particular the special situation of women, children, the elderly and other vulnerable groups;

2. *Also calls upon* all States, regional organizations, intergovernmental and non-governmental organizations and other relevant bodies to offer support to the Government of the Federal Republic of Yugoslavia in its efforts to ensure the transition from relief to the long-term goals of the rehabilitation, reconstruction and development of the country;

3. *Welcomes* the continued commitment of the Federal Republic of Yugoslavia, and encourages it to cooperate further with the United Nations system and humanitarian organizations to address the humanitarian needs of the affected population, including refugees and internally displaced persons, and urges the relevant authorities and the international community to support programmes that will ensure that the humanitarian needs of refugees and internally displaced persons in the Federal Republic of Yugoslavia are met and to pursue durable solutions to their plight, in particular voluntary repatriation and reintegration, stresses the need to create conditions that are conducive to their safe return, and emphasizes in this regard the importance of regional cooperation in the search for solutions to the plight of refugees;

4. *Calls upon* the Secretary-General to continue to mobilize the timely provision of international humanitarian assistance to the Federal Republic of Yugoslavia;

5. *Emphasizes* the importance of strengthening the coordination of humanitarian assistance to the Federal Republic of Yugoslavia, inter alia, through the mechanisms of a consolidated inter-agency appeal, and recognizes in this regard especially the role of the Office

for the Coordination of Humanitarian Affairs of the Secretariat;

6. *Encourages* the Office of the United Nations High Commissioner for Refugees, the Organization for Security and Cooperation in Europe, the Council of Europe and other organizations to enhance their cooperation in the provision of humanitarian assistance to the Federal Republic of Yugoslavia;

7. *Requests* the United Nations and the specialized agencies to continue their efforts to assess the humanitarian needs, in cooperation with the Government of the Federal Republic of Yugoslavia, relevant international and regional organizations and bodies and interested States, with a view to ensuring effective links between relief and longer-term assistance to the Federal Republic of Yugoslavia, taking into account the work already carried out in this field and the need to avoid duplication and the overlapping of efforts;

8. *Requests* the Secretary-General to submit to it at its fifty-seventh session, under the item entitled "Strengthening of the coordination of humanitarian and disaster relief assistance of the United Nations, including special economic assistance", a report on the implementation of the present resolution.

Special economic assistance

African economic recovery and development

Economic and Social Council consideration

In accordance with Economic and Social Council decision 2000/303 [YUN 2000 p. 1372], the Council's high-level segment in 2001 (16-18 July) was devoted to "The role of the United Nations in supporting the efforts of African countries to achieve sustainable development" [A/56/3/Rev.1]. The high-level segment comprised a policy dialogue and exchange of views on important developments in the world economy and international economic cooperation; the African Forum for Investment Promotion, which included three round tables on the investment climate in African countries, financing of investment and infrastructure needs; a panel of eminent personalities on the theme "The nexus between peace and development"; and the high-level ministerial discussion on the high-level segment's theme. Following the segment, a panel discussion took place on the Charter for the Public Service in Africa, adopted at the third Biennial Pan-African Conference of Ministers of Civil Service (Windhoek, Namibia, 5-6 February) [A/56/63-E/2001/21].

The Council had before it an extract from the report of the Open-ended Ad Hoc Working Group on the Causes of Conflict and the Promotion of Durable Peace and Sustainable Development in Africa (see p. 111); the Charter for the Public Service in Africa; the report of the Inter-Agency Mission to West Africa [E/2001/56] (see p. 160); the *World Economic and Social Survey 2001* (see p. 765); the report of the Committee for Development Policy (CDP) on its third session (see p. 848); the report of the Secretary-General on the role of the United Nations in supporting the efforts of African countries to achieve sustainable development (see p. 848); and a statement submitted by the NGO African Services Committee [E/2001/NGO/2].

Ministerial declaration. On 18 July, the high-level segment adopted a ministerial declaration on the role of the United Nations in support of the efforts of African countries to achieve sustainable development. The Ministers called on the UN system and the international community to support the New African Initiative, adopted by the Assembly of Heads of State and Government of the Organization of African Unity at its thirty-seventh ordinary session (Lusaka, Zambia, 9-11 July) [A/56/457] (the Initiative was launched and its name changed to the New Partnership for Africa's Development at an implementation meeting of African leaders (Abuja, Nigeria, 23 October)) (see p. 899). They also called for UN efforts to integrate peace and development, develop human capital, strengthen measures to improve agricultural development and food security, support industrialization, mobilize resources for development, harmonize and coordinate development assistance to Africa, and strengthen public-private partnerships to support initiatives in health, education, science and technology, transport, energy supply, and information and communications. The Ministers emphasized the role that sustainable use and management of resources could play in achieving sustainable development. Expressing the belief that the preparatory process for the final review and appraisal in 2002 of the United Nations New Agenda for the Development of Africa in the 1990s (see p. 849) presented an opportunity for an assessment of the role of the United Nations and the international community in supporting Africa's priorities, including a comprehensive review of initiatives on Africa, the Ministers suggested that the General Assembly, in considering the final review, should take into account how best to improve the effectiveness of UN support for Africa's priorities and initiatives. The Secretary-General was requested to review the structures charged with follow-up at the Secretariat level.

In a statement made at the opening of the high-level segment, the Secretary-General stated that the United Nations would fully support the New African Initiative and expressed the need to put an end to the multiplicity of initiatives on Africa.

CDP action. In response to Economic and Social Council resolution 2000/34 [YUN 2000, p. 807], CDP, at its third session (New York, 2-6 April) [E/2001/33], examined the role of the UN system in supporting the efforts of African countries to achieve sustainable development. The Committee was of the view that the main challenge for Africa was to reappropriate its own development strategy and policies. Sustained growth would be possible if a majority of African people became empowered in the development process. The Committee recommended that the UN system coordinate closely its own activities in order to assist African countries in developing their indigenous coordination capabilities by strengthening appropriate mechanisms at the local, national and regional levels. It urged the UN system to resolve existing coordination failures by establishing clear priorities aimed at implementing carefully designed and integrated development programmes and projects; ensuring the active participation of the African countries in the selection, design, implementation, monitoring and evaluation phases of programmes and projects; developing partnerships among donor agencies, technical assistance experts, host government agencies at the national and local levels, and the recipient countries' civil society; and introducing transparent and publicly accountable monitoring and evaluation procedures. The UN system should also play a leading role in facilitating the inflow of foreign direct investment (FDI) and other long-term private flows to Africa, and re-examine the effectiveness of the current official development assistance (ODA) system based on voluntary contributions by Member countries. Efforts should be made to design innovative mechanisms to reverse the decline in voluntary contributions, possibly through some form of mandatory contributions, and to increase aid effectiveness.

Report of Secretary-General. In a June report on the role of the UN system in supporting the efforts of African countries to achieve sustainable development [E/2001/83], the Secretary-General stated that the United Nations had to play a key role in forging a partnership between Africa and the international community in order to put the continent on the path to sustained growth and improved living conditions. The challenge was to build on African ownership and sound economic policies, which could be achieved with an adequate mix of resource flows, debt relief and much-improved market access for African exports, combined with support for the diversification of the region's economies and the replication of success stories implemented by, or in collaboration with, the UN system.

Having described the current situation in Africa, the UN role in forging a new partnership for growth in Africa and the challenges of sustainable development in Africa, the Secretary-General presented a series of policy conclusions and recommendations to assist the high-level segment of the Economic and Social Council in its deliberations (see p. 847). He stated that there should be better integration of UN system support with national development policies and programmes and a shift of inter-agency coordination increasingly to the regional level; further reinforcement of system-wide support for capacity-building in Africa; consistency and harmonization of the country programming framework of the United Nations and of the Bretton Woods institutions (the World Bank Group and the International Monetary Fund); urgent mobilization of resources to address the HIV/AIDS pandemic and other diseases and to strengthen health systems; encouragement of public-private partnerships; improved governance; and UN support for national and regional strategies to diversify African economies.

Follow-up to the Millennium Summit

In response to General Assembly resolution 55/162 [YUN 2000, p. 62] on the follow-up to the outcome of the Millennium Summit (the United Nations Millennium Declaration contained in resolution 55/2 [ibid., p. 49]), the Secretary-General submitted, in September, the "road map" towards the Declaration's implementation [A/56/326] (see p. 1278). Section VII of the road map dealt with meeting the special needs of Africa, one of the key objectives identified in the Declaration; the road map addressed the challenges posed by extreme poverty, devastating debt burdens, disease, conflict and wavering international interest. Although some of those problems were general to developing countries, Africa suffered particularly from its marginalization in the process of globalization. However, African leadership had galvanized local and international support in the following areas: supporting the New African Initiative; strengthening democratic governance; building peacekeeping capacity further, in cooperation with regional organizations; working for sustainable development; and forming partnerships to combat HIV/AIDS. The Assembly took action on the road map in **resolution 56/95** (see p. 1279).

New Agenda for the Development of Africa

The United Nations New Agenda for the Development of Africa in the 1990s (UN-NADAF), adopted by the General Assembly in resolution 46/151 [YUN 1991, p. 402], continued to be implemented by the United Nations Conference on Trade and Development (UNCTAD), among others.

During the year, consideration of UN-NADAF centred on its final review and appraisal, scheduled to take place in 2002 in accordance with Assembly resolution 51/32 [YUN 1996, p. 832].

UNCTAD action. At its twenty-seventh executive session (Geneva, 19 July) [A/56/15], the UNCTAD Trade and Development Board (TDB) considered a report by the UNCTAD Secretary-General on UNCTAD's contribution to the implementation of UN-NADAF [TD/B/EX(27)/2]. The report summarized specific UNCTAD activities, including advisory services and technical cooperation, in each of UNCTAD's mandated sectors—international trade, services development, debt and debt management, international investment and enterprise development, the UNCTAD/UNDP Global Programme on Globalization, Liberalization and Sustainable Human Development, and the United Nations System-wide Special Initiative on Africa.

Final review and appraisal (2002)

CPC action. At its forty-first session (New York, 11 June–6 July) [A/56/16], the Committee for Programme and Coordination (CPC) requested that the final evaluation of UN-NADAF should, among other things, present an assessment of the activities carried out by all partners concerned in the areas covered by the New Agenda and provide a critical analysis, which would make it possible to identify successes, obstacles and failures; highlight lessons learned; and indicate the impact and implications of UN-NADAF activities on Africa's development. It also requested that concrete proposals on the successor arrangements to UN-NADAF be put forward and include effective coordination measures at the international, regional, subregional and national levels.

Note of Secretary-General. In an August note [A/56/270], the Secretary-General discussed preparations for the UN-NADAF final review and appraisal.

As part of the independent evaluation of UN-NADAF and related initiatives requested by the Assembly in resolution 55/216 [YUN 2000, p. 875], the Secretary-General had established a panel of 12 independent personalities from Africa and the international community to oversee the evaluation (see p. 850). The Secretary-General proposed that the Assembly establish an ad hoc committee of the whole to carry out the final review and appraisal. The Assembly did so by resolution 56/218 (see p. 850).

UNCTAD action. At its forty-eighth session (Geneva, 1-12 October) [A/56/15], TDB had before it an UNCTAD secretariat report entitled *Economic Development in Africa: Performance, Prospects and Policy Issues* [TD/B/48/12], which stated that poverty had increased in the continent and that gross domestic product growth rates were half the annual average growth target of 6 per cent set by UN-NADAF; real per capita incomes were currently 10 per cent below the levels reached in 1980; savings and investment rates remained far below levels required for sustainable growth in the region and for attaining the objective of reducing poverty by half by the year 2015; Africa's share of world trade had fallen dramatically in the past decade, and the continent's terms of trade were 50 per cent lower than in 1980, owing mainly to commodity dependence; FDI remained at less than 1 per cent of world totals and was not expected to fill the resource gap; despite the Enhanced Heavily Indebted Poor Countries (HIPC) Initiative, African countries remained highly indebted; and ODA had fallen to historically low levels, representing about one third of UN targets.

In agreed conclusions of 12 October [A/56/15 (agreed conclusions 468(XLVIII))], TDB stated that only a few African countries had met the UN-NADAF targets. Greater coherence among policies regarding African development was needed in order to place the continent on a sustainable growth path to achieve the internationally agreed target of reducing poverty by half by the year 2015. The Board called for renewed and strengthened efforts by developed countries to meet as soon as possible the agreed ODA target of 0.7 per cent of their gross national product (GNP) and the agreed target of earmarking 0.15 per cent to 0.20 per cent of GNP for the least developed countries. Over the longer term, private capital flows and domestic savings should replace official financing, thereby reducing aid dependence. Regarding Africa's debt burden, the Board urged the effective implementation of the Enhanced HIPC Initiative for eligible African countries. Measures to deal with resource requirements should be incorporated into a comprehensive development approach, which could increase considerably the capacity of African countries to export and to augment their share in international trade transactions. Improved market access should be supplemented with specific capacity development programmes to help countries diversify exports and improve competitiveness. The international community should study ways to deal with the problem of declining commodity prices and their impact on African development. The Board encouraged continued attention to external factors and to the shortcomings of domestic markets and enterprises, human capital and physical infrastructure, institutions and income distribution.

Panel meeting. The Panel of Eminent Personalities on the Independent Evaluation of UN-NADAF held its first meeting (New York, 27-28 November) to discuss and endorse the plans and the methodology of the evaluation. A support team to the Panel had visited seven African countries (Botswana, Egypt, Ethiopia, Kenya, Nigeria, South Africa, United Republic of Tanzania), where they met with government officials and representatives of regional and subregional organizations and UN system organizations with a view to obtaining information on the extent of implementation of UN-NADAF priorities and the reasons for the slow or lack of progress in certain priority areas. The Panel was briefed by representatives of African missions, the donor community and UN system organizations on recent developments in Africa and on various initiatives that might have contributed to implementing UN-NADAF priorities. The support team was scheduled to carry out additional field missions in Asia, Latin America, Europe and North America to collect information on the role of the donor community in implementing UN-NADAF.

GENERAL ASSEMBLY ACTION

On 21 December [meeting 91], the General Assembly adopted **resolution 56/218** [draft: A/56/L.61 & Add.1] without vote [agenda item 22].

Final review and appraisal of the United Nations New Agenda for the Development of Africa in the 1990s

The General Assembly,

Having considered the note by the Secretary-General on the final review and appraisal of the implementation of the United Nations New Agenda for the Development of Africa in the 1990s,

Reaffirming its resolutions 46/151 of 18 December 1991, the annex to which contains the New Agenda, and 51/32 of 6 December 1996, which states that the final review and appraisal of the New Agenda will be conducted in 2002,

Reaffirming also its resolutions 48/214 of 23 December 1993, 49/142 of 23 December 1994, 53/90 of 7 December 1998 and 55/216 of 21 December 2000 on the implementation of the New Agenda,

Reaffirming further its resolutions 54/234 of 22 December 1999 and 55/217 of 21 December 2000 on the causes of conflict and the promotion of durable peace and sustainable development in Africa, and recalling its requests in resolutions 54/234 and 55/216 to conduct the final review and appraisal of the New Agenda and related initiatives on the basis of a report by the

Secretary-General on an independent high-level quality evaluation,

Mindful of the ministerial declaration of the high-level segment of the substantive session of 2001 of the Economic and Social Council on the role of the United Nations in support of the efforts of African countries to achieve sustainable development, adopted on 18 July 2001, with particular reference to paragraph 26, and the agreed conclusions 1999/2 adopted by the Economic and Social Council, at its substantive session of 1999, on coordination of the policies and activities of the specialized agencies and other bodies of the United Nations system related to the theme "Development of Africa: implementation and coordinated follow-up by the United Nations system of initiatives on African development",

Mindful also of the report of the Secretary-General on the causes of conflict and the promotion of durable peace and sustainable development in Africa, in particular paragraph 60,

1. *Decides* to establish an ad hoc committee of the whole of the General Assembly as the most appropriate mechanism to conduct the final review and appraisal of the implementation of the United Nations New Agenda for the Development of Africa in the 1990s and related initiatives;

2. *Decides also* to convene an organizational session of the Ad Hoc Committee of the Whole in June 2002 for one working day to consider and adopt the necessary arrangements for its work regarding, inter alia, the final review and appraisal of the implementation of the New Agenda and related initiatives on Africa, and decides that the Ad Hoc Committee should establish its bureau at the highest appropriate level, to be composed of a chairman, the President of the General Assembly, assisted by three vice-chairmen and a rapporteur, appointed by the President in consultation with Member States;

3. *Decides further* that the Ad Hoc Committee of the Whole should meet in substantive session for a period of five working days, from 9 to 13 September 2002, and for three working days from 7 to 9 October 2002, during the fifty-seventh session of the General Assembly, to conduct the final review and appraisal of the implementation of the New Agenda and related initiatives on the basis of the report of the Secretary-General on the independent high-level quality evaluation, as mandated in Assembly resolutions 54/234 and 55/216 and in agreed conclusions 1999/2 of the Economic and Social Council, and on other documents that the Ad Hoc Committee will have decided to make use of at its organizational session in June 2002, as well as on proposals by the Secretary-General on the modalities of the United Nations future engagement with the New Partnership for Africa's Development;

4. *Decides* that a high-level plenary meeting of the General Assembly should be held on 16 September 2002 to consider how to support the New Partnership for Africa's Development, in line with paragraph 5 of the ministerial declaration of the high-level segment of the substantive session of 2001 of the Economic and Social Council, which called on the United Nations system and the international community to support the New African Initiative, now called the New Partnership for Africa's Development, adopted by the Assembly of Heads of State and Government of the Organization of

African Unity, at its thirty-seventh ordinary session, held at Lusaka from 9 to 11 July 2001, and that preparations for the plenary meeting should be made during the fifty-sixth session of the General Assembly;

5. *Urges* Member States and organs and bodies of the United Nations system to ensure that they are represented at the highest appropriate level on, and to participate actively in the work of, the Ad Hoc Committee of the Whole and in the plenary meeting;

6. *Requests* the Secretary-General, in consultation with the organs and organizations of the United Nations system concerned, to ensure the necessary preparations for the meeting of the Ad Hoc Committee of the Whole;

7. *Also requests* the Secretary-General to submit to the General Assembly at its fifty-seventh session a report on the work of the Ad Hoc Committee of the Whole, including on the plenary meeting, and on the implementation of the present resolution.

On 24 December, the Assembly decided that the item on the UN-NADAF final review and appraisal would remain for consideration during its resumed fifth-sixth (2002) session (**decision 56/464**).

UN System-wide Special Initiative on Africa

CPC action. In response to a 2000 CPC request [YUN 2000, p. 877], the Secretary-General transmitted to CPC's forty-first session (New York, 11 June–6 July) [A/56/16] the independent evaluation [E/AC.51/2001/6 & Corr.1] of the United Nations System-wide Special Initiative on Africa, covering activities since the Initiative's launch in March 1996 [YUN 1996, p. 832]. The evaluation, prepared by three independent experts, concluded that the Initiative had achieved only modest success as a vehicle to encourage coordination among UN agencies. The Initiative's more lasting value was its role in encouraging cooperation within the UN system, and especially with the World Bank. Among other things, the experts said that the Initiative was overly ambitious and too imprecise; the lack of incentives, combined with inadequate consultation, left the Initiative without a sense of ownership from key constituencies; and it was subject to uncertain support from top UN leadership. The experts recommended that the United Nations might support a set of interlocking dialogues involving African countries and regional institutions, donors, the agencies and programmes of the UN system and other multilateral development agencies. The existence of the Initiative as a continuing special initiative should be brought to a close at a time considered appropriate by UN decision-making bodies.

In June comments on the independent experts' report [E/AC.51/2001/7], the Secretary-General stated that, with the exception of the

United Nations Educational, Scientific and Cultural Organization, which considered the implications of the report to be far-reaching and indicated that it might refer the matter to its Governing Body before making any comments, UN system organizations—FAO, UNDP, the United Nations Population Fund, the United Nations Children's Fund (UNICEF), the United Nations Industrial Development Organization, the World Health Organization (WHO) and the World Bank—agreed that the Initiative should be brought to a close. Those organizations generally agreed that, since the objectives of the Initiative were being absorbed more effectively by existing and planned coordinating mechanisms that were more country-based and responded to Africa's development challenges, the continuation of a special initiative did not provide any value-added. Regarding the framework for a new approach, a number of agencies agreed on the need for dialogue, but cautioned against the creation of yet another structure, and suggested the establishment of benchmarks and indicators to gauge progress in inter-agency coordination.

CPC members raised doubts about the quality and validity of the evaluation report. It was felt that the duration of two months for the evaluation was inadequate and only 6 of 53 countries in Africa had been visited. While the report referred to the Initiative's inability to bring in additional financial resources, it had failed to mention those resources that had actually been mobilized through its efforts. Referring to the comments provided by the Secretary-General on the evaluation, the Committee noted that only eight agencies had submitted comments, although 17 agencies had provided inputs and favourable comments in 2000 [YUN 2000, p. 877]. The Committee requested that a more detailed examination of the Initiative be conducted in the context of the final evaluation of UN-NADAF.

Democratic Republic of the Congo

In response to General Assembly resolution 55/166 [YUN 2000, p. 878], the Secretary-General, in an August report [A/56/269], described assistance provided by the UN system to the DRC in its economic recovery and reconstruction process in the context of recent political change and continuing conflict (see p. 116).

Against a background of limited resources, UN system agencies had continued their cooperation programmes by focusing on humanitarian activities to benefit the most vulnerable groups. Development efforts were targeted at various aspects of poverty reduction in the areas of health, agriculture, local development and employment generation, HIV/AIDS control and the promotion of good governance, including human rights and national capacity-building. An appropriate response to the crisis had been hampered by inadequate funding, difficult access to displaced persons for security reasons and past decisions of the national authorities, some of which had been overturned by the new President, Joseph Kabila. In agriculture, FAO and UNDP collaborated on food security, and, in the context of an emergency agriculture programme in Bas-Congo, FAO, UNHCR and the World Food Programme (WFP) developed synergies in their support for refugees, displaced persons and host populations. UNICEF provided assistance to the most vulnerable groups in the areas of health, food, child protection and assistance to displaced persons. In the health sector, WHO and UNDP helped to rehabilitate the health system in six health zones of several provinces, national immunization days were realized through a broad partnership and HIV/AIDS control was supported. Integration programmes were organized by UNHCR.

GENERAL ASSEMBLY ACTION

On 14 December [meeting 87], the General Assembly adopted **resolution 56/100** [draft: A/56/L.39 & Add.1] without vote [agenda item 20 (b)].

Special assistance for the economic recovery and reconstruction of the Democratic Republic of the Congo

The General Assembly,

Recalling its resolutions 52/169 A of 16 December 1997, 53/1 L of 7 December 1998, 54/96 B of 8 December 1999 and 55/166 of 14 December 2000,

Recalling also all resolutions of the Security Council and all statements by its President relating to the situation in the Democratic Republic of the Congo,

Recalling further the Ceasefire Agreement signed in Lusaka and the Kampala disengagement plan and the obligations of all signatories to those agreements and the obligations deriving from Security Council resolution 1304(2000),

Reaffirming the sovereignty, territorial integrity and political independence of the Democratic Republic of the Congo and all States in the region,

Alarmed at the plight of the civilian population throughout the country, and calling for its protection,

Gravely concerned at the deteriorating economic, social and humanitarian situation in the Democratic Republic of the Congo, in particular in the eastern Congo, and at the effect of the continued fighting on the inhabitants of the country, especially women and children,

Deeply concerned at the increased rate of infection with the human immunodeficiency virus/acquired immunodeficiency syndrome (HIV/AIDS), in particular among women and girls in the Democratic Republic of the Congo,

Expressing its deep concern at the dire consequences of the conflict for the humanitarian and human rights situations,

Gravely concerned at the negative impact of war on the promotion of the sustainable and overall development of the country,

Urging all parties to respect and protect human rights and respect international humanitarian law, in particular, the Geneva Conventions of 1949 and the additional Protocols thereto, of 1977,

Deeply concerned at the continued extensive destruction of life and property and the severe damage to infrastructure and the environment suffered by the Democratic Republic of the Congo, as well as the reports of the illegal exploitation of its natural resources,

Bearing in mind the fact that the Democratic Republic of the Congo hosts thousands of refugees from neighbouring countries, which places a great burden on its limited resources, and hoping that conditions will be created that will facilitate a safe and voluntary return of refugees,

Recalling that the Democratic Republic of the Congo is a least developed country with severe economic and social problems arising from its weak economic infrastructure and aggravated by the ongoing conflict,

Bearing in mind the close interrelationship between ensuring peace and security and the ability of the country to meet the humanitarian needs of its people and to take effective steps towards the rapid revitalization of the economy, and reaffirming the urgent need to assist the Democratic Republic of the Congo in the rehabilitation and reconstruction of its damaged economy and in its efforts to restore basic services and the infrastructure of the country,

1. *Takes note* of the report of the Secretary-General;
2. *Welcomes* the opening of the Inter-Congolese Dialogue on 15 October 2001, and calls upon all Congolese parties to make every effort to promote the process and ensure the success of a fully inclusive dialogue in a spirit of consensus;
3. *Urges* all parties concerned in the region to cease military activities, cease any support for armed groups and any recruitment, training and use of child soldiers, calls upon those States which have not done so to withdraw from the territory of the Democratic Republic of the Congo, in accordance with the Lusaka Ceasefire Agreement, the Kampala disengagement plan and relevant Security Council resolutions, and urges all parties to engage in a process of political dialogue and negotiation and to create the conditions necessary for the speedy and peaceful resolution of the crisis;
4. *Encourages* the Government of the Democratic Republic of the Congo to continue and develop its cooperation with the United Nations, its specialized agencies and other organizations in addressing the need for rehabilitation and reconstruction;
5. *Also encourages* the Government of the Democratic Republic of the Congo to pursue sound macro-economic policies and to promote good governance and the rule of the law, and urges it to exert all efforts for economic recovery and reconstruction despite the ongoing armed conflict;
6. *Stresses* the link between the peace process and the economic recovery of the Democratic Republic of the Congo, welcomes economic reforms undertaken by its Government, and encourages it to carry on with this process for the benefit of the entire Congolese people;
7. *Also stresses* the importance of the restoration of river traffic, welcomes in this regard the reopening of

the Congo and the Oubangi Rivers, and expresses its support for the establishment of the Congo River Basin Commission;

8. *Renews its urgent appeal* to the executive boards of the United Nations funds and programmes to continue to keep under consideration the special needs of the Democratic Republic of the Congo;

9. *Welcomes* the continued and increased efforts of the Secretary-General, the United Nations system and its agencies, programmes and funds in ensuring that the gender perspective is mainstreamed in the reconstruction agenda of the Democratic Republic of the Congo;

10. *Urges* all parties to respect fully international humanitarian law and to ensure the safe and unhindered access of humanitarian personnel to all affected populations throughout the territory of the Democratic Republic of the Congo and the safety of United Nations and humanitarian personnel, and in that regard stresses that the reopening of the Kisangani-Kindu rail and river link would facilitate the delivery of humanitarian assistance, as well as the resupplying of humanitarian personnel;

11. *Calls upon* the international community to continue to provide support to the humanitarian relief activities within the Democratic Republic of the Congo;

12. *Invites* Governments to continue to provide support to the Democratic Republic of the Congo;

13. *Requests* the Secretary-General:

(*a*) To continue to consult urgently with regional leaders, in coordination with the Secretary-General of the Organization of African Unity, about ways to bring about a peaceful and durable solution to the conflict, in accordance with the Lusaka Ceasefire Agreement and relevant Security Council resolutions;

(*b*) To continue to consult with regional leaders, in coordination with the Secretary-General of the Organization of African Unity, in order to convene, when appropriate, an international conference on peace, security and development in Central Africa and in the Great Lakes region, under the auspices of the United Nations and the Organization of African Unity, to address the problems of the region in a comprehensive manner;

(*c*) To keep under review the economic situation in the Democratic Republic of the Congo with a view to promoting participation in and support for a programme of financial and material assistance to the country to enable it to meet its urgent needs in terms of economic recovery and reconstruction;

(*d*) To submit to the General Assembly at its fifty-seventh session a report on the actions taken pursuant to the present resolution.

Djibouti

In response to General Assembly resolution 54/96 C [YUN 1999, p. 851], the Secretary-General submitted an August report [A/56/264] in which he described the situation in Djibouti and progress made in providing assistance for reconstruction and development. The country's development challenges were related to the economic and financial crisis, and recurring emergency situations, including drought, flood and epidemics, combined with large-scale destruction of livestock, water points, health and educational facilities as a result of the internal conflict in the country, had led to the need for further emergency and humanitarian assistance. UN agencies increasingly focused on social development in Djibouti, through activities related to health, food security, rehabilitation and reconstruction, environmental conservation, refugee repatriation, governance, human rights, gender mainstreaming and the integration of NGOs and civil society in development. The Secretary-General called on the international community for financial support to enable him to provide technical assistance to implement urgent socio-economic programmes.

GENERAL ASSEMBLY ACTION

On 14 December [meeting 87], the General Assembly adopted **resolution 56/108** [draft: A/56/L.56 & Add.1] without vote [agenda item 20 (*b*)].

Economic assistance for the reconstruction and development of Djibouti

The General Assembly,

Recalling its resolution 54/96 C of 8 December 1999 and its previous resolutions on economic assistance to Djibouti,

Recalling also the United Nations Millennium Declaration,

Recalling further the Brussels Declaration and the Programme of Action for the Least Developed Countries for the Decade 2001-2010, adopted by the Third United Nations Conference on the Least Developed Countries on 20 May 2001, as well as the mutual commitments undertaken on that occasion and the importance attached to follow-up and the implementation of the Programme of Action,

Aware that Djibouti is included in the list of least developed countries and that it is ranked 137th out of the 162 countries studied in the *Human Development Report 2001,*

Noting that the economic and social development efforts of Djibouti are constrained by the extremes of the local climate, in particular cyclical droughts, and that the implementation of reconstruction and development programmes requires the deployment of substantial resources which exceed the capacity of the country,

Noting also that the situation in Djibouti has been made worse by the drought situation in the Horn of Africa, and noting further the presence of tens of thousands of refugees and persons displaced from their countries, which has placed serious strains on the fragile economic, social and administrative infrastructure of Djibouti and caused security problems in the country, in particular in the city of Djibouti,

Noting with satisfaction that the Government of Djibouti is continuing to implement a structural adjustment programme, and convinced of the necessity to support that financial recovery programme and to take effective measures to alleviate the consequences, in particular the social consequences, of that adjustment policy, so that the country may achieve lasting economic results,

Noting with gratitude the support provided to relief, demobilization and rehabilitation operations by various countries and by intergovernmental and non-governmental organizations,

1. *Takes note* of the report of the Secretary-General;

2. *Declares its solidarity* with the Government and the people of Djibouti, who continue to face critical challenges owing, in particular, to the scarcity of natural resources, harsh climatic conditions and the continuing critical situation in the Horn of Africa;

3. *Notes with concern* the cyclical drought phenomenon in Djibouti, which is wreaking a major humanitarian disaster upon tens of thousands of people, particularly those who are vulnerable, and requests the international community to respond to the appeal launched by the Government;

4. *Encourages* the Government of Djibouti, despite difficult economic and regional situations, to continue its serious efforts towards the consolidation of democracy;

5. *Notes with satisfaction* the implementation of a structural adjustment programme by Djibouti, and in that context appeals to all Governments, international financial institutions, the specialized agencies and non-governmental organizations to respond adequately to the financial and material needs of the country;

6. *Also notes with satisfaction* the general peace agreement concluded between the Government and the opposition on 12 May 2001;

7. *Considers* that the process of demobilization, reintegration and employment of demobilized soldiers is essential not only for national rehabilitation but also for the success of agreements with the international financial institutions and for the consolidation of peace, and that it requires substantial resources that exceed the capacity of the country;

8. *Expresses its gratitude* to the intergovernmental organizations and the specialized agencies of the United Nations for their contributions to the national rehabilitation of Djibouti, and invites them to continue their efforts;

9. *Expresses its appreciation* to the Secretary-General for his continued efforts to make the international community aware of the difficulties faced by Djibouti;

10. *Notes with gratitude* Djibouti's support for regional peace efforts and its commitment to worldwide efforts to fight terrorism;

11. *Requests* the Secretary-General to continue, in close cooperation with the Government of Djibouti, his efforts to mobilize resources necessary for an effective programme of financial, technical and material assistance to Djibouti;

12. *Also requests* the Secretary-General to report to the General Assembly at its fifty-eighth session on the progress made with regard to economic assistance to Djibouti and the implementation of the present resolution.

Other economic assistance

Central America

In a July report [A/56/158], submitted in response to General Assembly resolution 54/96 E [YUN 1999, p. 852], the Secretary-General described

the activities of UNDP and other UN organs, organizations and programmes carried out between August 1999 and April 2001 to support the efforts of Central American countries to implement a new sustainable development strategy in the region. The report also discussed efforts made by the Central American Governments and people to recover from natural disasters and to utilize the reconstruction process as an opportunity to transform their societies within the context of the Alliance for the Sustainable Development of Central America (ALIDES), established in 1994 [YUN 1994, p. 389].

The UNDP programme for subregional cooperation in Central America, which was launched in 1996 within the ALIDES framework [YUN 1996, p. 154], focused on peace and democratic governance, economic and social development, and environmental sustainable development. The UNDP programme and the national programmes of UN agencies were reviewed during the preparations and conclusions of the Regional Consultative Group for strengthening integration and cooperation in Central America (Madrid, Spain, 8-9 March). With regard to peace and democratic governance, at the regional level the UNDP project entitled "State of the region" continued to carry out systematic follow-up on the process of human development and integration in Central America. At the national level, the UN system in El Salvador, Guatemala and Nicaragua continued to promote the consolidation of peace and consensus-building on the reforms needed to address the root causes of the Central American conflict. UNDP support was also provided to Costa Rica, Honduras and Panama. Bilateral donors had granted financial resources to UNDP to strengthen democratic institutions at the national level in Guatemala and Honduras. UNDP/Guatemala initiated programmes in the area of human rights, justice and reconciliation. Economic and social development programmes were carried out throughout the region to alleviate poverty, improve agricultural development, health and nutrition, public finance and economic growth and reduce environmental vulnerability.

GENERAL ASSEMBLY ACTION

On 14 December [meeting 87], the General Assembly adopted **resolution 56/105** [draft: A/56/L.53 & Add.1] without vote [agenda item 20 *(b)*].

International assistance to and cooperation with the Alliance for the Sustainable Development of Central America

The General Assembly,

Reaffirming the resolutions in which it emphasizes and acknowledges the importance of international, bilateral and multilateral economic, financial and technical support, cooperation and assistance for peace-keeping and peace-building in Central America following the armed conflicts in the region, in particular its resolutions 49/21 I of 20 December 1994, 50/58 B of 12 December 1995, 50/132 of 20 December 1995, 52/169 G of 16 December 1997 and 54/96 E of 15 December 1999, which provide a frame of reference for international assistance to and cooperation with the Alliance for the Sustainable Development of Central America, in support of national efforts to make the region a zone of peace, freedom, democracy and development,

Noting that the Central American countries have achieved significant progress towards the consolidation of democracy and good governance, the strengthening of civilian Governments, respect for human rights and the rule of law and the promotion of State and economic reforms, sustainable development and regional integration, reflecting the desire of the Central American peoples to live and prosper in a climate of peace and solidarity,

Stressing the importance and effectiveness of the commitments undertaken by the Central American Presidents at various regional presidential summits, in particular those which constitute the global framework for promoting and consolidating peace, freedom, democracy and sustainable human development in Central America,

Stressing also the consolidation of the Centre for Coordination of the Prevention of Natural Disasters in Central America, which is of great value for the sub-region in the development of more effective strategies to mitigate the impact of natural disasters,

Recognizing the extreme vulnerability of the poorest sectors of the population, in particular women and children, and the inadequacy of existing local and national institutions to deal with recurrent natural disasters,

Noting that the various natural phenomena which have affected the region are one of the factors that have put at risk the biodiversity of Central America,

Noting also the holding of the meeting of the Regional Consultative Group for the transformation and modernization of Central America, co-hosted by the Inter-American Development Bank and the Government of Spain, in Madrid on 8 and 9 March 2001, at which the main theme was the revision of the regional strategy for strengthening regional integration and cooperation and their contribution to poverty reduction and the acceleration of sustainable growth,

Taking into account that the Governments of the region have designated the period 2000-2004 as the Quinquennium for the Reduction of Vulnerability to and the Impact of Natural Disasters in Central America and that the Presidents of the region adopted the Strategic Framework for the Reduction of Vulnerability and Disasters in Central America, on 19 October 1999, in the Declaration of Guatemala II which contains guidelines for the elaboration, updating, improvement and development of regional plans for the reduction of vulnerability to and the impact of natural disasters, the integrated management and conservation of water resources and the prevention and control of forest fires,

Stressing that the achievement of the national priorities in the political, economic, social, cultural, environmental, public safety and regional integration fields, which are set out in the programme of the Alliance for the Sustainable Development of Central America, is essential for reducing the vulnerability of the region to natural disasters and for promoting sustainable development,

Considering the necessity of ensuring the elimination of anti-personnel mines from Central American territory as well as the rehabilitation and reintegration of mine victims in their communities in order to restore normal conditions for the integral development of that region,

Recognizing the valuable and effective contribution made by the organs, organizations and programmes of the United Nations system and by the various governmental and non-governmental mechanisms, the donor community and the Regional Consultative Group for the transformation and modernization of Central America and the importance of the political dialogue and cooperation taking place between the European Union and Central America and the joint initiative of the industrialized countries of the Group of Twenty-four and the Group of Three (Colombia, Mexico and Venezuela) in the progress made towards consolidating peace, freedom, democracy and the implementation of the Alliance for the Sustainable Development of Central America,

Reaffirming the need to continue focusing attention on the situation in Central America, with a view to overcoming the underlying causes of the armed conflicts which have impeded the development of the region and avoiding a reversal of the achievements,

1. *Takes note with satisfaction* of the report of the Secretary-General;

2. *Reiterates* the importance of supporting and strengthening the efforts of the Central American countries to implement the Strategic Framework for the Reduction of Vulnerability and Disasters in Central America, and the projects and programmes of the Quinquennium for the Reduction of Vulnerability to and the Impact of Natural Disasters in Central America, in accordance with the process of transformation and sustainable development for the region, which contain basic guidelines for the prevention and mitigation of damage, with special emphasis on the most vulnerable groups and sectors, as identified by levels of poverty and marginality;

3. *Notes* the efforts and achievements relating to mine clearance in Central America, and appeals to the organs of the United Nations system, in particular the Mine Action Service of the Department of Peacekeeping Operations of the Secretariat, the Organization of American States, as well as the international community, to continue providing the material, technical and financial support needed by the Central American Governments to complete mine-clearance, mine-awareness and victim assistance activities in the region, in conformity with the relevant resolutions of the United Nations and with the provisions of the Convention on the Prohibition of the Use, Stockpiling, Production and Transfer of Anti-personnel Mines and on Their Destruction that relate to international cooperation and assistance;

4. *Stresses* the need for the international community to maintain its cooperation and assistance, including provision of financial resources, both bilateral and multilateral, with the Central American countries to support the promotion of sustainable development and the consolidation of peace, freedom and democracy in the region;

5. *Notes with appreciation* the revision of the subregional cooperation programme in Central America of the United Nations Development Programme, launched in 1996, and of the national programmes of other United Nations agencies on the basis of the regional strategy entitled "Strategy for the transformation and modernization of Central America", the main objectives of which are the reduction of social, economic and environmental vulnerabilities, the transformation of productive sectors, sustainable management of natural resources, and the increased participation of civil society in development;

6. *Notes with satisfaction* the progress achieved in the establishment of a Meso-American Biological Corridor, which is being developed with assistance from the United Nations Development Programme's own funds, the Global Environment Facility through the World Bank, the United Nations Environment Programme, the Inter-American Development Bank, the German Agency for Technical Cooperation and the United States Agency for International Development;

7. *Supports* the decision of the Central American Governments to concentrate their efforts on the implementation of updated programmes with strategies to achieve sustainable human development in previously determined priority areas, which help to consolidate democracy and resolve social inequalities and extreme poverty;

8. *Requests* the Secretary-General, the organs, organizations and programmes of the United Nations system and all States, international financial institutions and regional and subregional organizations to continue providing the support needed to attain the objectives of the programme for the sustainable development of Central America, including those which are being pursued within the framework of the Quinquennium for the Reduction of Vulnerability to and the Impact of Natural Disasters in Central America;

9. *Requests* the Secretary-General to report to the General Assembly at its fifty-eighth session on the implementation of the present resolution;

10. *Decides* to consider at its fifty-eighth session the question of international assistance to and cooperation with the Alliance for the Sustainable Development of Central America.

Haiti

In response to Economic and Social Council decision 2000/235 [YUN 2000, p. 879], the Secretary-General submitted a May report [E/2001/67] on steps taken by the Haitian Government, the UN system and the international community towards elaborating a long-term programme of support for Haiti and on practical modalities for its implementation.

The Secretary-General described the UN development system's principal activities in Haiti in 2000 and observed that significant progress had been achieved in terms of preparing instruments to improve the coordination of UN operational activities with the Government of Haiti. The UN system country team had concluded in April the United Nations Development Assistance Framework for the period 2002-2006. Its overall objective was to promote sustainable human development through action to combat poverty and social exclusion, the strengthening of the rule of law, and the protection, observance and achievement of human rights. At the same time, the Government had focused on formulating its medium- and long-term strategic development framework, using, among other sources, the UN system's common country assessment document to provide data and indicators for planning Haiti's development programmes. The resident coordinator would continue to advocate action to strengthen the operational links between the UN system, the Bretton Woods institutions and the donor community.

ECONOMIC AND SOCIAL COUNCIL ACTION

On 26 July [meeting 43], the Economic and Social Council adopted **resolution 2001/25** [draft: E/2001/L.35] without vote [agenda item 7 *(f)*].

Long-term programme of support for Haiti

The Economic and Social Council,

Recalling its resolution 1999/11 of 27 July 1999 and its decision 2000/235 of 27 July 2000,

Taking note of the comprehensive report of the Secretary-General on the long-term programme of support for Haiti,

Welcoming the key role being played by the Organization of American States and the Caribbean Community in supporting the efforts of the Haitian Government and people to resolve the political, social and economic crisis,

Requests the Secretary-General to report to it at its substantive session of 2002 on progress achieved in elaborating a long-term programme of support for Haiti and on the practical modalities for its implementation.

Third States affected by sanctions

In a June note [E/2001/90], submitted in response to Economic and Social Council resolution 2000/32 [YUN 2000, p. 879] and General Assembly resolution 55/157 [ibid., p. 1271], the Secretary-General drew attention to his 2000 report on the implementation of the provisions of the Charter of the United Nations related to assistance to third States affected by the application of sanctions [ibid., p. 1270].

On 26 July, the Council took note of the Secretary-General's note (**decision 2001/315**).

States affected in the Balkans

In response to General Assembly resolution 55/170 [YUN 2000, p. 880], the Secretary-General submitted a November report on economic assistance to the Eastern European States affected by the consequences of severing their economic relations with FRY [A/56/632]. The report summarized information provided by seven States and 11 UN organizations, programmes and funds describing action they had taken to assist the affected States.

Although the limited number of replies was insufficient to make a conclusive assessment, the Secretary-General noted that recent analyses by international bodies in the region indicated that the affected countries continued to face varying economic difficulties and adjustment problems. Those difficulties stemmed from internal and external factors, including the long-term consequences of the developments in the Balkans during the preceding decade. The recent democratic changes in FRY (see p. 345) had strengthened the prospects for resuming and enhancing regional cooperation, particularly with regard to traditional economic links throughout the Balkans and the rest of Europe. However, ensuring the lasting stability and sustainable development of South-Eastern Europe would require the continued and concerted efforts of the countries of the region and the international development actors.

GENERAL ASSEMBLY ACTION

On 14 December [meeting 87], the General Assembly adopted **resolution 56/110** [draft: A/56/L.58 & Add.1] without vote [agenda item 20 (*b*)].

Economic assistance to the Eastern European States affected by the developments in the Balkans

The General Assembly,

Recalling its resolutions 54/96 G of 15 December 1999 and 55/170 of 14 December 2000,

Recalling also the Stability Pact for South-Eastern Europe, adopted in Cologne, Germany, on 10 June 1999, and endorsed at the Sarajevo Summit of 30 July 1999, and emphasizing the crucial importance of its implementation,

Stressing the importance of the regional cooperation initiatives, assistance arrangements and organizations, such as the South-East European Cooperative Initiative, the South-East European Cooperation Process, the Central European Initiative, the Black Sea Economic Cooperation Organization and the Danube Commission, as well as the Stabilization and Association process and other arrangements for the Eastern European States with the European Union,

Noting the leading role played by the high-level steering group for South-Eastern Europe, under the joint chairmanship of the European Commission and the World Bank, in guiding the donor coordination process for the economic reconstruction, stabilization, reform and development of the region, in close cooperation with the Stability Pact,

Mindful of the positive results of the two regional funding conferences for South-Eastern Europe organized by the European Commission and the World Bank in cooperation with the Stability Pact, held in Brussels on 29 and 30 March 2000 and in Bucharest on 25 and 26 October 2001, and of the progress achieved in mobilizing and coordinating support of the donor community and international financial institutions for reconstruction and development efforts in South-Eastern Europe,

Welcoming the democratic changes in the Federal Republic of Yugoslavia and their positive effects on peace, stability and development in South-Eastern Europe,

Welcoming also the positive results of the International Donors Conference for the Federal Republic of Yugoslavia, co-hosted by the World Bank and the European Commission in Brussels on 29 June 2001, and the progress achieved in mobilizing and coordinating support of the donor community and international financial institutions for the reconstruction and development of Yugoslavia,

Taking note of the report of the Secretary-General and the conclusions contained therein,

1. *Expresses concern* at the persistence of special economic problems confronting the Eastern European States affected by the developments in the Balkans, in particular their impact on regional trade and economic relations and on the navigation along the Danube and on the Adriatic Sea;

2. *Welcomes* the support already provided by the international community, in particular by the European Union and other major donors, to the affected States to assist them in coping with their special economic problems during the transition period following the developments in the Balkans, as well as in the longer-term process of economic recovery, structural adjustment and development in the region;

3. *Also welcomes* the progress made in the implementation of the Stability Pact for South-Eastern Europe, the objective of which is to strengthen countries in South-Eastern Europe in their efforts to foster peace, democracy, respect for human rights and economic prosperity, in order to achieve stability in the whole region, and in its follow-up activities, aimed, inter alia, at economic reconstruction, development and cooperation, including economic cooperation in the region and between the region and the rest of Europe;

4. *Invites* all States and the relevant international organizations, both within and outside the United Nations system, in particular the international financial institutions, to continue to take into account the special needs and situations of the affected States in providing support and assistance to their efforts for economic recovery, structural adjustment and development;

5. *Emphasizes* the importance of a well-coordinated and timely donor response to the external funding requirements of the process for economic reconstruction, stabilization, reform and development in the Balkans, as well as financial support to other affected countries of Eastern Europe;

6. *Encourages* the affected States of the region to continue and enhance the process of multilateral re-

gional cooperation in the fields of transport and infrastructure development, including the resumption of full navigation on the Danube, as well as to foster conditions favourable to trade, in such areas as customs, investment and private sector development, including privatization, in all the countries of the region;

7. *Invites* the relevant international organizations to take appropriate steps, consistent with the principle of efficient and effective procurement and with the agreed measures for procurement reform, in order to broaden access for interested local and regional vendors and to facilitate their participation in the international assistance efforts for the reconstruction, recovery and development of the region;

8. *Requests* the Secretary-General to report to the General Assembly at its fifty-eighth session on the implementation of the present resolution.

Disaster relief

The scale and number of natural disasters continued to grow in 2001. Asia was struck by more natural disasters than any other continent during the year, among them consecutive dzuds, or periods of devastating cold, in Mongolia, a devastating earthquake in India, serious floods in Bangladesh, Cambodia and Viet Nam, and a volcanic eruption in the Philippines. In the first 10 months of the year, natural disasters killed 20,871 people and affected 57.8 million others in the region.

Southern Africa witnessed a series of extensive floods and droughts in 2001. Heavy rains caused severe flooding in Angola, Malawi, Mozambique, Zambia and Zimbabwe, while other areas of Mozambique, Zambia and Zimbabwe were parched by drought after long spells without rain. Flooding in southern Angola added to the disruption caused by the civil war, and nearly 50 per cent of Malawi's 27 districts were flooded and 130,000 people were displaced. When the rivers Shire (Malawi) and Zambezi (Zimbabwe) burst their banks, flood waters rose drastically in the four central and southern provinces of Mozambique and more than 500,000 people were affected, of whom more than 230,000 were displaced. Central and East Africa were affected by both man-made and natural disasters that caused appalling levels of human suffering. West Africa experienced climatic changes manifested in natural disasters, including flooding and drought, and forced migration southwards from the Sahel, due to desertification and lack of cultivable land.

The Latin America and Caribbean region was hit hard in 2001. Within one month, two earthquakes shook El Salvador, followed by an earthquake in Peru, then drought affected Central America, and, during the hurricane season, hurricanes Iris and Michelle wrought havoc in Central America and the Caribbean.

The year was relatively calm in the Pacific in terms of natural disasters, reflecting the prolonged but weakening La Niña phase. However, at the end of February, tropical cyclone Paula adversely affected Fiji and Vanuatu. Five weeks later, tropical cyclone Sose struck the same islands of central and southern Vanuatu. Outer-island communities in Vanuatu were again affected by the eruption of Lopevi Volcano in June.

During the year, the Office for the Coordination of Humanitarian Affairs (OCHA), through the Response Coordination Branch and the Emergency Services Branch, mobilized and coordinated assistance to 67 natural disasters.

GENERAL ASSEMBLY ACTION

On 14 December [meeting 87], the General Assembly adopted **resolution 56/99** [draft: A/56/L.14 & Add.1] without vote [agenda item 20 *(a)*].

Emergency response to disasters

The General Assembly,

Reaffirming its resolution 46/182 of 19 December 1991 on the strengthening of the coordination of emergency humanitarian assistance of the United Nations, including the guiding principles of humanitarian assistance contained therein,

Recalling its resolutions 44/236 of 22 December 1989, 54/30 of 22 November 1999 and 54/219 of 22 December 1999,

Welcoming the International Strategy for Disaster Reduction,

Deeply concerned by the fact that natural disasters in every corner of the globe continue to claim high numbers of casualties and cause immense material damage and that the frequency and magnitude of these catastrophes place an ever-increasing material and moral burden on nations,

Reiterating the importance of mounting prompt and effective relief operations in the aftermath of such deadly calamities in the future,

Welcoming the ongoing efforts, led by the Office for the Coordination of Humanitarian Affairs of the Secretariat, aimed at promoting preparedness for disaster response at the international, regional and national levels, including, in collaboration with the International Search and Rescue Advisory Group, initiatives to improve the efficiency and effectiveness of international urban search and rescue assistance in the aftermath of natural disasters,

1. *Expresses its solidarity* with the peoples of the countries that have been struck by natural calamities as they cope with the consequences of these disasters;

2. *Expresses its appreciation* to all States of the international community, international agencies and organizations and non-governmental organizations and individuals that are providing emergency relief to the areas affected by natural disasters;

3. *Notes with satisfaction* the progress achieved by the Governments of Turkey and Greece, in cooperation with the Office for the Coordination of Humanitarian Affairs of the Secretariat, on the formation of a joint Hellenic-Turkish standby disaster response unit, which will be operational in the near future, with no financial implications for the programme budget of the United Nations;

4. *Requests* the Secretary-General, through the Office for the Coordination of Humanitarian Affairs, to continue work on the modalities for the utilization of the standby disaster relief unit by the United Nations system;

5. *Also requests* the Secretary-General to report to the General Assembly at its fifty-seventh session on the progress made in the implementation of the present resolution.

International cooperation

In response to General Assembly resolution 55/163 [YUN 2000, p. 848], the Secretary-General submitted an August report [A/56/307] in which he described international cooperation to mitigate the effects of natural disasters. OCHA, the focal point within the UN system to promote and coordinate disaster response preparedness among the UN humanitarian agencies and other partners, had carried out an independent review of the UN disaster assessment and coordination system, which had engendered useful recommendations to improve the system further. To strengthen response preparedness, OCHA established offices for regional disaster response advisers in South America, Asia and the Pacific. In response to an increase in disasters affecting entire regions, UN agencies with mitigation responsibilities, such as UNDP, FAO, WFP, the World Meteorological Organization (WMO) and the World Bank, had increased their disaster reduction capacities and funding. The UN disaster assessment and coordination team system remained one of the most effective and participatory international rapid response tools available to the Emergency Relief Coordinator. In the first half of 2001, six missions were undertaken, including in response to the severe winter in Mongolia, floods in the Russian Federation and earthquakes in El Salvador, India and Peru. The International Search and Rescue Advisory Group took major steps during the year to speed up the response of international urban search and rescue teams in the event of an earthquake.

With regard to the transition from relief to recovery after a major emergency, external strengthening of capacities from an early stage was necessary to ensure a smooth process. The concept of transitional recovery teams had been introduced by UNDP, which had further strengthened the capacity of its country offices and the resident coordinator system to initiate support to the early recovery efforts of national authorities. At the country level, UNDP had supported more than 50 national capacity-building programmes in natural disaster prevention, preparedness and mitigation.

The Secretary-General recommended that the secretariat of the International Strategy for Disaster Reduction (see p. 861), in collaboration with OCHA, UNDP and other partners, take the lead in developing an inventory of existing disaster mitigation capacity and inform the Assembly of progress made.

GENERAL ASSEMBLY ACTION

On 14 December [meeting 87], the General Assembly adopted **resolution 56/103** [draft: A/56/L.51 & Corr.1 & Add.1] without vote [agenda item 20 (a)].

International cooperation on humanitarian assistance in the field of natural disasters, from relief to development

The General Assembly,

Reaffirming its resolution 46/182 of 19 December 1991, the annex to which contains the guiding principles for the strengthening of the coordination of emergency humanitarian assistance of the United Nations system, and its resolutions 52/12 B of 19 December 1997, 54/219 and 54/233 of 22 December 1999 and 55/163 of 14 December 2000, and recalling agreed conclusions 1999/1 of the Economic and Social Council and Council resolution 1999/63 of 30 July 1999,

Recognizing the importance of the principles of neutrality, humanity and impartiality for the provision of humanitarian assistance,

Emphasizing that the affected State has the primary responsibility in the initiation, organization, coordination and implementation of humanitarian assistance within its territory, and in the facilitation of the work of humanitarian organizations in mitigating the consequences of natural disasters,

Emphasizing also the responsibility of all States to undertake disaster preparedness and mitigation efforts in order to minimize the impact of natural disasters,

Welcoming the International Strategy for Disaster Reduction,

Emphasizing the importance of raising awareness among developing countries of the capacities existing at the national, regional and international levels that could be deployed to assist them,

Emphasizing also the importance of international cooperation in support of the efforts of the affected States in dealing with natural disasters in all their phases, including prevention, preparedness, mitigation and recovery and reconstruction, and of strengthening the response capacity of affected countries,

1. *Takes note* of the report of the Secretary-General on international cooperation on humanitarian assistance in the field of natural disasters, from relief to development and on strengthening the coordination of emergency humanitarian assistance of the United Nations;

2. *Expresses deep concern* at the increasing number and scale of natural disasters, resulting in massive losses of life and property worldwide, in particular in vulnerable societies lacking adequate capacity to mitigate effectively the long-term negative social, economic and environmental consequences of natural disasters;

3. *Calls upon* all States to adopt, where required, and to continue to implement effectively necessary legislative and other appropriate measures to mitigate the effects of natural disasters, inter alia, by disaster prevention, including building regulations and appropriate land use, as well as disaster preparedness and capacity-building in disaster response, and requests the international community in that context to continue to assist developing countries, where appropriate;

4. *Stresses*, in that context, the importance of strengthening international cooperation in the provision of humanitarian assistance in support of the efforts of the affected States in dealing with natural disasters in all their phases, from relief and mitigation to development, including through the provision of adequate resources, and encourages the effective use of multilateral mechanisms;

5. *Also stresses* that humanitarian assistance for natural disasters should be provided in accordance with and with due respect for the guiding principles contained in the annex to resolution 46/182, and should be determined on the basis of the human dimension and needs arising out of the particular natural disasters;

6. *Recognizes* that economic growth and sustainable development contribute to improving the capacity of States to mitigate, respond to and prepare for natural disasters;

7. *Reaffirms* that disaster reduction forms an integral part of sustainable development strategies and needs to be considered in the development plans of all vulnerable countries and communities, and also reaffirms that within such preventive strategies, disaster preparedness and early warning systems must be strengthened further at the country and regional levels, inter alia, through better coordination among relevant United Nations bodies and cooperation with Governments of affected countries and regional and other relevant organizations with the aim of maximizing the effectiveness of natural disaster response and reducing the impact of natural disasters, particularly in developing countries;

8. *Emphasizes* the importance of enhanced international cooperation, including with the United Nations and regional organizations, to assist developing countries in their efforts to build capacities, and to predict, prepare and respond to natural disasters;

9. *Stresses* the need for partnership among Governments of the affected countries, relevant humanitarian organizations and specialized companies to promote training in, access to and use of technologies to strengthen preparedness for and response to natural disasters, and to enhance the transfer of current technologies and corresponding know-how, in particular to developing countries, on concessional and preferential terms, as mutually agreed;

10. *Encourages* the further use of space-based and ground-based remote-sensing technologies for the prevention, mitigation and management of natural disasters, where appropriate;

11. *Also encourages* in such operations the sharing of geographical data, including remotely sensed images and geographic information system and global positioning system data among Governments, space agencies and relevant international humanitarian organizations, as appropriate, and notes in that context the work being done by the International Charter on Space and Major Disasters and the Global Disaster Information Network;

12. *Stresses* that particular international cooperation efforts should be undertaken to enhance and broaden further the utilization of national and local capacities and, where appropriate, regional and subregional capacities of developing countries for disaster preparedness and response, which may be made available in closer proximity to the site of a disaster, more efficiently and at lower cost;

13. *Welcomes* the role of the Office for the Coordination of Humanitarian Affairs of the Secretariat as the focal point within the overall United Nations system for the promotion and coordination of disaster response preparedness among the United Nations humanitarian agencies and other humanitarian partners;

14. *Also welcomes* the establishment of the positions of regional disaster response advisers by the Office for the Coordination of Humanitarian Affairs, as well as the initiative of the United Nations Development Programme to establish regional disaster reduction adviser positions, and encourages the further development of those initiatives in a coordinated and complementary manner in order to assist developing countries in capacity-building for disaster prevention, preparedness mitigation and response;

15. *Takes note* of the initiatives taken by the Office for the Coordination of Humanitarian Affairs and by the International Search and Rescue Advisory Group to improve the efficiency and effectiveness of international urban search and rescue assistance in the aftermath of natural disasters;

16. *Encourages* the Office for the Coordination of Humanitarian Affairs to continue its efforts to promote greater international cooperation to improve the efficiency and effectiveness of urban search and rescue assistance;

17. *Encourages* further cooperation between the United Nations system and regional organizations in order to increase the capacity of those organizations to respond to natural disasters;

18. *Encourages* States that have not signed or ratified the Tampere Convention on the Provision of Telecommunication Resources for Disaster Mitigation and Relief Operations, adopted at Tampere, Finland, on 18 June 1998, to consider doing so;

19. *Invites* the United Nations system to explore further the concept of transitional recovery teams for providing assistance for bridging relief assistance and development cooperation;

20. *Requests* the Secretary-General, in collaboration with relevant organization partners, to continue progress on compiling a directory of disaster mitigation capacity existing at the national, regional and international levels and developing the Directory of Advanced Technologies for Disaster Response as a new part of the Central Register of Disaster Management Capacities;

21. *Also requests* the Secretary-General to complete the project of issuing a global report on disaster reduction as undertaken by the International Strategy for Disaster Reduction;

22. *Further requests* the Secretary-General to continue to consider mechanisms to improve the international response to natural disasters, inter alia, by addressing any geographical and sectoral imbalances in such a response, where they exist, as well as by more effective use of national emergency response agencies, taking into account their comparative advantages and specializations, as well as existing arrangements, and to report thereon to the General Assembly at its fifty-seventh session under the item entitled "Strengthening of the coordination of humanitarian and disaster relief assistance of the United Nations, including special economic assistance", with a view, inter alia, to contributing towards the comprehensive report on the implementation of the International Strategy for Disaster Reduction, to be submitted to the Assembly at that session under the item entitled "Environment and sustainable development".

International Strategy for Disaster Reduction

In response to General Assembly resolution 54/219 [YUN 1999, p. 861], the Secretary-General submitted a May report [A/56/68-E/2001/63 & Corr.1] on the implementation of the International Strategy for Disaster Reduction (ISDR). The Inter-Agency Task Force for Disaster Reduction and the ISDR secretariat served as the main mechanisms for the implementation of the Strategy.

The Inter-Agency Task Force (Geneva, 3-4 May) identified priority issues in disaster reduction to be addressed by the international community. A review of the Task Force working groups [YUN 2000, p. 882] suggested that start-up activities in terms of the identification of their membership, agreement on their work programme and the determination of the substantive issues to be addressed required considerable effort on the part of the lead agencies. Moreover, the convening of meetings had been constrained by the lack of resources.

The ISDR secretariat had developed a framework for action to implement the Strategy, which identified four main objectives: increasing public awareness; promoting commitment on the part of public authorities; stimulating interdisciplinary and intersectoral partnerships, and expanding risk reduction networking; and improving scientific knowledge of the causes of natural disasters and the effects of natural hazards and related technological and environmental disasters on societies. The framework also incorporated the continuation of international cooperation to reduce the impact of El Niño and other climatic variables and the strengthening of disaster re-

duction capacities through the development of early warning systems. The Task Force, which had endorsed the framework, had succeeded in identifying priority areas for action relevant to disaster reduction, including climate variability, early warning, vulnerability and risk, as well as wild land fires. It had also sought to launch initiatives on those areas through its working groups.

The report described activities taken by partner agencies and organizations to support the Strategy.

The Secretary-General recommended that the framework serve as the basic guide to implement the Strategy. He proposed that the Economic and Social Council and the Assembly launch a 10-year review of the implementation of the outcome of the 1994 Yokohama World Conference on Natural Disaster Reduction [YUN 1994, p. 851], beginning in 2002, to ensure that a comprehensive assessment was made of progress in disaster reduction, with a view to identifying ways to further strengthen the efforts of the international community in support of that objective. The formula for constituting the Inter-Agency Task Force should be modified in order to provide for increased participation of regional organizations and ensure the continued membership of key UN agencies. The key strategic agencies that participated in the Task Force should be increased from eight to a maximum of 14. Similarly, the number of regional organizations should be increased to a maximum of eight. Half of the members representing regional organizations and NGOs should be rotated on a biennial basis, beginning in January 2002. Donors were urged to increase their contributions to the Trust Fund for the International Strategy for Disaster Reduction. The Secretary-General intended to report to the Assembly's sixty-first session in 2006 on the implementation of his recommendations to determine what modifications might be necessary in the Strategy, taking into account the recommendations emanating from the proposed 10-year review of the Yokohama conference process.

A further meeting of the Inter-Agency Task Force (Geneva, 15-16 November) reviewed achievements made in implementing its work plan for 2001.

ECONOMIC AND SOCIAL COUNCIL ACTION

On 26 July [meeting 43], the Economic and Social Council adopted **resolution 2001/35** [draft: E/2001/L.19/Rev.1] without vote [agenda item 13 (h)].

International Strategy for Disaster Reduction

The Economic and Social Council,

Recalling General Assembly resolutions 44/236 of 22 December 1989, 49/22 A of 2 December 1994, 49/22 B of 20 December 1994, 53/185 of 15 December

1998, 54/219 of 22 December 1999 and 55/163 of 14 December 2000, and reiterating its resolution 1999/63 of 30 July 1999 entitled "International Decade for Natural Disaster Reduction: successor arrangements",

Recalling also the forward-looking platform for international concerted disaster reduction, as developed by the World Conference on Natural Disaster Reduction and as expressed in the Yokohama Strategy for a Safer World: Guidelines for Natural Disaster Prevention, Preparedness and Mitigation and its Plan of Action, as well as the Geneva mandate on disaster reduction and the strategy document entitled "A safer world in the twenty-first century: risk and disaster reduction",

Emphasizing the multisectoral, interdisciplinary and cross-cutting nature of natural disaster reduction, and stressing that continued interaction, cooperation and partnerships among the institutions concerned are considered essential to achieve jointly agreed objectives and priorities,

Having considered the report of the Secretary-General, including the conclusions and recommendations contained therein,

Having also considered the current institutional arrangements, as established by the General Assembly in its resolution 54/219, with the Inter-Agency Task Force for Disaster Reduction and the inter-agency secretariat for the implementation of the International Strategy for Disaster Reduction, and taking into account the assessment after the first period of operations,

Recognizing that disaster reduction is an important element contributing to the achievement of sustainable development and that it should be taken into account in the preparatory process of the World Summit on Sustainable Development to be held at Johannesburg, South Africa, in 2002,

Reiterating that natural disasters damage the social and economic infrastructure of all countries, although the long-term consequences of natural disasters are especially severe for developing countries and hamper their sustainable development,

Welcoming the emphasis placed on natural disaster reduction in the Programme of Action for the Least Developed Countries for the Decade 2001-2010, adopted at Brussels in May 2001,

Recognizing that disaster reduction should be regarded as an important function of the United Nations and should receive continued attention,

Stressing the need for the international community to demonstrate the firm political determination required to utilize scientific and technical knowledge to reduce the vulnerability to natural disasters and environmental hazards, taking into account the particular needs of developing countries,

1. *Expresses its deep concern* at the increasing number and scale of natural disasters, which have resulted in massive loss of life and long-term negative social, economic and environmental consequences for vulnerable societies worldwide, in particular in developing countries;

2. *Reaffirms* that the Inter-Agency Task Force for Disaster Reduction should perform the functions as indicated in the report of the Secretary General, in particular to serve as a main forum within the United Nations system for devising strategies and policies for disaster reduction and to ensure complementary action by agencies involved in disaster reduction, mitigation and preparedness, and decides to review the activities of the Task Force in 2003;

3. *Decides* that the Task Force should be modified in order to provide for the increased participation of regional organizations and to ensure the continued membership of key United Nations agencies;

4. *Recognizes* that the framework for action for the implementation of the International Strategy for Disaster Reduction, as endorsed by the Task Force, constitutes the basic guide for the implementation of the Strategy, and that the framework shall be periodically reviewed, according to the evolving needs in the field of natural disaster reduction;

5. *Urges* all relevant bodies within the United Nations system to cooperate fully within the context of the framework;

6. *Stresses* that the inter-agency secretariat for the implementation of the Strategy should be consolidated to perform its functions effectively, in particular to serve as the focal point within the United Nations system for the coordination of disaster reduction and to ensure synergies among disaster-reduction activities of the United Nations system and regional organizations and activities in socio-economic and humanitarian fields;

7. *Calls upon* Governments to continue to cooperate and coordinate their efforts with the United Nations system, other international organizations, regional organizations, non-governmental organizations and other partners, as appropriate, in order to ensure effective synergies in the field of natural disasters, and urges the Strategy secretariat to develop such synergies, as appropriate;

8. *Underlines* the importance of adequate financial and administrative resources for the effective functioning of the Task Force and the Strategy secretariat, under the direct authority of the Under-Secretary-General for Humanitarian Affairs;

9. *Calls upon* Governments to establish national platforms or focal points for disaster reduction, urges the United Nations system to provide appropriate support for those mechanisms, and invites the Secretary-General to strengthen the regional outreach of the Strategy secretariat in order to ensure such support;

10. *Invites* Governments and relevant organizations of the United Nations system to strengthen national participation, in particular of disaster-prone countries, in the Strategy, including through national multisectoral and interdisciplinary platforms, in order to achieve sustainable development goals and objectives, with the full utilization of scientific and technical knowledge, including through capacity-building at all levels and the development and strengthening of global and regional approaches that take into account regional, subregional, national and local circumstances and needs, as well as the need to strengthen coordination of national emergency response agencies;

11. *Recognizes* the urgent need to develop further and make use of the existing scientific and technical knowledge to reduce vulnerability to natural disasters, and emphasizes the need for developing countries to have access to technology to tackle natural disasters effectively;

12. *Encourages* the international community to provide the necessary financial resources to the Trust

Fund for the International Strategy for Disaster Reduction and to provide adequate scientific, technical, human and other resources to ensure adequate support for the Strategy secretariat and for the Task Force and its working groups;

13. *Requests* the relevant organizations of the United Nations system to support the implementation of the goals of the Strategy, including by seconding technical staff to the Strategy secretariat;

14. *Also requests* the Secretary-General to submit a report on disaster reduction to the preparatory process for the World Summit on Sustainable Development to be held at Johannesburg, South Africa, in 2002;

15. *Takes note* of the proposal of the Secretary-General to review the implementation of the Yokohama Strategy for a Safer World: Guidelines for Natural Disaster Prevention, Preparedness and Mitigation and its Plan of Action, within the context of the framework for action for the implementation of the Strategy;

16. *Reiterates* the need to continue international cooperation to reduce the impact of the El Niño phenomenon, within the framework for the Strategy, as requested by the Council in its resolutions 1999/46 of 28 July 1999 and 2000/33 of 28 July 2000 and by the General Assembly in its resolutions 52/200 of 18 December 1997, 53/185, 54/220 of 22 December 1999 and 55/197 of 20 December 2000;

17. *Recognizes* the importance of early warning as an essential element in the culture of prevention, and encourages renewed efforts at all levels to contribute to natural hazard monitoring and impact prediction, the development and transfer of technology, capacity-building for disaster preparedness, the detection of natural hazards and the issuance and communication of early warning, as well as education and professional training, public information and awareness-raising activities, and stresses the need for appropriate action in response to early warning;

18. *Reaffirms* the need to strengthen the international framework for the improvement of early warning systems and disaster preparedness by developing an effective international mechanism for early warning, including the transfer of technology related to early warning to developing countries, which ensures that vulnerable people receive appropriate and timely information, and by expanding and improving existing systems, in particular those under the auspices of the United Nations, as an integral part of the Strategy;

19. *Decides* to maintain the annual observance of the International Day for Natural Disaster Reduction on the second Wednesday of October, as a vehicle to promote a global culture of natural disaster reduction, including prevention, mitigation and preparedness;

20. *Invites* the General Assembly to give full consideration to the report of the Secretary-General at its fifty-sixth session, under the item entitled "Environment and sustainable development".

GENERAL ASSEMBLY ACTION

On 21 December [meeting 90], the General Assembly, on the recommendation of the Second (Economic and Financial) Committee [A/56/561/Add.2], adopted **resolution 56/195** without vote [agenda item 98 *(b)*].

International Strategy for Disaster Reduction

The General Assembly,

Recalling its resolutions 44/236 of 22 December 1989, 49/22 A of 2 December 1994, 49/22 B of 20 December 1994, 53/185 of 15 December 1998 and 54/219 of 22 December 1999 and Economic and Social Council resolution 1999/63 of 30 July 1999, and taking note of Council resolution 2001/35 of 26 July 2001,

Recalling also the forward-looking platform for international concerted disaster reduction, as developed by the World Conference on Natural Disaster Reduction and as expressed in the Yokohama Strategy for a Safer World: Guidelines for Natural Disaster Prevention, Preparedness and Mitigation and its Plan of Action, as well as the Geneva mandate on disaster reduction and the strategy document entitled "A safer world in the twenty-first century: risk and disaster reduction",

Emphasizing the multisectoral, interdisciplinary and cross-cutting nature of natural disaster reduction, and stressing that continued interaction, cooperation and partnerships among the institutions concerned are considered essential to achieve jointly agreed objectives and priorities,

Having considered the current institutional arrangements, as established in its resolution 54/219, with the Inter-Agency Task Force for Disaster Reduction and the inter-agency secretariat for the International Strategy for Disaster Reduction, and taking into account the assessment after the first period of operations,

Recognizing that disaster reduction is an important element that contributes to the achievement of sustainable development and that it should be taken into account in the preparatory process for the World Summit on Sustainable Development, to be held at Johannesburg, South Africa, from 26 August to 4 September 2002,

Reiterating that natural disasters damage the social and economic infrastructure of all countries, although the long-term consequences of natural disasters are especially severe for developing countries and hamper their sustainable development,

Welcoming the emphasis placed on natural disaster reduction in the Programme of Action for the Least Developed Countries for the Decade 2001-2010, adopted by the Third United Nations Conference on the Least Developed Countries, held at Brussels from 14 to 20 May 2001,

Recognizing that disaster reduction should be regarded as an important function of the United Nations and should receive continued attention,

Stressing the need for the international community to demonstrate the firm political determination required to utilize scientific and technical knowledge to reduce vulnerability to natural disasters and environmental hazards, taking into account the particular needs of developing countries,

1. *Takes note* of the report of the Secretary-General on the implementation of the International Strategy for Disaster Reduction;

2. *Expresses its deep concern* at the increasing number and scale of natural disasters, which have resulted in massive loss of life and long-term negative social, economic and environmental consequences for vulnerable societies throughout the world, in particular in developing countries;

3. *Reaffirms* that the Inter-Agency Task Force for Disaster Reduction should perform the functions as indicated in the report of the Secretary-General, in particular those of serving as a main forum within the United Nations system for devising strategies and policies for disaster reduction and ensuring complementarity of action by agencies involved in disaster reduction, mitigation and preparedness, decides to review the activities of the Task Force in 2003, and decides also that the inter-agency secretariat for the International Strategy for Disaster Reduction should develop collaborative links with appropriate regional disaster reduction organizations;

4. *Decides* that the Task Force should be modified in order to provide for the increased participation and continued membership of regional intergovernmental organizations and key United Nations agencies;

5. *Recognizes* that the framework for action for the implementation of the Strategy, as endorsed by the Task Force, constitutes the basic guide for the implementation of the Strategy, and that the framework shall be periodically reviewed, according to the evolving needs in the field of natural disaster reduction, and urges all relevant bodies within the United Nations system to cooperate fully within the context of the framework;

6. *Stresses* that the inter-agency secretariat for the Strategy should be consolidated and enhanced to perform its functions effectively, in particular to serve as the focal point in the United Nations system for the coordination of disaster reduction and to ensure synergies among the disaster-reduction activities of the United Nations system and regional organizations and activities in socio-economic and humanitarian fields;

7. *Calls upon* Governments to continue to cooperate and coordinate their efforts with the United Nations system, other international organizations, regional organizations, non-governmental organizations and other partners, as appropriate, in order to ensure effective synergies in the field of natural disasters, and urges the inter-agency secretariat for the Strategy to develop such synergies, as appropriate;

8. *Invites*, therefore, all Governments and relevant international organizations to give appropriate consideration to the issue of natural disaster reduction in their preparations for the World Summit on Sustainable Development;

9. *Underlines* the importance of adequate financial and administrative resources for the effective functioning of the Task Force and the inter-agency secretariat for the Strategy, under the direct authority of the Under-Secretary-General for Humanitarian Affairs;

10. *Calls upon* Governments to establish national platforms or focal points for disaster reduction, urges the United Nations system to provide appropriate support for those mechanisms, and invites the Secretary-General to strengthen the regional outreach of the inter-agency secretariat for the Strategy in order to ensure such support;

11. *Invites* Governments and relevant organizations of the United Nations system to strengthen national participation, in particular of disaster-prone countries, in the implementation of the Strategy, including through national multisectoral and interdisciplinary platforms, in order to achieve sustainable development

goals and objectives, with the full utilization of scientific and technical knowledge, including through capacity-building at all levels and the development and strengthening of global and regional approaches that take into account regional, subregional, national and local circumstances and needs, as well as the need to strengthen the coordination of national emergency response agencies;

12. *Calls upon* Governments to continue to cooperate and coordinate their efforts in the field of natural disasters within the framework for action for the implementation of the Strategy, in line with their respective skills and capacities, from prevention to early warning, response, mitigation, rehabilitation and reconstruction, including through capacity-building at all levels, and the development and strengthening of global and regional approaches that take into account regional, subregional, national and local circumstances and needs, as well as the need to strengthen the coordination of national emergency response agencies in natural disasters;

13. *Recognizes* the urgent need to develop further and make use of the existing scientific and technical knowledge to reduce vulnerability to natural disasters, and emphasizes the need for developing countries to have access to technology so as to tackle natural disasters effectively;

14. *Calls upon* Governments and United Nations agencies to collaborate more closely in the sharing of disaster response and mitigation information, to take full advantage of United Nations emergency information services such as ReliefWeb, as well as the Internet, and to consider other methods for the sharing of information;

15. *Calls upon* the inter-agency secretariat for the Strategy and the Office for the Coordination of Humanitarian Affairs of the Secretariat to facilitate the development of better linkages with all relevant actors, including the private sector and financial institutions, in the development of disaster management strategies;

16. *Encourages* the international community to provide the necessary financial resources to the Trust Fund for the International Strategy for Disaster Reduction and to provide adequate scientific, technical, human and other resources to ensure adequate support for the inter-agency secretariat for the Strategy and for the Task Force and its working groups;

17. *Requests* the relevant organizations of the United Nations system to support the implementation of the goals of the Strategy, including by seconding technical staff to the inter-agency secretariat for the Strategy;

18. *Endorses* the proposal of the Secretary-General to review the implementation of the Yokohama Strategy for a Safer World: Guidelines for Natural Disaster Prevention, Preparedness and Mitigation and its Plan of Action, within the context of the framework for action for the implementation of the Strategy;

19. *Requests* the Secretary-General to optimize further and disseminate through all available channels, including handbooks and information systems, the information necessary for the effective management of international cooperation in the fields of disaster prevention, early warning, response, mitigation, rehabilitation and reconstruction;

20. *Reiterates* the need to continue international cooperation to reduce the impact of the El Niño phe-

nomenon, within the framework for action for the implementation of the Strategy, as requested by the Economic and Social Council in its resolutions 1999/46 of 28 July 1999 and 2000/33 of 28 July 2000 and by the Assembly in its resolutions 52/200 of 18 December 1997, 53/185 of 15 December 1998, 54/220 of 22 December 1999 and 55/197 of 20 December 2000;

21. *Recognizes* the importance of early warning as an essential element in the culture of prevention, and encourages renewed efforts at all levels to contribute to natural hazard monitoring and impact prediction, the development and transfer of technology, capacity-building for disaster preparedness, the detection of natural hazards and the issuance and communication of early warning, as well as education and professional training, public information and awareness-raising activities, and stresses the need for appropriate action in response to early warning;

22. *Reaffirms* the need to strengthen the international framework for the improvement of early warning systems and disaster preparedness by developing an effective international mechanism for early warning, including the transfer of technology related to early warning to developing countries, which ensures that vulnerable people receive appropriate and timely information, and by expanding and improving existing systems, in particular those under the auspices of the United Nations, as an integral part of the Strategy;

23. *Decides* to maintain the annual observance of the International Day for Natural Disaster Reduction on the second Wednesday of October, as a vehicle to promote a global culture of natural disaster reduction, including prevention, mitigation and preparedness;

24. *Requests* the Secretary-General to submit to the General Assembly at its fifty-seventh session a report on the implementation of the present resolution, including criteria and modalities for the selection of the non-permanent members of the Task Force, and on the progress made in the implementation of the International Strategy for Disaster Reduction, under the item entitled "Environment and sustainable development".

El Niño

In response to General Assembly resolution 55/197 [YUN 2000, p. 884], the Secretary-General, in a May report [A/56/76-E/2001/54], reviewed ongoing activities designed to reduce the impact of the El Niño phenomenon, a disruption of the ocean-atmosphere system in the tropical Pacific that had important consequences for weather and climate worldwide.

The Working Group on Climate and Disasters of the Inter-Agency Task Force for Disaster Reduction (Geneva, 10-11 April), set up in 2000 [YUN 2000, p. 882] and led by WMO, established two priority areas: a review of sectoral monitoring and warning systems and the continuation of the mandate of the Inter-Agency Task Force on El Niño. Pursuant to Assembly resolution 52/200 [YUN 1997, p. 927], a number of activities were carried out at the global, regional and national levels, aimed at reducing the impact of future El Niño phenomena and similar climatic variables.

The Secretary-General recommended that the Working Group continue to gather information on how climate information was generated and distributed and consider how to improve distribution and transfer of the information. It should also continue advocacy and education activities and ensure that the experience gained from the 1998 intergovernmental meeting of experts in Guayaquil, Ecuador [YUN 1998, p. 873], and other events be made available to interested parties. The Working Group should continue to support studies to establish shortfalls in the coverage of climate monitoring, and explore further applications of climate monitoring information and forecasts.

Communication. On 2 October [A/C.2/56/2], Ecuador transmitted to the Secretary-General the text of a memorandum of cooperation it had signed with WMO to strengthen cooperation and to initiate activities relating to the establishment of the International Research Centre for the El Niño/Southern Oscillation Phenomenon. The Government of Ecuador would deposit $385,000 in a WMO trust fund account as a contribution to the activities leading to the establishment of the centre.

GENERAL ASSEMBLY ACTION

On 21 December [meeting 90], the General Assembly, on the recommendation of the Second Committee [A/56/561/Add.2], adopted **resolution 56/194** without vote [agenda item 98 (*b*)].

International cooperation to reduce the impact of the El Niño phenomenon

The General Assembly,

Recalling its resolutions 52/200 of 18 December 1997, 53/185 of 15 December 1998, 54/220 of 22 December 1999 and 55/197 of 20 December 2000 and Economic and Social Council resolutions 1999/46 of 28 July 1999 and 1999/63 of 30 July 1999, and taking note of Council resolution 2000/33 of 28 July 2000,

Noting that the signing of the memorandum of cooperation between Ecuador and the World Meteorological Organization constitutes a major step in the process for the establishment of an international centre for the study of the El Niño phenomenon,

Noting also the contributions made by regional and global climate-study organizations and specialized Internet information services, which have led to improved scientific understanding and prediction capabilities in the area of climate variability,

Reaffirming the importance of developing strategies at the national, subregional, regional and international levels that aim to prevent, mitigate and repair the damage caused by natural disasters that result from the El Niño phenomenon,

1. *Takes note with appreciation* of the report of the Secretary-General;

2. *Commends* the measures adopted by the host country for the establishment of an international centre for the study of the El Niño phenomenon, and en-

courages the Government of Ecuador to continue its efforts aimed at the completion of that process;

3. *Encourages* the centre, once established, to strengthen its links with other relevant regional and global climate-study organizations, as well as with Internet information services, in order to ensure an effective and efficient use of the available resources;

4. *Calls upon* the Secretary-General and the relevant United Nations organs, funds and programmes, in particular those taking part in the implementation of the International Strategy for Disaster Reduction, and encourages the international community, to adopt, as appropriate, the necessary measures to support the establishment of the above-mentioned research centre at Guayaquil, Ecuador, and invites the international community to provide scientific, technical and financial assistance and cooperation for that purpose, as well as to strengthen, as appropriate, other centres devoted to the study of the El Niño phenomenon;

5. *Welcomes* the establishment of the working group on climate and disasters, and invites the Inter-Agency Task Force for Disaster Reduction and the inter-agency secretariat for the International Strategy for Disaster Reduction to ensure functional synergies among the working groups dealing with climate variability, social and economic vulnerability, and the effectiveness of early warning systems;

6. *Requests* the Secretary-General to continue the full implementation of its resolutions 52/200, 53/185, 54/220 and 55/197 and Economic and Social Council resolutions 1999/46, 1999/63 and 2000/33;

7. *Also requests* the Secretary-General to report to the General Assembly at its fifty-seventh session on the implementation of the present resolution, under the item entitled "Environment and sustainable development".

Disaster assistance

Africa

Central African Republic

A UN inter-agency flash appeal for the Central African Republic, launched in June, sought $4.9 million to cover the period 1 July to 30 September for emergency needs resulting from the torrential rainfall of 26 February to 1 March. The population of Bangui and surrounding areas had been hard-hit by the floods and were facing additional hardship caused by continuing armed conflict between loyalist forces and those supporting a coup attempt. The target population was set at 80,000 people.

Horn of Africa

The situation in the drought-affected areas in the Horn of Africa (Djibouti, Eritrea, Ethiopia, Kenya, Somalia and northern parts of the United Republic of Tanzania) remained critical in 2001 following three consecutive years of poor rains and the total failure of rains in April 2000. In Ethiopia, while recent rains in the Somali region had been encouraging, the import ban on livestock from the Horn imposed by Gulf countries represented a potentially serious setback for the prospect of a quick economic recovery in the mainly pastoral lowlands. In many areas of Kenya, significant rains were still required, as the short season rains were largely below normal and poorly distributed in time and space. Important food aid relief operations were needed in some areas of Tanzania following four years of inadequate harvests. Insufficient rainfall in drought-affected areas of Djibouti and Eritrea in 2000 justified continued humanitarian assistance in 2001. Although the rains were satisfactory in Somalia, it was important that recovery efforts be sustained to enable those affected to rebuild their livelihood.

OCHA issued a UN emergency consolidated appeal for the region totalling $353 million for January to December 2001 to cover the basic needs of 12.8 million drought-affected people.

Djibouti

A UN inter-agency donor alert for the drought in Djibouti, prepared by the UN country team to complement the emergency appeal for the Horn of Africa (above), sought $11.2 million.

Kenya

In 2001, over 4 million people were suffering from the effects of the drought in Kenya. A majority of the population in pastoral, agro-pastoral and marginal agricultural areas had been reduced to near destitution and dependence on food aid.

A UN inter-agency donor alert for the drought in Kenya, issued in February and seeking $123 million for January to December 2001, was revised in July to $184 million.

Mozambique

Mozambique entered 2001 under the threat of floods in Zambezia province due to heavy rain in Zambia, which forced the authorities to release water from the Kariba dam. The Zambezi River burst its banks on 3 January, flooding farmland in the north-western province of Tete. Later in January, a tropical storm brought heavy rain to Quelimane, the capital of Zambezia, and other areas of the province. Further heavy rain in neighbouring countries and high discharges from dams led to 52 deaths, 81,394 persons displaced and 406,565 people affected around the Zambezi River valley by the end of February.

In March, a UN inter-agency appeal for flood relief in Mozambique was launched for $10.7 million to cover the period March to May 2001.

Asia

Democratic People's Republic of Korea

The UN Consolidated Inter-Agency Appeal for the Democratic People's Republic of Korea (DPRK), launched in November 2000, which sought $384 million for January to December 2001, received 67.4 per cent ($248.4 million) of requirements.

Improvements in the political climate between the DPRK and the Republic of Korea did not have a significant impact on the humanitarian situation in the DPRK in 2001, which was still critical following a period of economic decline and a series of natural disasters and erratic weather patterns. Large sectors of the population of 23 million people were vulnerable due to inadequate food availability, which was compounded by the poor quality of and limited access to basic health, water, sanitation and education services. A further appeal was launched to cover 2002.

Mongolia

Two consecutive dzuds—a Mongolia-specific winter disaster caused by extreme cold and heavy snowfall—in 1999/2000 and 2000/01 undermined the welfare and food security of the Mongolian herding community through large-scale death and debilitation of livestock. The indirect causes of the disaster were mainly over-concentration of stock and overgrazing of pastures in some areas and inadequate winter hay preparation. The continuing dzuds seriously increased the level of malnutrition and rates of morbidity and mortality among more vulnerable groups, the health and education systems had come under strain and the massive mortality of livestock had caused huge socio-economic and financial damage, not only to herders but to the whole country.

A UN appeal sought contributions worth $7.1 million in cash and $4.7 million in kind to assist beneficiaries in 73 counties.

Latin America and the Caribbean

Belize

On 8 October, category-four strength hurricane Iris swept through Belize, with highly destructive 233 kilometre (km) per hour winds. The hurricane took its highest toll on the poorest part of the country where, in a matter of days, it deprived many of the vulnerable Mayan and Garinagu families living in the districts of Toledo and Stann Creek of their traditional means of livelihood, their homes, schools and health centres. A UN international appeal launched on 17 October sought $1.4 million for assistance projects.

On 27 November [meeting 65], the General Assembly adopted **resolution 56/11** [draft: A/56/L.16 & Add.1] without vote [agenda item 20 (b)].

Emergency assistance to Belize

The General Assembly,

Recalling its resolutions 42/169 of 11 December 1987, 43/202 of 20 December 1988, 44/236 of 22 December 1989, 45/185 of 21 December 1990, 46/149 of 18 December 1991, 46/182 of 19 December 1991, 48/188 of 21 December 1993, 49/22 A of 2 December 1994 and 55/165 of 14 December 2000,

Having been made aware of the extensive damage caused by powerful hurricane Iris during its landfall and passage through Belize on 8 October 2001,

Mindful of the human suffering caused by the displacement of thousands of people and the disrupted delivery of health and social services,

Aware of the devastation to the infrastructure of southern Belize and to the agricultural, fisheries and tourism sectors of Belize,

Conscious of the negative ecological impact of the hurricane on the coastal region and the inland rainforest,

Noting the enormous efforts required to alleviate the devastation caused by this natural disaster,

Cognizant of the efforts of the Government and people of Belize to relieve the suffering of the victims of hurricane Iris,

Conscious of the rapid response being made by the Government of Belize, the agencies and bodies of the United Nations system, international and regional agencies, non-governmental organizations and private individuals to provide relief,

Recalling the International Strategy for Disaster Reduction, and in this regard underlining the importance of efforts aimed at strengthening early warning, prevention and preparedness mechanisms for natural disasters and measures to strengthen capacity-building at the local, national and regional levels, with an emphasis on risk reduction,

Aware that the extent of the disaster and its medium-term and long-term effects will require, as a complement to the efforts being made by the Government and people of Belize, a demonstration of international solidarity and humanitarian concern to ensure broad multilateral cooperation in order to facilitate the transition from the immediate emergency situation in the affected areas to the process of reconstruction,

1. *Expresses its solidarity and support* to the Government and people of Belize;

2. *Expresses its appreciation* to all States of the international community, international agencies and intergovernmental and non-governmental organizations that are providing emergency relief assistance to Belize;

3. *Urges* Member States, as a matter of urgency, to contribute generously to the relief, rehabilitation and reconstruction efforts of Belize;

4. *Requests* the Secretary-General, in collaboration with the international financial institutions, agencies and bodies of the United Nations system, to assist the Government of Belize in identifying medium-term and long-term needs and in mobilizing resources, as well as to help with the efforts towards rehabilitation and reconstruction of the affected areas in Belize;

5. *Encourages* the Government of Belize, in conjunction with relevant partners, further to develop strategies aimed at preventing and mitigating natural disasters, in accordance with the International Strategy for Disaster Reduction;

6. *Requests* the Secretary-General to make all necessary arrangements to continue mobilizing and coordinating humanitarian assistance from the specialized agencies and other organizations and bodies of the United Nations system with a view to supporting the efforts of the Government of Belize.

Bolivia

Heavy rains during the first half of 2001 caused floods and landslides in the western and northern regions of Bolivia, affecting some 357,250 people and causing serious damage to roads, crops and houses. The floods also destroyed important agricultural productive infrastructure, such as productive land, small irrigation systems and roads, and caused crop damage estimated at $121 million.

GENERAL ASSEMBLY ACTION

On 14 February [meeting 91], the General Assembly adopted **resolution 55/241** [draft: A/55/L.74 & Add.1] without vote [agenda item 20 *(b)*].

Assistance to Bolivia as a result of the flooding experienced in recent months

The General Assembly,

Distressed by the floods, torrents, cave-ins, landslides and inundation caused mainly by the torrential rains that have fallen in recent months, resulting in severe economic damage and loss of human lives in the territory of Bolivia,

Recognizing the large-scale relief and humanitarian assistance efforts being made by the Government and people of Bolivia to alleviate the suffering of the disaster victims and meet their immediate needs,

Noting the enormous efforts that have been made by the people and Government of Bolivia to build peace and democracy and achieve a favourable environment for promoting economic growth and furthering human development,

Aware of the grave consequences of natural disasters, which may present a serious obstacle to economic and social development in the developing countries, and which require considerable amounts of human and financial resources to overcome their negative effects, and considering it essential that the international community offer all its technical and financial support and assistance in order to supplement national efforts to undertake, as soon as possible, the process of rehabilitation, reconstruction and development in the areas afflicted by these natural disasters,

1. *Expresses its solidarity and support* to the Government and people of Bolivia in these difficult times;

2. *Welcomes* the valuable support of the international community in the work of rescuing and providing emergency relief to the stricken population;

3. *Urges* all Member States, specialized agencies and other organizations and organs of the United Nations system, together with international financial institutions and non-governmental organizations, to continue responding generously to Bolivia in its emergency, rehabilitation and reconstruction tasks and programmes, in order to maintain the present political stability and prevent the effects of this natural disaster from becoming an impediment to the economic and social development of Bolivia;

4. *Requests* the Secretary-General to make every effort to continue mobilizing and coordinating the humanitarian assistance being provided by the specialized agencies and other organizations and organs of the United Nations system in support of the efforts of the Government of Bolivia.

El Salvador

An earthquake measuring 7.6 on the Richter scale shook El Salvador on 13 January, affecting some 1.1 million people, of whom 43 per cent were under 18 years of age. By 24 January, the death toll had reached 726 and 360 people were still missing. Over 114,000 homes were damaged and close to 75,000 were totally destroyed. The agricultural and fishing sectors were greatly affected, especially the infrastructure that supported production and processing. The affected population in rural areas needed assistance to rehabilitate 30,772 farm dwellings.

An appeal for humanitarian assistance and initial rehabilitation activities, launched in February, requested $35 million to benefit some 200,000 people.

GENERAL ASSEMBLY ACTION

On 26 January [meeting 90], the General Assembly adopted **resolution 55/240** [draft: A/55/L.72 & Add.1] without vote [agenda item 20 *(b)*].

Assistance to El Salvador as a result of the earthquake of 13 January 2001

The General Assembly,

Deeply distressed by the lamentable loss of hundreds of human lives and the thousands of victims wounded and left homeless, together with the serious damage to infrastructure in El Salvador, as a result of the earthquake of 13 January 2001,

Recognizing the large-scale relief and humanitarian assistance efforts being made by the Government and people of El Salvador to alleviate the suffering of the disaster victims and meet their immediate needs,

Recognizing also the demonstrations of support and solidarity offered by the international community to the people and Government of El Salvador in this emergency situation,

Noting the enormous efforts that have been made by the people and Government of El Salvador to build peace and democracy and achieve a favourable environment for promoting economic growth and furthering human development,

Aware of the grave consequences of natural disasters, which may present a serious obstacle to economic and social development in the developing countries, and which require considerable amounts of human and financial resources to overcome their negative effects, and considering it essential that the international community offer all its technical and financial support and assistance in order to supplement national efforts to undertake, as soon as possible, the process of rehabilitation, reconstruction and development in the areas afflicted by these natural disasters,

1. *Expresses its solidarity and support* to the Government and people of El Salvador in these difficult times;

2. *Welcomes* the valuable support of the international community in the work of rescuing and providing emergency relief to the stricken population;

3. *Urges* all Member States, specialized agencies and other organizations and organs of the United Nations system, together with international financial institutions and non-governmental organizations, to continue responding generously to El Salvador in its emergency, rehabilitation and reconstruction tasks and programmes, in order to maintain the present political stability and prevent the effects of this natural disaster from becoming an impediment to the economic and social development of El Salvador;

4. *Requests* the Secretary-General to make every effort to continue mobilizing and coordinating the humanitarian assistance being provided by the specialized agencies and other organizations and organs of the United Nations system in support of the efforts of the Government of El Salvador.

Peru

On 23 June, an earthquake measuring 6.9 on the Richter scale hit southern Peru. The epicentre of the quake was offshore, causing a tsunami to hit 100 km of coastline between Ocoña and Quilca, flooding low-lying areas as far as 1 km inland. On 5 July, after more than 100 aftershocks, a second earthquake measuring 6 on the Richter scale hit the same area, and several aftershocks later, on 7 July, there was a third earthquake, measuring 6.5 on the Richter scale, with an epicentre 100 km to the south-west of Ocoña. As at 16 July, an estimated 222,423 people were affected by the disaster, with 78 dead, 2,723 injured and 64 missing. A total of 24,973 homes had been destroyed and 36,374 damaged. The disaster affected the health and education infrastructure, communications and the agriculture and fishery sectors.

A UN inter-agency appeal for the victims of the earthquake, issued in July, sought $4.4 million for immediate support and rehabilitation for six to eight months.

Chernobyl aftermath

In response to General Assembly resolution 54/97 [YUN 1999, p. 870], the Secretary-General, in an October report [A/56/447], described the activities undertaken by UN funds, programmes and specialized agencies during the preceding two years to optimize the international humanitarian response to the evolving consequences of the 1986 Chernobyl disaster [YUN 1986, p. 584]. The report also analysed the continuing consequences of the nuclear accident 15 years after it had occurred.

International assistance efforts were ongoing in the areas of health, socio-psychological rehabilitation, economic rehabilitation and employment, and environmental protection. Public awareness of the consequences of the disaster was a central focus of UN activities throughout the reporting period, culminating in a series of events to commemorate the fifteenth anniversary of the disaster. UN efforts to assist the victims continued to be plagued by a persistent lack of resources. In an attempt to enhance international funding, the UN Coordinator of International Cooperation on Chernobyl in March 2001 appealed to the Member States contributors to the Chernobyl Shelter Fund to support assistance programmes. A set of new projects aimed at providing developmental assistance (see below) would be presented to the donor community.

An inter-agency mission to study the human consequences of Chernobyl was carried out in July and August. The mission was deployed jointly by UNDP and UNICEF, with support from WHO, OCHA and others. On the basis of the best available data, the mission concluded that there was clear evidence of direct health effects due to radiation exposure, including 2,000 cases to date of thyroid cancer. There was little consensus on what the full effects would be, and many cancers were not expected to occur for several decades. The conditions of life of a significant portion of the rural population continued to decline due to a complex interaction between environmental, health, psychosocial and economic disadvantages. The accident imposed a heavy burden on national budgets through the cost of clean-up, compensation and recovery. During the reporting period, it became evident that the needs related to Chernobyl had gradually passed the emergency response stage and were of a developmental nature. The mission proposed a strategy for a new phase of activities, aimed to help restore life to normal for the majority of the inhabitants over a 10-year period. An overarching development strategy, as well as projects focused on affected communities, would emphasize sustainable household incomes, community-based primary health care and environmental education. The goal was, as far as possible, to give people control over their lives and communities control over their own futures.

GENERAL ASSEMBLY ACTION

On 14 December [meeting 87], the General Assembly adopted **resolution 56/109** [draft: A/56/L.57 & Add.1] without vote [agenda item 20 *(c)*].

Strengthening of international cooperation and coordination of efforts to study, mitigate and minimize the consequences of the Chernobyl disaster

The General Assembly,

Reaffirming its resolutions 45/190 of 21 December 1990, 46/150 of 18 December 1991, 47/165 of 18 December 1992, 48/206 of 21 December 1993, 50/134 of 20 December 1995, 52/172 of 16 December 1997 and 54/97 of 8 December 1999, as well as resolution 55/171 of 14 December 2000 on closure of the Chernobyl nuclear power plant, and taking note of the decisions adopted by the organs, organizations and programmes of the United Nations system in the implementation of those resolutions,

Recalling Economic and Social Council resolutions 1990/50 of 13 July 1990, 1991/51 of 26 July 1991 and 1992/38 of 30 July 1992 and Council decision 1993/232 of 22 July 1993,

Conscious of the long-term nature of the consequences of the disaster at the Chernobyl nuclear power plant, which was a major technological catastrophe in terms of its scope and complexity and created humanitarian, environmental, social, economic and health consequences and problems of common concern, requiring for their solution wide and active international cooperation and coordination of efforts in this field at the international and national levels,

Expressing profound concern at the ongoing effects of the consequences of the accident on the lives and health of people, in particular children, in the affected areas of Belarus, the Russian Federation and Ukraine, as well as in other affected countries,

Acknowledging the importance of the national efforts being undertaken by the Governments of Belarus, the Russian Federation and Ukraine to mitigate and minimize the consequences of the Chernobyl disaster,

Emphasizing that it is important for the authorities of the affected countries to cooperate fully in and facilitate efforts to mitigate the consequences of the Chernobyl catastrophe, including the efforts by non-governmental organizations in providing humanitarian assistance, and appreciating the progress already made in this regard,

Noting with appreciation the contribution made by States and by organizations of the United Nations system to the development of cooperation to mitigate and minimize the consequences of the Chernobyl disaster, the activities of regional and other organizations and those of non-governmental organizations, as well as bilateral activities,

Recognizing the importance of continuing international support to the national efforts of the Governments and civil societies of Belarus, the Russian Federation and Ukraine, as the most affected countries, to mitigate and minimize the persisting negative effects of the Chernobyl disaster on the sustainable development of the affected areas as a result of the radiological, health, socio-economic, psychological and environmental consequences of the disaster,

Welcoming the increased role played by the United Nations Development Programme, the United Nations resident coordinators and the United Nations country teams in Belarus, the Russian Federation and Ukraine in helping to address both the developmental and the humanitarian consequences of the catastrophe,

Noting the United Nations needs-assessment mission to the affected areas of Belarus, the Russian Federation and Ukraine in July and August 2001, as well as the visit of the Deputy United Nations Coordinator of International Cooperation on Chernobyl to those countries in October 2001, and emphasizing the need to consider incorporation of their findings and outcomes into the new United Nations strategy to mitigate the consequences of the Chernobyl disaster,

Taking note of the report of the Secretary-General concerning the implementation of resolution 54/97,

1. *Reaffirms* that the United Nations plays an important catalytic and coordinating role in the strengthening of international cooperation to study, mitigate and minimize the consequences of the Chernobyl disaster, and commends the contribution made by all other relevant multilateral mechanisms to this end;

2. *Welcomes* the practical measures that have been taken by the Secretary-General and the United Nations Coordinator of International Cooperation on Chernobyl to strengthen coordination of the international efforts in that area, especially the appointment by the Secretary-General of the Assistant Administrator of the United Nations Development Programme and Regional Director for Europe and the Commonwealth of Independent States as Deputy United Nations Coordinator of International Cooperation on Chernobyl;

3. *Also welcomes* the efforts undertaken by the agencies of the United Nations system, members of the Inter-Agency Task Force on Chernobyl to implement a new developmental approach to studying, mitigating and minimizing the consequences of the Chernobyl disaster, and requests the Inter-Agency Task Force on Chernobyl to continue further its activities to that end;

4. *Emphasizes* the importance of full cooperation and assistance by the authorities of the affected countries in facilitating the work of humanitarian organizations, including non-governmental organizations, to mitigate the humanitarian consequences of the Chernobyl catastrophe, notes the measures already taken by the Governments of the affected countries in this regard, and encourages them to take further measures to simplify their relevant internal procedures and to identify ways in which their systems of granting exemption from customs and other duties can be made more effective with regard to goods provided free of charge as humanitarian assistance by humanitarian organizations, including non-governmental organizations;

5. *Acknowledges* the difficulties faced by the most affected countries in minimizing the consequences of the Chernobyl disaster, and invites States, in particular donor States and all relevant agencies, funds and programmes of the United Nations system, in particular the Bretton Woods institutions, as well as non-governmental organizations, to continue to provide support to the ongoing efforts of Belarus, the Russian Federation and Ukraine to mitigate the consequences of the Chernobyl disaster, including through the allocation of additional funds to support medical, social, economic and ecological programmes related to the disaster;

6. *Notes* the appeal by the United Nations Coordinator to the donor community to consider allocating

additional resources to the humanitarian aspects of the Chernobyl disaster;

7. *Stresses* the need for coordinated international cooperation in studying the consequences of the Chernobyl catastrophe, and invites Member States and all interested parties to take part in and to promote the activities of the International Chernobyl Centre for nuclear safety, radioactive waste and radioecology as an important mechanism of scientific research in the unique conditions of the Chernobyl zone and the Shelter facility;

8. *Requests* the Secretary-General to continue his efforts in the implementation of the relevant General Assembly resolutions and, through existing co-ordination mechanisms, in particular the United Nations Coordinator, to continue to maintain close cooperation with the agencies of the United Nations system, as well as with regional and other relevant organizations, while implementing specific Chernobyl-related programmes and projects;

9. *Also requests* the Secretary-General to consider possible ways to strengthen further the coordination, analytical and technical capacities of the United Nations in the field, as well as at Headquarters, as described in the report of the Secretary-General, with due regard to the existing administrative and budgetary procedures of the Organization;

10. *Further requests* the Secretary-General to submit to the General Assembly at its fifty-eighth session, under a separate sub-item, a report containing a comprehensive assessment of the implementation of all aspects of the present resolution and proposals for innovative measures for optimizing the effectiveness of the response of the international community to the Chernobyl disaster.

Chapter IV

International trade, finance and transport

The collapse in growth of international trade, exacerbated by the disruption caused by the 11 September terrorist attacks in the United States, was the key feature of the economic slowdown of 2001. The international economic environment deteriorated, particularly for many developing countries and countries in transition. Net financial flows to those countries remained at a low level, the external financing conditions for them were more stringent and total flows of foreign direct investment fell. Developments during the year underlined the high degree of interdependence between developed and developing countries, as well as the need for further reforms in the international trade and financial systems.

Preparations for the International Conference on Financing for Development gathered momentum. In March, the General Assembly accepted Mexico's offer to host the Conference and, in July, decided that it would be held in Monterrey from 18 to 22 March 2002. Also in July, the Assembly decided that, in addition to States Members and observers of the United Nations and specialized agencies, Conference participation should include all relevant stakeholders, the business sector and civil society.

In other action on financial issues, the Assembly, in December, stressed the importance of continued substantive consideration of the international financial system and the external debt crisis in the context of development.

The high-level meeting between the Economic and Social Council and the Bretton Woods institutions (the World Bank Group and the International Monetary Fund), which took place in May, considered development financing, in particular poverty eradication, official development assistance and debt; and public and private responsibility in the prevention of financial crises. In November, the Ministerial Conference of the World Trade Organization (WTO) launched a work programme addressing the challenges facing the multilateral trading system.

The United Nations Conference on Trade and Development (UNCTAD) issued a number of publications during the year, including the *Trade and Development Report, 2001*, which focused on the reform of the international financial architecture. Other major publications included *World In-vestment Report 2001: Promoting Linkages* and the *E-Commerce and Development Report 2000*. The Trade and Development Board, UNCTAD's governing body, reviewed the work of its three subsidiary bodies—the Commission on Trade in Goods and Services, and Commodities; the Commission on Investment, Technology and Related Financial Issues; and the Commission on Enterprise, Business Facilitation and Development. It also carried out a review of UNCTAD's technical cooperation activities.

The International Trade Centre, operated jointly by UNCTAD and WTO, increased its technical cooperation activities, providing support to 124 developing countries and transitional economies, including 42 least developed countries. It extended capacity-building to national networks and launched an e-facilitated trade development strategy.

International trade

The *Trade and Development Report, 2001* [Sales No. E.01.II.D.10] observed that world trade in 2000 grew at twice the rate for 1999 and considerably faster than world output, stimulated by the resilience of the United States economy, a pickup in economic activity in the European Union (EU) and Japan, strong recovery in Latin America and the transition economies, and sustained growth in Asia. All regions recorded an expansion in trade volumes, which was particularly marked in the developing countries, where the volume of imports increased by more than 11 per cent. In Latin America and the transition economies, imports grew by more than 10 per cent; in Asia they continued to grow; and in Africa, less affected by the volatility in global markets, imports grew at a slower rate. Import growth also accelerated, but more slowly, in the developed countries. Imports into the United States again grew faster than into other developed economies and demand picked up significantly in some EU countries despite the weakness of the euro; overall growth for the euro zone exceeded 10 per cent in 2000. Japan also had an accelerated growth in import volume, due in part to a rebound in investment spending, especially on equipment related to information and communication technology (ICT). The strong expansion in global import demand in 2000 was accompanied by a correspondingly robust global export performance, with the exception of countries in Africa and Latin America whose exports were concentrated in a small number of non-oil primary commodities. A rapid turnaround in export volume growth was registered in the Middle East and the transition economies, and higher growth to other regions continued to power recovery in Asia and parts of Latin America, aided by currency depreciation. For Asian economies, an additional factor was the revival of intraregional trade, which also contributed to the fast growth of Chinese exports. Export volume also accelerated in developed countries, particularly in the euro zone, which benefited from the competitive edge given by the weakness of the euro. Strong growth also helped to revive the Japanese economy in 2000. The trade imbalances among major economic regions, due to growth differentials between the United States and other developed countries and to the strong dollar, increased in 2000. However, world trade expansion was expected to moderate, due to the slowdown in world industrial production towards the end of 2000 and the beginning of 2001 and more stable oil prices.

The *World Economic and Social Survey 2001* [Sales No. E.01.II.C.1] noted that international trade continued to play an important role in the recovery from the 1997-1998 financial crises for most of 2000. However, the same trade linkages also globalized the slowdown that began in the last part of the year. The deceleration in economic growth and import demand of the developed economies, led by retrenchment in the United States, had an adverse impact on their trading partners and its negative effects were multiplied through trade to a widening circle of developing and transition economies. The strong momentum of international trade in 1999 lasted throughout much of 2000 and lifted world trade growth from 5.2 to 12.3 per cent, despite the deceleration during the last quarter of the year.

In a joint report on the world economic situation and prospects [Sales No. E.02.II.C.2] issued by the Department of Economic and Social Affairs (DESA) and UNCTAD and based on information available as at 30 November, it was observed that world trade had decelerated dramatically over the course of 2001, growing by less than 1 per cent in terms of export volume, from growth of over 11 per cent in 2000. The slowdown emanated primarily from the decline in global demand for ICT-related products, particularly in major developed economies. As the weakness in the global econ-

omy intensified in the second half of the year, exacerbated by the terrorist attacks in the United States of 11 September, a general reciprocal reduction in import demand across nations led to a sharp dwindling in all trade categories: manufactured goods, primary commodities and services. The aggregated imports of developed countries' economies registered virtually no growth and there was a sharp decline in the growth of imports in many developing countries. However, import demand was robust in most economies in transition. Export performance was weak across major developed countries. Although it varied in developing countries, a large number of them suffered a decline in the volume of exports combined with a drop in the prices of their exports. Many transition economies maintained a double-digit growth of exports, partly because of the relatively low exposure of their exports to the markets of major developed countries.

Report of Secretary-General. In response to General Assembly resolution 55/182 [YUN 2000, p. 895], the Secretary-General submitted a September report [A/56/376], prepared in collaboration with UNCTAD, on international trade and development. It discussed developments in the multilateral trading system and other issues raised in resolution 55/182, including: the Third United Nations Conference on the Least Developed Countries (LDCs) (LDC-III) (see p. 770) and improved market access for LDCs; landlocked countries; small island developing States; the Integrated Framework for Trade-related Technical Assistance to LDCs (IF); regional integration developments; Africa; volatility of short-term capital flows and effects of financial crises on the international trading system; debt; electronic commerce (e-commerce); trade supporting services; and investment.

With regard to preparations by Governments for the Fourth Ministerial Conference of WTO to be held in November (see p. 874), the report stated that the meeting of the Organisation for Economic Cooperation and Development (OECD) Council at ministerial level (Paris, 16-17 May) recognized that efforts to strengthen the multilateral trading system required broad-based and balanced negotiations and the strengthening of WTO as a rules-based institution. The eleventh Group of 15 (G-15) summit of developing countries (Jakarta, Indonesia, 25-31 May) called for greater inclusiveness, internal transparency and effective participation of all members in the WTO decision-making process, and urged developed countries to promote substantial liberalization in agriculture, textiles and other sectors. A Meeting of the Ministers Responsible for Trade of LDCs (Zanzibar, United Republic of Tanzania,

22-24 July) called on the Fourth Ministerial Conference to agree on: binding commitment on duty-free and quota-free market access for all products from LDCs; facilitating the accession of LDCs into WTO; implementation of the commitments made in the Marrakesh Declaration [YUN 1994, p. 868] and other ministerial decisions; and full implementation of the commitments undertaken at LDC-III in May (see p. 770).

With regard to WTO work, the report gave the status of negotiations on agriculture and services, and described implementation of WTO agreements, discussions on the interaction between trade and competition policy, and the outcome of consultations on trade-related investment measures. As to UNCTAD activities, the report stated that the secretariat had assisted developing countries in understanding the key trade and development-related issues in multilateral trade and organized a series of expert meetings (see below).

WTO Ministerial Conference. On 19 November [A/C.2/56/7], Qatar transmitted to the Secretary-General the Ministerial Declaration of the Fourth Ministerial Conference of WTO (Doha, Qatar, 9-13 November). The Conference discussed its work programme regarding implementation-related issues and concerns; agriculture; services; market access for non-agricultural products; trade-related aspects of intellectual property rights; the relationship between trade and investment; interaction between trade and competition policy; transparency in government procurement; trade facilitation; WTO rules; dispute settlement understanding; trade and environment; e-commerce; small economies; trade, debt and finance; trade and transfer of technology; technical cooperation and capacity-building; LDCs; and special and differential treatment (see also p. 1432).

GENERAL ASSEMBLY ACTION

On 21 December [meeting 90], the General Assembly, on the recommendation of the Second (Economic and Financial) Committee [A/56/558/ Add.1], adopted **resolution 56/178** without vote [agenda item 95 (a)].

International trade and development

The General Assembly,

Reaffirming its resolution 55/182 of 20 December 2000 on international trade and development,

Taking into account the ongoing preparations for the International Conference on Financing for Development, to be held at Monterrey, Mexico, from 18 to 22 March 2002, which will consider, inter alia, trade in the context of financing for development,

Noting the outcome of the Fourth Ministerial Conference of the World Trade Organization, held at Doha from 9 to 13 November 2001,

Welcoming the outcome of the Third United Nations Conference on the Least Developed Countries, held at Brussels from 14 to 20 May 2001, in particular with regard to trade and development,

Taking note of the report of the Secretary-General of the United Nations on international trade and development, the report of the Secretary-General of the United Nations on unilateral economic measures as a means of political and economic coercion against developing countries, the report of the Secretary-General of the United Nations and the Secretary-General of the United Nations Conference on Trade and Development on the specific actions related to the particular needs and problems of landlocked developing countries, the report of the Trade and Development Board on its forty-eighth session and the report of the Secretary-General of the United Nations on measures taken to initiate the preparatory process for the final review and appraisal of the implementation of the United Nations New Agenda for the Development of Africa in the 1990s,

1. *Welcomes* the decision by the Trade and Development Board to conduct the midterm review of the outcome of the tenth session of the United Nations Conference on Trade and Development at Bangkok from 29 April to 3 May 2002, and, in this regard, expresses deep appreciation to the Government of Thailand for offering to host the meeting;

2. *Stresses* the importance of continued substantive consideration of the sub-item on trade and development, under the item entitled "Macroeconomic policy questions";

3. *Decides* to include in the provisional agenda of its fifty-seventh session, under the item entitled "Macroeconomic policy questions", a sub-item entitled "International trade and development";

4. *Requests* the Secretary-General, in collaboration with the secretariat of the United Nations Conference on Trade and Development, to report to the General Assembly at its fifty-seventh session on the implementation of the present resolution and developments in the multilateral trading system.

Trade policy

Trade in goods and services, and commodities

The Commission on Trade in Goods and Services, and Commodities held its fifth session in Geneva from 19 to 23 February and on 23 March [TD/B/48/6].

At its twenty-sixth executive session in April [A/56/15], the UNCTAD Trade and Development Board (TDB) took note of the Commission's report and approved the recommendations.

Agriculture. For its consideration of major agricultural concerns of developing countries: impact of the reform process in agriculture on LDCs and net food-importing developing countries (NFIDCs) and ways to address their concerns in multilateral trade negotiations, the Commission had before it the report of the 2000 Expert Meeting on the subject [YUN 2000, p. 898] and an

UNCTAD secretariat note on the outcome of the Meeting and comments on the Meeting's report from the EU, Morocco and Saudi Arabia [TD/B/COM.1/36 & Add.1].

In agreed recommendations, the Commission stated that LDCs and NFIDCs should identify specific areas where technical cooperation was required from development partners, particularly with regard to enhancing agricultural productivity, infrastructure-building, market information dissemination and export market development. It encouraged financial institutions to ensure coherence between their programmes and WTO reform commitments in LDCs and NFIDCs, and invited them and bilateral donors to examine the establishment of a special fund for technical and financial assistance. International organizations were invited to examine the long-term impact of food aid on domestic production and trading opportunities of agricultural products in LDCs and NFIDCs. The Commission recommended that UNCTAD provide analysis and technical assistance to developing countries to facilitate their participation in the WTO negotiations on agriculture and analyse the impact of new developments in world agricultural trade and of the reform process on key staples of developing countries, as well as ways to reduce the cost disadvantages in agricultural trade faced by landlocked developing countries and small island developing States.

Services. For its analysis of ways to enhance the contribution of specific services sectors to the development perspectives of developing countries: national experiences with regulation and liberalization: examples in the construction services sector and its contribution to the development of developing countries, the Commission had before it the report of the 2000 Expert Meeting on the subject [YUN 2000, p. 899] and an UNCTAD secretariat note containing policy proposals based on the expert discussions and comments by Mauritius on the Expert Meeting report [TD/B/COM.1/37 & Add.1].

In agreed recommendations, the Commission underlined the importance of the ongoing General Agreement on Trade in Services (GATS) negotiations in addressing problems faced by developing country construction and engineering firms in competing in world markets. It recommended to Governments that consideration be given to regional and subregional trade and cooperation promotion among developing countries in the construction services sector, and invited international funding agencies and bilateral donors to address the measures impeding local firms, in particular small and medium-sized enterprises (SMEs), from participating in their projects. The Commission agreed that UNCTAD

should promote establishment of linkages among stakeholders in the international market for construction services and work with the United Nations Commission on International Trade Law to assess the feasibility of model laws supporting the functioning of domestic construction services sectors. UNCTAD should also continue supporting the participation of developing countries in multilateral trade negotiations on trade in services and assist African countries in identifying the impact of further liberalization in that sector.

Resources. For its consideration of the sustainable use of biological resources: systems and national experiences for the protection of traditional knowledge (TK), innovations and practices, the Commission had before it the report of the 2000 Expert Meeting on the subject [YUN 2000, p. 899] and an UNCTAD secretariat note that highlighted important areas for policy action that had emerged from the Meeting's discussions [TD/B/COM.1/38].

In agreed recommendations, the Commission encouraged Governments to raise awareness of the role and value of TK and implement national legislation for its protection; promote the commercialization of TK-based products and services and the sustainable use of genetic resources; and support local and indigenous communities. It recommended that cooperation between intergovernmental organizations working in the field of TK protection be promoted, in particular in LDCs, and agreed that UNCTAD should organize workshops to exchange national experiences and examine strategies on TK-related issues; support initiatives to protect the development of traditional medicine; and assist member States and local and indigenous communities in exploring policies to harness TK for trade and development.

Market access. For its analysis of market access issues facing developing countries: impact of anti-dumping and countervailing actions, the Commission had before it the report of the 2000 Expert Meeting on the subject [YUN 2000, p. 899] and an UNCTAD secretariat note containing recommendations for further action based on the experts' discussions and comments from Malaysia and the United States on the Expert Meeting report [TD/B/COM.1/39 & Add.1,2].

The Commission recommended that UNCTAD should conduct comparative analyses on the technical difficulties identified by developing countries regarding anti-dumping and countervailing measures. It should also design and implement a technical assistance programme to support developing countries in improving understanding of anti-dumping and countervailing duty rules and procedures and capacity to administer anti-dumping and countervailing remedies.

Subsidiary bodies. In 2001, a number of expert meetings took place, all in Geneva, on issues to be considered by the Commission in 2002.

The Expert Meeting on Ways to Enhance the Production and Export Capacities of Developing Countries of Agriculture and Food Products, including Niche Products, such as Environmentally Preferable Products (16-18 July) [TD/B/COM.1/41] had before it an UNCTAD background note on the subject [TD/B/COM.1/EM.15/2], which discussed trends in world trade in food and agricultural products; production and export constraints of developing countries; quality and product differentiation; specialty and other niche products; organic products; and steps required to enhance production and export capacities.

The Meeting recommended that: Governments should support the development of the agriculture sector and promote organic agriculture and trade; the business sector should, among other things, emphasize professional organizations and cooperation among producers and exporters; the international community should support the efforts of developing countries, particularly LDCs, to develop supply capacities, improve market access and entry conditions and derive benefits from organic agriculture and trade; and UNCTAD should contribute to the development of the supply capacity of developing countries and assist them in deriving advantage from growing markets for agricultural products.

The Expert Meeting on Energy Services in International Trade: Development Implications (23-25 July) [TD/B/COM.1/42] had before it an UNCTAD note on the subject [TD/B/COM.1/EM.16/2], which addressed sectoral markets of energy and energy services; international trade in energy services and trade barriers; energy services in GATS; the ongoing debate in WTO; and the implications for developing countries. Noting the role of energy in sustainable development and the limited access to commercial energy of many developing countries, the Expert Meeting made suggestions with regard to policy strategies, international trade negotiations, analytical work and follow-up actions.

The Expert Meeting on Consumer Interests, Competitiveness, Competition and Development (17-19 October) [TD/B/COM.1/43] had before it an UNCTAD secretariat note transmitting the report of four regional meetings on the subject (Cartagena, Colombia, 23-25 July; Accra, Ghana, 20-21 August; Goa, India, 10-11 September; Bishkek, Kyrgyzstan, 1-2 October) [TD/B/COM.1/EM.17/2 & Add.1-4]. The Expert Meeting made a number of recommendations for action by Governments at the national and regional levels. It also made recommendations for action by UNCTAD, including the convening of expert meetings on the protection of consumers and regulation of public services.

Trade promotion and facilitation

In 2001, UN bodies continued to assist developing countries and transition economies in promoting their exports and facilitating their integration into the multilateral trading system. The International Trade Centre was the main originator of technical cooperation projects in that area.

International Trade Centre

During 2001, the International Trade Centre (ITC), under the joint sponsorship of UNCTAD and WTO, increased the scale of technical cooperation in terms of value, by 11 per cent to $12.6 million, and number of partner countries, to 124 developing countries and transition economies, including 42 LDCs [ITC/AG(XXXV)/189 & Add.1 & Add.1/Corr.1 & Add.2]. The Centre's goals during the year were to: facilitate the integration of developing and transition economy enterprises into the multilateral trading system; support national efforts to design and implement trade development strategies; strengthen key trade support services, both public and private; improve export performance in sectors of critical importance and opportunity; and foster international competitiveness within the business community as a whole and the SME sector in particular. ITC increased technical support to LDCs through a more active participation in IF at both the planning and implementation stages, extended capacity-building to national networks, upgraded support to the strategy aspect of export development and supported e-trade capacity-building by launching an e-facilitated trade development strategy. The Centre's activities relating to facilitating integration into the multilateral trading system continued to be directed towards clarifying the business implications of the system from the developing country perspective through the implementation of two multi-year programmes: the World Trade Net Programme and the Joint ITC/UNCTAD/WTO Integrated Technical Assistance Programme in Selected Least Developed and Other African Countries.

During the year, ITC delivered technical assistance through a three-track approach: the development of specialized tools for global use and national product-networks; multi-agency, capacity development programmes; and tailor-made trade development projects. Institutions, trade support professionals and enterprise managers from an increasing number of countries joined its specialized trade support networks. With regard to Africa, a major new effort was launched to increase the participation of African suppliers in the procurement programmes of African-based aid agencies, and the Centre laid the foundation for the development of intra-African trade in business and professional services. Under a partnership with the Agence intergouvernementale de la francophonie, ITC extended initial capacity-building support to Burundi, the Central African Republic, Chad, the Comoros, Djibouti, Equatorial Guinea, Guinea, Mali, Sao Tome and Principe, Senegal and Togo. At the national level in Africa, ITC provided technical support in quality certification, public procurement, export-led poverty reduction, national and sectoral strategy development, training and consultancy development.

Trade development projects in the Arab region were directed towards specific national capacity-building requirements: integration into the multilateral trading system (Tunisia) and trade information (Algeria and Egypt). ITC's programme in Central and Eastern Europe and the Commonwealth of Independent States highlighted enterprise-level support, and export-readiness assistance was provided to enterprises in Armenia, Kazakhstan, Kyrgyzstan and Romania. Export-led poverty reduction was a central area of activity in the Asia region and a major programme of training and consultancy capacity-building in international purchasing and supply chain management was under way. Under ITC's South-South Trade Promotion Programme, in Latin America and the Caribbean, funding possibilities for trade-related technical assistance were limited; trade development projects were active only in Bolivia, Brazil and Central America. Priority was therefore given to developing small, regional projects involving trade-related poverty reduction programmes that generated replicable models. Long-term initiatives to promote technical and economic cooperation among developing countries were begun and the development of commercial relationships within the Asian business community, and between Asia and Africa, was promoted.

The ITC State Secretariat for Economic Affairs (Switzerland) Executive Forum on National Export Strategies (Montreux, Switzerland, 26-29 September) highlighted the theme "Is your trade support network working?" The Forum, which was attended by teams from 23 developing and transition economies, focused on such issues as resource rationalization, client segmenting and prioritizing, network leadership and coordination and performance measurement. ITC's first

Regional Executive Forum (Nairobi, Kenya, 26-28 November), which was attended by eight national teams from Eastern and Southern Africa, focused on the theme "Rethinking export strategy".

JAG action. The ITC Joint Advisory Group (JAG) held its thirty-fourth session in Geneva from 30 April to 4 May [ITC/AG(XXXIV)/188]. It had before it reports on ITC activities in 2000 [YUN 2000, p. 900], a summary of technical cooperation projects operational in 2000 [ITC/AG(XXXIV)/185/Add.1] and the report of the ITC Global Trust Fund's Consultative Committee [ITC/AG(XXXIV)/186].

The Group fully endorsed the three-track approach to providing technical assistance, emphasized ITC's efforts to join other organizations in trade development programmes, and encouraged ITC to remain an active advocate of coordination and partnership building and to continue its work as the key link between UNCTAD and WTO technical assistance programmes. The Group reiterated that it was important for ITC to continue its support to enterprise competitiveness, maintain its focus on the needs of the SME sector and remain responsive to changes in the international commercial environment. Stressing the need of the business community to acquire e-competency and e-trade capability, several representatives welcomed the ITC e-facilitated trade development strategy. While commending ITC on the effective management of its limited resource base, the Group expressed concern about its overall resource situation and the number of demand-driven projects that remained unimplemented owing to the absence of funds. Some representatives recommended that the Centre be more active and structured in its efforts to develop new sources of funding.

Pledges of trust fund contributions to ITC were announced by Canada, China, Denmark, Finland, France, India, the Netherlands, Norway, Sweden and Switzerland.

TDB, at its twenty-seventh executive session in July [A/56/15], took note of the JAG report.

ITC administrative arrangements

In accordance with the arrangements approved in General Assembly decision 53/411 B [YUN 1998, p. 888], the Secretary-General, in February, submitted an outline of the proposed programme budget for ITC for the 2002-2003 biennium [A/55/797], which contained the ITC budget for the first year of activities for the biennium and a projection of requirements for the second year. Requirements, expressed in Swiss francs (SwF) at 2002-2003 rates, were estimated at SwF 30,221,800 for 2002 and SwF 30,322,800 for

2003. Since SwF 500,000 from various sources was expected to be available to ITC annually, the annual contribution of each organization (the United Nations and WTO) was estimated at SwF 14,860,900 and SwF 14,911,400 for 2002 and 2003, respectively.

Having considered the Secretary-General's report, the Advisory Committee on Administrative and Budgetary Questions (ACABQ), in May [A/55/7/Add.10], recommended approval of the budget outline for ITC.

By **decision 55/483** of 14 June, the Assembly took note of the proposed 2002-2003 programme budget and concurred with ACABQ's observations and recommendations.

ACABQ, having considered the proposed programme budget for 2002-2003 for ITC [A/56/6/Add.1 (Sect. 11 B)], submitted to the Assembly a December report [A/56/7/Add.3] in which it noted that the ITC requirements for 2002-2003 had been updated to an estimated SwF 60,555,700, representing an increase in real terms of 3.1 per cent instead of the 3.7 per cent indicated in the outline. The biennial contribution of each organization was SwF 30,277,900 ($17,203,350 for the UN contribution, $287,250 more than the figure in the outline).

The Assembly, in **resolution 56/255**, section IX (see p. 1320), approved an amount of $18,022,600 for the 2002-2003 biennium.

Enterprise, business facilitation and development

The Commission on Enterprise, Business Facilitation and Development held its fifth session in Geneva from 22 to 26 January [TD/B/48/3].

At its twenty-sixth executive session in April [A/56/15], TDB took note of the Commission's report and approved the recommendations.

Small and medium-sized enterprises. For its consideration of enhancing the competitiveness of SMEs in the context of foreign direct investment in developing countries, the Commission had before it an UNCTAD secretariat report on the subject [TD/B/COM.3/34], which reviewed the mandates of UNCTAD in the area of enterprise development and internationalization and identified topics for the Commission to take up during the four years leading to the eleventh session of UNCTAD. The topics identified explored ways and means for Governments and international organizations to promote the survival and competitiveness of domestic firms, by targeting foreign investors; using innovative financial mechanisms; adopting enterprise policies consistent with international commitments on trade and investment; and assisting SMEs to acquire information and communication technologies to enter global markets. The Commission also considered the report of the Expert Meeting on the Relationships Between SMEs and Transnational Corporations (TNCs) to Ensure the Competitiveness of SMEs [YUN 2000, p. 901].

The Commission's discussion highlighted the positive impact of TNC-SME linkages on national growth and development. It agreed that SMEs should be more competitive and TNCs should contribute to the local economy of developing countries by working with SMEs for their managerial and technological upgrading and by entering into public-private partnerships to work together with Governments, other TNCs and local business organizations to create support institutions. It called on Governments and the international community to take various actions to assist SMEs and TNCs to form linkages. The Commission recommended that UNCTAD collect and disseminate national best practices stimulating TNC-SME linkages in collaboration with other development actors; conduct regional workshops on successful linkage programmes; promote TNC-SME linkages within the framework of existing technical assistance programmes in order for SMEs to become more competitive; and undertake further research on financing SMEs.

Electronic commerce. For its consideration of capacity-building in electronic commerce: impact of the new economy on traditional sectors of developing countries: electronic commerce and tourism, the Commission had before it an UNCTAD secretariat note on the subject [TD/B/COM.3/35], which outlined the main reasons why e-commerce should continue to be a major issue on UNCTAD's development agenda and discussed specific policy questions in e-tourism and e-commerce in general. It also considered the report of the 2000 Expert Meeting on Electronic Commerce and Tourism [YUN 2000, p. 901].

The Commission, noting the low level of participation in e-commerce by developing countries and the importance of e-tourism, stressed that attention should be given to e-tourism development. It made a number of recommendations for action by Governments and the international community. The Commission stated that UNCTAD should contribute to strengthening the ability of developing countries to develop and implement policies on e-commerce by carrying out studies, disseminating information, organizing expert meetings and assisting them in capacity-building. It should also assist transition economies in studying e-commerce issues and implementing policies.

Human resources development. For its consideration of human resources development (HRD) and training in trade-supporting services:

key to growth with special potential for LDCs, the Commission had before it an UNCTAD secretariat note on the subject [TD/B/COM.3/36], which outlined the main reasons why HRD in trade-supporting services should continue to be a major issue on the UNCTAD development agenda, focused on specific policy questions and presented areas of future work for UNCTAD. It also considered the report of the 2000 Expert Meeting on Human Resources Development and Training in Trade-supporting Services: Key to Growth with Special Potential for LDCs [YUN 2000, p. 901].

The Commission recognized the need to accord the highest priority to the HRD issue, agreed that HRD initiatives should be consistent with broader national policies for education and training and the overall trade strategy, and emphasized that exchange of national experiences and dissemination of best practices would enhance cooperation among countries. It called on Governments and the international community to take specific actions in the area of HRD and training in trade-supporting services and stated that UNCTAD should promote awareness-raising and dissemination of best practices among government officials, private sector companies, business associations and academic institutions through holding workshops, producing and disseminating printed materials and maintaining web pages on HRD in trade-supporting services, among other initiatives.

Subsidiary bodies. In 2001, a number of expert meetings took place, all in Geneva, on issues to be considered by the Commission in 2002.

The Expert Meeting on Electronic Commerce and International Transport Services: Best Practices for Enhancing the Competitiveness of Developing Countries (26-28 September) [TD/B/COM.3/38] examined the impact of e-commerce on international transport services. It had before it an UNCTAD secretariat report on the subject [TD/B/COM.3/EM.12/2]. In agreed conclusions and recommendations, the Meeting, emphasizing the importance of e-commerce to transport services and developing countries' participation in global trade, urged Governments and enterprises to adapt their legal infrastructure to the requirements of e-transactions, taking into account international rules and guidelines, and to improve access to the Internet. It requested the international community to develop transport and telecommunications infrastructures and strengthen services providers, and recommended that UNCTAD monitor developments related to e-commerce and international transport services and disseminate information on best practices for developing countries.

The Expert Meeting on Improving the Competitiveness of SMEs in Developing Countries: The Role of Finance, including E-Finance, to Enhance Enterprise Development (22-24 October) [TD/B/COM.3/39] had before it an UNCTAD note on the subject [TD/B/COM.3/EM.13/2]. The Meeting discussed opportunities for e-finance and highlighted solutions for the supply side (banks and other financial institutions) and the demand side (SMEs). It examined best practices facilitating SME access to finance and made recommendations to Governments, the public and private sectors, development agencies, international financial institutions and UNCTAD. It also recommended that the Commission on Enterprise, Business Facilitation and Development select a topic for the following two years to develop coherent approaches to SME finance, e-finance and non-financial business support services.

The Expert Meeting on Mainstreaming Gender in Order to Promote Opportunities (14-16 November) [TD/B/COM.3/40] had before it an UNCTAD note on the subject [TD/B/COM.3/EM.14/2]. The Meeting made recommendations and suggested policy options to Governments, the international community and UNCTAD on mainstreaming gender in commodities, trade in services, FDI policy, enterprise development and ICT policy.

Commodities

The *Trade and Development Report, 2001* [Sales No. E.01.II.D.10] stated that in 2000 world non-oil commodity prices recovered slightly from sharp declines in 1998 and 1999. Faster growth in the major economic regions resulted in increases in demand for a large number of commodities, leading to lower stock levels and higher prices in some cases. Those increases were sufficient to offset acute declines in the prices of certain key commodities, notably cocoa, coffee and rice. The combined adverse effects of the persistent weakening of some non-oil commodity prices and the increase in oil prices generated severe balance-of-payments problems and welfare losses for oil-importing developing countries heavily dependent on the production and export of a few commodities.

Underlying the improvement in prices were divergent trends among various commodity groups. The lingering effects of the decline in demand during 1998-1999 left producers and exporters of a number of commodities—including cocoa, coffee, rice and tropical logs—with a large stock overhang. For some commodities, particularly nickel and zinc, the fall in stocks that began in late 1999 continued throughout 2000, as a result of strong demand. Changes in the stock levels of agricultural commodities, on the other hand, were mixed.

Prices of minerals, ores and metals as a group increased by 12 per cent from 1999, on account of nickel, copper, aluminium and tungsten. The marked rebound in prices of base metals and other industrial raw materials was the outcome of strong demand, cutbacks in production and a reduction in inventories. The prices of agricultural commodities in 2000 showed large variations, reflecting changes in the balance of supply and demand as well as in stock levels. Prices of key agricultural products remained weak owing to production increases and large inventories. Continued high output of commodities such as coffee, cocoa and rice resulted in a further build-up of stocks and exerted downward pressure on prices. Despite an increase in demand, cocoa prices reached a record low because of a large oversupply, which led to a further build-up of stocks. The 7 per cent increase in tea prices was due to a reduction in supply volumes, particularly from India and Kenya. The 6 per cent rise in food prices, the first increase since 1996, reflected a sharp recovery in sugar prices, which rose more than expected because of a large drawdown in stocks. Although wheat prices recovered slightly, the prices of rice and vegetable oilseeds and oils fell.

The annual average price of crude oil increased by 58 per cent to $27.6 a barrel in 2000, the highest level since 1985, and monthly average oil prices reached a peak of $31.5 a barrel in September 2000. As the price hikes began to be felt in many oil-importing countries, the Organization of Petroleum Exporting Countries (OPEC) increased its production quota by 1.7 million barrels per day (BPD) in April 2000 and adopted a production scheme to keep the price per barrel within the $22-$28 range. Thus, as prices rose above the $28 limit, OPEC raised its production target in July and October. Prices reached a peak in September and again in November, but dropped sharply in December to their lowest level in eight months. To prevent a slide below its target price band, OPEC cut production quotas of members, on a pro rata basis, by 1.5 million BPD as of February 2001.

A joint UNCTAD/DESA report on the world economic situation and prospects [Sales No. E.02.II.C.2], prepared on the basis of information available as at 30 November 2001, observed that oil prices had exhibited considerable volatility in the final months of the year. For the year as a whole, the price of Brent crude oil averaged $24.5 per barrel but was expected to decline to about $20 in 2002. Prior to the terrorist attacks of 11 September, oil

prices in 2001 fluctuated within the OPEC target of $22 and $28 per barrel.

Non-oil commodity prices fell by 2.5 per cent on average in 2001. The recovery in the prices of foods and grains, which began in the second quarter of 2000, ended towards the end of 2001. Trends, however, were divergent: sugar prices fell in the third quarter of 2001 due to increased stocks; banana prices increased by about 45 per cent; maize and wheat rose; rice declined; tropical beverages continued to slide; cocoa recovered; tea and coffee were weak; and vegetable oilseeds and oils weakened during the first half of 2001 but improved in the third quarter. The combined price index of agricultural raw materials recorded a 5 per cent decrease in the third quarter of the year, with cotton declining by about 12 per cent in 2001 and natural rubber declining significantly. Prices of minerals, ores and metals declined by at least 8 per cent during the year.

Individual commodities

Cocoa. On 2 March, the United Nations Conference on Cocoa, 2000, at its second session (Geneva, 26 February–2 March 2001), adopted the International Cocoa Agreement, 2001 [TD/COCOA.9/7]. The Agreement was opened for signature in New York on 1 May and would remain open until 31 December 2002. As at 31 December 2001, Brazil, Cameroon, Côte d'Ivoire and Togo had signed the Agreement.

Jute. On 13 March, the United Nations Conference on Jute and Jute Products (Geneva, 12-13 March) adopted the Agreement establishing the Terms of Reference of the International Jute Study Group, 2001 [TD/JUTE.4/6]. On 11 October, the International Jute Organization completed the process of its liquidation and would be succeeded by the International Jute Study Group in early 2002. As at 31 December, Bangladesh had indicated its definitive acceptance of the Agreement and Switzerland had indicated that it would apply it provisionally.

Common Fund for Commodities

The 1980 Agreement establishing the Common Fund for Commodities [YUN 1980, p. 621], a mechanism intended to stabilize the commodities market by helping to finance buffer stocks of specific commodities, as well as commodity development activities such as research and marketing, entered into force in 1989 and the Fund became operational later that year.

As at 31 December 2001, the number of parties to the Agreement stood at 108.

Finance

Financial policy

The *Trade and Development Report, 2001* [Sales No. E.01.II.D.10] stated that the second half of 2000 was marked by crises and financial support packages for Argentina and Turkey and by movements of financial indicators such as increases in yield spreads on the international bonds of some developing countries, pointing to perceptions of increased risk. In emerging markets, shifts in monetary conditions and pressures on exchange rates were gradual or absent, except during periods of political unrest in some countries. However, the year was also notable for sharp falls in equity prices. In Asia, there were few major changes since early 2000 in exchange-rate policy or regimes of exchange control, but in Latin America there was a trend towards full dollarization. The range of currency regimes in developing and transition economies continued to span the spectrum from rigid pegs (in Argentina and Hong Kong (China)) and dollarization (in Ecuador and El Salvador) to various types of floating.

Among major financial indicators, sharp falls in indices of equity prices were reported in 2000 after rises of more than 50 per cent for all major regions in 1999; the decline was largest in Asia. While those declines were partly fuelled by increased economic uncertainty, they also reflected a strengthening of the links between equity prices in emerging markets and in major developed countries, which was evident, for example, in increased correlations between emerging-market indices and the NASDAQ (National Association of Securities Dealers Automated Quotation System) index. In part, that was a response to the growing importance in emerging stock markets of firms belonging to the technology, media and telecommunications sector.

In Asian emerging-market economies, there was little change in monetary conditions. The main exceptions were Indonesia and the Philippines, where conditions tightened slightly; several countries in the region experienced currency depreciations. In Latin American emerging markets, monetary conditions were subject to great variation; there was a sharp tightening in Argentina in response to its financial crisis, monetary conditions eased in Brazil and Chile, while in Colombia gradual tightening was followed by stabilization and in Mexico short-term interest rates were subject to substantial fluctuation. Turkey was struck by a financial crisis in the last quarter of 2000, as creditors' confidence broke down in an exchange-rate-based stabilization programme that relied heavily on capital inflows. In other emerging-market economies, exchange and interest rates were subject to only small movements. The principal exception was South Africa, where the rand depreciated more than 20 per cent during the year.

The *World Economic and Social Survey 2001* [Sales No. E.01.II.C.1] said the slowdown of the world economy in 2000 was triggered by escalating monetary tightening in major developed economies, particularly the United States. In mid-1999, the United States Federal Reserve began to tighten monetary policy with the aim of moderating demand in order to pre-empt a resurgence of inflation. Central banks in most other developed economies followed suit and interest rates were raised by 150 to 200 basis points within a year. Monetary policy in most developed economies maintained that stance until at least the end of 2000 and in the euro zone until May 2001. As more signs of a sharp slowdown emerged in the beginning of 2001, many developed countries started to ease monetary policy by reducing policy interest rates. The United States Federal Reserve led that adjustment with five cuts in interest rates, totalling 250 basis points, in the first five months of the year.

The majority of world equity markets registered substantial losses in 2000 and during the first quarter of 2001. By March 2001, the NASDAQ index had fallen by more than 65 per cent from its peak a year earlier. The downturn also spread to broader United States stock indices, to most other developed country stock markets and to smaller equity markets, with many Asian emerging-market countries suffering the most. The declining values in global equity markets had an adverse impact on consumer and investment sentiment, leading to reduced consumption and corporate investment. In the second half of 2000, corporate borrowing tightened up as yield spreads in bond markets rose and banks raised their standards for business loans, particularly in the United States. Yield spreads for external borrowing by developing countries also widened markedly. International bond issuances by major developing countries and transition economies faltered in the last quarter of 2000, largely because of the economic and political turmoil in Argentina and Turkey.

In a joint DESA/UNCTAD report on the world economic situation and prospects [Sales No. E.02.II.C.2], based on information available as at 30 November 2001, it was observed that the lower exposure of developing countries to short-term capital flows and the adoption of more flexible exchange-rate regimes meant that external shocks through international financial channels in 2001 were smaller than in the 1997-1998 international financial crises. Nevertheless, a few countries, notably Argentina and Turkey, suffered from a combination of, and interaction between, domestic and international financial difficulties in 2001. Despite some large depreciations, there was a greater degree of stability in the exchange rates of developing countries and transition economies than in the previous few years. However, the adverse developments on both the current and capital accounts meant that a number of developing economies in Latin America, highly dependent on external financing, were facing a balance-of-payments shock.

Financial flows

The *World Economic and Social Survey 2001* [Sales No. E.01.II.C.1] stated that there was a sharp rise in the net outward transfer of financial resources from developing countries as a group in 2000. The net outward transfer from countries in Eastern and Southern Asia moderated significantly and the net inward transfer of financial resources to Latin America increased. There was a swing to a large outward net transfer from Western Asia, which substantially exceeded the increase in import demand. The net inward transfer of resources to Africa as a whole was also reversed. Inward resource transfers to oil-importing African countries to finance their trade deficits continued, while the net transfer to the heavily indebted poor countries (HIPCs) was the smallest in several years. Those developments were mirrored in the subdued net financial flows to developing countries, with both private and official flows declining.

The *Trade and Development Report, 2001* [Sales No. E.01.II.D.10] said that a major factor in the decline in net private financial flows to developing and transition economies since 1997 was the contraction of bank lending. The contraction in lending of the banks reporting to the Bank for International Settlements slowed in the first two quarters of 2000, reflecting developments in East and South Asia, net repayments by which were responsible for a larger part of the decline in net total lending to developing and transition economies in 1999. After a period of relative buoyancy in the aftermath of the financial crises of the late 1990s, net flows of foreign direct investment (FDI) to developing and transition economies decreased in 2000. However, much of the contraction was accounted for by a limited number of recipients; for some Asian countries, the rise in FDI that followed the region's financial crisis largely had run its course and the figures for the Republic of Korea were reduced by an increase in outward FDI. For Argentina, the figure

fell back from a level boosted in the previous year by the proceeds of a single privatization project. FDI flows to Brazil remained high. Capital flows to developing and transition economies in the form of private equity took two forms: international equity issues and foreign investment in local equity markets.

A joint DESA/UNCTAD report on the world economic situation and prospects [Sales No. E.02.II.C.2], based on information available as at 30 November 2001, noted that there was a net financial flow to developing countries and transition economies of almost $37 billion in 2001. Almost all of the net inflow was accounted for by net official financial flows, mainly because of the rise in assistance to countries in financial difficulties. FDI remained the mainstay of net private financial inflows, although it declined from its 2000 level, mainly as the result of the drop in world economic growth and, in particular, in cross-border mergers and acquisitions (M&As). The M&As-led decline in FDI flows affected mostly developed countries, with flows to developing countries relatively unchanged. Portfolio investment and other investment, mainly bank credit, were the sources of substantial net private financial outflows from developing countries and transition economies.

The issue of the net transfer of resources between developing and developed countries was also addressed by the Secretary-General in a July report to the General Assembly (see p. 883).

International financial system

High-level meeting of Economic and Social Council and Bretton Woods institutions. In accordance with General Assembly resolution 55/186 [YUN 2000, p. 908] and Economic and Social Council **decision 2001/207** of 31 January, the fourth special high-level meeting between the Council and the Bretton Woods institutions (the World Bank Group and the International Monetary Fund (IMF)) took place in New York on 1 May [A/56/3/Rev.1]. The meeting addressed two themes: development financing, in particular poverty eradication, official development assistance (ODA) and debt; and towards a development-friendly international financial system: public and private responsibility in the prevention of financial crises. It had before it a note by the Secretary-General on selected aspects of international cooperation in strengthening financing for development [E/2001/45], which also presented some questions on the two themes for discussion. In an informal summary of the high-level meeting [E/2001/72], the Secretary-General summarized the main aspects of the statements made and exchanges of views that took place and provided a synopsis of the discussions, from which the following main themes emerged: global economic outlook and achievement of goals of the Millennium Summit [YUN 2000, p. 47]; poverty eradication: the role of ODA, debt relief and trade; growth sustainability; strengthening the international financial system; participation in decision-making; and financing for development.

In concluding remarks, the IMF Deputy Managing Director observed that a balance needed to be struck between the multiple goals and priorities and the insufficient resources and limited instruments available, and that greater coherence and accountability were needed. He stated that IMF reform efforts placed an emphasis on: realigning the conditionality review process to make it more efficient and open; adapting the Fund's facilities to make them more conducive to pressing needs; and strengthening its role in surveillance and assessment of external vulnerability.

The Managing Director of the World Bank highlighted key constraints to development and the Bank's efforts in addressing them. He noted that the HIPC Initiative, combined with traditional debt relief and bilateral debt forgiveness, would provide $55 billion in debt relief for 22 countries, and that the Bank was also taking action in other areas that posed constraints to development, such as post-conflict reconstruction and HIV/AIDS. He further observed that, to take advantage of trade as a lever for development, market access needed to be improved and the capacity of developing countries to participate in trade negotiations strengthened.

In his closing remarks, the President of the Council stated that financial and monetary issues and the integration of developing and transition economies into the global economy remained crucial questions to be addressed for economic growth and development. Increased ODA, sound national policies and unhindered market access also remained critical issues. He observed that responsibility for development was incumbent upon a larger number of stakeholders, beyond Governments and international institutions, and the potentially devastating contagion effect of financial crises made it imperative to seek new ways of interaction, of sharing responsibility and of broadening participation between the public and the private sector.

By **decision 2001/305** of 26 July, the Council took note of the Secretary-General's note on the special high-level meeting [E/2001/72].

Report of Secretary-General. In response to General Assembly resolution 55/186 [YUN 2000, p. 908], the Secretary-General submitted a July report on international financial architecture and development, including net transfer of resources between developing and developed countries [A/56/173]. The report summarized recent developments in financial flows and net transfer of financial resources to developing countries and examined the main actions taken and concerns raised on policy issues addressed in resolution 55/186. It also sought to consolidate further a broader global agenda for a new international financial architecture, situating it within the preparatory process for the International Conference on Financing for Development, to be held in 2002 (see p. 886). In that regard, the report discussed international standards and codes; exchange-rate and capital account regimes; multilateral surveillance and monitoring; terms and conditions for international assistance; and private sector involvement in crisis prevention and resolution.

The Secretary-General stated that amid dramatic increases in global trade, direct investment and capital flows, there had been a growing tendency for economic changes in any country to reflect developments worldwide. The responsibility for achieving a more stable international financial system lay with national policy makers; developing and transition economies should be encouraged in their efforts to strengthen their financial sectors and pursue sound macroeconomic policies, and the major industrialized countries, which played a key role in setting the international economic environment for development, should pay more attention to the coherence of their policies with the global development objectives and priorities that they endorsed. The effectiveness of international institutions would be fundamental to a stable global economic and financial system, and emphasis should be placed on enhancing consistency, coherence and complementarity among different bodies dealing with financial, trade and developmental issues. More effective cooperation among international bodies required improved coordination at the national level among different ministries of government; and cooperation among regional groups of countries could complement activities at the global level. As the private sector accounted for the overwhelming share of international financial flows, it had important responsibilities in crisis prevention and resolution. In that regard, enhanced dialogue and active and regular contact on policy issues aimed at more stable private sector activity, particularly in emerging markets, could be developed, and a closer collaboration with civic groups and nongovernmental organizations (NGOs) representing civil society was vital. Enhanced global governance required complementary and enhanced exchanges among all parties concerned, and the United Nations should bring its own perspective to identifying emerging issues and policy gaps and facilitate dialogue and consensus-building on global economic, financial and development problems.

By an addendum [A/56/173/Add.1], the Secretary-General transmitted a note by the United Nations Development Programme (UNDP) on financial stability and market efficiency: a global public goods (GPG) perspective. The paper suggested four concrete ways to achieve more successful cooperation in the finance area: to root the design of international cooperation in national policy goals and conditions and look at GPGs as public goods that required international cooperation but still should have positive utility for all nationally; to encourage broader participation in international financial policy-making as a means to reduce collective action and information as well as burden-sharing problems; to engage more actively the epistemic community in exploring possible production paths of the GPG financial stability and market efficiency; and to finance needed capacity-building in developing countries out of the seigniorage earned by the central banks of industrial countries as an integral part of their efforts to provide sound money.

By a second addendum [A/56/173/Add.2], the Secretary-General transmitted information on work undertaken by UNCTAD in support of the promotion of long-term private financial flows, especially FDI. The report noted that UNCTAD activities aimed to improve the understanding of developing and transition economies about policy options in international investment flows, and to strengthen their abilities to formulate and implement measures and action programmes to attract and benefit from FDI.

GENERAL ASSEMBLY ACTION

On 21 December [meeting 90], the General Assembly, on the recommendation of the Second Committee [A/56/558/Add.2], adopted **resolution 56/181** without vote [agenda item 95 (b)].

Towards a strengthened and stable international financial architecture responsive to the priorities of growth and development, especially in developing countries, and to the promotion of economic and social equity

The General Assembly,

Recalling its resolution 55/186 of 20 December 2000, entitled "Towards a strengthened and stable international financial architecture responsive to the priorities of growth and development, especially in developing countries, and to the promotion of economic and social equity",

1. *Takes note* of the report of the Secretary-General entitled "International financial architecture and development, including net transfer of resources between developing and developed countries";

2. *Takes note also* of the deliberations of the Preparatory Committee for the International Conference on Financing for Development, which is to be held at Monterrey, Mexico, from 18 to 22 March 2002;

3. *Stresses* the importance of continued substantive consideration of the sub-item on the international financial system and development;

4. *Requests* the Secretary-General to submit to the General Assembly at its fifty-seventh session a report on the international financial system and development, bearing in mind, inter alia, the outcome of the International Conference on Financing for Development;

5. *Decides* to include in the provisional agenda of its fifty-seventh session, under the item entitled "Macroeconomic policy questions", the sub-item entitled "International financial system and development".

Debt problems of developing countries

In response to General Assembly resolution 55/184 [YUN 2000, p. 912], the Secretary-General submitted an August report on the external debt and debt-servicing problems of developing countries, including those resulting from global financial instability [A/56/262]. The report described the overall debt situation of developing and transition economies, the recent evolution of conventional debt indicators and changes in the pattern of external financing of developing countries and in the nature of their external debt problems. It also considered developments in external debt owed to official creditors and progress made in the context of the IMF/World Bank HIPC Initiative and the Paris Club (group of creditor countries). It also described developments in financial obligations of developing country debtors vis-à-vis private creditors and international capital markets, and discussed how to involve the private sector in the prevention and resolution of financial crises.

The Secretary-General observed that the year 2000 had seen some improvements in the external debt situation of developing countries and transition economies. With the total stock of debt virtually unchanged in nominal terms and gross national product (GNP) growth rates exceeding 5 per cent in both developed and transition economies, debt to GNP ratios improved in all regions. However, cross-country differences in growth in export earnings were particularly large in 2000 owing to the differential effects of commodity price developments, strong growth in the United States and recovery in East Asia. Moreover, debt service continued to represent a heavy burden for many developing countries, in particular in sub-Saharan Africa and Latin America, as well as among transition economies, and arrears on interest payments actually rose in Latin America and East Asia. For all developing and transition economies taken together, the stock of reserves rose by $67 billion, or more than 9 per cent, in 2000, entailing considerable costs because they were borrowed at rates well above the interest earned on them.

As to official debt, of the 41 HIPCs, only two (Bolivia and Uganda) had reached completion point (receiving the full extent of debt relief possible under the Initiative) by mid-2001. Twenty-three countries, 19 from Africa and 4 from Latin America, reached the decision point (entitled to interim assistance); the majority of them were receiving enhanced debt relief from Paris Club creditors. Most of the countries that had not reached decision point by mid-2001 were engaged in armed conflicts, and consideration was being given to accommodating their circumstances by shortening the time required for reaching the decision and completion points of the Initiative. In the Brussels Declaration adopted at LDC-III (see p. 770), Governments undertook to make progress towards cancelling outstanding official bilateral debt within the enhanced HIPC Initiative. In 2000, the first countries to conclude new Paris Club flow rescheduling agreements on Cologne terms [YUN 1999, p. 896] were Mauritania and the United Republic of Tanzania. Cameroon, Chad, Guinea, Guinea-Bissau, Madagascar, Malawi and the Niger followed in the first half of 2001. Four HIPCs (Benin, Burkina Faso, Mali and Senegal) had their existing Paris Club agreements topped up to Cologne terms through supplementary debt relief, and two HIPCs, Honduras and Mozambique, benefited from a moratorium on debt service. Of the HIPCs that had yet to reach decision point, Ethiopia obtained a flow rescheduling in April 2001. Operations in connection with the provision of enhanced debt relief under the HIPC Initiative accelerated the pace of debt renegotiations in the Paris Club during the second half of 2000 and first half of 2001. New Paris Club agreements on non-concessional terms were concluded for eight countries (Ecuador, Gabon, Georgia, Kenya, Nigeria, Pakistan, the former Yugoslav Republic of Macedonia and Ukraine) up to July 2001.

As to commercial debt, the report analysed private capital flows, recent bond restructuring exercises, and official lending and private sector involvement in crisis resolution.

The Secretary-General stated that while some progress had been made, problems remained unresolved in most areas. While the enhancement of HIPC had brought some improvement in its

implementation, fundamental changes were needed, including measures to accelerate the provision of debt relief by facilitating the process of preparing and implementing Poverty Reduction Strategy Papers, which constituted a high hurdle for many countries. Some Governments of the Group of Seven major industrialized countries (G-7) had proposed or taken action to impose a moratorium on debt-service payments by HIPCs that had reached decision point; such action deserved further consideration. The Secretary-General underscored the importance of an independent assessment of debt sustainability that was not restricted to HIPCs but also encompassed other debt-distressed low-income and middle-income countries. He also stressed the need for contingency measures and safeguards for countries about to reach completion points in order to prevent them from falling back into the debt trap because of adverse changes in exogenous factors, including their export and borrowing prospects. A crucial factor for the success of the HIPC Initiative was the additionality of debt relief in comparison with overall pre-debt-relief transfers. That required ODA to be raised in accordance with the needs of recipient countries. Moreover, to ensure that the Initiative did not lead to reduction in multilateral financing to other poor countries, donors should provide the resources to maintain past levels of lending to those countries. Although Paris Club practices had evolved over time, they still fell short of addressing debt problems in a way that would ensure graduation from lengthy and repetitive rescheduling. An important step towards a rethinking of approaches of official debt relief in the Paris Club context could be to broaden the debt eligible for write-off.

The Secretary-General concluded that the international community had not yet made significant progress in providing orderly debt workout mechanisms to ensure that creditors and investors bore the consequences of the risks they had taken, and that the burden of crises was distributed equitably between debtors and creditors and among different classes of creditors.

GENERAL ASSEMBLY ACTION

On 21 December [meeting 90], the General Assembly, on the recommendation of the Second Committee [A/56/558/Add.4], adopted **resolution 56/184** without vote [agenda item 95 (d)].

Enhancing international cooperation towards a durable solution to the external debt problems of developing countries

The General Assembly,

Recalling its resolutions 51/164 of 16 December 1996, 52/185 of 18 December 1997, 53/175 of 15 December 1998, 54/202 of 22 December 1999 and 55/184 of 20 December 2000 on enhancing international co-operation towards a durable solution to the external debt problems of developing countries,

1. *Takes note* of the report of the Secretary-General on the external debt and debt-servicing problems of developing countries, including those resulting from global financial instability;

2. *Takes note also* of the deliberations of the Preparatory Committee for the International Conference on Financing for Development, which is to be held at Monterrey, Mexico, from 18 to 22 March 2002;

3. *Stresses* the importance of the continued substantive consideration of the sub-item on external debt crisis and development;

4. *Requests* the Secretary-General to report to the General Assembly at its fifty-seventh session on the external debt crisis and development, bearing in mind, inter alia, the outcome of the International Conference on Financing for Development;

5. *Decides* to include in the provisional agenda of its fifty-seventh session, under the item entitled "Macroeconomic policy questions", the sub-item entitled "External debt crisis and development".

Financing for development

International Conference on Financing for Development (2002)

The Preparatory Committee for the High-level International Intergovernmental Event on Financing for Development held two sessions and a resumed session in 2001. On the Committee's recommendation, the General Assembly, in March, decided that the event would be named the International Conference on Financing for Development and accepted Mexico's offer to host the Conference; in July, it decided that the Conference would be held in Monterrey from 18 to 22 March 2002.

Preparatory Committee meetings. The Preparatory Committee held two sessions in 2001, all in New York: the second (12-23 February) [A/55/28/Add.1], the third (2-8 May) [A/55/28/Add.2 & Corr.1] and the resumed third (15-19 October) [A/56/28 & Corr.1]. The Committee's organizational and first sessions were held in 2000 [YUN 2000, p. 916].

At its second session, convened in accordance with General Assembly resolution 55/213 [YUN 2000, p. 917], the Committee had before it the reports of the five regional consultative meetings on financing for development [ibid., p. 916] and the reports of the Committee's two hearings, one with civil society organizations and the other with the business community [ibid.]. It also considered a report of the Secretary-General [A/AC.257/12] containing recommendations for consideration by the Committee on: mobilizing domestic financial resources for development; mobilizing inter-

national resources for development: FDI and other private flows; trade; increasing international financial cooperation for development through, inter alia, ODA; debt; and addressing systemic issues: enhancing the coherence and consistency of the international monetary, financial and trading systems in support of development.

In addition to recommending to the Assembly the adoption of a draft resolution on the preparations for the substantive preparatory process and the Conference itself (see below), the Preparatory Committee decided to accredit 10 additional NGOs not in consultative status with the Economic and Social Council to the high-level intergovernmental event, including its preparatory process.

GENERAL ASSEMBLY ACTION

On 21 March [meeting 97], the General Assembly, on the recommendation of the Preparatory Committee for the High-level International Intergovernmental Event on Financing for Development [A/55/L.77], adopted **resolution 55/245 A** without vote [agenda item 101].

Preparations for the substantive preparatory process and the International Conference on Financing for Development

The General Assembly,

Recalling its resolutions 54/196 of 22 December 1999 and 55/186 and 55/213 of 20 December 2000,

Taking note with appreciation of the report of the Secretary-General and all other inputs submitted to the Preparatory Committee for the High-level International Intergovernmental Event on Financing for Development for consideration at its second session,

Welcoming the continuous and important progress made in consultations with the major institutional stakeholders, in particular the World Bank, the International Monetary Fund and the World Trade Organization, with regard to their involvement in the process of financing for development,

Encouraging Governments and all other relevant stakeholders to continue considering concrete initiatives in support of the financing for development preparatory process and the high-level international intergovernmental event, within the framework of the substantive agenda,

Further encouraging the deepening of the efforts of all relevant stakeholders, including at the regional level, as well as by civil society and the business sector, in support of the financing for development preparatory process and the high-level international intergovernmental event, within the framework of the substantive agenda,

Recalling the holistic nature of the financing for development preparatory process and the need to take into account other ongoing processes of relevance to the substantive agenda for the financing for development process,

Reiterating its appreciation to Governments for the support provided to the Trust Fund for extrabudgetary contributions to the financing for development process,

1. *Decides* that the high-level international intergovernmental event on financing for development will take the form of an international conference, under the auspices of the United Nations, at the highest political level, including at the summit level, and accepts with gratitude the generous offer of Mexico to host this conference, to be named the International Conference on Financing for Development, on the understanding that the specific timing and location of the Conference will be announced by the host country during the third session of the Preparatory Committee for the High-level International Intergovernmental Event on Financing for Development;

2. *Stresses* the importance of effective preparations for the Conference, and welcomes the preparatory activities carried out so far, including the substantive interactive dialogue and contribution of all stakeholders during the second session of the Preparatory Committee;

3. *Decides* that the Preparatory Committee will hold its third session for a period of one week from 2 to 8 May 2001, and that it will hold a resumed third session for a period of another full week during October or November 2001;

4. *Invites* Governments to submit to the coordinating secretariat, not later than 15 April 2001, a concise identification of possible initiatives or themes, consideration of which may serve as a means to focus further the substantive preparatory work, within the framework of the substantive agenda, on the understanding that a compilation of such submissions should be available to the Preparatory Committee at its third session;

5. *Decides* that the Preparatory Committee, at its third session, from 2 to 8 May 2001, taking into account all inputs submitted to it at its second session and the dialogue held therein, as well as the above-mentioned compilation of submissions and other relevant inputs, will consider in greater depth issues contained in a working paper prepared by the Facilitator, which will serve as a means to focus further the discussions of the substantive preparatory work, within the framework of the substantive agenda, and in this regard encourages active participation by all relevant stakeholders in the consideration of these issues;

6. *Also decides* that the Preparatory Committee, at its resumed third session, in October or November 2001, will consider a concise first draft prepared by the Facilitator, reflecting the progress made at its third session and taking into account all other relevant inputs received thereafter by the Preparatory Committee, within the framework of the substantive agenda;

7. *Requests* the Bureau of the Preparatory Committee to explore ways and means to deepen the efforts of all relevant stakeholders, including at the regional level, as well as those made by civil society and the business sector, in support of the financing for development preparatory process, within the framework of the substantive agenda, and to submit proposals for consideration and a decision by the Preparatory Committee.

At its third session, convened in accordance with resolution 55/245 A, the Committee (renamed the Preparatory Committee for the International Conference on Financing for Develop-

ment), in addition to the documents considered at its second session, had before it the third report of its Bureau [A/AC.257/22 & Corr.1], which addressed modalities for participation of key institutional and non-institutional stakeholders, arrangements for the Conference and other organizational matters; the report of the Bureau's task force on modalities for engaging the business community in the financing for development process [A/AC.257/22/Add.1]; a working paper by the Facilitator on issues related to the six headings of the Conference's substantive agenda and interlinkages between them [A/AC.257/24]; and a note by the Secretary-General transmitting a compilation of initiatives or themes submitted by Governments to further focus the discussions of the preparatory work within the framework of the substantive agenda [A/AC.257/23 & Add.1].

The Preparatory Committee recommended to the Assembly the adoption of a draft resolution (see below). It also decided to accredit an additional 13 NGOs not in consultative status with the Economic and Social Council to the Conference.

GENERAL ASSEMBLY ACTION

On 25 July [meeting 109], the General Assembly, on the recommendation of the Preparatory Committee for the International Conference on Financing for Development [A/55/L.82], adopted **resolution 55/245 B** without vote [agenda item 101].

Preparations for the substantive preparatory process and the International Conference on Financing for Development

The General Assembly,

Recalling its resolutions 54/196 of 22 December 1999, 55/186 and 55/213 of 20 December 2000 and 55/245 A of 21 March 2001, and decision 1/1 of the Preparatory Committee for the International Conference on Financing for Development,

Taking note with appreciation of the report of the Bureau of the Preparatory Committee as well as all other inputs submitted to date for the consideration of the Preparatory Committee at its third session,

Welcoming the progress made in consultations with the major institutional stakeholders, in particular the World Bank, the International Monetary Fund and the World Trade Organization, with regard to their involvement in the process of financing for development,

Encouraging Governments and all other relevant stakeholders to continue considering concrete initiatives in support of the financing for development preparatory process and the International Conference on Financing for Development, within the framework of the substantive agenda,

Further encouraging the deepening of the efforts of all relevant stakeholders, including at the regional level, as well as by civil society and the business sector, in support of the financing for development preparatory process and the Conference, within the framework of the substantive agenda,

Recalling the holistic nature of the financing for development preparatory process and the need to take into account other ongoing processes of relevance to the substantive agenda for the financing for development process,

Reiterating its appreciation to Governments for the support provided to the Trust Fund for extrabudgetary contributions to the financing for development process,

1. *Stresses* the importance of a successful outcome of the International Conference on Financing for Development, as reflected by the heads of State and Government in the United Nations Millennium Declaration, and expresses appreciation to those heads of State and Government who responded to the letter addressed to them by the Secretary-General in compliance with resolution 55/213;

2. *Also stresses* the importance of effective preparations for the Conference, and welcomes the preparatory activities carried out so far, including the substantive interactive dialogue and contribution of all stakeholders during the third session of the Preparatory Committee for the Conference;

3. *Expresses its gratitude* to the host country, Mexico, for its announcement regarding the venue and timing of the Conference, and decides that the International Conference on Financing for Development shall be held in Monterrey, capital of the state of Nuevo León, Mexico, from 18 to 22 March 2002;

4. *Requests* the Secretary-General to continue to provide the preparatory process and the Conference with all the support needed, including a secretariat commensurate with the level of the event and adequate staff and other resources, and including the launching of a global public awareness campaign with as much support as possible from public/private partnerships in order to ensure, in collaboration with the authorities of the host country, the successful realization of the Conference and public awareness of its outcome;

5. *Requests* the coordinating secretariat to provide the Preparatory Committee on a regular basis with all relevant information on the progress of the global public awareness campaign;

6. *Invites* all relevant stakeholders to continue their active involvement in support of the financing for development preparatory process, including through staff support from the major institutional stakeholders to the financing for development coordinating secretariat, and in this context invites the coordinating secretariat to continue to provide support to the Facilitator, including in the preparation of the concise first draft of the outcome document mandated in resolution 55/245 A, taking into account the substantive interactive dialogue and all other relevant inputs received by the Preparatory Committee within the framework of the substantive agenda;

7. *Requests* that the first draft of the outcome document be submitted to the Preparatory Committee in mid-September 2001 for its consideration at its resumed third session, to be held from 15 to 19 October 2001;

8. *Encourages* Governments, as well as all relevant stakeholders, including the World Bank, the International Monetary Fund, the World Trade Organization, the United Nations Conference on Trade and Development, the United Nations Development Programme, the regional development banks and all other relevant regional bodies, to continue considering concrete initiatives in support of the financing for development preparatory process and the International Conference on Financing for Development, within the framework of the substantive agenda, including through the organization of expert panels and round tables, and in that regard requests the coordinating secretariat to bring information on such work to the attention of the Preparatory Committee at its resumed third session;

9. *Reaffirms* the importance of continuing to strengthen ways and means to deepen the efforts of all relevant stakeholders, including at the regional level, as well as by civil society and the business sector, in support of the financing for development preparatory process and the Conference, within the framework of the substantive agenda, and in that regard, having considered the report of the task force established by the Bureau of the Preparatory Committee to consider modalities for engaging the business community in the financing for development process:

(*a*) Expresses its satisfaction with the informal discussion with business sector interlocutors on 2 May 2001, and in that context requests the coordinating secretariat, in full consultation with the Bureau, to advise on, assist in and monitor a programme of work developed with the business sector that draws on its perspectives relevant to the substantive agenda items. This programme of work may run from May 2001 until the Conference, and may include workshops, seminars, round tables, forums and other forms of input. The secretariat should bring the outcomes to the attention of the Preparatory Committee;

(*b*) Decides to invite the participation of business sector entities, as follows:

(i) Business sector entities that are in consultative status with the Economic and Social Council as non-governmental organizations will participate according to the existing rules;

(ii) Business sector entities that are not in consultative status with the Economic and Social Council will be accredited on an ad hoc basis in a similar manner to non-governmental organizations, using the following procedure. They shall provide the name of and information about the company or organization, such as annual reports and a business prospectus, to the coordinating secretariat which shall distribute the names of and information about these entities to members of the Preparatory Committee which will decide accreditation on a non-objection basis;

(*c*) Decides that the modalities for their participation in the Conference shall be finalized when the format of the Conference is decided upon by the Preparatory Committee at its resumed third session;

(*d*) Encourages other initiatives to involve the business sector at national and regional levels and to inform the Preparatory Committee thereof;

10. *Decides* that the format of the Conference should include a high-level official meeting, to be held on 18 March 2002; a segment at the ministerial level, to which delegations shall be invited to send fully integrated delegations, with representatives from all relevant national ministries, to be held on 19 and 20 March 2002; and a segment at the summit level, with the par-

ticipation of heads of State or Government, to be held on 21 and 22 March 2002;

11. *Decides also* that the Conference shall include the participation of States Members of the United Nations, States members of the specialized agencies and observers, in accordance with the established practice of the General Assembly;

12. *Decides further* that the Conference shall also include the participation of all relevant stakeholders, including the business sector and civil society;

13. *Requests*, in reference to paragraphs 11 and 12 above, that the Bureau of the Preparatory Committee prepare a proposal for the consideration and decision of the Preparatory Committee, at its resumed third session, on the specific format and rules of procedure of the Conference, as well as possible round tables or other suitable arrangements for the various segments;

14. *Agrees* that the Preparatory Committee, taking into account the dialogue held during its third session, will decide on the nature of the outcome of the International Conference on Financing for Development no later than at its resumed third session in order to guide the Facilitator in the continued intergovernmental negotiations and in the preparation of the draft outcome documents.

At its resumed third session, convened in accordance with resolution 55/245 A (see p. 886), the Committee had before it the final report of the High-level Panel on Financing for Development [A/55/1000]; the list of additional NGOs recommended for accreditation to the preparatory process and the Conference [A/AC.257/10/Add.4]; a list of business entities/organizations recommended for accreditation [A/AC.257/30]; a draft outcome document prepared by the Facilitator [A/AC.257/25]; a note by the Secretary-General on technical notes related to issues falling under the Conference's substantive agenda [A/AC.257/27 & Add.1-10]; the fourth report of the Committee's Bureau on preparations for the Conference [A/AC.257/29 & Add.1 & Add.1/Corr.1]; and a September note by the Secretary-General [A/AC.257/26] updating activities planned or undertaken pursuant to Assembly resolution 55/245 B, including the launch of a global public awareness campaign, initiatives by Governments and other relevant stakeholders and the development of a programme of work with the business sector.

The Panel recommended strategies for the mobilization of resources required to accelerate equitable and sustainable growth in developing countries and transition economies, and to fulfil the poverty and development commitments enshrined in the United Nations Millennium Declaration [YUN 2000, p. 49]. It discussed domestic resource mobilization, private capital flows, trade, international development cooperation and systemic issues.

The Preparatory Committee recommended to the Assembly for adoption draft decisions on the

format of the Conference and on the provisional rules of procedure (see below). It also adopted and brought to the Assembly's attention decisions on the accreditation of intergovernmental organizations [dec. 3/1], additional NGOs [dec. 3/2] and business entities/organizations [dec. 3/3]; and decisions on the provisional agenda for its fourth session, to be held in January 2002 [dec. 3/4], and on the preparation of the draft outcome document of the Conference [dec. 3/5].

GENERAL ASSEMBLY ACTION

On 21 December [meeting 90], the General Assembly, on the recommendation of the Second Committee [A/56/570], adopted **resolution 56/210** without vote [agenda item 107].

International Conference on Financing for Development

The General Assembly,

Recalling its resolutions 46/205 of 20 December 1991, 48/187 of 21 December 1993, 50/93 of 20 December 1995, 52/179 of 18 December 1997, 53/173 of 15 December 1998, 54/196 of 22 December 1999 and 55/213 of 20 December 2000 on the high-level international intergovernmental consideration of financing for development,

Recalling also its resolution 55/245 A of 21 March 2001, on convening an International Conference on Financing for Development, in which it accepted with gratitude the generous offer of Mexico to host the Conference, which is to be held at Monterrey from 18 to 22 March 2002,

1. *Takes note* of the deliberations of the Preparatory Committee for the International Conference on Financing for Development at its first, second and third substantive sessions;

2. *Stresses* the importance of continued substantive consideration of the item on financing for development;

3. *Requests* the Secretary-General to report to the General Assembly at its fifty-seventh session on the outcome of the International Conference on Financing for Development;

4. *Decides* to include in the provisional agenda of its fifty-seventh session the item entitled "High-level international intergovernmental consideration of financing for development".

On the same date, the Assembly decided that the format of the International Conference on Financing for Development would be as set out in the annex to its decision (**decision 56/445**) and recommended for adoption by the Conference the provisional rules of procedure, which were annexed to its decision (**decision 56/446**). On 24 December, the Assembly decided that the item on high-level international intergovernmental consideration of financing for development would remain for consideration during its resumed fifty-sixth (2002) session (**decision 56/464**).

Investment, technology and related financial issues

The UNCTAD Commission on Investment, Technology and Related Financial Issues held its fifth session in Geneva from 12 to 16 February [TD/B/48/4].

At its twenty-sixth executive session in April [A/56/15], TDB took note of the Commission's report and approved its recommendations.

Mergers and acquisitions. For its consideration of the impact of international investment flows on development: mergers and acquisitions (M&As)—policies aimed at maximizing the positive and minimizing the possible negative impact of international investment, the Commission had before it the report of an Expert Meeting on the subject [YUN 2000, p. 917]; an UNCTAD secretariat note transmitting the outcome of that Expert Meeting [TD/B/COM.2/29]; and a note submitted to that Meeting by the UNCTAD secretariat on the impact of cross-border M&As on development and policy issues [TD/B/COM.2/EM.7/2 & Corr.1].

In a series of recommendations, to Governments, the international community and UNCTAD, the Commission stated that national policies or guidelines on M&As should reflect a long-term developmental perspective and measures should be considered to maximize their benefits and minimize their social cost. International cooperation should be strengthened in the area of competition policies and consideration should be given to assisting developing countries, particularly LDCs, in developing and implementing national and regional policies and formulating policies and measures concerning cross-border M&As. UNCTAD should continue to analyse trends in cross-border M&As and their share in FDI flows and related policy responses and their impact on development. It should also elaborate guidelines, with a view to providing recommendations to deal with the challenges posed by the impact of cross-border M&As on national market structures, level of employment and competition policy.

Home country measures. For its consideration of home country measures, the Commission had before it the report of the 2000 Expert Meeting on the subject [YUN 2000, p. 917] and an UNCTAD secretariat note [TD/B/COM.2/30], which summarized that Meeting's key issues and policy proposals. In recommendations to Governments and the international community, the Commission stated that Governments should emulate best practices in the area of home country measures (measures aimed at promoting outward investment and technology transfer) and apply them in a cooperative spirit. Home countries, particularly developed ones, should further develop efforts to encourage FDI flows, particularly to and between developing countries and especially to LDCs; and host countries should take advantage of opportunities arising from home country measures and seek to develop linkages between their own investment promotion efforts and home country measures offered by home countries. The international community should further examine what measures Governments should take to implement the provisions of international agreements on transfer of technology, and international support measures could be useful in facilitating FDI flows to developing countries, including through the improvement of the enabling environment. UNCTAD, within the mandate from UNCTAD X [YUN 2000, p. 891], should analyse all aspects of agreements relevant to transfer of technology and design technical cooperation activities to assist countries in making effective use of home country measures.

Investment policy reviews. For its consideration of investment policy reviews: exchange of national experience, the Commission had before it the Investment and Innovation Policy Review of Ethiopia [UNCTAD/ITE/IPC/Misc.4] and the Investment Policy Reviews of Ecuador [UNCTAD/ITE/IPC/Misc.2], Mauritius [UNCTAD/ITE/IPC/Misc.1] and Peru [UNCTAD/ITE/IIP/Misc.19].

Subsidiary bodies. In 2001, two expert meetings took place, both in Geneva. The Expert Meeting on International Arrangements for Transfer of Technology: Best Practices for Access to and Measures to Encourage Transfer of Technology with a View to Capacity-building in Developing Countries, Especially in LDCs (27-29 June) [TD/B/COM.2/33] had before it an UNCTAD secretariat note on the subject [TD/B/COM.2/EM.9/2] and the Compendium of International Arrangements on Transfer of Technology: Selected Instruments [Sales No. E.01.II.D.28]. The experts highlighted the important role of technology in economic development and noted that more should be done to implement international instruments to enhance the transfer of technology and technological capabilities to developing countries, in particular to LDCs. They examined best practices that could contribute to technology transfer and capacity-building and recommended that UNCTAD provide assistance to developing countries to negotiate technology transfer provisions in international instruments and explore ways to implement international commitments effectively.

The Expert Meeting on the Impact of FDI Policies on Industrialization, Local Entrepreneurship and the Development of Supply Capacity (5-7 November) [TD/B/COM.2/35] had before it an UNCTAD secretariat note on the subject

[TD/B/COM.2/EM.10/2], which explored policy issues for countries wishing to attract and benefit from FDI. The experts examined policy issues related to: the link between FDI and industrialization, export competitiveness and supply capacity development; the role of corporate strategies and other considerations of foreign investors; targeting FDI in the context of development strategies; and local entrepreneurship and supply capacity development. They made recommendations on the role of Governments and the international community and agreed that UNCTAD should continue to analyse the international systems of production and assist developing countries in assessing their capabilities to define policy goals in line with their situation in the international market, and in implementing FDI targeting and linkage programmes consistent with their industrialization and development strategies.

Competition law and policy

The Intergovernmental Group of Experts on Competition Law and Policy held its third session in Geneva from 2 to 4 July [TD/B/COM.2/32]. It considered consultations on competition law and policy, including the model law and studies related to the provisions of the 1980 Set of Multilaterally Agreed Equitable Principles and Rules for the Control of Restrictive Business Practices (known as the Set) [YUN 1980, p. 626]; and the UNCTAD work programme on competition law and policy, including technical assistance, advisory and training programmes. It had before it a report on the model law [TD/B/COM.2/CLP/23] containing possible elements for a new article on competition and regulation, as requested by the Fourth United Nations Conference to Review All Aspects of the Set [YUN 2000, p. 901], and UNCTAD secretariat reports on: technical assistance, advisory and training programmes [TD/B/COM.2/CLP/20]; experiences gained on international cooperation on competition policy issues and the mechanisms used [TD/B/COM.2/CLP/21]; and competition policy and the exercise of intellectual property rights [TD/B/COM.2/CLP/22].

In agreed conclusions, the Group of Experts recommended the strengthening of UNCTAD's work programme and the intergovernmental machinery addressing competition law and policy issues. It invited member States to assist UNCTAD on a voluntary basis in its activities by providing experts, training facilities or financial resources, and requested the UNCTAD secretariat to study the possibility of formulating a model cooperation agreement on competition law and policy, based on the Set, and to expand its activities. The secretariat was also asked to prepare for the Group's next session: a study on the relationship between competition, competitiveness and development; an updated review of technical assistance; a preliminary report on ways in which international agreements on competition might apply to developing countries, enabling them to introduce and enforce competition law and policy; and a study of the roles of dispute mediation mechanisms and alternative arrangements.

International standards of accounting and reporting

The Intergovernmental Working Group of Experts on International Standards of Accounting and Reporting held its eighteenth session in Geneva from 10 to 12 September [TD/B/COM.2/34]. Having considered the report of the ad hoc consultative group of experts on accounting by small and medium-sized enterprises (SMEs) [TD/B/COM.2/ISAR/12], the Group, in agreed conclusions, stated that the report needed further refinement and requested the ad hoc consultative group to continue its work. It reconfirmed the need for guidance on an accounting framework for SMEs that took into consideration the fact that one uniform set of accounting rules would not suit the needs of large, medium-sized and small enterprises. The Group also made recommendations on environmental accounting and reporting and on the assessment of professional qualification requirements. The secretariat was encouraged to work with the members of the Group during the intersessional periods to identify topics for discussion.

Taxation

By **decision 2001/208** of 31 January, the Economic and Social Council approved the holding of the tenth meeting of the Ad Hoc Group of Experts on International Cooperation in Tax Matters in Geneva from 10 to 14 September instead of in New York from 23 to 27 April.

By **decision 2001/314** of 26 July, the Council deferred to its resumed session of 2001 consideration of the sub-item "International cooperation in tax matters".

The tenth meeting of the Ad Hoc Group of Experts on International Cooperation in Tax Matters was held in Geneva from 10 to 14 September [E/2002/6]. It discussed revision and updating of the United Nations Model Double Taxation Convention between Developed and Developing Countries and the *Manual for the Negotiation of Bilateral Tax Treaties between Developed and Developing Countries;* transfer pricing; new financial instruments; taxation of e-commerce; mutual assistance in tax collection; and technical training.

The Group of Experts recognized the need for developing countries and transitional economies to improve their ability to develop, implement and administer transfer-pricing rules in accordance with article 9 of the United Nations and OECD Model Conventions, and, to that end, recommended enhancing policy advice, technical assistance and international cooperation on transfer-pricing issues. It also recommended steps whereby developing countries and economies in transition could avoid or reduce the cost of resolving disputes with multinational companies over the arm's-length principle. In the light of the potential importance of e-commerce taxation for developing countries and economies in transition, the Group recommended that the United Nations undertake a study of the tax issues involved.

By **decision 2001/325** of 20 December, the Council deferred to its substantive session of 2002 consideration of the report of the Ad Hoc Group of Experts on its tenth meeting.

Transport

Maritime transport

The *Review of Maritime Transport 2001* [Sales No. E.01.II.D.26] stated that world seaborne trade recorded its fifteenth consecutive annual increase in 2000, reaching a record high of 5.88 billion tons. The annual growth rate increased to 3.6 per cent compared to 0.9 per cent in 1999. Global maritime trade growth in 2001 was expected to decline to 2 per cent. Total maritime activities measured in ton-miles increased to 22,940 billion in 2000, from 21,930 billion in 1999.

The world merchant fleet expanded to 808.4 million deadweight tons (dwt) at the end of 2000, a 1.2 per cent increase over 1999. New-building deliveries were up by 9.6 per cent to 44.4 million dwt and tonnage broken up and lost declined by 27.7 per cent to 22.2 million dwt, leaving a net gain of 9.4 million dwt. The fleet of oil tankers and dry bulk carriers, which together made up 70.1 per cent of the total world fleet, increased by 1.1 per cent and 2 per cent respectively. There was an 8.8 per cent increase to 69.2 million dwt in the container ship fleet and a 6.9 per cent increase to 18.5 million dwt in the liquefied gas carrier fleet. Registration of ships by developed market-economy countries and major open-registry countries accounted for 25.2 and 48.5 per cent of the world fleet, respectively. Open registries increased their tonnage by 1.9 per cent and two thirds of that beneficially owned fleet was owned by market economies and developing countries. Developing countries' share reached 19.4 per cent or 157 million dwt, 115.7 million of which was registered in Asia.

Transport of dangerous goods

In response to Economic and Social Council resolution 1999/62 [YUN 1999, p. 905], the Secretary-General submitted an April report on the work during 1999-2000 of the Committee of Experts on the Transport of Dangerous Goods [E/2001/44]. In accordance with Council resolution 1999/65 [YUN 1999, p. 906], the Committee, as from 1 January 2001, had been reconfigured into the Committee of Experts on the Transport of Dangerous Goods and on the Globally Harmonized System of Classification and Labelling of Chemicals.

The report stated that the Committee had adopted amendments to the eleventh revised edition of the *Recommendations on the Transport of Dangerous Goods: Model Regulations* and the third revised edition of the *Recommendations on the Transport of Dangerous Goods: Manual of Tests and Criteria*, published by the secretariat in accordance with resolution 1999/62. Those amendments concerned packaging and tank provisions; listing and classification; new provisions for carriage in bulk in tanks; and new provisions for construction, testing and approval of gas receptacles and multiple-element gas containers. All main legal instruments or codes governing the international transport of dangerous goods were amended, with effect from 1 July 2001, and many Governments transposed the provisions of the *Model Regulations* into their own legislation for domestic traffic for application as from 2001.

The Committee adopted a programme of work for the biennium 2001-2002, and continued to contribute to the development of a globally harmonized system of classification and labelling of chemicals in cooperation with other organizations, in particular the International Labour Organization (ILO) and OECD. It recommended a draft resolution on its work for adoption by the Council (see below).

In 2001, in accordance with resolution 1999/65, the Committee's two subsidiary bodies held two sessions each, in Geneva: the Subcommittee of Experts on the Transport of Dangerous Goods held its nineteenth (2-6 July) [ST/SG/AC.10/C.3/38] and twentieth (3-11 December) [ST/SG/AC.10/C.3/40 & Add.1,2] sessions; the Subcommittee of Experts on the Globally Harmonized System of Classification and Labelling of Chemicals held its first (9-11 July) [ST/SG/AC.10/

C.4/2] and second (12-14 December) [ST/SG/AC.10/ C.4/4] sessions.

ECONOMIC AND SOCIAL COUNCIL ACTION

On 26 July [meeting 43], the Economic and Social Council adopted **resolution 2001/34** [draft: proposed orally] without vote [agenda item 13 (*g*)].

Report of the Secretary-General on the work of the Committee of Experts on the Transport of Dangerous Goods and on the Globally Harmonized System of Classification and Labelling of Chemicals

The Economic and Social Council,

Having considered the report of the Secretary-General on the work of the Committee of Experts on the Transport of Dangerous Goods and on the Globally Harmonized System of Classification and Labelling of Chemicals during the biennium 1999-2000,

1. *Expresses its appreciation* for the work of the Committee of Experts on the Transport of Dangerous Goods and on the Globally Harmonized System of Classification and Labelling of Chemicals;

2. *Decides* to approve the programme of work of the Committee for the biennium 2001-2002 as contained in paragraph 31 of the report of the Secretary-General;

3. *Urges* the Secretary-General to publish the eleventh revised edition of the *Recommendations on the Transport of Dangerous Goods: Model Regulations* in Arabic, as well as the third revised edition of the *Recommendations on the Transport of Dangerous Goods: Manual of Tests and Criteria* in Arabic, French and Spanish, without delay;

4. *Requests* the Secretary-General:

(*a*) To circulate the new and amended recommendations to the Governments of member States, the specialized agencies, the International Atomic Energy Agency and other international organizations concerned;

(*b*) To publish the twelfth revised edition of the *Recommendations on the Transport of Dangerous Goods: Model Regulations,* and amendments to the third revised edition of the *Recommendations on the Transport of Dangerous Goods: Manual of Tests and Criteria* in all the official languages of the United Nations, in the most cost-effective manner, not later than the end of 2001;

(*c*) To give further consideration to the possibility of publishing the *Recommendations on the Transport of Dangerous Goods* on CD-ROM, if possible as a navigable version, for example, by commercial arrangement with external contractors;

5. *Decides* to defer further consideration of the report of the Secretary-General to its resumed substantive session of 2001.

On 20 December [meeting 46], the Council adopted **resolution 2001/44** [draft: E/2001/L.52] without vote [agenda item 13 (*g*)].

Work of the Committee of Experts on the Transport of Dangerous Goods and on the Globally Harmonized System of Classification and Labelling of Chemicals

The Economic and Social Council,

Recalling its resolution 2001/34 of 26 July 2001,

1. *Takes note* of the report of the Secretary-General on the work of the Committee of Experts on the Transport of Dangerous Goods and on the Globally Harmonized System of Classification and Labelling of Chemicals during the biennium 1999-2000, in particular regarding the adoption of new and amended provisions for inclusion in the eleventh revised edition of the *Recommendations on the Transport of Dangerous Goods: Model Regulations* and in the third revised edition of the *Recommendations on the Transport of Dangerous Goods: Manual of Tests and Criteria;*

2. *Invites* all Governments, the specialized agencies, the International Atomic Energy Agency and other international organizations concerned to transmit to the secretariat of the Committee their views on the work of the Committee, together with any comments that they may wish to make on the amended recommendations;

3. *Invites* all interested Governments, the regional commissions, the specialized agencies and international organizations concerned, when developing or updating appropriate codes and regulations, to consider taking into account the recommendations of the Committee;

4. *Requests* the Secretary-General to submit a report to it in 2003 on the implementation of its resolution 2001/34 and the present resolution.

UNCTAD institutional and organizational questions

UNCTAD programme

In 2001, the Trade and Development Board (TDB)—the executive body of UNCTAD—held three sessions, all in Geneva: the twenty-sixth (10 April) and twenty-seventh (19 July) executive sessions and the forty-eighth regular session (1-12 October) [A/56/15]. In April, the Board took note of the reports of its subsidiary bodies; reviewed experience in implementing the recommendations on improving the functioning and the structure of the intergovernmental machinery of UNCTAD; and considered a progress report on the preparatory process for LDC-III (see p. 770). In July, TDB considered UNCTAD's contribution to the implementation of the United Nations New Agenda for the Development of Africa in the 1990s (NADAF) (see p. 849); the report of the Working Party on the Medium-term Plan and the Programme Budget on its thirty-seventh session (see p. 895); and the report of the Joint Advisory Group on ITC on its thirty-fourth session (see p. 877). In October, the Board adopted a decision on the Programme of Action for LDCs for the Decade 2001-2010 [dec. 467(XLVIII)] (see p. 771) and agreed conclusions on UNCTAD's contribution to the final review and appraisal of the implementation of NADAF: economic development in Africa: performance, prospects and policy issues [agreed conclusions 468(XLVIII)] (see p. 849). It also adopted a decision on UNCTAD's technical cooperation activities and their financing [dec. 469(XLVIII)] (see below) and took action on the preparatory process for the 2002 midterm review of UNCTAD X (see p. 896).

Technical cooperation

In a July report [TD/B/48/5 & Add.1,2], the UNCTAD Secretary-General provided an overview of technical cooperation activities in 2000, noting that the main features were the emphasis on capacity-building; closer interaction with research and deliberative work; a continuation of focus on LDCs; and an increased level of contributions. UNCTAD's expenditures amounted to $24.1 million in 2000, a small decrease from the previous year, which was attributable to a decreased level of expenditures in Europe due to completion of a number of projects. Of that amount, $5.8 million was financed by UNDP, $15.8 million was from trust fund contributions and $2.5 million was from the programme budget.

By region, approximately $5.2 million went to Africa, $4.5 million to Asia and the Pacific, $1.4 million to Latin America and the Caribbean, $0.8 million to Europe and $12.2 million went to the interregional programme. The LDCs' share of technical cooperation expenditures in 2000 amounted to 43 per cent, up from 40 per cent in 1999.

By programme, the Division for Services Infrastructure for Development and Trade Efficiency accounted for 40.2 per cent of total expenditures. The Divisions on International Trade in Goods and Services, and Commodities, on Globalization and Development Strategies, and on Investment, Technology and Enterprise Development represented, respectively, 17.6, 9.7 and 13.7 per cent of total expenditures. The balance (18.7 per cent) was represented by the Office of the Special Coordinator for Least Developed, Landlocked and Island Developing Countries (10.1 per cent) and by activities reported for the secretariat as a whole (8.6 per cent).

As requested in the Plan of Action [TD/386] adopted at UNCTAD X [YUN 2000, p. 890], the UNCTAD secretariat, in an August note [TD/B/48/8 & Add.1], submitted the indicative plan of technical cooperation programmes for 2002, including information on: ongoing projects expected to continue in 2002; projects proposed by the secretariat to implement the mandates of UNCTAD X and LDC-III and mandates given to UNCTAD by the General Assembly; and projects proposed as a result of specific requests received from beneficiaries. All projects included in the plan placed emphasis on capacity-building, in accordance with paragraph 166 of the Plan of Action.

In an October decision [A/56/15 (dec. 469 (XLVIII)], TDB requested the UNCTAD secretariat to continue to work on consolidation and clustering of technical cooperation activities and, in combined international efforts, to assist developing countries to derive full benefits from trade and reduce poverty through mainstreaming trade into development strategies and enhanced partnership with other agencies involved in delivering trade-related technical assistance, especially for LDCs. It invited bilateral and multilateral donors to consider increasing their contributions to UNCTAD trust funds for developing countries, particularly in favour of Africa, and called for further geographical diversification of consultants and experts. TDB requested that comments made by the Working Party at its thirty-eighth session (see below) be taken into account in the preparation of future reports on technical cooperation activities.

Evaluations

A July progress report on the implementation of the three-year Trade Point Programme Strategy [TD/B/WP/143], approved in 1999 [YUN 1999, p. 911], stated that further progress had been achieved in the gradual externalization of the Programme, including by building capacities and structures in the Trade Point community that would enable them to take over the Trade Point Programme and transferring the Electronic Trading Opportunities (ETO) system to a non-profit entity. The World Trade Point Federation was formally created and was in the process of defining its future directions, and extrabudgetary funding was made available for the preparation of a business development plan aimed at facilitating that task.

In July, an independent evaluation team submitted an evaluation of the Trainmar programme [TD/B/WP/144], which was in its twenty-second year. The evaluation stated that, although the Trainmar methodology of course design and delivery was sound, it failed to take into account modern developments in pedagogic technology and the flexibility required by changes in the organization of international commerce and supply chain management, and by the differences in the development of the various parts of the network. Most of the courses were outdated and the basic curriculum needed restructuring. Effective implementation would depend on multidisciplinary support of the programme in maritime transport, global logistics and commerce. After more than 20 years, programme implementation had little managerial foundation and the recommendations that followed from previous reviews had been implemented only to a limited extent. Moreover, there was overlap of purpose and contents between Trainmar and other UNCTAD training programmes, as well as with those of other organizations. The evaluation team saw no prospects for effective UNCTAD management and support of the Trainmar network as a stand-alone programme, but saw possibilities for merging certain Trainmar components with other UNCTAD capacity-building programmes.

With regard to the 2000 in-depth evaluation of the EMPRETEC programme [YUN 2000, p. 920], a July UNCTAD secretariat report [TD/B/WP/145] stated that, although most of the recommendations had been implemented, limited financial resources were a key factor in determining the gradual implementation of the remaining ones. Most of the resources came from savings and the regular budget, and the availability of extrabudgetary resources was of vital importance in that regard. The Programming, Planning and Assessment Unit of UNCTAD had facilitated the identification of in-house technical solutions and encouraged cooperation among divisions within UNCTAD. All national EMPRETEC centres had offered support to the process.

Medium-term plan and programme budget

The UNCTAD Working Party on the Medium-term Plan and the Programme Budget held two sessions in 2001, both in Geneva.

At the first part of its thirty-seventh session (15-19 January) [TD/B/48/2], the Working Party reviewed the draft programme budget for the 2002-2003 biennium [UNCTAD/EDM/Misc.148/Rev.1]. In agreed conclusions, it concurred with the amended text and recommended that the subprogramme on LDCs, landlocked developing countries and small island developing States be reviewed in the light of the outcome of LDC-III (see p. 770) and decided to reconvene for that purpose. It reiterated the need for the subprogramme on the development of Africa to develop its analytical capacity in line with the provisions of the UNCTAD X Plan of Action, and recommended that appropriate resources be devoted to that area. With regard to the follow-up to the implementation of paragraph 166 of the UNCTAD X Plan of Action, which dealt with the strengthening of UNCTAD's capacity-building programmes, the Working Party welcomed the presentation of the detailed costed proposals for training courses [TD/B/WP/137] and recommended that UNCTAD implement a pilot phase of the training programme in a timely manner. It urged the UNCTAD Secretary-General to maximize synergies existing in the secretariat for the implementation

of paragraph 166. The Working Party welcomed the decision to establish the Debt Management and Financial Analysis System (DMFAS) Trust Fund and took note of the UNCTAD secretariat report on the subject [TD/B/WP/136]. It urged the secretariat to prepare a detailed project document on the funding of the Trust Fund, and recommended that the UNCTAD Secretary-General organize the second DMFAS Advisory Group meeting in June and report thereon to the Working Party.

At its resumed thirty-seventh session (11-12 June) [TD/B/48/7], the Working Party reviewed the draft programme budget for the 2002-2003 biennium [A/56/6 (Sect. 11A)] and concurred with the programmatic content of the section on trade and development, which took into account comments made by the Party at its January session. In agreed conclusions, the Working Party emphasized UNCTAD's role in the implementation of the Programme of Action for LDCs for the Decade 2001-2010 (see p. 770). It decided to review at a resumed thirty-eighth session the impact on the system-wide coordination aspects of the General Assembly's decisions, based on recommendations to be made by the UN Secretary-General to its fifty-sixth session, for a follow-up mechanism for the implementation of the Programme of Action. The Working Party invited the UNCTAD Secretary-General to explore further possibilities for financing the participation of experts from developing countries and economies in transition in UNCTAD expert meetings.

In July [A/56/15], TDB endorsed the report of the Working Party on its thirty-seventh session and its agreed conclusions on the draft programme budget for the 2002-2003 biennium.

At its thirty-eighth session (17-20 September) [TD/B/48/19], the Working Party approved a draft decision for adoption by TDB on the evaluation of technical cooperation activities (see p. 894). It stressed the importance of in-depth evaluations and follow-up action on the recommendations arising from them, and encouraged the UNCTAD secretariat to pay attention to the process and explore ways to foresee financing for in-depth evaluations of technical cooperation programmes. It welcomed the in-depth evaluation of the Trainmar programme [TD/B/WP/144], urged the UNCTAD Secretary-General to implement its recommendations and took note of progress made in the implementation of the Trade Point Programme Strategy [TD/B/WP/143] and the EMPRETEC programme [TD/B/WP/145].

In other action, the Working Party took note of the UNCTAD secretariat note on financing the participation of experts from developing countries and economies in transition in UNCTAD intergovernmental expert meetings [TD/B/WP/146], which covered the period from 1 January 1999 to 31 July 2001.

In October [A/56/15], TDB endorsed the outcome of the thirty-eighth session of the Working Party and adopted the decision on technical cooperation activities (see p. 894).

Midterm review (2002)

At its forty-eighth session in October [A/56/15], TDB considered the preparatory process for the midterm review of the work of UNCTAD, to be held in the second quarter of 2002, midway between UNCTAD X [YUN 2000, p. 890] and UNCTAD XI (2005). The Board endorsed Thailand's offer to host the midterm review in Bangkok and approved the basic modalities of the review process, namely: a review of the efficiency and functioning of the intergovernmental machinery; stocktaking in respect of the implementation of the commitments and work programme agreed to in the Bangkok Plan of Action [ibid., p. 891]; and interactive debates and policy dialogue in the context of opportunities and challenges of new policy developments since UNCTAD X. The Board also agreed on a number of procedures for the preparatory process.

Chapter V

Regional economic and social activities

The five regional commissions continued to provide technical cooperation, including advisory services, to their member States, promote programmes and projects, and provide training to enhance national capacity-building in various sectors. Four of them held regular sessions during the year: the Economic Commission for Africa (ECA), the Economic Commission for Europe (ECE), the Economic and Social Commission for Asia and the Pacific (ESCAP) and the Economic and Social Commission for Western Asia (ESCWA). The Economic Commission for Latin America and the Caribbean (ECLAC) did not meet in 2001 but was scheduled to meet in May 2002.

In 2001, ECA took the lead in promoting an African-developed and -led programme for development, which was adopted by African heads of State and Government as the New Partnership for Africa's Development, designed to eradicate poverty and to place African countries on a path of sustainable growth and development. The General Assembly endorsed the Partnership and called on the international community to provide financial support for its implementation. It also reviewed implementation of the programme for the Second Industrial Decade for Africa (1993-2002).

The Assembly recommended the promotion of further cooperation between the United Nations and a number of regional organizations. The Economic and Social Council established the Consultative Committee on Scientific and Technological Development and Technological Innovation of ESCWA, and further encouraged the investigation into a Europe-Africa permanent link through the Strait of Gibraltar.

Regional cooperation

Efforts continued in 2001 to improve cooperation among the United Nations regional commissions and between them and other UN entities, and with regional and international organizations.

On 3 May (**decision 2001/211**), the Economic and Social Council decided that the theme of its 2001 substantive session for the item on regional cooperation would be "Regional perspective on globalization: an opportunity for catching up or a risk of falling behind in the development process".

Meeting of executive secretaries. The executive secretaries of the regional commissions met from 12 to 14 February and on 21 November in New York, and from 18 to 20 July in Geneva.

At their February 2001 meeting and meetings held in the latter half of 2000 [YUN 2000, p. 923], they exchanged views on globalization and other development issues relating to their respective regions; areas of cooperation among the commissions; and their relationships with other relevant partners within and outside the United Nations system. The executive secretaries reviewed the commissions' input and participation in the common country assessment/United Nations Development Assistance Framework (CCA/UNDAF) process, and the strengthening of the relationship between the commissions and relevant regional and subregional organizations working in peace-building in their respective regions. The executive secretaries also reviewed preparations for follow-up to the implementation of the Millennium Declaration [YUN 2000, p. 49], and agreed on a common approach regarding their inputs to the Secretary-General's report to the General Assembly's fifty-sixth session on that issue (see p. 1278). They underlined the need for follow-up action on issues relating to financing for development and on others that emerged from the regional consultative meetings organized by the commissions.

The executive secretaries noted that, despite disparities between and within regions, some salient features had emerged in the five regional consultations organized by the regional commissions in 2000, and the updated report on those issues should be utilized as input to the International Conference on Financing for Development in 2002 (see p. 886).

Review and reform of the regional commissions

Reports of Secretary-General. In a May report [E/2001/18], the Secretary-General outlined steps taken by the regional commissions to implement the guidance given in Economic and Social Council resolution 1998/46 [YUN 1998, p. 1262] with respect to their dual role as UN outposts and the regional expression of the Organization. The report also discussed interregional cooperation, including regional perspectives on globalization; further measures undertaken by the commissions to achieve greater effectiveness; and the report on meetings of the executive secretaries (see p. 897).

In an addendum to his report [E/2001/18/Add.1], the Secretary-General reviewed regional follow-up to world conferences and other global meetings. A second addendum examined cooperation with other regional bodies [E/2001/18/Add.2], and, in a third addendum, the Secretary-General submitted resolutions and decisions adopted at recent sessions of the regional commissions calling for action by the Council [E/2001/18/Add.3 & Corr.1].

By **decision 2001/306** of 26 July, the Council took note of the Secretary-General's reports on regional cooperation (see above) and the summaries of the economic and social situation in Africa, 2000 [E/2001/13]; the economic and social survey of Asia and the Pacific, 2001 [E/2001/14]; the economic survey of Europe, 2000 [E/2001/12]; the economic survey of Latin America and the Caribbean, 2000 [E/2001/15]; and the survey of economic and social developments in the ESCWA region, 2000-2001 [E/2001/16].

The Council also adopted resolutions on the proposed Europe-Africa permanent link through the Strait of Gibraltar (resolution 2001/29), and on the establishment of the Consultative Committee on Scientific and Technological Development and Technological Innovation of ESCWA (resolution 2001/30).

(Summaries of the surveys and the texts of the resolutions are found in the relevant sections of this chapter.)

Africa

The Economic Commission for Africa (ECA) held its thirty-fourth session/twenty-fifth meeting of the Conference of Ministers/ninth session of the Conference of African Ministers of Finance (Algiers, Algeria, 8-10 May) [E/2001/38].

The Conference considered the implementation of the Millennium Partnership for the African Recovery Programme and the Omega Plan (see p. 900); mobilizing resources for a major response to AIDS in Africa; and the second United Nations Development Programme (UNDP) regional cooperation framework. It also discussed the special thematic issues of economic governance and attracting foreign investment to Africa.

The Conference was preceded by the twentieth meeting of the Technical Preparatory Committee of the Whole/ninth meeting of the Intergovernmental Group of Experts (Algiers, 2-7 May), which discussed the items on the Commission's agenda, as well as the promotion of good governance, peace and security; tackling diseases that deepened poverty—HIV/AIDS, malaria and tuberculosis; issues related to financing for development; bridging the digital divide; accelerating regional integration for infrastructure development; external debt issues for highly indebted middle-income and poor countries; transforming partnerships in Africa; and the ECA proposed programme of work and priorities for the 2002-2003 biennium [E/ECA/CM.25/5].

The Conference of Ministers adopted the Technical Preparatory Committee's report as amended [E/ECA/CM.25/7]. It also adopted a draft resolution on the development of an African initiative, which it brought to the attention of the Economic and Social Council.

On 11 December [A/56/708], Japan transmitted to the Secretary-General the Chairman's statement on the ministerial-level meeting of the Tokyo International Conference on African Development (Tokyo, 3-4 December), and, on 13 December [A/56/726-S/2001/1231], Japan and South Africa transmitted a joint communiqué entitled "Japan–South Africa partnership in the new century", issued after a meeting on 2 October between the South African President and the Japanese Prime Minister.

On 9 October [A/56/457], the Sudan transmitted to the Secretary-General the decisions of the Assembly of Heads of State and Government of the Organization of African Unity (OAU) at its thirty-seventh ordinary session (Lusaka, Zambia, 9-11 July), including one on the implementation of the Sirte Declaration establishing the African Union, adopted by the Assembly in 1999 (Sirte, Libyan Arab Jamahiriya, 8-9 September 1999) [YUN 1999, p. 1364]. The decision urged OAU member States to ratify the Constitutive Act before the inaugural session of the African Union, and established a one-year period of transition from OAU to the African Union to allow for the creation of the organs of the Union.

Economic trends

Africa's economy grew at an average 4.3 per cent in 2001, compared to the 2000 figure of 3.5 per cent, according to the ECA summary of the economic and social situation in Africa [E/2002/17]. Some 37 countries achieved gross domestic product (GDP) growth of more than 3 per cent, a significant increase from 26 in 2000, and just 16 experienced GDP growth of less than 3 per cent, compared to 27 in 2000. That performance, achieved amid the turbulence created by the global economic slowdown and the 11 September terrorist attacks in the United States (see p. 60), reflected better macroeconomic management, improvements in agricultural production, higher than expected exports under the United States African Growth and Opportunity Act, which eliminated duties on a range of commodities, especially textiles, lower oil prices, currency devaluation in South Africa and the cessation of conflicts in several countries.

By subregion, Southern Africa's GDP grew by only 2.4 per cent, mainly because of negative growth in Zimbabwe and slower growth in South Africa, reflecting poor harvests, while West Africa's GDP grew by 3.3 per cent and East Africa's by 5 per cent, driven by cheaper oil imports and higher prices for agricultural exports.

Africa's five largest economies (Algeria, Egypt, Morocco, Nigeria, South Africa), which accounted for 59 per cent of African GDP, grew by 4.3 per cent, up from 3.2 per cent in 2000, due to rapid economic growth in Algeria, Egypt and Morocco. Growth in the continent's 11 oil-exporting countries averaged 5.8 per cent, compared to 4.1 per cent in 2000, and among its 42 non-oil exporters, growth averaged 3.7 per cent, up from 2.9 per cent in 2000, due mainly to the lower oil prices.

At the sectoral level, primary commodity prices fell in the first 11 months of 2001, averaging, in September, 17 per cent below their cyclical peak a year earlier. However, the drop in oil prices freed resources for other imports, minimized inflationary and other pressures, and enabled oil exporters to sustain growth.

Export earnings fell by 0.2 per cent in 2001, while higher prices and volume were responsible for a 6.7 per cent increase in import costs. In 2001, Africa's terms of trade fell by 2.1 per cent due to falling oil prices, after having appreciated by 18.1 per cent in 2000. The continent's service balance (foreign freight, insurance and banking services) remained in deficit, falling to $11.4 billion. Its current account deficit also fell, from 4.8 per cent of Africa's GDP in 1998 to 0.9 per cent in 2001.

Africa's average per capita income grew by an estimated 1.9 per cent in 2001—better than the 0.7 per cent increase in 2000 but still not sufficient to achieve the international development goal of cutting poverty in half by 2015. Thirty African countries achieved per capita income growth above 1.5 per cent.

Net private flows to Africa's emerging financial markets—especially in Algeria, Egypt, Morocco, South Africa and Tunisia—nearly doubled, from $4.9 billion in 2000 to $9.5 billion in 2001. Net direct equity grew from $3.5 billion to $4.8 billion, driven by privatizations in Algeria and Morocco, and, despite weakness in global equity markets, net portfolio equity flows increased from $1.7 billion to $4.5 billion. Private credit flows increased slightly, from a net outflow of $400 million in 2000 to an inflow of $200 million in 2001. Emerging market equity prices fell particularly hard after the 11 September attacks in the United States. Except for South Africa's stock exchange, which rose 26 per cent, Africa's emerging equity markets lost value in 2001.

Activities in 2001

ECA activities in 2001 were undertaken through the following subprogrammes: facilitating economic and social policy analysis; fostering sustainable development; strengthening development management; harnessing information for development; promoting regional cooperation and integration; and promoting the advancement of women.

Development policy and regional economic cooperation

African recovery and development

In 2001, ECA undertook activities that contributed to sustainable growth and poverty reduction in Africa through, among other actions, in-depth analysis of development strategy, human resources development, poverty analysis, and assessing and recommending effective anti-poverty policies. It undertook studies on development issues to estimate the resources required for attaining Africa's development goal, measures for enhancing the mobilization of resources, and the relationship between saving and investment rates in a sample of countries.

New Partnership for Africa's Development

The Joint Conference of African Ministers of Finance and Ministers of Economic Development and Planning (Algiers, 8-10 May) considered the ECA document "Compact for African Recovery: operationalizing the Millennium Partnership for the African Recovery Programme (MAP)" [E/ECA/CM.25/2]. MAP, initiated by South African President Thabo Mbeki, Nigerian President Olusegun Obasanjo and Algerian President Abdelaziz Bouteflika, was emerging as the African initiative for development, bringing together all partnership initiatives within a single framework. The Compact for African Recovery, proposed by the Ministers of Finance at their 2000 meeting [YUN 2000, p. 924], would provide technical and analytical support to MAP.

On 10 May, the Conference of Ministers issued a statement setting out its overall vision for Africa's development and adopted a resolution [E/2001/38 (res. 837(XXXIV))] recognizing the MAP initiative; the Omega Plan, a proposal by Senegalese President Abdoulaye Wade to develop physical capital and human capital for sustained growth; and the Compact for African Recovery. The Conference resolved that the two initiatives should be consolidated through a process of consultation involving technical experts of each initiative towards a common vision of Africa's future growth and poverty reduction. It requested ECA to assist in the process by making its resources and expertise available and to draft a single African initiative from that process. It also requested the ECA Executive Secretary to submit the draft programme of the African initiative to the OAU Assembly of Heads of State and Government for review and approval.

Commending the efforts to formulate and consolidate those two initiatives, the OAU Assembly, at its thirty-seventh session (Lusaka, 9-11 July) [A/56/457], adopted the Strategic Policy Framework and the New African Initiative, as well as its Programme of Action. It decided to present the Initiative to the UN General Assembly for endorsement and to convene a summit with international economic and financial institutions, as well as the private sector (Dakar, Senegal, 15-17 November), to consider the financing of the Initiative. It established a follow-up committee consisting of 15 heads of State to ensure continuous follow-up, particularly the establishment of management institutions.

The Economic and Social Council, on 18 July [A/56/3/Rev.1], following consideration of the item "The role of the United Nations in supporting the efforts of African countries to achieve sustainable development" at the high-level segment of its 2001 substantive session, adopted a ministerial declaration in which it welcomed the efforts of African leaders to develop an African-owned and -led framework for action towards the continent's sustainable development, and called on the UN system and the international community to support the New African Initiative adopted by OAU. It invited the Secretary-General to ensure an effective and coordinated UN system response and acknowledged the call by African heads of State for a special session of the General Assembly to consider the best way of supporting the Initiative.

The Assembly, in **resolution 56/218** of 21 December (see p. 850), decided to hold a high-level plenary meeting on 16 September 2002 to consider how to support the Initiative, renamed the New Partnership for Africa's Development, and, in **resolution 56/207** of the same date (see p. 754), called on the developed countries and the UN system to support it and complement Africa's efforts to overcome the challenges it faced.

In related developments, the Summit of Heads of State and Government of the Group of Eight industrialized countries (Genoa, Italy, 20-22 July) [A/56/222-S/2001/736] adopted the Genoa Plan for Africa, designed to forge a new partnership to address African development issues, support the key themes of the New Partnership for Africa's Development and develop a plan of action.

Information technology

ECA efforts in information and communication technology (ICT) were focused on raising the awareness of member States to the realities of the information society and how to use ICT to build the competitiveness of national economies and enhance human development by assisting member States in developing their national information and communication infrastructure and plans.

ECA organized the annual meeting of the African Technical Advisory Committee of the African Information Society Initiative (Addis Ababa, Ethiopia, 11-12 May) and the meeting of Partners for Information and Communication Technologies in Africa (Addis Ababa, 7-8 September) to discuss strategies to accelerate African development through increased ICT use. The Information Technology Centre for Africa was at the forefront of building skills and capacity for the information age through workshops and training programmes. It organized a workshop on the use of ICTs by small and medium-sized enterprises (Addis Ababa, September) and national information and communications infrastructure workshops for Southern (Windhoek, Namibia, 11-14 April) and East (Addis Ababa, 19-21 June) Africa. ECA forged closer collaboration with key international development agencies and provided advisory services to countries and regional economic bodies and institutions in Africa. It emphasized strengthening the statistical infrastructure and the capacity for collecting, processing, analysing and disseminating data in Africa. Member States were made aware of new technologies for database development and data dissemination for decision-making.

ECA implemented a fully integrated library and technical information system. The second meeting of the Committee on Development Information (Addis Ababa, 4-7 September) mandated ECA to develop the African Virtual Library and Information Network as a platform for sharing development information and knowledge. Its main objective was to help bridge the digital divide between Africa and the developed world by focusing on capacity-building at the institutional, national and regional levels.

Transportation and communications

ECA's secretariat carried out a number of activities to develop transport and communications infrastructure and services, with the aim of promoting an efficient, safe, reliable and affordable transport and communications system in Africa. A workshop on implementation of air services liberalization policies in the West and Central Africa subregions (Bamako, Mali, 12-14 March) discussed implementation of the Yamoussoukro Declaration on a new air transport policy [YUN 1988, p. 273]. The meeting adopted an action plan based on the legal framework and institutions, economic regulation and financing of the sector. A publication was released in March on best practices in developing rural transport policies that took into account the empowerment of women. In February, a report was published on measuring the impact of the gradual liberalization of traffic rights on the air transport industry within the Common Market for Eastern and Southern Africa region. A study on the status of the Trans-East African Highway was published in June with the objective of revitalizing the highway network and the missing links that would play a role in developing intergovernmental road infrastructure and promote economic cooperation.

Europe-Africa permanent link

The ECA and ECE Executive Secretaries, in their April report on a Europe-Africa permanent link through the Strait of Gibraltar [E/2001/19], submitted by the Secretary-General pursuant to Economic and Social Council resolution 1999/37 [YUN 1999, p. 918], stated that the study "Evaluation of technological approaches to offshore geological coring in the Strait of Gibraltar", intended to compare drilling techniques, was completed in February. It favoured the "vessel with dynamic positioning" option as being more technically feasible, safer and more economical. The study confirmed the directive of the Joint Committee for the project concerning the technological approach to the drilling, and allowed research companies to prepare a new work plan for the resumption of investigations.

ECONOMIC AND SOCIAL COUNCIL ACTION

On 26 July [meeting 43], the Economic and Social Council adopted **resolution 2001/29** [draft: E/2001/L.15/Rev.1] without vote [agenda item 10].

Europe-Africa permanent link through the Strait of Gibraltar

The Economic and Social Council,

Recalling its resolutions 1982/57 of 30 July 1982, 1983/62 of 29 July 1983, 1984/75 of 27 July 1984, 1985/70 of 26 July 1985, 1987/69 of 8 July 1987, 1989/119 of 28 July 1989, 1991/74 of 26 July 1991, 1993/60 of 30 July 1993, 1995/48 of 27 July 1995, 1997/48 of 22 July 1997 and 1999/37 of 28 July 1999,

Referring to resolution 912(1989) adopted on 1 February 1989 by the Parliamentary Assembly of the Council of Europe regarding measures to encourage the construction of a major traffic artery in southwestern Europe and to study thoroughly the possibility of a permanent link through the Strait of Gibraltar,

Referring also to the Barcelona Declaration adopted at the Euro-Mediterranean Conference, held in Barcelona, Spain, in November 1995, and to the work programme annexed thereto, aimed at connecting the Mediterranean transport networks to the trans-European transport network so as to ensure their interoperability,

Referring further to the Lisbon Declaration adopted at the Conference on Transport in the Mediterranean, held at Lisbon in January 1997, and to the conclusions of the Pan-European Transport Conference, held at Helsinki in June 1997, on corridors in the Mediterranean incorporating the permanent link,

Taking note of the follow-up report prepared jointly by the Economic Commission for Africa and the Economic Commission for Europe, in accordance with resolution 1999/37,

Taking note also of the conclusions of the second and third meetings of the Western Mediterranean Transport Group, held at Rabat in September 1995 and at Madrid in January 1997, respectively, and of the conclusions of the study on transport infrastructure in the western Mediterranean, which included the permanent link among the priority corridors in the extension of the trans-European network,

1. *Welcomes* the cooperation on the project for the link through the Strait of Gibraltar established between the Economic Commission for Africa, the Economic Commission for Europe, the Governments of Morocco and Spain and specialized international organizations;

2. *Also welcomes* the organization by the International Tunnelling Association, under the auspices of the Economic Commission for Africa and the Economic Commission for Europe, of the seminar held at Rabat in April 1999 on the modelling of tunnel costs;

3. *Further welcomes* the progress achieved with project studies, especially the deep-sea drilling work, which has provided a decisive impetus to geological and geotechnical knowledge of undersea formations;

4. *Commends* the Economic Commission for Africa and the Economic Commission for Europe on the work done in preparing the project follow-up report requested by the Council in its resolution 1999/37;

5. *Renews its invitation* to the competent organizations of the United Nations system and to non-

governmental organizations, in particular the International Tunnelling Association and the International Union of Railways, to participate in the studies and work on the permanent link through the Strait of Gibraltar;

6. *Also renews its invitation* to the European Commission to consider the possibility of participating in the consolidation of the studies and the development of the project, both institutionally and financially, within the framework of the Euro-Mediterranean transport cooperation being developed under the Barcelona process;

7. *Requests* the Executive Secretaries of the Economic Commission for Africa and the Economic Commission for Europe to continue to take an active part in the follow-up to the project and to report to the Council at its substantive session of 2003;

8. *Requests* the Secretary-General to provide formal support and, to the extent that priorities permit, the resources necessary, within the regular budget, to the Economic Commission for Africa and the Economic Commission for Europe, to enable them to carry out the activities mentioned above.

Industrial development

Second Industrial Development Decade

In response to General Assembly resolution 54/203 [YUN 1999, p. 919], the Secretary-General submitted a July report on the implementation of the programme for the Second Industrial Decade for Africa (1993-2002) (IDDA-II) [A/56/139], endorsed by the Economic and Social Council in resolution 1992/44 [YUN 1992, p. 468]. The report examined economic and industrial development trends in Africa, including major challenges, and support programmes for implementing the programme for the Decade, including those implemented by the United Nations Industrial Development Organization (UNIDO).

The Secretary-General said that the programme for IDDA-II, due to end on 31 December 2002, was falling short of expectations. Given the underdeveloped state of industry in Africa, combined with the heavy debt burden facing the majority of African countries, UN system support for Africa's industrialization was still needed. The entire process by which the first Decade was prepared, implemented and evaluated needed to be reviewed, and a process identified that could easily be adapted to major policy shifts.

The first step in industrializing Africa was to strengthen its private sector. That could be achieved by finding an appropriate and constructive nexus between the State, industry and business, civil society organizations and individuals; investing heavily in education and other human resources development, particularly targeted areas of science and technology; motivating industrial entrepreneurs and minimizing start-up costs by providing economic and physical infrastructure to facilitate the mobility of production factors, goods and services; improving access by African entrepreneurs and small and medium-scale enterprises to financing by promoting and harnessing internal investment resources, especially domestic savings, and new sources of financing, such as pension funds; putting in place mechanisms to attract foreign direct investment; and developing national and subregional capital markets.

The Secretary-General concluded that economic development and industrialization in Africa should take into account the need for subregional and regional cooperation in all sectors of development. African Governments should therefore establish new and/or strengthen existing subregional and regional structures to lay the foundation for economic and industrial cooperation and integration.

Conference of African Ministers of Industry. The fifteenth meeting of the Conference of African Ministers of Industry (Yaoundé, Cameroon, 20-30 October) [A/57/175], organized by ECA and OAU, called upon African States: to implement sound macroeconomic policies and sectoral programmes to encourage competitiveness and good governance; to continue in 2002 to establish Industrial Partnership Councils as a platform for dialogue and cooperation between Governments and the private sector; and to formulate under their auspices national long- and medium-term industrial development plans. In addition, the Conference addressed a number of recommendations to UNIDO, and mandated the executive heads of ECA, OAU and UNIDO, in cooperation with other agencies, to pursue the relevant objectives set out in the New Partnership for Africa's Development (see p. 899). It was also decided to proceed, under the auspices of the Conference, ECA and UNIDO, with subregional meetings in Africa to come up with new regional development policies and strategies.

GENERAL ASSEMBLY ACTION

On 21 December [meeting 90], the General Assembly, on the recommendation of the Second (Economic and Financial) Committee [A/56/559], adopted **resolution 56/187** without vote [agenda item 96 (b)].

Second Industrial Development Decade for Africa (1993-2002)

The General Assembly,

Recalling the United Nations Millennium Declaration, the outcomes of major United Nations conferences and summits, the United Nations New Agenda for the Development of Africa in the 1990s and its resolutions 54/203 of 22 December 1999, 55/187 of 20 December 2000 and 55/216 of 21 December 2000,

Recalling also Economic and Social Council decision 1999/270 of 28 July 1999 concerning the implementation and coordinated follow-up by the United Nations system of initiatives on African development, and taking note of the ministerial declaration of the high-level segment of the substantive session of 2001 of the Economic and Social Council on the role of the United Nations in support of the efforts of African countries to achieve sustainable development, adopted on 18 July 2001,

Taking note of the Plan of Action of the Alliance for Africa's Industrialization, adopted by the Conference of African Ministers of Industry at its thirteenth meeting, held at Accra in May 1997, the outcome of the Conference on Industrial Partnerships and Investment in Africa, held at Dakar on 20 and 21 October 1999, and the outcome of the fifteenth meeting of the Conference of African Ministers of Industry, held at Yaoundé on 29 and 30 October 2001,

Taking note also of the statement of the Conference of African Ministers of Trade, held at Abuja in September 2001, to the Fourth Ministerial Conference of the World Trade Organization, and recalling resolution 2(XIV) on the African common position on globalization, adopted by the fourteenth meeting of the Conference of African Ministers of Industry, held at Dakar on 22 and 23 October 1999, both of which recognize the critical need for support for African countries in addressing the supply-side constraints on their integration into the world economy,

Welcoming the New Partnership for Africa's Development, which is a pledge by African leaders, based on a common vision and a firm and shared conviction, that they have a pressing duty to eradicate poverty and to place their countries, both individually and collectively, on a path of sustainable growth and development and at the same time to participate actively in the world economy and body politic, bearing in mind that the Partnership is anchored in the determination of Africans to extricate themselves and the continent from the malaise of underdevelopment and exclusion in a globalizing world, and urging that further steps be taken to operationalize it,

Recognizing the importance of industrialization as a key element in promoting sustained economic growth and sustainable development in Africa and its role in facilitating efforts to eradicate poverty, inter alia, through the enhancement of agro-based industries, the promotion of competitiveness, productive employment, capacity-building, gender mainstreaming and the empowerment of women and effective and efficient management systems,

Recognizing also the commendable efforts of African countries to engage their respective private sectors and civil society in policy dialogue at the highest levels and the need to continue such efforts to improve further the capacity of the private sector, including micro, small and medium-sized enterprises,

Recognizing further the need for African countries to continue their efforts to create a climate favourable to private sector development and foreign direct investment and the commitment of African countries to using both human and financial resources more efficiently in the process of industrialization, and emphasizing the continuing need for the mobilization of adequate resources through domestic initiatives and international support, inter alia, through enhanced official development assistance, investment guarantees, debt relief, as appropriate, and enhanced market access,

Recognizing the opportunities for and challenges of exploiting information and communication technologies and e-commerce for the overall industrial development of Africa, and in that regard noting the establishment of the Information and Communication Technologies Task Force,

Welcoming the progress made in the consolidation and programmatic reform of the United Nations Industrial Development Organization, including through the instrument of integrated programmes to promote sustainable industrial development in African countries, and its approach to field activities through joint programming with the United Nations resident coordinator system in the United Nations Development Assistance Framework,

1. *Takes note* of the report of the Secretary-General on the implementation of the programme for the Second Industrial Development Decade for Africa (1993-2002);

2. *Notes with concern* that, despite the Second Industrial Development Decade for Africa, which ends in 2002, little progress has been made in the overall industrialization of the continent and in some countries industrialization has regressed, and in that regard reaffirms the need for continuing domestic and international efforts towards Africa's industrialization;

3. *Reaffirms* the need for the African countries that have not yet done so to integrate the objectives of the Alliance for Africa's Industrialization, as appropriate, into their national plans for the establishment of institutional capacity for monitoring programmes and related projects;

4. *Emphasizes* the need for support for the implementation of the sectoral priorities in the New Partnership for Africa's Development concerning diversification of African production and exports, specifically with regard to promotion of the manufacturing sector and agro-based industries and for enhancing productive capacities and enabling African countries to participate more effectively in global trade;

5. *Underlines* the need for national Governments to improve the regulatory and policy environment in which micro, small and medium-sized enterprises operate, inter alia, to facilitate their access to credit and improve transport, energy and communications infrastructures, in order to foster their economic performance and competitiveness, and in that regard invites development partners to provide the appropriate technical assistance;

6. *Invites* the Economic Commission for Africa to work in cooperation with the Information and Communication Technologies Task Force and to play a more active role in the promotion of new information and communication technologies and e-commerce;

7. *Also invites* the Economic Commission for Africa to play a more active role in the development of African micro, small and medium-sized enterprises and industries, in coordination with the United Nations Industrial Development Organization and other United Nations bodies concerned with the development of

such enterprises, paying particular attention to enterprises owned by women and to women entrepreneurs;

8. *Invites* the international community, the World Bank, United Nations funds and programmes, the African Development Bank and other relevant regional institutions, in accordance with their respective mandates, to give full effect to the relevant provisions of the New Partnership for Africa's Development by supporting the implementation of the programme for the Second Industrial Development Decade for Africa and the Plan of Action of the Alliance for Africa's Industrialization, as well as the outcome of the Conference on Industrial Partnerships and Investment in Africa and the outcome of the fifteenth meeting of the Conference of African Ministers of Industry;

9. *Appeals* to the international community, the World Bank, the African Development Bank and United Nations funds and programmes, in accordance with their respective mandates, to support the efforts of the African countries to intensify and expand industrial cooperation among themselves;

10. *Commends* the United Nations Industrial Development Organization for its work related to the provision of technical assistance to African countries, in particular the least developed among them, so as to enhance their capacity to overcome technical barriers to trade in industrial and other products, including improving quality standards to alleviate supply-side constraints, and to promote industrial competitiveness, and calls upon the United Nations Industrial Development Organization to continue to work closely with the World Trade Organization, the United Nations Development Programme, the World Bank, the United Nations Conference on Trade and Development and other relevant multilateral institutions in the provision of technical assistance to African countries, in order to enable them to integrate fully into the world economy;

11. *Calls upon* the international community to support Africa in strengthening its private sector through, in particular, the promotion of investment and exports, the promotion and creation of small and medium-sized enterprises, increased productivity, improved quality assurance and standardization, and financing, and welcomes in that context the trade facilitation initiatives of the United Nations Industrial Development Organization;

12. *Also calls upon* the international community to support the efforts of African countries to enhance the development of their human resources in the fields of health, basic education and vocational and technical training through, inter alia, South-South cooperation utilizing triangular arrangements;

13. *Requests* the Secretary-General to complete a review of the implementation of the programme for the Decade, including identification of lessons learned, before the end of the fifty-sixth session of the General Assembly, with a view to including the outcome of such a review in the overall review and appraisal of the United Nations New Agenda for the Development of Africa in the 1990s and the ongoing processes under the New Partnership for Africa's Development and the establishment of the African Union;

14. *Decides* to include in the provisional agenda of its fifty-seventh session under an item entitled "United Nations New Agenda for the Development of Africa", a sub-item entitled "Implementation of the programme for the Second Industrial Development Decade for Africa";

15. *Requests* the Secretary-General to submit to the General Assembly at its fifty-seventh session a report on the implementation of the present resolution.

Food security and sustainable development

In 2001, ECA's Food Security and Sustainable Development Division promoted better understanding and management of the interrelationships among food security, population and environment sustainability by making information available for decision-making, and through its analytical and operational work aimed at promoting strategies for integrating those issues into development policies and programmes. The Division promoted environmentally sustainable development in Africa, including modern science and technology for food security. It offered policy and advisory services to member States and implemented capacity- and institution-building activities with regard to population, agriculture and the environment.

ECA organized the second meeting of its Committee on Sustainable Development (Addis Ababa, 26-29 November) on the theme "Agricultural intensification: feeding ourselves and sustaining Africa's land resources in the new millennium". The Committee also reviewed the implementation of plans of action emanating from global and regional conferences and other substantive reports.

It requested ECA to develop a mechanism for information exchange and experience sharing, collaborate with African Governments on a pilot project for accelerated agricultural intensification, and establish partnership programmes/agreements with donors and development financing institutions to implement activities emanating from the New Partnership for Africa's Development (see p. 899).

Development management

ECA activities in development management, designed to strengthen good governance, were devoted to public sector management, private sector development and encouraging civil society participation in governance. It organized a sub-regional workshop on the development of codes and indicators to monitor administrative governance (Addis Ababa, April) and the first meeting of the Committee on Industry and Private Sector Development to examine strategies for enhancing the competitiveness of Africa's private sector and to review Africa's industrialization process (Yaoundé, October), and organized or participated in other meetings in support of private sector development. Its African Centre for Civil Society organized jointly with OAU a conference on building partnerships for peace and development in Africa (Addis Ababa, June), which stressed the role of civil society organizations in Africa's development process; and, with the World Bank and the African Development Bank, a workshop on the participation of civil society in the development and implementation of Poverty Reduction Strategy Papers (Addis Ababa, July). Studies were prepared on issues relevant to the development of civil society, and training workshops and seminars were organized for Cameroon, Egypt, Namibia and Senegal to facilitate dialogue and build consensus on the best approaches for broadening participation in governance and development.

On 11 April [A/56/63-E/2001/21], Namibia transmitted to the General Assembly and the Economic and Social Council the texts of the Windhoek Declaration and the Charter for the Public Service in Africa, adopted at the third biennial Pan-African Conference of Ministers of Civil Service (Windhoek, 5-6 February).

Integration of women in development

ECA's mission to promote the advancement of women, conducted through its African Centre for Gender and Development, was devoted to influencing a gender perspective in policies developed and adopted by decision makers at the national, subregional and regional levels on socio-economic development. Towards that end, the Centre's activities included monitoring and evaluation of the Dakar [YUN 1994, p. 696] and Beijing [YUN 1995, p. 1170] Platforms for Action; producing the *African Women's Report* on the development of an African gender and development index; monitoring the status of women through country gender profiles for the 53 African countries; and promoting information and communication outreach.

In November, the Committee on Women and Development endorsed a monitoring and evaluation programme, which was being implemented in partnership with other institutions. One of its aims was building member States' capacity to implement that programme. Other activities to promote women's advancement included building a conceptual framework to support strategies for measuring women's unpaid work and time use, and an analytical framework to provide insight into and ways to measure and integrate that factor into national accounts and budgets; and developing a gender-aware macroeconomic model to demonstrate how gender inequality in national accounts and budgets impacted on women's welfare, growth and pov-

erty reduction. As part of its information and communication programme, the Centre embarked on a plan to make national policies more gender-sensitive. Its advisory services were centred on gender mainstreaming, focusing on gender policy and programme development and capacity-building for gender analysis. Technical advisory services for the economic empowerment of women were also provided to women's non-governmental organizations (NGOs).

Subregional Development Centres

The five Subregional Development Centres, based in Central, East, North, Southern and West Africa, continued to promote regional cooperation and integration through technical support to collective approaches in tackling common developmental problems at the subregional level. They also facilitated networking, information-sharing and the dissemination of ECA policy recommendations and technical publications; engaged in advocacy and capacity-building; and provided technical advisory services. The Centres also collaborated with UNDP and the UN resident coordinator system in implementing UN operational activities.

Programme, administration and organizational questions

ECA reform

The African Ministers of Finance and of Economic Development and Planning, in a statement issued at the end of their Joint Conference (see p. 899), said that the Joint Conferences were useful and appropriate forums and decided that they should be merged and that the new body should meet annually [E/2001/38]. The Ministers called on ECA to schedule the next Joint Conference.

Regional cooperation

Cooperation between the UN and SADC

Responding to General Assembly resolution 54/227 [YUN 1999, p. 923], the Secretary-General, in July [A/56/134 & Add.1], summarized information received from 20 Member States, 23 UN organizations and one regional organization on measures they had taken to cooperate with the Southern African Development Community (SADC).

By **decision 56/443** of 21 December, the General Assembly took note of the Secretary-General's report on cooperation between the United Nations and SADC. It decided to include in the provisional agenda of its fifty-seventh

(2002) session, under the item "Cooperation between the United Nations and regional and other organizations", a sub-item entitled "Cooperation between the United Nations and the Southern African Development Community", and requested the Secretary-General to submit an updated report on the question at that session.

Cooperation between the UN and ECCAS

The Secretary-General, responding to General Assembly resolution 55/22 [YUN 2000, p. 232], submitted an August report [A/56/301] outlining action taken by UN departments, offices, bodies, programmes and agencies to promote cooperation between the United Nations and the Economic Community of Central African States (ECCAS).

GENERAL ASSEMBLY ACTION

On 7 December [meeting 80], the General Assembly adopted **resolution 56/39** [draft: A/56/L.25/Rev.2 & Add.1] without vote [agenda item 21 (*g*)].

Cooperation between the United Nations and the Economic Community of Central African States

The General Assembly,

Recalling its resolutions 55/22 of 10 November 2000 and 55/161 of 12 December 2000 on cooperation between the United Nations and the Economic Community of Central African States,

Bearing in mind the charter establishing the Economic Community of Central African States, by which the Central African countries have agreed to work for the economic development of their subregion, to promote economic cooperation and to establish a Common Market of Central Africa,

Recalling the United Nations Millennium Declaration, adopted on 8 September 2000 by the heads of State and Government at the Millennium Summit of the United Nations, and especially chapter VII thereof,

Noting that, at the ninth regular session of the Economic Community of Central African States, held in Malabo on 24 June 1999, the heads of State and Government of the member States decided to resume the activities of the Community by providing it with sufficient financial and human resources to enable it to become a real tool for the integration of their economies and to foster the development of cooperation between their peoples, with the ultimate aim of making it one of the five pillars of the African Economic Community and of helping Central Africa to meet the challenges of globalization,

Bearing in mind the report of the Secretary-General on the causes of conflict and the promotion of durable peace and sustainable development in Africa,

Welcoming the establishment of the Council for Peace and Security in Central Africa with a view to creating a climate of peace and security in the subregion and strengthening the rule of law essential to its development,

Welcoming also the launching of the activities of the Subregional Centre for Human Rights and Democracy in Central Africa, in accordance with the recommendations of the General Assembly in its resolutions 53/78 A of 4 December 1998 and 54/55 A of 1 December 1999, with a view to strengthening democracy, respect for human rights and the rule of law in the subregion,

Commending the States members of the Economic Community of Central African States for their undertaking to strengthen arrangements for cooperation within the Community,

Noting that, owing to the conflicts, loss of human lives and destruction of the economic and social infrastructure in Central Africa, it is essential to continue and strengthen the recovery programmes in order to restart the economy of the countries of the subregion,

Noting with deep concern the danger of an increase in poverty, in particular in rural areas, due to the conflicts, loss of human lives and destruction of the economic and social infrastructure,

Stressing the need for continued and strengthened recovery programmes in order to restart the economy of the countries of the subregion,

Welcoming the contribution made by the United Nations system to supplement the efforts made at the national and subregional levels with a view to promoting the process of democratization, recovery and development in Central Africa,

Aware of the opportunities and challenges which may result from the process of globalization and liberalization for the economies of the countries of the subregion,

Noting with satisfaction the measures taken by the Economic Community of Central African States to combat the human immunodeficiency virus/acquired immunodeficiency syndrome (HIV/AIDS),

Noting the important contribution of women in the development process,

1. *Takes note* of the report of the Secretary-General on cooperation between the United Nations and the Economic Community of Central African States;

2. *Commends* those States Members of the United Nations and United Nations organs, organizations and agencies which have maintained or strengthened their cooperation with the Economic Community of Central African States or have begun to cooperate with it with a view to achieving peace, security and development;

3. *Invites* those States Members of the United Nations and United Nations organs, organizations and agencies which have not yet established contact or relations with the Economic Community of Central African States to consider doing so;

4. *Welcomes* the financial, technical and material support given to the Economic Community of Central African States by the international community;

5. *Emphasizes* the importance of appropriate cooperation between the United Nations system, including the Bretton Woods institutions, and the Economic Community of Central African States;

6. *Once again requests* the international community to consider seriously increases in its financial, technical and material support to the Economic Community of Central African States to enable it to implement fully its programme of action and to respond to the needs of the subregion for reconstruction and recovery;

7. *Urges* all Member States and the international community to contribute to the efforts of the Economic Community of Central African States to achieve economic integration and development, promote democracy and human rights and consolidate peace and security in Central Africa and to implement the goals, targets and commitment of the United Nations conferences and the United Nations Millennium Declaration, in particular, to strengthen the role of women in the development process;

8. *Welcomes* the reforms which the Economic Community of Central African States is carrying out, in particular the implementation of its programme of action, so that it may be in a better position to tackle the problems of cooperation and regional integration;

9. *Urges* the international community and the United Nations agencies to continue to provide those countries of the Economic Community of Central African States in which a process of national reconstruction is taking place with appropriate assistance to consolidate their efforts towards democratization and the consolidation of the rule of law and to support their national development programmes;

10. *Declares itself convinced* of the importance of well-conceived global development strategies in order to avoid conflicts and disturbances and aware of the value of international cooperation and efforts to restore and maintain peace, and emphasizes that the international community should continue to help those countries which receive refugees to meet the resulting economic, social, humanitarian and environmental challenges;

11. *Urges* the United Nations and the international community to help to strengthen the means existing in the region to ensure that the Economic Community of Central African States has the necessary capacity with regard to prevention, monitoring, early warning and peacekeeping operations;

12. *Invites* the international community to consider supporting the creation of special economic zones and development corridors in the Economic Community of Central African States, with the active participation of the private sector;

13. *Requests* the Secretary-General to continue to enhance contacts with the Economic Community of Central African States, with a view to encouraging and harmonizing cooperation between the United Nations and the Community;

14. *Also requests* the Secretary-General to report to it at its fifty-seventh session on the implementation of the present resolution.

Asia and the Pacific

The Economic and Social Commission for Asia and the Pacific (ESCAP), at its fifty-seventh session (Bangkok, Thailand, 19-25 April) [E/2001/39], had as its theme "Balanced development of urban and rural areas and regions within the countries of Asia and the Pacific". The Commission reviewed regional policy issues, ESCAP management issues, emerging issues and developments at the regional level, and programme planning. It also considered ESCAP's technical cooperation activities and programme and organizational questions.

The Commission decided that the theme of its 2002 session would be "Sustainable social development in a period of rapid globalization: challenges, opportunities and policy options".

Economic trends

According to the summary of the economic and social survey of Asia and the Pacific [E/2002/18], GDP growth declined sharply globally and in the ESCAP region in 2001. The decline, which averaged 3.9 percentage points in the region's developing economies and 2 per cent in the developed countries, was due mainly to a sharp downturn in world trade growth, from 12 per cent in 2000 to 1 per cent in 2001, and was triggered by a decline in information and communication technology (ICT) imports by the United States. The events of 11 September (see p. 60) significantly intensified the downturn. Economies with high trade-to-GDP ratios were especially vulnerable to the downturn in external demand. Of the various subregions, South-East Asia was the most severely affected, experiencing a 4 percentage point reduction in aggregate growth, with Singapore's GDP actually contracting. Viet Nam was a notable exception, maintaining GDP growth of 6.8 per cent. In East and North-East Asia, China remained largely immune to the global slowdown, achieving GDP growth of 7.3 per cent, compared to 8 per cent in 2000. In contrast, the Republic of Korea, Hong Kong, China, and Taiwan Province of China were significantly affected, with the latter two economies sliding into recession. The global slowdown, combined with continuing domestic constraints, impacted negatively on the economies of South and South-West Asia, with the notable exceptions of Bangladesh, whose GDP increased from 5.9 to 6 per cent, and India, with a growth rate of 5.4 per cent. The worst affected were Sri Lanka and Turkey. The Pacific island economies were adversely affected also, though to a lesser extent than the least developed countries (LDCs) of the region.

Policy issues

The global slowdown was expected to have an adverse social impact through higher unemployment and the constrained capacity of Governments to address emerging social problems and alleviate poverty through higher public expenditure. However, there was some leeway available in a number of economies of the region to tackle the emerging issues because of the benign inflationary environment and comfortable external position in the form of current account surpluses and stabilized levels of foreign debt. Against that background, stronger policy initiatives could be taken to enhance growth in the short run and mitigate the effects of the current slowdown in the medium term. However, the varying characteristics of each subregion suggested that policy approaches would need to be more nuanced to reflect the differences between and within the various subregions or within a particular group of countries. At the national level, most Governments would need to implement measures to preserve or enhance the momentum of growth through counter-cyclical fiscal and monetary policies; the latter would take precedence where public debt was already at a high level. Such a policy approach was not without some risk.

At the same time, Governments needed to reiterate their commitment to addressing and reforming the financial and corporate sectors and improving transparency and governance. In trade, it was imperative that countries avoid taking restrictive measures and thus risk a downward spiral in output. Developed countries should accelerate trade liberalization, especially in textiles and agricultural commodities, while developing countries could increase the flow of trade by enhancing trade facilitation.

ESCAP, at its 2001 session, considered a March report on the current economic situation in the region and related policy issues [E/ESCAP/1198]. The Commission stressed the need to continue improving financial and economic surveillance mechanisms, including the establishment of early warning mechanisms. ESCAP should be involved in strengthening those mechanisms and in exploring new, non-traditional modalities to reduce the risks involved in the financial and commodity markets. The region's reform agenda needed to be sustained, including measures to stabilize exchange rates, strengthen stock markets and promote regional trade liberalization. Human resources development was an important strategy for poverty reduction and for enabling the region to address the challenges, and reap the opportunities, of globalization. The Commission recommended that commodity markets be strengthened through further liberalization within the World Trade Organization (WTO) framework. It urged that concerted efforts, particularly in upgrading human resources development in ICT, be directed towards ensuring that the developing countries had affordable access to such technology and opportunities to participate in the new knowledge economy.

Activities in 2001

ESCAP activities in 2001 were carried out under seven thematic subprogrammes: regional economic cooperation; development research and policy analysis; social development; population and rural and urban development; environment and natural resources development; transportation, communications, tourism and infrastructure development; and statistics.

Development policy and regional economic cooperation

The Commission had before it the report of the Committee for Regional Economic Cooperation on its eighth session (Bangkok, 14-16 March) [E/ESCAP/1201]; a secretariat note on emerging issues and developments relevant to the subprogramme on regional economic cooperation [E/ESCAP/1202]; a secretariat note on the implementation of Commission resolution 56/1 [YUN 2000, p. 931] on the Decade of Greater Mekong Subregion Development Cooperation, 2000-2009 [E/ESCAP/1230]; a report on the Asian and Pacific Centre for Transfer of Technology [E/ESCAP/1203] (see p. 910); a report on the Regional Network for Agricultural Engineering and Machinery [E/ESCAP/1204] (see p. 912); and a report on policy issues for the ESCAP region: balanced development of urban and rural areas and regions within the countries of Asia and the Pacific [E/ESCAP/1199].

The Commission endorsed the recommendations, conclusions and decisions of the Committee for Regional Economic Cooperation and urged the secretariat to accord priority to assisting developing countries and countries with economies in transition to integrate more effectively into the multilateral trading system, with particular attention to capacity-building and training for trade negotiations, implementation of WTO agreements, enhanced understanding of WTO accession procedures and the integration of WTO agreements into national legal frameworks. The Commission welcomed the ESCAP/WTO Memorandum of Understanding and their joint training programme on WTO issues. Noting the abuse of anti-dumping and safeguards measures as hidden forms of protectionism, the Commission requested the secretariat to study the implications of protectionism for national economic development. The secretariat was also asked to continue to monitor and analyse the economic recovery process following the 2001 slowdown in world economic growth, so that developing countries could participate more effectively in the globalization process, to assist regional and subregional mechanisms for monitoring cross-border financial flows and to support the application of information technology in small manufacturing companies and businesses.

The Commission adopted a resolution [E/2001/39 (res. 57/5)], in which it noted the report of the Meeting of Eminent Persons ("Friends of the Chair") on the Integration of Asian Developing Countries into the International Trading System (Tehran, Iran, 10-11 March) and requested the Executive Secretary to further assist developing countries and economies in transition in their attempts at national capacity-building for the integration and implementation of multilateral trade agreements through policy advocacy, advisory services and training under the ESCAP/WTO programme.

The Commission also adopted a resolution on regional cooperation in ICTs for development [res. 57/4], in which it identified numerous areas where the Executive Secretary should accord priority assistance to member States in the region to support their work in strengthening regional cooperation in ICTs.

Least developed, landlocked and island developing countries

Special Body on Least Developed and Landlocked Developing Countries

The Commission endorsed the recommendations contained in the report of the Special Body on Least Developed and Landlocked Developing Countries on its fifth session (Bangkok, 20-21 February) [E/ESCAP/1216], which would serve as the regional input to the Third United Nations Conference on the Least Developed Countries (Brussels, Belgium, 14-20 May) (see p. 770). Noting with concern that the development goals of the Programme of Action for the Least Developed Countries for the 1990s [YUN 1990, p. 369] remained largely unmet, the Commission recommended that the new programme of action to be adopted at the May Conference address that issue with a fresh approach to improve economic and social conditions in LDCs.

The Commission asked the secretariat to incorporate the report's recommendations in its work programme, and to prepare a comprehensive results-oriented action plan tailored to the needs of each LDC. It urged the international community to grant LDCs better access to its markets, to provide increased financial and technical assistance and to consider ways to better distribute and enhance its assistance in helping those countries to sustain their development efforts.

The Commission asked the secretariat to implement activities to improve access by island developing countries to international markets, increase their ICT use, enhance their absorptive capacity for major investments and strengthen their institutional capacity, and address issues dealing with the threat of climate change and rising sea level.

Economic and technical cooperation

In 2001, ESCAP received $15.7 million for technical cooperation activities, an increase of 6 per cent over the 2000 figure. Of that amount, $4.7 million came from within the UN system and $11 million from donors and participating developing countries and other intergovernmental organizations and NGOs [E/ESCAP/1255]. Contributions from nine developed donor countries (Australia, Canada, France, Germany, Japan, Netherlands, New Zealand, Norway, Sweden) accounted for 77.2 per cent of the total bilateral assistance received. Japan continued to be the largest bilateral donor, followed by the Netherlands and Germany. Among the developing country members and associate members, China, India and the Republic of Korea were the largest contributors. In addition to cash contributions, donors and developing country members provided 244 work-months of services of experts on a non-reimbursable loan basis. Sixty-two projects, amounting to some $7.2 million, were approved under the programme of work.

Technical cooperation among developing countries

In 2001 [E/ESCAP/1255], the secretariat developed and implemented some 90 promotional programmes of technical cooperation among developing countries and economic cooperation among developing countries (TCDC/ECDC). TCDC activities were concentrated on capacity-building and on increasing TCDC focal points' understanding of the TCDC modality and its benefits to development efforts.

The Commission [E/2001/39] noted the lack of sufficient resources to implement TCDC activities, and urged ESCAP to continue to mobilize extrabudgetary resources from both traditional and non-traditional donors. It also urged that TCDC sensitization workshops and in-country consultations be organized annually to reinforce the TCDC national focal points, update information on TCDC opportunities and facilitate the exchange of TCDC experience and related matters among participating countries.

Transport, communications, tourism and infrastructure development

The Commission endorsed the recommendations of the Committee on Transport, Communications, Tourism and Infrastructure Development on its third session [YUN 2000, p. 934]. It also considered the report [E/ESCAP/1213] on the implementation of the New Delhi Action Plan on Infrastructure Development in Asia and the Pacific [YUN 1995, p. 1012]. The Commission underscored the importance of the commitment and participation of members and associate members for the implementation of the Action Plan, and urged them to provide information on the status of projects under phase I of the Plan. It noted that 61 of 64 phase I projects had been implemented or were being implemented, and asked the secretariat to assist countries in creating an environment conducive to private sector participation in the infrastructure sector. Members and associate members were invited to identify project areas for phase II of the Action Plan and to provide information on national activities so as to facilitate regular review of implementation. The Commission reaffirmed its support for the Asian land transport infrastructure development (ALTID) project and recommended that it be a priority under phase II.

The Commission welcomed the Ministerial Conference on Infrastructure to be held in November (below) as an opportunity to focus on emerging trends in infrastructure development. It requested that priority be given to multimodal transport and logistics to create a better understanding of the industry among government agencies and to enhance the knowledge of logistics service planners and operators. The secretariat was asked to promote the adoption of a harmonized legal framework for the freight-forwarding industry and multimodal transport operations in the region.

The Commission reiterated that priority should be given to tourism in the ESCAP programme, and urged the secretariat to intensify its activities in that sector, including the organization of forums for sharing information on best practices, studies on the development of tourism facilities for persons with disabilities, and the development of community- and village-based tourism.

Ministerial Conference on Infrastructure

The Ministerial Conference on Infrastructure (Seoul, Republic of Korea, 12-17 November) [E/ESCAP/1249] adopted the Seoul Declaration on Infrastructure Development in Asia and the Pacific, including phase II of the regional action programme (2002-2006) of the New Delhi Action Plan. Priority areas of the programme included development and improvement of integrated/intermodal international transport; establishment of working groups on the development of the Asian Highway and the Trans-Asian Railway to facilitate the development of the networks; private sector participation and foreign direct investment in infrastructure development; development of transport infrastructure and services to enhance access to markets, facilities and services for social development and poverty alleviation; and development of sustainable transport for effective management of the impacts of rising transport demand related to the environment, health and safety. The Conference recommended that the Commission endorse phase V (2002-2003) of the ALTID Plan of Action, with priority accorded to the container transport demonstration project of the Trans-Asian Railway Northern Corridor and implementation of the joint ESCAP/ECE programme on the development of Asia/Europe land transport links.

Science and technology

In 2001, the activities of the Asian and Pacific Centre for Transfer of Technology (APCTT) were directed towards technology capacity-building and innovation, as well as subregional and regional networking to support countries in responding to the challenges of integration with the new global economy. It organized 47 technology transfer–related events in 14 countries in cooperation with 51 partner institutions, and established strategic alliances with more than 100 industrial associations, chambers of commerce and business development organizations in 33 countries. A major endeavour in 2001 was the launch of a project to develop a subregional training centre on hazardous waste management for the South Asian Association for Regional Cooperation region under the 1989 Basel Convention on the Control of Transboundary Movements of Hazardous Wastes and their Disposal [YUN 1989, p. 420].

The APCTT Governing Board held its sixteenth session in Shanghai, China, on 26 and 27 November [E/ESCAP/1242].

The Commission endorsed the recommendations of the APCTT Governing Board's fifteenth session [YUN 2000, p. 935], and encouraged APCTT to proceed with establishing a subregional network for promoting technology transfer, and with implementing a regional cooperative policy mechanism to promote the transfer of environmentally sound technologies. APCTT was directed to expand its activities with respect to technology management, technology capacity-building and human resources development in knowledge-based technologies to enhance the competitiveness of small and medium-sized enterprises. It should also strengthen its activities for upgrading technologies in traditional areas and pursue programmes aimed at converging traditional and new and emerging technologies.

Environment and sustainable development

The Commission considered the report of the Ministerial Conference on Environment and Development in Asia and the Pacific, 2000 [YUN 2000, p. 936]. In a resolution [E/2001/39 (res. 57/2)], it welcomed the Conference's recommendations and requested members and associate members to participate in their implementation by ensuring the formulation of programmes to implement the Regional Action Programme for Environmentally Sound and Sustainable Development, 2001-2005 [YUN 2000, p. 936]; encouraging local governments to participate in implementing the Kitakyushu Initiative for a Clean Environment [ibid.]; and assisting the secretariat in assessing progress in the implementation of the Conference's recommendations. The Commission noted the progress made in implementing the second phase of the Regional Space Application Programme for Sustainable Development in Asia and the Pacific, launched by the Second Ministerial Conference on Space Applications for Sustainable Development in Asia and the Pacific [YUN 1999, p. 930], and called for implementation of that Conference's recommendations.

In preparation for the 2002 World Summit on Sustainable Development (see p. 749), the High-level Regional Meeting for the World Summit (Phnom Penh, Cambodia, 27-29 November) [E/ESCAP/1234] adopted the Phnom Penh Regional Platform on Sustainable Development for Asia and the Pacific, which outlined a number of initiatives to address sustainable development in the region.

Natural resources development

The Commission, having considered the report of the High-level Regional Meeting on Energy for Sustainable Development [YUN 2000, p. 937], adopted a resolution [E/2001/39 (res. 57/6)], in which it noted the adoption of the Bali Declaration on Asia-Pacific Perspectives on Energy and Sustainable Development, and the Sustainable Energy Development Action Programme, Strategies and Implementation Modalities for the Asian and Pacific Region, 2001-2005 [YUN 2000, p. 937]. It called on members and associate members to fulfil their commitments made in the Bali Declaration, and to implement the Action Programme. It asked donors, financial insti-

tutions, UN bodies, NGOs and the private sector to assist developing countries in enhancing their national capacity, mobilizing resources and facilitating technology transfer. Among its recommendations to the Executive Secretary was a request that he undertake a programme to assist countries of the region, particularly developing countries, in formulating strategies on the efficient use of energy and the application of renewable and clean energy technologies.

The Commission also considered a report [E/ESCAP/1207] on issues related to the environment and sustainable development of natural resources and endorsed in general the conclusions and recommendations made by the secretariat regarding emerging issues and developments at the regional level. It stressed the importance of adopting an integrated approach to water resources management, and supported ESCAP activities in capacity-building in the strategic planning of natural resources and the preparation of national water visions for action, as well as involvement in the preparation of the World Water Assessment Programme and in the Third World Water Forum, to be held in Japan in 2003.

The Commission also considered the report of the Mekong River Commission (MRC), established in 1995 [YUN 1995, p. 1017], on its 2000 activities [E/ESCAP/1224]. It noted that MRC had initiated a revision of the Strategic Plan for 1999-2003 [YUN 1999, p. 931], with a view to reflecting fully emerging needs and new strategic objectives in the period 2001-2005.

Having considered the report of the Coordinating Committee for Coastal and Offshore Geoscience Programmes in East and South-East Asia [E/ESCAP/1223], the Commission noted the progress made in the development of the human resources and technology of its member countries in the energy, minerals, coastal management and geohazards, and geodata and information management sectors. It requested the Committee to cooperate more closely with the private sector to generate income in support of its activities.

The Committee on Environment and Natural Resources Development held its third session in Bangkok from 16 to 18 October [E/ESCAP/1244].

Agriculture and development

The Commission endorsed the report of the Regional Coordination Centre for Research and Development of Coarse Grains, Pulses, Roots and Tuber Crops in the Humid Tropics of Asia and the Pacific [E/ESCAP/1211 & Corr.1]. Acknowledging the Centre's research on the effects of trade liberalization on agriculture and on food security strategies for the southern Pacific island countries, it recommended that the Centre strengthen research and development programmes as well as human resources development and information services with ESCAP members and associate members. Concerned over the Centre's unstable financial condition, the Commission called for a substantial increase in funding and the provision of experts to ensure implementation of the Centre's activities. The ESCAP secretariat was asked to assist the Centre in mobilizing financial resources.

The Commission endorsed the recommendations of the twentieth session of the Governing Body of the Regional Network for Agricultural Engineering and Machinery (RNAEM) [YUN 2000, p. 938]. It also endorsed further activities in post-harvest food processing technology, the mechanization of horticultural crops, low-cost surface-covered cultivation, and agricultural waste and by-product utilization. The Commission recommended that RNAEM provide technical assistance and consultancy services in agro-industries in rural areas.

Social development

The Commission endorsed the report of the Committee on Socio-economic Measures to Alleviate Poverty in Rural and Urban Areas on its third session [YUN 2000, p. 938], and the secretariat note [E/ESCAP/1210] on progress in the implementation of resolutions and decisions relating to socio-economic measures to alleviate poverty in rural and urban areas.

It requested the ESCAP secretariat to continue to play an advocacy and catalytic role in poverty alleviation efforts, and to develop mechanisms for formulating regional integrated development plans and cooperation on technology transfer, human resources development and capacity-building. The secretariat should also continue its research and dissemination of information on demographic issues and their relationship to development and provide policy guidance and technical assistance in areas related to demographic dynamics. Other proposed areas of work included human resources development training in poverty alleviation and rural development programmes, and social protection, including social safety nets, social security benefits and social services. The Commission recommended that the social and economic consequences of ageing in the region should be studied and analysed, as should ageing-related issues. The secretariat was urged to implement and coordinate activities in preparation for the UN Second World Assembly on Ageing, to be held in 2002 (see p. 1102).

The Commission endorsed the recommendations of the Regional High-level Meeting for Asia and the Pacific in Preparation for Istanbul+5 [YUN 2000, p. 938] (see p. 973), which reviewed implementation of the Habitat Agenda, adopted by the United Nations Conference on Human Settlements (Habitat II) [YUN 1996, p. 992]. Noting progress in achieving the goals of the Habitat Agenda, especially those related to adequate shelter for all and sustainable human settlements in an urbanizing world, the Commission remarked that low levels of economic and technological development and inadequate international cooperation had hindered further achievements. The Commission recognized the need to localize the Habitat Agenda and institutionalize its implementation through national, subnational and municipal Habitat committees.

Women in development

The Commission, on 25 April [E/2001/39 (res. 57/3)], reaffirmed its commitment and role in implementing the Beijing Platform for Action, adopted by the Fourth World Conference on Women [YUN 1995, p. 1170], the recommendations of the High-level Intergovernmental Meeting to Review Regional Implementation of the Beijing Platform for Action [YUN 1999, p. 933] and the outcome of the twenty-third special session of the General Assembly [YUN 2000, p. 1082]. It called on members and associate members to ensure that the momentum derived from the Assembly's twenty-third special session was maintained to achieve the full implementation of the Beijing Platform for Action, and urged donors, the private sector and regional and international financial institutions to assist developing countries, particularly least developed, landlocked and island developing economies and economies in transition, to implement the Beijing Platform for Action and the outcome of the special session. The Commission addressed a number of recommendations to the Executive Secretary for action.

Human resources development

The Third Asia-Pacific Intergovernmental Meeting on Human Resources Development for Youth was held in Bangkok from 4 to 8 June [E/ESCAP/1263] on the theme "Integrated approaches to youth health: focus on sexual and reproductive health, substance abuse and HIV/AIDS". The meeting adopted recommendations for national follow-up and subregional and regional cooperation on integrated approaches to youth health, focusing on the prevention of substance abuse and HIV/AIDS among youth and the promotion of their sexual and reproductive health.

Regional action to fight HIV/AIDS

The Commission had before it a document on regional preparations for the special session of the General Assembly on HIV/AIDS [E/ESCAP/1229] (see p. 1125).

In a resolution on a regional call for action to fight HIV/AIDS in Asia and the Pacific [E/2001/39 (res. 57/1)], the Commission, among other recommendations, called for a regional commitment to enhancing coordination and strengthening community, national, regional and international efforts to prevent the spread of HIV/AIDS and to address its social and economic impact; a political commitment on a response to HIV/AIDS; the mainstreaming of HIV/AIDS into national economic and social development processes; and an increase in government and financial resources at the country level to address the epidemic. It called on members and associate members to be actively involved in the preparatory activities and ensure representation at the highest political level at the Assembly's special session on HIV/AIDS. The Commission requested the Executive Secretary to strengthen UN regional coordination mechanisms under the aegis of ESCAP, and, with the Joint United Nations Programme on HIV/AIDS, promote accelerated action, including increased political engagement at the highest level, and support the United Nations Regional Coordination Meeting thematic working group on HIV/AIDS and intergovernmental working groups on HIV/AIDS. He should seek extrabudgetary resources to provide technical assistance and other support for efforts to combat the spread of HIV/AIDS in ESCAP countries, particularly the developing and least developed among them.

Natural disasters

The Commission, having considered the report of the Typhoon Committee [E/ESCAP/1225], noted the progress of work in 2000 on meteorological components, including observations, forecasts and warnings of typhoons; on hydrological components, including flood forecasts and warnings as well as storm surge forecasts; and on natural disaster reduction. It noted, in particular, the Committee's decisions to undertake a comprehensive review of the hydrological and disaster prevention and preparedness components, to restructure the Regional Cooperation Programme Implementation Plan, and to reestablish the Typhoon Research Coordination Group.

The Commission also considered the report of the Panel on Tropical Cyclones at its twenty-eighth session (Bangkok, 14-20 March) [E/ESCAP/1226]. It noted the Panel's proposal to the World Meteorological Organization (WMO), ESCAP and the Panel's Technical Support Unit to increase interaction among the national and subregional institutions involved in the mitigation of tropical cyclone disasters. It noted that a trust fund had been established with WMO for the Panel's activities and encouraged Panel members and others to contribute.

Statistics

The Commission endorsed the conclusions and decisions contained in the report of the Committee on Statistics on its twelfth session [YUN 2000, p. 940], including the secretariat's programme of work for 2002-2003 and the priority areas identified: the 1993 System of National Accounts, and statistics on poverty, gender, environment and the informal sector. It decided that ICT and the knowledge-based economy should be included as an additional priority item. It urged the secretariat to assist in building national capabilities and to develop projects in ICT, statistical classifications, the International Comparison Programme and statistics on social issues. The Commission recognized the need to develop concepts and methodologies for measuring the informal sector activities. Stressing the importance of better poverty statistics, it believed that the Committee on Statistics should develop standard methods for facilitating international comparison of those statistics. It recognized the need for timely and comprehensive environmental statistics in the national development planning process, and the importance of harmonizing and rationalizing the basic development indicators used for measuring the goals set by global conferences. The Commission endorsed the Statistics Committee's recommendations on the impact of information technology (IT) on statistical work, and agreed with its suggestion that the United Nations Statistics Division or ESCAP should prepare a manual on measuring IT-related activities. The secretariat should facilitate the sharing of experiences on the measurement of the digital economy and produce a document on best practices for measuring electronic commerce activities in the region.

The Commission also had before it a report on the Statistical Institute for Asia and the Pacific [E/ESCAP/1215], which included a summary of the deliberations of the sixth session of the Institute's Governing Board (Tokyo, 29-30 August 2000).

The Commission noted the revised content of the Institute's training courses and approved the shift in emphasis to specialized statistical topics in its outreach training programme. It endorsed the Institute's initiatives to collaborate with the national statistical offices in its outreach programme, and the Institute's 2001-2002 work programme.

Programme and organizational questions

The Commission noted the secretariat's report on the implementation of the programme of work for 2000-2001 [E/ESCAP/1217] and endorsed the programme changes for 2001 [E/ESCAP/1218]. It was satisfied with the overall implementation of the programme of work and with the shift in its focus from producing publications to increasing training activities and the dissemination of information and data through ESCAP web sites. It suggested that all recurrent publications be shifted to those web sites and that the sites be hyperlinked with related sites of other UN bodies.

The Commission endorsed ESCAP's draft programme of work for 2002-2003 [E/ESCAP/1219 & Corr.1] and approved a tentative calendar of meetings and training programmes for the period from April 2001 to March 2002 [E/ESCAP/1220].

ESCAP reform

The Commission considered the Executive Secretary's report [E/ESCAP/1200] on the implementation of a 1997 Commission resolution on ESCAP reform [YUN 1997, p. 993]. The Executive Secretary reported that he had invited the United Nations Office for Project Services to undertake a management consultancy of ESCAP, which was expected to provide practical recommendations on structural and work process adjustments to revitalize ESCAP.

Also before the Commission was the report of the Advisory Committee of Permanent Representatives and Other Representatives Designated by Members of the Commission (ACPR) and its Open-ended Informal Working Group [E/ESCAP/1227 & Add.1]; the latter had been convened to assist ACPR in its work on ESCAP reform. The Commission recognized the importance of ACPR in maintaining constructive dialogue between member countries and the secretariat, and recommended that its advisory role be strengthened with regard to development and implementation of the Commission's programmes and its resolutions and decisions.

Subregional activities

Cooperation with the Economic Cooperation Organization

In response to General Assembly resolution 55/42 [YUN 2000, p. 941], the Secretary-General reported in June on cooperation between the United Nations and the Economic Cooperation Organization (ECO) [A/56/122]. The report described the cooperative relationship of ECO with various UN organizations.

GENERAL ASSEMBLY ACTION

On 7 December [meeting 80], the General Assembly adopted **resolution 56/44** [draft: A/56/L.32] without vote [agenda item 21 (h)].

Cooperation between the United Nations and the Economic Cooperation Organization

The General Assembly,

Recalling its resolution 48/2 of 13 October 1993, by which it granted observer status to the Economic Cooperation Organization,

Recalling also the resolutions previously adopted by the General Assembly on cooperation between the United Nations and the Economic Cooperation Organization, and inviting various specialized agencies and other organizations and programmes of the United Nations system and relevant international financial institutions to join in their efforts towards implementation of economic programmes and projects of the Economic Cooperation Organization,

Bearing in mind the progress attained by the Economic Cooperation Organization both in its reorganization endeavours and in launching and implementing various regional development projects and programmes over the past decade,

Welcoming the endeavours of the Economic Cooperation Organization in regard to consolidating its ties with the United Nations system and with relevant international and regional organizations towards the furtherance of its objectives,

Recalling that one of the main objectives of the United Nations and the Economic Cooperation Organization is to promote international cooperation in solving international problems of an economic, social, cultural or humanitarian character,

Expressing grave concern at the prevalent drought and its devastating impact on the socio-economic situation of some States members of the Economic Cooperation Organization,

1. *Takes note with appreciation* of the report of the Secretary-General on the implementation of General Assembly resolution 55/42 of 21 November 2000, and expresses satisfaction at the enhanced pace of mutually beneficial interaction between the two organizations;

2. *Takes note* of the Dushanbe communiqué, issued at the eleventh meeting of the Ministers for Foreign Affairs of the States members of the Economic Cooperation Organization, held on 4 May 2001, in which the States members reiterated their common aspirations and resolve for a prosperous region of the Economic Cooperation Organization;

3. *Stresses* the importance of cooperation between the United Nations system and the Economic Cooperation Organization to address the challenges and opportunities of globalization in the region of the Economic Cooperation Organization by promoting the integration of States members of the Economic Cooperation Organization, as appropriate, into the world economy, particularly in areas of concern to

States members of the Economic Cooperation Organization, inter alia, trade, finance and transfer of technology;

4. *Notes* the holding in Islamabad on 8 November 2000 of a ministerial-level meeting on energy and petroleum, which, inter alia, resulted in a joint statement and the adoption of a plan of action for energy/petroleum cooperation in the region of the Economic Cooperation Organization for 2001–2005;

5. *Notes with satisfaction* the ongoing cooperation between the United Nations Development Programme and the Economic Cooperation Organization through the implementation of the capacity-building project of the secretariat of the Economic Cooperation Organization, and welcomes the decision of the two institutions to expand the scope of existing cooperation in priority areas of the Economic Cooperation Organization;

6. *Notes* the concern of the Economic Cooperation Organization with respect to agriculture, industry and the health sector in the region, and appreciates the due cognizance taken by the organization of the development of the region, and in this regard welcomes the fact that the Economic Cooperation Organization decided to hold a ministerial meeting on agriculture in Islamabad in October 2001;

7. *Welcomes* the signing in March 2001 of a memorandum of understanding between the Economic Cooperation Organization and the International Trade Centre, expresses its confidence that their mutual cooperation will add impetus to the ongoing trade transactions among States members of the Economic Cooperation Organization, and notes with appreciation the successful implementation of the ongoing project of the Economic Cooperation Organization and the International Trade Centre on expanding intraregional trade;

8. *Notes with satisfaction* the increasing cooperation between the Economic Cooperation Organization and the World Trade Organization, including the fact that the latter has accorded observer status to the former, and the increasing involvement of the Economic Cooperation Organization in relevant forums and ministerial conferences of the World Trade Organization, and appreciates the holding in Bishkek in 2002 of a joint Economic Cooperation Organization and World Trade Organization seminar on regionalism;

9. *Welcomes* the growing cooperation between the Economic Cooperation Organization and relevant international financial institutions in regard to financial assistance extended by them in the fields of transport, trade, energy, agriculture and privatization, particularly by the Islamic Development Bank in the joint projects of the Economic Cooperation Organization, the Islamic Development Bank, the Economic and Social Commission for Asia and the Pacific and the United Nations Conference on Trade and Development on the introduction of multimodal transport operations in the region of the Economic Cooperation Organization and the interconnection and parallel functioning of power systems in the region;

10. *Also welcomes* the efforts of the States members of the Economic Cooperation Organization in opening international passenger traffic and the launching of a demonstration container train on the Almaty-Tashkent-Tehran-Istanbul route of the Trans-Asian Railway main line;

11. *Appreciates* the fact that General Assembly resolution 55/181 of 20 December 2000, on the transit environment in landlocked States in Central Asia and their transit developing neighbours, has implications for the whole region of the Economic Cooperation Organization;

12. *Welcomes* the holding in Tehran in June 2001 of a joint Economic Cooperation Organization and United Nations Industrial Development Organization training course on technology management and technology transfer negotiations, which will enhance cooperation among the States members of the Economic Cooperation Organization in industry, particularly in the development of small and medium-sized enterprises;

13. *Notes* the increasing problem of the production, transit and abuse of narcotic drugs and their ill effects in the region of the Economic Cooperation Organization, notes with appreciation the commencement of phase II of the joint project of the Economic Cooperation Organization and the United Nations International Drug Control Programme on the Drug Control Coordination Unit established in the secretariat of the Economic Cooperation Organization in July 1999, and calls upon the other international and regional organizations to assist, as appropriate, the Economic Cooperation Organization in its efforts against the drug menace in the region;

14. *Appreciates* the cooperation of the Economic Cooperation Organization with the Centre for International Crime Prevention of the Office for Drug Control and Crime Prevention of the Secretariat in jointly organizing the regional seminar on the fight against supranational organized crime;

15. *Notes with satisfaction* the expansion of cultural ties in the region under the auspices of the Cultural Institute of the Economic Cooperation Organization, and supports the endeavours to promote the rich cultural and literary heritage of the region through the launching of appropriate projects and programmes, with possible assistance from the United Nations Educational, Scientific and Cultural Organization and other relevant entities;

16. *Also notes with satisfaction* the efforts of the States members of the Economic Cooperation Organization in the field of science and technology for the development of the region and endeavours in this regard, including the establishment of the Science Foundation of the Economic Cooperation Organization;

17. *Accentuates* the significance of environmental issues, such as air and water pollution, in the region of the Economic Cooperation Organization, and calls upon the relevant United Nations bodies to cooperate, as appropriate, with the Economic Cooperation Organization to implement joint plans and projects to improve the situation in the region;

18. *Invites* the United Nations system, its relevant bodies and the international community to continue to provide technical assistance, as appropriate, to the States members of the Economic Cooperation Organization and its secretariat in strengthening their early warning systems, preparedness, capacity for timely response and rehabilitation, with a view to reducing human casualties and mitigating the socio-economic impact of natural disasters;

19. *Expresses its appreciation* for the efforts of the Economic Cooperation Organization in the implementation of the United Nations programmes for the development of transit transport facilities in the landlocked countries of the region;

20. *Requests* the Secretary-General to submit to the General Assembly at its fifty-seventh session a report on the implementation of the present resolution;

21. *Decides* to include in the provisional agenda of its fifty-seventh session the sub-item entitled "Cooperation between the United Nations and the Economic Cooperation Organization".

Cooperation with the Pacific Islands Forum

On 14 September [A/56/388], Nauru transmitted the communiqué of the thirty-second meeting of the Pacific Islands Forum (Yaren, Nauru, 16-18 August), containing the decision of its heads of Government to pursue a closer and cooperative relationship between the United Nations and the Forum.

GENERAL ASSEMBLY ACTION

On 7 December [meeting 80], the General Assembly adopted **resolution 56/41** [draft: A/56/L.29 & Add.1] without vote [agenda item 21 *(m)*].

Cooperation between the United Nations and the Pacific Islands Forum

The General Assembly,

Recalling its resolution 49/1 of 17 October 1994, by which it granted observer status to the South Pacific Forum,

Taking note of the communiqué of the thirtieth meeting of the Pacific Islands Forum, held in Koror from 3 to 5 October 1999, which, inter alia, agreed to change the name of the organization from the "South Pacific Forum" to the "Pacific Islands Forum",

Recalling that one of the purposes of the United Nations is to achieve international cooperation in addressing international problems of an economic, social, cultural or humanitarian character,

Bearing in mind that one of the purposes of the Pacific Islands Forum, established in 1971, is to promote regional cooperation among its members through trade, investment, economic development and political and international affairs,

Welcoming the ongoing efforts towards closer cooperation between the United Nations and the Pacific Islands Forum,

Bearing in mind the provisions of Chapter VIII of the Charter of the United Nations on the existence of regional arrangements or agencies for dealing with such matters relating to the maintenance of international peace and security as are appropriate for regional action and other activities consistent with the purposes and principles of the United Nations,

Welcoming the assistance given by the United Nations towards the maintenance of peace and security in the Pacific Islands Forum region,

Welcoming also the fact that in the United Nations Millennium Declaration, adopted by resolution 55/2 of 8 September 2000, heads of State and Government resolved to address the special needs of small island developing States by implementing the Programme of Action for the Sustainable Development of Small Island Developing States and the outcome of the twenty-second special session of the General Assembly,

Taking note of the communiqué of the thirty-second meeting of the Pacific Islands Forum, held in Yaren from 16 to 18 August 2001,

Affirming the need to strengthen the cooperation that already exists between entities of the United Nations system and the Pacific Islands Forum in the areas of economic and social development, as well as in political and humanitarian affairs,

Mindful of the need for the coordinated utilization of available resources to promote the common objectives of the two organizations,

1. *Takes note* of the decision of the heads of Government of the Pacific Islands Forum on the pursuit of a closer and cooperative relationship between the United Nations and the Pacific Islands Forum;

2. *Invites* the Secretary-General of the United Nations to take the necessary measures, in consultation with the Secretary-General of the Pacific Islands Forum, to promote and expand cooperation and coordination between the two secretariats in order to increase the capacity of the organizations to attain their common objectives;

3. *Requests* the Secretary-General of the United Nations, in consultation with the Secretary-General of the Pacific Islands Forum, to promote, as a matter of priority, meetings between their representatives for consultations on policies, projects and procedures that will facilitate, broaden and, if necessary, formalize, cooperation and coordination between the two organizations;

4. *Calls upon* the Secretary-General of the United Nations, in consultation with the Secretary-General of the Pacific Islands Forum, to assist in the development of long-term peace-building programmes to address new security threats in the Pacific Islands Forum region;

5. *Urges* specialized agencies and other organizations and programmes of the United Nations system to cooperate with the Secretary-General of the United Nations in order to initiate, maintain and increase consultations and programmes with the Pacific Islands Forum and its associated institutions in the attainment of their objectives;

6. *Invites* initiatives from Member States to assist in the cooperation efforts between the United Nations and the Pacific Islands Forum;

7. *Requests* the Secretary-General to submit to the General Assembly at its fifty-seventh session a report on the implementation of the present resolution;

8. *Decides* to include in the provisional agenda of its fifty-seventh session the item entitled "Cooperation between the United Nations and the Pacific Islands Forum".

Europe

The Economic Commission for Europe (ECE), at its fifty-sixth session (Geneva, 8-11 May) [E/2001/37], focused on strengthening regional cooperation and establishing its strategic directions.

During its debate on the theme "Business enterprise and economic growth in the Central Asian and the Caucasian countries: creating a supportive and secure environment", discussions centred on progress and problems in the transition process since 1991; privatization, regulatory reform and enterprise development; and living standards and social policy. The Commission underlined the priority needs of those regions and encouraged the Executive Secretary to strengthen assistance to them through regional and subregional cooperation, and with other international institutions, in particular through the special programmes and projects for the southern Caucasus and Central Asia.

The Commission was briefed on preparations for the ECE Ministerial Conference on Ageing (Berlin, Germany, September 2002), which was expected to produce an implementation scheme for the plan to be developed by the UN Second World Assembly on Ageing (see p. 1102).

The Commission also considered strengthening links within the ECE region in environment, energy and transport. Its principal subsidiary bodies were invited to develop linkages in various areas and to examine the most efficient, flexible and cost-effective modalities to address those intersectoral issues, review annually intersectoral cooperation and consider potential new issues for such cooperation. They were encouraged to find new ways to secure the means of implementing intersectoral activities, including setting aside regular resources and seeking extrabudgetary funding for those activities.

The Commission discussed key policy concerns of the Millennium Declaration [YUN 2000, p. 49] relevant to the ECE region. Attention was focused on identifying the most relevant economic and social objectives for ECE member States, and on progress made and further efforts needed to achieve those objectives. The Chairman proposed a number of measures for assisting ECE member countries in implementing the Declaration and for monitoring progress.

In terms of ECE's strategic directions, the Executive Secretary reported to the Commission on an informal brainstorming session on 9 May, which discussed ways to meet the growing demands on ECE in an environment of zero-growth budget and the need to strengthen overall policy coherence and communication in ECE. It was suggested that a steering group be established to discuss and articulate the overall policy and direction for consideration by the Commission. The Commission also requested the Group of Experts on the Programme of Work to continue discussions on ECE's strategic directions.

Economic trends

According to ECE's summary of the economic survey of Europe, 2001 [E/2002/16], there was a progressive slowdown in the rate of expansion of the global economy in 2001, with world output increasing by 2.5 per cent, compared with a 4.7 per cent rise in 2000. Meanwhile, real GDP in the ECE region rose by only 1.7 per cent, compared to 4.2 per cent in 2000. However, that slowdown masked the resilience of the transition economies, especially in Eastern Europe where real GDP rose on average by 3.2 per cent. Global economic developments were overshadowed by the terrorist attacks in the United States on 11 September (see p. 60), which occurred at a time when the United States economy and the other major economic regions were in a fragile state and close to a cyclical downturn. The general effect of the attacks was to worsen the economic outlook, which was already uncertain, not least because of the large domestic and external imbalances in the United States economy.

Western Europe and North America

In the United States, real GDP fell between the second and third quarters of 2001. Economic activity in that period was influenced by the impact of the terrorist attacks of 11 September on consumer and business spending. Business activity peaked in March, and the economic expansion that started in March 1991 ended after exactly 10 years. However, real GDP did not decline further in the final quarter of 2001, as economic activity edged up by 0.3 per cent, just offsetting the fall in aggregate output in the third quarter. For the year as a whole, GDP rose by 1.2 per cent, due to growth of personal and government consumption expenditures, although they were largely offset by falling investment and exports. Manufacturing production declined by 4.4 per cent compared with 2000. Because of the sluggish economic activity, inflationary pressures weakened markedly. Core inflation remained broadly steady at 2.6 per cent for the year as a whole.

The current account deficit fell to some $415 billion or 4.1 per cent of GDP, compared to 4.5 per cent in 2000. The progressive easing of monetary policy since the beginning of 2001, designed to arrest and reverse the cyclical downturn, continued in the aftermath of the 11 September attacks. Between mid-September and early December, the target for the federal funds rate was reduced in four steps from 3.5 per cent to 1.75 per cent. The expansionary stance of fiscal policy, in combination with the cyclical downturn, resulted in a large fall in the federal budget surplus from 2.4 per cent of GDP in 2000 to 1.2 per cent ($127 billion) in 2001. The federal budget was forecast to move into deficit in 2002.

Canada's economy was adversely affected by the sharp downturn in the United States and the slowdown in the world economy, leading to a marked fall in exports. Real GDP rose by 1.5 per cent, down from 4.4 per cent in 2000. Unemployment rose to 8 per cent in December, the highest in almost three years. Core consumer price inflation was 2 per cent, well within the Bank of Canada's target of 1 to 3 per cent. In response to weakening domestic activity and low inflation, the Bank of Canada continued to loosen monetary policy.

In Western Europe, there was a marked slowdown in economic expansion, with real GDP rising by only 1.3 per cent, compared with 3.5 per cent the previous year. That outcome partly reflected the slump in Turkey, where GDP fell by more than 7 per cent. In the European Union (EU), real GDP rose by only 1.7 per cent, half the annual rate in 2000. In the euro area, between the third and final quarters of 2001, real GDP fell by 0.2 per cent and was only 0.75 of a percentage point above the level in the same period of 2000. The tendency for rapidly weakening growth was general. The falls in average annual growth rates of real GDP were particularly sharp in Finland and Ireland. Among the three major euro-area economies, France's long economic upswing petered out into a decline of real GDP by 0.1 per cent between the third and fourth quarters of 2001, mainly due to the slowdown in the rate of growth of private consumption and falling consumer confidence. In Germany, the economy moved into recession in the second half of 2001, with real GDP falling by 0.2 per cent between the second and third quarters and by 0.3 per cent in the final quarter, while in Italy, economic growth was very uneven. For the year, the average rate of economic growth was 1.8 per cent, down from nearly 3 per cent in 2000.

Outside the euro area, real GDP in the United Kingdom rose by 2.3 per cent, fuelled by buoyant private consumption. In contrast, business investment weakened in the course of the year. Fiscal policy supported economic activity in 2001 and the Bank of England reduced its base lending rate by 2 percentage points. The Government launched a massive investment programme designed to improve infrastructure (transport, health, education).

Eastern Europe, Baltic States and CIS

According to the summary of the economic survey of Europe, 2001 [E/2002/16], despite the global economic slowdown, 2001 turned out to be a relatively successful year for the ECE transition economies. With the exception of the former Yugoslav Republic of Macedonia (FYROM), all of them posted positive GDP growth. Aggregate GDP increased by 5 per cent, making them one of the fastest-growing regions in the world. The main factor behind that outcome was buoyant growth in the Commonwealth of Independent States (CIS), where a strong recovery continued for a third consecutive year. The Russian Federation remained the principal engine of growth for the CIS countries in 2001, with a 5 per cent increase in GDP. Two of the larger economies, Kazakhstan and Ukraine, showed strong recovery, registering some of the highest GDP growth rates in 2001, 13.2 per cent and 9.1 per cent, respectively. In most of those countries, strong growth was underpinned by export expansion. However, the surge in economic activity was mostly confined to the first half of 2001; in the second half of the year, there was a notable deceleration in both output and export performance throughout CIS.

Strong rates of growth also prevailed in most of the Eastern European and Baltic States. In Croatia, the Czech Republic, Latvia, Lithuania, Romania and Slovakia, GDP growth accelerated above expectations at the start of the year. Economic activity remained high, and, in line with expectations, in Albania, Bosnia and Herzegovina, Bulgaria and Estonia. In contrast, growth decelerated in Hungary and especially in Slovenia.

Two economies, Poland and FYROM, had encountered serious economic difficulties. After nine years of expansion, the Polish economy came to a near standstill in 2001. FYROM was the only transition economy with falling GDP in 2001, due to widespread disruption caused by the internal military conflict (see p. 368). A relatively strong post-war recovery continued in the Federal Republic of Yugoslavia, although that economy still faced formidable difficulties in implementing much-needed but painful economic reforms.

Thanks to the successful implementation of reforms which bolstered consumer and investor confidence, domestic demand in the transition economies had generally grown steadily in recent years, and helped to cushion them from the effects of the deteriorating external environment. In many countries in 2001, there was a shift from external towards predominantly domestic sources of growth. Moreover, the flow of inward foreign direct investment to the transition economies was unabated, and because of recent productivity gains, most Eastern European transition economies had been able to improve their cost competitiveness, helping exporters to perform better in Western European markets in 2001 than some of their competitors. While the total volume of Western European imports in 2001 increased by a little over 1 per cent, the volume of total exports from the Central European and Baltic countries increased by some 11 per cent. The gains in competitiveness and export performance led to an increase in Eastern Europe's share of the EU's extra-EU imports from 9.9 per cent in 2000 to 11.1 per cent in 2001.

Activities in 2001

Trade, industry and enterprise development

The Committee for Trade, Industry and Enterprise Development, at its fifth session (Geneva, 13-15 June) [ECE/TRADE/280], approved activities in support of greater policy coherence and cross-sectoral activities, including a request to subsidiary bodies to explore cross-sectoral activities in trade, transport facilitation and sustainable timber trade. It adopted the recommendations of its Round Table on Services in Transition Economies and those of its Forum on e-Services for Trade, Investment and Enterprise. The Committee also approved its new terms of reference, policy objectives and strategic goals. It requested that a task force be established to plan for a forum on trade facilitation to take place in Geneva in May 2002, and approved the establishment of ad hoc teams on metrology, business advisory, counselling and information services, gender and entrepreneurship, and poverty alleviation through enterprise and entrepreneurship. The Committee approved the 2001-2002 programme of work, the development of the *Trade, Industry and Enterprise Development Directory* and the holding of a preparatory meeting to finalize an optional protocol revising the 1961 European Convention on International Commercial Arbitration [YUN 1961, p. 272].

Transport

The Inland Transport Committee, at its sixty-third session (Geneva, 13-15 February) [ECE/TRANS/136], discussed follow-up to the 1997 Regional Conference on Transport and the Environment [YUN 1997, p. 1005] and to the London Charter on Transport, Environment and Health, adopted by the 1999 London Ministerial Conference on Environment and Health. It reviewed the transport situation in ECE member countries, emerging development trends, assistance to countries with economies in transition, and the status of application of international UN/ECE transport agreements and conventions. The Committee also considered transport trends and policies, transport economics, road transport, road traffic safety, safety in tunnels, harmonization of vehicle regulations, rail transport, inland water transport, customs questions affecting transport, the transport of dangerous goods and perishable foodstuffs, and transport statistics. It approved the report of the Working Party on Transport Trends and Economics and endorsed its decision to coordinate with the ESCAP secretariat action on land transport links between Europe and the Central Asian/Caucasian region. The Committee also approved the reports of the Working Party on Road Transport and encouraged proposals for amending the European Agreement on Main International Traffic Arteries.

The Committee noted that the Agreement Concerning the Establishment of Global Technical Regulations for Wheeled Vehicles, Equipment and Parts which can be fitted and/or be used on Wheeled Vehicles entered into force on 25 August, and that amendments to the European Agreement on Main International Railway Lines had entered into force on 15 November 2000.

Energy

The Committee on Sustainable Energy, at its eleventh session (Geneva, 21-22 November) [ECE/ENERGY/47], adopted the report of the Task Force on the United Nations International Framework Classification for Reserves and Resources (UNFC) and welcomed its widespread implementation. It recommended further ECE assistance for UNFC implementation within the new project on harmonizing definitions for reserve/resource classification of energy commodities—petroleum, natural gas, coal and uranium. The Committee established an Ad Hoc Group of Experts on Harmonization of Energy Reserves/Resources to apply the UNFC Codification System within existing commodities definitions. It took note of progress in the joint ECE/European Commission project on energy efficiency standards and labels, and welcomed the establishment of the Task Force on Environment and Energy (2002-2005), together with the Committee on Environmental Policy, to produce guidelines on reforming energy prices to support sustainable energy development. The Committee also welcomed progress made in the project on indicators of sustainable energy development, and recommended that the secretariat explore modalities to continue cooperation on that project with partner international organizations.

Agriculture

The Working Party on Standardization of Perishable Produce and Quality Development (fifty-seventh session, Geneva, 12-14 November) [TRADE/WP.7/2001/9] adopted revised standards for beans, sweet peppers, lettuce and onions, recommendations for avocados for a one-year trial period and for table grapes for a two-year trial period, and revised standards for walnut kernels.

The Timber Committee, at its fifty-ninth session (Geneva, 2-5 October) [ECE/TIM/97], approved proposals emerging from the review of its joint programme with the European Forestry Commission. It discussed strengthening intersectoral cooperation in trade, timber, environment and energy and agreed on synergies for implementation. The Committee endorsed the general direction of ECE/Food and Agriculture Organization of the United Nations activities in support of the international dialogue on forests, and reviewed the markets for forest products in 2001 and prospects for 2002.

Environment

The Committee on Environmental Policy, at its eighth session (Geneva, 25-27 September) [ECE/CEP/80], considered the outcome [ECE/AC.22/2001/2] of the Regional Ministerial Meeting for the 2002 World Summit on Sustainable Development (see p. 749) and requested that a comprehensive analysis highlighting the challenges and emerging orientations of environmental policies in the region be prepared for its future work. It adopted new terms of reference for the Expert Group on Environmental Performance. The Committee further supported ECE multilateral environmental agreements and requested that the question of interlinkages be included in the agenda of its meetings. It welcomed the entry into force of the ECE Convention on Access to Information, Public Participation in Decision-making and Access to Justice in Environmental Matters and the decision of the governing bodies of the ECE Conventions on the Protection and Use of Transboundary Watercourses and International Lakes and on the Transboundary Effects of Industrial Accidents to launch an intergovernmental negotiation process to draw up a legally binding instrument on civil liability for transboundary damage caused by hazardous activities. The Committee discussed its substantive input to the fifth "Environment for Europe" Ministerial Conference and cross-sectoral activities, in particular developments related to transport, environment and health.

The Executive Body for the Convention on Long-range Transboundary Air Pollution held its nineteenth session in Geneva from 11 to 14 December [ECE/EB.AIR/75].

Human settlements

The Committee on Human Settlements (sixty-second session, Geneva, 17-19 September) [ECE/HBP/122] discussed the implementation of the ECE Strategy for a Sustainable Quality of Life in Human Settlements in the 21st Century and the Ministerial Declaration adopted by ECE Ministers of Housing and Spatial Planning [YUN 2000, p. 946], and their implications for its future programme of work. The Committee agreed to take into account the decisions of the General Assembly's special session to review implementation of the Habitat Agenda [YUN 1996, p. 994] (Istanbul+5) (see p. 973) when formulating and implementing its programme of work. It discussed the facilitation of social cohesion and security through urban development and decided to draw up guidelines on social housing.

The Committee confirmed the high priority of the country profile project for the housing sector and the activities related to land registration and land markets. It approved the draft guidelines on housing condominiums, and agreed to consider the preparation of practical, policy-oriented statistical data on housing and urban development.

Statistics

The Conference of European Statisticians (forty-ninth session, Geneva, 11-13 June) [ECE/CES/60] considered the implications of the meetings of its parent bodies—the May session of ECE and the March session of the UN Statistical Commission (see p. 1173). The Conference agreed to review the Integrated Presentation of international statistical work in the ECE region, especially the growing use of the Internet for the collection and dissemination of statistics; new manuals and standards in economic statistics and their interrelationship with the 1993 System of National Accounts; and methods for measuring the new economy and adapting to it.

The Committee discussed small-area statistics and statistics for small countries. It agreed that substantial research, development and innovations were necessary to meet the increasing demand for detailed small-area statistics and that special support should be given to countries in transition and small national economies to help them develop such statistics.

Operational activities

The Executive Secretary submitted an August note [E/ECE/1390 & Add.1,2], which reviewed operational activities in 2000 in energy, enterprise development, entrepreneurship and small and medium-sized enterprise (SME) development, environment, investment promotion, trade facilitation, transport and statistics. It also described technical assistance to a number of subregional organizations.

Lack of financial resources continued to be a major obstacle to expanding operational activities and responding to the needs and requests of member States, especially from CIS. Other problems that hindered the efficiency of operational activities included frequent changes of Governments and instability of countries' managerial systems; the lack of national experts; poor communication systems; complications of internal procedures; and the complexity of UN rules and procedures. In an attempt to meet the growing demand for operational activities from economies in transition, some ECE divisions had stretched their capacity thinly, in particular the Energy and Transport Divisions. In the light of those obstacles, the Executive Secretary suggested that the Commission consider shifting resources to those two Divisions, and provide more systematic financial support and technical assistance for operational activities in poverty eradication and entrepreneurship and SME development.

Intersectoral activities and cross-sectoral concerns

The Commission considered a note by the Executive Secretary on intersectoral cooperation in ECE [E/ECE/1385], which described the rationale for the intersectoral approach and presented the areas of intersectoral work in ECE: transport and environment; energy and environment; trade, environment and timber; and statistics. Mechanisms for fostering intersectoral cooperation and potential areas for future activities were proposed.

Latin America and the Caribbean

The Economic Commission for Latin America and the Caribbean (ECLAC) did not meet in 2001. The Commission's twenty-ninth session was to be held in Brasilia, Brazil, from 6 to 10 May 2002.

Economic trends

According to the 2001 summary of the economic survey of Latin America and the Caribbean [E/2002/19], regional output grew at a very slow pace and GDP growth amounted to a scant 0.4 per cent. The severe slowdown in the world economy cut short the regional recovery that had begun in 2000, and that was compounded by a number of regional factors, including the financial crisis in Argentina and its repercussions for other economies in the region, the energy crisis in Brazil, natural disasters that forced authorities to undertake unbudgeted public expenditures, and a new outbreak of foot-and-mouth disease in the southern part of the continent which curtailed meat exports. Brazil's promising recovery was cut short by its energy crisis, the Chilean economy also lost momentum and Uruguay moved into its third consecutive year of recession. The economies of Bolivia, Colombia, Mexico and Peru stagnated, while the Dominican Republic, Paraguay and Venezuela experienced only moderate growth and Cuba's growth rate fell to 3 per cent. The exception was Ecuador, whose economy expanded rapidly in the first half of the year.

The region's inflation rate continued to abate, falling to 6.8 per cent, which was mainly attributable to stable exchange rates in most countries, the end of the escalation in oil prices, prudent monetary policies and the recessionary conditions in the region. The inflation rate decreased in 18 of the 22 countries for which information was available. Brazil and Guatemala registered inflation of three or four percentage points above 2000 figures, while Ecuador made the greatest improvement, with a drop of almost 70 percentage points. Only three economies had double-digit inflation.

The recessionary climate in the global economy led to declines in the value of the region's exports and the value of its imports. Those decreases reflected a steep drop in United States orders for Latin American and Caribbean products, which was compounded by a downward trend in raw materials prices. Export earnings also decreased, with the regional total for both goods and services slipping to little more than $390 billion, 3.7 per cent less than a year earlier. Regional consumption stagnated, gross fixed investment was reduced by 1 per cent, exports increased by just over 2 per cent and imports held steady.

Autonomous capital inflows to Latin America and the Caribbean plunged sharply, from $61.5 billion in 2000 to $34 billion in 2001, with Argentina witnessing a sharp turnaround that resulted in outflows of over $20 billion, followed by a contraction in flows to Brazil. Foreign direct investment diminished for the second year in a row, from $64.8 billion to $58.3 billion, but was still high compared to historical averages.

The current account deficit climbed to nearly $52 billion (around 3 per cent of regional GDP) from the 2000 level of $46 billion (2.4 per cent of GDP). The increases in the deficit remained within the bounds of each country's external financing capacity, however. Almost all countries saw a downturn in government income, especially in tax revenues, with the exceptions of Colombia, the Dominican Republic and Ecuador where tax reforms were instituted. Expenditure, on the other hand, increased, particularly for debt servicing.

The steep reduction in growth hurt the labour market, and the employment rate fell by over half a percentage point. Sluggish production activity in 2001 also hurt wages, which stagnated or fell in real terms. The regional unemployment rate held steady at 8.4 per cent of the economically active population.

External debt

The region's gross external debt declined moderately, from $740 billion in 2000 to $726 billion in 2001. Small variations were observed in most of the countries' external liabilities. Among the most heavily indebted nations, Bolivia, Brazil and Peru continued to report debt/export ratios of around 350 per cent; Argentina's ratio fell to 450 per cent from its 1999-2000 average of 500 per cent, while Nicaragua's held at around 700 per cent.

As Argentina was unable to obtain financing on voluntary debt markets, the Government swapped $30 billion in securities in June at very high interest rates to lighten its public debt service burden in 2002-2003. As the country's difficulties in securing financing persisted, it attempted to implement a new, comprehensive plan to restructure the public debt at an annual rate of no more than 7 per cent. By the end of November, it had completed a swap involving $50 billion in domestic obligations.

Activities in 2001

Development policy and regional economic cooperation

In 2001, ECLAC continued to implement its programme of work, which combined activities deriving from its role as a forum for regional dialogue, facilitating the emergence of common regional positions that could contribute to the world debate on development issues, with nor-

mative activities, comprehensive analysis of development and public policy-making processes and other operational activities, such as technical assistance, specialist information provision and training [LC/G.2160(SES.29/6)].

ECLAC expanded and strengthened collaboration and coordination with UN bodies and specialized agencies, as well as other regional intergovernmental organizations. It convened the second inter-agency coordination meeting for the Caribbean subregion (Port of Spain, Trinidad and Tobago, 8-9 March) and the first inter-agency technical coordination meeting on regional statistical information (Santiago, Chile, 8 May). ECLAC developed an information system on UN world conferences in order to disseminate the contributions and activities in those areas by different organizations in the region.

In addition, ECLAC, the Banco del Desarrollo de Chile, the Latin American Association of Development Financing Institutions and the Inter-American Development Bank (IDB) organized the first colloquium on development banks (Santiago, 27 August) where experts from the region, the United States and Europe discussed the role played by development banking in financing investment projects.

The Latin American and Caribbean Institute for Economic and Social Planning (ILPES) carried out activities related to the strategic management and reform of the State, regulation of public services, development and land-use management, national systems of public investment and basic planning functions. ILPES held the fifth Interparliamentary Conference on Mining and Energy in Latin America (CIME 2001) (Santiago, 18-20 July) and the fourth European–Latin American Dialogue for Sustainable Development of the Energy Sector (Santiago, 20 July), organized jointly with Chile's Energy and Mining Commission of the Chamber of Deputies and ECLAC's Natural Resources and Infrastructure Division. An international seminar was also organized on national systems of public investment in Latin America and the Caribbean (Santiago, 5-6 November). At the end of the year, ILPES signed an agreement with IDB to help Venezuela to review its national system of public investment and prepare a plan for strengthening it.

During the 2000-2001 biennium, the Institute organized training activities on issues associated with its areas of work for State and private sector officials and the teaching staff of universities and academic centres in the region. Fourteen international courses, six subregional courses and six national courses were held for 904 participants.

JIU report. In September [A/56/370], the Secretary-General transmitted to the General Assembly a Joint Inspection Unit (JIU) report entitled "United Nations system support for science and technology in Latin America and the Caribbean", which assessed the relevance and effectiveness of technical cooperation provided by UN organizations to endogenous capacity-building in science and technology in the region. JIU recommended that the United Nations Commission on Science and Technology for Development (see p. 757) discuss the feasibility of developing a UN system joint programme for science and technology for recommendation to the Economic and Social Council.

International trade and integration

The ECLAC Division of International Trade and Integration continued to monitor intraregional trade and investment flows, examine regulatory and institutional aspects of regional integration and assess the process of negotiation and the implications of the various regional and subregional integration schemes. Various expert meetings were organized. One (São Paulo, Brazil, 5-6 November) reviewed an agenda for research and policies on globalization, technological change and gender, while another (Santiago, 3-4 December) focused on international competitiveness and the influence of Governments, enterprises and multilateral institutions on the capacity of enterprises and nations to participate in the global economy. Another meeting (Santiago, 14 March), organized jointly with the Latin American Integration Association and the Latin American Economic System, considered the cooperation mechanism between the three agencies and its effectiveness in the context of the ongoing negotiations between the various regional and subregional integration schemes.

Social development and equity

ECLAC's Social Development Division, in the 2000-2001 biennium, concentrated on social needs related to the process of globalization and economic development to ensure that both had positive effects on the conditions of employment and on the well-being of the population. In that context, it supported countries in reforming social policies and provided technical assistance to Argentina, the Dominican Republic, Mexico and Paraguay. In a joint effort with the Statistics and Economic Projections Division, it prepared the 2000-2001 edition of the *Social Panorama of Latin America*. The Division participated in a regional conference on social capital and poverty reduction in Latin America and the Caribbean: towards a new paradigm (Santiago, 24-26 September) and in the World Conference against Racism, Racial

Discrimination, Xenophobia and Related Intolerance (Durban, South Africa, 31 August–8 September) (see p. 615).

Human rights were included in the subprogramme on social development and equity. The Human Rights Unit, created in the Social Development Division in conjunction with the Office of the United Nations High Commissioner for Human Rights, began its activities in November.

Environment and human settlements

ECLAC, in collaboration with the United Nations Environment Programme, the Sustainable Development Division of the UN Department of Economic and Social Affairs and UNDP, supported Latin American and Caribbean countries in regional preparations for the 2002 World Summit on Sustainable Development (see p. 749). Four subregional meetings were held to formulate proposals that would reflect the peculiarities of each subregion: Southern Cone (Santiago, 14-15 June), Caribbean (Havana, Cuba, 28-29 June), Andean area (Quito, Ecuador, 2-3 July) and Meso-America (San Salvador, El Salvador, 16-17 July). The Regional Preparatory Conference of Latin America and the Caribbean (Rio de Janeiro, Brazil, 23-24 October) adopted the Rio de Janeiro Platform of Action on the road to Johannesburg 2002, which reaffirmed previously adopted principles and agreements, identified obstacles encountered and lessons learned during the past decade and made other commitments for confronting challenges and exploring new forms of cooperation.

ECLAC's Environment and Human Settlements Division organized or collaborated in organizing expert meetings on ecotourism, trade, intellectual property and biological and genetic resources in Latin America. In October, it took part in the Regional Meeting of Ministers and High-level Authorities of the Housing and Urban Development Sector in Latin America and the Caribbean, and in November organized a seminar on transgenic agricultural products, jointly with the Division of Production, Productivity and Management. It also helped to organize the fourth European–Latin American Dialogue for Sustainable Development of the Energy Sector (Santiago, 20 July), the fifth Inter-parliamentary Conference on Mining and Energy in Latin America (Santiago, 18-20 July) and workshops in preparation for the Conference of Ministers of Mining of the Americas (Santiago, 19-22 June).

Population and development

The ECLAC secretariat pursued activities relating to the implementation of the Programme of Action of the International Conference on Population and Development (ICPD) [YUN 1994, p. 955], oriented towards supporting national systems and preparing a regional system of indicators for the follow-up of goals set at the Conference. In that regard, ECLAC, in conjunction with the United Nations Population Fund, organized a subregional workshop for Central America and Panama on those indicators (Managua, Nicaragua, 26-27 February).

The open-ended meeting of the Presiding Officers of the ECLAC sessional Ad Hoc Committee on Population and Development (Santiago, 4-5 December) reviewed progress in fulfilling the goals of the ICPD Programme of Action in countries of the region through the use of an appropriate system of indicators and agreed to adopt a basic system of indicators proposed by the secretariat, which would be revised and presented at the Committee's next meeting. It also agreed that the system should be implemented in 2004 in order to assess the fulfilment of the Programme of Action one decade after ICPD.

Three meetings of experts were held in Santiago to consider: the 2000-2001 census results and their use in formulating social policies (8 May); the sociodemographic analysis of social vulnerability in the region (20-21 June); and advances made in applying the recommendations of the Regional Plan of Action on Population and Development [YUN 1994, p. 740] (4-5 December).

Integration of women in development

The Presiding Officers of the Regional Conference on Women in Latin America and the Caribbean, at their thirty-second meeting (San José, Costa Rica, 19-20 April), agreed to request the assistance of national statistical institutes in each country in proposing the establishment, under the Statistical Conference of the Americas (below), of a special working group on gender statistics in all spheres. At their thirty-third meeting (Port of Spain, Trinidad and Tobago, 9-11 October), the Presiding Officers, in view of the need to harmonize the regional processes in follow-up to the Regional Programme of Action for the Women of Latin America and the Caribbean, 1995-2001 [YUN 1994, p. 739], and the 10-year review of the Beijing Platform for Action [YUN 1995, p. 1170], recommended that the ninth meeting of the Regional Conference on Women in Latin America and the Caribbean be postponed to 2004 to fit in with the global process.

Economic statistics and technical cooperation

During the 2000-2001 biennium, the Statistics and Economics Projections Division conducted activities on statistical databanks, the dissemination of statistics and regional indicators, national accounts and economic development, technical cooperation, evaluation and prospective analysis of ECLAC countries' development processes, and statistics and quantitative analysis of social trends. The Division expanded and strengthened its databank system, particularly with regard to current economic trends, household surveys, foreign trade and national accounting. ECLAC activities in social statistics were designed to strengthen countries' capacities to create integrated systems of household surveys under a programme for improving surveys and measuring living conditions, jointly sponsored with IDB and the World Bank.

In accordance with Economic and Social Council resolution 2000/7 [YUN 2000, p. 951], the secretariat organized the first meeting of the ECLAC Statistical Conference of the Americas (Santiago, 9-11 May). The Conference adopted the programme of international statistical work for Latin America and the Caribbean for the biennium June 2001 to June 2003, which was a comprehensive compendium of the international and regional cooperation activities to be carried out by all ECLAC Governments and relevant institutions. The programme, based on flexible institutional forms to take advantage of government capacity, included four subprogrammes: adaptation and production of basic statistics within the framework of a regional strategy for the implementation of the 1993 System of National Accounts; environmental statistics and statistics on science, technology and innovation; statistics and indicators on social variables and well-being; and dissemination of statistical information. The Conference also considered the adoption of measures for constructing gender indicators so that gender equity policies could be designed.

The first United Nations Inter-Agency Technical Coordination Meeting on Regional Statistical Information was held on 8 May.

Subregional activities

Caribbean

The ECLAC subregional headquarters for the Caribbean—the secretariat of the Caribbean Development and Cooperation Committee (CDCC) in Port of Spain—stepped up its efforts to provide technical support in operational and sectoral areas with a view to achieving sustained growth in the economies of member States and associate members of the Caribbean subregion.

The tenth meeting of CDCC's Monitoring Committee (Port of Spain, 6-7 March) reviewed CDCC secretariat activities between May 1999 and February 2001 and considered a secretariat document reviewing CDCC objectives, structure and mechanisms. In addition, a document on Caribbean perspectives on the implementation of the Programme of Action for the Sustainable Development of Small Island Developing States [YUN 1994, p. 783] was presented to the Subregional Preparatory Meeting of the Caribbean for the World Summit on Sustainable Development (Havana, June).

Mexico and Central America

The ECLAC subregional headquarters in Mexico City placed emphasis on the review of structural reform policies, trends in foreign direct investment, social marginalization, the wider participation of women, economic integration and sectoral competitiveness. Advisory services provided included support for the preparatory work for the meeting of the Regional Consultative Group for Central America (Madrid, Spain, 8-9 March). Cooperation was extended to the Consultative Group for Smaller Economies in the negotiations for the Free Trade Area of the Americas. Some countries of the subregion received advisory services relating to fiscal policy, competitiveness policies, priorities in the electric power industry and harmonization of the hydrocarbons markets. Among its other activities were projects financed by multilateral cooperation, such as those financed by UNDP to assess flood damage in Venezuela, to support the preparation of El Salvador's human development report, to provide agricultural training, to collaborate in the programme on violence in society and to support the Mexican Institute for International Cooperation in project management and multilateral cooperation. Other projects were financed by the United Nations Fund for International Partnerships, IDB and Germany.

The subregional headquarters also undertook activities on economic reform; public administration; foreign investment; agricultural modernization; industrial competitiveness; labour markets, gender and equity; international trade, economic integration and regional cooperation; and energy integration.

Cooperation between the United Nations and the Latin American Economic System

In accordance with General Assembly resolution 54/8 [YUN 1999, p. 947], the Secretary-General reported in July on cooperation between the United Nations and the Latin American Economic System [A/56/171]. The report summarized information from four UN organizations that had responded to the Secretary-General's request for a description of joint activities and coordination.

On 14 December [meeting 86], the General Assembly adopted **resolution 56/98** [draft: A/56/L.43 & Add.1] without vote [agenda item 21 *(a)*].

Cooperation between the United Nations and the Latin American Economic System

The General Assembly,

Recalling its resolution 54/8 of 25 October 1999 on cooperation between the United Nations and the Latin American Economic System,

Having considered the report of the Secretary-General,

Bearing in mind the Agreement between the United Nations and the Latin American Economic System, in which the parties agree to strengthen and expand their cooperation in matters that are of common concern in the field of their respective competence pursuant to their constitutional instruments,

Considering that the Latin American Economic System is developing joint activities with the specialized agencies and other organizations and programmes of the United Nations system, in particular the United Nations Conference on Trade and Development, the United Nations Educational, Scientific and Cultural Organization, the Food and Agriculture Organization of the United Nations, the World Intellectual Property Organization, the United Nations Industrial Development Organization and the Economic Commission for Latin America and the Caribbean,

Welcoming the continued monitoring of changes in the treatment of topics relating to the United Nations system, in close contact with the delegations of the Member States participating in such deliberations,

1. *Takes note with satisfaction* of the report of the Secretary-General;

2. *Urges* the Economic Commission for Latin America and the Caribbean to continue deepening its coordination and mutual support activities with the Latin American Economic System;

3. *Urges* the United Nations Development Programme, within its new overall framework and high-priority development objectives in support of sustainable development, to continue its financial and technical cooperation with the programmes that the Permanent Secretariat of the Latin American Economic System is carrying out in areas of mutual interest and concern, aimed at complementing the technical assistance activities conducted by the Latin American Economic System;

4. *Urges* the specialized agencies and other organizations, funds and programmes of the United Nations system to continue and intensify their support for, and cooperation in the activities of, the Latin American Economic System;

5. *Reiterates its request* to both the Secretary-General of the United Nations and the Permanent Secretary of

the Latin American Economic System to assess, at the appropriate time, the implementation of the Agreement between the United Nations and the Latin American Economic System and to report thereon to the General Assembly at its fifty-seventh session;

6. *Requests* the Secretary-General to submit to the General Assembly at its fifty-seventh session a report on the implementation of the present resolution.

Western Asia

The Economic and Social Commission for Western Asia (ESCWA) held its twenty-first session in Beirut, Lebanon, on 10 and 11 May [E/2001/41]. The Commission adopted a resolution for submission to the Economic and Social Council recommending the establishment of an ESCWA Consultative Committee on Scientific and Technological Development and Technological Innovation. It also adopted resolutions relating to election of officers, adoption of reports and the timing of sessions of its six subsidiary bodies, as well as resolutions on the sessions of the Committee on Transport and the Preparatory Committee, the programme of work and priorities for 2000-2001, the programme budget for 2002-2003, cooperation on shared water resources, energy, transport, a biennial pledging conference and rehabilitating the economic sectors in Palestine.

Economic and social trends

Economic trends

Economic growth was relatively meagre in the ESCWA region in 2001, according to the summary of the survey of economic and social developments in the region [E/2002/20]. Its estimated combined real GDP, excluding Iraq, grew by 2.1 per cent, substantially lower than the 4.5 per cent registered in 2000. Moreover, given the region's annual population growth rate of 2.4 per cent, the real GDP per capita was a negative 0.3 per cent in 2001, compared with 2.1 per cent the preceding year.

The deterioration was attributed mainly to the sharp slowdown in world economic growth, which adversely affected the demand for oil. Furthermore, the attacks of 11 September in the United States (see p. 60) intensified the world economic slowdown and therefore negatively affected the non-oil sectors in the region, particularly tourism and transport. The violence in the West Bank and Gaza Strip also had an adverse impact on the region's foreign direct investment.

The region's oil sector performed poorly in 2001, as both production levels and prices fell. Total oil revenue declined from $165.6 billion in 2000 to an estimated $128.6 billion in 2001. For most of the ESCWA members with more diversified economies, labour-market conditions remained generally unfavourable and, in most cases, deteriorated.

Inflation rates remained low in the region, at an estimated 3 per cent, because both Gulf Cooperation Council (GCC) States and ESCWA member countries with more diversified economies were able to keep inflation under control. Fiscal positions deteriorated in most of the region. The sharp decline in oil revenue, which was far greater than previously projected, had an extremely negative effect on budgetary positions in the region. The budgets of member countries with more diversified economies continued to be deflationary, with budget expenditures increasing at a rate lower than the rate of inflation, thus reducing expenditures in real terms.

Most stock markets in ESCWA member countries were affected by the events of 11 September, with some of them losing most of the gains recorded since the beginning of the year. The performance of the region's external sector deteriorated considerably, as a result of developments in the international oil market. Oil prices fell by 16.2 per cent and demand for the region's oil exports fell significantly, thereby drastically reducing the combined balance-of-trade surpluses of the GCC States and widening the balance-of-trade deficits of most of the countries with more diversified economies. Furthermore, the attacks carried out on 11 September dealt an additional blow to the external sector accounts of the region, particularly those of the more diversified economies, tourism revenue was sharply lowered and current accounts negatively affected. While such accounts in GCC States deteriorated, mainly because of significantly lower balance-of-trade surpluses, the current account positions of the other group of countries in the region deteriorated because of increased balance-of-trade deficits, decreased revenue from tourism and lower remittances from expatriates.

Oil

In 2001, the region's oil sector performed poorly, mainly because of reduced international demand for oil, caused by lower world economic growth, which depressed oil prices, production and revenue in the ESCWA region. World oil prices declined by an estimated 16.2 per cent, from an average of $27.6 a barrel in 2000 to $23.1 in 2001, while the region's oil production fell by 3.3 per cent, causing revenue to fall by 22.4 per cent, to $128.6 billion. Combined oil revenue in the GCC States was estimated at $106.3 billion. Saudi Arabia's oil revenue, at $59.4 billion, declined by over 20 per cent but remained the largest in the region by far.

Trade

Overall trade performance in 2001 remained tied to fluctuating oil export revenues. Export growth rates declined for all ESCWA member States relative to the previous year's gains. GCC countries on average experienced a 2.5 per cent decline in export growth. However, Qatar achieved an export growth of 18 per cent, the highest in the region. For the more diversified economies, the trade record was mixed. For oil-exporting States, such as Egypt, the Syrian Arab Republic and Yemen, strong oil revenues and efforts to diversify exports helped to steady trade performance, with Egypt leading the group with a 13 per cent export growth between 2000 and 2001, while that of the Syrian Arab Republic and Yemen declined by 0.1 per cent and 8 per cent, respectively. Non-oil-based economies had a more difficult time, with Lebanon registering an 18 per cent decline and Jordan 0.2 per cent.

Intraregional export growth fell by 12.8 per cent, when comparing the first and second quarters of 2000 and 2001. Moreover, the share of intraregional exports as part of the region's total exports fell by more than 1 per cent during the same period. The GCC countries continued to contribute over 80 per cent of intraregional exports. Non-GCC countries were among the hardest hit by the decline in intraregional exports, with Yemen, Jordan and Lebanon experiencing declines of 44, 27 and 15 per cent, respectively.

On the import side, GCC countries increased imports by 13 per cent, while imports by the more diversified economies fell on average by 5 per cent. Qatar recorded the highest annual increase in imports (23 per cent). Imports into the West Bank and Gaza fell dramatically, while Lebanese imports increased by almost 2 per cent.

Social trends

The population of the ESCWA region grew fairly rapidly, increasing from 94 million in 1980 to 166 million in 2000. A large youth population characterized the region, with an estimated 19 per cent of the total population between 15 and 24 years old. Unemployment among the youth in many member countries, especially in the more diversified economies, was a critical issue, as most of them were first-time job seekers, reflecting a swelling of the youth labour supply, as the Arab baby-boomer generation entered the labour market.

Health conditions in the region had continued to improve over the past several years, owing primarily to successful public-health campaigns. In addition, nutrition improved in all member countries except Iraq and Yemen, where improvement remained limited. At the regional level, life expectancy at birth, as the primary health indicator, reached an average of 70 years (71 for women and 68 for men) for 2000-2005.

However, while the level of education and enrolment rates in most of the member countries had improved significantly since the 1970s, the rates of illiteracy were still alarmingly high, particularly in the less developed countries of the region and conflict-stricken ones. That was evident from a relatively high adult illiteracy rate, especially for women, in several countries of the region. Moreover, poverty was still a serious problem in several countries. Meanwhile, public spending on social services, as a percentage of GDP, had not increased in the past 10 years, and had even declined in some countries. Political instability in the Middle East continued to dictate that large amounts of resources had to be allocated to defence expenditures, leaving an inadequate amount for social services, education and poverty alleviation. In spite of the considerable progress made in the status of women in the region over the decades, the gender gap in socio-economic status persisted in many countries in terms of educational opportunities, employment, land ownership and inheritance.

Activities in 2001

During 2001, ESCWA activities under the 2000-2001 work programme [YUN 1999, p. 954] focused on regional follow-up to global conferences, environment, poverty, civil society institutions, gender, trade and related concerns on globalization, electronic commerce and free trade in the region, and human rights.

Economic development and cooperation

The second session of the Technical Committee on Liberalization of Foreign Trade and Economic Globalization in the Countries of the ESCWA Region (Manama, Bahrain, 7-8 April) [E/ESCWA/C.1/21/6/Add.6] discussed issues related to the liberalization of foreign trade and economic globalization and the forthcoming World Trade Organization (WTO) negotiations and their impact on ESCWA countries.

The Committee, among other recommendations to the Commission, proposed that: information be exchanged on the issues to be discussed at the fourth WTO Ministerial Conference (Doha, Qatar, November) (see p. 1432); workshops and seminars be organized on new issues to be raised at future international negotiations; and technical assistance be provided to member States in implementing WTO agreements, with special attention paid to the mechanism for settling disputes. ESCWA should continue to provide countries with technical expertise for WTO accession negotiations and the review of trade policies. It should approach international and regional funding bodies for resources to support national and regional capacity-building programmes in world and regional trade.

Transportation

The Committee on Transport, at its second session (Beirut, 6-7 February) [E/ESCWA/C.1/21/6/Add.3], considered the draft agreement on international roads in the Arab Mashreq and proposals for facilitating transport in the ESCWA region. The Committee recommended that the draft agreement be submitted for approval at ESCWA's 2001 session, and it adopted a number of other recommendations for submission to the Commission. The Committee considered the report of the second meeting of the heads of UN regional committees responsible for transport (Beirut, 23-24 January) and noted, in particular, the joint project for capacity-building through cooperation between regions to develop land and land-sea transportation. The Committee, while noting Economic and Social Council resolution 1999/41 [YUN 1999, p. 957] on the biennialization of meetings of the Commission's subsidiary bodies, recommended that its meetings be held yearly to allow it to discuss new transport developments in and the priorities of regional States and follow up on implementation of the agreement on international roads in the Arab Mashreq and the recommendations for facilitation of transport in the region.

On 11 May [E/2001/41 (res. 235(XXI))], the Commission adopted the draft agreement on international roads in the Arab Mashreq and requested the secretariat to give priority to the development of the integrated transport system in the Arab Mashreq and facilitation of traffic so as to benefit from the increased volume of regional and international commercial and tourist exchanges.

On the same date [res. 229(XXI)], the Commission decided that, with effect from 2002, the Committee on Transport would hold its sessions annually rather than biennially.

Statistics

The Statistical Committee, at its fourth session (Beirut, 3-5 April) [E/ESCWA/C.1/21/6/Add.5], adopted the work programme of ESCWA's Statistics Division for 2002-2003. Other objectives of the session included development and support of cooperation between ESCWA countries and the Statistics Division in statistical activities and programmes, and examination of the status of the 1993 System of National Accounts in those countries. It also examined the status of a project on developing national gender statistics programmes in the Arab countries and suggested that a regional working group on the development of gender statistics in the region should be formed. The Committee highlighted activities of special importance, including technical cooperation in statistics, social indicators in the framework of the implementation and follow-up by Arab countries of UN global conferences, surveys and statistics on employment and unemployment, civil registration and vital statistics. The Committee urged ESCWA to hold more seminars, workshops and meetings of experts in the field of national accounts, and to carry out industrial and construction surveys.

Among other action, the Committee recommended that a regional commission for civil registration and vital statistics be formed for the purpose of exchanging experience and data, and that the Cairo Declaration on Civil Registration and Vital Statistics, adopted by the regional workshop on vital statistics and civil registration Systems in ESCWA member States [YUN 1999, p. 952], be implemented. The Committee approved a project on strengthening statistical capacity in the ESCWA region, and proposed that ESCWA determine the steps required for building the ESCWA Statistical Information System.

Natural resources, energy and environment

The Committee on Water Resources, at its fourth session (Beirut, 14-17 November) [E/ESCWA/C.1/21/6/Add.2], reviewed the proposed programme of work of the ESCWA Energy, Natural Resources and Environment Division and agreed on its general orientation and objectives. It decided to form a working group for the rational management of water resources to deal with policies for reform of the water sector in member States. It also recommended that ESCWA focus more on technical studies on desalinated water and the protection of groundwater from depletion and pollution, and that the technical cooperation carried out by ESCWA and Germany continue to be implemented and ongoing activities completed, especially the database of shared groundwater resources.

The Commission, on 11 May [E/2001/41 (res. 233(XXI))], urged member countries to increase cooperation in water resources, in particular shared groundwater, water-related legislation and management of demand, by creating working parties within the Committee on Water Resources to harmonize methodology on managing such resources.

The Commission also considered the report of the Committee on Energy at its second session [YUN 1999, p. 952]. On 11 May [E/2001/41 (res. 234(XXI))], the Commission urged member countries to include in their energy-related programmes policies and measures to increase the efficiency of, and rationalize the energy use of and promote renewable sources of, energy. Institutional frameworks should be devised to achieve that end. Member countries were asked to support activities related to the renewable energy promotion mechanism, with a view to strengthening regional cooperation in that field.

Quality of life

The third session of the Committee on Social Development (Beirut, 27-28 March) [E/ESCWA/C.1/21/6/Add.4] reviewed progress made by the Social Development Issues and Policies Division in 1999-2000 in implementing the subprogramme on improving the quality of life, and heard reports of member States on their plans and activities in social development areas, including human development, population, housing, women's issues and follow-up to global conferences.

The Commission had before it a paper on efforts to combat HIV/AIDS in the ESCWA region [E/ESCWA/21/7], in which it was recommended that the region face up to the need to care for and treat the thousands of HIV/AIDS patients in ESCWA countries and seek the best way of assuring that society accepted such persons and provided them with appropriate support. Resources should also be made available for preventing the spread of infection and reducing its effects. Countries of the region were requested to support the measures being taken by the Regional Office, including the assurance of a high level of political commitment and leadership, and strengthening national mechanisms for acquiring reliable data and institutional capacity.

Programme and organizational questions

On 11 May, the Commission decided that, with effect from 2002, member States would assume the chairmanship of the Commission's sessions and subsidiary bodies on a rotating basis, in Arabic alphabetical order [E/2001/41 (res. 226(XXI))], and sessions of ESCWA subsidiary bodies would be held not later than the end of the year prior to the Commission's session [res. 228(XXI)]; and with

effect from the twenty-second session, meetings of the Preparatory Committee would be an integral part of the Commission's sessions [res. 230(XXI)]. The Commission also adopted the recommendations contained in the reports of its subsidiary bodies, and requested the Executive Secretary to report on progress made in their implementation within the context of the 2000-2001 work programme [res. 227(XXI)].

Establishment of scientific and technological development and innovation committee

On 11 May [E/2001/41 (res. 225(XXI))], the Commission decided to submit a resolution establishing a Consultative Committee on Scientific and Technological Development and Technological Innovation for adoption by the Economic and Social Council.

ECONOMIC AND SOCIAL COUNCIL ACTION

On 26 July [meeting 43], the Economic and Social Council, on the recommendation of ESCWA [E/2001/18/Add.3 & Corr.1], adopted **resolution 2001/30** without vote [agenda item 10].

Establishment of the Consultative Committee on Scientific and Technological Development and Technological Innovation of the Economic and Social Commission for Western Asia

The Economic and Social Council,

Recognizing the vital role played by the development of scientific and technological capabilities and technological innovation in achieving the goals of sustainable development,

Recognizing also the need to integrate and coordinate the endeavours of all the parties concerned with the development of scientific and technological capabilities, including bodies from the public, joint and private sectors and the institutions of civil society, to employ technological innovation in order to promote the productivity and competitiveness of the production and services sectors in member countries of the Economic and Social Commission for Western Asia,

Noting the possibilities which technological innovation capabilities offer with regard to facing the challenges and demands of globalization and the new systems and measures relating to the quality of products, the preservation of intellectual property rights and environmental protection,

1. *Decides* to establish the Consultative Committee on Scientific and Technological Development and Technological Innovation of the Economic and Social Commission for Western Asia, the main responsibility of which will be to sponsor endeavours aimed at scientific and technological development and technological innovation. The Committee shall be composed of distinguished experts in the field, and shall have the following duties:

(a) To advise member countries on their efforts in acquiring modern technology, and to support such efforts with regional and international expertise, with particular reference to information and communica-

tions technologies, biotechnology and new materials technology;

(b) To propose ways of integrating and coordinating efforts aimed at transferring, adapting and mastering this technology, and promoting regional cooperation in these fields;

(c) To advise on priorities related to the programmes of work and medium-term plans adopted by the Commission in the fields of developing scientific and technological capabilities and technological innovation;

(d) To follow up on the resolutions and recommendations of international and regional conferences relating to the development of scientific and technological capabilities and technological innovation which are attended by member countries of the Commission, and to coordinate efforts related to the implementation of such resolutions and recommendations;

2. *Also decides* that the Committee shall hold its meetings at least once every two years, with effect from 2002;

3. *Requests* the Executive Secretary of the Commission to follow up implementation of the present resolution and to submit a report to the Commission at its twenty-second session on the progress achieved in this regard.

Programme of work, 1998-1999

The Commission had before it a report [E/ESCWA/C.1/21/3] on the implementation of the programme of work for the 1998-1999 biennium.

Despite the high vacancy rate among Professional staff and the scarcity of extrabudgetary resources, 99 per cent of the work programme activities were carried out. Only one output was postponed to the 2000-2001 biennium. Thirteen quantifiable outputs were added by legislation and four at the initiative of the secretariat, in addition to four operational activities. The high rate of performance was made possible through, among other measures, the use of consultants, short-term recruitment and extra time put in by Professional staff.

Programme of work, 2000-2001

The Commission considered reports on progress made in 2000 in implementing the programme of work for the 2000-2001 biennium [E/ESCWA/C.1/21/4 (Parts I-III)].

By the end of 2000, ESCWA had completed 35 per cent of its planned outputs and another 39 per cent were in progress. The vacancy rate in the Professional category had dropped to 25 per cent

from 29 per cent in 1999. Work-months utilized through short-term recruitment accounted for only 16 per cent of available work-months due to vacancies.

On 11 May [E/2001/41 (res. 231(XXI))], the Commission approved the changes introduced to the 2000-2001 programme of work and asked the Executive Secretary to include any further modifications to the programme and priorities in the report to be submitted in the years between Commission sessions.

Programme of work and budget, 2002-2003

The Commission considered the draft programme of work and priorities for the 2002-2003 biennium [E/ESCWA/C.1/21/7]. The five subprogrammes were: management of water, energy and the environment for sustainable development; promoting social change for sustainable development; economic development and regional cooperation during the evolution of a globalized economy; coordination of sectoral policies and harmonization of norms and standards for sustainable development within global changes; and development, coordination and harmonization of statistics.

On 11 May [E/2001/41 (res. 232(XXI))], the Commission approved the programme budget for the 2002-2003 biennium. On the same date [res. 236(XXI)], the Commission, concerned about the decline in extrabudgetary resources, decided to hold a pledging conference during each of its sessions. It invited member States to increase contributions to finance the Commission's extrabudgetary activities and requested the Executive Secretary to seek contributions from non-ESCWA States, organizations and individuals and to provide member States with proposals regarding specific activities to be funded from extrabudgetary resources.

The Commission also noted the difficult economic situation in Palestine as a result of the confrontation with Israel (see p. 428) and the damage to the Palestinian infrastructure [res. 237(XXI)]. It requested the Executive Secretary to include in the budget activities to be planned by the secretariat and implemented in consultation with relevant Palestinian institutions, and to ensure that the extrabudgetary resources to finance such activities were available.

Chapter VI

Energy, natural resources and cartography

The conservation, development and use of natural resources and energy were considered by several United Nations bodies in 2001, including the Commission on Sustainable Development, which held a high-level segment during its ninth session that gave special attention to energy issues. The Committee on Energy and Natural Resources for Development did not meet in 2001.

During the year, action was taken to promote new and renewable sources of energy, including the effective implementation of and mobilization of resources for the World Solar Programme 1996-2005. In December, the General Assembly encouraged Governments and relevant stakeholders to make more use of the Programme to boost the development and utilization of solar energy and all forms of new and renewable energy.

Addressing the Assembly in October, the Director General of the International Atomic Energy Agency noted that nuclear power was the principal alternative to fossil fuels that could in the foreseeable future provide electricity on a large scale with practically no greenhouse gas emissions. In December, the Assembly affirmed its confidence in the Agency's role in the application of nuclear energy for peaceful purposes.

Preparations for the International Year of Freshwater, 2003 continued through the interagency coordinating body for the Year, the Administrative Committee on Coordination (ACC) Subcommittee on Water Resources, which met in September.

The recommendations of the Seventh United Nations Regional Cartographic Conference for the Americas, which was held in New York in January, were endorsed by the Economic and Social Council in July.

Energy and natural resources

The Committee on Energy and Natural Resources for Development did not meet in 2001. The subject of energy and sustainable development was discussed at the ninth session of the Commission on Sustainable Development (see below and p. 747).

The Economic and Social Council had before it the Committee's report on its second session [YUN 2000, p. 959], containing a draft decision by which the Council would have taken note of the report [E/2000/32] and approved the provisional agenda for the Committee's third (2002) session.

By **resolution 2001/36** of 26 July (see below), the Council decided to transmit the Committee's report on its second session to the Commission on Sustainable Development and to defer to its next resumed session approval of the provisional agenda of the Committee's third session. On the same date, the Council decided, in the light of its adoption of resolution 2001/36 and in accordance with rule 57 of its rules of procedure, to reconsider the draft decision contained in the Committee's report on its second session (**decision 2001/312**).

By **decision 2001/324** of 20 December, the Council again deferred, to its resumed organizational session for 2002, consideration of the draft decision recommended by the Committee at its second session.

ECONOMIC AND SOCIAL COUNCIL ACTION

On 26 July [meeting 43], the Economic and Social Council adopted **resolution 2001/36** [draft introduced orally] without vote [agenda item 13 (*j*)].

Report of the Committee on Energy and Natural Resources for Development on its second session

The Economic and Social Council,

Having considered the report of the Committee on Energy and Natural Resources for Development on its second session,

1. *Decides* to transmit the report of the Committee on Energy and Natural Resources for Development to the Commission on Sustainable Development;

2. *Also decides* to defer the approval of the provisional agenda of the third session of the Committee on Energy and Natural Resources for Development to its next resumed session, bearing in mind that the third session of the Committee is to take place from 8 to 20 December 2002.

Energy

Commission on Sustainable Development

The ninth session of the Commission on Sustainable Development (CSD) (New York, 16-27

April) [E/2001/29] (see also p. 747) had as one of its sectoral themes the question of energy. In addition, a special panel discussed financing energy and transportation for sustainable development and a multi-stakeholder dialogue was held on sustainable energy and transport. The General Assembly, in resolution S/19-2 [YUN 1997, p. 792], adopted at its nineteenth special session [ibid., p. 790], had emphasized that in line with the objectives of Agenda 21, adopted by the 1992 United Nations Conference on Environment and Development [YUN 1992, p. 672], the ninth session of CSD should contribute to a sustainable energy future for all. Several meetings were held in 2000 in preparation for the session [YUN 2000, p. 960].

The Commission had before it a February report of the Secretary-General on the sustainable production, distribution and use of energy: trends in national implementation [E/CN.17/2001/12 & Corr.1]. Based on national information submitted by 78 Member States and Switzerland, the report comprised an overall assessment of progress made towards sustainable production, distribution and use of energy by region; a review of national implementation and regional trends; a summary of findings from the national information received, which presented in table form some of the key regional issues related to energy production, distribution and use; and a discussion of future challenges for sustainable energy.

Also before the Commission was the report of the second session of the Ad Hoc Open-ended Intergovernmental Group of Experts on Energy and Sustainable Development (New York, 26 February–2 March) [E/CN.17/2001/15], which contained for the Commission's consideration a draft decision on the key issues pertaining to energy for sustainable development that the Expert Group had identified at its first session [YUN 2000, p. 960]. Those issues were: accessibility of energy, energy efficiency, renewable energy, advanced fossil fuel technologies, nuclear energy technologies, rural energy, and energy and transport. The draft decision, in the form of a negotiated text, contained unresolved issues for consideration and appropriate action by CSD. With the transmission of the report, the Expert Group was deemed to have fulfilled the mandate entrusted to it by General Assembly resolution S/19-2 to prepare the work of the Commission's ninth session on energy issues.

The Expert Group had before it a report of the Secretary-General on options and strategies for action on the key issues relating to energy and sustainable development [E/CN.17/ESD/2001/2].

By a 3 April note verbale [E/CN.17/2001/18], Kenya transmitted to the Commission the statement and programme of action adopted at the African High-level Regional Meeting on Energy and Sustainable Development (Nairobi, 10-13 January).

In a 27 April decision [E/2001/29 (dec. 9/1)], CSD stated that energy was central to achieving the goals of sustainable development, noting that nearly one third of the global population of 6 billion, mostly living in developing countries, continued to lack access to energy and transportation services. Wide disparities in energy consumption existed within and between developed and developing countries and current patterns of energy production, distribution and utilization were unsustainable. Ensuring adequate and affordable access to energy for present and future generations, in an environmentally sound, socially acceptable and economically viable way, would require substantial investments, including from the private sector, and attention would have to be given to promoting an enabling environment. CSD invited Governments, regional and international organizations and other relevant stakeholders to consider a number of issues and options on the key issues identified by the Ad Hoc Open-ended Intergovernmental Group of Experts (see above). It also identified a number of overarching issues, including research and development; capacity-building; technology transfer; information-sharing and dissemination; mobilization of financial resources; making markets work effectively for sustainable development; and the multi-stakeholder approach and public participation. CSD recognized the critical role that international cooperation, including regional cooperation, could play in assisting countries, particularly developing countries, in their efforts to achieve the goals of sustainable development.

High-level segment. The Special Panel on Financing Energy and Transportation for Sustainable Development was held during the high-level segment of CSD's ninth session. In addition to discussing financing opportunities, the Panel addressed decentralized rural energy, expansion of the contribution of renewable energy and energy efficiency, and energy and infrastructure for poverty alleviation. During the high-level meeting, ministers noted that the main goal of energy for sustainable development should be poverty eradication, guided by the principle of common but differentiated responsibilities. Countries should be free to choose their energy policies, taking into account their special conditions, needs and national priorities for sustainable development.

It was stressed, however, that financing was critical for energy systems because of high upfront investment costs. An estimated $100 billion to \$300 billion would be required annually over the next 20 years to build adequate infrastructure to meet the energy needs of developing countries. The potential for gains in energy efficiency ranged from 25 to 45 per cent over the next 20 years. Governments should therefore promote investment in new energy-efficient technologies to replace outdated equipment and adopt a broad range of measures to manage energy demand, and energy efficiency improvements could also reduce the need for investments in new electricity-generation capacity. Wide-scale development and deployment of renewable energy technologies was recognized as another key to sustainable energy use. While some experts, organizations and countries believed that no energy option should be foreclosed, many participants expressed strong opposition to any further development and deployment of nuclear technology.

Multi-stakeholder dialogue. During its ninth session, CSD held a multi-stakeholder dialogue on energy and transport (16-18 April), involving representatives of business and industry, workers and trade unions, local authorities, scientific and technological communities, and non-governmental organizations (NGOs). The dialogue focused on four themes: achieving equitable access to sustainable energy; sustainable choices for producing, distributing and consuming energy; public-private partnerships to achieve sustainable energy for transport; and sustainable transport planning: choices and models for human settlements designs and vehicle alternatives. To achieve equitable access to sustainable energy, the various stakeholders included among their proposals to Governments: support for decentralized energy production, local and institutional capacity-building, and rational energy pricing; the elimination of subsidies for fossil fuels and the creation of subsidies for renewables; the establishment of a moratorium on fossil fuel exploration and large-scale dam construction; and continued market reforms. To provide sustainable choices for producing, distributing and consuming energy, they proposed, among other things, the promotion of energy efficiency through government programmes and policies; the development of a UN web-site database for information-sharing on sustainable energy sources; and the establishment of an international forum for stakeholders. One of the other proposals with regard to fostering public-private partnerships to achieve sustainable energy for transport was the establishment of a clean technology fund to provide preferential and affordable rates for transport alternatives. As to sustainable transport planning,

the stakeholders included among their proposals an increase in government research on transportation policies; inclusion of local knowledge in planning processes; and the development of partnership solutions for sustainable transport alternatives.

World Solar Programme (1996-2005)

In response to General Assembly resolution 55/205 [YUN 2000, p. 960], the Secretary-General submitted a July report on concrete action being taken for the promotion of new and renewable sources of energy, including the effective implementation of the World Solar Programme 1996-2005 [A/56/129]. He stated that growing environmental and social concerns had brought a new dimension to the perception of the significant contribution renewable energy could make in the long term and outlined the recommendations for action by Governments that had been made at CSD's ninth session (see p. 932).

As to activities being carried out at the international level to implement the World Solar Programme 1996-2005, the Secretary-General said that the United Nations Educational, Scientific and Cultural Organization was continuing its strategy of encouraging discussions on investment opportunities for renewable energy and energy efficiency projects, as well as stimulating advocacy and mobilizing functions and promoting training, education and information efforts. It continued to implement the Global Renewable Energy Education and Training Programme, with special attention to Africa. Other areas of the UN system that were undertaking initiatives in new and renewable sources of energy included the UN Department of Economic and Social Affairs; the Global Environment Facility, through its three implementing agencies (the World Bank, the United Nations Development Programme and the United Nations Environment Programme); the United Nations Industrial Development Organization; the Food and Agriculture Organization of the United Nations; and the UN regional commissions.

The Secretary-General outlined a number of obstacles and constraints impeding the promotion of new and renewable sources of energy and put forward options for action to overcome them. He called for an enabling policy environment and the introduction of innovative financing to accelerate the development and application of new and renewable sources of energy.

GENERAL ASSEMBLY ACTION

On 21 December [meeting 90], the General Assembly, on the recommendation of the Second (Economic and Financial) Committee [A/56/561/

Add.7], adopted **resolution 56/200** without vote [agenda item 98 *(g)*].

Promotion of new and renewable sources of energy, including the implementation of the World Solar Programme 1996-2005

The General Assembly,

Recalling its resolutions 53/7 of 16 October 1998, 54/215 of 22 December 1999 and 55/205 of 20 December 2000 on the World Solar Programme 1996-2005,

Recalling also resolution 14 concerning the World Solar Programme 1996-2005, adopted by the General Conference of the United Nations Educational, Scientific and Cultural Organization at its twenty-ninth session in November 1997,

Reaffirming that the convening at Harare on 16 and 17 September 1996 of the World Solar Summit, at which the Harare Declaration on Solar Energy and Sustainable Development was adopted and preparations for the World Solar Programme 1996-2005 approved, was a step in pursuance of the implementation of Agenda 21, which is a multifaceted and, at the same time, fundamental programme of action for achieving sustainable development,

Emphasizing that the World Solar Programme 1996-2005 is aimed at encompassing all forms of new and renewable energy, including solar, thermal, photovoltaic, biomass, wind, mini-hydro, tidal, ocean and geothermal forms,

Recalling resolution 19 adopted by the General Conference of the United Nations Educational, Scientific and Cultural Organization at its thirtieth session in November 1999, concerning the Global Renewable Energy Education and Training Programme 1996-2005, which constitutes one of the major programmes of universal value of the World Solar Programme 1996-2005,

Reiterating that mutually supportive efforts at the national and international levels are imperative in the pursuit of sustainable development, which includes the provision of financial resources and the transfer of technology for the application of cost-effective energy and the wider use of environment-friendly, renewable energies,

Acknowledging that the General Assembly continues to play an important role in promoting the World Solar Programme 1996-2005,

Acknowledging also that the Commission on Sustainable Development and the Economic and Social Council continue to play a pivotal role as forums for the discussion of new and renewable sources of energy and sustainable development,

Noting the role that the United Nations Educational, Scientific and Cultural Organization continues to play in the implementation of the World Solar Programme 1996-2005, in particular its efforts, in association with multilateral partners and national specialized institutions, to enhance bilateral and regional cooperation through the joint organization of regional and subregional business and investment forums,

Welcoming the recommendations of the Commission on Sustainable Development at its ninth session, in particular the references to renewable energy,

Expressing its appreciation for the continued efforts of the Secretary-General in bringing the World Solar Programme 1996-2005 to the attention of relevant sources of funding and technical assistance,

Calling for further action to ensure that the World Solar Programme 1996-2005 is fully integrated into the mainstream of the efforts of the United Nations system towards attaining the objective of sustainable development,

Emphasizing that the achievement of more substantive results in the implementation of the World Solar Programme 1996-2005 will require the active involvement of all concerned parties, including Governments, multilateral funding agencies and relevant bodies in the United Nations system,

1. *Takes note with appreciation* of the report of the Secretary-General concerning concrete action being taken to implement General Assembly resolutions 53/7, 54/215 and 55/205, and welcomes, in particular, the attempt therein to analyse and discuss the obstacles and constraints impeding the promotion of new and renewable sources of energy and options for action to overcome them;

2. *Notes with appreciation* the role that the World Solar Commission continues to play in the mobilization of international support and assistance for the implementation of many of the national high-priority projects on renewable sources of energy included in the World Solar Programme 1996-2005, many of which are being executed with national funding;

3. *Notes* that although significant financial support has been provided by some developed countries that are Members of the United Nations and some intergovernmental organizations, within and outside the United Nations system, in the implementation of the World Solar Programme 1996-2005, more action still needs to be taken in this regard;

4. *Encourages* national Governments and relevant stakeholders to make more use of the World Solar Programme 1996-2005 as one of the vehicles to boost the development and utilization of solar energy technologies and all forms of new and renewable energy, including biomass, wind, mini-hydro, tidal, ocean and geothermal forms;

5. *Invites* the international community to support, as appropriate, by, inter alia, providing financial resources, the efforts of developing countries to move towards sustainable patterns of energy production and consumption;

6. *Recognizes* that rural energy services, including their financing, should be designed to maximize local ownership, as appropriate;

7. *Reiterates its call upon* all relevant funding institutions and bilateral and multilateral donors, as well as regional funding institutions and non-governmental organizations, to support, as appropriate, the efforts being made for the development of the renewable energy sector in developing countries on the basis of environment-friendly renewable sources of energy of demonstrated viability, while taking fully into account the development structure of energy-based economies of developing countries, and to assist in the attainment of the levels of investment necessary to expand energy supplies beyond urban areas;

8. *Encourages* the Secretary-General to continue his efforts to promote the mobilization of adequate technical assistance and funding and to enhance the effectiveness and the full utilization of existing international funds for the effective implementation of national and regional high-priority projects in the area of renewable sources of energy;

9. *Emphasizes* the need to intensify research and development in support of energy for sustainable development, which will require increased commitment on the part of all stakeholders, including Governments and the private sector, to deploy financial and manpower resources for accelerating research efforts;

10. *Recognizes* that the wider use of available renewable energy technologies requires the diffusion of available technologies on a global scale, including through North-South and South-South cooperation;

11. *Takes note* of the decision of the General Conference of the United Nations Educational, Scientific and Cultural Organization regarding the contribution of the Global Renewable Energy Education and Training Programme 1996-2005 in attaining the objective of sustainable development, and in this context encourages the Director-General of the United Nations Educational, Scientific and Cultural Organization to mobilize resources, both human and financial, as mandated, to ensure the effective implementation of the Programme and to make efforts to promote public awareness in all Member States in this regard, with the support of international, regional and national institutions, both public and private;

12. *Invites* the Director-General of the United Nations Educational, Scientific and Cultural Organization to make effective the implementation of the Global Renewable Energy Education and Training Programme 1996-2005 in the various regions and to strengthen the implementation of its African chapter;

13. *Requests* the Secretary-General, in consultation with the United Nations Educational, Scientific and Cultural Organization and in cooperation with the United Nations Development Programme, the Global Environment Facility, the United Nations Environment Programme and other relevant organizations, to submit to the General Assembly at its fifty-eighth session a report on the concrete action being taken for the promotion of new and renewable sources of energy, including the effective implementation of and the mobilization of resources for the World Solar Programme 1996-2005;

14. *Decides* to include in the provisional agenda of its fifty-eighth session, under the item entitled "Environment and sustainable development", the sub-item entitled "Promotion of new and renewable sources of energy, including the implementation of the World Solar Programme 1996-2005".

Nuclear energy

1999 IAEA report. In accordance with decision 55/458 [YUN 2000, p. 962], the General Assembly considered the 1999 report of the International Atomic Energy Agency (IAEA) at its resumed fifty-fifth session in 2001.

GENERAL ASSEMBLY ACTION

On 16 March [meeting 96], the General Assembly adopted **resolution 55/244** [draft: A/55/L.75] without vote [agenda item 14].

Report of the International Atomic Energy Agency
The General Assembly,

Having received the report of the International Atomic Energy Agency to the General Assembly for the year 1999,

Noting the statement by the Director General of the Agency,

Recognizing the importance of the work of the Agency, and reaffirming its confidence in the role of the Agency,

Recognizing also the cooperation between the United Nations and the Agency and the Agreement covering the relationship between the United Nations and the Agency as approved by the General Conference of the Agency on 23 October 1957 and by the General Assembly in the annex to its resolution 1145(XII) of 14 November 1957,

Taking note of the resolutions and decisions adopted by the General Conference of the Agency at its forty-fourth regular session,

1. *Takes note* of the report of the International Atomic Energy Agency;

2. *Requests* the Secretary-General to transmit to the Director General of the Agency the records of the fifty-fifth session of the General Assembly relating to the activities of the Agency.

2000 IAEA report. By an August note [A/56/313], the Secretary-General transmitted to the General Assembly the 2000 report of IAEA. Presenting and updating the report in the Assembly on 22 October [A/56/PV.30], the IAEA Director General said that nuclear power, which in 2000 supplied about one sixth of global electricity, was the principal alternative to fossil fuels that could in the foreseeable future provide electricity on a large scale with practically no greenhouse gas emissions. The preceding 12 months had seen strong safety practices, reduced generating costs and the first extensions of power plant licences to 60 years. Six new plants were connected to national electricity grids, and 33 more were under construction by the end of 2000. Views on nuclear power, however, were still mixed because of safety and non-proliferation concerns and three crucial questions would determine its future: whether it would continue to prove itself a safe technology; whether it could be effectively safeguarded against non-peaceful purposes; and whether it could be an economically competitive technology. IAEA had established the International Project on Innovative Nuclear Reactors and Fuel Cycles to look into those and other questions.

The Director General noted that although IAEA had been at the forefront of encouraging States to make security an integral part of the management of their overall nuclear programmes, the 11 September attacks in the United States were a wake-up call that more could and must be done. Immediately following that tragedy, IAEA began a thorough review of its activities and programmes on preventing acts of terrorism involving nuclear and other radioactive materials. The Agency was engaged in a variety of activities, including programmes to ensure physical security, help prevent and respond to illicit trafficking of nuclear material and other radioactive sources, promote the safety of nuclear facilities, safeguard nuclear material against non-peaceful uses and respond to emergencies.

Through its research projects and technical cooperation programme, IAEA was working to strengthen the scientific and technological capacities of its Member States and functioned as a vehicle for the transfer of nuclear technologies to combat disease and child malnutrition, manage water resources, increase food production and protect the environment, the Director General said. In each of those areas of nuclear application, the Agency sought to promote the development and transfer of techniques that served the priorities of its Member States, with a focus on the special needs of developing countries.

The Director General noted that the development and adoption of international legally binding norms under the auspices of the Agency had significantly contributed to the enhancement of nuclear safety worldwide. To date, conventions had been developed covering the safety of power reactors, radioactive waste and spent fuel management, early notification and assistance in case of a nuclear accident or radiological emergency, and the physical protection of nuclear material. The Agency also maintained a comprehensive body of safety standards, which were being used by an increasing number of States for their national nuclear safety regulations. The Director General also discussed IAEA's inability to implement its nuclear inspection mandate in the Democratic People's Republic of Korea and in Iraq (see pp. 317, 292).

GENERAL ASSEMBLY ACTION

On 14 December [meeting 86], the General Assembly adopted **resolution 56/94** [draft: A/56/L.10 & Add.1] by recorded vote (150-1-2) [agenda item 14].

Report of the International Atomic Energy Agency

The General Assembly,

Having received the report of the International Atomic Energy Agency for the year 2000,

Taking note of the statement of the Director General of the International Atomic Energy Agency, in which he provided additional information on the main developments in the activities of the Agency during 2001,

Recognizing the importance of the work of the Agency in promoting the further application of nuclear energy for peaceful purposes as envisaged in the statute of the Agency and in accordance with the inalienable right of States parties to the Treaty on the Non-Proliferation of Nuclear Weapons and other relevant internationally legally binding agreements that have concluded relevant safeguards agreements with the Agency to develop research, production and use of nuclear energy for peaceful purposes without discrimination and in conformity with articles I and II and other

relevant articles of the Treaty, and with the objectives and purposes thereof,

Conscious of the importance of the safeguards system of the Agency and of the importance of the work of the Agency in the implementation of the safeguards provisions of the Treaty on the Non-Proliferation of Nuclear Weapons and other international treaties, conventions and agreements designed to achieve similar objectives, as well as in ensuring, as far as it is able, that the assistance provided by the Agency or at its request or under its supervision or control is not used in such a way as to further any military purpose, as stated in article II of its statute,

Reaffirming that the Agency is the competent authority responsible for verifying and assuring, in accordance with the statute and the safeguards system of the Agency, compliance with its safeguards agreements with States parties undertaken in fulfilment of their obligations under article III, paragraph 1, of the Treaty on the Non-Proliferation of Nuclear Weapons, with a view to preventing diversion of nuclear energy from peaceful uses to nuclear weapons or other nuclear explosive devices, and also reaffirming that nothing should be done to undermine the authority of the Agency in this regard and that States parties that have concerns regarding non-compliance with the safeguards agreement of the Treaty by the States parties should direct such concerns, along with supporting evidence and information, to the Agency to consider, investigate, draw conclusions and decide on necessary actions in accordance with its mandate,

Stressing the need for the highest standards of safety in the design and operation of nuclear installations and in peaceful nuclear activities so as to minimize risks to life, health and the environment, and recognizing that a good safety record relies on good technology, good regulatory practices and well-qualified and trained staff, as well as international cooperation,

Noting that a demonstrated global record of safety is a key element for the peaceful uses of nuclear energy and that continuous efforts are necessary to ensure that the human and technical elements of safety are maintained at the optimal level, and also noting that, although safety is a national responsibility, international cooperation on safety-related matters is indispensable,

Considering that an expansion of technical cooperation activities relating to the peaceful uses of nuclear energy will contribute to the well-being of the peoples of the world, recognizing the special needs of the developing countries for technical assistance from the Agency and the importance of funding in order to benefit effectively from the transfer and application of nuclear technology for peaceful purposes as well as from the contribution of nuclear energy to their economic development, and desiring that the resources of the Agency for technical cooperation activities be assured, predictable and sufficient to meet the objectives mandated in article II of its statute,

Conscious that the work done by the Agency in the field of nuclear sciences and applications in the non-power sector contributes to sustainable development, especially with programmes aimed at enhancing agricultural productivity and food security, improving human health, increasing the availability of drinking water supplies and protecting the terrestrial and marine environment,

Recognizing the importance of the work of the Agency on nuclear power, the fuel cycle and nuclear science, nuclear techniques for development and environmental protection and nuclear safety and protection against radiation, including its work directed towards assisting developing countries in all these fields,

Welcoming the convening of the fourth Scientific Forum, on the theme "Serving human needs: nuclear technology for sustainable development", during the forty-fifth regular session of the General Conference of the Agency,

Taking note of the report of the Director General to the General Conference of the International Atomic Energy Agency on the implementation of Security Council resolutions relating to Iraq, of his reports to the Security Council of 10 December 1999 and 11 October 2000, of 9 January, 12 February, 6 April and 5 October 2001, and of resolution GC(45)/RES/17 of 21 September 2001 of the General Conference,

Taking note also of resolution GC(45)/RES/16 in connection with the implementation of the Agreement between the Government of the Democratic People's Republic of Korea and the International Atomic Energy Agency for the application of safeguards in connection with the Treaty on the Non-Proliferation of Nuclear Weapons, the statements by the President of the Security Council of 31 March, 30 May and 4 November 1994 and the authorization of the Board of Governors, on 11 November 1994, to the Director General, to carry out all the tasks requested of the Agency in the statement by the President of the Security Council of 4 November 1994, noting recent political developments in northeast Asia, and expressing the hope that they will open the way to progress towards full implementation of the relevant agreements,

Taking note further of resolutions GC(45)/RES/10A on measures to strengthen international cooperation in nuclear, radiation and waste safety, GC(45)/RES/10B on transport safety, GC(45)/RES/10C on education and training, GC(45)/RES/11 on the strengthening of the technical cooperation activities of the Agency, GC(45)/RES/12A on the plan for producing potable water economically using small and medium-sized nuclear reactors, GC(45)/RES/12B on the use of isotope hydrology for water resources management, GC(45)/RES/12C on servicing immediate human needs, GC(45)/RES/12D on support to the Pan African Tsetse and Trypanosomiasis Eradication Campaign of the Organization of African Unity, GC(45)/RES/12E on drought in Central America, GC(45)/RES/12F on Agency activities in the development of innovative nuclear technology, GC(45)/RES/13 on strengthening the effectiveness and improving the efficiency of the safeguards system and the application of the Model Additional Protocol, GC(45)/RES/14A on measures against illicit trafficking in nuclear materials and other radioactive materials, GC(45)/RES/14B on the physical protection of nuclear material and nuclear facilities and GC(45)/RES/18 on the application of Agency safeguards in the Middle East, adopted on 21 September 2001 by the General Conference of the Agency at its forty-fifth regular session,

Taking note of resolution GC(45)/RES/15A on the staffing of the secretariat of the Agency, in which the General Conference called on developing and underrepresented member States to encourage well-qualified candidates to apply for vacant posts in the Agency, and considering the related resolution GC(45)/RES/15B on women in the secretariat, in which the General Conference called on the Director General to make every effort to rectify the present gender imbalance,

Recalling resolution GC(43)/RES/19 on the amendment to article VI of the statute and the statement by the President of the forty-third regular session of the General Conference of the Agency with respect to article VI, adopted on 1 October 1999 by the General Conference,

Taking note of the statement by the President of the forty-fifth regular session of the General Conference of the Agency, that:

"During the Conference, widespread condolences were expressed to the victims and their families as well as to the Government of the United States of America for the terrorist attacks that took place on 11 September 2001 in New York, Washington, D.C., and Pennsylvania. The delegates were unequivocal in their condemnation of these terrorists acts. As called for in General Assembly resolution 56/1 and Security Council resolution 1368(2001), the urgent need to work together to bring to justice the perpetrators, organizers and sponsors of these terrorist attacks and to hold accountable those responsible for aiding, supporting or harbouring the perpetrators, organizers and sponsors of these acts was supported. With particular regard to the Agency's mandate, the Conference expressed its concern about the possible impact of terrorism on the security of nuclear material and other radioactive materials. In this regard, the Conference requested the Director General to review thoroughly the activities and programmes of the Agency with a view to strengthening the Agency work relevant to preventing acts of terrorism involving nuclear materials and other radioactive materials. It further urged all member States to cooperate fully with the Director General and to support the Agency's efforts in this regard",

Taking note also of the statement by the President of the forty-fifth regular session of the General Conference of the Agency, which was endorsed by the General Conference at its tenth plenary meeting and issued under the item concerning Israeli nuclear capabilities and threat, that:

"The General Conference recalls the statement by the President of the thirty-sixth session in 1992 concerning the item entitled 'Israeli nuclear capabilities and threat'. That statement considered it desirable not to consider that item at the thirty-seventh session. The General Conference also recalls the statement by the President of the forty-third session, in 1999, concerning the same agenda item. At the forty-fourth and forty-fifth sessions, the item was, at the request of certain member States, included again in the agenda. The item was discussed. The President notes that certain member States intend to include the item in the provisional agenda of the forty-sixth regular session of the General Conference",

Noting with appreciation that the General Conference, in resolution GC(45)/RES/3, approved the appointment of Mr. Mohamed ElBaradei as the Director General until 30 November 2005,

1. *Takes note* of the report of the International Atomic Energy Agency;

2. *Affirms its confidence* in the role of the Agency in the application of nuclear energy for peaceful purposes;

3. *Encourages* all States members of the Agency that have not yet done so to ratify the amendment to article VI of the statute of the Agency, recalling the adoption by the General Conference of the Agency of resolution GC(43)/RES/19 on the amendment to article VI of the statute and the accompanying statement by the President of the forty-third regular session of the General Conference;

4. *Also encourages* all States members of the Agency that have not yet done so to ratify the amendment of article XIV.A of the statute of the Agency, recalling the adoption by the General Conference of the Agency of resolution GC(43)/RES/8 on the amendment of article XIV.A of the statute, which will provide for biennial budgeting by the Agency;

5. *Consistent* with the respective safeguards undertakings of member States and bearing in mind the importance of achieving the universal application of the safeguards system of the Agency, urges all States which have yet to bring into force comprehensive safeguards agreements to do so as soon as possible, affirms that measures to strengthen the effectiveness and improve the efficiency of the safeguards system with a view to detecting undeclared nuclear material and activities must be implemented rapidly and universally by all concerned States and other parties in compliance with their respective international commitments, stresses the importance of the safeguards system of the Agency, including comprehensive safeguards agreements and the Model Additional Protocol, which are among the essential elements of the system, requests all concerned States and other parties to safeguards agreements which have not yet done so promptly to sign additional protocols, requests the States and other parties to safeguards agreements having signed additional protocols to take the necessary measures to bring them into force as soon as their national legislation allows, and recommends that the Director General, the Board of Governors and member States continue to consider implementing the elements of the plan of action outlined in resolution GC(44)/RES/19, as appropriate and subject to available resources, with the aim of facilitating the entry into force of safeguards agreements and additional protocols and review the progress in this regard, and notes the important work being undertaken by the Agency, on an ongoing priority basis, in the conceptualization and development of integrated and cost-effective safeguards;

6. *Urges* all States to strive for effective and harmonious international cooperation in carrying out the work of the Agency, pursuant to its statute, in promoting the use of nuclear energy and the application of the necessary measures to strengthen further the safety of nuclear installations and to minimize risks to life, health and the environment, in strengthening technical assistance and cooperation for developing countries and in ensuring the effectiveness and efficiency of the safeguards system of the Agency;

7. *Recalls* resolution GC(45)/RES/12F on the activities of the Agency in the development of innovative nuclear technology, emphasizes the unique role that the Agency can play in developing user requirements and in addressing safeguards, safety and environmental questions for innovative reactors and their fuel cycles, within available extrabudgetary resources, and stresses the need for international collaboration in the development of innovative nuclear technology;

8. *Stresses* the need, in conformity with the statute of the Agency, to continue to pursue activities in the areas of nuclear science, technology and applications for meeting the basic sustainable development needs of member States, and also stresses the need to strengthen technical cooperation activities, including the provision of sufficient resources, and to enhance continually the effectiveness and efficiency of the programmes;

9. *Recalls* resolution GC(45)/RES/11 on the strengthening of the technical cooperation activities of the Agency, welcomes the measures and decisions taken by the Agency to strengthen and fund its technical cooperation activities, which should contribute to achieving sustainable development in developing countries, and calls upon States to cooperate in contributing to and in implementing the measures and decisions pursuant thereto;

10. *Reaffirms* the importance of all the measures contained in resolution GC(45)/RES/18 on the application of Agency safeguards in the Middle East, and calls upon all States in the region to implement all the provisions contained therein, including the application of full-scope Agency safeguards to all their nuclear activities, adherence to international non-proliferation regimes and the establishment of a nuclear-weapon-free zone in the region;

11. *Commends* the Director General and the secretariat of the Agency for their continuing, impartial efforts to implement the safeguards agreement still in force between the Agency and the Democratic People's Republic of Korea, recognizes the important role of the Agency in monitoring the freeze of nuclear facilities in that country as requested by the Security Council, notes with continuing concern that, although the Democratic People's Republic of Korea is a party to the Treaty on the Non-Proliferation of Nuclear Weapons, the Agency continues to be unable to verify the accuracy and completeness of the initial declaration of nuclear material it made and is therefore unable to conclude that there has been no diversion of nuclear material in the Democratic People's Republic of Korea, expresses deep concern about the continuing non-compliance of the Democratic People's Republic of Korea with the safeguards agreement between that country and the Agency, again urges the Democratic People's Republic of Korea to comply fully with its safeguards agreement, including all steps the Agency deems necessary to preserve all information relevant to verifying the accuracy and completeness of its initial declaration, and strongly encourages the Democratic People's Republic of Korea to respond positively and at an early date to the detailed proposal of the Agency for the first concrete steps needed for the implementation of the generic requirements for the verification of the accuracy and completeness of its initial declaration;

12. *Also commends* the Director General of the Agency and his staff for their strenuous efforts to implement Security Council resolutions 687(1991) of 3 April 1991, 707(1991) of 15 August 1991, 715(1991) of

11 October 1991, 1051(1996) of 27 March 1996, 1060 (1996) of 12 June 1996, 1115(1997) of 21 June 1997, 1154(1998) of 2 March 1998, 1194(1998) of 9 September 1998, 1205(1998) of 5 November 1998 and 1284(1999) of 17 December 1999, and calls upon Iraq to implement in full all relevant Security Council resolutions, including resolution 1284(1999), and in this regard to cooperate fully with the Agency and to provide the necessary access to enable it to carry out its mandate;

13. *Welcomes* the entry into force on 24 October 1996 of the Convention on Nuclear Safety, appeals to all States, particularly those operating, constructing, or planning nuclear power reactors, which have not yet taken the necessary steps to become parties to the Convention to do so, and looks forward to the second review meeting, due to take place in April 2002, expecting safety improvements in all areas, particularly in areas where the first review meeting found that there was room for improvement;

14. *Notes with satisfaction* that the Joint Convention on the Safety of Spent Fuel Management and on the Safety of Radioactive Waste Management entered into force on 18 June 2001, and appeals to all States which have not yet taken the necessary steps to become parties to it to do so in time to attend the first review meeting of the contracting parties;

15. *Recalls* resolution GC(45)/RES/10B on transport safety, and urges States to ensure that their national regulatory documents governing the transport of radioactive material are in conformity with the latest edition of the Agency's Transport Regulations;

16. *Welcomes* the measures taken by the Agency in support of efforts to prevent illicit trafficking in nuclear materials and other radioactive materials, and in this context decides to bear in mind, in its continued elaboration of an international convention on the suppression of acts of nuclear terrorism, those activities of the Agency, and urges all States to cooperate fully with the Director General and to support the efforts of the Agency in reviewing thoroughly the activities and programmes of the Agency with a view to strengthening its work relevant to preventing acts of terrorism involving nuclear materials and other radioactive materials;

17. *Appeals* to States that have not yet done so to accede to the Convention on the Physical Protection of Nuclear Material, also appeals to States to apply relevant physical protection recommendations and introduce and enforce appropriate measures and legislation to combat illicit trafficking in nuclear materials and other radioactive materials, welcomes the endorsement of the Physical Protection Objectives and Fundamental Principles referred to in document GC(45)/INF/14 by the Board of Governors of the Agency, encourages States to apply these principles in designing, implementing and regulating their national systems for the physical protection of nuclear material and nuclear facilities used for peaceful purposes, and welcomes the decision of the Director General to convene an open-ended group of legal and technical experts in order to prepare a draft of a well-defined amendment, to be subsequently reviewed by the States parties, aimed at strengthening the Convention on the Physical Protection of Nuclear Material and encouraging States to become parties to the Convention;

18. *Requests* the Secretary-General to transmit to the Director General of the Agency the records of the fifty-sixth session of the General Assembly relating to the activities of the Agency.

RECORDED VOTE ON RESOLUTION 56/94:

In favour: Albania, Algeria, Andorra, Angola, Antigua and Barbuda, Argentina, Armenia, Australia, Austria, Bahrain, Bangladesh, Belarus, Belgium, Benin, Bhutan, Bolivia, Bosnia and Herzegovina, Botswana, Brazil, Brunei Darussalam, Bulgaria, Burkina Faso, Cambodia, Canada, Cape Verde, Chile, China, Colombia, Comoros, Congo, Costa Rica, Croatia, Cuba, Cyprus, Czech Republic, Democratic Republic of the Congo, Denmark, Djibouti, Dominican Republic, Ecuador, Egypt, El Salvador, Equatorial Guinea, Eritrea, Estonia, Ethiopia, Fiji, Finland, France, Gabon, Georgia, Germany, Ghana, Greece, Grenada, Guatemala, Guyana, Haiti, Honduras, Hungary, Iceland, India, Indonesia, Iran, Ireland, Israel, Italy, Jamaica, Japan, Jordan, Kazakhstan, Kenya, Kuwait, Latvia, Lebanon, Libyan Arab Jamahiriya, Liechtenstein, Lithuania, Luxembourg, Madagascar, Malaysia, Maldives, Mali, Malta, Marshall Islands, Mauritius, Mexico, Micronesia, Monaco, Mongolia, Morocco, Mozambique, Myanmar, Nauru, Nepal, Netherlands, New Zealand, Nicaragua, Nigeria, Norway, Oman, Pakistan, Panama, Papua New Guinea, Paraguay, Peru, Philippines, Poland, Portugal, Qatar, Republic of Korea, Republic of Moldova, Romania, Russian Federation, Saint Lucia, Samoa, San Marino, Senegal, Seychelles, Sierra Leone, Singapore, Slovakia, Slovenia, Solomon Islands, South Africa, Spain, Sri Lanka, Sudan, Suriname, Sweden, Syrian Arab Republic, Thailand, The former Yugoslav Republic of Macedonia, Togo, Tonga, Trinidad and Tobago, Tunisia, Turkey, Ukraine, United Arab Emirates, United Kingdom and Northern Ireland, United Republic of Tanzania, United States, Uruguay, Vanuatu, Venezuela, Viet Nam, Yemen, Yugoslavia, Zambia.

Against: Democratic People's Republic of Korea.

Abstaining: Côte d'Ivoire, Lao People's Democratic Republic.

Natural resources

Water resources

Communication. Germany transmitted to the Secretary-General the Ministerial Declaration adopted at the International Conference on Freshwater (Bonn, 3-7 December) [E/CN.17/2002/PC.2/10]. Also transmitted were the Bonn Recommendations for Action and the Bonn Keys, which identified the main actions required to manage water better in order to achieve sustainable development.

International Year of Freshwater (2003)

In response to General Assembly resolution 55/196 [YUN 2000, p. 963], the Secretary-General submitted a July report on the status of preparations for the International Year of Freshwater, 2003 [A/56/189]. The report described potential activities, initiatives and networking at the international, national and local levels and gave examples of fund-raising activities that could be undertaken at the international and national levels. It also explored issues that would require greater attention during the Year and proposed further steps to be taken in preparation for it. The report was prepared by the ACC Subcommittee on Water Resources, which served as the coordinating body for the observance of the Year (see p. 940), in collaboration with its member UN entities and interested NGOs, such as the World Water Council, the Global Water Partnership and the Water Supply and Sanitation Collaborative Council.

On 21 December [meeting 90], the General Assembly, on the recommendation of the Second Committee [A/56/561/Add.8], adopted **resolution 56/192** without vote [agenda item 98].

Status of preparations for the International Year of Freshwater, 2003

The General Assembly,

Recalling its resolution 55/196 of 20 December 2000, in which it proclaimed 2003 as the International Year of Freshwater,

Recalling also the provisions of Agenda 21, the Programme for the Further Implementation of Agenda 21 adopted at its nineteenth special session and decisions of the Economic and Social Council and those of the Commission on Sustainable Development at its sixth session, relating to freshwater,

Recalling further its resolution 53/199 of 15 December 1998 on the proclamation of international years,

Reaffirming the goal of reducing by half, between 2000 and 2015, the proportion of people who are unable to reach or to afford safe drinking water,

Noting the efforts for the preparations for the Third World Water Forum, to be held in Japan in March 2003, and for the elaboration of the World Water Development Report,

Taking note of the report of the Secretary-General,

1. *Welcomes* the activities undertaken by States, the Secretariat, organizations of the United Nations system that are engaged in inter-agency work related to freshwater and major groups in preparation for the observance of the International Year of Freshwater, 2003, and encourages them to continue their efforts;

2. *Encourages* all Member States, the United Nations system and major groups to take advantage of the Year to raise awareness of the essential importance of freshwater resources for satisfying basic human needs and for health and food production and the preservation of ecosystems, as well as for economic and social development in general, and to promote action at the local, national, regional and international levels, and in this context calls for high priority to be given to the serious freshwater problems facing many regions, especially in the developing countries;

3. *Also encourages* all States, relevant international organizations and major groups to support activities related to the Year, inter alia, through voluntary contributions;

4. *Requests* the Secretary-General to submit to the General Assembly at its fifty-seventh session an interim report on the activities undertaken in preparation for the International Year of Freshwater, 2003.

Inter-agency action

The ACC Subcommittee on Water Resources, at its twenty-second session (Geneva, 24-28 September) [ACC/2001/18], discussed preparations for the World Summit on Sustainable Development, to be held in 2002 (see p. 749); preparations for the World Water Assessment Programme and the World Water Development Report (to be issued in 2003); groundwater assessment and manage-ment; activities related to preventing the use of arsenic-contaminated groundwater; regional activities; water supply and sanitation, including the possible terrorist threat to water supply systems; preparations of the International Year of Freshwater, 2003 (see above); activities undertaken for World Water Day 2001 (22 March) and those planned for World Water Day 2002; and the ongoing review process of the ACC structure and subsidiary bodies (see p. 1365).

With regard to the last issue, the Subcommittee stressed the need for a continued well-recognized and formal inter-agency coordination mechanism in the field of water resources.

Cartography

UN Regional Cartographic Conference for the Americas

In accordance with Economic and Social Council decision 1997/292 [YUN 1997, p. 1038], the Seventh United Nations Regional Cartographic Conference for the Americas was held in New York from 22 to 26 January [E/2001/11]. The Conference established three technical committees, which dealt with development needs and institutional capacity-building; fundamental data collection and management; and spatial data infrastructure (SDI) development in the Americas. The committees' deliberations confirmed that the concept of national SDI was gaining recognition as a fundamental asset of a society, equal to roads, communications networks, and other public utilities. The challenge for the cartographic/SDI community was not only knowing how to harness the enormous potential of geographic information/SDI technologies but also having the ability to restructure national mapping agencies and other governmental organizations to cooperate and to create regional and global data infrastructure standards.

The Conference recommended that the Economic and Social Council endorse its proposal that the Eighth Conference be convened no later than early 2005, with a primary focus on the continued and strengthened contribution of cartography and geographic information in support of the implementation of Agenda 21, adopted by the United Nations Conference on Environment and Development in 1992 [YUN 1992, p. 672]; and requested the Secretary-General to take measures, where appropriate and within available resources, to implement the other recommendations of the Conference, in particular, that the United Nations should continue to support surveying, mapping and spatial data infrastructure activities in the Americas region and continue, within available resources, to facilitate the participation of the least developed countries and the small island developing States of the region.

By **decision 2001/232** of 19 July, the Council endorsed the recommendations contained in the Secretary-General's report on the Conference. On the same date, it took note of the Secretary-General's report (**decision 2001/233**).

Chapter VII

Environment and human settlements

In 2001, the United Nations and the international community continued efforts to protect the environment through legally binding instruments and the activities of the United Nations Environment Programme (UNEP).

The second Global Ministerial Environment Forum/twenty-first session of the UNEP Governing Council (Nairobi, Kenya, 5-9 February) adopted decisions related to various aspects of the global ecosystem. During the Council's session, Governments expressed increasing concern that the current governance structures did not meet the needs of the environmental agenda. Thus, the Council initiated a review process on international environmental governance, which was aimed at a new model predicated on the need for sustainable development that met the inter-related social, economic and environmental requirements.

The United Nations Forum on Forests, a subsidiary body of the Economic and Social Council established to promote the management, conservation and sustainable development of all types of forests and to strengthen long-term political commitment to that end, at its first session (New York, 11-12 June), adopted its multi-year programme of work for 2001-2005 and plan of action, and outlined the functions of the Collaborative Partnership on Forests.

The Stockholm Convention on Persistent Organic Pollutants, which was adopted at a meeting of the Conference of Plenipotentiaries (Stockholm, Sweden, 22-23 May), was opened for signature on 23 May in Stockholm and at UN Headquarters from 24 May 2001 to 22 May 2002. The Convention set out control measures on the production, import, export, disposal and use of an initial list of 12 persistent organic pollutants (POPs) and included measures to reduce or eliminate the production and use of intentionally produced POPs; eliminate unintentionally produced POPs; and manage stockpiles and dispose of POP waste in an environmentally sound manner. The resumed sixth session of the Conference of the Parties to the United Nations Framework Convention on Climate Change (Bonn, Germany, 16-27 July) adopted the core elements for the implementation of the 1998 Buenos Aires Plan of Action to reduce the risk of global climate change (the Bonn Agreements), which provided for the establishment of two new funds to assist developing countries in adaptation, technology transfer and emissions reduction, and assist least developed countries in Convention implementation. At its seventh session (Marrakesh, Morocco, 29 October–10 November), the Conference adopted the Marrakesh Accords on modalities, guidelines and mechanisms to facilitate the entry into force of the 1997 Kyoto Protocol, which aimed to reduce industrialized countries' greenhouse gas emissions. The Thirteenth Meeting of the Parties to the 1985 Montreal Protocol (Colombo, Sri Lanka, 16-19 October) adopted the Colombo Declaration on Renewed Commitment to the Protection of the Ozone Layer to Mark the Forthcoming World Summit on Sustainable Development, in 2002, the Fifteenth Anniversary of the Montreal Protocol and the Tenth Anniversary of the Establishment of the Multilateral Fund.

The Millennium Ecosystem Assessment, a four-year international collaborative effort to evaluate the state of the major ecosystems (forests, freshwater systems, grasslands, coastal areas, agroecosystems) was launched in 2001 as part of the observance of World Environment Day on 5 June.

The General Assembly declared 6 November of each year as the International Day for Preventing the Exploitation of the Environment in War and Armed Conflict and invited Member States, UN system entities and other organizations to observe the Day.

The General Assembly convened its twenty-fifth special session (New York, 6-9 June) to review and appraise the implementation of the Habitat Agenda, a global call to action that offered a vision of adequate shelter for all and the sustainable development of human settlements, adopted by the 1996 United Nations Conference on Human Settlements (Habitat II). The Assembly adopted the Declaration on Cities and Other Human Settlements in the New Millennium, by which participants reaffirmed their commitment to the Habitat Agenda, presented an assessment of the implementation of the Habitat Agenda and proposed further action. In February, the Commission on Human Settlements, acting as the Preparatory Committee for the special session, held its second session and also convened its eighteenth regular session, during which it adopted 12 resolutions.

In December, the Assembly transformed the Commission on Human Settlements and its secretariat, the United Nations Centre for Human Settlements (Habitat), including the United Nations Habitat and Human Settlements Foundation, with effect from 1 January 2002, into the United Nations Human Settlements Programme (UN-Habitat), which would function as a subsidiary organ of the Assembly. The former Commission would serve as the UN-Habitat Governing Council.

Environment

UN Environment Programme

Governing Council/Ministerial Forum

The second Global Ministerial Environment Forum, also serving as the twenty-first session of the Governing Council of the United Nations Environment Programme (UNEP), was held at UNEP headquarters in Nairobi, Kenya, from 5 to 9 February [A/56/25]. It decided to convene the Governing Council's seventh special session in Cartagena, Colombia, from 13 to 15 February 2002 to consider preparations for the 2002 World Summit on Sustainable Development (see p. 749) and to discuss further the question of international environmental governance (see p. 944). The Council's twenty-second session would take place in Nairobi from 3 to 7 February 2003.

Ministerial consultations held on 8 and 9 February [UNEP/GC.21/9] focused on the implementation and development of the Nairobi Declaration on the Role and Mandate of the United Nations Environment Programme [YUN 1997, p. 1040], which declared UNEP the principal UN body and the leading global authority concerned with the environment, and on the Malmö Ministerial Declaration [YUN 2000, p. 968] (see p. 945). Other issues discussed were poverty and the environment, and health and the environment. A January paper of the UNEP Executive Director [UNEP/GC.21/5 & Corr.1] provided background information for the discussions.

The Committee of the Whole considered the programme of work, the Environment Fund and administrative and other budgetary matters [UNEP/GC.21/9].

Subsidiary bodies

The 36-member High-level Committee of Ministers and Officials, an intersessional subsidiary organ of the Governing Council established in 1997 [YUN 1997, p. 1040], during its fifth meeting (Nairobi, 4 February) [UNEP/HLC/5/3 & Corr.1], reviewed its role and mandate, in accordance with a 1997 Governing Council decision [YUN 1997, p. 1040]. Following consideration of a report of the Executive Director [UNEP/HLC/5/2] and a debate on the subject, the Committee concluded that it was no longer needed, as the Governing Council/Global Ministerial Environment Forum had assumed the functions expected of the Committee at the time it was established.

On 9 February [A/56/25 (dec. 21/20)], the Governing Council decided to discontinue the Committee.

In 2001, the Committee of Permanent Representatives, which was open to representatives of all UN Member States and members of specialized agencies, held a series of meetings, all in Nairobi. The Committee's seventy-fourth to seventy-seventh meetings were held on 30 March [UNEP/CPR/75/2], 27 June [UNEP/CPR/76/2], 19 September [UNEP/CPR/77/2] and 10 December [UNEP/CPR/78/2]; extraordinary meetings were convened on 24 January [UNEP/CPR/74/3] and 12 March [UNEP/CPR/74/4]. Over the course of the meetings, the Committee discussed, among other things, preparations for the Governing Council/Global Ministerial Environment Forum 2001 session, its contribution to the implementation of Council decision 21/21 on international environmental governance (see p. 944), UNEP relations with the United Nations Office at Nairobi (UNON), and preparations for the Council's seventh special session in 2002 and for the 2002 World Summit on Sustainable Development (see p. 749).

UNEP governance

In decision 21/20 [A/56/25] on UNEP governance and related aspects of General Assembly resolution 53/242 [YUN 1999, p. 975], the Governing Council decided, subject to the availability of an offer from a host country, to hold its sessions in alternate years in the UN regions, where possible, on a rotational basis. It called on Governments in a position to do so to provide financial resources to facilitate the participation of developing countries and countries with economies in transition in all meetings of the Governing Council/Global Ministerial Environment Forum. The Council decided that the proceedings of the Committee of Permanent Representatives would be conducted in all official languages, following the installation of full interpretation services in Nairobi. It requested the

Executive Director to provide all documentation for Council sessions to the Committee eight weeks in advance of the session and that the Committee endeavour to finish its work four weeks prior to the actual session. The Executive Director was also asked to notify designated focal points of upcoming UNEP meetings.

GENERAL ASSEMBLY ACTION

On 21 December [meeting 90], the General Assembly, on the recommendation of the Second (Economic and Financial) Committee [A/56/561/Add.8], adopted **resolution 56/193** without vote [agenda item 98].

Report of the Governing Council of the United Nations Environment Programme on its twenty-first session

The General Assembly,

Recalling its resolution 2997(XXVII) of 15 December 1972, by which it decided to establish the Governing Council of the United Nations Environment Programme,

Recalling also its resolution 55/200 of 20 December 2000 on the report of the Governing Council of the United Nations Environment Programme on its sixth special session,

Recalling further the Nairobi Declaration on the Role and Mandate of the United Nations Environment Programme and the United Nations Millennium Declaration,

Taking note with appreciation of the progress being made by the United Nations Environment Programme in the preparations for the World Summit on Sustainable Development,

1. *Takes note* of the report of the Governing Council of the United Nations Environment Programme on its twenty-first session;

2. *Welcomes* the efforts already made to realize the objectives of the Nairobi Declaration on the Role and Mandate of the United Nations Environment Programme, supports the early and full implementation of General Assembly resolution 53/242 of 28 July 1999, and requests that the reports on the work of the Environmental Management Group be made available to Member States and members of specialized agencies;

3. *Reiterates* the invitation to the international environmental governance process initiated by decision 21/21 of 9 February 2001 of the Governing Council of the United Nations Environment Programme to submit its progress report to the Preparatory Committee for the World Summit on Sustainable Development at its second session, to be held in New York from 28 January to 8 February 2002, and to submit the final results to the Committee at its third session, to be held in New York from 25 March to 5 April 2002, so that it may be fully considered in the preparatory process, and notes with interest the ongoing work of the open-ended intergovernmental group of ministers or their representatives on international environmental governance with respect to the comprehensive policy-oriented assessment of existing institutional weaknesses, as well as future needs and options for strengthened international environmental governance;

4. *Underlines* the need for sufficient financial resources on a stable and predictable basis to ensure the full implementation of the mandate of the Programme, and, within this context, notes ongoing related deliberations;

5. *Notes* the proposal of the Secretary-General to increase United Nations funding for the cost of servicing the Programme secretariat and the Governing Council from the regular budget;

6. *Requests* the Secretary-General to keep the resource needs of the United Nations Environment Programme and the United Nations Office at Nairobi under continuous review and to make proposals as needed in the context of the United Nations regular budget, with a view to strengthening the Programme and the Office.

International environmental governance

During the Governing Council's 2001 session, Governments expressed increasing concern that the current governance structures did not meet the needs of the environmental agenda. Thus, the Council initiated a review process on international environmental governance, which was aimed at a new model predicated on the need for sustainable development that met the inter-related social, economic and environmental requirements.

Council action. On 9 February [dec. 21/21], the Governing Council called on UNEP and UN Members and specialized agencies to implement General Assembly resolution 53/242 [YUN 1999, p. 975] as a basis for further institutional strengthening. It decided to establish an open-ended intergovernmental group of ministers or their representatives (see p. 945), with the Executive Director as an ex-officio member, to undertake a policy-oriented assessment of existing institutional weaknesses, as well as future needs and options to strengthen international environmental governance, including the financing of UNEP, and to present a report on analysis and options to the next session of the Governing Council/Global Ministerial Environment Forum. The Committee of Permanent Representatives was requested to provide its input for the process. The Council/Forum should provide its input on future requirements of international environmental governance in the broader context of sustainable development to the tenth session of the Commission on Sustainable Development (CSD), acting as the preparatory body for the World Summit on Sustainable Development (see p. 749), at its ministerial-level meeting in May 2002. The Council's President was requested to inform CSD of its decision and of the views expressed at the Council's current session by the Ministers of the Environment on international environmental governance. The Executive Director was requested, in consultation with Governments, to review the state of international environmental governance and to report to the intergovernmental group at its first meeting. He was also asked to seek additional resources from Governments in a position to do so to support the process, particularly to facilitate the participation of developing country representatives.

Intergovernmental group. In 2001, the Open-ended Intergovernmental Group of Ministers or Their Representatives on International Environmental Governance met four times: New York, 18 April [UNEP/IGM/1/3]; Bonn, 17 July [UNEP/IGM/2/6]; Algiers, Algeria, 9-10 September [UNEP/IGM/3/3]; and Montreal, Canada, 30 November-1 December [UNEP/IGM/4/6]. At its first meeting, the Group considered an April report of the Executive Director [UNEP/IGM/1/2], which described the current state of international environmental governance, reviewed the strengths and weaknesses of the existing arrangements, presented information on financing for the global environment, assessed the needs of the current environmental agenda and put forward options to strengthen international environmental governance. The Executive Director updated the report in August [UNEP/IGM/3/2] and revised it in November [UNEP/IGM/4/3] to include a sustainable development perspective and capacity-building, technology transfer and financing issues. In order to receive input on the issues raised in the Executive Director's report from expert institutions, major groups and individuals outside the UN system, civil society consultations (Nairobi, 22-23 May) and expert consultations (Cambridge, United Kingdom, 28-29 May) were held [UNEP/IGM/2/2]. The Intergovernmental Group had before it contributions on the governance process provided by the Environmental Management Group (EMG), an advisory group set up to coordinate UN system activities in addressing the major challenges in the UNEP work programme [UNEP/IGM/2/INF/4], and by the Committee of Permanent Representatives [UNEP/IGM/2/3]. The Group considered the concept of enhancing the coordination of international activities related to chemicals and waste through a chemicals and waste cluster [UNEP/IGM/2/INF/2 & Add.1]; a policy paper on improving international environmental governance among multilateral environment agreements (MEAs) [UNEP/IGM/2/4]; a report on the status of MEAs [UNEP/IGM/2/INF/3]; a proposal for a systematic approach to coordinate MEAs [UNEP/IGM/2/5]; and clustering as a policy and management strategy for enhancing coordination and policy coherence among MEAs [UNEP/IGM/4/4]. Based on proposals of the Governing Council President [UNEP/IGM/4/2], the Group established working groups to discuss improving coherence in policy-making (the role and structure of the Global Ministerial Environment Forum); strengthening UNEP's role, authority and financial situation; and improved coordination and coherence between MEAs, capacity-building, technology transfer and country-level coordination for environment and sustainable development, as well as enhanced coordination across the UN system (the role of EMG). The Group would present its final report in 2002.

Malmö Ministerial Declaration

The Malmö Ministerial Declaration, adopted by the Governing Council in 2000 [YUN 2000, p. 968], identified the major environmental challenges of the twenty-first century, as well as ways for the international community to address those challenges.

In a report on the Declaration's implementation [UNEP/GC.21/3], the Executive Director stated that the challenges and opportunities articulated in the Declaration were being actively addressed by UNEP to turn them into concrete action. Fragmented sectoral policy responses were being made more coherent and integrated in order to address effectively the multifaceted environmental dimensions of sustainable development. Areas of implementation covered in the report were: access to environment and environment-related information; environmental law; integrating environmental dimensions into economic policies; promoting environmental accountability; the engagement of civil society; the new ethics concerning respect for nature; programmatic responses to environmental threats; and the 10-year review of progress achieved in the implementation of the outcome of the United Nations Conference on Environment and Development (UNCED) [YUN 1992, p. 670] (see p. 749).

On 9 February [dec. 21/18], the Governing Council decided to transmit the Declaration to other UN system intergovernmental bodies and conferences, including international financial institutions, and to invite them to promote its implementation. The Council invited CSD to consider the integration of the Declaration's commitments into its work, especially in preparation for the 2002 World Summit on Sustainable Development (see p. 749). The Executive Director was asked to take further steps regarding the Declaration as it related to the mandate of UNEP, and to monitor the Declaration's implementation and report thereon to the Committee of Permanent Representatives and to the Governing Council at its next session.

UNEP activities

A report of the Executive Director [UNEP/GC.21/2] described action taken in UNEP areas of activities, as defined by the Governing Council in a 1998 decision [YUN 1998, p. 982], including environmental assessment and information; the development and implementation of environmental policy instruments; support to Africa; and technology transfer and industry.

A January policy statement of the Executive Director [UNEP/GC.21/8] provided information on the global context for UNEP's work, and on progress in the five areas of UNEP concentration (environmental information, assessment and early warning; enhanced coordination of environmental conventions and the development of environmental policy instruments; freshwater; technology transfer and industry; and support to Africa).

Support to Africa

On 9 February [dec. 21/15], the Governing Council, noting the escalating and emerging environmental problems in Africa, requested the Executive Director to: develop and promote understanding of the linkages between poverty and the environment, means of making people's livelihoods more productive and environmentally sustainable, and policy options for Governments that aimed at integrating the environment in central social and economic processes, including poverty reduction strategies and development frameworks; continue to support the implementation of a 1999 Governing Council decision on support to Africa [YUN 1999, p. 980], particularly within the context of the African Ministerial Conference on the Environment (AMCEN), which was established in 1985 [YUN 1985, p. 793] and scheduled to hold a special session in October 2001 [AMCEN/ SS/2001/12], as well as other African regional and subregional organizations; and assist African countries in the preparations for the seventh (2001) Conference of the Parties to the United Nations Framework Convention on Climate Change (see p. 955) and for the 2002 World Summit on Sustainable Development (see p. 749). Donor countries, international financial institutions and the UN system, including UNEP, were called on to provide financial support and expertise.

The Council asked the Executive Director to support the implementation of the 1981 Abidjan Convention for Cooperation in the Protection and Development of the Marine and Coastal Environment of the West and Central African Region [YUN 1981, p. 840], the 1985 Nairobi Convention for the Protection, Management and Development of the Marine and Coastal Environ-

ment of the Eastern African Region [YUN 1985, p. 816] and the 1991 Bamako Convention on the Ban of the Import of All Forms of Hazardous Waste into Africa and the Control of Transboundary Movements of such Wastes Generated in Africa [YUN 1991, p. 627]; to strengthen the Abidjan and Nairobi Conventions; and to report on progress made to the Committee of Permanent Representatives and the Council in 2003.

In a November report [UNEP/GCSS.VII/4], the Executive Director described UNEP activities in support of Africa, including a meeting of climate change negotiators from Africa; support for the participation of African countries in meetings on biodiversity and biosafety; and support for the implementation of the United Nations Convention to combat desertification [YUN 1994, p. 944] (see p. 959), especially for preparing national action plans. In the area of regional agreements and conventions, UNEP made efforts to mobilize African Governments to revitalize the 1981 Abidjan Convention and helped develop a funding mechanism to ensure the financial reliability, predictability and sustainability of the Convention's budget. UNEP facilitated the participation by African countries in expert meetings held in Geneva (August) and in Nairobi (October) to develop guidelines on compliance with and enforcement of MEAs. The African Preparatory Conference for the World Summit on Sustainable Development (Nairobi, 15-18 October) was organized by UNEP, working with the Economic Commission for Africa (ECA), the African Development Bank and the United Nations Development Programme (UNDP) as the joint expanded secretariat for the preparation of the Summit. In association with the African Preparatory Conference, UNEP organized an industry workshop as an input to the ministerial segment of the Conference, as well as a meeting of nongovernmental organizations (NGOs). UNEP continued to provide secretariat functions for AMCEN. Other areas of support related to cleaner production centres; sustainable energy; rural energy development; renewable energy projects; industry outreach activities; climate change; biodiversity; international waters; and the emerging priority areas of land degradation, persistent organic pollutants and biosafety.

The UNEP/Global Environment Facility (GEF) portfolio in Africa in 2001 included 61 activities with a total budget of some $48 million. During the year, 14 activities in the Africa portfolio were approved, with total funding of $8.4 million, including $4.7 million in GEF resources.

At the subregional level, UNEP established in June a liaison office in Addis Ababa, Ethiopia, to further enhance cooperation with ECA and the

Organization of African Unity. Under the United Nations System-wide Special Initiative on Africa (see p. 851), UNEP assisted African countries in reinforcing environmental management capacities; in formulating and implementing key water resource policies and management programmes; and in creating a "water forum".

Water policy and strategy

On 9 February [dec. 21/11], the Governing Council, taking note of a report of the Executive Director [UNEP/GC.21/INF/21] on progress made to implement Council decisions adopted in 1999 on freshwater [YUN 1999, p. 981] and in 2000 on UNEP's water policy and strategy [YUN 2000, p. 969], accepted UNEP's refined water policy and strategy as contained in a further report of the Executive Director [UNEP/GC.21/2/Add.1]. Expressing appreciation for the establishment of an expert group on exchange of information on best practices in freshwater management, the Council decided that UNEP should prioritize the identification of available expertise and knowledge relating to the environmental aspects of water quality; facilitate the establishment of partnerships between countries that had expertise and countries that needed it; and promote intergovernmental collaboration at the request of the Governments concerned. The Executive Director was asked to enhance, through the International Environmental Technology Centre, the transfer of environmentally sound technologies for water management; intensify collaboration with Governments, upon request, as well as with other organizations and agencies to further water policy and strategy implementation; and take measures to implement the water policy and strategy and to review it in 2003. He was further requested to identify key policy issues for the environmental aspects of water and to propose policy options in 2003. The Governing Council requested the Executive Director to report to the Council in 2003 on progress made to implement its decision.

Environment and sustainable development

In 2001, CSD, acting as the Preparatory Committee for the World Summit on Sustainable Development (see p. 749), began preparations for the 10-year review in 2002 of the implementation of Agenda 21—a programme of action for sustainable development worldwide, which was adopted by UNCED in 1992 [YUN 1992, p. 672].

The Preparatory Committee considered reports relating to the transfer of environmentally sound technologies, cooperation and capacity-building and environmentally sound manage-

ment of biotechnology; sustainable mountain development; the global status of biodiversity; oceans and seas; protection of the atmosphere; agriculture, land and desertification; progress in forestry since UNCED; and management of toxic chemicals and hazardous and radioactive wastes (see p. 749).

A report of the Executive Director [UNEP/GC.21/2] highlighted UNEP's contribution to future sessions of CSD in the areas related to the protection of the atmosphere (see p. 963), energy, transport (see below), information for decision-making and participation, and international cooperation for an enabling environment.

Commission action. CSD, at its ninth session (New York, 5 May 2000 and 16-27 April 2001) [E/2001/29] (see p. 747), considered a report of the Secretary-General on transport and sustainable development [E/CN.17/2001/3]. The report reviewed the environmental impact of transport systems and the problems of current transport technology. It recommended policy options to promote sustainability in the transport sector at the national, regional and international levels. Annexed to the report was information on the Global Initiative on Transport Emissions, a joint project of the United Nations and the World Bank, with the cooperation of the private sector, to facilitate cooperation among the automotive and petroleum industries, developing countries and relevant international agencies to promote energy efficiency and reduce environmental problems.

The Intersessional Ad Hoc Working Group on Transportation and Atmosphere (New York, 6-9 March) [E/CN.17/2001/16], which served as a preparatory body for the ninth session of CSD, submitted possible elements for a draft decision on transport.

On 27 April [E/2001/29 (dec. 9/3)], the Commission, emphasizing the importance of international cooperation in ensuring that transport was considered within the general framework of sustainable development, recommended a series of measures to the international community regarding the transfer of cleaner technologies, energy efficiency and the improvement of transport systems; partnerships between the public and private sectors to introduce environmentally sound technologies; and the use of technology transfer of cleaner fuels. Regional cooperation was encouraged through the better utilization of the regional commissions and existing regional development banks, organizations and mechanisms. At the national level, Governments were encouraged to develop transportation systems that were responsive to development needs and, where affordable, would reduce negative environmental impacts. They were also encouraged to involve the private sector in improvements in efficiency and vehicle emission control.

By **decision 56/439** of 21 December, the General Assembly took note of the report of the Second Committee on environment and sustainable development [A/56/561]; by **decision 56/464** of 24 December, the Assembly decided that the agenda item on environment and sustainable development would remain for consideration at its resumed fifty-sixth (2002) session.

Policy and advisory services

Institution-building

A report of the Executive Director [UNEP/GC.21/4] stated that, in accordance with Governing Council decisions adopted in 1999 [YUN 1999, pp. 973 & 998], UNEP continued to provide developing countries and those with economies in transition with policy and advisory services, particularly technical, legal and policy advice to develop national environmental legislation and relevant institutions. It supported African countries in developing environmental policy and policy instruments and in enhancing their national environmental legislation and related institutions. UNEP had strengthened its regional presence to ensure effective government participation in its work and to take into account regional concerns, priorities and perspectives in the development of policies, planning and implementation. It provided Governments and other parties with information on the state of the global environment and global environmental issues and with advisory services, and provided technical assistance to Governments upon request. Financial limitations had been the deciding factor in determining the amount of UNEP assistance provided; extrabudgetary resources had allowed the provision of assistance to more countries than otherwise would have been possible.

In response to a 1999 Governing Council decision [YUN 1999, p. 973], the Council considered a January report [UNEP/GC.21/INF/15] on the provision of policy and advisory services in key areas of institution-building. UNEP contributed to institution-building in countries at the national and regional levels by providing advisory services on scientific and technical matters, legal advisory services and information on legal, economic and policy instruments and tools, and by convening forums for policy dialogue. Specific activities covered environmental information, assessment and research, including environmental emergency response capacity and strengthening early warning and assessment; enhanced coordination of

environmental conventions and the development of environmental policy instruments; freshwater initiatives, technology transfer and industry; and support to Africa.

On 9 February [A/56/25 (dec. 21/24)], the Governing Council requested the Executive Director to strengthen further the provision of technical, legal and policy advice to Governments and regional and subregional institutions dealing with environmental matters, to continue to improve public access to information on environmental matters and policy instruments, and to promote the development of relevant skills and the capacity of key stakeholders and partners. He was asked to report in 2002 on international legal instruments reflecting the provisions contained in principle 10 of the Rio Declaration on Environment and Development [YUN 1992, p. 670], which underlined the fact that environmental issues were best handled with the participation of all concerned citizens and that, at the national level, individuals should have access to information concerning the environment that was held by public authorities.

Economics, trade and financial services

A January note of the Executive Director [UNEP/GC.21/INF/22] described UNEP's activities in the areas of economics, trade and finance, which were aimed at improving countries' understanding of the interlinkages and complementarities between environment, trade and development; enhancing countries' capacities in integrating environmental considerations into macroeconomic policies, including trade policies; and promoting sustainable development policies in the financial services sector. The note covered key challenges and UNEP's responses to them, including enhancing awareness and understanding, capacity-building, developing innovative policy tools, fostering partnerships and building consensus, promoting the role of financial services in sustainable development, and increasing international cooperation.

On 9 February [dec. 21/14], the Governing Council requested the Executive Director to further strengthen the secretariat to assist countries, particularly developing countries and countries with economies in transition, to enhance their capacities to develop and implement mutually supportive trade and environmental policies. It agreed that the Executive Director, in close cooperation with the World Trade Organization and the United Nations Conference on Trade and Development, should develop national capacities to assess the environmental effects of trade; study the effectiveness of market-based incentives in achieving the objectives of MEAs; and continue to promote understanding, dialogue and the dissemination of information about MEAs. The Executive Director was requested to further promote the national development and application of environmental impact assessment, environmental valuation, methodologies for natural resource accounting and relevant economic instruments, in accordance with the socio-economic and development priorities of individual countries; to continue to collaborate with the private sector, including the financial services sector, to enhance its contribution to the achievement of sustainable development through cleaner and more resource-efficient technologies for a life-cycle economy and the transfer of environmentally sound technologies to developing countries; and to consult and brief Governments and to report in 2003.

Coordination and cooperation

Implementation of resolution 53/242

The Governing Council addressed the implementation of various aspects of General Assembly resolution 53/242 [YUN 1999, p. 975], which dealt with issues related to coordination and cooperation, including strengthening UN activities in the area of environment and human settlements.

On 9 February [dec. 21/20], the Council asked the Executive Director to propose to relevant UN system organizations a joint review of their roles in the area of the environment, aimed at identifying and analysing the need for strengthened coordination and cooperation; to continue efforts to enhance policy coherence and synergy among international legal instruments related to the environment and sustainable development at the inter-agency and intergovernmental levels; to promote further international action to enhance synergy between UNEP programmes and multilateral environmental conventions; to promote further the engagement of the private sector in addressing environmental challenges; and to ensure that capacity-building and technical assistance, as well as research and scientific studies in the area of the environment, remained important components of UNEP's work programme. It encouraged the Executive Director to strengthen UNEP's collaboration with the United Nations Centre for Human Settlements. He was asked to report in 2003.

The Council asked EMG to publish a benchmark report on progress in its work at regular intervals, urged the Secretary-General to secure resources to ensure the proper functioning of the EMG secretariat and invited Governments in a position to do so to contribute resources.

The Secretary-General was urged to provide resources from the UN regular budget to UNEP for 2002-2003 and to consider other ways of lending support to strengthening UNEP, in view of preparations for and the outcome of the World Summit on Sustainable Development (see p. 749).

Environmental emergencies

On 9 February [dec. 21/17], the Governing Council, having considered a report of the Executive Director containing a draft strategic framework on emergency prevention, preparedness, assessment, response and mitigation [YUN 2000, p. 969], welcomed the Strategic Framework (see p. 950) and requested the Executive Director to establish a process for comments on it and thereafter to support its implementation within UNEP's mandate. It asked the Executive Director to enhance long-term strategic cooperation with the Office for the Coordination of Humanitarian Affairs (OCHA), including the International Strategy for Disaster Reduction (see p. 861), through the joint UNEP/OCHA Environment Unit; to present in 2003 an analysis of the causes and long-term environmental effects of emergencies and the possible policy implications for Governments and the international community; to strengthen cooperation between UNEP and other relevant international organizations in order to assess whether gaps existed in protecting the environment from accidents and man-made disasters; and to support the parties to the Convention on Biological Diversity (see p. 957) in their efforts to consider the issue of non-economic environmental harm, notably by encouraging and promoting cooperation with other relevant international organizations and institutions.

In 2001, the joint UNEP/OCHA Unit established the Core Group of the Advisory Group on Environmental Emergencies (AGEE-CG), which met between full meetings of the Advisory Group on Environmental Emergencies (AGEE) that took place every two years, to discuss selected issues in more substantive detail than could be allowed for in the larger AGEE meetings. At its first meeting (Paris, 5 November), AGEE-CG focused on terrorism and the specific elements that made it a unique threat compared to other environmental and human threats and considered the potential role of the joint Unit. Much of the discussion took place against the background of the terrorist attacks of 11 September in the United States (see p. 60). The Group made a series of recommendations for the work of the joint Unit regarding the environmental components of terrorism, and information gathering and sharing.

During the year, the joint Unit coordinated responses to the environmental aspects of emergencies resulting from floods in Iran, a dump site collapse in the Philippines and drought in Uzbekistan.

Strategic Framework

The 2001 UNEP Strategic Framework on Emergency Prevention, Preparedness, Assessment, Mitigation and Response provided guidance for UNEP's future work in the area of emergencies by identifying the institutional and global contexts for action, as well as its role and key partners within the UN system. It defined environmental emergencies as sudden-onset disasters or accidents resulting from natural, technological or human-induced factors, or a combination thereof, that caused or threatened to cause severe environmental damage, as well as loss of human lives and property. The Framework noted that there was increasing global attention to emergencies, reflecting a complex interplay of economic, social, political and environmental conditions.

Global Environment Facility

The Global Environment Facility (GEF), a joint programme of UNDP, UNEP and the World Bank, was established in 1991 [YUN 1991, p. 505] to forge international cooperation and finance activities to address global environmental problems.

On 9 February [dec. 21/25], the Governing Council, having considered a report of the Executive Director containing information on UNEP's participation in GEF from 1999 to 2000 [UNEP/GC/21/4] and a note by the secretariat [YUN 2000, p. 970] on the status of the implementation of the Action Plan on Complementarity between the activities undertaken by UNEP under GEF and its regular programme of work [YUN 1999, p. 977], welcomed the progress made by the Executive Director in strengthening UNEP's role as an implementing agency of GEF and progress achieved in implementing the Action Plan. The Executive Director was requested to keep Governments informed of further progress achieved in enhancing UNEP's role in GEF.

The UNEP portfolio of ongoing activities in 2001 was valued at $369 million, including $194 million in GEF financing. In addition, UNEP was co-implementing, with partner agencies, 15 projects whose UNEP component was worth $30 million. The overall work programme involved the participation of 144 countries.

Regarding the development of the UNEP/GEF portfolio, between January and December 2001, 53 new activities valued at $95 million, including $41 million in GEF financing, were approved. They included five full-size projects, 15 medium-size projects, 13 Project Preparation and Development Facility grants and 20 enabling activities, including those on persistent organic pollutants (POPs). The newly approved activities addressed conserving agro-biodiversity, climate change, POPs, land degradation and integrated catchment management.

Memorandums of understanding

In 2001 [UNEP/GC.22/INF/6], UNEP signed memorandums of understanding (MOUs) with the United Nations Office for Project Services (UNOPS) (February) to establish the terms and conditions for UNOPS to provide services to UNEP; and with the United Nations University (April) to collaborate and consult on issues of common interest, including research and capacity-building projects and other activities at the global, regional and national levels, in order to coordinate their work and to strengthen cooperation.

Participation of civil society

On 9 February [dec. 21/19], the Governing Council requested the Executive Director to further the consultative process with Governments, civil society, the private sector and other major groups on ways to enhance the active engagement and participation of civil society in UNEP's work. It also asked him to submit a report on the outcome of the consultations, as well as a draft strategy for the active engagement of civil society, the private sector and other major groups in UNEP's work, to the Committee of Permanent Representatives, and subsequently to the Council in 2002. The Council decided to include the item in the provisional agenda of its special session in 2002.

Pursuant to the Council's decision, the Executive Director held global and regional consultations and, in December [UNEP/GCSS.VII/4/Add.1], issued a draft strategy for enhanced civil society participation in UNEP's work, particularly in relation to programme implementation, institutional structures and outreach. Specific strengths and weaknesses related to policy, programme, institutional aspects, outreach, consultation and finance were examined during the consultations and brought to the attention of the Committee of Permanent Representatives in August.

Involvement of youth

On 9 February [dec. 21/22], the Governing Council, recalling aspects relating to the involvement of youth in environmental issues contained in the World Programme of Action for Youth to the Year 2000 and Beyond, adopted by the General Assembly in resolution 50/81 [YUN 1995, p. 1211], and also in Agenda 21, a global plan of action for sustainable development adopted at

UNCED [YUN 1992, p. 672], requested the Executive Director to develop a long-term strategy on how UNEP intended to engage and involve young people in environmental issues and debates; declare the engagement and involvement of young people a priority by undertaking a series of activities; and seek extrabudgetary resources to facilitate those activities. It decided to discuss ways of engaging and involving young people in UNEP's work in 2003.

The Youth Conference on Environment and Sustainable Development (Borgholm, Sweden, 23-27 May) marked the beginning of the Youth for Sustainable Development process, launched by UNEP in cooperation with Sweden and Nature and Youth of Denmark in preparation for the 2002 World Summit on Sustainable Development (see p. 749). A joint UNEP/United Nations Educational, Scientific and Cultural Organization (UNESCO) project on youth and sustainable consumption, designed to provide insight on consumption trends and motives of young people aged between 18 and 25 and to open a dialogue with the future decision makers, was under way.

UNEPnet/Mercure

In response to a 1999 Governing Council request [YUN 1999, p. 979], the Executive Director presented, in January [UNEP/GC.21/7/Add.2], a comprehensive review and cost-benefit analysis, conducted by independent external consultants, of the Mercure satellite communications system, UNEPnet (Internet mechanisms for environmental information access and exchange) and the UNEPnet Implementation Centre. The Mercure system was designed by the European Space Agency in response to an Agenda 21 call to utilize modern electronic telecommunications to improve access to, and the exchange of, environmental data and information for responsible decision-making concerning the environment. The consultants found that UNEPnet had played an important role in the functioning of UNEP's environmental information systems, ensuring electronic connectivity for many UNEP-sponsored establishments; had helped UNEP centres to gather and distribute data sets and services contributing to UNEP's programmatic goals; and had been effective in building environmental information capacity for some programme-targeted locations, allowing some sites to post and receive environmental data and information from the broader global Internet. The consultants reported that the Mercure satellite capacity was rapidly becoming saturated, which could be avoided by the full use of the system's technical capacity, and that there was a financial argument for making more use of Mercure. Due to the

growth of Internet sites supplying environmental data, UNEP no longer needed to provide its own, expensive networking capacity, and should seek alternative means of information-sharing and data dissemination using existing Internet-based solutions.

Based on the consultants' findings and recommendations, the Division of Early Warning and Assessment, the Office of the Deputy Executive Director, UNON and the consultants developed a plan of action to address institutional developments intended to streamline the strategic management of UNEP's information and communication technology requirements; operational development designed to meet UNEP's telecommunications requirements through commercial contract provisions, with possible components to assist less developed nations in bridging the "digital divide"; and environmental information services developments emphasizing closer coordination, leadership and collaborative efforts with major developers and providers of environmental information.

The report contained a history of funding sources for UNEPnet/Mercure, which indicated that the total cost of the programme to the Environment Fund for 2000 and 2001 amounted to $213,200 per annum.

On 9 February [dec. 21/34], the Governing Council requested the Executive Director to implement the action plan, while ensuring the continuity of services currently provided by UNEPnet/Mercure to UNEP and other UN bodies and agencies in Nairobi. It authorized him to make direct donation of the Mercure ground station facilities implemented at partner sites in Bolivia, China, Costa Rica, Cuba, Kazakhstan, Mozambique, Nepal, the Niger and Viet Nam effective as at the end of 2001, and asked him to invite those countries, as well as other UN bodies and agencies at UNON, to continue participating in Mercure on a cost-sharing basis. The Executive Director was further requested to report biannually to the Committee of Permanent Representatives on the further development of the Mercure telecommunications system for UNON, with special emphasis on its costs and cost recovery, and to report in 2003 on the implementation of the action plan.

Global Environment Outlook

As requested by the Governing Council in 1999 [YUN 1999, p. 979], the Executive Director submitted a user profile and impact study [UNEP/GC.21/INF/8] of the first (GEO-1) [YUN 1997, p. 1043] and second (GEO-2) [YUN 1999, p. 979] Global Environment Outlook (GEO) reports, which assessed the state of the environment, and of the GEO process. Data compiled through questionnaires, interviews and case studies indicated that ministers, senior advisers and permanent representatives found GEO-2 to be useful as an overview of the environmental situation at the global and regional levels, providing policy guidance at the national or regional levels, identifying emerging issues and putting national issues in a broader perspective. It was used as an authoritative source for environmental information by both the United Nations and the media, and was being used as course-related material by universities and other academic institutions. The GEO-2 report and process were contributing to regional and national policy development around the world, most identifiably in the growing adoption of the GEO methodology for the production and improvement of state-of-the-environment reports. The report contained sales and distribution data for GEO-2.

A report of the Executive Director [UNEP/GC.21/2] contained UNEP proposals regarding the optimal frequency and production schedule for future GEO and other related reports. It stated that GEO reports should be published every two years, and that those reports falling on the 10-year anniversaries of the 1972 Stockholm Conference on the Human Environment [YUN 1972, p. 317] and the review of progress on Agenda 21 (see p. 749) should include a comprehensive, integrated assessment of the state of the global environment. Publication of the GEO report should alternate with publication of the *World Resources Report*, produced jointly with UNDP, the World Bank and the World Resources Institute. UNEP should also produce at least one major environmental outlook report (technical, regional, subregional, thematic or targeted at specific meetings, forums or audiences) in interim years of the GEO report.

UNEP secretariat

OIOS audit and inspection activities

In September, the Secretary-General transmitted the seventh annual Office of Internal Oversight Services (OIOS) report [A/56/381], which included UNEP audit information and covered activities during the period from 1 July 2000 to 30 June 2001. OIOS conducted audits of the UNEP International Environmental Technology Centre and reviewed seven UNEP offices in Canada, Europe and Japan. The Office issued six critical audit recommendations concerning the Centre: five dealt with type II gratis personnel (those seconded to UN organizations by Governments) and one concerned accountability of the offices away from headquarters. The report

stated that those issues represented a continuing problem and UNEP should take further action to resolve them and to fully implement the OIOS recommendations. OIOS would continue to monitor UNEP's implementation of its recommendations.

OIOS audits of UNEP offices away from headquarters showed that, overall, they were well run but that their accountability had not been clearly established, which was attributed to the lack of clearly defined delegation of authority from UNEP headquarters and failure to distinguish their responsibilities from those of UNON for delivering financial and administrative services. OIOS was also concerned that some of the offices still had not completed host country agreements and were experiencing problems in obtaining exemptions from indirect taxes.

Regarding recommendations made in its 1999 follow-up inspection report to the General Assembly [YUN 2000, p. 971], OIOS stated that UNEP management had provided concrete evidence of actions taken to address most of the recommendations. Those actions related to, among other things, further clarifying the new functional structure of UNEP, enhancing dialogue with its Committee of Permanent Representatives, establishing mechanisms for the delegation of authority and improving programme delivery.

Misdirection of contributions

Following up on a 2000 case in which a private individual had received and refused to return 13 misdirected contributions made by Member States totalling $701,998.94 to the UNEP Trust Fund account [YUN 2000, p. 971], OIOS reported in September [A/56/381] that its investigators had assisted United States law enforcement authorities in preparing criminal proceedings against the individual in question. That individual was subsequently found guilty by a United States court jury, sentenced in April to 24 months in prison and required to make restitution of the misdirected funds to the Trust Fund bank.

UNEP Fund

Following consideration of the Executive Director's report on the proposed biennial programme and support budget for 2002-2003 [UNEP/GC.21/6 & Corr.1] and the related report of the Advisory Committee on Administrative and Budgetary Questions (ACABQ) [UNEP/GC.21/6/Add.1], the Governing Council, on 9 February [dec. 21/31], approved appropriations of Environment Fund resources of $14.9 million for the biennial budget, $100 million for the programme of work and $5 million for the Fund programme reserve, totalling $119.9 million. It noted that the $14.9 million for management and administrative support costs was conditional on an increase in funding from the UN regular budget for UNON and/or UNEP in the 2002-2003 biennium. The Council reconfirmed the authority of the Executive Director to reallocate resources between programmes up to a maximum of 20 per cent of the appropriation to which the resources were reallocated, and urged him to further increase the level of the financial reserve to $20 million as and when carry-over resources became available over and above those needed to implement the programme approved for the 2000-2001 and 2002-2003 bienniums. It requested the Committee of Permanent Representatives to consult with the Executive Director on ways to provide the Council and the Committee with further information on the distribution of work programme activities at the regional level. It noted with concern that the level of funding from the UN regular budget to UNEP was not sufficient to provide for the core functions of the Programme as stipulated by the General Assembly in resolution 2997(XXVII) [YUN 1972, p. 331], and appealed to the Assembly at its fifty-sixth (2001) session to consider a substantial increase in the UN regular budget allocation to UNEP and UNON for 2002-2003. The Executive Director was requested to provide financial details of work programmes to Governments in accordance with article VI of the General Procedures governing the operations of the Fund, if requested, and to make available to Governments, twice yearly, information on progress made in the implementation of the work programme; and to ensure that earmarked contributions to UNEP, apart from those for which UNEP acted as treasurer, funded activities that were in line with the work progamme. The Council authorized him to enter into forward commitments not exceeding $20 million for Fund programme activities for the 2004-2005 biennium, and requested him to prepare a work programme consisting of Fund programme activities with a cost of $120 million for the 2004-2005 biennium. The Executive Director was requested to submit a finalized draft budget and work programme for consideration and approval by the Council in 2003. A February note of the Executive Director [UNEP/GC.21/INF/24] contained the estimated distribution of Environment Fund resources by subprogramme objective.

A later report of the Executive Director [UNEP/GCSS.VII/INF/8] contained information on the status of the Environment Fund and other sources of funding for UNEP for the 2000-2001 biennium. The total projected resources for the biennium amounted to $274.84 million.

Trust funds

A secretariat note [UNEP/GC.21/INF/2] contained programmatic descriptions and actual, estimated or projected expenditures of UNEP trust funds for the 1998-1999, 2000-2001 and 2002-2003 bienniums.

On 9 February [dec. 21/32 B], the Governing Council approved the establishment of 12 trust funds and the extension of 27 others.

For the UNEP trust funds, which numbered 100, the projected income and expenditures as at 31 December 2001 were $816.86 million and $650.71 million, respectively.

Resource mobilization strategy

Pursuant to a 1999 Governing Council decision [YUN 1999, p. 982], the Executive Director reported on initial action taken to develop a strategy on stable, adequate and predictable funding for UNEP [UNEP/GC.21/7]. In an addendum [UNEP/GC.21/7/Add.1], the Executive Director presented the draft resource mobilization strategy, which was aimed at stabilizing, increasing and making more predictable the financing of UNEP activities from traditional resources; broadening the donor base within governmental and non-governmental sectors; and stimulating creative fund-raising, including through collaboration with the business community and the general public and the use of the Internet.

On 9 February [dec. 21/32 A], the Governing Council expressed support for the resource mobilization strategy and requested the Executive Director to make renewed and additional efforts towards improving UNEP's financial situation, especially towards increasing the number of countries contributing to the Environment Fund. It called on Governments and other relevant parties, including non-State actors, to provide stable and predictable financial and other resources to UNEP, taking the strategy into account. It also requested the Executive Director to implement the strategy and to keep Governments informed of progress through the Committee of Permanent Representatives, especially on fund-raising from non-State actors and on responses to special initiatives and emergency actions.

Financial reserve loan

The Governing Council, on 9 February [dec. 21/33], authorized the Executive Director to approve an advance of up to $8 million from the Environment Fund financial reserve to the UN Secretariat on a loan basis for the construction of additional office accommodation at UNON, subject and without prejudice to final approval by ACABQ and, as appropriate, by other competent authorities. It requested the Executive Director to ensure that the agreement between the Secretariat and UNEP included a provision that there should be an immediate repayment if requested by him. The Executive Director was asked to submit regular status reports to the Committee of Permanent Representatives and to report in 2003 on the decision's implementation.

International conventions and mechanisms

Implementation of environmental conventions

Following consideration of a report of the Executive Director on UNEP action to support and promote collaboration among multilateral environmental conventions [UNEP/GC.21/4] and a secretariat note on changes to the status of existing conventions and protocols from 1 March 1999 to 31 January 2001 [UNEP/GC.21/INF/16], the Governing Council, on 9 February [dec. 21/26], authorized the Executive Director to transmit the reports, together with comments made by delegations and relevant information received by the secretariat as at 31 May, to the General Assembly at its fifty-sixth (2001) session.

A January note of the Executive Director [UNEP/GC.21/INF/19], describing UNEP efforts to harmonize national reporting by parties to MEAs, noted that EMG had decided to establish an issue management group on the harmonization of national reporting and had implemented a pilot project, which would be presented to the World Summit on Sustainable Development in 2002 (see p. 749).

A secretariat note [UNEP/GC.21/INF/5] reviewed UNEP's initiative to develop guidelines relating to compliance with and enforcement of MEAs to ensure their effective implementation.

On 9 February [dec. 21/27], the Governing Council requested the Executive Director to continue to prepare the draft guidelines and to ensure the open-ended and transparent nature of the process. It encouraged him to complete the process and submit the draft guidelines in 2002.

The UNEP Intergovernmental Working Group of Experts on the Development of Guidelines on Compliance and Enforcement of Multilateral Environmental Agreements, at its first meeting (Nairobi, 22-26 October), adopted draft guidelines on the subject [UNEP/(DEPI)/MEAs/WG.1/3], which were to be submitted to the Governing Council for its consideration in 2002.

On 29 November, the General Assembly reaffirmed that international disarmament forums should take into account the relevant environmental norms in negotiating treaties and agreements (**resolution 56/24 F**) (see p. 518).

Climate change convention

As at 31 December, 186 States were parties to the United Nations Framework Convention on Climate Change (UNFCCC), which was opened for signature in 1992 [YUN 1992, p. 681] and entered into force in 1994 [YUN 1994, p. 938]. During the year, the Federal Republic of Yugoslavia (FRY) acceded to the Convention, replacing the Socialist Federal Republic of Yugoslavia.

At year's end, 46 States were parties to the Kyoto Protocol to the Convention [YUN 1997, p. 1048]. During the year, Argentina, the Cook Islands, Malta, Romania and Uruguay ratified it; Bangladesh, Burundi, Colombia, the Gambia, Malawi, Mauritius, Nauru, Senegal and Vanuatu acceded to it; and the Czech Republic approved it.

Conference of Parties

The Conference of the Parties to UNFCCC, at its resumed sixth session (Bonn, Germany, 16-27 July) [FCCC/CP/2001/5 & Add.1,2], adopted the core elements for the implementation of the 1998 Buenos Aires Plan of Action to reduce the risk of global climate change [YUN 1998, p. 987] (the Bonn Agreements). The Bonn Agreements provided for the establishment of two new funds under the Convention, to be managed by GEF: a special climate change fund to finance adaptation, technology transfer, emission reduction and assistance to developing country parties in diversifying their economies; and a least developed countries (LDCs) fund to support their implementation of the Convention, particularly in their adaptation needs. An adaptation fund, also to be managed by GEF, was to be established under the Kyoto Protocol to finance adaptation projects/programmes. An expert group on technology transfer was also established. Other decisions that gave effect to the Bonn Agreements related to capacity-building in developing countries and in countries with economies in transition, the development and transfer of technologies, the impact of single projects on emissions, and administrative and budgetary questions. Further decisions dealt with the potential of clean energy to contribute to global environmental benefits and the review of various articles of the Kyoto Protocol. As the Conference was unable to complete its work on the issue of land use, land-use change and forestry, its work programme on mechanisms, procedures and mechanisms on compliance under the Kyoto Protocol and best practices in policies and measures among parties, it forwarded those items to its seventh session (see below) for further consideration. In other action, following consideration of a June report of the Executive Secretary of the Convention on the institutional linkage of the UNFCCC secretariat to the United Nations [FCCC/SBI/2001/5], the Conference approved the continuation of the current institutional linkage, which was adopted by the Conference in 1995 and endorsed by the General Assembly in resolution 50/115 [YUN 1995, p. 1071], for a further five-year period, to be reviewed by the Assembly and the Conference not later than 31 December 2006. In September [A/56/385], the Secretary-General recommended that the Assembly approve the continuation of the institutional linkage; the Assembly did so in resolution 56/199 (see below).

On 10 November, the seventh session of the Conference (Marrakesh, Morocco, 29 October–10 November) [FCCC/CP/2001/13 & Add.1-4, Add.1/Corr.1, Add.3/Corr.1 & Add.4/Corr.1] adopted the Marrakesh Ministerial Declaration, which emphasized the linkage between sustainable development and climate change; reaffirmed development and poverty eradication as the overriding priorities of developing countries; and called on countries to explore synergies between the Convention and the Conventions on biodiversity (see p. 957) and desertification (see p. 959). The Declaration noted that the decisions adopted by the seventh session, constituting the Marrakesh Accords (see below), would facilitate the timely entry into force of the Kyoto Protocol. The President of the Conference and the UNFCCC Executive Secretary were requested to continue to participate actively in the preparations for the 2002 World Summit on Sustainable Development and in the Summit itself (see p. 749) and to report to the Conference at its eighth (2002) session.

The Marrakesh Accords, which set new emissions reduction targets for developed countries, with an average reduction of 5.2 per cent from 1990 levels by 2012, comprised a set of decisions spelling out rules for implementing the Kyoto Protocol. Major areas covered in the Accords were operating rules for international emissions trading and the Protocol's two other flexibility mechanisms (the clean development mechanism and joint implementation) and rules defining a party's eligibility to participate in the mechanisms; accounting procedures that provided for fungibility—meaning that emissions units under all three mechanisms could be transferred several times as equal units; a compliance regime; and the creation of a new type of emissions unit for "sink credits"—credits towards emissions targets for carbon absorbed by forests, soils and other so-called sinks.

The Conference adopted decisions on the items forwarded to it by the resumed sixth session (see p. 954). The eighth session of the Conference was scheduled to take place from 23 October to 1 November 2002 in India.

The Subsidiary Body for Scientific and Technological Advice (SBSTA) held its fourteenth session (24-27 July) [FCCC/SBSTA/2001/2] in Bonn, as did the Subsidiary Body for Implementation (SBI) [FCCC/SBI/2001/9]. The fifteenth sessions of SBSTA (29 October–6 November) [FCCC/SBSTA/2001/8] and SBI (29 October–8 November) [FCCC/SBI/2001/18] were held in Marrakesh.

Note by Secretary-General. Pursuant to General Assembly decision 55/443 [YUN 2000, p. 972], the Secretary-General, in October [A/56/509], transmitted a report of the UNFCCC Executive Secretary on the outcome of the fourth (1998) [YUN 1998, p. 987], fifth (1999) [YUN 1999, p. 984] and sixth (2000) [YUN 2000, p. 972] sessions of the Conference of the Parties. The report also discussed the institutional linkage of the Convention's secretariat to the United Nations (see above).

GENERAL ASSEMBLY ACTION

On 21 December [meeting 90], the General Assembly, on the recommendation of the Second Committee [A/56/561/Add.6], adopted **resolution 56/199** without vote [agenda item 98 *(f)*].

Protection of global climate for present and future generations of mankind

The General Assembly,

Recalling its resolutions 50/115 of 20 December 1995, 51/184 of 16 December 1996, 52/199 of 18 December 1997 and 54/222 of 22 December 1999, its decision 55/443 of 20 December 2000 and other resolutions relating to the protection of the global climate for present and future generations of mankind,

Noting that most States and one regional economic integration organization have ratified or acceded to the United Nations Framework Convention on Climate Change,

Remaining deeply concerned that all countries, in particular developing countries, including the least developed countries and small island States, face increased risk from the negative impacts of climate change,

Noting that, to date, the Kyoto Protocol to the United Nations Framework Convention on Climate Change has attracted forty-five ratifications,

Expressing its deep appreciation to the Government of Morocco for hosting the seventh session of the Conference of the Parties to the United Nations Framework Convention on Climate Change at Marrakesh, Morocco, from 29 October to 9 November 2001,

Noting the adoption of the Bonn Agreements on the implementation of the Buenos Aires Plan of Action by the Conference of the Parties to the Convention, at the second part of its sixth session, held at Bonn, Germany, from 16 to 27 July 2001,

Expressing its appreciation to the Intergovernmental Panel on Climate Change for its excellent work in preparing the Third Assessment Report, and encouraging parties to make full use of the information contained therein,

Taking note of the decision of the Conference of the Parties at its sixth session to approve the continuation of the current institutional linkage of the secretariat of the Convention to the United Nations and related administrative arrangements for a further five-year period, to be reviewed by both the General Assembly and the Conference of the Parties no later than 31 December 2006,

Taking note also of the report of the Secretary-General on the continuation of the institutional linkage of the secretariat of the Convention to the United Nations,

Taking note further of the decision of the Conference of the Parties inviting the General Assembly to decide at its fifty-sixth session on the question of meeting the conference-servicing expenses of the Convention from its regular budget, taking into account the views expressed by Member States,

Noting that, by paragraph *(c)* of its decision 55/443, it decided to include in the calendar of conferences and meetings for the biennium 2002-2003 the sessions of the Conference of the Parties and its subsidiary bodies envisaged for the biennium, in accordance with the decisions adopted by the Conference of the Parties,

Taking note of the report of the Executive Secretary of the United Nations Framework Convention on Climate Change, which was prepared in response to the invitation of the General Assembly in paragraph *(d)* of its decision 55/443,

1. *Recalls* the United Nations Millennium Declaration, in which heads of State and Government resolved to make every effort to ensure the entry into force of the Kyoto Protocol to the United Nations Framework Convention on Climate Change, preferably by the tenth anniversary of the United Nations Conference on Environment and Development in 2002, and to embark on the required reduction of emissions of greenhouse gases, and calls upon States to work cooperatively towards achieving the ultimate objective of the United Nations Framework Convention on Climate Change;

2. *Calls upon* all States parties to continue to take effective steps to implement their commitments under the Convention, in accordance with the principle of common but differentiated responsibilities;

3. *Stresses* the importance of capacity-building, as well as of developing and disseminating innovative technologies in respect of key sectors of development, in particular energy, and of investment in that regard, including through private sector involvement, market-oriented approaches and supportive public policies, as well as international cooperation, emphasizes that climate change and its adverse impacts have to be addressed through cooperation at all levels, and welcomes the efforts of all parties to implement the Convention;

4. *Takes note* of the Marrakesh Accords, adopted by the Conference of the Parties to the United Nations Framework Convention on Climate Change at its seventh session, complementing the Bonn Agreements on the implementation of the Buenos Aires Plan of Ac-

tion, paving the way for the timely entry into force of the Kyoto Protocol;

5. *Takes note with appreciation* of the Marrakesh Ministerial Declaration, adopted by the Conference of the Parties at its seventh session as a contribution to the preparatory process for the World Summit on Sustainable Development;

6. *Encourages* the conferences of the parties to and the secretariats of the United Nations Framework Convention on Climate Change, the Convention on Biological Diversity and the United Nations Convention to Combat Desertification in those Countries Experiencing Serious Drought and/or Desertification, particularly in Africa and other international instruments related to the environment and sustainable development, as well as relevant organizations, especially the United Nations Environment Programme, including, as appropriate, the involvement of the Environmental Management Group, to continue their work for enhancing mutual complementarities with full respect for the status of the secretariats of the conventions and the autonomous decision-making prerogatives of the conferences of the parties to the conventions concerned, to strengthen cooperation with a view to facilitating progress in the implementation of those conventions at the international, regional and national levels and to report thereon to their respective conferences of the parties;

7. *Approves* the continuation of the institutional linkage of the secretariat of the United Nations Framework Convention on Climate Change to the United Nations, and related administrative arrangements, for a further five-year period;

8. *Requests* the Secretary-General to review the functioning of that institutional linkage not later than 31 December 2006, in consultation with the Conference of the Parties to the United Nations Framework Convention on Climate Change, with a view to making such modifications as may be considered desirable by both parties, and to report thereon to the General Assembly;

9. *Invites* the conferences of the parties to the multilateral environmental conventions, when setting the dates of their meetings, to take into consideration the schedule of meetings of the General Assembly and the Commission on Sustainable Development so as to ensure the adequate representation of developing countries at those meetings;

10. *Invites* the Executive Secretary of the United Nations Framework Convention on Climate Change to report to the General Assembly at its fifty-seventh session on the work of the Conference of the Parties to the Convention;

11. *Decides* to include in the provisional agenda of its fifty-seventh session the sub-item entitled "Protection of global climate for present and future generations of mankind".

Vienna Convention and Montreal Protocol

As at 31 December, 183 States and the European Community (EC) were parties to the 1985 Vienna Convention for the Protection of the Ozone Layer [YUN 1985, p. 804], which entered into force in 1998 [YUN 1998, p. 810]. In 2001, Cambodia, Cape Verde, Nauru, Palau, Rwanda, Sao Tome and Principe, Sierra Leone and Somalia acceded to the Convention; FRY succeeded to it, replacing the Socialist Federal Republic of Yugoslavia.

Parties to the Montreal Protocol on Substances that Deplete the Ozone Layer, which was adopted in 1987 [YUN 1987, p. 686], numbered 182 States and the EC; to the 1990 Amendment to the Protocol, 159 and the EC; to the 1992 Amendment, 136 and the EC; to the 1997 Amendment, 75 and the EC; and to the 1999 Amendment, 24.

The Thirteenth Meeting of the Parties to the Montreal Protocol (Colombo, Sri Lanka, 16-19 October) [UNEP/OzL.Pro.13/10] adopted decisions on the 2003-2005 replenishment of the Multilateral Fund for the Implementation of the Protocol and its operation, the assessment of the ozone-depleting potential of new substances, the use of n-propyl bromide, the production of chlorofluoro-carbon-free metered-dose inhalers, critical-use exemptions for methyl bromide, illegal trade in ozone-depleting substances (ODS), and compliance by a number of parties. The Meeting adopted, and annexed to its report, the Colombo Declaration on Renewed Commitment to the Protection of the Ozone Layer to Mark the Forthcoming World Summit on Sustainable Development, in 2002, the Fifteenth Anniversary of the Montreal Protocol and the Tenth Anniversary of the Establishment of the Multilateral Fund. It decided to convene the Fourteenth Meeting of the Parties in Nairobi in November 2002.

Convention on air pollution

As at 31 December, 47 States and the EC were parties to the 1979 Convention on Long-Range Transboundary Air Pollution [YUN 1979, p. 710], which entered into force in 1983 [YUN 1983, p. 645]. Eight protocols to the Convention dealt with the programme for monitoring and evaluation of the pollutants in Europe (1984), the reduction of sulphur emissions or their transboundary fluxes by at least 30 per cent (1985), the control of emissions of nitrogen oxides or their transboundary fluxes (1988), the control of volatile organic compounds or their transboundary fluxes (1991), further reduction of sulphur emissions (1984), heavy metals (1998), POPs (1998) and the abatement of acidification, eutrophication and ground-level ozone (1999).

The nineteenth session of the Executive Body for the Convention (Geneva, 11-14 December) [ECE/EB.AIR/75] adopted decisions related to compliance, the facilitation of participation of countries with economies in transition and various budgetary questions. It adopted its work plan for 2002.

Convention on Biological Diversity

At year's end, 181 States and the EC were parties to the 1992 Convention on Biological Diversity [YUN 1992, p. 683], which entered into force in 1993 [YUN 1993, p. 810]. During 2001, the Convention was ratified by the Libyan Arab Jamahiriya and acceded to by Saudi Arabia.

As at 31 December, nine States were parties to the Cartagena Protocol on Biosafety, which was adopted in 2000 [YUN 2000, p. 973]. During the year, the Czech Republic, Fiji, Norway and Uganda ratified the Protocol and Lesotho, Nauru, and Saint Kitts and Nevis acceded to it.

The sixth (12-16 March) [UNEP/CBD/COP/6/3] and seventh (12-16 November) [UNEP/CBD/COP/6/4] meetings of the Subsidiary Body on Scientific, Technical and Technological Advice (SBSTTA), both held in Montreal, Canada, adopted recommendations for consideration by the sixth (2002) meeting of the Conference of the Parties to the Convention. A recommendation on forest biological diversity was among those adopted by SBSTTA in November.

The Ad Hoc Open-ended Working Group on Access and Benefit-sharing (Bonn, 22-26 October) [UNEP/CBD/COP/6/6] adopted the draft Bonn Guidelines on access to genetic resources and fair and equitable sharing of the benefits arising out of their utilization and recommended that the Conference of the Parties to the Convention finalize and adopt them. The Open-ended Intersessional Meeting on the Strategic Plan, National Reports and Implementation of the Convention on Biological Diversity (Montreal, 19-21 November) [UNEP/CBD/COP/6/5] agreed upon a structure and draft elements of the strategic plan for submission to the sixth (2002) meeting of the Conference of the Parties.

In November, the Convention secretariat published *Global Biodiversity Outlook*, a periodic report on biological diversity. A workshop on the strategic plan had been held from 28 to 30 May in Seychelles.

Note by Secretary-General. In accordance with General Assembly resolution 55/201 [YUN 2000, p. 974], the Secretary-General transmitted, in July [A/56/126], a report of the Executive Secretary of the Convention on ongoing work and cooperation with the Assembly and other relevant institutions.

Cartagena Protocol on Biosafety

The second meeting of the Intergovernmental Committee for the Cartagena Protocol on Biosafety (ICCP) (Nairobi, 1-5 October) [UNEP/CBD/ICCP/2/15] considered the preparations for the first meeting of the Conference of the Parties to the Convention serving as the meeting of the parties to the Protocol.

Governing Council action. The Governing Council considered a January report of the Executive Director [UNEP/GC.21/INF/18] describing the implementation of a 1999 Council decision on biosafety [YUN 1999, p. 987] and drawing attention to the need to promote capacity-building for safety in biotechnology to prepare countries for the entry into force of the Cartagena Protocol. It presented a new UNEP/GEF biosafety programme as follow-up to a UNEP/GEF pilot biosafety enabling activity project. Annexed to the report was the Montpellier Declaration on the Cartagena Protocol, adopted by the first meeting of ICCP [YUN 2000, p. 973].

On 9 February [dec. 21/8], the Council encouraged countries that had not yet signed the Cartagena Protocol to do so, followed by ratification thereof. It commended GEF's approval of the UNEP/GEF Development of National Biosafety Frameworks Project to benefit up to 100 GEF-eligible developing countries and countries with economies in transition. The Executive Director was requested to continue to mobilize resources for capacity-building initiatives in the area of biosafety, to mobilize resources and support, as appropriate, for the establishment and/or further strengthening of subregional and regional biosafety risk-assessment capabilities, considering the capacity need at the national level, and to report in 2003.

GENERAL ASSEMBLY ACTION

On 21 December [meeting 90], the General Assembly, on the recommendation of the Second Committee [A/56/561/Add.4], adopted **resolution 56/197** without vote [agenda item 98 (d)].

Convention on Biological Diversity

The General Assembly,

Recalling its resolution 55/201 of 20 December 2000 on the Convention on Biological Diversity, in which it, inter alia, decided to proclaim 22 May, the date of the adoption of the text of the Convention, as the International Day for Biological Diversity,

Recognizing the importance of the adoption by the Conference of the Parties to the Convention, in its decision EM-I/3 of 29 January 2000, of the Cartagena Protocol on Biosafety to the Convention on Biological Diversity, the subsequent signature of the Protocol by one hundred and three parties to the Convention by 5 June 2001, and the ratification thereof or accession thereto by nine parties to date,

Expressing its appreciation for the generous offer of the Government of the Netherlands to host the sixth meeting of the Conference of the Parties, and the third meeting of the Intergovernmental Committee for the Cartagena Protocol, which will be held at The Hague from 8 to 26 April 2002,

Urging the parties to the Convention to undertake thorough preparations to advance progress on all issues that are included in the agenda of the sixth meeting of the Conference of the Parties,

1. *Takes note* of the report of the Executive Secretary of the Convention on Biological Diversity, as submitted by the Secretary-General to the General Assembly at its fifty-sixth session;

2. *Notes* the outcome of the first meeting of the Ad Hoc Open-ended Working Group on Access and Benefit-sharing, which addresses the appropriate access to genetic resources and the fair and equitable sharing of benefits arising out of its utilization, hosted by the Government of Germany from 22 to 26 October 2001;

3. *Also notes* the outcome of the second meeting of the Intergovernmental Committee for the Cartagena Protocol on Biosafety, held at Nairobi from 1 to 5 October 2001;

4. *Welcomes* the fact that one hundred and eighty-one States and one regional economic integration organization have become parties to the Convention on Biological Diversity, and urges States that have not joined the Convention to become parties to it, without further delay;

5. *Calls upon* parties to the Convention to become parties to the Cartagena Protocol on Biosafety as soon as possible;

6. *Encourages* the conferences of the parties to, and the secretariats of, the United Nations Framework Convention on Climate Change, the Convention on Biological Diversity and the United Nations Convention to Combat Desertification in those Countries Experiencing Serious Drought and/or Desertification, particularly in Africa, and other international instruments related to the environment and sustainable development, as well as relevant organizations, especially the United Nations Environment Programme, including, as appropriate, the involvement of the Environmental Management Group, to continue their work on enhancing mutual complementarities, with full respect for the status of the secretariats of the conventions and the autonomous decision-making prerogatives of the conferences of the parties to the conventions concerned, to strengthen cooperation with a view to facilitating progress in the implementation of those conventions at the international, regional and national levels and to report thereon to their respective conferences of the parties;

7. *Welcomes* the decision of the Conference of the Parties to the Convention on Biological Diversity regarding its programme of work for forest biological diversity, and encourages the parties to and the secretariat of the Convention to cooperate with the United Nations Forum on Forests, inter alia, with regard to respecting, preserving and maintaining the knowledge, innovations and practices of indigenous and local communities embodying traditional lifestyles, in accordance with article 8 (j) and related provisions of the Convention;

8. *Takes note* of the fact that the provisions of the Agreement on Trade-related Aspects of Intellectual Property Rights and the Convention on Biological Diversity are interrelated, in particular with respect to intellectual property rights and relevant provisions of the Convention, and invites the World Trade Organization

and the World Intellectual Property Organization, within their respective mandates, to continue to explore this relationship, taking into account the ongoing work in other relevant forums and bearing in mind decision V/26 B of the Conference of the Parties;

9. *Invites* all funding institutions and bilateral and multilateral donors, as well as regional funding institutions and non-governmental organizations, to cooperate with the secretariat of the Convention on Biological Diversity in the implementation of the programme of work;

10. *Requests* the conferences of the parties to the multilateral environmental conventions, when setting the dates of their meetings, to take into consideration the schedule of meetings of the General Assembly and the Commission on Sustainable Development so as to ensure the adequate representation of developing countries at those meetings;

11. *Calls upon* parties to the Convention on Biological Diversity to settle urgently any arrears and to pay their contributions in full and in a timely manner so as to ensure continuity in the cash flows required to finance the ongoing work of the Conference of the Parties, the subsidiary bodies and the Convention secretariat;

12. *Looks forward* to the contribution of the Convention on Biological Diversity to the preparations for the World Summit on Sustainable Development, bearing in mind the decisions taken by the Commission on Sustainable Development at its tenth session;

13. *Invites* the Executive Secretary of the Convention on Biological Diversity to report to the General Assembly on the ongoing work regarding the Convention;

14. *Decides* to include in the provisional agenda of its fifty-seventh session the sub-item entitled "Convention on Biological Diversity".

Convention to combat desertification

In 2001, Belarus, Bulgaria, Poland, Slovenia and Thailand acceded to the 1994 United Nations Convention to Combat Desertification in those Countries Experiencing Serious Drought and/or Desertification, particularly in Africa [YUN 1994, p. 944], which entered into force in 1996 [YUN 1996, p. 958], bringing the total number of parties to 177.

The Conference of the Parties, at its fifth session (Geneva, 1-12 October) [ICCP/COP(5)/11 & Corr.1 & Add.1], decided to establish the Committee for the Review of the Implementation of the Convention (CRIC) as a subsidiary body of the Conference. The first session of CRIC was scheduled for November 2002 in Bonn. The Conference took note of the report of its ad hoc working group (AHWG) on the review of implementation [ICCD/COP(4)/AHWG/6], following its intersessional meeting (Bonn, 19 March–6 April), at which the group reviewed 114 national and subregional reports and discussed new strategies and policy frameworks, the implementation review process, the financial mechanism for the Convention and

cooperation between regions. In other action, the Conference decided to submit, as inputs to the preparatory process of the World Summit on Sustainable Development (see p. 749), the Chairman's summary of the Ministerial and High-level Interactive Dialogue sessions held during the Conference and AHWG reports. Other decisions related to regional approaches and coordination; contributions to and participation in the World Summit; traditional knowledge; the promotion and strengthening of relationships with other relevant conventions, international organizations, institutions and agencies; early warning systems; dryland degradation and the Millennium Ecosystem Assessment (see p. 961); and administrative issues. The sixth session was scheduled for October 2003 in Bonn. Within the context of the Regional Annex for Latin America and the Caribbean of the Convention, country parties of the region held their seventh meeting (La Serena, Chile, 21-24 August) [ICCD/COP(5)/INF.10] to identify priority actions and to establish and develop subregional and regional cooperation through a regional action programme to combat desertification.

The Committee on Science and Technology, a subsidiary body of the Conference (Geneva, 2-4 October), considered, among other things, reports on a proposal of the Government of Italy for a pilot project to create a network of institutions, bodies and experts on traditional knowledge [ICCD/COP(5)/CST/2], on communication strategies to generate best practices for combating desertification and mitigating the effects of drought [ICCD/COP(5)/CST/6], and on benchmarks and indicators [ICCD/COP(5)/CST/7].

Governing Council action. In response to a 1999 Governing Council request [YUN 1999, p. 989], the Executive Director submitted a review of UNEP support for the implementation of the Convention [UNEP/GC.21/INF/10] during the period 1999-2000. A further report of the Executive Director described the implementation of the Convention in relation to land degradation [UNEP/GC.21/2].

On 9 February [dec. 21/1], the Council requested the Executive Director to strengthen UNEP's capability to respond to global land issues in order to fulfil its mandate as Task Manager for chapter 12 of Agenda 21, on combating desertification and drought [YUN 1992, p. 672], and to support the Conference of the Parties to the Convention on desertification; to further strengthen the functional integration of UNEP's land resource management and soil conservation policy, and to strengthen UNEP's collaboration with the World Bank and UNDP, with a view to enhancing GEF assistance to countries for activities related to land degradation; to strengthen collaboration with relevant UN organizations and agencies and other organizations concerned with assistance for mitigating land degradation and for the implementation of the Convention; and to continue to assist countries affected by land degradation in the development of a pipeline of projects for financing by GEF and other relevant financial mechanisms.

Report of Secretary-General. As requested in General Assembly resolution 55/204 [YUN 2000, p. 976], the Secretary-General, in a July report [A/56/175], discussed the work of AHWG; an adjustment to the Convention's 2000-2001 programme budget; procedures for the review of the Convention's implementation; action by States; and regional implementation. The report reviewed the functioning of the institutional linkage, including financial arrangements, between the secretariat of the Convention and the United Nations, as approved by the Assembly in resolution 52/198 [YUN 1997, p. 1053]. No significant changes had taken place in the substantive linkage, and it was considered to have provided a sound basis for the day-to-day functioning of the Convention secretariat. The Secretary-General proposed that the Assembly approve the continuation of the institutional linkage for a further five-year period, to be reviewed by the Assembly and the Conference not later than 31 December 2006; the Assembly did so in resolution 56/196 (below).

GENERAL ASSEMBLY ACTION

On 21 December [meeting 90], the General Assembly, on the recommendation of the Second Committee [A/56/561/Add.3], adopted **resolution 56/196** without vote [agenda item 98 *(c)*].

Implementation of the United Nations Convention to Combat Desertification in those Countries Experiencing Serious Drought and/or Desertification, particularly in Africa

The General Assembly,

Recalling its resolution 55/204 of 20 December 2000 and other resolutions relating to the United Nations Convention to Combat Desertification in those Countries Experiencing Serious Drought and/or Desertification, particularly in Africa,

Expressing its deep appreciation to the Government of Germany for the generous manner in which it hosted and provided facilities for the fourth session of the Conference of the Parties to the Convention,

Noting with satisfaction that the fifth session of the Conference of the Parties was held at the United Nations Office at Geneva from 1 to 12 October 2001,

Expressing its deep appreciation to the Government of Switzerland for the organization of the fifth session of the Conference of the Parties and its special events in Geneva,

Welcoming the decision taken by the Council of the Global Environment Facility at its May 2001 session to pursue the designation of land degradation, primarily desertification and deforestation, as a focal area of the Facility, as a means of enhancing its support for the successful implementation of the Convention,

Acknowledging that desertification and drought are problems of a global dimension in that they affect all regions of the world and that joint actions of the international community are needed to combat desertification and/or mitigate the effects of drought, including the integration of strategies for poverty eradication,

1. *Takes note* of the report of the Secretary-General;

2. *Welcomes* the outcome of the fourth session of the Conference of the Parties to the United Nations Convention to Combat Desertification in those Countries Experiencing Serious Drought and/or Desertification, particularly in Africa, in particular the adoption of the Declaration on the Commitments to Enhance the Implementation of the Obligations under the Convention;

3. *Also welcomes* the outcome of the fifth session of the Conference of the Parties;

4. *Notes* the establishment of the Committee for the Review of the Implementation of the Convention as a subsidiary body of the Conference of the Parties, and invites parties and other actors to participate in the first session of the Committee, which shall be held at Bonn, Germany, from 18 to 29 November 2002, in accordance with Conference of the Parties decision 2/COP.5 of 12 October 2001;

5. *Also notes* that the mandate and functions of the Committee shall be subject to renewal at the seventh session of the Conference of the Parties, in the light of lessons learned during the overall review of the Committee;

6. *Encourages* the conferences of the parties to and the secretariats of the United Nations Framework Convention on Climate Change, the Convention on Biological Diversity, the Convention to Combat Desertification and other international instruments related to environment and sustainable development, as well as relevant organizations, especially the United Nations Environment Programme, with, as appropriate, the involvement of the Environmental Management Group, to continue their work on enhancing mutual complementarities, with full respect for the status of the secretariats of the conventions and the autonomous decision making prerogatives of the conferences of the parties to the conventions concerned, to strengthen cooperation with a view to facilitating progress in the implementation of those conventions at the international, regional and national levels and to report thereon to their respective conferences of the parties;

7. *Welcomes* the decision of the Conference of the Parties to the Convention to Combat Desertification to submit to the preparatory process of the World Summit on Sustainable Development, as inputs, the Chairman's summary of the Ministerial and High-level Interactive Dialogue sessions held at the fifth session of the Conference of the Parties, including the challenges of and opportunities in combating desertification, controlling land degradation and mitigating the effects of drought in affected developing countries, as well as those relating to financial resources and achieving sustainable development, and the comprehensive report of the Ad Hoc Working Group for the in-depth review

and analysis of reports submitted at the third and fourth sessions of the Conference of the Parties;

8. *Also welcomes* the decision taken by the Council of the Global Environment Facility, under item 7 of the agenda of its meeting in December 2001, to consider at its next meeting proposed amendments to the Instrument for the Establishment of the Restructured Global Environment Facility to designate land degradation, primarily desertification and deforestation, as a focal area of the Facility, as a means of enhancing its support for the successful implementation of the Convention, with a view to the Council recommending approval of such amendments by the Assembly of States participating in the Facility at its meeting in October 2002;

9. *Encourages* the Conference of the Parties and the Council and Assembly of the Global Environment Facility to work cooperatively and effectively to facilitate the financing of the full implementation of the Convention by the Facility to achieve the objectives of the Convention in the area of land degradation, primarily desertification and deforestation;

10. *Notes with appreciation* that some affected developing countries have adopted their national, subregional and regional action programmes, and urges affected developing countries that have not yet done so to accelerate the process of elaboration and adoption of their action programmes, with a view to finalizing them as soon as possible;

11. *Calls upon* the international community to contribute to the implementation of those programmes through, inter alia, the conclusion of partnership agreements and through the bilateral and multilateral cooperation programmes that are available to implement the Convention, including contributions from non-governmental organizations and the private sector, and to support the efforts of the developing countries to implement the Convention;

12. *Invites* affected developing countries to place the implementation of their action programmes to combat desertification high among their priorities in their dialogue with their development partners;

13. *Notes with satisfaction* the steps being taken by affected developing countries that are parties to the Convention, with the assistance of international organizations and bilateral development partners, to implement the Convention, and the efforts being made to promote the participation of all actors of civil society in the elaboration and implementation of national action programmes to combat desertification, and in that regard encourages countries to cooperate at the subregional and regional levels, as appropriate;

14. *Welcomes* the strengthened cooperation between the secretariat of the Convention and the Global Mechanism, and encourages further efforts in that regard for the effective implementation of the Convention;

15. *Invites* all parties to pay promptly and in full the contributions required for the core budget of the Convention for the biennium 2002-2003, and urges all parties that have not yet paid their contributions for the year 1999 and/or the biennium 2000-2001 to do so as soon as possible in order to ensure continuity in the cash flow required to finance the ongoing work of the Conference of the Parties, the secretariat and the Global Mechanism;

16. *Calls upon* Governments, multilateral financial institutions, regional development banks, regional economic integration organizations and all other interested organizations, as well as non-governmental organizations and the private sector, to contribute generously to the General Fund, the Supplementary Fund and the Special Fund, in accordance with the relevant paragraphs of the financial rules of the Conference of the Parties, and welcomes the financial support already provided by some countries;

17. *Decides* to include in the calendar of conferences and meetings for the biennium 2002-2003 the sessions of the Conference of the Parties and its subsidiary bodies, including the sixth ordinary session of the Conference of the Parties and the meetings of its subsidiary bodies;

18. *Encourages* the United Nations Development Programme to continue implementing decision 2000/23 of 29 September 2000 of its Executive Board pertaining to the cooperation between the secretariat of the Convention and the United Nations Development Programme in order to mainstream activities to combat desertification at the national, subregional and regional levels;

19. *Approves* the continuation of the current institutional linkage and related administrative arrangements between the United Nations Secretariat and the secretariat of the Convention for a further five-year period, to be reviewed by the General Assembly and the Conference of the Parties not later than 31 December 2006;

20. *Requests* the Secretary-General to report to the General Assembly at its fifty-seventh session on the implementation of the present resolution;

21. *Decides* to include in the provisional agenda of its fifty-seventh session the sub-item entitled "Implementation of the United Nations Convention to Combat Desertification in those Countries Experiencing Serious Drought and/or Desertification, particularly in Africa".

Environmental activities

Follow-up to Millennium Summit

The Millennium Ecosystem Assessment, proposed by the Secretary-General in his report to the United Nations Millennium Summit [YUN 2000, p. 977], was launched in 2001 as part of the observance of World Environment Day on 5 June. The Assessment was a four-year international collaborative effort to evaluate the state of the major ecosystems (forests, freshwater systems, grasslands, coastal areas, agroecosystems), designed by UNDP, UNEP, the World Bank and the World Resources Institute and its partners. At the time of the launch, assessments were under way for Southern Africa, South-East Asia, Central America, western China and Norway.

In a September report [A/56/326] on the implementation of the United Nations Millennium Declaration, adopted by the General Assembly in resolution 55/2 [YUN 2000, p. 49], the Secretary-General proposed strategies to protect the environment. He called for efforts to ensure the entry into force of the 1997 Kyoto Protocol [YUN 1997, p. 1048] to the United Nations Framework Convention on Climate Change, which was opened for signature in 1992 [YUN 1992, p. 681] and entered into force in 1994 [YUN 1994, p. 938] (see p. 954). Collective efforts needed to be intensified towards the management, conservation and sustainable development of all types of forests, and towards reducing the number and effects of natural and man-made disasters. The Secretary-General appealed for support to implement the 1994 United Nations Convention to Combat Desertification in those Countries Experiencing Serious Drought and/or Desertification, particularly in Africa [YUN 1994, p. 944], which entered into force in 1996 [YUN 1996, p. 958] (see p. 959), by taking measures to prevent land degradation and focusing on new participatory approaches to solving the problem of desertification. The Secretary-General called for the universal ratification of the 1992 Convention on Biological Diversity [YUN 1992, p. 683], which entered into force in 1993 [YUN 1993, p. 810], and the Cartagena Protocol on Biosafety [YUN 2000, p. 973] (see p. 957); a halt to unsustainable exploitation of water resources by developing water management strategies; and free access to information on the human genome sequence (for information on the human rights aspect of the human genome, see p. 674).

The General Assembly, in **resolution 56/95** of 14 December (see p. 1279), took note of the Secretary-General's report.

The atmosphere

In 2001, UNEP reported that while the battle against chlorofluorocarbons was being won, new challenges were emerging. Bromine concentrations, more effective at destroying ozone than chlorine, were increasing. New chemicals such as n-propyl bromide and halon-1202, which were not controlled by the 1987 Montreal Protocol on Substances that Deplete the Ozone Layer [YUN 1987, p. 686] (see p. 957), were being used as substitutes for banned ODS. The new substances threatened the UNEP-estimated recovery of the ozone layer to pre-1980 levels by 2050, including the closure of the ozone hole over Antarctica which, in September, extended over 24 million square kilometres.

The Secretary-General, in his message marking the International Day for the Preservation of the Ozone Layer (16 September), warned of a thriving illegal trade in ODS and other products controlled by the Montreal Protocol.

During the year, UNEP provided services to help countries curb illegal trading in ODS.

Intergovernmental Panel on Climate Change

The Intergovernmental Panel on Climate Change (IPCC), at its seventeenth session (Nairobi, 4-6 April), discussed the interlinkages between biodiversity and climate change, a proposed report on climate change and sustainable development, information and outreach activities, and IPCC's future work programme and 2002-2004 budget.

At its eighteenth session (Wembley, United Kingdom, 23-29 September), the Panel completed and approved its Third Assessment Report, which showed that changes in the climate system had occurred, hydrological systems and terrestrial and marine ecosystems had been affected by temperature increases, climate change would have either beneficial or adverse effects on environmental and socio-economic systems, and climate change would exacerbate water shortages in many water-scarce areas. Overall, climate change was projected to increase threats to human health and its impacts would fall disproportionately on the developing countries. The Panel decided to continue to prepare comprehensive assessment reports; it adopted several other decisions regarding its work and mandate, including its 2002-2004 work programme and budget.

Governing Council action. Following consideration of a report of the Executive Director [UNEP/GC.21/2], the Governing Council adopted a series of climate-related decisions.

Regarding the implementation of thrust 3 of the Climate Agenda on studies of climate impact assessment and response strategies to reduce vulnerability [YUN 1995, p. 1077] and the World Climate Impact Assessment and Response Strategies Programme of the World Meteorological Organization (WMO) [YUN 1991, p. 992], the Council, on 9 February [dec. 21/9 A], requested UNEP to continue to carry out activities related to climate impact assessment and response strategies in partnership with other agencies participating in the Climate Agenda. It asked the Executive Director to further promote technical assistance to developing countries in order to implement MEAs. The Council urged UNEP to continue to collaborate with international organizations to further the objectives of the Climate Agenda.

In a decision on IPCC [dec. 21/9 B], the Governing Council requested the Executive Director to disseminate the findings of IPCC's Third Assessment Report (see above), following publication, with a view to raising awareness among civil society and policy makers. It requested IPCC to continue to update its assessments and to report, through its Chair, to the Council in 2003.

As to the Global Climate Observing System (GCOS)—co-sponsored by WMO, the UNESCO Intergovernmental Oceanographic Commission (IOC), UNEP and the International Council of Scientific Unions—the Council [dec. 21/9 C] requested the Executive Director to continue to support the activities of the GCOS joint planning office in facilitating the participation of experts from developing countries and countries with economies in transition in GCOS activities. It urged Governments to address deficiencies in the climate-observing networks and invited them, in consultation with the GCOS secretariat, to bring to the attention of the Conference of the Parties to the United Nations Framework Convention on Climate Change (UNFCCC), which entered into force in 1994 [YUN 1994, p. 938], any capacity-building needs.

A Council decision on programmatic support to atmosphere-related conventions [dec. 21/9 D] urged the Executive Director to continue programmatic activities in support of UNFCCC, the 1995 Vienna Convention for the Protection of the Ozone Layer [YUN 1985, p. 804], which entered into force in 1998 [YUN 1998, p. 810], and the Montreal Protocol [YUN 1987, p. 686], in particular to encourage synergies between those instruments, and called on the Executive Director to continue to liaise with relevant UN agencies and international organizations, with a view to addressing the issue of systematic observations and assessment of the ozone layer.

Commission action. CSD, at its ninth session in April (see p. 747), had before it a report of the Secretary-General on the protection of the atmosphere [E/CN.17/2001/2], which discussed modifications in the atmosphere as a result of global factors, such as greenhouse gases, and regional and local factors, including transboundary and urban air pollution. The report stated that if emissions of greenhouse gases continued increasing, the expected rise in global temperature would not be steady and uniform. Recent climate models had predicted variable patterns of climate change across the Earth's surface and throughout the atmosphere and oceans, in response to emissions scenarios. The report examined the impact of climate change and variability on health due to temperature, humidity, wind, solar radiation and air pollution. Considering the long lifespan of greenhouse gases in the atmosphere, adaptation to climate change, based on a precautionary approach, would be required, along with mitigation of the greenhouse gas emissions. A series of recommendations was made for reducing vulnerability, strengthening resilience and building adaptive capacity.

In a 27 April decision [E/2001/29 (dec. 9/2)], the Commission recommended that the international community assist developing countries and countries with economies in transition to prevent and combat air pollution; improve the compilation, evaluation and analysis of data on the state of the atmosphere and air pollution; develop and introduce cleaner fuels and air pollution abatement technologies; and promote the transfer of technologies and sustainable consumption and production patterns, as well as the identification of financial, technological and institutional barriers and constraints to combating air pollution. At the regional level, the Commission encouraged cooperation on issues aimed at supporting regional arrangements, improving methods to quantify and assess air pollution, and enhancing capacity-building, institutional strengthening and involvement of stakeholders to improve air quality. National measures were aimed at improving data compilation and monitoring air quality; further developing and implementing air quality strategies, which included pollution control and air quality management; identifying, assessing and addressing the adverse effects of air pollution on human health, socio-economic development, ecosystems and cultural heritage; and enhancing capacity-building, institutional strengthening and involvement of all relative stakeholders to improve air quality.

Terrestrial ecosystems

Land degradation

In 2001, drylands occupied one third of the world's land area. Over 100 countries, 80 of them in the developing world, were affected by land degradation.

In order to address the consequences of land degradation and desertification in Africa, UNEP, together with the World Bank and UNDP, carried out the Special Initiative for Africa on Land and Water, which was implemented within the context of GEF.

Deforestation and forest degradation

United Nations Forum on Forests

The United Nations Forum on Forests (UNFF) was established by Economic and Social Council resolution 2000/35 [YUN 2000, p. 979] as a subsidiary body of the Council to promote the management, conservation and sustainable development of all types of forests and to strengthen long-term political commitment to that end. It was also mandated to promote the implementation of internationally agreed actions on forests, to provide a coherent, transparent and participatory global framework for policy implementation, coordination and development, and to carry out principal functions, based on the Rio Declaration on Environment and Development [YUN 1992, p. 670] and chapter 11 of Agenda 21 [ibid., p. 672] relating to forest principles, both adopted by UNCED [ibid., p. 670]. It was further mandated to promote the outcomes of the Intergovernmental Panel on Forests, established in 1995 [YUN 1995, p. 1080] to develop coordinated proposals for action towards the management, conservation and sustainable development of all types of forests, and the Intergovernmental Forum on Forests, created in 1997 [YUN 1997, p. 1057] to work towards the development of a legally binding instrument on the management, conservation and sustainable development of all types of forests.

Governing Council action. On 9 February [A/56/25 (dec. 21/2)], the Governing Council requested the Executive Director to support UNFF's programme of work. Governments, financial institutions and other organizations were called on to contribute resources to facilitate UNEP's participation and support to the implementation of UNFF's multi-year programme of work and plan of action.

UNFF session. UNFF held its first session (New York, 11-22 June), which was preceded by an organizational session (New York, 12 and 16 February) [E/2001/42/Rev.1].

In February, the Forum recommended a draft decision for adoption by the Economic and Social Council regarding the venue of its sessions (see below). It decided to locate the UNFF secretariat in New York [E/2001/42/Rev.1 (dec. ORG/1)] and to elect members of its Bureau for a one-year term, immediately following the closure of a regular session, during the first meeting of its subsequent regular session [dec. ORG/2]. The Forum elected its officers, adopted its provisional agenda and considered a report of an expert consultation on shaping its programme of work (Bonn, 27 November–1 December 2000) [E/CN.18/2001/2]. It also discussed progress towards setting up a collaborative partnership on forests, which was established in April.

In June, the Forum adopted three resolutions and one decision, which it brought to the Council's attention. The Forum adopted its multi-year programme of work for 2001-2005 [res. 1/1] and a plan of action [res. 1/2], outlined the functions of the Collaborative Partnership on Forests [res. 1/3] and accorded observer status to three intergovernmental organizations [dec. 1/1]. Documents

before the Forum included April reports of the Secretary-General on the mandate for the multi-year programme of work [E/CN.18/2001/5 & Corr.1] and on the plan of action [E/CN.18/2001/6 & Corr.1], and notes by the Secretariat on the Collaborative Partnership on Forests [E/CN.18/2001/7] and on the accreditation of intergovernmental organizations [E/CN.18/2001/9]. A May letter from Brazil, Denmark, Malaysia, Norway, South Africa and the United Kingdom transmitted the report of the International Workshop of Experts on Financing Sustainable Forest Management (Oslo, Norway, 22-25 January) [E/CN.18/2001/8].

ECONOMIC AND SOCIAL COUNCIL ACTION

On 3 May, the Economic and Social Council decided that UNFF's first and fifth substantive sessions would be held in New York, that two of the three intervening sessions would be held in Geneva and one in San José, Costa Rica, and that any ministerial segment to be convened during the intervening period would be held during the session in San José (**decision 2001/218**).

On 25 July, the Council decided that UNFF's first high-level ministerial segment would be held during the second session of the Forum, and welcomed Costa Rica's offer to host the session in San José from 4 to 15 March 2002 (**decision 2001/292**). On the same date, the Council, taking note of the report of the Forum on its first session, approved the provisional agenda for the second session (**decision 2001/293**).

Marine ecosystems

Oceans and seas

Global waters assessment

Governing Council action. On 9 February [dec. 21/13], the Governing Council took note of reports of the UN-sponsored Joint Group of Experts on the Scientific Aspects of Marine Environmental Protection (GESAMP) entitled "A sea of troubles", which recognized ineffective communication between scientists, policy makers and the public as a reason for the lack of commitment and the inability of the international community to address and solve the environmental problems of the seas, and "Protecting the oceans from land-based activities—Land-based sources and activities affecting the quality and uses of the marine, coastal and associated freshwater environment". It requested the Executive Director to assist in implementing General Assembly resolutions 54/33 [YUN 1999, p. 994] and 55/7 [YUN 2000, p. 1258] by participating in the United Nations Open-ended Informal Consultative Process on Oceans and the

Law of the Sea, an annual review and evaluation of developments in ocean affairs and the law of the sea (see below). It also requested him, in cooperation with UNESCO and the secretariat of the Convention on Biological Diversity, and in consultation with the regional seas programmes, to explore the establishment of a regular process to assess the state of the marine environment, with active involvement by Governments and regional agreements. He was further requested to present the matter to the Open-ended Informal Consultative Process at its May session, and to report in 2003.

Consultative process. During the second meeting of the UN Open-ended Informal Consultative Process on Oceans and the Law of the Sea (New York, 7-11 May) [A/56/121] (see p. 1236), the UNEP Assistant Executive Director presented an overview of the Programme's work in the area of the marine and coastal environment, highlighting the relevant decisions of the Governing Council's 2001 session.

Global assessment. In order to implement Council decision 21/13 (see p. 964), the first meeting on a feasibility study for establishing a regular process for a global assessment of the state of the marine environment was held (Reykjavik, Iceland, 12-14 September) [UNEP/GC.22/INF/19/Rev.1]. Participants from international bodies, regional organizations, Governments and other concerned organizations agreed that a global marine assessment (GMA) was urgently needed. It recommended that the GMA process be aimed at policy makers and determined four key criteria for the suitability of existing mechanisms and to guide the global assessment, namely cost-effectiveness, credibility, sustainability and the ability to address policy issues. The meeting proposed a workshop for GMA technical development.

The Global International Waters Assessment (GIWA), which was inaugurated in 2000 [YUN 2000, p. 982] to assess international waters and causes of environmental problems in 66 water regions and to focus on the aquatic environment in transboundary waters, held its first General Assembly (Kalmar, Sweden, 9-11 October). The Assembly considered work in the GIWA subregions and improving methodology, and highlighted the decline of the Black Sea due to overfishing, pollution and alien species. Following the Black Sea assessment, the three GEF members (UNEP, UNDP and the World Bank) joined with the European Union in the Black Sea Basin Strategic Partnership.

Global Programme of Action

On 9 February [dec. 21/10], following consideration of a report of the Executive Director [UNEP/GC.21/2] containing information on the Global Programme of Action (GPA) for the Protection of the Marine Environment from Land-based Activities [YUN 1995, p. 1081], the Governing Council requested him to organize in November the first intergovernmental review meeting on the status of the implementation of GPA (see below). He was also asked to pay due attention to activities in UNEP's work programme aimed at addressing the negative effects of sewage, physical alteration and destruction of habitats, nutrients and sediment mobilization on the marine, coastal and associated freshwater environment, and to submit a progress report on UNEP's activities as GPA secretariat to the Council in 2003.

Review meeting. The first Intergovernmental Review Meeting on the Implementation of GPA (Montreal, 26-30 November) [UNEP/GPA/IGR.1/9], convened by UNEP, adopted the Montreal Declaration, which provided a strategic direction for further implementing GPA. The meeting endorsed the work programme of the GPA Coordination Office, which focused on moving the implementation of GPA from the planning to the action phase by developing tool kits, facilitating partnerships and initiating demonstration and capacity-building projects.

The meeting reviewed issues relating to municipal waste water, integrated coastal and oceans governance, building partnerships and financing GPA implementation. It noted steady but slow progress in implementing GPA. A GESAMP report identified the most serious global threats as the alteration and destruction of habitats and ecosystems; the environmental and health effects of sewage; eutrophication; and altered sediment flows caused by hydrological modification. An annex to the report contained summaries of presentations describing experience in the development and implementation of GPA in relation to programmes in 12 regional seas areas.

On 28 November, the General Assembly, taking note of the intergovernmental meeting, called on States to continue to prioritize action on marine pollution from land-based sources as part of their national sustainable development strategies and programmes as a means of implementing GPA (**resolution 56/12**) (see p. 1236).

Coral reefs

Recalling its decisions of 1997 [YUN 1997, p. 1064] and 1999 [YUN 1999, p. 996] on the International Coral Reef Initiative (ICRI)—a programme to protect coral reefs [YUN 1995, p. 1084]—the Governing Council, on 9 February [dec. 21/12], noted the establishment of the UNEP Coral Reef Unit, as well as UNEP's continuing role in ICRI and its coordinating role in the International Coral Reef Action Network (ICRAN) (see below). It decided to support UNEP's continued participation and cooperation in the Global Coral Reef Monitoring Network. The Council underscored the need to strengthen the role of regional seas conventions and action plans as partners for implementing ICRI's Framework for Action, including ICRAN's action phase, and requested the Executive Director to ensure that the regional seas programmes worked as ICRI partners to prepare and implement programmes for the conservation and sustainable use of coral reefs. It also asked him to increase existing collaborative efforts between UNEP's coral-related activities and various multilateral environmental conventions; to develop collaborative approaches with UN agencies, to achieve sustainability in the management and use of coral reefs; to increase fund-raising efforts and work with partners such as ICRI to maximize the contributions of existing and new funding mechanisms; and to submit a progress report in 2003.

UNEP and the World Fish Centre (ICLARM), supported by the United Nations Foundation, through the United Nations Fund for International Partnerships, developed ICRAN. The project, set up in March, addressed the state of the declining coral reefs by facilitating the implementation of the priorities identified by ICRI. The network—which comprised UNEP and its Regional Seas Programme, the UNEP World Conservation Monitoring Centre (WCMC), ICLARM, the World Resources Institute, the ICRI secretariat, the Coral Reef Alliance, the Global Coral Reef Monitoring Network and the South Pacific Regional Environment Programme—supported coral reef management in regional seas programmes in the wider Caribbean, East Africa, East Asia and the South Pacific. Following start-up and bridging phases, the four-year ICRAN action phase was launched in June.

The *World Atlas of Coral Reefs*, which presented the most detailed assessment of coral reefs to date, was prepared by WCMC and launched in September.

Regional Seas Programme

In January [UNEP/GC.21/4/Add.1 & Corr.1], the Executive Director, in response to a 1999 Governing Council decision [A/54/25 (dec. 20/19 A], reported on UNEP's progress in strengthening the Regional Seas Programme as its central mechanism for implementation of its activities relevant to chapter 17 of Agenda 21, on oceans. Support to regional seas programmes focused largely on land-based sources of pollution, integrated coastal areas management, coral reefs, and the development or revision of regional seas conventions and

protocols. Attention was also given to the regional priorities of the respective regional seas conventions and action plans, and resources were assigned for strengthening the regional coordination units (RCUs). Incremental GEF funding had been mobilized for activities in various regions. Progress was made in strengthening the implementation of the Action Plan for the Protection, Management and Development of the Marine and Coastal Environment of the Northwest Pacific Region (NOWPAP).

In February, the Governing Council adopted a series of decisions regarding the Regional Seas Programme. It requested the Executive Director to establish NOWPAP and to enter into negotiations with Japan and the Republic of Korea for the host country agreements for co-hosting a single RCU and, if necessary, to consult with other member States [dec. 21/30]. The Council approved the extension of the duration of the NOWPAP trust fund through 2003. Regarding the further development and strengthening of the programmes [dec. 21/28], the Council requested the Executive Director to continue to use global meetings of the regional seas conventions and action plans and other cost-effective mechanisms for UNEP's work, and to invite, as the secretariat of the Regional Seas Programme, representatives of the shipping, chemical and tourism industries to the Fourth Global Meeting (see p. 967) to discuss possible roles and collaboration in support of the programmes. As to the revitalization of the Regional Seas Programme [dec. 21/28 A], the Council requested the Executive Director to focus on priority issues such as land-based sources of pollution, integrated coastal areas management, coral reefs and the development or revision of regional seas conventions and protocols. He was also asked to support the preparation of a strategic approach to financing the programmes and to assist them in the mobilization of resources. In a decision on horizontal cooperation among regional seas conventions and action plans [dec. 21/28 B], the Council requested the Executive Director to support the implementation of a series of twinning arrangements and to facilitate new arrangements for horizontal cooperation among regional seas programmes. The Council invited the Rotterdam Convention on the Prior Informed Consent Procedure for Certain Hazardous Chemicals and Pesticides in International Trade [YUN 1998, p. 997] (see p. 968), the future convention on POPs (see p. 971) and the Regional Seas Programme to work together to implement capacity-building and information exchange activities to assist countries in meeting their obligations under those conventions, and to collaborate on mutually supportive activities [dec. 21/28 C]. The Executive Director was requested to prepare an inventory of the work in chemicals undertaken by the regional seas programmes as an information base for collaboration with the Rotterdam Convention and the convention on POPs; to support cooperative initiatives aimed at the harmonization of work plans of the regional seas conventions and the 1992 Convention on Biological Diversity [YUN 1992, p. 683], which entered into force in 1993 [YUN 1993, p. 810], and the development of harmonized national reporting; to facilitate cooperative arrangements between the Convention on International Trade in Endangered Species of Wild Fauna and Flora and the regional seas programmes; and to continue with the restructuring of the UNEP Marine Mammal Action Plan through a greater coordinated effort among the regional seas programmes and relevant conventions and partner organizations. With regard to partnerships with international organizations [dec. 21/28 D], the Council requested the Executive Director to promote a more active involvement of the regional seas conventions and action plans in the UN Open-ended Informal Consultative Process on Oceans and the Law of the Sea, and in subregional preparatory activities for the 2002 UNCED review (see p. 749). He was requested to follow up on the endorsement by the Third Global Meeting [YUN 2000, p. 983] of a joint UNEP/Food and Agriculture Organization of the United Nations (FAO) paper on ecosystem-based fisheries management, including support to a series of actions to enhance cooperation. The Executive Director was further requested to support the establishment of a joint International Maritime Organization (IMO)/UNEP forum on emergency response to marine pollution; follow up on a recommendation that UNEP work closely with the Coastal Global Ocean Observing System, directed by IOC/UNESCO; work with the Marine Environment Laboratory of the International Atomic Energy Agency (IAEA) in supporting marine pollution sampling, monitoring and assessment in developing countries and countries with economies in transition that were members of regional seas programmes; and continue to strengthen partnerships with members of the Administrative Committee on Coordination (ACC) Subcommittee on Oceans and Coastal Areas in support of regional seas programmes. The Council welcomed the Reykjavik Conference on Responsible Fisheries in the Marine Ecosystem (Reykjavik, 1-4 October). Endorsing action taken to establish a regional seas programme of the Central-East Pacific region, the Council invited further efforts by Colombia, Costa Rica, El Salvador, Guatemala, Honduras, Mexico, Nicaragua and Panama to negotiate and adopt a convention

and action plan for the protection and sustainable development of the region, and requested the Executive Director to assist those Governments in the process [dec. 21/29]. It called for close cooperation between the proposed Central-East Pacific Regional Seas Programme, the South-East Pacific Action Plan and the Caribbean Action Plan. The Executive Director was requested to invite multilateral funding institutions, including the World Bank and GEF, to future meetings of the Central-East Pacific Regional Seas Programme, and to submit a progress report in 2003.

The second session of the High-level Government-designated Expert Meeting of the Proposed Central-East Pacific Regional Seas Programme (Managua, Nicaragua, 19-23 March) agreed on 25 of the 28 articles of a convention for the protection and sustainable development of the marine and coastal environment in the region. During the session, it was decided to retain the term "North-East Pacific" instead of "Central-East Pacific" within the title of the convention. The session approved the draft plan of action for the North-East Pacific and decided to hold a third session in August.

At the third session (Panama City, 6-9 August), the title of the proposed convention was modified to "convention for cooperation in the protection and sustainable development of the marine and coastal environment of the North-East Pacific". The full text of the convention was agreed upon, as was the full text of the convention's plan of action, including the regional programme of work on land-based sources of pollution 2001-2006 (annex I) and the strategy for the plan's operationalization (annex II). The formal signing of the convention and plan of action would take place in 2002.

The Fourth Global Meeting of Regional Seas Conventions and Action Plans (Montreal, 21-23 November) [UNEP/GCSS.VII/INF/5] adopted a series of recommendations on: implementation of joint programmes by UNEP and the International Ocean Institute; further collaboration between UNEP and IMO; an ecosystem-based approach to the management of fisheries and the marine and coastal environment; cooperation with the 1989 Basel Convention on the Control of Transboundary Movements of Hazardous Wastes and their Disposal [YUN 1989, p. 420], which entered into force in 1992 [YUN 1992, p. 685]; cooperation between regional seas programmes and IOC/UNESCO; a regular process to assess the state of the marine environment (see p. 965); cooperation between the regional seas programmes and the IAEA Marine Environment Laboratory (Monaco); compensation for environmental damage; strengthening relations between regional seas programmes and the oil and shipping industries; and international ocean governance. Other recommendations related to publications and resource mobilization. The fifth meeting would take place in 2002 in Toyama, Japan.

Conservation of wildlife

As at 31 December, the 1994 Lusaka Agreement on Cooperative Enforcement Operations Directed at Illegal Trade in Wild Fauna and Flora [YUN 1994, p. 951], which entered into force in 1996 [YUN 1996, p. 970], had been ratified or acceded to by six States (Congo, Kenya, Lesotho, Uganda, United Republic of Tanzania, Zambia). The Agreement aimed to reduce, and ultimately eliminate, illegal trafficking in African wildlife.

The fourth meeting of the Governing Council of the Parties to the Lusaka Agreement (Nairobi, 23-24 July) called on States parties, assisted by the Lusaka Agreement Task Force in collaboration with UNEP, to review, develop and strengthen their national wildlife management laws and regulations and to incorporate provisions of the Agreement.

ECONOMIC AND SOCIAL COUNCIL ACTION

On 24 July [meeting 40], the Economic and Social Council, on the recommendation of the Commission on Crime Prevention and Criminal Justice [E/2001/30/Rev.1], adopted **resolution 2001/12** without vote [agenda item 14 (c)].

Illicit trafficking in protected species of wild flora and fauna

The Economic and Social Council,

Aware that the conservation of wild flora and fauna and of genetic resources is essential for the maintenance of biological diversity and sustainable development, these being of fundamental importance, in particular, for local and indigenous communities with traditional lifestyles based on biological resources, and that concerns have been expressed with respect to illicit access to genetic resources,

Taking note of the principles on which are founded the Convention on International Trade in Endangered Species of Wild Fauna and Flora, an agreement regulating international trade in endangered species and establishing recommendations for combating illicit trafficking therein, and the Convention on Biological Diversity,

Deeply concerned about the existence of groups, in particular those operating transnationally, dedicated to illicit trafficking in protected species of wild flora and fauna, that are increasingly employing sophisticated technologies,

Recognizing the links between transnational organized crime and illicit trafficking in protected species of wild flora and fauna, as well as the need to prevent, combat and eradicate this form of illicit traffic,

Aware of the adverse environmental, economic, social and scientific repercussions of transnational organized criminal activities devoted to illicit trafficking in protected species of wild flora and fauna,

Recognizing that international cooperation, especially mutual assistance against illicit trafficking in protected species of wild flora and fauna, is essential,

Taking into account General Assembly resolution 55/25 of 15 November 2000, in which it is stated that the United Nations Convention against Transnational Organized Crime constitutes an effective tool and the necessary legal framework for international cooperation in combating such criminal activities as illicit trafficking in protected species of wild flora and fauna, in furtherance of the principles of the Convention on International Trade in Endangered Species of Wild Fauna and Flora,

1. *Urges* Member States to adopt, in accordance with the Convention on International Trade in Endangered Species of Wild Fauna and Flora, the legislative or other measures necessary for establishing illicit trafficking in protected species of wild flora and fauna as a criminal offence in their domestic legislation;

2. *Encourages* Member States to explore possible means of promoting law enforcement cooperation and information exchange aimed at preventing, combating and eradicating illicit trafficking in protected species of wild flora and fauna;

3. *Requests* the Secretary-General to prepare, within existing resources or drawing upon extrabudgetary contributions, in coordination with other competent entities of the United Nations system, a report analysing domestic, bilateral, regional and multilateral legal provisions and other relevant documents, resolutions and recommendations dealing with the prevention, combating and eradication of illicit trafficking in protected species of wild flora and fauna by organized criminal groups and to present its report to the Commission on Crime Prevention and Criminal Justice at its eleventh session;

4. *Also requests* the Secretary-General to prepare, within existing resources or drawing upon extrabudgetary contributions, in coordination with other competent entities of the United Nations system, a report analysing the domestic, bilateral, regional and multilateral legal provisions and other relevant documents, resolutions and recommendations dealing with illicit access to genetic resources and also the extent to which organized criminal groups are involved therein and to present its report to the Commission on Crime Prevention and Criminal Justice at its eleventh session.

Protection against harmful products and waste

Chemical safety

As at 31 December, 72 States and the EC had signed and 17 States (Bulgaria, Czech Republic, El Salvador, Germany, Guinea, Hungary, Kyrgyzstan, Mongolia, Netherlands, Nigeria, Norway, Oman, Panama, Saudi Arabia, Senegal, Slovenia, Suriname) had ratified, approved or acceded to the 1998 Rotterdam Convention on the Prior Informed Consent (PIC) Procedure for Certain Hazardous Chemicals and Pesticides in International Trade [YUN 1998, p. 997]. The Convention was to enter into force 90 days following the deposit of the fiftieth instrument of ratification.

Pending the entry into force of the Convention, the PIC procedure, which aimed to promote a shared responsibility between exporting and importing countries in protecting human health and the environment from the harmful effects of certain hazardous chemicals that were traded internationally, was applied voluntarily by Governments.

The eighth session of the Intergovernmental Negotiating Committee (INC) for an International Legally Binding Instrument for the Application of the PIC Procedure (Rome, 8-12 October) [UNEP/FAO/PIC/INC.8/19] considered issues associated with the implementation of the interim PIC procedure, and prepared for the Convention's entry into force. It resolved various questions associated with discontinuation of the interim PIC procedure and on conflict of interest in the Interim Chemical Review Committee, although some contentious issues, such as treatment of non-parties after discontinuation of the interim procedure and composition of the PIC regions, had been forwarded for consideration at INC's ninth session, scheduled for 2002 in Bonn.

The 29-member Interim Chemical Review Committee, a subsidiary body established by INC in 1999 [YUN 1999, p. 997] to make recommendations on the inclusion of banned and severely restricted chemicals or hazardous pesticide formulations in the PIC procedure, held its second session (Rome, 19-23 March) [UNEP/FAO/PIC/ICRC.2/11]. The Committee decided that maleic hydrazide would not become subject to the PIC procedure and a decision guidance document would not be developed. However, the Committee would review the potassium salt of maleic hydrazide, which was more water-soluble and more readily taken up by the target organisms. The Committee recommended to INC that chemical monocrotophos become subject to the interim PIC procedure.

Governing Council action. The Governing Council considered a January note of the Executive Director transmitting a report of an independent consultant on options for enhanced coherence and efficiency among international activities related to chemicals [UNEP/GC.21/INF/20], submitted in response to a 1997 Council decision [YUN 1997, p. 1066] and in the light of a 1999 decision [YUN 1999, p. 997].

In February, the Governing Council adopted a series of decisions relating to the 1998 Rotterdam Convention and chemical safety and management.

The Council called on States and regional economic integration organizations entitled to do so to ratify, accept, approve or accede to the Rotterdam Convention, to contribute to the trust fund established by UNEP to support interim arrangements and the operation of the Conference of the Parties, and to ensure the full participation of developing countries and those with economies in transition in the work of INC [dec. 21/3]. The Executive Director was requested to report in 2003.

Regarding chemicals management [dec. 21/7], the Council invited countries to share their experiences with the Executive Director to assist in capacity-building efforts as outlined in the Bahia Declaration on Chemical Safety and the Priorities for Action beyond 2000, adopted by the Intergovernmental Forum on Chemical Safety (IFCS) (Bahia, Brazil, 15-20 October 2000) [IFCS/FORUM III/23w]. The Executive Director was requested to report on UNEP's contribution to the implementation of the Declaration and Priorities in 2003, and examine the need for a strategic approach to international chemicals management and prepare a report thereon for consideration in 2002.

The Council, recalling the Programme for the Further Implementation of Agenda 21, annexed to General Assembly resolution S/19-2 [YUN 1997, p. 792], called on Governments that had not yet done so to eliminate the use of lead in gasoline, and urged Governments, intergovernmental organizations, IFCS and civil society to assist actively in the phase-out, by making available information, technical assistance, capacity-building and funding necessary for the participation of developing countries, especially LDCs and countries with economies in transition [dec. 21/6].

Mercury assessment

In a 31 January letter to the Director of UNEP Chemicals [UNEP/GC.21/INF/26], the Secretary to the Executive Body for the 1979 Convention on Long-Range Transboundary Air Pollution (see p. 957) emphasized the adverse environmental and health effects of mercury and its related compounds and invited UNEP to initiate an assessment of mercury.

Following consideration of a January note of the Executive Director [UNEP/GC.21/INF/20], the Governing Council, on 9 February [dec. 21/5], invited the Executive Director, in cooperation with other members of the Inter-Organization Programme for the Sound Management of Chemicals, which served as a mechanism to coordinate efforts of intergovernmental organizations in chemicals assessment and management, to initiate a global assessment of mercury and its compounds. The assessment should include, among other elements, a summary of existing information on chemical processes, toxicology, and impacts of mercury on human health and the environment, and should outline, for consideration in 2002, options addressing any significant global adverse impacts of mercury. The Council requested the Executive Director to report on the assessment's results in 2003, and agreed to consider the need for assessments of other heavy metals.

Harmful products

In June [A/56/115-E/2001/92 & Corr.1], the Secretary-General submitted a report covering the sixth triennial review of the Consolidated List of Products Whose Consumption and/or Sale Have Been Banned, Withdrawn, Severely Restricted or Not Approved by Governments. The report updated developments since the submission of the Secretary-General's last report in 1998 [YUN 1998, p. 998].

The Secretary-General noted that there had been marked progress in activities carried out in the area of products harmful to health and the environment. He presented a series of recommendations to the Economic and Social Council relating to the publication of the List in all UN official languages, the capacity-building of developing countries regarding the sound management of toxic chemicals and dangerous pharmaceutical products, cooperation by Member States, intergovernmental organizations and other members of civil society with the Secretariat on an indepth analysis of the utilization of the List to be undertaken following the publication of the seventh (2004) triennial review, and ratification, acceptance, approval or accession by Member States to the Rotterdam Convention (see p. 968).

By **decision 56/440** of 21 December, the General Assembly took note of the Secretary-General's report.

ECONOMIC AND SOCIAL COUNCIL ACTION

On 26 July [meeting 43], the Economic and Social Council adopted **resolution 2001/33** [draft: E/2001/L.37] without vote [agenda item 13 (e)].

Protection against products harmful to health and the environment

The Economic and Social Council,

Recalling General Assembly resolutions 37/137 cf 17 December 1982, 38/149 of 19 December 1983, 39/229 of 18 December 1984 and 44/226 of 22 December 1989, General Assembly decisions 47/439 of 22 December 1992 and 50/431 of 20 December 1995, and Council resolution 1998/41 of 30 July 1998,

Having considered the report of the Secretary-General on products harmful to health and the environment, which contains a review of the Consolidated List of Products Whose Consumption and/or Sale Have Been Banned, Withdrawn, Severely Restricted or Not Approved by Governments,

Taking note of the fact that an increasing number of countries participate in the preparation of the Consolidated List,

Noting with satisfaction the continued close collaboration between the United Nations, the Food and Agriculture Organization of the United Nations, the World Health Organization, the United Nations Environment Programme and the World Trade Organization in the preparation and dissemination of the Consolidated List,

1. *Expresses its appreciation* for the cooperation extended by Governments in the preparation of the Consolidated List of Products Whose Consumption and/or Sale Have Been Banned, Withdrawn, Severely Restricted or Not Approved by Governments, and urges all Governments, in particular those that have not yet done so, to provide the necessary information to relevant organizations for inclusion in future issues of the Consolidated List;

2. *Requests* the Secretary-General to prepare each of the two issuances of the Consolidated List, pharmaceuticals and chemicals, in all official languages—the English version in the already established format, and the versions in the other languages as a text file. In this connection, the Consolidated List should continue to include previously collected data, while at the same time making distinct entries for those products covered in the interim prior informed consent procedure, in line with the Rotterdam Convention on the Prior Informed Consent Procedure for Certain Hazardous Chemicals and Pesticides in International Trade, and should consequently keep updating the information contained therein, in accordance with relevant action being taken by the Convention;

3. *Invites* multilateral and bilateral agencies to continue to strengthen and coordinate their activities for improving the capacity-building of developing countries, particularly the least developed countries, including innovative methodologies for earmarking, assessing and monitoring technical assistance in the area of the sound management of hazardous chemicals and dangerous pharmaceutical products;

4. *Emphasizes* the need to continue to utilize the work being undertaken by relevant organizations of the United Nations system and other intergovernmental organizations in this area, as well as that being carried out under international agreements and conventions in related areas in updating the Consolidated List;

5. *Requests* the Secretary-General to continue to report every three years, in accordance with General Assembly resolution 39/229, on the implementation of the present resolution and of previous Assembly resolutions on the same subject;

6. *Requests* the Secretary-General, within existing resources, to continue to disseminate the Consolidated List as widely as possible and to look at the possibility of using online dissemination in collaboration with the World Trade Organization, the Food and Agriculture Organization of the United Nations, the World Health Organization and the United Nations Environment Programme.

Persistent organic pollutants

The Intergovernmental Negotiating Committee (INC) for an International Legally Binding Instrument for Implementing International Action on Certain Persistent Organic Pollutants, meeting in 2000 [YUN 2000, p. 988], had agreed on an international legally binding instrument, the Stockholm Convention on Persistent Organic Pollutants, for adoption by the Conference of Plenipotentiaries in 2001.

Following consideration of a report of the Executive Director [UNEP/GC.21/2] on international action to protect human health and the environment through measures that would reduce and/or eliminate emissions and discharges of POPs, including the development of a legally binding instrument, the Governing Council, on 9 February [dec. 21/4], called on Governments and regional economic integration organizations to adopt and thereafter sign the Stockholm Convention (see below), and encouraged countries to ratify, accept, approve or accede to the Convention with a view to its entry into force as soon as possible, preferably by 2004. It authorized the participation of UNEP's secretariat in an interim secretariat and in a secretariat to the Convention, if so decided by the Conference of Plenipotentiaries and provided that the arrangements were satisfactory to the Executive Director and costs were met through extrabudgetary resources. The Council requested the Executive Director to promote full cooperation between the secretariat and those of other relevant conventions, and urged him to assist in the implementation of relevant resolutions of the Conference of Plenipotentiaries with a view to facilitating capacity-building, early entry into force and financing. The Executive Director was invited to take action to facilitate the voluntary implementation of the Convention prior to its entry into force if the Conference of Plenipotentiaries called for such action. The Council appealed to Governments, as well as intergovernmental organizations, NGOs and the private sector, to provide sufficient financial resources to implement interim arrangements for the Convention prior to the first meeting of its Conference of the Parties, and encouraged financial and in-kind contributions for supporting implementation of the immediate actions called for in a 1997 Council decision [YUN 1997, p. 1065] on measures to reduce and/or eliminate POPs. The Executive Director was requested to continue taking actions as requested in the 1997 decision, and was asked to invite the GEF Council to take into account the relevant resolutions of the Stockholm Conference of Plenipotentiaries and consider ways and means to implement them.

A preparatory meeting (Stockholm, Sweden, 21 May) for the Conference of Plenipotentiaries [UNEP/POPS/CONF/PM/3/Rev.1] finalized resolutions that INC did not consider in 2000 [YUN 2000, p. 988]. The resolutions dealt with, among other things, interim arrangements to protect human health and the environment pending the Convention's entry into force and for its effective operation thereafter; the provision of assistance for capacity-building related to the implementation of the obligations of the Convention for developing countries and countries with economies in transition, and the development of a capacity assistance network with the cooperation of UNEP, as the interim secretariat of the Convention, and GEF; and liability and redress concerning the use and international introduction of POPs into the environment, including the organization of a workshop on the subject no later than 2002.

The Conference of Plenipotentiaries (Stockholm, 22-23 May) [UNEP/POPS/CONF/4] adopted the resolutions of the preparatory meeting, as well as those relating to interim financial arrangements, cooperation with the Basel Convention on the Control of Transboundary Movements of Hazardous Wastes and their Disposal (see p. 972), and proposals for the location of the Convention secretariat. The Final Act of the Conference of Plenipotentiaries was signed on 22 May by 114 States and the EC. On the same date, the Conference adopted the Stockholm Convention on Persistent Organic Pollutants, which was annexed to the meeting's report. The Convention was opened for signature on 23 May in Stockholm and at UN Headquarters from 24 May 2001 to 22 May 2002. It would enter into force 90 days after the deposit of the fiftieth instrument of ratification, acceptance, approval or accession. As at 31 December, 110 States and the EC had signed the Convention; Canada and Fiji had ratified it.

The Stockholm Convention set out control measures on the production, import, export, disposal and use of an initial list of 12 POPs, including 8 pesticides (aldrin, chlordane, DDT, dieldrin, endrin, heptachlor, mirex and toxaphene); 2 industrial chemicals (hexachlorobenzene (HCB) and polychlorinated biphenyls (PCBs)); and 2 unintended by-products (dioxins and furans). It included measures to reduce or eliminate the production and use of intentionally produced POPs; eliminate unintentionally produced POPs; and manage stockpiles and dispose of POP waste in an environmentally sound manner. A register of parties with specific exemptions was established. Parties were to promote the development or require the use of safer substitute or modified materials, and promote best available techniques for replacing existing POPs and preventing the development of new sources. Governments were to develop action plans to meet their obligations under the Convention. Procedures and criteria for listing new POPs were annexed to the Convention.

Hazardous wastes

As at 31 December, the number of parties to the 1989 Basel Convention on the Control of Transboundary Movements of Hazardous Wastes and their Disposal [YUN 1989, p. 420], which entered into force in 1992 [YUN 1992, p. 685], rose to 149, with the accession of Azerbaijan, Bosnia and Herzegovina, Cambodia, Cameroon, Guyana, the Libyan Arab Jamahiriya and Nauru. The 1995 amendment to the Convention [YUN 1995, p. 1333], not yet in force, had been ratified, accepted or approved by 27 parties. The 1999 Basel Protocol on Liability and Compensation for Damage Resulting from Transboundary Movements of Hazardous Wastes and their Disposal [YUN 1999, p. 998] had 13 signatories at year's end.

The Technical Working Group of the Convention, at its eighteenth session (Geneva, 18-20 June) [UNEP/CHW/TWG/18/14], considered, among other things, the preparation of draft technical guidelines on the environmentally sound management of lead acid battery wastes, metal and metal compounds, plastic wastes and their disposal, the dismantling of ships and POPs as waste.

The First Continental Conference for Africa on the environmentally sound management of unwanted stocks of hazardous wastes and their prevention (Rabat, Morocco, 8-12 January), organized jointly by Morocco and the Basel Convention secretariat, adopted the Rabat Declaration, by which participants pledged to implement national and regional solutions to deal with the unwanted stocks. It also adopted a Programme of Action and the necessary mechanisms, under the aegis of the United Nations, with a view to ensuring follow-up of recommendations relating to guidelines for undertaking inventories of unwanted stocks of pesticides and PCBs; transboundary movements of unwanted products; treatment technologies, including the use of cement kilns to incinerate pesticides; approaches for national policies and a regulatory framework regarding POPs; and strategies for the management of used oils.

Cleaner production and sustainable consumption patterns

The UNEP International Environmental Technology Centre organized workshops on eutrophication in lakes, advisory services on waste management and round tables on air quality and on trenchless technologies.

Under the UNEP Collaborating Centre on Energy and Environment, a sustainable energy advisory facility was established to provide advice to developing countries, including Botswana, Ghana and Mali.

Other matters

Environmental law

On 9 February [dec. 21/23], the Governing Council adopted the Programme for the Development and Periodic Review of Environmental Law for the First Decade of the Twenty-first Century (Montevideo Programme III) [YUN 2000, p. 989], to serve as a broad strategy for UNEP activities in that area. The Council requested the Executive Director to implement the Programme, within available resources, through UNEP's programmes of work and in close collaboration with States, conferences of the parties and secretariats of multilateral environmental agreements and other international organizations and actors. The Council decided to review the implementation of the Programme not later than its regular session in 2005. The Council had adopted previous Programmes in 1982 [YUN 1982, p. 1030] and 1993 [YUN 1993, p. 820].

Occupied Palestinian and other Arab territories

On 9 February [dec. 21/16], the Governing Council, gravely concerned by reports of environmental violations in the occupied Palestinian territories, requested the Executive Director to assess the repercussions of those violations and to assist the Palestinian Authority (PA) to address urgent environmental challenges. He was also asked to report on the environmental situation in the territories, in accordance with the Council's 1999 decision [YUN 1999, p. 999], and to include the findings of the assessment. The Executive Director was requested to report to the Committee of Permanent Representatives as soon as possible and, through it, to the Council in 2002.

In a November report [UNEP/GCSS.VII/4], the Executive Director stated that Governments were informed that circumstances in the Middle East prevented the preparation of the report requested in 1999. Due to the continued deterioration in the situation during the year (see p. 406), UNEP was still unable to collect the necessary information. It had requested Israel, the PA, the office of the UN Special Coordinator in the Occupied Territories and relevant agencies for advice and inputs to the report.

International Day for Preventing the Exploitation of the Environment in War and Armed Conflict

On 5 November [meeting 37], the General Assembly adopted **resolution 56/4** [draft: A/56/L.8 & Add.1] without vote [agenda item 171].

Observance of the International Day for Preventing the Exploitation of the Environment in War and Armed Conflict

The General Assembly,

Recalling the United Nations Millennium Declaration, which emphasized the necessity of safeguarding nature for the sake of future generations and working for the protection of our common environment,

Considering that damage to the environment in times of armed conflict impairs ecosystems and natural resources long beyond the period of conflict, and often extends beyond the limits of national territories and the present generation,

Recalling Article 2, paragraph 4, of the Charter of the United Nations, which states that all Member States shall refrain from the threat or use of force against the territorial integrity of any State in their international relations,

1. *Declares* 6 November each year as the International Day for Preventing the Exploitation of the Environment in War and Armed Conflict;

2. *Invites* Member States, entities of the United Nations system and other international and regional organizations to observe 6 November each year as the International Day for Preventing the Exploitation of the Environment in War and Armed Conflict;

3. *Requests* the Secretary-General to ensure the implementation of the present resolution and to promote it in the international community.

Human settlements

Follow-up to the 1996 UN Conference on Human Settlements (Habitat II)

Twenty-fifth special session

The twenty-fifth special session of the General Assembly to review and appraise the implementation of the Habitat Agenda [YUN 1996, p. 994], adopted by the 1996 United Nations Conference on Human Settlements (Habitat II) [ibid., p. 992], was held in New York from 6 to 9 June [A/S-25/9], in accordance with Assembly resolution 52/190 [YUN 1997, p. 1092]. The Assembly adopted the Declaration on Cities and Other Human Settlements in the New Millennium (**resolution S-25/2**) (see p. 974), by which participants reaffirmed their commitment to the Habitat Agenda, a global call to action that offered a vision of adequate shelter for all and the sustainable development of human settlements, and the Istanbul Declaration on Human Settlements—a high-level political statement that committed Governments to the Habitat Agenda's recommendations [YUN 1996, p. 993]—presented an assessment of the implementation of the Habitat Agenda and proposed further action.

In other action, the Assembly approved the report of the Credentials Committee [A/S-25/6] on 8 June (**resolution S-25/1**). Regarding procedural matters, the Assembly, on 6 June, appointed the members of the Credentials Committee (**decision S-25/11**) and selected its President (**decision S-25/12**), Vice-Presidents (**decision S-25/13**), Chairpersons of the Main Committees (**decision S-25/14**) and officers of the newly established Thematic Committee (**decision S-25/16**) (see p. 980) and of the Ad Hoc Committee of the Whole of the Twenty-fifth Special Session (**decision S-25/15**); made arrangements with regard to the organization of the session (**decision S-25/21**); approved eight speakers in the debate for the last two speaking slots at each plenary meeting, with the exception of the first and last plenary meetings (**decision S-25/23**); and adopted the agenda for the special session (**decision S-25/24**). On 6 June, the Assembly decided that 11 representatives of local authorities, NGOs and other Habitat Agenda partners might make statements in the plenary debate (**decision S-25/22**).

(For information on the preparatory process for the session, see p. 979.)

In an opening statement before the Assembly session [A/S-25/PV.1], the Secretary-General, recalled the Millennium Declaration, adopted by the Assembly in resolution 55/2 [YUN 2000, p. 49], in which world leaders pledged to achieve significant improvement in the lives of at least 100 million slum-dwellers by 2020. He stated that the challenge of the special session was to create lasting momentum for action on housing issues. Five years along the path of implementing the Habitat Agenda, a few points stood out. Two thirds of the world's cities had established new public-private partnerships. States had adapted housing and other policies to reflect internationally agreed principles in partnership with local authorities, NGOs, women's organizations and other civil society groups. The role of women needed to be strengthened and decision makers should address the issues that affected them. The lack of secure tenure led to the enlargement of the informal sector; action in that area had the potential to provide a major route out of poverty. The world's cities faced a long list of common challenges, and all partners—ministers and mayors responsible for urban policy, NGOs, women's groups and others in civil society—were responsible to the inhabitants of slums, favelas, barrios, ghettos, shanty towns and squatter settlements.

The Assembly considered an April note by the Secretary-General [A/S-25/3] transmitting the final report of the Executive Director of the United Nations Centre for Human Settlements (UNCHS) on the review and appraisal of progress made in the implementation of the Habitat Agenda. The report was based on a draft submitted in 2000 [YUN 2000, p. 990]. The report had been amended in response to Assembly resolution 55/194 [ibid., p. 991] to include information on the implementation of the twin goals of the Habitat Agenda—adequate shelter for all and sustainable human settlements development—as well as on the actions and achievements of the Global Campaign for Secure Tenure [YUN 2000, p. 995] and the Global Campaign for Urban Governance [ibid.], and in response to Assembly resolution 55/195 [ibid., p. 993], to include information on the Cities Alliance initiative (see below). The report included illustrative boxes that corresponded to the cases selected for presentation and discussion by the Thematic Committee of the special session.

A May addendum [A/S-25/3/Add.1] contained the Executive Director's progress report on the Cities Alliance, a joint initiative of the Centre, the World Bank and bilateral agencies, which provided financial and technical assistance for activities to facilitate the implementation of the Habitat Agenda, particularly activities relating to city development strategies and improving slum upgrading.

GENERAL ASSEMBLY ACTION

On 9 June [meeting 6], the General Assembly, on the recommendation of the Ad Hoc Committee of the Whole [A/S-25/7/Rev.1], adopted **resolution S-25/2** without vote [agenda item 10].

Declaration on Cities and Other Human Settlements in the New Millennium

The General Assembly

Adopts the Declaration on Cities and Other Human Settlements in the New Millennium annexed to the present resolution.

ANNEX
Declaration on Cities and Other Human Settlements in the New Millennium

We, the representatives of Governments, being guided by the purposes and principles of the Charter of the United Nations, meeting at the special session of the General Assembly to review the implementation of the Habitat Agenda, to recognize progress and to identify obstacles and emerging issues, reaffirm our will and commitment to implement fully the Istanbul Declaration on Human Settlements and the Habitat Agenda and decide on further initiatives, in the spirit of the United Nations Millennium Declaration. The Istanbul Declaration and the Habitat Agenda will remain the basic framework for sustainable human settlements development in the years to come.

Therefore, we:

A. Renewing the commitments made at the United Nations Conference on Human Settlements (Habitat II)

1. Reaffirm that human beings are at the centre of our concern for sustainable development and that they are the basis for our actions taken in the implementation of the Habitat Agenda;

2. Wish to stress that this is a special moment in the development of human settlements, when half of the world's 6 billion people will be living in cities and the world is facing the unprecedented growth of urban population, mainly in the developing world. The decisions we make now will have far-reaching consequences. We note with great concern that one fourth of the world's urban population is living below the poverty line. In many cities, which are confronted with rapid growth, environmental problems and the slow pace of economic development, it has not been possible to meet the challenges of generating sufficient employment, providing adequate housing and meeting the basic needs of citizens;

3. Re-emphasize that rural and urban areas are economically, socially and environmentally interdependent and that cities and towns are engines of growth contributing to the development of both rural and urban human settlements. Half of the world's inhabitants live in rural settlements and in Africa and Asia the population in the rural areas represents a majority. Integrated physical planning and balanced attention to rural and urban living conditions are of crucial importance for all nations. Full advantage must be taken of the complementary contributions and linkages between rural and urban areas by giving appropriate attention to their different economic, social and environmental requirements. While addressing urban poverty, it is also essential to eradicate rural poverty and to improve living conditions, as well as to create employment and educational opportunities in rural settlements and small and medium-sized cities and towns in rural areas;

4. Reconfirm our determination to address at all levels the deteriorating environmental conditions that threaten the health and quality of life of billions of people. Some activities at the local level that degrade the environment have implications at the global level and need to be addressed in the context of human settlements;

5. Reconfirm the goals and principles of adequate shelter for all and sustainable human settlements development in an urbanizing world, as set out in the Habitat Agenda, which form the basis of our commitments;

6. Renew and reaffirm the commitments we made in the Habitat Agenda concerning adequate shelter for all, sustainable human settlements, enablement and participation, gender equality, financing shelter and human settlements, international cooperation and assessing progress;

B. Welcoming progress in implementing the Habitat Agenda

7. Commend the efforts by all levels of government, the United Nations, other intergovernmental organizations and Habitat Agenda partners, as well as those by the Executive Director of the United Nations Centre for Human Settlements (Habitat), and welcome the progress made thus far towards the implementation

of the Habitat Agenda. We note with appreciation the national and regional reports on the implementation of the Habitat Agenda and the report of the Executive Director of the United Nations Centre for Human Settlements (Habitat) on the review and appraisal of progress made in the implementation of the Habitat Agenda, taking into account the specific priorities and objectives of each region, and in conformity with the legal framework and national policies of each country;

8. Welcome the decision by the Commission on Human Rights at its fifty-sixth session that the Special Rapporteur whose mandate would focus on adequate housing as a component of the right to an adequate standard of living should, as a part of his mandate, develop a regular dialogue and discuss possible areas of collaboration with Governments, relevant United Nations bodies, specialized agencies, international organizations in the field of housing rights, including the United Nations Centre for Human Settlements (Habitat), non-governmental organizations and international financial institutions, and should make recommendations on the realization of the rights relevant to the mandate;

9. Also take note with satisfaction of the growing awareness of the need to address, in an integrated manner, poverty, homelessness, unemployment, lack of basic services, exclusion of women and children and of marginalized groups, including indigenous communities, and social fragmentation, in order to achieve better, more liveable and inclusive human settlements worldwide. Governments, international organizations and members of civil society have made continuous efforts to address those problems;

10. Take note of the development of integrated and participatory approaches to urban environmental planning and management in relation to the implementation of Agenda 21. In this regard, we welcome the support provided by many Governments to mechanisms for consultations and partnerships among interested parties to prepare and implement local environmental plans and local Agenda 21 initiatives;

11. Welcome the increasing economic role of cities and towns in our globalizing world and the progress made in forging public-private partnerships and strengthening small enterprises and microenterprises. Cities and towns hold the potential to maximize the benefits and to offset the negative consequences of globalization. Well-managed cities can provide an economic environment capable of generating employment opportunities, as well as offering a diversity of goods and services;

12. Welcome the efforts made so far by many developing countries in effecting decentralization in the management of cities as a means of strengthening the operation of local authorities in the implementation of the Habitat Agenda;

13. Welcome the contributions of national and other Governments, which have the primary responsibility for the implementation of the Habitat Agenda through their laws, policies and programmes;

14. Appreciate the important contributions made by local authorities worldwide in the implementation of the Habitat Agenda through concerted efforts and strengthened partnerships between Governments at all levels, resulting in the improved condition of human settlements, including improved urban governance. Broad-based participation in decision-making, together with accountability, simplicity of procedures and transparency, is imperative to prevent corruption and to promote public interests. In this regard, we note with satisfaction the increased priority given to the implementation of the Habitat Agenda and to the principles of good governance at all levels;

15. Recognize the important work done by the Global Parliamentarians on Habitat in the implementation of the Habitat Agenda. At the same time, we encourage them to continue to promote the implementation of the Habitat Agenda;

16. Recognize that the overall thrust of the new strategic vision of the United Nations Centre for Human Settlements (Habitat) and its emphasis on the two global campaigns on secure tenure and urban governance are strategic points of entry for the effective implementation of the Habitat Agenda, especially for guiding international cooperation on adequate shelter for all and sustainable human settlements development. In this regard, we welcome the establishment of the Advisory Committee of Local Authorities and express our appreciation for its contributions to the work of the United Nations Centre for Human Settlements (Habitat) and to the preparations for the special session of the General Assembly;

C. Recognizing gaps and obstacles

17. Take note with great concern of the current conditions of human settlements worldwide, especially as documented in the third global report on human settlements. Although Governments and their Habitat Agenda partners have continued efforts to fulfil their commitments, widespread poverty remains the core obstacle, and environmental conditions need significant improvement in many countries. Critically, the majority of people living in poverty still lack legal security of tenure for their dwellings, while others lack even basic shelter. Thus, serious impediments to sustainable human settlements development still persist;

18. Note with concern that one of the basic obstacles to the implementation of the Habitat Agenda is the discrepancy between the commitments made at Istanbul and the political will to fulfil them. We also acknowledge the gaps in both public information and awareness-raising as impediments;

19. Recognize that serious financial constraints give rise to acute problems of adequate shelter, housing and human settlements in countries that receive an influx of refugees as a result of ongoing conflicts, human-made and natural disasters and other calamities taking place in neighbouring countries;

20. Acknowledge the gaps in shelter and urban policies that have limited the opportunities for participation and partnership and have made it difficult to convert best practices into good policies. We are also deeply concerned that many women still do not participate fully, on the basis of equality, in all spheres of society, while at the same time suffering to a greater extent the effects of poverty;

21. Also acknowledge the fact that the urbanization process in the world has resulted in metropolitan concentrations that extend over the administrative boundaries of the original cities, expand over two or more administrative units, have local authorities with

different capacities and priorities and suffer from an absence of coordination;

22. Recognize major obstacles that prevent the efficient functioning of land and housing markets to ensure an adequate supply of shelter. Actions recommended in paragraph 76 of the Habitat Agenda have not been fully implemented;

23. Have identified considerable obstacles associated with limited economic, technological and institutional capacities at all levels of government, in particular in the developing and the least developed countries. We recognize the absence of comprehensive and inclusive policies for capacity-building institutions and their networking;

24. Have also identified economic policies and financial market constraints at all levels that have prevented the mobilization of adequate resources to meet the sustainable human settlements needs of many countries;

25. Recognize that the mobilization of domestic resources as well as sound national policies are crucial for financing shelter and human settlements. Although Governments have the primary responsibility for the implementation of the Habitat Agenda, international support is likewise essential. We regret that international cooperation in shelter and human settlements development has not been enhanced significantly since 1996, which is a growing cause for concern. We also regret that many countries have been unable to make sufficient use of market mechanisms in support of their financial needs for shelter and human settlements development;

26. Recognize that there is unequal access to information and communication technologies, in particular in the developing countries, which has resulted in the inability of Governments and Habitat Agenda partners to make the best use of those resources in implementing the Habitat Agenda;

27. Further resolve to take concerted action against international terrorism, which causes serious obstacles to the implementation of the Habitat Agenda;

28. Recognize that the consequences of those gaps and obstacles are serious: for the first time in human history a majority of the world's 6 billion people will live in cities. Many people have experienced a deterioration in their living environment, not an improvement. The gaps and obstacles encountered in the past five years have slowed down global progress towards sustainable human settlements development. It is essential that actions are taken to ensure that the Habitat Agenda is now translated into policy and practice in every country;

D. Taking further actions

29. Affirm our commitment to overcoming obstacles encountered in the implementation of the Habitat Agenda, especially poverty, which we consider to be the major underlying factor, and to strengthening and safeguarding national and international enabling environments, and to that end pledge to accelerate our efforts to ensure the full and effective implementation of the Habitat Agenda. Determined to give new momentum to our efforts to improve the condition of human settlements, we here set out further initiatives for achieving those ends. At the start of the new millennium, aware of our responsibilities towards future generations, we are strongly committed to adequate shelter for all and sustainable human settlements development in an urbanizing world. We invite people from all countries and all walks of life, as well as the international community, to join in renewed dedication to our shared vision for a more just and equitable world;

30. Reaffirm that the family is the basic unit of society and as such should be strengthened. It is entitled to receive comprehensive protection and support. In different cultural, political and social systems, various forms of the family exist. Marriage must be entered into with the free consent of the intending spouses and husband and wife should be equal partners. The rights, capabilities and responsibilities of family members must be respected. Human settlements planning should take into account the constructive role of the family in the design, development and management of such settlements. Society should facilitate, as appropriate, all necessary conditions for its integration, reunification, preservation, improvement and protection within adequate shelter and with access to basic services and a sustainable livelihood;

31. Resolve, within the framework, inter alia, of a poverty eradication strategy, to encourage social and economic policies that are designed to meet the housing needs of families and their individual members, with particular attention to the care of children;

32. Also resolve to promote changes in attitudes, structures, policies, laws and other practices relating to gender in order to eliminate all obstacles to human dignity and equality in family and society and to promote the full and equal participation of women and men, inter alia, in the formulation and implementation of and follow-up to public policies and programmes;

33. Invite Governments, the United Nations and other international organizations to strengthen the quality and consistency of their support for poverty eradication and sustainable human settlements development, in particular in the least developed countries. This in turn requires not only renewed political will, but also the mobilization and allocation of new and additional resources at both the national and international levels. We urge the strengthening of international assistance to developing countries in their efforts to alleviate poverty, including by creating an enabling environment that would facilitate the integration of developing countries into the world economy, improving their market access, facilitating the flow of financial resources and implementing fully and effectively all initiatives already launched regarding debt relief;

34. Emphasize that the international community should consider further measures, as appropriate, that would lead to durable solutions to the external debt burden of developing countries;

35. Express, in this connection, our appreciation to the developed countries that have agreed to and have reached the target of 0.7 per cent of their gross national product for overall official development assistance, and call upon developed countries that have not yet done so to strengthen their efforts to achieve the agreed target of 0.7 per cent as soon as possible and, where agreed, within that target, to earmark 0.15 to 0.20 per cent of their gross national product for the least developed countries;

36. Request the international community to support strongly poverty eradication, and welcome the ongoing consultations by the Secretary-General on the establishment of a world solidarity fund for poverty eradication to finance and realize, inter alia, the social policies and programmes of the Habitat Agenda to address the challenges of poverty eradication and sustainable development in developing countries, especially the least developed countries, bearing in mind the voluntary nature of the contributions;

37. Resolve to raise awareness about human settlements challenges and solutions through full and open dissemination of information, and commit ourselves to renew and foster political will at all levels;

38. Also resolve to empower the poor and vulnerable, inter alia, by promoting greater security of tenure and enabling better access to information and good practices, including awareness of legal rights. We aim to develop specific policies to overcome growing urban poverty;

39. Further resolve to empower local authorities, non-governmental organizations and other Habitat Agenda partners, within the legal framework and according to the conditions of each country, to play a more effective role in the provision of shelter and in sustainable human settlements development. This can be achieved through effective decentralization, where appropriate, of responsibilities, policy management, decision-making authority and sufficient resources, where possible including revenue-collection authority to local authorities, through participation and local democracy as well as through international cooperation and partnerships. In particular, the effective role of women in decision-making in local authorities should be ensured, if necessary through appropriate mechanisms. In this context, we agree to intensify our dialogue, where possible, including through the Commission on Human Settlements, on all issues related to effective decentralization and the strengthening of local authorities, in support of the implementation of the Habitat Agenda, in conformity with the legal framework and policies of each country;

40. Encourage authorities within metropolitan areas to develop mechanisms and to foster, where appropriate, legal, financial, administrative, planning and coordination instruments, in order to achieve more equitable, ordered and functional cities;

41. Resolve to build capacities and networks to enable all partners to play an effective role in shelter and human settlements development. The management of urbanization processes requires strong and accountable public institutions able to provide an effective framework in which everybody has access to basic services. Capacity-building needs to be directed towards, inter alia, supporting decentralization and participatory urban management processes. We also pledge to strengthen the institutions and legal frameworks that assist and allow broad-based participation in decision-making and in the implementation of human settlements strategies, policies and programmes;

42. Acknowledge, value and support volunteer work and the work of community-based organizations. Voluntary practices offer an important contribution to the development of human settlements, as they help to build strong, cohesive communities as well as to develop a sense of social solidarity, in the process generating significant economic outputs;

43. Are committed to improving prevention, preparedness, mitigation and response capacities, with the contribution of national and international cooperation networks, in order to reduce the vulnerability of human settlements to natural and human-made disasters and to implement effective post-disaster programmes for the affected human settlements, aimed, inter alia, at meeting immediate needs, reducing future disaster risks and making rebuilt human settlements accessible to all;

44. Commit ourselves to the goal of gender equality in human settlements development and resolve to promote gender equality and the empowerment of women as effective ways to combat poverty and to stimulate the development of human settlements that are truly sustainable. We further commit ourselves to formulating and strengthening policies and practices to promote the full and equal participation of women in human settlements planning and decision-making;

45. Also commit ourselves to strengthening existing financial mechanisms and to identifying and developing appropriate innovative approaches for financing shelter and human settlements development at all levels. Furthermore, we resolve to continue to undertake legislative and administrative reforms giving women full and equal access to economic resources, including the right to inheritance and the ownership of land and other property, credit, natural resources and appropriate technologies, and to ensure their right to security of tenure and their right to enter into contractual agreements. We resolve to promote increased and equal access for all people to open, efficient, effective and appropriate housing finance, to support savings mechanisms in the informal sector, where appropriate, and to strengthen regulatory and legal frameworks and financial management capacity at all appropriate levels;

46. Resolve to promote the upgrading of slums and the regularization of squatter settlements, within the legal framework of each country. In particular, we reiterate the aim of the "Cities without Slums" initiative to make a significant improvement in the lives of at least 100 million slum-dwellers by 2020;

47. Affirm that, in the interest of affordable housing for the poor, it is necessary to promote cooperation among countries in order to popularize the use of adequate low-cost and sustainable building materials and appropriate technology for the construction of adequate low-cost housing and services within the reach of the poor, especially in slums and unplanned settlements;

48. Resolve to intensify efforts to include countries with economies in transition in the system of multilateral cooperation in the sustainable development of human settlements by developing the support for those countries to determine an adequate level of decentralization in the governance of urban and rural human settlements. We reiterate our commitment to involve in those efforts the United Nations financial institutions, international and national foundations, the private sector and other partners of the Habitat Agenda;

49. Take note with satisfaction of the ongoing formulation of housing policy by many countries. We resolve to undertake the legislative and administrative

reforms needed to support the efforts of people, individually and collectively, to produce affordable shelter, to adopt proactive planning of land supply, to promote the efficient functioning of land markets and administration, to eradicate legal and social barriers to equal and equitable access to land and to ensure that the equal rights of women and men to land and property are protected under the law. In implementing the above, we acknowledge the need for vigorously promoting affordable shelter and basic services for the homeless, preventing forced evictions that are contrary to the law and facilitating the access of all people, in particular the poor and vulnerable groups, to information on housing legislation, including any legal rights, and to remedies when those laws are violated. In this connection, we note with appreciation and support the initial approach and activities of the Global Campaign for Secure Tenure;

50. See the implementation of the Habitat Agenda as an integral part of the overall fight for the eradication of poverty. The implementation of the Habitat Agenda and the pursuit of sustainable development are intimately linked and interdependent, and human settlements development is a key factor for sustainable development. The World Summit on Sustainable Development, to be held at Johannesburg, South Africa, from 2 to 11 September 2002, provides a good opportunity to pursue further and intensify that relationship;

51. Resolve to intensify efforts to ensure the transparent, responsible, accountable, just, effective and efficient governance of cities and other human settlements. We recognize that good governance, within each country and at the international level, is essential to addressing the challenges of urban poverty and environmental degradation and to harnessing the potential opportunities offered by globalization. Cities need specific approaches and methodologies to improve governance, to plan and act strategically in order to reduce urban poverty and social exclusion and to improve the economic and social status of all citizens and protect the environment in a sustainable way. In this connection, we note the importance of promoting sustainable livelihoods through education and training, in particular for the poor and vulnerable groups;

52. The human immunodeficiency virus/acquired immunodeficiency syndrome (HIV/AIDS) pandemic has developed in a much faster and much more dramatic way than could have been foreseen at Istanbul. We resolve to intensify efforts at the international and national levels against HIV/AIDS and, in particular, to formulate and implement appropriate policies and actions to address the impact of HIV/AIDS on human settlements. We recognize the problem of accessing financial resources for housing by HIV/AIDS victims and the need for shelter solutions for accommodating HIV/AIDS victims, especially the orphans and the terminally ill;

53. Resolve to intensify efforts to enhance the role of youth and civil society and to increase cooperation with parliamentarians in human settlements development;

54. Also resolve to promote more determined action against urban crime and violence, in particular violence against women, children and the elderly, through a coordinated response at all levels, in accordance, as appropriate, with integrated crime prevention action plans. Those plans might include a diagnostic survey of crime phenomena, the identification of all the relevant actors in crime prevention and the fight against crime, the establishment of consultation mechanisms for the design of a coherent strategy and the elaboration of possible solutions to those problems;

55. Further resolve to address seriously the challenges to human settlements posed by wars, conflicts, refugees and human-made disasters, and commit ourselves, through enhanced international cooperation mechanisms, to support post-conflict and post-disaster countries, with special emphasis on the provision of shelter and other basic services, in particular to vulnerable groups, refugees and internally displaced persons, as well as to facilitate restoring security of tenure and property rights;

56. Resolve to take further effective measures to remove obstacles to the full implementation of the Habitat Agenda as well as obstacles to the realization of the rights of peoples living under colonial and foreign occupation, which are incompatible with the dignity and worth of the human person and must be combated and eliminated;

57. Also resolve to expand and to strengthen the protection of civilians in conformity with international humanitarian law, in particular the Geneva Convention relative to the Protection of Civilian Persons in Time of War, of 12 August 1949, including article 49 thereof;

58. Resolve to strengthen international cooperation, including burden-sharing in, and the coordination of humanitarian assistance to, the countries hosting refugees, and to help all refugees and displaced persons to return voluntarily to their homes, in safety and dignity, and to be reintegrated smoothly into their societies;

59. Resolve to promote access to safe drinking water for all and to facilitate the provision of basic infrastructure and urban services, including adequate sanitation, waste management and sustainable transport that is integrated and accessible to all, including people with disabilities. To that end, we need to promote transparent and accountable management of public services, as well as partnerships with the private sector and non-profit organizations, for the delivery of those services;

60. Commit ourselves to intensifying efforts to improve sustainable environmental planning and management practices and to promote sustainable production and consumption patterns in human settlements in all countries, in particular in industrialized countries. Integrated approaches addressing social, economic and environmental issues should be taken more systematically at all levels. Agenda 21 and the local Agenda 21 initiatives provide important inputs to the process;

61. Reiterate the need to integrate the local Agenda 21 process, as mentioned above, in the global plan of action for the implementation of the Habitat Agenda. The aims, policies and strategies of both agendas should be harmonized in order to promote sustainable urban planning and management;

62. Also reiterate that Governments, local authorities and other Habitat Agenda partners should regularly monitor and evaluate their own performances and that, in the implementation of the Habitat Agenda, Governments at all levels should identify and

disseminate best practices and apply shelter and human settlements development indicators. To this end, we need to strengthen the capacity among all Habitat Agenda partners to handle and analyse information as well as to communicate with each other;

63. A further goal is to translate best practices into policies and to permit their replication. In this respect, the international community should ensure the effective formatting and dissemination of proven best practices and policies;

64. Recognizing that those living in poverty are in fact rich in innovative faculties and that microcredit plays an important role in eradicating poverty and improving human settlements, and, following success stories of some countries in this field, we encourage Governments, within their legal framework, and both national and international financial institutions, to strengthen the institutional frameworks by which it would be possible to extend microcredit, without collateral or security, to those living in poverty, in particular women;

65. Reiterate that international cooperation takes on added significance and importance in the light of recent trends towards the increased globalization and interdependence of the world economy. There is a need for the political will of all States and for specific action at the international level, including among cities, to inspire, to encourage and to strengthen existing and innovative forms of cooperation and partnership, coordination at all levels and increased investment from all sources, including the private sector, in order to contribute effectively to the improvement of shelter conditions, especially in developing countries. In this regard, we also resolve to pay particular attention to cities and other human settlements in critical natural environments, such as arid and semi-arid areas, for the purpose of providing assistance to and support for their development;

66. Reconfirm the role of the Commission on Human Settlements and the United Nations Centre for Human Settlements (Habitat) in advocating, promoting, monitoring and assessing the progress made in implementing the goals of adequate shelter for all by providing legal security of tenure and sustainable human settlements development in all countries and in combining best practices, enabling policies, and compiling legislation and action plans for identifying illustrative cities for the two global campaigns and advancing further the normative debate and operational action on major human settlements issues, inter alia, by timely and regular publication of global flagship reports. We also support the establishment of the Habitat Agenda Task Manager System, designed to allow better monitoring and mutual reinforcement of actions taken by international agencies in support of the implementation of the Habitat Agenda;

67. Reaffirm our commitment to international cooperation as an essential element in the implementation of the Istanbul Declaration and the Habitat Agenda. In this regard, we invite the Secretary-General to report to the General Assembly at its fifty-sixth session on options for reviewing and strengthening the mandate and status of the Commission on Human Settlements and the status, role and function of the United Nations Centre for Human Settlements (Habitat), in accordance with the relevant decisions of the General Assembly, the Economic and Social Council and the United Nations Conference on Human Settlements (Habitat II);

68. Agree to review regularly the further implementation of the Habitat Agenda, with a view to assessing progress and considering new initiatives.

Preparatory process

The Commission on Human Settlements, acting as the Preparatory Committee for the twenty-fifth special session of the General Assembly, held its second session in Nairobi from 19 to 23 February [A/S-25/2]. The first preparatory session was held in 2000 [YUN 2000, p. 989]. The Committee decided to transmit the draft declaration on cities and other human settlements in the new millennium to the Assembly's special session [A/S-25/2 (dec. 2/1)]. Taking into account Assembly resolution 55/195 on preparations for the special session [YUN 2000, p. 993], the Committee decided to bring Economic and Social Council agreed conclusions 2000/1 [ibid., p. 991] on the coordinated implementation by the UN system of the Habitat Agenda to the Assembly's attention for further consideration. The Committee decided to establish the Thematic Committee, a new structure intended to recount the development of human settlements since Habitat II and to guide the search for solutions through presentations by Member States and accredited Habitat Agenda partners. The Preparatory Committee established criteria for the selection of presentations to ensure equitable geographical representation and thematic coverage. The five thematic meetings of the Committee would focus on the two main Habitat Agenda themes of adequate shelter for all and sustainable human settlements development in an urbanizing world. Sub-themes and cross-cutting elements would also be addressed. In other action, the Preparatory Committee decided to accredit the local authorities, NGOs and other Habitat Agenda partners [dec. 2/2], as listed in an annex to a February note by the Chair of the Committee [HS/CPC.2/4/Add.2], and that accreditation of Agenda partners would be open to members of the Advisory Committee of Local Authorities [dec. 2/3], established in 1999 [YUN 1999, p. 1000].

The Committee had before it a January note by the secretariat [HS/C.PC.2/BD/2], which stated that, in accordance with Assembly resolution 55/195, the report *Cities in a Globalizing World: Global Report on Human Settlements* would be issued every two years. *The State of the World's Cities Report*, a shorter and popular version of the *Global Report*, would also be issued biennially. (See p. 981.)

On 21 March [meeting 97], the General Assembly, on the recommendation of the Commission on Human Settlements acting as the Preparatory Committee for the Assembly's special session [draft: A/55/L.78], adopted **resolution 55/246** without vote [agenda item 94 (e)].

Organizational arrangements for the Thematic Committee for the special session of the General Assembly for an overall review and appraisal of the implementation of the outcome of the United Nations Conference on Human Settlements (Habitat II)

The General Assembly,

Recalling its resolution 55/195 of 20 December 2000, in which it decided that the special session of the General Assembly for an overall review and appraisal of the implementation of the outcome of the United Nations Conference on Human Settlements (Habitat II) should have a plenary, an ad hoc committee of the whole and a thematic committee, the details of which were to be worked out at the second session of the Preparatory Committee for the special session,

Decides to adopt the organizational arrangements for the Thematic Committee contained in the annex to the present resolution.

ANNEX
Organizational arrangements for the Thematic Committee

1. The Thematic Committee shall hold five meetings, as follows:

Wednesday, 6 June 2001, from 11 a.m. to 1 p.m. and from 3 p.m. to 7 p.m.

Thursday, 7 June 2001, from 9 a.m. to 1 p.m. and from 3 p.m. to 7 p.m.

Friday, 8 June 2001, from 9 a.m. to 1 p.m.

2. The five meetings shall focus on the two main themes of the Habitat Agenda: "adequate shelter for all" and "sustainable human settlements development in an urbanizing world".

3. The Bureau of the Thematic Committee shall consist of one Chairperson, three Vice-Chairpersons and one Rapporteur. The Chair of the Thematic Committee shall be assisted by facilitators who are representatives of Member States.

4. The Thematic Committee shall be open to Member States, observer States and observers, entities of the United Nations system, including programmes, funds, specialized agencies and regional commissions with expertise in the subject matter of the special session, and accredited Habitat Agenda partners.

5. To facilitate the presentations, the United Nations Centre for Human Settlements (Habitat), in consultation with Governments and accredited Habitat Agenda partners, shall be entrusted with the selection of thematic experiences. Submissions may come from the full range of Governments of Member States and accredited Habitat Agenda partners. Presentations may be made only by members of governmental delegations or accredited Habitat Agenda partners.

6. The Chairman of the Thematic Committee shall present a summary of the deliberations at the concluding plenary meeting of the special session.

Follow-up to the special session

An October report of the Secretary-General [A/56/477], submitted pursuant to General Assembly resolution 55/195 [YUN 2000, p. 993], presented an overview of the work of the session.

Referring to the Declaration on Cities and Other Human Settlements in the New Millennium, the Secretary-General said that the UNCHS 2002-2003 work programme addressed the main topics contained therein. In accordance with the Declaration, UNCHS would advocate, promote, monitor and assess progress made by combining best practices and enabling policies, and compiling legislation and plans of action to identify illustrative cities for the Global Campaign for Urban Governance and the Global Campaign for Secure Tenure (see p. 985) and further advancing the debate and operational action on major human settlements issues. Governments endorsed the establishment of the Habitat Agenda task manager system, designed to allow better monitoring and mutual reinforcement of action taken by international agencies in support of the implementation of the Habitat Agenda (see p. 989). In the plenary, most participants underlined the need for decentralization, more balanced regional development, promotion of participatory approaches and utilization of potential public and/or private partnerships. The Ad Hoc Committee of the Whole considered progress made in implementing the Habitat Agenda and the draft declaration, which it recommended for adoption by the Assembly (see p. 974). In the Thematic Committee, 16 case studies were presented from four cluster areas: shelter and services; environmental management; urban governance; and eradication of poverty. Cross-cutting themes were also addressed, such as participation, partnership and cooperation, gender, equality, social inclusion, the scaling up of local practice and exchange of knowledge. The studies indicated that progress was being made in many countries towards the Agenda goal of adequate shelter for all, through neighbourhood improvement and new construction, and demonstrated that countries were seeking to improve the governance of their cities. Overall, the review and appraisal process showed that Member States had taken steps towards incorporating the human settlements issues contained in the Istanbul Declaration [YUN 1996, p. 993] and the Habitat Agenda [ibid., p. 994] into national policies. Civil society, parliamentarians, local authorities, women and youth groups, the private sector and other actors had also played an important role in the implementation of the established goals and in the preparatory process.

Two major reports prepared by UNCHS, *The State of the World's Cities Report 2001* [HS/619/01E] and *Cities in a Globalizing World: Global Report on Human Settlements* [Sales No. E.01.III.Q.1], were launched during the special session. *The State of the World's Cities Report* presented a region-by-region description of urbanization trends and issues. Studies presented in *Cities in a Globalizing World* indicated that, while some population groups had improved their housing conditions, a disproportionate share of the world's population had seen its housing situation deteriorate further. One billion urban inhabitants lived in inadequate housing, mostly in the slums and squatter settlements in developing countries.

GENERAL ASSEMBLY ACTION

On 21 December [meeting 90], the General Assembly, on the recommendation of the Second Committee [A/56/565], adopted **resolution 56/205** without vote [agenda item 102].

Special session of the General Assembly for an overall review and appraisal of the implementation of the outcome of the United Nations Conference on Human Settlements (Habitat II)

The General Assembly,

Recalling the Habitat Agenda and the Istanbul Declaration on Human Settlements adopted in Istanbul in 1996,

Recalling also the report of the Ad Hoc Committee of the Whole of the twenty-fifth special session of the General Assembly, on an overall review and appraisal of the implementation of the outcome of the United Nations Conference on Human Settlements (Habitat II), held in New York from 6 to 8 June 2001,

Stressing the importance of the Declaration on Cities and Other Human Settlements in the New Millennium, which was adopted by the General Assembly at its twenty-fifth special session,

Recognizing the need for renewed political will and for the mobilization and allocation of new and additional resources at the national and international levels in order to achieve full and accelerated implementation of the Habitat Agenda and the Declaration on Cities and Other Human Settlements in the New Millennium,

Reiterating that strengthened international cooperation is an essential element for the effective implementation of the Habitat Agenda and the Declaration on Cities and Other Human Settlements in the New Millennium,

Recalling the goal contained in the United Nations Millennium Declaration of achieving a significant improvement in the lives of at least 100 million slum-dwellers by the year 2020, as proposed in the "Cities without Slums" initiative,

1. *Takes note* of the report of the Secretary-General;

2. *Reaffirms* the importance of the full implementation of all the commitments undertaken in the Habitat Agenda;

3. *Emphasizes* the importance, at all levels of policy-making and in the context of sustainable development,

of giving high priority to the implementation of the Habitat Agenda and the Declaration on Cities and Other Human Settlements in the New Millennium, including achieving the goals of adequate shelter for all and sustainable human settlements development in an urbanizing world, particularly in developing countries;

4. *Recognizes* that the overall thrust of the new strategic vision of the United Nations Human Settlements Programme (UN-Habitat) and its emphasis on the two global campaigns on secure tenure and urban governance are strategic points of entry for the effective implementation of the Habitat Agenda, especially for guiding international cooperation in respect of adequate shelter for all and sustainable human settlements development;

5. *Recognizes also* that Governments have the primary responsibility for the implementation of the Habitat Agenda and the Declaration on Cities and Other Human Settlements in the New Millennium, and stresses that the international community should fully implement its commitments to support Governments of developing countries and countries with economies in transition in their efforts, by providing the requisite means of implementation and through the creation of an international enabling environment;

6. *Requests* the relevant bodies of the United Nations system, including the specialized agencies, programmes, funds and regional commissions, as well as the World Bank and regional development banks, consistent with their respective mandates, to support fully the effective implementation at all levels of the Habitat Agenda and the Declaration on Cities and Other Human Settlements in the New Millennium;

7. *Invites* local authorities and other Habitat Agenda partners to contribute to the implementation of the Habitat Agenda and the Declaration on Cities and Other Human Settlements in the New Millennium, and encourages them to participate, as appropriate, in the Urban Forum and the Advisory Committee of Local Authorities, in their roles as advisory bodies to the Executive Director of the United Nations Human Settlements Programme (UN-Habitat), bearing in mind the decisions of the Commission on Human Settlements on the establishment of those two bodies;

8. *Urges* the Executive Director of the Programme to assess the role and funding of the regional programme activity centres of the Programme with a view to providing improved technical cooperation services to Governments to implement the Habitat Agenda and the Declaration on Cities and Other Human Settlements in the New Millennium at all levels;

9. *Invites* Governments and the Habitat Agenda partners, including local authorities, to facilitate the dissemination of the Declaration on Cities and Other Human Settlements in the New Millennium;

10. *Invites* the Executive Director of the Programme to transmit the outcomes of the relevant intergovernmental processes relating to sustainable human settlements development to the preparatory processes of the International Conference on Financing for Development and the World Summit on Sustainable Development, bearing in mind the relevant decisions of the preparatory processes of those two conferences;

11. *Decides* to include in the provisional agenda of its fifty-seventh session an item entitled "Implementation of the outcome of the United Nations Conference on

Human Settlements (Habitat II) and of the twenty-fifth special session of the General Assembly", and requests the Secretary-General to submit to the Assembly at its fifty-seventh session a report on the implementation of the present resolution.

By **decision 56/464** of 24 December, the Assembly decided that the agenda item on the implementation of the Habitat Agenda and the outcome of its twenty-fifth special session would remain for consideration during its resumed fifty-sixth (2002) session.

Coordination mechanisms to implement Habitat Agenda

A report of the UNCHS Executive Director [HS/C/18/11] covered coordination and cooperation, since the Commission's 1999 session [YUN 1999, p. 1001], between UNCHS, the UN system, intergovernmental organizations and NGOs to implement the Habitat Agenda [YUN 1996, p. 994].

In May [E/2001/62], the Secretary-General reviewed the implementation of Economic and Social Council agreed conclusions 2000/1 [YUN 2000, p. 991] on the coordinated implementation of the Habitat Agenda. He stated that the Commission on Human Settlements, in February [A/56/8 (res. 18/5)], had called on UN organizations and agencies to use, where possible, the existing coordinating mechanisms of the United Nations Development Group and the United Nations Development Assistance Framework to demonstrate their capacity and complementary action and to make such efforts visible at all levels. The Commission requested the UNCHS Executive Director to establish an Urban Forum, with a view to strengthening the coordination of international support to the implementation of the Habitat Agenda. She had taken steps to do so by merging, as at 2002, the existing Urban Environment Forum and the International Forum on Urban Poverty into the World Urban Forum, which she intended to convene biennially, alternating with Commission sessions. The substantive focus of the World Urban Forum would be international cooperation in shelter and urban development. It would serve as an advisory body to the Executive Director and UNCHS and be open to representatives from national Governments and Habitat Agenda partners. With regard to the Council's request to the Secretary-General to review the matter of UNCHS participation in all aspects of the work of ACC, the Centre was invited to participate in the ACC High-level Committee on Programmes and the High-level Committee on Management. The Commission on Human Settlements, acting as Preparatory Committee for the General Assembly's twenty-fifth special ses-

sion, transmitted to the Assembly for further consideration the text of the draft declaration on cities and other human settlements in the new millennium, which supported the establishment of the Habitat Agenda task manager system to facilitate coordinated implementation of the Habitat Agenda by the UN system (see also p. 984), and to streamline reporting to the Commission and the Council. Accordingly, UNCHS was taking steps through the ACC High-level Committee on Programmes to launch the system.

ACC action. In October [ACC/2001/11], ACC decided that UNCHS should be encouraged to pursue the launch of the Habitat Agenda task manager system.

ECONOMIC AND SOCIAL COUNCIL ACTION

On 26 July [meeting 43], the Economic and Social Council adopted **resolution 2001/22** [draft: E/2001/L.41 & E/2001/SR.43] without vote [agenda item 6].

Integrated and coordinated implementation of and follow-up to major United Nations conferences and summits: coordinated implementation of the Habitat Agenda

The Economic and Social Council,

Taking note with appreciation of the report of the Secretary-General on the implementation of agreed conclusions 2000/1 of the Economic and Social Council on the coordinated implementation of the Habitat Agenda,

Welcoming the actions taken by the Secretary-General in response to agreed conclusions 2000/1 of the Council, including the appointment of a full-time Executive Director of the United Nations Centre for Human Settlements (Habitat),

Recalling General Assembly resolution 35/77 C of 5 December 1980,

1. *Reiterates* once again the need for the United Nations Centre for Human Settlements (Habitat), as the United Nations focal point for the implementation of the Habitat Agenda, to participate in all aspects of the Administrative Committee on Coordination and its subsidiary machinery;

2. *Looks forward* to the report of the Secretary-General to the General Assembly at its fifty-sixth session on options for reviewing and strengthening the mandate and status of the Commission on Human Settlements and the status, role and function of the Centre, in accordance with the relevant resolutions of the General Assembly and the Economic and Social Council and decisions of the United Nations Conference on Human Settlements (Habitat II);

3. *Invites* the Secretary-General to implement, within the framework of the Administrative Committee on Coordination and in accordance with paragraph 66 of the Declaration on Cities and Other Human Settlements in the New Millennium adopted by the General Assembly at its twenty-fifth special session, the establishment of the Habitat Agenda task manager system in order to allow better monitoring and mutual reinforcement of actions taken by international agen-

cies in support of the implementation of the Habitat Agenda;

4. *Also invites* the Secretary-General to submit a report to the Council at its substantive session of 2002 on the implementation of the present resolution.

Commission on Human Settlements

The Commission on Human Settlements, at its eighteenth session (Nairobi, 12-16 February) [A/56/8], adopted 12 resolutions, of which one, on the establishment of the Committee of Permanent Representatives as a subsidiary body of the Commission [res. 18/1], recommended a resolution for adoption by the Economic and Social Council (see p. 984). A resolution on countries with economies in transition [res. 18/7] requested the UNCHS Executive Director to use pilot projects to launch cooperative programmes to promote the implementation of the Habitat Agenda [YUN 1996, p. 994], to initiate meetings and workshops to exchange experience in housing sector reform, and to report in 2003. The Commission asked UNCHS to continue to work with youth organizations in implementing the Habitat Agenda [res. 18/8]. A further resolution on the Habitat Agenda reviewed implementation mechanisms [res. 18/5] (see p. 984). Having considered a report of the Executive Director [HS/C/18/13], the Commission decided that the special themes of its nineteenth (2003) session would be urban development and shelter strategies for the poor, and the rural dimension of sustainable urban development [res. 18/2]. By a vote of 22 to 1, with 21 abstentions [res. 18/12], the Commission called on Israel to enable residents in the occupied Palestinian territories to ensure their housing needs, and asked the Executive Director to organize a meeting on the establishment of a human settlements fund for Palestinians and to report in 2003 (see p. 984). Following consideration of the Executive Director's reports on the global campaigns for secure tenure [HS/C/18/6] and urban governance [HS/C/18/7], the Commission took note of the need for technical and legal expertise to carry out the Campaign for Secure Tenure and, with regard to urban governance, of the initiative to illustrate and promote Inclusive Cities—formerly designated Illustrative Cities—as a means of advocacy and capacity-building [res. 18/3]; the Executive Director was asked to establish legal advisory capacity within UNCHS, to ensure continued expansion of the global campaigns and to report in 2003. The Commission called on the Executive Director to continue to involve local authorities in the Centre's work programme, to expand best practices, good policies and enabling legislation and action plans [res. 18/10] and to report in 2003. It also called on her to intensify dialogue among Governments on issues related to effective decentralization and the strengthening of local authorities [res. 18/11] and to report in 2003. Resolutions were adopted on cooperation between UNCHS and UNEP [res. 18/4] (see p. 986) and the revitalization of UNCHS [res. 18/9] (see p. 986).

On 16 February [res. 18/6], the Commission approved the 2002-2003 draft work programme [HS/C/18/8] and approved a budget of $24.9 million for 2002-2003, as presented by the Executive Director [HS/C/18/9], and following a review by ACABQ of the 2002-2003 budget [HS/C/18/9/Add.1]. It endorsed, in principle, the work programme and organizational and budget refinements as presented by the Executive Director [HS/C/18/8/Add.1, HS/C/18/9/Add.3] and by the Bureau of the Commission [HS/C/18/2/Add.4], and authorized the Executive Director, subject to the availability of additional resources, to make commitments up to $31.7 million.

The Commission considered reports of the Executive Director on follow-up to Commission resolutions and decisions [HS/C/18/2] adopted in 1999 [YUN 1999, p. 1001], international cooperation and the mechanisms to monitor the implementation of the Habitat Agenda [HS/C/18/4], lessons learned from best practices and partnerships to achieve adequate shelter for all and sustainable human settlements [HS/C/18/5], and the role of local authorities [HS/C/18/3 & Add.1].

On 26 July, the Economic and Social Council deferred consideration of the Commission's report to its resumed 2001 session (**decision 2001/311**) (see p. 984).

By resolution 56/206 (see p. 987), the General Assembly transformed the Commission into the Governing Council of UN-Habitat (formerly UNCHS), with effect from 1 January 2002.

Committee of Permanent Representatives

In a report on the role of the UNCHS Committee of Permanent Representatives [HS/C/18/2/Add.2 & Corr.1,2], submitted in response to a 1999 Commission request [YUN 1999, p. 1001], the Executive Director stated that there was no formal relationship between the Committee and the Commission. The Commission would have to decide whether it wished to enter into such a relationship and, if it did, submit a decision for the consideration and approval of the Economic and Social Council. When approval was given, the Committee would come into existence as an intersessional subsidiary organ of the Commission. The report presented the financial implication estimates for institutionalizing the Committee.

On 16 February [res. 18/1], the Commission recommended to the Economic and Social Council the establishment of the UNCHS Committee of Permanent Representatives as an intersessional subsidiary body of the Commission on Human Settlements and decided that, upon approval by the Council, the Committee would constitute an intersessional governing body of UNCHS, with the Centre functioning as the secretariat of the Committee. The Committee's terms of reference would be to review and monitor the implementation of the Centre's work programme and Commission decisions; review the Centre's draft work programme and budget; prepare draft decisions and resolutions for consideration by the Commission; and meet at least four times a year, with the participation of the UNCHS Executive Director. The Committee would consist of all Member States and members of the specialized agencies accredited to the Centre, and would elect a bureau composed of a chair, three vice-chairs and a rapporteur for a period of two years, taking into account the principles of rotation and equitable geographical representation. The Commission resolved to review the question of the use of languages in the Committee in 2003, based on the outcome of deliberations in the Council. The Chair of the Committee was requested to report to the Commission on the Committee's work. The Commission requested the Executive Director to take action regarding the Committee's establishment as a subsidiary body within the existing framework of expenditures for the informal operation of the Committee without prejudice to any new resources that might be made available, and to report in 2003.

ECONOMIC AND SOCIAL COUNCIL ACTION

On 24 October [meeting 45], the Economic and Social Council, on the recommendation of the Commission on Human Settlements [A/56/8], adopted **resolution 2001/48** without vote [agenda item 13 *(d)*].

Establishment of the Committee of Permanent Representatives as an intersessional subsidiary body of the Commission on Human Settlements

The Economic and Social Council,

Recalling its rules of procedure, especially rules 24 and 27,

Having considered the recommendation of the Commission on Human Settlements concerning the establishment of the Committee of Permanent Representatives as an intersessional subsidiary body of the Commission as contained in Commission resolution 18/1 of 16 February 2001,

Recognizing the need for a properly mandated subsidiary body that can act during the intersessional period in terms of review and monitoring of the implementation of the resolutions and decisions adopted by the Commission,

1. *Approves* the establishment of the Committee of Permanent Representatives as an intersessional subsidiary body of the Commission on Human Settlements and endorses the terms of reference given to it by the Commission;

2. *Decides* that the Committee may set up working groups without prior decision of the Economic and Social Council or the Commission;

3. *Asks* the Commission to amend its rules of procedure in order to take into account the establishment of the Committee as an intersessional subsidiary body of the Commission;

4. *Requests* the Commission on Human Settlements and the Secretary-General to report to the Council on the implementation of the present resolution.

Occupied Palestinian territories

In response to a 1999 Commission resolution [YUN 1999, p. 1001], the Executive Director submitted a January report [HS/C/18/2/Add.1] on the housing situation in the occupied Palestinian territories. UNCHS had launched an appeal to Member States to raise funds to produce a report on the situation, but contributions fell short of the estimated $30,000 required. A consultant was commissioned in 2000 and work began pending anticipated additional funds. Due to the eruption of violence in the region, however, the report could not be completed. On 16 February, by a vote of 22 to 1, with 21 abstentions, the Commission adopted a resolution on illegal human settlements in the occupied Palestinian territories [res. 18/12], taking note of the Executive Director's explanation on the status of the report. The international donor community and all financial institutions were called on to increase financial assistance to alleviate the housing problems faced by the Palestinian people. The Executive Director was requested to organize a meeting on the establishment of a human settlements fund for the same purpose, and to conclude and update a comprehensive report for the Commission in 2003.

Implementation

A report of the Executive Director on international cooperation and the review of mechanisms for monitoring implementation of the Habitat Agenda [HS/C/18/4] stated that further attention was required to strengthen partnerships between the UN system and its civil society partners in mobilizing resources; promote the exchange of technology and access to information; raise the priority of adequate shelter and sustainable urban development; and strengthen strategic and operational partnerships with local authorities, organizations and the private sector. Increased attention was also called for to improve the coordination of international aid programmes to ensure a global impact on urban poverty reduction. The report provided an outline for the proposed Habitat Agenda task manager system (see also p. 982), and suggested the merging of the Urban Environment Forum (a coalition of cities, support programmes and businesses) and the International Forum on Urban Poverty (a partnership of local authorities, academic institutions and agencies). The task manager system would address the gap in the information and reporting framework through an information-sharing system, and would establish information and communication protocols and modalities to strengthen cooperation and collaboration. Its substantive focus would be the twin goals of the Habitat Agenda: adequate shelter for all and sustainable urban development. On 16 February [res. 18/5], the Commission called on UN organizations and agencies to use the United Nations Development Group and the United Nations Development Assistance Framework coordinating mechanisms in the implementation of the Agenda, and called on Governments and international financial institutions to increase their support of the Cities Alliance. The Executive Director was requested to take appropriate steps to implement Economic and Social Council agreed conclusions 2000/1 [YUN 2000, p. 991], to promote the merger of the Urban Environment Forum and the International Forum on Urban Poverty, and to report to the Commission in 2003.

UN Centre for Human Settlements

The year 2001 was marked by renewed focus on the Global Campaign for Secure Tenure, an advocacy instrument launched in 2000 [YUN 2000, p. 995] to improve the human rights and living conditions of the urban poor. Special focus was given to the follow-up to local and regional campaigns in Europe, India, the Kosovo province of FRY, Latin America and South Africa, with a view to ensuring proper implementation, as well as drawing lessons for better preparation for future campaigns. Governments and NGOs in Brazil, Burkina Faso, Jamaica and Senegal had initiated situation analyses and consultation processes in preparation for the Global Campaign.

During 2001, UNCHS, together with the Office of the United Nations High Commissioner for Human Rights (OHCHR), developed the United Nations Housing Rights Programme (see p. 672).

As part of the Global Campaign for Urban Governance, which supported sustainable human settlements development in urban areas by eradicating poverty through improved urban governance, the "Inclusive Cities" initiative replaced the "Illustrative Cities" approach launched in 2000 [YUN 2000, p. 996]. An "Inclusive City" promoted growth with equity, and enabled and empowered all groups to participate fully in the social, economic and political opportunities offered by cities. National campaigns were under way or were planned in the Balkan region, Brazil, Burkina Faso, Cuba, India, Jamaica, Nicaragua, Nigeria, Peru, the Philippines and the United Republic of Tanzania. UNDP, UNCHS, OHCHR, the UN Department of Economic and Social Affairs and the United Nations Children's Fund (New York, June) agreed to integrate into their work equity, effectiveness, accountability, participation and security as five core principles of good urban governance.

Phase 3 (1996-2001) of the Urban Management Programme, a technical assistance programme initiative of UNDP, UNCHS, the World Bank and other bilateral partners, saw activities in 120 cities in 57 developing countries in Africa, the Arab States, Asia and Latin America and the Caribbean. In all regions, working papers and good practice guides were developed and disseminated.

The joint UNCHS/UNEP Sustainable Cities Programme, together with the Centre's Localizing Agenda 21 capacity-building programme, had more than 40 local projects either ongoing or completed in Chile, China, Egypt, Ghana, India, Malawi, Nigeria, the Philippines, Poland, the Republic of Korea, the Russian Federation, Senegal, Sri Lanka, Tunisia, the United Republic of Tanzania and Zambia.

In 2001, the Safer Cities Programme supported the development and implementation of local crime prevention strategies in Durban and Johannesburg (South Africa), Dar-es-Salaam (United Republic of Tanzania), Antananarivo (Madagascar), Abidjan (Côte d'Ivoire), Nairobi and Yaoundé (Cameroon). It was expanding its activities in Asia and Latin America, and in Hungary.

Through its Disaster Management Programme, the Centre was active in Afghanistan, China, East Timor, FRY (including Kosovo), Guatemala, Iraq, Mozambique and Somalia. Legal frameworks in post-conflict/disaster situations were developed, along with specific tools addressing participatory planning for emergencies, disaster vulnerability, flood assessment, programme development for emergencies, and disaster evaluation and response.

The Regional Office for Africa and the Arab States was active in 35 countries with 67 projects/programmes to assist areas suffering from disasters and ongoing conflicts and political unrest, environmental degradation, low productivity and high levels of economic and social exclusion in cities. In the Asia and Pacific region, the Centre's projects involved governance, urban management, institutional strengthening, capacity-building, and social and economic development. A safer city initiative was launched in Port Moresby, Papua New Guinea. At the end of the year, the Centre started a strategic planning exercise in Afghanistan to enable a quick and effective response to the anticipated need for social, institutional and physical rehabilitation when hostilities ceased (see p. 255). The Centre's Office in Japan organized activities linked to Habitat Agenda issues and hosted, jointly with Fukuoka City and the Fukuoka Prefecture, the World Habitat Day 2001 Global Observance. The Centre's operational activities in Latin America and the Caribbean experienced a decrease in terms of accrued revenue. However, efforts were made to build a new pipeline in countries where major national cost-sharing appeared feasible. Technical cooperation activities were carried out in Brazil, Colombia, Ecuador, Nicaragua, Panama and Paraguay. In Central and Eastern Europe, activities were under way in Kosovo, Poland and the Russian Federation and across the region. Projects in Kosovo, based on collaboration with the United Nations Interim Administration Mission in Kosovo (UNMIK), focused on rehabilitating the municipal administration, developing new spatial planning legislation, regularizing housing and property rights, and restoring property and land registries. The Habitat Kosovo Programme included training of local government-elected officials in collaboration with the Organization for Security and Cooperation in Europe and the European Union. The Centre continued to support UNMIK in further developing and implementing the Housing and Property Directorate and the Housing and Property Claims Commission (see p. 348).

Cooperation with UNEP

A joint progress report of the UNEP and UNCHS Executive Directors [HS/C/18/10] highlighted cooperation between the two entities in subject areas established by the joint bureaux. Within the area of assessing environmental conditions in human settlements, the joint UNCHS/UNEP Sustainable Cities Programme supported the development of environmental profiles in cities preparing to become participants in the Programme. Regarding environmental aspects of policies, planning and management of human settlements, UNEP and UNCHS had strengthened their collaborative activities in disaster manage-

ment, focusing on environmental and human settlement interactions, and were developing a flood vulnerability assessment tool and index to assist decision-making on settlements and environmental management and vulnerability reduction. Cooperation in the UNCHS/UNEP Sustainable Cities Programme promoted system-wide collaboration in urban environmental management at all levels; through the Joint UNEP/UNCHS Task Force on the Balkans, UNEP recommended action in areas of environmental concern and UNCHS assessed housing rights, property registration and local government sectors in Kosovo; and cooperation in the Managing Water for African Cities Programme addressed the growing urban water crisis and protection of Africa's threatened water resources and aquatic ecosystems from the increasing volume of land-based pollution from cities. Under the subject area of environmentally sound and appropriate human settlements technology, UNEP's International Environmental Technology Centre continued to cooperate with the Sustainable Cities Programme by supporting capacity-building activities. UNEP and UNCHS cooperated on research, training and the dissemination of information on environmentally sound human settlements planning and management through the Sustainable Cities Programme, particularly the development of products to address the city demonstration process, thematic support, and training requirements for strengthening city officials and stakeholders in their respective roles.

On 16 February [res. 18/4], the Commission requested the UNCHS Executive Director to continue to implement General Assembly resolution 53/242 [YUN 1999, p. 975]. It urged the Secretary-General to provide the necessary resources from the UN regular budget to the Centre for the 2002-2003 biennium. The Executive Director was requested to strengthen the Centre's core activities; to expand joint work in the Managing Water for African Cities Programme and to establish a mechanism for coordinated decision-making and oversight; to continue collaboration in the joint assessment of human settlements vulnerability to natural and human-made disasters, and in the joint formulation and implementation of vulnerability reduction strategies; and to report in 2003.

Revitalization

A February note by the secretariat [HS/C/18/2/Add.4] contained a progress report of the Bureau of the Commission on Human Settlements on the revitalization of UNCHS, as requested in a 1999 Commission resolution [YUN 1999, p. 1004], and a report of the Executive Director, intended to assist the Bureau in preparing its report. The Bureau stated that revitalization had not been completed, and cited the scarcity of resources, particularly non-earmarked resources, as an impediment to successful reform. Despite the absence of growth in contributions, which had restrained the implementation of the strategic vision adopted in 1999 [ibid., p. 1003], the concepts of the strategic vision had been fully developed, and there were positive signs that the Centre would be able to fully implement its Global Campaigns for Urban Governance and for Secure Tenure [YUN 2000, p. 995]. The Bureau welcomed the Executive Director's intention to strengthen the implementation tools for the strategic vision, such as steps taken to enter into strategic partnerships, and called for continued development of strategic planning. Despite substantial progress in 1999 and 2000, finance and administration required continued reform efforts. Administrative reform of UNCHS depended partly on the commitment of the United Nations Office at Nairobi (UNON). The Bureau was of the view that the relationship of UNCHS with UNON needed to be reviewed. The lack of clarity with regard to the delegation of authority from UN Headquarters to UNCHS imposed a restriction on the use of funds, and the Bureau suggested that the Executive Director take up the matter with the relevant authorities.

On 16 February [res. 18/9], the Commission on Human Settlements, welcoming the progress reports of the Commission's Bureau and the Executive Director on revitalization, endorsed measures taken by the Executive Director to rectify the identified weaknesses of the Centre. It called on Governments to continue their support for the Centre's revitalization. The Commission decided to review progress in 2003 and requested the Executive Director to submit a report.

Report of Secretary-General. Pursuant to General Assembly resolution S-25/2 (see p. 974), the Secretary General submitted a November report [A/56/618] on options for reviewing and strengthening the mandate and status of the Commission and the status, role and function of UNCHS (Habitat). The report presented measures to enhance the Commission's policy-making role and suggested that the Assembly might wish to consider either conferring on the Commission the status of a full-fledged functional commission of the Economic and Social Council or having the Commission function as an organ of the General Assembly, reporting to the Council.

The report suggested that UNCHS could be enhanced by upgrading its capacity to offer technical assistance in the implementation of the Habitat Agenda [YUN 1996, p. 994], and by strengthening its normative and operational activities in the areas of training and capacity-building, knowledge-building and research, urban economic analysis and housing finance. It could also identify and increase synergies in policy and operational activities related to shelter and human settlements. The proposed Habitat Agenda task manager system (see p. 982) would function as a working group on the implementation of the Habitat Agenda. Additional efforts could be made to forge partnership initiatives with UN system organizations. The report suggested that the Centre could promote the recognition of cities and local authorities as UN partners and enhance dialogue among Governments and Habitat Agenda partners on decentralization and the strengthening of local authorities. Other measures included support to NGOs in advocacy work; strengthening partnerships with civil society organizations; and identifying new strategies to involve the private sector. Efforts should be made to enhance the Centre's role in providing advisory services and implementing human settlements programmes at the request of Member States; diversify sources of financing for technical cooperation projects and programmes; and identify new avenues for inter-agency collaboration. An option was proposed to revitalize the United Nations Habitat and Human Settlements Foundation, a revolving fund set up to support shelter programmes and housing finance institutions. Other steps involving technical cooperation, local institution-building, mainstreaming the experiences of the Centre's Best Practices and Local Leadership Programme facility and strengthening involvement with the United Nations Development Group were also suggested.

GENERAL ASSEMBLY ACTION

On 21 December [meeting 90], the General Assembly, on the recommendation of the Second Committee [A/56/565], adopted **resolution 56/206** without vote [agenda item 102].

Strengthening the mandate and status of the Commission on Human Settlements and the status, role and functions of the United Nations Centre for Human Settlements (Habitat)

The General Assembly,

Recalling relevant resolutions on human settlements, in particular its resolutions 3327(XXIX) of 16 December 1974, 32/162 of 19 December 1977 and 34/115 of 14 December 1979,

Recalling also the Habitat Agenda and the Istanbul Declaration on Human Settlements,

Aware of rapid urbanization trends in developing countries and related challenges in shelter provision, eradicating poverty and sustainable human settlements development,

Convinced of the need for urgent action to advance the quality of life of all people in cities and other human settlements,

Conscious of the need to achieve greater coherence and effectiveness in the implementation of the Habitat Agenda within the United Nations system,

Recognizing that urgent steps should be taken to ensure a better mobilization of financial resources at all levels, to enhance the implementation of the Habitat Agenda, particularly in developing countries, with a view to improving human settlements,

Recalling the commitments of Governments to, inter alia, promoting broad access to appropriate housing financing, increasing the supply of affordable housing and creating an enabling environment for sustainable development that will attract investment,

Recalling also its resolution 51/177 of 16 December 1996, in which it, inter alia, designated the United Nations Centre for Human Settlements (Habitat) as a focal point for the implementation of the Habitat Agenda and called for a comprehensive and in-depth assessment of the Centre with a view to its revitalization,

Recalling further its resolutions 52/220 of 22 December 1997, 53/242 of 28 July 1999 and 55/195 of 20 December 2000, in which it requested the Secretary-General to consider further strengthening the Centre through the provision of requisite support and stable, adequate and predictable financial resources, including additional regular budget and human resources,

Recalling agreed conclusions 2000/1 of the Economic and Social Council adopted at the coordination segment of the substantive session of 2000 of the Council, and taking note of the conclusions of the Council at its substantive session of 2001 regarding improving inter-agency coordination in the implementation of the Habitat Agenda,

Bearing in mind the responsibilities of the Centre, as set out in paragraph 228 of the Habitat Agenda, and the establishment of the Habitat task manager system,

Recalling the Declaration on Cities and Other Human Settlements in the New Millennium, in particular paragraph 67 thereof, in which the Secretary-General was invited to report to the General Assembly at its fifty-sixth session on options for reviewing and strengthening the mandate and status of the Commission on Human Settlements and the status, role and functions of the United Nations Centre for Human Settlements (Habitat), in accordance with the relevant decisions of the General Assembly, the Economic and Social Council and the United Nations Conference on Human Settlements (Habitat II),

Encouraged by the resumption by several Member States of voluntary contributions to the United Nations Habitat and Human Settlements Foundation in response to the work undertaken by the management of the Centre to revitalize the Centre and give it a new impetus to advance the Habitat Agenda,

Taking note of the report of the Secretary-General on options for reviewing and strengthening the mandate and status of the Commission on Human Settlements and the status, role and functions of the United Nations Centre for Human Settlements (Habitat), including their financial implications,

I
United Nations Human Settlements Programme

Decides to transform the Commission on Human Settlements and its secretariat, the United Nations Centre for Human Settlements (Habitat), including the United Nations Habitat and Human Settlements Foundation, with effect from 1 January 2002, into the United Nations Human Settlements Programme, to be known as UN-Habitat, which will have the elements described below:

A. Governing body

Status, composition, objectives, functions and responsibilities

1. *Decides* to transform, with effect from 1 January 2002, the Commission on Human Settlements into the Governing Council of the United Nations Human Settlements Programme, to be known as UN-Habitat, a subsidiary organ of the General Assembly;

2. *Also decides* that the Governing Council shall propose its rules of procedure on the basis of the rules of procedure of the Commission on Human Settlements, bearing in mind the provisions of the present resolution, for consideration by the General Assembly;

3. *Further decides* that the practices regarding the participation of Habitat Agenda partners shall be according to the relevant rules of the Economic and Social Council with regard to participation and accreditation, that the established practices of the Commission on Human Settlements shall be utilized and that such practices shall in no way create a precedent for other governing bodies of the subsidiary organs of the General Assembly;

4. *Decides* that the Governing Council shall be composed of fifty-eight members, to be elected by the Economic and Social Council for four-year terms on the following basis:

    (a) Sixteen seats for African States;

    (b) Thirteen seats for Asian and Pacific States;

    (c) Six seats for Eastern European States;

    (d) Ten seats for Latin American and Caribbean States;

    (e) Thirteen seats for Western European and other States;

5. *Confirms* that the Governing Council shall have the objectives, functions and responsibilities set out in resolution 32/162 and in paragraph 222 of the Habitat Agenda;

6. *Decides* that the Governing Council shall be the intergovernmental decision-making body for the Programme;

7. *Also decides* that the Governing Council shall meet biennially and report to the General Assembly through the Economic and Social Council;

8. *Further decides* that the Committee of Permanent Representatives to UN-Habitat shall serve as the Governing Council's intersessional subsidiary body;

B. Secretariat of the Programme

1. *Decides* to transform, with effect from 1 January 2002, the United Nations Centre for Human Settlements (Habitat) into the secretariat of the United Nations Human Settlements Programme (UN-Habitat), and confirms that the secretariat of the Programme, under the direction of the Executive Director, shall be entrusted with the responsibilities set out in paragraph

228 of the Habitat Agenda and in resolution 32/162. The UN-Habitat secretariat shall service the Governing Council and serve as the focal point for human settlements and for the coordination of human settlements activities within the United Nations system;

2. *Also decides*, bearing in mind General Assembly resolution 54/249 of 23 December 1999, that the UN-Habitat secretariat shall be headed by an Executive Director at the level of Under-Secretary-General, to be elected by the General Assembly for a term of four years upon nomination by the Secretary-General after consultation with Member States;

3. *Affirms* that the Urban Forum is a non-legislative technical forum in which experts can exchange views in the years when the Governing Council does not meet, and that the Advisory Committee of Local Authorities is an advisory body to the Executive Director;

4. *Decides* that the resources for managing the Programme shall comprise the posts and budgetary resources of the Centre, without prejudice to additional regular budget and extrabudgetary resources that may become available;

II
Financing human settlements

1. *Confirms* that the Executive Director of the United Nations Human Settlements Programme (UN-Habitat) shall be responsible for the management of the United Nations Habitat and Human Settlements Foundation, with due regard to the terms of reference of the Foundation as stipulated in General Assembly resolution 3327(XXIX);

2. *Encourages* the Executive Director to strengthen the Foundation in order to achieve its primary operative objective, as set out in resolution 3327(XXIX), of supporting the implementation of the Habitat Agenda, including supporting shelter, related infrastructure development programmes and housing finance institutions and mechanisms, particularly in developing countries;

3. *Invites* all Governments to increase their contributions to the Foundation to enhance the capacity of the Programme to support the implementation of the Habitat Agenda and the Declaration on Cities and Other Human Settlements in the New Millennium;

4. *Encourages* the Executive Director of the Programme to continue her fund-raising appeals and initiatives for a substantial increase of Foundation resources;

5. *Calls* for the active participation and collaboration of organizations and bodies within and outside the United Nations system, including the World Bank and regional development banks, in the activities of the Programme and its Foundation, in particular with regard to the provision of seed capital and the financing of operational human settlements projects and programmes, as well as developing appropriate and innovative approaches for financing its projects and programmes;

6. *Requests* the Secretary-General to continue to support the Programme through the provision of adequate regular budget resources;

III
Policy coordination

1. *Reaffirms* that the General Assembly and the Economic and Social Council, in accordance with relevant provisions of the Charter of the United Nations and relevant resolutions, including General Assembly resolutions 48/162 of 20 December 1993 and 50/227 of 24 May 1996, together with the Governing Council of the United Nations Human Settlements Programme (UN-Habitat), constitute the three-tiered intergovernmental mechanism to oversee the coordination of the implementation of the Habitat Agenda;

2. *Emphasizes* the role and importance of the implementation of the Habitat Agenda, in particular achieving the goals of adequate shelter for all and sustainable human settlements, in the activities and programmes of the United Nations system, in particular in the context of common country assessments and the United Nations Development Assistance Framework, as well as the poverty reduction strategy papers process led by the World Bank and the International Monetary Fund;

3. *Welcomes* the fact that the Programme, as the United Nations focal point for the implementation of the Habitat Agenda, will participate in the United Nations System Chief Executives Board for Coordination at all levels of its machinery;

4. *Decides* that the Programme should strengthen its collaboration with the Commission on Sustainable Development and other relevant bodies in the implementation of the Habitat Agenda as it relates to sustainable development;

5. *Requests* the Secretary-General to submit a report to the General Assembly at its fifty-seventh session on the implementation of the present resolution.

OIOS review

In September, the Secretary-General transmitted the seventh annual report of the Office of Internal Oversight Services (OIOS) [A/56/381], which covered activities during the period from 1 July 2000 to 30 June 2001, and included UNCHS audit information. During the reporting period, OIOS issued 17 critical audit recommendations to UNCHS, of which eight, regarding an audit of the Habitat settlement rehabilitation programme in northern Iraq (see p. 990), had been implemented, while nine critical recommendations remained open. UNCHS also implemented one of the nine OIOS recommendations made in its 1999 follow-up inspection [YUN 2000, p. 994], dealing with information management, and had initiated action to address the remaining recommendations.

An OIOS investigation of allegations of mismanagement in UNCHS operations in north-west Somalia established that the allegations were unfounded, but revealed that the senior officer had not strictly adhered to UN rules and regulations. OIOS recommended holding him accountable for some $50,000 in losses that resulted from his actions. The Office recommended improving the internal controls of the use of money vendors to make local payments in the region, in order to achieve cost reductions and avoid the risk of financial losses. UNCHS agreed with the recommendations and was implementing them. OIOS identified accounting errors and other adjustments totalling about $1.6 million on projects funded by a Danish aid organization. To prevent a recurrence, OIOS recommended establishing formal project management procedures and training for staff involved in UN accounting and budgeting. With regard to numerous individual construction contracts, an OIOS audit of UNCHS systems and procedures for implementing activities in northern Iraq, valued at about $245 million, revealed that the segregation of duties in the tender preparation stage, bidding process and evaluation of bids was inadequate. The contractor selection process needed to be strengthened and procedures for evaluating contractor performance had not been established. OIOS considered cash payments of some $500,000 annually to local personnel for inspecting Habitat construction projects to be inappropriate, since UNCHS used its own personnel to inspect contractors' work. The Office recommended that the United Nations Office of the Humanitarian Coordinator in Iraq (UNOHCI) review the basis for those payments. UNOHCI had done so, with other concerned UN organizations.

Chapter VIII

Population

As the world's population reached 6.1 billion in 2001, the population activities of the United Nations continued to be guided by the Programme of Action adopted at the 1994 International Conference on Population and Development (ICPD) and the key actions for the further implementation of the Programme of Action adopted at the twenty-first special session of the General Assembly in 1999.

The United Nations Population Fund (UNFPA), the largest internationally funded source of population assistance, was the lead UN organization for advancing the ICPD Programme of Action. UNFPA's third Executive Director, Thoraya Ahmed Obaid, took office in January and developed a transition plan that had five principal aims: to develop and implement a strategic vision of the Fund's goals and operations; to realign the Fund's structure to provide greater and more effective support to the field; to invest in and develop UNFPA staff; to improve knowledge sharing and communications, both within UNFPA and between the Fund and its partners; and to increase the visibility of UNFPA and its achievements.

The Commission on Population and Development, in April, considered the central theme of population, environment and development. It adopted a resolution on the subject, which it brought to the attention of the Economic and Social Council. Other matters before the Commission included the flow of financial resources to implement the ICPD Programme of Action, world demographic trends and the activities of the UN Population Division.

The Population Division continued to analyse world demographic trends and population policies. New publications included *World Population Prospects: The 2000 Revision*.

Follow-up to the 1994 Conference on Population and Development

Implementation of the Programme of Action

Commission on Population and Development action. In follow-up to the recommendations of the 1994 International Conference on Population and Development (ICPD) [YUN 1994, p. 956], the Commission on Population and Development, at its thirty-fourth session (New York, 2-6 April) [E/2001/25], considered the central theme of population, environment and development. That subject was a key action for the further implementation of the ICPD Programme of Action, contained in resolution S-21/2 [YUN 1999, p. 1006], adopted at the 1999 special session of the General Assembly (ICPD+5). The Commission also discussed the flow of financial resources for assisting in the Programme of Action's implementation.

Population, environment and development

As decided at its 2000 session [YUN 2000, p. 1007], the central theme for the Commission's 2001 session was "Population, environment and development". For the Commission's discussion of the theme, the Secretary-General submitted a concise report on world population monitoring, 2001 [E/CN.9/2001/2], which analysed recent information and policy perspectives on population, environment and development. The report investigated the topics of: temporal trends in population, environment and development; government views and policies concerning population, environment and development; population size and growth, environment and development; migration, population change and the rural environment; health, mortality, fertility and the environment; and population, environment and development in urban settings.

The report concluded that, while all the environmental problems identified were largely or entirely the result of human activities, they varied in the extent to which they could be linked directly to population size, growth or distribution. For example, growth in some types of pollution was primarily the by-product of rising per capita production and consumption in industrialized economies, where population had generally been growing slowly. Even for environmental problems that were concentrated in countries with relatively rapid population growth, it was not necessarily the case that population increase was the main root cause, nor that halting population growth would resolve the problem. Nevertheless, continued population increase played an important role by increasing aggregate economic demand and, hence, the volume of pollution-causing production.

With globalization, new and emerging technologies and modes of production and consumption, the relationships among population, environment and development had become issues of heightened concern for Governments, the international community and the average citizen. Although population growth, structure and distribution were important aspects of environmental stress, that stress was a matter not just of population change, but also of how and what people produced and consumed, both currently and in the future.

The Commission, by a 6 April resolution [E/2001/25 (res. 2001/1)], which it brought to the attention of the Economic and Social Council, requested the UN Population Division to continue its research on the linkages among population, consumption and production, the environment and natural resources, and human health. Particular attention was given to levels, trends and differentials of mortality, fertility, distribution and mobility, and the role of population and development policies, as well as mainstreaming of a gender perspective. The Division was also asked to contribute its research findings to the preparatory processes for the special session of the General Assembly for the review and appraisal of the United Nations Conference on Human Settlements (Habitat II) (see p. 973), the 2002 World Summit on Sustainable Development and other relevant intergovernmental meetings and conferences. The Commission also requested that the findings from that and related research on population, environment and development should contribute to the next review and appraisal of the implementation of the ICPD Programme of Action, scheduled for 2004. The Division was encouraged to disseminate widely the results of its research, as a contribution to greater understanding and awareness of the interrelationships among population, environment and development.

Financial resources

In accordance with General Assembly resolutions 49/128 [YUN 1994, p. 963] and 50/124 [YUN 1995, p. 1094], the Secretary-General submitted to the Commission a report on the flow of financial resources for assisting in the implementation of the ICPD Programme of Action [E/CN.9/2001/3]. The report examined trends in bilateral, multilateral and foundation/non-governmental assistance to population activities in developing countries for 1998 and provisional figures for 1999, and also provided estimates of domestic expenditures reported by developing countries for 1999. International population assistance increased to just over $2.1 billion in 1998 and to almost $2.2 billion in 1999, but was far below the agreed target of $5.7 billion by 2000.

Developing countries continued to commit domestic resources to population programmes, the report stated. In 1999, domestic government and non-governmental expenditures were estimated at $8.9 billion, an increase over the 1998 level of $8.6 billion, but also below the agreed target. There was a significant and sizeable increase in the 1999 level of funding from the private sector, especially foundations, compared to 1998. Development banks also increased their loan commitments in 1999.

International population assistance was just over 38 per cent of the $5.7 billion target agreed upon at ICPD as the international community's share in financing the Programme of Action by 2000.

International migration and development

In response to General Assembly resolution 54/212 [YUN 1999, p. 1021], the Secretary-General submitted a July report on international migration, including the question of convening a UN conference on international migration and development to address migration issues [A/56/167]. The report summarized national policies on international migration and the views of Governments regarding the convening of a conference on the subject. It also described activities carried out by relevant organizations at the regional and international levels, taking account of the lessons on migration management and policies that they had learned through their activities. Also addressed were the possible mechanisms within the UN system for examining issues related to international migration and development.

Quoting the Population Policy Database of the Population Division, the report stated that, in recent decades, the number of Governments that had adopted measures to control international migration flows had increased to 35 per cent by 1995, compared to only 6 per cent in 1976. During the same period, the percentage of Governments that had adopted measures to maintain their levels of immigration or non-intervention policies decreased from 87 per cent to 61 per cent. In particular, developed countries showed the strongest inclination towards restricting immigration. Regarding emigration policies, between 1976 and 1995, the percentage of countries seeking to lower emigration increased from 13 per cent to 20 per cent. As at 1995, 75 per cent of countries aimed to maintain their existing level of emigration or not to intervene, a decline from 83 per cent in 1976. Both developed and developing countries showed similar trends in the evolution of their views.

Since 1995, the Population Division had on three occasions solicited views of Governments on the possibility of convening a conference on international migration and development as a follow-up to ICPD. Of the 78 Governments (41 per cent of UN membership) that had expressed their views since 1995, a majority appeared to favour holding a conference. However, there was a lack of consensus on objectives, funding and composition of the conference secretariat. Furthermore, a number of Governments expressed serious reservations about convening a conference, given the Organization's financial constraints. Those Governments appeared more in favour of a regional or subregional approach to the consideration of issues related to international migration and development.

In addition to providing an overview of the activities of different UN departments and programmes, specialized agencies and other bodies in various aspects of international migration, the report described the activities of a number of intergovernmental organizations that dealt with migration issues and provided assistance to migrants of different categories.

The report noted that the interlinkages between international migration and development were extremely complex. Efforts continued to explore to what extent international migration was a response to the dynamics of development and the extent to which migration itself could affect the development process. The experience gained by various organizations within and outside the UN system pointed to some mechanisms that might be used to better address and examine the issue of international migration and development. First, migration issues needed to be integrated in a more coherent way within a broader context of economic and social development frameworks, especially when designing strategies and programmes for development. Second, the Organization, in collaboration with other relevant bodies and agencies, could intensify its efforts to support the multilateral forums in which Governments, international organizations and civil society participated to address the issue. Thirdly, the dynamics of international migration could not be fully understood without the guidance of migration statistics. The United Nations continued to pursue and broaden its efforts to collect reliable data. To assist in those efforts, the Organization could further promote the implementation of the 1998 *Recommendations on Statistics of International Migration: Revision 1* [Sales No. E.98.XVII.14]. Finally, the United Nations could continue to exercise its leadership in promoting the ratification of various existing international instruments related to international migration.

GENERAL ASSEMBLY ACTION

On 21 December [meeting 90], the General Assembly, on the recommendation of the Second (Economic and Financial) Committee [A/56/563], adopted **resolution 56/203** without vote [agenda item 100].

International migration and development

The General Assembly,

Recalling the Programme of Action of the International Conference on Population and Development adopted at Cairo, in particular chapter X on international migration, and the key actions for the further implementation of the Programme of Action, set out in the annex to General Assembly resolution S-21/2 of 2 July 1999, in particular section II.C on international migration, as well as the relevant provisions contained in the Copenhagen Declaration on Social Development, the Programme of Action of the World Summit for Social Development, the Platform for Action adopted by the Fourth World Conference on Women and the outcome documents of the twenty-fourth and twenty-fifth special sessions of the General Assembly,

Recalling also its resolutions 49/127 of 19 December 1994, 50/123 of 20 December 1995, 52/189 of 18 December 1997 and 54/212 of 22 December 1999 on international migration and development, as well as Economic and Social Council decision 1995/313 of 27 July 1995,

Reaffirming the continuing validity of the principles set forth in the international instruments regarding the protection of human rights, in particular the Universal Declaration of Human Rights, the International Convention on the Elimination of All Forms of Racial Discrimination, the Convention on the Elimination of All Forms of Discrimination against Women and the Convention on the Rights of the Child,

Recalling that heads of State and Government, gathered at the United Nations Millennium Summit from 6 to 8 September 2000, committed themselves to respect for all internationally recognized human rights and fundamental freedoms, including the right to development,

Recalling also that heads of State and Government at the United Nations Millennium Summit resolved to take measures, inter alia, to ensure respect for and protection of the human rights of migrants, migrant workers and their families, to eliminate the increasing acts of racism and xenophobia in many societies and to promote greater harmony and tolerance in all societies,

Reaffirming that the General Assembly and the Economic and Social Council should carry out their respective responsibilities as entrusted to them in the Charter of the United Nations, as well as by the relevant United Nations conferences of the 1990s, in the formulation of policies and the provision of guidance to and coordination of United Nations activities in the field of population and development, including activities on international migration,

Noting the need for the relevant United Nations organizations and other international organizations to enhance their financial and technical support to developing countries as well as countries with economies in transition to ensure that migration contributes to development,

Recognizing the diversity of views expressed by the respondents to the survey regarding the question of convening a United Nations conference on international migration, its scope, form and agenda, which represented 41 per cent of the full United Nations membership, and that forty-seven respondents were in favour of convening a conference, five were partially in favour and twenty-six were against,

Noting in particular the need for more migration data, analysis of factors influencing international migration and of its impact, and a better understanding of the complex interrelationships between migration and development,

Noting the critical role of the existing forums within the United Nations system in addressing the issues of international migration and development, including through the Commission on Population and Development, the Commission on Human Rights, the Committee for Development Policy, the International Labour Organization and other relevant key organizations,

Noting with appreciation the numerous meetings and conferences convened relating to migration and development, in particular in the context of regional cooperation,

Noting the work undertaken, under the International Migration Policy Programme, by the United Nations Institute for Training and Research, the International Organization for Migration and the United Nations Population Fund, in partnership with the International Labour Office, the Office of the United Nations High Commissioner for Refugees, the Office of the United Nations High Commissioner for Human Rights and other relevant international and regional institutions, with a view to strengthening the capacity of Governments to manage migration flows at national and regional levels and thus to foster greater cooperation among States towards orderly migration,

Noting also the work of the Secretariat in the field of migration and development,

Aware that, among other important factors, both domestic and international, the widening economic and social gap between and among many countries and the marginalization of some countries in the global economy, due in part to the uneven impact of the benefits of globalization and liberalization, have contributed to large flows of people between and among countries and to the intensification of the complex phenomenon of international migration,

Aware also that, in spite of the existence of an already established body of principles, there is a need to make further efforts to ensure that the human rights and dignity of all migrants and their families are respected and protected and that it is desirable to improve the situation of all documented migrants and their families,

Recognizing the importance, from an analytical and operational point of view, of identifying the existing linkages among the social, economic, political and cultural factors related to international migration and development and of the need for comprehensive, coherent and effective policies on international migration based on the spirit of genuine partnership and common understanding,

1. *Takes note* of the report of the Secretary-General;

2. *Urges* Member States and the United Nations system to strengthen international cooperation in the area of international migration and development in order

to address the root causes of migration, especially those related to poverty, and to maximize the benefits of international migration to those concerned;

3. *Encourages*, where relevant, interregional, regional and subregional mechanisms to continue to address the question of migration and development;

4. *Calls upon* all relevant bodies, agencies, funds and programmes of the United Nations system and other relevant intergovernmental, regional and subregional organizations, within their continuing mandated activities, to continue to address the issue of international migration and development and to provide appropriate support for interregional, regional and subregional processes and activities on international migration and development, with a view to integrating migration issues in a more coherent way within the broader context of the implementation of agreed economic and social development programmes;

5. *Encourages* Governments of countries of origin, countries of transit and countries of destination to increase cooperation on issues related to migrations and to engage in further dialogue, including through relevant subregional, regional and international processes and organizations, as appropriate, including on the question of the convening of a United Nations conference on international migration and development;

6. *Calls upon* the United Nations, in collaboration with other relevant organizations and agencies, to provide support for dialogue involving Governments and other relevant stakeholders on international migration and development issues;

7. *Encourages* the international community, including donor countries, relevant United Nations bodies and other relevant international organizations and the private sector to provide support, including financial and technical support, for data collection and greater empirical research by Member States, in particular developing countries, and the relevant bodies of the United Nations system and other relevant international organizations on the causes and patterns of migration, including on irregular migration and trafficking, as well as its social, economic and demographic impacts, and for documenting and disseminating information on the successful management of all aspects of migration;

8. *Invites* Governments, with the assistance of the international community, where appropriate, to seek to make the option of remaining in one's country viable for all people, in particular through efforts to achieve sustainable development, leading to a better economic balance between developed and developing countries;

9. *Requests* the Secretary-General to solicit, one additional time, the views of Member States that have not responded to the survey requested in pursuance of resolution 52/189, as well as those of the International Labour Organization, the International Organization for Migration and other relevant organizations, both within and outside the United Nations system, and their views on his report submitted to the General Assembly at its fifty-sixth session, bearing in mind various regional processes, and to report thereon to the General Assembly at its fifty-eighth session;

10. *Also requests* the Secretary-General to initiate or continue appropriate action in consultation with regional commissions in order to ensure the carrying out

of interregional activities, with the contribution of the relevant actors on issues relating to international migration and development, taking into account, inter alia, the report of the Secretary-General, and encourages the United Nations bodies and other appropriate international organizations to provide support to such activities;

11. *Further requests* the Secretary-General to submit to the General Assembly at its fifty-eighth session a report on the implementation of the present resolution that will, inter alia, update the lessons learned, as well as best practices on migration management and policies, from the various activities relating to international migration and development that have been carried out at the regional and interregional levels, and submit action-oriented recommendations for the consideration of the Assembly;

12. *Decides* to include in the provisional agenda of its fifty-eighth session a sub-item entitled "International migration and development".

UN Population Fund

Thoraya Ahmed Obaid became UNFPA's third Executive Director on 1 January 2001. In her first statement to the United Nations Development Programme (UNDP)/UNFPA Executive Board, she identified three main challenges facing the Fund: ensuring a financially stable UNFPA; strengthening its institutional capacity; and addressing the sociocultural context of programme development and delivery.

In her annual report covering 2001 [DP/FPA/2002/4 (Part I)], the Executive Director stated that implementation of country programmes accounted for the majority of UNFPA's activities during the year. At the end of 2001, the Fund implemented projects in approximately 150 countries, including two subregional programmes for countries in the Caribbean and Pacific islands. A total of $144 million was spent on country programmes and an additional $27.7 million on regional and interregional programmes. Activities were carried out in the Fund's three core programme areas: reproductive health, including family planning and sexual health; population and development strategies; and advocacy.

The Fund's work in adolescent reproductive health, a programming priority, focused on providing young people with critical information, empowering girls, providing youth-friendly services, fostering supportive communities and encouraging youth participation. The Fund played a leading role in reproductive health commodity security by helping countries to procure quality, low-cost reproductive health supplies. Some 44

urgent requests for supplies were met through the Fund's Global Contraceptive Commodities Programme, a revolving fund designed to maintain stocks of reproductive health commodities for emergency situations. Notwithstanding generous contributions by the Netherlands and the United Kingdom, the Fund's activities in 2001 included a vigorous advocacy effort to raise awareness of the severe shortfall in funding in that critical area. The Executive Director estimated that the funding required for contraceptive commodities in the developing world would rise to $1.8 billion per year by 2015.

UNFPA responded to the HIV/AIDS pandemic on various fronts. It identified HIV prevention as an institutional priority, formulated a strategic direction for addressing HIV in its three core programme areas, and developed guidelines for national capacity-building. At the country and regional levels, efforts were intensified to integrate prevention into the reproductive health component of country programmes, especially in the context of adolescent reproductive health. The Fund was a key contributor to the special session of the General Assembly on HIV/AIDS in June (see p. 1125). The UNFPA strategic plan for HIV/AIDS for 2001-2005 was submitted to the UNDP/UNFPA Executive Board in June (see p. 996).

As the lead agency for implementing the ICPD Programme of Action, UNFPA continued its advocacy work for universal access to reproductive health care, the right to family planning, empowerment of women, the importance of engaging men as partners in the promotion of reproductive and sexual health and gender equity, the need for reproductive health information and services for adolescents, and the need for national Governments to adopt and implement sustainable population policies.

In other activities, UNFPA worked at the global level to raise awareness about fistula, a preventable and treatable condition caused by damage to the tissues of the bladder and rectum as a result of prolonged and obstructed labour. It also expanded its Goodwill Ambassador programme, through which celebrities helped to raise awareness of reproductive health needs in developing countries. Furthermore, it intensified the Face to Face Campaign, conducted in partnership with the International Planned Parenthood Federation, to contribute to resource mobilization by creating greater public and political awareness of population issues and organizations by engaging celebrities to help focus attention on advocacy initiatives. Another important advocacy tool, the Fund's annual *The State of World Population* report, called for greater efforts to balance human and environmental needs. Entitled *Footprints and Milestones: Population and Environmental Change,* the 2001 report argued that unbalanced consumption and environmental destruction were having a disproportionate impact on the poor, and noted that the world's population had doubled since 1960 and was projected to increase by another 3 billion by 2050.

UNFPA launched a dialogue on the role of religion and culture in the context of globalization and development and continued to prioritize gender mainstreaming in its core programme areas, in operations in emergency situations, and within the organization itself. It also increased its emphasis on emergency response and humanitarian assistance and focused attention on the speed of population ageing.

The Fund was committed to developing national capacities to integrate reproductive health, population and gender into policy-making and development planning, and for the effective design and implementation of reproductive health programmes. In that regard, it increased its emphasis in 2001 on building national capacity in efficient and effective programme management by strengthening a results-based approach in its programming, invested considerable resources in building human capacity by training health and community workers at all levels of the health-care system in reproductive health-care service provision, strengthened national capacities to monitor and analyse population trends and integrate population and gender issues into development programmes, and supported activities to build the capacity of country offices, Governments, NGOs and health workers to respond more quickly and effectively to humanitarian crises.

Upon taking office in January, the Executive Director initiated an organization-wide transition process to ensure that UNFPA and its operations remained relevant and effective in the face of new opportunities and challenges. That process had five principal aims: to develop and implement a strategic vision of the Fund's goals and operations; to realign the structure of the Fund to provide greater and more effective support to the field; to invest in and develop UNFPA staff; to improve knowledge sharing and communications within UNFPA and between the Fund and its partners; and to increase the visibility of UNFPA and its achievements. The Executive Director established thematic working groups to cover the five main transition components, plus finance. A field needs-assessment study was conducted in June/July, in which four teams travelled to 14 programme countries to solicit detailed information on wide-ranging issues from country office staff, country technical service teams, government rep-resentatives, bilateral agencies, NGOs and other UN system field staff. The resulting study yielded a large number of recommendations and formed the primary basis for the transition exercise. The Fund designated 2002 as the year for implementing and testing the new strategies and systems developed by the working groups. Planned transition outputs included: a positioning statement defining a common strategic direction for achieving greater progress with regard to the ICPD Programme of Action; finalization of a new human resources development strategy; the piloting and implementation of new strategies for knowledge sharing; the introduction of more streamlined administrative and financial systems for simpler and more reliable monitoring; and the launch of a new organizational identity to ensure that UNFPA would become better known for its work and to counter harmful misinformation.

By **decision 2001/226** of 10 July, the Economic and Social Council took note of the annual reports of the UNDP Administrator and of the UNFPA Executive Director to the Council [E/2001/10].

Strategic plan for HIV/AIDS

In response to Economic and Social Council resolution 1999/36 [YUN 1999, p. 1149], UNFPA, as one of the co-sponsors of the Joint United Nations Programme on HIV/AIDS (UNAIDS) (see p. 1125), submitted to the UNDP/UNFPA Executive Board an April report [DP/FPA/2001/9] on the Fund's contribution to the UN system strategic plan for HIV/AIDS for 2001-2005. The report described major UNFPA HIV-prevention activities before 2001 and lessons learned from its efforts.

The UNFPA strategic plan for 2001-2005 would continue to focus on HIV prevention through advocacy and information, education and communication and through integrating attention to HIV prevention in national reproductive health programmes. The country programmes for 2001-2005, including those for Burkina Faso, Cambodia, Chad, Ghana, Indonesia, Namibia and Uganda, already reflected those emphases. As the designated focal point within UNAIDS for condom programming, UNFPA had developed a plan on reproductive health commodities to be integrated into all programmes it supported. It would continue to collaborate with UNAIDS, the United Nations Children's Fund and the World Health Organization on activities related to preventing HIV infection in mothers and its transmission to children, and would give increased attention to reaching men with regard to their critical role in the spread of AIDS. In addition, efforts to prevent sexually transmitted HIV infection, as an integral component of the package of support in emergency and conflict situations, would be continued. The report went on to describe UNFPA's involvement in global, regional and national partnerships with regard to HIV/AIDS prevention and the institutional changes planned to reinforce its capacity to address the HIV epidemic and to strengthen national capacities in dealing with the problem.

Executive Board action. On 14 June [E/2001/35 (dec. 2001/9)], the Executive Board endorsed the Fund's focus and overall approach with respect to HIV/AIDS for the years 2001-2005. Recognizing UNFPA's experience and comparative advantage in fulfilling its lead role in implementing the goals of ICPD and the benchmarks of ICPD+5, and in making use of its extensive networks at the country level, the Board requested the Fund to intensify its efforts and to take a more visible leadership role in HIV prevention, especially among young people. It encouraged UNFPA to build further on its experience in addressing gender issues, including the role of men, as an integral part of HIV-prevention activities. Governments were encouraged to support UNFPA's efforts by increasing their commitment, including financial commitment, to curb and reverse the spread of HIV/AIDS in programme countries.

Humanitarian assistance

In a section of her annual report covering 2001 [DP/FPA/2002/4 (Part III)], the Executive Director stated that the Fund's humanitarian assistance activities in 2001 focused on reproductive health support; training and capacity-building; advocacy; data collection, analysis and information synthesis; inter-agency coordination and programme planning; tools development; and project development.

In 2001, through direct donor contributions or the use of other emergency resources, UNFPA supported UN consolidated appeal process activities in Afghanistan, Angola, Burundi, the Democratic People's Republic of Korea, the Democratic Republic of the Congo, Eritrea, Indonesia (for the Maluku crisis), the Russian Federation (northern Caucasus), Sierra Leone, Somalia, South-Eastern Europe, Tajikistan, Uganda and West Africa. The funds were utilized to save lives, including through the provision of emergency obstetric care and reproductive health services for refugees and internally displaced persons. UNFPA's achievements in assessing reproductive health needs, technical assistance in restoring basic and reproductive health services, provision of emergency supplies, safe delivery training, capacity-building, research activities and advocacy efforts had gone a long way

in helping development partners and the general public to understand the critical importance of reproductive health issues during emergencies and in post-disaster situations.

Reproductive health commodities

In a section of her annual report covering 2001 [DP/FPA/2002/4 (Part III)], the Executive Director stated that, during the year, UNFPA continued to consolidate and expand its work in reproductive health commodity security. As it had done for more than a decade, the Fund provided leadership in that field through its Global Initiative on Contraceptive Requirements and Logistics Management Needs in Developing Countries. In April, the Fund published *Reproductive Health Commodity Security: Partnerships for Change, A Global Call to Action*, which outlined the challenges developing countries faced in achieving reproductive health commodity security.

In 2001, UNFPA worked closely with 81 countries experiencing commodity shortfalls and programmed $76 million contributed by Canada, the Netherlands and the United Kingdom to meet requests for commodities. The least developed countries received the most support and countries with high HIV prevalence received approximately three times as many condoms per capita as those with HIV prevalence below 2 per cent. To avert reproductive health commodity shortfalls in developing countries, the Fund planned to establish a framework for adequate and predictable donor support. To that end, it was conducting a survey on the supply situation in developing countries; the information would be used to provide reproductive health commodities in 2002 and beyond.

Country and intercountry programmes

UNFPA's provisional project expenditures for country and intercountry (regional and interregional) programmes in 2001 totalled $171.7 million, compared to $127.5 million in 2000, according to the Executive Director's statistical overview report for the year [DP/FPA/2002/4 (Part I)/Add.1]. The 2001 figure included $144 million for country programmes and $27.7 million for intercountry programmes. In accordance with the procedure for allocating resources according to categorization of countries into groups, laid down in a 1996 UNDP/UNFPA decision [YUN 1996, p. 989] and updated in 2000 [YUN 2000, p. 1005], total expenditures in 2001 to Group A countries (those most in need) amounted to $98.1 million, compared to $72.3 million in 2000.

Africa. Provisional expenditures for UNFPA programmes in sub-Saharan Africa totalled $57 million in 2001, compared to $42.7 million in 2000. Most of the resources (70.2 per cent) went to reproductive health and family planning, followed by population and development strategies (25.1 per cent) and advocacy (3.9 per cent).

On 5 February [E/2001/35 (dec. 2001/7)], the UNDP/UNFPA Executive Board approved programmes of assistance to Burkina Faso, Chad, Ghana, Namibia and Uganda. On 14 September [dec. 2001/17], the Board approved programmes of assistance to Eritrea, Ethiopia, the Gambia, Mozambique, the Niger and Senegal.

Arab States and Europe. Provisional expenditures for UNFPA programmes in the Arab States and Europe totalled $22.6 million in 2001, compared with $17.4 million in 2000. Most of the resources (76.5 per cent) went to reproductive health and family planning, followed by population and development strategies (16.4 per cent) and advocacy (4 per cent).

On 5 February [dec. 2001/7], the UNDP/UNFPA Executive Board approved programmes of assistance to the Palestinian people and Turkey. On 14 September [dec. 2001/17], the Board approved programmes of assistance to Morocco, the Sudan and the Syrian Arab Republic.

Asia and the Pacific. Provisional expenditures for UNFPA programmes in Asia and the Pacific totalled $55.9 million in 2001, compared with $41.5 million in 2000. Most of the resources (77 per cent) went to reproductive health and family planning, followed by population and development strategies (14.8 per cent) and advocacy (7.3 per cent).

On 5 February [dec. 2001/7], the UNDP/UNFPA Executive Board approved a programme of assistance to Indonesia. On 14 September [dec. 2001/17], it approved programmes of assistance to Bhutan, Mongolia, Sri Lanka and Thailand. The Board also approved the programme of assistance to Myanmar and requested the Executive Director to report annually on its implementation.

Latin America and the Caribbean. Provisional expenditures for UNFPA programmes in Latin America and the Caribbean totalled $16.9 million in 2001, compared to $14.8 million in 2000. Most of the resources (72.2 per cent) went to reproductive health and family planning, followed by population and development strategies (21.9 per cent) and advocacy (4.7 per cent).

On 5 February [dec. 2001/7], the UNDP/UNFPA Executive Board approved programmes of assistance to Ecuador, Guatemala and Peru. It also approved a request for additional resources for the UNFPA programme for the English- and Dutch-speaking Caribbean countries.

Interregional programmes. Provisional expenditures for UNFPA's interregional and global programmes totalled $19.3 million in 2001, compared to $11.1 million in 2000. Of that total, 41.5 per cent went to advocacy, 34.6 per cent to reproductive health and family planning, 21.8 per cent to population and development strategies and 2.1 per cent to multisectoral activities.

On 5 February [dec. 2001/7], the UNDP/UNFPA Executive Board took note of an oral report on progress in implementing the 2000-2003 intercountry programme.

UNFPA information and communication strategy

In response to a 1997 Executive Board request [YUN 1997, p. 1083], the Executive Director submitted a May report in which she reviewed the implementation of the information and communication strategy between 1997 and 2000 [DP/FPA/2001/6]. The report examined the strategy in the light of experience gained since 1997 and of changes in population and development, notably the 1999 ICPD+5 review conference [YUN 1999, p. 1005]. The major finding of the review was that the strategy had proved to be effective in addressing many of the basic challenges facing UNFPA, such as ensuring sound and stable funding; increasing awareness and understanding of the role and relevance of population in the development process; building support for the Fund's activities; strengthening its capacity for international policy advocacy; and working towards ICPD goals successfully within national social and cultural realities. The strategy had also helped UNFPA to expand its outreach to key audiences and the general public and to expand its partnerships with governmental and non-governmental organizations. One of the best indicators of its success was the increase in extrabudgetary funding for specific activities.

UNFPA's web site was an important tool for implementing the Fund's information and communication strategy. In September 2000, 1.5 million hits by 107,000 users were reported. The content of and traffic on the Fund's web site had grown steadily since 1997 and nearly all of UNFPA's publications and reports had been posted online. With regard to video productions and broadband outreach, innovative technologies and new media techniques had been employed to promote the ICPD message to a broad range of audiences. The challenge for UNFPA's information and communication strategy was, among other things, to continue the process of consensus-building; counter unprincipled opposition while responding to legitimate concerns; and pay close attention to institutional positioning and promotion, especially among key donors, to meet the ICPD financial goals.

On 12 June [E/2001/35 (dec. 2001/8)], the Executive Board endorsed UNFPA's actions to strengthen its ability to carry out its information and communications strategy and urged the Fund to continue to build on its past experience and to develop innovative ways to implement the strategy. The international community was urged to increase financial support for the promotion of the goals of ICPD and ICPD+5.

Financial and administrative questions

UNFPA's income from all sources totalled $396.4 million in 2001, compared to $414.1 million in 2000 [DP/FPA/2002/12]. That comprised $268.6 million of Regular Funds and $127.8 million from Other Funds. Expenditures totalled $254.2 million from Regular Funds and $123.5 million from Other Funds, resulting in a net surplus of $14.4 million to Regular Funds and of $4.3 million to Other Funds. The Regular Funds surplus would be fully utilized in 2002 and the Other Funds surplus related mostly to trust-fund projects lasting for more than one year. Income to Regular Funds remained largely unchanged at $268.6 million, compared to $264 million in 2000. However, the strong United States dollar hid the underlying trend, which was a substantial increase in donor contributions. In local currency terms, donors increased their funding by $10.8 million.

Project expenditure increased by 35 per cent to $171.7 million in 2001, compared to $127.5 million in 2000.

2002-2003 support budget

In a July report [DP/FPA/2001/10], the Executive Director submitted to the UNDP/UNFPA Executive Board the proposed biennial support budget for 2002-2003, which assumed a total income of $702.5 million ($580 million in Regular Resources and $122.5 million in Other Resources). Of that estimated amount, $168.3 million gross ($146.5 million net) would be used for programme support (headquarters and country offices, agency programme support costs, and the management and administration of UNFPA). The proposed budget represented an increase of 15 per cent over the 2000-2001 net figure of $127.4 million and 12.6 per cent higher than the gross figure of $149.4 million.

Several strategic considerations were taken into account in structuring the proposals for the biennial support budget. They included the need to reach the goals of ICPD and the ICPD+5 review; combat the spread of HIV/AIDS, especially by helping to ensure reproductive health commodity security; build national capacity to design and implement population and reproductive health policies; and strengthen the Fund's field operations and relations with partners, both inside and outside the UN system.

Commenting on the 2002-2003 support budget in August [DP/FPA/2001/12], the Advisory Committee on Administrative and Budgetary Questions (ACABQ) stated that, prior to the adoption of the budget estimates, UNFPA should submit to the Executive Board, through ACABQ, a report on the implementation of a human resources strategy, in conjunction with the revised estimates for the biennial support budget for 2002-2003.

By a 14 September decision [E/2001/35 (dec. 2001/16)], the Executive Board approved gross appropriations of $168.3 million for the support budget for 2002-2003 and resolved that income estimates of $21.8 million should be used to offset the gross appropriations, resulting in estimated net appropriations of $146.5 million. It authorized the Executive Director to redeploy resources between appropriation lines, up to a maximum of 5 per cent of the appropriation to which the resources were redeployed. The Executive Director was urged to implement the foreseen reclassification of posts with the highest possible prudence and transparency, especially as to possible contradictions with requirements deriving from the field needs-assessment survey.

The Board requested the Executive Director to submit in 2002 a comprehensive human resources development strategy and proposed revisions to the biennial support budget for 2002-2003 arising from further review of organizational requirements, including the field needs-assessment survey.

Also on 14 September [dec. 2001/17], the Board took note of ACABQ's August report.

Multi-year funding commitments

In a May report [DP/FPA/2001/5], the Executive Director submitted to the UNDP/UNFPA Executive Board updated estimates of regular and supplementary resources for 2001-2003. As at 31 March, 53 countries had submitted written pledges to UNFPA for the year 2001; 20 had done so for 2002 and 17 for 2003. In 2000, UNFPA achieved its pledging target of 100 donor countries: 29 from Europe, 25 from Asia and the Pacific, 22 from Africa, 15 from Latin America and the Caribbean, 8 from the Arab States and 2 from North America. For 2001, the target had been increased to 110 donors. Total contributions received from donor Governments, as well as interest from the Mars Trust for UNFPA's general resources in 2000, amounted to $258.3 million (provisionally). As at 31 March 2001, $268.5 million had been pledged for 2001, including a projected additional amount of $6.5 million to be raised; $100.2 million had been pledged for 2002; and $100.6 million had been pledged for 2003. Total payments received from donor Governments for general resources in 2001 amounted to approximately $40.8 million as at 31 March.

Of UNFPA's 16 major donors (those contributing $1 million or more), which together provided an estimated 97 per cent of the total contributions to general resources, only five countries were in a position to make multi-year pledges, the report said. Noting that general resources were invaluable to its country programmes, UNFPA appealed to Executive Board members and the Fund's donors to consider increasing their contributions for 2001 and future years and to ensure the early and timely payment of those pledges.

On 22 June [E/2001/35 (dec. 2001/12)], the Executive Board took note of the Executive Director's report.

Programming process

In response to a 2000 Executive Board request [YUN 2000, p. 1006], the UNDP Administrator and the UNFPA Executive Director submitted an April report [DP/FPA/2001/7-DP/2001/12] on decentralizing programme development exercises (see p. 799). The Executive Board took action on the report in a 22 June decision [dec. 2001/11].

Audit reports

The Executive Director submitted to the UNDP/UNFPA Executive Board a status report [DP/FPA/2001/2] describing follow-up measures taken on the recommendations of the Board of Auditors on UNFPA for the 1998-1999 biennium.

On 1 February [E/2001/35 (dec. 2001/5)], the Executive Board took note of the report.

In a May report [DP/FPA/2001/8], the Executive Director described UNFPA's internal audit and oversight activities in 2000, stating that management audits had been carried out in 15 country offices and compliance audits undertaken in 11 country offices. Of 27 reports issued in 2000 (including 14 on 1999 audits), the level of internal controls and compliance with financial and administrative requirements were found to be satisfactory in 12 offices. Nine country offices were rated marginally deficient, four were deficient and two were seriously deficient.

The UNFPA Office of Oversight and Evaluation analysed the midterm reviews undertaken in 1999 and 2000 of 55 UNFPA-supported country programmes. It also conducted policy application reviews of two country programmes and continued to follow up on the implementation of recommendations of policy reviews conducted in previous years.

On 22 June [dec. 2001/12], the Executive Board took note of the Executive Director's report.

UN Population Award

The 2001 United Nations Population Award was presented to Dr. Nafis Sadik, former UNFPA Executive Director, in the individual category, and to the Japanese Organization for International Cooperation in Family Planning in the institutional category. Dr. Sadik was selected for her tremendous impact on population and development issues during her tenure as Executive Director between 1987 and 2000. During that time, she made significant contributions to the 1994 International Conference on Population and Development [YUN 1994, p. 955], which resulted in enormous changes in the field of population, including the global consensus that placed human rights, specifically women's rights, at the heart of the population debate. The Japanese Organization for International Cooperation in Family Planning was selected for its outstanding contribution to population issues in the developing world, as well as in Japan. It was active in the field of population and reproductive health, with projects in 26 countries in Asia, Latin America and Africa. Its major contributions were in the community-operated integrated approach to family planning; the sharing of Japanese expertise through human resources development; and advocacy in population and reproductive health issues.

The Award was established by the General Assembly in resolution 36/201 [YUN 1981, p. 792], to be presented annually to individuals or institutions for outstanding contributions to increased awareness of population problems and to their solutions. In October, the Secretary-General transmitted to the Assembly the report of the UNFPA Executive Director on the Population Award [A/56/459]. By **decision 56/447** of 21 December, the Assembly took note of the report.

Other population activities

Commission on Population and Development

The Commission on Population and Development, at its thirty-fourth session (New York, 2-6

April) [E/2001/25], considered as its central theme "Population, environment and development", which was discussed in the context of the follow-up to ICPD [YUN 1994, p. 955]. Documents before the Commission focusing on the theme were reports of the Secretary-General on world population monitoring [E/CN.9/2001/2] and on the flow of financial resources for assisting in implementing the ICPD Programme of Action [E/CN.9/2001/3] (see p. 991). The Commission also had before it reports of the Secretary-General on world demographic trends [E/CN.9/2001/4] (see p. 1002) and on programme implementation and progress of work in the field of population in 2000 [E/CN.9/2001/5] [YUN 2000, p. 1007], and a note by the Secretariat on the draft programme of work of the Population Division for the 2002-2003 biennium [E/CN.9/2001/6] (see p. 1002).

In addition to adopting a resolution on population, environment and development [E/2001/25 (res. 2001/1)] (see p. 992), the Commission recommended to the Economic and Social Council for adoption a draft decision on the Commission's report on its thirty-fourth session and the provisional agenda for its thirty-fifth (2002) session. It also took note of the documents it had considered [dec. 2001/1].

By **decision 2001/231** of 19 July, the Economic and Social Council took note of the report of the Commission on its thirty-fourth session and approved the provisional agenda and documentation for the thirty-fifth session.

In preparation for the thirty-fifth session, the Commission's Bureau held an intersessional meeting in New York on 7 and 8 November [E/CN.9/2002/CRP.1].

2001 UN activities

In a report on programme implementation and progress of work of the UN Population Division in 2001 [E/CN.9/2002/5], the Secretary-General described the Division's activities dealing with the analysis of demographic variables at the world level; world population estimates and projections; population policy and socio-economic development; monitoring, coordination and dissemination of population information; and technical cooperation in population.

The Population Division's work in fertility and family planning analysis included the completion of a wallchart on *World Contraceptive Use, 2001*, which showed the most recent data available from surveys on contraceptive prevalence, including methods used. A report on world marriage patterns was under preparation. A workshop on prospects for fertility decline in high-fertility countries (New York, 9-11 July) cited the low status of women, especially their lagging educational attainment—one of the main obstacles to fertility decline—together with high family size preferences and the lack of accessible and affordable contraceptives.

The manual on the estimation of adult mortality was finalized for publication in 2002. At the end of 2001 a completed database on infant and child mortality, which incorporated data on under-five mortality in developing countries, became available. The data and accompanying documentation were also available on diskettes.

With regard to international migration, the Population Division prepared the report of the Secretary-General to the General Assembly on the subject (see p. 992) and issued, on a set of three diskettes, the "International Migration from Countries with Economies in Transition, 1980-2000" database. It also updated the "Flows in International Migration from South to North" database and finalized the reports "Levels and Trends of International Migration in Asia" and "Replacement Migration: Is It a Solution to Declining and Ageing Populations?" [Sales No. E.01.XIII.19]. As to internal migration, work was completed on gathering data for Latin America and the Caribbean, and North America, while the report "The Components of Urban Growth in Developing Countries" was published.

The results of the *2000 Revision* of population estimates and projections to 2050 were published in two volumes. Volume I, *World Population Prospects: The 2000 Revision, Comprehensive Tables* [Sales No. E.01.XIII.8], was issued in July and volume II, *World Population Prospects: The 2000 Revision, Sex and Age Distribution of the World Population* [Sales No. E.01.XIII.9], was released in August. The data from the publication were also issued on CD-ROM. The *2000 Revision* incorporated the impact of HIV/AIDS for 45 countries and used a revised methodology to project the epidemic's effect. The *Analytical Report*, which completed the series of publications related to the *2000 Revision*, was finalized and would be published in 2002 under the title *World Population Prospects: The 2000 Revision*, volume III. The results of the *2001 Revision of World Urbanization Prospects* were issued in draft form and the urban and rural part of the projections were made available on the Population Division's web site.

In the area of population policy and socio-economic development, the three-volume monograph *Abortion Policies: A Global Review* [Sales No. E.02.XIII.13] presented a country-by-country examination of national policies concerning induced abortion and the context within which it took place. The report *Results of the Eighth United Nations Inquiry among Governments on Population and Development* [Sales No. E.01.XIII.2] was published as part of the Population Division's effort to ensure proper monitoring of the implementation of the ICPD Programme of Action. A wallchart, *Population, Environment and Development, 2001* [Sales No. E.01.XIII.5], presented statistical data on countries' population size and growth, economic development and selected areas of environmental concern, including the supply of freshwater, deforestation, food and agriculture and greenhouse gas emissions. The *Population, Resources, Environment and Development (PRED Bank, version 3)* database was released on CD-ROM. A new publication, *World Population Ageing, 1950-2050*, provided an overview of the world ageing process and detailed indicators of population ageing for the world, regions and countries. It showed that the ageing of populations was a pervasive, unprecedented and enduring process with profound social and economic implications.

In 2001, the Population Division prepared the latest edition of its annual report, "World Population Monitoring", which had as its topic reproductive rights and reproductive health, with special reference to HIV/AIDS. The Division continued to update and expand its web site, providing information about new research publications. The Population Information Network (POPIN) web site continued to provide users with a continuous source of population information, particularly links to material within the UN system.

The Population Division continued to focus its technical cooperation programme on activities to strengthen population research and teaching institutions in developing countries. The major objectives of its activities were: to build capacity in developing countries for effective use of the Internet for population research and training and to encourage proper institutionalization of new technologies of information and communication in population centres; to promote cooperation among population institutions in the South and enhance the visibility of their work; and to ensure that the results of the Division's analytical and normative activities were relayed to stakeholders in developing countries. The Division continued to support and develop three networks of population research and training institutions, each of them having a web site and an electronic discussion group. It also continued its Outreach Programme, which sought to associate promising students and young researchers from developing countries with some of its analytical activities. In 2001, five young scholars from Burkina Faso, Cameroon, Côte d'Ivoire, Morocco and Togo participated in a special training programme on the prospects for fertility decline in high-fertility countries.

World demographic trends

In a March report to the Commission on Population and Development [E/CN.9/2001/4], prepared in accordance with Economic and Social Council resolution 1996/2 [YUN 1996, p. 977], the Secretary-General provided an overview of the latest demographic trends worldwide for major areas and selected countries. It was estimated that the world population—some 6.1 billion in 2001—was growing at a rate of 1.2 per cent annually, implying a net addition of 77 million people per year. Six countries (Bangladesh, China, India, Indonesia, Nigeria, Pakistan) accounted for half of that annual increment. By 2050, the world population was expected to be between 7.9 billion (low variant) and 10.9 billion (high variant), with 9.3 billion as the medium variant.

Programme of work, 2002-2003

The Secretariat submitted to the Commission on Population and Development a February note [E/CN.9/2001/6] containing the Population Division's draft programme of work for 2002-2003. The Commission was invited to comment and make recommendations on the draft programme. On 6 April [E/2001/25 (dec. 2001/1)], the Commission took note of the draft.

Chapter IX

Social policy, crime prevention and human resources development

In 2001, the United Nations continued to promote the advancement of social, cultural and human resources development, and to strengthen its crime prevention and criminal justice programme.

In February, the Commission for Social Development considered measures for implementing the further initiatives for social development adopted by the General Assembly at its twenty-fourth (2000) special session to review and appraise implementation of the outcome of the 1995 World Summit for Social Development. The Assembly, in 2001, addressed follow-up to the World Summit and the special session and took action regarding other social issues, including the implementation of the 1982 World Programme of Action concerning Disabled Persons and preparations for the tenth anniversary of the 1994 International Year of the Family.

The Assembly devoted two plenary meetings to the observance of the International Year of Dialogue among Civilizations (2001), at the close of which it proclaimed the Global Agenda for Dialogue among Civilizations. The Assembly also proclaimed 2002 as the United Nations Year for Cultural Heritage and addressed the question of the return or restitution of cultural properties. As part of UN efforts to enhance respect for cultural diversity, the Assembly adopted resolutions on the protection of religious sites, the destruction of relics and monuments in Afghanistan and the building of a better world through sports and the Olympic ideal.

The Commission on Crime Prevention and Criminal Justice finalized draft plans of action for the implementation of the 2000 Vienna Declaration on Crime and Justice, which the Economic and Social Council endorsed and recommended to the Assembly for adoption. An intergovernmental expert group commenced work on drafting an international legal instrument against corruption. In May, the Assembly adopted and opened for signature the Protocol against the Illicit Manufacturing of and Trafficking in Firearms, Their Parts and Components and Ammunition to the 2000 United Nations Convention on Transnational Organized Crime.

In December, the Assembly called for the early ratification of the Convention and related protocols.

In continuing efforts to achieve the global goal of education for all, the Assembly, in December, proclaimed the 10-year period beginning 1 January 2003 the United Nations Literacy Decade. In its resolution on the University for Peace, it invited all peoples to celebrate One Day in Peace on 1 January 2002 and every year thereafter.

Social policy and cultural issues

Social development

Follow-up to 1995 World Summit and to General Assembly special session

In July [A/56/140], the Secretary-General, in accordance with General Assembly resolution 55/46 [YUN 2000, p. 1034], reported on follow-up to the Assembly's twenty-fourth (2000) special session [YUN 2000, p. 1012], which reviewed and appraised implementation of the Copenhagen Declaration on Social Development and the Programme of Action adopted at the 1995 World Summit for Social Development [YUN 1995, p. 1113]. The report focused on follow-up activities undertaken by relevant intergovernmental bodies within the UN system to implement the further initiatives for social development adopted at the special session by resolution S/24-2 [YUN 2000, p. 1013]. Following the special session, the Secretariat initiated efforts to improve coordination of UN system activities for implementing the outcomes of the World Summit and the further initiatives for social development. Subsequent progress reports from the heads of UN agencies, funds and programmes indicated that nearly all UN system bodies had initiated follow-up activities. Given that many of the activities reported were in existence prior to the adoption of the further initiatives, the special session provided an important political endorsement of the UN system's ongoing efforts to promote social development for all.

The principal themes and main areas for follow-up action included: reducing the proportion of people living in extreme poverty by one half by 2015; monitoring the social impact of macroeconomic policies; strengthening the international financial architecture and reducing the negative social and economic impacts of international financial turbulence; supporting developing countries' integration into the multilateral trading system; promoting efforts to mobilize additional resources for social development; sharing best practices in the field of social protection; minimizing undesirable humanitarian consequences of sanctions; strengthening mechanisms for conflict prevention and peacebuilding; elaborating a coordinated international strategy on employment; promoting initiatives on education for all; employing health policy as a proactive instrument for poverty reduction and economic and social development; strengthening the fight against money-laundering and corruption; promoting efforts to stop the HIV/AIDS pandemic; and finding durable solutions to the problems of refugees and returnees.

GENERAL ASSEMBLY ACTION

On 19 December [meeting 88], the General Assembly, on the recommendation of the Third (Social, Humanitarian and Cultural) Committee [A/56/585], adopted **resolution 56/177** without vote [agenda item 27].

Implementation of the outcome of the World Summit for Social Development and of the twenty-fourth special session of the General Assembly

The General Assembly,

Recalling the World Summit for Social Development, held at Copenhagen from 6 to 12 March 1995, and the twenty-fourth special session of the General Assembly, entitled "World Summit for Social Development and beyond: achieving social development for all in a globalizing world", held at Geneva from 26 June to 1 July 2000,

Reaffirming that the Copenhagen Declaration on Social Development and the Programme of Action and the further initiatives for social development adopted by the General Assembly at its twenty-fourth special session constitute the basic framework for the promotion of social development for all at the national and international levels,

Recalling the United Nations Millennium Declaration,

Recalling also and reaffirming the commitments made at major United Nations conferences, special sessions, summit conferences and their follow-up processes, and the principles expressed in relevant United Nations declarations,

Recalling further its resolution 55/46 of 29 November 2000 on the implementation of the outcome of the World Summit for Social Development and of the twenty-fourth special session of the General Assembly,

1. *Reaffirms* the commitments made by heads of State and Government at the World Summit for Social Development, contained in the Copenhagen Declaration on Social Development and the Programme of Action, which established a new consensus to place people at the centre of the concerns for sustainable development and pledged to eradicate poverty, promote full and productive employment and foster social integration so as to achieve stable, safe and just societies for all;

2. *Also reaffirms* the decisions on further action and initiatives to accelerate social development for all, adopted by the General Assembly at its twenty-fourth special session and contained in the further initiatives for social development;

3. *Stresses* the vital importance of placing the goals of social development, as contained in the Copenhagen Declaration and the Programme of Action and in the further initiatives for social development, at the centre of economic policy-making, including in policies that influence domestic and global market forces and the global economy;

4. *Encourages* coordinated and mutually reinforcing follow-up to the Copenhagen Declaration and the Programme of Action, the further initiatives for social development and the United Nations Millennium Declaration, emphasizing the strong interrelatedness in respect of social development issues;

5. *Invites* the Secretary-General, the Economic and Social Council, the Commission for Social Development, the regional commissions, the relevant agencies, funds and programmes of the United Nations system and other relevant intergovernmental forums, within their respective mandates, to take on a priority basis and in a coordinated manner all steps necessary to ensure the effective implementation of all commitments and undertakings contained in the Copenhagen Declaration and the Programme of Action and in the further initiatives for social development, and to continue to be actively involved in their follow-up;

6. *Recognizes* that the implementation of the outcome of the World Summit for Social Development and of the twenty-fourth special session of the General Assembly calls for the strengthening of cooperation at the regional level through, inter alia, the promotion of dialogue among regional and subregional groups and organizations, encouragement of the implementation of regional social development agendas where they exist, and encouragement of recipient countries, donor Governments and agencies and multilateral financial institutions to take greater account of the regional social development agendas of the regional commissions and of regional and subregional organizations, inter alia, in their funding policies and programmes;

7. *Reaffirms* that a strong political commitment by the international community is needed to implement strengthened and effective international cooperation and assistance for development, including social development, and that the mobilization of domestic and international resources for development from all sources is an essential component of the implementation of the Copenhagen Declaration and the Programme of Action and of the further initiatives for social development;

8. *Welcomes* the convening of the International Conference on Financing for Development, to be held at

Monterrey, Mexico, from 18 to 22 March 2002, which will consider the mobilization of national and international resources for social development, and the World Summit on Sustainable Development, to be held at Johannesburg, South Africa, from 2 to 11 September 2002, and encourages their preparatory committees and other relevant intergovernmental bodies involved in the preparations for and follow-up to those conferences to give consideration to the outcome of the World Summit for Social Development and of the twenty-fourth special session of the General Assembly;

9. *Reaffirms* that the follow-up to the World Summit for Social Development and the twenty-fourth special session of the General Assembly will be undertaken on the basis of an integrated approach to social development and within the framework of a coordinated follow-up to major international and summit conferences in the economic, social and related fields, and in this regard takes note of Economic and Social Council resolution 2001/21 of 26 July 2001 on integrated and coordinated implementation of and follow-up to the outcomes of the major United Nations conferences and summits;

10. *Also reaffirms* the need for effective partnership and cooperation between Governments and the relevant actors of civil society, including non-governmental organizations and the private sector, in the implementation of and follow-up to the Copenhagen Declaration and the Programme of Action and the further initiatives for social development, and the need for ensuring their involvement in the planning, elaboration, implementation and evaluation of social policies at the national level;

11. *Further reaffirms* that the Commission for Social Development, as a functional commission of the Economic and Social Council, will continue to have the primary responsibility for the follow-up to and review of the further implementation of the commitments made at Copenhagen and the outcome of the twenty-fourth special session of the General Assembly;

12. *Invites* Governments to support the work of the Commission for Social Development, inter alia, through the participation of high-level representatives on social development issues and policies, and to continue to assess on a regular basis the progress made at the national level towards the implementation of the outcome of the World Summit for Social Development and of the twenty-fourth special session of the General Assembly, and to submit such information on a voluntary basis to the Commission;

13. *Takes into account* the fact that the Commission for Social Development will consider the priority theme "Integration of social and economic policy" at its fortieth session, in 2002, and emphasizes the importance of the active participation in and contribution to the work of the Commission by the relevant funds and programmes and the specialized agencies of the United Nations system;

14. *Takes note* of the *Report on the World Social Situation, 2001*, and requests the Secretary-General to submit future reports on a biennial basis;

15. *Also takes note* of the report of the Secretary-General;

16. *Decides* to include in the provisional agenda of its fifty-seventh session the item entitled "Implementa-tion of the outcome of the World Summit for Social Development and of the twenty-fourth special session of the General Assembly", and requests the Secretary-General to submit a report on this question to the General Assembly at its fifty-seventh session.

An overview of the *Report on the World Social Situation, 2001* [Sales No. E.01.IV.5], noted by the Assembly above, had been presented by the Secretary-General to the Economic and Social Council the previous year [YUN 2000, p. 1034].

Commission for Social Development

The Commission for Social Development, at its thirty-ninth session (New York, 13-23 February) [E/2001/26 & Corr.1], recommended a multi-year work programme for 2002-2006 (see p. 1006) built around follow-up to the 1995 World Summit for Social Development and the twenty-fourth (2000) special session of the General Assembly, and considered preparations for the observance of the tenth anniversary of the International Year of the Family (1994) (see p. 1008). The Commission convened expert panels and adopted resolutions on the priority theme "Enhancing social protection and reducing vulnerability in a globalizing world" and on the sub-theme "The role of volunteerism in the promotion of social development".

The Commission considered an analytical report of the Secretary-General [E/CN.5/2001/2] on the priority theme, which drew on the deliberations of two expert group meetings, held in 2000 [YUN 2000, p. 1034], that explored ways to develop social protection systems and mechanisms to ensure their sustainability. The report defined the terrain of social protection policy in terms of: its objectives and functions; its relation to human rights and the political economy; the role of Government, the private sector, the community and the family; and multilateral efforts, including those of the UN system and the European Union (EU). It reviewed the challenges to social protection in the face of globalization; outlined key elements in a broad policy and institutional framework; and made recommendations for national and international action to promote human development and effective social protection systems, to be considered as part of the broader strategies adopted to achieve that goal.

Having discussed the foregoing report, the Commission decided to consider ways of further examining the issue at a future session [E/2001/26 (res. 39/1)].

The Commission also considered the Secretary-General's note [E/CN.5/2001/6] on the sub-theme of the role of volunteerism in the promotion of social development, which discussed the spirit of volunteering to recapture its human and community dimension, as well as its constituent and irreducible diversity; dealt with the crucial challenge of linking voluntary action with social development strategies; and explored possible avenues for government support of volunteering in the context of the unprecedented opportunities offered by the International Year of Volunteers (2001) (see p. 814). The Commission welcomed the Secretary-General's note and requested him to report to the General Assembly's fifty-sixth (2001) session on ways for Governments and the UN system to support volunteering (see p. 815) and to propose recommendations for discussion at that session [E/2001/26 (dec. 39/2)].

In preparation for the Commission's 2002 session, the Secretariat organized three expert group meetings (San José, Costa Rica, 11-13 June; Sofia, Bulgaria, 30 October–1 November; and New York, 5-7 November) on the social aspects of macroeconomic policies, expenditures in the social sector as a productive factor and social assessment as a policy tool. On the basis of the meetings' outcomes, the Secretary-General prepared a December report [E/CN.5/2002/3], which reviewed the framework for the integration of economic and social policy—the priority theme for the 2002 session—provided an overview of the major challenges facing that policy, highlighted the major conclusions of the expert meetings and presented recommendations for action at the national and international levels.

On 24 July, the Economic and Social Council took note of the Commission's report [E/2001/26 & Corr.1], endorsed its resolutions and decisions, and approved the provisional agenda and documentation for its fortieth (2002) session (**decision 2001/235**). On the same date, the Council took note of the report of the Commission acting as the Preparatory Committee for the Second World Assembly on Ageing on its first and resumed sessions and approved the provisional agenda for its second session (**decision 2001/239**) (see p. 1102).

Work programme

On 24 July [meeting 40], the Economic and Social Council, on the recommendation of the Commission for Social Development [E/2001/26 & Corr.1], adopted **resolution 2001/7** without vote [agenda item 14(*b*)].

Proposals for a multi-year programme of work of the Commission for Social Development for 2002-2006

The Economic and Social Council,

Recalling its resolution 1996/7 of 22 July 1996 by which it decided on the structure of the agenda and

work programme of the Commission for Social Development,

Decides that the multi-year programme of work of the Commission for the period 2002-2006 shall be the following:

2002: Follow-up to the World Summit for Social Development and the twenty-fourth special session of the General Assembly

(*a*) Priority theme: "Integration of social and economic policy". Under this theme, the following specific topics will be considered:

(i) Social aspects of macroeconomic policies;

(ii) Social assessment as a policy tool;

(iii) Expenditures in the social sector as a productive factor;

(*b*) Review of relevant United Nations plans and programmes of action pertaining to the situation of social groups:

(i) Preparatory Committee for the Second World Assembly on Ageing (second session);

(ii) Report of the Third Mandate of the Special Rapporteur on Disability.

2003: Follow-up to the World Summit for Social Development and the twenty-fourth special session of the General Assembly

(*a*) Priority theme: "National and international cooperation for social development". Under this theme, the following specific topics will be considered:

(i) Sharing of experiences and practices in social development;

(ii) Forging partnerships for social development;

(iii) Social responsibility of the private sector;

(iv) Impact of employment strategies on social development;

(v) Policies and role of international financial institutions and their effect on national social development strategies;

(*b*) Review of relevant United Nations plans and programmes of action pertaining to the situation of social groups:

Review of the global situation of youth.

2004: Follow-up to the World Summit for Social Development and the twenty-fourth special session of the General Assembly

(*a*) Priority theme: "Improving public sector effectiveness";

(*b*) Review of relevant United Nations plans and programmes of action pertaining to the situation of social groups:

Comprehensive review on the occasion of the tenth anniversary of the International Year of the Family.

2005: Follow-up to the World Summit for Social Development and the twenty-fourth special session of the General Assembly

(*a*) Priority theme: "Review of further implementation of the World Summit for Social Development and the outcome of the twenty-fourth special session of the General Assembly";

(*b*) Review of relevant United Nations plans and programmes of action pertaining to the situation of social groups.

2006: Follow-up to the World Summit for Social Development and the twenty-fourth special session of the General Assembly

(*a*) Priority theme: "Review of the first United Nations Decade for the Eradication of Poverty (1997-2006)";

(*b*) Review of relevant United Nations plans and programmes of action pertaining to the social groups.

Role of cooperatives

In response to General Assembly resolution 54/123 [YUN 1999, p. 1039], the Secretary-General submitted a May report with a later addendum [A/56/83-E/2001/68 & Add.1] summarizing information received from 18 Governments and 21 specialized agencies, international organizations, and national and international cooperative organizations on their activities in utilizing and developing cooperatives, as well as their views on the draft guidelines aimed at creating a supportive environment for the development of cooperatives, previously sent to them for comment.

In general, the Governments reported their continuing support for and recognition of the cooperative movement's potential for and contribution to the attainment of social development goals. On the basis of the information received, in particular the specific comments on and suggested revisions to the draft guidelines, the Secretary-General made a series of recommendations and annexed a revised draft text of the guidelines for the Assembly's consideration.

GENERAL ASSEMBLY ACTION

On 19 December [meeting 88], the General Assembly, on the recommendation of the Third Committee [A/56/572], adopted **resolution 56/114** without vote [agenda item 108].

Cooperatives in social development

The General Assembly,

Recalling its resolutions 47/90 of 16 December 1992, 49/155 of 23 December 1994 and 51/58 of 12 December 1996 and its resolution 54/123 of 17 December 1999, in which it requested the Secretary-General to seek the views of Governments on the draft guidelines aimed at creating a supportive environment for the development of cooperatives and to provide, if necessary, a revised version for adoption,

Recognizing that cooperatives, in their various forms, promote the fullest possible participation in the economic and social development of all people, including women, youth, older persons and people with disabilities, and are becoming a major factor of economic and social development,

Recognizing also the important contribution and potential of all forms of cooperatives to the follow-up to the World Summit for Social Development, held at Copenhagen from 6 to 12 March 1995, the Fourth World Conference on Women, held at Beijing from 4 to 15 September 1995, and the second United Nations Conference on Human Settlements (Habitat II), held at Istanbul, Turkey, from 3 to 14 June 1996, and their five-year reviews, as well as the World Food Summit, held at Rome from 13 to 17 November 1996,

1. *Takes note* of the report of the Secretary-General;

2. *Draws the attention* of Member States to the draft guidelines aimed at creating a supportive environment for the development of cooperatives, to be considered by them in developing or revising their national policies on cooperatives;

3. *Encourages* Governments to keep under review, as appropriate, the legal and administrative provisions governing the activities of cooperatives, with a view to ensuring a supportive environment for them and to protecting and advancing the potential of cooperatives to help them to achieve their goals;

4. *Urges* Governments, relevant international organizations and specialized agencies, in collaboration with national and international cooperative organizations, to give due consideration to the role and contribution of cooperatives in the implementation of and follow-up to the outcomes of the World Summit for Social Development, the Fourth World Conference on Women and the second United Nations Conference on Human Settlements (Habitat II) and their five-year reviews, as well as the World Food Summit, by, inter alia:

(a) Utilizing and developing fully the potential and contribution of cooperatives for the attainment of social development goals, in particular the eradication of poverty, the generation of full and productive employment and the enhancement of social integration;

(b) Encouraging and facilitating the establishment and development of cooperatives, including taking measures aimed at enabling people living in poverty or belonging to vulnerable groups to engage on a voluntary basis in the creation and development of cooperatives;

(c) Taking appropriate measures aimed at creating a supportive and enabling environment for the development of cooperatives by, inter alia, developing an effective partnership between Governments and the cooperative movement;

5. *Invites* Governments, in collaboration with the cooperative movement, to develop programmes to promote and strengthen the education of members, the elected leadership and professional cooperative management, where appropriate, and to create or improve statistical databases on the development of cooperatives and on their contribution to national economies;

6. *Invites* Governments, relevant international organizations, specialized agencies and local, national and international cooperative organizations to continue to observe the International Day of Cooperatives annually, on the first Saturday of July, as proclaimed by the General Assembly in its resolution 47/90;

7. *Requests* the Secretary-General, in cooperation with the relevant United Nations and other international organizations and national, regional and international cooperative organizations, to render support to Member States, as appropriate, in their efforts to create a supportive environment for the development of cooperatives and to promote an exchange of experience and best practices, through, inter alia, conferences, workshops and seminars at the national and regional levels;

8. *Also requests* the Secretary-General to submit a report on the implementation of the present resolution to the General Assembly at its fifty-eighth session.

UN Research Institute for Social Development

During 2001, the United Nations Research Institute for Social Development (UNRISD) continued to conduct research into the social dimensions of development issues. The report of the UNRISD Board [E/CN.5/2003/2] detailing the year's activities noted that, in September, the Institute contributed to the World Conference against Racism, Racial Discrimination, Xenophobia and Related Intolerance (see p. 615) and jointly organized a conference with the Ford Foundation on reviving development economics as a discipline that could improve the understanding of the acute problems facing developing countries. It also noted the commissioning of four papers on globalization and equity, in preparation for a meeting of high-level UN officials in 2002 on that theme. The report described the range of projects that were ongoing, completed or initiated under the UNRISD research programmes on social policy and development; democracy, governance and human rights; civil society and social movements; and technology, business and society.

UNRISD continued to carry out advisory activities for UN agencies, multilateral and bilateral organizations, Governments, non-governmental organizations (NGOs), other research institutes and universities. In addition, it maintained a steady output of publications, which were made available at many relevant events worldwide, and focused attention on a comprehensive redevelopment of its web site.

In February [E/2001/26 (dec. 39/105)], the Commission for Social Development took note of the report of the UNRISD Board for 1999 and 2000 [YUN 1999, p. 1040, & YUN 2000, p. 1035]. Following consideration of a January note by the Secretary-General with a later addendum [E/CN.5/2001/8 & Add.1], the Commission renominated three Board members, whose terms would expire on 30 June, for a further two-year term and nominated six new replacement members for four years, to be confirmed by the Economic and Social Council [dec. 39/101]. The Commission also took note of the Secretary-General's note [dec. 39/105].

On 24 July, the Council confirmed the three renominations and six new nominations to the UNRISD Board (**decision 2001/236**).

Follow-up to International Year of the Family

In response to General Assembly resolution 54/124 [YUN 1999, p. 1041] and decision 54/437 [ibid., p. 1346], the Secretary-General, by an August note [A/56/57-E/2001/5], transmitted to the Assembly and the Economic and Social Council the fourth biennial report [E/CN.5/2001/4] on follow-up activities during 1995-1999 to the International Year of the Family (1994), proclaimed by

Assembly resolution 44/82 [YUN 1989, p. 612]. According to the report, those activities resulted in significant accomplishments at all levels, among them a greater awareness of the role of families and family issues, new initiatives and long-term activities in support of families worldwide, strengthening and development of mechanisms devoted to family policy and research, and mobilization of a global network of partners, particularly NGOs.

Nonetheless, some crucial issues were left unresolved and gaps in policies remained. In particular, consensus was not achieved on definitions and terminology related to the family, family policies and family-sensitive considerations. Partly for that reason, a long-term global action plan on families, similar to those on the advancement of women, ageing, youth or disability, had not been developed.

The report also suggested appropriate ways to observe the Year's tenth anniversary in 2004, as well as national and international preparatory activities to be undertaken, and made a number of recommendations in that context. As the lead entity for the anniversary, the UN Department of Economic and Social Affairs (DESA) would stimulate and coordinate activities on five main themes: approaches to family policy development; technology and its impact on the family; parental roles and intra-familial support systems; statistics and indicators for family well-being; and HIV/AIDS and its impact on families.

ECONOMIC AND SOCIAL COUNCIL ACTION

On 24 July [meeting 40], the Economic and Social Council, on the recommendation of the Commission for Social Development [E/2001/26 & Corr.1], adopted **resolution 2001/6** without vote [agenda item 14 (*b*)].

Preparations for and observance of the tenth anniversary of the International Year of the Family

The Economic and Social Council

Recommends to the General Assembly the adoption of the following draft resolution:

[For text, see General Assembly resolution 56/113 below.]

GENERAL ASSEMBLY ACTION

On 19 December [meeting 88], the General Assembly, on the recommendation of the Third Committee [A/56/572], adopted **resolution 56/113** without vote [agenda item 108].

Preparations for and observance of the tenth anniversary of the International Year of the Family

The General Assembly,

Recalling its resolutions 44/82 of 8 December 1989, 47/237 of 20 September 1993, 50/142 of 21 December 1995, 52/81 of 12 December 1997 and 54/124 of 17 December 1999 concerning the proclamation, preparations for and observance of the International Year of the Family,

Recognizing that the preparation for and observance of the tenth anniversary of the International Year of the Family provides a useful opportunity for drawing further attention to the objectives of the Year for increasing cooperation at all levels on family issues and for undertaking concerted actions to strengthen family-centred policies and programmes as part of an integrated comprehensive approach to development,

Recognizing also that the follow-up to the International Year of the Family is an integral part of the agenda and of the multi-year programme of work of the Commission for Social Development until 2004,

Recognizing further that the family-related provisions of the outcomes of the world conferences of the 1990s continue to provide policy guidance on ways to strengthen family-centred components of policies and programmes as part of an integrated comprehensive approach to development,

Noting with concern the devastating effects of difficult social and economic conditions, armed conflicts, natural disasters and infectious diseases such as tuberculosis and malaria and of the human immunodeficiency virus/acquired immunodeficiency syndrome (HIV/AIDS) pandemic on family life,

Emphasizing that equality between women and men and respect for the human rights of all family members is essential to family well-being and to society at large,

Noting the active role of the United Nations in enhancing international cooperation in family-related issues, in particular in the area of research and information,

Emphasizing that it is necessary to intensify and improve coordination of the activities of the United Nations system on family-related issues so as to contribute fully to the effective preparation for and celebration of the tenth anniversary of the International Year of the Family,

1. *Takes note* of the report of the Secretary-General on the follow-up to the International Year of the Family and the preparations for the tenth anniversary of the International Year of the Family and the recommendations contained therein;

2. *Urges* Governments to view 2004 as a target year by which concrete achievements should be made to identify and elaborate issues of direct concern to families and also to set up and strengthen, where appropriate, mechanisms to plan and coordinate activities of governmental bodies and non-governmental organizations;

3. *Encourages* the regional commissions, within their respective mandates and resources, to participate in the preparatory process of the tenth anniversary of the International Year of the Family and to play an active role in facilitating regional cooperation in this regard;

4. *Requests* the Commission for Social Development to continue to review annually the preparations for the tenth anniversary of the International Year of the Family as part of its agenda and of its multi-year programme of work until 2004;

5. *Invites* Member States to consider organizing activities in preparation for the celebration of the tenth anniversary of the International Year of the Family at the national level;

6. *Requests* the Secretary-General, in order to facilitate contributions by Governments, to include the United Nations Trust Fund on Family Activities, on an annual basis, among the programmes for which funds are pledged at the United Nations Pledging Conference for Development Activities;

7. *Also requests* the Secretary-General to report to the General Assembly at its fifty-seventh session through the Commission for Social Development and the Economic and Social Council on the implementation of the present resolution, including a description of the state of preparation for the observance of the tenth anniversary of the International Year of the Family at all levels.

Report of Secretary-General. In an interim report [E/CN.5/2002/2] covering the period from February to December, the Secretary-General described initiatives undertaken in preparation for the tenth anniversary of the International Year of the Family in 2004.

DESA convened a consultative meeting on regional and global coordination in the promotion of social integration (New York, 1-5 October) to develop a focused approach to preparations for the observance, and initiated collaborative links with other UN organizations and consultations with intergovernmental organizations on family issues. The Secretariat organized the third consultative meeting of regional and international NGOs on the family (New York, 9 February) in conjunction with the February session of the Commission for Social Development to share information on planned activities. The United Nations Trust Fund on Family Activities provided financial assistance to Governments and NGOs for projects on the well-being of families. The UN family programme web site provided, in addition to other information, the bimonthly newsletter, *Family Matters.* The Secretariat prepared background information for use by Governments, the UN system and NGOs in the observance of the International Day of Families (15 May).

The report suggested that Governments might set up national coordinating committees, promote public information on the anniversary's objectives and encourage grass-roots involvement in related activities. It called on the Department of Public Information to develop an information strategy, on the UN regional commissions and intergovernmental organizations to participate in the preparations, and for contributions to the Trust Fund.

Persons with disabilities

Follow-up to World Programme of Action

In response to General Assembly resolution 54/121 [YUN 1999, p. 1043], the Secretary-General issued two reports on the implementation of the 1982 World Programme of Action concerning Disabled Persons, adopted by Assembly resolution 37/52 [YUN 1982, p. 981]. The first was an interim report [E/CN.5/2001/7], which reviewed progress in implementing equalization of opportunities by, for and with persons with disabilities in the light of the priorities for action identified in resolution 54/121, described selected experiences in regional cooperation and presented a perspective framework for the fourth review and appraisal of the World Programme of Action in 2002. In February, the Commission for Social Development took note of the interim report [E/2001/26 (dec. 39/104)].

The second report, issued in July [A/56/169 & Corr.1], described recent policy and programme initiatives related to persons with disabilities, based on information received from Governments, UN system organizations and intergovernmental and non-governmental organizations. Activities of the 27 reporting Governments concerned accessibility, health and social services, employment and sustainable livelihoods, national efforts to promote more inclusive societies, and national awareness campaigns on disability issues. Within the UN system, the International Labour Organization focused on promoting decent work for persons with disabilities; the Food and Agriculture Organization of the United Nations organized discussions on the integration of such persons in its field projects; the United Nations Educational, Scientific and Cultural Organization (UNESCO) directed attention to inclusive education as a strategy to achieve the goal of education for all; the International Initiative against Avoidable Disablement, jointly sponsored by the World Health Organization, the United Nations Development Programme and the United Nations Children's Fund, had 13 foundations in Asia and East Africa and funded a disability programme of the Palestinian Authority; and the World Bank introduced disability concerns into its poverty reduction projects.

The report examined progress in equalization of opportunities in terms of the establishment of international norms and standards to promote the rights of persons with disabilities, the improvement of accessibility of the United Nations for such persons and the compilation of global statistics and indicators on disability. In addition, the United Nations Voluntary Fund on Disability provided $159,676 in grants to six disability-related projects in Africa and in Central and Eastern Europe between November 2000 and June 2001.

The report further considered substantive aspects of a framework for the fourth review and appraisal of the World Programme of Action to be submitted to the Assembly in 2002. Five critical aspects were identified for review: the extent to which countries had specific policies and programmes designed to facilitate both community-based rehabilitation and equalization of opportunities for persons with disabilities; inclusion of the disability perspective in policies and programmes to foster social and economic development; elaboration of specific criteria for evaluation of progress towards full participation and equality; periodic data gathering based on those evaluation criteria; and monitoring systems to obtain indicators for measuring progress.

GENERAL ASSEMBLY ACTION

On 19 December [meeting 88], the General Assembly, on the recommendation of the Third Committee [A/56/572], adopted **resolution 56/115** without vote [agenda item 108].

Implementation of the World Programme of Action concerning Disabled Persons: towards a society for all in the twenty-first century

The General Assembly,

Recalling the purposes and principles of the Charter of the United Nations, and reaffirming the obligations contained in relevant human rights instruments, including the Convention on the Elimination of All Forms of Discrimination against Women and the Convention on the Rights of the Child,

Recalling also its resolutions 37/52 of 3 December 1982, by which it adopted the World Programme of Action concerning Disabled Persons, 48/96 of 20 December 1993, by which it adopted the Standard Rules on the Equalization of Opportunities for Persons with Disabilities, 49/153 of 23 December 1994, 50/144 of 21 December 1995, 52/82 of 12 December 1997 and 54/121 of 17 December 1999,

Recalling further all of its relevant resolutions on the equalization of opportunities for and the human rights of persons with disabilities, and those of the Economic and Social Council and its functional commissions,

Recalling the United Nations Millennium Declaration adopted on 8 September 2000 by the heads of State and Government at the Millennium Summit of the United Nations, and recognizing the need to promote and protect all human rights and fundamental freedoms of people with disabilities,

Noting with appreciation the actions of Governments to implement relevant sections of the Standard Rules and of relevant resolutions that give special attention to accessible environments and information and communications technologies, health, education and social services, employment and sustainable livelihoods, including the relevant activities of intergovernmental and non-governmental organizations,

Reaffirming the outcomes of the major United Nations conferences and summits and their respective follow-up reviews,

Noting with appreciation the assessment by the Secretary-General of the implementation of the outcomes of major United Nations conferences and summits to promote the rights and well-being of persons with disabilities, ensuring their full participation and equality, as well as the measures undertaken by the United Nations system aimed at preventing disabling conditions,

Noting the invitation made to the General Assembly by the World Conference against Racism, Racial Discrimination, Xenophobia and Related Intolerance, held at Durban, South Africa, from 31 August to 8 September 2001, to consider elaborating an integral and comprehensive international convention to protect and promote the rights and dignity of disabled people, including, in particular, provisions that address the discriminatory practices and treatment affecting them,

Acknowledging the important role of non-governmental organizations in the promotion and protection of the human rights of persons with disabilities, and noting in this regard their work in promoting the elaboration of an international convention on the rights of disabled persons,

Noting with appreciation the valuable work of the United Nations Voluntary Fund on Disability in supporting the building of national capacities to promote the Standard Rules in order to create opportunities for sustainable livelihoods by, for and with persons with disabilities,

Noting with appreciation also the important contributions of subregional, regional and international seminars and conferences related to persons with disabilities,

Mindful of the need to adopt and implement effective policies and strategies to promote the rights and the full and effective participation of persons with disabilities in economic, social, cultural and political life, on the basis of equality, to achieve a society for all,

Welcoming initiatives to hold international conferences relating to persons with disabilities, including the Sixth World Assembly of Disabled Peoples' International, to be held in Japan in 2002,

Concerned that improvement of awareness of and sensitivity to disability issues and respect for the human rights of disabled persons has not been significant enough to improve the quality of life of persons with disabilities worldwide,

Expressing grave concern that situations of armed conflict continue to have especially devastating consequences for the human rights of persons with disabilities,

Recognizing the importance of timely and reliable data on disability-sensitive topics, programme planning and evaluation and the need for further development of practical statistical methodology for the collection and compilation of data on populations with disabilities,

Reiterating that technology, in particular information and communications technology, provides new possibilities for improving accessibility and employment for persons with disabilities and for facilitating their full and effective participation and equality, and welcoming the initiatives of the United Nations in promoting information and communications technology as a means of achieving the universal goal of a society for all,

1. *Takes note with appreciation* of the report of the Secretary-General on the implementation of the World Programme of Action concerning Disabled Persons;

2. *Welcomes* the many initiatives and actions of Governments and relevant United Nations bodies and organizations, including relevant Bretton Woods institutions, as well as non-governmental organizations, to enhance the rights of persons with disabilities and the further equalization of opportunities by, for and with persons with disabilities in all sectors of society;

3. *Notes with appreciation* the valuable work undertaken by the Special Rapporteur on disability of the Commission for Social Development in monitoring the implementation of the Standard Rules on the Equalization of Opportunities for Persons with Disabilities under his third mandate for the period 2000-2002, and also notes with appreciation the work of the United Nations High Commissioner for Human Rights in supporting the work of the Special Rapporteur;

4. *Encourages* Governments, intergovernmental and non-governmental organizations and the private sector, as appropriate, to continue to take concrete measures to promote the implementation of relevant United Nations resolutions and agreed international standards concerning persons with disabilities, in particular the Standard Rules, and for the further equalization of opportunities for persons with disabilities by focusing on accessibility, health, education, social services, including training and rehabilitation, safety nets, employment and sustainable livelihoods, in the design and implementation of strategies, policies and programmes to promote a more inclusive society;

5. *Calls upon* Governments to undertake all necessary measures to advance beyond the adoption of national plans for people with disabilities through, inter alia, the creation or reinforcement of arrangements for the promotion and awareness of disability issues and the allocation of sufficient resources for the full implementation of existing plans and initiatives, and emphasizes in this regard the importance of supporting national efforts through international cooperation;

6. *Encourages* Governments and intergovernmental and non-governmental organizations to continue to take practical actions, including public information campaigns, by, for and with persons with disabilities, with a view to increasing awareness of and sensitivity to disability issues, combating and overcoming discrimination against persons with disabilities and furthering their full and effective participation in society;

7. *Encourages* Governments to continue their support to non-governmental organizations contributing to the fulfilment of the implementation of the World Programme of Action concerning Disabled Persons;

8. *Also encourages* Governments to involve persons with disabilities in the formulation of strategies and plans aimed at eradicating poverty, promoting education and enhancing employment;

9. *Urges* relevant bodies and organizations of the United Nations system, including relevant human rights treaty bodies and the regional commissions, as well as intergovernmental and non-governmental organizations and institutions, to continue to work closely with the programme on disability of the Division for Social Policy and Development of the Secretariat in the promotion of the rights of persons with disabilities, in-

cluding activities at the field level, by sharing experiences, findings and recommendations on persons with disabilities;

10. *Urges* Governments to cooperate with the Statistics Division of the Secretariat in the continued development of global statistics and indicators on disability, and encourages them to avail themselves of the technical assistance of the Division to build national capacities for national data collection systems, including the compilation and dissemination of data on disabled persons, as well as the development of methods for data collection and disability statistics, as appropriate;

11. *Urges* Governments, intergovernmental organizations and non-governmental organizations to provide special protection to girls and women with disabilities, elderly people with disabilities and persons with developmental and psychiatric disabilities, with special emphasis on integrating them into society and protecting and promoting their human rights;

12. *Urges* Governments, in collaboration with the United Nations system, to give special attention to the rights, needs and well-being of children with disabilities and their families in the development of policies and programmes, including the implementation of the Standard Rules;

13. *Encourages* Governments, intergovernmental organizations, concerned non-governmental organizations and the private sector to continue to support the United Nations Voluntary Fund on Disability with a view to strengthening its capacity to support catalytic and innovative activities to implement fully the World Programme of Action and the Standard Rules, including the work of the Special Rapporteur, and to support activities to build national capacities, with emphasis on priorities for action identified in the present resolution;

14. *Requests* the Secretary-General to continue to support initiatives of relevant bodies and organizations of the United Nations system, as well as those of regional, intergovernmental and non-governmental organizations and institutions, for the promotion of all human rights of, and non-discrimination in respect of, persons with disabilities and the further implementation of the World Programme of Action, as well as their efforts to integrate persons with disabilities in technical cooperation activities, both as beneficiaries and as decision makers;

15. *Expresses its appreciation* to the Secretary-General for his efforts in improving the accessibility of the United Nations for persons with disabilities, and urges him to continue to implement plans to provide a barrier-free environment;

16. *Welcomes* the preparations proposed by the Secretary-General in his current report for the fourth quinquennial review and appraisal of the World Programme of Action in 2002, including the proposed framework for that review, and requests the Secretary-General to submit to the General Assembly at its fifty-eighth session, through the Commission for Social Development and the Economic and Social Council, a report on the findings and recommendations based on the review and appraisal, including a report on the implementation of the present resolution.

Also on 19 December [meeting 88], the Assembly, on the recommendation of the Third Committee

[A/56/583/Add.2], adopted **resolution 56/168** without vote [agenda item 119 *(b)*].

Comprehensive and integral international convention to promote and protect the rights and dignity of persons with disabilities

The General Assembly,

Reaffirming the purposes and principles of the Charter of the United Nations and the obligations contained in the relevant human rights instruments,

Reaffirming also that the Universal Declaration of Human Rights proclaims that all human beings are born free and equal in dignity and rights, and that everyone is entitled to all the rights and freedoms set out therein, without distinction of any kind, such as race, colour, sex, language, religion, political or other opinion, national or social origin, property, birth or other status,

Recalling its resolution 37/52 of 3 December 1982, by which it adopted the World Programme of Action concerning Disabled Persons, its resolution 48/96 of 20 December 1993, by which it adopted the Standard Rules on the Equalization of Opportunities for Persons with Disabilities, and its resolution 54/121 of 17 December 1999,

Recalling also Economic and Social Council resolution 2000/10 of 27 July 2000 on further promotion of equalization of opportunities by, for and with persons with disabilities, as well as other relevant resolutions of the General Assembly, the Economic and Social Council and the functional commissions of the Council,

Reaffirming the outcomes of the major United Nations conferences and summits and their respective follow-up reviews, in particular as they pertain to the promotion of the rights and well-being of persons with disabilities on an equal and participatory basis,

Noting with satisfaction that the Standard Rules play an important role in influencing the promotion, formulation and evaluation of policies, plans, programmes and actions at the national, regional and international levels to further the equalization of opportunities by, for and with persons with disabilities,

Recognizing that, despite different efforts made to increase cooperation and integration and increasing awareness of and sensitivity to disability issues since the adoption of the World Programme of Action by Governments, bodies and relevant organizations of the United Nations system and non-governmental organizations, these efforts have not been sufficient to promote full and effective participation by and opportunities for persons with disabilities in economic, social, cultural and political life,

Encouraged by the increasing interest of the international community in the promotion and protection of the rights and dignity of persons with disabilities in the world under a comprehensive and integral approach,

Deeply concerned about the disadvantaged and vulnerable situation faced by 600 million persons with disabilities around the world, and conscious of the need to advance in the elaboration of an international instrument,

Looking forward to the final reports of the Special Rapporteur on disability of the Commission for Social Development to be presented to that Commission, and also the outcome of the study currently being undertaken pursuant to Commission on Human Rights resolution 2000/51 of 25 April 2000 on the adequacy of instruments in respect of the protection and monitoring of the human rights of persons with disabilities,

Taking into account the recommendation of the World Conference against Racism, Racial Discrimination, Xenophobia and Related Intolerance, held in Durban, South Africa, from 31 August to 8 September 2001, to the General Assembly to consider elaborating a comprehensive and integral international convention to promote and protect the rights and dignity of persons with disabilities, including special provisions that address the discriminatory practices and treatment that affect them,

1. *Decides* to establish an Ad Hoc Committee, open to the participation of all Member States and observers of the United Nations, to consider proposals for a comprehensive and integral international convention to promote and protect the rights and dignity of persons with disabilities, based on the holistic approach in the work done in the fields of social development, human rights and non-discrimination and taking into account the recommendations of the Commission on Human Rights and the Commission for Social Development;

2. *Also decides* that, prior to the fifty-seventh session of the General Assembly the Ad Hoc Committee shall hold at least one meeting of a duration of ten working days;

3. *Invites* States, relevant bodies and organizations of the United Nations system, including relevant human rights treaty bodies, the regional commissions, the Special Rapporteur on disability of the Commission for Social Development, as well as intergovernmental and non-governmental organizations with an interest in the matter to make contributions to the work entrusted to the Ad Hoc Committee, based on the practice of the United Nations;

4. *Requests* the Secretary-General, with the support of the Office of the United Nations High Commissioner for Human Rights and the Division for Social Policy and Development of the Department of Economic and Social Affairs of the Secretariat, to submit to the Ad Hoc Committee prior to its first session a compilation of existing international legal instruments, documents and programmes which directly or indirectly address the situation of persons with disabilities, including, inter alia, those of conferences, summits, meetings or international or regional seminars convened by the United Nations and intergovernmental and non-governmental organizations;

5. *Also requests* the Secretary-General to provide the Ad Hoc Committee with the outcome of the study undertaken pursuant to Commission on Human Rights resolution 2000/51 and the final reports that will be presented by the Special Rapporteur on disability of the Commission for Social Development to that Commission;

6. *Calls upon* States, in cooperation with regional commissions, the United Nations High Commissioner for Human Rights, the Division for Social Policy and Development and the Special Rapporteur on disability of the Commission for Social Development, to hold regional meetings or seminars to contribute to the work of the Ad Hoc Committee by making recommendations regarding the content and practical measures that should be considered in the international convention;

7. *Requests* the Secretary-General to provide the Ad Hoc Committee with the facilities necessary for the performance of its work;

8. *Also requests* the Secretary-General to submit a comprehensive report to the General Assembly at its fifty-seventh session on the progress made by the Ad Hoc Committee.

Cultural development

United Nations Year of Dialogue among Civilizations

General Assembly action. By **resolution 56/3** of 30 October, the General Assembly decided to convene its plenary meetings devoted to the United Nations Year of Dialogue among Civilizations (2001) not on the dates designated by resolution 55/23 [YUN 2000, p. 1039], but on 8 and 9 November. Accordingly, the Assembly devoted its meetings on those dates to the observance of the Year, aimed at promoting tolerance, trust, understanding and respect for cultural diversity. Proclaimed by resolution 53/22 [YUN 1998, p. 1031], the Year was intended to encourage initiatives by Governments, the UN system and other relevant international and non-governmental organizations to celebrate mutual respect, defuse the fear of diversity and underline the importance of inclusion.

Report of Secretary-General. Pursuant to Assembly resolution 55/23, the Secretary-General reported in November on activities pertaining to the Year [A/56/523]. A dialogue among civilizations had engendered wide interest among academic and international institutions and NGOs. UNESCO, instrumental in fostering that interest, carried out a broad range of activities in cooperation with Member States, intergovernmental organizations and NGOs, including the holding of conferences and seminars, together with Governments, civil society and other UN organizations. The United Nations University also organized conferences, workshops and other events, such as an essay contest for children entitled "Dialogue beyond Borders". A substantive contribution to the dialogue was the publication of a book entitled *Crossing the Divide, Dialogue among Civilizations,* the result of collaboration among the Secretary-General's Personal Representative for the Year, the UNESCO Director-General and the Group of Eminent Persons established by the Secretary-General.

Among major events launched in celebration and support of the Year were the Salzburg Dialogue among Civilizations: a New Paradigm of International Relations, hosted by Austria in Schloss Fuschl (28 August), which issued a document entitled "Salzburg Reflections" [A/56/419];

a UNESCO-sponsored international conference in Vilnius, Lithuania (24-26 April); and another conference in Tokyo and Kyoto, Japan (31 July-3 August). The Secretary-General remarked that the conferences and activities had shown that the United Nations remained the natural home of dialogue among civilizations, essential for achieving one of the main UN objectives, namely, conflict prevention.

Communications. Several other countries addressed communications to the Secretary-General reporting their activities in observance of the Year. The Czech Republic transmitted the text of the Prague Declaration adopted by the Fifth Forum 2000 Conference (14-17 October 2001) [A/56/498]; Iran forwarded the Tehran Declaration, adopted by the International Seminar on Environment, Religion and Culture (18-20 June) [A/56/458]; and China submitted a summary of the Twenty-first Century Forum—Symposium on Dialogue among Civilizations (Beijing, 11-12 September) [A/56/471].

GENERAL ASSEMBLY ACTION

On 9 November [meeting 43], the General Assembly adopted **resolution 56/6** [draft: A/56/L.3 & Add.1] without vote [agenda item 25].

Global Agenda for Dialogue among Civilizations

The General Assembly,

Recalling its resolutions 53/22 of 4 November 1998, 54/113 of 10 December 1999 and 55/23 of 13 November 2000 entitled "United Nations Year of Dialogue among Civilizations",

Reaffirming the purposes and principles embodied in the Charter of the United Nations, which are, inter alia, to develop friendly relations among nations based on respect for the principle of equal rights and self-determination of peoples, to take other appropriate measures to strengthen universal peace, and to achieve international cooperation in solving international problems of an economic, social, cultural or humanitarian character, and in promoting and encouraging respect for human rights and for fundamental freedoms for all without distinction as to race, sex, language or religion,

Underlining the fact that all Members have undertaken to refrain in their international relations from the threat or use of force against the territorial integrity or political independence of any State, or in any other manner inconsistent with the purposes of the United Nations,

Reaffirming their commitment to the fulfilment of the Universal Declaration of Human Rights as a common standard of achievement for all peoples and all nations and as a source of inspiration for the further promotion and protection of all human rights and fundamental freedoms—political, social, economic, civil and cultural—including the right to development,

Underlining the fact that all civilizations celebrate the unity and diversity of humankind and are enriched and have evolved through dialogue with other civiliza-

tions and that, despite obstacles of intolerance and aggression, there has been constructive interaction throughout history among various civilizations,

Emphasizing that a common humanity unites all civilizations and allows for the celebration of the variegated splendour of the highest attainments of this civilizational diversity, and reaffirming that the civilizational achievements constitute the collective heritage of humankind,

Recalling the United Nations Millennium Declaration of 8 September 2000, which considers, inter alia, that tolerance is one of the fundamental values essential to international relations in the twenty-first century and should include the active promotion of a culture of peace and dialogue among civilizations, with human beings respecting one another, in all their diversity of belief, culture and language, neither fearing nor repressing differences within and between societies but cherishing them as a precious asset of humanity,

Noting that globalization brings greater interrelatedness among people and increased interaction among cultures and civilizations, and encouraged by the fact that the celebration of the United Nations Year of Dialogue among Civilizations, at the beginning of the twenty-first century, has underscored that globalization is not only an economic, financial and technological process which could offer great benefit but that it also presents the challenge of preserving and celebrating the rich intellectual and cultural diversity of humankind and of civilization,

Bearing in mind the valuable contribution that dialogue among civilizations can make to an improved awareness and understanding of the common values shared by all humankind,

Recognizing that human rights and fundamental freedoms derive from the dignity and worth inherent in the human person and are thus universal, indivisible, interdependent and interrelated, and that the human person is the central subject of human rights and fundamental freedoms and, consequently, should be the principal beneficiary and should participate actively in the realization of these rights and freedoms,

Reaffirming that all peoples have the right of self-determination, by virtue of which they freely determine their political status and freely pursue their economic, social and cultural development,

Emphasizing that promotion and protection of freedom of opinion and expression and a collective commitment to listen to and learn from each other and to respect cultural heritage and diversity are essential for dialogue, progress and human advancement,

Underlining the fact that tolerance and respect for diversity and universal promotion and protection of human rights are mutually supportive, and recognizing that tolerance and respect for diversity effectively promote and are supported by, inter alia, the empowerment of women,

Recalling its resolution 55/254 of 31 May 2001, which calls upon all States to exert their utmost efforts to ensure that religious sites are fully respected and protected,

Emphasizing the need to acknowledge and respect the richness of all civilizations and to seek common ground among civilizations in order to address comprehensively common challenges facing humanity,

Welcoming the endeavours of Governments, international organizations, civil society organizations and countless individuals to enhance understanding through constructive dialogue among civilizations,

Welcoming also the efforts of the Personal Representative of the Secretary-General for the United Nations Year of Dialogue among Civilizations and of the Group of Eminent Persons established by the Secretary-General,

Expressing its firm determination to facilitate and promote dialogue among civilizations,

Proclaims the Global Agenda for Dialogue among Civilizations:

A. Objectives, principles and participants

Article 1

Dialogue among civilizations is a process between and within civilizations, founded on inclusion, and a collective desire to learn, uncover and examine assumptions, unfold shared meaning and core values and integrate multiple perspectives through dialogue.

Article 2

Dialogue among civilizations constitutes a process to attain, inter alia, the following objectives:

- Promotion of inclusion, equity, equality, justice and tolerance in human interactions;
- Enhancement of mutual understanding and respect through interaction among civilizations;
- Mutual enrichment and advancement of knowledge and appreciation of the richness and wisdom found in all civilizations;
- Identification and promotion of common ground among civilizations in order to address common challenges threatening shared values, universal human rights and achievements of human society in various fields;
- Promotion and protection of all human rights and fundamental freedoms and enrichment of common understanding of human rights;
- Development of a better understanding of common ethical standards and universal human values;
- Enhancement of respect for cultural diversity and cultural heritage.

Article 3

Pursuit of the above-mentioned objectives will be enhanced by collective commitment to the following principles:

- Faith in fundamental human rights, in the dignity and worth of the human person, in the equal rights of men and women and of nations large and small;
- Fulfilment in good faith of the obligations under the Charter of the United Nations and the Universal Declaration of Human Rights;
- Respect for fundamental principles of justice and international law;
- Recognition of diversified sources of knowledge and cultural diversity as fundamental features of human society and as indispensable and cherished assets for the advancement and material and spiritual welfare of humanity at large;
- Recognition of the right of members of all civilizations to preserve and develop their cultural heritage within their own societies;

- Commitment to inclusion, cooperation and the search for understanding as the mechanisms for the promotion of common values;
- Enhancement of participation by all individuals, peoples and nations in local, national and international decision-making processes.

Article 4

Dialogue among civilizations provides important contributions to progress in the following areas:

- Promotion of confidence-building at local, national, regional and international levels;
- Enhancing mutual understanding and knowledge among different social groups, cultures and civilizations in various areas, including culture, religion, education, information, science and technology;
- Addressing threats to peace and security;
- Promotion and protection of human rights;
- Elaboration of common ethical standards.

Article 5

Participation in dialogue among civilizations shall be global in scope and shall be open to all, including:

- People from all civilizations;
- Scholars, thinkers, intellectuals, writers, scientists, people of arts, culture and media and the youth, who play an instrumental role in initiation and sustainment of dialogue among civilizations;
- Individuals from civil society and representatives of non-governmental organizations, as instrumental partners in promoting dialogue among civilizations.

Article 6

Governments shall promote, encourage and facilitate dialogue among civilizations.

Article 7

Regional and international organizations should take appropriate steps and initiatives to promote, facilitate and sustain dialogue among civilizations.

Article 8

The media has an indispensable and instrumental role in the promotion of dialogue among civilizations and in the fostering of greater understanding among various civilizations and cultures.

Article 9

The United Nations should continue to promote and strengthen the culture of dialogue among civilizations.

B. Programme of Action

1. States, the United Nations system and other international and regional organizations and civil society, including non-governmental organizations, are invited to consider the following as a means of promoting dialogue among civilizations in all domains, within existing resources and also drawing upon voluntary contributions:

- Facilitating and encouraging interaction and exchange among all individuals, inter alia, intellectuals, thinkers and artists of various societies and civilizations;
- Promoting of mutual visits and meetings of experts in various fields from different civilizations, cultures and backgrounds, which provide an op-

portunity for discovering commonalities among various civilizations and cultures;

- Exchange of visits among representatives of the arts and culture and the organization of cultural festivals through which people will have a chance of getting acquainted with other cultures;
- Sponsorship of conferences, symposiums and workshops to enhance mutual understanding, tolerance and dialogue among civilizations;
- Planning sports competitions, Olympiads and scientific competitions, with a view to encouraging positive interaction among youth from different backgrounds and cultures;
- Reinvigorating and encouraging translation and dissemination of basic manuscripts and books and studies representing different cultures and civilizations;
- Promotion of historical and cultural tourism;
- Incorporation of programmes to study various cultures and civilizations in educational curriculums, including the teaching of languages, history and socio-political thoughts of various civilizations, as well as the exchange of knowledge, information and scholarship among academia;
- Advancement of research and scholarship to achieve an objective understanding of the characteristics of each civilization and the differences, as well as ways and means to enhance constructive interaction and understanding among them;
- Utilization of communication technologies, including audio, video, printed press, multimedia and the Internet, to disseminate the message of dialogue and understanding throughout the globe and depict and publicize historical instances of constructive interaction among different civilizations;
- Provision of equitable opportunities for participation in the dissemination of information, with a view to achieving an objective understanding of all civilizations and enhancing constructive interaction and cooperative engagement among civilizations;
- Implementation of programmes to enhance the spirit of dialogue, understanding and rejection of intolerance, violence and racism among people, particularly the youth;
- Utilizing the existence of migrants in various societies in bridging the gap of understanding between cultures;
- Consultation to articulate effective mechanisms to protect the rights of all people to maintain their cultural identity, while facilitating their integration into their social environment.

2. States should encourage and support initiatives taken by civil society and non-governmental organizations for the promotion of dialogue among civilizations.

3. States, international and regional organizations and civil society, including non-governmental organizations, are invited to develop appropriate ways and means at the local, national, regional and international levels to further promote dialogue and mutual understanding among civilizations, and to report their activities to the Secretary-General of the United Nations.

4. Governments, funding institutions, civil society organizations and the private sector are invited to mobilize the necessary resources to promote dialogue among civilizations, including by contributing to the Trust Fund established by the Secretary-General in 1999 for that purpose.

5. The United Nations system, including, in particular, the Personal Representative of the Secretary-General for the United Nations Year of Dialogue among Civilizations and the United Nations Educational, Scientific and Cultural Organization, are invited to continue to encourage and facilitate dialogue among civilizations and formulate ways and means to promote dialogue among civilizations in the activities of the United Nations in various fields.

6. The Secretary-General is requested to report to the General Assembly at its sixtieth session on the implementation of this Global Agenda and Programme of Action.

Human rights and cultural diversity

In December, by **resolution 56/156**, the General Assembly asked the Secretary-General to prepare a report on human rights and cultural diversity, taking into account the views of Member States, relevant UN agencies and NGOs regarding the recognition and importance of cultural diversity among all peoples and nations of the world, and to submit it to the Assembly at its fifty-seventh (2002) session.

(For further information on human rights and cultural diversity, see p. 621.)

United Nations Year for Cultural Heritage, 2002

By a letter of 20 September [A/56/231], 11 States requested the inclusion in the agenda of the General Assembly's fifty-sixth (2001) session of an additional item entitled "United Nations Year for Cultural Heritage, 2002". Annexed to the letter was an explanatory memorandum.

GENERAL ASSEMBLY ACTION

On 21 November [meeting 61], the General Assembly adopted **resolution 56/8** [draft: A/56/L.13 & Add.1] without vote [agenda item 177].

United Nations Year for Cultural Heritage, 2002
The General Assembly,

Recalling the international conventions dealing with the protection of cultural and natural heritage, including the Convention for the Protection of Cultural Property in the Event of Armed Conflict adopted at The Hague in 1954 and the two Protocols thereto, the 1970 Convention on the Means of Prohibiting and Preventing the Illicit Import, Export and Transfer of Ownership of Cultural Property, and the 1972 Convention for the Protection of the World Cultural and Natural Heritage, and recalling also the 1989 Recommendation on the Safeguarding of Traditional Culture and Folklore,

Welcoming the ratification of the Convention for the Protection of the World Cultural and Natural Heritage by one hundred and sixty-seven States parties, and noting the inscription of more than six hundred and ninety sites on the World Heritage List,

Mindful of the importance of protecting the world cultural tangible and intangible heritage as a common ground for the promotion of mutual understanding and enrichment among cultures and civilizations,

Noting the work already undertaken to protect the world cultural and natural heritage by the United Nations Educational, Scientific and Cultural Organization, including international campaigns,

Welcoming the decisions adopted at the twenty-ninth and thirty-first sessions of the General Conference of the United Nations Educational, Scientific and Cultural Organization and the one hundred and sixty-first session of the Executive Board of the United Nations Educational, Scientific and Cultural Organization envisaging and calling for the proclamation of a United Nations year for cultural heritage,

Taking into consideration the thirtieth anniversary of the Convention for the Protection of the World Cultural and Natural Heritage in 2002,

1. *Proclaims* 2002 as the United Nations Year for Cultural Heritage;

2. *Invites* the United Nations Educational, Scientific and Cultural Organization to serve as the lead agency for the year;

3. *Also invites* the United Nations Educational, Scientific and Cultural Organization, in collaboration with States, observers, relevant United Nations bodies, within their respective mandates, other international organizations and relevant non-governmental organizations, to intensify the implementation of programmes, activities and projects aimed at the promotion and protection of the world cultural heritage;

4. *Invites* Member States and observers to promote education and raise public awareness to foster respect for the national and world cultural heritage;

5. *Calls upon* Member States, observers, national and international organizations, non-governmental organizations and the private sector to make voluntary contributions to finance and support activities aimed at the promotion and protection of the national and world cultural heritage, including relevant activities of the United Nations Educational, Scientific and Cultural Organization;

6. *Decides* to devote one day of plenary meetings at the fifty-seventh session of the General Assembly, on 4 December 2002, to mark the end of the United Nations Year for Cultural Heritage, and encourages Member States and observers to be represented in those meetings at the highest level possible;

7. *Requests* the Secretary-General to report to the General Assembly at its fifty-eighth session on the activities carried out during the United Nations Year for Cultural Heritage;

8. *Decides* to include in the provisional agenda of its fifty-seventh session an item entitled "United Nations Year for Cultural Heritage".

Cultural property

The Secretary-General, in September [A/56/413], transmitted the UNESCO Director-General's report on action taken by the organization to implement the 1999 recommendations of the Intergovernmental Committee for Promoting the Return of Cultural Property to its Countries of Origin or its Restitution in Case of Illicit Appropriation [YUN 1999, p. 1045]. Submitted in response to General Assembly resolution 54/190 [ibid.], the report also contained 10 recommendations adopted by the Committee at its eleventh session (Phnom Penh, Cambodia, 6-9 March 2001).

Addressed mainly to UNESCO and its Director-General, the recommendations called for: initiatives to promote ongoing bilateral discussions on the question of restitution of works of art and for steps to search for illicitly exported cultural and archaeological objects for return to their countries of origin; technical and financial support for the prohibition of the sale of illegally acquired artifacts and protection of archaeological sites; measures to promote the adoption and dissemination of the International Code of Ethics for Dealers in Cultural Property [YUN 2000, p. 1417] and Object-ID, the international standard for recording data on movable cultural property and identifying cultural objects; a strategy to promote the Committee's voluntary international fund for the return and restitution of cultural property [ibid.]; and support to Member States for the inventory of their cultural heritage so as to guarantee better national conservation and information dissemination on cultural property in the event of theft. Member States were asked to prevent trade in forged cultural objects not identified as replicas and to ensure that customs and border officials were fully trained to apply the rules of the 1970 UNESCO Convention on the Means of Prohibiting and Preventing the Illicit Import, Export and Transfer of Ownership of Cultural Property.

GENERAL ASSEMBLY ACTION

On 14 December [meeting 86], the General Assembly adopted **resolution 56/97** [draft: A/56/L.41/Rev.1 & Add.1] without vote [agenda item 33].

Return or restitution of cultural property to the countries of origin

The General Assembly,

Reaffirming the relevant provisions of the Charter of the United Nations,

Recalling its resolutions 3026 A (XXVII) of 18 December 1972, 3148(XXVIII) of 14 December 1973, 3187 (XXVIII) of 18 December 1973, 3391(XXX) of 19 November 1975, 31/40 of 30 November 1976, 32/18 of 11 November 1977, 33/50 of 14 December 1978, 34/64 of 29 November 1979, 35/127 and 35/128 of 11 December 1980, 36/64 of 27 November 1981, 38/34 of 25 November 1983, 40/19 of 21 November 1985, 42/7 of 22 October 1987, 44/18 of 6 November 1989, 46/10 of

22 October 1991, 48/15 of 2 November 1993, 50/56 of 11 December 1995, 52/24 of 25 November 1997 and 54/190 of 17 December 1999,

Bearing in mind its resolution 56/8 of 21 November 2001 on the proclamation of 2002 as the United Nations Year for Cultural Heritage,

Recalling the Convention for the Protection of Cultural Property in the Event of Armed Conflict, adopted at The Hague on 14 May 1954,

Recalling also the Convention on the Means of Prohibiting and Preventing the Illicit Import, Export and Transfer of Ownership of Cultural Property, adopted on 14 November 1970 by the General Conference of the United Nations Educational, Scientific and Cultural Organization,

Recalling further the Convention concerning the Protection of the World Cultural and Natural Heritage, adopted on 16 November 1972 by the General Conference of the United Nations Educational, Scientific and Cultural Organization,

Recalling the Convention on Stolen or Illegally Exported Cultural Objects, adopted in Rome on 24 June 1995 by the International Institute for the Unification of Private Law,

Recalling also the Medellin Declaration for Cultural Diversity and Tolerance and the Plan of Action on Cultural Cooperation, adopted at the first Meeting of the Ministers of Culture of the Movement of Non-Aligned Countries, held in Medellin, Colombia, on 4 and 5 September 1997,

Noting the adoption of the Universal Declaration on Cultural Diversity and the Action Plan for its implementation, adopted by the General Conference of the United Nations Educational, Scientific and Cultural Organization on 2 November 2001,

Welcoming the report of the Secretary-General submitted in cooperation with the Director-General of the United Nations Educational, Scientific and Cultural Organization,

Aware of the importance attached by some countries of origin to the return of cultural property that is of fundamental spiritual and cultural value to them, so that they may constitute collections representative of their cultural heritage,

Expressing concern at the illicit traffic in cultural property and its damage to the cultural heritage of nations,

Expressing concern also at the loss, destruction, removal, theft, pillage, illicit movement or misappropriation of and any acts of vandalism or damage directed against cultural property in areas of armed conflict and territories that are occupied, whether such conflicts are international or internal,

1. *Commends* the United Nations Educational, Scientific and Cultural Organization and the Intergovernmental Committee for Promoting the Return of Cultural Property to its Countries of Origin or its Restitution in Case of Illicit Appropriation on the work they have accomplished, in particular through the promotion of bilateral negotiations, for the return or restitution of cultural property, the preparation of inventories of movable cultural property and the implementation of the Object-ID standard related thereto, as well as for the reduction of illicit traffic in cultural property and the dissemination of information to the public;

2. *Reaffirms* the importance of the provisions of the Convention for the Protection of Cultural Property in the Event of Armed Conflict, and invites Member States that have not already done so to become parties to the Convention and to promote its implementation;

3. *Welcomes* the adoption of the Second Protocol to the Convention for the Protection of Cultural Property in the Event of Armed Conflict, adopted at The Hague on 26 March 1999, and invites all States Parties to the Convention to consider becoming parties to the Second Protocol;

4. *Invites* Member States to consider adopting and implementing the Convention on the Means of Prohibiting and Preventing the Illicit Import, Export and Transfer of Ownership of Cultural Property;

5. *Reaffirms* the importance of the provisions of the Convention on Stolen or Illegally Exported Cultural Objects, and invites Member States that have not already done so to consider becoming parties to it;

6. *Urges* Member States to introduce effective national and international measures to prevent and combat the illicit trafficking in cultural property;

7. *Calls upon* all relevant bodies, agencies, funds and programmes of the United Nations system and other relevant intergovernmental organizations to work in coordination with the United Nations Educational, Scientific and Cultural Organization, within their mandates and in cooperation with Member States, in order to continue to address the issue of return or restitution of cultural property to the countries of origin, and to provide appropriate support accordingly;

8. *Invites* Member States to continue drawing up, in cooperation with the United Nations Educational, Scientific and Cultural Organization, systematic inventories of their cultural property;

9. *Reaffirms* the efforts of the United Nations Educational, Scientific and Cultural Organization to promote the use of identification systems, in particular the application of the Object-ID standard, and to encourage the linking of identification systems and existing databases, including the one developed by the International Criminal Police Organization, to allow for the electronic transmission of information in order to reduce the illicit trafficking in cultural property, and encourages the United Nations Educational, Scientific and Cultural Organization to make further efforts in this regard in cooperation with Member States, where appropriate;

10. *Welcomes* the adoption of the International Code of Ethics for Dealers in Cultural Property by the General Conference of the United Nations Educational, Scientific and Cultural Organization on 16 November 1999, and takes note of the creation by the General Conference at the same session of the International Fund for the Return of Cultural Property to its Countries of Origin or its Restitution in Case of Illicit Appropriation, which was launched in November 2000 on the occasion of the thirtieth anniversary of the Convention on the Means of Prohibiting and Preventing the Illicit Import, Export and Transfer of Ownership of Cultural Property;

11. *Encourages* the Director-General of the United Nations Educational, Scientific and Cultural Organization to define and implement a strategy for the effective promotion of the International Fund, and invites

Member States, intergovernmental bodies, the private sector and other interested donors of the international community to make voluntary contributions to the Fund;

12. *Requests* the Secretary-General to cooperate with the United Nations Educational, Scientific and Cultural Organization in its efforts to develop all possibilities, including any further initiatives, for bringing about the attainment of the objectives of the present resolution;

13. *Also requests* the Secretary-General, in co-operation with the Director-General of the United Nations Educational, Scientific and Cultural Organization, to submit to the General Assembly at its fifty-eighth session a report on the implementation of the present resolution;

14. *Decides* to include in the provisional agenda of its fifty-eighth session the item entitled "Return or restitution of cultural property to the countries of origin".

Protection of cultural sites

Destruction of relics and monuments in Afghanistan

The Security Council, at its 6 March meeting held in private [meeting 4286], was briefed by the Secretariat on the destruction of statues, including the colossal Buddhas at Bamian, and other non-Islamic shrines and artifacts in Afghanistan. The Council condemned the 26 February Taliban edict ordering the wanton acts of violence on Afghanistan's cultural heritage and joined calls by States, the United Nations Special Mission to Afghanistan, UNESCO, the Islamic Educational, Scientific and Cultural Organization and others urging the Taliban to halt the destruction [S/2001/730] (see also p. 256).

Communications. Sweden forwarded a 1 March statement [A/55/831] by the EU Presidency expressing the EU's dismay at the Taliban edict. Qatar, on 4 March [A/55/822-S/2001/192], appealed to those concerned to reconsider the edict. The Republic of Korea, on 6 March [A/55/824], called on the Taliban leadership to put an immediate end to the destruction.

GENERAL ASSEMBLY ACTION

On 9 March [meeting 94], the General Assembly adopted **resolution 55/243** [draft: A/55/L.79 & Add.1] without vote [agenda item 46].

The destruction of relics and monuments in Afghanistan

The General Assembly,

Recalling its resolutions 53/203 A of 18 December 1998, 54/189 A of 17 December 1999 and 55/174 A of 19 December 2000,

Bearing in mind the International Covenant on Economic, Social and Cultural Rights and the need to respect the common heritage of humankind,

Respecting the multicultural, multi-ethnic and historical heritage of Afghanistan,

Deeply concerned and appalled by the Taliban edict of 26 February 2001, ordering the destruction of all statues and non-Islamic shrines in Afghanistan, and by the deliberate ongoing destruction of these relics and monuments which belong to the common heritage of humankind,

Recalling the several appeals made by the General Assembly to all Afghan parties to protect the cultural and historic relics and monuments in Afghanistan, and welcoming recent calls by the Security Council, the United Nations Special Mission to Afghanistan, the United Nations Educational, Scientific and Cultural Organization, the Islamic Educational, Scientific and Cultural Organization and others, urging the Taliban to halt their destruction,

Noting that the destruction of the statues in Afghanistan, in particular of the unique Buddhist sculptures in Bamiyan, would be an irreparable loss for humanity as a whole,

1. *Strongly calls upon* the Taliban to abide by their previous commitments to protect the cultural heritage of Afghanistan from all acts of vandalism, damage and theft;

2. *Strongly urges* the Taliban to review their edict of 26 February 2001 and to stop its implementation;

3. *Also strongly urges* the Taliban to take immediate action to prevent the further destruction of the irreplaceable relics, monuments or artefacts of the cultural heritage of Afghanistan;

4. *Calls upon* Member States to help, through appropriate technical measures, to safeguard the sculptures, including, if necessary, their temporary relocation or removal from public view.

Protection of religious sites

On 31 May [meeting 101], the General Assembly adopted **resolution 55/254** [draft: A/55/L.81 & Add.1] without vote [agenda item 32].

Protection of religious sites

The General Assembly,

Recalling its resolutions 53/22 of 4 November 1998, 54/113 of 10 December 1999 and 55/23 of 18 November 2000, entitled "United Nations Year of Dialogue among Civilizations",

Recalling also its resolution 36/55 of 25 November 1981, by which it proclaimed the Declaration on the Elimination of All Forms of Intolerance and of Discrimination Based on Religion or Belief, and its resolution 55/97 of 4 December 2000 on the elimination of all forms of religious intolerance,

Recalling further its resolutions 47/124 of 18 December 1992, 48/126 of 20 December 1993, 49/213 of 23 December 1994 and 51/95 of 12 December 1996, on the United Nations Year for Tolerance,

Bearing in mind the Universal Declaration of Human Rights, the International Covenant on Economic, Social and Cultural Rights and the International Covenant on Civil and Political Rights, as well as the pertinent universal and regional human rights instruments,

Bearing in mind also the relevant provisions of the Geneva Conventions of 1949 and the Additional Protocols thereto, of 1977, as well as the relevant provisions of the Hague Convention for the Protection of

Cultural Property in the Event of Armed Conflict of 1954,

Recalling the Vienna Declaration and Programme of Action adopted by the World Conference on Human Rights on 25 June 1993, which emphasizes the need to counter intolerance and related violence based on religion or belief, including the desecration of religious sites,

Recalling also the appeal of the United Nations Millennium Declaration of 8 September 2000 to respect the diversity of belief, culture and language, to cherish differences within and between societies as a precious asset of humanity and to promote a culture of peace and dialogue among all civilizations,

1. *Condemns* all acts or threats of violence, destruction, damage or endangerment, directed against religious sites as such, that continue to occur in the world;

2. *Calls upon* all States to exert their utmost efforts to ensure that religious sites are fully respected and protected in conformity with international standards and in accordance with their national legislation and to adopt adequate measures aimed at preventing such acts or threats of violence, and invites relevant intergovernmental and non-governmental organizations to contribute to those efforts by developing appropriate initiatives in this field;

3. *Encourages* all States, relevant intergovernmental and non-governmental organizations and the media to promote, inter alia, through education, a culture of tolerance and respect for the diversity of religions and for religious sites, which represent an important aspect of the collective heritage of humankind;

4. *Requests* the Secretary-General to devote, in consultation with the relevant bodies of the United Nations system, attention to the issue of protection of religious sites in his forthcoming reports related to the United Nations Year of Dialogue among Civilizations;

5. *Decides* to continue consideration of the question of the protection of religious sites under the item entitled "United Nations Year of Dialogue among Civilizations".

Olympic truce

On 11 December [meeting 83], the General Assembly adopted **resolution 56/75** [draft: A/56/L.47 & Add.1] without vote [agenda item 23].

Building a peaceful and better world through sport and the Olympic ideal

The General Assembly,

Recalling its decision to include in the provisional agenda of its fifty-sixth session the item entitled "Building a peaceful and better world through sport and the Olympic ideal" and to consider this item every two years in advance of each Summer and Winter Olympic Games,

Recalling also its resolution 48/11 of 25 October 1993, which, inter alia, revived the ancient Greek tradition of *ekecheiria* or "Olympic Truce" with the aim of ensuring the safe passage and participation of athletes and others at the Games,

Taking into account the inclusion in the United Nations Millennium Declaration of an appeal for the observance of the Olympic Truce now and in the future and support for the International Olympic Committee in its efforts to promote peace and human understanding through sport and the Olympic ideal,

Recognizing that the goal of the Olympic movement is to build a peaceful and better world by educating the youth of the world through sport, practised without discrimination of any kind and in the Olympic spirit, which requires mutual understanding, promoted by friendship, solidarity and fair play,

Recognizing also the valuable contribution that the appeal launched by the International Olympic Committee for an Olympic Truce, with which the National Olympic Committees of the Member States are associated, could make towards advancing the purposes and principles of the Charter of the United Nations,

Noting with satisfaction the flying of the United Nations flag at all competition sites of the Olympic Games, and the joint endeavours of the International Olympic Committee and the United Nations system in fields such as development, humanitarian assistance, health promotion, education, women, the eradication of poverty, the fight against the human immunodeficiency virus/acquired immunodeficiency syndrome (HIV/AIDS), drug abuse and juvenile delinquency,

Noting also with satisfaction the organization by the International Olympic Committee, with the cooperation of the Secretary-General, of round tables on sport for a culture of peace on different continents for countries that have been or are still in a conflict situation, in the framework of the International Year for the Culture of Peace and in accordance with General Assembly resolution 52/13 of 20 November 1997,

Welcoming the setting up by the International Olympic Committee, with the adherence of Member States and intergovernmental organizations, of a World Anti-Doping Agency,

1. *Requests* Member States to observe, within the framework of the Charter of the United Nations, the Olympic Truce during the XIX Olympic Winter Games to be held in Salt Lake City, United States of America, from 8 to 24 February 2002, by ensuring the safe passage and participation of athletes at the Games;

2. *Welcomes* the decision of the International Olympic Committee to mobilize all international sports organizations and that of the National Olympic Committees of the Member States to undertake concrete action at the local, national, regional and world levels to promote and strengthen a culture of peace based on the spirit of the Olympic Truce;

3. *Requests* the Secretary-General to promote the observance of the Olympic Truce among Member States, drawing the attention of world public opinion to the contribution such a truce would make to the promotion of international understanding, peace and goodwill, and to cooperate with the International Olympic Committee in the realization of this objective;

4. *Welcomes* the participation of the President in office of the General Assembly and also the representatives of the Secretary-General and the Director-General of the United Nations Educational, Scientific and Cultural Organization in the International Olympic Truce Foundation;

5. *Urges* the International Olympic Committee to devise a special programme of assistance for the development of physical education and sport for countries affected by conflicts and poverty;

6. *Decides* to include in the provisional agenda of its fifty-eighth session the item entitled "Building a peaceful and better world through sport and the Olympic ideal" and to consider this item before the Games of the XXVIII Olympiad, to be held in Athens in 2004.

On 24 December, the Assembly decided that the agenda item on building a peaceful and better world through sport and the Olympic ideal would remain for consideration during its resumed fifty-sixth (2002) session (**decision 56/464**).

Crime prevention and criminal justice

Commission on Crime Prevention and Criminal Justice

The Commission on Crime Prevention and Criminal Justice, at its tenth session (Vienna, 8-17 May and 6-7 September) [E/2001/30/Rev.1], recommended to the Economic and Social Council approval of four draft resolutions for adoption by the General Assembly and three draft resolutions and one draft decision for adoption by the Council. The draft texts included action against illicit trafficking in protected species of wild flora and fauna (see p. 968). In accordance with a 2000 Commission resolution [YUN 2000, p. 1044], a thematic discussion was held on progress made in global action against corruption, with particular focus on government initiatives and asset recovery (see p. 1042).

On 24 July, the Council took note of the Commission's report on its tenth session and approved the provisional agenda and documentation for the eleventh (2002) session (**decision 2001/240**). On 3 May, it had elected Chad and Zimbabwe to fill postponed vacancies on the Commission for a term expiring on 31 December 2003 (**decision 2001/201 B**).

On the question of capital punishment, the Secretary-General, in March, issued his sixth quinquennial report on the subject [E/CN.15/2001/10 & Corr.1], which reviewed trends in the application of the death penalty during 1994-2000. The report was considered by the Commission on Human Rights (see p. 638).

Follow-up to Tenth UN Crime Congress

As a follow-up to the Tenth (2000) United Nations Congress on the Prevention of Crime and the Treatment of Offenders [YUN 2000, p. 1040], the Commission on Crime Prevention and Criminal Justice, in May, considered the Secretary-General's March report [E/CN.15/2001/5] on draft plans of action for implementation during 2001-2005 of the Vienna Declaration on Crime and Justice: Meeting the Challenges of the Twenty-first Century, adopted by General Assembly resolution 55/59 [YUN 2000, p. 1041]. The plans outlined actions to be undertaken by Member States and the UN system in 11 areas: transnational organized crime; corruption; trafficking in persons; smuggling of migrants; illicit manufacturing of and trafficking in firearms; money-laundering; terrorism; crime prevention; witnesses and victims of crime; treatment of offenders; and criminal misuse of information technologies. Each draft plan was divided into national and international actions, with emphasis on the former.

Consideration of the draft plans continued at the Commission's intersessional meeting (Vienna, 3-5 September) on the basis of revised draft plans transmitted by a Secretariat note [E/CN.15/2001/14/Rev.2], which took account of the May discussions on the first six plans above and contained four additional draft plans of action submitted by Finland and Canada, covering juvenile justice; the special needs of women in the criminal justice system; standards and norms in crime prevention; and restorative justice.

ECONOMIC AND SOCIAL COUNCIL ACTION

On 20 December [meeting 46], the Economic and Social Council, on the recommendation of the Commission on Crime Prevention and Criminal Justice [E/2001/30/Rev.1], adopted **resolution 2001/47** without vote [agenda item 14 *(c)*].

Plans of action for the implementation of the Vienna Declaration on Crime and Justice: Meeting the Challenges of the Twenty-first Century

The Economic and Social Council

Recommends to the General Assembly the adoption of the following draft resolution:

"*The General Assembly*,

"*Recalling* its resolution 55/59 of 4 December 2000, in which it endorsed the Vienna Declaration on Crime and Justice: Meeting the Challenges of the Twenty-first Century, adopted by the Tenth United Nations Congress on the Prevention of Crime and the Treatment of Offenders,

"*Noting* that, in paragraph 29 of the Vienna Declaration, the Tenth Congress invited the Commission on Crime Prevention and Criminal Justice to design specific measures for the implementation of and follow-up to the commitments undertaken in the Declaration,

"*Recalling* that, in its resolution 55/60 of 4 December 2000, it urged Governments, in their efforts to prevent and combat crime, to be guided by the results of the Tenth Congress, and requested the Secretary-General to prepare, in consultation with Member States, draft plans of action for the implementation of and follow-up to the commitments undertaken in the Vienna Declaration for consideration and action by the Commission on Crime Prevention and Criminal Justice at its tenth session,

"1. *Takes note with appreciation* of the plans of action for the implementation of the Vienna Declaration on Crime and Justice: Meeting the Challenges of the Twenty-first Century, which are contained in the annex to the present resolution;

"2. *Notes with appreciation* the work of the Commission on Crime Prevention and Criminal Justice at its ninth and tenth sessions on the preparation of the plans of action for the implementation of the Vienna Declaration;

"3. *Requests* the Secretary-General to ensure the widest possible circulation of the plans of action;

"4. *Invites* Governments to consider carefully and use, as appropriate, the plans of action as a guide in their efforts to formulate legislation, policies and programmes in the field of crime prevention and criminal justice, for the purpose of implementing and following up on the commitments undertaken in the Vienna Declaration;

"5. *Invites* the Secretary-General, in close cooperation with relevant intergovernmental organizations and non-governmental organizations, to consider carefully and implement, as appropriate, the plans of action as a guide in developing policies and programmes in the field of crime prevention and criminal justice, in accordance with the medium-term plans and the programme budgets and subject to available resources;

"6. *Invites* the Secretariat to discuss with the institutes of the United Nations Crime Prevention and Criminal Justice Programme network their possible contribution to the implementation of the plans of action, under the coordination of the Commission on Crime Prevention and Criminal Justice;

"7. *Invites* Member States and regional and international institutions, including financial institutions, to strengthen the Programme through sustained funding and other technical support activities in order to assist interested States in the field of crime prevention and criminal justice, as appropriate;

"8. *Invites* the Commission to follow up the implementation of the plans of action and to make any recommendations, as appropriate.

"**Annex**
"**Plans of action for the implementation of the Vienna Declaration on Crime and Justice: Meeting the Challenges of the Twenty-first Century**

"**I. Action against transnational organized crime**

"1. In order to implement and follow up on the commitments undertaken in paragraphs 5, 6, 7 and 10 of the Vienna Declaration on Crime and Justice: Meeting the Challenges of the Twenty-first Century and to facilitate the signature, ratification, entry into force and progressive implementation of the United Nations Convention against Transnational Organized Crime and the Protocols thereto, the specific measures set out below are recommended.

"**A. National actions**

"2. States that have not signed the Convention and the protocols thereto should do so as soon as possible, and States that have signed those legal instruments should make every effort to ratify them as soon as possible. Each State will set priorities for the effective implementation of the Convention and the protocols thereto

and will proceed as appropriate and as expeditiously as possible until all the provisions of all of those legal instruments are in full force and operation. Individually and collectively, States will endeavour, as appropriate, to support the following actions:

"*(a)* The development of legislation creating or strengthening sanctions, investigative powers, criminal procedures and other matters;

"*(b)* Capacity-building, including for the purpose of cooperation, through the strengthening of crime prevention and criminal justice systems, and the establishment or expansion of agencies responsible for the prevention, detection and control of transnational organized crime;

"*(c)* The establishment or improvement of training programmes for judges, prosecutors, law enforcement personnel and other individuals or agencies responsible for the prevention, detection and control of transnational organized crime;

"*(d)* The development and sharing of information and analytical expertise on methods and activities and general trends in organized crime and on the identities, whereabouts and activities of specific individuals or groups suspected of involvement in organized crime, to the extent consistent with national laws and international agreements and arrangements;

"*(e)* The general promotion of effective crime control strategies.

"3. States will also endeavour, as appropriate:

"*(a)* To support the efforts of the Centre for International Crime Prevention of the Office for Drug Control and Crime Prevention of the Secretariat to promote ratification of the Convention and the protocols thereto through regional seminars and provide pre- and post-ratification assistance to signatory States by providing financial contributions, expertise and/or other forms of assistance;

"*(b)* To increase in a sustained manner their overall level of extrabudgetary contributions and strengthen and broaden the donor base of the Centre in order to ensure the availability of adequate material and technical resources for projects in support of the Convention and the protocols thereto, as well as other projects and programmes;

"*(c)* To strengthen international cooperation in order to create a conducive environment for the fight against organized crime, promoting growth and sustainable development and eradicating poverty and unemployment.

"**B. International actions**

"4. The Centre for International Crime Prevention will, in cooperation with other relevant international and regional organizations, as appropriate, and in accordance with the present resolution:

"*(a)* Organize high-level seminars to increase awareness of the Convention and the protocols thereto on the part of States, intergovernmental and non-governmental organizations and other key groups or individuals;

"*(b)* Assist States in the development of legislation and regulations and provide other expertise or technical cooperation to facilitate the ratification and implementation of the legal instruments, on request;

"*(c)* Assist States in the establishment or intensification of bilateral and multilateral cooperation in the areas covered by the Convention, in particular those involving the use of modern communication technologies, on request;

"(d) Carry out the regular collection and analysis of data on transnational organized crime, in consultation with interested States;

"(e) Maintain a database to permit a more comprehensive in-depth analysis of patterns and trends and geographical mapping of the strategies and activities carried out by organized criminal groups, and of best practices to combat transnational organized crime, in consultation with interested States;

"(f) Maintain a database of relevant national legislation;

"(g) Support the Ad Hoc Committee on the Elaboration of a Convention against Transnational Organized Crime in the development of rules and procedures for the Conference of the Parties to the Convention;

"(h) Provide secretariat and general support to the Conference of the Parties to the Convention.

"II. Action against corruption

"5. In order to implement and follow up on the commitments undertaken in paragraph 16 of the Vienna Declaration to develop an effective international legal instrument against corruption and to develop and implement other measures and programmes to prevent and combat corruption, the specific measures below are recommended.

"A. National actions

"6. Individually and collectively, States will endeavour, as appropriate, to support the following actions:

"(a) Full participation in sessions of the Ad Hoc Committee for the Negotiation of a Convention against Corruption established pursuant to General Assembly resolution 55/61 of 4 December 2000;

"(b) Promoting the full and effective participation of developing countries, in particular least developed countries, in the deliberations of the Ad Hoc Committee; this may be done through the provision of extrabudgetary resources to the Centre for International Crime Prevention;

"(c) Making efforts to finalize the future United Nations convention against corruption by the end of 2003, taking into consideration existing legal instruments against corruption and, whenever relevant, the United Nations Convention against Transnational Organized Crime;

"(d) Commencing, when appropriate, the development of domestic legislative, administrative and other measures to facilitate the ratification and effective implementation of the future United Nations convention against corruption, including both domestic measures against corruption and measures to support effective cooperation with other States.

"7. States will endeavour, as appropriate, to address domestic corruption through the following measures:

"(a) The assessment of domestic types, causes, effects and costs of corruption;

"(b) The development of national strategies and action plans against corruption, based on the broad participation of stakeholders from government and civil society;

"(c) The maintenance or establishment of adequate domestic offences, investigative powers and criminal procedures to deal with corruption and related problems;

"(d) The strengthening of national governance systems and institutions, in particular criminal justice institutions, to create and/or ensure greater independence from and resistance to corrupt influences;

"(e) The maintenance or establishment of institutions and structures to achieve transparency and public accountability in government, business and other key social and economic sectors;

"(f) The development of expertise in anti-corruption measures and the education and training of officials about the nature and consequences of corruption and how to combat it effectively.

"8. States will endeavour, as appropriate, to address transnational corruption with the following measures:

"(a) The signature, ratification and implementation of existing international instruments against corruption, as appropriate;

"(b) Proper follow-up to international anti-corruption measures and recommendations at the national level, in conformity with national law;

"(c) The development and enhancement of domestic capacity to provide international cooperation in anti-corruption matters, including addressing the question of the repatriation of proceeds of corruption;

"(d) Awareness-raising on the part of relevant government departments or ministries such as ministries of justice, the interior, foreign affairs and development cooperation as to the seriousness of the problems posed by transnational corruption and the need to support effective measures against it;

"(e) The provision of material, technical or other support to other States in anti-corruption programmes, both directly and through financial support to the global programme against corruption;

"(f) The reduction of opportunities for the transfer and concealment of proceeds of corruption and measures to address the question of returning such proceeds to their countries of origin; actions may include ensuring the implementation of measures against money-laundering, pursuant to the United Nations Convention against Transnational Organized Crime and other international legal instruments, and the development and implementation of new measures.

"B. International actions

"9. The Centre for International Crime Prevention will, in cooperation with other relevant international and regional organizations, as appropriate, and in accordance with the present resolution:

"(a) Provide substantive expertise and full secretariat services to the Ad Hoc Committee for the Negotiation of a Convention against Corruption in the course of its work;

"(b) Ensure, with the assistance of Member States, the full and effective participation of developing countries, in particular least developed countries, in the work of the Ad Hoc Committee, including by covering travel and local expenses;

"(c) Provide to States, on request, technical cooperation to facilitate the ratification and implementation of the future United Nations convention against corruption;

"(d) Assist States in the establishment or intensification of bilateral and multilateral cooperation in the areas to be covered by the future United Nations convention against corruption;

"(e) Maintain a database of existing national assessments of corruption in a standardized format and a kit of best practices against corruption;

"(f) Facilitate the sharing of experience and expertise among States;

"(g) Revise and update the manual on practical measures against corruption;

"(h) Develop technical cooperation projects to prevent and combat corruption in order to assist States, upon request, in implementing such projects under the global programme against corruption.

"III. Action against trafficking in persons

"10. In order to implement and follow up on the commitments undertaken in paragraph 14 of the Vienna Declaration to take immediate and effective measures to prevent and combat trafficking in persons, especially women and children, and to promote cooperation between States in this respect, the specific measures below are recommended.

"A. National actions

"11. Individually and collectively, States will endeavour, as appropriate, to support the following actions:

"(a) Developing and sharing information and analytical expertise on the nature and extent of domestic and regional trafficking activities and on the identities, means and methods of known traffickers or trafficking organizations, to the extent consistent with national laws and international agreements and arrangements;

"(b) Adopting or strengthening, as necessary, effective laws and procedures for the prevention and punishment of trafficking in persons and effective measures for the support and protection of victims and witnesses of such trafficking;

"(c) Considering implementing measures to provide for the protection and physical, psychological and social recovery of victims of trafficking in persons;

"(d) Supporting and cooperating with national and international non-governmental and other organizations and elements of civil society, as appropriate, in matters relating to trafficking in persons;

"(e) Reviewing and assessing the effectiveness of domestic measures against trafficking in persons, and considering making that information available for comparison and research into the development of more effective measures against such trafficking;

"(f) Developing and disseminating public information about trafficking in persons, to educate potential victims of such trafficking;

"(g) Strengthening capacity for international cooperation to develop and implement measures against trafficking in persons;

"(h) Considering providing voluntary contributions to support the implementation of the global programme against trafficking in human beings;

"(i) Providing increased resources to support the development and implementation of national and regional strategies against trafficking in persons.

"B. International actions

"12. The Centre for International Crime Prevention will, in cooperation with other relevant international and regional organizations, as appropriate, and in accordance with the present resolution:

"(a) Develop technical cooperation projects to prevent and combat trafficking in persons and to protect the victims and witnesses of such trafficking, in order to assist States, upon request, in implementing such projects under the global programme against trafficking in human beings;

"(b) Maintain a global database containing information about the nature and extent of trafficking in persons and best practices for preventing and controlling it, in cooperation with the United Nations Interregional Crime and Justice Research Institute;

"(c) Develop tools to assess the effectiveness of measures against trafficking in persons.

"IV. Action against smuggling of migrants

"13. In order to implement and follow up the commitments undertaken in paragraph 14 of the Vienna Declaration and to take immediate and effective measures to prevent and combat the smuggling of migrants, and to promote cooperation between States in this respect, the specific measures below are recommended.

"A. National actions

"14. Individually and collectively, States will endeavour, as appropriate, to support the following actions:

"(a) Developing and sharing information and analytical expertise on the nature and extent of domestic and regional activities relating to the smuggling of migrants and on the identities, means and methods of known smugglers or smuggling organizations, to the extent consistent with national laws and international agreements and arrangements;

"(b) Enacting and strengthening, as necessary, effective laws for the prevention and punishment of the smuggling of migrants, and measures for the support and protection of the rights of smuggled migrants and of witnesses in smuggling cases, in conformity with the Protocol against the Smuggling of Migrants by Land, Sea and Air, supplementing the United Nations Convention against Transnational Organized Crime;

"(c) Implementing measures to protect the basic rights of smuggled migrants and, within their means, of witnesses in smuggling cases, to protect them from violence and take appropriate measures in cases where, in the course of being smuggled, the lives, safety or human dignity of migrants are placed in jeopardy;

"(d) Supporting and cooperating with national and international non-governmental and other organizations and elements of civil society, as appropriate, in matters relating to the smuggling of migrants;

"(e) Reviewing and assessing the effectiveness of domestic measures against the smuggling of migrants, and considering making that information available for comparison and research into the development of more effective measures;

"(f) Developing and disseminating public information about the smuggling of migrants, to educate officials, the general public and potential migrants about the true nature of such smuggling, including the involvement of organized criminal groups and the risks posed to smuggled migrants;

"(g) Strengthening capacity for international cooperation to develop and implement measures against the smuggling of migrants.

"B. International actions

"15. The Centre for International Crime Prevention will, in cooperation with other relevant international and regional organizations, as appropriate, and in accordance with the present resolution, develop technical cooperation projects to prevent and combat the smuggling of migrants, while protecting the rights of smuggled migrants, in order to assist States, upon request, in implementing such projects.

"V. Action against the illicit manufacturing of and trafficking in firearms, their parts and components and ammunition

"16. In order to implement and follow up on the commitments undertaken in paragraph 15 of the Vienna Declaration and to take such immediate and effective measures as are appropriate to reduce the incidence of the illicit manufacturing of and trafficking in firearms, their parts and components and ammunition and related criminal activities, in accordance with the terms of the Protocol against the Illicit Manufacturing of and Trafficking in Firearms, Their Parts and Components and Ammunition, supplementing the United Nations Convention against Transnational Organized Crime, the specific measures below are recommended.

"A. National actions

"17. Individually and collectively, States will endeavour, as appropriate, to support the following actions:

"(a) Adopting and strengthening, as necessary, national legislation and procedures, and in particular procedures regarding criminal offences and procedures for the confiscation, seizure, forfeiture and disposal of firearms, their parts and components and ammunition;

"(b) Implementing requirements to keep records regarding firearms, the marking of firearms and the deactivation of firearms;

"(c) Establishing or maintaining effective systems for the licensing or authorization of the import, export and transit of firearms, their parts and components and ammunition;

"(d) Establishing appropriate legal and administrative measures with a view to preventing the loss, theft or diversion of firearms, for the exchange of relevant information relating to firearms and for bilateral, regional and international cooperation, including by means of information exchange and technical assistance;

"(e) Considering the establishment of an effective regulatory framework for the activities of those engaged in the brokering of transactions involving the import, export or transit of firearms.

"B. International actions

"18. The Centre for International Crime Prevention will, in cooperation with other relevant international and regional organizations, as appropriate, and in accordance with the present resolution:

"(a) Develop technical cooperation projects to prevent, combat and eradicate the illicit trafficking in firearms, their parts and components and ammunition and related activities, in order to assist requesting States, in particular developing countries and countries with economies in transition, in implementing such projects;

"(b) Establish and maintain a global database of existing national and regional firearms regulations and related law enforcement practices, as well as best practices relating to firearms control measures.

"VI. Action against money-laundering

"19. In order to implement and follow up the commitments undertaken in paragraph 17 of the Vienna Declaration and to develop, adopt and implement effective domestic legislation, regulations and administrative measures to prevent, detect and combat, in cooperation with other States, domestic and transnational money-laundering, in accordance with the relevant international instruments, in particular the United Nations Convention against Transnational Organized Crime, and using as a guideline the relevant initiatives of regional, interregional and multilateral organizations against money-laundering, the specific measures below are recommended.

"A. National actions

"20. Individually and collectively, States will endeavour, as appropriate, to support the following actions:

"(a) Adopting comprehensive measures to deal effectively with the problem of money-laundering in all its aspects, with the participation of all relevant ministries, departments and agencies and in consultation with representatives of the financial sector;

"(b) Making efforts to ensure that domestic legislation adequately criminalizes activities and methods used to conceal, convert or transfer the proceeds of crime in order to disguise the nature or origin of the proceeds, in accordance with article 6 of the United Nations Convention against Transnational Organized Crime;

"(c) Making efforts to ensure that adequate regulatory, inspection and investigative powers exist to detect and identify money-laundering activities;

"(d) Making efforts to ensure that adequate investigative and judicial powers exist to permit the identification, tracing, seizure, confiscation and disposal of proceeds of crime;

"(e) Making efforts to ensure that adequate legal powers exist and administrative resources are available to permit timely and effective responses to be made to requests from other States in cases involving money-laundering;

"(f) Supporting and participating in domestic and international research efforts to monitor and analyse trends in money-laundering and international policy responses;

"(g) Consistent with existing multilateral arrangements, developing projects or programmes to assist other States in developing, drafting or upgrading legislation, regulations and administrative procedures against money-laundering, including the Global Programme against Money-Laundering and other activities or projects that support the implementation of the United Nations Convention against Transnational Organized Crime;

"(h) Activities or programmes to train officials or share expertise in combating money-laundering, such as training workshops and seminars.

"B. International actions

"21. The Office for Drug Control and Crime Prevention will, in cooperation with other relevant international and regional organizations, as appropriate, and in accordance with the present resolution, develop technical cooperation activities to prevent and combat money-laundering and assist requesting States in implementing those activities.

"VII. Action against terrorism

"22. In order to implement and follow up on the commitments undertaken in paragraph 19 of the Vienna Declaration and to take effective, resolute and speedy measures to prevent and combat criminal activities carried out for the purpose of furthering terrorism in all its forms and manifestations, the specific measures below are recommended.

"A. National actions

"23. Individually and collectively, States will endeavour, as appropriate, to support the following actions:

"(a) Signing and ratifying the international instruments dealing with terrorism;

"(b) Conducting research and gathering information about criminal activities carried out for the purpose of furthering terrorism in all its forms and manifestations, including the identities, whereabouts and activities of specific individuals or groups involved in such activities, and supporting similar work at the international level, to the extent consistent with national laws and international agreements and arrangements;

"(c) Reviewing their relevant domestic laws and procedures with a view to achieving effective domestic measures against terrorism and related crime, an enhanced ability to cooperate in appropriate cases with other States and the effective implementation of relevant international instruments;

"(d) Fostering cooperation between anti-terrorism agencies and agencies fighting crimes; this may include the establishment of liaison offices or other channels of communication between anti-terrorism agencies and agencies fighting crime in order to enhance information exchange;

"(e) Considering voluntary contributions to support the implementation of the terrorism-prevention activities of the Centre for International Crime Prevention.

"B. International actions

"24. The Centre for International Crime Prevention will, in cooperation with other relevant international and regional organizations, in coordination with the Office of Legal Affairs of the Secretariat, as appropriate, and in accordance with the present resolution:

"(a) Take steps to raise awareness of the relevant international instruments, encourage States to sign and ratify such instruments and, where feasible, provide assistance in implementing such instruments to States, upon request;

"(b) In cooperation with Member States, take measures to raise public awareness of the nature and scope of international terrorism and its relationship to crime, including organized crime, where appropriate;

"(c) Continue to maintain existing databases on terrorism;

"(d) Offer analytical support to Member States by collecting and disseminating information on the relationship between terrorism and related criminal activities;

"(e) If further developments so require, draw up concrete proposals for consideration by Member States to strengthen the capacity of the Centre to develop, within its mandate, and administer the terrorism prevention component of its activities.

"VIII. Action on crime prevention

"25. In order to implement and follow up on the commitment undertaken in paragraph 25 of the Vienna Declaration to develop comprehensive international, regional, national and local crime prevention strategies, the specific measures below are recommended.

"A. National actions

"26. Individually and collectively, States will endeavour, as appropriate, to support the following actions:

"(a) Promotion of close cooperation between the various sectors of society, including justice, health, education, social services and housing, which are necessary to support effective community-based crime prevention;

"(b) Close cooperation with and assistance to elements of civil society in the development, adoption and promotion of crime prevention initiatives, taking into account the importance of proceeding on the basis of proven practices wherever possible and of selecting the appropriate balance between various approaches to community-based crime prevention;

"(c) Encouragement of assessment of the effectiveness of crime prevention programmes;

"(d) Development of practices that seek to prevent crime victims from being victimized once again;

"(e) Development and implementation of situational and other crime prevention programmes, bearing in mind the need to avoid any infringement of civil liberties;

"(f) Collaboration with other Governments and non-governmental organizations in the development and dissemination of successful and innovative crime prevention initiatives and specialized knowledge and expertise in crime prevention practices, including public awareness and education campaigns about effective crime prevention and the contributions that individuals, families, communities and all levels of government may make to contribute to safer and more peaceful communities;

"(g) Consideration of how to contribute to the collective efforts of countries to develop a comprehensive international strategy to advance community-based crime prevention;

"(h) Take steps to incorporate into their national crime prevention strategies measures to prevent and combat crime associated with racism, racial discrimination, xenophobia and related forms of intolerance.

"B. International actions

"27. The Centre for International Crime Prevention will, in cooperation with other relevant international and regional organizations, as appropriate, and in accordance with the present resolution:

"(a) Develop and promote crime prevention expertise that has been carefully adapted from proven practices to the conditions in the countries where those practices are to be implemented, using seminars, training programmes and other means;

"*(b)* Where requested to do so by the State or States involved, conduct public awareness and education campaigns about effective crime prevention and the respective contributions that individuals, families, communities and all levels of government may make towards safer and more peaceful communities;

"*(c)* Endeavour to contribute to the exchange of information and experience in crime prevention, for the purpose of encouraging new forms of collaboration between countries involving government, the community and non-governmental organizations;

"*(d)* Assess the evolution and globalization of crime and prepare responses to it through innovative and effective crime prevention initiatives that take account of the impact of new technologies on crime and crime prevention;

"*(e)* Continue to coordinate studies on crime in urban areas and measures for its effective prevention, including on the possible cultural and institutional differences in effective crime prevention;

"*(f)* Encourage Member States to incorporate into international crime prevention strategies and norms measures to prevent and combat crime associated with racism, racial discrimination, xenophobia and related forms of intolerance, taking into account measures already taken by Member States;

"*(g)* Develop technical cooperation projects in the area of crime prevention for requesting States and assist in their implementation;

"*(h)* Develop a guide for policy makers and a handbook on proven practices in the area of crime prevention.

"IX. Action on witnesses and victims of crime

"28. In order to implement and follow up on the commitments undertaken in paragraph 27 of the Vienna Declaration to review relevant practices by 2002 where possible, to develop action plans, support services and awareness campaigns for victims, to consider the establishment of funds for victims and to develop and implement witness protection policies, the specific measures below are recommended.

"A. National actions

"29. Individually and collectively, States will endeavour, as appropriate, to support the following actions:

"*(a)* The conduct of national and regional studies on victims of crime in national justice systems;

"*(b)* The use and application of the Declaration of Basic Principles of Justice for Victims of Crime and Abuse of Power, subject to the domestic legal systems of each State, taking into account the Handbook on Justice for Victims on the use and application of the Declaration and the Guide for Policy Makers on the implementation of the Declaration.

"B. International actions

"30. The Centre for International Crime Prevention will, in cooperation with other relevant international and regional organizations, as appropriate, and in accordance with the present resolution:

"*(a)* In its projects and programmes, take into account measures for the assistance and support of victims and witnesses, including those who are women, children or victims of trafficking in persons;

"*(b)* Promote the establishment of funds for victims of crime;

"*(c)* Promote proven practices in providing support and services for victims and witnesses using, for example, the International Victimology web site;

"*(d)* Translate into the official languages of the United Nations and widely disseminate the Guide for Policy Makers and the Handbook on Justice for Victims and assist requesting States in using those documents;

"*(e)* Upon request, assist States in the development of new legislation on victims, using, inter alia, the international database established by the Government of the Netherlands;

"*(f)* Where necessary, promote demonstration or pilot projects for the development, further development or establishment of victim services and other related operational activities.

"X. Action on prison overcrowding and alternatives to incarceration

"31. In order to implement and follow up on the commitments undertaken in paragraph 26 of the Vienna Declaration to promote safe and effective alternatives to incarceration, the specific measures below are recommended.

"A. National actions

"32. Individually and collectively, States will endeavour, as appropriate, to support the following actions:

"*(a)* The development of specific actions and time-bound targets to address prison overcrowding, recognizing that conditions in overcrowded prisons may affect the human rights of prisoners, including such actions as adopting effective measures to reduce pretrial detention as far as possible; the introduction of appropriate alternatives to imprisonment; preferring non-custodial measures to imprisonment where possible; dealing with minor offences using options such as customary practice, mediation between concerned parties or the payment of civil reparations or compensation; and conducting public awareness and education campaigns on alternatives to imprisonment and how they work;

"*(b)* Encouraging international and regional institutions, including financial institutions, to incorporate into their relevant technical cooperation programmes measures to reduce prison overcrowding, in accordance with national laws;

"*(c)* Promoting and implementing good prison practice, taking into account international standards;

"*(d)* Ensuring that national and international actions on prison overcrowding and alternatives to incarceration take into account and address any disparate impact that such actions may have on women and men.

"B. International actions

"33. The Centre for International Crime Prevention will, in cooperation with other relevant international and regional organizations, as appropriate, and in accordance with the present resolution:

"*(a)* Encourage international and regional institutions, including financial institutions, to incorporate into their relevant technical cooperation programmes measures to reduce prison overcrowding, in accordance with national laws;

"*(b)* Promote national and international actions on prison overcrowding and alternatives to incarceration that take into account any disparate impact on women and men, as well as any special needs;

"(c) Upon request, provide assistance in the form of advisory services, needs assessment, capacity-building, training or other assistance to States to enable them to improve prison conditions.

"XI. Action against high-technology and computer-related crime

"34. In order to implement and follow up on the commitments undertaken in paragraph 18 of the Vienna Declaration to develop action-oriented policy recommendations for the prevention and control of high-technology and computer-related crime, taking into account the ongoing work in other forums and to enhance abilities to detect, prevent, investigate and prosecute such crimes, the specific measures below are recommended.

"A. National actions

"35. Individually and collectively, States will endeavour, as appropriate, to support the following actions:

"(a) Criminalization of the misuse of information technologies, as appropriate and in accordance with national law, including, if necessary, reviewing crimes such as fraud, in order to ensure that they apply to offences in which computer and telecommunication media and networks are used;

"(b) The development and implementation of rules and procedures, including on the exercise of jurisdiction, that would ensure that computer- and telecommunication-related crimes can be effectively detected and investigated at the national level and that effective cooperation can be obtained in multinational cases, taking into account national sovereignty, the need for effective law enforcement and the need to maintain effective protections for privacy and other related basic rights;

"(c) Ensuring that law enforcement personnel are trained and equipped to be able to respond effectively and expeditiously to requests for assistance in the tracing of communications and other measures necessary for the detection and investigation of transnational high-technology and computer-related crimes;

"(d) Engaging in domestic and international discussions on actions against high-technology and computer-related crime and the effects of technological change with industries involved in the development and deployment of computers, telecommunication equipment, network software and hardware and other relevant products and services. These discussions could include such key areas as:

"(i) Issues relating to domestic and international regulation of the technologies and networks;

"(ii) Issues relating to the incorporation of elements into new technologies, which are intended to prevent crime or facilitate the detection, investigation or prosecution of crime;

"(e) Making voluntary contributions, both bilaterally and through international and regional organizations, as appropriate, including in cooperation with the private sector, inter alia, in the form of technical expertise to assist other States in developing and implementing effective measures against high-technology and computer-related crime, including the measures referred to in subparagraphs (c) and (d) above.

"B. International actions

"36. The Centre for International Crime Prevention will, in cooperation with other relevant international and regional organizations, as appropriate, and in accordance with the present resolution:

"(a) Support national and international research activities to identify new forms of computer-related criminality and to assess the effects of such criminality in key areas such as sustainable development, the protection of privacy and electronic commerce, and the measures taken in response;

"(b) Disseminate internationally agreed materials such as guidelines, legal and technical manuals, minimum standards, proven practices and model legislation to assist legislators and law enforcement and other authorities in the development, adoption and application of effective measures against high-technology and computer-related crime and offenders both in general and in specific cases;

"(c) Promote, support and implement, as appropriate, technical cooperation and assistance projects. Such projects would bring together experts in crime prevention, computer security, criminal legislation and procedures, prosecution, investigative techniques and related matters with States seeking information or assistance in those areas.

"XII. Action on juvenile justice

"37. In order to implement and follow up the commitments, undertaken in paragraph 24 of the Vienna Declaration, the specific measures below are recommended.

"A. National actions

"38. Individually and collectively, States will endeavour, as appropriate, to support the following actions:

"(a) Giving timely assistance to juveniles in difficult circumstances in order to prevent them from resorting to crime;

"(b) Supporting the development of crime prevention practices that are focused on juveniles who are at risk of becoming delinquent or who are easy candidates for recruitment by criminal groups, bearing in mind the rights of such juveniles;

"(c) Strengthening juvenile justice systems;

"(d) Incorporating an integrated strategy for the prevention of youth crime and for juvenile justice in their national development plans;

"(e) Promoting the re-education and rehabilitation of juvenile offenders;

"(f) Encouraging, and where necessary, supporting the participation of civil society in the implementation of practices for the prevention of juvenile crime.

"B. International actions

"39. The Centre for International Crime Prevention will, in cooperation with other relevant international and regional organizations, as appropriate, and in accordance with the present resolution:

"(a) Upon request, develop technical cooperation projects to prevent youth crime, to strengthen juvenile justice systems and to improve the rehabilitation and treatment of juvenile offenders and assist States in implementing those projects;

"(b) Ensure effective cooperation among the relevant United Nations entities and the other organizations mentioned in the Guidelines for Action on Children in the Criminal Justice System.

"XIII. Action on the special needs of women in the criminal justice system

"40. In order to implement and follow up on the commitments undertaken in paragraphs 11 and 12 of the Vienna Declaration, and to review crime prevention and criminal justice strategies in order to identify and address any disparate impact of programmes and policies on women and men, the specific measures below are recommended.

"A. National actions

"41. Individually and collectively, States will endeavour, as appropriate, to support the following actions:

"(a) Reviewing, evaluating and, if necessary, modifying their legislation, policies, procedures and practices relating to criminal matters, in a manner consistent with their legal systems, in order to ensure that women are treated fairly by the criminal justice system;

"(b) Developing national and international crime prevention and criminal justice strategies that take into account the special needs of women as criminal justice practitioners, victims, witnesses, prisoners and offenders;

"(c) Considering sharing with other States, via web sites or other media or forums, any proven practices concerning women as criminal justice practitioners, victims, witnesses, prisoners and offenders that take into account the special needs of women.

"B. International actions

"42. The Centre for International Crime Prevention will, in cooperation with other relevant international and regional organizations, as appropriate, and in accordance with the present resolution:

"(a) Collect and disseminate information and materials on violence against women in all of its forms and manifestations, as referred to in the Declaration on the Elimination of Violence against Women, for the purpose of implementing its crime prevention and criminal justice programme, including technical assistance at the request of States;

"(b) Work on issues relating to violence against women and to the removal of gender bias in the administration of criminal justice;

"(c) Cooperate with all other relevant entities of the United Nations system regarding activities on issues relating to violence against women and to the removal of gender bias in the administration of criminal justice, and coordinate work on such issues;

"(d) Consolidate and disseminate information on successful intervention models and preventive programmes at the national level;

"(e) Continue to improve training concerning criminal justice and crime-prevention aspects of the human rights of women and issues of gender bias and violence against women for relevant United Nations staff members;

"(f) Assist Member States, upon request, in utilizing the Model Strategies and Practical Measures on the Elimination of Violence against Women in the Field of Crime Prevention and Criminal Justice.

"XIV. Action on standards and norms

"43. In order to implement and follow up on the commitments undertaken in paragraph 22 of the Vi-

enna Declaration and to promote the use and application, as appropriate, of the United Nations standards and norms in crime prevention and criminal justice in national law and practice, the specific measures below are recommended.

"A. National actions

"44. Individually and collectively, States will endeavour, as appropriate, to use and apply in national law and practice the United Nations standards and norms in crime prevention and criminal justice and to publish the *Compendium of United Nations Standards and Norms in Crime Prevention and Criminal Justice* in the languages of their countries.

"B. International actions

"45. The Centre for International Crime Prevention will, in cooperation with other relevant international and regional organizations, as appropriate, and in accordance with the present resolution:

"(a) Update the *Compendium of United Nations Standards and Norms in Crime Prevention and Criminal Justice;*

"(b) Promote the use and application of United Nations standards and norms in crime prevention and criminal justice, inter alia, by providing advisory services and technical cooperation to Member States upon request, including assistance to Member States in criminal justice and law reform, organization of training for law enforcement and criminal justice personnel and support to the administration and management of penal and penitentiary systems, thus contributing to the upgrading of their efficiency and capabilities;

"(c) Coordinate activities relating to the use and application of United Nations standards and norms in crime prevention and criminal justice between the Centre for International Crime Prevention and other relevant United Nations entities, taking into account bilateral and regional assistance programmes.

"XV. Action on restorative justice

"46. In order to implement and follow up on the commitments undertaken in paragraph 28 of the Vienna Declaration and to encourage the development of restorative justice policies, procedures and programmes, the specific measures below are recommended.

"A. National actions

"47. Individually and collectively, States will endeavour, as appropriate, to support the following actions:

"(a) Taking into account Economic and Social Council resolution 2000/14 of 27 July 2000, entitled "Basic principles on the use of restorative justice programmes in criminal matters", when considering the desirability and the means of establishing common principles;

"(b) Dealing with offences, especially minor offences, according to customary practice in respect of restorative justice, where available and appropriate, provided that this meets human rights requirements and that those involved so agree;

"(c) Using amicable means as provided by national law to deal with offences, especially minor offences, for example by using mediation, reparation or agreements whereby the offender compensates the victim;

"(d) Promoting a culture favourable to mediation and restorative justice among law enforcement, judicial and social authorities and local communities;

"*(e)* Providing appropriate training for those involved in the development and implementation of restorative justice policies and programmes;

"*(f)* Promoting the re-education and rehabilitation of juvenile offenders by encouraging, where appropriate, the use of mediation, conflict resolution, conciliation and other methods of restorative justice as alternatives to judicial proceedings and custodial-based sanctions;

"*(g)* Developing and implementing restorative justice policies and programmes, taking into account existing international commitments with respect to victims, in particular the Declaration of Basic Principles of Justice for Victims of Crime and Abuse of Power;

"*(h)* Promoting cooperation between government and civil society, including relevant non-governmental organizations, to implement restorative justice programmes and to ensure public support for the use of restorative justice principles.

"B. International actions

"48. The Centre for International Crime Prevention will, in cooperation with other relevant international and regional organizations, as appropriate, and in accordance with the present resolution:

"*(a)* Exchange information on experiences and proven practices in the implementation and evaluation of programmes for restorative justice;

"*(b)* Assist the Commission on Crime Prevention and Criminal Justice in considering the desirability and the means of establishing common principles on the use of restorative justice programmes in criminal matters;

"*(c)* Convene a meeting of experts to examine proposals for further action in relation to restorative justice, including mediation."

Crime congresses

In response to General Assembly resolution 53/110 [YUN 1998, p. 1032], the Commission on Crime Prevention and Criminal Justice reviewed the role, function, periodicity and duration of the UN congresses on the prevention of crime and the treatment of offenders, including the issue of regional preparatory meetings, on the basis of a Secretariat note [E/CN.15/2001/6] prepared for the review.

ECONOMIC AND SOCIAL COUNCIL ACTION

On 24 July [meeting 40], the Economic and Social Council, on the recommendation of the Commission on Crime Prevention and Criminal Justice [E/2001/30/Rev.1], adopted **resolution 2001/9** without vote [agenda item 14 *(c)*].

Role, function, periodicity and duration of the United Nations congresses on the prevention of crime and the treatment of offenders

The Economic and Social Council

Recommends to the General Assembly the adoption of the following draft resolution:

[For text, see General Assembly resolution 56/119 below.]

GENERAL ASSEMBLY ACTION

On 19 December [meeting 88], the General Assembly, on the recommendation of the Third Committee [A/56/574], adopted **resolution 56/119** without vote [agenda item 110].

Role, function, periodicity and duration of the United Nations congresses on the prevention of crime and the treatment of offenders

The General Assembly,

Recalling that, in its resolution 53/110 of 9 December 1998, it requested the Commission on Crime Prevention and Criminal Justice to review the role, function, periodicity and duration of the United Nations congresses on the prevention of crime and the treatment of offenders, including the issue of regional preparatory meetings for the congresses,

Taking note with appreciation of the results of the Tenth United Nations Congress on the Prevention of Crime and the Treatment of Offenders,

Bearing in mind that the congresses are a consultative body of the United Nations Crime Prevention and Criminal Justice Programme, in accordance with paragraph 29 of the statement of principles and programme of action of the Programme, annexed to General Assembly resolution 46/152 of 18 December 1991,

Recognizing the significant contributions of the congresses to the promotion and strengthening of international cooperation in crime prevention and criminal justice,

Recognizing also that the congresses have been a forum for promoting the exchange of experiences in research, law and policy development and the identification of emerging trends and issues in crime prevention and criminal justice among States, intergovernmental organizations and individual experts representing various professions and disciplines,

Recognizing further the role played by the congresses in preparing suggestions, for consideration by the Commission, on possible subjects for its programme of work,

Aware of the need to review the functioning and method of work of the congresses in order to improve their effectiveness,

Noting with appreciation the offers made by the Governments of Mexico and Thailand to host the next congress,

1. *Decides* to continue holding the United Nations congresses in accordance with paragraphs 29 and 30 of the statement of principles and programme of action of the United Nations Crime Prevention and Criminal Justice Programme, following a dynamic, interactive and cost-effective method of work and a focused programme of work, and to call them the United Nations congresses on crime prevention and criminal justice;

2. *Also decides* that, beginning in 2005, the congresses, pursuant to paragraphs 29 and 30 of the statement of principles and programme of action of the Programme, shall be held in accordance with the following guidelines:

(a) Each congress shall discuss specific topics, including, where appropriate, a main topic, all of which shall be determined by the Commission on Crime Prevention and Criminal Justice;

(b) Each congress shall include one session of pre-congress consultations;

(c) Each congress shall include a high-level segment in which States will be represented at the highest possible level and will be given an opportunity to make statements on the topics of the congress;

(d) As part of the high-level segment, the heads of delegations or their representatives shall participate in a number of thematic interactive round tables in order to further the discussion on the topics of the congress through open dialogue;

(e) Panels of experts, to be selected by the Commission with due regard for the principle of equitable geographical distribution, shall hold workshops dealing with the topics of the congress, maintaining an open dialogue with the participants and avoiding the reading of statements;

(f) Institutes of the United Nations Crime Prevention and Criminal Justice Programme network shall be invited to assist in the preparations for the workshops;

(g) The Secretary-General shall facilitate, within existing resources, the organization of ancillary meetings of non-governmental organizations and professional organizations at each congress;

(h) Each congress shall adopt a single declaration containing recommendations derived from the deliberations of the high-level segment, the round tables and the workshops, to be submitted to the Commission for its consideration;

(i) Any action suggested to the Commission regarding its programme of work, contained in the declaration of the congress, shall be undertaken through individual resolutions of the Commission;

(j) The Commission, as the preparatory body for the congress, shall request the Secretary-General to prepare only those background documents which are absolutely necessary for implementing the programme of work of the congress;

(k) Each congress shall be preceded by regional preparatory meetings, when necessary, and the costs of the regional preparatory meetings for each congress shall be streamlined by holding them in conjunction with other regional meetings, shortening their duration and limiting the preparation of background documents;

3. *Requests* the Commission on Crime Prevention and Criminal Justice to continue to act as the preparatory body for the congresses and to follow the guidelines contained in paragraph 2 above in organizing future congresses;

4. *Requests* the Secretary-General to continue to provide the staff required to serve as secretariat for the congresses and the regional preparatory meetings for the congresses;

5. *Also requests* the Secretary-General to provide the Centre for International Crime Prevention of the Office for Drug Control and Crime Prevention of the Secretariat with the necessary resources, within the overall appropriations of the programme budget for the biennium 2002-2003, for the preparations for the Eleventh United Nations Congress on Crime Prevention and Criminal Justice and to ensure that adequate resources are provided in the programme budget for the biennium 2004-2005 to support the holding of the Eleventh Congress;

6. *Requests* the Commission on Crime Prevention and Criminal Justice to formulate, at its eleventh session, recommendations regarding the Eleventh Congress, including recommendations on the main topic, the organization of round tables and workshops to be held by panels of experts and the venue and duration of the Eleventh Congress, and to submit those recommendations, through the Economic and Social Council, to the General Assembly at its fifty-seventh session;

7. *Also requests* the Commission on Crime Prevention and Criminal Justice to formulate, at its eleventh session, appropriate recommendations to enable the Economic and Social Council to introduce the necessary amendments to the rules of procedure for the congresses to reflect the guidelines contained in paragraph 2 above;

8. *Requests* the Secretary-General to ensure the proper follow-up to the present resolution and to report thereon to the General Assembly, through the Commission on Crime Prevention and Criminal Justice at its eleventh session.

UN Crime Prevention and Criminal Justice Programme

Commission consideration. In May, the Commission on Crime Prevention and Criminal Justice considered the Secretariat's April note [E/CN.15/2001/11] on the proposed programme of work in crime prevention and criminal justice for the 2002-2003 biennium. The note set out the overall objective of the United Nations Crime Prevention and Criminal Justice Programme, namely, to strengthen international cooperation and assistance to Governments in tackling crime problems, such as those posed by transnational organized crime, trafficking in persons, economic and financial crime, including money-laundering and corruption, illicit manufacturing of and trafficking in firearms and terrorism in all its forms, as well as to promote fair and efficient criminal justice systems. The note also outlined the expected accomplishments, together with performance indicators, and the outputs to be delivered.

The Centre for International Crime Prevention (CICP) of the Office for Drug Control and Crime Prevention was responsible for the programme of work.

Report of Secretary-General. In a July report [A/56/155], the Secretary-General provided an overview of progress made in implementing General Assembly resolution 55/64 [YUN 2000, p. 1045] on strengthening the United Nations Crime Prevention and Criminal Justice Programme. It identified three basic requirements for sustaining and building upon the progress of the past years: action to reinforce the focus of the Programme's activities on achievable priority areas of engagement; continued efforts to provide resources to match existing mandates; and increased voluntary contributions for technical cooperation services.

The report described the status of work on a third protocol on illicit firearms (see p. 1036) to the 2000 United Nations Convention against Transnational Organized Crime, adopted by Assembly resolution 55/25 [YUN 2000, p. 1048], and on the elaboration of an international legal instrument against corruption (see p. 1041); it identified the main challenges relating to the criminal misuse of information technologies (see p. 1045) and noted the outcome of the first meeting of the expert group (Vienna, 12-16 March) charged with preparing a study on the illicit manufacturing of and trafficking in explosives and their use for criminal purposes. In addition, the report provided an overview of CICP's technical cooperation activities as at 30 June, as well as information on the United Nations Crime Prevention and Criminal Justice Fund. Contributions and pledges to the Fund in 2000 totalled $3.1 million; in 2001, as at 31 May, they totalled $446,000.

GENERAL ASSEMBLY ACTION

On 19 December [meeting 88], the General Assembly, on the recommendation of the Third Committee [A/56/574], adopted **resolution 56/123** without vote [agenda item 110].

Strengthening the United Nations Crime Prevention and Criminal Justice Programme, in particular its technical cooperation capacity

The General Assembly,

Recalling its resolution 46/152 of 18 December 1991 on the creation of an effective United Nations crime prevention and criminal justice programme, in which it approved the statement of principles and programme of action annexed to that resolution,

Emphasizing the role of the United Nations in the field of crime prevention and criminal justice, specifically the reduction of criminality, more efficient and effective law enforcement and administration of justice, respect for human rights and promotion of the highest standards of fairness, humanity and professional conduct,

Recognizing that action against global criminal activity is a common and shared responsibility,

Convinced of the desirability of closer coordination and cooperation among States in combating crime, including the smuggling of migrants and trafficking in persons, especially women and children, drug-related crimes such as money-laundering, illicit manufacturing of and trafficking in firearms, their parts and components and ammunition, and criminal activities carried out for the purpose of furthering terrorism in all its forms and manifestations, bearing in mind the role that could be played by both the United Nations and regional organizations in this respect,

Recognizing the urgent need to increase technical cooperation activities to assist countries, in particular developing countries and countries with economies in transition, with their efforts in translating United Nations policy guidelines into practice,

Recalling its resolution 55/25 of 15 November 2000, by which it adopted the United Nations Convention against Transnational Organized Crime, the Protocol to Prevent, Suppress and Punish Trafficking in Persons, Especially Women and Children, and the Protocol against the Smuggling of Migrants by Land, Sea and Air, and its resolution 55/255 of 31 May 2001, by which it adopted the Protocol against the Illicit Manufacturing of and Trafficking in Firearms, Their Parts and Components and Ammunition,

Welcoming the adoption of the United Nations Convention against Transnational Organized Crime and the Protocols thereto as a milestone to fight and prevent organized crime, one of the most serious contemporary threats to democracy and peace,

Emphasizing the importance of the expeditious entry into force of the Convention and the Protocols thereto,

Recognizing the need to maintain a balance in the technical cooperation capacity of the Centre for International Crime Prevention of the Office for Drug Control and Crime Prevention of the Secretariat between the immediate priority of the Convention and the Protocols thereto and other priorities identified by the Economic and Social Council,

Recalling its relevant resolutions, in which it requested the Secretary-General, as a matter of urgency, to provide the United Nations Crime Prevention and Criminal Justice Programme with sufficient resources for the full implementation of its mandate, in conformity with the high priority attached to the Programme,

Bearing in mind the Vienna Declaration on Crime and Justice: Meeting the Challenges of the Twenty-first Century, adopted by the General Assembly in its resolution 55/59 of 4 December 2000, and the plans of action for the implementation of the Vienna Declaration proposed by the Commission on Crime Prevention and Criminal Justice,

Welcoming the report of the Meeting of the Intergovernmental Open-ended Expert Group to Prepare Draft Terms of Reference for the Negotiation of an International Legal Instrument against Corruption, held at Vienna from 30 July to 3 August 2001,

1. *Takes note with appreciation* of the report of the Secretary-General on the progress made in the implementation of General Assembly resolution 55/64 of 4 December 2000;

2. *Reaffirms* the importance of the United Nations Crime Prevention and Criminal Justice Programme in promoting effective action to strengthen international cooperation in crime prevention and criminal justice, in responding to the needs of the international community in the face of both national and transnational criminality, and in assisting Member States in achieving the goals of preventing crime within and among States and improving the response to crime;

3. *Also reaffirms* the role of the Centre for International Crime Prevention of the Office for Drug Control and Crime Prevention of the Secretariat in providing to Member States, upon request, technical cooperation, advisory services and other forms of assistance in the field of crime prevention and criminal justice, including in the areas of prevention and control of transnational organized crime and terrorism;

4. *Welcomes* the programme of work of the Centre, including the three global programmes addressing, respectively, the trafficking in human beings, corruption and organized crime, formulated on the basis of

close consultations with Member States and review by the Commission on Crime Prevention and Criminal Justice, and calls upon the Secretary-General further to strengthen the Centre by providing it with the resources necessary for the full implementation of its mandate;

5. *Supports* the high priority given to technical cooperation and advisory services in the field of crime prevention and criminal justice, including in the areas of prevention and control of transnational organized crime and terrorism, and stresses the need to enhance the operational activities of the Centre to assist, in particular, developing countries and countries with economies in transition;

6. *Urges* States and relevant international organizations to develop national, regional and international strategies and other necessary measures which complement the work of the United Nations Crime Prevention and Criminal Justice Programme in addressing effectively the significant problems posed by the smuggling of migrants and trafficking in persons and related activities;

7. *Welcomes* the increased number of technical assistance projects in the field of juvenile justice, reflecting an increased awareness among Member States of the importance of juvenile justice reform in establishing and maintaining stable societies and the rule of law;

8. *Invites* all States to support, through voluntary contributions to the United Nations Crime Prevention and Criminal Justice Fund, the operational activities of the United Nations Crime Prevention and Criminal Justice Programme;

9. *Encourages* relevant programmes, funds and organizations of the United Nations system, in particular the United Nations Development Programme, international financial institutions, in particular the World Bank, and regional and national funding agencies, to support the technical operational activities of the Centre;

10. *Urges* States and funding agencies to review, as appropriate, their funding policies for development assistance and to include a crime prevention and criminal justice component in such assistance;

11. *Welcomes* the efforts undertaken by the Commission on Crime Prevention and Criminal Justice to exercise more vigorously its mandated function of resource mobilization, and calls upon the Commission to strengthen further its activities in this direction;

12. *Expresses its appreciation* to non-governmental organizations and other relevant sectors of civil society for their support to the United Nations Crime Prevention and Criminal Justice Programme;

13. *Welcomes* the efforts of the Office for Drug Control and Crime Prevention to enhance the synergies between the United Nations International Drug Control Programme and the Centre for International Crime Prevention, in conformity with the reform proposals of the Secretary-General;

14. *Requests* the Secretary-General to take all necessary measures to provide adequate support to the Commission on Crime Prevention and Criminal Justice, as the principal policy-making body in this field, in performing its activities, including cooperation and coordination with other relevant bodies;

15. *Invites* States to make adequate voluntary contributions to the United Nations Crime Prevention and Criminal Justice Fund in order to strengthen the capacity of the Centre to provide technical assistance to requesting States for the implementation of the commitments entered into at the Tenth United Nations Congress on the Prevention of Crime and the Treatment of Offenders, including the measures outlined in the plans of action to implement the Vienna Declaration on Crime and Justice: Meeting the Challenges of the Twenty-first Century;

16. *Urges* all States and regional economic organizations that have not yet done so to sign and ratify the United Nations Convention against Transnational Organized Crime and the Protocols thereto as soon as possible in order to ensure the speedy entry into force of the Convention and the Protocols thereto;

17. *Welcomes* the voluntary contributions already made, and encourages States to make adequate and regular voluntary contributions for the entry into force and implementation of the Convention and the Protocols thereto, through the United Nations funding mechanism specifically designed for that purpose in the Convention;

18. *Requests* the Secretary-General to take all necessary measures and provide adequate support to the Centre during the biennium 2002-2003 so as to enable it to promote the speedy entry into force of the Convention and the Protocols thereto;

19. *Invites* the Secretary-General to consider, in consultation with Member States and the Commission on Crime Prevention and Criminal Justice, the ways in which the Centre could contribute to the efforts of the United Nations system against terrorism, in accordance with relevant General Assembly and Security Council resolutions;

20. *Welcomes* the decision of the Commission on Crime Prevention and Criminal Justice to mainstream a gender perspective into its activities and its request to the Secretariat that a gender perspective be integrated into all activities of the Centre;

21. *Requests* the Secretary-General to submit a report on the implementation of the present resolution to the General Assembly at its fifty-seventh session.

On 24 December, the Assembly decided that the agenda item on crime prevention and criminal justice would remain for consideration during its resumed fifty-sixth (2002) session (**decision 56/464**).

Coordination

In May, the Commission considered the Secretary-General's March report [E/CN.15/2001/8], prepared in response to Economic and Social Council resolution 1999/23 [YUN 1999, p. 1054]. The report highlighted the research and technical assistance activities carried out in 1999 and 2000 by the UN interregional crime and justice research institutes, the affiliated regional institutes and associate institutes, and centres comprising the United Nations Crime Prevention and Criminal Justice Programme network. It underscored efforts to coordinate and integrate those activities. In addition, it provided information on the activities of the International Scientific and Professional Advisory Council.

The Commission also considered the Secretary-General's related report [E/CN.15/2001/7] containing information received from Member States and relevant international organizations and other entities on their projects involving international technical assistance and training in crime prevention and criminal justice. Submitted in response to Council resolution 1999/24 [YUN 1999, p. 1055], the report addressed the viability and usefulness of expanding globally a centralized database of international training and technical assistance projects in crime prevention and criminal justice. The Secretary-General concluded that the establishment of a centralized clearing house for such projects would not achieve the desired coordination objective, as the level of responses and usage would prove too low.

UN African crime prevention institute

In October, pursuant to General Assembly resolution 55/62 [YUN 2000, p. 1047], the Secretary-General updated information on the activities, operations and funding of the United Nations African Institute for the Prevention of Crime and the Treatment of Offenders (UNAFRI) [A/56/151].

UNAFRI implemented a regional survey on illicit firearms trafficking involving the participation of 24 African countries, which culminated in the convening of the African Regional Workshop on Illicit Trafficking in Firearms in Africa (Kampala, Uganda, 11-13 June). Project proposals, for which the Institute was seeking sponsors, had been developed on the themes of trafficking in women and children, cult and crime, prison conditions and human rights, crime and AIDS, juvenile justice, conflict resolution, mob justice, a databank on crime and UNAFRI institutional capacity-building.

In spite of continued political support, the Institute's financial situation remained precarious, limiting its capacity to deliver fully on its mandate to provide effective and comprehensive services to African countries. However, within its limited resources, the Institute executed some major programmes in crime prevention and control.

The Institute's total resources for the 2000-2001 period amounted to $593,530, which came from Member States' assessed contributions, a UN grant, specific project grants, income received from the rental of UNAFRI premises and facilities, and interest on deposits.

A later report of the Secretary-General [A/57/135] stated that the UNAFRI Governing Board, at its seventh session (Kampala, 5-6 December), approved the Institute's budget and work programme for 2002-2003, stressing that successful implementation of the work programme was intertwined with future funding. The Board endorsed the recommendations of the Meeting of African Heads of Missions resident in Kampala on resource mobilization for the Institute, convened by UNAFRI on 25 October.

GENERAL ASSEMBLY ACTION

On 19 December [meeting 88], the General Assembly, on the recommendation of the Third Committee [A/56/574], adopted **resolution 56/122** without vote [agenda item 110].

United Nations African Institute for the Prevention of Crime and the Treatment of Offenders

The General Assembly,

Recalling its resolution 55/62 of 4 December 2000 and all other relevant resolutions,

Taking note of the report of the Secretary-General,

Bearing in mind the urgent need to establish effective crime prevention strategies for Africa, as well as the importance of law enforcement agencies and the judiciary at the regional and subregional levels,

Noting that the financial situation of the United Nations African Institute for the Prevention of Crime and the Treatment of Offenders has greatly affected its capacity to deliver its services to African Member States in an effective and comprehensive manner,

1. *Commends* the United Nations African Institute for the Prevention of Crime and the Treatment of Offenders for its efforts to promote and coordinate regional technical cooperation activities related to crime prevention and criminal justice systems in Africa;

2. *Also commends* the Secretary-General for his efforts to mobilize the financial resources necessary to provide the Institute with the core professional staff required to enable it to function effectively in the fulfilment of its mandated obligations;

3. *Reiterates* the need to strengthen further the capacity of the Institute to support national mechanisms for crime prevention and criminal justice in African countries;

4. *Urges* the States members of the Institute to make every possible effort to meet their obligations to the Institute;

5. *Calls upon* all Member States and non-governmental organizations to adopt concrete practical measures to support the Institute in the development of the requisite capacity and implement its programmes and activities aimed at strengthening crime prevention and criminal justice systems in Africa;

6. *Requests* the Secretary-General to intensify efforts to mobilize all relevant entities of the United Nations system to provide the necessary financial and technical support to the Institute to enable it to fulfil its mandate;

7. *Also requests* the Secretary-General to deploy his efforts to mobilize the financial resources necessary to maintain the Institute with the core professional staff required to enable it to function effectively in the fulfilment of its mandated obligations;

8. *Calls upon* the United Nations Crime Prevention and Criminal Justice Programme and the United Nations International Drug Control Programme to work closely with the Institute;

9. *Requests* the Secretary-General to enhance the promotion of regional cooperation, coordination and collaboration in the fight against crime, especially in its transnational dimension, which cannot be dealt with adequately by national action alone;

10. *Also requests* the Secretary-General to make concrete proposals, including the provision of additional core professional staff, to strengthen the programmes and activities of the Institute and to report to the General Assembly at its fifty-seventh session on the implementation of the present resolution.

Transnational crime

International convention

In 2001, UN efforts to combat transnational crime focused on promoting the early entry into force of the United Nations Convention against Transnational Organized Crime and its two supplementary protocols: the Protocol to Prevent, Suppress and Punish Trafficking in Persons, Especially Women and Children and the Protocol against the Smuggling of Migrants by Land, Sea and Air, all adopted in 2000 by General Assembly resolution 55/25 [YUN 2000, p. 1048]. In May, a third supplementary protocol, the Protocol against the Illicit Manufacturing of and Trafficking in Firearms, Their Parts and Components and Ammunition, was adopted by the Assembly and opened for signature (see p. 1036). As requested by the Assembly in resolution 55/25, the Secretary-General transmitted in September [A/56/380] the report of the High-level Political Signing Conference for the United Nations Convention against Transnational Organized Crime and the Protocols Thereto [YUN 2000, p. 1048].

To help facilitate the Convention's ratification and early entry into force, regional and subregional meetings were convened in Hanoi, Viet Nam (8-10 August), Tehran, Iran (3-4 October), Ouagadougou, Burkina Faso (28-30 November), and Port of Spain, Trinidad and Tobago (20 November–1 December).

As at 31 December, the Convention had 140 signatories and 6 parties; the Protocol on illegal trafficking in persons had 101 signatories and 4 parties; the Protocol against smuggling migrants had 97 signatories and 4 parties; and the Protocol on the illicit manufacturing and trafficking in firearms had 21 signatories. The Convention would enter into force on the ninetieth day after the date of deposit of the fortieth instrument of ratification, acceptance, approval or accession. Each Protocol required the same number of parties for entry into force.

ECONOMIC AND SOCIAL COUNCIL ACTION

On 24 July [meeting 40], the Economic and Social Council, on the recommendation of the Commission on Crime Prevention and Criminal Justice [E/2001/30/Rev.1], adopted **resolution 2001/10** without vote [agenda item 14 *(c)*].

Action against transnational organized crime: assistance to States in capacity-building with a view to facilitating the implementation of the United Nations Convention against Transnational Organized Crime and the Protocols thereto

The Economic and Social Council

Recommends to the General Assembly the adoption of the following resolution:

[For text, see General Assembly resolution 56/120 below.]

GENERAL ASSEMBLY ACTION

On 19 December [meeting 88], the General Assembly, on the recommendation of the Third Committee [A/56/574], adopted **resolution 56/120** without vote [agenda item 110].

Action against transnational organized crime: assistance to States in capacity-building with a view to facilitating the implementation of the United Nations Convention against Transnational Organized Crime and the Protocols thereto

The General Assembly,

Deeply concerned at the impact of transnational organized crime on the political, social and economic stability and development of societies,

Bearing in mind that the fight against transnational organized crime is a common and shared responsibility of the international community, necessitating cooperation at the bilateral and multilateral levels,

Reaffirming its support and commitment to the goals of the United Nations in the field of crime prevention and criminal justice, in particular the objectives set forth in the Vienna Declaration on Crime and Justice: Meeting the Challenges of the Twenty-first Century,

Recalling its resolution 55/25 of 15 November 2000, in which it adopted the United Nations Convention against Transnational Organized Crime and the Protocols thereto and urged all States and regional economic organizations to sign and ratify those international legal instruments,

Noting with appreciation the initiative of those States which have pledged financial contributions to the United Nations Crime Prevention and Criminal Justice Fund in order to enable developing countries and countries with economies in transition to initiate measures to implement the Convention and the Protocols thereto,

1. *Welcomes* the signing of the United Nations Convention against Transnational Organized Crime and the Protocols thereto;

2. *Expresses its appreciation* for the offers of a number of Governments to host regional conferences at the ministerial level and for the financial contributions of a number of States for the purpose of holding preratification seminars on facilitating the entry into force

of the Convention and the Protocols thereto and their future implementation;

3. *Encourages* Member States to make adequate voluntary contributions to the United Nations Crime Prevention and Criminal Justice Fund for the provision to developing countries and countries with economies in transition of the technical assistance they may require for implementation of the Convention and the Protocols thereto, including assistance for the preparatory measures needed for that implementation, taking into account article 30 of the Convention;

4. *Requests* the Secretary-General to provide the Centre for International Crime Prevention of the Office for Drug Control and Crime Prevention of the Secretariat with the resources necessary to enable it to promote, in an effective manner, the entry into force and implementation of the Convention and the Protocols thereto, inter alia, through the provision of assistance to developing countries and countries with economies in transition for building capacity in the areas covered by the Convention and the Protocols thereto;

5. *Also requests* the Secretary-General to submit a report on the implementation of the present resolution to the Commission on Crime Prevention and Criminal Justice at its eleventh session.

Protocol on illicit firearms

In March, the Ad Hoc Committee on the Elaboration of a Convention against Transnational Organized Crime, at its twelfth session (Vienna, 26 February–2 March) [A/55/383/Add.2,3], finalized the text of the draft Protocol against the Illicit Manufacturing of and Trafficking in Firearms, Their Parts and Components and Ammunition, and recommended it to the General Assembly for adoption. The draft Protocol was supplementary to the Convention, which, together with two other supplementary protocols, had been finalized by the Ad Hoc Committee at its tenth and eleventh sessions in 2000 [YUN 2000, p. 1048] and adopted by General Assembly resolution 55/25 [ibid.].

GENERAL ASSEMBLY ACTION

On 31 May [meeting 101], the General Assembly, on the recommendation of the Ad Hoc Committee on the Elaboration of a Convention against Transnational Organized Crime [A/55/383/Add.2], adopted **resolution 55/255** without vote [agenda item 105].

Protocol against the Illicit Manufacturing of and Trafficking in Firearms, Their Parts and Components and Ammunition, supplementing the United Nations Convention against Transnational Organized Crime

The General Assembly,

Recalling its resolution 53/111 of 9 December 1998, in which it decided to establish an open-ended intergovernmental ad hoc committee for the purpose of elaborating a comprehensive international convention against transnational organized crime and of discussing the elaboration, as appropriate, of international instruments addressing trafficking in women and children, combating the illicit manufacturing of and trafficking in firearms, their parts and components and ammunition, and illegal trafficking in and transporting of migrants, including by sea,

Recalling also its resolution 54/126 of 17 December 1999, in which it requested the Ad Hoc Committee on the Elaboration of a Convention against Transnational Organized Crime to continue its work, in accordance with resolutions 53/111 and 53/114 of 9 December 1998, and to intensify that work in order to complete it in 2000,

Recalling further its resolution 55/25 of 15 November 2000, by which it adopted the United Nations Convention against Transnational Organized Crime, the Protocol to Prevent, Suppress and Punish Trafficking in Persons, Especially Women and Children, supplementing the United Nations Convention against Transnational Organized Crime, and the Protocol against the Smuggling of Migrants by Land, Sea and Air, supplementing the United Nations Convention against Transnational Organized Crime,

Reaffirming the inherent right to individual or collective self-defence recognized in Article 51 of the Charter of the United Nations, which implies that States also have the right to acquire arms with which to defend themselves, as well as the right of self-determination of all peoples, in particular peoples under colonial or other forms of alien domination or foreign occupation, and the importance of the effective realization of that right,

1. *Takes note* of the report of the Ad Hoc Committee on the Elaboration of a Convention against Transnational Organized Crime on its twelfth session, and commends the Ad Hoc Committee for its work;

2. *Adopts* the Protocol against the Illicit Manufacturing of and Trafficking in Firearms, Their Parts and Components and Ammunition, supplementing the United Nations Convention against Transnational Organized Crime, annexed to the present resolution, and opens it for signature at United Nations Headquarters in New York;

3. *Urges* all States and regional economic organizations to sign and ratify the United Nations Convention against Transnational Organized Crime and the protocols thereto as soon as possible in order to ensure the speedy entry into force of the Convention and the protocols thereto.

ANNEX

Protocol against the Illicit Manufacturing of and Trafficking in Firearms, Their Parts and Components and Ammunition, supplementing the United Nations Convention against Transnational Organized Crime

Preamble

The States Parties to this Protocol,

Aware of the urgent need to prevent, combat and eradicate the illicit manufacturing of and trafficking in firearms, their parts and components and ammunition, owing to the harmful effects of those activities on the security of each State, region and the world as a whole, endangering the well-being of peoples, their social and economic development and their right to live in peace,

Convinced, therefore, of the necessity for all States to take all appropriate measures to this end, including international cooperation and other measures at the regional and global levels,

Recalling General Assembly resolution 53/111 of 9 December 1998, in which the Assembly decided to establish an open-ended intergovernmental ad hoc committee for the purpose of elaborating a comprehensive international convention against transnational organized crime and of discussing the elaboration of, inter alia, an international instrument combating the illicit manufacturing of and trafficking in firearms, their parts and components and ammunition,

Bearing in mind the principle of equal rights and self-determination of peoples, as enshrined in the Charter of the United Nations and the Declaration on Principles of International Law concerning Friendly Relations and Cooperation among States in accordance with the Charter of the United Nations,

Convinced that supplementing the United Nations Convention against Transnational Organized Crime with an international instrument against the illicit manufacturing of and trafficking in firearms, their parts and components and ammunition will be useful in preventing and combating those crimes,

Have agreed as follows:

I. General provisions

Article 1
Relation with the United Nations Convention against Transnational Organized Crime

1. This Protocol supplements the United Nations Convention against Transnational Organized Crime. It shall be interpreted together with the Convention.

2. The provisions of the Convention shall apply, mutatis mutandis, to this Protocol unless otherwise provided herein.

3. The offences established in accordance with article 5 of this Protocol shall be regarded as offences established in accordance with the Convention.

Article 2
Statement of purpose

The purpose of this Protocol is to promote, facilitate and strengthen cooperation among States Parties in order to prevent, combat and eradicate the illicit manufacturing of and trafficking in firearms, their parts and components and ammunition.

Article 3
Use of terms

For the purposes of this Protocol:

(a) "Firearm" shall mean any portable barrelled weapon that expels, is designed to expel or may be readily converted to expel a shot, bullet or projectile by the action of an explosive, excluding antique firearms or their replicas. Antique firearms and their replicas shall be defined in accordance with domestic law. In no case, however, shall antique firearms include firearms manufactured after 1899;

(b) "Parts and components" shall mean any element or replacement element specifically designed for a firearm and essential to its operation, including a barrel, frame or receiver, slide or cylinder, bolt or breech block, and any device designed or adapted to diminish the sound caused by firing a firearm;

(c) "Ammunition" shall mean the complete round or its components, including cartridge cases, primers, propellant powder, bullets or projectiles, that are used in a firearm, provided that those components are themselves subject to authorization in the respective State Party;

(d) "Illicit manufacturing" shall mean the manufacturing or assembly of firearms, their parts and components or ammunition:

(i) From parts and components illicitly trafficked;

(ii) Without a licence or authorization from a competent authority of the State Party where the manufacture or assembly takes place; or

(iii) Without marking the firearms at the time of manufacture, in accordance with article 8 of this Protocol;

Licensing or authorization of the manufacture of parts and components shall be in accordance with domestic law;

(e) "Illicit trafficking" shall mean the import, export, acquisition, sale, delivery, movement or transfer of firearms, their parts and components and ammunition from or across the territory of one State Party to that of another State Party if any one of the States Parties concerned does not authorize it in accordance with the terms of this Protocol or if the firearms are not marked in accordance with article 8 of this Protocol;

(f) "Tracing" shall mean the systematic tracking of firearms and, where possible, their parts and components and ammunition from manufacturer to purchaser for the purpose of assisting the competent authorities of States Parties in detecting, investigating and analysing illicit manufacturing and illicit trafficking.

Article 4
Scope of application

1. This Protocol shall apply, except as otherwise stated herein, to the prevention of illicit manufacturing of and trafficking in firearms, their parts and components and ammunition and to the investigation and prosecution of offences established in accordance with article 5 of this Protocol where those offences are transnational in nature and involve an organized criminal group.

2. This Protocol shall not apply to state-to-state transactions or to state transfers in cases where the application of the Protocol would prejudice the right of a State Party to take action in the interest of national security consistent with the Charter of the United Nations.

Article 5
Criminalization

1. Each State Party shall adopt such legislative and other measures as may be necessary to establish as criminal offences the following conduct, when committed intentionally:

(a) Illicit manufacturing of firearms, their parts and components and ammunition;

(b) Illicit trafficking in firearms, their parts and components and ammunition;

(c) Falsifying or illicitly obliterating, removing or altering the marking(s) on firearms required by article 8 of this Protocol.

2. Each State Party shall also adopt such legislative and other measures as may be necessary to establish as criminal offences the following conduct:

(a) Subject to the basic concepts of its legal system, attempting to commit or participating as an accomplice in an offence established in accordance with paragraph 1 of this article; and

(b) Organizing, directing, aiding, abetting, facilitating or counselling the commission of an offence established in accordance with paragraph 1 of this article.

Article 6
Confiscation, seizure and disposal

1. Without prejudice to article 12 of the Convention, States Parties shall adopt, to the greatest extent possible within their domestic legal systems, such measures as may be necessary to enable confiscation of firearms, their parts and components and ammunition that have been illicitly manufactured or trafficked.

2. States Parties shall adopt, within their domestic legal systems, such measures as may be necessary to prevent illicitly manufactured and trafficked firearms, parts and components and ammunition from falling into the hands of unauthorized persons by seizing and destroying such firearms, their parts and components and ammunition unless other disposal has been officially authorized, provided that the firearms have been marked and the methods of disposal of those firearms and ammunition have been recorded.

II. Prevention

Article 7
Record-keeping

Each State Party shall ensure the maintenance, for not less than ten years, of information in relation to firearms and, where appropriate and feasible, their parts and components and ammunition that is necessary to trace and identify those firearms and, where appropriate and feasible, their parts and components and ammunition which are illicitly manufactured or trafficked and to prevent and detect such activities. Such information shall include:

(a) The appropriate markings required by article 8 of this Protocol;

(b) In cases involving international transactions in firearms, their parts and components and ammunition, the issuance and expiration dates of the appropriate licences or authorizations, the country of export, the country of import, the transit countries, where appropriate, and the final recipient and the description and quantity of the articles.

Article 8
Marking of firearms

1. For the purpose of identifying and tracing each firearm, States Parties shall:

(a) At the time of manufacture of each firearm, either require unique marking providing the name of the manufacturer, the country or place of manufacture and the serial number, or maintain any alternative unique user-friendly marking with simple geometric symbols in combination with a numeric and/or alphanumeric code, permitting ready identification by all States of the country of manufacture;

(b) Require appropriate simple marking on each imported firearm, permitting identification of the country of import and, where possible, the year of im-

port and enabling the competent authorities of that country to trace the firearm, and a unique marking, if the firearm does not bear such a marking. The requirements of this subparagraph need not be applied to temporary imports of firearms for verifiable lawful purposes;

(c) Ensure, at the time of transfer of a firearm from government stocks to permanent civilian use, the appropriate unique marking permitting identification by all States Parties of the transferring country.

2. States Parties shall encourage the firearms manufacturing industry to develop measures against the removal or alteration of markings.

Article 9
Deactivation of firearms

A State Party that does not recognize a deactivated firearm as a firearm in accordance with its domestic law shall take the necessary measures, including the establishment of specific offences if appropriate, to prevent the illicit reactivation of deactivated firearms, consistent with the following general principles of deactivation:

(a) All essential parts of a deactivated firearm are to be rendered permanently inoperable and incapable of removal, replacement or modification in a manner that would permit the firearm to be reactivated in any way;

(b) Arrangements are to be made for deactivation measures to be verified, where appropriate, by a competent authority to ensure that the modifications made to a firearm render it permanently inoperable;

(c) Verification by a competent authority is to include a certificate or record attesting to the deactivation of the firearm or a clearly visible mark to that effect stamped on the firearm.

Article 10
General requirements for export, import and transit licensing or authorization systems

1. Each State Party shall establish or maintain an effective system of export and import licensing or authorization, as well as of measures on international transit, for the transfer of firearms, their parts and components and ammunition.

2. Before issuing export licences or authorizations for shipments of firearms, their parts and components and ammunition, each State Party shall verify:

(a) That the importing States have issued import licences or authorizations; and

(b) That, without prejudice to bilateral or multilateral agreements or arrangements favouring landlocked States, the transit States have, at a minimum, given notice in writing, prior to shipment, that they have no objection to the transit.

3. The export and import licence or authorization and accompanying documentation together shall contain information that, at a minimum, shall include the place and the date of issuance, the date of expiration, the country of export, the country of import, the final recipient, a description and the quantity of the firearms, their parts and components and ammunition and, whenever there is transit, the countries of transit. The information contained in the import licence must be provided in advance to the transit States.

4. The importing State Party shall, upon request, inform the exporting State Party of the receipt of the

dispatched shipment of firearms, their parts and components or ammunition.

5. Each State Party shall, within available means, take such measures as may be necessary to ensure that licensing or authorization procedures are secure and that the authenticity of licensing or authorization documents can be verified or validated.

6. States Parties may adopt simplified procedures for the temporary import and export and the transit of firearms, their parts and components and ammunition for verifiable lawful purposes such as hunting, sport shooting, evaluation, exhibitions or repairs.

Article 11
Security and preventive measures

In an effort to detect, prevent and eliminate the theft, loss or diversion of, as well as the illicit manufacturing of and trafficking in, firearms, their parts and components and ammunition, each State Party shall take appropriate measures:

(a) To require the security of firearms, their parts and components and ammunition at the time of manufacture, import, export and transit through its territory; and

(b) To increase the effectiveness of import, export and transit controls, including, where appropriate, border controls, and of police and customs transborder cooperation.

Article 12
Information

1. Without prejudice to articles 27 and 28 of the Convention, States Parties shall exchange among themselves, consistent with their respective domestic legal and administrative systems, relevant case-specific information on matters such as authorized producers, dealers, importers, exporters and, whenever possible, carriers of firearms, their parts and components and ammunition.

2. Without prejudice to articles 27 and 28 of the Convention, States Parties shall exchange among themselves, consistent with their respective domestic legal and administrative systems, relevant information on matters such as:

(a) Organized criminal groups known to take part or suspected of taking part in the illicit manufacturing of or trafficking in firearms, their parts and components and ammunition;

(b) The means of concealment used in the illicit manufacturing of or trafficking in firearms, their parts and components and ammunition and ways of detecting them;

(c) Methods and means, points of dispatch and destination and routes customarily used by organized criminal groups engaged in illicit trafficking in firearms, their parts and components and ammunition; and

(d) Legislative experiences and practices and measures to prevent, combat and eradicate the illicit manufacturing of and trafficking in firearms, their parts and components and ammunition.

3. States Parties shall provide to or share with each other, as appropriate, relevant scientific and technological information useful to law enforcement authorities in order to enhance each other's abilities to prevent, detect and investigate the illicit manufacturing of and trafficking in firearms, their parts and compo-

nents and ammunition and to prosecute the persons involved in those illicit activities.

4. States Parties shall cooperate in the tracing of firearms, their parts and components and ammunition that may have been illicitly manufactured or trafficked. Such cooperation shall include the provision of prompt responses to requests for assistance in tracing such firearms, their parts and components and ammunition, within available means.

5. Subject to the basic concepts of its legal system or any international agreements, each State Party shall guarantee the confidentiality of and comply with any restrictions on the use of information that it receives from another State Party pursuant to this article, including proprietary information pertaining to commercial transactions, if requested to do so by the State Party providing the information. If such confidentiality cannot be maintained, the State Party that provided the information shall be notified prior to its disclosure.

Article 13
Cooperation

1. States Parties shall cooperate at the bilateral, regional and international levels to prevent, combat and eradicate the illicit manufacturing of and trafficking in firearms, their parts and components and ammunition.

2. Without prejudice to article 18, paragraph 13, of the Convention, each State Party shall identify a national body or a single point of contact to act as liaison between it and other States Parties on matters relating to this Protocol.

3. States Parties shall seek the support and cooperation of manufacturers, dealers, importers, exporters, brokers and commercial carriers of firearms, their parts and components and ammunition to prevent and detect the illicit activities referred to in paragraph 1 of this article.

Article 14
Training and technical assistance

States Parties shall cooperate with each other and with relevant international organizations, as appropriate, so that States Parties may receive, upon request, the training and technical assistance necessary to enhance their ability to prevent, combat and eradicate the illicit manufacturing of and trafficking in firearms, their parts and components and ammunition, including technical, financial and material assistance in those matters identified in articles 29 and 30 of the Convention.

Article 15
Brokers and brokering

1. With a view to preventing and combating illicit manufacturing of and trafficking in firearms, their parts and components and ammunition, States Parties that have not yet done so shall consider establishing a system for regulating the activities of those who engage in brokering. Such a system could include one or more measures such as:

(a) Requiring registration of brokers operating within their territory;

(b) Requiring licensing or authorization of brokering; or

(c) Requiring disclosure on import and export licences or authorizations, or accompanying documents, of the names and locations of brokers involved in the transaction.

2. States Parties that have established a system of authorization regarding brokering as set forth in paragraph 1 of this article are encouraged to include information on brokers and brokering in their exchanges of information under article 12 of this Protocol and to retain records regarding brokers and brokering in accordance with article 7 of this Protocol.

III. Final provisions

Article 16
Settlement of disputes

1. States Parties shall endeavour to settle disputes concerning the interpretation or application of this Protocol through negotiation.

2. Any dispute between two or more States Parties concerning the interpretation or application of this Protocol that cannot be settled through negotiation within a reasonable time shall, at the request of one of those States Parties, be submitted to arbitration. If, six months after the date of the request for arbitration, those States Parties are unable to agree on the organization of the arbitration, any one of those States Parties may refer the dispute to the International Court of Justice by request in accordance with the Statute of the Court.

3. Each State Party may, at the time of signature, ratification, acceptance or approval of or accession to this Protocol, declare that it does not consider itself bound by paragraph 2 of this article. The other States Parties shall not be bound by paragraph 2 of this article with respect to any State Party that has made such a reservation.

4. Any State Party that has made a reservation in accordance with paragraph 3 of this article may at any time withdraw that reservation by notification to the Secretary-General of the United Nations.

Article 17
Signature, ratification, acceptance, approval and accession

1. This Protocol shall be open to all States for signature at United Nations Headquarters in New York from the thirtieth day after its adoption by the General Assembly until 12 December 2002.

2. This Protocol shall also be open for signature by regional economic integration organizations provided that at least one member State of such organization has signed this Protocol in accordance with paragraph 1 of this article.

3. This Protocol is subject to ratification, acceptance or approval. Instruments of ratification, acceptance or approval shall be deposited with the Secretary-General of the United Nations. A regional economic integration organization may deposit its instrument of ratification, acceptance or approval if at least one of its member States has done likewise. In that instrument of ratification, acceptance or approval, such organization shall declare the extent of its competence with respect to the matters governed by this Protocol. Such organization shall also inform the depositary of any relevant modification in the extent of its competence.

4. This Protocol is open for accession by any State or any regional economic integration organization of which at least one member State is a Party to this Protocol. Instruments of accession shall be deposited with the Secretary-General of the United Nations. At the time of its accession, a regional economic integration organization shall declare the extent of its competence with respect to matters governed by this Protocol. Such

organization shall also inform the depositary of any relevant modification in the extent of its competence.

Article 18
Entry into force

1. This Protocol shall enter into force on the ninetieth day after the date of deposit of the fortieth instrument of ratification, acceptance, approval or accession, except that it shall not enter into force before the entry into force of the Convention. For the purpose of this paragraph, any instrument deposited by a regional economic integration organization shall not be counted as additional to those deposited by member States of such organization.

2. For each State or regional economic integration organization ratifying, accepting, approving or acceding to this Protocol after the deposit of the fortieth instrument of such action, this Protocol shall enter into force on the thirtieth day after the date of deposit by such State or organization of the relevant instrument or on the date this Protocol enters into force pursuant to paragraph 1 of this article, whichever is the later.

Article 19
Amendment

1. After the expiry of five years from the entry into force of this Protocol, a State Party to the Protocol may propose an amendment and file it with the Secretary-General of the United Nations, who shall thereupon communicate the proposed amendment to the States Parties and to the Conference of the Parties to the Convention for the purpose of considering and deciding on the proposal. The States Parties to this Protocol meeting at the Conference of the Parties shall make every effort to achieve consensus on each amendment. If all efforts at consensus have been exhausted and no agreement has been reached, the amendment shall, as a last resort, require for its adoption a two-thirds majority vote of the States Parties to this Protocol present and voting at the meeting of the Conference of the Parties.

2. Regional economic integration organizations, in matters within their competence, shall exercise their right to vote under this article with a number of votes equal to the number of their member States that are Parties to this Protocol. Such organizations shall not exercise their right to vote if their member States exercise theirs and vice versa.

3. An amendment adopted in accordance with paragraph 1 of this article is subject to ratification, acceptance or approval by States Parties.

4. An amendment adopted in accordance with paragraph 1 of this article shall enter into force in respect of a State Party ninety days after the date of the deposit with the Secretary-General of the United Nations of an instrument of ratification, acceptance or approval of such amendment.

5. When an amendment enters into force, it shall be binding on those States Parties which have expressed their consent to be bound by it. Other States Parties shall still be bound by the provisions of this Protocol and any earlier amendments that they have ratified, accepted or approved.

Article 20
Denunciation

1. A State Party may denounce this Protocol by written notification to the Secretary-General of the United Nations. Such denunciation shall become effective one

year after the date of receipt of the notification by the Secretary-General.

2. A regional economic integration organization shall cease to be a Party to this Protocol when all of its member States have denounced it.

Article 21
Depositary and languages
1. The Secretary-General of the United Nations is designated depositary of this Protocol.

2. The original of this Protocol, of which the Arabic, Chinese, English, French, Russian and Spanish texts are equally authentic, shall be deposited with the Secretary-General of the United Nations.

IN WITNESS WHEREOF, the undersigned plenipotentiaries, being duly authorized thereto by their respective Governments, have signed this Protocol.

Strategies for crime prevention

Corruption

In 2001, the United Nations commenced elaboration of an international convention against corruption and continued activities to prevent corrupt practices, including the illegal transfer of funds and the criminal misuse of information technologies. In May, the Commission on Crime Prevention and Criminal Justice discussed progress made in global action against corruption as the theme of its tenth session [E/2001/30/Rev.1].

Communications. Communications transmitted to the Secretary-General on corruption issues included: from the Netherlands, the Final Declaration of the Global Forum on Fighting Corruption and Safeguarding Integrity II (The Hague, 28-31 May) [A/56/493]; from the Republic of Korea, the summary of the Seoul Anti-Corruption Symposium (30-31 August) [A/C.3/56/6]; and from the United Arab Emirates, a description of a newly approved law on money-laundering [A/56/468].

International instrument against corruption

In response to General Assembly resolution 55/61 [YUN 2000, p. 1072], the Secretary-General submitted to the Commission on Crime Prevention and Criminal Justice an April report [E/CN.15/2001/3 & Corr.1], in which he analysed all relevant international instruments, other documents and recommendations addressing corruption, to serve as the basis for recommendations on the development of a legal instrument against corruption. The Secretary-General observed that all existing legal instruments against corruption, with the exception of the Convention on Combating Bribery of Foreign Public Officials in International Business Transactions, negotiated under the auspices of the Organisation for Economic Cooperation and Development, were regional rather than international in scope. He

concluded that the mandate given by the Assembly in resolutions 55/61 and 55/188 [YUN 2000, p. 1073] represented a unique opportunity to develop a global legal instrument against corruption that fully addressed the concerns of the international community as a whole and could include provisions and mechanisms applicable at the global level.

Intergovernmental Expert Group. The Intergovernmental Open-Ended Expert Group to Prepare Draft Terms of Reference for the Negotiation of an International Legal Instrument against Corruption, established in accordance with Assembly resolution 55/61, held its first meeting in Vienna from 30 July to 3 August [A/AC.260/2 & Corr.1]. In accordance with Assembly resolution 55/188, the Expert Group also examined the question of illegally transferred funds and their repatriation to the countries of origin. Having considered the Expert Group's report at its resumed tenth session in September, the Commission approved it and the draft resolution contained therein. The Commission decided to transmit the report, through the Economic and Social Council, to the Assembly for consideration and adoption. By a September note [A/56/402-E/2001/105], the Secretariat transmitted the report to the Council and the Assembly. The Council took action in December (below) and the Assembly was expected to take action in 2002.

On 20 December [meeting 46], the Economic and Social Council, on the recommendation of the Commission on Crime Prevention and Criminal Justice [E/2001/30/Rev.1], adopted **resolution 2001/46** without vote [agenda item 14 (c)].

Terms of reference for the negotiation of an international legal instrument against corruption

The Economic and Social Council

Recommends to the General Assembly the adoption of the following draft resolution:

"*The General Assembly,*

"*Concerned* at the seriousness of the problems posed by corruption, which may endanger the stability and security of societies, undermine the values of democracy and morality and jeopardize social, economic and political development,

"*Recalling* its resolution 51/59 of 12 December 1996, by which it adopted the International Code of Conduct for Public Officials and recommended the Code to Member States as a tool to guide their efforts against corruption,

"*Recalling also* its resolution 51/191 of 12 December 1996, by which it adopted the United Nations Declaration against Corruption and Bribery in International Commercial Transactions,

"*Recalling further* its resolution 55/61 of 4 December 2000, in which it established an ad hoc committee for the negotiation of an effective international legal instrument against corruption, and requested the Secretary-General to convene an intergovernmental open-ended expert group to examine and prepare draft terms of reference for the negotiation of such an instrument,

"*Recalling* its resolution 55/188 of 20 December 2000, in which it invited the Intergovernmental Open-Ended Expert Group to Prepare Draft Terms of Reference for the Negotiation of an International Legal Instrument against Corruption, convened pursuant to resolution 55/61, to examine the question of illegally transferred funds and the return of such funds to the country of origin,

"*Recalling also* Economic and Social Council resolution 2001/13 of 24 July 2001, entitled "Strengthening international cooperation in preventing and combating the transfer of funds of illicit origin, derived from acts of corruption, including the laundering of funds, and in returning such funds",

"*Reiterating* the need to prepare a broad and effective international legal instrument against corruption,

"*Taking note* of the report of the Secretary-General on existing international legal instruments, recommendations and other documents addressing corruption, submitted to the Commission on Crime Prevention and Criminal Justice at its tenth session and before the meeting of the Intergovernmental Open-Ended Expert Group,

"1. *Takes note with appreciation* of the report of the Intergovernmental Open-Ended Expert Group to Prepare Draft Terms of Reference for the Negotiation of an International Legal Instrument against Corruption, which met in Vienna from 30 July to 3 August 2001, as endorsed by the Commission on Crime Prevention and Criminal Justice at its resumed tenth session and by the Economic and Social Council;

"2. *Decides* that the Ad Hoc Committee for the Negotiation of a Convention against Corruption, established pursuant to General Assembly resolution 55/61, shall negotiate a broad and effective convention, which, subject to the final determination of its title, shall be referred to as the "United Nations Convention against Corruption";

"3. *Requests* the Ad Hoc Committee, in developing the draft convention, to adopt a comprehensive and multidisciplinary approach and to consider, inter alia, the following indicative elements: definitions; scope; protection of sovereignty; preventive measures; criminalization; sanctions and remedies; confiscation and seizure; jurisdiction; liability of legal persons; protection of witnesses and victims; promoting and strengthening international cooperation; preventing and combating the transfer of funds of illicit origin derived from acts of corruption, including the laundering of funds, and returning such funds; technical assistance; collection, exchange and analysis of information; and mechanisms for monitoring implementation;

"4. *Invites* the Ad Hoc Committee to draw on the report of the Intergovernmental Open-Ended Expert Group, the report of the Secretary-General, and the relevant parts of the report of the Commission on Crime Prevention and Criminal Justice on its tenth session, as well as in particular on paragraph 1 of Economic and Social Council resolution 2001/13, as resource materials in the accomplishment of its tasks;

"5. *Requests* the Ad Hoc Committee to take into consideration existing international legal instruments against corruption and, whenever relevant, the United Nations Convention against Transnational Organized Crime;

"6. *Decides* that the Ad Hoc Committee shall be convened in Vienna in 2002 and 2003, as required, and shall hold no fewer than three sessions of two weeks each per year, within the overall approved appropriations of the programme budget for the biennium 2002-2003, according to a schedule to be drawn up by its bureau, and requests the Committee to complete its work by the end of 2003;

"7. *Also decides* that the bureau of the Ad Hoc Committee shall be elected by the Committee itself and shall consist of two representatives from each of the five regional groups;

"8. *Invites* donor countries to assist the United Nations in ensuring the full and effective participation of developing countries, in particular least developed countries, in the work of the Ad Hoc Committee, including by covering travel and local expenses;

"9. *Urges* States to be fully involved in the negotiation of the convention and to endeavour to ensure continuity in their representation;

"10. *Invites* the Ad Hoc Committee to take into consideration the contributions of non-governmental organizations and civil society, in accordance with United Nations rules and following the practice established by the Ad Hoc Committee on the Elaboration of a Convention against Transnational Organized Crime;

"11. *Accepts with gratitude* the offer of the Government of Argentina to host an informal preparatory meeting of the Ad Hoc Committee prior to its first session;

"12. *Requests* the Ad Hoc Committee to submit progress reports on its work to the Commission on Crime Prevention and Criminal Justice at its eleventh and twelfth sessions, in 2002 and 2003, respectively;

"13. *Requests* the Secretary-General to provide the Ad Hoc Committee with the necessary facilities and resources to support its work."

Corrupt practices and illegal transfer of funds

In May, the Commission on Crime Prevention and Criminal Justice considered asset recovery as a sub-theme of its discussion on global action against corruption [E/2001/30/Rev.1]. Discussions highlighted the fact that strengthened international cooperation in asset recovery deserved urgent attention and that the issue could be addressed most effectively by an international legal instrument to provide a common basis for sharing information, conducting investigations, tracing assets, overcoming bank secrecy, confiscating and returning funds and extraditing offenders.

ECONOMIC AND SOCIAL COUNCIL ACTION

On 24 July [meeting 40], the Economic and Social Council, on the recommendation of the Commission on Crime Prevention and Criminal Justice [E/2001/30/Rev.1], adopted **resolution 2001/13** without vote [agenda item 14 *(c)*].

Strengthening international cooperation in preventing and combating the transfer of funds of illicit origin, derived from acts of corruption, including the laundering of funds, and in returning such funds

The Economic and Social Council,

Recalling General Assembly resolutions 51/191 of 16 December 1996 on the United Nations Declaration against Corruption and Bribery in International Commercial Transactions, 53/176 of 15 December 1998 on action against corruption and bribery in international commercial transactions, 54/205 of 22 December 1999 on the prevention of corrupt practices and illegal transfer of funds, 55/25 of 15 November 2000 on the United Nations Convention against Transnational Organized Crime, 55/61 of 4 December 2000 on an effective international legal instrument against corruption and 55/188 of 20 December 2000 on preventing and combating corrupt practices and illegal transfer of funds and repatriation of such funds to the countries of origin,

Concerned about the seriousness of problems posed by corruption, which may endanger the stability and security of societies, undermine the values of democracy and morality and jeopardize social, economic and political development,

Concerned also that funds of illicit origin derived from acts of corruption include public funds, whose diversion may seriously threaten economic and political progress, in particular in developing countries,

Alarmed at the fact that such funds are often being transferred from their countries of origin to international banking centres and financial havens,

Recognizing that the authorities of those countries wishing to recover funds of illicit origin, including funds obtained through acts of corruption and financial fraud, have a legitimate wish to obtain information on the whereabouts of those funds and that confidentiality, the right to privacy and bank secrecy cannot guarantee impunity,

Recognizing also the importance of strengthening international cooperation in combating the transfer of funds of illicit origin and in returning such funds,

Viewing with deep concern the increasing link between money-laundering and corruption, making it essential to promote national and international efforts in areas such as preventing and combating the transfer of funds of illicit origin and returning such funds,

1. *Requests* the intergovernmental open-ended expert group referred to in General Assembly resolution 55/61 to consider, within the context of its mandates, the following issues, inter alia, as possible items of work to be included in the draft terms of reference for the negotiation of a future legal instrument against corruption:

(a) Strengthening international cooperation in preventing and combating the transfer of funds of illicit origin, including the laundering of funds derived from acts of corruption, and promoting ways and means of enabling the return of such funds;

(b) Developing the measures necessary to ensure that those working in banking systems and other financial institutions contribute to the prevention of the transfer of funds of illicit origin derived from acts of corruption, for example, by recording transactions in a transparent manner, and to facilitate the return of those funds;

(c) Defining funds derived from acts of corruption as proceeds of crime and establishing that an act of corruption may be a predicate offence in relation to money-laundering;

(d) Establishing criteria for the determination of countries to which funds, referred to above, should be returned and the appropriate procedures for such return;

2. *Requests* the Office for Drug Control and Crime Prevention of the Secretariat to support Governments that request technical assistance in combating the transfer of funds of illicit origin and in returning such funds, including by providing the names of experts to assist such Governments;

3. *Urges* Governments, through voluntary contributions, and invites multilateral financial institutions and regional development banks, as appropriate, to support the Office for Drug Control and Crime Prevention in its efforts to assist Governments that request technical cooperation in combating the transfer of funds of illicit origin and in returning such funds, including by providing the names of the experts available to assist the Office;

4. *Requests* the Secretary-General, further to his analytical report on progress made in the implementation of resolution 55/188, to prepare, within existing resources or drawing upon through extrabudgetary contributions, for the ad hoc committee referred to in resolution 55/61, a global study on the transfer of funds of illicit origin, especially funds derived from acts of corruption, and its impact on economic, social and political progress, in particular in developing countries, and to include in his study innovative ideas regarding appropriate ways and means of enabling the States concerned to obtain access to information on the whereabouts of funds belonging to them and to recover such funds.

Report of the Secretary-General. In response to General Assembly resolution 55/188 [YUN 2000, p. 1073], the Secretary-General submitted a September report [A/56/403 & Add.1], prepared by CICP, on the prevention of corrupt practices and illegal transfer of funds. The report summarized information received from 29 States and two UN organizations on measures taken to prevent and combat the transfer of funds of illicit origin and on the issue of returning such funds. It also reviewed the outcomes of the tenth session of the Commission on Crime Prevention and Criminal Justice (see p. 1021) and the first meeting of the Intergovernmental Open-Ended Expert Group to Prepare Draft Terms of Reference for the Negotiation of an International Legal Instrument against Corruption (see p. 1041). The report, which included input from the United Nations Conference on Trade and Development, went on to describe the main problems involved in preventing and combating the transfer of funds of illicit origin and returning them, as well as the technical assistance activities of the UN Office for Drug Control and Crime Prevention in that regard.

The Secretary-General concluded that the dimensions of the problem demanded joint and conclusive action by the international community. An area where the UN system could assist Member States was in capacity-building for case management; such a programme could provide support to requesting States for specific multinational cases. The system could also assist individual countries to coordinate efforts and assemble cases at the national level before other countries became involved. Other recommendations concerned the creation of a civil recovery vehicle, the use of "mentors" in asset-recovery cases, the funding of assistance in asset-recovery cases and the possible long-term role of the United Nations.

GENERAL ASSEMBLY ACTION

On 21 December [meeting 90], the General Assembly, on the recommendation of the Second (Economic and Financial) Committee [A/56/559], adopted **resolution 56/186** without vote [agenda item 96 (*a*)].

Preventing and combating corrupt practices and transfer of funds of illicit origin and returning such funds to the countries of origin

The General Assembly,

Recalling its resolutions 54/205 of 22 December 1999 on the prevention of corrupt practices and illegal transfer of funds, 55/61 of 4 December 2000 on an effective international legal instrument against corruption and 55/188 of 20 December 2000 on preventing and combating corrupt practices and illegal transfer of funds and repatriation of such funds to the countries of origin, as well as the report of the meeting of the Intergovernmental Open-Ended Expert Group to Prepare Draft Terms of Reference for the Negotiation of an International Legal Instrument against Corruption, which will be considered by the Economic and Social Council at its next session,

Concerned about the seriousness of problems posed by corrupt practices and transfer of funds of illicit origin, which may endanger the stability and security of societies, undermine the values of democracy and morality and jeopardize social, economic and political development,

Recognizing the need to create an enabling environment for business at the national and international levels in order to promote economic growth and sustainable development, taking into account the development priorities of Governments,

Recognizing also the responsibilities of Governments to adopt policies at the national and international levels aimed at preventing and combating corrupt practices and transfer of funds of illicit origin and returning such funds to the countries of origin,

Mindful of the catalytic role of the United Nations system in facilitating the constructive participation and orderly interaction of the private sector in the development process by embracing universal principles and norms, such as honesty, transparency and accountability,

Underlining the fact that preventing and combating corrupt practices and transfer of funds of illicit origin and returning such funds is an important element in mobilizing resources for development,

Recognizing the importance of international cooperation and existing international and national laws for combating corruption in international commercial transactions,

Noting that the International Conference on Financing for Development will be held at Monterrey, Mexico, from 18 to 22 March 2002,

Stressing the need to prevent and combat corrupt practices and the transfer of funds of illicit origin and to return such funds so as to enable countries to design and fund development projects, in accordance with their national priorities,

Noting that such corrupt practices include State funds being illegally acquired, transferred and invested abroad,

Noting also that the problem of corrupt practices and the transfer of funds of illicit origin, as well as the need to prevent the transfer of such funds, and to return them, have social, economic and legal implications that require comprehensive, holistic examination at the national and international levels,

1. *Takes note* of the report of the Secretary-General on the prevention of corrupt practices and illegal transfer of funds;

2. *Reiterates its condemnation* of corruption, bribery, money-laundering and the transfer of funds of illicit origin, and stresses its belief that those practices need to be prevented and that funds of illicit origin transferred abroad need to be returned after request and due process;

3. *Calls*, while recognizing the importance of national measures, for increased international cooperation, inter alia, through the United Nations system, in support of efforts by Governments to prevent and address the transfer of funds of illicit origin as well as to return such funds to the countries of origin;

4. *Requests* the international community to support the efforts of all countries to strengthen institutional capacity and regulatory frameworks for preventing corruption, bribery, money-laundering and the transfer of funds of illicit origin, as well as for returning such funds to the countries of origin;

5. *Invites* the Economic and Social Council to finalize its consideration of the draft terms of reference for the negotiation of a United Nations convention against corruption, by which an ad hoc committee would be requested to consider, inter alia, the elements of prevention and combating the transfer of funds of illicit origin derived from acts of corruption, including the laundering and returning of such funds, expeditiously;

6. *Requests* the Secretary-General to submit to the General Assembly at its fifty-seventh session a report on the implementation of the present resolution, and also requests the Secretary-General, upon the completion of the work of the ad hoc committee referred to above, to submit recommendations on options for fur-

ther consideration by the Assembly regarding this question;

7. *Decides* to keep the matter under review and to include in the provisional agenda of its fifty-seventh session a sub-item entitled "Preventing and combating corrupt practices and transfer of funds of illicit origin and returning such funds to the countries of origin" under the item entitled "Sectoral policy questions".

Criminal misuse of information technologies

In response to Economic and Social Council resolution 1999/23 [YUN 1999, p. 1054], the Secretary-General submitted to the Commission on Crime Prevention and Criminal Justice a March report containing the conclusions of a study on effective measures to prevent and control high-technology and computer-related crime [E/CN.15/2001/4]. The report provided a preliminary examination of the problems, including crimes committed against the technologies and their users; conventional crimes committed using computer or communications technologies; and the use of technologies to support criminal organizations and activities. It also described the activities of relevant international and intergovernmental organizations, particularly the Council of Europe, in relation to the prevention and control of computer-related crime.

The Secretary-General proposed that a more detailed study of the problem be presented to the Commission at its eleventh (2002) session and recommended that the Commission consider a series of options for further action, such as the possible drafting of an international instrument against computer-related crime, and options for a shorter-term strategy, including the establishment of a United Nations global programme against high-technology and computer-related crime.

GENERAL ASSEMBLY ACTION

On 19 December [meeting 88], the General Assembly, on the recommendation of the Third Committee [A/56/574], adopted **resolution 56/121** without vote [agenda item 110].

Combating the criminal misuse of information technologies

The General Assembly,

Recalling the United Nations Millennium Declaration, in which Member States resolved to ensure that the benefits of new technologies, especially information and communications technologies, in conformity with the recommendations contained in the ministerial declaration of the high-level segment of the substantive session of 2000 of the Economic and Social Council, are available to all, and its resolution 55/63 of 4 December 2000, in which it invited Member States to take into account measures to combat the criminal misuse of information technologies,

Recognizing that the free flow of information can promote economic and social development, education and democratic governance,

Noting the significant advances in the development and application of information technologies and means of telecommunication,

Expressing concern that technological advances have created new possibilities for criminal activity, in particular the criminal misuse of information technologies,

Noting that reliance on information technologies, while it may vary from State to State, has resulted in a substantial increase in global cooperation and coordination, with the result that the criminal misuse of information technologies may have a grave impact on all States,

Recognizing that gaps in the access to and use of information technologies by States can diminish the effectiveness of international cooperation in combating the criminal misuse of information technologies, and recognizing also the need to facilitate the transfer of information technologies, in particular to developing countries,

Noting the necessity of preventing the criminal misuse of information technologies,

Recognizing the need for cooperation between States and the private sector in combating the criminal misuse of information technologies,

Underlining the need for enhanced coordination and cooperation among States in combating the criminal misuse of information technologies, and, in this context, stressing the role that can be played by the United Nations and other international and regional organizations,

Welcoming the work of the Tenth United Nations Congress on the Prevention of Crime and the Treatment of Offenders,

Recognizing with appreciation the work of the Commission on Crime Prevention and Criminal Justice at its ninth and tenth sessions and the subsequent preparation of a plan of action against high-technology and computer-related crime, which recognizes, inter alia, the need for effective law enforcement and the need to maintain effective protections for privacy and other related basic rights, as well as the need to take into account ongoing work in other forums,

Noting the work of international and regional organizations in combating high-technology crime, including the work of the Council of Europe in elaborating the Convention on Cybercrime, as well as the work of those organizations in promoting dialogue between government and the private sector on safety and confidence in cyberspace,

1. *Invites* Member States, when developing national law, policy and practice to combat the criminal misuse of information technologies, to take into account, as appropriate, the work and achievements of the Commission on Crime Prevention and Criminal Justice and of other international and regional organizations;

2. *Takes note* of the value of the measures set forth in its resolution 55/63, and again invites Member States to take them into account in their efforts to combat the criminal misuse of information technologies;

3. *Decides* to defer consideration of this subject, pending work envisioned in the plan of action against

high-technology and computer-related crime of the Commission on Crime Prevention and Criminal Justice.

UN standards and norms

In April, the Secretary-General submitted to the Commission on Crime Prevention and Criminal Justice a report on the use and application of UN standards and norms in crime prevention and criminal justice [E/CN.5/2001/9]. He provided an overview of CICP efforts to promote the use and application of UN standards and norms, and reviewed the process of information-gathering and analysis conducted over two years through 12 surveys on existing international instruments and on standard-setting activities designed to facilitate the drafting of new international instruments. The report recommended that the cost-benefit value of the resources expended in gathering information through surveys be weighed against the output and suggested that attention be focused on consolidating mandated work and reporting obligations, inclusive of surveys, and on keeping them to a minimum. A possible option would be to request consolidated reporting obligations; follow-up activities would be focused on clusters of cross-cutting issues, areas, sectors or professions, rather than on individual instruments.

ECONOMIC AND SOCIAL COUNCIL ACTION

On 24 July [meeting 40], the Economic and Social Council, on the recommendation of the Commission on Crime Prevention and Criminal Justice [E/2001/30/Rev.1], adopted **resolution 2001/11** without vote [agenda item 14 (c)].

Action to promote effective community-based crime prevention

The Economic and Social Council,

Bearing in mind its resolution 1996/16 of 23 July 1996, in which it requested the Secretary-General to continue to promote the use and application of United Nations standards and norms in crime prevention and criminal justice,

Recalling the "Elements of responsible crime prevention: standards and norms", annexed to its resolution 1997/33 of 21 July 1997, in particular those elements on community involvement in crime prevention contained in paragraphs 14 to 23,

Recalling also the revised draft elements of responsible crime prevention prepared by the Expert Group Meeting on Elements of Responsible Crime Prevention: Addressing Traditional and Emerging Crime Problems, held in Buenos Aires from 8 to 10 September 1999,

Noting that the revised draft elements of responsible crime prevention were annexed to the working paper prepared by the Secretariat on effective crime prevention: keeping pace with new developments, submitted

to the Tenth United Nations Congress on the Prevention of Crime and the Treatment of Offenders,

Acknowledging the need to update and finalize the draft elements of responsible crime prevention,

Noting the international colloquium of crime prevention experts held in Montreal, Canada, from 3 to 6 October 1999 in preparation for the Tenth Congress by the Governments of Canada, France and the Netherlands, in collaboration with the International Centre for the Prevention of Crime,

Noting with appreciation the workshop on community involvement in crime prevention, organized during the Tenth Congress by the International Centre for the Prevention of Crime,

Aware of the scope for significant reductions in crime and victimization through research-based approaches and of the contribution that effective crime prevention can make in terms of the safety and security of individuals and communities and their property,

Desirous that the commitments made in the Vienna Declaration on Crime and Justice: Meeting the Challenges of the Twenty-first Century, adopted by the Tenth Congress, in relation to crime prevention, especially those made in paragraphs 11, 13, 20, 21, 24 and 25 of the Vienna Declaration, be implemented nationally and internationally,

Convinced of the need to advance a collaborative agenda for action with respect to those commitments made in the Vienna Declaration,

1. *Requests* the Secretary-General to convene, subject to the availability of extrabudgetary resources, a meeting of experts selected on the basis of equitable geographical representation for the purposes of further revising the draft elements of responsible crime prevention, with a view to arriving at a version of the draft elements on which the Commission on Crime Prevention and Criminal Justice, at its eleventh session, will be able to reach consensus, and proposing priority areas for international action, including the identification of technical assistance issues, to promote effective community-based crime prevention;

2. *Welcomes* the offer of the Government of Canada to host the meeting of the expert group;

3. *Requests* the expert group, within the context of its meeting, to consider the results of the work of the recent United Nations meetings on this subject;

4. *Requests* the Secretary-General to submit a report on the results of the meeting of the expert group, including its revised version of the draft elements of responsible crime prevention and the priority areas for international action to promote effective community-based crime prevention, to the Commission on Crime Prevention and Criminal Justice at its eleventh session for its consideration and action.

Restorative justice

In accordance with Economic and Social Council resolution 2000/14 [YUN 2000, p. 1076], the Secretary-General convened a meeting of the Group of Experts on Restorative Justice (Ottawa, Canada, 29 October–1 November) [E/CN.15/2002/5/Add.1 & Corr.1]. The Group of Experts reviewed comments received from 37 Member States on the preliminary draft elements of a declaration of basic principles on the use of restorative justice programmes in criminal matters and proposed a revised text, which was annexed to its report. The experts suggested that a non-binding international instrument on restorative justice could provide guidance in the establishment of national programmes and agreed that restorative justice measures should be flexible in their adaptation to established criminal justice practices.

Human resources development

In response to General Assembly resolution 54/211 [YUN 1999, p. 1072], the Secretary-General submitted a July report on advancing human resources development in developing countries [A/56/162]. The report outlined the background and context of UN system activity in human resources development, in the light of the twin challenges of reducing poverty and advancing technology.

The Secretary-General recommended that future UN initiatives for human resources development should take a broader view of the issue, not only equating it with education and training, but also relating it to broader capability development through knowledge acquisition, institutional change and policy reforms. That would allow human resources to respond to new demands associated with the technology revolution, take advantage of emerging opportunities in a globalized world and participate in processes that influenced the lives of the poor.

On 19 July, the Economic and Social Council, by **decision 2001/299**, adopted "The contribution of human resources development, including in the areas of health and education, to the process of development" as the theme for its high-level segment in 2002.

GENERAL ASSEMBLY ACTION

On 21 December [meeting 90], the General Assembly, on the recommendation of the Second Committee [A/56/560/Add.2], adopted **resolution 56/189** without vote [agenda item 97 (b)].

Human resources development
The General Assembly,

Reaffirming its resolutions 45/191 of 21 December 1990, 46/143 of 17 December 1991, 48/205 of 21 December 1993, 50/105 of 20 December 1995, 52/196 of 18 December 1997 and 54/211 of 22 December 1999, as well as the relevant sections of the Agenda for Development,

Reaffirming also the United Nations Millennium Declaration adopted by heads of State and Government on 8 September 2000,

Recalling Economic and Social Council decision 2001/299 of 19 July 2001, by which the Council adopted "The contribution of human resources development, including in the areas of health and education, to the process of development" as the theme for the high-level segment of its substantive session of 2002,

Recognizing that human beings are at the centre of concern in sustainable development,

Stressing that Governments have the primary responsibility for defining and implementing appropriate policies for human resources development and that there is a need for continuing support from the international community to complement the efforts of developing countries,

Stressing also that there is a need for an enabling national and international environment that will enhance human resources development in developing countries and promote sustained economic growth and sustainable development,

Stressing further that health and education are at the core of human resources development, and the need to ensure that by 2015 children everywhere, boys and girls alike, will be able to complete a full course of primary schooling and that girls and boys will have equal access to all levels of education, as expressed at the World Education Forum, held at Dakar from 26 to 28 April 2000, and in the United Nations Millennium Declaration,

Emphasizing that human resources development should be an essential component of international development cooperation and that there is a need to promote continuous training and capacity-building within projects and programmes as a means of advancing such development,

Recognizing that there is a need to integrate human resources development into comprehensive strategies that mainstream a gender perspective, taking into account the needs of all people, in particular the needs of women and girls,

Recognizing also the vital role of South-South cooperation in supporting national efforts at human resources development,

Expressing concern at the increasing development gap between developed and developing countries, including the gap in knowledge, information and communication technologies, and the increasing disparity of income in and among nations and its adverse impact on the development of human resources, in particular in the developing countries,

Stressing that developing countries should be assisted in their efforts to develop capacity in and be well equipped with the knowledge of information technologies that would enable them to benefit from the opportunities offered by globalization and to avoid the risk of marginalization in the process of globalization,

Expressing deep concern at the devastating impact of the human immunodeficiency virus/acquired immunodeficiency syndrome (HIV/AIDS) pandemic, especially in sub-Saharan Africa, and of other major diseases on human resources development, in particular in developing countries,

Emphasizing the continuing need for coordination and integration among the organs and organizations of the United Nations system in assisting developing countries, in particular the least developed among them, to foster the development of their human resources, especially that of the most vulnerable groups, and for the United Nations to continue to give priority to human resources development in developing countries,

1. *Takes note* of the report of the Secretary-General;

2. *Recognizes* the importance of developing human resources as a means, inter alia, of promoting economic growth and eradicating poverty as well as of participating more effectively in the world economic system and benefiting from globalization;

3. *Urges* increased investments by all countries, the United Nations system, international organizations, the private sector, non-governmental organizations and civil society in all aspects of human development, such as health, nutrition, education, training and further capacity-building, with a view to achieving sustainable development and the well-being of all;

4. *Encourages* all countries to accord priority to human resources development in the context of the adoption of national economic and social policies, including their financing, taking into account their financial constraints;

5. *Urges* the adoption of comprehensive approaches to human resources development which combine, among other factors, economic growth, poverty eradication, provision of basic social services, sustainable livelihoods, empowerment of women, involvement of young people, the needs of vulnerable groups of society, the needs of local indigenous communities, political freedom, popular participation and respect for human rights, justice and equity, all of which are essential for enhancing human capacity to meet the challenge of development;

6. *Encourages* all countries to ensure local and community-level engagement in policy issues of human resources development;

7. *Emphasizes* the need to ensure the full participation of women in the formulation and implementation of national and local policies to promote human resources development;

8. *Recognizes* the need to direct concerted efforts at enhancing the technical skills and know-how of people living in rural and agricultural areas, with a view to improving their means of livelihood and material well-being, and in this regard encourages the allocation of more resources for that purpose so as to facilitate access to appropriate technology and know-how from within and from other countries, in particular the developed countries, as well as through South-South cooperation;

9. *Encourages* the adoption of policies, approaches and measures that serve to narrow the increasing gap between developed and developing countries in information and communication technologies in particular and in technology in general by, inter alia:

(a) Encouraging the private sector, in collaboration with the United Nations system and non-governmental organizations, to donate voluntarily to designated centres in developing countries literary materials, information and communications technology equipment and training which, together with the enabling policies and institutions both at the national and international levels, will facilitate improved access;

(b) Taking advantage of the rapid turnaround in both the educational institutions and corporations in developed countries of literary material and information and communications technology equipment, through coordinated efforts involving the United Nations system, non-governmental organizations and recipients in interested developing countries;

(c) Promoting transparent, efficient regulatory regimes and other policies that encourage investment;

(d) Supporting targeted investments in infrastructure that would establish the physical foundation for the operation of Internet services and pave the way for commercial and development applications;

(e) Developing training in information technologies for users such as non-governmental organizations, universities and business service organizations, as well as key governmental agencies;

10. *Calls upon* the United Nations system to harmonize further its collective human resources development efforts, in accordance with national policies and priorities;

11. *Encourages* the United Nations system to take a comprehensive view of human resources development in its initiatives, relating it to the acquisition of broader knowledge, with a view to enabling human resources to respond to the new demands associated with the technology revolution and to take advantage of emerging opportunities in a globalized world;

12. *Also encourages* the United Nations system to promote strategies for human resources development that facilitate access by developing countries to new information and communication technologies so as to bridge the digital divide;

13. *Further encourages* the United Nations system to focus in its cooperation activities on building human and institutional capacity, with specific attention given to women, girls and vulnerable groups;

14. *Encourages* the United Nations system to continue to engage, where appropriate, in partnerships with the private sector, in accordance with relevant United Nations resolutions, so as to contribute further to the building of human resources development capacity in developing countries;

15. *Invites* international organizations, including international financial institutions, to continue to give priority to supporting the objectives of human resources development and to integrating them into their policies, projects and operations;

16. *Calls upon* developed countries and the United Nations system to increase support to programmes and activities in developing countries for advancing human resources development and capacity-building, in particular those geared towards harnessing information and communication technologies;

17. *Requests* the Secretary-General to submit to the General Assembly at its fifty-eighth session a report on the implementation of the present resolution;

18. *Decides* to include in the provisional agenda of its fifty-eighth session, under the item entitled "Sustainable development and international economic cooperation", the sub-item entitled "Human resources development".

UN research and training institutes

UN Institute for Training and Research

In response to General Assembly resolution 55/208 [YUN 2000, p. 1078], the Secretary-General submitted a November report on the United Nations Institute for Training and Research (UNITAR) [A/56/615]. He noted that the conduct of the various UNITAR programmes was evolving smoothly following a restructuring phase, and activities remained steady and sustained. Each year since 1996, some 120 programmes, seminars and workshops had been organized throughout the world and more than 5,500 participants were benefiting from UNITAR training and capacity-building activities annually. Significant developments included fellowship programmes in preventive diplomacy, international law, international civil service and international affairs management, organized in Europe and the United States, which had largely met the expectations of participants. The Institute had made progress in attracting experts from developing countries and countries with economies in transition for the preparation of training materials and in concentrating its programming on development issues. Almost all UNITAR programmes were being designed and conducted in conjunction with one or more institutions within and outside the UN system and systematic utilization of UNITAR's services had increased.

The Secretary-General stated that UNITAR's financial situation had improved but remained fragile. Although contributions to the Special Purpose Grants Fund were satisfactory, the insufficiency of non-earmarked voluntary contributions made it difficult to maintain training programmes in Nairobi and Vienna and impossible to inaugurate new programmes in cities hosting UN regional commissions, as requested by the Assembly in resolution 55/208. The Secretary-General also discussed continuity in UNITAR management and the question of the classification of rental rates and of maintenance costs charged to the Institute.

GENERAL ASSEMBLY ACTION

On 21 December [meeting 90], the General Assembly, on the recommendation of the Second Committee [A/56/567], adopted **resolution 56/208** without vote [agenda item 104].

United Nations Institute for Training and Research

The General Assembly,

Recalling its resolutions 50/121 of 20 December 1995, 51/188 of 16 December 1996, 52/206 of 18 December 1997, 53/195 of 15 December 1998, 54/229 of 22 December 1999 and 55/208 of 20 December 2000,

Taking note of the report of the Secretary-General,

Welcoming the recent progress made by the United Nations Institute for Training and Research in its various programmes and activities, including the improved cooperation that has been established with other organizations of the United Nations system and with regional and national institutions,

Expressing its appreciation to the Governments and private institutions that have made or pledged financial and other contributions to the Institute,

Noting that contributions to the General Fund have not increased and that the participation of the developed countries in training programmes in New York and Geneva is increasing,

Noting also that the bulk of the resources contributed to the Institute are directed to the Special Purpose Grants Fund rather than to the General Fund, and stressing the need to address that unbalanced situation,

Noting further that the Institute receives no subsidy from the United Nations regular budget, that it provides training programmes to all Member States free of charge and that similar United Nations institutions based at Geneva are not charged rent or maintenance costs,

Welcoming the decisions taken by the Secretary-General to ensure continuity in the management of the Institute and to establish the proper grade for the post of Executive Director with the concurrence of the Advisory Committee on Administrative and Budgetary Questions,

Reiterating that training activities should be accorded a more visible and larger role in support of the management of international affairs and in the execution of the economic and social development programmes of the United Nations system,

1. *Reaffirms* the importance of a coordinated, United Nations system-wide approach to research and training based on an effective coherent strategy and an effective division of labour among the relevant institutions and bodies;

2. *Also reaffirms* the relevance of the United Nations Institute for Training and Research in view of the growing importance of training within the United Nations and the training requirements of States and the relevance of training-related research activities undertaken by the Institute within its mandate;

3. *Stresses* the need for the Institute to strengthen further its cooperation with other United Nations institutes and relevant national, regional and international institutes;

4. *Welcomes* the progress made in building partnerships between the Institute and other organizations and bodies of the United Nations system with respect to their training programmes, and in this context underlines the need to develop further and to expand the scope of those partnerships, in particular at the country level;

5. *Requests* the Board of Trustees of the United Nations Institute for Training and Research to continue to ensure fair geographical distribution and transparency in the preparation of the programmes and in the employment of experts, and in this regard stresses that the courses of the Institute should focus primarily on development issues;

6. *Renews its appeal* to all Governments, in particular those of developed countries, and to private institutions that have not yet contributed financially or

otherwise to the Institute, to give it their generous financial and other support, and urges the States that have interrupted their voluntary contributions to consider resuming them in view of the successful restructuring and revitalization of the Institute;

7. *Calls upon* developed countries, which are increasingly participating in the training programmes conducted in New York and Geneva, to make contributions or consider increasing their contributions to the General Fund;

8. *Encourages* the Board of Trustees of the Institute to continue its efforts to resolve the critical financial situation of the Institute, in particular with a view to broadening its donor base and increasing the contributions made to the General Fund;

9. *Also encourages* the Board of Trustees to consider diversifying further the venues of the events organized by the Institute and to include the cities hosting regional commissions, in order to promote greater participation and reduce costs;

10. *Requests* the Secretary-General, in consultation with the Institute and United Nations funds and programmes, to continue to explore ways and means of systematically utilizing the Institute in the execution of training and capacity-building programmes for the economic and social development of developing countries;

11. *Also requests* the Secretary-General to clarify the reason why the United Nations Institute for Training and Research does not benefit from rental rates and maintenance costs similar to those enjoyed by other organizations affiliated with the United Nations, such as the United Nations Institute for Disarmament Research and the United Nations Research Institute for Social Development, and further requests the Secretary-General to submit proposals on how to waive or reduce the rental rates and maintenance costs charged to the United Nations Institute for Training and Research with a view to alleviating its current financial difficulties, which are aggravated by the current practice of charging commercial rates;

12. *Requests* the Secretary-General to report to it at its fifty-seventh session on the implementation of the present resolution, including details on the status of contributions to, and the financial situation of, the United Nations Institute for Training and Research, as well as on the use of its services by Member States.

United Nations University

The report of the United Nations University (UNU) Council [A/57/31], which described activities in 2001, stated that UNU continued to work within two major thematic areas—peace and governance, and environment and sustainable development. Within those areas, UNU undertook research and training and developed networks on a broad range of issues, from the causes of conflict to leadership, debt relief and international environmental governance. The University disseminated the results of its research through high-level panels, conferences, workshops, books, journals, newsletters and the Internet. In 2001, UNU initiated a new programme on science and technology for sustainability with the Republic

of Korea and the Kwangja Institute of Science and Technology, and a new research and training programme on fragile ecosystems in wetland areas in Mato Grosso, Brazil, in cooperation with the Universidade Federal de Mato Grosso and the Mato Grosso government. The University also received endorsement for a new research and training centre on environment and human security in Germany, continued discussions with Qatar regarding a new centre in the Middle East and extended a fisheries training programme in Iceland.

UNU Council

At its annual session (Tokyo, 3-7 December), the UNU Council, the University's governing body, reviewed implementation of UNU activities; considered evaluations of the UNU World Institute for Development Economics Research and the University's capacity development activities; examined proposals for new research and training centres, programmes, networks and initiatives; assessed the University's financial situation; and reviewed and adopted the 2002-2003 academic programme and budget.

University for Peace

In response to General Assembly resolution 54/29 [YUN 1999, p. 1070], the Secretary-General submitted a September report [A/56/314], in which he detailed progress in revitalizing the Costa Rica–based University for Peace, especially concerning a strategy and programme for the development and management of its academic programme and other peace-related activities. The activities of the University, which was established in 1980 [YUN 1980, p. 1004], were being expanded and its academic programme enhanced in order to make it a focus of global efforts in the study of and education for peace. To that end, advisory meetings had been organized in all regions, with the participation of eminent international scholars, to address various aspects of the University's academic programme.

The Secretary-General concluded that the University could serve as a useful tool to support the peace and security objectives of the United Nations.

GENERAL ASSEMBLY ACTION

On 22 October [meeting 29], the General Assembly adopted **resolution 56/2** [draft: A/56/L.4 & Add.1] without vote [agenda item 31].

University for Peace

The General Assembly,

Recalling its resolution 54/29 of 18 November 1999, in which it recalled that, in its resolution 34/111 of 14

December 1979, it had approved the idea of establishing the University for Peace as a specialized international centre for postgraduate studies, research and the dissemination of knowledge specifically aimed at training and education for peace and its universal promotion within the United Nations system,

Recalling also that in its resolution 35/55 of 5 December 1980 it approved the establishment of the University for Peace in conformity with the International Agreement for the Establishment of the University for Peace,

Recalling further its resolutions 45/8 of 24 October 1990, 46/11 of 24 October 1991 and 48/9 of 25 October 1993,

Recalling that in its resolution 46/11 it decided to include in the agenda of its forty-eighth session and biennially thereafter an item entitled "University for Peace",

Recalling also its resolution 50/41 of 8 December 1995, in which it decided to request the Secretary-General to consider ways of strengthening cooperation between the United Nations and the University for Peace and to submit a report thereon to the General Assembly at its fifty-second session,

Recalling further its adoption on 13 September 1999 of the Declaration and Programme of Action on a Culture of Peace,

Noting that in 1991 the Secretary-General, with the assistance of the United Nations Development Programme, established a Trust Fund for Peace consisting of voluntary contributions in order to provide the University with the means necessary to extend its sphere of activity to the whole world, taking full advantage of its potential capacity for education, research and support of the United Nations and to carry out its mandate of promoting peace in the world,

Noting with appreciation that the Government of Uruguay, by agreement with the University for Peace, established in 1997 a World Centre for Research and Information on Peace as regional subheadquarters of the University for South America,

Noting also with appreciation the vigorous actions taken by the Secretary-General, in consultation with the Director-General of the United Nations Educational, Scientific and Cultural Organization and with the encouragement and support of the Government of Costa Rica, to revitalize the University,

Noting that the University has placed special emphasis on the area of conflict prevention, peacekeeping, peace-building and peaceful settlement of disputes, and that it has launched programmes in the areas of democratic consensus-building and training of academic experts in the techniques of peaceful settlement of conflicts, which is highly relevant to the promotion of universal peace,

Noting also that the University has launched a broad programme for building a culture of peace in Central America and the Caribbean in the context of the efforts being made by the United Nations and by the United Nations Educational, Scientific and Cultural Organization for the development and promotion of a culture of peace,

Noting with appreciation that the University organized a symposium in celebration of the International Year of Older Persons, 1999, at which it emphasized the valuable contribution that older persons can make to the promotion of peace, solidarity, tolerance and the culture of peace,

Recognizing the important and varied activities carried out by the University during the period 1999-2000, within its financial limitations and with the valuable assistance and contributions of Governments, foundations and non-governmental organizations,

Considering the importance of promoting education for peace that fosters respect for the values inherent in peace and universal coexistence among persons, including respect for the life, dignity and integrity of human beings, as well as friendship and solidarity among peoples irrespective of their nationality, race, sex, religion or culture,

Considering that, by its resolution 52/15 of 20 November 1997, the General Assembly proclaimed the year 2000 as the International Year for the Culture of Peace and that it should be ushered in with One Day in Peace, 1 January 2000,

1. *Takes note with appreciation* of the report of the Secretary-General submitted pursuant to resolution 54/29 on ways of strengthening cooperation between the United Nations and the University for Peace;

2. *Requests* the Secretary-General to consider using the services of the University in his conflict-resolution and peace-building efforts and in the promotion of the Declaration and Programme of Action on a Culture of Peace;

3. *Invites* Member States, intergovernmental bodies, non-governmental organizations and interested individuals to contribute directly to the Trust Fund for Peace or to the budget of the University;

4. *Invites* Member States to accede to the International Agreement for the Establishment of the University for Peace, thereby demonstrating their support for an educational institution devoted to the promotion of a universal culture of peace;

5. *Invites* Member States, intergovernmental and non-governmental organizations and all the peoples of the world to celebrate One Day in Peace, 1 January 2002, and every year thereafter;

6. *Decides* to include in the provisional agenda of its fifty-eighth session the item entitled "University for Peace".

Education for all

UN Literacy Decade

By a June note [A/56/114-E/2001/93 & Add.1], the Secretary-General transmitted to the General Assembly the report of the UNESCO Director-General containing the draft proposal and plan for a United Nations literacy decade, as envisaged by the Assembly in resolution 54/122 [YUN 1999, p. 1073]. The report noted that UNESCO estimates indicated that, if current trends continued, one in six adults (830 million people) would still be illiterate in 2010. There was, therefore, an urgent need for a major new worldwide initiative that focused on literacy as an integral component of the global commitment to Education for All.

The proposed decade would give greater thrust to achieving international development targets and give priority to making opportunities available for the poorest and most marginalized. The decade's outcomes would include a better understanding of the structure of illiteracy; a viable policy-making framework, with regional and international support for national initiatives; national prioritization of population groups; increased capacity in designing strategies; improved quality of teacher training; the promotion of functional literacy skills in order to reduce poverty; and the use of information technologies.

GENERAL ASSEMBLY ACTION

On 19 December [meeting 88], the General Assembly, on the recommendation of the Third Committee [A/56/572], adopted **resolution 56/116** without vote [agenda item 108].

United Nations Literacy Decade: education for all

The General Assembly,

Recalling that in the Universal Declaration of Human Rights, the International Covenant on Economic, Social and Cultural Rights and the Convention on the Rights of the Child the right of every individual to education is recognized as inalienable,

Recalling also its resolutions 42/104 of 7 December 1987, by which it proclaimed 1990 as International Literacy Year, and 54/122 of 17 December 1999, in which it requested the Secretary-General, in cooperation with the Director-General of the United Nations Educational, Scientific and Cultural Organization and Member States and with other relevant organizations and bodies, to submit to the General Assembly at its fifty-sixth session a proposal for a United Nations literacy decade, with a draft plan of action and possible time frame for such a decade, on the basis of the outcome of the World Education Forum and the special session of the General Assembly for the five-year review of the World Summit for Social Development,

Reaffirming its resolution 49/184 of 23 December 1994, by which it proclaimed the ten-year period beginning on 1 January 1995 the United Nations Decade for Human Rights Education and appealed to all Governments to intensify their efforts to eradicate illiteracy and to direct education towards the full development of the human personality and to the strengthening of respect for all human rights and fundamental freedoms,

Taking note of Commission on Human Rights resolution 2001/29 of 20 April 2001 on the right to education,

Recalling the United Nations Millennium Declaration of 8 September 2000 in which Member States resolved to ensure that, by the year 2015, children everywhere, boys and girls alike, would be able to complete a full course of primary schooling and that girls and boys would have equal access to all levels of education, which requires a renewed commitment to promote literacy for all,

Recalling also the Copenhagen Declaration on Social Development and the Programme of Action of the World Summit for Social Development and the outcome document of the twenty-fourth special session of the General Assembly entitled "World Summit for Social Development and beyond: achieving social development for all in a globalizing world",

Convinced that literacy is crucial to the acquisition, by every child, youth and adult, of essential life skills that enable them to address the challenges they can face in life, and represents an essential step in basic education, which is an indispensable means for effective participation in the societies and economies of the twenty-first century,

Affirming that the realization of the right to education, especially for girls, contributes to the eradication of poverty,

Acknowledging the activities undertaken at the national and regional levels for the Education for All 2000 assessment of progress towards achieving the goals of education for all, and stressing further the need to redouble efforts in order to meet the basic needs of people of all age groups, in particular girls and women,

Recognizing that, despite the significant progress in basic education, especially the increase in primary school enrolment coupled with a growing emphasis on the quality of education, major problems, both emerging and continuing, still persist, which require even more forceful and concerted action at the national and international levels so as to achieve the goal of education for all,

Deeply concerned about the persistence of the gender gap in education, which is reflected by the fact that nearly two thirds of the world's adult illiterates are women,

Urging Member States, in close partnership with international organizations, as well as non-governmental organizations, to promote the right to education for all and to create conditions for all for learning throughout life,

1. *Takes note* of the report of the Director-General of the United Nations Educational, Scientific and Cultural Organization entitled "Draft proposal and plan for a United Nations literacy decade";

2. *Proclaims* the ten-year period beginning on 1 January 2003 the United Nations Literacy Decade;

3. *Reaffirms* the Dakar Framework for Action adopted at the World Education Forum, in which commitments were made to achieve a 50 per cent improvement in levels of adult literacy by 2015 and to improve the quality of education;

4. *Appeals* to all Governments to redouble their efforts to achieve their own goals of education for all by developing national plans in accordance with the Dakar Framework for Action, setting firm targets and timetables, including gender-specific education targets and programmes, to eliminate gender disparities at all levels of education, to combat the illiteracy of women and girls and to ensure that girls and women have full and equal access to education, and by working in active partnership with communities, associations, the media and development agencies to reach those targets;

5. *Also appeals* to all Governments to reinforce political will and develop more inclusive policy-making environments and devise innovative strategies for reaching the poorest and most marginalized groups and for seeking alternative formal and non-formal approaches to learning with a view to achieving the goals of the Decade;

6. *Urges* all Governments to take the lead in the coordination of the Decade activities at the national level, bringing all relevant national actors together in sustained dialogue on policy formulation, implementation and evaluation of literacy efforts;

7. *Reaffirms* that literacy for all is at the heart of basic education for all and that creating literate environments and societies is essential for achieving the goals of eradicating poverty, reducing child mortality, curbing population growth, achieving gender equality and ensuring sustainable development, peace and democracy;

8. *Appeals* to all Governments and to economic and financial organizations and institutions, both national and international, to lend greater financial and material support to the efforts to increase literacy and achieve the goals of education for all and those of the Decade through, inter alia, the 20/20 initiative, as appropriate;

9. *Invites* Member States, the specialized agencies and other organizations of the United Nations system as well as relevant intergovernmental and non-governmental organizations to intensify further their efforts to implement effectively the World Declaration on Education for All, the Dakar Framework for Action and the relevant commitments and recommendations to promote literacy made at recent major United Nations conferences and at their five-year reviews with a view to better coordinating their activities and increasing their contribution to development within the framework of the Decade in a manner that is complementary to and coordinated with the ongoing education for all process;

10. *Decides* that the United Nations Educational, Scientific and Cultural Organization should take a co-ordinating role in stimulating and catalysing the activities at the international level within the framework of the Decade;

11. *Requests* the Secretary-General, in cooperation with the Director-General of the United Nations Educational, Scientific and Cultural Organization, to seek and take into account comments and proposals from Governments and the relevant international organizations on the draft plan for the Decade in order to develop and finalize a well targeted and action-oriented plan of action to be submitted to the General Assembly at its fifty-seventh session;

12. *Decides* to include in the provisional agenda of its fifty-seventh session a question entitled "United Nations Literacy Decade".

Chapter X

Women

During 2001, United Nations efforts to advance the status of women and ensure their rights continued to be guided by the Beijing Declaration and Platform for Action, adopted at the Fourth (1995) World Conference on Women. That guidance was augmented by the political declaration and further action and initiatives adopted in 2000 at the General Assembly's twenty-third special session to appraise and assess implementation of the Beijing Declaration and Platform for Action (Beijing+5).

The Commission on the Status of Women, the Economic and Social Council and the Assembly considered follow-up to the Fourth World Conference on Women and Beijing+5. In a December resolution, the Assembly called on Governments, the UN system and civil society, including non-governmental organizations (NGOs), to take action to achieve full and effective implementation of the outcomes of the Beijing Conference and the special session.

The Commission on the Status of Women, at its forty-fifth session in March and May, recommended to the Council for adoption agreed conclusions on its two thematic issues: women, the girl child and HIV/AIDS; and gender and all forms of discrimination, in particular racism, racial discrimination, xenophobia and related intolerance. The Council endorsed the agreed conclusions in July. Also on the Commission's recommendation, the Council adopted resolutions on the situation of and assistance to Palestinian women; discrimination against women and girls in Afghanistan; and mainstreaming a gender perspective into all policies and programmes in the UN system. It also adopted a multi-year programme of work for the Commission for 2002-2006. The Commission adopted and brought to the Council's attention resolutions on the release of women and children taken hostage, including those imprisoned during armed conflict, and the 2002-2005 system-wide medium-term plan for the advancement of women.

The United Nations Development Fund for Women continued to focus on women's economic and political empowerment and to advocate for gender equality. In December, the Assembly urged Member States, NGOs and the private sector to continue to contribute to the Fund. The Assembly also adopted resolutions on the situation

of older women; traditional and customary practices affecting the health of women and girls; women in development; and violence against migrant women, among others.

The International Research and Training Institute for the Advancement of Women, which announced the completion of phases I and II of the Gender Awareness Information and Networking System, and the initiation of phase III, continued to suffer from financial insecurity throughout the year. In December, the Assembly decided to establish a working group to consider the Institute's future operations.

Follow-up to the Fourth World Conference on Women and Beijing+5

During 2001, the Commission on the Status of Women, the Economic and Social Council and the General Assembly considered follow-up to the 1995 Fourth World Conference on Women, particularly the implementation of the Beijing Declaration and Platform for Action [YUN 1995, p. 1170], and the political declaration and further actions and initiatives to implement the Beijing Declaration and Platform for Action, adopted at the twenty-third special session of the Assembly (Beijing+5) by resolution S/23-2 [YUN 2000, p. 1084]. The political declaration had reaffirmed the commitment of Governments to the goals and objectives of the Fourth World Conference and to implementation of the 12 critical areas of concern set forth in the Platform for Action: women and poverty; education and training of women; women and health; violence against women; women and armed conflict; women and the economy; women in power and decision-making; institutional mechanisms for the advancement of women; human rights and women; women and the media; women and the environment; and the girl child.

Commission on the Status of Women. At its forty-fifth session (New York, 6-17 March and 9-11 May), the Commission on the Status of Women had before it the first annual report of the Secretary-General on follow-up to and implementation of the Beijing Declaration and Platform for Action [E/CN.6/2001/2], submitted in response to Assembly resolution 55/71 [YUN 2000, p. 1107]. The report emphasized the Secretariat's efforts in support of gender mainstreaming and follow-up activities, including those undertaken by NGOs. It also provided information, in accordance with specific mandates, on the situation of Palestinian women (see p. 1067) and on women and children taken hostage (see p. 1060). An addendum [E/CN.6/2001/2/Add.1] described the situation of women and girls in Afghanistan (see p. 1065).

Economic and Social Council. In a May report to the Economic and Social Council [E/2001/78], the Secretary-General discussed action taken by the Commission on the Status of Women, other functional commissions of the Council and the UN regional commissions towards the implementation of the Beijing Declaration and Platform for Action and the outcome of the twenty-third special session of the General Assembly. The report aimed to assist the Council in its coordination function.

On 26 July, the Council, by **decision 2001/317**, took note of the Secretary-General's report.

General Assembly. In response to General Assembly resolution 55/71, the Secretary-General submitted an August report [A/56/319] that provided updated information on follow-up to the Fourth World Conference on Women and Beijing+5 by intergovernmental bodies, the Economic and Social Council in particular, the UN system and NGOs.

The Secretary-General identified several resolutions adopted by the Council at its 2001 substantive session that addressed the situation of women. He drew particular attention to the fact that ministers at the Council's high-level segment on UN efforts to support the efforts of African countries to achieve sustainable development (see p. 847) had recognized the need to promote the role of women in social and economic development, including by ensuring their participation in the political and economic life of African countries.

In an addendum [A/56/319/Add.1], the Secretary-General described the full range of tasks of the Division for the Advancement of Women, including those that arose from the implementation of the outcome of Beijing+5, the greater acceptance of the Convention on the Elimination of All Forms of Discrimination against Women, and the entry into force of the Optional Protocol to the Convention (see p. 1075).

GENERAL ASSEMBLY ACTION

On 19 December [meeting 88], the General Assembly, on the recommendation of the Third (Social, Humanitarian and Cultural) Committee [A/56/577], adopted **resolution 56/132** without vote [agenda item 113].

Follow-up to the Fourth World Conference on Women and full implementation of the Beijing Declaration and Platform for Action and the outcome of the twenty-third special session of the General Assembly

The General Assembly,

Recalling its resolutions 50/203 of 22 December 1995, 51/69 of 12 December 1996, 52/100 of 12 December 1997, 53/120 of 9 December 1998, 54/141 of 17 December 1999 and 55/71 of 4 December 2000,

Welcoming the outcome of the twenty-third special session of the General Assembly entitled "Women 2000: gender equality, development and peace for the twenty-first century", and stressing the importance of the outcome of the special session, which has assessed the implementation of the Beijing Declaration and Platform for Action, identified obstacles and challenges thereto and proposed actions and initiatives to overcome them and achieve full and accelerated implementation,

Deeply convinced that the Beijing Declaration and Platform for Action and the outcome of the twenty-third special session are important contributions to the advancement of women worldwide in the achievement of gender equality and must be translated into effective action by all States, the United Nations system and other organizations concerned, as well as by non-governmental organizations,

Stressing the importance of strong, sustained political will and commitment at the national, regional and international levels in order to achieve full and accelerated implementation of the Beijing Declaration and Platform for Action and the outcome of the twenty-third special session,

Recognizing that the responsibility for the implementation of the Beijing Declaration and Platform for Action and the outcome of the twenty-third special session rests primarily at the national level and that strengthened efforts are necessary in this respect, and reiterating that enhanced international cooperation is essential for the effective implementation of the Beijing Declaration and Platform for Action and the outcome of the twenty-third special session,

Welcoming the increased integration of a gender perspective in the work of the United Nations, in particular in the outcomes of major United Nations conferences, special sessions, summit conferences and their follow-up processes,

Welcoming also the integration of a gender perspective in the outcome of the twenty-sixth special session of the General Assembly, on the human immunodeficiency virus/acquired immunodeficiency syndrome (HIV/AIDS), held in New York from 25 to 27 June 2001, in particular the emphasis on the gender dimensions of the epidemic, and the recognition that gender equality and the empowerment of women are fundamental elements in the reduction of the vulnerability of women and girls, who are disproportionately affected by HIV/AIDS,

Welcoming further the integration of a gender perspective in the World Conference against Racism, Racial Discrimination, Xenophobia and Related Intolerance, held at Durban, South Africa, from 31 August to

8 September 2001, which recognized, inter alia, the multiple forms of discrimination faced by women and the need to apply a gender perspective in measures to eradicate racism, racial discrimination, xenophobia and related intolerance,

Emphasizing the importance of the decision by the Economic and Social Council, in its resolution 2001/41 of 26 July 2001, to devote the coordination segment of one of its substantive sessions, before 2005, to the review and appraisal of the system-wide implementation of agreed conclusions 1997/2 on mainstreaming the gender perspective into all policies and programmes in the United Nations system, adopted by the Council on 18 July 1997,

Welcoming the ministerial declaration on the role of the United Nations system in support of the efforts of African countries to achieve sustainable development, adopted by the Economic and Social Council on 18 July 2001 at the high-level segment of its substantive session of 2001, in which the Council recognized, inter alia, the need to promote the role of women in social and economic development, including by assuring their participation in political and economic life,

Reaffirming the primary and essential role of the General Assembly and the Economic and Social Council in promoting the advancement of women and gender equality, while noting the importance of the open debate entitled "Women and peace and security", held in the Security Council on 24 October 2000, and its outcome,

Welcoming the adoption of the United Nations Convention against Transnational Organized Crime and the Protocols thereto,

1. _Reaffirms_ the goals, objectives and commitments contained in the Beijing Declaration and Platform for Action and also in the political declaration and further actions and initiatives to implement the Beijing Declaration and Platform for Action adopted by the General Assembly at its twenty-third special session;

2. _Takes note with appreciation_ of the report of the Secretary-General on the follow-up to and progress made in the implementation of the Beijing Declaration and Platform for Action and the outcome of the twenty-third special session of the General Assembly;

3. _Calls upon_ Governments, the relevant entities of the United Nations system within their respective mandates and all other relevant actors of civil society, including non-governmental organizations, to take effective action to achieve full and effective implementation of the Beijing Declaration and Platform for Action and the outcome of the twenty-third special session, as elaborated in the above-mentioned documents;

4. _Calls upon_ Governments, in collaboration with relevant actors of civil society, including non-governmental organizations, to continue to facilitate the translation and dissemination of the Beijing Declaration and Platform for Action and the outcome of the twenty-third special session as broadly and as accessibly as possible;

5. _Strongly encourages_ Governments to continue to support the role and contribution of civil society, in particular non-governmental organizations and women's organizations, in the implementation of the Beijing Declaration and Platform for Action and the outcome of the twenty-third special session;

6. _Welcomes_ the integration of a gender perspective in the United Nations Millennium Declaration, and emphasizes the importance of mainstreaming a gender perspective in the implementation of and follow-up to the Millennium Declaration and in future reports on this subject;

7. _Reaffirms_ its decision that the General Assembly, the Economic and Social Council and the Commission on the Status of Women, in accordance with their respective mandates and with General Assembly resolution 48/162 of 20 December 1993 and other relevant resolutions, constitute a three-tiered intergovernmental mechanism that plays the primary role in the overall policy-making and follow-up and in coordinating the implementation and monitoring of the Beijing Platform for Action and the outcome of the twenty-third special session;

8. _Also reaffirms_ that the follow-up to the Fourth World Conference on Women and the twenty-third special session will be undertaken within the framework of an integrated and coordinated follow-up to major international conferences and summits in the economic, social and related fields, and in this regard takes note of Economic and Social Council resolution 2001/21 of 26 July 2001 on integrated and coordinated implementation of and follow-up to the outcomes of the major United Nations conferences and summits;

9. _Requests_ the Economic and Social Council to intensify further its efforts to ensure that gender mainstreaming is an integral part of all United Nations activities, building upon agreed conclusions 1997/2 adopted by the Council on 18 July 1997;

10. _Invites_ the Council to continue to further policy coordination and inter-agency cooperation towards the achievement of the objectives of the Beijing Platform for Action and the outcome of the twenty-third special session, including by considering the dedication of specific segments of the Council to the advancement of women and implementation of the above-mentioned documents and by mainstreaming a gender perspective in all its work;

11. _Encourages_ the Council to request the regional commissions, within their respective mandates and resources, to intensify efforts to build up a database, to be updated regularly, in which all programmes and projects carried out in their respective regions by agencies or organizations of the United Nations system are listed, and to facilitate their dissemination, as well as the evaluation of their impact on the empowerment of women through the implementation of the Beijing Platform for Action;

12. _Reaffirms_ that the Commission on the Status of Women has a central role in assisting the Council in monitoring, assessing progress made in and accelerating, within the United Nations system, the implementation of the Beijing Platform for Action and the outcome of the twenty-third special session, and in advising the Council thereon, encourages the Commission, in this regard, further to enhance its working methods in order to improve the effectiveness of its work and its catalytic role in ensuring the integration of a gender perspective in United Nations activities, taking into consideration the adoption by the Council of the multi-year programme of work of the Commission for 2002-2006, and calls on the Commission and all involved to implement the programme of work;

13. *Recognizes* the importance attached to the regional and subregional monitoring of the global and regional platforms for action and of the implementation of the outcome of the twenty-third special session by regional commissions and other regional or subregional structures, within their mandates, in consultation with Governments, and calls for the promotion of further cooperation in that respect among Governments and, where appropriate, national machineries of the same region;

14. *Reaffirms* that, in order to implement the Beijing Platform for Action and the outcome of the twenty-third special session, adequate mobilization of resources at the national and international levels, as well as new and additional resources for the developing countries, in particular those in Africa and the least developed countries, from all available funding mechanisms, including multilateral, bilateral and private sources, will also be required;

15. *Recognizes* that the implementation of the Beijing Platform for Action and the outcome of the twenty-third special session in the countries with economies in transition requires continued national efforts and international cooperation and assistance;

16. *Reaffirms* that, in order to implement the Beijing Platform for Action and the outcome of the twenty-third special session, a reformulation of policies and reallocation of resources may be needed, but that some policy changes may not necessarily have financial implications;

17. *Recognizes* that the creation of an enabling environment at the national and international levels, including through the full participation of women at all levels of decision-making, is necessary to ensure the full participation of women in economic activities, and calls upon States to remove obstacles to the full implementation of the Beijing Declaration and Platform for Action and the outcome of the twenty-third special session;

18. *Reaffirms* that, in order to ensure the effective implementation of the strategic objectives of the Beijing Platform for Action and the outcome of the twenty-third special session, the United Nations system should promote an active and visible policy of mainstreaming a gender perspective, including through the work of the Special Adviser on Gender Issues and Advancement of Women and the maintenance of gender units and focal points;

19. *Also reaffirms* that United Nations bodies that focus on gender issues, such as the United Nations Population Fund, the United Nations Development Fund for Women and the International Research and Training Institute for the Advancement of Women, have an important role to play in the implementation of the objectives of the Beijing Declaration and Platform for Action and the outcome of the twenty-third special session;

20. *Welcomes* the convening, in 2002, of the International Conference on Financing for Development, to be held at Monterrey, Mexico, the World Summit on Sustainable Development, to be held at Johannesburg, South Africa, the Second World Assembly on Ageing, to be held at Madrid, and the special session of the General Assembly on children, and urges Governments to integrate a gender perspective in the respective processes and outcome documents;

21. *Expresses its appreciation* for the efforts made by all relevant organizations of the United Nations system in promoting the role of women in conflict prevention and resolution;

22. *Recognizes* the important role of women in the prevention and resolution of conflicts and in peace-building, the importance of their equal participation and full involvement in all efforts for the maintenance and promotion of peace and security and the need to increase their role in decision-making with regard to conflict prevention and resolution, and urges the United Nations system and Governments to make further efforts in this regard and to take steps to ensure and support the full participation of women at all levels of decision-making and implementation in development activities and peace processes, including conflict prevention and resolution, post-conflict reconstruction, peacemaking, peacekeeping and peace-building, as well as through the integration of a gender perspective into those United Nations processes;

23. *Requests* the Secretary-General to ensure that all United Nations personnel and officials at Headquarters and in the field, especially in field operations, receive training so that they mainstream a gender perspective in their work, including gender impact analysis, and to ensure appropriate follow-up to such training;

24. *Requests* all bodies that deal with programme and budgetary matters, including the Committee for Programme and Coordination, to ensure that all programmes, medium-term plans and programme budgets visibly mainstream a gender perspective;

25. *Invites* States parties to the Convention on the Elimination of All Forms of Discrimination against Women to include information on measures taken to implement the outcome of the twenty-third special session, as well as the Beijing Platform for Action, in their reports to the Committee on the Elimination of Discrimination against Women under article 18 of the Convention;

26. *Welcomes* the entry into force of the Optional Protocol to the Convention on the Elimination of All Forms of Discrimination against Women, and urges States parties to the Convention that have not yet done so to consider signing, ratifying or acceding to the Optional Protocol;

27. *Urges* Member States to consider signing, ratifying or acceding to the United Nations Convention against Transnational Organized Crime and the Protocols thereto, in particular the Protocol to Prevent, Suppress and Punish Trafficking in Persons, Especially Women and Children;

28. *Requests* the Secretary-General to continue to disseminate the Beijing Declaration and Platform for Action and the outcome of the twenty-third special session as widely as possible in all the official languages of the United Nations;

29. *Also requests* the Secretary-General to report annually to the General Assembly, the Economic and Social Council and the Commission on the Status of Women on follow-up to and progress in the implementation of the Beijing Declaration and Platform for Action and the outcome of the twenty-third special session, with an assessment of progress made in mainstreaming a gender perspective within the United Nations system, including by providing information on

key achievements, lessons learned and best practices, and to recommend further measures and strategies for future action within the United Nations system;

30. *Decides* to include in the provisional agenda of its fifty-seventh session the item entitled "Implementation of the outcome of the Fourth World Conference on Women and of the twenty-third special session of the General Assembly, entitled 'Women 2000: gender equality, development and peace for the twenty-first century' ".

Critical areas of concern

Violence against women

The Secretary-General transmitted to the Commission on the Status of Women and the Commission on Human Rights a January report of the United Nations Development Fund for Women (UNIFEM) on activities in 2000 to eliminate violence against women [E/CN.4/2001/126-E/CN.6/2001/6]. UNIFEM continued to build on advocacy campaigns established with UN partners in various regions. Beijing+5 [YUN 2000, p. 1082] gave strong reaffirmation to activities within the international community addressing gender-based violence and added specific forms of violence against women to the international agenda, namely so-called honour killings and dowry-related deaths.

Since it began operations in 1997 [YUN 1997, p. 1193], the Trust Fund in Support of Action to Eliminate Violence against Women had received over $5.4 million in contributions and funded 105 projects around the world. Grants of $1 million were allocated to 17 projects in 2000; requests, however, totalled more than $12.5 million. Projects in 2000 addressed diverse forms of violence against women, including domestic violence, trafficking and sexual exploitation, honour killings, sexual harassment and violence against girls and women with disabilities. Strategies applied in executing the projects ranged from public-awareness raising and education to advocacy, legal literacy, training for professionals, action-oriented research and service provision, and training and mobilization of women's groups.

To encourage projects with increased potential, the Fund implemented guidelines to raise grants from $50,000 to $150,000 for joint proposals; under that framework, six grants were awarded in 2000. With support from a United Nations Foundation grant, a call for project proposals focusing on media and documentation was issued. It generated over 250 proposals, from which four to eight projects would be selected.

The Trust Fund learning component, supported by the John D. and Catherine T. MacArthur Foundation, focused on reviewing and analysing lessons learned from Trust Fund initiatives.

Field visits to five countries highlighted effective strategies for changing attitudes, reversing stereotypes and eliminating harmful practices.

(For details of action on violence against women taken by the Commission on Human Rights, see p. 677.)

Women migrant workers

In response to General Assembly resolution 54/138 [YUN 1999, p. 1087], the Secretary-General submitted a September report [A/56/329], in which he summarized information received from 15 Member States, UN bodies, mechanisms and organizations, intergovernmental entities and NGOs to address the issue of violence against women migrant workers. The Secretary-General stated that data on the numbers of women migrant workers remained difficult to obtain and there was a lack of clarity about the scale of abuse and discrimination against them. Comprehensive information was needed on bilateral labour agreements between countries of origin and of destination and on labour and immigration legislation, as well as on the impact of such provisions, especially with respect to the enjoyment by women of the full range of human rights (see also p. 618).

GENERAL ASSEMBLY ACTION

On 19 December [meeting 88], the General Assembly, on the recommendation of the Third Committee [A/56/576], adopted **resolution 56/131** without vote [agenda item 112].

Violence against women migrant workers

The General Assembly,

Recalling all of its previous resolutions on violence against women migrant workers and those adopted by the Commission on the Status of Women, the Commission on Human Rights and the Commission on Crime Prevention and Criminal Justice, and the Declaration on the Elimination of Violence against Women,

Reaffirming the outcome of the World Conference on Human Rights, the International Conference on Population and Development, the Fourth World Conference on Women and the World Summit for Social Development and their five-year reviews, specifically as the results pertain to women migrant workers,

Noting the various activities initiated by entities in the United Nations system, such as the expert group meeting organized by the International Research and Training Institute for the Advancement of Women and the International Organization for Migration, held at Geneva in August 1999, the international workshop on best practices concerning migrant workers and their families initiated by the International Organization for Migration, held at Santiago in June 2000, and the seminar on women immigrants organized by the United Nations Development Fund for Women and the Argentine National Institute against Discrimination, Xenophobia and Racism, held at Buenos Aires in July 2001, as well as other activities that continue to assess and alleviate the plight of women migrant workers,

Emphasizing the need for objective, comprehensive, broad-based information, possibly including a database for research and analysis, and a wide exchange of experience and lessons learned by individual Member States and civil society in the formulation of policies and concrete strategies to address the problem of violence against women migrant workers,

Encouraging the continuing participation of civil society in developing and implementing appropriate measures to support innovative partnerships among public agencies, non-governmental organizations and other members of civil society for combating violence against women migrant workers,

Noting the large numbers of women from developing countries and some countries with economies in transition who continue to venture forth to more affluent countries in search of a living for themselves and their families as a consequence of poverty, unemployment and other socio-economic conditions, and acknowledging the duty of the countries of origin to try to create conditions that provide employment and economic security for their citizens,

Expressing deep concern at the continuing reports of grave abuses and acts of violence committed against women migrant workers,

Realizing that the movement of a significant number of women migrant workers may be facilitated and made possible by means of fraudulent or irregular documentation and sham marriages with the object of migration, that this may be facilitated through, among others, the Internet, and that these women migrant workers are more vulnerable to abuse and exploitation,

Acknowledging the economic benefits that accrue to both the country of origin and the country of destination from the employment of women migrant workers,

Recognizing the importance of joint and collaborative approaches and strategies at the bilateral, regional, interregional and international levels in protecting and promoting the rights and welfare of women migrant workers,

Recognizing also the importance of exploring the link between migration and trafficking,

Encouraged by some measures adopted by some countries of destination to alleviate the plight of women migrant workers residing in their areas of jurisdiction,

Underlining the important role of relevant United Nations treaty bodies in monitoring the implementation of human rights conventions and the relevant special procedures, within their respective mandates, in addressing the problem of violence against women migrant workers and in protecting and promoting their rights and welfare,

1. *Takes note* of the report of the Secretary-General;

2. *Also takes note* of the reports of the Special Rapporteur of the Commission on Human Rights on the human rights of migrants and of the Special Rapporteur of the Commission on Human Rights on violence against women, its causes and consequences, with regard to violence against women migrant workers, and encourages them to continue to address the issue of violence against women migrant workers and their human rights, in particular the problem of gender-based violence and of discrimination, and trafficking in women;

3. *Requests* all Governments to continue to cooperate fully with both Special Rapporteurs in the performance of their tasks and mandated duties and to furnish all information requested, including by reacting promptly to the urgent appeals of the Special Rapporteurs;

4. *Encourages* Governments, in particular those of the countries of origin and destination, to make available to the Special Rapporteur on the human rights of migrants information on violence against women migrant workers, with a view to requesting the Special Rapporteur to recommend concrete measures and actions to address the problem;

5. *Also encourages* Governments to give serious consideration to inviting the Special Rapporteur to visit their countries so as to enable her to fulfil the mandate effectively;

6. *Urges* concerned Governments, in particular those of the countries of origin and destination, to strengthen further their national efforts to protect and promote the rights and welfare of women migrant workers, including through sustained bilateral, regional, interregional and international cooperation, by developing strategies and joint action and taking into account the innovative approaches and experiences of individual Member States, and to establish and maintain continuing dialogues to facilitate the exchange of information;

7. *Also urges* concerned Governments, in particular those of the countries of origin and destination, to support and allocate appropriate resources for programmes aimed at strengthening preventive action, in particular information for target groups, education and campaigns to increase public awareness of this issue at the national and grass-roots levels, in cooperation with non-governmental organizations;

8. *Notes with appreciation* the adoption by Member States, including countries of origin, transit and destination, of measures to inform women migrant workers of their rights and the benefits to which they are entitled, and encourages other Member States to adopt appropriate measures in this regard;

9. *Calls upon* concerned Governments, in particular those of the countries of origin and destination, if they have not done so, to put in place penal and criminal sanctions to punish perpetrators of violence against women migrant workers and, to the extent possible, to provide, and to encourage non-governmental organizations to provide, victims of violence with the full range of immediate assistance and protection, such as counselling, legal and consular assistance, temporary shelter and other measures that will allow them to be present during the judicial process, as well as to establish reintegration and rehabilitation schemes for returning women migrant workers to their countries of origin;

10. *Encourages* concerned Governments, in particular those of the countries of origin and destination, to support and, if they have not done so, to formulate and implement training programmes for their law enforcers, prosecutors and service providers with a view to instilling among those public sector workers the necessary skills and attitude to ensure the delivery of proper and professional interventions for women migrant workers who are subjected to abuse and violence;

11. *Also encourages* concerned Governments, in particular those of the countries of origin and destination,

to adopt measures or strengthen existing ones to regulate the recruitment and deployment of women migrant workers, and to consider the adoption of appropriate legal measures against intermediaries who deliberately encourage the clandestine movement of workers and who exploit women migrant workers;

12. *Invites* Governments to identify the causes of undocumented migration and its economic, social and demographic impact, as well as its implications for the formulation and application of social, economic and migration policies, including those relating to women migrant workers;

13. *Encourages* concerned Governments, in particular those of the countries of origin, transit and destination, to avail themselves of the expertise of the United Nations, including the Statistics Division of the Secretariat and other relevant bodies, such as the International Research and Training Institute for the Advancement of Women, to develop appropriate national data-collection methodologies that will generate comparable data on violence against women migrant workers as bases for research and analyses of the subject;

14. *Encourages* Member States to consider signing and ratifying or acceding to relevant International Labour Organization conventions and to consider signing and ratifying or acceding to the International Convention on the Protection of the Rights of All Migrant Workers and Members of Their Families, as well as the Slavery Convention of 1926;

15. *Welcomes* the adoption by the General Assembly of the Protocol to Prevent, Suppress and Punish Trafficking in Persons, Especially Women and Children and the Protocol against the Smuggling of Migrants by Land, Sea and Air, supplementing the United Nations Convention against Transnational Organized Crime, and encourages Governments to consider signing and ratifying or acceding to the Protocols;

16. *Encourages* the Committee on the Elimination of Discrimination against Women to consider developing a general recommendation on the situation of women migrant workers;

17. *Requests* the Secretary-General to submit to the General Assembly at its fifty-eighth session a report on the problem of violence against women migrant workers and on the implementation of the present resolution, taking into account updated information from the organizations of the United Nations system, in particular the International Labour Organization, the United Nations Development Programme, the United Nations Development Fund for Women and the International Research and Training Institute for the Advancement of Women, as well as the International Organization for Migration and other relevant sources, including non-governmental organizations.

Women and children in armed conflict

Women and children taken hostage

In response to a 2000 Commission on the Status of Women request [YUN 2000, p. 1112], the Secretary-General, in a January report on follow-up to and implementation of the Beijing Declaration and Platform for Action [E/CN.6/2001/2], summarized information received from 17 Member States and 12 entities of the UN system on the release of women and children taken hostage, including those imprisoned during armed conflict.

By a 17 March resolution [E/2001/27 (res. 45/1)], the Commission condemned violent acts in contravention of international humanitarian law against civilian women and children in areas of armed conflict, and called for the immediate release of such women and children taken hostage. It strongly urged parties to armed conflicts to respect the norms of international humanitarian law and to take measures to protect those women and children and to secure their immediate release. All parties were urged to provide access to humanitarian assistance for those women and children and the Secretary-General and all relevant international organizations were asked to facilitate their release. The Secretary-General was also asked to prepare, taking into account information provided by States and relevant international organizations, a report on the subject for the Commission's 2002 session.

Communication. On 4 December [A/56/680-S/2001/1155], the Democratic Republic of the Congo transmitted to the Secretary-General the report of the subregional conference on the protection of women and children in armed conflict in Central Africa (Kinshasa, 14-16 November). Annexed to the report was a plan of action, which outlined measures to be taken at the national, subregional and international levels in order to find lasting solutions for the suffering of women and children in armed conflict in Central Africa.

(See also p. 677.)

Women, peace and security

On 8 March—the United Nations Day for Women's Rights and International Peace—the Security Council held informal consultations on women, peace and security (see p. 54).

On 31 October, the Council President made statement **S/PRST/2001/31**, in which members reaffirmed their commitment to the implementation of resolution 1325(2000) [YUN 2000, p. 1113] and support for increasing the role of women in decision-making with regard to conflict prevention and resolution (see p. 54).

Communication. On 27 November [A/C.3/56/9], Austria transmitted to the Secretary-General a document that emanated from a meeting of 15 women Foreign Ministers on the topic "Women and human security" (New York, 12 November).

The girl child

On 19 December [meeting 88], the General Assembly, on the recommendation of the Third

Committee [A/56/579], adopted **resolution 56/139** without vote [agenda item 115].

The girl child

The General Assembly,

Recalling its resolution 55/78 of 4 December 2000 and all relevant resolutions, including the agreed conclusions of the Commission on the Status of Women, in particular those relevant to the girl child,

Recalling also all relevant United Nations conferences and the Declaration and Agenda for Action adopted by the World Congress against Commercial Sexual Exploitation of Children, held at Stockholm from 27 to 31 August 1996, as well as the outcome documents of the recent five-year reviews of the implementation of the Programme of Action of the International Conference on Population and Development and the Programme of Action of the World Summit for Social Development,

Deeply concerned about discrimination against the girl child and the violation of the rights of the girl child, which often result in less access for girls to education, nutrition and physical and mental health care and in girls enjoying fewer of the rights, opportunities and benefits of childhood and adolescence than boys and often being subjected to various forms of cultural, social, sexual and economic exploitation and to violence and harmful practices, such as female infanticide, incest, early marriage, prenatal sex selection and female genital mutilation,

Recognizing the need to achieve gender equality so as to ensure a just and equitable world for girls,

Deeply concerned that, in situations of poverty, war and armed conflict, girl children are among the victims most affected and that thus their potential for full development is limited,

Concerned that the girl child has furthermore become a victim of sexually transmitted diseases and the human immunodeficiency virus, which affect the quality of her life and leave her open to further discrimination,

Reaffirming the equal rights of women and men as enshrined, inter alia, in the Preamble to the Charter of the United Nations, the Convention on the Elimination of All Forms of Discrimination against Women and the Convention on the Rights of the Child,

Reaffirming also the political declaration and further actions and initiatives to implement the Beijing Declaration and Platform for Action, adopted by the General Assembly at its twenty-third special session entitled "Women 2000: gender equality, development and peace for the twenty-first century",

Reaffirming further the Dakar Framework for Action adopted at the World Education Forum,

Reaffirming the Declaration of Commitment on HIV/AIDS adopted by the General Assembly at its twenty-sixth special session,

1. *Stresses* the need for full and urgent implementation of the rights of the girl child as guaranteed to her under all human rights instruments, including the Convention on the Rights of the Child and the Convention on the Elimination of All Forms of Discrimination against Women, as well as the need for universal ratification of those instruments;

2. *Urges* States to consider signing, ratifying or acceding to the Optional Protocol to the Convention on the Elimination of All Forms of Discrimination against Women;

3. *Welcomes* the adoption of the Optional Protocols to the Convention on the Rights of the Child on the involvement of children in armed conflict and on the sale of children, child prostitution and child pornography, and invites States to consider signing and ratifying the Optional Protocols as a matter of priority with a view to their entry into force as soon as possible;

4. *Welcomes also* the United Nations Girls' Education Initiative launched by the Secretary-General at the World Education Forum;

5. *Urges* all Governments and the United Nations system to strengthen efforts bilaterally and with international organizations and private sector donors in order to achieve the goals of the World Education Forum, in particular that of eliminating gender disparities in primary and secondary education by 2005, and to implement the United Nations Girls' Education Initiative as a means of reaching this goal, and reaffirms the commitment contained in the United Nations Millennium Declaration;

6. *Calls upon* all States to take measures to address the obstacles that continue to affect the achievement of the goals set forth in the Beijing Platform for Action, as contained in paragraph 33 of the further actions and initiatives to implement the Beijing Declaration and Platform for Action, where appropriate, including the strengthening of national mechanisms to implement policies and programmes for the girl child and, in some cases, to enhance coordination among responsible institutions for the realization of the human rights of girls, as indicated in the further actions and initiatives;

7. *Urges* all States to take all necessary measures and to institute legal reforms to ensure the full and equal enjoyment by the girl child of all human rights and fundamental freedoms, to take effective action against violations of those rights and freedoms and to base programmes and policies for the girl child on the rights of the child;

8. *Urges* States to enact and enforce strictly laws to ensure that marriage is entered into only with the free and full consent of the intending spouses, to enact and enforce strictly laws concerning the minimum legal age of consent and the minimum age for marriage and to raise the minimum age for marriage where necessary;

9. *Urges* all States to fulfil their obligations under the Convention on the Rights of the Child and the Convention on the Elimination of All Forms of Discrimination against Women, as well as the commitment to implement the Beijing Platform for Action;

10. *Also urges* all States to enact and enforce legislation to protect girls from all forms of violence, including female infanticide and prenatal sex selection, female genital mutilation, rape, domestic violence, incest, sexual abuse, sexual exploitation, child prostitution and child pornography, and to develop age-appropriate safe and confidential programmes and medical, social and psychological support services to assist girls who are subjected to violence;

11. *Calls upon* all States and international and non-governmental organizations, individually and collectively, to implement further the Beijing Platform for Action, in particular the strategic objectives relating to the girl child and including the further actions and

initiatives to implement the Beijing Declaration and Platform for Action;

12. *Urges* States to take special measures for the protection of war-affected girls and in particular to protect them from sexually transmitted diseases, such as the human immunodeficiency virus/acquired immunodeficiency syndrome (HIV/AIDS), and gender-based violence, including rape and sexual abuse, torture, sexual exploitation, abduction and forced labour, paying special attention to refugee and displaced girls, and to take into account the special needs of the war-affected girl child in the delivery of humanitarian assistance and disarmament, demobilization and reintegration processes;

13. *Urges* all States and the international community to respect, protect and promote the rights of the child, taking into account the particular vulnerabilities of the girl child in pre-conflict, conflict and post-conflict situations, and calls for special initiatives designed to address all of the rights and needs of war-affected girls;

14. *Welcomes* the holding of the International Conference on War-Affected Children at Winnipeg, Canada, from 10 to 17 September 2000, and takes note with appreciation of the Winnipeg Agenda for War-Affected Children;

15. *Urges* States to formulate comprehensive, multidisciplinary and coordinated national plans, programmes or strategies to eliminate all forms of violence against women and girls, which should be widely disseminated and should provide targets and timetables for implementation, as well as effective domestic enforcement procedures through the establishment of monitoring mechanisms involving all parties concerned, including consultations with women's organizations, giving attention to the recommendations relating to the girl child of the Special Rapporteur of the Commission on Human Rights on violence against women, its causes and consequences;

16. *Calls upon* Governments, civil society, including the media, and non-governmental organizations to promote human rights education and the full respect for and enjoyment of the human rights of the girl child, inter alia, through the translation, production and dissemination of age-appropriate information material on those rights to all sectors of society, in particular to children;

17. *Requests* the Secretary-General, as Chairman of the United Nations System Chief Executives Board for Coordination, to ensure that all organizations and bodies of the United Nations system, individually and collectively, in particular the United Nations Children's Fund, the United Nations Educational, Scientific and Cultural Organization, the World Food Programme, the United Nations Population Fund, the United Nations Development Fund for Women, the World Health Organization, the United Nations Development Programme and the Office of the United Nations High Commissioner for Refugees, take into account the rights and the particular needs of the girl child in the country programme of cooperation in accordance with the national priorities, including through the United Nations Development Assistance Framework;

18. *Requests* all human rights treaty bodies, special procedures and other human rights mechanisms of the Commission on Human Rights and its Subcommission on the Promotion and Protection of Human Rights to adopt regularly and systematically a gender perspective in the implementation of their mandates and to include in their reports information on the qualitative analysis of violations of the human rights of women and girls, and encourages the strengthening of cooperation and coordination in that regard;

19. *Calls upon* States and international and non-governmental organizations to mobilize all necessary resources, support and efforts to realize the goals, strategic objectives and actions set out in the Beijing Platform for Action and the further actions and initiatives to implement the Beijing Declaration and Platform for Action;

20. *Stresses* the importance of a substantive assessment of the implementation of the Beijing Platform for Action with a life-cycle perspective so as to identify gaps and obstacles in the implementation process and to develop further actions for the achievement of the goals of the Platform;

21. *Welcomes* the convening of the Second World Congress against Commercial Sexual Exploitation of Children, at Yokohama, Japan, from 17 to 20 December 2001, and the regional consultative meetings for the preparation thereof, which aim to review the progress made in implementing the Declaration and Agenda for Action adopted by the first World Congress and to strengthen actions to eradicate commercial sexual exploitation of children, and invites Member States and observers to ensure their representation at the Second World Congress at a high political level;

22. *Encourages* the regional commissions and other regional organizations to carry out activities in support of the Second World Congress;

23. *Stresses* the importance of integrating a gender perspective and of considering the needs and rights of the girl child in the work of the special session of the General Assembly on children.

(See also p. 680.)

Women's health

Traditional or customary practices affecting the health of women and girls

In response to General Assembly resolution 54/133 [YUN 1999, p. 1091], the Secretary-General submitted an August report on traditional or customary practices affecting the health of women and girls [A/56/316]. He summarized information received from 17 Member States concerning the formulation and revision of legislation and policy and awareness-raising programmes in order to protect women against such harmful traditional practices as female genital mutilation, early marriage and marriage by force or abduction. Information was also provided by NGOs and UN entities and mechanisms.

The Secretary-General stated that Member States had indicated that traditional or customary practices affecting the health of women and girls, particularly female genital mutilation, continued to be addressed through the adoption of legal and policy measures, educational programmes and awareness-raising campaigns. However, concrete measures to eliminate the practices needed to be strengthened. The adoption and enforcement of legal measures prohibiting the practices and the development of comprehensive national plans and public information campaigns remained crucial. Education and training should be reinforced to include behavioural change approaches, reach women and men in all communities engaged in such practices, and address the underlying values that supported the practices. Those efforts should involve community and religious leaders, educators, medical practitioners, the media and those responsible for enforcing laws and implementing policies, such as the police and judicial personnel. The sensitization of, and alternative career training programmes for, traditional practitioners, as well as the pursuit of alternatives where harmful practices constituted a ritual ceremony or rite of passage, should be intensified.

(See also p. 679.)

GENERAL ASSEMBLY ACTION

On 19 December [meeting 88], the General Assembly, on the recommendation of the Third Committee [A/56/576], adopted **resolution 56/128** without vote [agenda item 112].

Traditional or customary practices affecting the health of women and girls

The General Assembly,

Reaffirming its resolution 54/133 of 17 December 1999 and its other relevant resolutions and decisions, and bearing in mind those of the Economic and Social Council, the Commission on Human Rights and the Subcommission on the Promotion and Protection of Human Rights,

Taking note of the reports of the Special Rapporteur of the Subcommission on the Promotion and Protection of Human Rights on traditional practices affecting the health of women and the girl child and of the Special Rapporteur of the Commission on Human Rights on violence against women, its causes and consequences,

Reaffirming the obligation of all States to promote and protect human rights and fundamental freedoms as stated in the Charter of the United Nations, and emphasizing the obligations contained in human rights instruments, in particular articles 5 and 12 of the Convention on the Elimination of All Forms of Discrimination against Women, article 24 of the Convention on the Rights of the Child and article 12 of the International Covenant on Economic, Social and Cultural Rights,

Bearing in mind article 2 *(a)* of the Declaration on the Elimination of Violence against Women, and article 5, paragraph 5, of the Declaration on the Elimination of All Forms of Intolerance and of Discrimination Based on Religion or Belief,

Recalling the provisions pertaining to traditional or customary practices affecting the health of women and girls contained in the outcome of the World Conference on Human Rights, the International Conference on Population and Development, the Fourth World Conference on Women and the twenty-first, twenty-third and twenty-sixth special sessions of the General Assembly,

Recalling also general recommendation 14 concerning female circumcision adopted by the Committee on the Elimination of Discrimination against Women at its ninth session, paragraphs 11, 20 and 24 *(l)* of general recommendation 19 concerning violence against women adopted by the Committee at its eleventh session, paragraphs 15 *(d)* and 18 of general recommendation 24 concerning article 12 of the Convention on the Elimination of All Forms of Discrimination against Women on women and health adopted by the Committee at its twentieth session, and taking note of paragraphs 21, 35 and 51 of general comment No. 14 (2000) concerning article 12 of the International Covenant on Economic, Social and Cultural Rights adopted by the Committee on Economic, Social and Cultural Rights at its twenty-second session,

Reaffirming that harmful traditional or customary practices, including female genital mutilation, constitute a serious threat to the health of women and girls, and may have fatal consequences,

Expressing concern at the continuing large-scale existence of these practices,

Reaffirming that such harmful traditional or customary practices constitute a definite form of violence against women and girls and a serious violation of their human rights,

Emphasizing that the elimination of harmful traditional or customary practices will contribute to reducing the vulnerability of women and girls to the human immunodeficiency virus/acquired immunodeficiency syndrome (HIV/AIDS) and other sexually transmitted infections,

Stressing that the elimination of such practices requires greater efforts and commitment from Governments, the international community and civil society, including non-governmental and community-based organizations, and that fundamental changes in societal attitudes are required,

Noting with appreciation the work done in the context of the Organization of African Unity to prepare a draft protocol to the African Charter on Human and Peoples' Rights on the rights of women in Africa,

Welcoming the call for the elimination of all harmful traditional practices which are detrimental to girls' and women's rights and health made by the Pan-African Forum on the Future of Children, held in Cairo from 28 to 31 May 2001,

1. *Welcomes:*

(a) The report of the Secretary-General, which provides encouraging examples of national and international developments;

(b) The efforts undertaken by United Nations bodies, programmes and organizations, including the United Nations Children's Fund, the United Nations Population Fund, the World Health Organization, the Office of the United Nations High Commissioner for Refugees, the United Nations Development Fund for Women and the Joint United Nations Programme on HIV/AIDS, to address the issue of traditional or customary practices affecting the health of women and

girls, and encourages them to continue to coordinate their efforts;

(c) The work carried out by the Special Ambassador for the Elimination of Female Genital Mutilation of the United Nations Population Fund and her continuing contribution to the campaign to eliminate female genital mutilation;

(d) The work carried out by the Inter-African Committee on Traditional Practices Affecting the Health of Women and Children and other non-governmental and community organizations, including women's organizations, in raising awareness of the harmful effects of such practices, in particular of female genital mutilation;

(e) The fact that the elimination of harmful traditional or customary practices will be considered during the special session of the General Assembly on children;

2. *Emphasizes* the need for technical and financial assistance to those developing countries working to achieve the elimination of traditional or customary practices affecting the health of women and girls from United Nations funds and programmes, international and regional financial institutions and bilateral and multilateral donors, as well as the need for assistance to non-governmental organizations and community-based groups active in this field from the international community;

3. *Calls upon* all States:

(a) To ratify or accede to, if they have not yet done so, the relevant human rights treaties, in particular the Convention on the Elimination of All Forms of Discrimination against Women and the Convention on the Rights of the Child, to consider signing and ratifying or acceding to the Optional Protocol to the Convention on the Elimination of All Forms of Discrimination against Women and to respect and implement fully their obligations under any such treaties to which they are parties;

(b) To implement the international commitments made at relevant major United Nations conferences and special sessions and summit meetings of the General Assembly held since 1990 and their follow-up processes;

(c) To collect and disseminate basic data about the occurrence of traditional or customary practices affecting the health of women and girls, including female genital mutilation;

(d) To develop, adopt and implement national legislation, policies, plans and programmes that prohibit traditional or customary practices affecting the health of women and girls, including female genital mutilation, and to prosecute the perpetrators of such practices;

(e) To establish, if they have not done so, a concrete national mechanism for the implementation and monitoring of relevant legislation, law enforcement and national policies;

(f) To establish or strengthen support services to respond to the needs of victims by, inter alia, developing comprehensive and accessible sexual and reproductive health services and by providing training to health-care providers at all levels on the harmful health consequences of such practices;

(g) To address specifically in the training of health and other relevant personnel traditional or customary practices affecting the health of women and girls, also addressing the increased vulnerability of women and girls to HIV/AIDS and other sexually transmitted infections due to such practices;

(h) To take all necessary measures to empower women and strengthen their economic independence and protect and promote the full enjoyment of all human rights and fundamental freedoms in order to allow women and girls better to protect themselves from, inter alia, traditional or customary practices affecting the health of women and girls;

(i) To intensify efforts to raise awareness of and to mobilize international and national public opinion concerning the harmful effects of traditional or customary practices affecting the health of women and girls, including female genital mutilation, inter alia, by involving public opinion leaders, educators, religious leaders, chiefs, traditional leaders, medical practitioners, teachers, women's health and family planning organizations, social workers, childcare agencies, relevant non-governmental organizations, the arts and the media in awareness-raising campaigns, in order to achieve the total elimination of those practices;

(j) To address traditional or customary practices affecting the health of women and girls in education curricula, as appropriate;

(k) To promote men's understanding of their roles and responsibilities with regard to promoting the elimination of harmful practices, such as female genital mutilation;

(l) To continue to take specific measures to increase the capacity of communities, including immigrant and refugee communities, in which female genital mutilation is practised, to engage in activities aimed at preventing and eliminating such practices;

(m) To explore, through consultations with communities and religious and cultural groups and their leaders, alternatives to harmful traditional or customary practices, in particular where those practices form part of a ritual ceremony or rite of passage, as well as through alternative training and education possibilities for traditional practitioners;

(n) To cooperate closely with the Special Rapporteur of the Subcommission on the Promotion and Protection of Human Rights on traditional practices affecting the health of women and the girl child, in particular by supplying all necessary information requested by her and by giving serious consideration to inviting her to visit their countries;

(o) To cooperate closely with relevant specialized agencies and United Nations funds and programmes, as well as with regional intergovernmental organizations, as appropriate, and relevant community and non-governmental organizations, including women's organizations, in a joint effort to eradicate traditional or customary practices affecting the health of women and girls;

(p) To include in their reports to the Committee on the Elimination of Discrimination against Women, the Committee on the Rights of the Child and other relevant treaty bodies specific information on measures taken to eliminate traditional or customary practices affecting the health of women and girls, including female genital mutilation, and to prosecute the perpetrators of such practices;

4. *Invites*:

(*a*) Relevant specialized agencies, United Nations bodies, regional intergovernmental organizations and non-governmental organizations to exchange information on the subject of the present resolution, and encourages the exchange of such information between non-governmental organizations active in this field and the bodies monitoring the implementation of relevant human rights treaties;

(*b*) The Commission on the Status of Women to address this subject at its forty-seventh session under the priority theme "Women's human rights and elimination of all forms of violence against women and girls as defined in the Beijing Platform for Action and the outcome document of the twenty-third special session of the General Assembly";

(*c*) Governments, organizations and individuals that are in a position to do so to contribute to the trust fund that supports the work of the Special Ambassador for the Elimination of Female Genital Mutilation of the United Nations Population Fund;

5. *Requests* the Secretary-General:

(*a*) To continue to make his report available to relevant meetings within the United Nations system;

(*b*) To report to the General Assembly at its fifty-eighth session on the implementation of the present resolution, with a special focus on recent national and international developments, including examples of national best practices and international cooperation.

HIV/AIDS

One of the thematic issues for the 2001 session of the Commission on the Status of Women was women, the girl child and HIV/AIDS. On 8 March, the Commission held a panel discussion and a dialogue on the theme. On 11 May, the Commission adopted draft agreed conclusions on the thematic issue, which it recommended to the Economic and Social Council for adoption. The Council endorsed the agreed conclusions in **resolution 2001/5** (see p. 1076).

Women in Afghanistan

In response to Economic and Social Council resolution 2000/9 [YUN 2000, p. 1120], the Secretary-General submitted to the Commission on the Status of Women a January report on the situation of women and girls in Afghanistan [E/CN.6/2001/2/Add.1]. Having described the continuing conflict in Afghanistan (see p. 255) and the deteriorating socio-economic conditions, particularly as a result of the drought, the collapsed health-care and education systems and a lack of governance, the Secretary-General characterized Afghanistan as nearing a humanitarian disaster (see p. 838). Women were particularly vulnerable due to their social status in Afghan society, which historically had observed conservative cultural norms and traditions and a strong division of gender roles. With the Taliban takeover of Kabul in 1996, gender discrimination became institutionalized through the issuance of edicts placing severe restrictions on women's freedom of movement, association and participation in public life. The Taliban's ban on employment of women not only violated women's human rights but also presented formidable obstacles to humanitarian efforts by the United Nations and the assistance community to improve the status of women and girls.

Along with mechanisms to link gender policy to concrete actions, the United Nations had set up a monitoring mechanism to oversee compliance, particularly to identify inconsistencies among gender policies of humanitarian organizations, and to implement those policies in operational fieldwork. The Secretary-General stated that the overall situation of women in Afghanistan remained unacceptable and required sustained attention from the international community. He called on the UN system and the international community to facilitate continued dialogue on human rights and gender issues with the Taliban. (See also p. 680.)

ECONOMIC AND SOCIAL COUNCIL ACTION

On 24 July [meeting 40], the Economic and Social Council, on the recommendation of the Commission on the Status of Women [E/2001/27], adopted **resolution 2001/3** without vote [agenda item 14 (*a*)].

Discrimination against women and girls in Afghanistan

The Economic and Social Council,

Guided by the Charter of the United Nations, the Universal Declaration of Human Rights, the International Covenants on Human Rights, the Convention against Torture and Other Cruel, Inhuman or Degrading Treatment or Punishment, the Convention on the Elimination of All Forms of Discrimination against Women, the Declaration on the Elimination of Violence against Women, the Convention on the Rights of the Child and the optional protocols thereto on the involvement of children in armed conflict and on the sale of children, child prostitution and child pornography, the Beijing Declaration and Platform for Action, the further actions and initiatives to implement the Beijing Declaration and Platform for Action, adopted by the General Assembly at its twenty-third special session, accepted humanitarian rules as set out in the Geneva Conventions of 12 August 1949, and other instruments of human rights and international law,

Recalling that Afghanistan is party to the Convention on the Prevention and Punishment of the Crime of Genocide, the International Covenant on Civil and Political Rights, the International Covenant on Economic, Social and Cultural Rights, the Convention against Torture and Other Cruel, Inhuman or Degrading Treatment or Punishment, the Convention on the Rights of the Child and the Geneva Convention relative to the Protection of Civilian Persons in Time of War, and that it has signed the Convention on the Elimination of All Forms of Discrimination against Women,

Reaffirming that all States have an obligation to promote and protect human rights and fundamental freedoms and to fulfil the obligations they have freely undertaken under the various international instruments,

Welcoming the substantive report of the Secretary-General to the Commission on the Status of Women on the situation of women and girls in Afghanistan, and the conclusions contained therein, including the need to monitor and evaluate the promotion and protection of the human rights of women and girls who reside in all areas of Afghanistan,

Noting the report of the Special Rapporteur of the Commission on Human Rights on violence against women, and deploring the "official, widespread and systematic violation of the human rights of women in Taliban-controlled areas" as found in the report,

Deploring the deteriorating economic, social and cultural conditions of women and girls in all areas of Afghanistan, in particular in areas under the control of the Taliban, as documented by the continued and substantiated reports of grave violations to the security of the person and integrity as well as the human rights of women and girls, including discrimination in terms of access to health care, to levels and types of education, to employment outside the home, to freedom of movement and to freedom of association,

Also deploring the July 2000 edict of the Taliban barring Afghan women from working in foreign organizations and non-governmental organizations, as well as the August 2000 statute on the activities of the United Nations in Afghanistan,

Welcoming the fourth report of the Special Rapporteur of the Commission on Human Rights on the situation of human rights in Afghanistan, entitled "Interim report of the Special Rapporteur of the Commission on Human Rights on the situation of human rights in Afghanistan", in particular his special focus on violations of the human rights of women and girls, especially in territories under the control of the Taliban,

Deeply concerned about the detrimental impact of these harmful conditions on the well-being of Afghan women and the children in their care, and the detrimental effect of the restrictions to women's and girls' education and women's employment on the functions of Afghan society and the reconstruction and development of the country,

Expressing its appreciation to the international community for its support for, and solidarity with, the women and girls of Afghanistan, in particular the women of Afghanistan who protest against violations of their human rights, and encouraging women and men worldwide to continue efforts to draw attention to their situation and to promote the immediate restoration of their ability to enjoy their human rights,

1. *Strongly condemns* the continuing grave violations of the human rights of women and girls, including all forms of discrimination against them, in all areas of Afghanistan, in particular in areas under the control of the Taliban;

2. *Also condemns* the continued restrictions on the access of women to health care and the systematic violation of the human rights of women in Afghanistan, including the restrictions on access to education and to employment outside the home, freedom of movement and freedom from intimidation, harassment and

violence, which have a serious detrimental effect on the well-being of Afghan women and the children in their care;

3. *Urges* the Taliban and other Afghan parties to recognize, protect, promote and act in accordance with all human rights and fundamental freedoms, regardless of gender, ethnicity or religion, in accordance with international human rights instruments, and to respect international humanitarian law;

4. *Urges* all the Afghan parties, in particular the Taliban, to bring to an end, without delay, all human rights violations against women and girls, and to take urgent measures to ensure:

(a) The repeal of all legislative and other measures that discriminate against women and girls and those that impede the realization of all their human rights;

(b) The effective participation of women in civil, cultural, economic, political and social life throughout the country;

(c) Respect for the equal right of women to work and their reintegration into employment in all segments of Afghan society, as well as throughout the United Nations system and human rights and humanitarian organizations operating within Afghanistan;

(d) The equal right of women and girls to education without discrimination, the reopening of schools and the admission of women and girls to all levels of education;

(e) Respect for the right of women and girls to security of person, and that those responsible for physical attacks on women and girls are brought to justice;

(f) Respect for freedom of movement for women and girls;

(g) Respect for effective and equal access of women and girls to the facilities necessary to protect their right to the highest attainable standard of physical and mental health;

5. *Encourages* the continuing efforts of the United Nations and other international and non-governmental organizations and donors to ensure that all United Nations–assisted programmes in Afghanistan are formulated and coordinated in such a way as to promote and ensure the participation of women in those programmes, and that women benefit equally with men from such programmes, and to that end encourages such measures as the establishment of culturally sensitive programmes to sensitize Afghan officials, ministry staff and technical departments concerning international principles of human rights and gender equality;

6. *Appeals* to all States and to the international community to ensure that all humanitarian assistance to the people of Afghanistan, in conformity with the Strategic Framework for Afghanistan, is based on the principle of non-discrimination, integrates a gender perspective, and actively attempts to promote the participation of both women and men and to promote peace and respect for human rights and fundamental freedoms;

7. *Urges* States to continue to give special attention to the promotion and protection of the human rights of women and girls in Afghanistan and to mainstream a gender perspective in all aspects of their policies and actions related to Afghanistan;

8. *Welcomes* the overall efforts of the Secretary-General to address the situation of women and girls in Afghanistan, including the establishment of the posi-

tions of Gender Adviser and Human Rights Adviser in the United Nations Office of the Resident Coordinator for Afghanistan, in order to ensure more effective consideration and implementation of human rights and gender concerns in all United Nations programmes within Afghanistan, taking into account the recommendations contained in the report of the Inter-Agency Gender Mission to Afghanistan conducted by the Special Adviser to the Secretary-General on Gender Issues and Advancement of Women in November 1997;

9. *Urges* the Secretary-General to ensure that all United Nations activities in Afghanistan are carried out according to the principle of non-discrimination against women and girls, that a gender perspective and special attention to the human rights of women and girls are fully incorporated into the work of the Civil Affairs Unit established within the United Nations Special Mission to Afghanistan, including the training and selection of staff, and that efforts are made to enhance the role of women in preventative diplomacy, peacemaking and peacekeeping;

10. *Encourages* United Nations agencies to intensify their efforts to employ more women in their programmes in Afghanistan, particularly at the decision-making level, to ensure, inter alia, the functioning of all programmes in order to better address the needs of the female population;

11. *Stresses* the importance of the Special Rapporteur of the Commission on Human Rights on the situation of human rights in Afghanistan giving special attention to the human rights of women and girls and fully incorporating a gender perspective in his work;

12. *Appeals* to States and the international community to implement the recommendations of the Inter-Agency Gender Mission to Afghanistan under the leadership of the Special Adviser to the Secretary-General on Gender Issues and Advancement of Women, and urges all countries, international organizations and non-governmental organizations having influence in Afghanistan to continue to bring pressure to bear on all armed groups to respect the human rights of women and girls in all circumstances;

13. *Demands* that all Afghan factions, in particular the Taliban, ensure the safety and protection of all United Nations and humanitarian workers in Afghanistan and allow them, regardless of gender, to carry out their work unhindered;

14. *Requests* the Secretary-General to continue to review the situation of women and girls in Afghanistan and to submit to the Commission on the Status of Women at its forty-sixth session a report on progress made in the implementation of the present resolution.

Palestinian women

In a report to the Commission on the Status of Women on follow-up to and implementation of the Beijing Declaration and Platform for Action [E/CN.6/2001/2], the Secretary-General discussed the situation of Palestinian women and assistance provided by the UN system. Covering the period from September 1999 to September 2000 and based on reports from UN bodies monitor-

ing the situation in the occupied territories and refugee camps, the report stated that, despite continued UN system efforts to improve the economic and social conditions of Palestinian women and in spite of positive trends in the Palestinian economy during the review period, women continued to experience unequal access to the labour market and income-generating activities. Women living in the occupied territories were directly affected by Israeli policies, especially the closure of access routes that hindered efforts by the Palestinian Authority, civil society groups and UN organizations to advance women. It was particularly important that Palestinian women should continue to be given assistance in such areas as education, health, social services and microcredit and that efforts were made to increase their full and equal participation in decision-making and peace programmes.

On 24 July, the Economic and Social Council, in **resolution 2001/2**, called for measures for tangible improvements in the difficulties faced by Palestinian women and called on Israel to facilitate the return of displaced Palestinian women and children to their homes (see p. 427).

Gender and all forms of discrimination

One of the thematic issues for the 2001 session of the Commission on the Status of Women was gender and all forms of discrimination, in particular racism, racial discrimination, xenophobia and related intolerance. On 13 March, the Commission held a panel discussion and a dialogue on the theme. On 17 March, the Commission adopted draft agreed conclusions on the thematic issue, which it recommended to the Economic and Social Council for adoption. The Council endorsed the agreed conclusions in **resolution 2001/5** (see p. 1076).

Older women in society

On 19 December [meeting 88], the General Assembly, on the recommendation of the Third Committee [A/56/576], adopted **resolution 56/126** without vote [agenda item 112].

Situation of older women in society

The General Assembly,

Reaffirming the obligations of all States to promote and protect human rights and fundamental freedoms as stated in the Charter of the United Nations, and emphasizing also their obligations under the human rights instruments, in particular the Convention on the Elimination of All Forms of Discrimination against Women and the Optional Protocol thereto,

Recalling its resolution 44/76 of 8 December 1989 on elderly women, Economic and Social Council resolutions 1982/23 of 4 May 1982 on elderly women and the World Assembly on Ageing and 1986/26 of 23 May

1986 and 1989/38 of 24 May 1989 on elderly women, and resolution 36/4 of 20 March 1992 of the Commission on the Status of Women, on the integration of elderly women into development,

Recalling also the outcome of the twenty-third special session of the General Assembly entitled "Women 2000: gender equality, development and peace for the twenty-first century" and the Beijing Declaration and Platform for Action, in particular their provisions regarding older women,

Welcoming the convening of the Second World Assembly on Ageing, to be held at Madrid in April 2002,

Aware that women constitute the majority of older populations in all regions of the world and represent an important human resource, whose contribution to society has not been fully recognized,

Recognizing the increasing role of older women in taking the responsibility of providing care and assistance to victims of the human immunodeficiency virus/ acquired immunodeficiency syndrome (HIV/AIDS) in various regions of the world, particularly in developing countries,

Affirming the dual challenges of ageing and disability, and affirming also that older persons have specific health needs and that, with the increase in life expectancy and the growing number of older women, their health concerns require particular attention and further research,

Aware that few statistics are available on the situation of older women, and recognizing the importance of data, including data disaggregated by age and sex, as an essential element of planning and policy evaluations,

Recognizing that women of all ages, in particular older women, continue to suffer from discrimination and lack of opportunities,

Emphasizing that Governments bear the primary responsibility for creating an enabling environment for the economic and social development of their citizens, and noting with appreciation the valuable contributions of civil society, including non-governmental organizations, in calling attention to the specific needs of older women,

1. *Stresses* the importance of mainstreaming a gender perspective, taking into account the needs of older women, in policy and planning processes at all levels;

2. *Also stresses* the need to eliminate discrimination on the basis of gender and age and ensure equal rights and their full enjoyment for women of all ages;

3. *Urges* Governments and regional and international organizations, including the United Nations system in cooperation with civil society, including the non-governmental organizations concerned, to promote programmes for healthy active ageing that stress the independence, equality, participation and security of older women and undertake gender-specific research and programmes to address their needs;

4. *Emphasizes* the need for Governments and regional and international organizations, including the United Nations system and the international financial institutions, to develop and improve the collection, analysis and dissemination of data disaggregated by age and sex;

5. *Urges* Governments to take measures to enable all older women to be engaged actively in all aspects of life, as well as to assume a variety of roles in commu-

nities, public life and decision-making, and to develop and implement policies and programmes in cooperation with civil society, including the non-governmental organizations concerned, to ensure their full enjoyment of human rights and quality of life, as well as to address their needs, with a view to contributing to the realization of a society for all ages;

6. *Invites* Governments, the United Nations system and international organizations to consider, in their development planning, the increasing responsibilities of older women in providing care and assistance to victims of HIV/AIDS;

7. *Invites* Governments and the United Nations system to give attention to the situation of older women in the context of the Second World Assembly on Ageing, to be held at Madrid in April 2002, including the integration of a gender perspective into the outcome document.

Women and development

In an August report to the General Assembly on women in development: access to financial resources: a gender perspective [A/56/321 & Corr.1], the Secretary-General discussed, in the context of the International Conference on Financing for Development, to be held in 2002, the gender perspective of financing for development. He also provided statistics on women entrepreneurs and addressed the question of women's access to financial resources and instruments through bank financing, microcredit, equity financing and savings and insurance services. Other issues covered in the report were women's access to information through technology and empowerment of women.

The Secretary-General noted that the number of women-owned businesses had steadily increased worldwide and that women-owned small enterprises and microenterprises were increasingly contributing to the economic and social development of their countries. However, women's contributions were limited by the constraints that women entrepreneurs faced in obtaining financial resources. He therefore recommended that Governments develop accessible financial mechanisms responsive to women's needs; facilitate the access of young women and women entrepreneurs to education and training in business, administration and information and communications technologies; and change existing laws or formulate new laws and regulations on access to financial resources based on the principle of equality between women and men. Governments should encourage banks and other financial intermediaries to: explore viable venues to reach people living in poverty, in particular women, including through international public/private partnership funds; design savings schemes attractive to the poor and to poor women in particular; undertake research to learn more about the characteristics, financial needs and performance of women-owned businesses; and work towards equal treatment of women clients. The Secretary-General recommended that all aspects of financing for development should be examined from a gender perspective in order to ensure women's access to financial resources, and that gender-sensitive policies and programmes should be developed at the micro and macro levels.

GENERAL ASSEMBLY ACTION

On 21 December [meeting 90], the General Assembly, on the recommendation of the Second (Economic and Financial) Committee [A/56/560/Add.1], adopted **resolution 56/188** without vote [agenda item 97 (a)].

Women in development

The General Assembly,

Recalling its resolutions 52/195 of 18 December 1997, 54/210 of 22 December 1999 and all its other resolutions on the integration of women in development, and the relevant resolutions and agreed conclusions, including those on women in the economy, adopted by the Commission on the Status of Women,

Reaffirming the Beijing Declaration and Platform for Action and the outcome documents of the twenty-third special session of the General Assembly, entitled "Women 2000: gender equality, development and peace for the twenty-first century", as well as the outcomes of other recent major United Nations conferences and summits and other relevant special sessions of the General Assembly and their follow-up processes,

Reaffirming also the United Nations Millennium Declaration, which affirms that the equal rights and opportunities of women and men must be assured, and calls for, inter alia, the promotion of gender equality and the empowerment of women as effective ways to combat poverty, hunger and disease and to stimulate development that is truly sustainable,

Reaffirming further that gender equality is of fundamental importance for achieving sustained economic growth and sustainable development, in accordance with the relevant General Assembly resolutions and recent United Nations conferences, and that investing in the development of women and girls has a multiplier effect, in particular on productivity, efficiency and sustained economic growth,

Recognizing the significant contribution that women make to the economy and the major force that they represent for change and development in all sectors of the economy, especially in key areas such as agriculture, industry and services,

Reaffirming that women are key contributors to the economy and to combating poverty through both remunerated and unremunerated work at home, in the community and in the workplace, and that the empowerment of women is a critical factor in the eradication of poverty,

Recognizing that population and development issues, education and training, health, nutrition, the environment, water supply, sanitation, housing, communications, science and technology and employment opportunities are important elements for effective poverty eradication and the advancement and empowerment of women,

Recognizing also, in this context, the importance of respect for all human rights, including the right to development, and of a national and international environment that promotes, inter alia, justice, gender equality, equity, popular participation and political freedom for the advancement and empowerment of women,

Recognizing further that education and training, in particular in business, trade, administration, information and communication technologies and other new technologies, are essential for gender equality, the empowerment of women and poverty eradication,

Recognizing that the difficult socio-economic conditions that exist in many developing countries, in particular the least developed countries, have resulted in the acceleration of the feminization of poverty and that the empowerment of women is a critical factor in the eradication of poverty,

Recognizing also that poverty eradication and the achievement and preservation of peace are mutually reinforcing, and recognizing further that peace is inextricably linked to equality between women and men and to development,

Aware that, although globalization and liberalization processes have created employment opportunities for women in many countries, they have made women, especially in developing countries and in particular in the least developed countries, more vulnerable to problems caused by increased economic volatility,

Recognizing that some effects of market liberalization may deepen the socio-economic marginalization of women in the agricultural sector, including through the loss of employment among small-scale farmers who are more likely to be women than men, and emphasizing that women who are small-scale farmers need special support and empowerment so as to be able to meet the challenges and take advantage of the opportunities of agricultural market liberalization,

Recognizing also that enhanced trade opportunities for developing countries, including through trade liberalization, will improve the economic condition of those societies, including women, which is of particular importance in rural communities,

Aware that, while women represent an important and growing proportion of business owners, their contribution to economic and social development is constrained by, inter alia, the lack of equal access of women and men to, and control over, credit, technology, support services, land and information,

Concerned that the continuing discrimination against women, the denial or lack of equal rights and access to education, training and credit facilities and the lack of control over land, capital, technology and other areas of production impede their full and equal contribution to, and equal opportunity to benefit from, development,

Emphasizing the promotion of programmes aimed at financial intermediation with a view to ensuring the access of rural women to credit and to agricultural inputs and implements and, in particular, to easing collateral requirements for access to finance by women,

Expressing its concern about the underrepresentation of women in economic decision-making, and stressing the importance of mainstreaming a gender perspective in the formulation, implementation and evaluation of all policies,

Noting the importance of the organizations and bodies of the United Nations system, in particular its funds and programmes, including the United Nations Development Fund for Women, in facilitating the advancement of women in development, and recognizing the work done by the International Research and Training Institute for the Advancement of Women,

Welcoming the fact that the Commission on the Status of Women will take up the theme of eradicating poverty, including through the empowerment of women throughout their life cycle in a globalizing world, at its forty-sixth session, in 2002,

1. *Takes note* of the report of the Secretary-General entitled "Women in development: access to financial resources: a gender perspective";

2. *Calls* for the accelerated and effective implementation of the Beijing Declaration and Platform for Action and the relevant provisions of the outcome documents of the twenty-third special session of the General Assembly, as well as the outcomes of all other major United Nations conferences and summits and other relevant special sessions of the General Assembly and their follow-up processes;

3. *Stresses* that a favourable and conducive national and international environment in all fields of life is necessary for the effective integration of women in development;

4. *Urges* Governments to develop and promote methodologies for mainstreaming a gender perspective in all aspects of policy-making, including economic policy-making;

5. *Recognizes* the mutually reinforcing links between gender equality and poverty eradication, as well as the need to elaborate and implement, where appropriate, in consultation with civil society, comprehensive gender-sensitive poverty eradication strategies that address social, structural and macroeconomic issues;

6. *Stresses* the importance of developing national strategies for the promotion of sustainable and productive entrepreneurial activities that will generate income among disadvantaged women and women living in poverty;

7. *Urges* all Governments to ensure women's equal rights with men and their full and equal access to education, training, employment, technology and economic and financial resources, including credit, in particular for rural women and women in the informal sector, and to facilitate, where appropriate, the transition of women from the informal to the formal sector;

8. *Encourages* Governments, the private sector, non-governmental organizations and other actors of civil society to promote and protect the rights of women workers and to take action to remove structural and legal barriers as well as stereotypical attitudes to gender equality at work, and to initiate positive steps to promote equal pay for equal work or work of equal value;

9. *Urges* all Governments to take all appropriate measures to eliminate discrimination against women with regard to their access to bank loans, mortgages and other forms of financial credit, giving special attention to poor, uneducated women, and to support women's access to legal assistance;

10. *Calls upon* Governments and entrepreneurial associations to facilitate the access of women, including young women and women entrepreneurs, to education and training in business, administration and information and communication technologies;

11. *Recognizes* the role of microfinance, including microcredit, in the eradication of poverty, the empowerment of women and the generation of employment, and in this regard notes the importance of sound national financial systems and encourages the strengthening of existing and emerging microcredit institutions and their capacities, including through the support of international financial institutions;

12. *Stresses* the need for assistance to enable women in developing countries, particularly grass-roots women's groups, to have full access to and use of new technologies, including information technologies, for their empowerment;

13. *Urges* States to design and revise laws that ensure that women are accorded full and equal rights to own land and other property, including through inheritance, and to undertake administrative reforms and other necessary measures to give women the same right as men to credit, capital and appropriate technologies and access to markets and information;

14. *Calls upon* Governments to encourage the financial sector to mainstream a gender perspective in its policies and programmes, in particular by:

(a) Exploring viable options to reach people living in poverty, in particular women, including through international public and/or private funds;

(b) Designing savings schemes that are attractive to the poor and to poor women in particular;

(c) Undertaking research to learn more about the characteristics, financial needs and performance of businesses owned by women;

(d) Working towards equal treatment for women clients through comprehensive gender-awareness training for staff at all levels and better representation of women in decision-making positions;

15. *Requests* Governments to ensure the full participation of women in decision-making and in policy formulation and implementation at all levels so that their priorities, skills and potentials can be adequately reflected in national policy;

16. *Calls upon* Governments to promote, inter alia, through legislation, family-friendly and gender-sensitive work environments and also to promote the facilitation of breastfeeding for working mothers as well as the provision of the necessary care for working women's children and other dependants;

17. *Calls upon* the international community to make efforts to mitigate the effects of excess volatility and economic disruption, which have a disproportionately negative impact on women, and to enhance trade opportunities for developing countries in order to improve the economic conditions of women;

18. *Urges* the international community, the United Nations system and relevant organizations to give priority to assisting the efforts of developing countries to ensure the full and effective participation of women in deciding and implementing development strategies and integrating gender concerns into national programmes, including by providing adequate resources to operational activities for development in support of the efforts of Governments to ensure, inter alia, full and equal access of women to health care, capital, edu-

cation, training and technology, as well as full and equal participation in all decision-making;

19. *Expresses its appreciation* to the developed countries that have agreed to and have reached the target of 0.7 per cent of their gross national product for overall official development assistance, and calls upon the developed countries that have not yet done so to strengthen their efforts to achieve the agreed target as soon as possible and, where agreed, within that target, to earmark 0.15 to 0.20 per cent of gross national product for the least developed countries;

20. *Encourages* the international community, the United Nations system, the private sector and civil society to provide the necessary financial resources to assist national Governments in their efforts to meet the development targets and benchmarks agreed upon at the World Summit for Social Development, the Fourth World Conference on Women, the International Conference on Population and Development, the twenty-third and twenty-fourth special sessions of the General Assembly and other relevant United Nations conferences and summits;

21. *Encourages* the United Nations system and international and regional organizations, as appropriate, to assist Governments, at their request, in building institutional capacity and developing national action plans or further implementing existing action plans for the implementation of the Beijing Platform for Action;

22. *Urges* multilateral donors, international financial institutions and regional development banks to review and implement policies to support national efforts to ensure that a higher proportion of resources reach women, in particular in rural and remote areas;

23. *Encourages* the International Conference on Financing for Development, to be held at Monterrey, Mexico, from 18 to 22 March 2002, to examine all aspects of financing for development from a gender perspective;

24. *Encourages* Governments to integrate fully a gender perspective in their preparations for the World Summit on Sustainable Development, to be held at Johannesburg, South Africa, from 26 August to 4 September 2002;

25. *Calls upon* the United Nations system to integrate gender mainstreaming into all its programmes and policies, including in the integrated follow-up to United Nations conferences, in accordance with agreed conclusions 1997/2 on gender mainstreaming adopted by the Economic and Social Council at its substantive session of 1997;

26. *Reiterates its request* to the Secretary-General to update the *World Survey on the Role of Women in Development* for the consideration of the General Assembly at its fifty-ninth session; as in the past, the survey should focus on selective emerging development issues that have an impact on the role of women in the economy at the national, regional and international levels;

27. *Requests* the Secretary-General to submit to the General Assembly at its fifty-eighth session a report on the progress made in the implementation of the present resolution, including the impact of globalization on the empowerment of women and their integration in development;

28. *Decides* to include in the provisional agenda of its fifty-eighth session the sub-item entitled "Women in development".

Women in rural areas

In response to General Assembly resolution 54/135 [YUN 1999, p. 1089], the Secretary-General submitted a July report on improvement of the situation of women in rural areas [A/56/268]. The report was based on the analysis and conclusions of an expert group meeting on the situation of rural women in the context of globalization (Ulaanbaatar, Mongolia, 4-8 June). The expert group examined the impact of major global economic trends on rural women; proposed a research and policy agenda to maximize the beneficial effects of globalization for women; and made recommendations to Governments, the UN system, intergovernmental organizations, NGOs, the private sector and civil society.

In order to implement the findings of the expert group meeting, it was suggested that a high-level policy consultation be convened at the United Nations to set priorities and outline critical strategies that would meet the needs and objectives of rural women in the context of globalization. It was further suggested that the Commission on the Status of Women include consideration of the situation of rural women as a priority theme in its multi-year programme of work.

GENERAL ASSEMBLY ACTION

On 19 December [meeting 88], the General Assembly, on the recommendation of the Third Committee [A/56/576], adopted **resolution 56/129** without vote [agenda item 112].

Improvement of the situation of women in rural areas

The General Assembly,

Recalling its resolution 54/135 of 17 December 1999,

Recalling also the importance attached to the problems of rural women by the Nairobi Forward-looking Strategies for the Advancement of Women, the Beijing Declaration and Platform for Action and the Convention on the Elimination of All Forms of Discrimination against Women,

Welcoming the outcome of the twenty-third special session of the General Assembly entitled "Women 2000: gender equality, development and peace for the twenty-first century", namely, the political declaration and further actions and initiatives to implement the Beijing Declaration and Platform for Action,

Recalling the United Nations Millennium Declaration of 8 September 2000, in which Member States resolved, inter alia, to promote gender equality and the empowerment of women as effective ways to combat poverty, hunger and disease and to stimulate development that is truly sustainable,

Recognizing the critical role and contribution of rural women in enhancing agricultural and rural development, improving food security and eradicating rural poverty,

Noting that some effects of globalization may deepen the socio-economic marginalization of rural women,

Noting also that the globalization process has had some benefits by providing opportunities for wage employment for rural women in new sectors,

Mindful of the fact that the available data and existing tools of measurement and analysis are insufficient for a full understanding of the gender implications of the processes of globalization and rural change, and their impact on rural women,

Recognizing the urgent need to take appropriate measures aimed at further improving the situation of women in rural areas,

1. *Takes note* of the report of the Secretary-General;

2. *Welcomes* the holding, from 4 to 8 June 2001 at Ulaanbaatar, of the expert group meeting on the situation of rural women within the context of globalization;

3. *Requests* the Secretary-General to prepare a user-friendly publication based, inter alia, on case studies presented at the expert group meeting referred to in paragraph 2 above in order to raise awareness of the situation of rural women in the context of globalization;

4. *Also requests* the Secretary-General to seek the views of Member States on the desirability of convening a high-level policy consultation at the governmental level with a view to setting priorities and developing critical strategies that would meet the manifold challenges faced by rural women;

5. *Welcomes* the convening of the World Summit on Sustainable Development in South Africa in September 2002, including the review of chapter 24 of Agenda 21, entitled "Global action for women towards sustainable and equitable development", entailing, inter alia, measures to improve the situation of women in rural areas, and the World Food Summit: five years later, to be held in Italy in June 2002, and urges Governments to integrate a gender perspective, with attention to the improvement of the situation of women in rural areas, in the respective processes and outcome documents;

6. *Invites* Member States, in collaboration with the organizations of the United Nations and civil society, as appropriate, to continue their efforts to implement the outcome of and to ensure an integrated and coordinated follow-up to United Nations conferences and summits, including their five-year reviews, and to attach greater importance to the improvement of the situation of rural women in their national, regional and global development strategies by, inter alia:

(*a*) Creating an enabling environment for improving the situation of rural women, including integrating a gender perspective in macroeconomic policies and developing appropriate social support systems;

(*b*) Designing and revising laws to ensure that, where private ownership of land and property exists, rural women are accorded full and equal rights to own land and other property, including through the right to inheritance, and undertaking administrative reforms and other necessary measures to give women the same right as men to credit, capital, appropriate technologies and access to markets and information;

(*c*) Taking steps towards ensuring that women's unpaid work and contributions to on-farm and off-farm production, including income generated in the informal sector, are visible, and assessing the feasibility of developing and improving mechanisms, such as time-use studies, to measure in quantitative terms unpaid

work, recognizing the potential for it to be reflected in the formulation and implementation of policies and programmes at the national and regional levels;

(*d*) Investing in and strengthening efforts to meet the basic needs of rural women through capacity-building and human resources development measures and the provision of a safe and reliable water supply, health services, including family planning services, and nutritional programmes as well as education and literacy programmes and social support measures;

(*e*) Pursuing the political and socio-economic empowerment of rural women by supporting their full and equal participation in decision-making at all levels, including in rural institutions through, inter alia, the provision of training and capacity-building programmes, including legal literacy;

(*f*) Promoting programmes to enable rural women and men to reconcile their work and family responsibilities and to encourage men to share equally with women household and childcare responsibilities;

(*g*) Integrating a gender perspective into the design, implementation, monitoring and evaluation of development policies and programmes with an emphasis on reducing the disproportionate number of rural women living in poverty;

(*h*) Designing and implementing policies that promote and protect the enjoyment by women of all human rights and fundamental freedoms and creating an environment that does not tolerate violations of the rights of women and girls;

(*i*) Developing specific assistance programmes and advisory services to promote economic skills of rural women in banking, modern trading and financial procedures and providing microcredit and other financial and business services to a greater number of women in rural areas for their economic empowerment;

7. *Invites* the Commission on the Status of Women to pay due attention to the situation of rural women in the consideration of the priority themes identified in its multi-year programme of work for the period 2002-2006;

8. *Invites* the relevant organizations of the United Nations system dealing with issues of development to address and support the empowerment of rural women and their specific needs in their programmes and strategies, including in the context of globalization;

9. *Stresses* the need to identify the best practices for ensuring that rural women have access to and full participation in the area of information and communications technologies, inter alia, through specific studies, and invites the International Telecommunication Union to consider this matter in connection with the preparations for the World Summit on the Information Society;

10. *Requests* the Secretary-General to report to the General Assembly at its fifty-eighth session on the implementation of the present resolution.

Mainstreaming a gender perspective

Inter-Agency Meeting. The Inter-Agency Meeting on Women and Gender Equality of the Administrative Committee on Coordination (ACC) (New York, 27 February–2 March) [ACC/2001/3] held a one-day workshop on approaches and methodologies for gender mainstreaming. The workshop's recommendations included that ACC members should be invited to establish within their own organizations regular reporting mechanisms for all senior managers on gender mainstreaming and that ACC should be invited to undertake in 2002 a review of progress made in implementing Economic and Social Council agreed conclusions 1997/2 [YUN 1997, p. 1186].

Commission on the Status of Women. In his January report to the Commission on the Status of Women on follow-up to and implementation of the Beijing Declaration and Platform for Action [E/CN.6/2001/2], the Secretary-General stated that, in accordance with the Council's agreed conclusions 1997/2 on gender mainstreaming, the UN Special Adviser on Gender Issues and Advancement of Women had continued systematically to promote, facilitate and monitor the integration of gender perspectives into all areas of the work of the UN system. He noted that a framework had been developed for assessing progress towards gender mainstreaming, which would facilitate more systematic and effective reports and provide a monitoring tool for the Special Adviser in her efforts to promote and support gender mainstreaming throughout the system.

On 17 March [E/2001/27 (res. 45/2)], the Commission reaffirmed that the primary goal of mainstreaming a gender perspective was the achievement of gender equality. It called on the Secretary-General, in future reports on follow-up to and implementation of the Beijing Declaration and Platform for Action, to assess progress made on mainstreaming a gender perspective within the UN system, including by providing information on key achievements, lessons learned and best practices, and to recommend strategies for future action. The Commission recommended that the Economic and Social Council consider including a regular item in its agenda on mainstreaming a gender perspective in the UN system and devoting a future coordination segment, by 2005, to the review and appraisal of the system-wide implementation of Council agreed conclusions 1997/2. The Council was further asked to ensure that a gender perspective was mainstreamed into all its work.

ECONOMIC AND SOCIAL COUNCIL ACTION

On 26 July [meeting 43], the Economic and Social Council adopted **resolution 2001/41** [draft: E/2001/L.29] without vote [agenda item 14 (a)].

Mainstreaming a gender perspective into all policies and programmes in the United Nations system

The Economic and Social Council,

Affirming that gender mainstreaming constitutes a critical strategy in the implementation of the Beijing Platform for Action and the outcome of the twenty-third special session of the General Assembly, and for achieving the overall goal of gender equality,

Recalling its agreed conclusions 1997/2 on mainstreaming the gender perspective into all policies and programmes in the United Nations system,

Welcoming General Assembly resolution 55/71 of 4 December 2000, in which the Assembly, inter alia, invited the Council to continue to further policy coordination and inter-agency cooperation towards the achievement of the objectives of the Beijing Platform for Action and the outcome of the twenty-third special session of the General Assembly, including by considering the dedication of specific segments to the advancement of women and the implementation of the above-mentioned instruments and by mainstreaming a gender perspective in all its work,

Having considered resolution 45/2 of the Commission on the Status of Women,

Determined to further intensify its efforts to ensure that gender mainstreaming is an integral part of all its activities concerning integrated and coordinated follow-up to United Nations conferences,

1. *Decides* to include in its agenda, under the item entitled "Coordination, programme and other questions", a sub-item entitled "Mainstreaming a gender perspective into all policies and programmes of the United Nations system", in order to, inter alia, monitor and evaluate achievements made and obstacles encountered by the United Nations system, and to consider further measures to strengthen the implementation and monitoring of gender mainstreaming within the United Nations system;

2. *Calls upon* the Secretary-General, in future reports to the Commission on the Status of Women, the Economic and Social Council and the General Assembly on follow-up to and implementation of the Beijing Declaration and Platform for Action, to assess progress made on mainstreaming a gender perspective within the United Nations system, including by providing information on key achievements, lessons learned and best practices, and to recommend further actions and strategies for future action within the United Nations system;

3. *Also calls upon* the Secretary-General and all bodies reporting to the Economic and Social Council to address the gender aspects of issues before the Council in their reports;

4. *Decides* to devote the coordination segment of one of its substantive sessions, before 2005, to the review and appraisal of the system-wide implementation of agreed conclusions 1997/2 of the Council on mainstreaming the gender perspective into all policies and programmes in the United Nations system.

(See also p. 680.)

System-wide plan

In response to Economic and Social Council resolution 1999/16 [YUN 1999, p. 1099], the Secretary-General submitted to the Commission on the Status of Women the proposed system-wide medium-term plan for the advancement of women for the period 2002-2005 [E/CN.6/2001/4]. The plan outlined actions to be taken by each UN system organization to achieve the objectives set out in the Beijing Platform for Action and the outcome document of the General Assembly's twenty-third special session on women. The plan was structured around the activities of the system to mainstream a gender perspective in all of its activities, as well as in relation to the 12 critical areas of concern in the Platform for Action.

On 9 May [E/2001/27 (res. 45/3)], the Commission recommended the adoption of the proposed system-wide medium-term plan for the advancement of women 2002-2005 by the Economic and Social Council and that the Council, through the Commission, follow up the implementation of the plan and undertake a comprehensive midterm review in 2004. The Commission recommended that the Council request the formulation of a new system-wide medium-term plan to cover the period 2006-2010 and that the Secretary-General submit, in 2005, the new draft plan to the Council and a draft of the proposal to the Commission.

CPC action. By a 24 May letter [E/AC.51/2001/8], the Chairperson of the Commission on the Status of Women transmitted to the Committee for Programme and Coordination (CPC) the text of Commission resolution 45/3 (above) and summaries of the comments of Member States on the plan.

At its forty-first session (New York, 11 June-6 July) [A/56/16], CPC took note of the proposed system-wide medium-term plan for 2002-2005 and of the Commission Chairperson's letter.

By **decision 2001/326** of 20 December, the Economic and Social Council adopted the system-wide medium-term plan for the advancement of women 2002-2005.

UN machinery

Convention on elimination of discrimination against women

As at 31 December 2001, 168 States were parties to the 1979 Convention on the Elimination of All Forms of Discrimination against Women, adopted by the General Assembly in resolution 34/180 [YUN 1979, p. 895]. During the year, the Democratic Republic of Korea and Mauritania acceded to the Convention and the Federal Republic of Yugoslavia succeeded to it, replacing the former Socialist Federal Republic of Yugoslavia. At year's end, 26 States parties had also accepted the amendment to article 20, paragraph 1, of the Convention in respect of the meeting time of the Committee on the Elimination of Discrimination against Women (CEDAW), which was

adopted by the States parties in 1995 [YUN 1995, p. 1178]. The amendment would enter into force when accepted by a two-thirds majority of States parties.

The Optional Protocol to the Convention, adopted by the Assembly in resolution 54/4 [YUN 1999, p. 1100], which entered into force in 2000 [YUN 2000, p. 1123], had 28 States parties by the end of 2001. The Protocol entitled individuals or groups to submit directly to CEDAW complaints concerning alleged Convention violations and established procedures for inquiries into situations of grave or systematic violations of women's rights.

The Secretary-General submitted his annual report to the Assembly on the status of the Convention as at 1 August [A/56/328].

CEDAW

In 2001, the 23-member Committee on the Elimination of Discrimination against Women, established in 1982 [YUN 1982, p. 1149] to monitor compliance with the 1979 Convention, held two sessions in New York [A/56/38].

At its twenty-fourth session (15 January–2 February), CEDAW reviewed the initial or periodic reports of Burundi, Egypt, Finland, Jamaica, Kazakhstan, Maldives, Mongolia and Uzbekistan on measures they had taken to implement the Convention. CEDAW also considered a Secretariat report on ways of expediting the Committee's work [CEDAW/C/2001/I/4] and the Committee's revised rules of procedure [CEDAW/C/2001/I/WG.I/WP.1]. By three decisions, CEDAW adopted its rules of procedure [A/56/38 (dec. 24/I)]; adopted a statement on gender and racial discrimination to be forwarded to the Preparatory Committee for the World Conference against Racism, Racial Discrimination, Xenophobia and Related Intolerance (see p. 616) [dec. 24/II]; and decided to develop closer links with the Commission on the Status of Women [dec. 24/III].

At its twenty-fifth session (2-20 July), CEDAW reviewed the initial or periodic reports of Andorra, Guinea, Guyana, the Netherlands, Nicaragua, Singapore, Sweden and Viet Nam. It also considered Secretariat reports on ways of improving the Committee's work [CEDAW/C/2001/II/4] and on the Committee's approach to article 4, paragraph 1, of the Convention (on temporary special measures) [CEDAW/C/2001/II/5]. By three decisions, CEDAW requested approval from the General Assembly to hold, on an exceptional basis, a three-week session in August 2002, in order to consider the backlog of States parties' reports, and to enlarge the pre-sessional working group, to meet in February 2002, to prepare issues and questions relating to the backlog [A/56/38 (dec. 25/I)]; decided that the pre-sessional working group should formulate a short list of issues and questions, focusing on themes addressed by the Convention [dec. 25/II]; and adopted a statement to be forwarded to the special session of the Assembly on children in 2002 [dec. 25/III]. The Committee also adopted suggestions, one recommending that the Division for the Advancement of Women (UN Department of Economic and Social Affairs) establish a confidential electronic database for the registration of communications submitted under the Optional Protocol to the Convention [suggestion 25/1] and the other on the content of reports of UN bodies and specialized agencies submitted to CEDAW [suggestion 25/2].

GENERAL ASSEMBLY ACTION

On 24 December [meeting 92], the General Assembly, on the recommendation of the Third Committee [A/56/576], adopted **resolution 56/229** without vote [agenda item 112].

Convention on the Elimination of All Forms of Discrimination against Women

The General Assembly,

Recalling its resolution 55/70 of 4 December 2000 and its previous resolutions on the elimination of discrimination against women,

Bearing in mind that one of the purposes of the United Nations, as stated in Articles 1 and 55 of the Charter, is to promote universal respect for human rights and fundamental freedoms for all without distinction of any kind, including distinction as to sex,

Affirming that women and men should participate equally in social, economic and political development, should contribute equally to such development and should share equally in improved conditions of life,

Recalling the Vienna Declaration and Programme of Action adopted by the World Conference on Human Rights on 25 June 1993, in which the Conference reaffirmed that the human rights of women and the girl child were an inalienable, integral and indivisible part of universal human rights,

Acknowledging the need for a comprehensive and integrated approach to the promotion and protection of the human rights of women, which includes the integration of the human rights of women into the mainstream of United Nations activities system-wide,

Reaffirming the commitments made in the political declaration and the outcome document of the twenty-third special session of the General Assembly entitled "Women 2000: gender equality, development and peace for the twenty-first century", in particular paragraphs 68 *(c)* and *(d)* concerning the Convention on the Elimination of All Forms of Discrimination against Women and the Optional Protocol thereto,

Recalling that, in the United Nations Millennium Declaration, heads of State and Government resolved to implement the Convention,

Welcoming the progress made in the implementation of the Convention, but expressing concern about the remaining challenges,

Welcoming also the growing number of States parties to the Convention, which now stands at one hundred and sixty-eight,

Welcoming further the entry into force on 22 December 2000 of the Optional Protocol to the Convention on the Elimination of All Forms of Discrimination against Women,

Bearing in mind the recommendation of the Committee on the Elimination of Discrimination against Women that national reports should contain information on the implementation of the Beijing Platform for Action, in accordance with paragraph 323 of the Platform,

Having considered the report of the Committee on its twenty-fourth and twenty-fifth sessions,

Expressing concern at the great number of reports that are overdue and that continue to be overdue, in particular initial reports, which constitutes an obstacle to the full implementation of the Convention,

1. *Welcomes* the report of the Secretary-General on the status of the Convention on the Elimination of All Forms of Discrimination against Women;

2. *Expresses disappointment* that universal ratification of the Convention was not achieved by 2000, and urges all States that have not yet ratified or acceded to the Convention to do so;

3. *Emphasizes* the importance of full compliance by States parties with their obligations under the Convention and the Optional Protocol thereto;

4. *Welcomes* the rapidly growing number of State parties to the Optional Protocol, which now stands at twenty-eight, and urges other States parties to the Convention to consider signing and ratifying or acceding to the Optional Protocol;

5. *Also welcomes* the fact that the Committee on the Elimination of Discrimination against Women has adopted the rules governing its work under the Optional Protocol as part of its revised rules of procedure;

6. *Notes* that some States parties have modified their reservations, expresses satisfaction that some reservations have been withdrawn, and urges States parties to limit the extent of any reservations that they lodge to the Convention, to formulate any such reservations as precisely and as narrowly as possible, to ensure that no reservations are incompatible with the object and purpose of the Convention or otherwise incompatible with international treaty law, to review their reservations regularly with a view to withdrawing them and to withdraw reservations that are contrary to the object and purpose of the Convention or that are otherwise incompatible with international treaty law;

7. *Urges* States parties to the Convention to make every possible effort to submit their reports on the implementation of the Convention in accordance with article 18 thereof and with the guidelines provided by the Committee and to cooperate fully with the Committee in the presentation of their reports;

8. *Encourages* the Secretariat to extend further technical assistance to States parties, upon their request, in the preparation of reports, in particular initial reports, and invites Governments to contribute to these efforts;

9. *Commends* the Committee on its contributions to the effective implementation of the Convention;

10. *Strongly urges* States parties to the Convention to take appropriate measures so that acceptance of the amendment to article 20, paragraph 1, of the Convention by a two-thirds majority of States parties can be reached as soon as possible so that the amendment may enter into force;

11. *Expresses its appreciation* for the additional meeting time that allows the Committee to hold two sessions annually, each session of three weeks' duration and each preceded by a pre-sessional working group of the Committee;

12. *Also expresses its appreciation* for the efforts made by the Committee to improve the efficiency of its working methods, and encourages further efforts in this regard;

13. *Acknowledges* the number of reports awaiting consideration by the Committee, and in this regard decides to authorize the Committee to hold, on an exceptional basis, an extraordinary session of three weeks' duration in 2002 to be used entirely for the consideration of the reports of the States parties in order to reduce the backlog of reports, and to enlarge the membership of the pre-sessional working group in 2002 to prepare for the exceptional session of the Committee, taking into account decision 25/I of the Committee;

14. *Requests* the Secretary-General, in accordance with General Assembly resolution 54/4 of 6 October 1999, to provide the resources, including staff and facilities, necessary for the effective functioning of the Committee within its full mandate, in particular taking into account the entry into force of the Optional Protocol;

15. *Urges* Governments, agencies and organizations of the United Nations system and intergovernmental and non-governmental organizations to disseminate the Convention and the Optional Protocol thereto;

16. *Encourages* all relevant entities of the United Nations system, within their mandates, as well as Governments and intergovernmental and non-governmental organizations, in particular women's organizations, as appropriate, to continue to assist States parties, upon their request, in implementing the Convention, and in this regard encourages States parties to pay attention to the concluding comments as well as the general recommendations of the Committee;

17. *Encourages* all relevant entities of the United Nations system to continue to build women's knowledge and understanding of and capacity to utilize human rights instruments, in particular the Convention and the Optional Protocol thereto;

18. *Welcomes* the submission by the specialized agencies, at the invitation of the Committee, of reports on the implementation of the Convention in areas falling within the scope of their activities and the contribution of non-governmental organizations to the work of the Committee, and encourages the specialized agencies to continue to submit reports;

19. *Requests* the Secretary-General to submit to the General Assembly at its fifty-seventh session a report on the status of the Convention on the Elimination of All Forms of Discrimination against Women and the implementation of the present resolution.

Commission on the Status of Women

The Commission on the Status of Women, at its forty-fifth session (New York, 6-17 March and 9-11 May) [E/2001/27 & Corr.1], recommended four resolutions to the Economic and Social Council

for adoption on the situation of Palestinian women (see p. 1067); discrimination against women and girls in Afghanistan (see p. 1065); proposals for the Commission's multi-year programme of work for 2002-2006 (see p. 1084); and its agreed conclusions on thematic issues (women and HIV/AIDS; gender and all forms of discrimination) (below). The Commission also adopted and brought to the Council's attention resolutions on the release of women and children taken hostage, including those imprisoned during armed conflicts (see p. 1060); mainstreaming a gender perspective into all policies and programmes in the UN system (see p. 1072); and the proposed system-wide medium-term plan for the advancement of women (2002-2005) (see p. 1073). The Commission further adopted six decisions, by which it requested that a decision for enhancing the review of progress in implementing the Beijing Platform for Action and of the outcome documents of the General Assembly's twenty-third special session should be taken in coordination with the conference reviews of other functional commissions [E/2001/27 (dec. 45/101)]; requested its Bureau to undertake the preparatory work for a further discussion of the Commission's working methods at its forty-sixth (2002) session [dec. 45/102]; requested the Secretary-General to submit another report on the Commission's communications procedure to the forty-sixth session [dec. 45/103]; decided to meet in resumed session from 9 to 11 May [dec. 45/104]; recommended that CPC, when reviewing the proposed programme budget for 2002-2003, take into consideration the discussion on the subject in the Commission [dec. 45/105]; and took note of the documents before it [dec. 45/106].

By **decision 2001/317** of 26 July, the Economic and Social Council took note of the Commission's report on its forty-fifth session.

ECONOMIC AND SOCIAL COUNCIL ACTION

On 24 July [meeting 40], the Economic and Social Council, on the recommendation of the Commission on the Status of Women [E/2001/27 & Corr.1], adopted **resolution 2001/5** without vote [agenda item 14 *(a)*].

Agreed conclusions of the Commission on the Status of Women on thematic issues

The Economic and Social Council

Endorses the following agreed conclusions adopted by the Commission on the Status of Women with respect to the thematic issues addressed by the Commission at its forty-fifth session:

A. Women, the girl child and human immunodeficiency virus/acquired immunodeficiency syndrome

1. Women play a vital role in the social and economic development of their countries. It is a profound con-

cern that by the end of 2000, 36.1 million people were living with human immunodeficiency virus/acquired immunodeficiency syndrome (HIV/AIDS), and of those infected, 95 per cent were living in developing countries, and 16.4 million were women. The proportion of women infected with HIV is increasing and in sub-Saharan Africa women constitute 55 per cent of all adult HIV-infected, while teenage girls are infected at a rate of five to six times greater than their male counterparts.

2. Full enjoyment by women and girls of all human rights, civil, cultural, economic, political and social, including the right to development—which are universal, indivisible, interdependent and interrelated—is of crucial importance in preventing the further spread of HIV/AIDS. The majority of women and girls do not fully enjoy their rights, in particular to education, the highest attainable standard of physical and mental health and social security, especially in developing countries. These inequalities begin early in life and render women and girls more vulnerable in the area of sexual and reproductive health, thus increasing their risk and vulnerability to HIV infection and their disproportionate suffering from the consequences of the HIV/AIDS epidemic.

3. Poverty and the negative and harmful traditional and customary practices that subordinate women in the household, community and society render women especially vulnerable to HIV/sexually transmitted infections. Millions of women and girls lack access and/or have insufficient access to health care, medication and social support in general, including in the case of sexually transmitted infections/HIV/AIDS.

4. The Commission on the Status of Women has taken into account the recommendations on women, the girl child and HIV/AIDS as contained in the following documents: the Beijing Platform for Action, the Programme of Action of the International Conference on Population and Development, the Programme of Action of the World Summit for Social Development, the outcome documents of the twenty-first, twenty-third and twenty-fourth special sessions of the General Assembly, the United Nations Millennium Declaration, the agreed conclusions of the Commission on the Status of Women on women and health, and Commission resolution 44/2 of 2 March 2000.

5. The Commission recalls the internationally agreed targets as contained in the documents referred to in paragraph 4 above, and suggests that the outcome document of the special session of the General Assembly on HIV/AIDS should fully integrate a gender perspective, including in any new targets, and focus on actions needed to achieve existing targets.

6. The Commission welcomes the Abuja Declaration on HIV/AIDS, Tuberculosis and other Related Infectious Diseases, in particular its gender dimension, adopted by the Organization of African Unity at its Special Summit on HIV/AIDS, held at Abuja, on 26 and 27 April 2001.

7. The Commission notes with appreciation the efforts of the Joint United Nations Programme on HIV/AIDS (UNAIDS) and its co-sponsors, bilateral and multilateral donors, governmental, intergovernmental and non-governmental organizations to empower women through capacity-development programmes, as well as programmes that provide women with access to

development resources and strengthen their networks that offer care and support to women affected by HIV/AIDS.

8. The highest level of political commitment to the empowerment and advancement of women and to the prevention, research, care and treatment of sexually transmitted infections, especially HIV/AIDS, must be secured.

9. It is important to integrate fully a gender perspective in the preparatory process and in the outcome document of the special session of the General Assembly on HIV/AIDS, including, inter alia, the full integration of a gender perspective in any new targets and in actions needed to achieve internationally agreed targets that relate to women, the girl child and HIV/AIDS as contained in the documents referred to in paragraph 4 above.

10. In order to accelerate the implementation of the strategic objectives of the conferences and documents mentioned in paragraph 4 above, especially of those objectives related to women, the girl child and HIV/AIDS, the Commission recommends that the following actions be taken:

Actions to be taken by Governments, the United Nations system and civil society, as appropriate

1. Empowerment of women:

(a) The rapid progression of the HIV/AIDS pandemic, particularly in the developing world, has had a devastating impact on women. The unequal power relationships between women and men, in which women often do not have the power to insist on safe and responsible sex practices, and lack of communication and understanding between women and men on women's health needs, inter alia, endanger women's health, in particular by increasing their susceptibility to sexually transmitted infections, including HIV/AIDS;

(b) Responsible behaviour and gender equality are among the important prerequisites for its prevention;

(c) Ensure that the sexual health and reproductive rights of women of all ages as defined in paragraphs 94 to 96 of the Beijing Platform for Action is seen as an essential part in efforts to promote women's empowerment, bearing in mind that women and girls are disproportionately affected by HIV/AIDS and, in this context, further promote the advancement and empowerment of women and women's full enjoyment of all human rights, including the right to development and their right to have control over and decide freely and responsibly on matters related to their sexuality, in order to protect themselves from high risk and irresponsible behaviour leading to sexually transmitted infections, including HIV/AIDS, and access to health information and education, health care and health services, which are critical to increasing the ability of women and young girls to protect themselves from HIV infection;

(d) Focus national and international policies towards the eradication of poverty in order to empower women to better protect themselves from the spread of the pandemic and to deal more effectively with the adverse effects of HIV/AIDS;

(e) Alleviate the social and economic impact of HIV/AIDS on women who, in their roles as food suppliers and traditional caregivers, are primarily affected by the negative consequences of the pandemic, such as a reduced labour force and a breakdown of social service systems;

(f) Reaffirm the equal rights of women and the girl child infected and affected by sexually transmitted infections/HIV/AIDS to have access to health, education and social services and to be protected from all forms of discrimination, stigma, abuse and neglect;

(g) Also reaffirm the human rights of girls and women to equal access to education, skill training and employment opportunities as a means to reduce their vulnerability to sexually transmitted diseases/HIV;

(h) Urge Governments to take all necessary measures to empower women and strengthen women's economic independence and protect and promote full enjoyment of all human rights and fundamental freedoms in order to allow women and girls to better protect themselves from sexually transmitted infections/HIV;

(i) Address and reduce the increased HIV/AIDS risks, vulnerabilities and impact on women and girls, including in conflict situations, through gender-sensitive economic, legal and social services and programmes, including integration of HIV/AIDS prevention and care services into minimum essential health-care packages;

(j) Strengthen concrete measures to eliminate all forms of violence against women and girls, including harmful traditional and customary practices, abuse and rape, battering and trafficking in women and girls, which aggravate the conditions fostering the spread of HIV/AIDS, through, inter alia, the enactment and enforcement of laws, as well as public campaigns to combat violence against women and girls;

(k) Take steps to create an environment that promotes all human rights, compassion and support for people infected/affected by HIV/AIDS, including through introducing and/or reviewing legislation, with a view to striving to remove discriminatory provisions and provide the legal framework that will protect the rights of people living with HIV/AIDS, in particular of women and girls, and enable those who are vulnerable to have access to appropriate voluntary and confidential counselling services, and encourage efforts to reduce discrimination and stigmatization;

(l) Further develop and fully integrate a gender perspective into national, regional and international HIV/AIDS programmes and strategies, taking into account, inter alia, sex- and age-disaggregated data and statistics, with a particular focus on gender equality;

(m) Take measures to promote and implement women's equal access to and control over economic resources, including land, property rights and the right to inheritance, regardless of their marital status, in order to reduce the vulnerability of women in the context of the HIV/AIDS epidemic;

(n) Provide women and girls, including those in marginalized groups, with equal access to quality education, literacy programmes, health care and health services, social services, skills training and employment opportunities, support capacity-building and the strengthening of women's networks and protect them from all forms of discrimination, including racial discrimination, stigma, abuse and neglect, in order to reduce their risk and vulnerability to HIV/AIDS and alleviate the impact on those infected and affected by HIV/AIDS.

2. Prevention:

(a) Governments, relevant United Nations agencies, funds and programmes and intergovernmental and non-governmental organizations, individually and collectively, should make efforts to place combating HIV/AIDS as a priority on the development agenda and to implement multisectoral and decentralized effective preventive strategies and programmes, especially for the most vulnerable populations, including women, young girls and infants, also taking into account the prevention of mother-to-child transmission of HIV/AIDS;

(b) Governments, with the assistance of relevant United Nations agencies, funds and programmes, must adopt a long-term, timely, coherent and integrated AIDS prevention policy, with public information and life skills-based education programmes specifically tailored to the needs of women and girls, adapted to their social and cultural context and sensitivities, and the specific needs in their life cycle;

(c) Intensify efforts to determine the best policies and programmes to prevent women and young girls from becoming infected with HIV/AIDS, taking into account that women, in particular young girls, are socially, physiologically and biologically more vulnerable than men to sexually transmitted infections;

(d) Take measures to integrate, inter alia, a family-based approach in programmes aimed at providing prevention, care and support to women and girls infected and affected by HIV/AIDS and a community-based approach in policies and programmes aimed at providing prevention, care and support to women and girls infected and affected by HIV/AIDS;

(e) Ensure equal and non-discriminatory access to accurate, comprehensive information, prevention education on reproductive health, and voluntary testing and counselling services and technologies, within a cultural and gender-sensitive framework and with particular emphasis on adolescents and young adults;

(f) Request the Joint United Nations Programme on HIV/AIDS (UNAIDS) and its co-sponsors to continue in their efforts aimed at providing complete and accurate sexual and reproductive health education for young people, within a cultural and gender-sensitive framework, while, inter alia, encouraging them to delay sexual initiation, or/and to use condoms and, in this context, urge that greater attention be given to the education of men and boys about their roles and their responsibilities in preventing the transmission of sexually transmitted diseases, including HIV/AIDS, to their partners;

(g) Promote gender equality in relationships, and provide information and resources to promote informed, responsible and safe sexual behaviour and practices, mutual respect and gender equality in sexual relationships;

(h) Encourage all forms of media to promote non-discriminatory and gender-sensitive images and a culture of non-violence and respect for all human rights, in particular women's rights, in addressing HIV/AIDS;

(i) Encourage active involvement of men and boys through, inter alia, youth-led and youth-specific HIV education projects and peer-based programmes in challenging gender stereotypes and attitudes as well as gender inequalities in relation to HIV and AIDS, as well as their full participation in prevention, impact alleviation and care, and design and implement programmes to encourage and enable men to adopt safe and responsible sexual and reproductive behaviour and to use effectively methods to prevent unwanted pregnancies and sexually transmitted infections, including HIV/AIDS;

(j) Intensify, especially in the most affected countries, education, services, community-based mobilization and information strategies to protect women of all ages from HIV and other sexually transmitted infections, including through the development of safe, affordable, effective and easily accessible female-controlled methods, including such methods as microbicides and female condoms that protect against sexually transmitted infections and HIV/AIDS, as well as voluntary and confidential HIV testing and counselling and the promotion of sexually responsible behaviour, including abstinence and condom use;

(k) Strengthen sustainable, efficient and accessible primary health-care systems that serve to support prevention efforts;

(l) Special attention should be given to the prevention of HIV, in particular with regard to mother-to-child transmission and for victims of rape—on the basis of informed consent and voluntary and confidential testing, counselling and treatment—including through ensuring access to care and improving the quality and availability of affordable drugs and diagnostics, especially antiretroviral therapies, and by building on existing efforts, with special attention to the issue of breastfeeding;

(m) Strive to ensure that schools at all levels, other educational institutions and non-formal systems of education play a leading role in preventing HIV infection and preventing and combating stigmatization and discrimination by providing an environment free of all forms of violence that promotes compassion and tolerance, and provide gender-sensitive education, including on responsible sexual behaviour and practices, life skills and behaviour change;

(n) Work together with civil society, including traditional, community and religious leaders, to identify the customary and traditional practices that adversely influence gender relations and to eliminate those practices that increase the vulnerability of women and girls to HIV/AIDS.

3. Treatment, care and support:

(a) Request Governments to ensure universal and equal access for women and men throughout their life cycle to social services related to health care, including education, clean water and safe sanitation, nutrition, food security and health education programmes, especially for women and girls living with and affected by HIV/AIDS, including treatment for opportunistic diseases;

(b) Request Governments to work to provide comprehensive health care for women and girls living with HIV/AIDS, including dietary and food supplements and treatment for opportunistic infections and full, equal, non-discriminatory and prompt access to health care and health services, including sexual and reproductive health and voluntary and confidential counselling, taking into account the rights of the child to access to information, privacy, confidentiality, respect and in-

formed consent and the responsibilities, rights and duties of parents and legal guardians;

(c) Care and support for people living with HIV/AIDS, in particular women and girls, should have a comprehensive approach, involving medical, social, psychological, spiritual and economic needs, targeting the community and national levels;

(d) Collaborate to strengthen efforts to create an environment and the conditions necessary, with the assistance of relevant United Nations agencies, funds and programmes and intergovernmental and non-governmental organizations, upon request to address the challenges faced by women and girls infected and affected by HIV/AIDS, in particular orphans and widows, girls and older women who may also be primary caregivers for people living with HIV/AIDS, all of whom are particularly vulnerable to both economic and sexual exploitation; provide them with the necessary economic and psycho-social support; and encourage their economic independence through income-generating programmes and other methods;

(e) Provide support for the implementation of special programmes for the growing problems of children orphaned by AIDS, especially girls, who may easily become victims of sexual exploitation.

4. Enabling environment for regional and international cooperation:

(a) Call upon the international community, relevant agencies, funds and programmes of the United Nations system and intergovernmental and non-governmental organizations to intensify their support of national efforts against HIV/AIDS, in particular in favour of women and young girls, including efforts to provide affordable antiretroviral drugs, diagnostics and drugs to treat tuberculosis and other opportunistic infections; strengthening health systems, including reliable distribution and delivery systems; implementing a strong generic drug policy; bulk purchasing; negotiating with pharmaceutical companies to reduce prices; appropriate financing systems; and encouraging local manufacturing and import practices consistent with national laws and international agreements, in particular in the worst hit regions in Africa and where the epidemic is severely setting back national development gains;

(b) Take action to eradicate poverty, which is a major contributory factor in the spread of HIV infection and worsens the impact of the epidemic, in particular for women and girls, as well as depleting resources and incomes of families and endangering the survival of present and future generations;

(c) Identify and implement development-oriented and durable solutions that integrate a gender perspective to external debt and debt-servicing problems of developing countries, including least developed countries, inter alia, through debt relief, including the option of debt cancellation for official development assistance, in order to help them to finance programmes and projects targeted at development, including the advancement of women, inter alia, through facilitating the delivery of health care and health services and the provision of preventive programmes on HIV/AIDS, especially targeting women and girls; in this regard, welcome the Cologne initiative for the reduction of debt, in particular the speedy implementation

of the enhanced heavily indebted poor countries initiatives; and encourage Governments to ensure the provision of adequate funds for its implementation and implement the provision that funds saved should be used to support anti-poverty programmes that are gender sensitive and that address prevention, care and support of women and girls infected and affected;

(d) Ensure international, regional and South-South cooperation, including development assistance and additional adequate resources, to implement gender-sensitive policies and programmes aimed at halting the spread of the epidemic by providing affordable quality treatment and care of all people, especially women and girls living with HIV/AIDS;

(e) Encourage the Joint United Nations Programme on HIV/AIDS (UNAIDS) and its co-sponsors, bilateral and multilateral donors and intergovernmental and non-governmental organizations, to intensify their support to empower women and prevent HIV infection and to give urgent and priority attention to the situation of women and girls, especially in Africa, in particular through the International Partnership against AIDS in Africa;

(f) Increase investment in research on the development of HIV vaccines, microbicides and other female-controlled methods, simpler and less expensive diagnostic tests, single-dose treatments for sexually transmitted infections and quality low-cost drug combinations, including for opportunistic infections and sexually transmitted infections, as well as alternative medicine for HIV/AIDS, focusing on the needs of women and girls;

(g) Support and assist research and development centres, in particular at the national level, in the worst-hit regions, with a gender specific focus, in the field of vaccines and treatment for HIV/AIDS, as well as support the efforts by Governments in building and/or strengthening their national capacities in this area;

(h) Develop and implement as well as strengthen already existing training programmes for law enforcement officers, prison officers, medical officers and judicial personnel, as well as United Nations personnel, including peacekeeping staff, to be more sensitive and responsive to the needs of threatened and abused women and children infected with HIV/AIDS, including intravenous drug users, female inmates and orphans;

(i) Ensure that the needs of girls and women in relation to HIV/AIDS in all situations of conflict, post-conflict and peacekeeping, and in the immediate and reconstructive responses to emergencies and natural disasters, are addressed;

(j) Provide gender-sensitive prevention and treatment services for female substance abusers living with HIV/AIDS;

(k) Provide technical and financial support to networks of people living with HIV/AIDS, and non-governmental organizations and community-based organizations involved in implementing HIV/AIDS programmes, in particular women's groups, in order to strengthen their efforts;

(l) Adopt a balanced approach to prevention and comprehensive care, including treatment and support, for women and girls affected by HIV/AIDS, taking into account the role played by poverty, poor nutritional conditions and underdevelopment, which increases the vulnerability of women and girls to HIV/AIDS;

(m) Urge relevant United Nations entities to incorporate a gender perspective into their follow-up and evaluation of the progress made in the control of sexually transmitted infections and HIV/AIDS;

(n) Commend UNAIDS for its advocacy in successfully accelerating both increased prevention and improved access to care, urge Governments and the international community to continue advocating and lobbying, and encourage Governments to enter into negotiations with multinational drug companies for reduction in market prices of HIV/AIDS related drugs and diagnostics to ensure availability, affordability and sustainability to women and girls living with HIV/AIDS.

B. Gender and all forms of discrimination, in particular racism, racial discrimination, xenophobia and related intolerance

1. The Charter of the United Nations, the Universal Declaration of Human Rights, the International Convention on the Elimination of All Forms of Racial Discrimination, the Convention on the Elimination of All Forms of Discrimination against Women and other international instruments reaffirm the principles of equality and non-discrimination.

2. The consistent efforts of the international community in promoting gender equality through the convening of world conferences on women are recalled. It should also be recalled that the Vienna Declaration and Programme of Action adopted by the World Conference on Human Rights, the Beijing Declaration and Platform for Action adopted at the Fourth World Conference on Women and the outcome documents of the twenty-third special session of the General Assembly, entitled "Women 2000: gender equality, development and peace for the twenty-first century", emphasize that all human rights of women and of the girl child are an inalienable, integral and indivisible part of universal human rights. The Platform for Action reaffirms that all human rights—civil, cultural, economic, political and social, including the right to development—are universal, indivisible, interdependent and interrelated.

3. The Beijing Declaration and Platform for Action indicate that many women face additional barriers to the enjoyment of their human rights because of such factors as their race, language, ethnicity, culture, religion, disability or socio-economic class or because they are indigenous people, migrants, including women migrant workers, displaced women or refugees. Also, the outcome documents of the twenty-third special session indicate that in situations of armed conflict and foreign occupation, the human rights of women have been extensively violated. Among the further actions and initiatives to implement the platform adopted by the special session were several directed at the elimination of racially motivated violence against women and girls.

4. The efforts of the international community in combating racism, racial discrimination, xenophobia and related intolerance are recalled.

5. There has been growing recognition that various types of discrimination do not always affect women and men in the same way. Moreover, gender discrimination may be intensified and facilitated by all other forms of discrimination. It has been increasingly recognized

that without gender analysis of all forms of discrimination, including multiple forms of discrimination and, in particular, in this context, racial discrimination, xenophobia and related intolerance, violations of the human rights of women might escape detection and that remedies to address racism may also fail to meet the needs of women and girls. It is also important that efforts to address gender discrimination incorporate approaches to the elimination of all forms of discrimination, including racial discrimination.

6. By its resolution 52/111 of 12 December 1997, the General Assembly decided to convene a World Conference against Racism, Racial Discrimination, Xenophobia and Related Intolerance, to be held in Durban, South Africa, from 31 August to 8 September 2001. In its resolution 53/132 of 9 December 1998, the Assembly proclaimed 2001 as the International Year of Mobilization against Racism, Racial Discrimination, Xenophobia and Related Intolerance. It is therefore timely that the gender dimensions of racism, racial discrimination, xenophobia and related intolerance are addressed by the Commission on the Status of Women.

7. The increasing gravity of different manifestations of racism, racial discrimination and xenophobia in various parts of the world requires a more integrated and effective approach on the part of relevant mechanisms of the United Nations human rights machinery. These trends affect the implementation of the outcome documents of the twenty-third special session of the General Assembly entitled "Women 2000: gender equality, development and peace for the twenty-first century" and of the relevant international instruments against discrimination.

8. The Commission recommends that the following actions be taken:

Actions to be taken by Governments, the United Nations and civil society, as appropriate

1. **An integrated, holistic approach to address multiple forms of discrimination against women and girls, in particular racism, racial discrimination, xenophobia and related intolerance:**

   (a) Examine the intersection of multiple forms of discrimination, including their root causes, from a gender perspective, with special emphasis on gender-based racial discrimination, in order to develop and implement strategies, policies and programmes aimed at the elimination of all forms of discrimination against women and to increase the role that women play in the design, implementation and monitoring of gender-sensitive anti-racist policies;

   (b) Establish and strengthen effective partnerships with and provide support, as appropriate, to all relevant actors of civil society, including non-governmental organizations working to promote gender equality and the advancement of women, in particular women subject to multiple discrimination, in order to promote an integrated and holistic approach to the elimination of all forms of discrimination against women and girls;

   (c) Acknowledge the need to address the issues of racism, racial discrimination, xenophobia and related intolerance as and where they affect young women and men and boys and girls and recognize the role they play in the fight against racism, racial discrimination, xenophobia and related intolerance, including particular

forms of racism experienced by young women and girls, and support the fundamental role played by youth non-governmental organizations in educating young people and children to build a society based on respect and solidarity;

   (d) Promote respect for and the value of the full diversity of women's and girls' situations and conditions and recognize that some women face particular barriers to their empowerment, and ensure that the goals of achieving gender equality and the advancement of women, including marginalized women, are reflected in all strategies, policies and programmes aimed at the elimination of all forms of discrimination against women and girls; and mainstream a gender perspective into the preparation and implementation of policies integrating multiculturalism, ensuring the full enjoyment of all human rights and fundamental freedoms by all women and girls and reaffirming that human rights—civil, cultural, economic, political and social, including the right to development—are universal, indivisible, interdependent and interrelated;

   (e) Promote recognition that the empowerment of women is an essential component of a proactive strategy to fight racism, racial discrimination, xenophobia and other forms of related intolerance, and take measures to empower women subject to multiple discrimination to exercise fully their rights in all spheres of life and to play an active role in the design and implementation of policies and measures that affect their lives;

   (f) Take action to raise awareness and promote the eradication of all forms of discrimination, including multiple discrimination experienced by women, through, inter alia, education and mass media campaigns;

   (g) The Platform for Action recognized that women face barriers to full equality and advancement because of such factors as their race, age, language, ethnicity, culture, religion or disability, because they are indigenous women or of other status. Many women encounter specific obstacles related to their family status, particularly as single parents, and their socio-economic status, including their living conditions in rural, isolated or impoverished areas. Additional barriers also exist for refugee women, other displaced women, including internally displaced women, as well as for immigrant women and migrant women, including women migrant workers. Many women are also particularly affected by environmental disasters, serious and infectious diseases and various forms of violence against women;

   (h) Acknowledge that racism, racial discrimination, xenophobia and related intolerance manifest themselves in a differentiated manner for women, increasing poverty, causing their living conditions to deteriorate, generating violence and limiting or denying them the full enjoyment and exercise of all their human rights;

   (i) Ensure the full and equal opportunity for the sustained participation and representation of indigenous women and girls and of women and girls, as appropriate, from culturally diverse backgrounds, in all relevant decision-making processes;

   (j) Ensure that the Commission on the Status of Women takes into account in its work the impact of all forms of discrimination, including multiple discrimination, on the advancement of women;

(*k*) Acknowledge the ongoing work of the Committee on the Elimination of Discrimination against Women and the Committee on the Elimination of Racial Discrimination in taking into account the impact of multiple forms of discrimination on the advancement of women and the achievement of gender equality.

2. Policies, legal measures, mechanisms and machineries:

(*a*) Establish and/or strengthen, where appropriate, legislation and regulations against all forms of racism, racial discrimination, xenophobia and related intolerance, including their gender-based manifestations;

(*b*) Condemn all forms of racism and racial discrimination, including propaganda, activities and organizations based on doctrines of superiority of one race or group of persons, that attempt to justify or promote racism or racial discrimination in any form;

(*c*) Take concrete measures to promote equality based on the elimination of gender and racial prejudice in all fields, through, inter alia, better access to education, health care, employment and other basic services, to promote full enjoyment of economic, social and cultural rights for all women and girls;

(*d*) Take measures to address, through policies and programmes, racism and racially motivated violence against women and girls and to increase cooperation, policy responses, effective implementation of national legislation and other protective and preventive measures aimed at the elimination of all forms of violence against women and girls;

(*e*) Review, where appropriate, national legal and other mechanisms, including the criminal justice system, to ensure equality before the law so that women and girls can seek protection, shelter and remedies against all forms of discrimination, including intersectional discrimination;

(*f*) Review, where appropriate, policies and laws, including those on citizenship, immigration and asylum, for their impact on the elimination of all forms of discrimination against women and the achievement of gender equality;

(*g*) Design and implement policies and measures that address all forms of violence against women and girls, and empower victims of all forms of violence, in particular women and girls, to regain control over their lives, inter alia, through special protection and assistance measures;

(*h*) Devise, enforce and strengthen effective measures to combat and eliminate all forms of trafficking in women and girls through a comprehensive anti-trafficking strategy consisting of, inter alia, legislative measures, prevention campaigns, information exchange, assistance and protection for and reintegration of the victims and prosecution of all the offenders involved, including intermediaries;

(*i*) Develop and implement policies to ensure the full enjoyment of all human rights and fundamental freedoms by all women and girls, regardless of race, colour, descent or national or ethnic origin;

(*j*) Take measures, as appropriate, to promote and strengthen policies and programmes for indigenous women, with their full participation and respect for their cultural diversity, to combat discrimination based on gender and race and to ensure their full enjoyment of all human rights;

(*k*) Review and revise, as appropriate, emigration policies, with a view to eliminating all discriminatory policies and practices against migrants, especially women and children, and to protect fully all their human rights, regardless of their legal status, as well as to provide them with humane treatment;

(*l*) Take steps to eliminate any violations of the human rights of women refugees, asylum seekers and internally displaced persons, who are often subjected to sexual and other violence;

(*m*) Urge all States that have not yet done so to become parties to the International Convention on the Elimination of All Forms of Racial Discrimination, in order to achieve its universal ratification, and emphasize the importance of the full compliance of States parties with the obligations they have accepted under this Convention;

(*n*) Consider signing, ratifying or acceding to the International Convention on the Protection of the Rights of All Migrant Workers and Members of Their Families as a matter of priority, and consider promoting ratification of the relevant conventions of the International Labour Organization.

3. Change attitudes and eliminate stereotypes and prejudice:

(*a*) Develop gender-sensitive education and training programmes aimed at eliminating discriminatory attitudes towards women and girls, and adopt measures to address the intersection between racist and gender-based stereotypes;

(*b*) Develop and implement programmes and policies to raise awareness among all relevant actors at the national, regional and international levels to the issue of multiple discrimination against women and girls;

(*c*) Review and update educational materials, including textbooks, and take appropriate action to remove all elements promoting discrimination, in particular gender-based discrimination, racism, racial discrimination, xenophobia and related intolerance;

(*d*) Ensure that education and training, especially teacher training, promote respect for human rights, the culture of peace, gender equality and cultural, religious and other diversity, and encourage educational and training institutions and organizations to adopt policies of equal opportunities and follow up their implementation with the participation of teachers, parents, boys and girls and the community;

(*e*) Develop strategies to increase awareness among men and boys with respect to their shared responsibility in promoting gender equality and combating all forms of discrimination, in particular racism, racial discrimination, xenophobia and related intolerance as well as multiple discrimination;

(*f*) Develop anti-racist and gender-sensitive human rights training for personnel in the administration of justice, law enforcement agencies, security and health-care services, schools and migration authorities, paying particular attention to immigration officials, border police and staff of migrant detention centres, as well as for United Nations personnel;

(*g*) Bearing in mind gender perspective, encourage the mass media to promote ideas of tolerance and understanding among peoples and different cultures.

4. Research and collection of data and information:

(a) Develop methodologies to identify the ways in which various forms of discrimination converge and affect women and girls, and conduct studies on how racism, racial discrimination, xenophobia and related intolerance are reflected in laws, policies, institutions and practices and how this has contributed to the vulnerability, victimization, marginalization and exclusion of women and the girl child;

(b) Collect, analyse and disseminate quantitative, qualitative and gender-sensitive data regarding the impact of all forms of discrimination, including multiple discrimination, on women and girls, and sponsor, where appropriate, surveys and community-based research, including the collection of disaggregated data by sex, age and other variables, as appropriate.

5. Preventing conflict and promoting a culture of peace, equality, non-discrimination, respect and tolerance:

(a) Respect fully international human rights law and international humanitarian law applicable to the rights and protection of women and girls, and take special measures to protect women and girls from gender-based violence, in particular rape and all other forms of sexual violence during armed conflict, and end impunity and prosecute those responsible for genocide, crimes against humanity and war crimes, including those relating to sexual and other gender-based violence against women and girls;

(b) Violence against women and girls is a major obstacle to the achievement of the objectives of gender equality, development and peace. Violence against women both violates and impairs or nullifies the enjoyment by women of their human rights and fundamental freedoms. Gender-based violence, such as battering and other domestic violence, sexual abuse, sexual slavery and exploitation, international trafficking in women and children, forced prostitution and sexual harassment, as well as violence against women resulting from cultural prejudice, racism and racial discrimination, xenophobia, pornography, ethnic cleansing, armed conflict, foreign occupation, religious and anti-religious extremism and terrorism, are incompatible with the dignity and worth of the human person and must be combated and eliminated;

(c) Ensure the full and equal opportunity for sustained participation and representation of women at all levels and in all areas in conflict prevention, management and conflict resolution and in post-conflict peace-building.

6. World Conference against Racism, Racial Discrimination, Xenophobia and Related Intolerance:

The Commission on the Status of Women stresses the importance of mainstreaming a gender perspective into the preparations, work and outcome of the World Conference, and urges the inclusion of women in delegations to the Conference.

Communications on the status of women

Working group. At a closed meeting on 16 March [E/2001/27], the Commission took note of the report of the Working Group on Communications on the Status of Women, established in 1993 [YUN 1993, p. 1050] to consider ways of making the communications procedure more transparent and efficient. The Working Group considered 14 confidential and three non-confidential communications received directly by the Division for the Advancement of Women and 22 confidential communications received by the Office of the United Nations High Commissioner for Human Rights. The Working Group expressed deep concern about the continuing grave violations of women's human rights, as well as persistent and pervasive discrimination against women. In particular, the Working Group was concerned about discrimination against women in employment and in their enjoyment of the right to health; dowry-related crimes; the systematic use of physical and sexual violence against women, including rape as a weapon of armed conflict, torture, beatings, custodial killings, abduction, arbitrary arrests and harassment by military, paramilitary or police forces; the targeting of civilians in conflict situations and the mistreatment of persons internally displaced, especially women and girls; and the failure of authorities to take appropriate action in such cases. The Working Group was also gravely concerned about contemporary forms of slavery, which included domestic and sexual slavery and trafficking in women and girls for economic or sexual exploitation. It noted with concern the ongoing acts of violence, intimidation and death threats of women human rights defenders by members of the police and others in authority, and the lack of investigation by authorities. The Working Group noted with concern the continued discrimination against and systematic attacks, including killings, detention, torture, rape, forced sterilization and forced disappearances, on indigenous groups, and the discriminatory provisions against women in national legal systems. The Working Group expressed deep concern at the harmful traditional practice of female genital mutilation and recognized the urgent need for Governments to implement the relevant international commitments with regard to that practice. Having considered the responses from Governments, the Working Group recommended further public education campaigns and gender-awareness training for specific sectors directed at the elimination of stereotypic attitudes towards women and girls.

Communications procedure. The Commission on the Status of Women had before it a January report of the Secretary-General assessing the implications of the reforms of mechanisms in the human rights area (1503 procedure) for communications concerning the status of women [E/CN.6/2001/12]. The report gave an overview of the development of the Commission's confidential communications procedures and those of the Commission on Human Rights; discussed the operation of the two confidential procedures, the relationship between them and options for better coordination of the procedures; and presented options for more fundamental reform of the existing communications procedure of the Commission on the Status of Women. Among the options presented were: the transformation of the communications procedure into a "situations" mechanism, involving the Working Group on Communications or with a working group of independent experts; the appointment of a special rapporteur who would take over the function of the Working Group; and the appointment of a thematic special rapporteur with the primary task of collecting information and preparing a detailed report.

Programme of work

In a January report [E/CN.6/2001/7 & Corr.1], the Secretary-General presented proposals for the Commission on the Status of Women's multi-year programme of work (2002-2006), which took into account challenges identified in the outcome document of Beijing+5 that impacted on the implementation of the 12 critical areas of concern of the Beijing Platform for Action. In addition to thematic proposals, the Secretary-General suggested that the Commission be sufficiently flexible and dynamic so that it could address issues in addition to those adopted in the programme of work and revisit certain issues taken up at previous sessions.

ECONOMIC AND SOCIAL COUNCIL ACTION

On 24 July [meeting 40], the Economic and Social Council, on the recommendation of the Commission on the Status of Women [E/2001/27 & Corr.1], adopted **resolution 2001/4** without vote [agenda item 14 *(a)*].

Proposals for a multi-year programme of work for the Commission on the Status of Women for 2002-2006

The Economic and Social Council

1. *Adopts* a multi-year work programme for the effective implementation of the Beijing Platform for Action and the outcome documents of the twenty-third special session of the General Assembly, entitled "Women 2000: gender equality, development and peace for the twenty-first century", which will provide a framework to assess the progress achieved in the implementation of the Platform for Action and the outcome documents of the special session and will be in line with the coordinated follow-up to major forthcoming United Nations conferences and summits;

2. *Decides* that the work of the Commission on the Status of Women, as set out in the programme of work, shall be closely related to its mandate and to the relevant provisions of the Platform for Action and the outcome documents of the special session, with a view to ensuring their effective implementation through more practical and action-oriented initiatives and outcomes. To achieve effective implementation, the work of the Commission should take into account relevant cross-cutting issues, such as institutional capacity-building;

3. *Also decides* that the agenda for the sessions of the Commission shall consist of the following:

1. Election of officers
2. Adoption of the agenda and other organizational matters
3. Follow-up to the Fourth World Conference on Women and to the twenty-third special session of the General Assembly, entitled "Women 2000: gender equality, development and peace for the twenty-first century":
   (a) Review of gender mainstreaming in entities of the United Nations system
   (b) Emerging issues, trends and new approaches to issues affecting the situation of women or equality between women and men
   (c) Implementation of strategic objectives and actions in the critical areas of concern and further actions and initiatives
4. Communications concerning the status of women
5. Follow-up to Economic and Social Council resolutions
6. Provisional agenda for the next session of the Commission
7. Adoption of the report of the Commission on its present session;

4. *Further decides* on the following calendar:

2002
Item 1
Eradicating poverty, including through the empowerment of women throughout their life cycle in a globalizing world.
Item 2
Environmental management and mitigation of natural disasters: a gender perspective.

2003
Item 1
Participation and access of women to the media, and information and communication technologies and their impact on and use as an instrument for the advancement and empowerment of women.
Item 2
Human rights of women and elimination of all forms of violence against women and girls as defined in the Beijing Platform for Action and the outcome documents of the twenty-third special session of the General Assembly, entitled "Women 2000: gender equality, development and peace for the twenty-first century".

2004
Item 1
The role of men and boys in achieving gender equality.

Item 2

Equal participation of women in conflict prevention, management and resolution and in post-conflict peace-building.

2005

Item 1

Review of the implementation of the Beijing Platform for Action and the outcome documents of the twenty-third special session of the General Assembly, entitled "Women 2000: gender equality, development and peace for the twenty-first century".

Item 2

Current challenges and forward-looking strategies for the advancement and empowerment of women and girls.

2006

Item 1

Enhanced participation of women in development: an enabling environment for achieving gender equality and the advancement of women, taking into account, inter alia, the fields of education, health and work.

Item 2

Equal participation of women and men in decision-making processes at all levels.

UN Development Fund for Women (UNIFEM)

During 2001 [A/57/125], the United Nations Development Fund for Women (UNIFEM) continued to focus on strengthening women's economic security and rights; ensuring that women's leadership shaped governance and peace-building; and promoting women's human rights and eliminating violence against women. UNIFEM's work was undertaken in the context of its 2000-2003 strategy and business plan, endorsed by the Executive Board of the United Nations Development Programme/United Nations Population Fund in 2000 [YUN 2000, p. 1127].

Four key results emerged from UNIFEM's work on women's economic security and rights: new and strengthened institutions, laws and policies to facilitate women's equal ownership and access to economic resources; increased knowledge and understanding with respect to managing globalization and economic transition from the perspective of poor women; new commitments to incorporate gender perspectives in economic governance; and increased economic capacity for women entrepreneurs, producers and informal sector workers. Among notable results from UNIFEM's initiatives in the governance and peace-building area were: the creation of replicable models for increasing women's leadership in peace-building and reconstruction; and new and strengthened partnerships with UN agencies. Promoting women's human rights and eliminat-

ing violence against women continued to be a strong focus in all of the regions in which UNIFEM worked. Efforts resulted in: new and strengthened policies, legislation and commitments; the creation of new or strengthened institutional mechanisms to address gender-based violence; and scaled-up and replicable strategies based on UNIFEM-supported pilot projects and lessons learned about ending violence and addressing the gender dimensions of HIV/AIDS. Considerable progress was made in 2001 in strengthening UN system capacity to support women's empowerment and gender mainstreaming in its policies and programmes. Results included: stronger and more focused support to the resident coordinator system; the development of new agreements and strengthening of existing collaboration with UN funds, programmes and specialized agencies; and heightened visibility for field-based innovations for gender equality in the intergovernmental arena. The Fund's achievements in supporting learning and strategic partnerships included: more targeted and focused documentation and dissemination of experiences and lessons learned; increased collaboration with partners; and movement from isolated projects to thematic programmes.

UNIFEM's core resources increased by 8 per cent to $20.7 million in 2001 from $19.1 million in 2000. Total contributions rose to $27.9 million in 2001, an increase of $1.3 million over 2000. UNIFEM continued to enter into co-financing arrangements with various donors. In 2001, a total of $12.3 million was approved by donors for multi-years, compared with $8.2 million in 2000.

UNIFEM's Trust Fund in Support of Actions to Eliminate Violence against Women approved grants for 21 new projects in 2001 to address diverse forms of violence against women, including domestic violence, trafficking and sexual exploitation and female servitude.

Through an initiative to use media and communications strategies to address gender-based violence, UNIFEM awarded grants to five organizations for projects that included a soap opera in Nicaragua to reach young viewers with the message that they had a right to make their own decisions and confront discrimination; and a music video in India that focused on violence against women and its impact on women's livelihoods. The Trust Fund's learning component held regional strategic communications workshops in Mexico, Nepal, Slovakia and Zimbabwe for Trust Fund grantees. In addition, UNIFEM joined with Johns Hopkins University (Baltimore, Maryland, United States) to develop a catalogue, *Picturing a Life Free of Violence*, and a database of media and communications resources on violence against women.

Since its establishment in 1996, the Trust Fund had awarded $6.8 million in grants to 129 projects in over 73 countries.

In July [A/56/174], the Secretary-General transmitted to the General Assembly a report on UNIFEM's 2000 activities [YUN 2000, p. 1126]. The Assembly, by **decision 56/442** of 21 December, took note of the report.

GENERAL ASSEMBLY ACTION

On 19 December [meeting 88], the General Assembly, on the recommendation of the Third Committee [A/56/576], adopted **resolution 56/130** without vote [agenda item 112].

United Nations Development Fund for Women

The General Assembly,

Recalling its resolution 39/125 of 14 December 1984, in which it established the United Nations Development Fund for Women as a separate and identifiable entity in autonomous association with the United Nations Development Programme, as well as its resolutions 52/94 of 12 December 1997 and 54/136 of 17 December 1999,

Recalling also the Platform for Action adopted by the Fourth World Conference on Women, which recognizes the special role of the Fund in the promotion of the empowerment of women and calls upon the Fund to review and strengthen its work programme in the light of the Platform for Action, focusing on the political and economic empowerment of women,

Welcoming the contributions that the Fund has made in supporting initiatives of Member States, United Nations organizations and non-governmental organizations to formulate and implement activities that promote gender equality and the empowerment of women, concentrating on three thematic areas, namely, strengthening women's economic capacity, engendering governance and leadership and promoting women's human rights and the elimination of all forms of violence against women,

Recalling and reaffirming the commitments made at United Nations world conferences and summit meetings and special sessions of the General Assembly held since 1990 and their follow-up processes,

Noting the importance of the work of the Consultative Committee on the United Nations Development Fund for Women in policy and programme directions, as stipulated in the annex to resolution 39/125,

1. *Takes note with appreciation* of the note by the Secretary-General on the activities of the United Nations Development Fund for Women;

2. *Encourages* the Fund to continue to assist, in its areas of expertise, in the implementation of commitments made at the Fourth World Conference on Women and at the twenty-third special session of the General Assembly entitled "Women 2000: gender equality, development and peace for the twenty-first century";

3. *Commends* the focus by the Fund on strategic programmes in its three thematic areas and on supporting innovative and experimental activities in im-

plementing its strategy and business plan (2000-2003) within the context of the Beijing Platform for Action and the outcome document of the twenty-third special session of the General Assembly;

4. *Notes with appreciation* the increased synergy between the United Nations Development Fund for Women and other funds, programmes and organizations of the United Nations system, as well as the Office of the Special Adviser on Gender Issues and Advancement of Women and the Division for the Advancement of Women of the Secretariat, and calls upon these entities to continue their collaborative efforts;

5. *Notes* the ability of the Fund to execute projects and programmes on behalf of the United Nations Development Programme in order to fulfil their respective mandates as well as their individual and common purposes;

6. *Also notes* the activities undertaken by the Fund in follow-up to General Assembly resolution 54/136, including activities relating to the impact of armed conflict on women and the role of women in peacebuilding, and the support it provides for the participation of women in peace processes, and in this regard encourages the Fund to continue to consult with Member States on these activities;

7. *Emphasizes* the importance of the Trust Fund in Support of Actions to Eliminate Violence against Women and its learning component in extracting and sharing good practices with respect to the elimination of violence against women, and reiterates the call to Governments, non-governmental organizations and the public and private sectors to consider contributing or increasing contributions to the Trust Fund;

8. *Encourages* the Fund to continue to contribute to ensuring that a gender perspective is integrated into a comprehensive approach to the human immunodeficiency virus (HIV) and acquired immunodeficiency syndrome (AIDS) at all levels of the three thematic areas of the Fund, in particular in the follow-up to the special session of the General Assembly on HIV/AIDS, building on its partnerships within the United Nations system, in particular with the Joint United Nations Programme on HIV/AIDS;

9. *Also encourages* the Fund to support the development or strengthening of mechanisms to increase accountability for gender equality, at the request of countries, including by building the capacity of Governments to undertake gender-responsive budget analysis;

10. *Urges* the Fund to continue its efforts to mainstream a gender perspective in United Nations operational activities, including through the resident coordinator system and the common country assessment and United Nations Development Assistance Framework processes;

11. *Welcomes* the role of the Fund in promoting the strategic importance of the empowerment of women in all of the regions in which it operates, and notes with appreciation the enhanced programme activities of the Fund in the African region;

12. *Encourages* the Fund to continue to assist Governments in implementing the Convention on the Elimination of All Forms of Discrimination against Women, in order to advance gender equality at all levels, including by reinforcing the cooperation between

Governments and civil society, especially women's organizations;

13. *Recognizes* that the Fund has been able to secure increased contributions for its work, and expresses its appreciation to Member States and private organizations and foundations, whose increased contributions demonstrate their commitment to the issues on which the Fund is working;

14. *Expresses its appreciation* for the work of the national committees for the Fund, and encourages them, with appropriate support from the Fund, to increase their capacity and intensify their outreach to civil society and the private sector in terms of building broad-based visibility and mobilizing resources for the work of the Fund;

15. *Urges* Member States, non-governmental organizations and members of the private sector that have contributed to the Fund to continue to contribute and to consider increasing their financial contributions, and urges others to consider contributing to the Fund.

On 24 December, the Assembly decided that the agenda item on the advancement of women would remain for consideration at its resumed fifty-sixth (2002) session (**decision 56/464**).

International Research and Training Institute (INSTRAW)

The Board of Trustees of the International Research and Training Institute for the Advancement of Women (INSTRAW) held its twenty-first session (22-24 May) via the Internet. All Board Members were in their home countries, except for the outgoing and new Presidents of the Board, who were at the Institute's headquarters in Santo Domingo, Dominican Republic [E/2001/88]. An autonomous institution, INSTRAW undertook research and training programmes for the advancement and mobilization of women in development.

The Board stated that the United Nations should take measures to ensure INSTRAW's continuity by motivating Member States to contribute to its sustainability, taking into consideration the fact that phases I and II of the Gender Awareness Information and Networking System (GAINS), launched in 2000 [YUN 2000, p. 1127], had been completed, phase III had been initiated, and 50 per cent of the projected funds had been invested. It recommended that a new INSTRAW Director be appointed as soon as possible and that, if funds allowed, the new Director should assume functions while the current Director was still at the Institute in order to facilitate a smooth transition. The Board approved the proposed strategic focus, work plan and budgetary requirements for the year 2001, acknowledged the relevance of the GAINS methodology and recognized the need to secure INSTRAW's financial sustain-

ability beyond 2001 in order to implement the methodology fully. It requested the Economic and Social Council to recommend to the General Assembly the transfer of any funds remaining of the $800,000 supplement provided in 2000 [ibid., p. 1128] for 2001 as a reserve for the year 2002. The Board recommended that, if insufficient funds were received for INSTRAW's core operations for 2002, operations for that year should be adjusted to the level of funds available. It recommended the immediate implementation of INSTRAW's fund-raising strategy.

INSTRAW restructuring

In response to Economic and Social Council resolution 2000/24 [YUN 2000, p. 1127], the Secretary-General submitted a May report on the revitalization and strengthening of INSTRAW [E/2001/76]. He outlined efforts by the UN Secretariat and the Institute to improve the financial situation of the Institute and to explore new sources of funding. The report also assessed prospects for securing the Institute's sustainability beyond 31 December 2001.

INSTRAW, with a consulting firm's assistance, had developed and implemented a fund-raising strategy, which included developing a list of potential new funding sources and publicity and communications materials, expanding links and building partnerships with organizations within and outside the UN system, and raising public awareness of the capabilities of GAINS. To diversify its funding sources, the Institute prepared a portfolio of special projects for which it sought funding from non-government sources.

Secretariat efforts included the holding of a series of donor meetings, demonstrations of GAINS for delegations and NGOs, and continued appeals to Governments for contributions. Despite those efforts to improve INSTRAW's financial situation, reserves remained insufficient to assure the Institute's full transition in 2002 to the new working method mandated by the General Assembly and the Council. Without effective measures by Member States to ensure INSTRAW's financial stability beyond 2001, it would face closure by the end of the year.

ECONOMIC AND SOCIAL COUNCIL ACTION

On 26 July [meeting 43], the Economic and Social Council adopted **resolution 2001/40** [draft: E/2001/L.25] without vote [agenda item 14 *(a)*].

Revitalization and strengthening of the International Research and Training Institute for the Advancement of Women

The Economic and Social Council,

Recalling its resolution 2000/24 of 28 July 2000, in which, inter alia, it expressed grave concern that the level of contributions had not adequately increased to a level to enable, in particular, the full implementation of the Gender Awareness Information and Networking System nor the operational viability of the International Research and Training Institute for the Advancement of Women beyond 31 December 2000, and reiterating the importance of supporting traditional methods of information dissemination, research and training,

Recalling also General Assembly resolution 55/219 of 23 December 2000, in which it decided to provide the Institute with financial assistance on a non-recurrent basis, enabling the Institute to continue its activities throughout 2001,

1. *Takes note* of the report of the Secretary-General;

2. *Appreciates* the support of Member States in approving the advance to the International Research and Training Institute for the Advancement of Women of up to US $800,000 for 2001, pending receipt of voluntary contributions, on a one-time, exceptional and emergency basis;

3. *Takes note* of the report of the Board of Trustees of the Institute on its twenty-first session and of the recommendations and decisions contained therein;

4. *Expresses its appreciation* to the Director of the Institute for her efforts to revitalize the Institute through the Gender Awareness Information and Networking System vision and methodology, and urges the Secretary-General to ensure that a new Director is appointed immediately in order to ensure continuity in the leadership and direction of the Institute;

5. *Commends* the Institute for the implementation of successive phases I and II of the System;

6. *Expresses its appreciation* for the efforts made by the Director of the Institute as well as its Board of Trustees in developing a fund-raising strategy for the Institute, and urges that it be implemented as soon as possible;

7. *Expresses its concerns* that, due to the insufficient reserves in the United Nations Trust Fund for the International Research and Training Institute for the Advancement of Women at the current time, the Institute may be unable to continue its operations beyond 2001;

8. *Takes into account* that the Institute cannot anticipate the level of contributions that will be received during the course of 2001;

9. *Recommends* that the General Assembly consider transferring to the Institute any balance remaining of the sum of $800,000 advanced for 2001 by the Assembly as a reserve for the year 2002, and invites the Assembly to consider requesting the Joint Inspection Unit to conduct a review of the Institute's Trust Fund and an urgent evaluation of the activities of the Institute, including options for its future;

10. *Invites* the Institute to further intensify its campaign to raise funds and attract support from, inter alia, private sector foundations and corporations for its activities;

11. *Decides* to amend article V, paragraph 5, of the statute of the Institute with regard to the approval of focal points, to read:

"Correspondents and focal points in countries or regions may be used by the Institute to assist in maintaining contact with national or regional institutions and in carrying out or advising on studies and research";

12. *Urges* the Secretary-General:

(a) To continue to encourage Member States to make voluntary contributions to the Trust Fund so that it can continue to operate at an adequate level during 2002;

(b) To continue to encourage other relevant sources of funding within the United Nations, including the United Nations Foundation, to contribute to the restructuring of the Institute;

13. *Requests* the Secretary-General to report to the Economic and Social Council at its substantive session of 2002 as well as to the General Assembly at its fifty-sixth session on the implementation of the present resolution.

Critical situation

In response to General Assembly resolution 55/219 [YUN 2000, p. 1129], the Secretary-General submitted an August report on the critical situation of INSTRAW [A/56/279]. Having described the status of implementation of INSTRAW activities during 2001, reported on the use of the financial resources provided from the UN regular budget for the year, and provided detailed information on the financial flows of the INSTRAW Trust Fund, the Secretary-General discussed prospects for the Institute beyond 31 December 2001. He stated that, by the end of the year, it was anticipated that INSTRAW would have used approximately $369,000 of the $800,000 subvention approved by Assembly decision 55/457 [YUN 2000, p. 1128], resulting in an unspent balance of $431,000. He noted that the INSTRAW Board of Trustees had recommended that any unspent amounts be carried forward to 2002 to facilitate the Institute's initial operations for that year (see p. 1087). The Economic and Social Council, in resolution 2001/40, had recommended that the Assembly consider transferring the unspent balance from the subvention as a reserve for 2002, which would allow the Institute to initiate its 2002 operations. Given the flow of contributions received during 2000 and 2001, the Secretary-General estimated that during 2002 INSTRAW's core operations might need to be adjusted to a minimal budget level of $600,000, which would entail a considerable downsizing of the core staff and a significant reduction in operational activities. He observed that, despite the persistent difficulties and uncertainties that INSTRAW had confronted during the two preceding years, it had managed to secure minimal resources with which to respond to the mandates given by the Assembly and the Council. Given that the Institute had begun to achieve tangible results through GAINS, the Secretary-General suggested that the Assembly might wish to decide on the scope within which INSTRAW could operate beyond 2001 in a productive and cost-effective manner.

On 19 December [meeting 88], the General Assembly, on the recommendation of the Third Committee [A/56/576], adopted **resolution 56/125** without vote [agenda item 112].

Critical situation of the International Research and Training Institute for the Advancement of Women

The General Assembly,

Recalling its resolution 55/219 of 23 December 2000, in which it decided to provide the International Research and Training Institute for the Advancement of Women with financial assistance on a non-recurrent basis, enabling the Institute to continue its activities throughout 2001,

Taking note of Economic and Social Council resolution 2001/40 of 26 July 2001 and the recommendation contained therein that the General Assembly consider the transfer of any balance remaining from the $800,000 advance for 2001 to the Institute as a reserve for 2002,

Recognizing that, despite the persistent difficulties and uncertainties that the Institute has confronted during the past two years, it has managed to secure the minimal resources with which to respond to the mandates given by the General Assembly and the Economic and Social Council,

1. *Takes note* of the report of the Secretary-General;

2. *Commends* the International Research and Training Institute for the Advancement of Women for the successive implementation of phases I and II of the Gender Awareness Information and Networking System and the initiation of phase III;

3. *Expresses its concern* that, since the departure of the Director in July 2001, and notwithstanding the severe predicament of the Institute, a new Director has not yet been appointed;

4. *Decides*:

(*a*) To establish a working group composed of two governmental representatives from each of the five regional groups of the United Nations and one representative of the host country, the mandate of the working group being to make recommendations to the General Assembly before the end of the fifty-sixth session, for its consideration by the end of 2002, on the future operation of the Institute;

(*b*) To examine ways, within the framework of General Assembly resolution 55/219 and Economic and Social Council resolution 2001/40, in which the Institute could be provided with resources to enable it to continue its operation until the Assembly has considered the recommendations of the working group;

5. *Urges* the Secretary-General:

(*a*) To appoint a Director of the International Research and Training Institute for the Advancement of Women as soon as possible in order to provide the Institute with the required leadership;

(*b*) To continue to encourage Member States to support the Institute by making voluntary contributions to the United Nations Trust Fund for the International Research and Training Institute for the Advancement of Women;

6. *Requests* the Secretary-General to report to the General Assembly at its fifty-seventh session, through the Economic and Social Council at its substantive session of 2002, on the implementation of the present resolution.

Chapter XI

Children, youth and ageing persons

In 2001, the United Nations Children's Fund (UNICEF) continued its efforts to secure the best possible start in life for every child, collaborating with multisectoral partners to ensure that all children could begin life healthy and cared for and receive education, in order to develop to their optimal potential, safe from abuse and exploitation.

UNICEF spent much of the year preparing for the United Nations General Assembly's special session on children, which, because of the 11 September terrorist attacks in New York, had to be postponed from 2001 until May 2002. In the context of the Global Movement for Children, UNICEF and key partners galvanized the support of people around the world for the cause of children, so that their voices could be heard at the special session.

In addition to being guided by the 1989 Convention on the Rights of the Child, which established international standards of behaviour towards children, UNICEF's efforts were also in accordance with its medium-term plan for 1998-2001. The four core organizational priorities for that period were: enhancing partnerships and promoting advocacy on children's rights; enhancing the survival, development, protection and participation of children; improving the availability and use of data in critical areas; and strengthening management and operations. In 2001, the UNICEF Executive Board approved the medium-term strategic plan for the period 2002-2005, which established five organizational priorities: girls' education; fighting HIV/AIDS; integrated early childhood development; immunization "plus"; and improved protection of children from violence, exploitation, abuse and discrimination.

Important developments in favour of children's rights during 2001 included the deposit of sufficient ratifications of the two optional protocols to the Convention on the Rights of the Child, on the sale of children, child prostitution and child pornography, and on the involvement of children in armed conflict, for them to enter into force in 2002 (see p. 595).

United Nations policies and programmes focusing on youth in 2001 strengthened the implementation of the 1995 World Programme of Action for Youth to the Year 2000 and Beyond.

The Youth Employment Network, formed by the Secretary-General in collaboration with the International Labour Organization and the World Bank, appointed a high-level panel, which prepared policy recommendations for national action and established four top priorities: employability; equal opportunity for young men and women; entrepreneurship; and employment creation. The fourth session of the World Youth Forum of the United Nations System (Dakar, Senegal, August) adopted the Dakar Youth Empowerment Strategy, which set out priority areas of action and interest adopted by young people themselves.

In preparation for the Second World Assembly on Ageing, to be held in 2002, the Commission for Social Development, acting as preparatory committee, held three sessions. The central task of the Second World Assembly would be to revise the International Plan of Action on Ageing, adopted by the first World Assembly in 1982.

Children

United Nations Children's Fund

Because of the 11 September terrorist attacks in New York, the General Assembly special session on children, initially scheduled for 19 to 21 September 2001, was postponed until 8 to 10 May 2002. As the secretariat for the special session, UNICEF spent much of 2001 on preparations. It was a driving force for children's participation in the preparatory process and the special session, and hosted regional consultations and other events that rallied leadership around the cause of children. With UNICEF advice and support, 150 countries collected key information about children's rights and well-being to assess progress made for children since the 1990 World Summit for Children [YUN 1990, p. 797]. That effort amounted to the most comprehensive study ever completed on the situation of children around the world.

UNICEF and its key partners in the Global Movement for Children worked to ensure that children's voices could be heard at the special session. Under the "Say Yes for Children" campaign, which was launched in April, the partners devised a mechanism through which people from all walks of life could pledge their support for 10 essential actions to ensure children's rights to live in health, peace and dignity, promising to deliver the pledges to heads of State or Government attending the special session: leave no child out; put children first; care for every child; fight HIV/AIDS; stop harming and exploiting children; listen to children; educate every child; protect children from war; protect the earth for children; and fight poverty: invest in children. Nearly 100 million people in 155 countries pledged their support for those actions, indicating that the three top priority issues were educate every child, leave no child out and fight HIV/AIDS.

UNICEF's major achievements in 2001 included: a record 575 million children immunized against polio; an increase in school enrolment of girls in 21 countries; the provision of HIV/AIDS prevention support to young people in 71 countries; $14 million worth of emergency aid to children and their families in Afghanistan; UNICEF-organized opinion polls that permitted 40,000 children on three continents to speak out on key issues; the freeing of more than 8,000 child soldiers in Sierra Leone and the Sudan; and a birth registration campaign in Bangladesh that reached 1 million infants.

UNICEF continued to form strategic alliances to focus global attention on child-specific issues. In 2001, the Fédération Internationale de Football Association, the international governing body for football (soccer), announced that its 2002 World Cup would be dedicated to children and joined UNICEF in promoting the well-being of children through sports.

The State of the World's Children 2001, UNICEF's annual flagship publication, focused on early childhood development, noting that the earliest years, from birth to age 3, influenced how the rest of childhood and adolescence would unfold. Drawing on reports from around the world, *The State of the World's Children 2001* detailed the daily lives of parents and other caregivers who were striving—in the face of war, poverty and the HIV/AIDS epidemic—to protect the rights and meet the needs of the youngest children. It made the case for giving the highest-priority attention to the time of early childhood, highlighting how choices made during the early years affected not only how a child developed, but also how a country progressed.

In 2001, UNICEF cooperated with 162 countries, areas and territories: 46 in sub-Saharan Africa; 35 in Latin America and the Caribbean; 34 in Asia; 20 in the Middle East and North Africa;

and 27 in Central and Eastern Europe, the Commonwealth of Independent States (CIS) and the Baltic States.

Total expenditures, including write-offs, amounted to $1,246 million (compared with $1,103 million in 2000), of which 93 per cent ($1,157 million) was for country programmes of cooperation; 6 per cent ($81 million) for management and administration of the organization; and about 1 per cent ($8 million) for write-offs and other charges. Programme expenditures by priorities were: $364 million on integrated early childhood development; $240 million on immunization "plus"; $153 million on girls' education; $146 million on the improved protection of children; and $67 million on HIV/AIDS. UNICEF operations in 2001 were described in the *2002 UNICEF Annual Report* and the annual report of its Executive Director [E/ICEF/2002/4 (Part I) & (Part I)/Corr.1 & (Part II)].

The UNICEF Executive Board held its first regular session of 2001 (22-24 and 26 January), the annual session (4-6 June) and the second regular session (10-12 December), all in New York [E/2001/34]. The Board adopted 23 decisions during those sessions.

The Economic and Social Council, by **decision 2001/226** of 10 July, took note of the Board's report on its first regular session; an extract from the report on its annual session; and the annual report of the Executive Director covering the year 2000 [E/2001/20], which was transmitted in accordance with a January decision of the Board [dec. 2001/3].

On 12 December [dec. 2001/23], the Executive Board adopted the programme of work and dates for its 2002 sessions. The first regular session was to be held from 21 to 25 January, the annual session from 3 to 7 June and the second regular session from 16 to 20 September.

Programme policies

In decisions related to UNICEF's programme policies, the Executive Board, on 6 June [dec. 2001/9], took note of the report entitled "A good start for every child: UNICEF programming to improve immunization services and child health, reduce the burden of vaccine-preventable disease and eradicate polio" [E/ICEF/2001/9]. In another decision of the same date [dec. 2001/11], the Board, having considered a report on sector-wide approaches (SWAPs) [E/ICEF/2001/10], encouraged the Executive Director to strengthen further UNICEF participation in SWAPs, identified on the basis of national specific needs and priorities. It requested the continuation of adequate staff training on SWAPs to enable the full participation of UNICEF in the process.

General Assembly special session (2002)

In accordance with General Assembly resolution 54/93 [YUN 1999, p. 1113], preparations were made during 2001 for a special session of the General Assembly to review the achievement of the goals of the 1990 World Summit for Children [YUN 1990, p. 797], which was scheduled to be held in New York from 19 to 21 September. In the light of the terrorist attacks in New York on 11 September, it was decided to postpone the special session on children until 8 to 10 May 2002.

Preparatory Committee. The Preparatory Committee for the Special Session of the General Assembly on Children, established by General Assembly resolution 54/93, convened its second (29 January–2 February) and third (11-15 June) substantive sessions both in New York [A/S-27/2 & Add.1]. It had held an organizational session and its first substantive session in 2000 [YUN 2000, p. 1132].

The second session considered organizational arrangements for the preparatory process and the special session and authorized its Bureau to prepare a revised version of the draft outcome document for the third session. Panel discussions were held on adolescent development and participation and on the girl child.

Among other documents, the Committee considered a note by its Chairperson on the participation of children and adolescents in the special session [A/AC.256/8] and a 22 January letter from Jamaica [A/55/743], transmitting the Kingston Consensus, which was endorsed by the fifth Ministerial Meeting on Children and Social Policy in the Americas (Kingston, 9-13 October 2000).

The Committee recommended for adoption by the General Assembly three draft decisions regarding arrangements for the participation of non-governmental organizations (NGOs), the provisional agenda and organizational arrangements for the special session.

On 14 February (**decision 55/459**), the Assembly decided on arrangements for NGO participation in the special session.

In June, the Preparatory Committee considered the organizational arrangements for the preparatory process and the special session and the outcome document of the special session [A/AC.256/CRP.6/Rev.2 & Rev.3 (Parts I & II)], entitled "A world fit for children". It also had before it the report of the Secretary-General [A/S-27/3] entitled "We the Children: End-decade review of the follow-up to the World Summit for Children". The report, prepared in response to General Assembly resolutions 51/186 [YUN 1996, p. 1083], 54/93 [YUN 1999, p. 1113] and 55/26 [YUN 2000, p. 1133], reviewed the implementation and results of the 1990 World Declaration and Plan of Action

[YUN 1990, p. 797], including appropriate recommendations for further action, and also elaborated on the best practices noted and obstacles encountered in the implementation. Measures to overcome those obstacles were suggested. Major thematic issues discussed in the report included: health, nutrition, water and environmental sanitation; education and literacy; special child protection measures; civil rights and freedoms; and the role of the family.

Other documents considered included: a 23 January letter from Canada transmitting the *Machel Review 1996-2000* [A/55/749]; a 22 February letter from Canada transmitting documents of the International Conference on War-Affected Children (Winnipeg, 10-17 September 2000) [A/AC.256/14]; a 7 June letter from Germany transmitting the report of the Conference on Children in Europe and Central Asia (Berlin, 16-18 May 2001) [A/AC.256/16 & Corr.1]; and a note by the Preparatory Committee's Chairperson on participation. Panel discussions were held on children and armed conflict and on commercial sexual exploitation of children.

The Committee recommended to the General Assembly for adoption a draft resolution on the organizational arrangements for the round tables for the special session and a draft decision on the presentation of the outcome of the children's forum to the special session. It also decided to consider and take action on the draft outcome document "A world fit for children" at its resumed third session.

Pan-African Forum. Egypt transmitted to the Secretary-General on 11 June [A/S-27/4] the African Declaration and Plan of Action adopted at the Pan-African Forum on the Future of Children (Cairo, 28-31 May).

GENERAL ASSEMBLY ACTION

On 22 June [meeting 104], the General Assembly, on the recommendation of the Preparatory Committee [A/55/L.85], adopted **resolution 55/276** without vote [agenda item 42].

Organizational arrangements for the round tables for the special session of the General Assembly on children

The General Assembly,

Recalling its resolutions 54/93 of 7 December 1999 and 55/26 of 20 November 2000 on the preparations for the special session on children,

1. *Decides* that the special session on children shall include three interactive round-table sessions;

2. *Decides also* to adopt the organizational arrangements set out in the annex to the present resolution;

3. *Decides further* that these arrangements shall in no way create a precedent for other special sessions.

ANNEX

1. The round tables shall be held as follows:

Round table 1: Wednesday, 19 September 2001, from 3 p.m. to 6.30 p.m.
Round table 2: Thursday, 20 September 2001, from 9.30 a.m. to 1 p.m.
Round table 3: Friday, 21 September 2001, from 9.30 a.m. to 1 p.m.

2. The round tables shall have as their overarching theme "Renewal of commitment and future action for children in the next decade".

3. Each round table shall have two co-chairpersons, making a total of six co-chairpersons. The co-chairpersons shall be heads of State or Government. Five co-chairpersons shall be selected from the five regional groups by 31 July 2001. The sixth co-chairperson, who shall be the head of State of the country of the President of the fifty-sixth session of the General Assembly, will co-chair round table 3.

4. Each round table shall be limited to a maximum of 71 participants, of whom approximately 66 will be heads of delegation of Member States and approximately five will be participants representing observers and entities of the United Nations system.

5. Following the selection of the chairpersons of the round tables, each regional group should determine which of its members will participate in each round table, ensuring that equitable geographical distribution is maintained, allowing for some flexibility.

6. Thus, in order to allow for some flexibility, for each round table the maximum number of participants from each regional group shall be as follows:

African States	18 Member States
Asian States	18 Member States
Eastern European States	8 Member States
Latin American and Caribbean States	12 Member States
Western European and other States	10 Member States

7. Member States that are not members of any of the regional groups may participate in a round table of their choice.

8. For each round table, participants other than Member States, representing observers and entities of the United Nations system, will be selected by the President of the General Assembly, in consultation with Member States. In addition, the President of the Assembly, in consultation with the co-chairpersons of each round table and Member States, will choose, by 31 August 2001, two child delegates, taking into account equitable gender and geographical representation, who will each be permitted to present a brief introductory statement on the theme of the round tables in a language of their choice.

9. Each head of delegation attending a round table may be accompanied by two advisers.

10. The Holy See and Switzerland, in their capacity as observer States, and Palestine, in its capacity as observer, may also participate in different round tables, to be determined in consultation with the President of the General Assembly.

11. The co-chairpersons of each round table will be responsible for presenting orally their summary of the discussions during the concluding plenary meeting of the special session.

12. The round tables shall be closed to the media and the general public. Accredited delegates and observers will be able to follow the proceedings of the round tables via a closed-circuit television in an overflow room.

The Assembly, by **decision 56/401** of 12 September, decided to postpone the special session until a date to be decided by the Assembly at its fifty-sixth session.

Executive Board. The UNICEF Executive Board, on 12 December [dec. 2001/21], decided that, in the light of the postponement until 2002 of the special session on children, the Executive Director would provide a final report on the use of funds to the Board's first regular session of 2003. The Board urged that Member States contribute to the unfunded balance of $1,132,665 to ensure that UNICEF could adequately support the preparations and arrangements for the special session and the children's forum.

GENERAL ASSEMBLY ACTION

On 24 December [meeting 92], the General Assembly adopted **resolution 56/222** [draft: A/56/L.7] without vote [agenda item 26].

Special session of the General Assembly on children
The General Assembly,
Recalling its resolution 55/26 of 20 November 2000, in which it decided to convene the special session of the General Assembly for follow-up to the World Summit for Children from 19 to 21 September 2001, and refer to it as the "special session on children",
Recalling also its decision 56/401 of 12 September 2001, by which it decided to postpone the special session on children until a date to be decided by the General Assembly at its fifty-sixth session,
1. *Decides* to convene the special session of the General Assembly on Children from 8 to 10 May 2002;
2. *Also decides* to include in the provisional agenda of its fifty-seventh session the item entitled "Follow-up to the outcome of the special session on children".

Also on 24 December, the Assembly decided that the agenda item on follow-up to the special session would remain for consideration at its resumed fifty-sixth (2002) session (**decision 56/464**).

Medium-term strategic plan (2002-2005)

At its second regular session in December, the Executive Board had before it the medium-term strategic plan (MTSP) for the period 2002-2005 [E/ICEF/2001/13 & Corr.1], which combined a reinforced results-based management approach and a human rights–based approach to programming. Building on the lessons learned from the implementation of the medium-term plan for 1998-2001 [YUN 1998, p. 1093], the new plan established five organizational priorities, defined objectives and indicators more clearly, and strengthened the strategic use of the evaluation function. The MTSP was developed through a widespread consultation process, involving staff at all levels from headquarters and regional and country offices.

UNICEF's five organizational priorities during the programming period would be: girls' education; integrated early childhood development; immunization "plus" (protection from vaccine-preventable diseases and micronutrient deficiencies, with lifelong benefits); fighting HIV/AIDS; and improved protection of children from violence, exploitation, abuse and discrimination. UNICEF's strategies to pursue those organizational priorities would be: programme excellence; effective country programmes of cooperation; partnerships for shared success; influential information, communication and advocacy; and excellence in internal management and operations.

On 12 December [dec. 2001/22], the Board welcomed the MTSP for 2002-2005 and approved the five organizational priorities for action and financial expenditure set forth in it. It also approved the MTSP as a framework of projections for 2002-2005, including the preparation of up to $424 million in programme expenditures from regular resources to be submitted to the Board in 2002. The Executive Director was requested to review and, where necessary, propose adjustments to the MTSP, based on comments made by Board members, the results of the General Assembly's special session on children and experience in implementing the plan. She was further requested to assess progress towards the targets set within the five organizational priorities in her annual report to the Executive Board.

Emergency assistance

During 2001, UNICEF used its Emergency Programme Fund to retain emergency response capacity in Afghanistan, Angola, Burundi, Côte d'Ivoire, Cuba, Guinea, Liberia and the Sudan, and in the Central American and South-Eastern European regions.

It also accessed funding from the Central Emergency Revolving Fund to jump-start emergency actions for children and women affected by the protracted humanitarian situation in the Sudan and to address the acute needs of internally displaced persons and refugee women and children affected by the crisis in Afghanistan and its neighbouring countries.

During the year, UNICEF worked closely with the United Nations Mine Action Service, the United Nations Development Programme and other UN agencies to develop the United Nations Mine Action Strategy 2001-2005 and the United Nations Sectoral Policy on Information Management for Mine Action. It also developed its own mine action strategy, to be launched in 2002 (see also p. 828).

Maurice Pate Award

In January, the Bureau of the Executive Board asked the secretariat to review the selection process and criteria to ensure that the Maurice Pate Award, established in 1966 [YUN 1966, p. 385] in memory of UNICEF's first Executive Director, was continuing to meet its purpose. A working group held consultations throughout the year on the matter. The Board, which was to consider the group's proposals at its first regular session of 2002, decided not to make an Award for 2001 while the review was being undertaken.

UNICEF programmes by region

In 2001, UNICEF expenditures on regional programmes totalled $1,157 million, of which $444 million (38 per cent) went to programmes in sub-Saharan Africa; $344 million (30 per cent) to programmes in Asia; $101 million (9 per cent) to programmes in Central and Eastern Europe, CIS and the Baltic States; $99 million (9 per cent) to programmes in the Middle East and North Africa; and $94 million (8 per cent) to programmes in the Americas and the Caribbean. An additional $74 million (6 per cent) went to interregional programmes.

The majority of UNICEF resources continued to be spent in the 64 low-income countries with a per capita gross national product of $755 or less. Those countries had a total child population of 1.3 billion, or about 70 per cent of all children worldwide, and received 68 per cent of the total programme expenditure, which was 1 per cent higher than in 2000.

Field visits

Members of the UNICEF Executive Board visited the Republic of Moldova and Romania from 5 to 17 May to learn about the problems and needs of the two countries and about the countries in the region in general. It was noted that UNICEF-supported programmes of cooperation effectively complemented the countries' efforts to protect their children and women, and the lessons learned could be shared with other countries in similar situations. UNICEF was viewed as a reliable partner, with a good reputation with donors and highly skilled professional staff. It was felt that possibilities existed for improving cooperation with other agencies, especially with the Bretton Woods institutions (the World Bank Group and the International Monetary Fund).

Executive Board members who visited the Gambia and Senegal from 5 to 17 May were impressed by UNICEF's work in both countries. The challenge, which was to build true partnerships with local authorities, was being met in those countries, where the group witnessed frank, open and ongoing dialogue on all issues. It was noted that international NGOs were important partners, but the team observed that, in some cases, those organizations were competitors rather than true partners with UNICEF. Private sector support in both countries was limited, and more avenues needed to be explored to ensure more predictable funding. In the area of education, there appeared to be great progress, especially in providing separate sanitation facilities in schools and in working to harmonize Koranic schools with the mainstream education system.

In June [DEC. 2001/10], the Executive Board took note of the report [E/ICEF/2001/CRP.7] and oral presentation on the field visits.

UNICEF programmes by sector

As in previous years, the largest single share of total UNICEF programme expenditure of $1,157 million was in the area of health ($440 million or 38 per cent). Significant shares also went to basic education ($188 million or 16 per cent); programme support ($145 million or 13 per cent); child protection ($122 million or 11 per cent); water and environmental sanitation ($98 million or 8 per cent); community development and gender ($72 million or 6 per cent); nutrition ($48 million or 4 per cent); and assessment, analysis and monitoring ($45 million or 4 per cent).

A total of $25.7 million was made available to country programmes in 2001 from the global set-aside of 7 per cent of regular resources. Based on the criteria set out in a 1997 Executive Board decision establishing the set-aside [YUN 1997, p. 1220], the Executive Director made allocations for strategic programming efforts in support of programme priorities and for additional special needs. The largest segment of funds—40 per cent—went to the global polio eradication effort and the second largest (24 per cent) went to initiatives to fight HIV/AIDS. Stronger emphasis was placed on girls' education (14 per cent) and child protection (10 per cent). The balance of the funds was allocated to other areas, including malaria prevention, early childhood development and water and environmental sanitation. Programmes in sub-Saharan Africa received 51 per cent of the funds, those in Asia 38 per cent and other regions 11 per cent.

Child and adolescent health

UNICEF continued to assist Governments in immunizing children against the "basic six" diseases—polio, measles, diphtheria, pertussis, tuberculosis and tetanus—and against other diseases, such as hepatitis B, for which newer vaccines had been developed. In 2001, the immunization focus was primarily on polio, measles and tetanus, and on the introduction of new vaccines through the Global Alliance for Vaccines and Immunization (GAVI). During the year, UNICEF procured over 2 billion doses of vaccines for nearly 100 developing countries, including vaccines and immunization supplies on behalf of GAVI for 23 countries approved for support from GAVI's Vaccine Fund.

Spearheaded by UNICEF, the World Health Organization (WHO) and other members of the Global Polio Eradication Initiative, the campaign to eradicate polio vaccinated a record 575 million children against the disease in 2001, reducing the number of new polio cases globally by more than 80 per cent. The number of confirmed polio cases declined from 2,979 in 20 countries in 2000 to 537 in only 10 countries in 2001. UNICEF collaborated with WHO and other Initiative members on vaccine supply and delivery and the organization of national and subnational immunization days in endemic countries.

UNICEF fought measles in more than 30 countries in 2001, helping to save the lives of over 80,000 children. Efforts were particularly directed towards Africa, where most measles deaths occurred. The Measles Initiative, launched by UNICEF and a number of partners, immunized more than 20 million children in eight African countries and reduced annual deaths due to measles in those countries by more than 47,000.

UNICEF continued to be a major partner in the Roll-Back Malaria Initiative. Collaboration between the Initiative partnership and the integrated management of childhood illness (IMCI) increased. In partnership with WHO, UNICEF supported the IMCI approach in over 70 countries, emphasizing training of local health workers and strengthening family childcare practices. Community-based, family-oriented health and nutrition programmes registered achievements in Bangladesh and parts of Cambodia, India, Madagascar and Nepal, using such approaches as participatory assessment and monitoring of child development. In Malawi and other countries, SWAPs in health provided opportunities to increase the priority given to community-based approaches to child health and nutrition. However, the programmes tended to be slowed by funding shortfalls, poor-quality data and the impact of AIDS.

Consistent with IMCI and the integrated approach to early childhood development, UNICEF cooperation gave greater priority to improved sanitation and hygiene education, including through school programmes in some 55 countries. Although affected by funding shortages in some countries, UNICEF continued to support safe water programmes, notably in response to emergencies, or as part of multisectoral approaches in disadvantaged areas. UNICEF assistance to monitoring and improving the quality of water expanded to over 30 countries. With arsenic, fluoride and nitrates joining faecal contamination as serious threats to domestic drinking water supplies and child health—especially but not only in Asia—UNICEF was assisting the development of national standards for water quality and the introduction of community surveillance systems.

Since efforts to improve the lives of children were inseparable from actions to improve the lives of women, UNICEF supported programmes in 102 countries in 2001 to secure women's rights to quality health care and freedom from discrimination and violence. Those programmes helped to reduce the death toll from tetanus and unsafe practices during childbirth and to improve women's health and nutrition.

One urgent UNICEF goal was the prevention of mother-to-child transmission (PMTCT) of HIV/AIDS. In 2001 alone, more than 720,000 children contracted HIV from their mothers. UNICEF programmes provided women with voluntary and confidential counselling and testing, antiretroviral drugs where needed, and counselling and support in choosing the best feeding options for their infants. UNICEF supported prevention programmes in 47 countries and was the lead agency for those efforts in several countries, including Botswana, the only nation in Africa with a national PMTCT programme; by December 2001, UNICEF had helped all health facilities in 23 districts to implement programmes.

Basic education

In 2001, UNICEF emphasized girls' education and issues of quality. Several countries in sub-Saharan Africa and the Middle East and North Africa reported significantly increased numbers of children enrolled in primary schools, but problems of dropouts or very poor learning achievement became more apparent in other regions. Endemic weaknesses of educational systems continued to pose challenges for many poor and conflict-affected countries, including low teachers' salaries, unreliable data, population displacement and discrimination.

In 38 countries, UNICEF supported "child-friendly" schools, which provided a welcoming and effective learning environment. In the Philippines, it helped 200 schools to join the child-friendly schools programme, bringing the total number of children reached to 165,000. In Colombia, 11,000 children were enrolled in child-friendly schools for the first time, and Tajikistan began a new child-friendly school programme.

With regard to girls' education, UNICEF assisted 74 countries to break down the barriers that excluded girls. Programmes provided girls with scholarships and school supplies, constructed separate sanitation facilities for girls and boys, and promoted curricula and teaching methods free of gender bias. In 2001, 21 countries reported improvements in school enrolment and retention for girls. In Afghanistan, where girls were excluded from the official education system, UNICEF supported home schools for girls and boys. By the end of the year, such schools were teaching 58,000 children. During the year, Egypt undertook a major new push to end gender discrimination in schools, working with eight UN agencies in a partnership brokered by UNICEF. The UNICEF-assisted Africa Girls' Education Initiative covered 34 countries.

Educational interventions in emergencies were also a critical component of UNICEF efforts. Although the 2001 earthquake in the state of Gujarat, India, destroyed or damaged more than 12,000 primary schools, within five months UNICEF had helped the state authorities to set up and equip 2,000 tent schools for 400,000 children. In war-ravaged Sierra Leone, UNICEF's contribution of supplies, teacher training and rehabilitation of schools helped to enrol nearly 70,000 additional children in primary schools in 2001. Late in the year, there was a massive mobilization to support the commitment of the Afghan Interim Authority to re-establish educational opportunities for boys and girls throughout Afghanistan. Large-scale support was also given for the restoration of primary education in East Timor.

Protection from armed conflict, exploitation and abuse

UNICEF's support with regard to protecting children from exploitation, violence and abuse focused on child labour, reducing the impact of AIDS and conflict on children, prevention of sexual abuse and trafficking, and reform of juvenile justice systems.

During the year, UNICEF helped to expand Cambodia's community-based Child Protection Networks from 52 to 225 villages and facilitated two major cross-border agreements to halt child trafficking between China and Viet Nam and among Benin, Gabon, Nigeria and Togo. Sexual exploitation and the trafficking of children gained global attention when the Second World Congress against Commercial Sexual Exploitation of Children was convened in Yokohama in December, sponsored by the Government of Japan, and produced a new plan of action.

In the area of child labour, the rapid ratification of International Labour Organization (ILO) Convention 182 on the elimination of the worst forms of child labour [YUN 1999, p. 1388] was an important stimulus. In 2001, UNICEF supported education as a preventive strategy in some 30 countries. It also facilitated inter-country contacts for cross-border coordination in both West Africa and East Asia and participated, together with ILO, in discussions with producers to protect children on cocoa plantations.

UNICEF assisted in the care and reintegration of child soldiers in 16 countries, helped to negotiate the release of abducted child soldiers in Uganda and advocated against the recruitment of children in the Democratic Republic of the Congo. UNICEF assisted in the demobilization of over 3,500 child soldiers in the Sudan, and more than 3,600 child soldiers in Sierra Leone were helped to leave army life. With UNICEF support, thousands of former child soldiers in Sierra Leone and other countries were able to rejoin their families; obtain counselling, vocational training and education; and take other steps towards reintegrating into their communities.

Many UNICEF offices advocated or provided technical support for the better protection of children in conflict with the law and the broader reform of juvenile justice systems. The organization advocated against the detention of children except as a measure of last resort, and for the diversion of children away from the criminal justice system.

Prevention of gender discrimination

UNICEF continued to promote the elimination of discrimination against women, with emphasis on issues relating to girls. It supported the mainstreaming of gender-related concerns in consolidated appeals and emergency training materials, and participated in the gender subgroup for Afghanistan. The advancement of women was promoted in a number of countries—notably in West Africa—through training and support to small-scale enterprises, usually linked to basic service programmes.

Efforts to combat female genital mutilation received UNICEF support in more than a dozen countries through national workshops, information campaigns and partnerships with local leaders, health workers and youth clubs. Similar strategies were used to address other issues of gender-based violence, such as advocacy against "honour" killings in South Asia and partnerships with health services to assist victims of violence in Peru. There were also new initiatives to strengthen action against early marriage.

Organizational and administrative matters

UNICEF finances

UNICEF income in 2001 totalled $1,218 million, an increase of $86 million (8 per cent) over 2000 and of $58 million (5 per cent) over the target of $1,160 million established in the financial plan. As in previous years, UNICEF derived its 2001 income principally from two sources: Governments and intergovernmental organizations, which, on a net basis, contributed $782 million (64 per cent) of total income; and non-governmental or private sector sources, which provided $400 million (33 per cent). The balance of $36 million (3 per cent) was derived from other miscellaneous sources. Interest was the main component of miscellaneous income.

By a 12 December decision [dec. 2001/20], the Executive Board took note of UNICEF's interim financial report and statements for the year ended 31 December 2000 [E/ICEF/2001/AB/L.5].

Budget appropriations

In order to allow UNICEF to take full advantage of the conclusions and outcomes of the General Assembly special session on children (initially planned for 19-21 September 2001) in the finalization of the medium-term strategic plan, the Executive Board, on 6 June [dec. 2001/12], decided to merge its second regular session with the extraordinary budget session.

On 11 December [dec. 2001/14], at the second regular session, the Board approved the Executive Director's recommendations for funding from regular and other resources in 2001 for 57 country programmes, 4 multi-country or subregional programmes, and 3 programmes with other resources proposals only, of which 2 were of a multi-country nature [E/ICEF/2001/P/L.73], amounting to the following respective amounts for regular resources and other resources by region: Africa, $410,261,601 and $550,535,000; Americas and the Caribbean, $69,463,909 and $252,135,000; Asia, $58,159,363 and $117,675,000; Central and Eastern Europe, CIS and the Baltic States, $12,894,000 and $66,500,000; and the Middle East and North Africa, $82,535,229 and $123,091,000. The Board also approved the amount of $2,344,697 from regular resources to cover expenditures against write-off and overexpenditures due to revaluation.

Having considered the biennial support budget for 2002-2003 [E/ICEF/2001/AB/L.10], the Board, on 10 December [dec. 2001/13], approved gross appropriations in the amount of $566,169,000 for UNICEF programme support in the field and at headquarters, and for management and administration. It resolved that income estimates of $88,300,000 would be used to offset the gross appropriations, resulting in estimated net appropriations of $477,869,000. The Board authorized the Executive Director to redeploy resources between appropriation lines up to a maximum of 5 per cent of the appropriation to which the resources were redeployed.

On 11 December [dec. 2001/15], the Board approved the allocation of additional regular resources totalling $12,762,102 to fund the approved country programmes of 11 countries for 2001 and 11 countries for 2002, as recommended by the Executive Director [E/ICEF/2001/P/L.72]. It also approved the one-year extension of the Amazon subregional programme for social action to allow time to prepare a new programme proposal to start in 2003.

Also on 11 December [dec. 2001/16], the Board approved a regular resources programme budget of $19.67 million (other than the Emergency Programme Fund) for 2002-2003. The budget for that Fund for 2002-2003 was approved for $25 million. The Executive Director was authorized to transfer, if necessary, between the programme fields an amount not exceeding 10 per cent of the approved budget of the fund to which the transfer was made. The Board also approved a resources-funded programme budget of $203 million for the 2002-2003 biennium, subject to availability of specific-purpose contributions. Further, a total recommendation of $203 million for other resources funding was approved for the biennium.

Audits

On 24 January [dec. 2001/6], the Executive Board took note of the UNICEF financial report and audited financial statements for the biennium ended 31 December 1999 and the report of the Board of Auditors [A/55/5/Add.2], and the UNICEF report to the Board of Auditors and the Advisory Committee on Administrative and Budgetary Questions (ACABQ) [E/ICEF/2001/AB/L.2], which reported on steps taken in response to the recommendations of the Board of Auditors on UNICEF accounts for the 1998-1999 biennium and the status of implementation of the Board's recommendations on the 1996-1997 UNICEF accounts.

In its fourth annual report [E/ICEF/2001/AB/L.7], the Office of Internal Audit stated that in 2000 it had completed 34 audits of field offices and found that overall control in most locations was satisfactory. On 12 December [dec. 2001/18], the Executive Board took note of the report.

On 11 December [dec. 2001/17], the Board took note of the UNICEF report to the United Nations Board of Auditors and ACABQ [E/ICEF/2001/AB/L.8] on steps taken or to be taken in response to the Board's recommendations on the UNICEF accounts for the 1998-1999 and 1996-1997 bienniums.

Operational reserve

As recommended by ACABQ in 1999, UNICEF conducted a review of the advantages and disadvantages of establishing an operational reserve for both regular and other resources [E/ICEF/2001/AB/L.3], which it submitted to the Executive Board's first regular session in January. The review, having considered the existing financial management framework and liquidity policy, concluded that enhancements to UNICEF financial management systems, together with increased government and National Committee support, would enhance the Fund's ability to manage cash resources even more effectively. Therefore, the establishment of a funded operational reserve was unwarranted. In a related report [E/ICEF/2001/AB/L.4], ACABQ recommended that the Executive Board keep the issue of establishing an operational reserve under review.

On 24 January [dec. 2001/7], the Board took note of the UNICEF and ACABQ reports and decided that UNICEF should continue its current practice based on management of its short-term liquidity requirement on a cash-flow basis and should not establish a funded operating reserve. It also decided to keep the issue of establishing an operational reserve under review and to consider it further in 2003, taking into account the ACABQ report on the biennial support budget of UNICEF for 2002-2003 and the report of the Board of Auditors for 2000-2001.

Resource mobilization

During 2001, UNICEF developed new ways of collaborating with Governments for mobilizing regular and other resources, holding 15 formal and informal consultations with donor Governments and partners on various aspects of cooperation, including core financial support. UNICEF also entered into five new framework agreements with donor Governments.

At the pledging event in January, 66 Governments (28 donor and 38 programme Governments) pledged or indicated tentative pledges of $346 million; 11 more countries announced pledges than in 2000.

A total of 91 countries contributed to UNICEF regular resources in 2001, 27 of them members of the Organisation for Economic Cooperation and Development. The United States remained the largest government donor, contributing $216 million, followed by Japan ($97 million), the United Kingdom ($74 million) and the Netherlands ($69 million). Compared to prior years, 35 countries increased their contributions.

Private Sector Division

Net income from the UNICEF Private Sector Division (PSD) for the year ending 31 December 2001 totalled $161.1 million for regular resources, compared to $163.3 million in 2000 [E/ICEF/ 2002/AB/L.3]. That amount included $31.1 million from the sale of UNICEF cards and products, $147 million from private sector fund-raising activities, and an offset of $17 million for other charges and adjustments. In addition, $174.2 million ($146.2 million in 2000) was raised from private sector fund-raising activities that were earmarked for other resources. The net consolidated income, including both regular and other resources, amounted to $335.3 million ($309.5 million in 2000).

On 24 January [dec. 2001/5], the Executive Board approved budgeted expenditures of $87.7 million for the PSD work plan for 2001 [E/ICEF/ 2001/AB/L.1]. The Executive Director was authorized to redeploy resources between the various budget lines up to a maximum of 10 per cent of the amounts approved and to spend an additional amount between Executive Board sessions, when necessary, up to the amount caused by currency fluctuations, to implement the 2001 approved work plan. The Board approved changes in posts with a net decrease of four posts as indicated in the proposed budget; renewed the Market Development Programme ($3.4 million), the Fund-raising Development Programme ($7 million), the Central and Eastern National Committees Development Programme ($0.4 million) and the Nordic Investment Programme ($4.1 million). It also authorized the Executive Director to incur expenditures in 2001 related to the cost of goods delivered (production/purchase of raw materials, cards and other products) for 2002 up to $32.5 million.

In December [dec. 2001/19], the Board took note of the PSD financial report and statements for the year ended 31 December 2000 [YUN 2000, p. 1139].

JIU reports

In January, the Executive Board had before it a secretariat note on the reports of the Joint Inspection Unit (JIU) prepared between June 1999 and August 2000 of relevance to UNICEF [E/ICEF/ 2001/5].

On 22 January [dec. 2001/4], the Board requested the Executive Director to submit JIU reports to it along with a brief summary and recommendations for Board action. She was also asked to inform the Board of measures taken to implement JIU's recommendations.

Coordinating Committee on Health

At its third session (New York, 19-20 April) [E/ICEF/2001/11], the WHO/UNICEF/United Nations Population Fund (UNFPA) Coordinating Committee on Health reviewed progress in implementing its 2000 recommendations [YUN 2000, p. 1140], discussed the role of SWAPs for health and development at the country level, and reviewed the resolutions and decisions of the governing bodies of WHO, UNICEF and UNFPA adopted since the Committee's second session that were relevant to its work.

The Executive Board, on 5 June [dec. 2001/8], approved the Committee's report.

Youth

Implementation of the World Programme of Action for Youth

In 2001, UN policies and programmes on youth continued to focus on the implementation of the 1995 World Programme of Action for Youth to the Year 2000 and Beyond, adopted by the General Assembly in resolution 50/81 [YUN 1995, p. 1211]. The Programme of Action addressed the problems faced by youth worldwide and outlined ways to enhance youth participation in national and international policy- and decision-making.

Report of Secretary-General. In a July report [A/56/180], submitted in response to Assembly resolution 54/120 [YUN 1999, p. 1123], the Secretary-General reviewed progress in implementing the Programme of Action, which was based on information received from Member States, the UN system and statements made by Member States during the 2000 session of the Assembly, as well as on information collected by the Secretariat, and focused on priority youth issues for the twenty-first century: globalization and empowerment of youth.

The report summarized action taken at the national, regional and global levels to implement the Programme of Action and described youth participation at the United Nations. Annexed to the report was a table indicating the status of implementation of national youth policies, coordination mechanisms and programmes of action as at May 2001.

Follow-up to the
outcome of the Millennium Summit

In a 28 September letter to the President of the General Assembly [A/56/422], the Secretary-General referred to his report to the Millennium Summit in 2000 [YUN 2000, p. 55], in which he called the attention of world leaders to the urgency of addressing the problem of unemployment and underemployment of young people. That challenge had been taken up in the Millennium Declaration, contained in Assembly resolution 55/2 [ibid., p. 49], in which heads of State and Government resolved to develop and implement strategies that gave young people everywhere a real chance to find decent and productive work.

The Secretary-General, in collaboration with ILO and the World Bank, had formed the Youth Employment Network and appointed a high-level panel to prepare a set of policy recommendations. The recommendations of the Youth Employment Network and its High-level Panel were attached to his letter. The recommendations were based on a new approach and a new partnership between national Governments and global organizations for full employment: young people were an asset in building a better world, not a problem; heads of State and Government at the Millennium Summit had given a firm political commitment to developing and implementing strategies to give young people a real chance to find decent and productive work; and there was great potential for improving the employment situation through the integration of public policies for young women and men in overall employment policies. The Panel identified four top priorities for all national action plans: employability, equal opportunities for young men and women, entrepreneurship and employment creation.

Noting that translating those priorities into national action plans was only a start towards meeting the common goal of decent and productive employment for young people, the Panel recommended that the heads of the United Nations, the World Bank and ILO provide guidance and organize technical support for the policy-making process over the coming years, with ILO having lead responsibility for the effort. The Panel also made 12 recommendations to provide a guide to the range of actions to improve the position of young people in the labour market. They covered: a youth employment dimension integrated into comprehensive employment strategies; strong institutional support for youth employment poli-

cies; investment in education, training and life-long learning; a bridge between the informal and the mainstream economies; the potential of information and communication technologies; new sources of work in the service sector; entrepreneurship and enterprise development; access of youth to employment services and support; a social floor for working youth; partnership for youth employment; an enabling international environment; and the future of the Youth Employment Network.

Dakar Youth Empowerment Strategy

By a 4 October letter [A/C.3/56/2], Senegal submitted to the Secretary-General the Dakar Youth Empowerment Strategy, which was adopted by the fourth session of the World Youth Forum of the United Nations System (Dakar, 6-10 August). The document, designed to strengthen the Braga (Portugal) Youth Action Plan developed at the third (1998) session of the World Youth Forum [YUN 1998, p. 1103], set out priority areas of action and interest identified by young people themselves.

Several youth empowerment strategies were identified in the areas of education and information and communication technologies; employment; health and population; hunger, poverty and debt; human settlements and the environment; social integration; a culture of peace; youth policy, participation and rights; young women and girls; youth, sports and leisure-time activities; and the establishment of mechanisms for monitoring and implementing the Dakar Youth Empowerment Strategy and the Braga Youth Action Plan.

Annexed to the Strategy was a statement on HIV/AIDS by the young people attending the Forum.

GENERAL ASSEMBLY ACTION

On 19 December [meeting 88], the General Assembly, on the recommendation of the Third (Social, Humanitarian and Cultural) Committee [A/56/572], adopted **resolution 56/117** without vote [agenda item 108].

Policies and programmes involving youth

The General Assembly,

Recalling its resolution 50/81 of 14 December 1995, by which it adopted the World Programme of Action for Youth to the Year 2000 and Beyond, annexed thereto, as an integral part of that resolution,

Recalling also its resolutions 32/135 of 16 December 1977 and 36/17 of 9 November 1981, by which it adopted guidelines for the improvement of the channels of communication between the United Nations and youth and youth organizations, and 40/14 of 18 November 1985, entitled "International Youth Year: Participation, Development, Peace", by which it endorsed the guidelines for further planning and suitable follow-up in the field of youth as contained in the report of the Advisory Committee for the International Youth Year on its fourth session, held at Vienna from 25 March to 3 April 1985,

Recalling further its resolution 54/120 of 17 December 1999, in which it took note with appreciation of the Lisbon Declaration on Youth Policies and Programmes adopted at the World Conference of Ministers Responsible for Youth in 1998,

Welcoming the adoption of the Dakar Framework for Action at the World Education Forum,

Recalling the United Nations Millennium Declaration adopted by the heads of State and Government on 8 September 2000, and recognizing that the Declaration includes important goals and targets pertaining to youth,

Recalling and reaffirming the commitments made at the major United Nations conferences and summits since 1990 and their follow-up processes,

Noting in particular that, in the World Programme of Action, regional and interregional conferences of ministers responsible for youth affairs in Africa, Asia, Europe, Latin America and the Caribbean and Western Asia were invited to intensify their cooperation and to consider meeting regularly at the international level under the aegis of the United Nations to provide an effective forum for a focused global dialogue on youth-related issues,

Recalling that, in the World Programme of Action, the World Youth Forum of the United Nations System was invited to contribute to the implementation of the Programme through the identification and promotion of joint initiatives to further its objectives so that they could better reflect the interests of youth,

Welcoming the support of the Government of Senegal for the holding of the fourth session of the World Youth Forum at Dakar from 6 to 10 August 2001,

Acknowledging that poverty, among other factors, represents a serious challenge to the full and effective participation and contribution of young people to society,

Recognizing that global cross-sectoral youth policies should take into consideration the empowerment and full and effective participation of young people, and their role as a resource and as independent decision-makers in all sectors of society,

1. *Takes note with appreciation* of the report of the Secretary-General on the implementation of the World Programme of Action for Youth to the Year 2000 and Beyond;

2. *Calls upon* all States, all United Nations bodies, the specialized agencies, the regional commissions and the intergovernmental and non-governmental organizations concerned, in particular youth organizations, to make every possible effort towards the implementation of the World Programme of Action, aiming at cross-sectoral youth policies by integrating a youth perspective into all planning and decision-making processes relevant to youth;

3. *Also calls upon* all parties concerned, as mentioned in paragraph 2 above, within the framework of the World Programme of Action, to consider the appropriate ways and means to provide follow-up to the Lisbon Declaration on Youth Policies and Programmes adopted at the World Conference of Ministers Responsible for Youth;

4. *Takes note with appreciation* of the work by the regional commissions to implement the World Programme of Action and to follow up the World Conference in their respective regions, in coordination with regional meetings of ministers responsible for youth and regional non-governmental youth organizations, and to provide advisory services to support national youth policies and programmes in each region, and encourages them to continue to do so;

5. *Invites* all relevant programmes and funds, the specialized agencies and other bodies within the United Nations system, as well as other intergovernmental organizations and regional financial institutions, to give greater support to national youth policies and programmes within their country programmes as a way to follow up the World Conference;

6. *Calls upon* all States, all United Nations bodies, the specialized agencies, the regional commissions and intergovernmental and non-governmental organizations, in particular youth organizations, to exchange knowledge and expertise on youth-related issues, upon setting up the ways and means to do so;

7. *Welcomes* the public information activities organized by the Secretariat for International Youth Day, 12 August, as a way to promote better awareness, especially among youth, of the World Programme of Action;

8. *Recognizes* that information and communications technology plays a crucial role as a potential means of promoting participation, access to information and education and networking possibilities for young people;

9. *Welcomes* the fact that the special session of the General Assembly on children will also discuss issues relevant to youth;

10. *Expresses its appreciation* to the Government of Senegal for its support to the fourth session of the World Youth Forum of the United Nations System, held at Dakar from 6 to 10 August 2001, where, once again, youth delegates had the opportunity to meet and debate strategies for youth empowerment;

11. *Affirms* that future sessions of the World Youth Forum should integrate an active and representative involvement of youth organizations and young people into all planning, reviewing and decision-making processes, and invites the Secretary-General to conduct a thorough review of and provide recommendations on the Forum's structure, organization, participation, including to ensure that it is fully representative of all geographical regions and of a diversity of views, and processes, taking into account the views of Member States and youth organizations, and, in this context, to include this matter in his report to the General Assembly at its fifty-eighth session, through the Commission for Social Development at its forty-first session;

12. *Recognizes* the importance of the full and effective participation of youth and youth organizations at the local, national, regional and international levels in promoting and implementing the World Programme of Action and in evaluating the progress achieved and the obstacles encountered in its implementation and of the need to support the activities of youth mechanisms that have been set up by youth and youth organizations, bearing in mind that young people are active agents for positive change and development in society;

13. *Also recognizes* the great importance of the empowerment of youth through building the capacity of young people to achieve greater independence, overcoming constraints to their participation and providing them with opportunities to make decisions that affect their life and well-being;

14. *Reaffirms* the decision of the heads of State and Government, as contained in the United Nations Millennium Declaration, to develop and implement strategies that give young people everywhere a real chance to find decent and productive work, welcomes in this context the Secretary-General's initiative to create a Youth Employment Network, and invites the Secretary-General to continue with these initiatives;

15. *Expresses deep concern* over the fact that, currently, approximately half of new human immunodeficiency virus (HIV) infections are in youth aged 15 to 24 years and that no fewer than 6,500 young people are infected by the virus each day, and reiterates the need to achieve the goals and commitments contained in the Declaration of Commitment on HIV/AIDS adopted by the General Assembly at its twenty-sixth special session, held at Headquarters from 25 to 27 June 2001;

16. *Reaffirms* the importance of schooling and education, in particular for girls and young women, and recognizes the value of all forms of lifelong learning, including formal education and training and non-formal education;

17. *Calls upon* Member States, all United Nations bodies and non-governmental organizations to continue to implement fully the guidelines for further planning and suitable follow-up in the field of youth endorsed by the General Assembly in its resolution 40/14, and the guidelines for the improvement of the channels of communication between the United Nations and youth and youth organizations which the Assembly adopted by its resolutions 32/135 and 36/17, and in particular to facilitate, in accordance with these resolutions, the activities of youth mechanisms that have been set up by youth and youth organizations;

18. *Takes note with appreciation* of the important role of the United Nations Youth Fund in the implementation of agreed programmes and mandates on youth, including the provision of support for youth activities promoting South-South cooperation, and support for the participation of young delegates from the least developed countries at the fourth session of the World Youth Forum;

19. *Invites* all Governments and intergovernmental and non-governmental organizations to contribute to the Fund, and requests the Secretary-General to take appropriate actions to encourage contributions;

20. *Reiterates* the call made in the World Programme of Action to Member States to consider including youth representatives in their delegations to the General Assembly and other relevant United Nations meetings, thus broadening the channels of communication and enhancing the discussion of youth-related issues, and requests the Secretary-General to convey this invitation again to Member States;

21. *Welcomes* Economic and Social Council resolution 2001/7 of 24 July 2001, in which the Council decided that the Commission for Social Development would review the relevant United Nations plans and programmes of action pertaining to the situation of so-cial groups and the global situation of youth in 2003, and in this regard requests the Secretary-General to present a comprehensive report on this issue, with concrete and action-oriented recommendations, to the Commission at its forty-first session, bearing in mind the need for Member States to develop more holistic and cross-sectoral youth policies and the need to enhance, inter alia, the channels of communication between the United Nations system and youth and youth organizations;

22. *Requests* the Secretary-General to report to the General Assembly at its fifty-eighth session on the implementation of the present resolution, in particular on progress made in the implementation of the World Programme of Action.

Ageing persons

Second World Assembly on Ageing (2002)

In accordance with General Assembly resolution 54/262 [YUN 2000, p. 1141], the Commission for Social Development, during 2001, acted as the preparatory committee for the Second World Assembly on Ageing, which, as decided in Assembly resolution 55/58 [ibid., p. 1142], would be held in Madrid, Spain, from 8 to 12 April 2002.

Commission for Social Development (February/March and April/May). The Commission for Social Development acting as the preparatory committee held its first session in New York from 26 February to 2 March and on 30 April and 1 May 2001 [E/2001/71].

In addition to a number of documents on procedural and organizational questions, the Commission had before it the report of the Secretary-General entitled "Towards the Second World Assembly on Ageing" [E/CN.5/2001/PC/2 & Corr.1]. The Secretary-General stated that the World Assembly would be devoted to the overall review of the outcome of the first World Assembly on Ageing, which was held in 1982 [YUN 1982, p. 1182], and to the adoption of a revised plan of action and a long-term strategy on ageing in the context of a society for all ages, the theme of the 1999 International Year of Older Persons [YUN 1999, p. 1124]. His report reviewed the preparations for the Second World Assembly and included an extended draft framework for the revised International Plan of Action on Ageing. The main body of the revised Plan of Action identified three priority directions for policy action: sustaining development in an ageing world; advancing health and well-being into old age; and ensuring enabling and supportive environments for all ages.

The Commission, acting as the preparatory committee, recommended to the Economic and

Social Council the approval for adoption by the General Assembly (see below) of a draft resolution on the United Nations Trust Fund for Ageing and draft decisions on arrangements regarding participation of NGOs in the World Assembly and on its provisional rules of procedure. The Commission also recommended to the Council the adoption of a draft decision on its report and the provisional agenda for its second session (see below). In addition, the Commission adopted three decisions that it brought to the Council's attention. By a decision on abuse against older persons [dec. 2001/PC/1], the Commission requested the Secretary-General to submit a report on the subject to its second (2002) session. In the second decision [dec. 2001/PC/2], the Commission decided to meet in resumed session on 30 April and 1 May and for one week in November (subsequently changed to 10-14 December), in order to complete the work of its first session. In the third decision [dec. 2001/PC/3], the Commission established arrangements regarding the accreditation of NGOs to the Second World Assembly.

ECONOMIC AND SOCIAL COUNCIL ACTION

On 24 July [meeting 40], the Economic and Social Council took note of the report of the Commission for Social Development acting as the preparatory committee for the Second World Assembly on Ageing on its first session and approved the provisional agenda for the second session (**decision 2001/239**).

On the same date, the Council adopted **decision 2001/237**, recommending to the General Assembly a draft decision on arrangements regarding participation of NGOs in the Second World Assembly (see Assembly decision 56/426 below).

Also on the same date, the Council adopted **decision 2001/238**, recommending to the General Assembly, for adoption by the Second World Assembly, the provisional rules of procedure for the Second World Assembly (see General Assembly decision 56/427 below).

Report of Secretary-General. In response to resolution 54/262 [YUN 2000, p. 1141], the Secretary-General submitted a July report on preparations for the Second World Assembly [A/56/152]. In addition to describing the work of the preparatory committee (see above), the report outlined the format of the World Assembly, which would comprise a political segment, responsible for the central task of preparing the revised International Plan of Action on Ageing, and other associated events, including a series of round-table discussions under the sponsorship of the host Government; an NGO forum, to be held in Madrid prior to and during the Assembly;

and a research forum, to take place in Valencia the week before the Assembly.

Member States had been invited to submit additional comments on the draft revised Plan to the Secretariat by 25 June and the preparatory committee set the end of August as the deadline for the secretariat to complete the draft to allow Member States and the international community to review it before the preparatory committee's December meeting.

Activities in preparation for the Second World Assembly took place during the year: a meeting of UN system organizations (6-7 March) discussed preparations and opportunities for future collaboration; the Department of Public Information published the brochure *Building a Society for All Ages* and unveiled the Assembly's logo; and the UN programme on ageing published the *World Ageing Situation* [Sales No. E.00.IV.4], a compilation of studies on global trends and emerging issues on ageing. Planned events included a regional preparatory consultation, organized by the Economic and Social Commission for Asia and the Pacific (Macao, China, September) and an expert group meeting to explore approaches to alleviating urban and rural poverty in old age, especially among older women in developing countries and countries with economies in transition (October).

Commission for Social Development (December). The Commission for Social Development acting as the preparatory committee for the Second World Assembly on Ageing held its resumed first session from 10 to 14 December [E/2001/71/Add.1].

The Commission brought two decisions to the attention of the Economic and Social Council. The first [dec. 2001/PC/3] listed 26 NGOs that it had decided to accredit to the Second World Assembly; and the second [dec. 2001/PC/4] took note of the report of the Secretary-General entitled "Towards the Second World Assembly on Ageing" (see above).

By **decision 2001/327** of 20 December, the Economic and Social Council took note of the report of the Commission acting as the preparatory committee on its resumed first session.

GENERAL ASSEMBLY ACTION

On 19 December, the General Assembly adopted **decision 56/426**, by which it established the arrangements regarding participation of NGOs in the Second World Assembly on Ageing. On the same date, by **decision 56/427**, the Assembly recommended for adoption by the Second World Assembly the provisional rules of procedure, which were annexed to the decision.

On 24 December [meeting 92], the Assembly, on the recommendation of the Third Committee [A/56/573], adopted **resolution 56/228** without vote [agenda item 109].

Follow-up to the International Year of Older Persons: Second World Assembly on Ageing

The General Assembly,

Recalling its resolution 54/24 of 10 November 1999 and its resolution 54/262 of 25 May 2000, by which it decided to convene the Second World Assembly on Ageing, to be held in Spain in April 2002, as well as its resolution 55/58 of 4 December 2000 on the Second World Assembly on Ageing,

Bearing in mind that, in its resolution 54/262, the General Assembly decided that the Commission for Social Development would serve as the preparatory committee for the Second World Assembly on Ageing,

Reiterating that the Second World Assembly should give particular attention, inter alia, to linkages between ageing and development, with particular attention to the needs, priorities and perspectives of developing countries,

Reaffirming the necessity of ensuring that the Second World Assembly will provide an action-oriented follow-up to the International Year of Older Persons, and recognizing the importance of an adequate preparatory process,

Affirming that the long-term strategy and revised plan of action on ageing to be adopted at the Second World Assembly should be realistic and relevant so that its implementation can be followed up effectively,

Reaffirming that the strategy and plan of action will contain realistic financial recommendations for implementation,

Aware of the need for the relevant bodies and agencies of the United Nations system, within their respective mandates, to collaborate among themselves to support and follow up the implementation of the strategy and plan of action,

Recognizing the importance of the contributions of the relevant bodies and agencies of the United Nations system and non-governmental organizations to the preparations for the Second World Assembly,

1. *Takes note* of the report of the Secretary-General on preparations for the Second World Assembly on Ageing;

2. *Recommends* that the preparatory committee give due consideration to the period to be covered by the long-term strategy and revised plan of action on ageing to be adopted at the Second World Assembly;

3. *Requests* the Secretary-General to submit a report to the General Assembly at its fifty-seventh session on the full range of tasks of the United Nations programme on ageing of the Division for Social Policy and Development of the Department of Economic and Social Affairs of the Secretariat, with a view to ensuring, as a matter of urgency, that the programme can effectively fulfil its tasks, including those that might arise from the implementation of the outcome of the Second World Assembly;

4. *Invites* all relevant agencies and bodies of the United Nations system to coordinate better their response to the global ageing of populations and to integrate within their respective mandates their programmes and activities related to older persons, taking into account the importance of the perspective of older persons;

5. *Invites* the Second World Assembly to address, inter alia, the question of abuse of and discrimination against older persons;

6. *Invites* Member States, where appropriate, to consider extending the mandate of national committees or other mechanisms established on the occasion of the International Year of Older Persons in order to undertake national preparations for the Second World Assembly, and invites those Member States currently without such mechanisms to consider appropriate ways or mechanisms for their preparations for the Second World Assembly;

7. *Invites* the regional commissions, within their respective mandates, to explore the feasibility of undertaking regional activities with Member States, non-governmental organizations and other relevant actors of civil society in their region to participate in and follow up the Second World Assembly;

8. *Invites* the Department of Public Information of the Secretariat to continue, in cooperation with the Department of Economic and Social Affairs and the host country, the information campaign for the Second World Assembly;

9. *Requests* the Secretary-General to report to the General Assembly at its fifty-seventh session on the implementation of the present resolution.

On the same date (**decision 56/464**), the Assembly decided that the agenda item on follow-up to the International Year of Older Persons: Second World Assembly on Ageing would remain for consideration during its resumed fifty-sixth (2002) session.

Trust Fund

On 24 July [meeting 40], the Economic and Social Council, on the recommendation of the Commission for Social Development acting as the preparatory committee for the Second World Assembly on Ageing [E/2001/71], adopted **resolution 2001/8** without vote [agenda item 14 (*b*)].

United Nations Trust Fund for Ageing

The Economic and Social Council

Recommends to the General Assembly the adoption of the following draft resolution:
[For text, see General Assembly resolution 56/118 below.]

GENERAL ASSEMBLY ACTION

On 19 December [meeting 88], the General Assembly, on the recommendation of the Third Committee [A/56/573], adopted **resolution 56/118** without vote [agenda item 109].

United Nations Trust Fund for Ageing

The General Assembly,

Noting the importance of the participation of developing countries and the least developed countries in the preparatory process for the Second World Assembly on Ageing and in the World Assembly itself,

Recalling its resolution 54/262 of 25 May 2000, in which it encouraged Member States and other actors to, inter alia, provide voluntary contributions to the United Nations Trust Fund for Ageing in support of preparatory activities for the Second World Assembly, including the participation of the least developed countries,

1. *Urges* all Member States and other actors to contribute generously to the United Nations Trust Fund for Ageing, to support preparatory activities for the Second World Assembly on Ageing, in particular to facilitate the fullest participation of the least developed countries, and to support public information activities to promote the Second World Assembly and its outcome;

2. *Urges* all States and public and private organizations to contribute to the Trust Fund to support public information activities to promote the Second World Assembly and its outcome.

Chapter XII

Refugees and displaced persons

In 2001, the total number of persons of concern to the Office of the United Nations High Commissioner for Refugees (UNHCR) throughout the world fell to 19.8 million, from 21.1 million in 2000. Over 12 million (60 per cent) of the total were refugees, 5.3 million were internally displaced persons, 925,677 were asylum-seekers, 703,558 returned to their places of origin and the remaining 1 million included forced migrants and stateless people.

Although there were no major refugee emergencies on the scale of those of the 1990s, UNHCR still faced major challenges concerning refugee protection. The military action in Afghanistan following the 11 September terrorist attacks in the United States led to the return of hundreds of thousands of Afghan refugees from Iran and Pakistan. However, the impact of those events also fuelled intolerance and distrust of aliens, including refugees and asylum-seekers. In tackling those challenges, UNHCR emphasized the need to secure refugee protection by facilitating durable solutions, such as voluntary repatriation, local integration and resettlement whenever possible.

Although Africa's refugee population fell by almost 10 per cent in 2001, the continent's 3.1 million refugees still accounted for approximately 30 per cent of the global refugee population at the end of the year. The main countries of origin of refugees were Angola, Burundi and the Sudan, while the host countries of the largest refugee populations were the Democratic Republic of the Congo, the Sudan and the United Republic of Tanzania. The main refugee returns in the region in 2001 were Burundians, Eritreans, Sierra Leoneans and Somalis.

The prime focus in Central and South America remained the protracted armed conflict in Colombia, which had uprooted some 700,000 people, most of them forced into the neighbouring countries of Ecuador, Panama and Venezuela.

In South Asia, peace initiatives in Sri Lanka raised hopes for durable solutions for the estimated 700,000 internally displaced Sri Lankans and the 64,000 refugees in India. However, there was only minimal progress on the situation of the 110,000 Bhutanese, one of the largest refugee groups in the region, who had been in Nepalese camps for over 10 years. The protection of asylum-seekers was the dominant issue in East

Asia and the Pacific, where there was a general narrowing of access to asylum. As East Timor moved closer to independence, UNHCR initiated negotiations with the Indonesian Government for the local settlement of some 50,000 East Timorese remaining there. In Central and South-West Asia, UNHCR's main focus was on Afghanistan and surrounding countries following the military intervention. UNHCR provided relief for the estimated 200,000 Afghans who fled to Pakistan in 2001, in addition to the over 2 million who were already in camps in Iran and Pakistan.

The main challenge in Western Europe continued to be the maintenance of access for asylum-seekers. Close to 420,000 applications for asylum were made in a context of reinforced legislation against irregular migration, people smuggling and trafficking, and of security concerns. In Eastern Europe, UNHCR focused on finding durable solutions for those displaced by protracted conflicts in the Caucasus.

To mark the fiftieth anniversary of the adoption of the 1951 Convention relating to the Status of Refugees, UNHCR convened, in December, the first meeting of States parties to the Convention and its 1967 Protocol, which adopted a landmark declaration reinforcing commitment to those two instruments. During the course of the year, UNHCR continued to hold meetings within the framework of the Global Consultations on International Protection, launched in 2000. It also took steps to sharpen its focus and strengthen its capacity to meet future challenges. A review of priorities and fund-raising efforts resulted in the reduction of UNHCR's 2001 budget by some 10 per cent and the number of staff posts by 16 per cent.

Office of the United Nations High Commissioner for Refugees

Programme policy

Executive Committee action. At its fifty-second session (Geneva, 1-5 October) [A/56/12/Add.1], the Executive Committee of the UNHCR Programme, noting the fiftieth anniversary of the adoption of the 1951 Convention relating to the Status of Refugees [YUN 1951, p. 520], expressed satisfaction at the increasing number of parties to the Convention and/or its 1967 Protocol [YUN 1967, p. 477] and urged broader accession. Recognizing that some countries of asylum, particularly developing countries and countries in transition, bore a heavy burden by hosting large numbers of refugees, the Committee reiterated its strong commitment to international solidarity and cooperation to share responsibilities. It stressed the national and international responsibilities of countries of origin and reaffirmed UNHCR's role in assisting and supporting countries receiving refugees and in mobilizing assistance to address the impact of large-scale refugee populations. The Committee emphasized that the ultimate goal of international protection was to achieve a durable solution for refugees, notably voluntary repatriation and, where feasible, local integration and resettlement. Noting the global dimension of statelessness, the Committee encouraged States to cooperate with UNHCR in devising appropriate solutions for stateless persons. The trafficking of persons, which represented a grave violation of their human rights, was strongly condemned by the Committee, which also expressed concern that many trafficking victims were rendered effectively stateless due to an inability to establish their identity and nationality. It reiterated its call to States to accede to the 1954 Convention relating to the Status of Stateless Persons [YUN 1954, p. 416] and the 1961 Convention on the Reduction of Statelessness [YUN 1961, p. 533].

The Committee also adopted conclusions on the registration of refugees and asylum-seekers and follow-up to the 1996 Geneva Conference on the problems of refugees, displaced persons, migration and asylum issues. It also adopted decisions on administrative, financial and programme matters and institutional questions.

Since Ruud Lubbers began his first three-year term as High Commissioner on 1 January, the Committee decided to replace the traditional annual theme discussion with a debate on his perspective on the work of the Office.

Reflecting on UNHCR's challenges in 2001 in his opening statement to the Committee, the High Commissioner highlighted the large-scale refugee movements in Guinea and the former Yugoslav Republic of Macedonia (FYROM), and the unfolding humanitarian emergency in Afghanistan and surrounding countries. He observed that emergencies were hard to predict and UNHCR and its partners needed to be ready at all times to respond efficiently; measures taken towards that end included improved staff training, increased numbers of deployable emergency staff and emergency stockpiles, and new stand-

by arrangements with Governments and partners. Other major concerns included staff security, the management of complex population flows, the need to find durable solutions for refugees and the need to promote coexistence and reconciliation in divided communities.

Regarding organizational management, the High Commissioner stated that he had taken a number of measures to sharpen UNHCR's focus and strengthen its capacity to meet future challenges, including new appointments, changes to the organizational structure and new policy directives. In addition, further measures were taken to strengthen internal investigation and oversight mechanisms. As to the budget, the High Commissioner recalled that when he took up his appointment a 20 per cent budget freeze had been imposed on all operations because donors had stated that the 2001 budget of $955 million, approved by the Executive Committee only three months earlier [YUN 2000, p. 1150], was not fundable. However, through the "Actions 1, 2 and 3" exercise, UNHCR defined its strategic direction, reviewed its operations and priorities and had initiated an ongoing review of its fundraising efforts. Under that process, UNHCR reduced its budget for 2001 by approximately 10 per cent and the number of staff posts by 16 per cent.

Looking to the future, the High Commissioner said the Office faced many threats, including restrictive interpretation of the 1951 Convention relating to the Status of Refugees, the deteriorating quality and perceived abuse of asylum systems and the high costs and burdens of hosting refugees. To address the question of whether UNHCR was adequately positioned to address the problems it was mandated to tackle, the High Commissioner announced that he had launched the "UNHCR 2004" process to develop a concept to better position the Office to carry out its mandate. That process would be completed by 1 January 2004 when UNHCR's current mandate would be due for renewal.

By **decision 2001/317** of 26 July, the Economic and Social Council took note of the High Commissioner's report covering the period 1 January 2000 to 31 March 2001 [E/2001/46 & Corr.1].

Coordination of emergency humanitarian assistance

In 2001 [A/57/12], UNHCR placed renewed emphasis on strengthening existing partnerships to increase the level and quality of resources reaching refugees and returnees. A Task Force on Partnerships was established in September with two working groups: one examined partnerships with UN agencies and international organizations while the other considered partnerships with non-governmental organizations (NGOs) (see below). Within the context of the Global Consultations on International Protection (see also p. 1113), UNHCR and the International Organization for Migration (IOM) formed the Action Group on Asylum and Migration to further the understanding of the connection between migration and asylum, review policy issues and improve cooperation between UNHCR and IOM on related matters.

In June, the annual high-level UNHCR/International Committee of the Red Cross (ICRC) meeting considered issues relating to their respective mandates and activities, the security of refugees and staff, and the separation of armed elements. The 1969 memorandum of understanding with the Organization of African Unity (OAU) was amended to update the framework of cooperation between the two organizations in the areas of protection of and material assistance to refugees, internally displaced persons and persons of concern; promotion of refugee law; emergency preparedness; and public awareness of refugee rights. In November, UNHCR signed a memorandum of understanding with the Economic Community of West African States (ECOWAS) to ensure protection, repatriation and resettlement of refugees within ECOWAS countries.

Within the UN system, UNHCR participated in the Administrative Committee on Coordination and the Inter-Agency Standing Committee, among other bodies, and in the resident coordinator system and UN country team at the field level. At year's end, a senior UNHCR staff member was seconded to the Internal Displacement Unit within the Office for the Coordination of Humanitarian Affairs.

Following the 11 September terrorist attacks in the United States, UNHCR contributed to the work of the Security Council's Counter-Terrorism Committee (see p. 66) and participated at the senior level in meetings of the Executive Committee on Peace and Security, set up by the Secretary-General as the UN system-wide focal point on terrorism. UNHCR also participated in the Executive Committee on Humanitarian Affairs, established to develop an integrated UN strategy for humanitarian response, post-conflict rehabilitation and development in Afghanistan in the first months of the crisis following the advent of the war on terror.

During 2001, UNHCR concluded project agreements with 573 NGOs, covering operational activities favouring refugees and other populations of concern. Those partnerships mobilized $193 million, representing 21 per cent of UNHCR's total budget. Throughout the year, NGOs played an active role in UNHCR's Global Consultations on International Protection, participating in round-table meetings to examine trends in refugee law, with a view to informing decision makers who formulated refugee policy.

Evaluation plan and activities

UNHCR's evaluation policy, which was described in an August report [A/AC.96/947], included a three-year development plan that committed UNHCR to steadily increasing levels of evaluation activity, placed new responsibilities on regional and field offices to undertake and commission evaluations, and introduced new approaches to ensure that the findings and recommendations of evaluations were effectively utilized.

The work programme of the Evaluation and Policy Analysis Unit focused on a number of key policy issues, including refugee children, refugee women, statelessness, refugee education, protracted refugee situations, and incorporating protection and human rights issues into evaluations.

Evaluation projects initiated in 2001 included reviews of UNHCR's work on internal displacement issues in Angola and Sri Lanka, reintegration programmes in Liberia and South-East Asia, and refugees' physical security in Kenya and the United Republic of Tanzania. UNHCR's role in strengthening national and non-governmental organizations and in developing policy issues affecting urban-based refugees was also evaluated.

Inspections

In 2001 [A/57/12], inspections of operations by the Inspector General's Office (IGO) were conducted in Armenia, Azerbaijan, Botswana, Djibouti, Eritrea, India, Lebanon, Namibia, South Africa, Yemen and Zambia. In September, IGO oversaw the conduct of an inquiry into the violent death of a staff member in the Democratic Republic of the Congo (DRC). In the course of the year, IGO received 31 complaints of alleged wrongdoing and conducted nine investigations of 16 staff members accused of harassment, fraud, corruption regarding resettlement and misuse of UNHCR assets and facilities. Disciplinary measures were recommended against 12 staff members while the remaining four were cleared of the allegations against them. Two other investigations initiated during the year were ongoing, one of which was being conducted jointly with the Investigations Division of the UN Office of Internal Oversight Services (OIOS).

OIOS report. In December [A/56/733], the Secretary-General transmitted to the General Assembly an OIOS report on the investigation into allegations of refugee smuggling at the Nairobi Office of UNHCR, which resulted in the arrest of nine persons—three UNHCR staff members, two members of an affiliated NGO and four others who operated the alleged criminal enterprise. Criminal charges were pending against all nine, including conspiracy to threaten to kill the United States Ambassador and the UNHCR representative and for demanding money from refugees. OIOS noted that UNHCR had taken substantial measures to correct management lapses that provided the opportunity for such activities and had also improved operations in Kenya. However, it warned against the recurrence of such incidents wherever the demand for resettlement by refugees who could not return home exceeded the ability or willingness of other Governments to take them.

Commenting on the OIOS findings and recommendations, UNHCR stated that it had learned and implemented many lessons from the investigation and would, as a result, become a much more accountable organization with strengthened management and improved oversight and investigation capacity.

GENERAL ASSEMBLY ACTION

On 19 December [meeting 88], the General Assembly, on the recommendation of the Third (Social, Humanitarian and Cultural) Committee [A/56/578], adopted **resolution 56/137** without vote [agenda item 114].

Office of the United Nations High Commissioner for Refugees

The General Assembly,

Having considered the report of the United Nations High Commissioner for Refugees on the activities of his Office and the report of the Executive Committee of the Programme of the United Nations High Commissioner for Refugees on the work of its fifty-second session and the conclusions and decisions contained therein,

Recalling its annual resolutions on the work of the Office of the United Nations High Commissioner for Refugees adopted since its establishment by the General Assembly,

Expressing its appreciation for the leadership shown by the High Commissioner since he assumed office in January 2001, and commending the staff and implementing partners of the Office of the High Commissioner for the competent, courageous and dedicated manner in which they discharge their responsibilities,

1. *Endorses* the report of the Executive Committee of the Programme of the United Nations High Commissioner for Refugees on the work of its fifty-second session;

2. *Welcomes* the fiftieth anniversary of the 1951 Convention relating to the Status of Refugees, notes that the Convention and the 1967 Protocol thereto have continuously served as the cornerstone of the international refugee protection regime, and welcomes in this context the convening of a ministerial meeting of States parties as an expression of their collective commitment to full and effective implementation of the Convention and Protocol and the values they embody;

3. *Reaffirms* that the 1951 Convention and the 1967 Protocol remain the foundation of the international refugee regime and recognizes the importance of their full application by States parties, notes with satisfaction that one hundred and forty-one States are now parties to one or both instruments, encourages the Office of the United Nations High Commissioner for Refugees and States to strengthen their efforts to promote broader accession to those instruments and their full implementation, and underlines in particular the importance of full respect for the principle of non-refoulement;

4. *Notes* that fifty-three States are now parties to the 1954 Convention relating to the Status of Stateless Persons and that twenty-five States are parties to the 1961 Convention on the Reduction of Statelessness, and encourages the High Commissioner to continue his activities on behalf of stateless persons;

5. *Welcomes* the process of Global Consultations on International Protection launched by the Office of the High Commissioner, and acknowledges their importance as a forum for open discussion on complex legal and operational protection issues;

6. *Reiterates* that international protection is a dynamic and action-oriented function, carried out in cooperation with States and other partners, inter alia, to promote and facilitate the admission, reception and treatment of refugees and to ensure durable, protection-oriented solutions, bearing in mind the particular needs of vulnerable groups;

7. *Re-emphasizes* that the protection of refugees is primarily the responsibility of States, whose full and effective cooperation, action and political resolve are required to enable the Office of the High Commissioner to fulfil its mandated functions;

8. *Urges* all States and relevant non-governmental and other organizations, in conjunction with the Office of the High Commissioner, in a spirit of international solidarity and burden- and responsibility-sharing, to cooperate and to mobilize resources with a view to enhancing the capacity of States and reducing the heavy burden borne by them, in particular by developing countries and countries with economies in transition that have received large numbers of refugees and asylum-seekers, and calls upon the Office of the High Commissioner to continue to play its catalytic role in mobilizing assistance from the international community to address the root causes as well as the economic, environmental and social impact of large-scale refugee populations, especially in developing countries and countries with economies in transition;

9. *Strongly reaffirms* the fundamental importance and the purely humanitarian and non-political character of the function of the Office of the High Commissioner of providing international protection to refugees and seeking permanent solutions to refugee problems, recalls that these solutions include voluntary

repatriation and, where appropriate and feasible, local integration and resettlement in a third country, reaffirming that voluntary repatriation remains the preferred solution, supported by necessary rehabilitation and development assistance, to facilitate sustainable reintegration;

10. *Emphasizes* the obligation of all States to accept the return of their nationals, calls upon all States to facilitate the return of their nationals who have been determined not to be in need of international protection, and affirms the need for the return of persons to be undertaken in a safe and humane manner and with full respect for their human rights and dignity, irrespective of the status of the persons concerned;

11. *Recognizes* that adequate and timely resources are essential to the High Commissioner to discharge effectively his mandated functions on an equitable basis, and urges Governments and other donors to respond promptly to the global appeal issued by his Office for requirements under its annual programme budget;

12. *Requests* the Office of the High Commissioner, with that sustained support, to continue to fulfil the mandate conferred upon it by its statute and by subsequent General Assembly resolutions regarding refugees and other persons of concern, in close cooperation with its relevant partners;

13. *Requests* the High Commissioner to report on his activities to the General Assembly at its fifty-seventh session, and to include in his report the results of the Global Consultations on International Protection.

Enlargement of Executive Committee

On 3 May, the Economic and Social Council, by **decision 2001/217**, took note of Guinea's request [E/1999/13] for membership in the UNHCR Executive Committee and recommended that the General Assembly decide, at its fifty-sixth (2001) session, on the issue of enlarging the Committee's membership from 57 to 58 States.

In July, the Council had before it communications from Ecuador [E/2001/52], New Zealand [E/2001/4] and the Federal Republic of Yugoslavia (FRY) [E/2001/49] requesting membership in the Committee. By **decision 2001/298** of 25 July, the Council took note of those requests and recommended that the Assembly take a decision at its fifty-sixth session on the question of enlarging the Committee's membership from 58 to 61 States.

GENERAL ASSEMBLY ACTION

On 19 December [meeting 88], the General Assembly, on the recommendation of the Third Committee [A/56/578], adopted **resolution 56/133** without vote [agenda item 114].

Enlargement of the Executive Committee of the Programme of the United Nations High Commissioner for Refugees

The General Assembly,

Taking note of Economic and Social Council decisions 2001/217 of 3 May 2001 and 2001/298 of 25 July 2001 concerning the enlargement of the Executive Committee of the Programme of the United Nations High Commissioner for Refugees,

Taking note also of the requests regarding the enlargement of the Executive Committee contained in the annex to the note verbale dated 21 January 1999 from the Permanent Mission of Guinea to the United Nations addressed to the Secretary-General, in the letter dated 3 November 2000 from the Permanent Representative of New Zealand to the United Nations addressed to the Secretary-General, in the annex to the letter dated 20 April 2001 from the Permanent Representative of the Federal Republic of Yugoslavia to the United Nations addressed to the Secretary-General and in the note verbale dated 27 April 2001 from the Permanent Mission of Ecuador to the United Nations addressed to the Secretary-General,

1. *Decides* to increase the number of members of the Executive Committee of the Programme of the United Nations High Commissioner for Refugees from fifty-seven to sixty-one States;

2. *Requests* the Economic and Social Council to elect the additional members at its resumed organizational session for 2002.

Financial and administrative questions

UNHCR's initial annual programme budget target for 2001 was set at $898.5 million [A/57/12] by the Executive Committee in 2000 [YUN 2000, p. 1150]. In addition, during the course of 2001, some $117 million was added for operations in Afghanistan, Eritrea, Sierra Leone and FYROM. However, income from donors' contributions stood at only $779.2 million, considerably short of requirements, resulting in budget cuts that affected many operations. Expenditures during the year totalled $801 million, of which $677.6 million was from the annual programme budget. UNHCR expenditure by region was as follows: Africa, $307 million; Europe, $172 million; Central Asia, South-West Asia, North Africa and the Middle East, $105 million; Asia and the Pacific, $52 million; and the Americas, $23 million.

In October, the Executive Committee approved the revised 2001 annual programme budget amounting to $782.1 million, which, together with the UN regular budget contribution of $19.2 million, provisions for Junior Professional Officers of $7 million and the needs under supplementary programmes of $66.1 million, brought total requirements for the year to $874.4 million. For 2002, the Committee approved budgetary requirements of $801.7 million, including an operational reserve of $72.9 million (representing 10 per cent of programmed activities), which, together with the UN regular budget contribution of $19.9 million and provisions for Junior Professional Officers of $7 million, brought total requirements for 2002 to $828.6 million. The High Commissioner was requested, within the resources available, to respond flexibly and efficiently to the needs currently indicated under the annual programme budget for 2002, and authorized to create supplementary programmes and issue special appeals in the case of new emergency needs. Member States were urged to respond generously and promptly to such appeals.

Accounts (2000)

The audited financial statements of voluntary funds administered by UNHCR for the year ending 31 December 2000 [A/56/5/Add.5] showed total expenditures of some $784 million and total income of $709 million, with a reserve balance of $127 million.

The Board of Auditors recommended that UNHCR should: ensure that field offices verified project monitoring reports, including supporting documents and bank statements; ensure that field offices reviewed audit certificates and followed up significant issues that arose; establish realistic milestones against which the progress of projects could be monitored; establish a single line of project management for staff reports on all aspects of the integrated system project development; review the appropriateness of undertaking projects not directly related to assistance to refugees and routinely set clear milestones against which to measure progress and assess when its mission was complete; maintain accurate information on the size and characteristics of the refugee population; and include clearly stated and quantified objectives and outputs, incorporating key milestones and target dates.

UNHCR, in September [A/AC.96/949/Add.1], reported on measures taken or proposed to respond to the recommendations of the Board of Auditors.

In an October report [A/56/436], the Advisory Committee on Administrative and Budgetary Questions (ACABQ), while noting UNHCR's progress in reducing its level of expenditures, expressed the hope that further efforts would be made to address the $55.5 million outstanding in advances to implementing partners, covering the years 1994 to 2000. The Committee asked UNHCR to examine the problem of denial of access to the accounting records of implementing partners, requesting that it be brought to the attention of the Secretary-General if necessary. With regard to subproject monitoring, ACABQ recommended increased staff training and a stringent application of accountability requirements. UNHCR was asked to take measures to improve the performance of all country offices where significant gaps in the extent and quality of audit certificates existed and to take immediate steps to address the findings of the Board of Auditors and report

to the Committee not later than autumn 2002 on actions taken in that regard. ACABQ also reiterated its request that UNHCR report comprehensively on the implementation of all information technology projects, including relevant costs.

The Executive Committee, in a decision on administrative, financial and programme matters [A/56/12/Add.1], requested that it be kept regularly informed of the measures taken to address the recommendations and observations raised by the Board of Auditors and ACABQ.

OIOS reports

In July [A/56/128], the Secretary-General transmitted to the General Assembly the OIOS report on its November 1999 audit of UNHCR's emergency operations in Albania and on a follow-up audit in November 2000. The initial audit disclosed serious shortcomings in the management of the operation, owing to sub-standard procurement, improper tracking of assets and commodities, inadequate programme monitoring and budget control, unrefunded taxes paid on purchases and inadequate staffing.

Noting that the follow-up audit showed that UNHCR had made significant progress in addressing those shortcomings, OIOS found, however, that further improvement could be made in the following areas: staffing of emergency operations to ensure continuity and proper internal control; monitoring of implementing partners with proper and timely financial reporting; and asset management to more accurately reflect both assets on hand and those provided by partners.

OIOS recommended that UNHCR should: ensure that emergency operations were adequately staffed and that rotation was kept to a workable minimum; establish from the beginning of an emergency adequate tracking of assets and commodities; review rules and procedures for financial management, procurement and asset management; and renegotiate existing cooperation agreements with host Governments to ensure that tax exemptions granted to UNHCR were extended to purchases made by implementing partners using UNHCR funds.

In December [A/56/759], the Secretary-General transmitted to the Assembly an OIOS report on its audit of UNHCR's private sector fund-raising activities. It found that policies and procedures still needed to be more clearly defined or developed in some areas; self-sustainability, critical for any fund-raising operation, and the achievement of financial targets were not explicitly established as objectives in most cases; the methodology for calculating the return on investment should be determined to increase the value of analytical comparison and ensure better informed decision-making; complete data on the overall cost of UNHCR's private sector fund-raising were not readily available; contributions and associated fund-raising costs were understated; and the concept of using national associations, UNHCR's preferred tool for private sector fund-raising, had still to be proved effective. By year's end, OIOS stated, UNHCR had taken positive steps to address the issues raised.

By **decision 56/428** of 19 December, the Assembly took note of the report of OIOS on the audit of UNHCR operations in Albania. The Assembly, on 24 December, again took note of the report and looked forward to the full and expeditious implementation of the recommendations contained in it within the context of the annual OIOS report at the Assembly's fifth-seventh (2002) session (**decision 56/459**).

Standing Committee

The UNHCR Standing Committee held three meetings in 2001 (12-14 March [A/AC.96/945 & Corr.1], 25-27 June [A/AC.96/956] and 26 September [A/AC.96/958]). It reviewed UNHCR's programmes and activities in various regions, and considered updates on overall programme and funding issues; the Global Report on UNHCR's activities in 2000; programme/protection policy issues, including the safety and security of staff and the security of refugees; the economic and social impact of refugee populations on host countries; refugee women; the refugee situation in Afghanistan; international protection, statelessness and resettlement; coordination issues within the UN system; and issues relating to management, finance, oversight and human resources.

In October [A/56/12/Add.1], the Executive Committee adopted the following items for the Standing Committee's 2002 programme of work: international protection; programme/protection policy; programme and funding; governance; coordination; and management, financial, oversight and human resources. It authorized the Standing Committee to add items to and delete items from its intersessional programme of work.

Safety of staff

At its March meeting [A/AC.96/945 & Corr.1], the Standing Committee discussed the issue of staff safety, including action taken to reinforce and strengthen it, which had focused on three key areas: mainstreaming responsibilities and capacities for security within UNHCR; supporting proactive security management; and establishing and maintaining security standards in UNHCR's operations. The Committee emphasized the importance of the management aspects of staff security, clear lines of decision-making, increased accountability at all levels and inter-agency cooperation. While stressing the need for adequate funding from the UN regular budget, the Committee also acknowledged that UNHCR required extra funding for its increased security needs and proposed examining how best to provide that additional support.

Addressing the UNHCR Executive Committee in October [A/56/12/Add.1], the High Commissioner stated that a UNHCR staff member was murdered in the DRC in March and that six ICRC staff members had been killed a month later. He indicated that addressing the staff security issue would be one of his major priorities.

In **resolution 56/217** of 21 December, the General Assembly urged all States to ensure the safety and security of humanitarian personnel and UN and associated personnel (see p. 1349).

Refugee protection and assistance

Protection issues

In his annual report covering 2001 [A/57/12], the High Commissioner said the environment in which refugee protection had to be realized was increasingly affected by recurring cycles of violence and systematic human rights violations in many parts of the world, by the changing nature of armed conflict and of patterns of displacement, and by serious apprehensions about "uncontrolled" migration in an era of globalization. Additional compounding factors included the trafficking and smuggling of people, abuse of asylum procedures and difficulties in dealing with unsuccessful asylum-seekers. Countries of asylum in many parts of the world were concerned about the failure to resolve some long-standing refugee problems, urban refugee issues, irregular migration and a perceived imbalance in burden-sharing.

In a September note on international protection [A/AC.96/951], the High Commissioner focused on the fiftieth anniversary in 2001 of the 1951 UN Convention relating to the Status of Refugees [YUN 1951, p. 520] (see also p. 1113). He observed that while many States and regional organizations had reaffirmed their commitment to that Convention and its 1967 Protocol [YUN 1967, p. 477], many States still faced challenges in trying to reconcile their obligations under the Convention with problems arising from migratory movements, misuse of the asylum system, increasing costs, the growth in smuggling and trafficking of people and the struggle for international solidarity in resolving refugee situations.

UNHCR also faced considerable challenges. Over the preceding decade, States had asked the organization to take on a wider range of responsibilities. However, funding in recent years had not been commensurate, leading to the closure of some offices and the curtailing of a number of programmes and operations. UNHCR also had to contend with an increasingly restrictive application of the 1951 Convention, including diverging interpretations of its provisions and a waning quality of asylum offered worldwide.

The High Commissioner stated that security threats to refugees during the reporting period included, in particular, refoulement (forced return) and violence and intimidation in camps. Although the basic civil and political rights of refugees had generally been respected by States parties to the 1951 Convention, challenges remained in connection with documentation and certainty of status, non-discrimination, freedom of movement, freedom of association and religion, and access to courts. Moreover, States, often for resource-related reasons, had tended to curtail refugees' economic, social and cultural rights under the Convention.

The Executive Committee, in October [A/56/12/Add.1], re-emphasized that the protection of refugees was primarily the responsibility of States, whose full and effective cooperation was required to enable UNHCR to fulfil its mandated functions.

International instruments

In 2001, Belarus became party to the 1951 Convention relating to the Status of Refugees [YUN 1951, p. 520] and to its 1967 Protocol [YUN 1967, p. 477], bringing the number of parties to the Convention to 138 and to the Protocol to 137. Hungary became party to the 1954 Convention relating to the Status of Stateless Persons [YUN 1954, p. 416], increasing the number of States party to that instrument to 54. In March, FRY succeeded to those three instruments and all other treaties to which the Socialist Federal Republic of Yugoslavia had been a party, assuming the latter's responsibilities in that regard. Following the accession of the Czech Republic, Guatemala and Uruguay, the number of States party to the 1961 Convention on the Reduction of Statelessness [YUN 1961, p. 533] rose to 26.

Global Consultations

The Global Consultations on International Protection, launched in 2000 [YUN 2000, p. 1153], proceeded along three parallel tracks in 2001. The first track culminated in the Ministerial Meeting of States Parties to the 1951 Convention and its 1967 Protocol (see below). The second track provided a forum to consider developments in refugee law and examine a number of emerging legal issues. Four expert round tables discussed cessation and exclusion; the principle of non-refoulement and UNHCR's supervisory responsibility; membership of a particular social group; gender-related persecution; internal protection/relocation/flight alternative; illegal entry; and family unity. The third track was structured around a number of protection policy matters, including issues not adequately covered by the Convention. Four broad themes were selected for discussion: protection of refugees in mass influx situations; protection of refugees in the context of individual asylum systems; the search for protection-based solutions; and protection of refugee women and children. The first two themes were addressed at meetings held in March, June and September. The Global Consultations would conclude in 2002.

Ministerial Meeting of States Parties

On the occasion of the fiftieth anniversary of the 1951 Convention relating to the Status of Refugees, UNHCR and Switzerland co-convened the first Ministerial Meeting of States Parties to the Convention and/or its 1967 Protocol (Geneva, 12-13 December) [HCR/MMSP/2001/10]. Conceived as an integral part of the Global Consultations on International Protection, the meeting was preceded by a preparatory session (Geneva, 20-21 September) [HCR/MMSP/2001/03].

On 13 December, the meeting adopted by consensus a declaration in which States parties, acknowledging the continuing relevance of the international regime of rights and principles established by the Convention and its Protocol, reaffirmed their commitment to upholding the values embodied in them. They recognized the importance of promoting universal adherence to those instruments and reaffirmed UNHCR's importance as the institution mandated to provide international protection to refugees. Urging all States to consider ways to strengthen the Convention, ensure closer cooperation with UNHCR and respond promptly and adequately to its funding appeals, the States parties committed themselves to providing better refugee protection through comprehensive regional and international strategies.

Assistance measures

The global population of concern to UNHCR decreased from 21.1 million in 2000 to 19.8 million at the end of 2001, due mainly to a net decrease in the number of internally displaced persons. Those assisted included asylum-seekers, refugees, returning refugees in the early stages of their reintegration, internally displaced persons and other people of concern, mainly victims of conflict. Although there were no major refugee emergencies on the scale of those in the 1990s, persistent instability and strife, particularly in Africa and parts of South America, continued to cause population movements. In the course of the year, UNHCR facilitated the resettlement of some 33,400 refugees from 75 first asylum countries to 23 countries of permanent residence.

In 2001, UNHCR received a total of some $779.2 million in voluntary contributions towards its annual programme budget.

Refugees and the environment

In 2001, UNHCR reformulated its objectives for promoting environmental management in refugee and returnee situations and developed new and improved guidelines for the application and monitoring of sound practices in agriculture, land management and energy conservation. Parallel efforts were made in collaboration with the United Nations Educational, Scientific and Cultural Organization to promote environmental awareness in refugee communities through educational outreach programmes geared particularly towards children. Specific projects included those in Afghanistan, Rwanda, the Sudan and Zimbabwe to prevent soil erosion and reduce wood usage through reliance on alternative fuel sources. Permaculture systems were introduced to benefit environmental rehabilitation and income-generating activities, such as the sale of produce. Joint ventures with NGOs helped UNHCR to identify potential development partners for eventual handover of projects it had initiated. Monitoring and assessment missions were dispatched to the DRC, Djibouti, Kenya, Rwanda, the Sudan, Thailand and Uganda.

Refugee women

UNHCR's main objective with regard to refugee women in 2001 was to assess progress in advancing their rights and promoting gender equality, with a view to redefining a strategy for the future based on lessons learned and the views of refugees themselves. Other objectives included: developing and improving multisectoral activities to prevent and respond to sexual and gender-based violence; empowering refugee and returnee women as peace-builders; promoting the rights and equality of women; strengthening the protection of women through training of both staff and refugees; and disseminating good practices.

In March, UNHCR hosted an inter-agency lessons learned conference on prevention of and response to sexual and gender-based violence in refugee situations, which, among other things, identified where progress had been made towards developing a multisectoral approach and provided the basis for updating UNHCR's Guidelines on Prevention and Response to Sexual Violence. The Office also hosted a dialogue involving women of concern to UNHCR from over 20 locations across the world, which culminated in an international meeting (Geneva, June) where 50 refugee women shared their experiences. At the field level, the Office undertook and/or supported various activities to prevent and respond to sexual and gender-based violence against women and girls in Kenya and in Sierra Leone (see p. 678).

UNHCR efforts to mainstream gender equality included incorporating the experience of refugee women in various peace processes in East and West Africa. In Guinea, Kenya, Liberia and Uganda, it supported the training of refugee women in negotiation and conflict resolution skills. Gender awareness staff were deployed with emergency response teams sent to Afghanistan, Guinea and Sierra Leone, and that approach would become common practice in future emergency operations.

Refugee children and adolescents

UNHCR's key concerns regarding refugee children and adolescents, numbering an estimated 7.7 million in 2001, continued to be issues of separation, exploitation, sexual abuse and HIV/AIDS, military recruitment, access to education and the specific needs of adolescents. In most refugee and returnee situations, children, particularly girls, faced increasing risks of sexual abuse and violence because of their age and the social disruption surrounding them. A joint UNHCR/Save the Children (United Kingdom) assessment mission visited West Africa in October and November. It reported alleged sexual exploitation of refugee children, noting that some employees of NGOs and UN agencies, including UNHCR, could be involved. OIOS was immediately asked to investigate, and UNHCR put in place a comprehensive action plan to address programme, management and resource issues and to work on an effective code of conduct based on "zero tolerance" in the region and elsewhere.

The issue of unaccompanied and separated children continued to be a UNHCR priority and was the subject of a General Assembly resolution (see below). Resource materials on child protection continued to be produced and, by year's end, 10 packs of such materials, including one on child soldiers, were available on UNHCR's web site. UNHCR and its partners incorporated peace education into refugee assistance programmes in the DRC, Guinea, Kenya, Liberia and Uganda, with some 200,000 schoolchildren and many others in non-formal education receiving peace education as part of their learning during 2001.

Report of Secretary-General. In response to General Assembly resolution 54/145 [YUN 1999, p. 1138], the Secretary-General submitted a September report on assistance to unaccompanied refugee minors [A/56/333 & Corr.1]. The report reviewed new developments in family tracing and reunification and described the work of the Separated Children in Europe Programme and the Action for the Rights of Children training and capacity-building initiative. It also detailed action taken on behalf of internally displaced children and problems relating to the military recruitment of children and to sexual violence, exploitation and abuse. Efforts to strengthen UNHCR's field network were also described. Other issues of concern in the report included the girl child, adoption of separated children, and child-headed households and self-reliance of unaccompanied and separated children.

The Secretary-General noted that, despite some progress, many of the basic needs of unaccompanied and separated children remained unmet. A key challenge was the lack of adequate human and financial resources. Community-based strategies for addressing those needs required further emphasis and support in humanitarian interventions, and there was a need to strengthen inter-agency coordination and to pursue more effective registration and tracing systems. States were urged to accede to the two Optional Protocols to the 1989 Convention on the Rights of the Child [YUN 1989, p. 561], on the involvement of children in armed conflict and on the sale of children, child prostitution and child pornography, which were adopted by General Assembly resolution 54/263 [YUN 2000, p. 615].

GENERAL ASSEMBLY ACTION

On 19 December [meeting 88], the General Assembly, on the recommendation of the Third Committee [A/56/578], adopted **resolution 56/136** without vote [agenda item 114].

Assistance to unaccompanied refugee minors

The General Assembly,

Recalling its resolutions 49/172 of 23 December 1994, 50/150 of 21 December 1995, 51/73 of 12 December 1996, 52/105 of 12 December 1997, 53/122 of 9 December 1998 and 54/145 of 17 December 1999,

Aware of the fact that the majority of refugees are children and women,

Bearing in mind that unaccompanied refugee minors are among the most vulnerable refugees and the most at risk of neglect, violence, forced military recruitment and sexual assault and therefore require special assistance and care,

Mindful of the fact that the ultimate solution to the plight of unaccompanied minors is their return to and reunification with their families,

Noting the revised Guidelines on Refugee Children issued by the Office of the United Nations High Commissioner for Refugees in May 1994 and the development of an emergency kit to facilitate coordination and enhance the quality of responses to the needs of unaccompanied minors by the Office of the High Commissioner, the United Nations Children's Fund and non-governmental organizations,

Noting with appreciation the efforts of the Office of the High Commissioner and the United Nations Children's Fund in the identification and tracing of unaccompanied minors, and welcoming their efforts in reunifying families of refugees,

Welcoming the efforts exerted by the United Nations High Commissioner for Refugees to reunite refugees with their families,

Noting the efforts of the High Commissioner to ensure the protection of and assistance to refugees, including children and unaccompanied minors, and that further enhanced efforts need to be exerted to this effect,

Recalling the provisions of the Convention on the Rights of the Child, and the 1951 Convention and the 1967 Protocol relating to the Status of Refugees,

1. *Takes note* of the report of the Secretary-General;

2. *Also takes note* of the report of the Special Representative of the Secretary-General for Children and Armed Conflict;

3. *Expresses its deep concern* at the continuing plight of unaccompanied refugee minors, and emphasizes once again the urgent need for their early identification and for timely, detailed and accurate information on their number and whereabouts;

4. *Stresses* the importance of providing adequate resources for programmes of identification and tracing of unaccompanied minors;

5. *Calls upon* the Office of the United Nations High Commissioner for Refugees, in cooperation with other relevant United Nations bodies, to incorporate into its programmes policies that aim at preventing the separation of refugee families, conscious of the importance of family unity;

6. *Calls upon* all Governments, the Secretary-General, the Office of the High Commissioner, all United Nations organizations, other international organizations and non-governmental organizations concerned to exert the maximum effort to assist and protect refugee minors and to expedite the return and reunification with their families of unaccompanied refugee minors;

7. *Urges* the Office of the High Commissioner, all United Nations organizations, other international organizations and non-governmental organizations concerned to take appropriate steps to mobilize resources

commensurate with the needs and interests of unaccompanied refugee minors and for their reunification with their families;

8. *Calls upon* all States and other parties to armed conflict to respect international humanitarian law, and in this regard calls upon States parties to respect fully the provisions of the Geneva Conventions of 12 August 1949 and related instruments, bearing in mind resolution 2 adopted at the twenty-sixth International Conference of the Red Cross and Red Crescent, held at Geneva in December 1995, and to respect the provisions of the Convention on the Rights of the Child, which accord children affected by armed conflict special protection and treatment;

9. *Condemns* all acts of exploitation of unaccompanied refugee minors, including their use as soldiers or human shields in armed conflict and their forced recruitment into military forces, and any other acts that endanger their safety and personal security;

10. *Calls upon* the Secretary-General, the United Nations High Commissioner for Refugees, the Office for the Coordination of Humanitarian Affairs of the Secretariat, the United Nations Children's Fund, other United Nations organizations and other international organizations to mobilize adequate assistance to unaccompanied refugee minors in the areas of relief, education, health and psychological rehabilitation;

11. *Encourages* the Special Representative of the Secretary-General for Children and Armed Conflict in his efforts to raise awareness worldwide and mobilize official and public opinion for the protection of children affected by armed conflict, including refugee minors;

12. *Requests* the Secretary-General to report to the General Assembly at its fifty-eighth session on the implementation of the present resolution and to give special attention in his report to the girl-child refugee.

Refugees and HIV/AIDS

In recognition of the fact that the circumstances in which refugees and displaced persons lived offered fertile ground for the spread of HIV/AIDS, UNHCR accorded high priority to HIV/AIDS issues in 2001 and drafted a strategic plan for 2002-2004, aimed at strengthening prevention and care in refugee situations globally. The plan was discussed at the first meeting in February 2001 of a newly created UNHCR Advisory Group on HIV/AIDS, whose role covered advocacy, the promotion of partnerships, the provision of technical and financial support and the identification of potential support from existing bilateral and multilateral aid.

Within the context of a three-year joint initiative with the United Nations Population Fund, which began in 2000 with funding from the United Nations Foundation, UNHCR continued to support projects on HIV/AIDS and reproductive health. In 2001, projects that particularly targeted young people were executed in 12 countries, in cooperation with national and international NGOs.

Regional activities

Africa

Report of Secretary-General. In response to General Assembly resolution 55/77 [YUN 2000, p. 1158], the Secretary-General submitted a September report on assistance to refugees, returnees and displaced persons in Africa [A/56/335]. He stated that, although some repatriation had taken place, some 3.6 million refugees remained in Africa, representing 30 per cent of the global 12.1 million refugee population. The main refugee groups continued to originate from Angola (421,200), Burundi (567,000), the DRC (340,000), Eritrea (377,100), Sierra Leone (401,800), Somalia (441,600) and the Sudan (443,000). Substantial numbers also originated from Liberia and Rwanda.

In East Africa and the Horn of Africa, a tripartite agreement signed in March between Eritrea, the Sudan and UNHCR enabled the repatriation of Eritrean refugees from the Sudan to begin in May. Some 62,000 refugees were scheduled to return home by year's end and, by the end of July, 20,984 of them had done so. However, the protracted civil conflict in the Sudan itself made the repatriation of some 443,000 Sudanese refugees in exile unlikely. UNHCR, while caring for the Sudanese refugees, also pursued a policy of self-reliance for them and for host communities. It also pursued local integration as a possible durable solution for such protracted refugee situations. Kenya continued to receive a steady influx of asylum-seekers, mainly from Ethiopia and the Sudan. Some 11,000 Somalis fled to Kenya following the eruption of inter-factional fighting in the southern town of Bula Hawa in March; 4,000 of them returned to Somalia with UNHCR assistance. Several thousand other Somali refugees repatriated voluntarily from Ethiopia to north-west Somalia, bringing the number of those that had returned since 1997 to over 160,000. The return of 10,547 former Ethiopian refugees from the Sudan and 1,780 from Djibouti brought the number of Ethiopians that had repatriated since 1993 to over 84,000 and marked the end of one of the oldest refugee situations on the continent.

In West and Central Africa, although the situation in the Mano River Union countries of Guinea, Liberia and Sierra Leone remained complex and insecure, witnessing movements of 705,600 refugees, a decrease in the violence in Sierra Leone enabled 25,000 Sierra Leonean refugees in Guinea to return home voluntarily in May. More than 58,000 others were relocated to more secure sites further away from the volatile border area between the two countries. Ongoing conflict in northern Liberia forced several thousand refugees into neighbouring countries and remained a cause for concern. A total of 15,000 Liberians were scheduled to be relocated from border areas in Guinea to less violent sites, where UNHCR would further improve living conditions and consolidate assistance programmes. The repatriation of Chadian refugees from Cameroon entered its final stage, with a total of 5,530 repatriated during the year, while some 40,000 had integrated locally with UNHCR assistance. The Office also assisted Senegalese refugees in the Gambia, Central African Republic refugees in the DRC and Congolese ex-military refugees in Gabon.

In the Great Lakes region, despite some progress in the inter-Congolese dialogue in the DRC and the Arusha peace process in Burundi, many obstacles to peace and voluntary repatriation for Burundian and DRC refugees remained. Preparations were being made to repatriate Congolese refugees from the United Republic of Tanzania and a bilateral committee was to be established to discuss modalities for repatriating and resettling Burundian refugees living along Tanzania's western border.

In Southern Africa, the number of refugees increased by 7.8 per cent during the first half of the year to over 345,000. The conflict in Angola and the fragile peace process in the DRC dominated political activity in the region. Angola alone had 3.8 million internally displaced persons, with UNHCR providing assistance to over 200,000 of them in three northern provinces. Over 430,000 Angolan refugees were hosted mainly in the DRC and Zambia. In May, bilateral talks between Angola and Zambia established a mechanism to aid repatriation and UNHCR established a technical committee to further consider the possibilities of repatriation in the region, while also assisting some 20,600 refugees in Namibia.

The Secretary-General described inter-agency cooperation efforts to protect and assist refugees, returnees and displaced persons in Africa and discussed UNHCR's cooperation with continental and subregional initiatives.

Report of High Commissioner. In his report covering 2001 [A/57/12], the High Commissioner stated that the refugee population in Africa fell by almost 10 per cent to 3.1 million at year's end. While there were almost 190,000 new refugees, 260,000 others returned home, and another 14,500 were resettled by UNHCR in countries of permanent residence.

UNHCR's activities in West Africa covered 21 countries, focusing mainly on the Mano River Union countries. Throughout 2001, there were few opportunities for repatriation in the Great Lakes region owing to the prevailing security situation. The safety of humanitarian workers remained a major preoccupation, especially following the shooting in March of a UNHCR driver in south-eastern DRC and the assassination in May of six ICRC delegates in the north-east. In Burundi, UNHCR's access to populations of concern was often blocked by sporadic violence; as a result, only 28,000 Burundian refugees were able to return during the year. In the United Republic of Tanzania, which continued to witness an influx of refugees from neighbouring countries, UNHCR assisted 500,000 out of the 670,000 refugees in the country. Security in and around refugee camps remained a cause for concern and sexual and gender-based violence against women persisted. UNHCR facilitated the voluntary repatriation of 21,000 refugees to Rwanda, and it was anticipated that the target figure of 25,000 returns would be reached in 2002.

In Southern Africa, efforts to find lasting solutions for refugees through voluntary repatriation and resettlement were affected by the wars in Angola and the DRC. Elsewhere in the subregion, concerted efforts were made to develop self-sufficiency projects for refugees, including those in Malawi, where UNHCR provided land and loans to initiate income-generating agricultural activities, and in Swaziland, where animal husbandry and agricultural activities were initiated under a microcredit scheme.

By subregion, UNHCR assisted 888,392 persons in West and Central Africa, which received $85.2 million in agency expenditures. In East Africa, the Horn of Africa and the Great Lakes region, $185.9 million was spent on 2,445,822 persons of concern, while some $35.5 million was spent on programmes assisting 602,312 refugees, internally displaced persons, asylum-seekers and returnees in Southern Africa.

Communication. By a 9 October letter [A/56/457], the Sudan transmitted to the Secretary-General the decisions adopted by the Council of Ministers of OAU (Lusaka, Zambia, 5-8 July) and by the Assembly of Heads of State and Government of OAU (Lusaka, 9-11 July), which included decisions on the situation of refugees, returnees and displaced persons and on the fiftieth anniversary of the 1951 Convention relating to the Status of Refugees.

GENERAL ASSEMBLY ACTION

On 19 December [meeting 88], the General Assembly, on the recommendation of the Third

Committee [A/56/578], adopted **resolution 56/135**
without vote [agenda item 114].

Assistance to refugees, returnees and displaced persons in Africa

The General Assembly,

Recalling its resolution 55/77 of 4 December 2000,

Recalling also the provisions of its resolution 2312
(XXII) of 14 December 1967, by which it adopted the
Declaration on Territorial Asylum,

Recalling further the Organization of African Unity
Convention governing the specific aspects of refugee
problems in Africa of 1969 and the African Charter on
Human and Peoples' Rights,

Recalling the Khartoum Declaration and the Recommendations on Refugees, Returnees and Internally
Displaced Persons in Africa adopted by the Organization of African Unity at the ministerial meeting held at
Khartoum on 13 and 14 December 1998,

Welcoming decision CM/Dec.598(LXXIV) on the
situation of refugees, returnees and displaced persons
in Africa adopted by the Council of Ministers of the
Organization of African Unity at its seventy-fourth ordinary session, held at Lusaka from 5 to 8 July 2001,

Welcoming also decision AHG/Dec.165(XXXVII) on
the fiftieth anniversary of the adoption of the 1951 Convention relating to the Status of Refugees adopted by
the Assembly of Heads of State and Government of the
Organization of African Unity at its thirty-seventh ordinary session, held at Lusaka from 9 to 11 July 2001,

Noting that 2001 marks the fiftieth anniversary of the
1951 Convention relating to the Status of Refugees,
which, together with the 1967 Protocol thereto, as complemented by the Organization of African Unity Convention of 1969, remains the foundation of the international refugee protection regime in Africa,

Recognizing that the fundamental principles and
rights embodied in those Conventions have provided a
resilient protection regime within which millions of
refugees have been able to find safety from armed conflicts and persecution,

Recalling the Comprehensive Implementation Plan
adopted by the Special Meeting of Governmental and
Non-Governmental Technical Experts convened by the
Organization of African Unity and the Office of the
United Nations High Commissioner for Refugees at
Conakry from 27 to 29 March 2000 on the occasion of
the thirtieth anniversary of the adoption of the Organization of African Unity Convention, and noting its endorsement by the Council of Ministers of the Organization of African Unity at its seventy-second ordinary
session,

Commending the First Ministerial Conference on
Human Rights in Africa of the Organization of African
Unity, held at Grand-Baie, Mauritius, from 12 to 16
April 1999, and recalling the attention paid to issues
relevant to refugees and displaced persons in the Dec-
laration and Plan of Action adopted by the Conference,

Recognizing the contributions made by African States
to the development of regional standards for the protection of refugees and returnees, and noting with
appreciation that countries of asylum are hosting refugees in a humanitarian spirit and in a spirit of African
solidarity and brotherhood,

Recognizing also the need for States to address resolutely the root causes of forced displacement and to
create conditions that facilitate durable solutions for
refugees and displaced persons, and stressing in this
regard the need for States to foster peace, stability and
prosperity throughout the African continent,

Convinced of the need to strengthen the capacity of
States to provide assistance to and protection for refugees, returnees and displaced persons and of the need
for the international community, within the context of
burden-sharing, to increase its material, financial and
technical assistance to countries affected by refugees,
returnees and displaced persons,

Acknowledging with appreciation that some assistance
is already rendered by the international community to
refugees, returnees and displaced persons and host
countries in Africa,

Noting with great concern that, despite all the efforts
deployed so far by the United Nations, the Organization of African Unity and others, the situation of refugees and displaced persons in Africa remains precarious,

Stressing that the provision of relief and assistance to
African refugees by the international community
should be on an equitable, non-discriminatory basis,

Considering that, among refugees, returnees and internally displaced persons, women and children are
the majority of the population affected by conflict and
bear the brunt of atrocities and other consequences of
conflict,

1. *Takes note* of the reports of the Secretary-General
and the United Nations High Commissioner for Refugees;

2. *Notes with concern* that the declining socio-
economic situation, compounded by political instability, internal strife, human rights violations and natural
disasters, has led to increased numbers of refugees and
displaced persons in some countries of Africa, and remains particularly concerned about the impact of
large-scale refugee populations on the security, socio-
economic situation and environment of countries of
asylum;

3. *Encourages* African States to ensure the full implementation of and follow-up to the Comprehensive
Implementation Plan adopted by the Special Meeting
of Governmental and Non-Governmental Technical
Experts convened by the Organization of African
Unity and the Office of the United Nations High Commissioner for Refugees at Conakry on the occasion of
the thirtieth anniversary of the adoption of the Organization of African Unity Convention governing the specific aspects of refugee problems in Africa of 1969;

4. *Calls upon* States and other parties to armed conflict to observe scrupulously the letter and the spirit of
international humanitarian law, bearing in mind that
armed conflict is one of the principal causes of forced
displacement in Africa;

5. *Expresses its appreciation* for the leadership shown
by the United Nations High Commissioner for Refugees since he assumed office in January 2001, and commends the Office of the High Commissioner for the
ongoing efforts, with the support of the international
community, to assist African countries of asylum and
to respond to the protection and assistance needs of
refugees, returnees and displaced persons in Africa;

6. *Notes* the Ministerial Meeting of States Parties to
the 1951 Convention relating to the Status of Refugees,
to be held at Geneva on 12 and 13 December 2001, and

encourages African States parties to the Convention to participate actively in the event;

7. *Welcomes* the process of the Global Consultations on International Protection launched by the Office of the High Commissioner, which provides an important forum for open discussion on complex legal and operational protection issues, and in this context invites African States to continue to participate actively in this process so as to bring their regional perspective to bear, thus ensuring that adequate attention is paid to concerns that are specific to Africa;

8. *Reaffirms* that the 1951 Convention and the 1967 Protocol relating to the Status of Refugees, as complemented by the Organization of African Unity Convention of 1969, remain the foundation of the international refugee protection regime in Africa, encourages African States that have not yet done so to accede to those instruments, and calls upon States parties to the Conventions to reaffirm their commitment to their ideals and to respect and observe their provisions;

9. *Notes* the need for States to address the root causes of forced displacement in Africa, and calls upon African States, the international community and relevant United Nations organizations to take concrete action to meet the needs of refugees, returnees and displaced persons for protection and assistance and to contribute generously to national projects and programmes aimed at alleviating their plight;

10. *Notes also* the link, inter alia, between human rights violations, poverty, natural disasters and environmental degradation and population displacement, and calls for redoubled and concerted efforts by States, in collaboration with the Organization of African Unity, to promote and protect human rights for all and to address these problems;

11. *Encourages* the Office of the United Nations High Commissioner for Refugees to continue to cooperate with the Office of the United Nations High Commissioner for Human Rights and the African Commission on Human and Peoples' Rights, within their respective mandates, in the promotion and protection of the human rights and fundamental freedoms of refugees, returnees and displaced persons in Africa;

12. *Notes with appreciation* the ongoing mediation and conflict resolution efforts carried out by African States, the Organization of African Unity and subregional organizations, as well as the establishment of regional mechanisms for conflict prevention and resolution, and urges all relevant parties to address the humanitarian consequences of conflicts;

13. *Expresses its appreciation and strong support* for those African Governments and local populations that, in spite of the general deterioration of socio-economic and environmental conditions and overstretched national resources, continue to accept the additional burden imposed upon them by increasing numbers of refugees and displaced persons, in compliance with the relevant principles of asylum;

14. *Expresses its concern* about instances in which the fundamental principle of asylum is jeopardized by unlawful expulsion or refoulement or by threats to the life, physical security, integrity, dignity and well-being of refugees;

15. *Calls upon* States, in cooperation with international organizations, within their mandates, to take all necessary measures to ensure respect for the principles of refugee protection and, in particular, to ensure that the civilian and humanitarian nature of refugee camps is not compromised by the presence or the activities of armed elements;

16. *Deplores* the deaths and injuries and other forms of violence sustained by staff members of the Office of the United Nations High Commissioner for Refugees, and urges States, parties to conflict and all other relevant actors to take all necessary measures to protect activities related to humanitarian assistance, to prevent attacks on and kidnapping of national and international humanitarian workers and to ensure their safety and security, calls upon States to investigate fully any crimes committed against humanitarian personnel and bring to justice persons responsible for such crimes, and calls upon organizations and aid workers to abide by the national laws and regulations of the countries in which they operate;

17. *Calls upon* the Office of the High Commissioner, the Organization of African Unity, subregional organizations and all African States, in conjunction with organizations of the United Nations system, intergovernmental and non-governmental organizations and the international community, to strengthen and revitalize existing partnerships and forge new ones in support of the international refugee protection system;

18. *Calls upon* the Office of the High Commissioner, the international community and other concerned entities to intensify their support to African Governments through appropriate capacity-building activities, including training of relevant officers, disseminating information about refugee instruments and principles, providing financial, technical and advisory services to accelerate the enactment or amendment and implementation of legislation relating to refugees, strengthening emergency response and enhancing capacities for the coordination of humanitarian activities;

19. *Reaffirms* the right of return and also the principle of voluntary repatriation, appeals to countries of origin and countries of asylum to create conditions that are conducive to voluntary repatriation, and recognizes that, while voluntary repatriation remains the pre-eminent solution, local integration and third-country resettlement, as appropriate, are also viable options for dealing with the situation of African refugees who, owing to prevailing circumstances in their respective countries of origin, are unable to return home;

20. *Notes with satisfaction* the voluntary return of millions of refugees to their homelands following the successful repatriation and reintegration operations carried out by the Office of the High Commissioner with the cooperation and collaboration of countries hosting refugees and countries of origin, and looks forward to other programmes to assist the voluntary repatriation and reintegration of all refugees in Africa;

21. *Appeals* to the international community to respond positively, in a spirit of solidarity and burden-sharing, to the third-country resettlement requests of African refugees, and notes with appreciation that some African countries have offered resettlement places for refugees;

22. *Welcomes* the programmes carried out by the Office of the High Commissioner with host Governments, the United Nations, non-governmental organi-

zations and the international community to address the environmental impact of refugee populations;

23. *Calls upon* the international donor community to provide material and financial assistance for the implementation of programmes intended for the rehabilitation of the environment and infrastructure affected by refugees in countries of asylum;

24. *Expresses its concern* about the long stay of refugees in certain African countries, and calls upon the Office of the High Commissioner to keep its programmes under review, in conformity with its mandate in the host countries, taking into account the increasing needs of refugees;

25. *Emphasizes* the need for the Office of the High Commissioner to collate statistics, on a regular basis, on the number of refugees living outside refugee camps in certain African countries, with a view to evaluating and addressing the needs of those refugees;

26. *Urges* the international community, in a spirit of international solidarity and burden-sharing, to continue to fund generously the refugee programmes of the Office of the High Commissioner and, taking into account the substantially increased needs of programmes in Africa, to ensure that Africa receives a fair and equitable share of the resources designated for refugees;

27. *Requests* all Governments and intergovernmental and non-governmental organizations to pay particular attention to meeting the special needs of refugee women and children and displaced persons, including those with special protection needs;

28. *Calls upon* States and the Office of the High Commissioner to make renewed efforts to ensure that the rights, needs and dignity of elderly refugees are fully respected and addressed through appropriate programme activities;

29. *Expresses grave concern* about the plight of internally displaced persons in Africa, calls upon States to take concrete action to pre-empt internal displacement and to meet the protection and assistance needs of internally displaced persons, recalls in this regard the Guiding Principles on Internal Displacement, and urges the international community, led by relevant United Nations organizations, to contribute generously to national projects and programmes aimed at alleviating the plight of internally displaced persons;

30. *Invites* the Representative of the Secretary-General on internally displaced persons to continue his ongoing dialogue with Member States and the intergovernmental and non-governmental organizations concerned, in accordance with his mandate, and to include information thereon in his reports to the Commission on Human Rights and the General Assembly;

31. *Requests* the Secretary-General to submit a comprehensive report on assistance to refugees, returnees and displaced persons in Africa to the General Assembly at its fifty-seventh session, taking fully into account the efforts expended by countries of asylum, under the item entitled "Report of the United Nations High Commissioner for Refugees, questions relating to refugees, returnees and displaced persons and humanitarian questions", and to present an oral report to the Economic and Social Council at its substantive session of 2002.

The Americas

UNHCR's main focus in Central and South America in 2001 remained the protection of some 700,000 Colombians, a high percentage of whom were indigenous and Afro-Colombians, affected by four decades of armed conflict. Although the neighbouring countries of Ecuador, Panama and Venezuela, which were affected by cross-border movements of displaced Colombians, signed tripartite agreements to facilitate the repatriation of those refugees, voluntary returnee numbers remained small. UNHCR encouraged local integration as a durable solution for long-staying refugees. Within Colombia, UNHCR reinforced the response of national institutions that addressed internal displacement, working with 14 Colombian NGOs and with local authorities. Elsewhere in South America, UNHCR continued to build and strengthen national constituencies to which it could progressively hand over responsibility for refugee protection and local integration, as in Brazil and Chile, both of which received refugees from outside the subregion for resettlement. Following the events of 11 September in the United States (see p. 60), asylum-seekers in the region were affected by stricter immigration controls resulting from heightened security concerns in the so-called "triple frontier" abutting Argentina, Brazil and Paraguay.

In North America and the Caribbean, UNHCR's utmost concern was the suspension of the United States resettlement programme owing to security concerns after 11 September. Only about 800 out of 14,000 expected refugees were admitted for resettlement in the last quarter of the year, with over 20,000 approved cases put on hold. In Canada, where visa requirements were tightened for citizens of leading asylum-seeker countries, 12,250 refugees were resettled, which was slightly below the 2000 figure of 13,520. Working with NGOs and government partners, UNHCR addressed the issue of separated children seeking asylum in Canada and published a report with recommendations for improved practices. In the Caribbean, the Office increased its monitoring of key refugee-receiving countries, including the Bahamas, the Dominican Republic and Jamaica, and worked to build up asylum systems in the region.

Total UNHCR expenditure in the Americas and the Caribbean for the year was $22.6 million for a total population of concern numbering 1,850,836.

Asia and the Pacific and the Arab States

In 2001, UNHCR spent a total of $52.3 million on activities in Asia and the Pacific for a total population of concern of 1,662,166. For operations in Central Asia, South-West Asia, North Africa and the Middle East, a total of $105.5 million was spent for a population of concern of 6,342,768.

South Asia

The protracted armed conflict in Sri Lanka had resulted in the displacement of an estimated 700,000 people within the country and another 64,000 in refugee camps in southern India. As peace initiatives by the new Sri Lanka Government were being pursued, the United Nations Guiding Principles on Internal Displacement [YUN 1998, p. 675] were accepted as a likely basis for government policy and action by NGOs. With UNHCR's assistance, Bhutan and Nepal jointly assessed the eligibility of 12,000 out of the 110,000 Bhutanese refugees remaining in Nepal, one of the largest refugee groups in the region. Pending the outcome of future bilateral talks, the refugees remained in camps where they had lived for 10 years under temporary asylum. The plight of 22,000 refugees from Myanmar in Bangladesh remained a cause for concern. Although a population survey conducted by UNHCR and Bangladesh revealed that 7,500 of those in refugee camps were willing to return home without delay, fewer than 300 of them actually did so during the year, the lowest number since the resumption of repatriation in 1998. In Northern Rakhine State in Myanmar, UNHCR continued to protect a large number of Muslim returnees, while promoting their sustainable reintegration. To encourage self-reliance, UNHCR, in cooperation with the United Nations Development Programme, organized literacy programmes in the Myanmar language, particularly among women. In India, UNHCR welcomed the Government's September decision to reissue resident permits to a large number of Afghan refugees in the country. It was anticipated that many of them would be able to return home once conditions for their voluntary repatriation were met.

East Asia and the Pacific

In 2001, the protection of asylum-seekers was a dominant issue in East Asia and the Pacific. The matter was brought to a head by the rescue at sea of some 430 asylum-seekers from an Indonesian fishing vessel, seeking to reach Australia, which led to Australia's "Pacific Solution", whereby asylum-seekers would be taken elsewhere in the region to be processed. Following the 11 September terrorist attacks in the United States, States of the region felt justified in further tightening procedures. As East Timor prepared for independence, UNHCR played a major role assisting and

encouraging the return of Timorese refugees, including through the distribution of shelter units. Opportunities for the local resettlement of the 50,000 Timorese refugees still in Indonesia were being sought. Over 1,000 members of Vietnamese ethnic minorities (Montagnards) seeking asylum in north-eastern Cambodia were declared by UNHCR as persons of concern and provided with basic assistance. Measures were taken to prevent deportations and to monitor conditions for those who returned to Viet Nam.

Communication. On 26 November [A/C.3/56/8], the Democratic People's Republic of Korea (DPRK) rejected some of the information contained in UNHCR's annual report for 2000 [A/56/12], which suggested there were DPRK refugees in the north-eastern area of China. Many Koreans lived in that part of China and travelled across the border to visit relatives. However, it was preposterous to call such travellers refugees.

Central Asia, South-West Asia, North Africa and the Middle East

UNHCR's main focus in the region was on Afghanistan, where, following the military intervention, UNHCR and its partners initially prepared for an exodus of up to 1.5 million refugees and vigorously advocated an open-border policy with all neighbouring States. Some 200,000 Afghan refugees fled to Pakistan, which authorized UNHCR to establish a pre-registration camp near the border and to move new arrivals to new camps in Baluchistan. All of UNHCR's international staff members were withdrawn to offices in neighbouring countries, where, with the backing of emergency teams, they stockpiled relief items and identified and prepared campsites. Following the collapse of the Taliban, UNHCR's focus switched to preparing for a mass return into Afghanistan and assistance for internally displaced persons. The major challenge for UNHCR in Central Asia remained the advocacy of refugee issues and the promotion of effective asylum legislation. In Tajikistan, the Government's proposed new refugee law was a serious cause for concern, as were restrictions on Afghan refugees' right to freedom of movement and residence. In Kyrgyzstan, however, efforts to develop close working relations with governmental counterparts were rewarded as several hundred Tajik refugees acquired citizenship.

In North Africa, which did not experience any changes in the refugee situation, UNHCR continued to provide protection and material assistance to urban and camp-based refugees and asylum-seekers, mainly from sub-Saharan African countries. Protection and assistance was assured for the most needy of an estimated 165,000 refugees residing in the Tindouf camps in the Western Sahara region in south-west Algeria. Finding durable solutions for those refugees was hindered by the political impasse in Western Sahara and preparations for voluntary repatriation to enable them to participate in the referendum on independence or integration with Morocco remained at a standstill. In the Middle East, the international offensive against terrorism, combined with the deterioration of the situation over the Palestinian issue, led to mounting tension in countries thought to be harbouring terrorist groups. UNHCR updated contingency plans to ensure optimum emergency preparedness should there be renewed conflict.

Europe

In 2001, UNHCR's expenditure for activities in Europe (excluding South-Eastern Europe) was $59.7 million for a population of concern numbering 4,405,307.

Western, Central and Eastern Europe

Western Europe remained a major destination for asylum-seekers, with almost 420,000 applications made. UNHCR's main challenge in the region continued to be the maintenance of access for new arrivals both to the countries of destination and to their asylum systems. Such access became increasingly difficult due to reinforced legislation against irregular migration, smuggling and trafficking, as well as heightened concerns about the perceived or real misuse of the asylum system. Additional security concerns raised by the events of 11 September triggered more restrictions.

In Central Europe, the gradual improvement of asylum systems resulted in an increase in asylum-seekers, to 42,000 in 2001. UNHCR, together with concerned States, comprehensively addressed the problem of refugees and asylum-seekers who moved in an irregular manner from Central to Western Europe. The key reason for such movements was the absence of real opportunities for economic and social integration in most Central European countries. During the year, UNHCR assisted several States to formulate refugee legislation and asylum procedures and actively pursued a special programme for meeting the protection and assistance needs of separated asylum-seeking and refugee children.

In Eastern Europe, UNHCR's major challenge continued to be the need to find durable solutions to the plight of those displaced by the protracted conflicts in the Caucasus. As it provided humanitarian assistance, UNHCR also sought suitable interim solutions that would provide dis-

placed persons with clearly recognized legal status in the social and economic life of the host societies.

Partnerships with other agencies, including IOM, the Organization for Security and Co-operation in Europe and the Council of Europe, were an important feature of UNHCR's contribution to the implementation of the Programme of Action adopted at the 1996 Regional Conference to Address the Problems of Refugees, Displaced Persons, Other Forms of Involuntary Displacement and Returnees in the Countries of the Commonwealth of Independent States (CIS) and Relevant Neighbouring States [YUN 1996, p. 1117].

The UNHCR Executive Committee, in October [A/56/12/Add.1], welcomed the progress made in a number of CIS countries in implementing the 1996 Programme of Action and called on all CIS countries to strengthen their commitment to carrying out the 2000 recommendations [YUN 2000, p. 1163] of the Steering Group established to monitor the Programme of Action's implementation.

GENERAL ASSEMBLY ACTION

On 19 December [meeting 88], the General Assembly, on the recommendation of the Third Committee [A/56/578], adopted **resolution 56/134** without vote [agenda item 114].

Follow-up to the Regional Conference to Address the Problems of Refugees, Displaced Persons, Other Forms of Involuntary Displacement and Returnees in the Countries of the Commonwealth of Independent States and Relevant Neighbouring States

The General Assembly,

Recalling its resolutions 48/113 of 20 December 1993, 49/173 of 23 December 1994, 50/151 of 21 December 1995, 51/70 of 12 December 1996, 52/102 of 12 December 1997, 53/123 of 9 December 1998 and, in particular, 54/144 of 17 December 1999,

Taking note of the report of the Secretary-General,

Having considered the report of the United Nations High Commissioner for Refugees,

Reaffirming the importance and continuing validity of the Programme of Action, adopted in 1996 by the Regional Conference to Address the Problems of Refugees, Displaced Persons, Other Forms of Involuntary Displacement and Returnees in the Countries of the Commonwealth of Independent States and Relevant Neighbouring States, as a basic guiding tool for future activities,

Recognizing the ongoing acuteness of the migration and displacement problems in the countries of the Commonwealth of Independent States and the necessity to follow up the Conference,

Recalling the decision of the Steering Group of the Conference at its fifth meeting to continue activities in the process entitled "Follow-up to the 1996 Geneva Conference on the Problems of Refugees, Displaced Persons, Migration and Asylum Issues" for a period of five years,

Welcoming the Work Plan for the Thematic Issues, prepared jointly by the Office of the United Nations

High Commissioner for Refugees, the International Organization for Migration, the Organization for Security and Cooperation in Europe and the Council of Europe in accordance with the recommendations adopted by the Steering Group at its fifth meeting,

Welcoming also the convening, at Kiev from 11 to 13 December 2000, of the first meeting of experts within the framework of the newly launched thematic process on citizenship and statelessness, as well as international efforts aimed at improving migration and border management, with due respect to refugee protection matters, and encouraging all lead agencies to continue to implement the Work Plan,

Reaffirming the view of the Conference that the primary responsibility for tackling population displacement problems lies with the affected countries themselves and that these issues are to be regarded as national priorities, while at the same time recognizing the need for enhancing international support for the national efforts of the countries of the Commonwealth of Independent States aimed at the effective implementation of such responsibilities within the framework of the Programme of Action adopted by the Conference,

Noting with satisfaction the efforts of the Office of the United Nations High Commissioner for Refugees, the International Organization for Migration and the Organization for Security and Cooperation in Europe in developing strategies and practical tools for more effective capacity-building in countries of origin and enhancing programmes to address the needs of various categories of concern to the countries of the Commonwealth of Independent States,

Taking note of positive results emanating from the implementation of the Programme of Action,

Convinced of the necessity of further strengthening practical measures and of continuing to maintain the regional approach for the achievement of effective implementation of the Programme of Action,

Recalling that the protection and promotion of human rights and the strengthening of democratic institutions are essential to prevent mass population displacement,

Mindful that adherence to the principles and the recommendations contained in the Programme of Action should be facilitated and can be ensured only through cooperation and coordinated activities undertaken in this respect by all interested States, intergovernmental and non-governmental organizations and other actors,

1. *Takes note* of the report of the United Nations High Commissioner for Refugees;

2. *Calls upon* the Governments of the countries of the Commonwealth of Independent States, in cooperation with the Office of the United Nations High Commissioner for Refugees, the International Organization for Migration and the Organization for Security and Cooperation in Europe, to strengthen their efforts and mutual cooperation relating to the follow-up to the Regional Conference to Address the Problems of Refugees, Displaced Persons, Other Forms of Involuntary Displacement and Returnees in the Countries of the Commonwealth of Independent States and Relevant Neighbouring States, and welcomes the positive results achieved by them in the implementation of the Programme of Action adopted by the Conference;

3. *Invites* all States that have not yet done so to accede to and implement fully the 1951 Convention and the 1967 Protocol relating to the Status of Refugees;

4. *Calls upon* States and interested international organizations, in a spirit of solidarity and burden-sharing, to provide appropriate forms and levels of support for activities undertaken in follow-up to the Programme of Action;

5. *Invites* international financial and other institutions to contribute to the financing of projects and programmes within the framework of such follow-up activities;

6. *Invites* the countries of the Commonwealth of Independent States to intensify bilateral, subregional and regional cooperation in maintaining the balance of commitments and interests in such activities;

7. *Calls upon* the Governments of the countries of the Commonwealth of Independent States to continue to strengthen their commitment to the principles underpinning the Programme of Action, in particular principles of human rights and refugee protection, and to lend high-level political support to ensure the implementation of activities undertaken in follow-up to the Programme of Action;

8. *Invites* the Office of the United Nations High Commissioner for Refugees and the International Organization for Migration to enhance their mutual relationship with other key international actors, such as the Council of Europe, the European Commission and human rights, development and financial institutions, in order better to address the wide-ranging and complex issues in activities undertaken in follow-up to the Programme of Action;

9. *Welcomes* the progress made in building civil society, in particular through the development of the non-governmental sector and the development of cooperation between non-governmental organizations and the Governments of a number of countries of the Commonwealth of Independent States, and notes in this regard the relationship between adherence to the principles of the Programme of Action and success in promoting civil society, especially in the field of human rights;

10. *Encourages* the involvement of intergovernmental and non-governmental organizations in the follow-up to the Conference, and invites them to demonstrate stronger support for the process of multinational constructive dialogue among a wide range of countries concerned;

11. *Emphasizes* the necessity of undertaking follow-up activities to the Programme of Action in relation to ensuring respect for human rights as an important factor in the management of migration flows, the consolidation of democracy, the rule of law and stability;

12. *Recognizes* the importance of taking measures, on the basis of strict adherence to all of the principles of international law, including humanitarian, human rights and refugee law, to prevent situations that lead to new flows of refugees, displaced persons and other forms of involuntary displacement;

13. *Requests* the Secretary-General to report to the General Assembly at its fifty-eighth session on the progress achieved in the implementation of activities undertaken in follow-up to the Programme of Action;

14. *Decides* to continue its consideration of the question at its fifty-eighth session.

South-Eastern Europe

In 2001, conflicts in southern Serbia and in FYROM led to renewed population displacement in South-Eastern Europe. Some 75,000 people became internally displaced in FYROM and another 93,000 crossed the border into FRY, triggering an emergency deployment by UNHCR. By year's end, some 80 per cent of the refugees and internally displaced persons had returned to their homes. Significant progress was recorded on a number of refugee and returnee issues in other parts of the region. In FRY, where the refugee population had decreased to 400,000, new government initiatives favouring durable solutions created an opportunity for changing the status of some 60 per cent of those refugees who expressed a wish to stay in the country. In Bosnia and Herzegovina and Croatia, there were encouraging signs of minority returns, with some 92,000 returning to Bosnia and Herzegovina alone. The situation in the Kosovo province of FRY was less encouraging. Despite the prospects for stability evidenced by democratic elections in August, minorities remained in a precarious situation, with only 2,500 of the displaced among them returning to their homes. On the other hand, many displaced ethnic Albanians from southern Serbia were able to return from Kosovo, although the process of reconstruction and reconciliation remained fragile. Important UNHCR activities included a Regional Return Initiative, with an Agenda for Action, which was endorsed in June by Governments in the region. Other efforts were aimed at ensuring that bona fide asylum-seekers and refugees received the international protection they needed, which commanded particular importance due to increasing flows of irregular migrants and trafficking across the region towards Western Europe.

Chapter XIII

Health, food and nutrition

In 2001, the United Nations continued to promote human health, coordinate food aid and food security and support research in nutrition.

At the end of the year, some 40 million people were living with HIV/AIDS, about one third of whom were between the ages of 15 and 24. During the year, approximately 5 million people became infected, 800,000 of them children. The General Assembly's special session on HIV/AIDS (New York, 25-27 June) was seen as the first step in the realization of the commitments contained in the Millennium Declaration, adopted in 2000, in which the world's leaders resolved to halt and begin to reverse the spread of HIV/AIDS by 2015. The Declaration of Commitment, adopted at the special session, represented a watershed in the history of the epidemic, establishing, for the first time, time-bound targets on prevention, care, support and treatment, impact alleviation, and children orphaned and made vulnerable by HIV/AIDS.

In September, the Assembly proclaimed the period 2001-2010 the Decade to Roll Back Malaria in Developing Countries, Particularly in Africa. In July, the Economic and Social Council called for support to the Organization of African Unity plan of action to achieve the goal of the Pan-African Tsetse and Trypanosomiasis Eradication Campaign initiative. Regarding tobacco control, work progressed on the drafting of a framework convention on tobacco control and related protocols.

The World Food Programme—a joint undertaking of the United Nations and the Food and Agriculture Organization of the United Nations (FAO)—provided food aid to 77 million people, supplying a record level of 4.2 million tons of such aid. FAO continued to implement the plan of action adopted at the 1996 World Food Summit and the FAO Council approved a proposal to convene, in June 2002, a review of the 1996 Summit.

Health

AIDS prevention and control

In the Millennium Declaration [YUN 2000, p. 49], adopted by the Millennium Summit of the United Nations in 2000, the world's leaders com-

mitted themselves to halting and beginning to reverse the spread of HIV/AIDS by 2015; providing special assistance to children orphaned by HIV/AIDS; and helping Africa build its capacity to tackle the spread of the pandemic and other infectious diseases. The decision by the General Assembly to convene a special session to review the problem as a matter of urgency followed quickly after the Millennium Summit, and was seen as the first step in the realization of the commitments expressed in the Declaration. The special session, which called for an expanded global response, for the first time ever established time-bound targets relating to prevention, care, support and treatment, impact alleviation, and children orphaned and made vulnerable by HIV/AIDS.

General Assembly special session on HIV/AIDS

The twenty-sixth special session of the General Assembly to review and address the HIV/AIDS problem in all its aspects and to secure a global commitment to enhance coordination and intensify efforts to combat the epidemic was held in New York from 25 to 27 June, as decided by the Assembly in resolutions 54/283 [YUN 2000, p. 1166] and 55/13 [ibid., p. 1167]. On 27 June, the Assembly adopted a Declaration of Commitment entitled "Global Crisis—Global Action" (see p. 1126), in which Member States committed themselves to addressing the HIV/AIDS crisis at all levels, through strong leadership and effective responses in such areas as: prevention; care, support and treatment; human rights; reducing vulnerability; a supportive environment for orphaned children; alleviating the epidemic's social and economic impact; research and development; developing strategies in conflict and disaster-affected regions; and additional and sustained resources. On the same date, the Assembly approved the report of the Credentials Committee (**resolution S-26/1**).

In other action, the Assembly, on 25 June, appointed the Credentials Committee members (**decision S-26/11**), elected its President (**decision S-26/12**), Vice-Presidents (**decision S-26/13**) and Chairpersons of the Main Committees (**decision S-26/14**), and appointed the facilitators (**decision S-26/15**) and chairpersons of the round tables (**decision S-26/16**). The Assembly also approved the organizational arrangements for the session (**decision S-26/21**), adopted its agenda (**decision S-26/22**) and selected accredited civil society actors to participate in the plenary debate and in the round tables (**decision S-26/23**).

In addition to discussions in the Assembly, four interactive round tables, with the participation of Member States, observers, the UN system and accredited civil society actors, were held on: HIV/AIDS prevention and care [A/S-26/RT.1]; HIV/AIDS and human rights [A/S-26/RT.2]; the epidemic's social and economic impact and strengthening national capacities to combat HIV/AIDS [A/S-26/RT.3]; and international funding and cooperation to address the challenges of HIV/AIDS [A/S-26/RT.4]. The round-table chairpersons made oral presentations to the Assembly.

GENERAL ASSEMBLY ACTION

On 27 June [meeting 8], the General Assembly adopted **resolution S-26/2** [draft: A/S-26/L.2] without vote [agenda item 8].

Declaration of Commitment on HIV/AIDS

The General Assembly

Adopts the Declaration of Commitment on the human immunodeficiency virus/acquired immunodeficiency syndrome (HIV/AIDS) annexed to the present resolution.

ANNEX

Declaration of Commitment on HIV/AIDS

"Global Crisis—Global Action"

1. We, heads of State and Government and representatives of States and Governments, assembled at the United Nations, from 25 to 27 June 2001, for the twenty-sixth special session of the General Assembly, convened in accordance with resolution 55/13 of 3 November 2000, as a matter of urgency, to review and address the problem of HIV/AIDS in all its aspects, as well as to secure a global commitment to enhancing coordination and intensification of national, regional and international efforts to combat it in a comprehensive manner;

2. Deeply concerned that the global HIV/AIDS epidemic, through its devastating scale and impact, constitutes a global emergency and one of the most formidable challenges to human life and dignity, as well as to the effective enjoyment of human rights, which undermines social and economic development throughout the world and affects all levels of society—national, community, family and individual;

3. Noting with profound concern that by the end of 2000 36.1 million people worldwide were living with HIV/AIDS, 90 per cent in developing countries and 75 per cent in sub-Saharan Africa;

4. Noting with grave concern that all people, rich and poor, without distinction as to age, gender or race, are affected by the HIV/AIDS epidemic, further noting that people in developing countries are the most affected and that women, young adults and children, in particular girls, are the most vulnerable;

5. Concerned also that the continuing spread of HIV/AIDS will constitute a serious obstacle to the realization of the global development goals we adopted at the Millennium Summit of the United Nations;

6. Recalling and reaffirming our previous commitments on HIV/AIDS made through:
- The United Nations Millennium Declaration, of 8 September 2000;
- The political declaration and further actions and initiatives to implement the commitments made at the World Summit for Social Development, of 1 July 2000;
- The political declaration and further action and initiatives to implement the Beijing Declaration and Platform for Action, of 10 June 2000;
- Key actions for the further implementation of the Programme of Action of the International Conference on Population and Development, of 2 July 1999;
- The regional call for action to fight HIV/AIDS in Asia and the Pacific, of 25 April 2001;
- The Abuja Declaration and Framework for Action for the fight against HIV/AIDS, tuberculosis and other related infectious diseases in Africa, of 27 April 2001;
- The Declaration of the Tenth Ibero-American Summit of heads of State, of 18 November 2000;
- The Pan-Caribbean Partnership against HIV/AIDS, of 14 February 2001;
- The European Union Programme for Action: Accelerated action on HIV/AIDS, malaria and tuberculosis in the context of poverty reduction, of 14 May 2001;
- The Baltic Sea Declaration on HIV/AIDS Prevention, of 4 May 2000;
- The Central Asian Declaration on HIV/AIDS, of 18 May 2001;

7. Convinced of the need to have an urgent, coordinated and sustained response to the HIV/AIDS epidemic, which will build on the experience and lessons learned over the past 20 years;

8. Noting with grave concern that Africa, in particular sub-Saharan Africa, is currently the worst-affected region, where HIV/AIDS is considered a state of emergency which threatens development, social cohesion, political stability, food security and life expectancy and imposes a devastating economic burden, and that the dramatic situation on the continent needs urgent and exceptional national, regional and international action;

9. Welcoming the commitments of African heads of State or Government at the Abuja special summit in April 2001, particularly their pledge to set a target of allocating at least 15 per cent of their annual national budgets for the improvement of the health sector to help to address the HIV/AIDS epidemic; and recognizing that action to reach this target, by those countries whose resources are limited, will need to be complemented by increased international assistance;

10. Recognizing also that other regions are seriously affected and confront similar threats, particularly the Caribbean region, with the second-highest rate of HIV infection after sub-Saharan Africa, the Asia-Pacific region where 7.5 million people are already living with HIV/AIDS, the Latin American region with 1.5 million people living with HIV/AIDS and the Cen-

tral and Eastern European region with very rapidly rising infection rates, and that the potential exists for a rapid escalation of the epidemic and its impact throughout the world if no specific measures are taken;

11. Recognizing that poverty, underdevelopment and illiteracy are among the principal contributing factors to the spread of HIV/AIDS, and noting with grave concern that HIV/AIDS is compounding poverty and is now reversing or impeding development in many countries and should therefore be addressed in an integrated manner;

12. Noting that armed conflicts and natural disasters also exacerbate the spread of the epidemic;

13. Noting further that stigma, silence, discrimination and denial, as well as a lack of confidentiality, undermine prevention, care and treatment efforts and increase the impact of the epidemic on individuals, families, communities and nations and must also be addressed;

14. Stressing that gender equality and the empowerment of women are fundamental elements in the reduction of the vulnerability of women and girls to HIV/AIDS;

15. Recognizing that access to medication in the context of pandemics such as HIV/AIDS is one of the fundamental elements to achieve progressively the full realization of the right of everyone to the enjoyment of the highest attainable standard of physical and mental health;

16. Recognizing that the full realization of human rights and fundamental freedoms for all is an essential element in a global response to the HIV/AIDS pandemic, including in the areas of prevention, care, support and treatment, and that it reduces vulnerability to HIV/AIDS and prevents stigma and related discrimination against people living with or at risk of HIV/AIDS;

17. Acknowledging that prevention of HIV infection must be the mainstay of the national, regional and international response to the epidemic, and that prevention, care, support and treatment for those infected and affected by HIV/AIDS are mutually reinforcing elements of an effective response and must be integrated in a comprehensive approach to combat the epidemic;

18. Recognizing the need to achieve the prevention goals set out in the present Declaration in order to stop the spread of the epidemic, and acknowledging that all countries must continue to emphasize widespread and effective prevention, including awareness-raising campaigns through education, nutrition, information and health-care services;

19. Recognizing that care, support and treatment can contribute to effective prevention through an increased acceptance of voluntary and confidential counselling and testing, and by keeping people living with HIV/AIDS and vulnerable groups in close contact with health-care systems and facilitating their access to information, counselling and preventive supplies;

20. Emphasizing the important role of cultural, family, ethical and religious factors in the prevention of the epidemic and in treatment, care and support, taking into account the particularities of each country as well as the importance of respecting all human rights and fundamental freedoms;

21. Noting with concern that some negative economic, social, cultural, political, financial and legal factors are hampering awareness, education, prevention, care, treatment and support efforts;

22. Noting the importance of establishing and strengthening human resources and national health and social infrastructures as imperatives for the effective delivery of prevention, treatment, care and support services;

23. Recognizing that effective prevention, care and treatment strategies will require behavioural changes and increased availability of and non-discriminatory access to, inter alia, vaccines, condoms, microbicides, lubricants, sterile injecting equipment, drugs, including anti-retroviral therapy, diagnostics and related technologies, as well as increased research and development;

24. Recognizing also that the cost, availability and affordability of drugs and related technology are significant factors to be reviewed and addressed in all aspects and that there is a need to reduce the cost of these drugs and technologies in close collaboration with the private sector and pharmaceutical companies;

25. Acknowledging that the lack of affordable pharmaceuticals and of feasible supply structures and health systems continues to hinder an effective response to HIV/AIDS in many countries, especially for the poorest people, and recalling efforts to make drugs available at low prices for those in need;

26. Welcoming the efforts of countries to promote innovation and the development of domestic industries consistent with international law in order to increase access to medicines to protect the health of their populations, and noting that the impact of international trade agreements on access to or local manufacturing of essential drugs and on the development of new drugs needs to be evaluated further;

27. Welcoming the progress made in some countries to contain the epidemic, particularly through: strong political commitment and leadership at the highest levels, including community leadership; effective use of available resources and traditional medicines; successful prevention, care, support and treatment strategies; education and information initiatives; working in partnership with communities, civil society, people living with HIV/AIDS and vulnerable groups; and the active promotion and protection of human rights; and recognizing the importance of sharing and building on our collective and diverse experiences, through regional and international cooperation including North-South, South-South and triangular cooperation;

28. Acknowledging that resources devoted to combating the epidemic both at the national and international levels are not commensurate with the magnitude of the problem;

29. Recognizing the fundamental importance of strengthening national, regional and subregional capacities to address and effectively combat HIV/AIDS and that this will require increased and sustained human, financial and technical resources through strengthened national action and cooperation and increased regional, subregional and international cooperation;

30. Recognizing that external debt and debt-servicing problems have substantially constrained the capacity of many developing countries, as well as coun-

tries with economies in transition, to finance the fight against HIV/AIDS;

31. Affirming the key role played by the family in prevention, care, support and treatment of persons affected and infected by HIV/AIDS, bearing in mind that in different cultural, social and political systems various forms of the family exist;

32. Affirming that beyond the key role played by communities, strong partnerships among Governments, the United Nations system, intergovernmental organizations, people living with HIV/AIDS and vulnerable groups, medical, scientific and educational institutions, non-governmental organizations, the business sector including generic and research-based pharmaceutical companies, trade unions, the media, parliamentarians, foundations, community organizations, faith-based organizations and traditional leaders are important;

33. Acknowledging the particular role and significant contribution of people living with HIV/AIDS, young people and civil society actors in addressing the problem of HIV/AIDS in all its aspects, and recognizing that their full involvement and participation in the design, planning, implementation and evaluation of programmes is crucial to the development of effective responses to the HIV/AIDS epidemic;

34. Further acknowledging the efforts of international humanitarian organizations combating the epidemic, including the volunteers of the International Federation of Red Cross and Red Crescent Societies in the most affected areas all over the world;

35. Commending the leadership role on HIV/AIDS policy and coordination in the United Nations system of the Programme Coordinating Board of the Joint United Nations Programme on HIV/AIDS (UNAIDS); and noting its endorsement in December 2000 of the Global Strategy Framework on HIV/AIDS, which could assist, as appropriate, Member States and relevant civil society actors in the development of HIV/AIDS strategies, taking into account the particular context of the epidemic in different parts of the world;

36. Solemnly declare our commitment to address the HIV/AIDS crisis by taking action as follows, taking into account the diverse situations and circumstances in different regions and countries throughout the world;

Leadership

Strong leadership at all levels of society is essential for an effective response to the epidemic

Leadership by Governments in combating HIV/AIDS is essential and their efforts should be complemented by the full and active participation of civil society, the business community and the private sector

Leadership involves personal commitment and concrete actions

At the national level

37. By 2003, ensure the development and implementation of multisectoral national strategies and financing plans for combating HIV/AIDS that address the epidemic in forthright terms; confront stigma, silence and denial; address gender and age-based dimensions of the epidemic; eliminate discrimination and marginalization; involve partnerships with civil society and the business sector and the full participation

of people living with HIV/AIDS, those in vulnerable groups and people mostly at risk, particularly women and young people; are resourced to the extent possible from national budgets without excluding other sources, inter alia, international cooperation; fully promote and protect all human rights and fundamental freedoms, including the right to the highest attainable standard of physical and mental health; integrate a gender perspective; address risk, vulnerability, prevention, care, treatment and support and reduction of the impact of the epidemic; and strengthen health, education and legal system capacity;

38. By 2003, integrate HIV/AIDS prevention, care, treatment and support and impact-mitigation priorities into the mainstream of development planning, including in poverty eradication strategies, national budget allocations and sectoral development plans;

At the regional and subregional level

39. Urge and support regional organizations and partners to be actively involved in addressing the crisis; intensify regional, subregional and interregional cooperation and coordination; and develop regional strategies and responses in support of expanded country-level efforts;

40. Support all regional and subregional initiatives on HIV/AIDS including: the International Partnership against AIDS in Africa (IPAA) and the ECA–African Development Forum African Consensus and Plan of Action: Leadership to overcome HIV/AIDS; the Abuja Declaration and Framework for Action for the fight against HIV/AIDS, tuberculosis and other related infectious diseases in Africa; the CARICOM Pan-Caribbean Partnership against HIV/AIDS; the ESCAP regional call for action to fight HIV/AIDS in Asia and the Pacific; the Baltic Sea Initiative and Action Plan; the Horizontal Technical Cooperation Group on HIV/AIDS in Latin America and the Caribbean; and the European Union Programme for Action: Accelerated action on HIV/AIDS, malaria and tuberculosis in the context of poverty reduction;

41. Encourage the development of regional approaches and plans to address HIV/AIDS;

42. Encourage and support local and national organizations to expand and strengthen regional partnerships, coalitions and networks;

43. Encourage the United Nations Economic and Social Council to request the regional commissions, within their respective mandates and resources, to support national efforts in their respective regions in combating HIV/AIDS;

At the global level

44. Support greater action and coordination by all relevant organizations of the United Nations system, including their full participation in the development and implementation of a regularly updated United Nations strategic plan for HIV/AIDS, guided by the principles contained in the present Declaration;

45. Support greater cooperation between relevant organizations of the United Nations system and international organizations combating HIV/AIDS;

46. Foster stronger collaboration and the development of innovative partnerships between the public and private sectors, and by 2003 establish and strengthen mechanisms that involve the private sector and civil

society partners and people living with HIV/AIDS and vulnerable groups in the fight against HIV/AIDS;

Prevention

Prevention must be the mainstay of our response

47. By 2003, establish time-bound national targets to achieve the internationally agreed global prevention goal to reduce by 2005 HIV prevalence among young men and women aged 15 to 24 in the most affected countries by 25 per cent and by 25 per cent globally by 2010, and intensify efforts to achieve these targets as well as to challenge gender stereotypes and attitudes, and gender inequalities in relation to HIV/AIDS, encouraging the active involvement of men and boys;

48. By 2003, establish national prevention targets, recognizing and addressing factors leading to the spread of the epidemic and increasing people's vulnerability, to reduce HIV incidence for those identifiable groups, within particular local contexts, which currently have high or increasing rates of HIV infection, or which available public health information indicates are at the highest risk of new infection;

49. By 2005, strengthen the response to HIV/AIDS in the world of work by establishing and implementing prevention and care programmes in public, private and informal work sectors, and take measures to provide a supportive workplace environment for people living with HIV/AIDS;

50. By 2005, develop and begin to implement national, regional and international strategies that facilitate access to HIV/AIDS prevention programmes for migrants and mobile workers, including the provision of information on health and social services;

51. By 2003, implement universal precautions in health-care settings to prevent transmission of HIV infection;

52. By 2005, ensure: that a wide range of prevention programmes, which take account of local circumstances, ethics and cultural values, is available in all countries, particularly the most affected countries, including information, education and communication, in languages most understood by communities and respectful of cultures, aimed at reducing risk-taking behaviour and encouraging responsible sexual behaviour, including abstinence and fidelity; expanded access to essential commodities, including male and female condoms and sterile injecting equipment; harm-reduction efforts related to drug use; expanded access to voluntary and confidential counselling and testing; safe blood supplies; and early and effective treatment of sexually transmittable infections;

53. By 2005, ensure that at least 90 per cent, and by 2010 at least 95 per cent, of young men and women aged 15 to 24 have access to the information, education, including peer education and youth-specific HIV education, and services necessary to develop the life skills required to reduce their vulnerability to HIV infection, in full partnership with young persons, parents, families, educators and health-care providers;

54. By 2005, reduce the proportion of infants infected with HIV by 20 per cent, and by 50 per cent by 2010, by ensuring that 80 per cent of pregnant women accessing antenatal care have information, counselling and other HIV-prevention services available to them, increasing the availability of and providing access for HIV-infected women and babies to effective treatment to reduce mother-to-child transmission of HIV, as well as through effective interventions for HIV-infected women, including voluntary and confidential counselling and testing, access to treatment, especially antiretroviral therapy and, where appropriate, breast-milk substitutes and the provision of a continuum of care;

Care, support and treatment

Care, support and treatment are fundamental elements of an effective response

55. By 2003, ensure that national strategies, supported by regional and international strategies, are developed in close collaboration with the international community, including Governments and relevant intergovernmental organizations, as well as with civil society and the business sector, to strengthen health-care systems and address factors affecting the provision of HIV-related drugs, including anti-retroviral drugs, inter alia, affordability and pricing, including differential pricing, and technical and health-care system capacity. Also, in an urgent manner make every effort to provide progressively and in a sustainable manner, the highest attainable standard of treatment for HIV/AIDS, including the prevention and treatment of opportunistic infections, and effective use of quality-controlled anti-retroviral therapy in a careful and monitored manner to improve adherence and effectiveness and reduce the risk of developing resistance; and to cooperate constructively in strengthening pharmaceutical policies and practices, including those applicable to generic drugs and intellectual property regimes, in order further to promote innovation and the development of domestic industries consistent with international law;

56. By 2005, develop and make significant progress in implementing comprehensive care strategies to: strengthen family and community-based care, including that provided by the informal sector, and health-care systems to provide and monitor treatment to people living with HIV/AIDS, including infected children, and to support individuals, households, families and communities affected by HIV/AIDS; and improve the capacity and working conditions of health-care personnel, and the effectiveness of supply systems, financing plans and referral mechanisms required to provide access to affordable medicines, including anti-retroviral drugs, diagnostics and related technologies, as well as quality medical, palliative and psychosocial care;

57. By 2003, ensure that national strategies are developed in order to provide psychosocial care for individuals, families and communities affected by HIV/AIDS;

HIV/AIDS and human rights

Realization of human rights and fundamental freedoms for all is essential to reduce vulnerability to HIV/AIDS

Respect for the rights of people living with HIV/AIDS drives an effective response

58. By 2003, enact, strengthen or enforce, as appropriate, legislation, regulations and other measures to eliminate all forms of discrimination against and to ensure the full enjoyment of all human rights and fundamental freedoms by people living with HIV/AIDS and members of vulnerable groups, in particular to ensure their access to, inter alia, education, inheritance, employment, health care, social and health services, prevention, support and treatment, information and legal

protection, while respecting their privacy and confidentiality; and develop strategies to combat stigma and social exclusion connected with the epidemic;

59. By 2005, bearing in mind the context and character of the epidemic and that, globally, women and girls are disproportionately affected by HIV/AIDS, develop and accelerate the implementation of national strategies that promote the advancement of women and women's full enjoyment of all human rights; promote shared responsibility of men and women to ensure safe sex; and empower women to have control over and decide freely and responsibly on matters related to their sexuality to increase their ability to protect themselves from HIV infection;

60. By 2005, implement measures to increase capacities of women and adolescent girls to protect themselves from the risk of HIV infection, principally through the provision of health care and health services, including for sexual and reproductive health, and through prevention education that promotes gender equality within a culturally and gender-sensitive framework;

61. By 2005, ensure development and accelerated implementation of national strategies for women's empowerment, the promotion and protection of women's full enjoyment of all human rights and reduction of their vulnerability to HIV/AIDS through the elimination of all forms of discrimination, as well as all forms of violence against women and girls, including harmful traditional and customary practices, abuse, rape and other forms of sexual violence, battering and trafficking in women and girls;

Reducing vulnerability

The vulnerable must be given priority in the response

Empowering women is essential for reducing vulnerability
62. By 2003, in order to complement prevention programmes that address activities which place individuals at risk of HIV infection, such as risky and unsafe sexual behaviour and injecting drug use, have in place in all countries strategies, policies and programmes that identify and begin to address those factors that make individuals particularly vulnerable to HIV infection, including underdevelopment, economic insecurity, poverty, lack of empowerment of women, lack of education, social exclusion, illiteracy, discrimination, lack of information and/or commodities for self-protection, and all types of sexual exploitation of women, girls and boys, including for commercial reasons. Such strategies, policies and programmes should address the gender dimension of the epidemic, specify the action that will be taken to address vulnerability and set targets for achievement;

63. By 2003, develop and/or strengthen strategies, policies and programmes which recognize the importance of the family in reducing vulnerability, inter alia, in educating and guiding children and take account of cultural, religious and ethical factors, to reduce the vulnerability of children and young people by ensuring access of both girls and boys to primary and secondary education, including HIV/AIDS in curricula for adolescents; ensuring safe and secure environments, especially for young girls; expanding good-quality, youth-friendly information and sexual health education and counselling services; strengthening reproductive and sexual health programmes; and involving families and young people in planning, implementing and evaluating HIV/AIDS prevention and care programmes, to the extent possible;

64. By 2003, develop and/or strengthen national strategies, policies and programmes, supported by regional and international initiatives, as appropriate, through a participatory approach, to promote and protect the health of those identifiable groups which currently have high or increasing rates of HIV infection or which public health information indicates are at greatest risk of and most vulnerable to new infection as indicated by such factors as the local history of the epidemic, poverty, sexual practices, drug-using behaviour, livelihood, institutional location, disrupted social structures and population movements, forced or otherwise;

Children orphaned and made vulnerable by HIV/AIDS

Children orphaned and affected by HIV/AIDS need special assistance
65. By 2003, develop and by 2005 implement national policies and strategies to build and strengthen governmental, family and community capacities to provide a supportive environment for orphans and girls and boys infected and affected by HIV/AIDS, including by providing appropriate counselling and psychosocial support, ensuring their enrolment in school and access to shelter, good nutrition and health and social services on an equal basis with other children; and protect orphans and vulnerable children from all forms of abuse, violence, exploitation, discrimination, trafficking and loss of inheritance;

66. Ensure non-discrimination and full and equal enjoyment of all human rights through the promotion of an active and visible policy of de-stigmatization of children orphaned and made vulnerable by HIV/AIDS;

67. Urge the international community, particularly donor countries, civil society, as well as the private sector, to complement effectively national programmes to support programmes for children orphaned or made vulnerable by HIV/AIDS in affected regions and in countries at high risk and to direct special assistance to sub-Saharan Africa;

Alleviating social and economic impact

To address HIV/AIDS is to invest in sustainable development
68. By 2003, evaluate the economic and social impact of the HIV/AIDS epidemic and develop multisectoral strategies to address the impact at the individual, family, community and national levels; develop and accelerate the implementation of national poverty eradication strategies to address the impact of HIV/AIDS on household income, livelihoods and access to basic social services, with special focus on individuals, families and communities severely affected by the epidemic; review the social and economic impact of HIV/AIDS at all levels of society, especially on women and the elderly, particularly in their role as caregivers, and in families affected by HIV/AIDS, and address their special needs; and adjust and adapt economic and social development policies, including social protection policies, to address the impact of HIV/AIDS on economic growth, provision of essential economic services, labour productivity, government revenues, and deficit-creating pressures on public resources;

69. By 2003, develop a national legal and policy framework that protects in the workplace the rights and dignity of persons living with and affected by HIV/AIDS and those at the greatest risk of HIV/AIDS, in consultation with representatives of employers and workers, taking account of established international guidelines on HIV/AIDS in the workplace;

Research and development

With no cure for HIV/AIDS yet found, further research and development is crucial

70. Increase investment in and accelerate research on the development of HIV vaccines, while building national research capacity, especially in developing countries, and especially for viral strains prevalent in highly affected regions; in addition, support and encourage increased national and international investment in HIV/AIDS-related research and development, including biomedical, operations, social, cultural and behavioural research and in traditional medicine to improve prevention and therapeutic approaches; accelerate access to prevention, care and treatment and care technologies for HIV/AIDS (and its associated opportunistic infections and malignancies and sexually transmitted diseases), including female-controlled methods and microbicides, and in particular, appropriate, safe and affordable HIV vaccines and their delivery, and to diagnostics, tests and methods to prevent mother-to-child transmission; improve our understanding of factors which influence the epidemic and actions which address it, inter alia, through increased funding and public/private partnerships; and create a conducive environment for research and ensure that it is based on the highest ethical standards;

71. Support and encourage the development of national and international research infrastructures, laboratory capacity, improved surveillance systems, data collection, processing and dissemination, and the training of basic and clinical researchers, social scientists, health-care providers and technicians, with a focus on the countries most affected by HIV/AIDS, particularly developing countries and those countries experiencing or at risk of a rapid expansion of the epidemic;

72. Develop and evaluate suitable approaches for monitoring treatment efficacy, toxicity, side effects, drug interactions and drug resistance, and develop methodologies to monitor the impact of treatment on HIV transmission and risk behaviours;

73. Strengthen international and regional cooperation, in particular North-South, South-South and triangular cooperation, related to the transfer of relevant technologies suitable to the environment in the prevention and care of HIV/AIDS, the exchange of experiences and best practices, researchers and research findings and strengthen the role of UNAIDS in this process. In this context, encourage ownership of the end results of these cooperative research findings and technologies by all parties to the research, reflecting their relevant contribution and dependent upon their providing legal protection to such findings; and affirm that all such research should be free from bias;

74. By 2003, ensure that all research protocols for the investigation of HIV-related treatment, including anti-retroviral therapies and vaccines, based on international guidelines and best practices, are evaluated by independent committees of ethics, in which persons living with HIV/AIDS and caregivers for anti-retroviral therapy participate;

HIV/AIDS in conflict and disaster-affected regions

Conflicts and disasters contribute to the spread of HIV/AIDS

75. By 2003, develop and begin to implement national strategies that incorporate HIV/AIDS awareness, prevention, care and treatment elements into programmes or actions that respond to emergency situations, recognizing that populations destabilized by armed conflict, humanitarian emergencies and natural disasters, including refugees, internally displaced persons, and in particular women and children, are at increased risk of exposure to HIV infection; and, where appropriate, factor HIV/AIDS components into international assistance programmes;

76. Call on all United Nations agencies, regional and international organizations, as well as nongovernmental organizations involved with the provision and delivery of international assistance to countries and regions affected by conflicts, humanitarian crises or natural disasters, to incorporate as a matter of urgency HIV/AIDS prevention, care and awareness elements into their plans and programmes and provide HIV/AIDS awareness and training to their personnel;

77. By 2003, have in place national strategies to address the spread of HIV among national uniformed services, where this is required, including armed forces and civil defence forces, and consider ways of using personnel from these services who are educated and trained in HIV/AIDS awareness and prevention to assist with HIV/AIDS awareness and prevention activities, including participation in emergency, humanitarian, disaster relief and rehabilitation assistance;

78. By 2003, ensure the inclusion of HIV/AIDS awareness and training, including a gender component, into guidelines designed for use by defence personnel and other personnel involved in international peacekeeping operations, while also continuing with ongoing education and prevention efforts, including pre-deployment orientation, for these personnel;

Resources

The HIV/AIDS challenge cannot be met without new, additional and sustained resources

79. Ensure that the resources provided for the global response to address HIV/AIDS are substantial, sustained and geared towards achieving results;

80. By 2005, through a series of incremental steps, reach an overall target of annual expenditure on the epidemic of between 7 and 10 billion United States dollars in low- and middle-income countries and those countries experiencing or at risk of experiencing rapid expansion for prevention, care, treatment, support and mitigation of the impact of HIV/AIDS, and take measures to ensure that the resources needed are made available, particularly from donor countries and also from national budgets, bearing in mind that resources of the most affected countries are seriously limited;

81. Call on the international community, where possible, to provide assistance for HIV/AIDS prevention, care and treatment in developing countries on a grant basis;

82. Increase and prioritize national budgetary allocations for HIV/AIDS programmes as required, and en-

sure that adequate allocations are made by all ministries and other relevant stakeholders;

83. Urge the developed countries that have not done so to strive to meet the targets of 0.7 per cent of their gross national product for overall official development assistance and the targets of earmarking 0.15 per cent to 0.20 per cent of gross national product as official development assistance for least developed countries as agreed, as soon as possible, taking into account the urgency and gravity of the HIV/AIDS epidemic;

84. Urge the international community to complement and supplement efforts of developing countries that commit increased national funds to fight the HIV/AIDS epidemic through increased international development assistance, particularly those countries most affected by HIV/AIDS, particularly in Africa, especially in sub-Saharan Africa, the Caribbean, countries at high risk of expansion of the HIV/AIDS epidemic and other affected regions whose resources to deal with the epidemic are seriously limited;

85. Integrate HIV/AIDS actions in development assistance programmes and poverty eradication strategies as appropriate, and encourage the most effective and transparent use of all resources allocated;

86. Call on the international community, and invite civil society and the private sector to take appropriate measures to help to alleviate the social and economic impact of HIV/AIDS in the most affected developing countries;

87. Without further delay, implement the enhanced Heavily Indebted Poor Country (HIPC) Initiative and agree to cancel all bilateral official debts of HIPC countries as soon as possible, especially those most affected by HIV/AIDS, in return for demonstrable commitments by them to poverty eradication, and urge the use of debt service savings to finance poverty eradication programmes, particularly for prevention, treatment, care and support for HIV/AIDS and other infections;

88. Call for speedy and concerted action to address effectively the debt problems of least developed countries, low-income developing countries, and middle-income developing countries, particularly those affected by HIV/AIDS, in a comprehensive, equitable, development-oriented and durable way through various national and international measures designed to make their debt sustainable in the long term and thereby to improve their capacity to deal with the HIV/AIDS epidemic, including, as appropriate, existing orderly mechanisms for debt reduction, such as debt swaps for projects aimed at the prevention, care and treatment of HIV/AIDS;

89. Encourage increased investment in HIV/AIDS-related research nationally, regionally and internationally, in particular for the development of sustainable and affordable prevention technologies, such as vaccines and microbicides, and encourage the proactive preparation of financial and logistic plans to facilitate rapid access to vaccines when they become available;

90. Support the establishment, on an urgent basis, of a global HIV/AIDS and health fund to finance an urgent and expanded response to the epidemic based on an integrated approach to prevention, care, support and treatment and to assist Governments, inter alia, in their efforts to combat HIV/AIDS with due priority to the most affected countries, notably in sub-Saharan Africa and the Caribbean, and to those countries at high risk, and mobilize contributions to the fund from public and private sources with a special appeal to donor countries, foundations, the business community, including pharmaceutical companies, the private sector, philanthropists and wealthy individuals;

91. By 2002, launch a worldwide fund-raising campaign aimed at the general public as well as the private sector, conducted by UNAIDS with the support and collaboration of interested partners at all levels, to contribute to the global HIV/AIDS and health fund;

92. Direct increased funding to national, regional and subregional commissions and organizations to enable them to assist Governments at the national, regional and subregional level in their efforts to respond to the crisis;

93. Provide the UNAIDS co-sponsoring agencies and the UNAIDS secretariat with the resources needed to work with countries in support of the goals of the present Declaration;

Follow-up

Maintaining the momentum and monitoring progress are essential

At the national level

94. Conduct national periodic reviews with the participation of civil society, particularly people living with HIV/AIDS, vulnerable groups and caregivers, of progress achieved in realizing these commitments, identify problems and obstacles to achieving progress, and ensure wide dissemination of the results of these reviews;

95. Develop appropriate monitoring and evaluation mechanisms to assist with follow-up in measuring and assessing progress, and develop appropriate monitoring and evaluation instruments, with adequate epidemiological data;

96. By 2003, establish or strengthen effective monitoring systems, where appropriate, for the promotion and protection of human rights of people living with HIV/AIDS;

At the regional level

97. Include HIV/AIDS and related public health concerns, as appropriate, on the agenda of regional meetings at the ministerial and head of State and Government level;

98. Support data collection and processing to facilitate periodic reviews by regional commissions and/or regional organizations of progress in implementing regional strategies and addressing regional priorities, and ensure wide dissemination of the results of these reviews;

99. Encourage the exchange between countries of information and experiences in implementing the measures and commitments contained in the present Declaration, and in particular facilitate intensified South-South and triangular cooperation;

At the global level

100. Devote sufficient time and at least one full day of the annual session of the General Assembly to review and debate a report of the Secretary-General on progress achieved in realizing the commitments set out in the present Declaration, with a view to identifying

problems and constraints and making recommendations on action needed to make further progress;

101. Ensure that HIV/AIDS issues are included on the agenda of all appropriate United Nations conferences and meetings;

102. Support initiatives to convene conferences, seminars, workshops, training programmes and courses to follow up issues raised in the present Declaration, and in this regard encourage participation in and wide dissemination of the outcomes of the forthcoming Dakar Conference on access to care for HIV infection; the Sixth International Congress on AIDS in Asia and the Pacific; the Twelfth International Conference on AIDS and Sexually Transmitted Infections in Africa; the Fourteenth International Conference on AIDS, Barcelona, Spain; the Tenth International Conference on People Living with HIV/AIDS, Port-of-Spain; the Second Forum and Third Conference of the Horizontal Technical Cooperation Group on HIV/AIDS and Sexually Transmitted Infections in Latin America and the Caribbean, Havana; the Fifth International Conference on Home and Community Care for Persons Living with HIV/AIDS, Chiang Mai, Thailand;

103. Explore, with a view to improving equity in access to essential drugs, the feasibility of developing and implementing, in collaboration with non-governmental organizations and other concerned partners, systems for the voluntary monitoring and reporting of global drug prices;

We recognize and express our appreciation to those who have led the effort to raise awareness of the HIV/AIDS epidemic and to deal with its complex challenges;

We look forward to strong leadership by Governments and concerted efforts with the full and active participation of the United Nations, the entire multilateral system, civil society, the business community and private sector;

And finally, we call on all countries to take the necessary steps to implement the present Declaration, in strengthened partnership and cooperation with other multilateral and bilateral partners and with civil society.

Preparatory process

The General Assembly, acting as the preparatory committee for the special session, held open-ended informal consultations on the report of the Secretary-General (see below) and on the issues for consideration in the Declaration of Commitment. The Joint United Nations Programme on HIV/AIDS (UNAIDS) served as the substantive secretariat of the session.

Report of Secretary-General. In response to General Assembly resolution 55/13 [YUN 2000, p. 1167], the Secretary-General, in a report of 16 February [A/55/779], examined the spread of the epidemic and reviewed its impacts—demographic, social, economic and from the standpoint of the security of people and nations. The report outlined key lessons learned and successes achieved, and assessed the response to the epidemic through leadership, coordination and the need for adequate resources. Action by Govern-

ments to respond to critical challenges to combat HIV/AIDS were described. Annexed to the report were the goals set by global conferences in 1999 and 2000 and their follow-up processes, and the UN system response to HIV/AIDS.

Other action. Prior to the special session, Member States and various regional organizations held meetings and adopted declarations and calls for action. The second African Development Forum adopted the African Consensus and Plan of Action: Leadership to overcome HIV/AIDS (Addis Ababa, Ethiopia, 3-7 December 2000) [A/55/774]; the heads of State and Government of the Caribbean, on 14 February in Bridgetown, Barbados, signed the Pan-Caribbean Partnership against HIV/AIDS; on 25 April [E/2001/39], the Economic and Social Commission for Asia and the Pacific adopted a regional call for action to fight HIV/AIDS; the Organization of African Unity (OAU) (Abuja, Nigeria, 26-27 April) adopted the Abuja Declaration and Framework for Action for the fight against HIV/AIDS, tuberculosis and other related infectious diseases; Sweden, on 17 May [A/55/946], drew the Assembly's attention to a communication of 21 February from the Commission of the European Communities to the Council of the European Union (EU) and the European Parliament on the Programme for Action: Accelerated action on HIV/AIDS, malaria and tuberculosis in the context of poverty reduction, and on the same date [A/55/945] to the Programme as published by the EU; the Central Asian Conference on HIV/AIDS (Almaty, Kazakhstan, 16-18 May), attended by the representatives of Kazakhstan, Kyrgyzstan, Tajikistan and Uzbekistan, declared commitments to scale up national responses to HIV/AIDS; the Russian Federation, on behalf of members of the Commonwealth of Independent States (CIS), transmitted, on 22 June [A/S-26/4], an appeal of the Council on cooperation in the field of health of CIS members (Baku, Azerbaijan, 19 June); and Bolivia, on behalf of the Andean Community, transmitted the text of a political declaration (Valencia, Venezuela, 24 June) [A/S-26/6], expressing concern over the worldwide consequences of HIV/AIDS.

GENERAL ASSEMBLY ACTION

On 22 February [meeting 92], the General Assembly adopted **resolution 55/242** [draft: A/55/L.76] without vote [agenda item 179].

Organizational arrangements for the special session of the General Assembly on HIV/AIDS and its preparatory process

The General Assembly,

Recalling its resolution 54/283 of 5 September 2000, in which it decided, inter alia, to convene in 2001 a special session of the General Assembly for a duration of three days to review and address the problem of human immunodeficiency virus/acquired immunodeficiency syndrome (HIV/AIDS) in all its aspects and to coordinate and intensify international efforts to combat it,

Recalling also its resolution 55/13 of 3 November 2000, in which it decided, inter alia, to convene, as a matter of urgency, a special session of the General Assembly, from 25 to 27 June 2001, to review and address the problem of HIV/AIDS in all its aspects, as well as to secure a global commitment to enhancing coordination and intensification of national, regional and international efforts to combat it in a comprehensive manner,

Recalling further that, in its resolution 55/13, the General Assembly called for a comprehensive public information programme to raise global HIV/AIDS awareness while also building broad international support for the special session and its goals, and welcoming in this connection the offer of the President of the General Assembly to organize a number of side events to contribute to achieving these objectives and his intention to brief Member States during the second week of the open-ended informal consultations of the plenary on the results of these events,

Taking into account the further decisions taken by the General Assembly in its resolution 55/13 concerning the special session and its preparatory process,

Taking into account also the unique and exceptional nature of the special session and its preparatory process,

1. *Decides* that the special session shall be referred to as the "special session of the General Assembly on HIV/AIDS";

2. *Also decides* to adopt the organizational arrangements contained in the annex to the present resolution.

ANNEX

Organizational arrangements for the special session of the General Assembly on HIV/AIDS and its preparatory process

President

1. The special session shall take place under the presidency of the President of the fifty-fifth regular session of the General Assembly.

Vice-Presidents

2. The Vice-Presidents of the special session shall be the same as those of the fifty-fifth regular session of the General Assembly.

Credentials Committee

3. The Credentials Committee of the special session shall have the same membership as the Credentials Committee of the fifty-fifth regular session of the General Assembly.

General Committee

4. The General Committee shall consist of the President and the 21 Vice-Presidents of the special session, the Chairpersons of the six Main Committees of the fifty-fifth regular session of the General Assembly, the two facilitators and the chairpersons of the round tables.

Rules of procedure

5. The rules of procedure of the General Assembly shall apply to the special session.

Level of representation

6. In accordance with resolution 55/13, Member States and observers are invited to be represented at the special session at the highest political level.

Delegations to the special session

7. Member States and observers are encouraged to include representatives of civil society actors, people living with HIV/AIDS or representatives of their associations, as well as young people's organizations, and representatives of the business and private sector in their national delegations to the special session.

Accreditation of civil society actors

8. Pursuant to paragraph 13 of resolution 55/13, accreditation of civil society actors to the preparatory activities and the special session shall be open to:

(a) Non-governmental organizations which enjoy consultative status in accordance with Economic and Social Council resolution 1996/31 of 25 July 1996;

(b) Non-governmental organizations which are members of the Programme Coordinating Board of the Joint United Nations Programme on HIV/AIDS (UNAIDS);

(c) Those which are approved from the list as defined in resolution 55/13 of associations of people living with HIV/AIDS, non-governmental organizations and members of the business sector, including pharmaceutical companies, prepared by the Executive Director of UNAIDS, along with relevant background information, made available to Member States for consideration on a non-objection basis for decision by the General Assembly in a timely manner. A complementary list, prepared by the Executive Director of UNAIDS, along with relevant background information, made available to Member States, shall be submitted to Member States no later than 1 April 2001 for consideration by Member States, on a non-objection basis for decision by the Assembly in a timely manner.

Schedule of plenary meetings

9. The special session shall consist of a total of eight plenary meetings, as follows:

Monday, 25 June 2001, from 9 a.m. to 1 p.m., from 3 to 6 p.m. and from 7 to 9 p.m.
Tuesday, 26 June 2001, from 9 a.m. to 1 p.m., from 3 to 6 p.m. and from 7 to 9 p.m.
Wednesday, 27 June 2001, from 9 a.m. to 1 p.m. and from 3 to 6 p.m.

The last hour of the afternoon meeting on Wednesday will be devoted to the adoption of the outcome document and the closing of the special session, following oral presentations by the chairpersons of the four round tables of the summaries of the discussions.

Debate in the plenary of the special session

10. Statements in the debate in the plenary of the special session shall be limited to five minutes.

11. The list of speakers for the debate in plenary shall be established by a drawing of lots on the basis of the eight meetings.

12. Member States, the Holy See and Switzerland, in their capacity as observer States, and Palestine, in its capacity as observer, shall be invited to participate in the drawing of lots.

13. The order of precedence for the list of speakers for the debate in plenary will be as follows: (a) heads of State/heads of Government; (b) Vice-Presidents/

Crown Princes or Princesses; *(c)* Deputy Prime Ministers; *(d)* Ministers; *(e)* Vice-Ministers; *(f)* heads of delegations; and *(g)* the highest-ranking official of the delegations of the Holy See and Switzerland, in their capacity as observer States, and of Palestine, in its capacity as observer.

Participation of speakers other than Member States in the debate in the plenary of the special session

14.   Observers may make statements in the debate in plenary:

(a) A number of organizations and entities have received a standing invitation to participate as observers in the sessions and the work of the General Assembly;

(b) In accordance with resolution 55/13, States members of the specialized agencies that are not members of the United Nations may participate in the special session in the capacity of observers.

15.   Heads of entities of the United Nations system, including programmes, funds, the specialized agencies and the regional commissions, may make statements in the debate in plenary. The Executive Director of UNAIDS will be given the opportunity to make a statement early in the debate in plenary.

16.   Given the availability of time, a limited number of accredited civil society actors may make statements in the debate in plenary. The President of the General Assembly is requested, following appropriate consultations with Member States, to present the list of selected accredited civil society actors to Member States for consideration on a non-objection basis for final decision by the Assembly. The President is also requested to ensure that such selection is made on an equal and transparent basis, taking into account the principle of equitable geographical representation, relevant expertise and a wide variety of perspectives.

Round tables

17.   Pursuant to resolution 55/13, four interactive round tables shall be held, as follows:

Round table 1:   Monday, 25 June 2001,
              from 3 to 6 p.m.
Round table 2:   Tuesday, 26 June 2001,
              from 10 a.m. to 1 p.m.
Round table 3:   Tuesday, 26 June 2001,
              from 3 to 6 p.m.
Round table 4:   Wednesday, 27 June 2001,
              from 10 a.m. to 1 p.m.

18.   The chairpersons of the four round tables shall be from the four regional groups not represented by the President of the General Assembly. The four chairpersons shall be selected by their respective regional groups. The chairpersons of the round tables will present orally their summaries of the discussions, during the concluding plenary meeting of the special session.

19.   A number of issues to be discussed in the round tables are outlined in resolution 55/13. AIDS in Africa will be a cross-cutting theme in all four round tables. The overall themes to be discussed in the round tables will be the following:

Round table 1
HIV/AIDS prevention and care
Round table 2
HIV/AIDS and human rights

Round table 3
The social and economic impact of the epidemic and the strengthening of national capacities to combat HIV/AIDS
Round table 4
International funding and cooperation to address the challenges of the HIV/AIDS epidemic

20.   The round tables shall be open to Member States, observers, as well as entities of the United Nations system and accredited civil society actors.

21.   In order to ensure interactive and substantive discussions of high quality, participation in each round table shall be limited to a maximum of 65 participants, of which at least 48 will be representatives of Member States. In addition, each round table shall include a maximum of 17 participants, representing observers, entities of the United Nations system and accredited civil society actors.

22.   Following the selection of the chairpersons of the round tables, each regional group should determine which of its members will participate in each round table, ensuring that equitable geographical distribution will be maintained, allowing for some flexibility, and taking into account the importance of ensuring a mix of countries highly affected by the epidemic as well as countries that are less affected.

23.   Thus, in order to allow for some flexibility, for each round table the maximum number of participants from each regional group will be as follows:

(a) African States: 14 Member States;
(b) Asian States: 14 Member States;
(c) Eastern European States: six Member States;
(d) Latin American and Caribbean States: nine Member States;
(e) Western European and other States: eight Member States.

24.   The chairpersons of the regional groups will communicate to the President of the General Assembly the list of countries from their respective regions that will participate in each round table.

25.   Member States that are not members of any of the regional groups may participate in different round tables, to be determined in consultation with the President of the General Assembly.

26.   Each representative of a Member State attending the round tables may be accompanied by two advisers.

27.   The Holy See and Switzerland, in their capacity as observer States, and Palestine, in its capacity as observer, may also participate in different round tables, to be determined in consultation with the President of the General Assembly.

28.   A limited number of observers as defined in paragraph 14 above may also participate in each round table.

29.   Entities of the United Nations system with specific expertise in areas related to the themes of the round tables will be invited to participate in the round tables. The UNAIDS secretariat will provide to the President of the General Assembly a list of those entities that will participate in each round table.

30.   Accredited civil society actors with specific expertise in areas related to the themes of the round tables will also be invited to participate in the round tables. The President of the General Assembly is requested to conduct appropriate consultations with

Member States, and also with accredited civil society actors, before presenting a list of selected accredited civil society actors that may participate in each round table to Member States, in the last week of May 2001, for consideration on a non-objection basis for final decision by the General Assembly. When selecting civil society actors, due consideration shall be given to the principles of equitable geographical representation and gender, as well as to an adequate mix of national, regional and international civil society actors, and to the need to ensure that a variety of perspectives are represented.

31. The list of participants of each round table will be made available as soon as possible.

32. The round tables shall be closed to the general public. Representatives of Member States, observers, entities of the United Nations system and accredited civil society actors, as well as representatives of accredited media, will be able to follow the proceedings of the round tables via a closed-circuit television in an overflow room.

Outcome document of the special session

33. The General Assembly at its special session shall consider and adopt a declaration of commitment, taking into account the report of the Secretary-General and other relevant documents, as may be deemed necessary.

Preparatory process of the special session

34. During the preparatory process, one week, from 26 February to 2 March 2001, will be devoted to the discussion on the report of the Secretary-General and to open-ended informal consultations of the plenary.

35. A limited number of accredited civil society actors may make statements during the discussion devoted to the report of the Secretary-General, given the availability of time, and ensuring that equitable geographical representation and a wide variety of perspectives are represented.

36. The first draft outline of the declaration of commitment shall be made available by 12 March 2001, and a meeting of the open-ended informal consultations of the plenary shall be held at that time for its introduction.

37. During a second week, from 21 to 25 May 2001, the open-ended informal consultations of the plenary shall focus on the draft declaration of commitment.

38. The provisions outlined above shall in no way create a precedent for other special sessions of the General Assembly.

By **resolution 55/256** of 31 May, the Assembly adopted the special session's provisional agenda.

In a series of decisions, the Assembly took action regarding the accreditation of civil society organizations not in consultative status with the Economic and Social Council or not members of the Programme Coordinating Board of UNAIDS (see below) to participate in the special session (**decision 55/460 A** of 26 February, **decision 55/460 B** of 18 May, **decision 55/460 C** of 22 June).

Joint UN programme on HIV/AIDS

UNAIDS, which became fully operational in 1996 [YUN 1996, p. 1121], continued to coordinate UN activities for AIDS prevention and control. The Programme, which served as the main advocate for global action on HIV/AIDS, had seven co-sponsors: the United Nations Development Programme (UNDP), the United Nations Children's Fund (UNICEF), the United Nations Educational, Scientific and Cultural Organization (UNESCO), the United Nations International Drug Control Programme (UNDCP), the United Nations Population Fund (UNFPA), the World Bank and the World Health Organization (WHO). UNAIDS was mandated to lead, strengthen and support an expanded response to the epidemic, mainly through facilitation and coordination, best practice development and advocacy.

According to UNAIDS, at the end of 2001, an estimated 40 million people were living with HIV/AIDS, of whom about one third were between the ages of 15 and 24. During the year, some 5 million people became infected globally, 800,000 of them children. Sub-Saharan Africa remained the worst-affected region, with about 3.4 million new infections occurring in 2001, bringing to 28.1 million the total number of people living with HIV/AIDS; in 2001, AIDS killed 2.3 million people in Africa. In Asia and the Pacific, 1.07 million people were newly infected, bringing to 7.1 million the total number of people living with the disease. HIV incidence was rising faster in Eastern Europe and Central Asia than anywhere else; an estimated 250,000 new infections in 2001 raised to 1 million the number of people afflicted.

Report of UNAIDS Executive Director. In response to Economic and Social Council resolution 1999/36 [YUN 1999, p. 1149], the Secretary-General, by a June note [E/2001/82], transmitted a report of the UNAIDS Executive Director, which described the status of the HIV/AIDS epidemic, the UN system support to an expanded response, the country-level response and the efforts of the UNAIDS secretariat, co-sponsors and other partners towards more effective and coordinated action.

The period under review, July 1999 to May 2001, laid the groundwork for a more mature, focused and coordinated response to the epidemic from UN system organizations and from a wider set of national and international partners. Within the United Nations, HIV/AIDS received one of the highest priorities, which was reflected by Security Council deliberations on the epidemic [YUN 2000, p. 1169] (see also p. 77), the commitment of the Secretary-General and the co-sponsors and the General Assembly's special session on HIV/

AIDS in June (see p. 1125). The UNAIDS approach to the epidemic over the biennium was multifaceted, with progress achieved in advancing the prevention and the care agendas. Effective prevention was promoted through the dissemination of information, educational programmes, and drug abuse and HIV/AIDS prevention activities. UNAIDS continued to assist Governments and civil society in developing comprehensive care plans and increasing their capacities to provide anti-retroviral drugs. With the United Nations as facilitator and partner, major research and development pharmaceutical companies and generic competition combined to make HIV drugs available, at a significantly reduced price, to a greater number of people in developing countries.

UN theme groups on HIV/AIDS demonstrated increased effectiveness in supporting national co-ordination mechanisms, broadening their scope to include such areas as advocacy, resource mobilization and facilitating exchanges of experiences within regions. The theme groups also focused on integrating HIV/AIDS into the United Nations Development Assistance Framework and other development frameworks, such as the poverty reduction strategy papers process and the common country assessments. As mainstreaming HIV/AIDS into development frameworks was one of the priorities of the UNAIDS secretariat, the secretariat, UNDCP, UNDP, UNICEF, the World Bank and WHO worked to do so by giving it a prominent place analytically and operationally. UNAIDS strategic planning development funds continued to be channelled to programmes through the UN theme groups.

The United Nations System Strategic Plan [YUN 2000, p. 1166], developed to identify strategies and partnerships necessary for UN support to countries, incorporated the plans and strategies of 29 UN organizations working on HIV/AIDS. Progress was made in developing cooperation frameworks with non-co-sponsoring organizations, including FAO, OAU and the International Labour Organization (ILO).

The report identified some of the challenges that would confront UNAIDS in the next biennium, including promoting a shift from pilot projects and small-scale interventions to more comprehensive prevention programmes; promoting expanded access to existing HIV-related commodities; further strengthening coordination at the country level; promoting the development of comprehensive care strategies; enhancing UNAIDS capacity to support policy development and coordination at all levels; expanding the participation of civil society in the response; and mobilizing the financial resources necessary to counter the epidemic.

ECONOMIC AND SOCIAL COUNCIL ACTION

On 26 July [meeting 43], the Economic and Social Council adopted **resolution 2001/23** [draft: E/2001/L.28] without vote [agenda item 7 *(c)*].

Joint United Nations Programme on HIV/AIDS (UNAIDS)

The Economic and Social Council,

Recalling its resolution 1999/36 of 28 July 1999,

Having considered the report of the Executive Director of the Joint United Nations Programme on HIV/AIDS (UNAIDS),

Expressing concern about the continued global spread of human immunodeficiency virus (HIV) and resulting increase in cases of acquired immunodeficiency syndrome (AIDS),

Recalling the HIV/AIDS goals of the United Nations Millennium Declaration of 8 September 2000,

Also recalling the successful convening of the special session of the General Assembly on HIV/AIDS from 25 to 27 June 2001, and the Declaration of Commitment on HIV/AIDS adopted at the end of the session,

Encouraged by the resolve of Governments to implement, on an urgent basis, the goals and commitments contained in the Declaration of Commitment on HIV/AIDS in order to accelerate the response to the epidemic,

1. *Urges* all the organizations and bodies of the United Nations system, in particular the co-sponsors and secretariat of the Joint United Nations Programme on HIV/AIDS (UNAIDS), to give priority to the full implementation of the Declaration of Commitment on HIV/AIDS, including through support to Governments in their expanded national responses to the epidemic;

2. *Also urges* the co-sponsors of the Programme, other participating organizations and bodies of the United Nations system and the secretariat of the Programme to refine their respective strategic objectives on HIV/AIDS in the light of the goals of the special session of the General Assembly on HIV/AIDS and to monitor progress in implementation;

3. *Calls* upon the United Nations system, in collaboration with all relevant stakeholders, to strengthen further coordinated action at the country level;

4. *Encourages* the Executive Director of the Programme to draw upon the administrative and financial support systems of all co-sponsors of the Programme, as appropriate, so as to maximize the efficiency and effectiveness of support provided by the secretariat of the Programme;

5. *Requests* the Secretary-General to transmit to the Economic and Social Council, at its substantive session of 2003, a report prepared by the Executive Director of the Programme, in collaboration with other relevant organizations and bodies of the United Nations system, which should include the progress made in developing a coordinated response by the United Nations system to the HIV/AIDS pandemic.

On 24 December, the General Assembly decided that the item "Review of the problem of human immunodeficiency virus/acquired immunodeficiency syndrome in all its aspects" should remain for consideration during its resumed fifty-sixth (2002) session (**decision 56/464**).

Security Council action. In a statement of 28 June (**S/PRST/2001/16**), the Security Council, welcoming the fact that the Declaration of Commitment contained practical measures to reduce the impact of conflict and disasters on the spread of HIV/AIDS, recognized that further efforts were necessary to do so and to develop the capacity of peacekeepers to become advocates and actors for awareness and prevention of HIV transmission. The Council encouraged continued efforts with regard to relevant training for peacekeeping, pre-deployment orientation and increased international cooperation by Member States (see p. 78).

Tobacco

A report of the Secretary-General [E/2002/44] described the global tobacco epidemic and the activities of the Ad Hoc Inter-Agency Task Force on Tobacco Control.

An estimated 1.3 billion people used tobacco worldwide by 2000, and assuming no change in global prevalence, the global number of smokers was expected to reach 1.7 billion in 2020. Most tobacco users resided in developing countries or in transitional economies. It was predicted that the total number of female smokers would rise from 257.8 million in 2000 to 324 million in 2020; most of the increase would occur in developing countries.

The Ad Hoc Inter-Agency Task Force on Tobacco Control, established in 1999 [YUN 1999, p. 1151], at its third session (8 December 2000), organized in a global videoconference format, linked together eight UN organizations, as well as the World Bank and the World Trade Organization. The session provided an update on the work of each agency related to tobacco, focused on developing a work plan for inter-agency cooperation and discussed technical cooperation in support of the framework convention on tobacco control (see below). The fourth session of the Task Force (Kobe, Japan, 5 December), comprising seven UN organizations, the World Bank and the World Customs Organization, updated smoke-free policies in the UN system and discussed the recommendations and follow-up to the International Meeting on Economic, Social and Health Issues in Tobacco Control (Kobe, 3-4 December), hosted by WHO. Experts at the meeting reviewed the ongoing UN work in the area of international tobacco control, and explored the economic transition issues relevant to the technical mandates and ongoing work of the Task Force members, particularly FAO, ILO, WHO and the World Bank. WHO and the World Bank discussed effective collaboration between the health and financial sectors for tobacco control (Malta, 5-7 September).

The report contained tables presenting tobacco use prevalence by WHO regions and levels of development for the year 2000 and the projected number of smokers in 2020 and in 2050.

On 31 May, World No Tobacco Day was observed under the theme "Second-hand smoke kills. Let's clear the air".

Framework convention

During the second session of the Intergovernmental Negotiating Body (INB) (Geneva, 30 April–5 May), responsible for negotiating the text of the WHO framework convention on tobacco control and possible related protocols, a first Chair's text was discussed and the Co-Chairs of the three INB working groups developed a compendium of all the textual proposals on the Chair's text, which were submitted by member States. At the third session (22-28 November), significant progress was made in advancing the negotiations.

Inter-agency coordination in health policy

The WHO/UNICEF/UNFPA Coordinating Committee on Health, at its third session (New York, 19-20 April) [E/ICEF/2001/11], reviewed progress made in implementing the recommendations made during its second session [YUN 1999, p. 1151], particularly in the area of advocacy, and noted that work was continuing in the areas of programme development, implementation, monitoring and evaluation. Areas under review were maternal mortality and morbidity, adolescent health and development, HIV/AIDS, immunization and coordination of follow-up to the International Conference on Population and Development [YUN 1994, p. 955]. The Committee considered sector-wide approaches for health and development, and reviewed the resolutions and decisions adopted by the three organizations.

Other diseases

Roll Back Malaria initiative

Communications. On 8 March [A/55/240], Togo, representing OAU, requested the inclusion of an additional item on the General Assembly's agenda in 2001, for the purpose of proclaiming the decade 2001-2010 the "Decade to Roll Back Malaria in Africa". Also in March [A/55/240/Add.1], Togo transmitted the Declaration and

Plan of Action on "Roll Back Malaria in Africa", adopted by the Extraordinary Summit of the Assembly of Heads of State and Government of OAU (Abuja, Nigeria, 24-25 April 2000), which had called on the United Nations to declare the decade.

Report of Secretary-General. Pursuant to Economic and Social Council resolution 1998/36 [YUN 1998, p. 1129], the Secretary-General submitted a June report [E/2001/80], prepared by WHO and other UN system entities, on progress made over the past two years regarding the Roll Back Malaria Partnership. Roll Back Malaria, launched by WHO in 1998 [YUN 1998, p. 1384], aimed at establishing sustainable capacity within communities to combat malaria and worked through global partnerships for advocacy and technical and financial assistance and through country-level partnerships to implement the strategic plans of countries.

Since January, 12 African countries had conducted national round-table meetings in order to reach agreement on a shared strategy, obtain buy-in into the strategic plan by health partners active in the country, and determine budgetary gaps and quantify the additional global resources necessary to ensure scaled-up implementation. Ghana, Uganda and the United Republic of Tanzania had shown that prioritizing Roll Back Malaria could be accomplished through a sector-wide approach to health. Eritrea had decided that rolling back malaria was the Government's primary responsibility, which had allowed the country to move towards its goal of reducing malaria mortality and morbidity by 80 per cent by 2004.

The fourth meeting of Roll Back Malaria partners, hosted by the World Bank (Washington, D.C., 18-19 April), assessed progress and agreed on priorities for malaria control for the next few years.

The report recommended that the Council call on donors that had pledged support to Roll Back Malaria to initiate urgent disbursement procedures in favour of the high-quality country strategic plans that had been developed in many malaria-affected countries. It proposed that the Council might wish to endorse the concept of a global fund for HIV/AIDS and health and urge that the fund be capitalized in order to contribute to the estimated $1.5 billion per year needed for malaria control during the rest of the decade.

On 26 July, the Council took note of the report (**decision 2001/303**).

On 7 September [meeting 111], the General Assembly adopted **resolution 55/284** [draft: A/55/ L.84/Rev.1 & Rev.1/Add.1] without vote [agenda item 186].

2001-2010: Decade to Roll Back Malaria in Developing Countries, Particularly in Africa

The General Assembly,

Recalling its resolutions 49/135 of 19 December 1994 and 50/128 of 20 December 1995 concerning the struggle against malaria in the developing countries, particularly in Africa,

Bearing in mind the relevant resolutions of the Economic and Social Council relating to the struggle against malaria and diarrhoeal diseases, in particular its resolution 1998/36 of 30 July 1998,

Acknowledging that it is important and necessary for countries where malaria is endemic to adopt appropriate strategies to combat malaria, one of the most deadly of all tropical diseases, which annually causes approximately one million deaths in Africa, where nine out of every ten cases of malaria occur,

Taking note of the declarations and decisions on health issues adopted by the Organization of African Unity, in particular the declaration and plan of action on the "Roll Back Malaria" initiative adopted at the Extraordinary Summit of Heads of State and Government of the Organization of African Unity, held in Abuja on 24 and 25 April 2000, as well as decision AHG/Dec.155(XXXVI) concerning the implementation of that declaration and plan of action, adopted by the Assembly of Heads of State and Government of the Organization of African Unity at its thirty-sixth ordinary session, held in Lomé from 10 to 12 July 2000,

Acknowledging the efforts of the World Health Organization and other partners to fight malaria over the years, including the launching of the Roll Back Malaria Partnership in 1998,

Recognizing that malaria-related ill health and deaths throughout the world can be eliminated with political commitment and commensurate resources if the public is educated and sensitized about malaria and appropriate health services are made available in countries where the disease is endemic,

Emphasizing that the international community has an essential role to play in strengthening the support and assistance provided to developing countries, particularly African countries, in their efforts to reduce the incidence of malaria and mitigate its negative effects,

Emphasizing also the importance of implementing the United Nations Millennium Declaration, and welcoming, in this connection, the commitments of Member States to respond to the specific needs of Africa,

1. *Proclaims* the period 2001-2010 the Decade to Roll Back Malaria in Developing Countries, Particularly in Africa;

2. *Takes note with satisfaction* of the continuing efforts of developing countries, particularly those in African countries, to combat malaria through the formulation of plans and strategies at the national, regional and continental levels, despite their limited financial, technical and human resources;

3. *Stresses* that the proclamation of the Decade will stimulate the efforts of African countries and the international community not only to roll back malaria

worldwide, in particular in Africa where the burden is heaviest, but also to prevent its spread to previously malaria-free areas;

4. *Appeals* to the international community, United Nations bodies, international and regional organizations and non-governmental organizations to allocate substantial new and additional resources, including through the new global fund to fight HIV/AIDS, malaria and tuberculosis, launched by the Group of Eight Major Industrialized Countries at its Genoa Summit, held from 20 to 22 July 2001, and by the Secretary-General, for developing countries, particularly in Africa, with a view to enabling them to implement fully the plan of action adopted in Abuja for the "Roll Back Malaria" initiative;

5. *Commends* the World Health Organization and its partners, and urges them to provide the necessary support for its ongoing measures to combat malaria in developing countries, particularly in Africa, and to provide the assistance necessary for African States to meet their objectives;

6. *Calls* for joint comprehensive efforts between Africa and the international community to ensure that by 2005 the following targets are achieved:

(a) At least 60 per cent of those at risk for malaria, particularly pregnant women and children under five years of age, shall benefit from the most suitable combination of personal and community protective measures, such as insecticide-treated bednets and other interventions that are accessible and affordable, to prevent infection and suffering;

(b) At least 60 per cent of all pregnant women who are at risk for malaria, especially those in their first pregnancies, shall have access to chemoprophylaxis or presumptive intermittent treatment;

(c) At least 60 per cent of those suffering from malaria shall have prompt access to and shall be able to use correct, affordable and appropriate treatment within twenty-four hours of the onset of symptoms;

7. *Reiterates* the need to ensure that measures to reduce malaria transmission risks, including environmental management, are included in development planning and activities;

8. *Requests* the Secretary-General, acting in close collaboration with the Director-General of the World Health Organization, developing countries and regional organizations, including the Organization of African Unity, to conduct in 2005 an evaluation of the measures taken and progress made towards the achievement of the mid-term targets, the means of implementation provided by the international community in this regard and the overall goals of the Decade, and to report thereon to the General Assembly at its sixtieth session;

9. *Also requests* the Secretary-General to report to it at its fifty-seventh session on the implementation of the present resolution.

Trypanosomiasis

African animal trypanosomiasis, carried by the tsetse fly, remained a major constraint to food security in Africa. The vector, which also transmitted the parasites responsible for human sleeping sickness, killed livestock, depriving

farmers of the use of the animals for draft power for ploughing. It was found only in Africa.

Communication. The Sudan, as Chairman of the African Group, transmitted the decisions and declarations adopted by the OAU Assembly of Heads of State and Government at its thirty-seventh ordinary session and fifth ordinary session of the African Economic Community (Lusaka, Zambia, 9-11 July) [A/56/457], among them a decision on the implementation of the plan of action for the eradication of tsetse flies in Africa.

Report of Secretary-General. As part of discussions during the high-level segment of the Economic and Social Council on the role of the UN system in supporting the efforts of African countries to achieve sustainable development, the Council considered a June report of the Secretary-General [E/2001/83]. He observed that the gains made in human development in the 1960s and the 1970s were being reversed by various infectious diseases. The activities of the International Atomic Energy Agency and FAO to create tsetse-free zones in sub-Saharan Africa contributed to increasing agricultural productivity in rural areas. Support to control the vector would contribute to reducing rural poverty. The Secretary-General recommended the urgent mobilization of resources to strengthen health systems in the context of a broad development approach where health sector reforms went hand in hand with poverty reduction and community participation.

ECONOMIC AND SOCIAL COUNCIL ACTION

On 26 July [meeting 43], the Economic and Social Council adopted **resolution 2001/26** [draft: E/2001/L.34] without vote [agenda item 7 (g)].

Implementation of the plan of action for the eradication of tsetse flies from Africa

The Economic and Social Council,

Having considered the report of the Secretary-General on the role of the United Nations system in supporting the efforts of African countries to achieve sustainable development,

Taking note with appreciation of the ongoing efforts to fight sleeping sickness, in particular the programme for the surveillance and control of African trypanosomiasis,

1. *Calls attention* to the seriousness of the tsetse and trypanosomiasis problem and its increasing significance as a constraint to sustainable development in Africa and the alleviation of rural poverty;

2. *Takes note* of the decision of the Assembly of Heads of State and Government of the Organization of African Unity to free Africa of tsetse flies;

3. *Welcomes* the Organization of African Unity plan of action for a campaign to achieve the goal of the Pan-African Tsetse and Trypanosomiasis Eradication Campaign initiative;

4. *Calls upon* all Member States, organizations of the United Nations system and the international community to support fully this initiative.

Food and agriculture

Food aid

World Food Programme

In July, the Economic and Social Council examined two reports pertaining to the work of the World Food Programme (WFP): the annual report of the Executive Director of WFP for 2000 [E/2001/47] and a report of the WFP Executive Board containing the decisions and recommendations of its 2000 sessions [E/2001/36]. The Council, by **decision 2001/226** of 10 July, took note of the two reports.

The WFP Executive Board decided on organizational and programme matters and approved a number of projects at its 2001 sessions, all held in Rome, Italy: first regular session (13-16 February), second regular session (16-18 May), annual session (21-24 May) and third regular session (22-25 October). On 25 October, the Board approved the 2002-2003 provisional work programme.

WFP activities

During 2001 [E/2002/54], WFP assisted 77 million of the world's poorest in 82 countries, of whom 20 million benefited from development programmes in 55 countries, 43 million benefited from emergency operations in 50 countries and 14 million benefited from protracted relief operations in 41 countries. The beneficiaries included 8 million persons internally displaced and 3 million refugees.

Total quantities of food provided by WFP reached a record level of 4.2 million tons, an increase of some 20 per cent over 2000. Of the total food provided, 660,600 tons was for development projects, 2.7 million tons was for emergency operations and 818,700 tons was for protracted relief and recovery operations.

Global food aid deliveries amounted to 11 million tons in 2001, a decrease of nearly 3 percent from the 11.3 million tons delivered in 2000. Programme food aid provided bilaterally on a government-to-government basis decreased by 15 per cent, from 3.2 million to 2.7 million tons, which accounted for the decrease of global food aid deliveries in 2001. Nearly half of the food aid delivered during the year was emergency food aid provided as relief to people affected by man-

made or natural emergency situations. Compared with 2000, the portion of food aid channelled multilaterally increased from 36 per cent to 42 per cent in 2001. The decrease in Programme food aid resulted in an increase of the share of total food provided as targeted food aid. An important aspect of project food aid in 2001 was that some 27 per cent of the deliveries was monetized.

Even though the total number of beneficiaries decreased (83 million in 2000), WFP initiated 59 new operational activities and 16 country programmes worldwide.

Sub-Saharan Africa received the largest share of WFP assistance, with 51.7 per cent of its operational expenditures spent in 39 countries; Asia received 33.5 per cent for 15 countries; Eastern Europe and the Commonwealth of Independent States, 9.4 per cent for nine countries; Latin America and the Caribbean, 3.5 per cent for 13 countries; and the Middle East and North Africa, 1.8 per cent for nine countries.

Administrative and financial matters

Resources and financing

WFP operational expenditure for 2001 amounted to $1.7 billion for development and relief activities in the least developed countries and low-income, food-deficit countries. Contributions reached a record level of $1.9 billion, the highest amount in WFP's history, including a $1.2 billion contribution from the United States, the largest-ever amount from a single donor. Of the total contributed, $1.1 billion went to emergency operations, $270 million to development activities, $510 million to protracted relief and recovery operations and $20 million for other purposes.

Food security

Follow-up to 1996 World Food Summit

The Food and Agriculture Organization of the United Nations (FAO) continued to implement the Plan of Action adopted at the 1996 World Food Summit [YUN 1996, p. 1129], in which the organization committed itself to assisting developing countries on trade issues, particularly in preparing for multilateral trade negotiations in agriculture through studies, analyses and training. FAO reported in 2001 that progress had been made in reducing the absolute number of hungry people, but that was not happening fast enough to achieve the 1996 Summit goal of halving the number of hungry people by 2015. During the year, the FAO Director-General proposed to postpone the "World Food Summit: five years later", scheduled for November 2001. The FAO Council, at its one hundred and twenty-first session (Rome, 30 October–1 November), approved the proposal to convene the follow-up meeting from 10 to 13 June 2002.

The State of Food and Agriculture 2001, FAO's annual report on current developments and issues in world agriculture, stated that latest estimates suggested that the declining trend in the prevalence of hunger had come to a near standstill, with some 826 million people undernourished. Improvements in some subregions, notably East Asia, had been offset by a deterioration in others, especially sub-Saharan Africa and Central America and the Caribbean. The publication featured a review of the existing evidence on the link between nutrition and productivity and economic growth.

Nutrition

ACC activities

During its twenty-eighth session (Nairobi, Kenya, 2-6 April) [ACC/2001/9], the Administrative Committee on Coordination Subcommittee on Nutrition (ACC/SCN) reviewed the reports of working groups on such issues as the nutrition of school-age children; capacity development in food and nutrition; micronutrients; nutrition, ethics and human rights; breastfeeding; nutrition in emergencies; household food security; and prevention of foetal and infant malnutrition. During the session, a symposium on nutrition and HIV/AIDS took place, which was hosted by the WFP Nairobi office. An ACC/SCN statement on nutrition and HIV/AIDS, approved for wide dissemination, was annexed to the Subcommittee's report.

Projected SCN expenditure, as at 14 March 2001, to the end of the 2000-2001 biennium totalled $780,000, against income of $714,400. The deficit was partly due to UNDP's total suspension of its contributions for the biennium. The UN agencies approved unanimously the core and programme budget presented for the 2002-2003 biennium. The proposed core budget was set at $860,000, while the programme budget was estimated to total $920,000.

UNU activities

The United Nations University (UNU) food and nutrition programme assisted developing regions to enhance individual, organizational and institutional capacity, carried out research activities that required global efforts and served as the academic arm for the UN system in the areas of food and nutrition that were best addressed in a non-regulatory, non-normative environment.

In 2001 [A/57/31], the UNU food and nutrition programme worked with WHO to develop new growth references for infants and young children, and in its review of technical information relevant to international policies related to infant feeding. It partnered with WHO and FAO in developing updates for the evaluation of protein and energy requirements, and discussions were under way to review the harmonization of approaches for developing dietary standards published by individual countries.

Under its capacity development training programme, UNU organized a 12-month training programme on food science and technology at the National Food Research Institute (Tsukuba, Japan), in which five fellows took part. In the degree-oriented studies programme, two fellowships were awarded to students to participate in a two-year postgraduate training programme in nutrition planning at the Department of Food Technology and Nutrition of the University of Nairobi. In cooperation with FAO, work in the area of nutrition data management continued with two 3-week training courses, in the Caribbean and in the Netherlands, on the production and use of food composition data in nutrition. The programme continued its quarterly publication of *The Food and Nutrition Bulletin* and *The Journal of Food Composition and Analysis*.

Chapter XIV

International drug control

During 2001, the United Nations, through the Commission on Narcotic Drugs, the International Narcotics Control Board (INCB) and the United Nations International Drug Control Programme (UNDCP), renewed its commitment to strengthen international cooperation and increase efforts to counter the world drug problem, in accordance with the obligations of States under the United Nations drug control conventions and on the basis of the outcome of the General Assembly's twentieth special session, held in 1998. Activities focused mainly on implementation of the 1999 Action Plan for the Implementation of the Declaration on the Guiding Principles of Drug Demand Reduction, which served as a guide to Member States in adopting strategies and programmes for reducing illicit drug demand in order to achieve significant results by 2008.

UNDCP stimulated action at the national, regional and international levels through technical cooperation programmes and supported the international community in implementing the strategy agreed upon by the Assembly at its special session. It assisted States in complying with international treaties and supported national efforts and initiatives to reduce or eliminate illicit cultivation of opium poppy, coca bush and cannabis through alternative development, and to strengthen national capacities in demand reduction and institution-building.

The Commission on Narcotic Drugs—the main UN policy-making body dealing with drug control—addressed a number of issues and adopted resolutions on the reduction of the demand for illicit drugs, illicit drug trafficking and supply, and implementation of the Global Programme of Action and international treaties. In July, the Economic and Social Council urged Governments to continue contributing to the maintenance of a balance between the licit supply of and demand for opiate raw materials for medical and scientific needs, and to cooperate in preventing the proliferation of sources of production of opiate raw materials.

INCB continued to oversee the implementation of the three major international drug control conventions, to analyse the drug situation worldwide and to draw Governments' attention to weaknesses in national control and treaty compliance, making suggestions and recommendations for improvements at the national and international levels.

Follow-up to the twentieth special session

In response to General Assembly resolution 55/65 [YUN 2000, p. 1175], the Secretary-General, in a July report [A/56/157], presented an overview of the implementation of the outcome of the twentieth special session of the Assembly on the world drug problem, held in 1998 [YUN 1998, p. 1135], and of resolution 54/132 [YUN 1999, p. 1157], by which the Assembly adopted the Action Plan for the Implementation of the Declaration on the Guiding Principles of Drug Demand Reduction. The report reviewed 2003 and 2008 goals and targets set by the special session; the role of the Commission on Narcotic Drugs; the Action Plan for implementing the Declaration on the principles; the Action Plan on International Cooperation on the Eradication of Illicit Drug Crops and on Alternative Development [YUN 1998, p. 1148]; measures to promote judicial cooperation; the Action Plan against Illicit Manufacture, Trafficking and Abuse of Amphetamine-type Stimulants and Their Precursors [ibid., p. 1139]; control of precursors; countering money-laundering; and UNDCP as a catalyst for action by Member States and the UN system.

In March, the Commission on Narcotic Drugs considered the first biennial report of the UNDCP Executive Director on the implementation of the outcome of the special session [YUN 2000, p. 1174]. The report [E/CN.7/2001/2 & Add.1-3], presented an overview of Governments' efforts to meet the objectives and target dates set out in the action plans and measures adopted at the special session, drawing on information provided by Governments through biennial questionnaires and on other sources.

By a 28 March resolution [E/2001/28/Rev.1 (res. 44/2)], the Commission took note of the first biennial report of the UNDCP Executive Director on the implementation of the outcome of the special session [YUN 2000, p. 1174] and requested him to provide additional information in subsequent reports. Welcoming Governments' efforts to meet the goals and targets set out in the Political Declaration adopted at the special session [YUN 1998, p. 1136], it urged Member States to continue making every effort to meet those targets. Member States were also urged to transmit to the UNDCP Executive Director their replies to the second biennial questionnaire by 30 June 2002.

The Executive Director submitted to the Commission's resumed session (Vienna, 12-14 December) his consolidated first biennial report, which contained replies to the biennial questionnaires received after November 2000. A revised questionnaire was also included in the report.

GENERAL ASSEMBLY ACTION

On 19 December [meeting 88], the General Assembly, on the recommendation of the Third (Social, Humanitarian and Cultural) Committee [A/56/575], adopted **resolution 56/124** without vote [agenda item 111].

International cooperation against the world drug problem

The General Assembly,

Recalling its resolutions 52/92 of 12 December 1997, 53/115 of 9 December 1998, 54/132 of 17 December 1999 and 55/65 of 4 December 2000,

Recalling also its resolution 55/2 of 8 September 2000, entitled "United Nations Millennium Declaration", in which the world leaders resolved to redouble efforts to counter the world drug problem,

Reaffirming its commitment to the outcome of the twentieth special session of the General Assembly, devoted to countering the world drug problem together, held in New York from 8 to 10 June 1998, and welcoming the continued determination of Governments to overcome the world drug problem by a full and balanced application of national, regional and international strategies to reduce the demand for, production of and trafficking in illicit drugs, as reflected in the Political Declaration, the Action Plan for the Implementation of the Declaration on the Guiding Principles of Drug Demand Reduction and the measures to enhance international cooperation to counter the world drug problem,

Gravely concerned that, despite continued increased efforts by States, relevant international organizations, civil society and non-governmental organizations, the drug problem is still a challenge of a global dimension which constitutes a serious threat to the health, safety and well-being of all mankind, in particular young people, in all countries, undermines development, including efforts to reduce poverty, socio-economic and political stability and democratic institutions, entails an increasing economic cost for Governments, also threatens the national security and sovereignty of States, as well as the dignity and hope of millions of people and their families, and causes irreparable loss of human lives,

Concerned that the demand for, production of and trafficking in illicit drugs and psychotropic substances continue to threaten seriously the socio-economic and political systems, stability, national security and sovereignty of many States, especially those involved in conflicts and wars, and that trafficking in drugs could make conflict resolution more difficult,

Deeply alarmed by the violence and economic power of criminal organizations and terrorist groups engaged in drug-trafficking activities and other criminal activities, such as money-laundering and illicit traffic in arms, precursors and essential chemicals, and by the increasing transnational links between them, and recognizing the urgent need for enhanced international cooperation and implementation of effective strategies on the basis of the outcome of the twentieth special session of the General Assembly, which are essential to achieving results against all forms of transnational criminal activities,

Welcoming the call on States and appropriate international and regional organizations in a position to do so to provide assistance, upon request, to combat the illicit trade in small arms and light weapons linked to drug trafficking, transnational organized crime and terrorism, as expressed in the outcome document of the United Nations Conference on the Illicit Trade in Small Arms and Light Weapons in All Its Aspects,

Noting with grave concern the global increase in the use of minors in the illicit production of and trafficking in narcotic drugs and psychotropic substances, as well as in the number of children and young people starting to use drugs at an earlier age and in their access to substances not previously used,

Alarmed by the rapid and widespread increase in the illicit manufacture, trafficking and consumption, in particular by young people, of synthetic drugs in many countries and by the high probability that amphetamine-type stimulants, in particular methamphetamine and amphetamine, may become drugs of choice among abusers in the twenty-first century,

Deeply convinced that the special session made a significant contribution to a new comprehensive framework for international cooperation, based on an integrated and balanced approach with strategies, measures, methods, practical activities, goals and specific targets to be met, that all States, the United Nations system and other international organizations must implement them with concrete actions and that the international financial institutions, such as the World Bank, and the regional development banks should be invited to include action against the world drug problem in their programmes, taking into account the priorities of States,

Reaffirming the importance of the commitments of Member States in meeting the objectives targeted for 2003 and 2008, as set out in the Political Declaration adopted by the General Assembly at its twentieth special session, and welcoming the guidelines for reporting on the follow-up to the twentieth special session adopted by the Commission on Narcotic Drugs at its reconvened forty-second session, as well as the elements recommended to the Executive Director of the United Nations International Drug Control Programme by the Commission at its forty-fourth session for the preparation of subsequent reports,

Welcoming the inclusion in the provisional agenda of the forty-fifth session of the Commission on Narcotic Drugs of an item on the preparations for the ministerial segment to be held in 2003, in line with Economic and Social Council resolution 1999/30 of 28 July 1999, to focus on the progress made by States in implementing the action plan and measures adopted by the General Assembly at its twentieth special session,

Emphasizing the importance of the Action Plan for the Implementation of the Declaration on the Guiding Principles of Drug Demand Reduction, which introduces a global approach, recognizing a new balance between illicit supply and demand reduction, under the principle of shared responsibility, aims at preventing the use of drugs and at reducing the adverse consequences of drug abuse, ensuring that special attention is paid to vulnerable groups, in particular children and young people, and constitutes one of the pillars of the new global strategy, and reaffirming the need for demand reduction programmes,

Emphasizing equally the importance of supply reduction as an integral part of a balanced drug control strategy under the principles enshrined in the Action Plan on International Cooperation on the Eradication of Illicit Drug Crops and on Alternative Development, reaffirming the need for alternative development programmes that are sustainable, welcoming the achievements of some States on their way to eradicating illicit drug crops, and urging all other States to make similar efforts,

Underlining the role of the Commission on Narcotic Drugs as the principal United Nations policy-making body on drug control issues and as the governing body of the United Nations International Drug Control Programme, the leadership role and commendable work of the Programme as the main focus for concerted multilateral action and the important role of the International Narcotics Control Board as an independent monitoring authority, as set out in the international drug control treaties,

Recognizing the efforts of all countries, in particular those that produce narcotic drugs for scientific and medical purposes, and of the International Narcotics Control Board in preventing the diversion of such substances to illicit markets and in maintaining production at a level consistent with licit demand, in line with the Single Convention on Narcotic Drugs of 1961 and the Convention on Psychotropic Substances of 1971,

Recognizing also that the problem of the illicit production of and trafficking in narcotic drugs and psychotropic substances is often related to development problems and that those links and the promotion of the economic development of countries affected by the illicit drug trade require, within the context of shared responsibility, appropriate measures, including strengthened international cooperation in support of alternative and sustainable development activities, in the affected areas of those countries, that have as their objectives the reduction and elimination of illicit drug production,

Stressing that respect for all human rights is and must be an essential component of measures taken to address the drug problem,

Ensuring that women and men benefit equally, and without any discrimination, from strategies directed against the world drug problem, through their involvement in all stages of programmes and policy-making,

Recognizing that the use of the Internet poses new opportunities for and challenges to international cooperation in countering drug abuse and illicit production and trafficking, and recognizing also the need for increased cooperation among States and the exchange of information, including with reference to national experiences, on how to counter the promotion of drug abuse and illicit drug trafficking through this instrument and on ways to use the Internet for information concerning drug demand reduction,

Convinced that civil society, including non-governmental organizations and community-based organizations, play an active role and make an effective contribution to countering the world drug problem, and should be encouraged to continue to do so,

Acknowledging with appreciation the increased efforts and achievements of many States, relevant international organizations and civil society, including non-governmental organizations, in countering drug abuse and illicit production of and trafficking in drugs, and that international cooperation has shown that positive results can be achieved through sustained and collective efforts,

I

Respect for the principles enshrined in the Charter of the United Nations and international law in countering the world drug problem

1. *Reaffirms* that countering the world drug problem is a common and shared responsibility which must be addressed in a multilateral setting, requiring an integrated and balanced approach, and must be carried out in full conformity with the purposes and principles of the Charter of the United Nations and international law, and in particular with full respect for the sovereignty and territorial integrity of States, the principle of non-intervention in the internal affairs of States and all human rights and fundamental freedoms;

2. *Calls upon* all States to take further action to promote effective cooperation at the international and regional levels in the efforts to counter the world drug problem so as to contribute to a climate conducive to achieving that end, on the basis of the principles of equal rights and mutual respect;

3. *Urges* all States to ratify or accede to and implement all the provisions of the Single Convention on Narcotic Drugs of 1961 as amended by the 1972 Protocol, the Convention on Psychotropic Substances of 1971 and the United Nations Convention against Illicit Traffic in Narcotic Drugs and Psychotropic Substances of 1988;

II

International cooperation to counter the world drug problem

1. *Urges* all States to take appropriate action to address the linkages between the illicit traffic in small arms and light weapons and the illicit trade in narcotic drugs through, inter alia, increased international cooperation and by ensuring full implementation of the Programme of Action to Prevent, Combat and Eradicate the Illicit Trade in Small Arms and Light Weapons in All Its Aspects;

2. *Welcomes* the renewed commitment made in the United Nations Millennium Declaration to counter the world drug problem;

3. *Urges* competent authorities, at the international, regional and national levels, to implement the outcome of the twentieth special session, within the agreed time frames, in particular the high-priority practical measures at the international, regional or national level, as indicated in the Political Declaration, the Action Plan for the Implementation of the Declaration on the Guiding Principles of Drug Demand Reduction and the measures to enhance international cooperation to counter the world drug problem, including the Action Plan against Illicit Manufacture, Trafficking and Abuse of Amphetamine-type Stimulants and Their Precursors, the measures to prevent the illicit manufacture, import, export, trafficking, distribution and diversion of precursors used in the illicit manufacture of narcotic drugs and psychotropic substances, the measures to promote judicial cooperation, the measures to counter money-laundering and the Action Plan on International Cooperation on the Eradication of Illicit Drug Crops and on Alternative Development;

4. *Urges* all Member States to implement the Action Plan for the Implementation of the Declaration on the Guiding Principles of Drug Demand Reduction in their respective national, regional and international actions and to strengthen their national efforts to counter the abuse of illicit drugs among their population, in particular among children and young people;

5. *Recognizes* the role of the United Nations International Drug Control Programme in developing action-oriented strategies to assist Member States to implement the Action Plan for the Implementation of the Declaration, and requests the Executive Director of the Programme to report to the Commission on Narcotic Drugs at its forty-fifth session on the follow-up to the Action Plan;

6. *Reaffirms its resolve* to continue to strengthen the United Nations machinery for international drug control, in particular the Commission on Narcotic Drugs, the United Nations International Drug Control Programme and the International Narcotics Control Board, in order to enable them to fulfil their mandates, bearing in mind the recommendations contained in Economic and Social Council resolution 1999/30 and the measures taken and recommendations adopted by the Commission on Narcotic Drugs at its forty-fourth session aimed at the enhancement of its functioning, in particular regarding Commission resolution 44/16;

7. *Renews its commitment* to further strengthening international cooperation and substantially increasing efforts to counter the world drug problem, in accordance with the obligations of States under the United Nations drug control conventions, on the basis of the general framework given by the outcome of the special session, and taking into account experience gained;

8. *Calls upon* all States to adopt effective measures, including national laws and regulations, to implement the outcome and the goals of the special session, within the agreed time frame, to strengthen national judicial systems and to carry out effective drug control activities in cooperation with other States and in accordance with United Nations drug control conventions;

9. *Calls upon* the relevant United Nations bodies, the specialized agencies, the international financial institutions and other concerned intergovernmental and international organizations, within their mandates, and all actors of civil society, notably nongovernmental organizations, community-based organizations, sports associations, the media and the private sector, to continue their close cooperation with Governments in their efforts to promote and implement the outcome of the special session and the Action Plan for the Implementation of the Declaration on the Guiding Principles of Drug Demand Reduction, including through public information campaigns, resorting, inter alia, where available, to the Internet;

10. *Urges* Governments, the relevant United Nations bodies, the specialized agencies and other international organizations to assist and support States, upon request, in particular developing countries in need of such assistance and support, with the aim of enhancing their capacity to counter illicit trafficking of narcotic drugs and psychotropic substances, taking into account national plans and initiatives, and emphasizes the importance of subregional, regional and international cooperation in countering illicit drug trafficking;

11. *Reaffirms* that preventing the diversion of chemicals from legitimate commerce to illicit drug manufacture is an essential component of a comprehensive strategy against drug abuse and trafficking, which requires the effective cooperation of exporting, importing and transit States, notes the progress made in developing practical guidelines to prevent such diversion of chemicals, including those of the International Narcotics Control Board and the recommendations on implementing article 12 of the 1988 Convention, and calls upon all States to adopt and implement measures to prevent the diversion of chemicals to illicit drug manufacture, in cooperation with competent international and regional bodies and, if necessary and to the extent possible, with the private sector in each State, in accordance with the objectives targeted for 2003 and 2008 in the Political Declaration and the resolution on the control of precursors adopted at the special session;

12. *Calls upon* States in which cultivation and production of illicit drug crops occur to establish or reinforce, where appropriate, national mechanisms to monitor and verify illicit crops, and requests the Executive Director of the United Nations International Drug Control Programme to report to the Commission on Narcotic Drugs at its forty-fifth session, in March 2002, on the follow-up to the Action Plan on International Cooperation on the Eradication of Illicit Drug Crops and on Alternative Development;

13. *Encourages* States to open their markets to products that are the object of alternative development programmes, and which are necessary for the creation of employment and the eradication of poverty;

14. *Calls upon* States, the international community, international organizations, regional organizations, international financial institutions and regional development banks to support the implementation of the Action Plan on International Cooperation on the Eradication of Illicit Drug Crops and on Alternative Development by States affected by illicit crop cultivation to enable them to apply fully measures for drug eradication and sustainable alternative development;

15. *Encourages* States further to cooperate through bilateral, regional and multilateral means to avoid dis-

placement of illicit drug crop cultivation from one area, region or country to another;

16. *Calls upon* all States to report biennially to the Commission on Narcotic Drugs on their efforts to meet the goals and targets for 2003 and 2008, as set out in the Political Declaration adopted at the special session, in accordance with the terms established in the guidelines adopted by the Commission at its forty-second and forty-fourth sessions;

17. *Welcomes* the decision of the Commission on Narcotic Drugs to submit a report to the General Assembly in 2003 and 2008 on the progress achieved in meeting the goals and targets set out in the Political Declaration;

18. *Encourages* the Commission on Narcotic Drugs and the International Narcotics Control Board to continue their useful work on the control of precursors and other chemicals used in the illicit manufacture of narcotic drugs and psychotropic substances;

19. *Calls upon* the Commission on Narcotic Drugs to continue mainstreaming a gender perspective into all its policies, programmes and activities, and requests the Secretariat to continue integrating a gender perspective into all documentation prepared for the Commission;

20. *Recalls* the World Programme of Action for Youth to the Year 2000 and Beyond adopted by the General Assembly on 14 December 1995, notes with satisfaction the commitment of young people to a drug-free society made at various forums, and stresses the importance of young people continuing to contribute their experiences and to participate in the decision-making processes and, in particular, putting into effect the Action Plan for the Implementation of the Declaration on the Guiding Principles of Drug Demand Reduction;

21. *Urges* all States to assign priority to activities aimed at preventing drug and inhalant abuse among children and young people, inter alia, through the promotion of information and education programmes aimed at raising awareness of the risks of drug abuse with a view to giving effect to the Action Plan for the Implementation of the Declaration on the Guiding Principles of Drug Demand Reduction;

22. *Welcomes* the Declaration of Commitment on HIV/AIDS adopted on 27 June 2001 at the special session of the General Assembly on HIV/AIDS, including the acknowledgment of the link between drug-using behaviour and HIV infection;

23. *Calls upon* States to adopt effective measures, including possible national legislative measures, and to enhance cooperation to stem the illicit trade in small arms, which, as a result of its close link to the illicit drug trade, is generating extremely high levels of crime and violence within the societies of some States, threatening the national security and the economies of those States;

24. *Welcomes* the adoption of the United Nations Convention against Transnational Organized Crime and the three Protocols thereto, namely, the Protocol to Prevent, Suppress and Punish Trafficking in Persons, Especially Women and Children, the Protocol against the Smuggling of Migrants by Land, Sea and Air and the Protocol against the Illicit Manufacturing of and Trafficking in Firearms, Their Parts and Components

and Ammunition, and encourages universal signature and ratification of these legal instruments;

25. *Stresses* the need for coordinated action to reduce the demand for illicit drugs, in the context of a comprehensive, balanced and coordinated approach encompassing supply control and demand reduction, as set out in the Action Plan for the Implementation of the Declaration on the Guiding Principles of Drug Demand Reduction, noting, inter alia, the links between drug trafficking, organized crime and terrorism;

26. *Welcomes* the thematic debate on the theme "Building partnerships to address the world drug problem", which allowed a useful exchange of ideas on the topics "Approaches to building partnerships within and across sectors, including health, education, law enforcement and justice" and "Prevention, education and early intervention strategies and trends in drug abuse among children and young people" at the forty-fourth session of the Commission on Narcotic Drugs, and the continuation of a focused thematic debate;

27. *Recognizes* the desirability of providing support to the States that are most affected by the transit of drugs and are willing to implement plans to eliminate such transit, and in this regard requests the United Nations International Drug Control Programme to extend technical assistance, from available voluntary contributions for that purpose, to those States that are most affected by the transit of drugs, in particular developing countries in need of such assistance and support;

28. *Urges* all States to develop and implement policies and programmes for children, including adolescents, aimed at preventing the use of narcotic drugs, psychotropic substances and inhalants, except for medical purposes, and at reducing the adverse consequences of their abuse, as well as support preventive policies and programmes, especially against tobacco and alcohol;

29. *Also urges* all States to make appropriate treatment and rehabilitation accessible for children, including adolescents, dependent on narcotic drugs, psychotropic substances, inhalants and alcohol;

III
Action by the United Nations system

1. *Emphasizes* the role of the Commission on Narcotic Drugs as the principal United Nations policy-making body on drug control issues and as the governing body of the United Nations International Drug Control Programme;

2. *Reaffirms* the role of the Executive Director of the United Nations International Drug Control Programme in coordinating and providing effective leadership for all United Nations drug control activities so as to increase cost-effectiveness and ensure coherence of action, as well as coordination, complementarity and non-duplication of such activities throughout the United Nations system, and encourages further efforts in this regard;

3. *Emphasizes* that the multidimensional nature of the world drug problem calls for the promotion of integration and coordination of drug control activities throughout the United Nations system, including in the follow-up to major United Nations conferences;

4. *Invites* Governments and the United Nations International Drug Control Programme to attach high priority to the improvement of the coordination of

United Nations activities related to the world drug problem so as to avoid duplication of such activities, strengthen efficiency and accomplish the goals approved by Governments;

5. *Urges* the specialized agencies, programmes and funds, including humanitarian organizations, and invites multilateral financial institutions, to include action against the world drug problem in their programming and planning processes in order to ensure that the integral and balanced strategy that emerged from the special session devoted to countering the world drug problem together is being addressed;

IV
United Nations International Drug Control Programme

1. *Welcomes* the efforts of the United Nations International Drug Control Programme to implement its mandate within the framework of the international drug control treaties, the Comprehensive Multidisciplinary Outline of Future Activities in Drug Abuse Control, the Global Programme of Action, the outcome of the special session of the General Assembly devoted to countering the world drug problem together and relevant consensus documents;

2. *Expresses its appreciation* to the Programme for the support provided to different States in meeting the objectives of the Global Programme of Action and of the special session, especially in cases where significant and anticipated progress was achieved regarding the objectives targeted for 2003 and 2008;

3. *Requests* the Programme to continue:

(a) To strengthen dialogue with Member States and also to ensure continued improvement in management, so as to contribute to enhanced and sustainable programme delivery and further encourage the Executive Director to maximize the effectiveness of the Programme, inter alia, through the full implementation of resolution 44/16 of the Commission on Narcotic Drugs, in particular the recommendations contained therein;

(b) To strengthen cooperation with Member States and with United Nations programmes, funds and relevant agencies, as well as relevant regional organizations and agencies and non-governmental organizations, and to provide, on request, assistance in implementing the outcome of the special session;

(c) To increase its technical assistance, within the available voluntary resources, to countries that are deploying efforts to reduce illicit crop cultivation by, in particular, adopting alternative development programmes;

(d) To allocate, while keeping the balance between supply and demand reduction programmes, adequate resources to allow it to fulfil its role in the implementation of the Action Plan for the Implementation of the Declaration on the Guiding Principles of Drug Demand Reduction;

(e) To strengthen dialogue and cooperation with multilateral development banks and with international financial institutions so that they may undertake lending and programming activities related to drug control in interested and affected countries to implement the outcome of the special session, and to keep the Commission on Narcotic Drugs informed of further progress made in this area;

(f) To take into account the outcome of the special session, to include in its report on illicit traffic in drugs an updated, objective and comprehensive assessment of worldwide trends in illicit traffic and transit in narcotic drugs and psychotropic substances, including methods and routes used, and to recommend ways and means of improving the capacity of States along those routes to deal with all aspects of the drug problem;

(g) To publish the *World Drug Report*, with comprehensive and balanced information about the world drug problem, and to seek additional extrabudgetary resources for its publication in all official languages;

4. *Urges* all Governments to provide the fullest possible financial and political support to the Programme by widening its donor base and increasing voluntary contributions, in particular general-purpose contributions, to enable it to continue, expand and strengthen its operational and technical cooperation activities;

5. *Calls upon* the International Narcotics Control Board to increase efforts to implement all its mandates under international drug control conventions and to continue to cooperate with Governments, inter alia, by offering advice to Member States that request it;

6. *Notes* that the Board needs sufficient resources to carry out all its mandates, and therefore urges Member States to commit themselves in a common effort to assigning adequate and sufficient budgetary resources to the Board, in accordance with Economic and Social Council resolution 1996/20 of 23 July 1996, and emphasizes the need to maintain its capacity, inter alia, through the provision of appropriate means by the Secretary-General and adequate technical support by the Programme;

7. *Stresses* the importance of the meetings of Heads of National Drug Law Enforcement Agencies, in all regions of the world, and the Subcommission on Illicit Drug Traffic and Related Matters in the Near and Middle East of the Commission on Narcotic Drugs, and encourages them to continue to contribute to the strengthening of regional and international cooperation, taking into account the outcome of the special session;

8. *Takes note* of the report of the Secretary-General, and, taking into account the promotion of integrated reporting, requests the Secretary-General to submit to the General Assembly at its fifty-seventh session a report on the implementation of the outcome of the twentieth special session, including on the Action Plan for the Implementation of the Declaration on the Guiding Principles of Drug Demand Reduction, and the present resolution.

Conventions

In 2001, international efforts to control narcotic drugs were governed by three global conventions: the 1961 Single Convention on Narcotic Drugs [YUN 1961, p. 382], which, with some exceptions of detail, replaced earlier narcotics treaties and was amended in 1972 by a Protocol [YUN 1972, p. 397] intended to strengthen the role of INCB; the

1971 Convention on Psychotropic Substances [YUN 1971, p. 380]; and the 1988 United Nations Convention against Illicit Traffic in Narcotic Drugs and Psychotropic Substances [YUN 1988, p. 690].

As at 31 December 2001, 170 States were parties to the 1961 Convention, as amended by the 1972 Protocol. During the year, Albania, Belarus, Belize, the Central African Republic, Iran, Saint Vincent and the Grenadines, Turkey and Ukraine became parties. The Federal Republic of Yugoslavia (FRY) succeeded to it, replacing the Socialist Federal Republic of Yugoslavia.

The number of parties to the 1971 Convention stood at 171 as at 31 December 2001. Belize, the Central African Republic, Djibouti and Saint Vincent and the Grenadines became parties during the year. FRY succeeded to the Convention, replacing the Socialist Federal Republic.

At year's end, 162 States were parties to the 1988 Convention. Albania, the Central African Republic, Djibouti and Mauritius became parties in 2001. FRY succeeded to it, replacing the Socialist Federal Republic.

Commission action. At its forty-fourth session in March [E/2001/28/Rev.1], the Commission on Narcotic Drugs reviewed implementation of the international drug control treaties. It had before it a January note by the Secretariat on changes in the scope of substance control [E/CN.7/2001/6] and the INCB report covering 2000 [YUN 2000, p. 1181]. The Commission took note of the Board's recommendations to Governments to reduce overconsumption of controlled substances and to monitor their supply and consumption. Ensuring the availability of narcotic drugs and psychotropic substances for medical purposes, on the one hand, and preventing excessive consumption, on the other, were at the core of the Board's mandate. Education of both prescribers and consumers of controlled substances was an important element in achieving a reduction of excessive consumption of psychotropic substances. The Commission welcomed the Board's efforts to promote a balance between the supply of and demand for opiates used for medical and scientific purposes, as required under the 1961 Convention. While recognizing the benefits of modern information technology, it noted that the rapid growth of the Internet posed new challenges to international drug control, in particular the illicit advertisement and sale of controlled substances. With regard to implementation of article 12 of the 1988 Convention concerning the control of precursors, the Commission noted the continued success of Operation Purple, the international tracking programme for potassium permanganate used in the illicit manufacture of cocaine, and welcomed the actions of the Board to initiate a similar programme, Operation Topaz, for the international tracking of acetic anhydride, used in the manufacture of heroin.

On 20 March [E/2001/28/Rev.1 (dec. 44/1-6)], the Commission decided to include or transfer six narcotic drugs and psychotropic substances in various schedules or tables of the 1971 and 1988 Conventions.

The Commission, on 28 March [res. 44/13], recognized the usefulness and importance of benzodiazepines in therapy and believed that the risk-benefit ratio remained favourable, justifying their retention in the therapeutic armoury. It made several recommendations for consideration by health-care professionals when prescribing those drugs, and urged that health professionals receive training and patients receive relevant information on their use. Recommendations were also made to the pharmaceutical industry, national health authorities and others regarding research, appropriate dosage, marketing, withdrawal information, statistics, monitoring of abuse, dependence and control measures.

INCB action. In its report covering 2001 [E/INCB/2001/1], INCB stated that the implementation of the 1988 Convention could not be ensured without adherence to the other international drug control treaties. It welcomed the fact that the number of States that had taken steps to accede to the 1988 Convention and to implement it had increased steadily. The Board reiterated its request to States that had not done so to accede to the Conventions on drug control.

ECONOMIC AND SOCIAL COUNCIL ACTION

On 24 July [meeting 40], the Economic and Social Council, on the recommendation of the Commission on Narcotic Drugs [E/2001/28/Rev.1], adopted **resolution 2001/17** without vote [agenda item 14 (d)].

Demand for and supply of opiates for medical and scientific needs

The Economic and Social Council,

Recalling its resolution 2000/18 of 27 July 2000 and previous relevant resolutions,

Emphasizing that the need to balance the global licit supply of opiates against the legitimate demand for opiates for medical and scientific purposes is central to the international strategy and policy of drug control,

Noting the fundamental need for international cooperation with the traditional supplier countries in drug control to ensure universal application of the provisions of the Single Convention on Narcotic Drugs of 1961,

Considering that a balance between consumption and production of opiate raw materials has been achieved as a result of efforts made by the two traditional supplier countries, India and Turkey, together with other producing countries,

Noting the importance of opiates in pain relief therapy as advocated by the World Health Organization,

1. *Urges* all Governments to continue contributing to the maintenance of a balance between the licit supply of and demand for opiate raw materials for medical and scientific needs, the achievement of which would be facilitated by maintaining, insofar as their constitutional and legal systems permit, support to the traditional and legal supplier countries, and to cooperate in preventing the proliferation of sources of production of opiate raw materials;

2. *Urges* Governments of all producing countries to adhere strictly to the provisions of the Single Convention on Narcotic Drugs of 1961, and to take effective measures to prevent illicit production or diversion of opiate raw materials to illicit channels, especially when increasing licit production;

3. *Urges* consumer countries to assess their licit needs for opiate raw materials realistically and to communicate those needs to the International Narcotics Control Board, in order to ensure easy supply, and also urges the producing countries concerned and the Board to increase efforts to monitor the available supply and to ensure sufficient stocks of licit opiate raw materials;

4. *Requests* the Board to continue its efforts in monitoring the implementation of the relevant Economic and Social Council resolutions, in full compliance with the Single Convention on Narcotic Drugs of 1961;

5. *Commends* the Board for its efforts in monitoring the implementation of the relevant Council resolutions and, in particular:

(*a*) In urging the Governments concerned to adjust global production of opiate raw materials to a level corresponding to actual licit needs and to avoid unforeseen imbalances between licit supply of and demand for opiates caused by the exportation of products manufactured from seized and confiscated drugs;

(*b*) In inviting the Governments concerned to ensure that opiates imported into their countries for medical and scientific use do not originate from countries that transform seized and confiscated drugs into licit opiates;

(*c*) In arranging informal meetings, during sessions of the Commission on Narcotic Drugs, with the main States importing and producing opiate raw materials;

6. *Requests* the Secretary-General to transmit the text of the present resolution to all Governments for consideration and implementation.

On the same day [meeting 40], the Council, on the recommendation of the Commission [E/2001/28/Rev.1], adopted **resolution 2001/14** without vote [agenda item 14 (*d*)].

Prevention of diversion of precursors used in the illicit manufacture of synthetic drugs

The Economic and Social Council,

Reaffirming that the control of precursor chemicals is a key component in the prevention of diversion of such chemicals to the illicit manufacture of drugs,

Alarmed by the continued spread of the illicit manufacture of synthetic drugs, including amphetamine, methamphetamine and Ecstasy-type drugs, and by the health hazards associated with their abuse,

Noting that the global nature of both the problem of synthetic drugs and the trade in chemicals makes cooperation at all levels, with all relevant agencies and with the chemical industry and trade, essential in preventing diversion,

Recognizing that the United Nations Convention against Illicit Traffic in Narcotic Drugs and Psychotropic Substances of 1988 provides the foundation and framework for such cooperation,

Recalling the provisions of the Action Plan against Illicit Manufacture, Trafficking and Abuse of Amphetamine-type Stimulants and Their Precursors and the measures to control precursors adopted by the General Assembly at its twentieth special session, devoted to countering the world drug problem together, in resolutions S-20/4 A and B of 10 June 1998, including the application of the principle "know your customer",

Recognizing that further information is required about the identity of chemicals used in the illicit manufacture of synthetic drugs,

Recognizing also that many of the chemicals used in the illicit manufacture of synthetic drugs are also used in the licit industry and trade,

Bearing in mind the use of non-controlled and easily substitutable chemicals in the illicit manufacture of synthetic drugs,

Recognizing the importance of drug characterization and impurity profiling and of the results of forensic analysis of drugs in obtaining information on trends in, and on the chemicals used for, the illicit manufacture of synthetic drugs,

Recognizing also that large quantities of 3,4-methylenedioxyphenyl-2-propanone, also known as PMK (piperonyl methyl ketone), a controlled chemical included in table I of the 1988 Convention and an important precursor used in the illicit manufacture of Ecstasy-type drugs, are being seized, and that there is little legitimate trade in that chemical,

1. *Recommends* that concerned Governments and international and regional organizations make every effort to establish closer contact to facilitate the exchange of information between countries used as a source of key chemicals and those in which synthetic drugs are illicitly manufactured;

2. *Urges* Governments and international and regional organizations to make every effort to enhance cooperation at all levels, with all relevant agencies and with the chemical industry and trade, to ensure the rapid exchange of information, in particular relating to stopped shipments, suspicious transactions and new chemicals identified as being used in the illicit manufacture of drugs;

3. *Also urges* Governments to implement operating procedures for chemical control that would give effect, as a minimum, to the measures to control precursors, in particular those relating to pre-export notification, adopted by the General Assembly at its twentieth special session, devoted to countering the world drug problem together, in resolution S-20/4 B, and to articles 12 and 18 of the United Nations Convention against Illicit Traffic in Narcotic Drugs and Psychotropic Substances of 1988, as well as article 13 thereof, relating to the tracking of essential laboratory equipment used in the illicit manufacture of drugs;

4. *Recommends* that Governments and international and regional organizations collect and exchange the information needed to identify the chemicals used in the illicit manufacture of synthetic drugs and the sources of such chemicals. That information should be supplied to the International Narcotics Control Board and the United Nations International Drug Control Programme for analysis, interpretation and dissemination as necessary;

5. *Calls upon* Governments and international and regional organizations to use the information thus obtained as the basis for future initiatives to prevent the diversion of such chemicals;

6. *Urges* Governments and regional organizations to make use of the limited international special surveillance list of substances established by the Board, adapted or supplemented, where appropriate, by lists of chemicals subject to voluntary monitoring, to reflect national and regional situations and changing trends in the illicit manufacture of drugs;

7. *Calls upon* Governments and regional organizations to consider the establishment of early warning systems for suspicious key nationally non-controlled chemicals found to be used in the illicit manufacture of drugs, in order to allow the rapid dissemination of information to the chemical industry and trade and to the appropriate authorities;

8. *Urges* Governments to develop cooperation programmes, together with the chemical industry and trade, to ensure the regular exchange of information, thus promoting greater awareness of chemicals used in the illicit manufacture of drugs, and to encourage reporting of suspicious transactions;

9. *Recommends* that Governments and regional organizations consider drawing up guidelines for their chemical industry and trade, setting out indicators of suspicious transactions and allowing for the regular updating of regulations and procedures;

10. *Recommends also* that Governments consider facilitating, with the technical support of the United Nations International Drug Control Programme, if necessary, the development and distribution of analytical methods for drug characterization and impurity profiling, and the development of chemical tracers, as tools for the identification of manufacturing trends and new chemicals used in the illicit manufacture of drugs;

11. *Recommends further* that interested Governments and international and regional organizations consider the possibility of establishing a network of collaborating laboratories to serve as a source of primary information leading to a better understanding of illicit manufacturing trends, new drugs and the precursors used in illicit manufacture;

12. *Recommends* that Governments consider, if necessary, ways of improving the enforcement capacity, including the use of controlled delivery, where appropriate, available for investigation of illicit laboratories, stopped shipments and seized chemicals;

13. *Recommends also* that, in view of the very limited legitimate trade in PMK, all transactions involving that chemical be regarded with concern and that end-users be thoroughly verified before shipments are allowed to proceed in accordance with national legislation and procedures.

International Narcotics Control Board

The 13-member International Narcotics Control Board held its seventieth (5-9 February), seventy-first (21 May–1 June) and seventy-second (29 October–15 November) sessions, all in Vienna.

In performing the functions assigned to it under the international conventions, the Board maintained ongoing discussions with Governments. The information provided by them was used to evaluate whether Governments had enforced treaty provisions requiring them to limit to medical and scientific purposes the licit manufacture of, trade in and distribution and use of narcotic drugs and psychotropic substances. The Board, which was required by the international drug control treaties to report annually on the drug control situation worldwide, noted weaknesses in treaty compliance and made recommendations for improvements in national control through such means as strengthening legislation and enforcement.

In its 2001 report [Sales No. E.02.XI.1], the Board examined the challenges that globalization and the misuse of new technologies, such as the Internet, posed to drug law enforcement. According to the Board, Internet-based crime was easy to commit as it required few resources and was difficult to fight in a "virtual" environment, where national boundaries were irrelevant and personal risk to the criminals and likelihood of detection were low. The Board examined the impact that globalization and new technology had on drug-related crime, in particular organized crime and money-laundering, and on government structures and capabilities for combating such crime. Drug trafficking groups utilized new technologies to improve the efficiency of product delivery and distribution and to protect themselves from identification and prosecution. The Board analysed how the structural, legal, technical and resource challenges were being addressed in various countries, and urged that law enforcement agencies be given the technical and legislative means to develop an appropriate response capacity; at the same time, it acknowledged that concerns raised by civil liberty groups over the invasion of privacy and the potential to limit freedom of expression were genuine.

Among its recommendations, the Board called on Governments to ensure that appropriate laws were introduced and appropriate funding, resources and infrastructure provided to law enforcement agencies; to introduce specialized inter-agency high-tech drug units, provided with infrastructure to protect their information and intelligence databases from "cyber attack"; to proceed towards ratification of the 2001 Convention on Cybercrime; and to consider the development of a UN convention against cybercrime.

The Board analysed the operation of the international drug control system and the major developments in drug abuse and trafficking worldwide. The international and domestic movement of narcotic drugs and psychotropic substances was continuously monitored in order to identify any deficiencies in control mechanisms, particularly those that could facilitate the diversion of such drugs from licit to illicit channels. As in recent years, no cases involving the diversion of narcotic drugs from licit international trade into the illicit traffic were detected during 2001; however, several Governments reported domestic diversion and abuse. The Board invited Governments to monitor and prevent the diversion and abuse of narcotic drugs and to provide law enforcement authorities with adequate information, training and technical means to increase their capacity to detect such products. With controls on international trade in psychotropic substances having been strengthened, diversion of pharmaceutical products containing those substances from domestic distribution channels had become an increasingly important supply source for drug traffickers. The most frequently diverted pharmaceuticals from domestic distribution channels included stimulants, benzodiazepines, phenobarbital and buprenorphine. The Board reiterated its request to Governments to amend their national legislation to allow for the prosecution of the drug traffickers involved. It also recommended that Governments ensure that seized psychotropic substances were either destroyed or protected against diversion attempts.

With regard to chemicals used as precursors in the manufacture of illegal drugs, the Board called on Governments to investigate interceptions of smuggled consignments and seizures at illicit laboratories in order to identify the sources and determine the methods of diversion used by traffickers. Operation Purple, the voluntary international initiative to track individual shipments of potassium permanganate in international trade, continued to achieve success in preventing diversions into illicit traffic. The Board continued to verify the legitimacy of shipments of potassium permanganate to countries not participating in the Operation and noticed an increase in shipments, particularly to Asian countries. Operation Topaz, a comparable initiative for acetic anhydride, was launched in March and, as with Operation Purple, the Board, through its secretariat, served as the international focal point for the exchange of information. The Operation recorded successes through law enforcement activities to intercept smuggled

acetic anhydride, with large seizures being reported and new smuggling routes identified. In view of the increasing concern over the diversion of precursors used in the illicit manufacture of amphetamine-type stimulants, various initiatives resulted in proposals for preventive action, which formed the basis of Economic and Social Council resolution 2001/14 (see p. 1150). In June, the Board organized a round table in Beijing for competent authorities investigating the diversion and smuggling of precursors for methylenedioxymethamphetamine (MDMA), commonly known as Ecstasy.

While the Board welcomed sound scientific research into the possible therapeutic properties and medical uses of cannabis, it reminded the countries of the requirements set by the 1961 Convention to reduce the risk of its diversion and abuse. The Board invited Governments and relevant international bodies, in particular the Commission on Narcotic Drugs and the World Health Organization (WHO), to take note of new cannabis policies in a number of countries and to agree on ways to address that development within the framework of international law. The Board also requested Governments to ensure the prevention of trade in opium poppy seeds. It asked countries that did not yet control the import and export of psychotropic substances to introduce systems of import and export authorizations.

As to the supply of and demand for opiates used for medical and scientific purposes, the Board noted that since 1998, when commercial cultivation of the thebaine-rich variety of opium poppy began in Australia, the total area under such cultivation had been on the rise. The trend continued towards a larger proportion of the extraction of alkaloids from concentrate of poppy straw than from opium, mainly as the result of the increasing use of thebaine-rich poppy straw to respond to the growing demand for oxycodone for treating pain and for buprenorphine, used as an analgesic and in heroin substitution treatment. So far, however, the Board had not included any quantities related to thebaine in its analysis of the supply of and demand for opiates. Among its recommendations on methodologies for determining the supply of and demand for opiates for medical and scientific purposes, the Board proposed that additional opiates, such as thebaine, oxycodone, buprenorphine and hydrocodone, be included in calculations of supply and demand.

The Board requested Governments to monitor the consumption of stimulants used as anorectics in order to avoid their overprescription and to ensure adequate control of domestic distribution channels to avoid diversion to illicit markets. It reminded Governments of their commitment to give high priority to measures against the abuse of amphetamine-type stimulants.

By **decision 2001/242** of 24 July, the Economic and Social Council took note of the INCB report for 2000 [Sales No. E.01.XI.1].

ECONOMIC AND SOCIAL COUNCIL ACTION

On 24 July [meeting 40], the Economic and Social Council, on the recommendation of the Commission on Narcotic Drugs [E/2001/28/Rev.1], adopted **resolution 2001/15** without vote [agenda item 14 (*d*)].

International cooperation for the control of narcotic drugs

The Economic and Social Council,

Concerned with the health and welfare of humankind,

Recognizing that the medical use of narcotic drugs continues to be indispensable for the relief of pain and suffering and that adequate provision must be made to ensure the availability of narcotic drugs for such purposes,

Deeply concerned by the magnitude of and rising trend in the illicit production of, demand for and trafficking in opiates,

Emphasizing that the need to balance the global licit supply of opiates against the legitimate demand for opiates for medical and scientific purposes is central to the international strategy and policy of drug control,

Recognizing that the control of narcotic drugs is the collective responsibility of all States and that, to that end, coordinated action within the framework of international cooperation is necessary,

Taking into account the social and cultural aspects of poppy cultivation in the traditional supplier countries, India and Turkey, and the dependence of large segments of populations in rural areas of those countries on the licit production of opium poppy for a living,

Acknowledging the sacrifices and costly efforts made by the traditional supplier countries in order to ensure secure methods of poppy cultivation and to prevent diversion from licit to illicit channels,

Reaffirming the guiding principles of existing treaties in the field of narcotic drugs, in particular the provisions of the Single Convention on Narcotic Drugs of 1961, and the system of control that they embody,

Having considered the *Report of the International Narcotics Control Board for 1999*, in which the Board points to the overproduction of opiates,

1. *Calls upon* all Governments to support the traditional supplier countries in a spirit of international cooperation and solidarity in drug control;

2. *Underlines* that international trade in narcotic drugs, without distinction as to source or kind, is subject to the control provided for in the related international conventions, the implementation of which is essential in order to counter the world drug problem;

3. *Reconfirms* that the new variety of Papaver somniferum (opium poppy) with a high thebaine content comes under the international control regime established by the Single Convention on Narcotic Drugs of 1961, and must be controlled in the same way as other varieties of Papaver somniferum containing other alkaloids;

4. *Requests* the International Narcotics Control Board to monitor the cultivation of this new variety of Papaver somniferum, the production of thebaine from it and the international trade in thebaine accordingly;

5. *Commends* the Government of the United States of America for the 80/20 rule applied in its import of narcotic raw materials, which has contributed greatly to global efforts to maintain a lasting balance between the supply of and demand for opiates.

World drug situation

In its 2001 report [Sales No. E.02.XI.1], INCB provided a regional analysis of world drug abuse trends and control efforts, so that Governments would be kept aware of situations that might endanger the objectives of international drug control treaties.

Africa

Illicit cultivation and abuse of and trafficking in cannabis continued in several countries throughout Africa. Despite increased seizures and continued eradication efforts, cannabis remained the main drug of abuse. Cannabis cultivated within the region was also smuggled into Europe and North America. The main African source countries for cannabis smuggled into Europe continued to be Morocco (which accounted for 69 to 70 per cent of the cannabis seized in Europe) and South Africa and, to a lesser degree, Ghana, Nigeria and Senegal. According to Interpol, 22 per cent of the cannabis herb seizures worldwide in 2001 were effected in Africa.

The abuse of psychotropic substances continued to be a major problem in many countries in Africa, particularly in major cities in Southern, Eastern and Western Africa. Self-medication, the sale of licit drugs through unregulated channels (street hawkers, drug vendors, unauthorized retailers) and the sale of psychotropic substances without prescription were believed to have contributed to that development. While the abuse of amphetamine, benzodiazepine, ephedrine and pemoline was more pronounced in Western Africa, methaqualone continued to be abused mainly in Southern and Eastern Africa, in particular in South Africa. The abuse of Ecstasy was also on the rise in South Africa.

Opiate abuse remained relatively limited in the region, although it was rising in cities along the Indian Ocean. Cocaine continued to be mainly abused in cities and tourist centres in Southern and Western Africa, particularly in Côte d'Ivoire, Ghana, Lesotho, South Africa and

Swaziland, which were the major transit points for cocaine from South America into Europe.

Africa continued to be a major transit area for heroin trafficking. Côte d'Ivoire, Ghana and Nigeria were used as major transit points for smuggling and packaging heroin from South-East Asia and South-West Asia, which was then smuggled into Europe and North America. While heroin abuse continued to be relatively low in most countries in Africa, South Africa saw an increase of 40 per cent in the number of intravenous heroin abusers over the preceding three years, a development that raised concerns about the increased spread of HIV/AIDS there.

Regional cooperation in drug control improved in 2001. The Organization of African Unity (OAU) strengthened its focal point for drugs for more sustained cooperation with African Governments and enhanced its drug control cooperation and coordination with African subregional organizations. In January, the Ministers for Foreign Affairs of Kenya, Uganda and the United Republic of Tanzania signed a protocol on combating illicit drug trafficking in the East African Community. Those countries, together with Rwanda, strengthened their cooperation in drug control through biennial meetings of heads of departments of investigation and drug control units.

The Board noted with appreciation the progress made in the judicial system through training in drug-related cases in Southern and Eastern Africa. By October, a total of 92 investigators and prosecutors, 50 magistrates and 38 judges had completed training courses in South Africa and Zimbabwe. The Centre for Judicial Training was established in Maputo, Mozambique, in April to provide training for public prosecutors, drug law enforcement officials and judicial officials.

Many countries in Africa worked to update existing drug control laws and to prepare legislation to combat money-laundering, including the Central African Republic, Egypt, Mauritius, Morocco, Mozambique, Swaziland and the United Republic of Tanzania. The Board noted with concern that the Financial Action Task Force on Money-Laundering had included Egypt and Nigeria in the list of non-cooperative countries and urged them to expedite the drafting of relevant legislation. Kenya, the Libyan Arab Jamahiriya, Madagascar, Nigeria, Rwanda, Seychelles, South Africa, Togo and the United Republic of Tanzania adopted or worked on finalizing national strategies and plans of action on drug control. The Board noted with concern that resources were not always made available to implement plans made by some African countries.

In April, the Board sent a mission to Eritrea. Recognizing that accession to the three international drug control treaties might have been difficult for Eritrea in the early years following its independence, the Board urged the Government to accede to the treaties as peace returned to the country. Another mission was sent to Egypt in May, and the Board invited the Government to share with others its approaches to dealing with the drug problem and its experience in implementing the international drug control treaties. The Board expressed appreciation for Egypt's commitment to international drug control. It also visited Morocco in June to discuss the problems of national and international drug control, particularly cannabis cultivation and illicit trafficking. The Board urged the Government to elaborate a concrete plan for the eradication of cannabis cultivation.

In May, the Board reviewed the progress made by Gabon on recommendations by the Board pursuant to its 1998 mission to that country [YUN 1998; p. 1153]. It was pleased that, after nearly 10 years, Gabon had resumed submitting data related to the licit trade in narcotic drugs and psychotropic substances.

Americas

Central America and the Caribbean

Cannabis, the only drug crop cultivated in the Caribbean, remained an important source of income in Jamaica and other islands in the subregion. All countries in Central America reported some cannabis cultivation.

While cannabis trafficking and cocaine transit trafficking were predominant in the subregion, there was also evidence of the smuggling of synthetic drugs from Europe and heroin from South America, through Central America and the Caribbean, into the United States. It was estimated that nearly half of the cocaine that arrived in the United States each year (375 tons) came through Central America and the Mexican land corridor. Drug traffickers took advantage of the unstable political situation in Haiti by routing drugs through that country and the Dominican Republic to the United States. Reporting by countries of the subregion on illicit activities regarding psychotropic substances remained limited, but trafficking in such substances was increasing. Traffickers smuggling cocaine into Europe returned with Ecstasy, most of which was then smuggled into the United States. Amphetamines, Ecstasy and lysergic acid diethylamide (LSD) were seized in the Bahamas, the Cayman Islands, Costa Rica, the Dominican Republic and the Netherlands Antilles.

The smuggling of drugs, mostly cocaine hydrochloride, coca paste (basuco) and "crack", by land continued unabated. Ports on the Caribbean Sea and on the Pacific Ocean were increasingly used for the trans-shipment of illicit drugs. Costa Rica and Panama were important transit points for shipment, on a small scale, of illicit drug consignments by air to Europe.

There was a noticeable increase in firearms trafficking along drug trafficking routes, together with an increase in other criminal activities associated with the illicit drug trade, such as trafficking in persons and motor vehicle theft.

In March, the Board sent a mission to the Dominican Republic. It noted the recent success achieved in prosecuting money-laundering activities in that country and urged the Government to strengthen its prosecution capability. It also urged the Government formally to adopt the five-year national master plan against drugs, prepared some years earlier, including the modifications necessary to meet its criteria. Also in March, the Board sent a mission to Jamaica, where it noted the efforts made by law enforcement authorities to manually eradicate cannabis, the most widely available drug in the country. It expressed concern over the high cannabis-related crime rate, the smuggling of substantial quantities of cannabis out of the country, mainly into the United States, the increase in the smuggling of cocaine from South America through Jamaica into North America and the related flow of smuggled firearms in the opposite direction.

The Board, in May, reviewed action taken by Belize pursuant to its recommendations after a mission to that country in April 1998 [YUN 1998, p. 1154]. It noted the steps taken towards monitoring psychotropic substances, and urged Belize to become party to the 1961 and 1971 Conventions.

At the regional level, the Caribbean Drug Control Coordination Mechanism continued to monitor progress in implementing measures of the 1996 Plan of Action on Drug Control Coordination in the Caribbean. Improved communications technology and the use of electronic transfer of funds by drug traffickers made control efforts more challenging.

North America

In Canada and the United States, the use of cannabis, the most common drug of abuse in North America, remained stable though it was increasingly used in combination with stimulants. Cocaine abuse appeared to be stabilizing, even declining, in many parts of Canada and the United States. The abuse of "crack" continued to diminish as the addict population aged. After a period of stabilization, there seemed to be an increase in heroin abuse among young people in Canada and the United States, possibly due to lower prices and an increase in the level of purity, which made it easier to snort or smoke rather than inject the substance. In British Columbia, Canada, injection of heroin had led to high rates of overdose and HIV/AIDS and hepatitis C infection. In Mexico, data showed that the abuse of cannabis, cocaine and heroin increased, though it remained lower than the level of use in Canada and the United States. The level of drug abuse in Mexico was highest in the districts closest to the border with the United States. The availability and abuse of Ecstasy continued to spread beyond nightclub scenes into other settings, such as the military. In the United States, the abuse of benzodiazepines and other prescription drugs to alleviate Ecstasy's stimulant effects was noted among adolescents. There was also widespread abuse of the "club drugs"—ketamine, *gamma*-hydroxybutyric acid (GHB), *gamma*-butyrolactone (GBL) and methamphetamine. In Canada and the United States, the abuse of benzodiazepines continued to be common and the abuse of licit opiates, including hydrocodone, hydromorphone and, above all, oxycodone, also increased.

Mexico continued to be a major gateway for cocaine consignments from Colombia destined for Canada and the United States, and Mexican authorities had seized large consignments of cannabis that were in transit. On the west coast of Canada, much of the illicit heroin was smuggled into the country from South-East Asia. Criminal groups involved in those operations and in cocaine trafficking had become more organized. As law enforcement pressure increased in Mexico and the Caribbean, more cocaine was smuggled from South America into Canada and the United States via the eastern Pacific route, in containers and aboard "go-fast" boats and fishing vessels.

In July, Canada passed a regulation allowing individuals to access cannabis for medical purposes. The Board shared the concerns expressed by the Canadian Medical Association on the burden placed on physicians to approve the use of cannabis in the absence of conclusive research into its safety for medical use.

Mexico and the United States continued to cooperate in drug control policy. The Attorney-General of each of those countries and the National Security Adviser of Mexico led a working group on legal affairs and drug control cooperation. Mexico and the United States signed a memorandum of understanding allowing each Government an equal share of seized drug assets, to be used in the fight against drug trafficking. The law enforcement authorities of Canada and the United States cooperated in intelligence-sharing and conducted joint investigations and operations, which yielded positive results.

The Board expressed concern over legal loopholes in the United States that made it possible for public advertising of prescription drugs; in particular, methylphenidate, widely used for the treatment of attention deficit disorder, was being diverted for abuse by schoolchildren.

South America

Coca bush continued to be cultivated exclusively in South America. The overall levels of coca leaf production remained stable despite fluctuations in individual countries, and the abuse of cocaine increased, particularly in transit countries such as Argentina, Brazil, Chile, Ecuador and Venezuela. Bolivia and Peru were the only countries in the region in which the abuse of cocaine appeared to have decreased. Opium poppy cultivation and heroin production increased in some countries in the Andean subregion. Heroin abuse was low compared with other drugs and other regions, although it increased in Argentina, Colombia and Ecuador. Cannabis cultivation continued to be widespread in South America, mainly for local consumption.

In Colombia, increased interdiction efforts included aerial fumigation to eradicate coca bush and opium poppy where access by land was difficult. By midyear, 50,000 hectares had been sprayed. However, eradication efforts were offset by increased cultivation in other areas of Peru and Colombia.

Almost all countries in South America were used by traffickers as transit points for transporting illicit drug consignments destined for the region, Europe and North America. The precursors smuggled into South America were transported mainly to Colombia, where most drug-processing laboratories were located. Authorities, mainly in Colombia, continued to seize significant amounts of cocaine. Heroin seizures increased significantly in Colombia, and in June 67 kilograms of heroin were seized, the largest single heroin seizure ever made in the country. Colombian drug traffickers diversified their operations, as evidenced by the increased seizures of substances such as Ecstasy. South American cocaine was smuggled into Europe, where it was exchanged for Ecstasy that was then smuggled back into South America.

In March, the Board sent a mission to Venezuela, where it noted the active role played by the Venezuelan authorities in cooperating in drug control with their counterparts in other countries in South America and other regions.

In June, the Board sent a mission to Bolivia, where the production and chewing of coca leaf continued. Illicit production of coca leaf was currently taking place only to a limited extent, as the illicit manufacture of cocaine in Bolivia and in other countries with coca leaf of Bolivian origin had been reduced significantly. Controls over precursor chemicals had been implemented, but controls over narcotic drugs and psychotropic substances were insufficient.

The Board also sent a mission to Chile in June and noted with satisfaction that national policies concerning drug abuse and illicit trafficking provided for a balanced system of measures for the reduction of illicit drug demand and supply. Chile was an important manufacturer and importer of precursor chemicals, some of which were diverted for the illicit manufacture of cocaine, mainly in neighbouring countries. The Board welcomed a new law that dealt more effectively with offences related to precursors.

In May, the Board reviewed action taken by Argentina to implement its recommendations after the mission to that country in September 1998 [YUN 1998, p. 1157]; it expressed satisfaction that most recommendations had been implemented.

Asia

East and South-East Asia

A number of countries in East and South-East Asia, including Brunei Darussalam, Indonesia, Japan and Thailand, reported that the abuse of opiates such as raw opium, codeine and heroin had declined while the abuse of amphetamine-type stimulants had increased. In some countries, illicit manufacture of, trafficking in and abuse of amphetamine-type stimulants had become matters of greater concern than illicit activities relating to opiates. Amphetamine-type substances were the most popular drugs abused in several countries, particularly Japan, the Philippines, the Republic of Korea and Thailand. The spread of HIV infection was closely linked to drug abuse by injection. The Board expressed concern that Ecstasy, which was virtually unknown in the region a decade earlier, continued to gain popularity among youth.

Eradication efforts by Myanmar and alternative development activities resulted in a decrease in illicit opium poppy cultivation by one third from 1996 to 2000; however, there were indications that such cultivation had increased again in

2001. Myanmar accounted for most of the world's illicit opium poppy cultivation in 2001. In the Lao People's Democratic Republic, the total area under illicit opium poppy cultivation declined. Opium poppy cultivation in Thailand remained at negligible levels. In Viet Nam, illicit opium poppy cultivation had been significantly reduced in the preceding decade.

Cannabis was illicitly cultivated mainly in Cambodia, Indonesia, the Lao People's Democratic Republic, the Philippines and Thailand. In Indonesia, a marked increase in the illicit cultivation and trafficking in cannabis was reported. Since 1996, significant quantities of Cambodian cannabis had been seized in Australia, Europe and the United States. The level of cannabis abuse was low in most countries in East and South-East Asia.

Regionally, countries continued their multilateral drug control cooperation through the Association of South-East Asian Nations (ASEAN), the 1993 memorandum of understanding on drug control between the countries in the Mekong area (Cambodia, China, the Lao People's Democratic Republic, Myanmar, Thailand and Viet Nam) and UNDCP. East Asian countries, including Japan and the Republic of Korea, participated in drug control efforts throughout the region. In July, Cambodia and Thailand signed a memorandum of understanding and made arrangements for increased bilateral cooperation against a number of illicit activities, including drug trafficking.

The Board took note of the measures adopted by the Republic of Korea to strengthen its ability to deal with money-laundering by establishing a financial intelligence unit. The Board also noted adoption of a bill against money-laundering in the Philippines. Mongolia undertook a rapid situation assessment to ascertain the extent of problems related to drug injection and HIV prevalence. In Thailand, schools were instructed to set up drug control committees in order to curb the abuse of drugs and other illegal acts by youth.

In April, the Board sent a mission to Thailand. It expressed concern over the abuse of certain psychotropic substances, including phentermine and diazepam, and requested the Thai authorities to give further attention to controls over those substances, especially stimulants. It also noted the Government's efforts to establish programmes to strengthen prevention in communities and schools and to develop strategies to address addiction to amphetamine-type stimulants.

The Board sent a mission to Myanmar in September and, following a review of the progress on its recommendations following a 1998 mission to that country [YUN 1998, p. 1158], found that continuous implementation efforts were being made. It noted that Myanmar was committed to the eradication of illicit opium poppy cultivation, but that limited resources and the low level of external assistance had negatively impacted Myanmar's ability to achieve goals set out in its eradication programme and to consolidate gains.

The Board noted the ministerial meeting on drug control cooperation between China, the Lao People's Democratic Republic, Myanmar and Thailand held in Beijing on 28 August.

South Asia

The region's drug trafficking and abuse problems were largely related to transit traffic, as South Asia was situated between the world's two main opiate-producing areas. Illicit opium poppy cultivation and heroin manufacture had increased over several years and illicit cannabis cultivation and abuse continued unabated. There was an increase in polydrug abuse involving, in addition to illicitly manufactured drugs, a range of pharmaceutical products containing narcotic drugs and psychotropic substances.

Cannabis was the most widely abused drug in South Asia. In all countries in the region, except Bhutan and Maldives, there were reports of cannabis growing wild or being illicitly cultivated. Cocaine abuse remained very limited, though seizures of the drug increased, particularly in India. The incidence of heroin injection increased particularly in Bangladesh, India and Nepal, while in Maldives and Sri Lanka smoking and inhalation continued to be the most common methods of heroin abuse. In almost all South Asian countries, there was an increase in the abuse of prescription drugs that were either diverted from domestic distribution channels or smuggled out of neighbouring countries. Psychotropic substances were also abused in Bangladesh, India, Maldives, Nepal and Sri Lanka to varying degrees.

In Bangladesh, opium poppy was illicitly cultivated in the remote areas of the Chittagong Hill Tracts, where the movement of security forces was restricted. In India, cultivation and abuse posed problems in eastern Arunachal Pradesh, where plans for alternative development and income substitution projects were under way. India, a main licit producer of opium, designed an elaborate system to prevent the diversion of licitly produced opium into illicit channels, which involved control of licensing, demanding minimum qualifying yields, a government monopoly on purchasing and meeting strict monitoring requirements. Most of the heroin smuggled out of South-West Asia into South Asia was destined for countries in Western Europe and the United States.

India was an important producer of precursor chemicals, such as acetic anhydride, ephedrine, pseudoephedrine, anthranilic acid and N-acetyl-anthranilic acid. The diversion of precursor chemicals into Central Asia and Afghanistan dropped significantly as a result of India's strict controls and cooperation among manufacturing companies. In Nepal, an interdepartmental co-ordination committee on precursor control was established and regulatory measures and controls were introduced for all substances.

India was an important manufacturer and trader of pharmaceuticals, including a number of widely used psychotropic substances. Despite a control system for international trade in psychotropic substances and measures to control domestic distribution, problems were encountered in monitoring compliance. The growing abuse of psychotropic substances was one of the reasons for the increase in polydrug abuse in combination with other pharmaceuticals (opiates and non-opiates), illicit drugs and alcohol. In Nepal, many abusers of opiates reverted to the abuse of pharmaceutical products containing nitrazepam, diazepam and buprenorphine due to their easy availability and low prices. Benzodiazepines were abused in Maldives, mostly in combination with cannabis or heroin. In Bangladesh, the abuse of tranquillizers such as benzodiazepines was widespread and the availability of illicit buprenorphine caused an increase in the abuse by injection.

Among regional efforts in drug control, the Board noted the relaunching of the precursor control project for member States of the South Asian Association for Regional Cooperation, including a regional workshop on precursor control, held in Kathmandu, Nepal, at the beginning of 2001. A number of bilateral agreements were signed. For example, Bangladesh and Myanmar signed an agreement to combat illicit trafficking in narcotic drugs, psychotropic substances and precursors; and India and Tajikistan signed an agreement on the reduction of illicit drug demand and the prevention of trafficking in narcotic drugs, psychotropic substances and precursors.

In April, the Board visited India and welcomed additional efforts to strengthen measures at the Neemuch Opium and Alkaloid Factory, in line with earlier Board recommendations. The Board remained concerned about leakages from licit opium production, noting that there was still no adequate system for collecting information and that coordination among government agencies responsible for reporting was insufficient.

West and Central Asia

Developments in Afghanistan affected the drug abuse situation in West Asia. As a result of the prolonged drought and the ban on opium poppy cultivation issued in July 2000 by the Taliban, such cultivation was significantly reduced in the areas under Taliban control; however, illicit cultivation increased in other parts of Afghanistan and it appeared that the flow of illicit drugs in Central Asian countries, in particular heroin, from Afghanistan increased in 2001, marking a continuation of the trend in 2000. As in recent years, while a significant portion of the opiates produced in West Asia was destined for illicit markets in Europe and, to a lesser degree, Africa, East Asia and South Asia, a considerable amount remained in West Asia. Opiates originating in Afghanistan continued to be smuggled into and through Iran and Pakistan, where opiate addiction rates continued to be among the highest in the world. The smuggling of opiates in West Asia had become more organized, profitable and violent, and was jeopardizing the economic and social stability of some countries.

Most countries in West Asia were used as transit points for smuggling opiates into Europe and other regions. Precursors and chemicals used in the illicit manufacture of heroin continued to flow from outside the region into countries in West Asia where such manufacture was taking place. Seizure statistics for regional countries showed that opium had been increasingly processed into other opiates in Afghanistan.

The harvest in the crop year 2000/01 in Afghanistan was estimated to be less than one tenth of that in the previous crop year. As a result, opium and morphine were much less available on illicit markets in West Asia; however, in response to post-11 September developments (see p. 259), large quantities of opiates were made available from illicit stocks. The availability of heroin originating in Afghanistan remained high in the region. In Pakistan, only isolated cases involving illicit opium poppy cultivation were identified, and in Turkey, poppy straw from licit cultivation was used for the extraction of alkaloids. No diversion of opiates into illicit markets was reported.

Cannabis remained the most widely abused substance in West Asia. Huge quantities continued to be illicitly cultivated or grew wild in Afghanistan and, to a lesser degree, in Pakistan and Kazakhstan. Cannabis resin was smuggled into other countries in West Asia and Europe. The total amount of cannabis seized in West Asia increased during 2000 and the first half of 2001. In Lebanon, cannabis cultivation, which had been eradicated in the early 1990s, was resumed in 2001.

Data on the extent of drug abuse in Central Asia were limited; however, indications of an increase in drug abusers were reported. The most serious trend was the rapid increase in abuse by injection, which contributed to the spread of HIV infection.

Stimulants continued to be smuggled and abused in West Asia, mainly in the eastern Mediterranean area and on the Arabian peninsula. The abuse of benzodiazepines was widespread, indicating that controls over the licit distribution of such products were weak. In Afghanistan, Iran and Pakistan, benzodiazepines were often abused in conjunction with opium and heroin and they were added to heroin as adulterants. The abuse of LSD continued to be reported in Israel.

All of the countries in Central Asia, except Tajikistan and Uzbekistan, had adopted comprehensive national drug control strategies. Initiatives included measures by Kyrgyzstan to prevent drug addiction and halt drug traffickers; the establishment by Iran of an institute to monitor illicit drug demand; the setting-up by Turkmenistan of specialized clinics to treat addicts; Lebanon's adoption of a law on the control of narcotic drugs, psychotropic substances and precursors; and Bahrain's adoption of a law to combat money-laundering. Legislation on precursors was enacted in all Central Asian countries except Turkmenistan, where such legislation was before parliament.

The Board noted the cooperation that took place within the framework of the memorandum of understanding on drug control cooperation in Central Asia, involving Azerbaijan, Kazakhstan, Kyrgyzstan, the Russian Federation, Tajikistan, Turkmenistan and Uzbekistan, as well as UNDCP and the Aga Khan Development Network. It also noted that the European Union had adopted a Central Asian action plan on drugs, which aimed at, among other things, providing assistance in drug law enforcement and gathering drug-related information.

In March, the Board sent a mission to Jordan. It noted with satisfaction that the activities outlined in the 1999-2001 national plan for combating drugs and psychotropic substances were beginning to be implemented and encouraged Jordan to join efforts with neighbouring countries in strengthening the interdiction capacity of national institutions in order to improve border surveillance.

The Board sent a mission to Pakistan in April and noted with appreciation Pakistan's commitment to eradicate illicit opium poppy cultivation, which resulted in the effective clearance of opium-harvesting areas in the Dir district. Concern was expressed that control of licit activities related to narcotic drugs and psychotropic substances was inadequate in Pakistan.

The Board visited the Syrian Arab Republic in June and encouraged the Government to establish an information network to address trafficking in synthetic drugs, large amounts of which were seized annually in the country. The Board welcomed the Government's approval of a bank secrecy law and its efforts to develop mechanisms to prevent use of the financial system for money-laundering.

Europe

Europe remained a major source of illicitly manufactured synthetic drugs, abused widely by young people both within and outside the region. Western Europe remained the source of most of the Ecstasy seized throughout the world. The continent remained the second largest market for cocaine in the world, after North America. In Central and Eastern Europe, a noticeable increase in the illicit manufacture and abuse of amphetamine-type stimulants was reported. Most countries in Central and Eastern Europe, having been used for a long time as transit countries, were facing serious problems of heroin abuse.

Cannabis continued to be the most commonly abused drug in the region and much of it was grown there. Albania continued to be a major source for cannabis herb despite eradication efforts and large seizures by authorities. Indoor cannabis cultivation also continued, facilitated by unrestricted sale of cannabis seeds and growing accessories on the Internet and availability in shops in some countries. The availability of opiates originating in South-West Asia increased as well.

Illicit opium poppy cultivation was discovered for the first time in Albania and small-scale cultivation was reported in several other countries in Central and Eastern Europe. There was an increased flow of Afghan heroin into the Russian Federation. HIV infection and hepatitis C infection were spreading among injecting drug users in many countries in Central and Eastern Europe.

Most of the cocaine in Europe was smuggled through transit countries in South America or the Caribbean, with Spain continuing to be the most significant entry point, followed by the Netherlands and Portugal. Drug trafficking organizations also used countries in Central and Eastern Europe for transporting consignments of cocaine to Western Europe.

Trafficking in stimulants between Asia and Europe was conducted in both directions. In August, Switzerland's national law enforcement agency discovered and dismantled a major methamphetamine trafficking ring, the first of its kind in Europe, which had been smuggling the substance from South-East Asia into Europe. Illicit methamphetamine manufacture continued in the Czech Republic, despite action by the regulatory and law enforcement authorities. A clandestine laboratory manufacturing methamphetamine was also discovered in Bulgaria and the abuse of the substance had become more common, particularly among women and young people. In countries of the Commonwealth of Independent States (CIS), there was continued concern over the large-scale abuse of home-made ephedrone (a combination of ephedrine and plants of the genus *Ephedra*).

The Board noted action by a number of countries to reduce drug abuse, in particular Germany's increased control of drugs used in maintenance programmes, Slovakia's legislation on precursor control, and action by Poland and the Russian Federation against money-laundering. The Board welcomed government activities against organized crime and anti-corruption measures in several countries in Central and Eastern Europe.

The Board sent missions to Croatia, Finland, the Holy See, the Netherlands, Norway, Ukraine and Yugoslavia. It encouraged Croatian authorities to establish close cooperation with their counterparts in Bosnia and Herzegovina and Yugoslavia in order to develop a comprehensive regional approach to countering the increasing use of the Balkan route for trafficking in illicit drugs. The Board commended Finland for its comprehensive policy for drug control and a balance between law enforcement, prevention and treatment. In the Holy See, it expressed appreciation for the activities of the Roman Catholic Church in the area of drug demand reduction. The Board was concerned that seeds of cannabis varieties with a high tetrahydrocannabinol (THC) content from the Netherlands continued to be advertised via the Web and that authorities in the country appeared to have no legal instruments to deal with that problem. It was also concerned that the country remained the source of a significant proportion of the world's illicitly manufactured Ecstasy, despite efforts by law enforcement agencies. Norway was congratulated for its implementation of the international drug control conventions, Ukraine was urged to prevent the diversion of poppy straw from licensed farms cultivating poppy for culinary purposes, and Yugoslavia was encouraged to develop a drug control master plan, covering the trafficking and manufacturing of substances under international control.

Oceania

Hydroponically grown cannabis was the most popular form of cannabis abused in Australia, where that type of cannabis cultivation continued to increase and outdoor cultivation decreased. Significant cannabis cultivation also continued in Papua New Guinea for local consumption and for smuggling into other countries, mainly Australia, often in exchange for small arms. Reports were received of cannabis growing wild, being cultivated or seized in a number of smaller Pacific island States, such as Fiji and Tonga.

The availability of and demand for cocaine remained limited in all countries in Oceania except Australia. Seizure data indicated that for the preceding two to three years, New Zealand and many of the smaller Pacific island countries in Oceania were increasingly used as trans-shipment points for smuggling illicit drugs into Australia. Fiji and Vanuatu were used as transit points for large consignments of heroin originating in South-East Asia and destined for Australia, the main heroin abuse area in Oceania. Other countries in the region did not appear to have a significant heroin or cocaine abuse problem. Drug traffickers continued to move cocaine from South America to Australia through the Pacific islands. The quantity of cocaine seized at the border of Australia in 2001 was more than twice the figure for the preceding year.

An increased number of clandestine laboratories manufacturing amphetamine-type stimulants was detected in Australia, where police established chemical diversion units to monitor suspicious purchases of the precursor chemicals. Abusers in Australia increasingly injected methamphetamine with a high purity level, and in New Zealand it was reported that the illicit manufacture of methamphetamine was on the increase. Increased seizures and abuse of Ecstasy were reported in countries throughout Oceania.

In March, Australia launched the National Illicit Drugs Campaign aimed at motivating parents of teenagers to talk with their children about drugs. The Board noted that the Government had developed an international drug strategy to complement its National Drug Strategic Framework.

Regional organizations, including the Pacific Islands Forum and the Asia/Pacific Group on Money-Laundering, as well as the United Nations and the Commonwealth Secretariat, continued to coordinate action to implement the international drug control treaties.

UN action to combat drug abuse

UN International Drug Control Programme

The United Nations International Drug Control Programme (UNDCP), established in 1991 [YUN 1991, p. 721] to promote the application of international drug control treaties and the development of drug control strategies, was a catalyst in stimulating action at the national, regional and international levels. The Executive Director described UNDCP's 2001 activities in a report to the Commission on Narcotic Drugs [E/CN.7/2002/8 & Corr.1]. Through technical cooperation programmes supported by field offices in key regions and countries, it promoted subregional cooperation and furthered bilateral cooperation. In mounting a global response to the drug problem, UNDCP mobilized specialized agencies and other UN entities, international financial institutions, intergovernmental organizations and civil society, particularly non-governmental organizations (NGOs). In addition, UNDCP supported States in their efforts to comply with the international drug control treaties; supported their initiatives to meet the objectives agreed upon at the twentieth special session of the General Assembly [YUN 1998, p. 1135]; assisted in the prosecution of serious drug trafficking offences, including money-laundering; and provided support in improving judicial cooperation against drug-related offences, including by providing training to members of the judiciary, law enforcement personnel, prosecutors and personnel working in demand reduction. UNDCP continued to provide technical assistance for the development of crop-monitoring systems in countries affected by illicit crop cultivation, and, by the end of 2001, the activities covered all the main opium- and coca-producing countries, namely Afghanistan, Bolivia, Colombia, the Lao People's Democratic Republic, Myanmar and Peru.

UNDCP served as the substantive secretariat of INCB and, in close cooperation with the Board and Governments, it monitored the international drug control system and the flow of precursors. It provided legal advisory services, electronic support and laboratory services to the Board and implemented programmes that contributed to the establishment of mechanisms and procedures for precursor control, with emphasis given to law enforcement and operational issues. It also served as the substantive secretariat of the Commission on Narcotic Drugs and assisted the Commission in monitoring the implementation of the goals and targets for 2003 and 2008 set out in the Political Declaration adopted by the General Assembly

in resolution S-20/2 [YUN 1998, p. 1136]. In particular, the first consolidated biennial report on the progress achieved by Governments was prepared.

Income to the UNDCP Fund was estimated at $131.2 million for 2000-2001, which was 7.5 per cent less than in 1998-1999. The total estimated expenditure was $117.4 million for programmes, $28.6 million for programme support and $8.9 million for management and administration.

The UNDCP programme on scientific and technical support continued to develop, set and provide scientific and procedural standards in support of international drug control. Training for laboratory staff in the identification and analysis of drugs and precursors was organized at regional training centres in Africa, South-East Asia and Europe. Technical assistance for drug testing was provided to laboratories in Mexico, Pakistan and countries in Central America. Guidelines for testing drugs were prepared and revised. UNDCP continued to distribute field test kits for the rapid detection of drugs and precursors. During the year, 150 laboratories participated in the UNDCP International Collaborative Exercises of the International Quality Assurance Programme. In all regions, training in surveillance and research methods and other basic issues of drug abuse information collection and analysis was undertaken. The Global Assessment Programme on Drug Abuse aimed to disseminate methodological practices and encourage the adoption of harmonized indicators. A second global epidemiology network meeting was convened (Vienna, December) to assess existing data-collection networks and to develop a framework for harmonizing indicators and procedures.

UNDCP continued to work closely with organizations, including the International Monetary Fund, on money-laundering issues. It assisted a number of countries with the development of anti-money-laundering legal frameworks, including revision of legislation in several countries. It cooperated with Interpol and Canada to organize in Ottawa an international seminar on undercover financial investigative techniques; co-sponsored with the Egmont Group of Financial Intelligence Units a workshop for financial intelligence in Vienna; and co-organized in the Russian Federation the International Conference on Illegal Economy and Money-Laundering. UNDCP continued to collaborate with other UN entities on drug control issues and to interact with NGOs and encourage networking among them in order to promote the sharing of experiences in drug demand reduction activities. It organized the fourth interparliamentarian conference on drug control (Santa Cruz, Bolivia,

February) for officials from more than 25 countries, which focused on reducing illicit crops.

The Global Youth Network for the Prevention of Drug Abuse, initiated by UNDCP, expanded to include 70 groups from more than 40 countries.

Africa

UNDCP continued activities in Africa in demand reduction, suppression of illicit trafficking and drug control policy-making/advocacy involving international advisory functions with either full- or part-time local expertise. Multi-year priority programmes were prepared for Western Africa, Eastern Africa and Nigeria. UNDCP and OAU created the OAU focal unit for drugs, and UNDCP provided support for the establishment of a database on drug control experts and institutions in Africa. Following endorsement by the Economic Community of West African States for creating an Intergovernmental Task Force against Money-Laundering in West Africa, UNDCP supported the establishment of a secretariat in Dakar, Senegal, including establishing a library on money-laundering, setting up terms of reference for training courses and holding an expert meeting on money-laundering in West Africa. UNDCP and the Southern African Development Community (SADC) cooperated in harmonizing legislation at the regional level and conducting assessments and fact-finding events. At the country level, Governments in Southern, Central, Eastern and Western Africa were supported in establishing national drug control coordination bodies and formulating national policies. In North Africa, UNDCP provided expertise and played a catalytic role to effect changes in national drug control policies and programmes, and increased support for drug control activities by Governments, such as setting targets for cannabis elimination in Morocco and integrating licit control and demand reduction in the Libyan Arab Jamahiriya.

UNDCP introduced a new Africa-wide initiative on the development of regional expert networks (LEN) in Eastern Africa and held its first LEN workshop, bringing together 10 demand reduction experts from six countries. It provided LEN members with training and advice on good practice and models. In East Africa, country-level activities in support of prevention and education activities were undertaken in Ethiopia, Madagascar and the United Republic of Tanzania. In Kenya, training was given to more than 2,600 scout leaders in drug abuse awareness and prevention. In West Africa, rapid assessments of the drug abuse situation were conducted in Côte d'Ivoire, Ghana and Senegal. UNDCP initiated a joint project to integrate drug abuse prevention

into the United Nations Population Fund (UNFPA) healthy-lifestyle education programme for youth in Cape Verde, the Gambia and Senegal. In Nigeria, prevention activities, to be undertaken by demand reduction experts, were initiated and training provided. In South Africa, work was undertaken to expand community-based treatment centres to the remaining seven centres in other provinces.

Among efforts to suppress illicit drug trafficking, UNDCP supported national policy-making, the adoption of drug control measures and initiatives, the adoption and implementation of money-laundering legislation and training to improve control capacity. It supported the SADC national offices, workshops and assessments on money-laundering and judicial cooperation. Through the programme of legal assistance for 19 Southern and Eastern African countries, more than 180 judges, magistrates, prosecutors and senior investigators were trained in six regional training courses. A network of licit control officials covering all Eastern African countries was established. A new project with the Universal Postal Union was begun, aimed at addressing drug trafficking by post. At the country level, UNDCP provided training and basic detection, search and communications equipment to law enforcement agencies operating at borders and airports. In North Africa, UNDCP organized a two-week-long drugs investigation and surveillance training course in Abu Dhabi, United Arab Emirates, for drug enforcement officers from States members of the Gulf Cooperation Council.

Central and Eastern Europe

UNDCP supported Central and Eastern European countries in developing effective drug policies and measures, and in fostering cooperation among them to counter drug trafficking and reduce demand. Best practices in management, administration and operations were emphasized, as well as technical support in, among other things, computerized intelligence analysis, surveillance and computer-based training for law enforcement officers. Representatives of the Czech Republic, Hungary, Poland, Slovakia, Slovenia and UNDCP met in Bratislava, Slovakia, in May to identify new regional activities. UNDCP organized a legal workshop for the Danube Basin and Central European countries in Budapest, Hungary, in June. The Memorandum of Understanding on Cooperation in Drug Control and Activities against Money-Laundering, agreed by Azerbaijan, Georgia, Iran and UNDCP, was adopted in October.

UNDCP and the Pompidou Group of the Council of Europe jointly published materials on developing drug information systems in Central and Eastern Europe. UNDCP supported the initiation of school-based prevention activities in three Baltic States and organized a youth network training course for countries in Central and Eastern Europe in Riga, Latvia. It collaborated with the Joint United Nations Programme on HIV/AIDS (UNAIDS) on activities to diversify services for drug abusers in Belarus, the Republic of Moldova, the Russian Federation and Ukraine. As part of the UNDCP Global Assessment Programme, activities were initiated to assist in the collection of reliable and internationally comparable drug abuse data and to assess patterns in Belarus, the Republic of Moldova, the Russian Federation, Ukraine and the Central Asian States.

Among efforts to suppress drug trafficking, UNDCP strengthened cooperation with Interpol and supported drug intelligence units in Bulgaria, Romania and the former Yugoslav Republic of Macedonia. It also worked with law enforcement authorities in Albania and Bosnia and Herzegovina. In the Russian Federation, an Inter-Agency Drug Control Centre and 15 regional divisions were set up and equipped, and UNDCP supported the strengthening of the capacities of the Russian Federal Border troops at the Tajik-Afghan border. In Tajikistan and Uzbekistan, a modern automated telecommunications data system was established and 600 officers were trained.

South Asia

Efforts in South Asia focused on law enforcement, demand reduction and drug-related HIV/AIDS issues, though funding constraints limited the expansion of UNDCP activities. At the country level, support was provided to develop national strategies, with emphasis on strengthening technical capacity in drug law enforcement and on formulating methodologies for assessing the drug situation, and legal assistance for implementing national legislation. Legal advisory services were provided to the Governments of Bangladesh, Nepal and Sri Lanka for their national drug control strategies, and UNDCP participated in events with civil society to raise awareness of drug issues. In India, the national survey on the extent, patterns and trends in drug abuse was completed and a rapid assessment survey was conducted in 10 cities.

In collaboration with the International Labour Organization (ILO), UNDCP conducted over 50 training courses on community-based prevention and rehabilitation, and drug abuse monitoring. A regional project aimed at reducing drug abuse and drug-related HIV was elaborated for the South Asian Association for Regional Cooperation countries in late 2001. Five drop-in centres in Colombo, Sri Lanka, were assisted and staff were provided with the necessary training, in cooperation with WHO. Grants were approved for demand reduction work by NGOs in Bangladesh, India, Nepal and Sri Lanka, with support from Japan.

UNDCP assisted the region with the further development of measures to prevent the diversion of precursor chemicals and organized, in consultation with INCB, national and regional precursor control training programmes. Technical missions were undertaken to Bhutan, Maldives, Nepal, Pakistan and Sri Lanka to assess their precursor control situation and related law enforcement needs. UNDCP designed a survey, undertaken by ILO with United Nations Development Programme support, of four opium poppy-growing areas in Arunachal Pradesh state in India and assisted the Government in developing a comprehensive strategy for alternative development in the region.

East Asia and the Pacific

UNDCP continued its catalytic coordinating role in promoting drug control within the framework of the Subregional Action Plan developed under the 1993 memorandum of understanding between Cambodia, China, the Lao People's Democratic Republic, Myanmar, Thailand and Viet Nam. At a ministerial-level meeting (Yangon, Myanmar, May), representatives of the six countries reaffirmed their commitment to and satisfaction with the framework and the progress made in implementing the Subregional Action Plan programmes. At a meeting of all countries of ASEAN and China, representatives endorsed an inter-agency programme to implement the plan of action entitled "Association of South-East Asian Nations and China Cooperative Operations in Response to Dangerous Drugs" (ACCORD). UNDCP and the ASEAN secretariat convened the first task force meeting under the ACCORD Action Plan cooperation mechanism (Bali, Indonesia, November), during which the terms of reference and 2002 work plans for each task force were approved. A new programme on precursor control, aimed at halting the diversion and trafficking of precursors in East Asia, was agreed on in May, and UNDCP developed several computer-based training modules for the six countries that had signed the 1993 memorandum of understanding.

UNDCP worked in cooperation with the Economic and Social Commission for Asia and the Pacific in several drug demand reduction activities through regional youth forums and other consultation mechanisms. It developed a comprehensive demand reduction programme for amphetamine-type stimulants for the region, with activities aimed at developing national and regional data-collection and information systems, as well as primary prevention activities related to such substance abuse in the workplace and among youth. In the Lao People's Democratic Republic, a national drug demand reduction centre was under construction in Vientiane, and UNDCP carried out a major study on drug abuse in two cities. In Viet Nam, an initiative aimed at preventing drug abuse among ethnic minorities was started. UNAIDS-funded efforts to incorporate HIV/AIDS issues in drug demand reduction programmes in South-East Asia began in late 2001.

Seven regional law enforcement projects in East Asia were implemented during 2001, including a computer-based training project for law enforcement officers. Five resource centres under the training project were established in Cambodia, China, Thailand and Viet Nam. In an effort to reduce response time in countering drug trafficking across national borders, several cross-border meetings were held, for example, the fifth Myanmar-Thailand Cross-Border Meeting on Drug Law Enforcement (Phuket Province, Thailand, August). UNDCP initiated a process to strengthen synergies with the Pacific Islands Forum and the Asia-Pacific Group on Money-Laundering in their anti-drug/crime policies and activities. In the Lao People's Democratic Republic, UNDCP supported the Government's alternative development programmes under the national strategy for eliminating illicit cultivation of opium poppy. The National Opium Survey 2001, conducted in collaboration with UNDCP, estimated that 17,255 hectares were under cultivation in 2001, representing a 36 per cent reduction since 1998. In Viet Nam, UNDCP assisted with the development of a new master plan for drug control for the years 2001-2010. In Thailand, with the support of UNDCP, a report and book were published highlighting lessons learned in reducing opium poppy cultivation over the period 1970-2000.

West and Central Asia

UNDCP concentrated its efforts on assisting Central Asian Governments in strengthening their capacity in drug control, since the region had emerged as one of the major trafficking routes for illicit drugs from Afghanistan. While continuing to implement its programme on alternative development interventions and drug demand reduction activities, UNDCP was involved in the implementation of the Drug Prevention and Monitoring Project of the Greater Azro Initiative by the Office of the United Nations High Commissioner for Refugees. In Pakistan, UNDCP assisted in preparing a comprehensive framework to monitor the implementation of the National Drug Control Master Plan for 1998-2003, and cooperated in new activities in drug demand reduction. The third review meeting (Dushanbe, Tajikistan, 17-18 September) of the parties to the memorandum of understanding on subregional drug control cooperation, signed by five Central Asian countries, the Russian Federation, the Aga Khan Development Network and UNDCP, called for further cooperation in combating illicit trafficking in drugs, precursors and psychotropic substances, as well as drug abuse. The meeting also endorsed the accession of Azerbaijan to the memorandum of understanding. UNDCP continued its assistance to the secretariat of the Economic Cooperation Organization in coordinating the drug control activities of its member States (Afghanistan, Azerbaijan, Iran, Kazakhstan, Kyrgyzstan, Pakistan, Tajikistan, Turkey, Turkmenistan, Uzbekistan), including a drug control reporting system, training drug control coordinators and a drug control database.

UNDCP provided continued support in assessing the problem of drug abuse in Afghanistan and the Afghan refugee community in Pakistan and published two new studies on those issues. New drug demand reduction activities targeting Afghan refugee women in Pakistan began in August. In Iran, UNDCP supported four studies aimed at revising legislation on money-laundering, alternative punishments, international judicial cooperation, controlled delivery and precursor control. Within the framework of the subregional drug control cooperation programme for the Middle East, programmes in treatment and rehabilitation were initiated in Egypt and Jordan, and a national conference on demand reduction was convened in Cairo in April.

UNDCP released the results of its 2001 opium poppy survey in Afghanistan, which showed a 91 per cent reduction in the total area under cultivation compared to the previous year; however, the existence of large surplus stocks from the two previous harvests had mitigated the effect of the drop in production on the global heroin market. UNDCP organized a field mission to former opium poppy–growing areas in Afghanistan for experts from donor countries and organizations, which confirmed the Taliban's implementation of the ban on opium poppy cultivation but found that it had resulted in additional hardship for many small farmers. In August, UNDCP began supporting agricultural inputs and food-for-work schemes to former opium poppy–cultivating areas in Nangarhar province, but the initiative came to an end following the 11 September terrorist attacks in the United States (see p. 60).

UNDCP continued to support Pakistan's strategy for supply reduction, which aimed at maintaining virtually zero opium poppy cultivation and other activities in Central Asia, enhancing the operational effectiveness of drug enforcement bodies, establishing a system for collecting criminal intelligence, implementing systems for effective cross-border cooperation and enhancing capacities for precursor control.

Latin America and the Caribbean

The UNDCP Caribbean Drug Control Coordination Mechanism undertook assessments of the implementation of the 1996 Barbados Plan of Action for Regional Drug Control Coordination and Cooperation. In Central America, UNDCP supported the Permanent Central American Commission for the Eradication of the Illicit Production, Traffic, Consumption and Use of Drugs and Psychotropic Substances and agreed to assist with the development of a regional drug control action plan. UNDCP continued to support national drug control commissions in Bolivia, Colombia and Peru in policy coordination and fund-raising. In Central America, UNDCP organized regional meetings and workshops aimed at improving national planning capacities.

Among prevention activities, UNDCP supported Mexican authorities in launching a drug abuse and HIV/AIDS prevention campaign through the media, reaching some 1 million people. A regional advocacy programme in the Caribbean focused on the theme "Sports against drugs", and local athletes acted as advocates. A teacher training programme was carried out in the context of a multi-agency health and family-life education programme. UNDCP appointed a regional epidemiology adviser for the Caribbean and contributed to the drug abuse surveillance work implemented by the Caribbean Epidemiology Centre. UNDCP helped the Dominican Republic's national drug prevention programme to decentralize its mandate to the provincial level and to set up regional committees. In Haiti, a school and street youth survey was carried out in Port-au-Prince, and support was given to NGOs concerned with drug abuse prevention. UNDCP provided assistance to Cuba in demand reduction training, including toxicology and epidemiological surveillance. A UN inter-agency programme supported community-based demand reduction activities in Guyana, focusing on youth. In Bolivia, UNDCP, in cooperation with UNFPA and the World Bank, promoted the inclusion of drug abuse preventive education and healthy lifestyles in school curricula, reaching 700 schools. It supported the Brazilian national HIV/AIDS prevention programme, targeting specific groups, including drug abusers. UNDCP expanded the subregional drug abuse information system under the memorandum of understanding on drug control cooperation signed with Argentina, Bolivia, Chile, Peru and Uruguay.

UNDCP supported alternative development in Bolivia, Colombia and Peru, assisting in the implementation of 14 projects at a total value of $51 million, of which $10 million was implemented during 2001.

UNDCP continued to provide support to police, customs, judiciary and forensic laboratories in Bolivia, Brazil, Colombia, Ecuador and Mexico as well as to regional bodies. In Bolivia, it assisted in upgrading management and information systems and personnel training, and, in Brazil, it supported the modernization of police programmes and facilities. Precursor control assistance was given to Colombia, while the judiciary sector in Ecuador was provided with training and equipment. UNDCP supported the Caribbean Customs Law Enforcement Council in establishing a regional clearance system for control of the movement of vessels. Training in risk profiling and targeting techniques was provided to customs and port authorities from Aruba, the Dominican Republic, Guyana, Haiti, Jamaica, the Netherlands Antilles and Trinidad and Tobago. In Cuba, expert advice was provided for the planning of law enforcement training. UNDCP assisted 14 Caribbean countries in revising legislation on precursor control and, under the subregional forensic laboratory programmes for Mexico, Central America and the Caribbean, UNDCP provided equipment to analyse seized illicit drugs and their precursors.

Administrative and budgetary matters

The Commission on Narcotic Drugs, at its forty-fourth session in March (see p. 1168), had before it a report [E/CN.7/2001/10 & Corr.1] of the Advisory Committee on Administrative and Budgetary Questions (ACABQ), which considered and issued comments on the UNDCP Executive Director's reports on the proposed revised biennial support and programme budget for 2000-2001 for the UNDCP Fund [E/CN.7/2001/9] and on the proposed budget outline for 2002-2003 for the Fund [E/CN.7/2001/8].

In view of the decrease in income estimates for 2000-2001 ($144.2 million, compared to initial estimates of $156 million), ACABQ noted what appeared to be an overly positive description of income in the former report. Revised total expenditures were projected at $187.6 million for the biennium. It expressed concern that the report did not suggest proposals that could address the problem of a continued low-level general-purpose income and requested that, in future, the budget document should provide information on UNDCP efforts to attract voluntary contributions. It recommended that the adequacy of maintaining the operational reserve at the $12 million level be reviewed should the declining trend in income continue, and requested that future UNDCP budget documents contain background information on the operational reserve. ACABQ shared the view of the Executive Director on the need to concentrate on areas of intervention where UNDCP had the greatest comparative advantage, and welcomed the reduction in the number of projects from 260 in 2000 to 150 in 2001, which were consolidated into 25 national, regional and global programmes. The Committee welcomed the format of the budget outline for 2002-2003, in particular its presentation along the four main thematic areas of activity, together with programme support, management and administration.

By a 27 March resolution [E/2001/28/Rev.1 (res. 44/17)], the Commission approved an appropriation in the amount of $35,239,800 for the revised 2000-2001 biennial support budget funded by the UNDCP Fund. Of that amount, $26,480,600 was allocated for programme support (country offices, $19,698,000; headquarters, $6,782,600); and $8,759,200 for management and administration. The Commission authorized the Executive Director to redeploy resources between appropriation lines up to 5 per cent of the appropriation to which the resources were redeployed.

On the same date [res. 44/18], the Commission endorsed the programme and budget strategy for the 2000-2001 biennium and the revised resource allocation for programme activities in the amount of $148,298,000. It noted that implementation of the budget and additional priority programmes was subject to the availability of funding. In other action [res. 44/19], the Commission endorsed the programme and budget strategy for the 2002-2003 biennium and took note of the outline for that biennium totalling $198,254,600. It considered that the proposed outline provided a basis for the submission of the 2002-2003 proposed initial budget by the UNDCP Executive Director.

At its reconvened forty-fourth session in December, the Commission considered further reports on administrative and budgetary matters.

In an October report [E/CN.7/2001/14 & Corr.1 & Add.1] containing the proposed final budget for 2000-2001 and the proposed initial budget for 2002-2003 for the UNDCP Fund, the Executive Director stated that the final expenditure budget for 2000-2001 amounted to $154.9 million, compared to the proposed revised budget of $187.6 million. Of that amount, the final programme budget amounted to $117.4 million compared to the revised programme budget of $148.3 million; the final support budget amounted to $33.8 million, compared to the revised support budget of $35.2 million, reflecting a decrease in costing adjustments of $2.5 million (7.1 per cent) and an increase in volume changes of $1.1 million (3 per cent); and the final agency support costs were $3.8 million compared to the revised budget of $4.1 million.

The Executive Director stated that the initial budget proposal for 2002-2003 amounted to $168.4 million, compared to the outline projection of $198.3 million. Total resources budgeted were covered by fund balances and estimated income of $179.8 million for the same period. The initial Fund budget proposals for 2002-2003 were aligned, within the outline framework, with best estimates of income trends and updated projections, as compared to those one year earlier when the outline was prepared. There was a 10.2 per cent reduction in the total budget proposed for 2002-2003, as compared to the revised budget for 2000-2001, which was necessary to control the level of fund balances in order to maintain adequate cash flow. A small increase in total income of $5.1 million, or 3.9 per cent, was projected as compared to 2000-2001, attributable entirely to increased cost-sharing funds mainly for ongoing projects in Latin America. In the addendum to the budget, the Executive Director provided supplemental programme information narratives for 2002-2003, linked to the programme budget priorities and budgetary data, in a results-based budget framework.

In a November report [E/CN.7/2001/18], ACABQ commented on the Executive Director's proposed final budget for the 2000-2001 biennium for the UNDCP Fund and the proposed initial budget for the 2002-2003 biennium.

By a 13 December resolution [res. 44/20], the Commission approved an appropriation in the amount of $33,784,900 for the final budget for the 2000-2001 biennium. It also approved an appropriation of $35,386,400 for the initial budget for the 2002-2003 biennium funded under the UNDCP Fund. Among other action, the Commission also adopted guidelines for the use of general-purpose funds, which were annexed to the resolution.

Reviews by OIOS

In May, the Secretary-General, in response to General Assembly resolution 54/244 [YUN 1999, p. 1274], transmitted the report [E/AC.51/2001/4] of the Office of Internal Oversight Services (OIOS) on its triennial (1998-2000) review of the implementation of the recommendations made by the Committee for Programme and Coordination (CPC) on the 1998 in-depth evaluation of UNDCP [YUN 1998, p. 1168]. The report affirmed that UNDCP benefited from the outcome of the twentieth special session of the General Assembly in 1998, with the adopted action plans providing a strategic focus for drug control until 2008. Among CPC recommendations that needed further attention was the need for UNDCP to coordinate more with other organizations in developing information networks, to improve substantive dialogue with other organizations on drug abuse control and to promote appropriate methodologies for assessing the drug problem with reliability and comparability.

OIOS reported in June [A/56/83] on its inspection of programme management and administrative practices in the Office for Drug Control and Crime Prevention (ODCCP), an umbrella entity that included UNDCP and the United Nations Centre for International Crime Prevention (CICP). The report, also prepared in response to Assembly resolution 54/244, reviewed programme management, the outcome of consolidation, funding concerns, technical cooperation issues and overall management. While OIOS recognized the Executive Director's energetic efforts, which had heightened the global visibility of the Office and made it more action-oriented, it found that the overcentralized and arbitrary manner in which ODCCP was run by the Executive Director had concentrated authority and decision-making without institutional mechanisms to ensure that programmes were properly conceived and executed and that results were assessed. Inordinate delays in approving projects, programmes and specific actions were common. The absence of clearly defined delegation of authority from the Executive Director to programme managers clouded accountability and paralysed decision-making during his absence from Vienna. Of particular concern was the view expressed to OIOS by some Member States, including both donors and recipients of services, that the poor management of the Office had affected the fulfilment of its mandates and the proper implementation of some projects.

OIOS recommended that: management should develop comprehensive annual plans for both UNDCP and CICP; ODCCP should not undertake any large-scale, long-term commitments without feasibility research and assurances of donor support; ODCCP should put in place an organizational structure that delineated functions and responsibilities and reduced the lines of authority reporting directly to the top; immediate measures should be taken to strengthen financial and programme oversight at ODCCP; a review mechanism for projects and programmes drawing on best practices should be re-established; UNDCP should make efforts to establish a general-purpose fund margin at a level that would preclude a financial crisis; and ODCCP should ensure that its human resources management practices conformed to UN regulations and rules for fairness, transparency and objectivity.

In December, OIOS reported to the Assembly on its investigation into allegations of misconduct and mismanagement at ODCCP [A/56/689]. The investigation was begun in late 2000 after OIOS received reports alleging that the ODCCP Executive Director had engaged in misconduct by giving Office funds and equipment to a personal friend, who was the captain of a sailboat, in exchange for a favour. Although the investigation determined that the evidence did not support the allegation, OIOS did determine that multiple incidents of mismanagement of project operations and waste of ODCCP funds had occurred in connection with a related project, known as the "boat project". The report detailed the management failures and made recommendations for corrective action. The Secretary-General, in his transmittal note to the General Assembly, took note of the findings and concurred with the recommendations.

National database system

UNDCP, on the basis of the recommendations made by a meeting of the group of users of the national database system on drug control in November 2000, designed a work plan for the system's activities in 2001. The plan focused primarily on expanding the use of the system to as many competent authorities as possible, following a series of missions by the project team which installed the system and provided training in its use. The fourth meeting of the group of users (Vienna, 1 October) concluded that the system fully served the needs of national and international control of licit drugs and set standards for automating national and international drug control.

ECONOMIC AND SOCIAL COUNCIL ACTION

On 24 July [meeting 40], the Economic and Social Council, on the recommendation of the Commission on Narcotic Drugs [E/2001/28/Rev.1], adopted **resolution 2001/18** without vote [agenda item 14 (d)].

Implementation of the computer and telecommunication system for international and national drug control developed by the United Nations International Drug Control Programme

The Economic and Social Council,

Bearing in mind that, pursuant to the international drug control treaties, the States parties thereto are obliged to share with other States, the Secretary-General and the International Narcotics Control Board, on a regular basis, large amounts of information and data on narcotic drugs, psychotropic substances and precursor chemicals,

Aware of the increased administrative procedures that national drug control administrations must fulfil in implementing the international drug control treaties,

Bearing in mind the Political Declaration, the Declaration on the Guiding Principles of Drug Demand Reduction, and the measures to enhance international cooperation to counter the world drug problem, adopted by the General Assembly at its twentieth special session, devoted to countering the world drug problem together, whereby States were requested to use modern technology to improve procedures for, and the timeliness of, the collection and dissemination of information, in order to achieve the highest level of accuracy of the results obtained,

Recalling Commission on Narcotic Drugs resolution 8(XXXVII) of 20 April 1994, in which the United Nations International Drug Control Programme, in cooperation with the relevant bodies and authorities, was requested to establish standards to be used in the electronic transmission of data between the Programme and national authorities responsible for drug control,

Recalling also its resolution 1994/3 of 20 July 1994 and Commission on Narcotic Drugs resolution 43/1, in which the Programme was requested to integrate all annual reports questionnaires, using modern communication and presentation techniques,

Taking into account the report of the Secretary-General on the utilization of the development dividend and General Assembly resolution 53/220 of 7 April 1999, in which the Assembly approved the sum of 1.1 million United States dollars for the expansion of the computer and telecommunication system for international and national drug control (hereinafter referred to as the national database system) as an important development in building national capacities, in particular in developing countries,

Cognizant of the findings of the in-depth evaluation of the Programme carried out by the Office of Internal Oversight Services, in which the Programme is requested to strengthen its capacity for gathering information from Governments by expanding the national database system to cover other data-collection activities,

Taking note of the progress made by the Programme through the amendment of the Harmonized Commodity Description and Coding System of the Customs Cooperation Council, also known as the World Customs Organization, to establish a unique system for identifying narcotic drugs and psychotropic substances and precursor chemicals under international control,

1. *Notes with satisfaction* the report of the third meeting of the group of users of the national database system, held in Vienna from 1 to 3 November 2000, at which 25 Governments concluded unanimously that the national database system is a comprehensive and mature product that is highly user-friendly and ready for detailed testing and possible implementation in many countries;

2. *Commends* the United Nations International Drug Control Programme on its success to date in developing the national database system and on its responsiveness to the requirements of Member States in developing the system;

3. *Notes with satisfaction* that the national database system stresses ownership by the users of the system and that it is being implemented with the emphasis on building capacity within, and promoting cooperation between, developing countries;

4. *Recommends* that States that have not already done so consider implementing the national database system in cooperation with the Programme and the current group of user States or establishing systems compatible with the national database system;

5. *Urges* States that wish to adopt the national database system to cooperate with the Programme in that endeavour by assessing the implications of implementation of the system by their national drug control authorities and by informing the Programme of their needs with regard to initial implementation and training as well as ongoing support;

6. *Also urges* Governments to consider making additional resources available to the Programme to enable it to strengthen its capacity to implement, maintain and further develop the national database system in Member States;

7. *Requests* the United Nations International Drug Control Programme to report to the Commission on Narcotic Drugs at its forty-fifth session on the national database system.

Commission on Narcotic Drugs

The Commission on Narcotic Drugs held its forty-fourth session in Vienna from 20 to 29 March, during which it adopted 19 resolutions and six decisions and recommended to the Economic and Social Council for adoption five draft resolutions and three draft decisions. It held a reconvened forty-fourth session on 12 and 13 December, also in Vienna, at which it adopted a resolution on the 2000-2001 final budget and the initial budget for 2002-2003 for the UNDCP Fund (see p. 1166), and brought it to the attention of the Economic and Social Council.

Following the closure of the forty-fourth session on 13 December, the Commission opened its forty-fifth session to elect the new chairman and other bureau members.

The Commission considered a note by the Secretariat containing the revised part II of the annual reports questionnaire [E/CN.7/2001/3]. Following up on its request to the UNDCP Executive Director to streamline the questionnaire [YUN

2000, p. 1197], the Commission, by a 29 March resolution [E/2001/28/Rev.1 (res. 44/3)], approved the revised part II, entitled "Extent, patterns and trends of drug abuse", for use in the reporting on drug abuse. It called on the Executive Director to make the necessary changes to ensure that parts I and III benefited from the improvements to part II. The Commission requested the Executive Director to provide States with guidance in completing and submitting the revised questionnaire and to report to the Commission in 2002 on measures to improve the submission rate and the data quality of the questionnaire. At its reconvened forty-fourth session, the Commission examined proposals to amend the biennial questionnaire, including an improved layout and supporting notes for guidance [E/CN.7/2001/17].

The Commission also considered a Secretariat note [E/CN.7/2001/11], prepared in response to the Commission's 2000 request to include the question of the duration of its sessions in the 2001 agenda and to identify the daily operational and other budgetary cost implications of convening the Commission.

(Other action taken by the Commission is described in the relevant sections of this chapter.)

By **decision 2001/241** of 24 July, the Economic and Social Council took note of the Commission's report on its forty-fourth session [E/2001/28/Rev.1] and approved the provisional agenda and documentation for the forty-fifth (2002) session, on the understanding that intersessional meetings would be held in Vienna, at no additional cost, to finalize the items to be included in the provisional agenda and the documentation requirements for the forty-fifth session. By **decision 2001/243** of the same date, the Council outlined some parameters guiding the functioning and duration of the forty-fifth session.

Demand reduction

At its forty-fourth session, the Commission on Narcotic Drugs considered reduction of illicit demand for drugs. It had before it a note by the Secretariat describing the world situation with regard to drug abuse, in particular among children and youth [E/CN.7/2001/4].

By a 29 March resolution [res. 44/4], the Commission requested UNDCP to urge States that had effective demand reduction strategies to share them with other States and assist them in those strategies, where appropriate, in accordance with the Declaration on the Guiding Principles of Drug Demand Reduction [YUN 1998, p. 1137].

On the same date [res. 44/5], the Commission requested UNDCP to provide States with guidance and assistance in developing drug demand re-

duction strategies and programmes, in accordance with the Declaration, especially among young people in recreational areas. It encouraged UNDCP to gather information on successful experiences in prevention programmes and promote its exchange among States and practitioners. States were encouraged to promote proposals aimed at developing healthy recreational activities in coordination with local governments and civil society and invited to develop appropriate means of communicating and distributing prevention information aimed at young people. The Commission encouraged States to adapt and make compatible their research on drug addiction and treatment, and to develop information systems and prevention programmes aimed at raising public awareness of the risks associated with trends in drug use among young people, particularly in recreational areas. It requested the UNDCP Executive Director to report in 2002 on the implementation of the resolution.

Drug abuse

The Commission, in a 29 March resolution on measures to promote the exchange of information on new patterns of drug use and on substances consumed [res. 44/14], encouraged States to improve their understanding of drug abuse in terms of both the patterns of use and the substances consumed. It invited States and relevant regional organizations to foster the exchange of information among themselves and to pursue their efforts to develop a harmonized procedure for evaluating drug abuse and dependence, following the guidelines used by WHO. It requested INCB and UNDCP to provide technical support to those efforts, within available voluntary contributions.

On the same date [res. 44/15], the Commission considered provisions regarding travellers under treatment with medication containing narcotic drugs or psychotropic substances. Noting that INCB had reviewed problems encountered by travellers carrying medicines, the Commission invited Governments to inform INCB of restrictions involved in such cases and requested INCB to publish such information in its lists of narcotic drugs and psychotropic substances under international control. UNDCP was invited, in cooperation with INCB and WHO, to convene a meeting of experts to develop guidelines for national regulations concerning travellers under treatment.

Illicit cultivation and trafficking

In a 28 March resolution on enhancing multilateral cooperation in combating illicit traffic by sea [res. 44/6], the Commission took note of the report of the informal open-ended working group on maritime cooperation against illicit trafficking by sea (Vienna, 5-8 December 2000) [UNDCP/2000/MAR.3]. It requested UNDCP to provide technical assistance and training to interested States and to cooperate with States parties to the 1988 Convention against Illicit Traffic in Narcotic Drugs and Psychotropic Substances [YUN 1988, p. 690]. The UNDCP Executive Director was requested to report in 2003 on progress.

Also on 28 March [res. 44/9], the Commission invited the Secretary-General to inform all Member States, relevant specialized agencies and other UN entities of the resolutions adopted in 2000 by the Subcommission on Illicit Drug Traffic and Related Matters in the Near and Middle East [UNDCP/SUBCOM/2000/6]. It commended countries that had taken steps to prevent the trafficking and manufacturing of acetic anhydride, and INCB for implementing Operation Topaz, an international programme to monitor trade in acetic anhydride (see p. 1149). It urged States to take appropriate action to control trade in the substance and support Operation Topaz.

By another resolution of the same date [res. 44/7], the Commission requested parties to the 1988 Convention that had not done so to designate their authorities in accordance with article 7. It urged parties to use a designated authority as the mechanism for requests for mutual legal assistance. Parties were also encouraged to consider special measures for receiving urgent requests and urged to provide mutual legal assistance to respond to requests for information and evidentiary items. The Commission urged parties, when they exercised their right to postpone or refuse requests for mutual legal assistance under article 7, to inform the requesting State of their reasons. The Commission requested UNDCP to increase its technical assistance in order to strengthen the capacity for response of parties to the Convention.

On the same date [res. 44/8], the Commission drew the attention of States to the provisions of the United Nations Convention against Transnational Organized Crime [YUN 2000, p. 1050] and of the protocols thereto, which strengthened the countermeasures against transnational organized crime. It called on all States that had not done so to sign and ratify the Convention and stressed the need to enhance law enforcement cooperation strategies, especially in the exchange of intelligence and information in accordance with international law, in order to fight against criminal organizations involved in illicit drug and other trafficking.

On 29 March [res. 44/11], the Commission called on Member States to continue efforts to reduce illicit crop cultivation with a view to reintegrating the affected population groups into the licit economy. It requested multilateral financial institutions and regional development banks to provide financial assistance for alternative development programmes and encouraged UNDCP to increase its technical assistance to countries that were working to reduce illicit crop cultivation. The Commission urged the international community to undertake a greater financial and technical cooperation effort to promote alternative development projects and encouraged States to open their markets to products that were the object of alternative development programmes. The UNDCP Executive Director was requested to report in 2002 on the implementation of the resolution.

ECONOMIC AND SOCIAL COUNCIL ACTION

On 24 July [meeting 40], the Economic and Social Council, on the recommendation of the Commission on Narcotic Drugs [E/2001/28/Rev.1], adopted **resolution 2001/16** without vote [agenda item 14 (d)].

International assistance to the States most affected by the transit of drugs

The Economic and Social Council,

Bearing in mind the United Nations Convention against Illicit Traffic in Narcotic Drugs and Psychotropic Substances of 1988,

Recalling the Political Declaration adopted by the General Assembly at its twentieth special session, devoted to countering the world drug problem together, the Declaration on the Guiding Principles of Drug Demand Reduction and the Action Plan for the Implementation of the Declaration on the Guiding Principles of Drug Demand Reduction,

Taking into account the *Report of the International Narcotics Control Board for 2000,*

Considering that action against the world drug problem is a shared responsibility calling for coordinated and balanced measures consistent with the relevant multilateral instruments in force at the international level,

Deeply concerned by the continuing illicit traffic in narcotic drugs, psychotropic substances and substances listed in tables I and II of the 1988 Convention,

Aware that, in order to counter drug trafficking effectively, it is necessary to undertake appropriate initiatives against the transit of drugs,

Stressing the unswerving determination and commitment to resolve the world drug problem by means of national and international strategies aimed at reducing both the supply of and demand for illicit drugs,

Recognizing the desirability of providing support to the States that are most affected by the transit of drugs and are willing to implement plans to eliminate such transit,

Emphasizing the need for joint action to ensure that international cooperation and solidarity do not become merely empty notions,

1. *Requests* the United Nations International Drug Control Programme to extend technical assistance, from available voluntary contributions for that purpose, to those States that are most affected by the transit of drugs, and in particular developing countries in need of such assistance and support;

2. *Exhorts* the international financial institutions, as well as other potential donors, to provide financial assistance to such transit States in order to enable them to intensify their action against illicit drug trafficking;

3. *Requests* the Executive Director of the United Nations International Drug Control Programme to prepare a report on the implementation of the present resolution for submission to the Commission on Narcotic Drugs at its forty-fifth session.

Secretariat report. A December report by the Secretariat [E/CN.7/2002/4 & Corr.1] provided an overview of global trends and patterns in illicit drug production and trafficking and of the action taken by subsidiary bodies of the Commission. The report, which was based primarily on information received from Governments in the annual questionnaires submitted to UNDCP and reports on individual significant seizure cases, also drew on information received from Interpol, the Customs Cooperation Council, INCB and the Inter-American Drug Abuse Control Commission of the Organization of American States. The report stated that the global supply of heroin declined considerably during 2001, mainly because of the substantive reduction of opium production in Afghanistan during the year, with opium production in the country dropping from 3,276 tons in 2000 to 185 tons in 2001—a decrease of 94 per cent. Trafficking trends, which were assessed up to the year 2000 in the report, reflected a huge increase in heroin seizures at the global level, assumed to be the result of the enormous opium production peak in Afghanistan during 1999. Heroin prices continued to decrease in Western Europe and North America. It was estimated that cocaine production followed trends of previous years, with Colombia remaining the major producer country. In 2000, seizures of cocaine declined in both North America and Western Europe, two major consumer markets. Cannabis herb seizures greatly increased in 2000, while interceptions of cannabis resin continued to reflect stabilization. Production and trafficking of amphetamine-type stimulants showed levelling off for the first time in many years and, in some instances, trends in regard to methamphetamine in North America and amphetamine in Western Europe were decreasing. However, methamphetamine seizure trends continued to rise in East/South-East Asia. Trafficking of Ecstasy-type substances showed further increases worldwide, with Western Europe, mainly the Netherlands, remaining the primary supplier. The report also provided an overview of action taken by the Commission's subsidiary bodies (see p. 1172).

Regional cooperation

By a 28 March resolution on enhancing cooperation against the drug problem in Asia and the Pacific [res. 44/1], the Commission commended the convening of the meeting entitled "International Congress: In pursuit of a drug-free ASEAN 2015: Sharing the vision, leading the change" (Bangkok, Thailand, October 2000). It appreciated the strong political consensus to respond to the drug menace, expressed in the Bangkok Political Declaration adopted by 33 States at the International Congress, and welcomed the plan of action known as ACCORD (see p. 1163), endorsed by the Congress. The Commission supported the decision to establish a regional cooperative mechanism to execute and monitor the progress of the ACCORD plan and called on Member States and subregional, regional and international organizations, international financial institutions, the private sector and NGOs to consider making resources available to support its implementation. It requested UNDCP to assist in the implementation process and to report thereon to the Commission at its annual sessions.

By a resolution of the same date [res. 44/10] on enhancing regional cooperation on drug control through training, the Commission welcomed the opening of the Turkish International Academy against Drugs and Organized Crime in Ankara in June by the ODCCP Executive Director. It commended Turkey, the United States and ODCCP for their cooperation in establishing the Academy and urged other Governments, in particular those of the Near and Middle East, to support and contribute to its functioning.

The Commission, on 29 March [res. 44/12], commended ODCCP and the Chairmanship of the Organization for Security and Cooperation in Europe for convening the International Conference on Enhancing Security and Stability in Central Asia: An Integrated Approach to Counter Drugs, Organized Crime and Terrorism, held with the assistance of Uzbekistan in Tashkent on 19 and 20 October 2000. It took note of the endorsement given at the Conference by the States of Central Asia to a declaration and a document on priorities for cooperation and invited regional States to take further initiatives to continue and enhance multilateral cooperation. The Commission welcomed the efforts of donor countries and international and regional organizations to support control projects in Central Asia, and called on the donor community and UNDCP to continue activities in the region. The ODCCP Executive Director was requested to report to the Commission in 2003 on implementation of the resolution.

At its thirty-fifth session [E/CN.7/2001/5/Add.1], the Subcommission on Illicit Drug Traffic and Related Matters in the Near and Middle East recommended a draft resolution on international cooperation for the control of narcotic drugs for adoption by the Economic and Social Council, and another on enhancing regional cooperation on drug control through training for adoption by the Commission. It brought to the Commission's attention a resolution [res. 35/1] in which it urged Governments to take appropriate action to control acetic anhydride and to consider participating in regional and multilateral initiatives.

Four meetings of the subsidiary bodies of the Commission were held in 2001. Following a review of salient drug trafficking trends and regional and subregional cooperation, each meeting addressed drug law enforcement issues of priority concern to its region. The eleventh meeting of Heads of National Drug Law Enforcement Agencies (HONLEA), Latin America and the Caribbean (Panama City, 2-5 October) [UNDCP/HONLAC/2001/4] considered combating illicit drugs in the region, challenges for the new millennium, and funding of national drug control strategies and the role of international financial institutions in supporting the costs borne by Governments. The twenty-fifth meeting of HONLEA, Asia and the Pacific (Sydney, Australia, 15-18 October) [UNDCP/HONLAP/2001/5] examined illicit traffic in and abuse of heroin, control of stimulants and their precursors, cooperation in the exchange of criminal intelligence on trafficking, and trafficking by sea. The thirty-sixth session of the Subcommission on Illicit Drug Traffic and Related Matters in the Near and Middle East (Abu Dhabi, 4-7 November) [UNDCP/SUBCOM/2001/5] examined countering money-laundering, controlled delivery, precursor control and emerging trends in illicit trafficking. The eleventh meeting of HONLEA, Africa (Nairobi, Kenya, 26-29 November) [UNDCP/HONLAF/2001/4] considered the use of couriers to traffic illicit drugs, the use of commercial cargo containers for that purpose, national drug investigative capacities and regional cooperation in law enforcement, and control of stimulants and precursor control.

Strengthening UN mechanisms

The Commission on Narcotic Drugs, in response to UNDCP's 1999 suggestion that it provide guidance on UN action to strengthen UNDCP's role in drug control [YUN 1999, p. 1191], by a 29 March resolution [res. 44/16], encouraged strengthened dialogue between Member States and the Secretariat on UNDCP priorities and management, and requested the UNDCP Executive Director to facilitate that process. It also requested the Executive Director to convene joint meetings of donor and recipient countries on planning operational activities of the Programme. The Commission decided that it should, in cooperation with the Executive Director and donor and recipient countries, identify thematic areas and geographical regions that required UNDCP's special attention to ensure the implementation of the mandates established by the General Assembly at its twentieth special session. It requested the Executive Director to present all reports to Commission members in a timely manner and encouraged UNDCP's efforts to report on the implementation of independent evaluations of operational activities. The Commission welcomed the early implementation of the planned system of financial management to allow UNDCP and Member States to assess the cost, impact and effectiveness of operational activities in an open manner. It called for continued improvement in management and a strengthened dialogue with Member States to enhance programme delivery. It urged all Governments to provide financial support to UNDCP and requested the Executive Director to continue efforts to broaden the donor base. The Commission requested a preliminary report in 2001 on the progress made in implementing the resolution and a final report in 2002.

In response to that request, the Executive Director submitted a preliminary report in October [E/CN.7/2001/15], which outlined action taken in the areas of strengthening dialogue between Member States and UNDCP; improving the effectiveness of the Commission's work; UNDCP operations and management; and funding.

Chapter XV

Statistics

In 2001, the United Nations continued its statistical work programme. In March, the 24-member Statistical Commission endorsed the proposed new approach developed by the Intersecretariat Working Group on National Accounts for a better and more comprehensive assessment of the implementation of the System of National Accounts, 1993; welcomed the publication of a handbook on the measurement of capital stocks and flows; and adopted the draft manual on statistics of international trade in services. The Commission reviewed the work of a number of established bodies and international organizations in various areas of economic, social and environment statistics and made specific recommendations and suggestions.

The Commission agreed with the proposed time frame for updating the International Standard Industrial Classification of All Economic Activities and the Central Product Classification by 2002 and for planning their revision by 2007.

The Subcommittee on Statistical Activities of the Administrative Committee on Coordination met in September.

Work of Statistical Commission

The Statistical Commission held its thirty-second session in New York from 6 to 9 March [E/2001/24]. Action taken included the adoption of the draft manual on statistics of international trade in services; agreement on the work programme proposed by the United Nations Statistics Division to validate development indicators in the context of follow-up to UN conferences and summits; and acceptance of the invitation by the Economic and Social Council to serve as the intergovernmental focal point for the review of conference indicators.

Having considered the work that groups of countries and international organizations were undertaking in the fields of economic, social and environment statistics, the Commission endorsed the human settlements statistics programme presented by the United Nations Centre for Human Settlements (Habitat), including the

quinquennial cycle for data collection and dissemination, and encouraged the Centre to convene, in consultation with the Statistics Division, an expert group to evaluate existing methodologies and data-collection and dissemination instruments, as well as concepts and sources of city statistics. It welcomed the Division's initiatives in the measurement of paid and unpaid work, in particular the development of a guide to produce statistics on time use for measuring paid and unpaid work and the web site on time-use surveys; endorsed the outline for the guide; and further endorsed the proposed new approach developed by the Intersecretariat Working Group on National Accounts (ISWGNA) for the assessment of the extent to which the System of National Accounts (SNA), 1993, had been implemented. The Commission welcomed progress made in the areas of household income statistics, capital stock statistics, price statistics, social statistics and the labour statistics supplement to the tourism satellite account, and gave specific directions in several of those areas, in particular regarding presentational aspects of the International Labour Organization (ILO) Manual on Consumer Price Indices, the process and timing of revision of the System of Integrated Environmental and Economic Accounting, the long- and short-term goals of the Siena Group for Social Statistics, and the focus of ILO's work on a labour accounting system. It reaffirmed its support for a credible International Comparison Programme, welcomed the efforts of the World Bank in developing its project proposal for a global Programme, and restated its concerns about securing the necessary funding for the Programme's success.

The Commission agreed with the proposed work programme and time frame for updating the International Standard Industrial Classification of All Economic Activities and the Central Product Classification by 2002 and for planning their revision by 2007, and provided specific directions for the work of the Expert Group on International Economic and Social Classifications. It noted the Statistics Division's progress on three web sites on: the global integrated presentation of the work of the international organizations in statistical methodology; good practices in official statistics; and the United Nations Economic and

Social Information System common database for global statistics.

The Commission expressed appreciation for the report of the Friends of the Chair, entitled "An assessment of the statistical criticisms made of the *Human Development Report, 1999*", and welcomed the response to that report of the Human Development Report Office of the United Nations Development Programme (UNDP), in which a number of positive developments in relation to statistical aspects of the *Report* were outlined.

In relation to the planned work of the Statistics Division, the Commission endorsed the draft work programme for the 2002-2003 biennium and the 2001 schedule of expert group meetings and workshops. It noted the activities undertaken and planned under the Development Account and the new initiative in building capacity in household surveys, particularly in Africa.

By **decision 2001/230** of 19 July, the Council took note of the Commission's 2001 report, decided that the Commission's thirty-third session should be held in New York from 5 to 8 March 2002 and approved the provisional agenda and documentation for that session.

Economic statistics

National accounts

In response to a 2000 Statistical Commission request [YUN 2000, p. 1201], the Secretary-General submitted a January report on assessment of the implementation of the 1993 SNA [E/CN.3/2001/8]. The report provided background information on the ISWGNA proposal for a better and more comprehensive assessment of the implementation of the 1993 SNA (see below); described the implications of the introduction of the new UN national accounts questionnaire on the assessment of the scope of the accounts based on the UN national accounts database; and presented the results of the first assessment of the "minimum requirement data set" as the measurement for a country's scope of 1993 SNA implementation. In addition, the measurement of the minimum requirement data set was compared with the previous milestone assessment.

The Commission also had before it the report of the 2000 meeting of the Task Force on National Accounts (convened by ISWGNA) [YUN 2000, p. 1201].

The Commission welcomed and endorsed ISWGNA's proposed new approach for assessing the extent to which the 1993 SNA had been implemented. It supported the definition of the new scope of the accounts, consisting of three data

sets (minimum, recommended, other) for assessing the broad coverage of national accounts in various regions and agreed that those data sets should be referred to by more neutral names. While the Commission did not decide whether the three data sets should be considered as a replacement for or a supplement to the six milestones used before, it recognized that both methods provided sufficient information to identify countries and regions that needed technical assistance in 1993 SNA implementation. It also recognized that, for the time being, only an assessment of the first data set and after 2003 of the second data set could be conducted by the Statistics Division due to the transitional status of the new national accounts database.

Regarding electronic discussion groups, the Commission concluded that there was no simple solution to the problem of improving their effectiveness and noted that the existence of a special interest group and the method used to communicate updates appeared to be key factors in determining effectiveness.

The Commission encouraged ISWGNA to review the treatment of intangible assets and report back in 2002; expressed satisfaction with the proposed clearance of manuals or handbooks developed by "city groups" and containing concepts that diverged from those in the 1993 SNA; and requested ISWGNA to make a decision on the national accounting treatment of mobile phone licences.

Capital stocks

The Statistical Commission had before it the report of the Expert Group on Capital Stock Statistics [E/CN.3/2001/9], which indicated the topics considered at the Group's 1997, 1998 and 1999 meetings and described its products, future activities and expected future products. The Commission welcomed the publication of a handbook on the measurement of capital stocks and flows and noted that the Group would continue to function electronically to discuss concepts and practices.

Service statistics

The Statistical Commission considered the report of the Task Force on Statistics of International Trade in Services [E/CN.3/2001/10], which noted that the final draft of the proposed manual on statistics of international trade in services [PROV/ST/ESA/STAT/SER.M/86] was before the Commission for approval.

The Commission approved the manual as an international manual and commended the Task Force for its work. Noting a proposal by the World Tourism Organization regarding the manual, the Commission responded that the detail requested should be elaborated in satellite accounts but not in that particular manual. It recommended that the Task Force continue its work, focusing on the proposed users' manual on data collection as the next step. The Commission noted that the implementation of the manual would be a long-term process and agreed to the Task Force's proposal for international data collection on trade in services, observing that full coordination between agencies was required and that implementation of the data collection would also require a phased process.

International Comparison Programme

Having considered a background paper by the World Bank on the implementation plan for the International Comparison Programme (ICP), the Commission agreed on the fundamental importance of generating high-quality purchasing power parities through ICP for improved comparisons of living standards and recognized ICP's potential for building national statistical capacity in the areas of prices and national accounts. The Commission reaffirmed its support for a credible ICP programme and welcomed the efforts of the World Bank to develop its project proposal for a global ICP. It restated its concerns about securing the necessary funding for the programme's success and, in that context, requested the World Bank to follow up on its project proposal and reconsider the amount and duration of funding that was necessary. The Commission asked the international agencies to raise the visibility of the programme and stressed the need for secure funding at the highest levels of their agencies.

The Commission indicated the need to develop a comprehensive project plan for implementation of the proposed ICP strategy, and requested the World Bank to develop the plan in consultation with the Friends of the Chair; affirmed the critical importance of strong project management for the programme; requested the existing Friends of the Chair to continue their efforts until the Commission's thirty-third (2002) session; and urged members and specialized agencies to mobilize efforts at the political level to promote support for the project.

Other economic statistics

Ottawa Group and ISWGPS

Having considered the report of the Ottawa Group on Price Indexes [E/CN.3/2001/11] and that of the Intersecretariat Working Group on Price Statistics (ISWGPS) [E/CN.3/2001/12], the Commission welcomed progress made by the groups in their work programmes; supported the future work programme of the Ottawa Group and took note of its joint meeting with ISWGPS, planned for April 2001; and noted that the preparation of the Consumer Price Index manual was in its final stage.

Environmental accounting

The Statistical Commission considered the report of the London Group on Environmental Accounting [E/CN.3/2001/13], which had been requested by the Commission to revise *Integrated Environmental and Economic Accounting* (SEEA), published as an interim handbook in 1993. The Commission acknowledged the progress made in the SEEA revision and emphasized the need for it to be published as soon as possible. The Commission welcomed the announcement that the London Group would meet in May and requested the Group to reach consensus on issues that needed to be resolved and on changes to be made to the draft handbook. The Commission recommended that a group of friends of the Chair, composed of directors or deputy directors of national statistical offices or equivalent, be created to solve any outstanding issues and further steer the process after the final draft was delivered by the Group to the international agencies at the end of July. It agreed that an interim version of the handbook be published by all agencies and recommended that the revised SEEA be submitted to the Commission's 2002 session for approval.

The projected 31 July deadline for the final version of the draft SEEA, which was decided at the London Group's meeting (Voorburg, Netherlands, May), was not met and editing continued throughout 2001. A new deadline was set for January 2002 [E/CN.3/2002/17].

Demographic and social statistics

Human settlements

The Commission had before it a report of the United Nations Centre for Human Settlements (Habitat) [E/CN.3/2001/2], which outlined progress made in developing and improving human settlements statistical concepts, definitions and classifications; statistical support for UN global conferences on human settlements and the General Assembly's special session on the review and appraisal of the implementation of the outcome of the 1996 UN Conference on Human Settlements (Habitat II) (see p. 973); quantitative monitoring of the implementation of the Habitat Agenda, adopted at Habitat II [YUN 1996, p. 994];

and future activities to improve international human settlements statistics and national capacities.

The Commission endorsed the Centre's human settlements statistics programme, including the quinquennial cycle of data collection and dissemination; noted the necessity for and stressed the importance of reviewing and enhancing the quality of human settlements statistics; and pointed out the obstacles to international agreement on standards in housing, housing conditions and human settlements development. It encouraged the Centre to convene, in consultation with the Statistics Division, an expert group meeting to evaluate existing methodologies and data-collection and dissemination instruments, as well as concepts and sources of city statistics. The Commission recognized the work on the development of more dynamic city indicators on such topics as environment, urban poverty and informal sector economic activities.

Labour statistics

As agreed at its 2000 session [YUN 2000, p. 1203], the Statistical Commission considered a report prepared by the ILO Bureau of Statistics entitled "Developing a labour accounting system for tourism: issues and approaches" [E/CN.3/2001/3]. The report described work undertaken by ILO, which built on that carried out by the World Tourism Organization and the Organisation for Economic Cooperation and Development (OECD), to develop tourism satellite accounts (TSA) to SNA. ILO and some national statistical agencies had been working to develop a labour accounting system (LAS) and a labour accounting system for tourism (LAS-T).

LAS-T would represent a labour statistics–based extension of TSA, designed to produce TSA-consistent statistics to answer questions about how many and what kind of workers were participating in tourism-related activities; how compensation was being distributed among those workers; and what the impact would be on total employment of a change in tourism-related demand. The report provided an overview of the main concepts and principles of LAS and LAS-T linked to TSA.

The Commission expressed support for ILO's continued work on LAS, took note of the difficulties of applying the general framework of labour accounting to the tourism industry, and suggested that ILO focus first on the further development of the general LAS.

Gender statistics

The Statistical Commission had before it a report of the Secretary-General on the progress of a project developed by the Statistics Division, UNDP and the International Development Research Centre (Canada) on gender issues in the measurement of paid and unpaid work [E/CN.3/2001/4]. The report described project activities and presented an outline for a technical guide on methods for conducting time-use activities and the conclusions of a 2000 expert group meeting on the guide. The Commission welcomed the Statistics Division's initiatives in the measurement of paid and unpaid work, in particular the development of a guide to produce statistics on time use for measuring paid and unpaid work and the web site on time-use surveys. It noted the value of time-use statistics and endorsed the outline for the guide.

Siena Group

Having considered the report of the Siena Group for Social Statistics [E/CN.3/2001/5], the Commission requested the Group to provide a document stating the priority areas, covering both short- and long-term goals, to ensure that the Group's objectives were both clear and attainable.

The Group's 2001 meeting did not take place. Therefore, an intermediate meeting was held (Geneva, 3-4 December) to outline the Group's strategy for the next few years and set strategic medium-term goals [E/CN.3/2002/6].

Other statistical activities

International economic and social classifications

The Statistical Commission had before it a report of the Secretary-General on international economic and social classifications [E/CN.3/2001/14], which provided an overview of how the Commission's 2000 recommendations concerning international statistical classifications [YUN 2000, p. 1204] had been addressed and contained proposals for future work.

The Commission agreed with the proposed work programme and time frame for updating the International Standard Industrial Classification of All Economic Activities (ISIC) and the Central Product Classification (CPC) by 2002 and their revision by 2007, stressing the importance of reaching convergence of major activity classifications by 2007. It also agreed with suggestions regarding the scope of changes to ISIC and CPC.

The Commission suggested that the Expert Group on International Economic and Social Classifications consider the possibility of further synchronizing and coordinating the revision of classifications supporting production and trade statistics so that resulting data could become more comparable; emphasized the need for alternate industry aggregations for analytical purposes; and recommended that the Expert Group further consider the identification of a useful level of detail for an international classification, possibly expanding in the area of services.

The Commission noted the need to keep developing countries involved in the work process; recommended that the high costs of implementing a revised classification be considered in the revision process; noted the need for increased activities relating to implementation assistance and the need for monitoring country implementation of ISIC and CPC; and requested a more detailed work plan for the 2007 revision of ISIC and CPC.

Follow-up to UN conferences and summits

In accordance with Economic and Social Council resolution 2000/27 [YUN 2000, p. 1377], the Secretary-General submitted to the Statistical Commission a report on activities and plans of the Statistics Division and the Commission in support of the harmonization and rationalization of indicators [E/CN.3/2001/16] in the context of follow-up to international conferences and summits in the economic, social and related fields (see also p. 1366). Statistics Division activities in support of the implementation of resolution 2000/27 focused on developing an agreed process to rationalize and harmonize the various sets of conference indicators and on strengthening national capacity to produce relevant indicators for policy decision-making. As the Council had invited the Commission to take a lead role in acting as its technical advisory body on indicators, the Secretary-General proposed an action plan for the period 2001-2002, culminating in the submission of a report to the Council in 2002.

The Commission also had before it a report by the European Commission, the International Monetary Fund (IMF), OECD and the World Bank on strengthening cooperation for statistical capacity-building [E/CN.3/2001/24]. The report described the background to the establishment of the Partnership in Statistics for Development in the Twenty-first Century (PARIS 21) and its organization and work programme.

The Commission accepted the Council's invitation to serve as the intergovernmental focal point for the review of conference indicators and emphasized the importance of the needs for capacity-building, effective user-producer dialogue on indicators and reduction of the overburdening of countries with data requests. It agreed with the Statistics Division's work programme, in particular the formation of a friends of the Chair advisory group. With respect to the limited set of indicators, the Commission expressed doubts that a single set could satisfy the various national, regional and specialized sectoral needs, and emphasized the need for flexibility. It recommended that the Friends of the Chair consider the intersection of existing lists of indicators and explore a layered approach. The Commission took note of the information provided on PARIS 21 and noted the need for further discussions on its work programme, structure, financing and location. In that connection, some delegations suggested that the integration of the tasks of PARIS 21 into the UN system be investigated.

Human Development Report

The Commission had before it a report by its Friends of the Chair, entitled "An assessment of the statistical criticisms made of the *Human Development Report, 1999*" [E/CN.3/2001/18], which discussed the accuracy of the statistical information in that report, focusing on criticisms raised in a document authored by Ian Castles (Australia). Annexed to the report were Mr. Castles' document and the point-by-point response of the Human Development Report Office of UNDP to that document.

Also before the Commission was a report of that Office [E/CN.3/2001/19], which noted the observations of the Friends of the Chair and outlined steps being taken to improve the *Human Development Report*.

The Commission took note of a statement by the Chair of the Friends of the Chair, who emphasized the need to apply high statistical professional standards to the *Human Development Report*, particularly as it was so widely used by a variety of audiences. In that regard, he stressed that purchasing power parities–based comparisons should be used systematically for most of the analyses in the *Report* and more extensively than was the case in the 1999 edition. The Commission also took note of a statement by a representative of the Human Development Report Office, who noted that the Commission's interest in the *Report* had generated a variety of positive developments, including closer links between the Office and statistics-producing agencies, the involvement of a statistical advisory panel, the appointment of a senior statistical adviser and the rethinking of the structure of the statistical tables in the *Report*. The Commission warmly welcomed the response of the Office to the report of the Friends of the Chair and accepted the Office's proposal to submit to its thirty-third (2002) session a paper that would discuss the needs of users of statistics of human development and provide information on the implementation of the report of the Friends of the Chair.

Coordination and integration of international statistical programmes

Having considered the report of the Administrative Committee on Coordination (ACC) Subcommittee on Statistical Activities on its 2000 session [YUN 2000, p. 1205], the Commission noted the ongoing and planned work on the methodology and collection of electronic commerce statistics at the national and international levels. The Commission also restated its view that: the international statistical agencies should pay adequate attention to coordination and integration of their work; the integrated programme of the Economic Commission for Europe, OECD and Eurostat and the global integrated presentation of the work of the international organizations in statistical methodology were important tools for coordination and integration; and programme reviews of selected fields of statistics should be carried out.

Inter-agency cooperation

The ACC Subcommittee on Statistical Activities, at its thirty-fifth session (Vienna, 18-20 September) [ACC/2001/2], noted the six major new initiatives planned by organizations and the coordination involved in them—industrial statistics database according to ISIC, Revision 3 on CD-ROM (United Nations, Industrial Development Organization); technical report on surveys in developing and transition countries (Statistics Division); establishing a joint poverty-monitoring project (UNDP/Economic and Social Commission for Asia and the Pacific); IMF update: reports on the observance of standards and codes and the data quality assessment framework; strengthening statistical capacity in the Economic and Social Commission for Western Asia (ESCWA) region (Statistics Division and ESCWA Statistics Division); and progress towards the 1996 World Food Summit [YUN 1996, p. 1129] target on the numbers of undernourished (Food and Agriculture Organization of the United Nations). The Subcommittee also adopted a set of principles for disseminating statistical information on the Internet and noted that each organization should continue to set its own policies regarding the pricing of such information, including the extent to which data might be provided free of charge. In identifying issues that the Statistical Commission might wish to discuss, the Subcommittee suggested that items on information and communications technology statistics and the definition and measurement of the so-called information society be added to the multi-year programme of work.

Programme questions

Having reviewed major developments in the work programme of the Statistics Division, the Commission took note of and endorsed the draft programme of work for the biennium 2002-2003 [E/CN.3/2001/CRP.1], the list of expert group meetings and workshops in 2001 [E/CN.3/2001/CRP.2] and the priorities proposed by the Division's Director. The Commission also took note of the medium-term plan for 2002-2005 [A/55/6/Rev.1] and the report of the Secretary-General on the programme performance of the United Nations for the 1998-1999 biennium [A/55/73]; the activities undertaken and planned under the Development Account; the new initiative in household surveys capacity-building, particularly in Africa; and the discontinuation of the commodity trade statistics microfiche programme.

PART FOUR

Legal questions

Chapter I

International Court of Justice

In 2001, the International Court of Justice (ICJ) delivered three Judgments, made 18 Orders and had 25 contentious cases pending before it.

On 31 October, the ICJ President informed the General Assembly that the Court's docket remained overburdened and that solutions would have to be found to avoid excessive delays in examining cases that were ready to be heard. Noting that administrative and procedural efforts made by the Court to redress the situation would not be sufficient, he appealed to the Assembly to ensure the financial and human resources required for the Court to perform its duties properly. The President stated that ICJ could play an important role in preventing conflicts, particularly territorial ones, and encouraged States to refer their disputes to the Court by way of Special Agreement.

Judicial work of the Court

During 2001, the Court delivered its Judgment on the merits in the case concerning *Maritime Delimitation and Territorial Questions between Qatar and Bahrain (Qatar v. Bahrain)* and in the *LaGrand Case (Germany v. United States)*. It also delivered its Judgment on the Application of the Philippines for permission to intervene in the case concerning *Sovereignty over Pulau Ligitan and Pulau Sipadan (Indonesia/Malaysia)*.

The Court or its President made further Orders on the conduct of the proceedings in the cases concerning *Oil Platforms (Iran v. United States)*; *Application of the Convention on the Prevention and Punishment of the Crime of Genocide (Bosnia and Herzegovina v. Yugoslavia)*; *Land and Maritime Boundary between Cameroon and Nigeria (Cameroon v. Nigeria: Equatorial Guinea intervening)*; *Legality of Use of Force (Yugoslavia v. Belgium)*, *(Yugoslavia v. Canada)*, *(Yugoslavia v. France)*, *(Yugoslavia v. Germany)*, *(Yugoslavia v. Italy)*, *(Yugoslavia v. Netherlands)*, *(Yugoslavia v. Portugal)* and *(Yugoslavia v. United Kingdom)*; *Armed Activities on the Territory of the Congo (Democratic Republic of the Congo v. Burundi)*, *(Democratic Republic of the Congo v. Uganda)* and *(Democratic Republic of the Congo v. Rwanda)*; *Arrest Warrant of 11 April 2000 (Democratic Republic of the Congo v. Belgium)*; and *Certain Property (Liechtenstein v. Germany)*.

ICJ activities in 2001 were covered in two reports to the General Assembly, for the periods 1 August 2000 to 31 July 2001 [A/56/4] and 1 August 2001 to 31 July 2002 [A/57/4]. On 30 October, the Assembly took note of the 2000/01 report (**decision 56/407**).

Maritime delimitation and territorial questions (Qatar v. Bahrain)

Qatar instituted proceedings in 1991 [YUN 1991, p. 820] against Bahrain in respect of disputes relating to sovereignty over the Hawar Islands, sovereign rights over the shoals of Dibal and Qit'at Jaradah, and the delimitation of the maritime areas of the two States.

In 1992, a Memorial by Qatar and a Counter-Memorial by Bahrain were filed [YUN 1992, p. 982], as were their respective Reply and Rejoinder.

Following hearings, the Court delivered a Judgment on 1 July 1994 [YUN 1994, p. 1279].

The Court received a letter from Qatar on 30 November 1994 transmitting an "Act to comply with paragraphs (3) and (4) of the operative paragraph 41 of the Judgment of the Court dated 1 July 1994". On the same day, Bahrain transmitted a "Report of the State of Bahrain to the International Court of Justice on the Attempt by the Parties to Implement the Court's Judgment of 1 July 1994".

In 1995, the Court delivered a Judgment on jurisdiction and admissibility [YUN 1995, p. 1305], by which it found that it had jurisdiction and that the Application of Qatar as formulated on 30 November 1994 was admissible.

In 1996, each Party filed a Memorial on the merits [YUN 1996, p. 1176]. Counter-Memorials of the Parties were filed on 23 December 1997 [YUN 1997, p. 1312].

On 17 March 1998, the President held a meeting to ascertain the views of the Parties on a procedure concerning the authenticity of documents produced by Qatar in 1997 [YUN 1997, p. 1312]. By an Order of 30 March 1998 [YUN 1998, p. 1184], the Court fixed 30 September 1998 as the time limit for the filing of an interim report by Qatar on the authenticity of the documents and directed the filing of a Reply by each of the Parties within the time limit of 30 March 1999. In its interim report filed in September 1998, Qatar stated that it would not rely on the disputed documents for the purposes of the case so as to enable the Court to address the merits of the case without further procedural complications. In December 1998, Qatar requested "a two-month extension of the time limit for the filing of a Reply by each of the Parties, to 30 May 1999" [ibid.].

In February 1999 [YUN 1999, p. 1202], the Court placed on record Qatar's decision to disregard the 82 documents annexed to its written pleadings, which had been challenged by Bahrain, and decided that the Replies yet to be filed by Qatar and by Bahrain would not rely on those documents. After filing their Replies within the extended time limit, Qatar and Bahrain submitted, with the approval of the Court, certain additional expert reports and historical documents.

At the conclusion of sittings held from 29 May to 29 June 2000 [YUN 2000, p. 1210], Qatar requested the Court to adjudge and declare that it had sovereignty over the Hawar Islands, and Dibal and Qit'at Jaradah shoals; and that Bahrain had no sovereignty over the island of Janan or over Zubarah, and that any claim by it concerning archipelago baselines and areas for fishing for pearls and swimming fish would be irrelevant for the purpose of maritime delimitation. Qatar also requested that the Court draw a single maritime boundary between the areas of seabed, subsoil and superjacent waters appertaining to Qatar and Bahrain on the basis that Zubarah, the Hawar Islands and Janan appertained to it and not to Bahrain, that boundary being based on a delimitation agreement between Bahrain and Iran (1971), a 23 December 1947 decision of the United Kingdom, and a delimitation agreement between Bahrain and Saudi Arabia (1958). Bahrain's final submission asked the Court to adjudge and declare that it was sovereign over Zubarah and the Hawar Islands, including Janan and Hadd Janan, and that the maritime boundary between Bahrain and Qatar was as described in its Memorial.

At a public sitting of 16 March 2001, the Court delivered its Judgment. It unanimously found that Qatar had sovereignty over Zubarah and, by 12 votes to 5, that Bahrain had sovereignty over the Hawar Islands. By 13 votes to 4, the Court found that Qatar had sovereignty over Janan Island, including Hadd Janan and, by 12 votes to 5, that Bahrain had sovereignty over the island of Qit'at Jaradah. The Court unanimously found that the low-tide elevation of Fasht ad Dibal fell under the sovereignty of Qatar and, by 13 votes to 4, decided that the single maritime boundary dividing the various maritime zones of Qatar and Bahrain should be drawn as indicated in paragraph 250 of its Judgment.

Judge Oda appended a separate opinion to the Judgment; Judges Bedjaoui, Ranjeva and Koroma, a joint dissenting opinion; Judges Herczegh, Vereshchetin and Higgins, declarations; and Judges Parra-Aranguren, Kooijmans and Al-Khasawneh, separate opinions. Judge ad hoc Torres Bernárdez appended a dissenting opinion to the Judgment, and Judge ad hoc Fortier, a separate opinion.

Questions of interpretation and application of the 1971 Montreal Convention arising from the aerial incident at Lockerbie (Libyan Arab Jamahiriya v. United Kingdom) and (Libyan Arab Jamahiriya v. United States)

The Libyan Arab Jamahiriya instituted in 1992 [YUN 1992, p. 982] separate proceedings against the United Kingdom and the United States in respect of a dispute over the interpretation and application of the 1971 Montreal Convention for the Suppression of Unlawful Acts against the Safety of Civil Aviation [YUN 1971, p. 739], which arose from its alleged involvement in the crash of Pan Am flight 103 over Lockerbie, Scotland, on 21 December 1988. In the Applications, Libya referred to the charging and indictment of two of its nationals by the Lord Advocate of Scotland and by a United States Grand Jury for having caused a bomb to be placed aboard Pan Am flight 103, which exploded, caused the aircraft to crash and killed all 270 persons aboard.

The United Kingdom and the United States, on 16 and on 20 June 1995, respectively [YUN 1995, p. 1306], filed preliminary objections to the jurisdiction of the Court to entertain Libya's Applications. Libya presented a written statement of its observations and submissions on the preliminary objections raised by the United Kingdom and the United States within the prescribed time limits set by the Court. Public sittings to hear the oral arguments of the Parties on the preliminary objections raised by the United Kingdom and the United States were held in October 1997 [YUN 1997, p. 1313].

In February 1998 [YUN 1998, p. 1184], the Court delivered the two Judgments on the preliminary objections, by which it rejected the objection to jurisdiction raised by the United Kingdom and the United States on the basis of the alleged absence of a dispute between the Parties concerning the interpretation or application of the Montreal Convention; found that it had jurisdiction, on the basis of article 14, paragraph 1, of the Convention, to hear the disputes between Libya and the United Kingdom and Libya and the United States concerning the interpretation or application of the provisions of the Convention; rejected the objection to admissibility derived by the United Kingdom and the United States from Security Council resolutions 748(1992) [YUN 1992, p. 55] and 883(1993) [YUN 1993, p. 101]; found that the Applications filed by Libya on 3 March 1992 were admissible; and declared that the objection raised by both countries according to which the same Council resolutions had rendered the claims of Libya without object did not, in the circumstances of the case, have an excessively preliminary character.

The time limit of 30 December 1998 fixed by the Court [YUN 1998, p. 1185] for the filing of the Counter-Memorials of the United Kingdom and the United States was extended to 31 March 1999 following a proposal of the United Kingdom and the United States, which referred to diplomatic initiatives [ibid., p. 163], and after the views of Libya had been ascertained. The Counter-Memorials were filed within the time limit.

Taking account of the agreement of the Parties and the special circumstances of the case, the Court, by Orders of 29 June 1999 [YUN 1999, p. 1203], authorized the submission of a Reply by Libya and Rejoinders by the United Kingdom and the United States, which fixed 29 June 2000 as the time limit for the filing of the Reply. The Court fixed no date for the filing of the Rejoinders; the representatives of the Respondent States had expressed the desire that no such date be fixed at that stage of the proceedings, "in view of the new circumstances consequent upon the transfer of the two accused to the Netherlands for trial by a Scottish court". Libya's Reply was filed within the prescribed time limit.

By Orders of 6 September 2000 [YUN 2000, p. 1211], the President of the Court, taking account of the Parties' views, fixed 3 August 2001 as the time limit for filing the Rejoinders of the United Kingdom and the United States. The Rejoinders were filled within the prescribed time limit.

Oil platforms (Iran v. United States)

Iran instituted proceedings against the United States in 1992 [YUN 1992, p. 983] regarding a dispute in which Iran alleged that the destruction by United States warships, on 19 October 1987 and 18 April 1988, of three offshore oil production complexes owned and operated by the National Iranian Oil Company constituted a breach of international law and the 1955 Iran/United States Treaty of Amity, Economic Relations and Consular Rights. Iran requested the Court to rule on the matter.

Orders of the Court in 1992 [YUN 1992, p. 983] and 1993 [YUN 1993, p. 1183] fixed time limits for the filing of the Memorial by Iran and for a Counter-Memorial by the United States. Iran filed its Memorial, while the United States filed certain preliminary objections to the jurisdiction of the Court. In 1994 [YUN 1994, p. 1280], Iran presented a written statement of its observations and submissions on the United States objections, in accordance with an Order of the Court.

The Court delivered its Judgment in 1996 [YUN 1996, p. 1178], by which it rejected the preliminary objection of the United States and found that it had jurisdiction to entertain the claims made by Iran.

By an Order of 16 December 1996 [YUN 1996, p. 1178], the President of the Court fixed 23 June 1997 as the time limit for the filing of the Counter-Memorial of the United States. Within that time limit, the United States filed the Counter-Memorial and a counter-claim [YUN 1997, p. 1313].

In November and December 1997, respectively, Iran and the United States submitted written observations on the question of the admissibility of the United States counter-claim.

In 1998 [YUN 1998, p. 1185], the Court found that the counter-claim presented by the United States in its Counter-Memorial was admissible. It further directed Iran to submit a Reply and the United States to submit a Rejoinder, fixing the time limits for those pleadings at 10 September 1998 and 23 November 1999, respectively.

In May 1998 [YUN 1998, p. 1185], the Vice-President of the Court, Acting President, extended, at the request of Iran and taking into account the views expressed by the United States, the time limits for Iran's Reply and the United States Rejoinder to 10 December 1998 and 23 May 2000, respectively. In December 1998, the Court further extended those time limits to 10 March 1999 for Iran's Reply and 23 November 2000 for the United States Rejoinder. Iran's Reply was filed within the time limit thus extended.

In September 2000 [YUN 2000, p. 1211], the President of the Court extended, at the request of the United States and taking into account the agreement between the Parties, the time limit for filing the United States Rejoinder to 23 March 2001. The Rejoinder was filed within the time limit thus extended.

By an Order of 28 August 2001, the Vice-President of the Court, taking account of the agreement of the Parties, authorized the submission by Iran of an additional pleading relating solely to the counter-claim submitted by the United States and fixed 24 September 2001 as the time limit for the filing of that pleading. The additional pleading was filed by Iran within the prescribed time limit.

Application of the Convention on the Prevention and Punishment of the Crime of Genocide (Bosnia and Herzegovina v. Yugoslavia)

Bosnia and Herzegovina instituted proceedings in 1993 [YUN 1993, p. 1138] against the Federal

Republic of Yugoslavia (Serbia and Montenegro) (FRY) for alleged violations of the 1948 Convention on the Prevention and Punishment of the Crime of Genocide, adopted by the General Assembly in resolution 260 A (III) [YUN 1948-49, p. 959]. The time limits were fixed for the filing of a Memorial by Bosnia and Herzegovina and a Counter-Memorial by FRY [YUN 1993, p. 1138]. The Memorial by Bosnia and Herzegovina was filed within the prescribed time limit [YUN 1994, p. 1281].

The time limit for the filing of the Counter-Memorial by FRY was extended in 1995 [YUN 1995, p. 1307]. Within the time limit, FRY filed certain preliminary objections. The objections related, first, to the admissibility of the Application and, second, to the jurisdiction of the Court to deal with the case. By virtue of the Rules of Court, proceedings on the merits were suspended. Pursuant to an Order of the Court [ibid.], Bosnia and Herzegovina presented a written statement of its observations and submissions on the preliminary objections raised by FRY, within the prescribed time limit.

The Court delivered its Judgment on 11 July 1996 on the preliminary objections [YUN 1996, p. 1179], by which it rejected the objections raised by FRY. In accordance with an Order of 23 July 1996 [ibid.], FRY filed a Counter-Memorial that included counter-claims against Bosnia and Herzegovina [YUN 1997, p. 1315].

Both Parties accepted in 1997 that their respective Governments would submit written observations on the question of the admissibility of the FRY counter-claims and did so. The Court found that the counter-claims submitted by FRY in its Counter-Memorial were admissible and directed Bosnia and Herzegovina to submit a Reply and FRY to submit a Rejoinder, fixing the time limits for those pleadings at 23 January and 23 July 1998, respectively. In January 1998 [YUN 1998, p. 1186], those time limits were extended to 23 April 1998 and 22 January 1999, respectively. The Reply of Bosnia and Herzegovina was filed within the prescribed time limit. The Court, in December 1998 [ibid.], extended the time limit for the filing of FRY's Rejoinder to 22 February 1999, which was filed within the time limit [YUN 1999, p. 1204].

By an Order of 10 September 2001, the President of the Court placed on record the withdrawal by FRY of the counter-claims submitted in its Counter-Memorial. The Order was made after FRY had informed the Court that it intended to withdraw its counter-claims and Bosnia and Herzegovina had indicated to the latter that it had no objection to the withdrawal.

Application for Revision of the Judgment of 11 July 1996 concerning Application of the Convention on the Prevention and Punishment of the Crime of Genocide (Bosnia and Herzegovina v. Yugoslavia), Preliminary Objections (Yugoslavia v. Bosnia and Herzegovina)

On 24 April 2001, FRY filed an Application for revision of the Judgment delivered by the Court on 11 July 1996 in the case concerning the *Application of the Convention on the Prevention and Punishment of the Crime of Genocide (Bosnia and Herzegovina v. Yugoslavia), Preliminary Objections* [YUN 1996, p. 1179] (see above). FRY contended that a revision of the Judgment was necessary, since it had become clear that, before 1 November 2000 (the date on which it was admitted as a new Member of the United Nations), FRY did not continue the international legal and political personality of the Socialist Federal Republic of Yugoslavia, was not a UN Member State, was not a State party to the Statute of the Court, and was not a State party to the 1948 Convention on Genocide (which was open only to UN Member States or to non-member States invited by the General Assembly to sign or accede).

FRY based its Application for revision on Article 61 of the Court's Statute, which provided that an "application for revision of a judgment may be made only when it is based upon the discovery of some fact of such a nature as to be a decisive factor, which fact was, when the judgment was given, unknown to the Court and also to the party claiming revision, always provided that such ignorance was not due to negligence". FRY stated that its admission to the United Nations as a new Member on 1 November 2000 constituted "a new fact", which was "obviously unknown to both the Court and to [Yugoslavia] at the time of the 1996 Judgment". It added that "since membership in the United Nations, combined with the status of a party to the Statute [of the Court] and to the Genocide Convention represent the only basis on which jurisdiction over the FRY was assumed, and could be assumed, the disappearance of this assumption . . . [is] clearly of such a nature [as] to be a decisive factor".

FRY asserted that no alternative basis for the Court's jurisdiction existed or could have existed in the case. It further noted that, while on 8 March 2001 it submitted to the United Nations Secretary-General a notification seeking accession to the Genocide Convention, that instrument included a reservation to article IX. According to FRY, accession had no retroactive effect; even if it had such an effect, it could not encompass the compromissory clause in article IX of the Genocide Convention, because FRY never accepted article IX, and FRY's accession to the Convention did not encompass that article.

FRY requested the Court to declare that there was a "new fact of such a character as to lay the case open to revision under Article 61 of the Statute of the Court". It further asked the Court to suspend proceedings regarding the merits of the case until a decision on the Application was rendered.

Copies of the pleadings were made available to the Government of Croatia, at its request.

On 3 December 2001, within the time limit fixed by the President of the Court at a meeting with representatives of the Parties, Bosnia and Herzegovina filed written observations regarding the admissibility of FRY's Application, in accordance with Article 99, paragraph 2, of the Rules of Court.

Land and maritime boundary between Cameroon and Nigeria (Cameroon v. Nigeria: Equatorial Guinea intervening)

Cameroon instituted proceedings against Nigeria in March 1994 [YUN 1994, p. 1281] in a dispute concerning the question of sovereignty over the peninsula of Bakassi and requested the Court to determine the course of the maritime frontier between the two States insofar as that frontier had not already been established in 1975. The Application was amended by an Additional Application in June 1994. Cameroon's Memorial was filed in 1995 [YUN 1995, p. 1308]. In December 1995, within the time limit for the filing of its Counter-Memorial, Nigeria filed certain preliminary objections to the jurisdiction of the Court and to the admissibility of the claims of Cameroon.

In 1996 [YUN 1996, p. 1180], Cameroon presented a written statement of its observations and submissions on the preliminary objections raised by Nigeria. Following hearings in March 1996, the Court made an Order indicating that neither Party should take any action of any kind, and that both should lend every assistance to a fact-finding mission to be sent by the United Nations Secretary-General [ibid., p. 146].

In June 1998 [YUN 1998, p. 1187], the Court delivered its Judgment on the preliminary objections, by which it rejected seven of Nigeria's eight preliminary objections; declared that the eighth did not have, in the circumstances of the case, an exclusively preliminary character; and found that, on the basis of Article 36, paragraph 2, of the ICJ Statute, it had jurisdiction to adjudicate on the dispute and that the Application filed by Cameroon on 29 March 1994, as amended by the Additional Application of 6 June 1994, was admissi-

ble. The Court, having been informed of the views of the Parties, fixed 31 March 1999 as the time limit for the filing of the Counter-Memorial of Nigeria.

On 28 October 1998, Nigeria filed a request for an interpretation of the Court's Judgment on the preliminary objections [YUN 1998, p. 1187]. The request for interpretation formed a separate case, in which the Court delivered its Judgment in March 1999 [YUN 1999, p. 1205].

On 23 February 1999 [YUN 1999, p. 1204], Nigeria requested an extension of the time limit for the deposit of its Counter-Memorial; in March [ibid.], the Court extended to 31 May 1999 the time limit for the filing of Nigeria's Counter-Memorial, which was filed within the time limit. The Counter-Memorial included counter-claims. At the end of each section dealing with a particular sector of the frontier, Nigeria asked the Court to declare that the incidents referred to "engage the international responsibility of Cameroon, with compensation in the form of damages, if not agreed between the parties, then to be awarded by the Court in a subsequent phase of the case". The seventh and final submission set out by Nigeria in its Counter-Memorial read as follows: "as to Nigeria's counter-claims as specified in . . . of this Counter-Memorial, [the Court is asked to] adjudge and declare that Cameroon bears responsibility to Nigeria in respect of those claims, the amount of reparation due therefor, if not agreed between the parties within six months of the date of judgment, to be determined by the Court in a further judgment". In June 1999 [YUN 1999, p. 1204], the Court found that Nigeria's counter-claims were admissible and formed part of the proceedings; decided that Cameroon should submit a Reply and Nigeria a Rejoinder, relating to the claims of both Parties; and fixed the time limits for those pleadings at 4 April 2000 and 4 January 2001, respectively.

On 30 June 1999, Equatorial Guinea filed an Application for permission to intervene in the case, stating that the purpose was to protect its legal rights in the Gulf of Guinea and to inform the Court of Equatorial Guinea's legal rights and interests so that they might remain unaffected as the Court proceeded to address the question of the maritime boundary between Cameroon and Nigeria. Equatorial Guinea clarified that it did not seek to intervene in those aspects of the proceedings that related to the land boundary between Cameroon and Nigeria, or to become a Party to the case. It further stated that, although it would be open to a request to the Court from the three countries not only to determine the Cameroon-Nigeria maritime boundary but also to determine Equatorial Guinea's maritime boundary with those two States, Equatorial Guinea had made no such request and wished to continue to determine its maritime boundary with its neighbours by negotiation.

The Court fixed 16 August 1999 [YUN 1999, p. 1205] as the time limit for the filing of written observations by Cameroon and Nigeria on Equatorial Guinea's Application, which were filed within the prescribed time limits.

By an Order of 21 October 1999, the Court unanimously decided that Equatorial Guinea could intervene in the case, and fixed the time limits for the filing of the written statement and the written observations at 4 April 2001 for the written statement of Equatorial Guinea and 4 July 2001 for the written observations of Cameroon and Nigeria. Equatorial Guinea's written statement was filed within the prescribed time limit.

By an Order of 20 February 2001, the Court, at the request of Cameroon and taking into account the agreement of the Parties, authorized the submission by Cameroon of an additional pleading, relating solely to the counter-claims submitted by Nigeria, and fixed 4 July 2001 as the time limit for its filing. The various pleadings, which were due to be lodged on 4 July 2001, were filed within the prescribed time limit.

Sovereignty over Pulau Ligitan and Pulau Sipadan (Indonesia/Malaysia)

On 2 November 1998 [YUN 1998, p. 1189], Indonesia and Malaysia jointly notified the Court of a Special Agreement between them, signed at Kuala Lumpur on 31 May 1997, which entered into force on 14 May 1998, in which they requested the Court "to determine on the basis of the treaties, agreements and any other evidence furnished by the Parties, whether sovereignty over Pulau Ligitan and Pulau Sipadan belongs to the Republic of Indonesia or to Malaysia". By an Order of 10 November 1998 [ibid.], the Court fixed 2 November 1999 and 2 March 2000, respectively, as the time limits for the filing by each of the Parties of a Memorial and a Counter-Memorial. The time limit for filing the Counter-Memorials was extended to 2 July 2000, by an Order of 14 September 1999 [YUN 1999, p. 1206].

The Memorials were filed within the time limit of 2 November 1999, as fixed by the Court's Order of 10 November 1998.

The Counter-Memorials were filed within the time limit of 2 August 2000, as extended by an Order of 11 May 2000 [YUN 2000, p. 1213]. Replies were filed within the time limit of 2 March 2001, as fixed by the President in October 2000 [ibid.].

On 13 March 2001, the Philippines filed an Application for permission to intervene in the case

in order "to preserve and safeguard [its Government's] historical and legal rights . . . arising from its claim to dominion and sovereignty over the territory of North Borneo, to the extent that these rights are affected, or may be affected, by a determination of the Court of the question of sovereignty over Pulau Ligitan and Pulau Sipadan"; "to inform the . . . Court of the nature and extent of [those] rights"; and "to appreciate more fully the indispensable role of the . . . Court in comprehensive conflict prevention". The Philippines made it clear that it did not seek to become a party to the case, and further maintained that "[its] Constitution . . . as well as its legislation, ha[d] laid claim to dominion and sovereignty over North Borneo". According to the Philippines, "[t]his . . . claim . . . ha[d] been the subject of diplomatic negotiations, official international correspondence, and peaceful discussions which ha[d] not been concluded. A decision by the Court, or that incidental part of a decision by the Court, which [would] lay down an appreciation of specific treaties, agreements and other evidence bearing on the legal status of North Borneo [would] inevitably and most assuredly affect the outstanding territorial claim of . . . the Philippines to North Borneo, as well as the direct legal right and interest of the Philippines to settle that claim by peaceful means".

In their written observations, which were filed within the time limit fixed by the Court of 2 May 2001, Indonesia and Malaysia objected to the Application for permission to intervene submitted by the Philippines. Indonesia, among other things, stated that the Application should be rejected as untimely and that the Philippines had not demonstrated that it possessed an interest of a legal nature that might be affected by a decision of the Court. Malaysia stated that the Philippines had no interest of a legal nature in the dispute, and that its request had no proper object.

Pursuant to Article 84, paragraph 2, of its Rules, the Court held public sittings on 25, 26, 28 and 29 June 2001 in order to hear the arguments of the Philippines, Indonesia and Malaysia before deciding whether the Application for permission to intervene should be granted. Meanwhile, following the resignation of Mohamed Shahabuddeen, Indonesia chose Thomas Franck to sit as judge ad hoc.

At a public sitting on 23 October 2001, the Court delivered its Judgment on the Application of the Philippines to intervene. By 14 votes to 1, the Court found that the Application of the Philippines for permission to intervene in the proceedings could not be granted.

Judge Oda appended a dissenting opinion to the Judgment; Judge Koroma, a separate opinion;

and Judges Parra-Aranguren and Kooijmans, declarations. Judges ad hoc Weeramantry and Franck appended separate opinions to the Judgment.

Ahmadou Sadio Diallo
(Guinea v. Democratic Republic of the Congo)

In 1998 [YUN 1998, p. 1190], Guinea instituted proceedings against the Democratic Republic of the Congo (DRC) by an "Application with a view to diplomatic protection", in which it requested the Court to condemn the DRC for the grave breaches of international law perpetrated upon the person of a Guinean national, Ahmadou Sadio Diallo.

According to Guinea, Mr. Diallo, a businessman who had been a resident of the DRC for 32 years, was "unlawfully imprisoned by the authorities of that State" for two and a half months, "divested from his important investments, companies, bank accounts, movable and immovable properties, then expelled". The expulsion took place on 2 February 1996, as a result of his attempts to recover sums owed to him by the DRC (especially by Gécamines, a State enterprise and mining monopoly) and by oil companies operating in that country (Zaïre Shell, Zaïre Mobil and Zaïre Fina), by virtue of contracts concluded with businesses owned by him, namely Africom-Zaïre and Africontainers-Zaïre.

As a basis of the Court's jurisdiction, Guinea invoked its own declaration of acceptance of the compulsory jurisdiction of the Court of 11 November 1998 and the declaration of the DRC of 8 February 1989.

In November 1999 [YUN 1999, p. 1206], the Court, taking into account the agreement of the Parties, fixed 11 September 2000 as the time limit for the filing of a Memorial by Guinea and 11 September 2001 for the filing of a Counter-Memorial by the DRC.

By an Order of 8 September 2000 [YUN 2000, p. 1213], the President of the Court, at Guinea's request and after the views of the other Party had been ascertained, extended to 23 March 2001 and 4 October 2002 the respective time limits for the Memorial and Counter-Memorial. The Memorial was filed within the extended time limit.

Vienna Convention on Consular Relations
(Germany v. United States)

On 2 March 1999 [YUN 1999, p. 1206], Germany instituted proceedings against the United States in a dispute concerning alleged violations of the 1963 Vienna Convention on Consular Relations [YUN 1963, p. 510].

In its Application, Germany based the jurisdiction of the Court on Article 36, paragraph 1, of the Statute and on article I of the Optional Protocol concerning the Compulsory Settlement of Disputes [ibid., p. 512] to the Vienna Convention. Germany stated that in 1982 the authorities of Arizona (United States) detained two German nationals, Karl and Walter LaGrand; that the individuals were tried and sentenced to death without having been informed, as was required under article 36, subparagraph 1 *(b)*, of the Vienna Convention, of their rights under that provision (which required the competent authorities of a State party to advise, without delay, a national of another State party whom such authorities arrested or detained of the national's right to consular assistance). Germany also alleged that the failure to provide the required notification precluded it from protecting its nationals' interests in the United States, as provided for by the 1963 Convention, at both the trial and the appeal levels in United States courts.

The State Attorney admitted during proceedings before the Arizona Mercy Committee on 23 February 1999 that, contrary to a previous contention, the authorities of the State of Arizona had been aware since 1982 that the two detainees were German nationals. Germany further stated that the LaGrands, finally with the assistance of German consular officers, did claim violations of the Vienna Convention before the Federal District Court (the federal court of first instance). In addition, it claimed that the Court, applying the municipal law doctrine of "procedural default", decided that, because the individuals in question had not asserted their rights under the Vienna Convention in the previous legal proceedings at the state level, they could not assert them in the federal habeas corpus proceedings; and the intermediate federal appellate court, the last means of legal recourse in the United States available to them, had affirmed that decision.

Germany asked ICJ to adjudge and declare that: the United States, in arresting, detaining, trying, convicting and sentencing the LaGrands, had violated its international legal obligations to Germany, as provided by articles 5 and 36 of the Vienna Convention; Germany was therefore entitled to reparation; the United States was under an international legal obligation not to apply the doctrine of "procedural default", or any other doctrine of its internal law, so as to preclude the exercise of the rights accorded under the Vienna Convention; and the United States was under an international obligation to carry out in conformity with the foregoing international legal obligations any future detention of or criminal proceedings against the LaGrands or any other

German national in its territory. The foregoing international legal obligations held that: any criminal liability imposed on the LaGrands in violation of international legal obligations was void, and should be recognized as void by the United States legal authorities; the United States should provide reparation, in the form of compensation and satisfaction, for the execution of Karl LaGrand on 24 February 1999; the United States should restore the status quo ante in the case of Walter LaGrand, which meant re-establishing the situation that existed before the detention of, proceedings against and conviction and sentencing of Walter LaGrand, whose execution had been set for 3 March; and the United States should provide Germany a guarantee of the non-repetition of the illegal acts.

On 2 March 1999 [YUN 1999, p. 1207], Germany also submitted an urgent request for the indication of provisional measures, asking the Court to indicate that "the United States should take all measures at its disposal to ensure that Walter LaGrand is not executed pending the final decision in these proceedings, and should inform the Court of all the measures which it has taken in implementation of that Order"; it asked the Court, moreover, to consider its request as a matter of the greatest urgency "in view of the extreme gravity and immediacy of the threat of execution of a German citizen".

By a letter of the same date, the Vice-President of the Court drew the attention of the United States Government "to the need to act in such a way as to enable any Order the Court will make on the request for provisional measures to have its appropriate effects".

At a public sitting on 3 March 1999, the Court rendered its Order on the request for the indication of provisional measures by which it indicated that: the United States should take all measures at its disposal to ensure that Walter LaGrand was not executed pending the final decision in the proceedings, and should inform the Court of all the measures that it had taken in implementation of the Order; and the United States should transmit the Order to the Governor of the State of Arizona. It decided that, until the Court had given its final decision, it would remain seized of the matters which formed the subject of the Order. Walter LaGrand was executed later that day.

Judge Oda appended a declaration to the Order and President Schwebel a separate opinion.

By an Order of 5 March 1999 [YUN 1999, p. 1207], the Court, taking into account the views of the Parties, fixed 16 September 1999 and 27 March 2000 as the time limits for the filing of the Memorial of Germany and the Counter-Memorial of the United States, respectively. The Memorial was filed within the prescribed time limit.

Following oral proceedings held in November 2000 [YUN 2000, p. 1215], Germany requested the Court, in four submissions, to adjudge and declare that the United States had violated its international legal obligations to Germany (submissions 1 and 2); that the United States had violated its international legal obligations to comply with the Court's Order of 3 March 1999 (submission 3); and that the United States should assure Germany that it would not repeat the unlawful acts (submission 4). The United States asked the Court to adjudge and declare that there was a breach of the United States obligation to Germany under the Vienna Convention; that it had apologized to Germany for the breach and was taking substantial measures to prevent any recurrence; and that all other claims and submissions of Germany were dismissed. The Court held deliberations on its Judgment in 2000.

At a public sitting on 27 June 2001, the Court delivered its Judgment. By 14 votes to 1, the Court found that it had jurisdiction, on the basis of article I of the 1963 Optional Protocol concerning the Compulsory Settlement of Disputes, to entertain the Application filed by Germany on 2 March 1999. The Court found all four of Germany's submissions admissible: the first submission by 13 votes to 2; the second by 14 to 1; the third by 12 to 3; and the fourth by 14 to 1. By 14 votes to 1, the Court found that, by not informing the LaGrands without delay, following their arrest, of their rights under the 1963 Convention, and thereby depriving Germany of the possibility to render assistance to them, the United States breached its obligations to Germany and to the LaGrand brothers under the Convention's article 36, paragraph 1. The Court, by 14 votes to 1, found that, by not permitting the review and reconsideration, in the light of the rights set forth in the 1963 Convention, of the convictions and sentences of the LaGrand brothers after the violations referred to above had been established, the United States breached its obligation to Germany and to the LaGrand brothers under article 36, paragraph 2, of the Convention. Furthermore, by 13 votes to 2, the Court found that, by failing to take all measures at its disposal to ensure that Walter LaGrand was not executed pending ICJ's final decision in the case, the United States breached the obligation incumbent upon it under the Order indicating provisional measures issued by the Court on 3 March 1999. Unanimously, the Court took note of the United States commitment to ensure implementation of the specific measures adopted in performance of its obligations under article 36, paragraph 1 *(b)*, of the Convention; and found that the commitment must be regarded as meeting Germany's request for a general assurance of non-repetition. By 14 votes to 1, the Court found that should German nationals nonetheless be sentenced to severe penalties, without their rights under article 36, paragraph 1 *(b)*, of the Convention having been respected, the United States, by means of its own choosing, should allow the review and reconsideration of the conviction and sentence by taking account of the violation of the rights set forth in that Convention.

President Guillaume appended a declaration to the Judgment; Vice-President Shi, a separate opinion; Judge Oda, a dissenting opinion; Judges Koroma and Parra-Aranguren, separate opinions; and Judge Buergenthal, a dissenting opinion.

Use of force (Yugoslavia v. Belgium), (Yugoslavia v. Canada), (Yugoslavia v. France), (Yugoslavia v. Germany), (Yugoslavia v. Italy), (Yugoslavia v. Netherlands), (Yugoslavia v. Portugal), (Yugoslavia v. Spain), (Yugoslavia v. United Kingdom) and (Yugoslavia v. United States)

FRY instituted proceedings on 29 April 1999 [YUN 1999, p. 1207] against Belgium, Canada, France, Germany, Italy, the Netherlands, Portugal, Spain, the United Kingdom and the United States for alleged violation of the obligation not to use force. In the cases against Belgium, Canada, the Netherlands, Portugal, Spain and the United Kingdom, FRY invoked the jurisdiction of the Court based on Article 36, paragraph 2, of the Statute and on article IX of the 1948 Convention on the Prevention and Punishment of the Crime of Genocide, adopted by the General Assembly in resolution 260 A (III) [YUN 1948-49, p. 959], and, in the cases against France, Germany, Italy and the United States, on article IX of the Convention and Article 38, paragraph 5, of the Rules of Court.

In its Applications, FRY stated that the disputes involved "acts of the [respondent State concerned] by which it has violated the international obligation banning the use of force against another State, the obligation not to intervene in the internal affairs of another State, the obligation not to violate the sovereignty of another State, the obligation to protect the civilian population and civilian objects in wartime, the obligation to protect the environment, the obligation relating to free navigation on international rivers, the obligation regarding fundamental human rights and freedoms, the obligation not to use prohibited weapons, the obligation not to deliberately inflict conditions of life calculated to cause the physical destruction of a national group".

FRY requested the Court to adjudge and declare that the respondent State concerned had acted against it by taking part in the bombing of the territory of FRY, breaching its obligation not to use force against another State; by taking part in the training, arming, financing, equipping and supplying of terrorist groups, i.e., the Kosovo Liberation Army, breaching its obligation not to intervene in the affairs of another State; by taking part in attacks on civilian targets, breaching its obligation to spare the civilian population and civilian objects; by taking part in destroying or damaging monasteries and cultural monuments, breaching its obligation not to commit any act of hostility directed against historical monuments, works of art or places of worship that constituted people's cultural or spiritual heritage; by taking part in the use of cluster bombs, breaching its obligation not to use prohibited weapons, i.e., weapons calculated to cause unnecessary suffering; by taking part in the bombing of oil refineries and chemical plants, breaching its obligation not to cause considerable environmental damage; by taking part in the use of weapons containing depleted uranium, breaching its obligation not to use prohibited weapons and not to cause far-reaching health and environmental damage; by taking part in killing civilians, destroying enterprises, communications, health and cultural institutions, breaching its obligation to respect the rights to life, to work, to information and to health care, as well as other basic human rights; by taking part in destroying bridges on international rivers, breaching its obligation to respect freedom of navigation on international rivers; and by taking part in activities listed above, and in particular by causing enormous environmental damage and by using depleted uranium, breaching its obligation not to deliberately inflict on a national group conditions of life calculated to bring about its physical destruction, in whole or in part. In addition, the respondent State concerned was responsible for the violation of the above international obligations; was obliged to stop immediately the violation of the above obligations vis-à-vis FRY; and was obliged to provide compensation for the damage to FRY and to its citizens and juridical persons.

Also on 29 April 1999 [YUN 1999, p. 1208], FRY submitted, in each of the cases, a request for the indication of provisional measures, asking the Court to indicate that "the [respondent State concerned] shall cease immediately its acts of use of force and shall refrain from any act of threat or use of force" against FRY. Hearings on the requests for the indication of provisional measures were held between 10 and 12 May 1999.

At a public sitting on 2 June 1999, the Vice-President of the Court, Acting President, read the Orders, by which, in the cases *(Yugoslavia v. Belgium)*, *(Yugoslavia v. Canada)*, *(Yugoslavia v. France)*, *(Yugoslavia v. Germany)*, *(Yugoslavia v. Italy)*, *(Yugoslavia v. Netherlands)*, *(Yugoslavia v. Portugal)* and *(Yugoslavia v. United Kingdom)*, the Court rejected the requests for the indication of provisional measures and reserved the subsequent procedure for further decision. In the cases of *(Yugoslavia v. Spain)* and *(Yugoslavia v. United States of America)*, the Court—having found that it manifestly lacked jurisdiction to entertain FRY's Application; that it could not therefore indicate any provisional measure whatsoever in order to protect the rights invoked therein; and that, within a system of consensual jurisdiction, to maintain on the General List a case upon which it appeared certain that the Court would not be able to adjudicate on the merits would most assuredly not contribute to the sound administration of justice—rejected FRY's requests for the indication of provisional measures and ordered that those cases be removed from the List.

In each of the cases *(Yugoslavia v. Belgium)*, *(Yugoslavia v. Canada)*, *(Yugoslavia v. Netherlands)* and *(Yugoslavia v. Portugal)*, Judge Koroma appended a declaration to the Order of the Court; Judges Oda, Higgins, Parra-Aranguren and Kooijmans appended separate opinions; and Vice-President Weeramantry, Acting President, Judges Shi and Vereshchetin and Judge ad hoc Kreca appended dissenting opinions.

In each of the cases *(Yugoslavia v. France)*, *(Yugoslavia v. Germany)* and *(Yugoslavia v. Italy)*, Vice-President Weeramantry, Acting President, and Judges Shi, Koroma and Vereshchetin appended declarations to the Order of the Court; Judges Oda and Parra-Aranguren appended separate opinions; and Judge ad hoc Kreca appended a dissenting opinion.

In the case *(Yugoslavia v. Spain)*, Judges Shi, Koroma and Vereshchetin appended declarations to the Order of the Court; and Judges Oda, Higgins, Parra-Aranguren and Kooijmans and Judge ad hoc Kreca appended separate opinions.

In the case *(Yugoslavia v. United Kingdom)*, Vice-President Weeramantry, Acting President, and Judges Shi, Koroma and Vereshchetin appended declarations to the Order of the Court; Judges Oda, Higgins, Parra-Aranguren and Kooijmans appended separate opinions; and Judge ad hoc Kreca appended a dissenting opinion.

In the case *(Yugoslavia v. United States of America)*, Judges Shi, Koroma and Vereshchetin appended declarations to the Order of the Court; Judges Oda and Parra-Aranguren appended separate opinions; and Judge ad hoc Kreca appended a dissenting opinion.

By Orders of 30 June 1999 [YUN 1999, p. 1209], the Court, having ascertained the views of the Parties, fixed the time limits for the filing of the written pleadings in each of the eight cases maintained on the List as at 5 January 2000 for the Memorial of FRY and 5 July 2000 for the Counter-Memorial of the respondent State concerned.

On 5 July 2000 [YUN 2000, 1217], within the time limit for filing its Counter-Memorial, each of the respondent States in the eight cases maintained on the Court's List raised preliminary objections of lack of jurisdiction and admissibility. By virtue of Article 79, paragraph 3, of the Rules of Court, the proceedings on the merits were suspended; proceedings then had to be organized for the consideration of the preliminary objections in accordance with the Article's provisions.

By Orders of 8 September 2000 [ibid.], the Vice-President of the Court, Acting President, fixed 5 April 2001 as the time for filing, in each of the cases, of a written statement by FRY on the preliminary objections raised by the respondent State concerned. By an order of 21 February 2001, the Court, in each of the cases, taking into account the agreement of the Parties and the circumstances of the case, extended the time limit to 5 April 2002.

Armed activities on the territory of the Congo (Democratic Republic of the Congo v. Burundi), (Democratic Republic of the Congo v. Uganda) and (Democratic Republic of the Congo v. Rwanda)

The DRC instituted proceedings against Burundi, Uganda and Rwanda on 23 June 1999 [YUN 1999, p. 1209] for acts of armed aggression perpetrated in flagrant violation of the Charter of the United Nations and the Charter of the Organization of African Unity.

In its Applications, the DRC contended that "such armed aggression . . . involved inter alia violation of the sovereignty and territorial integrity of the [DRC], violations of international humanitarian law and massive human rights violations". The DRC sought the cessation of the aggression against it; reparation for acts of intentional destruction and looting; and restitution of national property and resources appropriated for the benefit of the respective respondent States.

In the cases against Burundi and Rwanda, the DRC invoked as bases for the jurisdiction of the Court Article 36, paragraph 1, of the Statute, which provided that the jurisdiction of the Court comprised all cases which the parties referred to it and all matters specially provided for in the UN Charter or in treaties and conventions in force;

the Convention against Torture and Other Cruel, Inhuman or Degrading Treatment or Punishment, adopted by the General Assembly in resolution 39/46 [YUN 1984, p. 813]; the Convention for the Suppression of Unlawful Acts against the Safety of Civil Aviation [YUN 1971, p. 739]; and Article 38, paragraph 5, of the Rules of Court, which contemplated the situation where a State filed an application against another State that had not accepted the jurisdiction of the Court. In the case against Uganda, the DRC based the jurisdiction on Article 36, paragraph 2, of the Statute.

The DRC requested the Court to adjudge and declare that: the respondent State concerned was guilty of an act of aggression as defined by article 1 of Assembly resolution 3314(XXIX) [YUN 1974, p. 847] and by the jurisprudence of the Court, contrary to Article 2, paragraph 4, of the UN Charter; the respondent State concerned committed repeated violations of the Geneva Conventions for the protection of war victims of 1949 and the two Additional Protocols of 1977 [YUN 1977, p. 706], in flagrant disregard of the elementary rules of international humanitarian law in conflict zones, and also was guilty of massive human rights violations in defiance of the most basic customary law; the respondent State concerned, by taking forcible possession of the Inga hydroelectric dam and deliberately and regularly causing massive electrical power cuts, in violation of the provisions of article 56 of Additional Protocol I of 1977, was responsible for very heavy loss of life in the city of Kinshasa (5 million inhabitants) and the surrounding area; and the respondent State concerned had violated the Convention on International Civil Aviation signed in Chicago on 7 December 1944, the 1970 Convention for the Suppression of Unlawful Seizure of Aircraft and the 1971 Convention for the Suppression of Unlawful Acts against the Safety of Civil Aviation by shooting down, on 9 October 1998 at Kindu, a Boeing 727, the property of Congo Airlines, thereby killing 40 civilians.

The DRC requested the Court to adjudge and declare that: all armed forces of the respondent State concerned participating in acts of aggression should forthwith vacate its territory; the respondent State concerned should secure the immediate and unconditional withdrawal from Congolese territory of its nationals, both natural and legal persons; and the DRC was entitled to compensation from the respondent State concerned in respect of all acts of looting, destruction, removal of property and persons and other unlawful acts attributable to the respondent State concerned, in respect of which the DRC reserved the right to determine at a later date the precise amount of the damage suffered, in addi-

tion to its claim for the restitution of all property removed.

In each of the cases against Burundi and Rwanda, the Court, by an Order of 21 October 1999 [YUN 1999, p. 1210], taking into account the agreement of the Parties, decided that the written proceedings should first address the questions of the jurisdiction of the Court to entertain the Application and of its admissibility, and fixed 21 April 2000 as the time limit for filing Memorials on those questions by Burundi and Rwanda, and 23 October 2000 for filing a Counter-Memorial by the DRC.

The DRC, by letters dated 15 January 2001, notified the Court that it wished to discontinue the proceedings against Burundi and Rwanda and stated that it "reserve[d] the right to invoke subsequently new grounds of jurisdiction of the Court". In each of the two cases, the respondent Party informed the Court that it concurred in the DRC's discontinuance. The President of the Court, in Orders of 30 January 2001, placed the discontinuance by the DRC on record and ordered the removal of the case from the List.

In the case against Uganda, the Court, taking into account the agreement of the Parties in 1999 [ibid.], fixed, by an Order of 21 October, 21 July 2000 as the time limit for the filing of a Memorial by the DRC and 21 April 2001 for the filing of a Counter-Memorial by Uganda. The Memorial of the DRC was filed within the prescribed time limit.

On 19 June 2000 [YUN 2000, p. 1218], the DRC requested the Court to indicate provisional measures requiring, among other things, the withdrawal of Uganda's army from Kisangani and the cessation of military and other activities by Uganda within the territory of the DRC. Public sittings to hear the oral observations of the Parties on the request for the indication of provisional measures were held on 26 and 28 June 2000.

On 1 July 2000 [ibid.], the Court rendered its Order on the DRC's request for provisional measures, which stated that both Parties must, forthwith, prevent and refrain from any action, particularly armed action, which might prejudice the rights of the other Party in respect of whatever judgment the Court might render, or which might aggravate or extend the dispute before the Court or make it more difficult to resolve; both Parties must, forthwith, take measures to comply with all their obligations under international law; and both Parties must, forthwith, take measures to ensure full respect within the zone of conflict for fundamental human rights and for the applicable provisions of humanitarian law. Judges Oda and Koroma appended declarations to the Order.

The DRC chose Joe Verhoeven and Uganda selected James L. Kateka to sit as judges ad hoc.

Uganda filed its Counter-Memorial, which contained counter-claims, within the time limit set by the Court's Order of 21 October 1999 (see p. 1191).

By an Order of 29 November 2001, the Court found that two of the counter-claims submitted by Uganda against the DRC were "admissible as such and [formed] part of the current proceedings", but that the third was not. In view of those conclusions, the Court considered it necessary for the DRC to file a Reply and Uganda a Rejoinder, addressing the claims of both Parties, and fixed 29 May 2002 as the time limit for the filing of the Reply and 29 November 2002 for the Rejoinder. Further, in order to ensure strict equality between the Parties, the Court reserved the right of the DRC to present its views in writing a second time on the Uganda counter-claims, in an additional pleading to be the subject of a subsequent Order. Judge ad hoc Verhoeven appended a declaration to the Order.

Application of the genocide convention (Croatia v. Yugoslavia)

Croatia instituted proceedings against FRY on 2 July 1999 [YUN 1999, p. 1210] for alleged violations of the 1948 Convention on the Prevention and Punishment of the Crime of Genocide, adopted by the General Assembly in resolution 260 A (III) [YUN 1948-49, p. 959], said to have been committed between 1991 and 1995.

In its Application, Croatia contended that by "directly controlling the activity of its armed forces, intelligence agents, and various paramilitary detachments, on the territory of . . . Croatia, in the Knin region, eastern and western Slovenia, and Dalmatia, [Yugoslavia] is liable [for] the 'ethnic cleansing' of Croatian citizens from these areas . . . and is required to provide reparation for the resulting damage". It further alleged that, "by directing, encouraging, and urging Croatian citizens of Serb ethnicity in the Knin region to evacuate the area in 1995, as . . . Croatia reasserted its legitimate governmental authority . . . [Yugoslavia] engaged in conduct amounting to a second round of 'ethnic cleansing'". Croatia invoked the jurisdiction of the Court based on Article 36, paragraph 1, of the Statute and on article IX of the Convention.

Croatia requested the Court to adjudge and declare that FRY breached its legal obligations towards Croatia under articles I, II (a, b, c, d), III (a, b, c, d, e), IV and V of the 1948 Convention; and that FRY had an obligation to pay to Croatia, in its own right and as *parens patriae* for its citizens, reparations for damages to persons and property, as well as to the Croatian economy and environment caused by the foregoing violations of international law, in a sum to be determined by the Court. Croatia reserved the right to introduce to the Court at a future date a precise evaluation of the damages.

By an Order of 14 September 1999, the Court took account of an agreement of the Parties expressed on 13 September and fixed 14 March 2000 as the time limit for the filing of the Memorial of Croatia and 14 September 2000 for the filing of the Counter-Memorial of FRY.

In 2000 [YUN 2000, p. 1219], at Croatia's request, the President of the Court extended the time limits twice: in March, to 14 September 2000 for the Memorial of Croatia and 14 September 2001 for the Counter-Memorial of FRY, and again in June, to 14 March 2001 for the Memorial and to 16 September 2002 for the Counter-Memorial. The Memorial of Croatia was filed within the time limit thus extended. Croatia chose Budislav Vukas to sit as judge ad hoc.

Maritime delimitation (Nicaragua v. Honduras)

On 8 December 1999 [YUN 1999, p. 1210], Nicaragua instituted proceedings against Honduras in respect of a dispute concerning the delimitation of the maritime zones appertaining to each of those States in the Caribbean Sea. In its Application, Nicaragua stated that it had maintained for decades the position that its maritime Caribbean border with Honduras had not been determined, while the position of Honduras allegedly was that a delimitation line was fixed by the King of Spain in an Arbitral Award of 23 December 1906, which was found valid and binding by ICJ on 18 November 1960 [YUN 1960, p. 536]. According to Nicaragua, the position adopted by Honduras had brought repeated confrontations and mutual capture of vessels of both nations in and around the general border area, and diplomatic negotiations had failed. Nicaragua founded jurisdiction of the Court on declarations under Article 36, paragraph 2, of the Court's Statute, by which both States accepted the compulsory jurisdiction of the Court, and also article XXXI of the American Treaty on Pacific Settlement (officially known as the "Pact of Bogotá"), signed on 30 April 1948, to which both Nicaragua and Honduras were parties.

Nicaragua requested the Court to determine the course of the single maritime boundary between areas of territorial sea, continental shelf and exclusive economic zone appertaining to Nicaragua and Honduras.

By an Order of 21 March 2000 [YUN 2000, p. 1219], the Court, taking into account the agreement of the Parties, fixed 21 March 2001 as the time limit for the filing of a Memorial by Nicaragua and 21 March 2002 for the filing of the Counter-Memorial by Honduras. The Memorial was filed within the prescribed time limit.

Copies of the pleadings and annexed documents were made available to Colombia, at its request.

Arrest warrant of 11 April 2000 (Democratic Republic of the Congo v. Belgium)

In October 2000 [YUN 2000, p. 1219], the DRC instituted proceedings against Belgium concerning an international arrest warrant issued on 11 April 2000 by a Belgian examining judge against the DRC's Acting Minister for Foreign Affairs, seeking his detention and subsequent extradition to Belgium for alleged crimes constituting grave violations of international humanitarian law. The warrant was transmitted to all States.

In its Application [ibid.], the DRC noted that the warrant characterized the alleged facts as crimes of international law committed by action or omission against persons or property protected by the Geneva Conventions of 12 August 1949 and Additional Protocols I and II to those Conventions [YUN 1977, p. 706], and as crimes against humanity, and cited the allegedly applicable Belgian Law of 16 June 1993 as amended by the Law of 10 February 1999 pertaining to the punishment of grave violations of international humanitarian law. The DRC maintained that certain articles of the Belgian Law and the warrant itself constituted "a violation of the principle whereby a State may not exercise its authority on territory of another State and the principle of sovereign equality among all members of the United Nations", as declared in Article 2, paragraph 1, of the UN Charter, and that they contravened international law, insofar as they claimed to derogate from the diplomatic immunity of the Minister for Foreign Affairs of a sovereign State, "deriving from article 41, paragraph 2, of the Vienna Convention of 18 April 1961 on Diplomatic Relations" [YUN 1961, p. 512]. Accordingly, the DRC asked the Court to declare that Belgium should annul the warrant, and filed a request for the indication of a provisional measure seeking to have the warrant withdrawn forthwith.

Following hearings on the request for an indication of provisional measures in November 2000 [YUN 2000, p. 1220], the DRC asked the Court to order Belgium to comply with international law; to cease and desist from any conduct that might exacerbate the dispute with the DRC; and to discharge the warrant issued against its acting Foreign Minister. Belgium asked the Court to refuse the DRC's request for an indication of provisional measures and to remove the case from its List.

By an Order of 8 December 2000 [ibid.], the Court unanimously rejected Belgium's request to remove the case from the List and found that the circumstances did not require it to exercise its power to indicate provisional measures. Judges Oda and Ranjeva appended declarations to the Order; Judges Koroma and Parra-Aranguren, separate opinions; Judge Rezek and Judge ad hoc Bula-Bula, dissenting opinions; and Judge ad hoc Van den Wijngaert, a declaration.

By an Order of 13 December 2000 [ibid.], the President of the Court, taking account of the agreement of the Parties, fixed 15 March 2001 and 31 May as the time limits for the filing of the Memorial of the DRC and the Counter-Memorial of Belgium, respectively. Subsequently, the Court extended those time limits to 17 April 2001 and 31 July 2001, respectively, and further extended them to 17 May 2001 and 17 September 2001, respectively. The DRC's Memorial was filed within the time limit thus extended.

By an Order of 27 June 2001, the Court rejected a request by Belgium seeking to derogate from the agreed procedure in the case and extended to 28 September 2001 the time limit for the filing of a Counter-Memorial by Belgium, addressing both questions of jurisdiction and admissibility and the merits of the dispute. It further fixed 15 October 2001 as the date for the opening of the hearings. The Counter-Memorial was filed within the prescribed time limit.

At the conclusion of public sittings to hear the oral arguments, held from 15 to 19 October 2001, the DRC requested the Court to adjudge and declare that by issuing and internationally circulating the arrest warrant of 11 April 2000, Belgium violated, in regard to the DRC, the rule of customary international law concerning the absolute inviolability and immunity from criminal process of incumbent foreign ministers and, in doing so, violated the principle of sovereign equality among States; a formal finding by the Court of the unlawfulness of that act constituted an appropriate form of satisfaction; the violations of international law underlying the issue and international circulation of the arrest warrant precluded any State, including Belgium, from executing it; and Belgium should be required to recall and cancel the arrest warrant of 11 April 2000 and to inform the foreign authorities to whom the warrant was circulated that Belgium renounced its request for cooperation in the warrant's execution. Belgium requested the Court to adjudge and declare that the Court lacked jurisdiction in the case and/or that the Application by the DRC against Belgium was inadmissible. If the Court concluded that it did have jurisdiction and the DRC's Application was admissible, Belgium requested the Court to reject the DRC's submissions on the merits of the case and to dismiss the Application.

The Court deliberated on a Judgment.

Certain property (Liechtenstein v. Germany)

On 1 June 2001, Liechtenstein filed an Application instituting proceedings against Germany concerning Germany's decisions to treat certain property of Liechtenstein nationals as German assets, seized for the purposes of reparation or restitution as a consequence of the Second World War, without ensuring any compensation.

In the Application, Liechtenstein alleged that in 1945, during the Second World War, Czechoslovakia—an allied country and a belligerent against Germany—through a series of decrees (the Beneš decrees) seized German and Hungarian property located on its territory. Czechoslovakia applied those decrees not only to German and Hungarian nationals but also to other persons allegedly of German or Hungarian origin or ethnicity. For that purpose, it treated the nationals of Liechtenstein as German nationals. The property of the Liechtenstein nationals seized under the decrees (the "Liechtenstein property") was never returned to its owners, nor had compensation been offered or paid. The application of the Beneš decrees to the Liechtenstein property remained unresolved between Liechtenstein and Czechoslovakia until the dissolution of the latter, and it continued to be an unresolved issue between Liechtenstein and the Czech Republic.

Liechtenstein further referred to the Convention on the Settlement of Matters arising out of the War and the Occupation, signed in Bonn on 26 May 1952 ("the Settlement Convention"), which stated that Germany agreed, among other things, that it would "in the future raise no objections against the measures which have been, or will be, carried out with regard to German external assets or other property, seized for the purpose of reparation or restitution, or as a result of the state of war". The Application alleged that the Settlement Convention was only concerned with German property, i.e., property of the German State or of its nationals, and that under international law, having regard to Liechtenstein's neutrality and the absence of any links between Liechtenstein and the conduct of the war by Germany, any Liechtenstein property that might have been affected by measures of an Allied Power could not be considered as "seized for the purpose of reparation or restitution, or as a result of the state of war". Liechtenstein maintained that subsequent to the conclusion of the Settlement Convention, it was accordingly understood between Germany and itself that the

Liechtenstein property did not fall within the scope of the Convention. As a corollary, Germany maintained the position that property falling outside the scope of the Convention was unlawfully seized, and that the German courts were not barred from considering claims affecting such property.

Following a Federal Constitutional Court ruling of Germany, pronounced in 1998, the property was treated as German external assets and could be used for payment of Germany's war-reparation debts. The Application of Liechtenstein claimed that the decision of the Federal Constitutional Court was unappealable, was attributable to Germany as a matter of international law, and was binding upon Germany.

Liechtenstein stated that it protested to Germany that the latter was treating as German assets that which belonged to Liechtenstein nationals. It further stated that Germany rejected the protest and that in subsequent consultations it became clear that Germany adhered to the position that Liechtenstein assets as a whole were "seized for the purpose of reparation or restitution, or as a result of the state of war" within the meaning of the Settlement Convention, even though the decision of the Federal Constitutional Court only concerned a single item. According to the Application of Liechtenstein, in taking that position, Germany remained faithful to the decision of its highest court in the matter; at the same time, it ignored and undermined the rights of Liechtenstein and its nationals in respect of the Liechtenstein property. Liechtenstein claimed that by its conduct with respect to the Liechtenstein property, in and since 1998, Germany failed to respect the rights of Liechtenstein with respect to that property; and by its failure to make compensation for losses suffered by Liechtenstein and/or its nationals, Germany was in breach of international law. Liechtenstein requested the Court to adjudge and declare that Germany had incurred international legal responsibility and was bound to make appropriate reparation to Liechtenstein for the damage and prejudice suffered. Liechtenstein further requested that the nature and amount of such reparation should, in the absence of agreement between the Parties, be assessed and determined by the Court, if necessary, in a separate phase of the proceedings.

As a basis for the Court's jurisdiction, Liechtenstein invoked article 1 of the European Convention for the Peaceful Settlement of Disputes, signed at Strasbourg, France, on 29 April 1957.

By an Order of 28 June 2001, the Court, taking account of the agreement of the Parties, fixed 28 March 2002 and 27 December 2002, respectively, as the time limits for the filing of a Memorial by Liechtenstein and of a Counter-Memorial by Germany.

Territorial and maritime dispute (Nicaragua v. Colombia)

On 6 December 2001, Nicaragua instituted proceedings against Colombia in respect of a dispute concerning "a group of related legal issues subsisting" between the two States "concerning title to territory and maritime delimitation".

In its Application, Nicaragua claimed that "the islands and keys of San Andres and Providencia pertain to those groups of islands and keys that in 1821 [date of independence from Spain] became part of the newly formed Federation of Central American States and, after the dissolution of the Federation in 1838, . . . came to be part of the sovereign territory of Nicaragua". It considered in this connection that the Barcenas-Esguerra Treaty of 24 March 1928 "lacks legal validity and consequently cannot provide a basis of Colombian title with respect to the Archipelago of San Andres". Nicaragua added that, in any case, the treaty was "not . . . a treaty of delimitation".

Nicaragua recalled that as early as 1948 its Constitution affirmed that the national territory included the continental platforms on both the Atlantic and Pacific Oceans and, by decrees of 1958, it had made clear that the resources of the continental shelf belonged to it. Moreover, in 1965 it declared a national fishing zone of 200 nautical miles. Nicaragua went on to state that, by claiming sovereignty over the islands of Providencia and San Andres and keys, which, according to it, had a total "land area of 44 square kilometers and an overall coastal length that is under 20 kilometers, Colombia claims dominion over more than 50,000 square kilometers of maritime space that appertain to Nicaragua", representing "more than half" the maritime spaces of Nicaragua in the Caribbean Sea. It contended that the current situation was "seriously imperiling the livelihood of the Nicaraguan people, particularly those of the Caribbean coast that traditionally have had a great dependence on natural resources of the sea", and claimed that the Colombian navy had been intercepting and capturing a number of fishing vessels "in areas as close as 70 miles off the Nicaraguan coast", east of the 82 meridian. Nicaragua maintained that diplomatic negotiations had failed.

Nicaragua requested the Court to adjudge and declare, first, that Nicaragua had sovereignty over the islands of Providencia, San Andres and Santa Catalina and all the appurtenant islands and keys, and also over the Roncador, Serrana, Serranilla and Quitasueño keys (insofar as they were capable of appropriation); and, second, in the light of the determinations concerning title requested above, the Court was asked further to determine the course of the single maritime boundary between the areas of continental shelf and exclusive economic zone appertaining to Nicaragua and Colombia, in accordance with equitable principles and relevant circumstances recognized by general international law as applicable to such a delimitation of a single maritime boundary.

Nicaragua reserved the right to claim compensation for elements of unjust enrichment consequent upon Colombian possession of the islands of San Andres and Providencia, as well as the keys and maritime spaces up to the 82 meridian, in the absence of lawful title. It also reserved the right to claim compensation for interference with fishing vessels of Nicaraguan nationality or vessels licensed by Nicaragua.

As a basis for the Court's jurisdiction, Nicaragua invoked article XXXI of the American Treaty on Pacific Settlement (officially known as the "Pact of Bogotá"), signed on 30 April 1948, to which both Colombia and Nicaragua were parties. Nicaragua also referred to the declarations under Article 36 of the Statute of the Court, by which Nicaragua and Colombia accepted the compulsory jurisdiction of the Court, in 1929 and 1937, respectively.

Other questions

Composition of the Court

On 21 June [S/2001/615], the Secretary-General informed the Security Council that Judge Mohammed Bedjaoui (Algeria), a member and former President of the Court, whose term was due to expire on 5 February 2006, intended to resign effective 30 September 2001. The Secretary-General drew the Council's attention to Article 14 of the Statute of the Court regarding fixing a date for the election to fill the vacancy. He noted that the date of the election was to be fixed by the Council and suggested that it might wish to consider the question at an early meeting.

Also in June [A/56/142], the Secretary-General informed the General Assembly of the vacancy.

SECURITY COUNCIL ACTION

On 5 July [meeting 4345], the Security Council adopted **resolution 1361(2001)** without vote. The draft [S/2001/663] was prepared during consultations among Council members.

The Security Council,

Noting with regret the resignation of Judge Mohammed Bedjaoui, taking effect on 30 September 2001,

Noting further that a vacancy in the International Court of Justice for the remainder of the term of office of Judge Mohammed Bedjaoui will thus occur and must be filled in accordance with the terms of the Statute of the Court,

Noting that, in accordance with Article 14 of the Statute, the date of the election to fill the vacancy shall be fixed by the Security Council,

Decides that the election to fill the vacancy shall take place on 12 October 2001 at a meeting of the Security Council and at a meeting of the General Assembly at its fifty-sixth session.

By notes of 17 September [A/56/373-S/2001/882], the Secretary-General submitted a list of three candidates nominated by national groups of States parties to the ICJ Statute to fill the vacancy left by Judge Bedjaoui and their curricula vitae [A/56/374-S/2001/883]. A 19 September memorandum by the Secretary-General [A/56/372-S/2001/881] provided information on the vacancy left by Judge Bedjaoui and ICJ's composition, and described the procedure in the General Assembly and the Security Council for the election of a new Member of the Court. On 6 October [A/56/373/Add.1-S/2001/882/Add.1], one of the candidates withdrew his candidature, and on 9 October [A/56/374/Corr.2-S/2001/883/Corr.2], the Secretary-General issued a corrigendum to the curricula vitae.

On 12 October, the Security Council [S/PV.4389] and the General Assembly [A/56/PV.24] elected, by secret ballot, Nabil Elaraby (Egypt) as a Member of the Court for the remainder of the term of office of Judge Bedjaoui (see p. 1463).

Rules of Court

Practice Directions

As from October 2001, the Court adopted certain Practice Directions for use by the States appearing before it. The Practice Directions, the result of an ongoing review of the Court's working methods to ensure that cases were adjudicated as expeditiously as possible, involved no alteration to the Rules of Court, but were additional thereto.

Amendments

Amendments to Article 79 of the Rules of Court, relating to preliminary objections, and Article 80 of the Rules, relating to counter-claims, entered into force on 1 February 2001. The amendments aimed to shorten the duration of proceedings. The Rules, which were adopted on 14 April 1978 [YUN 1978, p. 944], would continue to apply to all cases submitted to the Court prior to 1 February 2001, and to all phases of those cases.

Trust Fund to Assist States in the Settlement of Disputes

In October [A/56/456], the Secretary-General updated the activities and status of the Trust Fund to Assist States in the Settlement of Disputes through ICJ since the submission of his previous report in 1992 [YUN 1992, p. 986]. The Fund, established in 1989 [YUN 1989, p. 818], provided financial assistance to States for expenses incurred in connection with a dispute submitted to ICJ by way of a Special Agreement or the execution of a judgment resulting from such an Agreement.

In 1997, an award was made to two developing countries that had applied for assistance in 1996 and 1997 in connection with their submission to the Court of a boundary dispute with a neighbouring State. In both cases, the Secretary-General only approved limited financial assistance in order to strike a balance between encouraging recourse to the Court and the need to accommodate future applications.

During the period under review (1992-2001), 18 States had contributed to the Fund. As at 30 June, the total balance of the Fund, excluding awards already paid, amounted to $1,602,734.

JIU report

On 13 March [A/55/834], the Secretary-General transmitted the report of the Joint Inspection Unit (JIU) on its review of management and administration in the ICJ Registry. JIU concluded that, in addition to a shortage of staff and funds, the Court was experiencing institutional and administrative problems in the Registry, which needed attention. The Registry's personnel practices and procedures also needed to be examined.

JIU made a series of recommendations to the Court, among them, including in its 2002-2003 budget three posts for research assistants; reducing the Registrar's term of office to three years, with renewal subject to performance approved by the Court; amending its Rules regarding the appointment and term of office of the Deputy Registrar; increasing staff resources for translation; establishing more consistent, fair and transparent personnel management by aligning its practices and procedures with the staff rules and regulations of the UN Secretariat; and increasing cooperation and coordination with the International Tribunal for the Former Yugoslavia (see p. 1198) and the Organization for the Prohibition of Chemical Weapons (see p. 495).

ICJ's comments on the JIU report were annexed to a 14 March note of the Secretary-General [A/55/834/Add.1]. The Court accepted the greater part of JIU's analysis concerning the increase in the Court's workload and the inadequacy of the resources available to it, and stated that it would make proposals on those matters to the General Assembly in connection with the 2002-2003 budget. The Court did not see fit to adopt the recommendations related to shortening the terms of office of the Registrar and the Deputy Registrar. With regard to administrative practices, the Court stated that it was unable to accept all of the report's recommendations, but it was involved in a determined, ongoing effort to improve, rationalize and update the practices and procedures in question.

Also annexed to the note were the Secretary-General's comments on issues related to budgetary matters, including the establishment of posts to provide research assistance for the judges, increased staff resources for translation and the establishment of a Senior Administrative/Personnel Officer.

The comments and observations of the Advisory Committee on Administrative and Budgetary Questions on the report were contained in its August report on the 2002-2003 programme budget [A/56/7].

GENERAL ASSEMBLY ACTION

On 14 June [meeting 103], the General Assembly, on the recommendation of the Fifth (Administrative and Budgetary) Committee [A/56/982], adopted **resolution 55/257** without vote [agenda items 116 & 117].

Report of the Joint Inspection Unit on the review of management and administration in the Registry of the International Court of Justice

The General Assembly,

Recalling section V of its resolution 55/238 of 23 December 2000,

Having considered the report of the Joint Inspection Unit entitled "Review of management and administration in the Registry of the International Court of Justice" and the comments of the International Court of Justice and those of the Secretary-General thereon,

1. *Notes* that the problems in the management of the Registry of the International Court of Justice referred to in the report of the Joint Inspection Unit have been, to a large extent, resolved;

2. *Takes note* of recommendations 1 and 7 of the Unit concerning, respectively, research assistants and the post of a senior Administrative/Personnel Officer, and requests the Advisory Committee on Administrative and Budgetary Questions to consider the matter and make such recommendations as it deems appropriate in the context of its first report on the proposed programme budget for the biennium 2002-2003, for decision by the General Assembly at its fifty-sixth session;

3. *Emphasizes* the importance of consistent, fair and transparent management of personnel and the need for the introduction of an effective performance appraisal system for the staff of the Court, referred to in paragraph 85 of the report of the Unit;

4. *Invites* the Court to review the need to amend its own staff rules to enable the introduction and implementation of the performance appraisal system;

5. *Decides* to keep the matter under review at its fifty-sixth session.

Chapter II

International tribunals

In 2001, the International Tribunal for the Prosecution of Persons Responsible for Serious Violations of International Humanitarian Law Committed in the Territory of the Former Yugoslavia since 1991 (ICTY) increased its judicial activity and, for the first time, entered a conviction for genocide. The Tribunal implemented reforms to fulfil its mandate more expeditiously and, in that regard, the General Assembly, in June, elected 27 ad litem judges, who would serve with the permanent judges on a case-by-case basis. Permanent judges were elected for a four-year term commencing on 17 November.

The International Criminal Tribunal for the Prosecution of Persons Responsible for Genocide and Other Serious Violations of International Humanitarian Law Committed in the Territory of Rwanda and Rwandan Citizens Responsible for Genocide and Other Such Violations Committed in the Territory of Neighbouring States between 1 January and 31 December 1994 (ICTR) was actively engaged in conducting trials. It also adopted measures either to remedy perceived problems or to increase its efficiency. The Trial Chambers delivered one judgement and the Appeals Chamber gave final judgement in three cases.

International Tribunal for the Former Yugoslavia

In an effort to increase trial capacity to expedite the Tribunal's cases, the General Assembly, pursuant to Security Council resolution 1329 (2000) [YUN 2000, p. 1228], elected 27 ad litem judges in June (see p. 1203). The ad litem judges would serve with the permanent judges on a case-by-case basis; several of them were assigned to specific cases during the year. Further reforms were initiated to improve the organization, management methods and proceedings of the Appeals Chamber.

In November [meeting 4429], the ICTY President and the Chief Prosecutor proposed to the Security Council that the Tribunal should focus on prosecuting crimes that constituted the most se-

rious breaches of international public law and order, and, under certain conditions, refer cases of lesser importance to the courts of the States created out of the former Yugoslavia.

In other action, the Tribunal authorized Senior Legal Officers to manage certain aspects of the pre-trial phase to enable judges to devote more time to the merits of the cases. Several rules of procedure and evidence were amended to allow judges to set the number of witnesses the parties called to testify, determine the length of the cases and take measures required to preclude interlocutory appeals from interrupting the trials. In the same vein, a Coordination Council and a Management Committee ensured that the three organs of ICTY—the Chambers, the Office of the Prosecutor and the Registry—coordinated more closely in setting judicial priorities.

In 2001, the activities of ICTY, established by Security Council resolution 827(1993) [YUN 1993, p. 440], were covered in two reports to the Council and the General Assembly, for the periods 1 August 2000 to 31 July 2001 [A/56/352-S/2001/865] and 1 August 2001 to 31 July 2002 [A/57/379-S/2002/985]. On 26 November, the Assembly took note of the 2000/01 report (**decision 56/408**). On 24 December, it decided that the item on the report would remain for consideration at its resumed fifty-sixth (2002) session (**decision 56/464**).

The Chambers

The judicial activity of the three Trial Chambers and the Appeals Chamber of the Tribunal included trial and appeals proceedings, proceedings pertaining to the primacy of the Tribunal and cases of contempt of the Tribunal.

In accordance with Security Council resolution 1329(2000) [YUN 2000, p. 1228], two ICTR judges were assigned to the Appeals Chamber.

New trials and cases

Biljana Plavsic surrendered voluntarily to the Tribunal in January. On 23 February, the Trial Chamber joined her case with that of Momcilo Krajisnik, who pleaded not guilty in 2000 [YUN 2000, p. 1221]; on 9 March, the prosecution filed a consolidated indictment against the two co-accused. They were charged with genocide, crimes against humanity, violations of the laws and customs of war and grave breaches of the Geneva Conventions for the protection of war victims of 12 August 1949 (Geneva Conventions). Both were alleged to have been high-ranking members of the Serbian Democratic Party and, along with Radovan Karadzic— indicted in 1995 [YUN 1995, p. 1314] and not yet arrested—and others, were accused of committing those crimes in order to secure control of areas of Bosnia and Herzegovina that had been proclaimed as belonging to the Serb part of Bosnia and Herzegovina. Ms. Plavsic filed a motion for provisional release, which was withdrawn in March following a change of counsel. On 5 September, the Trial Chamber ordered her provisional release from detention under strict conditions.

Blagoje Simic, who surrendered voluntarily to the Tribunal on 12 March, entered a plea of not guilty on 15 March. He was the last of the five accused in the case of Simic and Others [YUN 2000, p. 1223] to come before the Tribunal. The trial began on 10 September.

Dr. Milomir Stakic, whose initial indictment in 1997 had been kept confidential until it was unsealed on 23 March, was transferred to the Tribunal's Detention Unit on the same day. At his initial appearance on 28 March, he pleaded not guilty to the charge of genocide committed in Bosnia and Herzegovina, the only count in the initial indictment. The Prosecutor filed an amended indictment twice during the year. On 5 October, Dr. Stakic pleaded not guilty to 14 counts in the second amended indictment. Following objections by the defence to the form of that indictment, it was reorganized and filed on 27 November; it included the charges of genocide or complicity in genocide, crimes against humanity (extermination, murder, persecution, torture, inhumane acts and deportation) and violations of the laws or customs of war (murder, torture, cruel treatment, plunder, wanton destruction of cities, towns or villages, or devastation not justified by military necessity, and destruction or wilful damage done to institutions dedicated to religion). The trial was scheduled for 2002.

On 6 September, the prosecution filed a motion seeking leave to join the cases of Dragan Obrenovic, Vidoje Blagojevic and Dragan Jokic for their alleged involvement in the events in and around Srebrenica in 1995 [YUN 1995, p. 529]. Mr. Obrenovic, arrested by the multinational Stabilization Force (SFOR) and transferred to the Detention Unit on 15 April, pleaded not guilty at his initial appearance on 18 April to charges of complicity in genocide, extermination, murder and persecution. Mr. Blagojevic, who was arrested by SFOR and transferred to the Detention Unit on 10

August, was charged with complicity in genocide, extermination, murder, persecution and other inhumane acts. Mr. Jokic, who surrendered to the jurisdiction of the Tribunal on 15 August, was charged with extermination, murder and persecution.

General Rahim Ademi voluntarily surrendered to the Tribunal on 25 July. At his initial appearance on 26 July, he pleaded not guilty to charges of persecutions, murder, plunder and wanton destruction.

On 26 July, an 8 June indictment against Ante Gotovina, a former high-ranking Croatian military official, was unsealed. He was charged with crimes against humanity and violations of the laws or customs of war, allegedly committed during and after a Croatian offensive in the Krajina region of Croatia in 1995 [YUN 1995, p. 580].

General Enver Hadzihasanovic, General Mehmed Alagic and Colonel Amir Kubura came into the custody of the Tribunal on 4 August and pleaded not guilty at their initial appearance on 9 August. On the basis of their command responsibility, they were charged with violations of the laws or customs of war and grave breaches of the Geneva Conventions for alleged crimes committed in central Bosnia between January 1993 and January 1994. The crimes alleged included executions and massacres following attacks on towns and villages; crimes allegedly committed in detention facilities involving killings, beatings, physical and psychological abuse, the use of detainees to dig trenches in combat conditions, and the use of detainees as hostages and human shields; and systematic plunder and destruction. On 15 and 16 November, the defendants applied for provisional release, which was ordered on 13 December, under strict terms and conditions. The Chamber considered that the accused had voluntarily surrendered to the Tribunal and that satisfactory guarantees had been provided by Bosnia and Herzegovina and by the accused to uphold the conditions of release. Bosnia and Herzegovina reported regularly on the compliance of the accused with the conditions of release.

On 25 September, following his voluntary surrender, Sefer Halilovic was transferred to the Detention Unit. At his initial appearance on 27 September, he pleaded not guilty to one charge of murder, a violation of the laws or customs of war. The indictment addressed the 1993 killing by Bosnian Muslim forces of 33 Bosnian Croat civilians in Grabovica and of 29 Bosnian Croat civilians and one Croatian prisoner of war in Uzdol. On 28 November, the accused filed a request for provisional release, to which the prosecution agreed on 6 December, provided that the accused supplied certain guarantees and undertakings. The Trial Chamber granted the request on 13 December.

On 2 October, the names of four persons (Miodrag Jokic, Vladimir Kovacevic, Pavle Strugar, Milan Zec) charged with crimes in connection with operations to secure control of areas of Croatia that were intended for inclusion in a so-called Dubrovnik Republic were made public. General Strugar surrendered voluntarily on 21 October and Admiral Jokic did so on 12 November; both filed a motion for provisional release, which General Strugar was granted on 30 November.

The initial indictment of Pasko Ljubicic on 27 September 2000 was kept confidential until it was unsealed on 30 October 2001. On 30 November, he pleaded not guilty to the charges against him relating to crimes against humanity, including persecution, and violations of the laws or customs of war in connection with events that occurred in the Lasva Valley in central Bosnia between June 1992 and July 1993.

The case against Nenad and Predrag Banovic, who were transferred to the Tribunal's Detention Unit on 9 November following their arrest by Belgrade authorities, arose from the same indictment (relating to the Keraterm camp in the municipality of Prijedor) as the case of Dusko Sikirica, Damir Dosen and Dragan Kolundzija [YUN 1999, p. 1215] (see p. 1201). The accused came into the Tribunal's custody after the close of those proceedings. On 16 November, Nenad Banovic pleaded not guilty to the 10 counts against him in the second amended indictment of 3 January, and Predrag Banovic pleaded not guilty to all 25 counts. The indictment charged each of them with crimes against humanity and with violations of the laws or customs of war.

During the year, a number of other indictments became public. In July, at the request of the Prosecutor, the Chambers ordered the unsealing of an indictment and the arrest warrant of Stojan Zupljanin, a co-accused of Radoslav Brdanin and Momir Talic (see p. 1201). An indictment against Savo Todovic and Mitar Rasevic was made public in November; the accused, who remained at large, were indicted with Milorad Krnoljelac (see p. 1201). An indictment against Vinko Pandurevic was made public in December. Mr. Pandurevic, who remained at large, was accused jointly with General Radislav Krstic (see p. 1201).

Two additional indictments involving the accused Slobodan Milosevic (see p. 1201) were confirmed on 8 October and 22 November. The first concerned his alleged responsibility for crimes committed in Croatia from August 1991 to June 1992; and the second related to crimes allegedly committed in Bosnia and Herzegovina, including genocide, from March 1992 to December 1995.

Ongoing trials

On 22 February, the Trial Chamber pronounced its judgement against the accused in the case of Kunarac and Others (Dragoljub Kunarac, Radomir Kovac, Zoran Vukovic) [YUN 1999, p. 1215]. Mr. Kunarac, who was found guilty on five counts of crimes against humanity (torture, rape and enslavement) and six counts of violations of the laws or customs of war (torture and rape), was sentenced to 28 years' imprisonment. Mr. Kovac, found guilty on two counts of crimes against humanity (rape and enslavement) and two counts of violations of the laws or customs of war (rape and outrages upon personal dignity), was sentenced to 20 years' imprisonment. Mr. Vukovic, who was found guilty on two counts of crimes against humanity (torture and rape) and two counts of violations of the laws or customs of war (torture and rape), was sentenced to 12 years' imprisonment. In March, the three defendants filed notices of appeal against their conviction and sentence. The filing of briefs in the appeal was completed in September and oral hearings took place in December.

On 26 February, the Trial Chamber issued its judgement in the case of Dario Kordic and Mario Cerkez, whose case began in 2000 [YUN 2000, p. 1223]. Mr. Kordic was found guilty by virtue of his individual responsibility for four counts of crimes against humanity (persecutions on political, racial or religious grounds, murder, inhumane acts and imprisonment), five counts of violations of the laws or customs of war (unlawful attack on civilians and on civilian objects, wanton destruction, plunder, and destruction or wilful damage to institutions dedicated to religion or education) and three counts of grave breaches of the Geneva Conventions (wilful killing, inhumane treatment and unlawful confinement of civilians). Mr. Cerkez was found guilty by virtue of his individual responsibility for four counts of crimes against humanity (persecutions on political, racial or religious grounds, murder, inhumane acts and imprisonment), five counts of violations of the laws or customs of war (unlawful attacks on civilians and on civilian objects, wanton destruction, plunder, and destruction or wilful damage to institutions dedicated to religion or education), and six counts of grave breaches of the Geneva Conventions (wilful killing, inhuman treatment, unlawful confinement of civilians, cruel treatment, and taking civilians as hostages). Furthermore, the Trial Chamber found Mr. Cerkez liable under article 7 (3) of the ICTY statute on the basis that, as a commander who exercised de jure and de facto control over his brigade, he failed to take the necessary measures to prevent a number of attacks and to punish those responsible for the attacks. Messrs. Kordic and Cerkez were sentenced to 25 and 15 years' imprisonment, respectively. Notices of appeal against the judgement and sentence were filed both by the defendants and by the prosecution. The filing of briefs in the appeal was completed on 20 October. However, the appellants had filed requests for access to additional evidence.

On 31 July, the Trial Chamber pronounced a sentence of 10 years' imprisonment against Stevan Todorovic, who had pleaded guilty to the count of persecution in the indictment in the case of Simic and Others in 2000 [YUN 2000, p. 1224]. During the course of events, the proceedings of Mr. Todorovic were separated from those against the other accused.

On 2 August, the Trial Chamber, for the first time in the Tribunal's history, entered a conviction for genocide. Radislav Krstic, whose trial began in 2000 [YUN 2000, p. 1222], was sentenced to 46 years' imprisonment in connection with events surrounding the attack on, and the fall of, Srebrenica [YUN 1995, p. 529]. General Krstic filed a notice of appeal on 14 August and the prosecution filed its notice of appeal on 16 August.

Simultaneously with the Krstic case, the Trial Chamber conducted the trial of the case of Kvocka and Others, which began in 2000 [YUN 2000, p. 1222]. In a 2 November judgement, Miroslav Kvocka was sentenced to a term of seven years' imprisonment, Dragoljub Prcac to five years and Milojica Kos to six years. Mlado Radic, who alone had been charged with rape, was sentenced to 20 years and Zoran Zigic to 25 years. Notices of appeal were filed by all of the convicted.

On 13 November, the Trial Chamber sentenced Dusko Sikirica to 15 years' imprisonment, Dragan Kolundzija to three years and Damir Dosen to five years; the Tribunal decided to try the three accused jointly in 2000 [YUN 2000, p. 1223]. As the sentences fell within the ranges agreed by the parties, no appeals were made.

Slobodan Milosevic, the former President of the Federal Republic of Yugoslavia (FRY), charged with crimes against humanity with respect to criminal conduct in Kosovo [YUN 1999, p. 1214], was transferred from FRY into the Tribunal's custody on 29 June and appeared before the Trial Chamber for the first time on 3 July. He was subsequently also indicted for crimes committed in Croatia and Bosnia and Herzegovina; his initial appearances on those indictments took place on 29 October and 11 December, respectively. Mr. Milosevic was charged alternatively as a commander and participant in a joint criminal enterprise for the commission of offences that included crimes against humanity, violations of the laws or customs of war and genocide. Following his refusal to plead to the charges, the Trial Chamber entered pleas of not guilty in respect of all charges against him. In December, the Trial Chamber denied a prosecution application to join the three indictments (Kosovo, Croatia, and Bosnia and Herzegovina) and to hear the cases in one trial, and ordered that the trial on the Kosovo indictment would proceed separately.

In other action, the case was opened against General Stanislav Galic, who had pleaded not guilty to charges against him in 1999 [YUN 1999, p. 1215] and had received new defence counsel in 2000 [YUN 2000, p. 1223]; the pre-trial phase continued in the case of Radoslav Brdanin and Momir Talic, both of whom had been charged with genocide and crimes against humanity in 1999 [YUN 1999, p. 1215] and had pleaded not guilty in 2000 [YUN 2000, p. 1222]; hearings were completed in the case of Milorad Krnojelac, who had pleaded not guilty to charges against him in 1999 [YUN 1999, p. 1216] and whose trial began in 2000 [YUN 2000, p. 1223]; the trial against Vinko Martinovic and Mladen Naletilic, who had pleaded not guilty in 1999 [YUN 1999, p. 1216] and 2000 [YUN 2000, p. 1223], began on 10 September, as did the trial of Mitar Vasiljevic, who pleaded not guilty to charges against him in 2000 [ibid., p. 1221]. Regarding the case of Dragan Nikolic, who was arrested by SFOR in 2000 and pleaded guilty to all charges against him [ibid.], agreement was reached to narrow the issues in dispute surrounding the defence counsel allegation of the illegality of his arrest.

During the year, the Appeals Chamber rendered a number of judgements on appeals against final trial judgements. In February, in the Celebici case, the Appeals Chamber remitted to a Trial Chamber the issue of what adjustment, if any, should be made to the original sentences imposed on Zdravko Mucic, Esad Landzo and Hazim Delic [YUN 1998, p. 1193]. The process had started in 2000 [YUN 2000, p. 1223]. Following hearings, the Trial Chamber rendered its sentencing judgement on 9 October. Mr. Mucic was sentenced to a single sentence of nine years' imprisonment, revised from three terms of seven years to run concurrently; Mr. Delic to 18 years' imprisonment, revised from 20 years; and Mr. Landzo's sentence of 15 years' imprisonment was left unchanged. The convicted persons filed notices of appeal in October. On 5 July, in the case against Goran Jelisic [YUN 2000, p. 1223], convicted and sen-

tenced in 1999 [YUN 1999, p. 1216], the Appeals
Chamber found that cumulative convictions
under articles 3 and 5 of the statute were permissible and his sentence of 40 years' imprisonment
was therefore upheld. In the case of Kupreskic
and Others [YUN 1998, p. 1194], the Appeals Chamber rendered its judgement on an appeal filed in
2000 [YUN 2000, p. 1222]. On 23 October, the convictions of Zoran and Mirjan Kupreskic on count 1
for persecution were reversed. The Chamber
found that the Trial Chamber had erred in relying on the identification evidence given by a single witness, an error that had caused a miscarriage of justice. The two were acquitted on all
counts and released. Similarly, with the addition
of new evidence, the circumstantial evidence on
which the conviction of Vlatko Kupreskic was
based could not be accepted; he was acquitted
and released. The sentences of Drago Josipovic
and Vladimir Santic were reduced from 15 to 12
years' imprisonment and from 25 to 18 years,
respectively.

Election of judges

Permanent judges

In January [S/2001/61] and February [A/55/773 &
Add.1], the Secretary-General forwarded to the
Security Council and the General Assembly,
respectively, the curricula vitae of candidates
nominated to replace 14 permanent judges of the
Tribunal whose terms would expire on 16 November. By a February memorandum [A/55/769],
the Secretary-General transmitted to the Assembly the list of the candidates and an explanation
of the procedure for electing them.

SECURITY COUNCIL ACTION

On 8 February [meeting 4274], the Security
Council unanimously adopted **resolution 1340
(2001)**. The draft [S/2001/108] was prepared in
consultations among Council members.

The Security Council,

Recalling its resolutions 808(1993) of 22 February
1993, 827(1993) of 25 May 1993, 1166(1998) of 13 May
1998 and 1329(2000) of 30 November 2000,

Having decided to consider the nominations for permanent judges of the International Tribunal for the
Prosecution of Persons Responsible for Serious Violations of International Humanitarian Law Committed
in the Territory of the Former Yugoslavia since 1991 received by the Secretary-General by 31 January 2001,

Forwards the following nominations to the General
Assembly in accordance with paragraph 1 *(d)* of article
13 bis of the statute of the International Tribunal:

    Mr. Carmel A. Agius (Malta)
    Mr. Richard Allen Banda (Malawi)
    Mr. Mohamed Amin El Abbassi Elmahdi (Egypt)
    Mr. Mohamed El Habib Fassi Fihri (Morocco)

    Mr. David Hunt (Australia)
    Mr. Claude Jorda (France)
    Mr. O-gon Kwon (Republic of Korea)
    Mr. Liu Daqun (China)
    Mr. Abderraouf Mahbouli (Tunisia)
    Mr. Richard George May (United Kingdom of Great
      Britain and Northern Ireland)
    Mr. Theodor Meron (United States of America)
    Mrs. Florence Ndepele Mwachande Mumba (Zambia)
    Mr. Rafael Nieto Navia (Colombia)
    Mr. Leopold Ntahompagaze (Burundi)
    Mr. Alphonsus Martinus Maria Orie (Netherlands)
    Mr. Fausto Pocar (Italy)
    Mr. Jonah Rahetlah (Madagascar)
    Mr. Patrick Lipton Robinson (Jamaica)
    Mr. Almiro Simões Rodrigues (Portugal)
    Ms. Miriam Defensor Santiago (Philippines)
    Mr. Wolfgang Schomburg (Germany)
    Mr. Mohamed Shahabuddeen (Guyana)
    Mr. Demetrakis Stylianides (Cyprus)
    Mr. Krister Thelin (Sweden)
    Mr. Volodymyr Vassylenko (Ukraine)
    Mr. Karam Chand Vohrah (Malaysia)

On the same day [A/55/771], the Council transmitted the text of its resolution to the General Assembly.

GENERAL ASSEMBLY ACTION

On 14 March [meeting 95], the General Assembly
adopted **decision 55/320 A** without vote [agenda
item 166].

By that decision, the Assembly, in accordance
with article 13 bis of the ICTY statute, elected the
following 14 permanent judges for a four-year
term of office beginning 17 November 2001:

    Mr. Carmel Agius (Malta)
    Mr. Mohamed Amin El Abbassi Elmahdi (Egypt)
    Mr. David Hunt (Australia)
    Mr. Claude Jorda (France)
    Mr. O-gon Kwon (Republic of Korea)
    Mr. Liu Daqun (China)
    Mr. Richard George May (United Kingdom of
      Great Britain and Northern Ireland)
    Mr. Theodor Meron (United States of America)
    Mrs. Florence Ndepele Mwachande Mumba
      (Zambia)
    Mr. Alphonsus Martinus Maria Orie (Netherlands)
    Mr. Fausto Pocar (Italy)
    Mr. Patrick Lipton Robinson (Jamaica)
    Mr. Wolfgang Schomburg (Germany)
    Mr. Mohamed Shahabuddeen (Guyana).

In November, the Appeals Chamber welcomed
two additional judges from ICTR, in accordance
with Security Council resolution 1329(2000)
[YUN 2000, p. 1228].

Ad litem judges

In April and May, the Secretary-General forwarded to the Security Council [S/2001/391] and the General Assembly [A/55/919 & Add.1,2] the curricula vitae of candidates nominated to serve as ad litem judges of the Tribunal, in accordance with Council resolution 1329(2000) [YUN 2000, p. 1228]. By an April memorandum [A/55/918], the Secretary-General transmitted to the Assembly a list of candidates and an explanation of the procedure for electing them.

SECURITY COUNCIL ACTION

On 27 April [meeting 4316], the Security Council unanimously adopted **resolution 1350(2001)**. The draft [S/2001/414] was prepared in consultations among Council members.

The Security Council,

Recalling its resolutions 808(1993) of 22 February 1993, 827(1993) of 25 May 1993, 1166(1998) of 13 May 1998 and 1329(2000) of 30 November 2000,

Having decided to consider the nominations for ad litem judges of the International Tribunal for the Prosecution of Persons Responsible for Serious Violations of International Humanitarian Law Committed in the Territory of the Former Yugoslavia since 1991 received by the Secretary-General,

Forwards the following nominations to the General Assembly in accordance with paragraph 1 (*d*) of article 13 ter of the statute of the International Tribunal:

Mr. Aydin Sefa Akay (Turkey)
Ms. Carmen María Argibay (Argentina)
Ms. Lucy Asuagbor (Cameroon)
Mr. Jeremy Badgery-Parker (Australia)
Mr. Chifumu Kingdom Banda (Zambia)
Mr. Roberto Bellelli (Italy)
Mr. Pierre G. Boutet (Canada)
Mr. Hans Henrik Brydensholt (Denmark)
Mr. Guibril Camara (Senegal)
Mr. Joaquin Martin Canivell (Spain)
Mr. Romeo T. Capulong (Philippines)
Mr. Oscar Ceville (Panama)
Mr. Isaac Chibulu Tantameni Chali (Zambia)
Mr. Arthur Chaskalson (South Africa)
Ms. Maureen Harding Clark (Ireland)
Ms. Fatoumata Diarra (Mali)
Mr. Cenk Alp Durak (Turkey)
Mr. Moise Ebongue (Cameroon)
Mr. Mathew Epuli (Cameroon)
Mr. Albin Eser (Germany)
Mr. Mohamed Al Habib Fassi Fihri (Morocco)
Mr. John Foster Gallop (Australia)
Mr. Joseph Nassif Ghamroun (Lebanon)
Mr. Michael Grotz (Germany)
Mr. Adbullah Mahamane Haidara (Mali)
Mr. Claude Hanoteau (France)
Mr. Hassan Bubacarr Jallow (Gambia)
Ms. Ivana Janu (Czech Republic)
Mr. Aykut Kiliç (Turkey)
Ms. Flavia Lattanzi (Italy)
Mr. Per-Johan Lindholm (Finland)
Mr. Augustin P. Lobejón (Spain)
Mr. Diadié Issa Maiga (Mali)
Ms. Irene Chirwa Mambilima (Zambia)
Mr. Dick F. Marty (Switzerland)
Ms. Jane Hamilton Mathews (Australia)
Ms. Suzanne Mengue Zomo (Cameroon)
Mr. Ghulam Mujaddid Mirza (Pakistan)
Mr. Ahmad Aref Moallem (Lebanon)
Mr. Mphanza Patrick Mvunga (Zambia)
Mr. Rafael Nieto-Navia (Colombia)
Mr. Léopold Ntahompagaze (Burundi)
Mr. André Ntahomvukiye (Burundi)
Mr. Cesar Pereira Burgos (Panama)
Mr. Mauro Politi (Italy)
Ms. Vonimbolana Rasoazanany (Madagascar)
Mr. Ralph Riachy (Lebanon)
Mr. Ingo Risch (Germany)
Mr. Robert Roth (Switzerland)
Mr. Zacharie Rwamaza (Burundi)
Mr. Sourahata Babouccar Semega-Janneh (Gambia)
Mr. Tom Farquhar Shepherdson (Australia)
Mr. Amarjeet Singh (Singapore)
Ms. Ayla Songor (Turkey)
Mr. Albertus Henricus Joannes Swart (Netherlands)
Mr. Gyorgy Szénási (Hungary)
Mr. Ahmad Takkieddine (Lebanon)
Ms. Chikako Taya (Japan)
Mr. Krister Thelin (Sweden)
Mr. Stefan Trechsel (Switzerland)
Ms. Christine Van Den Wyngaert (Belgium)
Mr. Volodymyr Vassylenko (Ukraine)
Mr. Lal Chand Vohrah (Malaysia)
Ms. Sharon A. Williams (Canada)

On the same date [A/55/917], the Council transmitted the text of its resolution to the General Assembly.

Memorandum of Secretary-General. On 11 June [A/55/918/Add.1], the Secretary-General informed the Assembly that Messrs. Ghamroun, Grotz, Haidara, Maiga, Mirza, Moallem, Risch and Takkieddine had withdrawn their candidatures.

GENERAL ASSEMBLY ACTION

On 12 June [meeting 102], the General Assembly adopted **decision 55/320 B** without vote [agenda item 166].

By that decision, the Assembly, in accordance with article 13 ter of the ICTY statute, elected the following 27 ad litem judges for a four-year term of office beginning on 12 June 2001:

Ms. Carmen María Argibay (Argentina)
Mr. Hans Henrik Brydensholt (Denmark)
Mr. Guibril Camara (Senegal)
Mr. Joaquin Martin Canivell (Spain)
Mr. Romeo Capulong (Philippines)
Mr. Arthur Chaskalson (South Africa)
Ms. Maureen Harding Clark (Ireland)
Ms. Fatoumata Diarra (Mali)
Mr. Albin Eser (Germany)
Mr. Mohamed Al Habib Fassi Fihri (Morocco)
Mr. Claude Hanoteau (France)
Mr. Hassan Bubacarr Jallow (Gambia)

Ms. Ivana Janu (Czech Republic)
Mr. Per-Johan Lindholm (Finland)
Mr. Rafael Nieto-Navia (Colombia)
Mr. Mauro Politi (Italy)
Ms. Vonimbolana Rasoazanany (Madagascar)
Mr. Ralph Riachy (Lebanon)
Mr. Amarjeet Singh (Singapore)
Mr. Albertus Henricus Joannes Swart (Netherlands)
Mr. Gyorgy Szénási (Hungary)
Ms. Chikako Taya (Japan)
Mr. Krister Thelin (Sweden)
Ms. Christine Van Den Wyngaert (Belgium)
Mr. Volodymyr Vassylenko (Ukraine)
Mr. Lal Chand Vohrah (Malaysia)
Ms. Sharon Williams (Canada).

Composition of the Chambers

By an 11 January letter [S/2001/47], the Secretary-General informed the Security Council that Judge Mohamed Bennouna (Morocco) had resigned effective 28 February. He considered that the appointment of Mohamed Al Habib Fassi Fihri (Morocco), whose curriculum vitae was annexed to the letter, would ensure adequate representation on the Tribunal of the world's principal legal systems. The Council supported the Secretary-General's proposal on 16 January [S/2001/48]. On 25 January [S/2001/88], the Secretary-General informed the Council President that he had received a letter from the General Assembly President in which he had also concurred. He had therefore appointed Mr. Fassi Fihri, effective 1 March, for the remainder of Mr. Bennouna's term, due to expire on 16 November. Also on 25 January [A/55/754], the Secretary-General informed the Assembly President that he had received a corresponding letter from the Council President.

Office of the Prosecutor

In 2001, the Prosecutor continued efforts to prosecute high-level leaders and notorious offenders responsible for the most serious crimes, with lower- and mid-level perpetrators being subject to local/domestic prosecutions.

Cooperation with Croatia continued to improve, although problems persisted in gaining access to specific documents and witnesses. Cooperation with FRY, where significant numbers of high-level accused were still at large, was complicated and varied, and was affected by the political instability within the coalition Government. Although Republika Srpska (Bosnia and Herzegovina) passed a law on cooperation with the Tribunal on 2 October, major obstacles remained, particularly regarding the surrender of indicted accused. In the light of allegations that war crimes were committed by both sides to an internal armed conflict in the former Yugoslav Republic of Macedonia (FYROM) between FYROM security forces and organized Albanian rebel groups in 2001 (see p. 368), the Prosecutor opened two investigations in November.

The Prosecutor's Office undertook an exhumation of four sites in a graveyard in Knin, Croatia. It also monitored exhumations in Bosnia and Herzegovina, which were relevant to ongoing ICTY prosecutions.

An advocacy training course covering the history of the conflict, the warring factions, violations covered by the Tribunal's statute, individual criminal responsibility and practice before the Tribunal was held in The Hague in January for ICTY and ICTR prosecutors.

The Office continued to maintain six field offices in the territory of the former Yugoslavia (Banja Luka, Belgrade, Pristina, Sarajevo, Skopje, Zagreb).

The Registry

The Registry of the Tribunal continued to exercise court management functions and provide administrative services to the Chambers and the Office of the Prosecutor. It also channelled information to the media and the public, administered the legal aid system and supervised the Detention Unit.

Legal support was provided in negotiations with individual States on enforcement of sentences and relocation of witnesses. In December, Stevan Todorovic (see p. 1201) was transferred to Spain to serve his imprisonment sentence under a 2000 agreement with the United Nations [YUN 2000, p. 1225]. Other States that had signed agreements were Austria, Finland, France, Italy, Norway and Sweden.

The ICTY Outreach Programme informed people in the former Yugoslavia about the work of the Tribunal and sought to ensure that the Tribunal's activities were transparent and accessible through publications, broadcasts, symposiums, workshops and round tables. The Outreach Programme opened new offices in Belgrade and Pristina, in addition to those in Sarajevo and Zagreb.

Temporal jurisdiction of ICTY

In response to Security Council resolution 1329(2000) [YUN 2000, p. 1228], the Secretary-General reported, in February [S/2001/154], on the terminal date of the temporal jurisdiction of ICTY. He noted that the Tribunal's statute did not specify any such terminal date, nor did it contain any provision as a result of which that date might be determined or otherwise become definite. In accordance with Council resolution 827(1993) [YUN 1993, p. 440], the date was left for subsequent determination by the Council "upon the restoration of peace". In view of the Council's repeated determinations that the situation in the region constituted a threat to international peace and security, most recently in resolution 1305(2000) regarding Bosnia and Herzegovina [YUN 2000, p. 342] and resolution 1244(1999) regarding Kosovo [YUN 1999, p. 353], the Secretary-General was not able to state that peace had been restored. He could not, therefore, recommend a date that the Council might, pursuant to resolution 827(1993), determine to be the terminal date of the Tribunal's temporal jurisdiction.

Financing

GENERAL ASSEMBLY ACTION (April)

Following consideration of reports submitted in 2000 on the financing of ICTY [YUN 2000, p. 1234], the General Assembly, on 12 April [meeting 98], on the recommendation of the Fifth (Administrative and Budgetary) Committee [A/55/691/ Add.1], adopted **resolution 55/225 B** without vote [agenda item 127].

Financing of the International Tribunal for the Prosecution of Persons Responsible for Serious Violations of International Humanitarian Law Committed in the Territory of the Former Yugoslavia since 1991

The General Assembly,

Having considered the report of the Secretary-General on the financing of the International Tribunal for the Prosecution of Persons Responsible for Serious Violations of International Humanitarian Law Committed in the Territory of the Former Yugoslavia since 1991 and the related report of the Advisory Committee on Administrative and Budgetary Questions,

Recalling its resolution 47/235 of 14 September 1993 on the financing of the International Tribunal for the Former Yugoslavia and its subsequent resolutions thereon, the latest of which was resolution 55/225 A of 23 December 2000,

Recalling also its resolution 55/249 of 12 April 2001 on the conditions of service and compensation of the ad litem judges of the International Tribunal for the Former Yugoslavia,

1. *Takes note* of the report of the Secretary-General on the financing of the International Tribunal for the Prosecution of Persons Responsible for Serious Violations of International Humanitarian Law Committed in the Territory of the Former Yugoslavia since 1991 and the recommendations made by the Advisory Committee on Administrative and Budgetary Questions in paragraph 19 of its report;

2. *Authorizes* the Secretary-General to enter into commitments in an amount not to exceed 5,280,900 United States dollars gross (4,899,400 dollars net) for

the resource requirements of the International Tribunal for the Former Yugoslavia to support ad litem judges for the year 2001, and requests the Secretary-General to report thereon to the General Assembly at its fifty-sixth session.

Reports of Secretary-General. In response to General Assembly resolution 55/225 A [YUN 2000, p. 1234], the Secretary-General, in October [A/56/ 495 & Corr.1 & Add.1], submitted proposed resource requirements for ICTY for 2002-2003, which, after recosting, amounted to $254,198,300 gross ($225,645,600 net).

Pursuant to Assembly resolution 54/239 B [YUN 2000, p. 1232], the Secretary-General, in October [A/56/501], presented the sixth annual financial performance report of ICTY for the year ended 31 December 2000, including actual performance indicators. Expenditures totalled $100,465,700 gross ($89,561,100 net), resulting in a reduction in requirements of $5,683,700 gross ($6,381,500 net). Savings were mainly attributed to reductions under salaries and in contractual services.

Revised estimates presented to the Fifth Committee in December [A/C.5/56/30] proposed an additional appropriation of $167,550 for the 2002-2003 budget to expand internal oversight coverage of the Tribunal, initially for a six-month period from 1 January to 30 June 2002.

ACABQ action. In November [A/56/665], the Advisory Committee on Administrative and Budgetary Questions (ACABQ) recommended that the General Assembly approve an appropriation of $249,013,600 gross ($223,233,100 net) for the operations of ICTY during the 2002-2003 biennium. ACABQ summarized its recommendations regarding post reductions.

In December [A/56/717], ACABQ recommended that the Assembly approve the additional appropriation of $167,550 to strengthen internal oversight services.

GENERAL ASSEMBLY ACTION (December)

On 24 December [meeting 92], the General Assembly, on the recommendation of the Fifth Committee [A/56/730], adopted **resolution 56/247** without vote [agenda item 131].

Financing of the International Tribunal for the Prosecution of Persons Responsible for Serious Violations of International Humanitarian Law Committed in the Territory of the Former Yugoslavia since 1991

The General Assembly,

Taking note of the reports of the Secretary-General on the financing of the International Tribunal for the Prosecution of Persons Responsible for Serious Violations of International Humanitarian Law Committed in the Territory of the Former Yugoslavia since 1991 and the related reports of the Advisory Committee on Administrative and Budgetary Questions,

Recalling its resolution 47/235 of 14 September 1993 on the financing of the International Tribunal for the Former Yugoslavia and its subsequent resolutions thereon, the latest of which were resolutions 55/225 A of 23 December 2000 and 55/225 B of 12 April 2001,

Taking note of the report of the Secretary-General on the budget performance of the International Tribunal for the Former Yugoslavia for the period from 1 January to 31 December 2000 and the comments of the Advisory Committee thereon in its report,

Taking note also of Security Council resolution 1329(2000) of 30 November 2000 concerning the establishment of a pool of ad litem judges in the International Tribunal for the Former Yugoslavia,

1. *Endorses* the conclusions and recommendations contained in the reports of the Advisory Committee on Administrative and Budgetary Questions, subject to the provisions of the present resolution;

2. *Deeply regrets* the delay in the submission of the reports of the Secretary-General on the financing of the International Tribunal for the Former Yugoslavia;

3. *Reaffirms* paragraph 3 of its resolution 54/239 A of 23 December 1999, and emphasizes that future reports on the financing of the International Tribunal for the Former Yugoslavia should be submitted by 1 October of the year in which they are to be considered;

4. *Notes* that gratis personnel were still used in the International Tribunal for the Former Yugoslavia in 2000, and emphasizes that the provisions of General Assembly resolution 51/243 of 15 September 1997 on this issue must be strictly adhered to;

5. *Notes also* that a large total number of interns were used, and stresses that the acceptance of such interns should be consistent with the established guidelines, rules and regulations, in particular as regards the exceptional nature of a six-month assignment;

6. *Notes with great concern* the high vacancy rate in the International Tribunal for the Former Yugoslavia;

7. *Notes with concern* the absence of a firm exit strategy for the completion of the work of the International Tribunal for the Former Yugoslavia;

8. *Welcomes* all efforts that contribute to the determination of a firm exit strategy for the International Tribunal for the Former Yugoslavia, and, in this context, notes the comment of the Advisory Committee on empowering special national courts to undertake trials, as stated in paragraph 5 of the report of the Advisory Committee;

9. *Notes* the issues raised by the Advisory Committee in paragraphs 32, 80 and 82 of its report, and decides to revert to these issues at the resumed fifty-sixth session of the General Assembly;

10. *Decides* that the staffing table for the International Tribunal for the Former Yugoslavia shall remain at levels approved for 2001 until the General Assembly at its resumed fifty-sixth session in March 2002 determines appropriate levels for the biennium 2002-2003;

11. *Authorizes* the International Tribunal for the Former Yugoslavia to utilize the general temporary assistance resources necessary to provide the equivalent of up to the ninety new posts recommended by the Advisory Committee for the purposes and functions intended, it being understood that this utilization of general temporary assistance is to ensure the ability of the Court to assume an accelerated schedule of trials, as foreseen in the budget proposal, and would be without prejudice to the decisions adopted by the General Assembly at its resumed fifth-sixth session as regards an authorized staffing table for the biennium 2002-2003;

12. *Welcomes* recent improvements in the functioning of the International Tribunal for the Former Yugoslavia, and encourages continued efforts to address areas where improvement is needed;

13. *Decides* to appropriate, on a provisional basis, subject to further review at its resumed fifty-sixth session, to the Special Account for the International Tribunal for the Former Yugoslavia, a total amount of 242,791,600 United States dollars gross (218,216,300 dollars net) for the biennium 2002-2003;

14. *Requests* the International Tribunal for the Former Yugoslavia to submit, on an annual basis, a financial and programme performance report to the General Assembly;

15. *Decides* that the financing of the appropriation for the biennium 2002-2003 under the Special Account shall take into account the unused unencumbered balance of 3,183,700 dollars gross (4,154,500 dollars net) for 2000, interest and miscellaneous income of 3,559,600 dollars recorded for the biennium 2000-2001, the estimated additional requirements of 4,854,700 dollars gross (3,571,900 dollars net) for 2001 and the estimated income of 154,400 dollars for the biennium 2002-2003, which shall be set off against the aggregate amount of the appropriation, as detailed in the annex to the present resolution;

16. *Decides also* to apportion for the year 2002 the amount of 60,187,150 dollars gross (53,518,525 dollars net) among Member States in accordance with the scale of assessments applicable to the regular budget of the United Nations for the biennium 2002-2003 as set out in its resolution 55/5 B of 23 December 2000;

17. *Decides further* to apportion for the year 2002 the amount of 60,187,150 dollars gross (53,518,525 dollars net) among Member States in accordance with the rates of assessment applicable to peacekeeping operations for 2002;

18. *Decides* that, in accordance with the provisions of its resolution 973(X) of 15 December 1955, there shall be set off against the apportionment among Member States, as provided for in paragraphs 16 and 17 above, their respective share in the Tax Equalization Fund in the amount of 13,337,250 dollars, being half of the estimated staff assessment income approved for the International Tribunal for the Former Yugoslavia for the biennium 2002-2003.

ANNEX

Financing of the International Tribunal for the Prosecution of Persons Responsible for Serious Violations of International Humanitarian Law Committed in the Territory of the Former Yugoslavia since 1991

	Gross	Net
	(United States dollars)	
Estimated appropriation for the biennium 2002-2003 (after recosting)	256,241,300	229,787,800
Revised estimates (after recosting)[a]	156,300	156,300
Reductions made by the Advisory Committee on Administrative and Budgetary Questions (after recosting)	(7,227,700)	(6,554,700)

	Gross	Net
	(United States dollars)	
Reductions proposed by the Fifth Committee	(6,378,300)	(5,173,100)
Revised estimated appropriation for the biennium 2002-2003 (after recosting)	242,791,600	218,216,300
Prior credits and debits	(1,888,600)	(4,142,200)
Estimated income for the biennium 2002-2003	(154,400)	—
Balance to be assessed for the biennium 2002-2003	240,748,600	214,074,100
Assessment for 2002,[b]	120,374,300	107,037,050
Of which:		
Contributions assessed on Member States in accordance with the scale of assessments applicable to the regular budget of the United Nations for 2002	60,187,150	53,518,525
Contributions assessed on Member States in accordance with the scale of assessments applicable to peace-keeping operations of the United Nations for 2002	60,187,150	53,518,525

[a]To provide for internal oversight functions for the first six months of 2002 as detailed in document A/C.5/56/30.
[b]For the year 2003 equivalent amounts will be assessed by the General Assembly at its fifty-seventh session.

Also on 24 December, the Assembly decided that the item on the financing of ICTY would remain for consideration at its resumed fifty-sixth (2002) session (**decision 56/464**) and that the Fifth Committee would continue to consider it at that session (**decision 56/458**).

International Tribunal for Rwanda

In 2001, ICTR continued to identify areas for improvement, particularly in efficiency and judicial economy, and to adopt measures either to remedy perceived problems or to increase the Tribunal's output.

The lengthy period of pre-trial detention, in some cases as long as three years, was a matter of grave concern. Thus, the President proposed the creation of a pool of ad litem judges, similar to the solution adopted for ICTY (see p. 1203), to move the trials forward. In addition, the Prosecutor provided a revised investigation programme, which projected that the Tribunal would be able to complete its mandate by 2007-2008, contingent upon a number of variables.

On 31 May, the ICTR judges re-elected Judge Navanethem Pillay (South Africa) for a second and final two-year term as President of the Tribunal. They also re-elected Judge Erik Møse (Norway) as Vice-President.

In 2001, the activities of ICTR, established by Security Council resolution 955(1994) [YUN 1994,

p. 299], were covered in two reports to the Council and the General Assembly, for the periods 1 July 2000 to 30 June 2001 [A/56/351-S/2001/863 & Corr.1,2] and 1 July 2001 to 30 June 2002 [A/57/163-S/2002/733]. On 26 November, the Assembly took note of the 2000/01 report (**decision 56/409**) and, on 24 December, decided that the item would remain for consideration at its resumed fifty-sixth (2002) session (**decision 56/464**).

The Chambers

New trials and cases

On 26 April, Samuel Musabyimana, former Anglican Bishop of Shyogwe in Gitarama prefecture, was arrested in Kenya and transferred immediately to the Tribunal. On 2 May, he appeared before the Tribunal and pleaded not guilty to charges of genocide and crimes against humanity (extermination).

Simeon Nshamihigo, former Deputy Prosecutor of Cyangugu, was arrested in the United Republic of Tanzania on 19 May and transferred to the Tribunal on 25 May. On 29 June, he pleaded not guilty to three counts of genocide or complicity in genocide, extermination or murder as a crime against humanity, and violations of the Geneva Conventions.

Sylvestre Gacumbitsi, former Bourgmestre of Rusumo commune in Kibungo prefecture, was arrested in Tanzania on 20 June and immediately transferred to ICTR. On 26 June, he pleaded not guilty to charges of genocide or complicity in genocide, and crimes against humanity (extermination, murder and rape).

On 21 June, Jean Mpambara, former Bourgmestre of Rukara commune in Kibungo prefecture, was arrested in Tanzania and transferred to the Tribunal on 23 June. On 27 July, he pleaded not guilty to one count of genocide.

On 12 July, Emmanuel Ndindabahizi, former Minister of Finance, was arrested in Belgium and transferred to ICTR on 25 September. On 19 October, he pleaded not guilty to charges of genocide, direct and public incitement to commit genocide, and crimes against humanity (extermination, murder and rape).

Emmanuel Rukundo, former Military Chaplain in Ruhengeri prefecture, was arrested in Switzerland on 12 July and transferred to the Tribunal on 20 September. He pleaded not guilty to charges of genocide and crimes against humanity (murder and extermination) on 26 September.

Protais Zigiranyirazo, a former member of the Akazu, the inner circle of the late President of Rwanda, Juvenal Habyarimana, and the President's brother-in-law, was arrested in Belgium on 26 July. He was transferred to ICTR on 3 October and on 10 October pleaded not guilty to two counts of extermination or murder as a crime against humanity.

François Karera, former Prefect of Kigali-rural prefecture, was arrested in Kenya on 20 October and immediately transferred to ICTR. On 26 October, he pleaded not guilty to charges of genocide or complicity in genocide and crimes against humanity (extermination or murder).

On 27 November, Aloys Simba, former Lieutenant Colonel in the Rwanda Armed Forces, was arrested in Senegal under a warrant issued by the Tribunal.

Joseph Nzabirinda, former organizer of youth movements in Ngoma commune (Butare prefecture), was arrested in Belgium on 21 December under a warrant issued by the Tribunal.

Ongoing trials

In 2001, the Trial Chamber delivered one judgement involving the acquittal of Ignace Bagilishema, former Bourgmestre of Mabanza commune, Kibuye prefecture, whose trial concluded in 2000 [YUN 2000, p. 1226]. On 7 June, the Chamber acquitted Mr. Bagilishema of all charges (genocide, complicity in genocide, serious violations of the Geneva Conventions and crimes against humanity). The Prosecutor, on 9 July, filed a notice of appeal, seeking a warrant of arrest for further detention of the accused. Alternatively, the Prosecutor submitted that the accused could be provisionally released subject to certain conditions, such as compelling the accused to report his presence to the police authorities in the host country and to surrender his passport. The Chamber decided that Mr. Bagilishema should be released subject to certain conditions.

The trial of Juvénal Kajelijeli, former Bourgmestre of Mukingo commune, Ruhengeri prefecture, who pleaded guilty to charges against him in 1999 [YUN 1999, p. 1223], began on 13 March. Mr. Kajelijeli was charged with genocide, conspiracy to commit genocide and crimes against humanity (rape and extermination). After two days of hearings and following the death of Judge Laïty Kama on 6 May, the trial was suspended and reopened before a reconstituted Trial Chamber on 4 July. The trial was conducted in two phases (4-25 July and 26 November–13 December), with the third phase scheduled for 2002.

On 17 April, the trial of Jean de Dieu Kamuhanda, former Minister of Higher Education, Research and Culture who pleaded not guilty to charges in 2000 [YUN 2000, p. 1225], opened before the Trial Chamber. After a one-day hearing and following the death of Judge Kama, the trial was suspended until 3 September, when it was reopened before a reconstituted Trial Chamber.

In the Butare case [YUN 1999, p. 1222], which comprised six persons charged with genocide, crimes against humanity and serious violations of the Geneva Conventions, the joint trial began on 12 June and would continue in 2002. The accused were Pauline Nyiramasuhuko, former Rwandan Minister for Family and Women's Affairs [YUN 1997, p. 1328; YUN 1999, p. 1223]; her son and former leader of the Interahamwe militia, Arsène Shalom Ntahobali [YUN 1997, p. 1328]; Sylvain Nsabimana, former Prefect of Butare [ibid.]; Alphonse Nteziryayo, former Commanding Officer of the Military Police and former Prefect of Butare; Joseph Kanyabashi, former Bourgmestre of Ngoma [YUN 1999, p. 1222]; and Elie Ndayambaje, former Bourgmestre of Muganza.

The joint trial of Elizaphan Ntakirutimana, former clergyman who was transferred to the Tribunal in 2000 [YUN 2000, p. 1225], and his son, Gérard Ntakirutimana, began on 18 September. The accused jointly faced charges of genocide or complicity in genocide, conspiracy to commit genocide, crimes against humanity and violations of the Geneva Conventions. The trial would continue in 2002.

Other ongoing trials included the "Media" case (the joint trial of Ferdinand Nahimana, former Director of Radio Télévision Libre des Mille Collines, Jean-Bosco Barayagwiza, a former Director of Political Affairs in the Ministry of Foreign Affairs, and Hassan Ngeze, a former editor of *Kangura* newspaper), which began in 2000 [YUN 2000, p. 1226]; the joint trial of Lieutenant Samuel Imanishimwe, former Commander of the Cyangugu Barracks, Emmanuel Bagambiki, former Prefect of Cyangugu, and André Ntagerura, former Minister of Transport and Communication (the Cyangugu case), which began in 2000 [ibid.] and in which the prosecution closed its case on 21 November 2001; and the trial of Laurent Semanza, former Bourgmestre of Bicumbi commune, which also began in 2000 [ibid.] and in which the prosecution closed its case in April and the defence commenced the presentation of its case in October.

On 9 December, the Tribunal marked a milestone in its history when six individuals it had convicted were transferred from the UN Detention Facility in Arusha to Bamako, Mali, to begin serving their sentences. The Tribunal had agreements for the execution of its sentences with Benin, Mali and Swaziland. The six included Jean Kambanda, former Prime Minister of Rwanda, who was sentenced to life imprisonment in 1998

[YUN 1998, p. 1202]. The others were Jean-Paul Akayesu, Clément Kayishema, Alfred Musema, Obed Ruzindana (see below) and Omar Serushago, a former Interahamwe militia leader who was sentenced in 1999 [YUN 1999, p. 1221].

During the year, the Appeals Chamber continued to alleviate the outstanding roll of appeals. Several interlocutory appeals were lodged raising issues of the Tribunal's lack of jurisdiction, wrongful arrests and defects in indictments. Of those, several were disposed of: nine in the Ignace Bagilishema case (see p. 1208); two in the Jean-Bosco Barayagwiza case (see p. 1208); one in a joint case, consolidated as the "Military" case in 1999 [YUN 1999, p. 1222], of Théoneste Bagosora, Gratien Kabiligi, Anatole Nsengiyumva and Aloys Ntabakuze; four in the Laurent Semanza case (see p. 1208); and one in the case of Joseph Nzirorera [YUN 1999, p. 1222].

During the year, the Appeals Chamber delivered its final judgement in three cases. On 1 June, the Chamber dismissed an appeal by the defence and affirmed a decision of a Trial Chamber in the case of Jean-Paul Akayesu, former Bourgmestre of Taba, who had appealed against his conviction and sentence of life imprisonment rendered in 1998 [YUN 1998, p. 1201]. On the same date, the Chamber dismissed an appeal by the defence and affirmed a decision of a Trial Chamber in the joint trial of Clément Kayishema and Obed Ruzindana, who had lodged appeals against sentences of life imprisonment and 25 years in jail, respectively, in 1999 [YUN 1999, p. 1221]. On 16 November, the Chamber confirmed the conviction, in 2000 [YUN 2000, p. 1226], of Alfred Musema for genocide and for extermination as a crime against humanity and upheld the sentence of imprisonment for life for those crimes. On the basis of new evidence, the Chamber quashed his conviction for rape as a crime against humanity.

Election of judges

In accordance with Security Council resolution 1329(2000) [YUN 2000, p. 1228], the General Assembly elected two new judges to ICTR and two Trial Chamber judges were assigned to the Appeals Chamber.

In a 22 March letter to the Security Council President [S/2001/262], the Secretary-General, recalling that the Council, in resolution 1329 (2000), had decided that two additional judges should be elected to ICTR and that the terms of all ICTR judges should expire on 24 May 2003, forwarded the names of four candidates for the two additional judges. Member States and non-member States maintaining permanent observer missions in New York had been invited in January to submit nominations.

On the same date, the Legal Counsel forwarded an additional nomination to the Council President.

SECURITY COUNCIL ACTION

On 30 March [meeting 4307], the Security Council unanimously adopted **resolution 1347(2001)**. The draft [S/2001/294] was prepared in consultations among Council members.

The Security Council,
Recalling its resolutions 955(1994) of 8 November 1994, 1165(1998) of 30 April 1998 and 1329(2000) of 30 November 2000,
Having considered the nominations for judges of the International Tribunal for Rwanda received by the Secretary-General,
Forwards the following nominations to the General Assembly in accordance with paragraph 2 (d) of article 12 of the statute of the International Tribunal for Rwanda:
Mr. Mouinou Aminou (Benin)
Mr. Frederick Mwela Chomba (Zambia)
Mr. Winston Churchill Matanzima Maqutu (Lesotho)
Mr. Harris Michael Mtegha (Malawi)
Ms. Arlette Ramaroson (Madagascar)

On the same date [A/55/871], the Council President transmitted the Council's resolution to the President of the General Assembly.

Memorandum and note of Secretary-General. By a 3 April memorandum [A/55/872], the Secretary-General presented to the General Assembly the list of candidates and described the procedure for electing additional judges. On the same date [A/55/873], he transmitted the curricula vitae of the candidates.

GENERAL ASSEMBLY ACTION

On 24 April [meeting 99], the General Assembly adopted **decision 55/321** without vote [agenda item 185].

By that decision, the Assembly, in accordance with article 12 of the ICTR statute, elected the following two judges to serve in the Tribunal until the date of expiry of the terms of office of the judges currently serving in the Tribunal, that is, until 24 May 2003:
Mr. Winston Churchill Matanzima Maqutu (Lesotho)
Ms. Arlette Ramaroson (Madagascar).

The General Assembly was informed that the terms of office of the two judges would commence as soon as possible; the terms of office commenced on 29 May.

Composition of the Chambers

On 23 May [S/2001/550], the Secretary-General informed the Security Council of the death of

Judge Laïty Kama (Senegal) and indicated that the Government of Senegal had proposed the candidacy of Andrésia Vaz to replace him. He stated that Ms. Vaz met the qualifications that were prescribed in the ICTR statute. Annexed to the letter was her curriculum vitae. On 30 May [S/2001/551], the Council supported the Secretary-General's intention to appoint Ms. Vaz. On 31 May [S/2001/552], the Secretary-General informed the Council President that he had received a letter from the General Assembly President supporting his intention to appoint Ms. Vaz. She had therefore been appointed, effective 31 May, for the remainder of the term of Judge Kama, which was due to expire on 24 May 2003.

In identical letters of 14 September to the Council and the General Assembly [A/56/265- S/2001/764 & Corr.1], the Secretary-General transmitted a 9 July letter from the ICTR President containing a proposal to amend the Tribunal's statute to allow for the creation of a pool of 18 ad litem judges in order to complete current and future trials.

Office of the Prosecutor

In 2001, investigations carried out by the Office of the Prosecutor continued to target persons who occupied positions of authority at the time of the genocide, especially those who conspired to commit genocide. It also continued to combine cases under one indictment to reflect the various areas where such joinder applied at the national and prefecture levels. Following the judgement rendered in the case of Jean-Paul Akayesu (see p. 1209), investigations of sexual violence were expanded. The team in charge of sexual assault had been decentralized, but a central core of investigators continued to ensure coordination and the supervision of operations. The Office strengthened its cooperation with the authorities of other countries in the conduct of investigations and the prosecution of offences. The team in charge of tracking suspects still at large was divided into sub-teams along geographical lines, one covering Europe and North America, the other, Africa.

In February, the Prosecutor prepared an estimate of the investigative workload for the coming years, involving a total of 136 new accused persons. She projected that the Investigations Section should have finished most, or all, of its work on new cases by the end of 2004. The completion of the trials of the new 136 accused would depend on the arrest rate.

The Registry

The Registry continued to administer and service the Chambers and the Office of the Prosecutor in the performance of their functions. In addition to court management, the Registry's Judicial and Legal Services Division managed a legal aid system of assigning defence counsel to indigent accused. The Registry's Division of Administration was responsible for personnel, finance, language services, security and general services and for managing and running the Detention Facility in Arusha.

The Information and Documentation Centre, Umuzanzu mu Bwiyunge, in Kigali, which was the focal point of the Registry's Outreach Programme to Rwanda, attracted more than 21,000 visitors during the year. Facilities included a law library, a collection of videos of trial proceedings, ICTR public documents, Internet access and a public meeting room.

Financing

Reports of Secretary-General. In October [A/56/497 & Add.1], the Secretary-General submitted the proposed ICTR resources requirements for 2002-2003, amounting to $198,523,800 gross ($179,015,300 net) after recosting. The total included an amount of $19,516,500 required for staff assessment, to be offset by income from staff assessment of the same amount.

In response to General Assembly resolution 49/251 [YUN 1995, p. 1324], the Secretary-General, in October [A/56/500], submitted the sixth annual financial performance report of ICTR for the year ended 31 December 2000, including actual performance indicators. Expenditures for 2000 amounted to $83,144,800 gross ($75,817,300 net), resulting in an unencumbered balance of $3,010,100 gross ($2,352,900 net).

In a December report to the Fifth Committee [A/C.5/56/30], an additional appropriation of $219,850 to the 2002-2003 budget was proposed to expand internal oversight coverage of ICTR, initially for a six-month period from 1 January to 30 June 2002.

ACABQ action. In November [A/56/666], ACABQ recommended that the General Assembly approve an appropriation of $196,444,800 gross ($177,151,400 net) for the operation of ICTR in 2002-2003, representing a reduction of $2,079,000 gross ($1,863,900 net) from the estimate in the Secretary-General's proposal. The Committee also recommended 24 post reductions for the biennium.

In December [A/56/717], ACABQ recommended that the Assembly approve the proposed appropriation of $219,850 to the 2002-2003 budget to strengthen the role of internal oversight services.

On 24 December [meeting 92], the General Assembly, on the recommendation of the Fifth Committee [A/56/731], adopted **resolution 56/248** without vote [agenda item 132].

Financing of the International Criminal Tribunal for the Prosecution of Persons Responsible for Genocide and Other Serious Violations of International Humanitarian Law Committed in the Territory of Rwanda and Rwandan Citizens Responsible for Genocide and Other Such Violations Committed in the Territory of Neighbouring States between 1 January and 31 December 1994

The General Assembly,

Taking note of the reports of the Secretary-General on the financing of the International Criminal Tribunal for the Prosecution of Persons Responsible for Genocide and Other Serious Violations of International Humanitarian Law Committed in the Territory of Rwanda and Rwandan Citizens Responsible for Genocide and Other Such Violations Committed in the Territory of Neighbouring States between 1 January and 31 December 1994 and the related reports of the Advisory Committee on Administrative and Budgetary Questions,

Recalling its resolution 49/251 of 20 July 1995 on the financing of the International Tribunal for Rwanda and its subsequent resolutions thereon, the latest of which was resolution 55/226 of 23 December 2000,

Taking note of the report of the Secretary-General on the budget performance of the International Tribunal for Rwanda for the period from 1 January to 31 December 2000 and the comments of the Advisory Committee thereon in its report,

Taking note also of Security Council resolution 1329(2000) of 30 November 2000 concerning the election of two judges of the International Tribunal for Rwanda and the assignment of two of the judges elected or appointed in accordance with article 12 of the statute of the International Tribunal for Rwanda to be members of the Appeals Chamber of the International Tribunal for Rwanda and the International Tribunal for the Prosecution of Persons Responsible for Serious Violations of International Humanitarian Law Committed in the Territory of the Former Yugoslavia since 1991,

1. *Endorses* the conclusions and recommendations contained in the reports of the Advisory Committee on Administrative and Budgetary Questions, subject to the provisions of the present resolution;

2. *Deeply regrets* the delay in the submission of the reports of the Secretary-General on the financing of the International Tribunal for Rwanda;

3. *Reaffirms* paragraph 3 of its resolution 54/240 A of 23 December 1999, and emphasizes that future reports on the financing of the International Tribunal for Rwanda should be submitted by 1 October of the year in which they are to be considered;

4. *Notes* that a large total number of interns were used, and stresses that the acceptance of such interns should be consistent with the established guidelines, rules and regulations, in particular as regards the exceptional nature of a six-month assignment;

5. *Notes with great concern* that the high vacancy rate, particularly at the higher level of the administrative hierarchy, affects the effectiveness of the activities of the International Tribunal for Rwanda;

6. *Notes* the issues raised by the Advisory Committee in paragraphs 12, 16, 18, 29, 30, 44 and 49 of its report, and decides to revert to these issues at the resumed fifty-sixth session of the General Assembly;

7. *Decides* that the staffing table for the International Tribunal for Rwanda shall remain at levels approved for 2001 until the General Assembly at its resumed fifty-sixth session in March 2002 determines appropriate levels for the biennium 2002-2003;

8. *Authorizes* the International Tribunal for Rwanda to utilize the general temporary assistance resources necessary to provide the equivalent of up to seventy-seven new posts recommended by the Advisory Committee for the purposes and functions intended, it being understood that this utilization of general temporary assistance is to ensure the ability of the Tribunal to assume an accelerated schedule of trials, as foreseen in the budget proposal, and would be without prejudice to the decisions adopted by the General Assembly at its resumed fifty-sixth session as regards an authorized staffing table for the biennium 2002-2003;

9. *Decides* to appropriate, on a provisional basis, subject to further review at its resumed fifty-sixth session, to the Special Account for the International Tribunal for Rwanda, a total amount of 192,312,400 United States dollars gross (173,611,600 dollars net) for the biennium 2002-2003;

10. *Decides also* that the financing of the appropriation for the biennium 2002-2003 under the Special Account shall take into account the actual unencumbered balance of 3,010,100 dollars gross (2,352,900 dollars net) as at the end of 2000 and the estimated unencumbered balance of 4,237,100 dollars gross (3,851,900 dollars net), which was taken into account in resolution 55/226, as well as the amount of 2,160,000 dollars gross (2,160,000 dollars net), being the interest and other miscellaneous income recorded for the biennium 2000-2001, which shall be set off against the aggregate amount of the appropriation, as detailed in the annex to the present resolution;

11. *Requests* the International Tribunal for Rwanda to submit, on an annual basis, a financial and programme performance report to the General Assembly;

12. *Notes* the proposed maintenance costs for prisoners, and requests the Secretary-General to include this item in the context of the requested report on the long-term financial implications of the International Tribunal for Rwanda at the resumed fifty-sixth session;

13. *Decides* to apportion for the year 2002 the amount of 47,844,850 dollars gross (43,237,650 dollars net) among Member States in accordance with the scale of assessments applicable to the regular budget of the United Nations for the biennium 2002-2003 as set out in its resolution 55/5 B of 23 December 2000;

14. *Decides also* to apportion for the year 2002 the amount of 47,844,850 dollars gross (43,237,650 dollars net) among Member States in accordance with the rates of assessment applicable to peacekeeping operations for 2002;

15. *Decides further* that, in accordance with the provisions of its resolution 973(X) of 15 December 1955, there shall be set off against the apportionment among Member States, as provided for in paragraphs 13 and 14

above, their respective share in the Tax Equalization Fund in the amount of 9,214,400 dollars, being half of the estimated staff assessment income approved for the International Tribunal for Rwanda for the biennium 2002-2003.

ANNEX

Financing of the International Criminal Tribunal for the Prosecution of Persons Responsible for Genocide and Other Serious Violations of International Humanitarian Law Committed in the Territory of Rwanda and Rwandan Citizens Responsible for Genocide and Other Such Violations Committed in the Territory of Neighbouring States between 1 January and 31 December 1994

	Gross	Net
	(United States dollars)	
Estimated appropriation for the biennium 2002-2003 (after recosting)	198,523,800	179,015,300
Additional appropriations (after recosting)[a]	189,200	189,200
Reduction made by the Advisory Committee on Administrative and Budgetary Questions (after recosting)	(2,079,000)	(1,863,900)
Reductions proposed by the Fifth Committee	(4,321,600)	(3,729,000)
Revised estimated appropriation for the biennium 2002-2003 (after recosting)	192,312,400	173,611,600
Add:		
Estimated unencumbered balance for 2000 that was taken into account and reduced from the assessment for 2001 (see resolution 55/226)	4,237,100	3,851,900
Less:		
Actual unencumbered balance for the year 2000	(3,010,100)	(2,352,900)
Interest and other miscellaneous income for the biennium 2000-2001 as at 30 June 2001	(2,160,000)	(2,160,000)
Balance to be assessed for the biennium 2002-2003	191,379,400	172,950,600
Assessment for 2002,[b]	95,689,700	86,475,300
Of which:		
Contributions assessed on Member States in accordance with the scale of assessments applicable to the regular budget of the United Nations for 2002	47,844,850	43,237,650
Contributions assessed on Member States in accordance with the scale of assessments applicable to peacekeeping operations for 2002	47,844,850	43,237,650

[a]Includes resources for internal oversight functions as detailed in documents A/C.5/56/30 and A/56/717.

[b]For the year 2003 equivalent amounts will be assessed by the General Assembly at its fifty-seventh session.

Also on 24 December, the Assembly decided that the item on the financing of ICTR would remain for consideration at its resumed fifty-sixth (2002) session (**decision 56/464**) and that the Fifth Committee would continue to consider it at that session (**decision 56/458**).

Functioning of the Tribunals

OIOS

GENERAL ASSEMBLY ACTION

Having considered a report of the Office of Internal Oversight Services (OIOS) on an investigation in 2000 [YUN 2000, p. 1233] into possible fee-splitting arrangements between defence counsel and indigent detainees at both ICTY and ICTR, the General Assembly, on 12 April [meeting 98], on the recommendation of the Fifth Committee [A/55/877], adopted **resolution 55/250** without vote [agenda items 127 & 128].

Report of the Office of Internal Oversight Services on the investigation into possible fee-splitting arrangements between defence counsel and indigent detainees at the International Tribunal for Rwanda and the International Tribunal for the Former Yugoslavia

The General Assembly,

Having considered the report of the Office of Internal Oversight Services on the investigation into possible fee-splitting arrangements between defence counsel and indigent detainees at the International Criminal Tribunal for the Prosecution of Persons Responsible for Genocide and Other Serious Violations of International Humanitarian Law Committed in the Territory of Rwanda and Rwandan Citizens Responsible for Genocide and Other Such Violations Committed in the Territory of Neighbouring States between 1 January and 31 December 1994 and the International Tribunal for the Prosecution of Persons Responsible for Serious Violations of International Humanitarian Law Committed in the Territory of the Former Yugoslavia since 1991 and the information provided that the investigation will be ongoing to ensure the highest standards of propriety and effectiveness of the two Tribunals,

Having also considered the recommendations of the Office of Internal Oversight Services, which should be implemented expeditiously, taking into account the observations expressed by the Tribunals in this regard,

Requests the Secretary-General to ensure that the Office of Internal Oversight Services continues its investigation on the question of the possible fee-splitting arrangements between defence counsel and indigent detainees at the International Tribunal for Rwanda and the International Tribunal for the Former Yugoslavia, and other related matters, in consultation with the Registrars of the two Tribunals, and to report thereon to the General Assembly, including on the implementation of the recommendations of the Office of Internal Oversight Services, at its fifty-sixth session.

On the same date, the Assembly took note of a 1999 OIOS report on the audit and investigation of ICTY [A/54/120] (**decision 55/477**) and of a 1998 OIOS report on ICTR [YUN 1998, p. 1208] (**decision 55/478**).

Chapter III

Legal aspects of international political relations

During 2001, the Preparatory Commission for the International Criminal Court, created by the 1998 United Nations Diplomatic Conference of Plenipotentiaries on the Establishment of an International Criminal Court to make arrangements for the coming into operation of the Court, made significant progress in drafting the instruments essential for the Court's functioning. Its report for the year contained the draft texts of the Relationship Agreement between the Court and the United Nations, the Financial Regulations, the Agreement on the Privileges and Immunities of the Court, and the Rules of Procedure of the Assembly of States Parties. The Netherlands, host country of the Court, had chosen a site for the Court's future headquarters and was making temporary premises ready for its use in the interim. The General Assembly welcomed the progress made and called on all States that had signed the 1998 Rome Statute of the International Criminal Court to consider ratifying or acceding to it without delay.

The Assembly expressed appreciation to the International Law Commission (ILC) for the work it had accomplished during its 2001 session in the codification and progressive development of international law, in particular for its completion of the final draft articles on "Responsibility of States for internationally wrongful acts", which it commended to the attention of Governments. The Assembly further expressed appreciation for ILC's valuable work on the prevention of transboundary harm from hazardous activities (a sub-topic of international liability for injurious consequences arising out of acts not prohibited by international law), the draft texts of the preamble and 19 articles, which ILC had also completed and adopted.

The Ad Hoc Committee on the convention for suppression of nuclear terrorism continued, within the framework of a working group of the Assembly's Sixth (Legal) Committee, to elaborate a comprehensive convention on international terrorism, to resolve outstanding issues relating to the preparation of a draft international convention for the suppression of acts of nuclear terrorism, and to keep on its agenda the possible convening of a high-level conference under UN auspices to formulate a joint international response to terrorism.

The Security Council and the Assembly strongly condemned the 11 September terrorist attacks in the United States, and called for international cooperation to bring to justice the perpetrators, organizers and sponsors of those outrages. Subsequently, the Council specified a number of measures addressed to States to help eliminate international terrorism. Disturbed by the persistence of terrorist acts worldwide, the Assembly also urged all States that had not done so, to consider, as a matter of priority, becoming parties to relevant conventions and protocols relating to the prevention, suppression and financing of terrorism.

Concerned by the increasing dangers and security risks faced by UN and associated personnel in the field, the Assembly also called on all States to consider becoming parties to the relevant international instruments, in particular the 1994 Convention on the Safety of United Nations and Associated Personnel.

Establishment of the International Criminal Court

The 1998 Rome Statute of the International Criminal Court [YUN 1998, p. 1209], which established the Court as a permanent institution with the power to exercise jurisdiction over persons for the most serious crimes of international concern—genocide, crimes against humanity, war crimes and the crime of aggression—had closed for signature on 31 December 2000.

As at 31 December 2001, the Statute had 139 signatories and 48 States parties. It would enter into force after 60 States had become parties to it.

Preparatory Commission

In accordance with General Assembly resolution 55/155 [YUN 2000, p. 1239], the Preparatory Commission for the International Criminal Court, established by the 1998 United Nations Diplomatic Conference of Plenipotentiaries on the Establishment of an International Criminal Court [YUN 1998, p. 1209], held two sessions in New York in 2001: its seventh (26 February–9 March) and eighth (24 September–5 October), at which it continued drafting the instruments essential for the Court's functioning.

At the February/March session, the Preparatory Commission considered five items: the Relationship Agreement between the Court and the United Nations, the Financial Regulations, the Agreement on the Privileges and Immunities of the Court, the Rules of Procedure of the Assembly of States Parties, and the crime of aggression. At the closing meeting, the Chairman indicated that, given the rapid pace of ratifications and the considerable workload still to be accomplished, the Bureau would draw up a road map to assist in the timely completion of the Commission's work.

At the September/October session, the Commission considered, in addition to the five items above, the basic principles governing a headquarters agreement to be negotiated between the Court and the host country (Netherlands), and the budget for the first financial year, for which two working groups were established.

The road map presented at the session [PCNICC/2001/L.2 & Corr.1] outlined the documents and activities needed for the smooth operation of the Assembly of States Parties and for the most efficient establishment of the Court. Activities would begin with the deposit of the sixtieth instrument of ratification of the Statute. The first session of the Assembly of States Parties would be held between 60 and 90 days thereafter, at which it would set up its Bureau, elect its President and adopt nomination and election procedures for the judges and the Prosecutor, as well as documents recommended by the Preparatory Commission. The Court's inaugural meeting would swear in the judges and the Prosecutor, elect its Presidency, establish the Chambers, and draw up a list of candidates for the position of Registrar for transmission to the Assembly so as to expedite the Court's election of the Registrar.

The road map listed the documents to be prepared for the Assembly's adoption, including those relating to the Court's provisional internal rules and regulations, grouped under three categories: human resources and administration; budget and finance; and operational issues. It pointed to the need for an interlocutor mechanism between the Preparatory Commission and the host country, which a subcommittee of the Commission's Bureau could fill, for the management of practical issues related to the permanent and interim premises and infrastructure that had to be addressed before the Court was established.

The Netherlands, as future host State, informed the session that a site for the Court's headquarters had been chosen and preparations were under way for an international architectural competition for its design [PCNICC/2001/INF/3]. It would cover some 30,000 square metres of office space, courtrooms, service areas, areas for the public and detention facilities; construction should be finished by 2007. In the interim, temporary premises were being readied for the Court's use from the day of its inception.

The Preparatory Commission adopted a report on its work from the sixth (2000) session [YUN 2000, p. 1238] to the eighth [PCNICC/2001/1 & Add.1-4], which contained the draft texts of the Relationship Agreement between the Court and the United Nations, the Financial Regulations, the Agreement on the Privileges and Immunities of the Court, the Rules of Procedure of the Assembly of States Parties and two draft resolutions of the Assembly of States Parties, one on the establishment of the Committee on Budget and Finance, and the other on relevant criteria for voluntary contributions to the International Criminal Court.

Communications. Among the documents before the Commission's seventh session was the final report and recommendations of a subregional seminar on information and awareness-raising with regard to the International Criminal Court (Yaoundé, 13-15 February) [PCNICC/2001/INF/1], submitted by Cameroon.

On 24 July [A/55/1020], Belgium transmitted to the Secretary-General the English, French and Spanish texts of the Common Position concerning the Court adopted by the Council of the European Union in Luxembourg on 11 June.

On 12 December [meeting 85], the General Assembly, on the recommendation of the Sixth (Legal) Committee [A/56/591], adopted **resolution 56/85** without vote [agenda item 164].

Establishment of the International Criminal Court

The General Assembly,

Recalling its resolutions 47/33 of 25 November 1992, 48/31 of 9 December 1993, 49/53 of 9 December 1994, 50/46 of 11 December 1995, 51/207 of 17 December 1996, 52/160 of 15 December 1997, 53/105 of 8 December 1998, 54/105 of 9 December 1999 and 55/155 of 12 December 2000,

Noting that the Rome Statute of the International Criminal Court was adopted on 17 July 1998, and taking note of the Final Act of the United Nations Diplomatic Conference of Plenipotentiaries on the Establishment of an International Criminal Court done at Rome on 17 July 1998,

Recalling the United Nations Millennium Declaration adopted at the Millennium Assembly, in which heads of State and Government stressed the importance of the International Criminal Court,

Noting in particular that the Conference decided to establish a Preparatory Commission for the Court, and that the Commission held two sessions in 2001, from 26 February to 9 March and from 24 September to 5 October,

Bearing in mind the mandate of the Preparatory Commission, as set out in resolution F adopted by the Conference, with regard to the preparation of the proposals for practical arrangements for the establishment and coming into operation of the Court,

Noting, with regard to the work of the Preparatory Commission and related working groups, the adoption by the Commission on 5 October 2001 of the report on its sixth to eighth sessions, containing the draft texts of the Relationship Agreement between the Court and the United Nations, the Financial Regulations, the Agreement on the Privileges and Immunities of the Court and the Rules of Procedure of the Assembly of States Parties,

Noting also the progress made in regard to the necessary arrangements for the commencement of the functions of the International Criminal Court in order to ensure its effective operation, and taking note in particular of the statement of the Minister for Foreign Affairs of the Kingdom of the Netherlands to the Preparatory Commission at its eighth session, on the preparatory work that the Government of the Netherlands was undertaking for the establishment of the Court,

Recognizing the continuing need for making available adequate resources and secretariat services to the Preparatory Commission in order to enable it to discharge its functions efficiently and expeditiously,

Noting in particular that one hundred and thirty-nine States have signed the Rome Statute and that the number of States that have deposited their instruments of ratification has grown significantly,

Taking into consideration the probability that the first meeting of the Assembly of States Parties will be held by September 2002, as well as article 112, paragraph 1, of the Rome Statute,

1. *Reiterates* the historic significance of the adoption of the Rome Statute of the International Criminal Court;

2. *Calls upon* all States that have signed the Rome Statute to consider ratifying or acceding to it, as appropriate, without delay, and encourages efforts aimed at promoting awareness of the results of the United Nations Diplomatic Conference of Plenipotentiaries on the Establishment of an International Criminal Court, held in Rome from 15 June to 17 July 1998, and of the provisions of the Statute;

3. *Welcomes* the important work accomplished by the Preparatory Commission for the International Criminal Court in the completion of a great number of parts of its mandate under resolution F adopted by the Conference, and notes in this respect in particular the importance of the growing participation in the work of the working group on the crime of aggression;

4. *Requests* the Secretary-General to reconvene the Preparatory Commission, in accordance with resolution F, from 8 to 19 April and from 1 to 12 July 2002, to continue to carry out the mandate of that resolution and, in that connection, to discuss ways to enhance the effectiveness and acceptance of the Court;

5. *Also requests* the Secretary-General to make available to the Preparatory Commission secretariat services, including the preparation of working documents if so requested by the Commission, to enable it to perform its functions;

6. *Further requests* the Secretary-General to invite, as observers to the Preparatory Commission, representa-

tives of organizations and other entities that have received a standing invitation from the General Assembly, pursuant to its relevant resolutions, to participate in the capacity of observers in its sessions and work, and also to invite as observers to the Commission representatives of interested regional intergovernmental organizations and other interested international bodies, including the International Tribunal for the Prosecution of Persons Responsible for Serious Violations of International Humanitarian Law Committed in the Territory of the Former Yugoslavia since 1991 and the International Criminal Tribunal for the Prosecution of Persons Responsible for Genocide and Other Serious Violations of International Humanitarian Law Committed in the Territory of Rwanda and Rwandan Citizens Responsible for Genocide and Other Such Violations Committed in the Territory of Neighbouring States, between 1 January 1994 and 31 December 1994;

7. *Notes* that non-governmental organizations may participate in the work of the Preparatory Commission by attending its plenary and its other open meetings, in accordance with the rules of procedure of the Commission, receiving copies of the official documents and making available their materials to delegates;

8. *Encourages* States to make voluntary contributions to the trust funds established pursuant to General Assembly resolutions 51/207 and 52/160, the mandates of which were expanded pursuant to Assembly resolution 53/105, towards meeting the costs of the participation in the work of the Preparatory Commission of the least developed countries and of those developing countries not covered by the trust fund established pursuant to resolution 51/207;

9. *Requests* the Secretary-General to undertake the preparations necessary to convene, in accordance with article 112, paragraph 1, of the Rome Statute, the meeting of the Assembly of States Parties to be held at United Nations Headquarters upon the entry into force of the Statute in accordance with article 126, paragraph 1, of the Statute;

10. *Decides* that expenses that may accrue to the United Nations as a result of the implementation of the request contained in paragraph 9 above, as well as expenses resulting from the provision of facilities and services for the meeting of the Assembly of States Parties and any consequent follow-up shall be paid in advance to the Organization, for which an appropriate mechanism will be set up in the near future;

11. *Notes* that the United Nations and the Secretary-General may participate, without the right to vote, in the work of the Assembly of States Parties;

12. *Requests* the Secretary-General to invite, as observers to the meeting of the Assembly of States Parties, representatives of intergovernmental organizations and other entities that have received a standing invitation from the General Assembly, pursuant to its relevant resolutions, to participate in the capacity of observers in its sessions and work, and also to invite as observers to the Assembly representatives of interested regional intergovernmental organizations and other international bodies invited to the Rome Conference or accredited to the Preparatory Commission for the International Criminal Court;

13. *Notes* that non-governmental organizations invited to the Rome Conference, registered to the Preparatory Commission for the International Criminal

Court or having consultative status with the Economic and Social Council of the United Nations whose activities are relevant to the activities of the Court may participate in the work of the Assembly of States Parties in accordance with agreed rules;

14. *Requests* the Secretary-General to report to the General Assembly at its fifty-seventh session on the implementation of the present resolution;

15. *Decides* to include in the provisional agenda of its fifty-seventh session the item entitled "Establishment of the International Criminal Court".

International Law Commission

The International Law Commission (ILC) held its fifty-third session in Geneva in two parts: from 23 April to 1 June and from 2 July to 10 August [A/56/10 & Corr.1]. During the second part, the thirty-seventh session of the International Law Seminar was held. It was attended by 24 participants, mostly from developing countries, who observed Commission meetings, attended specially arranged lectures and participated in working groups on specific topics.

ILC, assisted by working groups and a Drafting Committee, continued to consider the Special Rapporteurs' proposals related to draft articles or draft guidelines for the formulation of instruments on State responsibility, international liability for injurious consequences arising out of acts not prohibited by international law (prevention of transboundary damage from hazardous activities), unilateral acts of States, diplomatic protection and reservations to treaties (see below for details under those topics). Draft articles proposed by the Special Rapporteurs assigned to report on those topics were reproduced in ILC's report on the work of its 2001 session [A/56/10 & Corr.1].

In furtherance of cooperation with other bodies concerned with international law, ILC continued its traditional information exchanges with the Inter-American Juridical Committee, the Asian-African Legal Consultative Organization—formerly the Asian-African Legal Consultative Committee—the European Committee on Legal Cooperation, the Committee of Legal Advisers on Public International Law of the Council of Europe, the International Court of Justice and the International Committee of the Red Cross.

In response to General Assembly resolution 55/152 [YUN 2000, p. 1240], ILC decided to hold its fifty-fourth session, the first of its next five-year mandate (2002-2006), in Geneva in two parts: from 6 May to 7 June and from 8 July to 9 August 2002. To continue to enhance its efficiency and productivity, ILC, on the recommendation of its

Planning Group, decided to give priority during the first part of that session to the appointment of Special Rapporteurs on two of the five topics considered suitable for codification, which included its long-term programme of work adopted in 2000 [ibid.]. ILC also indicated specific issues relating to reservations to treaties, diplomatic protection and unilateral acts of States on which the views of Governments or the Sixth Committee could provide guidance for its further work.

GENERAL ASSEMBLY ACTION

On 12 December [meeting 85], the General Assembly, on the recommendation of the Sixth Committee [A/56/589 & Corr.1], adopted **resolution 56/82** without vote [agenda item 162].

Report of the International Law Commission on the work of its fifty-third session

The General Assembly,

Having considered the report of the International Law Commission on the work of its fifty-third session,

Emphasizing the importance of furthering the codification and progressive development of international law as a means of implementing the purposes and principles set forth in the Charter of the United Nations and in the Declaration on Principles of International Law concerning Friendly Relations and Cooperation among States in accordance with the Charter of the United Nations,

Recognizing the desirability of referring legal and drafting questions to the Sixth Committee, including topics that might be submitted to the International Law Commission for closer examination, and of enabling the Sixth Committee and the Commission to further enhance their contribution to the progressive development of international law and its codification,

Wishing to enhance further the interaction between the Sixth Committee as a body of governmental representatives and the International Law Commission as a body of independent legal experts, with a view to improving the dialogue between the two organs,

Recalling the need to keep under review those topics of international law which, given their new or renewed interest for the international community, may be suitable for the progressive development and codification of international law and therefore may be included in the future programme of work of the International Law Commission,

Welcoming the holding of the International Law Seminar, and noting with appreciation the voluntary contributions made to the United Nations Trust Fund for the International Law Seminar,

Stressing the usefulness of structuring the debate on the report of the International Law Commission in the Sixth Committee in such a manner that conditions are provided for concentrated attention to each of the main topics dealt with in the report,

1. *Takes note* of the report of the International Law Commission on the work of its fifty-third session;

2. *Expresses its appreciation* to the International Law Commission for the work accomplished at its fifty-third session, in particular for the completion of the final draft articles on "Responsibility of States for

internationally wrongful acts" and for the valuable work done on the issue of prevention on the topic of "International liability for injurious consequences arising out of acts not prohibited by international law (prevention of transboundary harm from hazardous activities)";

3. *Requests* the International Law Commission, taking into consideration its decision at its forty-ninth session to proceed with its work on the topic of "International liability for injurious consequences arising out of acts not prohibited by international law", undertaking, as a first step, the issue of prevention, to resume, during its fifty-fourth session, its consideration of the liability aspects of the topic, bearing in mind the interrelationship between prevention and liability and taking into account the developments in international law and comments by Governments;

4. *Draws the attention* of Governments to the importance for the International Law Commission of having their views on the various aspects involved in the topics on the agenda of the Commission, in particular on all the specific issues identified in chapter III of its report;

5. *Reiterates its invitation* to Governments, within the context of paragraph 4 above, to respond, to the extent possible, in writing by 28 February 2002 to the questionnaire and requests for materials on unilateral acts of States circulated by the Secretariat to all Governments on 31 August 2001;

6. *Also reiterates its invitation* to Governments to submit the most relevant national legislation, decisions of domestic courts and State practice relevant to diplomatic protection in order to assist the International Law Commission in its work on the topic "Diplomatic protection";

7. *Recommends* that the International Law Commission, taking into account the comments and observations of Governments, whether in writing or expressed orally in debates in the General Assembly, continue its work on the topics in its current programme;

8. *Requests* the International Law Commission, taking into account paragraph 259 of its report, to begin its work on the topic "Responsibility of international organizations" and to give further consideration to the remaining topics to be included in its long-term programme of work, having due regard to comments made by Governments;

9. *Invites* the International Law Commission to continue taking measures to enhance its efficiency and productivity;

10. *Takes note* of paragraph 260 of the report of the International Law Commission with regard to the cost-saving measures taken by the Commission in organizing its programme of work, and encourages the Commission to continue taking such measures at its future sessions;

11. *Takes note also* of paragraph 261 of the report, and decides that the next session of the International Law Commission shall be held at the United Nations Office at Geneva from 29 April to 7 June and from 22 July to 16 August 2002;

12. *Stresses* the desirability of further enhancing the dialogue between the International Law Commission and the Sixth Committee, and in this context encourages, inter alia, the holding of informal discussions between the members of the Sixth Committee and those

members of the Commission attending the fifty-seventh session of the General Assembly;

13. *Requests* the International Law Commission to continue to pay special attention to indicating in its annual report, for each topic, any specific issues on which expressions of views by Governments, either in the Sixth Committee or in written form, would be of particular interest in providing effective guidance for the Commission in its further work;

14. *Also requests* the International Law Commission to continue the implementation of article 16, paragraph *(e)*, and article 26, paragraphs 1 and 2, of its statute in order to further strengthen cooperation between the Commission and other bodies concerned with international law, having in mind the usefulness of such cooperation;

15. *Notes* that consulting with national organizations and individual experts concerned with international law may assist Governments in considering whether to make comments and observations on drafts submitted by the International Law Commission and in formulating their comments and observations;

16. *Reaffirms* its previous decisions concerning the role of the Codification Division of the Office of Legal Affairs of the Secretariat and those concerning the summary records and other documentation of the International Law Commission;

17. *Expresses the hope* that the International Law Seminar will continue to be held in connection with the sessions of the International Law Commission and that an increasing number of participants, in particular from developing countries, will be given the opportunity to attend the Seminar, and appeals to States to continue to make urgently needed voluntary contributions to the United Nations Trust Fund for the International Law Seminar;

18. *Requests* the Secretary-General to provide the International Law Seminar with adequate services, including interpretation, as required, and encourages him to continue considering ways to improve the structure and content of the Seminar;

19. *Also requests* the Secretary-General to forward to the International Law Commission, for its attention, the records of the debate on the report of the Commission at the fifty-sixth session of the General Assembly, together with such written statements as delegations may circulate in conjunction with their oral statements, and to prepare and distribute a topical summary of the debate, following established practice;

20. *Requests* the Secretariat to circulate to States, as soon as possible after the conclusion of the session of the International Law Commission, chapter II of its report containing a summary of the work of that session and the draft articles adopted on either first or second reading by the Commission;

21. *Recommends* that the debate on the report of the International Law Commission at the fifty-seventh session of the General Assembly commence on 28 October 2002.

State responsibility

ILC, at its fifty-third session [A/56/10 & Corr.1], considered comments received from Governments on the draft articles on State responsibility as provisionally adopted by the Drafting Committee in 2000 [YUN 2000, p. 1245]. It also considered the fourth report of the Special Rapporteur, James Crawford (Australia), which addressed the main issues relating to the draft articles and recommended specific amendments in the light of comments received [A/CN.4/517 & Add.1]. Two working groups were established: an open-ended one to deal with outstanding issues and another to consider commentaries to the draft articles.

ILC, which began studying the issue of State responsibility in 1955 and had completed the first reading of the draft articles in 1996 [YUN 1996, p. 1207], finalized the second reading at the 2001 session. Its deliberations were preceded by a debate on four main outstanding issues: serious breaches of obligations to the international community as a whole (part two, chapter III); countermeasures (part two bis, chapter II); dispute settlement provisions (part three); and the form of the draft articles. On the recommendation of its open-ended working group, ILC reached understanding on each of those issues and agreed, as an exception to its long-standing practice of adopting draft articles on second reading, to include a brief summary of the debate in the light of the topic's importance and complexity.

Concerned that the title "State responsibility" was not sufficiently clear to distinguish it from the responsibility of a State under internal law, ILC, after considering different connotations, decided on "Responsibility of States for internationally wrongful acts".

The amended draft texts were again referred to the Drafting Committee. Following its consideration of the Committee's final report, ILC adopted the entire draft articles with the commentaries thereto. It recommended to the Assembly that it take note of the draft articles in a resolution and annex them to it, and consider at a later stage, in the light of the importance of the topic, the possibility of convening an international conference of plenipotentiaries to examine the draft articles, with a view to concluding a convention.

GENERAL ASSEMBLY ACTION

On 12 December [meeting 85], the General Assembly, on the recommendation of the Sixth Committee [A/56/589 & Corr.1], adopted **resolution 56/83** without vote [agenda item 162].

Responsibility of States for internationally wrongful acts

The General Assembly,

Having considered chapter IV of the report of the International Law Commission on the work of its fifty-third session, which contains the draft articles on responsibility of States for internationally wrongful acts,

Noting that the International Law Commission decided to recommend to the General Assembly that it should take note of the draft articles on responsibility of States for internationally wrongful acts in a resolution and annex the draft articles to that resolution, and that it should consider at a later stage, in the light of the importance of the topic, the possibility of convening an international conference of plenipotentiaries to examine the draft articles with a view to concluding a convention on the topic,

Emphasizing the continuing importance of the codification and progressive development of international law, as referred to in Article 13, paragraph 1 *a*, of the Charter of the United Nations,

Noting that the subject of responsibility of States for internationally wrongful acts is of major importance in the relations of States,

1. *Welcomes* the conclusion of the work of the International Law Commission on responsibility of States for internationally wrongful acts and its adoption of the draft articles and a detailed commentary on the subject;

2. *Expresses its appreciation* to the International Law Commission for its continuing contribution to the codification and progressive development of international law;

3. *Takes note* of the articles on responsibility of States for internationally wrongful acts, presented by the International Law Commission, the text of which is annexed to the present resolution, and commends them to the attention of Governments without prejudice to the question of their future adoption or other appropriate action;

4. *Decides* to include in the provisional agenda of its fifty-ninth session an item entitled "Responsibility of States for internationally wrongful acts".

ANNEX

Responsibility of States for internationally wrongful acts

Part one
The internationally wrongful act of a State

Chapter I
General principles

Article 1
Responsibility of a State for its internationally wrongful acts

Every internationally wrongful act of a State entails the international responsibility of that State.

Article 2
Elements of an internationally wrongful act of a State

There is an internationally wrongful act of a State when conduct consisting of an action or omission:

(a) Is attributable to the State under international law; and

(b) Constitutes a breach of an international obligation of the State.

Article 3
Characterization of an act of a State as internationally wrongful

The characterization of an act of a State as internationally wrongful is governed by international law. Such characterization is not affected by the characterization of the same act as lawful by internal law.

Chapter II
Attribution of conduct to a State

Article 4
Conduct of organs of a State

1. The conduct of any State organ shall be considered an act of that State under international law, whether the organ exercises legislative, executive, judicial or any other functions, whatever position it holds in the organization of the State, and whatever its character as an organ of the central Government or of a territorial unit of the State.

2. An organ includes any person or entity which has that status in accordance with the internal law of the State.

Article 5
Conduct of persons or entities exercising elements of governmental authority

The conduct of a person or entity which is not an organ of the State under article 4 but which is empowered by the law of that State to exercise elements of the governmental authority shall be considered an act of the State under international law, provided the person or entity is acting in that capacity in the particular instance.

Article 6
Conduct of organs placed at the disposal of a State by another State

The conduct of an organ placed at the disposal of a State by another State shall be considered an act of the former State under international law if the organ is acting in the exercise of elements of the governmental authority of the State at whose disposal it is placed.

Article 7
Excess of authority or contravention of instructions

The conduct of an organ of a State or of a person or entity empowered to exercise elements of the governmental authority shall be considered an act of the State under international law if the organ, person or entity acts in that capacity, even if it exceeds its authority or contravenes instructions.

Article 8
Conduct directed or controlled by a State

The conduct of a person or group of persons shall be considered an act of a State under international law if the person or group of persons is in fact acting on the instructions of, or under the direction or control of, that State in carrying out the conduct.

Article 9
Conduct carried out in the absence or default of the official authorities

The conduct of a person or group of persons shall be considered an act of a State under international law if the person or group of persons is in fact exercising elements of the governmental authority in the absence or default of the official authorities and in circumstances such as to call for the exercise of those elements of authority.

Article 10
Conduct of an insurrectional or other movement

1. The conduct of an insurrectional movement which becomes the new Government of a State shall be considered an act of that State under international law.

2. The conduct of a movement, insurrectional or other, which succeeds in establishing a new State in part of the territory of a pre-existing State or in a territory under its administration shall be considered an act of the new State under international law.

3. This article is without prejudice to the attribution to a State of any conduct, however related to that of the movement concerned, which is to be considered an act of that State by virtue of articles 4 to 9.

Article 11
Conduct acknowledged and adopted by a State as its own

Conduct which is not attributable to a State under the preceding articles shall nevertheless be considered an act of that State under international law if and to the extent that the State acknowledges and adopts the conduct in question as its own.

Chapter III
Breach of an international obligation

Article 12
Existence of a breach of an international obligation

There is a breach of an international obligation by a State when an act of that State is not in conformity with what is required of it by that obligation, regardless of its origin or character.

Article 13
International obligation in force for a State

An act of a State does not constitute a breach of an international obligation unless the State is bound by the obligation in question at the time the act occurs.

Article 14
Extension in time of the breach of an international obligation

1. The breach of an international obligation by an act of a State not having a continuing character occurs at the moment when the act is performed, even if its effects continue.

2. The breach of an international obligation by an act of a State having a continuing character extends over the entire period during which the act continues and remains not in conformity with the international obligation.

3. The breach of an international obligation requiring a State to prevent a given event occurs when the event occurs and extends over the entire period during which the event continues and remains not in conformity with that obligation.

Article 15
Breach consisting of a composite act

1. The breach of an international obligation by a State through a series of actions or omissions defined in aggregate as wrongful occurs when the action or omission occurs which, taken with the other actions or omissions, is sufficient to constitute the wrongful act.

2. In such a case, the breach extends over the entire period starting with the first of the actions or omissions of the series and lasts for as long as these actions or omissions are repeated and remain not in conformity with the international obligation.

Chapter IV
Responsibility of a State in connection with the act of another State

Article 16
Aid or assistance in the commission of an internationally wrongful act

A State which aids or assists another State in the commission of an internationally wrongful act by the latter is internationally responsible for doing so if:

(a) That State does so with knowledge of the circumstances of the internationally wrongful act; and

(b) The act would be internationally wrongful if committed by that State.

Article 17
Direction and control exercised over the commission of an internationally wrongful act

A State which directs and controls another State in the commission of an internationally wrongful act by the latter is internationally responsible for that act if:

(a) That State does so with knowledge of the circumstances of the internationally wrongful act; and

(b) The act would be internationally wrongful if committed by that State.

Article 18
Coercion of another State

A State which coerces another State to commit an act is internationally responsible for that act if:

(a) The act would, but for the coercion, be an internationally wrongful act of the coerced State; and

(b) The coercing State does so with knowledge of the circumstances of the act.

Article 19
Effect of this chapter

This chapter is without prejudice to the international responsibility, under other provisions of these articles, of the State which commits the act in question, or of any other State.

Chapter V
Circumstances precluding wrongfulness

Article 20
Consent

Valid consent by a State to the commission of a given act by another State precludes the wrongfulness of that act in relation to the former State to the extent that the act remains within the limits of that consent.

Article 21
Self-defence

The wrongfulness of an act of a State is precluded if the act constitutes a lawful measure of self-defence taken in conformity with the Charter of the United Nations.

Article 22
Countermeasures in respect of an internationally wrongful act

The wrongfulness of an act of a State not in conformity with an international obligation towards another State is precluded if and to the extent that the act constitutes a countermeasure taken against the latter State in accordance with chapter II of part three.

Article 23
Force majeure

1. The wrongfulness of an act of a State not in conformity with an international obligation of that State is precluded if the act is due to force majeure, that is the occurrence of an irresistible force or of an unforeseen event, beyond the control of the State, making it materially impossible in the circumstances to perform the obligation.

2. Paragraph 1 does not apply if:

(a) The situation of force majeure is due, either alone or in combination with other factors, to the conduct of the State invoking it; or

(b) The State has assumed the risk of that situation occurring.

Article 24
Distress

1. The wrongfulness of an act of a State not in conformity with an international obligation of that State is precluded if the author of the act in question has no other reasonable way, in a situation of distress, of saving the author's life or the lives of other persons entrusted to the author's care.

2. Paragraph 1 does not apply if:

(a) The situation of distress is due, either alone or in combination with other factors, to the conduct of the State invoking it; or

(b) The act in question is likely to create a comparable or greater peril.

Article 25
Necessity

1. Necessity may not be invoked by a State as a ground for precluding the wrongfulness of an act not in conformity with an international obligation of that State unless the act:

(a) Is the only way for the State to safeguard an essential interest against a grave and imminent peril; and

(b) Does not seriously impair an essential interest of the State or States towards which the obligation exists, or of the international community as a whole.

2. In any case, necessity may not be invoked by a State as a ground for precluding wrongfulness if:

(a) The international obligation in question excludes the possibility of invoking necessity; or

(b) The State has contributed to the situation of necessity.

Article 26
Compliance with peremptory norms

Nothing in this chapter precludes the wrongfulness of any act of a State which is not in conformity with an obligation arising under a peremptory norm of general international law.

Article 27
Consequences of invoking a circumstance precluding wrongfulness

The invocation of a circumstance precluding wrongfulness in accordance with this chapter is without prejudice to:

(a) Compliance with the obligation in question, if and to the extent that the circumstance precluding wrongfulness no longer exists;

(b) The question of compensation for any material loss caused by the act in question.

Part two
Content of the international responsibility of a State

Chapter I
General principles

Article 28
Legal consequences of an internationally wrongful act

The international responsibility of a State which is entailed by an internationally wrongful act in accordance with the provisions of part one involves legal consequences as set out in this part.

Article 29
Continued duty of performance

The legal consequences of an internationally wrongful act under this part do not affect the continued duty of the responsible State to perform the obligation breached.

Article 30
Cessation and non-repetition

The State responsible for the internationally wrongful act is under an obligation:

(a) To cease that act, if it is continuing;

(b) To offer appropriate assurances and guarantees of non-repetition, if circumstances so require.

Article 31
Reparation

1. The responsible State is under an obligation to make full reparation for the injury caused by the internationally wrongful act.

2. Injury includes any damage, whether material or moral, caused by the internationally wrongful act of a State.

Article 32
Irrelevance of internal law

The responsible State may not rely on the provisions of its internal law as justification for failure to comply with its obligations under this part.

Article 33
Scope of international obligations set out in this part

1. The obligations of the responsible State set out in this part may be owed to another State, to several States, or to the international community as a whole, depending in particular on the character and content of the international obligation and on the circumstances of the breach.

2. This part is without prejudice to any right, arising from the international responsibility of a State, which may accrue directly to any person or entity other than a State.

Chapter II
Reparation for injury

Article 34
Forms of reparation

Full reparation for the injury caused by the internationally wrongful act shall take the form of restitution, compensation and satisfaction, either singly or in combination, in accordance with the provisions of this chapter.

Article 35
Restitution

A State responsible for an internationally wrongful act is under an obligation to make restitution, that is, to re-establish the situation which existed before the wrongful act was committed, provided and to the extent that restitution:

(a) Is not materially impossible;

(b) Does not involve a burden out of all proportion to the benefit deriving from restitution instead of compensation.

Article 36
Compensation

1. The State responsible for an internationally wrongful act is under an obligation to compensate for the damage caused thereby, insofar as such damage is not made good by restitution.

2. The compensation shall cover any financially assessable damage including loss of profits insofar as it is established.

Article 37
Satisfaction

1. The State responsible for an internationally wrongful act is under an obligation to give satisfaction for the injury caused by that act insofar as it cannot be made good by restitution or compensation.

2. Satisfaction may consist in an acknowledgement of the breach, an expression of regret, a formal apology or another appropriate modality.

3. Satisfaction shall not be out of proportion to the injury and may not take a form humiliating to the responsible State.

Article 38
Interest

1. Interest on any principal sum due under this chapter shall be payable when necessary in order to ensure full reparation. The interest rate and mode of calculation shall be set so as to achieve that result.

2. Interest runs from the date when the principal sum should have been paid until the date the obligation to pay is fulfilled.

Article 39
Contribution to the injury

In the determination of reparation, account shall be taken of the contribution to the injury by wilful or negligent action or omission of the injured State or any person or entity in relation to whom reparation is sought.

Chapter III
Serious breaches of obligations under peremptory norms of general international law

Article 40
Application of this chapter

1. This chapter applies to the international responsibility which is entailed by a serious breach by a State of an obligation arising under a peremptory norm of general international law.

2. A breach of such an obligation is serious if it involves a gross or systematic failure by the responsible State to fulfil the obligation.

Article 41
Particular consequences of a serious breach of an obligation under this chapter

1. States shall cooperate to bring to an end through lawful means any serious breach within the meaning of article 40.

2. No State shall recognize as lawful a situation created by a serious breach within the meaning of article 40, nor render aid or assistance in maintaining that situation.

3. This article is without prejudice to the other consequences referred to in this part and to such further consequences that a breach to which this chapter applies may entail under international law.

Part three
The implementation of the international responsibility of a State

Chapter I
Invocation of the responsibility of a State

Article 42
Invocation of responsibility by an injured State

A State is entitled as an injured State to invoke the responsibility of another State if the obligation breached is owed to:

(a) That State individually; or

(b) A group of States including that State, or the international community as a whole, and the breach of the obligation:

(i) Specifically affects that State; or

(ii) Is of such a character as radically to change the position of all the other States to which the obligation is owed with respect to the further performance of the obligation.

Article 43
Notice of claim by an injured State

1. An injured State which invokes the responsibility of another State shall give notice of its claim to that State.

2. The injured State may specify in particular:

(a) The conduct that the responsible State should take in order to cease the wrongful act, if it is continuing;

(b) What form reparation should take in accordance with the provisions of part two.

Article 44
Admissibility of claims

The responsibility of a State may not be invoked if:

(a) The claim is not brought in accordance with any applicable rule relating to the nationality of claims;

(b) The claim is one to which the rule of exhaustion of local remedies applies and any available and effective local remedy has not been exhausted.

Article 45
Loss of the right to invoke responsibility

The responsibility of a State may not be invoked if:

(a) The injured State has validly waived the claim;

(b) The injured State is to be considered as having, by reason of its conduct, validly acquiesced in the lapse of the claim.

Article 46
Plurality of injured States

Where several States are injured by the same internationally wrongful act, each injured State may separately invoke the responsibility of the State which has committed the internationally wrongful act.

Article 47
Plurality of responsible States

1. Where several States are responsible for the same internationally wrongful act, the responsibility of each State may be invoked in relation to that act.

2. Paragraph 1:

(a) Does not permit any injured State to recover, by way of compensation, more than the damage it has suffered;

(b) Is without prejudice to any right of recourse against the other responsible States.

Article 48
Invocation of responsibility by a State other than an injured State

1. Any State other than an injured State is entitled to invoke the responsibility of another State in accordance with paragraph 2 if:

(a) The obligation breached is owed to a group of States including that State, and is established for the protection of a collective interest of the group; or

(b) The obligation breached is owed to the international community as a whole.

2. Any State entitled to invoke responsibility under paragraph 1 may claim from the responsible State:

(a) Cessation of the internationally wrongful act, and assurances and guarantees of non-repetition in accordance with article 30; and

(b) Performance of the obligation of reparation in accordance with the preceding articles, in the interest of the injured State or of the beneficiaries of the obligation breached.

3. The requirements for the invocation of responsibility by an injured State under articles 43, 44 and 45 apply to an invocation of responsibility by a State entitled to do so under paragraph 1.

Chapter II
Countermeasures

Article 49
Object and limits of countermeasures

1. An injured State may only take countermeasures against a State which is responsible for an internationally wrongful act in order to induce that State to comply with its obligations under part two.

2. Countermeasures are limited to the non-performance for the time being of international obligations of the State taking the measures towards the responsible State.

3. Countermeasures shall, as far as possible, be taken in such a way as to permit the resumption of performance of the obligations in question.

Article 50
Obligations not affected by countermeasures

1. Countermeasures shall not affect:

(a) The obligation to refrain from the threat or use of force as embodied in the Charter of the United Nations;

(b) Obligations for the protection of fundamental human rights;

(c) Obligations of a humanitarian character prohibiting reprisals;

(d) Other obligations under peremptory norms of general international law.

2. A State taking countermeasures is not relieved from fulfilling its obligations:

(a) Under any dispute settlement procedure applicable between it and the responsible State;

(b) To respect the inviolability of diplomatic or consular agents, premises, archives and documents.

Article 51
Proportionality

Countermeasures must be commensurate with the injury suffered, taking into account the gravity of the internationally wrongful act and the rights in question.

Article 52
Conditions relating to resort to countermeasures

1. Before taking countermeasures, an injured State shall:

(a) Call upon the responsible State, in accordance with article 43, to fulfil its obligations under part two;

(b) Notify the responsible State of any decision to take countermeasures and offer to negotiate with that State.

2. Notwithstanding paragraph 1 *(b)*, the injured State may take such urgent countermeasures as are necessary to preserve its rights.

3. Countermeasures may not be taken, and if already taken must be suspended without undue delay if:

(a) The internationally wrongful act has ceased; and

(b) The dispute is pending before a court or tribunal which has the authority to make decisions binding on the parties.

4. Paragraph 3 does not apply if the responsible State fails to implement the dispute settlement procedures in good faith.

Article 53
Termination of countermeasures

Countermeasures shall be terminated as soon as the responsible State has complied with its obligations under part two in relation to the internationally wrongful act.

Article 54
Measures taken by States other than an injured State

This chapter does not prejudice the right of any State, entitled under article 48, paragraph 1, to invoke the responsibility of another State, to take lawful measures against that State to ensure cessation of the breach and reparation in the interest of the injured State or of the beneficiaries of the obligation breached.

Part four
General provisions

Article 55
Lex specialis

These articles do not apply where and to the extent that the conditions for the existence of an internationally wrongful act or the content or implementation of the international responsibility of a State are governed by special rules of international law.

Article 56
Questions of State responsibility not regulated by these articles

The applicable rules of international law continue to govern questions concerning the responsibility of a State for an internationally wrongful act to the extent that they are not regulated by these articles.

Article 57
Responsibility of an international organization

These articles are without prejudice to any question of the responsibility under international law of an international organization, or of any State for the conduct of an international organization.

Article 58
Individual responsibility

These articles are without prejudice to any question of the individual responsibility under international law of any person acting on behalf of a State.

Article 59
Charter of the United Nations

These articles are without prejudice to the Charter of the United Nations.

International liability

ILC, in accordance with its 1997 decision [YUN 1997, p. 1336] to deal separately with the issues of prevention and international liability under the main topic of international liability for injurious consequences arising out of acts prohibited by international law, continued at its 2001 session [A/56/10 & Corr.1] to consider the sub-topic on prevention. It examined the report of the Drafting Committee containing the final version of the draft texts of a preamble and a set of 19 articles on prevention of transboundary harm from hazardous activities referred to it at the 2000 session [YUN 2000, p. 1246]. ILC adopted the final draft texts and recommended to the General Assembly the elaboration of a convention on the subject on the basis of those texts.

Unilateral acts of States

ILC, at its 2001 session [A/56/10 & Corr.1], considered the fourth report on unilateral acts of States [A/CN.4/519] by Special Rapporteur Victor Rodríguez Cedeño (Venezuela). The Special Rapporteur noted that his report was prepared on the basis of a wide range of literature and comments by ILC and Governments, as well as jurisprudence and some State practice referred to therein. He sought ILC guidance on issues relating to the causes of invalidity of unilateral acts, the determination of the moment when the legal effects of a unilateral act came into being, in turn leading to determining the moment when it was opposable or enforceable. He addressed the issues of silence regarding unilateral acts, interpretative declarations, countermeasures, the classification of unilateral acts and the rules for their interpretation. He proposed two draft articles on a general rule of interpretation and on supplementary means of interpretation, which were based on the 1969 Vienna Convention on the Law of Treaties [YUN 1969, p. 730], but modified to the specificity of the unilateral act.

ILC established an open-ended working group chaired by the Special Rapporteur, who orally reported on the group's work. On the recommendation of the group, ILC requested the Secretariat to circulate a questionnaire to Governments inviting further information regarding their practice of formulating and interpreting unilateral acts.

International State relations and international law

Jurisdictional immunities of States and their property

ILC [A/56/10 & Corr.1], in continuation of its work on the future form of the draft articles it had adopted in 1991 on jurisdictional immunities of States and their property [YUN 1991, p. 829], considered a 14 August report of the Secretary-General, with later addenda [A/56/291 & Add.1,2], which reproduced comments received from four States in response to General Assembly resolution 55/150 [YUN 2000, p. 1246]. The comments related to reports on the subject by the open-ended working group of ILC and of the Sixth Committee, established under resolution 53/98 [YUN 1998, p. 1215].

Pursuant to Assembly resolution 55/150, the agenda item entitled "Convention on jurisdictional immunities of States and their property" was included in the agenda of the Assembly's fifty-sixth (2001) session, in order to decide on the session dates of the Ad Hoc Committee established by the same resolution to consolidate areas of agreement and resolve outstanding issues, with a view to elaborating a generally acceptable instrument based on the 1991 draft articles on the topic.

GENERAL ASSEMBLY ACTION

On 12 December [meeting 85], the General Assembly, on the recommendation of the Sixth Committee [A/56/587 & Corr.1], adopted **resolution 56/78** without vote [agenda item 160].

Convention on jurisdictional immunities of States and their property

The General Assembly,

Recalling its resolution 55/150 of 12 December 2000, wherein it was decided to establish an Ad Hoc Committee on Jurisdictional Immunities of States and Their Property, open also to participation by States members of the specialized agencies, to further the work done, consolidate areas of agreement and resolve outstanding issues with a view to elaborating a generally acceptable instrument based on the draft articles on jurisdictional immunities of States and their property adopted by the International Law Commission at its forty-third session, and also on the discussions of the open-ended working group of the Sixth Committee and their results,

1. *Decides* that the Ad Hoc Committee on Jurisdictional Immunities of States and Their Property shall meet from 4 to 15 February 2002;

2. *Requests* the Secretary-General to make available to the Ad Hoc Committee the comments submitted by States in accordance with General Assembly resolution 49/61 of 9 December 1994 and on the reports of the open-ended working group of the Sixth Committee established under Assembly resolutions 53/98 of 8 December 1998 and 54/101 of 9 December 1999;

3. *Requests* the Ad Hoc Committee to report to the General Assembly at its fifty-seventh session on the outcome of its work;

4. *Decides* to include in the provisional agenda of its fifty-seventh session the item entitled "Convention on jurisdictional immunities of States and their property".

International terrorism

Convention for suppression of nuclear terrorism

Ad Hoc Committee

The Ad Hoc Committee on the convention for suppression of nuclear terrorism, established by General Assembly resolution 51/210 [YUN 1996, p. 1208], convened its fifth session (New York, 12-23 February) [A/56/37]. It continued, within the framework of a working group of the Sixth Committee, to elaborate a comprehensive convention on international terrorism, to resolve outstanding issues relating to the elaboration of a draft international convention for the suppression of acts of nuclear terrorism, and to address the question of the convening of a high-level conference under UN auspices to formulate a joint international response to terrorism in all its forms and manifestations.

The Ad Hoc Committee, in a working group of the whole, first discussed the revised texts of a number of articles, following which its Bureau prepared a discussion paper containing the texts of articles 3, 8 and 11, annexed to the Committee's report to provide a basis for consideration in the Sixth Committee's working group. India also prepared a reference paper containing the texts of articles 4, 5, 9, 10, 12 and 13, reproduced in annex II. The working group then discussed the revised texts of articles 1 and 2, contained in annexes IA and B to the report of the Sixth Committee working group [A/C.6/56/L.9], as well as the definition of terrorism, the relationship of the draft convention to existing and future instruments on international terrorism, and differentiating between terrorism and the right of peoples to self-determination and to combat foreign occupation.

The report contained written amendments and proposals submitted by delegations at the current session (annex III), a list of written amendments and proposals submitted by delegations to the Sixth Committee working group at the Assembly's fifty-fifth (2000) session (annex IV), an informal summary of the general exchange of views prepared by the Ad Hoc Committee Chairman (annex V) and the coordinator's report on the results of the informal consultations (annex VI).

Sixth Committee working group

During the General Assembly's fifty-sixth (2001) session, the Sixth Committee, on 8 October, established an open-ended working group, which held five meetings (New York, 15-26 October) [A/C.6/56/L.9] to continue the elaboration of a draft comprehensive convention on international terrorism, with appropriate time allocated to the continued consideration of outstanding issues related to the draft international convention for the suppression of acts of nuclear terrorism. Before the working group were the reports of the Ad Hoc Committee on the work of its fifth session (see p. 1224) and the 1998 report of the Sixth Committee working group [YUN 1998, p. 1216], which contained a revised text of the draft convention on the suppression of acts of nuclear terrorism.

Informal consultations on the draft articles, based on the texts submitted by the Ad Hoc Committee, led to the preparation of a discussion paper on articles 3-17, 17 bis, 20 and 22, which were further reviewed, together with article 23. The working group heard oral reports on the consultations by the coordinators of those consultations and received oral and written proposals by delegations, following which the Friends of the Chairman prepared revised texts of articles 3-17, 17 bis and 20-27, while the consultations coordinator prepared informal texts for articles 2 and 2 bis, reproduced in annexes IA and B to the working group's report.

At its last meeting, the working group decided to refer its report to the Sixth Committee, recommending that work continue as a matter of urgency on the elaboration of a draft comprehensive convention on international terrorism and that the coordinator for the draft international convention for the suppression of acts of nuclear terrorism should continue consultations on that draft.

Measures to eliminate terrorism

Report of Secretary-General. In accordance with General Assembly resolution 50/53 [YUN 1995, p. 1330], the Secretary-General, in July, issued his annual report with a later addendum [A/56/160 & Corr.1 & Add.1], containing information on measures taken at the national and international levels by 26 States and six international organizations and UN agencies and bodies to implement the 1994 Declaration on Measures to Eliminate International Terrorism, approved by Assembly resolution 49/60 [YUN 1994, p. 1294], and Security Council resolution 1269(1999) [YUN 1999, p. 1240]. It listed 19 international instruments pertaining to terrorism, indicating the status of State participation in each, and provided information on workshops and training courses on combating terrorist crimes. It also listed the States that had submitted texts of their laws and regulations to prevent and suppress terrorism for inclusion in the Secretariat's compendium of such laws. The report noted in that regard the publication in February of the *International Instruments related to the Prevention and Suppression of International Terrorism* [Sales No. E.01.V.3], containing the texts of global and regional instruments.

Communications. A number of communications were addressed to the General Assembly and the Security Council by individual Member States or groups, condemning the 11 September terrorist attacks in the United States (see pp. 61 and 63).

Other communications concerned a United Arab Emirates law against terrorist activities and related money-laundering [A/56/468]; a decision by Saudi Arabia to sever diplomatic relations with the Taliban Government of Afghanistan for, among other reasons, its alleged harbouring of suspected terrorists [A/56/424]; the Moscow Declaration between the Russian Federation and India on international terrorism [A/56/631]; and a number of other communications circulated under various Assembly agenda items, including measures to eliminate international terrorism [A/56/118, A/56/446-S/2001/944, A/56/634-S/2001/1087].

Further measures to eliminate terrorism

On 12 September, the Security Council, by **resolution 1368(2001)**, and the General Assembly, by **resolution 56/1**, condemned the previous day's terrorist attacks in the United States (see p. 60). In that connection, the Council, in **resolutions 1373(2001)** and **1377(2001)**, specified a number of measures to be taken by States to eliminate international terrorism. In addition, in conjunction with the Assembly's 1-5 October debate in plenary on that subject (see p. 63), the

United Nations held a treaty event—Multilateral Treaties on Terrorism (New York, 10-16 November) (see p. 69)—which resulted in 180 treaty actions by 79 countries.

(see p. 69)

GENERAL ASSEMBLY ACTION

On 12 December [meeting 85], the General Assembly, on the recommendation of the Sixth Committee [A/56/593], adopted **resolution 56/88** without vote [agenda item 166].

Measures to eliminate international terrorism

The General Assembly,

Guided by the purposes and principles of the Charter of the United Nations,

Recalling the Declaration on the Occasion of the Fiftieth Anniversary of the United Nations,

Recalling also the United Nations Millennium Declaration,

Recalling further all General Assembly and Security Council resolutions on measures to eliminate international terrorism,

Convinced of the importance of the consideration of measures to eliminate international terrorism by the General Assembly as the universal organ having competence to do so,

Deeply disturbed by the persistence of terrorist acts, which have been carried out worldwide,

Reaffirming its strong condemnation of the heinous acts of terrorism that caused enormous loss of human life, destruction and damage in the cities of New York, host city of the United Nations, and Washington, D.C., and in Pennsylvania, which prompted the adoption of General Assembly resolution 56/1 of 12 September 2001, as well as Security Council resolutions 1368(2001) of 12 September 2001, 1373(2001) of 28 September 2001 and 1377(2001) of 12 November 2001,

Recalling its debate on the item entitled "Measures to eliminate international terrorism", held in plenary meeting from 1 to 5 October 2001,

Stressing the need to strengthen further international cooperation among States and among international organizations and agencies, regional organizations and arrangements and the United Nations in order to prevent, combat and eliminate terrorism in all its forms and manifestations, wherever and by whomsoever committed, in accordance with the principles of the Charter, international law and relevant international conventions,

Mindful of the need to enhance the role of the United Nations and the relevant specialized agencies in combating international terrorism, and of the proposals of the Secretary-General to enhance the role of the Organization in this respect,

Recalling the Declaration on Measures to Eliminate International Terrorism, contained in the annex to resolution 49/60 of 9 December 1994, wherein the General Assembly encouraged States to review urgently the scope of the existing international legal provisions on the prevention, repression and elimination of terrorism in all its forms and manifestations, with the aim of ensuring that there was a comprehensive legal framework covering all aspects of the matter,

Taking note of the final document of the Thirteenth Ministerial Conference of the Movement of Non-Aligned Countries, held at Cartagena, Colombia, on 8 and 9 April 2000, which reiterated the collective position of the Movement of Non-Aligned Countries on terrorism and reaffirmed the previous initiative of the Twelfth Conference of Heads of State or Government of Non-Aligned Countries, held at Durban, South Africa, from 29 August to 3 September 1998, calling for an international summit conference under the auspices of the United Nations to formulate a joint organized response of the international community to terrorism in all its forms and manifestations, and other relevant initiatives,

Recalling its decision in resolutions 54/110 of 9 December 1999 and 55/158 of 12 December 2000 that the Ad Hoc Committee established by General Assembly resolution 51/210 of 17 December 1996 should address, and keep on its agenda, the question of convening a high-level conference under the auspices of the United Nations to formulate a joint organized response of the international community to terrorism in all its forms and manifestations,

Noting regional efforts to prevent, combat and eliminate terrorism in all its forms and manifestations, wherever and by whomsoever committed, including through the elaboration of and adherence to regional conventions,

Having examined the report of the Secretary-General, the report of the Ad Hoc Committee and the report of the Working Group of the Sixth Committee established pursuant to resolution 55/158,

1. *Strongly condemns* all acts, methods and practices of terrorism as criminal and unjustifiable, wherever and by whomsoever committed;

2. *Reiterates* that criminal acts intended or calculated to provoke a state of terror in the general public, a group of persons or particular persons for political purposes are in any circumstances unjustifiable, whatever the considerations of a political, philosophical, ideological, racial, ethnic, religious or other nature that may be invoked to justify them;

3. *Reiterates its call* upon all States to adopt further measures in accordance with the Charter of the United Nations and the relevant provisions of international law, including international standards of human rights, to prevent terrorism and to strengthen international cooperation in combating terrorism and, to that end, to consider in particular the implementation of the measures set out in paragraphs 3 *(a)* to *(f)* of resolution 51/210;

4. *Also reiterates its call* upon all States, with the aim of enhancing the efficient implementation of relevant legal instruments, to intensify, as and where appropriate, the exchange of information on facts related to terrorism and, in so doing, to avoid the dissemination of inaccurate or unverified information;

5. *Further reiterates its call* upon States to refrain from financing, encouraging, providing training for or otherwise supporting terrorist activities;

6. *Reaffirms* that international cooperation as well as actions by States to combat terrorism should be conducted in conformity with the principles of the Charter, international law and relevant international conventions;

7. *Urges* all States that have not yet done so to consider, as a matter of priority, and in accordance with Security Council resolution 1373(2001), becoming parties

to relevant conventions and protocols as referred to in paragraph 6 of General Assembly resolution 51/210, as well as the International Convention for the Suppression of Terrorist Bombings and the International Convention for the Suppression of the Financing of Terrorism, and calls upon all States to enact, as appropriate, domestic legislation necessary to implement the provisions of those conventions and protocols, to ensure that the jurisdiction of their courts enables them to bring to trial the perpetrators of terrorist acts, and to cooperate with and provide support and assistance to other States and relevant international and regional organizations to that end;

8. *Urges* States to cooperate with the Secretary-General and with one another, as well as with interested intergovernmental organizations, with a view to ensuring, where appropriate within existing mandates, that technical and other expert advice is provided to those States requiring and requesting assistance in becoming parties to the conventions and protocols referred to in paragraph 7 above;

9. *Notes with appreciation and satisfaction* that, consistent with the call contained in paragraph 7 of General Assembly resolution 55/158, a number of States became parties to the relevant conventions and protocols referred to therein, thereby realizing the objective of wider acceptance and implementation of those conventions;

10. *Reaffirms* the Declaration on Measures to Eliminate International Terrorism, contained in the annex to resolution 49/60, and the Declaration to Supplement the 1994 Declaration on Measures to Eliminate International Terrorism, contained in the annex to resolution 51/210, and calls upon all States to implement them;

11. *Urges* all States and the Secretary-General, in their efforts to prevent international terrorism, to make best use of the existing institutions of the United Nations;

12. *Welcomes* the efforts of the Terrorism Prevention Branch of the Centre for International Crime Prevention in Vienna, after reviewing existing possibilities within the United Nations system, to enhance, through its mandate, the capabilities of the United Nations in the prevention of terrorism;

13. *Invites* States that have not yet done so to submit to the Secretary-General information on their national laws and regulations regarding the prevention and suppression of acts of international terrorism;

14. *Invites* regional intergovernmental organizations to submit to the Secretary-General information on the measures they have adopted at the regional level to eliminate international terrorism;

15. *Welcomes* the important progress attained in the elaboration of the draft comprehensive convention on international terrorism during the meetings of the Ad Hoc Committee established by General Assembly resolution 51/210 of 17 December 1996 and the Working Group of the Sixth Committee established pursuant to General Assembly resolution 55/158;

16. *Decides* that the Ad Hoc Committee shall continue to elaborate a comprehensive convention on international terrorism as a matter of urgency, and shall continue its efforts to resolve the outstanding issues relating to the elaboration of a draft international convention for the suppression of acts of nuclear terrorism

as a means of further developing a comprehensive legal framework of conventions dealing with international terrorism, and that it shall keep on its agenda the question of convening a high-level conference under the auspices of the United Nations to formulate a joint organized response of the international community to terrorism in all its forms and manifestations;

17. *Also decides* that the Ad Hoc Committee shall meet from 28 January to 1 February 2002 to continue the elaboration of a draft comprehensive convention on international terrorism, with appropriate time allocated to the continued consideration of outstanding issues relating to the elaboration of a draft international convention for the suppression of acts of nuclear terrorism, that it shall keep on its agenda the question of convening a high-level conference under the auspices of the United Nations to formulate a joint organized response of the international community to terrorism in all its forms and manifestations, and that the work shall continue, if necessary, during the fifty-seventh session of the General Assembly, within the framework of a working group of the Sixth Committee;

18. *Requests* the Secretary-General to continue to provide the Ad Hoc Committee with the necessary facilities for the performance of its work;

19. *Requests* the Ad Hoc Committee to report to the General Assembly at its fifty-sixth session in the event of the completion of the draft comprehensive convention on international terrorism or the draft international convention for the suppression of acts of nuclear terrorism;

20. *Also requests* the Ad Hoc Committee to report to the General Assembly at its fifty-seventh session on progress made in the implementation of its mandate;

21. *Decides* to include in the provisional agenda of its fifty-seventh session the item entitled "Measures to eliminate international terrorism".

Safety and security of United Nations and associated personnel

In November, the Sixth Committee considered the report of the Secretary-General [YUN 2000, p. 1347] on the scope of legal protection under the 1994 Convention on the Safety of United Nations and Associated Personnel, adopted by General Assembly resolution 49/59 [YUN 1994, p. 1288].

GENERAL ASSEMBLY ACTION

On 12 December [meeting 85], the General Assembly, on the recommendation of the Sixth Committee [A/56/594 & Corr.1], adopted **resolution 56/89** without vote [agenda item 167].

Scope of legal protection under the Convention on the Safety of United Nations and Associated Personnel

The General Assembly,

Recalling its resolution 55/175 of 19 December 2000 on the safety and security of humanitarian personnel and protection of United Nations personnel,

Recalling also its resolution 49/59 of 9 December 1994, by which it adopted the Convention on the Safety of United Nations and Associated Personnel,

Recalling further the letter dated 24 October 2000 addressed to the President of the Security Council on behalf of the global staff of the United Nations system, drawing attention to the safety and security problems faced by United Nations and associated personnel,

Reaffirming the need to promote and ensure respect for the principles and rules of international law, including international humanitarian law, as well as the relevant provisions of human rights and refugee law,

Deeply concerned by the increasing dangers and security risks faced by United Nations and associated personnel at the field level, and mindful of the need to provide the fullest possible protection for their security,

Expressing concern that locally recruited personnel are particularly vulnerable to attacks,

Welcoming the recent increase in the number of States that have become parties to the Convention, which entered into force on 15 January 1999, and noting that the Convention has been ratified or acceded to by fifty-five States as at the date of the present resolution,

Mindful of the need to promote the universality of the Convention,

1. *Expresses its appreciation* to the Secretary-General for his report on the scope of legal protection under the Convention on the Safety of United Nations and Associated Personnel, and takes note of the recommendations contained therein;

2. *Calls upon* all States to consider becoming parties to and to respect fully their obligations under the relevant international instruments, in particular the Convention on the Safety of United Nations and Associated Personnel;

3. *Takes note* of the report of the Special Committee on Peacekeeping Operations with regard to the safety and security of United Nations and associated personnel and the scope of existing legal protection and its recommendations;

4. *Recommends* that the Secretary-General continue to seek the inclusion of relevant provisions of the Convention in the status-of-forces or status-of-mission agreements concluded by the United Nations;

5. *Encourages* the Secretary-General and relevant bodies within the United Nations system to continue to take such other practical measures as are within their authority and existing institutional mandates to strengthen protection for United Nations and associated personnel;

6. *Recognizes* the need to consider the safety and security of locally recruited personnel, who are particularly vulnerable and account for the majority of casualties;

7. *Decides* to establish an Ad Hoc Committee open to all States Members of the United Nations or members of the specialized agencies or of the International Atomic Energy Agency to consider the recommendations made by the Secretary-General in his report on measures to strengthen and enhance the protective legal regime for United Nations and associated personnel;

8. *Requests* the Secretary-General to invite the International Committee of the Red Cross to participate as an observer in the deliberations of the Ad Hoc Committee;

9. *Decides* that the Ad Hoc Committee shall meet from 1 to 5 April 2002, and recommends that, following the submission of the report of the Ad Hoc Committee, the Sixth Committee consider whether to continue this work during the fifty-seventh session of the General Assembly from 7 to 11 October 2002 within the framework of a working group of the Sixth Committee;

10. *Requests* the Ad Hoc Committee to submit a report on its work to the General Assembly at its fifty-seventh session;

11. *Decides* to include in the provisional agenda of its fifty-seventh session the item entitled "Scope of legal protection under the Convention on the Safety of United Nations and Associated Personnel".

Diplomatic relations

Protection of diplomatic and consular missions and representatives

As at 31 December 2001, the States parties to the following conventions relating to the protection of diplomats and diplomatic and consular relations were: 180 States parties to the 1961 Vienna Convention on Diplomatic Relations [YUN 1961, p. 512], 49 parties to the Optional Protocol concerning acquisition of nationality [ibid., p. 516] and 62 parties to the Optional Protocol concerning the compulsory settlement of disputes [ibid.].

The 1963 Vienna Convention on Consular Relations [YUN 1963, p. 510] had 165 parties, the Optional Protocol concerning acquisition of nationality [ibid., p. 512] had 38 and the Optional Protocol concerning the compulsory settlement of disputes [ibid.] had 45.

Parties to the 1973 Convention on the Prevention and Punishment of Crimes against Internationally Protected Persons, including Diplomatic Agents [YUN 1973, p. 775], numbered 113.

Report of Secretary-General. Pursuant to General Assembly resolution 55/149 [YUN 2000, p. 1252], the Secretary-General, in a June report [A/INF/56/6], reproduced reports received from six States (four from one of them) detailing instances of serious violations of the protection, security and safety of diplomatic and consular missions and representatives. The Secretary-General also reproduced the comments received from one State on measures taken to enhance security at foreign diplomatic and consular offices, in response to Assembly resolution 42/154 [YUN 1987, p. 1068], and updated the status of State participation in the conventions named above.

ILC consideration. ILC, at its fifty-third session [A/56/10 & Corr.1], had before it an addendum to the first report of Special Rapporteur John R.

Dugard (South Africa) on diplomatic protection, consideration of which was deferred in 2000 [YUN 2000, p. 1252], as well as his second report on the subject. The addendum dealt with draft article 9 on continuous nationality and transferability of claims, which was debated in an open-ended informal consultation chaired by the Special Rapporteur, as were draft articles 10 and 11 on the rule of exhaustion of local remedies covered in the second report. Following various suggestions relating to drafting and further issues to be considered, ILC referred those articles to the Drafting Committee. It deferred consideration of draft articles 12 and 13 on other aspects of the local remedies rule to the 2002 session.

Treaties and agreements

Reservations to treaties

ILC, at its 2001 session [A/56/10 & Corr.1], considered the second part of the fifth report of Special Rapporteur Alain Pellet (France) relating to questions of procedure regarding reservations to treaties and interpretative declarations. Following deliberations on draft guidelines 2.2.1 to 2.2.4 and 2.3.1 to 2.3.4 on the formulation of reservations and 2.4.3 to 2.4.8 on interpretative declarations, ILC referred them to the Drafting Committee. The resulting revised draft guidelines were provisionally adopted by ILC and reproduced in its report.

ILC also considered the sixth report of the Special Rapporteur on the modalities of formulating reservations and interpretative declarations, particularly their form and notification, and the publicity of reservations and interpretative declarations, including their communication, recipients and obligations of the depositary. The Special Rapporteur introduced draft guidelines 2.1.1 to 2.1.4, 2.4.1 and 2.4.2 (including 2.1.3 bis and 2.4.1 bis, and two alternatives for guideline 2.1.3) on the form and notification of reservations; 2.1.5 to 2.1.8 on procedures for the communication and publicity of reservations; and 2.4.2 (third paragraph) and 2.4.9 (second paragraph) on interpretative declarations. Having considered those draft guidelines, ILC also referred them to the Drafting Committee.

Treaties involving international organizations

The 1986 Vienna Convention on the Law of Treaties between States and International Organizations or between International Organizations [YUN 1986, p. 1006], which had not entered into force, had 34 parties as at 31 December 2001.

Registration and publication of treaties by the United Nations

During 2001, the Secretariat received 1,091 international agreements and 1,388 subsequent actions, which were registered or filed and recorded. In addition, 929 formalities concerning agreements in relation to which the Secretary-General performed depositary functions were registered. Twelve issues of the *Monthly Statement of Treaties and International Agreements* were published.

Additionally, the texts of international agreements registered or filed and recorded by the Secretary-General from 1993 to 1999 were published in the United Nations *Treaty Series* in 126 volumes during 2001 in the original languages, with translations into English and French where necessary. Volumes 29 to 34 of the *Cumulative Index to the Treaty Series*, published in English and French, covered up to volume 2,000, bringing the *Index* abreast with the published volumes of the *Treaty Series*.

Multilateral treaties

The UN *Treaty Series* (2,000 printed volumes) and the regularly updated status of multilateral treaties deposited with the Secretary-General were available on the Internet at the UN Treaty Collection web site (http://untreaty.un.org).

New multilateral treaties concluded under UN auspices

The following treaties, concluded under UN auspices, were deposited with the Secretary-General during 2001:

Amendment to the Convention on Environmental Impact Assessment in a Transboundary Context (adopted in Espoo, Finland, on 25 February 1991), adopted in Sofia, Bulgaria, on 27 February 2001

Amendment to the Convention on Prohibitions or Restrictions on the Use of Certain Conventional Weapons Which May Be Deemed to Be Excessively Injurious or to Have Indiscriminate Effects (with Protocols I, II and III) (adopted in Geneva on 10 October 1980), adopted in Geneva on 21 December 2001

United Nations Convention on the Assignment of Receivables in International Trade, adopted by General Assembly resolution 56/81 of 12 December 2001

Agreement on Succession Issues, adopted at the Conference on Succession Issues, held at the Hofburg Palace, Vienna, on 29 June 2001

Protocol against the Illicit Manufacturing of and Trafficking in Firearms, Their Parts and Components and Ammunition, supplementing the United Nations Convention against Transnational Organized Crime, adopted by General Assembly resolution 55/255 of 31 May 2001

Stockholm Convention on Persistent Organic Pollutants, adopted at the Conference of Plenipotentiaries on the Stockholm Convention on Persistent Organic Pollutants, Stockholm, Sweden, 22-23 May 2001

Agreement on International Roads in the Arab Mashreq, adopted by resolution 235(XXI) of the Economic and Social Commission for Western Asia, Beirut, Lebanon, 10 May 2001

Agreement establishing the Terms of Reference of the International Jute Study Group, 2001, adopted by the United Nations Conference on Jute and Jute Products in Geneva on 13 March 2001

International Cocoa Agreement, 2001, adopted in Geneva on 2 March 2001 by the United Nations Conference on Cocoa, 2000

Multilateral treaties
deposited with the Secretary-General

The number of multilateral treaties for which the Secretary-General performed depositary functions was over 500 at the end of 2001. During the year, 429 signatures were affixed to treaties for which he performed depositary functions and 1,435 instruments of ratification, accession, acceptance and approval were deposited.

The following multilateral treaties, among others, in respect of which the Secretary-General acted as depositary came into force in 2001:

Agreement concerning the Adoption of Uniform Conditions for Periodical Technical Inspections of Wheeled Vehicles and the Reciprocal Recognition of Such Inspections, adopted in Vienna on 13 November 1997

Regulation No. 112. Uniform provisions concerning the approval of motor vehicle headlamps emitting an asymmetrical passing beam or a driving beam or both and equipped with filament lamps, annexed to the 1958 Motor Vehicle Agreement

Regulation No. 113. Uniform provisions concerning the approval of motor vehicle headlamps emitting a symmetrical passing beam or a driving beam or both and equipped with filament lamps, annexed to the 1958 Motor Vehicle Agreement

International Convention against the Recruitment, Use, Financing and Training of Mercenaries, adopted by General Assembly resolution 44/34 of 4 December 1989

International Convention for the Suppression of Terrorist Bombings, adopted by General Assembly resolution 52/164 of 15 December 1997

International Coffee Agreement 2001, approved in London on 28 September 2000

Agreement for the Implementation of the Provisions of the United Nations Convention on the Law of the Sea of 10 December 1982 relating to the Conservation and Management of Straddling Fish Stocks and Highly Migratory Fish Stocks, adopted in New York on 4 August 1995

Agreement on the Privileges and Immunities of the International Tribunal for the Law of the Sea, adopted in New York on 23 May 1997

Amendments to the Agreement establishing the Asia-Pacific Institute for Broadcasting Development, adopted in Islamabad, Pakistan, on 21 July 1999

Convention on Access to Information, Public Participation in Decision-Making and Access to Justice in Environmental Matters, adopted in Aarhus, Denmark, on 25 June 1998

Information for 2001 regarding all multilateral treaties deposited with the Secretary-General was contained in *Multilateral Treaties Deposited with the Secretary-General: Status as at 31 December 2001*, Vols. I & II [ST/LEG/SER.E/20], Sales No. E.02.V.4.

Chapter IV

Law of the sea

During 2001, the United Nations continued to promote the universal acceptance of the 1982 United Nations Convention on the Law of the Sea and the two related Agreements. The three institutions created by the Convention—the International Seabed Authority, the International Tribunal for the Law of the Sea and the Commission on the Limits of the Continental Shelf—held sessions during the year.

Two Agreements dealing with aspects of the Convention entered into force in 2001, one on the conservation and management of straddling fish stocks and highly migratory fish stocks and the other on privileges and immunities of the International Tribunal for the Law of the Sea.

UN Convention on the Law of the Sea

Signatures and ratifications

In 2001, Bangladesh and Madagascar ratified the United Nations Convention on the Law of the Sea (UNCLOS), bringing the number of parties to 137. The Convention, which was adopted by the Third United Nations Conference on the Law of the Sea in 1982 [YUN 1982, p. 178], entered into force on 16 November 1994 [YUN 1994, p. 1301].

Meeting of States Parties. The eleventh Meeting of States Parties to the Convention (New York, 14-18 May) [SPLOS/73 & Corr.1] discussed the 2000 activities of the International Tribunal for the Law of the Sea [YUN 2000, p. 1257] and its draft budget for 2002 and other financial matters. Also discussed were the 2000 International Seabed Authority activities [ibid.]; the 2000 activities of the Commission on the Limits of the Continental Shelf [ibid.] and other Commission-related matters, including its possible observer status in the Meetings of States Parties; the responsibility of the Secretary-General under article 319 of the Convention to report on matters of a general nature relevant to the Convention; the rules of procedure for Meetings of States Parties; and the proposal to establish an open-ended working group to review budgetary and financial matters. That proposal was adopted by consensus [SPLOS/71] as a new rule (53 bis) of the rules of procedure.

With respect to article 4 of annex II to the Convention on the Law of the Sea, which dealt with the 10-year limit for coastal States to submit to the Commission data supporting claims to establish the outer limit of their continental shelf beyond 200 nautical miles, the Meeting considered a background paper by the Secretariat [SPLOS/64]; a position paper on the time frame for submissions put forward by some members of the Pacific Islands Forum (Australia, Fiji, Marshall Islands, Micronesia, Nauru, New Zealand, Papua New Guinea, Samoa, Solomon Islands, Tonga, Vanuatu) [SPLOS/67]; and a Secretariat note [SPLOS/66], transmitting two notes verbales from Seychelles (6 October 1998 and 29 December 2000) on its position. The Meeting, on 29 May [SPLOS/72], decided that in the case of a State party for which the Convention entered into force before 13 May 1999, the 10-year time limit would have begun from that date. The issue of the ability of States, particularly developing States, to fulfil the requirements of the article would be kept under review.

On 16 May, the Meeting elected Xu Guangjian (China) to fill the vacancy in the Tribunal for the remainder of the term (until 30 September 2002) of Judge Lihai Zhao (China), who had passed away on 10 October 2000. On 11 September, Judge Edward A. Laing (Belize) passed away; the election to fill the vacancy would take place during the twelfth (2002) Meeting of States Parties.

Agreement relating to the
Implementation of Part XI of the Convention

During 2001, the number of States parties to the Agreement relating to the Implementation of Part XI of the Convention (governing exploitation of seabed resources beyond national jurisdiction), which was adopted by the General Assembly in 1994 by resolution 48/263 [YUN 1994, p. 1301], reached 103. The Agreement, which entered into force on 28 July 1996 [YUN 1996, p. 1215], was to be interpreted and applied together with the Convention as a single instrument, and in the event of any inconsistency between the Agreement and Part XI of the Convention, the provisions of the Agreement would prevail. Any ratification of or accession to the Convention after 28 July 1994 represented consent to be bound by the Agreement as well. States that were parties to the

Convention prior to the Agreement's adoption had to deposit an instrument of ratification of or accession to the Agreement separately.

Agreement on the conservation and management of straddling fish stocks and highly migratory fish stocks

Report of Secretary-General. In response to General Assembly resolution 54/32 [YUN 1999, p. 1243], the Secretary-General submitted a September report [A/56/357] on the Agreement for the Implementation of the Provisions of the United Nations Convention on the Law of the Sea of 10 December 1982 relating to the Conservation and Management of Straddling Fish Stocks and Highly Migratory Fish Stocks (the Agreement) [YUN 1995, p. 1334].

As requested in resolution 54/32, the Secretary-General brought that resolution to the attention of all States, relevant intergovernmental organizations, members of the UN system, regional and subregional fisheries organizations and non-governmental organizations. He provided summaries of information received and observed that a review of those responses indicated that genuine efforts were being made to implement the Agreement, in particular its key provisions, even before its entry into force. He further noted that the entry into force of the Agreement, which was expected to take place in the very near future (see below), would create a new situation with important implications for all States. While non-States parties would continue to submit information to the Secretary-General on a voluntary basis, States parties might wish to decide whether the existing report of the Secretary-General should evolve into one that monitored compliance with the Agreement and whether a meeting of the States parties to the Agreement would be necessary to consider that and other issues.

On 11 December, 30 days after the deposit of the thirtieth instrument of ratification by Malta, the Agreement entered into force.

Reykjavik Declaration. On 6 November [E/CN.17/2002/PC.2/3], Iceland transmitted to the Secretary-General the text of the Reykjavik Declaration on Responsible Fisheries in the Marine Ecosystem, adopted by the Reykjavik Conference on the subject (1-4 October).

GENERAL ASSEMBLY ACTION

On 28 November [meeting 67], the General Assembly adopted **resolution 56/13** [draft: A/56/L.18 & Add.1] without vote [agenda item 30 (b)].

Agreement for the Implementation of the Provisions of the United Nations Convention on the Law of the Sea of 10 December 1982 relating to the Conservation and Management of Straddling Fish Stocks and Highly Migratory Fish Stocks

The General Assembly,

Recalling the relevant provisions of the United Nations Convention on the Law of the Sea ("the Convention"), including Part VII, section 2,

Recognizing that, in accordance with the Convention, the Agreement for the Implementation of the Provisions of the United Nations Convention on the Law of the Sea of 10 December 1982 relating to the Conservation and Management of Straddling Fish Stocks and Highly Migratory Fish Stocks ("the Agreement") sets forth provisions concerning the conservation and management of straddling fish stocks and highly migratory fish stocks, including provisions on subregional and regional cooperation in enforcement, binding dispute settlement and the rights and obligations of States in authorizing the use of vessels flying their flags for fishing on the high seas,

Recognizing also the duty provided in the Agreement and reiterated as a principle in the Agreement to Promote Compliance with International Conservation and Management Measures by Fishing Vessels on the High Seas ("the Compliance Agreement") and the Code of Conduct for Responsible Fisheries of the Food and Agriculture Organization of the United Nations for flag States to exercise effective control over fishing vessels flying their flag and vessels flying their flag which provide support to such vessels, and to ensure that the activities of such vessels do not undermine the effectiveness of conservation and management measures taken in accordance with international law and adopted at the national, subregional, regional or global levels,

Noting with satisfaction the imminent entry into force of the Agreement due to the fact that thirty States have ratified or acceded to it, and noting also that the entry into force of the Agreement entails responsibilities for States parties and other important considerations as outlined in the Agreement,

Noting the obligation of all States, pursuant to the provisions of the Convention, to cooperate in the conservation and management of straddling fish stocks and highly migratory fish stocks,

Conscious of the need to promote and facilitate international cooperation, in particular at the regional and subregional levels, in order to ensure the conservation, management and long-term sustainability of the living marine resources of the world's oceans and seas, consistent with the present resolution, and deploring the fact that the straddling fish stocks and highly migratory fish stocks in many parts of the world are overfished or subject to heavy and sparsely regulated fishing efforts, mainly as a result of, inter alia, unauthorized fishing, inadequate regulatory measures and excess fishing capacity,

Conscious also that the Agreement requires States and entities to pursue cooperation in relation to straddling fish stocks and highly migratory fish stocks either directly or through appropriate subregional or regional fisheries management organizations or arrangements, taking into account the specific characteristics of the subregion or region, to ensure the effective conservation, management and long-term sustainability of such stocks, and to establish such organizations or arrangements where none exist,

Recognizing the importance of the Agreement for the conservation and management of straddling fish stocks and highly migratory fish stocks and the need for the regular consideration by the General Assembly and review by the parties to the Agreement pursuant to the provisions of the Agreement, once in force, of developments relating thereto,

Welcoming the conclusion of negotiations, and the commencement of preparatory work, to establish new regional instruments, arrangements and organizations in several heretofore unmanaged fisheries, and noting the role of the Convention and the Agreement in the elaboration of these instruments, arrangements and organizations,

Welcoming also the fact that a growing number of States and other entities, as well as regional and subregional fisheries management organizations and arrangements, have enacted legislation, established regulations, adopted conventions or taken other measures as steps towards implementation of the provisions of the Agreement, even before its entry into force,

Taking into account that, in accordance with the Convention, the Code of Conduct for Responsible Fisheries and the Agreement, States fishing for straddling fish stocks or highly migratory fish stocks on the high seas, and relevant coastal States, shall give effect to their duty to cooperate by becoming members of the subregional or regional fisheries management organizations or participants in arrangements of that nature, or by agreeing to apply the conservation and management measures established by such organizations or arrangements, and that States having a real interest in the fisheries concerned may become members of such organizations or participants in such arrangements,

Recognizing the obligation of States to cooperate, either directly or through subregional, regional or global organizations, to enhance the ability of developing States, in particular the least developed among them and small island developing States, to conserve and manage straddling fish stocks and highly migratory fish stocks and to develop their own fisheries for such stocks,

Recognizing also the importance of the Compliance Agreement, which builds upon the legal framework established by the Convention, and noting that while twenty-two States have accepted it, the Compliance Agreement has not yet entered into force,

Concerned that illegal, unreported and unregulated fishing, including that noted in the report of the Secretary-General, threatens seriously to deplete populations of certain fish species, and in that regard urging States and entities to collaborate in efforts to address these types of fishing activities,

Welcoming the adoption by the Food and Agriculture Organization of the United Nations of an International Plan of Action to Prevent, Deter and Eliminate Illegal, Unreported and Unregulated Fishing, which focuses on the primary responsibility of the flag State and the use of all available jurisdiction in accordance with international law, including port State measures, coastal State measures, market-related measures and measures to ensure that nationals do not support or engage in illegal, unreported and unregulated fishing,

Noting that the objective of the International Plan of Action is to prevent, deter and eliminate illegal, unreported and unregulated fishing by providing all States with comprehensive, effective and transparent measures by which to act, including through appropriate regional fisheries management organizations established in accordance with international law,

Recalling that the Food and Agriculture Organization of the United Nations in 1999 adopted international plans of action for the management of fishing capacity, for reducing the incidental catch of seabirds in longline fisheries and for the conservation and management of sharks,

Noting the importance of the wide application of the precautionary approach to the conservation, management and exploitation of straddling fish stocks and highly migratory fish stocks, in accordance with the Agreement,

Noting also the importance of implementing the principles elaborated in article 5 of the Agreement, including ecosystem considerations, in the conservation and management of straddling fish stocks and highly migratory fish stocks,

Noting further the Reykjavik Declaration on Responsible Fisheries in the Marine Ecosystem, adopted on 4 October 2001,

Welcoming the report of the Secretary-General on recent developments and the current status of the Agreement,

1. *Calls upon* all States and other entities referred to in article 1, paragraph 2 *(b)*, of the Agreement that have not done so to ratify or accede to it and to consider applying it provisionally;

2. *Calls upon* all States that have not done so, in order to achieve the goal of universal participation, to become parties to the Convention, which sets out the legal framework within which all activities in the oceans and seas must be carried out, taking into account the relationship between the Convention and the Agreement;

3. *Emphasizes* the importance of the entry into force and effective implementation of the provisions of the Agreement, including those provisions relating to bilateral, regional and subregional cooperation in enforcement, and urges continued efforts in this regard;

4. *Urges* all States and other entities referred to in the Agreement to pursue cooperation in relation to straddling fish stocks and highly migratory fish stocks, either directly or through appropriate subregional or regional fisheries management organizations or arrangements, to ensure the effective conservation, management and long-term sustainability of such stocks, to agree upon measures necessary to coordinate and, where there are no subregional or regional fisheries management organizations or arrangements in respect of particular straddling or highly migratory fish stocks, to cooperate to establish such organizations or enter into other appropriate arrangements;

5. *Welcomes* the initiation of negotiations to establish regional and subregional fisheries management organizations or arrangements in several fisheries, and urges participants in those negotiations to apply provisions of the Convention and the Agreement to their work;

6. *Anticipates* the entry into force of the Agreement, and requests the Secretary-General, once the Agreement enters into force, to consult with States that have

either ratified or acceded to the Agreement, for the purposes and objectives of, inter alia, considering the regional, subregional and global implementation of the Agreement; making any appropriate recommendation to the General Assembly on the scope and content of the annual report of the Secretary-General relating to the Agreement; and preparing for the review conference to be convened by the Secretary-General pursuant to article 36 of the Agreement;

7. *Calls upon* States to provide assistance to developing States as outlined in the Agreement, notes the importance of participation by representatives of developing States in forums in which fisheries issues are discussed, and once the Agreement enters into force, agrees to review the implementation of the provisions calling for assistance to developing States and to facilitate the establishment of a programme of assistance within the Agreement;

8. *Requests* the Secretary-General to include in his next report on the status and implementation of the Agreement a background study on the provisions of Part VII of the Agreement concerning requirements of developing States, taking into account existing arrangements and assistance to developing States that may be relevant under the Agreement, as well as suggesting possible forms of assistance;

9. *Invites* States and international financial institutions and organizations of the United Nations system to provide assistance according to Part VII of the Agreement, including, if appropriate, the development of special financial mechanisms or instruments to assist developing States, in particular the least developed among them and small island developing States, to enable them to develop their national capacity to exploit fishery resources, including developing their domestically flagged fishing fleet, value-added processing and expansion of their economic base in the fishing industry, consistent with the duty to ensure the proper conservation and management of those fisheries resources;

10. *Calls upon* all States and other entities referred to in article X, paragraph 1, of the Compliance Agreement that have not done so to accept that instrument and afterwards to implement it effectively;

11. *Calls upon* all States to ensure that their vessels comply with the conservation and management measures in accordance with the Agreement that have been adopted by subregional and regional fisheries management organizations and arrangements;

12. *Calls upon* States not to permit vessels flying their flag to engage in fishing on the high seas without having effective control over their activities and to take specific measures, in accordance with the relevant provisions of the Convention, the Agreement and the Compliance Agreement, to control fishing operations by vessels flying their flag;

13. *Takes note* of the outcome of the first meeting of the Joint Ad Hoc Working Group on Illegal, Unreported and Unregulated Fishing and Related Matters of the Food and Agriculture Organization of the United Nations and the International Maritime Organization, held in Rome from 9 to 11 October 2000, which contained a number of recommendations aimed at enhancing flag State and port State control over fishing vessels, with a view to eliminating the roots of illegal, unreported and unregulated fishing;

14. *Calls upon* the Food and Agriculture Organization of the United Nations and its members, in cooperation with States and entities, with regional fisheries management organizations and arrangements and other competent international organizations, such as the International Maritime Organization, to address possible key issues constituting effective fishery-related flag State control of a fishing vessel;

15. *Urges* States, as a matter of priority, to coordinate their activities and cooperate directly and, as appropriate, through relevant regional fisheries management organizations, in the implementation of the International Plan of Action to Prevent, Deter and Eliminate Illegal, Unreported and Unregulated Fishing recently adopted by the Food and Agriculture Organization of the United Nations, to develop national plans of action on illegal, unreported and unregulated fishing and management of fishing capacity, to promote information-sharing, to encourage the full participation of all stakeholders, and in all efforts to coordinate all the work of the Food and Agriculture Organization of the United Nations with other international organizations, including the International Maritime Organization;

16. *Encourages* States and other entities to integrate in an appropriate manner, including through subregional or regional fisheries management organizations or arrangements to which they are party or in which they are participants, the requirements for the protection of the environment, in particular those resulting from multilateral environmental agreements, in the management of straddling fish stocks and highly migratory fish stocks;

17. *Encourages* States to give effect to the principles elaborated in article 5 of the Agreement, including ecosystem considerations, in the conservation and management of straddling fish stocks and highly migratory fish stocks, and to incorporate those principles in fisheries management at the national level and in subregional or regional fisheries management organizations or arrangements to which they are party or in which they are participants, or as appropriate at the global level;

18. *Urges* all States to apply the precautionary approach widely to the conservation, management and exploitation of straddling fish stocks and highly migratory fish stocks, and calls upon States parties to the Agreement to implement fully the provisions of article 6 of the Agreement as a matter of priority;

19. *Requests* the Secretary-General to submit to the General Assembly at its fifty-eighth session a report on the status and implementation of the Agreement and on the impact of the entry into force of the Agreement on related or proposed instruments and programmes throughout the United Nations system relating to straddling fish stocks and highly migratory fish stocks, taking into account information provided by States, relevant specialized agencies, in particular the Food and Agriculture Organization of the United Nations, and other appropriate organs, organizations and programmes of the United Nations system, regional and subregional organizations and arrangements for the conservation and management of straddling fish stocks and highly migratory fish stocks, as well as other relevant intergovernmental bodies and non-governmental organizations, and including further de-

velopments relating to the conservation and management of straddling fish stocks and highly migratory fish stocks and other aspects of the present resolution;

20. *Decides* to include in the provisional agenda of its fifty-seventh session, under the item entitled "Oceans and the law of the sea", the sub-item entitled "Agreement for the Implementation of the Provisions of the United Nations Convention on the Law of the Sea of 10 December 1982 relating to the Conservation and Management of Straddling Fish Stocks and Highly Migratory Fish Stocks".

Institutions created by the Convention

International Seabed Authority

Through the International Seabed Authority, established by UNCLOS and the 1994 Implementation Agreement [YUN 1994, p. 1301], States organized and conducted exploration and exploitation of the resources of the seabed and ocean floor and subsoil beyond the limits of national jurisdiction. In 2001, the Authority, which had 137 members as at 31 December, held its seventh session (Kingston, Jamaica, 2-13 July) [ISBA/8/A/5].

On 29 March, the Authority entered into the first 15-year contracts for exploration for polymetallic nodules in the deep seabed, in accordance with the 2000 Regulations on Prospecting and Exploration for Polymetallic Nodules in the Area [YUN 2000, p. 1257], signing contracts with a State enterprise of the Russian Federation and with a consortium formed by Bulgaria, Cuba, the Czech Republic, Poland, the Russian Federation and Slovakia. Further exploration contracts were signed in 2001 with governmental agencies or companies of China, France, Japan and the Republic of Korea.

No notable progress was made between the Authority and its host country, the Government of Jamaica, in securing a supplementary agreement for the Authority's continued use of its headquarters.

As at 31 December, the Protocol on the Privileges and Immunities of the International Seabed Authority, adopted in 1998 [YUN 1998, p. 1226], had 28 signatories and six ratifications/accessions. The Protocol would enter into force 30 days after the date of deposit of the tenth instrument of ratification or accession.

International Tribunal for the Law of the Sea

The International Tribunal for the Law of the Sea held its eleventh (5-16 March) and twelfth (17-28 September) sessions, both in Hamburg, Germany [SPLOS/74].

Regarding its judicial work, the Tribunal, on 20 April, delivered its judgement in the *Grand Prince* case (*Belize v. France*) and its Order in the

MOX Plant case (*Ireland v. United Kingdom*). Following a provisional arrangement between Chile and the European Community in the case concerning the conservation and sustainable exploitation of swordfish stocks in the south-eastern Pacific Ocean, the Chamber suspended the proceedings by a 15 March Order. On 3 July, Panama filed against Yemen for the prompt release of the *Chaisiri Reefer 2*, a vessel flying the Panamanian flag, its cargo and crew. Following an agreement between the parties, the Tribunal, by a 13 July Order, discontinued the proceedings. Regarding the *M/V Saiga (No. 2)* case between Saint Vincent and the Grenadines and Guinea, Saint Vincent and the Grenadines informed the Tribunal on 12 April that the parties to the case had reached an amicable agreement on outstanding issues in respect of the Tribunal's judgement of 1 July 1999 [YUN 1999, p. 1246]. In the *Monte Confurco* case between Seychelles and France, Seychelles informed the Tribunal on 12 January of developments concerning judicial proceedings with respect to the vessel and the Master before French courts [YUN 2000, p. 1257].

The Agreement on the Privileges and Immunities of the International Tribunal for the Law of the Sea, adopted by the seventh Meeting of States Parties to the Convention on 23 May 1997 [YUN 1997, p. 1361], entered into force on 30 December 2001, 30 days after the deposit of the tenth instrument of ratification or accession.

The eleventh Meeting of States Parties to the Convention, in May, approved the Tribunal's budget for 2002, in the amount of $7,807,500.

Commission on the Limits of the Continental Shelf

In 2001, the Commission on the Limits of the Continental Shelf, established in 1997 [YUN 1997, p. 1362], held its ninth session (New York, 21-25 May) [CLCS/29]. The 21-member Commission reviewed existing training projects, the outline of a five-day training course for delineation of the outer limits of the continental shelf beyond 200 nautical miles, and the basic flow chart for preparation of submissions by coastal States to the Commission. It also discussed the decision of the eleventh Meeting of States Parties to the Convention regarding the date of commencement of the 10-year period for making submissions to the Commission (see p. 1231), and examined the Secretariat's technical and logistical preparedness to provide the Commission with assistance in respect to submissions of coastal States. The Commission reiterated its request to the Secretariat to issue a training manual on the preparation of a submission to assist the States concerned, particularly developing States.

Other developments related to the Convention

Report of Secretary-General. In response to resolution 55/7 [YUN 2000, p. 1258], the Secretary-General submitted to the General Assembly in March his annual report on oceans and the law of the sea [A/56/58 & Add.1], in which he described developments relating to the implementation of the Convention and its related Agreements. The Secretary-General drew attention to the continuing deterioration in the seas, citing such problems as the explosive growth of coastal cities, pollution, the exhaustion of fishing stocks, the destruction of marine habitats, the increase in shipping and crimes committed at sea, the registration of ships under a foreign flag and the ageing of the world's shipping fleet.

In addition to describing the issue of maritime space, including national claims to maritime zones and delimitation of maritime boundaries, the Secretary-General discussed shipping and navigation, and crimes at sea; marine resources, marine environment and sustainable development; the settlement of disputes; marine science and technology; capacity-building; international cooperation and coordination; and the Open-ended Informal Consultative Process on Oceans and the Law of the Sea (see below).

United Nations Open-ended Informal Consultative Process

The second meeting of the United Nations Open-ended Informal Consultative Process on Oceans and the Law of the Sea (New York, 7-11 May) [A/56/121] considered the annual report of the Secretary-General on oceans and the law of the sea and, as recommended by General Assembly resolution 55/7 [YUN 2000, p. 1258], discussed two topics: marine science and the development and transfer of marine technology as mutually agreed, including capacity-building in that regard; and coordination and cooperation in combating piracy and armed robbery at sea. The Consultative Process, which was established by Assembly resolution 54/33 [YUN 1999, p. 994], made a number of proposals on those topics for the Assembly's consideration. With regard to the third (2002) meeting of the Consultative Process, there was broad support for including capacity-building and the regional approach in oceans management and development, among other topics, as the focus of discussions.

GENERAL ASSEMBLY ACTION

On 28 November [meeting 67], the General Assembly adopted **resolution 56/12** [draft: A/56/L.17 & Add.1] by recorded vote (121-1-4) [agenda item 30 (a)].

Oceans and the law of the sea

The General Assembly,

Recalling its resolutions 49/28 of 6 December 1994, 52/26 of 26 November 1997, 54/33 of 24 November 1999, 55/7 of 30 October 2000 and other relevant resolutions adopted subsequent to the entry into force of the United Nations Convention on the Law of the Sea ("the Convention") on 16 November 1994,

Recalling also its resolution 2749(XXV) of 17 December 1970, and considering that the Convention, together with the Agreement relating to the Implementation of Part XI of the United Nations Convention on the Law of the Sea of 10 December 1982 ("the Agreement"), provides the regime to be applied to the Area and its resources as defined in the Convention,

Emphasizing the universal and unified character of the Convention and its fundamental importance for the maintenance and strengthening of international peace and security, as well as for the sustainable development of the oceans and seas,

Reaffirming that the Convention sets out the legal framework within which all activities in the oceans and seas must be carried out and is of strategic importance as the basis for national, regional and global action in the marine sector, and that its integrity needs to be maintained, as recognized also by the United Nations Conference on Environment and Development in chapter 17 of Agenda 21,

Conscious of the importance of increasing the number of States parties to the Convention and the Agreement in order to achieve the goal of universal participation,

Conscious also that the problems of ocean space are closely interrelated and need to be considered as a whole through an integrated, interdisciplinary and intersectoral approach,

Convinced of the need, building on arrangements established in accordance with the Convention, to improve coordination at the national level and cooperation and coordination at both intergovernmental and inter-agency levels, in order to address all aspects of oceans and seas in an integrated manner,

Recognizing the important role that the competent international organizations have in relation to ocean affairs, in implementing the Convention and in promoting the sustainable development of the oceans and seas,

Recalling that the role of international cooperation and coordination on a bilateral basis and, where applicable, within a subregional, interregional, regional or global framework is to support and supplement the national efforts of all States, including coastal States, to promote the integrated management and sustainable development of coastal and marine areas,

Mindful of the importance of the oceans and seas for the earth's ecosystem and for providing the vital resources for food security and for sustaining economic prosperity and the well-being of present and future generations,

Bearing in mind the contribution that major groups, as identified in Agenda 21, can make to raising awareness of the goal of the sustainable development of the oceans and seas,

Underlining once again the essential need for capacity-building to ensure that all States, especially developing countries, in particular least developed countries and small island developing States, are able both to implement the Convention and to benefit from the sustainable development of the oceans and seas, as well as to participate fully in global and regional forums and processes dealing with oceans and law of the sea issues,

Taking note of the report of the Secretary-General, and reaffirming the importance of the annual consideration and review of developments relating to ocean affairs and the law of the sea by the General Assembly as the global institution having the competence to undertake such a review,

Taking note also of the report on the work of the United Nations Open-ended Informal Consultative Process ("the Consultative Process") established by the General Assembly in its resolution 54/33 in order to facilitate the annual review by the Assembly of developments in ocean affairs at its second meeting,

Bearing in mind that marine science, by improving knowledge, through sustained research efforts and the evaluation of monitoring results, and applying such knowledge to management and decision-making, is important for eradicating poverty, contributing to food security, conserving the world's marine environment and resources, helping to understand, predict, mitigate the effects of and respond to natural events, and promoting the sustainable development of the oceans and seas,

Reaffirming the need to achieve the effective application of marine scientific knowledge and technology, through cooperation at the regional and global levels, by ensuring access of decision makers to relevant advice and information, as well as to the transfer of technology and support for the production and diffusion of factual data and knowledge for end-users, as appropriate, taking fully into account socio-economic factors and traditional ecological knowledge,

Emphasizing the urgent need for cooperation at the international level to address the issue of the acquisition, generation and transfer of marine scientific data to assist coastal developing States,

Convinced of the need to develop, where appropriate, a strong regional focus in marine scientific research and technology, through existing regional organizations, arrangements and programmes, so as to ensure the most effective use of the available resources and the protection and preservation of the marine environment, particularly by avoiding duplication and by achieving a holistic approach to the scientific study of the oceans and their resources,

Expressing deep concern once again at the continued increase in the number of incidents of piracy and armed robbery at sea, the harm they cause to seafarers, and the threats they pose to the safety of shipping and to the other uses of the sea, including marine scientific research and, consequently, to the marine and coastal environment, which are exacerbated further by the involvement of transnational organized crime,

Emphasizing, in this context, the need for the capacity-building and cooperation of all States and relevant international bodies at both the regional and global levels, as well as the business sectors, to prevent and combat piracy and armed robbery at sea,

Recognizing the importance of enhancing the safety of navigation, the need to provide accurate and up-to-date charts of world oceans in order to promote maritime safety, and the need to build hydrographic capacity, in particular for those States that do not yet have adequate hydrographic services,

Reiterating its serious concern at the increase in illegal, unreported and unregulated fishing, and recognizing the importance of combating such activities, particularly by strengthening bilateral cooperation, as well as through the relevant regional fisheries management organizations and arrangements, and through the implementation of appropriate enforcement measures,

Expressing its deep concern once again at the degradation of the marine environment, particularly from land-based activities, and emphasizing the need for international cooperation and for a coordinated approach at the national and regional levels to this problem, bringing together the many different economic sectors involved in protecting the ecosystems, and in this context reaffirming the importance of ensuring the full implementation of the Global Programme of Action for the Protection of the Marine Environment from Land-based Activities,

Reiterating its concern also at the adverse impacts on the marine environment from ships, including pollution, in particular through the illegal release of oil and other harmful substances and by the dumping of hazardous waste, including radioactive materials, nuclear waste and dangerous chemicals, as well as the physical impacts on coral,

Welcoming resolution GC(45)/RES/10 adopted on 21 September 2001 by the General Conference of the International Atomic Energy Agency at its forty-fifth regular session, concerning measures to strengthen international cooperation in nuclear, radiation, transport and waste safety, including those aspects relating to maritime transport safety,

Bearing in mind the World Summit on Sustainable Development, to be held in Johannesburg, South Africa, in 2002, and emphasizing the importance, in the preparations for the Summit, of addressing the sustainable development of oceans and seas,

Noting the responsibilities of the Secretary-General under the Convention and related resolutions of the General Assembly, in particular resolutions 49/28, 52/26 and 54/33, and in this context the expected increase in responsibilities of the Division for Ocean Affairs and the Law of the Sea of the Office of Legal Affairs of the Secretariat in view of the progress in the work of the Commission on the Limits of the Continental Shelf ("the Commission") and the anticipated receipt of submissions from States,

I. Implementation of the Convention

1. *Calls upon* all States that have not done so, in order to achieve the goal of universal participation, to become parties to the Convention and the Agreement;

2. *Reaffirms* the unified character of the Convention;

3. *Calls upon* States to harmonize, as a matter of priority, their national legislation with the provisions of the Convention, to ensure the consistent application of those provisions and to ensure also that any declarations or statements that they have made or make when signing, ratifying or acceding to the Convention are in conformity therewith and, otherwise, to withdraw any of their declarations or statements that are not in conformity;

4. *Encourages* States parties to the Convention to deposit with the Secretary-General charts and lists of geographical coordinates, as provided for in the Convention;

5. *Takes note* of the imminent entry into force of the Agreement for the Implementation of the Provisions of the United Nations Convention on the Law of the Sea of 10 December 1982 relating to the Conservation and Management of Straddling Fish Stocks and Highly Migratory Fish Stocks;

II. Capacity-building

6. *Urges* the international community to assist, as appropriate, developing countries, in particular least developed countries and small island developing States, in the acquisition of data and the preparation of charts or lists of geographical coordinates for publication under articles 16, 22, 47, 75 and 84 of the Convention and in the preparation of information under article 76 and annex II to the Convention;

7. *Calls upon* bilateral and multilateral donor agencies to keep their programmes systematically under review to ensure the availability in all States, particularly in developing States, of the economic, legal, navigational, scientific and technical skills necessary for the full implementation of the Convention and the sustainable development of the oceans and seas nationally, regionally and globally, and in so doing to bear in mind the rights of landlocked developing States;

8. *Requests* the Secretary-General, in cooperation with the competent international organizations and programmes, including the Food and Agriculture Organization of the United Nations, the International Labour Organization, the International Hydrographic Organization, the International Maritime Organization, the United Nations Development Programme, the United Nations Industrial Development Organization, the Intergovernmental Oceanographic Commission of the United Nations Educational, Scientific and Cultural Organization, the United Nations Environment Programme, the United Nations Conference on Trade and Development, the World Meteorological Organization and the World Bank, as well as representatives of regional development banks and the donor community, to review the efforts being made to build capacity as well as to identify the duplications that need to be avoided and the gaps that may need to be filled for ensuring consistent approaches, both nationally and regionally, with a view to implementing the Convention, and to include a section on this subject in his annual report on oceans and the law of the sea;

III. Meeting of States Parties

9. *Requests* the Secretary-General to convene the twelfth Meeting of States Parties to the Convention in New York from 16 to 26 April 2002 and to provide the services required;

IV. Settlement of disputes

10. *Notes with satisfaction* the continued contribution of the International Tribunal for the Law of the Sea ("the Tribunal") to the peaceful settlement of disputes in accordance with Part XV of the Convention, underlines its important role and authority concerning the interpretation or application of the Convention and the Agreement, encourages States parties to the Convention to consider making a written declaration choosing from the means set out in article 287 for the settlement of disputes concerning the interpretation or application of the Convention and the Agreement, and invites States to note the provisions of annexes V, VI, VII and VIII to the Convention concerning, respectively, conciliation, the Tribunal, arbitration and special arbitration;

11. *Recalls* the obligations of parties under article 296 of the Convention, in cases before a court or a tribunal referred to in article 287 of the Convention, to ensure prompt compliance with the decisions rendered by such court or tribunal;

12. *Encourages* States that have not yet done so to nominate conciliators and arbitrators in accordance with annexes V and VII to the Convention, and requests the Secretary-General to continue to update and circulate lists of these conciliators and arbitrators on a regular basis;

V. The Area

13. *Notes with satisfaction* the ongoing work of the International Seabed Authority ("the Authority"), including the issuance of contracts for exploration in accordance with the Convention, the Agreement and the Regulations on Prospecting and Exploration for Polymetallic Nodules in the Area;

14. *Notes* the ongoing elaboration of recommendations for the guidance of contractors to ensure the effective protection of the marine environment from harmful effects that may arise from activities in the Area, and notes that the Council of the Authority will continue to consider issues relating to regulations for prospecting and exploration for polymetallic sulphides and cobalt-rich crusts in the Area at the next session of the Authority, to be held in Kingston from 5 to 16 August 2002;

VI. Effective functioning of the Authority and the Tribunal

15. *Appeals* to all States parties to the Convention to pay their assessed contributions to the Authority and to the Tribunal in full and on time, and appeals also to all former provisional members of the Authority to pay any outstanding contributions;

16. *Calls upon* States that have not done so to consider ratifying or acceding to the Agreement on the Privileges and Immunities of the Tribunal and to the Protocol on the Privileges and Immunities of the Authority;

VII. The continental shelf

17. *Notes with satisfaction* the work of the Commission and its readiness to receive submissions by coastal States regarding the establishment of the outer limits of their continental shelf beyond 200 nautical miles, and encourages concerned States and relevant international organizations and institutions to consider developing and making available training courses to assist States in the preparation of such submissions;

18. *Takes note* of the decision of the eleventh Meeting of States Parties to the Convention that, in the case of a State party for which the Convention entered into force before 13 May 1999, it is understood that the ten-year time period referred to in article 4 of annex II to the Convention shall be taken to have commenced on 13 May 1999;

19. *Encourages* States parties that are in a position to do so to make every effort to make submissions to the

Commission within the time period established by the Convention;

20. *Approves* the convening by the Secretary-General of the tenth session of the Commission in New York starting on 25 March 2002, of a duration of three weeks in the event of a submission being filed, or of one week, depending on the workload of the Commission, of the eleventh session from 24 to 28 June 2002, and of the twelfth session from 26 to 30 August 2002;

VIII.   Marine science and technology

21. *Stresses* the importance of the issues of marine science and technology and the need to focus on how best to implement the many obligations of States and competent international organizations under Parts XIII and XIV of the Convention, and calls upon States to adopt, as appropriate and in accordance with international law, such national laws, regulations, policies and procedures as are necessary to promote and facilitate marine scientific research and cooperation, especially those relating to consent for marine scientific research projects as provided for in the Convention;

22. *Calls upon* States, through national and regional institutions, to ensure that, in respect of marine scientific research conducted pursuant to Part XIII of the Convention in areas over which a coastal State has jurisdiction, the rights of the coastal State under the Convention are respected and that, at the request of the coastal State, information, reports, results, conclusions and assessments of data, samples and research results are made available, and access to data and samples are provided, to that coastal State;

23. *Invites* the Intergovernmental Oceanographic Commission of the United Nations Educational, Scientific and Cultural Organization to request its Advisory Body of Experts on the Law of the Sea to work, in close cooperation with the Division for Ocean Affairs and the Law of the Sea of the Office of Legal Affairs of the Secretariat and in consultation with relevant regional or subregional organizations as appropriate, on the development of procedures under Part XIII of the Convention;

24. *Invites* the relevant United Nations agencies to continue to promote various ocean science programmes, strengthen the coordination among such programmes and develop rules, regulations and procedures within the framework of the Convention so as to facilitate the effective implementation of the programmes;

25. *Urges* relevant bodies of the United Nations system to develop, with the Intergovernmental Oceanographic Commission acting as a focal point, appropriate interactions in the field of marine science with regional fisheries organizations, environmental and scientific bodies or regional centres foreseen by Part XIV of the Convention, and encourages States to establish, where appropriate, such regional centres;

26. *Calls upon* States, through national and regional institutions engaged in marine scientific research, to ensure that the knowledge resulting from marine scientific research and monitoring is made available in a user-friendly data format, especially to developing countries, so that it can be employed by decision makers and resource managers with a view to the effective application of marine research knowledge and technology;

27. *Stresses* the importance of increasing the scientific understanding of the oceans/atmosphere interface and other factors required for an integrated ecosystem-based approach to the management of oceans and coastal areas, including through participation in ocean observing programmes and geographic information systems;

28. *Calls upon* States, through bilateral, regional and international financial organizations and technical partnerships, to continue to strengthen capacity-building activities, in particular in developing countries, in the field of marine scientific research by, inter alia, training the necessary skilled personnel, providing the necessary equipment, facilities and vessels, and transferring environmentally sound technologies;

IX.   Piracy and armed robbery

29. *Urges* all States and relevant international bodies to prevent and combat piracy and armed robbery at sea by adopting measures, including assisting with capacity-building, for prevention, for reporting and investigating incidents, and for bringing the alleged perpetrators to justice, in accordance with international law, in particular through training seafarers, port staff and enforcement personnel, providing enforcement vessels and equipment and guarding against fraudulent ship registration;

30. *Welcomes* initiatives of the International Maritime Organization and Governments aimed at enhancing international cooperation, particularly at the regional level, and encourages the development by Governments, based on mutual trust, of a common approach to enforcement, investigation and prosecution in dealing with piracy and armed robbery at sea;

31. *Calls upon* States and private entities concerned to cooperate fully with the International Maritime Organization, including by submitting reports on incidents to the organization and by implementing its guidelines on preventing attacks of piracy and armed robbery;

32. *Urges* States to become parties to the Convention for the Suppression of Unlawful Acts against the Safety of Maritime Navigation and its Protocol, and to ensure its effective implementation, in particular through the adoption of legislation, where appropriate, aimed at ensuring that there is a proper framework for responses to incidents of armed robbery at sea;

X.   Safety of navigation

33. *Invites* the International Hydrographic Organization, in cooperation with other relevant international organizations and interested Member States, to provide the necessary assistance to States, in particular to developing countries, in order to enhance hydrographic capability to ensure, in particular, the safety of navigation and the protection of the marine environment;

XI.   Marine environment, marine resources and sustainable development

34. *Welcomes* the adoption by the Committee on Fisheries of the Food and Agriculture Organization of the United Nations of the International Plan of Action to Prevent, Deter and Eliminate Illegal, Unreported and Unregulated Fishing, and urges States to take, as a matter of priority, all necessary steps to implement it effectively, including through relevant regional and

subregional fisheries management organizations and arrangements;

35. *Emphasizes once again* the importance of the implementation of Part XII of the Convention in order to protect and preserve the marine environment and its living marine resources against pollution and physical degradation, and calls upon all States to cooperate and take measures, directly or through competent international organizations, for the protection and preservation of the marine environment;

36. *Calls upon* States to continue to prioritize action on marine pollution from land-based sources as part of their national sustainable development strategies and programmes, in an integrated and inclusive manner, as a means of implementing the Global Programme of Action for the Protection of the Marine Environment from Land-based Activities, and takes note of the review by the intergovernmental meeting in Montreal, Canada, from 26 to 30 November 2001;

37. *Calls upon* United Nations agencies and programmes identified in General Assembly resolution 51/189 of 16 December 1996 to continue to fulfil their roles in support of the Global Programme of Action, as well as to consult with Governments, representatives of the private sector, financial institutions and bilateral and multilateral donor agencies to review their involvement in the implementation of the Global Programme of Action and to consider, inter alia, what international support is needed to help overcome the obstacles to the preparation and implementation of national and local action programmes and how they can participate actively in partnership-building with developing countries for the transfer of the requisite technology in accordance with the Convention, and taking into account the relevant parts of Agenda 21, capacity-building and funding for the implementation of the Global Programme of Action;

38. *Calls upon* States to take measures for the protection and preservation of coral reefs and to support international efforts in this regard, in particular the measures outlined in the 1998 Renewed Call to Action of the International Coral Reef Initiative and in decision V/3 adopted by the Conference of the Parties to the Convention on Biological Diversity at its fifth meeting, held in Nairobi from 15 to 26 May 2000;

39. *Emphasizes* the importance of ensuring that adverse impacts on the marine environment are taken into account when assessing and evaluating development programmes and projects;

40. *Once again urges* States to take all practicable steps, in accordance with the International Convention for the Prevention of Pollution from Ships, 1973, as modified by the Protocol of 1978 relating thereto, to prevent pollution of the marine environment from ships and, in accordance with the 1972 Convention on the Prevention of Marine Pollution by Dumping of Wastes and Other Matter, to prevent pollution of the marine environment by dumping, and further calls upon States to become parties to and to implement the 1996 Protocol to the 1972 Convention;

41. *Urges* States to continue to work, through the International Maritime Organization, on issues relating to the protection of the marine environment from degradation resulting from ship-based activities, including the transfer of harmful aquatic organisms and pathogens through ships' ballast water, and notes the adop-

tion of the International Convention on the Control of Harmful Anti-fouling Systems on Ships;

42. *Encourages* coastal States to enhance their national capacity and establish or improve their marine management systems in order to promote integrated marine management, the protection of the marine environment and ecosystem, and the sustainable development and utilization of marine resources, and invites the relevant agencies of the United Nations system and regional organizations to take effective measures to assist the coastal States in this regard;

XII. Underwater cultural heritage

43. *Takes note* of the adoption by the United Nations Educational, Scientific and Cultural Organization of the Convention on the Protection of the Underwater Cultural Heritage;

XIII. Activities of the Division for Ocean Affairs and the Law of the Sea

44. *Invites* Member States and others in a position to do so to contribute to the further development of the Hamilton Shirley Amerasinghe Memorial Fellowship Programme on the Law of the Sea established by the General Assembly in its resolution 35/116 of 10 December 1980 and to support the training activities under the TRAIN-SEA-COAST Programme of the Division for Ocean Affairs and the Law of the Sea;

45. *Expresses its appreciation* to the Secretary-General for the annual comprehensive report on oceans and the law of the sea, prepared by the Division for Ocean Affairs and the Law of the Sea, as well as for the other activities of the Division, in accordance with the provisions of the Convention and the mandate set forth in resolutions 49/28, 52/26 and 54/33;

46. *Requests* the Secretary-General to continue to carry out the responsibilities entrusted to him in the Convention and related resolutions of the General Assembly, including resolutions 49/28 and 52/26, and to ensure that appropriate resources are made available to the Division for Ocean Affairs and the Law of the Sea for the performance of such responsibilities under the approved budget for the Organization;

XIV. International coordination and cooperation

47. *Reaffirms* its decision to undertake an annual review and evaluation of the implementation of the Convention and other developments relating to ocean affairs and the law of the sea, taking into account resolution 54/33 establishing the consultative process to facilitate the review of developments in ocean affairs, and requests the Secretary-General to convene the third meeting of the Consultative Process in New York from 8 to 15 April 2002;

48. *Recommends* that, in view of the forthcoming World Summit on Sustainable Development, in its deliberations on the report of the Secretary-General on oceans and the law of the sea at its third meeting, the Consultative Process organize its discussions around the following areas:

(*a*) Protection and preservation of the marine environment;

(*b*) Capacity-building, regional cooperation and coordination, and integrated ocean management, as important cross-cutting issues to address ocean affairs, such as marine science and the transfer of technology, sustainable fisheries, the degradation of the marine environment and the safety of navigation;

49. *Requests* the Secretary-General to ensure more effective collaboration and coordination between the relevant parts of the Secretariat of the United Nations and the United Nations as a whole, in particular in ensuring the effectiveness, transparency and responsiveness of the mechanism for coordination on ocean issues, and also requests the Secretary-General to include in his report specific suggestions on initiatives to improve coordination, in particular at the inter-agency level, in accordance with resolution 54/33, and encourages all United Nations bodies to help this process by drawing to the attention of the Secretariat and the Subcommittee on Oceans and Coastal Areas of the Administrative Committee on Coordination those areas of their work which may, directly or indirectly, affect the work of other United Nations bodies;

50. *Also requests* the Secretary-General to bring the present resolution to the attention of heads of intergovernmental organizations, the specialized agencies and funds and programmes of the United Nations engaged in activities relating to ocean affairs and the law of the sea, drawing their attention to paragraphs of particular relevance to them, and underlines the importance of their constructive and timely input for the report of the Secretary-General on oceans and the law of the sea and of their participation in relevant meetings and processes;

51. *Invites* the competent international organizations, as well as funding institutions, to take specific account of the present resolution in their programmes and activities, and to contribute to the preparation of the comprehensive report of the Secretary-General on oceans and the law of the sea;

XV. Trust funds

52. *Recognizes* the importance of the trust funds established by the Secretary-General pursuant to General Assembly resolution 55/7 for the purpose of assisting States in the settlement of disputes through the Tribunal, and of assisting developing countries, in particular the least developed countries and small island developing States, in the preparation of submissions to the Commission in compliance with article 76 of the Convention, in defraying the cost of participation of Commission members in the meetings of the Commission, and in attending the meetings of the Consultative Process; and invites States, intergovernmental organizations and agencies, national institutions, nongovernmental organizations and international financial institutions, as well as natural and juridical persons, to make voluntary financial or other contributions to these trust funds;

XVI. Fifty-seventh session of the General Assembly

53. *Decides* to devote two days of plenary meetings at the fifty-seventh session of the General Assembly, on 9 and 10 December 2002, to the consideration of the item entitled "Oceans and the law of the sea" and the commemoration of the twentieth anniversary of the opening for signature of the Convention, and encourages Member States and observers to be represented at the highest possible level;

54. *Requests* the Secretary-General to report to the General Assembly at its fifty-seventh session on the implementation of the present resolution, including other developments and issues relating to ocean affairs and the law of the sea, in connection with his annual comprehensive report on oceans and the law of the sea, and to provide the report in accordance with the modalities set out in resolution 54/33;

55. *Decides* to include in the provisional agenda of its fifty-seventh session the item entitled "Oceans and the law of the sea".

RECORDED VOTE ON RESOLUTION 56/12:

In favour: Afghanistan, Algeria, Andorra, Angola, Argentina, Armenia, Australia, Austria, Bahamas, Bahrain, Bangladesh, Barbados, Belgium, Belize, Bolivia, Botswana, Brazil, Brunei Darussalam, Bulgaria, Cameroon, Canada, Chile, China, Comoros, Croatia, Cuba, Cyprus, Czech Republic, Denmark, Dominican Republic, Egypt, Equatorial Guinea, Eritrea, Estonia, Fiji, Finland, France, Georgia, Germany, Ghana, Greece, Guatemala, Guyana, Hungary, Iceland, India, Iran, Ireland, Israel, Italy, Jamaica, Japan, Kazakhstan, Kenya, Kuwait, Lao People's Democratic Republic, Lebanon, Libyan Arab Jamahiriya, Liechtenstein, Lithuania, Luxembourg, Madagascar, Malaysia, Maldives, Mali, Malta, Mauritius, Mexico, Micronesia, Monaco, Mongolia, Morocco, Mozambique, Myanmar, Nauru, Nepal, Netherlands, New Zealand, Nicaragua, Nigeria, Norway, Oman, Pakistan, Panama, Papua New Guinea, Philippines, Poland, Portugal, Qatar, Republic of Korea, Republic of Moldova, Romania, Russian Federation, Saint Kitts and Nevis, Saint Lucia, Samoa, San Marino, Saudi Arabia, Senegal, Sierra Leone, Singapore, Slovakia, Slovenia, Spain, Sri Lanka, Suriname, Sweden, Thailand, The former Yugoslav Republic of Macedonia, Togo, Tonga, Trinidad and Tobago, Tuvalu, Ukraine, United Kingdom, United Republic of Tanzania, United States, Uruguay, Viet Nam, Yugoslavia, Zambia.

Against: Turkey.

Abstaining: Colombia, Ecuador, Peru, Venezuela.

Division for Ocean Affairs and the Law of the Sea

During 2001, the Division for Ocean Affairs and the Law of the Sea of the Office of Legal Affairs continued to fulfil its role as the substantive unit of the Secretariat responsible for reviewing and monitoring all developments related to the law of the sea and ocean affairs, as well as for the implementation of the Convention and related General Assembly resolutions.

The Division provided input for two training courses under its TRAIN-SEA-COAST (TSC) programme [YUN 1998, p. 1232], designed to build up in-country capacity to improve skills in integrated ocean and coastal management. Environmental officers, government officials and environmental specialists attended the courses on pollution control in the Benguela current ecosystem and on the management of marine protected areas in the Red Sea and Gulf of Aden region.

The sixteenth Hamilton Shirley Amerasinghe Memorial Fellowship, established in 1981 [YUN 1981, p. 139], was presented to Kamran Hashemi of Iran, and the fourth Special Fellowship award, funded by a grant from the United Kingdom, was presented to Boris Danailov of Bulgaria.

Chapter V

Other legal questions

The Special Committee on the Charter of the United Nations and on the Strengthening of the Role of the Organization continued in 2001 to consider, among its other standing agenda items, proposals relating to the maintenance of international peace and security in order to strengthen the Organization and, as a priority, the implementation of Charter provisions on assistance to third States affected by the application of sanctions under Chapter VII. In that connection, the Security Council, in October, discussed general issues relating to sanctions aimed at, not only improving the effectiveness of UN sanctions, but also reducing their negative effects on civilian populations and on third States.

The Committee on Relations with the Host Country continued to address complaints raised by permanent missions to the United Nations relating to the maintenance of conditions for the proper functioning of those missions. The General Assembly requested the host country (the United States) to consider, among other measures, removing travel controls on permanent mission and Secretariat staff of certain nationalities, issuing entry visas in a timely manner to representatives of Member States for the purpose of attending UN official meetings and taking steps to resolve the problem relating to the parking of diplomatic vehicles.

During the year, two instruments emanated from the continuing work of the United Nations Commission on International Trade Law (UNCITRAL) aimed at the global unification and harmonization of international trade law: the draft Convention on the Assignment of Receivables in International Trade; and the UNCITRAL Model Law on Electronic Signatures, together with the Guide to Enactment of the Model Law. On 12 December, the Assembly took note of UNCITRAL's completion and adoption of those instruments, recommended that all States give favourable consideration to the Model Law and Guide to Enactment when enacting or revising their laws, and adopted and opened the Convention for signature or accession.

In other action, the Assembly, concerned at the recently disclosed information on ongoing research into the reproductive cloning of human beings, established an ad hoc committee to consider the elaboration of an international convention against such cloning.

International organizations and international law

Strengthening the role of the United Nations

Special Committee on UN Charter

In accordance with General Assembly resolution 55/156 [YUN 2000, p. 1268], the Special Committee on the Charter of the United Nations and on the Strengthening of the Role of the Organization, during its meetings in New York from 2 to 12 April 2001 [A/56/33], continued to consider proposals relating to: the maintenance of international peace and security, according priority to the implementation of the provisions of the Charter of the United Nations on assistance to third States affected by the application of sanctions; the peaceful settlement of disputes between States; the future of the Trusteeship Council; the improvement of the Committee's working methods; and the publications *Repertory of Practice of United Nations Organs* and *Repertoire of the Practice of the Security Council.*

Under the first item, the working group of the whole, established by the Committee, completed the first paragraph-by-paragraph reading of the proposed revised basic conditions and standard criteria for the imposition of sanctions and other coercive measures submitted by the Russian Federation (2000), requested a recasting of five paragraphs and indicated that the text might require further readings. A paper on strengthening principles concerning the impact and application of sanctions was presented by the Libyan Arab Jamahiriya (2001), which addressed sanctions as a last resort, the financial or economic burdens sustained by the target State beyond those resulting from direct sanctions application, and that State's right to claim for damages resulting from sanctions imposed or applied illegally. The sponsor raised specific problems with regard to current sanctions regimes, which it said were not immutable, and was interested in answers to those problems.

Debate continued on the Russian Federation's working paper (1998), aimed at the elaboration of legal parameters for peacekeeping operations in the context of Chapter VI (pacific settlement of disputes) of the Charter. It was pointed out that the issues raised in the proposal, for years on the Committee's agenda, could be addressed by other more competent bodies that had already covered those issues thoroughly. The sponsor could therefore withdraw the proposal and submit it to another body; or, if it had acquired the status of a Committee document, the Committee could request the Assembly, through the Sixth (Legal) Committee, to submit it to another body.

Cuba reiterated the viability of its proposal for strengthening the role and effectiveness of the United Nations (1998), which was concerned with the revitalization of the Assembly's role in terms not only of efficiency but also of democratization, stating that the Assembly was the only body with universal membership and no veto power. While that proposal and a Libyan revised proposal (2001) were aimed at enhancing coordination between the Assembly and the Security Council and focused on issues on which both bodies had a common responsibility, the Libyan proposal was more concerned with improving the Council's working methods to ensure objectivity, effectiveness and transparency. The view was expressed that double standards in the application of the Charter provisions in Chapter VII (action with respect to threats to the peace, breaches of the peace and acts of aggression), particularly with regard to sanctions imposition and implementation, undermined the Council's credibility. The need to restore balance between the Council and the Assembly, which could be achieved only through structural reforms of the Council, was pointed out, as was the fact that some of the proposal's aspects had been subsumed in the work of the body currently considering the Council's reform (see p. 1287).

Discussion of the joint Belarus and Russian Federation working paper requesting an advisory opinion from the International Court of Justice (ICJ) (1999) on the legal consequences of the resort to the use of force by States, either without prior Council authorization or outside the context of self-defence, resulted in a revised draft text by the sponsors reiterating the importance of an ICJ advisory opinion. The point was made that, if consensus could not be reached in the Committee, the request could be submitted directly to the Assembly, which would, however, require explicit Council authorization. On the other hand, the Assembly was empowered by Article 96 of the Charter to request an advisory opinion from ICJ on any legal question.

As to the item on the peaceful settlement of disputes, a working paper, jointly submitted by Sierra Leone and the United Kingdom (2000) containing a revised draft resolution on dispute prevention and settlement, was further revised and submitted (2001) by the sponsors. The working group undertook a paragraph-by-paragraph reading of the preambular section; the operative paragraphs were not taken up, however, due to lack of time.

On the future of the Trusteeship Council, Malta reiterated its proposal (1995) that a revised Trusteeship Council would act in trust to safeguard the environment, protect the global commons and monitor the governance of the oceans, providing impetus for international environmental governance and coordination. Such a change, it was pointed out, would entail an amendment to the Charter, which should be considered in the context of the Charter's revision and reform of the Organization. One view held that serious consideration should be given to removing the Trusteeship Council from the UN books.

The Special Committee's working methods were debated on the basis of a revised working paper submitted by Japan (2000), which included proposals for making the best use of the Committee's conference resources; the advance submission of action-oriented proposals; avoiding duplication of discussions that were ongoing in other forums; a preliminary evaluation of new proposals; a mechanism to enable the Committee to decide whether to continue discussion of proposals already debated; and the duration of the Committee's meetings, the periodic review of its working methods, including the consideration of proposals on a biennial basis, and procedural improvements for the adoption of its reports. Following an exchange of views on the paper, Japan said it would consult with the Bureau and interested delegations on the working paper's future, taking account of the suggestions made.

With respect to the identification of new subjects for the Committee's consideration, the following topics were proposed for inclusion in a possible middle-term work programme: basic conditions of "provisional measures" employed by the Council under Article 40 of the Charter; clarification of the term "threat to international peace and security"; ways to overcome the negative consequences of globalization and ensure the supremacy of law in international relations; and applicability of the Charter provisions to the concept of "humanitarian intervention".

As to the *Repertory of Practice of United Nations Organs* and *Repertoire of the Practice of the Security Council,* the Secretary-General's ongoing efforts to reduce the backlog in their publication were commended. According to one view, the Assembly should consider further ways of providing financial and other assistance to the Secretariat to enable the speedy updating of those publications.

Report of Secretary-General. As called for by General Assembly resolution 55/156 [YUN 2000, p. 1268], the Secretary-General reported in September [A/56/330] on steps taken by the Secretariat to expedite the preparation of the Supplements to the *Repertory* and *Repertoire,* on the up-to-date status of those publications and on ongoing action to eliminate the existing production backlogs. The report indicated that a pilot project, begun in 2000, to place the *Repertory* on the Internet continued and a web site for it would be established during the 2002-2003 biennium; the *Repertoire* was available on the Internet on the UN Department of Political Affairs web site. In addition, contributions in the amount of $364,181 to the trust fund for the updating of the *Repertoire* were received from six Member States and one Permanent Observer.

GENERAL ASSEMBLY ACTION

On 12 December [meeting 85], the General Assembly, on the recommendation of the Sixth Committee [A/56/592], adopted **resolution 56/86** without vote [agenda item 165].

Report of the Special Committee on the Charter of the United Nations and on the Strengthening of the Role of the Organization
The General Assembly,
Recalling its resolution 3499(XXX) of 15 December 1975, by which it established the Special Committee on the Charter of the United Nations and on the Strengthening of the Role of the Organization, and its relevant resolutions adopted at subsequent sessions,
Recalling also its resolution 47/233 of 17 August 1993 on the revitalization of the work of the General Assembly,
Recalling further its resolution 47/62 of 11 December 1992 on the question of equitable representation on and increase in the membership of the Security Council,
Taking note of the report of the Open-ended Working Group on the Question of Equitable Representation on and Increase in the Membership of the Security Council and Other Matters Related to the Security Council,
Recalling the elements relevant to the work of the Special Committee contained in its resolution 47/120 B of 20 September 1993,
Recalling also its resolution 51/241 of 31 July 1997 on the strengthening of the United Nations system and its resolution 51/242 of 15 September 1997, entitled "Supplement to an Agenda for Peace", by which it adopted

the texts on coordination and the question of sanctions imposed by the United Nations, which are annexed to that resolution,
Recalling further that the International Court of Justice is the principal judicial organ of the United Nations, and reaffirming its authority and independence,
Considering the desirability of finding practical ways and means to strengthen the Court, taking into consideration, in particular, the needs resulting from its increased workload,
Taking note of the report of the Secretary-General on the *Repertory of Practice of United Nations Organs* and the *Repertoire of the Practice of the Security Council,*
Recalling its resolution 55/156 of 12 December 2000,
Having considered the report of the Special Committee on the work of its session held in 2001,
1. *Takes note* of the report of the Special Committee on the Charter of the United Nations and on the Strengthening of the Role of the Organization;
2. *Decides* that the Special Committee shall hold its next session from 18 to 28 March 2002;
3. *Requests* the Special Committee, at its session in 2002, in accordance with paragraph 5 of General Assembly resolution 50/52 of 11 December 1995:
(*a*) To continue its consideration of all proposals concerning the question of the maintenance of international peace and security in all its aspects in order to strengthen the role of the United Nations and, in this context, to consider other proposals relating to the maintenance of international peace and security already submitted or which may be submitted to the Special Committee at its session in 2002;
(*b*) To continue to consider on a priority basis the question of the implementation of the provisions of the Charter of the United Nations related to assistance to third States affected by the application of sanctions under Chapter VII of the Charter by commencing a substantive debate on all of the related reports of the Secretary-General, the proposals submitted on this subject, taking into consideration the debate on the question held by the Sixth Committee at the fifty-sixth session of the General Assembly and the text on the question of sanctions imposed by the United Nations contained in annex II to Assembly resolution 51/242, and also the implementation of the provisions of Assembly resolutions 50/51 of 11 December 1995, 51/208 of 17 December 1996, 52/162 of 15 December 1997, 53/107 of 8 December 1998, 54/107 of 9 December 1999 and 55/157 of 12 December 2000;
(*c*) To continue its work on the question of the peaceful settlement of disputes between States and, in this context, to continue its consideration of proposals relating thereto, including the proposal on the establishment of a dispute settlement service offering or responding with its services early in disputes and those proposals relating to the enhancement of the role of the International Court of Justice, with a view to completing, if possible, its consideration of these proposals;
(*d*) To continue to consider proposals concerning the Trusteeship Council in the light of the report of the Secretary-General submitted in accordance with General Assembly resolution 50/55 of 11 December 1995, the report of the Secretary-General entitled "Renewing the United Nations: a programme for reform" and

the views expressed by States on this subject at previous sessions of the General Assembly;

(e) To continue to consider, on a priority basis, ways and means of improving its working methods and enhancing its efficiency with a view to identifying widely acceptable measures for future implementation;

4. *Takes note* of paragraph 47 of the report of the Secretary-General, commends the Secretary-General for his continued efforts to reduce the backlog in the publication of the *Repertory of Practice of United Nations Organs*, and endorses the efforts of the Secretary-General to eliminate the backlog in the publication of the *Repertoire of the Practice of the Security Council*;

5. *Invites* the Special Committee at its session in 2002 to continue to identify new subjects for consideration in its future work with a view to contributing to the revitalization of the work of the United Nations;

6. *Takes note* of the readiness of the Special Committee, in the context of its consideration of the subject of assistance to working groups on the revitalization of the work of the United Nations and coordination between the Special Committee and other working groups dealing with the reform of the Organization, to provide, within its mandate, such assistance as may be sought at the request of other subsidiary bodies of the General Assembly in relation to any issues before them;

7. *Requests* the Special Committee to submit a report on its work to the General Assembly at its fifty-seventh session;

8. *Decides* to include in the provisional agenda of its fifty-seventh session the item entitled "Report of the Special Committee on the Charter of the United Nations and on the Strengthening of the Role of the Organization".

Charter provisions relating to sanctions

Special Committee consideration. At the Special Committee's discussion on the implementation of the Charter provisions related to assistance to third States affected by the application of sanctions [A/56/33], it was noted that little headway had been made on the item despite its having been on the agenda for several years. In view of the great hardship endured by those States, it was emphasized that an urgent and permanent solution had to be found. In that regard, support was voiced for the proposals to establish a trust fund and a permanent consultation mechanism.

Attention was again drawn to the 1998 ad hoc expert group proposals [YUN 1998, p. 1235] on developing a methodology for assessing the impact on third States of preventive or enforcement measures and on exploring innovative and practical measures of international assistance to those States. It was suggested that in 2002 the Committee should establish which of those recommendations had overall support, which ones required additional clarification and which ones drew divergent views, thereby allowing the Committee to endorse some of the recommendations and submit them for the General Assembly's consideration.

The Committee recommended that the Assembly, at its 2001 session, should continue to consider the results of the ad hoc expert group meeting, taking account of, among other information, the Committee's current debate; the related views presented by the Secretary-General in his 1999 [YUN 1999, p. 1252] and 2000 [YUN 2000, p. 1270] reports; his views on the expert group's deliberations and main findings to be submitted pursuant to Assembly resolutions 54/107 [YUN 1999, p. 1252] and 55/157 [YUN 2000, p. 1271]; and information he was also to submit on the follow-up to the 1999 Security Council note [YUN 1999, p. 1252], proposing improvements to the work of the sanctions committees related to assistance to third States affected by the application of sanctions. The Committee encouraged the Secretary-General to expedite his report as requested by the resolutions named above for consideration by the Sixth Committee at the 2001 Assembly session.

Reports of Secretary-General (August and September). The Secretary-General, in his August report [A/56/303], prepared in response to General Assembly resolution 55/157 [YUN 2000, p. 1271], noted that the informal working group established by the Security Council in 2000 to examine issues from which to develop general recommendations on how to improve the effectiveness of UN sanctions [ibid., p. 1270] had yet to reach consensus on all of the recommendations put forward. Those issues, which related to the development of adequate capacity and appropriate modalities by the competent units of the Secretariat to coordinate information about international assistance available to third States affected by sanctions, to develop a methodology for assessing adverse consequences actually incurred by those States and to explore practical measures of assistance to them, were being reviewed by several intergovernmental bodies. The Secretary-General would continue to support that review process to ensure the timely and efficient implementation of relevant intergovernmental mandates.

The Secretary-General also reported on action taken by the General Assembly, the Economic and Social Council and the Committee for Programme and Coordination to assist third States affected by sanctions imposition and enforcement.

In his September report [A/56/326] on the road map towards the implementation of the UN Millennium Declaration [YUN 2000, p. 49], the Secretary-General addressed each of the Declaration's goals and commitments, including the goal to minimize the adverse effects of UN economic sanctions on innocent populations, to subject such sanctions regimes to regular reviews and to eliminate the adverse effects of sanctions on third parties. He noted that, although sanctions were an important tool in maintaining or restoring international peace and security, further progress had to be made in developing targeted sanctions and improving their effectiveness, while seeking to minimize their humanitarian impact on civilian populations and on affected third States. Moreover, such sanctions had to be integrated into a comprehensive conflict resolution or prevention strategy and complemented by inducement measures. A permanent sanctions-monitoring mechanism needed to be developed to ensure better targeting and enforcement of smart sanctions and to draw to the Council's attention information on non-cooperation and non-compliance.

Security Council consideration (October). The Security Council met on 22 and 25 October [meeting 4394] to discuss general issues relating to sanctions. At their request, Germany, Sweden and the Permanent Observer of Switzerland were invited to participate; the Secretariat's Assistant Secretary-General for Political Affairs was also invited.

The Permanent Observer stated that, in cooperation with the United Nations, Switzerland had organized a series of international expert meetings (Interlaken, Switzerland; and New York, 1998-1999) to examine the feasibility of targeted financial sanctions. Referred to as the Interlaken process, the key recommendations called for a better understanding of the specific technical requirements of targeted financial sanctions and the preconditions necessary for them to be effective; standardized language for Council resolutions on sanctions; identification of the basic legal and administrative requirements for national implementation of financial sanctions; and development of greater UN capabilities for administering and monitoring financial sanctions. The Permanent Observer said the Interlaken process showed that the conceptual, technical and practical elements to make targeted financial sanctions effective were available, but required political will to translate them into reality. He presented to the Council a handbook on the results of the process, which would also be distributed to all permanent missions to the United Nations.

Germany also presented a handbook containing the results of the Bonn-Berlin process, a series of conferences, seminars and workshops (Bonn and Berlin, 1999-2000) organized by the Bonn International Center for Conversion, an organization with considerable sanctions exper-

tise, which addressed two types of sanctions: arms embargoes and travel restrictions. The handbook, which would be sent to all UN Member States, set out model resolutions on arms embargoes and travel-related sanctions, with extensive commentary. It also reflected national implementation of those types of sanctions and offered suggestions for monitoring and enforcement.

Sweden announced that it was ready to continue the work accomplished by Switzerland and Germany through what it called the Stockholm process, to take place in 2002 and to which would be invited a broad range of government representatives, NGOs, regional organizations, academics and UN actors. It would focus on the implementation and monitoring of targeted sanctions and on finding a clearer understanding of their scope and limitations.

The UN Assistant Secretary-General for Political Affairs, Ibrahima Fall, stated that efforts to develop the concept of smart sanctions, pressuring regimes rather than peoples and thereby reducing their humanitarian costs, were to be welcomed in view of concerns over the negative effects that comprehensive sanctions regimes could have on civilian populations and on neighbouring and other affected States. Sanctions needed continual refining to strengthen their effectiveness and to ease their negative impact, thus consolidating support by the international community. He noted that some of the Interlaken recommendations were being put into practice and hoped the knowledge gained there could be successfully put to use within the Counter-Terrorism Committee established by Security Council resolution 1373(2001) (see p. 61). Many of the suggestions of the Bonn-Berlin process, also discussed in the Council's working group on general issues on sanctions [YUN 2000, p. 1371], had contributed to the improvement of sanctions resolutions.

Mr. Fall advanced a number of suggestions for effective sanctions implementation and monitoring so that sanctions might continue to be a useful tool in the maintenance of international peace and security. Pointing out that monitoring was the primary responsibility of Member States, he suggested that assistance could be provided to help them carry out that responsibility by a duly augmented sanctions secretariat and competent regional organizations. State compliance could be encouraged by greater Council attention to mitigating the negative effects of sanctions on civilian populations and third States, as well as providing support and inducements for neighbouring States. The Council could also consider assisting Member States to develop greater legal authority and administrative capacity for implementing sanctions. Model legislation could be provided to enable interested Member States to make adjustments in their domestic laws and regulations to permit compliance with sanctions.

As to the suggested establishment of a permanent sanctions-monitoring mechanism to ensure better targeting and implementation of smart sanctions, such a framework, in addition to allowing a systematic follow-up of violations or noncooperation, would provide a point of contact between the Council and relevant regional and international organizations. The Council could make more frequent use of humanitarian assessments before imposing sanctions and, once they had been imposed, continue to monitor their humanitarian impact.

Mr. Fall said that targeted sanctions could have important deterrent and preventive roles and urged the Council to consider using sanctions in that context. Stating that making sanctions smarter was not enough, he reiterated that it was imperative to provide the sanctions committees and the Secretariat with the means necessary for the effective administration of sanctions regimes and of a credible monitoring system: technical expertise, enhanced analytical capacity and commitment of adequate resources.

GENERAL ASSEMBLY ACTION

On 12 December [meeting 85], the General Assembly, on the recommendation of the Sixth Committee [A/56/592], adopted **resolution 56/87** without vote [agenda item 165].

Implementation of the provisions of the Charter of the United Nations related to assistance to third States affected by the application of sanctions

The General Assembly,

Concerned about the special economic problems confronting certain States arising from the carrying out of preventive or enforcement measures taken by the Security Council against other States, and taking into account the obligation of Members of the United Nations under Article 49 of the Charter of the United Nations to join in affording mutual assistance in carrying out the measures decided upon by the Security Council,

Recalling the right of third States confronted with special economic problems of that nature to consult the Security Council with regard to a solution of those problems, in accordance with Article 50 of the Charter,

Recognizing the desirability of the consideration of further appropriate procedures for consultations to deal in a more effective manner with the problems referred to in Article 50 of the Charter,

Recalling:

(*a*) The report of the Secretary-General entitled "An Agenda for Peace", in particular paragraph 41 thereof,

(*b*) Its resolution 47/120 A of 18 December 1992 entitled "An Agenda for Peace: preventive diplomacy and related matters", its resolution 47/120 B of 20 Sep-

tember 1993, entitled "An Agenda for Peace", in particular section IV thereof, entitled "Special economic problems arising from the implementation of preventive or enforcement measures", and its resolution 51/242 of 15 September 1997, entitled "Supplement to an Agenda for Peace", in particular annex II thereto, entitled "Question of sanctions imposed by the United Nations",

(*c*) The position paper of the Secretary-General entitled "Supplement to an Agenda for Peace",

(*d*) The statement by the President of the Security Council of 22 February 1995,

(*e*) The report of the Secretary-General prepared pursuant to the statement by the President of the Security Council regarding the question of special economic problems of States as a result of sanctions imposed under Chapter VII of the Charter,

(*f*) The annual overview reports of the Administrative Committee on Coordination for the period from 1992 to 2000, in particular the sections therein on assistance to countries invoking Article 50 of the Charter,

(*g*) The reports of the Secretary-General on economic assistance to States affected by the implementation of the Security Council resolutions imposing sanctions against the Federal Republic of Yugoslavia and General Assembly resolutions 48/210 of 21 December 1993, 49/21 A of 2 December 1994, 50/58 E of 12 December 1995, 51/30 A of 5 December 1996, 52/169 H of 16 December 1997, 54/96 G of 15 December 1999 and 55/170 of 14 December 2000,

(*h*) The reports of the Special Committee on the Charter of the United Nations and on the Strengthening of the Role of the Organization on the work of its sessions held in the years 1994 to 2001,

(*i*) The reports of the Secretary-General on the implementation of the provisions of the Charter related to assistance to third States affected by the application of sanctions under Chapter VII of the Charter,

(*j*) The report of the Secretary-General to the Millennium Assembly of the United Nations, in particular section IV.E thereof, entitled "Targeting sanctions",

(*k*) The United Nations Millennium Declaration, in particular paragraph 9 thereof,

(*l*) The report of the Secretary-General entitled "Road map towards implementation of the United Nations Millennium Declaration", in particular paragraphs 56 to 61 thereof,

Taking note of the most recent report of the Secretary-General, submitted in accordance with General Assembly resolution 55/157 of 12 December 2000,

Taking note also of the report of the Office of Internal Oversight Services on the in-depth evaluation of United Nations programmes relating to global development trends, issues and policies and global approaches to social and microeconomic issues and policies, and the corresponding subprogrammes in the regional commissions, in particular recommendation 3 contained therein, as approved by the Committee for Programme and Coordination at its fortieth session,

Recalling that the question of assistance to third States affected by the application of sanctions has been addressed recently in several forums, including the General Assembly, the Security Council, the Economic and Social Council and their subsidiary organs,

Recalling also the measures taken by the Security Council, in accordance with the statement by the President of the Security Council of 16 December 1994, that, as part of the effort of the Council to improve the flow of information and the exchange of ideas between members of the Council and other States Members of the United Nations, there should be increased recourse to open meetings, in particular at an early stage in its consideration of a subject,

Recalling further the measures taken by the Security Council in accordance with the note by the President of the Security Council of 29 January 1999 aimed at improving the work of the sanctions committees, including increasing the effectiveness and transparency of those committees,

Stressing that, in the formulation of sanctions regimes, due account should be taken of the potential effects of sanctions on third States,

Stressing also, in this context, the powers of the Security Council under Chapter VII of the Charter and the primary responsibility of the Council under Article 24 of the Charter for the maintenance of international peace and security in order to ensure prompt and effective action by the United Nations,

Recalling that, under Article 31 of the Charter, any Member of the United Nations that is not a member of the Security Council may participate, without vote, in the discussion of any question brought before the Council whenever the latter considers that the interests of that Member are specially affected,

Recognizing that the imposition of sanctions under Chapter VII of the Charter has been causing special economic problems in third States and that it is necessary to intensify efforts to address those problems effectively,

Taking into consideration the views of third States which could be affected by the imposition of sanctions,

Recognizing that assistance to third States affected by the application of sanctions would further contribute to an effective and comprehensive approach by the international community to sanctions imposed by the Security Council,

Recognizing also that the international community at large and, in particular, international institutions involved in providing economic and financial assistance should continue to take into account and address in a more effective manner the special economic problems of affected third States arising from the carrying out of preventive or enforcement measures taken by the Security Council under Chapter VII of the Charter, in view of their magnitude and of the adverse impact on the economies of those States,

Recalling the provisions of its resolutions 50/51 of 11 December 1995, 51/208 of 17 December 1996, 52/162 of 15 December 1997, 53/107 of 8 December 1998, 54/107 of 9 December 1999 and 55/157 of 12 December 2000,

1. *Renews its invitation* to the Security Council to consider the establishment of further mechanisms or procedures, as appropriate, for consultations as early as possible under Article 50 of the Charter of the United Nations with third States which are or may be confronted with special economic problems arising from the carrying out of preventive or enforcement measures imposed by the Council under Chapter VII of the Charter, with regard to a solution of those problems, including appropriate ways and means for increasing the effectiveness of its methods and procedures applied in the consideration of requests by the affected States for assistance;

2. *Welcomes* the measures taken by the Security Council since the adoption of General Assembly resolution 50/51, most recently the note by the President of the Security Council of 17 April 2000, whereby the members of the Security Council decided to establish an informal working group of the Council to develop general recommendations on how to improve the effectiveness of United Nations sanctions, looks forward to the adoption of the Chairman's proposed outcome of the working group, in particular those provisions thereof regarding the issues of the unintended impact of sanctions and assistance to States in implementing sanctions, and strongly recommends that the Council continue its efforts to enhance further the effectiveness and transparency of the sanctions committees, to streamline their working procedures and to facilitate access to them by representatives of States that find themselves confronted with special economic problems arising from the carrying out of sanctions;

3. *Invites* the Security Council, its sanctions committees and the Secretariat to continue to ensure, as appropriate, that:

(a) Both pre-assessment reports and ongoing assessment reports include as part of their analysis the likely and actual unintended impact of the sanctions on third States and recommend ways in which the negative impact of sanctions can be mitigated;

(b) Sanctions committees provide opportunities for third States affected by sanctions to brief them on the unintended impact of sanctions they are experiencing and on assistance needed by them to mitigate the negative impact of sanctions;

(c) The Secretariat continues to provide, upon request, advice and information to third States to help them to pursue means to mitigate the unintended impact of sanctions, for example, on invoking Article 50 of the Charter for consultation with the Security Council;

(d) Where economic sanctions have had severe effects on third States, the Security Council is able to request the Secretary-General to consider appointing a special representative or dispatching, as necessary, fact-finding missions on the ground to undertake necessary assessments and to identify, as appropriate, possible means of assistance;

(e) The Security Council is able, in the context of situations referred to in subparagraph (d) above, to consider establishing working groups to consider such situations;

4. *Requests* the Secretary-General to pursue the implementation of General Assembly resolutions 50/51, 51/208, 52/162, 53/107, 54/107 and 55/157 and to ensure that the competent units within the Secretariat develop the adequate capacity and appropriate modalities, technical procedures and guidelines to continue, on a regular basis, to collate and coordinate information about international assistance available to third States affected by the implementation of sanctions, to continue developing a possible methodology for assessing the adverse consequences actually incurred by third States and to explore innovative and practical measures of assistance to the affected third States;

5. *Welcomes* the report of the Secretary-General containing a summary of the deliberations and main findings of the ad hoc expert group meeting on developing a methodology for assessing the consequences incurred by third States as a result of preventive or enforcement measures and on exploring innovative and practical measures of international assistance to the affected third States, and renews its invitation to States and relevant international organizations within and outside the United Nations system which have not yet done so to provide their views regarding the report of the ad hoc expert group meeting;

6. *Requests* the Secretary-General to expedite the preparation of a report to the General Assembly containing his views on the deliberations and main findings, including the recommendations, of the ad hoc expert group on the implementation of the provisions of the Charter related to assistance to third States affected by the application of sanctions, taking into account the views of States, the organizations of the United Nations system, international financial institutions and other international organizations, as well as the Chairman's proposed outcome of the informal working group of the Security Council on general issues relating to sanctions;

7. *Reaffirms* the important role of the General Assembly, the Economic and Social Council and the Committee for Programme and Coordination in mobilizing and monitoring, as appropriate, the economic assistance efforts of the international community and the United Nations system on behalf of States confronted with special economic problems arising from the carrying out of preventive or enforcement measures imposed by the Security Council and, as appropriate, in identifying solutions to the special economic problems of those States;

8. *Takes note* of the decision of the Economic and Social Council, in its resolution 2000/32 of 28 July 2000, to continue its consideration of the question of assistance to third States affected by the application of sanctions, invites the Council, at its organizational session for 2002, to make appropriate arrangements for this purpose within its programme of work for 2002, and decides to transmit the most recent report of the Secretary-General on the implementation of the provisions of the Charter related to assistance to third States affected by the application of sanctions, together with the relevant background materials, to the Council at its substantive session of 2002;

9. *Invites* the organizations of the United Nations system, international financial institutions, other international organizations, regional organizations and Member States to address more specifically and directly, where appropriate, the special economic problems of third States affected by sanctions imposed under Chapter VII of the Charter and, for this purpose, to consider improving procedures for consultations to maintain a constructive dialogue with such States, including through regular and frequent meetings as well as, where appropriate, special meetings between the affected third States and the donor community, with the participation of United Nations agencies and other international organizations;

10. *Requests* the Special Committee on the Charter of the United Nations and on the Strengthening of the Role of the Organization, at its session in 2002, to continue to consider on a priority basis the question of the implementation of the provisions of the Charter related to assistance to third States affected by the application of sanctions under Chapter VII of the Charter by commencing a substantive debate on all of the related reports of the Secretary-General, in particular the 1998 report containing a summary of the deliberations and main findings of the ad hoc expert group meeting convened pursuant to paragraph 4 of General Assembly resolution 52/162, together with the most recent report of the Secretary-General on this question, taking into consideration the forthcoming report of the informal working group of the Security Council on general issues relating to sanctions, the proposals submitted on the question, the debate on the question in the Sixth Committee during the fifty-sixth session of the Assembly and the text on the question of sanctions imposed by the United Nations contained in annex II to Assembly resolution 51/242, as well as the implementation of the provisions of Assembly resolutions 50/51, 51/208, 52/162, 53/107, 54/107, 55/157 and the present resolution;

11. *Decides* to consider, within the Sixth Committee or a working group of the Committee, at the fifty-seventh session of the General Assembly, further progress in the elaboration of effective measures aimed at the implementation of the provisions of the Charter related to assistance to third States affected by the application of sanctions under Chapter VII of the Charter;

12. *Requests* the Secretary-General to submit a report on the implementation of the present resolution to the General Assembly at its fifty-seventh session, under the agenda item entitled "Report of the Special Committee on the Charter of the United Nations and on the Strengthening of the Role of the Organization".

UN Programme for the teaching and study of international law

In response to General Assembly resolution 54/102 [YUN 1999, p. 1258], the Secretary-General submitted an October report [A/56/484] on the implementation of the United Nations Programme of Assistance in the Teaching, Study, Dissemination and Wider Appreciation of International Law during 2000 and 2001. The report gave an account of UN activities and described contributions made by the United Nations Institute for Training and Research (UNITAR) and the United Nations Educational, Scientific and Cultural Organization (UNESCO). The Advisory Committee on the Programme held its thirty-fifth and thirty-sixth sessions on 22 November 2000 and 17 October 2001, respectively.

During the biennium, the UN Office of Legal Affairs (OLA) continued to perform various functions connected with the Programme's goals. The United Nations Audio-Visual Library in International Law established a web site on the UN home page. OLA's Codification Division continued to catalogue the tapes received for the Library and to assist in disseminating information regarding UN work on the codification and progressive development of international law, as well as on some aspects regarding its application.

UN fellowship programmes for the study of international law included the Fellowship Programme in International Law, provided by OLA in cooperation with UNITAR. Under the Programme, lectures and courses on private and public international law were given at The Hague Academy of International Law. Special lectures and seminars were also organized by OLA and UNITAR. Twenty-one international law fellowships were awarded in 2000 and 18 in 2001. Other programmes included the Hamilton Shirley Amerasinghe Memorial Fellowship on the Law of the Sea (see p. 1241), awarded annually by OLA, and the Fellowship Programme on the International Civil Service, organized by UNITAR in cooperation with other organizations.

The International Law Seminar, designed for advanced students specializing in international law and young professors or government officials dealing with that subject, held its thirty-sixth and thirty-seventh sessions (Geneva, 10-28 July 2000 and 2-20 July 2001). Funded by voluntary contributions from Member States and through national fellowships, the Seminars were organized by OLA through the United Nations Office at Geneva in conjunction with the annual sessions of the International Law Commission to allow seminar participants to observe its plenary meetings, attend specially arranged lectures and participate in working groups on specific topics.

UNESCO continued to disseminate international standards on human rights through its publications and partners. The network of UNESCO Chairs on Human Rights, Democracy, Peace and Tolerance was further expanded in 2001 with the establishment of new Chairs in Germany and the United States.

The report also provided guidelines and recommendations for the execution of the Programme in the 2002-2003 biennium, formulated to take account of the fact that the Assembly provided no new budgetary resources for it.

GENERAL ASSEMBLY ACTION

On 12 December [meeting 85], the General Assembly, on the recommendation of the Sixth Committee [A/56/586], adopted **resolution 56/77** without vote [agenda item 159].

United Nations Programme of Assistance in the Teaching, Study, Dissemination and Wider Appreciation of International Law

The General Assembly,

Taking note with appreciation of the report of the Secretary-General on the implementation of the United Nations Programme of Assistance in the Teaching, Study, Dissemination and Wider Appreciation of International Law and the guidelines and recommendations on future implementation of the Programme which were adopted by the Advisory Committee on the Programme and are contained in section III of the report,

Considering that international law should occupy an appropriate place in the teaching of legal disciplines at all universities,

Noting with appreciation the efforts made by States at the bilateral level to provide assistance in the teaching and study of international law,

Convinced, nevertheless, that States and international organizations and institutions should be encouraged to give further support to the Programme and increase their activities to promote the teaching, study, dissemination and wider appreciation of international law, in particular those activities which are of special benefit to persons from developing countries,

Reaffirming its resolutions 2464(XXIII) of 20 December 1968, 2550(XXIV) of 12 December 1969, 2838 (XXVI) of 18 December 1971, 3106(XXVIII) of 12 December 1973, 3502(XXX) of 15 December 1975, 32/146 of 16 December 1977, 36/108 of 10 December 1981 and 38/129 of 19 December 1983, in which it stated or recalled that in the conduct of the Programme it was desirable to use as far as possible the resources and facilities made available by Member States, international organizations and others, as well as its resolutions 34/144 of 17 December 1979, 40/66 of 11 December 1985, 42/148 of 7 December 1987, 44/28 of 4 December 1989, 46/50 of 9 December 1991 and 48/29 of 9 December 1993, in which, in addition, it expressed or reaffirmed the hope that, in appointing lecturers for the seminars to be held within the framework of the fellowship programme in international law, account would be taken of the need to secure the representation of major legal systems and balance among various geographical regions,

Welcoming the establishment of the United Nations Audio-Visual Library in International Law,

1. *Approves* the guidelines and recommendations contained in section III of the report of the Secretary-General and adopted by the Advisory Committee on the United Nations Programme of Assistance in the Teaching, Study, Dissemination and Wider Appreciation of International Law, in particular those designed to achieve the best possible results in the administration of the Programme within a policy of maximum financial restraint;

2. *Authorizes* the Secretary-General to carry out in 2002 and 2003 the activities specified in his report, including the provision of:

(*a*) A number of international law fellowships in both 2002 and 2003, to be determined in the light of the overall resources for the Programme and to be awarded at the request of Governments of developing countries;

(*b*) A minimum of one scholarship in both 2002 and 2003 under the Hamilton Shirley Amerasinghe Memorial Fellowship on the Law of the Sea, subject to the availability of new voluntary contributions made specifically to the fellowship fund;

(*c*) Subject to the overall resources for the Programme, assistance in the form of a travel grant for one participant from each developing country, who would be invited to possible regional courses to be organized in 2002 and 2003;

and to finance the above activities from provisions in the regular budget, when appropriate, as well as from voluntary financial contributions earmarked for each of the activities concerned, which would be received as a result of the requests set out in paragraphs 12 to 14 below;

3. *Expresses its appreciation* to the Secretary-General for his constructive efforts to promote training and assistance in international law within the framework of the Programme in 2000 and 2001, in particular for the organization of the thirty-sixth and thirty-seventh sessions of the International Law Seminar, held at Geneva in 2000 and 2001, respectively, and for the activities of the Office of Legal Affairs of the Secretariat related to the fellowship programme in international law and to the Hamilton Shirley Amerasinghe Memorial Fellowship on the Law of the Sea, carried out, respectively, through its Codification Division and its Division for Ocean Affairs and the Law of the Sea;

4. *Requests* the Secretary-General to consider the possibility of admitting, for participation in the various components of the Programme, candidates from countries willing to bear the entire cost of such participation;

5. *Also requests* the Secretary-General to consider the relative advantages of using available resources and voluntary contributions for regional, subregional or national courses, as against courses organized within the United Nations system;

6. *Further requests* the Secretary-General to continue to provide the necessary resources to the programme budget for the Programme for the next and the future bienniums with a view to maintaining the effectiveness of the Programme;

7. *Welcomes* the efforts undertaken by the Office of Legal Affairs to bring up to date the United Nations *Treaty Series* and the *United Nations Juridical Yearbook*, as well as efforts made to place on the Internet the *Treaty Series* and other legal information;

8. *Expresses its appreciation* to the United Nations Institute for Training and Research for its participation in the Programme through the activities described in the report of the Secretary-General;

9. *Also expresses its appreciation* to the United Nations Educational, Scientific and Cultural Organization for its participation in the Programme through the activities described in the report of the Secretary-General;

10. *Further expresses its appreciation* to The Hague Academy of International Law for the valuable contribution it continues to make to the Programme, which has enabled candidates under the fellowship programmes in international law to attend and participate in the Programme in conjunction with the Academy courses;

11. *Notes with appreciation* the contributions of The Hague Academy to the teaching, study, dissemination and wider appreciation of international law, and calls upon Member States and interested organizations to give favourable consideration to the appeal of the Academy for a continuation of support and a possible increase in their financial contributions, to enable the Academy to carry out its activities, particularly those relating to the summer courses, regional courses and programmes of the Centre for Studies and Research in International Law and International Relations;

12. *Requests* the Secretary-General to continue to publicize the Programme and periodically to invite Member States, universities, philanthropic foundations and other interested national and international institutions and organizations, as well as individuals, to make voluntary contributions towards the financing of the Programme or otherwise to assist in its implementation and possible expansion;

13. *Reiterates its request* to Member States and to interested organizations and individuals to make voluntary contributions, inter alia, for the International Law Seminar, the fellowship programme in international law, the Hamilton Shirley Amerasinghe Memorial Fellowship on the Law of the Sea and the United Nations Audio-Visual Library in International Law, and expresses its appreciation to those Member States, institutions and individuals which have made voluntary contributions for this purpose;

14. *Urges* in particular all Governments to make voluntary contributions for the organization of regional refresher courses in international law by the United Nations Institute for Training and Research, especially with a view to covering the amount needed for the financing of the daily subsistence allowance for up to twenty-five participants in each regional course, thus alleviating the burden on prospective host countries and making it possible for the Institute to continue to organize the regional courses;

15. *Requests* the Secretary-General to report to the General Assembly at its fifty-eighth session on the implementation of the Programme during 2002 and 2003 and, following consultations with the Advisory Committee on the Programme, to submit recommendations regarding the execution of the Programme in subsequent years;

16. *Decides* to include in the provisional agenda of its fifty-eighth session the item entitled "United Nations Programme of Assistance in the Teaching, Study, Dissemination and Wider Appreciation of International Law".

Host country relations

At four meetings held in New York between 22 February and 26 October, the Committee on Relations with the Host Country continued to consider the following aspects of relations between the UN diplomatic community and the United States, the host country: exemption from taxation; housing for diplomatic personnel; host country travel regulations; acceleration of immigration and customs procedures; transportation issues; and a letter from the Permanent Mission of Cuba to the United Nations concerning an order to seize the Mission's bank accounts and the United States response. The recommendations and conclusions on those items, approved by the Committee at its 26 October meeting, were incorporated in its report [A/56/26].

The working group established in 1997 [YUN 1997, p. 1376] on the use of diplomatic motor vehicles, parking and related matters and the working group on indebtedness did not meet in 2001.

Exemption from taxation

On 22 February, the United States clarified the regime governing the payment of property tax by permanent missions in New York. It said permanent missions that owned their buildings and rented, leased or otherwise made available additional space therein to other entities were engaging in commercial transactions and were therefore responsible for the property tax on that portion of the building so used even if the tenant was another diplomatic mission. Buildings occupied by permanent missions that were owned by their Governments and used by various organizations affiliated with those Governments were considered mixed-use buildings. The Governments of such properties were advised to discuss their tax status through normal bilateral channels. The United States also clarified that water, sewage and frontage taxes were not in fact taxes but charges for public utility services provided by the local government; therefore, permanent missions were obligated to pay for those services. The United States would communicate the foregoing information to all diplomatic missions.

Housing for diplomatic personnel

On 22 February, Iraq drew attention to the difficulty facing its Mission staff in obtaining housing due to the refusal of many landlords to rent to diplomats. It requested the United States Mission's assistance in resolving that problem. Acknowledging the host country's position that it could not interfere with personal and commercial transactions in a free market, Iraq nonetheless maintained that the problem had to be considered in the light of the host country's obligations vis-à-vis the permanent missions and their staff, including their housing. Cuba expressed support for Iraq's concerns and suggested that the New York City Commissioner for the United Nations might consider measures to improve the housing situation for diplomats accredited to the United Nations.

Host country travel regulations

On 22 February, the Committee heard complaints from Cuba, Iraq and the Russian Federation regarding the host country's policy of restricting the movement and travel of mission personnel and Secretariat officials of certain nationalities. They said that policy, in addition to hampering the work of the affected missions, was unfair, arbitrary, discriminatory and politically motivated. It violated not only human rights, the Charter and international law, but also the Agreement between the United Nations and the United States of America regarding the Headquarters of the United Nations, contained in General Assembly resolution 169(II) [YUN 1947-48, p. 199]. Referring to the denial of its travel authorization requests beyond the 25-mile zone on behalf of its Mission officials, Cuba called on the host country to put an end to such unjustified practice.

The United States responded that such politically motivated allegations, which had not been legally supported, were undermining the Committee's effectiveness. It said the host country had continuously acted within its treaty obligations to the United Nations and challenged Member States to provide evidence to substantiate their allegations in writing to facilitate an appropriate response. As to Cuba's travel-related complaints, the United States recalled its position set out in a letter (that it had no obligation to permit unrestricted travel outside the UN Headquarters district for personal reasons or for travel not related to the sending State at the United Nations). It questioned Cuba's definition of what constituted official UN business and doubted that a personal recreational tourist trip could be defined as UN official business.

The Committee continued to urge the host country to remove the remaining travel restrictions as soon as possible.

Acceleration of immigration and customs procedures

On 1 June, Iraq raised the issue of the host country's three-week requirement for processing visa applications of accredited Iraqi diplomats, which caused official and personal difficulties for them. It drew attention to the inability of the Permanent Representative of Iraq to obtain a re-entry visa in connection with his departure to his country to visit his ailing mother. Cuba said its Mission also had suffered under the same visa regime, complaining that, often, entry visas would be issued to its delegates after the UN meetings they had to attend had ended or were about to end. It claimed that, despite its cooperative approach, it continued to suffer from the host country's selective and discriminatory treatment.

The United States reiterated that the host country's obligations under the Headquarters Agreement related to access to official meetings; it had always constructively responded to cases involving specific problems. Regarding Iraq's complaint, the Permanent Representative's passport had been returned to him to allow his immediate departure, which could not have been prevented by United States policy dealing with re-entry visas. As for delays in the issuance of visas to Cuban representatives, the host country recalled that UN meetings and conferences were scheduled months, sometimes years, in advance and questioned Cuba's tendency to wait for the last minute to apply for visas for those purposes.

Cuba commented that if submitting a visa application 21 days in advance constituted "waiting for the last minute", there was clearly a problem of definition. Iraq acknowledged that, while the host country did not prevent its Permanent Representative's departure, it was not advisable for him to leave without ensuring his ability to return. Since the accreditation of permanent mission representatives had been formally accepted by the United States, there appeared no compelling reason to restrict and/or delay issuance of their return visas.

The Committee anticipated that the host country would continue to ensure the issuance, in a timely manner, of entry visas to representatives of Member States pursuant to article IV, section 11, of the Headquarters Agreement, including to attend official UN meetings.

Transportation

On 1 June, Cuba raised the subject of diplomatic parking and stated that the number of reserved parking spaces had been reduced in the area of the Permanent Mission of Cuba to the United Nations. The diplomatic parking sign had been removed without prior notification and fines had been imposed on the Mission's personnel who had parked where they had always parked. The United States replied that Cuba should have brought the matter to its attention so that remedial action, if warranted, could have been taken.

The Committee requested the host country to continue to take steps, in conjunction with the City of New York, to resolve that problem in order to maintain appropriate conditions for the functioning of the delegations and missions accredited to the United Nations in a manner that was fair, non-discriminatory, efficient and consistent with international law.

Bank accounts

On 17 August, Cuba reported that notice of a restraining order had been served on Chase Manhattan Bank on 7 August in respect to two accounts maintained by its Permanent Mission to the United Nations. That was a serious violation of Cuba's diplomatic immunity and hence of its bank accounts, which were immune from attach-

ment and execution under international law; the notice was therefore in and of itself illegal. Following an exchange of letters between Cuba's lawyers and Chase Manhattan Bank, the bank decided on 8 August not to implement the restraining notice and to continue the operation of the accounts. On 9 August, Cuba notified the United States about the matter and, on 10 August, Cuban and United States representatives met in Washington, D.C. On 14 August, the United States, acknowledging that the situation was clearly a violation of diplomatic immunity, said it wished to remove any misunderstanding on Cuba's part. Cuba said that a restraining order by a private plaintiff had the same practical and legal effect as a court ruling and, although the bank had not given effect to the notice, the notice itself was a violation of Cuba's immunity. Cuba was satisfied with the United States recognition that diplomatic accounts were immune from attachment and execution; it was not pleased that the host country would intervene only if the operation of such accounts were interfered with. It did not address the heart of Cuba's position: that the restraining notice was illegal and should not be enforced.

Cuba said it had requested the meeting of the Committee to elicit a more detailed statement of the host country's position; to clarify the misunderstanding to which it had referred; to conduct a debate in the proper exercise of the Committee's competence; and to seek guarantees against the recurrence of such violations. Cuba also sought clarification regarding measures to be taken in the event the restraining notice was not rescinded and compensation for its legal expenses and interruption of its Mission's normal functioning.

The United States explained that the restraining notice was issued by an individual lawyer on behalf of a private plaintiff. Chase Manhattan Bank, realizing it was not a court order, never honoured the notice. Such notices were issued all the time, and while the United States could not prevent private individuals from taking such actions, it had done and would continue to do whatever was necessary to protect permanent mission assets and accounts.

On 26 October, Cuba said it had informed the United States on 23 August that the restraining notice was still in place. On 15 October, it set out its legal position in response to the arguments advanced by the United States at the Committee's 17 August meeting. The only acceptable solution, Cuba asserted, was for the restraining notice to be withdrawn; it would not deem the matter settled until its accounts were under full and normal operation.

Although the host country said it was not obliged to respond to the questions of the law firm representing the Permanent Mission of Cuba, it gave the following clarifications. With regard to a court action to vacate the restraining notice, efforts under United States law were not relevant as long as the host country had fulfilled its obligations under international law. To the assertion that the restraining notice was a form of legal process, it emphasized that it was for the host country authorities to uphold the immunity and to determine the manner in which they did so. It recalled that the notice had been issued to Chase Manhattan Bank, not to the Permanent Mission of Cuba. The bank had been advised, and was well aware, of the invalidity of the notice. Cuba might of course raise its legal concerns in the Sixth Committee; in the meantime, the host country maintained that the Cuban accounts had been fully protected.

As to the Libyan Arab Jamahiriya's reference to unwarranted ceilings and restrictions imposed on its Mission's bank accounts, the host country explained that the licence permitting the Libyan Mission to maintain a United States–based account was an exception to the United States law precluding Libyan accounts in the country. The exception had been granted in recognition of the host country's obligations under the Headquarters Agreement. It invited the Libyan representative to discuss bilaterally the question of the ceiling imposed on such accounts.

GENERAL ASSEMBLY ACTION

On 12 December [meeting 85], the General Assembly, on the recommendation of the Sixth Committee [A/56/590 & Corr.1], adopted **resolution 56/84** without vote [agenda item 163].

Report of the Committee on Relations with the Host Country

The General Assembly,

Having considered the report of the Committee on Relations with the Host Country,

Expressing deep condolences to the families of the victims of the heinous acts of terrorism of 11 September 2001, as well as solidarity with the Government and people of the host country,

Recalling Article 105 of the Charter of the United Nations, the Convention on the Privileges and Immunities of the United Nations, the Agreement between the United Nations and the United States of America regarding the Headquarters of the United Nations and the responsibilities of the host country,

Recalling also that, in accordance with paragraph 7 of General Assembly resolution 2819(XXVI) of 15 December 1971, the Committee should consider, and advise the host country on, issues arising in connection with the implementation of the Agreement between the United Nations and the United States of America regarding the Headquarters of the United Nations,

Recognizing that effective measures should continue to be taken by the competent authorities of the host country, in particular to prevent any acts violating the security of missions and the safety of their personnel,

1. *Endorses* the recommendations and conclusions of the Committee on Relations with the Host Country contained in paragraph 37 of its report;

2. *Considers* that the maintenance of appropriate conditions for the normal work of the delegations and the missions accredited to the United Nations and the observance of their privileges and immunities, which is an issue of great importance to them, are in the interest of the United Nations and all Member States, and requests the host country to continue to take all measures necessary to prevent any interference with the functioning of missions;

3. *Expresses its appreciation* for the efforts made by the host country, and hopes that the issues raised at the meetings of the Committee will continue to be resolved in a spirit of cooperation and in accordance with international law;

4. *Notes* that during the reporting period the travel controls previously imposed by the host country on staff of certain missions and staff members of the Secretariat of certain nationalities remained in effect, and requests the host country to consider removing such travel controls, and in this regard notes the positions of affected States, of the Secretary-General and of the host country;

5. *Notes also* that the Committee anticipates that the host country will continue to ensure the issuance, in a timely manner, of entry visas to representatives of Member States, pursuant to article IV, section 11, of the Agreement between the United Nations and the United States of America regarding the Headquarters of the United Nations, inter alia, for the purpose of their attending official United Nations meetings;

6. *Requests* the host country to continue to take steps to resolve the problem relating to the parking of diplomatic vehicles in a fair, balanced and non-discriminatory way, with a view to responding to the growing needs of the diplomatic community, and to continue to consult with the Committee on this important issue;

7. *Requests* the Secretary-General to remain actively engaged in all aspects of the relations of the United Nations with the host country;

8. *Requests* the Committee to continue its work in conformity with General Assembly resolution 2819 (XXVI);

9. *Decides* to include in the provisional agenda of its fifty-seventh session the item entitled "Report of the Committee on Relations with the Host Country".

International law

International bioethics law

Convention against cloning of human beings

In view of the latest technological advances regarding the human genome, the Commission on

Human Rights adopted a resolution in April on human rights and bioethics (see p. 674). In November, the General Conference of the United Nations Educational, Scientific and Cultural Organization (UNESCO), as a follow-up to its resolutions calling on UNESCO to promote a programme of bioethics based on respect for human rights, adopted a resolution on bioethics, by which it invited the UNESCO Director-General to submit to it in 2002 the technical and legal studies undertaken regarding the possibility of elaborating universal norms on bioethics.

GENERAL ASSEMBLY ACTION

On 12 December [meeting 85], the General Assembly, on the recommendation of the Sixth Committee [A/56/599], adopted **resolution 56/93** without vote [agenda item 174].

International convention against the reproductive cloning of human beings

The General Assembly,

Recalling the Universal Declaration on the Human Genome and Human Rights, adopted by the General Conference of the United Nations Educational, Scientific and Cultural Organization on 11 November 1997, in particular article 11 thereof, in which the Conference specified that practices which are contrary to human dignity, such as reproductive cloning of human beings, shall not be permitted and invited States and international organizations to cooperate in taking, at the national or international level, the measures necessary in that regard,

Recalling also its resolution 53/152 of 9 December 1998, by which it endorsed the Universal Declaration on the Human Genome and Human Rights,

Bearing in mind Commission on Human Rights resolution 2001/71 of 25 April 2001, entitled "Human rights and bioethics", adopted at the fifty-seventh session of the Commission,

Noting the resolution on bioethics adopted by the General Conference of the United Nations Educational, Scientific and Cultural Organization on 2 November 2001, in which the Conference approved the recommendations by the Intergovernmental Bioethics Committee towards the possible elaboration, within the United Nations Educational, Scientific and Cultural Organization, of universal norms on bioethics,

Aware that the rapid development of the life sciences opens up tremendous prospects for the improvement of the health of individuals and mankind as a whole, but also that certain practices pose potential dangers to the integrity and dignity of the individual,

Particularly concerned, in the context of practices which are contrary to human dignity, at recently disclosed information on the research being conducted with a view to the reproductive cloning of human beings,

Determined to prevent such an attack on the human dignity of the individual,

Aware of the need for a multidisciplinary approach to the elaboration by the international community of an appropriate response to this problem,

1. *Decides* to establish an Ad Hoc Committee, open to all States Members of the United Nations or members of specialized agencies or of the International Atomic Energy Agency, for the purpose of considering the elaboration of an international convention against the reproductive cloning of human beings;

2. *Requests* the Secretary-General to invite the specialized agencies that work and have substantial interest in the field of bioethics, including, in particular, the United Nations Educational, Scientific and Cultural Organization and the World Health Organization, to participate as observers in the work of the Ad Hoc Committee;

3. *Decides* that the Ad Hoc Committee shall meet from 25 February to 1 March 2002 to consider the elaboration of a mandate for the negotiation of such an international convention, including a list of the existing international instruments to be taken into consideration and a list of legal issues to be addressed in the convention, with the understanding that the Ad Hoc Committee will open with an exchange of information and technical assessments provided by experts on genetics and bioethics, and recommends that the work continue during the fifty-seventh session of the General Assembly from 23 to 27 September 2002, within the framework of a working group of the Sixth Committee;

4. *Requests* the Secretary-General to provide the Ad Hoc Committee with the necessary facilities for the performance of its work;

5. *Requests* the Ad Hoc Committee to report on its work to the General Assembly at its fifty-seventh session;

6. *Recommends* that, upon the adoption of a negotiation mandate by the General Assembly, it may decide, taking into account the acute nature of the problem, to reconvene the Ad Hoc Committee, in order to open negotiations on the international convention referred to in paragraph 1 above;

7. *Decides* to include in the provisional agenda of its fifty-seventh session the item entitled "International convention against the reproductive cloning of human beings".

International economic law

In 2001, legal aspects of international economic law continued to be considered by the United Nations Commission on International Trade Law (UNCITRAL) and by the Sixth Committee of the General Assembly.

International trade law

At its thirty-fourth session (Vienna, 25 June–13 July), UNCITRAL considered and adopted a draft Convention on the Assignment of Receivables in International Trade and a draft UNCITRAL Model Law on Electronic Signatures, together with a draft Guide to Enactment of the Model Law. In addition, it considered its future work in electronic commerce, several aspects of international commercial arbitration, insolvency law, security interests, training and technical assistance, the enlargement of UNCITRAL's membership and its working methods, and coordination and cooperation with other legal bodies. The report on the session [A/56/17 & Corr.3] described action taken on those topics and annexed a list of related documents.

On 12 December [meeting 85], the General Assembly, on the recommendation of the Sixth Committee [A/56/588 & Corr.1], adopted **resolution 56/79** without vote [agenda item 161].

Report of the United Nations Commission on International Trade Law on the work of its thirty-fourth session

The General Assembly,

Recalling its resolution 2205(XXI) of 17 December 1966, by which it established the United Nations Commission on International Trade Law with a mandate to further the progressive harmonization and unification of the law of international trade and in that respect to bear in mind the interests of all peoples, in particular those of developing countries, in the extensive development of international trade,

Reaffirming its conviction that the progressive harmonization and unification of international trade law, in reducing or removing legal obstacles to the flow of international trade, especially those affecting the developing countries, would contribute significantly to universal economic cooperation among all States on a basis of equality, equity and common interest and to the elimination of discrimination in international trade and, thereby, to the well-being of all peoples,

Emphasizing the need for higher priority to be given to the work of the Commission in view of the increasing value of the modernization of international trade law for global economic development and thus for the maintenance of friendly relations among States,

Stressing the value of the participation by States at all levels of economic development and from different legal systems in the process of harmonizing and unifying international trade law,

Having considered the report of the Commission on the work of its thirty-fourth session,

Concerned that activities undertaken by other bodies of the United Nations system in the field of international trade law without coordination with the Commission might lead to undesirable duplication of efforts and would not be in keeping with the aim of promoting efficiency, consistency and coherence in the unification and harmonization of international trade law, as stated in its resolution 37/106 of 16 December 1982,

Stressing the importance of the further development of case law on United Nations Commission on International Trade Law texts in promoting the uniform application of the legal texts of the Commission and its value for government officials, practitioners and academics,

1. *Takes note with appreciation* of the report of the United Nations Commission on International Trade Law on the work of its thirty-fourth session;

2. *Takes note with satisfaction* of the completion and adoption by the Commission of the draft Convention on the Assignment of Receivables in International Trade and of the United Nations Commission on International Trade Law Model Law on Electronic Signatures;

3. *Takes note* of the progress made in the work of the Commission on arbitration and insolvency law and of its decision to commence work on electronic contracting, privately financed infrastructure projects, security interests and transport law, and expresses its appreciation to the Commission for its decision to adjust its working methods in order to accommodate its increased workload without endangering the high quality of its work;

4. *Expresses its appreciation* to the secretariat of the Commission for the publication and distribution of the *Legislative Guide on Privately Financed Infrastructure Projects,* calls upon the secretariat to ensure, in a joint effort with intergovernmental organizations such as the regional commissions of the United Nations, the United Nations Development Programme, the United Nations Industrial Development Organization, organizations of the World Bank Group and regional development banks, wide dissemination of the *Legislative Guide,* and invites States to give favourable consideration to its provisions when revising or adopting legislation in that area;

5. *Appeals* to Governments that have not yet done so to reply to the questionnaire circulated by the Secretariat in relation to the legal regime governing the recognition and enforcement of foreign arbitral awards and, in particular, to the legislative implementation of the Convention on the Recognition and Enforcement of Foreign Arbitral Awards, done at New York on 10 June 1958;

6. *Invites* States to nominate persons to work with the private foundation established to encourage assistance to the Commission from the private sector;

7. *Reaffirms* the mandate of the Commission, as the core legal body within the United Nations system in the field of international trade law, to coordinate legal activities in this field and, in this connection:

(*a*) Calls upon all bodies of the United Nations system and invites other international organizations to bear in mind the mandate of the Commission and the need to avoid duplication of effort and to promote efficiency, consistency and coherence in the unification and harmonization of international trade law;

(*b*) Recommends that the Commission, through its secretariat, continue to maintain close cooperation with the other international organs and organizations, including regional organizations, active in the field of international trade law;

8. *Also reaffirms* the importance, in particular for developing countries, of the work of the Commission concerned with training and technical assistance in the field of international trade law, such as assistance in the preparation of national legislation based on legal texts of the Commission;

9. *Expresses the desirability* of increased efforts by the Commission, in sponsoring seminars and symposia, to provide such training and technical assistance, and in this connection:

(*a*) Expresses its appreciation to the Commission for organizing seminars and briefing missions in Belarus, Burkina Faso, China, Colombia, Croatia, Cuba, the Dominican Republic, Egypt, Kenya, Lithuania, Peru, the Republic of Korea, Tunisia, Ukraine and Uzbekistan;

(*b*) Expresses its appreciation to the Governments whose contributions enabled the seminars and briefing missions to take place, and appeals to Governments, the relevant bodies of the United Nations system, organizations, institutions and individuals to make voluntary contributions to the United Nations Commission on International Trade Law Trust Fund for Symposia and, where appropriate, to the financing of special projects, and otherwise to assist the secretariat of the Commission in financing and organizing seminars and symposia, in particular in developing countries, and in the award of fellowships to candidates from developing countries to enable them to participate in such seminars and symposia;

10. *Appeals* to the United Nations Development Programme and other bodies responsible for development assistance, such as the International Bank for Reconstruction and Development and the European Bank for Reconstruction and Development, as well as to Governments in their bilateral aid programmes, to support the training and technical assistance programme of the Commission and to cooperate and coordinate their activities with those of the Commission;

11. *Appeals* to Governments, the relevant bodies of the United Nations system, organizations, institutions and individuals, in order to ensure full participation by all Member States in the sessions of the Commission and its working groups, to make voluntary contributions to the trust fund established to provide travel assistance to developing countries that are members of the Commission, at their request and in consultation with the Secretary-General;

12. *Decides*, in order to ensure full participation by all Member States in the sessions of the Commission and its working groups, to continue, in the competent Main Committee during the fifty-sixth session of the General Assembly, its consideration of granting travel assistance to the least developed countries that are members of the Commission, at their request and in consultation with the Secretary-General;

13. *Reiterates*, in view of the increased work programme of the Commission, its request to the Secretary-General to strengthen the secretariat of the Commission within the bounds of the resources available in the Organization so as to ensure and enhance the effective implementation of the programme of the Commission;

14. *Requests* the Secretary-General to adjust the terms of reference of the United Nations Commission on International Trade Law Trust Fund for Symposia so as to make it possible for the resources in the Trust Fund to be used also for the financing of training and technical assistance activities undertaken by the Secretariat;

15. *Stresses* the importance of bringing into effect the conventions emanating from the work of the Commission for the global unification and harmonization of international trade law, and to this end urges States that have not yet done so to consider signing, ratifying or acceding to those conventions.

Electronic commerce

Model law on electronic signatures and draft guide

UNCITRAL, at its June/July session, had for its consideration the draft model law on electronic signatures, which the Working Group on Electronic Commerce had completed at its thirty-seventh session (18-19 September 2000); the comments received from Governments and international organizations on that draft; and the revised draft guide to the enactment of the UNCITRAL model law, prepared by the Secretariat based on the Working Group's deliberations and decisions during its thirty-eighth session (12-23 March 2001).

Having debated the proposals for amending draft articles 2, 5 and 7-12 of the draft model law in the light of the comments submitted by Governments and international organizations, UNCITRAL conducted a systematic review of the entire set of draft model law articles, as well as of the draft guide to enactment, which, it found, adequately implemented its intent to assist States in enacting and applying the model law. UNCITRAL requested the Secretariat to prepare the definitive version of the guide and to publish it, together with the text of the draft model law.

On 5 July, having completed consideration of the revised text of the draft model law and the definitive draft guide to enactment, UNCITRAL adopted the UNCITRAL Model Law on Electronic Signatures as it appeared in annex II to its report [A/56/17], together with the Guide to Enactment of the Model Law; requested the Secretary-General to transmit the texts to Governments and other interested bodies; and recommended that all States give favourable consideration to them, as well as to the 1996 Model Law on Electronic Commerce [YUN 1996, p. 1236], when enacting or revising their relevant laws.

Future work

For its discussion of possible future work on electronic commerce, UNCITRAL considered its Working Group's recommendations arrived at following the Group's 2001 review of proposals based on notes dealing with a possible convention to remove obstacles to electronic commerce in existing international conventions, dematerialization of documents of title and electronic contracting.

Those recommendations called for the preparation, on a priority basis, of an international instrument dealing with selected issues on electronics contracting and for the Secretariat to prepare studies on three other topics: a comprehensive survey of possible legal barriers to the development of electronic commerce in international instruments; a further study of the issues related to transfer of rights, in particular rights in tangible goods, by electronic means and mechanisms for publicizing and keeping a record of acts of transfer or the creation of security interests in such goods; and a study of the UNCITRAL Model Law on International Commercial Arbitration (1985) [YUN 1985, p. 1192] and the UNCITRAL Arbitration Rules [YUN 1976, p. 823], to assess their appropriateness for meeting the specific needs of online arbitration.

Taking note of the exchange of views on those recommendations, UNCITRAL decided that they should be reconsidered during deliberations on its overall work programme by the Working Group in 2002.

GENERAL ASSEMBLY ACTION

On 12 December [meeting 85], the General Assembly, on the recommendation of the Sixth Committee [A/56/588 & Corr.1], adopted **resolution 56/80** without vote [agenda item 161].

Model Law on Electronic Signatures of the United Nations Commission on International Trade Law

The General Assembly,

Recalling its resolution 2205(XXI) of 17 December 1966, by which it established the United Nations Commission on International Trade Law, with a mandate to further the progressive harmonization and unification of the law of international trade and in that respect to bear in mind the interests of all peoples, particularly those of developing countries, in the extensive development of international trade,

Noting that an increasing number of transactions in international trade are carried out by means of communication commonly referred to as electronic commerce, which involves the use of alternatives to paper-based forms of communication, storage and authentication of information,

Recalling the recommendation on the legal value of computer records adopted by the Commission at its eighteenth session, in 1985, and paragraph 5 *(b)* of General Assembly resolution 40/71 of 11 December 1985, in which the Assembly called upon Governments and international organizations to take action, where appropriate, in conformity with the recommendation of the Commission, so as to ensure legal security in the context of the widest possible use of automated data processing in international trade,

Recalling also that the Model Law on Electronic Commerce was adopted by the Commission at its twenty-ninth session, in 1996, and complemented by an additional article, 5 bis, adopted by the Commission at its thirty-first session, in 1998, and recalling paragraph 2 of General Assembly resolution 51/162 of 16 December 1996, in which the Assembly recommended that all States should give favourable consideration to the Model Law when enacting or revising their laws, in view of the need for uniformity of the law applicable to alternatives to paper-based methods of communication and storage of information,

Convinced that the Model Law on Electronic Commerce is of significant assistance to States in enabling or facilitating the use of electronic commerce, as demonstrated by the enactment of the Model Law in a number of countries and its universal recognition as an essential reference in the field of electronic commerce legislation,

Mindful of the great utility of new technologies used for personal identification in electronic commerce and commonly referred to as electronic signatures,

Desiring to build on the fundamental principles underlying article 7 of the Model Law on Electronic Commerce with respect to the fulfilment of the signature function in an electronic environment, with a view to promoting reliance on electronic signatures for producing legal effect where such electronic signatures are functionally equivalent to handwritten signatures,

Convinced that legal certainty in electronic commerce will be enhanced by the harmonization of certain rules on the legal recognition of electronic signatures on a technologically neutral basis and by the establishment of a method to assess in a technologically neutral manner the practical reliability and the commercial adequacy of electronic signature techniques,

Believing that the Model Law on Electronic Signatures will constitute a useful addition to the Model Law on Electronic Commerce and significantly assist States in enhancing their legislation governing the use of modern authentication techniques and in formulating such legislation where none currently exists,

Being of the opinion that the establishment of model legislation to facilitate the use of electronic signatures in a manner acceptable to States with different legal, social and economic systems could contribute to the development of harmonious international economic relations,

1. *Expresses its appreciation* to the United Nations Commission on International Trade Law for completing and adopting the Model Law on Electronic Signatures contained in the annex to the present resolution, and for preparing the Guide to Enactment of the Model Law;

2. *Recommends* that all States give favourable consideration to the Model Law on Electronic Signatures, together with the Model Law on Electronic Commerce adopted in 1996 and complemented in 1998, when they enact or revise their laws, in view of the need for uniformity of the law applicable to alternatives to paper-based forms of communication, storage and authentication of information;

3. *Recommends also* that all efforts be made to ensure that the Model Law on Electronic Commerce and the Model Law on Electronic Signatures, together with their respective Guides to Enactment, become generally known and available.

ANNEX

Model Law on Electronic Signatures of the United Nations Commission on International Trade Law

Article 1
Sphere of application

This Law applies where electronic signatures are used in the context of commercial activities. It does not override any rule of law intended for the protection of consumers.

Article 2
Definitions

For the purposes of this Law:

(a) "Electronic signature" means data in electronic form in, affixed to or logically associated with, a data message, which may be used to identify the signatory in relation to the data message and to indicate the signatory's approval of the information contained in the data message;

(b) "Certificate" means a data message or other record confirming the link between a signatory and signature creation data;

(c) "Data message" means information generated, sent, received or stored by electronic, optical or similar means including, but not limited to, electronic data interchange (EDI), electronic mail, telegram, telex or telecopy;

(d) "Signatory" means a person that holds signature creation data and acts either on its own behalf or on behalf of the person it represents;

(e) "Certification service provider" means a person that issues certificates and may provide other services related to electronic signatures;

(f) "Relying party" means a person that may act on the basis of a certificate or an electronic signature.

Article 3
Equal treatment of signature technologies

Nothing in this Law, except article 5, shall be applied so as to exclude, restrict or deprive of legal effect any method of creating an electronic signature that satisfies the requirements referred to in article 6, paragraph 1, or otherwise meets the requirements of applicable law.

Article 4
Interpretation

1. In the interpretation of this Law, regard is to be had to its international origin and to the need to promote uniformity in its application and the observance of good faith.

2. Questions concerning matters governed by this Law which are not expressly settled in it are to be settled in conformity with the general principles on which this Law is based.

Article 5
Variation by agreement

The provisions of this Law may be derogated from or their effect may be varied by agreement, unless that agreement would not be valid or effective under applicable law.

Article 6
Compliance with a requirement for a signature

1. Where the law requires a signature of a person, that requirement is met in relation to a data message if an electronic signature is used that is as reliable as was appropriate for the purpose for which the data message was generated or communicated, in the light of all the circumstances, including any relevant agreement.

2. Paragraph 1 applies whether the requirement referred to therein is in the form of an obligation or whether the law simply provides consequences for the absence of a signature.

3. An electronic signature is considered to be reliable for the purpose of satisfying the requirement referred to in paragraph 1 if:

(a) The signature creation data are, within the context in which they are used, linked to the signatory and to no other person;

(b) The signature creation data were, at the time of signing, under the control of the signatory and of no other person;

(c) Any alteration to the electronic signature, made after the time of signing, is detectable; and

(d) Where a purpose of the legal requirement for a signature is to provide assurance as to the integrity of the information to which it relates, any alteration made to that information after the time of signing is detectable.

4. Paragraph 3 does not limit the ability of any person:

(a) To establish in any other way, for the purpose of satisfying the requirement referred to in paragraph 1, the reliability of an electronic signature; or

(b) To adduce evidence of the non-reliability of an electronic signature.

5. The provisions of this article do not apply to the following: [. . .].

Article 7
Satisfaction of article 6

1. [*Any person, organ or authority, whether public or private, specified by the enacting State as competent*] may determine which electronic signatures satisfy the provisions of article 6 of this Law.

2. Any determination made under paragraph 1 shall be consistent with recognized international standards.

3. Nothing in this article affects the operation of the rules of private international law.

Article 8
Conduct of the signatory

1. Where signature creation data can be used to create a signature that has legal effect, each signatory shall:

(a) Exercise reasonable care to avoid unauthorized use of its signature creation data;

(b) Without undue delay, utilize means made available by the certification service provider pursuant to article 9 of this Law, or otherwise use reasonable efforts, to notify any person that may reasonably be expected by the signatory to rely on or to provide services in support of the electronic signature if:

  (i) The signatory knows that the signature creation data have been compromised; or

  (ii) The circumstances known to the signatory give rise to a substantial risk that the signature creation data may have been compromised;

(c) Where a certificate is used to support the electronic signature, exercise reasonable care to ensure the accuracy and completeness of all material representations made by the signatory that are relevant to the certificate throughout its life cycle or that are to be included in the certificate.

2. A signatory shall bear the legal consequences of its failure to satisfy the requirements of paragraph 1.

Article 9
Conduct of the certification service provider

1. Where a certification service provider provides services to support an electronic signature that may be used for legal effect as a signature, that certification service provider shall:

  (a) Act in accordance with representations made by it with respect to its policies and practices;

  (b) Exercise reasonable care to ensure the accuracy and completeness of all material representations made by it that are relevant to the certificate throughout its life cycle or that are included in the certificate;

  (c) Provide reasonably accessible means that enable a relying party to ascertain from the certificate:

   (i) The identity of the certification service provider;

   (ii) That the signatory that is identified in the certificate had control of the signature creation data at the time when the certificate was issued;

   (iii) That signature creation data were valid at or before the time when the certificate was issued;

  (d) Provide reasonably accessible means that enable a relying party to ascertain, where relevant, from the certificate or otherwise:

   (i) The method used to identify the signatory;

   (ii) Any limitation on the purpose or value for which the signature creation data or the certificate may be used;

   (iii) That the signature creation data are valid and have not been compromised;

   (iv) Any limitation on the scope or extent of liability stipulated by the certification service provider;

   (v) Whether means exist for the signatory to give notice pursuant to article 8, paragraph 1 *(b)*, of this Law;

   (vi) Whether a timely revocation service is offered;

  (e) Where services under subparagraph *(d)* (v) are offered, provide a means for a signatory to give notice pursuant to article 8, paragraph 1 *(b)*, of this Law and, where services under subparagraph *(d)*(vi) are offered, ensure the availability of a timely revocation service;

  (f) Utilize trustworthy systems, procedures and human resources in performing its services.

2. A certification service provider shall bear the legal consequences of its failure to satisfy the requirements of paragraph 1.

Article 10
Trustworthiness

For the purposes of article 9, paragraph 1 *(f)*, of this Law in determining whether, or to what extent, any systems, procedures and human resources utilized by a certification service provider are trustworthy, regard may be had to the following factors:

  (a) Financial and human resources, including existence of assets;

  (b) Quality of hardware and software systems;

  (c) Procedures for processing of certificates and applications for certificates and retention of records;

  (d) Availability of information to signatories identified in certificates and to potential relying parties;

  (e) Regularity and extent of audit by an independent body;

  (f) The existence of a declaration by the State, an accreditation body or the certification service provider

regarding compliance with or existence of the foregoing; or

  (g) Any other relevant factor.

Article 11
Conduct of the relying party

A relying party shall bear the legal consequences of its failure:

  (a) To take reasonable steps to verify the reliability of an electronic signature; or

  (b) Where an electronic signature is supported by a certificate, to take reasonable steps:

   (i) To verify the validity, suspension or revocation of the certificate; and

   (ii) To observe any limitation with respect to the certificate.

Article 12
Recognition of foreign certificates and electronic signatures

1. In determining whether, or to what extent, a certificate or an electronic signature is legally effective, no regard shall be had:

  (a) To the geographic location where the certificate is issued or the electronic signature created or used; or

  (b) To the geographic location of the place of business of the issuer or signatory.

2. A certificate issued outside [*the enacting State*] shall have the same legal effect in [*the enacting State*] as a certificate issued in [*the enacting State*] if it offers a substantially equivalent level of reliability.

3. An electronic signature created or used outside [*the enacting State*] shall have the same legal effect in [*the enacting State*] as an electronic signature created or used in [*the enacting State*] if it offers a substantially equivalent level of reliability.

4. In determining whether a certificate or an electronic signature offers a substantially equivalent level of reliability for the purposes of paragraph 2 or 3, regard shall be had to recognized international standards and to any other relevant factors.

5. Where, notwithstanding paragraphs 2, 3 and 4, parties agree, as between themselves, to the use of certain types of electronic signatures or certificates, that agreement shall be recognized as sufficient for the purposes of cross-border recognition, unless that agreement would not be valid or effective under applicable law.

Convention on assignment of receivables

In continuation of its work on uniform legislation on assignment in receivables financing, UN-CITRAL had before it the consolidated version of the draft convention on assignment of receivables in international trade [A/CN.9/486], a revised version of the analytical commentary on the draft convention prepared by the Secretariat, comments by Governments and international organizations, and a Secretariat report on pending and other issues.

UNCITRAL reviewed the draft convention texts of articles 18-47, the annex to the draft convention comprising articles 1-9, the title and preamble; and reconsidered articles 1-17, which had been adopted in 2000 [YUN 2000, p. 1278], as well as articles 37 and 38. UNCITRAL subsequently referred the revised draft texts to a Secretariat drafting group for review so as to ensure consistency among the various language versions and requested the Secretariat to prepare a revised version of the commentary.

On 2 July, following its adoption of the draft Convention and annex as a whole, as contained in the drafting group's report, UNCITRAL adopted a decision, submitting to the General Assembly the draft Convention, as set forth in annex I to its report [A/56/17], with a recommendation that the Assembly consider it with a view to concluding a UN Convention on the Assignment of Receivables in International Trade.

GENERAL ASSEMBLY ACTION

On 12 December [meeting 85], the General Assembly, on the recommendation of the Sixth Committee [A/56/588 & Corr.1], adopted **resolution 56/81** without vote [agenda item 161].

United Nations Convention on the Assignment of Receivables in International Trade

The General Assembly,

Recalling its resolution 2205(XXI) of 17 December 1966, by which it established the United Nations Commission on International Trade Law with a mandate to further the progressive harmonization and unification of the law of international trade and in that respect to bear in mind the interests of all peoples, in particular those of developing countries, in the extensive development of international trade,

Considering that problems created by uncertainties as to the content and the choice of the legal regime applicable to the assignment of receivables constitute an obstacle to international trade,

Convinced that the adoption of a convention on the assignment of receivables in international trade will enhance transparency, contribute to overcoming the problems of uncertainties in this field and promote the availability of capital and credit at more affordable rates, while protecting existing assignment practices and facilitating the development of new practices, as well as ensuring adequate protection of the interests of debtors in assignments of receivables,

Recalling that, at its twenty-eighth session in 1995, the Commission decided to prepare uniform legislation on assignment in receivables financing and entrusted the Working Group on International Contract Practices with the preparation of a draft,

Noting that the Working Group on International Contract Practices devoted nine sessions, from 1995 to 2000, to the preparation of the draft Convention on the Assignment of Receivables in International Trade, and that the Commission considered the draft Convention at its thirty-third session in 2000 and at its thirty-fourth session in 2001,

Being aware that all States and interested international organizations were invited to participate in the preparation of the draft Convention at all the sessions of the Working Group and at the thirty-third and thirty-fourth sessions of the Commission, either as members or as observers, with a full opportunity to speak and make proposals,

Noting with satisfaction that the text of the draft Convention was circulated for comments once before the thirty-third session of the Commission and a second time in its revised version before the thirty-fourth session of the Commission to all Governments and international organizations invited to attend the meetings of the Commission and the Working Group as observers, and that the comments received were before the Commission at its thirty-third and thirty-fourth sessions,

Taking note with satisfaction of the decision of the Commission at its thirty-fourth session to submit the draft Convention to the General Assembly for its consideration,

Taking note of the draft Convention adopted by the Commission,

1. *Expresses its appreciation* to the United Nations Commission on International Trade Law for preparing the draft Convention on the Assignment of Receivables in International Trade;

2. *Adopts and opens for signature or accession* the United Nations Convention on the Assignment of Receivables in International Trade, contained in the annex to the present resolution;

3. *Calls upon* all Governments to consider becoming party to the Convention.

ANNEX

United Nations Convention on the Assignment of Receivables in International Trade

Preamble

The Contracting States,

Reaffirming their conviction that international trade on the basis of equality and mutual benefit is an important element in the promotion of friendly relations among States,

Considering that problems created by uncertainties as to the content and the choice of legal regime applicable to the assignment of receivables constitute an obstacle to international trade,

Desiring to establish principles and to adopt rules relating to the assignment of receivables that would create certainty and transparency and promote the modernization of the law relating to assignments of receivables, while protecting existing assignment practices and facilitating the development of new practices,

Desiring also to ensure adequate protection of the interests of debtors in assignments of receivables,

Being of the opinion that the adoption of uniform rules governing the assignment of receivables would promote the availability of capital and credit at more affordable rates and thus facilitate the development of international trade,

Have agreed as follows:

Chapter I
Scope of application

Article 1
Scope of application

1. This Convention applies to:

(*a*) Assignments of international receivables and to international assignments of receivables as defined in this chapter, if, at the time of conclusion of the contract of assignment, the assignor is located in a Contracting State; and

(b) Subsequent assignments, provided that any prior assignment is governed by this Convention.

2. This Convention applies to subsequent assignments that satisfy the criteria set forth in paragraph 1 (a) of this article, even if it did not apply to any prior assignment of the same receivable.

3. This Convention does not affect the rights and obligations of the debtor unless, at the time of conclusion of the original contract, the debtor is located in a Contracting State or the law governing the original contract is the law of a Contracting State.

4. The provisions of chapter V apply to assignments of international receivables and to international assignments of receivables as defined in this chapter independently of paragraphs 1 to 3 of this article. However, those provisions do not apply if a State makes a declaration under article 39.

5. The provisions of the annex to this Convention apply as provided in article 42.

Article 2
Assignment of receivables

For the purposes of this Convention:

(a) "Assignment" means the transfer by agreement from one person ("assignor") to another person ("assignee") of all or part of or an undivided interest in the assignor's contractual right to payment of a monetary sum ("receivable") from a third person ("the debtor"). The creation of rights in receivables as security for indebtedness or other obligation is deemed to be a transfer;

(b) In the case of an assignment by the initial or any other assignee ("subsequent assignment"), the person who makes that assignment is the assignor and the person to whom that assignment is made is the assignee.

Article 3
Internationality

A receivable is international if, at the time of conclusion of the original contract, the assignor and the debtor are located in different States. An assignment is international if, at the time of conclusion of the contract of assignment, the assignor and the assignee are located in different States.

Article 4
Exclusions and other limitations

1. This Convention does not apply to assignments made:

(a) To an individual for his or her personal, family or household purposes;

(b) As part of the sale or change in the ownership or legal status of the business out of which the assigned receivables arose.

2. This Convention does not apply to assignments of receivables arising under or from:

(a) Transactions on a regulated exchange;

(b) Financial contracts governed by netting agreements, except a receivable owed on the termination of all outstanding transactions;

(c) Foreign exchange transactions;

(d) Inter-bank payment systems, inter-bank payment agreements or clearance and settlement systems relating to securities or other financial assets or instruments;

(e) The transfer of security rights in, sale, loan or holding of or agreement to repurchase securities or other financial assets or instruments held with an intermediary;

(f) Bank deposits;

(g) A letter of credit or independent guarantee.

3. Nothing in this Convention affects the rights and obligations of any person under the law governing negotiable instruments.

4. Nothing in this Convention affects the rights and obligations of the assignor and the debtor under special laws governing the protection of parties to transactions made for personal, family or household purposes.

5. Nothing in this Convention:

(a) Affects the application of the law of a State in which real property is situated to either:

(i) An interest in that real property to the extent that under that law the assignment of a receivable confers such an interest; or

(ii) The priority of a right in a receivable to the extent that under that law an interest in the real property confers such a right; or

(b) Makes lawful the acquisition of an interest in real property not permitted under the law of the State in which the real property is situated.

Chapter II
General provisions

Article 5
Definitions and rules of interpretation

For the purposes of this Convention:

(a) "Original contract" means the contract between the assignor and the debtor from which the assigned receivable arises;

(b) "Existing receivable" means a receivable that arises upon or before conclusion of the contract of assignment and "future receivable" means a receivable that arises after conclusion of the contract of assignment;

(c) "Writing" means any form of information that is accessible so as to be usable for subsequent reference. Where this Convention requires a writing to be signed, that requirement is met if, by generally accepted means or a procedure agreed to by the person whose signature is required, the writing identifies that person and indicates that person's approval of the information contained in the writing;

(d) "Notification of the assignment" means a communication in writing that reasonably identifies the assigned receivables and the assignee;

(e) "Insolvency administrator" means a person or body, including one appointed on an interim basis, authorized in an insolvency proceeding to administer the reorganization or liquidation of the assignor's assets or affairs;

(f) "Insolvency proceeding" means a collective judicial or administrative proceeding, including an interim proceeding, in which the assets and affairs of the assignor are subject to control or supervision by a court or other competent authority for the purpose of reorganization or liquidation;

(g) "Priority" means the right of a person in preference to the right of another person and, to the extent relevant for such purpose, includes the determination whether the right is a personal or a property right, whether or not it is a security right for indebtedness or other obligation and whether any requirements necessary to render the right effective against a competing claimant have been satisfied;

(*h*) A person is located in the State in which it has its place of business. If the assignor or the assignee has a place of business in more than one State, the place of business is that place where the central administration of the assignor or the assignee is exercised. If the debtor has a place of business in more than one State, the place of business is that which has the closest relationship to the original contract. If a person does not have a place of business, reference is to be made to the habitual residence of that person;

(*i*) "Law" means the law in force in a State other than its rules of private international law;

(*j*) "Proceeds" means whatever is received in respect of an assigned receivable, whether in total or partial payment or other satisfaction of the receivable. The term includes whatever is received in respect of proceeds. The term does not include returned goods;

(*k*) "Financial contract" means any spot, forward, future, option or swap transaction involving interest rates, commodities, currencies, equities, bonds, indices or any other financial instrument, any repurchase or securities lending transaction, and any other transaction similar to any transaction referred to above entered into in financial markets and any combination of the transactions mentioned above;

(*l*) "Netting agreement" means an agreement between two or more parties that provides for one or more of the following:

(i) The net settlement of payments due in the same currency on the same date whether by notation or otherwise;

(ii) Upon the insolvency or other default by a party, the termination of all outstanding transactions at their replacement or fair market values, conversion of such sums into a single currency and netting into a single payment by one party to the other; or

(iii) The set-off of amounts calculated as set forth in subparagraph (*l*) (ii) of this article under two or more netting agreements;

(*m*) "Competing claimant" means:

(i) Another assignee of the same receivable from the same assignor, including a person who, by operation of law, claims a right in the assigned receivable as a result of its right in other property of the assignor, even if that receivable is not an international receivable and the assignment to that assignee is not an international assignment;

(ii) A creditor of the assignor; or

(iii) The insolvency administrator.

Article 6
Party autonomy

Subject to article 19, the assignor, the assignee and the debtor may derogate from or vary by agreement provisions of this Convention relating to their respective rights and obligations. Such an agreement does not affect the rights of any person who is not a party to the agreement.

Article 7
Principles of interpretation

1. In the interpretation of this Convention, regard is to be had to its object and purpose as set forth in the preamble, to its international character and to the need to promote uniformity in its application and the observance of good faith in international trade.

2. Questions concerning matters governed by this Convention that are not expressly settled in it are to be settled in conformity with the general principles on which it is based or, in the absence of such principles, in conformity with the law applicable by virtue of the rules of private international law.

Chapter III
Effects of assignment

Article 8
Effectiveness of assignments

1. An assignment is not ineffective as between the assignor and the assignee or as against the debtor or as against a competing claimant, and the right of an assignee may not be denied priority, on the ground that it is an assignment of more than one receivable, future receivables or parts of or undivided interests in receivables, provided that the receivables are described:

(*a*) Individually as receivables to which the assignment relates; or

(*b*) In any other manner, provided that they can, at the time of the assignment or, in the case of future receivables, at the time of conclusion of the original contract, be identified as receivables to which the assignment relates.

2. Unless otherwise agreed, an assignment of one or more future receivables is effective without a new act of transfer being required to assign each receivable.

3. Except as provided in paragraph 1 of this article, article 9 and article 10, paragraphs 2 and 3, this Convention does not affect any limitations on assignments arising from law.

Article 9
Contractual limitations on assignments

1. An assignment of a receivable is effective notwithstanding any agreement between the initial or any subsequent assignor and the debtor or any subsequent assignee limiting in any way the assignor's right to assign its receivables.

2. Nothing in this article affects any obligation or liability of the assignor for breach of such an agreement, but the other party to such agreement may not avoid the original contract or the assignment contract on the sole ground of that breach. A person who is not party to such an agreement is not liable on the sole ground that it had knowledge of the agreement.

3. This article applies only to assignments of receivables:

(*a*) Arising from an original contract that is a contract for the supply or lease of goods or services other than financial services, a construction contract or a contract for the sale or lease of real property;

(*b*) Arising from an original contract for the sale, lease or licence of industrial or other intellectual property or of proprietary information;

(*c*) Representing the payment obligation for a credit card transaction; or

(*d*) Owed to the assignor upon net settlement of payments due pursuant to a netting agreement involving more than two parties.

Article 10
Transfer of security rights

1. A personal or property right securing payment of the assigned receivable is transferred to the assignee without a new act of transfer. If such a right, under the law governing it, is transferable only with a new act of transfer, the assignor is obliged to transfer such right and any proceeds to the assignee.

2. A right securing payment of the assigned receivable is transferred under paragraph 1 of this article notwithstanding any agreement between the assignor and the debtor or other person granting that right, limiting in any way the assignor's right to assign the receivable or the right securing payment of the assigned receivable.

3. Nothing in this article affects any obligation or liability of the assignor for breach of any agreement under paragraph 2 of this article, but the other party to that agreement may not avoid the original contract or the assignment contract on the sole ground of that breach. A person who is not a party to such an agreement is not liable on the sole ground that it had knowledge of the agreement.

4. Paragraphs 2 and 3 of this article apply only to assignments of receivables:

(a) Arising from an original contract that is a contract for the supply or lease of goods or services other than financial services, a construction contract or a contract for the sale or lease of real property;

(b) Arising from an original contract for the sale, lease or licence of industrial or other intellectual property or of proprietary information;

(c) Representing the payment obligation for a credit card transaction; or

(d) Owed to the assignor upon net settlement of payments due pursuant to a netting agreement involving more than two parties.

5. The transfer of a possessory property right under paragraph 1 of this article does not affect any obligations of the assignor to the debtor or the person granting the property right with respect to the property transferred existing under the law governing that property right.

6. Paragraph 1 of this article does not affect any requirement under rules of law other than this Convention relating to the form or registration of the transfer of any rights securing payment of the assigned receivable.

Chapter IV
Rights, obligations and defences

Section I
Assignor and assignee

Article 11
Rights and obligations of the assignor and the assignee

1. The mutual rights and obligations of the assignor and the assignee arising from their agreement are determined by the terms and conditions set forth in that agreement, including any rules or general conditions referred to therein.

2. The assignor and the assignee are bound by any usage to which they have agreed and, unless otherwise agreed, by any practices they have established between themselves.

3. In an international assignment, the assignor and the assignee are considered, unless otherwise agreed, implicitly to have made applicable to the assignment a usage that in international trade is widely known to, and regularly observed by, parties to the particular type of assignment or to the assignment of the particular category of receivables.

Article 12
Representations of the assignor

1. Unless otherwise agreed between the assignor and the assignee, the assignor represents at the time of conclusion of the contract of assignment that:

(a) The assignor has the right to assign the receivable;

(b) The assignor has not previously assigned the receivable to another assignee; and

(c) The debtor does not and will not have any defences or rights of set-off.

2. Unless otherwise agreed between the assignor and the assignee, the assignor does not represent that the debtor has, or will have, the ability to pay.

Article 13
Right to notify the debtor

1. Unless otherwise agreed between the assignor and the assignee, the assignor or the assignee or both may send the debtor notification of the assignment and a payment instruction, but after notification has been sent only the assignee may send such an instruction.

2. Notification of the assignment or a payment instruction sent in breach of any agreement referred to in paragraph 1 of this article is not ineffective for the purposes of article 17 by reason of such breach. However, nothing in this article affects any obligation or liability of the party in breach of such an agreement for any damages arising as a result of the breach.

Article 14
Right to payment

1. As between the assignor and the assignee, unless otherwise agreed and whether or not notification of the assignment has been sent:

(a) If payment in respect of the assigned receivable is made to the assignee, the assignee is entitled to retain the proceeds and goods returned in respect of the assigned receivable;

(b) If payment in respect of the assigned receivable is made to the assignor, the assignee is entitled to payment of the proceeds and also to goods returned to the assignor in respect of the assigned receivable; and

(c) If payment in respect of the assigned receivable is made to another person over whom the assignee has priority, the assignee is entitled to payment of the proceeds and also to goods returned to such person in respect of the assigned receivable.

2. The assignee may not retain more than the value of its right in the receivable.

Section II
Debtor

Article 15
Principle of debtor protection

1. Except as otherwise provided in this Convention, an assignment does not, without the consent of the debtor, affect the rights and obligations of the debtor, including the payment terms contained in the original contract.

2. A payment instruction may change the person, address or account to which the debtor is required to make payment, but may not change:

(a) The currency of payment specified in the original contract; or

(b) The State specified in the original contract in which payment is to be made to a State other than that in which the debtor is located.

Article 16
Notification of the debtor

1. Notification of the assignment or a payment instruction is effective when received by the debtor if it is in a language that is reasonably expected to inform the debtor about its contents. It is sufficient if notification of the assignment or a payment instruction is in the language of the original contract.

2. Notification of the assignment or a payment instruction may relate to receivables arising after notification.

3. Notification of a subsequent assignment constitutes notification of all prior assignments.

Article 17
Debtor's discharge by payment

1. Until the debtor receives notification of the assignment, the debtor is entitled to be discharged by paying in accordance with the original contract.

2. After the debtor receives notification of the assignment, subject to paragraphs 3 to 8 of this article, the debtor is discharged only by paying the assignee or, if otherwise instructed in the notification of the assignment or subsequently by the assignee in a writing received by the debtor, in accordance with such payment instruction.

3. If the debtor receives more than one payment instruction relating to a single assignment of the same receivable by the same assignor, the debtor is discharged by paying in accordance with the last payment instruction received from the assignee before payment.

4. If the debtor receives notification of more than one assignment of the same receivable made by the same assignor, the debtor is discharged by paying in accordance with the first notification received.

5. If the debtor receives notification of one or more subsequent assignments, the debtor is discharged by paying in accordance with the notification of the last of such subsequent assignments.

6. If the debtor receives notification of the assignment of a part of or an undivided interest in one or more receivables, the debtor is discharged by paying in accordance with the notification or in accordance with this article as if the debtor had not received the notification. If the debtor pays in accordance with the notification, the debtor is discharged only to the extent of the part or undivided interest paid.

7. If the debtor receives notification of the assignment from the assignee, the debtor is entitled to request the assignee to provide within a reasonable period of time adequate proof that the assignment from the initial assignor to the initial assignee and any intermediate assignment have been made and, unless the assignee does so, the debtor is discharged by paying in accordance with this article as if the notification from the assignee had not been received. Adequate proof of an assignment includes but is not limited to any writing emanating from the assignor and indicating that the assignment has taken place.

8. This article does not affect any other ground on which payment by the debtor to the person entitled to payment, to a competent judicial or other authority, or to a public deposit fund discharges the debtor.

Article 18
Defences and rights of set-off of the debtor

1. In a claim by the assignee against the debtor for payment of the assigned receivable, the debtor may raise against the assignee all defences and rights of set-off arising from the original contract, or any other contract that was part of the same transaction, of which the debtor could avail itself as if the assignment had not been made and such claim were made by the assignor.

2. The debtor may raise against the assignee any other right of set-off, provided that it was available to the debtor at the time notification of the assignment was received by the debtor.

3. Notwithstanding paragraphs 1 and 2 of this article, defences and rights of set-off that the debtor may raise pursuant to article 9 or 10 against the assignor for breach of an agreement limiting in any way the assignor's right to make the assignment are not available to the debtor against the assignee.

Article 19
Agreement not to raise defences or rights of set-off

1. The debtor may agree with the assignor in a writing signed by the debtor not to raise against the assignee the defences and rights of set-off that it could raise pursuant to article 18. Such an agreement precludes the debtor from raising against the assignee those defences and rights of set-off.

2. The debtor may not waive defences:

(a) Arising from fraudulent acts on the part of the assignee; or

(b) Based on the debtor's incapacity.

3. Such an agreement may be modified only by an agreement in a writing signed by the debtor. The effect of such a modification as against the assignee is determined by article 20, paragraph 2.

Article 20
Modification of the original contract

1. An agreement concluded before notification of the assignment between the assignor and the debtor that affects the assignee's rights is effective as against the assignee, and the assignee acquires corresponding rights.

2. An agreement concluded after notification of the assignment between the assignor and the debtor that affects the assignee's rights is ineffective as against the assignee unless:

(a) The assignee consents to it; or

(b) The receivable is not fully earned by performance and either the modification is provided for in the original contract or, in the context of the original contract, a reasonable assignee would consent to the modification.

3. Paragraphs 1 and 2 of this article do not affect any right of the assignor or the assignee arising from breach of an agreement between them.

Article 21

Recovery of payments

Failure of the assignor to perform the original contract does not entitle the debtor to recover from the assignee a sum paid by the debtor to the assignor or the assignee.

Section III
Third parties

Article 22

Law applicable to competing rights

With the exception of matters that are settled elsewhere in this Convention and subject to articles 23 and 24, the law of the State in which the assignor is located governs the priority of the right of an assignee in the assigned receivable over the right of a competing claimant.

Article 23

Public policy and mandatory rules

1. The application of a provision of the law of the State in which the assignor is located may be refused only if the application of that provision is manifestly contrary to the public policy of the forum State.

2. The rules of the law of either the forum State or any other State that are mandatory irrespective of the law otherwise applicable may not prevent the application of a provision of the law of the State in which the assignor is located.

3. Notwithstanding paragraph 2 of this article, in an insolvency proceeding commenced in a State other than the State in which the assignor is located, any preferential right that arises, by operation of law, under the law of the forum State and is given priority over the rights of an assignee in insolvency proceedings under the law of that State may be given priority notwithstanding article 22. A State may deposit at any time a declaration identifying any such preferential right.

Article 24

Special rules on proceeds

1. If proceeds are received by the assignee, the assignee is entitled to retain those proceeds to the extent that the assignee's right in the assigned receivable had priority over the right of a competing claimant in the assigned receivable.

2. If proceeds are received by the assignor, the right of the assignee in those proceeds has priority over the right of a competing claimant in those proceeds to the same extent as the assignee's right had priority over the right in the assigned receivable of that claimant if:

(a) The assignor has received the proceeds under instructions from the assignee to hold the proceeds for the benefit of the assignee; and

(b) The proceeds are held by the assignor for the benefit of the assignee separately and are reasonably identifiable from the assets of the assignor, such as in the case of a separate deposit or securities account containing only proceeds consisting of cash or securities.

3. Nothing in paragraph 2 of this article affects the priority of a person having against the proceeds a right of set-off or a right created by agreement and not derived from a right in the receivable.

Article 25

Subordination

An assignee entitled to priority may at any time subordinate its priority unilaterally or by agreement in favour of any existing or future assignees.

Chapter V
Autonomous conflict-of-laws rules

Article 26

Application of chapter V

The provisions of this chapter apply to matters that are:

(a) Within the scope of this Convention as provided in article 1, paragraph 4; and

(b) Otherwise within the scope of this Convention but not settled elsewhere in it.

Article 27

Form of a contract of assignment

1. A contract of assignment concluded between persons who are located in the same State is formally valid as between them if it satisfies the requirements of either the law which governs it or the law of the State in which it is concluded.

2. A contract of assignment concluded between persons who are located in different States is formally valid as between them if it satisfies the requirements of either the law which governs it or the law of one of those States.

Article 28

Law applicable to the mutual rights and obligations of the assignor and the assignee

1. The mutual rights and obligations of the assignor and the assignee arising from their agreement are governed by the law chosen by them.

2. In the absence of a choice of law by the assignor and the assignee, their mutual rights and obligations arising from their agreement are governed by the law of the State with which the contract of assignment is most closely connected.

Article 29

Law applicable to the rights and obligations of the assignee and the debtor

The law governing the original contract determines the effectiveness of contractual limitations on assignment as between the assignee and the debtor, the relationship between the assignee and the debtor, the conditions under which the assignment can be invoked against the debtor and whether the debtor's obligations have been discharged.

Article 30

Law applicable to priority

1. The law of the State in which the assignor is located governs the priority of the right of an assignee in the assigned receivable over the right of a competing claimant.

2. The rules of the law of either the forum State or any other State that are mandatory irrespective of the law otherwise applicable may not prevent the application of a provision of the law of the State in which the assignor is located.

3. Notwithstanding paragraph 2 of this article, in an insolvency proceeding commenced in a State other than the State in which the assignor is located, any preferential right that arises, by operation of law, under the

law of the forum State and is given priority over the rights of an assignee in insolvency proceedings under the law of that State may be given priority notwithstanding paragraph 1 of this article.

Article 31
Mandatory rules

1. Nothing in articles 27 to 29 restricts the application of the rules of the law of the forum State in a situation where they are mandatory irrespective of the law otherwise applicable.

2. Nothing in articles 27 to 29 restricts the application of the mandatory rules of the law of another State with which the matters settled in those articles have a close connection if and insofar as, under the law of that other State, those rules must be applied irrespective of the law otherwise applicable.

Article 32
Public policy

With regard to matters settled in this chapter, the application of a provision of the law specified in this chapter may be refused only if the application of that provision is manifestly contrary to the public policy of the forum State.

Chapter VI
Final provisions

Article 33
Depositary

The Secretary-General of the United Nations is the depositary of this Convention.

Article 34
Signature, ratification, acceptance, approval, accession

1. This Convention is open for signature by all States at the Headquarters of the United Nations in New York until 31 December 2003.

2. This Convention is subject to ratification, acceptance or approval by the signatory States.

3. This Convention is open to accession by all States that are not signatory States as from the date it is open for signature.

4. Instruments of ratification, acceptance, approval and accession are to be deposited with the Secretary-General of the United Nations.

Article 35
Application to territorial units

1. If a State has two or more territorial units in which different systems of law are applicable in relation to the matters dealt with in this Convention, it may at any time declare that this Convention is to extend to all its territorial units or only one or more of them, and may at any time substitute another declaration for its earlier declaration.

2. Such declarations are to state expressly the territorial units to which this Convention extends.

3. If, by virtue of a declaration under this article, this Convention does not extend to all territorial units of a State and the assignor or the debtor is located in a territorial unit to which this Convention does not extend, this location is considered not to be in a Contracting State.

4. If, by virtue of a declaration under this article, this Convention does not extend to all territorial units of a State and the law governing the original contract is the law in force in a territorial unit to which this Convention does not extend, the law governing the original contract is considered not to be the law of a Contracting State.

5. If a State makes no declaration under paragraph 1 of this article, the Convention is to extend to all territorial units of that State.

Article 36
Location in a territorial unit

If a person is located in a State which has two or more territorial units, that person is located in the territorial unit in which it has its place of business. If the assignor or the assignee has a place of business in more than one territorial unit, the place of business is that place where the central administration of the assignor or the assignee is exercised. If the debtor has a place of business in more than one territorial unit, the place of business is that which has the closest relationship to the original contract. If a person does not have a place of business, reference is to be made to the habitual residence of that person. A State with two or more territorial units may specify by declaration at any time other rules for determining the location of a person within that State.

Article 37
Applicable law in territorial units

Any reference in this Convention to the law of a State means, in the case of a State which has two or more territorial units, the law in force in the territorial unit. Such a State may specify by declaration at any time other rules for determining the applicable law, including rules that render applicable the law of another territorial unit of that State.

Article 38
Conflicts with other international agreements

1. This Convention does not prevail over any international agreement that has already been or may be entered into and that specifically governs a transaction otherwise governed by this Convention.

2. Notwithstanding paragraph 1 of this article, this Convention prevails over the Unidroit Convention on International Factoring ("the Ottawa Convention"). To the extent that this Convention does not apply to the rights and obligations of a debtor, it does not preclude the application of the Ottawa Convention with respect to the rights and obligations of that debtor.

Article 39
Declaration on application of chapter V

A State may declare at any time that it will not be bound by chapter V.

Article 40
Limitations relating to Governments and other public entities

A State may declare at any time that it will not be bound or the extent to which it will not be bound by articles 9 and 10 if the debtor or any person granting a personal or property right securing payment of the assigned receivable is located in that State at the time of conclusion of the original contract and is a Government, central or local, any subdivision thereof, or an entity constituted for a public purpose. If a State has made such a declaration, articles 9 and 10 do not affect the rights and obligations of that debtor or person. A State may list in a declaration the types of entity that are the subject of a declaration.

Article 41
Other exclusions

1. A State may declare at any time that it will not apply this Convention to specific types of assignment or to the assignment of specific categories of receivables clearly described in a declaration.

2. After a declaration under paragraph 1 of this article takes effect:

(a) This Convention does not apply to such types of assignment or to the assignment of such categories of receivables if the assignor is located at the time of conclusion of the contract of assignment in such a State; and

(b) The provisions of this Convention that affect the rights and obligations of the debtor do not apply if, at the time of conclusion of the original contract, the debtor is located in such a State or the law governing the original contract is the law of such a State.

3. This article does not apply to assignments of receivables listed in article 9, paragraph 3.

Article 42
Application of the annex

1. A State may at any time declare that it will be bound by:

(a) The priority rules set forth in section I of the annex and will participate in the international registration system established pursuant to section II of the annex;

(b) The priority rules set forth in section I of the annex and will effectuate such rules by use of a registration system that fulfils the purposes of such rules, in which case, for the purposes of section I of the annex, registration pursuant to such a system has the same effect as registration pursuant to section II of the annex;

(c) The priority rules set forth in section III of the annex;

(d) The priority rules set forth in section IV of the annex; or

(e) The priority rules set forth in articles 7 and 9 of the annex.

2. For the purposes of article 22:

(a) The law of a State that has made a declaration pursuant to paragraph 1 *(a)* or *(b)* of this article is the set of rules set forth in section I of the annex, as affected by any declaration made pursuant to paragraph 5 of this article;

(b) The law of a State that has made a declaration pursuant to paragraph 1 *(c)* of this article is the set of rules set forth in section III of the annex, as affected by any declaration made pursuant to paragraph 5 of this article;

(c) The law of a State that has made a declaration pursuant to paragraph 1 *(d)* of this article is the set of rules set forth in section IV of the annex, as affected by any declaration made pursuant to paragraph 5 of this article; and

(d) The law of a State that has made a declaration pursuant to paragraph 1 *(e)* of this article is the set of rules set forth in articles 7 and 9 of the annex, as affected by any declaration made pursuant to paragraph 5 of this article.

3. A State that has made a declaration pursuant to paragraph 1 of this article may establish rules pursuant to which contracts of assignment concluded before the declaration takes effect become subject to those rules within a reasonable time.

4. A State that has not made a declaration pursuant to paragraph 1 of this article may, in accordance with priority rules in force in that State, utilize the registration system established pursuant to section II of the annex.

5. At the time a State makes a declaration pursuant to paragraph 1 of this article or thereafter, it may declare that:

(a) It will not apply the priority rules chosen under paragraph 1 of this article to certain types of assignment or to the assignment of certain categories of receivables; or

(b) It will apply those priority rules with modifications specified in that declaration.

6. At the request of Contracting or Signatory States to this Convention comprising not less than one third of the Contracting and Signatory States, the depositary shall convene a conference of the Contracting and Signatory States to designate the supervising authority and the first registrar and to prepare or revise the regulations referred to in section II of the annex.

Article 43
Effect of declaration

1. Declarations made under articles 35, paragraph 1, 36, 37 or 39 to 42 at the time of signature are subject to confirmation upon ratification, acceptance or approval.

2. Declarations and confirmations of declarations are to be in writing and to be formally notified to the depositary.

3. A declaration takes effect simultaneously with the entry into force of this Convention in respect of the State concerned. However, a declaration of which the depositary receives formal notification after such entry into force takes effect on the first day of the month following the expiration of six months after the date of its receipt by the depositary.

4. A State that makes a declaration under articles 35, paragraph 1, 36, 37 or 39 to 42 may withdraw it at any time by a formal notification in writing addressed to the depositary. Such withdrawal takes effect on the first day of the month following the expiration of six months after the date of the receipt of the notification by the depositary.

5. In the case of a declaration under articles 35, paragraph 1, 36, 37 or 39 to 42 that takes effect after the entry into force of this Convention in respect of the State concerned or in the case of a withdrawal of any such declaration, the effect of which in either case is to cause a rule in this Convention, including any annex, to become applicable:

(a) Except as provided in paragraph 5 *(b)* of this article, that rule is applicable only to assignments for which the contract of assignment is concluded on or after the date when the declaration or withdrawal takes effect in respect of the Contracting State referred to in article 1, paragraph 1 *(a)*;

(b) A rule that deals with the rights and obligations of the debtor applies only in respect of original contracts concluded on or after the date when the declaration or withdrawal takes effect in respect of the Contracting State referred to in article 1, paragraph 3.

6. In the case of a declaration under articles 35, paragraph 1, 36, 37 or 39 to 42 that takes effect after the entry into force of this Convention in respect of the State concerned or in the case of a withdrawal of any such declaration, the effect of which in either case is to cause a rule in this Convention, including any annex, to become inapplicable:

(a) Except as provided in paragraph 6 (b) of this article, that rule is inapplicable to assignments for which the contract of assignment is concluded on or after the date when the declaration or withdrawal takes effect in respect of the Contracting State referred to in article 1, paragraph 1 (a);

(b) A rule that deals with the rights and obligations of the debtor is inapplicable in respect of original contracts concluded on or after the date when the declaration or withdrawal takes effect in respect of the Contracting State referred to in article 1, paragraph 3.

7. If a rule rendered applicable or inapplicable as a result of a declaration or withdrawal referred to in paragraph 5 or 6 of this article is relevant to the determination of priority with respect to a receivable for which the contract of assignment is concluded before such declaration or withdrawal takes effect or with respect to its proceeds, the right of the assignee has priority over the right of a competing claimant to the extent that, under the law that would determine priority before such declaration or withdrawal takes effect, the right of the assignee would have priority.

Article 44
Reservations

No reservations are permitted except those expressly authorized in this Convention.

Article 45
Entry into force

1. This Convention enters into force on the first day of the month following the expiration of six months from the date of deposit of the fifth instrument of ratification, acceptance, approval or accession with the depositary.

2. For each State that becomes a Contracting State to this Convention after the date of deposit of the fifth instrument of ratification, acceptance, approval or accession, this Convention enters into force on the first day of the month following the expiration of six months after the date of deposit of the appropriate instrument on behalf of that State.

3. This Convention applies only to assignments if the contract of assignment is concluded on or after the date when this Convention enters into force in respect of the Contracting State referred to in article 1, paragraph 1 (a), provided that the provisions of this Convention that deal with the rights and obligations of the debtor apply only to assignments of receivables arising from original contracts concluded on or after the date when this Convention enters into force in respect of the Contracting State referred to in article 1, paragraph 3.

4. If a receivable is assigned pursuant to a contract of assignment concluded before the date when this Convention enters into force in respect of the Contracting State referred to in article 1, paragraph 1 (a), the right of the assignee has priority over the right of a competing claimant with respect to the receivable to the extent that, under the law that would determine

priority in the absence of this Convention, the right of the assignee would have priority.

Article 46
Denunciation

1. A Contracting State may denounce this Convention at any time by written notification addressed to the depositary.

2. The denunciation takes effect on the first day of the month following the expiration of one year after the notification is received by the depositary. Where a longer period is specified in the notification, the denunciation takes effect upon the expiration of such longer period after the notification is received by the depositary.

3. This Convention remains applicable to assignments if the contract of assignment is concluded before the date when the denunciation takes effect in respect of the Contracting State referred to in article 1, paragraph 1 (a), provided that the provisions of this Convention that deal with the rights and obligations of the debtor remain applicable only to assignments of receivables arising from original contracts concluded before the date when the denunciation takes effect in respect of the Contracting State referred to in article 1, paragraph 3.

4. If a receivable is assigned pursuant to a contract of assignment concluded before the date when the denunciation takes effect in respect of the Contracting State referred to in article 1, paragraph 1 (a), the right of the assignee has priority over the right of a competing claimant with respect to the receivable to the extent that, under the law that would determine priority under this Convention, the right of the assignee would have priority.

Article 47
Revision and amendment

1. At the request of not less than one third of the Contracting States to this Convention, the depositary shall convene a conference of the Contracting States to revise or amend it.

2. Any instrument of ratification, acceptance, approval or accession deposited after the entry into force of an amendment to this Convention is deemed to apply to the Convention as amended.

Annex to the Convention

Section I
Priority rules based on registration

Article 1
Priority among several assignees

As between assignees of the same receivable from the same assignor, the priority of the right of an assignee in the assigned receivable is determined by the order in which data about the assignment are registered under section II of this annex, regardless of the time of transfer of the receivable. If no such data are registered, priority is determined by the order of conclusion of the respective contracts of assignment.

Article 2
Priority between the assignee and the insolvency administrator or creditors of the assignor

The right of an assignee in an assigned receivable has priority over the right of an insolvency administrator and creditors who obtain a right in the assigned receivable by attachment, judicial act or similar act of a competent authority that gives rise to such right, if the receivable was assigned, and data about the assignment were registered under section II of this annex, before the commencement of such insolvency proceeding, attachment, judicial act or similar act.

Section II
Registration

Article 3
Establishment of a registration system

A registration system will be established for the registration of data about assignments, even if the relevant assignment or receivable is not international, pursuant to the regulations to be promulgated by the registrar and the supervising authority. Regulations promulgated by the registrar and the supervising authority under this annex shall be consistent with this annex. The regulations will prescribe in detail the manner in which the registration system will operate, as well as the procedure for resolving disputes relating to that operation.

Article 4
Registration

1. Any person may register data with regard to an assignment at the registry in accordance with this annex and the regulations. As provided in the regulations, the data registered shall be the identification of the assignor and the assignee and a brief description of the assigned receivables.

2. A single registration may cover one or more assignments by the assignor to the assignee of one or more existing or future receivables, irrespective of whether the receivables exist at the time of registration.

3. A registration may be made in advance of the assignment to which it relates. The regulations will establish the procedure for the cancellation of a registration in the event that the assignment is not made.

4. Registration or its amendment is effective from the time when the data set forth in paragraph 1 of this article are available to searchers. The registering party may specify, from options set forth in the regulations, a period of effectiveness for the registration. In the absence of such a specification, a registration is effective for a period of five years.

5. Regulations will specify the manner in which registration may be renewed, amended or cancelled and regulate such other matters as are necessary for the operation of the registration system.

6. Any defect, irregularity, omission or error with regard to the identification of the assignor that would result in data registered not being found upon a search based on a proper identification of the assignor renders the registration ineffective.

Article 5
Registry searches

1. Any person may search the records of the registry according to identification of the assignor, as set forth in the regulations, and obtain a search result in writing.

2. A search result in writing that purports to be issued by the registry is admissible as evidence and is, in the absence of evidence to the contrary, proof of the registration of the data to which the search relates, including the date and hour of registration.

Section III
Priority rules based on the time of the contract of assignment

Article 6
Priority among several assignees

As between assignees of the same receivable from the same assignor, the priority of the right of an assignee in the assigned receivable is determined by the order of conclusion of the respective contracts of assignment.

Article 7
Priority between the assignee and the insolvency administrator or creditors of the assignor

The right of an assignee in an assigned receivable has priority over the right of an insolvency administrator and creditors who obtain a right in the assigned receivable by attachment, judicial act or similar act of a competent authority that gives rise to such right, if the receivable was assigned before the commencement of such insolvency proceeding, attachment, judicial act or similar act.

Article 8
Proof of time of contract of assignment

The time of conclusion of a contract of assignment in respect of articles 6 and 7 of this annex may be proved by any means, including witnesses.

Section IV
Priority rules based on the time of notification of assignment

Article 9
Priority among several assignees

As between assignees of the same receivable from the same assignor, the priority of the right of an assignee in the assigned receivable is determined by the order in which notification of the respective assignments is received by the debtor. However, an assignee may not obtain priority over a prior assignment of which the assignee had knowledge at the time of conclusion of the contract of assignment to that assignee by notifying the debtor.

Article 10
Priority between the assignee and the insolvency administrator or creditors of the assignor

The right of an assignee in an assigned receivable has priority over the right of an insolvency administrator and creditors who obtain a right in the assigned receivable by attachment, judicial act or similar act of a competent authority that gives rise to such right, if the receivable was assigned and notification was received by the debtor before the commencement of such insolvency proceeding, attachment, judicial act or similar act.

DONE at . . . , this . . . day of . . . two thousand one, in a single original, of which the Arabic, Chinese, English, French, Russian and Spanish texts are equally authentic.

IN WITNESS WHEREOF the undersigned plenipotentiaries, being duly authorized by their respective Governments, have signed the present Convention.

International commercial arbitration

Privately financed infrastructure projects

UNCITRAL took note of the results of the Colloquium on Privately Financed Infrastructure: Legal Framework and Technical Assistance (Vienna, 2-4 July), organized by the Secretariat with the co-sponsorship of the Public-Private Infrastructure Advisory Facility, a multi-donor technical assistance facility aimed at helping developing countries improve the quality of their infrastructure through private sector involvement. UNCITRAL agreed that the Colloquium's proceedings should be published by the United Nations and endorsed its recommendation that the Secretariat, in coordination with other organizations, should undertake joint initiatives to ensure widespread awareness of the 2000 UNCITRAL Legislative Guide on Privately Financed Infrastructure Projects [YUN 2000, p. 1278].

In the light of the views expressed as to the desirability and feasibility of further work in privately financed infrastructure projects, UNCITRAL agreed that a working group should be entrusted with the task of drafting core model legislative provisions in that field.

Implementation of the 1958 New York Convention

UNCITRAL noted that, at the beginning of its June/July session, the Secretariat had received replies from 59 States parties (out of the current 125) to its questionnaire relating to the legal regime governing the recognition and enforcement of foreign awards in States parties to the 1958 Convention on the Recognition and Enforcement of Foreign Arbitral Awards (New York Convention) [YUN 1958, p. 390]. The Commission repeated its appeal to States parties to the Convention that had not replied to the questionnaire to do so as soon as possible, and requested the Secretariat to prepare, for a future UNCITRAL session, a note presenting the findings based on the analysis of the information gathered.

Commercial dispute settlement

UNCITRAL considered the report of the Working Group on Arbitration on its thirty-third (Vienna, 20 November–1 December 2000) and thirty-fourth (New York, 21 May–1 June 2001) sessions. It commended the Working Group for the progress accomplished regarding the three main issues under discussion, namely, the requirement of the written form for the arbitration agreement, interim measures of protection and the preparation of a model law on conciliation.

Regarding the first issue, it was pointed out that, while the Working Group should not lose sight of the importance of providing certainty as to the intent of the parties to arbitrate, it was equally important to work towards facilitating a more flexible interpretation of the strict form requirement contained in the 1958 New York Convention so as not to frustrate the parties' expectations when they agreed to arbitrate. In that respect, UNCITRAL took note of the possibility that the Working Group could examine further the meaning and effect of the more-favourable-right provision of article VII of the New York Convention. As to the second issue, the Working Group was requested to continue its work on the basis of revised draft provisions of the 1985 UNCITRAL Model Law on International Commercial Arbitration to be prepared by the Secretariat. On the third issue, it was requested to complete the examination of articles 1-16 of the draft model legislative provisions on conciliation as a matter of priority, with a view to presenting a draft model law on conciliation for review and adoption by UNCITRAL at its 2002 session.

Case law on UNCITRAL texts

UNCITRAL noted the ongoing work under the established system for the collection and dissemination of case law on UNCITRAL texts (CLOUT). It was noted that CLOUT was an important means of promoting the uniform interpretation and application of UNCITRAL texts by enabling interested persons, such as judges, arbitrators, lawyers or parties to commercial transactions, to take into account decisions and awards of other jurisdictions when rendering their own judgements or opinions or adjusting their actions to the prevailing interpretation of those texts. The Commission expressed appreciation to national correspondents for their work in the collection of relevant decisions and arbitral awards and the preparation of case abstracts, as well as to the Secretariat for compiling, editing, issuing and distributing abstracts.

Transport law

As requested by UNCITRAL, the Secretary-General submitted a report on possible future work in transport law, describing in particular the scope of and issues to be dealt with in a future legislative instrument on the carriage of goods by sea. Those issues included the scope of application of the instrument, the period of responsibility of the carrier, its obligations and liability, obligations of the shipper, transport documents, freight, delivery to the consignee, right of control of parties interested in the cargo during carriage, transfer of rights in goods, the party that had the right to bring an action against the carrier and the time bar for action against the carrier.

To consider the issues outlined in the report, UNCITRAL established a working group for which the Secretariat would prepare a preliminary working document containing drafts on possible solutions for a future instrument, and the International Maritime Committee would prepare alternatives and comments. UNCITRAL decided that the work should include issues of liability and that the working group should initially cover port-to-port transport operations, although it would be free to study the desirability and feasibility of dealing with door-to-door transport operations.

Model law on corporate insolvency

UNCITRAL considered the report on the UNCITRAL-INSOL-IBA Global Insolvency Colloquium (Vienna, 4-6 December 2000), which provided a forum for dialogue among insolvency practitioners and experts, international organizations and government representatives on the work carried out by other organizations—the World Bank, the International Monetary Fund (IMF), the Asian Development Bank (ADB), the International Federation of Insolvency Professionals (INSOL) and the International Bar Association (IBA)—in the area of insolvency law reform. The report noted the key elements that an insolvency regime should address: eligibility and access criteria; bankruptcy estate; application of automatic stay; role of management; role of creditors/creditor committees; treatment of contractual obligations; avoidance actions; distribution priorities; and additional issues specific to reorganization (relationship between liquidation and reorganization; business operations and financing; and provisions specific to the reorganization plan).

UNCITRAL discussed the Colloquium's recommendations, in particular the form that future work might take and the interpretation of the mandate given to the Working Group in 2000 [YUN 2000, p. 1280]. The recommendations outlined three key areas for organizing the material for future work: the first would reflect the key component of the reports from the World Bank, IMF and ADB, setting out the core elements of an effective insolvency regime and considering alternative policy options and approaches to the different issues identified, including the impact of social and economic factors; the second would be a comparative analysis of some of the provisions and precedents already in existence in national legislation and international instruments;

and the third would set forth recommendations or outlines of legislative provisions. UNCITRAL confirmed that the Working Group's mandate should be broadly interpreted to ensure an appropriately flexible work product in the form of a legislative guide.

Security interests

UNCITRAL considered a Secretariat note containing a study on the issue of security interests, requested by UNCITRAL to facilitate its consideration of future work in the area of secured transaction law. The study discussed the relationship between insolvency law and the law on security rights. It addressed issues pertaining to the development of model legislative solutions on security rights in general; the drafting of asset-specific model legislation, in particular securities and intellectual property rights; and private international law.

Following discussion of the foregoing study, UNCITRAL established a Working Group on Security Interests to develop an efficient legal regime for security rights in goods involved in a commercial activity, including inventory; and to identify the issues to be addressed, such as the form of the instrument, the exact scope of the assets that could serve as collateral, the perfection of security, the degree of formalities to be complied with, the need for an efficient and well-balanced enforcement regime, the scope of the debt that might be secured, the means of publicizing the existence of security rights, the limitations, if any, on the creditors entitled to the security right, the effects of bankruptcy on the enforcement of that right and the certainty and predictability of the creditor's priority over competing interests.

Emphasizing the importance of the subject matter and the need to consult with practitioners and organizations with the relevant expertise, UNCITRAL recommended that a two- or three-day colloquium be held before the first session of the Working Group in 2002.

Training and technical assistance

UNCITRAL had before it a Secretariat note indicating training and technical assistance activities undertaken since its 2000 session and the direction of future activities. It reported that five seminars/briefing missions and a symposium were held, and that for the remainder of 2001 only some requests from Africa, Asia, Latin America and Eastern Europe could be met due to insufficient resources.

UNCITRAL recommended that the General Assembly should request the Secretary-General to increase substantially the human and financial resources of its secretariat to enable it to implement fully its training and technical assistance programme. It reiterated its appeal to all States, international organizations and other interested entities for contributions to the UNCITRAL trust funds so as to enable its secretariat to meet the increasing demands in developing countries for training and assistance.

UNCITRAL membership

UNCITRAL consideration. On the question of the enlargement of its membership, UNCITRAL took note of the relevant background information prepared by the Secretariat to enable States to formulate a recommendation to the General Assembly. In that connection, it was observed that an enlarged UNCITRAL would, among other advantages, ensure representation of all legal traditions and economic systems, assist in better implementing its mandate by drawing on a correspondingly larger pool of experts, reflect the increased importance of international trade law for economic development and foster participation of those States that could not justify the resources for the preparation and attendance of UNCITRAL meetings unless they were members. In addition, no impact was foreseen on conference servicing by an increased membership.

A common theme in the debate on the size of the increase was the need to make UNCITRAL more representative of the Organization's membership without affecting its efficiency or working methods.

On 11 July, UNCITRAL recommended that the Assembly approve an increase in its membership from the current 36 States to 72, with the following distribution among the regional groups of the additional seats: 18 from the Group of African States, 14 from the Group of Asian States, 10 from the Group of Eastern European States, 12 from the Group of Latin American and Caribbean States and 18 from the Group of Western European and Other States; and elect the new members as soon as possible.

Report of Secretary-General. In response to General Assembly resolution 55/151 [YUN 2000, p. 1276], the Secretary-General submitted a report in August [A/56/315] on the implications of increasing UNCITRAL's membership. The report contained comments from 22 States in reply to his request for their views on the question. All supported an enlarged UNCITRAL, citing the need to align it with the increased UN membership so as to preserve its representative character, to make possible the participation of States in its work, the cost of which they could not justify unless they were members, and to promote the acceptability of UNCITRAL's work by broadening the spectrum of representation. The suggested increase ranged from 50 to at least 60 seats, which took into account the need to preserve UNCITRAL's efficiency.

By **decision 56/422** of 12 December, the Assembly deferred further consideration of and a decision on the enlargement of UNCITRAL's membership until its fifty-seventh (2002) session, under the item entitled "Report of the United Nations Commission on International Trade Law on the work of its thirty-fifth session".

PART FIVE

Institutional, administrative and budgetary questions

Chapter 1

Strengthening and restructuring of the United Nations system

In 2001, further progress was made in implementing the Secretary-General's programme of reform of the Organization, as Member States endorsed proposals in the priority areas of human resources reform, information technology policy and the capital master plan for refurbishing the UN Headquarters complex. Procurement reform had been completed successfully, the streamlining of the Organization's rules and procedures progressed, efforts continued to shift to a more results-based mode of operation and performance indicators were being introduced at all levels.

As follow-up to the outcome of the 2000 Millennium Summit, the Secretary-General presented a "road map" towards the implementation of the goals and commitments made by Member States in the Millennium Declaration, which the General Assembly recommended should be considered as a useful guide when formulating plans for implementing those goals. The Assembly also took up the issue of revitalizing its work through improvement of its procedures and working methods and adopted a text addressing relevant issues concerning its agenda, consideration of reports, organization of work, role of the Assembly President and the use of modern technology.

The Secretary-General reported on the restructuring and revitalization of the United Nations in the economic, social and related fields, describing progress in the implementation of relevant resolutions of the Assembly and the Economic and Social Council and recommending measures for further progress. He also reviewed the work of UN oversight bodies—the Office of Internal Oversight Services and the Joint Inspection Unit—and reported continuing progress in ongoing discussions on increasing the membership of the Security Council within the Open-ended Working Group on the Question of Equitable Representation on and Increase in the Membership of the Security Council and Other Matters related to the Security Council. A review of the outcome of the consolidation of the three former economic and social departments into the Department of Economic and Social Affairs confirmed that the emergent Department had made notable progress in implementing the goals for which it was established.

Programme of reform

General aspects

The Secretary-General continued to implement his programme for UN reform, first introduced in 1997 [YUN 1997, p. 1389]. In his annual report on the work of the Organization (see p. 3), he said Member States had endorsed proposals in three priority areas for management reform: human resources reform, information technology policy and the capital master plan. The comprehensive human resources reform introduced would change the Organization's management culture, modernize its management standards and strengthen its capacity to recruit, develop and manage its staff. The information technology strategy, designed to promote access to and sharing of information, and to support field operations, strengthen technical infrastructure, build human resources capacity and launch an electronic administration, would ensure a coordinated approach to technical challenges. In that regard, the Integrated Management Information System (IMIS), an electronic administration system for human resources, finance, accounts and procurement, was being installed throughout the Secretariat, and there were plans to further develop and extend its use, including to all major duty stations and peacekeeping missions (see p. 1390). A comprehensive design plan and a detailed cost analysis were being prepared for the capital master plan for refurbishing the Headquarters complex (see p. 1394).

Other initiatives included the successful completion of procurement reform, the progressive simplification and streamlining of the Organization's rules and procedures, the shifting to a more results-based mode of operation, leading to the introduction of performance indicators at all levels, the introduction and refinement of performance measurements, through the performance appraisal system, and the introduction of results-based budgeting (see p. 1317) designed to ensure the delivery of high-priority services. The Secretariat would continue to implement comprehensive management reform, introducing best management practices and technologies to ensure that the limited resources were made available for priorities. It would complete and implement a Key Item Management Reporting System and make productivity a managerial responsibility. Innovations would continue to be introduced in the overall information technology strategy, and human resources management reform would also go on.

By **decision 56/464** of 24 December, the General Assembly decided that the item entitled "United Nations reform: measures and proposals" would remain for consideration during its resumed fifty-sixth (2002) session.

Road map for implementing the Millennium Declaration

The Secretary-General, as requested in General Assembly resolution 55/162 [YUN 2000, p. 62], submitted a September report [A/56/326], in which he outlined his road map for the implementation of the United Nations Millennium Declaration, adopted by the Assembly in resolution 55/2 [YUN 2000, p. 49]. The report set out in detail how the commitments made by Member States in the Declaration could be fulfilled. It examined the interaction of the different goals with each other, highlighting cross-cutting issues, and outlined potential strategies for action, with suggested paths to follow for meeting each goal, and shared information on best practices. The report examined the Millennium Declaration goals related to peace, security and disarmament (see p. 47); development and poverty eradication (see p. 753); protecting the environment (see p. 961); human rights, democracy and good governance (see p. 640); protecting the vulnerable; meeting the special needs of Africa (see p. 848); and strengthening the United Nations.

In terms of strengthening the United Nations, the Secretary-General argued that, for the Organization to continue being a catalyst for change and a forum for dialogue and effective action, it would have to be renewed and modernized to cope with the challenges of the millennium. Strategies for strengthening the Organization would be directed towards continuing efforts to revitalize and streamline the Assembly's work and strengthen the office of its President (see p. 1287); consideration in the Assembly of expanding the size and composition of the Security Council, the reform of its methods of work and enhancing its ability to anticipate, prevent and react to events on short notice; and consideration of how best the Economic and Social Council could fulfil its mandate and streamline its work. States would be encouraged to use the International Court of Justice more frequently for the resolution of their disputes and the number of

organizations entitled to request advisory opinions of the Court increased. Other strategies included ensuring that all States paid their dues in full, on time and without preconditions and reform of the budget methodology and practice progressed; information technologies were allocated sufficient resources and were strategically developed throughout the Secretariat; and the modernization of human resources policies and procedures and the streamlining of administrative procedures continued. Greater attention would be paid to the safety of UN and associated personnel, building a stronger relationship among the United Nations, the Bretton Woods institutions (the World Bank Group and the International Monetary Fund) and the World Trade Organization, deepening the relationship with the Inter-Parliamentary Union, and engaging the private sector, non-governmental organizations and the rest of civil society through the United Nations Fund for International Partnerships (see p. 810) and the Global Compact [YUN 2000, p. 989]. The Secretary-General concluded that the road map attempted to carry forward the vision of world leaders at the Millennium Summit and offered suggestions for the future. He would submit a yearly report charting progress made in fulfilling the millennium commitments and highlighting specific themes of special significance for each year, and a comprehensive progress report every five years. He proposed that the Assembly consider as themes, for 2002, preventing armed conflict and the treatment and prevention of diseases, including HIV/AIDS and malaria; for 2003, financing for development and strategies for sustainable development; and for 2004, bridging the digital divide and curbing transnational crime. Annexed to the report was a comprehensive set of indicators to assess progress in achieving development goals.

ACC consideration. The High-level Committee on Programmes of the Administrative Committee on Coordination (ACC), at its second regular session of 2001 (Geneva, 25-26 September) [ACC/2001/11], considered the Secretary-General's road map and ways to enhance coordination and coherence in the UN system to assist Member States to realize the goals of the Millennium Declaration. In that context, it discussed an inventory exercise to help it devise a potential action plan, identify gaps, overlaps and areas of inter-agency cooperation, and monitor progress in the implementation of UN system actions and initiatives. The Committee recommended to ACC that consideration be given to identifying a limited set of initiatives in the areas relating to the themes proposed in the Secretary-General's report for the years 2002 to 2004 (see above), elaborating action plans and aiming for concrete results within a five-year time-span, taking into account the principles of joint accountability and continuous learning. Special efforts should continue to help countries implement programmes and monitor goals and targets.

GENERAL ASSEMBLY ACTION

On 14 December [meeting 86], the General Assembly adopted **resolution 56/95** [draft: A/56/L.48] without vote [agenda item 29].

Follow-up to the outcome of the Millennium Summit

The General Assembly,

Recalling its resolution 55/2 of 8 September 2000, by which it adopted the United Nations Millennium Declaration as the outcome of the Millennium Summit of the United Nations, held at Headquarters from 6 to 8 September 2000,

Recalling also its resolution 55/162 of 14 December 2000, in which it, inter alia, requested the Secretary-General to prepare a long-term "road map" towards the implementation of the Millennium Declaration within the United Nations system and to submit it to the General Assembly at its fifty-sixth session,

Reaffirming the need to maintain the will and momentum of the Millennium Summit, as well as the importance of a comprehensive and balanced approach in the implementation of and follow-up to the Millennium Declaration,

1. *Takes note with appreciation* of the report of the Secretary-General entitled "Road map towards the implementation of the United Nations Millennium Declaration";

2. *Recommends* that the "road map" be considered as a useful guide in the implementation of the Millennium Declaration by the United Nations system, and invites Member States, as well as the Bretton Woods institutions, the World Trade Organization and other interested parties to consider the "road map" when formulating plans for implementing goals related to the Declaration;

3. *Requests* the Secretary-General to prepare an annual report and a comprehensive report every five years on progress achieved by the United Nations system and Member States towards implementing the Millennium Declaration, drawing upon the "road map" and in accordance with resolution 55/162, and requests that the annual reports focus on cross-cutting and cross-sectoral issues, as well as on the major areas set forth in the "road map", while the quinquennial comprehensive reports examine progress achieved towards implementing all the commitments made in the Declaration;

4. *Invites* the United Nations system, in cooperation with Member States, to adopt specific measures to give widespread publicity to the Millennium Declaration and to increase the dissemination of information on the Declaration;

5. *Decides* to include in the provisional agenda of its fifty-seventh session the item entitled "Follow-up to the outcome of the Millennium Summit".

On 24 December, the Assembly decided that the item on follow-up to the outcome of the Millennium Summit would remain for consideration during its resumed fifty-sixth (2002) session (**decision 56/464**).

Managerial reform and oversight

Procurement

The General Assembly, at its resumed fifty-fifth session, continued consideration of the Secretary-General's reports on procurement reform [YUN 2000, p. 1286], measures taken to improve procurement activities in the field [ibid., p. 111], procurement-related arbitration [YUN 1999, p. 1315] and the related reports of the Advisory Committee on Administrative and Budgetary Questions (ACABQ) [YUN 2000, p. 1286] (see p. 1280), and the March report of the Office of Internal Oversight Services (OIOS) on the follow-up audit of the implementation of procurement reform (see below).

OIOS report. The OIOS report [A/55/746], transmitted by the Secretary-General pursuant to Assembly resolutions 48/218 B [YUN 1994, p. 1362] and 54/244 [YUN 1999, p. 1274], aimed to verify that the recommendations of the High-level Group of Experts on Procurement [YUN 1996, p. 1381] and of various oversight bodies had been satisfactorily implemented, and to identify areas requiring further improvement, as well as any new issues. The follow-up audit, carried out at UN Headquarters from November 1999 to May 2000, included a review of 51 procurement cases valued at $116 million.

The OIOS audit found that its 1998 recommendations on procurement reform [YUN 1998, p. 1253] had been satisfactorily implemented, and overall there had been a significant improvement in the systems and procedures used by the Procurement Division. However, the UN procurement system needed further improvement and a number of issues had to be resolved, including that of the application of financial rule 110.17 (a) relating to contract requisitions exceeding $200,000, and decisions concerning the procurement of air transport services through letters of assist. It also found that the Procurement Division did not adequately monitor low-value procurement cases assigned to procurement assistants and that the procurement processing time for those cases appeared excessive.

To improve the procurement process, OIOS recommended, among other actions, that the Assistant Secretary-General for Central Support Services should re-examine the current interpretation of financial rule 110.17 (a) to ensure that all cases requiring verification by the Headquarters Committee on Contracts were submitted for review, and that the Procurement Division should review the implications of changing the period of reference under that rule. The Under-Secretary-General for Management should review and approve all formal interpretations of the procurement-related financial regulations and rules, and the Under-Secretary-General for Peacekeeping Operations should ensure that decisions to contract with Governments were made only after determining that the conditions for using letters of assist had been met and the basis for those decisions fully documented. The Assistant Secretary-General for Central Support Services should ensure that recommendations of the Office of Legal Affairs and the Headquarters Committee on Contracts concerning procurement were fully implemented. The Procurement Division should conduct a market survey of air transportation services contractors by region and encourage them to register as prospective vendors, and ensure that the assignments given to procurement assistants included target completion dates and that major departures from those dates were approved and remaining cases were followed up in a timely manner.

ACABQ report. ACABQ, in a March report [A/55/829], considered the Secretary-General's 1999 report on procurement arbitration [YUN 1999, p. 1315] and a report on the examination of practices and procedures in the handling of arbitration/claim cases conducted by the UN Board of Auditors at ACABQ's request. ACABQ noted the lack of coordination between the Office of Legal Affairs and the Office of Central Support Services, which exposed the Organization to claims because of the lack of sufficient rigour in negotiating, reviewing and managing contracts. ACABQ endorsed the Board's recommendations, which it believed would, if fully implemented, eliminate the shortcomings identified and strengthen the Secretariat's capacity, thereby minimizing the Organization's exposure to claims and litigation. It requested a comprehensive report on the results of the implementation of the Board's recommendations by February 2002, in the context of the review of the 2002/03 budgets for peacekeeping operations, indicating actions taken and the changes, effects and results of those actions.

ACABQ also recommended that all claims, names of claimants and amounts claimed be fully disclosed in peacekeeping performance reports and that information on the circumstances of those claims be submitted to it. It emphasized that all procedures designed to prevent a conflict of interest, or the appearance of such, should be rigorously applied. The administration needed to

make greater efforts to monitor more effectively the cost to the United Nations of fees to outside counsel, and contracts awarded should contain provisions to ensure strict adherence to fee caps.

GENERAL ASSEMBLY ACTION

On 12 April [meeting 98], the General Assembly, on the recommendation of the Fifth (Administrative and Budgetary) Committee [A/55/532/Add.2], adopted **resolution 55/247** without vote [agenda item 116].

Procurement reform

The General Assembly,

Recalling its resolutions 52/214 B and 52/220 of 22 December 1997, 52/212 B of 31 March 1998, 52/252 of 8 September 1998, 53/204 and 53/208 B of 18 December 1998 and 54/14 of 29 October 1999,

Having considered the reports of the Secretary-General on procurement reform, on measures taken to improve procurement activities in the field and on procurement-related arbitration and the related reports of the Advisory Committee on Administrative and Budgetary Questions, as well as the report of the Office of Internal Oversight Services on the follow-up audit of the implementation of procurement reform,

1. *Takes note* of the reports of the Secretary-General and of the comments and observations contained in the reports of the Advisory Committee on Administrative and Budgetary Questions;

2. *Welcomes* the progress achieved so far in addressing the concerns expressed in General Assembly resolution 54/14, and urges the Secretary-General to continue the full implementation of the resolution;

3. *Stresses* the need for the procurement process to be efficient, transparent and cost-effective and to reflect fully the international character of the Organization;

4. *Endorses* the observations of the Advisory Committee in paragraph 6 of its report concerning procurement reform, and requests the Secretary-General to ensure proper accountability and training of all those involved in the procurement process at Headquarters and in the field;

5. *Stresses* the need for adequate training of all personnel involved in the procurement process at Headquarters and in the field;

6. *Takes note* of the experiences of the United Nations Educational, Scientific and Cultural Organization and the Office of the United Nations High Commissioner for Refugees referred to in the report of the Secretary-General on procurement reform, and reaffirms the need for the Secretary-General to continue to explore ways to increase procurement opportunities for vendors from developing countries and countries with economies in transition;

7. *Reiterates its request* to the Secretary-General for the expeditious dissemination of information relating to procurement in developing countries and countries with economies in transition, and requests the Secretary-General to pursue his efforts to sensitize the business community and United Nations offices in the developing countries and countries with economies in transition to procurement opportunities with the United Nations;

8. *Requests* the Secretary-General to continue to encourage the use of procurement from developing countries within the region for the requirements of missions when this is more efficient and cost-effective;

9. *Welcomes* the initiative taken by the Procurement Division to make procurement officials directly accountable to substantive departments that they support;

10. *Requests* the Secretary-General to determine if similar tracking mechanisms can be introduced in other areas of the Secretariat;

11. *Looks forward* to the issuance of a revised version of the Procurement Manual before the end of 2001;

12. *Encourages* the Secretary-General to continue to improve annual procurement planning for all offices and departments and to make such plans publicly available, including to all permanent missions to the United Nations;

13. *Reaffirms its request* to the Secretary-General to develop a comprehensive system to measure the efficiency and cost-effectiveness of the procurement function, by taking into account the best practices of other organizations of the United Nations system, reaffirms the need for the completion of the exercise, and requests the Secretary-General to submit to the General Assembly the results when completed;

14. *Expresses its concern* about delays in payments to vendors, and requests the Secretary-General to ensure that terms of contracts are respected;

15. *Requests* the Secretary-General to continue to monitor the discussions of the World Trade Organization on rules of origin and to keep the General Assembly informed of the progress achieved;

16. *Notes* that the detailed information requested in paragraph 20 of its resolution 54/14 was not included in the current report of the Secretary-General on procurement reform, and requests the Secretary-General to submit in future reports, as an annex, detailed information on the awarding of contracts for procurement at Headquarters and in the field to all countries, in particular to developing, least developed and African countries and countries with economies in transition;

17. *Also notes* the increase in the delegation of authority to the field in procurement activities, as mentioned in paragraph 6 of the report of the Advisory Committee concerning procurement reform, and requests the Secretary-General to ensure that there is capacity in field missions to perform the procurement functions properly as well as effective and efficient mechanisms at Headquarters for monitoring procurement in the field, including:

(*a*) Remedial measures taken to address problems identified with regard to the United Nations peacekeeping missions;

(*b*) Standardization of the corrective measures taken for existing and future peacekeeping operations;

(*c*) A description of how accountability was pursued in the cases of individuals found to have engaged in fraud, mismanagement or abuse and how accountability measures would be applied in the future;

18. *Requests* the Secretary-General to assess the workload and functions of all relevant units involved in the procurement process in order to guarantee that each is planning and performing with optimum efficiency and to ensure proper training for improving the skills of personnel involved in the procurement process;

19. *Reiterates* that the criteria for an exigency, as outlined in its decision 54/468 of 7 April 2000, must be met before making emergency procurements as an exigency provision, so that all procurements follow set procedures;

20. *Requests* the Secretary-General to submit to the General Assembly, through the Advisory Committee, proposals for revision of the Financial Regulations and Rules of the United Nations, which may facilitate the implementation of procurement reform;

21. *Also requests* the Secretary-General, pursuant to recommendation 4 made by the Office of Internal Oversight Services in its report, to ensure that the criteria contained in the Procurement Manual for the use of letters of assist are strictly adhered to, and in this connection requests that a report on the subject be submitted to the General Assembly;

22. *Reiterates* the need for executive heads of the funds and programmes of the United Nations to improve their procurement practices by simplifying the registration process for vendors who have already registered with another organization of the United Nations system, with a view to a more streamlined and transparent process, utilizing, among other things, the Internet;

23. *Requests* the Secretary-General to submit to the General Assembly at its fifty-seventh session a report on all aspects of procurement reform at Headquarters and in the field, including improvements to the procurement process within the United Nations funds and programmes, as well as on the implementation of the present resolution.

Oversight

Internal oversight

The Secretary-General, in transmitting a report on the activities of OIOS (see p. 1282), noted the accomplishments of the Office, as well as its continuing efforts to improve its relationships with management and all governing bodies, and to coordinate its programme with other oversight bodies, including the Board of External Auditors and the Joint Inspection Unit (JIU).

The General Assembly, by **decision 55/476** of 12 April, deferred until the second part of its resumed fifty-fifth (2001) session consideration of the report of the Secretary-General on OIOS activities. By **decision 55/461 A** of the same date, it took note of the OIOS reports on the follow-up to the 1997 review of the programme and administrative practices of the United Nations Centre for Human Settlements (Habitat) [YUN 2000, p. 994]; the follow-up to the 1996 review of the programme and administrative practices of the United Nations Environment Programme [ibid., p. 971]; the audit of the Office of the United Nations High Commissioner for Human Rights Field Operation in Rwanda [ibid., p. 600]; and the inspection of the outcome of the consolidation of the three former economic and social departments into the Department of Economic and Social Affairs (DESA) [A/55/750] (see p. 1291).

The Assembly considered reports of the Secretary-General on enhancing the internal oversight mechanisms in operational funds and programmes [YUN 1997, p. 855] and the updated version thereof [A/55/826 & Corr.1] (see p. 790); and rules and procedures to be applied for the investigation functions performed by OIOS [YUN 2000, p. 1289]. The Assembly also considered OIOS annual reports covering its activities from 1 July 1995 to 30 June 1996 [YUN 1996, p. 1268], 1 July 1996 to 30 June 1997 [YUN 1997, p. 1398], 1 July 1997 to 30 June 1998 [YUN 1998, p. 1258], 1 July 1998 to 30 June 1999 [YUN 1999, p. 1275] and 1 July 1999 to 30 June 2000 [YUN 2000, p. 1288]. Also considered were JIU comments on OIOS reports [YUN 1996, p. 1269; YUN 1997, p. 1400] and the Secretary-General's note on enhancing the internal oversight mechanisms in operational funds and programmes [A/C.5/55/23] (see p. 790).

GENERAL ASSEMBLY ACTION

On 14 June [meeting 103], the General Assembly, on the recommendation of the Fifth Committee [A/55/888/Add.1], adopted **resolution 55/259** without vote [agenda item 126].

Report of the Secretary-General on the activities of the Office of Internal Oversight Services

The General Assembly,

Having considered the following documents:

(a) Annual report of the Office of Internal Oversight Services for the period from 1 July 1995 to 30 June 1996,

(b) Note by the Secretary-General transmitting the comments of the Joint Inspection Unit on the final reports produced by the Office of Internal Oversight Services,

(c) Annual report of the Office of Internal Oversight Services for the period from 1 July 1996 to 30 June 1997,

(d) Note by the Secretary-General transmitting the comments of the Joint Inspection Unit on the final reports produced by the Office of Internal Oversight Services,

(e) Annual report of the Office of Internal Oversight Services for the period from 1 July 1997 to 30 June 1998,

(f) Annual report of the Office of Internal Oversight Services for the period from 1 July 1998 to 30 June 1999,

(g) Report of the Secretary-General on the rules and procedures to be applied for the investigation functions performed by the Office of Internal Oversight Services,

1. *Requests* the Secretary-General to ensure that future reports of the Office of Internal Oversight Services would be in accordance with the provisions of General Assembly resolutions 48/218 B of 29 July 1994 and 54/244 of 23 December 1999 and the relevant provi-

sions of the Charter of the United Nations and the rules of procedure of the General Assembly;

2. *Decides* to defer until its fifty-sixth session consideration of the updated version of the report of the Secretary-General on enhancing the internal oversight mechanisms in operational funds, and requests the Secretary-General to seek updated views from the funds and programmes on this report and to transmit them to the General Assembly during the main part of its fifty-sixth session;

3. *Also decides* to defer until its fifty-sixth session consideration of the sixth annual report of the Office of Internal Oversight Services, covering activities for the period from 1 July 1999 to 30 June 2000.

On the same date, the Assembly noted the OIOS report on the inspection of the consolidation of technical support services in the Department of General Assembly Affairs and Conference Services [A/55/803] (see p. 1383) (**decision 55/461 B**).

OIOS report. In September, the Secretary-General transmitted the seventh annual report of OIOS covering its activities from 1 July 2000 to 30 June 2001 [A/56/381].

During the reporting period, OIOS issued 12 reports to the General Assembly. Those transmitted in 2001 were on: experiences learned from the use of resident auditors at peacekeeping missions [A/55/735]; follow-up audit of the implementation of procurement reform [A/55/746]; inspection of the outcome of the consolidation of the three former economic and social departments into DESA [A/55/750]; investigation into possible fee-splitting arrangements between defence counsel and indigent detainees at the International Criminal Tribunal for Rwanda and the International Tribunal for the Former Yugoslavia [A/55/759]; inspection of the consolidation of technical support services in the Department of General Assembly Affairs and Conference Services [A/55/803]; management audit of UN civilian police operations [A/55/812]; enhancing the internal oversight mechanisms in operational funds and programmes, updated version [A/55/826 & Corr.1]; and inspection of programme management and administrative practices in the Office for Drug Control and Crime Prevention [A/56/83].

Reporting on the status of its recommendations, OIOS stated that it had modified its reporting format to include qualitative assessments of clients' implementation of recommendations defined as critical. It had also established a client profile database that integrated all client information and provided assessments of their efforts to implement oversight recommendations. During the reporting period, OIOS issued 2,105 recommendations, of which 577 (27 per cent) were classified as critical. The significantly higher number of recommendations, compared to previous years, was due to the decision to include recommendations issued through observations made at the operating level in the field. The overall implementation rate for all recommendations was 53 per cent, compared with 50 per cent during the previous reporting period [YUN 2000, p. 1288]. Comparatively, the implementation rate for critical recommendations was 46 per cent, reflecting their more complex nature and the longer time required to implement them. The critical recommendations addressed areas that had the most far-reaching consequences for the Organization's performance. As such, 43 per cent of them were meant to improve operational efficiency and effectiveness, 30 per cent to improve management controls, 19 per cent to improve accuracy and reliability of reports, and the remaining 8 per cent related to administrative improvements.

OIOS recommended savings and recoveries of approximately $58 million resulting from audits, inspections and investigations, which was substantially higher than the $17 million reported in 2000. It recommended $50.8 million in reduced expenditures, $4.8 million for recovery and $2.9 million as either additional income to the Organization or loss/waste of resources. As a result of implementing OIOS recommendations issued during the current and prior reporting periods, the Organization reduced expenditures by $8 million and recovered $2.5 million.

The report gave an overview of activities of oversight priority areas for the reporting period: human rights and humanitarian affairs, political affairs, international justice and law, international cooperation for development, regional cooperation for development, and UN Headquarters activities and those of offices away from Headquarters. Regarding human rights and humanitarian affairs, OIOS audited the operations of the Office of the United Nations High Commissioner for Refugees in 30 countries in Africa, Asia and the Pacific and Europe.

In reviewing international cooperation for development, OIOS conducted an inspection of DESA and reported satisfactory progress in the implementation of its recommendations. OIOS also audited many related offices and programmes and made recommendations for addressing irregularities found. Regarding regional cooperation for development, it reviewed the activities of the Economic Commission for Africa (ECA) and the Economic Commission for Latin America and the Caribbean (ECLAC). A comprehensive audit of ECA's payroll services revealed weaknesses in the arrangements for verifying, processing and recording payments

and allowances. The Commission was already implementing recommendations to improve the situation. OIOS found that ECLAC had yet to develop guidelines to ensure the proper and efficient conduct of self-evaluations by substantive divisions, and it needed to ensure that budgeted resources for planned activities were not used to finance unplanned programmes. OIOS also investigated telephone usage and book publishing at the Economic and Social Commission for Western Asia, which resulted in corrective action against fraudulent practices.

At UN Headquarters, the audit of selected activities of the Public Affairs and News and Media Divisions of the Department of Public Information (DPI) indicated the absence of an effective system for tracking and monitoring audit recommendations, and although DPI had accepted OIOS recommendations, it had yet to implement them. The OIOS review of the Department of Management showed that, although further attention needed to be paid to cost-sharing between offices and although the Office of Human Resources Management had yet to undertake a customer satisfaction survey, most of its previous recommendations relating to the Department's services had been implemented in New York, Geneva and Vienna. Other OIOS activities relating to the Department of Management included follow-up audits of the implementation of procurement reform and of the recruitment process, and audits of the contributions management system, processing of inter-office vouchers through IMIS and education grants.

The Investigations Section received 433 cases, 51 per cent more than the 287 it dealt with in the previous reporting period. As at 30 June, the Section had 274 open cases, 15 per cent of which were located at UN Headquarters, 29 per cent in Africa, 29 per cent in Europe, 23 per cent in the Middle East and Asia and 4 per cent in North America outside UN Headquarters and in South America. Overall, the cases located at duty stations away from Headquarters rose to 85 per cent in 2001, compared to 75 per cent since the inception of the Section.

In-depth evaluations were undertaken of sustainable development [E/AC.51/2001/2] and the population programme [E/AC.51/2001/3]. Triennial reviews were conducted of the implementation of the recommendations made by the Committee for Programme and Coordination (CPC) at its thirty-eighth session [YUN 1998, p. 1336] on the in-depth evaluation of the United Nations International Drug Control Programme [E/AC.51/2001/4] and on the in-depth evaluation of the United Nations Crime Prevention and Criminal Justice Programme [E/AC.51/2001/5]. The OIOS report on enhancing the internal oversight mechanisms in operational funds and programmes [A/C.5/55/23] was also submitted to CPC.

On 24 December [meeting 92], the General Assembly, on the recommendation of the Fifth Committee [A/56/739], adopted **resolution 56/246** without vote [agenda item 130].

Report of the Secretary-General on the activities of the Office of Internal Oversight Services

The General Assembly,

Recalling its resolutions 48/218 B of 29 July 1994 and 54/244 of 23 December 1999,

Recalling also its decision 55/488 of 7 September 2001,

Having considered the annual reports of the Office of Internal Oversight Services of the Secretariat for the periods from 1 July 1999 to 30 June 2000 and from 1 July 2000 to 30 June 2001,

1. *Notes with appreciation* the work of the Office of Internal Oversight Services;

2. *Takes note* of the annual reports of the Office of Internal Oversight Services for the periods from 1 July 1999 to 30 June 2000 and from 1 July 2000 to 30 June 2001;

3. *Requests* the Secretary-General to ensure that the Office of Internal Oversight Services includes in its annual reports information regarding the implementation rate of the recommendations of the previous three reporting periods;

4. *Also requests* the Secretary-General to ensure that the Office of Internal Oversight Services includes, in its next annual report, information regarding the impact of its reorganization on its work;

5. *Welcomes* the initiative to include in the report of the Office of Internal Oversight Services qualitative assessments of the implementation of recommendations defined as critical, and invites the Secretary-General to entrust the Office with refining the criteria referred to in paragraph 8 of that report, taking into account the relevant provisions of resolutions 48/218 B and 54/244, and to report thereon in the context of the next annual report of the Secretary-General on the activities of the Office;

6. *Requests* the Secretary-General to ensure that the Office of Internal Oversight Services, when providing information on the implementation rate of critical recommendations in its future annual reports, deals separately with those recommendations which have been implemented, those which are in the process of being implemented and those for which no implementation process is under way, and the reasons for their non-implementation;

7. *Also requests* the Secretary-General to present an update on the implementation of the recommendations of the Office of Internal Oversight Services on mission liquidation activities at the United Nations, in particular with regard to write-offs, to the General Assembly at its resumed fifty-sixth session;

8. *Further requests* the Secretary-General to ensure that the recommendations of the Office of Internal Oversight Services, with regard to the new mission subsistence allowance referred to in paragraphs 88 and 89 of its report are fully and expeditiously implemented, and to report on the matter in the context of the budget performance reports of the relevant peacekeeping operations;

9. *Requests* the Secretary-General to ensure that the Office of Internal Oversight Services submits an update on the status of the oversight activities referred to in paragraphs 71 to 81 and in paragraphs 52 to 60, respectively, of its two most recent annual reports, for further consideration by the General Assembly at its resumed fifty-sixth session;

10. *Recalls* section III, paragraph 7, of its resolution 55/222 of 23 December 2000, by which it reiterated that all documents submitted to legislative organs by the Secretariat and expert bodies for consideration and action should have conclusions and recommendations in bold print.

Also on 24 December, the Assembly decided that the item on the report of the Secretary-General on the activities of OIOS would remain for consideration during its resumed fifty-sixth (2002) session (**decision 56/464**) and that the Fifth Committee should continue consideration of the item at that session (**decision 56/458**).

Strengthening the investigations function

By an August note [A/56/282], the Secretary-General transmitted to the General Assembly a JIU report on strengthening the investigations function in UN system organizations. JIU stated that, although that function had become an increasingly important component of internal oversight for most UN organizations, because it was relatively new in the system, some major issues needed to be resolved. JIU found that the investigations function, intended to deter wrong-doing, assure proper accountability and maintain the confidence of Member States and stakeholders in the integrity of the organizations they supported, was subject to fragmentation within UN system organizations, and significant differences existed among them regarding the location and lines of reporting for those units specifically mandated to conduct investigations. Among the major issues to be addressed were: the lack of recognized standards and procedures for conducting investigations; the need to train programme and administrative support managers in the recognized standards and procedures to minimize the risk to the investigative process that could result from their involvement in it; meeting the need for access to a professional investigations capability; options for small organizations regarding the financing of such access; the need for preventive measures to reduce vulnerability to wrongdoing by use of proactive investigations and lessons learned from completed investigations; and inter-agency cooperation.

To enhance the capability of UN system organizations to meet the need for investigations, JIU recommended that the forthcoming Third Conference of Investigators of United Nations Organizations and Multilateral Financial Institutions should develop and adopt standards and procedures for conducting investigations in UN system organizations. It should also continue to develop opportunities for fostering inter-agency cooperation regarding the investigations function. Executive heads of organizations should ensure that managers involved in investigations had sufficient training in the use of established standards and procedures for conducting investigations; conduct a risk profile of their respective organizations as a basis for reporting to their legislative organs on the need for access to professionally trained and experienced investigators, including recommendations to meet that need; present to their respective legislative organs options for financing that access; and ensure that work programmes of units responsible for investigations included the development of preventive measures based on proactive investigations and lessons learned from completed investigations.

Annexed to the JIU report was a brief description of the investigation capabilities in UN system organizations.

External oversight

Joint Inspection Unit

In its thirty-third report to the General Assembly [A/57/34], JIU gave an overview of its activities in 2001, during which it issued reports on: the management of buildings: practices of selected UN system organizations relevant to the renovation of United Nations Headquarters [A/56/274]; UN system support for science and technology in Latin America and the Caribbean [A/56/370]; review of management and administration in the International Telecommunication Union [JIU/REP/2001/3]; enhancing governance oversight role: structure, working methods and practices on handling oversight reports [A/57/58]; review of management and administration in the World Health Organization [JIU/REP/2001/5]; and reforming the Field Service category of personnel in UN peace operations [JIU/REP/2001/6].

JIU continued to enhance its functioning and impact. It maintained comprehensive reviews of the administration and management of its participating organizations and issued reports, which were useful in comparing the policies and practices of the management and administration of organizations confronted with similar problems, thereby encouraging best practices. It noted that the relatively small number of reports

it had issued in the current reporting period was due, in part, to high staff turnover. Also, several reports could not be finalized because of the delays of some of its participating organizations in providing it with the requisite information and/or comments. However, the 2002-2003 programme budget provided for the reallocation of staff resources and increased resources for individual contractors, which should reinforce its research and related capacity.

The Secretary-General, in a June report [A/56/84], transmitted to the Assembly JIU's 2001 work programme and preliminary list of potential reports for 2002 and beyond.

The Secretary-General, in a July report [A/56/135], transmitted information on the status of implementation of the recommendations contained in JIU reports on: common services at UN Headquarters; the challenge of outsourcing for the UN system; enhancing the relevance and effectiveness of the United Nations University; a review of ACC and its subsidiary machinery; an evaluation of the International Research and Training Institute for the Advancement of Women; and the experience of UN system organizations with results-based budgeting.

In a September note [A/56/356], the Secretary-General transmitted the JIU report on experience with the follow-up system on JIU reports and recommendations, prepared in response to General Assembly resolution 54/16 [YUN 1999, p. 1277]. JIU found that the major obstacle to the implementation of the follow-up system [YUN 1997, p. 1401], approved by Assembly resolution 54/16, was the lack of specific legislative action on its recommendations. Legislative organs usually contented themselves with "taking note" of JIU's conclusions and recommendations, without a clear indication as to their approval or otherwise. That prevented effective follow-up action, since article 12 of the JIU statute relating to the implementation of JIU recommendations was usually interpreted as referring only to those recommendations approved through legislative action, and the action of "take note" did not legally bind the secretariats to ensuring effective implementation or follow-up. Moreover, participating organizations were divided as to whether the term "recommendations . . . approved by . . . competent organs" legally included those addressed to and accepted by the executive heads and whether "competent organs" included the secretariats.

In response to a JIU request, several participating organizations indicated that there were no approved recommendations that had not been implemented, while others declared their inability to report in the absence of a clearly agreed follow-up system. The system had so far been formally acted upon only by the United Nations and the legislative organs of four specialized agencies. Eight others were in discussion with JIU on the adoption of a similar follow-up system, which would have to be tailored to take account of the specific character of each organization.

JIU concluded that legislative bodies should avoid vague expressions such as "take note". To that end, secretariats should indicate clearly, when submitting JIU reports to legislative organs, those recommendations that needed specific legislative action and those that could be implemented directly by the executive heads, without prejudice to the authority of the legislative body to review all recommendations. It was also important to reach a common understanding that recommendations addressed to and accepted by the executive heads should be implemented and were subject to follow-up. It was expected that the term "recommendations . . . approved by . . . competent organs" would be clarified and the term "take note" eliminated. That should allow JIU to report with greater ease and accuracy on the implementation of its reports and recommendations or the lack thereof.

The Assembly, by **decision 55/488** of 7 September (see p. 1362), clarified that "takes note of" and "notes" were neutral terms and did not constitute approval or disapproval.

GENERAL ASSEMBLY ACTION

On 24 December [meeting 92], the General Assembly, on the recommendation of the Fifth Committee [A/56/655], adopted **resolution 56/245** without vote [agenda item 128].

Joint Inspection Unit

The General Assembly,

Reaffirming its previous resolutions on the Joint Inspection Unit, in particular resolutions 50/233 of 7 June 1996, 54/16 of 29 October 1999 and 55/230 of 23 December 2000,

1. *Takes note with appreciation* of the report of the Joint Inspection Unit for 2000;

2. *Takes note* of the note by the Secretary-General transmitting the programme of work of the Unit for 2001 and the preliminary listing of potential reports for 2002 and beyond, as well as the note by the Secretary-General transmitting the report of the Unit on experience with the follow-up system on Joint Inspection Unit reports and recommendations;

3. *Also takes note* of the report of the Secretary-General on the implementation of the recommendations of the Unit;

4. *Takes note in particular* that, as noted in the preliminary listing of potential reports for 2002 and beyond and reaffirmed by the Chairman of the Unit, the preliminary listing is of a tentative nature and does not necessarily imply that the Unit is committed to taking up these subjects;

5. *Invites* the Unit to improve the presentation of the listing of potential reports for the following year

and beyond by providing information on the source, including legislative basis, objectives, problems to be addressed, duration and expected date of completion, and to present such information before the final quarter of each year;

6. *Requests* the executive heads of participating organizations to observe fully the time frame for submitting their comments, as called for in article 11, paragraphs 4 *(d)* and *(e)*, of the statute of the Unit;

7. *Requests* the Unit to consider including in its reports, where possible, the comments of the participating organizations on its findings and recommendations and to report thereon to the General Assembly at its fifty-seventh session;

8. *Stresses* the need for the Unit to place emphasis in its work on well-defined and timely items of high priority, identifying concrete managerial, administrative and programming questions aimed at providing the General Assembly and other legislative organs of participating organizations with practical and action-oriented recommendations;

9. *Stresses also* that the compliance with the provisions of paragraph 4 of the system of follow-up to the reports of the Unit, endorsed by the General Assembly in its resolution 54/16 and contained in the annual report of the Unit for the period from 1 July 1996 to 30 June 1997, is a responsibility of the Unit as a whole, and, in this regard, requests the Unit to exercise fully its collective wisdom in accordance with article 11, paragraph 2, of the statute;

10. *Requests* the Chairman of the Unit, in accordance with article 18 of the statute, to ensure compliance by the Unit with the provisions of its statute as well as the internal standards, guidelines and procedures as approved by the Unit;

11. *Requests* the Secretary-General and the executive heads of the other participating organizations to ensure that the Unit is provided with the information requested by it in due time, in accordance with article 6, paragraph 2, of the statute;

12. *Welcomes* the initial steps taken by the Unit with other external and internal oversight bodies of the United Nations system to develop interaction and intensify relations with a view to achieving better coordination among them with respect, in particular, to the oversight coverage and sharing of best practices, thus enhancing the impact of oversight activities as a whole and endeavouring to avoid duplication, and requests the Unit to report thereon, in the context of its report for 2001, to the General Assembly at its fifty-seventh session;

13. *Requests* the executive heads of those participating organizations that have not yet done so to take the necessary steps to facilitate the consideration of and action on the system of follow-up to the reports of the Unit, and invites the legislative organs concerned to consider and act upon it;

14. *Requests* the Unit to submit, as part of its annual report, additional comments and recommendations on its experience with the system of follow-up to the reports of the Unit, focusing in particular on legislative actions and implementation of the approved recommendations, to the General Assembly at its fifty-seventh session, including measures the Unit has taken to achieve a punctual and systematic follow-up of its

recommendations as approved by the legislative organs of participating organizations;

15. *Decides* to review the current state of coordination and cooperation among the United Nations oversight bodies with a view to ensuring greater synergy and mutual complementarity in their joint efforts to improve the efficiency of the administrative and financial functioning of the United Nations;

16. *Requests* that the Unit place more emphasis on the evaluation aspects of its work, in accordance with recommendation 63 contained in the report of the Group of High-level Intergovernmental Experts to Review the Efficiency of the Administrative and Financial Functioning of the United Nations, as endorsed by the General Assembly in its resolution 41/213 of 19 December 1986;

17. *Underlines* the fact that the evaluation function is envisaged in the statute of the Unit, and stresses the need for the Unit to pay special attention to the preparation of reports that are more evaluation-oriented;

18. *Requests* the Secretary-General to transmit the present resolution to the executive heads of the other participating organizations for their attention.

Also on 24 December, the Assembly decided that the item entitled "Joint Inspection Unit" would remain for consideration during its resumed fifty-sixth (2002) session (**decision 56/464**).

Intergovernmental machinery

Strengthening of the UN system

By **decision 56/464** of 24 December, the General Assembly decided that the item entitled "Strengthening of the United Nations system" would remain for consideration during its resumed fifty-sixth (2002) session.

Revitalization of the work of the General Assembly

In 2001, the General Assembly took up the item on the revitalization of its work, through improvement of its procedures and working methods, to enable it to play its role effectively as the chief deliberative, policy-making and representative body of the United Nations. In that regard, it adopted a text (below) addressing relevant issues relating to the rationalization and streamlining of its agenda, its consideration of reports, organization of work, the work of the General Committee, the role of the Assembly President and the use of modern technology.

GENERAL ASSEMBLY ACTION

On 7 September [meeting 111], the General Assembly adopted **resolution 55/285** [draft: A/56/L.93] without vote [agenda items 61 & 62].

Revitalization of the General Assembly; improving the efficiency of the General Assembly

The General Assembly,

Recalling its resolutions 47/233 of 17 August 1993, 48/264 of 29 July 1994 and 51/241 of 31 July 1997 and other relevant resolutions,

1. *Decides* to adopt the text contained in the annex to the present implementing resolution;

2. *Decides also* to continue its consideration of the items entitled "Strengthening of the United Nations system" and "Revitalization of the work of the General Assembly" at its fifty-sixth session.

ANNEX

I. Purpose

1. The process of revitalizing the General Assembly and improving its efficiency focuses on the implementation of existing Assembly resolutions and decisions, in particular resolution 51/241 of 31 July 1997, and also taking into account other resolutions such as resolutions 47/233 of 17 August 1993 and 48/264 of 29 July 1994. Improvement of the procedures and working methods of the Assembly is only a first step towards more substantive improvements in and revitalization of the Assembly. The goal of this ongoing process is to enable the Assembly to play its role effectively as the chief deliberative, policy-making and representative body of the United Nations.

II. The agenda of the General Assembly

2. The rationalization and streamlining of the agenda of the General Assembly should continue in order to enable the Assembly to focus its work on priority issues. Any change or suggestion concerning the agenda is made with the understanding that Member States may at any time propose any issue or item for the attention and consideration of the Assembly.

A. Clustering and biennialization of items

Cooperation item

3. All cooperation items shall be clustered under an item entitled "Cooperation between the United Nations and regional and other organizations" and individual cooperation items shall become sub-items of that item.

4. Practical measures to implement the clustering shall be taken in September 2001 by the General Assembly in conjunction with the adoption of the agenda of its fifty-sixth session.

5. The cooperation item shall be biennialized, starting at the fifty-seventh session, and shall appear in the agenda of the General Assembly thereafter at odd-numbered sessions.

6. Pursuant to the above decision, the biennialization shall be reflected in each related resolution, starting at the fifty-sixth session, as appropriate.

7. A joint debate shall be held on the cooperation item, during which all or some aspects of cooperation between the United Nations and regional and other organizations may be addressed.

8. Any resolution under individual sub-items shall remain separate.

9. The cooperation item and its sub-items shall read as follows:

"Cooperation between the United Nations and regional and other organizations:

"*(a)* Cooperation between the United Nations and the Organization of African Unity;

"*(b)* Cooperation between the United Nations and the Organization of the Islamic Conference;

"*(c)* Cooperation between the United Nations and the Asian-African Legal Consultative Organization;

"*(d)* Cooperation between the United Nations and the League of Arab States;

"*(e)* Cooperation between the United Nations and the Latin American Economic System;

"*(f)* Cooperation between the United Nations and the Organization of American States;

"*(g)* Cooperation between the United Nations and the Organization for Security and Cooperation in Europe;

"*(h)* Cooperation between the United Nations and the Caribbean Community;

"*(i)* Cooperation between the United Nations and the Economic Cooperation Organization;

"*(j)* Cooperation between the United Nations and the Inter-Parliamentary Union;

"*(k)* Cooperation between the United Nations and the International Organization of la Francophonie;

"*(l)* Cooperation between the United Nations and the Preparatory Commission for the Comprehensive Nuclear-Test-Ban Treaty Organization;

"*(m)* Cooperation between the United Nations and the Council of Europe;

"*(n)* Cooperation between the United Nations and the Economic Community of Central African States;

"*(o)* Cooperation between the United Nations and the Organization for the Prohibition of Chemical Weapons;

"*(p)* Cooperation between the United Nations and the Black Sea Economic Cooperation Organization."

B. Biennialization of items

10. The following items shall be considered by the General Assembly at its fifty-sixth session and thereafter biennially:

(a) "Zone of peace and cooperation of the South Atlantic";

(b) "Support by the United Nations system of the efforts of Governments to promote and consolidate new or restored democracies";

(c) "United Nations reform: measures and proposals";

(d) "The situation of democracy and human rights in Haiti";

(e) "Restructuring and revitalization of the United Nations in the economic, social and related fields".

11. The following item shall continue to be considered biennially, at even-numbered sessions: "Elimination of coercive measures as a means of political and economic compulsion".

C. Items for consideration by a Main Committee

12. The following item shall be considered by the Third Committee, starting at the fifty-sixth session: "Implementation of the outcome of the World Summit for Social Development and of the twenty-fourth special session of the General Assembly".

III. General Assembly consideration of reports

A. Report of the Secretary-General on the work of the Organization

13. The General Assembly stresses the importance of fulfilling the mandates given by it to the Secretary-General, pursuant to section II of the annex to resolution 51/241, in particular paragraphs 5, 6 and 9 thereof.

14. As regards implementation of paragraph 7 of the annex to resolution 51/241, the President of the General Assembly, after consideration by the Assembly of the report of the Secretary-General on the work of the Organization, shall inform the Assembly of his assessment of the debate on the report in order for the Assembly to determine the need for further action.

B. Efforts towards more concise reports, issued and submitted on time

15. Member States need to take concrete action to implement paragraph 32 of the annex to resolution 51/241, including by requesting more integrated reports.

16. In preparing the annual memorandum concerning the implementation of the resolutions and decisions of the General Assembly, the secretariat of the Assembly, in consultation with the substantive departments of the Secretariat, should look for synergies and integration of reports.

17. Member States and entities of the United Nations system should make a serious effort to submit their replies and inputs to requests for information or views pursuant to resolutions of the General Assembly within the prescribed deadlines.

18. The Secretary-General is requested to make further suggestions as to how to speed up the preparation of reports and to rationalize the scheduling of meetings. The Secretary-General shall keep the President of the General Assembly and the General Committee informed on this issue on a regular basis throughout the sessions of the Assembly.

IV. Organization of work

19. In order to implement fully paragraph 28 of the annex to resolution 51/241, the President of the General Assembly is encouraged to make greater use of facilitators, where appropriate.

V. The General Committee

20. In order to enhance the capacity of the General Committee to assist the President of the General Assembly in the conduct of the business of the Assembly and to improve continuity between its different sessions, at the outset of each session, each Vice-President of the Assembly shall designate a liaison person for the duration of the session. This designation may be made informally, without any amendment to rule 39 of the rules of procedure of the Assembly, by means of a letter to its President.

VI. Role of the President of the General Assembly

A. Consultations

21. In order to make more use of the regular consultations provided for in paragraph 43 of the annex to resolution 51/241, including between the President of the General Assembly and the Presidents of the Secu-

rity Council and the Economic and Social Council, the Secretary-General should provide these meetings with secretarial support, as appropriate, including written information to Member States through the chairmen of the regional groups.

B. Strengthening the office of the President of the General Assembly

22. Additional measures are required to implement paragraph 44 of the annex to resolution 51/241, in particular in the area of substantive support for the President of the General Assembly. Therefore, adequate support should be made available to the office of the President in the substantive areas of its work. To this end, the Secretary-General is requested to take appropriate measures and to submit proposals to the relevant committees for their consideration during the fifty-sixth session of the Assembly.

VII. Enhancing the use of modern technology

23. There is a need to enhance the use of modern technology and information technology within the United Nations, including in the process of negotiation within the Organization.

24. Taking into account the general support in this regard, the Secretary-General is requested to submit proposals to the General Assembly for its consideration:

(a) Introduction of a system to read ballot papers electronically, taking due account of the security requirements in this regard;

(b) Wiring of the main conference rooms at Headquarters to provide members of delegations and the Secretariat with access to the Official Document System and other databases of the Organization, as well as to the Internet, together with electronic access to texts of statements and reports and, in the case of reports, simultaneous access to texts in all official languages;

(c) Other areas of the work of the Assembly in which the use of modern technology and information technology would contribute to enhancing efficiency in its working methods.

On 24 December, the Assembly decided that the item entitled "Revitalization of the work of the General Assembly" would remain for consideration during its resumed fifty-sixth (2002) session (**decision 56/464**).

Review of Security Council membership and related matters

The Open-ended Working Group on the Question of Equitable Representation on and Increase in the Membership of the Security Council and Other Matters related to the Security Council submitted a report on its work during five substantive sessions held between 5 February and 20 July [A/55/47]. Discussions continued on the items under cluster I: decision-making, including the veto, the Council's expansion and periodic review of the enlarged Council; and on those under cluster II: the Council's working methods and the transparency of its work. The

Working Group had before it conference room papers prepared by its Bureau.

At its first session (5 February), the Working Group adopted its work programme. At its second session (12-16 March), it began its consideration of clusters I and II issues, which it continued at the third (7-11 May), fourth (11 and 13-14 June) and fifth (16-20 July) sessions, on the basis of related conference room papers before it. In addition, the then President of the Council (Bangladesh), Colombia and the United Kingdom, at the invitation of the Group, spoke at the fourth session on steps taken by the Council to ensure greater openness and transparency in its procedures. Many members of the Group found such interactive exchange with Council members useful and asked that it continue in future. Grenada and Pakistan submitted proposals on cluster I issues at the fifth session, during which the Secretariat circulated a note concerning record-keeping practices in the Council. The Director of the Security Council Affairs Division of the Department of Political Affairs, at the Group's request, answered questions raised on the Secretariat's note and on services provided to the informal consultations of the whole, meetings of subsidiary organs and working groups, and the Council's fact-finding missions. The Group also considered and adopted its report to the Assembly.

The Assembly, by **decision 55/503** of 10 September, took note of the Working Group's report, welcomed progress made so far, as provisional agreement had been recorded on a large number of issues, and urged the Group to continue efforts during its fifty-sixth session to achieve progress in all aspects of equitable representation on and increase in the membership of the Security Council and other related matters. The Assembly decided to continue consideration of the item during its fifty-sixth session and that the Working Group should continue its work, taking into account progress achieved during the Assembly's forty-eighth (1993) to fifty-fifth (2000) sessions, as well as the views to be expressed at the fifty-sixth session, and report before the end of that session, including any agreed recommendations.

By **decision 56/464** of 24 December, the Assembly decided that the item would remain for consideration during its resumed fifty-sixth (2002) session.

Revitalization of the United Nations in the economic, social and related fields

In an April note [E/2001/INF/3], the Secretary-General updated information provided in 1996

[YUN 1996, p. 1258] and 1997 [YUN 1997, p. 1408] on the establishment, terms of reference, membership and composition, term of office of members, reporting procedure, frequency of meetings and working methods of subsidiary bodies of the Economic and Social Council and the General Assembly in the economic, social and related fields.

On 3 May (**decision 2001/212**), the Economic and Social Council, having considered the Secretary-General's 2000 report on restructuring and revitalization of the United Nations in the economic, social and related fields and cooperation between the United Nations and the Bretton Woods institutions [YUN 2000, p. 1292] and his consolidated report on the work of the functional commissions of the Council [ibid., p. 1373], decided to examine the subject at its 2001 substantive session. It requested the Secretary-General to report during that session on the implementation of General Assembly resolutions 50/227 [YUN 1996, p. 1249] and 52/12 B [YUN 1997, p. 1392] and Council resolutions 1998/46 [YUN 1998, p. 1262] and 1999/51 [YUN 1999, p. 1281], and to submit a consolidated report on the work of the functional commissions.

Reports of Secretary-General. As requested by the Council, the Secretary-General, in May [A/56/77-E/2001/69], reported on progress in the implementation of relevant resolutions of the Assembly and the Council, aimed at assisting the Council in exploring ways to streamline its efforts in restructuring and revitalizing the United Nations in the economic, social and related fields. The report summarized how the implementation of those resolutions was monitored and discussed by the Assembly and the Council, with suggestions for streamlining the review of their implementation. The Secretary-General noted that most of their provisions had been implemented and incorporated into practices over the last few years. For further progress in that regard, he recommended that the Council could streamline its consideration of the restructuring and revitalization process by focusing on its management responsibilities in relation to its subsidiary bodies. To that end, the consolidated report on the outcomes of the functional commissions (see below) should be examined more closely, with a view to giving guidance to those commissions.

The Secretary-General, responding to Council resolution 1998/46 [YUN 1998, p. 1262], submitted in June [E/2001/95] the consolidated report on the work of the functional commissions. He analysed the commissions' follow-up action to policy guidance provided by the Council and identified the common themes, issues and approaches that emerged during the reporting period, designed to provide the Council with a holistic view of matters of common interest to the commissions in 2001 and to facilitate its overall policy guidance. He also reviewed the methods of work of the commissions, including multi-year work programmes, in relation to the guidance provided in relevant Council resolutions and made recommendations regarding key issues on which the Council should consider taking action.

ECONOMIC AND SOCIAL COUNCIL ACTION

On 26 July [meeting 43], the Economic and Social Council adopted **resolution 2001/27** [draft: E/2001/L. 40] without vote [agenda item 8].

Implementation of General Assembly resolutions 50/227 and 52/12 B: improving the working methods of the functional commissions of the Economic and Social Council

The Economic and Social Council,

Recalling General Assembly resolutions 50/227 of 24 May 1996 and 52/12 B of 19 December 1997, and its resolutions 1996/43 of 26 July 1996, 1998/46 and 1998/47 of 31 July 1998, 1998/49 of 16 December 1998, 1999/1 of 2 February 1999 and 1999/51 of 29 July 1999,

Having considered the consolidated report of the Secretary-General on the work of the functional commissions of the Economic and Social Council,

1. *Welcomes* the progress made in implementing the provisions of resolutions 50/227 and 52/12 B;

2. *Recognizes* that the consolidated report of the outcomes of the functional commissions, that looks at the linkages between them and highlights the key points on which the Council needs to consider taking action, is a useful tool with respect to its coordination function;

3. *Invites* its functional commissions to provide concise, action-oriented input to its annual high-level and/or coordination segments, for example by utilizing, as applicable, their standing agenda item on new trends and emerging issues affecting the overall goals within their mandates;

4. *Requests* the Secretary-General to include, in the next consolidated report, an analysis of the practice of its functional commissions in the preparation of draft resolutions for action by the Council or the General Assembly, with a view to elaborating guidelines addressed to the functional commissions on the submission of draft proposals to the Council;

5. *Encourages* its functional commissions to consider how best to ensure continuity in the work of their successive bureaux, and to that end requests the Secretary-General to include a summary of the views of the functional commissions, if any, in the next consolidated report;

6. *Requests* the Secretary-General to provide the functional commissions with comprehensive information on all existing multi-year work programmes and special themes in order for them to maintain and increase their coordination and collaboration at the planning and formulation stage of such programmes, and encourages those functional commissions that choose annual themes for a special debate to take into consideration the work of other commissions;

7. *Also requests* the Secretary-General to submit to the Council, when it considers the themes for its high-level and coordination segments, information about the multi-year work programmes of the functional commissions;

8. *Encourages* the functional commissions to continue to keep their working methods under review;

9. *Urges* its functional commissions to further develop opportunities for sharing national experience during annual sessions, in particular with regard to the implementation of conference outcomes, and to allocate an appropriate amount of time for that purpose at their annual sessions;

10. *Encourages* its functional commissions to consider, as appropriate and within existing resources, holding joint bureaux meetings to discuss coordination on issues that are addressed by two or more commissions, using information technology, as required;

11. *Also encourages* its functional commissions, within existing resources, to share more systematically the outcome of their work, including through communications among chairpersons or through briefings by the Secretariat;

12. *Further encourages* its functional commissions to identify similar or related topics, and, in this context, requests the Secretary-General, inter alia, to present a joint report on such topics, where appropriate;

13. *Requests* the Secretary-General, where this is not yet being done, to provide each of the functional commissions, for their consideration, with concise notes on actions already planned or undertaken by them, or to propose steps they could take to follow up the policy guidance of the Council;

14. *Welcomes* the attention given by its functional commissions to the follow-up to the outcome of the substantive session of 2000 of the Council and to a number of main themes, issues and approaches, which has facilitated policy coherence and effectiveness in these areas;

15. *Invites* its relevant functional commissions to assess, in greater depth, the impact of particular policies on achieving poverty eradication goals and to identify good practices and lessons learned so as to increase the sharing of knowledge, including among the functional commissions themselves;

16. *Also invites* its functional commissions to increase their attention to the role of information and communication technologies for development in their areas of responsibility;

17. *Welcomes* the efforts of its functional commissions to mainstream a gender perspective in their work;

18. *Encourages* its functional commissions to continue to coordinate their work, in particular in areas of common interest, by, for example, biennializing items or making use of joint reports;

19. *Agrees* to take steps to integrate the outcome of the special session of the General Assembly on human immunodeficiency virus/acquired immunodeficiency syndrome (HIV/AIDS) into its own work, based on the decision taken by the Assembly at that special session, and requests the functional commissions to do the same for effective implementation and follow-up;

20. *Welcomes* the attention given by several of its functional commissions to cross-cutting dimensions in relation to all aspects of human settlements, and invites relevant commissions to seek greater interaction on those issues;

21. *Invites* its functional commissions to provide further inputs into the Council's own work on means of implementation, including the role of resource mobilization, capacity-building, research and data collection, and information- and knowledge-sharing in their respective areas, with a particular focus on impact, gaps, good practices and lessons learned, and the types of capacity-building most commonly sought in the implementation of the outcomes of the major United Nations conferences and summits, including the Millennium Summit;

22. *Also invites* its functional commissions to continue to explore opportunities for effective and productive contributions to their work by relevant stakeholders;

23. *Requests* the Secretary-General to submit to the Council at its substantive session of 2002 a consolidated report on the work of the functional commissions.

GENERAL ASSEMBLY ACTION

By **decision 55/490** of 7 September, the General Assembly decided to include in the draft agenda of its fifty-sixth (2001) session the item entitled "Restructuring and revitalization of the United Nations in the economic, social and related fields". By **decision 56/464** of 24 December, it decided that the item would remain for consideration during its resumed fifty-sixth (2002) session.

Department of Economic and Social Affairs

Pursuant to General Assembly resolutions 48/218 B [YUN 1994, p. 1362] and 54/244 [YUN 1999, p. 1274], the Secretary-General, in January [A/55/750], transmitted an OIOS report on the inspection of the outcome of the consolidation of the three former economic and social departments into the Department of Economic and Social Affairs (DESA). The review assessed whether the reform had achieved its strategic goals of enhancing the Department's coherence of normative, analytical and operational functions; providing more effective policy support to intergovernmental bodies; and achieving greater effectiveness in coordinating UN activities in the socio-economic field.

OIOS confirmed that DESA had made significant progress in implementing those goals. However, more needed to be done, as the commitment to excellence, coherence and innovation was not always well replicated at the Department's divisional and working levels. In some instances, the strategies for change had lost their momentum or were distorted into pro forma exercises, and, in some other areas, compartmentalization still existed, with interdisciplinary teamwork remaining an exception rather than the norm.

OIOS recommended that DESA should draw up a long-term comprehensive plan of action to strengthen its substantive support to the work of the Economic and Social Council's functional commissions, ensure that the commissions' work was mutually reinforcing in advancing cross-cutting goals of UN conferences and summits on socio-economic issues, and establish a viable mechanism for promoting mutually supportive policies among UN agencies and organizations in the pursuit of those goals. Measures should be introduced to secure sufficient resources for the evaluation of UN operational activities for development, including extrabudgetary funding, and in-house research and evaluation capacity developed through training, streamlining work processes and applying more effective research methodologies. DESA should develop modalities to monitor the implementation of the decisions of the Executive Committee for Economic and Social Affairs and report to it on the status of that implementation. The Department should provide leadership in fostering innovative, timely and cost-effective inter-agency collaboration for problem-specific tasks and projects in other sub-programmes. It should also review monitoring, evaluation and reporting arrangements on the Development Account projects (see p. 809) and ensure that those functions were carried out comprehensively and effectively. DESA should ensure that interdisciplinary interaction was a permanent feature of its work culture and discourage managerial obstruction to horizontal professional interaction. It should also develop the Information Support Unit into an effective, forward-looking centre for the solution of information and communication technology problems, skills promotion and the exchange of experience and as a facilitator for creating access to technological information. It should take urgent action to mobilize resources to restore the UN Population Information Network to full capacity and to ensure the network's long-term sustainability. The Secretary-General concurred with those recommendations.

Chapter II

United Nations financing and programming

The overall financial situation of the United Nations during 2001 was significantly more positive than for a number of years, reflecting higher aggregate cash, lower unpaid assessments and reduced debt owed by the Organization to Member States. Unpaid assessments were 7 per cent lower than in 2000, at $2,106 million, and amounts due to Member States for troops and contingent-owned equipment, at $748 million, were down 18 per cent from 2000.

The General Assembly, in December, adopted revised budget appropriations for the 2000-2001 biennium of $2,561,578,000, an increase of $28,452,600 over the initial approved appropriations of $2,533,125,400. It approved appropriations of $2,625,178,700 for the 2002-2003 biennium.

The Committee on Contributions continued to review the methodology for preparing the scale of assessments of Member States' contributions to the UN budget, including a methodology for assessing contributions of non-member States, as well as measures to encourage the timely payment of assessed contributions. It also continued to examine proposals relating to the procedural aspects for considering requests for exemptions under Article 19 of the Charter of the United Nations. In December, the Secretary-General brought to the Assembly's attention the question of the payment of the arrears of the former Socialist Federal Republic of Yugoslavia, following the admission in 2000 of the Federal Republic of Yugoslavia to UN membership.

The Assembly accepted the audited financial statements of the Board of Auditors on UN peacekeeping operations. It also accepted the financial reports and audited financial statements and audit opinions of the Board on the voluntary funds administered by the United Nations High Commissioner for Refugees, the United Nations Development Programme, the United Nations Population Fund and the Fund of the United Nations International Drug Control Programme. The Assembly changed the term of office of the members of the Board of Auditors from the current three years to a non-consecutive term of six years' duration starting on 1 July 2002.

Financial situation

The overall financial situation of the United Nations in 2001 was better than in 2000. The Secretary-General's October report [A/56/464] attributed the improvement mainly to the expected payments by the United States of $1,459 million in the last quarter of 2001, which, together with current payments and credits of $207 million, would bring its total 2001 payments and credits to $1,666 million. Those payments and payments by other Member States were expected to reach a total of $4,716 million, exceeding projected assessments of $4,246 million in 2001. That would allow the United Nations, for the first time in many years, to have a more solid financial base on which to do business and to tackle issues long held in abeyance, including delayed reimbursements for peacekeeping troops and equipment, cash deficits and cross-borrowing from peacekeeping accounts.

As at 30 September, unpaid assessments for the regular budget, peacekeeping and the international tribunals totalled $3.9 billion (an increase over the figure a year earlier of just over $3 billion). That total included $541 million for the regular budget, $3,281 million for peacekeeping (compared with $2,507 million in 2000), and $71 million for the tribunals (compared to $54 million in 2000). Member States paying their regular budget assessments in full for 2001 and prior years numbered 122 at the end of September, down from 131 at the same date in 2000.

In his end-of-year review of the financial situation [A/56/464/Add.1], the Secretary-General confirmed the more positive financial picture than in 2000: aggregate cash was higher, unpaid assessments were lower and debt owed by the Organization to Member States had been reduced. Aggregate cash, including in the regular budget, and that for peacekeeping and the tribunals, was up 32 per cent at $1,326 million; unpaid assessments were 7 per cent lower at $2,106 million; and amounts due to Member States for troops and contingent-owned equipment were down 18 per cent at $748 million. However, the number of Member States paying in full and on time as at 31

December 2001 had decreased to 135, as against 141 by the end of 2000.

By **decision 55/493** of 7 September, the General Assembly included in the draft agenda of its fifty-sixth (2001) session the item entitled "Improving the financial situation of the United Nations". On 24 December, the Assembly decided that the item would remain for consideration at its resumed fifty-sixth (2002) session (**decision 56/464**) and that the Fifth (Administrative and Budgetary) Committee should continue to consider the item at that session (**decision 56/458**).

UN budget

Budget for 2000-2001

Final appropriations

In 2001, the General Assembly adopted final budget appropriations for the 2000-2001 biennium, increasing the amount of $2,533.1 million approved in 2000 by resolution 55/239 A [YUN 2000, p. 1298] by $28.5 million, to $2,561.6 million, and reducing approved income estimates of $380.8 million approved by resolution 55/239 B [ibid., p. 1299] by $1.1 million, to $379.7 million.

Report of Secretary-General. In his second performance report on the 2000-2001 programme budget [A/56/674 & Corr.1], the Secretary-General provided estimates of the anticipated final levels of expenditure and income for the biennium based on actual expenditures for the first 20 months and projections for the last four months, as well as changes in inflation and exchange rates and cost-of-living adjustments.

The proposed revised estimates represented a net increase in requirements of $28.9 million, reflecting increases of $10.4 million for changes in exchange rates, $9.1 million for changes in inflation and $14.5 million for commitments entered into under the provisions of General Assembly resolution 54/252 [YUN 1999, p. 1309]; a reduction of $6.2 million attributable to variations in post costs and adjustments to other objects of expenditure, based on actual anticipated requirements; and a decrease in income of $1.1 million.

Taking account of the revised budget appropriations of $2,533.1 million approved in 2000, together with the increases ($34 million) and reductions ($6.2 million) noted above, the resultant revised expenditure amounted to $2,560.9 million, an increase of $27.8 million over the 2000 figure. Income was revised to an estimated $379.7 million.

The Advisory Committee on Administrative and Budgetary Questions (ACABQ), in its related December report [A/56/694], said it had requested the data annexed to its report showing a breakdown of savings under travel, which indicated variances in travel expenses relating to staff and to representatives appointed by the Secretary-General. ACABQ advised that such information should be included in future performance reports.

On 24 December [meeting 92], the General Assembly, on the recommendation of the Fifth Committee [A/56/735], adopted **resolutions 56/240 A and B** without vote [agenda item 122].

Programme budget for the biennium 2000-2001

A

Final budget appropriations for the biennium 2000-2001

The General Assembly

1. *Takes note* of the second performance report of the Secretary-General on the programme budget for the biennium 2000-2001 and the related report of the Advisory Committee on Administrative and Budgetary Questions;

2. *Requests* the Secretary-General to keep Member States informed of regular budget expenditures on a quarterly basis;

3. *Decides*, in the light of the critical financial situation of the International Research and Training Institute for the Advancement of Women, to retain in the programme budget for the biennium 2000-2001, 650,000 United States dollars of the original provision of 800,000 dollars made pursuant to General Assembly resolution 55/219 of 23 December 2000, and requests the Secretary-General to disburse the provision in December 2001 as a subvention to be credited to the United Nations Trust Fund for the Institute, so as to ensure the continuation of its operations in 2002;

4. *Resolves* that, for the biennium 2000-2001, the amount of 2,533,125,400 United States dollars appropriated under its resolution 55/239 A of 23 December 2000 shall be augmented by a commitment authority of 28,452,600 dollars, as follows:

Section	Amount approved by the General Assembly in its resolution 55/239 A	Provisional increase/ decrease	Revised appropriation and commitment authority
	(United States dollars)		
Part I. *Overall policy-making, direction and coordination*			
1. Overall policy-making, direction and coordination	48,013,100	(2,543,300)	45,469,800
2. General Assembly affairs and conference services	409,024,100	36,844,600	445,868,700
Total, part I	**457,037,200**	**34,301,300**	**491,338,500**

Section	Amount approved by the General Assembly in its resolution 55/239 A	Provisional increase/ decrease	Revised appropriation and commitment authority
	(United States dollars)		
Part II. *Political affairs*			
3. Political affairs	167,844,700	(6,095,700)	161,749,000
4. Disarmament	13,820,900	345,000	14,165,900
5. Peacekeeping operations	74,884,000	(4,067,600)	70,816,400
6. Peaceful uses of outer space	3,313,500	136,400	3,449,900
Total, part II	**259,863,100**	**(9,681,900)**	**250,181,200**
Part III. *International justice and law*			
7. International Court of Justice	20,606,700	1,642,000	22,248,700
8. Legal affairs	33,880,600	(343,200)	33,537,400
Total, part III	**54,487,300**	**1,298,800**	**55,786,100**
Part IV. *International cooperation for development*			
9. Economic and social affairs	112,431,800	1,718,600	114,150,400
10. Africa: New Agenda for Development	5,859,800	(641,200)	5,218,600
11A. Trade and development	81,373,600	1,126,200	82,499,800
11B. International Trade Centre UNCTAD/WTO	17,009,800	247,000	17,256,800
12. Environment	8,100,900	495,900	8,596,800
13. Human settlements	12,297,300	2,607,900	14,905,200
14. Crime prevention and criminal justice	4,821,300	3,900	4,825,200
15. International drug control	13,718,200	309,500	14,027,700
Total, part IV	**255,612,700**	**5,867,800**	**261,480,500**
Part V. *Regional cooperation for development*			
16. Economic and social development in Africa	80,645,000	(9,163,500)	71,481,500
17. Economic and social development in Asia and the Pacific	54,411,200	(511,300)	53,899,900
18. Economic development in Europe	37,414,600	1,748,500	39,163,100
19. Economic and social development in Latin America and the Caribbean	75,584,100	1,287,900	76,872,000
20. Economic and social development in Western Asia	48,581,400	(2,883,200)	45,698,200
21. Regular programme of technical cooperation	41,254,800	(44,400)	41,210,400
Total, part V	**337,891,100**	**(9,566,000)**	**328,325,100**

Section	Amount approved by the General Assembly in its resolution 55/239 A	Provisional increase/ decrease	Revised appropriation and commitment authority
	(United States dollars)		
Part VI. *Human rights and humanitarian affairs*			
22. Human rights	39,067,700	(102,400)	38,965,300
23. Protection of and assistance to refugees	38,838,900	1,546,400	40,385,300
24. Palestine refugees	23,175,400	1,139,300	24,314,700
25. Humanitarian assistance	18,447,900	(53,800)	18,394,100
Total, part VI	**119,529,900**	**2,529,500**	**122,059,400**
Part VII. *Public information*			
26. Public information	142,534,500	(1,252,400)	141,282,100
Total, part VII	**142,534,500**	**(1,252,400)**	**141,282,100**
Part VIII. *Common support services*			
27. Management and central support services	433,569,100	4,391,900	437,961,000
A. Office of the Under-Secretary-General for Management	11,380,200	(6,100)	11,374,100
B. Office of Programme Planning, Budget and Accounts	22,209,800	552,700	22,762,500
C. Office of Human Resources Management	47,977,900	1,188,700	49,166,600
D. Office of Central Support Services	229,817,700	903,800	230,721,500
E. Administration, Geneva	84,412,400	485,300	84,897,700
F. Administration, Vienna	23,553,500	298,400	23,851,900
G. Administration, Nairobi	14,217,600	969,100	15,186,700
Total, part VIII	**433,569,100**	**4,391,900**	**437,961,000**
Part IX. *Internal oversight*			
28. Internal oversight	18,750,700	(493,900)	18,256,800
Total, part IX	**18,750,700**	**(493,900)**	**18,256,800**
Part X. *Jointly financed administrative activities and special expenses*			
29. Jointly financed administrative activities	8,020,500	(415,400)	7,605,100
30. Special expenses	54,511,700	(1,135,500)	53,376,200
Total, part X	**62,532,200**	**(1,550,900)**	**60,981,300**
Part XI. *Capital expenditures*			
31. Construction, alteration, improvement and major maintenance	49,767,300	(365,700)	49,401,600
Total, part XI	**49,767,300**	**(365,700)**	**49,401,600**

Section	Amount approved by the General Assembly in its resolution 55/239 A	Provisional increase/ decrease	Revised appropriation and commitment authority
	(United States dollars)		
Part XII. *Staff assessment*			
32. Staff assessment	328,485,300	2,974,100	331,459,400
Total, part XII	328,485,300	2,974,100	331,459,400
Part XIII. *Develop-ment Account*			
33. Development Account	13,065,000	—	13,065,000
Total, part XIII	13,065,000	—	13,065,000
Grand total	2,533,125,400	28,452,600	2,561,578,000

5. *Notes* the request of the Secretary-General that the revised appropriation should be increased by 28,452,600 dollars, and decides, keeping in mind the need for precision in determining the required final level of appropriations and assessments, that it will revert to consideration of the final appropriation at its resumed fifty-sixth session in March 2002;

6. *Resolves* that:

(*a*) The Secretary-General shall be authorized to transfer credits between sections of the budget, with the concurrence of the Advisory Committee;

(*b*) In addition to the commitment authority approved under paragraph 4 above, an amount of 250,000 dollars is appropriated for each year of the biennium 2000-2001 from the accumulated income of the Library Endowment Fund for the purchase of books, periodicals, maps and library equipment and for such other expenses of the Library at the Palais des Nations as are in accordance with the objects and provisions of the endowment.

B
Final income estimates for the biennium 2000-2001

The General Assembly

Resolves that for the biennium 2000-2001:

(*a*) The estimates of income of 380,822,700 United States dollars approved under its resolution 55/239 B of 23 December 2000 shall provisionally be decreased by 1,149,200 dollars, as follows:

Income section	Amount approved by the General Assembly in its resolution 55/239 B	Provisional increase/ decrease	Provisional income estimate
	(United States dollars)		
1. Income from staff assessment	333,125,200	1,903,900	335,029,100
Total, income section 1	333,125,200	1,903,900	335,029,100
2. General income	42,728,600	997,100	43,725,700
3. Services to the public	4,968,900	(4,050,200)	918,700
Total, income sections 2 and 3	47,697,500	(3,053,100)	44,644,400
Grand total	380,822,700	(1,149,200)	379,673,500

(*b*) The income from staff assessment shall be credited to the Tax Equalization Fund in accordance with the provisions of General Assembly resolution 973(X) of 15 December 1955;

(*c*) Direct expenses of the United Nations Postal Administration, services to visitors, catering and related services, garage operations, television services and the sale of publications, not provided for under the budget appropriations, shall be charged against the income derived from those activities.

Also on 24 December, the Assembly decided that the agenda item "Programme budget for the biennium 2000-2001" would remain for consideration at its resumed fifty-sixth (2002) session (**decision 56/464**) and that the Fifth Committee should continue to consider the item at that session (**decision 56/458**).

Budget for 2002-2003

In introducing the proposed programme budget for the 2002-2003 biennium [A/56/6 & Corr.1 & Add.1] before the Fifth Committee on 15 October, the Secretary-General said that the proposed budget of $2,519 million represented a 0.5 per cent real resource reduction compared with the 2000-2001 biennium. It called for small but important increases in priority areas, such as international peace and security; the promotion of sustained economic growth and sustainable development; the development of Africa; the promotion of human rights; the coordination of humanitarian assistance efforts; the promotion of justice and international law; disarmament; and drug control, crime prevention and combating international terrorism. A modest increase for internal oversight and a provision for expenditure for special political missions that would be extended or approved in the next biennium were also included. Resources had been allocated also for events to be held in 2002, notably the International Conference on Financing for Development. The budget also reflected the ongoing reform effort, including, for the first time, indicators of expected achievements.

The Secretary-General noted that in the past six years, the United Nations had had absolutely no budgetary growth. Even in dollar terms, its total budget was currently lower than it had been in 1994-1995. The Organization had been able, thus far, to absorb the effects of inflation and a large number of unfunded mandates through careful management of resources and prioritization, various reforms, and efficiency measures and new technologies. Further budgetary constraints would seriously compromise its ability to deliver the services expected of it, particularly if Member States imposed new mandates without adding new resources. It was time to review carefully the UN programme of work and to ask whether all the meetings being held were really indispensable; whether some of the reports requested duplicated others; and whether resources were allocated in the most productive way or could be applied more usefully to priorities in keeping with the Millennium Declaration [YUN 2000, p. 49]. Member States should ask themselves if all the mandates entrusted to the United Nations were really important and, above all, should ensure the availability of resources for what they considered to be high-priority areas. Noting that the General Assembly had not yet accepted his proposal for time limits or sunset provisions for new initiatives involving organizational structures or major commitments of funds, the Secretary-General urged the Fifth Committee to give that proposal serious thought.

The Committee for Programme and Coordination (CPC) considered the proposed programme budget at its 2001 session (New York, 11 June–6 July) [A/56/16] and recommended that the Assembly approve the narratives of the majority of the budget sections. It requested the Secretary-General to realign the expected accomplishments and indicators of achievement of section 8, Legal affairs, in conformity with the medium-term plan for submission to the Assembly's fifty-sixth (2001) session. CPC took note of the preliminary estimate for section 11 B, International Trade Centre (ITC) United Nations Conference on Trade and Development (UNCTAD)/World Trade Organization (WTO), and of the fact that the detailed proposed ITC programme budget for 2002-2003 would be submitted directly to the Assembly. It recommended that the Assembly review section 22, Human rights, as well as the location and level of the Ombudsman post under section 27, Management and central support services. The activities of section 27 should be presented in terms of objectives, expected accomplishments and indicators of achievement, where possible; the Secretary-General should reformulate the programme narrative of section 27C, Office of Human Resources Management (OHRM), and submit it for the Assembly's consideration at its fifty-sixth session. CPC noted the narrative of section 29, Jointly financed administrative activities, and recommended that those activities be presented in terms of objectives, expected accomplishments and indicators of achievement.

As requested, the Secretary-General submitted the reformulated narratives of section 27C, OHRM [A/C.5/56/10/Rev.1], and of section 8, Legal affairs [A/C.5/56/11/Rev.2]. Section 11 B, ITC [A/56/6/Add.1], was submitted to the Assembly on 3 December.

GENERAL ASSEMBLY ACTION

On 24 December [meeting 92], the General Assembly, on the recommendation of the Fifth Com-

mittee [A/56/736], adopted **resolution 56/253** without vote [agenda item 123].

Questions relating to the proposed programme budget for the biennium 2002-2003

The General Assembly,

I

Reaffirming its resolutions 41/213 of 19 December 1986, 42/211 of 21 December 1987 and section VI of its resolution 45/248 B of 21 December 1990,

Recalling its resolution 55/233 of 23 December 2000,

Recalling also its resolutions 54/249 of 23 December 1999 and 55/234 of 23 December 2000,

Recalling the relevant paragraphs of resolutions 52/12 A and 52/12 B of 12 November and 19 December 1997, respectively, as well as resolutions 52/235 of 26 June 1998, 53/220 A of 7 April 1999, 53/220 B of 8 June 1999 and 54/15 of 29 October 1999, relating to the Development Account,

Recalling also paragraph 2 *(a)* of its resolution 1798(XVII) of 11 December 1962,

Reaffirming the respective mandates of the Advisory Committee on Administrative and Budgetary Questions and the Committee for Programme and Coordination in the consideration of the proposed programme budget,

Reaffirming also the requirement of all Member States to fulfil their financial obligations as set out in the Charter of the United Nations on time, in full and without conditions,

Having considered the proposed programme budget for the biennium 2002-2003, the relevant reports of the Advisory Committee and the report of the Committee for Programme and Coordination on the work of its forty-first session,

Recognizing the detrimental effect of the withholding of assessed contributions on the administrative and financial functioning of the United Nations,

Recognizing also that late payments of assessed contributions adversely affect the financial situation of the Organization,

Stressing that the established procedures for the formulation, implementation and approval of the programme budget must be maintained and strictly followed,

1. *Reaffirms* that the Fifth Committee is the appropriate Main Committee of the General Assembly entrusted with responsibilities for administrative and budgetary matters;

2. *Reaffirms also* rule 153 of its rules of procedure;

3. *Reaffirms further* the Regulations and Rules Governing Programme Planning, the Programme Aspects of the Budget, the Monitoring of Implementation and the Methods of Evaluation and the Financial Regulations and Rules of the United Nations;

4. *Recalls* section III, paragraph 13, of its resolution 55/222 of 23 December 2000, and requests the Secretary-General to submit, in a consolidated form, the long overdue and delayed revisions to the Financial Regulations and Rules of the United Nations approved by the General Assembly;

5. *Requests* the Secretary-General to take steps to ensure proper compliance with all regulations and rules of the Regulations and Rules Governing Programme Planning, the Programme Aspects of the Budget, the Monitoring of Implementation and the Methods

of Evaluation, as well as the relevant resolutions that establish the budgetary procedures, as part of the preparation of the proposed programme budget for the biennium 2004-2005, reporting thereon to the Committee for Programme and Coordination at its forty-second session;

6. *Decides* that no changes to the budget methodology, to established budgetary procedures and practices or to the financial regulations may be implemented without prior review and approval by the General Assembly, in accordance with established budgetary procedures;

7. *Reaffirms* the role of the General Assembly in carrying out a thorough analysis and approval of posts and financial resources, as well as of human resources policies, with a view to ensuring the full implementation of all mandated programmes and activities and the implementation of policies in this regard;

8. *Welcomes* the timely submission of the proposed programme budget and the continued efforts made by the Secretary-General to improve the format of the proposed programme budget;

9. *Notes with satisfaction* the clarity of the presentation of the proposed programme budget, including through the provision of organization charts, and requests the Secretary-General to ensure that, in the presentation of such charts in the future, complete information on proposals for additional posts, conversions and reclassifications is reflected;

10. *Decides* that the staffing table for each year of the biennium 2002-2003 shall be as contained in annex II to the present resolution;

11. *Notes with concern* the late submission of section 11 B, International Trade Centre (UNCTAD/WTO), of the proposed programme budget for the biennium 2002-2003;

12. *Commends* the efforts and initiatives of the Secretary-General aimed at reforming the United Nations;

13. *Requests* the Secretary-General to ensure that, in the implementation of approved reform proposals, there is no adverse impact on the fulfilment of legislative mandates;

14. *Also requests* the Secretary-General to review the format currently used for the presentation of estimates, gross and net, of staff assessment, with a view to enhancing comparability with other organizations of the United Nations system, and to report on options in this regard to the General Assembly at its fifty-seventh session;

15. *Further requests* the Secretary-General, in preparing the proposed programme budget for the biennium 2004-2005, to ensure full compliance with the provisions of General Assembly resolution 55/231 of 23 December 2000 and with the relevant approved recommendations made by the Committee for Programme and Coordination in paragraphs 35 to 40 of its report, as well as those of the Advisory Committee in paragraphs 10 to 18 of its report, bearing in mind the intergovernmental, multilateral and international character of the United Nations;

16. *Requests* the Secretary-General to make proposals for the incorporation in the proposed revisions to the medium-term plan for the period 2002-2005, of a medium-term plan chapter to cover the activities of section 1 of the budget to be considered by the Committee for Programme and Coordination at its forty-second session;

17. *Reiterates* that indicators of achievement should be used, where appropriate, to measure the performance of the Secretariat and not of Member States;

18. *Emphasizes* that the resources proposed by the Secretary-General should be commensurate with all mandated programmes and activities in order to ensure their full, efficient and effective implementation;

19. *Renews its appeal* to Member States to demonstrate their commitment to the United Nations by, inter alia, meeting their financial obligations on time, in full and without conditions, in accordance with the Charter of the United Nations and the Financial Regulations and Rules of the United Nations;

II

20. *Reaffirms* that the medium-term plan, as approved by the General Assembly, shall continue to constitute the principal policy directive of the United Nations;

21. *Reiterates* that the priorities for the biennium 2002-2003 are the following:

(a) Maintenance of international peace and security;

(b) Promotion of sustained economic growth and sustainable development, in accordance with relevant General Assembly resolutions and recent United Nations conferences;

(c) Development of Africa;

(d) Promotion of human rights;

(e) Effective coordination of humanitarian assistance efforts;

(f) Promotion of justice and international law;

(g) Disarmament;

(h) Drug control, crime prevention and combating international terrorism in all its forms and manifestations;

22. *Endorses* the conclusions and recommendations of the Committee for Programme and Coordination on the programme narrative of the proposed programme budget for the biennium 2002-2003 contained in the report of the Committee on the work of its forty-first session, subject to the provisions of the present resolution;

23. *Emphasizes* that programmes and activities mandated by the General Assembly must be respected and implemented fully in the most effective and efficient manner;

24. *Reaffirms* that changes in mandated programmes and activities are the prerogative of the General Assembly;

25. *Notes with concern* that some sections of the proposed programme budget for the biennium 2002-2003 are not consistent with the medium-term plan for the period 2002-2005, and requests the Secretary-General to prepare the next biennial proposed programme budget in full conformity with the medium-term plan for the period 2002-2005, as adopted by the General Assembly in its resolution 55/234, in particular with regard to the expected accomplishments and indicators of achievement and taking into account mandates specific to the biennium;

26. *Reiterates* that the allocation of resources should reflect fully the priorities established in the medium-

term plan, and notes the importance of adopting efficient and effective management practices within the United Nations system, in particular by promoting cooperation, learning and comparison of experience between United Nations duty stations, so that optimal practices are widely adopted, as appropriate;

27. *Requests* the Secretary-General to pursue the necessary management improvement measures as indicated in paragraph 26 above, and to report thereon to the Committee for Programme and Coordination at its forty-second session;

28. *Recalls* paragraph 28 of General Assembly resolution 54/249, in which it requested the Secretary-General to provide a better explanation in the proposed programme budget for the biennium 2002-2003 on the use of standard costs and unit rates, notes with regret the absence of such explanations and requests the Secretary-General to address this matter in the context of the proposed programme budget for the biennium 2004-2005;

29. *Emphasizes* that cost accounting and the system of costing outputs are an important part of an effective and transparent decision-making process, and requests the Secretary-General to report to the General Assembly at its fifty-seventh session on this subject;

30. *Reaffirms* the Regulations and Rules Governing Programme Planning, the Programme Aspects of the Budget, the Monitoring of Implementation and the Methods of Evaluation, and requests the Secretary-General to implement regulation 5.6 of the regulations and rules and to report to the General Assembly on his effort, and also reaffirms that the application of rule 105.6 (a) should continue to reflect the understanding that approval of the medium-term plan and the programme budget constitute the reaffirmation of the mandate reflected therein;

31. *Notes with concern* the high cost of information technology–related equipment at some duty stations away from Headquarters;

32. *Recalls* its resolution 56/239 of 24 December 2001, in which it requested the Secretary-General to resubmit to the General Assembly at its fifty-seventh session his proposed information technology strategy to improve efficiency, clarify responsibilities in the Secretariat, improve decision-making and identify information technology priorities;

33. *Requests* the Secretary-General to ensure a more consistent presentation of proposed expenditure on information technology–related services and equipment for the biennium 2004-2005, detailing the maintenance and unit costs for equipment and making a full distinction between internal and external costs;

34. *Also requests* the Secretary-General to conduct a review of library services covering the Dag Hammarskjöld Library, the libraries of the United Nations Offices at Geneva and at Vienna, libraries in the regional commissions, departmental libraries, libraries at information centres and depositary libraries, with a view to defining the purpose of United Nations library services and identifying primary clients or users and the relationships and roles of the libraries, including the best way to achieve their mandates through the relevant intergovernmental bodies, and to report thereon to the General Assembly at its fifty-seventh session;

35. *Further requests* the Secretary-General to implement as soon as possible new and more efficient ways of providing library services;

36. *Decides* to make changes, as contained in annex I to the present resolution, to the programme narratives in the final published version of the proposed programme budget for the biennium 2002-2003, as reflected in the conclusions and recommendations of the Committee for Programme and Coordination at its forty-first session and the provisions of the present resolution;

37. *Requests* the Secretary-General to study the possibility of introducing a practice whereby user departments within the United Nations Secretariat are responsible from their own budgets for the consumption and payment of those central services currently borne centrally under section 27, Common support services, of the regular budget, and to report thereon to the General Assembly at its fifty-seventh session;

III

38. *Endorses* the conclusions and recommendations of the Advisory Committee contained in its reports on the proposed programme budget for the biennium 2002-2003, subject to the provisions of the present resolution;

39. *Reaffirms* paragraph 6 of its resolution 55/233, whereby the General Assembly decided, inter alia, that additional requirements in the amount of 93.7 million United States dollars (before recosting) included in the proposed programme budget for the financing of special political missions should be financed in conformity with the provisions of resolution 41/213;

40. *Reaffirms its support* for maintaining the international character of the Organization and for the principles of efficiency, competence and integrity enshrined in Article 101 of the Charter of the United Nations;

41. *Reaffirms* the role of the General Assembly with regard to the structure of the Secretariat, including the creation, conversion, suppression and redeployment of posts, and requests the Secretary-General to continue to provide the General Assembly with comprehensive information on all decisions involving established and temporary high-level posts, including equivalent positions financed from the regular budget and from extrabudgetary resources;

42. *Emphasizes* that there shall be no arbitrary ceiling on the budget of the United Nations, and that resources proposed by the Secretary-General, in the context of the proposed programme budget, should be commensurate with all mandated programmes and activities, in order to ensure their full, effective and efficient implementation;

43. *Requests* the Secretary-General, in the proposed programme budget for the biennium 2004-2005, to submit estimates of the total amount of resources, from all sources of financing, that he should have at his disposal to be able to implement fully the mandated programmes and activities efficiently and effectively;

44. *Also requests* the Secretary-General to submit to the General Assembly at its fifty-seventh session an updated study on a comprehensive solution to the problem of additional expenditures deriving from inflation and currency fluctuations, taking into account its resolution 41/213;

45. *Reaffirms* its role in carrying out a thorough analysis and approval of human and financial resources, with a view to ensuring the full, efficient and effective implementation of all mandated programmes and activities and the implementation of policies in this regard;

46. *Emphasizes* the need for Member States to provide adequate resources for the full, efficient and effective implementation of all mandated programmes and activities;

47. *Reiterates* the need for the Secretary-General to ensure that resources are utilized strictly for the purposes approved by the General Assembly;

48. *Notes* the substantial reliance on extrabudgetary resources in some sections of the proposed programme budget, in view of the mandated programmes and activities, of some programmes, and reiterates that core functions of the United Nations, as a principle, should be financed through apportionment among Member States;

49. *Notes with concern* the current and projected potential decreasing trend in extrabudgetary resources and that this decrease in some sections of the proposed programme budget for the biennium 2002-2003 could have an adverse impact on the effective implementation of programmes and activities, especially those programmes that are still heavily funded primarily through such resources;

50. *Notes* that the bulk of extrabudgetary funds are tied to specific operations and utilized on the basis of donor wishes, and requests the Secretary-General to ensure that this does not affect the nature of the programme or the orientation of its mandates;

51. *Requests* the Secretary-General to select consultants and experts, as well as staff charged against general temporary assistance, on as wide a geographical basis as possible, in accordance with the principles of the Charter and the provisions of General Assembly resolution 53/221 of 7 April 1999;

52. *Also requests* the Secretary-General to ensure that, in future programme budget proposals, requests for consultants and experts groups are clearly and separately identified in the programme narratives;

53. *Reaffirms* that the vacancy rate is a tool for budgetary calculations and should not be used to achieve budgetary savings;

54. *Also reaffirms* that deliberate management decisions should not be taken to keep a certain number of posts vacant, as this action makes the budget process less transparent and management of human and financial resources less efficient;

55. *Decides* that a vacancy rate of 6.5 per cent for Professional staff and 3.1 per cent for General Service staff shall be used as a basis for the calculation of the budget for the biennium 2002-2003;

56. *Notes* that, should the realized vacancy rates be lower than those budgeted, the General Assembly would provide additional resources, if required, in the first and/or second performance report, so as to preclude the need for any constraint on recruitment of staff;

57. *Requests* the Secretary-General to recruit staff expeditiously through proper planning and by streamlining personnel practices and procedures, in accordance with the provisions of General Assembly resolution 55/238 of 23 December 2000, in order to avoid any adverse impact of a high vacancy rate on the effective and efficient implementation and delivery of mandated programmes and activities;

58. *Also requests* the Secretary-General to ensure that posts are not deliberately left vacant to provide a cushion for absorbing the costs of special missions and other activities authorized "within available resources";

59. *Reaffirms* paragraphs 62 and 63 of the annex to its resolution 51/241 of 31 July 1997;

60. *Regrets* that the Secretary-General did not undertake a comprehensive review of the post structure of the Secretariat and did not make proposals in the proposed programme budget for the biennium 2002-2003 to address the top-heavy nature of the Organization;

61. *Decides* not to approve the upward reclassifications of the posts requested by the Secretary-General in the proposed budget for the biennium 2002-2003;

62. *Notes with concern* that the comprehensive review of the post structure of the Secretariat requested in its resolution 54/249 to address the top-heavy post structure of the Organization was not submitted, and reiterates that the comprehensive review be submitted to it at its fifty-seventh session;

63. *Also notes with concern* the number of reclassifications and new posts at senior levels proposed by the Secretary-General, which could lead to a further distortion in the pyramid staff structure of an Organization that is already top-heavy;

64. *Further notes with concern* the inadequacies of existing mechanisms for proposing and filling the reclassified posts, and requests the Secretary-General to establish a new mechanism centralizing within the auspices of the Office of Human Resources Management all proposals for reclassification, provided that all such proposals meet the following criteria:

(*a*) Proposals are of an exceptional nature;

(*b*) There is justification in terms of a change in the nature or scope of the work;

(*c*) There are full details outlining the increase in the responsibility;

(*d*) Such proposals are accompanied by justifiable and verifiable workload statistics;

(*e*) Any request involving the grading of a post must be justified solely in relation to the post itself and without reference to the incumbent or potential incumbent;

(*f*) The potential incumbent of the post being proposed for reclassification has encumbered that post for at least three years;

65. *Emphasizes* that the reclassification of posts should not be used as a promotion tool and that reclassified posts, as approved by the General Assembly, should be filled only in full conformity with the established procedures for recruitment and placement;

66. *Notes with concern* cases in which incumbents of posts are being paid at a level other than the one provided for in the budget, and requests the Secretary-General to provide a comprehensive report on this matter to the General Assembly at its fifty-seventh session;

67. *Requests* the Secretary-General to continue to comply strictly with the approved travel policies, standards, and regulations and rules, particularly with respect to ensuring that travel is undertaken by the most direct and economical route;

68. *Notes* the current use of videoconferencing as a means of communication within the United Nations, and requests the Secretary-General to study comprehensively this issue and to report thereon to the General Assembly at its fifty-seventh session;

69. *Requests* the Secretary-General to further enhance cooperation between relevant headquarters departments and regional commissions in order to ensure the quality of output and services to Member States and address the duplication and overlap of services, where they exist, and to improve the efficiency of programme support activities, and to report thereon to the General Assembly at its fifty-seventh session;

70. *Decides* to reduce the resources proposed by the Secretary-General for allocation for specific operational requirements, as follows:

(a) Travel of staff, by 2.8 million dollars;

(b) Contractual services, by 6.4 million dollars;

(c) General operating expenses, by 19.7 million dollars;

(d) Supplies and materials, by 1.4 million dollars;

(e) Furniture and equipment, by 7.2 million dollars;

(f) Consultants and experts, with exception of resources allocated under section 9 for the Department of Economic and Social Affairs, and under sections 1 to 20 for the regional commissions, by 2 million dollars;

(g) Information technology, with exception of resources for the Economic Commission for Africa allocated under section 16, by 10 million dollars;

IV

71. *Requests* the Secretary-General to ensure a more balanced proportion of staff costs devoted to programme support in comparison with those devoted to the programme of work itself in all the regional commissions, in particular in the Economic Commission for Africa;

72. *Notes with concern* the high proportion of General Service posts compared to Professional posts in the regional commissions, and requests the Secretary-General to report to the General Assembly at its fifty-seventh session on efforts undertaken, as appropriate;

73. *Notes* paragraph VI.14 of the report of the Advisory Committee, and requests the Secretary-General, as a general principle, to keep under review the ratio between General Service staff and Professional staff, taking into account the impact on the Organization of the investments in new technologies and bearing in mind the differentiated mandates and programmes of work of the various duty stations;

74. *Requests* the Secretary-General, in accordance with the Regulations and Rules Governing Programme Planning, the Programme Aspects of the Budget, the Monitoring of Implementation and the Methods of Evaluation, to review the publications and information materials of the United Nations to ensure that:

(a) They do not duplicate other United Nations publications;

(b) They have an identified target group;

(c) They are targeted to the appropriate audience;

(d) They have a significant impact on that audience;

(e) Recommendations are made on methods to strengthen the publication activities;

(f) The direct and indirect costs of producing, translating and disseminating the materials are identified;

and to report thereon to the General Assembly at its fifty-seventh session;

75. *Also requests* the Secretary-General to ensure equal treatment for the six official languages in the Dag Hammarskjöld Library in both the traditional means of publication and in the electronic media, including the Internet;

76. *Further requests* the Secretary-General to consider the importance of specialists available at the Dag Hammarskjöld Library to provide services in cataloguing and collection maintenance in all six official languages, to facilitate the use of reference works and documents by delegations and to upgrade the Library's holdings of reference works and books in all relevant categories in all six official languages;

77. *Requests* the Secretary-General to accelerate his efforts to fill all posts currently vacant in the Dag Hammarskjöld Library and to ensure the prompt and efficient processing of materials in all six official languages;

Part I
Overall policy-making, direction and coordination

Section 1
Overall policy-making, direction and coordination

78. *Notes with concern* the potential for duplication in some functions between sections of the Office of External Relations and the Department of Public Information, both of which have functions that include outreach, promotion and maintenance of the relations of the United Nations with important actors in civil society and non-governmental organizations;

79. *Decides* to establish the position of Ombudsman at the level of Assistant Secretary-General in the Office of the Secretary-General, to be supported by a legal officer at the P-4 level, in place of the D-2 and the P-4 posts originally proposed under section 27A, Office of the Under-Secretary-General for Management, and requests the Secretary-General to submit a report on the adequate level of the post in the future;

Section 2
General Assembly affairs and conference services

80. *Notes with concern* that productivity standards for interpreters have not been reviewed since 1974 and that workload standards and processes for translation have not changed substantially, as well as the complaints about the quality of the interpretation and translation;

81. *Requests* the Secretary-General to ensure that conference services are managed in an integrated manner throughout all duty stations in the Organization;

82. *Emphasizes* that all duty stations shall be given equal treatment in respect of conference services and, in this regard, requests the Secretary-General to provide adequate resources for the effective and efficient discharge of their mandates;

83. *Requests* the Secretary-General to submit to the General Assembly at its fifty-sixth session, or no later than its fifty-seventh session, through the relevant intergovernmental and expert bodies, specific proposals for the conversion of some of the temporary assistant posts requested in section 2 into established posts wherever that would measurably lead to higher efficiency and better quality of services;

84. *Also requests* the Secretary-General to submit a report to the General Assembly at its fifty-seventh ses-

sion on working methods, functions and productivity standards, and on the quality and quantity of those functions of the Department of General Assembly Affairs and Conference Services, and on the backstopping functions within the Secretariat, bearing in mind the need to make proposals for the efficient use of resources and to consider the best way to fulfil its mandates;

85. *Notes* the information contained in paragraph I.76 of the report of the Advisory Committee that the billing arrangement used by the United Nations Office at Nairobi for conference services was working fairly well, and requests the Secretary-General to take further measures to address instances of irregular cash flow;

86. *Requests* the Secretary-General to include in the budget performance reports comprehensive information (in tabular form) on the use of temporary assistance in the United Nations language services at duty stations under the responsibility of the Department of General Assembly Affairs and Conference Services, with the breakdown for languages, number of staff (local and non-local), number of workdays and expenditures (on local and non-local staff);

87. *Decides* to reduce the allocation of resources proposed for travel costs under subprogramme 2 in New York by 20,000 dollars;

Part II
Political affairs

Section 3
Political affairs

88. *Notes with concern* the potential for duplication of some activities under subprogramme 4 with the Department of Public Information;

89. *Decides* to reduce the allocation of resources proposed for travel of representatives under policy-making organs by 10,000 dollars;

Section 4
Disarmament

90. *Decides* to establish two new posts in the Professional category (one P-5 and one P-4) and one new General Service (Other level) post;

Part III
International justice and law

Section 7
International Court of Justice

91. *Recalls* its resolution 55/257 of 14 June 2001;

92. *Requests* the Secretary-General to invite the International Court of Justice to review its management functions, with a view to introducing a system of results-based budgeting, modernizing work-flow processes and enhancing the use of information technology for, inter alia, remote translation and the introduction of a performance appraisal system for staff;

Section 8
Legal affairs

93. *Requests* the Secretary-General to pursue increased timeliness and availability of international law codification documents and legal instruments in all six official languages of the United Nations;

Part IV
International cooperation for development

Section 9
Economic and social affairs

94. *Requests* the Secretary-General to consider, in consultation with relevant intergovernmental bodies, with respect to the delivery of advisory services to Member States, avoiding duplication and achieving optimum and effective use of resources, and to report thereon to the relevant intergovernmental bodies at the fifty-seventh session of the General Assembly;

95. *Decides* to establish seven new P-2 posts as recommended by the Advisory Committee as well as two further P-2 posts as submitted in the proposed programme budget;

Section 10
Africa: New Agenda for Development

96. *Reaffirms once again* the decision contained in paragraph 95 of its resolution 54/249 to assign priority to the development of Africa, and reiterates its previous request to the Secretary-General to continue his efforts to mobilize additional resources for the implementation of the programme of action contained in the United Nations New Agenda for the Development of Africa in the 1990s;

97. *Notes with appreciation* African-led and African-owned development plans, such as the New Partnership for Africa's Development;

Section 11A
Trade and development

98. *Emphasizes* that management restructuring should produce clearly defined gains in productivity and/or economies;

Section 12
Environment

99. *Notes* that the activities undertaken by the United Nations Environment Programme continue to depend heavily on extrabudgetary resources for their implementation, requests the Secretary-General to make every effort to ensure stability and predictability in funding the activities of the United Nations Environment Programme, and, in this regard, reiterates paragraph 110 of its resolution 54/249;

Section 13
Human settlements

100. *Notes* that the activities undertaken by the United Nations Centre for Human Settlements (Habitat) continue to depend heavily on extrabudgetary resources for their implementation, requests the Secretary-General to make every effort to ensure stability and predictability in funding the activities of the Centre, and, in this regard, reiterates paragraph 114 of its resolution 54/249;

101. *Emphasizes* the need for the Centre to be provided with adequate human and financial resources to enable it to implement effectively the Declaration on Cities and Other Human Settlements in the New Millennium, adopted by the General Assembly at its twenty-fifth special session;

102. *Reiterates* its request to the Secretary-General contained in paragraph 111 of its resolution 54/249, in accordance with paragraph 229 of the Habitat Agenda and in consultation with the Commission on Human Settlements, to continue to ensure more effective func-

tioning of the Centre by, inter alia, providing sufficient human and financial resources within the regular budget of the United Nations;

Section 14
Crime prevention and criminal justice

103. *Requests* the Secretary-General to make proposals to strengthen the Terrorism Prevention Branch at the United Nations Office at Vienna to enable it to carry out its mandate as approved by the General Assembly, and to report thereon to the General Assembly for its consideration;

Section 15
International drug control

104. *Notes with deep concern* the reports of serious management irregularities in the United Nations drug-control activities, as documented in recent reports of the Board of Auditors and the Office of Internal Oversight Services;

105. *Requests* the Secretary-General to take all necessary actions to correct immediately the management problems;

Part V
Regional cooperation for development

Section 16
Economic and social development in Africa

106. *Notes with concern* the high vacancy rate in the Economic Commission for Africa, and in this regard reiterates paragraph 50 of its resolution 54/249;

107. *Regrets* that the request contained in paragraph 123 of its resolution 54/249 to achieve a vacancy rate of no more than 5 per cent within the biennium 2000-2001 was not met and, in this regard, requests the Secretary-General to take immediate steps to decrease substantially the persistently high vacancy rate which negatively affects programme delivery in the Commission;

108. *Recalls* paragraph 123 of its resolution 54/249, in which it requested the Secretary-General to take the necessary measures, as a matter of priority, to achieve a vacancy rate of no more than 5 per cent;

109. *Expresses its deep concern* that the Economic Commission for Africa is still suffering from a significantly high vacancy rate at the Professional level, and requests the Secretary-General to ensure that all posts budgeted for the biennium 2002-2003 are filled;

110. *Reiterates its request* to the Secretary-General to redeploy to the subregional development centres any savings realized during the biennium as a result of reform measures and efficiency gains from within the Economic Commission for Africa;

111. *Also reiterates its request* to the Secretary-General to provide the African Institute for the Prevention of Crime and the Treatment of Offenders with the core Professional staff required to enable it to function effectively towards the fulfilment of its mandates;

112. *Expresses concern* about the inadequate connectivity between the headquarters of the Economic Commission for Africa and the five subregional development centres and between the Commission and the rest of the United Nations system, and, in this regard, decides to exempt the Commission from the proposed reductions in information technology referred to in paragraph 70 *(g)* of the present resolution;

113. *Emphasizes* the need to improve the capacity of the Economic Commission for Africa to disseminate information effectively through the use of electronic methods, and, in this regard, shares the opinion of the Advisory Committee contained in paragraph V.20 of its report that the programme of modernization of operations of the Commission is important and that the provision of resources therefor should not be dependent upon the possibility of absorption within the Commission's appropriations, and requests the Secretary-General to report in the context of the budget performance report on the additional expenditure that might be incurred;

114. *Requests* the Secretary-General to report on progress in implementing new communications technologies and resulting efficiencies in the context of the proposed programme budget for the biennium 2004-2005;

115. *Recognizes* that the Economic Commission for Africa will have a major role to play in the implementation of the new African initiatives, such as the New Partnership for Africa's Development;

Section 17
Economic and social development in Asia and the Pacific

116. *Requests* the Secretary-General to pursue his efforts to maximize the use of the Conference Centre, including its external use, and to report thereon to the General Assembly at its fifty-seventh session;

Section 18
Economic development in Europe

117. *Notes with concern* the lack of detail in the proposed programme budget of unit costs for the replacement or acquisition of information technology–related equipment;

118. *Notes* the increase in proposed resources for external support for strengthening the information technology platform;

Section 19
Economic and social development in Latin America and the Caribbean

119. *Commends* the Economic Commission for Latin America and the Caribbean for the implementation of the reform programme for the Commission;

120. *Expresses its deep concern* at the decreasing trend in extrabudgetary resources and at its impact on the level of technical cooperation activities;

121. *Requests* the Secretary-General to submit to the General Assembly at its fifty-seventh session concrete proposals to address the impact of declining extrabudgetary resources for the Economic Commission for Latin America and the Caribbean;

122. *Also requests* the Secretary-General to ensure that all the necessary means are provided for the full implementation of all subprogrammes and their respective activities;

123. *Notes with concern* that consultants and experts are also used for verifying the views of the Secretariat;

Section 20
Economic and social development in Western Asia

124. *Requests* the Secretary-General to ensure fully the issuance of all documents and publications of the Economic and Social Commission for Western Asia in Arabic, which is most relevant to the requirements of the Member States of the region, as well as in the other

working languages of the Commission, to meet the requirements of readers outside the region, as appropriate, and to report thereon to the General Assembly by its fifty-seventh session;

Part VI
Human rights and humanitarian affairs

Section 22
Human rights

125. *Notes with concern* that section 22 of the proposed programme budget for the biennium 2002-2003 was prepared prior to the adoption of the medium-term plan by the General Assembly and that it was not reformulated in its submission in accordance with the medium-term plan approved by the Assembly;

126. *Notes* that resources proposed for activities related to the right to development, research and analysis are not clearly differentiated in subprogramme 1, and requests the Secretary-General to submit concrete proposals to address this issue in the context of the revisions of the medium-term plan to be considered by the Committee for Programme and Coordination;

127. *Notes also* that there are twenty-two subcommissions, committees and other groups involved in the programme of work of human rights, and requests the Secretary-General to make proposals through the relevant intergovernmental bodies with a view to rationalizing and streamlining the human rights machinery, as well as the establishment of rapporteurs and the number of meetings, reports and publications, in order to avoid duplication and promote efficiency and effectiveness, and to report thereon in the context of the next programme budget;

128. *Requests* the Secretary-General to entrust to the Office of Internal Oversight Services a comprehensive management review of the Office of the United Nations High Commissioner for Human Rights, including its working methods and functions, bearing in mind the need to make proposals for the efficient and effective use of resources as well as its organizational structure, and to report to the General Assembly at its fifty-seventh session on the actions taken thereon;

129. *Notes* that the bulk of extrabudgetary funds are tied to specific operations and are utilized on the basis of donor wishes, and requests the Secretary-General to ensure that the practice of tied funds does not affect the policies of the Office of the United Nations High Commissioner for Human Rights or the Commission on Human Rights and its subsidiary bodies as impartial international instruments for the advancement of human rights;

130. *Decides* to establish one new P-3 post and one new General Service (Other level) post for the functions in the Office;

131. *Decides also* to reduce the proposed allocation of resources for furniture and equipment under programme support by 40,200 dollars;

132. *Requests* the Secretary-General to ensure that funding for the Centre for Human Rights and Democracy in Central Africa will be formally made an integral part of the regular budget for human rights in future bienniums;

Section 23
Protection of and assistance to refugees

133. *Deeply regrets* that some amounts previously funded under posts, other staff costs, general operat-

ing expenses and supplies and materials have been presented in a less transparent manner under the provision of grants and contributions;

134. *Requests* the Secretary-General to reinstate resource requirements by object of expenditure with provisions other than grants and contributions, and to report thereon to the General Assembly at its fifty-sixth session;

135. *Also requests* the Secretary-General to review the funding of the Office of the United Nations High Commissioner for Refugees from the regular budget in a transparent manner;

136. *Further requests* the Secretary-General to present resource requirements by object of expenditure with provisions other than grants and contributions in the proposed programme budget for the biennium 2004-2005;

Section 24
Palestine refugees

137. *Welcomes* the efforts of a number of donors during the past year to the programme;

138. *Notes with concern* the direct impact of the decrease in extrabudgetary resources on the quality of services provided by the United Nations Relief and Works Agency for Palestine Refugees in the Near East;

139. *Decides* to restore to the regular budget five additional international posts (one P-5 and four P-4) currently financed from the Agency's extrabudgetary resources, in line with General Assembly resolution 3331 B (XXIX) of 17 December 1974;

Section 25
Humanitarian assistance

140. *Decides* to establish three P-4 posts for the functions of the Office for the Coordination of Humanitarian Affairs;

Part VII
Public information

Section 26
Public information

141. *Decides* to establish a P-3 post in the News and Media Division for a Portuguese-language radio producer;

142. *Also decides* to establish a P-3 post at the United Nations Information Centre at Dar es Salaam;

143. *Requests* the Secretary-General to make available web site language assistance in the Information Technology Section of the Department of Public Information, in Arabic, Chinese, Russian and Spanish, and to make proposals as he deems appropriate so that all official languages are equally serviced;

144. *Emphasizes* the need for the United Nations to have a coordinated public information strategy in order to bring the activities of different parts of the Secretariat together in an integrated way;

145. *Requests* the Secretary-General to submit to the General Assembly at its fifty-sixth session concrete proposals on strengthening the Department of Public Information within the existing capacity in order to support and enhance the United Nations web site in all the official languages of the Organization;

146. *Emphasizes* that the public information resources of the Organization must be targeted properly to ensure that the United Nations delivers a consistent

message, through a variety of outlets, to the largest possible worldwide audience;

147. *Recognizes* the critical role of the Official Document System as a primary tool for accessing all forms of United Nations documentation and the United Nations web site as the public gateway to the activities of the Organization;

148. *Requests* the Secretary-General to improve the justification provided for the resources requested for the United Nations information centres in the context of the next proposed programme budget;

149. *Also requests* the Secretary-General to report to the General Assembly at its fifty-seventh session on the financial implications of redressing the imbalance among the six official languages of the United Nations on the United Nations web site;

150. *Further requests* the Secretary-General to conduct a comprehensive review of the management and operations of the Department of Public Information, taking into account the medium-term plan, and to report thereon to the General Assembly at its fifty-seventh session, addressing, among other things:

(*a*) Ways to carry out these activities in the most effective and efficient manner;

(*b*) Focusing of the activities of the Department to reflect better the substantive priorities and relevant mandates of the Organization;

(*c*) The need for greater coordination of public information activities among departments of the Secretariat to avoid duplication of efforts and to strengthen complementarity, where appropriate;

(*d*) Assessment of the impact of United Nations information centres, taking into account their mandates;

(*e*) The option and benefit of funding the United Nations information centres on a cost-shared basis with other United Nations entities that benefit from the services of the information centres in each location;

151. *Notes with concern* the fact that the post of the Director of the Office of the United Nations Information Centre for Central Africa is still vacant despite several appeals by Member States of the subregion to ensure that a person is appointed to fill it;

152. *Decides* to resume publication of the *United Nations Chronicle* in all official languages, as proposed by the Secretary-General, and allocates 700,000 dollars for this purpose, and welcomes the intention of using a co-publishing mechanism in publishing the *Chronicle*;

Part VIII
Common support services

Section 27
Management and central support services

153. *Requests* the Secretary-General to conduct an evaluation through the Office of Internal Oversight Services of the implementation of all provisions of resolutions 55/231 on results-based budgeting and 55/258 of 14 June 2001 on human resources management by the Department of Management, including the Office of the Under-Secretary-General for Management, and to report thereon to the General Assembly;

Section 27A
Office of the Under-Secretary-General for Management

154. *Expresses concern* about the large number of posts and amount of resources that are devoted to management activities and programme support in the De-

partment of Management and all the other departments;

155. *Stresses* the need for the Integrated Management Information System to be enabled to manage and execute its administrative tasks, as foreseen when it was first proposed to the General Assembly;

156. *Requests* the Secretary-General, with the assistance of the Office of Internal Oversight Services, to review administrative tasks, procedures and policies with a view to eliminating duplication, and unnecessary and complex bureaucratic procedures and practices within all departments and entities of the Secretariat, and to ensure that the Organization is managed in an integrated manner in order to eliminate duplication;

157. *Also requests* the Secretary-General to ensure that the necessary equipment is available for the work of the Main Committees of the General Assembly so as to make the Secretariat more efficient, effective and modern;

Section 27D
Office of Central Support Services

158. *Decides* to reduce general operating expenditures as explained in paragraph A.27D.16 of the proposed programme budget by 100,000 dollars and to eliminate the maintenance and support of Dictaphones in the Organization, as it is incompatible with the goals of an "e-Organization";

159. *Also decides* not to approve the increase of 2,116,800 dollars for furniture and equipment in the Information Technology Services Division;

160. *Invites* the Secretary-General to continue his efforts to expand free access to the Official Document System, taking into account the technical capacity of the Office on the Internet in the six official languages of the United Nations, without affecting the quality of the service provided;

Section 27G
Administration, Nairobi

161. *Welcomes* the commitment of the Secretary-General to increase gradually the regular budget component of the United Nations Office at Nairobi, with a view to easing the administrative costs levied on the substantive programmes of the United Nations Environment Programme and the United Nations Centre for Human Settlements (Habitat), and requests the Secretary-General to report to the General Assembly at its fifty-seventh session on his plan for the upcoming bienniums;

162. *Also welcomes* the establishment of a permanent interpretation service at the United Nations Office at Nairobi, and notes with satisfaction that the conference services facility at the United Nations Office at Nairobi is becoming organizationally, functionally and in terms of the budget an integral part of the Department of General Assembly Affairs and Conference Services and that the proposed programme budget for the biennium 2002-2003 for the Division of Conference Services is programmed in the context of section 2;

163. *Reaffirms* paragraph 178 of its resolution 54/249, in which it requested the Secretary-General to bring the financial arrangements of the United Nations Office at Nairobi into line with those of similar United Nations administrative offices;

164. *Notes* the recommendation of the Advisory Committee on the need to determine more accurately

the level of services that the United Nations Office at Nairobi is required to provide to the organizations at Nairobi and the rates for reimbursing the cost of those services, and requests the Secretary-General to expedite the completion of the agreements between the United Nations Environment Programme, the United Nations Centre for Human Settlements (Habitat) and the United Nations Office at Nairobi to this effect;

Part X
Jointly financed administrative activities and special expenses

Section 29
Jointly financed administrative activities

165. *Stresses* the need to ensure that the independence of the Joint Inspection Unit, as the only system-wide external oversight body, is not compromised through the budgetary process;

166. *Reiterates* its decision 54/454 of 23 December 1999;

167. *Reaffirms* the statute of the Unit, in particular article 20, paragraph 1;

Income section 2
General income

168. *Requests* the Secretary-General to continue with the current arrangement regarding rental charges for the Office of the Group of 77 and China located at United Nations Headquarters.

ANNEX I
Changes to the programme narratives of the proposed programme budget for the biennium 2002- 2003 as reflected in the conclusions and recommendations of the Committee for Programme and Coordination in its report on the work of its forty-first session, and additional modifications

Section 2
General Assembly affairs and conference services

1. In paragraph 2.7, at the end of the last sentence, replace "on an as-available basis from within the existing capacity of the Department" with "in accordance with paragraph 4 of section I of General Assembly resolution 55/222 of 23 December 2000".

2. In paragraph 2.8, at the end of the fourth sentence, insert ", without prejudice to the mandates of the General Assembly".

3. In paragraph 2.19 *(d)*, at the end of the subparagraph, replace "within available resources" with ", in accordance with the rules of procedure of the General Assembly and the relevant United Nations resolutions on decolonization."

4. In paragraph 2.46 *(a)*, after "Translation and writing of summary records." add "Translation and publishing of the *Repertoire of Practice of the Security Council* in the six official languages;".

5. In paragraph 2.48, at the end of the fourth sentence, insert ", in accordance with General Assembly resolutions 54/248 and 55/222".

Section 3
Political affairs

6. In paragraph 3.3, after "while fully respecting the sovereignty, territorial integrity and political independence of Member States", in accordance with paragraph 1.3 of the medium-term plan for 2002-2005, add the following:

"and the principles of non-intervention in matters that are essentially within the domestic jurisdiction of any State and of consent".

7. In table 3.12:

(a) At the end of the text under "Expected accomplishments", add ", in accordance with the relevant resolutions and decisions of the General Assembly and the Security Council";

(b) Under "Indicators of achievement", replace the existing text of subparagraph (i) with "Provision of electoral assistance to Member States in response to their request".

8. In paragraph 3.26:

(a) Replace "a fair and free" with "an";

(b) At the end of the paragraph add ", in accordance with relevant resolutions and decisions".

9. In paragraph 3.27:

(a) In subparagraph *(a)* (i) a., delete "the principle of periodic and genuine", and add at the end ", in accordance with relevant resolutions and decisions";

(b) In subparagraph *(d)* (ii), replace "authorities at the regional, national or local level" with "national electoral institutions".

10. In paragraph 3.38, after the first sentence, in accordance with paragraph 1.26 of the medium-term plan, add the following sentence:

"Assistance will be provided to the Committee in promoting a comprehensive, just and lasting settlement of the question of Palestine in accordance with all relevant United Nations resolutions, as well as the full and effective implementation of the Israeli-Palestinian peace agreements."

Section 4
Disarmament

11. Replace paragraph 4.1, with the following:

"General and complete disarmament under strict and effective international control remains the ultimate goal of all efforts exerted in the field of disarmament. The main responsibilities for disarmament lie with Member States, and the United Nations, in accordance with its Charter, has a central role and primary responsibility in supporting Member States in this sphere. The Department for Disarmament Affairs, headed by an Under-Secretary-General, is responsible for the implementation of the programme."

12. Replace paragraph 4.2 with the following:

"The mandate for the programme derives from the priorities established in General Assembly resolutions and decisions in the field of disarmament, including the Final Document of the Tenth Special Session of the General Assembly devoted to disarmament (resolution S-10/2). While weapons of mass destruction, in particular nuclear weapons, continue to be the primary concern, the Organization would also continue its work in the field of conventional disarmament."

13. In paragraph 4.4, in the first sentence, replace the phrase "as well as to expert groups on disarmament studies" with "as well as review conferences, other meetings of States parties to multilateral agreements on disarmament and related matters and expert groups assisting the Secretary-General in undertaking disarmament studies".

14. After paragraph 4.4, insert a new paragraph 4.5 to read as follows:

"4.5 Training and advisory services will continue to be provided through the United Nations disarmament fellowships, training and advisory services programme and the United Nations Institute for Disarmament Research for Member States, in particular developing countries, to enhance their expertise with a view to participating more effectively in international deliberating and negotiating forums. The Department will also assist Member States in increasing understanding among them of the relationship between disarmament and development."

and renumber the subsequent paragraphs.

15. In former paragraph 4.6, delete "and landmine issues".

16. In former paragraph 4.14:

(a) In the second sentence, after "international disarmament agenda", delete "in order to make them conform to the new international political and security environment";

(b) Replace the third and fourth sentences with the following:

"The Conference on Disarmament will be finalizing its work programme, which will include resuming negotiations on a number of disarmament issues and continuing the promotion of global disarmament, in accordance with its agenda."

17. In table 4.7:

(a) Under "Indicators of achievement":

(i) In paragraph (a), after "effectiveness of", add "the services provided by the Secretariat to facilitate";

(ii) Replace paragraph (c) with the following:

"An increase in the number of applicants for the United Nations disarmament fellowship, training and advisory services programme, wider representation of Member States in the programme and greater support for the disarmament fellowship programme from Member States."

18. In table 4.9:

(a) Under "Expected accomplishments":

(i) In paragraph (a), replace the text after "disarmament issues" with the following: "and on matters related to weapons of mass destruction, in particular nuclear weapons, by Member States,";

(ii) In paragraph (b), replace "including the issue of missiles" with "on specific issues related to weapons of mass destruction, in particular nuclear weapons";

(b) Under "Indicators of achievement", subparagraph (a) (i) should read:

"A record of appreciation for assistance provided, including substantive and organizational support, for the implementation of agreements in the field of weapons of mass destruction, in particular nuclear weapons. This would include sessions of the Preparatory Committee for the 2005 Review Conference and ad hoc meetings;".

19. In former paragraph 4.25:

(a) In subparagraph (a) (iv), delete "and the panel of governmental experts on missiles (2 sessions, 40 meetings, 2000)";

(b) In subparagraph (a) (v), after "2 sessions", add ", 40 meetings, 2002" within the parentheses;

(c) In all instances where the phrase "weapons of mass destruction" appears, if it has not already been done, add ", in particular nuclear weapons".

Section 5
Peacekeeping operations

20. In paragraph 5.3:

(a) Replace the first sentence with the entire text of paragraph 3.1 of the medium-term plan for the period 2002-2005, as follows:

"The overall purpose of the programme is the maintenance of peace and security through the deployment of peacekeeping operations in accordance with the principles and provisions of the Charter of the United Nations. The legislative authority for the programme derives from the principles and purposes of the Charter of the United Nations. The mandates of the programme are provided in resolutions of the Security Council and General Assembly resolutions on the comprehensive review of the whole question of peacekeeping operations in all their aspects on the administrative and budgetary aspects of the financing of United Nations peacekeeping operations and on assistance in mine clearance. In respect of peacekeeping operations, legislative authority derives from decisions and resolutions of the Security Council related to particular operations."

(b) In the seventh sentence, replace "on a broad geographic basis" with "and on as wide a geographical basis as possible";

(c) After the seventh sentence, add the following sentence:

"However, this will not affect the troop-contributing countries in taking their sovereign decisions on the composition of their units deployed to peacekeeping operations within the mission's specific guidelines, as agreed upon by troop-contributing countries."

21. In paragraph 5.8, at the end of the penultimate sentence, replace "peace operations" with "peacekeeping operations".

22. In paragraph 5.24, after "Security Council mandates", delete "and that other parties . . . their role".

23. In paragraph 5.25 (c), after "and provision of support to meetings with Member States," replace the remainder of the subparagraph with the following:

"by other Organizations within the United Nations system, as well as with other regional organizations and actors, in accordance with legislative mandates".

24. In table 5.11, under "Indicators of achievement" in paragraph (b), add two additional indicators, as follows:

"(i) Reduction in the duration of the liquidation process;

"(ii) Timeliness of the processing and settling of claims of troop-contributing countries by the Claims and Information Management Section of the Finance Management and Support Service."

25. In paragraph 5.32, after "required military and civilian police components", add "that meet the rele-

vant prerequisites of the peacekeeping missions", and delete the words "to peacekeeping missions".

26. In paragraph 5.33, in subparagraphs *(b)*, *(c)* and *(d)*, replace "peace operations" with "peacekeeping operation(s)".

Section 6
Peaceful uses of outer space

27. In table 6.3:

(a) Under "Expected accomplishments", paragraph *(c)* should read:

"Increased access and use of space technologies by developing countries in their efforts to promote economic, social and cultural development."

(b) Under "Indicators of achievement":

(i) Reletter paragraph *(c)* as *(c)*(i), which should read:

"*(c)* (i) An increase in the number of projects and activities carried out by developing countries to promote economic, social and cultural development through bilateral and multilateral cooperation, with access to and use of space technologies."

(ii) Insert the following text as paragraph *(c)* (ii):

"(ii) An increase in and further enhancement of training opportunities for developing countries, including fellowships provided to individuals from developing countries to participate in workshops, expert meetings and training courses on various topics of space science and technology and its application."

Section 8
Legal affairs

28. In table 8.8:

(a) Replace the entire text under "Expected accomplishments" with the following:

"Provision of quality legal advice to the principal and subsidiary organs of the United Nations, leading to an increased understanding of international law, including the United Nations legal regime."

(b) Replace the entire text under "Indicators of achievement" with the following:

"*(a)* Quality, timeliness and accuracy of advice.

"*(b)* Number of instruments finalized.

"*(c)* Number and impact of opinions rendered on violations of international legal instruments for the conduct of United Nations operations."

29. In table 8.10:

(a) Replace the entire text under "Expected accomplishments" with the following:

"*(a)* Greater protection of the Organization's legal rights and minimization of its legal liabilities, through the provision of quality legal advice to the principal and subsidiary organs of the United Nations, leading to an increased understanding of the Organization's legal rights and obligations.

"*(b)* Provision of legal advice and support aimed at enabling offices, departments and subsidiary organs to maximize their compliance with regulations, rules and administrative issuances consistent with the Organization's policies and purposes."

(b) Replace the entire text under "Indicators of achievement" with the following:

"*(a)* Quality, accuracy and timeliness of legal advice and support.

"*(b)* Number and impact of legal opinions and other legal advice such that the United Nations offices are in a better position to interpret and apply provisions of the United Nations legal regime to specific cases and to comply with such provisions."

30. In table 8.12:

Under "Indicators of achievement", replace paragraphs *(a)* and *(b)* with the following:

"*(a)* Increase in the number of new legal instruments emanating from the process of codification, adherence by States to existing instruments; and satisfaction expressed by Member States with the quality, volume and timeliness of documentation prepared by the Codification Division.

"*(b)* The quality of publications and seminars dealing with issues of international law and an increase in the number of visitors to the Division's web site."

31. In table 8.14:

(a) Replace the entire text under "Expected accomplishments" with the following:

"*(a)* Greater respect for and acceptance of the United Nations Convention on the Law of the Sea and the related Agreements and a higher degree of uniformity and consistency in their application.

"*(b)* Increased opportunities for States to derive benefits from the oceans and seas in conformity with the United Nations Convention on the Law of the Sea."

(b) Replace the entire text under "Indicators of achievement" with the following:

"*(a)* An increase in the number of legal instruments developed by States and international organizations in the field of the law of the sea and ocean affairs.

"*(b)* The degree of satisfaction on the part of Member States, reflected in:

"(i) Acknowledgement by Member States that the products and services provided through the subprogramme assisted their maritime programmes;

"(ii) Increased participation of Member States in bodies and processes relating to oceans and the law of the sea."

32. In table 8.16:

(a) Replace the entire text under "Expected accomplishments" with:

"*(a)* Modernization of trade practices.

"*(b)* Reduction of legal uncertainties and obstacles posed by inadequate and disparate laws.

"*(c)* More efficient trade negotiations.

"*(d)* Simplification of the administration of transaction and lower transaction costs.

"*(e)* Reduction of disputes in international trade."

(b) Replace the entire text under "Indicators of achievement" with the following:

"*(a)* A higher number of transactions or a higher volume of international trade carried out under the regime of UNCITRAL legislative and non-legislative texts.

"*(b)* An increase in the number of legislative decisions based on UNCITRAL texts.

"(c) An increase in the number of merchants using or relying on harmonized international trade law in conducting trade."

33. In table 8.18:

(a) Replace the entire text under "Expected accomplishments" with the following:

"(a) Improved access to international treaties deposited with the Secretary-General, including their status, and to treaties registered with the Secretariat.

"(b) Respect for the international treaty framework and the advancement of the international rule of law."

(b) Replace the entire text under "Indicators of achievement" with the following:

"(a) Timely processing, registration and publication of international treaties deposited with the Secretary-General in accordance with Article 102 of the Charter, and of actions relating to treaties deposited with the Secretary-General, including the United Nations *Treaty Series*, multilateral treaties deposited with the Secretary-General, the monthly Statement of Treaties and International Agreements and the United Nations *Treaty Series* Cumulative Index; and the timely availability of such information through electronic services.

"(b) Increased application of information obtained through services provided under this subprogramme, including electronic services.

"(c) Greater satisfaction of users with the services provided by the Treaty Section, including electronic services."

Section 9
Economic and social affairs

34. In table 9.9:

(a) Under "Expected accomplishments", add new paragraphs (e), (f) and (g) as follows:

"(e) Establishment of an expanded framework for information exchange and communication with Governments and civil society.

"(f) Increased efficiency and effectiveness of the Inter-Agency Committee on Women and Gender Equality.

"(g) An increased number of ratifications of the Convention on the Elimination of All Forms of Discrimination against Women and the Optional Protocol thereto, increased compliance by States parties with reporting obligations under the Convention and improved coordination between the Division for the Advancement of Women and the Office of the United Nations High Commissioner for Human Rights in contributing to the development and strengthening of human rights mechanisms to ensure the enjoyment by women of their human rights."

(b) Under "Indicators of achievement", add new paragraphs (e) and (f) as follows:

"(e) The number of ratifications of the Convention and the Optional Protocol thereto, the number of States parties submitting their reports to the Committee on the Elimination of Discrimination against Women on time and the number of reports examined by the Committee.

"(f) The development of tools and methodologies and the promotion of good practices with respect to system-wide gender mainstreaming by the Inter-Agency Committee on Women and Gender Equality of the United Nations System Chief Executive Board for Coordination, including enhancement of the capabilities of the regional economic commissions to work as focal points for inter-agency coordination on gender issues within the United Nations system."

35. In paragraph 9.62 (a) (iii) b.:

After "Reports on:" add "existing studies, information and documentation on abuse against older persons;".

36. In table 9.13:

(a) Under "Expected accomplishments", reletter paragraph (c) as (c) (i) and insert a new subparagraph (c) (ii), reading as follows:

"(ii) Improved coordination of the implementation of the World Solar Programme."

(b) Under "Indicators of achievement", paragraph (c), after the phrase "sustainable development", insert the phrase ", including the World Solar Programme".

37. In paragraph 9.69 (a) (vi), in the last sentence, after the word, "development", add ", including solar energy".

38. In table 9.21, under "Expected accomplishments", replace paragraph (e) with the following text:

"Improved access by Governments and international bodies to analytical tools, options and adequate methodologies regarding the linkages between political and economic issues and policies, such as economic sanctions, imposition of coercive economic measures, the relationship between disarmament and development and relevant aspects of post-conflict rehabilitation and reconstruction."

Section 10
Africa: New Agenda for Development

39. In table 10.4:

(a) Under "Expected accomplishments", replace paragraph (b) with the following:

"Greater awareness and understanding of African development issues, including those related to post-conflict situations."

(b) Under "Indicators of achievement":

(i) In paragraph (b), after "The contribution" add "and impact";

(ii) After paragraph (d), add the following paragraphs (e) to (i):

"(e) An assessment of the quality and timeliness of reports submitted to intergovernmental policy-making and review bodies to facilitate deliberations on Africa.

"(f) The number and usefulness of briefing sessions on issues concerning African development.

"(g) The number and usefulness of South-South forums sponsored or co-sponsored.

"(h) The number of visits to the Africa web page.

"(i) The use of databases on the activities of non-governmental organizations and other non-governmental partners contributing to African development."

40. In table 10.6:

(a) Under "Expected accomplishments", add paragraphs (d) and (e) as follows:

"*(d)* Improved reporting on and dissemination of experiences in the implementation of programmes and initiatives on Africa.

"*(e)* Strengthened national economic management capacity as an integral component of peacebuilding and post-conflict resolution."

(b) Under "Indicators of achievement":

(i) Add the following paragraph *(a)* and reletter the subsequent paragraphs accordingly:

"*(a)* Expression of satisfaction over the support provided to Member States in implementing the programme of action."

(ii) In new paragraphs *(c)* and *(d)*, add "and impact" after "The number";

(iii) Add paragraphs *(e)* and *(f)* after paragraph *(d)* as follows:

"*(e)* The number and impact of forums and expert meetings organized to access and monitor the rate of implementation of the action programme.

"*(f)* The number and impact of training activities organized and development personnel benefiting from them."

41. In table 10.8, replace the two indicators of achievement with the following:

"*(a)* Assessment by users of the quality and volume of information disseminated regionally and internationally through the print and electronic media outlets.

"*(b)* The timely and regular issuance of *Africa Recovery*.

"*(c)* The number and quality of informational materials prepared and media events organized in order to maintain the international spotlight on Africa."

Section 11A
Trade and development

42. In paragraph 11A.2, after the last sentence, insert the following sentence:

"It is foreseen that the Trade and Development Board will mainstream the implementation of the Programme of Action for the Least Developed Countries for the Decade 2001-2010 within the work programme of UNCTAD, as well as in the UNCTAD intergovernmental process. It is also foreseen that similar efforts will be undertaken by the governing bodies of all United Nations system organizations, as appropriate."

Section 12
Environment

43. In paragraph 12.21:

(a) In the second sentence, replace "collection, analysis and interpretation of data" with the words "collection and analysis of data";

(b) In the third sentence, after "reporting arrangements", add "invited it to submit its programme of work to the Assembly".

44. In paragraph 12.22, at the end of the last sentence, add "in consultation with scientists and experts from interested Member States".

45. In table 12.10:

(a) Insert a new expected accomplishment *(e)* as follows:

"*(e)* The implementation of a new strategic environmental law programme for the first decade of the millennium."

(b) Insert a new indicator of achievement *(e)* as follows:

"*(e)* The adoption by the Governing Council of a new strategic environmental law programme."

46. In table 12.14:

(a) Insert a new expected accomplishment *(f)* as follows:

"*(f)* Adherence to the goals of the International Declaration on Cleaner Production."

(b) Insert a new indicator of achievement *(f)* as follows:

"*(f)* The number of signatures to the International Declaration on Cleaner Production."

Section 13
Human settlements

47. In table 13.9, under "Expected accomplishments", replace "city authorities" with "local authorities".

Section 14
Crime prevention and criminal justice

48. In table 14.5:

(a) Under "Expected accomplishments", replace paragraph *(b)* with paragraph 12.7 *(b)* of the medium-term plan for the period 2002-2005, as follows:

"The expansion of global knowledge of and expertise to deal with crime problems such as those posed by transnational organized crime, trafficking in persons, economic and financial crime, including money-laundering, corruption, illicit manufacturing and trafficking in firearms and terrorism in all its forms and manifestations, as well as to promote fair and efficient criminal justice systems."

(b) Under "Indicators of achievement":

(i) Replace paragraph *(b)* with paragraph 12.8 *(b)* of the medium-term plan, as modified below:

"Awareness of best practices and information disseminated, research undertaken and new techniques developed and shared among Member States to respond to crime problems as well as to promote fair and efficient criminal justice systems."

(ii) In subparagraphs *(c)* (i) and (iii), replace "transnational organized crime, trafficking in persons, corruption and terrorism in all its forms and manifestations" with the words "crime problems".

49. In paragraph 14.18 *(a)*, replace "Readiness of Governments to ratify" with "Cooperation of Member States in ratifying".

50. In paragraph 14.18 *(b)*, delete "including from sensitive government data sources".

51. In paragraph 14.19 *(a)*, add a new subparagraph (vi), reading:

"(vi) Ad Hoc Committee for the negotiation of a legal instrument against corruption:

"a. Substantive servicing of meetings. Six sessions of two weeks' duration (120 meetings);

"b. Parliamentary documentation. Six reports to the Ad Hoc Committee, including annotated agendas with the transmission of a draft text, contributions and proposals by States; six reports on each session of the Ad Hoc Committee."

52. Paragraph 14.19 *(a)* (v) should read:
"Ad hoc expert groups (RB/XB): Four regional expert group meetings on technical issues of common regional concern on the ratification and/or implementation of the Convention against Transnational Organized Crime and its three protocols; one expert group meeting each on: the criminal misuse of information technologies; best practices to combat trafficking in human beings and smuggling of migrants by land, sea and air, with attention given to the gender dimensions; best practices in combating corruption, with attention given to the gender dimensions; hostage situations and rescue operations; recognizing early warning signals of terrorist escalation; and legal approaches to combating terrorism;".

53. Delete paragraph 14.19 *(d)* (ii).

Section 15
International drug control

54. In table 15.7:
(a) Under "Expected accomplishments", add new paragraphs *(e)* and *(f)*, as follows:
"*(e)* Improved coordination of drug control-related activities throughout the United Nations system, with UNDCP providing leadership.
"*(f)* Progress made towards the adoption and implementation of measures to strengthen national legislation and progress giving effect to the action plan against the illicit manufacture, trafficking and abuse of amphetamine-type stimulants and their precursors; measures to eliminate or reduce significantly the illicit manufacture, marketing and trafficking of other psychotropic substances, including synthetic drugs, and the diversion of precursors; national legislation and programmes to counter money-laundering; and measures to promote and strengthen judicial cooperation."
(b) Under "Indicators of achievement", add new paragraphs *(e)* and *(f)*, as follows:
"*(e)* The completion of needs assessments for multilateral cooperation on drug control.
"*(f)* Measures taken to strengthen national legislation and to give effect to the action plan against the illicit manufacture, trafficking and abuse of amphetamine-type stimulants and their precursors; to eliminate or reduce significantly the illicit manufacture, marketing and trafficking of other psychotropic substances, including synthetic drugs, and the diversion of precursors; and national legislation and programmes to counter money-laundering; and to promote and strengthen judicial cooperation."

55. In table 15.10, under "Indicators of achievement", delete in paragraph *(c)* "(conclusion of agreements and memoranda of understanding)".

56. In table 15.12:
(a) Under "Expected accomplishments", in paragraph *(a)*, between "meeting" and "goals", insert "by 2003 the";
(b) Under "Indicators of achievement":
(i) In paragraph *(a)*, add "by 2003" after "society"
(ii) Paragraph *(e)* should read:
"Number of guides on prevention and treatment issues developed during seminars and workshops and expert group meetings, and actually in use by Member States, to determine what constitutes effective prevention among school-based youth, youth at risk and women, and the design of treatment responses based on needs assessment and evaluation results."

57. In table 15.14, objective 2, under "Expected accomplishments", in paragraph *(a)*, add "by 2003" between "to meet" and "the goals".

58. In paragraph 15.35 *(a)* (iv), delete "one ad hoc expert group meeting on international cooperation against drug trafficking at sea; and".

Section 16
Economic and social development in Africa

59. In paragraph 16A.1, the last sentence of the paragraph should read:
"The main objective of development in Africa is the reduction of poverty, an objective that was reaffirmed in Copenhagen in 1995 at the World Summit for Social Development, which set a target of reducing poverty by half by 2015."

60. In table 16A.9:
(a) Under "Expected accomplishments", add the following: "Increased mobilization of financial resources for the development of Africa."
(b) Under "Indicators of achievement", add new subparagraphs (iii) and (iv) as follows:
"(iii) A substantial increase in financial flows to the countries of the region;
"(iv) The number of countries that have adopted investment and trade liberalization policies, including the removal of physical and non-physical barriers."

61. In table 16A.13, at the beginning of paragraph *(b)* under "Indicators of achievement", add the words "An increase in".

62. In table 16A.15:
(a) Under "Expected accomplishments", add the following paragraph *(d)*:
"*(d)* Increased Internet connectivity of African countries."
(b) Under "Indicators of achievement":
(i) At the end of paragraph *(b)*, add the following:
"Number of countries that, with the support of ECA, have improved their statistical systems, leading to the collection and dissemination of timely and reliable data."
(ii) Add paragraph *(d)* as follows:
"*(d)* An increase in the number of African Internet hosts and countries with direct connections."

63. In table 16A.17:
(a) Under "Expected accomplishments", add the following paragraphs *(c)* and *(d)*:
"*(c)* Increased, effective and harmonized utilization of transboundary water resources.
"*(d)* Substantial implementation of the Framework for Action adopted by the Conference of African Ministers of Transport and Communications."
(b) Under "Indicators of achievement", add paragraph *(c)* as follows:
"*(c)* An increase in positive results of the implementation of the Framework for Action for transport and communications."

Section 19

Economic and social development in Latin America and the Caribbean

64. In table 19.7, under "Indicators of achievement", in paragraph *(a)*, delete the phrase "in particular with respect to the ongoing negotiations on a Free Trade Area of the Americas".

65. In table 19.19, under "Expected accomplishments", in paragraph *(b)*, delete the phrase "democratic governance".

66. In table 19.21, under "Expected accomplishments", paragraph *(b)* should read:

"Increased technical capacity to incorporate an environmental dimension into the design of economic policies and the innovative use of economic instruments in environmental management, including a better understanding of the uneven effects of such policies on men and women."

Section 22

Human rights

67. Replace paragraphs 22.1 to 22.8 with paragraphs 19.1 to 19.3 of the medium-term plan for the period 2002-2005, as follows:

"22.1 The purpose of the United Nations human rights programme is to promote universal enjoyment of all human rights by giving practical effect to the will and resolve of the world community as expressed by the United Nations. Its mandate derives from Articles 1, 13 and 55 of the Charter of the United Nations, the Vienna Declaration and Programme of Action adopted by the World Conference on Human Rights on 25 June 1993 (A/CONF.157/24 (Part I), chap. III) and subsequently endorsed by the General Assembly in its resolution 48/121 of 20 December 1993, the mandate of the United Nations High Commissioner for Human Rights as defined in Assembly resolution 48/141 of the same date, international human rights instruments adopted by the United Nations and the resolutions and decisions of policy-making bodies. The programme is based on the principles and recommendations of the Vienna Declaration and Programme of Action.

"22.2 The programme is under the responsibility of the United Nations High Commissioner for Human Rights, who performs her or his functions under the direction and authority of the Secretary-General in accordance with General Assembly resolution 48/141. Its objectives are to provide the leading role on human rights issues and to emphasize the importance of human rights on the international and national agendas; to promote international cooperation for human rights; to stimulate and coordinate action across the whole United Nations system; to promote universal ratification and implementation of international standards and to assist in the development of new norms; to support human rights organs and treaty monitoring bodies; to anticipate serious violations and react to violations; to emphasize preventive human rights action and to promote the establishment of national human rights infrastructures; to undertake human rights field activities and operations; and to provide educa-

tion, information, advisory services and technical assistance in the field of human rights.

"22.3 By the end of the period covered by the medium-term plan for the period 2002-2005, it is expected that the following will have been accomplished:

"*(a)* A significant enhancement and strengthening of international cooperation in the field of human rights leading to increased effectiveness of international machinery, improved respect for human rights at the national level, through, inter alia, universal ratification of all international human rights treaties, the incorporation of those standards into the domestic legislation of States and the continuing adaptation of the United Nations human rights machinery to current and future needs in the promotion and protection of human rights, as reflected in the Vienna Declaration and Programme of Action;

"*(b)* Major strengthening of coordination for human rights across the United Nations system, leading to a comprehensive and integrated approach to the promotion and protection of human rights based on the contribution of each of the United Nations organs, bodies and specialized agencies whose activities deal with human rights and on improved inter-agency cooperation and coordination;

"*(c)* The adoption and implementation of an integrated and multidimensional strategy for the promotion and protection of the right to development, accompanied by a significant enhancement of support from relevant United Nations bodies for that purpose;

"*(d)* Provision of the appropriate assistance by the Secretariat and the Office of the United Nations High Commissioner for Human Rights to ensure that the promotion and protection of all human rights are guided by the principles of impartiality, objectivity and non-selectivity, in the spirit of constructive international dialogue and cooperation;

"*(e)* Compliance by the Office of the High Commissioner with the paramount consideration of securing the highest standards of efficiency, competence and integrity, and with due regard to the importance of recruiting the staff on as wide a geographical basis as possible, bearing in mind that the principle of equitable geographical distribution is compatible with the highest standards of efficiency, competence and integrity;

"*(f)* A significant increase in the recognition of economic, social and cultural rights and in activities for their protection, including the integration of economic, social and cultural rights as human rights into the strategies and programmes of international organizations, agencies and financial and developmental institutions, the identification of measurements of achievement showing success in respecting those rights and the adoption of a communication procedure relating to non-compliance with economic, social and cultural rights;

"*(g)* The adoption and progressive implementation of an improved treaty monitoring system dealing with multiple reporting obligations and based on a comprehensive national approach;

"*(h)* The implementation of a strengthened system of special procedures based on harmonization and rationalization of work;

"*(i)* The reinforcement of the United Nations as the unique worldwide forum for the discussion and resolution of human rights matters of international concern, with the participation of all relevant actors;

"*(j)* The adoption of more efficient methods within the United Nations to promote and protect human rights, including by preventing human rights violations throughout the world and removing obstacles to the full realization of human rights;

"*(k)* The implementation of a comprehensive United Nations programme to assist States, at their request, in developing and implementing national human rights plans of action strengthening, inter alia, national structures having an impact on democracy and the rule of law; to establish national institutions to give effect to the right to development and economic, social and cultural rights; and also to assist States, at their request, within the respective mandates of the Secretariat and the Office of the High Commissioner, in the process of ratifying United Nations human rights instruments;

"*(l)* Fulfilment of the mandates given to the Secretariat for giving appropriate assistance, according to the resolutions and decisions of the General Assembly, the Economic and Social Council and the Commission on Human Rights, to treaty bodies, intergovernmental and expert bodies, as well as the existing relevant voluntary trust funds;

"*(m)* The full integration of the human rights of women and the girl child into the activities of the United Nations system as a whole and its human rights machinery in particular;

"*(n)* The implementation of effective measures to promote equality, dignity and tolerance, to fight racism and xenophobia, and to protect minorities, indigenous populations, migrant workers, the disabled and others, taking into account also the outcome of the World Conference against Racism, Racial Discrimination, Xenophobia and Related Intolerance, to be held in 2001;

"*(o)* The establishment of effective programmes of education and public information and the strengthened contribution of non-governmental organizations, national institutions, grass-roots organizations and civil society in United Nations human rights activities at all levels, according to the legislative mandates in effect regarding those issues;

"*(p)* The provision to States, United Nations bodies, experts and the academic community of high-quality research and analysis on human rights issues, including that dealing with emerging problems and the development of new standards and instruments."

and renumber the subsequent paragraphs accordingly.

68. In former paragraph 22.27, after the words "the Council also decided that", insert the phrase ", once the

Permanent Forum had been established and had held its first annual session," and replace the words "that it would" with "to".

69. In table 22.7:

(a) Replace the text of Objectives 1 and 2 with paragraphs 19.4 and 19.5 of the medium-term plan, as follows:

"**Objective 1:** The primary objectives of this subprogramme will include the promotion and protection of the right to development. In this regard, the objectives will be to develop an integrated and multidimensional strategy for the implementation, coordination and promotion of the right to development in accordance with the Declaration on the Right to Development (General Assembly resolution 41/128, annex) and subsequent mandates and the Vienna Declaration and Programme of Action, aimed at facilitating action to be taken by relevant bodies of the United Nations system, including treaty bodies, international development and financial institutions and non-governmental organizations, for the implementation of the right to development as an integral part of fundamental human rights, ensuring the realization of the right to development across the human rights programme and by specialized agencies and United Nations treaty bodies; to promote national implementation of the right to development through coordination with State-appointed officials; to identify obstacles at the national and international levels; and to promote awareness about the content and importance of the right to development, including through information and educational activities.

"**Objective 2:** With regard to research and analysis, the objectives will be to strengthen respect for human rights by increasing knowledge, awareness and understanding of human rights issues through data collection, research and analysis. These objectives will be pursued within the framework of the indivisibility, interdependence and interrelatedness of all human rights and will be aimed at facilitating the implementation of standards, the work of treaty bodies, special rapporteurs and other bodies and the preparation of new standards; ensuring the recognition on the national and international levels of economic, social and cultural rights; promoting democracy and strengthening national human rights institutions and procedures for the rule of law; contributing to the elimination of racism, racial discrimination, xenophobia and new forms of discrimination; and strengthening the recognition of the human rights of women and children and the protection of vulnerable groups such as minorities, migrant workers and indigenous people."

(b) Under "Expected accomplishments", replace the existing text with paragraph 19.6 of the medium-term plan, as follows:

"Expected accomplishments of the Secretariat would include:

"*(a)* Wider integration and/or inclusion of the promotion and protection of the right to development, in particular across the human rights programme and the relevant programmes of work of the United Nations departments and/or offices and specialized agencies and of major international organizations and forums related to this issue;

"*(b)* Major strengthening of coordination for human rights across the United Nations system, leading to a comprehensive and integrated approach to the promotion and protection of human rights based on the contribution of each of the United Nations organs, bodies and specialized agencies whose activities deal with human rights and also based on improved inter-agency cooperation and coordination;

"*(c)* Strengthened efforts that will contribute to the elimination of racism, racial discrimination, xenophobia and related intolerance;

"*(d)* Enhanced awareness, knowledge and understanding of all human rights, including the right to development;

"*(e)* Wider recognition of the rights of women, children and persons belonging to minorities, migrant workers, indigenous people and persons with disabilities, and strengthening the protection of vulnerable groups."

(c) Under "Measurements of achievement", replace the existing text with paragraphs 19.7 and 19.8 of the medium-term plan, as modified below:

"Measures of achievement are elements used as tools for determining, where possible, the extent to which the objectives and/or expected accomplishments have been achieved.

"Measures of achievement of the Secretariat to be applied to each expected accomplishment, as appropriate, would include:

"*(a)* The extent to which the right to development had been included in the work programmes of the departments and offices of the United Nations, the specialized agencies and other relevant intergovernmental organizations, providing compiled examples of concrete steps in that regard;

"*(b)* The extent to which the mandates given to the Secretariat contained in resolutions and decisions adopted by the General Assembly, the Economic and Social Council and the Commission on Human Rights had been fulfilled;

"*(c)* The holding of seminars and workshops organized by the Office of the United Nations High Commissioner for Human Rights, in accordance with the relevant resolutions and decisions adopted by the General Assembly, the Economic and Social Council and the Commission on Human Rights, or in cooperation with the Office of the High Commissioner, and the extent to which they contributed to the fulfilment of the objectives of the subprogramme;

"*(d)* The extent to which the activities of the Office of the High Commissioner contributed to increasing knowledge, awareness and understanding in order to advance the full realization of the right to development, in accordance with the Declaration on the Right to Development;

"*(e)* An increased number of visitors to the web site of the Office of the High Commissioner;

"*(f)* The number of new publications of the Office of the High Commissioner as well as their distribution, and the assessment by users of their quality and usefulness."

70. In table 22.9:

(a) Replace the text of the objective with paragraph 19.9 of the medium-term plan, as follows:

"**Objective:** The objectives are to support the United Nations human rights bodies and organs and to facilitate their deliberations by ensuring and enhancing their effective functioning; to contribute to increasing the knowledge, expanding the awareness and promoting the importance of all international human rights treaties; to improve existing procedures through rationalization and streamlining, and the coordination of the participation of Governments, experts, specialized agencies, other international organizations, national institutions and non-governmental organizations in their work; and to ensure the analytical capacity of human rights treaty bodies for the review of State party reports under international treaties and for the processing of communications."

(b) Under "Expected accomplishments", replace the existing text with paragraph 19.10 of the medium-term plan, as follows:

"Expected accomplishments of the Secretariat would include:

"*(a)* The timely delivery of required and appropriate support to intergovernmental bodies, expert bodies and treaty bodies, inter alia, in order to contribute to reducing the backlog in the consideration by the reviewing mechanisms of the States parties' reports;

"*(b)* The timely delivery of required and appropriate support to intergovernmental bodies, expert bodies and treaty bodies, inter alia, in order to contribute to reducing the backlog in the consideration by the reviewing mechanisms of complaints."

(c) Under "Measurements of achievement", replace the existing text with paragraphs 19.11 and 19.12 of the medium-term plan, as modified below:

"Measures of achievement are elements used as tools for determining, where possible, the extent to which the objectives and/or expected accomplishments have been achieved.

"Measures of achievement of the Secretariat to be applied to each expected accomplishment, as appropriate, would include:

"*(a)* The quality and timeliness of services provided by the Office of the High Commissioner;

"*(b)* A reduction in the time lag between the submission of a State party report and its examination by the relevant treaty body;

"*(c)* A reduction in the time lag between the submission of a complaint and its review, as appropriate, by the relevant mechanisms;

"*(d)* The number of reports prepared by the Secretariat in accordance with resolutions and decisions of the General Assembly, the Economic and Social Council and the Commission on Human Rights, and the extent to which they were presented in a timely manner, in compliance with the six-week rule for the issuance of documentation, for consideration by organs dealing with human rights."

71. In table 22.11:

(*a*) Replace the text of Objective 1 with paragraphs 19.13 to 19.15 of the medium-term plan, as follows:

"**Objective:** In the area of advisory services and technical cooperation, the objectives are to assist countries, at their request, in developing comprehensive national plans of action to promote and protect human rights and to provide advice and support to specific projects to promote respect for human rights; to develop a comprehensive and coordinated United Nations programme to help States in building and strengthening national structures for human rights promotion and protection; and to raise awareness and promote specialized knowledge about human rights through the organization of training courses, seminars and workshops, and the production of a wide range of educational, training and information material.

"In the area of support to fact-finding bodies, the objectives are to ensure the effective functioning of human rights monitoring mechanisms by assisting special rapporteurs and representatives, experts and working groups mandated by policy-making bodies, including through the preparation of information regarding alleged violations and situations for review and the provision of support for missions and meetings; and to enhance the efficiency of action by policy-making bodies by providing analytical information on human rights situations.

"With respect to field activities, the objective is to ensure the efficiency of field missions and presences through the maintenance of contacts with Governments, appropriate sectors of the United Nations system, international and regional organizations and others by supporting and developing such activities through the development of training programmes and materials for human rights field staff and training in human rights for the appropriate components of other United Nations field operations."

and delete the text of Objectives 2 and 3.

(*b*) Under "Expected accomplishments", replace the existing text with paragraph 19.16 of the medium-term plan, as follows:

"Expected accomplishments of the Secretariat would include:

"(*a*) Provision of advisory services and technical and financial assistance, at the request of the State concerned and, where appropriate, the regional human rights organizations, with a view to supporting actions and programmes in the field of human rights;

"(*b*) Fulfilment of the mandates given to the Office of the High Commissioner in resolutions and decisions of the General Assembly, the Economic and Social Council and the Commission on Human Rights to support human rights monitoring mechanisms, such as special rapporteurs and representatives and expert and working groups mandated by policy-making bodies;

"(*c*) Enhanced awareness, knowledge and understanding of all human rights, including the right to development."

(*c*) Under "Measurements of achievement", replace the existing text with paragraphs 19.17 and 19.18 of the medium-term plan, as modified below:

"Measures of achievement are elements used as tools for determining, where possible, the extent to which the objectives and/or expected accomplishments have been achieved.

"Measures of achievement of the Secretariat to be applied to each expected accomplishment, as appropriate, would include:

"(*a*) The number of seminars, workshops and training courses held or supported by the Office of the High Commissioner; and the number of persons trained, participants in seminars and workshops and fellowships granted as well as data on their geographical distribution and the extent to which they contributed to the fulfilment of the objectives of the subprogramme;

"(*b*) The number of requests from Member States and, where appropriate, from the regional human rights organizations, received and fulfilled by the Office of the High Commissioner for the provision of advisory services and technical and financial assistance, with a view to supporting actions and programmes in the field of human rights;

"(*c*) The timeliness, significance and relevance of the advisory services and technical cooperation."

Section 23
Protection of and assistance to refugees

72. In paragraph 23.2, after the first sentence, insert the following sentence, based on the last sentence of paragraph 21.1 of the medium-term plan for the period 2002-2005: "The pursuit of permanent solutions to the problems of refugees is at the heart of protection and the principal purpose of this section."

73. In paragraph 23.3, in paragraph (*e*), replace "in these activities, due consideration will be given to the interests both of Member States and of the United Nations" with the following text from the end of paragraph 21.5 (*f*) of the medium-term plan:

"in this regard, due consideration should be given to the obligation of United Nations officials, in the conduct of their duties, to observe fully both the laws and regulations of Member States and their duties and responsibilities to the Organization".

74. In table 23.4, under "Indicators of achievement" at the end of paragraph (*e*), add the following phrase, based on paragraph 21.17 (*d*) of the medium-term plan: "; the number of refugees repatriated and resettled".

75. In paragraph 23.11 delete paragraph (*a*), "UNHCR staff are trained as to the need for, and most effective design of, programme initiatives;" and reletter the remaining paragraphs accordingly.

76. In paragraph 23.14, paragraph (*c*) should read: "a sufficient level of extrabudgetary funding is raised to allow for the funding of planned capacity-building projects."

Section 24
Palestine refugees

77. In paragraph 24.14 (*b*), insert the word "some" between "by" and "host" in the first line.

Section 25
Humanitarian assistance

78. In table 25.6:

(a) Delete paragraphs *(b)* and *(c)* under "Expected accomplishments";

(b) Delete paragraphs *(b)* and *(c)* under "Indicators of achievement";

(c) Delete "Increased attention to and respect for an active and visible policy of" in paragraph *(d)* under "Expected accomplishments".

79. In paragraph 25.18:

(a) In subparagraph *(b)* (iii), replace the words "human rights and international humanitarian law" with "international humanitarian law and human rights instruments";

(b) Subparagraph *(b)* (vi) should read "Paper requested by the Security Council on protection for humanitarian assistance to refugees and others in conflict situations (1);"

(c) Subparagraph *(b)*(vii) should read: "Study on the application of the guiding principles of humanitarian assistance to all populations in need, as contained in the annex to General Assembly resolution 46/182 (1);"

(d) At the end of subparagraph *(b)* (viii), add "in strict conformity with the principles of humanity, neutrality and impartiality and to ensure that they are not working at cross-purposes";

(e) Subparagraph *(c)* (iv) should read: "Production of inter-agency training package on enhancing the provision of humanitarian assistance to all populations in need;"

(f) Add a new subparagraph after *(c)* (iv), reading:

"(v) Collaboration with other agencies to support and to promote the efforts of Governments of affected countries upon their request to assist and to protect internally displaced persons;"

(g) Delete subparagraph *(c)* (vi) and reletter the subsequent subparagraphs accordingly.

80. In paragraph 25.27, in the second sentence, add "where appropriate" after "Framework".

81. In table 25.10:

(a) Under "Expected accomplishments":

(i) Paragraph *(a)* should read: "Increased capacity of developing countries for preparedness in disaster prevention and mitigation."

(ii) Add a new paragraph *(b)*, reading: "*(b)* Increased participation by developing countries in disaster reduction–related training and seminars."

(b) Under "Indicators of achievement":

(i) Paragraph *(a)* should read: "Increase in the number of developing countries having the technical capacity to deal with disaster prevention and mitigation."

(ii) Add a new paragraph *(b)*, reading: "The number of experts from developing countries participating in training seminars on disaster prevention."

(c) Reletter former paragraphs *(b)* and *(c)* as *(c)* and *(d)* respectively.

(d) Under "Expected accomplishments":

(i) Delete *(d)*;

(ii) Add a new paragraph *(e)* reading:

"*(e)* Better and more effective coordination in the mobilization of international support to contribute to preventive management and rehabilitation related to natural disasters."

(e) Under "Indicators of achievement", reletter former paragraph *(d)* as *(e)*.

82. At the end of paragraph 25.30 *(c)* (i), add a new item, reading: "n. Update inventory of the resources available to help deal with natural disasters;".

83. In table 25.12:

(a) Delete *(a)* under "Expected accomplishments";

(b) Delete *(a)* under "Indicators of achievement";

(c) Under both headings, reletter paragraphs *(b)* and *(c)* as *(a)* and *(b)* respectively;

(d) Under "Expected accomplishments", add a new paragraph *(c)*, as follows:

"*(c)* Increased capacity of developing countries to deal with disaster relief."

(e) Under "Indicators of achievement" add a new paragraph *(c)*, as follows:

"*(c)* Increased participation in training seminars on disaster management, improved field and regional cooperation in disaster management and increased donor response to inter-agency appeals."

(f) Under "Expected accomplishments", in paragraphs *(a)* and *(d)*, after "environmental disasters", add "as well as technological accidents".

84. In table 25.14, under "Expected accomplishments", in paragraph *(b)*, after "United Nations", delete the remainder of the paragraph.

Section 27C
Office of Human Resources Management

85. In paragraph 27C.1, at the end of the last sentence, add the following text:

", as well as meet the expectations of Member States as set forth in General Assembly resolution 55/258 of 14 June 2001".

86. After paragraph 27C.4, add a new paragraph, reading:

"27C.5. At its fifty-fifth session, the General Assembly considered the report of the Secretary-General and adopted resolution 55/258. In implementing all the activities under this subprogramme, the Office of Human Resources Management will take fully into account the provisions of resolution 55/258."

and renumber subsequent paragraphs accordingly.

87. In former paragraph 27C.5:

(a) In the first line, replace "resolution 53/221" with "resolution 55/258";

(b) In the fourth line, insert the word "robust" before the word "monitoring".

88. In former paragraph 27C.6 *(a)*, replace "monitoring" with "robust monitoring mechanisms".

89. In former paragraph 27C.12, replace the second sentence with the following text:

"In accordance with the decisions of the General Assembly contained in its resolution 55/258, the Division will concentrate on the implementation of human resources management reform in the areas of its expertise and will work on improving and enhancing its control and monitoring mechanisms and procedures."

90. In former paragraph 27C.16, at the beginning of the paragraph, insert the following text:

"In line with the provisions of General Assembly resolution 55/258 and".

91. In former paragraph 27C.20, at the beginning of the paragraph, insert the following text:

"In line with the provisions of General Assembly resolution 55/258,".

92. In former paragraph 27C.21, at the beginning of the paragraph, insert the following text:
"In accordance with the decisions of the General Assembly, including resolution 55/258,".

93. In former paragraph 27C.26, at the beginning of the paragraph, insert the following text:
"In line with the provisions of General Assembly resolution 55/258,".

Section 28
Internal oversight

94. In table 28.6, under Objective 1, replace paragraph *(b)* under "Indicators of achievement" with the following: "The number of joint meetings, agreements and assignments with external oversight bodies."

95. In table 28.8:

(a) Under "Indicators of achievement":

(i) Merge subparagraphs *(b)* (i) and (ii) to read *"(b)* Clear delegation of authority and the existence and effective use of mechanisms to ensure accountability at all levels of the Organization."

(ii) Replace paragraph *(d)* with the following: "The number of joint meetings, agreements and assignments with external oversight bodies."

ANNEX II

Staffing table for 2002 and 2003

	2002	*2003*
Professional category and above		
Deputy Secretary-General	1	1
Under-Secretary-General	26	26
Assistant Secretary-General	19	19
D-2	80	80
D-1	244	244
P-5	687	687
P-4/3	2,300	2,300
P-2/1	457	457
Subtotal	**3,814**	**3,814**
General Service category		
Principal level	269	269
Other level	2,653	2,653
Subtotal	**2,922**	**2,922**
Other categories		
Security Services	181	181
Local level	1,632	1,632
Field Service	185	185
Trades and Crafts	185	185
Subtotal	**2,183**	**2,183**
Total	**8,919**	**8,919**

On 24 December, the Assembly decided that the item on the proposed programme budget for the 2002-2003 biennium would remain for consideration at its resumed fifty-sixth (2002) session **(decision 56/464)** and that the Fifth Committee should continue to consider it at that session **(decision 56/458)**.

Appropriations

In his proposed programme budget for the 2002-2003 biennium [A/56/6 & Corr.1 & Add.1], the Secretary-General proposed expenditures amounting to $2,648.7 million and income totalling $51.8 million, as well as staff assessment income of $348.4 million, an increase of $15.3 million, resulting in a net estimate of $2,248.5 million. The proposed budget represented a 4.5 per cent real growth from the 2000-2001 budget.

Extrabudgetary resources for the 2002-2003 biennium were estimated at $3,834.4 million, comprising $286.8 million for support activities, $238.4 million for substantive activities and $3,309.2 million for operational activities.

ACABQ, in its first report on the 2002-2003 proposed programme budget [A/56/7], noted that the difference (before recosting) between the 2002-2003 estimates and the revised 2001-2002 estimates amounted to a nominal decrease of $13.7 million. As such, it had, except for proposals relating to new posts and reclassifications, refrained in most cases from making specific recommendations for reductions or additions, although there were a number of areas where one or the other was possible. It regarded the introduction in the 2002-2003 programme budget of results-based budgeting [YUN 1999, p. 1284] as the first fundamental change to the budget presentation since the introduction of programme budgeting in 1973 and recommended that its development be managed with care. In that connection, ACABQ recalled Assembly resolution 53/205 [YUN 1998, p. 1273], which stressed that results-based budgeting should not be a budget- and staff-reduction exercise, and its own 2000 report on such budgeting [YUN 2000, p. 1295]. ACABQ reiterated its comments on the 2000-2001 programme budget [YUN 1999, p. 1302] relating to continued budget stringency and restraint and recalled the Secretary-General's 7 May statement to ACABQ that, for a number of years, the Secretariat had been expected to do more with less; adhering to such a course was becoming increasingly untenable and greatly strained the ability of the Organization to fulfil its mandates.

In November [A/56/659], the Secretary-General recommended revised estimates to reflect the latest data on actual inflation experience, the outcome of salary surveys, the movement of post adjustment indices in 2001, salary expenditure experience and the effect of the evolution of operational rates of exchange on the proposed programme budget for 2002-2003. The recosted level of expenditures amounted to $2,681 million and total income was revised to $408.3 million.

ACABQ, in its fifth report on the 2002-2003 programme budget [A/56/7/Add.4], found no technical basis for objecting to the Secretary-General's revised estimates and transmitted them to the Fifth Committee.

On 24 December [meeting 92], the General Assembly, on the recommendation of the Fifth Committee [A/56/736], adopted **resolutions 56/254 A-C** without vote [agenda item 123].

Programme budget for the biennium 2002-2003

A

Budget appropriations for the biennium 2002-2003
The General Assembly
Resolves that for the biennium 2002-2003:

1. Appropriations totalling 2,625,178,700 United States dollars are hereby approved for the following purposes:

Section		*Thousands of United States dollars*
	Part I. *Overall policy-making, direction and coordination*	
1.	Overall policy-making, direction and coordination	49,365.8
2.	General Assembly affairs and conference services	449,775.3
	Total, part I	**499,141.1**
	Part II. *Political affairs*	
3.	Political affairs	155,016.3
4.	Disarmament	15,432.3
5.	Peacekeeping operations	73,600.7
6.	Peaceful uses of outer space	4,044.8
	Total, part II	**248,094.1**
	Part III. *International justice and law*	
7.	International Court of Justice	23,837.3
8.	Legal affairs	35,265.8
	Total, part III	**59,103.1**
	Part IV. *International cooperation for development*	
9.	Economic and social affairs	121,043.4
9A.	Office of the High Representative for the Least Developed Countries	3,055.6
10.	Africa: New Agenda for Development	5,932.7
11A.	Trade and development	84,858.4
11B.	International Trade Centre UNCTAD/WTO	18,022.6
12.	Environment	7,660.2
13.	Human settlements	11,541.8
14.	Crime prevention and criminal justice	5,733.8
15.	International drug control	15,289.1
	Total, part IV	**273,137.6**
	Part V. *Regional cooperation for development*	
16.	Economic and social development in Africa	80,760.1
17.	Economic and social development in Asia and the Pacific	52,804.5
18.	Economic development in Europe	40,605.9
19.	Economic and social development in Latin America and the Caribbean	69,167.4
20.	Economic and social development in Western Asia	49,095.2
21.	Regular programme of technical cooperation	42,749.6
	Total, part V	**335,182.7**
	Part VI. *Human rights and humanitarian affairs*	
22.	Human rights	44,727.1
23.	Protection of and assistance to refugees	42,890.4
24.	Palestine refugees	24,828.4
25.	Humanitarian assistance	20,011.6
	Total, part VI	**132,457.5**

Section		*Thousands of United States dollars*
	Part VII. *Public information*	
26.	Public information	144,719.2
	Total, part VII	**144,719.2**
	Part VIII. *Common support services*	
27.	Management and central support services	428,530.5
	Total, part VIII	**428,530.5**
	Part IX. *Internal oversight*	
28.	Internal oversight	20,296.9
	Total, part IX	**20,296.9**
	Part X. *Jointly financed administrative activities and special expenses*	
29.	Jointly financed administrative activities	8,436.6
30.	Special expenses	69,340.5
	Total, part X	**77,777.1**
	Part XI. *Capital expenditures*	
31.	Construction, alteration, improvement and major maintenance	45,423.6
	Total, part XI	**45,423.6**
	Part XII. *Staff assessment*	
32.	Staff assessment	348,250.3
	Total, part XII	**348,250.3**
	Part XIII. *Development Account*	
33.	Development Account	13,065.0
	Total, part XIII	**13,065.0**
	Total, expenditure sections	**2,625,178.7**

2. The Secretary-General shall be authorized to transfer credits between sections of the budget with the concurrence of the Advisory Committee on Administrative and Budgetary Questions;

3. The total net provision made under the various sections of the budget for contractual printing shall be administered as a unit under the direction of the United Nations Publications Board;

4. In addition to the appropriations approved under paragraph 1 above, an amount of 125,000 dollars is appropriated for each year of the biennium 2002-2003 from the accumulated income of the Library Endowment Fund for the purchase of books, periodicals, maps and library equipment and for such other expenses of the Library at the Palais des Nations as are in accordance with the objects and provisions of the endowment.

B

Income estimates for the biennium 2002-2003
The General Assembly
Resolves that for the biennium 2002-2003:

1. Estimates of income other than assessments on Member States totalling 404,295,400 United States dollars are approved as follows:

Income section		*Thousands of United States dollars*
1.	Income from staff assessment	352,537.8
2.	General income	47,283.2
3.	Services to the public	4,474.4
	Total, income sections	**404,295.4**

2. The income from staff assessment shall be credited to the Tax Equalization Fund in accordance with

the provisions of General Assembly resolution 973(X) of 15 December 1955;

3. Direct expenses of the United Nations Postal Administration, services to visitors, sales of statistical products, catering operations and related services, garage operations, television services and the sale of publications not provided for under the budget appropriations, shall be charged against the income derived from those activities.

C
Financing of appropriations for the year 2002
The General Assembly

Resolves that for the year 2002:

1. Budget appropriations consisting of 1,312,589,350 United States dollars, being half of the appropriations of 2,625,178,700 dollars approved for the biennium 2002-2003 by the General Assembly under paragraph 1 of resolution A above, shall be financed in accordance with regulations 5.1 and 5.2 of the Financial Regulations of the United Nations, as follows:

(a) 25,878,800 dollars, being the net of half of the estimated income other than staff assessment approved for the biennium 2002-2003 under resolution B above;

(b) 1,286,710,550 dollars, being the assessment on Member States in accordance with its resolution 55/5 B of 23 December 2000 on the scale of assessments for the year 2002;

2. There shall be set off against the assessment on Member States, in accordance with the provisions of General Assembly resolution 973(X) of 15 December 1955, their respective share in the Tax Equalization Fund in the total amount of 176,268,900 dollars, being half of the estimated staff assessment income approved for the biennium 2002-2003 under resolution B above.

Other questions related to the 2002-2003 programme budget

The Fifth Committee considered a number of special subjects relating to the 2002-2003 programme budget, among them the request for a subvention to the United Nations Institute for Disarmament Research (UNIDIR); revised estimates relating to Security Council actions and Economic and Social Council resolutions and decisions in 2001; administrative expenses of the United Nations Joint Staff Pension Fund; the contingency fund; and the effect of changes in rates of exchange or inflation (see sections below).

Other subjects concerned the Joint Inspection Unit (see p. 1285); the International Civil Service Commission (see p. 1330); special political missions (see p. 58); the safety and security of UN personnel (see p. 1347); the comprehensive review of peacekeeping operations (see p. 74); and ITC UNCTAD/WTO (see p. 876).

GENERAL ASSEMBLY ACTION

On 24 December [meeting 92], the General Assembly, on the recommendation of the Fifth Com-

mittee [A/56/736], adopted **resolution 56/255** without vote [agenda item 123].

Special subjects relating to the proposed programme budget for the biennium 2002-2003
The General Assembly

I
Request for subvention to the United Nations Institute for Disarmament Research resulting from the recommendations of the Board of Trustees of the Institute contained in the report of the Director of the Institute

Approves the recommendation of a subvention of 213,000 United States dollars from the regular budget of the United Nations for 2002, on the understanding that no additional appropriation would be required under section 4, Disarmament, of the proposed programme budget for the biennium 2002-2003;

II
Joint Inspection Unit

Approves a gross budget for the Joint Inspection Unit for the biennium 2002-2003 in the amount of 7,546,100 dollars;

III
International Civil Service Commission

Approves a gross budget for the International Civil Service Commission for the biennium 2002-2003 in the amount of 12,813,400 dollars;

IV
Revised estimates resulting from resolutions and decisions adopted by the Economic and Social Council at its substantive session of 2001

Takes note of the report of the Secretary-General and the related report of the Advisory Committee on Administrative and Budgetary Questions on the revised estimates resulting from resolutions and decisions adopted by the Economic and Social Council at its substantive session of 2001, on the understanding that such appropriations as may be necessary (and not exceeding 1,444,200 dollars) will be requested by the Secretary-General in the context of a consolidated statement of programme budget implications and revised estimates to be submitted to the General Assembly;

V
Administrative expenses of the United Nations Joint Staff Pension Fund

Having considered the report of the Standing Committee of the United Nations Joint Staff Pension Board to the General Assembly and to the member organizations of the Fund, and the related report of the Advisory Committee,

1. *Concurs* with the recommendations contained in the report of the Advisory Committee on the administrative expenses of the United Nations Joint Staff Pension Fund;

2. *Approves* expenses, chargeable directly to the Fund, totalling 74,322,400 dollars net for the biennium 2002-2003, and a decrease of 3,098,900 dollars net for the biennium 2000-2001;

3. *Authorizes* the United Nations Joint Staff Pension Board to supplement voluntary contributions to the

Emergency Fund for the biennium 2002-2003 by an amount not exceeding 200,000 dollars;

VI
Contingency fund

Notes that a balance of 2,192,100 dollars remains in the contingency fund;

VII
Special political missions

1. *Takes note* of the reports of the Secretary-General on the estimates in respect of matters of which the Security Council is seized, and concurs with the observations and recommendations of the Advisory Committee contained in its reports;

2. *Approves* the charge of 8 million dollars for the period from 1 January to 31 March 2002 for the 15 missions dealt with in the report of the Secretary-General against the provision for special political missions requested under section 3, Political affairs, of the proposed programme budget for the biennium 2002-2003;

3. *Also approves* the charge of 1.7 million dollars for the period from 1 January to 31 March 2002 for the United Nations Office in Burundi against the provision for special political missions requested under section 3, Political affairs, of the proposed programme budget for the biennium 2002-2003;

4. *Further approves* the charge of 1,413,400 dollars for the period from 1 January to 31 December 2002 for the Special Adviser to the Secretary-General on Cyprus against the provision for special political missions requested under section 3, Political affairs, of the proposed programme budget for the biennium 2002-2003;

5. *Decides* to resume its consideration of the reports of the Secretary-General on the estimates in respect of which the Security Council is seized in March 2002;

6. *Notes* that an unallocated balance of 64,648,400 dollars remains against the provision of 98,338,700 dollars for special political missions;

VIII
Safety and security of United Nations personnel

Recalling section II of its resolution 55/238 of 23 December 2000,

Having considered the report of the Secretary-General entitled "Inter-organizational security measures: implementation of section II, Safety and security of United Nations personnel, of General Assembly resolution 55/238 of 23 December 2000", and the related report of the Advisory Committee,

1. *Endorses* the recommendations contained in the report of the Advisory Committee;

2. *Welcomes* the agreed inter-agency cost-sharing arrangement, and requests that the apportionment of expenses be updated in 2003;

3. *Notes with concern* the lack of an accountability and responsibility mechanism in the area of field security, and requests the Secretary-General to submit to the General Assembly at its fifty-seventh session a comprehensive report on the establishment of a clear mechanism of accountability and responsibility, including such provisions as its scope, depth and common standards and methods of enforcing them in an inter-agency structure;

4. *Requests* the Secretary-General to conduct an evaluation of the United Nations security system, including the new security arrangements and the rela-

tionship and interaction between the Department of Peacekeeping Operations of the Secretariat and the Office of the United Nations Security Coordinator, and to report his findings and recommendations to the General Assembly at its fifty-eighth session;

IX
International Trade Centre UNCTAD/WTO

Having considered section 11B, International Trade Centre UNCTAD/WTO, of the proposed programme budget for the biennium 2002-2003, and the related report of the Advisory Committee,

Decides to approve the resources in the amount of 18,022,600 dollars proposed for the biennium 2002-2003 under section 11B;

X
Effect of changes in rates of exchange and inflation

Having considered the report of the Secretary-General on the revised estimates of the effect of changes in rates of exchange and inflation and the related report of the Advisory Committee,

Takes note of the revised estimates arising from the recosting of the effects of changes in the rates of exchange and inflation;

XI
Comprehensive review of the whole question of peacekeeping operations in all their aspects

Having considered the statement of the Secretary-General on the comprehensive review of the whole question of peacekeeping operations in all their aspects and the related report of the Advisory Committee,

Decides to appropriate an additional amount of 1,575,700 dollars under the following sections of the proposed programme budget for the biennium 2002-2003: 376,400 dollars under section 3, Political affairs; 888,800 dollars under section 22, Human rights; 127,900 dollars under section 27, Management and central support services; and 182,600 dollars under section 32, Staff assessment, to be offset by a corresponding amount (182,600 dollars) under income section 1, Income from staff assessment, of the proposed programme budget for the biennium 2002-2003.

Contingency fund

The contingency fund, established by General Assembly resolution 41/213 [YUN 1986, p. 1024], accommodated additional expenditures relating to each biennium that derived from legislative mandates not provided for in the proposed programme budget or from revised estimates. Guidelines for its use were annexed to Assembly resolution 42/211 [YUN 1987, p. 1098].

The Fifth Committee considered the Secretary-General's December report [A/C.5/56/33] containing a consolidated statement of all programme budget implications and revised estimates falling under the guidelines for use of the fund. The consolidated amount of $16,707,900 was within the available balance of the fund.

Revised estimates in respect of matters of which the Security Council was seized

As a result of certain actions taken by the Security Council in 2001, the Secretary-General submitted in December estimated resource requirements of: $29,519,400 for 15 political missions [A/C.5/56/25]; $6,925,800 for the United Nations Office in Burundi (UNOB) [A/C.5/56/25/Add.1]; and $1,413,400 for the Special Adviser of the Secretary-General on Cyprus for one year [A/C.5/56/25/Add.2]. Those amounts were to be charged against the $93.7 million (before costing) proposed for special political missions under section 3, Political affairs, of the 2002-2003 proposed programme budget.

Pending its detailed review of those requests in 2002, ACABQ recommended approval of charges against the proposed provision above of: $8 million for the 15 political missions [A/56/7/Add.5] and $1,700,000 for UNOB [A/56/7/Add.6] during the period 1 January to 31 March 2002; and $1,413,400 for the Special Adviser on Cyprus [A/56/7/Add.7] for the period 1 January to 31 December 2002.

Revised estimates resulting from Economic and Social Council action

By an October report [A/C.5/56/4], the Secretary-General submitted estimates of requirements totalling $1,964,000 additional to the resources proposed in the programme budget for the 2002-2003 biennium, resulting from Economic and Social Council decisions 2001/293 (see p. 964) and 2001/316 (see p. 693), and from a decision of the Committee on Economic, Social and Cultural Rights to revert, during a two-year experimental period, to holding only two sessions a year [E/2001/L.8]. Those requirements related to section 9, Economic and social affairs ($1,572,800); section 22, Human rights (a net reduction of $286,000); section 27D, Office of Central Support Services ($519,800); and section 32, Staff assessment ($157,400). The provision would be charged against the contingency fund, requiring increases or decreases in appropriations for that biennium.

ACABQ, in its related report [A/56/518], was of the opinion that the requirements of $519,800 under section 27D should continue to be met in the 2002-2003 biennium in the same manner as in the 2000-2001 biennium. Accordingly, it recommended that the Fifth Committee take note of the estimate of $1,444,200, on the understanding that any required appropriations would be requested by the Secretary-General in the context of the consolidated statement of programme budget implications and revised estimates to be submitted to the General Assembly.

Subvention to UNIDIR

The Secretary-General, in September [A/56/359], transmitted for the General Assembly's approval a request for a subvention of $213,000 from the UN regular budget to UNIDIR for 2002. The request was based on a recommendation by the UNIDIR Board of Trustees, following its review of the Director's report on UNIDIR's activities from July 2000 to July 2001 and proposed work programme and budget for the 2001-2002 biennium.

Working Capital Fund

In December, the General Assembly established the Working Capital Fund for the 2002-2003 biennium at $100 million, the same level as during 2000-2001. As in the past, the Fund was to be used to finance appropriations pending the receipt of assessed contributions, pay for unforeseen and extraordinary expenses, as well as for miscellaneous self-liquidating purchases and advance insurance premiums, and to enable the Tax Equalization Fund to meet current commitments pending the accumulation of credits.

GENERAL ASSEMBLY ACTION

On 24 December [meeting 92], the General Assembly, on the recommendation of the Fifth Committee [A/56/736], adopted **resolution 56/257** without vote [agenda item 123].

Working Capital Fund for the biennium 2002-2003

The General Assembly

Resolves that:

1. The Working Capital Fund shall be established for the biennium 2002-2003 in the amount of 100 million United States dollars;

2. Member States shall make advances to the Working Capital Fund in accordance with the scale adopted by the General Assembly for contributions of Member States to the budget for the year 2002;

3. There shall be set off against this allocation of advances:

(a) Credits to Member States resulting from transfers made in 1959 and 1960 from the surplus account to the Working Capital Fund in an adjusted amount of 1,025,092 dollars;

(b) Cash advances paid by Member States to the Working Capital Fund for the biennium 2000-2001 in accordance with General Assembly resolution 54/253 of 23 December 1999;

4. Should the credits and advances paid by any Member State to the Working Capital Fund for the biennium 2000-2001 exceed the amount of that Member State's advance under the provisions of paragraph 2 above, the excess shall be set off against the amount of the contributions payable by the Member State in respect of the biennium 2002-2003;

5. The Secretary-General is authorized to advance from the Working Capital Fund:

(*a*) Such sums as may be necessary to finance budgetary appropriations pending the receipt of contributions; sums so advanced shall be reimbursed as soon as receipts from contributions are available for that purpose;

(*b*) Such sums as may be necessary to finance commitments that may be duly authorized under the provisions of the resolutions adopted by the General Assembly, in particular resolution 56/256 of 24 December 2001 relating to unforeseen and extraordinary expenses; the Secretary-General shall make provision in the budget estimates for reimbursing the Working Capital Fund;

(*c*) Such sums as may be necessary to continue the revolving fund to finance miscellaneous self-liquidating purchases and activities, which, together with net sums outstanding for the same purpose, do not exceed 200,000 dollars; advances in excess of the total of 200,000 dollars may be made with the prior concurrence of the Advisory Committee on Administrative and Budgetary Questions;

(*d*) With the prior concurrence of the Advisory Committee, such sums as may be required to finance payments of advance insurance premiums where the period of insurance extends beyond the end of the biennium in which payment is made; the Secretary-General shall make provision in the budget estimates of each biennium, during the life of the related policies, to cover the charges applicable to each biennium;

(*e*) Such sums as may be necessary to enable the Tax Equalization Fund to meet current commitments pending the accumulation of credits; such advances shall be repaid as soon as credits are available in the Tax Equalization Fund;

6. Should the provision in paragraph 1 above prove inadequate to meet the purposes normally related to the Working Capital Fund, the Secretary-General is authorized to utilize, in the biennium 2002-2003, cash from special funds and accounts in his custody, under the conditions approved by the General Assembly in its resolution 1341(XIII) of 13 December 1958, or the proceeds of loans authorized by the Assembly.

Unforeseen and extraordinary expenses

Under very specific circumstances, the Secretary-General was authorized by the General Assembly to enter into commitments for activities of an urgent nature, without reverting to it for approval under the terms of resolution 54/252 [YUN 1999, p. 1309].

GENERAL ASSEMBLY ACTION

On 24 December [meeting 92], the General Assembly, on the recommendation of the Fifth Committee [A/56/736], adopted **resolution 56/256** without vote [agenda item 123].

**Unforeseen and extraordinary expenses
for the biennium 2002-2003**

The General Assembly

1. *Authorizes* the Secretary-General, with the prior concurrence of the Advisory Committee on Administrative and Budgetary Questions and subject to the Financial Regulations of the United Nations and the provisions of paragraph 3 below, to enter into commitments in the biennium 2002-2003 to meet unforeseen and extraordinary expenses arising either during or subsequent to the biennium, provided that the concurrence of the Advisory Committee shall not be necessary for:

(*a*) Such commitments, not exceeding a total of 8 million United States dollars in any one year of the biennium 2002-2003, as the Secretary-General certifies relate to the maintenance of peace and security;

(*b*) Such commitments as the President of the International Court of Justice certifies relate to expenses occasioned by:

(i) The designation of ad hoc judges (Statute of the International Court of Justice, Article 31), not exceeding a total of 330,000 dollars;

(ii) The calling of witnesses and the appointment of experts (Statute, Article 50) and the appointment of assessors (Statute, Article 30), not exceeding a total of 50,000 dollars;

(iii) The maintenance in office for the completion of cases of judges who have not been re-elected (Statute, Article 13, paragraph 3), not exceeding a total of 40,000 dollars;

(iv) The payment of pensions and travel and removal expenses of retiring judges, and travel and removal expenses and installation grant of members of the Court (Statute, Article 32, paragraph 7), not exceeding a total of 410,000 dollars;

(v) The work of the Court or its Chambers away from The Hague (Statute, Article 22), not exceeding a total of 25,000 dollars;

(*c*) Such commitments, not exceeding a total of 500,000 dollars in the biennium 2002-2003, as the Secretary-General certifies are required for inter-organizational security measures pursuant to section IV of General Assembly resolution 36/235 of 18 December 1981;

2. *Resolves* that the Secretary-General shall report to the Advisory Committee and to the General Assembly at its fifty-seventh and fifty-eighth sessions all commitments made under the provisions of the present resolution, together with the circumstances relating thereto, and shall submit supplementary estimates to the Assembly in respect of such commitments;

3. *Decides* that for the biennium 2002-2003, if a decision of the Security Council results in the need for the Secretary-General to enter into commitments relating to the maintenance of peace and security in an amount exceeding 10 million dollars in respect of the decision, that matter shall be brought to the General Assembly, or, if the General Assembly is suspended or not in session, a resumed or special session of the Assembly shall be convened by the Secretary-General to consider the matter.

Contributions

Unpaid assessed contributions from Member States to the UN budget at the end of 2001 totalled $2.1 billion (slightly lower than the 2000 figure of $2.2 billion); unpaid regular budget assessments totalled $240 million (compared to $222 million in 2000); outstanding peacekeeping arrears aggregated $1,823 million ($166 million less than in 2000); and unpaid assessments for the international tribunals aggregated $44 million ($3 million less than in 2000).

The number of Member States paying their regular budget assessment in full decreased from a high of 141 in 2000 to 135 at 31 December 2001.

Assessments

Report of Secretary-General. In response to General Assembly resolution 55/5 A [YUN 2000, p. 1310], the Secretary-General submitted a February report [A/55/789] reviewing the implications of the calculation of assessed contributions in arrears for the purpose of the application of Article 19 of the Charter, whereby a Member State would lose its vote in the Assembly if the amount of its arrears should equal or exceed the amount of contributions due from it for the preceding two full years.

The report examined current procedures for applying Article 19, including interpretations of the terms "arrears", "contributions due for the preceding two full years", and the use of "net" and "gross" assessments in the calculation of "arrears" and "contributions due". It also examined the implications of annual and biannual calculations (at the beginning of each calendar year and at the beginning of the peacekeeping financial period on 1 July) for the application of Article 19. Annexes I and II to the report contained tables illustrating the practical implications of changes in the current approach, using data on gross and net assessments, payments, credits and outstanding assessed contributions from 1 January 1998 to 31 December 2000 to show the results of the current and various alternative approaches on 1 January, 1 July and 31 December 2000.

The illustrative information indicated that calculations for and application of Article 19 on a biannual basis would tend to bring some Member States under its provisions sooner than the current annual exercise. Calculations based on a "net to net" comparison would tend to produce the same result or by a larger margin than the current "gross to net" comparison. Pending further consideration of issues relating to that Article's application by the Committee on Contributions at its sixty-first session (see below), the Secretary-General recommended that the Assembly take note of the foregoing information and either take final decisions on the procedures for applying Article 19 or provide guidance to the Com-

mittee in its consideration of the matter. In the case of a revision to those procedures, the Assembly might also consider a corresponding revision of the UN financial regulations.

On 9 April [A/55/521/Add.2], the Fifth Committee took note of the view of a large majority of delegations that it should defer a decision on the subject, pending consideration of the report by the Committee on Contributions.

By **decision 55/473 A** of 12 April, the Assembly took note of the Fifth Committee's report.

Committee on Contributions. The Committee on Contributions, at its sixty-first session (New York, 11-28 June) [A/56/11], considered the application of Article 19, measures to encourage the timely, full and unconditional payment of assessed contributions, the methodology for preparing future scales of assessments, the assessment of non-member States and appeals by Member States for a change in rate of assessment.

The Committee noted that the information provided in the Secretary-General's February report supported its earlier conclusions. Should the General Assembly move to biannual calculations of arrears for the application of Article 19, some Member States might be prompted to pay their contributions earlier in the year, while more of them might be subject to the application of that Article should the pattern of payments in 2000 continue. The two changes proposed—biannual calculations and net to net comparisons—would potentially affect a significant number of Members, and could lead to an increase in the number and frequency of requests for Article 19 exemptions, affect the Committee's timetable and programme of work, and have consequences for decisions under Article 108 concerning amendments to the Charter.

The Committee recommended that, should the Assembly decide to proceed with those changes in the current practices for the application of Article 19, it should do so gradually. It might begin with the net to net comparison and later implement biannual calculations of arrears, taking into account the results of the first change. It might provide a grace period before implementation to give Members time to make adjustments.

Following its examination of requests from four Member States for exemptions under Article 19, the Committee took no action on Burundi's request since it was not submitted within the required two-week period prior to the Committee's session. It determined that the failure by the Comoros, Georgia and the Republic of Moldova to pay the full minimum amount of their arrears necessary to avoid the application of Article 19 was due to conditions beyond their control, as explained in their letters to the Chairman [A/C.5/

55/44], and therefore recommended that they be permitted to vote in the Assembly until 30 June 2002. The Comoros' intention to consider a payment schedule was noted, as were the payment schedules proposed by Georgia and the Republic of Moldova.

At the conclusion of the Committee's session, nine Member States (Central African Republic, Guinea, Guinea-Bissau, Iraq, Liberia, Niger, Seychelles, Somalia, Uzbekistan) were in arrears in the payment of their assessed contributions under the terms of Article 19. Seven others (Burundi, Comoros, Georgia, Kyrgyzstan, Republic of Moldova, Sao Tome and Principe, Tajikistan), similarly in arrears, had been permitted to vote until 30 June 2001, pursuant to Assembly resolution 55/5 A [YUN 2000, p. 1310].

The Committee noted that, in 2000, Cyprus and Pakistan had availed themselves of the opportunity afforded by Assembly resolution 52/215 A [YUN 1997, p. 1442] of paying the equivalent of $976,276.02 in currencies other than United States dollars.

In its consideration of measures to encourage the timely, full and unconditional payment of assessed contributions, including applying indexation or interest to arrears, the Committee concluded that indexation would pose more complex technical issues than would charging interest. Should the Assembly decide on the latter, the Committee recommended that it be applied only to arrears arising after adoption of that decision, that the interest rate be low and that the measure be delayed to allow Member States to make appropriate adjustments. The Committee would consider the question further in 2002, including the date from which indexation or interest charges should accrue; the rates to be applied; the periodicity; the basis for calculating the charges; whether charges should be compounded for continued non-payment; and the appropriate use for the resulting income.

The Committee also considered the question of multi-year payment plans as useful tools for reducing unpaid assessed contributions. It recommended that the Assembly should decide on the matter, on the basis of proposed guidelines for such plans to be put forward by the Secretary-General. An addendum to the Committee's report [A/56/11/Add.1 & Corr.1] provided information on some multi-year payment plans and incentives and disincentives applied by UN system organizations and other multilateral and regional organizations.

Regarding other possible measures, the Committee agreed to continue to consider at a future session, on the basis of further Assembly guidance, the positive impact that early UN reimbursement of amounts owed to troop-contributing Member States could have on the payment of their assessed contributions; crediting budgetary surpluses to Members current with their financial obligations; and incentive payments keyed to payments status.

The Committee decided not to consider further: the proposals for the establishment of a new assessed fund to which each Member State's contribution would depend on its payment record, as it was overly complicated; redeemable peacekeeping certificates; the ineligibility of Members in arrears for election to committees and other bodies, as it was not in keeping with Article 19; and restricting access of such Members to opportunities for recruitment and procurement, as being outside the Committee's competence.

On the methodology for preparing future scales of assessments, the Committee focused on technical issues not addressed by Assembly resolution 55/5 B [YUN 2000, p. 1311] but of importance for its review of the next scale of assessments. As requested by resolution 54/237 D [ibid., p. 1306], the Committee examined a report on the consequences of sharply depressed levels of primary commodity prices on commodity-dependent economies, but felt it was not clear how that factor could fit into the scale methodology; it thus decided against considering it further unless asked to do so by the Assembly. The Committee would again review the problem of the socio-economic impact of refugee flows on host countries when specific and detailed data were made available and would continue to take that factor into account in its review of requests for exemption under Article 19. It decided to keep the matter of the implementation of the 1993 System of National Accounts [YUN 1993, p. 1112] under review and encouraged Members to adopt it and to respond promptly to the National Accounts Questionnaire to ensure the availability of accurate information for the preparation of the next scale of assessments. After reviewing the revised method of price-adjusted rates of exchange, the Committee decided to continue to consider the matter in 2002, based on a further report on the subject by the Statistics Division, in order to agree on an approach to the issue of identifying excessive income fluctuations or distortions due to the use of market exchange rates and to choose the most appropriate alternative conversion rate.

The Committee deferred to its 2003 session the question of the assessment of non-member States and requested the Secretariat to consult with those States on a possible simplified assessment methodology. It noted that four Member States (Democratic People's Republic of Korea, Kiribati, Tonga, Viet Nam) still had outstanding non-member State contributions assessed prior to their membership in the Organization, and requested the Chairman to seek the Legal Counsel's opinion about the possibility of adding those arrears to their current arrears as Member States.

The Committee took note of the information provided by the United Arab Emirates in support of its request for a change in its rate of assessment. The Committee recommended no change, but encouraged that Member State to make available full and accurate data to the Statistics Division before the next consideration of the assessment scale in 2003. The Committee took no action on Afghanistan's request for a reduction in its rate of assessment as the time available did not allow a complete review of that request.

During the Fifth Committee's consideration of the agenda item on the scale of assessments on 20 July, Burundi reported that, despite its ongoing civil war, it had paid $136,565 on 12 June. That amount had been reduced, however, due to the rapid depreciation of the national currency during the delayed release of the funds so that the final payment was not enough to prevent the loss of Burundi's voting rights. Burundi therefore requested an exemption under Article 19, while it sought to meet its obligation in full.

By **decision 55/473 B** of 14 June, the Assembly deferred consideration of the proposal for the re-establishment of the Ad Hoc Intergovernmental Working Group on the Implementation of the Principle of Capacity to Pay until the main part of its fifty-sixth session.

By **decision 55/473 C** of 25 July, the Assembly endorsed the Committee on Contributions' recommendation in respect of the Comoros, Georgia and the Republic of Moldova. In welcoming Burundi's undertaking and assurances, the Assembly also decided to permit Burundi to vote in the Assembly until 30 June 2002.

Reports of Secretary-General. During the year, the Secretary-General reported to the Assembly on payments made by certain Member States to reduce their level of arrears below that specified in Article 19, so that they could vote in the Assembly. As at 24 January [A/55/745], 38 Member States remained below the gross amount assessed for the preceding two full years (1999-2000). By 22 June [A/S-26/3], that number had been reduced to 16 and to 15 by 10 September [A/56/345].

GENERAL ASSEMBLY ACTION

On 24 December [meeting 92], the General Assembly, on the recommendation of the Fifth Committee [A/56/728], adopted **resolution 56/243** without vote [agenda item 125].

Scale of assessments for the apportionment of the expenses of the United Nations

The General Assembly,

Having considered the report of the Committee on Contributions,

1. *Recalls* its resolution 55/5 A of 26 October 2000;

2. *Requests* the Secretary-General to update the information contained in the annexes to his report on the application of Article 19 of the Charter of the United Nations;

3. *Recognizes* that multi-year payment plans, subject to careful formulation, could be helpful in allowing Member States to demonstrate their commitment under Article 19 of the Charter to pay their arrears, thereby facilitating consideration of applications for exemption by the Committee on Contributions, and requests the Secretary-General to propose guidelines for such multi-year payment plans through the Committee on Contributions;

4. *Recognizes also* that it would be helpful for the Secretariat to be equipped with input from Member States on a schedule of payments or other information about their intentions to clear their accumulated arrears, and encourages Member States in a position to do so to provide such information;

5. *Urges* all Member States to pay their assessed contributions in full, on time and without imposing conditions, in order to avoid the difficulties being experienced by the United Nations;

6. *Requests* the Secretary-General to propose or consider further measures to encourage Member States in arrears to reduce and eventually pay their arrears, and to report thereon to the General Assembly during the main part of its fifty-seventh session for subsequent consideration at its resumed fifty-seventh session.

Also on 24 December, the Assembly decided that the item on the scale of assessments for the apportionment of expenses of the United Nations would remain for consideration at its resumed fifty-sixth (2002) session **(decision 56/464)**.

Communication. In a 27 December letter [A/56/767] to the Assembly President, to which a Secretariat note was annexed, the Secretary-General drew attention to the admission of the Federal Republic of Yugoslavia (FRY) to membership in the United Nations on 1 November 2000 [YUN 2000, p. 1365], which automatically terminated the membership of the former Socialist Federal Republic of Yugoslavia (SFRY) and raised the consequential issue of the payment of its outstanding assessed contributions of $16,218,555, as at 31 October 2000, adjusted for credits in 2001. The Secretary-General concluded that, since the arrears were not collectable from SFRY and consistent with the position of the five successor States (Bosnia and Herzegovina, Croatia, Slovenia, the former Yugoslav Republic of Macedonia, FRY), as set out in their letters appended to the Secretariat note, the Assembly might wish to approve the write-off of the amounts in question, or seek payment from the five successor States of all or part of those arrears. The Secretary-General outlined a number of payment methods if the Assembly took the latter course of action.

Accounts and auditing

The General Assembly, at its resumed fifty-fifth (2001) session, considered the report of the Board of Auditors on UN peacekeeping operations for the period 1 July 1999 to 30 June 2000 [A/55/5, vol. II], together with the Secretary-General's March report on implementation of the Board's recommendations thereon [A/55/380/Add.2] and ACABQ's related comments and recommendations [A/55/878].

On 14 June, the Assembly, in **resolution 55/220 C**, endorsed the Board's report (see p. 98).

Board of Auditors report. The Assembly had before it a March note by the Secretary-General [A/55/820], submitted pursuant to resolution 55/220 A [YUN 2000, p. 1317], transmitting the comments of the Board of Auditors concerning action taken by the United Nations Development Programme, the United Nations Population Fund and the Fund of the United Nations International Drug Control Programme towards removing the reasons that led to the qualified audit opinion on their financial statements for the biennium ended 31 December 1999 [ibid., p. 1316].

ACABQ, in March [A/55/836], welcomed the measures taken to address the reasons for the qualified audit opinions, as well as the three organizations' progress in obtaining additional audit reports. It recommended their careful review of those reports with a view to taking any required remedial action. ACABQ noted the Board's satisfaction that the plans developed by the three organizations provided an adequate basis for improving the extent to which national execution expenditure was covered by audit reports, which, if achieved, should result in steady progress towards removing the reasons for the qualified audit. It would follow up on such progress and inform the Assembly accordingly. In the meantime, ACABQ would not object to the Assembly's approval of the financial statements of the three organizations for the biennium ended 31 December 1999.

GENERAL ASSEMBLY ACTION

On 12 April [meeting 98], the General Assembly, on the recommendation of the Fifth Committee [A/55/689/Add.1], adopted **resolution 55/220 B** without vote [agenda item 115].

Financial reports and audited financial statements, and reports of the Board of Auditors

The General Assembly,

Recalling its resolution 55/220 A of 23 December 2000,

Having considered the note by the Secretary-General transmitting the comments of the Board of Auditors concerning action taken by the United Nations Development Programme, the United Nations Population Fund and the Fund of the United Nations International Drug Control Programme towards removing the reasons that led to the qualified audit opinion on their financial statements for the biennium ended 31 December 1999,

Having also considered the related report of the Advisory Committee on Administrative and Budgetary Questions,

1. *Takes note* of the comments of the Board of Auditors contained in the note by the Secretary-General;

2. *Endorses* the observations and recommendations contained in the report of the Advisory Committee on Administrative and Budgetary Questions;

3. *Accepts* the financial reports and audited financial statements and the reports and qualified audit opinions of the Board of Auditors regarding the United Nations Development Programme, the United Nations Population Fund and the Fund of the United Nations International Drug Control Programme for the biennium ended 31 December 1999;

4. *Requests* the United Nations Development Programme, the United Nations Population Fund and the Fund of the United Nations International Drug Control Programme to adhere to the plans they submitted to the Board of Auditors to correct the deficiencies which led to the qualified audit opinions of the financial statements for the biennium ended 31 December 1999 and to take all the necessary steps to prevent such shortcomings from occurring again.

The Assembly, at its fifty-sixth (2001) session, had before it the Board of Auditors' report on the audited financial statements of the voluntary funds administered by the United Nations High Commissioner for Refugees (UNHCR) for the year ended 31 December 2000 [A/56/5/Add.5]; the Secretary-General's second report [A/56/66] on the implementation of the Board's recommendations on UN accounts for the biennium ended 31 December 1999 [YUN 2000, p. 1316], as well as replies from the executive heads of organizations and programmes relating to the implementation of its recommendations on UN funds and programmes for the same biennium [A/56/66/Add.1]; and the Board's report [A/56/132] on implementation of its recommendations relating to the 1998-1999 biennium, submitted in response to Assembly resolution 52/212 B [YUN 1998, p. 1288].

ACABQ, in its comments on those reports [A/56/436], noted with concern that the Board had qualified its audit opinion on UNHCR's financial statements (see p. 1111).

ACABQ requested that the Board of Auditors, in its reports on the implementation of its recommendations, should indicate the extent to which such recommendations had been implemented and on their impact, and that similar reports by the Secretary-General should focus less on describing how the administration intended to implement the Board's recommendations, and instead indicate briefly the actions taken and results achieved.

GENERAL ASSEMBLY ACTION

On 24 December [meeting 92], the General Assembly, on the recommendation of the Fifth Committee [A/56/651], adopted **resolution 56/233** without vote [agenda item 120].

Financial reports and audited financial statements, and reports of the Board of Auditors

The General Assembly,

Having considered the audited financial statements and the report of the Board of Auditors on voluntary funds administered by the United Nations High Commissioner for Refugees for the year ended 31 December 2000, the report of the Board of Auditors on the implementation of its recommendations relating to the biennium 1998-1999, the second report of the Secretary-General on the implementation of the recommendations of the Board of Auditors on the accounts of the United Nations and on the United Nations funds and programmes for the biennium ended 31 December 1999, and the related report of the Advisory Committee on Administrative and Budgetary Questions,

1. *Accepts* the financial report and audited financial statements and the report and audit opinion of the Board of Auditors regarding the voluntary funds administered by the United Nations High Commissioner for Refugees for the period from 1 January to 31 December 2000;

2. *Endorses* the recommendations of the Board of Auditors contained in its report and the recommendations and conclusions contained in the report of the Advisory Committee on Administrative and Budgetary Questions;

3. *Welcomes* the second report of the Secretary-General on the implementation of the recommendations of the Board of Auditors on the accounts of the United Nations and on the United Nations funds and programmes for the biennium ended 31 December 1999 and the report of the Board of Auditors on the implementation of its recommendations;

4. *Requests* the audited organizations to take all necessary steps to implement expeditiously the outstanding audit recommendations;

5. *Notes with concern* the qualified audit opinion on the financial statements of the United Nations High Commissioner for Refugees, and requests the audited organizations to cooperate fully with the Board of Auditors and to submit the requested information and documentation in a comprehensive and timely manner so that this does not lead in future to similar qualified opinions.

On 24 December, the Assembly decided that the item on the financial reports and audited financial statements, and reports of the Board of Auditors, would remain for consideration at its resumed fifty-sixth (2002) session (**decision 56/464**) and that the Fifth Committee should continue consideration of the item at that session (**decision 56/458**).

Term of office of Board of Auditors

In response to General Assembly resolution 55/220 A [YUN 2000, p. 1317], the Secretary-General submitted in February [A/55/796] his review of the question of extending the current three-year term of office of members of the Board of Auditors to six years. As the Board had noted in 1994 [YUN 1994, p. 1370], the UN move to a biennial accounting period meant one member had to step down in the middle of each biennial audit cycle, thus disrupting the Board's work when that member was not reappointed. A six-year term of office would ensure a smooth pattern of rotation by synchronizing the Board's appointment with the two-year financial reporting cycle, and still maintain the rule that members be appointed for three (two-year) financial periods. It was further proposed that appointments be effective from 1 July, by which time all financial reports would have been submitted.

To facilitate a smooth transition from the current annual appointments to the Board to a two-year appointment cycle, starting on 1 July 2002, the Secretary-General proposed two approaches. One would achieve the six-year cycle with immediate effect by extending South Africa's term of office, due to expire in 2003, to 2006, as the terms of office of the two other members were due to expire in 2002 and 2004. The alternative approach would require that, in 2002, 2003 and 2004, Board members be appointed for four, five and six years, respectively. The Board preferred the first approach, since it would affect only one member, South Africa. Accordingly, each member would cover three full financial cycles; at the end of each audit cycle of the biennium, the term of office of one member would expire, and the term of the new member would commence on 1 July and expire on 30 June six years later.

GENERAL ASSEMBLY ACTION

On 12 April [meeting 98], the General Assembly, on the recommendation of the Fifth Committee [A/55/532/Add.2], adopted **resolution 55/248** without vote [agenda item 116].

Review of the question of the term of office of the Board of Auditors

The General Assembly,

Recalling its resolutions 48/216 D of 23 December 1993 and 55/220 A of 23 December 2000,

Recalling also its resolution 74(I) of 7 December 1946,

Having considered the report of the Secretary-General on the review of the question of the term of office of the Board of Auditors,

1. *Decides* that the term of office of the Board of Auditors shall be a non-consecutive term of office of six years' duration starting on 1 July 2002;

2. *Decides also,* for the transitional arrangements, to approve alternative 1 in the report of the Secretary-General, whereby only the appointment of the Auditor-General of South Africa will be extended until 30 June 2006 and the other members elected under the current procedure shall be eligible for re-election;

3. *Decides further* to amend the first sentence of regulation 12.2 of the Financial Regulations and Rules of the United Nations as follows:

"The members of the Board of Auditors shall be elected for a non-consecutive term of office of six years' duration."

The Secretary-General, in October [A/C.5/56/7], following his notification in June [A/56/103] of the expiration on 30 June 2002 of the term of a member of the Board of Auditors, transmitted the nomination by the Philippines of the Chairman of its Commission on Audit for reappointment.

The Assembly, by **decision 56/315** of 26 November 2001, approved that appointment for a six-year term of office beginning on 1 July 2002.

Administrative and budgetary coordination

By **decision 55/472** of 12 April, the General Assembly took note of the 2000 statistical report of the Administrative Committee on Coordination on the budgetary and financial situation of the UN system organizations [YUN 2000, p. 1319].

In June [A/56/82], the Secretary-General, in response to Assembly resolution 54/236 [YUN 1999, p. 1317], submitted a progress report on the review of the efficiency and the administrative functioning of the United Nations, including human resources management reforms, budget-related issues, and simplification of procurement, finance

and human resources processing work, among others.

CPC, in June [A/56/16], took note of the Secretary-General's report and recommended that the Assembly strengthen the role of the Joint Inspection Unit in programme evaluation, and review the state of coordination and cooperation among oversight bodies with a view to ensuring greater mutual complementarity in their efforts to improve the efficiency of the administrative and financial functioning of the United Nations.

On 24 December, the Assembly decided that the agenda item on the review of the efficiency of the administrative and financial functioning of the United Nations would remain for consideration at its resumed fifty-sixth (2002) session (**decision 56/464**) and that the Fifth Committee should continue to consider the item at that session (**decision 56/458**).

Programme planning

Evaluation and programme planning

The Secretary-General transmitted to CPC a number of evaluation reports of the Office of Internal Oversight Services: in-depth evaluation of sustainable development [E/AC.51/2001/2]; in-depth evaluation of the population programme [E/AC.51/2001/3]; triennial review of the implementation of CPC recommendations made at its thirty-eighth (1998) session on the in-depth evaluation of the United Nations International Drug Control Programme [E/AC.51/2001/4]; and the triennial review of the implementation of CPC recommendations made at its thirty-eighth session on the in-depth evaluation of the United Nations crime prevention and criminal justice programme [E/AC.51/2001/5].

CPC's comments and recommendations on those reports were contained in the report on its 2001 session [A/56/16].

Chapter III

United Nations staff

In 2001, United Nations Secretary-General Kofi Annan (Ghana) was appointed for a second five-year term, effective 1 January 2002. In October, the Secretary-General and the United Nations were awarded the 2001 Nobel Peace Prize (see p. 46), which, according to the Security Council President, reflected the high esteem shared by people throughout the world for the Secretary-General and honoured his exceptional achievements and those of the United Nations itself.

The General Assembly, through the International Civil Service Commission (ICSC), reviewed the conditions of service of the staff of the UN common system. It adopted ICSC recommendations relating to the draft standards of conduct for the international civil service, the implications for the UN system of the introduction in 2002 of the euro as the national currency in the 12 euro-zone countries of the European Union and the base/floor salary scale. The Assembly also took action on the conditions of service for ad litem judges of the International Tribunal for the Former Yugoslavia (ICTY), and continued to consider the proposed review and strengthening of ICSC as part of ongoing initiatives for UN reform.

The Secretary-General reported on the comprehensive review of the conditions of service of judges of the International Court of Justice, ICTY and the International Criminal Tribunal for Rwanda, staff composition, gratis personnel, consultants and individual contractors, the status of women in the Secretariat, multilingualism, regulations governing the status, rights and duties of non-Secretariat officials and experts on mission, staff rules and regulations, staff safety and security, young professionals, mandatory age of separation, the United Nations System Staff College and adherence to regulations governing standards of accommodation for air travel of UN officials.

The Joint Inspection Unit examined policies and practices regarding the recruitment and management of entry-level professionals in selected organizations of the common system.

In continuing efforts to enhance the security and safety of UN staff and associated humanitarian personnel, the Assembly underlined the need to allocate adequate and predictable resources towards that end and requested the Secretary-General to ensure the human rights, privileges and immunities of UN and other personnel carrying out activities in fulfilment of the mandate of a UN operation. In other action, the Assembly adopted the statute of the United Nations System Staff College.

Appointment of Secretary-General

On 29 June, Kofi Annan (Ghana), first appointed Secretary-General of the United Nations on 17 December 1996 [YUN 1996, p. 1312], was appointed for a second five-year term, effective 1 January 2002.

SECURITY COUNCIL ACTION

On 27 June [meeting 4337], the Security Council, at a private meeting, unanimously adopted **resolution 1358(2001)**. The draft [S/2001/635] was co-sponsored by all Council members.

The Security Council,

Having considered the question of the recommendation for the appointment of the Secretary-General of the United Nations,

Recommends to the General Assembly that Mr. Kofi Annan be appointed Secretary-General of the United Nations for a second term of office from 1 January 2002 to 31 December 2006.

GENERAL ASSEMBLY ACTION

By **decision 55/402 B** of 22 June, the General Assembly, following a request by Nigeria [A/55/242], as chairman of the African Group, included in the agenda of its fifty-fifth session an additional item entitled "Appointment of the Secretary-General of the United Nations".

On 29 June [meeting 105], the Assembly adopted **resolution 55/277** [draft: A/55/L.87] without vote [agenda item 187].

Appointment of the Secretary-General of the United Nations

The General Assembly,

Having considered the recommendation contained in Security Council resolution 1358(2001) of 27 June 2001,

Expressing its appreciation for the effective and dedicated service rendered to the United Nations by Mr. Kofi Annan during his first term of office,

Appoints Mr. Kofi Annan Secretary-General of the United Nations for a second term of office beginning on 1 January 2002 and ending on 31 December 2006.

Assembly President Harri Holkeri (Finland), in a statement congratulating the Secretary-General, noted that the Member States' decision to reappoint him demonstrated their strong support and trust for his second term of office and testified to their continued support for his ideas and actions.

Conditions of service

International Civil Service Commission

The International Civil Service Commission (ICSC), a 15-member body established in 1974 by General Assembly resolution 3357(XXIX) [YUN 1974, p. 875], continued in 2001 to regulate and coordinate the conditions of service of the UN common system of salaries and allowances. The ICSC statute had been accepted by the United Nations and 12 related organizations: the International Labour Organization (ILO); the Food and Agriculture Organization of the United Nations; the United Nations Educational, Scientific and Cultural Organization; the World Health Organization; the International Civil Aviation Organization; the Universal Postal Union; the International Telecommunication Union; the World Meteorological Organization; the International Maritime Organization; the World Intellectual Property Organization; the United Nations Industrial Development Organization; and the International Atomic Energy Agency. One other organization, the International Fund for Agricultural Development, had not formally accepted the statute but participated fully in ICSC work.

ICSC held its fifty-third session (Montreal, Canada, 11-29 June), at which it considered, in addition to organizational matters, the conditions of service applicable to both Professional and General Service categories of staff, and those relating specifically to the Professional and higher categories and to the General Service and other locally recruited categories.

The deliberations, recommendations and decisions of ICSC on those matters were detailed in its twenty-seventh annual report to the Assembly [A/56/30] (see sections below).

In an October statement on the administrative and financial implications of ICSC decisions and recommendations for the 2000-2001 programme budget and for the 2002-2003 proposed programme budget [A/56/485], the Secretary-General estimated the resultant requirements at \$1,779,200 and \$7,817,700, respectively, net of staff assessment.

The General Assembly, in **resolution 56/255**, section III (see p. 1319), approved the amount of \$12,813,400 for ICSC for the 2002-2003 biennium.

GENERAL ASSEMBLY ACTION

On 24 December [meeting 92], the General Assembly, on the recommendation of the Fifth (Administrative and Budgetary) Committee [A/56/729], adopted **resolution 56/244** without vote [agenda item 127].

United Nations common system: report of the International Civil Service Commission

The General Assembly,

Having considered the report of the International Civil Service Commission for the year 2001 and the statement submitted by the Secretary-General on the administrative and financial implications of the decisions and recommendations contained in the report of the Commission,

Reaffirming its commitment to a single, unified United Nations common system as the cornerstone for the regulation and coordination of the conditions of service of the United Nations common system,

Convinced that the common system constitutes the best instrument to secure staff of the highest standards of efficiency, competence and integrity for the international civil service, as stipulated under the Charter of the United Nations,

Reaffirming the statute of the Commission and the central role of the Commission in the regulation and coordination of the conditions of service of the United Nations common system,

Takes note of the report of the International Civil Service Commission for the year 2001;

I
Conditions of service applicable to both categories of staff

A. **Standards of conduct for the international civil service**

Recalling its resolutions 52/252 of 8 September 1998, 54/238 of 23 December 1999 and 55/223 of 23 December 2000,

Welcomes the standards of conduct as set out in annex II to the report of the Commission;

B. **Introduction of the euro**

1. *Approves* the recommendation of the Commission that:

(a) Effective 1 January 2002, the euro should be used as the official currency for those emoluments which are currently set in the national currencies of the twelve euro-zone countries, and that the national currency amounts would be converted by applying the respective fixed conversion rates and then rounded up or down to the nearest euro;

(b) The converted values of the education grant for nine currency areas, and of the children's and secondary dependant's allowances for nine locations, will change over to the euro effective 1 January 2002, as reflected in annexes I and II to the present resolution;

2. *Invites* organizations to convert officially into euros, where applicable, their respective General Service salary scales and allowances effective 1 January 2002, on the basis of the approach referred to in paragraph 1 *(a)* above;

II
Conditions of service of staff in the Professional and higher categories

A. Evolution of the margin

Recalling section I.B of its resolution 52/216 of 22 December 1997 and the standing mandate from the General Assembly, in which the Commission is requested to continue its review of the relationship between the net remuneration of the United Nations staff in the Professional and higher categories in New York and that of the comparator civil service (the United States federal civil service) employees in comparable positions in Washington, D.C. (referred to as "the margin"),

Recalling also section IX, paragraph 3, of its resolution 46/191 A of 20 December 1991, in which it requested the Commission to include in its work programme a review of the differences between the United Nations and the United States net remuneration at individual grade levels,

1. *Notes* that the margin between the net remuneration of United Nations staff in grades P-1 to D-2 in New York and that of officials in comparable positions in the United States federal civil service for 2001 is 111.0, as reflected in annex III to the present resolution;

2. *Also notes* that the United Nations/United States net remuneration ratios range from 117.1 at the P-2 level to 104.4 at the D-2 level, and considers that this imbalance should be addressed in the context of the overall margin considerations established by the General Assembly;

B. Base/floor salary scale

Recalling section I.H of its resolution 44/198 of 21 December 1989, by which it established a floor net salary level for staff in the Professional and higher categories by reference to the corresponding base net salary levels of officials in comparable positions serving at the base city of the comparator civil service (the United States federal civil service),

1. *Notes* the increasing number of duty stations where the post adjustment classification is equal or close to zero, and requests the Commission to review the methodology to ensure that purchasing power equivalence is appropriately reflected;

2. *Approves*, with effect from 1 March 2002, as recommended by the Commission, the revised base scale of gross and net salaries for staff in the Professional and higher categories, as contained in annex IV to the present resolution;

III
Strengthening of the international civil service

Having considered the note by the Secretary-General on the review of the International Civil Service Commission and the report of the Secretary-General on strengthening the international civil service,

Requests the Secretary-General, in close consultation with the Chairman of the International Civil Service Commission, to submit a timetable for the implementation of the review of the strengthening of the international civil service to the General Assembly at the main part of its fifty-seventh session.

ANNEX I

Education grant amounts for euro-zone currency areas effective 1 January 2002

(In euros)

Country	Maximum admissible educational expenses and maximum grant for disabled children	Maximum education grant	Normal flat rate when boarding not provided	Additional flat rate when boarding (at designated duty stations)
Austria	12,159	9,119	3,170	4,755
Belgium	12,898	9,673	2,929	4,394
Finland	9,082	6,812	2,229	3,343
France	9,330	6,997	2,500	3,751
Germany	15,736	11,802	3,592	5,389
Ireland	9,997	7,498	2,404	3,606
Italy	12,289	9,217	2,558	3,838
Netherlands	13,085	9,814	3,170	4,755
Spain	9,452	7,089	2,456	3,684

ANNEX II

Children's and secondary dependant's allowance amounts for euro-zone currency areas effective 1 January 2002

(In euros)

Country	Children's allowance	Secondary dependant's allowance
Austria	2,298	849
Belgium	1,947	623
France	1,730	574
French Guyana	1,730	574
Germany	2,321	832
Ireland	1,627	533
Luxembourg	1,947	623
Monaco	1,730	574
Netherlands	2,271	773

ANNEX III (see next page)

Also on 24 December, the Assembly decided that the agenda item on the UN common system would remain for consideration during its resumed fifty-sixth (2002) session (**decision 56/464**).

Functioning of ICSC

Strengthening of ICSC

On 12 April, the General Assembly deferred consideration of the Secretary-General's reports on the composition and terms of reference of the group established to examine the mandate, membership and functioning of ICSC [YUN 1999, p. 1319] and on the review of ICSC [YUN 2000, p. 1334], with a view to taking a decision at its fifty-sixth (2001) session (**decision 55/475**).

ANNEX III

Comparison of average net remuneration of United Nations officials in the Professional and higher categories in New York and United States officials in Washington, D.C., by equivalent grades (margin for calendar year 2001)

Grade	Net remuneration (United States dollars) United Nations[a, b]	United States	United Nations/ United States ratio (United States, Washington, D.C. = 100)	United Nations/ United States ratio adjusted for cost-of-living differential	Weights for calculation of overall ratio[c]
D-2	130,560	108,975	119.8	104.4	3.7
D-1	121,881	101,797	119.7	104.3	9.9
P-5	112,001	89,924	124.6	108.5	26.8
P-4	97,243	75,896	128.1	111.6	32.0
P-3	81,742	61,551	132.8	115.7	21.8
P-2	67,416	50,170	134.4	117.1	5.6
P-1	50,821	38,355	132.5	115.4	0.2
Weighted average ratio before adjustment for New York/Washington, D.C., cost-of-living differential				127.4	
New York/Washington, D.C., cost-of-living ratio				114.8	
Weighted average ratio, adjusted for cost-of-living difference				111.0	

[a]Average United Nations salary at dependency level by grade reflecting two months at multiplier 48.4 (on the basis of the salary scale effective through 28 February 2001), eight months at multiplier 41.2 and two months at multiplier 46.4 (on the basis of the salary scale in effect from 1 March 2001).

[b]For the calculation of the average United Nations salaries, Personnel Statistics of the Consultative Committee on Administrative Questions as at 31 December 1999 were used.

[c]These weights correspond to United Nations common system staff in grades P-1 to D-2 inclusive, serving at headquarters and established offices as at 31 December 1999.

ANNEX IV (see next page)

Remuneration issues

Pursuant to the standing mandate in General Assembly resolution 52/216 [YUN 1992, p. 1055] and to resolution 55/223 [YUN 2000, p. 1331], ICSC continued to review the relationship between the net remuneration of UN staff in the Professional and higher categories (grades P-1 to D-2) in New York and that of the current comparator, the United States federal civil service employees in comparable positions in Washington, D.C. (referred to as the margin). ICSC, in its 2001 report to the Assembly [A/56/30], noted that a net remuneration margin of 112.2 was forecast for 2001, based on current grade equivalencies between United Nations and United States officials in comparable positions, as shown in annex VII to its report. ICSC acknowledged that the United States Administration, in a bid to close a 32 per cent pay gap between its public and non-public sectors, had increased salaries in 2001 as an alternative to pre-existing recommended pay reforms. The Commission noted that the level of the margin reported to it did not reflect recent retroactive tax changes introduced by the United States

Administration. Once full details of those changes were known and taken into account, it was expected that a revised margin would be reported to the Assembly.

In view of the rise in the comparator's civil service salaries as at 1 January 2001, ICSC recommended that, with effect from 1 March 2002, the current base/floor salary scale for Professional and higher categories in the UN common system be increased by 3.87 per cent, through standard consolidation procedures, on a no-loss/no-gain basis. The proposed revised salary scale and staff assessment rates were set out in annexes V and VI to the ICSC report.

Based on the 1997 revised methodology for surveys of best prevailing conditions of employment at headquarters and non-headquarters duty stations [YUN 1997, p. 1453], ICSC conducted a survey of best prevailing conditions of service for General Service and other locally recruited categories of staff in Rome, with a reference date of November 2000. It recommended a new salary scale for Rome-based staff, as reproduced in annex VIII to its report, which was, on average, 4.25

ANNEX IV

Salary scale for the Professional and higher categories, showing annual gross salaries and net equivalents after application of staff assessment[a] effective 1 March 2002

(United States dollars)

Level		I	II	III	IV	V	VI	VII	VIII	IX	X	XI	XII	XIII	XIV	XV
Under-Secretary-General																
USG	Gross	174,137														
	Net D	118,165														
	Net S	106,342														
Assistant Secretary-General																
ASG	Gross	158,353														
	Net D	108,379														
	Net S	98,141														
Director																
D-2	Gross	129,834	132,689	135,540	138,392	141,245	144,097									
	Net D	90,697	92,467	94,235	96,003	97,772	99,540									
	Net S	83,322	84,805	86,286	87,768	89,250	90,733									
Principal Officer																
D-1	Gross	114,784	117,226	119,669	122,106	124,550	126,994	129,437	131,877	134,319						
	Net D	81,366	82,880	84,395	85,906	87,421	88,936	90,451	91,964	93,478						
	Net S	75,209	76,539	77,868	79,195	80,526	81,845	83,115	84,384	85,652						
Senior Officer																
P-5	Gross	101,084	103,294	105,505	107,715	109,924	112,132	114,344	116,553	118,761	120,974	123,185	125,392	127,602		
	Net D	72,872	74,242	75,613	76,983	78,353	79,722	81,093	82,463	83,832	85,204	86,575	87,943	89,313		
	Net S	67,698	68,955	70,159	71,362	72,565	73,767	74,970	76,173	77,376	78,579	79,781	80,983	82,162		
First Officer																
P-4	Gross	83,255	85,283	87,306	89,329	91,442	93,597	95,752	97,906	100,065	102,216	104,371	106,529	108,682	110,837	112,994
	Net D	61,548	62,887	64,222	65,557	66,894	68,230	69,566	70,902	72,240	73,574	74,910	76,284	77,583	78,919	80,256
	Net S	57,316	58,546	59,770	60,994	62,220	63,443	64,669	65,894	67,118	68,342	69,540	70,717	71,888	73,062	74,235
Second Officer																
P-3	Gross	68,306	70,208	72,112	74,011	75,915	77,815	79,715	81,620	83,523	85,423	87,326	89,226	91,202	93,226	95,250
	Net D	51,682	52,937	54,194	55,447	56,704	57,958	59,212	60,469	61,725	62,979	64,235	65,489	66,745	68,000	69,255
	Net S	48,242	49,396	50,553	51,706	52,862	54,015	55,169	56,324	57,477	58,632	59,782	60,933	62,083	63,233	64,384
Associate Officer																
P-2	Gross	55,346	56,907	58,465	60,027	61,729	63,429	65,130	66,829	68,532	70,233	71,932	73,636			
	Net D	42,849	43,973	45,095	46,218	47,341	48,463	49,586	50,707	51,831	52,954	54,075	55,200			
	Net S	40,191	41,210	42,226	43,244	44,260	45,279	46,313	47,344	48,379	49,412	50,444	51,479			
Assistant Officer																
P-1	Gross	42,944	44,444	45,942	47,442	48,939	50,438	51,938	53,436	54,932	56,432					
	Net D	33,920	35,000	36,078	37,158	38,236	39,315	40,395	41,474	42,551	43,631					
	Net S	31,997	32,992	33,986	34,980	35,974	36,967	37,962	38,944	39,921	40,899					

D = Rate applicable to staff members with a dependent spouse or child.

S = Rate applicable to staff members with no dependent spouse or child.

[a]This scale will be implemented in conjunction with a consolidation of 3.87 per cent of post adjustment. There will be consequential adjustments in post adjustment indices and multipliers at all duty stations effective 1 March 2002. Thereafter, changes in post adjustment classifications will be implemented on the basis of the movement of the consolidated post adjustment indices.

per cent higher than the current scale. It also recommended revised rates for dependency allowances, determined on the basis of tax abatements provided by the Italian Government and supplementary payments provided by surveyed employers. The financial implications of the recommendations were estimated at $1.9 million yearly.

ICSC also conducted surveys of employment conditions for staff in the Trades and Crafts and Language Teachers categories in New York, which resulted in increases of 3.78 per cent for those in the Trades and Crafts category, as outlined in annex IX, and of 5.8 per cent for the Language Teachers category, as reflected in the recommended salary scale contained in annex X.

Introduction of the euro

ICSC considered the effect on the UN common system of the introduction of the euro as the official currency of participating member States of the European Union, with effect from 1 January 2002. To facilitate the transition, common system organizations had introduced, or were to introduce, changes in budgeting, accounting, payroll and procurement. However, to ensure a consistent approach in dealing with those changes, some issues required ICSC's attention, including some common system emoluments set in the national currencies of the euro-zone countries, such as education grant levels, children's and secondary dependant's allowances for the Professional and higher categories, General Service salary scales for Vienna, Rome and Paris, and daily subsistence allowance rates. The Commission therefore considered a uniform procedure for expressing those emoluments in euros.

ICSC recommended to the Assembly and/or organizations that, as at 1 January 2002, the euro be used as the official currency for emoluments currently set in the national currencies of the 12 euro-zone countries. The national currency amounts would be converted by applying the respective rates, and then rounded up or down to the nearest euro. It also recommended converted values of education grant for nine currency areas, as set out in annex III to its report, and proposed that organizations convert into euros, where applicable, their General Service salary scales and allowances, as at 1 January 2002.

Post adjustment

ICSC continued its periodic surveys of the operation of the post adjustment system, designed to measure cost-of-living differences. The results of those cost-of-living (place to place) surveys conducted in 2000 were examined by ICSC's Advisory Committee on Post Adjustment Questions

at its March 2001 session. ICSC, in considering the Committee's recommendations, concluded that increases in post adjustment at all headquarters duty stations were attributable to a combination of factors. It approved the survey results, to the effect that the Geneva post adjustment index should continue to be applied to Berne, and that the survey results for London, Montreal, Paris, Rome, Vienna and Washington, D.C., should be taken into account in determining their post adjustment classifications from 1 July 2001. The estimated financial implications of the implementation of the survey results were $15 million.

Other remuneration issues

Conditions of service and compensation for non-Secretariat officials serving the General Assembly

Ad litem judges of the International Tribunal for the Former Yugoslavia

Report of Secretary-General. In February [A/55/756], the Secretary-General submitted a report on the conditions of service of the ad litem judges of the International Tribunal for the Former Yugoslavia (ICTY) (see p. 1198), approved by Security Council resolution 1329(2000) [YUN 2000, p. 1228]. He recommended that the conditions of service and travel and subsistence regulations he had proposed in 1997 [YUN 1997, p. 1452], which were approved by the General Assembly in resolution 53/214 [YUN 1998, p. 1301], for the judges of ICTY and of the International Criminal Tribunal for Rwanda (ICTR) should be applied to the ad litem judges. They included an annual salary of $160,000 prorated for the length of service, travel costs and subsistence benefits, education allowance, disability payments, survivors' lump-sum benefit and medical insurance. All entitlements and allowances would be conditional on residence at The Hague and ad litem judges would not be entitled to pension benefits or relocation allowance owing to the limitation on the length of their appointment. However, in the light of the Assembly's decision in resolution 53/214 to review in 2001 the emoluments, pensions and other conditions of service of members of the International Court of Justice (ICJ) and of ICTY and ICTR judges, the Secretary-General proposed that any adjustments to those conditions of service and compensation should also be applied, as appropriate, to ad litem judges.

ACABQ report. In February [A/55/806], the Advisory Committee on Administrative and Budgetary Questions (ACABQ) noted that the Secretary-General's suggestion that the same conditions of service for judges of the tribunals be applied to ad litem judges was not entirely consistent with the provision in article 13 quater of ICTY's statute that the terms and conditions of service be applied mutatis mutandis. Nonetheless, it did not object to his proposals concerning salary, travel and subsistence regulations, relocation allowance and pension benefits. It was of the opinion, however, that the requirement for actual residence of the judges at The Hague might be onerous, pointing out that the ICJ Statute required only the President and Registrar to reside at the seat of the Court. Therefore, ad litem judges should be required to hold themselves at the disposal of the Court only during the period of their appointment. Also, ACABQ saw no need to apply to ad litem judges the education allowance and lump-sum survivor benefit, given the uncertainty as to the length of their service and the probability of breaks in service. It recommended that their disability benefit entitlement be limited to injury or illness attributable to service with ICTY.

GENERAL ASSEMBLY ACTION

On 12 April [meeting 98], the General Assembly, on the recommendation of the Fifth Committee [A/55/691/Add.1], adopted **resolution 55/249** without vote [agenda item 127].

Conditions of service and compensation for the ad litem judges of the International Tribunal for the Prosecution of Persons Responsible for Serious Violations of International Humanitarian Law Committed in the Territory of the Former Yugoslavia since 1991

The General Assembly,

Recalling its resolution 53/214 of 18 December 1998, in particular paragraphs 4 to 6 of section VIII entitled "Conditions of service and compensation for officials other than Secretariat officials: members of the International Court of Justice, judges of the International Tribunal for the Prosecution of Persons Responsible for Serious Violations of International Humanitarian Law Committed in the Territory of the Former Yugoslavia since 1991 and judges of the International Criminal Tribunal for the Prosecution of Persons Responsible for Genocide and Other Serious Violations of International Humanitarian Law Committed in the Territory of Rwanda and Rwandan Citizens Responsible for Genocide and Other Such Violations Committed in the Territory of Neighbouring States between 1 January and 31 December 1994", and paragraph 8 of its resolution 55/225 of 23 December 2000 on the financing of the International Tribunal for the Prosecution of Persons Responsible for Serious Violations of International Humanitarian Law Committed in the Territory of the Former Yugoslavia since 1991,

Having considered the report of the Secretary-General on the conditions of service of the ad litem judges of the International Tribunal for the Former Yugoslavia

and the related report of the Advisory Committee on Administrative and Budgetary Questions,

1. *Endorses* the observations and recommendations of the Advisory Committee on Administrative and Budgetary Questions on the emoluments, travel and subsistence regulations and disability payments for the ad litem judges of the International Tribunal for the Prosecution of Persons Responsible for Serious Violations of International Humanitarian Law Committed in the Territory of the Former Yugoslavia since 1991;

2. *Decides* to review, in conjunction with the comprehensive review of the emoluments, pensions and other conditions of service for the members of the International Court of Justice, the judges of the International Tribunal for the Former Yugoslavia and the judges of the International Criminal Tribunal for the Prosecution of Persons Responsible for Genocide and Other Serious Violations of International Humanitarian Law Committed in the Territory of Rwanda and Rwandan Citizens Responsible for Genocide and Other Such Violations Committed in the Territory of neighbouring States between 1 January and 31 December 1994, to be undertaken at its fifty-sixth session, in accordance with its resolution 53/214, the emoluments and other conditions of service for the ad litem judges of the International Tribunal for the Former Yugoslavia.

Judges of ICJ and international tribunals

Report of Secretary-General. In November [A/C.5/56/14], the Secretary-General submitted his comprehensive review of the emoluments, pensions and other conditions of service of members of ICJ and judges of ICTR and ICTY, including the ad litem judges. He recommended that the annual emoluments of ICJ, ICTR and ICTY judges and the ad litem judges should be maintained at their current level of $160,000. Noting the introduction of the euro as the national currency of the Netherlands as at 1 January 2002, he proposed that the floor/ceiling mechanism used for protecting the value of the level of salary of the judges against the weakening/strengthening of the United States dollar against the Dutch guilder should continue to be applied to the emoluments of the judges based on the euro. The Secretary-General also proposed increasing the special allowance of the Presidents of ICJ, ICTR and ICTY from $15,000 to $20,000, with a commensurate increase in the daily special allowance of their respective Vice-Presidents when acting as President from $94 per day to $125, subject to a maximum of $12,500 per year. The increase in the level of education grant, including that for disabled children, approved by General Assembly resolution 55/223 [YUN 2000, p. 1331], should be extended to ICJ members and ICTY and ICTR judges as from 1 January 2001. The reference to "installation grant" in the travel and subsistence regulations applicable to members of the Court and the tribunals, respectively, should be revised to make reference to the "assignment grant" provisions applicable to senior officials of the United Nations Secretariat. Concerning health insurance, the Secretary-General noted that, for the duration of their appointment, arrangements would be made for the ICJ, ICTR and ICTY judges and eligible dependants to participate in the official UN health plan on the same conditions as those of other non-staff members. He recommended that the issues of increasing pension payments to remove the disparity in payments to former members of ICJ, and of the existing disparity between the pension benefits of ICTY and ICJ judges, should be brought to the Assembly's attention, in the light of arguments put forward by the Registrar and the President of ICTY.

Concerning the benefits of ad litem judges, which were addressed in his February report (see p. 1334), the Secretary-General stated that the issue of providing them educational assistance should be also brought to the Assembly's attention. Acknowledging that guidance had been requested on the question of disability benefits for ad litem judges and the interpretation of service-related injuries and illnesses, he stated that entitlements in that regard would be determined in accordance with the guidelines set out in his bulletin ST/SGB/103/Rev.1.

ACABQ report. In December [A/56/7/ Add.2], ACABQ stated that it had no objections to the proposals contained in the Secretary-General's November report (see p. 1335) regarding annual emoluments, education grant, travel and subsistence regulations, and entitlements relating to the hardship classification of duty stations and related home leave travel of ICJ members and judges of the international tribunals. It did not, however, recommend the proposed increases in the special allowance for their Presidents and Vice-Presidents. Noting the Secretary-General's comments concerning health insurance, ACABQ reiterated its view that ICJ members should cover the total cost of their participation in the Organization's health insurance plans. It also did not recommend any changes to pension benefits for ICJ members, recalling that its previous recommendations, approved in Assembly resolution 53/214 [YUN 1998, p. 1301], continued to provide protection for pensions against a cost-of-living increase. ACABQ did not recommend any change in the current arrangements with regard to pension benefits of judges of the tribunals. Regarding educational assistance to ad litem judges, it found no justification for changing its February recommendations (see p. 1334).

Payment of honorariums

In August [A/56/311], the Secretary-General recalled that, although his 1998 report on the pay-ment of honorariums to members of subsidiary organs of the United Nations and the practice followed by other UN system organizations [YUN 1998, p. 1304] was before the General Assembly at its fifty-fourth (1999) session, it had been neither formally introduced nor debated. However, ACABQ's comments and recommendations on that report were contained in its reports to the Assembly on the 2000-2001 programme budget. While the Assembly, in resolution 54/249 [YUN 1999, p. 1289], did endorse in general ACABQ's conclusions and recommendations on the proposed 2000-2001 programme budget, it made no specific reference to the question of honorariums. The Secretariat was, therefore, not in a position to provide a precise indication as to whether the Assembly had endorsed the Secretary-General's recommendations on the subject.

The Secretary-General was therefore requesting the Assembly to provide a clear indication of its intentions, including an effective date for the application of the proposals, either retroactive to January 2000, or prospectively to January 2002. In either case, a budgetary provision would be required to meet the additional expenses.

Other staff matters

Personnel policies and practices

Human resources management

The General Assembly, at its resumed fifty-fifth (2001) session, considered the agenda item "Human resources management", which it had deferred by **decision 55/474** of 12 April. The Assembly had before it reports of the Secretary-General on developments in the UN Secretariat post structure [YUN 1999, p. 1330] and staff composition [ibid., p. 1331], notes on the delegation of authority in human resources management and the related ACABQ report [ibid., p. 1338], on personnel practices [ibid.] and on the competitive examinations for promotion to the Professional category of staff and the related ACABQ report [ibid.]. It also considered reports on a comprehensive human resources management implementation programme [YUN 2000, p. 1337] and on delineating the continuum between responsibility, authority and accountability [ibid.] and ACABQ's related comments and recommendations [ibid., p. 1338]; a report by the Office of Internal Oversight Services on the UN recruitment process [ibid., p. 1351]; a report of the Secretary-General reviewing the status of women in the Secretariat [ibid., p. 1341]; Joint Inspection Unit (JIU) reports on the implementation of policy directives on the use of consultants [ibid., p. 1340] and the Secretary-General's comments thereon [ibid., p. 1341], and on senior-level appointments [ibid., p. 1352] together with the Secretary-General's comments thereon [A/55/423/Add.1]; reports of the Secretary-General on staff composition [YUN 2000, p. 1338] and on the use of retirees [ibid., p. 1352]; a JIU report on the administration of justice in the Secretariat and related comments of the Secretary-General [ibid., p. 1359] and ACABQ [ibid., p. 1360]; a report of the Secretary-General on management irregularities causing financial loss to the Organization [ibid., p. 1318]; and lists of the Secretariat's staff.

GENERAL ASSEMBLY ACTION

On 14 June [meeting 103], the General Assembly, on the recommendation of the Fifth Committee [A/55/890/Add.1], adopted **resolution 55/258** without vote [agenda item 123].

Human resources management

The General Assembly,

Recalling Articles 8, 97, 100 and 101 of the Charter of the United Nations,

Reaffirming its resolutions 49/222 A and B of 23 December 1994 and 20 July 1995, 51/226 of 3 April 1997, 52/219 of 22 December 1997, 52/252 of 8 September 1998 and 53/221 of 7 April 1999, as well as its other relevant resolutions and decisions, and subject to the provisions of the present resolution,

Having considered the relevant reports on human resources management questions submitted by the Secretary-General to the General Assembly for consideration during its fifty-fifth session and the related reports of the Advisory Committee on Administrative and Budgetary Questions,

Reaffirming that the staff of the United Nations is an invaluable asset of the Organization, and commending its contribution to furthering the purposes and principles of the United Nations,

Aware of the views expressed by the staff representatives in the Fifth Committee, in accordance with General Assembly resolution 35/213 of 17 December 1980,

Paying tribute to the memory of all staff members who have lost their lives in the service of the Organization,

I

Principles and role of the Office of Human Resources Management of the Secretariat

Reaffirms the principles set out in section I of its resolution 53/221 concerning human resources management and the role of the Office of Human Resources Management of the Secretariat as set out in section II of that resolution;

II

Human resources planning

Reaffirms the provisions contained in section III of its resolution 53/221;

III

Contractual arrangements

Having considered the proposals of the Secretary-General on new contractual arrangements,

1. *Decides* to revert to this issue at its fifty-seventh session;

2. *Requests* the Secretary-General to submit his definitive proposals, in accordance with the steps outlined in paragraph 50 of his report, on new contractual arrangements, spelling out the differences between existing and proposed types of appointments, for consideration by the General Assembly;

IV

Recruitment and placement

Recognizing the value of a transparent process of recruitment, placement and promotion in the Organization,

Having considered the proposals of the Secretary-General concerning changes to the system of recruitment, placement and promotion,

1. *Endorses* the views and recommendations of the Advisory Committee on Administrative and Budgetary Questions in paragraphs 8 to 11 and annex VIII of its report, subject to the provisions of the present resolution;

2. *Requests* the Secretary-General to ensure that the highest standards of efficiency, competence and integrity serve as the paramount consideration in the employment of staff, with due regard to the principle of equitable geographical distribution, in accordance with Article 101, paragraph 3, of the Charter of the United Nations;

3. *Reiterates* that all external vacancy announcements should be submitted to the permanent missions of Member States and be displayed on the notice boards in United Nations premises, as well as posted on the United Nations home page, decides that they should be effectively circulated on the date of issue and that the deadline for the submission of applications should be at least two months from the date of issue and, for unplanned vacancies, such as, inter alia, death or sudden departure of staff, the Secretary-General may reduce the deadline for applications for external vacancies to 30 days if he deems it to be in the best interests of the Organization, and requests the Secretary-General to report to the General Assembly thereon;

4. *Requests* the Secretary-General to circulate internal vacancy announcements to permanent missions when issued;

5. *Requests* the Secretary-General to issue a monthly bulletin electronically that would encompass all Professional and General Service vacancies in the United Nations, including peacekeeping operations, without prejudice to the traditional means of dissemination of vacancy announcements;

6. *Reaffirms* that the Secretary-General may consider external candidates for posts at the P-4 level, with due regard to geographical distribution, while giving fullest regard in filling those posts to candidates with the requisite qualifications and experience already in the service of the United Nations;

7. *Requests* the Secretary-General to have the Office of Human Resources Management maintain and supervise the recruitment process to ensure that the principle of equitable geographical distribution and the

goal of gender balance are respected, in accordance with General Assembly resolutions 42/220 A of 21 December 1987, 51/226 and 53/221, including through the appropriate screening of candidates from such a viewpoint;

8. *Emphasizes* the need to increase the number of staff recruited from unrepresented and under-represented Member States, requests the Secretary-General to make further efforts to reduce the level of under-representation of Member States and the number of unrepresented Member States, and also requests the Secretary-General to develop a programme and set specific targets as soon as possible for achieving equitable geographical representation for all unrepresented and under-represented Member States, bearing in mind the need to increase the number of staff recruited from Member States below the mid-point of their desirable ranges and to report to the General Assembly thereon at its fifty-seventh session;

9. *Requests* the Secretary-General, while filling vacant posts in the language services of the Secretariat, to ensure the highest performance of translation and interpretation in all six official languages;

10. *Reaffirms* that the national competitive examination programme is a useful tool for selecting the best-qualified candidates from inadequately represented Member States, and requests the Secretary-General to continue to hold the examinations for posts subject to geographical distribution at the P-2 and, if necessary, P-3 levels;

11. *Requests* the Secretary-General to continue to offer probationary appointments to all staff members who have passed a competitive recruitment examination and to consider such staff members for conversion to permanent appointment after successful completion of the probationary service;

12. *Regrets* that despite section V, paragraph 19, of its resolution 53/221 and according to paragraph 52 of the report of the Office of Internal Oversight Services of the Secretariat on the follow-up audit of the recruitment process in the Office of Human Resources Management, some programme managers are still reluctant to recruit candidates selected through national competitive examinations, leaving many P-2 posts vacant, and requests the Secretary-General to take concrete measures to fill those posts expeditiously from the existing roster of successful candidates;

13. *Urges* the Secretary-General to strictly comply with the principle that appointment to P-2 posts and to posts requiring special language competence for conference services be made exclusively through competitive examinations, and requests, in this context, that he include in his future reports the information justifying non-compliance with that principle;

14. *Reaffirms* the policy that appointments at the P-3 level shall normally be made through competitive examinations;

15. *Requests* the Secretary-General to ensure that candidates selected through national competitive examinations are placed in a timely fashion and that special efforts are made to recruit candidates from the national competitive examinations roster against existing vacancies until these rosters are cleared;

16. *Regrets* that the provisions of section V, paragraph 22, of its resolution 53/221 were not fully complied with, which led to candidates from over-represented countries taking the General Service to Professional category examination in February 2000, and decides, as a one-time exception, to allow the movement of successful candidates from the G to P examination of 2000 from the General Service to the Professional category;

17. *Notes* the efforts made by the Secretary-General to align the General Service to the Professional category examinations with the national competitive examinations, as required under section V, paragraph 22, of resolution 53/221, and decides that henceforth recruitment of qualified staff from the General Service to the Professional category should be limited to the P-1 and P-2 levels and be permitted up to 10 per cent of the appointments at those levels;

18. *Emphasizes* the need for a systematic rejuvenation of the Secretariat and for retaining younger Professional staff, particularly in the light of the age profile of the staff in the Organization;

19. *Reaffirms* that secondment from government service is consistent with Articles 100 and 101 of the Charter and is beneficial to both the Organization and Member States, and urges the Secretary-General to pursue this practice on a wider scale;

20. *Takes note* of the recommendations of the report of the Joint Inspection Unit on senior-level appointments in the United Nations and its programmes and funds, and notes the comments of the Secretary-General thereon;

21. *Reiterates* that the recruitment, appointment and promotion of staff shall be made without distinction as to race, sex or religion, in accordance with principles of the Charter and the provisions of the Staff Regulations and Rules of the United Nations;

22. *Requests* the Secretary-General to ensure, without exception, the uniform application of the regulations and rules of the Organization in all departments of the Secretariat, in accordance with the relevant resolutions of the General Assembly;

23. *Notes* paragraphs 62 to 66 of the report of the Secretary-General, and requests the Secretary-General to conduct an inspection through the Office of Internal Oversight Services on the issue of possible discrimination due to nationality, race, sex, religion and language in recruitment, promotion and placement, and to report thereon to the General Assembly at its fifty-sixth session;

V
Mobility

Recognizing the value of staff mobility in the Organization,

Recognizing also that the requirement for mobility is one of the essential elements of contractual status of staff,

Having considered the recommendations of the Secretary-General and the related views of the Advisory Committee on Administrative and Budgetary Questions,

1. *Requests* the Secretary-General to develop further criteria for mobility to maximize its benefits for the Organization and to ensure the fair and equitable treatment of all staff and to avoid its possible abuse as an instrument of coercion against staff, taking into account job security in the Organization and other relevant fac-

tors, such as an appropriate incentive scheme and assurances of onward assignment;

2. *Requests* the International Civil Service Commission to conduct a comprehensive review of the question of mobility and its implications on career development of staff members in the United Nations system and report to the General Assembly during the course of its fifty-seventh session;

3. *Notes* the difference between mobility within a duty station and mobility across duty stations, and considers that the latter should be a more important factor in career development;

4. *Requests* the Secretary-General to develop further appropriate mechanisms for promotion with a view to introducing adequate incentives for mobility between duty stations, including the possibility of promotion for staff subject to such mobility;

5. *Also requests* the Secretary-General to ensure that lateral mobility does not negatively affect the continuity and quality of the services required for the implementation of mandated programmes and activities;

6. *Stresses* that mobility of staff should not lead to the transfer or abolition of posts as a result of vacancy;

7. *Requests* the Secretary-General for proposals to solve problems resulting from increasing staff mobility;

8. *Also requests* the Secretary-General to encourage and recognize outstanding job performance of United Nations staff, especially in exceptional circumstances;

VI
Proposed amendment to staff rule 104.14

Decides to approve the proposed amendment to staff rule 104.14, subject to the following provisions:

(a) The central review bodies shall review the recruitment process for compliance with the pre-approved selection criteria and shall offer recommendations. Where these recommendations are not in line with those of the relevant manager, it shall transmit its recommendations to the Secretary-General for a final decision who shall give due consideration to the recommendations of the central review bodies;

(b) The three staff representatives and the alternates shall be selected by the appropriate staff representative body;

(c) One additional member of the Central Review Boards shall be selected jointly by the representatives of the Secretary-General and the staff members appointed to the Boards;

(d) Members of the Central Review Boards, and alternates if any, shall be appointed for a period of two years and shall serve for a maximum of four years;

(e) Delete the last phrase in the proposed amendment to staff rule 104.14 in paragraph (i)(ii) "in accordance with procedures established by the Secretary-General", dealing with the review function of the Central Review Boards/bodies;

VII
Delegation of authority and accountability

Reiterating section IV of its resolution 53/221, by which the General Assembly requested the Secretary-General, inter alia, to ensure, before delegating authority to programme managers, that well-designed mechanisms of accountability, including the necessary internal monitoring and control procedures, as well as training, are put in place,

1. *Endorses* the views and recommendations of the Advisory Committee on Administrative and Budgetary Questions in paragraphs 22 and 23 of its report on accountability and responsibility and on management irregularities;

2. *Emphasizes* that the administrative and managerial discretionary powers of the Secretary-General should be in conformity with the relevant provisions of the Charter of the United Nations and the staff, financial and programme planning regulations and mandates given by the General Assembly;

3. *Reiterates* that every staff member of the United Nations shall be responsible and accountable to the Secretary-General, in accordance with financial rule 114.1 and staff rule 112.3;

4. *Emphasizes* that any delegation of authority should be in accordance with the Charter and the regulations and rules of the Organization and should entail clear lines of authority and accountability as well as improvements in the administration of justice, taking into account the central role played by the Office of Human Resources Management in setting the policies and guidelines in respect of the human resources management of the Organization and monitoring their observance and implementation;

5. *Stresses* that rules and regulations governing separation from service shall be followed strictly;

6. *Recalls its request* to the Secretary-General in section II, paragraph 2, of its resolution 51/226, as reiterated in section IV, paragraph 10, of its resolution 53/221, to enhance managerial accountability with respect to human resources management decisions, including imposing sanctions in cases of demonstrated mismanagement of staff and wilful neglect of, or disregard for, established rules and procedures, while safeguarding the right of due process of all staff members, including managers, and urges the Secretary-General to continue to seek improvements in this area;

7. *Requests* the Secretary-General to continue to improve accountability and responsibility in the reform of human resources management as well as the monitoring and control mechanisms and procedures and to report on the implementation of his proposals to the General Assembly at its fifty-seventh session;

8. *Requests* the Secretary-General to report to the General Assembly at its fifty-seventh session on the progress achieved, including with regard to management irregularities;

9. *Reaffirms* that, in accordance with staff regulation 1.2, staff members shall not be actively associated with the management of, or hold a financial interest in, any profit-making, business or other concern, if it were possible for the staff member or the profit-making, business or other concern to benefit from such association or financial interest by reason of his or her position with the United Nations;

10. *Decides* to further consider the issue of a robust monitoring capacity in the Office for Human Resources Management for the monitoring of all relevant activities in the Secretariat, regardless of the source of their funding, and requests the Secretary-General to provide an analytical and thorough report thereon to the General Assembly at its fifty-sixth session;

VIII
Streamlined rules and procedures

Notes the ongoing efforts of the Secretary-General mentioned in paragraphs 27 to 32 of his report regarding the elimination of documentation relating to obsolete and redundant rules and procedures, and requests that the General Assembly be informed at its fifty-sixth session on the details of the documentation being eliminated;

IX
Consultants

Decides to consider the question of the use of consultants and individual contractors at its fifty-sixth session, and requests the Advisory Committee on Administrative and Budgetary Questions to present its reports to the General Assembly at the main part of its fifty-sixth session on the relevant reports of the Secretary-General and the Joint Inspection Unit;

X
Composition of the Secretariat

Noting that the relative weight of the population factor in the calculation of desirable ranges for the implementation of posts was reduced to 5 per cent from 7.2 per cent in section III of General Assembly resolution 42/220 A of 21 December 1987,

Also noting that posts subject to geographical distribution have witnessed a decrease, from 3,350 to 2,700 to the current 2,600,

Further noting the increase in the number of Member States and the gradual decrease in the number of non-represented and under-represented Member States in the United Nations Secretariat,

Bearing in mind that the new scales of assessment, which will have a direct bearing on the desirable ranges currently being followed, have been adopted by the General Assembly on 23 December 2000,

1. *Reaffirms* that, in accordance with its resolutions 41/206 A of 11 December 1986 and 53/221 of 7 April 1999, no post should be considered the exclusive preserve of any Member State or group of States, including at the highest levels, and requests the Secretary-General to ensure that, as a general rule, no national of a Member State succeeds a national of that State in a senior post and that there is no monopoly on senior posts by nationals of any State or group of States;

2. *Requests* the Secretary-General to take all the necessary measures to ensure, at the senior and policy-making levels of the Secretariat, equitable representation of Member States, especially those with inadequate representation at those levels, unrepresented and under-represented, in particular developing countries, in accordance with the relevant resolutions of the General Assembly, and to continue to include relevant information thereon in all future reports on the composition of the Secretariat;

3. *Reiterates its request* to the Secretary-General to increase further his efforts to improve the composition of the Secretariat by ensuring a wide and equitable geographical distribution of staff in all departments;

4. *Requests* the Secretary-General to undertake a study, in the context of the report on the composition of the Secretariat as of 30 June 2002, on the ramifications of changing the relative weights of the population factor from the current level of 5 per cent, the member-ship factor (from 40 per cent) and the contribution factor (from 55 per cent);

XI
Administration of justice

1. *Decides* to inscribe the item entitled "Administration of justice" in the provisional agenda of its fifty-sixth session;

2. *Notes with concern* that the present system for the administration of justice at the United Nations is slow and cumbersome;

3. *Welcomes* the proposal of the Secretary General to establish a function of ombudsman;

4. *Requests* the Secretary-General to submit a report, after consultations with the staff, on the possible amendments to the staff rules and regulations to review the role of the Joint Appeals Board, taking into account the following four options:

    (a) The current nature of the Joint Appeals Board (JAB) as an advisory body, with the following changes:

      (i) Members representing the staff shall be elected solely by the staff without prejudice to the right of the Secretary-General to appoint members representing the administration;

      (ii) Jointly selecting the chairpersons and examining the need for a full-time chairperson;

      (iii) The current power of the JAB to suspend action on a contested decision;

      (iv) Limiting the time available for the JAB to produce its report and recommendations to three months from the date of receipt of the application;

    (b) The current nature of the JAB;

    (c) Changing the nature of the JAB from an advisory body to a semi-judicial body with the power to take decisions;

    (d) Other changes that might flow from these consultations;

5. *Requests* the Secretary-General to report to the General Assembly on an annual basis on the outcome of the work of the Joint Appeals Board;

6. *Welcomes* the intention of the Secretary-General to organize basic legal training courses for new members of the Joint Appeals Board and joint disciplinary committees;

7. *Takes note* of the observations of the Advisory Committee on Administrative and Budgetary Questions that there is a gap between the statutes of the United Nations Administrative Tribunal and the Administrative Tribunal of the International Labour Organization with respect to specific performance of an obligation and compensation limits, and requests the Secretary-General to take necessary measures to close the gap as appropriate between the statutes of the two Tribunals;

8. *Requests* the Secretary-General to establish a clear linkage between the administration of justice and the system of accountability when the decisions of the Administrative Tribunal result in losses to the Organization due to management irregularities;

9. *Requests* the Secretary-General to take urgent measures in accordance with financial rule 114.1 and staff rule 112.3 to recover financial losses caused to the Organization by wrongful actions or gross negligence of senior officials of the United Nations, particularly as a result of the judgements of the Administrative Tri-

bunal, and to report thereon to the General Assembly at its fifty-seventh regular session, taking into account section IV, paragraph 10, of General Assembly resolution 53/221;

10. *Takes note* of the intention of the Joint Inspection Unit to continue its study of the possible need for higher-level jurisdiction in consultation with all organizations of the United Nations system, bearing in mind the national legal systems of Member States of the United Nations, and requests the Joint Inspection Unit to report thereon to the General Assembly at its fifty-seventh session;

11. *Requests* the Secretary-General to present a report on the implementation of this section to the General Assembly at its fifty-sixth session;

XII
Conditions of service

1. *Endorses* the recommendation of the Advisory Committee on Administrative and Budgetary Questions in paragraph 19 of its report that a competitive package of conditions of service is a prerequisite for the successful achievement of goals of human resources management reform, and requests the Secretary-General to transmit to the International Civil Service Commission these recommendations having direct impact on the United Nations common system, with the request that it report to the General Assembly at its fifty-seventh session, so as to enable the Assembly to make a final decision;

2. *Requests* the Secretary-General to study the implications of fixing the mandatory age of separation for staff members appointed prior to 1 January 1990 to the current age of sixty-two years and to report thereon to the General Assembly at its fifty-sixth session;

3. *Emphasizes* that the Organization requires a good working environment and a comprehensive compensation package to attract and retain high-quality staff;

XIII
Competencies, performance management and career development

1. *Emphasizes* the necessity for the United Nations to develop a culture of continuous learning, and welcomes the progress made in this regard, and stresses the role of the United Nations Staff College to this effect as an institution for system-wide knowledge management, training and continuous learning for the staff of the United Nations system, aimed, in particular, at the areas of economic and social development, peace and security and internal management of the United Nations system;

2. *Agrees* with the goal of the Secretary-General to create a fair, equitable, transparent and measurable system of performance management throughout the Secretariat, and underlines the importance of creating a comprehensive career development system;

3. *Endorses* the proposals of the Secretary-General concerning performance management and career development, bearing in mind the provisions of the present resolution, and requests the Secretary-General to report to the General Assembly at its fifty-seventh session regarding the implementation of his proposals;

XIV
Status of women in the Secretariat

Reaffirming that the Fifth Committee is the appropriate Main Committee of the General Assembly entrusted with responsibility for administrative and budgetary matters related to the question of the status of women in the Secretariat,

1. *Reaffirms* the provisions of section X of its resolution 53/221, and recalls its resolution 55/69;

2. *Urges* the Secretary-General to intensify his efforts to achieve the goal of 50/50 gender distribution reaffirmed in section X, paragraph 3, of resolution 53/221;

XV
Reports of the Office of Internal Oversight Services

1. *Takes note* of the report of the Office of Internal Oversight Services on the follow-up audit of the recruitment process in the Office of Human Resources Management;

2. *Also takes note* of the report of the Office of Internal Oversight Services on the proactive investigation of the education grant entitlement;

XVI
Requests the Secretary-General to submit to the General Assembly for consideration at its fifty-seventh session a detailed report on the results of the implementation of the provisions of the present resolution.

The General Assembly, on 24 December, decided that the agenda item entitled "Human resources management" would remain for consideration during its resumed fifty-sixth (2002) session (**decision 56/464**), and that the Fifth Committee would continue to consider it at that session (**decision 56/458**).

Pay and benefits system

ICSC, at its fifty-third session, reviewed the pay and benefits system, one of the principal elements of the integrated framework for human resources management [YUN 2000, p. 1337], adopted by ICSC in 2000 and approved by the General Assembly in resolution 55/223, section I [ibid., p. 1331]. The objective of the review was to design a competitive system that would enable organizations to attract, develop and retain high-quality staff, reward them on the basis of merit and competence, recognize team as well as individual performance and simplify the system with a view to ease of administration and greater cost-effectiveness. That would be achieved through improved organizational performance: linking remuneration to performance; strengthened management capacity; increased flexibility; greater competitiveness; improved work/life policies; and streamlining, simplification, greater transparency and accountability.

ICSC, functioning as an open-ended working group of the whole, discussed the challenges faced by the organizations of the common system, especially the need for competitiveness and improved organizational performance. It examined possible new approaches to the pay and benefits system, including updating and streamlining job classification standards and procedures, a remuneration system that included tools to recognize and reward contribution, and mechanisms to strengthen management's capacity to meet organizational goals and enhance performance and effectiveness. Also examined were the treatment of allowances and related issues, diversity among organizations, the pension scheme and the need for a strategic approach.

ICSC, pending submission of its report to the General Assembly in 2002, requested the Assembly to take note of progress made and the ideas and approaches explored, which it would further consider and develop. It decided to continue in 2002 the biennial review of the level of the education grant; the amount of children's and secondary dependant's allowance for the Professional and higher categories; and the common scale of staff assessment.

Contractual arrangements

ICSC considered the issue of contractual arrangements, one of the core elements identified in the integrated framework for human resources management [YUN 2000, p. 1337]. It had before it an analysis of recent employment trends, by type of contractual arrangement, in common system organizations, as well as information on recent developments in employment in the national civil services of a selected number of countries.

ICSC decided that future work on the subject should be integrated into the review of the pay and benefits system (see above). In that context, it requested the Secretariat to: update available statistics; take further inventory of the various types of contracts in use and the numbers of staff against each type of contract, together with descriptions of the types of appointment; collect information on the administrative policies of common system organizations and of selected national civil services on career versus time-limited appointments; and propose a compendium of contracts from which organizations could select and adapt, according to their specific needs.

Draft standards of conduct
for the international civil service

At its fifty-third session [A/56/30], ICSC, after considering the views of the Administrative Committee on Coordination (ACC) and of the common system's organizations and staff representatives, finalized and adopted the draft standards of conduct for the international civil service and recommended them to the General Assembly and other organizations of the system. The draft, which was updated by a working group and further revised by ICSC in 2000 [YUN 2000, p. 1338], was set out in annex II to its report.

The General Assembly, in section I of **resolution 56/244** (see p. 1330), welcomed the standards of conduct for the international civil service.

Staff composition

In his October annual report on the Secretariat's staff composition [A/56/512 & Corr.1], the Secretary-General updated information on changes in the desirable range of posts for Member States and described measures taken to ensure equitable representation at the senior and policy-making levels. As at 30 June 2001, Secretariat staff numbered 14,874, higher by 1,710 than at 30 June 2000. Of that number, 5,508 were in the Professional and higher categories, 8,530 were in the General Service and related categories and 836 were project personnel; 7,485 were paid from the regular budget and 7,389 from extrabudgetary sources. Staff in posts subject to geographical distribution numbered 2,445, of whom 983 were female (an increase of 1 per cent compared to 2000). Eighteen Member States remained unrepresented in all staff categories, while 10 were underrepresented, compared to 21 and 8, respectively, in 2000. Appointments to posts subject to geographical distribution between 1 July 2000 and 30 June 2001 totalled 159. Of those, 5 (3.1 per cent) were nationals of unrepresented Member States, 38 (33.9 per cent) of underrepresented Member States, 109 (68.6 per cent) of within-range Member States and 6 (3.8 per cent) of overrepresented Member States. Changes in representation status resulted from appointments or separation from service, adjustments to desirable ranges owing to an increase or decrease in the number of posts subject to geographical distribution and changes in the number of Member States, the scale of assessments, the population of Member States and the status of individual staff members.

The report also detailed information on the demographic profile of Secretariat staff, Secretariat staff movement between 1 July 2000 and 30 June 2001 and forecasts of anticipated retirements between 2001 and 2005.

Gratis personnel

By **decision 55/462** of 12 April, the General Assembly took note of the Secretary-General's 2000 reports on the situation of gratis personnel provided by Governments and other entities

[YUN 2000, p. 1339] and the related oral report of the ACABQ Chairman, and decided that future reports on that item should be submitted annually.

Report of Secretary-General. The Secretary-General, in his annual report [A/56/839] on the status of types I and II gratis personnel for the period 1 January to 31 December 2001, submitted pursuant to General Assembly resolution 51/243 [YUN 1997, p. 1469], provided information on, among other things, their nationality, duration of service and functions. Type I gratis personnel serving under an established regime included interns, associate experts and technical cooperation experts obtained on non-reimbursable loans. Type II gratis personnel included a hydrology expert, a health economist and an indigenous people's rights lawyer. The Secretary-General stated that, between 31 December 2000 and 31 December 2001, the total number of type I gratis personnel decreased from 265 to 187 (29.4 per cent), owing mainly to a 51.8 per cent decrease in the number of associate experts (from 218 to 105). On the other hand, the number of interns and technical cooperation experts increased from 39 to 68 (74 per cent) and from 8 to 14 (75 per cent), respectively. During the same period, the number of type II gratis personnel decreased from 43 to 3 (93 per cent), as the engagement of 40 forensic investigators by ICTY was discontinued in 2001. Among the remaining three, one was engaged by the Office of the United Nations High Commissioner for Human Rights, one by the Economic and Social Commission for Western Asia and one by the Economic Commission for Africa.

Consultants and individual contractors

Report of Secretary-General. Pursuant to section VIII of General Assembly resolution 53/221 [YUN 1999, p. 1328] and section IX of resolution 55/258 (see p. 1340), the Secretary-General submitted his annual report on the hiring and use of consultants and individual contractors in 2000 [A/56/834]. He noted that, while the necessary data were available for Headquarters through the Integrated Management Information System (IMIS), comparable information regarding the type and nature of their contracts on a worldwide basis would not be available until the full deployment in 2001 of IMIS (Release III) at all duty stations. Therefore, the data were collated from both the legacy systems and from IMIS, resulting in their delayed issuance.

The report included statistical tables giving the number of persons engaged and the number and types of contracts, their status as retired or not retired, gender, levels of education and performance, nationality, purpose of engagement, occupational groups, duration of contracts, number of days worked, hiring departments, fees, source of funding and total expenditure. In 2000, 3,054 consultants and 1,314 individual contractors were engaged, accounting for 4,173 and 2,471 contracts, respectively. Fees for both totalled $41.9 million, an increase of $13 million over the total reported for 1999 [YUN 2000, p. 1340].

ACABQ report. ACABQ, in its first report on the proposed programme budget for the 2002-2003 biennium [A/56/7], considered a JIU report on the use of consultants and the related report of the Secretary-General on the hiring and use of consultants and individual contractors in 1999 [YUN 2000, p. 1340]. In its comments on JIU's recommendations concerning geographical balance for consultancy, ACABQ, while acknowledging the importance of the geographical mix of consultants, noted the Secretary-General's observations on the increased costs and delays in project execution such restrictions would cause, and questioned the utility of using desirable ranges in procuring that type of expertise. As to the Secretary-General's related report, ACABQ pointed out that the weaknesses in record keeping, data collection and processing it had earlier identified [YUN 1998, p. 1311] persisted, as a system for accurate data collection had yet to be established. It noted that, while information could be obtained relatively easily from Headquarters through IMIS, data from offices away from Headquarters were less reliable. The installation of IMIS in those offices would facilitate data collection and analysis. Moreover, at the beginning of a financial period, areas where consultancy would be required should be identified. Thus, the estimates in the proposed programme budget for the 2002-2003 biennium should have contained more precise information on requirements and full justification for the use of outside expertise. To facilitate that process, ACABQ urged the speedy establishment in the Secretariat of a viable inventory of skills, taking into account the expertise of agencies, funds and programmes of the UN system.

CPC consideration. The Committee for Programme and Coordination (CPC), at its forty-first session (11 June–6 July) [A/56/16], also considered the JIU report on the use of consultants as well as the Secretary-General's related comments [YUN 2000, p. 1341]. CPC expressed disappointment over the lack of progress in establishing mechanisms to avoid duplication of activities and in developing norms to attract consultants on a wider geographical base, and the lack of a gender perspective in the JIU report. It requested the Secretary-General to study different methodologies for correcting the geographical imbalance in hiring consultants and to report on workable options to enable Member States to make an informed choice among alternative systems.

The General Assembly, by **decision 56/460** of 24 December, endorsed CPC's conclusions and recommendations on the use of consultants and ACABQ's observations contained in its first report on the proposed programme budget for the 2002-2003 biennium. It requested the Secretary-General to report on the implementation of the decision at its fifty-seventh (2002) session.

Status of women in the Secretariat

In a January report [E/CN.6/2001/5] to the Commission on the Status of Women, the Secretary-General provided a statistical update, as at 30 November 2000, of the gender distribution of staff at the Professional and higher levels in the UN Secretariat and in the organizations of the UN common system. He also outlined the 2001 work programme, highlighting his strategy for achieving gender equality in the Secretariat. Priority would be assigned to evaluating progress made in improving women's representation, based on the implementation of action plans for achieving gender balance in individual departments and offices, and to developing strategies for improving women's representation in peacekeeping and other special missions.

In response to General Assembly resolution 55/69 [YUN 2000, p. 1342], the Secretary-General submitted an October report [A/56/472] reviewing the status of women in the UN system. The number of appointments of Professional and higher-level staff for one year or more increased from 1,601 (36.5 per cent) in 2000 to 1,906 (34.6 per cent) in 2001; the higher figure was attributable to the significant increase in the number of appointments to peacekeeping missions. The largest increase was at the D-1 level, rising from 81 (29.3 per cent) in 2000 to 97 (30.1 per cent) in 2001. The highest concentration of women remained at the P-3 and P-4 levels, despite the decline from 40.2 per cent in 2000 to 36.9 per cent in 2001 at the P-3 level, and from 33.5 per cent to 31.4 per cent at the P-4 level during the same period. The percentage of women at the P-5 level also declined (from 32.6 per cent in June 2000 to 29.5 per cent in June 2001). Only at the P-2 level was the goal of 50/50 gender distribution met (48 per cent). While the percentage of women at the D-1 level had reached critical mass, the overall increase in the percentage of women at the senior and policy-making levels (D-1 and above) had been negligible, from ' per cent to 24.8 per cent.

he proportion of women appointed in the ssional and higher categories between 2000 and 30 June 2001 remained steady at 'r cent, despite a considerable increase in

the overall number of appointments to 378, compared to 279 in the previous year. The proportion of women promoted during the same period increased from 43.1 per cent to 47.1 per cent but still fell short of the goal of 50 per cent.

The Secretary-General, while acknowledging that the General Assembly's goal of gender balance in the appointment and promotion of Professional and higher-level staff had not yet been met, stated that there were signs of progress, as 14 departments and offices had met that goal in the preceding year. Heads of departments and offices had set targets for the selection of women candidates under the 2001-2002 Human Resources Action Plans, and their performance would be monitored and evaluated. The endorsement by the Assembly in resolution 55/258 (see p. 1337) of the Secretary-General's human resources management reform programme would require the introduction of a new recruitment, promotion and placement system. Priority would be given to developing strategies to expand the supply of women candidates for vacancies to be filled under the new system, particularly in terms of identifying sources of such candidates in Member States that were unrepresented or underrepresented in the Secretariat. The special measures for women would be reviewed to determine how they might be enhanced and made more effective under the new selection system.

GENERAL ASSEMBLY ACTION

On 19 December [meeting 88], the General Assembly, on the recommendation of the Third (Social, Humanitarian and Cultural) Committee [A/56/576], adopted **resolution 56/127** without vote [agenda item 112].

Improvement of the status of women in the United Nations system

The General Assembly,

Recalling Articles 1 and 101 of the Charter of the United Nations, as well as Article 8, which provides that the United Nations shall place no restrictions on the eligibility of men and women to participate in any capacity and under conditions of equality in its principal and subsidiary organs,

Recalling also the goal, contained in the Platform for Action adopted by the Fourth World Conference on Women, of achieving overall gender equality, particularly at the Professional level and above, by 2000 and the further actions and initiatives set out in the outcome document adopted by the General Assembly at its twenty-third special session entitled "Women 2000: gender equality, development and peace for the twenty-first century",

Recalling further its resolution 55/69 of 4 December 2000 on the improvement of the status of women in the United Nations system,

Taking note of Commission on Human Rights resolution 2001/50 of 24 April 2001 on integrating the human rights of women throughout the United Nations system, in particular paragraph 13, in which the Commission recognizes that gender mainstreaming will strongly benefit from the enhanced and full participation of women, including at the higher levels of decision-making in the United Nations system,

Welcoming the decision of the Secretary-General to include, in the performance appraisal of managers, information on the opportunities presented for the selection of women candidates and on progress made in improving women's representation, including efforts made to identify women candidates,

Welcoming also the proposed system-wide medium-term plan for the advancement of women, 2002-2005, as recommended to the Economic and Social Council by the Commission on the Status of Women at its forty-fifth session,

Taking into account the continuing lack of representation or underrepresentation of women from certain countries, in particular from developing countries, including least developed countries and small island developing States, and from countries with economies in transition,

Noting with appreciation those departments and offices that have achieved the goal of gender balance, as well as those departments that have met or exceeded the goal of 50 per cent in the selection of women candidates for vacant posts in the past year,

Welcoming the progress made in maintaining and improving the representation of women at some levels of the Secretariat, in particular in the category of geographical appointments, and welcoming the fact that the percentage of women appointed and promoted in the Secretariat has been maintained or increased, but expressing concern that progress in improving the representation of women at the senior and policy-making levels has been negligible,

Expressing concern that there are currently no women acting as special representatives or envoys,

Noting that the statistics on the representation of women in the organizations of the United Nations system are not fully up to date,

1. *Takes note with appreciation* of the report of the Secretary-General and the actions described therein;

2. *Reaffirms* the urgent goal of achieving 50/50 gender distribution in all categories of posts within the United Nations system, especially at senior and policy-making levels, with full respect for the principle of equitable geographical distribution, in conformity with Article 101, paragraph 3, of the Charter of the United Nations, and also taking into account the continuing lack of representation or underrepresentation of women from certain countries, in particular from developing countries and countries with economies in transition;

3. *Welcomes*:

(*a*) The ongoing personal commitment of the Secretary-General to meeting the goal of gender equality and his assurance that gender balance will be given the highest priority in his continuing efforts to bring about a new management culture in the Organization, including full implementation of the special measures for the achievement of gender equality;

(*b*) The pledge of the executive heads of the organizations of the United Nations system to intensify their efforts to meet the gender equality goals set out in the Beijing Declaration and Platform for Action;

(*c*) The inclusion of the objective of improving gender balance in action plans on human resources management for individual departments and offices, and encourages further cooperation, including the sharing of best-practice initiatives, between heads of departments and offices, the Special Adviser on Gender Issues and Advancement of Women and the Office of Human Resources Management of the Secretariat in the implementation of those plans, which include specific targets and strategies for improving the representation of women in individual departments;

(*d*) The continuing designation of focal points for women in United Nations peacekeeping operations, and requests the Secretary-General to ensure that the focal points are designated at a sufficiently high level and enjoy full access to senior management in the mission area and at Headquarters;

(*e*) The continued provision of specific training programmes on gender mainstreaming and gender issues in the workplace, tailored to meet the special needs of individual departments, commends those heads of departments and offices who have launched gender training for their managers and staff, and strongly encourages those who have not yet organized such training to do so by the end of the biennium;

4. *Regrets* that the goal of 50/50 gender distribution was not met by the end of 2000, and urges the Secretary-General to redouble his efforts to realize significant progress towards this goal in the near future;

5. *Expresses concern* that, in five departments and offices of the Secretariat, women still account for less than 30 per cent of staff, and encourages the Secretary-General to intensify his efforts to meet the goal of gender balance within all departments and offices of the Secretariat;

6. *Requests* the Secretary-General, in order to achieve and maintain the goal of 50/50 gender distribution with full respect for the principle of equitable geographical distribution, in conformity with Article 101, paragraph 3, of the Charter:

(*a*) To develop innovative recruitment strategies to identify and attract suitably qualified women candidates, particularly from and in developing countries and countries with economies in transition and other Member States that are unrepresented or underrepresented in the Secretariat, and in occupations in which women are underrepresented;

(*b*) To encourage the United Nations system and its agencies and departments to make more effective use of existing information technology resources and systems and other established methods to disseminate information about employment opportunities for women and to better coordinate rosters of potential women candidates;

(*c*) To continue to monitor closely the progress made by departments and offices in meeting the goal of gender balance, to ensure that the appointment and promotion of suitably qualified women will be no less than 50 per cent of all appointments and promotions until the goal of 50/50 gender distribution is met, including through full implementation of the special measures for women, and to effectively encourage, monitor and assess the performance of managers in meeting targets for improving women's representation;

(d) To enable the Office of the Special Adviser on Gender Issues and Advancement of Women to monitor effectively and facilitate progress in the implementation of the strategic action plans for the achievement of gender balance and the special measures for women, including by ensuring access to the information required to carry out that work;

(e) To intensify his efforts to create, within existing resources, a gender-sensitive work environment supportive of the needs of his staff, both women and men, including through the development of policies for flexible working time, flexible workplace arrangements and childcare and elder-care needs, as well as through the provision of more comprehensive information to prospective candidates and new recruits on employment opportunities for spouses, the provision of support for the activities of women's networks and organizations within the United Nations system and the expansion of gender-sensitivity training in all departments, offices and duty stations;

(f) To strengthen further the policy against harassment, including sexual harassment, by, inter alia, ensuring the full implementation of the guidelines for its application at Headquarters and in the field, including in peacekeeping operations;

7. *Strongly encourages* the Secretary-General to renew his efforts to appoint more women as special representatives and envoys to pursue good offices on his behalf, especially in matters related to peacekeeping, peacebuilding, preventive diplomacy and economic and social development, as well as in operational activities, including appointment as resident coordinators, and to appoint more women to other high-level positions;

8. *Encourages* the Secretary-General and the executive heads of the organizations of the United Nations system to continue to develop common approaches for retaining women, promoting inter-agency mobility and improving career development opportunities;

9. *Encourages* the United Nations and Member States to continue to implement the outcome of the twenty-third special session of the General Assembly entitled "Women 2000: gender equality, development and peace for the twenty-first century" pertaining to the improvement of the status of women in the United Nations system;

10. *Strongly encourages* Member States:

(a) To support the efforts of the United Nations and the specialized agencies to achieve the goal of 50/50 gender distribution, especially at senior and policy-making levels, by identifying and regularly submitting more women candidates for appointment to positions in the United Nations system, by identifying and proposing national recruitment sources that will assist the organizations of the United Nations system in identifying suitable women candidates, in particular from developing countries and countries with economies in transition, and by encouraging more women to apply for positions within the Secretariat, the specialized agencies, funds and programmes and the regional commissions, including in areas in which women are underrepresented, such as peacekeeping, peacebuilding and other non-traditional areas;

(b) To identify women candidates for assignment to peacekeeping missions and to improve the representation of women in military and civilian police contingents;

(c) To identify and submit regularly more women candidates for appointment or election to intergovernmental, expert and treaty bodies;

(d) To identify and nominate more women candidates for appointment or election as judges or other senior officials in international courts and tribunals;

11. *Requests* the Secretary-General to report on the implementation of the present resolution, including by providing up-to-date statistics on the number and percentage of women in all organizational units and at all levels throughout the United Nations system, and on the implementation of departmental action plans for the achievement of gender balance, to the Commission on the Status of Women at its forty-sixth session and to the General Assembly at its fifty-seventh session.

Multilingualism

In response to General Assembly resolution 54/64 [YUN 1999, p. 1335], the Secretary-General submitted a November report on efforts to promote multilingualism in the Secretariat [A/56/656]. The Secretary-General had appointed the Assistant Secretary-General of the UN Department of General Assembly Affairs and Conference Services as Coordinator for Multilingualism. The Coordinator would propose strategies for addressing weaknesses in the pattern of language use in the Organization, as identified in Assembly resolution 50/11 [YUN 1995, p. 1416], and serve as the focal point for multilingualism in the Secretariat. Recognizing that efforts to promote multilingualism should be Secretariat-wide, the Coordinator involved all Secretariat departments and/or offices, conferring regularly with departmental focal points on how to reinforce multilingualism.

The Secretary-General said that the key issues identified during the consultations related to: the working languages of the Secretariat and efforts made to improve their use by staff, through vacancy announcements and recruitment, incentives and training; the use of official languages in documents and meetings and actions required to improve related activities; and public information, through the efforts of the UN Department of Public Information (DPI) to promote the work of the Organization. The Secretary-General concluded that effective actions to promote multilingualism would require policy guidance from the General Assembly, concerted efforts from Member States and the Secretariat, as well as adequate resources, particularly regarding public information activities.

Communications. On 11 April [A/56/93], the 20 Spanish-speaking Member States at the United Nations drew the attention of the Secretary-General to the growing tendency throughout the UN system to favour the use of only one language in the secretariats and governing bodies of its organizations, and expressed their concern over the failure to accord equal treatment to the Spanish language in the area of public information. They cited, in particular, the content of the Organization's web site, noting that the gulf between public information available in Spanish and in English was widening. They urged that measures be taken to correct the imbalance, that the Organization's language policy be rigorously applied to public information, and that Spanish sections be established in DPI's information and news services, as well as in all departments publishing official information on the Internet.

In an 18 June reply [A/56/176], the Secretary-General assured those States of his commitment to a multilingual approach to information dissemination. However, he noted that the creation of public information and other materials in the six official languages, when resources had been provided for their production in only one or two languages, was problematic, requiring an infusion of substantial additional resources and/or a reduction in mandates. Initiatives to improve linguistic balance in the Organization's published output within existing resources included broadening the cadre of creators of web sites in official languages, notably in Spanish, through its training programmes. Also, UN information centres were active in creating web sites in local official and non-official languages, especially in Spanish-speaking countries, where a wide range of information material was produced in Spanish. Certain Member States had offered substantive assistance to the Organization in that regard through the Associate Expert Programme, and the Secretary-General invited other interested Member States to do likewise.

On 31 July [A/56/261], Qatar, on behalf of the League of Arab States, informed the Secretary-General that the Arab Group was deeply concerned by declining standards in Arabic language services, both in the conference services context and in UN information activities. The deterioration confirmed that there was, within the UN system, discrimination in the treatment accorded the Organization's official languages on the one hand, and the working languages on the other hand, particularly English. (For General Assembly action on multilingualism, see section III of **resolution 56/64 B** (p. 561)).

Proposed regulations governing the status, basic rights and duties of non-Secretariat officials and experts on mission

As requested in General Assembly resolution 55/221 [YUN 2000, p. 1344], the Secretary-General, in May [A/55/928], reported on consultations he had held with the Chairmen of ACABQ, ICSC, JIU and the International Law Commission, as well as

the Executive Chairman of the United Nations Monitoring, Verification and Inspection Commission (UNMOVIC), on proposed draft regulations governing the status, basic rights and duties of officials other than Secretariat officials and of experts on mission. He also expected to receive comments from the group of special rapporteurs of the Commission on Human Rights on the application of the proposed draft regulations to human rights experts on mission. Based on the comments received, the Secretary-General proposed adjustments to the proposed draft regulations and explanatory commentary, set out in annexes I and II to the report, which he intended to recommend to the Assembly for consideration.

By **decision 55/482** of 14 June, the Assembly deferred consideration of the Secretary-General's report until its fifty-sixth session.

In an October report [A/56/437], the Secretary-General submitted the comments received from the eighth meeting of special rapporteurs, special representatives, independent experts and chairpersons of working groups of the Commission on Human Rights on the proposed draft regulations. He recommended the consolidated draft regulations, annexed to the report, to the Assembly for consideration.

Staff rules and regulations

In accordance with staff regulation 12.3 stipulating that the full text of provisional staff rules and amendments should be reported annually to the General Assembly, the Secretary-General, in a July report [A/56/227], outlined amendments to the 100, 200 and 300 series of Staff Rules, together with the rationale for the changes.

The Secretary-General recommended that the Assembly take note of the amendments in the annex to the report, which he proposed to implement as from 1 January 2002.

Note by Secretariat. As requested in section VIII of Assembly resolution 55/258 (see p. 1340), the Secretariat, in October [A/C.5/56/3], provided details on the Secretary-General's elimination of documentation on obsolete or redundant rules and procedures, as part of ongoing efforts at human resources management reform. Altogether, 460 documents, dating from 1 June 1997 to 31 August 2001, had been abolished or had lapsed or expired.

Safety and security

In response to General Assembly resolution 55/175 [YUN 2000, p. 1348], the Secretary-General issued an interim report in September [A/56/384 & Corr.1] on the safety and security of humanitarian personnel and the protection of UN personnel, which provided information on threats against

UN personnel and measures taken to enhance staff security. The Secretary-General stated that continued incidents of violence against UN and humanitarian personnel had resulted in the death of three more UN civilian staff members, bringing the total number lost since 1992 to 201, and four cases of hostage-taking involving 10 UN system personnel, bringing that number to 255 since 1994. They, together with staff from non-governmental organizations (NGOs), also continued to be targets of rape and sexual assault, ambushes, armed robbery and other attacks, including carjackings, harassment and arrest and detention. The alarming increase in the danger to humanitarian personnel over the past decade was largely attributable to the proliferation and enlargement of irregular armed groups that often did not respect the neutrality and impartiality of such personnel and/or rejected the international agreements providing for them. The majority of perpetrators of attacks upon humanitarian workers had gone unpunished, while the few that had been apprehended received only light penalties.

The Secretary-General drew attention to the measures he was proposing to enhance staff security, including the appointment of a full-time UN Security Coordinator at the Assistant Secretary-General level to provide the leadership required for increasing the efficacy of UN security management. The Office of the Security Coordinator was being strengthened by the recruitment of additional staff to enable it to respond more effectively to new crises, develop and undertake more security training, initiate inspection and compliance missions, ensure better coordination and exercise greater authority in the security management system. UN agencies, programmes and funds had also shown greater commitment to security management and training, enabling staff serving at 29 high-risk duty stations to benefit from such training provided by the Office during 2001. The rigorous training had reinforced significantly the overall competence of the UN security management system as an inter-agency and integrated initiative. At the field level, the primary aim was to strengthen the security management system through improved coordination and collaboration on security between the United Nations and its partners.

Other measures taken to enhance security arrangements included increased stress management training, stress counselling, the development of minimum operating security and minimum telecommunications standards. UN/NGO security collaboration was also enhanced.

The Secretary-General recommended that greater efforts be made to prevent violence against humanitarian personnel and to bring perpetrators to justice. It should be made clear that violence towards humanitarian workers undermined the legitimacy of any group seeking political recognition or entitlements. In addition, UN and humanitarian personnel had to be provided with the tools and ability to minimize their exposure to risks. Member States should ensure, when establishing mandates, that proper and adequate means were placed at the disposal of UN system organizations to safely fulfil those mandates, and should insist on a universally accepted and respected system of security coordination, with appropriate funding for personnel, training and equipment. Inter-agency collaboration should be improved and strengthened through the harmonization of security management. Personnel, on their part, should ensure that they were well informed about the security conditions in their areas of assignment. The Secretary-General was therefore instructing senior officials to provide security training and awareness to every staff member. He would also pursue the implementation of preventive risk management. The Secretary-General called on Member States to contribute generously to the security proposals contained in UN consolidated appeals and to the Trust Fund for Security of Staff Members of the United Nations System.

The Secretary-General, in a 15 October report [A/56/469 & Corr.1,2], submitted in response to Assembly resolution 55/238, section II [YUN 2000, p. 1300], outlined the evolution of the current security management system, presented comprehensive proposals for strengthening the Office of the Security Coordinator at Headquarters and for improving the safety of UN personnel in the field, and outlined the agreed modalities for cost-sharing of the total resource requirements for safety and security among UN agencies, funds and programmes. His proposals included maintaining the Office of the Security Coordinator as a separate organizational structure, the appointment of a full-time Security Coordinator at the Assistant Secretary-General level, and the establishment of 92 additional field security offices in the most critical locations to replace the existing organizational field structure. In that regard, the Secretary-General further proposed the recruitment of 98 Professional and 10 General Service staff, 184 local-level staff and 92 field security officers. Estimated resource requirements for the new security management system for the 2002-2003 biennium totalled $53,366,400, to be apportioned among the participating organizations on the basis of the cost-sharing formula outlined by the Secretary-General. The UN share of that cost amounted to $11,987,100, resulting in revised budget estimates of $10,421,200, an increase of $7,996,400 over the original estimates of $2,424,000

proposed for inter-organizational security measures under section 30, Special expenses, of the
proposed 2002-2003 programme budget.

ACABQ report. ACABQ, in November [A/56/
619], recommended acceptance of the Secretary-
General's staffing proposals. Noting that some of
the posts established in Assembly resolution
55/238 [YUN 2000, p. 1300], effective 1 January 2001,
had not been filled, ACABQ asked that the recruitment process be expedited. ACABQ stated that it
did not see the need for a P-4 post in the Department of Peacekeeping Operations (DPKO) to serve
as liaison with the Office of the Security Coordinator, and asked that further efforts be made to
clarify the relationship and interaction between
the two offices. Regarding the Office's proposed
new organizational structure and the disposition
of the field security offices, ACABQ said it expected that the arrangement would not compromise the role of the Security Coordinator in performing security functions on behalf of the United
Nations and its specialized agencies, funds and
programmes. ACABQ stressed the need to define
expeditiously clear lines of responsibility and
accountability in ensuring staff safety and security, and asked the Secretary-General to report to
the General Assembly in 2002 on progress made
in that regard.

On the question of the cost-sharing arrangement, ACABQ stressed that participating entities
should share fully in all costs and adhere to
the shared financial responsibilities in the coordinated management of the safety and security
of UN personnel. It requested the Secretary-
General to ensure that the funds of participating
organizations were transferred for that purpose as
at 1 January of each year, and that the UN share
was not exceeded without the Assembly's prior approval. He should also report on the implementation of the cost-sharing agreement to facilitate a
better assessment of the security-related funds involved and the benefits of the proposed arrangement. (For General Assembly action on the
Secretary-General's human resource and financing proposals for the UN security management
system and ACABQ's recommendations thereon,
see section VIII of **resolution 56/255** (p. 1320).)

GENERAL ASSEMBLY ACTION

On 21 December [meeting 91], the General Assembly adopted **resolution 56/217** [draft: A/56/L.64
& Add.1] without vote [agenda item 20].

**Safety and security of humanitarian personnel and
protection of United Nations personnel**

The General Assembly,

Reaffirming its resolution 46/182 of 19 December
1991 on strengthening of the coordination of humanitarian emergency assistance of the United Nations,

Recalling its resolutions 53/87 of 7 December 1998,
54/192 of 17 December 1999 and 55/175 of 19 December 2000 on safety and security of humanitarian personnel and protection of United Nations personnel, as
well as resolutions 52/167 of 16 December 1997 on
safety and security of humanitarian personnel and
52/126 of 12 December 1997 on protection of United
Nations personnel,

Taking note of the report of the Secretary-General
on the protection of civilians in armed conflict and of
Security Council resolutions 1265(1999) of 17 September 1999 and 1296(2000) of 19 April 2000 and the recommendations made therein, as well as the statements
by the President of 30 November 1999, on the role of
the Security Council in the prevention of armed conflicts, 13 January 2000, on humanitarian assistance to
refugees in Africa, 9 February 2000, on protection of
United Nations personnel, associated personnel and
humanitarian personnel in conflict zones, and
9 March 2000, on humanitarian aspects of issues before the Security Council, and in this context also noting the range of views expressed during all open debates of the Security Council on these issues,

Taking note also of the report of the Special Committee on Peacekeeping Operations, as well as the report
of the Special Committee on the report of the Panel on
United Nations Peace Operations and the report of the
Secretary-General on the implementation of the report of the Panel,

Reaffirming the need to promote and ensure respect
for the principles and rules of international humanitarian law,

Deeply concerned by the growing number of complex
humanitarian emergencies in the past few years, in
particular in armed conflicts and in post-conflict situations, which have dramatically increased the loss of human lives, in particular of civilians, the suffering of
victims, flows of refugees and internally displaced persons, as well as material destruction, which disrupt the
development efforts of the countries affected, in particular those of developing countries,

Concerned by the increasingly difficult context in
which humanitarian assistance takes place in some
areas, in particular the continuous erosion, in many
cases, of respect for the principles and rules of international humanitarian law,

Deeply concerned by the dangers and security risks
faced by humanitarian personnel and United Nations
and associated personnel at the field level, and mindful
of the need to improve the current security management system in order to improve their safety and security,

Strongly deploring the rising toll of casualties among
national and international humanitarian personnel
and United Nations and associated personnel in complex humanitarian emergencies, in particular in
armed conflicts and in post-conflict situations,

Strongly condemning the acts of murder and other
forms of violence, rape and sexual assault, intimidation, armed robbery, abduction, hostage-taking, kidnapping, harassment and illegal arrest and detention
to which those participating in humanitarian operations are increasingly exposed, as well as attacks on humanitarian convoys and acts of destruction and looting
of their property,

Strongly condemning also all incidents in many parts of the world in which humanitarian personnel have been deliberately targeted, and expressing profound regret at the deaths of all United Nations and other personnel involved in the provision of humanitarian assistance,

Reaffirming that ensuring the safety and security of United Nations personnel constitutes an underlying duty of the Organization, which must be based on a necessary cost-sharing arrangement with the relevant agencies, funds and programmes within the United Nations system,

Recalling that primary responsibility under international law for the security and protection of humanitarian personnel and United Nations and associated personnel lies with the Government hosting a United Nations operation conducted under the Charter of the United Nations or its agreements with relevant organizations,

Urging all other parties involved in armed conflicts, in compliance with international humanitarian law, in particular their obligations under the Geneva Conventions of 12 August 1949 and the obligations applicable to them under the Additional Protocols thereto, of 8 June 1977, to ensure the security and protection of all humanitarian personnel and United Nations and associated personnel,

Expressing concern that the occurrence of attacks and threats against humanitarian personnel and United Nations and associated personnel is a factor that increasingly restricts the ability of the Organization to provide assistance and protection to civilians in fulfilment of its mandate and Charter,

Recalling the inclusion of attacks intentionally directed against personnel involved in a humanitarian assistance or peacekeeping mission in accordance with the Charter as a war crime in the Rome Statute of the International Criminal Court, adopted on 17 July 1998, and noting the role that the Court could play in appropriate cases in bringing to justice those responsible for serious violations of international humanitarian law,

Noting that the Convention on the Safety of United Nations and Associated Personnel, which entered into force on 15 January 1999, has been ratified by fifty-five Member States as at the present date,

Mindful of the need to promote universality of the Convention on the Safety of United Nations and Associated Personnel,

Reaffirming the fundamental requirement that appropriate modalities for the safety and security of humanitarian personnel and United Nations and associated personnel be incorporated into all new and ongoing United Nations field operations,

Increasingly concerned at the need to ensure adequate levels of safety and security for United Nations personnel and humanitarian personnel and a culture of accountability at all levels, from the highest to the lowest, throughout the United Nations system, and in this regard commending the recent efforts by the United Nations agencies, funds and programmes aimed at the improvement of security management and training of their personnel,

Commending the courage and commitment of those who take part, often at great personal risk, in humanitarian operations, especially of locally recruited staff,

Guided by the relevant provisions on protection contained in the Convention on the Privileges and Immunities of the United Nations of 13 February 1946, the Convention on the Privileges and Immunities of the Specialized Agencies of 21 November 1947, the Convention on the Safety of United Nations and Associated Personnel, the Geneva Convention relative to the Protection of Civilian Persons in Time of War of 12 August 1949 and the Additional Protocols to the Geneva Conventions, and Amended Protocol II of 3 May 1996 to the Convention on Prohibitions and Restrictions on the Use of Certain Conventional Weapons Which May Be Deemed to Be Excessively Injurious or to Have Indiscriminate Effects of 10 October 1980,

1. *Takes note with appreciation* of the report of the Secretary-General on the safety and security of humanitarian personnel and protection of United Nations personnel;

2. *Urges* all States to take the necessary measures to ensure the full and effective implementation of the relevant principles and rules of international law, including international humanitarian law, as well as the relevant provisions of human rights and refugee law related to the safety and security of humanitarian personnel and United Nations personnel;

3. *Also urges* all States to take the necessary measures to ensure the safety and security of humanitarian personnel and United Nations and associated personnel and to respect and ensure respect for the inviolability of United Nations premises, which are essential to the continuation and successful implementation of United Nations operations;

4. *Calls upon* all Governments and parties in complex humanitarian emergencies, in particular in armed conflicts and in post-conflict situations, in countries in which humanitarian personnel are operating, in conformity with the relevant provisions of international law and national laws, to cooperate fully with the United Nations and other humanitarian agencies and organizations and to ensure the safe and unhindered access of humanitarian personnel in order to allow them to perform efficiently their task of assisting the affected civilian population, including refugees and internally displaced persons;

5. *Strongly condemns* any act or failure to act, contrary to international law, which obstructs or prevents humanitarian personnel and United Nations personnel from discharging their humanitarian functions, or which entails being subjected to threats, the use of force or physical attack, frequently resulting in injury or death, and affirms the need to hold accountable those who commit such acts and, for that purpose, the need to enact national legislation, as appropriate;

6. *Urges* all States to ensure that any threat or act of violence committed against humanitarian personnel on their territory is fully investigated and to take all appropriate measures, in accordance with international law and national law, to ensure that the perpetrators of such acts are duly prosecuted;

7. *Requests* the Secretary-General to take the necessary measures to ensure full respect for the human rights, privileges and immunities of United Nations and other personnel carrying out activities in fulfilment of the mandate of a United Nations operation and to continue to consider ways and means in which to strengthen the protection of United Nations and other

personnel carrying out activities in fulfilment of the mandate of a United Nations operation, notably by seeking the inclusion, in negotiations of headquarter and other mission agreements concerning United Nations and associated personnel, of the applicable conditions contained in the Convention on the Privileges and Immunities of the United Nations, the Convention on the Privileges and Immunities of the Specialized Agencies and the Convention on the Safety of United Nations and Associated Personnel;

8. *Emphasizes* the importance of paying special attention to the safety and security of United Nations and associated personnel engaged in United Nations peacekeeping and peace-building operations;

9. *Recommends* that the Secretary-General continue to seek the inclusion of relevant provisions of the Convention on the Safety of United Nations and Associated Personnel in the status-of-forces or status-of-mission agreements concluded by the United Nations;

10. *Calls upon* all States to provide adequate and prompt information in the event of arrest or detention of humanitarian personnel or United Nations personnel, to afford them the necessary medical assistance and to allow independent medical teams to visit and examine the health of those detained, and urges them to take the necessary measures to ensure the speedy release of United Nations and other personnel carrying out activities in fulfilment of the mandate of a United Nations operation who have been arrested or detained in violation of their immunity, in accordance with the relevant conventions referred to in the present resolution and applicable international humanitarian law;

11. *Underlines* the need to allocate adequate and predictable resources to the safety and security of United Nations personnel;

12. *Calls upon* all other parties involved in armed conflicts, in compliance with international humanitarian law, in particular their obligations under the 1949 Geneva Conventions and the obligations applicable to them under the Additional Protocols thereto, to ensure the safety and protection of humanitarian personnel and United Nations and associated personnel, to refrain from abducting or detaining them in violation of their immunity under relevant conventions referred to in the present resolution and applicable international humanitarian law, and speedily to release, without harm, any abductee or detainee;

13. *Encourages* all States to become parties to and respect fully their obligations under the relevant international instruments, including the Convention on the Safety of United Nations and Associated Personnel;

14. *Calls upon* all States to consider becoming parties to the Rome Statute of the International Criminal Court;

15. *Reaffirms* the obligation of all humanitarian personnel and United Nations and associated personnel to observe and respect the national laws of the country in which they are operating, in accordance with international law and the Charter of the United Nations;

16. *Calls upon* all States to promote a climate of respect for the security of United Nations and humanitarian personnel;

17. *Requests* the Secretary-General to take the necessary measures, falling within his responsibilities, to ensure that security matters are an integral part of the planning for existing and newly mandated United Nations operations and that such precautions extend to all United Nations and associated personnel;

18. *Also requests* the Secretary-General to take the necessary measures to ensure that United Nations and other personnel carrying out activities in fulfilment of the mandate of a United Nations operation are properly informed about the conditions under which they are called upon to operate, including relevant customs and traditions in the host country, and the standards that they are required to meet, including those contained in relevant domestic and international law, and that adequate training in security, human rights and international humanitarian law is provided so as to enhance their security and effectiveness in accomplishing their functions, and reaffirms the necessity for all other humanitarian organizations to provide their personnel with similar support;

19. *Emphasizes* the need to give further consideration to the safety and security of locally recruited humanitarian personnel, who account for the majority of casualties, and United Nations and associated personnel;

20. *Requests* the Office of the United Nations Security Coordinator to continue to play a central role in promoting increased cooperation and collaboration among agencies, funds and programmes in the planning and implementation of measures aimed at improving staff security training and awareness;

21. *Stresses* the need to ensure that all United Nations staff members receive adequate security training, including physical and psychological training, prior to their deployment to the field, the need to attach a high priority to the improvement of stress and trauma counselling services available to United Nations staff members, including through the implementation of a comprehensive security and stress and trauma management training, support and assistance programme for United Nations staff throughout the system, before, during and after missions, and the need to make available to the Secretary-General the means for this purpose;

22. *Encourages* all States to contribute to the Trust Fund for Security of Staff Members of the United Nations System;

23. *Reaffirms* the need to strengthen the Office of the United Nations Security Coordinator, and in this regard reiterates the need for the appointment of a full-time Security Coordinator, at the appropriate level, so as to enable the Office to enhance its capacity in the discharge of its duties, in consultation with the Office for the Coordination of Humanitarian Affairs of the Secretariat and appropriate agencies within the Inter-Agency Standing Committee, and calls for expeditious consideration of this recommendation;

24. *Recognizes* the need for a strengthened and comprehensive security management system for the United Nations system, both at the headquarters and the field level, and requests the United Nations system, as well as Member States, to take all appropriate measures needed to that end;

25. *Also recognizes* the need for enhanced coordination and cooperation, both at the headquarters and the field level, between the United Nations security management system and non-governmental organizations on matters relating to the safety and se-

curity of humanitarian personnel and United Nations and associated personnel, with a view to addressing mutual security concerns in the field;

26. *Welcomes* the establishment, in accordance with resolution 56/89 of 12 December 2001, of an Ad Hoc Committee open to all Member States or members of the specialized agencies or of the International Atomic Energy Agency, to consider the recommendations made by the Secretary-General in his report on measures to strengthen and enhance the protective legal regime for United Nations and associated personnel;

27. *Calls upon* all States to consider becoming parties to and to respect fully their obligations under the Convention on the Privileges and Immunities of the United Nations and the Convention on the Privileges and Immunities of the Specialized Agencies, which have been ratified so far by one hundred and forty-five States and one hundred and seven States, respectively;

28. *Recalls* the essential role of telecommunication resources in facilitating the safety of humanitarian personnel and United Nations and associated personnel, calls upon States to consider signing and ratifying the Tampere Convention on the Provision of Telecommunication Resources for Disaster Mitigation and Relief Operations of 18 June 1998, and encourages them, pending the entry into force of the Convention, to facilitate, consistent with their national laws and regulations, the use of communications equipment in such operations;

29. *Requests* the Secretary-General to submit to it at its fifty-seventh session a comprehensive, updated report on the safety and security situation of humanitarian personnel and protection of United Nations personnel and on the implementation of the present resolution, including the progress made by the Secretary-General in pursuing accountability and assessing responsibility for all individual security incidents that involve United Nations and associated personnel at all levels throughout the United Nations system, as well as an account of the measures taken by Governments and the United Nations to prevent and respond to such incidents.

In other action, the Assembly, in section VIII of **resolution 56/255** of 24 December (see p. 1320), endorsed ACABQ's recommendations and requested that the apportionment of expenses be updated in 2003. It requested the Secretary-General to submit in 2002 a report on the establishment of a clear mechanism of accountability and responsibility. He should evaluate the UN security system and report his findings and recommendations to the Assembly at its fifty-eighth (2003) session.

In related action, the Assembly, by **resolution 56/89** (see p. 1227), established an Ad Hoc Committee to consider the Secretary-General's recommendations on measures to strengthen and enhance the protective legal regime for UN and associated personnel.

Delegation of authority

The General Assembly, by **decision 55/481** of 14 June, welcomed the 2000 JIU report [YUN 2000, p. 1350] on the delegation of authority for the management of human and financial resources in the UN Secretariat and endorsed its recommendations. It also took note of the comments of the Secretary-General thereon. The Assembly decided to consider the relevant ACABQ report during the main part of its fifty-sixth (2001) session.

ACABQ report. In its first report on the proposed programme budget for the 2002-2003 biennium [A/56/7], ACABQ expressed concern that the delegation of authority to programme managers and their accountability for the recruitment and placement of staff, performance management and career development were not among the areas in which the Office of Human Resources Management (OHRM) expected to progress in furthering reforms during the coming biennium. Pointing out that delegation of authority was not synonymous with abdication of responsibility, ACABQ emphasized that, for orderly and efficient functioning and for managers to be held accountable for actions under delegated authority, what was being delegated should be clearly spelled out in writing. Monitoring of its implementation needed to be streamlined to avoid excessive reporting and other costly bureaucratic processes. ACABQ requested that the issue be addressed immediately, and information on the proposed course of action be provided to the General Assembly at its fifty-sixth session. Noting the dual delegation to the same programme manager at different levels for regular budget and extrabudgetary posts, ACABQ recommended that the implementation of delegation of authority in personnel action be reviewed and steps taken to ensure that it did not contribute to undue delays in personnel action, especially at the main duty stations.

By **decision 56/461** of 24 December, the Assembly requested the Secretary-General, in the implementation of JIU recommendations on the delegation of authority for the management of human and financial resources in the UN Secretariat, to take fully into account ACABQ's observations (above).

Young professionals

JIU report. The Secretary-General, in February [A/55/798], transmitted to the General Assembly a JIU report comparing and analysing policies and practices on the recruitment and management of entry-level professionals in selected UN system organizations, with a view to recommending ways to retain dedicated and competent professionals.

JIU observed that, in most organizations of the system, up to half of the staff were scheduled to retire during the decade, which called for the revitalization of human resources and careful succession planning. The large numbers of scheduled retirements should be seen as an opportunity not only to reduce workforces and budgets, but also to recruit younger staff with expert knowledge in such emerging fields as information management and technology, governance, sustainable development and capacity-building. Factors hampering such recruitment included the growing tendency to hire a significant proportion of the workforce at the P-4 and higher levels, insufficient competitiveness of salaries at the lowest levels of the Professional scale, the steady increase in the entry-level age as people stayed in school longer and requisite qualifications became stricter, and a steady outflow of young professionals through resignation, as the UN system appeared to be losing part of its appeal as an employer. Of particular concern was the situation at the UN Secretariat, where, between July 1998 and June 1999, more staff resigned (298) than retired (176), including 113 in the Professional category, of whom a third were staff at the P-2 level. Other factors hampering the recruitment and career prospects of young professionals included delays in placing candidates successful at the National Competitive Recruitment Examination (NCRE) and the protracted bureaucratic processes involved in other recruitment systems; insufficient structures for staff integration, orientation and development; limited opportunities for lateral or upward mobility; failure of management to provide enough support and attention to staff concerns; and conditions of service, including salaries, benefits and family-related matters.

JIU recommended that efforts be made to reduce the entry-level age for recruitment to all Professional-level posts, particularly for P-1 to P-3 posts. In that context, the UN Secretariat might wish to review the age-limit imposed on NCRE candidates. The separation of Professional staff should be more carefully monitored through the annual publication of data on grade and type of separation and from exit questionnaires to better identify the causes. Recruitment processes in all organizations of the common system, including under NCRE, should be speeded up. Member States should cooperate more effectively in organizing and publicizing NCRE examinations and the Secretary-General could include in regular reports on human resources management examples of good practices in that regard. Other recommendations related to measures to facilitate the successful integration of young professionals and

their career development, through assistance with practical problems and appropriate orientation courses, as well as through such incentives as mentoring programmes, study schemes and opportunities for upward or lateral mobility, and, in addition to job satisfaction, support on family-related issues, such as spouse employment.

Report of Secretary-General. In March [A/55/798/Add.1], the Secretary-General submitted to the General Assembly his comments and those of ACC on the JIU report on young professionals (above). Underlining that significant differences existed between organizations' mandates, structures and size of workforce, among other features, the Secretary-General noted that there was no single "best practice" in human resources management to which UN agencies could look as a universal model. Best practice was what worked best in the context and interest of each organization. Similarly, human resources requirements and strategies, which should be matched to the programme needs of an organization, had to be determined by each organization rather than subjected to any form of common prescription across the UN system, as recognized by ICSC in its framework for human resources management [YUN 2000, p. 1337]. Instead of organizations appointing mostly young persons who would rise through the ranks, as had been the practice, organizations were inclined to seek high-level specialists with global experience, owing to demands for immediate advice on such highly complex issues as nuclear safety, the spread of HIV/AIDS or industrial restructuring. Consequently, "entry level" for many specialized agencies might often refer to someone in midcareer, recruited for senior specialist responsibilities at the P-4 or P-5 level. At the same time, organizations had to compete with other global employers for a talented workforce. To recruit and retain good performers, reduce turnover and promote institutional loyalty, competitive employment conditions were of paramount importance.

There was overall agreement with most of JIU's recommendations (see above). However, on the question of recruitment, including through NCRE, it was clarified that each organization had to meet its own requirements and procedures, and opportunities for attracting and retaining a quality workforce should be managed within budgetary constraints and in the light of an organization's projected skill/competence requirements.

The General Assembly, by **decision 55/480** of 14 June, deferred until its fifty-sixth (2001) session consideration of the JIU report on young professionals, as well as the Secretary-General's comments and those of ACC thereon (above).

ACABQ report. ACABQ, in its first report on the proposed programme budget for the 2002-2003 biennium [A/56/7], considered the JIU report on young professionals (see p. 1352) as a valuable contribution to the debate on the best means of adopting a realistic personnel management and planning strategy for the rejuvenation of the Secretariat. It noted, however, that in the Secretary-General's comments no mention was made of the issue of rejuvenation among the outputs to be delivered by OHRM during the 2002-2003 biennium, which was surprising in view of the growing importance of information technology and of the obvious expertise of young professionals in that field.

By **decision 56/462** of 24 December, the Assembly requested the Secretary-General to submit in 2002 a progress report on the question of young professionals in the context of his report on human resources management, taking into account ACABQ's observations.

Mandatory age of separation

As requested in General Assembly resolution 55/258 (see p. 1337), the Secretary-General, in December [A/56/701], reported on his study of the implications of changing the mandatory age of separation for staff members appointed prior to 1 January 1990 from 60 years to 62 years, as was currently applicable to staff appointed on or after that date. He examined the potential number of staff members affected and the possible implications for the age profile of the Organization, geographical distribution, gender balance, career development opportunities, the United Nations Joint Staff Pension Fund (UNJSPF) and related matters. He noted that, as at 30 June 2001, of the 11,244 staff members with appointments of one year or more serving under the 100 series, 5,944 would potentially be affected by a change in the mandatory age of separation (4,061, or two thirds, in the General Service and related categories and Field Service category; 1,883, or one third, in the Professional and higher categories). To examine the implications of a change in the mandatory age of separation, the Secretary-General studied four scenarios for projected separations during the period 2002-2006 when some 1,571 (26 per cent) of the 5,944 staff members appointed prior to 1 January 1990 would reach the current mandatory age of separation of 60. The most likely scenario projected that two thirds of them would separate at 60 as scheduled, with the remaining one third opting for 62 years, which would result in the separation of a total of 1,339 staff members between 2002 and 2006, as against 1,571 retirements under the current policy. Those numbers could be considerably lower because of separations due to early retirement, resignation, expiration of contract, disability and death in service.

The Secretary-General concluded that, in view of the numbers involved, fixing the mandatory age of separation at 62 years for those appointed prior to 1 January 1990 would have a minimal impact on such critical characteristics as the age profile of the Organization, geographical distribution, gender balance and career development opportunities. He projected some positive impact on the actuarial situation of UNJSPF (see p. 1357), especially if other common system organizations adopted the same policy, and on staff morale, considering that all staff members would be treated equally regardless of their date of entrance on duty.

Staff college

ACC action. ACC, at its first regular session of 2001 (Nairobi, Kenya, 2-3 April) [ACC/2001/4], considered arrangements for the institutionalization of the United Nations System Staff College, established by General Assembly resolution 55/207 [YUN 2000, p. 1354]. ACC endorsed the functioning of the College as a system-wide and demand-driven institution dedicated to innovation and reform across the UN system, endorsed the governance structure and funding arrangements for the College, and approved the convening of an inter-agency consultation to finalize a business plan and a draft statute.

Report of Secretary-General. In response to General Assembly resolution 55/207 [YUN 2000, p. 1354], the Secretary-General, in June [A/55/989], presented the final draft of the statute of the United Nations System Staff College, which was annexed to his report.

A key feature of the draft were principles intended to establish true ownership of the Staff College by specialized agencies and other organizations of the UN system. The College would carry out its activities on the basis of the needs of the agencies. Its Board of Governors would be composed of ACC member organizations and would report to ACC. The draft statute also envisaged regular reporting to the Assembly on the activities of the College so that Member States could assess progress and provide overall policy guidance. The principle of system-wide ownership also guided the financing arrangements set out in the draft statute, under which the main part of the College's budget would be met on a cost-sharing basis by the organizations of the system, with further support obtained from fees for courses and voluntary contributions.

While Turin, Italy, would remain the base of the College, it would continue to carry out its activities in different UN system headquarters and field locations through distance learning, in order to reach out to the largest possible number of UN system staff. As part of the United Nations, the College would enjoy the status, privileges and immunities pertaining to the Organization, and the relevant parts of the draft statute would be reflected in the host country agreement to be entered into by the United Nations and the Italian authorities following the adoption of the statute by the Assembly.

The Secretary-General recommended that the Assembly, in adopting the draft statute, reaffirm the objectives of the institution as set out in relevant Assembly resolutions, invite ACC to identify innovative ways of enhancing cooperation and coherence throughout the UN system and express the expectation that the College would contribute to the system's capacity to meet those objectives in a cost-effective way.

GENERAL ASSEMBLY ACTION

On 12 July [meeting 107], the General Assembly adopted **resolution 55/278** [draft: A/55/L.89] without vote [agenda item 97].

Statute of the United Nations System Staff College in Turin, Italy

The General Assembly,

Recalling its resolutions 54/228 of 22 December 1999, 55/207 of 20 December 2000 and 55/258 of 14 June 2001,

Having considered the report of the Secretary-General,

1. *Reaffirms* the role of the United Nations System Staff College as an institution for system-wide knowledge management, training and continuous learning for the staff of the United Nations system, in particular in the areas of economic and social development, peace and security and internal management;

2. *Welcomes* the consultations, held in the framework of the Administrative Committee on Coordination, on the functions, governance and funding of the Staff College aimed, inter alia, at making the new College an innovative instrument to enhance cooperation and coherence throughout the United Nations system, including in system-wide coordination to assist with the implementation of the United Nations Millennium Declaration, as requested in resolution 55/162 of 14 December 2000;

3. *Approves* the statute of the Staff College, as contained in the annex to the present resolution;

4. *Requests* all relevant bodies to expedite those administrative, organizational and logistic arrangements needed to ensure a smooth start of operations of the Staff College as from 1 January 2002;

5. *Invites* the Secretariat to keep the General Assembly informed of the implementation of the present resolution, inter alia, of the activities of the Staff College, its funding situation and its planned work programme, including through informal briefings;

6. *Decides* that the first biennial report on the work, activities and accomplishments of the Staff College, including on collaboration with other relevant United Nations institutions, should be submitted to the General Assembly for its consideration at its fifty-eighth session.

ANNEX
Statute of the United Nations System Staff College

Article I
Establishment

The General Assembly of the United Nations, by adopting the present statute, establishes the United Nations System Staff College as from 1 January 2002 as an institution for system-wide knowledge management, training and continuous learning for the staff of the United Nations system, aimed in particular at the areas of economic and social development, peace and security and internal management of the United Nations system.

Article II
Objectives

1. The Staff College shall serve as a distinct system-wide knowledge-management and learning institution, with a view to fostering a cohesive management culture across the United Nations system. It shall provide strategic leadership and management development for international civil servants with a view to strengthening collaboration within the system in areas of common organizational responsibility; increasing operational effectiveness; enhancing cooperation with States Members and observers of the United Nations, the specialized agencies, regional organizations, nongovernmental organizations and civil society; and developing a more cohesive system-wide management culture.

2. The Staff College shall carry out its activities on the basis of the needs expressed by the agencies of the United Nations system and in close cooperation with training and learning institutes and similar bodies within the United Nations system. It may also collaborate with relevant entities outside the system.

Article III
Location

The Staff College shall be located in Turin, Italy.

Article IV
Governance

1. The Staff College shall have a Board of Governors composed of representatives of the member organizations of the Administrative Committee on Coordination. The Director of the Staff College shall participate as an ex officio member in the work of the Board and shall arrange for secretarial support for the Board.

2. The Board shall meet at least once a year and shall adopt its own rules of procedure, which shall be consistent with the provisions of the present statute.

3. The Board shall be responsible for:

(a) Formulating general policy for the activities of the Staff College;

(b) Considering the work programme and budget, on the basis of proposals submitted by the Director, and making recommendations thereon to the Administrative Committee on Coordination;

(c) Considering ways and means of enhancing the financial resources of the Staff College with a view to ensuring the effectiveness and continuity of its operations;

(*d*) Evaluating the activities of the Staff College and their impact and reporting thereon to the Administrative Committee on Coordination;

(*e*) Submitting an annual report to the Administrative Committee on Coordination.

4. The Board shall establish an expert technical review panel to advise on the development of the activities of the Staff College, to review its performance and to report thereon to the Board. The technical review panel shall be composed of expert staff of the common system organizations who shall be selected by the Board.

5. The Secretary-General, in his capacity as Chairman of the Administrative Committee on Coordination, shall submit a biennial report to the General Assembly on the activities of the Staff College.

Article V
Director and staff

1. The Director of the Staff College shall be appointed by the Secretary-General after consultation with the Administrative Committee on Coordination in the light of criteria recommended by the Board.

2. The Director shall be responsible for the management of the Staff College and accountable for its results in accordance with directives issued by the Board. The Director shall in consultation, as appropriate, with the technical review panel, inter alia:

(*a*) Submit the work programme and budget of the Staff College to the Board for its consideration;

(*b*) Oversee the execution of the work programme and budget of the Staff College;

(*c*) Submit to the Board annual and ad hoc reports on the activities of the Staff College and the execution of its work programme;

(*d*) Manage the staff of the Staff College in accordance with the Staff Regulations and Rules of the United Nations and the terms of the present statute;

(*e*) Coordinate the work of the Staff College with that of related organs of the United Nations system and of relevant institutions outside the system;

(*f*) Negotiate such arrangements, including those with Governments, as may be appropriate with a view to offering and receiving services related to the activities of the Staff College;

(*g*) Seek appropriate funding for the implementation of the work programme of the Staff College;

(*h*) Accept, subject to the provisions of article VII below, voluntary contributions to the Staff College.

3. The staff of the Staff College shall be appointed by the Director on behalf of the Secretary-General, under letters of appointment signed by him or her, and limited to service with the College. The staff shall be responsible to the Director in the exercise of their functions.

4. The terms and conditions of service of the Director and the staff shall be those provided for in the Staff Regulations and Rules of the United Nations, subject to such administrative arrangements as are approved by the Secretary-General in his capacity as Chairman of the Administrative Committee on Coordination.

5. The Director and the staff of the Staff College shall be officials of the United Nations within the meaning of Article 105 of the Charter of the United Nations.

Article VI
Associate collaborators and consultants

1. The Director may designate a limited number of well-qualified persons to serve as associate collaborators of the Staff College. Associate collaborators shall be permitted to pursue their work at the College and shall be expected to provide advice and assistance in matters related to the work programme of the College.

2. Associate collaborators shall be designated for a fixed period in accordance with their qualifications and with the criteria and procedures established by the Director and approved by the Board. Associate collaborators shall be neither staff members of the Staff College nor consultants or officials of the United Nations.

3. The Director may arrange for the services of consultants for special assignments in connection with the work programme of the Staff College.

Article VII
Finance

1. The Financial Regulations and Rules of the United Nations, as well as the financial procedures of the United Nations, shall apply to the financial operations of the Staff College.

2. The Staff College shall have a biennial budget approved by the Administrative Committee on Coordination. A core portion of this budget shall be met by the members of the Committee in accordance with the cost-sharing formula decided upon by it.

3. The Staff College may also receive voluntary contributions from Governments, intergovernmental organizations and foundations and other non-governmental sources.

4. The Director may accept contributions on behalf of the Staff College, provided that no contribution for a specific purpose is accepted if the purpose is inconsistent with the purposes and policies of the College and the Financial Regulations and Rules of the United Nations. Contributions that may directly or indirectly involve an immediate or ultimate financial liability for the College may be accepted only with the approval of the Board, after consultation with the Controller of the United Nations.

5. The Staff College shall organize courses and other activities related to its mandates on a fee basis.

6. The Director of the Staff College shall prepare budgets on a biennial basis. The budget shall show separately the core portion of the budget and projected income and expenditures in respect of voluntary contributions. The Director shall submit the proposed budget to the Board at least six weeks before the session of the Board at which it is to be considered.

7. The Board shall consider the proposed budget and make recommendations thereon to the Administrative Committee on Coordination. The budget, as approved by the Committee, shall be forwarded to the participating agencies. The United Nations shall bill the agencies for their share of the core budget.

8. The funds of the Staff College shall be kept in a separate account to be established by the Secretary-General in accordance with the Financial Regulations and Rules of the United Nations.

9. The funds of the Staff College shall be administered solely for the purposes of the College. The United Nations shall perform all necessary financial and accounting functions for the College, including

acting as custodian of its funds, and shall prepare and certify its biennial accounts.

10. The Director may enter into commitments only if the total amount of such commitments does not exceed the core portion of the budget and the amount of voluntary contributions received.

11. The Staff College shall be subject to audit by the United Nations Board of Auditors in accordance with the Financial Regulations and Rules of the United Nations.

Article VIII
Administrative support

The United Nations shall provide the Staff College with appropriate administrative support. The College shall reimburse such support at a level that shall be determined from time to time in consultations between the United Nations and the Board.

Article IX
Status and authority

1. The Staff College, as part of the United Nations, shall enjoy the status, privileges and immunities provided for in Articles 104 and 105 of the Charter of the United Nations, the Convention on the Privileges and Immunities of the United Nations and other international agreements and United Nations resolutions relating to the status, privileges and immunities of the Organization.

2. The Staff College may, under the authority of the Director, enter into contracts with organizations, institutions or firms for the purpose of carrying out its programmes. The College may acquire and dispose of real and personal property and may take other legal action necessary for the performance of its functions.

Article X
Amendments

Amendments to the present statute may be made by the General Assembly on the recommendation of the Administrative Committee on Coordination.

UN Joint Staff Pension Fund

During the biennium ended 31 December 2001, the number of participants in the United Nations Joint Staff Pension Fund (UNJSPF) increased from 68,935 to 80,082 (16.2 percent); the number of periodic benefits in award increased from 46,199 to 49,416 (7 per cent). On 31 December, the breakdown of the periodic benefits in award was: 15,558 retirement benefits; 10,726 early retirement benefits; 6,509 deferred retirement benefits; 7,687 widows' and widowers' benefits; 8,049 children's benefits; 845 disability benefits; and 42 secondary dependants' benefits. In the course of the biennium, 8,630 lump-sum withdrawal and other settlements were paid.

The Fund was administered by the 33-member United Nations Joint Staff Pension Board, which did not meet in 2001 owing to the biennialization of the work of the Fifth Committee. Instead, the Board's Standing Committee met on its behalf (New York, 9-13 July) [A/56/289] and discussed,

among other subjects, matters relating to the administration and operation of the Fund, revised budget estimates for the 2000-2001 biennium, budget estimates for the 2002-2003 biennium and the authorization for contributions to the Emergency Fund for 2002-2003.

ACABQ, commenting in October [A/56/7/Add.1] on the Standing Committee's report, concurred with its recommendation for revised appropriations for administrative expenses amounting to $59,202,200 for the 2000-2001 biennium and $74,322,400 for the 2002-2003 biennium. It also agreed with the Committee's proposal to supplement voluntary contributions to the Emergency Fund by an amount not exceeding $200,000 for 2002-2003.

Those recommendations were approved by the General Assembly in **resolution 56/255**, section V, of 24 December (see p. 1319).

Pension Fund investments

The market value of UNJSPF assets as at 31 December 2001 was $21.8 billion, a decrease of $2.3 billion from the previous year. The total investment return for the year was -8.4 per cent, which, after adjusting for inflation, represented a "real" rate of return of -9.8 per cent. Investment income from interest and dividends amounted to $614 million. New funds that became available for investment (contributions plus investment income, less benefit payment and administrative expenses) totalled $1.9 billion. The Fund's investment income during the 2000-2001 biennium amounted to $2.2 billion, comprising $1.4 billion in interest and dividends and $810 million in net profit on sales of investments. Investment management costs amounted to $38 million.

The Fund remained one of the most diversified pension funds in the world, with 45.2 per cent of its assets exposed to currencies other than the United States dollar, which was the Fund's unit of account.

Travel-related matters

In October, the Secretary-General submitted his annual report on standards of accommodation for air travel [A/56/426], listing exceptions to those standards from 1 July 2000 to 30 June 2001.

During the period under review, the Secretary-General authorized 37 cases of first-class and 30 of business-class air travel, as exceptions to the standards of accommodation, compared with 78 in the previous reporting period. Included in the first-class group were the Deputy Secretary-General, the President of the General Assembly's fifty-fourth session and the Secretary-General's personal aide/security officer. The Secretary-General noted that, while continuous administrative oversight had kept exceptions at a minimum, they were unavoidable in certain cases.

ACABQ report. ACABQ, in November [A/56/630], welcomed the reduction in the overall number of exceptions to the standards of accommodation for air travel and their related costs. Regarding exceptions on medical grounds, it recommended that they should continue to be made on the merits of each case. ACABQ reiterated the need for clear criteria to determine the level of "eminency" of travellers and that such criteria should be applied to individuals rather than groups.

Administration of justice

The General Assembly, at its resumed fifty-fifth (2001) session, considered certain aspects of the administration of justice in the Secretariat, on which it took a number of decisions, in section XI of **resolution 55/258** of 14 June (see p. 1340), including the establishment of an ombudsman function, the role of the Joint Appeals Board, and the difference between the statutes of the United Nations Administrative Tribunal and the ILO Administrative Tribunal. It also decided to include the item "Administration of justice" in the provisional agenda of its fifty-sixth session.

The General Assembly, on 24 December, decided that the agenda item entitled "Administration of justice at the United Nations" would remain for consideration during its resumed fifty-sixth (2002) session (**decision 56/464**), and that the Fifth Committee would consider the item at that session (**decision 56/458**).

Communication. Guinea-Bissau, in a 22 January note verbale [A/55/751], referred to its previous communication [YUN 2000, p. 1360] concerning the treatment of its national on the Secretariat staff and to the response from the Under-Secretary-General for Management, stating that the staff member had been treated fairly and in full conformity with the applicable rules and policies of the Organization. If that were the case, in the interest of justice, the Department of Management should express support for the detailed investigation being sought. The investigation requested concerned the manner in which the case had been handled by the Departments of Public Information and Management and by the Joint Appeals Board. Guinea-Bissau requested an immediate public trial of the case or, if that was not possible, the staff member in question should be placed on special leave with pay until the matter was resolved.

UN Administrative Tribunal

In its annual note to the General Assembly [A/INF/56/5], the United Nations Administrative Tribunal reported in December, through the Secretary-General, that it had delivered 51 judgements during 2001, relating to cases brought by staff against the Secretary-General or the executive heads of other UN bodies to resolve disputes involving terms of appointment and related issues and regulations. The Tribunal met in plenary in New York on 22 October and held two panel sessions (Geneva, 25 June–27 July; New York, 22 October–30 November).

Chapter IV

Institutional and administrative matters

In 2001, the United Nations addressed a number of institutional and administrative matters to ensure its efficient functioning. The General Assembly commenced its fifty-sixth session on 12 September. Earlier in the year, the Assembly resumed its fifty-fifth session, convened its twenty-fifth (6-9 June) and twenty-sixth (25-27 June) special sessions and resumed its tenth emergency special session. The Assembly granted observer status to the International Development Law Institute, the International Hydrographic Organization and the Community of Sahelo-Saharan States. It also adopted a number of measures to improve its efficiency.

During the year, the Security Council held 192 formal meetings to deal with regional conflicts, peacekeeping operations and a wide variety of other issues related to the maintenance of international peace and security. The Assembly again examined the question of expanding the Council's membership.

The Economic and Social Council held its 2001 organizational session in New York in January and a resumed organizational session in March, May and June. It also held a special high-level meeting with the Bretton Woods institutions in May, its substantive session in Geneva in July and a resumed substantive session in New York in October and December. The Council agreed to change the name of the Administrative Committee on Coordination (ACC) to the United Nations System Chief Executives Board for Coordination (CEB).

The work of UN bodies concerned with administrative and coordination matters, including ACC, the Committee for Programme and Coordination and the Joint Inspection Unit, was also reviewed. ACC continued to give high priority to security issues, adopting a new cost-sharing formula for security-related matters at Headquarters and in the field.

The Committee on Conferences examined requests for changes to the calendar of conferences and meetings for 2001, and again recommended measures to improve the use of conference-servicing resources. The Committee welcomed the establishment of permanent interpretation services at the United Nations Office at Nairobi and was pleased that its conference-servicing facility was becoming organizationally, functionally and budgetarily an integral part of the UN Department of General Assembly Affairs and Conference Services. The Committee commended the re-engineering of the Official Document System that was made available to UN staff and the permanent missions to the United Nations, but expressed serious concern about the growing disparities on the UN web site between English and the other official languages of the Organization.

Other issues addressed included the promotion of information technology, the further development and streamlining of common services, especially at the United Nations Office at Geneva, the use of private management consulting firms, measures to enhance the profitability of UN commercial activities and questions relating to the construction, management and maintenance of UN buildings and facilities.

Institutional machinery

General Assembly

The General Assembly met throughout 2001; it resumed and concluded its fifty-fifth session and held the major part of its fifty-sixth session. The fifty-fifth session was resumed in plenary meetings on 26 January, 14, 22 and 26 February, 9, 14, 16 and 21 March, 12 and 24 April, 18 and 31 May, 12, 14, 22 and 29 June, 12, 13 and 25 July, 1 August and 7 and 10 September. The fifty-sixth session opened on 12 September and continued until its suspension on 24 December.

The Assembly also held its twenty-fifth special session on "Implementation of the outcome of the United Nations Conference on Human Settlements (Habitat II)" from 6 to 9 June (see p. 973) and the twenty-sixth special session on the problem of HIV/AIDS in all its aspects from 25 to 27 June (see p. 1125). It resumed the tenth emergency special session on 20 December to discuss "Illegal Israeli actions in Occupied East Jerusalem and the rest of the Occupied Palestinian Territory" (see p. 414).

The Assembly, by **decision 56/401** of 12 September, postponed its special session on children, scheduled to be held from 19 to 21 September, until a date to be decided by the Assembly at its fifty-sixth session (see p. 1093).

Organization of Assembly sessions

Fifty-sixth session

On 12 September, by **decision 56/400**, the General Assembly, on the recommendation of the General Committee [A/56/250], adopted a number of provisions concerning the organization of its fifty-sixth session. By the same decision, the Assembly postponed the two-day high-level dialogue on strengthening international economic cooperation for development through partnership from 17 and 18 September to 20 and 21 September.

The Assembly authorized the following bodies to meet during its fifty-sixth session: the Committee on the Exercise of the Inalienable Rights of the Palestinian People, the Executive Board of the United Nations Development Programme (UNDP) and the United Nations Population Fund (UNFPA), and the Working Group on the Financing of the United Nations Relief and Works Agency for Palestine Refugees in the Near East (**decision 56/403 A** of 13 September); and the Committee on Relations with the Host Country, the Executive Board of the United Nations Children's Fund (UNICEF) and the Commission for Social Development (**decision 56/403 B** of 19 September).

Credentials

The Credentials Committee, at its first meeting on 18 December [A/56/724], had before it a memorandum by the Secretary-General indicating that, as at 14 December, 119 Member States had submitted the formal credentials of their representatives. Information concerning the representatives of 70 Member States had been communicated also.

The Assistant Secretary-General for Legal Affairs reported that the Secretary-General had received an informal communication from the Interim Authority of Afghanistan indicating that the formal credentials of its representatives would be submitted after it took office on 22 December.

The Committee adopted a resolution accepting the credentials received and recommended a draft resolution to the Assembly for adoption. On 24 December, the Assembly, by **resolution 56/221**, approved the report of the Credentials Committee.

Agenda

During its resumed fifty-fifth session, the General Assembly took a number of actions relating to its agenda, which were listed in **decision 55/402 B**: it decided to consider, in plenary, an additional item on the election of judges of the International Criminal Tribunal for Rwanda; to reopen the item "High-level international intergovernmental consideration of financing for development" in plenary, so as to consider the recommendation of the Preparatory Committee for the High-level International Intergovernmental Event on Financing for Development [A/55/L.77]; to consider in plenary a sub-item on the implementation of the outcome of the United Nations Conference on Human Settlements (Habitat II), so as to consider the recommendation of the Commission on Human Settlements acting as the preparatory committee for the special session of the General Assembly for an overall review and appraisal of the implementation of the outcome of Habitat II [A/55/L.78]; to reopen the item "Report of the Economic and Social Council" so as to consider a draft resolution [A/55/L.80]; to consider in plenary an additional item entitled "2001-2010: Decade to Roll Back Malaria in Africa"; to reopen the item on the United Nations Year of Dialogue among Civilizations so as to consider a draft resolution [A/55/L.81 & Add.1]; to consider, in plenary, the sub-item on the high-level dialogue on strengthening international economic cooperation for development through partnership, so as to consider a letter from the Chairman of the Second (Economic and Financial) Committee [A/55/955]; to include the item on the appointment of the Secretary-General for consideration in plenary; to consider, in plenary, the item on training and research, so as to consider a draft resolution [A/55/L.89]; to consider, in plenary, the item on the Third United Nations Conference on the Least Developed Countries, so as to consider a draft resolution [A/55/L.88 & Add.1]; to reopen the item on support by the UN system of the efforts of Governments to promote and consolidate new or restored democracies, so as to consider a draft resolution [A/55/L.90 & Add.1]; to include an additional item on observer status for Partners in Population and Development in the Assembly; and to reopen the item on the culture of peace, so as to consider a draft resolution [A/55/L.95 & Add.1].

On 12 April, the Assembly deferred until the second part of its resumed fifty-fifth session the items on human resources management (**decision 55/474**) and the Secretary-General's report on the activities of the Office of Internal Oversight Services (OIOS) (**decision 55/476**). It also deferred to its fifty-sixth session consideration of the Secretary-General's reports on strengthening the international civil service (**decision 55/475**), and decided to revert to the question of measures to improve the profitability of the commercial activities of the United Nations at that session (**decision 55/466**).

On 14 June, the Assembly deferred until the main part of its fifty-sixth session consideration of the proposal for the re-establishment of the Ad Hoc Intergovernmental Working Group on the Implementation of the Principle of Capacity to Pay (**decision 55/473 B**); the document entitled "Progress in the implementation of the field assets control system: a module of the field mission logistics system", the Joint Inspection Unit (JIU) report on "Young professionals in selected organizations of the United Nations system: recruitment, management and retention" and the comments of the Secretary-General and of the Administrative Committee on Coordination thereon, and the Secretary-General's report on the participation of United Nations Volunteers in peacekeeping operations (**decision 55/480**); and the Secretary-General's report on the proposed regulations governing the status, basic rights and duties of officials other than Secretariat officials and experts on mission and regulations governing the status, basic rights and duties of the Secretary-General (**decision 55/482**).

On 7 September, the Assembly decided to include in the draft agenda of its fifty-sixth session the following items: the situation of democracy and human rights in Haiti (**decision 55/489**), restructuring and revitalization of the United Nations in the economic, social and related fields (**decision 55/490**), question of Cyprus (**decision 55/491**), comprehensive review of the whole question of peacekeeping operations in all their aspects (**decision 55/492**), improving the financial situation of the United Nations (**decision 55/493**), financing of the United Nations Mission in East Timor (**decision 55/494**), financing and liquidation of the United Nations Transitional Authority in Cambodia (**decision 55/495**), financing of the United Nations Operation in Somalia II (**decision 55/496**), financing of the United Nations Operation in Mozambique (**decision 55/497**), financing of the United Nations Mission in Haiti (**decision 55/498**), financing of the United Nations Observer Mission in Liberia (**decision 55/499**), financing of the United Nations Assistance Mission for Rwanda (**decision 55/500**), financing of the United Nations Transitional Administration for Eastern Slavonia, Baranja and Western Sirmium and the Civilian Police Support Group (**decision 55/501**) and armed aggression against the Democratic Republic of the Congo (**decision 55/502**).

On 10 September, the Assembly decided that the item on the question of equitable representation on and increase in the membership of the Security Council and related matters should be considered during the fifty-sixth session (**decision 55/503**).

On 19 September, by **decision 56/402**, the Assembly, on the recommendation of the General Committee [A/56/250], adopted the agenda [A/56/251 & Add.1] and the allocation of agenda items [A/56/252 & Add.1-3] for the fifty-sixth session.

On 30 October, by the same decision, the Assembly, on the recommendation of the General Committee [A/56/250/Add.1], included in the agenda of the fifty-sixth session an additional item entitled "United Nations Year for Cultural Heritage, 2002" and decided to consider it in plenary.

On 9 November, by the same decision, the Assembly, on the recommendation of the General Committee [A/56/250/Add.2], allocated the item on the administration of justice at the United Nations to the Fifth (Administrative and Budgetary) Committee, on the understanding that any decision requiring amendment to the statute of the United Nations Administrative Tribunal or relating to the establishment of a higher-level jurisdiction would be subject to the advice of the Sixth (Legal) Committee; and decided to consider the report of the Economic and Social Council in plenary, on the understanding that the Second, Third (Social, Humanitarian and Cultural) and Fifth Committees would remain seized of the chapters of the report already referred to them.

On 16 November, by the same decision, the Assembly, on the recommendation of the General Committee [A/56/250/Add.3], decided to allocate to the Sixth Committee the sub-item entitled "Cooperation between the United Nations and the Inter-Parliamentary Union".

On 19 September and 26 November, respectively, the Assembly decided to defer consideration of and include in the provisional agenda of its fifty-seventh (2002) session the question of the Malagasy islands of Glorieuses, Juan de Nova, Europa and Bassas da India (**decision 56/402**) and the item "Question of the Falkland Islands (Malvinas)" (**decision 56/410**).

On 21 December, it took the same action in respect of the following items: "Declaration of the Assembly of Heads of State and Government of the Organization of African Unity on the aerial and naval attack against the Socialist People's Libyan Arab Jamahiriya by the present United States Administration in April 1986" (**decision 56/449**); armed Israeli aggression against the Iraqi nuclear installations and its grave consequences for the established international system concerning the peaceful uses of nuclear energy, the non-proliferation of nuclear weapons and international peace and security (**decision 56/450**); consequences of the Iraqi occupation of and aggression against Kuwait (**decision 56/451**); implementation of the resolutions of the United Nations (**decision 56/452**); launching of global negotiations on international economic cooperation for development (**decision 56/453**); and the question of the Comorian island of Mayotte (**decision 56/454**).

On 29 November, the Assembly decided, on the recommendation of the First (Disarmament and International Security) Committee, to include the following items in the provisional agenda of its fifty-seventh session: towards a nuclear-weapon-free world: the need for a new agenda (**decision 56/411**); establishment of a nuclear-weapon-free zone in Central Asia (**decision 56/412**); United Nations conference to identify ways of eliminating nuclear dangers in the context of nuclear disarmament (**decision 56/413**); Convention on the Prohibition of the Development, Production and Stockpiling of Bacteriological (Biological) and Toxin Weapons and on Their Destruction (**decision 56/414**); Comprehensive Nuclear-Test-Ban Treaty (**decision 56/415**); and review of the implementation of the Declaration on the Strengthening of International Security (**decision 56/417**).

On 21 December, the Assembly took the same action in respect of the sub-item on cooperation between the United Nations and the Southern African Development Community (**decision 56/443**), and the item on the elimination of unilateral extraterritorial coercive economic measures as a means of political and economic compulsion, and decided to consider it at odd-numbered sessions, thereby correcting paragraph 11 of the annex to resolution 55/285 (see p. 1287) (**decision 56/455**).

On 24 December, the Assembly decided to retain 81 items for consideration during its resumed fifty-sixth (2002) session (**decision 56/464**).

Second, Third and Fifth Committees

The General Assembly, by **decision 56/433** of 19 December, approved the organization of work of the Third Committee and its 2002-2003 biennial programme of work. By **decision 56/432** of the same date, the Assembly decided that the Committee should meet during the Assembly's resumed fifty-sixth (2002) session to consider the item on the elimination of racism and racial discrimination, following the issuance of the report of the World Conference against Racism, Racial Discrimination, Xenophobia and Related Intolerance (see p. 615).

The Assembly, by **decision 56/448** of 21 December, approved the biennial programme of work of the Second Committee for 2002-2003. By **decision 56/457** of 24 December, it approved the biennial programme of work of the Fifth Committee for 2002-2003.

Resolutions and decisions of the General Assembly

On 7 September, by **decision 55/488**, the General Assembly adopted the following text: "The General Assembly, while reaffirming paragraph 28 of annex VI to the rules of procedure of the Assembly, reiterates that the terms 'takes note of' and 'notes' are neutral terms that constitute neither approval nor disapproval."

By **decision 56/452** of 21 December, the Assembly deferred consideration of the agenda item "Implementation of the resolutions of the United Nations" and included it in the provisional agenda of its fifty-seventh (2002) session.

Revitalization of the General Assembly

The General Assembly, in **resolution 55/285** of 7 September (see p. 1287), adopted a number of measures to improve its efficiency relating to its agenda, consideration of reports, organization of work, the General Committee, the role of the Assembly President and enhancing the use of modern technology.

Security Council

The Security Council held 192 formal meetings in 2001, adopted 52 resolutions and issued 39 presidential statements. It considered 52 agenda items (see APPENDIX IV). In a September note [A/56/366], the Secretary-General, in accordance with Article 12, paragraph 2, of the Charter of the United Nations and with the consent of the Council, notified the General Assembly of 48 matters relative to the maintenance of international peace and security that the Council had discussed since his previous annual notification [YUN 2000, p. 1371]. The Secretary-General also listed 63 matters that the Council had not discussed since then. On 15 October, the Assembly, by **decision 56/405**, took note of the Secretary-General's note.

By **decision 56/406** of 16 October, the Assembly took note of the Council's report for the period 16 June 2000 to 15 June 2001 [A/56/2].

By **decision 56/464** of 24 December, the Assembly decided that the item on the report of the Council would remain for consideration during its resumed fifty-sixth (2002) session.

Documentation

Working methods and procedures

The Security Council President, in a June note [S/2001/640], indicated that Council members had agreed to continue and strengthen the current practice for disseminating Council resolutions and presidential statements. They had also agreed to disseminate press statements made by the President on behalf of its members as follows: the President should, as requested, draw the attention of the representative(s) of the Member State(s) as well as regional organizations and arrangements concerned to relevant statements made by the President on the Council's behalf or to Council decisions; the Secretariat should continue to inform those concerned, including non-State actors, of Council resolutions, presidential statements and press statements by the President to ensure their promptest communication and widest possible dissemination; and it should also issue, as UN press releases, all press statements made by the President on the Council's behalf, once cleared by the President.

The Council, by presidential statement **S/PRST/2001/3** of 31 January (see p. 79), established a Working Group of the whole on UN peacekeeping operations to address generic peacekeeping issues relevant to the Council's responsibilities.

Membership

The General Assembly continued to examine the question of expanding the Security Council's membership. It considered the report of the Open-ended Working Group on the Question of Equitable Representation on and Increase in the Membership of the Security Council and Other Matters related to the Security Council [A/55/47] (see p. 1289), established by Assembly resolution 48/26 [YUN 1993, p. 212].

In February [A/55/791], Brazil proposed that the Group's working methods be reviewed to ensure that it was not paralysed into inaction by the lack of absolute unanimity on issues of such complexity. It should serve as a catalyst in helping to identify those elements of a reform package that met the broad expectations of the international community for effective and expeditious action in a matter that was central to international peace and security.

The Assembly, by **decision 55/503** of 10 September, took note of the Working Group's report and decided that it should continue its work and report before the end of the Assembly's fifty-sixth session. On 24 December, the Assembly decided that the item on the question of equitable representation on and increase in the membership of the Council and related matters would remain for consideration at its resumed fifty-sixth (2002) session (**decision 56/464**).

Economic and Social Council

The Economic and Social Council held its organizational session for 2001 on 29 and 31 January, a resumed organizational session on 8, 13 and 22 March, 3 May and 4 June, and a special high-level meeting with the Bretton Woods institutions (the World Bank Group and the International Monetary Fund) on 1 May, all in New York. The Council held its substantive session from 2 to 26 July in Geneva, and a resumed substantive session on 10 and 24 October and 26 December in New York.

On 29 January, the Council elected five members of its Bureau for 2001—the President and four Vice-Presidents (see APPENDIX III). The Council also adopted the agenda of its organizational session [E/2001/2 & Add.1].

On 31 January, the Council adopted the provisional agenda of its substantive session [E/2001/1] (**decision 2001/202**) and decided on the working arrangements for that session (**decision 2001/204**). On 2 July, the Council adopted the agenda of its 2001 substantive session [E/2001/100 & E/2001/51 & Add.1], and approved the organization of work of that session [E/2001/L.10 & Corr.1] and requests by non-governmental organizations (NGOs) to be heard [E/2001/81] (**decision 2001/223**).

(For agenda lists, see APPENDIX IV.)

Sessions and segments

During 2001, the Economic and Social Council adopted 48 resolutions and 129 decisions. By **decision 2001/204** of 31 January, the Council decided that the coordination segment of its substantive session should be held from 2 to 4 July; the operational activities segment from 5 to 10 July; the humanitarian affairs segment from 11 to 13 July; the high-level segment from 16 to 18 July; and the general segment from 19 to 25 July. By **decision 2001/207** of the same date, the Council decided that the high-level meeting with the Bretton Woods institutions should be held on 1 May.

The work of the Council in 2001 was summarized in its report to the General Assembly [A/56/3/Rev.1]. On 19 (**decision 56/434**) and 24 (**decision 56/463**) December, the Assembly took note of various chapters of the report and, by **decision 56/464** of 24 December, decided that the item would remain for consideration at its resumed fifty-sixth (2002) session.

2001 and 2002 sessions

On 31 January, the Council decided that the theme of the operational activities segment of its 2001 substantive session should be "Triennial policy review of operational activities for development" (**decision 2001/205**); and for the humanitarian affairs segment the theme would be "Strengthening the coordination of the emergency humanitarian assistance of the United Nations". The Council also decided to hold panel discussions during the segment, details on the organization of which would be worked out at the intersessional informal consultations, on the understanding that various challenges, including gender perspective, would be considered in the panel discussions (**decision 2001/206**). The Council adopted the working arrangements for that segment on 2 July (**decision 2001/225**).

The Council decided on 3 May that the theme for the agenda item on regional cooperation would be "Regional perspective on globalization: an opportunity for catching up or a risk of falling behind in the development process" (**decision 2001/211**).

On 26 July, the Council, by **decision 2001/299**, decided that the theme for the high-level segment of the 2002 substantive session would be "The contribution of human resources development, including in the areas of health and education, to the process of development", and that the theme for the coordination segment would be "Strengthening further the Economic and Social Council, building on its recent achievements, to help it fulfil the role ascribed to it in the Charter of the United Nations as contained in the United Nations Millennium Declaration".

On 24 July, the Council, by **decision 2001/234**, approved the calendar of conferences and meetings for 2002 and 2003 in the economic, social and related fields [E/2001/L.9 & Add.1].

On 20 December, the Council, by **decision 2001/322**, decided that its organizational session for 2002, which had been scheduled from 29 January to 1 February 2002, would instead be held from 12 to 15 February.

Work programme

On 31 January, the Economic and Social Council considered its basic programme of work for 2001 and 2002 [E/2001/1]. By **decision 2001/203**, the Council took note of the list of questions for inclusion in the programme of work for the 2002 substantive session.

Restructuring issues

The Economic and Social Council, on 3 May (**decision 2001/212**), decided to continue consideration of the implementation of General Assembly resolutions 50/227 [YUN 1996, p. 1249] and 52/12 B [YUN 1997, p. 1392] on the restructuring and revitalization of the United Nations in the economic, social and related fields (see p. 1289). It had before it the Secretary-General's report on the subject [A/56/77-E/2001/69], the Secretary-General's note on the special high-level meeting of the Council with the Bretton Woods institutions [E/2001/72], the Secretary-General's report on the work of the functional commissions of the

Council in 2001 [E/2001/95] and the Secretary-General's note on the subsidiary bodies of the Council and the Assembly in the economic, social and related fields [E/2001/INF/3].

On 26 July, the Council adopted **resolution 2001/27** on improving the working methods of its functional commissions (see p. 1290); **decision 2001/304** on confidentiality of the 1503 (confidential communications) procedure (see p. 579); and **decision 2001/305**, in which it noted the Secretary-General's note on the special high-level meeting of the Council with the Bretton Woods institutions.

Office of the President

On 24 October, the Economic and Social Council, by **decision 2001/319**, submitted a draft decision entitled "Office of the President of the Economic and Social Council" for adoption by the General Assembly.

In December, the Assembly, on the recommendation of the Second Committee [A/56/571], adopted **decision 56/456** without vote [agenda item 12].

Office of the President of the Economic and Social Council

At its 92nd plenary meeting, on 24 December 2001, the General Assembly, on the recommendation of the Second Committee, recognizing the important functions entrusted to the Economic and Social Council in the Charter of the United Nations and reaffirming the United Nations Millennium Declaration, in which the General Assembly called, inter alia, for the further strengthening of the Council, building on its recent achievements, to help in fulfilling the role ascribed to it in the Charter, decided that the Office of the President of the Economic and Social Council should be provided with the means to carry out its important functions, taking into account the different arrangements made for the principal organs of the United Nations listed in Article 7, paragraph 1, of the Charter.

Coordination, monitoring and cooperation

Institutional mechanisms

Change of name

The Economic and Social Council, by **decision 2001/321** of 24 October, agreed to the proposal to rename the Administrative Committee on Coordination (ACC) the United Nations System Chief Executives Board for Coordination (CEB), without any change in its mandate, and requested

ACC to submit a comprehensive report on the reform of its machinery to the Council's next session, bearing in mind the relevant reports of the Committee for Programme and Coordination.

ACC (CEB) activities

During 2001, ACC focused its attention on orchestrating closer inter-agency cooperation towards the attainment of the millennium development goals [YUN 2000, p. 49]. In its annual overview report for 2001 [E/2002/55], ACC stated that to ensure a systematic and effective follow-up to the United Nations Millennium Declaration and, in particular, a concerted system-wide response to the achievement of the millennium development goals, it had addressed the follow-up to the outcome of the Millennium Summit (see p. 1278) through a two-pronged strategy: resource mobilization to attain the millennium development goals at the national and international levels, and its review and monitoring process. To enhance the coordination effort in the implementation of the Declaration, the High-level Committee on Programmes (HLCP), along with the United Nations Industrial Development Organization, undertook the preparation of an inventory of ongoing actions and initiatives intended to provide quantitative and qualitative data on UN system activities and to serve as a management tool for helping to locate gaps, overlaps and areas for inter-agency cooperation.

ACC also devoted attention to strengthening system-wide support for the sustainable development of Africa, particularly through the New Partnership for Africa's Development (NEPAD) (see p. 899). In line with NEPAD's priorities, ACC identified areas where urgent action was required. It agreed that the Economic Commission for Africa should continue to act as the system's key interlocutor with African countries at the regional level on NEPAD, and UNDP at the national level, and that the UN system should pursue a deliberate strategy to engender support for NEPAD.

ACC continued to study globalization and its interrelated dimensions, noting the need to remedy the negative aspects in such areas as poverty, hunger, health, education, employment, the environment and the links between migration and problems posed by refugees and internally displaced persons.

ACC continued to give high priority to staff security and safety, endorsing a new cost-sharing formula for security-related costs both at Headquarters and in the field (see p. 1347). It considered arrangements for the institutionalization of the United Nations Staff College, endorsing HLCP's recommendations. ACC also considered

assistance to countries invoking Article 50 of the Charter on assistance to third States affected by the application of sanctions.

Concerning the continuing reform of its own functioning, ACC considered that the networking among agency specialists in different sectors had reached a sufficient level of maturity and that the two new High-level Committees on Programmes and on Management, established in 2000 [YUN 2000, p. 1373], had sufficiently consolidated their work to make it possible to replace the rest of the inter-agency machinery—a rigid hierarchical system of inter-agency committees and subcommittees—by a more flexible system of "networks" of specialists in different areas and by ad hoc inter-agency groups. The secretariats of the former subsidiary bodies were invited to consult on how best the ACC decisions could be implemented.

ACC held two regular sessions during the year (Nairobi, Kenya, 2-3 April; New York, 19-20 October). Its principal subsidiary bodies met as follows:

> High-level Committee on Management, second session (Geneva, 10-11 September); High-level Committee on Programmes, first (Vienna, 26-27 February) and second (Geneva, 25-26 September) sessions.

Bodies on specific subjects met as follows:

> Subcommittee on Oceans and Coastal Areas, tenth session (Paris, 9-11 January); Subcommittee on Nutrition, twenty-eighth session (Nairobi, Kenya, 2-6 April); Subcommittee on Statistical Activities, thirty-fifth session (Vienna, 18-20 September); Inter-Agency Committee on Women and Gender Equality, sixth session (New York, 27 February–2 March); Inter-Agency Committee on Sustainable Development, seventeenth meeting (New York, 22-23 March); Ad Hoc Inter-Agency Meeting on Security (Paris, 14-18 May); Joint United Nations Information Committee, twenty-seventh session (Geneva, 10-12 July).

Report for 2000

ACC's annual report for 2000 [E/2001/55] was considered on 25 June by the Committee for Programme and Coordination (CPC) [A/56/16], which took note of the report. CPC recommended that ACC continue to coordinate the implementation of intergovernmental mandates and report on progress in its annual overview reports, which should place more emphasis on ACC's role in ensuring effective coordination among the organizations of the UN system. CPC noted the reform measures adopted by ACC during 2000 [YUN 2000, p. 1373] and requested that it report on the practical outcomes of those measures in its next annual overview report.

The Economic and Social Council, by **decision 2001/302** of 26 July, took note of ACC's report. It invited ACC to ensure that the reform of its subsidiary machinery strengthened inter-agency bodies and processes with specific mandates from intergovernmental bodies, particularly those related to the coordinated implementation of outcomes of UN conferences and summits, as well as those adopted by the Council and the General Assembly. ACC should keep the Council informed on its reform process. The Council deferred consideration of the ACC report to its resumed substantive session.

By **decision 2001/321** of 24 October, the Council requested a comprehensive report on the reform of ACC's subsidiary machinery at its next (2002) session, bearing in mind the relevant CPC reports.

Programme coordination

The Committee for Programme and Coordination held an organizational meeting in New York on 2 May and its forty-first session from 11 June to 6 July [A/56/16].

The Committee reviewed the efficiency of the administrative and financial functioning of the United Nations. It considered the proposed programme budget for the 2002-2003 biennium, in-depth evaluations of sustainable development and the population programme undertaken by OIOS, and triennial reviews of the implementation of CPC recommendations on the drug control and crime prevention and criminal justice programmes, and suggested themes for future evaluation reports. On coordination questions, the Committee considered ACC's annual report for 2000 [YUN 2000, p. 1373], implementation of the special initiative for the implementation of the United Nations New Agenda for the Development of Africa in the 1990s (see p. 849) and the draft system-wide medium-term plan for the advancement of women (2002-2005) (see p. 1073). It examined JIU's report on the use of consultants in the United Nations [A/55/59] and the Secretary-General's comments thereon [A/55/59/Add.1] and discussed the improvement of its working methods and procedures and its provisional agenda for the forty-second session.

By **decision 2001/303** of 26 July, the Economic and Social Council took note of CPC's report on its forty-first session.

Joint Inspection Unit

The Joint Inspection Unit (JIU), in its thirty-second report to the General Assembly, covering the period 1 January to 31 December 2000 [A/56/34 & Corr.1], examined relations and cooperation with participating organizations and other oversight bodies and follow-up on its reports and recommendations. JIU continued to enhance its functioning and impact, undertaking reviews of the administration and management of the United Nations and that of its participating organizations.

The Unit noted that the goal of having its reports issued in advance of meetings of legislative organs of participating organizations to facilitate their thorough and effective consideration had been hindered by, among other reasons, the tardiness of some secretariats in providing the Unit with timely information and/or comments requested by it. JIU had enhanced interaction with Member States and legislative organs, especially on the question of the handling of its reports. It held informal meetings with Member States represented in Geneva on a number of issues, including its programme of work, and developed and coordinated interaction with other UN oversight bodies and those of participating organizations. Although the majority of executive heads of participating organizations submitted JIU reports to their legislative organs, there were not many instances of specific action being taken on the recommendations contained therein. To improve the situation, the Unit had been enhancing dialogue with a number of participating organizations, which had so far resulted in agreement with the World Health Organization secretariat on follow-up procedures.

(For General Assembly action on the JIU report, see **resolution 56/245**, p. 1286.)

Other coordination matters

Follow-up to international conferences

The Secretary-General submitted, in May [E/2001/73], his report on the implementation of agreed conclusions 2000/2 of the Economic and Social Council's coordination segment [YUN 2000, p. 1376] on the integrated and coordinated conference follow-up, in particular the views of the functional commissions. The report reviewed follow-up to those conclusions, addressing specifically the recommendations on options for ensuring an effective and comprehensive review, at the intergovernmental level, of major UN conferences and summits, and on the functional commissions' capacity to conduct their follow-up.

The Secretary-General said that follow-up to the implementation of agreed conclusions 2000/2 required the commitment of the Council, its functional commissions and UN system entities to adhere to the guidance provided. The Council's monitoring of the various elements of those conclusions should therefore be a regular part of its reporting under the related agenda item. While the Council's focus on integrated follow-up to conferences was part of its ongoing work, further concrete action was required, such as the Council's role in addressing cross-cutting themes common to major UN conferences and summits, promoting integrated and coordinated follow-up, progress towards quantified goals and targets agreed at conferences and those underlined in the Millennium Declaration [YUN 2000, p. 49], including the urgency of charting a course for their achievement and regular monitoring, and the Council's ongoing work on basic indicators for the integrated and coordinated follow-up to conferences at all levels.

In terms of ensuring an effective and comprehensive review at the intergovernmental level of major UN conferences and summits, since the five-year reviews of the conferences of the 1990s had been completed, the challenge was to achieve a balance between continuing implementation and follow-up as part of regular work programmes and the periodic reviews through intergovernmental preparatory processes. Moreover, there was no clear preference for any of the options recommended by the Secretary-General in 2000 [YUN 2000, p. 1375] for conducting the conference reviews.

The Secretary-General recommended that regular assessments by the Council of the Millennium Declaration's goals and targets should include progress in implementing decisions of major UN conferences and summits of the 1990s and their quinquennial reviews, as well as progress in implementing the outcome of the International Conference on Financing for Development (see p. 886), to be held in 2002, in support of those goals. The Council and its functional commissions should specify their role in monitoring those goals and in advising the Assembly on obstacles, constraints and new challenges to progress.

As to the periodic conference reviews, the Council could examine the options proposed by the Secretary-General in 2000 and assume a greater role in the 10-year reviews with the focus on an integrated or multisectoral approach to assessing progress. The commissions should use the agenda item on new trends and emerging issues to elaborate input into the Council's high-level and/or coordination segment, especially when they related to conference follow-up. In the light of the proposed 10-year comprehensive reviews by some commissions, the Council could develop its own forward-looking multi-year programme of work for its coordination segment to reinforce the commissions' work. The Assembly should focus on overall policy issues and consider new and emerging issues and trends that might require in-depth attention.

Also before the Council were the Secretary-General's progress report on the implementation of the ministerial declaration of its 2000 high-level segment (see p. 763) and the report of the UNDP/UNFPA Executive Board on the work of its first regular session of 2001 (see p. 793). Those reports were noted by the Council in **decision 2001/301** of 26 July.

ECONOMIC AND SOCIAL COUNCIL ACTION

On 26 July [meeting 43], the Economic and Social Council adopted **resolution 2001/21** [draft: E/2001/L.41] without vote [agenda item 6].

Integrated and coordinated implementation of and follow-up to the outcomes of the major United Nations conferences and summits

The Economic and Social Council,

Welcoming the resolve, expressed by heads of State and Government in the United Nations Millennium Declaration, to strengthen further the Economic and Social Council, building on its recent achievements, to help it fulfil the role ascribed to it in the Charter of the United Nations,

Recalling that the goals and targets in the economic, social and related fields contained in the Millennium Declaration and the outcomes of the major United Nations conferences and summits, supplemented by the outcomes of their reviews, constitute a comprehensive basis for actions at the national, regional and international levels,

Reaffirming its commitment to promote an integrated and coordinated implementation of and follow-up to the outcomes of the major United Nations conferences and summits and the reviews of their implementation,

Recalling its agreed conclusions 1995/1 and 2000/2 and its relevant resolutions on the integrated and coordinated implementation of and follow-up to the outcomes of the major United Nations conferences and summits,

Having considered the report of the Secretary-General on the implementation of agreed conclusions 2000/2 of the coordination segment of the Council on the integrated and coordinated conference follow-up, in particular the views expressed by functional commissions,

Recognizing the need to continue to enhance its contribution to the coordination and implementation of the outcomes of the major United Nations conferences and summits by bringing together relevant cross-cutting issues in a comprehensive and holistic assessment of progress achieved,

1. *Recalls* that the General Assembly, the Economic and Social Council and the relevant functional commissions or, as appropriate, other relevant bodies of the United Nations system, will continue to play, within their respective mandates, the primary role with regard to the coordinated implementation of and follow-up to the outcomes of the United Nations conferences and summits;

2. *Reiterates its commitment* to assist the General Assembly in its overall responsibilities in follow-up to the United Nations Millennium Declaration, in compliance with General Assembly resolution 55/162 of 14 December 2000, and to the outcomes of the major

United Nations conferences and summits and the reviews of their implementation, as well as in achieving the international development targets;

3. *Underlines* the specific responsibilities of the relevant functional commissions and, as appropriate, other relevant bodies of the United Nations system, in reviewing and assessing progress achieved, lessons learned and problems encountered in the implementation of the outcomes of the major United Nations conferences and summits;

4. *Recommends* that the General Assembly examine how best to address the reviews of the implementation of the outcomes of the major United Nations conferences and summits of the 1990s, including their format and periodicity;

5. *Decides* to strengthen the links with relevant functional commissions and other relevant bodies of the United Nations system, including regional commissions, in the follow-up to conferences and summits, by reviewing progress in the implementation of cross-cutting issues, and to strengthen links with the General Assembly by bringing to its attention overall policy issues that might emerge from such follow-up and might require the consideration of the Assembly;

6. *Encourages* the participation of all relevant stakeholders, including the private sector, in maintaining and strengthening the momentum for building partnerships in pursuit of the goals of the Millennium Summit and of other conferences;

7. *Requests* the Secretary-General to submit a report to the Council at its substantive session of 2002 on the implementation of the present resolution, ensuring full integration between the review and follow-up processes of the Millennium Summit and of other conferences and summits.

GENERAL ASSEMBLY ACTION

On 21 December [meeting 90], the General Assembly, on the recommendation of the Second Committee [A/56/571], adopted **resolution 56/211** without vote [agenda item 12].

Integrated and coordinated implementation of and follow-up to the outcomes of the major United Nations conferences and summits in the economic and social fields

The General Assembly,

Welcoming Economic and Social Council resolution 2001/21 of 26 July 2001,

1. *Decides* to examine how best to address the reviews of the implementation of the outcomes of the major United Nations conferences and summits of the 1990s, in the economic and social fields, including their format and periodicity;

2. *Also decides* to include in the provisional agenda of its fifty-seventh session an item entitled "Integrated and coordinated implementation of and follow-up to the outcomes of the major United Nations conferences and summits in the economic and social fields";

3. *Requests* the Secretary-General to make available to the Assembly the report requested by the Economic and Social Council for consideration at its substantive session of 2002 on the implementation of Council resolution 2001/21.

The UN and other organizations

Cooperation with organizations

Economic Cooperation Organization

In a June report [A/56/122], the Secretary-General described cooperation between the Economic Cooperation Organization and various UN bodies during 2000 and 2001. The General Assembly took action on the report in **resolution 56/44** (see p. 914).

Council of Europe

In response to General Assembly resolution 55/3 [YUN 2000, p. 410], the Secretary-General submitted an August report [A/56/302], which described the cooperation between the United Nations and the Council of Europe. Noting that it would be more useful to report on such cooperation every two years, the Secretary-General recommended that his next report be submitted to the Assembly's fifty-eighth (2003) session.

The Assembly took action on that report in **resolution 56/43** (see p. 399).

Organization of the Islamic Conference

In response to General Assembly resolution 55/9 [YUN 2000, p. 1379], the Secretary-General submitted a September report detailing the cooperation between the United Nations and the Organization of the Islamic Conference (OIC) [A/56/398]. The two organizations continued to work closely in the political, economic, social, cultural and humanitarian fields and to seek solutions to global problems, especially in peace-making and diplomacy. The report outlined follow-up action by UN system organizations on the recommendations of the meetings between the UN system and OIC.

GENERAL ASSEMBLY ACTION

On 7 December [meeting 80], the General Assembly adopted **resolution 56/47** [draft: A/56/L.36 & Add.1] without vote [agenda item 21 (d)].

Cooperation between the United Nations and the Organization of the Islamic Conference

The General Assembly,

Recalling its resolutions 37/4 of 22 October 1982, 38/4 of 28 October 1983, 39/7 of 8 November 1984, 40/4 of 25 October 1985, 41/3 of 16 October 1986, 42/4 of 15 October 1987, 43/2 of 17 October 1988, 44/8 of 18 October 1989, 45/9 of 25 October 1990, 46/13 of 28 October 1991, 47/18 of 23 November 1992, 48/24 of 24 November 1993, 49/15 of 15 November 1994, 50/17 of 20 November 1995, 51/18 of 14 November 1996, 52/4 of 22 October 1997, 53/16 of 29 October 1998, 54/7 of 25 October 1999 and 55/9 of 30 October 2000,

Recalling also its resolution 3369(XXX) of 10 October 1975, by which it decided to invite the Organization of the Islamic Conference to participate in the sessions and the work of the General Assembly and of its subsidiary organs in the capacity of observer,

Having considered the report of the Secretary-General,

Taking into account the desire of both organizations to continue to cooperate closely in the political, economic, social, humanitarian, cultural and scientific fields and in their common search for solutions to global problems, such as questions relating to international peace and security, disarmament, self-determination, decolonization, fundamental human rights and economic and social development,

Recalling the Articles of the Charter of the United Nations that encourage activities through regional cooperation for the promotion of the purposes and principles of the United Nations,

Noting the strengthening of cooperation between the United Nations, its funds and programmes and specialized agencies and the Organization of the Islamic Conference, its subsidiary organs and its specialized and affiliated institutions,

Noting also the encouraging progress made in the ten priority areas of cooperation between the two organizations,

Convinced that the strengthening of cooperation between the United Nations and other organizations of the United Nations system and the Organization of the Islamic Conference and its organs and institutions contributes to the promotion of the purposes and principles of the United Nations,

Noting with appreciation the determination of both organizations to strengthen further the existing cooperation by developing specific proposals in the designated priority areas of cooperation, as well as in the political field,

1. *Takes note with satisfaction* of the report of the Secretary-General;

2. *Notes with satisfaction* the active participation of the Organization of the Islamic Conference in the work of the United Nations towards the realization of the purposes and principles embodied in the Charter of the United Nations;

3. *Requests* the United Nations and the Organization of the Islamic Conference to continue to cooperate in their common search for solutions to global problems, such as questions relating to international peace and security, disarmament, self-determination, decolonization, fundamental human rights, social and economic development and technical cooperation;

4. *Welcomes* the efforts of the United Nations and the Organization of the Islamic Conference to continue to strengthen cooperation between the two organizations in areas of common concern and to review the ways and means of enhancing the actual mechanisms of such cooperation;

5. *Welcomes with appreciation* the continuing cooperation between the United Nations and the Organization of the Islamic Conference in the field of peacemaking and preventive diplomacy, and notes the close cooperation between the two organizations in continuing the search for a peaceful and lasting solution to the conflict in Afghanistan;

6. *Welcomes* the efforts of the secretariats of the two organizations to strengthen information exchange, coordination and cooperation between them in areas of mutual interest in the political field and their ongoing consultations with a view to developing the modalities of such cooperation;

7. *Also welcomes* the periodic high-level meetings between the Secretary-General of the United Nations and the Secretary-General of the Organization of the Islamic Conference, as well as between senior secretariat officials of the two organizations, and encourages their participation in important meetings of the two organizations;

8. *Recommends* that, in accordance with its resolution 50/17, in order to enhance cooperation and for the purpose of review and appraisal of progress, a general meeting of representatives of the secretariats of the United Nations system and the Organization of the Islamic Conference be held in 2002;

9. *Also recommends* that, in accordance with its resolution 50/17, coordination meetings of focal points of the organizations and agencies of the United Nations system and the Organization of the Islamic Conference and its subsidiary organs and specialized and affiliated institutions be held concurrently with the general meeting in 2002;

10. *Encourages* the specialized agencies and other organizations of the United Nations system to continue to expand their cooperation with the subsidiary organs and specialized and affiliated institutions of the Organization of the Islamic Conference in priority areas of interest to the United Nations and the Organization of the Islamic Conference;

11. *Urges* the United Nations and other organizations of the United Nations system, especially the lead agencies, to provide increased technical and other forms of assistance to the Organization of the Islamic Conference and its subsidiary organs and specialized and affiliated institutions in order to enhance cooperation;

12. *Expresses its appreciation* to the Secretary-General for his continued efforts to strengthen cooperation and coordination between the United Nations and other organizations of the United Nations system and the Organization of the Islamic Conference and its subsidiary organs and specialized and affiliated institutions to serve the mutual interests of the two organizations in the political, economic, social, humanitarian, cultural and scientific fields;

13. *Requests* the Secretary-General to report to the General Assembly at its fifty-seventh session on the state of cooperation between the United Nations and the Organization of the Islamic Conference;

14. *Decides* to include in the provisional agenda of its fifty-seventh session the sub-item entitled "Cooperation between the United Nations and the Organization of the Islamic Conference".

League of Arab States

In response to General Assembly resolution 55/10 [YUN 2000, p. 1380], the Secretary-General submitted an October report [A/56/474] on cooperation between the United Nations and the League of Arab States (LAS). The report summarized follow-up action on proposals agreed to at meetings between the UN system and LAS. At a general meeting on cooperation between the representatives of the secretariats of the UN system and of the LAS General Secretariat (Vienna, 17-19 July), LAS confirmed that enhancing cooperation and coordination with the UN system was high on its list of priorities and it hoped to benefit from and draw upon UN capacity-building and training expertise in the areas of conflict prevention, peace-building and disarmament. The United Nations expressed its willingness to explore the possibility of cooperation in those areas.

The meeting recommended strengthening cooperation between the two organizations on humanitarian issues, particularly building capacity for monitoring emergencies and coordinating regional relief operations.

GENERAL ASSEMBLY ACTION

On 7 December [meeting 80], the General Assembly adopted **resolution 56/40** [draft: A/56/L.26 & Add.1] without vote [agenda item 21 *(e)*].

Cooperation between the United Nations and the League of Arab States

The General Assembly,

Recalling its previous resolutions on cooperation between the United Nations and the League of Arab States,

Having considered the report of the Secretary-General on cooperation between the United Nations and the League of Arab States,

Recalling article 3 of the Pact of the League of Arab States, which entrusts the Council of the League with the function of determining the means whereby the League will collaborate with the international organizations which may be created in the future to guarantee peace and security and organize economic and social relations,

Noting the desire of both organizations to consolidate, develop and enhance further the ties existing between them in the political, economic, social, humanitarian, cultural, technical and administrative fields,

Taking into account the report of the Secretary-General entitled "An Agenda for Peace", in particular section VII, concerning cooperation with regional arrangements and organizations, and the "Supplement to An Agenda for Peace",

Convinced of the need for more efficient and coordinated utilization of available economic and financial resources in order to promote the common objectives of the two organizations,

1. *Takes note with satisfaction* of the report of the Secretary-General;

2. *Commends* the continued efforts of the League of Arab States to promote multilateral cooperation among Arab States, and requests the United Nations system to continue to lend its support;

3. *Expresses its appreciation* to the Secretary-General for the follow-up action taken by him to implement the proposals adopted at the meetings between the representatives of the secretariats of the United Nations and

other organizations of the United Nations system and the General Secretariat of the League of Arab States and its specialized organizations, including the general meeting on cooperation between the United Nations system and the League of Arab States and its specialized organizations held in Vienna, from 17 to 19 July 2001;

4. *Requests* the Secretariat of the United Nations and the General Secretariat of the League of Arab States, within their respective fields of competence, to intensify further their cooperation for the realization of the purposes and principles embodied in the Charter of the United Nations, the strengthening of international peace and security, economic and social development, disarmament, decolonization, self-determination and the eradication of all forms of racism and racial discrimination;

5. *Requests* the Secretary-General to continue his efforts to strengthen cooperation and coordination between the United Nations and other organizations and agencies of the United Nations system and the League of Arab States and its specialized organizations in order to enhance their capacity to serve the mutual interests and objectives of the two organizations in the political, economic, social, humanitarian, cultural and administrative fields;

6. *Calls upon* the specialized agencies and other organizations and programmes of the United Nations system:

(a) To continue to cooperate with the Secretary-General and among themselves, as well as with the League of Arab States and its specialized organizations, in the follow-up of multilateral proposals aimed at strengthening and expanding cooperation in all fields between the United Nations system and the League of Arab States and its specialized organizations;

(b) To strengthen the capacity of the League of Arab States and of its institutions and specialized organizations to benefit from globalization and information technology and to meet the development challenges of the new millennium;

(c) To step up cooperation and coordination with the specialized organizations of the League of Arab States in the organization of seminars and training courses and in the preparation of studies;

(d) To maintain and increase contacts and improve the mechanism of consultation with the counterpart programmes, organizations and agencies concerned regarding projects and programmes in order to facilitate their implementation;

(e) To participate whenever possible with organizations and institutions of the League of Arab States in the execution and implementation of development projects in the Arab region;

(f) To inform the Secretary-General, not later than 30 June 2002, of the progress made in their cooperation with the League of Arab States and its specialized organizations and, in particular, of the follow-up action taken on the multilateral and bilateral proposals adopted at the previous meetings between the two organizations;

7. *Also calls upon* the specialized agencies and other organizations and programmes of the United Nations system to increase their cooperation with the League of Arab States and its specialized organizations in the pri-

ority sectors of energy, rural development, desertification and green belts, training and vocational education, technology, environment and information and documentation;

8. *Requests* the Secretary-General of the United Nations, in cooperation with the Secretary-General of the League of Arab States, to encourage periodic consultation between representatives of the Secretariat of the United Nations and of the General Secretariat of the League of Arab States in order to review and strengthen coordination mechanisms with a view to accelerating implementation of, and follow-up action on, the multilateral projects, proposals and recommendations adopted at the meetings between the two organizations;

9. *Recommends* that the United Nations and all organizations of the United Nations system make the greatest possible use of Arab institutions and technical expertise in projects undertaken in the Arab region;

10. *Reaffirms* that, in order to enhance cooperation and for the purpose of the review and appraisal of progress, a general meeting between representatives of the United Nations system and the League of Arab States should be held once every two years and that joint inter-agency sectoral meetings should also be convened on a biennial basis to address priority areas of major importance to the development of the Arab States, on the basis of agreement between the United Nations system and the League of Arab States and its specialized organizations;

11. *Recommends* that a sectoral meeting between the United Nations and the League of Arab States be held at the headquarters of the League of Arab States in Cairo during 2002 on the use of information technology in development;

12. *Also recommends* that the next general meeting on cooperation between the representatives of the secretariats of organizations of the United Nations system and of the General Secretariat of the League of Arab States and its specialized organizations be held during 2003;

13. *Requests* the Secretary-General to submit to the General Assembly at its fifty-seventh session a report on the implementation of the present resolution;

14. *Decides* to include in the provisional agenda of its fifty-seventh session the sub-item entitled "Cooperation between the United Nations and the League of Arab States".

Inter-Parliamentary Union

The Secretary-General, in June [A/55/996], reviewed efforts to strengthen cooperation between the United Nations and the Inter-Parliamentary Union (IPU). He said that IPU had consistently contributed to major governmental commitments of the preceding decade through its world conferences. However, its current classification as an NGO in consultative status with the Economic and Social Council no longer corresponded to its status as the world organization of parliaments and limited its ability to give full meaning to the Millennium Declaration [YUN 2000, p. 49] and that of the Conference of Presiding

Officers of National Parliaments [ibid., p. 67]. In April, the IPU Council made suggestions for strengthening cooperation between the United Nations and national parliaments, including identifying elements of a programme of work for IPU to promote parliamentary debate and action in specific areas of jointly identified priorities. The Secretary-General said that he agreed with the IPU suggestions, and, in view of the General Assembly's desire to establish a strengthened and formalized relationship with IPU, recommended that the Assembly grant IPU a standing invitation to participate in its sessions and work and in international conferences convened under UN auspices, decide on the circulation of IPU documents in the Assembly, and invite UN specialized agencies to adopt similar modalities for cooperation with IPU. Depending on the Assembly's decision, the Secretary-General would initiate a joint review of the 1996 Cooperation Agreement between the two organizations.

In October [A/56/449], responding to Assembly resolution 55/19 [YUN 2000, p. 1382], the Secretary-General described actions taken by the United Nations and IPU to secure parliamentary input to recent major UN events, as well as IPU action to support or complement the work of the United Nations in peace and security, economic and social development, international law and human rights, democracy, governance and gender issues. He was pleased with efforts currently under way to act on his suggestions concerning a new relationship between IPU and the Assembly (see above) and looked forward to the strengthening of the parliamentary dimension of UN work. (For more information on UN/IPU relations, see p. 1375.)

GENERAL ASSEMBLY ACTION

On 7 December [meeting 80], the General Assembly adopted **resolution 56/46** [draft: A/56/L.35 & Add.1] without vote [agenda item 21 (*f*)].

Cooperation between the United Nations and the Inter-Parliamentary Union

The General Assembly,

Recalling its resolution 55/19 of 8 November 2000, in which it expressed the wish that the cooperation between the United Nations and the Inter-Parliamentary Union be strengthened further,

Having considered the report of the Secretary-General, which takes stock of such cooperation over the last twelve months,

Noting with appreciation the resolutions adopted by the Inter-Parliamentary Union and its activities during the past year in support of the United Nations,

Recalling with satisfaction the United Nations Millennium Declaration, in which Member States resolved to strengthen further cooperation between the United Nations and national parliaments through their world organization, the Inter-Parliamentary Union, in various fields, including peace and security, economic and social development, international law and human rights and democracy and gender issues,

Welcoming the report of the Secretary-General of 26 June 2001,

Taking into consideration the Cooperation Agreement between the United Nations and the Inter-Parliamentary Union of 1996, which provides the foundation for current cooperation between the two organizations,

Recalling the unique inter-State character of the Inter-Parliamentary Union,

1. *Welcomes* the ongoing efforts to explore ways in which a new and strengthened relationship may be established between the General Assembly and its subsidiary organs on the one hand and the Inter-Parliamentary Union on the other, and encourages Member States to continue their consultations with a view to adopting a decision thereon during the fifty-seventh session of the Assembly;

2. *Also welcomes* the efforts made by the Inter-Parliamentary Union to provide for a greater parliamentary contribution and enhanced support to the United Nations, and calls for the cooperation between the two organizations to be consolidated further;

3. *Requests* the Secretary-General to submit a report to the General Assembly at its fifty-seventh session on the various aspects of cooperation between the United Nations and the Inter-Parliamentary Union;

4. *Decides* to include in the provisional agenda of its fifty-seventh session the sub-item entitled "Cooperation between the United Nations and the Inter-Parliamentary Union".

Economic Community of Central African States

In response to General Assembly resolution 55/22 [YUN 2000, p. 232], the Secretary-General submitted an August report [A/56/301] on cooperation between the United Nations and the Economic Community of Central African States (ECCAS). Interaction between the two organizations focused on how UN experience and expertise could best serve ECCAS in such areas as peacekeeping, disarmament, human rights and development. The Assembly, in **resolution 56/39** (see p. 906), took note of the Secretary-General's report.

Organization for Security and Cooperation in Europe

In response to General Assembly resolution 55/179 [YUN 2000, p. 408], the Secretary-General submitted a June report [A/56/125] describing cooperation between the United Nations and the Organization for Security and Cooperation in Europe. The General Assembly, by **resolution 56/216** (see p. 397), took note of the report.

Organization of African Unity

The Secretary-General submitted an October report [A/56/489] on activities undertaken to promote cooperation between the United Nations and the Organization of African Unity. The General Assembly, by **resolution 56/48** (see p. 236), took action on the report.

Southern African Development Community

In response to General Assembly resolution 54/227 [YUN 1999, p. 923], the Secretary-General, in July [A/56/134], summarized information received from Member States and UN organizations and bodies on measures taken to cooperate with the Southern African Development Community. The General Assembly, by **decision 56/443** (see p. 905), took action on the report.

Latin American Economic System

In response to General Assembly resolution 54/8 [YUN 1999, p. 947], the Secretary-General submitted a July report [A/56/171] on activities undertaken to promote cooperation between the United Nations and the Latin American Economic System. The General Assembly, by **resolution 56/98** (see p. 925), noted the report.

International Organization of la Francophonie

In response to General Assembly resolution 54/25 [YUN 1999, p. 1356], the Secretary-General submitted a September report [A/56/390] on activities undertaken in 2000 and 2001 to promote cooperation between the United Nations and the International Organization of la Francophonie in preventive diplomacy, peacemaking and peace-building, human rights, and economic, social and cultural development.

GENERAL ASSEMBLY ACTION

On 7 December [meeting 80], the General Assembly adopted **resolution 56/45** [draft: A/56/L.34 & Add.1] without vote [agenda item 21 (b)].

Cooperation between the United Nations and the International Organization of la Francophonie

The General Assembly,

Recalling its resolutions 33/18 of 10 November 1978, 50/3 of 16 October 1995, 52/2 of 17 October 1997 and 54/25 of 15 November 1999, as well as its decision 53/453 of 18 December 1998,

Recalling also the Articles of the Charter of the United Nations which encourage the promotion of the purposes and principles of the United Nations through regional cooperation,

Having considered the report of the Secretary-General,

Noting the desire of the two organizations to consolidate, develop and tighten the ties that exist between them in the political, economic, social and cultural fields,

Noting with satisfaction the substantial progress achieved in cooperation between the United Nations, the specialized agencies and other United Nations bodies and programmes and the International Organization of la Francophonie,

Convinced that strengthening cooperation between the United Nations and the International Organization of la Francophonie serves the purposes and principles of the United Nations,

Considering that the International Organization of la Francophonie brings together a considerable number of States Members of the United Nations, among which it promotes multilateral cooperation in areas of interest to the United Nations,

Noting with appreciation the will shown by the heads of State and Government of countries that use French as a common language at their eighth summit session, held in Moncton, Canada, from 3 to 5 September 1999, to play an active part in resolving the main political and economic problems of the contemporary world and to consolidate the partnership with the United Nations to that end,

1. *Takes note* of the report of the Secretary-General;

2. *Notes with satisfaction* the positive evolution and development of cooperation between the two organizations;

3. *Expresses its appreciation* to the Secretary-General of the United Nations and the Secretary-General of the International Organization of la Francophonie for their sustained efforts to strengthen cooperation and coordination between the two organizations, thereby serving their mutual interests in the political, economic, social and cultural fields;

4. *Notes with satisfaction* that the International Organization of la Francophonie is participating more frequently in the work of the United Nations, to which it makes a valuable contribution;

5. *Welcomes* the involvement of the countries that use French as a common language, particularly through the International Organization of la Francophonie, in United Nations activities, including the preparation for, conduct of and follow-up to international conferences organized under United Nations auspices;

6. *Emphasizes* the importance of the steps taken by the International Organization of la Francophonie during the past two years to promote dialogue between cultures and civilizations;

7. *Commends* the International Organization of la Francophonie for its efforts in relation to conflict prevention, management and resolution, the promotion of human rights and the strengthening of democracy and the rule of law, as well as its action in favour of the development of multilateral cooperation among countries with French as a common language, particularly in the areas of economic, social and cultural development, and the promotion of new information technologies, and requests United Nations bodies to give it their support;

8. *Also commends* the high-level meetings held periodically between the secretariats of the United Nations and the International Organization of la Francophonie, and advocates the participation of those secretariats in major meetings of the two organizations;

9. *Expresses its appreciation* to the Secretary-General for including the International Organization of la Francophonie in the periodic meetings he holds with the heads of regional organizations, and invites him to continue to do so, taking into account the role played by the International Organization of la Francophonie in conflict prevention and support for democracy and the rule of law;

10. *Recommends* to the United Nations and the International Organization of la Francophonie that they should continue and intensify their consultations with a view to ensuring greater coordination in the areas of conflict prevention, peace-building, support for the rule of law and democracy and the promotion of human rights;

11. *Notes with satisfaction* the strengthening of collaboration between the United Nations and the International Organization of la Francophonie in the area of electoral monitoring and assistance, and advocates the strengthening of cooperation between the two organizations in that area;

12. *Requests* the Secretary-General of the United Nations, acting in cooperation with the Secretary-General of the International Organization of la Francophonie, to encourage the holding of periodic meetings between representatives of the United Nations Secretariat and representatives of the secretariat of the International Organization of la Francophonie in order to promote the exchange of information, coordination of activities and identification of new areas of cooperation;

13. *Invites* the Secretary-General to take the necessary steps, in consultation with the Secretary-General of the International Organization of la Francophonie, to continue to promote cooperation between the two organizations;

14. *Invites* the specialized agencies, funds and programmes of the United Nations, as well as the regional commissions, including the Economic Commission for Africa, to collaborate to this end with the Secretary-General of the International Organization of la Francophonie by identifying new synergies in favour of development, in particular in the areas of poverty elimination, energy, sustainable development, education, training and the development of new information technologies;

15. *Requests* the Secretary-General to submit to the General Assembly at its fifty-seventh session a report on the implementation of the present resolution;

16. *Decides* to include in the provisional agenda of its fifty-seventh session the sub-item entitled "Cooperation between the United Nations and the International Organization of la Francophonie".

Pacific Islands Forum

On 14 September [A/56/388], Nauru transmitted to the Secretary-General a letter from the President of Nauru and Chairman of the Pacific Islands Forum, annexed to which was a communiqué adopted at the Forum's thirty-second meeting (Nauru, 16-18 August). The Forum welcomed the inclusion of the item "Cooperation between the United Nations and the Pacific Islands Forum" in the General Assembly's provisional agenda. The Assembly, in **resolution 56/41** (see p. 916), took note of the communiqué.

Organization for the Prohibition of Chemical Weapons

The General Assembly, by **resolution 55/283** of 7 September (see p. 495), approved the Agreement concerning the Relationship between the United Nations and the Organization for the Prohibition of Chemical Weapons [A/55/988], submitted by the Secretary-General in response to resolution 51/230 [YUN 1997, p. 499].

In December, by **resolution 56/42** (see p. 498), the Assembly noted the annual report of the Organization for the Prohibition of Chemical Weapons [A/56/490].

Preparatory Commission for the Comprehensive Nuclear-Test-Ban Treaty Organization

By an August note [A/56/317], the Secretary-General transmitted to the General Assembly the report of the Executive Secretary of the Preparatory Commission for the Comprehensive Nuclear-Test-Ban Treaty Organization for the year 2000 on cooperation between the United Nations and that organization, pursuant to resolution 54/280 [YUN 2000, p. 501]. In December, by **resolution 56/49** (see p. 483), the Assembly took note of the report.

Cooperation with UN partners

In response to General Assembly resolution 55/215 [YUN 2000, p. 785], the Secretary-General submitted an August report [A/56/323], which presented the views of Member States and relevant partners on ways to enhance cooperation between the United Nations and all relevant partners, in particular the private sector. The General Assembly, by **resolution 56/76** (see p. 744), took note of the report.

Observer status

International Development Law Institute

In June [A/56/141], Austria requested the inclusion in the provisional agenda of the General Assembly's fifty-sixth session of an item entitled "Observer status for the International Development Law Institute in the General Assembly". In an explanatory memorandum, Austria said that the Institute, founded in 1987, promoted and assisted in the use of legal resources in the development process. Its activities included legal development training, technical assistance, research, publications and the operation of a legal documentation centre. Its membership as at 31 March stood at 15 States. A closer link with the Institute would provide the United Nations with a further

resource in its work in development and international law and allow the Institute closer interaction with all relevant UN system organs in the furtherance of the common aims of both organizations.

GENERAL ASSEMBLY ACTION

On 12 December [meeting 85], the General Assembly, on the recommendation of the Sixth Committee [A/56/596], adopted **resolution 56/90** without vote [agenda item 170].

Observer status for the International Development Law Institute in the General Assembly

The General Assembly,

Wishing to promote cooperation between the United Nations and the International Development Law Institute,

1. *Decides* to invite the International Development Law Institute to participate in the sessions and the work of the General Assembly in the capacity of observer;

2. *Requests* the Secretary-General to take the necessary action to implement the present resolution.

International Hydrographic Organization

In July [A/56/145], Monaco requested the inclusion in the provisional agenda of the General Assembly's fifty-sixth session of the item entitled "Observer status for the International Hydrographic Organization in the General Assembly". In an explanatory memorandum, Monaco indicated that the objective of the organization, established in 1967 and comprising 69 members, was to coordinate the activities of national hydrographic offices, achieve uniformity of nautical charts and documents, adopt reliable hydrographic survey methods and develop hydrography and oceanography techniques. It had been associated on a regular basis with the work of the States parties to the United Nations Convention on the Law of the Sea [YUN 1982, p. 181] and the Assembly's review of ocean affairs. Observer status would enable it to increase cooperation and coordination with UN system programmes and institutions in marine science activities and develop training and capacity-building in those areas.

GENERAL ASSEMBLY ACTION

On 12 December [meeting 85], the General Assembly, on the recommendation of the Sixth Committee [A/56/597 & Corr.1], adopted **resolution 56/91** without vote [agenda item 172].

Observer status for the International Hydrographic Organization in the General Assembly

The General Assembly,

Wishing to promote cooperation between the United Nations and the International Hydrographic Organization,

1. *Decides* to invite the International Hydrographic Organization to participate in its sessions and its work in the capacity of observer;

2. *Requests* the Secretary-General to take the necessary action to implement the present resolution.

Community of Sahelo-Saharan States

In July [A/56/191], the Sudan requested the inclusion in the agenda of the General Assembly's fifty-sixth session of the item "Observer status for the Community of Sahelo-Saharan States". The Community, an intergovernmental organization with 16 members (Burkina Faso, Central African Republic, Chad, Djibouti, Egypt, Eritrea, Gambia, Libyan Arab Jamahiriya, Mali, Morocco, Niger, Nigeria, Senegal, Somalia, Sudan, Tunisia), established in 1998, was concerned with the economic, cultural, political and social integration of its member States. It had concluded a partnership and cooperation agreement with the UN Economic Commission for Africa. Observer status in the Assembly would greatly enhance future cooperation and ensure more effective results, as well as strengthen the efforts of both organizations in economic development.

GENERAL ASSEMBLY ACTION

On 12 December [meeting 85], the General Assembly, on the recommendation of the Sixth Committee [A/56/598 & Corr.1], adopted **resolution 56/92** without vote [agenda item 173].

Observer status for the Community of Sahelo-Saharan States in the General Assembly

The General Assembly,

Considering the importance of the Community of Sahelo-Saharan States, an intergovernmental organization that addresses the common interests of its members and takes account of the diverse links that unite their peoples, and given the determination of the organization to confront the factors that have caused economic backwardness and instability in its member States, its conviction that joint action in a framework of complementarity is the best way to integrate its countries and peoples, its commitment to the maintenance of international peace and security in the Sahelo-Saharan region and its determination to satisfy the wish for economic, cultural, political and social integration in accordance with the Charter of the United Nations, the Charter of the Organization of African Unity, the Charter of the Organization of the Islamic Conference, the Treaty Establishing the African Economic Community of 3 June 1991 (the Abuja Treaty) and the constitutive documents of the regional organizations to which its member States belong,

Considering also the need, frequently noted by the United Nations, to promote and support every effort towards the development of bilateral and multilateral cooperation on the basis of international law,

Noting that the treaty establishing the Community of Sahelo-Saharan States stresses regional cooperation as part of the process of achieving African unity on the basis of human rights and fundamental freedoms and the promotion of social justice and stability,

Wishing to promote cooperation between the United Nations and the Community of Sahelo-Saharan States,

1. *Decides* to invite the Community of Sahelo-Saharan States to participate in the sessions and the work of the General Assembly in the capacity of observer;

2. *Requests* the Secretary-General to take the necessary action to implement the present resolution.

International Institute for Democracy and Electoral Assistance

The General Assembly, by **decision 56/423** of 12 December, deferred further consideration of and a decision on the 2000 request [YUN 2000, p. 1383] for observer status for the International Institute for Democracy and Electoral Assistance in the General Assembly until its fifty-seventh (2002) session.

Partners in Population and Development

In April [A/55/241], the States members of Partners in Population and Development requested inclusion in the agenda of the General Assembly's fifty-fifth session of the item on observer status for that organization in the Assembly. The organization, established in 1994, comprised 16 members (Bangladesh, China, Colombia, Egypt, Gambia, India, Indonesia, Kenya, Mali, Mexico, Morocco, Pakistan, Thailand, Tunisia, Uganda, Zimbabwe). It promoted South-South cooperation in population and development, and had made much progress in the transfer of knowledge, expertise and skills in population and reproductive health. It wished to share its experience with other countries, and believed that its involvement with the United Nations would enable it to enrich the Organization's work in that area.

On 7 September, by **decision 55/402 B**, the Assembly included the item in the agenda of its fifty-sixth session. On 12 December, by **decision 56/424**, the Assembly deferred consideration of and a decision on the request until its fifty-seventh (2002) session.

Inter-Parliamentary Union

In a 7 November letter to the General Assembly President [A/56/614], India recalled the Secretary-General's reports on cooperation between the Inter-Parliamentary Union (IPU) and the United Nations and on a new relationship between the two organizations (see p. 1371). India, in its capacity as current President of IPU, was proposing that IPU be granted observer status on a par with other international bodies that had similar status in the Assembly. However, since the Assembly's procedural requirements would delay action on the request, it was asking that the agenda item on cooperation between the United Nations and IPU be referred immediately to the Sixth Committee and that the Committee's recommendation be sent to the Assembly's plenary session before 6 December. On 16 November [A/C.6/56/2], the Assembly President informed the Sixth Committee Chairman that the Assembly had agreed to allocate the item to the Sixth Committee solely to consider the question of granting observer status to IPU in the Assembly.

The Assembly, by **decision 56/425** of 12 December, deferred to its fifty-seventh (2002) session consideration of and a decision on observer status for IPU.

Participation of organizations in UN work

Intergovernmental organizations

On 10 October, the Economic and Social Council, by **decision 2001/318**, having considered the application of the International Association of Economic and Social Councils and Similar Institutions, decided that the organization might participate on a continuing basis, without the right to vote, in the deliberations of the Council on questions within the scope of its activities.

Non-governmental organizations

Committee on NGOs

The Committee on Non-Governmental Organizations, at its resumed 2000 session (New York, 15-26 January 2001) [E/2000/8], considered 147 applications for consultative status with the Economic and Social Council, including those deferred from its 1998, 1999 and 2000 sessions, as well as seven requests for reclassification. It recommended 52 organizations for consultative status, two for reclassification and one to maintain its current status. Due to time constraints, the Committee deferred consideration of the quadrennial reports. It recommended two draft decisions for action by the Council.

The Committee also considered implementation of Council decision 1996/302 [YUN 1996, p. 1368] on NGOs on the Roster, reviewed its working methods as they related to implementation of Council resolution 1996/31 [ibid., p. 1360], including the process of accreditation of NGO representatives, and Council decision 1995/304 [YUN 1995, p. 1445] on arrangements for consultation with NGOs.

On 3 May (**decision 2001/215**), the Council noted the Committee's report on its resumed

2000 session. On the same date (**decision 2001/214**), the Council granted special consultative status to 44 NGOs; placed eight on the Roster; and reclassified two organizations from special to general consultative status. The Council noted that the Committee did not recommend granting consultative status to six organizations; had closed consideration of the applications of two; and had also closed three cases of complaints from Member States.

At its 2001 session (New York, 7-25 May) [E/2001/86], the Committee recommended 44 organizations for consultative status, deferred consideration of 101 applications, closed consideration of one, reviewed four requests for reclassification and deferred consideration of three. The Committee also considered 172 quadrennial reports and deferred consideration of another 56, pending responses from those organizations to Committee questions. It adopted four draft decisions for action by the Council.

The Committee resumed consideration of the items it had discussed at its 2000 resumed session (above). Concerning its working methods, the Committee continued consideration of its accreditation procedures and proposals on additional coordination mechanisms with the secretariat of the Commission on Human Rights. It also exchanged views on two complementary draft proposals by India and Germany on a new application questionnaire for consultative status to better meet the Committee's information criteria. The Committee agreed that the contents of the questionnaire should be better focused to bring more clarity to the Committee's review of new applications.

On the issue of strengthening the NGO Section of the Department of Economic and Social Affairs of the UN Secretariat, the Committee was informed about the Section's achievements in improving its methods of work; however, it expressed concern about the increased workload of the Section, as the increase in new applications for consultative status had outpaced its capacity to deal with them.

On the implementation of Council decision 1996/302 relating to NGOs on the Roster, the Committee was of the view that the procedure for applying for Roster consultative status should be reviewed and streamlined to correct the discrepancy between applications from NGOs on the Roster for the purpose of the work of the Commission on Sustainable Development and those from other organizations. Following consultation with the Office of Legal Affairs, the Committee expressed the view that NGOs on the Roster of the Commission should go through the same channels of application for consultative status with the Council as any other organization.

On 25 July, by **decision 2001/294**, the Council granted special consultative status to 38 NGOs and placed six on the Roster. The Council noted that the Committee had closed consideration of the application of one organization, the complaint submitted against one organization, and one request for reclassification.

On the same date, by **decision 2001/295**, the Council decided that requests by NGOs referred to in its decision 1993/220 [YUN 1993, p. 668] to expand their participation in other fields of the Council's work would be considered expeditiously by the Committee on NGOs.

Also on the same date (**decision 2001/296**), the Council authorized the Committee to hold a resumed session from 14 to 25 January 2002 to complete the work of its 2001 session. It took note of the Committee's report on its 2001 session [E/2001/86] and approved the provisional agenda and documentation for its 2002 session (**decision 2001/297**).

Requests for hearing

On 15 May, the Committee on NGOs approved requests from NGOs in consultative status to address the Economic and Social Council in connection with items on its agenda. It approved the requests of the Organization for Industrial, Spiritual and Cultural Advancement International, the Conference of Non-Governmental Organizations in Consultative Relationship with the United Nations and the Centro de Ricerca e Documentazione Febbraio 74 to be heard by the Council at the high-level segment of its substantive session. In addition, the Committee approved the request of the Asia Crime Prevention Foundation to present a written statement to the general segment of the Council on the agenda item "Social and human rights questions: crime prevention and criminal justice".

Participation of NGOs not in consultative status

By **decisions 55/460 A-C** of 26 February, 18 May and 22 June, the General Assembly approved the list of civil society organizations not in consultative status with the Council and not members of the Programme Coordinating Board of the Joint United Nations Programme on Human Immunodeficiency Virus/Acquired Immunodeficiency Syndrome for accreditation to the Assembly's special session on HIV/AIDS (see p. 1125), including its preparatory process.

Conferences and meetings

The Committee on Conferences held organizational meetings on 19 April and 22 June and its substantive session from 27 to 29 August [A/56/32]. The Committee examined requests for additions and changes to the approved calendar of conferences and meetings for 2001 [A/AC.172/2001/2] and the draft revised calendar for 2002-2003. It considered the utilization of conference-servicing resources and facilities, requests for exceptions to General Assembly resolution 40/243 [YUN 1985, p. 1256] concerning the holding of meetings of subsidiary bodies, documentation- and publication-related matters, translation- and interpretation-related matters, information technology and the proposed programme budget for 2002-2003 for the UN Department of General Assembly Affairs and Conference Services. (The deliberations and recommendations of the Committee on those matters are detailed in the sections below.)

The Committee approved requests from the International Civil Service Commission to convene its fifty-third session (11-29 June) in Montreal, Canada, rather than New York; the Intergovernmental Preparatory Committee for the Third United Nations Conference on the Least Developed Countries to convene its second session for five days in February, in New York instead of Geneva; the Ad Hoc Group of Experts on International Cooperation in Tax Matters to convene its tenth meeting in Geneva from 10 to 14 September rather than from 23 to 27 April in New York; the Commission for Social Development acting as the preparatory committee for the Second World Assembly on Ageing to convene a resumed session (30 April-1 May); the Commission on the Status of Women to convene a resumed session (9-11 May) to complete the work of its forty-fifth session; the Advisory Board on Disarmament Matters to convene its thirty-seventh session (25-27 July) in Geneva rather than New York; the Meeting of Government Experts of Landlocked and Transit Developing Countries and Representatives of Donor Countries and Financial and Development Institutions to convene its fifth session (30 July- 3 August) in New York rather than Geneva; the Commission on Human Rights acting as preparatory committee for the World Conference against Racism, Racial Discrimination, Xenophobia and Related Intolerance to convene a third session in Geneva (30 July-10 August) to continue drafting of the declaration and programme of action of the Conference; and the Committee on Information to convene a resumed session (5-7 September) to take a final decision on the mandate and allocation of the necessary resources for the establishment of a permanent international radio broadcasting capacity for the United Nations during the main part of the General Assembly's fifty-sixth session.

The Committee recommended that the Assembly adopt the draft calendar of conferences and meetings for 2002-2003 and authorize the Committee to make adjustments to the calendar as a result of Assembly action. The Committee noted that the Secretariat had taken into account the arrangements in resolutions 54/248 [YUN 1999, p. 1368] and 55/222 [YUN 2000, p. 1387] regarding Orthodox Good Friday observed on 3 May 2002 and 25 April 2003. It recommended that, when planning the calendar of conferences and meetings, every effort should be made to avoid simultaneous peak periods at the various duty stations and welcomed efforts at effective coordination in achieving that objective.

GENERAL ASSEMBLY ACTION

On 24 December [meeting 92], the General Assembly, on the recommendation of the Fifth Committee [A/56/737], adopted **resolution 56/242** without vote [agenda item 124].

Pattern of conferences

The General Assembly,

Recalling its relevant resolutions, including resolutions 40/243 of 18 December 1985, 41/213 of 19 December 1986, 43/222 A to E of 21 December 1988, 50/11 of 2 November 1995, 54/248 of 23 December 1999 and 55/222 of 23 December 2000,

Having considered the report of the Committee on Conferences and the reports of the Secretary-General,

Having also considered the report of the Advisory Committee on Administrative and Budgetary Questions,

Reiterates the provisions of its resolutions 51/211 A to E of 18 December 1996, 52/214 of 22 December 1997, 53/208 A to E of 18 December 1998, 54/248 and 55/222;

I
Calendar of conferences and meetings

1. *Notes with appreciation* the work of the Committee on Conferences, and endorses the recommendations contained in its report, subject to the provisions of the present resolution;

2. *Approves* the draft biennial calendar of conferences and meetings of the United Nations for 2002-2003, as submitted by the Committee on Conferences, taking into account the observations of the Committee, and subject to the provisions of the present resolution;

3. *Authorizes* the Committee on Conferences to make any adjustments to the calendar of conferences and meetings for 2002-2003 that may become necessary as a result of actions and decisions taken by the General Assembly at its fifty-sixth session;

4. *Notes with satisfaction* that the Secretariat took into account the arrangements referred to in General Assembly resolutions 53/208 A, 54/248 and 55/222 concerning Orthodox Good Friday and the official holidays of Id al-Fitr and Id al-Adha, and requests all intergovernmental bodies to observe those decisions when planning their meetings;

5. *Reaffirms* its decision that the headquarters rule shall be adhered to by all bodies, and decides that waivers to the headquarters rule shall be granted solely on the basis of the calendar of conferences and meetings of the United Nations as recommended by the Committee on Conferences for adoption by the General Assembly;

6. *Also reaffirms* the general principle established in the headquarters rule and, in particular, that all meetings related to the environment and to human settlements that are organized by the United Nations Environment Programme and the United Nations Centre for Human Settlements (Habitat), respectively, should be held at Nairobi, headquarters of the Programme and Habitat;

7. *Further reaffirms* the relevant provisions established by the General Assembly in its resolution 50/11 on multilingualism;

8. *Requests* the Committee on Conferences and the Secretary-General, when planning the calendar of conferences and meetings, to avoid simultaneous peak periods at the various duty stations and to avoid scheduling meetings of related intergovernmental bodies too closely together;

II
Utilization of conference-servicing resources and facilities

1. *Approves* the guidelines on limiting meeting duration contained in the annex to the present resolution;

2. *Requests* the Secretary-General to enhance further the established practice of workload sharing among duty stations in documentation services as a means to improve the utilization of conference-servicing resources, and to include information on these efforts in the context of a single, comprehensive report to be submitted to the General Assembly at its fifty-eighth session;

3. *Also requests* the Secretary-General, bearing in mind the recent organizational changes, to ensure that the Department of General Assembly Affairs and Conference Services of the Secretariat is considered the appropriate executive authority to oversee, coordinate and enhance the global management and delivery of United Nations conference services, under the legislative authority of the General Assembly and through oversight and examination by the Committee on Conferences;

4. *Reaffirms* the terms of reference and main functions of the Committee on Conferences as formulated in section I, paragraph 1, of resolution 41/213 and in resolution 43/222 B;

5. *Welcomes* the improved participation of observers in the work of the Committee on Conferences, the changes in the procedure governing the participation of observers and the decision of the Committee to keep this procedure under review;

6. *Requests* the Secretary-General to submit a report to the General Assembly at its fifty-seventh session on the mechanisms available for addressing the concerns of Member States about the efficiency, quality and de-

livery of conference services, including information about the way in which the concerns of Member States are recorded and reported, and on the grouping of these issues in reports to the General Assembly;

7. *Welcomes* the establishment of a permanent interpretation service at the United Nations Office at Nairobi, and notes with satisfaction that the conference-servicing facility at the United Nations Office at Nairobi is becoming organizationally, functionally and in terms of the budget an integral part of the Department of General Assembly Affairs and Conference Services;

8. *Notes with appreciation* the increase in the number of multilingual meetings to be held at the United Nations Office at Nairobi and with the participation of the Nairobi interpretation team elsewhere in 2001 and 2002, as well as the cost-saving effect of the establishment of the Nairobi interpretation service for the regular budget in terms of temporary assistance;

9. *Emphasizes* the importance of providing adequate conference-servicing resources to all United Nations conference centres, for the effective and efficient discharge of their mandates;

10. *Notes* the improvement in the rate of utilization of conference facilities at the United Nations Office at Nairobi, as recorded during the most recent reporting period;

11. *Urges* all subsidiary bodies of the Governing Council of the United Nations Environment Programme and the Commission on Human Settlements, and encourages Member States, intergovernmental bodies and regional and other major groupings, to increase their use of the conference facilities at Nairobi;

12. *Reiterates its request* to the Secretary-General to assist the bodies mentioned in paragraph 11 of the present section in improving this situation, and requests the Secretary-General to report to the General Assembly at its fifty-seventh session, through the Committee on Conferences, on the actions taken to that end;

13. *Encourages* all United Nations bodies and expert groups not subject to the headquarters rule to hold some of their meetings at the United Nations Office at Nairobi;

14. *Strongly discourages* any invitation for hosting meetings which would violate the headquarters rule, in particular for United Nations centres with a low utilization level;

15. *Encourages* the Secretary-General to continue to intensify efforts being made by the United Nations Office at Nairobi to attract more meetings to its facilities;

16. *Reiterates its request* to the Committee on Conferences to consult with those bodies that consistently utilized less than the applicable benchmark figure of their allocated resources for the past three sessions with a view to making appropriate recommendations in order to achieve the optimum utilization of conference-servicing resources;

17. *Reiterates* that meetings of Charter and mandated bodies must be serviced as a priority;

18. *Decides* to include all necessary resources in the budget for the biennium 2002-2003 to provide interpretation services for meetings of regional and other major groupings of Member States upon request by those groups, on an ad hoc basis, in accordance with established practice, and requests the Secretary-General

to submit to the General Assembly at its fifty-seventh session, through the Committee on Conferences, a report on the implementation of this decision;

19. *Notes* the importance of meetings of regional and other major groupings of Member States for the smooth functioning of the sessions of intergovernmental bodies, and requests the Secretary-General to ensure that, as far as possible, all requests for conference services for meetings of regional and other major groupings of Member States are met;

20. *Notes with concern* the difficulties experienced by some Member States owing to the lack of conference services for some meetings of regional and other major groupings of Member States;

21. *Requests* the Secretary-General to provide information on meetings of regional and other major groupings of Member States not serviced by conference services in the context of the proposed programme budget for the biennium 2002-2003;

22. *Also requests* the Secretary-General, when preparing budget proposals for conference services, to ensure that the level of resources proposed for temporary assistance is commensurate with the full demand for services, estimated on the basis of current experience;

23. *Further requests* the Secretary-General to continue to report on the utilization rates of interpretation services and conference facilities at all duty stations;

24. *Reiterates its request* to the Secretary-General to consider improving and modernizing the conference facilities at the United Nations Office at Nairobi in order to accommodate adequately major meetings and conferences, and to report thereon to the General Assembly at its resumed fifty-sixth session, through the Committee on Conferences;

III
Documentation- and publication-related matters

1. *Notes with deep concern* the low rate of compliance with the six-week rule for the issuance of documentation, and encourages the Secretary-General, in view of the impact of late submissions on the timely issuance of documents, to deal with this alarming situation;

2. *Reiterates its request* to the Secretary-General to ensure that documentation is available in accordance with the six-week rule for the distribution of documents simultaneously in the six official languages of the General Assembly;

3. *Deeply regrets* the failure of author departments to abide by section III, paragraph 5, of its resolution 55/222, and in this regard requests the Secretary-General to take corrective measures to ensure the full implementation of this provision and to report to the General Assembly in the first part of its resumed fifty-sixth session;

4. *Notes* that the failure to abide by that provision also connotes failure to abide by the six-week rule for the availability of documents as well as General Assembly resolution 50/11 on multilingualism, in which the Assembly recalled the need to ensure the simultaneous distribution of documents in the six official languages of the United Nations;

5. *Reiterates its request* to the Secretary-General to direct all departments to include, where appropriate, the following elements in reports originating in the Secretariat:

(a) A summary of the report;

(*b*) Consolidated conclusions, recommendations and other proposed actions;

(*c*) Relevant background information;

6. *Reiterates* that all documents submitted to legislative organs by the Secretariat and expert bodies for consideration and action should have conclusions and recommendations in bold print;

7. *Requests* the Office of Internal Oversight Services to submit its reports in accordance with paragraph 12 of General Assembly resolution 53/208 B;

8. *Regrets* that, if a report is issued late, some departments of the Secretariat still do not indicate the reasons for the delay when the report is introduced;

9. *Reiterates its decision* that, if a report is submitted late to conference services, the reasons therefor should be included in a footnote to the document;

10. *Decides* to approve the report of the Secretary-General on measures taken by the Secretariat to strengthen responsibility and accountability in the submission of documentation, with the exception of those described in paragraph 12 of the present section, and requests the Secretary-General to submit a comprehensive report to the General Assembly at its fifty-seventh session on measures taken to ensure full implementation of the report;

11. *Requests* the Secretary-General to develop an effective accountability and responsibility system within the Secretariat in order to ensure timely submission of documents for processing, and to report thereon, through the Committee on Conferences, to the General Assembly at its fifty-seventh session;

12. *Also requests* the Secretary-General to bring to the attention of the organs concerned, when they are taking action on draft resolutions and decisions, rules 78 and 120 of the rules of procedure of the General Assembly;

13. *Notes with concern* the delay in the issuance of verbatim and summary records, and in this regard requests the Secretary-General to take appropriate measures to ameliorate the situation;

14. *Requests* the Secretary-General to study the possibility of further measures in this regard, including enhanced cooperation between the production of press releases by the Department of Public Information of the Secretariat and the preparation of summary records by the Department of General Assembly Affairs and Conference Services, bearing in mind the different nature of press releases and summary records;

15. *Also requests* the Secretary-General to ensure the communication of resolutions adopted by the General Assembly to the States Members of the United Nations within fifteen days of the close of each session;

16. *Welcomes* the new format for the issuance of the *Official Records* of the resolutions and decisions adopted by the General Assembly at its fifty-fifth session, in accordance with the request contained in resolution 54/248, section C, paragraph 3;

17. *Requests* the Secretary-General to ensure fully the issuance of all documents and publications of the Economic and Social Commission for Western Asia in Arabic, which is most relevant to the requirements of the Member States of the region, as well as in the other working languages of the Commission to meet the requirements of readers outside the region, as appropriate, and to report thereon to the General Assembly by its fifty-seventh session;

IV
Translation- and interpretation-related matters

1. *Requests* the Secretary-General not to conduct further pilot projects on remote interpretation until technological developments so warrant;

2. *Also requests* the Secretary-General to provide a comprehensive comparative cost-benefit analysis on the use of remote interpretation at all United Nations duty stations, as recipients and as providers of that service, covering, inter alia, direct and indirect related costs and utilization rates, as well as issues pertaining to the working conditions of interpreters;

3. *Decides* to approve, for an initial period of one year, the training initiative for interpreters who, on the first competitive examination, scored higher than the benchmark of 55 per cent and who possess those language combinations that are insufficiently represented on the roster of successful candidates, subject to the submission to the General Assembly at its fifty-seventh session of information on the results of the training activities, the continuing need for the programme and related financial arrangements;

4. *Requests* the Secretary-General to provide updated information to the General Assembly at its fifty-seventh session, under the agenda item entitled "Human resources management", on current practices related to the special ceiling on the United Nations annual earnings for United Nations retirees employed on a short-term basis in language services, as established by the Assembly in its decision 51/408 of 4 November 1996, with a view to reviewing this issue;

5. *Decides* to conduct a comprehensive review of the current norms and standards of productivity in the language services and the impact of ongoing technological innovations on their work, and requests the Secretary-General to submit a detailed report on the subject, through the Committee on Conferences, to the General Assembly at its fifty-seventh session;

6. *Reiterates its concern* at the high rate of self-revision in the translation services, which exceeded the benchmark, and in this regard requests the Secretary-General to accord high priority to the post of reviser and to reduce reliance on self-revision to the maximum extent, and to take these considerations into account when filling vacancies in the translation services;

7. *Notes with deep concern* that some official documents are not translated into all the official languages of the Organization;

8. *Requests* the Secretary-General to ensure that the Secretariat undertakes to translate all United Nations documents into all the other official languages of the Organization simultaneously, including documents for which circulation is requested under agenda items of the principal deliberative bodies of the United Nations, regardless of their length;

9. *Also requests* the Secretary-General to fill expeditiously the remaining vacancies in the interpretation service at the United Nations Office at Nairobi and to report thereon to the General Assembly at its resumed fifty-sixth session;

10. *Further requests* the Secretary-General to accelerate his efforts to fill vacant posts in interpretation and translation at Headquarters and at all other United Nations duty stations;

11. *Requests* the Secretary-General to refrain from using the terms "different languages" or "multilin-

gual" in official documents when referring to the six official languages of the United Nations;

12. *Expresses concern* about the quality of interpretation services provided to intergovernmental meetings, and requests the Secretary-General to ensure the highest standards of quality for interpretation services provided to these meetings;

13. *Reiterates its request* to the Secretary-General to ensure that training opportunities in the six official languages are equally available to all language staff, including those at duty stations away from Headquarters;

14. *Requests* the Secretary-General to ensure that efforts continue to be made to improve the quality control of language services at all duty stations;

15. *Reiterates its request* to the Secretary-General to ensure that translation, in principle, reflects the specificity of each language;

16. *Also reiterates its request* to the Secretary-General, in order to improve further the quality of translation of documents issued in the six official languages, to ensure continuous dialogue between translation staff and interpretation staff, among United Nations headquarters at New York, Geneva, Vienna and Nairobi, and between translation divisions and Member States with regard to the standardization of the terminology used;

17. *Further reiterates its request* to the Secretary-General to hold informational meetings in order to brief Member States periodically on the terminology used;

18. *Requests* the Secretary-General to conduct consultations, with Member States concerned, on the improvement of translation services;

V
Information technology

1. *Requests* the Secretary-General to submit to the General Assembly at its fifty-seventh session a progress report on the use of information technology in the Department of General Assembly Affairs and Conference Services, including voice recognition, remote translation, computer-assisted translation, the Electronic Documents Registration, Information and Tracking System, the new stock control system for documents and publications, digitization of meeting recording systems, electronic planning and servicing of meetings, and computerized terminology data banks, specifying in particular the impact of these technologies on the working methods and productivity of the personnel of the Department;

2. *Notes with concern* the content of paragraph 7 of the report of the Secretary-General, which stresses that progress in the development of the United Nations web site on the Internet in the six official languages has been slower than expected, and that the realization of a truly equal multilingual web site will remain elusive.

ANNEX
Guidelines on limiting meeting duration

1. Meetings normally should be held during regular meeting hours, namely, from 10 a.m. to 1 p.m. and from 3 p.m. to 6 p.m., on working days;

2. The Secretariat should intensify coordination between its relevant units with a view to planning for the provision of conference services;

3. Intergovernmental bodies should undertake a review of their meeting patterns and, in coordination with the Department of General Assembly Affairs and Conference Services of the Secretariat, adjust their meeting requests for subsequent sessions accordingly;

4. Requests for the extension of sessions beyond the originally scheduled dates, resumed sessions and other intersessional departures would continue to be submitted to the Committee on Conferences and handled in accordance with General Assembly resolution 43/222 B and with past practice as agreed by the Committee.

On 24 December, the Assembly decided that the item entitled "Pattern of conferences" would remain for consideration at its resumed fifty-sixth (2002) session (**decision 56/464**) and that the Fifth Committee would continue consideration of the item at that session (**decision 56/458**).

Intergovernmental meetings

At the request of host Governments, the main documents of intergovernmental conferences held in 2001 were transmitted to the Secretary-General for circulation to the General Assembly, the Security Council or both, as follows:

Seventy-fourth ordinary session of the Council of Ministers of the Organization of African Unity (OAU) and ninth ordinary session of the African Economic Community (Lusaka, Zambia, 5-8 July) and thirty-seventh ordinary session of the Assembly of Heads of State and Government of OAU and fifth ordinary session of the African Economic Community (Lusaka, 9-11 July) [A/56/457]; Summit of Heads of State and Government of the G-8 (Genoa, Italy, 20-22 July) [A/56/222-S/2001/736]; thirty-second Pacific Islands Forum (Nauru, 16-18 August) [A/56/388]; ninth extraordinary session of Foreign Ministers of the Organization of the Islamic Conference (OIC) (Doha, Qatar, 10 October) [A/56/462-S/2001/962]; twenty-fifth annual meeting of Ministers for Foreign Affairs of the Group of 77 (New York, 16 November) [A/56/647]; tenth extraordinary session of Foreign Ministers of OIC (Doha, 10 December) [A/56/703-S/2001/1192]; twenty-fifth session of the Authority of Heads of State and Government of the Economic Community of West African States (Dakar, Senegal, 20-21 December) [A/56/849-S/2002/219]; twenty-second Summit of the Supreme Council of the Gulf Cooperation Council (Muscat, Oman, 30-31 December) [A/56/797-S/2002/125].

Use of conference services

The Committee on Conferences considered a July report of the Secretary-General on improved utilization of conference-servicing resources, including meeting statistics of UN organs for 2000 [A/AC.172/2001/3] and a conference room paper containing statistical information on and analysis of extended meetings and sessions, with proposals for limiting meeting duration.

The Committee noted that the 2000 utilization factor exceeded the benchmark of 80 per cent. In Vienna, it decreased by 5 percentage points, while it increased by 3 percentage points in Geneva and 16 percentage points in Nairobi. The Committee recommended that chairpersons institute time limits for the presentation of standard documents by the Secretariat. It expressed concern at the increased number of extended meetings and sessions, and suggested that the secretariats of the bodies concerned be informed, in advance, of the overtime costs involved. It endorsed the guidelines on limiting meetings and recommended them to the General Assembly for adoption.

The Committee requested the Chairman to consult with bodies that consistently utilized less than the applicable benchmark figure of their allocated resources over the preceding three sessions with a view to making recommendations on achieving the optimum utilization of conference-servicing resources. It noted the concerns of intergovernmental bodies on the methodology for calculating the utilization factor and looked forward to receiving a further analysis and review of the indices, including possible benchmark figures for the planning accuracy factor and the meeting ratio, among others, and a measurement of the degree to which unutilized services were reallocated.

Use of regional conference facilities

Bangkok and Addis Ababa

In August, pursuant to General Assembly resolution 55/222 [YUN 2000, p. 1387], the Committee on Conferences considered the Secretary-General's report on the utilization of the UN conference centres in Bangkok, Thailand, and Addis Ababa, Ethiopia [A/56/293].

The report indicated that, as a result of the measures introduced in 2000 [YUN 2000, p. 1393], the utilization of the conference centre in Bangkok had increased steadily. In 2000, a total of 499 events were organized, compared to 423 in 1999, and, for the first five months of 2001, the centre was the venue for 219 events. The constraints to the use of the centre remained, in particular the fixed meeting-style configuration of meeting rooms that did not satisfy the requirements of events not held by the Economic and Social Commission for Asia and the Pacific (ESCAP). To maximize the commercial use of the centre, one of the large conference rooms would therefore have to be converted into a multi-purpose room with a flexible seating arrangement at an estimated cost of $273,000. Attempts were continuing to cooperate with professional conference organizers in bringing business to the centre, and Member States, specialized agencies and related UN entities, regional and other organizations and the private sector were being encouraged to hold events there.

At the Addis Ababa conference centre, utilization of the facilities increased significantly, from 356 events in 1999 to 491 in 2000. The utilization rate increased from 29.92 per cent in 1999 to 41.26 per cent in 2000, attributable to marketing and advertising strategies, both locally and internationally, as well as an increase in events held by the Economic Commission for Africa (ECA). Additional measures were being taken to improve the centre's functioning, including the loan of staff from the Nairobi conference centre to Addis Ababa, recruitment of a Chief of the Conference Coordination Unit and the redeployment of additional staff. A favourable catering service contract was negotiated to provide quality catering at all events. Efforts also continued to encourage all UN and other bodies to use the centre.

The Committee on Conferences [A/56/32] encouraged ESCAP and ECA to continue their efforts to improve the utilization of their conference centres and to keep the Committee informed of developments. Conference services managers of the Secretariat and regional commissions were also encouraged to share their experience and expertise.

Nairobi

In July, pursuant to General Assembly resolution 55/222 [YUN 2000, p. 1387], the Secretary-General submitted a report on the improved utilization of conference facilities at the United Nations Office at Nairobi (UNON) [A/56/133 & Corr.1]. The report examined meeting activity, including statistical information, in Nairobi in 2000 and January-June 2001, and projections for the remainder of 2001.

The number of meetings with interpretation held in Nairobi in 2000 was 242, a slight decrease from the 254 in 1999. Non-calendar meetings increased to 72, surpassing the 65 planned for the biennium. From January to June 2001, 43 non-calendar meetings were held. During 2000, 560 meetings were held without interpretation, an increase of more than 200 over 1999; and 122 multilingual meetings with remote translation were held outside Nairobi. During 2000, 13 major meetings were serviced by UNON but held at locations outside Nairobi, and five meetings between January and June 2001.

The establishment of a permanent interpretation service in Nairobi in January had already had a positive effect on the work of the United Nations Environment Programme (UNEP) and the United Nations Centre for Human Settlements (Habitat), and the committees of permanent representatives, which, since May, had had access to multilingual interpretation.

The Committee on Conferences [A/56/32] expressed satisfaction that the conference-servicing facility of Nairobi was becoming organizationally, functionally and budgetarily an integral part of the UN Department of General Assembly Affairs and Conference Services (DGAACS). It noted the increase in the number of multilingual meetings held and the cost-saving effect of the establishment of the Nairobi interpretation service for the regular budget in terms of the reduced need for temporary assistance. The Committee recommended that the Assembly request UNEP and Habitat to comply with the headquarters rule and hold all their meetings at UNON to further increase conference facilities utilization.

Conference services for regional and other major groupings

In July, pursuant to General Assembly resolutions 54/248 [YUN 1999, p. 1368] and 55/222 [YUN 2000, p. 1387], the Secretary-General reported on the provision of interpretation services to meetings of regional and other major groupings of Member States from 1 July 2000 to 30 June 2001 [A/56/213 & Corr.1]. During that period, 100 per cent of requests for services by such States were met in New York, Geneva, Vienna and Nairobi. Ninety-one per cent of requests for interpretation services were met in New York and 100 per cent in Geneva.

The Committee on Conferences [A/56/32] recommended that duty stations should continue to keep statistics of requests for servicing of meetings. It urged intergovernmental bodies, at the planning stage, to take into account meetings of regional and other major groupings of Member States; to make provision for such meetings in their programmes of work; and to notify DGAACS of cancellations, so that conference-servicing resources could be reassigned.

Coordination of conference services

The Committee on Conferences [A/56/32] considered an oral report on improved coordination of conference services. Concerning meetings held away from established headquarters, the Committee was told that the responsibility for conferences services coordination was assigned to the headquarters location of the substantive secretariat. Discussions had taken place on broad policy aspects, such as coordinating clearance procedures for the headquarters agreement, establishing teams of staff from all locations, financial arrangements and the inclusion of smaller duty stations. Trials of coordinated workload-

sharing pointed to potential efficiency gains. As to the coordination of technology advances, to avoid duplication and make the most efficient use of limited resources, a working group was established to formulate specific projects of the ongoing programme and elements of an information technology strategy. A working group was also established to develop guidelines for the preparation of financial reports and to analyse procedures for their clearance. The DGAACS Executive Office at Headquarters would analyse the experience gained in the common examinations for written language functions so as to address further the lack of functional mobility of language staff, to move staff to meet peak workloads and to improve career prospects.

The Committee noted the oral report and encouraged further steps by the Secretariat to coordinate conference services globally. It concluded that the Inter-Agency Meeting on Language Arrangements, Documentation and Publications should promote cooperation between the United Nations and other international organizations on the use of conference services and make proposals for sharing translation, interpretation, editorial and printing services. It recommended that the General Assembly study the possibility of strengthening the Committee's oversight and supervisory functions to, among other objectives, increase the effectiveness of its work and strengthen its role as one of the Assembly's subsidiary bodies.

OIOS report. The Secretary-General transmitted to the General Assembly in February [A/55/803] the report of the UN Office of Internal Oversight Services (OIOS) on the inspection of the consolidation of technical support services in DGAACS. Established in 1997 as part of the Secretary-General's programme of reform [YUN 1997, p. 1390], DGAACS integrated the major technical support services for the General Assembly, the Economic and Social Council and their subsidiary bodies. The inspection assessed how DGAACS's establishment and the consolidation of the technical support services contributed to the Secretary-General's overall reform objectives.

The inspection found that DGAACS had enhanced the efficiency of the services provided to Member States. Meetings scheduling and document processing were currently part of a coordinated process under the guidance of a single Department head, and the time-consuming interdepartmental consultations of previous years had been reduced. That had allowed for improved planning in the allocation of services and facilities, resulting in a more rational use of resources. However, continuous high-level collaboration between DGAACS and other departments was needed to further clarify technical and substantive functions.

OIOS recommended that the Under-Secretaries-General for General Assembly Affairs and Conference Services and for Disarmament Affairs should ensure that decisions taken to enhance the provision of technical and substantive services to the Assembly and its subsidiary committees were fully complied with and monitored, and any necessary corrective action taken.

The Under-Secretary-General of DGAACS should discuss with the senior management group the enforcing of compliance with document submission requirements and issue a directive on electronic submission standards, including the non-acceptance of documents in hard-copy form only. He should collaborate with Geneva and Vienna, as well as the Department of Management, in the budget preparation process to ensure that conference resources were optimally utilized. The Advisory Panel on Information Technology should prioritize DGAACS information technology needs and present a clear and coordinated strategy in 2001.

All section/unit chiefs should establish performance criteria and prepare operational guidelines to safeguard institutional memory and for efficient management. DGAACS should work towards ensuring client satisfaction, including the conduct of customer surveys. Lessons learned should be reviewed after each major conference and best practices exchanged among the technical secretariats on a regular basis.

The Under-Secretary-General should, with the Committee on Conferences, identify meeting demands in order to adjust servicing capacity and limit meeting duration. Mechanisms or guidelines for meetings or conferences should be established to ensure that extended meetings were an exception and not the rule, bearing in mind their budgetary implications, as well as the toll on the well-being of staff.

The Advisory Committee on Administrative and Budgetary Questions (ACABQ), in its first report on the 2002-2003 proposed programme budget [A/56/7], commented on various issues raised in the OIOS report.

Documents control

In response to General Assembly resolution 55/222 [YUN 2000, p. 1387], the Secretary-General submitted an interim report on the availability of documentation for the proper functioning of intergovernmental bodies [A/56/299], which compiled information from those bodies on the availability of their pre-session documentation and the review process with author departments. A comprehensive picture of the situation would be obtained, upon the completion of the biennial cycle of meetings, when more responses from intergovernmental bodies were expected. However, at the current stage, distinctions could be made between the various organs and the degree to which their work was affected by the availability of pre-session documentation. It was clear that the level of coordination between intergovernmental bodies and the Secretariat and conference services could have a significant impact on the availability of documentation. Reducing the number of reports requested could also contribute to timely issuance of pre-session documentation.

The Committee on Conferences took note of the report and looked forward to obtaining a comprehensive review. It recommended that the Assembly ask the Secretary-General to provide a detailed report on the Secretariat's capacity for efficient and effective delivery of conference services and ways of enhancing the timely availability of documentation to Member States.

The Committee on Conferences also considered the Secretary-General's report on the submission of documentation consistent with the six-week rule [A/56/300], in response to Assembly resolutions 55/222 [YUN 2000, p. 1387] and 54/248 [YUN 1999, p. 1368]. The report described measures taken by the Secretariat to strengthen responsibility and accountability in that regard and proposed measures that could lead to the timely issuance of documentation. The Committee took note of those measures and recommended that the Assembly invite the Secretary-General to develop an effective accountability and responsibility system to ensure the timely submission of documents for processing. The Committee encouraged the Secretariat to continue making concerted efforts to remedy the situation of late issuance of documentation and to analyse more extensively the reasons for it and the resulting additional costs.

ACABQ report. In October [A/56/475], ACABQ said that, given the close relationship of the issues and in the interest of streamlining documentation, those two reports should have been consolidated into one. The availability of documentation for intergovernmental bodies could not be properly considered without also considering compliance with the six-week rule. It welcomed the replacement of the traditional paper-based management system for the coordination of the submission of documentation with a computerized database application and encouraged its further development.

Official Document System

The Committee on Conferences considered the Secretary-General's June report on the re-engineering of the optical disk system (ODS) [A/56/120], submitted in response to General Assembly resolution 55/222 [YUN 2000, p. 1387]. The system was renamed the Official Document System, retaining the old acronym. The report stated that the re-engineered ODS, replacing the old optical disk system, developed in 1991, with faster, more reliable and inexpensive magnetic media (disks), would be delivered in two phases: phase 1 (one-to-one migration) in which the old system would be migrated to the new system, and phase 2 (non-Roman language support function), which would facilitate search and retrieval in the six official languages. In February, developmental work of phase 1 was completed and the new software and converted database were installed and tested.

The Committee welcomed the efforts to update the ODS and the introduction of the new system. It encouraged the Secretary-General to continue those efforts and requested that a report on progress achieved, as well as on the impact of the re-engineering on ODS access at all duty stations, be submitted for consideration at the Assembly's fifty-sixth (2001) session.

In an October revised report [A/56/120/Rev.1], the Secretary-General said that phase 1 was concluded in September and the new system was running smoothly. It was web technology–based, and could be accessed from anywhere in the world using a standard web browser. It was available to all UN staff and permanent missions in New York and at all offices away from Headquarters, with the exception of ECA. Efforts were being made to establish a connectivity for ECA and for all peace-keeping missions. Implementation of phase 2 was expected to start in December and would provide for a full multilingual support function. Because of the high maintenance required for the new system, the restriction on the number of users by each Member State remained, but was raised from 10 to 20 in August. The Secretariat hoped to gradually remove that restriction.

ACABQ reports. In October [A/56/475], ACABQ welcomed the progress made and encouraged the Secretariat to continue to work towards unrestricted and free access to the system for all accredited NGOs. The availability of the system should be advertised as widely as possible. In its first report on the 2002-2003 proposed programme budget [A/56/7], ACABQ requested a review of the cost-effectiveness of the level of fees currently being charged for access by public users to the ODS.

Availability of electronic documents

In November [A/C.5/56/12], the Secretary-General reported on the simultaneous availability of parliamentary documentation in electronic form in the six official languages on the UN web site. He said that currently only limited parliamentary documents were made available on the UN web site. To ensure simultaneous availability of all parliamentary documents, it would be most practical to make the ODS free to the public and modify the UN web site to provide direct hyperlink access to documents on the ODS, instead of the current practice of copying them to the web site.

However, the degree to which the performance of the ODS would be impacted by the implementation of the full multilingual support function, expected to be fully operational in January 2002, was unknown. Therefore, after carefully monitoring the impact during 2002, the Secretariat would address the feasibility of free access to the ODS and submit proposals for revising the current ODS subscription policy guided by General Assembly resolution 51/211 F [YUN 1997, p. 1503], including its financial implications.

Cost-effectiveness of UN publications

In September, responding to General Assembly resolution 54/259 [YUN 2000, p. 1392], the Secretary-General reported on the implementation of recommendations contained in resolution 52/220 [YUN 1997, p. 1421] regarding the publication of the *UN Chronicle* in all official languages [A/56/339]. Since the adoption of that resolution, the UN Department of Public Information (DPI) had been exploring several options to resume publication of the *UN Chronicle* in Arabic, Chinese, Russian and Spanish, suspended in 1996 due to the Organization's financial crisis. DPI conducted a pilot project in each of the four languages to assess the costs and feasibility of resuming regular production of those language editions. The pilot project showed that the lengthy period of time required to carry out, through an external contractor, the entire publication process in those languages could result in the publication losing its value. Moreover, it reflected the necessity to base the production of those editions on a secure financial basis so as to ensure the greatest possible parity in quality and timeliness among all editions. Bearing in mind the difficulties experienced by DPI in producing the publication in the manner and frequency requested by the Assembly, $1.3 million was included in the proposed programme budget of the Department for the 2002-2003 biennium for producing the *UN Chronicle* four times a year in all six official languages.

ACABQ report. ACABQ, in October [A/56/475], recommended that a critical assessment be undertaken by the relevant intergovernmental bodies of the utility of the *UN Chronicle* in general, including an analysis of its demand in the various languages, the merits of its distribution online and the method of its publication and printing.

UN web sites

The Committee on Conferences, having heard a presentation by a DPI representative on the multilingual development, maintenance and enrichment of the UN web site and received a report of the Secretary-General on the subject [A/AC.198/2001/8] (see p. 557), expressed serious concern about the growing disparities on the web site between English and the other official languages. It requested the Secretariat to include Nairobi and Vienna, together with New York and Geneva, on the web site entitled "About the United Nations".

Interpretation and translation matters

Remote interpretation

In July [A/56/188], the Secretary-General, responding to General Assembly resolutions 54/248 [YUN 1999, p. 1368] and 55/222 [YUN 2000, p. 1387], reported on the second remote interpretation experiment conducted at UN Headquarters from 16 to 27 April during the ninth session of the Commission on Sustainable Development, the first having been held in 1999 [YUN 1999, p. 1367]. The experiment tested the suitability of satellite links for remote interpretation purposes; designed and tested the best possible configuration of video technology; assessed the impact of remote interpretation on interpreters' working conditions; and gathered information on the costs of remote interpretation systems.

The Secretary-General concluded that bringing remote interpretation as close as possible to normal on-site conditions was only partially successful. Deficient synchronization between sound and image and the inability to obtain the visual information available on-site were two problems for which technological solutions had not yet been found. Satellite links proved reliable and could make service between Nairobi and New York financially viable, but it would be costly in Geneva and Vienna, which were not covered by the UN satellite communications system. As to the comparative cost-effectiveness of each servicing modality, comparing the likely costs of daily subsistence allowance for interpreters with the cost for integrated services digital network (ISDN) communications showed that the ratio between the two varied widely depending on the meeting location. In addition, the combination of available technical and human resources was not conducive to effective simultaneous interpretation.

There were also uncertainties and trade-offs between the volume of data transmitted via ISDN lines and the stability of the transmissions, and interpreters did not perform with the same efficiency when working remotely.

Future advances in videoconferencing and communications should be continually assessed to determine whether they could offer solutions to the outstanding technical problems of remote interpretation. Potential financial advantages of remote interpretation in certain cases, together with the additional flexibility in the use of interpretation services that it could offer, justified further work along those lines.

Committee consideration. The Committee on Conferences [A/56/32] noted the report and supported the Secretariat's intention to foster the accumulation of experience among interpreters working on-site at meetings with a videoconferencing component so as to facilitate their adaptation to the new working environment. It asked the Secretariat to assess future advances in videoconferencing and communications to determine whether they could solve the outstanding technical problems of remote interpretation. It noted that the Secretariat did not foresee conducting further experiments. The Committee also asked that a report on developments in those areas, as well as on activities in remote interpretation carried out by other international organizations, be submitted to the Assembly's fifty-seventh (2002) session through the Committee on Conferences.

ACABQ report. In October [A/56/475], ACABQ reiterated its encouragement of the continued exploration of the feasibility of large-scale remote interpretation. It urged the Secretariat to intensify its efforts to find solutions to the technical problems involved, as well as to issues pertaining to the working conditions of interpreters, and requested that a progress report be submitted to the Assembly's fifty-seventh session.

Recruitment in language services

In August [A/56/277], the Secretary-General, in response to General Assembly resolution 55/222 [YUN 2000, p. 1387], submitted a report on excessive vacancy rates in language services at some duty stations and issues relating to the recruitment of language staff.

A review of the vacancy rates at the four main UN conference-servicing centres (Headquarters, the UN Office at Geneva (UNOG), the UN Office at Nairobi (UNON) and the UN Office at Vienna (UNOV)), as well as at the regional commissions, showed, as at 30 June 2001, a decrease in the total number of vacancies for all language services, with the aggregate vacancy rate falling from 10.3 per cent to 9 per cent. However, decreasing but still fairly high aggregate vacancy rates at duty stations with large language services could only be explained by recruitment difficulties and the non-availability of suitable candidates. There were language-specific difficulties in matching the "yield" of recruitment exercises with high depletion rates resulting from early or normal retirement, and the system of mobility incentives proposed in 1999 [YUN 1999, p. 1367] for reducing excessive vacancy rates was limited, given the need to ensure uniform treatment of language and non-language staff.

In terms of recruitment, there was a downward trend in the yield of language examinations for some languages or language combinations. However, increasing the frequency of those examinations was too costly and likely to produce diminishing returns. In addition, the nature of the training received by language specialists in educational institutions seemed to be ill-suited to the special and stringent requirements of the United Nations and other international organizations. As for interpretation, the Secretary-General recommended that the Assembly approve the reinstatement of the training programme to address recruitment difficulties for one year, subject to the submission of a report in 2002 on its results, the continuing need for the programme and related financial arrangements. In the case of translators, on-the-job training was an option that was often resorted to. The abolition of the common examinations for recruiting editors, translators and verbatim reporters from a common roster in favour of jointly held examinations for the three functions producing three different rosters would save costs, help alleviate recruitment difficulties in some editorial units and attract more candidates.

The Inter-Agency Meeting on Language Arrangements, Documentation and Publications (Geneva, 3-6 July) examined the option of dealing with the problem of recruitment at its root rather than through remedial action. It established a working group to promote cooperation between international organizations and major educational institutions engaged in the training of language specialists, to better inform them about language professions in international organizations and to launch pilot projects aimed at adjusting curricula or establishing special training paths.

The Committee on Conferences remained concerned about the persistence of excessive vacancy rates at most duty stations with small or medium-sized language services, and at the lack of success in filling vacant interpreter posts in some languages at UNON. It recommended that priority be given to filling such posts, as well as those at UNOV, from the 2001 competitive examinations for Arabic and English interpreters, and at UNON and UNOV from the January 2002 competitive examinations for French and Spanish interpreters. The Secretariat should continue to monitor the vacancy situation at duty stations with chronic vacancy problems.

The Committee also expressed concern about the low yield of some competitive language examinations and that successful candidates often refused offers of employment by the Organization. It recommended that the Secretariat advertise competitive language examinations more effectively by focusing on language schools, other educational institutions and professional associations, and that the in-house training programme for interpreters be reinstated. It welcomed the inter-agency initiative to address training issues at their source and asked the General Assembly to initiate a comprehensive review of the norms and standards of productivity in the language services in the light of ongoing technological innovations.

ACABQ report. In October [A/56/475], ACABQ, in its comments on the Secretary-General's report, noted that it had not been possible to implement the non-monetary mobility incentives for language staff that had been envisaged in Assembly resolution 53/208 A [YUN 1998, p. 1348].

ACABQ expressed concern at the downward trend in the yield of language examinations in the past few years. It recommended approval of the training initiative for interpreters for an initial period of one year, subject to the submission of information on its results to the Assembly in 2002. It welcomed the on-the-job training for translators.

In a related matter, ACABQ called attention to the need to ensure cost-effectiveness in arrangements for contractual translation, and requested that information be provided to the Fifth Committee on comparative costs of commercial translation, current arrangements for contractual translation at the United Nations and the experience of Member States in that field. It suggested that the question of assuring quality control should also be addressed.

UN information systems

Information technology

In response to General Assembly resolution 54/249 [YUN 1999, p. 1289], the Secretary-General submitted a February report on a plan of action for information technology in the Secretariat

[A/55/780]. The report, which also responded to his programme of reform of the United Nations in information and communication technology (ICT) [YUN 1997, p. 1389], reviewed the status of technology in the Secretariat, described the objectives that had been established and outlined a strategy to achieve them. It also presented a description of planned action in each area and those already undertaken, and expected results. According to the report, a survey undertaken by the Information Technology Services Division in 2000 revealed that, while all duty stations had or were in the process of setting up modern and reliable ICT infrastructure, it was adequate to meet current needs but major upgrades would be needed to meet the increasing demand. There was also duplication of systems in certain areas and no standard methodology had been followed throughout the Secretariat in the development of those systems. The Secretariat needed to build its ability to take advantage of new technologies and keep up to date with rapid developments in the field.

Based on that review and at the directive of the Secretary-General, specific objectives were established to ensure the integration of the ICT dimension into the strategic component of programme delivery. Those included access to and sharing of information, ICT field support, technical infrastructure, capacity-building and the achievement of electronic administration. To achieve those objectives, the Secretariat adopted a strategy of parallel and coordinated activities in five areas: sharing internally and externally the knowledge of the Secretariat; management of ICT activities in the Secretariat; methodologies for the development and integration of systems; ICT human resources policies; and technical administrative aspects. Implementation of the strategy would include a detailed inventory of ICT infrastructure, systems and organizational structures within the Secretariat; a high-level ICT governance structure, defined by the Steering Committee on Reform and Management Policy; and the establishment of an ICT coordination body at Headquarters and the creation of similar ancillary bodies at offices away from Headquarters.

ACABQ report. ACABQ, in its first report on the proposed programme budget for the 2002-2003 biennium [A/56/7], was in broad agreement with the approach to the management of ICT activities, but stressed that successful implementation of the proposals would require effective central leadership for policy, strategic guidance and standard setting, as well as the commitment of departmental heads to implement decisions at the operational level. It pointed out that the experience of past technological boards and com-

mittees had not been very encouraging, and trusted that the Steering Committee on Reform and Management Policy and the Information and Communication Technology Board would develop into effective policy-setting instruments that could establish and monitor clear, unambiguous guidelines.

Since the 2002-2003 budget was prepared before the ICT strategy was defined, ACABQ noted the lack of information on long-term requirements to implement the strategy and requested that a comprehensive progress report that encompassed peacekeeping information systems be prepared for the Assembly's fifty-seventh (2002) session, in conjunction with the proposed programme budget. Recognizing that more attention needed to be devoted to system-wide coherence and coordination, the Committee requested that the possibility of linking the various stand-alone systems be reviewed and the results included in the comprehensive progress report. Efforts should also be enhanced to adapt the Integrated Management Information System (see p. 1390) to the needs of field and country offices and peacekeeping operations wherever possible.

GENERAL ASSEMBLY ACTION

On 24 December [meeting 92], the General Assembly, on the recommendation of the Fifth Committee [A/56/653], adopted **resolution 56/239** without vote [agenda item 122].

Information technology

The General Assembly,

Recalling its resolution 54/249 of 23 December 1999, by which it requested the Secretary-General to develop a comprehensive strategy for the development and implementation of information technology,

1. *Takes note* of the report of the Secretary-General entitled "Information technology in the Secretariat: a plan of action", and endorses the observations and recommendations of the Advisory Committee on Administrative and Budgetary Questions thereon;

2. *Requests* the Secretary-General to resubmit the plan of action, taking into account the provisions of paragraph 1 above and:

(*a*) Developing a specific plan to improve efficiency through the application of information technology in the Secretariat and the action required to implement it;

(*b*) Defining clearly the responsibilities of the different bodies in the application and integration of information technology within the United Nations;

(*c*) Addressing the objective of improving decision-making with respect to information technology in the Secretariat by improving coordination and reducing duplication;

(*d*) Developing a cost-benefit analysis for use in identifying information technology priorities;

(*e*) Developing an implementation plan for those priorities;

3. *Also requests* the Secretary-General to submit for the consideration of the General Assembly at its fifty-seventh session a single report containing the information requested in the present resolution.

International cooperation in informatics

In response to Economic and Social Council resolution 1999/58 [YUN 1999, p. 1372], the Secretary-General submitted a June report on international cooperation in the field of informatics [E/2001/96], summarizing activities undertaken by the Ad Hoc Open-ended Working Group on Informatics and the UN Secretariat. The Working Group and the Association for Information Technology co-sponsored meetings in January, April and June at the permanent missions of Australia, Denmark and Germany to engage the UN diplomatic community in investigating the impact of ICT on various economic and social agendas, and organized a conference on information security (New York, 30 March). The Working Group continued to establish relationships with UN agencies and, in cooperation with the Secretariat, worked on stabilizing and improving the Internet service offered to Member States. The report also contained information on activities carried out by Secretariat departments.

ECONOMIC AND SOCIAL COUNCIL ACTION

On 26 July [meeting 43], the Economic and Social Council adopted **resolution 2001/24** [draft: E/2001/L.39] without vote [agenda item 7 *(e)*].

The need to harmonize and improve United Nations informatics systems for optimal utilization and accessibility by all States

The Economic and Social Council,

Recognizing the interest of Member States in taking full advantage of information and communications technologies for the acceleration of economic and social development,

Recalling its previous resolutions on the need to harmonize and improve United Nations information systems for optimal utilization and access by all States, with due regard to all official languages,

Stressing the need to ensure complementarities between the mandates of the Ad Hoc Open-ended Working Group on Informatics and of the Information and Communication Technologies Task Force,

Welcoming the report presented by the Chairman of the Working Group on the progress achieved so far in fulfilling its mandate,

1. *Reiterates* the high priority that it attaches to easy, economical, uncomplicated and unhindered access for States Members of the United Nations and observers, as well as non-governmental organizations accredited to the United Nations, to the computerized databases and information systems and services of the United Nations, provided that the unhindered access of non-governmental organizations shall not prejudice the access of Member States and that it shall not impose an additional financial burden for the use of databases and other systems;

2. *Requests* the President of the Economic and Social Council to convene the Ad Hoc Open-ended Working Group on Informatics for one more year to enable it to carry out, from within existing resources, its work of facilitating the successful implementation of the initiatives being taken by the Secretary-General with regard to the use of information technology and of continuing the implementation of measures required to achieve its objectives. In this regard, the Working Group is requested to continue:

(a) To improve electronic connectivity via the Internet for all Member States in their capitals and at major United Nations locations, inter alia, through the enhanced connectivity of permanent missions to the Internet and United Nations databases;

(b) To improve the access of Member States to a wider database of United Nations information on economic and social, development and political issues and other substantive programming areas, and to have all official documents available via the Internet;

(c) To improve electronic links among Member States, the United Nations and the specialized agencies;

(d) To provide training for the staff of permanent missions to enable them to take full advantage of the facilities being developed for Member States;

(e) To enhance the capacity of Member States to access United Nations data online, using low-cost telecommunications links or providing other modalities, such as CD-ROM, whereby Member States can have access to specialized databases not available on the Internet;

(f) To make arrangements, as appropriate, to provide permanent missions of developing countries with hardware platforms to utilize Internet technology;

(g) To use videoconferencing on a more frequent basis, as appropriate, to further communication and interaction within the United Nations system and between the United Nations, permanent missions and academic institutions;

(h) To intensify contacts with the private sector so as to bring its wealth of experience to contribute positively to the work of the Working Group;

(i) To make greater use of projector/screen units for negotiations;

(j) To establish a password-protected system of mailing lists and bulletin boards on the United Nations web site to facilitate the dissemination of information among the United Nations missions;

(k) To explore ways to fully use the potential of information and communication technologies in order to speed up translation processes;

3. *Supports* the efforts of the Working Group to keep intact the network of national focal points that was established in connection with the year 2000 problem, as a vehicle for the diffusion of best practices and lessons learned, in particular for the exchange of information on locally and regionally appropriate solutions, and in this regard appeals once again to countries and other sources to provide the extrabudgetary resources necessary to maintain the mailing list of the national focal points;

4. *Requests* the Secretary-General to extend full cooperation to the Working Group and to give priority to implementing its recommendations;

5. *Also requests* the Secretary-General to report to the Council at its substantive session of 2002 on the action taken in follow-up to the present resolution, including the findings of the Working Group.

Integrated Management Information System

The General Assembly, by **decision 55/463** of 12 April, took note of the Secretary-General's twelfth progress report on the Integrated Management Information System (IMIS) and endorsed ACABQ's observations and recommendations thereon [YUN 2000, p. 1399].

In his thirteenth progress report on IMIS [A/56/602], the Secretary-General said that the system was currently installed at eight major duty stations and was also being used by UNDP, UNFPA and the United Nations Office for Project Services and, as far as human resources were concerned, by the secretariat of the United Nations Framework Convention on Climate Change, the International Labour Organization, the International Trade Centre and UNICEF. Implementation of the finance functionality had been completed in all major duty stations and usage of the system continued to increase. Payroll processing was extended to all Secretariat staff payrolled from Headquarters in January, including staff in field missions, and in July at the Economic and Social Commission for Western Asia, as well as in Vienna.

Major enhancements to the system included the consolidation of data with the full implementation of the consolidated extracts reporting database used in the preparation of financial reports; a technical and business study of options for full system consolidation in 2002; work on the processes for accounts' closing and opening balances, completion of which would allow for the finalization of archiving requirements; upgrading of the technical platform of the IMIS application to the latest version, making it possible for the entire application to be designed in web format; implementation of the use of electronic forms; and research into "personal accounts" in order to make some IMIS personal data available online. Other enhancements included re-engineering of the user-interface with the upgrade of application software; research into replacing the current reporting tool; and discussion with the Department of Management on integration of IMIS with other programme budgeting and reporting systems.

The long-term strategy for IMIS functioning addressed the need for a technological upgrade of the system to ensure that it met the needs of the Organization. That would require a significant enhancement effort, involving its re-engineering, finance and human resources transactions requiring more than one IMIS site with the required software component, the creation of global security, auditing and administrative controls and the streamlining of UN administrative procedures. The scope of those enhancements to IMIS would require additional budgetary resources in the amount of $5,634,700.

ACABQ, in a December report [A/56/684], said that it had no objection to the detailed work programme for the proposed technological updates, which was annexed to its report, and recommended approval of the amount requested for those enhancements, to be provided from investment income of $5,956,000 reported under the IMIS Fund as at 30 June. It requested that, after the submission of the Secretary-General's final report on lessons learned (see below), information on maintenance and future enhancements to the system should be provided in the context of the proposed programme budget, including information on integrating IMIS with other programme budgeting and reporting systems being developed by the Secretariat.

ACABQ recommended that the Secretary-General report in 2002 on the strategy for deploying IMIS to peacekeeping operations and the international tribunals, and on the enhancements required to make it viable for possible programme applications by UN funds and programmes.

In a December addendum [A/56/602/Add.1], the Secretary-General focused on lessons learned from the development and implementation of IMIS. He said that the project's scope and its impact on the Organization were underestimated. Insufficient resources assigned to the design stages resulted in delays, flaws and omissions that made costly changes necessary. Initially, no budgetary provision was made for training or to cover other implementation activities, and insufficient provision had been made for implementing the system at offices away from Headquarters. The Secretary-General concluded that major lessons learned from the IMIS project included establishing a realistic scope for a project; comprehensive planning; commitment and support of the Organization; and a staged implementation of the system, a realistic approach that allowed for corrective steps. The implementation of IMIS accelerated the upgrade and enhancement of information technologies at all duty stations, and changed the Secretariat's management culture and working habits of staff members.

Other matters

Common services

Communication for
UN development programmes

In a July note, the Secretary-General transmitted to the General Assembly a report prepared by the United Nations Educational, Scientific and Cultural Organization (UNESCO) [A/56/221], in response to Assembly resolution 51/172 [YUN 1996, p. 1352]. The report included the recommendations of the seventh Inter-Agency Round Table on Communication and Development, organized by UNICEF (Salvador de Bahia, Brazil, 1998), and reviewed the communication and development activities of UNESCO, UNICEF, UNFPA, UNEP, the World Health Organization, the Joint United Nations Programme on HIV/AIDS, the Food and Agriculture Organization of the United Nations and the World Bank. UNFPA organized the eighth Round Table (Managua, Nicaragua, 26-29 November) on evaluating the information programmes designed to halt the HIV/AIDS pandemic, development of methodologies to evaluate current communication programmes and using community radio to reach disadvantaged persons.

By **decision 56/437** of 21 December, the Assembly took note of the Secretary-General's note transmitting UNESCO's report.

Common services at Geneva

By **decision 55/469** of 12 April, the General Assembly, having considered the Secretary-General's 2000 report on common services [YUN 2000, p. 1399], endorsed ACABQ's recommendations thereon [ibid., p. 1400] and requested that the Secretary-General report at its fifty-seventh (2002) session on progress made and decisions taken on the future of the Task Force on Common Services.

JIU report. In March [A/55/856], the Secretary-General transmitted a JIU report on the UN system common services at Geneva, part II, on case studies of the International Computing Centre (ICC), the Joint Medical Service (JMS), the Training and Examination Section (TES), the Diplomatic Pouch Service (DPS) and the Joint Purchase Service (JPS). The report identified key strengths and constraints of some existing common services, in accordance with the plan of action for Geneva common services 2000-2010, recommended in part I of its report [YUN 1999, p. 1376].

JIU stated that the facilities and potential of some of the services at the UN Office at Geneva (UNOG) were not being harnessed fully to trim costs, and the fact that some agencies had pulled out of the common services suggested inadequate understanding in some secretariats of the legislative and legal architecture of the UN common system.

JIU recommended the development of a closer association between ICC and the Information Systems Coordination Committee, and that information on the reasons why organizations opted not to use ICC services should be regularly provided and compiled so as to enable the Centre to adjust its operations accordingly. Independent technical auditors should be commissioned to conduct comparisons of quality, efficiency and unit costs of the Centre's services with those of similar services. Those ICC members that intended to reduce their recourse to its services should review their decisions.

JMS should be reorganized into four units, with a more structured management committee, and take measures to enhance its independence and ensure its effective oversight. Staff insurance policies and rules of member organizations should be harmonized and a single staff insurance programme created. The UN system at Geneva should have its own Advisory Board on Compensation Claims and develop a long-term vision for JMS.

The TES mandate should be revised to make it a fully fledged common service, its service rates reviewed to reflect real direct and indirect costs and its budget consolidated.

A review should be conducted of JPS statutes, including its staffing and structure. The Management Board should ensure that its budget reflected all costs and establish annually combined purchase value objectives or targets, including annual quotas of information technology items and contractual services.

UNOG should play an enhanced role in promoting and facilitating increased administrative cooperation and coordination in Geneva. Accordingly, the Secretary-General should change the names of the Divisions of Administration and Conference Services, respectively, to the Division of Common Administrative Services and the Division of Common Conference Services to underline their potential for wider inter-organizational coverage and the need for efficiency improvements.

The Secretary-General, in May [A/55/856/Add.1], transmitting his comments and those of ACC on the JIU report (part II), reiterated that an expansion of common services might be difficult to reconcile with the policy of further decentralization in the context of management reform. Nevertheless, some steps had been taken to underline UNOG's capacity to take the lead in common services, particularly through the establishment of the Management Ownership Committee (below) and the implementation of separate memorandums of understanding between UNOG and all the entities it serviced.

ACABQ, in its first report on the 2002-2003 proposed programme budget [A/56/7], took note of the Secretary-General's comment. It pointed out that printing operations in Geneva was a particular case where economies of scale should be possible, and requested that a comprehensive analysis of the comparative costing for internal and external printing in Geneva be provided to the Fifth Committee during consideration of the 2002-2003 proposed programme budget. ACABQ welcomed the ongoing discussions on cooperation in the further development of Internet services to link major organizations in Geneva and permanent missions there and to establish greater transmission capacity. UN system organizations in Geneva should cooperate fully in the planning, design, development, implementation and maintenance of infrastructure for a variety of information technology services from vendors.

Report of Secretary-General. Responding to Assembly resolution 54/255 [YUN 2000, p. 1375], the Secretary-General, in October [A/56/417/Rev.1], provided information on cooperation among UN specialized agencies based in Geneva in budget and finance, telecommunications, information technology, travel and transportation, medical services and insurance, security services, procurement and contracting, library and archiving services, management of human resources and facilities, mail and diplomatic pouch services and conference facilities.

In terms of the common services structure, the Secretary-General reported the establishment of a Geneva Management Ownership Committee, under the chairmanship of UNOG's Director-General. The Committee, with its three-tier structure (the Committee, a Task Force on Common Services and technical working groups), would establish and maintain high-level support for and commitment to common services initiatives among UN system organizations based in Geneva, provide executive direction to its Task Force on Common Services and take decisions on related recommendations.

The Task Force on Common Services, composed of heads of administration of participating organizations and agencies, would make recommendations for the establishment of a common service or reinforcement of existing ones; review proposals and recommendations by the working groups on common services; and define the commitment, participation and human and financial resources required from participating organizations.

The working groups would assess critical central, shared or common services to identify areas for improving quality and cost-effectiveness; review the potential for expanding common services; and recommend action, with the timetable, resource estimate and definition of accountability for implementation, including the lead agency.

The Management Ownership Committee had identified JPS, the banking, travel and cleaning services, as well as the provision of electricity, as priority areas for strengthening common services tools or developing new approaches.

Use of private management consulting firms

In June [A/55/979], the Secretary-General transmitted his comments, as well as those of ACC, on a JIU report entitled "Policies and practices in the use of the services of private management consulting firms in the organizations of the United Nations system" [YUN 2000, p. 1401]. Many organizations believed that the report lacked rigorous analysis and a clear methodology. Statements in the report were either too general or could not be substantiated, thus eroding the validity of some of the report's conclusions and recommendations. Some organizations felt that the basic objective of the report's findings was to reduce cost without due regard to "quality", which in their view was a simplistic approach. JIU proposed regulating the use of management consulting firms but without any substantial argument or evidence to support such a proposal. There was general agreement on the recommendations relating to policy framework, and agreement on monitoring and control, follow-up actions, interorganization cooperation and coordination, and conflicts of interest. Recommendations on using regionally based consulting firms, a policy of rotating consulting firms and utilizing as many official languages and countries in the bidding process were not fully accepted.

GENERAL ASSEMBLY ACTION

On 24 December [meeting 92], the General Assembly, on the recommendation of the Fifth Committee [A/56/652], adopted **resolution 56/235** without vote [agenda items 121 & 128].

Report of the Joint Inspection Unit on policies and practices in the use of the services of private management consulting firms in the organizations of the United Nations system

The General Assembly,

Recalling its resolutions 55/232 of 23 December 2000 and 55/247 of 12 April 2001,

Having considered the report of the Joint Inspection Unit on policies and practices in the use of the services of private management consulting firms in the organizations of the United Nations system and the note by the Secretary-General transmitting his comments as well as those of the Administrative Committee on Coordination thereon,

1. *Endorses* the elements contained in paragraphs *(b)* and *(d)* of recommendation 1, and recommendations 2, 3, 4 and 5 of the Joint Inspection Unit;

2. *Invites* the Secretary-General and participating organizations of the United Nations system, when addressing the issues raised in paragraphs *(a)* and *(c)* of recommendation 1, and in recommendations 6, 7 and 8 of the Unit and using the services of private management consulting firms, to take fully into account the relevant provisions of General Assembly resolutions 55/232 and 55/247.

Internal and external printing

By **decision 55/470** of 12 April, the General Assembly, having considered the Secretary-General's report on internal and external printing practices of the Organization [YUN 2000, p. 1402], endorsed ACABQ's comments and observations on the report [ibid.] and requested the Secretary-General to continue his efforts to improve the Organization's printing practices and expand the use of the UN printing facilities as a common service for the needs of the UN funds and programmes based at Headquarters and the specialized agencies based in Geneva.

Measures to increase profitability of UN commercial activities

By **decision 55/466** of 12 April, the General Assembly took note of ACABQ's intention to review the Secretary-General's report on the proposed measures to improve the profitability of UN commercial activities [YUN 2000, p. 1402] and decided to revert to that question during the main part of its fifty-sixth session on the basis of the ACABQ report.

ACABQ, in its first report on the proposed programme budget for the 2002-2003 biennium [A/56/7], said that the Secretariat proposals were too general and should be followed by a blueprint with specific commercial goals and an implementation plan. With respect to the United Nations Postal Administration, ACABQ said that, in view of the continuing decline in income from the sale of stamps, the possibility of outsourcing that activity should be explored, as well as negoti-ating more favourable reimbursement rates paid to the United States Postal Service.

In connection with the United Nations Bookshop, ACABQ agreed with the recommendation that the United Nations use a contractor with book and/or retail experience. The pricing of United Nations publications should take into account the target audience's ability to pay and every effort should be made to minimize cost and maximize offsetting revenue, and perhaps even to make a profit. To ascertain the true cost of the preparation, production and dissemination of publications, the Committee recommended that a pilot project be undertaken, using one or more publications of the Department of Economic and Social Affairs. Consideration should also be given to greater use of joint arrangements for production and distribution with publishers of scholarly and institutional materials.

The operation and cost of the catering services and their actual cost to the United Nations should be re-examined. Contractual arrangements should be financially attractive to both the contractor and the United Nations. ACABQ requested that it be consulted before the conclusion of any new contract arrangement. It also recommended that contractual arrangements include a provision for annual independent auditing at the contractor's expense, and be based on a fair market return to the United Nations for space occupied by the contractors.

GENERAL ASSEMBLY ACTION

On 24 December [meeting 92], the General Assembly, on the recommendation of the Fifth Committee [A/56/653], adopted **resolution 56/238** without vote [agenda item 122].

Proposed measures to improve the profitability of the commercial activities of the United Nations

The General Assembly,

Recalling its resolution 55/232 of 23 December 2000,

Recalling also the international and non-commercial character of the Organization,

Having considered the report of the Secretary-General on the proposed measures to improve the profitability of the commercial activities of the United Nations and the related report of the Advisory Committee on Administrative and Budgetary Questions,

1. *Notes with satisfaction* the report of the Secretary-General, and endorses the recommendations of the Advisory Committee on Administrative and Budgetary Questions thereon;

2. *Notes* the proposal to separate the management of the commercial activities from the other activities of the Organization, and requests the Secretary-General to submit detailed information on this proposal and its administrative and financial implications;

3. *Requests* the Secretary-General to elaborate on this proposal by means of a blueprint concerning the specific commercial goals of the Organization and the

steps that should be taken to achieve them, in particular the use of outsourcing, in accordance with the provisions of its resolution 55/232 and its resolution 55/247 of 12 April 2001, and the optimum use of space within the United Nations buildings;

4. *Also requests* the Secretary-General to make proposals to streamline and simplify the administration and management structure underpinning those activities;

5. *Further requests* the Secretary-General to submit for the consideration of the General Assembly at its fifty-seventh session a single report containing the information requested in the present resolution.

Enhancing the UN experience for visitors

In March, the Secretary-General submitted to the General Assembly a proposal for enhancing the UN experience for visitors [A/55/835], which aimed at modernizing and improving the experience of visitors to Headquarters and envisaged the construction of new visitors' facilities and the introduction of an interactive, multimedia programme of exhibits. The capital cost of the proposed new facilities was estimated at $50 million to $60 million to be funded entirely from private sources and in-kind contributions. The associated improvements to the General Assembly building would be part of the Secretary-General's proposed capital master plan [YUN 2000, p. 1405]. It was expected that the proposed new visitors' facilities would enhance the financial viability of the guided tour programme and improve the profitability of commercial activities.

Projected revenue was estimated at $15.8 million in the first biennium, compared to almost $5 million realized in the 1998-1999 biennium. Budgetary implications during construction were estimated at $1.6 million. The Secretary-General recommended that the Assembly endorse the proposal and authorize him, in close coordination with prospective donors, to proceed with it.

ACABQ report. ACABQ, in its first report on the proposed programme budget for the biennium 2002-2003 [A/56/7], stressed the need for close coordination of the new visitors' experience project and the capital master plan [YUN 2000, p. 1405]. Noting that the capital cost was to be entirely funded from private sources, ACABQ trusted that the dignity and image of the United Nations would not be compromised through commercialization. While welcoming the interest of the United Nations Association of the United States of America (UNA/USA), the Committee said that the number of potential contributors should be expanded to include UNAs of other countries. It requested the Secretary-General to report on that issue in his next report on that matter.

While ACABQ had no objection in principle to the establishment of a visitors' experience capital improvement fund to be financed from 20 per cent of gross revenues, it was concerned that deficits might become a potential burden to the Organization and requested that consideration be given to the management of the fund and that the rules governing its replenishment, operation and management should be submitted to it for review, in conjunction with the final proposals for the project.

GENERAL ASSEMBLY ACTION

On 24 December [meeting 92], the General Assembly, on the recommendation of the Fifth Committee [A/56/653], adopted **resolution 56/236** without vote [agenda item 122].

Enhancing the United Nations experience for visitors

The General Assembly,

Having considered the report of the Secretary-General containing his proposal for enhancing the United Nations experience for visitors,

Having also considered the related report of the Advisory Committee on Administrative and Budgetary Questions,

1. *Welcomes* the initiatives of the United Nations Association of the United States of America, the prospective donor, as described in the report of the Secretary-General, to mobilize resources in order to provide new facilities for the visitors' experience in the form of a donation in kind to the United Nations;

2. *Endorses* the observations and recommendations of the Advisory Committee on Administrative and Budgetary Questions contained in its report;

3. *Requests* the Secretary-General to ensure that the development of the proposed visitors' experience project is fully integrated with the capital master plan, including necessary security measures;

4. *Decides* that a decision on this question should be taken in the light of any further decision on the capital master plan;

5. *Authorizes* the Secretary-General to invite the United Nations Association of the United States of America to proceed with the preparation of a schematic design for the new visitors' experience, taking into account the four conditions set out in the report of the Secretary-General, which are highlighted in the report of the Advisory Committee, on the understanding that it will be for the General Assembly to declare itself satisfied with the fulfilment of these conditions;

6. *Notes* the desirability of expanding the number of potential contributors to the project by including the United Nations Associations of other countries;

7. *Requests* the Secretary-General to evaluate the proposed financial and fiscal aspects of the donation, in view of the Financial Regulations and Rules of the United Nations and in the light of the capital master plan, taking into account the eventual financial implications for the Organization, and to report thereon to the General Assembly;

8. *Also requests* the Secretary-General to submit, when practicable, for the consideration of the General Assembly, a comprehensive report on the outcome of

the schematic design; options for deciding on the final scale of the project; projected revenues and the cost of operating and maintaining the new visitors' experience; proposals for expanded commercial activities; options for operating methodologies; means of adjusting to changing situations; procedures for the operation of the proposed capital improvement fund; and a time-line for implementation.

UN premises and property

Facilities management

By **decision 55/465** of 12 April, the General Assembly took note of the Secretary-General's report on facilities management [YUN 1999, p. 1379] and endorsed ACABQ's observations thereon [YUN 2000, p. 1403]. The Assembly also took note of the Secretary-General's report entitled "Overseas Properties Management and Information Exchange Network (OPMIEN): a globally coordinated collaborative approach to facilities management" [ibid.] and endorsed the related observations and recommendations of ACABQ [ibid., p. 1404].

JIU report. In August [A/56/274], the Secretary-General transmitted to the General Assembly a JIU report entitled "Management of buildings: practices of selected United Nations system organizations relevant to the renovation of the United Nations Headquarters". JIU reviewed the operational and financial issues of buildings management at the UN Headquarters building to assist Member States and the Secretariat in considering measures for the timely and systematic maintenance and capital improvements at UN Headquarters.

JIU concluded that ensuring adequate provision for systematic building maintenance and capital expenditure was a problem that most UN system organizations faced. The United Nations needed to review its budgeting policy on building maintenance costs and capital expenditure against its prolonged budget stringency and competing demands for its scarce resources. The Organization also needed an institutionalized financial framework to handle substantive capital expenditure, which the biennial regular programme budget could not handle.

JIU recommended that, in the context of the capital master plan [YUN 2000, p. 1405], the Assembly should establish a policy on management and maintenance of UN buildings. The Secretariat should fully comply with local building codes and seek financial and other support from the host Government and local authorities towards the UN renovation project. The Secretary-General should prepare a feasibility study for establishing a building/real estate fund to cover the costs of major repairs, renovation, upgrading and replacement of equipment.

In September [A/56/274/Add.1], the Secretary-General, in his comments on the JIU report, stated that JIU's observations and recommendations were pertinent and important for the efficient, safe and reliable management of the extensive real estate owned or managed by the United Nations. However, certain JIU findings required further assessment, especially those regarding the need for a large expenditure for the capital master plan, the observation that programme managers were not fully aware of the financial implications of building maintenance and use of office space, and that financial considerations were not taken into account in the decision-making process in the allocation of office space.

On 24 December [meeting 92], the General Assembly, on the recommendation of the Fifth Committee [A/56/652], adopted **resolution 56/234** without vote [agenda items 121 & 128].

Management of buildings: practices of selected United Nations system organizations relevant to the renovation of the United Nations Headquarters

The General Assembly,

Having considered the report of the Joint Inspection Unit entitled "Management of buildings: practices of selected United Nations system organizations relevant to the renovation of the United Nations Headquarters" and the comments of the Secretary-General thereon,

1. *Welcomes* the comprehensive and timely preparation of the report of the Joint Inspection Unit;

2. *Endorses* the report of the Unit, and requests the Secretary-General to take full account of its recommendations and findings when elaborating the capital master plan, without prejudice to the future consideration by the General Assembly of the report of the Secretary-General on the capital master plan;

3. *Decides* to revert to the consideration of the report of the Unit and the comments of the Secretary-General thereon within the context of its consideration of the report of the Secretary-General on the capital master plan, requested by the General Assembly in section IV of its resolution 55/238 of 23 December 2000.

Asbestos problem

The General Assembly, by **decision 55/464** of 12 April, took note of the report of the Secretary-General on the review and assessment of the asbestos problem at UN Headquarters and the management of asbestos-containing materials at UN buildings in Geneva, Vienna, Nairobi and the locations of the regional commissions; and ACABQ's observations [YUN 2000, p. 1404]. The Assembly welcomed the continuing efforts of the Secretary-General to solve the problem.

Addis Ababa conference and office facilities

By **decision 55/467** of 12 April, the General Assembly took note of the Secretary-General's report on the construction of additional conference facilities in Addis Ababa and the related ACABQ report [YUN 2000, p. 1405]. The Assembly decided to retain the remaining balance in the construction-in-progress account pending its consideration of all related matters.

In December [A/56/672], the Secretary-General submitted proposals for the construction of additional office facilities at ECA in Addis Ababa. That had become necessary due to the serious shortage of office space resulting from the relocation of regional, subregional and country offices of UN specialized agencies, funds and programmes to the UN compound for security reasons and in the context of the UN common house concept, as well as the considerable expansion of UN humanitarian and development activities in the region. The Secretary-General's proposal entailed the construction of a new four-storey office building with an area of 6,770 square metres at a total cost of $7,711,800, to be financed from the balance in the construction-in-progress account following the completion of the ECA conference facilities ($8,253,000 as at 30 June 2001), which the Assembly by decision 55/467 (see above) had decided to retain.

ACABQ, in its report on the Secretary-General's proposals [A/56/711], recommended that the Assembly authorize the construction and approve an appropriation of $7,711,800, to be funded from the construction-in-progress account. It recommended that ECA consider leasing any unoccupied office space. It trusted that an agreement with the host Government for tax exemption with regard to materials for the project would be concluded soon. ACABQ also requested that a progress report be submitted annually until the completion of the project in 2005.

UN Office at Nairobi

Office facilities

The Governing Council of the United Nations Environment Programme (UNEP), at its twenty-first session (5-9 February) [A/56/25 (dec. 21/33)], having considered a conference room paper submitted by the Executive Director containing proposals for the construction of additional office accommodation at the UN complex in Nairobi, authorized the Executive Director to approve an advance of up to $8 million from the Environment Fund financial reserve to the UN Secretariat on a loan basis towards the construction, subject to ACABQ's approval and that of other competent authorities according to UN rules and procedures. The Executive Director should ensure that the agreement between the UN Secretariat and UNEP on the loan included a provision that there should be an immediate repayment, upon request.

Administrative and management practices

In November [A/56/620], the Secretary-General transmitted the report of the UN Office of Internal Oversight Services (OIOS) on its inspection of the administrative and management practices of the United Nations Office at Nairobi (UNON), which assessed the level of satisfaction with the services provided by UNON to its clients in administration, financial management, human resources, security and safety, support and information technologies services.

The review found that, although the authority delegated to UNEP and the United Nations Centre for Human Settlements (Habitat) had been clarified by the Department of Management, the relationship of the two entities with UNON remained unclear, especially UNON's functional responsibilities and reporting lines, in particular, accountability for the delivery of services in the absence from Nairobi of the Director-General and the reporting lines and level of accountability of the Division of Administrative Services. Diplomatic missions were not adequately informed of UNON's responsibilities and their relationship with it. There was no effective system in place for UNEP or Habitat to monitor the quality and effective delivery of services by UNON.

OIOS recommended that UNON's Division of Administrative Services should assess the areas in which UNON had delegated authority and compile a manual outlining the authority delegated to UNON and that retained by UNEP and Habitat for each service, including the responsible agency official. It should assess problem areas and explain to UNEP and Habitat officials the reporting lines and functional responsibilities as outlined in the Secretary-General's bulletin [ST/SGB/2000/13]. The Director-General should explain that, during his absence, representational duties would be carried out by the next highest-ranking UN official in Nairobi, and confirm that the Chief of the Division of Administrative Services was accountable for the operational activities of UNON and was also the Chief Administrator for Habitat. The Director-General should establish mechanisms to ensure the quality and timeliness of UNON's services, consult Headquarters regarding the request of the permanent representatives in Nairobi to be accredited to UNON as a separate entity from UNEP and Habitat, and institutionalize regular consultative meetings with the Committee of Permanent Representatives.

UNEP and Habitat should establish a system for monitoring the delivery of services provided by UNON and, with UNON, finalize the basis, formula and performance indicators for those services. They should also clarify remaining questions regarding the costing of those services. The Division of Administrative Services should review its staffing requirements and develop a plan to achieve it, as well as a training programme.

The Secretary-General concurred with the OIOS recommendations and noted that measures were being taken to correct the issues addressed.

Security

The Ad Hoc Inter-Agency Meeting on Security (Paris, 14-18 May) [ACC/2001/10] made recommendations to ACC on security training, Field Security Officers, Minimum Operating Safety Standards, collaboration with NGOs, evacuation entitlements and accountability. The Meeting recommended that resources be pooled to facilitate joint training in security and stress management. It endorsed the Minimum Operating Safety Standards and the Minimum Telecommunications Standards and recommended that a full implementation plan with time frame and costing be made available before the ACC High-level Committee on Management meeting (Geneva, 10-11 September). Common inter-agency standards/procedures should be developed also for stress counsellors and be forwarded to the High-level Committee on Management. The Meeting agreed in principle to the 16 recommendations put forward by the Inter-Agency Standing Committee Working Group Staff Security Task Force on UN-NGO field collaboration on security for "humanitarian actors" and decided that they should be reviewed by the UN Office of Legal Affairs (OLA) prior to implementation.

The Meeting supported UNDP's proposal to simplify evacuation entitlements and called on all agencies to adhere to them. It recommended that organizations take urgent action to implement the Secretary-General's decision [A/55/494] that security responsibilities be included in the job descriptions of all staff in the field, taking into account the duties and responsibilities already contained in the revised Field Security Handbook, and that UNICEF continue to discuss with interested organizations the further development of the Field Reporting System. The Meeting revised the Field Security Handbook, subject to review by OLA.

Security arrangements in Geneva

In March [A/C.5/55/SR.44], the ACABQ Chairman, commenting on the Secretary-General's report on security arrangements at the United Nations Office at Geneva (UNOG) [YUN 2000, p. 1406], noted that the preliminary estimated cost of those arrangements was some $2 million higher than the amounts allocated for 1998-1999 and 2000-2001. ACABQ decided to revert to the matter in the context of the Secretary-General's 2002-2003 budget proposals.

By **decision 55/468** of 12 April, the General Assembly took note of the Secretary-General's report and the related ACABQ observations, and requested the Secretary-General to keep the security arrangements at UNOG under review to ensure full protection of delegates, staff and visitors in the UN premises and the safety of UN property.

In its first report on the proposed programme budget for 2002-2003 [A/56/7], ACABQ said it had no objection to the provision of $2,439,100 requested for upgrading security arrangements at UNOG, which the Assembly approved in **resolution 56/253**.

PART SIX

Intergovernmental organizations related to the United Nations

Chapter I

International Atomic Energy Agency (IAEA)

In 2001, the International Atomic Energy Agency (IAEA) continued to focus on bringing about the development and transfer of peaceful nuclear technologies; building and maintaining a global nuclear safety regime; and guarding against the proliferation of nuclear weapons and strengthening the security of nuclear material and facilities. After the terrorist attacks of 11 September in the United States, IAEA intensified its action to upgrade nuclear safety and security.

The forty-fifth session of the IAEA General Conference (Vienna, 17-21 September) adopted resolutions on improving the security of nuclear and other radioactive materials; strengthening international cooperation in nuclear, radiation, transport and waste safety; improving the effectiveness and efficiency of the safeguards system; strengthening IAEA technical cooperation activities; applying safeguards in the Middle East; implementing the safeguards agreement between IAEA and the Democratic People's Republic of Korea; and implementing UN Security Council resolutions relating to Iraq.

In 2001, IAEA membership rose to 133 with the admission of Botswana and the Federal Republic of Yugoslavia.

Activities

Nuclear safety

IAEA continued to provide nuclear safety services and assistance worldwide. A safety guide, *Safety Assessment and Verification for Nuclear Power Plants*, was published in 2001, while another, *Instrumentation and Control Systems Important to Safety in Nuclear Power Plants*, was in the process of being published. The Agency also drafted safety requirements for fuel cycle and isotope production facilities and two safety guides covering mixed oxide and uranium fuel production facilities. Design safety review missions were carried out in the Czech Republic, the Democratic People's Republic of Korea and Iran. An international action plan was developed to improve the safety of research reactors. In September, the Agency convened a conference on the safety of nuclear power, which focused on risk-informed decision-making, influence of external factors on safety, safety of fuel cycle facilities, safety of research reactors and safety performance indicators.

Radiation safety

In 2001, the safety and security of radioactive sources emerged as an increasingly important issue. The Agency took account of the recommendations of the 2000 Buenos Aires conference of national regulators [YUN 2000, p. 1409] and updated the action plan on the safety of radiation sources and the security of radioactive materials. In March, IAEA held a conference in Málaga, Spain, on the radiological protection of patients in diagnostic and interventional radiology and nuclear medicine. It was agreed to convene a group of experts to develop an international action plan in that area in 2002. A panel meeting on the safe transport of radioactive material held in November recommended the publication in 2003 of the Agency's revised Transport Regulations, which would take effect in 2005.

In May, the Agency participated in an international nuclear emergency exercise, JINEX 1, involving 55 States, which aimed to test existing national and international procedures and arrangements for responding to a nuclear emergency. A new occupational radiation protection appraisal service was launched and the first review was conducted. A key objective of the appraisal was to provide member States with an objective assessment of the provisions for occupational radiation protection.

Nuclear power

In 2001, the Agency continued to assist member States in planning and implementing programmes for the utilization of nuclear power, as well as to support them in achieving improved safety, reliability and economic cost-effectiveness of their nuclear power plants. Publications were issued on quality assurance standards, risk management, managing change in nuclear utilities, economic performance indicators, personnel training and evaluating outside contractors. Updated versions of Agency databases and the Power Reactor Information System were released to member States, and a third module on steam generators was added to the Agency's database on nuclear power plant life management. In May, a major international seminar was convened in Cairo, Egypt, to review innovative small to medium-sized reactor designs. In the area of metal cooled reactors, the Agency completed a coordinated research project on the verification of analysis methods for predicting seismically isolated nuclear structures, and harmonization and validation of analysis methods for fast reactor thermal-hydraulic codes and relations using experimental data. In response to requests from member States, the Agency conducted information exchange activities with regard to heavy liquid metal coolants for fast reactors.

Nuclear fuel cycle

In 2001, IAEA and the Nuclear Energy Agency of the Organisation for Economic Cooperation and Development (OECD/NEA) published *Country Nuclear Fuel Cycle Profiles* in response to changes in nuclear fuel markets, and *Uranium 2001: Resources, Production and Demand,* the foremost world reference on uranium supplies. A complementary study, *Analysis of Uranium Supply to 2050,* was also published. Key milestones were achieved by the Agency in the areas of mixed oxide fuel technology, water chemistry and corrosion control in nuclear power plants and zirconium alloy degradation by hydrogen. IAEA also focused on issues connected with long-term dry storage, the implications for fuel fabrication and burn-up credit. Initiatives to address the issue of geological repositories and the lack of infrastructure and resources to implement available technologies in many developing member States included the creation of an International Network of Centres of Excellence for Demonstration and Training in Geological Disposal, and an international conference on the management of radioactive waste from non-power applications (Malta, November).

Radioactive waste management

An important new development in 2001 was the entry into force of the Joint Convention on the Safety of Radioactive Waste Management and on the Safety of Spent Fuel Management. The Convention was one of several safety-related agreements under the Agency's auspices. A specialists' meeting in June addressed a number of topics, including a common framework for radioactive waste disposal. The meeting helped to clarify and document the areas of agreement that could be reflected in safety standards. The Agency finalized a report assessing the implications of the recommendations from a 2000 conference on the safety of radioactive waste management on its work programme. The report highlighted seven actions, including the development of a common framework for the disposal of different types of radioactive waste and the development of a programme to ensure adequate application of the Agency's waste safety standards. Together with OECD/NEA, the Agency organized a peer review of the performance assessment being developed for a proposed waste disposal site at Yucca Mountain, Nevada, United States.

Marine environment and water resources

In 2001, IAEA developed several new techniques and facilities that provided significantly improved methods for the detection and study of both nuclear and non-nuclear marine pollutants in the laboratory and in the field. In water resources management, IAEA assessed the current status and future directions for isotope applications in water-cycle modelling, groundwater sustainability and the impacts of climate change on water resources. Efforts were made to link the Agency's research and development and technical cooperation activities to water sector programmes of the United Nations and bilateral agencies. IAEA was invited to be the UN system's lead organization to mark World Water Day in March 2002, in recognition of the impact of its work in water resources. An international conference organized by the Agency (Vienna, April) discussed how isotopes could be used in environmental change studies. IAEA also played a major role in building a cadre of trained isotope hydrologists worldwide, a profession in short supply in many developing countries.

Food and agriculture

Significant achievements were made by the Agency in applying radiation and isotope techniques in research, leading to the optimum use of water and nutrients by plants, and ultimately ensuring sustainable crop and livestock productivity and environmental preservation. The 1964 arrangements between the Directors General of the Food and Agriculture Organization of the United Nations (FAO) and IAEA for the joint FAO/IAEA Division of Nuclear Techniques in Food and Agriculture (which planned and implemented the food and agriculture programme at the Agency) were revised to include redefinition of responsibilities and the establishment of a steering committee to oversee the programme. IAEA also developed standard operating and good laboratory procedures, manuals and guidelines for scientists and technicians of its member States.

Human health

A priority during 2001 was the development of diagnostic methods and treatment procedures for coronary artery disease, liver cancer, thyroid cancer, bacterial infection, and infectious and childhood diseases. A critical part of the Agency's human health programme was the application of nuclear and related techniques in the treatment of cancer and infectious diseases. Several analyses and projects were directed at the evaluation of the economics of radiation therapy for cancer. Models to derive the cost of cancer treatment using brachytherapy and cobalt and Linac teletherapy in different countries were developed and implemented. IAEA provided developing member States with a link to international standards for measuring radiation and the quality assurance techniques necessary for the calibration of radiation therapy machines and industrial radiation facilities.

Technical cooperation

IAEA's secretariat delivered a record $71 million worth of training, expert services, equipment and other assistance to member States under its technical cooperation programme in 2001—up by $3.1 million from 2000. Extrabudgetary resources reached $7.1 million, the highest amount in more than 10 years, including government cost-sharing of $2.6 million. In June, the Agency's Board recommended increasing the regular budget allocation for the management of technical cooperation activities. The Agency began "upstream" work for the 2003-2004 technical cooperation programme, emphasizing projects that enjoyed government support and commitment. The preparation of thematic plans, one of the three major instruments of the Agency's technical cooperation strategy, was under way. Two thematic plans were completed in 2001, one on coastal zone management and the other on area-wide tsetse control. Technology transfer was the focus of the scientific forum at the 2001 regular session of the General Conference. The forum looked at several technical cooperation projects as case studies and discussed factors that contributed to the projects' success.

Safeguards responsibilities

All information available to IAEA in 2001 led to the conclusion that nuclear material and related items placed under safeguards remained in peaceful nuclear activities or were otherwise adequately accounted for. As at 31 December, 225 safeguards agreements with 141 States (and with Taiwan Province of China) were in force. During 2001, 2,487 inspections were carried out at 592 facilities and other locations. The number of States parties to the Treaty on the Non-Proliferation of Nuclear Weapons, adopted by the General Assembly in resolution 2373(XXII) [YUN 1968, p. 17], that had not fulfilled their legal obligation to bring into force the required Treaty safeguards agreements stood at 52, compared to 54 at the end of 2000. Protocols additional to safeguards agreements [YUN, 1997, p. 1519] for 61 States had been approved by the IAEA Board of Governors; 24 such protocols were in force. An additional protocol with Ghana was being implemented provisionally pending entry into force.

Nuclear information

Interest in nuclear matters at the global level was particularly strong after the 11 September attacks in the United States, when issues such as the physical protection of nuclear material, illicit trafficking and the possible use by subnational groups of unconventional weapons came to the fore. IAEA launched a press campaign on combating nuclear terrorism. IAEA's WorldAtom web site was further enhanced and expanded, resulting in a significant increase in the number of visits to the site. A notable event in April was multimedia coverage of the fifteenth anniversary of the Chernobyl accident.

The International Nuclear Information System, with 122 participating members, continued to collect and distribute scientific information in all areas of nuclear science and technology.

Secretariat

At the end of 2001, IAEA secretariat staff totalled 2,205, including 950 in the Professional and higher categories and 1,255 in the General Service category.

Budget

The 2001 regular budget amounted to $197.2 million, of which $189.1 million was financed from assessed contributions by member States, $4.1 million from income from reimbursable work and $4 million from miscellaneous income. Actual budget expenditure amounted to $196.8 million. A total of $51.7 million in extrabudgetary funds was provided by member States, the United Nations, international organizations and other sources.

NOTE: For further information, see *Annual Report 2001*, published by IAEA.

HEADQUARTERS AND OTHER OFFICE

HEADQUARTERS

International Atomic Energy Agency
(P. O. Box 100, Vienna International Centre)
Wagramerstrasse 5
A-1400 Vienna, Austria
  Telephone: (43) (1) 2600-0
  Fax: (43) (1) 2600-7
  E-mail: Official.Mail@iaea.org

LIAISON OFFICE

International Atomic Energy Agency Liaison Office at the United Nations
1 United Nations Plaza, Room 1155
New York, NY 10017, United States
  Telephone: (1) (212) 963-6012
  Fax: (1) (917) 367-7046

Chapter II

International Labour Organization (ILO)

In 2001, the International Labour Organization (ILO) continued to promote social justice and economic stability and improve labour conditions. ILO's strategic objectives were to promote and realize fundamental principles and rights at work; create greater opportunities for women and men to secure decent employment and income; enhance the coverage and effectiveness of social protection; and strengthen tripartism and social dialogue.

In 2001, ILO membership remained at 175.

Meetings

The eighty-ninth session of the International Labour Conference (ILC) (Geneva, 5-21 June) adopted the first international standard on safety in agriculture, in an effort to ensure that member States established an adequate system of inspection for agricultural workplaces. The Conference also recognized the importance of social security and broadly endorsed established social security principles. It was acknowledged, however, that within the framework of those principles each country would need to determine its own social security system coverage.

ILO's International Programme on the Elimination of Child Labour launched a new initiative at the Conference, aimed at accelerating the removal of millions of children from the most abusive forms of child labour in participating countries in 10 years or less.

The Director-General submitted to the Conference a global report on forced labour, as a follow-up to the 1998 ILO Declaration on Fundamental Principles and Rights at Work [YUN 1998, p. 1375]. He also submitted a report on ILO programme implementation in 2000-2001, which identified the achievements, difficulties and constraints faced by the organization during the biennium.

An ILO informal meeting (Geneva, 25-26 October) discussed the global and social impacts of the 11 September terrorist attacks in the United States (see p. 60) on the tourist sector. On 30 October, ILO called for a series of operational measures to rebuild the devastated aviation sector.

Sectoral and other meetings convened in Geneva during 2001 included: meeting of ILO declaration expert-advisers (29 January–2 February);

tripartite meeting on the employment impact of mergers and acquisitions in the banking and financial services sector (5-9 February); meeting of experts on ILO guidelines on occupational safety and health management systems (19-27 April); international symposium to strengthen workers' participation in the UN system and impact on Bretton Woods institutions (24-28 September); tripartite meeting of experts on the management of disability at the workplace (3-12 October); tripartite meeting on the construction industry in the twenty-first century: its image, employment prospects and skill requirements (10-14 December); and high-level tripartite working group on maritime labour standards (first meeting) (17-21 December).

International standards

During 2001, ILO activities with regard to Conventions and Recommendations included standard-setting and the supervision and promotion of the application of standards. Supervisory bodies reviewed existing procedures and standard-setting policy.

In June, ILC adopted the Safety and Health in Agriculture Convention (No. 184) and Recommendation (No. 192). During 2000-2001, the follow-up of ILO's Declaration of Fundamental Principles and Rights at Work [YUN 1998, p. 1375] became operational, and action programmes on freedom of association and the promotion of the right to collective bargaining were launched.

Employment and development

ILO continued in 2001 to help constituents combat unemployment and poverty through the creation of employment opportunities and improvement of existing jobs. It provided advice and guidance on employment and labour market policies, as well as on their labour market information and statistical systems. Activities to promote employment included support to constituents to develop entrepreneurship through the creation of cooperatives and small and micro-enterprises.

On 3 November, a Global Employment Forum, held in Geneva, launched a 10-point plan (Global Agenda for Employment), aimed at reversing mounting unemployment and poverty due to the dual impact of global recession and the September terrorist attacks in the United States.

Regarding human resources development, ILO emphasized the adaptation of training policy and delivery to the rapidly changing skill requirements and the special needs of vulnerable groups. It also responded to the needs of countries affected by conflict.

Field activities

In 2001, expenditure on technical cooperation programmes totalled $121.7 million compared to $91 million in 2000. The leading field of activity was the employment sector with 38 per cent ($47.2 million), followed by international labour standards (30 per cent), and social dialogue- and social protection–related activities (15 and 11 per cent respectively).

In terms of regional distribution, Africa accounted for 26.9 per cent of total expenditure ($32.8 million), Asia and the Pacific for 22 per cent ($26.8 million), Latin America and the Caribbean 16.5 per cent ($20 million), Europe 4.9 per cent ($5.9 million) and the Arab States 1.9 per cent ($2.2 million). Interregional and global activities accounted for the greatest share (27.8 per cent), an increase of some 5 per cent over 2000.

Educational activities

The Turin Centre and the International Institute for Labour Studies, both autonomous institutions within ILO, reported to the ILO Governing Body. The Centre continued to carry out training and related activities in a wide range of technical areas as an integral part of ILO technical cooperation activities. The Institute continued to carry out research and encouraged networking related to emerging labour policy issues, and acted as catalyst for future ILO programme development.

Secretariat

As at 31 December 2001, ILO employed a total of 2,273 full-time staff. Of those, 988 were in the Professional and higher categories and 1,285 were in the General Service category.

Budget

ILC had adopted a budget of $467 million for the 2000-2001 biennium in June 1999. At its 2001 session, ILC adopted a budget of $434 million for the 2002-2003 biennium.

NOTE: For further information on ILO, see *Report of the Director-General, ILO programme implementation, 2000-2001.*

HEADQUARTERS, LIAISON AND OTHER OFFICES

HEADQUARTERS
International Labour Organization
4 Route des Morillons
CH-1211 Geneva 22, Switzerland
Telephone: (41) (22) 799-6111
Fax: (41) (22) 798-8685
Internet: http://www.ilo.org
E-mail: doscom@ilo.org

LIAISON OFFICE
International Labour Organization
Liaison Office with the United Nations
220 East 42nd Street, Suite 3101
New York, NY 10017, United States
Telephone: (1) (212) 697-0150
Fax: (1) (212) 697-5218
E-mail: newyork@ilo.org

ILO maintained regional offices in Abidjan, Côte d'Ivoire; Bangkok, Thailand; Geneva, Switzerland; and Lima, Peru.

Chapter III

Food and Agriculture Organization of the United Nations (FAO)

The Food and Agriculture Organization of the United Nations (FAO) continued to work towards achieving sustainable global food security by raising nutrition levels and living standards, improving agricultural productivity and advancing the condition of rural populations.

The FAO Conference, the agency's governing body, held its thirty-first session (Rome, Italy, 2-13 November). It approved a budget of $651.8 million for 2002-2003—an increase of $1.8 million over the previous biennium. The Conference approved an International Treaty on Plant Genetic Resources for Food and Agriculture intended to ensure access to plant genetic diversity while considering the needs of farmers and plant breeders. It adopted a new FAO Plan of Action on Gender and Development (2002-2007) with four priorities: food and nutrition, natural resources, agricultural support systems, and agricultural and rural development policy and planning.

The FAO Council, in November, decided that the World Food Summit: five years later, originally planned as part of the Conference, would instead take place in Rome in June 2002.

In March, FAO announced that more than 110 countries had adopted a new plan of action against illegal, unregulated and unreported fishing. The voluntary agreement was aimed at eliminating those practices, which were blamed for overfishing of several high-value fish stocks.

In 2001, FAO membership rose to 183 countries, plus the European Community.

World food situation

World cereal output in 2001 was estimated at 1,880 million tonnes (including rice in milled equivalent), 22 million tonnes, or 1.2 per cent, above the previous year's level, representing the first increase since 1996. World coarse grain production rose by around 3 per cent compared to 2000, despite declines in North America. World wheat production reached 582 million tonnes, about the same as in 2000. World rice output was estimated at 591 million tonnes (395 million tonnes in milled equivalent), 7 million tonnes less than in 2000. Much of that contraction concentrated in China. With overall cereal utilization ex-

ceeding world production for the second year in a row, world cereal reserves by the close of the 2001/02 season were expected to decline sharply. World cereal stocks were forecast to reach 587 million tonnes by the end of 2002, down 8 per cent from the previous season's level.

FAO's Global Information and Early Warning System (GIEWS), in cooperation with the World Food Programme (WFP), fielded crop and food-supply assessment missions to affected countries. The GIEWS Workstation, an integrated information system, maintained a reference database for global crop monitoring and early warning.

Activities

FAO's Emergency Operations and Rehabilitation Division responded to requests for emergency assistance in the agricultural, livestock, fisheries and forestry sectors submitted by developing countries affected by natural or human-induced calamities. The value of FAO's emergency assistance reached $335 million in 2000-2001, including emergency relief and early rehabilitation programmes around the globe and the agricultural component of the oil-for-food programme in Iraq, FAO's largest emergency and rehabilitation programme.

Through its field programmes, FAO provided technical advice and support in all areas of food and agriculture, fisheries, forestry and rural development. In 2001, $201 million was spent on 1,428 field projects. FAO's Investment Centre assisted developing and transition countries to identify and assess investment opportunities, and formulated 90 agricultural and rural development projects for some $3.7 billion. The Special Programme for Food Security continued to assist developing countries, particularly through its South-South Cooperation initiative, to improve national and household food security on an economically and environmentally sustainable basis.

In 2001, FAO participated in activities related to the conservation and use of plant biological diversity, crop management and diversification, seed production and improvement, crop protection, agricultural engineering, prevention of food losses, and food and agricultural industries. It developed programmes and strategies for livestock production and health, and supported improved smallholder, specialized and mixed livestock farming through better resource utilization, improved processing and commercialization, and better control of animal diseases. Through its Emergency Prevention System for Transboundary Animal and Plant Pests and Diseases, FAO promoted cooperation among countries on early warning, control of and research on the desert locust, the prevention and control of significant transboundary diseases, and the global eradication of rinderpest by 2010.

The FAO Forestry Department continued its work in forest resource management, forest policy and planning, and forest products. At its fifteenth session in March, the FAO Committee on Forestry (COFO) was informed about the main findings of the Forest Resources Assessment (FRA) 2000, according to which the total estimated global forest area in 2000 was nearly 3.9 billion hectares (95 per cent natural forest and 5 per cent plantations). COFO made a number of recommendations, in particular that the global FRA programme continue to be a priority for the Forestry Department.

FAO promoted long-term sustainable development and utilization of the world's fisheries and aquaculture. Its priorities included the implementation of the FAO Code of Conduct for Responsible Fisheries, with particular attention to the problem of excess fishing capacity, strengthening of regional fisheries bodies, and the promotion of an increased contribution of responsible fisheries and aquaculture to world food supplies and food security.

In 2001, the Codex Alimentarius Commission, responsible for implementing the joint FAO/World Health Organization Food Standards Programme, agreed on the first global principles for the safety assessment of genetically modified foods, on maximum levels of certain food toxins and on guidelines for organic livestock production. FAO continued to provide member countries with information and technical assistance in the formulation and implementation of national food policies and nutrition programmes.

FAO continued to implement the Plan of Action of the 1996 World Food Summit [YUN 1996, p. 1129]. In addition, it engaged in activities to enhance the capacity of developing countries to analyse the implications of the Uruguay Round of multilateral trade agreements [YUN 1994, p. 1474] in agriculture, forestry and fisheries, and to take advantage of new trading opportunities.

FAO activities to achieve more productive and efficient use of the Earth's natural resources to meet current and future food and agricultural needs in a sustainable manner concentrated on six areas: natural resources assessment and planning; farming systems development; plant nutrition development and management; water development, management and conservation; soil management, conservation and reclamation; and sustaining the potential of natural resources.

FAO continued to provide technical assistance in plant breeding and the safe movement of germ plasm and associated systems. Its Global Strategy for the Management of Farm Animal Genetic Resources supported projects in Asia, sub-Saharan Africa and Europe. FAO assisted members to comply with the World Trade Organization Agreement on Trade-Related Aspects of Intellectual Property Rights as it related to plant varieties, animal breeds, related technology and germ plasm.

FAO continued to function as an information centre, collecting, analysing, interpreting and disseminating information through various media. The World Agricultural Information Centre provided immediate access to FAO's bibliographical information documents and multimedia resources through the Internet and on CD-ROM.

Secretariat

As at 31 December 2001, FAO staff numbered 3,542, of whom 1,499 were in the Professional or higher categories and 2,043 in the General Service category.

Budget

The regular programme budget for the 2000-2001 biennium was $650 million.

NOTE: For further information, see *The State of Food and Agriculture 2001.*

HEADQUARTERS AND OTHER OFFICES

HEADQUARTERS

Food and Agriculture Organization of the United Nations
Viale delle Terme di Caracalla
00100 Rome, Italy
  Telephone: (39) (06) 57051
  Fax: (39) (06) 5705 3152
  Internet: http://www.fao.org
  E-mail: FAO-HQ@fao.org

NEW YORK LIAISON OFFICES

Food and Agriculture Organization Liaison
  Office with the United Nations
1 United Nations Plaza, Room 1125
New York, NY 10017, United States
  Telephone: (1) (212) 963-6036
  Fax: (1) (212) 963-5425
  E-mail: LONY-Registry@un.org

FAO also maintained liaison offices in Brussels, Geneva, Washington, D.C., and Yokohama, Japan; regional offices in Accra, Ghana; Bangkok, Thailand; Cairo, Egypt; and Santiago, Chile; and subregional offices in Apia, Samoa; Bridgetown, Barbados; Budapest, Hungary; Harare, Zimbabwe; and Tunis, Tunisia.

Chapter IV

United Nations Educational, Scientific and Cultural Organization (UNESCO)

The United Nations Educational, Scientific and Cultural Organization (UNESCO) continued in 2001 to promote cooperation in education, science, culture and communication among its member States.

The General Conference convened its thirty-first session (Paris, 15 October–3 November), at which it adopted the organization's 2002-2003 programme budget and 2002-2007 medium-term strategy. The 58-member Executive Board held its one hundred and sixty-first (28 May–13 June), one hundred and sixty-second (2-12 October) and one hundred and sixty-third (5-6 November) sessions, all in Paris.

The Bureau of Field Coordination launched the first phase of a streamlining exercise to enhance programme delivery and cost-effectiveness of the organization's network of field offices. It created 27 cluster offices to serve groups of member States and closed 18 national offices.

UNESCO membership remained at 188 in 2001.

Activities

Education

As follow-up to the 2000 World Education Forum [YUN 2000, p. 1416], UNESCO initiated steps to develop and publish generic criteria for assessing the credibility of national education for all (EFA) plans. The first EFA monitoring report was circulated at UNESCO's first high-level group meeting on EFA (Paris, 29-30 October), which adopted a communiqué requesting all partners to redouble their efforts to meet EFA goals. In addition, the development of an inter-agency cooperative programme on "Teachers and Quality" was approved, and, as part of the World Teachers' Day campaign, focus was placed on the issue of teacher shortages.

UNESCO continued to play a major convening role with regard to Chapter 36 of Agenda 21 [YUN 1992, p. 672], which addressed education for sustainable development. It participated in the preparations for the 2002 World Summit on Sustainable Development (see p. 749), worked with teachers and students worldwide, and developed partnerships that linked those concerned with sustainable development to the EFA movement. It

also implemented national and subregional projects in Africa, Latin America and South-East Europe, with a view to mainstreaming education for human rights, peace and democracy within education systems.

Sciences

Under its programme of sciences in the service of development, UNESCO continued to promote the advancement, sharing and transfer of knowledge. It emphasized the fostering of synergies between the exact and natural sciences and the social and human sciences.

Natural sciences

In 2001, UNESCO's activities continued to focus on the advancement, sharing and transfer of scientific and technological knowledge, the training of scientists and the provision of advisory services and training programmes on science and technology policy-making and planning.

In conjunction with partners, UNESCO inaugurated the Arab Academy of Sciences (Beirut, Lebanon) and the Euro-Arab Research Network centre at Ajman University of Science and Technology (United Arab Emirates), and launched the Arab Open University and the Virtual University of Science and Technology (Jakarta, Indonesia).

In other activities, UNESCO designated 10 November as World Science Day for Peace and Development, in an effort to strengthen public support for science; awarded the first Great Man-Made River International Prize for Water Resources in Arid and Semi-Arid Areas, sponsored by the Libyan Arab Jamahiriya; and signed an agreement with the Latin American Centre of Physics in Havana, Cuba, to create a regional laboratory.

UNESCO also organized and/or supported major conferences in Africa, including the African Conference on Scientific Education for Girls (Lusaka, Zambia, 18-22 June), which resulted in a 2001-2005 action plan on education for girls, and the African Forum on the Promotion of Renewable Energy in Africa (Niamey, Niger, 22-25 January).

UNESCO implemented the Urban Pollution of Superficial and Groundwater Aquifers programme in seven African cities within the framework of hydrology and water resources development in vulnerable environments. It approved the creation of the UNESCO/International Institute for Infrastructural, Hydraulic and Environmental Engineering Institute for Water Education in Delft, Netherlands; the Regional Centre for Urban Water Management in Tehran, Iran; and the Regional Centre on Water Resources Management in Arid Zones in Cairo, Egypt.

Social and human sciences

UNESCO continued to promote foresight and future-oriented studies, in particular through its publications *Keys to the 21st Century*, a first anthology of the *21st Century Talks* series, and *The World Ahead: Our Future in the Making*, a forward-looking report on 20 major world issues. In 2001, the General Conference listed science and technology ethics among the five principal priorities of UNESCO's programme. UNESCO also participated in the World Conference against Racism, Racial Discrimination, Xenophobia and Related Intolerance (Durban, South Africa) (see p. 615), and drew attention to its 1993 Slave Route Project, which aimed to break the silence and tackle the denial of the plight of millions of victims of the slave trade.

In promoting women's human rights, UNESCO translated and distributed its "Passport to Equality" in several national languages. The Passport illustrated all 30 articles of the Convention on the Elimination of All Forms of Discrimination against Women [YUN 1979, p. 889]. In that connection, a conference on women and human rights was organized (Mali), the aim of which was to introduce women to legislative instruments on human rights. UNESCO also launched the publication *Education for a Culture of Peace* by Betty Reardon, which received honourable mention in the UNESCO Prize for Peace Education in 2001, and organized a preview of the film "Kandahar" in an effort to raise awareness of women's condition in Afghanistan.

Youth-related activities included the General Conference Youth Forum (October) and the promotion of the International Year of Volunteers 2001 (see p. 814), an innovative approach to youth voluntary service.

Culture

At its 2001 session, the General Conference adopted the UNESCO Universal Declaration on Cultural Diversity and its Action Plan, which emphasized respect for and revitalization of cultural diversity. It also adopted the UNESCO Convention on the Protection of the Underwater Cultural Heritage, as UNESCO continued to assert its role as coordinator of complex operations to safeguard heritage damaged by conflicts.

The General Conference launched the "Global Alliance for Cultural Diversity", a partnership initiative between public, private and civil society sectors that would build local capacity in creative industries to increase competitive participation in domestic and international markets and develop effective mechanisms to prevent piracy.

Communication

UNESCO promoted activities in favour of press freedom, notably the worldwide celebration of World Press Freedom Day on 3 May. It continued to implement some 180 operational communication projects. UNESCO also held regional workshops on its Programme for Creative Television, providing training, distribution and production opportunities.

Secretariat

As at 31 December 2001, UNESCO had 2,140 full-time staff, of whom 1,005 were in the Professional or higher categories and 1,135 were in the General Service category.

Budget

The UNESCO General Conference, in 1999, had approved a budget of $544,367,250 for the 2000-2001 biennium. In 2001, it approved the same amount for the 2002-2003 biennium.

HEADQUARTERS AND OTHER OFFICES

HEADQUARTERS

UNESCO House
7, Place de Fontenoy
75352 Paris 07-SP, France
  Telephone: (33) (1) 45-68-10-00
  Fax: (33) (1) 45-67-16-90
  Internet: http://www.unesco.org

UNESCO also maintained a liaison office in Geneva.

NEW YORK LIAISON OFFICE

United Nations Educational, Scientific and Cultural Organization
2 United Nations Plaza, Room 900
New York, NY 10017, United States
  Telephone: (1) (212) 963-5995
  Fax: (1) (212) 963-8014
  E-mail: newyork@unesco.org

Chapter V

World Health Organization (WHO)

In 2001 the World Health Organization (WHO) continued to implement its corporate strategy by addressing the burden of ill-health among poor populations; tracking and assessing risks to health and helping societies take action to reduce them; improving the performance of health systems and encouraging national policies that promoted health. The strategy also included WHO's core functions of eradicating epidemics and other diseases, research, the establishment of international conventions and regulations, partnership-building, innovation and the development and monitoring of norms and standards.

The World Health Assembly, WHO's governing body, at its fifty-fourth session (Geneva, 14-22 May), adopted resolutions on, among other issues, the global response to HIV/AIDS, infant and young child nutrition, a WHO medicines strategy, and epidemic alert and response. The one hundred and seventh session of the WHO Executive Board (Geneva, 15-23 January) discussed infant and child feeding, assessment of health systems performance, new international health regulations, nursing and midwifery, and schistosomiasis. The Board adopted a resolution calling for protection, promotion and support of breast-feeding and complementary feeding practices. The year 2001 marked the twentieth anniversary of the adoption of the International Code of Marketing of Breast-milk Substitutes, and the Board called for the strengthening of national mechanisms to ensure global compliance with the Code. At the one hundred and eighth session (23-24 May), Board members discussed the need for transparency and participation in governing body meetings, in addition to other management matters.

The World Health Report 2001—Mental Health: New Understanding, New Hope focused on mental disorders, and was intended to help dismantle many of the barriers that prevented millions of people worldwide from receiving the necessary treatment. WHO also launched the mental health global action programme, a five-year initiative to close the gap between the resources needed to reduce the burden of mental disorders and those currently available.

In 2001, WHO membership remained at 191, with two associate members and four observers.

Health and development

In 2001, WHO continued to work with national health authorities around the world to achieve progress in health care policies, establish better health systems and provide improved health care, especially to those in greatest need. It emphasized health problems and diseases on the global level, especially in developing countries, offering strong support to the Stop Tuberculosis (TB) Partnership and the Global Plan to Stop TB. The Global TB Drug Facility was launched in 2001 and operated as a unique mechanism to ensure the uninterrupted provision of quality-assured anti-TB drugs for implementing DOTS (Directly Observed Treatment Short Course). In pursuing access to essential medicines and health care technologies for all countries, WHO worked in strong cooperation with the World Trade Organization, which discussed the question at its Fourth Ministerial Conference in November in Doha, Qatar.

The Commission on Macroeconomics and Health submitted a ground-breaking report in December, showing that a few health conditions were responsible for a high proportion of the avoidable deaths in poor countries and that well-targeted measures, using existing technologies, could save the lives of about 8 million people per year and generate yearly economic benefits of more than \$360 billion by 2015-2020. The Commission was made up of 18 leading economic and health experts. WHO reached agreement with publishing houses to make many medical and scientific journals available on the Internet at no or low cost to developing countries.

Disease trends and control efforts

A record number of 168 member States participated in November in the third session of negotiations on the framework convention on tobacco control. The convention, which would provide a set of rules and regulations to govern the spread of tobacco and tobacco products, was scheduled to be ready for adoption by August 2003.

WHO continued to support countries in fighting malaria, offering technical guidance and helping local institutions undertake the applied research necessary to assess the national malaria situation. With WHO support, the Roll Back Malaria Partnership had enabled over 30 countries to draw up strategies for increasing their investment in support of halting the spread of the disease. WHO also provided a range of technical and administrative services to the Global Fund to Fight AIDS, TB and Malaria.

Secretariat

At the end of 2001, WHO had a staff of 3,436, including 1,351 in the Professional and higher categories and 2,085 in the General Service category.

Budget

The World Health Assembly adopted a budget of $842.6 million for the 2002-2003 biennium, the same as the previous biennium. Extra budgetary resources for 2002-2003 were expected to grow by 25 per cent.

NOTE: For further details of WHO activities, see the *World Health Report 2001* and *2002*, published by the organization.

HEADQUARTERS AND OTHER OFFICES

HEADQUARTERS

World Health Organization
20, Avenue Appia
CH-1211 Geneva 27, Switzerland
  Telephone: (41) (22) 791-21-11
  Fax: (41) (22) 791-31-11
  Internet: http:// www.who.int
  E-mail: info@who.ch

WHO OFFICE AT THE UNITED NATIONS

2 United Nations Plaza, Room 970
New York, NY 10017, United States
  Telephone: (1) (212) 963-4388
  Fax: (1) (212) 963-8565

WHO also maintained regional offices in Alexandria, Egypt; Brazzaville, Congo; Copenhagen, Denmark; Harare, Zimbabwe; Manila, Philippines; New Delhi, India; and Washington, D.C.

Chapter VI

World Bank (IBRD and IDA)

The World Bank consisted of the International Bank for Reconstruction and Development (IBRD) and the International Development Association (IDA) (see below). Collectively, the following five institutions were known as the World Bank Group: IBRD, IDA, the International Finance Corporation, the Multilateral Investment Guarantee Agency (MIGA) and the International Centre for Settlement of Investment Disputes (ICSID).

In fiscal 2001 (1 July 2000–30 June 2001), the World Bank continued to promote sustainable economic development by providing loans, guarantees and related technical assistance for projects and programmes in developing nations. Within the context of the Bank's central objective of poverty reduction, key focal points of its assistance were human development, infrastructure, finance and private sector development, agriculture and environment, and public sector management.

In collaboration with partners, the Bank launched the multi-country HIV/AIDS programme (MAP) for Africa, the first of its kind. Under MAP, flexible and rapid funding would be committed, on IDA terms, to individual HIV/AIDS projects developed by countries. The Bank also developed and presented to the Board of Executive Directors in 2001 a new Strategic Framework Paper and a Strategic Directions Paper that set out two inter-related objectives: building the climate for investment, jobs and sustainable growth; and empowering poor people to participate in development.

By the end of fiscal 2001, IBRD membership had increased to 183 countries.

Lending operations

In 2001, IBRD continued to promote sustainable development through loans, guarantees and non-lending, including analytical and advisory services. As at 30 June 2001, its cumulative lending totalled $360 billion.

Gross IBRD disbursement in fiscal 2001 totalled $11.8 billion, a decrease of nearly 12 per cent from fiscal 2000. The Bank's loan commitment decreased to $10.5 billion in 2001 for 91 new operations compared to $10.9 billion in 2000 for 97 new operations. The share of adjustment lending declined to 38 per cent in fiscal 2001, down

from 41 per cent in 2000 and 63 per cent in 1999, approaching pre–East Asia crisis levels. However, the quality of IBRD operations continued to improve, with fewer ongoing projects at risk of not achieving their development objectives.

IBRD lending commitments in fiscal 2001 were highest in Latin America and the Caribbean ($4.8 billion), followed by Europe and Central Asia ($2.2 billion). The share of education, health/nutrition/population and social protection lending increased to 21 per cent ($2.2 billion) from 16 per cent ($1.7 billion) in fiscal 2000. Lending also helped to strengthen the financial sector ($1.7 billion), improve public sector management ($1.4 billion), meet infrastructure needs ($2.7 billion, including $2.4 billion in the transport sector) and support the environment and rural development ($1.3 billion).

The five largest borrowers were China ($19.1 billion), Mexico ($14.7 billion), Indonesia ($13.4 billion), India ($11.3 billion) and Argentina ($11.1 billion).

International Development Association

Established in 1960 as the Bank's concessional lending arm, IDA provided interest-free loans and other services to low-income countries to reduce poverty and improve the quality of life. In 2001, 78 countries were eligible for IDA assistance; IDA credits totalled $6.8 billion for 134 new operations in 57 countries compared with $4.4 billion in 2000. Contributing to that rise was $1.4 billion in new commitments to three countries (Ethiopia, Kenya, Pakistan) that had not received new IDA financing in fiscal 2000. In 2001, adjustment lending increased to 27 per cent from 16 per cent in 2000 as a result of large adjustment loans, including the first two poverty reduction support credits (PRSCs) approved for Uganda and Viet Nam. The Bank introduced PRSCs to help low-income countries implement policy and institutional reforms drawn from their poverty reduction strategy papers (PRSPs).

At the end of fiscal 2001, IDA membership had increased to 162 countries.

Fiscal 2001, was the second of the three years of the twelfth replenishment of IDA, which provided resources for new financing commitments during fiscal 2000-2002 [YUN 2000, p. 1421].

In fiscal 2001, lending increased in all regions except the Middle East and North Africa. Of the total new commitments of $6.8 billion, the African region received 50 per cent ($3.4 billion), as a result of several new programmes that included a concerted response to HIV/AIDS and post-conflict reconstruction support. Ethiopia was the largest IDA borrower ($667 million), followed by Viet Nam ($629 million) and India ($520 million). IDA support for human development, including education, health/nutrition/population and social protection, reached $2.2 billion, representing a $600 million increase compared to fiscal 2000. Other priorities were economic reform and public sector management ($1.3 billion), infrastructure development ($0.9 billion), finance and private sector development ($1 billion) and rural development and the environment ($1 billion).

International Centre for Settlement of Investment Disputes

ICSID, established in 1966, continued to encourage foreign investment by providing international facilities for conciliation and arbitration of investment disputes. In 2001, 12 new cases were registered with the Centre. ICSID also undertook research and publishing activities in arbitration and foreign investment law.

In 2001, ICSID membership totalled 134.

Multilateral Investment Guarantee Agency

MIGA, established in 1988, continued to encourage the flow of foreign direct investment to its developing member countries by providing investment guarantees against non-commercial risks. The Agency also provided technical assistance to help developing countries disseminate information on investment opportunities.

In fiscal 2001, MIGA had 154 members and issued $2 billion in guarantee coverage, for a cumulative total of $9.1 billion.

World Bank Institute

In 2001, the World Bank Institute reached some 48,000 participants in nearly 150 countries through some 600 training activities in its efforts to empower people through knowledge- and capacity-building. It scaled up its programmes through distance learning, global knowledge networks and extended partnerships, and by harnessing the newest learning technologies. A new initiative, the Attacking Poverty Programme, supported the building of national capacity to prepare and implement PRSPs.

Scholarships

The joint Japan/World Bank Graduate Scholarship Programme awarded 130 scholarships to individuals applying for advanced studies in fields related to public policy-making.

In 2001, the Robert S. McNamara Fellowship Programme awarded 25 postgraduate fellowships for study in such areas as collaborative approaches to forest management in Indonesia and options for developing educational opportunities for the disabled in urban communities in Bangladesh.

Co-financing

In fiscal 2001, co-financing amounted to $5.47 billion, a decrease of $3.83 billion compared to the previous year. Bilateral and multilateral partners continued to be the largest source of co-financing, accounting for 85 per cent of the total share. Major co-financing partners included the Inter-American Development Bank ($1.9 billion), the Japan Bank for International Cooperation ($0.53 billion) and Kreditanstalt für Wiederaufbau ($0.3 billion). By region, the majority of co-financing went to Latin America and the Caribbean ($3.4 billion), followed by Africa ($1.12 billion) and Europe and Central Asia ($0.46 billion). The major sectors that attracted co-financing were public sector management ($1.2 billion), finance ($1 billion) and oil and gas ($0.9 billion).

In addition to co-financing of $5.47 billion, $2 billion was committed under the Strategic Partnership with Africa Framework.

Financing activities

During fiscal 2001, IBRD raised $17 billion in medium- and long-term debt, compared to $15.8 billion the previous year. It issued debt in nine currencies and in a wide range of maturities and structures. Diversification helped lower borrowers' funding costs and expanded IBRD's investor base.

As at 30 June 2001, outstanding borrowings totalled $111.5 billion, after swaps.

Capitalization

As at 30 June 2001, the total subscribed capital of IBRD was $189.5 billion, or 99 per cent of its authorized capital of $190.8 billion. Outstanding loans and callable guarantees totalled $118.9 billion, or 62 per cent of IBRD's statutory lending limit.

Income, expenditures and reserves

IBRD's gross revenues totalled $10 billion in fiscal 2001, equalling fiscal 2000. Net income amounted to $1.49 billion, down from $1.99 billion in fiscal 2000. Expenses increased to $8.9 billion, compared to $8.1 billion a year earlier. Administrative costs fell to $859 million, from $935 million in 2000. At the end of fiscal 2001, the Bank's liquid asset portfolio was $24.2 billion, equalling fiscal year 2000.

Secretariat

As at 30 June 2001, IBRD's regular, fixed-term and long-term consultants, and long-term temporary staff in Washington, D.C., and local offices numbered 8,507.

NOTE: For further details regarding the Bank's activities, see *The World Bank Annual Report 2001.*

HEADQUARTERS AND OTHER OFFICES

The World Bank
1818 H Street, NW
Washington, DC 20433, United States
 Telephone: (1) (202) 477-1234
 Fax: (1) (202) 477-6391
 Internet: http://www.worldbank.org
 E-mail: feedback@worldbank.org

The World Bank Mission to the United Nations
1 Dag Hammarskjöld Plaza
885 Second Avenue, 26th floor
New York, NY 10017, United States
 Telephone: (1) (212) 355-5112
 Fax: (1) (212) 355-4523

The World Bank also maintained offices in Brussels, Frankfurt, Geneva, London, Paris, Sydney and Tokyo.

Chapter VII

International Finance Corporation (IFC)

The International Finance Corporation (IFC), part of the World Bank Group, continued in fiscal 2001 (1 July 2000–30 June 2001) to promote growth in developing countries, by financing private sector investments, helping to mobilize capital in the international financial markets and providing technical assistance and advice to Governments and businesses.

IFC pursued investment in fiscal 2001 under challenging circumstances—private capital flows to emerging markets continued to be depressed, private debt flows declined and lenders tended to be short-term oriented while concentrating on large, well-established businesses. Since demand for IFC services remained high under those conditions, IFC focused its resources where it could promote the strongest development impact. Over 40 per cent of its investments for its own account were in low-income or high-risk countries and over 70 per cent in its priority sectors.

During fiscal 2001, IFC membership increased to 175.

Financial and advisory services

In fiscal 2001, IFC's Board of Directors approved $5.4 billion in financing for 240 new projects in 75 countries, compared with $5.8 billion for 259 projects in 81 countries in fiscal 2000. Total project cost of the enterprises supported by IFC amounted to more than $16.4 billion, down from $21.1 billion the previous year.

Direct investment in small and medium-sized enterprises (SMEs) was de-emphasized in favour of mobilization and intermediary investment that could create models to leverage resources more effectively. IFC committed or approved support for SMEs through corporate-linked transactions, credit lines and other loans to banks in all regions. As part of its financial focus on SMEs, IFC launched a global initiative in e-finance.

In fiscal 2001, 117 advisory assignments, in more than 50 countries and regions received some $17 million. IFC continued to provide advisory services towards building institutional capacity, establishing commercial microfinance institutions, developing secondary mortgage markets and leasing, legal and regulatory market assessments.

The Private Sector Advisory Services, established in 2000 when IFC and World Bank advisory services were integrated, advised Government and State-owned enterprises on privatization transactions and projects that were commercially viable and environmentally and socially responsible. In fiscal 2001, focus was placed on developing activities in Eastern Europe and Southern Africa.

Cumulative contributions to the IFC-managed technical assistance trust fund (TATF) programme totalled $582 million in fiscal 2001, compared to $525 million in fiscal 2000. Projects supported by TATF in 2001 included advice on privatization, environmental policy, capacity-building and corporate governance practices.

Regional projects

IFC approved 240 new projects in 75 countries in fiscal 2001.

In sub-Saharan Africa, IFC focused on the financial sector, infrastructure, SMEs, and tourism. It approved 45 projects in 17 countries in fiscal 2001, compared to 80 projects in 25 countries in fiscal 2000. As at 30 June 2001, IFC's committed portfolio, including loans and investments, totalled $1.8 billion, up from $1.5 billion in fiscal 2000.

In Asia and the Pacific in fiscal 2001, IFC provided credit enhancement, completed restructuring transactions, and supported financial institutions in crisis-affected countries. It approved 65 projects in 15 countries compared to 54 projects in 12 countries in fiscal 2000. As at 30 June 2001, IFC's committed portfolio, including loans and investments, totalled $6.5 billion, down from $6.8 billion in fiscal 2000.

In Europe and Central Asia, IFC increased its emphasis on sectors and countries with the most acute need, providing assistance in legal and regulatory reform and in the improvement of management capabilities and governance practices. IFC established a regional hub in Istanbul, Turkey, to enhance operations in Southern Europe and Central Asia. The particularly difficult constraints on private sector development in the former Soviet Union countries were addressed through a technical assistance unit, the Private Enterprise Partnership. IFC established a regional programme in Central Asia to assist borrowers in developing management information and automated accounting systems, and invested in the Central Asian Early Stage Investment Fund, a venture capital fund. As European Union accession neared for many Central European countries, IFC modified its regional strategy; it withdrew from sectors and lines of business where the private sector was ready to take over, focused on socially and environmentally sensitive sectors and stressed its catalytic role in attracting foreign direct investments (FDI) into the region. It approved 58 projects in 23 countries in fiscal 2001, compared to 47 projects in 19 countries in fiscal 2000. As at 30 June 2001, IFC's committed portfolio, including loans and investments, totalled $3.3 billion, down from $3.7 billion in fiscal 2000.

In Latin America and the Caribbean, with the demand for services far exceeding financial resources, IFC financed businesses where private sector participation could provide a visible impact on living standards, SMEs and firms with high growth and employment impact. Project areas included education, health and housing. IFC also provided credit lines and loans to banking institutions to build their capacity to serve small and mid-size companies. An IFC regional office was opened in Bogotá, Colombia. IFC approved 54 projects in 14 countries in fiscal 2001, compared to 58 projects in 15 countries in fiscal 2000. As at 30 June 2001, IFC's committed portfolio, including loans and investments, totalled $8.5 billion, down from $8.9 billion in fiscal 2000.

In the Middle East and North Africa, IFC promoted broader private sector participation, particularly in infrastructure and financial markets. In fiscal 2001, it participated in large infrastructure projects, small information technology companies, large capital market investments and institution-building investments in the financial sector. It approved 15 projects in 6 countries in fiscal 2001, compared to 16 projects in 10 countries in fiscal 2000. As at 30 June 2001, IFC's committed portfolio, including loans and investments, totalled $1.6 billion, up from $997 million in fiscal 2000.

Foreign Investment Advisory Service

The Foreign Investment Advisory Service (FIAS), jointly operated by IFC and the World Bank, continued to assist Governments in policy design and institution development, in order to attract FDI.

In fiscal 2001, FIAS completed 48 advisory projects, of which 10 dealt with reviewing the legal framework for FDI, nine with reducing the administrative barriers to FDI, and five with diagnosing and identifying a country's main policy impediments to attracting productive FDI. FIAS also conducted six regional projects for groups of countries to coordinate their FDI strategies and investment promotion activities.

Financial performance

In fiscal 2001, IFC's net income was $345 million, compared to $380 million in fiscal 2000. The loan portfolio recorded a net loss of $11 million. The equity and quasi-equity portfolios also recorded a net operating loss of $10 million, compared to net operating income of $191 million in fiscal 2000. Net operating income from IFC's invested net worth and treasury activities totalled $280 million.

IFC's committed portfolio at the end of the fiscal year was $14.3 billion, up from $13.5 billion in fiscal 2000. The portfolio consisted of loans, equity investments, guarantees and risk management products in 1,378 companies in 117 countries.

Capital and retained earnings

As at 30 June 2001, IFC's net worth reached $6.1 billion, compared to $5.8 billion at the end of fiscal 2000.

Secretariat

As at 31 December 2001, IFC employed almost 2,000 staff, of whom about 70 per cent worked at its headquarters and about 30 per cent were stationed in over 80 IFC field offices.

NOTE: For further details of IFC activities, see *International Finance Corporation 2001 Annual Report*, published by the Corporation.

HEADQUARTERS AND OTHER OFFICE

HEADQUARTERS
International Finance Corporation
2121 Pennsylvania Avenue, NW
Washington, DC 20433, United States
 Telephone: (1) (202) 473-1000
 Fax: (1) (202) 974-4384
 Internet: http://www.ifc.org
 E-mail: webmaster@ifc.org

NEW YORK OFFICE
International Finance Corporation
809 UN Plaza, 9th floor
New York, NY 10017, United States
 Telephone: (1) (212) 963-6008
 Fax: (1) (212) 697-7020

Chapter VIII

International Monetary Fund (IMF)

During 2001, the International Monetary Fund (IMF) engaged in a process of reform, while advancing its operational work, by establishing an Independent Evaluation Office to enhance transparency and accountability of its activities; strengthening its surveillance work, notably in the area of financial sector assessments through the joint IMF–World Bank Financial Sector Assessment Programme; disseminating international standards and codes of good practice; and updating its lending policies. IMF focused on financial crisis prevention among its members, and established a new International Capital Markets Department to improve its understanding of financial markets and financial flows. It also made some progress towards a framework agreement on the involvement of the private sector in crisis prevention and management. IMF continued to implement the strategy for poverty reduction and growth facility (PRGF) for its low-income member countries, and to assist the Heavily Indebted Poor Countries (HIPCs) through debt relief. In addition, it assessed offshore financial centres and enhanced its contribution to international efforts to combat money-laundering.

During fiscal 2001 (1 May 2000–30 April 2001), IMF membership increased to 183.

IMF facilities and policies

In fiscal 2001, IMF updated its lending policies and policy conditionality to ensure that they met member country needs. Regular lending facilities were restructured to allow more effective support in crisis resolution, prevent crises arising from contagion and ensure a more efficient use of IMF financial resources; policy conditionality was streamlined to increase effectiveness and promote strong country ownership of IMF-supported programmes. IMF also reaffirmed its role in promoting good governance in member countries.

The IMF Executive Board agreed on several measures to sharpen the focus of IMF lending on crisis resolution and prevention by making the contingent credit line facility more attractive to potential users; encouraging early repayment and discouraging excessive use of IMF loans; and by strengthening the monitoring of countries' economic policies after conclusion of IMF-supported programmes.

IMF provided concessional financing to help low-income countries to boost their economic growth through PRGF and the HIPC Initiative.

Financial assistance

New IMF lending commitments in fiscal 2001 totalled 14.5 billion special drawing rights (SDR) compared with SDR 23.5 billion in fiscal 2000, reflecting favourable global economic and financial conditions. Members' drawings of IMF general resources amounted to SDR 9.5 billion compared with SDR 6.3 billion in fiscal 2000.

IMF approved nine new standby arrangements totalling SDR 2.1 billion and one new extended fund facility arrangement for the former Yugoslav Republic of Macedonia for SDR 24 million. Drawings under PRGF for poor countries increased to SDR 0.6 billion, compared with SDR 0.5 billion in fiscal 2000. Emergency post-conflict assistance was provided to the Congo, Sierra Leone and the Federal Republic of Yugoslavia (FRY) in the amount of SDR 138 million.

As at 30 April 2001, 25 standby arrangements, 12 extended arrangements and 43 PRGF arrangements were in effect with members, while outstanding IMF credit amounted to SDR 48.7 billion, compared with SDR 50.4 billion a year earlier.

Liquidity

The Fund's liquidity position continued to improve due to the 1999 increases in members' quotas under the Eleventh General Review [YUN 1999, p. 1404].

As at 30 April, IMF's usable resources totalled SDR 112.1 billion, an increase of SDR 3.9 billion over 2000. Net uncommitted usable resources totalled SDR 78.7 billion at the end of fiscal 2001, compared with SDR 74.8 billion in fiscal 2000.

The Fund's liquid liabilities totalled SDR 46.7 billion, compared with SDR 48.8 billion a year earlier, while the ratio of the Fund's net uncommitted resources to its liabilities increased to 168.4 per cent at the end of April 2001, from 153 per cent a year earlier.

SDR activity

In fiscal 2001, total transfers of SDRs declined to SDR 18.7 billion from SDR 22.9 billion in fiscal 2000. Transfers of SDRs among participants and prescribed holders fell to SDR 6.8 billion in 2001, from SDR 7.8 billion a year earlier.

Transfers from participants to the general resources account (GRA) declined to SDR 5.8 billion from SDR 7.1 billion in 2000, reflecting a fall in quota payments, lower use of SDRs in repayments of IMF credit and a decline in charges. Drawings from IMF in SDRs decreased to SDR 3.2 billion from SDR 3.6 billion in fiscal 2000, representing the largest category of transfers from the GRA, followed by remuneration payments of SDR 1.8 billion to members with creditor positions.

IMF holdings of SDRs in the GRA declined to SDR 2.4 billion at the end of fiscal 2001, from SDR 2.7 billion a year earlier. SDRs held by prescribed holders decreased by SDR 0.2 billion. SDR holdings by participants increased slightly to SDR 18.6 billion, from SDR 18.1 billion in fiscal 2000. SDR holdings of industrial countries and net creditor countries relative to their net cumulative allocation increased from a year earlier, mainly due to large interest (remuneration) payments made to those members. SDR holdings of non-industrial members decreased to 54.6 per cent of their net cumulative allocations from 62.5 per cent a year earlier, mainly as a result of repayments and payments of interest charges on loans from the GRA.

Policy on arrears

As at 30 April 2001, obligations to IMF declined slightly to SDR 2.24 billion from SDR 2.32 billion a year earlier. Afghanistan, the Democratic Republic of the Congo (DRC), Iraq, Liberia, Somalia and the Sudan remained ineligible to use IMF's general resources. Declarations of non-cooperation were still in effect for the DRC and Liberia. IMF reinstated the Sudan's voting rights upon its compliance with payment commitments, while FRY cleared its arrears in December, prior to succeeding to the membership in IMF of the former Socialist Federal Republic of Yugoslavia.

Technical assistance and training

In fiscal 2001, technical assistance and training accounted for some 18.5 per cent of IMF's total administrative expenses. Demand for such assistance remained strong and continued to focus on fiscal, monetary, statistical and legal aspects. New guidelines on planning and monitoring technical assistance were issued during fiscal 2001 to ensure adherence to management's priorities for allocating and delivering technical assistance. As part of its information dissemination programme, IMF also published comprehensive annual reports on technical assistance activities.

The IMF Institute continued to expand its training in different parts of the world, delivering 108 courses and seminars to some 3,464 officials. In May, it established a regional training centre for Latin American countries and Portuguese-speaking African countries in Brasilia, Brazil, in collaboration with the Brazilian Government. The Institute also increased the number of distance learning courses on financial programming and policies, and courses on financial sector issues, introduced in fiscal 2000, had become part of the regular curriculum.

Secretariat

As at December 2001, IMF employed 2,633 staff members, of whom 1,846 were Professional staff and 787 assistant staff.

Budget

The Fund's administrative budget for fiscal 2001 was approved at $689.9 million ($650.9 million net of estimated reimbursements). The approved capital budget of $50.6 million included $23.5 million for building facility projects and $27.1 million for information technology projects. Actual administrative expenses during the fiscal year totalled $638 million and capital project disbursements totalled $34.6 million.

NOTE: For further details of IMF activities, see *International Monetary Fund Annual Report 2001*, published by the Fund.

HEADQUARTERS AND OTHER OFFICES

HEADQUARTERS
International Monetary Fund
700 19th Street, NW
Washington DC 20431, United States
 Telephone: (1) (202) 623-7000
 Fax: (1) (202) 623-4661
 Internet: http://www.imf.org
 E-mail: publicaffairs@imf.org

 IMF also maintained offices in Geneva, Paris and Tokyo.

IMF OFFICE, UNITED NATIONS, NEW YORK
International Monetary Fund
885 Second Avenue, 26th floor
New York, NY 10017, United States
 Telephone: (1) (212) 893-1700
 Fax: (1) (212) 893-1715

Chapter IX

International Civil Aviation Organization (ICAO)

The International Civil Aviation Organization (ICAO) continued in 2001 to promote the safety and efficiency of civil air transport by prescribing standards and recommending practices and procedures for facilitating civil aviation operations. Its objectives were set forth in annexes to the Convention on International Civil Aviation, adopted in Chicago, Illinois, United States, in 1944, known as the Chicago Convention.

In 2001, domestic and international scheduled traffic of the world's airlines decreased to some 385.4 billion tonne-kilometres, the first decrease since 1991. The airlines carried about 1.62 billion passengers and some 28.7 million tonnes of freight. The passenger load factor on scheduled services in 2001 decreased to 69 per cent. Airfreight decreased by 6 per cent to 110.7 billion tonne-kilometres, and airmail traffic decreased by 13 per cent to 5.3 billion tonne-kilometres. Reported monthly figures suggested that, up to September 2001, there had been little change in overall passenger/freight/mail tonne-kilometres over the same period in 2000; however, following the 11 September terrorist attacks in the United States (see p. 60), data for 2001 showed a total traffic decrease.

The thirty-third ICAO Assembly (Montreal, Canada, 25 September–5 October) elected a new Council and adopted 31 resolutions dealing with safety and security and other issues of international civil aviation. In the light of the 11 September terrorist attacks, the Assembly adopted a resolution strongly condemning the misuse of civil aircraft as weapons of destruction and calling for strengthened programmes of aviation security measures by States and ICAO.

The Council of ICAO held three regular sessions in 2001. In September, it made preparations for the ICAO Assembly's review of the organization's current policy regarding aviation security. On 22 October, the Council established a Special Group on Aviation War Risk Insurance, which held its first meeting in Montreal on 6 and 7 December. At the Assembly's request, the Council decided in November to convene a ministerial conference on aviation security in February 2002.

ICAO celebrated International Civil Aviation Day (7 December) under the theme "Flight Between Nations—Dialogue Between Peoples".

In 2001, ICAO membership increased to 187 countries.

Activities

Air navigation

ICAO continued to update and implement international specifications and regional plans, with particular emphasis on the introduction of communications, navigation and surveillance/air traffic management (CNS/ATM) systems. The specifications consisted of International Standards and Recommended Practices (SARPs) contained in 18 technical annexes to the 1944 Chicago Convention and Procedures for Air Navigation Services (PANS). Following the 11 September attacks in the United States, further efforts were made to better integrate safety and security aspects of civil aviation in the specifications.

The fifth meeting of the Committee on Aviation Environmental Protection (8-17 January) and the eighteenth meeting of the Dangerous Goods Panel (15-25 October) made recommendations to amend ICAO standards. ICAO introduced new requirements for certification of aerodromes by States, which placed greater emphasis on compliance with the applicable SARPs to ensure safety of aircraft operations at aerodromes. The certification requirement would facilitate expansion of ICAO's Universal Safety Oversight Audit Programme to aerodromes, as authorized by the ICAO Assembly's thirty-third session.

Other projects that were given special attention in 2001 included accident investigation; accident and incident data reporting; accident prevention; aerodrome rescue and fire fighting; the aeronautical electromagnetic spectrum, with particular regard to the development of ICAO's position for the International Telecommunication Union's World Radiocommunication Conference (2003); aeronautical information services; aeronautical meteorology; assistance to aircraft accident victims and their families; aviation environmental matters; certification of aerodromes; satellite navigation; and flight safety and human factors.

Air transport

ICAO's air transport programmes were directed towards economic analysis, policy, forecasting and planning; collection and publication of air transport statistics; airport and route facility management; economic and organizational aspects of CNS/ATM systems coordination; economic aspects of environmental protection; the promotion of greater facilitation in international air transport; and aviation security.

The Council, and subsequently the Assembly, endorsed the establishment of an International Financial Facility for Aviation Safety with the objective of financing safety-related projects for which States could not otherwise provide or obtain the financial resources. It also adopted an amendment to annex 17 (security) to the Chicago Convention, which would become effective and applicable in 2002. The amendment included the introduction of various definitions and new provisions in relation to, among others, international cooperation relating to threat information, passengers and their cabin baggage, and in-flight security personnel and protection of the cockpit.

ICAO continued to provide secretariat services to three regional aviation bodies—the African Civil Aviation Commission, the European Civil Aviation Conference and the Latin American Civil Aviation Commission.

Legal matters

On 24 December, ICAO deposited an act with the United Nations, formally confirming the 1986 Vienna Convention on the Law of Treaties between States and International Organizations or between International Organizations [YUN 1986, p. 1006].

The Secretariat Study Group on Unruly Passengers, at its fifth meeting (Montreal, 19-20 April), finalized its work on the draft Model Legislation on Certain Offences Committed on Board Civil Aircraft and the guidance material accompanying the legislation. The model legislation was adopted at the thirty-third session of the ICAO Assembly.

The Diplomatic Conference to Adopt a Mobile Equipment Convention and an Aircraft Protocol (Cape Town, South Africa, 29 October-16 November), adopted the Convention on International Interests in Mobile Equipment and the Protocol to the Convention on International Interests in Mobile Equipment on Matters Specific to Aircraft Equipment.

Technical cooperation

In 2001, the ICAO technical cooperation programme undertook 125 projects in 88 developing countries. The programme, financed by the United Nations Development Programme (UNDP), trust funds, management service agreements and the Civil Aviation Purchasing Service, had total expenditures of $100.7 million. Some 51 per cent of that amount was provided by Governments to fund their own projects on the basis of cost sharing with UNDP.

A total of 583 fellowships were awarded in 2001, of which 548 were implemented. Under a joint programme with Singapore, 100 training awards were provided for 2001-2003 in the area of safety. In addition, 41 scholarships in air navigation services were provided by the Czech Republic.

ICAO employed 414 experts from 35 countries, of whom 94 were on assignment under UNDP and 320 on trust fund projects. There were 89 Governments and organizations registered with ICAO in 2001 under its Civil Aviation Purchasing Service. Equipment purchases in 2001 totalled $89.3 million, compared to $20.5 million in 2000. ICAO had resident missions in 34 countries.

Secretariat

As at 31 December 2001, ICAO employed 778 staff members, including 336 in the Professional and higher categories and 442 in the General Service and related categories.

Budget

Appropriations for the ICAO budget in 2001 were $55,174,000.

NOTE: For further details on the activities of ICAO in 2001, see *Annual Report of the Council, 2001.*

HEADQUARTERS AND REGIONAL OFFICES

International Civil Aviation Organization
999 University Street
Montreal, Quebec, Canada H3C 5H7
Telephone: (1) (514) 954-8219
Fax: (1) (514) 954-6077
Internet: http://www.icao.int
E-mail: icaohq@icao.int

ICAO maintained regional offices in Bangkok, Thailand; Cairo, Egypt; Dakar, Senegal; Lima, Peru; Mexico, D.F.; Nairobi, Kenya; and Paris, France.

Chapter X

Universal Postal Union (UPU)

In 2001, the Universal Postal Union (UPU) continued to promote a fast and reliable universal postal service at affordable prices through international collaboration among its member countries. Activities focused on postal reform and the future development of the Union, with special attention to the needs of developing countries.

UPU's 189 member countries remained the largest physical distribution network in the world, with more than 5 million postal employees working in some 600,000 post offices worldwide.

Activities of UPU organs

Universal Postal Congress

The Universal Postal Congress, UPU's supreme legislative authority, met every five years. It last convened in 1999 [YUN 1999, p. 1408]. In 2001, the High Level Group on the Future Development of UPU (HLG) presented a two-year study on the reform of UPU's structure and on its mission, decision-making process and financing. HLG concluded that a consultative committee should be created for private-sector postal stakeholders—private express couriers, international mailers, equipment manufacturers and suppliers, trade unions and non-governmental organizations—and that committee members should be permitted to participate in UPU's major governing bodies.

Council of Administration

The Council of Administration, which ensured the continuity of UPU's work between Congresses and studied regulatory, administrative and legal issues, held its annual session in Berne, Switzerland (18-26 October). It took action on HLG recommendations and on combating terrorism.

Postal Operations Council

The Postal Operations Council (POC) dealt with the operational, economic and commercial aspects of international postal services, assisting them to modernize and upgrade their products, including letter post, express mail service, postal parcels and postal financial services. At its annual session (Berne, 18-27 April), POC adopted decisions concerning amendments to the Letter Post and Parcel Post Regulations, the election of the new Quality of Service Fund Board of Trustees and the Fund's management and secretariat functions.

International Bureau

The International Bureau provided support, liaison, information and consultation to the postal administrations of member countries. It continued to act as a clearing house for the settlement of various inter-administration charges related to the exchange of postal items and international reply coupons and studied developments in the postal environment, monitored the global quality of postal service and published information and statistics on international postal services. Its Postal Technology Centre managed the postal application of electronic data interchange.

As at 31 December 2001, the permanent staff members of the Bureau numbered 170, of whom 78 were in the Professional and higher categories and 92 were in the General Service category.

Budget

Under UPU's self-financing system, contributions were payable in advance by member States based on the following year's budget. The Council of Administration approved a budget of 71.4 million Swiss francs for the 2001-2002 biennium.

HEADQUARTERS

Universal Postal Union
Weltpoststrasse 4
3015 Berne, Switzerland
Postal address: Union postale universelle
Case postale
3000 Berne 15, Switzerland
Telephone: (41) (31) 350 31 11
Fax: (41) (31) 350 31 10
Internet: http://www.upu.int
E-mail: ib.info@upu.int

Chapter XI

International Telecommunication Union (ITU)

The International Telecommunication Union (ITU) continued in 2001 to promote development and efficient operation of telecommunication systems and to provide technical assistance.

At its annual session (Geneva, 18-29 June), the ITU Council discussed, among other things, ITU reform, the 2003-2007 ITU strategic plan and satellite network filings. It also adopted a resolution endorsing the proposal by the ITU Secretary-General to hold the World Summit on the Information Society in two phases, with the first phase to be held in Geneva in 2003 and the second in Tunis, Tunisia, in 2005. The General Assembly, in resolution 56/183 of 21 December, welcomed the Council's resolution (see p. 764).

During the year, the Union staged the third World Telecommunication Policy Forum (Geneva, 7-9 March) on the topic of voice-over internet protocol (IP) and ITU TELECOM AFRICA 2001 (Johannesburg, South Africa, 12-16 November), the fifth regional telecommunication exhibition and forum for Africa. The exhibition attracted over 15,000 professionals from more than 100 countries, and more than 200 exhibitors from the telecommunication, information technology and audio-visual entertainment fields. Other conferences included the fourth meeting of the Working Group on ITU Reform (Salvador de Bahia, Brazil, 2-6 April); the second annual Global Symposium for Regulators (Geneva, 3-5 December); and the Joint ITU/World Intellectual Property Organization Multilingual Domain Names Symposium (Geneva, 6-7 December).

The Internet Training Centres Initiative for Developing Countries was launched; by the end of the year, 20 of the 50 planned centres were operational, providing training to engineers.

ITU membership remained at 189 in 2001.

Radiocommunication Sector

ITU's Radiocommunication Sector (ITU-R) continued in 2001 to develop operational procedures and technical characteristics for terrestrial and space-based wireless services and systems. ITU-R study groups prepared new and revised recommendations for many services, including spectrum management, fixed-satellite and broadcasting, and held preparatory meetings for the 2003 World Radiocommunication Conference (WRC) and Radiocommunication Assembly.

An ITU-R study group was chosen to focus on revising the 1961 Stockholm Agreement [YUN 1961, p. 651] to enable the introduction of digital sound and television broadcasting. ITU-R finalized the contents of the 2001 edition of the Radio Regulations, including all 2000 WRC [YUN 2000, p. 1433] amendments and decisions. A major achievement for ITU-R was the completion of a two-year (2002-2003) operational plan for improved linkages between strategic, financial and operational planning. The plan would result in a more effective management of the Radiocommunication Bureau's limited resources.

Telecommunication Standardization Sector

During 2001, the Telecommunication Standardization Sector (ITU-T) continued to ensure an efficient and on-time production of high-quality standards covering all fields of telecommunications. It streamlined its work in data networks, open system communications and telecommunication software; organized an informal forum summit (Geneva, 3-4 December) to improve cooperation with forums and consortia; and organized workshops, seminars and study group meetings worldwide.

ITU-T launched the Alternative Approval Process, a fast-track approval procedure for technical standards. Of 244 recommendations received in 2001, 69 per cent were approved in less than six weeks, compared with previous approval times of nine months to four years. Other initiatives included an IP project aimed at addressing the provision of voice, video and data, and a quality-of-service project, designed to establish best practices for service providers.

Telecommunication Development Sector

The Telecommunication Development Sector (ITU-D) continued in 2001 to promote investment and foster expansion of telecommunication infrastructure in developing countries. The Telecommunication Development Advisory Group met twice in 2001, in February and October. At its first meeting, it discussed ITU-D reform, the 2002 World Telecommunication Development Conference (WTDC), digital divide initiatives, and gender issues, among other topics. At its second meeting, it discussed various issues, including the analysis of the implementation of the Valetta Action Plan [YUN 1998, p. 1400] and priority objectives of the 2002 operational plan.

The Telecommunication Development Bureau (BDT), the administrative arm of ITU-D, continued to provide assistance to countries in reforming and restructuring of their telecommunication sectors by introducing new technologies, developing the human resources necessary to ensure sustainability in management and operations, and promoting financing and partnerships as a strategy to attract investment into the sectors. BDT also organized a global symposium for regulators (Geneva, 3-5 December), which resulted in a four-point action plan to assist regulators in developing the tools needed for effective regulation: a focus on skills training, developing benchmarks and models, bolstering regional and subregional initiatives, and broadening input beyond the community of regulators. To engage the global regulatory community in sharing best practices and learning, ITU, through BDT, launched the Global Regulators Exchange.

In preparation for the 2002 WTDC, BDT also held regional preparatory meetings in Asia and the Pacific, Africa and Europe and the Commonwealth of Independent States.

Secretariat

As at 31 December, ITU had 783 staff members, comprising 5 elected officials, 314 in the Professional and higher categories and 464 in the General Service category.

Budget

The budget for ITU in 2000-2001 amounted to 332,621,000 Swiss francs (SwF). The ITU Council set the 2002-2003 budget at 341,947,736 SwF.

NOTE: For further details regarding ITU activities, see *ITU 2001 Annual Report*, published by the Union.

HEADQUARTERS

International Telecommunication Union
Place des Nations
CH-1211, Geneva 20, Switzerland
Telephone: (41) (22) 730-6039
Fax: (41) (22) 733-7256
Internet: http://www.itu.int
E-mail: pressinfo@itu.int

Chapter XII

World Meteorological Organization (WMO)

In 2001, the World Meteorological Organization (WMO) continued to facilitate worldwide cooperation in the generation and exchange of meteorological and hydrological information and the application of meteorology to aviation, shipping, water problems and agriculture. It also promoted operational hydrology and encouraged research and training in meteorology.

The WMO Executive Council, at its fifty-third session (Geneva, 5-15 June), reviewed the organization's programmes and activities, including coordination in the UN system of geosciences and their applications for the benefit of humankind; free and unrestricted exchange of international meteorological and hydrological data and products; climate-related matters; hydrology and water resources; and the role and operation of national meteorological and hydrological services.

WMO's membership remained at 179 States and six Territories in 2001.

World Weather Watch Programme

The World Weather Watch (WWW) Programme, the backbone of WMO scientific and technical programmes, provided meteorological data and products to member States. WWW offered up-to-the-minute worldwide weather information, analyses and forecasts through its Global Observing System (GOS), Global Telecommunications System (GTS), Global Data-processing System and data management and system support activities, collectively known as the basic systems. It also included the Tropical Cyclone Programme, the Instruments and Methods of Observation Programme and WMO satellite and environmental emergency response activities.

WMO's main objectives in implementing WWW continued to be the redesign of GOS and the strengthening of the system's infrastructure in developing countries, particularly in Africa. The implementation of GTS components continued, and efforts were made to consolidate the Regional Meteorological Data Communication Strategy in Africa and improve Asia's meteorological telecommunication network. A similar effort was under way in the Americas.

An expert meeting on rainfall intensity measurements (Bratislava, Slovakia, 23-25 April) developed proposals on the standardization of such measurements. In May/June, the WMO Inter-comparison of Global Positioning System Radiosondes was held at the Brazilian Air Force Satellite/Rocket Launch Centre in Alcantara. A working group on surface measurements (Geneva, 27-31 August) addressed the increasing automation of observations. To strengthen collaboration between instrument manufacturers and WMO, the Association of Hydrometeorological Equipment Industry was being established.

During 2001, the Tropical Cyclone Programme helped to restructure or update the technical plans of the five tropical cyclone regional centres—Miami, Florida (United States), Nadi (Fiji), New Delhi (India), Réunion and Tokyo (Japan). The Typhoon Committee, in close coordination with WMO, organized a workshop on typhoon forecasting research (Cheju Island, Republic of Korea, 25-28 September) and awarded three research fellowships. A workshop on hurricane forecasting and warning and public weather services was held (Miami, 23 April–5 May).

World Climate Programme

The Executive Council's Advisory Group on Climate and Environment (Tehran, Iran, March) recognized, among other things, the need for country-focused approaches when seeking funds for climate and environmental activities.

The Commission for Climatology (Geneva, 21-30 November) agreed to focus its activities for the next four years on climate data and data management, analysis of climate variability and change, and climate applications, information and prediction services.

The World Climate Research Programme, undertaken jointly by WMO, the International Council of Scientific Unions and the Intergovernmental Oceanographic Commission (IOC) of the United Nations Educational, Scientific and Cultural Organization, continued studies to provide the scientific basis for predictions of global and regional climate variations and made projections of the magnitude and rate of human-induced climate change. A principal project was an appraisal of the concentration, distribution and variability of water vapour in the upper troposphere and lower straposphere. Work began on large-format atlases of the physical and chemical properties of the global ocean.

Progress continued in the climate variability and predictability study, which included an investigation of the variability of the American monsoon system, among others. Two regional workshops were organized (Kingston, Jamaica, January; Casablanca, Morocco, February) to prepare climate-change indices for the Caribbean and North Africa, respectively.

Atmospheric Research and Environment Programme

The Atmospheric Research and Environment Programme coordinated and encouraged research in atmospheric and related sciences. The tenth session of the Commission for Atmospheric Sciences (CAS) Advisory Working Group met (Guilin, China, May) to prepare for the thirteenth session of CAS in February 2002. The World Weather Research Programme organized a workshop on verification of quantitative precipitation forecasts (Prague, Czech Republic, 14-16 May) to review existing verification methodologies for high-impact weather events associated with flooding, and to develop recommendations for use by the expert community. The Science Steering Committee (Geneva, October) reviewed research and development projects and made recommendations on those in the planning stage. Several workshops organized by the Tropical Meteorology Research Programme provided forums for interaction between researchers and forecasters from developed and developing countries.

Applications of meteorology

The Applications of Meteorology Programme continued to support member States in a wide range of socio-economic activities, including the protection of life and property and safeguarding the environment. Commission for Agricultural Meteorology meetings included that of its Advisory Working Group (Florence, Italy 2-5 April), which discussed a proposed new structure of the Commission.

The Aeronautical Meteorology Programme held training events on, among other things, the application of numerical weather prediction products to aviation and to pilots' coordination. The final phase of the World Area Forecast System was being implemented with the execution of transition plans for the transfer of responsibility of the remaining regional area forecast centres to the London and Washington centres.

The first session of the Joint WMO/IOC Technical Commission for Oceanography and Marine Meteorology (Akureyri, Iceland, 19-29 June) agreed that a major priority for the intersessional period would be the implementation and maintenance of an operational ocean observing system to provide data for global climate studies. The Automated Shipboard Aerological Programme continued to provide WWW with high-quality upper-air profile data.

Hydrology and water resources

The Hydrology and Water Resources Programme focused on worldwide cooperation in the evaluation of water resources and the development of hydrological networks and services. An Associated Programme on Flood Management was launched in collaboration with the Global Water Partnership.

Technical cooperation

In 2001, WMO technical assistance, valued at $25.31 million, was financed by trust funds ($10.99 million), the WMO Voluntary Cooperation Programme ($8.37 million), the United Nations Development Programme ($5.01 million) and the WMO regular budget ($1 million).

Secretariat

As at 31 December 2001, the number of full-time staff employed by WMO totalled 267. Of those, 118 were in the Professional and higher categories, 146 were in the General Service category, and 3 were unclassified members of the Secretariat.

Budget

A regular budget of 126,150,000 Swiss francs (SwF) for the 2000-2001 biennium was approved by the WMO Executive Council in 1999. The Thirteenth World Meteorological Congress, also in 1999, approved a maximum expenditure of SwF 252,300,000 for the thirteenth financial period (2000-2003).

NOTE: For further details regarding WMO activities, see *World Meteorological Organization Annual Report 2001*, published by WMO.

HEADQUARTERS AND LIAISON OFFICE

World Meteorological Organization
7 bis, avenue de la Paix
(Case postale No. 2300)
CH-1211 Geneva 2, Switzerland
 Telephone: (41) (22) 730-8111
 Fax: (41) (22) 730-8181
 Internet: http://www.wmo.ch
 E-mail: ipa@gateway.wmo.ch

WMO Liaison Office at the United Nations
2 United Nations Plaza, Room 980
New York, NY 10017
 Telephone: (1) (212) 963-9444
 Fax: (1) (212) 963-6997
 E-mail: DDC DonNanjira@un.org

Chapter XIII

International Maritime Organization (IMO)

In 2001, the International Maritime Organization (IMO) continued to improve the safety and security of international shipping and prevent marine pollution from ships.

The IMO Assembly, the organization's governing body, at its twenty-second session (London, 19-30 November), adopted 34 resolutions on measures and procedures to strengthen maritime security. It also elected a new Council for the 2002-2003 biennium.

In 2001, IMO membership increased to 160 with the admission of Comoros, Saint Kitts and Nevis and the Federal Republic of Yugoslavia.

Activities in 2001

The IMO Council awarded the International Maritime Prize for 2000 to Heikki Juhani Valkonen, Director of the Maritime Safety Department of the Finnish Maritime Administration.

On 27 September, IMO observed World Maritime Day under the theme "Globalization and the role of the seafarer" and, at its London headquarters, unveiled an international memorial to the world's seafarers.

Prevention of pollution

At its forty-sixth session (London, 23-27 April), IMO's Marine Environment Protection Committee agreed to a timetable for the elimination of single-hull oil tankers by 2015 or earlier. The new phase-out timetable would enter into force in September 2002 and would be enshrined in a revised regulation of the International Convention for the Prevention of Pollution from Ships, 1973, as modified by the Protocol of 1978 relating thereto (MARPOL 73/78). New draft guidelines for designating environmentally important areas as Particularly Sensitive Sea Areas were also adopted.

A diplomatic conference (London, 19-23 March) adopted the International Convention on Civil Liability for Bunker Oil Pollution Damage, which would establish a liability and compensa-

tion regime for spills of oil carried as fuel in ships' bunkers. The Convention applied to ships over 1,000 gross tonnage.

The International Convention on the Control of Harmful Anti-fouling Systems on Ships was adopted in October. The Convention would prohibit the use of harmful organotins in anti-fouling paints used on ships and would establish a mechanism to prevent the potential future use of other harmful substances in anti-fouling systems.

Ship security and safety at sea

The IMO Assembly agreed to hold a conference on maritime security in December 2002 to adopt new regulations to enhance ship and port security and to reduce the possibility of shipping becoming a target for international terrorism. The Assembly also agreed to a significant boost to the organization's technical cooperation programme of 1.5 million pounds sterling to help developing countries address maritime security issues, adopted a resolution dealing with the plight of asylum-seekers shipwrecked at sea, and recommended a comprehensive review of safety measures and procedures for the treatment of rescued persons. IMO began work on guidelines for cases where damaged or disabled ships required a place of refuge.

As at December 2001, parties to the revised Convention on Standards of Training, Certification and Watch-keeping for Seafarers had risen to 102 States and one IMO associate member.

Secretariat

As at 31 December, IMO had 272 staff members, of whom 114 were in the Professional and higher categories and 158 were in the General Service category.

Budget

The IMO Assembly, in 2001, approved budgetary appropriations of 39,531,100 pounds sterling for the 2002-2003 biennium.

HEADQUARTERS

International Maritime Organization
4 Albert Embankment
London SE1 7SR, United Kingdom
Telephone: (44) (207) 735-7611
Fax: (44) (207) 587-3210
Internet: http://www.imo.org
E-mail: info@imo.org

Chapter XIV

World Intellectual Property Organization (WIPO)

The World Intellectual Property Organization (WIPO) continued development cooperation, norm-setting and registration activities to promote respect for the protection and use of intellectual properties. WIPO focused on strengthening the intellectual property systems of developing countries; promoting new or revised norms for the protection of intellectual property at the national, regional and multilateral levels; and facilitating the acquisition of intellectual property protection through international registration systems.

The governing bodies of WIPO and the Unions administered by the organization held their thirty-sixth series of meetings (Geneva, 24 September–3 October).

During 2001, WIPO membership increased to 177 States, with the accession of Myanmar and Tonga to the 1967 Convention establishing WIPO, amended in 1979. The number of States adhering to treaties administered by WIPO also increased: as at 31 December 2001, 162 States were parties to the Paris Convention for the Protection of Industrial Property, 148 to the Berne Convention for the Protection of Literary and Artistic Works, and 115 to the Patent Cooperation Treaty (PCT).

On 26 April, World Intellectual Property Day was observed for the first time, under the theme "Creating the Future Today".

Activities in 2001

Development cooperation

In 2001, WIPO continued to assist developing countries in building infrastructures, developing human resources and implementing laws that enabled them to utilize effectively the intellectual property system for their economic, social and cultural development. To help bring developing countries into compliance with international standards, in particular the Agreement on Trade-related Aspects of Intellectual Property Rights (TRIPS Agreement) administered by the World Trade Organization, WIPO prepared 28 draft laws for 14 developing countries. Efforts to strengthen administrative infrastructures, training and the preparation and implementation of laws reached a new level of efficiency with the in-

troduction of the Cooperation for Development web site in 2001. The site provided up-to-date access to information about intellectual property developments, training and regional events. During the year, six new nationally focused action plans (NFAPs) were launched in order to help developing countries to improve their management and use of the national intellectual property system.

WIPO continued to focus on the intellectual property needs of small and medium-sized enterprises (SMEs). In cooperation with the Ministry of Industry and Foreign Trade of Italy, it organized the International Forum on Intellectual Property and SMEs (Milan, 9-10 February). The Plan of Action adopted at the Forum served as a blueprint for helping SMEs to benefit fully from the intellectual property system.

In 2001, the WIPO Worldwide Academy trained 4,344 men and women, an increase of 86 per cent over 2000. It also awarded 15 fellowships, enrolled 3,842 students in the Distance Learning (DL) programme delivered via the Internet, and launched a joint diploma course with the University of South Africa on intellectual property law via DL. The Chinese version of DL was also launched, joining the English, French and Spanish versions.

Intellectual property law

WIPO continued to promote the progressive development and harmonization of intellectual property laws, standards and practices among its member States.

In 2001, the Standing Committee on the Law of Patents began discussions on harmonization of substantive patent law, with the aim of reaching common worldwide standards for examining patent applications and granting patents. At the end of the year, the Patent Law Treaty on the harmonization of patent formalities, adopted in 2000 [YUN 2000, p. 1440], had been signed by 53 States and the European Patent Organization.

For the third year in a row, WIPO member States adopted a set of treaty provisions aimed at providing a clear, harmonized and simplified legal framework for the trademark community. After two years of intensive discussions within the Standing Committee on the Law of Trademarks, Industrial Designs and Geographical Indications, WIPO Assemblies adopted, as a Joint Recommendation, provisions concerning the protection of marks and other industrial property rights on the Internet, which would provide a legal framework for those who wished to use their marks on the Internet and to participate in electronic commerce.

The Standing Committee on Copyright and Related Rights continued to consider the enhancement of protection for broadcasting organizations and of non-original databases.

The Advisory Committee on Enforcement of Industrial Property Rights and the Advisory Committee on Management and Enforcement of Copyright and Related Rights in Global Information Networks held a joint meeting and discussed issues such as training needs and techniques, information exchange on national experiences and the development of enforcement guidelines.

Arbitration and Mediation Centre

In 2001, the Arbitration and Mediation Centre expanded its position as the pre-eminent provider of services for domain name and other intellectual property disputes. Throughout the year, the Centre received 3,192 domain name cases. The Uniform Domain Name Dispute Resolution Policy continued to provide trademark owners with an administrative remedy against bad-faith registration and use of domain names corresponding to those trademark rights. Arbitration and mediation workshops contributed to the increased prominence of WIPO dispute procedures tailored to the needs of intellectual property owners and users worldwide.

International registration activities

PCT. During the year, 103,947 international patent applications were filed, representing an increase of 14.3 per cent over 2000.

Madrid Agreement. In the trademark system under the Madrid Agreement concerning the International Registration of Trademarks and its 1989 Protocol, the number of international registrations reached almost 24,000 in 2001, a 4.4 per cent increase over 2000.

Hague Agreement. The international deposits recorded under the Hague Agreement concerning the International Deposit of Industrial Designs totalled 4,183, representing a decrease of 3.5 per cent from the 2000 figure.

Secretariat

As at 31 December 2001, WIPO employed 858 staff members representing 86 countries; 367 were in the Professional or higher categories and 491 were in the General Service category.

Budget

The approved programme and budget for 2002-2003 amounted to 678.4 million Swiss francs (SwF), an increase of 19.9 per cent over the revised budget for 2000-2001 of SwF 565.9 million. The portion of the budget funded by member States' contributions represented less than 6 per cent of the overall budget. WIPO remained largely a self-funding agency, financing its activities from revenues acquired through the provision of services to the private sector.

NOTE: For further information, see *WIPO Annual Report 2001*, published by WIPO.

HEADQUARTERS AND OTHER OFFICE

HEADQUARTERS

World Intellectual Property Organization
34, Chemin des Colombettes (P.O. Box 18)
CH-1211 Geneva 20, Switzerland
  Telephone: (41) (22) 338-9111
  Fax: (41) (22) 733-5428
  Internet: http://www.wipo.int
  E-mail: wipo.mail@wipo.int

WIPO OFFICE AT THE UNITED NATIONS

2 United Nations Plaza, Suite 2525
New York, NY 10017, United States
  Telephone: (1) (212) 963-6813
  Fax: (1) (212) 963-4801
  E-mail: wipo@un.org

Chapter XV

International Fund for Agricultural Development (IFAD)

The International Fund for Agricultural Development (IFAD) continued in 2001 to promote the economic advancement of the rural poor by improving the productivity of on- and off-farm activities and by designing and implementing innovative, cost-effective and replicable programmes.

The twenty-fourth session of the Governing Council (Rome, 20-22 February) approved a document entitled "Partnerships for eradicating rural poverty: report of the Consultation to Review the Adequacy of the Resources Available to IFAD 2000-2002". The document contained a plan of action for improvement of the Fund's operations with respect to project portfolio performance and impact assessment, knowledge management, policy and institutional environment and strategic partnerships. The Executive Board held three regular sessions (April, September, December); it approved loans for 25 projects and programmes, 15 grants and 13 contributions to debt reduction within the framework of the Heavily Indebted Poor Countries Initiative.

IFAD membership increased to 162 during 2001, with the admission of Iceland. Of its member countries, 23 were in List A (developed countries), 12 in List B (oil-exporting developing countries) and 127 in List C (other developing countries); 49 were in Sub-List C1 (Africa), 47 were in Sub-List C2 (Europe, Asia and the Pacific) and 31 in Sub-List C3 (Latin America and the Caribbean).

Resources

The fifth replenishment of IFAD's resources, totalling about $470 million, became effective on 7 September 2001. That amount was expected to cover almost one third of IFAD's lending programme for the fifth replenishment period, 2002-2003. Other resources used for lending, the grant programme and operating expenses came from lending reflows and investment income. The 2001 programme of work was approved for about $440 million, and the administrative budget at about $50 million.

Activities in 2001

Loans approved in 2001 and financed through IFAD totalled $403.1 million; another $30.8 million was in grants. The total cost of the 25 projects was estimated at $996.8 million, of which $270.3 million would be provided by other external financiers and $323.1 million by financiers in the recipient countries—primarily Governments.

Regular Programme lending was distributed as follows: Asia and the Pacific, $107.1 million for six projects (26.6 per cent); Western and Central Africa, $73.5 million for five projects (18.2 per cent); Eastern and Southern Africa, $100.5 million for six projects (24.9 per cent); Latin America and the Caribbean, $69.2 million for four projects (17.2 per cent); and the Near East and North Africa, $52.9 million for four projects (13.1 per cent).

During 2001, 25 projects were completed; 206 projects remained effective at the end of the year.

Secretariat

As at 31 December 2001, the IFAD secretariat had 315 staff members, comprising 134 staff in the Professional and higher categories and 181 in the General Service category.

Income and expenditure

At the end of 2001, IFAD's net income on loans was $42.3 million and on investments was minus $42.8 million, representing an annual income of minus $0.5 million. Operating expenses for the year totalled $148.9 million.

NOTE: For further details on IFAD activities in 2001, see *Annual Report 2001*, published by the Fund.

HEADQUARTERS AND OTHER OFFICES

HEADQUARTERS
International Fund for Agricultural Development
Via del Serafico, 107
00142 Rome, Italy
  Telephone: (39) (06) 54591
  Fax: (39) (06) 5043463
  Internet: http://www.ifad.org
  E-mail: ifad@ifad.org

  IFAD also maintained offices in Eschborn, Germany, and in Washington, DC.

IFAD LIAISON OFFICE
1 United Nations Plaza, Room DC1-1464
New York, NY 10017, United States
  Telephone: (1) (212) 963-0546
  Fax: (1) (212) 963-2787

Chapter XVI

United Nations Industrial Development Organization (UNIDO)

The United Nations Industrial Development Organization (UNIDO) continued to promote the sustainable industrial development of developing countries and countries with economies in transition. As a global forum on industrialization, UNIDO facilitated the spread of industrial information, knowledge, technology and investment.

The Industrial Development Board, at its twenty-fourth session (Vienna, 19-22 June), considered, among other things, UNIDO's programme and budget for the 2002-2003 biennium, new initiatives for funds mobilization, field representation and its contribution to technical cooperation delivery, and environment-related activities.

The ninth session of the General Conference (Vienna, 3-7 December) adopted the programme and budget for 2002-2003 and reappointed the incumbent Director-General, Carlos Magariños, for a second term. The adoption of a resolution on the medium-term programme framework (MTPF) 2002-2005 placed emphasis on technical cooperation and confirmed UNIDO's global forum function. MTPF represented the response of UNIDO's 1997 Business Plan [YUN 1997, p. 1564] to the lessons learned from the process of transformation within UNIDO, in the UN system and in the development community at large. The Conference also agreed to deposit with the United Nations Secretary-General UNIDO's instrument of accession to the 1986 Vienna Convention on the Law of Treaties between States and International Organizations or between International Organizations [YUN 1986, p. 1007]. The Convention offered a specific legal framework governing formal treaties between international organizations and States and would thus provide stability and predictability in the best interest of UNIDO treaty relations.

UNIDO membership remained at 169 in 2001.

Global forum activities

In 2001, UNIDO, through its global forum activities, continued to promote industrial development and cooperation between countries, partnerships, knowledge-sharing, technology and investment. It also assisted developing countries and countries in transition in the implementation of multilateral environmental agreements.

Within the framework of its General Conference, UNIDO organized a forum on the theme "Fighting marginalization through sustainable industrial development: challenges and opportunities in a globalized world" (Geneva, 5 December). Two groups of issues were addressed: one on technology, investment and trade, and the other on the environment.

In other activities, UNIDO launched a portfolio of special initiatives focusing on energy and market access, formulated renewable energy projects promoting solar, wind and biomass energy in rural areas and, in cooperation with Hungary, extended its technology foresight initiative and convened a regional conference on that issue for Eastern European countries and newly independent States (Vienna, 4-5 April). It also continued to cooperate with the Bretton Woods institutions and UN organizations in a concerted response to the development goals of the Millennium Declaration, adopted by the General Assembly in 2000 [YUN 2000, p. 49].

Integrated programmes

UNIDO continued to provide technical cooperation through its integrated programmes, the major components of which were training, investment promotion, quality and standardization, and activities promoting cleaner industrial production and waste management. As at 31 December, 44 integrated programmes had been approved. Africa accounted for 39.5 per cent of the countries covered by integrated programmes, of which 75 per cent were in sub-Saharan Africa.

Investment promotion
and institutional capacity-building

In 2001, the Investment Promotion and Institutional Capacity-building Division focused its activities on poverty reduction by strengthening the capacity of industries in developing countries and countries in transition to benefit from globalization. Technical cooperation and research activities aimed to strengthen the capabilities of and cooperation among public and private stakeholders in industrial development for formulating and implementing industrial strategies. Operational support continued to strengthen the role of the private sector in economic and industrial development, while investment promotion activities were enhanced with the development and launching of sustainable subregional investment and technology promotion networks.

Activities in Africa concentrated on strengthening public-private consultative mechanisms and, in the Arab region, on the formulation of a long-term industrial vision and policy response to new challenges and opportunities. In Asia, activities included the preparation of a long-term industrial development perspective plan for Nepal, and the tracking of manufacturing performance in Thailand. In Latin America, industrial policy advisory services were, in some cases, channelled directly to the private sector. That marked a new departure for UNIDO, which had traditionally worked mainly with Governments.

Environmental sustainability

In 2001, UNIDO's Sectoral Support and Environmental Sustainability Division focused on the formulation and implementation of integrated programmes and country service frameworks, and on increased cooperation with other UN organizations, as well as with international protocols, conventions and funds, particularly within the framework of environmental protection.

As at 31 December, UNIDO had implemented 778 projects in 66 countries, at a net value of $251 million, under the 1987 Montreal Protocol on Substances that Deplete the Ozone Layer [YUN 1987, p. 686]. Those activities corresponded to a phase-out of over 32,000 tons of ozone-depleting pollutants, of which 20,000 had already been eliminated. The National Cleaner Production Centres continued to promote cleaner production capacities and the transfer and development of ecologically sound technologies.

Secretariat

As at 31 December 2001, UNIDO employed a total of 643 staff members: 239 were in the Professional or higher categories, 393 were in the General Service category and 11 were national officers.

Budget

The eighth (1999) session of the UNIDO General Conference approved the organization's 2000-2001 regular budget in the amount of $167.7 million. In 2001, new project approvals totalled $85.6 million, compared to $76.9 million in 2000. In December 2001, the ninth session of the General Conference approved UNIDO's 2002-2003 regular budget in the amount of 133,689,800 euros. The estimated volume of UNIDO operations for the biennium was 349,239,400 euros.

NOTE: For further information on UNIDO, see *Annual Report of UNIDO 2001*.

HEADQUARTERS AND OTHER OFFICES

HEADQUARTERS
United Nations Industrial Development Organization
Vienna International Centre
P.O. Box 300
A-1400 Vienna, Austria
  Telephone: (43) (1) 26026-0
  Fax: (43) (1) 269-26-69
  Internet: http://www.unido.org
  E-mail: unido@unido.org

LIAISON OFFICES

UNIDO Office at Geneva
Le Bocage
Pavillion 1/Palais des Nations
CH-1211 Geneva 10, Switzerland
  Telephone: (41) (22) 917-3364
  Fax: (41) (22) 917-0059

UNIDO Office in New York
1 United Nations Plaza, Room DC1-1110
New York, NY 10017, United States
  Telephone: (1) (212) 963-6891
  Fax: (1) (212) 963-7904

Chapter XVII

World Trade Organization (WTO)

In 2001, the World Trade Organization (WTO), the legal and institutional foundation of the multilateral trading system, continued to oversee the rules of international trade, settle trade disputes and organize trade negotiations.

The Fourth WTO Ministerial Conference, WTO's highest authority, which comprised all of its members, was held in Doha, Qatar, from 9 to 14 November. It adopted the Doha Development Agenda, which set out WTO's work programme for the coming years. Specifically, it incorporated expanded negotiations and other activities and decisions designed to address the challenges facing the trading system and the needs and interests of WTO's diverse membership. The Conference also adopted a declaration on the WTO Agreement on Trade-related Aspects of Intellectual Property Rights (TRIPS) and public health, which clarified specific segments of the TRIPS Agreement, thereby allaying concerns about the possible implications of the Agreement for access to drugs.

WTO's General Council, the body entrusted with overseeing the organization's work in the interval between Conferences, continued to monitor the implementation and operation of the multilateral trading system embodied in the WTO Agreement [YUN 1995, p. 1515]. It oversaw progress in electronic commerce and examined, among other things, the internal transparency and effective participation of member States.

During the year, WTO membership increased to 143 with the admission of China, Lithuania and the Republic of Moldova.

General activities

The three working groups set up by the 1996 Ministerial Conference [YUN 1996, p. 1441] met during 2001. The Working Group on the Relationship between Trade and Investment continued to examine the implications of the relationship between trade and investment for development and economic growth, and for stocktaking and analysis of related international instruments and activities. The Working Group on Transparency in Government Procurement discussed the definition and scope of government procurement; procurement methods; publication of information on national legislation and procedures; information on procurement qualifications; contract awards; domestic review procedures; main-

tenance of records; information technology; language; bribery and corruption; notifications to other Governments; dispute settlement procedures; and technical cooperation and special and differential treatment for developing countries. The Working Group on the Interaction between Trade and Competition Policy continued to discuss the relevance of fundamental WTO principles of national treatment, transparency and most-favoured-nation treatment to competition policy and vice versa; approaches to promoting technical cooperation; and the contribution of competition policy in achieving WTO objectives, including the promotion of international trade.

During the year, the Trade Policy Review Body carried out reviews of Brunei Darussalam, Cameroon, Costa Rica, the Czech Republic, Gabon, Ghana, Macao (China), Madagascar, Malaysia, Mauritius, Mozambique, Slovakia, Uganda, the United States and WTO members of the Organisation of Eastern Caribbean States.

WTO provided technical cooperation and training to developing countries and economies in transition through courses, seminars and symposiums to widen understanding of trade policy, the multilateral trading system, international law and other trade and development issues.

Trade in goods

During 2001, the Council for Trade in Goods continued to monitor implementation of agreements and examined and approved requests for waivers and waiver extensions from members in connection with the transposition of their schedules into the Harmonized System. It reviewed the operation of the Trade-related Investment Measures Agreement; adopted terms of reference under which 18 regional agreements were to be examined in the Committee on Regional Trade Agreements; and continued work on trade facilitation. It extended the transition period for application of the Trade-related Investments Measures Agreement for Argentina, Colombia, Malaysia, Mexico, Pakistan, the Philippines and Romania.

The Committee on Agriculture carried out negotiations under article 20 of the Agreement on Agriculture on the continuation of the reform process, as agreed in 2000 [YUN 2000, p. 1445]. During the first phase (March 2000–March 2001), 121 members submitted 45 negotiating proposals. A programme for the second phase of the negotiations up to early 2002 was also adopted. The Committee continued to review progress in the implementation of commitments under the Uruguay Round agricultural reform programme, or resulting from WTO accession negotiations.

The Committee on Sanitary and Phytosanitary Measures monitored implementation of the Agreement on the Application of Sanitary and Phytosanitary Measures, which set out the rights and obligations of members to ensure food safety, protect humans from plant- or animal-spread diseases, or protect plants and animals from pests and diseases. In 2001, the Committee discussed trade concerns of members and considered the difficulties faced by developing countries regarding the need for technical assistance.

The Committee on Safeguards continued its review of national safeguard legislation.

Trade in services

In 2001, the Council for Trade in Services held five formal meetings and, among other things, held a stocktaking exercise to consider progress made in negotiations to progressively liberalize trade in services. It also held one special meeting to review the Annex on Air Transport Services.

Intellectual property

The TRIPS Agreement provided for minimum international standards of protection in copyright, trademarks, geographic indications, industrial designs, patents, layout designs of integrated circuits and undisclosed information. In 2001, the Council for TRIPS continued to review the national implementing legislation of developing countries and WTO members with economies in transition.

Regional trade agreements

As at December 2001, the Committee on Regional Trade Agreements had completed factual examination of 82 of the more than 100 regional trade agreements under its purview.

Trade and development

In 2001, the Committee on Trade and Development continued to examine, among other things, special and differential treament in favour of developing countries and their participation in world trade; technical cooperation and training; market access for least developed countries; the development dimension of electronic commerce; and implementation of WTO agreements.

Plurilateral agreements

The Committee on Government Procurement continued to carry out work relating to negotiations on expanding the coverage of the Agreement on Government Procurement; its simplification and improvement, especially with regard to advances in information technology; and the elimination of discriminatory measures and practices that distorted open procurement.

The Agreement on Trade in Civil Aircraft eliminated customs duties and other charges on imports of civil aircraft products and repairs, bound them at zero level, and required the adoption of end-use customs administration. Although part of the WTO Agreement, it remained outside the organization's framework. The Committee on Trade in Civil Aircraft adopted the Protocol (2001) Amending the Annex to the Agreement on Trade in Civil Aircraft and a decision on interim application of duty-free treatment to aircraft ground maintenance simulators.

International Trade Centre

The International Trade Centre (ITC), operated jointly by WTO and the United Nations Conference on Trade and Development (see p. 876), played a crucial role in trade-related technical cooperation and trade-related capacity-building. It was also responsible for the day-to-day management of the Integrated Technical Assistance Programme in Selected Least Developed Countries and Other African Countries.

Budget

The WTO budget for 2001 totalled 143 million Swiss francs.

Secretariat

At the end of 2001, WTO staff numbered 550.

NOTE: For further information on WTO activities, see the organization's *Annual Report 2001.*

HEADQUARTERS

World Trade Organization
Centre William Rappard
154, rue de Lausanne
CH-1211 Geneva, 21, Switzerland
Telephone: (41) (22) 739-5111
Fax: (41) (22) 731-4206
Internet: www.wto.org
E-mail: enquiries@wto.org

Appendices

Appendix I

Roster of the United Nations

There were 189 Member States as at 31 December 2001.

MEMBER	DATE OF ADMISSION	MEMBER	DATE OF ADMISSION	MEMBER	DATE OF ADMISSION
Afghanistan	19 Nov. 1946	El Salvador	24 Oct. 1945	Mauritania	27 Oct. 1961
Albania	14 Dec. 1955	Equatorial Guinea	12 Nov. 1968	Mauritius	24 Apr. 1968
Algeria	8 Oct. 1962	Eritrea	28 May 1993	Mexico	7 Nov. 1945
Andorra	28 July 1993	Estonia	17 Sep. 1991	Micronesia (Federated	
Angola	1 Dec. 1976	Ethiopia	13 Nov. 1945	States of)	17 Sep. 1991
Antigua and Barbuda	11 Nov. 1981	Fiji	13 Oct. 1970	Monaco	28 May 1993
Argentina	24 Oct. 1945	Finland	14 Dec. 1955	Mongolia	27 Oct. 1961
Armenia	2 Mar. 1992	France	24 Oct. 1945	Morocco	12 Nov. 1956
Australia	1 Nov. 1945	Gabon	20 Sep. 1960	Mozambique	16 Sep. 1975
Austria	14 Dec. 1955	Gambia	21 Sep. 1965	Myanmar	19 Apr. 1948
Azerbaijan	2 Mar. 1992	Georgia	31 July 1992	Namibia	23 Apr. 1990
Bahamas	18 Sep. 1973	Germany[3]	18 Sep. 1973	Nauru	14 Sep. 1999
Bahrain	21 Sep. 1971	Ghana	8 Mar. 1957	Nepal	14 Dec. 1955
Bangladesh	17 Sep. 1974	Greece	25 Oct. 1945	Netherlands	10 Dec. 1945
Barbados	9 Dec. 1966	Grenada	17 Sep. 1974	New Zealand	24 Oct. 1945
Belarus	24 Oct. 1945	Guatemala	21 Nov. 1945	Nicaragua	24 Oct. 1945
Belgium	27 Dec. 1945	Guinea	12 Dec. 1958	Niger	20 Sep. 1960
Belize	25 Sep. 1981	Guinea-Bissau	17 Sep. 1974	Nigeria	7 Oct. 1960
Benin	20 Sep. 1960	Guyana	20 Sep. 1966	Norway	27 Nov. 1945
Bhutan	21 Sep. 1971	Haiti	24 Oct. 1945	Oman	7 Oct. 1971
Bolivia	14 Nov. 1945	Honduras	17 Dec. 1945	Pakistan	30 Sep. 1947
Bosnia and Herzegovina	22 May 1992	Hungary	14 Dec. 1955	Palau	15 Dec. 1994
Botswana	17 Oct. 1966	Iceland	19 Nov. 1946	Panama	13 Nov. 1945
Brazil	24 Oct. 1945	India	30 Oct. 1945	Papua New Guinea	10 Oct. 1975
Brunei Darussalam	21 Sep. 1984	Indonesia[4]	28 Sep. 1950	Paraguay	24 Oct. 1945
Bulgaria	14 Dec. 1955	Iran (Islamic Republic of)	24 Oct. 1945	Peru	31 Oct. 1945
Burkina Faso	20 Sep. 1960	Iraq	21 Dec. 1945	Philippines	24 Oct. 1945
Burundi	18 Sep. 1962	Ireland	14 Dec. 1955	Poland	24 Oct. 1945
Cambodia	14 Dec. 1955	Israel	11 May 1949	Portugal	14 Dec. 1955
Cameroon	20 Sep. 1960	Italy	14 Dec. 1955	Qatar	21 Sep. 1971
Canada	9 Nov. 1945	Jamaica	18 Sep. 1962	Republic of Korea	17 Sep. 1991
Cape Verde	16 Sep. 1975	Japan	18 Dec. 1956	Republic of Moldova	2 Mar. 1992
Central African Republic	20 Sep. 1960	Jordan	14 Dec. 1955	Romania	14 Dec. 1955
Chad	20 Sep. 1960	Kazakhstan	2 Mar. 1992	Russian Federation[6]	24 Oct. 1945
Chile	24 Oct. 1945	Kenya	16 Dec. 1963	Rwanda	18 Sep. 1962
China	24 Oct. 1945	Kiribati	14 Sep. 1999	Saint Kitts and Nevis	23 Sep. 1983
Colombia	5 Nov. 1945	Kuwait	14 May 1963	Saint Lucia	18 Sep. 1979
Comoros	12 Nov. 1975	Kyrgyzstan	2 Mar. 1992	Saint Vincent and the	
Congo	20 Sep. 1960	Lao People's Democratic		Grenadines	16 Sep. 1980
Costa Rica	2 Nov. 1945	Republic	14 Dec. 1955	Samoa	15 Dec. 1976
Côte d'Ivoire	20 Sep. 1960	Latvia	17 Sep. 1991	San Marino	2 Mar. 1992
Croatia	22 May 1992	Lebanon	24 Oct. 1945	Sao Tome and Principe	16 Sep. 1975
Cuba	24 Oct. 1945	Lesotho	17 Oct. 1966	Saudi Arabia	24 Oct. 1945
Cyprus	20 Sep. 1960	Liberia	2 Nov. 1945	Senegal	28 Sep. 1960
Czech Republic[1]	19 Jan. 1993	Libyan Arab Jamahiriya	14 Dec. 1955	Seychelles	21 Sep. 1976
Democratic People's		Liechtenstein	18 Sep. 1990	Sierra Leone	27 Sep. 1961
Republic of Korea	17 Sep. 1991	Lithuania	17 Sep. 1991	Singapore[5]	21 Sep. 1965
Democratic Republic of		Luxembourg	24 Oct. 1945	Slovakia[1]	19 Jan. 1993
the Congo	20 Sep. 1960	Madagascar	20 Sep. 1960	Slovenia	22 May 1992
Denmark	24 Oct. 1945	Malawi	1 Dec. 1964	Solomon Islands	19 Sep. 1978
Djibouti	20 Sep. 1977	Malaysia[5]	17 Sep. 1957	Somalia	20 Sep. 1960
Dominica	18 Dec. 1978	Maldives	21 Sep. 1965	South Africa	7 Nov. 1945
Dominican Republic	24 Oct. 1945	Mali	28 Sep. 1960	Spain	14 Dec. 1955
Ecuador	21 Dec. 1945	Malta	1 Dec. 1964	Sri Lanka	14 Dec. 1955
Egypt[2]	24 Oct. 1945	Marshall Islands	17 Sep. 1991	Sudan	12 Nov. 1956

MEMBER	DATE OF ADMISSION	MEMBER	DATE OF ADMISSION	MEMBER	DATE OF ADMISSION
Suriname	4 Dec. 1975	Turkmenistan	2 Mar. 1992	Vanuatu	15 Sep. 1981
Swaziland	24 Sep. 1968	Tuvalu	5 Sep. 2000	Venezuela	15 Nov. 1945
Sweden	19 Nov. 1946	Uganda	25 Oct. 1962	Viet Nam	20 Sep. 1977
Syrian Arab Republic[2]	24 Oct. 1945	Ukraine	24 Oct. 1945	Yemen[8]	30 Sep. 1947
Tajikistan	2 Mar. 1992	United Arab Emirates	9 Dec. 1971	Yugoslavia (Federal	
Thailand	16 Dec. 1946	United Kingdom of Great		Republic of)	1 Nov. 2000
The former Yugoslav		Britain and Northern		Zambia	1 Dec. 1964
Republic of Macedonia	8 Apr. 1993	Ireland	24 Oct. 1945	Zimbabwe	25 Aug. 1980
Togo	20 Sep. 1960	United Republic of			
Tonga	14 Sep. 1999	Tanzania[7]	14 Dec. 1961		
Trinidad and Tobago	18 Sep. 1962	United States of America	24 Oct. 1945		
Tunisia	12 Nov. 1956	Uruguay	18 Dec. 1945		
Turkey	24 Oct. 1945	Uzbekistan	2 Mar. 1992		

[1]Czechoslovakia, which was an original Member of the United Nations from 24 October 1945, split up on 1 January 1993 and was succeeded by the Czech Republic and Slovakia.

[2]Egypt and Syria, both of which became Members of the United Nations on 24 October 1945, joined together—following a plebiscite held in those countries on 21 February 1958—to form the United Arab Republic. On 13 October 1961, Syria, having resumed its status as an independent State, also resumed its separate membership in the United Nations; it changed its name to the Syrian Arab Republic on 14 September 1971. The United Arab Republic continued as a Member of the United Nations and reverted to the name of Egypt on 2 September 1971.

[3]Through accession of the German Democratic Republic to the Federal Republic of Germany on 3 October 1990, the two German States (both of which became United Nations Members on 18 September 1973) united to form one sovereign State. As from that date, the Federal Republic of Germany has acted in the United Nations under the designation Germany.

[4]On 20 January 1965, Indonesia informed the Secretary-General that it had decided to withdraw from the United Nations. By a telegram of 19 September 1966, it notified the Secretary-General of its decision to resume participation in the activities of the United Nations. On 28 September 1966, the General Assembly took note of that decision and the President invited the representatives of Indonesia to take their seats in the Assembly.

[5]On 16 September 1963, Sabah (North Borneo), Sarawak and Singapore joined with the Federation of Malaya (which became a United Nations Member on 17 September 1957) to form Malaysia. On 9 August 1965, Singapore became an independent State and on 21 September 1965 it became a Member of the United Nations.

[6]The Union of Soviet Socialist Republics was an original Member of the United Nations from 24 October 1945. On 24 December 1991, the President of the Russian Federation informed the Secretary-General that the membership of the USSR in all United Nations organs was being continued by the Russian Federation.

[7]Tanganyika was admitted to the United Nations on 14 December 1961, and Zanzibar, on 16 December 1963. Following ratification, on 26 April 1964, of the Articles of Union between Tanganyika and Zanzibar, the two States became represented as a single Member: the United Republic of Tanganyika and Zanzibar; it changed its name to the United Republic of Tanzania on 1 November 1964.

[8]Yemen was admitted to the United Nations on 30 September 1947 and Democratic Yemen on 14 December 1967. On 22 May 1990, the two countries merged and have since been represented as one Member.

Appendix II

Charter of the United Nations and Statute of the International Court of Justice

Charter of the United Nations

NOTE: The Charter of the United Nations was signed on 26 June 1945, in San Francisco, at the conclusion of the United Nations Conference on International Organization, and came into force on 24 October 1945. The Statute of the International Court of Justice is an integral part of the Charter.

Amendments to Articles 23, 27 and 61 of the Charter were adopted by the General Assembly on 17 December 1963 and came into force on 31 August 1965. A further amendment to Article 61 was adopted by the General Assembly on 20 December 1971 and came into force on 24 September 1973. An amendment to Article 109, adopted by the General Assembly on 20 December 1965, came into force on 12 June 1968.

The amendment to Article 23 enlarges the membership of the Security Council from 11 to 15. The amended Article 27 provides that decisions of the Security Council on procedural matters shall be made by an affirmative vote of nine members (formerly seven) and on all other matters by an affirmative vote of nine members (formerly seven), including the concurring votes of the five permanent members of the Security Council.

The amendment to Article 61, which entered into force on 31 August 1965, enlarged the membership of the Economic and Social Council from 18 to 27. The subsequent amendment to that Article, which entered into force on 24 September 1973, further increased the membership of the Council from 27 to 54.

The amendment to Article 109, which relates to the first paragraph of that Article, provides that a General Conference of Member States for the purpose of reviewing the Charter may be held at a date and place to be fixed by a two-thirds vote of the members of the General Assembly and by a vote of any nine members (formerly seven) of the Security Council. Paragraph 3 of Article 109, which deals with the consideration of a possible review conference during the tenth regular session of the General Assembly, has been retained in its original form in its reference to a "vote of any seven members of the Security Council", the paragraph having been acted upon in 1955 by the General Assembly, at its tenth regular session, and by the Security Council.

WE THE PEOPLES
OF THE UNITED NATIONS
DETERMINED

to save succeeding generations from the scourge of war, which twice in our lifetime has brought untold sorrow to mankind, and

to reaffirm faith in fundamental human rights, in the dignity and worth of the human person, in the equal rights of men and women and of nations large and small, and

to establish conditions under which justice and respect for the obligations arising from treaties and other sources of international law can be maintained, and

to promote social progress and better standards of life in larger freedom,

AND FOR THESE ENDS

to practice tolerance and live together in peace with one another as good neighbours, and

to unite our strength to maintain international peace and security, and

to ensure, by the acceptance of principles and the institution of methods, that armed force shall not be used, save in the common interest, and

to employ international machinery for the promotion of the economic and social advancement of all peoples,

HAVE RESOLVED TO
COMBINE OUR EFFORTS TO
ACCOMPLISH THESE AIMS

Accordingly, our respective Governments, through representatives assembled in the city of San Francisco, who have exhibited their full powers found to be in good and due form, have agreed to the present Charter of the United Nations and do hereby establish an international organization to be known as the United Nations.

Chapter I
PURPOSES AND PRINCIPLES

Article 1

The Purposes of the United Nations are:

1. To maintain international peace and security, and to that end: to take effective collective measures for the prevention and removal of threats to the peace, and for the suppression of acts of aggression or other breaches of the peace, and to bring about by peaceful means, and in conformity with the principles of justice and international law, adjustment or settlement of international disputes or situations which might lead to a breach of the peace;

2. To develop friendly relations among nations based on respect for the principle of equal rights and self-determination of peoples, and to take other appropriate measures to strengthen universal peace;

3. To achieve international co-operation in solving international problems of an economic, social, cultural or humanitarian character, and in promoting and encouraging respect for human rights and for fundamental freedoms for all without distinction as to race, sex, language or religion; and

4. To be a centre for harmonizing the actions of nations in the attainment of these common ends.

Article 2

The Organization and its Members, in pursuit of the Purposes stated in Article 1, shall act in accordance with the following Principles:

1. The Organization is based on the principle of the sovereign equality of all its Members.

2. All Members, in order to ensure to all of them the rights and benefits resulting from membership, shall fulfil in good faith the obligations assumed by them in accordance with the present Charter.

3. All Members shall settle their international disputes by peaceful means in such a manner that international peace and security, and justice, are not endangered.

4. All Members shall refrain in their international relations from the threat or use of force against the territorial integrity or political independence of any state, or in any other manner inconsistent with the Purposes of the United Nations.

5. All Members shall give the United Nations every assistance in any action it takes in accordance with the present Charter, and shall refrain from giving assistance to any state against which the United Nations is taking preventive or enforcement action.

6. The Organization shall ensure that states which are not Members of the United Nations act in accordance with these Principles so far as may be necessary for the maintenance of international peace and security.

7. Nothing contained in the present Charter shall authorize the United Nations to intervene in matters which are essentially within the domestic jurisdiction of any state or shall require the Members to submit such matters to settlement under the present Charter; but this principle shall not prejudice the application of enforcement measures under Chapter VII.

Chapter II
MEMBERSHIP

Article 3

The original Members of the United Nations shall be the states which, having participated in the United Nations Conference on International Organization at San Francisco or having previously signed the Declaration by United Nations of 1 January 1942, sign the present Charter and ratify it in accordance with Article 110.

Article 4

1. Membership in the United Nations is open to all other peace-loving states which accept the obligations contained in the present Charter and, in the judgment of the Organization, are able and willing to carry out these obligations.

2. The admission of any such state to membership in the United Nations will be effected by a decision of the General Assembly upon the recommendation of the Security Council.

Article 5

A Member of the United Nations against which preventive or enforcement action has been taken by the Security Council may be suspended from the exercise of the rights and privileges of membership by the General Assembly upon the recommendation of the Security Council. The exercise of these rights and privileges may be restored by the Security Council.

Article 6

A Member of the United Nations which has persistently violated the Principles contained in the present Charter may be expelled from the Organization by the General Assembly upon the recommendation of the Security Council.

Chapter III
ORGANS

Article 7

1. There are established as the principal organs of the United Nations: a General Assembly, a Security Council, an Economic and Social Council, a Trusteeship Council, an International Court of Justice, and a Secretariat.

2. Such subsidiary organs as may be found necessary may be established in accordance with the present Charter.

Article 8

The United Nations shall place no restrictions on the eligibility of men and women to participate in any capacity and under conditions of equality in its principal and subsidiary organs.

Chapter IV
THE GENERAL ASSEMBLY

Composition

Article 9

1. The General Assembly shall consist of all the Members of the United Nations.

2. Each Member shall have not more than five representatives in the General Assembly.

Functions and Powers

Article 10

The General Assembly may discuss any questions or any matters within the scope of the present Charter or relating to the powers and functions of any organs provided for in the present Charter, and, except as provided in Article 12, may make recommendations to the Members of the United Nations or to the Security Council or both on any such questions or matters.

Article 11

1. The General Assembly may consider the general principles of co-operation in the maintenance of international peace and security, including the principles governing disarmament and the regulation of armaments, and may make recommendations with regard to such principles to the Members or to the Security Council or to both.

2. The General Assembly may discuss any questions relating to the maintenance of international peace and security brought before it by any Member of the United Nations, or by the Security Council, or by a state which is not a Member of the United Nations in accordance with Article 35, paragraph 2, and, except as provided in Article 12, may make recommendations with regard to any such questions to the state or states concerned or to the Security Council or to both. Any such question on which action is necessary shall be referred to the Security Council by the General Assembly either before or after discussion.

3. The General Assembly may call the attention of the Security Council to situations which are likely to endanger international peace and security.

4. The powers of the General Assembly set forth in this Article shall not limit the general scope of Article 10.

Article 12

1. While the Security Council is exercising in respect of any dispute or situation the functions assigned to it in the present Charter, the General Assembly shall not make any recommendation with regard to that dispute or situation unless the Security Council so requests.

2. The Secretary-General, with the consent of the Security Council, shall notify the General Assembly at each session of any matters relative to the maintenance of international peace and security which are being dealt with by the Security Council and shall similarly notify the General Assembly, or the Members of the United Nations if the General Assembly is not in session, immediately the Security Council ceases to deal with such matters.

Article 13

1. The General Assembly shall initiate studies and make recommendations for the purpose of:
   a. promoting international co-operation in the political field and encouraging the progressive development of international law and its codification;
   b. promoting international co-operation in the economic, social, cultural, educational and health fields, and assisting in the realization of human rights and fundamental freedoms for all without distinction as to race, sex, language or religion.

2. The further responsibilities, functions and powers of the General Assembly with respect to matters mentioned in paragraph 1 (b) above are set forth in Chapters IX and X.

Article 14

Subject to the provisions of Article 12, the General Assembly may recommend measures for the peaceful adjustment of any situation, regardless of origin, which it deems likely to impair the general welfare or friendly relations among nations, including situations resulting from a violation of the provisions of the present Charter setting forth the Purposes and Principles of the United Nations.

Article 15

1. The General Assembly shall receive and consider annual and special reports from the Security Council; these reports shall include an account of the measures that the Security Council has decided upon or taken to maintain international peace and security.
2. The General Assembly shall receive and consider reports from the other organs of the United Nations.

Article 16

The General Assembly shall perform such functions with respect to the international trusteeship system as are assigned to it under Chapters XII and XIII, including the approval of the trusteeship agreements for areas not designated as strategic.

Article 17

1. The General Assembly shall consider and approve the budget of the Organization.
2. The expenses of the Organization shall be borne by the Members as apportioned by the General Assembly.
3. The General Assembly shall consider and approve any financial and budgetary arrangements with specialized agencies referred to in Article 57 and shall examine the administrative budgets of such specialized agencies with a view to making recommendations to the agencies concerned.

Voting

Article 18

1. Each member of the General Assembly shall have one vote.
2. Decisions of the General Assembly on important questions shall be made by a two-thirds majority of the members present and voting. These questions shall include: recommendations with respect to the maintenance of international peace and security, the election of the non-permanent members of the Security Council, the election of the members of the Economic and Social Council, the election of members of the Trusteeship Council in accordance with paragraph 1 (c) of Article 86, the admission of new Members to the United Nations, the suspension of the rights and privileges of membership, the expulsion of Members, questions relating to the operation of the trusteeship system, and budgetary questions.
3. Decisions on other questions, including the determination of additional categories of questions to be decided by a two-thirds majority, shall be made by a majority of the members present and voting.

Article 19

A Member of the United Nations which is in arrears in the payment of its financial contributions to the Organization shall have no vote in the General Assembly if the amount of its arrears equals or exceeds the amount of the contributions due from it for the preceding two full years. The General Assembly may, nevertheless, permit such a Member to vote if it is satisfied that the failure to pay is due to conditions beyond the control of the Member.

Procedure

Article 20

The General Assembly shall meet in regular annual sessions and in such special sessions as occasion may require. Special sessions shall be convoked by the Secretary-General at the request of the Security Council or of a majority of the Members of the United Nations.

Article 21

The General Assembly shall adopt its own rules of procedure. It shall elect its President for each session.

Article 22

The General Assembly may establish such subsidiary organs as it deems necessary for the performance of its functions.

Chapter V
THE SECURITY COUNCIL

Composition

Article 23[1]

1. The Security Council shall consist of fifteen Members of the United Nations. The Republic of China, France, the Union of Soviet Socialist Republics, the United Kingdom of Great Britain and Northern Ireland and the United States of America shall be permanent members of the Security Council. The General Assembly shall elect ten other Members of the United Nations to be non-permanent members of the Security Council, due regard being specially paid, in the first instance to the contribution of Members of the United Nations to the maintenance of international peace and security and to the other purposes of the Organization, and also to equitable geographical distribution.
2. The non-permanent members of the Security Council shall be elected for a term of two years. In the first election of the non-permanent members after the increase of the membership of the Security Council from eleven to fifteen, two of the four additional members shall be chosen for a term of one year. A retiring member shall not be eligible for immediate re-election.
3. Each member of the Security Council shall have one representative.

Functions and Powers

Article 24

1. In order to ensure prompt and effective action by the United Nations, its Members confer on the Security Council primary responsibility for the maintenance of international peace and security, and agree that in carrying out its duties under this responsibility the Security Council acts on their behalf.
2. In discharging these duties the Security Council shall act in accordance with the Purposes and Principles of the United Nations. The specific powers granted to the Security Council for the discharge of these duties are laid down in Chapters VI, VII, VIII and XII.
3. The Security Council shall submit annual and, when necessary, special reports to the General Assembly for its consideration.

Article 25

The Members of the United Nations agree to accept and carry out the decisions of the Security Council in accordance with the present Charter.

Article 26

In order to promote the establishment and maintenance of international peace and security with the least diversion for armaments of the world's human and economic resources, the Security Council shall be responsible for formulating, with the assistance of the Military Staff Committee referred to in Article

47, plans to be submitted to the Members of the United Nations for the establishment of a system for the regulation of armaments.

Voting

Article 27[2]

1.   Each member of the Security Council shall have one vote.

2.   Decisions of the Security Council on procedural matters shall be made by an affirmative vote of nine members.

3.   Decisions of the Security Council on all other matters shall be made by an affirmative vote of nine members including the concurring votes of the permanent members; provided that, in decisions under Chapter VI, and under paragraph 3 of Article 52, a party to a dispute shall abstain from voting.

Procedure

Article 28

1.   The Security Council shall be so organized as to be able to function continuously. Each member of the Security Council shall for this purpose be represented at all times at the seat of the Organization.

2.   The Security Council shall hold periodic meetings at which each of its members may, if it so desires, be represented by a member of the government or by some other specially designated representative.

3.   The Security Council may hold meetings at such places other than the seat of the Organization as in its judgment will best facilitate its work.

Article 29

The Security Council may establish such subsidiary organs as it deems necessary for the performance of its functions.

Article 30

The Security Council shall adopt its own rules of procedure, including the method of selecting its President.

Article 31

Any Member of the United Nations which is not a member of the Security Council may participate, without vote, in the discussion of any question brought before the Security Council whenever the latter considers that the interests of that Member are specially affected.

Article 32

Any Member of the United Nations which is not a member of the Security Council or any state which is not a Member of the United Nations, if it is a party to a dispute under consideration by the Security Council, shall be invited to participate, without vote, in the discussion relating to the dispute. The Security Council shall lay down such conditions as it deems just for the participation of a state which is not a Member of the United Nations.

Chapter VI
PACIFIC SETTLEMENT OF DISPUTES

Article 33

1.   The parties to any dispute, the continuance of which is likely to endanger the maintenance of international peace and security, shall, first of all, seek a solution by negotiation, enquiry, mediation, conciliation, arbitration, judicial settlement, resort to regional agencies or arrangements, or other peaceful means of their own choice.

2.   The Security Council shall, when it deems necessary, call upon the parties to settle their dispute by such means.

Article 34

The Security Council may investigate any dispute, or any situation which might lead to international friction or give rise to a dispute, in order to determine whether the continuance of the dispute or situation is likely to endanger the maintenance of international peace and security.

Article 35

1.   Any Member of the United Nations may bring any dispute, or any situation of the nature referred to in Article 34, to the attention of the Security Council or of the General Assembly.

2.   A state which is not a Member of the United Nations may bring to the attention of the Security Council or of the General Assembly any dispute to which it is a party if it accepts in advance, for the purposes of the dispute, the obligations of pacific settlement provided in the present Charter.

3.   The proceedings of the General Assembly in respect of matters brought to its attention under this Article will be subject to the provisions of Articles 11 and 12.

Article 36

1.   The Security Council may, at any stage of a dispute of the nature referred to in Article 33 or of a situation of like nature, recommend appropriate procedures or methods of adjustment.

2.   The Security Council should take into consideration any procedures for the settlement of the dispute which have already been adopted by the parties.

3.   In making recommendations under this Article the Security Council should also take into consideration that legal disputes should as a general rule be referred by the parties to the International Court of Justice in accordance with the provisions of the Statute of the Court.

Article 37

1.   Should the parties to a dispute of the nature referred to in Article 33 fail to settle it by the means indicated in that Article, they shall refer it to the Security Council.

2.   If the Security Council deems that the continuance of the dispute is in fact likely to endanger the maintenance of international peace and security, it shall decide whether to take action under Article 36 or to recommend such terms of settlement as it may consider appropriate.

Article 38

Without prejudice to the provisions of Articles 33 to 37, the Security Council may, if all the parties to any dispute so request, make recommendations to the parties with a view to a pacific settlement of the dispute.

Chapter VII
ACTION WITH RESPECT TO THREATS TO THE PEACE,
BREACHES OF THE PEACE, AND ACTS OF AGGRESSION

Article 39

The Security Council shall determine the existence of any threat to the peace, breach of the peace, or act of aggression and shall make recommendations, or decide what measures shall be taken in accordance with Articles 41 and 42, to maintain or restore international peace and security.

Article 40

In order to prevent an aggravation of the situation, the Security Council may, before making the recommendations or deciding upon the measures provided for in Article 39, call upon the parties concerned to comply with such provisional measures as it deems necessary or desirable. Such provisional measures shall be without prejudice to the rights, claims or position of the parties concerned. The Security Council shall duly take account of failure to comply with such provisional measures.

Article 41

The Security Council may decide what measures not involving the use of armed force are to be employed to give effect to its decisions, and it may call upon the Members of the United Nations to apply such measures. These may include complete or partial interruption of economic relations and of rail, sea, air, postal, telegraphic, radio and other means of communication, and the severance of diplomatic relations.

Article 42

Should the Security Council consider that measures provided for in Article 41 would be inadequate or have proved to be inadequate, it may take such action by air, sea or land forces as may be necessary to maintain or restore international peace and security. Such action may include demonstrations, blockade, and other operations by air, sea, or land forces of Members of the United Nations.

Article 43

1. All Members of the United Nations, in order to contribute to the maintenance of international peace and security, undertake to make available to the Security Council, on its call and in accordance with a special agreement or agreements, armed forces, assistance and facilities, including rights of passage, necessary for the purpose of maintaining international peace and security.

2. Such agreement or agreements shall govern the numbers and types of forces, their degree of readiness and general location, and the nature of the facilities and assistance to be provided.

3. The agreement or agreements shall be negotiated as soon as possible on the initiative of the Security Council. They shall be concluded between the Security Council and Members or between the Security Council and groups of Members and shall be subject to ratification by the signatory states in accordance with their respective constitutional processes.

Article 44

When the Security Council has decided to use force it shall, before calling upon a Member not represented on it to provide armed forces in fulfilment of the obligations assumed under Article 43, invite that Member, if the Member so desires, to participate in the decisions of the Security Council concerning the employment of contingents of that Member's armed forces.

Article 45

In order to enable the United Nations to take urgent military measures, Members shall hold immediately available national air-force contingents for combined international enforcement action. The strength and degree of readiness of these contingents and plans for their combined action shall be determined, within the limits laid down in the special agreement or agreements referred to in Article 43, by the Security Council with the assistance of the Military Staff Committee.

Article 46

Plans for the application of armed force shall be made by the Security Council with the assistance of the Military Staff Committee.

Article 47

1. There shall be established a Military Staff Committee to advise and assist the Security Council on all questions relating to the Security Council's military requirements for the maintenance of international peace and security, the employment and command of forces placed at its disposal, the regulation of armaments, and possible disarmament.

2. The Military Staff Committee shall consist of the Chiefs of Staff of the permanent members of the Security Council or their representatives. Any Member of the United Nations not permanently represented on the Committee shall be invited by the Committee to be associated with it when the efficient discharge of the Committee's responsibilities requires the participation of that Member in its work.

3. The Military Staff Committee shall be responsible under the Security Council for the strategic direction of any armed forces placed at the disposal of the Security Council. Questions relating to the command of such forces shall be worked out subsequently.

4. The Military Staff Committee, with the authorization of the Security Council and after consultation with appropriate regional agencies, may establish regional sub-committees.

Article 48

1. The action required to carry out the decisions of the Security Council for the maintenance of international peace and security shall be taken by all the Members of the United Nations or by some of them, as the Security Council may determine.

2. Such decisions shall be carried out by the Members of the United Nations directly and through their action in the appropriate international agencies of which they are members.

Article 49

The Members of the United Nations shall join in affording mutual assistance in carrying out the measures decided upon by the Security Council.

Article 50

If preventive or enforcement measures against any state are taken by the Security Council, any other state, whether a Member of the United Nations or not, which finds itself confronted with special economic problems arising from the carrying out of those measures shall have the right to consult the Security Council with regard to a solution of those problems.

Article 51

Nothing in the present Charter shall impair the inherent right of individual or collective self-defence if an armed attack occurs against a Member of the United Nations, until the Security Council has taken measures necessary to maintain international peace and security. Measures taken by Members in the exercise of this right of self-defence shall be immediately reported to the Security Council and shall not in any way affect the authority and responsibility of the Security Council under the present Charter to take at any time such action as it deems necessary in order to maintain or restore international peace and security.

Chapter VIII
REGIONAL ARRANGEMENTS

Article 52

1. Nothing in the present Charter precludes the existence of regional arrangements or agencies for dealing with such matters relating to the maintenance of international peace and security as are appropriate for regional action, provided that such arrangements or agencies and their activities are consistent with the Purposes and Principles of the United Nations.

2. The Members of the United Nations entering into such arrangements or constituting such agencies shall make every effort to achieve pacific settlement of local disputes through such regional arrangements or by such regional agencies before referring them to the Security Council.

3. The Security Council shall encourage the development of pacific settlement of local disputes through such regional arrangements or by such regional agencies either on the initiative of the states concerned or by reference from the Security Council.

4. This Article in no way impairs the application of Articles 34 and 35.

Article 53

1. The Security Council shall, where appropriate, utilize such regional arrangements or agencies for enforcement action under its authority. But no enforcement action shall be taken under regional arrangements or by regional agencies

without the authorization of the Security Council, with the exception of measures against any enemy state, as defined in paragraph 2 of this Article, provided for pursuant to Article 107 or in regional arrangements directed against renewal of aggressive policy on the part of any such state, until such time as the Organization may, on request of the Governments concerned, be charged with the responsibility for preventing further aggression by such a state.

2.   The term enemy state as used in paragraph 1 of this Article applies to any state which during the Second World War has been an enemy of any signatory of the present Charter.

Article 54

The Security Council shall at all times be kept fully informed of activities undertaken or in contemplation under regional arrangements or by regional agencies for the maintenance of international peace and security.

Chapter IX
INTERNATIONAL ECONOMIC AND SOCIAL CO-OPERATION

Article 55

With a view to the creation of conditions of stability and well-being which are necessary for peaceful and friendly relations among nations based on respect for the principle of equal rights and self-determination of peoples, the United Nations shall promote:

a.   higher standards of living, full employment, and conditions of economic and social progress and development;

b.   solutions of international economic, social, health, and related problems; and international cultural and educational co-operation; and

c.   universal respect for, and observance of, human rights and fundamental freedoms for all without distinction as to race, sex, language, or religion.

Article 56

All Members pledge themselves to take joint and separate action in co-operation with the Organization for the achievement of the purposes set forth in Article 55.

Article 57

1.   The various specialized agencies, established by intergovernmental agreement and having wide international responsibilities, as defined in their basic instruments, in economic, social, cultural, educational, health, and related fields, shall be brought into relationship with the United Nations in accordance with the provisions of Article 63.

2.   Such agencies thus brought into relationship with the United Nations are hereinafter referred to as specialized agencies.

Article 58

The Organization shall make recommendations for the co-ordination of the policies and activities of the specialized agencies.

Article 59

The Organization shall, where appropriate, initiate negotiations among the states concerned for the creation of any new specialized agencies required for the accomplishment of the purposes set forth in Article 55.

Article 60

Responsibility for the discharge of the functions of the Organization set forth in this Chapter shall be vested in the General Assembly and, under the authority of the General Assembly, in the Economic and Social Council, which shall have for this purpose the powers set forth in Chapter X.

Chapter X
THE ECONOMIC AND SOCIAL COUNCIL

Composition

Article 61[3]

1.   The Economic and Social Council shall consist of fifty-four Members of the United Nations elected by the General Assembly.

2.   Subject to the provisions of paragraph 3, eighteen members of the Economic and Social Council shall be elected each year for a term of three years. A retiring member shall be eligible for immediate re-election.

3.   At the first election after the increase in the membership of the Economic and Social Council from twenty-seven to fifty-four members, in addition to the members elected in place of the nine members whose term of office expires at the end of that year, twenty-seven additional members shall be elected. Of these twenty-seven additional members, the term of office of nine members so elected shall expire at the end of one year, and of nine other members at the end of two years, in accordance with arrangements made by the General Assembly.

4.   Each member of the Economic and Social Council shall have one representative.

Functions and Powers

Article 62

1.   The Economic and Social Council may make or initiate studies and reports with respect to international economic, social, cultural, educational, health, and related matters and may make recommendations with respect to any such matters to the General Assembly, to the Members of the United Nations, and to the specialized agencies concerned.

2.   It may make recommendations for the purpose of promoting respect for, and observance of, human rights and fundamental freedoms for all.

3.   It may prepare draft conventions for submission to the General Assembly, with respect to matters falling within its competence.

4.   It may call, in accordance with the rules prescribed by the United Nations, international conferences on matters falling within its competence.

Article 63

1.   The Economic and Social Council may enter into agreements with any of the agencies referred to in Article 57, defining the terms on which the agency concerned shall be brought into relationship with the United Nations. Such agreements shall be subject to approval by the General Assembly.

2.   It may co-ordinate the activities of the specialized agencies through consultation with and recommendations to such agencies and through recommendations to the General Assembly and to the Members of the United Nations.

Article 64

1.   The Economic and Social Council may take appropriate steps to obtain regular reports from the specialized agencies. It may make arrangements with the Members of the United Nations and with the specialized agencies to obtain reports on the steps taken to give effect to its own recommendations and to recommendations on matters falling within its competence made by the General Assembly.

2.   It may communicate its observations on these reports to the General Assembly.

Article 65

The Economic and Social Council may furnish information to the Security Council and shall assist the Security Council upon its request.

Article 66

1. The Economic and Social Council shall perform such functions as fall within its competence in connexion with the carrying out of the recommendations of the General Assembly.

2. It may, with the approval of the General Assembly, perform services at the request of Members of the United Nations and at the request of specialized agencies.

3. It shall perform such other functions as are specified elsewhere in the present Charter or as may be assigned to it by the General Assembly.

Voting

Article 67

1. Each member of the Economic and Social Council shall have one vote.

2. Decisions of the Economic and Social Council shall be made by a majority of the members present and voting.

Procedure

Article 68

The Economic and Social Council shall set up commissions in economic and social fields and for the promotion of human rights, and such other commissions as may be required for the performance of its functions.

Article 69

The Economic and Social Council shall invite any Member of the United Nations to participate, without vote, in its deliberations on any matter of particular concern to that Member.

Article 70

The Economic and Social Council may make arrangements for representatives of the specialized agencies to participate, without vote, in its deliberations and in those of the commissions established by it, and for its representatives to participate in the deliberations of the specialized agencies.

Article 71

The Economic and Social Council may make suitable arrangements for consultation with non-governmental organizations which are concerned with matters within its competence. Such arrangements may be made with international organizations and, where appropriate, with national organizations after consultation with the Member of the United Nations concerned.

Article 72

1. The Economic and Social Council shall adopt its own rules of procedure, including the method of selecting its President.

2. The Economic and Social Council shall meet as required in accordance with its rules, which shall include provision for the convening of meetings on the request of a majority of its members.

Chapter XI

DECLARATION REGARDING
NON-SELF-GOVERNING TERRITORIES

Article 73

Members of the United Nations which have or assume responsibilities for the administration of territories whose peoples have not yet attained a full measure of self-government recognize the principle that the interests of the inhabitants of these territories are paramount, and accept as a sacred trust the obligation to promote to the utmost, within the system of international peace and security established by the present Charter, the well-being of the inhabitants of these territories and, to this end:

a. to ensure, with due respect for the culture of the peoples concerned, their political, economic, social, and educational advancement, their just treatment, and their protection against abuses;

b. to develop self-government, to take due account of the political aspirations of the peoples, and to assist them in the progressive development of their free political institutions, according to the particular circumstances of each territory and its peoples and their varying stages of advancement;

c. to further international peace and security;

d. to promote constructive measures of development, to encourage research, and to co-operate with one another and, when and where appropriate, with specialized international bodies with a view to the practical achievement of the social, economic, and scientific purposes set forth in this Article; and

e. to transmit regularly to the Secretary-General for information purposes, subject to such limitation as security and constitutional considerations may require, statistical and other information of a technical nature relating to economic, social, and educational conditions in the territories for which they are respectively responsible other than those territories to which Chapters XII and XIII apply.

Article 74

Members of the United Nations also agree that their policy in respect of the territories to which this Chapter applies, no less than in respect of their metropolitan areas, must be based on the general principle of good-neighbourliness, due account being taken of the interests and well-being of the rest of the world, in social, economic, and commercial matters.

Chapter XII

INTERNATIONAL TRUSTEESHIP SYSTEM

Article 75

The United Nations shall establish under its authority an international trusteeship system for the administration and supervision of such territories as may be placed thereunder by subsequent individual agreements. These territories are hereinafter referred to as trust territories.

Article 76

The basic objectives of the trusteeship system, in accordance with the Purposes of the United Nations laid down in Article 1 of the present Charter, shall be:

a. to further international peace and security;

b. to promote the political, economic, social, and educational advancement of the inhabitants of the trust territories, and their progressive development towards self-government or independence as may be appropriate to the particular circumstances of each territory and its peoples and the freely expressed wishes of the peoples concerned, and as may be provided by the terms of each trusteeship agreement;

c. to encourage respect for human rights and for fundamental freedoms for all without distinction as to race, sex, language, or religion, and to encourage recognition of the interdependence of the peoples of the world; and

d. to ensure equal treatment in social, economic, and commercial matters for all Members of the United Nations and their nationals, and also equal treatment for the latter in the administration of justice, without prejudice to the attainment of the foregoing objectives and subject to the provisions of Article 80.

Article 77

1. The trusteeship system shall apply to such territories in the following categories as may be placed thereunder by means of trusteeship agreements:

a. territories now held under mandate;
b. territories which may be detached from enemy states as a result of the Second World War; and
c. territories voluntarily placed under the system by states responsible for their administration.

2. It will be a matter for subsequent agreement as to which territories in the foregoing categories will be brought under the trusteeship system and upon what terms.

Article 78

The trusteeship system shall not apply to territories which have become Members of the United Nations, relationship among which shall be based on respect for the principle of sovereign equality.

Article 79

The terms of trusteeship for each territory to be placed under the trusteeship system, including any alteration or amendment, shall be agreed upon by the states directly concerned, including the mandatory power in the case of territories held under mandate by a Member of the United Nations, and shall be approved as provided for in Articles 83 and 85.

Article 80

1. Except as may be agreed upon in individual trusteeship agreements, made under Articles 77, 79 and 81, placing each territory under the trusteeship system, and until such agreements have been concluded, nothing in this Chapter shall be construed in or of itself to alter in any manner the rights whatsoever of any states or any peoples or the terms of existing international instruments to which Members of the United Nations may respectively be parties.

2. Paragraph 1 of this Article shall not be interpreted as giving grounds for delay or postponement of the negotiation and conclusion of agreements for placing mandated and other territories under the trusteeship system as provided for in Article 77.

Article 81

The trusteeship agreement shall in each case include the terms under which the trust territory will be administered and designate the authority which will exercise the administration of the trust territory. Such authority, hereinafter called the administering authority, may be one or more states or the Organization itself.

Article 82

There may be designated, in any trusteeship agreement, a strategic area or areas which may include part or all of the trust territory to which the agreement applies, without prejudice to any special agreement or agreements made under Article 43.

Article 83

1. All functions of the United Nations relating to strategic areas, including the approval of the terms of the trusteeship agreements and of their alteration or amendment, shall be exercised by the Security Council.

2. The basic objectives set forth in Article 76 shall be applicable to the people of each strategic area.

3. The Security Council shall, subject to the provisions of the trusteeship agreements and without prejudice to security considerations, avail itself of the assistance of the Trusteeship Council to perform those functions of the United Nations under the trusteeship system relating to political, economic, social, and educational matters in the strategic areas.

Article 84

It shall be the duty of the administering authority to ensure that the trust territory shall play its part in the maintenance of international peace and security. To this end the administering authority may make use of volunteer forces, facilities, and assistance from the trust territory in carrying out the obligations towards the Security Council undertaken in this regard by the administering authority, as well as for local defence and the maintenance of law and order within the trust territory.

Article 85

1. The functions of the United Nations with regard to trusteeship agreements for all areas not designated as strategic, including the approval of the terms of the trusteeship agreements and of their alteration or amendment, shall be exercised by the General Assembly.

2. The Trusteeship Council, operating under the authority of the General Assembly, shall assist the General Assembly in carrying out these functions.

Chapter XIII
THE TRUSTEESHIP COUNCIL

Composition

Article 86

1. The Trusteeship Council shall consist of the following Members of the United Nations:
   a. those Members administering trust territories;
   b. such of those Members mentioned by name in Article 23 as are not administering trust territories; and
   c. as many other Members elected for three-year terms by the General Assembly as may be necessary to ensure that the total number of members of the Trusteeship Council is equally divided between those Members of the United Nations which administer trust territories and those which do not.

2. Each member of the Trusteeship Council shall designate one specially qualified person to represent it therein.

Functions and Powers

Article 87

The General Assembly and, under its authority, the Trusteeship Council, in carrying out their functions, may:
   a. consider reports submitted by the administering authority;
   b. accept petitions and examine them in consultation with the administering authority;
   c. provide for periodic visits to the respective trust territories at times agreed upon with the administering authority; and
   d. take these and other actions in conformity with the terms of the trusteeship agreements.

Article 88

The Trusteeship Council shall formulate a questionnaire on the political, economic, social, and educational advancement of the inhabitants of each trust territory, and the administering authority for each trust territory within the competence of the General Assembly shall make an annual report to the General Assembly upon the basis of such questionnaire.

Voting

Article 89

1. Each member of the Trusteeship Council shall have one vote.

2. Decisions of the Trusteeship Council shall be made by a majority of the members present and voting.

Procedure

Article 90

1. The Trusteeship Council shall adopt its own rules of procedure, including the method of selecting its President.

2. The Trusteeship Council shall meet as required in accordance with its rules, which shall include provision for the convening of meetings on the request of a majority of its members.

Article 91

The Trusteeship Council shall, when appropriate, avail itself of the assistance of the Economic and Social Council and of the specialized agencies in regard to matters with which they are respectively concerned.

Chapter XIV

THE INTERNATIONAL COURT OF JUSTICE

Article 92

The International Court of Justice shall be the principal judicial organ of the United Nations. It shall function in accordance with the annexed Statute, which is based upon the Statute of the Permanent Court of International Justice and forms an integral part of the present Charter.

Article 93

1. All Members of the United Nations are *ipso facto* parties to the Statute of the International Court of Justice.
2. A state which is not a Member of the United Nations may become a party to the Statute of the International Court of Justice on conditions to be determined in each case by the General Assembly upon the recommendation of the Security Council.

Article 94

1. Each Member of the United Nations undertakes to comply with the decision of the International Court of Justice in any case to which it is a party.
2. If any party to a case fails to perform the obligations incumbent upon it under a judgment rendered by the Court, the other party may have recourse to the Security Council, which may, if it deems necessary, make recommendations or decide upon measures to be taken to give effect to the judgment.

Article 95

Nothing in the present Charter shall prevent Members of the United Nations from entrusting the solution of their differences to other tribunals by virtue of agreements already in existence or which may be concluded in the future.

Article 96

1. The General Assembly or the Security Council may request the International Court of Justice to give an advisory opinion on any legal question.
2. Other organs of the United Nations and specialized agencies, which may at any time be so authorized by the General Assembly, may also request advisory opinions of the Court on legal questions arising within the scope of their activities.

Chapter XV

THE SECRETARIAT

Article 97

The Secretariat shall comprise a Secretary-General and such staff as the Organization may require. The Secretary-General shall be appointed by the General Assembly upon the recommendation of the Security Council. He shall be the chief administrative officer of the Organization.

Article 98

The Secretary-General shall act in that capacity in all meetings of the General Assembly, of the Security Council, of the Economic and Social Council, and of the Trusteeship Council, and shall perform such other functions as are entrusted to him by these organs. The Secretary-General shall make an annual report to the General Assembly on the work of the Organization.

Article 99

The Secretary-General may bring to the attention of the Security Council any matter which in his opinion may threaten the maintenance of international peace and security.

Article 100

1. In the performance of their duties the Secretary-General and the staff shall not seek or receive instructions from any government or from any other authority external to the Organization. They shall refrain from any action which might reflect on their position as international officials responsible only to the Organization.
2. Each Member of the United Nations undertakes to respect the exclusively international character of the responsibilities of the Secretary-General and the staff and not to seek to influence them in the discharge of their responsibilities.

Article 101

1. The staff shall be appointed by the Secretary-General under regulations established by the General Assembly.
2. Appropriate staffs shall be permanently assigned to the Economic and Social Council, the Trusteeship Council, and, as required, to other organs of the United Nations. These staffs shall form a part of the Secretariat.
3. The paramount consideration in the employment of the staff and in the determination of the conditions of service shall be the necessity of securing the highest standards of efficiency, competence, and integrity. Due regard shall be paid to the importance of recruiting the staff on as wide a geographical basis as possible.

Chapter XVI

MISCELLANEOUS PROVISIONS

Article 102

1. Every treaty and every international agreement entered into by any Member of the United Nations after the present Charter comes into force shall as soon as possible be registered with the Secretariat and published by it.
2. No party to any such treaty or international agreement which has not been registered in accordance with the provisions of paragraph 1 of this Article may invoke that treaty or agreement before any organ of the United Nations.

Article 103

In the event of a conflict between the obligations of the Members of the United Nations under the present Charter and their obligations under any other international agreement, their obligations under the present Charter shall prevail.

Article 104

The Organization shall enjoy in the territory of each of its Members such legal capacity as may be necessary for the exercise of its functions and the fulfilment of its purposes.

Article 105

1. The Organization shall enjoy in the territory of each of its Members such privileges and immunities as are necessary for the fulfilment of its purposes.
2. Representatives of the Members of the United Nations and officials of the Organization shall similarly enjoy such privileges and immunities as are necessary for the independent exercise of their functions in connexion with the Organization.
3. The General Assembly may make recommendations with a view to determining the details of the application of paragraphs 1 and 2 of this Article or may propose conventions to the Members of the United Nations for this purpose.

Chapter XVII
TRANSITIONAL SECURITY ARRANGEMENTS

Article 106

Pending the coming into force of such special agreements referred to in Article 43 as in the opinion of the Security Council enable it to begin the exercise of its responsibilities under Article 42, the parties to the Four-Nation Declaration, signed at Moscow, 30 October 1943, and France, shall, in accordance with the provisions of paragraph 5 of that Declaration, consult with one another and as occasion requires with other Members of the United Nations with a view to such joint action on behalf of the Organization as may be necessary for the purpose of maintaining international peace and security.

Article 107

Nothing in the present Charter shall invalidate or preclude action, in relation to any state which during the Second World War has been an enemy of any signatory to the present Charter, taken or authorized as a result of that war by the Governments having responsibility for such action.

Chapter XVIII
AMENDMENTS

Article 108

Amendments to the present Charter shall come into force for all Members of the United Nations when they have been adopted by a vote of two thirds of the members of the General Assembly and ratified in accordance with their respective constitutional processes by two thirds of the Members of the United Nations, including all the permanent members of the Security Council.

Article 109[1]

1. A General Conference of the Members of the United Nations for the purpose of reviewing the present Charter may be held at a date and place to be fixed by a two-thirds vote of the members of the General Assembly and by a vote of any nine members of the Security Council. Each Member of the United Nations shall have one vote in the conference.

2. Any alteration of the present Charter recommended by a two-thirds vote of the conference shall take effect when ratified in accordance with their respective constitutional processes by two thirds of the Members of the United Na-

tions including all the permanent members of the Security Council.

3. If such a conference has not been held before the tenth annual session of the General Assembly following the coming into force of the present Charter, the proposal to call such a conference shall be placed on the agenda of that session of the General Assembly, and the conference shall be held if so decided by a majority vote of the members of the General Assembly and by a vote of any seven members of the Security Council.

Chapter XIX
RATIFICATION AND SIGNATURE

Article 110

1. The present Charter shall be ratified by the signatory states in accordance with their respective constitutional processes.

2. The ratifications shall be deposited with the Government of the United States of America, which shall notify all the signatory states of each deposit as well as the Secretary-General of the Organization when he has been appointed.

3. The present Charter shall come into force upon the deposit of ratifications by the Republic of China, France, the Union of Soviet Socialist Republics, the United Kingdom of Great Britain and Northern Ireland and the United States of America, and by a majority of the other signatory states. A protocol of the ratifications deposited shall thereupon be drawn up by the Government of the United States of America which shall communicate copies thereof to all the signatory states.

4. The states signatory to the present Charter which ratify it after it has come into force will become original Members of the United Nations on the date of the deposit of their respective ratifications.

Article 111

The present Charter, of which the Chinese, French, Russian, English, and Spanish texts are equally authentic, shall remain deposited in the archives of the Government of the United States of America. Duly certified copies thereof shall be transmitted by that Government to the Governments of the other signatory states.

IN FAITH WHEREOF the representatives of the Governments of the United Nations have signed the present Charter.

DONE at the city of San Francisco the twenty-sixth day of June, one thousand nine hundred and forty-five.

---

[1] Amended text of Article 23, which came into force on 31 August 1965.
(The text of Article 23 before it was amended read as follows:
1. The Security Council shall consist of eleven Members of the United Nations. The Republic of China, France, the Union of Soviet Socialist Republics, the United Kingdom of Great Britain and Northern Ireland and the United States of America shall be permanent members of the Security Council. The General Assembly shall elect six other Members of the United Nations to be non-permanent members of the Security Council, due regard being specially paid in the first instance to the contributions of Members of the United Nations to the maintenance of international peace and security and to the other purposes of the Organization, and also to equitable geographical distribution.
2. The non-permanent members of the Security Council shall be elected for a term of two years. In the first election of the non-permanent members, however, three shall be chosen for a term of one year. A retiring member shall not be eligible for immediate re-election.
3. Each member of the Security Council shall have one representative.)

[2] Amended text of Article 27, which came into force on 31 August 1965.
(The text of Article 27 before it was amended read as follows:
1. Each member of the Security Council shall have one vote.
2. Decisions of the Security Council on procedural matters shall be made by an affirmative vote of seven members.
3. Decisions of the Security Council on all other matters shall be made by an affirmative vote of seven members including the concurring votes of the permanent members; provided that, in decisions under Chapter VI, and under paragraph 3 of Article 52, a party to a dispute shall abstain from voting.)

[3] Amended text of Article 61, which came into force on 24 September 1973.
(The text of Article 61 as previously amended on 31 August 1965 read as follows:
1. The Economic and Social Council shall consist of twenty-seven Members of the United Nations elected by the General Assembly.
2. Subject to the provisions of paragraph 3, nine members of the Economic and Social Council shall be elected each year for a term of three years. A retiring member shall be eligible for immediate re-election.
3. At the first election after the increase in the membership of the Economic and Social Council from eighteen to twenty-seven members, in addition to the members elected in place of the six members whose term of office expires at the end of that year, nine

additional members shall be elected. Of these nine additional members, the term of office of three members so elected shall expire at the end of one year, and of three other members at the end of two years, in accordance with arrangements made by the General Assembly.

4. Each member of the Economic and Social Council shall have one representative.)

[4] Amended text of Article 109, which came into force on 12 June 1968.
(The text of Article 109 before it was amended read as follows:

1. A General Conference of the Members of the United Nations for the purpose of reviewing the present Charter may be held at a date and place to be fixed by a two-thirds vote of the members of the General Assembly and by a vote of any seven members of the Security Council. Each Member of the United Nations shall have one vote in the conference.

2. Any alteration of the present Charter recommended by a two-thirds vote of the conference shall take effect when ratified in accordance with their respective constitutional processes by two thirds of the Members of the United Nations including all the permanent members of the Security Council.

3. If such a conference has not been held before the tenth annual session of the General Assembly following the coming into force of the present Charter, the proposal to call such a conference shall be placed on the agenda of that session of the General Assembly, and the conference shall be held if so decided by a majority vote of the members of the General Assembly and by a vote of any seven members of the Security Council.)

Statute of the International Court of Justice

Article 1

The International Court of Justice established by the Charter of the United Nations as the principal judicial organ of the United Nations shall be constituted and shall function in accordance with the provisions of the present Statute.

Chapter I

ORGANIZATION OF THE COURT

Article 2

The Court shall be composed of a body of independent judges, elected regardless of their nationality from among persons of high moral character, who possess the qualifications required in their respective countries for appointment to the highest judicial offices, or are jurisconsults of recognized competence in international law.

Article 3

1. The Court shall consist of fifteen members, no two of whom may be nationals of the same state.

2. A person who for the purposes of membership in the Court could be regarded as a national of more than one state shall be deemed to be a national of the one in which he ordinarily exercises civil and political rights.

Article 4

1. The members of the Court shall be elected by the General Assembly and by the Security Council from a list of persons nominated by the national groups in the Permanent Court of Arbitration, in accordance with the following provisions.

2. In the case of Members of the United Nations not represented in the Permanent Court of Arbitration, candidates shall be nominated by national groups appointed for this purpose by their governments under the same conditions as those prescribed for members of the Permanent Court of Arbitration by Article 44 of the Convention of The Hague of 1907 for the pacific settlement of international disputes.

3. The conditions under which a state which is a party to the present Statute but is not a Member of the United Nations may participate in electing the members of the Court shall, in the absence of a special agreement, be laid down by the General Assembly upon recommendation of the Security Council.

Article 5

1. At least three months before the date of the election, the Secretary-General of the United Nations shall address a written request to the members of the Permanent Court of Arbitration belonging to the states which are parties to the present Statute, and to the members of the national groups appointed under Article 4, paragraph 2, inviting them to undertake, within a given time, by national groups, the nomination of persons in a position to accept the duties of a member of the Court.

2. No group may nominate more than four persons, not more than two of whom shall be of their own nationality. In no case may the number of candidates nominated by a group be more than double the number of seats to be filled.

Article 6

Before making these nominations, each national group is recommended to consult its highest court of justice, its legal faculties and schools of law, and its national academies and national sections of international academies devoted to the study of law.

Article 7

1. The Secretary-General shall prepare a list in alphabetical order of all the persons thus nominated. Save as provided in Article 12, paragraph 2, these shall be the only persons eligible.

2. The Secretary-General shall submit this list to the General Assembly and to the Security Council.

Article 8

The General Assembly and the Security Council shall proceed independently of one another to elect the members of the Court.

Article 9

At every election, the electors shall bear in mind not only that the persons to be elected should individually possess the qualifications required, but also that in the body as a whole the representation of the main forms of civilization and of the principal legal systems of the world should be assured.

Article 10

1. Those candidates who obtain an absolute majority of votes in the General Assembly and in the Security Council shall be considered as elected.

2. Any vote of the Security Council, whether for the election of judges or for the appointment of members of the conference envisaged in Article 12, shall be taken without any distinction between permanent and non-permanent members of the Security Council.

3. In the event of more than one national of the same state obtaining an absolute majority of the votes both of the General Assembly and of the Security Council, the eldest of these only shall be considered as elected.

Article 11

If, after the first meeting held for the purpose of the election, one or more seats remain to be filled, a second and, if necessary, a third meeting shall take place.

Article 12

1. If, after the third meeting, one or more seats still remain unfilled, a joint conference consisting of six members, three appointed by the General Assembly and three by the Security Council, may be formed at any time at the request of either the General Assembly or the Security Council, for the purpose of choosing by the vote of an absolute majority one name for each seat still vacant, to submit to the General Assembly and the Security Council for their respective acceptance.

2. If the joint conference is unanimously agreed upon any person who fulfils the required conditions, he may be included in its list, even though he was not included in the list of nominations referred to in Article 7.

3. If the joint conference is satisfied that it will not be successful in procuring an election, those members of the Court who have already been elected shall, within a period to be fixed by the Security Council, proceed to fill the vacant seats by selection from among those candidates who have obtained votes either in the General Assembly or in the Security Council.

4. In the event of an equality of votes among the judges, the eldest judge shall have a casting vote.

Article 13

1. The members of the Court shall be elected for nine years and may be re-elected; provided, however, that of the judges elected at the first election, the terms of five judges shall expire at the end of three years and the terms of five more judges shall expire at the end of six years.

2. The judges whose terms are to expire at the end of the above-mentioned initial periods of three and six years shall be chosen by lot to be drawn by the Secretary-General immediately after the first election has been completed.

3. The members of the Court shall continue to discharge their duties until their places have been filled. Though replaced, they shall finish any cases which they may have begun.

4. In the case of the resignation of a member of the Court, the resignation shall be addressed to the President of the Court for transmission to the Secretary-General. This last notification makes the place vacant.

Article 14

Vacancies shall be filled by the same method as that laid down for the first election, subject to the following provision: the Secretary-General shall, within one month of the occurrence of the vacancy, proceed to issue the invitations provided for in Article 5, and the date of the election shall be fixed by the Security Council.

Article 15

A member of the Court elected to replace a member whose term of office has not expired shall hold office for the remainder of his predecessor's term.

Article 16

1. No member of the Court may exercise any political or administrative function, or engage in any other occupation of a professional nature.

2. Any doubt on this point shall be settled by the decision of the Court.

Article 17

1. No member of the Court may act as agent, counsel, or advocate in any case.

2. No member may participate in the decision of any case in which he has previously taken part as agent, counsel, or advocate for one of the parties, or as a member of a national or international court, or of a commission of enquiry, or in any other capacity.

3. Any doubt on this point shall be settled by the decision of the Court.

Article 18

1. No member of the Court can be dismissed unless, in the unanimous opinion of the other members, he has ceased to fulfil the required conditions.

2. Formal notification thereof shall be made to the Secretary-General by the Registrar.

3. This notification makes the place vacant.

Article 19

The members of the Court, when engaged on the business of the Court, shall enjoy diplomatic privileges and immunities.

Article 20

Every member of the Court shall, before taking up his duties, make a solemn declaration in open court that he will exercise his powers impartially and conscientiously.

Article 21

1. The Court shall elect its President and Vice-President for three years; they may be re-elected.

2. The Court shall appoint its Registrar and may provide for the appointment of such other officers as may be necessary.

Article 22

1. The seat of the Court shall be established at The Hague. This, however, shall not prevent the Court from sitting and exercising its functions elsewhere whenever the Court considers it desirable.

2. The President and the Registrar shall reside at the seat of the Court.

Article 23

1. The Court shall remain permanently in session, except during the judicial vacations, the dates and duration of which shall be fixed by the Court.

2. Members of the Court are entitled to periodic leave, the dates and duration of which shall be fixed by the Court, having in mind the distance between The Hague and the home of each judge.

3. Members of the Court shall be bound, unless they are on leave or prevented from attending by illness or other serious reasons duly explained to the President, to hold themselves permanently at the disposal of the Court.

Article 24

1. If, for some special reason, a member of the Court considers that he should not take part in the decision of a particular case, he shall so inform the President.

2. If the President considers that for some special reason one of the members of the Court should not sit in a particular case, he shall give him notice accordingly.

3. If in any such case the member of the Court and the President disagree, the matter shall be settled by the decision of the Court.

Article 25

1. The full Court shall sit except when it is expressly provided otherwise in the present Statute.

2. Subject to the condition that the number of judges available to constitute the Court is not thereby reduced below eleven, the Rules of the Court may provide for allowing one or more judges, according to circumstances and in rotation, to be dispensed from sitting.

3. A quorum of nine judges shall suffice to constitute the Court.

Article 26

1. The Court may from time to time form one or more chambers, composed of three or more judges as the Court may determine, for dealing with particular categories of cases; for example, labour cases and cases relating to transit and communications.

2. The Court may at any time form a chamber for dealing with a particular case. The number of judges to constitute such a chamber shall be determined by the Court with the approval of the parties.

3. Cases shall be heard and determined by the chambers provided for in this Article if the parties so request.

Article 27

A judgment given by any of the chambers provided for in Articles 26 and 29 shall be considered as rendered by the Court.

Article 28

The chambers provided for in Articles 26 and 29 may, with the consent of the parties, sit and exercise their functions elsewhere than at The Hague.

Article 29

With a view to the speedy dispatch of business, the Court shall form annually a chamber composed of five judges which, at the request of the parties, may hear and determine cases by summary procedure. In addition, two judges shall be selected for the purpose of replacing judges who find it impossible to sit.

Article 30

1. The Court shall frame rules for carrying out its functions. In particular, it shall lay down rules of procedure.

2. The Rules of the Court may provide for assessors to sit with the Court or with any of its chambers, without the right to vote.

Article 31

1. Judges of the nationality of each of the parties shall retain their right to sit in the case before the Court.

2. If the Court includes upon the Bench a judge of the nationality of one of the parties, any other party may choose a person to sit as judge. Such person shall be chosen preferably from among those persons who have been nominated as candidates as provided in Articles 4 and 5.

3. If the Court includes upon the Bench no judge of the nationality of the parties, each of these parties may proceed to choose a judge as provided in paragraph 2 of this Article.

4. The provisions of this Article shall apply to the case of Articles 26 and 29. In such cases, the President shall request one or, if necessary, two of the members of the Court forming the chamber to give place to the members of the Court of the nationality of the parties concerned, and, failing such, or if they are unable to be present, to the judges specially chosen by the parties.

5. Should there be several parties in the same interest, they shall, for the purpose of the preceding provisions, be reckoned as one party only. Any doubt upon this point shall be settled by the decision of the Court.

6. Judges chosen as laid down in paragraphs 2, 3 and 4 of this Article shall fulfil the conditions required by Articles 2, 17 (paragraph 2), 20, and 24 of the present Statute. They shall take part in the decision on terms of complete equality with their colleagues.

Article 32

1. Each member of the Court shall receive an annual salary.

2. The President shall receive a special annual allowance.

3. The Vice-President shall receive a special allowance for every day on which he acts as President.

4. The judges chosen under Article 31, other than members of the Court, shall receive compensation for each day on which they exercise their functions.

5. These salaries, allowances, and compensation shall be fixed by the General Assembly. They may not be decreased during the term of office.

6. The salary of the Registrar shall be fixed by the General Assembly on the proposal of the Court.

7. Regulations made by the General Assembly shall fix the conditions under which retirement pensions may be given to members of the Court and to the Registrar, and the conditions under which members of the Court and the Registrar shall have their travelling expenses refunded.

8. The above salaries, allowances, and compensation shall be free of all taxation.

Article 33

The expenses of the Court shall be borne by the United Nations in such a manner as shall be decided by the General Assembly.

Chapter II

COMPETENCE OF THE COURT

Article 34

1. Only states may be parties in cases before the Court.

2. The Court, subject to and in conformity with its Rules, may request of public international organizations information relevant to cases before it, and shall receive such information presented by such organizations on their own initiative.

3. Whenever the construction of the constituent instrument of a public international organization or of an international convention adopted thereunder is in question in a case before the Court, the Registrar shall so notify the public international organization concerned and shall communicate to it copies of all the written proceedings.

Article 35

1. The Court shall be open to the states parties to the present Statute.

2. The conditions under which the Court shall be open to other states shall, subject to the special provisions contained in treaties in force, be laid down by the Security Council, but in no case shall such conditions place the parties in a position of inequality before the Court.

3. When a state which is not a Member of the United Nations is a party to a case, the Court shall fix the amount which that party is to contribute towards the expenses of the Court. This provision shall not apply if such state is bearing a share of the expenses of the Court.

Article 36

1. The jurisdiction of the Court comprises all cases which the parties refer to it and all matters specially provided for in the Charter of the United Nations or in treaties and conventions in force.

2. The states parties to the present Statute may at any time declare that they recognize as compulsory *ipso facto* and without special agreement, in relation to any other state accepting the same obligation, the jurisdiction of the Court in all legal disputes concerning:

a. the interpretation of a treaty;

b. any question of international law;

c. the existence of any fact which, if established, would constitute a breach of an international obligation;

d. the nature or extent of the reparation to be made for the breach of an international obligation.

3. The declarations referred to above may be made unconditionally or on condition of reciprocity on the part of several or certain states, or for a certain time.

4. Such declarations shall be deposited with the Secretary-General of the United Nations, who shall transmit copies thereof to the parties to the Statute and to the Registrar of the Court.

5. Declarations made under Article 36 of the Statute of the Permanent Court of International Justice and which are still in force shall be deemed, as between the parties to the present Statute, to be acceptances of the compulsory jurisdiction of the International Court of Justice for the period which they still have to run and in accordance with their terms.

6. In the event of a dispute as to whether the Court has jurisdiction, the matter shall be settled by the decision of the Court.

Article 37

Whenever a treaty or convention in force provides for reference of a matter to a tribunal to have been instituted by the League of Nations, or to the Permanent Court of International Justice, the matter shall, as between the parties to the present Statute, be referred to the International Court of Justice.

Article 38

1. The Court, whose function is to decide in accordance with international law such disputes as are submitted to it, shall apply:
    a. international conventions, whether general or particular, establishing rules expressly recognized by the contesting states;
    b. international custom, as evidence of a general practice accepted as law;
    c. the general principles of law recognized by civilized nations;
    d. subject to the provisions of Article 59, judicial decisions and the teachings of the most highly qualified publicists of the various nations, as subsidiary means for the determination of rules of law.
2. This provision shall not prejudice the power of the Court to decide a case *ex aequo et bono*, if the parties agree thereto.

Chapter III
PROCEDURE

Article 39

1. The official languages of the Court shall be French and English. If the parties agree that the case shall be conducted in French, the judgment shall be delivered in French. If the parties agree that the case shall be conducted in English, the judgment shall be delivered in English.
2. In the absence of an agreement as to which language shall be employed, each party may, in the pleadings, use the language which it prefers; the decision of the Court shall be given in French and English. In this case the Court shall at the same time determine which of the two texts shall be considered as authoritative.
3. The Court shall, at the request of any party, authorize a language other than French or English to be used by that party.

Article 40

1. Cases are brought before the Court, as the case may be, either by the notification of the special agreement or by a written application addressed to the Registrar. In either case the subject of the dispute and the parties shall be indicated.
2. The Registrar shall forthwith communicate the application to all concerned.
3. He shall also notify the Members of the United Nations through the Secretary-General, and also any other states entitled to appear before the Court.

Article 41

1. The Court shall have the power to indicate, if it considers that circumstances so require, any provisional measures which ought to be taken to preserve the respective rights of either party.
2. Pending the final decision, notice of the measures suggested shall forthwith be given to the parties and to the Security Council.

Article 42

1. The parties shall be represented by agents.
2. They may have the assistance of counsel or advocates before the Court.
3. The agents, counsel, and advocates of parties before the Court shall enjoy the privileges and immunities necessary to the independent exercise of their duties.

Article 43

1. The procedure shall consist of two parts: written and oral.

2. The written proceedings shall consist of the communication to the Court and to the parties of memorials, counter-memorials and, if necessary, replies; also all papers and documents in support.
3. These communications shall be made through the Registrar, in the order and within the time fixed by the Court.
4. A certified copy of every document produced by one party shall be communicated to the other party.
5. The oral proceedings shall consist of the hearing by the Court of witnesses, experts, agents, counsel, and advocates.

Article 44

1. For the service of all notices upon persons other than the agents, counsel, and advocates, the Court shall apply direct to the government of the state upon whose territory the notice has to be served.
2. The same provision shall apply whenever steps are to be taken to procure evidence on the spot.

Article 45

The hearing shall be under the control of the President or, if he is unable to preside, of the Vice-President; if neither is able to preside, the senior judge present shall preside.

Article 46

The hearing in Court shall be public, unless the Court shall decide otherwise, or unless the parties demand that the public be not admitted.

Article 47

1. Minutes shall be made at each hearing and signed by the Registrar and the President.
2. These minutes alone shall be authentic.

Article 48

The Court shall make orders for the conduct of the case, shall decide the form and time in which each party must conclude its arguments, and make all arrangements connected with the taking of evidence.

Article 49

The Court may, even before the hearing begins, call upon the agents to produce any document or to supply any explanations. Formal note shall be taken of any refusal.

Article 50

The Court may, at any time, entrust any individual, body, bureau, commission, or other organization that it may select, with the task of carrying out an enquiry or giving an expert opinion.

Article 51

During the hearing any relevant questions are to be put to the witnesses and experts under the conditions laid down by the Court in the rules of procedure referred to in Article 30.

Article 52

After the Court has received the proofs and evidence within the time specified for the purpose, it may refuse to accept any further oral or written evidence that one party may desire to present unless the other side consents.

Article 53

1. Whenever one of the parties does not appear before the Court, or fails to defend its case, the other party may call upon the Court to decide in favour of its claim.
2. The Court must, before doing so, satisfy itself, not only that it has jurisdiction in accordance with Articles 36 and 37, but also that the claim is well founded in fact and law.

Article 54

1. When, subject to the control of the Court, the agents, counsel, and advocates have completed their presentation of the case, the President shall declare the hearing closed.

2. The Court shall withdraw to consider the judgment.

3. The deliberations of the Court shall take place in private and remain secret.

Article 55

1. All questions shall be decided by a majority of the judges present.

2. In the event of an equality of votes, the President or the judge who acts in his place shall have a casting vote.

Article 56

1. The judgment shall state the reasons on which it is based.

2. It shall contain the names of the judges who have taken part in the decision.

Article 57

If the judgment does not represent in whole or in part the unanimous opinion of the judges, any judge shall be entitled to deliver a separate opinion.

Article 58

The judgment shall be signed by the President and by the Registrar. It shall be read in open court, due notice having been given to the agents.

Article 59

The decision of the Court has no binding force except between the parties and in respect of that particular case.

Article 60

The judgment is final and without appeal. In the event of dispute as to the meaning or scope of the judgment, the Court shall construe it upon the request of any party.

Article 61

1. An application for revision of a judgment may be made only when it is based upon the discovery of some fact of such a nature as to be a decisive factor, which fact was, when the judgment was given, unknown to the Court and also the party claiming revision, always provided that such ignorance was not due to negligence.

2. The proceedings for revision shall be opened by a judgment of the Court expressly recording the existence of the new fact, recognizing that it has such a character as to lay the case open to revision, and declaring the application admissible on this ground.

3. The Court may require previous compliance with the terms of the judgment before it admits proceedings in revision.

4. The application for revision must be made at latest within six months of the discovery of the new fact.

5. No application for revision may be made after the lapse of ten years from the date of the judgment.

Article 62

1. Should a state consider that it has an interest of a legal nature which may be affected by the decision in the case, it may submit a request to the Court to be permitted to intervene.

2. It shall be for the Court to decide upon this request.

Article 63

1. Whenever the construction of a convention to which states other than those concerned in the case are parties is in question, the Registrar shall notify all such states forthwith.

2. Every state so notified has the right to intervene in the proceedings; but if it uses this right, the construction given by the judgment will be equally binding upon it.

Article 64

Unless otherwise decided by the Court, each party shall bear its own costs.

Chapter IV
ADVISORY OPINIONS

Article 65

1. The Court may give an advisory opinion on any legal question at the request of whatever body may be authorized by or in accordance with the Charter of the United Nations to make such a request.

2. Questions upon which the advisory opinion of the Court is asked shall be laid before the Court by means of a written request containing an exact statement of the question upon which an opinion is required, and accompanied by all documents likely to throw light upon the question.

Article 66

1. The Registrar shall forthwith give notice of the request for an advisory opinion to all states entitled to appear before the Court.

2. The Registrar shall also, by means of a special and direct communication, notify any state entitled to appear before the Court or international organization considered by the Court, or, should it not be sitting, by the President, as likely to be able to furnish information on the question, that the Court will be prepared to receive, within a time limit to be fixed by the President, written statements, or to hear, at a public sitting to be held for the purpose, oral statements relating to the question.

3. Should any such state entitled to appear before the Court have failed to receive the special communication referred to in paragraph 2 of this Article, such state may express a desire to submit a written statement or to be heard; and the Court will decide.

4. States and organizations having presented written or oral statements or both shall be permitted to comment on the statements made by other states or organizations in the form, to the extent, and within the time limits which the Court, or, should it not be sitting, the President, shall decide in each particular case. Accordingly, the Registrar shall in due time communicate any such written statements to states and organizations having submitted similar statements.

Article 67

The Court shall deliver its advisory opinions in open court, notice having been given to the Secretary-General and to the representatives of Members of the United Nations, of other states and of international organizations immediately concerned.

Article 68

In the exercise of its advisory functions the Court shall further be guided by the provisions of the present Statute which apply in contentious cases to the extent to which it recognizes them to be applicable.

Chapter V
AMENDMENT

Article 69

Amendments to the present Statute shall be effected by the same procedure as is provided by the Charter of the United Nations for amendments to that Charter, subject however to any provisions which the General Assembly upon recommendation of the Security Council may adopt concerning the participation of states which are parties to the present Statute but are not Members of the United Nations.

Article 70

The Court shall have power to propose such amendments to the present Statute as it may deem necessary, through written communications to the Secretary-General, for consideration in conformity with the provisions of Article 69.

Appendix III

Structure of the United Nations

General Assembly

The General Assembly is composed of all the Members of the United Nations.

SESSIONS
Resumed fifty-fifth session: 26 January–10 September 2001.
Twenty-fifth special session: 6-9 June 2001.
Twenty-sixth special session: 25-27 June 2001.
Fifty-sixth session: 12 September–24 December 2001 (suspended).
Resumed tenth emergency special session: 20 December 2001 (suspended).

OFFICERS
Resumed fifty-fifth and twenty-fifth and twenty-sixth[1] special sessions
President: Harri Holkeri (Finland).[2]
Vice-Presidents:[3] Belarus, Bhutan, Burkina Faso, China, Comoros, El Salvador, France, Gabon, Guinea, Haiti, Kuwait, Maldives, Mozambique, Russian Federation, Suriname, Tunisia, Turkey, United Kingdom, United States, Uzbekistan, Yemen.

Fifty-sixth and resumed tenth emergency special sessions
President: Han Seung-soo (Republic of Korea).[4]
Vice-Presidents:[5] Cambodia, China, Democratic Republic of the Congo, Ethiopia, France, Greece, Guatemala, Kyrgyzstan, Libyan Arab Jamahiriya, Malta, Mauritania, Nepal, Nicaragua, Paraguay, Republic of Moldova, Russian Federation, Saudi Arabia, Sierra Leone, South Africa, United Kingdom, United States.

The Assembly has four types of committees: (1) Main Committees; (2) procedural committees; (3) standing committees; (4) subsidiary and ad hoc bodies. In addition, it convenes conferences to deal with specific subjects.

Main Committees

Six Main Committees have been established as follows:

Disarmament and International Security Committee (First Committee)
Special Political and Decolonization Committee (Fourth Committee)
Economic and Financial Committee (Second Committee)
Social, Humanitarian and Cultural Committee (Third Committee)
Administrative and Budgetary Committee (Fifth Committee)
Legal Committee (Sixth Committee)

The General Assembly may constitute other committees, on which all Members of the United Nations have the right to be represented.

OFFICERS OF THE MAIN COMMITTEES

Resumed fifty-fifth session

Fifth Committee[6]
Chairperson: Gert Rosenthal (Guatemala).

Vice-Chairpersons: Jasminka Dinic (Croatia), Collen Vixen Kelapile (Botswana), Park Hae-yun (Republic of Korea).
Rapporteur: Eduardo Manuel da Fonseca Fernandes Ramos (Portugal).

Twenty-fifth and twenty-sixth special sessions[7]

First Committee
Chairperson: U Mya Than (Myanmar).
Acting Chairperson: Abdelkader Mesdoua (Algeria) (twenty-fifth special session), Alberto Guani (Uruguay) (twenty-sixth special session).

Fourth Committee
Chairperson: Matia Mulumba Semakula Kiwanuka (Uganda).
Acting Chairperson: Patrick Albert Lewis (Antigua and Barbuda).

Second Committee
Chairperson: Alexandru Niculescu (Romania).

Third Committee
Chairperson: Yvonne Gittens-Joseph (Trinidad and Tobago).

Fifth Committee
Chairperson: Gert Rosenthal (Guatemala).

Sixth Committee
Chairperson: Mauro Politi (Italy).
Acting Chairperson: Marcelo Vasquez (Ecuador).

Fifty-sixth session[8]

First Committee
Chairperson: André Erdös (Hungary).
Vice-Chairpersons: Milos Alcalay (Venezuela), Lie Kie-Cheon (Republic of Korea), Stephane De Loecker (Belgium).
Rapporteur: Sylvester Ekundayo Rowe (Sierra Leone).

Fourth Committee
Chairperson: Hasmy Agam (Malaysia).
Vice-Chairpersons: Anna-Maija Korpi (Finland), Alexandrina Livi Rusu (Romania), Christian Streeter (Chile).
Rapporteur: Graham Maitland (South Africa).

Second Committee
Chairperson: Fransisco Seixas da Costa (Portugal).
Vice-Chairpersons: Garfield Barnwell (Guyana), Dharmansjah Djumala (Indonesia), Felix Mbayu (Cameroon).
Rapporteur: Jana Simonova (Czech Republic).

Third Committee
Chairperson: Fuad Mubarak al-Hinai (Oman).
Vice-Chairpersons: Carlos Enrique García González (El Salvador), Carina Mårtensson (Sweden), Yehia Oda (Egypt).
Rapporteur: Juraj Priputen (Slovakia).

Fifth Committee
Chairperson: Nana Effah-Apenteng (Ghana).
Vice-Chairpersons: Durga P. Bhattarai (Nepal), Olexsii V. Ivaschenko (Ukraine), John Orr (Canada).

Rapporteur: Santiago Wins (Uruguay).

Sixth Committee

Chairperson: Pierre Lelong (Haiti).
Vice-Chairpersons: Siddig M. Abdalla (Sudan), Zsolt Hetesy (Hungary), Alexander Marschik (Austria).
Rapporteur: Mahmoud M. Al-Naman (Saudi Arabia).

Additional committees and round tables of the special sessions

OFFICERS

Twenty-fifth special session

Ad Hoc Committee of the Whole

Chairperson: Germán García Durán (Colombia).[9]
Vice-Chairpersons: Manfred Konukiewitz (Germany), Andrzej Olszoka (Poland), Seydou Sy Sall (Senegal).
Rapporteur: Alireza Esamaeilzadeh (Iran).

Thematic Committee

Chairperson: Slaheddine Belaid (Tunisia).[10]
Vice-Chairpersons: Luis Garcia Cerezo (Spain), Jose Maria Matamoros (Venezuela), Erna Witoelar (Indonesia).
Rapporteur: Elena Szolgayova (Slovakia).

Twenty-sixth special session

Round tables[11]

Chairperson, round table 1: Denzil Douglas (Saint Kitts and Nevis).
Chairperson, round table 2: Grzegorz Opala (Poland).
Chairperson, round table 3: Abdul Malik Kasi (Pakistan).
Chairperson, round table 4: Benjamin William Mkapa (United Republic of Tanzania).

Procedural committees

General Committee

The General Committee consists of the President of the General Assembly, as Chairperson, the 21 Vice-Presidents and the Chairpersons of the six Main Committees [at the twenty-fifth special session, the Chairpersons of the Ad Hoc Committee of the Whole and of the Thematic Committee were also members of the General Committee (dec. S-25/15 & S-25/16); at the twenty-sixth special session, the two facilitators and the Chairpersons of the round tables were also members of the General Committee (dec. S-26/15 & S-26/16)].

Credentials Committee

The Credentials Committee consists of nine members appointed by the General Assembly on the proposal of the President.

Resumed fifty-fifth and twenty-fifth and twenty-sixth special sessions[12]
Bahamas, China, Ecuador, Gabon, Ireland, Mauritius, Russian Federation, Thailand, United States.

Fifty-sixth and resumed tenth emergency special sessions[13]
China, Denmark, Jamaica, Lesotho, Russian Federation, Senegal, Singapore, United States, Uruguay.

Standing committees

The two standing committees consist of experts appointed in their individual capacity for three-year terms.

Advisory Committee on Administrative and Budgetary Questions (ACABQ)

To serve until 31 December 2001: Nazareth A. Incera (Costa Rica); Ahmad Kamal (Pakistan); Rajat Saha (India); Juichi Takahara (Japan); Nicholas A. Thorne (United Kingdom); Giovanni Luigi Valenza (Italy).
To serve until 31 December 2002: Gérard Biraud (France); Norma Goicochea Estenoz (Cuba); Vladimir V. Kuznetsov (Russian Federation); Susan M. McLurg (United States); Roger Tchoungui (Cameroon).
To serve until 31 December 2003: Andrzej T. Abraszewski (Poland); Manlan Narcisse Ahounou (Côte d'Ivoire); Felipe Mabilangan (Philippines); E. Besley Maycock, *Vice-Chairman* (Barbados); C. S. M. Mselle, *Chairman* (United Republic of Tanzania).

On 26 November 2001 (dec. 56/313), the General Assembly appointed the following for a three-year term beginning on 1 January 2002 to fill the vacancies occurring on 31 December 2001: Michiel W. H. Crom (Netherlands), Nazareth A. Incera (Costa Rica), Rajat Saha (India), Sun Minqin (China), Juichi Takahara (Japan), Nicholas A. Thorne (United Kingdom).

Committee on Contributions

To serve until 31 December 2001: Pieter Johannes Bierma (Netherlands); Uldis Blukis (Latvia); Paul Ekorong A Ndong (Cameroon); Neil Hewitt Francis (Australia); Bernardo Greiver (Uruguay); Henry Hanson-Hall, *Vice-Chairman* (Ghana); Eduardo Iglesias (Argentina).
To serve until 31 December 2002: Alvaro Gurgel de Alencar Netto (Brazil); Sergei I. Mareyev (Russian Federation); Angel Marrón (Spain); Hae-yun Park (Republic of Korea); Ugo Sessi, *Chairman* (Italy); Wu Gang (China).
To serve until 31 December 2003: Petru Dumitriu (Romania); Chinmaya Gharekhan (India); Ihor V. Humenny (Ukraine); Gebhard Benjamin Kandanga (Namibia); David A. Leis (United States); Kazuo Watanabe (Japan).

On 26 November 2001 (dec. 56/314), the General Assembly appointed the following for a three-year term beginning on 1 January 2002 to fill the vacancies occurring on 31 December 2001: Henry S. Fox (Australia), Bernardo Greiver (Uruguay), Hassan Mohammed Hassan (Nigeria), Eduardo Iglesias (Argentina), Omar Kadiri (Morocco), Eduardo Manuel da Fonseca Fernandes Ramos (Portugal).

Subsidiary and ad hoc bodies

The following is a list of subsidiary and ad hoc bodies functioning in 2001, including the number of members, dates of meetings/sessions in 2001, document numbers of 2001 reports (which generally provide specific information on membership), and relevant decision numbers pertaining to elections. (For other related bodies, see p. 1464.)

Ad Hoc Committee on the Elaboration of a Convention against Transnational Organized Crime

Sessions: Twelfth, Vienna, 26 February–2 March
Chairman: Luigi Lauriola (Italy) (acting in his personal capacity)
Membership: Open to all States
Reports: A/55/383/Add.2, A/AC.254/L.280

Ad Hoc Committee established by General Assembly resolution 51/210 of 17 December 1996

Session: Fifth, New York, 12-23 February
Chairman: Rohan Perera (Sri Lanka)
Membership: Open to all States Members of the United Nations or members of the specialized agencies or of IAEA
Report: A/56/37

Ad Hoc Committee on the Indian Ocean

Meeting: New York, 5 July
Chairman: John de Saram (Sri Lanka)

Membership: 43
Report: A/56/29

Advisory Committee on the United Nations Programme of Assistance in the Teaching, Study, Dissemination and Wider Appreciation of International Law

Session: Thirty-sixth, New York, 17 October
Chairman: Thomas Kwesi Quartey (Ghana)
Membership: 25
Report: A/56/484

Board of Auditors

Sessions: Fifty-fifth, New York, 27-29 June; fourteenth special, Geneva, 28 November
Chairman: Guillermo N. Carague (Philippines)
Membership: 3
Decision: GA 56/315

Committee on Conferences

Sessions: New York, 19 April and 22 June (organizational), 27-29 August (substantive)
Chairman: Abdelmalek Bouheddou (Algeria)
Membership: 21
Report: A/56/32
Decision: GA 56/309

Committee on the Exercise of the Inalienable Rights of the Palestinian People

Meetings: Throughout the year
Chairman: Ibra Deguène Ka (Senegal)
Membership: 25
Report: A/56/35

Committee on Information

Session: Twenty-third, New York, 30 April–11 May
Chairman: Milos Alcalay (Venezuela)
Membership: 96 (98 from 10 December)
Report: A/56/21
Decision: GA 56/318

Committee on the Peaceful Uses of Outer Space

Session: Forty-fourth, Vienna, 6-15 June
Chairman: Raimundo González (Chile)
Membership: 61 (64 from 10 December)
Report: A/56/20 & Corr.1

Committee on Relations with the Host Country

Meetings: New York, 22 February, 1 June, 17 August, 26 October
Chairman: Sotirios Zackheos (Cyprus)
Membership: 19 (including the United States as host country)
Report: A/56/26

Committee for the United Nations Population Award

Meetings: New York, 7 March, 10 May
Chairman: José Luis Barbosa Leao Monteiro (Cape Verde) (March), Pierre Lelong (Haiti) (May)
Membership: 10 (plus 5 honorary members, the Secretary-General and the UNFPA Executive Director)
Report: A/56/459
Decision: ESC 2001/201 B

Disarmament Commission

Sessions: New York, 9 April (organizational), 9-27 April (substantive), 2 November (organizational)
Chairman: Diane Quarless (Jamaica)
Membership: All UN Members
Reports: A/56/42, A/57/42

High-level Committee on the Review of Technical Cooperation among Developing Countries

Sessions: 8 May (organizational), 29 May–1 June (substantive)

President: Alounkèo Kittikhoun (Lao People's Democratic Republic)
Membership: All States participating in UNDP
Report: A/56/39

Intergovernmental Preparatory Committee for the Third United Nations Conference on the Least Developed Countries

Sessions: Second, New York, 5-9 February; third (final), New York, 2-6 April
Chairman: Jacques Scavee (Belgium)
Membership: Open to all States members of UNCTAD
Reports: A/CONF.191/3, A/CONF.191/5

International Civil Service Commission (ICSC)

Session: Fifty-third, Montreal, Canada, 11-29 June
Chairman: Mohsen Bel Hadj Amor (Tunisia)
Membership: 15
Report: A/56/30
Decision: GA 56/317

ADVISORY COMMITTEE ON POST ADJUSTMENT QUESTIONS
Session: Twenty-fourth, New York, 12-20 March
Chairman: Eugeniusz Wyzner (Poland)
Membership: 6

International Law Commission

Session: Fifty-third, Geneva, 23 April–1 June and 2 July–10 August
Chairman: Peter C. R. Kabatsi (Uganda)
Membership: 34
Report: A/56/10 & Corr.1,2
Decision: GA 56/311

Investments Committee

Meetings: Singapore, 19-20 February; New York, 7-8 May, 30-31 July and 5-6 November
Chairman: Emmanuel Noi Omaboe (Ghana)
Membership: 9
Decision: GA 56/316

Joint Advisory Group on the International Trade Centre UNCTAD/WTO

Session: Thirty-fourth, Geneva, 30 April–4 May
Chairperson: A. Filip (Romania)
Membership: Open to all States members of UNCTAD and all members of WTO
Report: ITC/AG(XXXIV)/188

Joint Inspection Unit (JIU)

Chairman: Sumihiro Kuyama (Japan)
Membership: 11
Report: A/57/34

Office of the United Nations High Commissioner for Refugees (UNHCR)

EXECUTIVE COMMITTEE OF THE HIGH COMMISSIONER'S PROGRAMME
Session: Fifty-second, Geneva, 1-5 October
Chairman: Johan Molander (Sweden)
Membership: 58
Report: A/56/12/Add.1
Decision: ESC 2001/201 B

High Commissioner: Ruud Lubbers

Panel of External Auditors

Membership: Members of the UN Board of Auditors and the appointed external auditors of the specialized agencies and IAEA

Preparatory Committee for the International Conference on Financing for Development

Sessions: Second, New York, 12-23 February; third and resumed third, New York, 2-8 May and 15-19 October
Co-Chairmen: Shamshad Ahmad (Pakistan) (from 15 October), Jørgen Bøjer (Denmark) (to 8 May), Ruth Jacoby (Sweden) (from 8 May), Asda Jayanama (Thailand) (to 15 October)
Membership: Open to all States
Reports: A/55/28/Add.1, A/55/28/Add.2 & Corr.1, A/56/28 & Corr.1

Preparatory Committee for the Special Session of the General Assembly on Children

Sessions: Second, New York, 29 January–2 February; third, New York, 11-15 June
Chairperson: Patricia Durrant (Jamaica)
Membership: Open to all States Members of the United Nations and members of the specialized agencies
Reports: A/S-27/2 & Add.1 (Part I)

Preparatory Committee for the World Conference against Racism, Racial Discrimination, Xenophobia and Related Intolerance

Sessions: Second, Geneva, 21 May–1 June; third (final), Geneva, 30 July–10 August
Chairperson: Absa Claude Diallo (Senegal)
Membership: Open to all States Members of the United Nations and members of the specialized agencies
Reports: A/CONF.189/PC.2/30, A/CONF.189/PC.3/11

Special Committee on the Charter of the United Nations and on the Strengthening of the Role of the Organization

Meetings: New York, 2-12 April
Chairman: Mirza Cristina Gnecco (Colombia)
Membership: Open to all States Members of the United Nations
Report: A/56/33

Special Committee to Investigate Israeli Practices Affecting the Human Rights of the Palestinian People and Other Arabs of the Occupied Territories

Meetings: Geneva, 17 and 18 May; Cairo, Egypt, 26-29 July; Amman, Jordan, 30 July–1 August; Damascus, Syrian Arab Republic, 2-4 August
Chairperson: John de Saram (Sri Lanka)
Membership: 3
Report: A/56/491

Special Committee on Peacekeeping Operations

Meetings: New York, 18-19 June, 31 July (general debate); 19 June–30 July (open-ended working group)
Chairman: Arthur C. I. Mbanefo (Nigeria)
Membership: 110
Report: A/55/1024 & Corr.1

Special Committee to Select the Winners of the United Nations Human Rights Prize

Meeting: Did not meet in 2001
Membership: 5

Special Committee on the Situation with regard to the Implementation of the Declaration on the Granting of Independence to Colonial Countries and Peoples

Session: New York, 21 February and 12 March (first part); 18-19 June, 21 June, 28-29 June and 2-3 July (second part)
Chairman: Julian R. Hunte (Saint Lucia)
Membership: 23
Report: A/56/23

United Nations Administrative Tribunal

Sessions: Geneva, 25 June–27 July; New York, 22 October–30 November
President: Mayer Gabay (Israel)
Membership: 7
Report: A/INF/56/5

United Nations Capital Development Fund (UNCDF)

EXECUTIVE BOARD

The UNDP/UNFPA Executive Board acts as the Executive Board of the Fund.

Managing Director: Mark Malloch Brown (UNDP Administrator)

United Nations Commission on International Trade Law (UNCITRAL)

Session: Thirty-fourth, New York, 25 June–13 July
Chairman: Alejandro Ogarrio Ramirez-España (Mexico)
Membership: 36
Report: A/56/17 & Corr.1-3

United Nations Conciliation Commission for Palestine

Membership: 3
Reports: A/56/290, A/57/294

United Nations Conference on Trade and Development (UNCTAD)

Membership: Open to all States Members of the United Nations or members of the specialized agencies or of IAEA
Secretary-General of UNCTAD: Rubens Ricupero

TRADE AND DEVELOPMENT BOARD

Sessions: Twenty-sixth and twenty-seventh executive, Geneva, 10 April, 19 July; forty-eighth, Geneva, 1-12 October
President: Camilo Reyes Rodriguez (Colombia) (executive sessions), Ali Said Mchumo (United Republic of Tanzania) (forty-eighth session)
Membership: Open to all States members of UNCTAD
Report: A/56/15

SUBSIDIARY ORGANS OF THE TRADE AND DEVELOPMENT BOARD

COMMISSION ON ENTERPRISE, BUSINESS FACILITATION AND DEVELOPMENT
Session: Fifth, Geneva, 22-26 January
Chairperson: Martin Pavelsons (Latvia)
Membership: Open to all States members of UNCTAD
Report: TD/B/48/3

COMMISSION ON INVESTMENT, TECHNOLOGY AND RELATED FINANCIAL ISSUES
Session: Fifth, Geneva, 12-16 February
Chairperson: Jean-Luc Le Bideau (France)
Membership: Open to all States members of UNCTAD
Report: TD/B/48/4

Intergovernmental Group of Experts on Competition Law and Policy
Session: Third, Geneva, 2-4 July
Chairperson: Fernando Heftye (Mexico)
Membership: Open to all States members of UNCTAD
Report: TD/B/COM.2/32

Intergovernmental Working Group of Experts on International Standards of Accounting and Reporting
Session: Eighteenth, Geneva, 10-12 September
Chairperson: Richard Martin (United Kingdom)
Membership: 34
Report: TD/B/COM.2/34
Decisions: ESC 2001/201 A & B

COMMISSION ON TRADE IN GOODS AND SERVICES, AND COMMODITIES
Session: Fifth, Geneva, 19-23 February, 23 March
Chairperson: Boniface G. Britto Chidyausiku (Zimbabwe)
Membership: Open to all States members of UNCTAD
Report: TD/B/48/6

WORKING PARTY ON THE
MEDIUM-TERM PLAN AND THE PROGRAMME BUDGET
Sessions: Thirty-seventh, Geneva, 15-19 January, 11-12 June; thirty-eighth, Geneva, 17-20 September
Chairperson: Mussie Delelegnarega (Ethiopia) (thirty-seventh session), Arnaldo Abeti (Italy) (thirty-eighth session)
Membership: Open to all States members of UNCTAD
Reports: TD/B/48/7, TD/B/48/19

United Nations Development Fund for Women (UNIFEM)

CONSULTATIVE COMMITTEE
Session: Forty-first, New York, 26-27 January
Chairperson: Victoria Sandru (Romania)
Membership: 5

Director of UNIFEM: Noeleen Heyzer
Acting Deputy Director: Joanne Sandler

United Nations Environment Programme (UNEP)

GOVERNING COUNCIL
Session: Twenty-first/Global Ministerial Environment Forum, Nairobi, Kenya, 5-9 February
President: David Anderson (Canada)
Membership: 58
Report: A/56/25
Decisions: GA 56/307, 56/312

Executive Director of UNEP: Klaus Töpfer

United Nations Institute for Disarmament Research (UNIDIR)

BOARD OF TRUSTEES
Sessions: Thirty-sixth, New York, 31 January–2 February; thirty-seventh, Geneva, 25-27 July
Chairman: Nabil Fahmy (Egypt)
Membership: 20, plus 1 ex-officio member (Director of UNIDIR)
Report: A/56/418

Director of UNIDIR: Patricia Lewis
Deputy Director: Christophe Carle

United Nations Institute for Training and Research (UNITAR)

BOARD OF TRUSTEES
Session: Thirty-ninth, Geneva, 30 April–2 May
Chairman: Arthur C. I. Mbanefo (Nigeria)
Membership: Not less than 11 and not more than 30, plus 4 ex-officio members
Report: A/56/615

Executive Director of UNITAR: Marcel A. Boisard

United Nations Joint Staff Pension Board
Session: Did not meet in 2001
Membership: 33

United Nations Relief and Works Agency for Palestine Refugees in the Near East (UNRWA)

ADVISORY COMMISSION OF UNRWA
Meeting: Amman, Jordan, 25 September
Chairperson: Mohamed Higazy (Egypt)
Membership: 10
Report: A/56/13

WORKING GROUP ON THE FINANCING OF UNRWA
Meetings: New York, 14 September, 3 October
Chairman: Mehmet U. Pamir (Turkey)
Membership: 9
Report: A/56/430

Commissioner-General of UNRWA: Peter Hansen
Deputy Commissioner-General: Karen Koning AbuZayd

United Nations Scientific Committee on the Effects of Atomic Radiation
Session: Fiftieth, Vienna, 23-27 April
Chairman: J. Lipsztein (Brazil)
Membership: 21
Report: A/56/46

United Nations Staff Pension Committee
Meetings: New York and Geneva (via teleconference), 17 May, 6 December
Chairperson: Jean-Michel Jakobowicz (France)
Membership: 12 members and 8 alternates

United Nations University (UNU)

COUNCIL OF THE UNITED NATIONS UNIVERSITY
Session: Forty-eighth, Tokyo, Japan, 3-7 December
Chairperson: Jairam Reddy (South Africa)
Membership: 24 (plus 3 ex-officio members and the UNU Rector)
Report: A/57/31

Rector of the University: Johannes A. van Ginkel

United Nations Voluntary Fund for Indigenous Populations

BOARD OF TRUSTEES
Session: Fourteenth, Geneva, 28-30 March
Chairperson: Victoria Tauli-Corpuz (Philippines)
Membership: 5
Report: E/CN.4/Sub.2/AC.4/2001/4

United Nations Voluntary Fund for Victims of Torture

BOARD OF TRUSTEES
Session: Twentieth, Geneva, 18 May–1 June
Chairman: Jaap Walkate (Netherlands)
Membership: 5
Report: A/56/181

United Nations Voluntary Trust Fund on Contemporary Forms of Slavery

BOARD OF TRUSTEES
Session: Sixth, Geneva, 22-26 January
Chairperson: Swami Agnivesh (India)
Membership: 5
Report: A/56/205

Conferences

Third United Nations Conference on the Least Developed Countries
Session: Brussels, Belgium, 14-20 May
President: Göran Persson (Sweden)
Attendance: 159 States, PLO (as observer), plus UN offices and bodies, specialized agencies, intergovernmental organizations and non-governmental organizations
Report: A/CONF.191/3

United Nations Conference on the Illicit Trade in Small Arms and Light Weapons in All Its Aspects
Session: New York, 9-20 July
President: Camilo Reyes Rodriguez (Colombia)
Attendance: 171 States, Palestine (as observer), plus intergovernmental and non-governmental organizations
Report: A/CONF.192/15

World Conference against Racism, Racial Discrimination, Xenophobia and Related Intolerance
Session: Durban, South Africa, 31 August–7 September

President: Nkosazana Dlamini Zuma (South Africa)
Attendance: 170 States plus Palestine, UN offices and bodies, specialized agencies, intergovernmental and non-governmental organizations, and national human rights institutions
Report: A/CONF.189/12

Security Council

The Security Council consists of 15 Member States of the United Nations, in accordance with the provisions of Article 23 of the United Nations Charter as amended in 1965.

MEMBERS

Permanent members: China, France, Russian Federation, United Kingdom, United States.
Non-permanent members: Bangladesh, Colombia, Ireland, Jamaica, Mali, Mauritius, Norway, Singapore, Tunisia, Ukraine.

On 8 October 2001 (dec. 56/305), the General Assembly elected Bulgaria, Cameroon, Guinea, Mexico and the Syrian Arab Republic for a two-year term beginning on 1 January 2002, to replace Bangladesh, Jamaica, Mali, Tunisia and Ukraine whose terms of office were to expire on 31 December 2001.

PRESIDENT

The presidency of the Council rotates monthly, according to the English alphabetical listing of its member States. The following served as President during 2001:

Month	Member	Representative
January	Singapore	Kishore Mahbubani Shunmugam Jayakumar
February	Tunisia	Saïd Ben Mustapha
March	Ukraine	Valery Kuchinsky Volodymyr Yel'chenko Anatoliy Zlenko
April	United Kingdom	Sir Jeremy Quentin Greenstock, KCMG
May	United States	James B. Cunningham
June	Bangladesh	Anwarul Karim Chowdhury Alhaj Abdus Smad Azad
July	China	Wang Yingfan
August	Colombia	Alfonso Valdivieso Guillermo Fernández de Soto
September	France	Jean-David Levitte
October	Ireland	Richard Ryan Brian Cowen, TD
November	Jamaica	Mignonette Patricia Durrant Percival James Patterson, PC, QC, MP K. D. Knight, MP
December	Mali	Moctar Ouane

Military Staff Committee

The Military Staff Committee consists of the chiefs of staff of the permanent members of the Security Council or their representatives. It meets fortnightly.

Standing committees

Each of the three standing committees of the Security Council is composed of representatives of all Council members:

Committee of Experts (to examine the provisional rules of procedure of the Council and any other matters entrusted to it by the Council)
Committee on the Admission of New Members
Committee on Council Meetings Away from Headquarters

Subsidiary body

United Nations Monitoring, Verification and Inspection Commission (UNMOVIC)

Executive Chairman: Hans Blix.

Peacekeeping operations

United Nations Truce Supervision Organization (UNTSO)

Chief of Staff: Major General Franco Ganguzza.

United Nations Military Observer Group in India and Pakistan (UNMOGIP)

Chief Military Observer: Major General Manuel Saavedra.

United Nations Peacekeeping Force in Cyprus (UNFICYP)

Special Adviser to the Secretary-General on Cyprus: Alvaro de Soto.
Acting Special Representative of the Secretary-General and Chief of Mission: Zbigniew Wlosowicz.
Force Commander: Major General Victory Rana (until December), Lieutenant General Jin Ha Hwang (from December).

United Nations Disengagement Observer Force (UNDOF)

Force Commander: Major General Bo Wranker.

United Nations Interim Force in Lebanon (UNIFIL)

Personal Representative of the Secretary-General for Southern Lebanon: Staffan de Mistura (from 15 January).
Force Commander: Major General Seth Kofi Obeng (until 15 May), Major General Lalit Mohan Tewari (from 19 August).

United Nations Iraq-Kuwait Observation Mission (UNIKOM)

Force Commander: Major General John Augustine Vize (until 30 November), Major General Miguel Angel Moreno (from 1 December).

United Nations Mission for the Referendum in Western Sahara (MINURSO)

Personal Envoy of the Secretary-General: James A. Baker III.
Special Representative of the Secretary-General and Head of Mission: William Eagleton (until 30 November), William Lacy Swing (from 1 December).
Force Commander: Brigadier General Claude Buze.

United Nations Observer Mission in Georgia (UNOMIG)

Special Representative of the Secretary-General and Head of Mission: Dieter Boden.
Chief Military Observer: Major General Anis Ahmed Bajwa.

United Nations Mission in Bosnia and Herzegovina (UNMIBH)

Special Representative of the Secretary-General and Coordinator of United Nations Operations in Bosnia and Herzegovina: Jacques Paul Klein.
Commissioner of the United Nations International Police Task Force: General Vincent Coeurderoy.

United Nations Mission of Observers in Prevlaka (UNMOP)

Chief Military Observer: Lieutenant Colonel Graeme Williams (until 15 September), Colonel Rodolfo Sergio Mujica (from 15 September).

United Nations Interim Administration Mission in Kosovo (UNMIK)

Special Representative of the Secretary-General: Hans Haekkerup (from 15 January).
Principal Deputy Special Representative: Gary L. Mathews (until 31 October), Charles Brayshaw (from 1 November).

United Nations Mission in Sierra Leone (UNAMSIL)

Special Representative of the Secretary-General and Head of Mission: Oluyemi Adeniji.
Force Commander: Lieutenant General Daniel Ishmael Opande.

United Nations Transitional Administration in East Timor (UNTAET)

Personal Representative of the Secretary-General for East Timor: Jamsheed K. A. Marker.
Special Representative of the Secretary-General and Transitional Administrator: Sergio Vieira de Mello.
Force Commander: Lieutenant General Boonsrang Niumpradit (until 31 August), Lieutenant General Winai Phattiyakul (from 31 August).

United Nations Organization Mission in the Democratic Republic of the Congo (MONUC)

Special Representative of the Secretary-General and Head of Mission: Kamel Morjane (until August), Amos Namanga Ngongi (from September).
Force Commander: Major General Mountaga Diallo.

United Nations Mission in Ethiopia and Eritrea (UNMEE)

Special Representative of the Secretary-General: Legwaila Joseph Legwaila.
Force Commander: Major General Patrick Cammaert.

Political, peace-building and other missions

United Nations Office in Burundi (UNOB)

Representative of the Secretary-General and Head of UNOB: Jean Arnault (until August).
Officer-in-Charge: Amadou Keita (from 1 September).

United Nations Political Office for Somalia (UNPOS)

Representative of the Secretary-General and Head of UNPOS: David Stephen.

United Nations Peace-building Support Office in Liberia (UNOL)

Representative of the Secretary-General and Head of UNOL: Felix-Cyril Downes-Thomas.

Office of the Special Representative of the Secretary-General for the Great Lakes Region

Special Representative: Berhanu Dinka.

United Nations Political Office in Bougainville (UNPOB)

Head of Office: Noel Sinclair.

United Nations Peace-building Support Office in Guinea-Bissau (UNOGBIS)

Representative of the Secretary-General and Head of UNOGBIS: Samuel C. Nana-Sinkam.

Office of the United Nations Special Coordinator for the Middle East (UNSCO)

Special Coordinator for the Middle East Peace Process and Personal Representative of the Secretary-General to the Palestine Liberation Organization and the Palestinian Authority: Terje Roed-Larsen.

United Nations Office in Angola (UNOA)

Representative of the Secretary-General and Head of UNOA: Mussagy Jeichande.

United Nations Peace-building Office in the Central African Republic (BONUCA)

Representative of the Secretary-General and Head of BONUCA: Cheikh Tidiane Sy (until May), General Lamine Cissé (from 16 July).

United Nations Tajikistan Office of Peace-building (UNTOP)

Special Representative of the Secretary-General: Ivo Petrov.

Economic and Social Council

The Economic and Social Council consists of 54 Member States of the United Nations, elected by the General Assembly, each for a three-year term, in accordance with the provisions of Article 61 of the United Nations Charter as amended in 1965 and 1973.

MEMBERS

To serve until 31 December 2001: Bolivia, Bulgaria, Canada, China, Czech Republic, Democratic Republic of the Congo, Denmark, Guinea-Bissau, Honduras, Indonesia, Morocco, Norway, Russian Federation, Rwanda, Saudi Arabia, Syrian Arab Republic, United Kingdom, Venezuela.
To serve until 31 December 2002: Angola, Austria, Bahrain, Benin, Burkina Faso, Cameroon, Costa Rica, Croatia, Cuba, Fiji, France, Germany, Greece, Japan, Mexico, Portugal, Sudan, Suriname.
To serve until 31 December 2003: Andorra, Argentina, Brazil, Egypt, Ethiopia, Georgia, Iran, Italy, Nepal, Netherlands, Nigeria, Pakistan, Peru, Republic of Korea, Romania, South Africa, Uganda, United States.

On 26 October 2001 (dec. 56/310), the General Assembly elected the following for a three-year term beginning on 1 January 2002 to fill the vacancies occurring on 31 December 2001: Australia, Bhutan, Burundi, Chile, China, El Salvador, Finland, Ghana, Guatemala, Hungary, India, Libyan Arab Jamahiriya, Qatar, Russian Federation, Sweden, Ukraine, United Kingdom, Zimbabwe.

By the same decision, the Assembly elected Spain for the remaining term of office of Portugal, beginning on 1 January 2002.

SESSIONS

Organizational session for 2001: New York, 29 and 31 January.
Resumed organizational session for 2001: New York, 8, 13 and 22 March, 3 May and 4 June.
Special high-level meeting with the Bretton Woods institutions: New York, 1 May.
Substantive session of 2001: Geneva, 2-26 July.
Resumed substantive session of 2001: New York, 10 and 24 October and 26 December.

OFFICERS

President: Martin Belinga-Eboutou (Cameroon).
Vice-Presidents: Antonio Monteiro (Portugal), Bernd Niehous (Costa Rica), Ivan Šimonovic (Croatia), Mikhail Wehbe (Syrian Arab Republic).

Subsidiary and other related organs

SUBSIDIARY ORGANS

The Economic and Social Council may, at each session, set up committees or working groups, of the whole or of limited membership, and refer to them any items on the agenda for study and report.

Other subsidiary organs reporting to the Council consist of functional commissions, regional commissions, standing committees, expert bodies and ad hoc bodies.

The inter-agency Administrative Committee on Coordination also reports to the Council.

Functional commissions

Commission on Crime Prevention and Criminal Justice
Session: Tenth, Vienna, 8-17 May and 6-7 September
Chairman: Shaukat Umer (Pakistan)
Membership: 40
Report: E/2001/30/Rev.1
Decision: ESC 2001/201 B

Commission on Human Rights
Session: Fifty-seventh, Geneva, 19 March–27 April
Chairperson: Leandro Despouy (Argentina)
Membership: 53
Report: E/2001/23
Decisions: ESC 2001/201 A & B

SUBCOMMISSION ON THE PROMOTION
AND PROTECTION OF HUMAN RIGHTS
Session: Fifty-third, Geneva, 30 July–17 August
Chairperson: David Weissbrodt (United States)
Membership: 26
Report: E/CN.4/2002/2

Commission on Narcotic Drugs
Session: Forty-fourth, Vienna, 20-29 March and 12-13 December
Chairman: Pavel Vacek (Czech Republic)
Membership: 53
Report: E/2001/28/Rev.1
Decisions: ESC 2001/201 B & C

Commission on Population and Development
Session: Thirty-fourth, New York, 2-6 April
Chairman: Makoto Atoh (Japan)
Membership: 47
Report: E/2001/25
Decision: ESC 2001/201 B

Commission on Science and Technology for Development
Session: Fifth, Geneva, 28 May–1 June
Chairperson: Stefan Moravek (Slovakia)
Membership: 33
Report: E/2001/31
Decisions: ESC 2001/201 A-C

Commission for Social Development
Session: Thirty-ninth, New York, 13-23 February
Chairperson: Faith Innerarity (Jamaica)
Membership: 46
Report: E/2001/26
Decision: ESC 2001/201 A

Commission on the Status of Women
Session: Forty-fifth, New York, 6-17 March and 9-11 May
Chairperson: Dubravka Šimonovic (Croatia)
Membership: 45
Report: E/2001/27
Decision: ESC 2001/201 B

Commission on Sustainable Development
Session: Ninth (second part), New York, 16-27 April
Chairperson: Bedrich Moldan (Czech Republic)
Membership: 53
Report: E/2001/29
Decision: ESC 2001/201 B

Statistical Commission
Session: Thirty-second, New York, 6-9 March
Chairman: Shigeru Kawasaki (Japan)
Membership: 24
Report: E/2001/24
Decision: ESC 2001/201 B

United Nations Forum on Forests
Sessions: Organizational, New York, 12 and 16 February; first, New York, 11-22 June
Chairman: Mubarak Hussein Rahmtalla (Sudan)
Membership: Open to all States Members of the United Nations and members of the specialized agencies
Report: E/2001/42/Rev.1

Regional commissions

Economic Commission for Africa (ECA)
Session: Thirty-fourth (twenty-fifth meeting of Conference of Ministers), Algiers, Algeria, 8-10 May
Chairman: Algeria
Membership: 53
Report: E/2001/38

Economic Commission for Europe (ECE)
Session: Fifty-sixth, Geneva, 8-11 May
Chairman: Harald Kreid (Austria)
Membership: 55
Report: E/2001/37

Economic Commission for Latin America and the Caribbean (ECLAC)
Session: Did not meet in 2001
Membership: 41 members, 6 associate members

Economic and Social Commission for Asia and the Pacific (ESCAP)
Session: Fifty-seventh, Bangkok, Thailand, 19-25 April
Chairperson: Ismail Shafeeu (Maldives)
Membership: 52 members, 9 associate members
Report: E/2001/39

Economic and Social Commission for Western Asia (ESCWA)
Session: Twenty-first, Beirut, Lebanon, 10-11 May
Chairman: Basil Fulayhan (Lebanon)
Membership: 13
Report: E/2001/41

Standing committees

Commission on Human Settlements
Session: Eighteenth, Nairobi, Kenya, 12-16 February
Chairperson: Sid-Ali Ketrandji (Algeria)
Membership: 58
Report: A/56/8
Decisions: ESC 2001/201 A & B

Committee on Non-Governmental Organizations
Sessions: Resumed 2000, New York, 15-26 January; 2001 regular, New York, 7-25 May
Chairman: Levent Bilman (Turkey)
Membership: 19
Reports: E/2001/8, E/2001/86

Committee for Programme and Coordination (CPC)
Sessions: Forty-first, New York, 2 May (organizational), 11 June–6 July (substantive)
Chairperson: Sharon Brennen-Haylock (Bahamas)
Membership: 34
Report: A/56/16
Decisions: ESC 2001/201 B, GA 56/308

Expert bodies

Ad Hoc Group of Experts on International Cooperation in Tax Matters

Meeting: Tenth, Geneva, 10-14 September
Membership: 25
Report: E/2002/6

Committee for Development Policy

Session: Third, New York, 2-6 April
Chairman: Riyokichi Hirono (Japan)
Membership: 24
Report: E/2001/33
Decision: ESC 2001/201 A

Committee on Economic, Social and Cultural Rights

Sessions: Twenty-fifth, twenty-sixth and twenty-seventh, Geneva, 23 April–11 May, 13-31 August, 12-30 November
Chairman: Virginia Bonoan-Dandan (Philippines)
Membership: 18
Report: E/2002/22

Committee on Energy and Natural Resources for Development

Session: Did not meet in 2001
Membership: 24

Committee of Experts on the Transport of Dangerous Goods and on the Globally Harmonized System of Classification and Labelling of Chemicals

Session: Did not meet in 2001
Membership: 31
Decision: ESC 2001/201 B

Permanent Forum on Indigenous Issues

Session: Did not meet in 2001
Membership: 16
Decision: ESC 2001/201 C

United Nations Group of Experts on Geographical Names

Session: Did not meet in 2001
Membership: Representatives of the 22 geographical/linguistic divisions of the Group of Experts

Ad hoc bodies

Commission on Human Settlements acting as the preparatory committee for the special session of the General Assembly for an overall review and appraisal of the implementation of the outcome of the United Nations Conference on Human Settlements (Habitat II)

Session: Second (final), Nairobi, Kenya, 19-23 February
Chairperson: Germán García Durán (Colombia)
Membership: Open to all States
Report: A/S-25/2

Commission for Social Development acting as the preparatory committee for the Second World Assembly on Ageing

Sessions: First and resumed first, New York, 26 February–2 March and 30 April–1 May, 10-14 December
Chairman: Felipe Paolillo (Uruguay)
Membership: Open to all States Members of the United Nations, members of the specialized agencies and observers
Reports: E/2001/71 & Add.1

Commission on Sustainable Development acting as the preparatory committee for the World Summit on Sustainable Development

Session: Organizational, New York, 30 April–2 May
Chairman: Emil Salim (Indonesia)
Membership: Open to all States Members of the United Nations and members of the specialized agencies
Report: A/56/19

Administrative Committee on Coordination (ACC)[14]

Sessions: Nairobi, Kenya, 2-3 April; New York, 19-20 October
Chairman: The Secretary-General
Membership: Organizations of the UN system
Reports: ACC/2001/4, ACC/2001/5

Other related bodies

International Research and Training Institute for the Advancement of Women (INSTRAW)

BOARD OF TRUSTEES

Session: Twenty-first, through the Internet, 22-24 May
President: Ana Maria Braga da Cruz (Portugal)
Membership: 11
Report: E/2001/88
Decision: ESC 2001/201 B

Director of INSTRAW: Eleni Stamiris (until July)

Joint United Nations Programme on Human Immunodeficiency Virus/Acquired Immunodeficiency Syndrome (UNAIDS)

PROGRAMME COORDINATING BOARD

Meeting: Eleventh, Geneva, 30 May–1 June
Chairperson: Dr. C. P. Thakur (India)
Membership: 22
Report: UNAIDS/PCB(11)/01.7
Decisions: ESC 2001/201 A & B

Executive Director of the Programme: Dr. Peter Piot

United Nations Children's Fund (UNICEF)

EXECUTIVE BOARD

Sessions: First and second regular, New York, 22-24 and 26 January, 10-12 December; annual, New York, 4-6 June
President: Movses Abelian (Armenia)
Membership: 36
Report: E/2001/34
Decisions: ESC 2001/201 B & C

Executive Director of UNICEF: Carol Bellamy

United Nations Development Programme (UNDP)/ United Nations Population Fund (UNFPA)

EXECUTIVE BOARD

Sessions: First and second regular, New York, 26 January and 29 January–6 February, 10-14 September; annual, New York, 11-22 June
President: Gert Rosenthal (Guatemala)
Membership: 36
Report: E/2001/35
Decisions: ESC 2001/201 A & B

Administrator of UNDP: Mark Malloch Brown
Associate Administrator: Zéphirin Diabré
Executive Director of UNFPA: Thoraya Obaid

United Nations Research Institute for Social Development (UNRISD)

BOARD OF DIRECTORS

Session: Thirty-ninth, Geneva, 25-26 June
Chairperson: Emma Rothschild (United Kingdom)
Membership: 11 (plus 7 ex-officio members)
Decision: ESC 2001/236

Director of the Institute: Thandika Mkandawire

World Food Programme (WFP)

EXECUTIVE BOARD

Sessions: First, second and third regular, Rome, Italy, 13-16 February, 16-18 May, 22-25 October; annual, Rome, 21-24 May
President: Ulla-Maija Finskas-Aho (Finland)
Membership: 36
Report: E/2002/36
Decisions: ESC 2001/201 A-C

Executive Director of WFP: Catherine A. Bertini

Conference

Seventh United Nations Regional Cartographic Conference for the Americas

Session: New York, 22-26 January
President: Mexico
Attendance: 136 representatives and observers of 34 countries and territories and 18 intergovernmental/international scientific organizations
Report: E/2001/11

Trusteeship Council

Article 86 of the United Nations Charter lays down that the Trusteeship Council shall consist of the following:

Members of the United Nations administering Trust Territories;
Permanent members of the Security Council that do not administer Trust Territories;
As many other members elected for a three-year term by the General Assembly as will ensure that the membership of the Council is equally divided between United Nations Members that administer Trust Territories and those that do not.[15]

Members: China, France, Russian Federation, United Kingdom, United States.

International Court of Justice

Judges of the Court

The International Court of Justice consists of 15 Judges elected for nine-year terms by the General Assembly and the Security Council.

The following were the Judges of the Court serving in 2001, listed in the order of precedence:

Judge	Country of nationality	End of term[16]
Gilbert Guillaume, *President*	France	2009
Shi Jiuyong, *Vice-President*	China	2003
Shigeru Oda	Japan	2003
Mohammed Bedjaoui[17]	Algeria	2006
Raymond Ranjeva	Madagascar	2009
Géza Herczegh	Hungary	2003
Carl-August Fleischhauer	Germany	2003
Abdul G. Koroma	Sierra Leone	2003
Vladlen S. Vereshchetin	Russian Federation	2006
Rosalyn Higgins	United Kingdom	2009
Gonzalo Parra-Aranguren	Venezuela	2009
Pieter H. Kooijmans	Netherlands	2006
Francisco Rezek	Brazil	2006
Awn Shawkat Al-Khasawneh	Jordan	2009
Thomas Buergenthal	United States	2006

Registrar: Philippe Couvreur.
Deputy Registrar: Jean-Jacques Arnaldez.

Chamber of Summary Procedure

Members: Gilbert Guillaume (ex officio), Shi Jiuyong (ex officio), Géza Herczegh, Abdul G. Koroma, Gonzalo Parra-Aranguren.
Substitute members: Rosalyn Higgins, Awn Shawkat Al-Khasawneh.

Chamber for Environmental Matters

Members: Gilbert Guillaume (ex officio), Shi Jiuyong (ex officio), Mohammed Bedjaoui (until 30 September), Raymond Ranjeva, Géza Herczegh, Francisco Rezek, Awn Shawkat Al-Khasawneh, Nabil Elaraby (from 12 October).

Parties to the Court's Statute

All Members of the United Nations are ipso facto parties to the Statute of the International Court of Justice. Also party to it was the following non-member: Switzerland.

States accepting the compulsory jurisdiction of the Court

Declarations made by the following States, a number with reservations, accepting the Court's compulsory jurisdiction (or made under the Statute of the Permanent Court of International Justice and deemed to be an acceptance of the jurisdiction of the International Court) were in force at the end of 2001:[18]

Australia, Austria, Barbados, Belgium, Botswana, Bulgaria, Cambodia, Cameroon, Canada, Costa Rica, Côte d'Ivoire,[19] Cyprus, Democratic Republic of the Congo, Denmark, Dominican Republic, Egypt, Estonia, Finland, Gambia, Georgia, Greece, Guinea, Guinea-Bissau, Haiti, Honduras, Hungary, India, Japan, Kenya, Lesotho, Liberia, Liechtenstein, Luxembourg, Madagascar, Malawi, Malta, Mauritius, Mexico, Nauru, Netherlands, New Zealand, Nicaragua, Nigeria, Norway, Pakistan, Panama, Paraguay, Philippines, Poland, Portugal, Senegal, Somalia, Spain, Sudan, Suriname, Swaziland, Sweden, Switzerland, Togo, Uganda, United Kingdom, Uruguay, Yugoslavia.

United Nations organs and specialized and related agencies authorized to request advisory opinions from the Court

Authorized by the United Nations Charter to request opinions on any legal question: General Assembly, Security Council.

Authorized by the General Assembly in accordance with the Charter to request opinions on legal questions arising within the scope of their activities: Economic and Social Council, Trusteeship Council, Interim Committee of the General Assembly, ILO, FAO, UNESCO, ICAO, WHO, World Bank, IFC, IDA, IMF, ITU, WMO, IMO, WIPO, IFAD, UNIDO, IAEA.

Committees of the Court

BUDGETARY AND ADMINISTRATIVE COMMITTEE

Members: Gilbert Guillaume (ex officio) (Chair), Shi Jiuyong (ex officio), Mohammed Bedjaoui (until 30 September), Raymond Ranjeva, Carl-August Fleischhauer, Vladlen S. Vereshchetin, Pieter H. Kooijmans, Nabil Elaraby (from 12 October).

COMMITTEE ON THE COURT'S MUSEUM
Members: Pieter H. Kooijmans (Chair), Shigeru Oda, Raymond Ranjeva, Vladlen S. Vereshchetin.

COMMITTEE ON RELATIONS
Members: Gonzalo Parra-Aranguren (Chair), Géza Herczegh, Francisco Rezek, Awn Shawkat Al-Khasawneh.

COMPUTERIZATION COMMITTEE
Members: Rosalyn Higgins (Chair); open to all interested members of the Court.

LIBRARY COMMITTEE
Members: Abdul G. Koroma (Chair), Rosalyn Higgins, Pieter H. Kooijmans, Francisco Rezek.

RULES COMMITTEE
Members: Carl-August Fleischhauer (Chair), Shigeru Oda, Mohammed Bedjaoui (until 30 September), Géza Herczegh, Abdul G. Koroma, Rosalyn Higgins, Thomas Buergenthal, Nabil Elaraby (from 12 October).

Other United Nations–related bodies

The following bodies are not subsidiary to any principal organ of the United Nations but were established by an international treaty instrument or arrangement sponsored by the United Nations and are thus related to the Organization and its work. These bodies, often referred to as "treaty organs", are serviced by the United Nations Secretariat and may be financed in part or wholly from the Organization's regular budget, as authorized by the General Assembly, to which most of them report annually.

Commission against Apartheid in Sports
Session: Has not met since 1992
Membership: 15

Committee on the Elimination of Discrimination against Women (CEDAW)
Sessions: Twenty-fourth, New York, 15 January–2 February; twenty-fifth, New York, 2-20 July
Chairperson: Charlotte Abaka (Ghana)
Membership: 23
Report: A/56/38

Committee on the Elimination of Racial Discrimination (CERD)
Sessions: Fifty-eighth, Geneva, 6-23 March; fifty-ninth, Geneva, 30 July–17 August
Chairman: Michael E. Sherifis (Cyprus)
Membership: 18
Report: A/56/18

Committee on the Rights of the Child
Sessions: Twenty-sixth, twenty-seventh and twenty-eighth, Geneva, 8-26 January, 21 May–8 June, 24 September–12 October
Chairperson: Jacob Egbert Doek (Netherlands)
Membership: 10

Reports: A/57/41, CRC/C/103, CRC/C/108, CRC/C/111

Committee against Torture
Sessions: Twenty-sixth, Geneva, 30 April–18 May; twenty-seventh, Geneva, 12-23 November
Chairman: Peter Burns (Canada)
Membership: 10
Reports: A/56/44, A/57/44

Conference on Disarmament
Meetings: Geneva, 22 January–30 March, 14 May–29 June, 30 July–14 September
President: Canada, Chile, China, Colombia, Cuba, Ecuador (successively)
Membership: 61
Report: A/56/27

Human Rights Committee
Sessions: Seventy-first, New York, 19 March–6 April; seventy-second, Geneva, 9-27 July; seventy-third, Geneva, 15 October–2 November
Chairperson: Prafullachandra Natwarlal Bhagwati (India)
Membership: 18
Reports: A/56/40, vol. I, A/57/40, vol. I

International Narcotics Control Board (INCB)
Sessions: Seventieth, seventy-first and seventy-second, Vienna, 5-9 February, 21 May–1 June, 29 October–15 November
President: Hamid Ghodse (Iran)
Membership: 13
Report: E/INCB/2001/1
Decision: ESC 2001/201 B

Principal members of the United Nations Secretariat

(as at 31 December 2001)

Secretariat
The Secretary-General: Kofi A. Annan
Deputy Secretary-General: Louise Fréchette

Executive Office of the Secretary-General
Under-Secretary-General, Chef de Cabinet: S. Iqbal Riza
Under-Secretary-General, Special Adviser to the Secretary-General: Dr. Nafis I. Sadik
Under-Secretary-General, Special Adviser to the Secretary-General and Rector of the University for Peace: Maurice F. Strong
Assistant Secretary-General, Special Adviser: Michael Doyle
Assistant Secretary-General for External Relations: Gillian M. Sorensen

Office of Internal Oversight Services
Under-Secretary-General: Dileep Nair

Office of Legal Affairs
Under-Secretary-General, Legal Counsel: Hans Corell
Assistant Secretary-General: Ralph Zacklin

Department of Political Affairs
Under-Secretary-General: Kieran Prendergast
Under-Secretary-General, Adviser for Special Assignments in Africa: Ibrahim A. Gambari
Assistant Secretaries-General: Ibrahima Fall, Danilo Türk

Department for Disarmament Affairs
Under-Secretary-General: Jayantha Dhanapala

Department of Peacekeeping Operations
Under-Secretary-General: Jean-Marie Guéhenno
Assistant Secretaries-General: Hédi Annabi, Michael Sheehan

Office for the Coordination of Humanitarian Affairs
Under-Secretary-General for Humanitarian Affairs, Emergency Relief Coordinator: Kenzo Oshima
Assistant Secretary-General, Deputy Emergency Relief Coordinator: Carolyn McAskie

Department of Economic and Social Affairs
Under-Secretary-General: Nitin Desai
Assistant Secretaries-General: Angela E. V. King, Patrizio M. Civili

Department of General Assembly Affairs and Conference Services
Under-Secretary-General: Jian Chen
Assistant Secretary-General: Miles Stoby

Department of Public Information
Interim Head: Shashi Tharoor

Department of Management
Under-Secretary-General: Joseph E. Connor

OFFICE OF PROGRAMME PLANNING, BUDGET AND ACCOUNTS
Assistant Secretary-General, Controller: Jean-Pierre Halbwachs

OFFICE OF HUMAN RESOURCES MANAGEMENT
Assistant Secretary-General: Rafiah Salim

OFFICE OF CENTRAL SUPPORT SERVICES
Assistant Secretary-General: Toshiyuki Niwa

Office of the Iraq Programme
Under-Secretary-General, Executive Director: Benon V. Sevan
Under-Secretary-General, High-level Coordinator: Yuli Vorontsov
Assistant Secretary-General, Humanitarian Coordinator: Tun Myat

Economic Commission for Africa
Under-Secretary-General, Executive Secretary: K. Y. Amoako

Economic Commission for Europe
Under-Secretary-General, Executive Secretary: Danuta Hübner

Economic Commission for Latin America and the Caribbean
Under-Secretary-General, Executive Secretary: Jose Antonio Ocampo

Economic and Social Commission for Asia and the Pacific
Under-Secretary-General, Executive Secretary: Hak-Su Kim

Economic and Social Commission for Western Asia
Under-Secretary-General, Executive Secretary: Mervat Tallawy

United Nations Centre for Human Settlements (Habitat)
Assistant Secretary-General, Executive Director: Anna Kajumulo Tibaijuka

United Nations Office at Geneva
Under-Secretary-General, Director-General of the United Nations Office at Geneva: Vladimir Petrovsky

Office of the High Commissioner for Human Rights
Under-Secretary-General, High Commissioner: Mary Robinson
Assistant Secretary-General, Deputy High Commissioner: Bertrand Gangapersaud Ramcharan

United Nations Office at Vienna
Under-Secretary-General, Director-General of the United Nations Office at Vienna and Executive Director of the United Nations Office for Drug Control and Crime Prevention: Giuseppe Arlacchi

International Court of Justice Registry
Assistant Secretary-General, Registrar: Philippe Couvreur

Secretariats of subsidiary organs, special representatives and other related bodies

International Trade Centre UNCTAD/WTO
Executive Director: J. Denis Bélisle

Office of the Secretary-General in Afghanistan and Pakistan
Under-Secretary-General, Special Representative of the Secretary-General for Afghanistan: Lakhdar Brahimi
Assistant Secretary-General, Head of the Special Mission in Afghanistan: Francesc Vendrell

Office of the Special Adviser to the Secretary-General on International Assistance to Colombia
Under-Secretary-General, Special Adviser: Jan Egeland

Office of the Special Envoy of the Secretary-General for Myanmar
Under-Secretary-General, Special Envoy: Ismail Razali

Office of the Special Representative of the Secretary-General for Children and Armed Conflict
Under-Secretary-General, Special Representative: Olara A. Otunnu

Office of the Special Representative of the Secretary-General for the Great Lakes Region
Assistant Secretary-General, Special Representative: Berhanu Dinka

Office of the United Nations High Commissioner for Refugees
Under-Secretary-General, High Commissioner: Ruud Lubbers

Office of the United Nations Security Coordinator
Under-Secretary-General, United Nations Security Coordinator: Benon V. Sevan

Office of the United Nations Special Coordinator for the Middle East
Under-Secretary-General, Special Coordinator for the Middle East Peace Process and Personal Representative of the Secretary-General to the Palestine Liberation Organization and the Palestinian Authority: Terje Roed-Larson

Special Adviser to the Secretary-General on Africa
Under-Secretary-General, Special Adviser: Mohamed Sahnoun

Special Adviser to the Secretary-General on European Issues
Under-Secretary-General, Special Adviser: Jean-Bernard Merimée

Special Adviser to the Secretary-General on Latin American Issues
Under-Secretary-General, Special Adviser: Diego Cordovez

Special Envoy of the Secretary-General for the Commonwealth of Independent States
Under-Secretary-General, Special Envoy: Yuli Vorontsov

Special Envoy of the Secretary-General for Humanitarian Affairs for the Sudan
Under-Secretary-General, Special Envoy: Tom Vraalsen

United Nations Children's Fund
Under-Secretary-General, Executive Director: Carol Bellamy
Assistant Secretaries-General, Deputy Executive Directors: Kul Gautam, Karin Holmgrunn Sham Poo, André Roberfroid

United Nations Compensation Commission
Assistant Secretary-General, Executive Secretary: Rolf Goran Knutsson

United Nations Conference on Trade and Development

Under-Secretary-General, Secretary-General of the Conference: Rubens Ricupero

Assistant Secretary-General, Deputy Secretary-General of the Conference: Carlos Fortin Cabezas

United Nations Convention to Combat Desertification

Assistant Secretary-General, Executive Secretary: Hama Arba Diallo

United Nations Development Programme

Administrator: Mark Malloch Brown

Under-Secretary-General, Associate Administrator: Zéphirin Diabré

Assistant Administrator and Director, Bureau for Crisis Prevention and Recovery: Julia V. Taft

Assistant Administrator and Director, Bureau of Management: Jan Mattson

Assistant Administrator and Director, Bureau for Development Policy: Eimi Watanabe

Assistant Administrator and Regional Director, UNDP Africa: Abdoulie Janneh

Assistant Administrator and Regional Director, UNDP Arab States: Rima Khalaf Hunaidi

Assistant Administrator and Regional Director, UNDP Asia and the Pacific: Hafiz Ahmed Pasha

Assistant Administrator and Regional Director, UNDP Europe and the Commonwealth of Independent States: Kalman Mizsei

Associate Administrator and Regional Director, UNDP Latin America and the Caribbean: Elena Martinez

United Nations Disengagement Observer Force

Assistant Secretary-General, Force Commander: Major General Bo Wranker

United Nations Environment Programme

Under-Secretary-General, Executive Director: Klaus Töpfer

Assistant Secretary-General, Deputy Executive Director: Shafqat S. Kakakhel

United Nations Institute for Training and Research

Executive Director: Marcel A. Boisard

United Nations Interim Administration Mission in Kosovo

Under-Secretary-General, Special Representative of the Secretary-General: Hans Haekkerup

Assistant Secretary-General, Principal Deputy Special Representative of the Secretary-General: Charles Brayshaw

Assistant Secretaries-General, Deputy Special Representatives of the Secretary-General: Jean-Christian Cady, Tom Koenigs

United Nations Interim Force in Lebanon

Assistant Secretary-General, Personal Representative of the Secretary-General: Staffan de Mistura

Assistant Secretary-General, Force Commander: Major General Lalit Mohan Tewari

United Nations Iraq-Kuwait Observation Mission

Assistant Secretary-General, Force Commander: Major General Miguel Angel Moreno

United Nations Joint Staff Pension Fund

Assistant Secretary-General, Chief Executive Officer: Bernard G. Cochemé

United Nations Military Observer Group in India and Pakistan

Chief Military Observer: Major General Manuel Saavedra

United Nations Mission in Bosnia and Herzegovina

Under-Secretary-General, Special Representative of the Secretary-General and Coordinator of United Nations Operations in Bosnia and Herzegovina: Jacques Paul Klein

Commissioner of the United Nations International Police Task Force: General Vincent Coeurderoy

United Nations Mission in Ethiopia and Eritrea

Under-Secretary-General, Special Representative of the Secretary-General: Legwaila Joseph Legwaila

Assistant Secretaries-General, Deputy Special Representatives of the Secretary-General: Cheikh Tidiane Gaye, Ian Martin

Force Commander: Major General Patrick Cammaert

United Nations Mission of Observers in Prevlaka

Chief Military Observer: Colonel Rodolfo Sergio Mujica

United Nations Mission for the Referendum in Western Sahara

Under-Secretary-General, Personal Envoy of the Secretary-General: James A. Baker III

Under-Secretary-General, Special Representative of the Secretary-General: William Lacy Swing

Force Commander: Brigadier General Claude Buze

United Nations Mission in Sierra Leone

Under-Secretary-General, Special Representative of the Secretary-General and Head of Mission: Oluyemi Adeniji

Assistant Secretaries-General, Deputy Special Representatives of the Secretary-General: Alan Claude Doss, Behrooz Sadry

Assistant Secretary-General, Force Commander: Lieutenant General Daniel Ishmael Opande

United Nations Monitoring, Verification and Inspection Commission

Executive Chairman: Hans Blix

United Nations Observer Mission in Georgia

Assistant Secretary-General, Special Representative of the Secretary-General and Head of Mission: Dieter Boden

Chief Military Observer: Major General Anis Ahmed Bajwa

United Nations Office in Angola

Representative of the Secretary-General and Head of Office: Mussagy Jeichande

United Nations Office in Burundi

Officer-in-Charge: Amadou Keita

United Nations Office for Project Services

Assistant Secretary-General, Executive Director: Reinhart Helmke

United Nations Organization Mission in the Democratic Republic of the Congo

Under-Secretary-General, Special Representative of the Secretary-General and Head of Mission: Amos Namanga Ngongi

Force Commander: Major General Mountaga Diallo

United Nations Peace-building Office in the Central African Republic

Representative of the Secretary-General and Head of Office: General Lamine Cissé

United Nations Peace-building Support Office in Guinea-Bissau

Representative of the Secretary-General and Head of Office: Samuel C. Nana-Sinkam

United Nations Peace-building Support Office in Liberia

Representative of the Secretary-General and Head of Office: Felix-Cyril Downes-Thomas

United Nations Peacekeeping Force in Cyprus

Under-Secretary-General, Special Adviser to the Secretary-General on Cyprus: Alvaro de Soto
Force Commander: Lieutenant General Jin Ha Hwang

United Nations Political Office in Bougainville

Head of Office: Noel Sinclair

United Nations Political Office for Somalia

Representative of the Secretary-General and Head of Office: David Stephen

United Nations Population Fund

Under-Secretary-General, Executive Director: Thoraya Obaid
Deputy Executive Director, Management: Imelda Henkin
Deputy Executive Director, Programme: Kunio Waki

United Nations Relief and Works Agency for Palestine Refugees in the Near East

Under-Secretary-General, Commissioner-General: Peter Hansen
Assistant Secretary-General, Deputy Commissioner-General: Karen Koning AbuZayd

United Nations Tajikistan Office of Peace-building

Assistant Secretary-General, Special Representative of the Secretary-General: Ivo Petrov

United Nations Transitional Administration in East Timor

Under-Secretary-General, Special Representative of the Secretary-General for East Timor: Jamsheed K. A. Marker
Under-Secretary-General, Special Representative of the Secretary-General and Transitional Administrator: Sergio Vieira de Mello
Assistant Secretary-General, Deputy Special Representative of the Secretary-General: Dennis McNamara
Assistant Secretary-General, Force Commander: Lieutenant General Winai Phattiyakul
Assistant Secretary-General, Chief of Staff: Parameswaran Nagalingam

United Nations Truce Supervision Organization

Assistant Secretary-General, Chief of Staff: Major General Franco Ganguzza

United Nations University

Under-Secretary-General, Rector: Johannes A. van Ginkel
Director, World Institute for Development Economics Research: Anthony F. Shorrocks

United Nations Verification Mission in Guatemala

Special Representative of the Secretary-General and Chief of Mission: Gerd D. Merrem

---

On 31 December 2001, the total number of staff of the United Nations Secretariat with continuous service or expected service of a year or more was 15,287. Of these, 5,651 were in the Professional and higher categories, 849 were experts (200-series Project Personnel staff) and 8,787 were in the General Service and related categories.

[1]In addition, on 25 June 2001 (dec. S-26/15), the Assembly appointed Penny Wensley (Australia) and Ibra Deguène Ka (Senegal) as co-facilitators of the twenty-sixth special session.

[2]On 6 and 25 June 2001 (dec. S-25/12 and S-26/12), the Assembly decided that the President at its fifty-fifth session would serve in the same capacity at the twenty-fifth and twenty-sixth special sessions.

[3]On 6 and 25 June 2001 (dec. S-25/13 and S-26/13), the Assembly decided that the Vice-Presidents at its fifty-fifth session would serve in the same capacity at the twenty-fifth and twenty-sixth special sessions.

[4]Elected on 12 September 2001 (dec. 56/302).

[5]Elected on 13 September 2001 (dec. 56/304).

[6]The only Main Committee to meet at the resumed session.

[7]On 6 and 25 June 2001 (dec. S-25/14 and S-26/14), the Assembly decided that the Chairpersons of the Main Committees of the fifty-fifth session would serve in the same capacity at the twenty-fifth and twenty-sixth special sessions. In the absence of the First, Fourth and Sixth Committee Chairpersons at the twenty-fifth and twenty-sixth special sessions, a Vice-Chairperson from the respective Committee served as Acting Chairperson.

[8]Chairpersons elected by the Committees; announced by the Assembly President on 13 September 2001 (dec. 56/303).

[9]Elected by the Assembly on 6 June 2001 (dec. S-25/15); other officers elected by the Ad Hoc Committee.

[10]Elected by the Assembly on 6 June 2001 (dec. S-25/16); other officers elected by the Thematic Committee.

[11]Chairpersons appointed by the Assembly on 25 June 2001, except for Abdul Malik Kasi, appointed on 26 June (dec. S-26/16).

[12]On 6 and 25 June 2001 (dec. S-25/11 and S-26/11), the Assembly decided that the Credentials Committee for the twenty-fifth and twenty-sixth special sessions would have the same composition as that for the fifty-fifth session.

[13]Appointed on 12 September 2001 (dec. 56/301).

[14]Name changed on 24 October 2001 to United Nations System Chief Executives Board for Coordination.

[15]During 2001, no Member of the United Nations was an administering member of the Trusteeship Council, while five permanent members of the Security Council continued as non-administering members.

[16]Term expires on 5 February of the year indicated.

[17]Resigned on 30 September 2001; Nabil Elaraby (Egypt) was elected by the General Assembly (dec. 56/306) and the Security Council on 12 October to fill the resultant vacancy.

[18]Colombia withdrew its declaration on 5 December 2001.

[19]Declaration deposited on 29 August 2001.

Appendix IV

Agendas of United Nations principal organs in 2001

This appendix lists the items on the agendas of the General Assembly, the Security Council and the Economic and Social Council during 2001. For the Assembly, the column headed "Allocation" indicates the assignment of each item to plenary meetings or committees.

Agenda item titles have been shortened by omitting mention of reports, if any, following the subject of the item. Where the subject matter of an item is not apparent from its title, the subject is identified in square brackets; this is not part of the title.

General Assembly

Agenda items considered at the resumed fifty-fifth session
(26 January–10 September 2001)

Item No.	Title	Allocation
2.	Minute of silent prayer or meditation.	Plenary
8.	Adoption of the agenda and organization of work.	Plenary
10.	Report of the Secretary-General on the work of the Organization.	Plenary
12.	Report of the Economic and Social Council.	Plenary[1]
14.	Report of the International Atomic Energy Agency.	Plenary
17.	Appointments to fill vacancies in subsidiary organs and other appointments:	
	(j) Approval of the appointment of the United Nations High Commissioner for Human Rights.	Plenary
20.	Strengthening of the coordination of humanitarian and disaster relief assistance of the United Nations, including special economic assistance:	
	(b) Special economic assistance to individual countries or regions.	Plenary
32.	United Nations Year of Dialogue among Civilizations.	Plenary
33.	Culture of peace.	Plenary
39.	Support by the United Nations system of the efforts of Governments to promote and consolidate new or restored democracies.	Plenary
42.	Special session of the General Assembly in 2001 for follow-up to the World Summit for Children.	Plenary
46.	The situation in Afghanistan and its implications for international peace and security.	Plenary
48.	The situation of democracy and human rights in Haiti.	Plenary
59.	Question of equitable representation on and increase in the membership of the Security Council and related matters.	Plenary
61.	Strengthening of the United Nations system.	Plenary
62.	Revitalization of the work of the General Assembly.	Plenary
63.	Restructuring and revitalization of the United Nations in the economic, social and related fields.	Plenary
64.	Question of Cyprus.	[2]
86.	Comprehensive review of the whole question of peacekeeping operations in all their aspects.	4th
94.	Sustainable development and international economic cooperation:	
	(d) High-level dialogue on strengthening international economic cooperation for development through partnership;	[3]
	(e) Implementation of the outcome of the United Nations Conference on Human Settlements (Habitat II).	[3]
97.	Training and research.	[3]
101.	High-level international intergovernmental consideration of financing for development.	[3]
102.	Third United Nations Conference on the Least Developed Countries.	[3]
105.	Crime prevention and criminal justice.	Plenary[4]
115.	Financial reports and audited financial statements, and reports of the Board of Auditors.	5th
116.	Review of the efficiency of the administrative and financial functioning of the United Nations.	5th
117.	Programme budget for the biennium 2000-2001.	5th
119.	Improving the financial situation of the United Nations.	[5]
120.	Administrative and budgetary coordination of the United Nations with the specialized agencies and the International Atomic Energy Agency.	5th

Item No.	Title	Allocation
122.	Scale of assessments for the apportionment of the expenses of the United Nations.	5th
123.	Human resources management.	5th
124.	United Nations common system.	5th
126.	Report of the Secretary-General on the activities of the Office of Internal Oversight Services.	5th
127.	Financing of the International Tribunal for the Prosecution of Persons Responsible for Serious Violations of International Humanitarian Law Committed in the Territory of the Former Yugoslavia since 1991.	5th
128.	Financing of the International Criminal Tribunal for the Prosecution of Persons Responsible for Genocide and Other Serious Violations of International Humanitarian Law Committed in the Territory of Rwanda and Rwandan Citizens Responsible for Genocide and Other Such Violations Committed in the Territory of Neighbouring States between 1 January and 31 December 1994.	5th
129.	Financing of the United Nations Angola Verification Mission and the United Nations Observer Mission in Angola.	5th
130.	Financing of the activities arising from Security Council resolution 687(1991):	
	(a) United Nations Iraq-Kuwait Observation Mission.	5th
131.	Financing of the United Nations Mission in East Timor.	5
132.	Financing of the United Nations Mission in Sierra Leone.	5th
133.	Financing of the United Nations Interim Administration Mission in Kosovo.	5th
134.	Financing of the United Nations Transitional Administration in East Timor.	5th
135.	Financing of the United Nations Mission for the Referendum in Western Sahara.	5th
136.	Financing of the United Nations Mission of Observers in Tajikistan.	5th
137.	Financing of the United Nations Preventive Deployment Force.	5th
138.	Financing of the United Nations peacekeeping forces in the Middle East:	
	(a) United Nations Disengagement Observer Force;	5th
	(b) United Nations Interim Force in Lebanon.	5th
139.	Financing and liquidation of the United Nations Transitional Authority in Cambodia.	5
140.	Financing of the United Nations Protection Force, the United Nations Confidence Restoration Operation in Croatia, the United Nations Preventive Deployment Force and the United Nations Peace Forces headquarters.	5th
141.	Financing of the United Nations Operation in Somalia II.	5
142.	Financing of the United Nations Operation in Mozambique.	5
143.	Financing of the United Nations Peacekeeping Force in Cyprus.	5th
144.	Financing of the United Nations Observer Mission in Georgia.	5th
145.	Financing of the United Nations Mission in Haiti.	5
146.	Financing of the United Nations Observer Mission in Liberia.	5
147.	Financing of the United Nations Assistance Mission for Rwanda.	5
148.	Financing of the United Nations Mission in Bosnia and Herzegovina.	5th
149.	Financing of the United Nations Transitional Administration for Eastern Slavonia, Baranja and Western Sirmium and the Civilian Police Support Group.	5
150.	Financing of the United Nations Support Mission in Haiti, the United Nations Transition Mission in Haiti and the United Nations Civilian Police Mission in Haiti.	5
151.	Financing of the Military Observer Group of the United Nations Verification Mission in Guatemala.	5
152.	Financing of the United Nations Mission in the Central African Republic.	5th
153.	Administrative and budgetary aspects of the financing of the United Nations peacekeeping operations:	
	(a) Financing of the United Nations peacekeeping operations.	5th
166.	Election of judges of the International Tribunal for the Prosecution of Persons Responsible for Serious Violations of International Humanitarian Law Committed in the Territory of the Former Yugoslavia since 1991.	Plenary
167.	Financing of the United Nations Organization Mission in the Democratic Republic of the Congo.	5th
168.	Programme budget for the biennium 1998-1999.	5th
169.	Scale of assessments for the apportionment of the expenses of United Nations peacekeeping operations.	5th
176.	Financing of the United Nations Mission in Ethiopia and Eritrea.	5th
178.	Armed aggression against the Democratic Republic of the Congo.	Plenary
179.	Review of the problem of human immunodeficiency virus/acquired immunodeficiency syndrome in all its aspects.	Plenary
181.	Cooperation between the United Nations and the Organization for the Prohibition of Chemical Weapons.	Plenary
185.	Election of judges of the International Criminal Tribunal for the Prosecution of Persons Responsible for Genocide and Other Serious Violations of International Humanitarian Law Committed in the Territory of Rwanda and Rwandan Citizens Responsible for Genocide and Other Such Violations Committed in the Territory of Neighbouring States between 1 January and 31 December 1994.[6]	Plenary

Item No.	*Title*	*Allocation*
186.	2001-2010: Decade to Roll Back Malaria in Africa.[6]	Plenary
187.	Appointment of the Secretary-General of the United Nations.[6]	Plenary

Agenda of the twenty-fifth special session
(6-9 June 2001)

Item No.	*Title*	*Allocation*
1.	Opening of the session by the Chairman of the delegation of Finland.	Plenary
2.	Minute of silent prayer or meditation.	Plenary
3.	Credentials of representatives to the twenty-fifth special session of the General Assembly:	
	(a) Appointment of the members of the Credentials Committee;	Plenary
	(b) Report of the Credentials Committee.	Plenary
4.	Election of the President.	Plenary
5.	Report of the Commission on Human Settlements acting as the preparatory committee for the special session of the General Assembly for an overall review and appraisal of the implementation of the outcome of the United Nations Conference on Human Settlements (Habitat II).	Plenary
6.	Organization of the session.	Plenary
7.	Adoption of the agenda.	Plenary
8.	Review and appraisal of progress made in the implementation of the Habitat Agenda.	Plenary[7]
9.	Further actions and initiatives for overcoming obstacles to the implementation of the Habitat Agenda.	Plenary[7]
10.	Declaration on cities and other human settlements in the new millennium.	Plenary[7]
11.	Adoption of the final document.	Plenary

Agenda of the twenty-sixth special session
(25-27 June 2001)

Item No.	*Title*	*Allocation*
1.	Opening of the session by the Chairman of the delegation of Finland.	Plenary
2.	Minute of silent prayer or meditation.	Plenary
3.	Credentials of representatives to the twenty-sixth special session of the General Assembly:	
	(a) Appointment of the members of the Credentials Committee;	Plenary
	(b) Report of the Credentials Committee.	Plenary
4.	Election of the President.	Plenary
5.	Organization of the session.	Plenary
6.	Adoption of the agenda.	Plenary
7.	Review of the problem of human immunodeficiency virus/acquired immunodeficiency syndrome (HIV/AIDS) in all its aspects.	Plenary
8.	Adoption of the final document.	Plenary

Agenda of the fifty-sixth session
(first part, 12 September–24 December 2001)

Item No.	*Title*	*Allocation*
1.	Opening of the session by the Chairman of the delegation of Finland.	Plenary
2.	Minute of silent prayer or meditation.	Plenary
3.	Credentials of representatives to the fifty-sixth session of the General Assembly:	
	(a) Appointment of the members of the Credentials Committee;	Plenary
	(b) Report of the Credentials Committee.	Plenary
4.	Election of the President of the General Assembly.	Plenary
5.	Election of the officers of the Main Committees.	Plenary
6.	Election of the Vice-Presidents of the General Assembly.	Plenary
7.	Notification by the Secretary-General under Article 12, paragraph 2, of the Charter of the United Nations.	Plenary
8.	Adoption of the agenda and organization of work.	Plenary
9.	General debate.	Plenary

Item No.	Title	Allocation
10.	Report of the Secretary-General on the work of the Organization.	Plenary
11.	Report of the Security Council.	Plenary
12.	Report of the Economic and Social Council.	Plenary, 4th, 2nd, 3rd, 5th
13.	Report of the International Court of Justice.	Plenary
14.	Report of the International Atomic Energy Agency.	Plenary
15.	Elections to fill vacancies in principal organs:	
(a)	Election of five non-permanent members of the Security Council;	Plenary
(b)	Election of eighteen members of the Economic and Social Council;	Plenary
(c)	Election of a member of the International Court of Justice.	Plenary
16.	Elections to fill vacancies in subsidiary organs and other elections:	
(a)	Election of the members of the International Law Commission;	Plenary
(b)	Election of twenty-nine members of the Governing Council of the United Nations Environment Programme;	Plenary
(c)	Election of seven members of the Committee for Programme and Coordination;	Plenary
(d)	Election of the Executive Director of the United Nations Environment Programme.	Plenary
17.	Appointments to fill vacancies in subsidiary organs and other appointments:[8]	
(a)	Appointment of members of the Advisory Committee on Administrative and Budgetary Questions;	5th
(b)	Appointment of members of the Committee on Contributions;	5th
(c)	Appointment of a member of the Board of Auditors;	5th
(d)	Confirmation of the appointment of members of the Investments Committee;	5th
(e)	Appointment of members of the United Nations Administrative Tribunal;	5th
(f)	Appointment of members of the International Civil Service Commission;	5th
(g)	Appointment of members of the Joint Inspection Unit;	Plenary
(h)	Appointment of members of the Committee on Conferences;	Plenary
(i)	Approval of the appointment of the United Nations High Commissioner for Human Rights.	Plenary
18.	Implementation of the Declaration on the Granting of Independence to Colonial Countries and Peoples.	Plenary, 4th
19.	Admission of new Members to the United Nations.	Plenary
20.	Strengthening of the coordination of humanitarian and disaster relief assistance of the United Nations, including special economic assistance:	
(a)	Strengthening of the coordination of emergency humanitarian assistance of the United Nations;	Plenary
(b)	Special economic assistance to individual countries or regions;	Plenary
(c)	Strengthening of international cooperation and coordination of efforts to study, mitigate and minimize the consequences of the Chernobyl disaster;	Plenary
(d)	Participation of volunteers, "White Helmets", in the activities of the United Nations in the field of humanitarian relief, rehabilitation and technical cooperation for development;	Plenary
(e)	Assistance to the Palestinian people;	Plenary
(f)	Emergency international assistance for peace, normalcy and reconstruction of war-stricken Afghanistan.	Plenary
21.	Cooperation between the United Nations and regional and other organizations:	
(a)	Cooperation between the United Nations and the Latin American Economic System;	Plenary
(b)	Cooperation between the United Nations and the International Organization of la Francophonie;	Plenary
(c)	Cooperation between the United Nations and the Council of Europe;	Plenary
(d)	Cooperation between the United Nations and the Organization of the Islamic Conference;	Plenary
(e)	Cooperation between the United Nations and the League of Arab States;	Plenary
(f)	Cooperation between the United Nations and the Inter-Parliamentary Union;	Plenary, 6th
(g)	Cooperation between the United Nations and the Economic Community of Central African States;	Plenary
(h)	Cooperation between the United Nations and the Economic Cooperation Organization;	Plenary
(i)	Cooperation between the United Nations and the Organization for Security and Cooperation in Europe;	Plenary
(j)	Cooperation between the United Nations and the Organization of African Unity;	Plenary
(k)	Cooperation between the United Nations and the Preparatory Commission for the Comprehensive Nuclear-Test-Ban Treaty Organization;	Plenary
(l)	Cooperation between the United Nations and the Organization for the Prohibition of Chemical Weapons;	Plenary
(m)	Cooperation between the United Nations and the Pacific Islands Forum.	Plenary

Item No.	Title	Allocation
22.	Final review and appraisal of the implementation of the United Nations New Agenda for the Development of Africa in the 1990s.	Plenary
23.	Building a peaceful and better world through sport and the Olympic ideal.	Plenary
24.	Review of the problem of human immunodeficiency virus/acquired immunodeficiency syndrome in all its aspects.	Plenary
25.	United Nations Year of Dialogue among Civilizations.	Plenary
26.	Follow-up to the outcome of the special session on children.	Plenary
27.	Implementation of the outcome of the World Summit for Social Development and of the twenty-fourth special session of the General Assembly.	3rd
28.	Culture of peace.	Plenary
29.	Follow-up to the outcome of the Millennium Summit.	Plenary
30.	Oceans and the law of the sea:	
	(a) Oceans and the law of the sea;	Plenary
	(b) Agreement for the Implementation of the Provisions of the United Nations Convention on the Law of the Sea of 10 December 1982 relating to the Conservation and Management of Straddling Fish Stocks and Highly Migratory Fish Stocks.	Plenary
31.	University for Peace.	Plenary
32.	Multilingualism.	Plenary
33.	Return or restitution of cultural property to the countries of origin.	Plenary
34.	Necessity of ending the economic, commercial and financial embargo imposed by the United States of America against Cuba.	Plenary
35.	Support by the United Nations system of the efforts of Governments to promote and consolidate new or restored democracies.	Plenary
36.	Zone of peace and cooperation of the South Atlantic.	Plenary
37.	The role of diamonds in fuelling conflict.	Plenary
38.	Assistance in mine action.	Plenary
39.	Towards global partnerships.	Plenary
40.	The situation in Bosnia and Herzegovina.	Plenary
41.	Question of Palestine.	Plenary
42.	The situation in the Middle East.	Plenary
43.	The situation in Afghanistan and its implications for international peace and security.	Plenary
44.	The situation in Central America: procedures for the establishment of a firm and lasting peace and progress in fashioning a region of peace, freedom, democracy and development.	Plenary
45.	Question of the Falkland Islands (Malvinas).	Plenary, 4th
46.	The situation in East Timor during its transition to independence.	Plenary
47.	The situation of democracy and human rights in Haiti.	Plenary
48.	Causes of conflict and the promotion of durable peace and sustainable development in Africa.	Plenary
49.	Question of equitable representation on and increase in the membership of the Security Council and related matters.	Plenary
50.	Report of the International Tribunal for the Prosecution of Persons Responsible for Serious Violations of International Humanitarian Law Committed in the Territory of the Former Yugoslavia since 1991.	Plenary
51.	Report of the International Criminal Tribunal for the Prosecution of Persons Responsible for Genocide and Other Serious Violations of International Humanitarian Law Committed in the Territory of Rwanda and Rwandan Citizens Responsible for Genocide and Other Such Violations Committed in the Territory of Neighbouring States between 1 January and 31 December 1994.	Plenary
52.	Declaration of the Assembly of Heads of State and Government of the Organization of African Unity on the aerial and naval military attack against the Socialist People's Libyan Arab Jamahiriya by the present United States Administration in April 1986.	Plenary
53.	Armed Israeli aggression against the Iraqi nuclear installations and its grave consequences for the established international system concerning the peaceful uses of nuclear energy, the non-proliferation of nuclear weapons and international peace and security.	Plenary
54.	Consequences of the Iraqi occupation of and aggression against Kuwait.	Plenary
55.	Implementation of the resolutions of the United Nations.	Plenary
56.	Launching of global negotiations on international economic cooperation for development.	Plenary
57.	Question of the Comorian island of Mayotte.	Plenary
58.	United Nations reform: measures and proposals.	Plenary
59.	Strengthening of the United Nations system.	Plenary
60.	Revitalization of the work of the General Assembly.	Plenary

Item No.	Title	Allocation
61.	Restructuring and revitalization of the United Nations in the economic, social and related fields.	Plenary 9
62.	Question of Cyprus.	
63.	Armed aggression against the Democratic Republic of the Congo.	Plenary
64.	Reduction of military budgets:	
	(a) Reduction of military budgets;	1st
	(b) Objective information on military matters, including transparency of military expenditures.	1st
65.	Verification in all its aspects, including the role of the United Nations in the field of verification.	1st
66.	Implementation of the Declaration of the Indian Ocean as a Zone of Peace.	1st
67.	African Nuclear-Weapon-Free Zone Treaty.	1st
68.	Maintenance of international security—good-neighbourliness, stability and development in South-Eastern Europe.	1st
69.	Developments in the field of information and telecommunications in the context of international security.	1st
70.	Role of science and technology in the context of international security and disarmament.	1st
71.	Establishment of a nuclear-weapon-free zone in the region of the Middle East.	1st
72.	Conclusion of effective international arrangements to assure non-nuclear-weapon States against the use or threat of use of nuclear weapons.	1st
73.	Prevention of an arms race in outer space.	1st
74.	General and complete disarmament:	
	(a) Notification of nuclear tests;	1st
	(b) Further measures in the field of disarmament for the prevention of an arms race on the seabed and the ocean floor and in the subsoil thereof;	1st
	(c) Prohibition of the dumping of radioactive wastes;	1st
	(d) Missiles;	1st
	(e) Preservation of and compliance with the Treaty on the Limitation of Anti-Ballistic Missile Systems;	1st
	(f) Towards a nuclear-weapon-free world: the need for a new agenda;	1st
	(g) Assistance to States for curbing the illicit traffic in small arms and collecting them;	1st
	(h) Consolidation of peace through practical disarmament measures;	1st
	(i) Implementation of the Convention on the Prohibition of the Development, Production, Stockpiling and Use of Chemical Weapons and on Their Destruction;	1st
	(j) Nuclear-weapon-free southern hemisphere and adjacent areas;	1st
	(k) Observance of environmental norms in the drafting and implementation of agreements on disarmament and arms control;	1st
	(l) Relationship between disarmament and development;	1st
	(m) Convening of the fourth special session of the General Assembly devoted to disarmament;	1st
	(n) Reducing nuclear danger;	1st
	(o) Regional disarmament;	1st
	(p) Conventional arms control at the regional and subregional levels;	1st
	(q) Illicit traffic in small arms and light weapons;	1st
	(r) Nuclear disarmament;	1st
	(s) Transparency in armaments;	1st
	(t) Implementation of the Convention on the Prohibition of the Use, Stockpiling, Production and Transfer of Anti-personnel Mines and on Their Destruction;	1st
	(u) Establishment of a nuclear-weapon-free zone in Central Asia;	1st
	(v) Follow-up to the advisory opinion of the International Court of Justice on the *Legality of the Threat or Use of Nuclear Weapons*;	1st
	(w) Small arms.	1st
75.	Review and implementation of the Concluding Document of the Twelfth Special Session of the General Assembly:	
	(a) Regional confidence-building measures: activities of the United Nations Standing Advisory Committee on Security Questions in Central Africa;	1st
	(b) United Nations Regional Centre for Peace and Disarmament in Africa;	1st
	(c) United Nations Regional Centre for Peace, Disarmament and Development in Latin America and the Caribbean;	1st
	(d) United Nations regional centres for peace and disarmament;	1st
	(e) Convention on the Prohibition of the Use of Nuclear Weapons;	1st
	(f) United Nations Regional Centre for Peace and Disarmament in Asia and the Pacific.	1st

Item No.	Title	Allocation
76.	Review of the implementation of the recommendations and decisions adopted by the General Assembly at its tenth special session:	
	(a) Advisory Board on Disarmament Matters;	1st
	(b) United Nations Institute for Disarmament Research;	1st
	(c) Report of the Conference on Disarmament;	1st
	(d) Report of the Disarmament Commission.	1st
77.	The risk of nuclear proliferation in the Middle East.	1st
78.	Convention on Prohibitions or Restrictions on the Use of Certain Conventional Weapons Which May Be Deemed to Be Excessively Injurious or to Have Indiscriminate Effects.	1st
79.	Strengthening of security and cooperation in the Mediterranean region.	1st
80.	Consolidation of the regime established by the Treaty for the Prohibition of Nuclear Weapons in Latin America and the Caribbean (Treaty of Tlatelolco).	1st
81.	Convention on the Prohibition of the Development, Production and Stockpiling of Bacteriological (Biological) and Toxin Weapons and on Their Destruction.	1st
82.	Comprehensive Nuclear-Test-Ban Treaty.	1st
83.	Compliance with arms limitation and disarmament and non-proliferation agreements.	1st
84.	Review of the implementation of the Declaration on the Strengthening of International Security.	1st
85.	Effects of atomic radiation.	4th
86.	International cooperation in the peaceful uses of outer space.	4th
87.	United Nations Relief and Works Agency for Palestine Refugees in the Near East.	4th
88.	Report of the Special Committee to Investigate Israeli Practices Affecting the Human Rights of the Palestinian People and Other Arabs of the Occupied Territories.	4th
89.	Comprehensive review of the whole question of peacekeeping operations in all their aspects.	4th
90.	Questions relating to information.	4th
91.	Information from Non-Self-Governing Territories transmitted under Article 73 *e* of the Charter of the United Nations.	4th
92.	Economic and other activities which affect the interests of the peoples of the Non-Self-Governing Territories.	4th
93.	Implementation of the Declaration on the Granting of Independence to Colonial Countries and Peoples by the specialized agencies and the international institutions associated with the United Nations.	4th
94.	Offers by Member States of study and training facilities for inhabitants of Non-Self-Governing Territories.	4th
95.	Macroeconomic policy questions:	
	(a) Trade and development;	2nd
	(b) International financial system and development;	2nd
	(c) Science and technology for development;	2nd
	(d) External debt crisis and development.	2nd
96.	Sectoral policy questions:	
	(a) Business and development;	2nd
	(b) Industrial development cooperation.	2nd
97.	Sustainable development and international economic cooperation:	
	(a) Women in development;	2nd
	(b) Human resources development;	2nd
	(c) High-level dialogue on strengthening international economic cooperation for development through partnership;	Plenary, 2nd
	(d) Implementation of the commitments and policies agreed upon in the Declaration on International Economic Cooperation, in particular the Revitalization of Economic Growth and Development of the Developing Countries, and implementation of the International Development Strategy for the Fourth United Nations Development Decade.	2nd
98.	Environment and sustainable development:	
	(a) Implementation of Agenda 21 and the Programme for the Further Implementation of Agenda 21;	2nd
	(b) International strategy for disaster reduction;	2nd
	(c) Implementation of the United Nations Convention to Combat Desertification in Those Countries Experiencing Serious Drought and/or Desertification, particularly in Africa;	2nd
	(d) Convention on Biological Diversity;	2nd
	(e) Further implementation of the Programme of Action for the Sustainable Development of Small Island Developing States;	2nd
	(f) Protection of global climate for present and future generations of mankind;	2nd
	(g) Promotion of new and renewable sources of energy, including the implementation of the World Solar Programme 1996-2005.	2nd

Item No.	*Title*	*Allocation*
99.	Operational activities for development:	
	(a) Triennial policy review of operational activities for development of the United Nations system;	2nd
	(b) Economic and technical cooperation among developing countries.	2nd
100.	International migration and development, including the question of the convening of a United Nations conference on international migration and development to address migration issues.	2nd
101.	Permanent sovereignty of the Palestinian people in the Occupied Palestinian Territory, including Jerusalem, and of the Arab population in the occupied Syrian Golan over their natural resources.	2nd
102.	Implementation of the Habitat Agenda and outcome of the special session of the General Assembly on this topic.	2nd
103.	Implementation of the first United Nations Decade for the Eradication of Poverty (1997-2006).	2nd
104.	Training and research.	2nd
105.	Globalization and interdependence.	2nd
106.	Third United Nations Conference on the Least Developed Countries:	
	(a) Third United Nations Conference on the Least Developed Countries;	2nd
	(b) Implementation of the Programme of Action for the Least Developed Countries for the Decade 2001-2010.	2nd
107.	High-level international intergovernmental consideration of financing for development.	2nd
108.	Social development, including questions relating to the world social situation and to youth, ageing, disabled persons and the family.	Plenary, 3rd
109.	Follow-up to the International Year of Older Persons: Second World Assembly on Ageing.	3rd
110.	Crime prevention and criminal justice.	3rd
111.	International drug control.	3rd
112.	Advancement of women.	3rd
113.	Implementation of the outcome of the Fourth World Conference on Women and of the twenty-third special session of the General Assembly, entitled "Women 2000: gender equality, development and peace for the twenty-first century".	3rd
114.	Report of the United Nations High Commissioner for Refugees, questions relating to refugees, returnees and displaced persons and humanitarian questions.	3rd
115.	Promotion and protection of the rights of children.	3rd
116.	Programme of activities of the International Decade of the World's Indigenous People.	3rd
117.	Elimination of racism and racial discrimination.	3rd
118.	Right of peoples to self-determination.	3rd
119.	Human rights questions:	
	(a) Implementation of human rights instruments;	3rd
	(b) Human rights questions, including alternative approaches for improving the effective enjoyment of human rights and fundamental freedoms;	3rd
	(c) Human rights situations and reports of special rapporteurs and representatives;	3rd
	(d) Comprehensive implementation of and follow-up to the Vienna Declaration and Programme of Action;	3rd
	(e) Report of the United Nations High Commissioner for Human Rights.	3rd
120.	Financial reports and audited financial statements, and reports of the Board of Auditors:	
	(a) United Nations peacekeeping operations;	5th
	(b) Voluntary funds administered by the United Nations High Commissioner for Refugees.	5th
121.	Review of the efficiency of the administrative and financial functioning of the United Nations.	5th
122.	Programme budget for the biennium 2000-2001.	5th
123.	Proposed programme budget for the biennium 2002-2003.	5th
124.	Pattern of conferences.	5th
125.	Scale of assessments for the apportionment of the expenses of the United Nations.	5th
126.	Human resources management.	5th
127.	United Nations common system.	5th
128.	Joint Inspection Unit.	5th
129.	Improving the financial situation of the United Nations.	5th
130.	Report of the Secretary-General on the activities of the Office of Internal Oversight Services.	5th
131.	Financing of the International Tribunal for the Prosecution of Persons Responsible for Serious Violations of International Humanitarian Law Committed in the Territory of the Former Yugoslavia since 1991.	5th
132.	Financing of the International Criminal Tribunal for the Prosecution of Persons Responsible for Genocide and Other Serious Violations of International Humanitarian Law Committed in the Territory of Rwanda and Rwandan Citizens Responsible for Genocide and Other Such Violations Committed in the Territory of Neighbouring States between 1 January and 31 December 1994.	5th

Item No.	*Title*	*Allocation*
133.	Administrative and budgetary aspects of the financing of the United Nations peacekeeping operations.	5th
134.	Financing of the United Nations peacekeeping forces in the Middle East:	
	(a) United Nations Disengagement Observer Force;	5th
	(b) United Nations Interim Force in Lebanon.	5th
135.	Financing of the United Nations Interim Administration Mission in Kosovo.	5th
136.	Financing of the United Nations Transitional Administration in East Timor.	5th
137.	Financing of the United Nations Mission in Ethiopia and Eritrea.	5th
138.	Financing of the United Nations Angola Verification Mission and the United Nations Observer Mission in Angola.	5th
139.	Financing of the activities arising from Security Council resolution 687(1991):	
	(a) United Nations Iraq-Kuwait Observation Mission;	5th
	(b) Other activities.	5th
140.	Financing of the United Nations Mission in East Timor.	5th
141.	Financing of the United Nations Mission in Sierra Leone.	5th
142.	Financing of the United Nations Mission for the Referendum in Western Sahara.	5th
143.	Financing of the United Nations Mission of Observers in Tajikistan.	5th
144.	Financing of the United Nations Preventive Deployment Force.	5th
145.	Financing and liquidation of the United Nations Transitional Authority in Cambodia.	5th
146.	Financing of the United Nations Protection Force, the United Nations Confidence Restoration Operation in Croatia, the United Nations Preventive Deployment Force and the United Nations Peace Forces headquarters.	5th
147.	Financing of the United Nations Operation in Somalia II.	5th
148.	Financing of the United Nations Operation in Mozambique.	5th
149.	Financing of the United Nations Peacekeeping Force in Cyprus.	5th
150.	Financing of the United Nations Observer Mission in Georgia.	5th
151.	Financing of the United Nations Mission in Haiti.	5th
152.	Financing of the United Nations Observer Mission in Liberia.	5th
153.	Financing of the United Nations Assistance Mission for Rwanda.	5th
154.	Financing of the United Nations Mission in Bosnia and Herzegovina.	5th
155.	Financing of the United Nations Transitional Administration for Eastern Slavonia, Baranja and Western Sirmium and the Civilian Police Support Group.	5th
156.	Financing of the United Nations Support Mission in Haiti, the United Nations Transition Mission in Haiti and the United Nations Civilian Police Mission in Haiti.	5th
157.	Financing of the United Nations Mission in the Central African Republic.	5th
158.	Financing of the United Nations Organization Mission in the Democratic Republic of the Congo.	5th
159.	United Nations Programme of Assistance in the Teaching, Study, Dissemination and Wider Appreciation of International Law.	6th
160.	Convention on jurisdictional immunities of States and their property.	6th
161.	Report of the United Nations Commission on International Trade Law on the work of its thirty-fourth session.	6th
162.	Report of the International Law Commission on the work of its fifty-third session.	6th
163.	Report of the Committee on Relations with the Host Country.	6th
164.	Establishment of the International Criminal Court.	6th
165.	Report of the Special Committee on the Charter of the United Nations and on the Strengthening of the Role of the Organization.	6th
166.	Measures to eliminate international terrorism.	Plenary, 6th
167.	Scope of legal protection under the Convention on the Safety of United Nations and Associated Personnel.	6th
168.	Observer status for the International Institute for Democracy and Electoral Assistance in the General Assembly.	6th
169.	Administration of justice at the United Nations.	5th
170.	Observer status for the International Development Law Institute in the General Assembly.	6th
171.	Observance of the International Day for Preventing the Exploitation of the Environment in War and Armed Conflict.	Plenary
172.	Observer status for the International Hydrographic Organization in the General Assembly.	6th
173.	Observer status for the Community of Sahelo-Saharan States in the General Assembly.	6th
174.	International convention against the reproductive cloning of human beings.	6th

Item No.	Title	Allocation
175.	Peace, security and reunification on the Korean peninsula.	Plenary
176.	Observer status for Partners in Population and Development in the General Assembly.	6th
177.	United Nations Year for Cultural Heritage, 2002.	Plenary

Agenda item considered at the resumed tenth emergency special session
(20 December 2001)

Item No.	Title	Allocation
5.	Illegal Israeli actions in occupied East Jerusalem and the rest of the Occupied Palestinian Territory.	Plenary

Security Council

Agenda items considered during 2001

Item No.[10]	Title

1. The situation in Somalia.
2. The situation in Croatia.
3. Strengthening cooperation with troop-contributing countries.
4. Security Council resolutions 1160(1998), 1199(1998), 1203(1998), 1239(1999) and 1244(1999) [Kosovo].
5. The responsibility of the Security Council in the maintenance of international peace and security: HIV/AIDS and international peacekeeping operations.
6. International Tribunal for the Prosecution of Persons Responsible for Serious Violations of International Humanitarian Law Committed in the Territory of the Former Yugoslavia since 1991.
7. Situation in the Central African Republic.
8. The situation in Angola.
9. The situation in Sierra Leone.
10. The situation in East Timor.
11. Briefing by His Excellency Mr. Mircea Geoana, Minister for Foreign Affairs of Romania, Chairman-in-Office of the Organization for Security and Cooperation in Europe.
12. The situation in the Middle East.
13. The situation in Georgia.
14. The situation concerning the Democratic Republic of the Congo.
15. Peace-building: towards a comprehensive approach.
16. The situation in the Great Lakes region.
17. The situation between Eritrea and Ethiopia.
18. The situation in Guinea following recent attacks along its borders with Liberia and Sierra Leone; the situation in Liberia; the situation in Sierra Leone.
19. The situation concerning Western Sahara.
20. The situation in Burundi.
21. The situation in Liberia.
22. Ensuring an effective role of the Security Council in the maintenance of international peace and security, particularly in Africa.
23. Letter dated 4 March 2001 from the Permanent Representative of the former Yugoslav Republic of Macedonia to the United Nations addressed to the President of the Security Council.
24. The situation along the borders of Guinea, Liberia and Sierra Leone.
25. The situation in the Middle East, including the Palestinian question.
26. The situation in Bosnia and Herzegovina.
27. International Criminal Tribunal for the Prosecution of Persons Responsible for Genocide and Other Serious Violations of International Humanitarian Law Committed in the Territory of Rwanda and Rwandan Citizens Responsible for Genocide and Other Such Violations Committed in the Territory of Neighbouring States between 1 January and 31 December 1994.
28. Protection of civilians in armed conflict.
29. The situation in Guinea following recent attacks along its borders with Liberia and Sierra Leone; the situation in Sierra Leone.
30. The situation between Iraq and Kuwait.
31. The situation in Afghanistan.

*Item
No.*[10]   *Title*

32. The situation in Cyprus.
33. Role of the Security Council in the prevention of armed conflicts.
34. Recommendation for the appointment of the Secretary-General of the United Nations.
35. Wrap-up discussion on the work of the Security Council for the current month [June, August, November, December].
36. Date of election to fill a vacancy in the International Court of Justice.
37. Small arms.
38. The situation in the former Yugoslav Republic of Macedonia.
39. Security Council resolution 1160(1998) of 31 March 1998 [Kosovo].
40. Meeting of the Security Council with the troop-contributing countries to the United Nations Mission in Ethiopia and Eritrea pursuant to resolution 1353(2001), annex II, section A.
41. Threats to international peace and security caused by terrorist acts.
42. Briefing by His Excellency Mr. Nebojša Covic, Deputy Prime Minister of Serbia, Federal Republic of Yugoslavia.
43. Consideration of the draft report of the Security Council to the General Assembly.
44. Security Council resolution 1054(1996) of 26 April 1996 [lifting of sanctions against the Sudan].
45. Election of a member of the International Court of Justice.
46. Nobel Peace Prize.
47. General issues relating to sanctions.
48. Briefing by Judge Gilbert Guillaume, President of the International Court of Justice.
49. Women and peace and security.
50. Children and armed conflict.
51. International Tribunal for the Prosecution of Persons Responsible for Serious Violations of International Humanitarian Law Committed in the Territory of the Former Yugoslavia since 1991; International Criminal Tribunal for the Prosecution of Persons Responsible for Genocide and Other Serious Violations of International Humanitarian Law Committed in the Territory of Rwanda and Rwandan Citizens Responsible for Genocide and Other Such Violations Committed in the Territory of Neighbouring States between 1 January and 31 December 1994.
52. Letter dated 30 April 2001 from the Secretary-General addressed to the President of the Security Council [report of Inter-Agency Mission to West Africa].

Economic and Social Council

Agenda of the organizational and resumed organizational sessions for 2001
(29 and 31 January; 8, 13 and 22 March, 3 May and 4 June)

*Item
No.*   *Title*

1. Election of the Bureau.
2. Adoption of the agenda and other organizational matters.
3. Basic programme of work of the Council.
4. Elections, nominations and confirmations.

Agenda of the substantive and resumed substantive sessions of 2001
(2-26 July; 10 and 24 October and 26 December)

*Item
No.*   *Title*

1. Adoption of the agenda and other organizational matters.

High-level segment

2. The role of the United Nations system in supporting the efforts of African countries to achieve sustainable development.

Operational activities of the United Nations for international development cooperation segment

3. Operational activities of the United Nations for international development cooperation:
    (a) Follow-up to policy recommendations of the General Assembly and the Council;
    (b) Reports of the Executive Boards of the United Nations Development Programme/United Nations Population Fund, the United Nations Children's Fund and the World Food Programme;
    (c) Economic and technical cooperation among developing countries.

Item
No.

Title

Coordination segment

4. Coordination of the policies and activities of the specialized agencies and other bodies of the United Nations system related to the following theme: the role of the United Nations in promoting development, particularly with respect to access to and transfer of knowledge and technology, especially information and communication technologies, inter alia, through partnerships with relevant stakeholders, including the private sector.

Humanitarian affairs segment

5. Special economic, humanitarian and disaster relief assistance.

General segment

6. Integrated and coordinated implementation of and follow-up to major United Nations conferences and summits.
7. Coordination, programme and other questions:
    (a) Reports of coordination bodies;
    (b) Proposed programme budget for the biennium 2002-2003;
    (c) Joint United Nations Programme on Human Immunodeficiency Virus/Acquired Immunodeficiency Syndrome (UNAIDS);
    (d) Calendar of conferences and meetings in the economic, social and related fields;
    (e) International cooperation in the field of informatics;
    (f) Long-term programme of support for Haiti;
    (g) Malaria and diarrhoeal diseases, in particular cholera.
8. Implementation of General Assembly resolutions 50/227 and 52/12 B.
9. Implementation of the Declaration on the Granting of Independence to Colonial Countries and Peoples by the specialized agencies and the international institutions associated with the United Nations.
10. Regional cooperation.
11. Economic and social repercussions of the Israeli occupation on the living conditions of the Palestinian people in the occupied Palestinian territory, including Jerusalem, and the Arab population in the occupied Syrian Golan.
12. Non-governmental organizations.
13. Economic and environmental questions:
    (a) Sustainable development;
    (b) Science and technology for development;
    (c) Statistics;
    (d) Human settlements;
    (e) Environment;
    (f) Women in development;
    (g) Transport of dangerous goods;
    (h) International Decade for Natural Disaster Reduction;
    (i) Population and development;
    (j) Energy and natural resources for development;
    (k) Public administration and development;
    (l) Cartography;
    (m) International cooperation in tax matters;
    (n) United Nations Forum on Forests;
    (o) Assistance to third States affected by the application of sanctions;
    (p) Global Code of Ethics for Tourism.
14. Social and human rights questions:
    (a) Advancement of women;
    (b) Social development;
    (c) Crime prevention and criminal justice;
    (d) Narcotic drugs;
    (e) United Nations High Commissioner for Refugees;
    (f) Implementation of the Programme of Action for the Third Decade to Combat Racism and Racial Discrimination;
    (g) Human rights;
    (h) Discrimination and genetic privacy;
    (i) Permanent Forum on Indigenous Issues.

[1]   Also allocated to the Fourth, Second, Third and Fifth Committees at the first part of the session in 2000.

[2]   Not allocated; consideration deferred to the fifty-sixth session.

[3]   Allocated to the Second Committee at the first part of the session in 2000 but considered only in plenary meeting at the resumed session.

[4]   Also allocated to the Third Committee at the first part of the session in 2000.

[5]   Allocated to the Fifth Committee at the first part of the session in 2000 but considered only in plenary meeting at the resumed session.

[6]   Item added at the resumed session.

[7]   Also allocated to the Ad Hoc Committee of the Whole of the Twenty-fifth Special Session.

[8]   On 24 December 2001, the General Assembly decided that the item would remain for consideration at the resumed fifty-sixth (2002) session (dec. 56/464).

[9]   On 19 September 2001, the General Assembly adopted the General Committee's recommendation that the item be allocated at an appropriate time during the session.

[10] Numbers indicate the order in which items were taken up in 2001.

Appendix V

United Nations information centres and services

(as at 21 May 2003)

ACCRA. United Nations Information Centre
Gamel Abdul Nassar/Liberia Roads
(P.O. Box GP 2339)
Accra, Ghana
    Serving: Ghana, Sierra Leone

ADDIS ABABA. United Nations Information
  Service, Economic Commission for Africa
P.O. Box 3001
Addis Ababa, Ethiopia
    Serving: Ethiopia, ECA

ALGIERS. United Nations Information Centre
9A rue Emile Payen, Hydra
(Boîte postale 823, Alger-Gare)
Algiers, Algeria
    Serving: Algeria

ANKARA. United Nations Information Centre
Birlik Mahallesi, 2 Cadde No. 11
06610 Cankaya
(P.K. 407)
Ankara, Turkey
    Serving: Turkey

ANTANANARIVO. United Nations Information Centre
22 rue Rainitovo, Antasahavola
(Boîte postale 1348)
Antananarivo, Madagascar
    Serving: Madagascar

ASUNCION. United Nations Information
  Centre
Avda. Mariscal López esq. Saraví
Edificio Naciones Unidas
(Casilla de Correo 1107)
Asunción, Paraguay
    Serving: Paraguay

ATHENS. United Nations Information
  Centre
36 Amalias Avenue
GR-10558 Athens, Greece
    Serving: Cyprus, Greece, Israel

BANGKOK. United Nations Information
  Service, Economic and Social Commis-
  sion for Asia and the Pacific
United Nations Building
Rajdamnern Nok Avenue
Bangkok 10200, Thailand
    Serving: Cambodia, China, Lao Peo-
ple's Democratic Republic, Malaysia, Sin-
gapore, Thailand, Viet Nam, ESCAP

BEIRUT. United Nations Information Cen-
  tre/United Nations Information Service,
  Economic and Social Commission for
  Western Asia
UN House
Riad El-Solh Square
(P.O. Box 11-8575-4656)
Beirut, Lebanon
    Serving: Jordan, Kuwait, Lebanon,
Syrian Arab Republic, ESCWA

BOGOTA. United Nations Information Centre
Calle 100 No. 8A-55, Piso 10
Edificio World Trade Center - Torre "C"
(Apartado Aéro 058964)
Bogotá 2, Colombia
    Serving: Colombia, Ecuador, Vene-
zuela

BONN. United Nations Information Centre
United Nations Premises in Bonn
Martin-Luther-King Strasse 8
D-53175 Bonn, Germany
    Serving: Germany

BRAZZAVILLE. United Nations Informa-
  tion Centre
Avenue Foch, Case Ortf 15
(P.O. Box 13210 or 1018)
Brazzaville, Congo
    Serving: Congo

BRUSSELS. United Nations Information
  Centre
UN House
14 rue Montoyer, 7th floor
B-1000 Brussels, Belgium
    Serving: Belgium, Luxembourg, Neth-
erlands, European Union

BUCHAREST. United Nations Information
  Centre
16 Aurel Vlaicu
Bucharest 79362, Romania
    Serving: Romania

BUENOS AIRES. United Nations Information Centre
Junín 1940, 1er piso
1113 Buenos Aires, Argentina
    Serving: Argentina, Uruguay

BUJUMBURA. United Nations Information Centre
117 Avenue de la Révolution
(P.O. Box 2160)
Bujumbura, Burundi
    Serving: Burundi

CAIRO. United Nations Information
  Centre
1 Osiris Street, Garden City
(P.O. Box 262)
Cairo, Egypt
    Serving: Egypt, Saudi Arabia

COLOMBO. United Nations Information
  Centre
202/204 Bauddhaloka Mawatha
(P.O. Box 1505)
Colombo 7, Sri Lanka
    Serving: Sri Lanka

COPENHAGEN. United Nations Informa-
  tion Centre
Midtermolen 3
DK-2100 Copenhagen East, Denmark
    Serving: Denmark, Finland, Iceland,
Norway, Sweden

DAKAR. United Nations Information
  Centre
Rues de Thann x Dagorne
(Boîte postale 154)
Dakar, Senegal
    Serving: Cape Verde, Côte d'Ivoire,
Gambia, Guinea, Guinea-Bissau, Maurita-
nia, Senegal

DAR ES SALAAM. United Nations Infor-
  mation Centre
Morogoro Road/Sokoine Drive
Old Boma Building (ground floor)
(P.O. Box 9224)
Dar es Salaam, United Republic of Tanzania
    Serving: United Republic of Tanzania

DHAKA. United Nations Information
  Centre
IDB Bhaban (14th floor)
Begum Rokeya Sharani
Sher-e-Bangla Nagar
(G.P.O. Box 3658, Dhaka-1000)
Dhaka-1207, Bangladesh
    Serving: Bangladesh

GENEVA. United Nations Information Service, United Nations Office at Geneva
Palais des Nations
1211 Geneva 10, Switzerland
Serving: Bulgaria, Switzerland

HARARE. United Nations Information Centre
Sanders House (2nd floor)
First Street/Jason Moyo Avenue
(P.O. Box 4408)
Harare, Zimbabwe
Serving: Zimbabwe

ISLAMABAD. United Nations Information Centre
House No. 26, Street 88, G-6/3
(P.O. Box 1107)
Islamabad, Pakistan
Serving: Pakistan

JAKARTA. United Nations Information Centre
Gedung Surya (14th floor)
Jl. M. H. Thamrin Kavling 9
Jakarta 10350, Indonesia
Serving: Indonesia

KATHMANDU. United Nations Information Centre
UN House
Pulchowk, Patan
(P.O. Box 107)
Kathmandu, Nepal
Serving: Nepal

KHARTOUM. United Nations Information Centre
United Nations Compound
Gamma'a Avenue
(P.O. Box 1992)
Khartoum, Sudan
Serving: Somalia, Sudan

KINSHASA. United Nations Information Centre
Immeuble Losonia
Boulevard du 30 juin
B.P. 7248
Kinshasa 1, Democratic Republic of the Congo
Serving: Democratic Republic of the Congo

LAGOS. United Nations Information Centre
17 Kingsway Road, Ikoyi
(P.O. Box 1068)
Lagos, Nigeria
Serving: Nigeria

LA PAZ. United Nations Information Centre
Calle 14 esq. S. Bustamante
Edificio Metrobol II, Calacoto
(Apartado Postal 9072)
La Paz, Bolivia
Serving: Bolivia

LIMA. United Nations Information Centre
Lord Cochrane 130
San Isidro (L-27)
(P.O. Box 14-0199)
Lima, Peru
Serving: Peru

LISBON. United Nations Information Centre
Rua Latino Coelho 1
Edificio Aviz, Bloco A-1, 10°
1050-132 Lisbon, Portugal
Serving: Portugal

LOME. United Nations Information Centre
107 boulevard du 13 janvier
(Boîte postale 911)
Lomé, Togo
Serving: Benin, Togo

LONDON. United Nations Information Centre
Millbank Tower (21st floor)
21-24 Millbank
London SW1P 4QH, United Kingdom
Serving: Ireland, United Kingdom

LUSAKA. United Nations Information Centre
Revenue House (ground floor)
Cairo Road (Northend)
(P.O. Box 32905)
Lusaka 10101, Zambia
Serving: Botswana, Malawi, Swaziland, Zambia

MADRID. United Nations Information Centre
Avenida General Perón, 32-1
(P.O. Box 3400, 28080 Madrid)
28020 Madrid, Spain
Serving: Spain

MANAGUA. United Nations Information Centre
Palacio de la Cultura
(Apartado Postal 3260)
Managua, Nicaragua
Serving: Nicaragua

MANAMA. United Nations Information Centre
United Nations House
Bldg. 69, Road 1901
(P.O. Box 26004)
Manama 319, Bahrain
Serving: Bahrain, Qatar, United Arab Emirates

MANILA. United Nations Information Centre
NEDA sa Makati Building
106 Amorsolo Street
Legaspi Village, Makati City, 1229
(P.O. Box 7285 ADC (DAPO), Pasay City)
Metro Manila, Philippines
Serving: Papua New Guinea, Philippines, Solomon Islands

MASERU. United Nations Information Centre
United Nations Road
UN House
(P.O. Box 301, Maseru 100)
Maseru, Lesotho
Serving: Lesotho

MEXICO CITY. United Nations Information Centre
Presidente Masaryk 29 (2do piso)
Col. Chaputelpec Morales
11570 México D.F., Mexico
Serving: Cuba, Dominican Republic, Mexico

MONROVIA. United Nations Information Centre
UNDP—Simpson Building
P.O. Box 0274
Mamba Point
Monrovia, Liberia
(UNDP Liberia, Grand Central Station, P.O. Box 1608, New York, NY 10163)
Serving: Liberia

MOSCOW. United Nations Information Centre
4/16 Glazovsky Pereulok
Moscow 121002, Russian Federation
Serving: Russian Federation

NAIROBI. United Nations Information Centre
United Nations Office
Gigiri
(P.O. Box 30552)
Nairobi, Kenya
Serving: Kenya, Seychelles, Uganda

NEW DELHI. United Nations Information Centre
55 Lodi Estate
New Delhi 110 003, India
Serving: Bhutan, India

OUAGADOUGOU. United Nations Information Centre
14 Avenue Georges Konseiga
Secteur no. 4
(Boîte postale 135)
Ouagadougou 01, Burkina Faso
Serving: Burkina Faso, Chad, Mali, Niger

PANAMA CITY. United Nations Information Centre
Calle Gerardo Ortega y Ave. Samuel Lewis
Banco Central Hispano Building (1st floor)
(P.O. Box 6-9083 El Dorado)
Panama City, Panama
Serving: Panama

PARIS. United Nations Information Centre
1 rue Miollis
75732 Paris cedex 15, France
Serving: France

PORT OF SPAIN. United Nations Information Centre
2nd floor, Bretton Hall
16 Victoria Avenue
(P.O. Box 130)
Port of Spain, Trinidad, W.I.

Serving: Antigua and Barbuda, Bahamas, Barbados, Belize, Dominica, Grenada, Guyana, Jamaica, Netherlands Antilles, Saint Kitts and Nevis, Saint Lucia, Saint Vincent and the Grenadines, Suriname, Trinidad and Tobago

PRAGUE. United Nations Information Centre
nam. Kinskych 6
15000 Prague 5, Czech Republic

Serving: Czech Republic

PRETORIA. United Nations Information Centre
Metro Park Building
351 Schoeman Street
(P.O. Box 12677)
Pretoria, South Africa

Serving: South Africa

RABAT. United Nations Information Centre
6 Angle avenue Tarik Ibnou Ziyad et Ruet Roudana
(Boîte postale 601, Casier ONU, Rabat-Chellah)
Rabat, Morocco

Serving: Morocco

RIO DE JANEIRO. United Nations Information Centre
Palácio Itamaraty
Av. Marechal Floriano 196
20080-002 Rio de Janeiro, RJ Brazil

Serving: Brazil

ROME. United Nations Information Centre
Palazzetto Venezia
Piazza San Marco 50
00186 Rome, Italy

Serving: Holy See, Italy, Malta, San Marino

SANA'A. United Nations Information Centre
Street 5, off Al-Bonyia Street
Handlal Zone, beside Handhal Mosque
(P.O. Box 237)
Sana'a, Yemen

Serving: Yemen

SANTIAGO. United Nations Information Service, Economic Commission for Latin America and the Caribbean
Edificio Naciones Unidas
Avenida Dag Hammarskjöld, Vitacura
(Avenida Dag Hammarskjöld s/n, Vitacura Casilla 179-D)
Santiago, Chile

Serving: Chile, ECLAC

SYDNEY. United Nations Information Centre
46-48 York Street (5th floor)
(G.P.O. Box 4045, Sydney, N.S.W. 2001)
Sydney, N.S.W. 2000, Australia

Serving: Australia, Fiji, Kiribati, Nauru, New Zealand, Samoa, Tonga, Tuvalu, Vanuatu

TEHRAN. United Nations Information Centre
185 Gheammagham-Farahani St.
(P.O. Box 15875-4557)
Tehran 15868, Iran

Serving: Iran

TOKYO. United Nations Information Centre
UNU Building (8th floor)
53-70 Jingumae 5-chome, Shibuya-Ku
Tokyo 150-0001, Japan

Serving: Japan

TRIPOLI. United Nations Information Centre
Muzzafar Al-Aftas St.
Hay El-Andalous (2)
(P.O. Box 286)
Tripoli, Libyan Arab Jamahiriya

Serving: Libyan Arab Jamahiriya

TUNIS. United Nations Information Centre
61 boulevard Bab-Benath
(Boîte postale 863)
Tunis, Tunisia

Serving: Tunisia

VIENNA. United Nations Information Service, United Nations Office at Vienna
Vienna International Centre
Wagramer Strasse 5
(P.O. Box 500, A-1400 Vienna)
A-1220 Vienna, Austria

Serving: Austria, Hungary, Slovakia, Slovenia

WARSAW. United Nations Information Centre
A. Niepodleglosci 186
(UN Centre P.O. Box 1, 02-514 Warsaw 12)
00-608 Warsaw, Poland

Serving: Poland

WASHINGTON, D.C. United Nations Information Centre
1775 K Street, N.W., Suite 400
Washington, D.C. 20006, United States

Serving: United States

WINDHOEK. United Nations Information Centre
372 Paratus Building
Independence Avenue
(Private Bag 13351)
Windhoek, Namibia

Serving: Namibia

YANGON. United Nations Information Centre
6 Natmauk Road
(P.O. Box 230)
Yangon, Myanmar

Serving: Myanmar

YAOUNDE. United Nations Information Centre
Immeuble Tchinda, Rue 2044, derrière camp SIC TSINGA
(Boîte postale 836)
Yaoundé, Cameroon

Serving: Cameroon, Central African Republic, Gabon

For more information on UNICs, access the Internet: http://www.un.org/aroundworld/unics

Indexes

USING THE SUBJECT INDEX

To assist the researcher in reading and searching the *Yearbook* index, three typefaces have been employed.

ALL BOLD CAPITAL LETTERS are used for major subject entries, including chapter topics (e.g., **DEVELOPMENT, DISARMAMENT**), as well as country names (e.g., **TAJIKISTAN**), region names (e.g., **AFRICA**) and principal UN organs (e.g., **GENERAL ASSEMBLY**).

CAPITAL LETTERS are used to highlight major sub-topics (e.g., POVERTY), territories (e.g., MONTSERRAT), subregions (e.g., CENTRAL AMERICA) and official names of specialized agencies (e.g., UNIVERSAL POSTAL UNION) and regional commissions (e.g., ECONOMIC COMMISSION FOR EUROPE).

Regular body text is used for single entries and cross-reference entries, e.g., armed conflict, juvenile detention, social development.

1—An asterisk (*) next to a page number indicates the presence of a text (reproduced in full) of General Assembly, Security Council or Economic and Social Council resolutions and decisions, or Security Council presidential statements.

2—Entries, which are heavily cross-referenced, appear under key substantive words, as well as under the first word of official titles.

3—United Nations bodies are listed under major subject entries and alphabetically.

Subject index

Index of resolutions and decisions

Resolution/decision numbers in italics indicate that the text is summarized rather than reprinted in full. (For dates of sessions, refer to Appendix III.)

GENERAL ASSEMBLY,
  56th SESSION *(cont.)*

Index of 2001 Security Council presidential statements

How to obtain volumes of the *Yearbook*

Recent volumes of the *Yearbook* may be obtained in many bookstores throughout the world, as well as from United Nations Publications, Room DC2-853, United Nations, New York, N.Y. 10017, or from United Nations Publications, Palais des Nations, CH-1211 Geneva 10, Switzerland.

Older editions are available in microfiche.

Yearbook of the United Nations, 2000
Vol. 54. Sales No. E.02.I.1 $150.

Yearbook of the United Nations, 1999 Vol. 53. Sales No. E.01.I.4 $150.	**Yearbook of the United Nations, 1991** Vol. 45. Sales No. E.92.I.1 $115.
Yearbook of the United Nations, 1998 Vol. 52. Sales No. E.01.I.1 $150.	**Yearbook of the United Nations, 1990** Vol. 44. Sales No. E.98.I.16 $150.
Yearbook of the United Nations, 1997 Vol. 51. Sales No. E.00.I.1 $150.	**Yearbook of the United Nations, 1989** Vol. 43. Sales No. E.97.I.11 $150.
Yearbook of the United Nations, 1996 Vol. 50. Sales No. E.97.I.1 $150.	**Yearbook of the United Nations, 1988** Vol. 42. Sales No. E.93.I.100 $150.
Yearbook of the United Nations, 1995 Vol. 49. Sales No. E.96.I.1 $150.	**Yearbook of the United Nations, 1987** Vol. 41. Sales No. E.91.I.1 $105.
Yearbook of the United Nations, 1994 Vol. 48. Sales No. E.95.I.1 $150.	**Yearbook of the United Nations, 1986** Vol. 40. Sales No. E.90.I.1 $95.
Yearbook of the United Nations, 1993 Vol. 47. Sales No. E.94.I.1 $150.	**Yearbook of the United Nations, 1985** Vol. 39. Sales No. E.88.I.1 $95.
Yearbook of the United Nations, 1992 Vol. 46. Sales No. E.93.I.1 $150.	**Yearbook of the United Nations, 1984** Vol. 38. Sales No. E.87.I.1 $90.

Yearbook of the United Nations
Special Edition
UN Fiftieth Anniversary
1945-1995
Sales No. E.95.I.50 $95

The first 54 volumes of the *Yearbook of the United Nations* (1946-2000) are now available on CD-ROM in both single-user and network versions. Institutions can subscribe at $500 (single-user version) or $1,000 (network version). Special rates are available for individuals and least developed countries. For more information, contact United Nations Publications at the above address.

NOTES

NOTES